PRENTICE HALL

UNITED STATES HISTORY
MODERN AMERICA

Emma J. Lapsansky-Werner

Peter B. Levy

Randy Roberts

Alan Taylor

PEARSON

Upper Saddle River, New Jersey   Boston, Massachusetts   Chandler, Arizona   Glenview, Illinois

Cover Images: TR, © Josef Scaylea/CORBIS; TL, © Bettmann/CORBIS; TR, © Bettmann/CORBIS; MR, Carr Clifton/Minden Pictures; BR, Pearson Curriculum; Bkgd Corbis Royalty-Free; BL, Getty Images; BFL, Fox Photos/Getty Images; BM, © Ted Streshinsky/CORBIS; BR, © Michael Macor/San Francisco Chronicle/Corbis; **Title page** Corbis Royalty-Free; **Spine:** Corbis Royalty-Free; **Back cover:** Corbis Royalty-Free

Acknowledgments appear on page 802, which constitutes an extension of this copyright page.

ISBN-13: 978-0-13-3189063
ISBN-10:   0-13-3189066

PEARSON

2 3 4 5 6 7 8 9 10   V092   17 16 15 14 13

AUTHORS

Emma J. Lapsansky-Werner

Emma J. Lapsansky-Werner is Professor of History and Curator of the Quaker Collection at Haverford College. After receiving her doctorate from the University of Pennsylvania, she taught at Temple University for almost two decades. Dr. Lapsansky-Werner's recent publications include *Quaker Aesthetics,* coauthored with Ann Verplanck, and *Back to Africa: Benjamin Coates and the Colonization Movement in America, 1848–1880,* coedited with Margaret Hope Bacon.

Peter B. Levy

Peter B. Levy is a Full Professor in the Department of History at York College of Pennsylvania, where he teaches a wide variety of courses in American history. He received his B.A. from the University of California, Berkeley, and his Ph.D. from Columbia University. Dr. Levy is the author of eight books and many articles, including: *The New Left and Labor in the 1960s; Civil War on Race Street: The Civil Rights Movement in Cambridge, Maryland;* and *100 Key Documents in American Democracy.* He lives in Towson, Maryland, with his wife, two children, and a yellow Labrador.

Randy Roberts

Randy Roberts, Professor of History at Purdue University, specializes in twentieth-century American history and the history of popular culture. He has written, cowritten, or edited more than 20 books, including biographies of John Wayne, Jack Johnson, and Oscar Robertson. Dr. Roberts has also written histories of American sports and of the Vietnam War. His books have been nominated for and won a number of national prizes. At Purdue University, he has won the University Teacher of the Year award. Dr. Roberts has also appeared frequently on the History Channel and in documentaries for HBO, NBC, ESPN, and PBS.

Alan Taylor

Alan Taylor, Professor of History at the University of California, Davis, earned his Ph.D. in history from Brandeis University and did a postdoctoral fellowship at the Institute of Early American History and Culture in Williamsburg, Virginia. He teaches courses in early American history and the history of the American West. Dr. Taylor is the author of five books, including *American Colonies* and *William Cooper's Town,* which won the Bancroft and Beveridge prizes, as well as the 1996 Pulitzer Prize for American history. He is a contributing editor for *The New Republic.*

Program Consultant

Grant Wiggins, Ed.D., is the President of Authentic Education in Hopewell, New Jersey. He earned his Ed.D from Harvard University and his B.A. from St. John's College in Annapolis. Dr. Wiggins consults with schools, districts, and state education departments on a variety of reform matters. He organizes conferences, workshops, and develops print materials and Web resources on curricular change. He is the co-author, with Jay McTighe, of *Understanding by Design* and *The Understanding by Design Handbook,* the award-winning and highly successful materials on curriculum.

The Association for Supervision of Curriculum Development (ASCD), publisher of the "Understanding by Design Handbook" co-authored by Grant Wiggins and registered owner of the trademark "Understanding by Design", has not authorized, approved, or sponsored this work and is in no way affiliated with Pearson or its products.

Senior Consultants

John R. Chávez is Professor of History at Southern Methodist University, Clements Department of History. He earned his Ph.D. from the University of Michigan, with a specialty in Mexican American history. Dr. Chávez's publications include *Eastside Landmark: A History of the East Los Angeles Community Union, The Lost Land: The Chicano Image of the Southwest,* and *Teaching Mexican American History,* co-authored with Neil Foley.

Herman J. Viola specializes in the history of the American West, the American Indian, and the Civil War. He has published books on historic subjects, including *After Columbus* and *Little Bighorn Remembered: The Untold Indian Story of Custer's Last Stand.* Dr. Viola earned his Ph.D. from Indiana University and currently serves as curator emeritus at the Smithsonian's National Museum of Natural History.

Senior Reading Consultants

Kate Kinsella, Ed.D., Adjunct faculty member, Department of Secondary Education at San Francisco State University. A specialist in second-language and adolescent literacy, she teaches coursework addressing language and literacy development across the secondary curricula. Dr. Kinsella earned her M.A. in TESOL from San Francisco State University and her Ed.D. in Second Language Acquisition from the University of San Francisco.

Kevin Feldman, Ed.D., is the Director of Reading and Early Intervention with the Sonoma County Office of Education (SCOE) and an independent educational consultant. At the SCOE, he develops, organizes, and monitors programs related to K–12 literacy. Dr. Feldman has an M.A. from the University of California, Riverside, in Special Education, Learning Disabilities, and Instructional Design. He earned his Ed.D. in Curriculum and Instruction from the University of San Francisco.

Differentiated Instruction Consultants

Don Deshler

Don Deshler, Ph.D., is the director of the Center for Research on Learning (CRL) at the University of Kansas. Dr. Deshler's expertise centers on adolescent literacy, learning strategic instruction, and instructional strategies for teaching content areas to academically diverse classes. He is the author of *Teaching Content to All: Evidence-Based Inclusive Practices in Middle and Secondary Schools,* a text which presents the instructional practices that have been tested and validated through his research at CRL.

Anthony S. Bashir
Director, Academic and Disability Services
Emerson College
Boston, Massachusetts

Cathy Collins Block, Ph.D.
Professor of Curriculum and Instruction
Texas Christian University
Fort Worth, Texas

Anna Uhl Chamot
Professor of Secondary Education (ESL)
The George Washington University
Washington, D.C.

John Guthrie
Professor of Human Development
University of Maryland
College Park, Maryland

Susan P. Miller
Professor of Special Education
University of Nevada, Las Vegas
Las Vegas, Nevada

Jennifer Platt
Executive Associate Dean for Academic Affairs
College of Education
University of Central Florida
Orlando, Florida

Reviewers

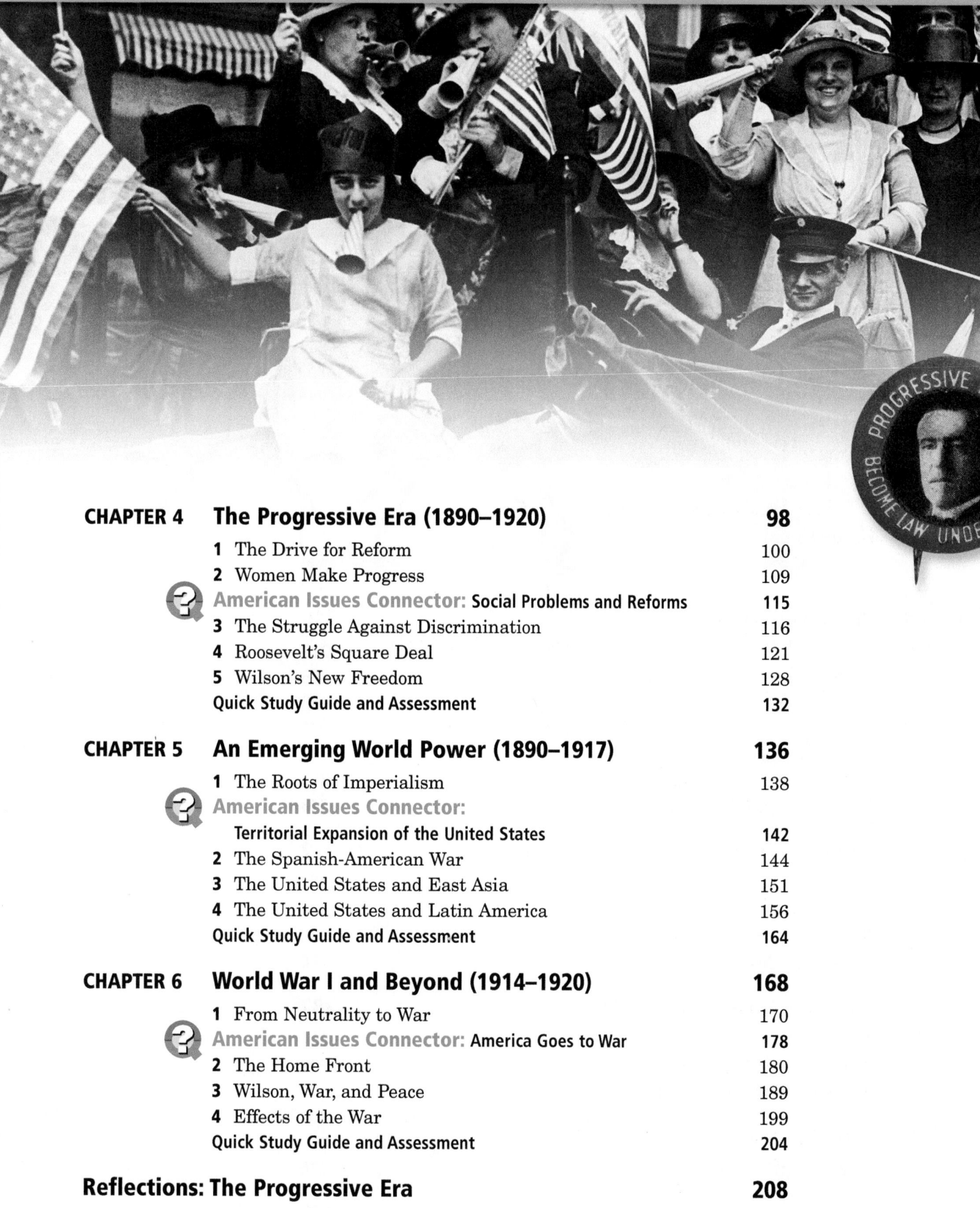

EMERGENCE OF THE MODERN UNITED STATES (1890–1920)

CHALLENGES AND CHANGE (1945–1980)

CHANGING AND ENDURING ISSUES (1980–Today)

SPECIAL FEATURES AND MULTIMEDIA

Witness History: The Latest Fad

As baby boomers went to school, new fads came and went with amazing speed. One such fad revolved around a popular television show about the American folk hero Davy Crockett. Steven Spielberg, who later would become one of Hollywood's most successful movie directors, recalled the craze.

“I was in third grade at the time. Suddenly, the next day, everybody in my class but me was Davy Crockett. And because I didn't have my coonskin cap and my powder horn, or Old Betsy, my rifle, and my chaps, I was deemed the Mexican leader, Santa Anna. And they chased me home from school until I got my parents to buy me a coonskin cap.”

—Steven Spielberg, recalling the Davy Crockett craze of 1955

WITNESS HISTORY

Primary source accounts throughout the text bring the voices of history to life.

History *Interactive*

Audio, video, and animation-filled features help you explore major turning points in history.

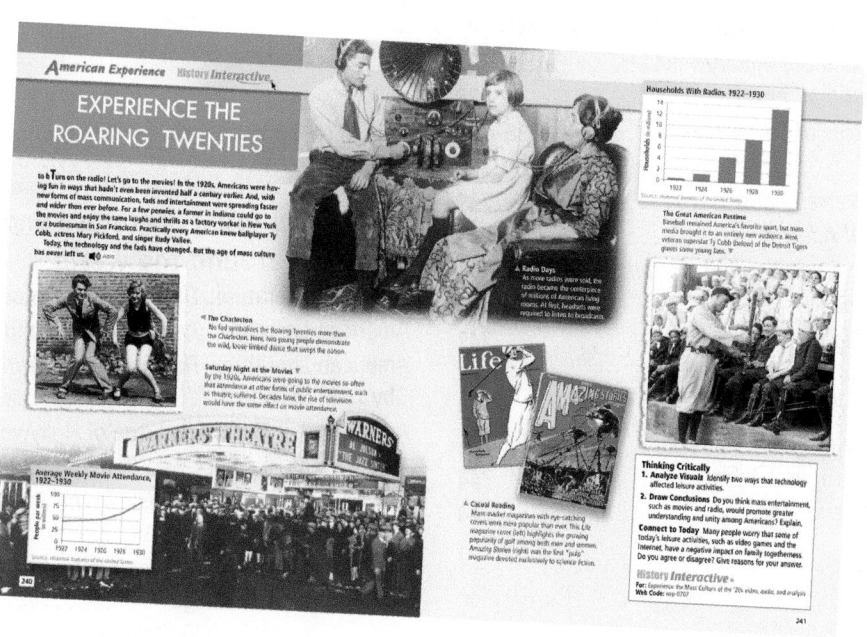

Primary Source

Full-page excerpts allow you to relive history through eyewitness accounts and documents.

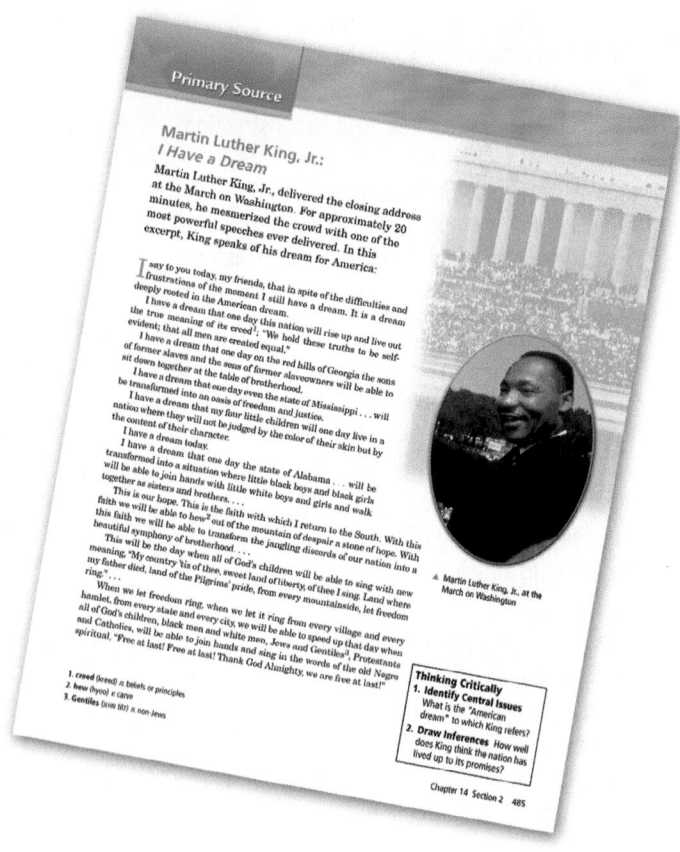

American Humanities

Experience great literature and arts from around the world.

In-Text Primary Source

Gain insights as you read by reading the words of people who were there.

Comparing Viewpoints

Explore issues by analyzing two opposing viewpoints.

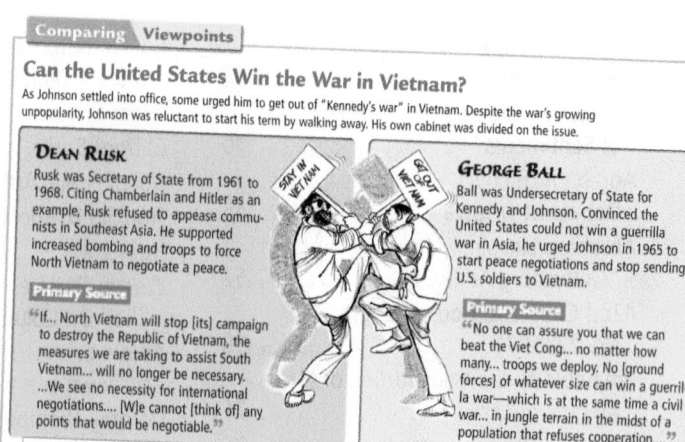

Decision Point

Consider how you would have decided key questions in American history.

Cause and Effect

**Diagrams help you see the short- and long-term causes
and effects of history's most important events.**

HISTORY MAKERS

Meet many fascinating people.

HISTORY MAKERS

Cesar Chavez (1927–1993)

Cesar Chavez spent his childhood and youth toiling, like his parents, as a migrant farmworker. In the 1950s, he trained to be a community organizer. His skills led him to be named chief of the group doing the training. In 1962, he formed the National Farm Workers Association. Migrant workers had tried to form unions before and failed; Chavez made the effort succeed. In an impassioned letter to the grape industry, he expressed the workers' suffering and determination. "We are men and women who have suffered and endured much," he wrote. "Generation after generation have sought to demoralize us, to break our human spirit. But God knows that we are not beasts of burden, agricultural implements or rented slaves; we are men."

American Issues
Connector

Examine key issues that have endured throughout American history.

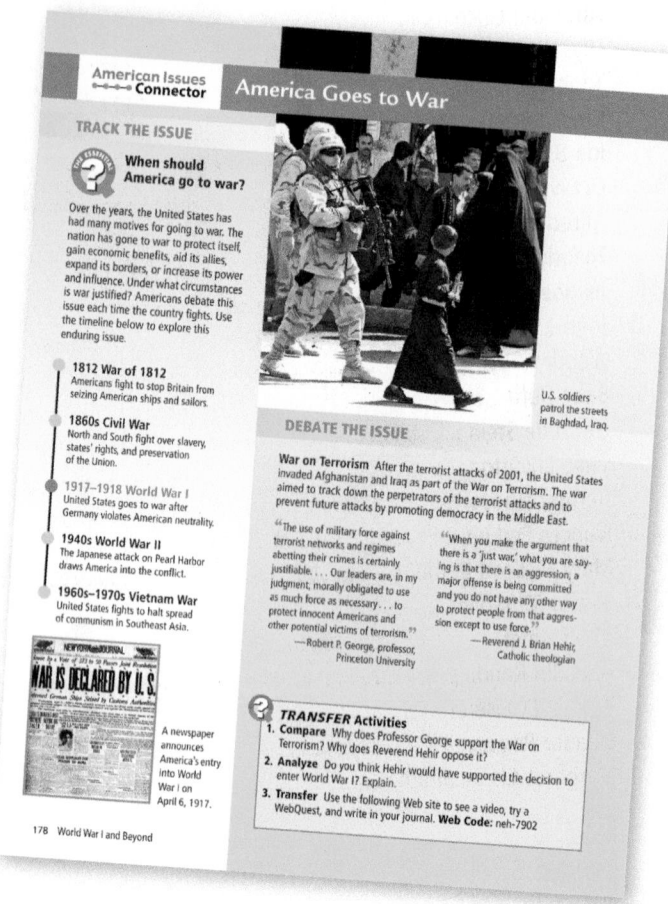

INFOGRAPHIC

Photographs, maps, charts, illustrations, and text help you understand the significance of important historical events and developments.

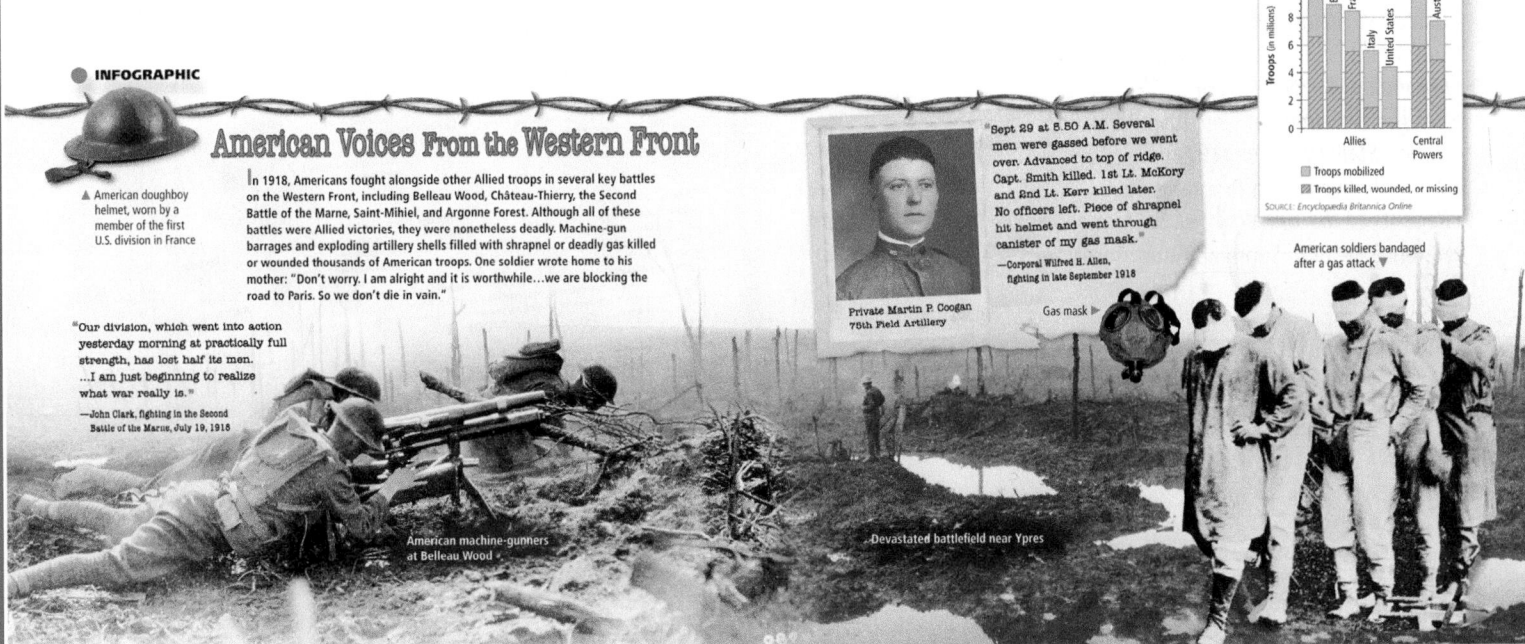

Document-Based Assessment

Practice the art and science of a historian by analyzing an event through multiple historical documents, data, and images.

Landmark Decisions of the Supreme Court

Explore key Supreme Court cases and link the decisions to today.

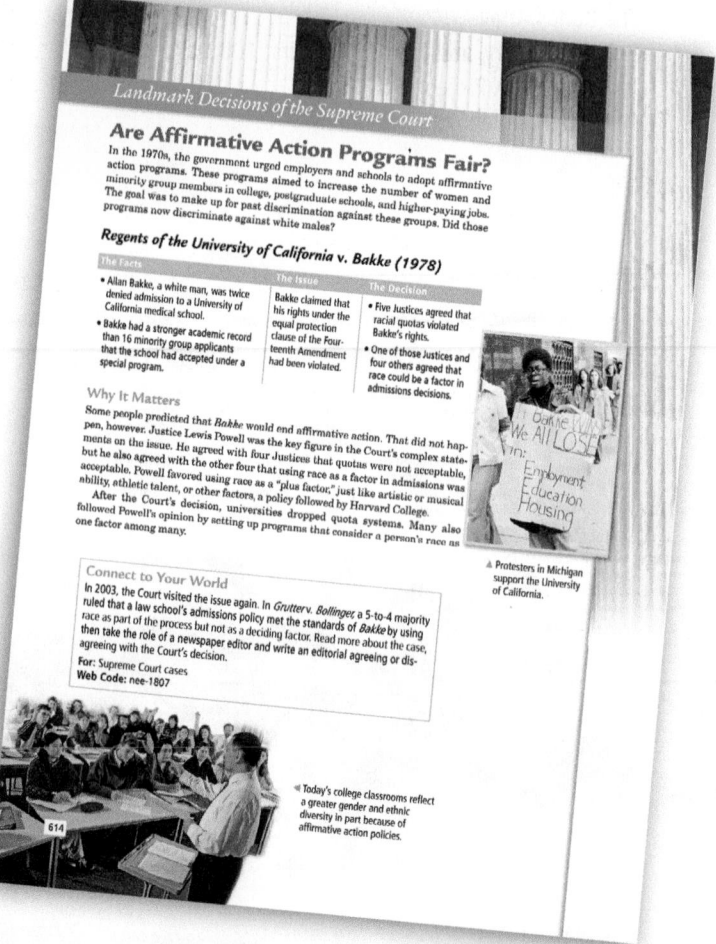

☑ Quick Study

Review key information and concepts to prepare for tests.

Charts and Graphs

Diagrams and data help you understand history through visuals.

Maps Geography *Interactive*

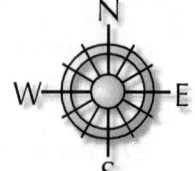

Interactive maps help you understand where history happened.

☑ Quick Study Timeline

Review key events from each chapter on illustrated timelines.

Political Cartoons

Examine how artists have expressed their points of view about events of their day.

IN THE HANDS OF HIS PHILANTHROPIC FRIENDS. 1897

Focus On Geography

See how geography has affected events in American history.

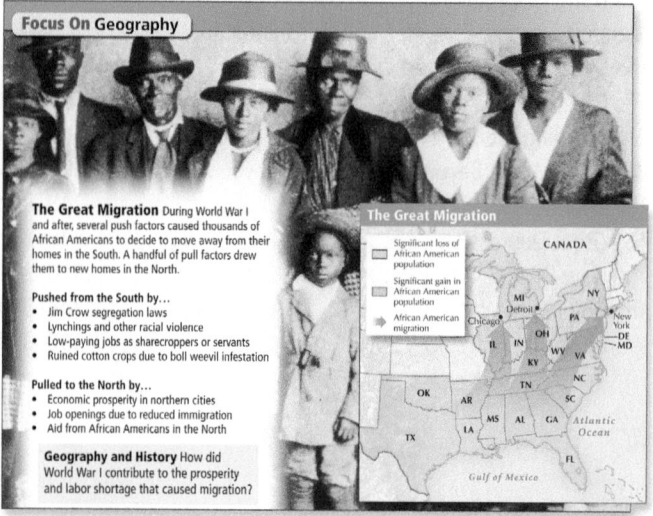

Focus On Geography

The Great Migration During World War I and after, several push factors caused thousands of African Americans to decide to move away from their homes in the South. A handful of pull factors drew them to new homes in the North.

Pushed from the South by...
- Jim Crow segregation laws
- Lynchings and other racial violence
- Low-paying jobs as sharecroppers or servants
- Ruined cotton crops due to boll weevil infestation

Pulled to the North by...
- Economic prosperity in northern cities
- Job openings due to reduced immigration
- Aid from African Americans in the North

Geography and History How did World War I contribute to the prosperity and labor shortage that caused migration?

The Great Migration

- Significant loss of African American population
- Significant gain in African American population
- African American migration

Events That Changed America

See how certain events changed the course of our nation's history.

Events That Changed America

SURPRISE ATTACK! PEARL HARBOR

December 7, 1941, dawned an overcast day in Pearl Harbor, Hawaii. The members of the U.S. military stationed there went about their usual Sunday activities. About half of the United States Navy's Pacific Fleet, including eight huge battleships, sat clustered in the harbor. At nearby Hickam Field and other airfields, American planes sat quietly wing-to-wing in perfect rows.

Just before 8 A.M., the Japanese attack on the unsuspecting Americans below had begun. Over the next several hours, Japanese bombers torpedoed the moored ships, while fighters and dive-bombers machine-gunned and bombed ship decks and airfields. American military forces, caught completely by surprise, attempted to ward off the attackers with little effect. The scene was one of utter destruction.

Sailors at Ford Island Naval Air Station are stunned by the wreckage around them. ▼

◄ The USS Arizona sank during the attack. Nearly 1,200 sailors and marines died on this ship alone.

Damage at Pearl Harbor

- Sunk or capsized
- Damaged
- Undamaged
- Battleship
- Cruiser
- Destroyer
- Submarine
- Other

▲ As the map shows, Japanese torpedoes sank or capsized six huge battleships and several smaller ships at Pearl Harbor. Most of the damaged ships were eventually repaired.

Soon, newspapers such as the *Honolulu Star-Bulletin* (below) spread grief and outrage around the country. Pearl Harbor inspired motivation for the U.S. war effort. ▼

Why It Matters

When the smoke cleared, nearly 2,500 people, including military personnel and civilians, were dead. The Pacific Fleet had taken a big hit—and there was no longer any question that the United States would enter World War II. The war would change the lives of all Americans, and its effects would ripple across the globe for decades after the last shot was fired.

Female firefighters try to douse fires after the attack. ▼

WAR! OAHU BOMBED BY JAPANESE PLANES

AVENGE December 7

Thinking Critically
How did Pearl Harbor change American opinion about the war?
History Interactive

For: More information about Pearl Harbor
www.pearsonschool.com/ushist

Discover

the enduring issues of our nation's history

The **American Issues Connector** explores the enduring questions that frame our American past, present, and future.

Here's how it works:

1 **Highlight issues as you learn**
Review issues in every chapter using the American Issues Connector Cumulative Review.

2 **Study issues in depth**
The American Issues Connector feature focuses on a modern debate about an enduring issue.

3 **Track issues over time**
Take notes in the Study Guide to prepare for thematic essays on enduring issues.

Here's an example:
What is the proper balance between national security and civil liberties?

Patrick Henry addressing Congress

1

American Issues •——•——• Connector

By connecting prior knowledge with what you have learned in this chapter, you can gradually build your understanding of enduring questions that still affect America today. Answer the questions below. Then, use your American Issues Connector study guide (or go online: www.PHSchool.com **Web Code:** neh-8503).

Issues You Learned About

● **Civil Liberties and National Security** From the beginning of the American republic, Americans have debated to what extent individual freedom should be limited when the safety of the nation is at stake.

1. How does the Bill of Rights guarantee the rights of people accused of crimes?

2. During the Civil War, what action did President Lincoln take that limited these guaranteed rights? Why?

3. During the Cold War, what effect did the actions of HUAC and Senator McCarthy have on individual rights?

● **America Goes to** debate whether U.S. er

7. What were argumen against North Korea

8. What were argumen

Connect to You

America and the Wo
when dealing with thre

2

American Issues •——•——• Connector | Civil Liberties and National Security

TRACK THE ISSUE

What is the proper balance between national security and civil liberties?

The Constitution guarantees rights and freedoms to all American citizens. But during war and other crises, government leaders have limited such civil liberties in order to protect citizens' lives. Should they? Use the timeline below to explore this enduring issue.

1790s Undeclared War With France
Alien Act allows President to imprison or deport resident aliens. Sedition Act limits freedoms of speech and press.

1860s Civil War
Lincoln suspends the right of habeas corpus.

1940s World War II
Government sends more than 100,000 Japanese Americans into internment camps.

1950s Cold War

A traveler has his baggage searched at an airport security checkpoint.

DEBATE THE ISSUE

Terrorism and the Patriot Act After the devastating terrorist attacks of September 11, 2001, the United States declared a "War on Terrorism." Congress passed the Patriot Act to help law enforcement agencies prevent future terrorist attacks. The Act was to expire in 2005. In spite of controversy regarding it, Congress voted to extend the provisions of the Patriot Act to 2009.

"I have a lot of problems with the   "Right after 9-11, the President

---

3

Name _____
Class _____ Date _____

American Issues Journal

Civil Liberties and National Security

Essential Question: What is the proper balance between national security and civil liberties?

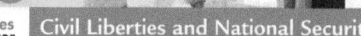

1790s Undeclared War with France Alien and Sedition Acts	**1860s Civil War** Habeas Corpus suspended	**1940s World War II** Internment of Japanese Americans	**2001 War on Terror** Patriot Act
1780	1820 1860	1900 1940	1980 2020
		1950s Cold War Red Scare	

...UP

...is history, the U.S. government has faced moments when the safety of the ...d more important than preserving all the rights and liberties of its citizens. ...n this page shows when this issue surfaced in U.S. history. ...ween national security and civil liberties in U.S. history. ...ce between safety and liberty surface in your life?

...you define the term "safe?"   **1. (b)** How do you define the term "freedom?"

...where students assemble to learn, discuss ideas, and acquire essential ...ve citizens. Schools are also organizations with rules and regulations ...fety.

...e things that you think   **2. (b)** What three freedoms do you think

Make Connections

Historians do more than study about the past as a series of separate, isolated events. They often look at key issues that Americans have grappled with throughout our history. Historians try to understand how Americans have defined and addressed each of these enduring issues at various times. The American Issues Connector system will help you recognize and trace enduring American issues across time. A list of the American Issues Connector topics can be found on page xviii.

• **American Issues Connector Features**
Each of the 21 issues that you'll be tracking this year is described in a feature in the textbook. Timelines point out important historical events. Debate the Issue and Transfer Activities show why the issue is still relevant today.

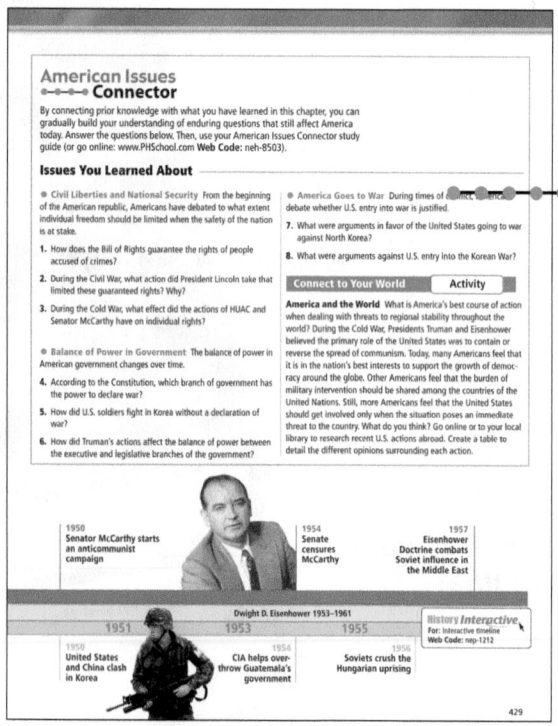

American Issues Connector Review
You can review American Issues on the American Issues Connector page at the end of each chapter. First, you can activate your prior knowledge by answering the Issues You Learned About questions. Then, through research, you will learn more by completing the Connect to Your World Activity.

• **American Issues Study Guides**
There are 21 study guides, one for each enduring issue discussed in your textbook. You can access and print the American Issues Connector Study Guides at www.pearsonschool.com/ushist. At the end of each chapter, the American Issues Connector page will remind you to record information on the study guides. Completing these study guides will help you develop a note-taking system to answer the enduring questions that still affect America today. At the end of the course, your completed study guides will prepare you for essays that may appear on tests.

Develop Key Skills

Geography *Interactive*

Historical maps are important for understanding where events took place, so we've created easy-to-read maps for your exploration. To make sure you get the most out of each map, we've also provided you with an opportunity to interact with each map online. You can access these interactive maps through www.pearsonschool.com/ushist.

Some of the maps in your textbook have interactive-online versions that will allow you to see how events shown on the map unfolded over time or will give you additional images and information to make the places shown on the map come alive.

Go Online at pearsonschool.com/ushist

Geography *Interactive*

For: Interactive Map
Visit: www.pearsonschool.com/ushist
1. Go to www.pearsonschool.com/ushist
2. Log onto your online course.
3. Go to the Interactivities folder and select your Geography Interactive map.

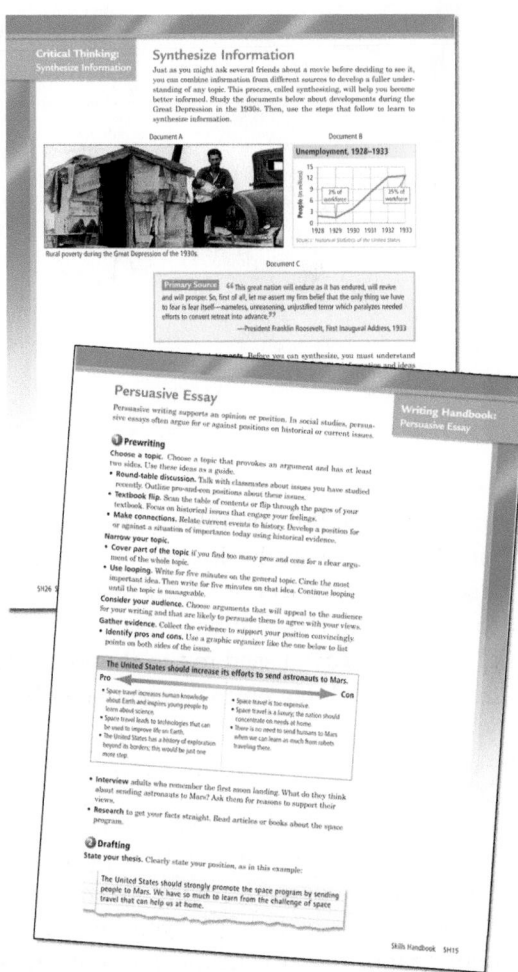

SKILLS Handbook

The Skills Handbook at the front of this textbook allows you to brush up on important skills at the beginning of the course or at any time you need help.

- **Reading Informational Text**
  Make the most of the time you spend reading the text, and improve your reading comprehension by looking at some proven reading strategies to use before you read, while you read, and after you read.

- **Writing Handbook**
  Learning to be a good writer is key to your success in this class, on tests, and in life. Use this part of the Skills Handbook to study models of good writing and to learn hints for writing various types of essays, including expository and persuasive essays.

- **Critical Thinking About Visuals and Text**
  As a practicing historian, you need to train yourself to think critically about everything you read, see, and hear. Is what you are reading accurate? Biased? Use this part of the Skills Handbook to practice your critical thinking skills.

- **Speaking and Listening**
  Speaking is another way to demonstrate what you've learned. Good listening is another key to success in every classroom. In this part of the Skills Handbook, look for key tips on how to prepare a presentation and how to listen actively.

Prepare for Tests

NoteTaking

Throughout this course, you'll be reading and studying information as it occurred chronologically. In each section of the textbook, you'll find suggestions for how to take notes using graphic organizers, timelines, and outlines. Complete these graphic organizers in your own notebook, in your Reading and Note Taking Study Guide, or on the Note Taking Worksheets for each section, which you can download at pearsonschool.com/ushist. If you complete all of the suggested notetaking strategies, your notes will prepare you for chapter, midterm, and high-stakes end-of-course tests.

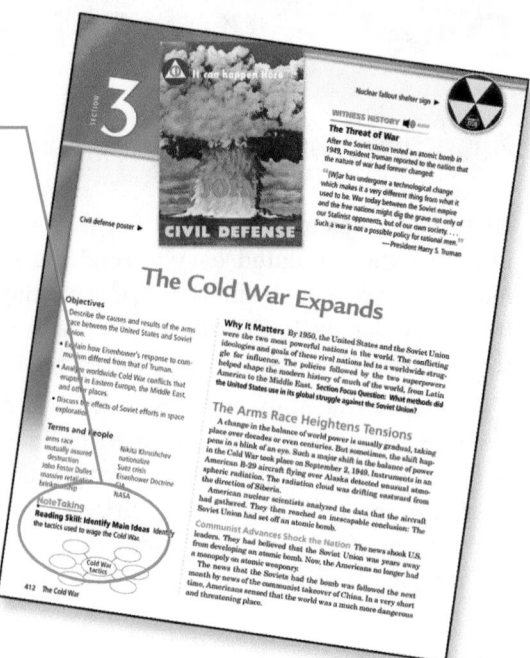

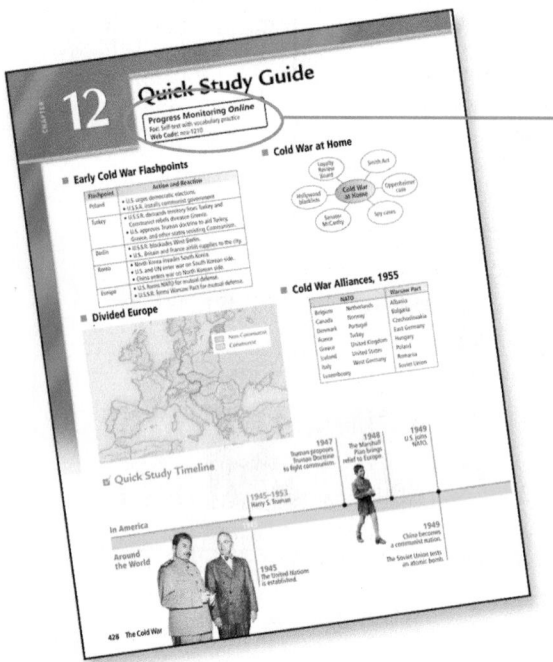

Progress Monitoring *Online*

At the end of every section, you can take an online quiz with multiple-choice questions on section content and vocabulary. At the end of every chapter, you'll find an online self-test on chapter content and a crossword puzzle to test your vocabulary mastery. Both quizzes and tests provide you with instant help so you can be sure you have grasped key content.

Go Online at pearsonschool.com/ushist

Progress Monitoring *Online*
For: Self-test with vocabulary practice
www.pearsonschool.com/ushist

Quick Study Guide

In addition to the notetaking graphics that you create yourself, we've provided some for each chapter on the end-of-chapter Quick Study pages. Use these pages to review for tests and to make sure you have mastered the content in the chapter. The Quick Study pages also include a timeline of key events discussed in the chapter. Interactive versions of these timelines are available online at pearsonschool.com/ushist.

Document-Based Assessment

To prepare you for document-based questions on in-class and high-stakes tests, each chapter ends with a page of Document-Based Assessment. Each of these pages contains several documents followed by multiple-choice questions that help you analyze documents and practice your map, graph, visual learning, and critical reading skills. A writing task helps you analyze and draw conclusions about the various documents.

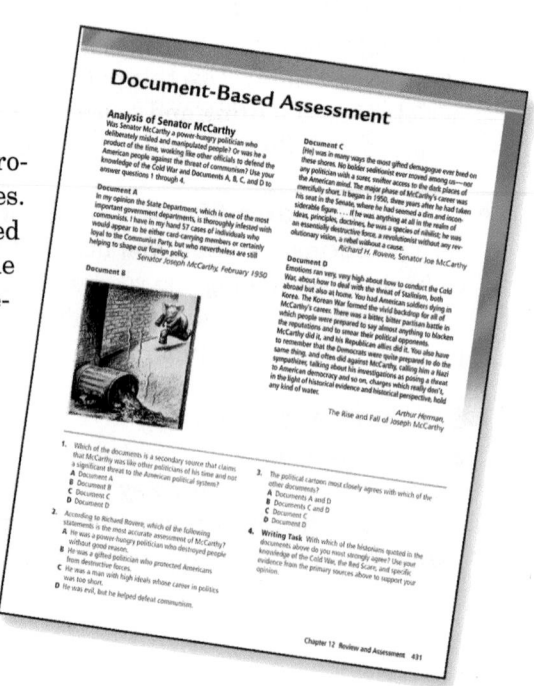

Common Core State Standards for Literacy in History/Social Studies, Grades 9–10, 11–12

© Common Core State Standards for Literacy in History/Social Studies, Grades 9–10, 11–12	PRENTICE HALL UNITED STATES HISTORY

History/Social Studies, Grades 9–10

Key Ideas and Details

1. Cite specific textual evidence to support analysis of primary and secondary sources, attending to such features as the date and origin of the information.	Primary Sources, pages 198, 339, 405, 485, 638, 725–744 Document-Based Assessment Questions, pages 31, 63, 95, 135, 167, 207, 251, 281, 319, 351, 395, 431, 463, 501, 529, 567, 595, 623, 653, 687
2. Determine the central ideas or information of a primary or secondary source; provide an accurate summary of how key events or ideas develop over the course of the text.	Primary Sources, pages 198, 339, 405, 485, 638, 725–744 In-Text Primary Source, pages 14, 40, 45, 52, 58, 71, 76, 86, 90, 102, 111, 122, 129, 139, 148, 152, 161, 174, 179, 187, 193, 217, 220, 228, 230, 238, 239, 245, 246, 255, 262, 265, 269, 276, 285, 291, 295, 297, 298, 302, 304, 306, 313, 328, 332, 334, 341, 357, 365, 371, 374, 379, 385, 389, 391, 402, 404, 407, 414, 426, 450, 456, 457, 473, 478, 481, 489, 492, 493, 507, 512, 518, 521, 534, 541, 542, 545, 553, 555, 562, 571, 575, 584, 589, 601, 604, 605, 613, 618, 631, 635, 641, 664, 675 Decision Point, pages 18, 196, 378, 410 Political Cartoons, pages 46, 88, 101, 122, 127, 160, 167, 175, 196, 207, 219, 225, 281, 289, 298, 319, 336, 394, 421, 431, 513, 543, 595, 623, 641, 667, 687
3. Analyze in detail a series of events described in a text; determine whether earlier events caused later ones or simply preceded them.	Cause-and-Effect Charts, pages 28, 59, 60, 204, 278, 308, 390 Events That Changed America, pages 112, 294, 342, 372, 482, 602, 642, 674

Craft and Structure

4. Determine the meaning of words and phrases as they are used in a text, including vocabulary describing political, social, or economic aspects of history/social science.	Chapter Assessments, Terms and People sections, pages 30, 62, 94, 134, 166, 206, 250, 280, 318, 350, 394, 430, 462, 500, 528, 566, 594, 622, 652, 686
5. Analyze how a text uses structure to emphasize key points or advance an explanation or analysis.	Primary Sources, pages 198, 339, 405, 485, 638, 725–744
6. Compare the point of view of two or more authors for how they treat the same or similar topics, including which details they include and emphasize in their respective accounts.	Comparing Viewpoints, pages 117, 225, 290, 399, 506, 548, 577 American Issues Connector, pages 7, 19, 26, 37, 44, 57, 70, 77, 83, 91, 115, 142, 178, 226, 305, 424, 491, 519, 558, 590, 682

Integration of Knowledge and Ideas

7. Integrate quantitative or technical analysis (e.g., charts, research data) with qualitative analysis in print or digital text.	Infographic features, pages 10, 38, 46, 51, 68, 75, 102, 122, 146, 152, 162, 176, 183, 192, 214, 228, 235, 256, 263, 275, 286, 306, 326, 358, 382, 403, 414, 422, 436, 442, 451, 474, 479, 494, 514, 520, 540, 549, 556, 572, 582, 612, 618, 636, 659, 668
	Maps Geography Interactive, pages 5, 11, 13, 24, 28, 40, 46, 53, 85, 114, 125, 129, 141, 149, 158, 160, 162, 164, 172, 176, 191, 195, 200, 214, 266, 281, 286, 306, 328, 333, 343, 346, 372, 374, 376, 388, 401, 403, 408, 409, 416, 428, 438, 444, 460, 470, 479, 509, 533, 539, 547, 550, 564, 565, 588, 601, 611, 632, 648, 650, 672, 676, 684, 692, 694, 695, 696, 697, 698, 699, 700
	Charts and Graphs, pages 20, 28, 29, C3, C6, C9, C13, 35, 54, 57, 59, 60, 92, 105, 129, 130, 132, 135, 140, 147, 149, 159, 164, 165, 166, 171, 174, 181, 183, 191, 193, 198, 204, 213, 216, 217, 221, 224, 235, 238, 240, 241, 248, 256, 257, 260, 262, 263, 266, 274, 278, 280, 286, 293, 295, 296, 297, 299, 303, 305, 308, 309, 316, 318, 325, 337, 344, 348, 350, 351, 358, 365, 377, 390, 392, 395, 402, 411, 413, 414, 428, 430, 435, 436, 438, 441, 458, 460, 463, 476, 490, 494, 496, 498, 505, 508, 518, 526, 528, 529, 539, 545, 549, 550, 553, 564, 566, 572, 578, 581, 583, 589, 592, 594, 599, 601, 603, 605, 609, 610, 611, 620, 629, 632, 634, 640, 648, 650, 652, 653, 658, 659, 660, 663, 664, 668, 672, 680, 681, 682, 684
8. Assess the extent to which the reasoning and evidence in a text support the author's claims.	Primary Sources, pages 198, 339, 405, 485, 638, 725–744
	Comparing Viewpoints, pages 117, 225, 290, 399, 506, 548, 577
	American Issues Connector, pages 7, 19, 26, 37, 44, 57, 70, 77, 83, 91, 115, 142, 178, 226, 305, 424, 491, 519, 558, 590, 682
9. Compare and contrast treatments of the same topic in several primary and secondary sources.	Document-Based Assessment Questions, pages 31, 63, 95, 135, 167, 207, 251, 281, 319, 351, 395, 431, 463, 623
	Comparing Viewpoints, pages 117, 225, 290, 399, 506, 548, 577

Range of Reading and Level of Text Complexity

10. By the end of grade 10, read and comprehend history/social studies texts in the grades 9–10 text complexity band independently and proficiently.	This objective is met throughout, *Prentice Hall United States History,* including:
	American Humanities, pages 108, 247, 277, 315, 454, 497, 579
	American Issues Connectors, pages 7, 19, 26, 37, 44, 57, 70, 77, 83, 91, 115, 142, 178, 226, 305, 424, 491, 519, 558, 590, 682
	Landmark Decisions of the Supreme Court, pages 188, 367, 476, 516, 525, 606, 614, 714

Writing, Grades 9–10

Text Types and Purposes

1. Write arguments focused on *discipline-specific content*. **a.** Introduce precise claim(s), distinguish the claim(s) from alternate or opposing claims, and create an organization that establishes clear relationships among the claim(s), counterclaims, reasons, and evidence. **b.** Develop claim(s) and counterclaims fairly, supplying data and evidence for each while pointing out the strengths and limitations of both claim(s) and counterclaims in a discipline-appropriate form and in a manner that anticipates the audience's knowledge level and concerns. **c.** Use words, phrases, and clauses to link the major sections of the text, create cohesion, and clarify the relationships between claim(s) and reasons, between reasons and evidence, and between claim(s) and counterclaims. **d.** Establish and maintain a formal style and objective tone while attending to the norms and conventions of the discipline in which they are writing. **e.** Provide a concluding statement or section that follows from and supports the argument presented.	Section Assessment Writing About History Activities, pages 8, 14, 20, 27, 41, 47, 54, 59, 72, 79, 86, 90, 107, 114, 120, 127, 131, 143, 150, 155, 163, 179, 187, 197, 203, 217, 222, 230, 239, 246, 260, 269, 276, 291, 299, 309, 314, 330, 338, 347, 360, 366, 379, 385, 391, 404, 411, 417, 427, 439, 447, 453, 459, 475, 484, 496, 510, 515, 524, 536, 543, 551, 559, 563, 573, 578,585, 591, 605, 613, 619, 632, 637, 644, 649, 660, 665, 670, 678, 683 Chapter Assessment Writing About History Activities, pages 30, 62, 94, 134, 166, 206, 250, 280, 318, 350, 394, 430, 462, 462, 500, 528, 566, 594, 622, 652, 686
2. Write informative/explanatory texts, including the narration of historical events, scientific procedures/ experiments, or technical processes. **a.** Introduce a topic and organize ideas, concepts, and information to make important connections and distinctions; include formatting (e.g., headings), graphics (e.g., figures, tables), and multimedia when useful to aiding comprehension. **b.** Develop the topic with well-chosen, relevant, and sufficient facts, extended definitions, concrete details, quotations, or other information and examples appropriate to the audience's knowledge of the topic. **c.** Use varied transitions and sentence structures to link the major sections of the text, create cohesion, and clarify the relationships among ideas and concepts. **d.** Use precise language and domain-specific vocabulary to manage the complexity of the topic and convey a style appropriate to the discipline and context as well as to the expertise of likely readers. **e.** Establish and maintain a formal style and objective tone while attending to the norms and conventions of the discipline in which they are writing. **f.** Provide a concluding statement or section that follows from and supports the information or explanation presented (e.g., articulating implications or the significance of the topic).	Section Assessment Writing About History Activities, pages 8, 14, 20, 27, 41, 47, 54, 59, 72, 79, 86, 90, 107, 114, 120, 127, 131, 143, 150, 155, 163, 179, 187, 197, 203, 217, 222, 230, 239, 246, 260, 269, 276, 291, 299, 309, 314, 330, 338, 347, 360, 366, 379, 385, 391, 404, 411, 417, 427, 439, 447, 453, 459, 475, 484, 496, 510, 515, 524, 536, 543, 551, 559, 563, 573, 578,585, 591, 605, 613, 619, 632, 637, 644, 649, 660, 665, 670, 678, 683 Chapter Assessment Writing About History Activities, pages 30, 62, 94, 134, 166, 206, 250, 280, 318, 350, 394, 430, 462, 462, 500, 528, 566, 594, 622, 652, 686
3. (See note; not applicable as a separate requirement)	Not applicable.

Production and Distribution of Writing

4. Produce clear and coherent writing in which the development, organization, and style are appropriate to task, purpose, and audience.	Section Assessment Writing About History Activities, pages 8, 14, 20, 27, 41, 47, 54, 59, 72, 79, 86, 90, 107, 114, 120, 127, 131, 143, 150, 155, 163, 179, 187, 197, 203, 217, 222, 230, 239, 246, 260, 269, 276, 291, 299, 309, 314, 330, 338, 347, 360, 366, 379, 385, 391, 404, 411, 417, 427, 439, 447, 453, 459, 475, 484, 496, 510, 515, 524, 536, 543, 551, 559, 563, 573, 578, 585, 591, 605, 613, 619, 632, 637, 644, 649, 660, 665, 670, 678, 683
	Chapter Assessment Writing About History Activities, pages 30, 62, 94, 134, 166, 206, 250, 280, 318, 350, 394, 430, 462, 462, 500, 528, 566, 594, 622, 652, 686
	Document-Based Assessment Writing Task, pages 31, 63, 95, 135, 167, 207, 251, 281, 319, 351, 395, 431, 463, 501, 529, 567, 595, 623, 653, 687
5. Develop and strengthen writing as needed by planning, revising, editing, rewriting, or trying a new approach, focusing on addressing what is most significant for a specific purpose and audience.	Chapter Assessment Writing About History Activities, pages 30, 62, 94, 134, 166, 206, 250, 280, 318, 350, 394, 430, 462, 462, 500, 528, 566, 594, 622, 652, 686
6. Use technology, including the Internet, to produce, publish, and update individual or shared writing products, taking advantage of technology's capacity to link to other information and to display information flexibly and dynamically.	History Interactive features (pearsonschool.com/ushist), pages 10, 28, 38, 60, 68, 92, 102, 132, 152, 164, 192, 204, 214, 240, 248, 266, 270, 278, 294, 316, 342, 348, 368, 372, 392, 403, 418, 428, 442, 454, 460, 482, 486, 498, 520, 526, 540, 564, 572, 592, 602, 620, 642, 650, 684

Research to Build and Present Knowledge

7. Conduct short as well as more sustained research projects to answer a question (including a self-generated question) or solve a problem; narrow or broaden the inquiry when appropriate; synthesize multiple sources on the subject, demonstrating understanding of the subject under investigation.	History Interactive features (pearsonschool.com/ushist), pages 10, 28, 38, 60, 68, 92, 102, 132, 152, 164, 192, 204, 214, 240, 248, 266, 270, 278, 294, 316, 342, 348, 368, 372, 392, 403, 418, 428, 442, 454, 460, 482, 486, 498, 520, 526, 540, 564, 572, 592, 602, 620, 642, 650, 684
8. Gather relevant information from multiple authoritative print and digital sources, using advanced searches effectively; assess the usefulness of each source in answering the research question; integrate information into the text selectively to maintain the flow of ideas, avoiding plagiarism and following a standard format for citation.	Primary Sources, pages 198, 339, 405, 485, 638, 725–744
	Section Assessment Writing About History Activities, pages 8, 14, 20, 27, 41, 47, 54, 59, 72, 79, 86, 90, 107, 114, 120, 127, 131, 143, 150, 155, 163, 179, 187, 197, 203, 217, 222, 230, 239, 246, 260, 269, 276, 291, 299, 309, 314, 330, 338, 347, 360, 366, 379, 385, 391, 404, 411, 417, 427, 439, 447, 453, 459
	Connect to Your World Activities, pages 29, 61, 93, 133, 165, 205, 249, 279, 317, 349, 393, 429, 461, 499, 527, 565, 593, 621, 651, 685
	Chapter Assessment Writing About History Activities, pages 30, 62, 94, 134, 166, 206, 250, 280, 318, 350, 394, 430, 462, 462
9. Draw evidence from informational texts to support analysis, reflection, and research.	Primary Sources, pages 198, 339, 405, 485, 638, 725, 734
	Landmark Decisions of the Supreme Court pages 188, 367, 476, 516, 525, 606, 614, 714
	Document-Based Assessment Writing Task, pages 31, 63, 95, 135, 167, 207, 251, 281, 319, 351, 395, 431, 463, 501, 529, 567, 595, 623, 653, 687

Range of Writing

10. Write routinely over extended time frames (time for reflection and revision) and shorter time frames (a single sitting or a day or two) for a range of discipline-specific tasks, purposes, and audiences.	Section Assessment Writing About History Activities, pages 8, 14, 20, 27, 41, 47, 54, 59, 72, 79, 86, 90, 107, 114, 120, 127, 131, 143, 150, 155, 163, 179, 187, 197, 203, 217, 222, 230, 239, 246, 260, 269, 276, 291, 299, 309, 314, 330, 338, 347, 360, 366, 379, 385, 391, 404, 411, 417, 427, 439, 447, 453, 459, 475, 484, 496, 510, 515, 524, 536, 543, 551, 559, 563, 573, 578,585, 591, 605, 613, 619, 632, 637, 644, 649, 660, 665, 670, 678, 683
	Chapter Assessment Writing About History Activities, pages 30, 62, 94, 134, 166, 206, 250, 280, 318, 350, 394, 430, 462, 462, 500, 528, 566, 594, 622, 652, 686

History/Social Studies, Grades 11–12

Key Ideas and Details

1. Cite specific textual evidence to support analysis of primary and secondary sources, connecting insights gained from specific details to an understanding of the text as a whole.	Primary Sources, pages 198, 339, 405, 485, 638, 725–744 Document-Based Assessment Questions, pages 31, 63, 95, 135, 167, 207, 251, 281, 319, 351, 395, 431, 463, 501, 529, 567, 595, 623, 653, 687
2. Determine the central ideas or information of a primary or secondary source; provide an accurate summary that makes clear the relationships among the key details and ideas.	Primary Sources, pages 198, 339, 405, 485, 638, 725–744 In-Text Primary Source, pages 14, 40, 45, 52, 58, 71, 76, 86, 90, 102, 111, 122, 129, 139, 148, 152, 161, 174, 179, 187, 193, 217, 220, 228, 230, 238, 239, 245, 246, 255, 262, 265, 269, 276, 285, 291, 295, 297, 298, 302, 304, 306, 313, 328, 332, 334, 341, 357, 365, 371, 374, 379, 385, 389, 391, 402, 404, 407, 414, 426, 450, 456, 457, 473, 478, 481, 489, 492, 493, 507, 512, 518, 521, 534, 541, 542, 545, 553, 555, 562, 571, 575, 584, 589, 601, 604, 605, 613, 618, 631, 635, 641, 664, 675 Decision Point, pages 18, 196, 378, 410 Political Cartoons, pages 46, 88, 101, 122, 127, 160, 167, 175, 196, 207, 219, 225, 281, 289, 298, 319, 336, 394, 421, 431, 513, 543, 595, 623, 641, 667, 687
3. Evaluate various explanations for actions or events and determine which explanation best accords with textual evidence, acknowledging where the text leaves matters uncertain.	Cause-and-Effect Charts, pages 28, 59, 60, 204, 278, 308, 390

Craft and Structure

4. Determine the meaning of words and phrases as they are used in a text, including analyzing how an author uses and refines the meaning of a key term over the course of a text (e.g., how Madison defines *faction* in *Federalist* No. 10).	Chapter Assessments, Terms and People sections, pages 30, 62, 94, 134, 166, 206, 250, 280, 318, 350, 394, 430, 462, 462, 500, 528, 566, 594, 622, 652, 686
5. Analyze in detail how a complex primary source is structured, including how key sentences, paragraphs, and larger portions of the text contribute to the whole.	Primary Sources, pages 198, 339, 405, 485, 638, 725–744
6. Evaluate authors' differing points of view on the same historical event or issue by assessing the authors' claims, reasoning, and evidence.	Comparing Viewpoints, pages 117, 225, 290, 399, 506, 548, 577

Integration of Knowledge and Ideas

7. Integrate and evaluate multiple sources of information presented in diverse formats and media (e.g., visually, quantitatively, as well as in words) in order to address a question or solve a problem.	Infographic features, pages 10, 38, 46, 51, 68, 75, 102, 122, 146, 152, 162, 176, 183, 192, 214, 228, 235, 256, 263, 275, 286, 306, 326, 358, 382, 403, 414, 422, 436, 442, 451, 474, 479, 494, 514, 520, 540, 549, 556, 572, 582, 612, 618, 636, 659, 668
	Maps Geography Interactive, pages 5, 11, 13, 24, 28, 40, 46, 53, 85, 114, 125, 129, 141, 149, 158, 160, 162, 164, 172, 176, 191, 195, 200, 214, 266, 281, 286, 306, 328, 333, 343, 346, 372, 374, 376, 388, 401, 403, 408, 409, 409, 416, 428, 438, 444, 460, 470, 479, 509, 533, 539, 547, 550, 564, 565, 588, 601, 611, 632, 648, 650, 672, 676, 684, 692, 694, 695, 696, 697, 698, 699, 700
	Charts and Graphs, pages 20, 28, 29, C3, C6, C9, C13, 35, 54, 57, 59, 60, 92, 105, 129, 130, 132, 135, 140, 147, 149, 159, 164, 165, 166, 171, 174, 181, 183, 191, 193, 198, 204, 213, 216, 217, 221, 224, 235, 238, 240, 241, 248, 256, 257, 260, 262, 263, 266, 274, 278, 280, 286, 293, 295, 296, 297, 299, 303, 305, 308, 309, 316, 318, 325, 337, 344, 348, 350, 351, 358, 365, 377, 390, 392, 395, 402, 411, 413, 414, 428, 430, 435, 436, 438, 441, 458, 460, 463, 476, 490, 494, 496, 498, 505, 508, 518, 526, 528, 529, 539, 545, 549, 550, 553, 564, 566, 572, 578, 581, 583, 589, 592, 594, 599, 601, 603, 605, 609, 610, 611, 620, 629, 632, 634, 640, 648, 650, 652, 653, 658, 659, 660, 663, 664, 668, 672, 680, 681, 682, 684
8. Evaluate an author's premises, claims, and evidence by corroborating or challenging them with other information.	Primary Sources, pages 198, 339, 405, 485, 638, 725–744
	Comparing Viewpoints, pages 117, 225, 290, 399, 506, 548, 577
	American Issues Connector, pages 7, 19, 26, 37, 44, 57, 70, 77, 83, 91, 115, 142, 178, 226, 305, 424, 491, 519, 558, 590, 682
9. Integrate information from diverse sources, both primary and secondary, into a coherent understanding of an idea or event, noting discrepancies among sources.	Document-Based Assessment Questions, pages 31, 63, 95, 135, 167, 207, 251, 281, 319, 351, 395, 431, 463, 501, 529, 567
	Comparing Viewpoints, pages 117, 225, 290, 399, 506, 548, 577

Range of Reading and Level of Text Complexity

10. By the end of grade 12, read and comprehend history/social studies texts in the grades 11–CCR text complexity band independently and proficiently.	This objective is met throughout *Prentice Hall United States History,* including:
	American Humanities, pages 108, 247, 277, 315, 454, 497, 579
	American Issues Connectors, pages 7, 19, 26, 37, 44, 57, 70, 77, 83, 91, 115, 142, 178, 226, 305, 424, 491, 519, 558, 590
	Landmark Decisions of the Supreme Court, pages 188, 367, 476, 516, 525, 606, 614, 714–723

Common Core State Standards for Literacy in
History/Social Studies, Grades 9–10, 11–12

PRENTICE HALL
UNITED STATES
HISTORY

Common Core State Standards Program Correlation

Writing, Grades 11-12

Text Types and Purposes

1. Write arguments focused on discipline-specific content. **a.** Introduce precise, knowledgeable claim(s), establish the significance of the claim(s), distinguish the claim(s) from alternate or opposing claims, and create an organization that logically sequences the claim(s), counterclaims, reasons, and evidence. **b.** Develop claim(s) and counterclaims fairly and thoroughly, supplying the most relevant data and evidence for each while pointing out the strengths and limitations of both claim(s) and counterclaims in a discipline-appropriate form that anticipates the audience's knowledge level, concerns, values, and possible biases. **c.** Use words, phrases, and clauses as well as varied syntax to link the major sections of the text, create cohesion, and clarify the relationships between claim(s) and reasons, between reasons and evidence, and between claim(s) and counterclaims. **d.** Establish and maintain a formal style and objective tone while attending to the norms and conventions of the discipline in which they are writing. **e.** Provide a concluding statement or section that follows from and supports the argument presented.	Section Assessment Writing About History Activities, pages 8, 14, 20, 27, 41, 47, 54, 59, 72, 79, 86, 90, 107, 114, 120, 127, 131, 143, 150, 155, 163, 179, 187, 197, 203, 217, 222, 230, 239, 246, 260, 269, 276, 291, 299, 309,314, 330, 338, 347, 360, 366, 379, 385, 391, 404, 411, 417, 427, 439, 447, 453, 459, 475, 484, 496, 510, 515, 524, 536, 543, 551, 559, 563, 573, 578,585, 591, 605, 613, 619, 632, 637, 644, 649, 660, 665, 670, 678, 683 Chapter Assessment Writing About History Activities, pages 30, 62, 94, 134, 166, 206, 250, 280, 318, 350, 394, 430, 462, 462, 500, 528, 566, 594, 622, 652, 686
2. Write informative/explanatory texts, including the narration of historical events, scientific procedures/ experiments, or technical processes. **a.** Introduce a topic and organize complex ideas, concepts, and information so that each new element builds on that which precedes it to create a unified whole; include formatting (e.g., headings), graphics (e.g., figures, tables), and multimedia when useful to aiding comprehension. **b.** Develop the topic thoroughly by selecting the most significant and relevant facts, extended definitions, concrete details, quotations, or other information and examples appropriate to the audience's knowledge of the topic. **c.** Use varied transitions and sentence structures to link the major sections of the text, create cohesion, and clarify the relationships among ideas and concepts. **d.** Use varied transitions and sentence structures to link the major sections of the text, create cohesion, and clarify the relationships among complex ideas and concepts. **e.** Use precise language, domain-specific vocabulary and techniques such as metaphor, simile, and analogy to manage the complexity of the topic; convey a knowledgeable stance in a style that responds to the discipline and context as well as to the expertise of likely readers. **f.** Provide a concluding statement or section that follows from and supports the information or explanation provided (e.g., articulating implications or the significance of the topic).	Section Assessment Writing About History Activities, pages 8, 14, 20, 27, 41, 47, 54, 59, 72, 79, 86, 90, 107, 114, 120, 127, 131, 143, 150, 155, 163, 179, 187, 197, 203, 217, 222, 230, 239, 246, 260, 269, 276, 291, 299, 309,314, 330, 338, 347, 360, 366, 379, 385, 391, 404, 411, 417, 427, 439, 447, 453, 459, 475, 484, 496, 510, 515, 524, 536, 543, 551, 559, 563, 573, 578,585, 591, 605, 613, 619, 632, 637, 644, 649, 660, 665, 670, 678, 683 Chapter Assessment Writing About History Activities, pages 30, 62, 94, 134, 166, 206, 250, 280, 318, 350, 394, 430, 462, 462, 500, 528, 566, 594, 622, 652, 686
3. (See note; not applicable as a separate requirement)	Not applicable.

Production and Distribution of Writing

4. Produce clear and coherent writing in which the development, organization, and style are appropriate to task, purpose, and audience.	Section Assessment Writing About History Activities, pages 8, 14, 20, 27, 41, 47, 54, 59, 72, 79, 86, 90, 107, 114, 120, 127, 131, 143, 150, 155, 163, 179, 187, 197, 203, 217, 222, 230, 239, 246, 260, 269, 276, 291, 299, 309, 314, 330, 338, 347, 360, 366, 379, 385, 391, 404, 411, 417, 427, 439, 447, 453, 459, 475, 484, 496, 510, 515, 524, 536, 543, 551, 559, 563, 573, 578,585, 591, 605, 613, 619, 632, 637, 644, 649, 660, 665, 670, 678, 683
	Chapter Assessment Writing About History Activities, pages 30, 62, 94, 134, 166, 206, 250, 280, 318, 350, 394, 430, 462, 462, 500, 528, 566, 594, 622, 652, 686
	Document-Based Assessment Writing Task, pages 31, 63, 95, 135, 167, 207, 251, 281, 319, 351, 395, 431, 463, 501, 529, 567, 595, 623, 653, 687
5. Develop and strengthen writing as needed by planning, revising, editing, rewriting, or trying a new approach, focusing on addressing what is most significant for a specific purpose and audience.	Chapter Assessment Writing About History Activities, pages 30, 62, 94, 134, 166, 206, 250, 280, 318, 350, 394, 430, 462, 500, 528, 566, 594, 622, 652, 686
6. Use technology, including the Internet, to produce, publish, and update individual or shared writing products in response to ongoing feedback, including new arguments or information.	History Interactive features (pearsonschool.com/ushist), pages 10, 28, 38, 60, 68, 92, 102, 132, 152, 164, 192, 204, 214, 240, 248, 266, 270, 278, 294, 316, 342, 348, 368, 372, 392, 403, 418, 428, 442, 454, 460, 482, 486, 498, 520, 526, 540, 564, 572, 592, 602, 620, 642, 650, 684

Research to Build and Present Knowledge

7. Conduct short as well as more sustained research projects to answer a question (including a self-generated question) or solve a problem; narrow or broaden the inquiry when appropriate; synthesize multiple sources on the subject, demonstrating understanding of the subject under investigation.	History Interactive features (pearsonschool.com/ushist), pages 10, 28, 38, 60, 68, 92, 102, 132, 152, 164, 192, 204, 214, 240, 248, 266, 270, 278, 294, 316, 342, 348, 368, 372, 392, 403, 418, 428, 442, 454, 460, 482, 486, 498, 520, 526, 540, 564, 572, 592, 602, 620, 642, 650, 684
8. Gather relevant information from multiple authoritative print and digital sources, using advanced searches effectively; assess the strengths and limitations of each source in terms of the specific task, purpose, and audience; integrate information into the text selectively to maintain the flow of ideas, avoiding plagiarism and overreliance on any one source and following a standard format for citation.	Primary Sources, pages 198, 339, 405, 485, 638, 725–744
	Section Assessment Writing About History Activities, pages 8, 14, 20, 27, 41, 47, 54, 59, 72, 79, 86, 90, 107, 114, 120, 127, 131, 143, 150, 155, 163, 179, 187, 197, 203, 217, 222, 230, 239, 246, 260, 269, 276, 291, 299, 309, 314, 330, 338, 347, 360, 366, 379, 385, 391, 404, 411, 417, 427, 439, 447, 453, 459
	Connect to Your World Activities, pages 29, 61, 93, 133, 165, 205, 249, 279, 317, 349, 393, 429, 461, 499, 527, 565, 593, 621, 651, 685
	Chapter Assessment Writing About History Activities, pages 62, 94, 134, 166, 206, 250, 280, 318, 350, 394, 430, 462
9. Draw evidence from informational texts to support analysis, reflection, and research.	Primary Sources, pages 198, 339, 405, 485, 638, 725–744
	Landmark Decisions of the Supreme Court; Era Reflections, pages 188, 367, 476, 516, 525, 606, 614, 714-723; SH32, 96, 208, 320, 464, 624, 688
	Document-Based Assessment Writing Task, pages 31, 63, 95, 135, 167, 207, 251, 281, 319, 351, 395, 431, 463, 501, 529, 567, 595, 623, 653, 687

Range of Writing

10. Write routinely over extended time frames (time for reflection and revision) and shorter time frames (a single sitting or a day or two) for a range of discipline-specific tasks, purposes, and audiences.	Section Assessment Writing About History Activities, pages 8, 14, 20, 27, 41, 47, 54, 59, 72, 79, 86, 90, 107, 114, 120, 127, 131, 143, 150, 155, 163, 179, 187, 197, 203, 217, 222, 230, 239, 246, 260, 269, 276, 291, 299, 309, 314, 330, 338, 347, 360, 366, 379, 385, 391, 404, 411, 417, 427, 439, 447, 453, 459, 475, 484, 496, 510, 515, 524, 536, 543, 551, 559, 563, 573, 578, 585, 591, 605, 613, 619, 632, 637, 644, 649, 660, 665, 670, 678, 683
	Chapter Assessment Writing About History Activities, pages 30, 62, 94, 134, 166, 206, 250, 280, 318, 350, 394, 430, 462, 462, 500, 528, 566, 594, 622, 652, 686

Common Core Reading Skills Alignment

Prentice Hall US History Modern Reading Skills	Common Core Standards for ELA Reading Informational Text, Grades 9–10/11–12
Chapter 1 **Section 1:** • Identify Causes and Effects **Section 2:** • Recognize Sequence **Section 3:** • Recognize Sequence **Section 4:** • Categorize	**RI.9-10.3** Analyze how the author unfolds an analysis or series of ideas or events, including the order in which the points are made, how they are introduced and developed, and the connections that are drawn between them. **RI.9-10.7** Analyze various accounts of a subject told in different mediums, determining which details are emphasized in each account. **RI.11-12.2** Determine two or more central ideas of a text and analyze their development over the course of the text, including how they interact and build on one another to provide a complex analysis; provide an objective summary of the text. **RI.11-12.3** Analyze a complex set of ideas or sequence of events and explain how specific individuals, ideas, or events interact and develop over the course of the text.
Chapter 2 **Section 1:** • Identify Main Ideas **Section 2:** • Recognize Main Ideas **Section 3:** • Recognize Sequence **Section 4:** • Categorize	**RI.9-10.2** Determine a central idea of a text and analyze its development over the course of the text, including how it emerges and is shaped and refined by specific details; provide an objective summary of the text. **RI.9-10.3** Analyze how the author unfolds an analysis or series of ideas or events, including the order in which the points are made, how they are introduced and developed, and the connections that are drawn between them. **RI.9-10.7** Analyze various accounts of a subject told in different mediums, determining which details are emphasized in each account. **RI.11-12.2** Determine two or more central ideas of a text and analyze their development over the course of the text, including how they interact and build on one another to provide a complex analysis; provide an objective summary of the text. **RI.11-12.3** Analyze a complex set of ideas or sequence of events and explain how specific individuals, ideas, or events interact and develop over the course of the text.
Chapter 3 **Section 1:** • Identify Causes and Effects **Section 2:** • Understand Effects **Section 3:** • Summarize **Section 4:** • Recognize Multiple Causes	**RI.9-10.3** Analyze how the author unfolds an analysis or series of ideas or events, including the order in which the points are made, how they are introduced and developed, and the connections that are drawn between them. **RI.11-12.2** Determine two or more central ideas of a text and analyze their development over the course of the text, including how they interact and build on one another to provide a complex analysis; provide an objective summary of the text. **RI.11-12.3** Analyze a complex set of ideas or sequence of events and explain how specific individuals, ideas, or events interact and develop over the course of the text.
Chapter 4 **Section 1:** • Identify Details **Section 2:** • Identify Main Ideas **Section 3:** • Main Idea and Details **Section 4:** • Identify Main Ideas **Section 5:** • Identify Details	**RI.9-10.2** Determine a central idea of a text and analyze its development over the course of the text, including how it emerges and is shaped and refined by specific details. **RI.9-10.7** Analyze various accounts of a subject told in different mediums, determining which details are emphasized in each account. **RI.11-12.1** Cite strong and thorough textual evidence to support analysis of what the text says explicitly as well as inferences drawn from the text. **RI.11-12.2** Determine two or more central ideas of a text and analyze their development over the course of the text, including how they interact and build on one another to provide a complex analysis.

Prentice Hall US History Modern Reading Skills	Common Core Standards for ELA Reading Informational Text, Grades 9–10/11–12
Chapter 5 **Section 1:** • Identify Main Ideas **Section 2:** • Identify Causes and Effects **Section 3:** • Recognize Sequence **Section 4:** • Identify Supporting Details	**RI.9-10.1** Cite strong and thorough textual evidence to support analysis of what the text says explicitly as well as inferences drawn from the text. **RI.9-10.2** Determine a central idea of a text and analyze its development over the course of the text, including how it emerges and is shaped and refined by specific details. **RI.9-10.3** Analyze how the author unfolds an analysis or series of ideas or events, including the order in which the points are made, how they are introduced and developed, and the connections that are drawn between them. **RI.11-12.1** Cite strong and thorough textual evidence to support analysis of what the text says explicitly as well as inferences drawn from the text. **RI.11-12.2** Determine two or more central ideas of a text and analyze their development over the course of the text, including how they interact and build on one another to provide a complex analysis. **RI.11-12.3** Analyze a complex set of ideas or sequence of events and explain how specific individuals, ideas, or events interact and develop over the course of the text.
Chapter 6 **Section 1:** • Identify Causes **Section 2:** • Summarize **Section 3:** • Sequence **Section 4:** • Identify Main Ideas	**RI.9-10.2** Determine a central idea of a text and analyze its development over the course of the text, including how it emerges and is shaped and refined by specific details. **RI.9-10.3** Analyze how the author unfolds an analysis or series of ideas or events, including the order in which the points are made, how they are introduced and developed, and the connections that are drawn between them. **RI.11-12.2** Determine two or more central ideas of a text and analyze their development over the course of the text, including how they interact and build on one another to provide a complex analysis. **RI.11-12.3** Analyze a complex set of ideas or sequence of events and explain how specific individuals, ideas, or events interact and develop over the course of the text.
Chapter 7 **Section 1:** • Identify Supporting Details **Section 2:** • Compare and Contrast **Section 3:** • Contrast **Section 4:** • Summarize **Section 5:** • Identify Main Ideas	**RI.9-10.1** Cite strong and thorough textual evidence to support analysis of what the text says explicitly as well as inferences drawn from the text. **RI.9-10.2** Determine a central idea of a text and analyze its development over the course of the text, including how it emerges and is shaped and refined by specific details; provide an objective summary of the text. **RI.9-10.7** Analyze various accounts of a subject told in different mediums, determining which details are emphasized in each account. **RI.11-12.1** Cite strong and thorough textual evidence to support analysis of what the text says explicitly as well as inferences drawn from the text. **RI.11-12.2** Determine two or more central ideas of a text and analyze their development over the course of the text, including how they interact and build on one another to provide a complex analysis; provide an objective summary of the text. **RI.11-12.3** Analyze a complex set of ideas or sequence of events and explain how specific individuals, ideas, or events interact and develop over the course of the text.
Chapter 8 **Section 1:** • Recognize Multiple Causes **Section 2:** • Categorize **Section 3:** • Identifying Supporting Details	**RI.9-10.1** Cite strong and thorough textual evidence to support analysis of what the text says explicitly as well as inferences drawn from the text. **RI.9-10.3** Analyze how the author unfolds an analysis or series of ideas or events, including the order in which the points are made, how they are introduced and developed, and the connections that are drawn between them. **RI.11-12.1** Cite strong and thorough textual evidence to support analysis of what the text says explicitly as well as inferences drawn from the text. **RI.11-12.3** Analyze a complex set of ideas or sequence of events and explain how specific individuals, ideas, or events interact and develop over the course of the text.

Prentice Hall *US History Modern* Reading Skills	Common Core Standards for ELA Reading Informational Text, Grades 9–10/11–12
Chapter 9 **Section 1:** • Connect Ideas **Section 2:** • Connect Ideas **Section 3:** • Identify Main Ideas **Section 4:** • Identify Main Ideas and Details	**RI.9-10.2** Determine a central idea of a text and analyze its development over the course of the text, including how it emerges and is shaped and refined by specific details. **RI.9-10.3** Analyze how the author unfolds an analysis or series of ideas or events, including the order in which the points are made, how they are introduced and developed, and the connections that are drawn between them.**RI.11-12.2** Determine two or more central ideas of a text and analyze their development over the course of the text, including how they interact and build on one another to provide a complex analysis. **RI.11-12.3** Analyze a complex set of ideas or sequence of events and explain how specific individuals, ideas, or events interact and develop over the course of the text.
Chapter 10 **Section 1:** • Summarize **Section 2:** • Sequence **Section 3:** • Identify Causes and Effects	**RI.9-10.2** Determine a central idea of a text and analyze its development over the course of the text, including how it emerges and is shaped and refined by specific details; provide an objective summary of the text. **RI.9-10.3** Analyze how the author unfolds an analysis or series of ideas or events, including the order in which the points are made, how they are introduced and developed, and the connections that are drawn between them.**RI.11-12.2** Determine two or more central ideas of a text and analyze their development over the course of the text, including how they interact and build on one another to provide a complex analysis; provide an objective summary of the text. **RI.11-12.3** Analyze a complex set of ideas or sequence of events and explain how specific individuals, ideas, or events interact and develop over the course of the text.
Chapter 11 **Section 1:** • Summarize **Section 2:** • Identify Main Ideas **Section 3:** • Recognize Sequence **Section 4:** • Recognize Sequence **Section 5:** • Understand Effects	**RI.9-10.2** Determine a central idea of a text and analyze its development over the course of the text, including how it emerges and is shaped and refined by specific details; provide an objective summary of the text. **RI.9-10.3** Analyze how the author unfolds an analysis or series of ideas or events, including the order in which the points are made, how they are introduced and developed, and the connections that are drawn between them. **RI.11-12.2** Determine two or more central ideas of a text and analyze their development over the course of the text, including how they interact and build on one another to provide a complex analysis; provide an objective summary of the text. **RI.11-12.3** Analyze a complex set of ideas or sequence of events and explain how specific individuals, ideas, or events interact and develop over the course of the text.
Chapter 12 **Section 1:** • Contrast **Section 2:** • Categorize **Section 3:** • Identify Main Ideas **Section 4:** • Identify Causes and Effects	**RI.9-10.2** Determine a central idea of a text and analyze its development over the course of the text, including how it emerges and is shaped and refined by specific details. **RI.9-10.3** Analyze how the author unfolds an analysis or series of ideas or events, including the order in which the points are made, how they are introduced and developed, and the connections that are drawn between them. **RI.9-10.7** Analyze various accounts of a subject told in different mediums, determining which details are emphasized in each account.**RI.11-12.2** Determine two or more central ideas of a text and analyze their development over the course of the text, including how they interact and build on one another to provide a complex analysis. **RI.11-12.3** Analyze a complex set of ideas or sequence of events and explain how specific individuals, ideas, or events interact and develop over the course of the text.

Prentice Hall US History Modern Reading Skills	Common Core Standards for ELA Reading Informational Text, Grades 9–10/11–12
Chapter 13 **Section 1:** • Understand Effects **Section 2:** • Identify Main Ideas **Section 3:** • Identify Main Ideas **Section 4:** • Identify Main Ideas	**RI.9-10.2** Determine a central idea of a text and analyze its development over the course of the text, including how it emerges and is shaped and refined by specific details. **RI.9-10.3** Analyze how the author unfolds an analysis or series of ideas or events, including the order in which the points are made, how they are introduced and developed, and the connections that are drawn between them. **RI.11-12.2** Determine two or more central ideas of a text and analyze their development over the course of the text, including how they interact and build on one another to provide a complex analysis. **RI.11-12.3** Analyze a complex set of ideas or sequence of events and explain how specific individuals, ideas, or events interact and develop over the course of the text.
Chapter 14 **Section 1:** • Summarize **Section 2:** • Summarize **Section 3:** • Summarize	**RI.9-10.2** Determine a central idea of a text and analyze its development over the course of the text, including how it emerges and is shaped and refined by specific details; provide an objective summary of the text. **RI.11-12.2** Determine two or more central ideas of a text and analyze their development over the course of the text, including how they interact and build on one another to provide a complex analysis; provide an objective summary of the text.
Chapter 15 **Section 1:** • Understand Effects **Section 2:** • Identify Main Ideas **Section 3:** • Identify Main Ideas	**RI.9-10.2** Determine a central idea of a text and analyze its development over the course of the text, including how it emerges and is shaped and refined by specific details. **RI.9-10.3** Analyze how the author unfolds an analysis or series of ideas or events, including the order in which the points are made, how they are introduced and developed, and the connections that are drawn between them. **RI.11-12.2** Determine two or more central ideas of a text and analyze their development over the course of the text, including how they interact and build on one another to provide a complex analysis. **RI.11-12.3** Analyze a complex set of ideas or sequence of events and explain how specific individuals, ideas, or events interact and develop over the course of the text.
Chapter 16 **Section 1:** • Summarize **Section 2:** • Identify Supporting Details **Section 3:** • Recognizing Sequence **Section 4:** • Compare and Contrast **Section 5:** • Categorize	**RI.9-10.1** Cite strong and thorough textual evidence to support analysis of what the text says explicitly as well as inferences drawn from the text. **RI.9-10.2** Determine a central idea of a text and analyze its development over the course of the text, including how it emerges and is shaped and refined by specific details; provide an objective summary of the text. **RI.9-10.3** Analyze how the author unfolds an analysis or series of ideas or events, including the order in which the points are made, how they are introduced and developed, and the connections that are drawn between them. **RI.9-10.7** Analyze various accounts of a subject told in different mediums, determining which details are emphasized in each account.**RI.11-12.1** Cite strong and thorough textual evidence to support analysis of what the text says explicitly as well as inferences drawn from the text. **RI.11-12.2** Determine two or more central ideas of a text and analyze their development over the course of the text, including how they interact and build on one another to provide a complex analysis. **RI.11-12.3** Analyze a complex set of ideas or sequence of events and explain how specific individuals, ideas, or events interact and develop over the course of the text.
Chapter 17 **Section 1:** • Identify Main Ideas **Section 2:** • Identify Causes and Effects **Section 3:** • Compare and Contrast **Section 4:** • Recognize Sequence	**RI.9-10.2** Determine a central idea of a text and analyze its development over the course of the text, including how it emerges and is shaped and refined by specific details. **RI.9-10.3** Analyze how the author unfolds an analysis or series of ideas or events, including the order in which the points are made, how they are introduced and developed, and the connections that are drawn between them. **RI.9-10.7** Analyze various accounts of a subject told in different mediums, determining which details are emphasized in each account.**RI.11-12.2** Determine two or more central ideas of a text and analyze their development over the course of the text, including how they interact and build on one another to provide a complex analysis. **RI.11-12.3** Analyze a complex set of ideas or sequence of events and explain how specific individuals, ideas, or events interact and develop over the course of the text

Prentice Hall *US History Modern* Reading Skills	Common Core Standards for ELA Reading Informational Text, Grades 9–10/11–12
Chapter 18 **Section 1:** • Identify Main Ideas **Section 2:** • Identify Main Ideas **Section 3:** • Identify Supporting Details	**RI.9-10.1** Cite strong and thorough textual evidence to support analysis of what the text says explicitly as well as inferences drawn from the text. **RI.9-10.2** Determine a central idea of a text and analyze its development over the course of the text, including how it emerges and is shaped and refined by specific details. **RI.11-12.1** Cite strong and thorough textual evidence to support analysis of what the text says explicitly as well as inferences drawn from the text. **RI.11-12.2** Determine two or more central ideas of a text and analyze their development over the course of the text, including how they interact and build on one another to provide a complex analysis.
Chapter 19 **Section 1:** • Summarize **Section 2:** • Identify Main Ideas **Section 3:** • Sequence **Section 4:** • Summarize	**RI.9-10.2** Determine a central idea of a text and analyze its development over the course of the text, including how it emerges and is shaped and refined by specific details; provide an objective summary of the text. **RI.9-10.3** Analyze how the author unfolds an analysis or series of ideas or events, including the order in which the points are made, how they are introduced and developed, and the connections that are drawn between them. **RI.11-12.2** Determine two or more central ideas of a text and analyze their development over the course of the text, including how they interact and build on one another to provide a complex analysis; provide an objective summary of the text. **RI.11-12.3** Analyze a complex set of ideas or sequence of events and explain how specific individuals, ideas, or events interact and develop over the course of the text.
Chapter 20 **Section 1:** • Categorize **Section 2:** • Summarize **Section 3:** • Identify Main Ideas **Section 4:** • Recognize Sequence **Section 5:** • Identify Supporting Details	**RI.9-10.1** Cite strong and thorough textual evidence to support analysis of what the text says explicitly as well as inferences drawn from the text. **RI.9-10.2** Determine a central idea of a text and analyze its development over the course of the text, including how it emerges and is shaped and refined by specific details; provide an objective summary of the text. **RI.9-10.3** Analyze how the author unfolds an analysis or series of ideas or events, including the order in which the points are made, how they are introduced and developed, and the connections that are drawn between them. **RI.11-12.1** Cite strong and thorough textual evidence to support analysis of what the text says explicitly as well as inferences drawn from the text. **RI.11-12.2** Determine two or more central ideas of a text and analyze their development over the course of the text, including how they interact and build on one another to provide a complex analysis; provide an objective summary of the text. **RI.11-12.3** Analyze a complex set of ideas or sequence of events and explain how specific individuals, ideas, or events interact and develop over the course of the text.

Professional DEVELOPMENT **Contents**

Raising the achievement level of all students is the number one challenge facing teachers today. To assist in meeting this challenge, we've enlisted a team of respected authors and consultants who specialize in American history education, reading in the content areas, and Differentiated Instruction. In the following pages, you'll find the key elements woven throughout this program that assure teaching and learning success.

Pacing GUIDE

Choose your course from the chart below. Then use the **Daily Pacing Guide** on this and the following pages to help plan the number of days that can be allotted to chapters or sections to meet your curriculum needs.

Chapter/ Section	American History (Survey)		Reconstruction		20th Century	
	Periods	Blocks	Periods	Blocks	Periods	Blocks
Many Cultures Meet (Prehistory–1550)						
1 The American Indians	1	.5				
2 The Europeans	1	.5				
3 The West Africans	1	.5				
4 First Encounters	1	.5				
TOTAL	4	2				
Europeans Establish Colonies (1492–1752)						
1 Spain's Empire in the Americas	1	.5				
2 The French Empire	1	.5				
3 England's Southern Colonies	1	.5				
4 The New England Colonies	1.5	.75				
5 The Middle Colonies	1	.5				
TOTAL	5.5	2.75				
The American Colonies Take Shape (1607–1765)						
1 Immigration and Slavery	1	.5				
2 The American Colonies and England	1.5	.75				
3 Comparing Regional Cultures	1	.5				
4 Wars of Empire	1	.5				
TOTAL	4.5	2.25				
The American Revolution (1765–1783)						
1 Causes of the Revolution	1.5	.75				
2 Declaring Independence	1.5	.75				
3 Turning Points of the War	1.5	.75				
4 War's End and Lasting Effects	1	.5				
TOTAL	5.5	2.75				
Creating the Constitution (1781–1789)						
1 A Confederation of States	1	.5				
2 Drafting the Constitution	1.5	.75				
3 Ratifying the Constitution	1.5	.75				
The Constitution	1	.5				
The Bill of Rights	1	.5				
TOTAL	6	3				

1 Period = 50 minutes   1 block = 100 minutes

Reconstruction and 20th Century users:
Pacing Guide begins on page T4.

Chapter/ Section	American History (Survey)		Reconstruction		20th Century	
	Periods	**Blocks**	**Periods**	**Blocks**	**Periods**	**Blocks**
The New Republic (1789–1816)						
1 Government and Party Politics	1.5	.75				
2 The Struggle Over Foreign Policy	1	.5				
3 The Age of Jefferson	1	.5				
4 The War of 1812	1	.5				
TOTAL	**4.5**	**2.25**				
Nationalism and Sectionalism (1812–1855)						
1 Industry and Transportation	1	.5				
2 Sectional Differences	1	.5				
3 An Era of Nationalism	1	.5				
4 Democracy and the Age of Jackson	1	.5				
5 Constitutional Disputes and Crises	1	.5				
TOTAL	**5**	**2.5**				
Religion and Reform (1812–1860)						
1 A Religious Awakening	1	.5				
2 A Reforming Society	1	.5				
3 The Antislavery Movement	1.5	.75				
4 The Women's Movement	1.5	.75				
TOTAL	**5**	**2.5**				
Manifest Destiny (1800–1850)						
1 Migrating to the West	1	.5				
2 Texas and the Mexican-American War	1	.5				
3 Effects of Territorial Expansion	1	.5				
TOTAL	**3**	**1.5**				
The Union in Crisis (1846–1861)						
1 Slavery, States' Rights, and Western Expansion	1	.5				
2 A Rising Tide of Protest and Violence	1	.5				
3 Political Realignment Deepens the Crisis	1.5	.75				
4 Lincoln, Secession, and War	1.5	.75				
TOTAL	**5**	**2.5**				

Pacing GUIDE

* Survey users: Pacing Guide continues on page T5.

** 20th Century users: Pacing Guide continues on page T5.

Chapter/ Section	American History (Survey)		Reconstruction		20th Century	
	Periods	Blocks	Periods	Blocks	Periods	Blocks
The Civil War (1861–1865)						
1 Resources, Strategies, and Early Battles	1	.5				
2 African Americans and the War	1	.5				
3 Life During the War	1	.5				
4 Turning Points of the War	1.5	.75				
5 The War's End and Impact	1	.5				
TOTAL	**5.5**	**2.75**				
The Reconstruction Era (1865–1877)						
1 Rival Plans for Reconstruction	1	.5				
2 Reconstruction in the South	1	.5				
3 The End of Reconstruction	1	.5				
TOTAL	**3***	**1.50***				
The Nation's Beginnings (Prehistory–1824)						
1 Many Cultures Meet			2	1	2	1
2 The American Revolution			2	1	2.5	1.25
3 The Constitution			2	1	2.5	1.25
4 The New Republic			2	1	2	1
TOTAL			**8**	**4**	**9****	**4.5****
Growth and Reform (1800–1850)						
1 Democracy, Nationalism, and Sectionalism			2	1		
2 Religion and Reform			2	1		
3 The Antislavery Movement			2	1		
4 The Women's Movement			2	1		
5 Manifest Destiny			2	1		
TOTAL			**10**	**5**		
Crisis, Civil War, and Reconstruction (1846–1877)						
1 The Union in Crisis			2	1		
2 Lincoln, Secession, and War			2	1		
3 The Civil War			2	1		
4 The Reconstruction Era			2	1		
TOTAL			**8**	**4**		

Chapter/ Section	American History (Survey)		Reconstruction		20th Century	
	Periods	Blocks	Periods	Blocks	Periods	Blocks
The Triumph of Industry (1865–1914)						
1 Technology and Industrial Growth	1.5	.75	2	1		
2 The Rise of Big Business	1	.5	2	1		
3 The Organized Labor Movement	1	.5	1.5	.75		
TOTAL	**3.5**	**1.75**	**5.5**	**2.75**		
Immigration and Urbanization (1865–1914)						
1 The New Immigrants	1	.5	1.5	.75		
2 Cities Expand and Change	1	.5	1.5	.75		
3 Social and Cultural Trends	1.5	.75	1.5	.75		
TOTAL	**3.5**	**1.75**	**4.5**	**2.25**		
The South and West Transformed (1865–1900)						
1 The New South	1.5	.75	2	1		
2 Westward Expansion and the American Indians	2	1	2	1		
3 Transforming the West	1.5	.75	2	1		
TOTAL	**5**	**2.5**	**6**	**3**		
Issues of the Gilded Age (1877–1900)						
1 Segregation and Social Tensions	1.5	.75	1.5	.75		
2 Political and Economic Challenges	1	.5	1.5	.75		
3 Farmers and Populism	1	.5	1.5	.75		
TOTAL	**3.5**	**1.75**	**4.5**	**2.25**		
Manifest Destiny, Civil War, and Reconstruction (1800–1877)						
1 Reform and Westward Expansion					2.5	1.25
2 The Union in Crisis					2.5	1.25
3 The Civil War					2.5	1.25
4 The Reconstruction Era					2	1
TOTAL					**9.5**	**4.75**
The Development of Industrial America (1865–1914)						
1 The Triumph of Industry					2.5	1.25
2 Immigration and Urbanization					2.5	1.25
3 The South and West Transformed					2.5	1.25
4 Issues of the Gilded Age					2.5	1.25
TOTAL					**10**	**5**

Pacing GUIDE

Chapter/Section	American History (Survey)		Reconstruction		20th Century	
	Periods	**Blocks**	**Periods**	**Blocks**	**Periods**	**Blocks**
The Progressive Era (1890–1920)						
1 The Drive for Reform	1.5	.75	1.5	.75	2	1
2 Women Make Progress	1.5	.75	1.5	.75	2	1
3 The Struggle Against Discrimination	1.5	.75	1.5	.75	2	1
4 Roosevelt's Square Deal	1	.5	1	.5	1.5	.75
5 Wilson's New Freedom	1	.5	1	.5	1.5	.75
TOTAL	**6.5**	**3.25**	**6.5**	**3.25**	**9**	**4.5**
An Emerging World Power (1890–1917)						
1 The Roots of Imperialism	1	.5	1.5	.75	2	1
2 The Spanish American War	1	.5	1.5	.75	2	1
3 The United States and East Asia	1	.5	1.5	.75	2	1
4 The United States and Latin America	1	.5	1.5	.75	2	1
TOTAL	**4**	**2**	**6**	**3**	**8**	**4**
World War I and Beyond (1914–1920)						
1 From Neutrality to War	2	1	2	1	2.5	1.25
2 The Home Front	1	.5	1.5	.75	2	1
3 Wilson, War, and Peace	2	1	2	1	2.5	1.25
4 Effects of the War	1	.5	1.5	.75	2.5	1.25
TOTAL	**6**	**3**	**7**	**3.5**	**9.5**	**4.75**
The Twenties (1919–1929)						
1 A Booming Economy	1	.5	2	1	2	1
2 The Business of Government	1.5	.75	2	1	2	1
3 Social and Cultural Tensions	1.5	.75	1.5	.75	2	1
4 A New Mass Culture	1.5	075	1.5	.75	1.5	.75
5 The Harlem Renaissance	1	.5	1.5	.75	1.5	.75
TOTAL	**6.5**	**3.25**	**8.5**	**4.25**	**9**	**4.50**
The Great Depression (1928–1932)						
1 Causes of the Depression	1.5	.75	1.5	.75	2	1
2 Americans Face Hard Times	2	1	2	1	2	1
3 Hoover's Response Fails	1	.5	1	.5	1.5	.75
TOTAL	**4.5**	**2.25**	**4.5**	**2.25**	**5.5**	**2.75**

Chapter/ Section	American History (Survey)		Reconstruction		20th Century	
	Periods	Blocks	Periods	Blocks	Periods	Blocks
The New Deal (1932–1941)						
1 FDR Offers Relief and Recovery	1.5	.75	1.5	.75	2	1
2 The Second New Deal	1	.5	1.5	.75	2	1
3 Effects of the New Deal	1.5	.75	1.5	.75	2	1
4 Culture of the 1930s	1	.5	1	.5	1.5	.75
TOTAL	**5**	**2.5**	**5.5**	**2.75**	**7.5**	**3.75**
The Coming of War (1931–1942)						
1 Dictators and Wars	1	.5	1.5	.75	2	1
2 From Isolation to Involvement	1.5	.75	2	1	2	1
3 America Enters the War	1.5	.75	2	1	2	1
TOTAL	**4**	**2**	**5.5**	**2.75**	**6**	**3**
World War II (1941–1945)						
1 The Allies Turn the Tide	1.5	.75	2	1	2	1
2 The Home Front	1	.5	1.5	.75	1.5	.75
3 Victory in Europe and the Pacific	1.5	.75	2	1	2.5	1.25
4 The Holocaust	1.5	.75	1.5	.75	2	1
5 Effects of the War	1	.5	1.5	.75	2	1
TOTAL	**6.5**	**3.25**	**8.5**	**4.25**	**10**	**5**
The Cold War (1945–1960)						
1 The Cold War Begins	1	.5	1.5	.75	2	1
2 The Korean War	1.5	.75	2	1	2	1
3 The Cold War Expands	1.5	.75	2	1	2	1
4 The Cold War at Home	1	.5	1.5	0.75	1.5	.75
TOTAL	**5**	**2.5**	**7**	**3.50**	**7.5**	**3.75**
Postwar Confidence and Anxiety (1945–1960)						
1 An Economic Boom	1.5	.75	1.5	.75	2	1
2 A Society on the Move	1	.5	1.5	.75	2	1
3 Mass Culture and Family Life	1.5	.75	1.5	.75	1.5	.75
4 Dissent and Discontent	1	.5	1.5	.75	2	1
TOTAL	**5**	**2.5**	**6**	**3**	**7.5**	**3.75**

Pacing GUIDE

Chapter/ Section	American History (Survey)		Reconstruction		20th Century	
	Periods	Blocks	Periods	Blocks	Periods	Blocks
The Civil Rights Movement (1945–1975)						
1 Early Demands for Equality	2	1	2	1	2	1
2 The Movement Gains Ground	2	1	2	1	2	1
3 New Successes and Challenges	1	.5	1.5	.75	2	1
TOTAL	**5**	**2.5**	**5.5**	**2.75**	**6**	**3**
The Kennedy and Johnson Years (1960–1968)						
1 Kennedy and the Cold War	1.5	.75	2	1	2	1
2 Kennedy's New Frontier	1.5	.75	2	1	2	1
3 Johnson's Great Society	1.5	.75	2	1	2	1
TOTAL	**4.5**	**2.25**	**6**	**3**	**6**	**3**
The Vietnam War Era (1954–1975)						
1 Origins of the Vietnam War	1	.5	1.5	.75	1.5	.75
2 U.S. Involvement Grows	1	.5	2	1	2	1
3 The War Divides America	1.5	.75	2	1	2	1
4 The War's End and Impact	1	.5	1.5	.75	2	1
5 Nixon and the Cold War	1	.5	2	1	2	1
TOTAL	**5.5**	**2.75**	**9**	**4.5**	**9.5**	**4.75**
An Era of Protest and Change (1960–1980)						
1 The Counterculture	1	.5	1.5	.75	2	1
2 The Women's Rights Movement	2	1	2	1	2	1
3 The Rights Revolution Expands	2	1	2	1	2	1
4 The Environmental Movement	1	.5	1.5	.75	2	1
TOTAL	**6**	**3**	**7**	**3.5**	**8**	**4**
A Crisis in Confidence (1968–1980)						
1 Nixon and the Watergate Scandal	1.5	.75	2	1	2	1
2 The Ford and Carter Years	1	.5	2	1	2	1
3 Foreign Policy Troubles	1	.5	1.5	.75	2	1
TOTAL	**3.5**	**1.75**	**5.5**	**2.75**	**6**	**3**

Chapter/ Section	American History (Survey)		Reconstruction		20th Century	
	Periods	Blocks	Periods	Blocks	Periods	Blocks
The Conservative Resurgence (1980–1993)						
1 The Conservative Movement Grows	1	.5	1.5	.75	2	1
2 The Reagan Revolution	1	.5	2	1	2	1
3 The End of the Cold War	1	.5	1.5	.75	2	1
4 Foreign Policy After the Cold War	1	.5	2	1	2	1
TOTAL	**4**	**2**	**7**	**3.5**	**8**	**4**
Into a New Century (1992–Today)						
1 The Computer and Technology Revolutions	1	.5	1.5	.75	1.5	.75
2 The Clinton Presidency	1	.5	2	1	2	1
3 Global Politics and Economics	1.5	.75	2	1	2	1
4 The Bush and Obama Presidencies	2	1	2	1	2	1
5 Americans Look to the Future	1	.5	1	.5	1	.5
TOTAL	**6.5**	**3.25**	**8.5**	**4.25**	**8.5**	**4.25**

Differentiated INSTRUCTION

Research on Differentiated Instruction

Why Do We Need Differentiated Instruction?

The wide range of academic diversity in schools today presents both a challenge and an opportunity to all teachers. Because the challenge of accommodating all students is so urgent, we need to plan and teach to include all learners in a new way.

The importance of differentiated instruction Why is it so important to modify our planning and instruction in light of the increased diversity in our classes? First, each of our students is expected to master the key content that is tied to district or state outcome examinations. In other words, if students are in our classes, we are expected to teach to enable them to be successful on these high-stakes exams.

Second, when adolescents encounter failure in meeting rigorous curriculum demands, they often lose hope in their ability to be successful—they may mentally disengage from school, seek out "success" by acting out inappropriately, or even drop out of school. Thus, when we work with struggling learners, the costs for not successfully meeting their needs can be significant.

Meeting the needs of highly capable students is equally challenging. They must be "stretched" to learn new materials and engage in higher order thinking about the curriculum.

In short, the most successful teachers understand the complexity of the academic diversity in their classes and design their lessons and learning experiences accordingly.

What the research tells us
The literature on differentiated instruction tells us that active instruction is that which increases the achievement levels of four major subgroups of students—special needs, low, average, and high-achieving—equally. If one sub-group benefits significantly more than another from a teacher's attempt to differentiate instruction for the entire class, eventually the attempt will be dropped because a significant portion of the class is not making gains.

To reach the needs of low-achieving students in any class, steps must be taken to ensure that instruction is systematic and explicit. That is, to the degree that the sequence of learning is not clear and new information to be mastered is not clearly taught, the students who struggle most in learning will continue to struggle and will fall further behind their classmates.

Finally, the long-term effects of any instructional practice will be enhanced if a majority of teachers use and reinforce that practice. For example, if Teacher A teaches her class to use a particular learning strategy to master new vocabulary, students will better learn and apply that strategy if it is used and reinforced by all teachers. Effective differentiated instruction instruction is in part dependent on teachers having an opportunity to coordinate the use of similar materials and reinforce critical learning strategies.

How Do We Provide Inclusive Instruction?

One of the most important roles that teachers play in effectively providing differentiated instruction is to see themselves as "mediators" in the learning process. That is, the chances of students learning complex content is greatly enhanced if teachers understand a) the specific difficulties of learners in their class, b) why the curriculum content they are teaching is difficult (Is it abstract, dense, etc.?), and c) the unique features of the curriculum materials and the particular challenges they present in learning. In light of these three factors, the most effective teachers are those who help "mediate" (or manipulate or transform) the content in such a way as to make it understandable and memorable to all their students.

What Is the Result of Differentiated Instruction?

While improving student outcomes is a major goal of differentiated instruction, it is important to remember that when teachers are successful in reaching a majority of students in their classes, an environment of cooperation, learning, and respect emerges. Teachers intent on successfully differentiating their instruction communicate a message that the "work" of this community is learning for everyone. Everyday practices and routines are based on cooperation in accomplishing this work, and the interests and learning needs of everyone in the community are taken seriously.

Don Deshler

Don Deshler, Ph.D., is the Chair of Prentice Hall's Differentiated Instruction Board. He assembled a distinguished panel of national experts to serve on the board, who offer extensive experience in educating special needs students, English language learners, less proficient readers, and gifted and talented students. This team informs Prentice Hall's approach to Differentiated Instruction and offers guidance on the development of new materials based on this approach. Deshler is the Director of the Center for Research on Learning at the University of Kansas.

Effective Classroom Implementation

The mission of *Prentice Hall United States History* is to provide standards-based instruction in ways that allow all learners to participate and to achieve. Because not all students learn in the same manner nor have the same abilities, our program provides options so that all learners work toward the same essential understandings and skills, but use different content, processes, and products to get there. Our effective support helps you close the achievement gap.

Teaching Support Helps You Modify Instruction

The ***Teacher's Edition*** provides continuous professional development throughout the program, starting with strategies for specific populations at the beginning of this textbook. Differentiated Instruction boxes throughout each chapter offer specific suggestions for modifying instruction to accommodate all learners. Direct instruction creates opportunities to build a community of learners who can learn from and about one another. Together, these tools help you provide all learners with meaningful access to the curriculum.

Varied Resources Address Different Populations

Prentice Hall United States History resources are designed to help students of all abilities master core content. The ***Reading and Note Taking Study Guide*** is one such aid that encourages literacy and provides a framework for vocabulary development and learning. With three versions (On-level, Adapted, and Spanish), this note-taking system provides the required support for all levels. The program also delivers content through a wide variety of formats—including text, transparencies, audio, video, and interactive text—that will appeal to all of your students.

Leveled Review and Assessments Give You More Options

The On-level, Adapted, and Spanish Study Guides review content in different formats. The ***ExamView*®** Test Bank CD-ROM offers leveled tests and makes it easy to adapt tests based on individual needs.

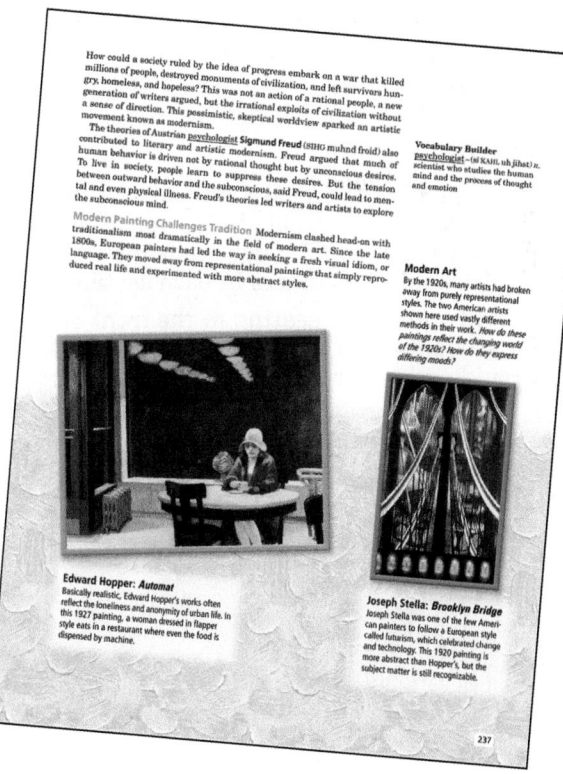

How could a society ruled by the idea of progress embark on a war that killed millions of people, destroyed monuments of civilization, and left survivors hungry, homeless, and hopeless? This was not an action of a rational people, a new generation of writers argued, but the irrational exploits of civilization without a sense of direction. This pessimistic, skeptical worldview sparked an artistic movement known as modernism.

The theories of Austrian psychologist Sigmund Freud (SIHG muhnd froid) also contributed to literary and artistic modernism. Freud argued that much of human behavior is driven not by rational thought but by unconscious desires. To live in society, people learn to suppress these desires. But the tension between outward behavior and the subconscious, said Freud, could lead to mental and even physical illness. Freud's theories led writers and artists to explore the subconscious mind.

Vocabulary Builder
psychologist—(sī KAHL uh jihst) *n.* scientist who studies the human mind and the process of thought and emotion

Modern Painting Challenges Tradition Modernism clashed head-on with traditionalism most dramatically in the field of modern art. Since the late 1800s, European painters had led the way in seeking a fresh visual idiom, or language. They moved away from representational paintings that simply reproduced real life and experimented with more abstract styles.

Modern Art
By the 1920s, many artists had broken away from purely representational styles. The two American artists shown here used vastly different methods in their work. *How do these paintings reflect the changing world of the 1920s? How do they express differing moods?*

Edward Hopper: *Automat*
Basically realistic, Edward Hopper's works often reflect the loneliness and anonymity of urban life. In this 1927 painting, a woman dressed in flapper style eats in a restaurant where even the food is dispensed by machine.

Joseph Stella: *Brooklyn Bridge*
Joseph Stella was one of the few American painters to follow a European style called futurism, which celebrated change and technology. This 1920 painting is more abstract than Hopper's, but the subject matter is still recognizable.

237

Differentiated INSTRUCTION

Strategies for Differentiated Instruction

Differentiated instruction can be fostered through modifying instruction to address individual needs. Lesson plans in this *Teacher's Edition* provide differentiated instruction strategies and suggest ancillary support such as the three levels of the *Reading and Note Taking Study Guide.* The following pages provide general guidelines for modifying instruction for special needs students, English Language Learners, less proficient readers, gifted and talented students, and advanced readers.

SPECIAL NEEDS

Students with special education needs require unique cognitive, behavioral, social, and physical strategies. To help create a classroom that supports the participation and achievement of all students, set clear expectations and provide reasonable choices. Plan lessons with individual adaptations and modifications. Offer instructional activities that foster the development of relationships among students and between students and teachers.

Preteach

Preteaching helps prepare students for learning.
- Preteach critical social studies terms, people, and places as well as high-use academic words using the Vocabulary Builders in each section.
- Provide preferred seating in the front of the class for students who read lips or for interpreters. Provide space for a guide dog as necessary.

Teach

Using a variety of approaches enhances lessons.
- Provide an overview of key ideas and concepts presented in the text using outlines, maps, or the text summaries and graphic organizers provided in the *Adapted Reading and Note Taking Study Guide.*
- Present all ideas orally and visually and, when possible, incorporate tactile and kinesthetic experiences as well.
- Require students to demonstrate that they are listening and following along (e.g., taking notes, running a finger along the text).
- Incorporate active reading strategies (e.g., choral reading, paired reading).
- Provide adaptive materials as appropriate (e.g., enlarged print, Braille editions, captions for the video program).
- Incorporate the same comprehension and learning strategies over time to allow for mastery.

Assess

Students need to know what is expected.
- Assess students' understanding by asking them to write questions about what they have learned, identify what they find unclear or confusing, or complete short quick writes of key points.
- When students work in groups or pairs, set up procedures that maintain each student's accountability (e.g., writing, drawing, or response).
- Make sure that you have adequately scaffolded tasks for special needs students and have equipped them with writing instruction and practice that builds spoken prerequisite skills.
- When appropriate, have students manage and chart their academic performance, homework and assignment completion, and behavior.
- Provide outlines of what is to be done, with suggested dates and timelines for project completion.

ENGLISH LANGUAGE LEARNERS

Students who are learning English are the fastest-growing segment of the school-age population. These students require frontloading, or preteaching, in order to grasp challenging literacy tasks, such as those encountered in a social studies textbook. Since English Language Learners may be approaching an assignment with limited background knowledge and weak English vocabulary, concentrate on activities that build strong conceptual and linguistic foundations, guide them through the text's organization, and model appropriate comprehension strategies.

Preteach

English Language Learners require extra preparation.

- Introduce new words in meaningful contexts, through simple sentences drawing on familiar issues, scenarios, and vocabulary. Ask students to write the definitions in their own words and then define the words when they occur within the reading.

- Utilize realia and visuals (e.g., photographs, objects from everyday life, color transparencies) to make concepts less abstract.

- Lead a quick "text tour," focusing students' attention on illustrations, titles and subtopics, and boldfaced words.

Teach

Many of these techniques will benefit all learners.

- Get students physically involved with the page, using sticky notes to focus and guide their reading.

- Encourage students to read while listening to a recording of the same passage as it is read aloud, such as on the *Student Edition Audio.* Spanish-language speakers can also listen to section summaries on the *Spanish Guided Reading Audio.*

- Use the text summaries and graphic organizers provided in the *Spanish Reading and Note Taking Study Guide.*

- Have students read the same brief passage several times to build word recognition, fluency, and reading rate.

- Praise students' efforts to experiment with new language in class, both in writing and in speaking.

Assess

Students will demonstrate learning in different ways.

- Ask students to demonstrate their understanding by drawing on different language skills: formal and informal writing assignments, posters, small group tasks, and oral presentations.

- Make sure students understand assessment criteria in advance. Distribute rubrics provided in the *Assessment Rubrics.* Whenever possible, provide models of work for students to emulate, along with a non-model that fails to meet the specified assessment criteria.

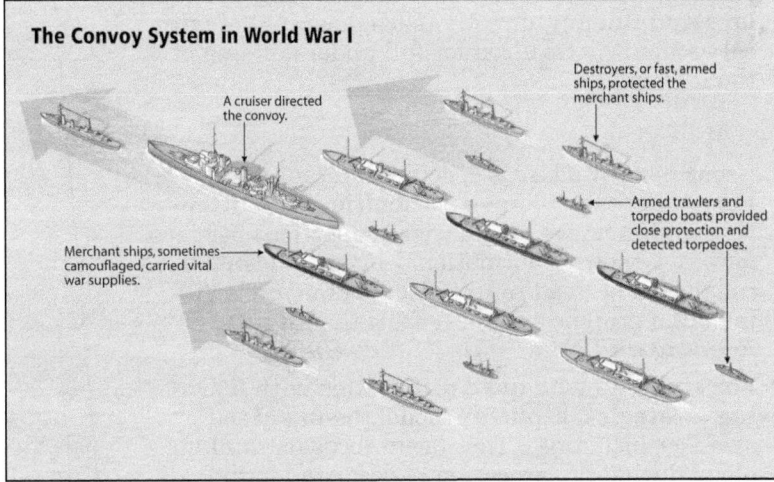

The Convoy System in World War I

A cruiser directed the convoy.

Destroyers, or fast, armed ships, protected the merchant ships.

Armed trawlers and torpedo boats provided close protection and detected torpedoes.

Merchant ships, sometimes camouflaged, carried vital war supplies.

Differentiated INSTRUCTION

LESS PROFICIENT READERS

Less proficient readers are students who begin the year one or more years below grade level, yet do not qualify for special education services. They may or may not be English Language Learners. They may be underprepared for academic challenges due to difficulties with attention and memory, learning strategies, or vocabulary and reading fluency. It is especially important to engage these students in challenging lessons while incorporating support or instructional scaffolding to increase their likelihood of success.

Preteach

Preteaching helps build students' confidence.

- **For students who have difficulties with attention and memory,** gain attention by requesting a simple physical response (e.g., "Everyone, eyes on me, please"). Then, keep the lesson pace brisk—a "perky not pokey" pace is helpful.

- **For students who have difficulties with learning strategies,** clarify the rationale for learning a new strategy. Directly teach any prerequisite skills needed to perform the strategy. Make strategies concrete by having students fill out a K-W-L chart.

- **For students who have difficulties with vocabulary and fluency,** directly teach meanings of critical vocabulary required for full understanding of the lesson.

Teach

Lessons have to address specific, different needs.

- **For students who have difficulties with attention and memory,** emphasize connections between new and known information. Engage students in a collaborative "read/reflect/discuss/note" cycle, filling out a graphic organizer from the *Adapted Reading and Note Taking Study Guide.*

- **For students who have difficulties with learning strategies,** explicitly model the use of the strategy, including a significant focus on thinking aloud during the execution of each step in the strategy. Discuss where else in or out of school students could use the strategy.

- **For students who have difficulties with vocabulary and fluency,** revisit newly acquired vocabulary during discussion. Suggest that students use the Vocabulary Builder Online.

Assess

Assessment must accommodate unique needs.

- **For students who have difficulties with attention and memory,** ask students to reorganize, prioritize, and otherwise reflect on the key aspects of the lesson. Have them explain their graphic organizers to a partner. Monitor and reteach as necessary.

- **For students who have difficulties with learning strategies,** explicitly include strategies as part of quizzes, reports, projects, and other formal assessments.

- **For students who have difficulties with vocabulary and fluency,** randomly call on students to provide examples of the vocabulary word under examination.

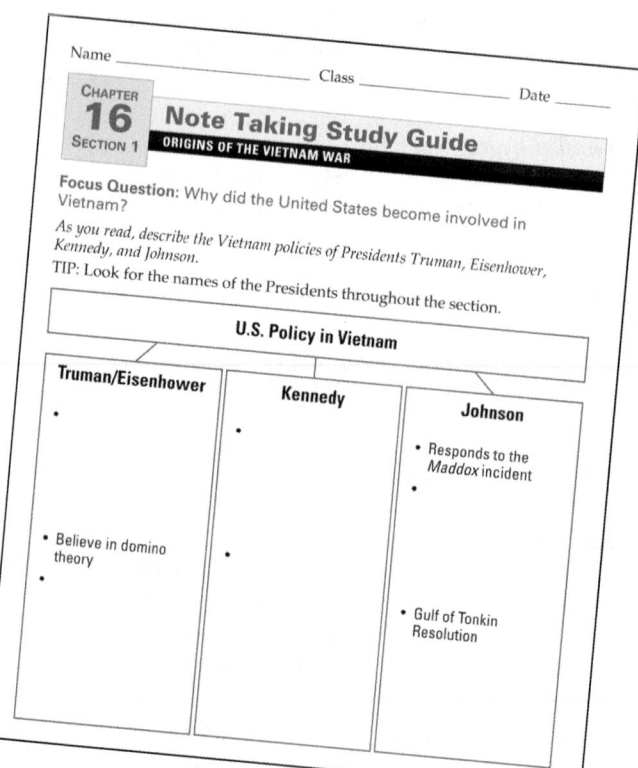

GIFTED AND TALENTED STUDENTS AND ADVANCED READERS

Gifted and talented students and advanced readers need modified instruction to achieve their highest potential. They tend to understand complex concepts quickly, learn more rapidly and in greater depth, and may have interests that are different from those of their peers. Teachers can modify pacing and offer enrichment to allow for exploring topics in-depth, manipulating ideas in novel ways, and making connections to other disciplines.

Preteach

These students may have an extensive background.
- Before beginning a new unit, have students write, verbalize, or draw on what they know about the topic and present this information to peers.
- Ask students to discuss what they would like to learn, and then work with them to create a plan for advanced study based on their interests.

Teach

Activate students' ability to think creatively and see connections.
- Help students adjust the pace of their learning by speeding through concepts they master quickly or by slowing down to study content in depth. The *Teacher's Edition* provides ideas for ways to extend content in the Extend part of the lesson plan.
- Challenge students to tackle more complex topics and offer frequent opportunities to focus on abstract ideas.
- Provide opportunities for in-depth research on student-directed topics. Have students explore topics on the Internet and under your direction.
- Encourage students to make connections between content they are learning and other disciplines such as language arts, science, and math. For example, students might want to read fiction about the historical period they are studying.

Assess

Assessment can take many forms.
- Have students be responsible for part of the assessment of their learning. Allow them to plan, design, and monitor the project or assignment.
- Encourage students to apply standards-based understandings to new situations. Challenge them to take information and use it in novel ways.

Name _____ Class _____ Date _____

THE VIETNAM WAR ERA

Enrichment: Build a Model

The Vietnam Veterans Memorial

Use this worksheet to guide your research by finding the information indicated.

1. Criteria for the design:_____
   _____
   _____

2. Purpose of the memorial:_____
   _____
   _____

3. Controversy about the memorial: _____
   _____
   _____

4. Shape and size of the memorial: _____
   _____
   _____

5. Materials used in the construction: _____
   _____
   _____

6. Maya Lin's vision or reasoning behind the design: _____
   _____
   _____

7. Criteria for and arrangement of the names on the wall: _____
   _____
   _____

8. Meaning of symbols and dates on the memorial: _____
   _____
   _____

9. Other details or statistics about the memorial: _____
   _____
   _____

10. Legacy or significance of the memorial: _____
    _____
    _____

14

Understanding The Common Core State Standards: What They Mean for Social Studies Teachers

The Common Core State Standards Initiative was organized by the National Governors Association and the Council of Chief State School Officers to develop college and career readiness through K-12 standards in English language arts and mathematics. This enterprise is meant to be comprehensive and will ultimately include a set of social studies standards as well. The underlying principle behind the Common Core is that today's students need to develop the skills and knowledge to make them ready for college or careers after high school.

Jeff Passe

Jeff Passe, former president of NCSS; current Chair, Department of Secondary Education, Towson University

Literacy Standards for Social Studies

A surprising twist in the language arts standards is the inclusion of literacy standards in history and social studies. This means that not only should historical and political texts be included in the language arts classroom, but language arts and reading teachers need to teach students how to apply their reading skills to primary and secondary social studies sources. Further, the Common Core standards in Language Arts set expectations for writing. Writing standards include presenting and supporting arguments, writing informative or explanatory texts, and conducting and presenting the results of research.

Writing should build in sophistication, clarity, and organization through the students' secondary years.

The inclusion of literacy standards in social studies could lead to collaboration between language arts and social studies colleagues. Consider the reading standard that requires students to determine "how Madison defines *faction* in *Federalist* No. 10." Standards such as this will challenge most language arts teachers, who may have only cursory knowledge of political and historical documents. So social studies teachers may be called upon to collaborate with their language arts colleagues.

> *The Common Core State Standards provide a consistent, clear understanding of what students are expected to learn, so teachers and parents know what they need to do to help them. The standards are designed to be robust and relevant to the real world, reflecting the knowledge and skills that our young people need for success in college and careers. With American students fully prepared for the future, our communities will be best positioned to compete successfully in the global economy.*
> —*Common Core State Standards Initiative*

**For more information about how Pearson can help you implement the
Common Core State Standards, go to http://commoncore.pearsoned.com/**

Helping Students Master the Common Core State Standards

Language arts teachers will not be the only ones
affected by the Common Core Standards initiative.
To help students master the new standards, social
studies teachers will have to teach some reading and
writing skills. In the pages that follow, you will find
helpful suggestions for incorporating literacy skills
in your instruction. Success in reading social studies sources will require a curricular plan based on
gradual increases in text complexity. Without such
a plan, students might have difficulty reaching the
level of reading proficiency required by college and
the workplace. Language arts teachers can be partners in achieving the right balance.

Toward College and Career Readiness

In many ways, this is a welcome development.
Secondary teachers who collaborate will share in
helping their students develop skills that are essential to citizenship in a democracy. Proficiency in
reading historical and political texts is required for
college success and effective citizenship. Obviously,
college social science courses are filled with those
types of reading, but so are courses in business,
nursing, and other professions. Because subjects like
history, economics, and law are relevant in many
workplace decisions, career success depends on
one's ability to process texts from those disciplines.
Implementation may transform the curriculum,
and it may alter the very essence of how secondary
teachers work together to achieve educational goals.
Social Studies teachers can play a key role in this
transformation.

READING

Research on Reading

Why do many students have difficulty reading textbooks? How can we help students read to learn social studies? In the pages that follow, we examine the research on the challenge of reading textbooks, show how Prentice Hall has responded to this research, and offer direct, systematic, and explicit strategies to help your students.

What Is Skilled Reading?

Recent research (Snow et al., 2002) suggests that skillful and strategic reading is a long-term developmental process in which "readers learn how to simultaneously extract and construct meaning through interaction with written language." In other words, successful readers know how to decode all types of words, read with fluency and expression, have well-developed vocabularies, and possess various comprehension strategies such as note taking and summarizing to employ as the academic reading task demands.

Many Students Lack Reading Skills

Sadly, many secondary students do not have solid reading skills. Even students quite skilled in reading novels, short stories, and adolescent magazines typically come to secondary school ill-equipped for the rigors of informational texts, or reading to learn.

Many students tend to dive right into a social studies chapter as if reading a recreational story. They don't first preview the material to create a mental outline and establish a purpose in reading. They have not yet learned other basic strategies, such as reading a section more than once, taking notes as they read, and reading to answer specific questions.

Kate Kinsella
Kate Kinsella, Ed.D., is a faculty member in the Department of Secondary Education at San Francisco State University and specializes in second language acquisition and adolescent literacy.

Kevin Feldman
Kevin Feldman, Ed.D., is Director of Reading and Early Intervention with the Sonoma County Office of Education and an independent educational consultant.

The Unique Demands of Textbooks

The differences between textbooks and the stories of adolescent magazines are dramatic. The most distinctive challenges include:

1. **Conceptual content** Content-area textbooks are laden with new and largely unfamiliar concepts (such as *human-environment interaction* and *nationalism*).

2. **Vocabulary load** The unique vocabulary used in academic texts is often referred to as *academic language*. Academic language consists of high-use academic words, such as *currency* and *restore,* and discipline-specific vocabulary (or "Key Terms"), such as *agrarian* and *legislature.*

3. **Paragraph and organizational patterns** Academic texts are constructed using unfamiliar organizational patterns such as cause-effect, problem-solution, categorization, chain of events, or comparison and contrast.

4. **Sentence structures** Because the purpose of textbooks is to communicate complex information as efficiently as possible, readers will come across sophisticated sentence structures.

Academic texts present such a significant challenge to most students that linguists and language researchers liken them to learning a foreign language (Schleppegrell, 2002). In other

words, most secondary students are second-language learners: they are learning the academic language of informational texts.

The Need for Vocabulary Instruction

There is a clear consensus among literacy researchers that accelerating vocabulary growth is a vital and often neglected component of a comprehensive reading program (Baumann and Kameenui, 2004). Numerous studies have documented the strong and reciprocal relationship between vocabulary knowledge and reading comprehension. Research focused on school-age second-language learners similarly concludes that vocabulary knowledge is the single best predictor of their academic achievement across subject matter domains.

Educators therefore need to make robust intentional vocabulary instruction a high priority. Intensive instruction should be focused on words related to central lesson concepts (or "Key Terms") and high-use academic words. Academic word lists developed by researchers can help educators determine appropriate high-use academic words (Coxhead, 2000; Xue and Nation, 1984).

Effective Classroom Implementation

Research illustrates that virtually all students benefit from direct, systematic, and explicit instruction in reading informational texts (Baker and Gersten, 2000). *Prentice Hall United States History* accomplishes this task in three steps: 1) Before reading—instructional frontloading; 2) During reading—guided instruction; 3) After reading—reflection and study.

Before Reading

If you emphasize preteaching, or "frontloading," your instruction, you will help structure learning to ensure student success.

Build Vocabulary To prepare students to read, introduce the key terms, people, and places at the beginning of each section. Vocabulary Builder terms are located in the margins next to where they appear in the student text and at the beginning of each section in the *Teacher's Edition.*

Set a Purpose Setting a purpose asks students to predict and anticipate what they will read. The Set a Purpose section at the beginning of each chapter in the *Teacher's Edition* includes a number of strategies for accomplishing this goal. These strategies are supported in the *Skills Handbook* and in the *Note Taking Transparencies.*

Additional Reading Strategies At the beginning of each section, the Note Taking activity asks students to focus on one reading skill, such as identifying the main idea, or recognizing sequence. It then provides a graphic organizer to help students apply the skill to the content. Detailed graphic organizers are located in the *Reading and Note Taking Study Guides.*

Prepare to Read

Background Knowledge L3

Ask students to recall how Truman and Eisenhower confronted the challenges of the Cold War. Tell them to predict whether subsequent Presidents will follow earlier policies or work out new approaches to the conflict.

Set a Purpose L3

- **WITNESS HISTORY** Read the selection aloud.

  Ask **Why might Kennedy's faith have concerned voters?** *(Possible answer: All previous Presidents had been Protestants. The Catholic Church has a strong central authority—the papacy—and voters may have been anxious about how Kennedy might be influenced by the pope.)*

- **Focus** Point out the Section Focus Question, and write it on the board. Tell students to refer to this question as they read. *(Answer appears with Section 1 Assessment answers.)*

- **Preview** Have students preview the Section Objectives and the list of Terms and People.

- NoteTaking Using the Structured Read Aloud strategy (TE, p. T20), have students read this section. As they read, have students list the results of the Cold War crises. Reading and Note Taking Study Guide

---

During Reading

As you read each section, use the direct instruction provided in the *Teacher's Edition* to help guide students through the text. Further practice in reading skills is located in the *Skills Handbook* and in the *Note Taking Transparencies.*

Active Reading To encourage active reading, the student text builds in questions for students to self-test their comprehension at the end of every section of text under a red heading.

> ✓ **Checkpoint** What strategies did Kennedy use to improve relations between the United States and developing countries?

Guided Instruction In the *Teacher's Edition,* the lesson plan introduces a variety of strategies to teach the lesson, including Quick Activities to help keep students interested and engaged.

Note Taking To promote active reading, ask students to fill in the graphic organizers located at the beginning of each section and throughout the chapters as they read. This not only gives students practice in taking notes, but also reinforces content and reading skills introduced at the beginning of the section.

Cold War Crisis	Result
Bay of Pigs Invasion	

After Reading

During the reflection and study phases, formally check for student understanding. If necessary provide remediation. Provide activities that challenge students to apply content in a new way.

Provide Review Direct students to the Quick Study Guide at the end of every chapter. Encourage students to use the Note Taking graphic organizers and American Issues Journal worksheets for additional review.

Assess Learning Use the Assess and Reteach portion of the lesson plan to check for student understanding. At the end of each section, the assessment returns to the Focus Question to reinforce key concepts. Students should use their completed graphic organizers to answer it. Encourage students to take the self-quizzes and tests with vocabulary practice online.

READING

Reading and Discussion Strategies for Improving Comprehension

In response to the continued emphasis on reading literacy, testing reform, and NCLB legislation, Prentice Hall asked Dr. Kate Kinsella and Dr. Kevin Feldman to provide specific instructional strategies you can use to improve student comprehension. Their guidance informed the development of the ***Prentice Hall United States History Teacher's Edition.*** In addition to the materials and strategies outlined on the previous page, the lesson plans in this ***Teacher's Edition*** incorporate the following instructional strategies to enhance students' comprehension.

Reading Comprehension Strategies

There is no single, magical strategy that will solve all of the difficulties that students encounter in reading challenging content-area texts. Students in mixed-ability classrooms depend on teachers to use a consistent set of research-informed and classroom-tested strategies in a patient and recursive manner—not the occasional or random use of different strategies. Some strategies, such as Pre-Reading, are designed to become the responsibility of the student to use independently. These are coded as "student self-directed" (SSD). Other strategies meant always to be used with the guidance of the teacher, such as the discussion strategies, are coded as "Teacher Directed" (TD).

How to Teach a Reading Strategy

A strategy is a plan of action or a series of steps to accomplish a task. Strategy instruction essentially consists of a teacher showing less-skilled, younger readers how to tackle a reading "strategically." The essence of how to teach a strategy can be summed up in three phases as "I do it, We do it, You do it" (Archer, 2001).

I do it
1. Explain the rationale: What is the purpose? How can this help you?
2. Demonstrate how to perform the strategy.

We do it
3. Guide the students in the steps of the strategy.
4. Direct students in practicing the strategy with a partner.
5. Re-model, providing feedback as necessary.

You do it
6. Direct students to perform the strategy while clarifying a clear "evidence check" of strategy application (e.g., turn in your Pre-Reading Outline) for accountability.

The amount of teacher support at the "I do it" and "We do it" phases of strategy instruction will vary widely depending on the difficulty of the content and literacy levels of your students. It is important to realize that it will take several teacher-directed experiences with a new reading strategy before students will be able to successfully apply it on their own.

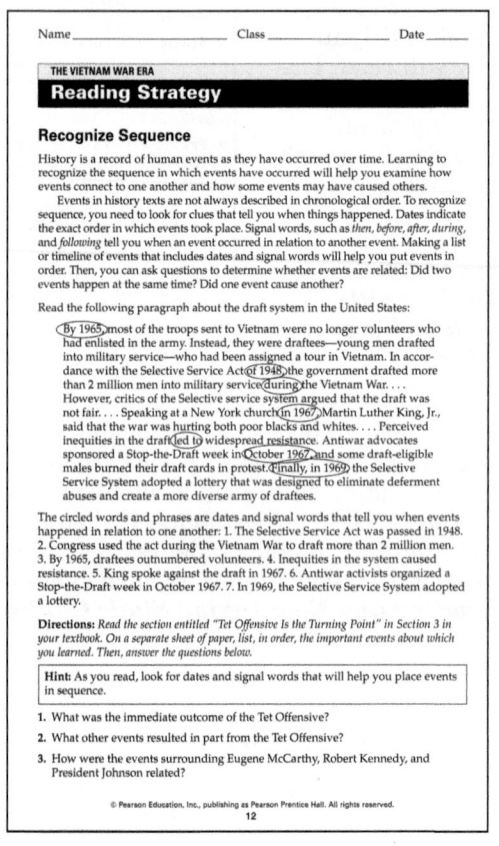

Before Reading

Three key strategies prepare students for the demands of reading and comprehending each chapter: Preread the Chapter: Why and How?, Word Knowledge Rating, and K-W-L.

Preread the Chapter: Why and How? (SSD)

Purpose: To build background knowledge, provide an overview of the topics, acquaint students with the structure and organization of the text, and establish the necessity of reading to learn from demanding text in more than one way.

1. Distribute the Preread the Chapter: Why and How? worksheet from the *Skills Handbook* to help focus students' attention on each step in the prereading process. Later, this guide can serve as a written record that students have preread when assigned to do so independently.

2. Model how to use the Why and How? checklist to preview chapter and section materials. You may also wish to read each heading and subheading aloud, clarify section structure (e.g., cause-effect relationships), frame the topics as questions to read to answer, and help students identify unfamiliar words and model ways to find clues to their meanings.

Word Knowledge Rating (TD)

Purpose: To teach students essential content terms and high-use academic words they will need to understand and be able to use in reading, discussion, and writing tasks.

1. Have students pronounce each new word and clarify the part of speech. For difficult or polysyllabic words, break them into syllables and pronounce them with the students.

2. Explain what the word means in common "student friendly" language using synonyms and antonyms when possible.

3. Provide concrete examples to clarify the meaning and rephrase the example, having students pronounce the target word as they fill in their form.

K-W-L (TD)

Purpose: Engage students in thinking about a topic before, during, and after reading by guiding them to reflect on what they **K**now, clarify what they **W**ant to learn (or expect to learn), and identify what they **L**earn as they read.

1. Make a three-column chart on the board labeling the columns What you already know, What you want to know, and What you've learned. Structure a brief discussion session with the group to identify what they already know (or think they know) about a topic. List the student's name and idea on the board and encourage students to generate questions at points of ambiguity. (Note: If the students have very limited background knowledge about a topic, focus on building background knowledge or providing key information directly rather than attempting to activate what is not present.)

2. Guide students to record key ideas from the brainstorming session under the What You Already Know section of the chart.

3. Teach students how to ask questions based on the topic they predict the chapter will address, even when they know very little about it (e.g., who, what, when, where, why, how, effects of, etc.). Have them record these questions in the second column of the chart.

4. After reading and/or at key junctures in the text, facilitate a discussion answering key questions and clarifying any lingering confusion about key concepts. Have students fill in the final column of the chart.

During Reading

This program supports student comprehension during reading by providing three key strategies: Paragraph Shrinking, Guided Questioning/Silent Reading, and Structured Reading Aloud.

Paragraph Shrinking (SSD)

Purpose: To teach students a basic strategy for summarizing essential information in each paragraph as they read.

1. Read the paragraph to yourself (you may choose to do this aloud if many students can't decode all of the words).

2. Identify the topic—what the paragraph is mainly about.

3. Clarify the two or three most essential details related to the topic.

4. Shrink the paragraph—state the topic and one or two key details in 15 words or less.

Guided Questioning/Silent Reading (TD)

Purpose: To ensure students' accountably, focus their attention on critical issues while reading silently.

1. Assign a section to read silently. Pose a question for the whole class to answer from their silent reading, such as the question at the end of each subsection. Model how one thinks while reading to find answers to a question.

2. When students get used to reading to answer the subsection questions, pose more in-depth questions, progressing from factual recall to questions that stimulate interpretative or applied thinking.

3. Teach students to ask and answer their own questions as they read. Model this process by reading a section aloud and answering your own questions as you read.

4. After students have read the section, direct them to share answers with a partner before having a brief unified-class discussion to clarify issues, key vocabulary, and related concepts.

Structured Read Aloud (TD)

Purpose: To provide basic access to the text, build fluency, and ensure active reading by all students.

1. Choose a passage and direct students to "read aloud silently using their inner voices." Be sure students understand that reading is an active process and their job is to follow along—eyes riveted to each word, saying the words to themselves as you read aloud.

2. Tell students to be on their "reading toes," for you will be leaving out an occasional word and their task is to chorally supply the word.

3. Provide a simple focus question for students to think about while they are reading along silently and chiming in on words you leave out.

4. After reading a section aloud and filling in the words you've left out, briefly partner students to clarify their answers to the section focus question at the beginning of the section. Follow up with a whole section class discussion as the topic warrants.

Prepare to Read

Background Knowledge 🔞

Ask students to recall what they know about the American Revolution. Have students describe why the colonists went to war against the British.

Set a Purpose 🔞

- **WITNESS HISTORY** Read the selection aloud, or play the audio.

  🔊 AUDIO Witness History Audio CD, A Voice for Freedom

  Ask **Why do you think Patrick Henry mentions slavery?** (*It is a powerful image and it is relevant to his listeners, as many American colonies allowed slavery.*) **What does "give me liberty or give me death" mean?** (*Henry would rather die than live without freedom.*)

- **Focus** Point out the Section Focus Question, and write it on the board. Tell students to refer to this question as they read. (*Answer appears with Section 2 Assessment answers.*)

- **Preview** Have students read the Standards Preview.

- **Reading Skill** Have students use the *Reading Strategy: Recognize Sequence* worksheet. Teaching Resources, **p. 12**

- **NoteTaking** Using the Paragraph Shrinking strategy (TE, p. T20), have students read the section. As students read, have them complete the sequence chart. Reading and Note Taking Study Guide

After Reading

After reading strategies help students synthesize and consolidate key information and study for quizzes and tests. This program supports reading comprehension after reading by providing two key strategies: Vocabulary Study (below) and Responding to Chapter Questions.

Vocabulary Study (SSD)

Purpose: To teach students processes for reviewing and studying critical vocabulary terms.

1. **Read-Cover-Recite-Check (RCRC): Verbal Rehearsal**

   - **Read** Read the new vocabulary word and definition, thinking about examples of the word from your own experience.

   - **Cover** Cover the vocabulary word/definitions with your hand.

   - **Recite** Tell yourself the word–definition–examples–visualizations associated with the definition.

   - **Check** Lift your hand and check your study list. Tell yourself any corrections or changes.

2. **Vocabulary Study Cards (SSD)** Guide students in selecting a few essential terms, including key concepts, to create vocabulary study cards.

   - On the unlined side of a 5 x 7 card:
     a. write the part of speech next to the word;
     b. write a phonetic pronunciation that you understand;
     c. in the lower left-hand corner, write any related word forms introduced during vocabulary instruction. If you know the word in another language, note the translation.

   - On the lined side of the card:
     a. on the top line fill in any "reminder words" (e.g., synonyms);
     b. copy the sentence from the reading/lesson that contains the new word;
     c. copy the relevant dictionary/glossary definition;
     d. write an example sentence from your own experience if possible.

   - Use RCRC to independently study the cards.

   - Partner students for additional study, asking them to take turns asking and answering.

Vocabulary Builder

Use the information below and the following resource to teach students the high-use words from this section. Teaching Resources, Vocabulary Builder, p. 11

High-Use Word	Definition and Sample Sentence
compel, p. 35	*v.* to force The government had no choice but to **compel** the rebels to pay the new tax.
manifest, p. 41	*adj.* obvious; clear; plain The Revolutionary War made **manifest** to Europeans that Americans were determined to have their own government and nation.

THE VIETNAM WAR ERA

Vocabulary Builder

Make Connections

Your American history text deals with events that happened in the past. Many of the events discussed occurred long before you were even born. As you learn new vocabulary, you may find it helpful to connect words and meanings to current events in your community, the nation, and the world. Making connections in this way will help you remember and understand unfamiliar and difficult terms. The example below provides a sentence connecting the word *ensure* to modern circumstances.

> **Example**
> **Word** ensure
> **Definition** to guarantee; to secure
> **Connection to current events** The President of the United States says that he wants to ensure the security of all Americans.

Directions: Record the definition in your textbook for each word listed below. Then, write a sentence for each word that connects it to current events. If you need help making a connection between a word and current events, skim a newspaper or news magazine for ideas.

1. auspices _____
   Connection to current events _____

2. doctrine _____
   Connection to current events _____

3. assert _____
   Connection to current events _____

4. deferment _____
   Connection to current events _____

5. inevitable _____
   Connection to current events _____

6. induce _____
   Connection to current events _____

7. pragmatic _____
   Connection to current events _____

READING

Strategies for Structuring Academic Discussion

Every secondary teacher recognizes that active engagement in classroom activities is an essential prerequisite to academic success. Yet time and again research verifies that many students, especially those less academically prepared, sit passively watching the teacher and their higher-performing peers apply reading strategies and react to lesson content. The discussion strategies outlined below were designed to increase the odds that every student is actively and academically responding during every lesson phase.

Strategy 1: Idea Wave

Purpose: To support all students in actively listening and responding academically to a single, critical prereading (e.g., discussion) or postreading (e.g., review, application) question within a more elaborate unified-class discussion.

1. Pose an open-ended question or task *(e.g., Identify four factors that contributed to the start of the Great Depression.)*

2. Provide a model response on the board *(e.g., One cause of the Great Depression was stock speculation, which led to the stock market crash.)*

3. Give students time to consider what they know about the topic and record a number of responses.

4. Provide two or three sentence starters and ask students to write one or two of their ideas using a sentence starter. These starters should include key academic vocabulary and sentence structures that students wouldn't ordinarily use in casual conversation. *(e.g., Many factors converged to lead to the Great Depression, among them, stock speculation and the crash of the stock market.)*

5. As students are jotting down ideas, "nominate" a few volunteers to jumpstart the subsequent class discussion. Get a few answers from students who wouldn't ordinarily respond voluntarily and bolster their confidence by affirming their idea prior to the actual discussion.

6. Read aloud your model response and have students read along with you a second time to build reading fluency.

7. Have students "rehearse" their responses and build reading fluency and confidence by sharing it first with a partner. This partnering stage also ensures that every student has an opportunity and accountability to respond even if not included in the subsequent unifiedclass discussion.

8. Whip around the class in a relatively fast-paced and structured manner (e.g., down rows, around tables), directing several students to share an idea (i.e., reading aloud their complete academic statement). After this structured debriefing, call on a few volunteers.

9. Provide an active listening and notetaking task during the discussion. Hold students accountable for active listening by asking them to jot down two ideas, such as two perspectives with which you agree, two additional examples, etc.

10. After several contributions, if there tends to be repetition, ask students to point out similarities in responses rather than simply stating that their idea has already been mentioned. Require that students use language for acknowledging other ideas: e.g., *My idea builds upon ___ 's idea. I also believe that. . . .*

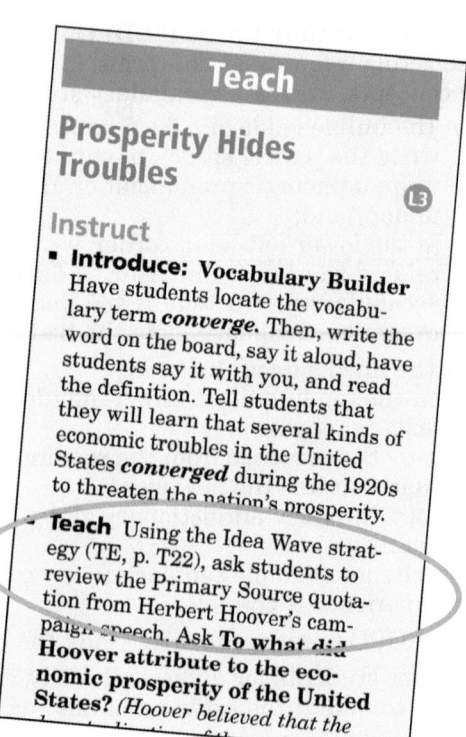

Teach

Prosperity Hides Troubles ③

Instruct

- **Introduce: Vocabulary Builder** Have students locate the vocabulary term *converge*. Then, write the word on the board, say it aloud, have students say it with you, and read the definition. Tell students that they will learn that several kinds of economic troubles in the United States *converged* during the 1920s to threaten the nation's prosperity.

- **Teach** Using the Idea Wave strategy (TE, p. T22), ask students to review the Primary Source quotation from Herbert Hoover's campaign speech. Ask **To what did Hoover attribute to the economic prosperity of the United States?** *(Hoover believed that the*

Strategy 2: Think-Write-Pair-Share

Purpose: To engage students in responding to instruction.

1. **Think** Students listen while the teacher poses a question or task related to the reading or classroom discussion. The level of questions should vary from lower level literal to higher order inferential or analytical.

2. **Write** Provide quiet thinking or writing time for students to deal with the question and go back to the text or review notes. Have students record their ideas in their notebooks. If you are only posing one or two more demanding and essential questions instead of several, consider providing academic sentence starters for students to complete as a means of encouraging more thoughtful and formal responses: *e.g., How did the financial collapse of the American economy change people's lives during the Great Depression? It ____ and forced people to ____.*

3. **Pair/Share** Cue students to find a partner and share their written response, noting similarities and differences. Teach students to encourage one another to clarify and justify their responses. To add more accountability for active listening, ask students to share their partner's idea during the structured debriefing and require that they begin their response with a citation expression: *e.g., My partner ____ pointed out/emphasized/indicated/ predicted that ___ forced people to ____ during the Great Depression.*

4. Randomly call on students to share during a unified-class discussion after they have all rehearsed answers with their partners.

5. Invite any volunteers to contribute additional ideas and points of view to the discussion after calling on a reasonable number of students.

6. Direct students to go back to their notes and add any important information garnered during the partner and class discussions.

Strategy 3: Numbered Heads

Purpose: To support and engage all students in responding to a series of questions to assess reading comprehension and/or review lesson content.

1. Seat students in groups of four and number off one through four.

2. After posing a particular question or task, specify the amount of time students have to discuss their response (allow only 30 seconds to 1 1/2 minutes or students wander off task) and monitor students' interactions to identify comprehension issues, probe thinking, etc.

3. Remind students to pay close attention to the comments of each group member because you will be randomly selecting one student to represent the best thinking of the entire group.

4. Call a number (one through four) and ask all students with that number to raise their hands, ready to respond to the topic at hand in a teacher-directed, whole-class discussion.

5. Add comments, extend key ideas, ask follow-up questions, and make connections between individual student's comments to create a lively whole-class discussion.

6. Provide any summary comments required to ensure that all students understand critical points.

> ■ **Teach** Show students *The Dust Bowl* from the Witness History DVD. Ask **How did depression era crop and livestock prices affect farmers?** *(During the 1930s, prices were so low that a large number of family farms could not survive.)* **What other disaster caused the collapse of many farms?** *(the Dust Bowl)* **What happened to families who lost their livelihoods in these ways?** *(Some remained on their land as tenant farmers, and others migrated to search for work elsewhere.)* Using the Numbered Heads strategy (TE, p. T23), ask students to consider the impact the Great Depression and the Dust Bowl had on rural America. **How did these calamities affect the agricultural industry?** *(Because large farming operations were the most likely to survive the Great Depression, the upheaval probably increased the average farm size. In addition, the government began to initiate large-scale irrigation projects.)* Display Color Transparency: *The Dust Bowl.* Use the transparency book to guide a discussion about the displacement of farmers because of the Dust Bowl. Color Transparencies

WRITING

Research on Writing

Teachers often assume that if they teach content effectively, their students will be able to communicate what they have learned in writing on state assessments. The performance of many students on the writing tasks found in state tests tells us that this isn't true. Many students falter when asked to write because they don't know how to construct a response that shows what they have learned. Teachers can help students improve their performance by embedding expository writing tasks in class activities, homework assignments, and tests throughout the year.

Bringing Writing Into the Social Studies Classroom

A good way to begin a writing program is with short-answer writing prompts. Because these questions can be answered in a sentence or two, they are less intimidating to students. Even so, short-answer does not mean easy. Good responses to such questions are clear, detailed, and complete.

From short-answer questions, move on to more complex constructed response prompts. Ideally these tasks should reflect what your students are likely to encounter on state assessments. These may be thematic essays, position papers, or document-based questions.

As you introduce each kind of prompt, take time with students to work through the process of analyzing the task and framing their response. To be successful, students will need to learn how to analyze the prompt, budget their time and answer space, plan and write their responses, and then edit their first drafts.

Embedding Writing in Assessment

As students become familiar with a type of writing prompt, embed similar tasks in your class assessments. A good prompt will:

- test what students have been taught, whether defined by state standards or your own course outline;
- communicate what is expected of students in terms of format, length, and level of detail, such as the number of examples or reasons; and
- be doable in the time and space allocated for the task.

> *Teachers can help students improve their performance by embedding expository writing tasks in class activities, homework assignments, and tests throughout the year.*

A good prompt provides multiple access points to help students with different learning styles, backgrounds, and abilities engage with the task. This may be done by breaking the task into parts that build from lower- to higher-order thinking skills. This sequencing provides a point of entry for weaker students who may not be capable of completing the entire task and enables them to respond in a limited way.

Bringing Students Into the Scoring Process

The goal of a writing program should be to empower students to assess and improve their own work. For this to happen, students need to have a clear vision of what good writing looks like and how to bring their own work up to that standard.

An effective way to communicate your expectations is through the consistent use of generic rubrics and/or scoring guides. Generic rubrics describe levels of performance on various aspects of a written task, such as writing mechanics or development of a clear thesis statement. Scoring guides, in contrast, describe levels of performance for each specific task. Teachers can use both of these tools to communicate efficiently with students about their written work.

More important, once students are trained in the use of rubrics and scoring guides, they can use these tools to evaluate their own and other students' work. As students take on this responsibility, they begin to internalize performance standards. Planning and implementing a writing program takes time and effort. But the potential payoffs are significant. Not only will students become more competent and confident writers, but their test scores will also reflect those gains.

Diane Hart

Diane Hart is a writer and consultant in history and social studies. She is a former teacher at the elementary, secondary, and college levels and is an active member of both the National and California Councils for the Social Studies.

Effective Classroom Implementation

Prentice Hall United States History provides a systematic approach to writing. It embeds detailed, step-by-step writing instructions so students can build their writing skills, and it provides opportunities for continuous practice throughout the course.

Teach the Steps

The ***Skills Handbook*** introduces the core steps of writing at the beginning of the Student Edition. It supplies students with the basic building blocks for writing different types of assignments—narrative, expository, research, persuasive, and assessment essays. Detailed worksheets and transparencies support the ***Skills Handbook.***

Practice the Steps

Quick Writes activities at the end of every section provide simple prompts that allow students to practice short-answer responses and practice each step of the writing process, such as writing a thesis, gathering details, and crafting a conclusion.

Put the Steps Together

Writing About History assignments in every chapter put the steps for writing an essay together to form a more complex writing assignment with scaffolded instruction. Each type of writing assignment appears multiple times to encourage mastery.

Prepare for Challenging Essays

The American Issues Connector pages help students prepare for the thematic essays that are common on both social studies exams and high-stakes assessments. Students may keep track of key concepts in the ***Note Taking Study Guide,*** which is also available online. Writing practice for Document-Based Assessment appears at the end of every chapter.

Provide Clear Expectations

Assessment Rubrics allow teachers to provide clear expectations and consistent grading. They will allow students to learn how to assess their own writing, edit their work, and internalize standards. Rubrics for evaluating essays on the SAT and ACT appear in the ***Skills Handbook.***

Writing About History

3. Quick Write: Organize the Material You need to give a speech describing environmental problems in your region and how they could affect the local economy. Outline topics and arguments, remembering to begin with a strong argument or a personal story and to end with your most compelling argument.

Writing About History

Writing a Persuasive Speech During the 1960s, many people used speeches to draw attention to their causes. Write a persuasive speech from the point of view of one of these people discussed in the chapter: Betty Friedan, Phyllis Schlafly, Cesar Chavez, Dennis Banks, Ralph Nader, or Rachel Carson. Deliver your completed speech to a classmate or to the entire class.

Prewriting
• Choose the person who most interests you. Take notes about the person's motivations and methods.
• Identify the venue where the speech will be delivered, as well as its audience.

Drafting
• Develop a thesis, and choose information to support it.
• List arguments that support your thesis, and answer opposing arguments.
• Write the speech, remembering to open with an attention-grabbing statement and to end with your strongest argument.

Revising
• Use the guidelines on page SH16 of the Writing Handbook to revise your speech.

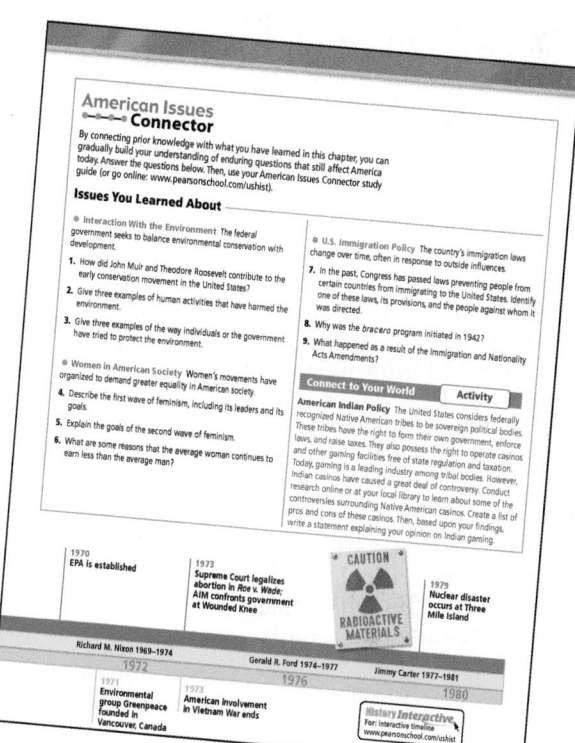

American Issues Connector

By connecting prior knowledge with what you have learned in this chapter, you can gradually build your understanding of enduring questions that still affect America today. Answer the questions below. Then, use your American Issues Connector study guide (or go online: www.pearsonschool.com/ushist).

Issues You Learned About

● **Interaction With the Environment** The federal government seeks to balance environmental conservation with development.

1. How did John Muir and Theodore Roosevelt contribute to the early conservation movement in the United States?

2. Give three examples of human activities that have harmed the environment.

3. Give three examples of the way individuals or the government have tried to protect the environment.

● **Women in American Society** Women's movements have organized to demand greater equality in American society.

4. Describe the first wave of feminism, including its leaders and its goals.

5. Explain the goals of the second wave of feminism.

6. What are some reasons that the average woman continues to earn less than the average man?

● **U.S. Immigration Policy** The country's immigration laws change over time, often in response to outside influences.

7. In the past, Congress has passed laws preventing people from certain countries from immigrating to the United States. Identify one of these laws, its provisions, and the people against whom it was directed.

8. Why was the *bracero* program initiated in 1942?

9. What happened as a result of the Immigration and Nationality Acts Amendments?

Connect to Your World | **Activity**

American Indian Policy The United States considers federally recognized Native American tribes to be sovereign political bodies. These tribes have the right to form their own government, enforce laws, and raise taxes. They also possess the right to operate casinos and other gaming facilities free of state regulation and taxation. Today, gaming is a leading industry among tribal bodies. However, Indian casinos have caused a great deal of controversy. Conduct research online or at your local library to learn about some of the controversies surrounding Native American casinos. Create a list of pros and cons of these casinos. Then, based upon your findings, write a statement explaining your opinion on Indian gaming.

1970
EPA is established

1973
Supreme Court legalizes abortion in *Roe v. Wade*; AIM confronts government at Wounded Knee

CAUTION RADIOACTIVE MATERIALS

1979
Nuclear disaster occurs at Three Mile Island

Richard M. Nixon 1969–1974

Gerald R. Ford 1974–1977

Jimmy Carter 1977–1981

1972 | **1976** | **1980**

1971
Environmental group Greenpeace founded in Vancouver, Canada

1973
American involvement in Vietnam War ends

History Interactive
For: Interactive timeline
www.pearsonschool.com/ushist

Research on Media Literacy

Defining Media Literacy

Research shows that social studies educators do not agree on a universal definition of the term media literacy (Hamot, Gregory, et. al., *Media Literacy in Social Studies Teacher Education: Relating Meaning to Practice,* 1997). Some understand it to mean teaching students how to *use technology*. Others see it as meaning teaching them how to *evaluate the media*. In fact, we need to teach students both the technical and the critical thinking aspects of media literacy in order to equip them with the skills they need to navigate today's electronic and media-rich era.

As every teacher and parent knows, not only are teenagers spending more time than ever before with more types of technologies, but they are "managing to pack increasing amounts of media content into the same amount of time each day" (Kaiser Family Foundation, 2005). In fact, a Senate report of the Committee on Commerce, Science, and Transportation found that "children spend, on average, 28 hours per week watching television [per year], which is more time than they spend in school [per year]" (S. Report. No. 171, 1995).

How do we as teachers channel this familiarity and time spent with technology toward technology that teaches and informs as well as entertains? How do we ensure that we and our students are taking full advantage of the opportunities for learning that technology in the classroom can provide? And how do we make sure that our students are critical consumers of the media with which they are surrounded on a daily basis?

Teaching With and About Technology

Studies indicate that students in "technology-rich environments" experience increased achievement in all major subject areas (Sivin-Kachela, 1998). By integrating technology into the classroom, teachers not only help students acquire the critical tools they need to thrive in a digital age, they also enhance social studies content.

Technology provides easily accessible ways to present core content and engage students. Audio and video bring dynamic moments to life. Primary sources provide the personal experience. The Internet unlocks a myriad array of materials. Together, these materials make history come alive in the classroom.

Teaching Critical Thinking About Media

Media can be a powerful tool not just to teach using technology, but also to teach critical thinking skills. Studies show that media literacy training increases students' ability to access, analyze, and evaluate media messages (Yates, 2001). Students need to learn to analyze what they see and hear as well as what they read. In a social studies course, primary sources and documents include quotations as well as

> *Studies indicate that students in "technology-rich environments" experience increased achievement in all major subject areas (Sivin-Kachela, 1998).*

political cartoons, fine art, and artifacts of all sorts. These are ideal instruments for fostering critical thinking skills, including:

- comparing viewpoints;
- identifying bias and prejudice;
- evaluating evidence;
- interpreting past events and issues within the context in which the event unfolded;
- understanding the meaning, implication, and impact of historical events.

By embedding these media skills into the course, teachers not only enhance key concepts, but also teach students key analysis skills, many of which are tested on high-stakes exams and in document-based assessments. In addition, media-literate students will become more effective consumers, decision makers, and citizens, who are able to succeed in the classroom and beyond.

Judith Mahnke

Judith Mahnke has been teaching in public schools in San Francisco for more than 20 years. She teaches Modern World Civilization, Advanced Placement United States History, Psychology, and Sociology. She is a teacher consultant for the California Geographic Alliance and has served on the board of the California Council for Social Studies for many years.

Effective Classroom Implementation

Media literacy is essential for students in today's classroom as well as in the world at large. ***Prentice Hall United States History*** supports media literacy in an exciting variety of ways, helping students at all levels become more active and engaged learners.

Before Reading

- **Witness History** uniquely engages students' interest with primary source quotes. The ***Teacher's Edition*** helps you use the ***Witness History*** to introduce every lesson.

During Reading

- **Geography Interactive** provides an audio-guided tour to improve geographic literacy. Each chapter also contains an Interactive map, timeline, or diagram to enhance learning.

- **History Interactive** timelines extend students' knowledge of events as they occurred chronologically and help students understand the world events that occurred simultaneously.

- **Political Cartoons** throughout the text challenge students with in-depth analysis questions.

- **Fine art, unique photos, posters, and artifacts** pique student interest and challenge their critical thinking skills.

- **Document-Based Assessment** provides a full page of primary sources, political cartoons, fine art, and charts and graphs followed by questions in a high-stakes exam format.

- **Note Taking Study Guide Online** contains   leveled Note Taking Graphic Organizers and American Issues Connector worksheets that students fill in as they read the text.

- **Extend Online** activities with step-by-step instruction appear in the ***Teacher's Edition*** in every chapter.

After Reading

- **Standards Monitoring Online** with vocabulary builder practice online allows students to interactively monitor their own learning.

- ***ExamView*®** **Test Bank CD-ROM** allows teachers to easily create customized tests from banks of thousands of questions. Questions can be sorted by difficulty level to provide leveled quizzes and tests for differentiated instruction.

ASSESSMENT

Research on Assessment

Frequent and numerous local, state, and federal mandates insist on systematic, ongoing assessment to assure that learning is targeted to outcomes and that students are indeed learning. We cannot expect this demand to be lifted or significantly altered.

A genuine strength of the texts we have assembled for your use is that learning outcomes (or objectives) that are specific to plan and guide instruction include companion assessments to monitor your instruction effort. Research demonstrates that reliance on assessment, especially formative assessment, is associated with greater learning. We have engaged in one of the time-honored procedures for sound, effective, and comprehensive instruction: teach-test-reteach and review and retest. This model works!

Assessment as a Process

Assessment should be viewed as a *process,* not merely an activity that independently evaluates instruction or student learning. As such, the goal of assessment is to assemble information from a variety of sources (unit tests, document assessments, AYP tests, locally crafted tests, specific instructor checklists, etc.), including professional judgment, to focus, guide, and support instruction and subsequently learning.

With the range of resources the series provides (both instructional supports and multiple diverse assessments), testing and assessment become a sequential and progressive process that provides the opportunity for regular assessments that inform both instructors and students. As information accumulates and you use this information to tailor your instruction, research shows that student learning advances and accelerates—making achievement a motivation in itself.

What Is Formative Assessment?

As you use assessments, become familiar with their different roles. First, plan for formative assessments across the school term. Formative assessment is self-assessment. It provides feedback to modify teaching and learning activities. As an integrated approach to assessment and instruction, formative assessments emphasize mastery of specific course material, as opposed to evaluation of performance or assignment of grades (summative assessment).

Formative assessments are conducted throughout the instructional process to monitor students' progress and provide feedback on strengths and weaknesses. The key is feedback. Feedback allows students to correct conceptual errors and encourages instructors to modify their methods. Since formative assessments are designed to guide learning and are not used as an outcome measure, they are generally considered a low-stakes assessment. Formative tests may be graded or not based on instructor purpose and preference. Such assessments become "formative" when the evidence gathered is actually used to guide and adapt teaching to meet the needs of students in meeting the targeted outcomes.

What Is Summative Assessment?

Instructors should also incorporate summative assessment into their instructional plan. Summative assessments are used to judge progress. A summative test "counts," and is comprehensive. Students are expected to prepare for it and to take it seriously. Nevertheless, from the instructor's perspective, summative testing, like formative, reveals areas that need review before moving on to new topics.

Assessment Today

We are in an age of assessment-driven reform. Teachers are expected to be data-driven decision makers. Formative and summative assessments are sound approaches to that end. Create a plan, use assessments to measure the successes and achievements of your students, and note the outcomes that do not meet your expectations. Gather diverse but complementary information, study it by the standards set by yourself, the parents, and the school, and then progress with lessons in the knowledge of your students' needs and accomplishments.

John Poggio

John Poggio, Ph.D., is co-Director of the Center for Educational Testing and Evaluation and a Professor of Educational Psychology and Research at the University of Kansas. He has authored more than 200 papers, articles, technical reports, book chapters, tests, and a text on topics relating to testing, assessment, evaluation, and statistical analysis in education.

Effective Classroom Implementation

In the past, it was common practice to teach a lesson, administer a test, grade it, and move on. Today, we know that continuous assessment of student progress with immediate intervention contributes to high performance (Just for Kids, 2001). ***Prentice Hall United States History*** helps you use data-driven assessment to inform teaching and point your students toward excellence.

Track Understanding

- ***Progress Monitoring Transparencies*** allow you to check student understanding of each section on a daily basis.
- **Progress Monitoring *Online*** lets students assess their understanding of content and get instant vocabulary practice.

Assess Progress, Report Results, and Prescribe Remediation

- ***ExamView*® Test Bank CD-ROM** allows teachers to create customized tests from banks of thousands of questions. Questions can be sorted by difficulty levels to provide leveled quizzes and tests for universal access.
- ***Assessment Rubrics*** includes reproducible rubrics for students and instruction for rubric use for teachers.

Prepare for Standardized Assessment

American Issues Connector and Document-Based Assessments get students ready for high-stakes American history assessments. Quick Study Guides enable students to check their understanding and prepare for test-taking success.

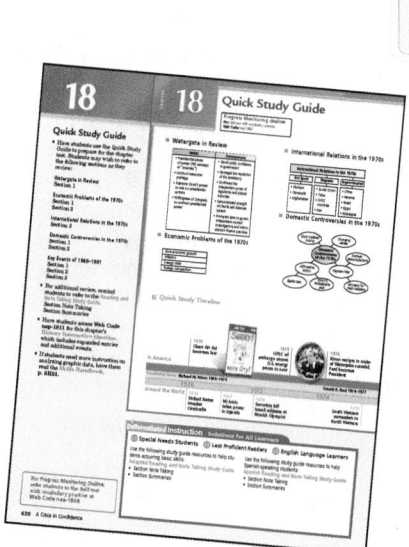

CHAPTER 1

The Nation's Beginnings, Prehistory–1824

Section	Core Instruction **L3**	Differentiated Instruction **L1 L2 L4**	
Section 1 100 minutes *Many Cultures Meet* **OBJECTIVES** • Discuss the migration of the first people to the Americas. • Explain why Europeans wanted to develop a sea route to India in the 1400s. • Describe the importance of trade in West Africa. • Identify the effects of Christopher Columbus's voyage to the Americas.	**Teaching Resources** Outline Map: North America, About 1450, p. 27 Issues Connector: Global Interdependence, pp. 15–18 Section 1 Quiz, p. 32 **Reading and Note Taking Study Guide** Section Note Taking, p. 1 Section 1 Summary, p. 2 American Issues Journal, pp. 173–175 **Progress Monitoring Transparencies,** 1 **Color Transparencies** Migration Across the Bering Strait, A-65	**L1 Adapted Reading and Note Taking Study Guide** Section Note Taking, p. 1 SN Section 1 Summary, p. 2 SN American Issues Connector, pp. 173–174 SN **L2 Adapted Reading and Note Taking Study Guide** Section Note Taking, p. 1 LPR Section 1 Summary, p. 2 LPR American Issues Journal, pp. 173–175 LPR **Spanish Reading and Note Taking Study Guide** Section Note Taking, p. 1 ELL Section 1 Summary, p. 2 ELL American Issues Journal, pp. 173–175 ELL	*Student Edition on Audio SN Differentiated Instruction Activity, Teacher's Edition, p. 5 SN *Guided Reading Audio, Spanish CD ELL *Student Edition on Audio LPR, ELL Differentiated Instruction Activity, Teacher's Edition, p. 5 LPR, ELL
Focus Question *What were the causes and effects of European arrival in the Americas?*		**L4 Differentiated Instruction Activity,** Teacher's Edition, p. 6 AR, GT	Extend Activity, Teacher's Edition, p. 8 AR, GT
Section 2 125 minutes *The American Revolution* **OBJECTIVES** • Describe the European colonial presence in North America. • Trace the development of democratic ideals in Europe and America. • Identify the causes of the American Revolution. • Discuss the results of the American Revolution.	**Teaching Resources** Reading Strategy: Recognizing Sequence, p. 12 Link to Literature: *Common Sense* and the Declaration of Independence, p. 29 Section 2 Quiz, p. 33 **Reading and Note Taking Study Guide** Section Note Taking, p. 3 Section 2 Summary, p. 4 **Progress Monitoring Transparencies,** 2 **Color Transparencies** English Colonies in North America, A-66	**L1 Adapted Reading and Note Taking Study Guide** Section Note Taking, p. 3 SN Section 2 Summary, p. 4 SN **L2 Adapted Reading and Note Taking Study Guide** Section Note Taking, p. 3 LPR Section 2 Summary, p. 4 LPR **Spanish Reading and Note Taking Study Guide** Section Note Taking, p. 3 ELL Section 2 Summary, p. 4 ELL	Differentiated Instruction Activities, Teacher's Edition, pp. 10, 11 SN **Teaching Resources Link to Literature: Thomas Paine's *Common Sense,* p. 28 LPR, ELL Differentiated Instruction Activities, Teacher's Edition, pp. 10, 11 LPR, ELL
Focus Question *What important ideas and major events led to the American Revolution?*		**L4 Differentiated Instruction Activity,** Teacher's Edition, p. 11 AR, GT	Extend Activity, Teacher's Edition, p. 14 AR, GT

Section	Core Instruction (L3)	Differentiated Instruction (L1)(L2)(L4)	
Section 3 125 minutes *The Constitution* **OBJECTIVES** • Identify the weaknesses of the Articles of Confederation. • Describe the role compromise played in the creation of the Constitution and the struggle for its ratification. • Define the principles expressed in the Constitution and Bill of Rights.	**Teaching Resources** Issues Connector: Expanding and Protecting Civil Rights, pp. 19–22 Viewpoints: The New Jersey Plan and the Virginia Plan, p. 30 Section 3 Quiz, p. 34 **Reading and Note Taking Study Guide** Section Note Taking, p. 5 Section 3 Summary, p. 6 American Issues Journal, pp. 176–178 **Progress Monitoring Transparencies**, 3 **Color Transparencies** The Constitutional Convention, A-67	**(L1) Adapted Reading and Note Taking Study Guide** Section Note Taking, p. 5 SN Section 3 Summary, p. 6 SN American Issues Journal, pp. 176–178 SN **(L2) Adapted Reading and Note Taking Study Guide** Section Note Taking, p. 5 LPR Section 3 Summary, p. 6 LPR American Issues Journal, pp. 176–178 LPR **Spanish Reading and Note Taking Study Guide** Section Note Taking, p. 5 ELL Section 3 Summary, p. 6 ELL American Issues Journal, pp. 176–178 ELL	**Differentiated Instruction Activity**, Teacher's Edition, p. 16 SN **Differentiated Instruction Activity**, Teacher's Edition, p. 16 LPR, ELL
Focus Question *What ideas and debates led to the Constitution and Bill of Rights?*		**(L4) Differentiated Instruction Activity**, Teacher's Edition, p. 17 AR, GT	**Extend Activity**, Teaching Resources, pp. 13–14 AR, GT
Section 4 100 minutes *The New Republic* **OBJECTIVES** • Discuss the structure of the federal government and the emergence of political parties. • Explore the major foreign policy issues that confronted the United States. • Describe the growing differences between the North and South.	**Teaching Resources** Biography: Thomas Jefferson, p. 31 Issues Connector: Sectionalism and National Politics, pp. 23–26 Section 4 Quiz, p. 35 **Reading and Note Taking Study Guide** Section Note Taking, p. 7 Section 4 Summary, p. 8 American Issues Journal, pp. 179–181 **Progress Monitoring Transparencies**, 4 **Color Transparencies** The Louisiana Purchase, A-68	**(L1) Adapted Reading and Note Taking Study Guide** Section Note Taking, p. 7 SN Section 4 Summary, p. 8 SN American Issues Journal, pp. 179–181 SN **(L2) Adapted Reading and Note Taking Study Guide** Section Note Taking, p. 7 LPR Section 4 Summary, p. 8 LPR American Issues Journal, pp. 179–181 LPR **Spanish Reading and Note Taking Study Guide** Section Note Taking, p. 7 ELL Section 4 Summary, p. 8 ELL American Issues Journal, pp. 179–181 ELL	**Differentiated Instruction Activity**, Teacher's Edition, p. 22 SN **Differentiated Instruction Activity**, Teacher's Edition, p. 22 LPR, ELL
Focus Question *How did the United States and its government change in the late 1700s and early 1800s?*		**(L4) Differentiated Instruction Activity**, Teacher's Edition, p. 23 AR, GT	**Extend Activity**, Teacher's Edition, p. 27 AR, GT

*Audio support is available for all sections.

**This worksheet also applies to L1.

Assessment Resources
• **Teaching Resources**, Tests A and B, pp. 36–41
• **AYP Monitoring Assessments**, Benchmark Test 1
• **Progress Monitoring Transparencies**, 1–4
• **Test Prep With Document-Based Assessment**
• *ExamView®* Test Bank CD-ROM
• **Progress Monitoring Online Quiz**
• **Assessment Rubrics**

Differentiated Instruction Key
(L1) Special Needs
(L2) Basic to Average
(L3) All Students
(L4) Average to Advanced

SN   Special Needs Students
ELL   English Language Learners
LPR   Less Proficient Readers
AR   Advanced Readers
GT   Gifted and Talented

Author's Note

The story of American history used to begin with the English colonies along the Atlantic Coast. According to that story, the "seeds" of the United States first appeared with the English colonists in 1607 at Jamestown in Virginia and in 1620 with the "Pilgrims" at Plymouth in New England. American historians neglected to discuss the earlier Spanish settlements in Florida or the French colonists in Canada. Those historians also treated the Indians only as primitive enemies to English civilization. And African slaves appeared as unfortunate exceptions in a happy story of Englishmen becoming freer and more prosperous as colonists in a new land of opportunity.

We now see colonial America more clearly with more diverse people. The colonial story now includes the Dutch along the Hudson, the Spanish in Florida, the southwest, and California, the French along the Great Lakes and in the Mississippi Valley, and even the Russians in Alaska. We also recognize the Indians as adaptable people whose trade and diplomacy helped determine the rise and fall of colonial empires. In addition, historians no longer treat slavery as some unfortunate exception. Instead, they see it as central to the economy and to the thinking of the colonists.

Colonization created a new world by mixing peoples, microbes, plants, and animals from four continents: Africa, Europe, and South and North America. This mixing was unprecedented in speed and scale in human history. Everyone—settler, native, and slave—had to adapt to a new world made by those combinations. The new societies offered new opportunities to some people, but greater exploitation to others. And we have inherited that mixed legacy.

—Alan Taylor

Extend Online

The First Presidency, 1789–1796

Have students conduct research on the first U.S. presidency under George Washington. Have them use information from both primary and secondary sources to write a journal entry from Washington's perspective. Use the steps below to help students conduct the activity.

Prepare for the Activity Explain that Washington had no one to look to for guidance in this new position for the new nation. Explain that diaries and journals are important sources for learning someone's thoughts and feelings at a particular time in history.

Conduct the Activity To help them get started, send students to **www.pearsonschool.com/ushist.** Students will read about the presidency of George Washington and the challenges he faced. Organize students in pairs. Have them analyze different periods of time during Washington's two-term administration. Ask each pair to choose a year or a time frame and write journal entries about the main issues that Washington dealt with as President during that time.

Follow-Up Conduct a class discussion by using the following questions: What kinds of issues did the first President face? How did Washington conduct himself in such a new and high-profile position? Do you think he was successful? Why or why not?

Shared Reading ⓛ ⓛ2

Depending on their skill level, some readers may be unable to complete a reading assignment at home or independently. They may understand the content sufficiently only if the selection of text is read aloud in class and the meaning is clarified by the teacher. You may address this situation in the following ways:

• In class, have each student read aloud a paragraph. Use strong readers for longer selections and less proficient readers for shorter selections. After each paragraph has been read, ask a question to check for understanding of key concepts, and wait for volunteers.

• Organize the class in small groups, assigning each group a small selection of text. Each group is responsible for extracting key information from that selection to present to the class. All members of the class should take notes as selections of texts are presented.

Creating a Dialogue ⓛ2

In addition to learning social studies content, English Language Learners face the more daunting challenge of developing proficiency in English. To encourage students to use both written and spoken English and to apply core content, have them create a dialogue. Follow these steps:

1. Organize students in groups, and assign each group a scenario.

2. On the board, list key terms and high-use words that must be included in the dialogue.

3. Require that every student in the group have a speaking role.

4. Have students submit a written copy of the script as part of the assessment in this activity.

Ask each group to perform its dialogue for the class to enhance the English language listening skills of students in the audience.

Modeling Reading and Writing Skills

Set a Purpose for Reading Tell students that setting a purpose for reading will help them know what information to look for in the text. Explain that their first step should be to preview the section headings and visuals. Next, they should use that information to set a purpose for their reading.

Model this skill by examining Section 1, noting the blue and red headings and the visuals. Point out that the images depict American Indians and their meeting with Europeans, that the map shows Native American cultures in North America about the year 1450, and that the headings list the cultures from around the world that met in North America during colonization. Explain that having previewed the chapter, students can now set an appropriate purpose for reading: to learn about the meetings of different cultures in North America during colonization. Ask students to list other purposes for reading this section. *(Possible response: to learn why Europeans came to North America)*

Gather Details Tell students that in this chapter, they will be writing a cause-and-effect essay. (See Writing About History at the end of the chapter.) Before they begin writing, students should list the causes and effects to help them organize the information. To gather details for each cause and each effect, create a concept web or a flowchart that shows the relationship between the facts. Remind students to make sure that all the details support either a cause or an effect. To avoid including unnecessary details, tell students to cross out circles that do not support the relationship.

Model this skill by writing *European arrival* on the board in the center of a web. Surround this cause with "effect" circles labeled *trade, cultural borrowing, conflict,* and *new nation.* Ask students to continue adding information to the webs as they gather more details. Remind students to avoid using details that do not help establish a cause-and-effect relationship. Point out that they may cross out details that prove to be unnecessary.

Manifest Destiny, Civil War, and Reconstruction, 1800–1877

Section	Core Instruction L3	Differentiated Instruction L1 L2 L4	
Section 1 125 minutes *Reform and Westward Expansion* **OBJECTIVES** • Analyze growing democratization, as well as limits on democracy, in the early 1800s. • Discuss the importance of the Second Great Awakening and the rise of various reform movements. • Explain how the nation expanded westward. **Focus Question** *What trends in democratization and reform had been taking shape in the United States by 1850?*	**Teaching Resources** Link to Literature: *Narrative of the Life of Frederick Douglass, an American Slave*, p. 27 American Issues Connector: Church and State, pp. 15–18 Section 1 Quiz, p. 33 **Reading and Note Taking Study Guide** Section Note Taking, p. 9 Section 1 Summary, p. 10 American Issues Journal, pp. 182–184 **Progress Monitoring Transparencies**, 14 **Color Transparencies** The Second Great Awakening, A-69	**L1 Adapted Reading and Note Taking Study Guide** Section Note Taking, p. 9 SN Section 1 Summary, p. 10 SN American Issues Journal, pp. 182–184 SN **L2 Adapted Reading and Note Taking Study Guide** Section Note Taking, p. 9 LPR Section 1 Summary, p. 10 LPR American Issues Journal, pp. 182–184 LPR **Spanish Reading and Note Taking Study Guide** Section Note Taking, p. 9 ELL Section 1 Summary, p. 10 ELL American Issues Journal, pp. 182–184 ELL **L4 Differentiated Instruction Activity,** Teacher's Edition, p. 39 AR, GT	***Student Edition on Audio** SN **Differentiated Instruction Activities,** Teacher's Edition, pp. 36, 40 SN ***Guided Reading Audio, Spanish CD** ELL ***Student Edition on Audio** LPR, ELL **Differentiated Instruction Activities,** Teacher's Edition, pp. 36, 40 LPR, ELL **Extend Activity,** Teacher's Edition, p. 41 AR, GT
Section 2 125 minutes *The Union in Crisis* **OBJECTIVES** • Trace the growing conflict over the issue of slavery in the western territories. • Analyze the importance of the Dred Scott decision. • Explain how the election of Abraham Lincoln in 1860 led to secession. **Focus Question** *How did the issue of slavery divide the Union?*	**Teaching Resources** Reading Strategy: Recognize Sequence, p. 12 Viewpoints: Douglas and Lincoln, p. 30 American Issues Connector: Federal Power and States' Rights, pp. 19–22 Section 2 Quiz, p. 34 **Reading and Note Taking Study Guide** Section Note Taking, p. 11 Section 2 Summary, p. 12 American Issues Journal, pp. 185–187 **Progress Monitoring Transparencies**, 15 **Color Transparencies** The Struggle Against Slavery, A-70	**L1 Adapted Reading and Note Taking Study Guide** Section Note Taking, p. 11 SN Section 2 Summary, p. 12 SN American Issues Journal, pp. 185–187 SN **L2 Adapted Reading and Note Taking Study Guide** Section Note Taking, p. 11 LPR Section 2 Summary, p. 12 LPR American Issues Journal, pp. 185–187 LPR **Spanish Reading and Note Taking Study Guide** Section Note Taking, p. 11 ELL Section 2 Summary, p. 12 ELL American Issues Journal, pp. 185–187 ELL **L4 Differentiated Instruction Activity,** Teacher's Edition, p. 46 AR, GT	**Differentiated Instruction Activities,** Teacher's Edition, pp. 43, 45 SN ****Teaching Resources,** Viewpoints: The Illinois Senate Campaign of 1858, pp. 28–29 LPR, ELL **Differentiated Instruction Activities,** Teacher's Edition, pp. 43, 45 LPR, ELL **Extend Activity,** Teacher's Edition, p. 47 AR, GT

*Audio support is available for all sections.   ****This worksheet also applies to L1.**

Assessment Resources
• **Teaching Resources**, Tests A and B, pp. 37–42
• **AYP Monitoring Assessments**, Benchmark Test 1
• **Progress Monitoring Transparencies**, 14–17
• **Test Prep With Document-Based Assessment**
• *ExamView*® Test Bank CD-ROM
• **Progress Monitoring Online Quiz**
• **Assessment Rubrics**

Differentiated Instruction Key		
L1 Special Needs	SN	Special Needs Students
L2 Basic to Average	ELL	English Language Learners
L3 All Students	LPR	Less Proficient Readers
L4 Average to Advanced	AR	Advanced Readers
	GT	Gifted and Talented

Section	Core Instruction (L3)	Differentiated Instruction (L1) (L2) (L4)	
Section 3 125 minutes *The Civil War* **OBJECTIVES** • Evaluate the advantages the North enjoyed in the Civil War. • Analyze the impact of the Civil War on the North and South, especially the impact of the Emancipation Proclamation. • Explore the outcome and aftermath of the Civil War. **Focus Question** *What factors and events led to the Union victory in the Civil War?*	**Teaching Resources** Reading a Chart: The Northern Economy During the Civil War, p. 31 Section 3 Quiz, p. 35 **Reading and Note Taking Study Guide** Section Note Taking, p. 13 Section 3 Summary, p. 14 **Progress Monitoring Transparencies,** 16 **Color Transparencies** The Civil War Ends, A-71	**(L1) Adapted Reading and Note Taking Study Guide** Section Note Taking, p. 13 SN Section 3 Summary, p. 14 SN **(L2) Adapted Reading and Note Taking Study Guide** Section Note Taking, p. 13 LPR Section 3 Summary, p. 14 LPR **Spanish Reading and Note Taking Study Guide** Section Note Taking, p. 13 ELL Section 3 Summary, p. 14 ELL **(L4) Differentiated Instruction Activity,** Teacher's Edition, p. 51 AR, GT	**Differentiated Instruction Activities,** Teacher's Edition, pp. 49, 52 SN **Differentiated Instruction Activities,** Teacher's Edition, pp. 49, 52 LPR, ELL **Extend Activity,** Teaching Resources, pp. 13–14 AR, GT
Section 4 100 minutes *The Reconstruction Era* **OBJECTIVES** • Explore how Congress and the President clashed over Reconstruction. • Describe the impact of Reconstruction on the South. • Explain how Reconstruction came to an end. **Focus Question** *What were the immediate and long-term effects of Reconstruction?*	**Teaching Resources** History Comics: Johnson's Impeachment, p. 32 American Issues Connector: Checks and Balances, pp. 23–26 Section 4 Quiz, p. 36 **Reading and Note Taking Study Guide** Section Note Taking, p. 15 Section 4 Summary, p. 16 American Issues Journal, pp. 188–190 **Progress Monitoring Transparencies,** 17 **Color Transparencies** Reconstruction and the New South, A-72	**(L1) Adapted Reading and Note Taking Study Guide** Section Note Taking, p. 15 SN Section 4 Summary, p. 16 SN American Issues Journal, pp. 188–190 SN **(L2) Adapted Reading and Note Taking Study Guide** Section Note Taking, p. 15 LPR Section 4 Summary, p. 16 LPR American Issues Journal, pp. 188–190 LPR **Spanish Reading and Note Taking Study Guide** Section Note Taking, p. 15 ELL Section 4 Summary, p. 16 ELL American Issues Journal, pp. 188–190 ELL **(L4) Differentiated Instruction Activity,** Teacher's Edition, p. 58 AR, GT	**Differentiated Instruction Activity,** Teacher's Edition, p. 56 SN **Differentiated Instruction Activity,** Teacher's Edition, p. 56 LPR, ELL **Extend Activity,** Teacher's Edition, p. 59 AR, GT

Author's Note

I have found that students love stories of the American West. These stories have symbolized mystery and adventure at least since Lewis and Clark began exploring new territory and sending home samples of its flora and fauna to a White House hungry for news of this exotic area. Since childhood, I myself was fascinated with Lewis and Clark, with the black explorer James Beckwourth, and a host of men and women who were lured by the unknown. Recently, I read Thomas P. Slaughter's *Exploring Lewis and Clark: Reflections on Men and Wilderness,* and then I assigned it in my early American history course. Students were just as stimulated as I was to explore questions of "how do we know what we know" about those early encounters between the Europeans and the people of the Pacific Northwest. And why were Lewis and Clark so intent on being the first to explore a wilderness that had in fact already been reached by the Europeans before them?

The answer is arrogance—though completely *understandable* arrogance—a quality that led Americans to name manifest destiny as the motivation that inspired them to "overspread the continent" with "yearly multiplying millions." And it was this same ambition that inspired historian Henry Nash Smith in his 1950 watershed work on American history and culture, *Virgin Land,* to examine the events, ideas, and people that pulled Americans west. Though works such as Smith's might be considered dated, notions of wide-open lands, romantic conquest, and daring exploration continue to linger and shape the American imagination.

—Emma Lapansky-Werner

Extend Online

Reconstruction Documents

Have students read and do background research on a document from the Reconstruction period. Use the steps below to help students complete the activity.

Prepare for the Activity Explain that the period called Reconstruction was a challenging time in our country's history. The South's infrastructure and economy had been devastated by the Civil War. Thousands of lives had been lost on both sides. Some people wanted to punish the South; others wanted to restore it.

Conduct the Activity Organize students in pairs and explain that they will be conducting research on a Reconstruction-period document, using resources provided by the Library of Congress (LOC). For help in starting the activity, send students to **www.pearsonschool.com/ushist.** Tell them to select a document from the list of documents on the LOC site and conduct additional research within the LOC site, on other Internet sites, or in the library. Students should then read the document and research the events and the context in which the document was written to create a slide-show presentation. Encourage students to include the following elements in their presentations: narrative, other primary sources, maps, dates and timelines, statistics, and images.

Follow-Up Conduct a class discussion based on these questions: What were the main points of the document? Do students support the document's argument or point of view? Was the document important to Reconstruction?

Peer Editing L2

Writing is a key component of any history-social science class. Many English Language Learners should not have great difficulty in developing an argument or finding factual information to support it, but they often struggle with the mechanics of writing. Peer editing can be a valuable tool because it allows students to see samples of writing so that they may internalize what is appropriate in an essay. As they read one another's essays, ask students to consider the following:

- Is a thesis statement evident in the first paragraph?
- Is appropriate and accurate historical information used to substantiate the thesis statement?
- Does the essay end with a logical conclusion that is supported by the evidence presented in the essay and that revisits the main argument?

Provide students with a rubric to use while critiquing their classmates' essays. Encourage students to be both constructive and specific in their feedback. Remind them to edit for grammar and spelling.

Debate L2

Debates challenge students by asking them to use higher-level thinking to consider, defend, and refute opposing arguments. In order to do this effectively, students need to have content knowledge on the topic. Debates can be structured in a variety of ways. Below is one model that can be particularly effective.

1. Provide students with an opinion-based question that can be logically answered in several different ways.
2. Organize students in two groups.
3. Have students discuss justifications for their positions. Make sure that students appoint one person to record the group members' ideas.
4. Provide time for students to research their position.
5. Instruct students on each side to prepare a compelling, two-minute opening statement.
6. Begin the debate. A student from each side should read the opening statement, which is to be followed by questions from the opposing side. Any member of the group can respond to questions.
7. Conclude the debate by giving each team several minutes to create a brief closing statement to be read to the class.

Modeling Reading and Writing Skills

Use Prior Knowledge Remind students that they already know something about many topics, both from reading previous materials and from their own experiences. Explain that building on this prior knowledge gives readers a head start on learning new information.

To demonstrate how students may use prior knowledge, have them read about social reform in Section 1. Ask **Do reformers today still seek improvement in areas targeted by nineteenth-century reformers?** *(Possible answer: Yes; reformers still struggle with issues related to alcohol abuse, the prison system, education, and care for the mentally ill.)* **Is civil disobedience, which Thoreau advocated, still a strategy used by people who seek social reform and change?** *(Yes; many groups continue to practice civil disobedience to effect social change.)* Tell students that by using what they already know, they can make connections between their own knowledge and the text, resulting in a greater understanding of the new content.

Use Facts and Details Explain that in this chapter, students will be writing a persuasive essay about a particular reform movement. (See Writing About History at the end of the chapter.) Review that in persuasive writing, students need to argue for a specific point of view or position. They must support their argument with evidence that fits the type of persuasive essay. They might use quotations, examples, or statistics as evidence. Write the following types of support on the board:

- Quotations: the exact words of a person, which are attributed both to the person and to the source in which you found it
- Examples: descriptions, specific details
- Statistics: numbers, figures that support the argument

Explain that if students are writing about educational reform, they might include a quotation from a historical figure who witnessed the movement's positive effects. They might list examples of these effects. Students might also include graphic information, such as a line graph showing increased literacy.

CHAPTER 3

The Development of Industrial America, 1870–1914

Section	Core Instruction L3	Differentiated Instruction L1 L2 L4	

Section 1 125 minutes
The Triumph of Industry

OBJECTIVES
- Analyze the growth of the United States as an industrial power.
- Summarize the rise of big business.
- Understand the plight of the industrial worker and how workers tried to improve their condition.
- Identify reasons that workers and big business clashed.

Focus Question *What factors led to the industrialization of America, and what impact did industrialization have on society?*

Teaching Resources
Reading Strategy: Identify Causes and Effects, p. 12
Issues Connector: Technology and Society, pp. 15–18
Biography: American Socialists, p. 32
Section 1 Quiz, p. 36

Reading and Note Taking Study Guide
Section Note Taking, pp. 17–18
Section Summary, p. 19
American Issues Journal, pp. 191–193

Progress Monitoring Transparencies, 18

Color Transparencies
The Robber Barons, A-73

L1 Adapted Reading and Note Taking Study Guide
Section Note Taking, pp. 17–18 SN
Section 1 Summary, p. 19 SN
American Issues Journal, pp. 191–193 SN

L2 Adapted Reading and Note Taking Study Guide
Section Note Taking, pp. 17–18 LPR
Section 1 Summary, p. 19 LPR
American Issues Journal, pp. 191–193 LPR

Spanish Reading and Note Taking Study Guide
Section Note Taking, pp. 17–18 ELL
Section 1 Summary, p. 19 ELL
American Issues Journal, pp. 191–193 ELL

L4 Differentiated Instruction Activity, Teacher's Edition, p. 67 AR, GT

Differentiated Instruction Activity, Teacher's Edition, p. 69 SN

****Teaching Resources**
Biography: Eugene V. Debs, p. 31 LPR, ELL

Differentiated Instruction Activity, Teacher's Edition, p. 69 LPR, ELL

Extend Activity,
Teaching Resources, pp. 13–14 AR, GT

Section 2 125 minutes
Immigration and Urbanization

OBJECTIVES
- Understand the reasons that immigrants came to America.
- Explain the immigrants' experience upon arriving in the United States.
- Identify the changes that took place in cities of the late nineteenth century.
- Describe the urban middle class.

Focus Question *Why did immigrants come to the United States, and how did they impact society?*

Teaching Resources
Issues Connector: Migration and Urbanization, pp. 19–22
Reading a Chart: Immigration, 1880–1920, p. 33
Section 2 Quiz, p. 37

Reading and Note Taking Study Guide
Section Note Taking, p. 20
Section Summary, p. 21
American Issues Journal, pp. 194–196

Progress Monitoring Transparencies, 19

Color Transparencies
New Immigrants, A-74

L1 Adapted Reading and Note Taking Study Guide
Section Note Taking, p. 20 SN
Section 2 Summary, p. 21 SN
American Issues Journal, pp. 194–196 SN

L2 Adapted Reading and Note Taking Study Guide
Section Note Taking, p. 20 LPR
Section 2 Summary, p. 21 LPR
American Issues Journal, pp. 194–196 LPR

Spanish Reading and Note Taking Study Guide
Section Note Taking, p. 20 ELL
Section 2 Summary, p. 21 ELL
American Issues Journal, pp. 194–196 ELL

L4 Differentiated Instruction Activity, Teacher's Edition, p. 74 AR, GT

***Student Edition on Audio** SN

Differentiated Instruction Activities, Teacher's Edition, pp. 76, 78 SN

***Guided Reading Audio, Spanish CD** ELL

***Student Edition on Audio** LPR, ELL

Differentiated Instruction Activities, Teacher's Edition, pp. 76, 78 LPR, ELL

Extend Activity,
Teacher's Edition, p. 79 AR, GT

Section	Core Instruction	Differentiated Instruction	
Section 3 125 minutes *The South and West Transformed* **OBJECTIVES** • Explain the development of the New South. • Understand the impact on Native Americans as settlers moved to the West. • Identify who moved to the West and their reasons for doing so.	**Teaching Resources** Issues Connector: American Indian Policy, pp. 23–26 Link to Literature: *Chief Joseph Surrenders,* p. 34 Section 3 Quiz, p. 38 **Reading and Note Taking Study Guide** Section Note Taking, p. 22 Section Summary, p. 23 American Issues Journal, pp. 197–199 **Progress Monitoring Transparencies,** 20 **Color Transparencies** Driving the Golden Spike, A-75	(L1) **Adapted Reading and Note Taking Study Guide** Section Note Taking, p. 22 SN Section 3 Summary, p. 23 SN American Issues Journal, pp. 197–199 SN	**Differentiated Instruction Activities,** Teacher's Edition, pp. 82, 85 SN
		(L2) **Adapted Reading and Note Taking Study Guide** Section Note Taking, p. 22 LPR Section 3 Summary, p. 23 LPR American Issues Journal, pp. 197–199 LPR **Spanish Reading and Note Taking Study Guide** Section Note Taking, p. 22 ELL Section 3 Summary, p. 23 ELL American Issues Journal, pp. 197–199 ELL	**Differentiated Instruction Activities,** Teacher's Edition, pp. 82, 85 LPR, ELL
Focus Question *What were the most important developments in the South and the West?*		(L4) **Differentiated Instruction Activity,** Teacher's Edition, p. 81 AR, GT	**Extend Activity,** Teacher's Edition, p. 86 AR, GT
Section 4 125 minutes *Issues of the Gilded Age* **OBJECTIVES** • Understand the segregation and social tensions that troubled the nation during the late 1800s. • Identify the political and economic challenges that existed during the Gilded Age. • Analyze the effects of the Populists' programs and activities.	**Teaching Resources** Issues Connector: Women in American Society, pp. 27–30 Interpreting a Political Cartoon: The Gilded Age, p. 35 Section 4 Quiz, p. 39 **Reading and Note Taking Study Guide** Section Note Taking, p. 24 Section Summary, p. 25 American Issues Journal, pp. 200–202 **Progress Monitoring Transparencies,** 21 **Color Transparencies** The Election of 1896, A-76	(L1) **Adapted Reading and Note Taking Study Guide** Section Note Taking, p. 24 SN Section 4 Summary, p. 25 SN American Issues Journal, pp. 200–202 SN	**Differentiated Instruction Activity,** Teacher's Edition, p. 88 SN
		(L2) **Adapted Reading and Note Taking Study Guide** Section Note Taking, p. 24 LPR Section 4 Summary, p. 25 LPR American Issues Journal, pp. 200–202 LPR **Spanish Reading and Note Taking Study Guide** Section Note Taking, p. 24 ELL Section 4 Summary, p. 25 ELL American Issues Journal, pp. 200–202 ELL	**Differentiated Instruction Activity,** Teacher's Edition, p. 88 LPR, ELL
Focus Question *What challenges arose for the nation during the Gilded Age?*		(L4) **Differentiated Instruction Activity,** Teacher's Edition, p. 89 AR, GT	**Extend Activity,** Teacher's Edition, p. 90 AR, GT

*Audio support is available for all sections.   **This worksheet also applies to L1.

Assessment Resources

- **Teaching Resources,** Tests A and B, pp. 40–45
- **AYP Monitoring Assessments,** Benchmark Test 1
- **Progress Monitoring Transparencies,** 18–21
- **Test Prep With Document-Based Assessment**
- *ExamView* ® **Test Bank CD-ROM**
- **Progress Monitoring Online Quiz**
- **Assessment Rubrics**

Differentiated Instruction Key

(L1) Special Needs		SN	Special Needs Students
(L2) Basic to Average		ELL	English Language Learners
(L3) All Students		LPR	Less Proficient Readers
(L4) Average to Advanced		AR	Advanced Readers
		GT	Gifted and Talented

Author's Note

Students (and their teachers) may think of the Gilded Age as a boring period in history, especially when compared to the Civil War and other action-packed eras. I know I felt this way when I was in high school and college. After all, if we judge an era by its presidents, the Gilded Age boasted the presidencies of three of our most lackluster leaders: Rutherford Hayes, Chester Arthur, and Benjamin Harrison.

We might begin our study of the Gilded Age by asking students to consider key developments of the time in which they live—political corruption, disruptive economic change, growing disparities between rich and poor, the immigration debate, urban decay, and terrorism—and then point out that these same issues predominated in the latter decades of the nineteenth century.

Or you might ask your students "Are we living through another Gilded Age now?" Then try outlining several of the basic similarities between then and now, and you might find that both you and your students have overcome your disinclination to cover this period.

If students need a bit more encouragement, mention that Karl Rove, George W. Bush's top political advisor, sees Mark Hanna, a Gilded Age senator considered the political rainmaker of the 1890s, as his idol. Or point out that just as the 2001 terrorist attacks shook our world, so too attacks by anarchists on leading industrialists and political leaders unsettled Americans during the Gilded Age.

If this doesn't get your students' attention, try natural disasters. Long before Hurricane Katrina, the United States experienced some of the worst natural disasters in its history during the Gilded Age: the Johnstown Flood of 1889, the Galveston Hurricane of 1900, and the San Francisco Earthquake of 1906. Encourage students to compare and contrast how America responded to these incidents, and they will see the true value to studying the past.

—Peter B. Levy

Extend Online

The Immigrant Experience

Have students prepare an oral presentation about the journey of an immigrant from his or her homeland to the United States. Use the steps below to help students complete the activity.

Prepare for the Activity
Remind students that most Americans are descended from ancestors who came here as immigrants centuries ago, decades ago, or recently. In the past, most immigrants arrived in the United States on ships and had to pass through immigration stations. In recent years, many immigrants have arrived by airplane. Still, one thing has not changed; each immigrant has a unique and interesting story to tell about his or her journey.

Conduct the Activity For help in starting the activity, send students to **www.pearsonschool.com/ushist.** Students will read about past immigration to the United States. The Web site will provide background and ideas for the types of information and visuals that students may include in their presentations. Have students work in small groups to research and develop a presentation about one immigrant's experience. Encourage students to include a combination of quotations from interviews, photographs, maps, and recordings to make each subject's experience come alive for classmates.

Follow-Up After the presentations, conduct a class discussion based on the following questions: What experiences or feelings did immigrants have in common? In what ways was the experience different for nineteenth-century immigrants than for immigrants of today?

Differentiated Instruction Solutions for All Learners

Using Images ⓛ ⓛ

The importance of images to an American history classroom cannot be overemphasized. Photographs, political cartoons, paintings, and artifacts can help students comprehend concepts addressed in the text. For example, a political cartoon can present the differing points of view of two candidates on an issue, and a painting can reveal the context of an era through the depiction of clothing or technology.

Suggest that students use visuals in this chapter to compare and contrast concepts. For example, refer students to the images in the "American Issues Connector: Migration and Urbanization," and have them compare the "streetcar suburb" University Park to the suburban neighborhood in Las Vegas, Nevada. Overall, visuals can make an individual, event, or era more vivid and memorable by giving students concrete examples of what they are studying. As you teach each visual, ask students to describe what they see, and ask them to make connections to the text.

Creating a Word Bank ⓛ

Research suggests that students will best learn new vocabulary words through frequent encounters. For this reason, the text continues to use high-use words after they are introduced. You can also encourage frequent encounters by asking students to create a word bank. A word bank can help students process, reflect, and integrate new terms into their personal vocabulary.

To begin, have students list key terms and high-use words from each chapter. Then, have students take the list home and see how many examples of these words they can find and copy from newspapers or periodicals. Have students present their examples to the class, and ensure that they are accurate. Then, have students tape or paste the examples on their lists next to the word and place the lists in their notebooks. Students may use the lists to refresh their knowledge and as a study guide.

Modeling Reading and Writing Skills

Cause and Effect Tell students that recognizing causes and effects helps them clarify the relationships among events or situations. Point out that noting signal words can help students identify these relationships. Clue words such as *reason, because, produce,* and *purpose* indicate possible causes. Words such as *brought about, effect, led to, outcome, produced, relation, result, so, then, therefore,* and *thus* indicate possible effects.

Model the way to identify cause-and-effect relationships by using this statement from Section 2: "Rapid growth led to a shortage of housing." Write the statement on the board, and read it aloud. Draw students' attention to the words *led to,* and point out that these words signal that a cause is leading to an effect. The cause of this shortage is *rapid growth.* The effect is *a shortage of housing.*

Oral Presentation Explain that in this chapter, students will deliver oral presentations. (See Writing About History at the end of the chapter.) Explain that an effective oral presentation engages listeners, holds their interest and includes various types of media—photos, illustrations, graphs, charts, maps, music, or video—that will both convey main ideas effectively and enliven the presentation for the audience. To help students prepare an oral presentation, instruct them to use these steps:

- Prewriting: Choose a topic that interests you; your enthusiasm will be evident as you give your presentation.
- Research: Gather information from school-approved Internet sources and from library sources.
- Outline: Prepare an outline that highlights your main points. Plan how you will use media to highlight key points or support your ideas.
- Make notes: Prepare numbered note cards that follow your outline. Use these to become familiar with your text and the sequence of information.

Tell students that most oral reports have time limits, so students should test for length as they practice their presentations. They should also have the proper equipment on hand and know how to use it.

The Progressive Era, 1890–1920

Section	Core Instruction L3	Differentiated Instruction L1 L2 L4	

Section 1 100 minutes
The Drive for Reform

OBJECTIVES
- Identify the causes of Progressivism and compare it to Populism.
- Analyze the role that journalists played in the Progressive Movement.
- Evaluate some of the social reforms that Progressives tackled.
- Explain what Progressives hoped to achieve through political reforms.

Focus Question *What areas did Progressives think were in need of the greatest reform?*

Teaching Resources
Reading Strategy: Main Ideas and Details, p. 13
Link to Literature: *The Octopus,* p. 20
Section 1 Quiz, p. 26

Reading and Note Taking Study Guide
Section Note Taking, p. 26
Section 1 Summary, p. 27

Progress Monitoring Transparencies, 82

Color Transparencies
City Commission, A-77

L1 Adapted Reading and Note Taking Study Guide
Section Note Taking, p. 26 SN
Section 1 Summary, p. 27 SN

L2 Adapted Reading and Note Taking Study Guide
Section Note Taking, p. 26 LPR
Section 1 Summary, p. 27 LPR

Spanish Reading and Note Taking Study Guide
Section Note Taking, p. 26 ELL
Section 1 Summary, p. 27 ELL

L4 Differentiated Instruction Activity, Teacher's Edition, pp. 103, 106 AR, GT

*Student Edition on Audio SN

Differentiated Instruction Activity, Teacher's Edition, p. 101 SN

*Guided Reading Audio, Spanish CD ELL

*Student Edition on Audio LPR, ELL

Differentiated Instruction Activities, Teacher's Edition, pp. 101, 105 LPR, ELL

Extend Activity
Teaching Resources, pp. 14–15 AR, GT

Section 2 100 minutes
Women Make Progress

OBJECTIVES
- Analyze the impact of changes in women's education on women's roles in society.
- Explain what women did to win workers' rights and to improve family life.
- Evaluate the tactics women used to win passage of the Nineteenth Amendment.

Focus Question *How did women of the Progressive Era make progress and win the right to vote?*

Teaching Resources
Issues Connector: Social Problems and Reform, pp. 16–19
Biography: Carrie Chapman Catt, p. 21
Section 2 Quiz, p. 27

Reading and Note Taking Study Guide
Section Note Taking, p. 28
Section 2 Summary, p. 29
American Issues Journal, pp. 203–205

Progress Monitoring Transparencies, 83

Color Transparencies
Women's Suffrage, A-78

L1 Adapted Reading and Note Taking Study Guide
Section Note Taking, p. 28 SN
Section 2 Summary, p. 29 SN
American Issues Journal, pp. 203–205 SN

L2 Adapted Reading and Note Taking Study Guide
Section Note Taking, p. 28 LPR
Section 2 Summary, p. 29 LPR
American Issues Journal, pp. 203–205 LPR

Spanish Reading and Note Taking Study Guide
Section Note Taking, p. 28 ELL
Section 2 Summary, p. 29 ELL
American Issues Journal, pp. 203–205 ELL

L4 Differentiated Instruction Activity, Teacher's Edition, p. 113 AR, GT

Differentiated Instruction Activity, Teacher's Edition, p. 110 SN

Differentiated Instruction Activity, Teacher's Edition, p. 110 LPR

Extend Activity,
Teacher's Edition, p. 114 AR, GT

*Audio support is available for all sections.

**This worksheet also applies to L1.

Assessment Resources
- **Teaching Resources,** Tests A and B, pp. 31–36
- **AYP Monitoring Assessments,** Benchmark Test 1
- **Progress Monitoring Transparencies,** 82–86
- **Test Prep With Document-Based Assessment**
- ***ExamView*® Test Bank CD-ROM**
- **Progress Monitoring Online Quiz**
- **Assessment Rubrics**

Differentiated Instruction Key
- L1 Special Needs
- L2 Basic to Average
- L3 All Students
- L4 Average to Advanced

- SN Special Needs Students
- ELL English Language Learners
- LPR Less Proficient Readers
- AR Advanced Readers
- GT Gifted and Talented

Section	Core Instruction L3	Differentiated Instruction L1 L2 L4	

Section 3 100 minutes
The Struggle Against Discrimination

OBJECTIVES
- Analyze Progressives' attitudes toward minority rights.
- Explain why African Americans organized.
- Examine the strategies used by members of other minority groups to defend their rights.

Focus Question *What steps did minorities take to combat social problems and discrimination?*

Teaching Resources
Viewpoints: Washington and Du Bois, p. 22
Section 3 Quiz, p. 28

Reading and Note Taking Study Guide
Section Note Taking, p. 30
Section 3 Summary, p. 31

Progress Monitoring Transparencies, 84

Color Transparencies
Organizing for Civil Rights, A-79

L1 Adapted Reading and Note Taking Study Guide
Section Note Taking, p. 30 SN
Section 3 Summary, p. 31 SN

Differentiated Instruction Activity, Teacher's Edition, p. 118 SN

L2 Adapted Reading and Note Taking Study Guide
Section Note Taking, p. 30 LPR
Section 3 Summary, p. 31 LPR

Spanish Reading and Note Taking Study Guide
Section Note Taking, p. 30 ELL
Section 3 Summary, p. 31 ELL

Differentiated Instruction Activity, Teacher's Edition, p. 118 LPR, ELL

L4 Differentiated Instruction Activity, Teacher's Edition, p. 117 AR, GT

Extend Activity, Teacher's Edition, p. 120 AR, GT

Section 4 75 minutes
Roosevelt's Square Deal

OBJECTIVES
- Discuss Theodore Roosevelt's ideas on the role of government.
- Analyze how Roosevelt changed the government's role in the economy.
- Explain the impact of Roosevelt's actions on natural resources.
- Compare and contrast Taft's policies with Roosevelt's.

Focus Question *What did Roosevelt think government should do for citizens?*

Teaching Resources
Outline Map: The National Parks System, p. 24
Section 4 Quiz, p. 29

Reading and Note Taking Study Guide
Section Note Taking, pp. 32–33
Section 4 Summary, p. 34

Progress Monitoring Transparencies, 85

L1 Adapted Reading and Note Taking Study Guide
Section Note Taking, pp. 32–33 SN
Section 4 Summary, p. 34 SN

Differentiated Instruction Activity, Teacher's Edition, p. 125 SN

L2 Adapted Reading and Note Taking Study Guide
Section Note Taking, pp. 32–33 LPR
Section 4 Summary, p. 34 LPR

Spanish Reading and Note Taking Study Guide
Section Note Taking, pp. 32–33 ELL
Section 4 Summary, p. 34 ELL

**Teaching Resources
Outline Map: National Land Conservation, p. 23 LPR, ELL

Differentiated Instruction Activities, Teacher's Edition, pp. 125, 126 LPR, ELL

L4 Differentiated Instruction Activity, Teacher's Edition, p. 122 AR, GT

Extend Activity, Teacher's Edition, p. 127 AR, GT

Section 5 75 minutes
Wilson's New Freedom

OBJECTIVES
- Evaluate what Wilson hoped to do with his "New Freedom" program.
- Describe Wilson's efforts to regulate the economy.
- Assess the legacy of the Progressive Era.

Focus Question *What steps did Wilson take to increase the government's role in the economy?*

Teaching Resources
Interpreting a Political Cartoon: Progressive Era Legislation, p. 25
Section 5 Quiz, p. 30

Reading and Note Taking Study Guide
Section Note Taking, p. 35
Section 5 Summary, p. 36

Progress Monitoring Transparencies, 86

Color Transparencies
The Election of 1912, A-80

L1 Adapted Reading and Note Taking Study Guide
Section Note Taking, p. 35 SN
Section 5 Summary, p. 36 SN

Differentiated Instruction Activity, Teacher's Edition, p. 129 SN

L2 Adapted Reading and Note Taking Study Guide
Section Note Taking, p. 35 LPR
Section 5 Summary, p. 36 LPR

Spanish Reading and Note Taking Study Guide
Section Note Taking, p. 35 ELL
Section 5 Summary, p. 36 ELL

Differentiated Instruction Activity, Teacher's Edition, p. 129 LPR, ELL

L4 Extend Activity, Teacher's Edition, p. 131 AR, GT

PROFESSIONAL DEVELOPMENT

Author's Note

I find the Progressive Era particularly fascinating because so much of the infrastructure that our students know today originated during this period: universal childhood education; the professions of social work, architecture, and city planning; dams, water management, and public control of utilities; and government concern for individuals' well-being, including protection for workers and families or concern for public health. Public policy that establishes protection for women and minorities is another legacy of these years, as is government intervention in environmental planning. These are great "handles" for getting students involved in the "what if" of history—what would be different if today's children did not attend school, but instead went to work in factories? Is it a good thing to have the government keep track of public health issues such as the safety of the food we eat? What *do* agencies such as the Centers for Disease Control and the Food and Drug Administration do, and how does their work benefit our daily lives?

Today, we take identity- and interest-group politics—and political lobbying—for granted. We might ask students to name interest groups that reflect their own concerns or sense of identity. We could discuss with them areas that work in American society today. Students might also enjoy speculating about how Progressives such as Jane Addams, Margaret Sanger, Woodrow Wilson, or Ida Wells Barnett might address today's areas of concern. And because we live in a democracy, we have to consider many unique variables and interests when considering how to fix any problem in today's society.

—Emma Lapsansky-Werner

Extend Online

African American Leaders of the Progressive Era

Have students research an African American leader who worked for reform during the Progressive Era. Ask students to present their findings to the class. Use the steps below to help students complete the activity.

Prepare for the Activity Explain that in the Progressive Era, the needs and problems of minority groups were often left out of reform movements. African American leaders worked to improve lives for their own people when their issues were ignored or even made worse by the Progressive Movement.

Conduct the Activity For help in starting this activity, send students to **www.pearsonschool.com/ushist**. Students will select one of the African American leaders from their textbook or from the Web site, and read the Web site for further information on the era. Have students find out about the life, challenges, and achievements of an individual leader. Have each student or group of students present the results of their research to the class and explain the significance of the subject's contributions to improving life and society for African Americans at this time.

Follow-Up Conduct a class discussion based on the following questions: What types of reforms did African Americans try to achieve during the Progressive Era? How were these reforms similar to or different from the reforms other Progressive leaders tried to achieve?

Ida B. Wells
Black Heritage USA 25

Mapping Concepts ⓛⓛ

Concept terms such as *intellectual strategy* and *rational* are not only complex, but they are also widely used in social studies. They warrant more extensive instruction than terms such as *referendum* or *suffrage*, which are less conceptually demanding. Model using the following steps:

1. On the board, create a concept organizer to be filled in as you teach each concept.

2. Pronounce the term—*strategy*.

3. Provide students with a contextually rich sentence— *The strategy of the generals was carefully developed to avoid fighting the war on two fronts.*

4. Guide students in coming up with synonyms for the term—*plan, policy, tactic, approach, line of attack.*

5. Guide students in analyzing the contextual sentence and synonyms, and clarify the essential attributes of the concept as they list them on their concept organizer form. *A strategy is a careful plan or approach, or a way to actively achieve something.*

6. Record examples of the new concept on the organizer, taking care to link directly to the attributes noted in the previous step—*planning how to win a war or make an attack, working out a way to win a football game, deciding how you will advance in the career you choose.*

7. Elicit from students additional examples of the concept. Be sure to insist that students justify their examples by using the attributes—*developing a strategy to excel in a difficult course.*

8. Provide non-examples that do NOT have all the attributes—*making unplanned, random moves in a chess game.*

9. Provide additional examples and non-examples, and coach students through the process of evaluating these until students are fairly proficient with the new concept. Coach students in writing in their organizer a "show you know" sentence that uses the new concept— *It is a good idea to have a strategy if you want to reach an important goal.*

10. When completed, the concept organizer provides students with information that can be used in a form to explain additional examples they may encounter.

Modeling Reading and Writing Skills

Identifying Supporting Details Remind students that the main idea of a text is supported by details that provide further information. These details may explain the main idea or give examples or reasons. A concept web is a useful tool for identifying supporting details and illustrating their connection to the main idea.

To model this, read aloud the first paragraph under *Progressives Share Common Beliefs* in Section 1. Point out that the main idea is that Progressives shared a belief that industrialization and urbanization had created serious problems. The supporting details are that they wanted to use logic and reason to make reforms and that many were motivated by religious faith.

Choosing a Topic Explain that in this chapter, students will be writing a narrative essay. (See Writing About History at the end of the chapter.) Remind students that this kind of essay tells a story complete with a beginning, a middle, and an end. Narrative essays should also have a climax, or point of greatest interest. Explain that

when writing a story about history, one way to choose a topic is to start with a point of interest. This could be an event or person from history. Model this skill by scanning the previous chapter and pointing out the following climactic events that could form the basis of a historical narrative:

A Thomas Edison invents the light bulb.

B Immigrant Irving Berlin arrives at Ellis Island.

C The Battle of the Little Bighorn is fought.

Discuss the fact that each topic has a central character and a climactic event. Model how to extend one topic into the frame of a narrative: *I could write a story about Irving Berlin arriving at Ellis Island, beginning when he steps off the boat and detailing his rise in show business. The climax could be Berlin's first big success in entertainment and his becoming famous.*

CHAPTER **5**

An Emerging World Power, 1890–1917

Section	Core Instruction L3	Differentiated Instruction L1 L2 L4	
Section 1 **100 minutes** *The Roots of Imperialism* **OBJECTIVES** • Identify the key factors that prodded America to expand. • Explain how the United States took its first steps toward increased global power. • Summarize the chain of events leading up to the U.S. annexation of Hawaii. **Focus Question** *How and why did the United States take a more active role in world affairs?*	**Teaching Resources** Reading Strategy: Main Idea and Details, p. 12 Issues Connector: Territorial Expansion of the United States, pp. 15–18 Biography: William Seward, p. 19 Section 1 Quiz, p. 25 **Reading and Note Taking Study Guide** Section Note Taking, p. 37 Section 1 Summary, p. 38 American Issues Journal, pp. 206–208 **Progress Monitoring Transparencies,** 87 **Color Transparencies** American Imperialism, A-81	**L1 Adapted Reading and Note Taking Study Guide** Section Note Taking, p. 37 SN Section 1 Summary, p. 38 SN American Issues Journal, pp. 206–208 SN **L2 Adapted Reading and Note Taking Study Guide** Section Note Taking, p. 37 LPR Section 1 Summary, p. 38 LPR American Issues Journal, pp. 206–208 LPR **Spanish Reading and Note Taking Study Guide** Section Note Taking, p. 37 ELL Section 1 Summary, p. 38 ELL American Issues Journal, pp. 206–208 ELL **L4 Extend Activity,** Teacher's Edition, p. 143 AR, GT	***Student Edition on Audio** SN **Differentiated Instruction Activities,** Teacher's Edition, pp. 139, 141 SN ***Guided Reading Audio, Spanish CD** ELL ***Student Edition on Audio** LPR, ELL **Differentiated Instruction Activities,** Teacher's Edition, pp. 139, 141 LPR, ELL
Section 2 **100 minutes** *The Spanish-American War* **OBJECTIVES** • Explain the causes of the Spanish-American War. • Identify the major battles of the war. • Describe the consequences of the war, including the debate over imperialism. **Focus Question** *What were the causes and effects of the Spanish-American War?*	**Teaching Resources** Interpreting a Political Cartoon: The Spanish-American War, p. 20 Section 2, Quiz, p. 26 **Reading and Note Taking Study Guide** Section Note Taking, p. 39 Section 2 Summary, p. 40 **Progress Monitoring Transparencies,** 88 **Color Transparencies** *Charge of the Rough Riders at San Juan Hill,* A-82	**L1 Adapted Reading and Note Taking Study Guide** Section Note Taking, p. 39 SN Section 2 Summary, p. 40 SN **L2 Adapted Reading and Note Taking Study Guide** Section Note Taking, p. 39 LPR Section 2 Summary, p. 40 LPR **Spanish Reading and Note Taking Study Guide** Section Note Taking, p. 39 ELL Section 2 Summary, p. 40 ELL **L4 Differentiated Instruction Activity,** Teacher's Edition, p. 147 AR, GT	**Differentiated Instruction Activities,** Teacher's Edition, pp. 145, 149 SN **Differentiated Instruction Activities,** Teacher's Edition, pp. 145, 149 LPR, ELL **Extend Activity,** Teaching Resources, pp. 13–14 AR, GT

*Audio support is available for all sections.

**This worksheet also applies to L1.

Assessment Resources
• **Teaching Resources,** Tests A and B, pp. 31–36
• **AYP Monitoring Assessments,** Benchmark Test 1
• **Progress Monitoring Transparencies,** 87–90
• **Test Prep With Document-Based Assessment**
• *ExamView*® **Test Bank CD-ROM**
• **Progress Monitoring Online Quiz**
• **Assessment Rubrics**

Differentiated Instruction **Key**

L1	Special Needs	SN	Special Needs Students
L2	Basic to Average	ELL	English Language Learners
L3	All Students	LPR	Less Proficient Readers
L4	Average to Advanced	AR	Advanced Readers
		GT	Gifted and Talented

Section	Core Instruction ③	Differentiated Instruction ① ② ④	
Section 3 100 minutes *The United States and East Asia* **OBJECTIVES** • Examine the causes and consequences of the Philippine insurrection. • Analyze the effects of the Open Door Policy. • Describe how the United States dealt with the rising power of Japan. **Focus Question** *How did the United States extend its influence in Asia?*	**Teaching Resources** Geography and History: Carving China: Spheres of Influence, pp. 21–22 Section 3 Quiz, p. 27 **Reading and Note Taking Study Guide** Section Note Taking, p. 41 Section 3 Summary, p. 42 **Progress Monitoring Transparencies,** 89 **Color Transparencies** The Boxer Rebellion, A-83	① **Adapted Reading and Note Taking Study Guide** Section Note Taking, p. 41 SN Section 3 Summary, p. 42 SN ② **Adapted Reading and Note Taking Study Guide** Section Note Taking, p. 41 LPR Section 3 Summary, p. 42 LPR **Spanish Reading and Note Taking Study Guide** Section Note Taking, p. 41 ELL Section 3 Summary, p. 42 ELL ④ **Extend Activity,** Teacher's Edition, p. 155 AR, GT	**Differentiated Instruction Activity,** Teacher's Edition, pp. 152, 154 SN ****Teaching Resources** Geography and History: Spheres of Influence, pp. 21–22 LPR, ELL **Differentiated Instruction Activity,** Teacher's Edition, pp. 152, 154 LPR, ELL
Section 4 100 minutes *The United States and Latin America* **OBJECTIVES** • Examine what happened to Puerto Rico and Cuba after the Spanish-American War. • Analyze the effects of Roosevelt's "big stick" diplomacy. • Compare Wilson's "moral diplomacy" with the foreign policies of his predecessors. **Focus Question** *What actions did the United States take to achieve its goals in Latin America?*	**Teaching Resources** Geography and History: The Panama Canal, pp. 23–24 Section 4 Quiz, p. 28 **Reading and Note Taking Study Guide** Section Note Taking, pp. 43–44 Section 4 Summary, p. 45 **Progress Monitoring Transparencies,** 90 **Color Transparencies** Building the Panama Canal, A-84	① **Adapted Reading and Note Taking Study Guide** Section Note Taking, pp. 43–44 SN Section 4 Summary, p. 45 SN ② **Adapted Reading and Note Taking Study Guide** Section Note Taking, pp. 43–44 LPR Section 4 Summary, p. 45 LPR **Spanish Reading and Note Taking Study Guide** Section Note Taking, pp. 43–44 ELL Section 4 Summary, p. 45 ELL ④ **Differentiated Instruction Activity,** Teacher's Edition, p. 158 AR, GT	**Differentiated Instruction Activities,** Teacher's Edition, pp. 160, 162 SN **Differentiated Instruction Activities,** Teacher's Edition, pp. 160, 161, 162 LPR, ELL **Extend Activity,** Teacher's Edition, p. 163 AR, GT

Author's Note

This chapter has special significance for me because, in a way, it helped launch my career as a professional historian. After I completed my Ph.D., I sought a full-time teaching position. The job market was tight, with each position receiving from 150 to 200 applications. Nonetheless, I made the cut at several institutions and, as part of the final winnowing process, was invited to present a guest lecture to a U.S. history class on the emergence of the United States as a world power.

Although I had teaching experience as a part-time lecturer, I worked hard to develop an especially concise and compelling lecture. At first, the task seemed daunting, if not impossible. I wondered how I was supposed to cover such a broad theme and, at the same time, connect with new students in a fifty-minute class period. Ultimately, I decided "less is more."

Rather than attempt to discuss the entire period of this country's emergence as a world power—from our earliest expansionist actions in the Pacific to Woodrow Wilson's decision to send troops to Mexico—I chose two specific topics: the economic, ideological, and political origins of imperialism and McKinley's decision to declare war on Spain. The former, I suggested, underlay virtually all U.S. actions in the Pacific and the Caribbean in the first two decades of the twentieth century (and in many ways ever since), and the latter served as an essential turning point in the nation's history.

As they say, the rest is history: I was awarded the position. I still use the "less is more" approach in my lectures, finding it as useful a tool as ever to cover broad topics. Of course, I also remind my students that in order to reach a fuller appreciation and understanding of the subject, they *are* expected to read the text.

—Peter Levy

Extend Online

The Panama Canal Route

Have students find out more about how the route of the Panama Canal was selected. Ask students to annotate a map that indicates the physical and political barriers to building a path between the Atlantic and Pacific oceans. Follow the steps below to help students complete the activity.

Prepare for the Activity Explain that canal builders considered routes in both Panama and Nicaragua before choosing the final location. Explain that both areas had advantages and disadvantages. The terrain in Panama, for example, included mountains that would have to be cut through. The land of Nicaragua, however, was prone to earthquakes and volcanoes.

Conduct the Activity For help in starting the activity, send students to **www.pearsonschool.com/ushist**. Students will view engineering documents supporting different routes across the isthmus and a discussion of the

politics involved in determining a route. Provide students with a map of Central America, or have them adapt one from the website. Tell students to suppose that they are making recommendations to people who will build the canal. Ask students to note on their maps the physical features that will have to be addressed by the canal builders. In addition, student annotations should include information about political alliances.

Follow-Up Conduct a class discussion based on the following questions: Do you think canal builders chose the best route to connect the Atlantic and Pacific oceans? Did politics or geography play the larger role in the selection of the final route? How does the decision to build the canal in Panama continue to affect people today?

Differentiated Instruction Solutions for All Learners

Responding to Chapter Questions

To teach students to answer chapter questions effectively, provide them with the following steps. These will also deepen their understanding of "study reading."

1. Read the chapter question silently, and ask yourself—based on the question—what type of information will I be looking for?

    Why? = For what reasons? What were the reasons?

    How? = What was the process? What was the sequence?

    What? = Definition (What is _____?)

    What + signal word =

    What were the benefits of _____?

    What was the reaction to _____?

2. Skim the headings to find the section that addresses the question.

3. Reread the section to find the answer.

4. Record the answer in your own words. If possible, turn the question into part of the answer; for example, you might ask, Why did William Randolph Hearst support the Spanish-American War?

Independent Research

Challenge advanced readers by asking them to research independently for material that goes beyond what is presented in the textbook. By honing their research skills, these advanced readers are learning to be independent thinkers and are developing skills that will aid them in future studies. The text provides an excellent base knowledge that can be used to encourage individual student research. You may assign students to research the personal backgrounds and biographies of historical individuals mentioned in a particular chapter. Students may also be asked to conduct in-depth research on events that receive only passing mention in the text. Students should present their research to the class through a multimedia presentation or an oral report.

Modeling Reading and Writing Skills

Predict Explain to students that making predictions can help them focus their reading and remember key content. Tell them that a prediction is an idea about what will come next. It can be based on information such as headings and visuals. Once students make their predictions, have them read the text to find out whether the predictions were accurate. If the predictions were not accurate, tell students to revise them.

To demonstrate this skill, begin by reading aloud the sections and describing the visuals from Section 1. Point out that the images show soldiers, warships, and flags. Tell students that you predict that the section will tell about the role that the military played on the road to U.S. imperialism.

Use Sensory Details Explain that in this chapter, students will be writing a narrative essay, or story. (See Writing About History at the end of the chapter.) After students have basic characters, settings, and plot events mapped out, they should brainstorm to identify sensory details that can bring these people, places, and events to life. One way to gather these details is with a sensory details web. Webs can be created for each main character or key event, with sections for sight, sound, smell, touch, and taste.

Model this skill by drawing a web on the board. Write "The Explosion of the USS *Maine*" in the center of a web. Add radiating spokes for sound, sight, and touch, and list the following details: sound: *heard blast*; sight: *saw flying metal*; touch: *felt rush of air*. Then post the topic "Spanish-American War" in the center of a new web, and ask students to complete the web with sensory details. Discuss how sensory details would create a vivid setting and help bring a narrative to life.

CHAPTER 6

World War I and Beyond, 1914–1920

Section	Core Instruction L3	Differentiated Instruction L1 L2 L4	
Section 1 125 minutes *From Neutrality to War* **OBJECTIVES** • Analyze the causes of World War I. • Describe the course and character of the war. • Explain why the United States entered the conflict on the side of the Allies.	**Teaching Resources** Issues Connector: America Goes to War, pp. 15–18 Interpreting a Political Cartoon: World War I, p. 19 Section 1 Quiz, p. 26 **Reading and Note Taking Study Guide** Section Note Taking, p. 46 Section 1 Summary, p. 47 American Issues Journal, pp. 209–211 **Progress Monitoring Transparencies,** 91 **Color Transparencies** German U-Boat, A-85	**L1 Adapted Reading and Note Taking Study Guide** Section Note Taking, p. 46 SN Section 1 Summary, p. 47 SN American Issues Journal, pp. 209–211 SN **L2 Adapted Reading and Note Taking Study Guide** Section Note Taking, p. 46 LPR Section 1 Summary, p. 47 LPR American Issues Journal, pp. 209–211 LPR **Spanish Reading and Note Taking Study Guide** Section Note Taking, p. 46 ELL Section 1 Summary, p. 47 ELL American Issues Journal, pp. 209–211 ELL	*Student Edition on Audio SN **Differentiated Instruction Activities,** Teacher's Edition, pp. 171, 172, 175, 176 SN *Guided Reading Audio, Spanish CD ELL *Student Edition on Audio LPR, ELL **Differentiated Instruction Activities,** Teacher's Edition, pp. 171, 172, 176 LPR, ELL
Focus Question *What caused World War I, and why did the United States enter the war?*		**L4 Differentiated Instruction Activity,** Teacher's Edition, p. 170 AR, GT	**Extend Activity,** Teaching Resources, pp. 13–14 AR, GT
Section 2 100 minutes *The Home Front* **OBJECTIVES** • Analyze how the American government mobilized the public to support the war effort. • Describe opposition to the war. • Outline significant social changes that occurred during the war.	**Teaching Resources** Geography and History: The Great Migration, p. 20 Landmark Decisions of the Supreme Court: What Are the Limits of Free Speech?, p. 21 Section 2 Quiz, p. 27 **Reading and Note Taking Study Guide** Section Note Taking, p. 48 Section 2 Summary, p. 49 **Progress Monitoring Transparencies,** 92 **Color Transparencies** Supporting the War, A-86; The Great Migration, A-87	**L1 Adapted Reading and Note Taking Study Guide** Section Note Taking, p. 48 SN Section 2 Summary, p. 49 SN **L2 Adapted Reading and Note Taking Study Guide** Section Note Taking, p. 48 LPR Section 2 Summary, p. 49 LPR **Spanish Reading and Note Taking Study Guide** Section Note Taking, p. 48 ELL Section 2 Summary, p. 49 ELL	**Differentiated Instruction Activities,** Teacher's Edition, pp. 183, 184, 186 SN **Differentiated Instruction Activities,** Teacher's Edition, pp. 183, 184, 186 LPR, ELL
Focus Question *How did the war affect Americans at home?*		**L4 Differentiated Instruction Activity,** Teacher's Edition, p. 182 AR, GT	**Extend Activity,** Teacher's Edition, p. 187 AR, GT

Section	Core Instruction (L3)	Differentiated Instruction (L1 L2 L4)	
Section 3 125 minutes *Wilson, War, and Peace* **OBJECTIVES** • Understand how the United States military contributed to the Allied victory in the war. • Describe the aims of the Fourteen Points. • Analyze the decisions made at the Paris Peace Conference. • Explain why the United States Senate refused to ratify the treaty ending World War I. **Focus Question** *How did Americans affect the end of World War I and its peace settlements?*	**Teaching Resources** Reading Strategy: Sequence, p. 12 Interpreting a Political Cartoon: The League of Nations, p. 22 Primary Source: *The Fourteen Points* and The League of Nations, p. 24 Section 3 Quiz, p. 28 **Reading and Note Taking Study Guide** Section Note Taking, pp. 50–51 Section 3 Summary, p. 52 **Progress Monitoring Transparencies**, 93	**L1 Adapted Reading and Note Taking Study Guide** Section Note Taking, pp. 50–51 SN Section 3 Summary, p. 52 SN **L2 Adapted Reading and Note Taking Study Guide** Section Note Taking, pp. 50–51 LPR Section 3 Summary, p. 52 LPR **Spanish Reading and Note Taking Study Guide** Section Note Taking, pp. 50–51 ELL Section 3 Summary, p. 52 ELL **L4 Differentiated Instruction Activities**, Teacher's Edition, pp. 190, 196 AR, GT	**Differentiated Instruction Activities**, Teacher's Edition, pp. 191, 193, 194 SN ****Teaching Resources** Primary Source: *The Fourteen Points*, p. 23 ELL, LPR **Differentiated Instruction Activities**, Teacher's Edition, pp. 191, 193, 194 LPR, ELL **Extend Activity**, Teacher's Edition, p. 197 AR, GT
Section 4 125 minutes *Effects of the War* **OBJECTIVES** • Describe the problems Americans faced immediately after the war. • Analyze how these problems contributed to the Red Scare. • Understand how the war changed America's role in world affairs. **Focus Question** *What political, economic, and social effects did World War I have on the United States?*	**Teaching Resources** Viewpoints: The Red Scare, p. 25 Section 4 Quiz, p. 29 **Reading and Note Taking Study Guide** Section Note Taking, p. 53 Section 4 Summary, p. 54 **Progress Monitoring Transparencies**, 94 **Color Transparencies** Reaction to Radicals, A-88	**L1 Adapted Reading and Note Taking Study Guide** Section Note Taking, p. 53 SN Section 4 Summary, p. 54 SN **L2 Adapted Reading and Note Taking Study Guide** Section Note Taking, p. 53 LPR Section 4 Summary, p. 54 LPR **Spanish Reading and Note Taking Study Guide** Section Note Taking, p. 53 ELL Section 4 Summary, p. 54 ELL **L4 Differentiated Instruction Activity**, Teacher's Edition, p. 202 AR, GT	**Differentiated Instruction Activity**, Teacher's Edition, p. 200 SN **Differentiated Instruction Activity**, Teacher's Edition, p. 200 ELL **Extend Activity**, Teacher's Edition, p. 203 AR, GT

*Audio support is available for all sections.   ****This worksheet also applies to L1.**

Assessment Resources
• **Teaching Resources**, Tests A and B, pp. 30–35
• **AYP Monitoring Assessments**, Benchmark Test 1
• **Progress Monitoring Transparencies**, 91–94
• **Test Prep With Document-Based Assessment**
• *ExamView*® Test Bank CD-ROM
• **Progress Monitoring Online Quiz**
• **Assessment Rubrics**

Differentiated Instruction Key
L1 Special Needs	SN	Special Needs Students
L2 Basic to Average	ELL	English Language Learners
L3 All Students	LPR	Less Proficient Readers
L4 Average to Advanced	AR	Advanced Readers
	GT	Gifted and Talented

Author's Note

I have a feel for certain times in history. Certain times and places attract my interest more than others—they just feel comfortable to me. One such period and place is Europe during World War I. Many times, I've walked in Paris, London, or Vienna, wandering through old streets where famous people once lived and visiting buildings where important documents were signed, and I feel the past bubbling all around me.

Nowhere is that sense stronger than on the battlefields of the Western Front. There is one place I've returned to often: the Somme, where in 1916 the British and French fought a long, deadly battle against the Germans. Between the last week in June and mid-November, more than 1,200,000 men fell in the Battle of the Somme. In fact, on one day, July 1, 1916, when Britain began its offensive, more than 60,000 troops from the British Empire were killed, wounded, or missing in action. By the end of the day, more than 19,000 were dead. And that battle was just beginning! Britain had not yet achieved any of its major objectives.

Today, the Somme region is tranquil farmland. The Somme River is little more than a slow-moving stream. The area is dotted by graves and markers where skirmishes took place, but it is so lovely that it is easy to forget that almost 100 years ago a terrible battle took place there that leveled villages, scarred the land, and destroyed lives.

There is one area that still retains the signs of battle. On the northern part of the Somme battle line is the village of Beaumont Hamel, where, on July 1, a Newfoundland Regiment made a disastrous assault against German forces. After the war the Newfoundland government purchased the land and kept the battle site intact. Today, you can walk through the trenches, cross "no man's land," and step on to the German position. It is the finest trench park on the Western Front, and on cold, foggy November days the past seems close at hand.

—Randy Roberts

Extend Online

Propaganda

Have students analyze posters from the Committee on Public Information (CPI) that were distributed during World War I. Ask them to compare posters from different nations and choose one poster to present to the class. Use the steps below to help students complete the activity.

Prepare for the Activity
Explain that each nation that fought in World War I used propaganda posters to influence public opinion. Governments designed posters to be seen by their own citizens to justify the war and by their enemies to instill fear. Some recruited men to enlist. Others, such as the one on this page, promoted patriotism and self-sacrifice or promoted the conservation of resources.

Conduct the Activity For help in starting the activity, send students to **www.pearsonschool.com/ushist.** Students will view propaganda posters from France, Germany, Italy, Russia, Australia, Britain, and the United States. Have them note similarities and differences

among the images that were chosen by the various countries. After students view the posters, have them choose one and present it to the class. Make sure that students explain the poster's audience, its message, and which propaganda techniques are used in the poster to persuade viewers.

Follow-Up Conduct a class discussion by using the following questions: What aspects of war are reflected in these propaganda posters? What methods do governments use to persuade people during wartime? What techniques are most effective? Do you think these posters would influence you? What might the Committee on Public Information do to influence public opinion today?

Layered Timelines L2

Often, high school students have difficulty placing important events in the correct context. They may not understand simultaneous developments across a continent. A large timeline at the front of the classroom can help students make these connections.

To help students sequence events, create a layered timeline. At the front of the classroom, display a timeline that shows the years 1914 through 1919. Students will make timelines that show events in different European countries leading up to and during World War I.

To begin, organize the class in groups, and have each group create a timeline for one country discussed in this chapter: Britain, France, Russia, Serbia, Germany, Austria-Hungary, Italy, the Ottoman Empire, or the United States. Have students list the important events and sequence them correctly on the timeline. Then, have each group place its timeline on the wall either above or below the one already displayed. Ask students to use this layered timeline to draw three to five conclusions about Europe in the early 1900s.

Descriptive Phrases L2

To further English Language Learners' acquisition of vocabulary, ask them to create descriptive phrases for key terms, people, and places. Assign students to work either individually or with a partner to find examples of the terms, people, and places listed at the beginning of each section in the chapter. Instruct students to create a bulleted list of descriptive phrases and adjectives for their given topic. Provide students with a thesaurus to assist them with the assignment. Then, ask students to read their list of descriptive phrases to the class. Allow members of the class to guess what is being described. Write the list of possible terms, people, and places on the board to assist students in guessing correctly.

Modeling Reading and Writing Skills

Cause and Effect Tell students that recognizing causes and effects helps them clarify the relationships between events or situations. Point out that noting signal words can help them identify these relationships. Clue words such as *reason, because, produced,* and *purpose* indicate possible causes. Words such as *brought about, effect, led to, outcome, reaction, result, so, then, therefore,* and *this* indicate possible effects.

Model how to identify cause and effect by reading aloud the first sentence under "German Submarines Violate Neutral Rights" in Section 1. Draw students' attention to the word *responded,* and point out that this word signals an effect. The effect is that Germany began using U-boats to sink English ships. The cause was the British blockade.

Choosing a Way of Organizing Explain that in this chapter, students will write a cause-and-effect essay. (See Writing About History at the end of the chapter.) Point out that this type of essay requires clear, consistent

organization that makes it easy to follow the connections among events. Encourage students to keep these ways of organizing in mind as they read. Write these two ways of organizing on the board:

A Chronological Order

B Order of Importance

Explain that in chronological order, events are presented in the order in which they occurred. In order of importance, events are presented in the order of their relative significance. Chronological order is effective when following a cause-and-effect chain, and order of importance is effective for prioritizing a series of causes of a single event. Help students match the types of organization with the following topics:

1. The events leading to World War I (A—Chronological)

2. The multiple effects of World War I (B—Order of Importance)

CHAPTER 7

The Twenties, 1919–1929

Section	Core Instruction L3	Differentiated Instruction L1 L2 L4
Section 1 100 minutes *A Booming Economy* **OBJECTIVES** • Explain the impact of Henry Ford and the automobile. • Analyze the consumer revolution and the bull market of the 1920s. • Compare the different effects of the economic boom on urban and rural America.	**Teaching Resources** Reading a Chart: Automobile Sales, p. 19 Section 1 Quiz, p. 25 **Reading and Note Taking Study Guide** Section Note Taking, p. 55 Section 1 Summary, p. 56 **Progress Monitoring Transparencies**, 95 **Color Transparencies** New York City Skyline, A-89	**L1 Adapted Reading and Note Taking Study Guide** Section Note Taking, p. 55 SN Section 1 Summary, p. 56 SN ∥ *Student Edition on Audio SN **Differentiated Instruction Activity**, Teacher's Edition, p. 213 SN
Focus Question *How did the booming economy of the 1920s lead to changes in American life?*		**L2 Adapted Reading and Note Taking Study Guide** Section Note Taking, p. 55 LPR Section 1 Summary, p. 56 LPR **Spanish Reading and Note Taking Study Guide** Section Note Taking, p. 55 ELL Section 1 Summary, p. 56 ELL ∥ *Guided Reading Audio, Spanish CD ELL *Student Edition on Audio LPR, ELL **Differentiated Instruction Activity**, Teacher's Edition, p. 213 LPR, ELL
		L4 Differentiated Instruction Activity, Teacher's Edition, p. 214 AR, GT ∥ **Extend Activity**, Teaching Resources, pp. 13–14 AR, GT
Section 2 100 minutes *The Business of Government* **OBJECTIVES** • Analyze how the policies of Presidents Harding and Coolidge favored business growth. • Discuss the most significant scandals during Harding's presidency. • Explain the role that the United States played in the world during the 1920s.	**Teaching Resources** Reading Strategy: Compare and Contrast, p. 12 History Comics: Albert Fall and the Teapot Dome Scandal, p. 21 Section 2 Quiz, p. 26 **Reading and Note Taking Study Guide** Section Note Taking, p. 57 Section 2 Summary, p. 58 **Progress Monitoring Transparencies**, 96 **Color Transparencies** A Booming Economy, A-90	**L1 Adapted Reading and Note Taking Study Guide** Section Note Taking, p. 57 SN Section 2 Summary, p. 58 SN ∥ **Teaching Resources** History Comics: The Teapot Dome Scandal, p. 20 ELL, LPR **Differentiated Instruction Activities**, Teacher's Edition, pp. 219, 220 SN
Focus Question *How did domestic and foreign policy change direction under Harding and Coolidge?*		**L2 Adapted Reading and Note Taking Study Guide** Section Note Taking, p. 57 LPR Section 2 Summary, p. 58 LPR **Spanish Reading and Note Taking Study Guide** Section Note Taking, p. 57 ELL Section 2 Summary, p. 58 ELL ∥ **Differentiated Instruction Activities**, Teacher's Edition, pp. 219, 220 LPR, ELL
		L4 Extend Activity, Teacher's Edition, p. 222 AR, GT

*Audio support is available for all sections.

**This worksheet also applies to L1.

Assessment Resources
• **Teaching Resources**, Tests A and B, pp. 30–35
• **AYP Monitoring Assessments**, Benchmark Test 1
• **Progress Monitoring Transparencies**, 95–99
• Test Prep With Document-Based Assessment
• *ExamView*® Test Bank CD-ROM
• Progress Monitoring Online Quiz
• Assessment Rubrics

Differentiated Instruction Key
L1	Special Needs	SN	Special Needs Students
L2	Basic to Average	ELL	English Language Learners
L3	All Students	LPR	Less Proficient Readers
L4	Average to Advanced	AR	Advanced Readers
		GT	Gifted and Talented

Section	Core Instruction L3	Differentiated Instruction L1 L2 L4	
Section 3 100 minutes *Social and Cultural Tensions* **OBJECTIVES** • Compare economic and cultural life in rural America to that in urban America. • Discuss the changes in U.S. immigration policy in the 1920s. • Analyze the goals and motives of the Ku Klux Klan in the 1920s. • Discuss the successes and failures of the Eighteenth Amendment. **Focus Question** *How did Americans differ on major social and cultural issues?*	**Teaching Resources** Issues Connector: U.S. Immigration Policy, pp. 15–18 Biography: John Scopes, p. 22 Section 3 Quiz, p. 27 **Reading and Note Taking Study Guide** Section Note Taking, p. 59 Section 3 Summary, p. 60 American Issues Journal, pp. 212–214 **Progress Monitoring Transparencies,** 97 **Color Transparencies** Prohibition, A-91	**L1 Adapted Reading and Note Taking Study Guide** Section Note Taking, p. 59 SN Section 3 Summary, p. 60 SN American Issues Journal, pp. 212–214 SN **L2 Adapted Reading and Note Taking Study Guide** Section Note Taking, p. 59 LPR Section 3 Summary, p. 60 LPR American Issues Journal, pp. 212–214 LPR **Spanish Reading and Note Taking Study Guide** Section Note Taking, p. 59 ELL Section 3 Summary, p. 60 ELL American Issues Journal, pp. 212–214 ELL **L4 Differentiated Instruction Activity,** Teacher's Edition, p. 225 AR, GT	**Differentiated Instruction Activities,** Teacher's Edition, pp. 224, 227 SN **Differentiated Instruction Activities,** Teacher's Edition, pp. 224, 227 LPR, ELL **Extend Activity,** Teacher's Edition, p. 230 AR, GT
Section 4 75 minutes *A New Mass Culture* **OBJECTIVES** • Trace the reasons that leisure time increased during the 1920s. • Analyze how the development of popular culture united Americans and created new activities and heroes. • Discuss the advancements of women in the 1920s. • Analyze the concept of modernism and its impact on writers and painters in the 1920s. **Focus Question** *How did the new mass culture reflect technological and social changes?*	**Teaching Resources** Viewpoints: The "New" Woman, p. 23 Section 4 Quiz, p. 28 **Reading and Note Taking Study Guide** Section Note Taking, pp. 61–62 Section 4 Summary, p. 63 **Progress Monitoring Transparencies,** 98	**L1 Adapted Reading and Note Taking Study Guide** Section Note Taking, pp. 61–62 SN Section 4 Summary, p. 63 SN **L2 Adapted Reading and Note Taking Study Guide** Section Note Taking, pp. 61–62 LPR Section 4 Summary, p. 63 LPR **Spanish Reading and Note Taking Study Guide** Section Note Taking, pp. 61–62 ELL Section 4 Summary, p. 63 ELL **L4 Differentiated Instruction Activities,** Teacher's Edition, pp. 233, 236, 238 AR, GT	**Differentiated Instruction Activities,** Teacher's Edition, pp. 232, 237 SN **Differentiated Instruction Activities,** Teacher's Edition, pp. 232, 237 LPR, ELL **Extend Activity,** Teacher's Edition, p. 239 AR, GT
Section 5 75 minutes *The Harlem Renaissance* **OBJECTIVES** • Analyze the racial and economic philosophies of Marcus Garvey. • Trace the development and impact of jazz. • Discuss the themes explored by writers of the Harlem Renaissance. **Focus Question** *How did African Americans express a new sense of hope and pride?*	**Teaching Resources** Link to Literature: *Their Eyes Were Watching God*, p. 24 Section 5 Quiz, p. 29 **Reading and Note Taking Study Guide** Section Note Taking, p. 64 Section 5 Summary, p. 65 **Progress Monitoring Transparencies,** 99 **Color Transparencies** The Harlem Renaissance, A-92	**L1 Adapted Reading and Note Taking Study Guide** Section Note Taking, p. 64 SN Section 5 Summary, p. 65 SN **L2 Adapted Reading and Note Taking Study Guide** Section Note Taking, p. 64 LPR Section 5 Summary, p. 65 LPR **Spanish Reading and Note Taking Study Guide** Section Note Taking, p. 64 ELL Section 5 Summary, p. 65 ELL **L4 Differentiated Instruction Activity,** Teacher's Edition, p. 245 AR, GT	**Differentiated Instruction Activity,** Teacher's Edition, p. 243 SN **Differentiated Instruction Activity,** Teacher's Edition, p. 243 LPR, ELL **Extend Activity,** Teacher's Edition, p. 246 AR, GT

Author's Note

The 1920s was a colorful era complete with a rising post–World War I economy, the spread of mass popular culture, and women challenging their traditional roles. Frederick Lewis Allen's influential popular history *Only Yesterday: An Informal History of the 1920s* (1931) vividly accounts this period leading to the stock market crash. Allen wrote his book at the beginning of the Great Depression, and through the fog of hard times the 1920s seemed a distant, exciting age. For Allen, the 1920s was largely a carefree decade that interrupted serious, trying episodes of history. Between the Great War and the Great Depression, Americans supposedly went to extremes, bathing in bathtub gin, sitting on flagpoles, dancing the Charleston, and watching Rudolph Valentino exude passion on the silver screen. The 1920s, to Allen, was simply one decade-long party.

The book's most quoted chapter asserts that the 1920s exemplified a "revolution in manners and morals": hemlines headed north, necklines moved south, and morals turned upside down. Allen also argues that mass circulation of "true confessions" magazines and unrated movies, the disregard for prohibition, and the ascendancy of the automobile all combined with a number of European forces to fuel the revolution.

Was Allen right? Was the 1920s a unique decade, different from what came before and what followed? Today, historians believe that the decade was more evolutionary than revolutionary. Certainly, Americans' social ideals were shifting, but most of the behavior Allen describes tended to be that of the urban and upper-middle class. Allen did not describe rural behavior, and he had little interest in working-class or minority practices.

Allen was right on one important point: the automobile changed American life. It altered transportation patterns, supported the growth of suburbs, and economic development. It is virtually impossible to imagine the United States without cars. From downtown offices to suburban homes, from drive-in theaters to drive-through restaurants, automobiles have changed this country's landscape.

—Randy Roberts

Extend Online

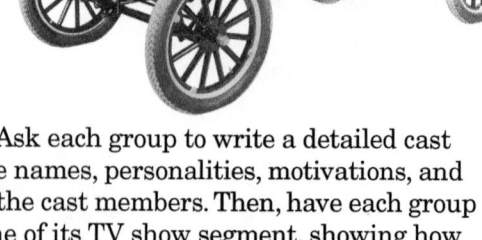

Race for Gold and Glory

Have students conduct research on participants in the Gold and Glory Sweepstakes; then, ask them to use this information to write a segment for a TV show about sports heroes in the 1920s. Use the steps below to help students conduct the activity.

Prepare for the Activity Explain that the 1920s were the decade of the "craze." New mass media created instant fashions and fads. One craze of the 1920s was unique: the Gold and Glory Sweepstakes. Explain that the African American drivers who participated in this competition faced the racism of Jim Crow laws and won the admiration of sports fans throughout the country.

Conduct the Activity For help in starting the activity, send students to **www.pearsonschool.com/ushist.** Students will hear popular music played by African American musicians, read newspaper articles by a celebrated African American journalist, learn about the drivers in the race, and feel the excitement of a craze that involved both automobiles and sports to create new heroes. Organize students in groups. Ask each group to write a detailed cast list, including the names, personalities, motivations, and achievements of the cast members. Then, have each group develop an outline of its TV show segment, showing how they would organize and present the story.

Follow-Up Conduct a class discussion by using the following questions: What was thrilling about being a Gold and Glory driver? What did the drivers have in common? How were they different? What challenges did they face? Why do you think that the sweepstakes is unknown to most Americans today?

Give One, Get One ⓛ2

Use the following steps to foster independent reflection and peer interaction before beginning a class discussion.

1. Pose a thought-provoking question to the class.
2. Allow students time to consider what they may already know about the topic and jot down potential responses.
3. Ask students to place a check mark next to the two or three ideas that they consider their strongest and then draw a line after their final idea to separate their own ideas from those that they will gather from classmates.
4. Give students a set amount of time (about eight to ten minutes) to get up from their seats and share ideas with a classmate. Have pairs of students exchange papers and quietly read each other's ideas. Then, direct pairs to discuss the ideas briefly. Ask each student to select one idea from the partner's list, and add it to his or her own, making sure to copy the idea accurately and note the partner's name. Then, tell students to find new partners and repeat the give one, get one process.
5. At the end of the exchange period, facilitate a unified class discussion. Call on a volunteer to share one new idea acquired from a conversation partner. The student whose idea has just been reported will then share the next idea, collected from a different conversation partner.

Modeling Reading and Writing Skills

Signal Words: Compare and Contrast Point out that comparing and contrasting helps students analyze information. Remind students that comparing involves examining similarities, and contrasting involves exploring differences. Signal words can help students identify these relationships. Words such as *despite, still, although, however, whereas, by contrast,* and *on the other hand* signal that ideas or items are being contrasted.

Model comparison and contrast by reading the first sentence of the last paragraph under the red heading "New Policies Favor Big Business." Draw students' attention to the word *still,* and point out that this word signals a contrast. The text is contrasting the Harding Administration's opposition to the business regulations favored by Progressives with the efforts of Harding's Secretary of Commerce Herbert Hoover to achieve social improvements through voluntary cooperation among interest groups.

Identify Causes/Effects Explain that in this chapter, students will write a compare-and-contrast essay. (See Writing About History at the end of the chapter.) Comparison and contrast essays focus on similarities and differences. Students can deepen their understanding of history by examining similarities and differences between cultures, or ways in which cultural differences have affected history. As students revise their writing, they can add details and transition words that clarify cause-and-effect relationships. To model the skill, write the following on the board:

because

Add the following sentence, and point out that it highlights the result of the difference stated: Many Americans had too much debt during the 1920s *because* they borrowed money to invest in the stock market. Ask students to brainstorm other cause-and-effect transition words.

CHAPTER 8

The Great Depression, 1928–1932

Section	Core Instruction L3	Differentiated Instruction L1 L2 L4	
Section 1 100 minutes *Causes of the Great Depression* **OBJECTIVES** • Discuss the weaknesses in the economy of the 1920s. • Explain how the stock market crash contributed to the coming of the Depression. • Describe how the Depression spread overseas. **Focus Question** *How did the prosperity of the 1920s give way to the Great Depression?*	**Teaching Resources** Reading Strategy: Recognize Multiple Causes, p. 11 Reading a Chart: Rising Unemployment and Business Closings, p. 15 Section 1 Quiz, p. 18 **Reading and Note Taking Study Guide** Section Note Taking, pp. 66–67 Section 1 Summary, p. 68 **Progress Monitoring Transparencies,** 100 **Color Transparencies** Stock Market Crash, A-93	**L1 Adapted Reading and Note Taking Study Guide** Section Note Taking, pp. 66–67 SN Section 1 Summary, p. 68 SN **L2 Adapted Reading and Note Taking Study Guide** Section Note Taking, pp. 66–67 LPR Section 1 Summary, p. 68 LPR **Spanish Reading and Note Taking Study Guide** Section Note Taking, pp. 66–67 ELL Section 1 Summary, p. 68 ELL **L4 Differentiated Instruction Activity,** Teacher's Edition, p. 259 AR, GT	**Differentiated Instruction Activities,** Teacher's Edition, pp. 255, 256, 259 SN ****Teaching Resources** Reading a Chart: Unemployment, p. 14 ELL, LPR **Differentiated Instruction Activities,** Teacher's Edition, pp. 255, 256, 259 LPR, ELL **Extend Activity,** Teacher's Edition, p. 260 AR, GT
Section 2 100 minutes *Americans Face Hard Times* **OBJECTIVES** • Examine the spread of unemployment in America's cities. • Discuss the impact of the Depression on rural America. • Explain the human and geographical factors that created the Dust Bowl. **Focus Question** *How did the Great Depression affect the lives of urban and rural Americans?*	**Teaching Resources** Geography and History: The Dust Bowl, p. 16 Section 2 Quiz, p. 19 **Reading and Note Taking Study Guide** Section Note Taking, p. 69 Section 2 Summary, p. 70 **Progress Monitoring Transparencies,** 101 **Color Transparencies** The Dust Bowl, A-94; The Great Depression, A-96	**L1 Adapted Reading and Note Taking Study Guide** Section Note Taking, p. 69 SN Section 2 Summary, p. 70 SN **L2 Adapted Reading and Note Taking Study Guide** Section Note Taking, p. 69 LPR Section 2 Summary, p. 70 LPR **Spanish Reading and Note Taking Study Guide** Section Note Taking, p. 69 ELL Section 2 Summary, p. 70 ELL **L4 Differentiated Instruction Activity,** Teacher's Edition, p. 265 AR, GT	***Student Edition on Audio** SN **Differentiated Instruction Activities,** Teacher's Edition, pp. 262, 263, 267 SN ***Guided Reading Audio, Spanish CD** ELL ***Student Edition on Audio** LPR, ELL **Differentiated Instruction Activities,** Teacher's Edition, pp. 262, 263, 267 LPR, ELL **Extend Activity,** Teaching Resources, pp. 12–13 AR, GT

Section	Core Instruction L3	Differentiated Instruction L1 L2 L4	
Section 3 75 minutes *Hoover's Response Fails* **OBJECTIVES** • Discuss how Hoover's initial conservative response to the Depression failed. • Explain the changes in the President's policies as the crisis continued. • Describe how Americans reacted to Hoover's relief programs.	**Teaching Resources** Viewpoints: Volunteerism, p. 17 Section 3 Quiz, p. 20 **Reading and Note Taking Study Guide** Section Note Taking, p. 71 Section 3 Summary, p. 72 **Progress Monitoring Transparencies,** 102 **Color Transparencies** Building the Hoover Dam, A-95	**L1** **Adapted Reading and Note Taking Study Guide** Section Note Taking, p. 71 SN Section 3 Summary, p. 72 SN **L2** **Adapted Reading and Note Taking Study Guide** Section Note Taking, p. 71 LPR Section 3 Summary, p. 72 LPR **Spanish Reading and Note Taking Study Guide** Section Note Taking, p. 71 ELL Section 3 Summary, p. 72 ELL	**Differentiated Instruction Activity,** Teacher's Edition, p. 273 SN **Differentiated Instruction Activity,** Teacher's Edition, p. 273 LPR, ELL
Focus Question *Why did Herbert Hoover's policies fail to solve the country's economic crisis?*		**L4** **Differentiated Instruction Activity,** Teacher's Edition, p. 275 AR, GT	**Extend Activity,** Teacher's Edition, p. 276 AR, GT

*Audio support is available for all sections.

**This worksheet also applies to L1.

Assessment Resources
• Teaching Resources, Tests A and B, pp. 21–26
• AYP Monitoring Assessments, Benchmark Test 2
• Progress Monitoring Transparencies, 100–102
• Test Prep With Document-Based Assessment
• *ExamView*® Test Bank CD-ROM
• Progress Monitoring Online Quiz
• Assessment Rubrics

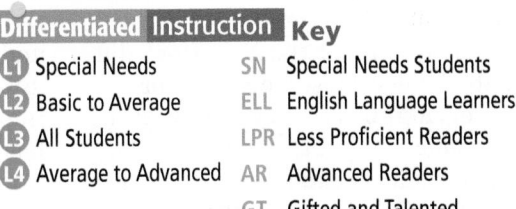

Differentiated Instruction Key
L1 Special Needs	SN Special Needs Students
L2 Basic to Average	ELL English Language Learners
L3 All Students	LPR Less Proficient Readers
L4 Average to Advanced	AR Advanced Readers
	GT Gifted and Talented

Author's Note

We tend to think of the Great Depression in purely economic terms; however, it had catastrophic political consequences and might very well have been the single greatest cause of World War II.

During the Depression, America experienced minimal political disruption. After the election of 1932, the transfer of presidential power from Republicans to Democrats went off without a hitch. And although Franklin D. Roosevelt could not take credit for ending the Depression—World War II, not the New Deal, did that—he does deserve praise for preserving the country's most vital economic and political systems. While radicals clamored that democracy had failed to meet the crisis,

FDR never wavered in his commitment to the constitutional process.

The same was not true in Japan and Germany. During the 1920s, Japan tried political liberalization. The Japanese initiated Western-style political parties and reduced the power of the military. However, the political atmosphere created by the Depression crippled the civilian government. The military insisted that the answer to Japan's economic troubles lay in expanding. During the 1930s, Japan invaded Manchuria and China and planned to expand into Southeast Asia, the Dutch East Indies, and the entire Western Pacific—this aggression resulted in war with the United States.

The 1920s was also a period of liberalization for Germany. Under the Weimar Republic, the government consisted of an elected president, a cabinet led by a chancellor, a two-house parliament, and free elections. A broad range of political parties flourished. One of these was the National Socialist German Workers' (Nazi) party, a fringe group that pushed a doctrine of hate and exclusion. Nazi numbers grew steadily until the 1933 appointment of Adolf Hitler as chancellor. Hitler systematically subverted the constitutional system until he became a German dictator. What had begun as economic problems associated with the Great Depression ended in world war.

—Randy Roberts

Extend Online

Hoover Dam

Have students research the history of the Hoover Dam. Then, ask them to use their research to develop a guided tour for visitors and tourists. Use the steps below to help students complete the activity.

Prepare the Activity Tell students that the Hoover Dam was built in the 1930s, during the Great Depression. The massive construction project brought much-needed jobs to the Southwest. The water collected in the reservoir created by the dam became a major source of electric power and water for the region.

Conduct the Activity For help in starting the activity, send students to **www.pearsonschool.com/ushist.** Students will explore different aspects of the dam and its history. Organize students in groups. Ask each group to use

its findings to create a guided tour of the Hoover Dam. The tour may be in the form of a brochure, Web site, or multimedia presentation. The tour should trace the history of the Hoover Dam, point out important mechanisms that help the dam function, and explain the significance of the dam to the West today. The tour also should explain how the planning and construction of the Hoover Dam fit into the story of the Great Depression. Have each group present its tour to the class.

Follow-Up Conduct a class discussion based on the following questions: Why was the Hoover Dam important to the West during the Great Depression? How do people today use the Hoover Dam? What positive and negative effects do dams have on the environment?

Experiential Learning

For learners struggling to grasp core concepts and generalizations presented in the text, help students "experience" what they read. Design an activity that enables students to get their hands on the content. Follow the guidelines below.

1. **Guide students through an experience.** Have students create a game to help them think about how different groups and individuals might have dealt with the challenges of the Great Depression. Begin by organizing the class in groups and asking them to create flashcards based on the following six categories: *race or ethnicity, age,* and *gender* (e.g., adult white man, adult white woman, adult African American man, adult African American woman); *employment status* (employed full-time, employed part-time, unemployed); *marital status* (single, married); *class* (upper, middle, lower); and *place of residence* (urban, rural). Have them write the category name on one side of a flashcard and a subcategory on the other. (Encourage students to create additional categories and subcategories.) Finally, have them separate the cards by category into six different piles.

To begin the exercise, have each student pick a card from each category. Ask each student to write the subcategories on a sheet of paper before shuffling the cards back into the appropriate pile. Next, each student should imagine that he or she were an individual with these characteristics living during the 1930s and write a paragraph or two explaining some of the experiences he or she might go through during the Great Depression.

2. **Reflect on that experience.** After all students have completed their paragraphs, have groups read and discuss their work together. Encourage them to identify which backgrounds and characteristics tended to most influence people's experiences. Have each group compile a list of additional information that might have helped it create more subtle profiles.

3. **Act on that experience.** Ask each group to follow-up on its discussions by making three generalizations about the Great Depression's impact on different groups. Although students cannot truly experience this type of crisis during the 1930s, using this learning strategy can help them make general connections to the economic and social upheaval that took place at that time.

Modeling Reading and Writing Skills

Ask Questions Explain to students that asking questions about the headings, subheadings, and visuals will help them understand and remember the text. Students should read to answer their own questions. This is another strategy to help students interact with the text and better comprehend it.

Model the process. Look at the first blue heading in Section 2, "Misery and Despair Grip America's Cities." Turn this into a question: When and why did misery and despair grip America's cities? Ask students to turn the next two blue headings into questions. Write these questions on the board. Then, as a class, read to find the answers to their questions.

Gather Information Tell students that in this chapter, they will be writing a problem-solution essay. (See Writing About History at the end of the chapter.) When proposing a solution to a problem, students must convince the audience that their solution is likely to work.

On the board, write the following types of evidence that can be used to present convincing detail:

A Statistics
B Expert opinion
C Comparable situations

Explain that statistics provide relevant numerical data that can support a claim. Expert opinion includes the advice of those who have experience related to the problem, and comparable situations describe the way that real-life scenarios were resolved. Ask students to brainstorm places where they might look to find each type of supporting detail for a problem-solution essay about one of the causes of the Great Depression.

CHAPTER 9

The New Deal, 1932–1941

Section	Core Instruction L3	Differentiated Instruction L1 L2 L4	
Section 1 100 minutes *FDR Offers Relief and Recovery* **OBJECTIVES** • Analyze the impact Franklin D. Roosevelt had on the American people after becoming President. • Describe the programs that were part of the First New Deal and their immediate impact. • Identify critical responses to the New Deal. **Focus Question** *How did the New Deal attempt to address the problems of the Great Depression?*	**Teaching Resources** Reading Strategy: Connect Ideas, p. 12 Interpreting a Political Cartoon: FDR and the New Deal, p. 20 Section 1 Quiz, p. 24 **Reading and Note Taking Study Guide** Section Note Taking, p. 73 Section 1 Summary, p. 74 **Progress Monitoring Transparencies,** p. 103 **Color Transparencies** Civilian Conservation Corps, A-97	**L1** **Adapted Reading and Note Taking Study Guide** Section Note Taking, p. 73 SN Section 1 Summary, p. 74 SN **L2** **Adapted Reading and Note Taking Study Guide** Section Note Taking, p. 73 LPR Section 1 Summary, p. 74 LPR **Spanish Reading and Note Taking Study Guide** Section Note Taking, p. 73 ELL Section 1 Summary, p. 74 ELL **L4** **Differentiated Instruction Activity,** Teacher's Edition, p. 287 AR, GT	**Differentiated Instruction Activities,** Teacher's Edition, pp. 286, 289, 290 SN ****Teaching Resources** Interpreting a Political Cartoon: The New Deal, p. 19 **Differentiated Instruction Activities,** Teacher's Edition, pp. 286, 289, 290 LPR, ELL **Extend Activity,** Teaching Resources, pp. 13–14 AR, GT
Section 2 100 minutes *The Second New Deal* **OBJECTIVES** • Discuss the programs of social and economic reform in the Second New Deal. • Explain how the New Deal legislation affected the growth of organized labor. • Describe the impact of Roosevelt's court-packing plan on the course of the New Deal. **Focus Question** *What major issues did the Second New Deal address?*	**Teaching Resources** Reading a Chart: New Deal Programs, p. 21 Section 2 Quiz, p. 25 **Reading and Note Taking Study Guide** Section Note Taking, p. 75 Section 2 Summary, p. 76 **Progress Monitoring Transparencies,** p. 104 **Color Transparencies** Critics of the New Deal, A-98	**L1** **Adapted Reading and Note Taking Study Guide** Section Note Taking, p. 75 SN Section 2 Summary, p. 76 SN **L2** **Adapted Reading and Note Taking Study Guide** Section Note Taking, p. 75 LPR Section 2 Summary, p. 76 LPR **Spanish Reading and Note Taking Study Guide** Section Note Taking, p. 75 ELL Section 2 Summary, p. 76 ELL **L4** **Differentiated Instruction Activity,** Teacher's Edition, p. 294 AR, GT	***Student Edition on Audio** SN **Differentiated Instruction Activities,** Teacher's Edition, pp. 295, 297 SN ***Guided Reading Audio, Spanish CD** ELL ***Student Edition on Audio** LPR, ELL **Differentiated Instruction Activities,** Teacher's Edition, pp. 285, 297 LPR, ELL **Extend Activity,** Teacher's Edition, p. 299 AR, GT

Section	Core Instruction L3	Differentiated Instruction L1 L2 L4	

Section 3 100 minutes
Effects of the New Deal

OBJECTIVES
- Describe how the New Deal affected different groups in American society.
- Analyze how the New Deal changed the shape of American party politics.
- Discuss the impact of Franklin D. Roosevelt on the presidency.

Focus Question *How did the New Deal change the social, economic, and political landscape of the United States for future generations?*

Teaching Resources
Biography: Eleanor Roosevelt, p. 22
Issues Connector: Governments Role in the Economy, pp. 15–18
Section 3 Quiz, p. 26

Reading and Note Taking Study Guide
Section Note Taking, p. 77
Section 3 Summary, p. 78
American Issues Journal, pp. 215–217

Progress Monitoring Transparencies, 105

Color Transparencies
The New Deal Provides Jobs, A-99

L1 Adapted Reading and Note Taking Study Guide
Section Note Taking, p. 77 SN
Section 3 Summary, p. 78 SN
American Issues Journal, pp. 215–217 SN

Differentiated Instruction Activities, Teacher's Edition, pp. 304, 306, 307 SN

L2 Adapted Reading and Note Taking Study Guide
Section Note Taking, p. 77 LPR
Section 3 Summary, p. 78 LPR
American Issues Journal, pp. 215–217 LPR

Spanish Reading and Note Taking Study Guide
Section Note Taking, p. 77 ELL
Section 3 Summary, p. 78 ELL
American Issues Journal, pp. 215–217 ELL

Differentiated Instruction Activities, Teacher's Edition, pp. 304, 306, 307 LPR, ELL

L4 Differentiated Instruction Activity, Teacher's Edition, p. 302 AR, GT

Extend Activity, Teacher's Edition, p. 309 AR, GT

Section 4 75 minutes
Culture of the 1930s

OBJECTIVES
- Trace the growth of radio and the movies in the 1930s and the changes in popular culture.
- Describe the major themes of literature of the New Deal era.

Focus Question *How did the men and women of the Depression find relief from their hardships in the popular culture?*

Teaching Resources
Link to Literature: "Roll On, Columbia," p. 23
Section 4 Quiz, p. 27

Reading and Note Taking Study Guide
Section Note Taking, p. 79
Section 4 Summary, p. 80

Progress Monitoring Transparencies, 106

Color Transparencies
Big Bands Swing, A-100

L1 Adapted Reading and Note Taking Study Guide
Section Note Taking, p. 79 SN
Section 4 Summary, p. 80 SN

Differentiated Instruction Activity, Teacher's Edition, p. 311 SN

L2 Adapted Reading and Note Taking Study Guide
Section Note Taking, p. 79 LPR
Section 4 Summary, p. 80 LPR

Spanish Reading and Note Taking Study Guide
Section Note Taking, p. 79 ELL
Section 4 Summary, p. 80 ELL

Differentiated Instruction Activity, Teacher's Edition, p. 311 LPR, ELL

L4 Differentiated Instruction Activity, Teacher's Edition, p. 313 AR, GT

Extend Activity, Teacher's Edition, p. 314 AR, GT

*Audio support is available for all sections.

**This worksheet also applies to L1.

Assessment Resources
- **Teaching Resources,** Tests A and B, pp. 28–33
- **AYP Monitoring Assessments,** Benchmark Test 2
- **Progress Monitoring Transparencies,** 103–106
- **Test Prep With Document-Based Assessment**
- *ExamView* ®Test Bank CD-ROM
- **Progress Monitoring Online Quiz**
- **Assessment Rubrics**

Differentiated Instruction Key
L1 Special Needs	SN	Special Needs Students
L2 Basic to Average	ELL	English Language Learners
L3 All Students	LPR	Less Proficient Readers
L4 Average to Advanced	AR	Advanced Readers
	GT	Gifted and Talented

Author's Note

Probably the best graduate school course I had was "America Between the Wars." Taught by William Leuchtenburg, one of the most respected scholars on Franklin D. Roosevelt, the course was both demanding and invigorating. Since I had applied to Columbia University primarily to study with Professor Leuchtenburg, I was especially interested in taking this class and doing well in it.

Structured as a seminar, the class centered on student-directed discussions of the most recent scholarship on the 1920s and the New Deal. Several weeks into the course, Leuctenburg added to our demanding reading list, requesting that we read Arthur Schlesinger's three-volume study of the Roosevelt years. He felt we needed a stronger sense of the time period before we could properly evaluate the strengths and weaknesses of the recent scholarship.

Initially, the class reacted with dismay. We were already reading at least a monograph a week, and some of these ran to more than 500 pages. How we were going to be able to complete this work along with the 1,000+ pages of Schlesinger's classic?

Somehow, we got the work done. Knowing that it was next to impossible to recall all this reading, we established our own study groups to prepare for exams. Indeed, I still have some of the study sheets I developed for this class, and I draw on them to prepare my lectures on the First and Second New Deal. I could never have guessed that those extra hours I put in for Professor Leuchtenburg's course would save me time and trouble today.

I never regretted taking that class for several reasons. First, I learned that if a teacher sets the bar high, student performance will rise to meet it. In addition, nothing about Leuchtenburg's methods were arbitrary or aimed to create busy work. His exams were fair and directly related to the readings. Perhaps most important, his enthusiasm for teaching and his warm personality made the class an enjoyable experience. These keys to good teaching, as well as what I learned about the New Deal, are lessons I will never forget.

—Peter B. Levy

Extend Online

Art's New Deal

Have small groups of students research and produce multimedia presentations on the works of government-sponsored New Deal artists. Use the steps below to help students complete the activity.

Prepare for the Activity "Always the heart and soul of our country will be the heart and soul of the common man." These words of President Franklin Roosevelt sum up one important theme in New Deal era art. The Depression left millions of Americans—including many artists—jobless and desperate. When federal projects were created to put people back to work, FDR saw to it that artists were not left out. For the first time in American history, the federal government paid painters to paint, writers to write, and musicians to play music.

Conduct the Activity For help in starting the activity, send students to **www.pearsonschool.com/ushist**. Students will select one type of art from the collection on the Web site that is characteristic of this period. Have students work in small groups to produce an oral presentation on the work of government-sponsored New Deal artists. It should include various multimedia elements, such as visuals of the art (from the Internet, books, magazines, posters, slides), music, or quotations from the period, and so on. Encourage students to be creative. They will find some background on the Web site itself but will have to supplement that information with additional research.

Follow-Up After each group has made its presentation, lead a classroom discussion based on the following questions: What themes were common in the art of the New Deal? Why were these common themes? Is the art of the New Deal different than art today?

Cornell Note Taking L1 L2

Learning to take notes efficiently will help students read the text and review key information. The Cornell Note Taking strategy provides students with a structured way to read and record core content.

1. Students draw a vertical line two and a half inches from the left-hand side of their notebook paper to create a Review Column.

2. Students take notes on the text material in the more spacious area to the right.

3. After taking notes on a section, students review their notes and in the Review Column write focused questions that elicit the specific content from the right-hand column. For example, if one section of the notes details New Deal programs initiated by Franklin Roosevelt during his first 100 days in office, the student would write the review questions "What New Deal programs did FDR initiate during his first 100 days in office?" Formulating such review questions forces students to review the section content carefully and clarify the information.

4. To study their notes, students cover the right side of the page, read the review questions, and quiz themselves by checking their understanding and recall of critical content, rather than passively rereading information.

5. Students can be encouraged or required to write a brief summary of each section in their own words at the end of their notes to strengthen their review and increase the likelihood that they will retain the information.

Modeling Reading and Writing Skills

Identify Implied Main Ideas Explain to students that main ideas do not have to be directly stated. They may be implied. To determine an implied main idea, readers must look for the idea that links all of the details in a section of text and then construct a sentence that states the main idea.

To model the skills, read aloud the text under the heading *The First Hundred Days Provide Instant Action,* in Section 1. Point out some of the details: Roosevelt uses fireside chats to restore public confidence, New Deal laws reform banking and the stock market, New Deal programs give help to farmers and provide jobs for the unemployed. The main idea, then, is that Roosevelt moved quickly to restore confidence, reform the economic system, and provide immediate relief to Americans suffering the worst effects of the Depression.

Synthesize Explain that in this chapter students will be writing an essay in which they must synthesize information that they have learned. (See Writing About History at the end of the chapter.) Point out that synthesizing information means that students will compare different pieces of historical evidence to draw their own conclusions about a topic.

On the board, write the following topics on which different information is available:

A Dress codes in schools

B Importance of college education

C Immigration to the United States

Explain to students that only one source of information about any of these topics will not provide sufficient evidence to draw a well-informed conclusion about it. Have students brainstorm places to find information on these topics, such as the Internet and encyclopedias. Also, have students list the types of information to look for, including charts, statistics, and personal narratives.

10 The Coming of War, 1931–1942

Section	Core Instruction **L3**	Differentiated Instruction **L1 L2 L4**	
Section 1 100 minutes *Dictators and War* **OBJECTIVES** • Explain how dictators and militaristic regimes arose in several countries in the 1930s. • Summarize the actions taken by aggressive regimes in Europe and Asia. • Analyze the responses of Britain, France, and the United States to the aggressive regimes. **Focus Question** *Why did totalitarian states rise after World War I, and what did they do?*	**Teaching Resources** Reading Strategy: Summarize, p. 11 Outline Map: German Aggression, p. 14 Section 1 Quiz, p. 19 **Reading and Note Taking Study Guide** Section Note Taking, pp. 81–82 Section 1 Summary, p. 83 **Progress Monitoring Transparencies, 107** **Color Transparencies** The Nazi Party, A-101	**L1 Adapted Reading and Note Taking Study Guide** Section Note Taking, pp. 81–82 SN Section 1 Summary, p. 83 SN **L2 Adapted Reading and Note Taking Study Guide** Section Note Taking, pp. 81–82 LPR Section 1 Summary, p. 83 LPR **Spanish Reading and Note Taking Study Guide** Section Note Taking, pp. 81–82 ELL Section 1 Summary, p. 83 ELL **L4 Differentiated Instruction Activity,** Teacher's Edition, p. 328 AR, GT	*Student Edition on Audio SN **Differentiated Instruction Activities,** Teacher's Edition, pp. 325, 326, 329 SN *Guided Reading Audio, Spanish CD ELL *Student Edition on Audio LPR, ELL **Differentiated Instruction Activities,** Teacher's Edition, pp. 325, 326, 329 LPR, ELL **Extend Activity,** Teacher's Edition, p. 330 AR, GT
Section 2 100 minutes *From Isolation to Involvement* **OBJECTIVES** • Understand the course of the early years of World War II in Europe. • Describe Franklin Roosevelt's foreign policy in the mid-1930s and the great debate between interventionists and isolationists. • Explain how the United States became more involved in the conflict. **Focus Question** *How did Americans react to events in Europe and Asia in the early years of World War II?*	**Teaching Resources** Interpreting a Political Cartoon: Neutrality, p. 15 Primary Source: The "Four Freedoms" Speech and George W. Bush's Address to a Joint Session of Congress, p. 17 Section 2 Quiz, p. 20 **Reading and Note Taking Study Guide** Section Note Taking, p. 84 Section 2 Summary, p. 85 **Progress Monitoring Transparencies, 108** **Color Transparencies** German Blitzkrieg, A-102	**L1 Adapted Reading and Note Taking Study Guide** Section Note Taking, p. 84 SN Section 2 Summary, p. 85 SN **L2 Adapted Reading and Note Taking Study Guide** Section Note Taking, p. 84 LPR Section 2 Summary, p. 85 LPR **Spanish Reading and Note Taking Study Guide** Section Note Taking, p. 84 ELL Section 2 Summary, p. 85 ELL **L4 Differentiated Instruction Activity,** Teacher's Edition, p. 335 AR, GT	**Differentiated Instruction Activities,** Teacher's Edition, pp. 332, 333, 337 SN **Teaching Resources** Primary Source: The "Four Freedoms" Speech, p. 16 ELL, LPR **Differentiated Instruction Activities,** Teacher's Edition, pp. 332, 333, 337 LPR, ELL **Extend Activity,** Teaching Resources, pp. 12–13 AR, GT

Section	Core Instruction L3	Differentiated Instruction L1 L2 L4

Section 3 100 minutes
America Enters the War

OBJECTIVES
- Explain why Japan decided to attack Pearl Harbor, and describe the attack itself.
- Outline how the United States mobilized for war after the attack on Pearl Harbor.
- Summarize the course of the war in the Pacific through the summer of 1942.

Focus Question *How did the United States react to the Japanese attack on Pearl Harbor?*

Core Instruction

Teaching Resources
Reading a Chart: Industry During World War II, p. 18
Section 3 Quiz, p. 21

Reading and Note Taking Study Guide
Section Note Taking, p. 86
Section 3 Summary, p. 87

Progress Monitoring Transparencies, 109

Color Transparencies
Women and the War Effort, A-103

Differentiated Instruction

L1 Adapted Reading and Note Taking Study Guide
Section Note Taking, p. 86 SN
Section 3 Summary, p. 87 SN

Differentiated Instruction Activities, Teacher's Edition, pp. 344, 345 SN

L2 Adapted Reading and Note Taking Study Guide
Section Note Taking, p. 86 LPR
Section 3 Summary, p. 87 LPR

Spanish Reading and Note Taking Study Guide
Section Note Taking, p. 86 ELL
Section 3 Summary, p. 87 ELL

Differentiated Instruction Activities, Teacher's Edition, pp. 344, 345 LPR, ELL

L4 Differentiated Instruction Activities, Teacher's Edition, pp. 342, 346 AR, GT

Extend Activity, Teacher's Edition, p. 347 AR, GT

*Audio support is available for all sections.

**This worksheet also applies to L1.

Assessment Resources
- **Teaching Resources,** Tests A and B, pp. 22–27
- **AYP Monitoring Assessments,** Benchmark Test 2
- **Progress Monitoring Transparencies,** 107–109
- **Test Prep With Document-Based Assessment**
- *ExamView* ® Test Bank CD-ROM
- **Progress Monitoring Online Quiz**
- **Assessment Rubrics**

Differentiated Instruction Key
L1 Special Needs	SN Special Needs Students
L2 Basic to Average	ELL English Language Learners
L3 All Students	LPR Less Proficient Readers
L4 Average to Advanced	AR Advanced Readers
	GT Gifted and Talented

Author's Note

The most popular course I teach is on the Second World War, and the question I always hear is "With so many battles in World War II, which are the most important?" I'm sometimes tempted to say the ones that are not on any maps: the battle to increase production on the home front, the battle to win the loyalty of citizens, the battle to maintain high-mindedness—these were all vital. Of course, what my students really want to know is "Which battles turned the tide of the war?"

In the Pacific Theater, the crucial action was the Battle of Midway in June 1942. For six months after Pearl Harbor, the Japanese took the offensive and enjoyed almost uninterrupted success, taking territory and defeating American, British, and Dutch forces. At Midway, however, they overplayed their hand: American code breakers learned of the Japanese plans to take Midway, and U.S. naval forces prepared a surprise for them, sinking four Japanese aircraft carriers. With that action, the advantage shifted to the Americans and the Allies. There was still much difficult fighting ahead—battles on coral reefs and in jungles—but Japan's hope for victory in the Pacific faded with almost every engagement.

The turning point in the European Theater was the Battle of Stalingrad. From 1939 to 1942, Germany had won a string of victories, conquering Poland, the Low Countries, and France. They had moved into Den-mark and Norway and invaded Eastern Europe and the Soviet Union. True, they had failed to invade Great Britain in 1940 and, while they had no success in routing the Soviet army in 1941, they hoped to complete the job at Stalingrad. Unprepared for the Russian winter, the German forces surrendered in February 1942 and the German momentum faltered. Still, the war was far from over. With American and Soviet advances on German forces in 1944 and 1945, Hitler's empire shrank considerably. What began at Stalingrad in the winter of 1943 ended in Berlin in the spring of 1945.

—Randy Roberts

Extend Online

Americans' Reactions to Pearl Harbor

Have students create their own oral history presentation on reactions to Pearl Harbor. Ask them to present their findings to the class. Use the steps below to help students complete the activity.

Prepare for the Activity Explain that the attack on Pearl Harbor shocked Americans. Those who were old enough to remember the event recall it as a defining aspect of their lives. Most recall the exact moment they heard the news and how they felt.

Conduct the Activity For help in starting the activity, send students to **www.pearsonschool.com/ushist**. Students will examine the interviews conducted and note the kinds of questions that people were asked and how they responded. Have students use their research to develop a series of questions to ask of someone who remembers December 7, 1941. Help students identify such a person and ask them to conduct an oral history interview with that person. If they cannot interview someone, have students search online or in the library for oral histories about Pearl Harbor. Then, have groups develop a presentation that notes any differences between responses to the event right after it happened and responses many years later. Have each group present its oral history to the class. Ask students to analyze how public reactions to the attack have changed over time.

Follow-Up Conduct a class discussion based on the following questions: How did the attack on Pearl Harbor affect the United States? What did the attack on Pearl Harbor reveal about the character of U.S. citizens? How do you think the passage of time affects a person's perception of an event such as the bombing of Pearl Harbor?

Creating a Dialogue L2

In addition to learning social studies content, English Language Learners face the additional challenge of developing proficiency in English. To encourage students to use both written and spoken English and apply core content, have them create a dialogue. Follow these steps:

1. Organize the class in groups, and assign each group a scenario.
2. List key terms and high-use words on the board that must be included in the dialogue.
3. Require that every student have a speaking role.
4. Have students submit a written copy of the script as part of the assessment for this activity.

Ask each group to perform its dialogues for the class to enhance the English language listening skills of students in the audience.

Comparing Historical Events L4

Comparing similar events in history helps students make connections, recognize change over time, and identify ways in which leaders either repeat or redeem mistakes that were made in the past. Suggest that students keep a running chart of comparisons between World War I and World War II. Categories for comparison might include:
• Long-term causes
• Immediate causes
• Major participants
• Major issues at stake

Students may work together to brainstorm other categories. When students are done, have them use their charts to answer the following question: Does the outbreak of World War II show that world leaders learned from the mistakes that led to World War I or merely repeated them?

Modeling Reading and Writing Skills

Use Prior Knowledge Remind students that they already know something about many topics, both from reading previous material and from their own experiences. By building on this prior knowledge, readers gain a head start in learning new information. To demonstrate this, have students look at the images and graphics throughout this chapter. Ask students what they already know about World War II. Tell them that by using what they know, they can make connections between their own knowledge and the text, which will give them a greater understanding of the new content.

Acknowledge Opposition Explain that in this chapter students will be writing a persuasive speech. (See Writing About History at the end of the chapter.) Point out that in persuasive speech, students need to acknowledge opposing arguments and make counter arguments to refute them. List the following arguments on the board, and ask students to provide opposing viewpoints. Remind them that arguments should be constructed logically.
A People should not be allowed to drive until they are 21.
B The U.S. government should provide financial aid to unemployed people during a national economic crisis.

As each opposing argument is presented, invite another student to counter it or do so yourself. Provide the following example as a guide:

A Opposing argument: Teenagers need to be able to drive to get to school or to work. **Counter argument:** They can use public transportation, which is safer, cheaper, and better for the environment.

CHAPTER 11 World War II, 1941–1945

Section	Core Instruction L3	Differentiated Instruction L1 L2 L4	
Section 1 100 minutes *The Allies Turn the Tide* **OBJECTIVES** • Analyze the reasons for and impact of the Allies' "Europe First" strategy. • Explain why the battles of Stalingrad and Midway were major turning points in the war. • Discuss how the Allies put increasing pressure on the Axis in North Africa and Europe.	**Teaching Resources** Geography and History: North Africa, p. 16 Section 1 Quiz, p. 23 **Reading and Note Taking Study Guide** Section Note Taking, p. 88 Section 1 Summary, p. 89 **Progress Monitoring Transparencies,** 110 **Color Transparencies** The Battle of Midway, A-104	L1 **Adapted Reading and Note Taking Study Guide** Section Note Taking, p. 88 SN Section 1 Summary, p. 89 SN	*Student Edition on Audio SN **Differentiated Instruction Activities,** Teacher's Edition, pp. 355, 356 SN
		L2 **Adapted Reading and Note Taking Study Guide** Section Note Taking, p. 88 LPR Section 1 Summary, p. 89 LPR **Spanish Reading and Note Taking Study Guide** Section Note Taking, p. 88 ELL Section 1 Summary, p. 89 ELL	*Guided Reading Audio, Spanish CD ELL *Student Edition on Audio LPR, ELL **Differentiated Instruction Activities,** Teacher's Edition, pp. 355, 356 LPR, ELL
Focus Question *How did the Allies turn the tide against the Axis?*		L4 **Differentiated Instruction Activity,** Teacher's Edition, p. 357 AR, GT	**Extend Activity,** Teacher's Edition, p. 360 AR, GT
Section 2 75 minutes *The Home Front* **OBJECTIVES** • Explain how World War II increased opportunities for women and minorities. • Analyze the effects of the war on civil liberties for Japanese Americans and others. • Examine how the need to support the war effort changed American lives.	**Teaching Resources** Biography: Navaho Code Talkers, p. 17 Landmark Decisions: Can government limit a group's liberties during wartime?, p. 18 Section 2 Quiz, p. 24 **Reading and Note Taking Study Guide** Section Note Taking, p. 90 Section 2 Summary, p. 91 **Progress Monitoring Transparencies,** 111 **Color Transparencies** Victory Gardens, A-105	L1 **Adapted Reading and Note Taking Study Guide** Section Note Taking, p. 90 SN Section 2 Summary, p. 91 SN	**Differentiated Instruction Activities,** Teacher's Edition, pp. 362, 364 SN
		L2 **Adapted Reading and Note Taking Study Guide** Section Note Taking, p. 90 LPR Section 2 Summary, p. 91 LPR **Spanish Reading and Note Taking Study Guide** Section Note Taking, p. 90 ELL Section 2 Summary, p. 91 ELL	**Differentiated Instruction Activities,** Teacher's Edition, pp. 362, 364 LPR, ELL
Focus Question *How did the war change America at home?*		L4 **Differentiated Instruction Activity,** Teacher's Edition, p. 364 AR, GT	**Extend Activity,** Teaching Resources, pp. 14–15 AR, GT

*Audio support is available for all sections.

**This worksheet also applies to L1.

Assessment Resources
• **Teaching Resources,** Tests A and B, pp. 28–33
• **AYP Monitoring Assessments,** Benchmark Test 2
• **Progress Monitoring Transparencies,** 110–114
• Test Prep With Document-Based Assessment
• *ExamView*® Test Bank CD-ROM
• Progress Monitoring Online Quiz
• Assessment Rubrics

Differentiated Instruction Key

L1	Special Needs	SN	Special Needs Students
L2	Basic to Average	ELL	English Language Learners
L3	All Students	LPR	Less Proficient Readers
L4	Average to Advanced	AR	Advanced Readers
		GT	Gifted and Talented

Section	Core Instruction L3	Differentiated Instruction L1 L2 L4	

Section 3 125 minutes
Victory in Europe and the Pacific

OBJECTIVES
- Analyze the planning and impact of the D-Day invasion of France.
- Understand how the Allies achieved final victory in Europe.
- Explore the reasons President Truman decided to use the atomic bomb against Japan.

Focus Question *How did the Allies defeat the Axis Powers?*

Teaching Resources
Reading Strategy: Recognize Sequence, p. 13
Biography: The Marines at Iwo Jima, p. 20
Section 3 Quiz, p. 25

Reading and Note Taking Study Guide
Section Note Taking, p. 92
Section 3 Summary, p. 93

Progress Monitoring Transparencies, 112

Color Transparencies
The Manhattan Project, A-106; The Allies Win the War, A-107

L1 Adapted Reading and Note Taking Study Guide
Section Note Taking, p. 92 SN
Section 3 Summary, p. 93 SN

L2 Adapted Reading and Note Taking Study Guide
Section Note Taking, p. 92 LPR
Section 3 Summary, p. 93 LPR

Spanish Reading and Note Taking Study Guide
Section Note Taking, p. 92 ELL
Section 3 Summary, p. 93 ELL

L4 Differentiated Instruction Activities, Teacher's Edition, pp. 374, 375, 378 AR, GT

Differentiated Instruction Activities, Teacher's Edition, pp. 371, 373, 376 SN

**Teaching Resources
Biography: Ira Hayes, p. 19 ELL, LPR

Differentiated Instruction Activities, Teacher's Edition, pp. 371, 373, 375, 376 LPR, ELL

Extend Activity, Teacher's Edition, p. 379 AR, GT

Section 4 100 minutes
The Holocaust

OBJECTIVES
- Trace the roots and progress of Hitler's campaign against the Jews.
- Explore the goals of Hitler's "final solution" and the nature of the Nazi death camps.
- Examine how the United States responded to the Holocaust.

Focus Question *How did the Holocaust develop and what were its results?*

Teaching Resources
Link to Literature: *Liberation*, p. 21
Section 4 Quiz, p. 26

Reading and Note Taking Study Guide
Section Note Taking, pp. 94–95
Section 4 Summary, p. 96

Progress Monitoring Transparencies, 113

L1 Adapted Reading and Note Taking Study Guide
Section Note Taking, pp. 94–95 SN
Section 4 Summary, p. 96 SN

L2 Adapted Reading and Note Taking Study Guide
Section Note Taking, pp. 94–95 LPR
Section 4 Summary, p. 96 LPR

Spanish Reading and Note Taking Study Guide
Section Note Taking, pp. 94–95 ELL
Section 4 Summary, p. 96 ELL

L4 Differentiated Instruction Activity, Teacher's Edition, p. 381 AR, GT

Differentiated Instruction Activities, Teacher's Edition, pp. 381, 382 SN

Differentiated Instruction Activities, Teacher's Edition, pp. 381, 382 LPR, ELL

Extend Activity, Teacher's Edition, p. 385 AR, GT

Section 5 100 minutes
Effects of the War

OBJECTIVES
- Evaluate the goals that the Allied leaders set for the postwar world.
- Describe the steps that the United States and other nations took toward international cooperation.
- Explain the impact of World War II on the postwar United States.

Focus Question *What were the major and immediate long-term effects of World War II?*

Teaching Resources
History Comics: Postwar Goals, p. 22
Section 5 Quiz, p. 27

Reading and Note Taking Study Guide
Section Note Taking, p. 97
Section 5 Summary, p. 98

Progress Monitoring Transparencies, 114

Color Transparencies
Dividing Germany, A-108

L1 Adapted Reading and Note Taking Study Guide
Section Note Taking, p. 97 SN
Section 5 Summary, p. 98 SN

L2 Adapted Reading and Note Taking Study Guide
Section Note Taking, p. 97 LPR
Section 5 Summary, p. 98 LPR

Spanish Reading and Note Taking Study Guide
Section Note Taking, p. 97 ELL
Section 5 Summary, p. 98 ELL

L4 Differentiated Instruction Activity, Teacher's Edition, p. 388 AR, GT

Differentiated Instruction Activity, Teacher's Edition, p. 389 SN

Differentiated Instruction Activity, Teacher's Edition, p. 389 LPR, ELL

Extend Activity, Teacher's Edition, p. 391 AR, GT

Author's Note

Winning World War II made demands on all Americans. Soldiers, sailors, and marines did their part, but so did farmers, doctors, nurses, and the millions of Americans who labored in defense-related industries. Even movie stars such as Jimmy Stewart, Clark Gable, Gene Autry, Tyrone Power, and Ronald Reagan served in the military. So did famous professional athletes, such as baseball players Joe DiMaggio, Ted Williams, and Bob Feller.

In the 1930s, world heavyweight boxing champion Joe Louis was the most visible and important African American celebrity in the country. His 1938 one-round knockout of the German challenger Max Schmeling was widely interpreted as America's first victory over Nazi Germany.

Newspaper journalist Heywood Broun commented, "[O]ne hundred years from now, some historian may theorize, in a footnote at least, that the decline of Nazi prestige began with a left hook delivered by a former unskilled automobile worker who had never studied the policies of Neville Chamberlain and had no opinion whatsoever in regard to the situation in Czechoslovakia."

After Pearl Harbor, Louis fought several fights for navy and army benefits and then enlisted. "I have only done what any red-blooded American would do," he told an audience at a pro-war rally. "We're going to do our part, and we will win, because we are on God's side." The idea of being "on God's side" became an important theme during the war. Louis himself

signified that white and black Americans were unified in the war effort.

Actor John Wayne also became a symbol of the American war effort, although he never enlisted. Before the war, Wayne had been a struggling movie actor, but, as other leading men went off to war, roles opened up for him. In 1942, he starred in seven films, and, by the end of the war, he had fought for justice—on the silver screen—in the Pacific, Europe, and America as a soldier, sailor, construction worker, cowboy, and steel tycoon. Even though he had never fought on an actual battlefield, his roles onscreen allowed movie fans on the home front to join in the heroic struggles of World War II.

—Randy Roberts

Extend Online

The Manhattan Project and the End of World War II

Have students research the Manhattan Project and the factors that led U.S. leaders to decide to use the bomb to end World War II. Ask students to present their findings to the class. Use the steps below to help students complete the activity.

Prepare for the Activity The Manhattan Project made the United States the first nation to develop a nuclear weapon—the atomic bomb. People debated whether the atomic bomb should be used. Some people, including prominent scientists, discouraged the U.S. government from using the bomb. Others believed that dropping the bomb on Japan would end the war quickly and save the lives of hundreds of thousands of U.S. soldiers. A few also thought that using the bomb in this way would demonstrate U.S. power to the Soviet Union, with whom the United States had a developing rivalry.

Conduct the Activity For help in starting this activity, send students to www.pearsonschool.com/ushist. Students will read background information on the topic, and formerly top-secret, primary-source documents about the Manhattan Project that discuss when, how, and whether to use the bomb. Have students use the information at this site to write a report that traces the decision-making process. Be sure that students correctly cite their sources. Have students present to the class the results of their investigations.

Follow-Up Conduct a class discussion based on the following questions: What factors led to Truman's decision to drop atomic bombs on Hiroshima and Nagasaki? Do you believe that Truman made the correct decision? Was Truman's decision inevitable? What other choices did he have? Explain.

Providing Appropriate Resource Materials L2

To maximize English Language Learners' success in your social studies class, make sure that your classroom is provisioned with materials that can assist students struggling with English as a second language. These materials can help students better decipher text and assigned readings, write more coherently, and feel confident in their understanding of the content being taught. Materials that a teacher of English Language Learners should try to make available include the following:

1. **An English dictionary** for looking up unfamiliar terms
2. **Two-way translation dictionaries** for looking up words in students' native language to obtain the equivalent word in English and for looking up unfamiliar words in English to find a definition in the native language.

3. **A thesaurus** to help students expand their English vocabulary. If a student essay repeatedly uses a basic vocabulary word such as *good,* encourage students to use the thesaurus to incorporate a wider variety of words in their writing.
4. **A grammar guide or textbook** to assist students in the mechanics of writing
5. **An encyclopedia** that provides brief and clear background information on a variety of topics. Often, full-length books on a subject from the library are daunting to an English Language Learner beginning his or her historical research. Encyclopedias, particularly those aimed at K–12 students, allow students to research information without becoming overwhelmed by lengthy and difficult passages in English.

Modeling Reading and Writing Skills

Sequence Tell students that when they see events in sequence, they can appreciate chronological order. Point out that noting the order of events can help them understand and remember the events.

Model recognizing sequence by reading aloud the first paragraph under the heading "Turning the Tide in the Pacific" in Section 1. Draw students' attention to the first word of the paragraph *(while)*, and point out that this word signals the introduction of a new sequence of events. The first event is the continued advance of Japanese forces through May 1942. Explain that dates also indicate a sequence. The fourth sentence in the paragraph begins with *Then,* which indicates an event that takes place after the occurance of the first one. The second event is the American victory in the Battle of Coral Sea.

Descriptive Essay Explain that in this chapter, students will be writing a descriptive essay. (See Writing About History at the end of the chapter.) Remind students that this type of essay describes an event by using sensory words. Descriptive essays should include precise adjectives and specific action verbs that vividly capture the

event and evoke a certain mood. These essays have an opening paragraph, in which the topic and setting are identified, and a conclusion, in which the topic is briefly summarized. As with all essays, students should follow these steps:

Prewriting: As students read about their topic, they should write words used to describe sights, sounds, tastes, and other aspects that appeal to the senses. For example, point out descriptive phrases in the Witness History feature in Section 1, such as *a mass of slops and stinks, foul scurrying,* and *inflamed flesh.* Students also should decide the mood they would like to convey to the reader.

Drafting: Remind students that a good essay starts with an outline. Also, to make their writing more vivid, students should consult a thesaurus for a wider word choice.

Revising: Have students reread their work to check for spelling and grammar errors, and tell them to consult a thesaurus again to further enhance descriptions.

Publishing: Students should create a final corrected version of their essays.

CHAPTER 12 The Cold War, 1945–1960

Section	Core Instruction L3	Differentiated Instruction L1 L2 L4	
Section 1 100 minutes *The Cold War Begins* **OBJECTIVES** • Trace the reasons that the war-time alliance between the United States and the Soviet Union unraveled. • Explain how President Truman responded to Soviet domination of Eastern Europe. • Describe the causes and results of Stalin's blockade of Berlin. **Focus Question** *How did U.S. leaders respond to the threat of Soviet expansion in Europe?*	**Teaching Resources** Reading Strategy: Contrast, p. 12 Reading a Chart: Causes and Effects of the Cold War, p. 19 Primary Source: *The Truman Doctrine and American Foreign Policy*, p. 21 Section 1 Quiz, p. 25 **Reading and Note Taking Study Guide** Section Note Taking, pp. 99–100 Section 1 Summary, p. 101 **Progress Monitoring Transparencies**, 115 **Color Transparencies** The Cost of Containment, A-109	**L1 Adapted Reading and Note Taking Study Guide** Section Note Taking, pp. 99–100 SN Section 1 Summary, p. 101 SN **L2 Adapted Reading and Note Taking Study Guide** Section Note Taking, pp. 99–100 LPR Section 1 Summary, p. 101 LPR **Spanish Reading and Note Taking Study Guide** Section Note Taking, pp. 99–100 ELL Section 1 Summary, p. 101 ELL **L4 Differentiated Instruction Activity,** Teacher's Edition, p. 402 AR, GT	**Differentiated Instruction Activities,** Teacher's Edition, pp. 399, 401 SN ****Teaching Resources** Primary Source: *The Truman Doctrine,* p. 20 ELL, LPR **Differentiated Instruction Activities,** Teacher's Edition, pp. 399, 400, 401 LPR, ELL **Extend Activity,** Teacher's Edition, p. 404 AR, GT
Section 2 100 minutes *The Korean War* **OBJECTIVES** • Explain how Mao Zedong and the communists gained power in China. • Describe the causes and progress of the war in Korea. • Identify the long-term effects of the Korean War. **Focus Question** *How did President Truman use the power of the presidency to limit the spread of communism in East Asia?*	**Teaching Resources** Viewpoints: MacArthur and Truman, p. 22 Section 2 Quiz, p. 26 **Reading and Note Taking Study Guide** Section Note Taking, p. 102 Section 2 Summary, p. 103 **Progress Monitoring Transparencies**, 116 **Color Transparencies** The Korean War, A-110	**L1 Adapted Reading and Note Taking Study Guide** Section Note Taking, p. 102 SN Section 2 Summary, p. 103 SN **L2 Adapted Reading and Note Taking Study Guide** Section Note Taking, p. 102 LPR Section 2 Summary, p. 103 LPR **Spanish Reading and Note Taking Study Guide** Section Note Taking, p. 102 ELL Section 2 Summary, p. 103 ELL **L4 Differentiated Instruction Activity,** Teacher's Edition, p. 410 AR, GT	***Student Edition on Audio** SN **Differentiated Instruction Activity,** Teacher's Edition, p. 408 SN ***Guided Reading Audio, Spanish CD** ELL ***Student Edition on Audio** LPR, ELL **Differentiated Instruction Activity,** Teacher's Edition, p. 408 LPR, ELL **Extend Activity,** Teacher's Edition, p. 411 AR, GT

*Audio support is available for all sections.

**This worksheet also applies to L1.

Assessment Resources
• **Teaching Resources,** Tests A and B, pp. 29–34
• **AYP Monitoring Assessments,** Benchmark Test 2
• **Progress Monitoring Transparencies,** 115–118
• **Test Prep With Document-Based Assessment**
• *ExamView*® **Test Bank CD-ROM**
• **Progress Monitoring Online Quiz**
• **Assessment Rubrics**

Differentiated Instruction Key

L1 Special Needs		SN	Special Needs Students
L2 Basic to Average		ELL	English Language Learners
L3 All Students		LPR	Less Proficient Readers
L4 Average to Advanced		AR	Advanced Readers
		GT	Gifted and Talented

Section	Core Instruction $L3$	Differentiated Instruction $L1$ $L2$ $L4$	

Section 3 100 minutes
The Cold War Expands

OBJECTIVES
- Describe the causes and results of the arms race between the United States and Soviet Union.
- Explain how Eisenhower's response to communism differed from that of Truman.
- Analyze worldwide Cold War conflicts that erupted in Eastern Europe, the Middle East, and other places.
- Discuss the effects of Soviet efforts in space exploration.

Focus Question *What methods did the United States use in its global struggle against the Soviet Union?*

Teaching Resources
Outline Map: Europe During the Cold War, p. 23
Section 3 Quiz, p. 27

Reading and Note Taking Study Guide
Section Note Taking, p. 104
Section 3 Summary, p. 105

Progress Monitoring Transparencies, 117

Color Transparencies
Cold War Initiatives, A-111

L1 Adapted Reading and Note Taking Study Guide
Section Note Taking, p. 104 SN
Section 3 Summary, p. 105 SN

Differentiated Instruction Activities, Teacher's Edition, pp. 414, 416 SN

L2 Adapted Reading and Note Taking Study Guide
Section Note Taking, p. 104 LPR
Section 3 Summary, p. 105 LPR

Spanish Reading and Note Taking Study Guide
Section Note Taking, p. 104 ELL
Section 3 Summary, p. 105 ELL

Differentiated Instruction Activities, Teacher's Edition, pp. 414, 416 LPR, ELL

L4 Differentiated Instruction Activity, Teacher's Edition, p. 415 AR, GT

Extend Activity, Teacher's Edition, p. 417 AR, GT

Section 4 75 minutes
The Cold War at Home

OBJECTIVES
- Describe the efforts of President Truman and the House of Representatives to fight communism at home.
- Explain how domestic spy cases increased fears of communist influence in the U.S. government.
- Analyze the rise and fall of Senator Joseph McCarthy and the methods of McCarthyism.

Focus Question *How did fear of domestic communism affect American society during the Cold War?*

Teaching Resources
Interpreting a Political Cartoon: McCarthyism, p. 24
Issues Connector: Civil Liberties and National Security, pp. 15–18
Section 4 Quiz, p. 28

Reading and Note Taking Study Guide
Section Note Taking, p. 106
Section 4 Summary, p. 107
American Issues Journal, pp. 218–220

Progress Monitoring Transparencies, 118

Color Transparencies
The Red Scare, A-112

L1 Adapted Reading and Note Taking Study Guide
Section Note Taking, p. 106 SN
Section 4 Summary, p. 107 SN
American Issues Journal, pp. 218–220 SN

Differentiated Instruction Activities, Teacher's Edition, pp. 422, 426 SN

L2 Adapted Reading and Note Taking Study Guide
Section Note Taking, p. 106 LPR
Section 4 Summary, p. 107 LPR
American Issues Journal, pp. 218–220 LPR

Spanish Reading and Note Taking Study Guide
Section Note Taking, p. 106 ELL
Section 4 Summary, p. 107 ELL
American Issues Journal, pp. 218–220 ELL

Differentiated Instruction Activities, Teacher's Edition, pp. 422, 426 LPR, ELL

L4 Differentiated Instruction Activities, Teacher's Edition, pp. 421, 425 AR, GT

Extend Activity, Teaching Resources, pp. 13–14 AR, GT

Author's Note

For more than forty years—from the pronouncement of the Truman Doctrine to the smashing of the Berlin Wall in 1989 and collapse of the Soviet Union in 1991—the Cold War between the United States and its allies and the Soviet Union and its allies dominated world history. On one level, it was an ideological war between East and West, communism and capitalism, totalitarianism and democracy. It was waged with propaganda, foreign aid, and weapons. The Berlin crisis, the Cuban Missile Crisis, the Korean War, and the Vietnam War were all events in the Cold War. But so, too, were the Marshall Plan, the World Bank, the North Atlantic Treaty Organization (NATO), the South-

east Asia Treaty Organization (SEATO), the Alliance for Progress, and dozens of other foreign policy and economic initiatives.

Yet the Cold War was more than just a political and economic reality. It was also the central cultural reality of the period. American popular culture revolved around the idea of "us" and "them." Hollywood directors turned out hundreds of films with Cold War themes—from such anti-communist films as *I Was a Communist for the FBI* and *My Son John* to movies that centered on the fear of a nuclear war as *Dr. Strangelove, Fail Safe,* and *On the Beach.* Novelists and television producers also trafficked in Cold War themes and settings. Ian Fleming's James Bond

series of novels were set in the Cold War. During the 1960s, "Mission Impossible" and "I Spy." were popular television series set amidst the Cold War rivalry between the American "us" and the Soviet "them."

Cold War competition between the United States and the Soviet Union even carried over into the running tracks and wrestling mats, boxing rings and basketball courts of the Olympic Games. Chants of "U.S.A., U.S.A., U.S.A.!" were as much products of the Cold War as the escalating arms race. Indeed, it is difficult to describe American culture between 1945 and 1990 without first talking about the Cold War.

—Randy Roberts

Extend Online

Cold War Crises

Have students research major crises of the early Cold War. Ask them to present their findings to the class. Use the steps below to help students complete the activity.

Prepare for the Activity
Explain that the Cold War gave rise to a series of crises in which tensions between the two superpowers increased. Key crises included the Korean War, the 1956 Polish and Hungarian crises, the launching of *Sputnik 1,* and the showdown in the Sinai.

Conduct the Activity For help in starting the activity, send students to **www.pearsonschool.com/ushist.** Students will select one of the Cold War crises listed above and research it. Students may work in groups, with each group researching one crisis. Have students find out how their crisis developed, the significance of the crisis in the history of the Cold War, the human impact of the crisis, and how the crisis was resolved.

Follow-Up Have each student or group of students present the results of their research to the class. Have students explain how the crisis illustrates a general feature of the Cold War.

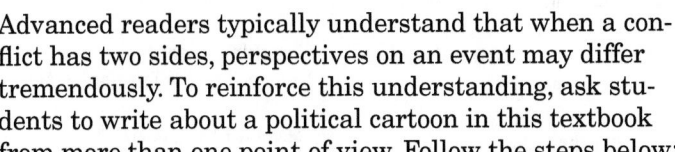

Oral History L1 L2

To help students become engaged in more recent historical events, have them conduct an oral history. First, have students select a focus for the oral history, suggested by the content of this chapter. As a class, brainstorm types of questions and specific questions for an interview. The class can use these questions with a guest speaker or with their own interviewee. Offer students a choice as to how they will report their findings: multimedia presentation, essay, poster, or skit. You may recommend that they record the interview with a camcorder, tape recorder, or MP3 player and then incorporate clips or sound bites into their presentation. To conclude the activity, have students compare and contrast their findings with a partner and with the information presented in this textbook. Remind students to analyze their sources when they compare findings. For example, a participant who experienced desegregation while serving in the army may view its success differently than someone who was a teacher in an inner-city public school.

Presenting Points of View L4

Advanced readers typically understand that when a conflict has two sides, perspectives on an event may differ tremendously. To reinforce this understanding, ask students to write about a political cartoon in this textbook from more than one point of view. Follow the steps below:

1. Assign a cartoon from this textbook to students.
2. Ask students to describe the cartoon in a way that represents the viewpoint of the cartoonist.
3. Students should then rewrite or revise their first description to reflect the opposite perspective. Revisions should include changes in the use of vocabulary that may make the reader more sympathetic to the other side and might mention events that support the second perspective but which were omitted from the first description.

Modeling Reading and Writing Skills

Interpret Nonliteral Meanings Explain to students that literal language means exactly what it says. Nonliteral language, on the other hand, uses images or comparisons to communicate an idea more vividly. When students come across such phrases, they should ask themselves what the phrase means and how it helps make the author's point.

Read aloud the excerpt from Winston Churchill's "Iron Curtain" speech in Section 1. Point out the phrase "an iron curtain has descended across the Continent." Explain that an iron curtain did not literally come down on Europe; the term iron curtain created a visual image that made Churchill's idea clearer to his listeners.

Gathering Information Tell students that in this chapter, they will be writing a research report. (See Writing About History at the end of the chapter.) When conducting research, it is important for students to evaluate the validity of their sources, especially those found on the Internet.

On the board, list some of the questions students should ask when evaluating Internet sources:

- Does the Web site provide information about the organization that sponsors the site? Is the organization reputable?
- What is the goal of the site? Does it aim to sell something? Provide information? Promote a cause?
- How often is the site updated? Is that often enough?

Explain that students must use judgment when using information from the Internet (as from books and articles). A source that may appear to be objective may, in fact, be promoting a cause or trying to sell something.

Have each student locate one site on the topic of Alger Hiss and use the questions at left to evaluate the source. Conduct a class discussion in which students provide examples from this exercise of both sources that seem reliable and sources that do not.

CHAPTER 13 Postwar Confidence and Anxiety, 1945–1960

Section	Core Instruction L3	Differentiated Instruction L1 L2 L4	
Section 1 100 minutes *An Economic Boom* **OBJECTIVES** • Describe how the United States made the transformation to a peacetime economy. • Discuss the accomplishments of Presidents Harry Truman and Dwight Eisenhower. • Analyze the 1950s economic boom. **Focus Question** *How did the nation experience recovery and economic prosperity after World War II?*	**Teaching Resources** Viewpoints: The Taft-Hartley Act, p. 16 Section 1 Quiz, p. 20 **Reading and Note Taking Study Guide** Section 1 Note Taking, p. 108 Section 1 Summary, p. 109 **Progress Monitoring Transparencies,** 119	**L1 Adapted Reading and Note Taking Study Guide** Section Note Taking, p. 108 SN Section 1 Summary, p. 109 SN **L2 Adapted Reading and Note Taking Study Guide** Section Note Taking, p. 108 LPR Section 1 Summary, p. 109 LPR **Spanish Reading and Note Taking Study Guide** Section Note Taking, p. 108 ELL Section 1 Summary, p. 109 ELL **L4 Differentiated Instruction Activity,** Teacher's Edition, p. 438 AR, GT	**Differentiated Instruction Activity,** Teacher's Edition, p. 437 SN ****Teaching Resources** Viewpoints: Labor Strikes, p. 15 LPR, ELL **Differentiated Instruction Activities,** Teacher's Edition, pp. 436, 437 LPR, ELL **Extend Activity,** Teacher's Edition, p. 439 AR, GT
Section 2 100 minutes *A Society on the Move* **OBJECTIVES** • Examine the rise of the suburbs and the growth of the Sunbelt. • Describe changes in the U.S. economy and education in the postwar period. **Focus Question** *What social and economic factors changed American life during the 1950s?*	**Teaching Resources** Reading Strategy: Identify Main Ideas and Supporting Details, p. 12 Outline Map: Interstate Highways, p. 17 Section 2 Quiz, p. 21 **Reading and Note Taking Study Guide** Section Note Taking, p. 110 SN Section Summary, p. 111 SN **Progress Monitoring Transparencies,** p. 120 **Color Transparencies** Levittown, A-113; The Interstate Highway System, A-114	**L1 Adapted Reading and Note Taking Study Guide** Section Note Taking, p. 110 SN Section 2 Summary, p. 111 SN **L2 Adapted Reading and Note Taking Study Guide** Section Note Taking, p. 110 LPR Section 2 Summary, p. 111 LPR **Spanish Reading and Note Taking Study Guide** Section Note Taking, p. 110 ELL Section 2 Summary, p. 111 ELL **L4 Differentiated Instruction Activities,** Teacher's Edition, pp. 443, 445 AR, GT	***Student Edition on Audio** SN **Differentiated Instruction Activities,** Teacher's Edition, pp. 442, 446 SN ***Guided Reading Audio, Spanish CD** ELL ***Student Edition on Audio** LPR, ELL **Differentiated Instruction Activities,** Teacher's Edition, pp. 442, 446 LPR, ELL **Extend Activity,** Teacher's Edition, p. 447 AR, GT

*Audio support is available for all sections.

**This worksheet also applies to L1.

Assessment Resources
• **Teaching Resources,** Tests A and B, pp. 24–29
• **AYP Monitoring Assessments,** Benchmark Test 3
• **Progress Monitoring Transparencies,** 119–122
• **Test Prep With Document-Based Assessment**
• *ExamView*® **Test Bank CD-ROM**
• **Progress Monitoring Online Quiz**
• **Assessment Rubrics**

Differentiated Instruction Key
L1 Special Needs		SN	Special Needs Students
L2 Basic to Average		ELL	English Language Learners
L3 All Students		LPR	Less Proficient Readers
L4 Average to Advanced		AR	Advanced Readers
		GT	Gifted and Talented

Section	Core Instruction ⬤L3	Differentiated Instruction ⬤L1 ⬤L2 ⬤L4	
Section 3 75 minutes *Mass Culture and Family Life* **OBJECTIVES** • Explain why consumer spending increased. • Discuss postwar changes in family life. • Describe the rise of new forms of mass culture.	**Teaching Resources** Biography: Rock-and-Roll Musicians, p. 18 Section 3 Quiz, p. 22 **Reading and Note Taking Study Guide** Section Note Taking, p. 112 SN Section Summary, p. 113 SN **Progress Monitoring Transparencies,** p. 121 **Color Transparencies** Television and the American Family, A-115	**L1 Adapted Reading and Note Taking Study Guide** Section Note Taking, p. 112 SN Section 3 Summary, p. 113 SN **L2 Adapted Reading and Note Taking Study Guide** Section Note Taking, p. 112 LPR Section 3 Summary, p. 113 LPR **Spanish Reading and Note Taking Study Guide** Section Note Taking, p. 112 ELL Section 3 Summary, p. 113 ELL	**Differentiated Instruction Activities,** Teacher's Edition, pp. 449, 452 SN **Differentiated Instruction Activities,** Teacher's Edition, pp. 449, 452 LPR, ELL
Focus Question *How did popular culture and family life change during the 1950s?*		**L4 Differentiated Instruction Activities,** Teacher's Edition, p. 450 AR, GT	**Extend Activity,** Teacher's Edition, p. 453 AR, GT
Section 4 100 minutes *Dissent and Discontent* **OBJECTIVES** • Summarize the arguments made by critics who rejected the culture of the fifties. • Describe the causes and effects of urban and rural poverty. • Explain the problems that many minority group members faced in the postwar era.	**Teaching Resources** Reading a Chart: Suburban Growth and Urban Decline, p. 19 Section 4 Quiz, p. 23 **Reading and Note Taking Study Guide** Section Note Taking, p. 114 SN Section Summary, p. 115 SN **Progress Monitoring Transparencies,** p. 122 **Color Transparencies** Native American Relocation, A-116	**L1 Adapted Reading and Note Taking Study Guide** Section Note Taking, p. 114 SN Section 4 Summary, p. 115 SN **L2 Adapted Reading and Note Taking Study Guide** Section Note Taking, p. 114 LPR Section 4 Summary, p. 115 LPR **Spanish Reading and Note Taking Study Guide** Section Note Taking, p. 114 ELL Section 4 Summary, p. 115 ELL	**Differentiated Instruction Activity,** Teacher's Edition, p. 457 SN **Differentiated Instruction Activity,** Teacher's Edition, p. 457 LPR, ELL
Focus Question *Why were some groups of Americans dissatisfied with conditions in postwar America?*		**L4 Differentiated Instruction Activity,** Teacher's Edition, p. 456 AR, GT	**Extend Activity,** Teaching Resources, pp. 13–14 AR, GT

Author's Note

Conventional wisdom states that the 1950s were the last "black and white decade." Television shows and many films were black and white; Jim Crow still ruled, *de jure* in the South and *de facto* in the North. And people tended to see the era in black and white terms, either as the best or worst of times, as "Happy Days" or as an era of repression McCarthyite paranoia.

As a historian, I have a propensity to see gray. When I approach the 1950s, I prod students to explore the contradictions of the era and to consider the ways in which seeming opposites were intertwined. For example, the discontent that women expressed about the narrow roles afforded them grew out of popular culture's glorification of the suburban housewife, a role that proved almost impossible to fulfill. Similarly, the affluence of the times created not only a basis for a burgeoning youth culture, but also served as a source of rebellion by the Beats and other counterculture types.

For teachers who want students to see and feel the contradictory and complex nature of history, the 1950s is an ideal place to start. Once students recognize that Happy Days were not happy for everyone, that underneath the surface there was much discontent, they will understand that every era has an underside.

This may not be an easy lesson for many students accustomed as they may be to thinking in black and white terms. Yet, once they grasp this lesson, they will begin to understand that history is much more than the memorization of arbitrary details about people, places, and things. Appreciating history's gray areas is where a real interest in and love of history begins.

—Peter B. Levy

Extend Online

The Roots of Rock-and-Roll

Have students write a report on one of the musical styles of the 1950s and early 1960s that continues to influence rock-and-roll musicians today. Use the steps below to help students complete the activity.

Prepare for the Activity Explain that the musical styles of early rock-and-roll music, which may not be well known to many students today, continue to influence today's musicians. This music, such as doowop, rockabilly, and rhythm and blues, were rooted in musical traditions as well as the changing times of the 1950s and early 1960s. Over many decades, "rock" music was gradually transformed by artists and other musical genres. Still, the music that teens danced to in the 1950s remains a foundation for much of the popular music teens listen to today.

Conduct the Activity For help in starting the activity, send students to **www.pearsonschool.com/ushist.** Students will choose a rock-and-roll musical style from the

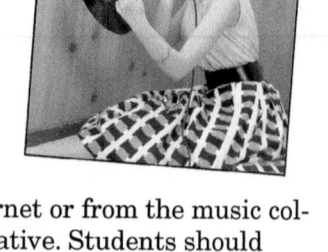

1950s or early 1960s from the Web site. Students will then work in pairs to research and write a report on the roots and characteristics of that music, as well as its place in the development of rock-and-roll. Encourage students to find a clip of music from the 1950s or early 1960s, either on the Internet or from the music collection of a family friend or relative. Students should integrate this sample into the report they present to the class.

Follow-Up After each pair of students has presented its report, lead a classroom discussion in which students analyze the following questions: What music spawned early rock-and-roll? What characterizes the sound of early rock-and-roll? What music today seems to have been influenced by early rock-and-roll? What musical genre of the 1950s and early 1960s is the most prevalent in today's music?

Finding High-Interest Ideas (L1) (L2)

Students will be more willing and interested in engaging in the discussion if the topic is of high interest to them. As students read the chapter, ask them to write down one idea that could be used to conduct an engaging discussion. Ideas could relate to something they do not understand, something they want to know more about, or something that relates to something else they already know but that provokes interest and more ideas.

Model the process by giving students both rich and poor ideas for a discussion.

Rich Idea: Why did the middle class grow during the 1950s?

Poor Idea: What color did most middle-class people choose for their houses?

Mapping Word Definitions (L2)

To help students learn unfamiliar words, introduce them to the strategy of mapping word definitions. Research shows that this technique helps students develop the ability to investigate word meanings independently and provide elaborated definitions (as opposed to simple one- or two-word definitions). Research also indicates that effective preliminary strategies require students to go beyond simply making up dictionary definitions or examining the context. Vocabulary learning must be based on the learner's dynamic engagement in constructing meaning. Model mapping word definitions by using the following steps for the high-use word *innovation.*

- Define the word in your own words—*something that is new or different.*
- Provide a synonym or example—*invention, new product.*
- Use the word in a sentence—*The window air conditioner was an important innovation.*
- Provide a non-example—*characteristic.*

Modeling Reading and Writing Skills

Vocabulary: Use Context Clues Explain that students can help determine the meaning of vocabulary words by looking for clues in the surrounding text. The word's context can provide clues to the word's meanings.

Model this skill by pointing out the word *enact* in the fourth paragraph under the blue heading "Truman Overcomes Huge Obstacles" in Section 1. The surrounding words explain that the word *enact* refers to a legislative body voting a bill into law.

Gather Details Explain that in this chapter, students will be conducting research and writing a report. (See Writing About History at the end of the chapter.) Point out that a helpful step in gathering information is to choose key words to guide research. Write the following topics on the board:

1. the effect of the baby boom on education
2. new U.S. settlement patterns in the 1950s
3. the U.S. culture of consumerism

Explain that searches, whether online or in a library, are driven by key words. These key words can be a subject, an author, or a title. For a research report, a subject or key word search works better than an author search. Model the skill by listing the following search terms for the first topic: *baby boom, education.* Ask students to suggest possible key word or subject entries for the remaining sample topics. Clarify that a search term may require adapting words or using words not in the topic. For example, a search term might be *Sunbelt, Levittown,* or *suburban United States, 1950s.*

CHAPTER

14 The Civil Rights Movement, 1945–1975

Section	Core Instruction L3	Differentiated Instruction L1 L2 L4	

Section 1 100 minutes
Early Demands for Equality

OBJECTIVES
- Describe efforts to end segregation in the 1940s and 1950s.
- Explain the importance of *Brown v. Board of Education*.
- Describe the controversy over school desegregation in Little Rock, Arkansas.
- Describe the Montgomery bus boycott and its impact.

Focus Question *How did African Americans challenge segregation after World War II?*

Teaching Resources
Reading Strategy: Summarize, p. 11
Biography: Jackie Robinson, p. 18
Landmark Decisions of the Supreme Court: How Does Segregation Affect Education?, p. 19
Section 1 Quiz, p. 24

Reading and Note Taking Study Guide
Section Note Taking, p. 116
Section 1 Summary, p. 117

Progress Monitoring Transparencies, 123

Color Transparencies
Working Toward Equal Rights, A-117

L1 Adapted Reading and Note Taking Study Guide
Section Note Taking, p. 116 SN
Section 1 Summary, p. 117 SN

L2 Adapted Reading and Note Taking Study Guide
Section Note Taking, p. 116 LPR
Section 1 Summary, p. 117 LPR

Spanish Reading and Note Taking Study Guide
Section Note Taking, p. 116 ELL
Section 1 Summary, p. 117 ELL

L4 Differentiated Instruction Activity, Teacher's Edition, p. 472 AR, GT

*Student Edition on Audio SN

Differentiated Instruction Activities, Teacher's Edition, pp. 469, 473 SN

*Guided Reading Audio, Spanish CD ELL

Differentiated Instruction Activities, Teacher's Edition, pp. 469, 473 LPR, ELL

Extend Activity, Teacher's Edition, p. 475 AR, GT

Section 2 100 minutes
The Movement Gains Ground

OBJECTIVES
- Describe the sit-ins, freedom rides, and the actions of James Meredith in the early 1960s.
- Explain how the protests at Birmingham and the March on Washington were linked to the Civil Rights Act of 1964.
- Summarize the provisions of the Civil Rights Act of 1964.

Focus Question *How did the civil rights movement gain ground in the 1960s?*

Teaching Resources
Viewpoints: Kennedy and Wallace, p. 20
Primary Source: Interpreting King's "I Have A Dream Speech," p. 22
Section 2 Quiz, p. 25

Reading and Note Taking Study Guide
Section Note Taking, p. 118
Section 2 Summary, p. 119

Progress Monitoring Transparencies, 124

Color Transparencies
The March on Washington, A-118

L1 Adapted Reading and Note Taking Study Guide
Section Note Taking, p. 118 SN
Section 2 Summary, p. 119 SN

L2 Adapted Reading and Note Taking Study Guide
Section Note Taking, p. 118 LPR
Section 2 Summary, p. 119 LPR

Spanish Reading and Note Taking Study Guide
Section Note Taking, p. 118 ELL
Section 2 Summary, p. 119 ELL

L4 Differentiated Instruction Activities, Teacher's Edition, pp. 480, 481 AR, GT

Differentiated Instruction Activities, Teacher's Edition, pp. 478, 482 SN

Teaching Resources
Primary Source: *I Have a Dream*, p. 21 LPR, ELL

Differentiated Instruction Activities, Teacher's Edition, pp. 478, 482, 483 LPR, ELL

Extend Activity, Teacher's Edition, p. 484 AR, GT

Section	Core Instruction L3	Differentiated Instruction L1 L2 L4	
Section 3 100 minutes *New Successes and Challenges* **OBJECTIVES** • Explain the significance of Freedom Summer, the march on Selma and why violence erupted in some American cities in the 1960s. • Compare the goals and methods of African American leaders. • Describe the social and economic situation of African Americans by 1975.	**Teaching Resources** Issues Connector: Voting Rights, pp. 14–17 Viewpoints: Carmichael and M.L. King, Jr., p. 23 Section 3 Quiz, p. 26 **Reading and Note Taking Study Guide** Section Note Taking, p. 120 ' Section 3 Summary, p. 121 American Issues Journal, pp. 221–223 **Progress Monitoring Transparencies**, 125 **Color Transparencies** Urban Riots, A-119; *The Lamp*, A-120	**L1 Adapted Reading and Note Taking Study Guide** Section Note Taking, p. 120 SN Section 3 Summary, p. 121 SN American Issues Journal, pp. 221–223 SN	**Differentiated Instruction Activities,** Teacher's Edition, pp. 489, 493, 494 SN
		L2 Adapted Reading and Note Taking Study Guide Section Note Taking, p. 120 LPR Section 3 Summary, p. 121 LPR American Issues Journal, pp. 221–223 LPR **Spanish Reading and Note Taking Study Guide** Section Note Taking, p. 120 ELL Section 3 Summary, p. 121 ELL American Issues Journal, pp. 221–223 ELL	**Differentiated Instruction Activities,** Teacher's Edition, pp. 489, 493, 494 LPR, ELL
Focus Question *What successes and challenges faced the civil rights movement after 1964?*		**L4 Differentiated Instruction Activity,** Teacher's Edition, p. 492 AR, GT	**Extend Activity,** Teaching Resources, pp. 12–13 AR, GT

*Audio support is available for all sections.   **This worksheet also applies to L1.

Assessment Resources
• Teaching Resources, Tests A and B, pp. 27–32
• AYP Monitoring Assessments, Benchmark Test 3
• Progress Monitoring Transparencies, 123–125
• Test Prep With Document-Based Assessment
• *ExamView*® Test Bank CD-ROM
• Progress Monitoring Online Quiz
• Assessment Rubrics

Differentiated Instruction Key

L1	Special Needs	SN	Special Needs Students
L2	Basic to Average	ELL	English Language Learners
L3	All Students	LPR	Less Proficient Readers
L4	Average to Advanced	AR	Advanced Readers
		GT	Gifted and Talented

Author's Note

I have spent the past 15 years engrossed in the history of the civil rights movement. I teach a special topics course on the period, have written a monograph of the battle for racial equality in Cambridge, Maryland, and have authored both a textbook and a documentary reader on the black freedom struggle. Needless to say, I have accumulated a virtual library of books, articles, and primary sources on the movement, though my "must read" list of works on the subject continues to grow.

In the course of this work, I have become convinced that one of the main challenges for teachers of the civil rights story is to make sure that students understand that ordinary men and women also fought for the case of racial equality, not just those we know well—Martin Luther King, Jr., Thurgood Marshall, and John F. Kennedy. By emphasizing the actions of everyday people—from the college students who initiated the Woolworth sit-down in Greensboro, North Carolina, to the hundreds of anonymous men and women who joined the bus boycott in Montgomery, Alabama—students can see that the efforts of average people can and do make a difference. While it is important for students to recognize King, Marshall, and other major figures of the movement, it is just as important for them to see the armies of ordinary people who protested for their rights.

One way that teachers can meet this challenge is to prompt their students to consider how the civil rights movement affected their own communities. They can interview parents, grandparents, and other relatives. They can examine local newspapers or visit local sites where the struggle for racial equality took place. They might even uncover some hometown heroes. By engaging students in such history projects, teachers can make the civil rights movement more relevant, and give them a taste of the excitement of historical research and discovery.

—Peter B. Levy

Extend Online

Youthful Civil Rights Activists

Have students analyze how young people fueled the post-World War II civil rights movement. Have them write journal entries from the point of view of a member of SNCC, the Student Nonviolent Coordinating Committee, chronicling their activities and the emotions they felt. Use the steps below to help students complete the activity.

Prepare for the Activity Explain that sit-ins and other nonviolent protests were organized and led by college students. SNCC began the sit-ins and took part in the Freedom Rides and in Freedom Summer. It published its own newspaper, *Student Voice*. The SNCC disbanded in the early 1970s, but several members later became prominent, including Julian Bond, state senator from Georgia.

Conduct the Activity For help in starting the activity, send students to **www.pearsonschool.com/ushist.** Students will view information about SNCC and its activities. Have them note the role of Ella Baker in the early

days of SNCC, as well as the organization's relationship with Martin Luther King, Jr., and the Southern Christian Leadership Conference (SCLC) and with the Black Power movement. Tell students to note the SNCC strategy in the sit-ins, Freedom Rides, and Freedom Summer and other voting programs. Ask students to write journal entries from the point of view of those involved in the various types of protest.

Follow-Up Conduct a class discussion based on the following questions: In what way did college students bring new energy to the civil rights movement? Why did members of SNCC want to remain independent of the SCLC? What factors led to the disintegration of SNCC?

Creating a Dialogue L2

In addition to learning social studies content, English Language Learners face the more daunting challenge of developing proficiency in English. To encourage students to use both written and spoken English and to apply core content, have them create a dialogue between people who hold different views about the values or strategies of the civil rights movement. Follow these steps:

1. Organize students into groups and assign each group a scenario.
2. On the board, list key terms and high-use words that must be included in the dialogue.
3. Require each student to have a speaking role.
4. Have students submit a written copy of the script as part of this activity's assessment.

Ask each group to perform its dialogue for the class to enhance the English language listening skills of students in the audience.

Historical Precedents L4

Events do not happen in a vacuum; they are usually shaped by many causes and situations. To better understand the greater context within American history of the conflicts studied in this chapter, ask students to draw on previously learned information to understand the motives and perspectives of those involved in the conflicts.

To help students develop an understanding of the continuum of history, ask them to formulate a list of causes of an event or condition being studied, such as the Selma March or the enforcement of Jim Crow laws. As a class, vote on which cause was the most significant. Ask **If this cause were removed or altered, might the event have changed or been prevented?**

Modeling Reading and Writing Skills

Vocabulary: Recognize Word Origins Tell students that by recognizing word origins, they can identify and understand many unfamiliar words. Point out that many words come from Greek or Latin. For example, the prefix *uni-*, which means "one," comes from the Latin word *unum,* which also means "one." This word part is found in the noun *unit* (the smallest whole number), the verb *unite* (to join into one, combine, make whole), and the adjective *universal* (covering the whole collectively).

To demonstrate this concept, write on the board: *vita, vitality*—based on the Latin root *vit/viv* meaning "life." Model the process aloud: If I know that *vita* means "life," I can add a meaning for the suffix *-ity* to build a word. Because *-ity* means "state or quality of," *vitality* must mean "full of life."

Evaluating Online Sources Explain that in this chapter, students will be writing a research paper. (See Writing About History at the end of the chapter.) Remind students that when conducting research, they must use credible, accurate sources. To improve accuracy of the information gathered on the Web, provide students with these guidelines:

1. Identify the sponsor of the Web site. Examine the sponsor's credentials and expertise. Determine any bias.
2. Check the time of the last update of the Web site to ensure that the information is current.
3. Use several sources to confirm information.

To model this skill, write the following sources on the board. Have students decide whether each one is a good source to use for a research paper.

- Personal home page updated daily (*No—the sponsor may not ensure that the information is accurate.*)
- Web site sponsored by a publisher of reference materials (*Yes—the group has an incentive to make sure that the information is accurate.*)
- Web site sponsored by a political group or business (*Possibly—students should examine the information carefully because the site may be biased.*)

CHAPTER 15 The Kennedy and Johnson Years, 1960–1968

Section	Core Instruction L3	Differentiated Instruction L1 L2 L4	
Section 1 100 minutes *Kennedy and the Cold War*	**Teaching Resources** Viewpoints: Two Presidents: Kennedy and Eisenhower, p. 19 Section 1 Quiz, p. 24 **Reading and Note Taking Study Guide** Section Note Taking, p. 122 Section 1 Summary, p. 123 **Progress Monitoring Transparencies,** 126 **Color Transparencies** The Cuban Missile Crisis, A-121	**L1 Adapted Reading and Note Taking Study Guide** Section Note Taking, p. 122 SN Section 1 Summary, p. 123 SN **L2 Adapted Reading and Note Taking Study Guide** Section Note Taking, p. 122 LPR Section 1 Summary, p. 123 LPR **Spanish Reading and Note Taking Study Guide** Section Note Taking, p. 122 ELL Section 1 Summary, p. 123 ELL	**Differentiated Instruction Activities,** Teacher's Edition, pp. 507, 508, 509 SN ****Teaching Resources** Viewpoints: Kennedy and Eisenhower, p. 18 LPR, ELL **Differentiated Instruction Activities,** Teacher's Edition, pp. 507, 508, 509 LPR, ELL

OBJECTIVES
- Explain the steps Kennedy took to change American foreign policy.
- Analyze the causes and effects of the Bay of Pigs invasion and the Cuban Missile Crisis.
- Assess the results of the Berlin Crisis and other foreign policy events of the 1960s.

L4 Differentiated Instruction Activity, Teacher's Edition, p. 505 AR; GT

Extend Activity, Teacher's Edition, p. 510 AR, GT

Focus Question *How did Kennedy respond to the continuing challenges of the Cold War?*

Section	Core Instruction	Differentiated Instruction	
Section 2 100 minutes *Kennedy's New Frontier*	**Teaching Resources** Reading Strategy: Identify Main Ideas, p. 11 Reading a Chart: Kennedy's Programs, p. 20 Landmark Decisions of the Supreme Court: Can a Poor Person Get a Fair Trial? p. 21 Section 2 Quiz, p. 25 **Reading and Note Taking Study Guide** Section Note Taking, pp. 124–125 Section 2 Summary, p. 126 **Progress Monitoring Transparencies,** 127 **Color Transparencies** The Kennedy Years, A-122	**L1 Adapted Reading and Note Taking Study Guide** Section Note Taking, pp. 124–125 SN Section 2 Summary, p. 126 SN **L2 Adapted Reading and Note Taking Study Guide** Section Note Taking, pp. 124–125 LPR Section 2 Summary, p. 126 LPR **Spanish Reading and Note Taking Study Guide** Section Note Taking, pp. 124–125 ELL Section 2 Summary, p. 126 ELL	***Student Edition on Audio** SN **Differentiated Instruction Activity,** Teacher's Edition, p. 514 SN ***Guided Reading Audio, Spanish CD** ELL ***Student Edition on Audio** LPR, ELL **Differentiated Instruction Activity,** Teacher's Edition, p. 514 LPR, ELL

OBJECTIVES
- Evaluate Kennedy's domestic policies.
- Assess the impact of the Kennedy assassination.

L4 Differentiated Instruction Activity, Teacher's Edition, p. 513 AR, GT

Extend Activity, Teaching Resources, pp. 12–13 AR, GT

Focus Question *What were the goals of Kennedy's New Frontier?*

Section 3 100 minutes
Johnson's Great Society

OBJECTIVES
- Evaluate Johnson's policies up to his victory in the 1964 presidential election.
- Analyze Johnson's goals and actions as seen in his Great Society programs.
- Assess the achievements of the Great Society.

Focus Question *How did Johnson's Great Society programs change life for most Americans?*

Core Instruction

Teaching Resources
Reading a Chart: The Great Society, p. 22
Issues Connector: Poverty and Prosperity, pp. 14–17
Viewpoints: Carmichael and M.L. King, Jr., p. 23
Section 3 Quiz, p. 26

Reading and Note Taking Study Guide
Section Note Taking, p. 127
Section 3 Summary, p. 128
American Issues Journal, pp. 224–226

Progress Monitoring Transparencies, 128

Color Transparencies
The Warren Court, A-123; Head Start, A-124

Differentiated Instruction

L1 Adapted Reading and Note Taking Study Guide
Section Note Taking, p. 127 SN
Section 3 Summary, p. 128 SN
American Issues Journal, pp. 224–226 SN

Differentiated Instruction Activities, Teacher's Edition, pp. 520, 521, 523 SN

L2 Adapted Reading and Note Taking Study Guide
Section Note Taking, p. 127 LPR
Section 2 Summary, p. 128 LPR
American Issues Journal, pp. 224–226 LPR

Spanish Reading and Note Taking Study Guide
Section Note Taking, p. 127 ELL
Section 2 Summary, p. 128 ELL
American Issues Journal, pp. 224–226 ELL

Differentiated Instruction Activities, Teacher's Edition, pp. 520, 521, 523 LPR, ELL

L4 Differentiated Instruction Activity, Teacher's Edition, p. 522 AR, GT

Extend Activity, Teacher's Edition, p. 524 AR, GT

*Audio support is available for all sections.

**This worksheet also applies to L1.

Assessment Resources
- **Teaching Resources,** Tests A and B, pp. 27–31
- **AYP Monitoring Assessments,** Benchmark Test 3
- **Progress Monitoring Transparencies,** 126–128
- **Test Prep With Document-Based Assessment**
- ***ExamView*® Test Bank CD-ROM**
- **Progress Monitoring Online Quiz**
- **Assessment Rubrics**

Differentiated Instruction Key
- L1 Special Needs
- L2 Basic to Average
- L3 All Students
- L4 Average to Advanced
- SN Special Needs Students
- ELL English Language Learners
- LPR Less Proficient Readers
- AR Advanced Readers
- GT Gifted and Talented

CHAPTER PLANNER

Author's Note

What makes presidential greatness? That was certainly a question that occupied the attention of John F. Kennedy. He believed that no President could achieve greatness without confronting and overcoming a crisis. George Washington had the American Revolution and the cradle years of the Republic. Abraham Lincoln had the dark days of the Civil War when secession threatened the Union. Franklin D. Roosevelt had the Great Depression and World War II—more than three terms of almost uninterrupted crises.

It is clear from his inaugural address and his handling of foreign policy issues that Kennedy welcomed his crisis—and greatness. "In the long history of the world," he intoned at his 1961 inauguration, "only a few generations have been granted the role of defending freedom in its hour of maximum danger. I will not shrink from the responsibility—I welcome it." Given that America was not at war when he spoke those words, and that the Cold War was not in a particularly hot period, Kennedy seemed more intent on giving the impression of a crisis atmosphere than of responding to any particular crisis.

Historians have long studied the subject of presidential greatness, and over the years they have rated Presidents. In 1948, 1962, and 1970, historians were asked to rate Presidents, and all three polls rated Lincoln, Washington, and Franklin D. Roosevelt at the top of the list. All three, of course, *were* Presidents or leaders during the nation's "hour of maximum danger," and all three were strong executives. Some other interesting insights can be taken from the polls. Historians generally rate practical Presidents over idealistic Presidents, movers and shakers over low-profile chief executives. Effective Presidents with more quiet styles, such as Dwight Eisenhower, do not rate as high as more dramatic and outspoken Presidents. I always find it interesting to ask my students what qualities they most prize in a President.

—Randy Roberts

Extend Online

Peace Corps

Have students familiarize themselves with the mission and history of the Peace Corps. Then, ask them to use their familiarity with the program to create a small exhibit. Use the steps below to help students complete the activity.

Prepare the Activity Tell students that the Peace Corps is a program that John F. Kennedy initiated during the Cold War. The program's aim is to provide technical, educational, and health services to developing countries. Explain that since the Peace Corps was established in March 1961, more than 180,000 volunteers and 138 different countries have participated in the program.

Conduct the Activity For help in starting the activity, send students to **www.pearsonschool.com/ushist**. Students will study the history, mission, and organization of the Peace Corps. They will also survey the variety of destinations to which volunteers travel and the services

they perform there. Ask students to read about notable former peace corps volunteers. Have them use their reading to develop an exhibit about at least five famous volunteers. The exhibit should include a poster or panel that gives a concise overview of the Peace Corps, a map that identifies the areas of service of the selected volunteers, individual photos or portraits of the volunteers with brief biographies and descriptions of their service, and a brochure with which to advertise the exhibit.

Follow-Up Conduct a class discussion based on the following questions: What are the main purposes of the Peace Corps? How well do you think the Peace Corps fulfills its stated purposes? How is the Peace Corps related to the Cold War? In what ways might the experiences of Peace Corps volunteers differ from those to whom the program provides assistance?

Mapping Word Definitions (L2)

To help students learn unfamiliar words, introduce them to the strategy of mapping word definitions. Research shows that this technique helps students develop the ability to investigate word meanings independently and provide extended definitions (as opposed to simple one- or two-word definitions).

Model mapping word definitions by using the following steps for the high-use word *advocate,* which is used in context in Section 2.

• Define the word simply—*to support or speak on behalf of something*

• Provide a synonym or example—*to support, to favor*

• Use the word in a sentence—*General MacArthur advocated the invasion of China as the best way for the United States to win the Korean War.*

• Provide an antonym—*dissuade, criticize*

Deciphering Idioms (L1) (L2)

Some vocabulary and idiomatic expressions are potentially problematic for English Language Learners and Less Proficient Readers. The meanings of statements such as "boiled down to" and "working behind the scenes" are not obvious to all students. To help students understand the meaning of these phrases, model these steps, using the phrase "behind the scenes."

1. Identify the origin of the phrase. This phrase seems to come from the theater.

2. Cite specific examples. To clarify the phrase, compare it with other sayings that high school students are likely to hear (for example, "behind closed doors" or "under cover").

3. Discuss the appeal of this phrase. We tend to think that someone who works "behind the scenes" has acquired some mastery of a craft or process.

4. Ask students to find two examples of this phrase in the text.

Modeling Reading and Writing Skills

Compare and Contrast Point out that comparing and contrasting helps students analyze information. Comparing examines similarities, while contrasting highlights differences. A Venn diagram provides an effective way to compare and contrast information. To make this graphic organizer, draw two overlapping circles. List differences in the outside portions and list similarities in the overlapping oval. Model this skill by going through the Infographic on Comparing Viewpoints: How Should the United States Fight the Cold War?

Acknowledge Opposition Explain that in this chapter, students will be writing a persuasive essay. (See Writing About History at the end of the chapter.) Point out that in a persuasive essay, students must acknowledge opposing arguments and make counter-arguments to refute these. List the following arguments on the board, and ask students to provide opposing arguments. Remind students that arguments should be constructed logically.

A Junk food should be banned from schools.

B Teenagers should be able to make their own curfews.

C Playing video games is a poor use of a teenager's free time.

As each opposing argument is presented, invite another student to counter it or do so yourself. Provide the following example as a guide:

A **Opposing argument:** Teenagers should be given information to make informed decisions about junk food because developing decision-making habits is important.

Counter-argument: Students can develop their decision-making habits as they choose between equally healthful options.

Remind students to use this process as they write their persuasive essays on the Warren Court and its decisions on the right of the accused.

CHAPTER

16 The Vietnam War Era, 1954–1975

Section	Core Instruction ③	Differentiated Instruction ① ② ④	
Section 1 75 minutes *Origins of the Vietnam War* **OBJECTIVES** • Describe the reasons that the United States helped the French fight the Vietnamese. • Identify ways in which the United States opposed communism in Southeast Asia. • Analyze how the United States increased its involvement in Vietnam. **Focus Question** *Why did the United States become involved in Vietnam?*	**Teaching Resources** Outline Map: Spread of Communism in Asia, p. 20 Section 1 Quiz, p. 25 **Reading and Note Taking Study Guide** Section Note Taking, p. 129 Section 1 Summary, p. 130 **Progress Monitoring Transparencies,** 129 **Color Transparencies** Rising U.S. Involvement in Vietnam, A-125	① **Adapted Reading and Note Taking Study Guide** Section Note Taking, p. 129 SN Section 1 Summary, p. 130 SN ② **Adapted Reading and Note Taking Study Guide** Section Note Taking, p. 129 LPR Section 1 Summary, p. 130 LPR **Spanish Reading and Note Taking Study Guide** Section Note Taking, p. 129 ELL Section 1 Summary, p. 130 ELL ④ **Differentiated Instruction Activity,** Teacher's Edition, p. 535 AR, GT	**Differentiated Instruction Activity,** Teacher's Edition, p. 533 SN ****Teaching Resources** Outline Map: Vietnam, p. 19 LPR, ELL **Differentiated Instruction Activities,** Teacher's Edition, p. 533 LPR, ELL **Extend Activity,** Teacher's Edition, p. 536 AR, GT
Section 2 100 minutes *U.S. Involvement Grows* **OBJECTIVES** • Identify the factors that caused President Johnson to increase American troop strength in Vietnam. • Assess the nature of the war in Vietnam and the difficulties faced by both sides. • Evaluate the effects of low morale on American troops and on the home front. **Focus Question** *What were the causes and effects of America's growing involvement in the Vietnam War?*	**Teaching Resources** Reading a Chart: War Weakens the Economy, p. 21 Section 2 Quiz, p. 26 **Reading and Note Taking Study Guide** Section Note Taking, p. 131 Section 2 Summary, p. 132 **Progress Monitoring Transparencies,** 130	① **Adapted Reading and Note Taking Study Guide** Section Note Taking, p. 131 SN Section 2 Summary, p. 132 SN ② **Adapted Reading and Note Taking Study Guide** Section Note Taking, p. 131 LPR Section 2 Summary, p. 132 LPR **Spanish Reading and Note Taking Study Guide** Section Note Taking, p. 131 ELL Section 2 Summary, p. 132 ELL ④ **Differentiated Instruction Activity,** Teacher's Edition, p. 538 AR, GT	***Student Edition on Audio** SN **Differentiated Instruction Activities,** Teacher's Edition, pp. 540, 541 SN ***Guided Reading Audio, Spanish CD** ELL ***Student Edition on Audio** LPR, ELL **Differentiated Instruction Activities,** Teacher's Edition, pp. 540, 541 LPR, ELL **Extend Activity,** Teacher's Edition, p. 543 AR, GT

*Audio support is available for all sections.   ****This worksheet also applies to L1.**

Assessment Resources
- **Teaching Resources,** Tests A and B, pp. 30–35
- **AYP Monitoring Assessments,** Benchmark Test 3
- **Progress Monitoring Transparencies,** 129–133
- **Test Prep With Document-Based Assessment**
- ***ExamView*® Test Bank CD-ROM**
- **Progress Monitoring Online Quiz**
- **Assessment Rubrics**

Differentiated Instruction Key

① Special Needs	SN	Special Needs Students	
② Basic to Average	ELL	English Language Learners	
③ All Students	LPR	Less Proficient Readers	
④ Average to Advanced	AR	Advanced Readers	
	GT	Gifted and Talented	

Section 3 100 minutes
The War Divides America

OBJECTIVES
- Describe the divisions within American society over the Vietnam War.
- Analyze the Tet Offensive and the American reaction to it.
- Summarize the factors that influenced the outcome of the 1968 presidential election.

Focus Question *How did the American war effort in Vietnam lead to rising protests and social divisions back home?*

Teaching Resources
Reading Strategy: Recognize Sequence, p. 12
Viewpoints: Can the United States Win the War in Vietnam? p. 22
Section 3 Quiz, p. 27

Reading and Note Taking Study Guide
Section Note Taking, p. 133
Section 3 Summary, p. 134

Progress Monitoring Transparencies, 131

Color Transparencies
Conflict on the Home Front, A-126

① Adapted Reading and Note Taking Study Guide
Section Note Taking, p. 133 SN
Section 3 Summary, p. 134 SN

Differentiated Instruction Activities, Teacher's Edition, pp. 546, 549 SN

② Adapted Reading and Note Taking Study Guide
Section Note Taking, p. 133 LPR
Section 3 Summary, p. 134 LPR

Spanish Reading and Note Taking Study Guide
Section Note Taking, p. 133 ELL
Section 3 Summary, p. 134 ELL

Differentiated Instruction Activities, Teacher's Edition, pp. 546, 549 LPR, ELL

④ Differentiated Instruction Activities, Teacher's Edition, pp. 545, 550 AR, GT

Extend Activity, Teacher's Edition, p. 551 AR, GT

Section 4 100 minutes
The War's End and Impact

OBJECTIVES
- Assess Nixon's new approach to the war, and explain why protests continued.
- Explain what led to the Paris Peace Accords and why South Vietnam eventually fell to the communists.
- Evaluate the impact of the Vietnam War on the United States.

Focus Question *How did the Vietnam War end, and what were its lasting effects?*

Teaching Resources
Link to Literature: *Night Patrol*, p. 23
Issues Connector: America and the World, pp. 15–18
Section 4 Quiz, p. 28

Reading and Note Taking Study Guide
Section Note Taking, pp. 135–136
Section 4 Summary, p. 137
American Issues Journal, pp. 227–229

Progress Monitoring Transparencies, 132

Color Transparencies
Protesting the Vietnam War, A-127; The Vietnam Veterans Memorial, A-128

① Adapted Reading and Note Taking Study Guide
Section Note Taking, pp. 135–136 SN
Section 4 Summary, p. 137 SN
American Issues Journal, pp. 227–229 SN

Differentiated Instruction Activity, Teacher's Edition, p. 557 SN

② Adapted Reading and Note Taking Study Guide
Section Note Taking, pp. 135–136 LPR
Section 4 Summary, p. 137 LPR
American Issues Journal, pp. 227–229 LPR

Spanish Reading and Note Taking Study Guide
Section Note Taking, pp. 135–136 ELL
Section 4 Summary, p. 137 ELL
American Issues Journal, pp. 227–229 ELL

Differentiated Instruction Activities, Teacher's Edition, pp. 553, 557 LPR, ELL

④ Differentiated Instruction Activity, Teacher's Edition, p. 554 AR, GT

Extend Activity, Teaching Resources, pp. 13–14 AR, GT

Section 5 100 minutes
Nixon and the Cold War

OBJECTIVES
- Explain the thinking behind Richard Nixon's foreign policy.
- Define Nixon's foreign policy toward China and the Soviet Union.

Focus Question *How did Richard Nixon change Cold War diplomacy during his presidency?*

Teaching Resources
History Comics: Nixon Goes to China, p. 24
Section 5 Quiz, p. 29

Reading and Note Taking Study Guide
Section Note Taking, p. 138
Section 5 Summary, p. 139

Progress Monitoring Transparencies, 133

① Adapted Reading and Note Taking Study Guide
Section Note Taking, p. 138 SN
Section 5 Summary, p. 139 SN

Differentiated Instruction Activity, Teacher's Edition, p. 561 SN

② Adapted Reading and Note Taking Study Guide
Section Note Taking, p. 138 LPR
Section 5 Summary, p. 139 LPR

Spanish Reading and Note Taking Study Guide
Section Note Taking, p. 138 ELL
Section 5 Summary, p. 139 ELL

Differentiated Instruction Activity, Teacher's Edition, p. 561 LPR, ELL

④ Differentiated Instruction Activity, Teacher's Edition, p. 562 AR, GT

Extend Activity, Teacher's Edition, p. 563 AR, GT

CHAPTER PLANNER

Author's Note

The Vietnam War had a dramatic impact on the way Americans thought about foreign policy and the way the world viewed the United States. It also affected American popular culture. Initially, Hollywood studios and movie producers were wary of spending millions of dollars to make a film about a war that had divided the country. They believed that if they made a film that supported American policy in Vietnam, they would alienate half of the potential viewing audience. On the other hand, if the film criticized American activities in Vietnam, they would lose another large group of moviegoers. In *Green Berets* (1968), John Wayne was bold enough to make a film that defended American policy, although most filmmakers still avoided the subject.

A decade later, a younger generation of filmmakers began to reexamine the war. *Coming Home* (1978) explores the problems confronted by returning soldiers. *Go Tell the Spartans* (1978) argues that the American effort was doomed from the start. *The Deer Hunter* (1978) shows how the war shattered lives of soldiers and loved-ones, and *Apocalypse Now* (1979) uses the war to underscore the fatal flaws in the American character. Although most of the films were critical of the U.S. involvement in Vietnam, several were quite sympathetic to the soldiers who fought in the war. However, filmmakers who had actually served in the war did not make most of these films.

Oliver Stone did serve in Vietnam, and he became the most important filmmaker of the war. In the course of a decade, he made a series of films that explored various aspects of the war. *Platoon* (1986) shows the physical nature of war in Vietnam, from the dust and the heat to the ants and the mosquitoes. It gives a sense of what it was like to serve in an infantry platoon in the war. *Born on the Fourth of July* (1989) explores the martial culture in the United States that leads men into wars. In *JFK* (1991) and *Nixon* (1995), Stone delved into the political roots of the war. Finally, in *Heaven and Earth* (1993), he portrayed the physical and psychological impact the war had on America and Vietnam. The films of Oliver Stone are highly personal and controversial, but they can be used to explore and to debate the causes, course, and impact of the war.

—Randy Roberts

Extend Online

Living Through the Vietnam War

Have students research first-person accounts from people who lived in Vietnam, and U.S. and Vietnamese soldiers who fought during the war. Ask students to read selections aloud to the class. Use the steps below to help students complete the activity.

Prepare for the Activity Tell students that as the United States escalated its involvement in the Vietnam War, few people realized the effect it would have on those who lived in Vietnam or who fought in the war. Explain that understanding the different perspectives and experiences of specific individuals involved in the war will help students understand the general hardships people faced in Vietnam.

Conduct the Activity For help in starting the activity, send students to **www.pearsonschool.com/ushist**. Students will read several first-person accounts of the Vietnam War. Then, each student will choose one account, write a paragraph summarizing it, and write another paragraph responding to the writer. Students may wish to conduct additional research about the writer to whom they have chosen to respond. Have students prepare oral reports to share their findings with the class.

Follow-Up Conduct a class discussion based on the following questions: What generalizations about the Vietnam War can you draw from the first-hand accounts? How did the war affect the people who lived in or fought in Vietnam? How was the Vietnam War different from and similar to the prior wars fought by the United States? Why do you think people chose to write about their experiences in Vietnam?

Using Images ⓛ1 ⓛ2

The importance of images in a United States history classroom cannot be stressed enough. Photographs, political cartoons, illustrations, and artifacts can help students comprehend concepts addressed in the text. For example, a political cartoon can visually represent the stances two candidates may have taken on an issue, and an artifact can give viewers an insight into everyday life that enhances understanding of trends and developments during a particular era.

Suggest that students use visuals to enter other eras in U.S. history and understand the activities and concerns of Americans at the time. For example, photographs of Americans protesting the Vietnam War can help students understand the depth of feeling that U.S. involvement in Vietnam evoked and how the war divided the American people. Overall, visuals can make an individual, event, or time period "come alive" by giving students concrete examples of what they are studying. As you come across each visual, ask students to describe what they are seeing and ask them to make connections to the text.

Identifying Viewpoints ⓛ4

As you present events in the text, ask students to consider how the accompanying visuals convey point of view. To begin, have students look at the visuals in the text and answer the following questions:

1. Who produced or sponsored the image?
2. Who is the target audience? How is the message tailored specifically to them?
3. What is implied in this image?
4. What tools are used to create the message?
5. What perspective is absent from the image? What is left out of the image that might be important to know?

Modeling Reading and Writing Skills

Interpret Nonliteral Meanings Explain that literal language means exactly what it says. Nonliteral language, on the other hand, uses images or comparisons to communicate an idea more vividly. When students come across such phrases, they should ask themselves what the phrase means and how it makes the author's point.

Model this skill by reading aloud the quotation from journalist Walter Cronkite at the beginning of Section 3. Point out the phrase "the silver linings they find in the dark clouds." Explain that American leaders did not literally find silver linings in dark clouds. The phrase creates a visual image that makes Cronkite's point clearer to his listeners. The image emphasizes the contrast between the optimistic statements of government leaders and what was actually happening in Vietnam.

Develop a Thesis Explain that in this chapter, students will be writing a persuasive essay. (See Writing About History at the end of the chapter.) Tell students that before an essay can be effective, it must have a strong thesis statement. Remind students that a thesis statement should provoke valid arguments and should then be supported and extended in the body of the essay. On the board, write the following thesis statements:

1. Many college students protested the war in Vietnam.
2. Protests led to the end of U.S. involvement in Vietnam.
3. Protesting while the country is at war is unpatriotic.

Point out that the second option is the best thesis statement because it is the only one that can be argued on the basis of facts. The first option is a straight fact, and the third option is a pure opinion.

17 An Era of Protest and Change, 1960–1980

Section	Core Instruction L3	Differentiated Instruction L1 L2 L4	
Section 1 **100 minutes** *The Counterculture* **OBJECTIVES** • Describe the rise of the counterculture. • List the major characteristics of the counterculture. • Evaluate the impact of the counterculture on American values and society.	**Teaching Resources** Link to Literature: *"Santa Barbara Declaration of Environmental Rights,"* p. 19 Section 1 Quiz, p. 24 **Reading and Note Taking Study Guide** Section Note Taking, p. 140 Section 1 Summary, p. 141 **Progress Monitoring Transparencies,** 134 **Color Transparencies** Changing Fashions, A-129	**L1 Adapted Reading and Note Taking Study Guide** Section Note Taking, p. 140 SN Section 1 Summary, p. 141 SN **L2 Adapted Reading and Note Taking Study Guide** Section Note Taking, p. 140 LPR Section 1 Summary, p. 141 LPR **Spanish Reading and Note Taking Study Guide** Section Note Taking, p. 140 ELL Section 1 Summary, p. 141 ELL **L4 Extend Activity,** Teaching Resources, pp. 13–14 AR, GT	***Student Edition on Audio** SN ***Guided Reading Audio, Spanish CD** ELL ***Student Edition on Audio** LPR, ELL **Differentiated Instruction Activity,** Teacher's Edition, p. 571 LPR, ELL
Focus Question *What was the counterculture, and what impact did it have on American society?*			
Section 2 **100 minutes** *The Women's Rights Movement* **OBJECTIVES** • Analyze how a movement for women's rights arose in the 1960s. • Explain the goals and tactics of the women's movement. • Assess the impact of the women's movement on American society.	**Teaching Resources** Reading Strategy: Identify Causes and Effects, p. 12 Biography: Women's Rights Activists, p. 21 Section 2 Quiz, p. 25 **Reading and Note Taking Study Guide** Section Note Taking, p. 142 Section 2 Summary, p. 143 **Progress Monitoring Transparencies,** 135 **Color Transparencies** The Equal Rights Amendment, A-130	**L1 Adapted Reading and Note Taking Study Guide** Section Note Taking, p. 142 SN Section 2 Summary, p. 143 SN **L2 Adapted Reading and Note Taking Study Guide** Section Note Taking, p. 142 LPR Section 2 Summary, p. 143 LPR **Spanish Reading and Note Taking Study Guide** Section Note Taking, p. 142 ELL Section 2 Summary, p. 143 ELL **L4 Differentiated Instruction Activity,** Teacher's Edition, p. 577 AR, GT	**Differentiated Instruction Activity,** Teacher's Edition, p. 575 SN ****Teaching Resources** Biography: Gloria Steinem, p. 20 LPR, ELL **Differentiated Instruction Activity,** Teacher's Edition, p. 575 LPR, ELL **Extend Activity,** Teacher's Edition, p. 578 AR, GT
Focus Question *What led to the rise of the women's movement, and what impact did it have on American society?*			

Section	Core Instruction (L3)	Differentiated Instruction (L1) (L2) (L4)	
Section 3 100 minutes *The Rights Revolution Expands* **OBJECTIVES** • Explain how the Latino population grew after World War I. • Analyze the Latino and Native American rights movements of the 1960s and 1970s. • Describe the expansion of rights for consumers and the disabled.	**Teaching Resources** History Comics: Cesar Chavez and the UFW, p. 22 Section 3 Quiz, p. 26 **Reading and Note Taking Study Guide** Section Note Taking, p. 144 Section 3 Summary, p. 145 **Progress Monitoring Transparencies,** 136 **Color Transparencies** The Latino Movement, A-131	(L1) **Adapted Reading and Note Taking Study Guide** Section Note Taking, p. 144 SN Section 3 Summary, p. 145 SN (L2) **Adapted Reading and Note Taking Study Guide** Section Note Taking, p. 144 LPR Section 3 Summary, p. 145 LPR **Spanish Reading and Note Taking Study Guide** Section Note Taking, p. 144 ELL Section 3 Summary, p. 145 ELL	**Differentiated Instruction Activity,** Teacher's Edition, p. 582 SN **Differentiated Instruction Activity,** Teacher's Edition, p. 582 LPR, ELL
Focus Question *How did the rights movements of the 1960s and 1970s expand rights for diverse groups of Americans?*		(L4) **Differentiated Instruction Activity,** Teacher's Edition, p. 583 AR, GT	**Extend Activity,** Teacher's Edition, p. 585 AR, GT
Section 4 100 minutes *The Environmental Movement* **OBJECTIVES** • Assess the causes and effects of the environmental movement. • Analyze why environmental protection became a controversial issue.	**Teaching Resources** Reading a Chart: Nuclear Energy, p. 23 Issues Connector: Interaction with the Environment, pp.15–18 Section 4 Quiz, p. 27 **Reading and Note Taking Study Guide** Section Note Taking, p. 146 Section 4 Summary, p. 147 American Issues Journal, pp. 230–232 **Progress Monitoring Transparencies,** 137 **Color Transparencies** Three Mile Island, A-132	(L1) **Adapted Reading and Note Taking Study Guide** Section Note Taking, p. 146 SN Section 4 Summary, p. 147 SN American Issues Journal, pp. 230–232 SN (L2) **Adapted Reading and Note Taking Study Guide** Section Note Taking, p. 146 LPR Section 4 Summary, p. 147 LPR American Issues Journal, pp. 230–232 LPR **Spanish Reading and Note Taking Study Guide** Section Note Taking, p. 146 ELL Section 4 Summary, p. 147 ELL American Issues Journal, pp. 230–232 ELL	**Differentiated Instruction Activity,** Teacher's Edition, p. 587 **Differentiated Instruction Activity,** Teacher's Edition, p. 587 LPR, ELL
Focus Question *What forces gave rise to the environmental movement, and what impact did it have?*		(L4) **Differentiated Instruction Activity,** Teacher's Edition, p. 588 AR, GT	**Extend Activity,** Teacher's Edition, p. 591 AR, GT

*Audio support is available for all sections.

**This worksheet also applies to L1.

Assessment Resources
• **Teaching Resources,** Tests A and B, pp. 28–33
• **AYP Monitoring Assessments,** Benchmark Test 4
• **Progress Monitoring Transparencies,** 134–137
• **Test Prep With Document-Based Assessment**
• *ExamView*® **Test Bank CD-ROM**
• **Progress Monitoring Online Quiz**
• **Assessment Rubrics**

Differentiated Instruction **Key**
(L1) Special Needs
(L2) Basic to Average
(L3) All Students
(L4) Average to Advanced

SN Special Needs Students
ELL English Language Learners
LPR Less Proficient Readers
AR Advanced Readers
GT Gifted and Talented

Author's Note

In *Travesties* (1974), playwright Tom Stoppard tells the story of the Russian revolutionary Lenin, the Irish author James Joyce, and the dadaist Tristan Tzara through the faltering memory of the English diplomat Henry Carr, who lived in Zurich during World War I. Not only does Carr misremember history, he does not understand the profound ways in which these three men shaped modern society.

Of course, historians are by definition outsiders. We can never intimately know the people or events of which we teach and write. Over time, I have come to recognize that there are distinct advantages to the outsider perspective. Time and distance allow one to look beyond the events that grabbed the headlines to see the long-term trends. This is an invaluable insight that I seek to pass on to my students. Each generation will contribute to our understanding of the past, and it is not just possible but probable that we will gain a clearer sense of events with the passage of time, not the other way around. Perhaps, I do not need to fear turning into another Henry Carr after all.

Sometimes, I feel like Henry Carr. I came of age in the San Francisco Bay area during the 1960s and 1970s. My sister attended some of the most famous rock concerts of the day. My neighbor attended U.C. Berkeley and participated in several protests that rocked the nation. The environmental, Chicano, and gay liberation movements were all born or at least blossomed in my backyard. What was I doing at the time—playing baseball, studying for exams, watching television?

One of the reasons I chose to attend U.C. Berkeley was because I intuited that I lived on the edge of momentous historical events, and I wanted to get closer to them. As a history major, I set out to learn as much about the Sixties as I could. I wrote my dissertation and first book on the New Left. Still, when I went to conferences and discussed my findings, I always worried that a veteran of the Sixties would stand up and declare that I did not know what I was talking about because I had not been there.

—Peter B. Levy

Extend Online

Environmental Issues of the 1960s and 1970s

Have students review photographs that depict environmental issues of concern in the 1960s and 1970s. Use the steps below to help students complete the activity.

Prepare for the Activity Explain that photographs of the environment can offer insights that are difficult to convey in words. To help students learn as much as possible from the photographs at the Web Code below, ask students to consider the following questions: What information does this photograph present? Why did the photographer choose the scene shown in this photograph? What conclusions can be drawn from this photograph?

Conduct the Activity For help in starting the activity, send students to **www.pearsonschool.com/ushist,** where they can access environmental photographs from this era. Have the students view the photographs and write a paragraph summarizing his or her observations.

Follow-Up Conduct a class discussion based on the following questions: How did these photographs expand your understanding of environmental issues in the 1960s and 1970s? What did you learn about environmental issues during this era? Are the environmental issues that were concerns then still important today?

Making Connections to Today L2

Students are more engaged when they understand why the information matters to them. To provide relevance, ask students to find examples of this chapter's themes in newspapers or magazines. Ask students to bring in their examples and share their findings with the class. This activity will not only encourage students to read more outside of class, but will also reinforce how this era changed our world today. Some possible themes include the following:

- Individual expression (free speech, nonconformity, popular culture, and so on)
- Women's rights
- Latino rights
- Rights of people with disabilities
- Consumer advocacy
- Environmental protection

Making Connections to Today L4

Strong readers have a keen interest in current world events that should be encouraged. Have students look through newspapers and magazines for examples of the themes listed in the left column. Then ask students to rewrite a section of the text, adding in the additional examples. Follow the steps below:

1. Ask students to choose a section of text from this chapter. Make sure the selection discusses an issue relevant to American society today.
2. Ask students to research further examples of the issue and develop a thorough understanding of its effects on American society.
3. Have students rewrite or revise the chosen selection of text to reflect the new information. Students should adjust the conclusion as needed.

Modeling Reading and Writing Skills

Cause and Effect Tell students that recognizing causes and effects helps them clarify the relationships among events or situations. Point out that noting signal words can help them identify these relationships. Clue words such as *reason, root, because, produced,* and *purpose* indicate possible causes. Words such as *brought about, effect, led to, outcome, produced, reaction, result, so, then, therefore,* and *this* indicate possible effects.

Model how to identify causes and effects by reading aloud the first sentence of "The Counterculture Rises" in Section 1. Draw students' attention to the phrase *was rooted in* and point out that this phrase signals a cause. The cause is the social and political events of the 1950s. The effect is the counterculture of the 1960s.

State Your Thesis Explain that in this chapter, students will be writing several speeches. (See Writing About History at the end of the chapter.) Remind students that every good persuasive speech should have a clear thesis that students can identify in a thesis statement. Remind them that a thesis statement should provoke valid arguments, and should be supported and defended in the body of the essay. On the board, write the following thesis statements:

1. Music from the 1960s was better than music from the 1950s.
2. Migrant farmworkers provided a major boost to the American economy during the 1960s.
3. Earth Day was launched to increase awareness of environmental issues.

Point out that the second thesis statement is the best choice because it is the only one that can be argued on the basis of facts. The first option is personal opinion, and the third is a known fact.

CHAPTER **18** A Crisis in Confidence, 1968–1980

Section	Core Instruction L3	Differentiated Instruction L1 L2 L4	
Section 1 100 minutes *Nixon and the Watergate Scandal* **OBJECTIVES** • Describe Richard Nixon's attitude toward "big" government. • Analyze Nixon's southern strategy. • Explain the Watergate incident and its consequences. **Focus Question** *What events led to Richard Nixon's resignation as President in 1974?*	**Teaching Resources** Reading Strategy: Identify Main Ideas, p. 10 Biography: Barbara Jordan, p. 13 Landmark Decisions of the Supreme Court: What Are the Limits of Executive Privilege? p. 14 Section 1 Quiz, p. 19 **Reading and Note Taking Study Guide** Section Note Taking, p. 148 Section 1 Summary, p. 149 **Progress Monitoring Transparencies,** 138 **Color Transparencies** The Watergate Scandal, A-133	**L1 Adapted Reading and Note Taking Study Guide** Section Note Taking, p. 148 SN Section 1 Summary, p. 149 SN **L2 Adapted Reading and Note Taking Study Guide** Section Note Taking, p. 148 LPR Section 1 Summary, p. 149 LPR **Spanish Reading and Note Taking Study Guide** Section Note Taking, p. 148 ELL Section 1 Summary, p. 149 ELL **L4 Differentiated Instruction Activity,** Teacher's Edition, p. 601 AR, GT	***Student Edition on Audio** SN **Differentiated Instruction Activities,** Teacher's Edition, pp. 599, 600, 603 SN ***Guided Reading Audio, Spanish CD** ELL ***Student Edition on Audio** LPR, ELL **Differentiated Instruction Activities,** Teacher's Edition, pp. 599, 600, 603 LPR, ELL **Extend Activity,** Teacher's Edition, p. 605 AR, GT
Section 2 100 minutes *The Ford and Carter Years* **OBJECTIVES** • Evaluate the presidency of Gerald Ford. • Assess the domestic policies of Jimmy Carter. • Analyze how American society changed in the 1970s. **Focus Question** *What accounted for the changes in American attitudes during the 1970s?*	**Teaching Resources** Geography and History: From Rust Belt to Sunbelt, p. 16 Landmark Decisions of the Supreme Court: Are Affirmative Action Programs Fair? p. 17 Section 2 Quiz, p. 20 **Reading and Note Taking Study Guide** Section Note Taking, p. 150 Section 2 Summary, p. 151 **Progress Monitoring Transparencies,** 139 **Color Transparencies** Rising Fuel Prices, A-134; Moving to the Sunbelt, A-136	**L1 Adapted Reading and Note Taking Study Guide** Section Note Taking, p. 150 SN Section 2 Summary, p. 151 SN **L2 Adapted Reading and Note Taking Study Guide** Section Note Taking, p. 150 LPR Section 2 Summary, p. 151 LPR **Spanish Reading and Note Taking Study Guide** Section Note Taking, p. 150 ELL Section 2 Summary, p. 151 ELL **L4 Differentiated Instruction Activities,** Teacher's Edition, pp. 609, 612 AR, GT	**Differentiated Instruction Activities,** Teacher's Edition, pp. 609, 611, 612 SN ****Teaching Resources** Geography and History: The Sunbelt, p. 15 LPR, ELL **Differentiated Instruction Activities,** Teacher's Edition, pp. 609, 611, 612 LPR, ELL **Extend Activity,** Teacher's Edition, p. 613 AR, GT

Section	Core Instruction L3	Differentiated Instruction L1 L2 L4	
Section 3 100 minutes *Foreign Policy Troubles* **OBJECTIVES** • Compare the policies of Gerald Ford and Jimmy Carter toward the Soviet Union. • Discuss changing U.S. foreign policy in the developing world. • Identify the successes and failures of Carter's foreign policy in the Middle East. **Focus Question** *What were the goals of American foreign policy during the Ford and Carter years, and how successful were Ford's and Carter's policies?*	**Teaching Resources** Biography: The American Hostages, p. 18 Section 3 Quiz, p. 21 **Reading and Note Taking Study Guide** Section Note Taking, p. 152 Section 3 Summary, p. 153 **Progress Monitoring Transparencies**, 140 **Color Transparencies** Camp David Accords, A-135	**L1** **Adapted Reading and Note Taking Study Guide** Section Note Taking, p. 152 SN Section 3 Summary, p. 153 SN **L2** **Adapted Reading and Note Taking Study Guide** Section Note Taking, p. 152 LPR Section 3 Summary, p. 153 LPR **Spanish Reading and Note Taking Study Guide** Section Note Taking, p. 152 ELL Section 3 Summary, p. 153 ELL **L4** **Differentiated Instruction Activities,** Teacher's Edition, pp. 614, 616 AR, GT	**Differentiated Instruction Activity,** Teacher's Edition, p. 618 SN **Differentiated Instruction Activities,** Teacher's Edition, pp. 616, 618 LPR, ELL **Extend Activity,** Teaching Resources, pp. 11–12 AR, GT

*Audio support is available for all sections.

**This worksheet also applies to L1.

Assessment Resources
- **Teaching Resources,** Tests A and B, pp. 22–27
- **AYP Monitoring Assessments,** Benchmark Test 4
- **Progress Monitoring Transparencies,** 138–140
- **Test Prep With Document-Based Assessment**
- *ExamView*® **Test Bank CD-ROM**
- **Progress Monitoring Online Quiz**
- **Assessment Rubrics**

Differentiated Instruction Key		
L1 Special Needs	SN	Special Needs Students
L2 Basic to Average	ELL	English Language Learners
L3 All Students	LPR	Less Proficient Readers
L4 Average to Advanced	AR	Advanced Readers
	GT	Gifted and Talented

Author's Note

On August 8, 1974, Richard Nixon resigned from the presidency. That same day, I quit my job as a Fuller Brush man, having spent hours walking door-to-door without a dime to show for my efforts. Historians have spent a great deal of time considering Nixon's action, depicting Watergate as a crisis in confidence that beset America during the 1970s. While my resignation did not attract anywhere near as much attention as the president's, in my capacity as a social historian, I can see that it too revealed much about the times.

America was at a crossroads in the mid-1970s. After a generation of sustained growth, the economy had become stagnant. At the same time it was beginning to experience profound structural shifts. For years, the Fuller Brush man traveled door-to-door taking orders for household items and then delivering them at no extra cost.

However, broad social and economic changes were making such occupations obsolete (though Fuller Brush has since evolved into a home-based business operation). By the mid-1970s, most housewives purchased these same items at their local supermarkets or drugstores and at a cheaper price. While a small group of affluent consumers continued to enjoy the luxury of purchasing mops and brooms from their personal Fuller Brush man, soaring prices and stalled wages left the majority of Americans looking for ways to save money and causing the virtual disappearance of door-to-door selling.

I could easily spend more time analyzing how my difficulties as a Fuller Brush man emanated from the social changes of the 1970s. But the point is that both teachers and students can gain much from their own experiences as they seek to shed light on the past (and the present).

For instance, consider the impact of online shopping and video-on-demand on shopping malls and megaplex movie theaters. Will these places go the way of the Fuller Brush man? Even if there is no clear answer to this question, students can look back to the 1970s for valuable lessons about their world now and the ways it continues to change around them.

—Peter B. Levy

Extend Online

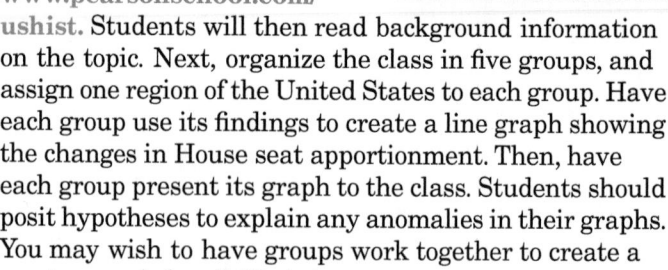

U.S. Demographics and Reapportionment Since 1900

Have students research shifts in U.S. demographics between 1900 and 2000 and create line graphs to show the reapportionment of the House of Representatives during that period. Ask students to present their findings in a class discussion. Use the steps below to help students complete the activity.

Prepare for the Activity Explain to students that the United States Constitution mandates a national census every ten years. The findings of the census are then used to reapportion the 435 seats in the House of Representatives to maintain fair representation. Explain to students that in 1900 there were 391 seats in the House, but that this number was increased to 435 in 1911, and then temporarily increased again to 437 with the addition of Hawaii and Alaska. After the 1960 census, the number returned to 435, where it has remained.

Conduct the Activity For help in starting this activity, send students to www.pearsonschool.com/ushist. Students will then read background information on the topic. Next, organize the class in five groups, and assign one region of the United States to each group. Have each group use its findings to create a line graph showing the changes in House seat apportionment. Then, have each group present its graph to the class. Students should posit hypotheses to explain any anomalies in their graphs. You may wish to have groups work together to create a master graph for all 50 states.

Follow-Up Conduct a class discussion based on the following questions: Which states in your graph gained representatives in the 100-year period? Which states lost representatives? How have these changes affected politics at the national level and at the state level?

Mapping Concepts L1 L2

Concept terms such as *contend* and *emphasis* are not only complex, but also pervasive in social studies. They warrant more extensive instruction than terms such as *executive privilege* or *sanctions,* which are less conceptually demanding. Model using the following steps.

1. Write the term on the board and pronounce it—*crucial.*

2. Provide students with a contextually rich sentence—*To win World War II, the Allies believed that it was crucial to defeat Hitler first.*

3. Guide students in suggesting synonyms for the term—*central, important, key, vital, essential.*

4. Guide students in analyzing the contextual sentence and synonyms, and clarify the essential attributes of the concept as students list the sentences and synonyms. *Essential attribute: Something is crucial when it is necessary for survival or success.*

5. Record examples of the new concept that relate to the students' experiences, taking care to link directly to the attributes noted in the previous step: *studying for a test, practicing for a game, eating a mixed diet for good health.*

6. Provide non-examples that do NOT have all of the attributes—*forgetting to bring a jacket on a warm day.*

7. Provide additional examples and non-examples, and coach students through the process of evaluating them until students are fairly proficient with the new concept.

8. Coach students in writing a "show you know" sentence by using the new concept on their organizer—*To make a great pizza, it is crucial that you get the crust just right.*

Modeling Reading and Writing Skills

Draw Inferences Tell students that when reading, they may need to recognize an implied message. By differentiating between what is stated explicitly and what is implied, they can draw inferences.

To model this skill, read aloud the Witness History Primary Source selection that opens Section 1. Point out the explicitly stated facts: There has been a break-in—a crime—and the President wants the FBI to stay out of it. What can be inferred is that President Nixon will try to use his power to force the FBI to ignore an illegal activity.

Apply for a Job Explain that in this chapter, students will write an essay or a letter of introduction in which they outline their qualifications for a specific job. (See Writing About History at the end of the chapter.) When applying for a job, students should point out how their qualifications match the needs of the job. Essays such as this have an opening paragraph, in which the student introduces himself or herself and identifies the job that is of interest, and a conclusion, in which the student briefly summarizes the reasons for believing that he or she is the best candidate for the job.

As with all essays, students should follow these steps:

Prewriting: Students should begin by doing research to list the job qualifications required by the employer. Then, students should list the skills that they possess and compare their skills with the list of job qualifications.

Drafting: Remind students that constructing a good essay starts with making an outline. Students should use their lists of qualifications as an outline. Students should use the outline to write a rough draft of the essay.

Revising: Have students reread their work and stress the importance of correct spelling and grammar when submitting a job application.

Publishing: Have students share their application with a partner for peer evaluation. Have evaluators consider how well the "candidate" fulfills the job's requirements.

19 The Conservative Resurgence, 1980–1993

Section	Core Instruction ⓛ₃	Differentiated Instruction ⓛ₁ ⓛ₂ ⓛ₄	
Section 1 100 minutes *The Conservative Movement Grows* **OBJECTIVES** • Describe the differences between liberal and conservative viewpoints. • Analyze the reasons behind the rise of conservatism in the early 1980s. • Explain why Ronald Reagan won the presidency in 1980.	**Teaching Resources** Reading Strategy: Summarize, p. 12 Viewpoints: Liberals and Conservatives, p. 15 Section 1 Quiz, p. 21 **Reading and Note Taking Study Guide** Section Note Taking, p. 154 Section 1 Summary, p. 155 **Progress Monitoring Transparencies,** 141 **Color Transparencies** Winning the South, A-137	ⓛ₁ **Adapted Reading and Note Taking Study Guide** Section Note Taking, p. 154 SN Section 1 Summary, p. 155 SN ⓛ₂ **Adapted Reading and Note Taking Study Guide** Section Note Taking, p. 154 LPR Section 1 Summary, p. 155 LPR **Spanish Reading and Note Taking Study Guide** Section Note Taking, p. 154 ELL Section 1 Summary, p. 155 ELL	*Student Edition on Audio SN **Differentiated Instruction Activity,** Teacher's Edition, p. 630 SN *Guided Reading Audio, Spanish CD ELL *Student Edition on Audio LPR, ELL **Differentiated Instruction Activity,** Teacher's Edition, p. 630 LPR, ELL
Focus Question *What spurred the rise of conservatism in the late 1970s and early 1980s?*		ⓛ₄ **Extend Activity,** Teacher's Edition, p. 632 AR, GT	
Section 2 100 minutes *The Reagan Revolution* **OBJECTIVES** • Analyze Reagan's economic policies as President. • Summarize how Reagan strengthened the conservative movement. • Evaluate the steps taken to address various problems in the 1980s and early 1990s.	**Teaching Resources** Reading a Chart: Social Security, p. 16 Primary Source: Understanding Reagan's "Tear Down This Wall" Speech, p. 18 Section 2 Quiz, p. 22 **Reading and Note Taking Study Guide** Section Note Taking, p. 156 Section 2 Summary, p. 157 **Progress Monitoring Transparencies,** 142	ⓛ₁ **Adapted Reading and Note Taking Study Guide** Section Note Taking, p. 156 SN Section 2 Summary, p. 157 SN ⓛ₂ **Adapted Reading and Note Taking Study Guide** Section Note Taking, p. 156 LPR Section 2 Summary, p. 157 LPR **Spanish Reading and Note Taking Study Guide** Section Note Taking, p. 156 ELL Section 2 Summary, p. 157 ELL	**Differentiated Instruction Activity,** Teacher's Edition, p. 636 SN **Teaching Resources** Primary Source: "Tear Down This Wall," p. 17 LPR, ELL **Differentiated Instruction Activity,** Teacher's Edition, p. 636 LPR, ELL
Focus Question *What were the major characteristics of the conservative Reagan Revolution?*		ⓛ₄ **Differentiated Instruction Activity,** Teacher's Edition, p. 634 AR, GT	**Extend Activity,** Teaching Resources, pp. 13–14 AR, GT

*Audio support is available for all sections.   **This worksheet also applies to L1.

Assessment Resources
• **Teaching Resources,** Tests A and B, pp. 25–30
• **AYP Monitoring Assessments,** Benchmark Test 4
• **Progress Monitoring Transparencies,** 141–144
• Test Prep With Document-Based Assessment
• *ExamView*® Test Bank CD-ROM
• Progress Monitoring Online Quiz
• Assessment Rubrics

Differentiated Instruction Key

ⓛ₁ Special Needs		SN	Special Needs Students
ⓛ₂ Basic to Average		ELL	English Language Learners
ⓛ₃ All Students		LPR	Less Proficient Readers
ⓛ₄ Average to Advanced		AR	Advanced Readers
		GT	Gifted and Talented Students

Section	Core Instruction L3	Differentiated Instruction L1 L2 L4	
Section 3 100 minutes *The End of the Cold War* **OBJECTIVES** • Analyze the ways that Ronald Reagan challenged communism and the Soviet Union. • Explain why communism collapsed in Europe and in the Soviet Union. • Describe other foreign policy challenges that faced the United States in the 1980s. **Focus Question** *What were Reagan's foreign policies, and how did they contribute to the fall of communism in Europe?*	**Teaching Resources** Reading a Chart: Military Spending, p. 19 Section 3 Quiz, p. 23 **Reading and Note Taking Study Guide** Section Note Taking, pp. 158–159 Section 3 Summary, p. 160 **Progress Monitoring Transparencies**, 143 **Color Transparencies** Reagan's Foreign Policy, A-138; The End of Communism, A-139	**L1 Adapted Reading and Note Taking Study Guide** Section Note Taking, pp. 158–159 SN Section 3 Summary, p. 160 SN **L2 Adapted Reading and Note Taking Study Guide** Section Note Taking, pp. 158–159 LPR Section 3 Summary, p. 160 LPR **Spanish Reading and Note Taking Study Guide** Section Note Taking, pp. 158–159 ELL Section 3 Summary, p. 160 ELL **L4 Differentiated Instruction Activity,** Teacher's Edition, p. 642 AR, GT	**Differentiated Instruction Activities,** Teacher's Edition, pp. 638, 643 SN **Differentiated Instruction Activities,** Teacher's Edition, pp. 638, 643 ELL, LPR **Extend Activity,** Teacher's Edition, p. 644 AR, GT
Section 4 100 minutes *Foreign Policy After the Cold War* **OBJECTIVES** • Analyze why George H.W. Bush decided to use force in some foreign disputes and not in others. • Summarize the Persian Gulf War and its results. **Focus Question** *What actions did the United States take abroad during George H.W. Bush's presidency?*	**Teaching Resources** Outline Map: World Oil Reserves, p. 20 Section 4 Quiz, p. 24 **Reading and Note Taking Study Guide** Section Note Taking, p. 161 Section 4 Summary, p. 162 **Progress Monitoring Transparencies**, 144 **Color Transparencies** Tiananmen Square Protests, A-140	**L1 Adapted Reading and Note Taking Study Guide** Section Note Taking, p. 161 SN Section 4 Summary, p. 162 SN **L2 Adapted Reading and Note Taking Study Guide** Section Note Taking, p. 161 LPR Section 3 Summary, p. 162 LPR **Spanish Reading and Note Taking Study Guide** Section Note Taking, p. 161 ELL Section 3 Summary, p. 162 ELL **L4 Differentiated Instruction Activity,** Teacher's Edition, p. 647 AR, GT	**Differentiated Instruction Activity,** Teacher's Edition, p. 648 SN **Differentiated Instruction Activity,** Teacher's Edition, p. 648 LPR, ELL **Extend Activity,** Teacher's Edition, p. 649 AR, GT

Author's Note

When I started teaching, Ronald Reagan was President. Not surprisingly, I did not spend much, if any, time discussing his presidency. Gradually, I sought to integrate Reagan and the conservative resurgence into my courses. One motivation to do this was that I had always believed that my teachers fell far short in covering the times in which I was lived. When it came time for me to teach this era, I was concerned as I had not formally studied it in school.

Then, in the early 1990s my publishers asked me to write an encyclopedia on the Reagan years. While the prospect of compiling 300 entries on topics ranging from Acid Rain to Boris Yeltsin sounded daunting, I looked at the offer as an opportunity to examine this era in a rigorous and balanced manner.

Indeed, this process of analyzing the Reagan years and arriving at my own conclusions about his presidency confirmed my belief in the valuable link between research and writing, for teachers and students alike. Today, I feel more comfortable lecturing about the 1980s than I do about those periods I studied in graduate school.

And my view of Reagan? I see him as a paradox. Often portrayed as an ideologue and as the consummate outsider, he acted in quite pragmatic and proficient ways. For instance, soon after he was elected, Reagan appointed as chief of staff James Baker, George H.W. Bush's campaign manager (Bush had run against Reagan for the Republican nomination), and Baker played a crucial role in getting the President's domestic policies through a Democratic congress.

Similarly, after some difficulties with Al Haig, his first Secretary of State, Reagan appointed George Shultz, another veteran of Washington, D.C., to serve in the most important foreign policy post, and it was Shultz who prodded Reagan to meet with Michael Gorbachev, bringing the Cold War to a rapid—and peaceful—end. Arguably, if he had not appointed Baker, but someone closer to him personally and ideologically, or had kept Haig, Reagan's legacy would have been very different. Interestingly, Reagan's pragmatism did not undermine his reputation as an ideologue, rather it cemented his legacy as a man for whom ideas and principles mattered the most.

—Peter B. Levy

Extend Online

The Berlin Wall

Have students research the political conflicts that led to the construction of the Berlin Wall and to its eventual fall. Use the steps below to help students complete the activity.

Prepare for the Activity
Explain that the Berlin Wall was raised because of the division of the city after World War II, which created British, French, Soviet, and American sectors. The Western sectors created an "island" of Western influence and freedom in a Soviet bloc country. The declining influence of the Soviet Union eventually brought down the artificial division of the city of Berlin.

Conduct the Activity For help in starting the activity, send students to **www.pearsonschool.com/ushist.** Where they can access information about the politicians who helped create the wall and the reasons behind their decision. Students may work in groups to explore the

wall's construction, its effect on the city of Berlin, and the events that led to its destruction. Have students present their findings to the class and discuss Berlin's role in the conflict between communist and democratic leaders.

Follow-Up Conduct a class discussion based on the following questions: Why would a government go to such an extreme as constructing a wall to control the movement of its citizens? What kind of controls would it take to keep such a wall in existence for more than 30 years? In the face of such a situation, what can citizens do to protect their rights and liberties?

Making Connections to Today L2

Students are more engaged when they understand why the information should matter to them. To prove relevancy, ask students to find examples of this chapter's themes in newspapers or magazines. Ask them to bring in their examples and share their findings with the class. This activity will not only encourage students to read more outside of class, but also reinforce why studying U.S. history matters today. Some possible themes include the following:

- the AIDS epidemic
- the role of government
- world drug trafficking
- fuel sources
- struggles against repressive governments
- the influence of political parties
- nuclear weapons
- conflict in the Middle East

Finding Patterns in History L4

Learning to find patterns in history helps students make connections among events and time periods and understand their relevance to the present. Comparing the Cold War and post–Cold War periods requires high-level thinking and presents an excellent opportunity for students to practice finding historical patterns.

Suggest that students keep a "Patterns Diary" in which they make comparisons between global tensions and problems before and after the Cold War. One column should be labeled "Cold War" and the other "post–Cold War." Categories may include the following:

- countries and leaders
- military technology
- freedom and repression
- struggles against communism

Students may also work together to brainstorm their own list of categories. When they have completed their reading, have students draw three to five conclusions from their Patterns Diaries.

Modeling Reading and Writing Skills

Distinguish Fact and Opinion Explain that when reading primary and secondary sources, students should distinguish between facts and opinions. Remind students that facts can be proven true, but that opinions are beliefs. Although they may be valid, they cannot be proved.

To model this skill, read aloud the Witness History Primary Source at the beginning of the chapter. Point out the facts: Ronald Reagan is running for President and is the Republican candidate. The quotation expresses his opinion that the crisis in the United States is "the failure of our leaders to establish rational goals."

Multimedia Presentation Explain that in this chapter, students will be creating multimedia presentations about the changes that happened in Europe during the late 1980s and early 1990s. (See Writing About History at the end of the chapter.) Discuss with students the number of resources they can include in creating a multimedia presentation. Encourage students to take an inventory

of the technology available to them as they begin looking for illustrations and other resources.

- Explain that students can add useful information without the use of computers. For example, students can enhance their presentations with images, illustrations, and interesting sources taken from newspaper articles and magazine pictures, as well as with their own illustrations or graphs. With these sources, they can create posters, flip charts, or news magazine reports.
- Students who wish to use overhead projectors can transfer their data onto transparencies for their presentations.
- If students are familiar with video cameras or videocassette players, they may want to conduct interviews to include in their presentations.
- Students with Internet access and graphics programs can incorporate their information into a Web site.
- If students are familiar with PowerPoint, they may use it to give their presentations.

Section	Core Instruction L3	Differentiated Instruction L1 L2 L4	
Section 1 75 minutes *The Computer and Technology Revolutions* **OBJECTIVES** • Describe the development of the computer and its impact on business and industry. • Analyze the impact of new technology on communications. • Explain how globalization and the rise of the service sector affected the American economy. **Focus Question** *How have technological changes and globalization transformed the American economy?*	**Teaching Resources** Reading Strategy: Categorize, p. 12 Reading a Chart: A Service Economy, p. 19 Section 1 Quiz, p. 25 **Reading and Note Taking Study Guide** Section Note Taking, p. 163 Section 1 Summary, p. 164 **Progress Monitoring Transparencies,** 145 **Color Transparencies** New Medical Technology, A-141	**L1 Adapted Reading and Note Taking Study Guide** Section Note Taking, p. 163 SN Section 1 Summary, p. 164 SN **L2 Adapted Reading and Note Taking Study Guide** Section Note Taking, p. 163 LPR Section 1 Summary, p. 164 LPR **Spanish Reading and Note Taking Study Guide** Section Note Taking, p. 163 ELL Section 1 Summary, p. 164 ELL **L4 Differentiated Instruction Activity,** Teacher's Edition, p. 657 AR, GT	***Student Edition on Audio** SN Section Note Taking **Differentiated Instruction Activity,** Teacher's Edition, p. 659 SN ***Guided Reading Audio, Spanish CD** ELL ***Student Edition on Audio** LPR, ELL **Differentiated Instruction Activity,** Teacher's Edition, p. 659 LPR, ELL **Extend Activity,** Teacher's Edition, p. 660 AR, GT
Section 2 100 minutes *The Clinton Presidency* **OBJECTIVES** • Explain why Bill Clinton won the presidency in 1992. • Assess the success of Clinton's domestic policies. • Describe the Contract With America and its impact. • Analyze the Clinton impeachment. **Focus Question** *What were the successes and failures of the Clinton presidency?*	**Teaching Resources** Viewpoints: Clinton and Gingrich, p. 20 Section 2 Quiz, p. 26 **Reading and Note Taking Study Guide** Section Note Taking, p. 165 Section 2 Summary, p. 166 **Progress Monitoring Transparencies,** 146 **Color Transparencies** Republicans Take Over Congress, A-142	**L1 Adapted Reading and Note Taking Study Guide** Section Note Taking, p. 165 SN Section 2 Summary, p. 166 SN **L2 Adapted Reading and Note Taking Study Guide** Section Note Taking, p. 165 LPR Section 2 Summary, p. 166 LPR **Spanish Reading and Note Taking Study Guide** Section Note Taking, p. 165 ELL Section 2 Summary, p. 166 ELL **L4 Differentiated Instruction Activity,** Teacher's Edition, p. 663 AR, GT	**Differentiated Instruction Activity,** Teacher's Edition, p. 662 SN **Differentiated Instruction Activity,** Teacher's Edition, p. 662 LPR, ELL **Extend Activity,** Teacher's Edition, p. 665 AR, GT

*Audio support is available for all sections.

**This worksheet also applies to L1.

Assessment Resources
• **Teaching Resources,** Tests A and B, pp. 30–35
• **AYP Monitoring Assessments,** Benchmark Test 4
• **Progress Monitoring Transparencies,** 145–149
• **Test Prep With Document-Based Assessment**
• ***ExamView*®** Test Bank CD-ROM
• **Progress Monitoring Online Quiz**
• **Assessment Rubrics**

Differentiated Instruction Key

L1 Special Needs	SN Special Needs Students
L2 Basic to Average	ELL English Language Learners
L3 All Students	LPR Less Proficient Readers
L4 Average to Advanced	AR Advanced Readers
	GT Gifted and Talented

Section	Core Instruction (L3)	Differentiated Instruction (L1) (L2) (L4)	
Section 3 100 minutes *Global Politics and Economics* **OBJECTIVES** • Analyze how the United States responded to changes in the global economy. • Assess the foreign policy goals and actions of the Clinton administration. • Describe U.S. relations with various Middle Eastern countries and groups. **Focus Question** *What role did the United States take on in global politics and economics following the Cold War?*	**Teaching Resources** Outline Map: Global Conflicts, p. 21 Section 3 Quiz, p. 27 **Reading and Note Taking Study Guide** Section Note Taking, p. 167 Section 3 Summary, p. 168 **Progress Monitoring Transparencies,** 147 **Color Transparencies** Ethnicity in Yugoslavia, A-143	(L1) **Adapted Reading and Note Taking Study Guide** Section Note Taking, p. 167 SN Section 3 Summary, p. 168 SN (L2) **Adapted Reading and Note Taking Study Guide** Section Note Taking, p. 167 LPR Section 3 Summary, p. 168 LPR **Spanish Reading and Note Taking Study Guide** Section Note Taking, p. 167 ELL Section 3 Summary, p. 168 ELL (L4) **Differentiated Instruction Activity,** Teacher's Edition, p. 668 AR, GT	**Differentiated Instruction Activity,** Teacher's Edition, p. 667 SN **Differentiated Instruction Activity,** Teacher's Edition, p. 667 LPR, ELL **Extend Activity,** Teacher's Edition, p. 670 AR, GT
Section 4 100 minutes *The Bush and Obama Presidencies* **OBJECTIVES** • Assess the outcome of the 2000 presidential election. • Explain the goals and achievements of George W. Bush's domestic policy. • Analyze the impact of terrorist attacks on the United States. • Summarize the policy goals and actions of the Obama administration. **Focus Question** *What was the impact of the terrorist attack against the United States and of the 2008 financial crisis?*	**Teaching Resources** History Comics: *Bush* v. *Gore*, p. 23 Section 4 Quiz, p. 28 **Reading and Note Taking Study Guide** Section Note Taking, p. 169 Section 4 Summary, p. 170 **Progress Monitoring Transparencies,** 148 **Color Transparencies** The Election of 2000, A-144	(L1) **Adapted Reading and Note Taking Study Guide** Section Note Taking, p. 169 SN Section 4 Summary, p. 170 SN (L2) **Adapted Reading and Note Taking Study Guide** Section Note Taking, p. 169 LPR Section 4 Summary, p. 170 LPR **Spanish Reading and Note Taking Study Guide** Section Note Taking, p. 169 ELL Section 4 Summary, p. 170 ELL (L4) **Differentiated Instruction Activities,** Teacher's Edition, pp. 673, 674 AR, GT	**Differentiated Instruction Activities,** Teacher's Edition, pp. 672, 676 SN ****Teaching Resources** History Comics: The 2000 Election, p. 22 LPR, ELL **Differentiated Instruction Activities,** Teacher's Edition, pp. 672, 676 LPR, ELL **Extend Activity,** Teacher's Edition, p. 678 AR, GT
Section 5 50 minutes *Americans Look to the Future* **OBJECTIVES** • Analyze the impact of immigration on American society. • Summarize the causes and effects of changing demographics. **Focus Question** *How was American society changing at the beginning of the twenty-first century?*	**Teaching Resources** Issues Connector: Education and American Society, pp. 15–18 Section 5 Quiz, p. 29 **Reading and Note Taking Study Guide** Section Note Taking, p. 171 Section 5 Summary, p. 172 American Issues Journal, pp. 233–235 **Progress Monitoring Transparencies,** 149	(L1) **Adapted Reading and Note Taking Study Guide** Section Note Taking, p. 171 SN Section 5 Summary, p. 172 SN American Issues Journal, pp. 233–235 SN (L2) **Adapted Reading and Note Taking Study Guide** Section Note Taking, p. 171 LPR Section 5 Summary, p. 172 LPR American Issues Journal, pp. 233–235 LPR **Spanish Reading and Note Taking Study Guide** Section Note Taking, p. 171 ELL Section 5 Summary, p. 172 ELL American Issues Journal, pp. 233–235 ELL (L4) **Differentiated Instruction Activity,** Teacher's Edition, p. 681 AR, GT	**Differentiated Instruction Activity,** Teacher's Edition, p. 681 SN **Differentiated Instruction Activity,** Teacher's Edition, p. 681 LPR, ELL **Extend Activity,** Teaching Resources, pp. 13–14 AR, GT

Author's Note

Historians package the past. In part, this is a distortion of the past, but it is also a way to make sense of it. As we teach the second half of an American history survey course, for example, we move from one "era" to the next: the era of the Civil War and Reconstruction to the Gilded Age, the Progressive Era to World War I, the Twenties to the Great Depression, and World War II to the Cold War. Of course, eras often overlap, and by providing time periods with neat labels we tend to prioritize some material and leave out other material.

Let me give one example. When we talk and write about the Progressive Era, we note that a reform impulse marked the period, and that the government improved the lot of many Americans. But this was also a period of racism in the South. Clearly for African Americans, the early twentieth century was not a time of progressivism.

The other problem with labels is how they frame the past. The labels I mentioned focus on political, economic, and military dates, but they slight many social and cultural issues. Labels often make it difficult to discuss changes in relationships among the sexes or intellectual evolution. Labels that impose order on the past, also impose a pattern.

I am not advocating abolishing labels because I believe that they do convey a rough truth about the past. However, by teaching history with labels, we have to be aware at the same time that there is no single "truth," that the past is complex and open to many interpretations.

Another difficulty with labels is that they break down as we approach the present. We need time and distance to see a pattern in the past and arrive at a label. But what label can we use for the years since the end of the Cold War? The Age of Terrorism? The Era of Freedom? This is not a question that historians can answer accurately or with confidence. Although we look into the past in search of patterns, we don't gaze into crystal balls searching for predictions.

—Randy Roberts

Extend Online

Understanding the Israeli-Palestinian Conflict

The ongoing Israeli-Palestinian conflict is important to the Middle East foreign policy of the United States. Using the steps below, have students research recent developments in the Israeli-Palestinian conflict, including current leaders, terrorist actions, and peace-making efforts with and without the help of the United States. Have students write a paragraph about their findings and prepare for a classroom discussion about the conflict.

Prepare for the Activity Tell students that there are many different perspectives on the Israeli-Palestinian conflict among Israelis, Palestinians, and people living outside the region, including Americans. Explain that understanding the different perspectives on the conflict can help in understanding the conflict itself.

Conduct the Activity For help in starting the activity, send students to www.pearsonschool.com/ushist. Each student will research recent developments in the Israeli-Palestinian conflict. You may assign students to work in groups or individually to focus on different aspects of the conflict. Have students write a one-paragraph summary of their findings and be prepared to discuss their findings in class.

Follow-Up Conduct a class discussion based on the following questions: What are the main concerns of Palestinians today? What are the main concerns of Israelis? Why is the Israeli-Palestinian conflict important to the United States? How might the conflict be resolved peacefully?

Oral History L1 L2

To help students become engaged in more recent historical events, have them conduct an oral history. First, have students select a focus for the oral history. The history could be based on a general topic, such as the growth of technology (how computers have changed life, for example) or a recollection-based history, such as remembering the September 11, 2001, terrorist attacks. As a class, draft specific questions for the interview. The class can use these questions with a guest speaker by conducting a one-on-one interview with a friend, relative, or family member. Offer students a choice as to how they will report their findings: multimedia presentation, essay, poster, or skit. You may recommend that they record the interview with a camcorder, tape recorder, or MP3 player and then incorporate clips or sound bites into their presentation.

After presenting their oral histories, students should discuss their findings with a partner. They may compare the information they learned with that of the text as well as other outside sources. In addition, students should consider the source of the oral history—the interviewee—taking into account how factors such as age or background might affect that person's outlook on the topic.

Historical Precedents L4

Modern events do not happen in a vacuum; they are often shaped by many preceding causes and situations. Students should place the events studied in this chapter within the greater context of United States history. Ask them to draw on previously learned information to understand the motives and perspectives of those involved in the events.

To help students develop an understanding of the continuum of history, ask them to formulate a list of causes of events being studied, such as the conflict in the Middle East or the war on terrorism. Then have them determine which cause was the most significant in ultimately shaping the outcome of the event. As a class, vote on which cause was the most significant. Ask students: If this cause were removed, how might the event have been altered? Could it have been prevented?

Modeling Reading and Writing Skills

Identify Evidence Remind students that before they accept an author's conclusion, they should identify the author's evidence. Then they should evaluate the evidence to ensure that it supports the conclusion.

To model this skill, read aloud the text under the Section 2 red heading "Healthcare Reform Fails." Point out the conclusion: Clinton's healthcare reform proposal failed because Americans did not want the government to run healthcare. Next, identify the evidence: The healthcare reform bill never won support in Congress despite highly publicized hearings and a detailed proposal. The proposal was met with criticism from diverse groups. Americans had a distrust of big government. Together, all those statements are credible evidence to support the conclusion: Clinton's healthcare reform proposal failed because Americans did not want the government to run healthcare.

Examine the Question Explain that in this chapter students will be writing for assessment. (See Writing About History at the end of the chapter.) Remind them

that a complete response to an assessment question will address every aspect of that question. As students read an essay question, they should look for key words that explain exactly what they should do to write a thorough answer. Key words include *explain, examine the causes, analyze, compare and contrast, defend, distinguish between, examine, explore, evaluate, identify,* and *show.*

Model how to identify key words by writing on the board the following sample essay question: Write an essay describing changes in America's foreign policy from Clinton's presidency through Bush's presidency. Point out the key word *describing.* The assignment is asking students to give details that tell about changes in America's foreign policy. Then, write on the board: President Bush declared war on terrorism in 2001. Write an essay justifying Bush's actions. Underline the key word *justifying.* Tell students that the assignment is asking them to demonstrate that Bush's actions were correct by using facts, reasoning, and examples, even if students do not agree with the statement.

Connect Students to the Drama of History

I do my research by shadowing teenagers through their day in high school to pinpoint the moments when they are genuinely engaged by what is transpiring in the classroom. My ultimate goal is to identify specific classroom episodes where young people find genuine meaning, worth, and value in their academic experiences, and to understand what teachers can do to cultivate engagement.

The students I shadow typically find their class time tedious. As one student put it, "Sitting in class is like being in the car with your parents on a long road trip without your CD player." They identified the chief culprits for their boredom: unwavering routine, relentless lecturing, detachment on the teacher's part, and content that mattered little to their world.

Despite this generally grim assessment, I have also witnessed numerous episodes where students experienced the classroom as provocative, enchanting, memorable, and enjoyable. Animated by the experience of learning, they would say, "I can't believe how fast class went" or "That was intense!" or the ubiquitous "today was cool." After watching hundreds of class sessions and analyzing the episodes with students and teachers who experienced them, I noted several commonalities.

Where students were engaged and motivated, the teachers viewed the students as unabashed and savvy consumers, and they saw themselves as marketers locked in a fierce competition to secure their students' attention. These teachers didn't show up to class expecting compliance and focus. Instead, they devoted themselves to devising approaches that would generate buzz and energy. Here is a sampling of approaches:

Manipulate the Pace and Rhythm of Classroom Experiences

One teacher veered between an almost frenetic pace of question-and-answer discussion followed by long spans of quiet journaling time. She told me that her model for pace was music television. "I try and jar them into paying attention with lots of transitions, quick back and forth, followed by some slow times. I see myself as a DJ at a party."

Teachers also manipulated routines to focus attention, taking students outside for class, introducing a subject with dramatic video footage, using music and gripping primary source materials to secure attention.

Frame the Curriculum in Ways That Provide Relevance

I almost never shadowed students who found intrinsic fascination with the subject matter at hand. In fact, the default response on the part of most students was a series of questions resembling, "Why should *I* care about the Industrial Revolution? Why—other than the fact you will test me on this—should I delve into a study of how World War I occurred?" Students responded enthusiastically to teachers who helped students make meaningful connections to the subject matter.

To make this happen, some teachers connected the past to the present. When studying the robber barons, students were asked to compare John D. Rockefeller and Standard Oil to Bill Gates and Microsoft. Other teachers evoked interest by having students take on the role of historical figures. For example, students studying the industrial revolution examined a series of photographs depicting children at work in factories and composed journal entries describing daily life as a child laborer. Other teachers utilized the principles of problem-based learning to create simulations where students had to resolve real historical knowledge and analytical skills. These varied approaches require intense preparation and pedagogical skill on the part of the teacher, but, done well, they provide stimulating ways for students to showcase their content knowledge and practice their emerging skills.

Infuse Your Classroom With Your Personal Presence

The students told me again and again: "Energy and passion matter." Teachers who connected with students told poignant personal stories, conveyed their own passion for the subject matter, expressed emotion, and conveyed their delight in what makes history puzzling and interesting. Their enthusiasm for the questions at the heart of the content modeled for students what it means to be a student of history. The episodes of inspired learning that I witnessed were always catalyzed by a teacher devoted to creating a space for students to express their emerging understandings.

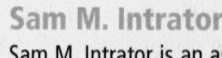

Sam M. Intrator

Sam M. Intrator is an associate professor of Education and Child Study at Smith College in Northampton, MA. His book ***Tuned in and Fired Up: How Teaching Can Inspire Genuine Learning*** (Yale University Press) explores how students experience their academic learning.

Contents

A series of handbooks provides skills instruction to help you read, learn, and demonstrate your knowledge of American history.

Objectives

- Learn how to read nonfiction critically by using prereading, during reading, and after-reading strategies.
- Use a systematic approach to write narrative, expository, research, persuasive, and assessment essays.
- Use a systematic approach to critically analyze and evaluate text and visual sources.
- Learn strategies for active participation in group discussions, for developing and presenting oral or multimedia presentations, and for active listening.

21st Century Skills

SKILLS HANDBOOK

Objective

As you teach this section, keep students focused on the following objective to help them master core content.

- Learn how to read informational materials critically by using prereading, during reading, and after reading strategies.

Prepare to Read

Background Knowledge

Ask students what types of reading they have done recently. List their responses on the board. For each response, ask students to consider the following questions: What kind of text is this? What information can I learn from it? What strategies can help me understand it? Explain that to fully understand what they read, readers must apply a variety of strategies before, during, and after reading.

Teach

Strategies to Use Before You Read

Instruct

- **Introduce** Read the black headings under *Strategies to Use Before You Read* and have students describe any strategies with which they are already familiar.

- **Teach** Point out that to set a purpose for reading, students should skim the text, reading headings and looking at illustrations. Have students fill in the *Set a Purpose for Reading* worksheet. Teaching Resources, Skills Handbook, **p. 1**

- Point out that asking questions is another key prereading strategy. Ask a volunteer to point to a passage anywhere in the student text, and then lead the class in asking and answers questions. Have students fill in the *Ask Questions* worksheet. Teaching Resources, Skills Handbook, **p. 2**

Reading Informational Texts

Reading a newspaper, a magazine, an Internet page, or a textbook differs from reading a novel. You read nonfiction texts to acquire new information. Researchers have shown that the reading strategies presented below will help you maximize your understanding of such informational texts.

Strategies to Use Before You Read

Before you read informational text, it's important to take the time to do some prereading. These strategies will help.

Set a Purpose for Reading

Try to focus on a goal when you're reading the text. Preview a section by reading the objectives and looking at the illustrations. Then, write a purpose for your reading, such as:

- "I'll learn about the development of the North and South and find ways to compare these regions."
- "I'll find out about the growth of railroads."

Ask Questions

Before you read a section, consider what you'd like to know about a topic. Then, ask questions that will yield relevant information. Scan the section headings and illustrations and write a few questions in a chart like the one below. As you read, try to answer each of your questions. Use phrases and words to fill in the chart.

Question	Answer
Why did immigrants come to the United States in the late 1800s?	To find religious freedom, to escape poverty, to flee persecution
What was life like for immigrants when they arrived?	It was hard at first, but opportunities opened up; sometimes they faced hostility and prejudice.

Predict

Engage in the reading process by making predictions about what you are preparing to learn. Scan the section headings and the visuals. Then, write a prediction, such as:

• "I will find out what caused the United States to fight Spain in 1898."

Keep your predictions in mind as you read—do they turn out to be accurate or do you need to revise them?

Use Prior Knowledge

Research shows that if you connect the new information in your reading to your prior knowledge, you'll be more likely to remember the new information. You'll also see the value of studying history if you see how it connects to the present. After previewing a section, create a chart like this one. Complete the chart as you read the section.

What I Know	What I Want to Know	What I Learned
Older Americans are worried about Social Security and whether it will provide for them when they retire.	When did Social Security start?	Social Security was a program that started during the Great Depression of the 1930s to help provide for older Americans when they retire.

Strategies to Use As You Read

It's important to be an active reader. Use these strategies as you read informational text.

Reread or Read Ahead

If you do not understand a certain passage, reread it to look for connections among the words and sentences. For example, look for cause-and-effect words that link ideas or sequence words that show when events took place. Or, try reading ahead to see if the ideas are clarified later on. Once you find new clarifying information, return to the confusing text and read it again with the new information in mind.

Paraphrase/Summarize

To paraphrase is to restate information in your own words. Summarizing—a version of paraphrasing—can also help you confirm your understanding of the text. Summarizing focuses on restating the main ideas of a passage, as you can see in the example below. Include a few important details, such as the time period, to orient yourself or other readers to the text.

Original Paragraph	Summary
During the 1920s, the National Women's Party took a more militant position, demanding complete economic, social, and political equality with men. Its primary goal was the passage of the Equal Rights Amendment. Most women, however, believed that a new constitutional amendment was premature.	In the 1920s, the National Women's Party demanded complete equality with men, working for passage of the Equal Rights Amendment. Most women thought it was too soon for such an amendment.

- Encourage students to predict what might happen in a given situation or what they might learn from a given text. For example, what do they predict might happen in the next presidential election? Ask **How might unfolding events affect their predictions?** Explain that predictions may need to be revised as new information becomes available. Have students fill in the *Predict* worksheet. Teaching Resources, Skills Handbook, **p. 3**

- Explain that students can use their own experiences and other history reading to make connections with new information. Model how to use the K-W-L chart on this page. Point out that the first column lists information that a reader knows before reading, that the second column lists the reader's questions, and that the third column is completed after reading. Have students fill in the *Use Prior Knowledge* worksheet. Teaching Resources, Skills Handbook, **p. 4**

Independent Practice

Ask students to choose a section of text from anywhere in their textbook. Have them use it to practice these prereading strategies.

Monitor Progress

Circulate to make sure that students are filling in their worksheets accurately.

Strategies to Use as You Read

Instruct

- **Introduce** Have students preview the black headings under *Strategies to Use as You Read.*

- **Teach** Explain that rereading or reading ahead to look for connections can help clarify a passage that is at first difficult to understand. Suggest a list of cause-and-effect and sequence words. Have students fill in the *Reread or Read Ahead* worksheet. Teaching Resources, Skills Handbook, **p. 5**

Differentiated Instruction   Solutions for All Learners

L1 Special Needs Students   **L2 Less Proficient Readers**   **L2 English Language Learners**

If students need extra practice paraphrasing and summarizing, have them choose a paragraph at random from their books. Using the steps in their text as a guide, students should paraphrase the selected paragraph. If students have omitted key information, point out the omission. Then, ask students to summarize the same text. Discuss how the paraphrases and summaries differ and the uses for each technique.

- Invite a volunteer to read aloud the original paragraph and summary about the Equal Rights Amendment, and discuss how the two versions differ. Then, ask **How are paraphrasing and summarizing different? How does each skill help you read critically?** *(Paraphrasing involves restating text in your own words. Summarizing is a version of paraphrasing and involves stating the main ideas of a passage. Both help you confirm your understanding of the text.)* Have students fill in the *Paraphrase/Summarize* worksheet. Teaching Resources, Skills Handbook, **p. 6**

- Ask students to look at the main ideas and details highlighted in the sample text and outline. **How is the main idea shown in the outline? How are the details shown?** *(The main idea is an outline section heading. The details are beneath that heading as subordinate entries.)* **How do the details support the main idea?** *(Each is an example of how the South changed economically.)* Have students fill in the *Identify Main Ideas and Details* worksheets. Teaching Resources, Skills Handbook, **p. 7**

- Explain that identifying the text structure helps the reader understand and remember its content. Ask students to summarize each type of structure (in the boxed text) in their own words and then discuss topics that lend themselves to each type. Have students fill in the *Analyze the Text's Structure* worksheet. Teaching Resources, Skills Handbook, **p. 8**

- Explain that understanding the author's purpose helps readers know how to approach a text. Discuss various approaches to reading different kinds of texts, such as a computer manual, an editorial, or a textbook. Have students fill in the *Analyze the Author's Purpose* worksheet. Teaching Resources, Skills Handbook, **p. 9**

Reading Informational Texts

Identify Main Ideas and Details

A main idea is the most important point in a paragraph or section of text. Some main ideas are stated directly, but others are implied. You must determine these yourself by reading carefully. Pause occasionally to make sure you can identify the main idea.

Main ideas are supported by details. Record main ideas and details in an outline format like the one shown here.

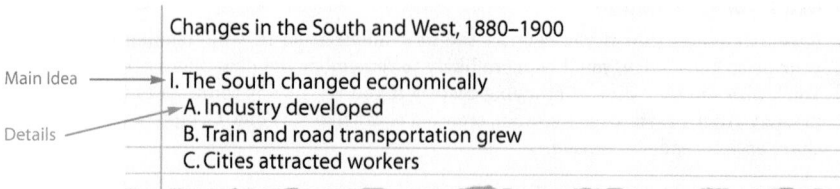

Changes in the South and West, 1880–1900

Main Idea → I. The South changed economically
Details → A. Industry developed
B. Train and road transportation grew
C. Cities attracted workers

Analyze the Text's Structure

Just as you might organize a story about your weekend to highlight the most important parts, authors will organize their writing to stress their key ideas. Analyzing text structure can help you tap into this organization. In a social studies textbook, the author frequently uses one of the structures listed in the chart at right to organize information. Learn to identify structures in texts and you'll remember text information more effectively.

Structures for Organizing Information

Compare and Contrast Here, an author highlights similarities and differences between two or more ideas, cultures, processes, people, etc. Look for clue words such as *on the other hand* or *similarly*.

Sequence Here, an author recounts the order in which events occurred or steps were taken. History is often told in chronological sequence but can also involve flashbacks from later times to earlier times. Look for sequence words such as *initially*, *later*, and *ultimately*.

Cause and Effect Here, an author highlights the impact of one event on another or the effects of key events. Cause and effect is critical to understanding history because events in one time often strongly influence those in later times. Look for clue words such as *because*, *so*, or *as a result*.

Analyze the Author's Purpose

Different reading materials are written with different goals, or purposes. For example, this textbook is written to teach you about American history. The technical manual that accompanies a cell phone is written to explain how to use the product.

An author's purpose influences not only how the material is presented but also how you read it. Thus you must identify the purpose, whether it is stated directly or merely suggested. If it is not directly stated, use clues in the text—such as opinion words in an editorial—to identify the author's purpose.

Differentiated Instruction Solutions for All Learners

L1 Special Needs Students **L2 Less Proficient Readers** **L2 English Language Learners**

Have students who need additional vocabulary practice choose a passage of text from anywhere in the Student Edition. Ask them to identify two or three unfamiliar words and then use context clues, word parts, or word origins to define the words. Next, have students check their definitions in a reference source and write sentences containing the words. Finally, have students share their sentences with the class.

Vocabulary

Here are several strategies to help you understand the meaning of a word you do not recognize.

Use Context Clues   You can often define an unfamiliar word with clues from the surrounding text. For example, in the sentence "One campaign of the Progressives had the goal of improving sanitation in cities," the words *campaign* and *improve* are clues that Progressives were reformers. Context clues can be in the same sentence as the unfamiliar word or in nearby sentences or paragraphs.

Analyze Word Parts   Use your knowledge of word parts to help you define unfamiliar words. Break the word into its parts—root, prefix, suffix. What do you know about these parts? For example, the prefix *inter* means "between" and the suffix *ism* means "belief in." The word *international* means "between nations" and *internationalism* means "belief in relations between nations."

Recognize Word Origins   Another way to figure out the meaning of an unfamiliar word is to understand the word's origins. Use your experience with Greek or Latin roots, for example, to build meaning. The word *bilingual* contains the Latin root *lingua,* which means "tongue." *Bilingual* means "two tongues" or "two languages."

Distinguish Between Facts and Opinions/Recognize Bias

It's important to read actively, especially when reading informational texts. Decide whether information is factual—which means it can be proven—or if it includes opinions or bias—that is, people's views or evaluations.

Anytime you read material that conveys opinions, such as an editorial, keep an eye out for author bias. This bias might be revealed in the use of emotionally charged words or faulty logic. For example, the newspaper editorial below includes factual statements (in blue) and opinion statements (in red). The emotionally charged words (underlined) will get a rise out of people. Faulty logic may include circular reasoning that returns to its beginning and either/or arguments that ignore other possibilities.

> **Editorial**
> Some day, Dwight Eisenhower will be remembered as the best President of the 20th century. He kept government small; he left the states alone to tend to their affairs; and the economy hummed. Any American with any sense will agree that these things contributed to the overall well-being of the nation.

Identify Evidence

Read critically. Do not accept an author's conclusion automatically. Identify and evaluate the author's evidence. Does it justify the conclusion in quantity and content? An author may present facts to support a claim, but there may be more to the story than facts. For example, what evidence does the writer of the editorial above present to support the claim that Eisenhower was a great President? Perhaps Americans who didn't prosper in the 1950s would disagree with the assertion.

- Review each vocabulary strategy with students. Model the strategies with the examples provided, and then help students find other examples in their textbooks or in other written materials. Have students fill in the following worksheets: *Vocabulary: Use Context Clues* worksheet. Teaching Resources, Skills Handbook, **p. 10** *Vocabulary: Analyze Word Parts* worksheet. Teaching Resources, Skills Handbook, **p. 11** *Vocabulary: Recognize Word Origins* worksheet. Teaching Resources, Skills Handbook, **p. 12**

- Explain that when evaluating informational text, students should be able to distinguish facts from opinions. Have students read the editorial in the text. Ask **How does the editorial show bias?** *(It uses emotionally charged language rather than facts to emphasize the author's opinions.)* Have students fill in the *Distinguish Between Facts and Opinions/Recognize Bias* worksheet. Teaching Resources, Skills Handbook, **p. 13**

- Tell students that identifying evidence is another way to read critically. Ask them to look again at the language highlighted in the sample editorial. **Does the evidence presented in this passage convince you that Eisenhower was a great President?** *(No; the evidence given is not detailed enough to support the idea that Eisenhower was the greatest President of the twentieth century.)* Have students fill in the *Identify Evidence* worksheet. Teaching Resources, Skills Handbook, **p. 14**

- Explain that *credible* means "believable and reliable." What makes an author credible? Explain that credibility is especially important in evaluating Internet sources. Discuss the list of questions for evaluating Web sites and ask students to consider the credibility of Web sites they have used. Have students fill in the *Evaluate Credibility* worksheet. Teaching Resources, Skills Handbook, **p. 15**

Independent Practice

Ask students to bring in an editorial from a local newspaper, or distribute copies of an appropriate editorial. Have students work in groups to apply *Strategies to Use as You Read* to the editorials.

Monitor Progress

Circulate to make sure that students are applying reading strategies correctly.

Strategies to Use After You Read

Instruct

- **Introduce** Explain that *Strategies to Use After You Read* allows readers to confirm understanding and organize information for future use.

- **Teach** Ask volunteers to read aloud each strategy under *Evaluate Understanding*. Discuss why each is useful. Ask students to identify which strategies are most important. Have them fill in the *Evaluate Understanding* worksheet. Teaching Resources, Skills Handbook, **p. 16**

- Ask volunteers to read each question under *Recall Information*. Explain that students should be able to answer these questions before continuing to read. Have students fill in the *Recall Information* worksheet. Teaching Resources, Skills Handbook, **p. 17**

Independent Practice

Have students choose one sample paragraph from their textbook. Ask them to write answers to the last three bulleted questions on this page on the basis of the sample.

Monitor Progress

If students cannot answer the *Strategies to Use After You Read* questions, urge them to reread the selected text and apply *Strategies to Use as You Read* again.

Evaluate Credibility

After you evaluate evidence, check an author's credentials. Consider his or her level of experience and expertise about the topic. Is he or she likely to be knowledgeable *and* objective about the topic? Evaluating credibility is especially important with Web sites you may visit on the Internet. Ask the following questions to determine if a Web site and its author are reliable.

- Who sponsors the Web site? Is it a respected organization, a discussion group of individuals, or a single person?
- What is the source of the Web site's information? Does the site list sources for facts and statements?
- Does the Web site creator include his or her name and credentials?
- Is the information on the Web site balanced and objective or biased to reflect only one point of view?
- Can you verify the Web site's information using two other sources, such as an encyclopedia or news agency?
- Is the information current? Is there a date on the Web site to show when it was created or last updated?

Strategies to Use After You Read

Evaluate Understanding

Evaluate how well you understand what you've read.
- Go back to the questions you asked yourself before reading. Try to answer each of them.
- Check the predictions you made and revise them if appropriate.
- Draw a conclusion about the author's evidence and credibility.
- Check meanings of unfamiliar words in the dictionary to confirm your definitions.

Recall Information

Before moving on to new material, you should be able to answer the following questions fully:
- What was the text about?
- What was the purpose of the text?
- How was the text structured?

You should also be able to place the information you have just read in the context of your prior knowledge of the topic.

Differentiated Instruction   Solutions for All Learners

L1 Special Needs   L2 Less Proficient Readers   L2 English Language Learners

If students are struggling, tell them to approach the task of reading informational text by asking themselves the following questions as they read: **What** is this text mainly about? **What** are the main ideas? **Which** words are unfamiliar, and **how** can I figure out their meanings? **Why** did the author write this? **How** has the author made his or her points—by

using facts, opinions, or biased text? **What** details or evidence has the author used to support the main idea? **Who** is the author, and what sources has he or she used? Have students practice asking and answering these questions with an editorial or newspaper article of your choice.

Writing Handbook

Writing is one of the most powerful communication tools you will use for the rest of your life. Research shows that writing about what you read actually helps you learn new information and ideas. A systematic approach to writing—including prewriting, drafting, revising, and proofreading—can always help you write better.

Narrative Essay

Narrative writing tells a story about a personal experience or a historical event. This story might also recount a person's life or tell about an important accomplishment.

1 Prewriting

Choose a topic. The focus of your essay will often be about a historical event from a particular point of view. Use these ideas as a guide.

- **Review the details of the event** you will be writing about.
- **Choose a person,** actual or fictional, who would have experienced the event.
- **List words** describing why the person caused the event or how he or she might have reacted to it.
- **Brainstorm** about the story you will write. Jot down ideas like the ones below.

> Teenager in the 1920s responds to hearing jazz music for the first time.
> • Circumstances: standing in the street outside an apartment building, overhearing a musician practicing
> • Reactions: startled at first because the music is different; intrigued; spellbound; wants to dance to the music; goes home and tries to play jazz

Consider audience and purpose.

- Keep your **audience's** knowledge and experience level in mind. Make sure you provide any necessary background information.
- Choose a **purpose** as well. If you want to entertain, include humorous details. You might also include more serious insights.

Gather details.

- Collect the facts and details you need to tell your story.
- Research any background about the historical event that readers might need to know about.

Step-by-Step Instruction

Objective

As you teach this section, keep students focused on the following objective to help them master core content.

- Use a systematic approach to write narrative, expository, research, persuasive, and assessment essays.

Prepare to Read

Background Knowledge

Ask students to name writing assignments that they have completed for school. Also, have them identify any outside writing they have done, such as letters, lists, or stories. Explain that all of these types of writing share certain writing purposes: to tell a story, to explain or share information about a topic or person, to persuade, or to demonstrate one's mastery of a topic.

Teach

Narrative Essay

Instruct

- **Introduce** Tell students that they will be asked to write narrative essays for school as a way of linking personal experience to a topic being studied. Point out that students are often asked to write a narrative essay in response to job or college applications that require information about how personal experiences have prepared candidates for the task ahead.

- **Teach** Discuss the *Prewriting* suggestions listed in the text, and ask volunteers to name specific instances in which they might apply each one. For example, a student may want to write about the struggles experienced by new immigrants to the United States, after reading about the life of a famous immigrant. Then, choose a topic such as "A New Immigrant's Experiences" and work through different scenarios for audience and purpose. Ask students to consider the prior knowledge of the intended audience and how that level of knowledge will affect the way the essay is written.

- Refer students to the *Writing Rubrics* on page SH20 so that they know what is expected.

- Students may find it helpful to write out the main events of their narratives in chronological order. They can then expand this list of events into an outline as they add details that will flesh out the story. They can also explore rearranging the events to allow for a flashback or other narrative break. Students might then organize sensory details in a concept web and apply them to enliven their narratives.

- Reassure students that dialogue will not suit every narrative. If their narrative has only one character, students may wish to use interior monologue to show the character's thoughts, or they may prefer to describe those thoughts through the narrative.

- Review the example under *First Draft* and *Revised Original*. Ask students to write simple sentences with general words on the board and then work together to replace that wording with more specific, descriptive, or active options. Have students fill in the *Narrative Essay* worksheet. Teaching Resources, Skills Handbook, p. 18

Independent Practice

Tell students to write a narrative essay about a recent experience that surprised them or changed their perspective in some way. Invite students to use one of the topic-generating ideas under *Prewriting* or to discuss topics with a peer. Remind students that you and their classmates may read their work, so they will want to make careful choices when sharing personal information.

Monitor Progress

Have students work in pairs to review each other's essays. Ask peer reviewers to identify at least two successful aspects of their partners' work before focusing on areas needing revision. Refer partners to the *Writing Rubrics* on page SH20 for formal evaluation criteria. Circulate to answer questions as needed.

---

2 Drafting

Identify the climax, or most interesting part of your story. Then, logically organize your story into a beginning, middle, and end. Narratives are often told in chronological order.

Open strongly with an engaging sentence, such as the one below, that will catch your reader's attention.

Use sensory details, such as sights, sounds, or smells, to make the story vivid for readers. Describe people's actions and gestures. Pinpoint and use detail to describe locations.

Write a conclusion that sums up the significance of the event or situation you are writing about.

Strong opening engages the reader.

Sensory details help the reader envision the experience.

Insight or significance tells the reader what this event means to the person in the narrative or to history.

> I never could have imagined how a simple stroll down the street would change my life. I was walking down the street yesterday, whistling to myself, when the most strange and enticing harmonies drifted toward me from an open third-floor window. Now, I'm pretty cool, but I've never heard such music before. It set me tingling; it set me to swaying. It made me want to dance right there on the spot. I emerged from the trance as the saxophonist let the last full note drift into the air. Then, I rushed home to see if I could replicate the smooth new sound on my clarinet. I know this chance encounter has changed my life forever.

3 Revising

Add dialogue or description. Dialogue, or conveying a person's thoughts or feelings in his or her own words, can make a narrative more effective. Look for places where the emotions are especially intense. In the model, this might be when the writer began to "feel" the music.

First Draft	Revised Original
The music made me feel very involved. It made me want to dance.	It set me tingling; it set me to swaying. It made me want to dance right there on the spot.

Revise word choice. Replace general words with more specific, colorful ones. Choose vivid action verbs, precise adjectives, and specific nouns to convey your meaning. Look at the example above. Notice how much more effective the revised version is at conveying the experience.

Read your draft aloud. Listen for grammatical errors and statements that are unclear. Revise your sentences as necessary.

4 Publishing and Presenting

Share by reading aloud. Highlight text you want to emphasize and then read your essay aloud to the class. Invite and respond to questions.

Differentiated Instruction   Solutions for All Learners

L4 Advanced Readers   L4 Gifted and Talented Students

Invite students to describe how they might change the narrative essay they wrote for *Independent Practice* if they wanted to include it in a job or college application. Ask whether they would change the topic, the tone, or any specific details. Challenge students to tell their stories to a partner orally, from memory, as they might do in a job interview. Have partners discuss how their stories changed in the oral retelling.

Expository Writing

Expository writing explains ideas or information in detail. The strategies on these pages examine each of several types of expository writing.

① Prewriting

Choose a topic. In social studies, the focus of your writing might be comparing and contrasting economic trends, explaining causes and effects of current events, or exploring problems the nation has faced and the solutions it has sought. These ideas are a guide.

- **Create a compare/contrast grab bag.** With a small group, write on separate slips of paper examples from each category: ideas, events, or time periods. Mix the slips in a bag and choose two. Compare and contrast the two ideas, events, or time periods.
- **Interview** someone who made a major change in lifestyle, such as moving from one part of the country to another. Find out how and why the person did this. Understanding why is the basis of any cause-and-effect essay.
- **Take a mental walk.** Study a map and envision taking a tour of the region. Think about problems each area you visit might face, such as economic challenges or natural disasters. Choose a problem and suggest solutions for it.

Consider audience and purpose. Consider how much your readers know about the problem, comparison, or event you will address. Suit your writing to your audience's knowledge or plan to give explanations of unfamiliar terms and concepts.

Gather details. Collect the facts and details you need to write your essay.

Research the topic. Use books, the Internet, or interviews of local experts. List facts, details, and other evidence related to your topic. Also consider your personal experience. For example, you might know about a problem from your own experience or have witnessed the effects of a historic legal decision.

Create a graphic organizer. For cause-and-effect or problem-solution essays, use a two-column chart. Process writing can be listed as a bulleted list of steps. A Venn diagram can help you compare and contrast.

World War I
- New weapons used: machine guns, poison gas, submarines
- 8.5 million military deaths

- Fought by two powerful alliances
- Began in Europe, then spread

World War II
- New weapon used: atomic bomb
- 20 million military deaths

Identify causes and effects. List possible explanations for events. Remember that many events result from multiple causes. Identify effects both large and small. Note that some events may have effects that in turn cause other events. Look for causes and effects in all your expository essays. But be aware that sometimes there are limitations on determining cause and effect.

Expository Writing

Instruct

- **Introduce** Tell students that expository writing may be the type they use most often in school. Expository writing assignments often require students to explain a process, make comparisons and contrasts, examine cause-and-effect relationships, or describe a problem and solution.

- **Teach** Lead students through the compare/contrast grab bag strategy by selecting time periods as your category. Then, use the Venn diagram on this page as a model to help students compare and contrast their chosen time periods. Have students fill in the *Expository Essay: Compare and Contrast* worksheet. Teaching Resources, Skills Handbook, **p. 19**

- Have students apply the "take a mental walk" strategy by using a U.S. or state map. Lead them through choosing a problem based on their "mental walk" and suggesting solutions to it. Have students complete the *Expository Essay: Problem and Solution* worksheet. Teaching Resources, Skills Handbook, **p. 21**

- Make a three-column chart on the board. Label the columns "Event," "Causes," and "Effects." Have students suggest a list of current events and fill in causes and effects for each. Have students fill in the *Expository Essay: Cause and Effect* worksheet. Teaching Resources, Skills Handbook, **p. 20**

- Refer students to the *Writing Rubrics* on page SH20 for clarification of writing expectations.

- Read the *Drafting* steps with students. Then, make two columns on the board: one listing types of essays mentioned in the text, such as cause-and-effect and problem-solution, and the other listing types of organization, such as sequence and block organization. Have students come to the board to match the type of essay with its corresponding style of organization. Discuss topics for each type of essay and ask students to create simple graphic organizers to show how the different essays could be structured.

- Encourage students to experiment with different organizational patterns for compare/contrast essays. Ask students to suppose that they are writing an essay comparing soccer and basketball. Ask **Which type of organization would you choose? Why?** *(Sample answers: There are advantages and disadvantages to both, but I prefer to organize my essay by subject because it is easier to make sure that I have included all the information./I prefer to organize my essay by point because it's easier to see connections.)*

- Model the steps in drafting an expository essay by working through the sample essay on changes in U.S. demographics in the twentieth century.

2 Drafting

Match structure to purpose. Typically, cause-and-effect essays are written in sequence order. Problem-solution essays benefit from block organization, which presents the entire problem and proposes a solution. For compare/contrast essays, you can organize by subject or by point.

By subject: Discuss the events and outcomes of World War I, and then compare and contrast these with those of World War II.
By point: Introduce a category, such as use of new weapons. Relate both wars to this category, comparing or contrasting them along the way.

Give background. To discuss events from history, first orient the reader to time and place. Choose the important facts but don't overwhelm the reader with detail. If you need to, return to prewriting to narrow your topic further.

Elaborate for interest and emphasis. Give details about each point in your essay. For example, add facts that make the link between events so that a cause-and-effect relationship is clear. Also, readers will support proposed solutions more if your details clearly show how these solutions will solve the stated problem. Use facts and human experiences to make your essay vivid.

Connect to today. Even when you write about historical events, you may find links to today. Explore these links in your essay.

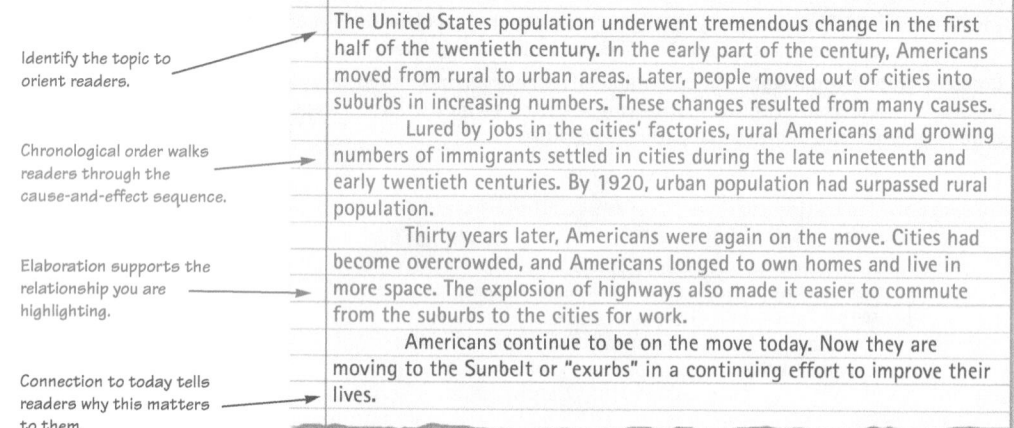

Identify the topic to orient readers.

The United States population underwent tremendous change in the first half of the twentieth century. In the early part of the century, Americans moved from rural to urban areas. Later, people moved out of cities into suburbs in increasing numbers. These changes resulted from many causes.

Chronological order walks readers through the cause-and-effect sequence.

Lured by jobs in the cities' factories, rural Americans and growing numbers of immigrants settled in cities during the late nineteenth and early twentieth centuries. By 1920, urban population had surpassed rural population.

Elaboration supports the relationship you are highlighting.

Thirty years later, Americans were again on the move. Cities had become overcrowded, and Americans longed to own homes and live in more space. The explosion of highways also made it easier to commute from the suburbs to the cities for work.

Connection to today tells readers why this matters to them.

Americans continue to be on the move today. Now they are moving to the Sunbelt or "exurbs" in a continuing effort to improve their lives.

Differentiated Instruction Solutions for All Learners

L1 Special Needs Students   **L2 Less Proficient Readers**   **L2 English Language Learners**

If students are struggling with writing essays, urge them to return to the *Prewriting* section and check their assumptions. Have students ask themselves the following questions: Is my topic narrow enough? Do I have enough information? Then encourage them to draft a brief outline of the main paragraphs or ideas they wish to cover before they begin to write. You may also want to encourage them to write for five or ten minutes on any subject as a warm-up to the more formal essay.

3 Revising

Add transition words. Make cause-and-effect relationships clear with words such as *because, as a result,* and so on. To compare or contrast ideas, use linking words, such as *similarly, both,* and *equally* or *in contrast, instead,* and *yet.* Use words such as *first, second, next,* and *finally* to help readers follow steps in a sequence or chain of causes. Look at the following examples. In the revised version, a reader knows the correct order in which to perform the steps.

First Draft	Revised
Historians form an educated guess called a hypothesis. They test that hypothesis with further research.	Next, historians form an educated guess called a hypothesis. Then, they test that hypothesis with further research.

Remember purpose. Shape your draft so that it answers the question or thesis you began with. For a problem-solution essay—in which your purpose is to sell your solution—that means anticipating opposing arguments and responding to them. For a cause-and-effect essay, you want to stress the way one event leads to the next. Always tell readers why they should care about your topic.

Review organization. Confirm that your ideas flow in a logical order. Write main points on index cards. Reorganize these until you are satisfied that the order best strengthens your essay.

Add details. Make sure you have not left out any steps in your essay, and do not assume readers will make the connections. For example, you might forget to state explicitly that your narrative represents a particular point of view. Add more background if necessary for clarity.

Revise sentences and words. Look at your sentence length. Vary it to include both short and long sentences. Then scan for vague words, such as *good.* Replace them with specific and vibrant words, such as *effective.* Use technical terms only when necessary, and then define them.

Peer review. Ask a peer to read your draft. Is it clear? Can he or she follow your ideas? Revise areas of confusion.

4 Publishing and Presenting

Contribute to a class manual. Include your comparison essay in a class History Journal.

Submit to a library. Find a specialized library, such as a presidential library. Mail your essay to the library's publications or public relations department.

Seek publication. If your historical events or issues are local, seek publication in a local historical magazine or contact a historical society. You might speak to its members.

Mail to an advocacy group. Find a local, national, or international organization that is concerned with your topic. Send it your essay and ask for comments on its ideas. Make sure to include a self-addressed stamped envelope and a note explaining your essay and offering thanks for its review.

- Read the *Revising* steps with students. Challenge students to use each transition word in the text in a sentence, as well as to add their own examples. Ask **Why is the Revised sample more effective than the First Draft?** *(It shows the order of events.)*

- Explain that even professional writers ask their peers to review their work. Explain that peers often use one another as "talking partners" to help clarify ideas that need further explanation.

- Read the *Publishing and Presenting* steps with students. Have students choose a publishing option from those listed or suggest one of their own. Ask them to explain why they believe that their essay is best suited to their chosen presentation format.

Independent Practice

Ask students to write an expository essay about a current issue related to American popular culture, such as music, films, books, video games, or fashion. Have students use one of the *Prewriting* steps listed and then choose the type of essay that best suits the topic.

Monitor Progress

Circulate to make sure that students are filling in their worksheets correctly and to provide guidance with essay planning and writing.

21st Century Skills

SKILLS HANDBOOK

Research Writing

Instruct

- **Introduce** Clarify that research writing results in an essay based heavily on information from outside sources beyond the writer's own knowledge. In addition to school work, research writing is often required in job settings, such as when an employer needs to learn about a new technology.

- **Teach** Read the steps for prewriting research essays with students. Invite students to share any questions they have.

- Point out several techniques for finding or refining a research topic. Urge students to choose topics that would interest general readers but that also interest them as writers. Research writing is time-consuming, and an interest in the topic will help students stay focused.

- Model dividing subjects into categories by working through the information on American agriculture in the 1800s found in the concept web on this page. Then, have students work in groups to choose a topic and create a web based on the one shown.

Research Writing

1 Prewriting

Choose a topic. Often, a teacher will assign your research topic. You may have flexibility in choosing your focus or you may have the opportunity to completely define your topic. These ideas are a guide.

- **Catalog scan.** Using a card or electronic catalog in a library, or Internet search engine, search for topics that interest you. When a title looks promising, find the book on the shelves. Or follow up on your Internet search results by reviewing the linked Web sites. You can use what you find to decide on your final topic.

- **Notes review.** Review your social studies notes from the last month or so. Jot down topics that you found interesting. Then repeat the process with your other classes. For example, you might find a starting point for research into an environmental issue from a biology experiment.

- **Social studies categories game.** With a group, brainstorm categories in social studies. For example, you might list key American leaders or important wars. Within each category, take turns adding subtopics. The chart below shows different topics related to agriculture.

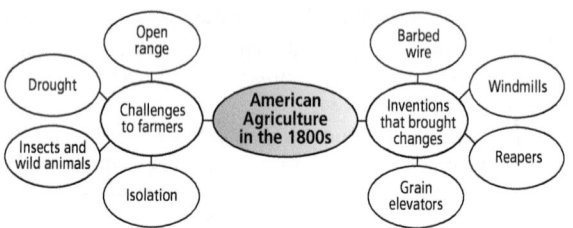

You can use sources such as newspapers to get ideas.

Analyze the audience. Your research and your paper should be strongly influenced by the audience. How much will readers know about this topic and how much will you have to teach them?

Gather details. Collect the facts and details you need to write your paper. Use resources beyond the typical history books. Look at nonfiction books such as memoirs or collections of letters. Also look at magazine and newspaper articles. Consider news magazines, as well as those focused on topics such as history or travel. Search the Internet, starting with online encyclopedias, news organizations, and history Web sites. Remember to check Web sites for reliability.

Organize evidence and ideas. Use note cards to record information and to help you organize your thoughts. Start with a general thesis statement in mind. Then begin reading and taking notes. Write a heading at the top of each note card to group it under a subtopic. Note a number or title to identify the information source. In the examples below, the number 3 is used. Use the same number for an additional source card containing the bibliographic information you will need.

Information source I.D. number

3   Background about barbed wire   **Heading**

p. 16
Invented in 1874

Bibliographic information for source 3

3
Razac, Oliver. *Barbed Wire: A Political History.* Cahners Business Information, Inc., 2002

Valley Regional High School Library

② Drafting

Fine-tune your thesis. Review your notes to find relationships between ideas. Shape a thesis that is supported by the majority of your information, then check that it is narrow enough to address thoroughly in the allotted time and space. Remember, you can fine-tune your thesis further as you draft or even when you revise.

Organize to fit your purpose. Do you want to persuade readers of a particular position about your topic, compare and contrast aspects of the topic, or show a cause-and-effect relationship? Organize appropriately.

Make an outline. Create an outline in which you identify each topic and subtopic in a single phrase. You can then turn these phrases into sentences and later into the topic sentences of your draft paragraphs. Study the example at the top of the next page to see how to do this well.

Write by paragraph. Write an introduction, at least three body paragraphs, and a conclusion. Address a subtopic of your main topic in each body paragraph. Support all your statements with the facts and details you gathered.

21st Century Skills

SKILLS HANDBOOK

- Review the sample note cards on this page. Have students identify and define each piece of information on the cards. Ask **How does the researcher identify his or her sources?** *(by numbering the cards)* Strongly encourage students to document facts as they research and write because to find one piece of information by returning to the source or to a stack of index cards can be very time-consuming.

- Refer students to the *Writing Rubrics* on page SH20 for clarification of writing expectations.

- Read the *Drafting* steps with students. To help students fine-tune a thesis, tell them to ask themselves questions such as the following: **According to my research, what are the main ideas I wish to communicate? Do I support or oppose the ideas and actions I have researched?** Urge students to discuss these questions with a peer if they are still struggling with a thesis statement. Have students fill in the *Research Writing* worksheet. Teaching Resources, Skills Handbook, **p. 22**

Differentiated Instruction   Solutions for All Learners

L1 Special Needs Students   **L2 Less Proficient Readers**   **L2 English Language Learners**

If students are having trouble starting their writing, tell them to skip the introduction and write a few paragraphs of the body of the essay. When the ideas in the body of the essay are more clearly expressed, students may find it easier to unite them in an introduction. Remind students that the ideas in the introduction must prepare readers for those in the body paragraphs.

- Review the sample outline on this page. Discuss each step in the outline, pointing out that the information is organized in a clear, logical fashion. Explain that each Roman numeral outline entry represents a paragraph of the essay. Point out that the Introduction puts the topic in context and conveys the thesis statement and that the Conclusion recaps key points and ends with a memorable statement.

- Read the *Revising* steps with students. Review the sample first draft, and discuss how the added details in the revision make the work of cowboys easier to understand.

- An important step in revising a research paper is rereading to confirm that each fact is documented. Stress the importance of documenting each fact, and point out that any undocumented fact should be deleted.

- Read the *Publishing and Presenting* suggestion with students. Point out that students should anticipate and prepare answers for questions that classmates are likely to ask.

Independent Practice

Have students consider and choose topics for a research paper. After they have selected a topic, have them work in groups to list possible sources of information.

Monitor Progress

Circulate to make sure that students are filling in their worksheets correctly and to provide guidance with selecting topics and searching for sources of information.

An outline helps you structure your information.

Each body paragraph looks at a part of the whole topic.

The introduction puts the topic in a context of time and place. The entire paragraph conveys the thesis: dividing up the Plains with barbed wire had lasting effects for the region.

The conclusion recaps key points and leaves readers with a final statement to remember.

The Importance of Barbed Wire
Outline

I. Introduction
II. Why barbed wire was invented
III. How barbed wire was used
IV. Effects of the use of barbed wire
    A. End of open grazing lands for cattle
    B. End of cowboys' way of life
    C. Increased importance of farming on the Plains
V. Conclusion

Introduction
No invention was more important to the development of the American Plains than barbed wire. Until its widespread use in the late 1800s, cattle herds roamed the Plains region and farmers worried about their crops getting trampled. With the advent of barbed wire, all of this changed.

Conclusion
By the end of the nineteenth century, the Plains had been sectioned off through the use of barbed wire. The earlier life on the Plains had been changed forever.

3 Revising

Add detail. Mark points where more details would strengthen your statements. Look at the following examples. Notice the added details in the revised version. When adding facts, make certain that they are accurate.

Make the connection for readers. Help readers find their way through your ideas. First, check that your body paragraphs and the information within them flow in a logical sequence. If they do not, revise to correct this. Then, add transition words to link ideas and paragraphs.

Give credit. Check that you have used your own words or given proper credit for borrowed words. You can give credit easily with parenthetical notes. These include the author's last name and the relevant page number from the source. For example, you could cite the note card on the previous page as "(Razac, 16)."

First Draft	Revised
Cowboys would ride the range with huge herds of cattle. Their goal was to bring the herd to Kansas for shipping to markets in Chicago and the East.	Cowboys worked long hours on the dusty Plains, keeping constant vigilance on their herd of hundreds of cattle. They always kept the goal in sight: reaching Kansas, a key shipping center, then taking a well-deserved rest.

4 Publishing and Presenting

Plan a conference. Gather a group of classmates and present your research projects. You may each wish to create visual materials to accompany your presentations. After you share your papers, hold a question-and-answer session.

Differentiated Instruction Solutions for All Learners

L1 Special Needs Students   L2 Less Proficient Readers   L2 English Language Learners

If students are struggling with research essays, urge them to return to the *Prewriting* phase and check their assumptions. Tell them to ask themselves questions like these: Is my topic narrow enough? Do I have enough information? If not, where can I find more information? Encourage students to draft a brief outline listing the main paragraphs or ideas they wish to cover and then to fill in supporting details as they do their research.

Persuasive Essay

Persuasive writing supports an opinion or position. In social studies, persuasive essays often argue for or against positions on historical or current issues.

❶ Prewriting

Choose a topic. Choose a topic that provokes an argument and has at least two sides. Use these ideas as a guide.

- **Round-table discussion.** Talk with classmates about issues you have studied recently. Outline pro-and-con positions about these issues.
- **Textbook flip.** Scan the table of contents or flip through the pages of your textbook. Focus on historical issues that engage your feelings.
- **Make connections.** Relate current events to history. Develop a position for or against a situation of importance today using historical evidence.

Narrow your topic.

- **Cover part of the topic** if you find too many pros and cons for a clear argument of the whole topic.
- **Use looping.** Write for five minutes on the general topic. Circle the most important idea. Then write for five minutes on that idea. Continue looping until the topic is manageable.

Consider your audience. Choose arguments that will appeal to the audience for your writing and that are likely to persuade them to agree with your views.

Gather evidence. Collect the evidence to support your position convincingly.

- **Identify pros and cons.** Use a graphic organizer like the one below to list points on both sides of the issue.

The United States should increase its efforts to send astronauts to Mars.	
Pro **Con**	
• Space travel increases human knowledge about Earth and inspires young people to learn about science.	• Space travel is too expensive.
• Space travel leads to technologies that can be used to improve life on Earth.	• Space travel is a luxury; the nation should concentrate on needs at home.
• The United States has a history of exploration beyond its borders; this would be just one more step.	• There is no need to send humans to Mars when we can learn as much from robots traveling there.

- **Interview** adults who remember the first moon landing. What do they think about sending astronauts to Mars? Ask them for reasons to support their views.
- **Research** to get your facts straight. Read articles or books about the space program.

❷ Drafting

State your thesis. Clearly state your position, as in this example:

> The United States should strongly promote the space program by sending people to Mars. We have so much to learn from the challenge of space travel that can help us at home.

Persuasive Essay ⓛ③

Instruct

- **Introduce** Show students an editorial from a current newspaper or magazine. Explain that it is a real-world example of persuasive writing. Invite students to suggest additional applications for persuasive writing, such as film reviews or advertisements.

- **Teach** Read the steps for prewriting persuasive essays with students. Tell them that the purpose of writing a persuasive essay is to persuade other people to share your viewpoint. However, clarify that persuasive essays must use solid, reliable evidence and arguments to support the writer's viewpoint.

- Review the suggestions for choosing a topic. On the basis of their prior knowledge, the textbook, and current events, lead students through an example of each strategy. Point out that students should write on a topic with which they can personally connect or that they can support. Writing persuasively is more effective when the writer has a distinct point of view.

- Direct students to scan the graphic organizer about U.S. exploration of Mars. Ask students to identify the side that makes the more persuasive points and explain their choice.

- Refer students to the *Writing Rubrics* on page SH20 for clarification of writing expectations. Have students fill in the *Persuasive Writing* worksheet. Teaching Resources, Skills Handbook, **p. 23**

- Read the *Drafting* steps with students. Invite a volunteer to read aloud the first sentence in the example under "State your thesis." This is the sample thesis statement. Point out that its strength is that it clearly states a position. Invite another volunteer to read aloud the second sentence in the example. Explain that this statement is the overarching reason to support the author's position. By using these two statements, readers then know what to expect from the essay to follow.

- Remind students to research to provide specific supporting information. Ask **Why is an argument supported with facts and examples more effective than one without these features?** (*Such an argument appeals to the reader's intelligence and reason, rather than stating an emotional position.*)

- Review the sample draft on this page. Ask **Where does the main argument appear?** (*in the third and fourth sentence of the first paragraph*) **Where else could it appear for equal effectiveness?** (*at the beginning of the first paragraph*)

- Walk students through the features of the sample draft, identifying the highlighted elements and confirming students' understanding.

- Read the *Revising* steps with students. Point out that to revise a persuasive essay, students should check for areas in which information should be added, areas of faulty logic, or places at which transition words could help guide readers through the argument.

- Discuss the sample first draft and revision. Ask **Why is the revision an improvement over the first draft?** (*It is more specific and contains more details.*)

- Read the *Publishing and Presenting* suggestion with students. Model the way speakers use emphasis, gesture, tone, volume, and speed in oral presentations. Stress that persuasive speech should be delivered with feeling, but should never involve shouting or emotional extremes. These distract listeners from the speaker's ideas.

Independent Practice

Ask students to write a persuasive essay about a topic that matters to them, such as restrictions on free speech, the length of the high-school day, the military draft age, or the value of competitive sports in high school. Have students discuss their positions in pairs; each partner will state his or her topic and position, and the other partner will refute it.

Monitor Progress

Circulate to make sure that students are filling in their worksheets correctly and are staying focused on their topics for a persuasive essay.

Writing Handbook:
Persuasive Essay

Use your introduction to provide a context for the issue. Tell your readers when and why the issue arose, and identify the important people involved.

Sequence your arguments. Open or close with your strongest argument. If you close with the strongest argument, open with the second-best argument.

Acknowledge opposition. State, and then refute, opposing arguments.

Use facts and details. Include quotations, statistics, or comparisons to build your case. Include personal experiences or reactions to the topic, such as those a family member might have shared when interviewed.

Write a conclusion that restates your thesis and closes with a strong, compelling argument.

Background orients readers. →

Thesis identifies your main argument. →

Supporting argument clarifies your thesis. →

Opposing argument, noted and refuted, adds to your position. →

> For a long time, the United States led the world in space exploration. But recently, the space program has become more limited. This situation should change. The United States should strongly promote the space program by sending people to Mars. We have so much to learn from meeting the challenge of space travel that can help us here at home.
>
> Sending people into space has already yielded great rewards in the development of technology and other advances. Improved computers, medicines, and GPS systems are all positive by-products of space exploration. Some people might argue that space exploration is too expensive and that we have problems to tackle right here at home. However, the benefits of space exploration will help us at home today and in the future. The benefits outweigh the costs....

---

3 Revising

Add information. Extra details can generate interest in your topic. For example, in the essay on space travel, add a quotation from a news article that assesses the importance of space exploration to solving problems on Earth.

Review arguments. Make sure your arguments are logically sound and clearly developed. Avoid faulty logic such as circular reasoning (arguing a point by merely restating it differently). Evidence is the best way to support your points. Look at the following examples. Notice how much more effectively the revised version supports the argument.

First Draft	Revised
Space exploration will help our nation in many ways.	Space exploration will provide jobs, new technologies, and inspiration to young scientists.

Use transition words to guide readers through your ideas.
- **To show contrast:** *however, although, despite*
- **To point out a reason:** *since, because, if*
- **To signal conclusion:** *therefore, consequently, so, then*

4 Publishing and Presenting

Persuasive Speech. Many persuasive essays are delivered orally. Prepare your essay as a speech, highlighting words for emphasis and adding changes in tone, volume, or speed.

Differentiated Instruction   Solutions for All Learners

L1 Special Needs Students   **L2 Less Proficient Readers**   **L2 English Language Learners**

If students are having trouble organizing their ideas, organize them in groups and assign each group a topic from the *Independent Practice* activity above. Ask each group member to write an important idea on a slip of paper or index card. Then, have group members work together to sort the ideas into categories. Point out that the ideas in each category belong together in one paragraph with its own topic sentence.

Writing for Assessment

Assessment writing differs from all other writing that you do. You have many fewer choices as a writer, and you almost always face a time limit. In social studies, you'll need to write both short answers and extended responses for tests. While these contrast in some ways, they share many requirements.

❶ Prewriting

Choose a topic. Short-answer questions seldom offer a topic choice. For extended-response questions, however, you may have a choice of more than one question. Use the following strategies to help you navigate that choice.

- **Examine the question.** To choose a question you can answer effectively, analyze what each question is asking. Use key words such as those listed below to help you choose topics and respond to short-answer questions in which the topic is given.

Key Words	What You Need in an Answer
Explain	Give a clear, complete account of how something works or why something happened.
Compare/Contrast	Show how two or more things are alike and different.
Define	Give examples to explain meaning.
Argue, Convince, Support, Persuade	Take a position on an issue and present strong reasons to support your side of the issue.
Summarize	Provide the most important elements of a subject.
Evaluate/Judge	Assign a value or explain an opinion.
Interpret	Support a thesis with examples from the text.

Notice in the examples below that the key words are underlined:

> **Short answer:** <u>Describe</u> one way that Chief Joseph showed his <u>military expertise</u>.
>
> **Extended response:** According to the author of this article, Chief Joseph was both a <u>peace chief</u> and a <u>military genius</u>. Use information from the article to <u>support this conclusion</u>.

- **Plot your answer.** After choosing a question, quickly plot the answer in your mind. Do you have the information to answer this question? If the answer is no, try another question.

Measure your time. Your goal is to show the instructor that you've mastered the material. To stay focused on this goal, divide your time: one-quarter on prewriting; half on drafting; one-quarter on revising. For short-answer questions, determine how much of the overall test time you can spend on each question. Don't spend more than that.

Gather details. Organize the facts and details you need to write your answer. For short-answer questions, this usually involves identifying exactly what information is required.

Writing for Assessment L3

Instruct

- **Introduce** Ask students to name the in-class and high-stakes tests they have completed recently. Discuss how many of these included writing components. Have students note how often they are asked to write for assessment. Explain that developing strategies for successful assessment writing will greatly enhance students' chances for school success.

- **Teach** With students, read the steps for prewriting assessment responses. Invite and answer any questions students may have.

- Highlight the issue of question choice. Ask **Why might choosing a particular question be important?** (*It allows me to focus on areas of greater knowledge or on structures I find easier.*)

- Review the boxed list of key words. Provide students with a few questions from a recent assessment, or discuss suitable questions on the board. Ask students to identify key words in each question by underlining them, as shown in the examples on this page.

- Remind students that prewriting for assessment includes quickly plotting the answer to make sure that they have chosen the best question, measuring their time, and gathering facts and details.

- Have students compare the extended-response question about Chief Joseph with the graphic organizer outlining an answer. Ask **How is the question reflected in the headings of the organizer? How will this help the writer plan a response?** *(Each underlined key element has a main heading in the organizer. This allows the writer to plan supporting details for each required point in the question.)*

- Refer students to the *Writing Rubrics* on page SH20 for clarification of writing expectations. Have students fill in the *Writing for Assessment* worksheet. Teaching Resources, Skills Handbook, **p. 24**

- Read the *Drafting* steps with students. Review the discussion about choosing an organization to fit the purpose. Ask **For which type of essay should you organize material in chronological order?** *(a summary or explanation)*

- Stress the value of restating the question at the beginning of the answer. Explain that doing so is immensely useful in focusing the response. Have students link the opening sentence of the sample response to the extended-response question about Chief Joseph. Ask them to circle words that appear in both texts. *(Chief Joseph, both, peace chief, military genius)*

Writing Handbook:
Writing for Assessment

Use a graphic organizer. For extended-response questions, divide your topic into subtopics that fit the type of question. Jot down facts and details for each. For the question on Chief Joseph, the following organizer would be effective:

Chief Joseph of the Nez Percés
Peace Chief
• traded peacefully with white settlers (1)
• reluctantly went to war (2)
• famous speech, "I will fight no more forever." (3)
Military Genius
• won battles with fewer warriors than opposing troops had (a)
• avoided capture for many months (b)
• led his people more than 1,000 miles (c)
• knew when to surrender for the good of his people (d)

2 Drafting

Choose an organization that fits the question. With a short-answer question, write one to three complete sentences. With extended responses, you'll need more elaborate organization. For the question on Chief Joseph, organize your points by importance within each subtopic. For a summary or explanation, use chronological order. For compare/contrast, present similarities first, then differences.

Open and close strongly. Start your answer by restating the question or using its language to state your position. This helps you focus and shows the instructor that you understand the question. Finish with a strong conclusion that restates your position. For short answers, include some language from the question in your response.

> One way that Chief Joseph showed his military expertise was by defeating U.S. Army troops despite having fewer warriors than they had.

Support your ideas. Each paragraph should directly or indirectly support your main idea. Choose facts that build a cohesive argument. The numbered sentences in the draft below show how this writer organized support.

The opening restates the question and presents the writer's main idea.

The writer uses information from the graphic organizer, in order of importance.

The writer supports the second subtopic in a separate paragraph.

The conclusion recaps the main idea and again references the question's language.

> Chief Joseph was both a peace chief and a military genius. He was a peace chief because he traded peacefully with white settlers for many years. (1) He went to war reluctantly after the government ordered his people to move to a reservation. (2) When he finally surrendered, he said in a famous speech, "I will fight no more forever." (3)
> Chief Joseph was also a military genius. He fought off U.S. Army forces with fewer warriors than they had, (a) and he avoided capture for many months. (b) He led his people more than 1,000 miles (c) before he made the decision to surrender. (d) Chief Joseph will long be remembered for his dual roles as peace chief and military genius.

Differentiated Instruction Solutions for All Learners

L1 Special Needs Students   **L2 Less Proficient Readers**   **L2 English Language Learners**

Emphasize the importance of reading directions and looking for key words in writing an assessment essay. Help students who need extra practice by having them copy the chart on the student page onto a sheet of notebook paper. Tell students to label the left side of the paper "key words" and the right side "What you need in an answer." Then, have students fold the paper in half. For each key word, have them describe what they need in an answer.

❸ Revising

Examine word choice. Replace general words with specific words. Add transitions where these improve clarity. Read the following examples. The revised version shows the relative importance of the writer's supporting evidence.

First Draft	Revised
Chief Joseph was both a peace chief and a military genius. He was a peace chief because he traded peacefully with whites for many years. He went to war reluctantly....	Chief Joseph was both a peace chief and a military genius. He was a peace chief for several reasons. First, he traded peacefully with whites for many years. Second, he went to war reluctantly....

Check organization. Make sure your introduction includes a main idea and defines subtopics. Review each paragraph for a single main idea. Check that your conclusion summarizes the information you've presented.

❹ Publishing and Presenting

Edit and proof. Check spelling, grammar, and mechanics. Make sure that tenses match, that subjects agree with verbs, and that sentences are not too long. Finally, confirm that you have responded to all the questions you were asked to answer.

- Read the *Revising* steps with students. Have them read the First Draft and Revised examples in the boxed text. Ask students to list words added to the Revised version and then explain how each addition or change makes the text about Chief Joseph more effective.

- Emphasize the importance of good time management. Tell students that revising can be a critical step in assessment writing and that they must resist the impulse to skip it. Have students complete the organizational check by circling the main idea in each paragraph of an essay that they have written or that you provide.

- Show students some samples of high-scoring assessment essays from previous years. Ask students to identify the strengths in each essay.

- Read the *Publishing and Presenting* step with students. Remind students to make all corrections neatly in the space between lines, using standard editing marks to indicate insertions and deletions.

Independent Practice

Give students a sample assessment question on a topic with which they are familiar. Allow them an appropriate amount of time to respond to the question.

Monitor Progress

Circulate to make sure that students are filling in their worksheets accurately. Make sure that they are staying on task and monitoring their time appropriately as they complete the *Independent Practice* activity. If students are spending too much time on planning, give them a discreet reminder to move on to the next step. If students appear stuck, refer them to the *Prewriting* steps and urge them to repeat their examination of the question.

Writing Rubrics

Instruct

- **Introduce** Poll students on how many plan to take the SAT or ACT exams. Explain that an important part of these exams now involves essay writing.

- **Teach** Explain that the *Writing Rubrics* on this page show students how their essays on the SAT and ACT exams will be scored. Ask volunteers to name the criteria that are used to rate essays for the SAT and the criteria used to rate the ACT. Then ask students to explain in their own words the qualities that distinguish a good essay from a weak one on both tests. Have students fill in the *Writing Rubrics* worksheet. Teaching Resources, Skills Handbook, **p. 25**

Independent Practice

Ask each student to choose the best essay that he or she has written so far and evaluate it by using the rubrics on this page.

Monitor Progress

Collect students' essays and self-evaluations. Meet with students individually to go over good points and areas for improvement.

Writing Rubrics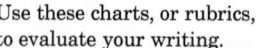

Use these charts, or rubrics, to evaluate your writing.

SAT	
SCORE OF 6 An essay in this category is **outstanding**, demonstrating **clear and consistent mastery**, although it may have a few minor errors. A typical essay • effectively and insightfully develops a point of view on the issue and demonstrates outstanding critical thinking, using clearly appropriate examples, reasons, and other evidence to support its position • is well organized and clearly focused, demonstrating clear coherence and smooth progression of ideas • exhibits skillful use of language, using a varied, accurate, and apt vocabulary • demonstrates meaningful variety in sentence structure • is free of most errors in grammar, usage, and mechanics	**SCORE OF 3** An essay in this category is **inadequate**, but demonstrates **developing mastery**, and is marked by **one or more** of the following weaknesses: • develops a point of view on the issue, demonstrating some critical thinking, but may do so inconsistently or use inadequate examples, reasons, or other evidence to support its position • is limited in its organization or focus, and may demonstrate some lapses in coherence or progression of ideas • displays developing facility in the use of language, but sometimes uses weak vocabulary or inappropriate word choice • lacks variety or demonstrates problems in sentence structure • contains an accumulation of errors in grammar, usage, and mechanics
SCORE OF 5 An essay in this category is **effective**, demonstrating **reasonably consistent mastery**, although it will have occasional errors or lapses in quality. A typical essay • effectively develops a point of view on the issue and demonstrates strong critical thinking, generally using appropriate examples, reasons, and other evidence to support its position • is well organized and focused, demonstrating coherence and progression of ideas • exhibits facility in the use of language, using appropriate vocabulary • demonstrates variety in sentence structure • is generally free of most errors in grammar, usage, and mechanics	**SCORE OF 2** An essay in this category is **seriously limited**, demonstrating **little mastery**, and is flawed by **one or more** of the following weaknesses: • develops a point of view on the issue that is vague or seriously limited, demonstrating weak critical thinking, providing inappropriate or insufficient examples, reasons, or other evidence to support its position • is poorly organized and/or focused, or demonstrates serious problems with coherence or progression of ideas • displays very little facility in the use of language, using very limited vocabulary or incorrect word choice • demonstrates frequent problems in sentence structure • contains errors in grammar, usage, and mechanics so serious that meaning is somewhat obscured
SCORE OF 4 An essay in this category is **competent**, demonstrating **adequate mastery**, although it will have lapses in quality. A typical essay • develops a point of view on the issue and demonstrates competent critical thinking, using adequate examples, reasons, and other evidence to support its position • is generally organized and focused, demonstrating some coherence and progression of ideas • exhibits adequate but inconsistent facility in the use of language, using generally appropriate vocabulary • demonstrates some variety in sentence structure • has some errors in grammar, usage, and mechanics	**SCORE OF 1** An essay in this category is **fundamentally lacking**, demonstrating **very little** or **no mastery**, and is severely flawed by **one or more** of the following weaknesses: • develops no viable point of view on the issue, or provides little or no evidence to support its position • is disorganized or unfocused, resulting in a disjointed or incoherent essay • displays fundamental errors in vocabulary • demonstrates severe flaws in sentence structure • contains pervasive errors in grammar, usage, or mechanics that persistently interfere with meaning
	SCORE OF 0 Essays not written on the essay assignment will receive a score of zero.

ACT	Scores of 4–6	Scores of 1–3
Purpose	shows a clear understanding of the essay's purpose by articulating a perspective and developing ideas	does not clearly articulate a perspective
Support	most generalizations developed with specific examples to support the perspective	demonstrates some development of ideas but may be overly general or repetitious
Focus	clear focus maintained throughout	focus maintained on general prompt topic but is not sufficiently specific
Language	shows competent use of language	language is mostly understandable, organization is clear but simple
Mechanics	minimal errors that only occasionally distract and do not interfere with meaning	errors frequently distract and interfere with meaning

Critical Thinking About Visuals and Text Sources

Analyze Graphic Data

The study of history requires that you think critically about the text you're reading as well as any visuals or media sources. This section will allow you to practice and apply some important skills for critical thinking.

Graphs show numerical facts in picture form. Bar graphs and line graphs compare things at different times or places, such as changes in school enrollment. Circle graphs show how a whole is divided into parts. To interpret a graph, look closely at its features. Use the graphs below and the steps that follow to practice analyzing graphic data.

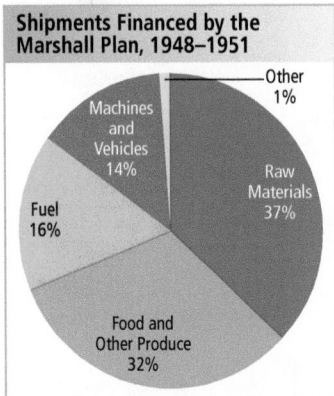

Shipments Financed by the Marshall Plan, 1948–1951
- Other 1%
- Machines and Vehicles 14%
- Raw Materials 37%
- Fuel 16%
- Food and Other Produce 32%

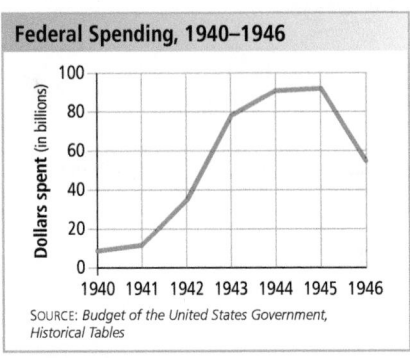

Federal Spending, 1940–1946

SOURCE: *Budget of the United States Government, Historical Tables*

Read the title to learn the main topic of the graph.

Use labels and the key to read the data given in the graph. The line graph is labeled in years, with single-year intervals. The different colors on the circle graph represent the different shipments.

Interpret the graph. Look for interesting patterns in the data. Look at changes over time or compare information for different categories.

Practice and Apply the Skill

Use the graphs above to answer the following questions:
1. What is the title of the line graph? What is its topic?
2. In which year did federal spending increase at the fastest rate? State two generalizations that are supported by the graph.
3. The Marshall Plan was a program under which the United States helped European countries devastated by World War II. According to the circle graph, what proportion of shipments contained fuel? What proportion of shipments contained items that could help factories run?
4. Could the information in the circle graph be shown as a line graph? Explain.

Independent Practice

Have students complete the Practice and Apply questions. Discuss their responses as a class.

Monitor Progress

As students answer the questions, circulate to confirm their understanding. Make sure that they can identify each feature of the graphs, and urge them to use the lesson suggestions for help.

Answers

1. Federal Spending, 1940–1946; billions of federal dollars spent between the years 1940 and 1946.
2. 1942; federal spending rose sharply during World War II; federal spending did not return to prewar levels directly following the war.
3. 16%; 68%—raw materials, fuel, and machines/vehicles combined
4. No; the information does not show change over time, which is the purpose of a line graph.

Step-by-Step Instruction

Objective

As you teach this section, keep students focused on the following objective to help them master core content.

- Use a systematic approach to critically analyze and evaluate visual and text sources.

Prepare to Read

Background Knowledge L3

Assign students to small groups and give them five minutes to list as many visual sources as they can. Then, write some examples on the board, such as political cartoons, newspapers, public records, advertisements, graphs and maps, and timelines. Explain that responding critically to these materials will help students become more active readers and achieve greater success in their assignments.

Teach

Analyze Graphic Data L3

Instruct

- **Introduce** Tell students that they will encounter graphs frequently in the study of both history and current events, whether in a textbook, on a test, or in a local newspaper. Explain that being able to read graphs quickly and accurately can help students maximize the information they learn from such sources.

- **Teach** Have students read the steps under Analyze Graphic Data and share any questions they have. Invite a student to read the graph titles and describe the main topic of each. Have students identify the labels and other information on both graphs. Have students fill in the *Analyze Graphic Data* worksheet. Teaching Resources, Skills Handbook, p. 26

Analyze Maps L3

Instruct

- **Introduce** Explain that maps can show different types of information. **What does the map on this page show?** *(explorations of the United States; territories claimed by different nations as of 1807)* Discuss different ways in which the focus on this same geographic area could be different. For example, it could show physical features, political boundaries at other times, weather, natural resources, economic activity, and so on.

- **Teach** Have students read the steps under *Analyze Maps* and share any questions they have. Emphasize the importance of using the key when analyzing special-purpose maps. Have students fill in the *Analyze Maps* worksheet. Teaching Resources, Skills Handbook, **p. 27**

Independent Practice

Have students complete the Practice and Apply questions. Discuss their responses as a class.

Monitor Progress

Circulate to make sure that students are answering the Practice and Apply questions accurately and to answer any additional questions they have.

Answers

1. to show early explorations across what would become the continental United States; most of North America
2. Lewis's return trip
3. Natchitoches
4. the Louisiana Purchase
5. Not explicitly; it does show how much the United States was enlarged by it, however.

Critical Thinking:
Analyze Maps

Analyze Maps

Maps can show many different types of information. A physical map represents what a region looks like by showing its major physical features, such as mountains and plains. A political map focuses on elements related to government, such as nations, borders, and cities.

A special-purpose map provides information on a specific subject—for example, land use, population distribution, natural resources, or trade routes. Road maps are special-purpose maps, as are weather maps. These maps often use a variety of colors and symbols to show different pieces of information, so the key is very important. Use the map below and the steps that follow to practice analyzing a special-purpose map.

Louisiana Purchase

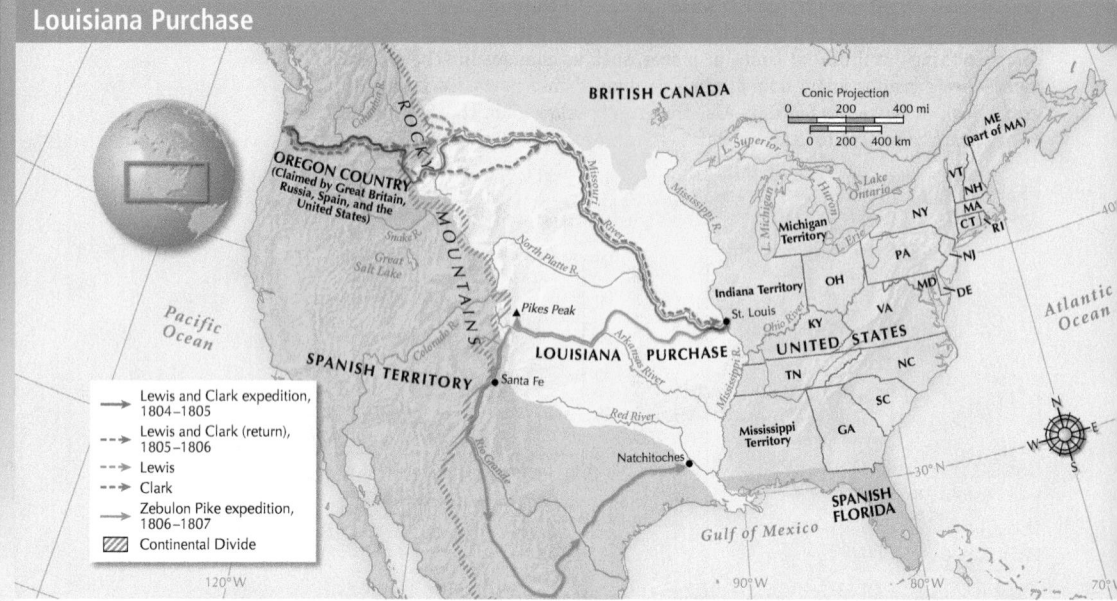

Study the title, locator globe, scale bar, and compass rose. Together, these features tell you the map's context—what part of the world it shows and why.

Read the key. Use the key to learn the specific details shown on the map.

Apply the key and labels to the map. Locate the symbols, lines, or colors from the key on the map. Also, read any labels on the map. Then, use the information given in the key and labels to understand what the map shows.

Practice and Apply the Skill

Use the map above to answer the following questions:

1. What is the purpose of this map? What part of the world does it show?
2. What does the red dotted line on the map represent?
3. Where did Zebulon Pike's expedition end?
4. Through which region did Lewis and Clark travel on their way to Oregon Country?
5. Does the map provide information about the effects of the Louisiana Purchase? Explain.

Differentiated Instruction   Solutions for All Learners

L4 Advanced Readers   L4 Gifted and Talented Students

Assign small groups to create a mini-atlas of special purpose maps on one region of the United States. Each group should be responsible for one of these regions: New England, the Middle Atlantic States, the Southeast, the Southwest, the Midwest, and the West. After students have chosen a region, have them suggest a list of special-purpose maps, such as

physical, political, trade routes, economic activities, national parks, and so on, that would be useful to someone studying the region. Then, have students collect data for their maps and create them. Finally, collect student maps in a United States Regions notebook to share with the class.

Analyze Images

Television, film, the Internet, and print media all carry images that seek to convey information or influence attitudes. To respond, you must develop the ability to understand and interpret visuals. Use the photograph below and the steps that follow to practice analyzing images.

In the 1950s, people everywhere worried about nuclear attacks. This 1952 image shows schoolchildren and their teacher ducking under desks during a nuclear air raid drill.

Identify the content. Look at all parts of the image and determine which are most important.

Note emotions. Study facial expressions and body positions. Consider the emotions they may suggest.

Read captions/credits. Gather information about the image, such as when it was produced.

Study purpose. Consider who might have created this image. Decide if the purpose was to entertain, inform, or persuade.

Consider context. Determine the context in which the image was created—in this case, the Cold War between the United States and the Soviet Union.

Respond. Decide if a visual's impact achieves its purpose—to inform, to entertain, or to persuade.

Practice and Apply the Skill

Use the photograph above to answer the following questions:

1. What is the focus of this photograph?
2. What feelings are conveyed by the children's facial expressions?
3. What do you think the photograph's purpose is?
4. When was this image produced? How did historical context influence its production?

Analyze Images

Instruct

- **Introduce** Write the saying "A picture is worth a thousand words" on the board, and discuss its meaning with students. Point out how important it is to recognize and critically evaluate the message in every visual image, especially if that message is meant to persuade viewers.

- **Teach** Have students read the steps under *Analyze Images* and share any questions they have. Then ask volunteers to complete one step to analyze the photograph for the class. Invite other students to add information or comment on the analysis. Reach consensus on the content, background, purpose, and context of the photograph, as well as on the emotions it conveys. Have students fill in the *Analyze Images* worksheet. Teaching Resources, Skills Handbook, **p. 28**

Independent Practice

Have students complete the Practice and Apply questions. Discuss their responses as a class.

Monitor Progress

As students complete the Practice and Apply questions, clarify any issues that are causing confusion. Remind students to look for key words in the questions that will help them identify the information that is being sought.

Differentiated Instruction   Solutions for All Learners

**Special Needs Students**   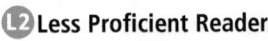**Less Proficient Readers**   **English Language Learners**

Help students who need more practice in analyzing graphic data and other visuals by having them skim their textbooks to choose a graph, chart, diagram, photograph, or painting for further analysis. Remind students of the steps in their text for analyzing graphic data and visuals, and then ask them to lead a small group in an analysis of their chosen piece.

Answers

1. schoolchildren ducking under their desks during a nuclear air raid drill
2. Sample answer: doubt, fear, apprehension
3. Possible response: Originally, it may have been to show children what to do during an air raid.
4. 1952; in the 1950s, people were worried about nuclear attacks and held drills such as these.

Analyze Primary Sources

Instruct

- **Introduce** Ask students to locate examples of primary sources in their textbooks, such as photographs, political cartoons, and quotations, and discuss why each is a primary source. Explain that writers often use the key ideas or facts in a primary source to support or amplify a point in the text.

- **Teach** Have students read the steps under *Analyze Primary Sources* and share any questions they have. Then, have a student read aloud the introduction to the primary source quotation and the quotation itself. Work as a group to paraphrase the quotation, and then help students work through the listed steps to analyze it. Have students fill in the *Analyze Primary Sources* worksheet. Teaching Resources, Skills Handbook, **p. 29**

Independent Practice

Have students complete the Practice and Apply questions. Discuss their responses as a class.

Monitor Progress

As students complete the questions, circulate to provide guidance. If necessary, ask additional questions to help facilitate understanding. For example: **Why is Europe shown in flames? What is the dome in the background? Who is "her" in the caption?**

Answers

1. World War II
2. democracy; the United States
3. Possible responses: the destruction of Europe; the consequences for democracy if the United States intervenes
4. that the United States should stay out of the war in Europe

SH24

Analyze Primary Sources

Primary sources include official documents and firsthand accounts of events or visual evidence such as photographs, paintings, and political cartoons. Such sources provide valuable information about the past. Use the excerpt below and the steps that follow to learn to analyze primary sources.

In 1914, a great war broke out in Europe. Americans debated whether the United States should take sides in the war. In this excerpt, President Wilson expresses his views:

> **Primary Source** ❝The people of the United States are drawn from many nations, and chiefly from the nations now at war. It is natural and inevitable that there should be the utmost variety of sympathy and desire among them. . . . Some will wish one nation, others another, to succeed in the momentous struggle. . . . The people of the United States, whose love of their country and whose loyalty to its government should unite them as Americans all, . . . may be divided in camps of hostile opinion. . . .
>
> Such divisions amongst us would be fatal to our peace of mind and might seriously stand in the way of the proper performance of our duty as the one great nation at peace.❞
>
> —speech by Woodrow Wilson, August 19, 1914

Read the headnote, caption, or attribution line. Determine the source's historical context—who wrote it, when, and why.

Read the primary source. Identify and define unfamiliar words. Then, look for the writer's main point.

Identify facts and opinions. Facts can be proven. Opinions reflect a person's views or feelings. Use clues to help identify opinion words: exaggeration, phrases such as *I think*, or descriptive words such as *gorgeous*.

The Only Way We Can Save Her

" STAY OUT! STAY OUT FOR MY SAKE, AS WELL AS YOUR OWN!"

DEMOCRACY

AMERICA THE LAST REFUGE OF DEMOCRACY

Identify bias and evaluate credibility. Consider whether the author's opinions suggest bias. Evaluate other factors that might lead to author bias, such as his or her previous experiences. Decide if the author knows enough to be credible and was objective enough to be reliable. Determine whether the source might be propaganda, that is, material published to promote a policy, an idea, or a cause.

Practice and Apply the Skill

Political cartoons reflect an artist's observations about events of the time. They often use symbols to represent things or exaggeration to make a point. Use the cartoon at left to answer the following questions.

1. What was happening in Europe when this cartoon was published?
2. What does the kneeling woman represent? the man?
3. What is exaggerated in this cartoon?
4. What opinion is the cartoonist expressing?

Differentiated Instruction   Solutions for All Learners

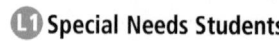**Special Needs Students**   **Less Proficient Readers**   **English Language Learners**

To help students who need further practice in analyzing primary sources, ask them to skim their textbooks to choose one primary source of interest. Ask students to read aloud the steps for analyzing primary sources and to explain each step in their own words. Then, have students work in pairs to analyze the primary sources that they have chosen.

Compare Viewpoints

A person's viewpoint is shaped by subjective influences such as feelings, prejudices, and past experiences. For example, two politicians may recommend two different policies to address the same problem. Likewise, historians often have different interpretations of past events, based on their research and review of other historians' work. Comparing such viewpoints will help you understand issues and develop your own interpretations. The excerpts below offer two different views on why the founders wrote a new U.S. Constitution in 1787. Use the excerpts and the steps that follow to learn about comparing viewpoints.

Comparing Viewpoints

> "[People who favored the Constitution] believed the slogans of 1776 were outmoded; . . . that certain political processes such as war, foreign affairs, and commerce, were national by nature; that the right to tax was essential to any government; and that powers wrested from king and parliament should not be divided among thirteen states, if the American government was to have any influence in the world."
>
> —Samuel E. Morison and Henry S. Commager, *The Growth of the American Republic.* New York: Oxford University Press, 1962.

> "The 55 delegates [to the Constitutional Convention] had much in common. All were white, male, and well educated, and many already knew one another. . . . Not surprisingly, all seemed to agree that the contagion of liberty had spread too far. . . . Most delegates hoped to replace the existing Confederation structure with a national government capable of controlling finances and creating [lender]-friendly [economic] policies. . . ."
>
> —Jacqueline Jones, Peter W. Wood, Elaine Tyler May, Thomas Borstelmann, and Vicki L. Ruiz, *Created Equal: A Social and Political History of the United States.* Boston: Pearson Education, 2003.

Identify the authors. Determine when the historians studied or wrote.

Examine the viewpoints. Identify each author's main idea and evaluate his or her supporting arguments. Determine whether the arguments are logical and the evidence is sufficient to support the main idea. Confirm that the evidence is valid by doing research if necessary.

Determine the author's frame of reference. Consider how the author's background and historical specialty might affect his or her viewpoint.

Recognize facts and opinions. Identify which statements are opinions and which are facts. Opinions represent the author's viewpoint.

Evaluate each viewpoint's validity. Decide whether the viewpoints are based on facts and/or reasonable arguments. Consider whether or not you agree with the viewpoints.

Practice and Apply the Skill

Use the excerpts above to answer the following questions.

1. Who are the authors of these two excerpts? When was each excerpt written?
2. What is each historian's main argument about the U.S. Constitution? What evidence or supporting arguments does each provide?
3. How might each historian's frame of reference affect the viewpoint?
4. Are these two viewpoints based on reasonable arguments? Explain.

Differentiated Instruction   Solutions for All Learners

L4 Advanced Readers   L4 Gifted and Talented Students

Ask students who need more of a challenge to find two viewpoints on a single topic currently in the news. Viewpoints may be from the editorial page of a newspaper, from news magazines, or from the Internet. Review students' choices, and help them make copies for the class. Then, have students lead the class in a discussion that works through the steps for comparing viewpoints in the text.

Compare Viewpoints L3

Instruct

- **Introduce** Recall with students a recent school, local, or national election. Identify a key issue in the candidates' debate and the differing viewpoints expressed. Clarify that, in order to be informed, voters needed to understand, compare, and choose among the different viewpoints expressed on the issue. Tell students that as citizens they, too, must often compare viewpoints.

- **Teach** Have students read the steps under *Compare Viewpoints,* and share any questions they have. Then, organize students in pairs. Have each partner read one of the primary sources and its source, explain its main idea, and list one supporting detail. Encourage partners to share ideas about the viewpoint with which they most agree and their reasoning. Have students fill in the *Compare Viewpoints* worksheet. Teaching Resources, Skills Handbook, **p. 29**

Independent Practice

Have students complete the Practice and Apply questions. Discuss their responses as a class.

Monitor Progress

As students complete the questions, circulate to provide assistance as needed. If students are struggling, read through the *Compare Viewpoints* steps with them. Confirm their understanding of the key concepts, and then urge them to try again to answer the questions.

Answers

1. Samuel E. Morison and Henry S. Commager, 1962; Jacqueline Jones et al., 2003

2. Morison and Commager state that the delegates to the Convention believed that the national government had to be powerful if it was to have any influence in the world; the other group states that the delegates thought that the idea of liberty had spread too far.

3. Sample: Historians' beliefs about the strength of national government as well as era in which they live affect perspective.

4. The views agree that delegates to the Constitutional Convention believed that certain powers should belong to a federal, or national, government; because of this consensus, the arguments seem reasonable.

Synthesize Information ⑬

Instruct

- **Introduce** Direct students' attention to a poster in the classroom or hall or to another piece of media containing both visual and textual information. Ask students to combine information from each part of the selected medium to explain the main idea of the entire item. Tell students that this process is known as synthesizing information.

- **Teach** Have students read the steps under *Synthesize Information* and share any questions they have. Invite volunteers to identify and describe each document on this page; for example, Document A is a photograph, Document B is a line graph, and Document C is a primary source quotation. Then, discuss the kind of information that each source provides, such as visual, firsthand account, or background. Discuss with students how together, all three documents contribute to a fuller understanding of life during the Great Depression than would one document alone. Have students fill in the *Synthesize Information* worksheet. Teaching Resources, Skills Handbook, p. 31

Independent Practice

Have students complete the Practice and Apply questions. Discuss their responses as a class.

Monitor Progress

If students are struggling to answer the questions, create a main-idea chart by making a column for each source and listing its main idea. Urge students to refer to this information as they answer the questions.

Synthesize Information

Just as you might ask several friends about a movie before deciding to see it, you can combine information from different sources to develop a fuller understanding of any topic. This process, called synthesizing, will help you become better informed. Study the documents below about developments during the Great Depression in the 1930s. Then, use the steps that follow to learn to synthesize information.

Document A

Rural poverty during the Great Depression of the 1930s.

Document B

Unemployment, 1928–1933

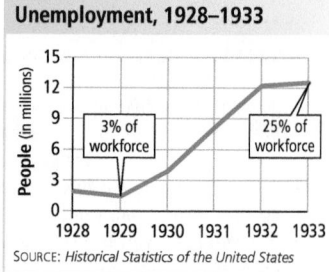

SOURCE: *Historical Statistics of the United States*

Document C

Primary Source ❝This great nation will endure as it has endured, will revive and will prosper. So, first of all, let me assert my firm belief that the only thing we have to fear is fear itself—nameless, unreasoning, unjustified terror which paralyzes needed efforts to convert retreat into advance.❞

—President Franklin Roosevelt, First Inaugural Address, 1933

Identify thesis statements. Before you can synthesize, you must understand the thesis, or main idea, of each source. Analyze how the information and ideas in the sources are the same or different. When several sources agree, the information is more reliable and thus more significant.

Draw conclusions and generalize. Look at all the information. Use it to draw conclusions that form a single picture of the topic. Make a generalization, or statement that applies to all the sources.

Construct and test hypotheses. As you learn new information about history, you can begin to form hypotheses, or educated guesses, about events and trends. You might form a hypothesis about why something happened or about the connection between two events. Then, as you learn more, you should test your hypothesis against new information. You should continue to refine your hypothesis based on the new information.

Practice and Apply the Skill

Use the documents above to answer the following questions.
1. What is the main idea of each source?
2. Which sources support the idea that the depression affected people throughout the United States?
3. Form a hypothesis about the Great Depression, based on the information presented.

Answers

1. Document A: People lived in great poverty at this time; Document B: Unemployment rose sharply at this time; Document C: People should not let fear stand in the way of achieving prosperity.

2. B and C

3. Sample answer: The Great Depression was a serious economic crisis in which many people lost their jobs and some fell into poverty.

Analyze Cause and Effect

One of a historian's main tasks is to understand the causes and effects of the event he or she is studying. Study the facts below, which are listed in random order. Then, use the steps that follow to learn how to analyze cause and effect.

> The United States, with other nations, fought a war in North and South Korea in the 1950s. This list shows key trends and events related to that war.
>
> - South Korea and its allies fight a 3-year war against North Korea and its allies.
> - At the end of World War II, Korea was divided into North Korea, a communist nation, and South Korea, a noncommunist nation, divided at the 38th parallel.
> - President Truman worried about the spread of communism in Europe and Asia.
> - Communists gained control of mainland China.
> - By the end of the Korean War, the border between North Korea and South Korea stood at about the 38th parallel, where it still is today.
> - North Korea invaded South Korea.
> - As a result of the north's invasion, the south and its allies pushed back.
> - The United States continues to station troops along the border dividing North Korea from South Korea.
> - Thousands of Americans were killed in the Korean War.
> - The United States stations thousands of troops in West Germany.

Identify the central event. Determine to what event or issue all the facts listed relate.

Locate clue words. Use words such as *because, so,* and *due to* to spot causes and effects.

Identify causes and effects. Causes precede the central event and contribute to its occurrence. Effects come after the central event. They occur or emerge as a result of it.

Consider time frame. Decide if causes have existed for a long period of time or if they emerged just prior to the central event. Short-term causes are usually single or narrowly defined events. Long-term causes usually arise from conditions that are ongoing.

Notice relationships that are not causal. Sometimes events are related, but the earlier event did not cause the later event. For example, although there are parallels, the Russian Revolution was not caused by the American Revolution.

Practice and Apply the Skill

Use the list above to answer the following questions:

1. Which item on the list describes the central event whose causes and effects can be determined?
2. Name two facts that are long-term effects.
3. Name two facts that are probably causes of the central event.
4. Name one fact that is not a cause or effect of the central event, though it is related.

Analyze Cause and Effect L3

Instruct

- **Introduce** Identify a recent school success, such as an athletic victory or a well-received play. Ask students what factors contributed to the success, and list these on the board. Then, ask students how the success affected the school community, and list those effects on the board. Explain that just as in the example illustrates, events in history are caused by actions and attitudes that, in turn, cause new effects.

- **Teach** Have students read the steps under *Analyze Cause and Effect* and share any questions they have. Tell students to read the bulleted items in the boxed text on the student page. Poll the class to identify the central event. Then, work through the bulleted items one at a time. Ask students whether they think each item is a cause or an effect and to explain their reasoning. Have students fill in the *Analyze Cause and Effect* worksheet. Teaching Resources, Skills Handbook, p. 32

Independent Practice

Have students complete the Practice and Apply questions. Discuss their responses as a class.

Monitor Progress

If students are struggling to answer the questions, review the steps in analyzing cause and effect and remind them of the definitions of long-term and short-term causes.

Differentiated Instruction Solutions for All Learners

 **L1 Special Needs Students**    **L2 Less Proficient Readers**   **L2 English Language Learners**

To help students who need further practice analyzing cause and effect, ask them to use the boxed list in the text to create their own cause-and-effect graphic organizers. Have students draw three large boxes on a sheet of paper, with arrows leading from the first box to the second and from the second box to the

third. Have students write the central event from the boxed list in the center box, with causes in the left-hand box and effects in the right-hand box. Explain that this type of graphic organizer can help them understand other causes and effects in history and current events.

Answers

1. North Korea invaded South Korea.
2. The United States still stations troops along the border between North and South Korea; the border between North and South Korea did not change after the war.
3. Korea was divided after World War II; communists gained control of China.
4. The United States stationed troops in West Germany.

Problem Solving and Decision Making

Instruct

- **Introduce** Invite volunteers to share a problem from their lives, such as too much homework or an annoying younger sibling. Ask students to contribute ideas for solving these problems.

- **Teach** Have students read the steps under *Problem Solving and Decision Making* and share any questions they have. Read the boxed text as a class. Ask **What is the main problem?** *(the Great Depression)* Ask students to identify the possible solutions listed on the chart and to identify additional advantages and disadvantages of each. Poll students on which option they think would be effective. Invite volunteers to explain their votes. Have students fill in the *Problem Solving and Decision Making* worksheet. Teaching Resources, Skills Handbook, **p. 33**

Independent Practice

Have students complete the Practice and Apply questions. Discuss their responses as a class.

Monitor Progress

If students are struggling to answer question 2, discuss a current nationwide problem that the government is trying to solve, and discuss the advantages and disadvantages of some of the solutions.

Answers

1. high unemployment, homelessness, business closings

2. Sample answer: Option 2: Advantage: The solutions would be widespread and would probably be well-funded; Disadvantage: Federal programs often do not solve specific, local problems. Option 3: Advantage: State and local governments could more accurately target needy individuals or specific, local problems; Disadvantage: States might not have enough money to provide relief; the depression was a national crisis, so it needed federal solutions.

3. Possible response: The Great Depression was a global economic crisis and needed more than governmental action to be solved, as well as more time.

SH28

Problem Solving and Decision Making

When you have a problem to solve or decision to make, you can find solutions if you think in a logical way. Study the situation outlined below. Then use the steps that follow to learn the skills of problem solving and decision making.

Ending the Woes of the Great Depression

In 1929, the United States entered a period of extreme economic difficulties, known as the Great Depression. Thousands of businesses closed, millions of people lost their jobs, and many people had to leave their homes because they couldn't afford the rent or other costs. When the Depression began, Herbert Hoover was President. Later, Franklin Roosevelt was elected to replace Hoover. Both Presidents tried strategies to solve the problems brought on by the Depression.

Options for Presidents Hoover and Roosevelt

Option	Advantages	Disadvantages
1. Allow the economy to correct itself.	• The economy works better when left alone. • The government does not have the right to intervene in local economic affairs.	• This could take a long time, while people continue to suffer. •
2. Let the federal government do whatever is necessary to relieve the effects of the Depression.	• •	• •
3. Take certain federal actions, but rely mainly on the states and on private economic activities.	• •	• •

The Decisions
- President Hoover decided to follow Option 3.
- President Roosevelt decided to follow Option 2.

Effects of the Decisions
- Hoover's actions did not relieve the problems of the Depression quickly enough and he lost his bid for reelection in 1932.
- Roosevelt's actions put some people back to work and relieved some hunger, but did not end the Depression.

Identify the problem. You cannot solve a problem until you examine it and understand it.

Gather information and identify options. Most problems have many solutions. Identify as many solution options as possible.

Consider advantages and disadvantages. Analyze each option by predicting benefits and drawbacks.

Decide on and implement the solution. Pick the option with the most desirable benefits and least important drawbacks.

Evaluate the decision. After awhile, reexamine your solution. If necessary, make a new decision.

Practice and Apply the Skill
Use information from the box above to answer the following questions:
1. What problems did Presidents Hoover and Roosevelt face?
2. Identify at least one advantage and one disadvantage of Options 2 and 3.
3. Why do you think that neither President was able to end the Depression?

Differentiated Instruction Solutions for All Learners

To help students who need further practice in problem solving and decision making, ask them to name a problem that they have solved or a decision that they have made in their own lives. Examples may include finding an after-school job or making a major purchase. Tell students to use the chart in the text as a model, and create a problem-solving and

decision-making chart that shows their own thinking as they solved their problem. Tell students that their charts should include a description of the problem, at least two solution options, and the advantages and disadvantages of each option. Finally, have each student write a sentence that indicates which option they chose and why.

Draw Inferences and Conclusions

Text and artwork may not contain all the facts and ideas you need to understand a topic. You may need to draw inferences, that is, to add information from your own experience or knowledge, or use information that is implied but not directly stated in the text or artwork. Study the biography below. Then, use the steps that follow to learn how to draw inferences and conclusions.

HISTORY MAKERS

Ida B. Wells (1862–1931)

Wells had gained fame for her campaign against the lynching of African Americans. But she was also a tireless worker for women's suffrage and joined in the famous 1913 march for universal suffrage that took place in Washington, D.C. Not able to tolerate injustice of any kind, Ida B. Wells, along with Jane Addams, successfully blocked the establishment of segregated schools in Chicago. In 1930, she ran for the Illinois State legislature, which made her one of the first black women to run for public office in the United States.

Study the facts. Determine what facts and information the text states.

Summarize information. Confirm your understanding of the text by briefly summarizing it.

Ask questions. Use who, what, when, where, why, and how questions to analyze the text and learn more. For example, you might compare and contrast, or look for causes or effects.

Add your own knowledge. Consider what you know about the topic. Use this knowledge to evaluate the information.

Draw inferences and conclusions. Use what you learned from the text and your own knowledge to draw inferences and conclusions about the topic.

Practice and Apply the Skill

Use the biography above to answer these questions.
1. Who is discussed in the biography? When did she live?
2. Briefly summarize the text.
3. How might Wells's activities have been unusual for her time?
4. What inferences can you draw about Wells's character from the information in the biography?

21st Century Skills

SKILLS HANDBOOK

Draw Inferences and Conclusions **L3**

Instruct

- **Introduce** Ask students to look out the window and describe what kind of day it is and what they would expect to feel outside. Discuss the clues students used to answer, such as previous experiences with similar weather or the presence of clouds or blowing leaves. Point out that people draw inferences and conclusions every day.

- **Teach** Have students read the steps under *Draw Inferences and Conclusions,* and share any questions they have. Then, guide students in using the boxed biography on this page to practice the skill. For example, invite students to suggest *who, what, when, where, why,* and *how* questions that could help them analyze the text. Ask **What do you know from the image(s)?** *(Ida B. Wells was honored on a stamp commemorating black history.)* **Given this information, what inferences and conclusions can you draw about Wells?** *(Wells probably worked successfully to help achieve civil rights.)* Have students fill in the *Drawing Inferences and Conclusions* worksheet. Teaching Resources, Skills Handbook, **p. 34**

Independent Practice

Have students complete the Practice and Apply questions. Discuss their responses as a class.

Monitor Progress

If students are struggling to answer the last question, have them review the biography and list all the words that describe what Wells was like as a person.

Answers

1. Ida B. Wells, 1862–1931
2. Wells worked for women's suffrage and for civil rights.
3. She was a black woman who spoke out against injustice at a time when white men held most of the power.
4. Possible response: She was strong-willed and courageous.

SH29

Step-by-Step Instruction

Objective

As you teach this section, keep students focused on the following objective to help them master core content.

- Learn strategies for active participation in group discussions and debates, for developing and presenting oral or multimedia presentations, and for active listening.

Prepare to Read

Background Knowledge L3

Review recent oral presentations or class discussions. Ask students to share the ways in which they felt prepared or effective and others with which they would have liked more practice.

Teach

Participate in Group Discussions L3

Instruct

- **Introduce** Ask students what they like and do not like about group discussions. Emphasize that discussions and debates are opportunities for students to share and discuss their views.

- **Teach** Have students read the steps under *Participate in Group Discussions*. Discuss any questions they have. Suggest that students keep a notepad and pen or pencil at hand during group discussions and debates so that they can jot down quick reminders of thoughts raised by others. Stress that taking notes should never interfere with active listening. Have students fill in the *Participate in Group Discussions* worksheet. Teaching Resources, Skills Handbook, **p. 35**

- Explain that a debate is a formal argument about a specific issue and that sometimes students will find themselves arguing positions with which they do not necessarily agree. Ask students why debates might be useful ways to compare political candidates or discuss controversial subjects. Have students fill in the *Debating Issues* worksheet. Teaching Resources, Skills Handbook, **p. 36**

Speaking and Listening

Speaking and listening are forms of communication you use every day. In certain situations, however, specific skills and strategies can increase the effectiveness of your communication. The strategies offered in this section will help you improve both your speaking and listening skills.

Participate in Group Discussions

A group discussion is an informal meeting of people that is used to openly discuss ideas and topics. You can express your views and hear those of others.

Identify Issues

Before you speak, identify the issues and main points you want to address. Incorporate what you already know about these issues into your views. Then find the best words to convey your ideas effectively.

Interact With the Group

As with persuasive writing, in a discussion it helps to accept the validity of opposing views, then argue your position. Always acknowledge the views of others respectfully, but ask questions that challenge the accuracy, logic, or relevance of those views.

Debating

A debate is a formal argument about a specific issue. Explicit rules govern the procedure of a debate, with each debater or team given an allotted time to make arguments and respond to opposing positions. You may also find yourself arguing a position you do not personally hold.

Prepare Your Arguments

If you support a position, use your existing knowledge of it to direct your research. If you personally oppose an assigned position, use that knowledge to identify likely opposing arguments. Generate an outline and then number note cards to highlight key information for each of your main points.

Avoid Common Pitfalls

Stay focused on your arguments. Be aware of words that may reveal bias, such as *unpatriotic*. Speak assertively, but avoid getting overly emotional. Vary the pitch and tone of your voice to keep listeners engaged. Try to speak actively, rather than just reading aloud, and use eye contact and gestures to emphasize your message.

Independent Practice

Organize students in groups. Help them choose an issue from their current studies to explore in a group discussion. Then, have groups identify two aspects of their topic or of another topic and carry out a debate.

Monitor Progress

If students are not fully participating in their groups or are displaying poor listening/speaking techniques, observe the behaviors and suggest ways in which techniques may be improved.

Give an Oral or Multimedia Presentation

An oral or multimedia presentation provides an audience with information through a variety of media.

Choose Media

If you are limited to speaking only, focus your time on developing a presentation that engages listeners. If you can include other media, consider what kind of information each form of media conveys most effectively.

Maps	Graphs/Charts	Pictures	Diagrams	Audio/Video
Clarify historical or geographical information	Show complicated information in an accessible format	Illustrate objects, scenes, or other details	Show links between parts and a whole or a process	Bring the subject to life and engage audiences

Prepare Your Presentation

Gather information using library and online sources. Develop your most important ideas in the body of your presentation. Back up assertions with solid facts and use multimedia examples to illustrate key points.

Present With Authority

Practice your presentation to gain comfort with the ideas and the presentation sequence. Experiment with the timing of how to include multimedia elements. Make sure you have the necessary equipment and know how to use it.

Active Listening

Active listening is a key component of the communication process. Like all communication, it requires your engaged participation.

Focus Your Attention on Ideas

Look at and listen to the speaker. Think about what you hear and see. Which ideas are emphasized or repeated? What gestures or expressions suggest strong feelings? Can you connect the speaker's ideas to your own experiences?

Listen to Fit the Situation

Active listening involves matching your listening to the situation. Listen critically to a speech given by a candidate for office. Listen empathetically to the feelings of a friend. Listen appreciatively to a musical performance.

Ask Questions

Try to think of questions while you're listening. Look at these examples:

Open-ended	Closed	Fact
Why do you think it is so important for young people to vote?	Do you support the current voting age of 18?	How many people between the ages of 18 and 25 voted in the most recent election?

Instruct

- **Introduce** Tell students that you give an oral presentation every day in the classroom. As you do, you must convey ideas orally but also listen actively so that you can respond to students' ideas and needs. Remind students that they, too, must use these presenting and speaking skills often in the classroom.

- **Teach** Have students read the suggestions under *Give an Oral or Multimedia Presentation*. Discuss any questions students may have. Then, review the types of media presented in the chart. Discuss examples with students, and invite their ideas about the advantages and disadvantages of each one in particular situations. Stress the importance of thorough preparation and sufficient practice before all oral presentations, including a rehearsal with visuals and equipment. Have students fill in the *Give an Oral or Multimedia Presentation* worksheet. Teaching Resources, Skills Handbook, **p. 37**

- **Teach** Point out the lesson title, "Active Listening." Ask **What does it mean to be an active listener?** *(Being an engaged participant by focusing one's attention and listening to others in ways that fit the situation).* Remind students of the importance of asking relevant questions. Have students fill in the *Active Listening* worksheet. Teaching Resources, Skills Handbook, **p. 38**

Independent Practice

Ask students to suggest a list of current topics of interest. Assign brief oral or multimedia presentations on these topics. Invite speakers to present their work as the other students listen actively.

Monitor Progress

Circulate to observe presenters and listeners. Redirect attention if any students are not focusing on the presentations. Develop and share with students a collection of nonverbal cues to indicate that time is running out or that they need to speak more slowly or more loudly, and so on.

Differentiated Instruction   Solutions for All Learners

 Special Needs Students    Less Proficient Readers   L2 English Language Learners

To help students who need further practice, review the steps for participating in group discussions, debating, giving presentations, and active listening. Then, have students evaluate their own performances in each of these areas by suggesting areas of strength and areas for improvement. Meet with individual students to review areas needing improvement that they noted or that you observed. Review listening and speaking skills as needed.

Background Knowledge

Have students discuss why it is true that knowing their own personal histories or their families' histories helps enrich their self-knowledge. Tell students that a nation, much like an individual or a family, depends on its history to form its identity and to help its citizens understand their country's role in the contemporary world.

Instruct

Have students read the essay, and then lead a class discussion about why history matters. Read aloud the quotation by David McCullough. Ask **To what does McCullough liken ignorance of history?** *(to rudeness or ingratitude)* **Do you agree with his assessment? Explain.** *(Possible answer: Yes; American citizens should learn history to appreciate the efforts of those who came before them and made the nation and the world—for better or worse— what it is today.)* Ask **Do you think history matters? Explain your response.** *(Possible answer: History matters because we can use the knowledge of the past to understand why society and the United States are as they are today. Knowledge of the past can help us avoid repeating mistakes and enable us to create a better future.)*

Looking Ahead

Tell students to keep in mind the questions of how and why the nation's history matters as they explore the events discussed in this textbook, beginning with the origins of the United States and the struggles that were overcome to build a new republic based on principles of democracy.

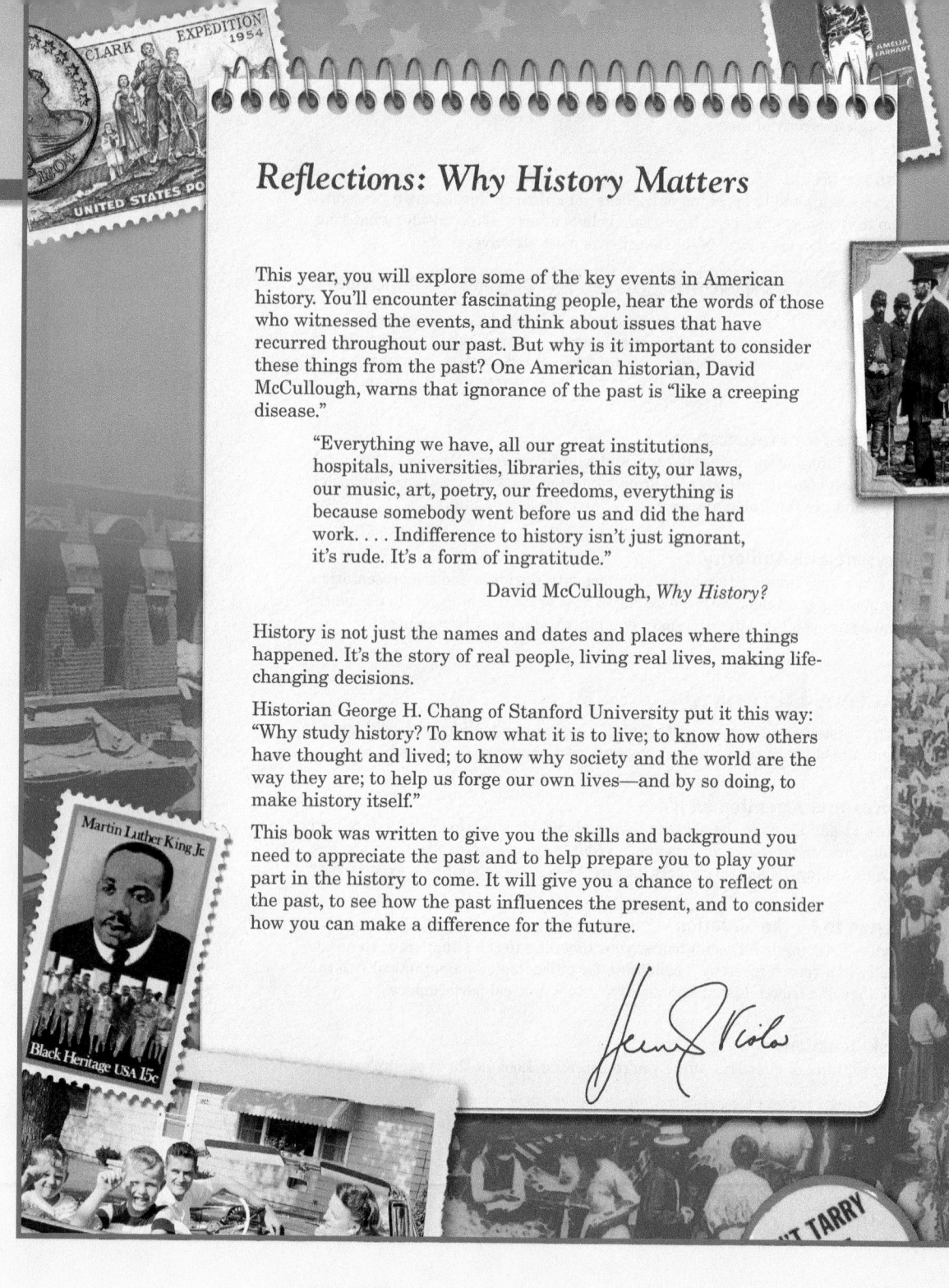

Reflections: Why History Matters

This year, you will explore some of the key events in American history. You'll encounter fascinating people, hear the words of those who witnessed the events, and think about issues that have recurred throughout our past. But why is it important to consider these things from the past? One American historian, David McCullough, warns that ignorance of the past is "like a creeping disease."

> "Everything we have, all our great institutions, hospitals, universities, libraries, this city, our laws, our music, art, poetry, our freedoms, everything is because somebody went before us and did the hard work. . . . Indifference to history isn't just ignorant, it's rude. It's a form of ingratitude."
>
> David McCullough, *Why History?*

History is not just the names and dates and places where things happened. It's the story of real people, living real lives, making life-changing decisions.

Historian George H. Chang of Stanford University put it this way: "Why study history? To know what it is to live; to know how others have thought and lived; to know why society and the world are the way they are; to help us forge our own lives—and by so doing, to make history itself."

This book was written to give you the skills and background you need to appreciate the past and to help prepare you to play your part in the history to come. It will give you a chance to reflect on the past, to see how the past influences the present, and to consider how you can make a difference for the future.

CONNECTING WITH PAST LEARNINGS

CONTENTS

The Spirit of '76, by Archibald M. Willard, honors the heroes of the American Revolution. ▶

Connecting With Past Learnings

Era Overview

Connecting With Past Learnings provides a brief overview of the history of North America and of the United States, beginning with the first peoples to live in North America and ending with the development of industry in the United States during the late 1800s and the early 1900s.

Chapter 1 summarizes the prehistory of North America, the colonial exploration and settlement of the continent, the birth of the United States, and the early challenges faced by the new nation. **Issues:** Expanding and Protecting Civil Rights, Global Interdependence, Territorial Expansion of the United States

Chapter 2 examines the factors that contributed to the westward expansion of the United States, the issues that divided the North and the South, the major events of the Civil War, and the measures taken by the U.S. government to reunify the nation during the Reconstruction Era. **Issues:** Checks and Balances, Federal Power and States' Rights, Church and State

Chapter 3 focuses on the development of American industry during the late 1800s and the early 1900s and the effects that industry had on immigration to and migration within the United States, the relationship between workers and big business, and the rise of the Populist Party. **Issues:** Migration and Urbanization, Technology and Society, American Indian Policy

CHAPTER 1

Teach With Technology

PresentationEXPRESS™ PREMIUM DVD

- Teach this chapter's core content by using PresentationExpress, which includes interactivities, video, lecture notes, and the *ExamView®* QuickTake assessment tool.
- To introduce this chapter by using PresentationExpress, ask students with which of the following statements they most agree: **A) The main theme of American history is conflict and change. B) The main theme of American history is exploration. C) The main theme of American history is the quest for liberty. D) The main theme of American history is new ideas and new identities.** Take a class poll or record students' answers by using the QuickTake feature, and discuss their responses. Point out that in this chapter, students will read about the history of North America from the first human migration to the creation of the United States. Continue introducing the chapter by using the chapter opener slide show.

Technology Resources

- Student**EXPRESS** CD-ROM
- Teacher Resource Library **DVD**
- Presentation**EXPRESS** **PREMIUM DVD**
- *ExamView®* **Test Bank CD-ROM** English and Spanish
- **Guided Reading Audio,** Spanish
- **Student Edition on Audio**

THE ESSENTIAL ? VIDEO By Students For Students
For videos on Amercian Issues, go to **www.pearsonschool.com/ushist**

CHAPTER 1 The Nation's Beginnings
Prehistory–1824

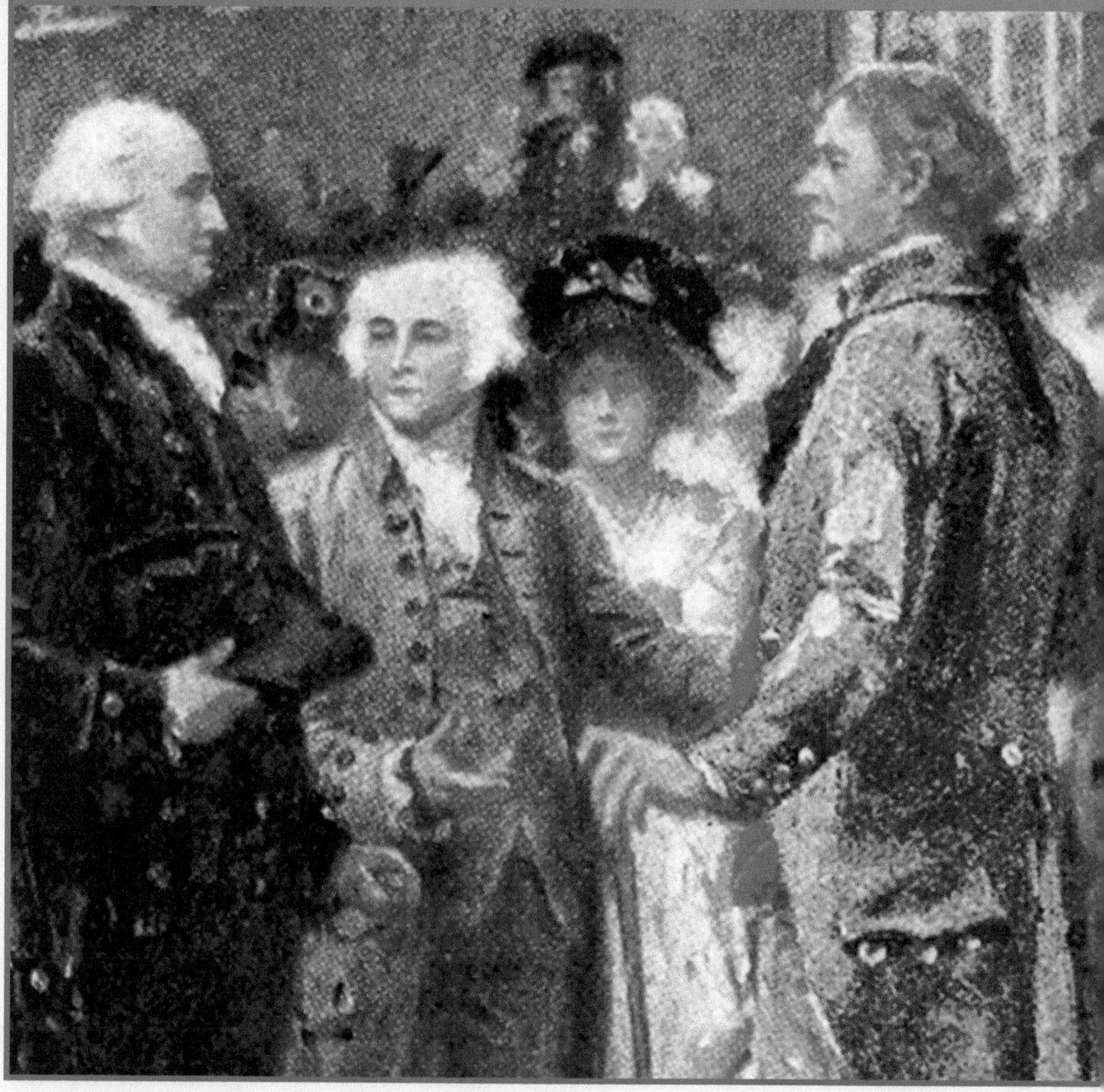

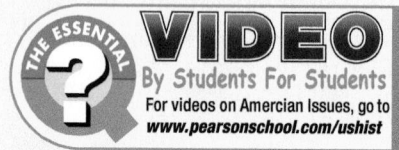

Bibliography

For the Teacher

Deetz, James, and Patricia Scott Deetz. *The Times of their Lives: Life, Love, and Death in Plymouth Colony.* Anchor, 2001.

Ellis, Joseph J. Founding Brothers: *The Revolutionary Generation.* Knopf, 2000.

Larson, Edward, and Michael P. Winship, eds. *The Constitutional Convention: A Narrative History from the Notes of James Madison.* Modern Library, 2005.

For the Student

L2 Jordan, Terry L. *The U.S. Constitution and Fascinating Facts About It.* Oak Hill, 1999.

L3 Least Heat-Moon, William. *Columbus in the Americas.* John Wiley and Sons, 2002.

L4 Weatherford, Jack. *Indian Givers: How the Indians of the Americas Transformed the World.* Random House, 1990.

WITNESS HISTORY

The Nation's First President

George Washington was elected President twice, serving from 1789 to 1797. Washington's second inauguration took place in Philadelphia, where he delivered the shortest inaugural speech ever given!

"I am again called upon by the voice of my country to execute the functions of its Chief Magistrate. . . . I shall endeavor to express the high sense I entertain of this distinguished honor, and of the confidence which has been reposed in me by the people of United America."
—George Washington, March 4, 1793

Navajo pottery

◄ This painting shows (from left to right) George Washington, John Adams, and Thomas Jefferson at Washington's second inauguration.

Chapter Preview

Chapter Focus Question: What factors led to the founding of the United States and its formation as a democratic republic?

Section 1
Many Cultures Meet

Section 2
The American Revolution

Section 3
The Constitution

Section 4
The New Republic

Three-cornered hat worn by Patriots during the American Revolution

Peace medal given to the Nez Percés in 1810 in honor of the expedition of Meriwether Lewis and William Clark

Use the ☑ **Quick Study Timeline** at the end of this chapter to preview chapter events.

Note Taking Study Guide Online
For: Note Taking and American Issues Connector
www.pearsonschool.com/ushist

Chapter-Level Resources

All In One Letter Home (English and Spanish), Preread the Chapter, Vocabulary Builder, Reading Strategy, Social Studies Skills Practice, Enrichment, Issues Connector, Chapter Tests

- Test Prep With Document-Based Assessment
- AYP Monitoring Assessments
- *ExamView*® Test Bank CD-ROM
- Guided Reading Audio (Spanish)
- Student Edition Audio

Previewing the Chapter

- **WITNESS HISTORY** Read the Witness History selection aloud. Ask students to restate the quotation in their own words. Ask **How did Washington define the role of President?** *(He calls himself a magistrate, so Washington probably believed that the President's role was to ensure that the law was obeyed.)*

- **Analyzing the Visuals** Ask students to study the painting and the photographs on these pages and discuss how they are related. Ask **What does Adams seem to be doing in the painting?** *(Possible response: He seems to be ushering Washington into the presidency; he is gesturing for Washington to walk forward.)* **How does the painting seem to show the Americans' views of Washington?** *(Washington is the focus of attention.)*

- **Focus** Write the Chapter Focus Question on the board. Tell students to keep this question in mind as they read the chapter. Then, have students preview the section titles in this chapter.

- **Preread** Have students complete the chapter's Preread the Chapter Worksheet, Teaching Resources, pp. 8–9

Differentiated Instruction Solutions for All Learners

The following Teacher's Edition strategies are suitable for students of varying abilities.

- **L1** Special Needs Students, pp. 5, 10, 11, 16, 22 SN
- **L2** English Language Learners, pp. 5, 10, 11, 16, 22 ELL
- **L2** Less Proficient Readers, pp. 5, 10, 11, 16, 22 LPR
- **L4** Advanced Readers, pp. 6, 11, 17, 23 AR
- **L4** Gifted and Talented Students, pp. 6, 11, 17, 23 GT

Have students access **www.pearsonschool. com/ushist** for the Note Taking Study Guide *Online* as an alternative to the *Reading and Note Taking Study Guide* booklet.

Step-by-Step Instruction

Objectives

As you teach this section, keep students focused on the following objectives to help them answer the Section Focus Question and master core content.

- Discuss the migration of the first people to the Americas.
- Explain why Europeans wanted to develop a sea route to India in the 1400s.
- Describe the importance of trade in West Africa.
- Identify the effects of Christopher Columbus's voyage to the Americas.

Prepare to Read

Background Knowledge **L3**

Ask students what they know about North America and its inhabitants before Columbus arrived in 1492. Ask them whether they can identify any specific Native American peoples.

Set a Purpose **L3**

- **WITNESS HISTORY** Read the selection aloud.

  Ask **Why did Columbus give the Native Americans gifts?** *(to show friendliness)* **Why do you think the Native Americans liked the "trifles of small value" that Columbus gave them?** *(Possible answer: They were unusual to the Native Americans.)*

- **Focus** Point out the Section Focus Question, and write it on the board. Tell students to refer to this question as they read. *(Answer appears with Section 1 Assessment answers.)*

- **Preview** Have students preview the Section Objectives and the list of Terms and People.

- **NoteTaking** Using the Guided Questioning strategy (TE, p. T20), have students read this section. As they read, have students fill in the causes and effects of European arrival in the Americas. Reading and Note Taking Study Guide

---

▼ An American Indian and a European exchange goods.

WITNESS HISTORY

Two Cultures Meet

In one of the great accidents of history, explorer Christopher Columbus sailed west from Spain and landed on an island he thought was in Asia. In fact, Columbus encountered lands and people that Europeans did not know existed. In an October 12, 1492, journal entry, Columbus describes his first encounter with the people who lived on the island.

❝As I saw that [the island residents] were very friendly to us, . . . I presented them with some red caps, and strings of beads to wear upon the neck, and many other trifles of small value. . . . Afterwards they came . . . bringing parrots, balls of cotton thread, javelins, and many other things which they exchanged for articles we gave them, such as glass beads, and hawk's bells; which trade was carried on with the utmost good will.❞

—Christopher Columbus, October 1492

Many Cultures Meet

Objectives

- Discuss the migration of the first people to the Americas.
- Explain why Europeans wanted to develop a sea route to India in the 1400s.
- Describe the importance of trade in West Africa.
- Identify the effects of Christopher Columbus's voyage to the Americas.

Terms and People

clan	conquistador
Middle Passage	Columbian Exchange
Christopher Columbus	

NoteTaking

Reading Skill: Identify Causes and Effects Identify the causes and effects of European arrival in the Americas.

Cause	Event	Effect
• Desire to find trade routes to Asia	Europeans arrive in the Americas	• Columbian Exchange
•		•

Why It Matters Europe's Age of Exploration began in the 1400s as a quest for a sea route to Asia. In 1492, Europeans crossed the Atlantic Ocean and began to explore North and South America. The arrival of European settlers and enslaved Africans brought traumatic changes to the Native Americans, who had developed many complex cultures in the Americas. **Section Focus Question: What were the causes and effects of European arrival in the Americas?**

The American Indians

North and South America are remarkable for the diversity of their landscapes and their climates. Tens of thousands of years ago, humans began arriving in these vast lands.

Ancient Peoples Migrate to the Americas Most scientists believe that the first inhabitants of the Americas migrated from the northeastern coast of Asia between 40,000 and 15,000 years ago. Some scientists believe that Asians came over a land bridge that appeared across the Bering Strait during the last ice age. Others suggest that the first Americans arrived in boats that traveled along the Pacific coastline.

Over the generations, the American Indians expanded southward, occupying North and South America. As they filled these two continents, they adapted to dramatically different climates and landscapes, developing great cultural diversity. By 1492, American Indians spoke at least 375 distinct languages.

Vocabulary Builder

Use the information below and the following resource to teach students the high-use word from this section. Teaching Resources, Vocabulary Builder, p. 11

High-Use Word	Definition and Sample Sentence
diverse	*adj.* different, varied The Native American peoples of North America were **diverse**, speaking hundreds of languages, living in different climates, making different clothes, and eating different foods.

Cultures Share Many Traits Despite their <u>diverse</u> cultures, many Indian groups shared a number of characteristics. Most cultures were based on extended family groups called **clans.** All members of a clan had a common ancestor and identified with the spirit of a powerful animal. Several clans combined to make up a roaming band of Indians or a stationary village.

Many American Indian cultures shared similar religious beliefs. They believed that powerful spiritual forces were part of nature. Some Indians became shamans, who conducted rituals to seek benefits from spirit beings.

Agriculture Leads to the Growth of Civilizations About 3,500 years ago in central Mexico, the Indians learned how to grow crops such as maize (corn), squash, and beans. These methods of cultivation spread northward into the American Southwest and Midwest. The expanded food supply allowed the population to grow, which led in turn to the growth of towns and cities sometimes guided by powerful chiefs.

Many Indians did not adopt an agricultural way of life and thrived on a mix of hunting, gathering, and fishing. Crops did not thrive in the arid Great Basin between the Sierra Nevada and Rocky Mountains. In the Pacific Northwest, Indians did not need to farm because fish and game were so plentiful.

✔ **Checkpoint** How did geography influence the American Indians' way of life?

Vocabulary Builder
<u>diverse</u>—(duh VERS) *adj.* different; varied

Geography *Interactive*
For: Interactive map
www.pearsonschool.com/ushist

Native American Culture Regions of North America in About 1450

Map Skills By 1450, a great variety of Native American groups lived in North America. Within each culture area shown on the map, groups shared similar ways of life.

1. **Locate:** (a) Gulf of Mexico, (b) Arctic Ocean, (c) Hudson Bay

2. **Regions** In which region do the Cheyennes live?

3. **Make Comparisons** Based on the characteristics of their regions, describe at least one way in which Inuit culture may have differed from Navajo culture.

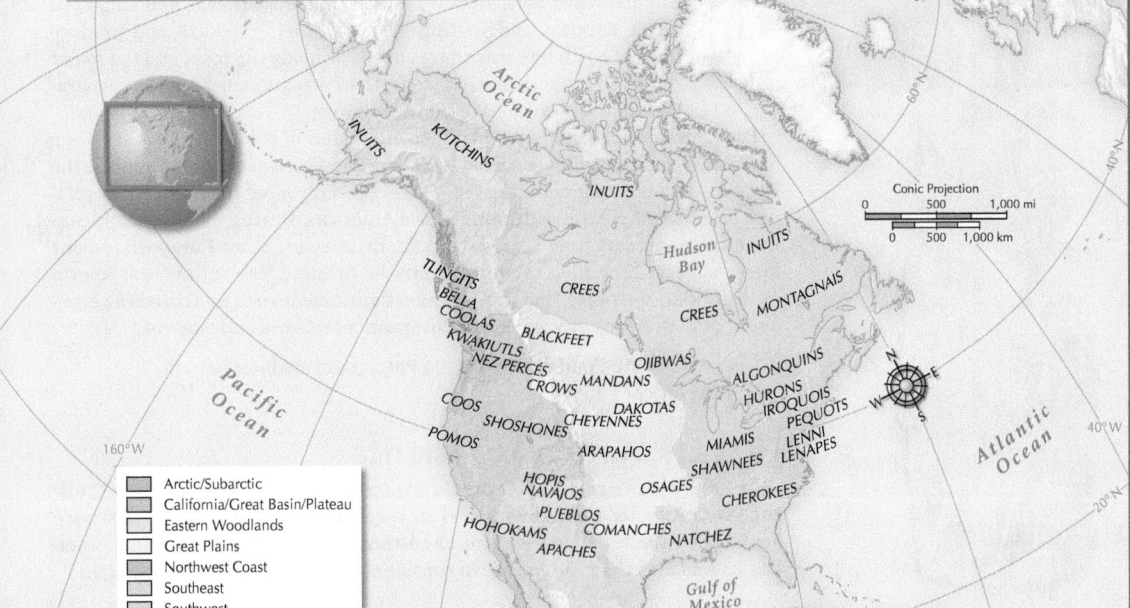

Arctic/Subarctic
California/Great Basin/Plateau
Eastern Woodlands
Great Plains
Northwest Coast
Southeast
Southwest

Differentiated Instruction   Solutions for All Learners

L1 Special Needs Students   L2 English Language Learners   L2 Less Proficient Readers

To help students understand the map on this page, model how to interpret the key, and explain that this key uses colors to represent the different regions of North America. Then, point out the scale, and explain how to use it. Have students locate a few of the highlighted regions, until they feel confident in using the key. Then, choose one region and ask students to name all the American Indian groups

labeled in that region. Explain that those peoples lived in that region. Tell students to find the region in which you live, and name the Native American groups who lived, or live, there. Ask students to describe the climate and geography in the region in which you live and decide whether the Native American groups listed on the map were farmers or hunter-gatherers. Have students explain their reasoning.

Teach

The American Indians   L3

Instruct

- **Introduce** Display Color Transparency: *Migration Across the Bering Strait.* Use the lesson suggested in the transparency book to lead a discussion about the routes that early humans might have taken to reach the Americas. Color Transparencies A-65

- **Teach** Ask **When did the first humans arrive in the Americas?** *(between 40,000 and 15,000 years ago)* **How were many Indian cultures similar?** *(They shared the belief in powerful spiritual forces that were part of nature.)* Using the Think-Write-Pair-Share strategy (TE, p. T23), have students describe ancient American Indian life. Ask **How did agriculture benefit Native Americans?** *(It expanded the food supply and allowed stable populations to grow.)*

Independent Practice

- Have students access **www.pearsonschool.com/ushist** to use the Geography Interactive map and answer the map skills questions in the text.

- Ask students to complete the worksheet *Outline Map: North America, About 1450.* Teaching Resources, **p. 27**

Monitor Progress

As students fill in their cause-and-effect charts, circulate to make sure that they note specific examples of the causes and effects of European arrival. For a completed version of the chart, see Note Taking Transparencies, **B-1.**

Answers

✔ Geography determined whether American Indians became farmers or remained hunter-gatherers.

Map Skills

1. Review locations with students.

2. the Great Plains

3. Sample answer: Because the Inuit lived in the Arctic/Subarctic region where the weather was cold and snowy most of the year, they could not grow crops and so relied on hunting and fishing. The Navajo lived in the warmer climate of the Southwest deserts and were hunter-gatherers.

The Europeans/The West Africans/First Encounters in America L3

Instruct

- **Introduce: Key Terms** Ask students to find the key terms *Middle Passage* and *Columbian Exchange* (in bold) in the text. Have students predict how the *Middle Passage* and the *Columbian Exchange* may have benefited Europeans, but harmed Africans and Native Americans.

- **Teach** Have students discuss the benefits and consequences of European colonization of the Americas. Ask **How did the Renaissance encourage European exploration?** (*Scientific advances and an increase in economic wealth led kingdoms to sponsor voyages of exploration.*) Have students examine the images on this page and describe the West African kingdoms as they were when European explorers arrived there. **What factor led to the expansion of the slave trade?** (*Europeans needed more people to work on new colonial plantations in the Americas.*) **What advantages did the conquistadors have over the Native Americans?** (*steel weapons, horses, immunity to European diseases*)

Independent Practice

Ask students to outline the information below the blue heading "First Encounters in America."

Monitor Progress

As students create their outlines, circulate to make sure that they understand the vast cultural differences between Native Americans and Europeans.

Answers

Caption Possible answer: Trade made the West African kingdoms wealthy and powerful, but trade with the Portuguese led to an increase in the slave trade, which ultimately weakened the region's economy.

✓ to increase trade with the merchants of Asia and Africa

✓ They expanded the African slave trade.

West African Kingdoms
Songhai and Benin were powerful African kingdoms. Pictured here are the city of Timbuktu, which reached its height under the Songhai empire, and a Benin ivory saltcellar with carvings of Portuguese traders. *How did trade affect West Africa?*

The Europeans

While Native American cultures thrived, life in Europe was changing rapidly. Changes in Europe that had begun in the fourteenth century would lead to increased contact between the cultures of Europe, Africa, and the Americas.

The Renaissance Changes Europe The period from the fourteenth to the sixteenth centuries saw great advances in science, economics, political thought, and art in Europe. This period is called the Renaissance. Scientific advances and an increase in economic wealth led some to sponsor early voyages of exploration. European kingdoms on the Atlantic coastline sent explorers out to sea. The monarchs and aristocrats who ruled these nations competed for access to the profitable trade in silks, gems, gold, ivory, and spices from Asia and Africa. This trade was dominated by Muslims who lived in North Africa, the Balkans, and Southwest Asia and by Italian merchants with access to the Mediterranean Sea.

The Age of Exploration Leads to Voyages of Discovery During the fifteenth century, the Portuguese took the lead in an era known as the Age of Exploration. By developing better ships and more advanced methods of navigation, the Portuguese regularly sailed the Atlantic Ocean far from the sight of land. Sailing farther south and then east, Portuguese mariner Bartolomeu Dias traveled around the southern tip of Africa to the Indian Ocean from 1487 to 1488. Then in 1498, Vasco da Gama reached India, opening a profitable trade.

✓ **Checkpoint** Why did Europeans seek a sea route to Asia?

The West Africans

Sailing south on the Atlantic Ocean, Portuguese mariners reached West African kingdoms below the Sahara. Highly civilized and densely populated, African kingdoms like Songhai and Benin had sophisticated agricultural systems, made iron tools, and employed draft animals and writing systems. Their products and produce moved north by caravans of camels or along the coast and the major rivers in large canoes. To trade, the Portuguese needed the cooperation of the powerful West African kings.

Portuguese merchants were not only interested in gold and salt, they were also interested in buying enslaved Africans. The Portuguese did not invent the slave trade, but they greatly expanded it—especially after 1500, when new colonial plantations created a demand in the Americas. During the next three centuries, slave traders from Portugal, Spain, Britain, and other European nations forced at least 11 million Africans across the Atlantic. The journey was known as the **Middle Passage.** This brutal transatlantic commerce weakened the economies of West Africa as it enriched European merchants and empires.

✓ **Checkpoint** What effects did the Portuguese mariners have in West Africa?

First Encounters in America

In 1492, Spain's rulers sponsored a voyage headed by Italian mariner **Christopher Columbus.** Columbus hoped to reach East Asia by sailing westward across the Atlantic. However, he underestimated the size of the world. Columbus had no idea that two American continents were there to block his ships.

Differentiated Instruction   Solutions for All Learners

L4 Advanced Readers   **L4 Gifted and Talented Students**

Have students prepare for and conduct a debate on the following topic: European explorers in Africa, Asia, and the Americas did more harm than good. Organize students into two groups, and assign one group to support this viewpoint and the second group to oppose it. Make sure that each group researches the European explorers and the peoples they encountered in Africa, Asia, and the Americas,

so that students can provide specific examples to support their points of view. Students should work together to research the topic and construct a persuasive argument. Have each group choose a speaker to conduct the debate. Allow each speaker ten minutes to make his or her argument, five minutes to make a rebuttal to the opposing viewpoint, and one minute to give a closing statement.

Global Interdependence

TRACK THE ISSUE

Is global interdependence good for the American economy?

Like many nations, the United States depends on trade and commerce with other countries to support its economy. Employment is a part of the global economy, as a growing number of U.S. companies outsource jobs overseas. Use the timeline below to explore this enduring issue.

1500s Columbian Exchange
Products and ideas are exchanged between the hemispheres.

1812 War of 1812
United States goes to war in part to protect its trade rights.

1944 World Bank
The World Bank and International Monetary Fund are established at Bretton Woods Conference.

1990s World Trade Increases
NAFTA joins the United States, Mexico, and Canada in a free-trade pact, and the World Trade Organization is founded.

2000s Globalization Debated
Critics and advocates debate benefits of globalization.

Europeans trade goods with Native Americans.

U.S. firms outsource work to such nations as India and Nigeria.

DEBATE THE ISSUE

Outsourcing Jobs Many American companies send work overseas where wages are lower. This is called "outsourcing." In the past, most of the jobs lost through outsourcing were factory jobs. Now office work and computer jobs are being sent abroad, too. How does outsourcing affect America?

"Sending jobs overseas is part of corporate America's quest for short-term profits at the expense of the well-being of our workers. In effect, forcing the middle class to compete with the cheapest foreign labor can only result in a decline in our nation's standard of living and a diminished quality of life."
—Lou Dobbs, News Anchor, CNN

"Will [the outsourcing of services] lead to jobs going overseas? You bet, but that is not a disaster. For a start, America runs a large and growing surplus in services with the rest of the world. The jobs lost will be low-paying ones. . . . By contrast, jobs will be created that demand skills to handle the deeper incorporation of information technology, and the pay for these jobs will be high."
—*The Economist* magazine

? **TRANSFER Activities**

1. **Compare** How do these two views on outsourcing differ?

2. **Analyze** Do you think either Lou Dobbs or the writer in *The Economist* would have considered the Columbian Exchange a danger to European or Native American economies? Explain.

3. **Transfer** Use the following Web site to see a video, try a WebQuest, and write in your journal. www.pearsonschool.com/ushist

Objectives

- Identify connections between historical events and movements.
- Analyze opposing arguments in primary sources.
- Formulate and support a point of view.

Background Knowledge L3

Explain that by the late twentieth century, many Americans had begun to worry that the U.S. economy was too dependent on foreign trade workers. Ask students to discuss whether America's increasing global interdependence is beneficial or harmful.

Instruct

Point out that the timeline shows the development of a global economy. Discuss the similarities and differences between NAFTA and the Columbian Exchange.

Monitor Progress

- Have students complete the Issues Connector worksheet, *Global Interdependence*. Teaching Resources, pp. 15–18

- Remind students to complete their American Issues Connector Journal worksheets notes. Review their work for accuracy. Reading and Note Taking Study Guide

Answers

Transfer Activities

1. Dobbs: the American standard of living will fall. *The Economist* writer: only low-paying jobs will move overseas, leaving high-paying, skilled jobs for Americans.

2. Sample answer: Neither would have considered the Columbian Exchange a danger. Both might have predicted that the trade in ideas would benefit Native Americans and that the trade in goods would help both economies.

3. For more information about outsourcing, have students access **www.pearsonschool.com/ushist**.

History Background

World Trade Protests In November 1999, the World Trade Organization (WTO) met in Seattle, Washington. Approximately 50,000 protesters disrupted the meeting, arguing that the WTO promoted free trade at the expense of democracy. The protesters also claimed that the WTO makes agreements with nations that increase trade but harm both the environment and workers. For five days, the protestors marched against the WTO. During one march, 240 people dressed in turtle suits to raise awareness about the environmental costs of trade. On the second day of the protests, WTO delegates were forced to stay in their hotel rooms as police battled huge crowds of protesters. Hundreds of protesters were jailed. The protests brought new attention to the WTO and its policies. Some Americans began to question whether continuous trade expansion was always positive. On the third day of the protest, President Bill Clinton said of the protesters, "I condemn the small number who were violent and who tried to prevent you from meeting, but I am glad the others showed up."

Columbus explored several Caribbean islands. Convinced that the islands were the Indies, he called the natives "Indians." (See the Witness History at the beginning of this section.) Columbus and those who followed worked to convert the Indians to Christianity. Europeans also enslaved Indians and took their lands.

The Conquistadores The Spanish rapidly conquered a vast empire around the Caribbean and in Central and South America. Known as **conquistadores,** Spanish invaders were brave, resourceful, ruthless, and destructive. Between 1519 and 1521, Hernando Cortés overpowered the Aztecs in Mexico.

Other Spanish conquistadores explored and conquered other parts of North America. Juan Ponce de Leon traveled through parts of Florida in 1513. Later, from 1539 to 1542, Hernando de Soto explored other portions of Florida and parts of the Southeast, reaching the Mississippi River. Francisco Coronado searched for legendary cities of gold in the Southwest. He explored present-day Arizona and New Mexico but found no gold.

The Columbian Exchange The conquistadores had the advantage of horses and steel weapons. But they had an unintentional weapon, too. Native Americans had no immunity to deadly European diseases such as smallpox, measles, and cholera. Indians died by the thousands.

These plagues made it easier for the Europeans to conquer and colonize North and South America. But they also thinned the number of possible Indian slaves. To make up the loss, the colonizers transported millions of enslaved Africans across the Atlantic to the Americas.

In addition to bringing new people into the Americas, the colonizers introduced new animals, including pigs, horses, mules, sheep, and cattle. The Europeans diversified their own agriculture by adopting crops pioneered by the Indians. Maize and potatoes helped to boost the population of Europe. The traffic of goods and ideas between Europe and the Americas is called the **Columbian Exchange.**

 Checkpoint How did European explorations affect life in the Americas, Africa, and Europe?

SECTION **1** Assessment

Progress Monitoring *Online*
For: Self-test with vocabulary practice
www.pearsonschool.com/ushist

Comprehension

1. Terms and People For each item below, write a sentence explaining its significance.
- clan
- Middle Passage
- Christopher Columbus
- conquistador
- Columbian Exchange

2. NoteTaking Reading Skill: Identify Causes and Effects Use your cause-and-effect chart to answer the Section Focus Question: What were the causes and effects of European arrival in the Americas?

Writing About History

3. Quick Write: Identify Effects Write a paragraph describing the effects of the European arrival in America from a Native American point of view. Your paragraph should state a main idea and include supporting details.

Critical Thinking

4. Draw Inferences How would the culture of Native American peoples who lived in a mountainous region differ from those who lived on a fertile plain? Which groups would be more likely to live in villages, and which would be more likely to hunt and gather?

5. Summarize What did the Europeans hope to gain by finding a sea route to Asia?

6. Analyze Information How did European contact with Africans affect the Africans?

7. Recognize Bias When Europeans and American Indians first encountered one another, they each must have been startled to see the other. What opinion do you think Columbus had of the Indians? What do you think American Indians thought of the Europeans?

DON'T TREAD ON ME

WITNESS HISTORY

A Voice for Freedom

In March 1775, the 13 colonies were on the brink of war with England. Delegates from across Virginia met to debate their options. Should they give Britain another chance to resolve the problem peacefully? Or were the colonists ready to fight for their freedom? Then, Patrick Henry urged the Virginia convention to prepare for war in a speech that roused the delegates. Based on recollections of men like Thomas Jefferson, Henry's biographer, William Wirt, included the text of the speech that is attributed to Patrick Henry.

"Gentlemen may cry peace, peace—but there is no peace. The war is actually begun! . . . Our brethren are already in the field! Why stand we here idle? . . . Is life so dear, or peace so sweet, as to be purchased at the price of chains and slavery? . . . I know not what course others may take; but as for me, give me liberty, or give me death!"

—Patrick Henry, March 23, 1775

▲ American colonists protest taxes levied by the Stamp Act.

The American Revolution

Objectives
- Describe the European colonial presence in North America.
- Trace the development of democratic ideals in Europe and America.
- Identify the causes of the American Revolution.
- Discuss the results of the American Revolution.

Terms and People

House of Burgesses	Enlightenment
Mayflower Compact	Great Awakening
Magna Carta	Thomas Jefferson
English Bill of Rights	George Washington

NoteTaking

Reading Skill: Recognize Sequence Note the sequence of events that led to the American Revolution by making a series-of-events chain.

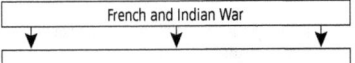
French and Indian War

Why It Matters European nations explored the Americas and began establishing colonies. England established 13 colonies along the mid-Atlantic coast of North America. Eventually, these colonies would declare their independence from England and become a new nation: the United States of America. **Section Focus Question: What important ideas and major events led to the American Revolution?**

European Colonies in the Americas

Wealth flowed into Spain from its colonies in Mexico, Central America, and South America. The population was thin and life was hard in the borderland regions in the present-day Southwest and in Florida. To encourage settlements and protect these outposts, Spain established presidios, or forts. Priests and nuns established dozens of missions to convert Native Americans to Christianity.

The French established colonies in Canada along the coast of Nova Scotia and the St. Lawrence River. Besides exploiting rich fishing off the coast, they found a fortune in furs. American Indians were eager to exchange beaver pelts for European-made metal axes, knives, and kettles. During the 1690s, the French founded Louisiana, along the Mississippi River valley and the Gulf Coast.

England Establishes Colonies in Virginia In 1607, the English established their first enduring settlement, Jamestown, in Virginia.

Vocabulary Builder

Use the information below and the following resource to teach students the high-use words from this section. Teaching Resources, Vocabulary Builder, p. 11

High-Use Words	Definitions and Sample Sentences
philosophy	*n.* theory or logical analysis of the fundamental principles of human conduct, thought, knowledge, and the nature of the universe Enlightenment **philosophy** stated that reason must be applied to all parts of human life, including politics and religion.
assert	*v.* to state positively; declare; affirm The Europeans **asserted** their right to explore the Americas to find riches and land.

Objectives

As you teach this section, keep students focused on the following objectives to help them answer the Section Focus Question and master core content.

- Describe the European colonial presence in North America.
- Trace the development of democratic ideals in Europe and America.
- Identify the causes of the American Revolution.
- Discuss the results of the American Revolution.

Prepare to Read

Background Knowledge L3

Ask students to recall what they know about the American Revolution. Have students describe why the colonists went to war against the British.

Set a Purpose L3

- **WITNESS HISTORY** Read the selection aloud.

  Ask **Why do you think Patrick Henry mentions slavery?** (*It is a powerful image and it is relevant to his listeners, as many American colonies allowed slavery.*) **What does "give me liberty or give me death" mean?** (*Henry would rather die than live without freedom.*)

- **Focus** Point out the Section Focus Question, and write it on the board. Tell students to refer to this question as they read. (*Answer appears with Section 2 Assessment answers.*)

- **Preview** Have students preview the Section Objectives and the list of Terms and People.

- **Reading Skill** Have students use the *Reading Strategy: Recognize Sequence* worksheet. Teaching Resources, **p. 12**

- **NoteTaking** Using the Paragraph Shrinking strategy (TE, p. T20), have students read the section. As students read, have them complete the sequence chart. Reading and Note Taking Study Guide

European Colonies in the Americas ⓛ3

Instruct

- **Introduce: Key Terms** Ask students to find the key terms **House of Burgesses** and **Mayflower Compact** (in bold) in the text. Ask students to predict how the two might have contributed to the American Revolution.

- **Teach** Ask **What countries had colonies in the Americas?** *(France, Spain, Portugal, the Netherlands, and England)* **How was the colony of Virginia governed?** *(by a royal governor and the elected House of Burgesses)* **How was the government of the New England colonies similar to that of Virginia?** *(Like Virginia, the New England colonies had a representative government.)* **How were the Southern colonies different from other English colonies in the Americas?** *(The economy was based on plantations operated with slave labor.)*

- **Quick Activity** Display Color Transparency: *English Colonies in North America.* Use the lesson in the transparency book to discuss each cluster of colonies. Color Transparencies **A-66**

Independent Practice

Have students study the map on the next page, and write paragraphs describing how the influence of each European nation can still be seen today in the area.

Monitor Progress

As students fill in their sequence charts, circulate to make sure that they sequence the events correctly. For a completed version of the sequence chart, see Note Taking Transparencies, **B-2**.

Answers

Thinking Critically

1. It reflects the traditions established by the Magna Carta and the English Bill of Rights, both of which guaranteed certain rights. Congress is modeled on the British Parliament.

2. Locke's ideas could lead to revolution if individuals believe that a goverment is disregarding their natural rights.

● **INFOGRAPHIC**

ROOTS of DEMOCRACY

Although the United States is more than 200 years old, the ideas of democracy and representative government are far older. The roots of democracy reach back to civilizations in southwest Asia and Europe.

THE ENLIGHTENMENT ▲

LOCKE   MONTESQUIEU

Two Enlightenment philosophers who influenced American ideas about government were John Locke and Baron de Montesquieu. Locke stated that all people have natural rights and that if a monarch violates those rights, then the people have the right to overthrow the monarch. Montesquieu declared that the powers of government should be clearly defined and limited.

JUDEO~CHRISTIAN ROOTS ▲

The values found in the Bible, including the Ten Commandments and the teachings of Jesus, inspired American ideas about government and morality.

DEMOCRACY

ENGLISH PARLIAMENTARY TRADITIONS ▼

Two key English documents inspired Americans. The Magna Carta (1215) and the English Bill of Rights (1689) guaranteed certain rights to citizens, including the right to trial by jury. The ideas of a two-house lawmaking body and voting rights also influenced Americans.

GRECO~ROMAN ROOTS ▶

Ancient Greek democracy and Roman republicanism have influenced American government.

ENGLISH BILL OF RIGHTS

MAGNA CARTA

ENGLAND

Thinking Critically

1. **Draw Conclusions** How does government in the United States reflect English Parliamentary traditions?

2. **Make Inferences** How might John Locke's ideas about natural rights lead to revolution?

History *Interactive* ✶
For: More about the roots of democracy
www.pearsonschool.com/ushist

Differentiated Instruction   **Solutions for All Learners**

ⓛ1 **Special Needs Students**   ⓛ2 **English Language Learners**   ⓛ2 **Less Proficient Readers**

Distribute blank outline maps of North America. Then, organize students into groups, and ask them to work together to locate on the map the Spanish colonies in Mexico, Central America, the American Southwest, and Florida; the French colonies in Canada (Nova Scotia and along the St. Lawrence River); and the English colonies along the Atlantic coast. Place a map of the United States as it appears today on the overhead to help students. Have students choose colors to represent the areas colonized by the three European countries, make map keys, and label the New England colonies, the Middle colonies, and the Southern colonies. Then, ask students to write sentences that summarize the information shown on their maps.

Despite enormous losses from disease, starvation, and war with the Indians, the English expanded around the Chesapeake Bay. The colonists prospered by raising tobacco for export. Claiming the political rights of Englishmen, the Virginia planters elected a legislature, known as the **House of Burgesses.** It governed the colony in partnership with a royal governor appointed by the king of England.

New England Colonies To the north, the English established more colonies, which they called New England. The first colonists were devout Protestants called "Puritans," who hoped to create model moral communities. They settled first in 1620 at Plymouth, where they adopted the **Mayflower Compact,** which provided a framework for self-government. By 1700, New England had four colonies: Massachusetts, Rhode Island, Connecticut, and New Hampshire.

Adapting to the cold climate and short growing season, the New Englanders supplemented farming with lumber harvested from the forests and fish from the sea. By building ships, they were able to trade with the other colonies and with Europe.

Middle and Southern Colonies The English developed a third cluster of colonies between Maryland and New England. They conquered Dutch New Netherland and renamed it New York, then added New Jersey and Pennsylvania, a haven for Quaker immigrants. The Middle Colonies offered religious toleration and a prospering economy based on exporting wheat.

South of Virginia, the English developed a fourth cluster of colonies. The Southern Colonies consisted of North Carolina, South Carolina, and Georgia. The colonists raised rice on coastal plantations and cattle on farms in the backcountry. The plantations relied on the labor of enslaved Africans.

✔ **Checkpoint** What were the major economic activities of the English colonies in America?

Democratic Ideals in the American Colonies

The English colonists brought ideas about democracy and republican government with them to America. Some of these ideas were from Southwest Asia while others came from Europe.

English Traditions As English citizens, the colonists believed that they were entitled to the same rights as English citizens in Britain. Many of these rights were contained in two important documents: the Magna Carta and the English Bill of Rights. The **Magna Carta,** signed by King John in 1215, limited the power of the English monarch. It protected the right of people to own private property and guaranteed the right to trial by jury. The **English Bill of Rights,** signed by King William and Queen Mary in 1688, was a written list of freedoms that the government promised to protect. The English Bill of Rights required Parliament, England's lawmaking body, to meet regularly. It also stated that the monarch could not raise taxes or build an army without Parliament's consent.

The Enlightenment and the Great Awakening During the 1700s, ideas based on the **Enlightenment** circulated among well-educated American colonists. The Enlightenment was a European intellectual movement. Enlightenment philosophers believed that all problems could be solved by human reason. Frenchman Baron de Montesquieu and Englishman John Locke were two thinkers who applied reason to government and politics.

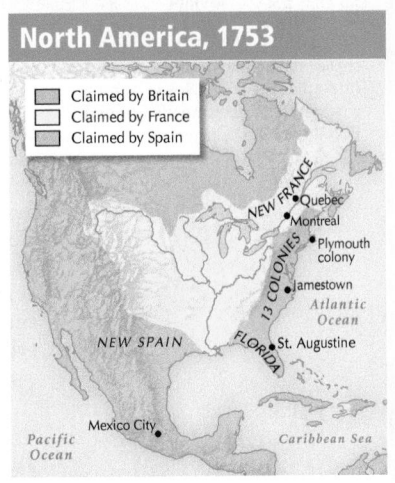

North America, 1753

Claimed by Britain
Claimed by France
Claimed by Spain

NEW FRANCE
Quebec
Montreal
13 COLONIES
Plymouth colony
Jamestown
Atlantic Ocean
NEW SPAIN
FLORIDA
St. Augustine
Pacific Ocean
Mexico City
Caribbean Sea

Colonial America

Three European nations controlled vast amounts of territory in North America in the mid-eighteenth century. *Which nation controlled territory that bordered the Pacific Ocean?*

Democratic Ideals in the American Colonies ⒀

Instruct

- **Introduce: Key Terms** Ask students to find the key terms ***Magna Carta, English Bill of Rights,*** and ***Enlightenment*** (in bold) in the text. Tell students that the American colonists viewed themselves as English citizens with the right to elect their own government representatives. Have students discuss how the key terms affect the way we view government today.

- **Teach** Ask **Which document seemed to guarantee colonists the right to reject laws that they had not approved?** *(the English Bill of Rights)* **How did the Great Awakening affect the colonists?** *(They began to form new churches, breaking away from established European churches, and became more independent in how they worshiped.)* **Describe the connection between the Enlightenment and the Great Awakening.** *(The Great Awakening was characterized by religious freedom that was part of the political freedom encouraged by Enlightenment ideas.)*

Independent Practice

To enrich the lesson, have students access the History Interactive at **www.pearsonschool.com/ushist.** After students experience the History Interactive, have them write a brief essay describing how each root of democracy is reflected in the U.S. government today.

Monitor Progress

As students write their essays, circulate to make sure that they understand how each root of democracy has influenced government in the United States.

Differentiated Instruction Solutions for All Learners

Ⓛ1 **Special Needs Students**
Ⓛ2 **English Language Learners**
Ⓛ2 **Less Proficient Readers**

Explain to students that *Common Sense* echoed the themes of the Enlightenment and called people to declare their independence from Britain. To help students understand the ideas presented in Paine's pamphlet, have them read and complete *Link to Literature: Thomas Paine's* Common Sense. Teaching Resources, **p. 28**

Ⓛ4 **Advanced Readers**
Ⓛ4 **Gifted and Talented Students**

Have students research the Magna Carta and the English Bill of Rights. Tell students to create outlines detailing examples of American colonists applying the principles in one or both documents. Then, have students create an outline to detail what could have happened differently in the American colonies if the two documents had not existed. Tell students to use their outlines to write alternative history stories.

Answers

✔ farming and trade in crops and other goods, such as lumber and fish, with England

Caption Spain

Causes of the American Revolution L3

Instruct

- **Introduce: Vocabulary Builder**
Ask students to find the term *assert* and its definition in the text. Have students predict the reasons why the British Parliament *asserted* that the American colonists must pay for the French and Indian War, and how this decision affected the relationship between Britain and the American colonies.

- **Teach** Ask **Why did the British Parliament raise taxes and tighten trade regulations for the American colonies?** *(to pay for the French and Indian War)* **How did many American colonists show their dissatisfaction with the new taxes?** *(They boycotted British goods and harassed tax collectors.)* **Why do you think some of the colonists remained loyal to Parliament and the king?** *(Sample response: They probably believed that the taxes were fair and that people who refused to pay were traitors.)*

Independent Practice

Have students research to find out why Americans refer to the war fought between 1754 and 1763 as the French and Indian War, and how the British and the French refer to that war. Tell students to present their findings in a couple of sentences. *(Sample answer: The British and the French refer to this conflict as the Seven Years' War because this conflict spilled over into Europe between 1756 and 1763. Americans helped the British fight the French and their Indian allies, so Americans call the conflict the French and Indian War.)*

Monitor Progress

As students write their sentences, circulate to make sure that students understand how the French and Indian War affected relations between Britain and the American colonies.

Answers

✔ Enlightenment thinkers championed freedom of thought, speech, the press, and religion.

✔ Parliament levied the taxes against the colonists without the approval of elected assemblies in the colonies.

Vocabulary Builder
philosophy–(fih LAHS uh fee) *n.* theory or logical analysis of the fundamental principles of human conduct, thought, knowledge, and the nature of the universe

Vocabulary Builder
assert–(uh SERT) *v.* to state positively; declare; affirm

Enlightenment philosophy affected religious beliefs in the colonies. Colonists who admired these ideas wanted a religion that was less emotional and more rational. At the same time, attendance at church services was in decline.

During the 1740s, concern about these trends led to a religious movement called the **Great Awakening.** Evangelical preachers such as Jonathan Edwards and George Whitefield toured the colonies promoting revivals where people felt a direct and transforming contact with an overwhelming Holy Spirit. The Great Awakening led to the birth of new churches. This eventually increased tolerance of religious differences. Many colonists also came to believe that if they could decide how to worship God, they could also decide how to govern themselves.

The Enlightenment and the Great Awakening would later combine to influence the American Revolution. The Enlightenment informed the writings of political leaders, while the Great Awakening inspired the common people.

✔ **Checkpoint** Which democratic ideas were expressed by Enlightenment thinkers?

Causes of the American Revolution

The tradition of a limited English monarchy, experience with self-government, and exposure to Enlightenment ideas influenced the leading American colonists. A European war and a spirit of independence in the colonies prompted the colonists to take action that would change the course of world history.

Between 1689 and 1763, the British and French fought a series of wars in Europe. These conflicts spread to America and involved the French and English colonists and their Native American allies.

The last of these wars, called the French and Indian War, erupted in 1754 and ended in 1763 with a British victory. The peace treaty gave Canada, Florida, and a portion of French Louisiana to Britain. British colonists were eager to move into Louisiana, but Britain wished to keep peace with the Indians who lived on this territory. British limits on westward expansion angered the colonists.

Taxes and Traditional Rights The British victory was expensive, nearly doubling Britain's national debt. During the 1760s, the British Parliament asserted that the colonists should pay new taxes to help the empire. The proposed taxes and tighter trade regulations shocked the colonists. Valuing the prosperity and protection of the empire, they did not immediately seek independence. Instead, they wanted to remain part of the empire that for so long had produced so many benefits at so little cost to them.

In resisting the taxes, colonists cited the traditional rights of Englishmen. They cited the Magna Carta and the English Bill of Rights, which blocked the king from levying taxes without the permission of Parliament. During the 1760s, their problem was with Parliament, rather than with King George III. Professing loyalty to the king, the colonists hoped to be free from Parliament's efforts to tax them. They would pay taxes levied only by their own elected assemblies in the colonies.

Colonial Resistance To pressure Parliament, colonists boycotted British goods. Local committees enforced this boycott, which threatened the British economy. Angry crowds harassed colonists who helped to collect the new taxes. Colonists who refused to honor the boycotts or who spoke out in favor of the taxes were considered Loyalists. Representing a large minority, the Loyalists preferred to pay the taxes and honor Parliament and the king. They also feared that the resistance would lead to a war that Britain seemed certain to win.

✔ **Checkpoint** Why did many American colonists object to paying taxes imposed by Parliament?

History Background

The French and Indian War The source of this conflict in North America was a dispute over which nation controlled the Upper Ohio River valley. In 1749, the governor-general of New France ordered that all British colonists be removed from the area. He wanted to restrict British settlement east of the Appalachian Mountains. In 1754, a small battle between French and British forces began the war. France, however, had fewer soldiers and colonists in North American than Britain did. In 1758, the British and American soldiers outnumbered the French and Canadian soldiers nearly 5 to 1. The French relied heavily on their Native American allies, who successfully employed guerilla tactics, to do much of the fighting. In 1759, the French engaged the British in a conventional battle at Quebec and were defeated. With the fall of Quebec, the French and Indian War was mostly over in North America, although battles continued in other places, such as the West Indies and the Philippines. The French and Indian War officially ended in 1763 with the signing of the Treaty of Paris.

Geography *Interactive*
For: Interactive map
www.pearsonschool.com/ushist

Original 13 colonies
Other British territories
★ American victory
★ British victory

Conic Projection
0   200   400 mi
0   200   400 km

Conflict With Great Britain

The American colonists opposed "taxation without representation"—or taxes levied by a Parliament to which the colonists had elected no representatives. Patriot leaders staged boycotts and anti-British propaganda campaigns in order to win support for independence.

Map Skills The American Revolution was fought in battles along the east coast of North America and along the Mississippi River in the West. This map shows the war's major battles in the fight for American independence from Great Britain.

1. Locate: (a) Saratoga, (b) Brandywine, (c) Yorktown

2. Place Which battles were fought along the Mississippi River?

3. Synthesize Information Based on the dates that appear on the map, in which region were the earlier battles fought? In which region were the later battles fought?

Roots of the American Revolution

1763 French and Indian War ends with a British victory. King George III signs the Proclamation of 1763, ending colonial expansion west of the Appalachian Mountains.

1764 To pay off war debt, Parliament passes the Sugar Act, imposing duties on imported sugar and other goods that colonists import from England.

1765 Stamp Act is passed by Parliament, directly taxing all legal documents, almanacs, and other items in the colonies. Colonists form the Sons of Liberty and the Daughters of Liberty to organize protests. One year later, the Stamp Act is repealed.

1767 Parliament passes the Townshend Acts, taxing a number of items the colonies import. Colonists boycott British goods.

1770 Boston Massacre results in death of five colonists. Townshend Acts are repealed.

1773 Protesting the tax on tea, colonists stage the Boston Tea Party, dumping crates of British tea into Boston Harbor.

1774 Parliament passes the Intolerable Acts, imposing harsh measures on the colonies. The First Continental Congress meets.

1775 First shots of the American Revolution are fired at Lexington and Concord.

Connect to Your World

The Declaration of Independence Despite its importance to U.S. history, the Declaration of Independence was not always preserved under ideal conditions. After it was written in 1776, the document was rolled up and transported from place to place during the American Revolution. In the early 1820s, it may have been copied using a wet paper process, causing the ink to fade. Later, it spent 35 years hanging near a window, where the sun caused it to fade still more. In 1870, one person stated that the Declaration was so "rapidly fading out that in a few years, only the naked parchment will remain. Already,

nearly all the signatures attached to the Declaration of Independence are entirely effaced."

In 1921, the Library of Congress took over care of the Declaration and created a "shrine" for it. For a short time during World War II, the Declaration was moved from Washington, D.C., to Fort Knox for safety. In 1952, the Declaration was sent to the National Archives, where it remains today. It is contained in a case of bulletproof glass with UV light filters to protect it from sunlight. Computer systems monitor the document for fading.

Assess and Reteach

Assess Progress

- Have students complete the Section Assessment.

- Administer the Section Quiz.
  Teaching Resources, **p. 33**

- To further assess student understanding, use Progress Monitoring Transparencies, **2.**

Reteach

If students need more instruction, have them read the section summary.

Reading and Note Taking
Study Guide

Adapted Reading and
Note Taking Study Guide

Spanish Reading and
Note Taking Study Guide

Extend

Have students research the creation of the Continental Congress and its debates over the wording of the Declaration of Independence. Ask students to prepare oral reports to present their findings to the class.

Answer

✓ Sample response: The British could declare war on the colonists and defeat them.

The War for Independence

In 1774, leading colonists held a convention, called the First Continental Congress. Delegates appealed to the British government to stop taxing the colonies. The British government refused.

Americans Declare Their Independence In 1775, war began when British troops tried to seize arms and ammunition stored at Concord, Massachusetts. New Englanders quickly organized an army, which the Continental Congress adopted as the army for all the colonies.

In 1776, Congress adopted a Declaration of Independence drafted by **Thomas Jefferson** of Virginia. This document declared American independence and expressed Enlightenment ideas about the natural rights of people. The Declaration stated that certain truths were "self-evident."

Primary Source "That all men are created equal; that they are endowed by their Creator with certain unalienable rights; that among these are life, liberty, and the pursuit of happiness. . . ."

—Declaration of Independence, July 4, 1776

The War Is Fought During the war, the British made many military mistakes because they underestimated the Patriots, who were highly motivated and benefited from the leadership of **George Washington.** Beginning in 1778, the Patriots also received military assistance from France. In 1781, a French fleet trapped the British army at Yorktown in Virginia, where Washington's army completed the victory. The treaty of Paris, signed in 1783, gave the new nation very favorable boundaries: Florida in the south; the Great Lakes to the north; and the Mississippi River to the west. The British retreated to Canada, while the Spanish claimed Florida and everything west of the Mississippi.

✓ **Checkpoint** What risks did declaring independence pose for the colonists?

Minuteman
This sculpture reminds Americans of the sacrifices made by minutemen, members of the Patriot militia who were ready to fight for freedom at a moment's notice.

SECTION **2** Assessment

Progress Monitoring Online
For: Self-test with vocabulary practice
www.pearsonschool.com/ushist

Comprehension

1. **Terms and People** For each term and person below, write a sentence explaining how each contributed to the development of U.S. democracy or to the Revolution.
   - House of Burgesses
   - Mayflower Compact
   - Enlightenment
   - Great Awakening
   - Magna Carta
   - English Bill of Rights
   - Thomas Jefferson
   - George Washington

2. **NoteTaking Reading Skill: Recognize Sequence** Use your series-of-events chain to answer the Section Focus Question: What important ideas and major events led to the American Revolution?

Writing About History

3. **Quick Write: Identify Effects** Make a list of one or two effects of each of the following events: the French and Indian War, the British decision to tax the colonists, the colonial boycott of British goods, and the American Revolution.

Critical Thinking

4. **Make Inferences** What Enlightenment values are reflected in the Declaration of Independence?

5. **Draw Conclusions** What effects did the Great Awakening have on American thought?

6. **Analyze Information** How did the peace treaty that marked the end of the American Revolution change the boundaries of the United States? Which countries controlled territory on the borders of the new nation?

Section 2 Assessment

1. Sentences should reflect an understanding of how each term or person contributed to U.S. democracy.

2. Ideas: the Magna Carta's and English Bill of Rights' limitation on the monarch's power and protection of rights, the Enlightenment belief in human reason, and the Great Awakening's trust in people to decide how to worship God and govern themselves; Events: Parliament's taxes on the colonists to pay for the French and Indian War, the British government's refusal to stop taxing the colonists without representation, and the British troops' attempt to seize arms stored at Concord, Massachusetts

3. Students should provide at least one effect of each event.

4. belief in the natural rights of individuals

5. the birth of new, organized churches; increased religious tolerance; the belief that if they could decide how to worship, they could also decide how to govern themselves

6. The western border of the new nation extended to the Mississippi River. Canada was controlled by Britain; Florida and lands west of the Mississippi were controlled by Spain.

For additional assessment, have students access **Progress Monitoring Online** at www.pearsonschool.com/ushist.

◄ Benjamin Franklin framed by the U.S. Constitution

WITNESS HISTORY

A New Constitution

Delegates to the Constitutional Convention met in 1787 at Independence Hall in Philadelphia. After intense debate and compromise, they created a document that has endured for more than 200 years. Benjamin Franklin, a great patriot, diplomat, and philosopher, urged his fellow delegates to ratify the Constitution:

❝I agree to this Constitution with all its faults . . . because I think a general government necessary for us, and there is no form of government but what may be a blessing to the people if well administered. . . . On the whole, sir, I can not help expressing a wish that every member of the convention who may still have objections to it, would, with me, . . . to make manifest our unanimity, put his name to this instrument.❞

—Benjamin Franklin, Constitutional Convention, 1787

The Constitution

Objectives

- Identify the weaknesses of the Articles of Confederation.
- Describe the role compromise played in the creation of the Constitution and the struggle for its ratification.
- Define the principles expressed in the Constitution and Bill of Rights.

Terms and People

bill of rights
Shays' Rebellion
James Madison
ratify

federalism
separation of powers
checks and balances

NoteTaking

Reading Skill: Recognize Sequence
Complete a timeline that includes important dates that led to the formation of the U.S. government.

```
     1781 Articles
     of Confederation

  |──────|──────|──────|──────|
 1780   1785   1790   1795
```

Why It Matters Dissatisfied with British rule, the American colonists rebelled and created the United States of America. The leaders of the new nation faced the task of creating a system of government. Their hard work resulted in the U.S. Constitution, an enduring document that has guided the nation for more than 200 years. **Section Focus Question: What ideas and debates led to the Constitution and Bill of Rights?**

A Confederation of States

The colonists declared their independence from Britain in 1776. After their 1781 victory in the American Revolution, the colonists faced many challenges, including the daunting task of creating and organizing a new government.

States Establish Constitutional Governments The former colonies became states in 1776, and each wrote a constitution that created republics, or governments in which officials are representatives elected by the people. Voters elected their state legislatures and their governors. Only white male property owners could vote, except in New Jersey where women had the right to vote until 1807. African Americans—whether free or enslaved—and Native Americans were not permitted to vote. Most state constitutions included a **bill of rights,** a list of freedoms guaranteed by the state government.

Vocabulary Builder

Use the information below and the following resource to teach students the high-use words from this section. Teaching Resources, Vocabulary Builder, p. 11

High-Use Words	Definitions and Sample Sentences
constrain	*v.* to hold back; restrain Americans did not want to be **constrained** to the Atlantic coast; they wanted to be able to move west.
advocate	*v.* to speak or write in support of; to be in favor of Many Americans **advocated** a revolution against Britain, but others opposed it.

A Confederation of States

Instruct

- **Introduce: Key Term** Ask students to find the key term *bill of rights* (in bold) in the text. Explain that a *bill of rights* guarantees basic rights. Ask students to speculate on why most of the first 13 state constitutions included a *bill of rights*.

- **Teach** Using the Idea Wave strategy (TE p. T22), have students discuss the principles of the Articles of Confederation. Ask **How did the new government obtain revenue?** *(The states contributed money to the federal government.)* Draw students' attention to the image on this page and discuss life in the Northwest Territory. **What laws did Congress pass to manage the Northwest Territory?** *(the Land Ordinance and the Northwest Ordinance)* Have students describe the provisions of each law. **What did Shays' Rebellion reveal about the government under the Articles of Confederation?** *(It demonstrated its weakness.)* **Why do you think most Americans did not want a strong central government?** *(Citizens were afraid of losing their liberties to a distant, all-powerful government.)*

Independent Practice

Ask students to suppose that they are living in the United States in 1785. Have them write paragraphs explaining their support for either a weak central government or a strong one.

Monitor Progress

As students fill in their timelines, circulate to make sure that they identify the important dates that led to the formation of the U.S. government. For a completed version of the timeline, see Note Taking Transparencies, **B-3a.**

Answer

✓ Weaknesses include a national government with no control over interstate commerce, no authority to levy taxes, and no direct income. Also, without a President, there was no leadership.

The Northwest Territory
Congress passed land ordinances to organize the Northwest Territory. Settlers then rushed in to build homes. Eventually, the states of Ohio, Indiana, Illinois, Michigan, Wisconsin, and part of Minnesota were carved out of this vast territory.

Vocabulary Builder
constrain–(kuhn STRAYN) *v.* to hold back; restrain

Many of them guaranteed freedom of religion, freedom of the press, and the right to trial by jury.

The Articles of Confederation In 1781, the 13 states adopted their first federal constitution. Under the Articles of Confederation, most power remained with the states. The Articles granted the federal government only certain limited powers. Congress had the power to declare and conduct war and could regulate trade with foreign countries and with Indian nations.

Under the Articles, each state set its own trade policy. Each state tried to protect its growing industry and agriculture from competition by taxing goods imported from other states. This practice discouraged trade among the states.

The national government had no say in interstate commerce and could not levy taxes. For money, Congress drew on contributions from the states, which were unreliable. Without a steady source of income, the federal government could not pay its immense war debt.

The government also suffered from structural weaknesses. There was no President. Each state, no matter how large or small, had a single vote in a unicameral, or one-house, Congress. On the major issues, including declaring war and making treaties, two thirds of the states (nine) had to approve. Amending the Articles was almost impossible, because all 13 states had to endorse any change.

The Northwest Territory Under the Articles, Congress had authority over the vast Northwest Territory, which lay north of the Ohio River and stretched west from Pennsylvania to the Mississippi River. In 1785 and 1787, Congress passed two laws to manage this land. The first, the Land Ordinance, created a system for surveying and selling the land to settlers. The second, the Northwest Ordinance, described how territories should be governed and how they could become full-fledged states. This law also banned slavery in the territory and provided for public education.

Troubles Grow in the 1780s Lacking an army, the weak Confederation could not defend American interests on the frontier. The Spanish in Louisiana tried to constrain western American settlements by closing the port of New Orleans. Along the Great Lakes, the British refused to abandon frontier forts on the American side of the boundary set by the terms of the peace treaty that ended the American Revolution.

During the mid-1780s, an economic depression reduced the prices paid to farmers for their produce. Unable to pay their debts, farmers faced losing their crops, livestock, and even their homes. In Massachusetts, matters worsened when the courts seized farms from farmers who did not pay taxes to the state or their loans. In rural Massachusetts in 1786, armed farmers led by Daniel Shays shut down the courts, blocking foreclosures. The state of Massachusetts sent troops to suppress this revolt, known as **Shays' Rebellion.** The rebellion highlighted the weaknesses of the federal government.

✓ **Checkpoint** What were the chief weaknesses of the Articles of Confederation?

Differentiated Instruction Solutions for All Learners

L1 Special Needs Students   **L2 English Language Learners**   **L2 Less Proficient Readers**

Have students read aloud the red headings under the blue heading "A Confederation of States." Write the title for each red heading on the board. Then, invite volunteers to the board to write details under each heading. For example, under "States Establish Constitutional Governments," students might write "Each state had its own constitution and government," or "Most state constitutions had a bill of rights." Discuss the details that the students wrote under each heading, and correct any misconceptions.

The Constitutional Convention

By 1787, many Americans agreed that the Articles of Confederation were flawed. To draft proposed amendments to the Articles, the states sent delegates to a special convention in Philadelphia, in May 1787. However, once delegates restructured the national government, the convention would be known as the Constitutional Convention.

Favored by the small states, the proposed New Jersey Plan would give Congress the power to regulate commerce and to tax, while keeping the basic structure of the Confederation. The plan retained a unicameral legislature representing the states as equals—no matter how large or small. The states remained sovereign except for those few powers specifically granted to the national government. Under the New Jersey Plan, the United States would stay a loose confederation of states, rather than become a unified nation.

James Madison of Virginia designed the Virginia Plan, which <u>advocated</u> a national union that was both strong and republican. He insisted that a large republic could be more stable than a small one, because in a large republic, the diverse interests would provide checks and balances to preserve the common good. In addition to securing the power to tax and to regulate commerce, this plan proposed major structural changes. The nation would have a bicameral legislature: a House of Representatives and a Senate. In both houses, the states with larger populations would have more members. The Virginia Plan also featured a President to command the armed forces and to manage foreign relations.

Vocabulary Builder

<u>advocate</u>–(AD vuh kayt) *v.* to speak or write in support of; be in favor of

The Great Compromise The delegates worked throughout the hot Philadelphia summer to resolve their differences. Roger Sherman proposed what has come to be called the Great Compromise. It settled the differences between the Virginia and the New Jersey plans by creating a bicameral, or two-house legislature. In a concession to the smaller states, the Senate would equally represent every state by allowing just two senators per state. In keeping with the Virginia Plan, the House of Representatives, which represented population, granted more power to the larger states.

Another major compromise appeased the southern states. Their delegates feared domination by the northern states, which had a larger white population. To reassure the South, the delegates adopted the three-fifths clause. It counted each enslaved person as three fifths of a person, to be added to a state's free population, which boosted the number of the South's seats in Congress. The three-fifths clause, however, gave no rights to enslaved African Americans.

✓ **Checkpoint** What key compromises did delegates to the Constitutional Convention make?

The Struggle Over Ratification

The Constitution was now written, but it was not yet the law of the land. Before it could go into effect, 9 of the 13 states had to **ratify,** or officially approve, it.

Federalists Argue for Ratification Supporters of the Constitution were called Federalists. They wanted the United States to have a strong central government. Three leading Federalists—James Madison, Alexander Hamilton, and John Jay—wrote a series

HISTORY MAKERS

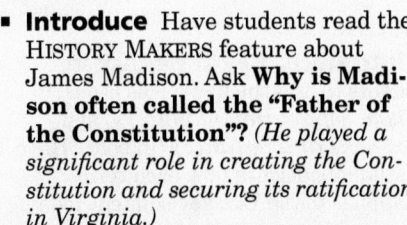

James Madison (1751–1836)
James Madison is aptly called the "Father of the Constitution" because he was so instrumental in creating that document and securing its ratification in Virginia. He agreed to add amendments that would guarantee basic freedoms, a promise he fulfilled by introducing the Bill of Rights when the House of Representatives first met. Later, Madison served as Secretary of State and was elected President for two terms.

The Struggle Over Ratification/Principles of the Constitution ⑬

Instruct

- **Introduce: Key Terms** Ask students to find the key terms *federalism, separation of powers,* and *checks and balances* (in bold). Have students discuss how each term applies to the U.S. government today.

- **Teach** Ask **What was the main point of *The Federalist Papers*?** *(The Constitution should be ratified because it was vital to the survival of the new nation.)* Have students read the Decision Point feature and discuss why the Antifederalists opposed ratification. Then, tell students to review the "Ideas Behind the Constitution" chart and discuss the principles listed. Ask **Why did the founders use flexible wording for the Constitution?** *(They could not anticipate the social, economic, or political events that the nation would face in the future.)* Have students predict how the flexible wording might cause conflict when interpreting the Constitution.

Independent Practice

NoteTaking Have students complete Venn diagrams comparing and contrasting the views of the Federalists and the Antifederalists. Reading and Note Taking Study Guide

Monitor Progress

As students complete their Venn diagrams, circulate to make sure that they understand the similarities and differences between the Federalists and the Antifederalists. For a complete version of the Venn diagram, see Note Taking Transparencies, **B-3b.**

Answers

✓ For: The United States needed a strong central government. Against: The Constitution gave too much power to the federal government.

You Decide

1. The majority of Americans supported the Constitution, and later a few powerful individuals might oppose it.
2. More time was needed to fix the objectionable parts; otherwise it would be dangerous.
3. Sample answer: The Constitution should be ratified because a strong national government would help the United States prosper as a new nation.

Reading Skill: Compare and Contrast As you read, identify similarities and differences between the Federalists and the Antifederalists.

Federalists		Anti-federalists
• For strong central government	•	• Against strong central government

of letters to newspapers in support of the Constitution. These letters, collectively called *The Federalist Papers,* explained why they believed the Constitution was vital to the survival of the new nation. Today, the *Federalist* essays are recognized as perhaps the most sophisticated explanation of the new American political system ever written.

Antifederalists Argue Against Ratification Opponents of the proposed Constitution were the Antifederalists. They included some leading Americans, such as Patrick Henry and Samuel Adams. The Antifederalists objected to the Constitution because they thought it gave the national government far too much power at the expense of the states. They believed that the President had too much power, that Congress was too small and could not represent voters, and that a federal court system interfered with local courts.

A Bill of Rights Leads to Ratification One of the most powerful arguments of the Antifederalists was that the proposed Constitution lacked a bill of rights. To secure ratification, the Federalists promised to add a bill of rights once the new government convened.

In 1789, Congress approved the ten constitutional amendments that became the federal Bill of Rights. States ratified the amendments in 1791. The protected rights included freedom of speech, freedom of religion, freedom of the press and of assembly, the right to bear arms as part of "a well-regulated militia," and judicial protections against arbitrary arrests and trials.

✓ **Checkpoint** What were the main arguments for and against ratification of the Constitution?

Decision ● Point

Should the states ratify the Constitution?

Delegates at the Constitutional Convention in 1787 debated the pros and cons of the new Constitution. In order for the Constitution to become law, at least 9 of the 13 states had to approve the document. Read the opinions below. Then, you decide.

Patrick Henry Opposes Ratifying the Constitution

Primary Source

"I review . . . the subject . . . and . . . the dangers . . . in this new plan of government, and compare . . . my poor abilities to secure our rights, it will take much more time to traverse the objectionable parts of it. . . . [T]he change is dangerous . . . and the experiment ought not be made. . . ."

—Patrick Henry, June 9, 1788

You Decide
1. Why did Hamilton favor ratifying the Constitution?
2. Why did Henry oppose ratifying the Constitution?
3. What decision would you have made? Why?

Alexander Hamilton Favors Ratifying the Constitution

Primary Source

"The establishment of a Constitution, . . . by the . . . consent of a whole people, is a prodigy, to the completion of which I look forward. . . . I dread . . . the consequences of new attempts, because I know that powerful individuals . . . are enemies to a general national government in every possible shape."

—Alexander Hamilton, *The Federalist Papers*

History Background

Constitutional Conflict The Constitutional Convention was held at a time when the new United States faced great challenges. The weak federal government was unable to pay its war debts either to France or to the Americans who had served as soldiers during the Revolution. Many Americans were angry about the lack of money and with what they saw as an uncaring government. When the delegates to the Constitutional Convention met in Philadelphia, many Americans opposed the creation of a federal government. Some feared that the union was about to dissolve. George Washington wrote, "Unless a remedy is soon applied, anarchy and confusion will inevitably ensue." Recognizing the seriousness of the situation, the delegates nominated Washington to lead the Constitutional Convention. But even Washington's prestige was insufficient to sway everyone—Rhode Island refused to send delegates because it feared that small states would be treated unfairly. Voters in Rhode Island refused to ratify the Constitution in March 1788 and for the next two years. The state was the thirteenth state to do so when its delegates finally voted for ratification on May 29, 1790.

Expanding and Protecting Civil Rights

TRACK THE ISSUE

What should the federal government do to expand and protect civil rights?

The U.S. Constitution guarantees equal rights for all Americans. However, in 1789, African Americans, women, and Native Americans did not have the same rights given white males. Over the years, rights have been extended to these groups. But a major question remains: How far should the government go to expand rights? Use the timeline below to explore this enduring issue.

1791 Bill of Rights
The first 10 amendments to the U.S. Constitution guarantee certain basic rights and freedoms.

1868 Fourteenth Amendment
Guarantees citizenship to everyone born or naturalized in the United States.

1920 Nineteenth Amendment
Women gain the right to vote.

1964 Civil Rights Act
Bans race or gender discrimination in public accommodations and jobs.

1990 Americans With Disabilities Act
Bans discrimination against people with disabilities.

The Bill of Rights

College graduates celebrate their achievements.

DEBATE THE ISSUE

Affirmative Action Some urge companies, colleges, and the government to use affirmative action programs to expand opportunities for women and minorities. Others argue that such steps are unfair.

❝You do not take a man who for years has been hobbled by chains, liberate him, bring him to the starting line of a race, saying 'you are free to compete with all the others,' and still justly believe you have been completely fair. . . . We seek not just freedom but opportunity . . . not just equality as a right and a theory, but equality as a fact and as a result.❞

—President Lyndon Johnson, speech, June 4, 1965

❝The civil rights laws themselves forbade employers to discriminate on the basis of race, sex, national origin, color, or religion. They didn't say anything about guaranteeing a certain number of slots to minorities or women. . . . The supporters of affirmative action everywhere seemed to believe that the only way to eliminate racial discrimination against blacks, Latinos, and women was to discriminate against white men.❞

—Linda Chavez, essay, October 2002

? TRANSFER Activities

1. **Compare** Choose a statement about affirmative action that you disagree with. Explain why you disagree.

2. **Analyze** Do you think either Johnson or Chavez believed that affirmative action is a basic right? Why or why not?

3. **Transfer** Use the following Web site to see a video, try a WebQuest, and write in your journal. www.pearsonschool.com/ushist

Objectives

- Identify measures the U.S. government has taken to expand and protect civil rights.
- Analyze opposing arguments regarding affirmative action.
- Formulate and support a point of view on a controversial issue.

Background Knowledge

Ask students to discuss which civil rights they believe are most important and explain why they think these rights are needed to make the nation free.

Instruct

Ask **What trend in civil rights does the timeline show?** *(that over time the U.S. government passed laws that extended civil rights to increasing numbers of people)* **How do the civil rights laws passed during the twentieth century differ from the Bill of Rights?** *(The civil rights laws apply to specific groups within the nation as a whole. The Bill of Rights guarantees basic rights to individuals.)*

Monitor Progress

- Have students complete the Issues Connector worksheet, *Expanding and Protecting Civil Rights.* Check their work to make sure that students grasp all aspects of the issue. Teaching Resources, **pp. 19–22**

- Remind students to complete their American Issues Connector Journal worksheets notes. Review their work for accuracy. Reading and Note Taking Study Guide

Answers

Transfer Activities

1. Sample answer: Chavez; because discrimination against nonwhites has been so severe for so long that passing laws requiring nonwhites to be treated fairly does not discriminate against white people.

2. Sample answer: Neither Johnson nor Chavez considered affirmative action a basic right. They saw it as a way to ensure equal treatment regardless of national origin, race, sex, and religion.

3. For more information about civil rights, have students access **www.pearsonschool. com/ushist.**

History Background

The Virginia Declaration of Rights At the conclusion of the Constitutional Convention, Virginia delegate George Mason was disappointed that the finished Constitution did not contain a bill of rights. Mason had written the Virginia Declaration of Rights, which was adopted in Virginia in 1776.

Mason did not remain disappointed for long. In 1789, James Madison used ideas from the Virginia Declaration of Rights to construct the Bill of Rights in the Constitution. Some of the ideas that Madison used from the Virginia Declaration of Rights included freedom of religion and the press, the right to bear arms, and the right to a trial by jury. In fact, the wording of Amendment VIII in the Bill of Rights is nearly identical to Virginia's Section 9: "Excessive bail shall not be required, nor excessive fines imposed, nor cruel and unusual punishments inflicted."

Assess Progress **L3**

- Have students complete the Section Assessment.

- Administer the Section Quiz.
  Teaching Resources, **p. 34**

- To further assess student understanding, use Progress Monitoring Transparencies, 3.

Reteach

If students need more instruction, have them read the section summary.

Reading and Note Taking **L3**
Study Guide

Adapted Reading and **L1 L2**
Note Taking Study Guide

Spanish Reading and **L2**
Note Taking Study Guide

Extend **L4**

Have students read and complete the Enrichment worksheet, *Document-Based Assessment: The Constitution.*
Teaching Resources, **pp. 13–14**

Answer

✓ the principles of federalism (a strong central government), separation of powers (three branches of government), and checks and balances on each branch of government

Ideas Behind the Constitution	☑ Quick Study
Principle	**Definition**
Popular sovereignty	People are the main source of the government's authority.
Limited government	The government has only the powers that the Constitution gives it.
Federalism	The federal government and the state governments share power.
Separation of powers	The government's power is divided among three branches: the legislative, the executive, and the judicial branch.
Checks and balances	Each branch of government has the power to limit the actions of the other two.
Representative government	Citizens elect representatives to government to make laws.
Individual rights	The Constitution protects citizens' individual rights, such as freedom of speech and freedom of religion.

Principles of the Constitution

The new Constitution divided power between the states and the nation, a division of sovereignty known as **federalism.** The states could no longer issue their own paper money. This was a delegated power belonging only to the federal government. Certain reserved powers belonged to the states, including the power to regulate elections. The federal and state governments also held some overlapping concurrent powers, among them parallel court systems.

The Constitution also promoted a **separation of powers** within the federal government by defining distinct executive, legislative, and judicial branches. Each branch had **checks and balances** on the others to prevent the emergence of a single center of power. For example, although Congress enacts laws, the President may veto them—but Congress may override the veto by a two-thirds majority. The President nominates judges, but the Senate must approve them.

The founders knew that they could not anticipate future social, economic, or political events, and so they worded parts of the Constitution to permit flexibility. For example, the Constitution gave Congress the power "to make all laws which shall be necessary and proper" to carry out its powers. This clause of the Constitution has been stretched to provide constitutional underpinning for so many laws that it is sometimes called the elastic clause. The ability to amend the Constitution also provides flexibility as well. Since its ratification, the Constitution has been amended 27 times.

✓ **Checkpoint** What major principles appear in the U.S. Constitution?

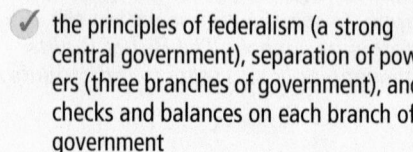

SECTION 3 Assessment

Progress Monitoring Online
For: Self-test with vocabulary practice
www.pearsonschool.com/ushist

Comprehension

1. **Terms and People** What do all of the terms and people listed below have in common? Explain.
   - bill of rights
   - Shays' Rebellion
   - James Madison
   - ratify
   - federalism
   - separation of powers
   - checks and balances

2. **NoteTaking Reading Skill: Recognize Sequence** Use your timeline to answer the Section Focus Question: What ideas and debates led to the Constitution and Bill of Rights?

Writing About History

3. **Quick Write: Make a Cause-and-Effect Flowchart** As you prepare a cause-and-effect essay, you need to decide how to organize it. To do so, create a flowchart that shows the causes and effects of Shays' Rebellion. Do you want to write about the events in chronological order or by the importance of each event?

Critical Thinking

4. **Draw Inferences** Under the Articles of Confederation, the federal government had limited power. Why do you think the states were reluctant to concede power to the federal government?

5. **Identify Central Issues** Why did delegates to the Constitutional Convention create a new Constitution rather than revise the Articles of Confederation?

6. **Recognize Ideologies** Does the following quotation express the views of a Federalist or an Antifederalist? Explain. "The entire separation of the States into thirteen unconnected sovereignties is a project too extravagant and too replete with danger to have many advocates."

1. Sentences should reflect an understanding of each term or person listed.

2. In 1776, the 13 states established individual governments. Most of their constitutions included a bill of rights. In 1781, the Articles of Confederation created a weak national government. Realizing that the Articles of Confederation were flawed, delegates met in 1787 to write a constitution. After the states ratified the Constitution, the Bill of Rights was added.

3. Students' flowcharts should organize information in a logical way and indicate how students will address the issue in their cause-and-effect essays.

4. Sample answer: The states did not want to be governed by a distant central government that might not be aware of each state's needs. Some delegates likened this to being governed by the British when the states were colonies.

5. They realized that they had very different ideas about how to fix the Articles and decided to write a new set of rules.

6. a Federalist point of view; the Federalists wanted one strong central government that had the power to make laws that applied to all the states.

For additional assessment, have students access **Progress Monitoring Online** at **www.pearsonschool.com/ushist**.

◀ Hard-working pioneers, like this woman, helped the new nation grow and prosper.

WITNESS HISTORY

Democracy in America

The French historian and politician, Alexis de Tocqueville, toured the United States for nine months in 1831 and 1832. After returning to France, he wrote *Democracy in America,* a highly regarded study of American life and customs. In one chapter, he discussed the importance of popular rule, or "sovereignty of the people," in America.

❝If there is a country in the world where the doctrine of the sovereignty of the people can be fairly appreciated, where it can be studied in its application to the affairs of society, and where its dangers and its advantages may be judged, that country is assuredly America. . . . The people reign in the American political world. . . . They are the cause and the aim of all things; everything comes from them, and everything is absorbed in them.❞

—Alexis de Tocqueville, *Democracy in America*

Objectives

As you teach this section, keep students focused on the following objectives to help them answer the Section Focus Question and master core content.

- Discuss the structure of the federal government and the emergence of political parties.
- Explore the major foreign policy issues that confronted the United States.
- Describe the growing differences between the North and South.

The New Republic

Objectives

- Discuss the structure of the federal government and the emergence of political parties.
- Explore the major foreign-policy issues that confronted the United States.
- Describe the growing differences between the North and the South.

Terms and People

Alien Act	impressment
Sedition Act	embargo
judicial review	cotton gin
Louisiana Purchase	Monroe Doctrine

NoteTaking

Reading Skill: Categorize Create a chart that lists the five Presidents in this chapter. List the major accomplishments of each President in the chart.

President	Accomplishments
George Washington	
John Adams	

Why It Matters The new U.S. Constitution promised a stronger federal government to guide the new republic through difficult times. During the 1790s and early 1800s, both internal political issues and international affairs tested the nation's strength. Despite these challenges, the nation continued to grow in size and power. Nevertheless, economic, political, and social differences began to divide the North and the South. **Section Focus Question: How did the United States and its government change in the late 1700s and early 1800s?**

Government and Party Politics

In 1789, a new federal government gathered in New York City. The nation was anxious as its first President took office. Washington's government set precedents of enduring importance to the nation's future. A good start would increase the strength of the nation. But early mistakes could doom it.

The Government Under Washington Fortunately, the United States enjoyed extraordinary leadership. Americans had the best of all possible Presidents in George Washington, whose dignity commanded respect. To conduct foreign policy, Washington appointed Thomas Jefferson as Secretary of State. To supervise domestic policy, the President depended on the Secretary of the Treasury, Alexander Hamilton.

Prepare to Read

Background Knowledge ⓛ

Ask students to recall that the new United States was trying to do two things: maintain the high ideals of the Revolution and assert itself as a new nation. Ask students to predict how these two goals might conflict.

Set a Purpose ⓛ

- **WITNESS HISTORY** Read the selection aloud.

  Ask **Do you think that Tocqueville approved of the way that the people "reigned" in American politics?** *(Possible answer: Tocqueville may have been skeptical about the wisdom of such a system and he probably found the situation highly unusual.)* Then, ask students to discuss how Americans may have responded to Tocqueville's report.

- **Focus** Point out the Section Focus Question, and write it on the board. Tell students to refer to this question as they read. *(Answer appears with Section 4 Assessment answers.)*

- **Preview** Have students preview the Section Objectives and the list of Terms and People.

- **NoteTaking** Using the Paragraph Shrinking strategy (TE, p. T20), have students read this section. As they read, have students fill in the chart. *Reading and Note Taking Study Guide*

Vocabulary Builder

Use the information below and the following resource to teach students the high-use word from this section. Teaching Resources, Vocabulary Builder, p. 11

High-Use Word	Definition and Sample Sentence
exploit	*v.* to make use of for one's own advantage or profit The Federalists tried to **exploit** any weaknesses in the Democratic Republican platform.

Government and Party Politics **L3**

Instruct

- **Introduce** Draw students' attention to the image of the American woman on the first page of this section. Explain that even in the late 1700s, the pioneer was a symbol of America. Ask students to discuss how the western settler represented American democracy to other Americans and to the world.

- **Teach** Ask **Why was Washington and his presidency so important to the nation?** *(He set precedents for the way that the nation would be governed.)* **What two political parties developed during Washington's presidency?** *(Federalists and Democratic Republicans)* **Why might Americans be opposed to a national bank?** *(Possible answer: It might have too much power; small farmers already feared bank foreclosures.)*

Independent Practice

Ask students to create a brief outline of the information under this blue heading to summarize what they have learned.

Monitor Progress

As students fill in their charts, circulate to make sure that they list the accomplishments of all five Presidents. For a completed version of the chart, see Note Taking Transparencies, **B-4.**

The Battle of Fallen Timbers
U.S. General Anthony Wayne led his troops against Indians in the Ohio Valley. Wayne's victory in 1794 opened the region to settlement and discouraged foreign nations from invading the region.

Hamilton and Jefferson belonged to a group of executive officers known as the President's Cabinet.

Hamilton's Financial Plan Stirs Debate

Alexander Hamilton wanted the United States to develop a commercial and industrial economy that could support a large federal government with a strong army and navy. He also wanted to pay off the nation's huge war debt. Hamilton proposed to pay off the debt by issuing government bonds, which paid interest to the bondholders. To pay the interest, Hamilton proposed new taxes on goods. To manage the debt, he asked Congress to charter a Bank of the United States with the power to regulate state banks.

To justify his ambitious program, Hamilton pointed to the Constitution's elastic clause empowering Congress to enact laws for the "general welfare." He reasoned that a national bank would promote the general welfare. In 1791, Hamilton's supporters in Congress—the Federalists—narrowly approved his program.

Democratic Republicans Challenge Hamilton

Hamilton's broad interpretation of the Constitution appalled critics who wanted to limit the federal government to powers explicitly granted by the Constitution. Favoring a "strict construction," Democratic Republicans led by Thomas Jefferson saw no grounds for a national bank.

The critics also pointed out that Hamilton's system favored merchants from northeastern cities who owed much of the debt. Why, southerners asked, should their tax dollars compensate creditors in the Northeast?

✓ **Checkpoint** How did Hamilton and Jefferson differ in their interpretations of the Constitution?

The Struggle Over Foreign Policy

President Washington and other federal government officials had their hands full dealing with domestic economic and political issues. But, as a sovereign country on the world stage, they also had to define and conduct foreign policy.

America Has Strained Relations With Europe In 1789, the French Revolution began. Many Americans, especially Democratic Republicans, sympathized with the French revolutionaries, whom they viewed as fighting for freedom from tyranny. Many Federalists, however, saw the revolutionaries as murderous mobs. Other nations of Europe shared this view, and they declared war on the new French government. Britain was among them.

The United States declared its neutrality in this war and continued to trade with Britain and France. In 1793, the British navy tested American neutrality by seizing U.S. merchant ships trading with the French colonies in the West Indies. This added to the U.S. outrage at British forts on the American side of the Great Lakes. To avoid war, Washington sent John Jay to London to negotiate with the British. In Jay's Treaty of 1794, the British gave up the forts but kept most of their restrictions on U.S. shipping. Washington had avoided war. However, the Democratic Republicans denounced Jay's Treaty as a sellout.

L1 Special Needs Students **L2 English Language Learners** **L2 Less Proficient Readers**

Ask students to find Jefferson and Hamilton below the blue heading "Government and Party Politics," and describe the governmental position that each man held. Then read the red heading titled "Democratic Republicans Challenge Hamilton" with students. Write the details on the board as you read. Help students understand that Jefferson believed that a national bank gave the government more power than was allowed by the Constitution. Write the phrase "strict construction" on the board, and ask students to find and read its definition. Refer students to a dictionary if they need additional support.

Answer

✓ Hamilton advocated a broad interpretation of the Constitution; Jefferson wanted a strict interpretation of the Constitution.

Meanwhile, the Americans were in conflict with Indians in the Ohio Country. In August 1794, General Anthony Wayne won the pivotal victory at Fallen Timbers. The Indians gave up two thirds of what is now Ohio as well as southern Indiana.

In 1795, the United States also benefited from a treaty negotiated by Thomas Pinckney with the Spanish. Pinckney's Treaty permitted Americans to export their produce through New Orleans. Recovering the forts, defeating the Indians, and opening New Orleans combined to encourage westward movement.

The Alien and Sedition Acts After two terms in office, George Washington retired. Federalist John Adams won the election of 1796. A foreign policy crisis with France dominated Adams's administration. Offended by Jay's Treaty, the French began seizing American merchant ships. In addition, the French demanded bribes from American diplomats. Soon, French and American ships were fighting a full-scale naval war on the high seas.

The Federalists exploited the crisis and tried to crush their political opponents by passing the Alien and Sedition Acts in 1798. Most immigrants voted Democratic Republican and the **Alien Act** made it more difficult for them to become citizens. The Alien Act also authorized the President to arrest and deport immigrants who criticized the federal government.

The **Sedition Act** made it a crime for citizens to publicly discredit federal leaders. The Federalists argued that criticism undermined trust in the government, which was dangerous at a time when the French might invade the country.

Vocabulary Builder
exploit—(ehk SPLOIT) v. to make use of for one's own advantage or profit

✔ **Checkpoint** Why did Jay's Treaty offend France?

Jefferson, Madison, and the War of 1812

By 1800, support for the Federalists and for fighting France declined. In the presidential election, Jefferson defeated Adams. The Democratic Republicans also won control of Congress and most of the state governments. The victors spoke of the election as the "Revolution of 1800."

Jefferson's election established the principle that the federal government should respect public opinion and allow public criticism. The new President encouraged Congress to abandon the Alien and Sedition Acts. He got rid of the Federalist taxes on stamps and on land. Despite reducing taxes, he cut the national debt from $80 million when he took office to $57 million in 1809. Jefferson achieved this budgetary miracle, in part, by reducing the size of the federal government, including major cuts in the army and the navy. He benefited from the French decision to seek peace and from increased federal revenue from customs duties.

The Supreme Court Issues a Landmark Decision
Thomas Jefferson's electoral revolution was limited by the growing power of the Supreme Court. In 1801, shortly before Jefferson became President, John Marshall became the Chief Justice of the Supreme Court.

Marshall served on the Supreme Court for 35 years—longer than any other Chief Justice. He had a lasting influence on the role of the Court. In 1803, Marshall first asserted **judicial review**—the power to decide the constitutionality of a federal law—in the celebrated case *Marbury* v. *Madison*. Judicial review gives the Court the power to review acts of the President or laws in Congress.

HISTORY MAKERS

Thomas Jefferson (1743–1826)
Thomas Jefferson was a writer, an inventor, an architect, and a politician. He served as the nation's first Secretary of State, second Vice President, and third President. Jefferson did not believe in a strong presidency or federal government. He thought the states should have relatively more strength. In 1798, he wrote the Virginia Resolutions, which said that states could leave the union if the federal government tried to take away their power.

The Struggle Over Foreign Policy

Instruct

- **Introduce** Ask students to find the key terms *Alien Act* and *Sedition Act* (in bold) in the text. Write these terms on the board, say them aloud, and have students say them with you. Ask **What is the definition of an alien?** *(an immigrant)* **What is the definition of sedition?** *(anti-government opinions)*

- **Teach** Using the Idea Wave strategy (TE, p. T22), have students discuss the events that took place in Europe during the administrations of George Washington and John Adams. Have students explore the U.S. response to these events. Record students' responses on the board under either *Washington* or *Adams.* Ask **How did Britain test U.S. authority in the 1790s?** *(by seizing U.S. ships and by maintaining forts on U.S. territory near the Great Lakes)* Draw students' attention to the image on the previous page and discuss the domestic issues the U.S. government faced. Point out to students that the Sedition Act has been held up as an example of the government interfering with the right to free speech. Ask **Why do you think the Federalist administration passed the Sedition Act?** *(to control or squash opposition to their policies)*

- **Quick Activity** Organize students into two groups, and assign one group to study the Alien Act and the other the Sedition Act. Then, have students present their findings and explain how each act affected the country.

Independent Practice

Have students write short essays explaining the challenges facing the U.S. government during the late 1790s.

Monitor Progress

As students write their essays, circulate to ensure that they are explaining the main challenges that the U.S. government faced and supporting their choices with evidence.

Answer

✔ because France was at war with Britain when the United States signed the treaty with Britain; the United States appeared to be taking Britain's side against France

Differentiated Instruction Solutions for All Learners

L4 Advanced Readers **L4 Gifted and Talented Students**

Have students research John Adams and his reasons for approving the Alien Act and the Sedition Act. Tell students to answer these questions: What was John Adams's role in the Revolution? What was his position on federal power during the Constitutional Convention? What was the main goal of his presidency?

Were the Alien and Sedition Acts in accordance with or at odds with Adams's political philosophy? After students have completed their research, have them organize and present the information in an oral report.

Instruct

- **Introduce** Display Color Transparency: *The Louisiana Purchase.* Use the lesson suggested in the transparency book to introduce the issues surrounding the *Louisiana Purchase.* Color Transparencies A-68

- **Teach** Have students examine the HISTORY MAKERS feature about Thomas Jefferson. Ask **How did the U.S. Supreme Court use judicial review during the Jefferson administration?** (*The Supreme Court tested the constitutionality of a federal law in* Marbury v. Madison.) **Why did Americans welcome the Louisiana Purchase?** (*France, which had been threatening war, would no longer hold territory adjoining the United States.*) **Why did the British step up their harassment of U.S. shipping?** (*because the United States was trading and conducting diplomatic relations with Britain's enemy, France*) **Did the United States benefit from the War of 1812?** (*No, the war was a draw and the nation lost its new Capitol and White House when the British burned them.*)

- **Analyzing the Visuals** Have students access **www.pearsonschool.com/ushist** to use the Geography Interactive map and answer the map skills questions in the text.

Independent Practice

For additional information on Thomas Jefferson, assign the *Biography: Thomas Jefferson* worksheet and have students answer the questions. Teaching Resources, **p. 31**

Monitor Progress

As students complete their charts, circulate to make sure that they list the correct accomplishments of each President.

Answers

Map Skills

1. Review locations with students.
2. The expedition began and ended in St. Louis, and crossed the Rocky Mountains and the Missouri and Columbia rivers.
3. Pike went directly west from St. Louis and then south into Mexico. Louis and Clark first traveled northwest and then west to the Pacific.

America Purchases Louisiana In 1803, Jefferson scored a great diplomatic coup when France's new ruler, Napoleon Bonaparte, agreed to sell the Louisiana Territory. In 1801, Napoleon had forced Spain to give the territory to France. That concession alarmed the Americans, who dreaded their powerful new neighbors. Fortunately, Napoleon needed money and decided to sell the territory.

In the **Louisiana Purchase,** Jefferson bought a vast territory extending from the Mississippi River to the Rocky Mountains. The Louisiana Territory nearly doubled the size of the United States and cost the country only $15 million. Explorers Meriwether Lewis and William Clark were sent west to the Pacific, while Zebulon Pike was sent southwest to explore the territory.

Jefferson's Embargo After the Louisiana Purchase, Jefferson's foreign policy faltered. The British navy resumed seizing American merchant ships trading with France. The British also seized sailors from U.S. ships to serve in the royal navy, a practice known as **impressment.**

As an alternative to war, in 1807 Jefferson persuaded Congress to declare an **embargo,** suspending trade by ordering American ships to stay in port. He expected that the embargo would pressure the British to make concessions. He reasoned that the British needed American food more than Americans needed to wear British-made clothing. In fact, however, the embargo hurt Americans more than it hurt the British.

Louisiana Purchase

Geography *Interactive*
For: Interactive map
www.pearsonschool.com/ushist

Map Skills The Louisiana Purchase of 1803 doubled the size of the United States. In exploring Louisiana Territory, Lewis and Clark were aided by Native American groups who lived in the region.

1. **Locate:** (a) Mississippi Territory, (b) Spanish Florida, (c) Missouri River

2. **Movement** Describe the journey of Lewis and Clark. Where did they begin and end their journey? What rivers and mountain ranges did they cross?

3. **Make Comparisons** How did Zebulon Pike's expedition differ from that of Lewis and Clark?

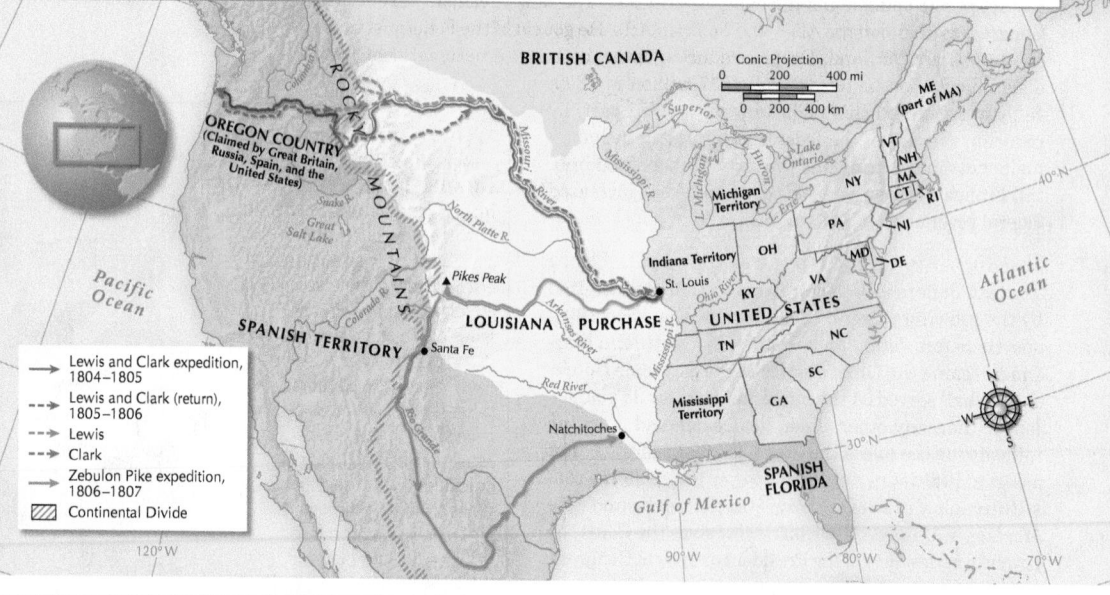

History Background

Jefferson's Compromise Many Americans consider the Louisiana Purchase to be Thomas Jefferson's greatest accomplishment as President.

However, in 1803, Jefferson's decision to purchase Louisiana posed a problem. The Constitution did not give the President the authority to buy foreign territory, but it did not say that the President could not buy foreign territory. Consequently, Jefferson used the "elastic" clause to justify the Louisiana Purchase, even though he had stated in the national bank debate that he did not believe in using this clause.

Jefferson had always insisted on a strict interpretation of the Constitution: if that document did not specifically assign a particular power to a branch of government, that branch could not use that power. By his own argument, Jefferson could not, therefore, justify the acquisition of the area.

However, the benefits of the Louisiana Purchase were so obvious to Jefferson that he decided to make the deal. The nation celebrated the great triumph, and Jefferson was never accused of overstepping his authority.

Industrial North and Agricultural South
In the North, industry relied on employing factory workers at low wages. In the South, agriculture often relied on the labor of enslaved Africans.

The War of 1812 Congress lifted the embargo in 1809, shortly before Jefferson's term ended. Another Democratic Republican, James Madison, became President. In 1812, he and Congress decided that there was no alternative to war with the British Empire.

During the first two years of war, the Americans failed in their attempts to invade British Canada. In 1814, the British invaded the United States. They briefly captured Washington, D.C., burning the Capitol and the White House. However, the Americans defeated the British in other major battles.

Weary of war, both sides agreed to a peace treaty that did not change any boundaries. Relieved at surviving the British counterattacks, the Americans celebrated the treaty as proving the stability of their republican form of government.

✓ **Checkpoint** What were the causes and effects of the War of 1812?

Growing Differences Between North and South

During the 1700s, a change took place that affected the way people worked. The gradual change from using mostly hand-held tools to using machines to produce goods is called the Industrial Revolution.

Industry Grows in the North The Industrial Revolution began in Great Britain, where inventors had built machines that revolutionized the way textiles were produced. Slowly, British textile workers came to the United States and built factories. Industrial growth was slow until after the War of 1812. The war cut off American access to British manufactured goods. Eager for substitutes, Americans built factories to produce textiles, shoes, guns, and tools.

Most of those new factories were in the northeastern states, which had more water power than any other region. Industrialization promoted urban growth and attracted European immigrants seeking work. Consequently, the Northeast became the most populous region in the nation.

Objectives

- Review the ideological differences of U.S. political parties over time.
- Analyze opposing arguments in primary sources.
- Formulate and support a point of view.

Background Knowledge ⓛ³

Have students discuss why geography can affect the way that people view political issues.

Instruct ⓛ³

Ask **What issues divided the North and the South in the eighteenth and nineteenth centuries?** *(The North had an industrial economy while the South's economy was based on agriculture with slave labor.)* Have students discuss issues that divide America regionally today and propose ways that people can resolve their disagreements.

Monitor Progress

- Have students complete the Issues Connector worksheet, *Sectionalism and National Politics.* Check their work to make sure that students grasp all aspects of the issue. Teaching Resources, **pp. 23–26**

- Remind students to complete their American Issues Connector Journal worksheets notes. Review their work for accuracy. Reading and Note Taking Study Guide

Answers

Transfer Activities

1. Bishop says that the nation has split into urban Democrats and suburban/rural Republicans. Abrams thinks most Americans share a set of core values.

2. Possible answer: Bishop might say that rural farmers would not care about how war would affect urban merchants. Abrams might say that all Americans had doubts about war, but that a slight majority of pro-war people in the South and West made others believe that they spoke for the South and the West.

3. For more information about national politics, have students access **www.pearsonschool.com/ushist**.

26 The Nation's Beginnings

TRACK THE ISSUE

How do regional differences affect national politics?

Throughout U.S. history, people in different parts of the country have had different views on important national issues. These differences have sometimes divided American politics along regional lines. Use the timeline below to explore this enduring issue.

1787 Three-fifths Compromise
North and South disagree over congressional representation of enslaved people.

1812 War of 1812
Western and southern farmers favor war.

1816–1832 Tariffs
North wants protective tariffs.

1861 Civil War
Disagreements between the North and the South lead to the Civil War.

1948 Dixiecrats
Southern Democrats split from their party over civil rights.

2004 Presidential Election
Election confirms division between Democratic and Republican states.

Henry Clay, a senator from the western state of Kentucky, supported the War of 1812.

Election of 2004
Candidate (Party)
☐ George W. Bush (Republican)
☐ John Kerry (Democratic)

The presidential election of 2004

DEBATE THE ISSUE

Red and Blue States Recent presidential elections have revealed an alleged political divide between the states. "Red" states in the South, West, and Midwest have generally voted Republican. "Blue" states in the Northeast and Pacific West have generally voted Democratic. Are regional or sectional differences affecting voting patterns?

❝Democrats and Republicans once came from the same kinds of communities. Now they don't. . . . The nation has gone through a big . . . sifting of people and politics into what is becoming two Americas. One is urban and Democratic, the other Republican, suburban and rural.❞
—Bill Bishop, *Austin American-Statesman*

❝Very little in politics, very little in life is black and white, or in this case, red and blue. There's an awful lot of gray. . . . Truth be told, if we ask about core American values and core beliefs, about opportunity, equity and how we should go about living our lives, we see very little [if] any difference.❞
—Samuel Abrams, Harvard University researcher

TRANSFER Activities

1. **Compare** In what way does Bishop believe the United States is split? How does Abrams see the red-blue divide?

2. **Analyze** How do you think each of the writers quoted above would respond to the regional differences of opinion regarding the War of 1812?

3. **Transfer** Use the following Web site to see a video, try a WebQuest, and write in your journal. www.pearsonschool.com/ushist

---

History Background

Why Red and Blue? In the twenty-first century, predominately Republican regions on a map of the United States are identified in red and predominately Democratic regions in blue. Why is this?

When television news programs began to broadcast election night results, they had to find a way to quickly identify which states' electoral votes had been won by Republicans and which had been won by Democrats. It was not until the 1970s, when most people had color televisions, that the major news networks began to use colors. At that time, each network chose the two colors that it would use to distinguish the two parties.

For the 2000 election returns, all of the networks chose red to represent Republican wins and blue to represent Democratic wins.

A week before the 2000 election, on NBC's *Today* show, a host asked how candidate George Bush could "get those remaining 61 electoral red states." This was the first time that the term "red states" was used. During the 36-day dispute over the election results, networks kept showing maps with red and blue areas, and the terms "red states" and "blue states" came into common use.

Cotton Boom in the South While the Northeast industrialized, the southern states had an agricultural economy that relied on enslaved labor. Slavery became more profitable as cotton became the South's leading crop. In 1793, Eli Whitney of Connecticut visited Georgia, where he invented the **cotton gin**. This simple machine reduced the time and cost of separating cotton fiber from its hard shell. American cotton production surged from 1.5 million pounds in 1790, to 167 million pounds in 1820.

Cotton farmers established new plantations in Tennessee, Alabama, Mississippi, Arkansas, Louisiana, and Texas. Taken from the Indians, the new lands proved more fertile for cotton than the longer-cultivated fields to the east.

Cotton was in great demand in textile factories in the northern United States and in Europe. By paying good prices for cotton, the mill owners encouraged southern planters to expand their fields and increase the number of enslaved African Americans to work them. However, as the North and South adopted different specializations, their political differences increased as well.

✔ **Checkpoint** How did the industrialization in the North and the spread of cotton in the South contribute to the spread of slavery?

The Monroe Doctrine

In 1817, James Monroe of Virginia succeeded James Madison as President. The Monroe administration hoped to ease sectional differences by cultivating national strength and ambition. The President and his Secretary of State, John Quincy Adams, wanted to prevent Spain from recovering her American colonies that had declared their independence. In 1823, Monroe and Adams announced a doctrine declaring that European monarchies had no business meddling with American republics. In return, the United States promised to stay out of European affairs.

The **Monroe Doctrine** meant little in 1823, when the Americans lacked the army and navy to enforce it. The Latin American republics kept their independence with British, rather than American, help. The doctrine became much more important later in the nineteenth century, when the United States began to intervene militarily in the Caribbean and Central America.

✔ **Checkpoint** How did the Monroe Doctrine assert American power in the Western Hemisphere?

Assess and Reteach

Assess Progress

- Have students complete the Section Assessment.

- Administer the Section Quiz. Teaching Resources, **p. 35**

- To further assess student understanding, use Progress Monitoring Transparencies, **4.**

Reteach
If students need more instruction, have them read the section summary.

Reading and Note Taking L3
Study Guide

Adapted Reading and L1 L2
Note Taking Study Guide

Spanish Reading and L2
Note Taking Study Guide

Extend L4
See the Professional Development pages for the Extend Online about the first presidency.

Answers

✔ The processing capability of the cotton gin had the effect of forcing slaves to increase cotton production. The North, with its growing number of factories, bought the cotton to make clothing and other textiles, supporting the growth of slavery.

✔ It united very different regions in the Western Hemisphere as "American republics" and confirmed the authority of the United States in the Americas.

SECTION 4 Assessment

Progress Monitoring Online
For: Self-test with vocabulary practice
www.pearsonschool.com/ushist

Comprehension

1. **Terms and People** For each item below, write a sentence explaining its significance.
   - Alien Act
   - Sedition Act
   - judicial review
   - Louisiana Purchase
   - impressment
   - embargo
   - cotton gin
   - Monroe Doctrine

2. **NoteTaking Reading Skill: Categorize** Use your completed chart to answer the Section Focus Question: How did the United States and its government change in the late 1700s and early 1800s?

Writing About History

3. **Quick Write: Rank Effects** Make a list of the effects of one of the following events: the Louisiana Purchase, the War of 1812, the Industrial Revolution. Then, rank the effects in order of importance.

Critical Thinking

4. **Identify Central Issues** Why did southerners object to Hamilton's plan to pay off America's war debt?

5. **Analyze Information** Why did the Democratic Republicans believe that Jay's Treaty did not serve American interests?

6. **Recognize Cause and Effect** What impact did the War of 1812 have on U.S. industrial growth? Explain.

Section 4 Assessment

1. Sentences should reflect an understanding of the significance of each term.

2. The federal government was strengthened, but many checks and balances to its power were included in the Constitution and in the Bill of Rights to make sure that federal power was not abused. As the United States dealt with international wars, the government's judgment was questioned and tested many times.

3. Sample answer: Louisiana Purchase: doubled the size of the nation; made western expansion possible; removed the French from North America

4. Southerners objected to Hamilton's using taxes on manufactured goods to help pay off the debt because northerners manufactured the goods and were making money on the deal, but southerners were not.

5. because it allowed the British to continue to restrict American shipping

6. Americans could no longer import British goods because of the boycott, so Americans built their own factories and manufactured their own goods, and these changes brought the Industrial Revolution to the nation.

For additional assessment, have students access **Progress Monitoring Online** at **www.pearsonschool.com/ushist**.

1 Quick Study Guide

Progress Monitoring Online
For: Self-test with Vocabulary Practice
www.pearsonschool.com/ushist

Quick Study Guide

- Have students use the Quick Study Guide to prepare for the chapter test. Students may wish to refer to the following sections as they review:

World in About 1500
Section 1

The Bill of Rights
Section 3

Causes of the American Revolution
Section 2
Section 3

The Growth of Federal Power
Section 3
Section 4

Key Events in the Nation's Beginnings
Section 1
Section 2
Section 3
Section 4

- For additional review, remind students to refer to the Reading and Note Taking Study Guide
Section Note Taking
Section Summaries

- Have students access **www.pearsonschool.com/ushist** for this chapter's History Interactive timeline, which includes expanded entries and additional events.

- If students need more instruction on analyzing graphic data, have them read the Skills Handbook, **p. SH21.**

■ World in About 1500

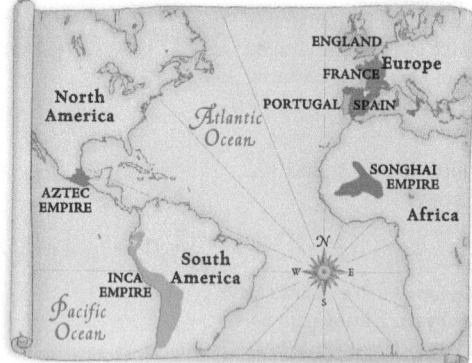

■ Causes of the American Revolution

The American Revolution	
Long-Term Causes	**Immediate Causes**
• Enlightenment	• British tax colonists
• Great Awakening	• Colonists protest and resist paying taxes
• French and Indian War	• British king refuses to compromise with colonists
	• Colonists declare independence

■ The Bill of Rights

1st:	Guarantees freedom of religion, speech, press, assembly, and petition
2nd:	Guarantees right to bear arms
3rd:	Prohibits quartering of troops in private homes
4th:	Protects people from unreasonable searches and seizures
5th:	Guarantees due process for accused persons
6th:	Guarantees the right to a speedy and public trial in the state where the offense was committed
7th:	Guarantees the right to jury trial for civil cases tried in federal courts
8th:	Prohibits excessive bail and cruel and unusual punishments
9th:	Provides that people have rights beyond those stated in the Constitution
10th:	Provides that powers not granted to the national government belong to the states and to the people

☑ Quick Study Timeline

In America

1492 Christopher Columbus sails to the Americas

1607 Jamestown established in Virginia

1740s Great Awakening sweeps through American colonies

Presidential Terms

1400–1600

1750

Around the World

1689 England's Glorious Revolution leads to English Bill of Rights

1707 Act of Union unites England and Scotland

Differentiated Instruction   Solutions for All Learners

L1 Special Needs Students   **L2 English Language Learners**   **L2 Less Proficient Readers**

Use the following study guide resources to help students acquiring basic skills:
Adapted Reading and Note Taking Study Guide
- Section Note Taking
- Section Summaries

Use the following study guide resources to help Spanish-speaking students:
Spanish Reading and Note Taking Study Guide
- Section Note Taking
- Section Summaries

American Issues
●—●—●—● Connector

By connecting prior knowledge with what you have learned in this chapter, you can gradually build your understanding of enduring questions that still affect America today. Answer the questions below. Then, use your American Issues Connector study guide (or go online: www.pearsonschool.com/ushist).

Issues You Learned About

● **Expanding and Protecting Civil Rights** The United States has long embraced the idea that citizens are entitled to certain rights.

1. What new ideas about citizenship were introduced during the Enlightenment?

2. Which groups of people were not afforded all the rights stated in the Bill of Rights? Why?

● **Global Interdependence** As Europeans explored and settled the Americas, these two regions became linked by culture and economics.

3. What caused European sailors to seek a sea route to Asia despite the dangers they faced?

4. Why were many American colonists dependent on trade with West Africa?

5. During the Industrial Revolution, Britain passed a law prohibiting textile workers from leaving the country or from sharing technological information on water-powered textile mills. Why would Britain do this?

Connect to Your World	Activity

Sectionalism and National Politics The Federalists and the Democratic Republicans were the first political parties in the United States. Today, the two main parties are the Democrats and the Republicans. Go online or to your local library and conduct research to learn more about each party. Then, use your findings to create a chart, similar to the one below, contrasting the two parties today.

Federalist Party	Democratic Republican Party
• Supported a powerful federal government	• Supported a weaker federal government and stronger state governments
• Promoted the growth of manufacturing and trade	• Promoted an economy based on agriculture
• Led by Hamilton and Adams	• Led by Madison and Jefferson

1775–1781	1788	1803	1823
American Revolution	U.S. Constitution is ratified	Louisiana Purchase	Monroe Doctrine issued

George Washington 1789–1797　John Adams 1797–1801　T. Jefferson 1801–1809　J. Madison 1809–1817　J. Monroe 1817–1825

1775 **1800** **1825**

1799	1805
Napoleon seizes control of France	Haiti declares independence from France

History Interactive
For: Interactive timeline
www.pearsonschool.com/ushist

American Issues
●—●—●—● Connector

Tell students that the main issues for this chapter are Expanding and Protecting Civil Rights, Global Interdependence, and Territorial Expansion of the United States. Then, ask students to answer the Issues You Learned About questions on this page. Discuss the Connect to Your World topics, and have students complete the project that follows.

American Issues Connector

1. the ideas that all people have natural rights, can overthrow the government if it violates those rights, and that the government should be clearly defined and limited

2. women, African Americans, and Native Americans; because only the rights of white males were recognized

3. The prospect of riches made up for the dangers of the exploration.

4. They relied on the labor of enslaved Africans.

5. Britain did not want the United States to be able to manufacture its own goods and stop paying for imported British goods.

Connect to Your World

Students' charts should include information about each party's history and its platforms.

For additional review of this chapter's enduring issues, remind students to refer to the Reading and Note Taking Study Guide American Issues Journal.

Chapter Assessment

Terms and People

1. a Spanish explorer who claimed lands in the Americas in the sixteenth century; affected Native American populations by enslaving them and accidentally giving them diseases to which they had no resistance

2. an intellectual movement during which philosophers believed that all problems could be solved by reason; most of the country's founders believed in Enlightenment ideals.

3. separation of powers: creating and defining distinct branches of a federal government; checks and balances: each branch of government limits the power of the other branches. Example: The courts can overturn laws that Congress passed.

4. a Virginia delegate who supported the Constitution and agreed to add amendments to guarantee basic freedoms; he was instrumental in creating the Constitution.

5. a machine that separated soft cotton fibers from the boll; made it possible to process cotton more quickly, increasing the number of slaves needed

Focus Questions

6. causes: the development of better ships and more advanced methods of navigation; scientific advances; an increase in economic wealth; competition for access to the profitable trade from Asia and Africa. effects: deaths from disease among Native Americans; an increase in the African slave trade; the Columbian Exchange

7. Important ideas: the Magna Carta's and English Bill of Rights' limitations of the power of the monarchy; the Enlightenment belief in natural rights. The Great Awakening instilled the idea that colonists could decide how to worship. Such ideas led many colonists to believe that they should govern themselves. Important events: the British taxes after the French and Indian War; the Boston Massacre, the Boston Tea Party; the Intolerable Acts

8. The Articles of Confederation were weak; delegates gathered in 1787

Terms and People

1. Define **conquistador.** What impact did conquistadores have on American Indian societies?

2. What is the **Enlightenment**? How did the Enlightenment influence American political thought?

3. Define **separation of powers** and **checks and balances.** Give an example of how these ideas work in U.S. government.

4. Who was **James Madison**? How did he contribute to the Constitutional Convention of 1787?

5. What was the **cotton gin**? What effect did it have on American economy and culture?

Focus Questions

The focus question for this chapter is **What factors led to the founding of the United States and its formation as a democratic republic?** Build an answer to this big question by answering the focus questions for Sections 1 through 4 and the Critical Thinking questions that follow.

Section 1
6. What were the causes and effects of European arrival in the Americas?

Section 2
7. What important ideas and major events led to the American Revolution?

Section 3
8. What ideas and debates led to the Constitution and Bill of Rights?

Section 4
9. How did the United States and its government change in the late 1700s and early 1800s?

Critical Thinking

10. **Identify Assumptions** What were some of the values held by North American Indian cultures?

11. **Analyze Information** What advantages did the Columbian Exchange bring to the people of the Americas? What disadvantages did it bring?

12. **Categorize** Identify four English colonial regions, and name their primary resources and economic activities.

13. **Recognize Cause and Effect** In what ways did Britain demonstrate its control over the American colonies? What result did these actions have on the colonists?

14. **Make Comparisons** How was the United States government under the Constitution different from the government under the Articles of Confederation?

15. **Draw Conclusions** Why do you think the Antifederalists demanded that a bill of rights be added to the Constitution?

16. **Summarize** Describe the accomplishments of Thomas Jefferson during his presidency.

17. **Problem Solving** Identify and evaluate one effort taken by the federal government prior to the War of 1812 to ease the problems caused by Britain's seizure of American vessels.

18. **Determine Relevance** How did the Monroe Doctrine demonstrate the increased presence of the United States in the world?

Writing About History

Expository Essay: Cause and Effect There were a number of reasons England established colonies on the eastern seaboard of North America. The founding of colonies had profound effects on Native Americans, Africans, and other European nations. Write an essay that explains the causes and effects of one of the 13 English colonies.

Prewriting
• Consider what you know about the founding of each colony, and choose one that you think best shows cause and effect.

• Take time to research facts, descriptions, and examples to clearly illustrate the causes and effects in your essay.

Drafting
• To organize the causes and effects in your essay, either show the chronological order of events or order the events from the least important to the most important.

• As you draft your essay, illustrate each cause and effect with supporting facts and details.

Revising
• Review your entire draft to ensure you show a clear relationship between the causes and effects.

• Analyze each paragraph to check that you have provided a thorough set of facts and details.

• Use the guidelines on page SH11 of the Writing Handbook to revise your essay.

to make revisions, but decided to write a new document. At the Constitutional Convention, delegates debated whether to make the federal government stronger. They also debated a bicameral legislature, the extent of presidential power, the size of Congress, and the federal court system. The Bill of Rights was added to the Constitution. Some believed that it gave too much power to the federal government.

9. The federal government became stronger. In the late 1790s, the government tried to protect itself from criticism, becoming less democratic. In the early 1800s, it restored

freedom of speech. By the 1820s, it was strong enough to set policy for all of the Americas.

Critical Thinking

10. valued family connections, worshiped animal spirits, and saw spiritual forces at work in the natural world

11. advantages: new ideas, goods, animals, and crops; disadvantages: disease, conflict, and enslavement

Document-Based Assessment

Religious Freedom in Early America

America was settled by colonists who had been subjected to religious discrimination in their native countries. How did their desire to protect their religious freedom influence the formation of state and federal governments? Use your knowledge of government and Documents A, B, and C to answer questions 1 through 4.

Document A

"Whereas Almighty God has created the mind free, so that all attempts to influence it by temporal punishments . . . are a departure from the plan of the Holy Author of our religion, . . . that to compel a man to furnish contributions of money for the propagation of opinions which he disbelieves is sinful and tyrannical; . . . that our civil rights have no dependence on our religious opinions, any more than our opinions in physics or geometry. . . .

Be it . . . enacted by the General Assembly that no man shall be compelled to frequent or support any religious worship, place, or ministry whatsoever, nor shall be enforced, restrained, molested, or burdened in his body or goods, nor shall otherwise suffer on account of his religious opinions or belief; but that all men shall be free to profess, and by argument to maintain, their opinion in matters of religion, and that the same shall in no wise diminish, enlarge, or affect their civil capacities. . . . [Y]et as we are free to declare, and do declare, that the rights hereby asserted are the natural rights of mankind, and that if any act shall hereafter be passed to repeal the present, or to narrow its operation, such act will be an infringement of natural right."

—Thomas Jefferson, Virginia Statute for Religious Freedom, 1779

Document B

"Congress shall make no law respecting an establishment of religion, or prohibiting the free exercise thereof; or abridging the freedom of speech, or of the press; or the right of the people peacefully to assemble, and to petition the government for a redress of grievances."

—First Amendment to the U.S. Constitution, 1791

Document C

Religion in the Colonies, 1776

Denomination	Number of Congregations
Congregational	668
Presbyterian	588
Baptist	497
Episcopal	495
Quaker	310
German Reformed	159
Lutheran	120
Methodist	65
Catholic	56
Moravian	31
Separatist and Independent	27
Dunker	24
Mennonite	16
Huguenot	7
Sandemanian	6
Jewish	5
Total	**3,074**

SOURCE: *The Churching of America, 1776–2005*, Roger Finke and Rodney Stark

1. What civil right is protected by Document A?
   A freedom of speech
   B freedom of the press
   C freedom of education
   D freedom of religion

2. What can you conclude about the growth of religion in the colonies based on Document C?
   A By 1776, there were fewer than 2,000 congregations in America.
   B There were a variety of religious denominations in colonial America.
   C Most colonists did not practice their religion on a regular basis.
   D Most colonists belonged to two establishment churches.

3. What is the relationship between Documents A and B?
   A Both established the right of assembly.
   B Both prohibited the government from imposing religious taxes.
   C Both guaranteed the separation of church and state.
   D Both guaranteed freedom of the press.

4. **Writing Task** What effect did the importance of religious liberty have on the social, moral, and political development of the new nation? Use your knowledge of the formation of the new national government and specific evidence from the primary and secondary sources above to support your answer.

12. Virginia: farmland; tobacco trade, slave labor; New England: timber and fish; merchant trade, shipbuilding, fishing. The Middle colonies: farmland; wheat trade; Southern colonies: farmland; slave labor

13. levied taxes without consent, fired on protesters, passed harsh laws to punish protesters; united many colonists in opposition to British rule, made people aware of their rights and eager to fight

14. Under the Articles of Confederation, the federal government was weak. Under the Constitution, the federal government was stronger.

15. They feared that a powerful federal government would trample on the rights of individuals unless its powers were limited.

16. Jefferson encouraged Congress to abandon the Alien and Sedition Acts, removed taxes on stamps and land, cut the national debt, and negotiated the Louisiana Purchase.

17. Possible response: an embargo, suspending trade by ordering U.S. ships to stay in port; however, it hurt Americans more than the British.

18. The United States was ready to claim the right to forbid European intervention in the Americas.

Objectives

- Describe the reasons that the colonists gave for wanting to break away from Britain.

- Identify the purpose and main ideas of the Declaration of Independence.

Prepare to Read

Background Knowledge ⓛ3

As a class, review the causes of the American Revolution and the events leading up to the writing of the Declaration of Independence. Then, as they read the Declaration, ask students to keep in mind the rights granted by the Magna Carta and English Bill of Rights.

By signing the Declaration of Independence, members of the Continental Congress sent a clear message to Britain that the American colonies were free and independent states. Starting with its Preamble, the document explains why the people of the United States have the right to break away from Britain.

The Declaration of Independence is made up of three parts: the Preamble and explanation of natural rights, which give the reasons for writing the Declaration; the list of grievances against British King George III; and the official statement of breaking away from Great Britain.

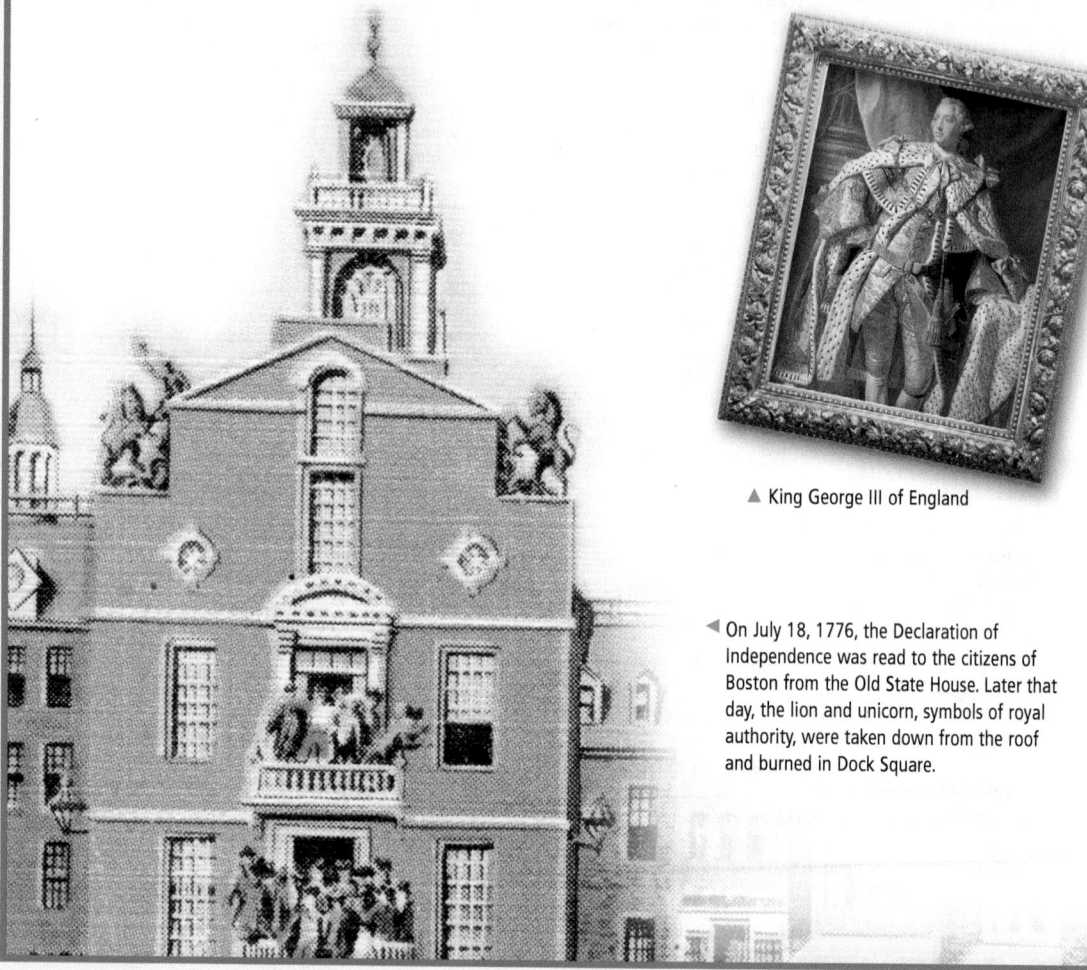

▲ King George III of England

◄ On July 18, 1776, the Declaration of Independence was read to the citizens of Boston from the Old State House. Later that day, the lion and unicorn, symbols of royal authority, were taken down from the roof and burned in Dock Square.

In Congress, July 4, 1776

THE UNANIMOUS DECLARATION OF THE THIRTEEN UNITED STATES OF AMERICA,

When in the Course of human events, it becomes necessary for one people to dissolve the political bands which have connected them with another, and to assume among the powers of the earth, the separate and equal station to which the Laws of Nature and of Nature's God entitle them, a decent respect to the opinions of mankind requires that they should declare the causes which impel them to the separation.

We hold these truths to be self-evident, that all men are created equal, that they are endowed by their Creator with certain unalienable Rights, that among these are Life, Liberty and the pursuit of Happiness.—That to secure these rights, Governments are instituted among Men, deriving their just powers from the consent of the governed,—That whenever any Form of Government becomes destructive of these ends, it is the Right of the People to alter or to abolish it, and to institute new Government, laying its foundation on such principles and organizing its powers in such form, as to them shall seem most likely to effect their Safety and Happiness. Prudence, indeed, will dictate that Governments long established should not be changed for light and transient causes; and accordingly all experience hath shewn, that mankind are more disposed to suffer, while evils are sufferable, than to right themselves by abolishing the forms to which they are accustomed. But when a long train of abuses and usurpations, pursuing invariably the same Object evinces a design to reduce them under absolute Despotism, it is their right, it is their duty, to throw off such Government, and to provide new Guards for their future security.—Such has been the patient sufferance of these Colonies; and such is now the necessity which constrains them to alter their former Systems of Government. The history of the present King of Great Britain is a history of repeated injuries and usurpations, all having in direct object the establishment of an absolute Tyranny over these States. To prove this, let Facts be submitted to a candid world.

He has refused his Assent to Laws, the most wholesome and necessary for the public good.

He has forbidden his Governors to pass Laws of immediate and pressing importance, unless suspended in their operation till his Assent should be obtained; and when so suspended, he has utterly neglected to attend to them.

He has refused to pass other Laws for the accommodation of large districts of people, unless those people would relinquish the right of Representation in the Legislature, a right inestimable to them and formidable to tyrants only.

He has called together legislative bodies at places unusual, uncomfortable, and distant from the depository of their public Records, for the sole purpose of fatiguing them into compliance with his measures.

Commentary

◄ **Preamble**
The document first lists the reasons for writing the Declaration.

◄ **Protection of Natural Rights**
People set up governments to protect their basic rights. These rights are unalienable; they cannot be taken away. The purpose of government is to protect these natural rights. When a government does not protect the rights of the people, the people must change the government or create a new one. The colonists feel that the king's repeated usurpations, or unjust uses of power, are a form of despotism, or tyranny, that has denied them their basic rights.

◄ **Grievances Against the King**
The list of grievances details the colonists' complaints against the British government and King George III. The colonists have no say in determining the laws that govern them, and they feel King George's actions show little or no concern for the well-being of the people.

The colonists refuse to relinquish, or give up, the right to representation, which they feel is inestimable, or priceless.

The Declaration of Independence ⓛ

Instruct

■ *Introduce* Tell students that the Declaration of Independence is a document that continues to influence our lives today. It is within this document that we read that "all men are created equal" and that everyone has a right to "Life, Liberty and the pursuit of Happiness." Help students understand that the equality, freedom, and other rights claimed in the Declaration of Independence may have started as political ideals, but today are embraced as part of American culture. Encourage students to consider the ways in which life in the United States would be different without the rights and freedoms spelled out in this document.

Differentiated Instruction Solutions for All Learners

ⓛ **Special Needs Students**   ⓛ **Less Proficient Readers**   ⓛ **English Language Learners**

Tell students that the Declaration of Independence contains words that are no longer common in modern English and that it is written in an old-fashioned, literary style. They will find reading it a challenge, but with concentration, they can understand the main ideas. Read aloud the first two complete sentences of the Declaration of Natural Rights (through "effect their Safety and Happiness"). Have students find the phrases that express cherished American

ideals and then discuss what they mean. *(Examples include all people are equal; people have certain rights that cannot be taken away; these rights include life, liberty, and the pursuit of happiness; governments are created to protect these rights; governments obtain their power from the people they govern; the people have a right to change or end a government that undermines these rights.)*

- **Teach** Ask students to read the Declaration of Independence silently and to refer to the Commentary to increase their comprehension. As students read the Declaration, have them record any unknown terms or unfamiliar phrasing. When students have finished reading, have them list those words and phrases on the board. Make sure that the list includes the words *impel* ("force"), *usurpations* ("unjust uses of power"), *despotism* ("tyranny"), *relinquish* ("give up"), and *inestimable* ("priceless"). Have students discuss each term, and allow them to refer to a dictionary to help decipher the eighteenth-century language. Then, discuss the document. Ask **Why did the colonists explain their reasons for declaring independence?** (*According to the Preamble, "a decent respect to the opinions of mankind" requires such a declaration.*) **Do you think that the colonists presented enough facts to support their case against the British king?** (*Yes—the List of Grievances runs on for more than two pages in this book.*) **Does this document work as a persuasive essay?** (*Students should note the introduction, the list of facts supporting the argument, and the conclusion—all of which are important parts of a persuasive essay.*) **How do you think King George III reacted to the Declaration upon first reading it?** (*with displeasure*)

Commentary

The king has refused to allow new legislators to be elected. As a result, the colonies have not been able to protect themselves against foreign enemies and convulsions, or riots, within the colonies.

The king has tried to stop foreigners from coming to the colonies by refusing to pass naturalization laws. Such laws set up the process for foreigners to become legal citizens.

The king alone has decided a judge's tenure, or term. This grievance later would result in Article 3, Section 1, of the Constitution, which states that federal judges hold office for life.

Forced by the king, the colonists have been quartering, or lodging, troops in their homes. This grievance found its way into the Constitution in the Third Amendment.

The king has taken away the rights of the people in a nearby province (Canada). The colonists feared he could do the same to the colonies if he so wished.

✓ Checkpoint

Why does the Declaration list the colonists' many grievances?

He has dissolved Representative Houses repeatedly, for opposing with manly firmness his invasions on the rights of the people.

He has refused for a long time, after such dissolutions, to cause others to be elected; whereby the Legislative powers, incapable of Annihilation, have returned to the People at large for their exercise; the State remaining in the mean time exposed to all the dangers of invasions from without, and convulsions within.

He has endeavored to prevent the population of these States; for that purpose obstructing the Laws for Naturalization of Foreigners; refusing to pass others to encourage their migration hither, and raising the conditions of new Appropriations of Lands.

He has obstructed the Administration of Justice, by refusing his Assent to Laws for establishing Judiciary powers.

He has made Judges dependent on his Will alone, for the tenure of their offices, and the amount and payment of their salaries.

He has erected a multitude of New Offices, and sent hither swarms of Officers to harass our people and eat out their substance.

He has kept among us in time of peace, Standing Armies, without the Consent of our legislatures.

He has affected to render the Military independent of and superior to the Civil power.

He has combined with others to subject us to a jurisdiction foreign to our constitutions, and unacknowledged by our laws; giving his Assent to their Acts of pretended Legislation:

For Quartering large bodies of armed troops among us:

For protecting them, by a mock Trial, from punishment for any Murders which they should commit on the Inhabitants of these States:

For cutting off our Trade with all parts of the world:

For imposing Taxes on us without our Consent:

For depriving us in many cases, of the benefits of Trial by Jury:

For transporting us beyond Seas to be tried for pretended offenses:

For abolishing the free System of English Laws in a neighbouring Province, establishing therein an Arbitrary government, and enlarging its Boundaries so as to render it at once an example and fit instrument for introducing the same absolute rule into these Colonies:

For taking away our Charters, abolishing our most valuable Laws, and altering fundamentally the Forms of our Governments:

For suspending our own Legislature, and declaring themselves invested with power to legislate for us in all cases whatsoever.

He has abdicated Government here, by declaring us out of his Protection, and waging War against us.

He has plundered our seas, ravaged our Coasts, burned our towns, and destroyed the lives of our people.

Differentiated Instruction Solutions for All Learners

L4 Advanced Readers   L4 Gifted and Talented Students

Encourage students to analyze the List of Grievances by assigning a topic to each complaint and then counting the number of times that each topic occurs. For example, one topic might be violence. Another might be legislative rights. Ask students to use their quantitative results, along with a more qualitative assessment of the signers' grievances, to draw a conclusion about what most irritated the colonists about British rule. Students should write out their conclusions, along with supporting evidence and reasoning.

Answer

✓ The Declaration lists the colonists' grievances so that King George III and the British government will know why the colonists find it necessary to declare their independence; they also hope to persuade others that their cause is just.

He is at this time transporting large Armies of foreign Mercenaries to compleat the works of death, desolation and tyranny, already begun with circumstances of Cruelty and perfidy scarcely paralleled in the most barbarous ages, and totally unworthy the Head of a civilized nation.

He has constrained our fellow Citizens taken Captive on the high Seas to bear Arms against their Country, to become the executioners of their friends and Brethren, or to fall themselves by their Hands.

He has excited domestic insurrections amongst us, and has endeavored to bring on the inhabitants of our frontiers the merciless Indian Savages, whose known rule of warfare, is an undistinguished destruction of all ages, sexes and conditions.

In every stage of these Oppressions We have Petitioned for Redress in the most humble terms: Our repeated Petitions have been answered only by repeated injury. A Prince, whose character is thus marked by every act which may define a Tyrant, is unfit to be the ruler of a free people.

Nor have We been wanting in attentions to our British brethren. We have warned them from time to time of attempts by their legislature to extend an unwarrantable jurisdiction over us. We have reminded them of the circumstances of our emigration and settlement here. We have appealed to their native justice and magnanimity, and we have conjured them by the ties of our common kindred to disavow these usurpations, which, would inevitably interrupt our connections and correspondence. They too have been deaf to the voice of justice and of consanguinity. We must, therefore, acquiesce in the necessity, which denounces our Separation, and hold them, as we hold the rest of mankind, Enemies in War, in Peace Friends.

We, therefore, the Representatives of the United States of America, in General Congress, Assembled, appealing to the Supreme Judge of the world for the rectitude of our intentions, do, in the Name, and by the Authority of the good People of these Colonies, solemnly publish and declare, That these United Colonies are, and of Right ought to be Free and Independent States; that they are Absolved from all Allegiance to the British Crown, and that all political connection between them and the State of Great Britain, is and ought to be totally dissolved; and that as Free and Independent States, they have full Power to levy War, conclude Peace, contract Alliances, establish Commerce, and to do all other Acts and Things which Independent States may of right do. And for the support of this Declaration, with a firm reliance on the protection of Divine Providence, we mutually pledge to each other our Lives, our Fortunes and our sacred Honor.

Commentary

The king has hired foreign mercenaries, or soldiers, to bring death and destruction to the colonists. The head of a civilized country should never act with the cruelty and perfidy, or dishonesty, that the king has.

The colonists have repeatedly asked the king to correct these wrongs. Each time, he has failed to do so. Because of the way he treats his subjects, the king is not fit to rule.

The colonists have appealed to the British people. They have asked their fellow British subjects to support them. However, like the king, the British people have ignored the colonists' requests.

◄ **Declaring Independence**
The resolution of independence boldly asserts that the colonies are now "free and independent states." The Declaration concludes by stating that these new states have the power to wage war, establish alliances, and trade with other countries.

✔ **Checkpoint**

What powers does the new nation have, now that it is independent?

Independent Practice

Assign each of four groups to one part of the Declaration (Preamble, Declaration of Natural Rights, List of Grievances, or Resolution of Independence). Vary the size of each group according to the length of each part (the List of Grievances being the longest by far). Ask group members to be prepared to "translate" and to explain the importance of any of the statements in their part of the Declaration. Also, ask groups to prepare an oral reading of their part of the Declaration. Remind students that the Declaration is a cherished piece of American literature, so they should apply their best oratorical skills.

Answer

 The new nation has the power to declare war, make peace, establish alliances with other countries, and trade with other nations.

Circulate to make sure that each group understands the amount of text for which it is responsible. Also, check that students understand that their tasks include "translating" and explaining the importance of the material as well as preparing to read aloud their part of the Declaration.

Signatories of the Declaration of Independence

JOHN HANCOCK
PRESIDENT OF THE CONTINENTAL CONGRESS 1775–1777

NEW HAMPSHIRE
Josiah Bartlett
William Whipple
Matthew Thornton

MASSACHUSETTS BAY
Samuel Adams
John Adams
Robert Treat Paine
Elbridge Gerry

RHODE ISLAND
Stephen Hopkins
William Ellery

CONNECTICUT
Roger Sherman
Samuel Huntington
William Williams
Oliver Wolcott

NEW YORK
William Floyd
Philip Livingston
Francis Lewis
Lewis Morris

NEW JERSEY
Richard Stockton
John Witherspoon
Francis Hopkinson
John Hart
Abraham Clark

DELAWARE
Caesar Rodney
George Read
Thomas McKean

MARYLAND
Samuel Chase
William Paca
Thomas Stone
Charles Carroll
of Carrollton

VIRGINIA
George Wythe
Richard Henry Lee
Thomas Jefferson
Benjamin Harrison
Thomas Nelson, Jr.
Francis Lightfoot Lee
Carter Braxton

PENNSYLVANIA
Robert Morris
Benjamin Rush
Benjamin Franklin
John Morton
George Clymer
James Smith
George Taylor
James Wilson
George Ross

NORTH CAROLINA
William Hooper
Joseph Hewes
John Penn

SOUTH CAROLINA
Edward Rutledge
Thomas Heyward, Jr.
Thomas Lynch, Jr.
Arthur Middleton

GEORGIA
Button Gwinnett
Lyman Hall
George Walton

▶ New Yorkers tear down a statue of King George III after a reading of the Declaration of Independence on Bowling Green. The statue was later melted down to make ammunition for the Continental Army.

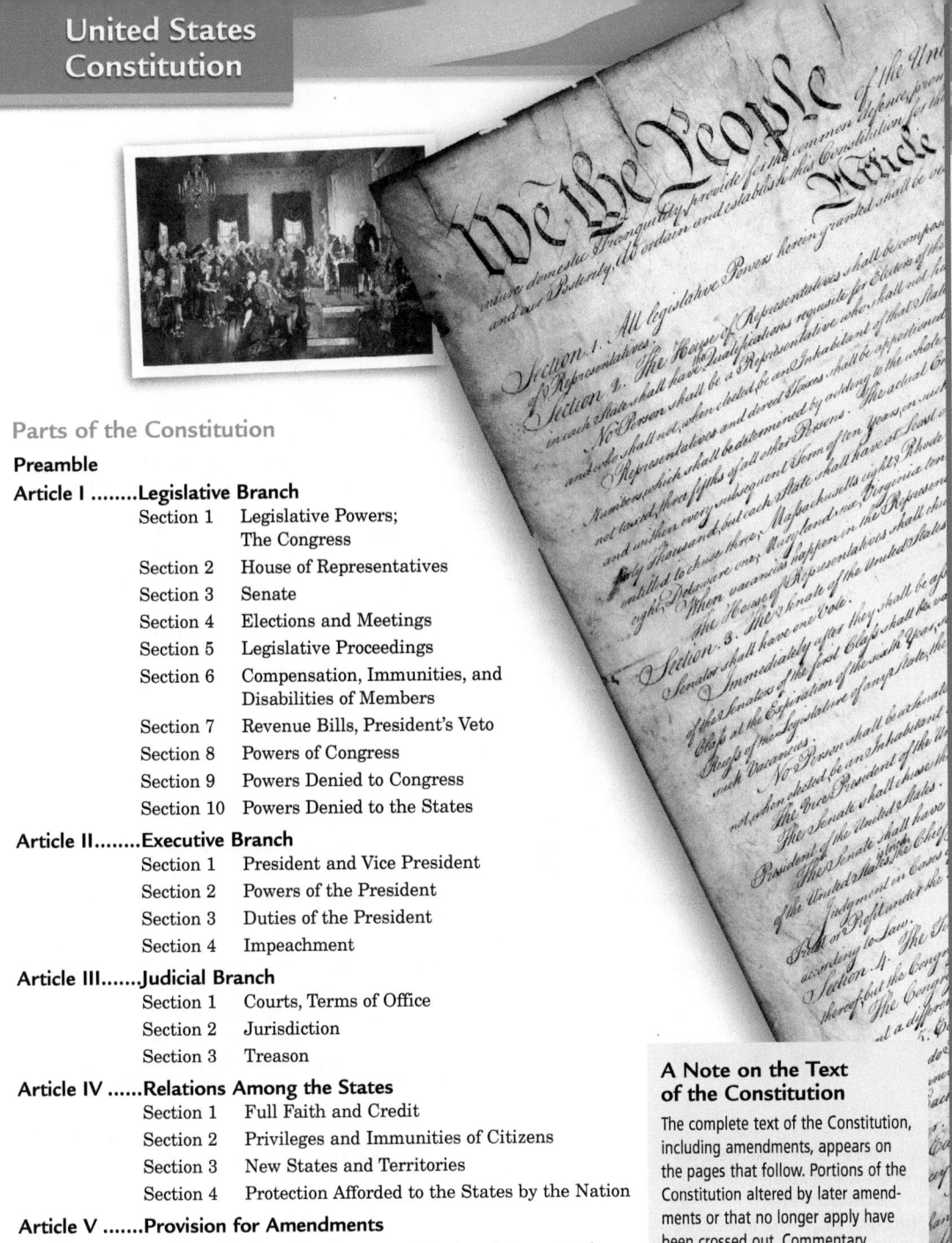

Parts of the Constitution

A Note on the Text of the Constitution

The complete text of the Constitution, including amendments, appears on the pages that follow. Portions of the Constitution altered by later amendments or that no longer apply have been crossed out. Commentary appears in the outside column of each page.

United States Constitution

Objectives

- Summarize the purpose of the U.S. Constitution.
- Discuss the powers granted to the executive, legislative, and judicial branches.
- List the rights provided by the Bill of Rights.
- Explain the provisions granted by the amendments to the Constitution.

Prepare to Read

Background Knowledge L3

Ask students to explain the importance of a written constitution. **Why is it vital that a nation have a constitution? What are the advantages of a written constitution? What might life be like in a country without a constitution?**

Article I
Legislative Branch

Instruct

- **Introduce** Remind students that the United States is a republic. Point out that the American people do not make laws directly; rather, they elect representatives to make laws for them. Representatives, therefore, have a vitally important job. Ask **If you wanted to be a member of Congress, could you run for office this year?** Tell students that the answer is in Article I of the Constitution. *(Qualifications for the House of Representatives include a minimum age of 25.)*

Commentary

The Preamble ▶
The Preamble describes the purpose of the government as set up by the Constitution. Americans expect their government to defend justice and liberty and provide peace and safety from foreign enemies.

Clause 4 ▶
Executive authority means the governor of a state. If a member of the House leaves office before his or her term ends, the governor must call a special election to fill the seat.

Preamble

We the People of the United States, in Order to form a more perfect Union, establish Justice, insure domestic Tranquility, provide for the common defence, promote the general Welfare, and secure the Blessings of Liberty to ourselves and our Posterity, do ordain and establish this Constitution for the United States of America.

Article I. Legislative Branch

Section 1. Legislative Powers; The Congress

All legislative Powers herein granted shall be vested in a Congress of the United States, which shall consist of a Senate and House of Representatives.

Section 2. House of Representatives

1. The House of Representatives shall be composed of Members chosen every second Year by the People of the several States, and the Electors in each State shall have the Qualifications requisite for Electors of the most numerous Branch of the State Legislature.

2. No Person shall be a Representative who shall not have attained to the Age of twenty-five Years, and been seven Years a Citizen of the United States, and who shall not, when elected, be an Inhabitant of that State in which he shall be chosen.

3. Representatives ~~and direct Taxes~~* shall be apportioned among the several States which may be included within this Union, according to their respective Numbers, ~~which shall be determined by adding to the whole Number of free Persons, including those bound to Service for a Term of Years and excluding Indians not taxed, three fifths of all other Persons.~~ The actual Enumeration shall be made within three Years after the first Meeting of the Congress of the United States, and within every subsequent Term of ten Years, in such Manner as they shall by Law direct. The Number of Representatives shall not exceed one for every thirty Thousand, but each State shall have at Least one Representative; ~~and, until such enumeration shall be made, the State of New Hampshire shall be entitled to choose three, Massachusetts eight, Rhode Island and Providence Plantations one, Connecticut five, New York six, New Jersey four, Pennsylvania eight, Delaware one, Maryland six, Virginia ten, North Carolina five, South Carolina five, and Georgia three.~~

4. When vacancies happen in the Representation from any State, the Executive Authority thereof shall issue Writs of Election to fill such Vacancies.

*Portions of the Constitution altered by later amendments or that no longer apply are crossed out.

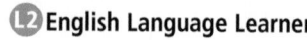

Differentiated Instruction Solutions for All Learners

L1 Special Needs Students   **L2 Less Proficient Readers**   **L2 English Language Learners**

Tell students that the Constitution begins with a brief Preamble, which states the broad reasons for forming a government, and that the rest of the document is broken into seven articles, or main parts. Have students find Article I. Tell them that most articles have several sections, each of which presents a particular topic. Point out that these topics, in turn, are often addressed in numbered subtopics called clauses. Ask **What is the subject of Article I, Section 2, Clause 2?** *(qualifications for election to the House of Representatives)*

5. The House of Representatives shall choose their Speaker and other Officers; and shall have the sole Power of Impeachment.

Section 3. Senate

1. The Senate of the United States shall be composed of two Senators from each State ~~chosen by the Legislature thereof~~ for six Years; and each Senator shall have one Vote.

2. Immediately after they shall be assembled in Consequences of the first Election, they shall be divided, as equally as may be, into three Classes. The Seats of the Senators of the first Class shall be vacated at the Expiration of the second Year; of the second Class, at the Expiration of the fourth Year; and of the third Class, at the Expiration of the sixth Year; so that one-third may be chosen every second Year; ~~and if Vacancies happen by Resignation, or otherwise, during the Recess of the Legislature of any State, the Executive thereof may make temporary Appointments until the next Meeting of the Legislature, which shall then fill such Vacancies.~~

3. No Person shall be a Senator who shall not have attained to the Age of thirty Years, and been nine Years a Citizen of the United States, and who shall not, when elected, be an Inhabitant of that State for which he shall be chosen.

Commentary

◀ **Clause 5** The House elects a Speaker. Also, only the House has the power to <u>impeach</u>, or accuse a federal official of wrongdoing.

◀ **Clause 1** Each State has two senators.

◀ **Clause 2** Every two years, one third of the senators run for reelection. The Seventeenth Amendment changed the way of filling <u>vacancies</u>, or empty seats. Today, the governor of a state must choose a senator to fill a vacancy that occurs between elections.

✓ **Checkpoint**

What is the main job of Congress?

■ **Teach** Have students read Article I. Ask **What is the main purpose of this article?** *(to present the rules related to the legislative branch of government)* **Why do you think the framers discussed the legislative branch first, and at such length?** *(To the framers, the legislative branch was the most important part of a democratic government.)* Now point out Section 8. Tell students that one problem with the Articles of Confederation, our first constitution, was that the federal government (also known as the national government or central government) did not have the power to tax the states for revenue to run the government. The federal government also lacked the power to regulate trade. **How did the Constitution correct these problems?** *(Clause 1 of Section 8 gives Congress the power to tax. Clause 3 gives it the power to regulate commerce among the states.)* **How did the Constitution affect the balance of power between the federal government and the states?** *(It increased federal power.)*

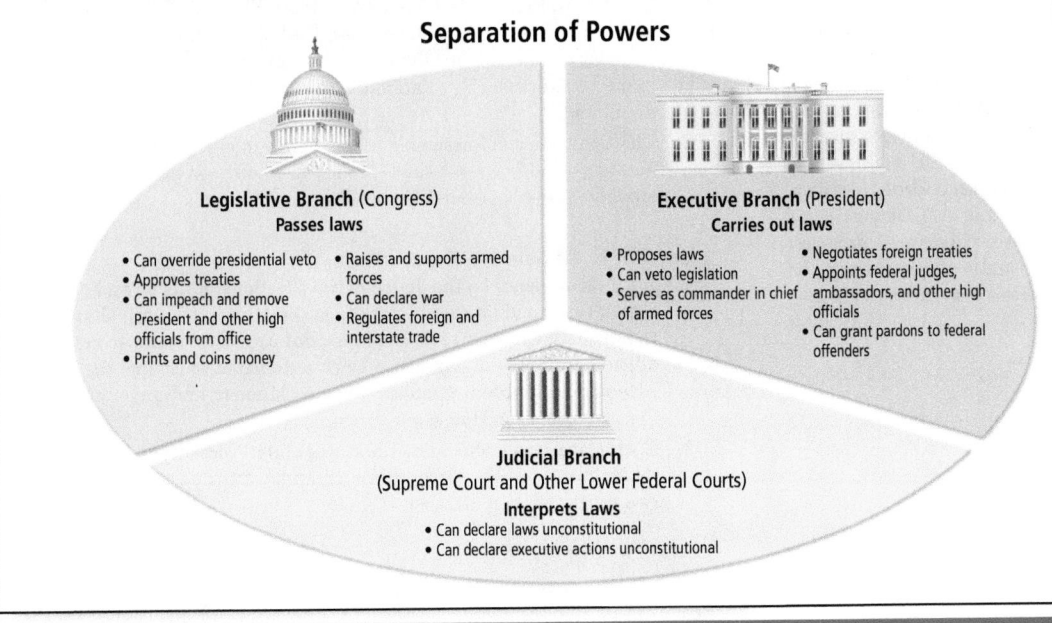

Separation of Powers

Legislative Branch (Congress)
Passes laws

- Can override presidential veto
- Approves treaties
- Can impeach and remove President and other high officials from office
- Prints and coins money
- Raises and supports armed forces
- Can declare war
- Regulates foreign and interstate trade

Executive Branch (President)
Carries out laws

- Proposes laws
- Can veto legislation
- Serves as commander in chief of armed forces
- Negotiates foreign treaties
- Appoints federal judges, ambassadors, and other high officials
- Can grant pardons to federal offenders

Judicial Branch
(Supreme Court and Other Lower Federal Courts)
Interprets Laws
- Can declare laws unconstitutional
- Can declare executive actions unconstitutional

Answer

✓ The main job of Congress is to pass national laws.

C3

Independent Practice

Have students create a table that summarizes the differences between the House and the Senate, according to Article I.

Monitor Progress

Circulate to make sure that students are creating a table with proper headings. Tables should be set up to compare rules related to the two houses of Congress and their members. Encourage students to make each entry as brief as possible, as they would if taking notes.

Commentary

Clause 5 ▶
The Vice President serves as President of the Senate. The Senate chooses its other officers.

Clause 6 ▶
The Senate acts as a jury if the House impeaches a federal official. The Chief Justice of the Supreme Court presides if the President is on trial. Two thirds of all senators present must vote for conviction, or finding the accused guilty. No President has ever been convicted.

 Checkpoint

Which branches are involved in presidential impeachment?

Clause 1 ▶
Each state legislature can decide when and how congressional elections take place, but Congress can overrule these decisions. In 1842, Congress required each state to set up congressional districts with one representative elected from each district. In 1872, Congress decided that congressional elections must be held in every state on the same date in even-numbered years.

4. The Vice President of the United States shall be President of the Senate but shall have no Vote, unless they be equally divided.

5. The Senate shall choose their other Officers, and also a President pro tempore, in the Absence of the Vice President, or when he shall exercise the Office of President of the United States.

6. The Senate shall have the sole Power to try all Impeachments. When sitting for that Purpose, they shall be on Oath or Affirmation. When the President of the United States is tried, the Chief Justice shall preside: And no Person shall be convicted without the Concurrence of two thirds of the Members present.

7. Judgment in Cases of Impeachment shall not extend further than to removal from Office, and disqualification to hold and enjoy any Office of honor, Trust, or Profit under the United States: but the Party convicted shall nevertheless be liable and subject to Indictment, Trial, Judgment and Punishment, according to Law.

Section 4. Elections and Meetings

1. The Times, Places and Manner of holding Elections for Senators and Representatives, shall be prescribed in each State by the Legislature thereof; but the Congress may at any time by law make or alter such Regulations, except as to the Places of choosing Senators.

2. The Congress shall assemble at least once in every Year, ~~and such Meeting shall be on the first Monday in December, unless they shall by Law appoint a different Day.~~

Section 5. Legislative Proceedings

1. Each House shall be the Judge of the Elections, Returns and Qualifications of its own Members, and a Majority of each shall constitute a Quorum to do Business; but a smaller Number may adjourn from day to day, and may be authorized to compel the Attendance of absent Members, in such Manner, and under such Penalties, as each House may provide.

2. Each House may determine the Rules of its Proceedings, punish its Members for disorderly Behavior, and, with the Concurrence of two thirds, expel a Member.

 Differentiated Instruction 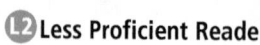 Solutions for All Learners

L1 Special Needs Students   **L2 Less Proficient Readers**   **L2 English Language Learners**

Ask students to list terms and phrases in Article I with which they are unfamiliar. They should note in which section and/or clause each term or phrase

appears. Have them work together to determine meanings and to restate phrases in their own words.

Answer

 Presidential impeachment involves the legislative branch and the judicial branch.

3. Each House shall keep a Journal of its Proceedings, and from time to time publish the same, excepting such Parts as may in their Judgment require Secrecy; and the Yeas and Nays of the Members of either House on any question shall, at the Desire of one fifth of those Present, be entered on the Journal.

4. Neither House, during the Session of Congress, shall, without the Consent of the other, adjourn for more than three days, nor to any other Place than that in which the two Houses shall be sitting.

Section 6. Compensation, Immunities, and Disabilities of Members

1. The Senators and Representatives shall receive a Compensation for their Services, to be ascertained by Law, and paid out of the Treasury of the United States. They shall in all Cases, except Treason, Felony, and Breach of the Peace, be privileged from Arrest during their Attendance at the Session of their respective Houses, and in going to and returning from the same; and for any Speech or Debate in either House, they shall not be questioned in any other Place.

2. No Senator or Representative shall, during the Time for which he was elected, be appointed to any civil Office under the Authority of the United States, which shall have been created, or the Emoluments whereof shall have been increased during such time; and no Person holding any Office under the United States, shall be a Member of either House during his Continuance in Office.

Section 7. Revenue Bills, President's Veto

1. All Bills for raising Revenue shall originate in the House of Representatives; but the Senate may propose or concur with amendments as on other Bills.

2. Every Bill which shall have passed the House of Representatives and the Senate, shall, before it become a Law, be presented to the President of the United States: If he approve he shall sign it, but if not he shall return it, with his Objections to that House in which it shall have originated, who shall enter the Objections at large on their Journal, and proceed to reconsider it. If after such Reconsideration two thirds of the House shall agree to pass the Bill, it shall be sent, together with the Objections, to the other House, by which it shall likewise be reconsidered, and if approved by two thirds of that House, it shall become a Law. But in all such Cases the Votes of both Houses shall be determined by Yeas and Nays, and the Names of the Persons voting for and against the Bill shall be entered on the Journal of each House respectively. If any Bill shall not be returned by the President within ten Days

Commentary

◄ **Clause 4** Neither house can adjourn, or stop meeting, for more than three days unless the other house approves. Both houses must meet in the same city.

◄ **Clause 1** Tax bills must be introduced in the House, but the Senate can make changes in those bills.

◄ **Clause 2** A bill, or proposed law, that is passed by a majority of the House and Senate is sent to the President. If the President signs the bill, it becomes law. The President can veto, or reject, a bill by sending it back to the house where it was introduced. Congress can override the President's veto if each house of Congress passes the bill again by a two-thirds vote.

(Sunday excepted) after it shall have been presented to him, the Same shall be a law, in like Manner as if he had signed it, unless the Congress by their Adjournment, prevent its Return, in which Case it shall not be a Law.

3. Every Order, Resolution, or Vote to which the Concurrence of the Senate and House of Representatives may be necessary (except on a question of adjournment) shall be presented to the President of the United States; and before the Same shall take Effect, shall be approved by him, or, being disapproved by him, shall be repassed by two thirds of the Senate and House of Representatives, according to the Rules and Limitations prescribed in the Case of a Bill.

 Checkpoint

What is the role of Congress and the President in making laws?

How a Bill Becomes a Law

Start: Senate

 Introduction
Bill introduced in Senate.

② Committee Action
Bill referred to standing committee. Moves to subcommittee for study, hearings, revisions, approval. Moves back to full committee for more hearings and revisions.

③ Floor Action
Bill is debated, then passed or defeated. If passed, the bill goes to the House of Representatives. If the bill has already passed in House, the bill goes to Conference Committee.

④ Conference Committee
Conference Committee resolves differences between House and Senate versions of the bill.

Congressional Approval
House and Senate vote on final passage. Approved bill is sent to the President.

⑤ Presidential Action
President signs, vetoes, or allows the bill to become a law without signing. Vetoed bill returns to Congress. Veto may be overridden by two-thirds majority vote of each house.

③ Floor Action
Bill is debated, then passed or defeated. If passed, the bill goes to Senate. If the bill has already passed through Senate, the bill goes to Conference Committee.

② Committee Action
Bill referred to standing committee. Moves to subcommittee for study, hearings, revisions, approval. Moves back to full committee for more hearings and revisions. Moves to Rules Committee to set conditions for debate and amendments.

① Introduction
Bill introduced in House

Start: House

 **Differentiated Instruction   Solutions for All Learners**

L1 Special Needs Students   L2 Less Proficient Readers   L2 English Language Learners

Ask students to study the diagram titled *How a Bill Becomes a Law*. Point out that the House and Senate follow similar steps in the process and help students follow the numbers and arrows on the diagram in order to understand the various steps. Then pair students and have them explain the process to each other. You may wish to have students create a board game based on the diagram in which players draw cards for the various possible outcomes at various stages. For example, players landing on step 3 in the Senate could draw a card that says that their bill has been defeated (in which case they drop out the game) or passed (in which case they move on to step 4).

Answer

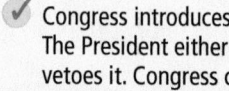 Congress introduces and passes a bill. The President either signs the bill or vetoes it. Congress can override the veto if two thirds of each house votes to pass it.

Section 8. Powers of Congress

The Congress shall have Power

1. To lay and collect Taxes, Duties, Imposts and Excises to pay the Debts and provide for the common Defence and general Welfare of the United States; but all Duties, Imposts and Excises, shall be uniform throughout the United States;
2. To borrow Money on the credit of the United States;
3. To regulate Commerce with foreign Nations, and among the several States, and with the Indian Tribes;
4. To establish an uniform Rule of Naturalization, and uniform Laws on the subject of Bankruptcies throughout the United States;
5. To coin Money, regulate the Value thereof, and of foreign Coin, and fix the Standard of Weights and Measures;
6. To provide for the Punishment of counterfeiting the Securities and current Coin of the United States;
7. To establish Post Offices and post Roads;
8. To promote the Progress of Science and useful Arts, by securing for limited Times to Authors and Inventors the exclusive Right to their respective Writings and Discoveries;
9. To constitute Tribunals inferior to the supreme Court;
10. To define and punish Piracies and Felonies committed on the high Seas, and Offences against the Law of Nations;

Commentary

◄ **Section 8** The Constitution is our social contract in which the people consent to the form and powers of government. An important part of the contract is the enumeration of legislative powers which sets the scope and limits of government authority over the people. Article I, Section 8, lists most of the expressed powers of Congress. Numbered from 1 to 18, these powers are also known as enumerated powers.

◄ **Clause 1** <u>Duties</u> are tariffs, or taxes on imports. Imposts are taxes in general. <u>Excises</u> are taxes on the production or sale of certain goods.

◄ **Clause 4** <u>Naturalization</u> is the process whereby a foreigner becomes a citizen. <u>Bankruptcy</u> is the condition in which a person or business cannot pay its debts. Congress has the power to pass laws on these two issues.

◄ **Clause 6** <u>Counterfeiting</u> is the making of imitation money. <u>Securities</u> are bonds. Congress can make laws to punish counterfeiters.

Commentary

Clause 11

Only Congress can declare war. Declarations of war are granted at the request of the President. Letters of marque and reprisal were documents issued by a government allowing merchant ships to arm themselves and attack ships of an enemy nation. They are no longer issued.

✓ **Checkpoint**

Which powers of Congress relate to taking in and spending money?

Clause 18 ▶

Congress has the power to make laws as needed to carry out the previous 17 clauses. It is sometimes known as the "Necessary and Proper Clause."

Clause 1 ▶

Such persons means slaves. In 1808, as soon as Congress was permitted to abolish the slave trade, it did so.

Clause 2 ▶

A writ of habeas corpus is a court order requiring government officials to bring a prisoner to court and explain why he or she is being held. A writ of habeas corpus protects people from unlawful imprisonment. The government cannot suspend this right except in times of rebellion or invasion.

11. To declare War, grant Letters of Marque and Reprisal, and make Rules concerning Captures on Land and Water;

12. To raise and support Armies, but no Appropriation of Money to that Use shall be for a longer Term than two Years;

13. To provide and maintain a Navy;

14. To make Rules for the Government and Regulation of the land and naval Forces;

15. To provide for calling forth the Militia to execute the Laws of the Union, suppress Insurrections and repel Invasions;

16. To provide for organizing, arming, and disciplining the Militia, and for governing such Part of them as may be employed in the Service of the United States, reserving to the States respectively, the Appointment of the Officers, and the Authority of training the Militia according to the discipline prescribed by Congress;

17. To exercise exclusive Legislation in all Cases whatsoever, over such District (not exceeding ten Miles square) as may, by Cession of Particular States, and the Acceptance of Congress, become the Seat of the Government of the United States, and to exercise like Authority over all Places purchased by the Consent of the Legislature of the State in which the Same shall be, for the Erection of Forts, Magazines, Arsenals, Dockyards and other needful Buildings;—And

18. To make all Laws which shall be necessary and proper for carrying into Execution the foregoing Powers and all other Powers vested by this Constitution in the Government of the United States, or in any Department or Officer thereof.

Section 9. Powers Denied to Congress

1. ~~The Migration or Importation of such Persons as any of the States now existing shall think proper to admit, shall not be prohibited by the Congress prior to the Year one thousand eight hundred and eight, but a Tax or duty may be imposed on such Importation, not exceeding ten dollars for each Person.~~

2. The Privilege of the Writ of Habeas Corpus shall not be suspended, unless when in Cases of Rebellion or Invasion the public Safety may require it.

Answer

 Congress has the power to set and collect taxes, borrow money on the credit of the United States, regulate foreign commerce, and coin and regulate money.

3. No Bill of Attainder or ex post facto Law shall be passed.

4. No Capitation, ~~or other direct, Tax~~ shall be laid, unless in Proportion to the Census of Enumeration hereinbefore directed to be taken.

5. No Tax or Duty shall be laid on Articles exported from any State.

6. No Preference shall be given by any Regulation of Commerce or Revenue to the Ports of one State over those of another: nor shall Vessels bound to, or from, one State, be obliged to enter, clear or pay Duties in another.

7. No Money shall be drawn from the Treasury, but in Consequence of Appropriations made by Law; and a regular Statement and Account of the Receipts and Expenditures of all public Money shall be published from time to time.

8. No Title of Nobility shall be granted by the United States: And no Person holding any Office of Profit or Trust under them, shall, without the Consent of the Congress, accept of any present, Emolument, Office, or Title, of any kind whatever, from any King, Prince, or foreign State.

Section 10. Powers Denied to the States

1. No State shall enter into any Treaty, Alliance, or Confederation; grant Letters of Marque and Reprisal; coin Money; emit Bills of Credit; make any Thing but gold and silver Coin a Tender in Payment of Debts; pass any Bill of Attainder, ex post facto Law, or Law impairing the Obligation of Contracts, or grant any Title of Nobility.

Commentary

◀ **Clause 3** A bill of attainder is a law declaring that a person is guilty of a particular crime without a trial. An ex post facto law punishes an act which was not illegal when it was committed.

◀ **Clause 1** The writers of the Constitution did not want the states to act like separate nations, so they prohibited states from making treaties or coining money. Some powers denied to the federal government are also denied to the states.

The Federal System

Powers of the National Government
- Regulate interstate and foreign trade
- Declare war
- Create and maintain armed forces
- Establish foreign policy
- Create federal courts
- Make copyright and patent laws
- Establish postal offices
- Coin money
- Set standard weights and measures
- Admit new states

Concurrent Powers
- Provide for public welfare
- Administer criminal justice
- Charter banks and borrow money
- Levy and collect taxes
- Borrow money

Powers Reserved to the States
- Regulate trade within state
- Maintain schools
- Establish local governments
- Make laws about marriage and divorce
- Conduct elections
- Provide for public safety
- Create corporation law

Differentiated Instruction   Solutions for All Learners

L1 Special Needs Students   **L2 Less Proficient Readers**   **L2 English Language Learners**

Ask students to study the chart titled *The Federal System.* Explain that the federal system determines how powers are divided and shared between the national and state governments. Then ask students to create a three column chart in their notebooks labeled *Powers of the National Government, Powers Reserved to the States,* and *Concurrent Powers.*

Read aloud the powers listed in the text and ask students to place each power in the correct column. Then have students point to powers under each column and explain why that power belongs there. (For example, the power to declare war belongs to the federal government because a war affects the entire country.)

Article II
Executive Branch

Instruct

- **Introduce** Ask **Who is the most powerful individual in the American government?** *(the President)* **Does the President's power include the right to rule over Congress and the courts?** *(No.)* **Why not?** *(The President heads a separate part of government—the executive branch. Through the principle of checks and balances, however, each branch's power is subject to some control by the other branches.)* Tell students that Article II of the Constitution establishes the powers of the President. Explain that later laws gave the President more specific powers.

- **Teach** Tell students that the President and the Vice President are the only elected officials in the executive branch. In fact, they are the only officials who are elected nationally, by all the people. Ask **Does the presidential candidate receiving the majority of the people's votes win the election?** *(No. The winner is the person who receives the greatest number of electoral votes.)* Have students read Section 1, Clauses 2 and 3, as well as Amendment XII. Explain that today, each political party with candidates in the election puts together a slate, or group, of people equal to the number of electors that the state is allowed. If a voter favors the candidate for President and Vice President from a particular party, he or she technically votes for that party's slate of electors. (The typical ballot lists the names of a party's candidates, preceded by the words "Electors for.") By tradition, each party's electors have pledged to vote for that party's candidates in the Electoral College—if their candidates win the state vote. **Do you think that the electoral college system is a good way to elect a President? Why or why not?** *(Students may point out that it is a difficult system to understand, that a candidate can win the popular vote nationally but still lose in the electoral college, or that direct election by all the people seems a simpler and fairer system.)*

Commentary

Clauses 2, 3 ▶
Powers listed here are forbidden to the states, but Congress can pass laws that give these powers to the states. Clause 2 forbids states from taxing imports and exports without the consent of Congress.

Clause 3 ▶
This clause forbids states from keeping an army or navy without the consent of Congress. States cannot make treaties or declare war unless an enemy invades or is about to invade.

Clauses 2, 3 ▶
Some writers of the Constitution were afraid to allow the people to elect the President directly. Therefore, the Constitutional Convention set up the electoral college. Clause 2 directs each state to choose <u>electors</u>, or delegates to the electoral college, to vote for President. A state's electoral vote is equal to the combined number of senators and representatives. Each state may decide how to choose its electors. Members of Congress and federal officeholders may not serve as electors. This part of the original electoral college system is still in effect.

Clause 3 ▶
This clause called upon each elector to vote for two candidates. The candidate who received a majority of the electoral votes would become President. The runner-up would become Vice President. If no candidate won a majority, the House

---

2. No State shall, without the Consent of the Congress, lay any Imposts or Duties on Imports or Exports, except what may be absolutely necessary for executing its inspection Laws; and the net Produce of all Duties and Imposts, laid by any State on Imports or Exports, shall be for the Use of the Treasury of the United States; and all such Laws shall be subject to the Revision and Control of the Congress.

3. No State shall, without the Consent of Congress, lay any Duty of Tonnage, keep Troops, or Ships of War in time of Peace, enter into any Agreement or Compact with another State, or with a foreign Power, or engage in War, unless actually invaded, or in such imminent Danger as will not admit of delay.

Article II Executive Branch

Section 1. President and Vice President

1. The executive Power shall be vested in a President of the United States of America. He shall hold his Office during the Term of four Years, and, together with the Vice President, chosen for the same Term, be elected as follows:

2. Each State shall appoint, in such Manner as the Legislature thereof may direct, a Number of Electors, equal to the whole Number of Senators and Representatives to which the State may be entitled in the Congress: but no Senator or Representative, or Person holding an Office of Trust or Profit, under the United States, shall be appointed an Elector.

3. ~~The Electors shall meet in their respective States, and vote by Ballot for two Persons, of whom one at least shall not be an Inhabitant of the same State with themselves. And they shall make a List of all the Persons voted for, and of the Number of Votes for each; which List they shall sign and certify, and transmit sealed to the Seat of the Government of the United States, directed to the President of the Senate. The President of the Senate shall, in the Presence of the Senate and House of Representatives, open all the Certificates, and the Votes shall then be counted. The Person having the greatest Number of Votes shall be the President, if such Number be a majority of the whole Number of Electors appointed; and if there be more than one who have such Majority, and have an equal Number of Votes, then, the House of Representatives shall immediately choose by Ballot one of them for President; and if no Person have a Majority, then from the five highest on the List the said House shall in like Manner choose the President. But in choosing the President, the Votes shall be taken by States, the Representatives from each State having one Vote; a quorum for this Purpose shall consist of a Member or Members from two thirds of the States, and a Majority of~~

L1 Special Needs Students   **L2 Less Proficient Readers**   **L2 English Language Learners**

Write the term *executive branch* on the board. Tell students that the verb *to execute* has several meanings. In Article II, it means "to carry out or enforce." Remind students that the legislative branch of government makes the laws. Explain that the executive branch has the power to enforce the laws and otherwise carry out the public policies of the United States. Encourage students to find and discuss any other unfamiliar terms in Article II.

~~all the States shall be necessary to a Choice. In every Case, after the Choice of the President, the Person having the greatest Number of Votes of the Electors shall be the Vice President. But if there should remain two or more who have equal Votes, the Senate shall choose from them by Ballot the Vice President.~~

4. The Congress may determine the Time of choosing the Electors, and the Day on which they shall give their Votes; which Day shall be the same throughout the United States.

5. No Person except a natural born Citizen, or a Citizen of the United States, at the time of the Adoption of this Constitution, shall be eligible to the Office of President; neither shall any person be eligible to that Office who shall not have attained to the Age of thirty-five Years, and been fourteen Years a Resident within the United States.

6. ~~In Case of the Removal of the President from Office, or of his Death, Resignation, or Inability to discharge the Powers and Duties of the said Office, the Same shall devolve on the Vice President,~~ and the Congress may by Law provide for the Case of Removal, Death, Resignation or Inability, both of the President and Vice President, declaring what Officer shall then act as President, and such Officer shall act accordingly, until the Disability be removed, or a President shall be elected.

7. The President shall, at stated Times, receive for his Services, a Compensation, which shall neither be increased nor diminished during the Period for which he shall have been elected, and he shall not receive within that Period any other Emolument from the United States, or any of them.

8. Before he enter on the Execution of his Office, he shall take the following Oath or Affirmation:

"I do solemnly swear (or affirm) that I will faithfully execute the Office of President of the United States, and will to the best of my Ability, preserve, protect and defend the Constitution of the United States."

Section 2. Powers of the President

1. The President shall be Commander in Chief of the Army and Navy of the United States, and of the Militia of the several States, when called into the actual Service of the United States; he may require the Opinion, in writing, of the principal Officer in each of the executive Departments, upon any Subject relating to the Duties of their respective Offices, and he shall have Power to Grant Reprieves and Pardons for Offences against the United States, except in Cases of Impeachment.

Commentary

would choose the President. The Senate would choose the Vice President. The election of 1800, however, ended in a tie in the electoral college between Thomas Jefferson and Aaron Burr. The Twelfth Amendment changed the electoral college system so that this could not happen again.

> ✔ **Checkpoint**
> **Who may become President?**

◀ **Clause 6** The powers of the President pass to the Vice President if the President leaves office or cannot discharge his or her duties. The Twenty-fifth Amendment clarifies this clause.

◀ **Clause 7** The President is paid a salary. It cannot be raised or lowered during his or her term in office. The President is not allowed to hold any other state or federal position while in office.

◀ **Clause 1** The President is the head of the armed forces and the state militias when they are called into national service. The military is under civilian, or nonmilitary, control. The President has the power to grant a reprieve, or pardon. A reprieve suspends punishment. A pardon prevents prosecution for a crime or overrides the judgment of a court.

Independent Practice

Assign each of the four sections of Article II to a group of students. (You may wish to assign a section to more than one group.) Have the groups prepare summaries of each section and research interesting examples of historical applications of specific sections or clauses. For Section 1, students might look for examples of elections in which a presidential candidate won the popular vote but lost the election or for examples of the death of a President. For Section 2, they might look for examples of how the President used his power as commander in chief of the army or as the government official who can make treaties. For Section 3, students might present a famous State of the Union message. For Section 4, they might explain impeachment procedures and describe an actual official's impeachment. Encourage students to use visual aids, such as charts and graphs, when they present their information to the class.

Monitor Progress

Observe each group to make sure that students realize that they must do research to find examples related to their section. Remind students that the goal of their presentations is to help their classmates better understand the sections of Article II.

Answer

 A natural-born citizen who is at least 35 years old and has lived in the United States for at least 14 years may become President.

Article III
Judicial Branch

Instruct

- **Introduce** Ask **Is it against the law for schools to use filtering software on computers?** (*no—United States v. American Library Association, 2003*) **Is it against the law for you to wear a black armband in school to protest some action by your government?** (*no—Tinker v. Des Moines, 1969*) Tell students that these and other controversial questions affecting student behavior in school have been answered by Supreme Court decisions. Point out that the Supreme Court is the highest court in the judicial branch of government—the branch that interprets the law.

- **Teach** Ask **How long is the term of a federal judge, according to Section 1?** (*"during good behavior"—In effect, federal judges are appointed for life.*) **Do federal courts have jurisdiction over all cases in our state?** (*No. State courts handle all cases except those that involve another state. Rarely, a case is appealed beyond the state court system to the Supreme Court, but only if the matter concerns a federal issue.*) **If a person committed a federal crime, would a federal judge determine that person's guilt or innocence?** (*No, a jury would—unless the accused gave up his or her right to a jury trial.*) **Could someone be tried for treason if he or she admitted thinking about stealing classified government documents?** (*No. Only a traitorous "overt act" is cause for arrest and trial.*) **Do you agree with scholars who claim that the judicial branch is the weakest of the three branches of government?** (*Students should support their answers with details that compare the power of the three branches. They may point out that the courts have no power to make laws or to enforce their decisions.*)

Commentary

Clause 2 ▶
The President has the power to make treaties with other nations. Under the system of checks and balances, all treaties must be approved by two thirds of the Senate. The President has the power to appoint ambassadors to foreign countries and to appoint other high officials. The Senate must confirm, or approve, these appointments.

Section 4 ▶
Civil officers include federal judges and members of the Cabinet. High crimes are major crimes. Misdemeanors are lesser crimes. The President, Vice President, and others can be forced out of office if impeached and found guilty of certain crimes.

2. He shall have Power, by and with the Advice and Consent of the Senate, to make Treaties, provided two thirds of the Senators present concur; and he shall nominate, and by and with the Advice and Consent of the Senate, shall appoint Ambassadors, other public Ministers and Consuls, Judges of the supreme Court, and all other Officers of the United States, whose Appointments are not herein otherwise provided for, and which shall be established by Law: but the Congress may by Law vest the Appointment of such inferior Officers, as they think proper, in the President alone, in the Courts of Law, or in the Heads of Departments.

3. The President shall have Power to fill up all Vacancies that may happen during the Recess of the Senate, by granting Commissions which shall expire at the End of their next Session.

Section 3. Duties of the President
He shall from time to time give to the Congress Information of the State of the Union, and recommend to their Consideration such Measures as he shall judge necessary and expedient; he may, on extraordinary Occasions, convene both Houses, or either of them, and in Case of Disagreement between them, with Respect to the Time of Adjournment, he may adjourn them to such Time as he shall think proper; he shall receive Ambassadors and other public Ministers; he shall take Care that the Laws be faithfully executed, and shall Commission all the Officers of the United States.

Section 4. Impeachment
The President, Vice President and all Civil Officers of the United States, shall be removed from Office on Impeachment for and Conviction of, Treason, Bribery, or other high Crimes and Misdemeanors.

Article III Judicial Branch

Section 1. Courts, Terms of Office
The judicial Power of the United States, shall be vested in one supreme Court, and in such inferior Courts as the Congress may from time to time ordain and establish. The Judges, both of the supreme and inferior Courts, shall hold their Offices during good Behavior, and shall, at stated Times, receive for their Services, a Compensation, which shall not be diminished during their Continuance in Office.

Section 2. Jurisdiction

1. The judicial Power shall extend to all Cases, in Law and Equity, arising under this Constitution, the Laws of the United States, and Treaties made, or which shall be made, under their Authority;— to all Cases affecting Ambassadors, other public Ministers, and Consuls;— to all Cases of Admiralty and maritime Jurisdiction;— to Controversies to which the United States shall be a Party;— to Controversies between two or more States;— ~~between a State and Citizens of another State;~~— between Citizens of different States;— between Citizens of the same State claiming Lands under Grants of different States, and between a State, or the Citizens thereof, and foreign States, Citizens, or Subjects.

2. In all Cases affecting Ambassadors, other public Ministers and Consuls, and those in which a State shall be a Party, the supreme Court shall have original Jurisdiction. In all the other Cases before mentioned, the supreme Court shall have appellate Jurisdiction, both as to Law and Fact, with such Exceptions, and under such Regulations as the Congress shall make.

3. The trial of all Crimes, except in Cases of Impeachment, shall be by Jury; and such Trial shall be held in the State where the said Crimes shall have been committed; but when not committed within any State, the Trial shall be at such Place or Places as the Congress may by Law have directed.

Commentary

◄ **Clause 1** Jurisdiction refers to the right of a court to hear a case. Federal courts have jurisdiction over cases that involve the Constitution, federal laws, treaties, foreign ambassadors and diplomats, naval and maritime laws, disagreements between states or between citizens from different states, and disputes between a state or citizen and a foreign state or citizen.

◄ **Clause 2** Original jurisdiction means the power of a court to hear a case when it first arises. The Supreme Court has original jurisdiction over only a few cases, such as those involving foreign diplomats. More often, the Supreme Court acts as an appellate court. An appellate court considers whether the trial judge made errors during the trial or incorrectly interpreted or applied the law in reaching a decision.

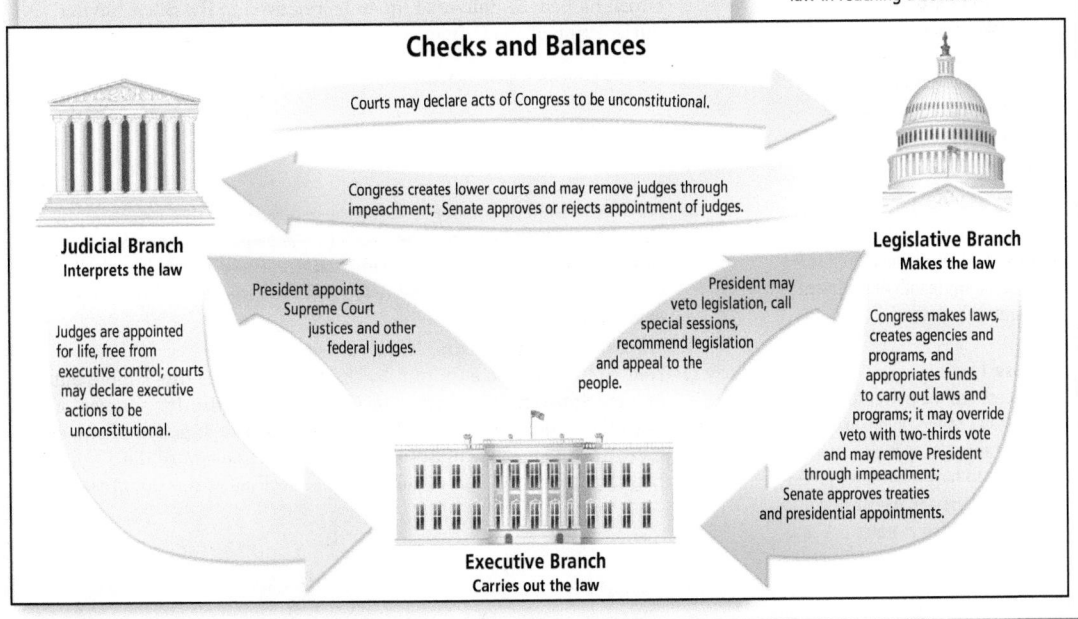

Checks and Balances

Courts may declare acts of Congress to be unconstitutional.

Congress creates lower courts and may remove judges through impeachment; Senate approves or rejects appointment of judges.

Judicial Branch
Interprets the law

Judges are appointed for life, free from executive control; courts may declare executive actions to be unconstitutional.

President appoints Supreme Court justices and other federal judges.

President may veto legislation, call special sessions, recommend legislation and appeal to the people.

Legislative Branch
Makes the law

Congress makes laws, creates agencies and programs, and appropriates funds to carry out laws and programs; it may override veto with two-thirds vote and may remove President through impeachment; Senate approves treaties and presidential appointments.

Executive Branch
Carries out the law

Instruct

- **Introduce** Invite students to imagine taking a family vacation to a neighboring state. They drive across the border and are soon stopped by a state police officer. The officer points out that it is illegal to drive a car there without a driver's license, registration, and plates issued by that state. Point out how inconvenient such a system would be. Then have students read Article IV, Section 1—often called the "full faith and credit clause." Point out that this constitutional provision eliminates the inconvenience and confusion of multiple licenses by making official licenses and other public records from one state valid in all states.

Commentary

> ✔ **Checkpoint**
>
> **How does the Constitution define treason?**

Clause 2 ▶
The act of returning a suspected criminal or escaped prisoner to a state where he or she is wanted is called <u>extradition</u>. State governors must return a suspect to another state. However, the Supreme Court has ruled that a governor cannot be forced to do so if he or she feels that justice will not be done.

Clause 3 ▶
<u>Persons held to service or labor</u> refers to slaves or indentured servants. The Thirteenth Amendment replaces this clause.

Clause 1 ▶
Congress has the power to admit new states to the Union. Existing states cannot be split up or joined together to form new states unless both Congress and the state legislatures approve. New states are equal to all other states.

Section 3. Treason

1. Treason against the United States shall consist only in levying War against them, or in adhering to their Enemies, giving them Aid and Comfort. No Person shall be convicted of Treason unless on the Testimony of two Witnesses to the same overt Act, or on Confession in open Court.

2. The Congress shall have Power to declare the Punishment of Treason, but no Attainder of Treason shall work Corruption of Blood, or Forfeiture except during the Life of the Person attainted.

Article IV Relations Among the States

Section 1. Full Faith and Credit

Full Faith and Credit shall be given in each State to the public Acts, Records, and judicial Proceedings of every other State. And the Congress may by general Laws prescribe the Manner in which such Acts, Records and Proceedings shall be proved, and the Effect thereof.

Section 2. Privileges and Immunities of Citizens

1. The Citizens of each State shall be entitled to all Privileges and Immunities of Citizens in the several States.

2. A Person charged in any State with Treason, Felony, or other Crime, who shall flee from justice, and be found in another State, shall on Demand of the executive Authority of the State from which he fled, be delivered up, to be removed to the State having Jurisdiction of the Crime.

3. ~~No Person held to Service or Labor in one State, under the Laws thereof, escaping into another, shall, in Consequence of any Law or Regulation therein, be discharged from Service or Labor, but shall be delivered up on Claim of the Party to whom such Service or Labor may be due.~~

Section 3. New States and Territories

1. New States may be admitted by the Congress into this Union; but no new State shall be formed or erected within the Jurisdiction of any other State; nor any State be formed by the Junction of two or more States, or Parts of States, without the Consent of the Legislatures of the States concerned as well as of the Congress.

Answer

 The Constitution defines treason as levying war against or aiding enemies of the United States.

2. The Congress shall have Power to dispose of and make all needful Rules and Regulations respecting the Territory or other Property belonging to the United States; and nothing in this Constitution shall be so construed as to Prejudice any Claims of the United States, or of any particular State.

Section 4. Protection Afforded to the States by the Nation
The United States shall guarantee to every State in this Union a Republican Form of Government, and shall protect each of them against Invasion; and on Application of the Legislature, or of the Executive (when the Legislature cannot be convened) against domestic Violence.

Article V Provision for Amendments
The Congress, whenever two thirds of both Houses shall deem it necessary, shall propose Amendments to this Constitution, or, on the Application of the Legislatures of two thirds of the several States, shall call a Convention for proposing Amendments, which, in either Case, shall be valid to all Intents and Purposes, as Part of this Constitution, when ratified by the Legislatures of three fourths of the several States, or by Conventions in three fourths thereof, as the one or the other Mode of Ratification may be proposed by the Congress; Provided that no Amendment which may be made prior to the Year One thousand eight hundred and eight shall in any Manner affect the first and fourth Clauses in the Ninth section of the first Article; and that no State, without its Consent, shall be deprived of its equal Suffrage in the Senate.

Article VI National Debts, Supremacy of National Law, Oath

Section 1.
All Debts contracted and Engagements entered into, before the Adoption of this Constitution, shall be as valid against the United States under this Constitution, as under the Confederation.

Section 2.
This Constitution, and the Laws of the United States which shall be made in Pursuance thereof; and all Treaties made, or which shall be made, under the Authority of the United States, shall be the supreme Law of the Land; and the Judges in every State shall be bound thereby, anything in the constitution or Laws of any State to the Contrary notwithstanding.

Commentary

◀ **Article V** The Constitution can be amended, or changed, if necessary. An amendment can be proposed by (1) a two-thirds vote of both houses of Congress or (2) a national convention called by Congress at the request of two thirds of the state legislatures. (This second method has never been used.) An amendment must be ratified, or approved, by (1) three fourths of the state legislatures or (2) special conventions in three fourths of the states. Congress decides which method will be used.

◀ **Section 2** The "supremacy clause" in this section establishes the Constitution, federal laws, and treaties that the Senate has ratified as the supreme, or highest, law of the land. Thus, they outweigh state laws. A state judge must overturn a state law that conflicts with the Constitution or with a federal law.

- **Teach** Tell students that the Constitution helped turn a group of independent-minded states into one country, the United States, and that Articles IV and VI played prominent roles in that transformation. Have them read Article IV, Section 2, Clauses 1 and 2. Ask **Which clause says that states must treat citizens of another state in the same way that they treat their own citizens?** *(Clause 1)* Direct students' attention to Article VI. Have students read Section 2, known as the "supremacy clause." Ask **If a state law conflicts with a federal law, which law is followed?** *(the federal law)* **Why was this section, along with Article IV, Sections 1 and 2, so important to the establishment of a united country?** *(These sections helped states establish friendly relations, and they also made clear that the national law, and by inference the national government, would have supremacy over the states.)* Now have students read Article V. Point out how amending the Constitution involves not only the federal government but also the state governments. Finally, direct students' attention to Article VII. Point out that the Constitution went into effect in 1788 and that all 13 states had ratified it by the end of May 1790.

Independent Practice

Have students study Articles IV through VII to find evidence to support this conclusion: The Constitution helped unify the states under a more powerful federal government. For each statement within these articles that supports this conclusion, students should write the article, section, and clause number, and a brief note about how the item supports the conclusion.

Monitor Progress

Circulate to make sure that students are studying the correct articles and that they have established a system for organizing information that supports the conclusion.

Commentary

Article VII

During 1787 and 1788, states held special conventions. By October 1788, the required nine states had ratified the United States Constitution.

> ✔ **Checkpoint**
>
> **What had to happen before the Constitution would go into effect?**

Section 3.

The Senators and Representatives before mentioned, and the Members of the several State legislatures, and all executive and judicial Officers, both of the United States and of the several States, shall be bound by Oath or Affirmation, to support this Constitution; but no religious Test shall ever be required as a Qualification to any Office or public Trust under the the United States.

Article VII Ratification of Constitution

The ratification of the Conventions of nine States, shall be sufficient for the Establishment of this Constitution between the States so ratifying the same.

Done in Convention by the Unanimous Consent of the States present the Seventeenth Day of September in the Year of our Lord one thousand seven hundred and Eighty seven and of the Independence of the United States of America the twelfth. In witness whereof We have hereunto subscribed our Names.

Attest: William Jackson, SECRETARY
　　　　George Washington, PRESIDENT and deputy from Virginia

New Hampshire
John Langdon
Nicholas Gilman

Massachusetts
Nathaniel Gorham
Rufus King

Connecticut
William Samuel Johnson
Roger Sherman

New York
Alexander Hamilton

New Jersey
William Livingston
David Brearley
William Paterson
Jonathan Dayton

Pennsylvania
Benjamin Franklin
Thomas Mifflin
Robert Morris
George Clymer
Thomas Fitzsimons
Jared Ingersoll
James Wilson
Gouverneur Morris

Delaware
George Read
Gunning Bedford, Jr.
John Dickinson
Richard Bassett
Jacob Broom

Maryland
James McHenry
Dan of St. Thomas Jenifer
Daniel Carroll

Virginia
John Blair
James Madison, Jr.

North Carolina
William Blount
Richard Dobbs Spaight
Hugh Williamson

South Carolina
John Rutledge
Charles Cotesworth Pinckney
Charles Pinckney
Pierce Butler

Georgia
William Few
Abraham Baldwin

Answer

 Nine of the thirteen states had to ratify the Constitution.

C16

AMENDMENTS

First Amendment Freedom of Religion, Speech, Press, Assembly, and Petition

Congress shall make no law respecting an establishment of religion, or prohibiting the free exercise thereof, or abridging the freedom of speech, or of the press; or the right of the people peaceably to assemble, and to petition the Government for a redress of grievances.

Second Amendment Bearing Arms

A well-regulated Militia being necessary to the security of a free State, the right of the people to keep and bear Arms, shall not be infringed.

Third Amendment Quartering of Troops

No Soldier shall, in time of peace be quartered in any house, without the consent of the Owner, nor, in time of war, but in a manner to be prescribed by law.

The Amendments The Amendments are changes made to the Constitution, which has been amended 27 times since it was originally ratified in 1788. The first 10 amendments are referred to as the Bill of Rights.

◄ **First Amendment** The First Amendment protects five basic rights: freedom of religion, speech, the press, assembly, and petition. Congress cannot set up an established, or official, church or religion for the nation, nor can it forbid the practice of religion.

Congress may not <u>abridge</u>, or limit, the freedom to speak or write freely. The government may not censor, or review, books and newspapers before they are printed. This amendment also protects the right to assemble, or hold public meetings. <u>Petition</u> means ask. <u>Redress</u> means to correct. <u>Grievances</u> are wrongs. The people have the right to ask the government for wrongs to be corrected.

◄ **Second Amendment** The Supreme Court decision in the case of *District of Columbia* v. *Heller* in 2008 ruled that a ban on handguns in the District of Columbia violated the Second Amendment. This is the first case since *U.S.* v. *Miller* in which the Court moved to interpret the Second Amendment.

◄ **Third Amendment** In colonial times, the British could quarter, or house, soldiers in private homes without permission of the owners. The Third Amendment prevents such abuses.

Instruct

- ***Introduce*** Ask **Is it legal to attend a meeting to discuss strategies for staging an antigovernment demonstration? Why or why not?** *(Yes. The First Amendment includes "the right of the people peaceably to assemble.")* Tell students that many of the rights and freedoms that Americans treasure most are found in the Constitution's first ten amendments, known collectively as the Bill of Rights.

Differentiated Instruction   Solutions for All Learners

L1 Special Needs Students   **L2 Less Proficient Readers**   **L2 English Language Learners**

Encourage students to read the commentary to help them understand the First Amendment. Then begin clarifying the meaning of the amendments by asking **What might happen if the freedoms recognized in the First Amendment were not protected?**

(Individuals might not be allowed to practice their religion, speak out in public, freely publish all information and opinions in newspapers, attend political meetings, or ask the government to correct wrongs.) Follow a similar procedure for other amendments.

■ **Teach** Point out that the Bill of Rights was ratified in 1789. Ask **What does the date of ratification suggest to you about these amendments?** *(They were ratified as a group.)* Remind students that the Constitution made the federal government much stronger than it had been. Tell them that several states, fearful of the federal government's power, refused to ratify the Constitution unless a list of basic individual rights and protections was attached. The delegates to the Constitutional Convention promised to make these amendments, and the Bill of Rights was the result. Have students read all ten amendments. **Which of these amendments are you most familiar with, and why?** *(Students are probably familiar with the important freedoms in the First Amendment. They might know of the controversy surrounding the Second Amendment. Phrases in other amendments may sound familiar.)* Ask students to reread the Ninth and Tenth Amendments, along with the related commentary. **Whose powers are these amendments intended to limit?** *(the federal government's powers)* Finally, ask **How might American life be different without the Bill of Rights?** *(In times of crisis, the federal government could have more easily trampled individual rights. Perhaps those rights would today be much less secure. Students may offer specific examples.)*

Commentary

Fourth Amendment ▶

This amendment protects Americans from unreasonable searches and seizures. Search and seizure are permitted only if a judge issues a <u>warrant</u>, or written court order. A warrant is issued only if there is probable cause. This means an officer must show that it is probable, or likely, that the search will produce evidence of a crime.

Fifth Amendment ▶

This amendment protects the rights of the accused. <u>Capital crimes</u> are those that can be punished with death. <u>Infamous crimes</u> are those that can be punished with prison or loss of rights. The federal government must obtain an <u>indictment</u>, or formal accusation, from a <u>grand jury</u> to prosecute anyone for such crimes. A grand jury is a panel of between 12 and 23 citizens who decide if the government has enough evidence to justify a trial.

<u>Double jeopardy</u> is forbidden by this amendment. This means that a person cannot be tried twice for the same crime. However, if a court sets aside a conviction because of a legal error, the accused can be tried again. A person on trial cannot be forced to <u>testify</u>, or give evidence, against himself or herself. A person accused of a crime is entitled to <u>due process of law</u>, or a fair hearing or trial.

The government cannot seize private property for public use without paying the owner a fair price for it.

Fourth Amendment Searches and Seizures

The right of the people to be secure in their persons, houses, papers, and effects, against unreasonable searches and seizures, shall not be violated, and no Warrants shall issue, but upon probable cause, supported by Oath or affirmation, and particularly describing the place to be searched, and the persons or things to be seized.

Fifth Amendment Criminal Proceedings; Due Process; Eminent Domain

No person shall be held to answer for a capital, or otherwise infamous crime, unless on a presentment or indictment of a Grand Jury, except in cases arising in the land or naval forces, or in the Militia, when in actual service in time of War or public danger; nor shall any person be subject for the same offence to be twice put in jeopardy of life or limb; nor shall be compelled in any criminal case to be a witness against himself, nor be deprived of life, liberty, or property, without due process of law; nor shall private property be taken for public use, without just compensation.

Sixth Amendment Criminal Proceedings

In all criminal prosecutions, the accused shall enjoy the right to a speedy and public trial, by an impartial jury of the State and district wherein the crime shall have been committed, which district shall have been previously ascertained by law, and to be informed of the nature and cause of the accusation; to be confronted with the witnesses against him; to have compulsory process for obtaining witnesses in his favor, and to have the Assistance of Counsel for his defence.

Seventh Amendment Civil Trials

In Suits at common law, where the value in controversy shall exceed twenty dollars, the right of trial by jury shall be preserved, and no fact tried by a jury, shall be otherwise re-examined in any Court of the United States, than according to the rules of the common law.

Eighth Amendment Punishment for Crimes

Excessive bail shall not be required, nor excessive fines imposed, nor cruel and unusual punishment inflicted.

Ninth Amendment Unenumerated Rights

The enumeration in the Constitution, of certain rights, shall not be construed to deny or disparage others retained by the people.

Tenth Amendment Powers Reserved to the States

The powers not delegated to the United States by the Constitution, nor prohibited by it to the States, are reserved to the States respectively, or to the people.

Commentary

◀ **Sixth Amendment** In criminal cases, the jury must be impartial, or not favor either side. The accused is guaranteed the right to a trial by jury. The trial must be speedy. The accused must be told the charges and be allowed to question all witnesses. The accused must be allowed a lawyer.

◀ **Seventh Amendment** Common law refers to rules of law established by judges in past cases. An appeals court can set aside a verdict only if legal errors make the trial unfair.

◀ **Eighth Amendment** <u>Bail</u> is money that the accused leaves with the court as a pledge to appear for trial. If the accused does not appear, the court keeps the money. This amendment prevents the court from imposing bail or fines that are <u>excessive</u>, or too high. The amendment also forbids cruel and unusual punishments, such as physical torture.

◀ **Ninth Amendment** The rights of the people are not limited to those listed in the Bill of Rights. In the Ninth Amendment, the government is prevented from claiming these are the only rights people have.

◀ **Tenth Amendment** Powers not given to the federal government belong to the states. Powers reserved to the states are not listed in the Constitution.

Independent Practice

Ask students to create a web diagram of the Bill of Rights. For each amendment, they should select each right or freedom and state it briefly within a separate circle. Most items can be introduced with the words *right to* or *freedom of*. When students have completed this task, work as a class to create a model web diagram on the board.

Monitor Progress

Circulate to make sure that students are constructing their web diagrams properly and are including the relevant rights and freedoms.

Amendments 11 and 12

Instruct

- **Introduce** Ask **On election day, after all voters have cast their ballots for President, how is the winner determined?** *(The winner is not necessarily the candidate with the most popular votes, but the candidate with the most electoral votes.)* Remind students that voters in a presidential election do not vote directly for the candidates but for a slate, or group, of state electors—one slate for each political party with candidates on the ballot. The voter's responsibility is to choose a slate of electors. Ask **How would you feel about having the state legislature, not the people, choose the electors?** *(Answers will vary.)* Tell students that most states, until around 1820, did just that. Citizens in those states did not cast votes for President or Vice President. By 1836, however, all but one state had opened the voting to its qualified citizens.

- **Teach** Start with the Eleventh Amendment, being aware that its phrasing makes the amendment difficult to comprehend. Have students read the commentary for clarification and refer to the related text in the Constitution—Article III, Section 2. Ask **What does the Eleventh Amendment prohibit?** *(lawsuits by citizens of one state against the government of another state in federal court)* **Why would states not want to be sued in federal court?** *(This would give the federal government yet more power over the states.)* Next, have students read the Twelfth Amendment and the text it replaced in Article II, along with both commentaries. **Why was this amendment adopted?** *(to eliminate the situation that occurred in 1800, when two candidates for President tied in the Electoral College.)* **Do either Article II or Amendment XII mention popular votes?** *(no)* **Who, then, do you think decided that the people in a state should vote for the slate of electors?** *(state legislatures—Article II of the Constitution says: "Each state shall appoint, **in such manner as the Legislature thereof may direct,** a number of electors . . .")*

Commentary

Eleventh Amendment ▶
A private citizen from one state cannot sue the government of another state in federal court. However, a citizen can sue a state government in a state court.

Twelfth Amendment ▶
This amendment changed the way the electoral college voted as outlined in Article II, Section 1, Clause 3. This amendment provides that each elector choose one candidate for President and one candidate for Vice President. If no candidate for President receives a majority of electoral votes, the House of Representatives chooses the President. If no candidate for Vice President receives a majority, the Senate elects the Vice President. The Vice President must be a person who is eligible to be President.

It is possible for a candidate to win the popular vote and lose the electoral college. This happened in 1888 and 2000.

Eleventh Amendment Suits Against States
The Judicial power of the United States shall not be construed to extend to any suit in law or equity, commenced or prosecuted against one of the United States by Citizens of another State, or by Citizens or Subjects of any Foreign State.

Twelfth Amendment Election of President and Vice President
The Electors shall meet in their respective States and vote by ballot for President and Vice President, one of whom, at least, shall not be an inhabitant of the same State with themselves; they shall name in their ballots the person voted for as President, and in distinct ballots the person voted for as Vice President, and they shall make distinct lists of all persons voted for as President, and of all persons voted for as Vice President, and of the number of votes for each, which lists they shall sign and certify, and transmit sealed to the seat of the government of the United States, directed to the President of the Senate;— The President of the Senate shall, in the presence of the Senate and the House of Representatives, open all the certificates and the votes shall then be counted;— the person having the greatest Number of votes for President shall be the President, if such number be a majority of the whole number of Electors appointed; and if no person have such a majority, then, from the persons having the highest numbers not exceeding three on the list of those voted for as President, the House of Representatives shall choose immediately, by ballot, the President. But in choosing the President, the votes shall be taken by States, the representation from each State having one vote; a quorum for this purpose shall consist of a member or members from two thirds of the States, and a majority of the States shall be necessary to a choice. ~~And if the House of Representatives shall not choose a President whenever the right of choice shall devolve upon them, before the fourth day of March next following, then the Vice President shall act as President, as in case of death or other constitutional disability of the President.~~ The person having the greatest number of votes as Vice President, shall be the Vice President, if such number be a majority of the whole number of Electors appointed, and if no person have a majority, then from the two highest numbers on the list, the Senate shall choose the Vice President; a quorum for the purpose shall consist of two thirds of the whole number of Senators, a majority of the whole number shall be necessary to a choice. But no person constitutionally ineligible to the office of President shall be eligible to that of Vice President of the United States.

Differentiated Instruction Solutions for All Learners

L1 Special Needs Students   **L2 Less Proficient Readers**   **L2 English Language Learners**

Write the word *elector* on the board. Circle or underline the *-or* ending, and remind students that this ending (like *-er*) usually means "person who." An elector is a person who elects. Explain that the earliest electors actually did elect the President and Vice President. Once chosen by their state, the elector had the constitutional right to vote for any candidate they wished. Electors still have this right today, although it is seldom used.

C20

Thirteenth Amendment Slavery and Involuntary Servitude

Section 1. Neither slavery nor involuntary servitude, except as a punishment for crime whereof the party shall have been duly convicted, shall exist within the United States, or any place subject to their jurisdiction.

Section 2. Congress shall have power to enforce this article by appropriate legislation.

Fourteenth Amendment Rights of Citizens

Section 1. All persons born or naturalized in the United States and subject to the jurisdiction thereof, are citizens of the United States and of the State wherein they reside. No State shall make or enforce any law which shall abridge the privileges or immunities of citizens of the United States; nor shall any State deprive any person of life, liberty, or property, without due process of law; nor deny to any person within its jurisdiction the equal protection of the laws.

Section 2. Representatives shall be apportioned among the several States according to their respective numbers, counting the whole number of persons in each State, excluding Indians not taxed. But when the right to vote at any election for the choice of electors for President and Vice President of the United States, Representatives in Congress, the Executive and Judicial officers of a State, or the members of the Legislature thereof, is denied to any of the male inhabitants of such State, being twenty-one years of age, and citizens of the United States, or in any way abridged, except for participation in rebellion, or other crime, the basis of representation therein shall be reduced in the proportion which the number of such male citizens shall bear to the whole number of male citizens twenty-one years of age in such State.

Section 3. No person shall be a Senator or Representative in Congress, or elector of President and Vice President, or hold any office, civil or military, under the United States, or under any State, who, having previously taken an oath, as a member of Congress, or as an officer of the United States, or as a member of any State legislature, or as an executive or judicial officer of any State, to support the Constitution of the United States, shall have engaged in insurrection or rebellion against the same, or given aid or comfort to the enemies thereof. But Congress may, by a vote of two thirds of each House, remove such disability.

Commentary

◀ **Thirteenth Amendment**
The Emancipation Proclamation (1863) freed slaves only in areas controlled by the Confederacy. This amendment freed all slaves. It also forbids involuntary servitude, or labor done against one's will. However, it does not prevent prison wardens from making prisoners work. Congress can pass laws to carry out this amendment.

◀ **Fourteenth Amendment, Section 1** This amendment defines citizenship for the first time in the Constitution. It was intended to protect the rights of the freed slaves by guaranteeing all citizens "equal protection under the law."

◀ **Fourteenth Amendment, Section 2** This section replaced the three-fifths clause. It provides that representation in the House of Representatives is decided on the basis of the number of people in the states. It also provides that states that deny the vote to male citizens aged 21 or over will be punished by losing part of their representation. This provision has never been enforced.

> ✓ **Checkpoint**
> What is one key provision of the Fourteenth Amendment?

Independent Practice
Have pairs of students work together to analyze the Twelfth Amendment. Students should determine how it changed the original functioning of the electoral college system, as set out in Article II, Section 1, Clauses 1–4 of the Constitution. Have students create a flowchart or diagram of the original and amended systems to clarify in what ways these differ.

Monitor Progress
Circulate to make sure that students are comparing the electoral rules that are crossed out in Article II, Section I, Clause 3 with the amended electoral rules. The two charts or diagrams should be similar, varying only as the original and amended systems vary.

Answer

 One key provision of the Fourteenth Amendment is the definition of citizenship as all people born or naturalized in the United States.

Amendments 13–15

Instruct

- **Introduce** Ask **What was the main cause of the American Civil War?** *(Some historians point to slavery while others contend that states' rights was the main cause.)* **Which form of involuntary servitude does the Thirteenth Amendment not forbid?** *(involuntary servitude of prisoners who have committed crimes.)* Tell students that the Thirteenth Amendment officially ended slavery and that the Fourteenth and Fifteenth Amendments were intended to protect freed slaves.

- **Teach** Direct students' attention to the Thirteenth, Fourteenth, and Fifteenth Amendments. Ask **Which of these amendments defines citizenship?** *(Section 1 of the Fourteenth Amendment)* Read this section aloud. What earlier amendment does this remind you of? *(the Fifth Amendment)* Have students find and read the similar wording in the Fifth Amendment. Tell students that this part of the Fourteenth Amendment was written to alert the states, especially the former Confederate states, that they had to treat freed slaves no differently than they treated other citizens. Ask **Who could vote after the Fourteenth Amendment was ratified?** *(all male citizens of the state who were 21 years of age or older, except for participants in rebellion or other crime)* **What is the subject of the Fifteenth Amendment?** *(voting rights)* Ask students to arrange these three amendments in order of importance. Use any differences of opinion to encourage a class discussion of the historic nature of all three amendments.

Independent Practice

Have students write a newspaper article about the 1870 ratification of the Fifteenth Amendment. Students should refer to the Thirteenth and Fourteenth Amendments, describing their content and explaining how all three amendments are related.

Monitor Progress

Circulate to make sure that students are formatting their information as a newspaper article and that it covers the main points of all three amendments.

Commentary

Fifteenth Amendment, ▶
Section 1 This amendment gave African Americans the right to vote. In the late 1800s, however, southern states used grandfather clauses, literacy tests, and poll taxes to keep African Americans from voting.

Fifteenth Amendment, ▶
Section 2 Congress can pass laws to carry out this amendment. The Twenty-fourth Amendment barred the use of poll taxes in national elections. The Voting Rights Act of 1965 gave federal officials the power to register voters where there was voting discrimination.

Sixteenth Amendment ▶
Congress has the power to collect taxes on people's income. An income tax can be collected without regard to a state's population. This amendment changed Article I, Section 9, Clause 4.

Section 4. The validity of the public debt of the United States, authorized by law, including debts incurred for payment of pensions and bounties for services in suppressing insurrection or rebellion, shall not be questioned. But neither the United States nor any State shall assume or pay any debt or obligation incurred in aid of insurrection or rebellion against the United States, or any claim for the loss or emancipation of any slave; but all such debts, obligations and claims shall be held illegal and void.

Section 5. The Congress shall have power to enforce, by appropriate legislation, the provisions of this article.

Fifteenth Amendment Right to Vote—Race, Color, Servitude
Section 1. The right of citizens of the United States to vote shall not be denied or abridged by the United States or by any State on account of race, color, or previous condition of servitude.

Section 2. The Congress shall have power to enforce this article by appropriate legislation.

Sixteenth Amendment Income Tax
The Congress shall have power to lay and collect taxes on incomes, from whatever source derived, without apportionment among the several States, and without regard to any census or enumeration.

Differentiated Instruction   Solutions for All Learners

L4 Advanced Readers   **L4 Gifted and Talented Students**

Invite students to investigate and report to the class about the ongoing influence on American society of the Fourteenth and Fifteenth amendments. Students may research how the Supreme Court interpreted the amendments in the decades following the Civil War and how those interpretations affected freed slaves and their descendants. Students might also examine how these amendments came into play during the civil rights movement that began in the 1950s. In addition, students might investigate how the Fourteenth Amendment's due process clause, with its extension of the Bill of Rights to the states, has been applied to various other issues.

Seventeenth Amendment Popular Election of Senators

Section 1. The Senate of the United States shall be composed of two Senators from each State, elected by the people thereof, for six years; and each Senator shall have one vote. The electors in each State shall have the qualifications requisite for electors of the most numerous branch of the State legislatures.

Section 2. When vacancies happen in the representation of any State in the Senate, the executive authority of such State shall issue writs of election to fill such vacancies: *Provided,* That the legislature of any State may empower the executive thereof to make temporary appointments until the people fill the vacancies by election as the legislature may direct.

Section 3. ~~This amendment shall not be so construed as to affect the election or term of any Senator chosen before it becomes valid as part of the Constitution.~~

Eighteenth Amendment Prohibition of Alcoholic Beverages

Section 1. ~~After one year from the ratification of this article the manufacture, sale, or transportation of intoxicating liquors within, the importation thereof into, or the exportation thereof from the United States and all territory subject to the jurisdiction thereof for beverage purposes is hereby prohibited.~~

Section 2. ~~The Congress and the several States shall have concurrent power to enforce this article by appropriate legislation.~~

Section 3. ~~This article shall be inoperative unless it shall have been ratified as an amendment to the Constitution by the legislatures of the several States, as provided in the Constitution, within seven years of the date of the submission hereof to the States by Congress.~~

Nineteenth Amendment Women's Suffrage

Section 1. The right of citizens of the United States to vote shall not be denied or abridged by the United States or by any State on account of sex.

Section 2. Congress shall have power to enforce this article by appropriate legislation.

Commentary

◄ **Seventeenth Amendment**
This amendment replaced Article I, Section 3, Clause 2. Before it was adopted, state legislatures chose senators. This amendment provides that senators are elected directly by the people of each state.

◄ **Eighteenth Amendment**
This amendment, known as Prohibition, banned the making, selling, or transporting of alcoholic beverages in the United States. Later, the Twenty-first Amendment repealed, or canceled, this amendment.

◄ **Nineteenth Amendment**
Neither the federal government nor state governments can deny the right to vote on account of sex.

Amendments 16–19 ⓛ³

Instruct

- **Introduce** Ask **Do you know anyone who pays federal income taxes?** *(relatives, friends, students themselves)* **Who receives this money?** *(the federal government)* **What does the federal government do with this revenue?** *(It funds government programs and activities.)* Tell students that no Americans paid federal income taxes until the Civil War, when the Union levied an emergency tax which the government repealed in 1872. In 1895, the Supreme Court struck down the second enaction of an income tax after just one year. The Sixteenth Amendment, ratified in 1913, met all constitutional tests and remains the basis for our present income tax laws.

- **Teach** Direct students' attention to the Sixteenth, Seventeenth, Eighteenth, and Nineteenth Amendments. Ask **What is the topic of each of these amendments?** *(Sixteenth Amendment, income tax; Seventeenth Amendment, election of senators; Eighteenth Amendment, prohibition of alcoholic beverages Nineteenth Amendment, women's suffrage)* **How were senators chosen before the Seventeenth Amendment was approved?** *(State legislatures chose them.)* **What year did Prohibition actually take effect?** *(Section 1 of the Eighteenth Amendment says "After one year from the ratification of this article," or 1920.)* **Which of these amendments expanded democracy in the United States?** *(The Seventeenth Amendment gave citizens the right to vote for senators, and the Nineteenth Amendment gave women the right to vote.)*

Independent Practice

Have students create pamphlets that might have circulated during the ratification period of one of these amendments. A pamphlet may praise or criticize the amendment. Students may want to do further research before they begin producing their pamphlets.

Monitor Progress

Circulate to make sure that each student's pamphlet takes a strong, persuasive position on one of the amendments.

Differentiated Instruction Solutions for All Learners

ⓛ⁴ Advanced Readers   ⓛ⁴ Gifted and Talented Students

Invite students to research the Progressive Era in the United States. Students should determine how this historical movement led to the reforms embodied by the Sixteenth, Seventeenth, Eighteenth, and Nineteenth Amendments. Have students report their findings to the class.

C23

Instruct

- *Introduce* Ask **Has anyone here ever seen a presidential inauguration in person or on television? Where does the ceremony take place?** *(in Washington, D.C., usually outdoors)* **What time of year does the inauguration take place?** *(winter; January)*

- *Teach* Ask **What does the Twentieth Amendment establish?** *(new dates for the start of the terms of the President and Vice President as well as those of senators and representatives)* **Why is the Twentieth Amendment popularly known as the "Lame Duck Amendment"?** *(The President and members of Congress who failed to be reelected in November nevertheless served until March of the next year. These officials were handicapped by a lack of power and influence.)* **What did the Twenty-first Amendment accomplish?** *(It repealed the Eighteenth Amendment, Prohibition.)* Have students read Section 2 carefully. **Explain the transfer of power from the federal government to the state governments that this section describes.** *(Section 2 gives each state the power to regulate the transportation, importation, delivery, and use of intoxicating liquors within its own borders.)*

Commentary

Twentieth Amendment, ▶
Section 1 The date for the inauguration of the President was changed to January 20, and the date for Congress to begin its term changed to January 3. Prior to this amendment, the beginning-of-term date was set in March. The outgoing officials with little or no influence on matters were not effective in office. Being so inactive, they were called "lame ducks."

Twentieth Amendment, ▶
Section 3 If the President-elect dies before taking office, the Vice President-elect becomes President. If no President has been chosen by January 20 or if the elected candidate fails to qualify for office, the Vice President-elect acts as President, but only until a qualified President is chosen. Finally, Congress has the power to choose a person to act as President if neither the President-elect nor the Vice President-elect is qualified to take office.

Twenty-first Amendment, ▶
Section 1 The Eighteenth Amendment is repealed, making it legal to make and sell alcoholic beverages. Prohibition ended on December 5, 1933.

Twentieth Amendment Presidential Terms; Sessions of Congress

Section 1. The terms of the President and Vice President shall end at noon on the 20th day of January, and the terms of Senators and Representatives at noon on the 3d day of January, of the years in which such terms would have ended if this article had not been ratified; and the terms of their successors shall then begin.

Section 2. The Congress shall assemble at least once in every year, and such meeting shall begin at noon on the 3d day of January, unless they shall by law appoint a different day.

Section 3. If, at the time fixed for the beginning of the term of the President, the President elect shall have died, the Vice President elect shall become President. If a President shall not have been chosen before the time fixed for the beginning of his term, or if the President elect shall have failed to qualify, then the Vice President elect shall act as President until a President shall have qualified; and the Congress may by law provide for the case wherein neither a President elect nor a Vice President elect shall have qualified, declaring who shall then act as President, or the manner in which one who is to act shall be selected, and such person shall act accordingly until a President or Vice President shall have qualified.

Section 4. The Congress may by law provide for the case of the death of any of the persons from whom the House of Representatives may choose a President whenever the right of choice shall have devolved upon them, and for the case of the death of any of the persons from whom the Senate may choose a Vice President whenever the right of choice shall have devolved upon them.

Section 5. ~~Sections 1 and 2 shall take effect on the 15th day of October following the ratification of this article.~~

Section 6. This article shall be inoperative unless it shall have been ratified as an amendment to the Constitution by the legislatures of three fourths of the several States within seven years from the date of its submission.

Twenty-first Amendment Repeal of Prohibition

Section 1. The eighteenth article of amendment to the Constitution of the United States is hereby repealed.

Section 2. The transportation or importation into any State, Territory, or possession of the United States for delivery or use therein of intoxicating liquors, in violation of the laws thereof, is hereby prohibited.

Differentiated Instruction   Solutions for All Learners

L1 Special Needs Students   **L2 Less Proficient Readers**   **L2 English Language Learners**

Direct students' attention to the Twentieth Amendment, Section 1. Have students read this section and the related commentary. Write *inauguration* on the board. Tell students that this term can be used to describe the act of beginning something and that it can apply to the ceremony beginning the term of a President. Then, write the term *President-elect*

on the board. Ask **In what month is the presidential election held?** *(November)* **When is the President inaugurated?** *(January 20)* Tell students that from election day in November to inauguration day in January, the winning presidential candidate is known as the President-elect.

Section 3. ~~This article shall be inoperative unless it shall have been ratified as an amendment to the Constitution by conventions in the several States, as provided in the Constitution, within seven years from the date of the submission hereof to the States by the Congress.~~

Twenty-second Amendment Presidential Tenure

Section 1. No person shall be elected to the office of the President more than twice, and no person who has held the office of President, or acted as President, for more than two years of a term to which some other person was elected President shall be elected to the office of the President more than once. ~~But this Article shall not apply to any person holding the office of President, when this Article was proposed by the Congress, and shall not prevent any person who may be holding the office of President, or acting as President, during the term within which this Article becomes operative from holding the office of President or acting as President during the remainder of such term.~~

Section 2. ~~This article shall be inoperative unless it shall have been ratified as an amendment to the Constitution by the legislatures of three fourths of the several states within seven years from the date of its submission to the States by the Congress.~~

Twenty-third Amendment Presidential Electors for The District of Columbia

Section 1. The District constituting the seat of Government of the United States shall appoint in such manner as the Congress may direct:

A number of electors of President and Vice President equal to the whole number of Senators and Representatives in Congress to which the District would be entitled if it were a State, but in no event more than the least populous State; they shall be in addition to those appointed by the States, they shall be considered, for the purposes of the election of President and Vice President, to be electors appointed by a State; and they shall meet in the District and perform such duties as provided by the twelfth article of amendment.

Section 2. The Congress shall have power to enforce this article by appropriate legislation.

Commentary

◄ **Twenty-second Amendment, Section 1** This amendment provides that no President may serve more than two terms. A President who has already served more than half of someone else's term can serve only one more full term. Before Franklin Roosevelt became President, no President served more than two terms in office. Roosevelt broke with this custom and was elected to four terms.

◄ **Twenty-third Amendment, Section 1** This amendment gives the residents of Washington, D.C., the right to vote in presidential elections. Until this amendment was adopted, people living in Washington, D.C., could not vote for President because the Constitution had made no provision for choosing electors from the nation's capital. Washington, D.C., has three electoral votes.

Independent Practice

Ask students to write a brief story exploring what might happen if a President-elect died or in some way proved unfit to assume the presidency (some qualifications appear in Article II, Section 1, Clause 6). Tell students that their stories should develop a hypothetical series of events based on the laws established in the Twentieth Amendment. Students may wish to reread related constitutional passages, specifically Article II, Section 1, and the Twelfth Amendment. Suggest that students start with a fictional election and work through the months until a President is finally inaugurated. They can make their stories straightforward or introduce any twists and turns they like, as long as they do not violate the Twentieth Amendment or any other constitutional provision.

Monitor Progress

Circulate to see that students understand that their stories are to be fictional, involve the inability of a President-elect to fulfill the duties of the office, and do not violate any constitutional provision.

Instruct

- **Introduce** Ask **How old must you be to vote in this country?** *(18 years old)* **Does that age limit make sense to you? Why or why not?** *(Some students may say that at age 18, people are considered mature enough to make other important decisions. Other students may point out that 18-year-olds have graduated or will soon graduate from high school, so they have the background in history and government necessary for a critical understanding of the politics surrounding elections.)*

- **Teach** Direct students' attention to the last six amendments. Ask **Which amendment says that you have to be 18 years of age or older to vote?** *(the Twenty-sixth Amendment)* **What is the difference between this amendment and the Twenty-fourth Amendment?** *(The subject of the Twenty-fourth Amendment relates to the poll tax, not to age, and it eliminates the poll tax as a bar to voting. The Twenty-sixth Amendment applies to the right to vote in **any** election. The Twenty-fourth Amendment applies only to presidential and congressional elections.)* **What possible events does the Twenty-fifth Amendment cover?** *(the death, resignation, or disability of a President)* **Which amendment came about in reaction to something that President Franklin Roosevelt did?** *(the Twenty-second)* **What did Roosevelt do?** *(He served four terms in office, the first and only President to serve more than two terms.)* **What do you think bothered Americans about Roosevelt's additional terms?** *(Historically, Americans have tried to limit the power of the President, seeking to avoid a tyrannical leader. A President who continues to run for office and wins could gain too much power and use that power to oppress the people.)* **Which amendment has to do with pay for members of Congress?** *(the Twenty-seventh)* **Why should members of Congress not get a pay increase immediately after they vote for it?** *(If members of Congress have the ability to vote themselves pay increases that take immediate effect, it would be a conflict of interest.)*

Commentary

Twenty-fourth Amendment, ▶
Section 1 A poll tax is a tax on voters. This amendment bans poll taxes in national elections. Some states used poll taxes to keep African Americans from voting. In 1966, the Supreme Court struck down poll taxes in state elections, also.

Twenty-fifth Amendment, ▶
Section 1 If the President dies or resigns, the Vice President becomes President. This section clarifies Article II, Section 1, Clause 6.

Twenty-fifth Amendment, ▶
Section 3 If the President declares in writing that he or she is unable to perform the duties of office, the Vice President serves as acting President until the President recovers.

Twenty-fifth Amendment, ▶
Section 4 Two Presidents, Woodrow Wilson and Dwight Eisenhower, fell gravely ill while in office. The Constitution contained no provision for this kind of emergency.

Twenty-fourth Amendment Right to Vote in Federal Elections

Section 1. The right of citizens of the United States to vote in any primary or other election for President or Vice President, for electors for President or Vice President, or for Senator or Representative in Congress, shall not be denied or abridged by the United States or any State by reason of failure to pay any poll tax or other tax.

Section 2. The Congress shall have power to enforce this article by appropriate legislation.

Twenty-fifth Amendment Presidential Succession; Vice Presidential Vacancy; Presidential Inability

Section 1. In case of the removal of the President from office or of his death or resignation, the Vice President shall become President.

Section 2. Whenever there is a vacancy in the office of the Vice President, the President shall nominate a Vice President who shall take office upon confirmation by a majority vote of both Houses of Congress.

Section 3. Whenever the President transmits to the President pro tempore of the Senate and the Speaker of the House of Representatives his written declaration that he is unable to discharge the powers and duties of his office, and until he transmits to them a written declaration to the contrary, such powers and duties shall be discharged by the Vice President as Acting President.

Section 4. Whenever the Vice President and a majority of either the principal officers of the executive departments or of such other body as Congress may by law provide, transmit to the President pro tempore of the Senate and the Speaker of the House of Representatives their written declaration that the President is unable to discharge the powers and duties of his office, the Vice President shall immediately assume the powers and duties of the office as Acting President.

Differentiated Instruction Solutions for All Learners

L1 Special Needs Students   L2 Less Proficient Readers

Ask students to create a chart to organize the information related to Amendments 22 through 27. For each amendment, the charts should include the amendment number, a summary description of the amendment, and any related constitutional clauses or amendments and how they are related. Discuss each amendment, and use information from students' work to create a finished chart on the board.

Thereafter, when the President transmits to the President pro tempore of the Senate and the Speaker of the House of Representatives his written declaration that no inability exists, he shall resume the powers and duties of his office unless the Vice President and a majority of either the principal officers of the executive department or of such other body as Congress may by law provide, transmit within four days to the President pro tempore of the Senate and the Speaker of the House of Representatives their written declaration that the President is unable to discharge the powers and duties of his office. Thereupon Congress shall decide the issue, assembling within forty-eight hours for that purpose if not in session. If the Congress, within twenty-one days after receipt of the latter written declaration, or, if Congress is not in session, within twenty-one days after Congress is required to assemble, determines by two-thirds vote of both Houses that the President is unable to discharge the powers and duties of his office, the Vice President shall continue to discharge the same as Acting President; otherwise, the President shall resume the powers and duties of his office.

Twenty-sixth Amendment Right to Vote—Age
   Section 1. The right of citizens of the United States, who are eighteen years of age or older, to vote shall not be denied or abridged by the United States or by any State on account of age.

   Section 2. The Congress shall have the power to enforce this article by appropriate legislation.

Twenty-seventh Amendment Congressional Pay
   No law varying the compensation for the services of the Senators and Representatives, shall take effect, until an election of Representatives shall have intervened.

Commentary

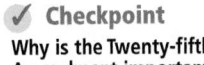

✓ Checkpoint
Why is the Twenty-fifth Amendment important?

◀ **Twenty-sixth Amendment, Section 1** In 1970, Congress passed a law allowing 18-year-olds to vote. However, the Supreme Court decided that Congress could not set a minimum age for state elections.

◀ **Twenty-seventh Amendment** If members of Congress vote themselves a pay increase, it cannot go into effect until after the next congressional election. This amendment was proposed in 1789. In 1992, Michigan became the thirty-eighth state to ratify it.

Independent Practice
Ask students to write a title, a nickname, or another brief identifier for each of the last six amendments. The titles should provide enough information to allow a classmate to identify the amendment. When students have finished, ask them to read aloud one of the titles, without giving the amendment number. After classmates guess the amendment, ask for additional titles for that amendment, and write these on the board. Have the class vote for the best and shortest title.

Monitor Progress
Circulate to make sure that students understand that their titles should be brief but should also carry enough information to identify the specific amendment.

Answer
✓ The Twenty-fifth Amendment is important because it determines who will lead the country if the President dies in office or is too ill to perform his or her duties.

CHAPTER 2

Teach With Technology

PresentationEXPRESS™ PREMIUM DVD

- Teach this chapter's core content by using PresentationExpress, which includes interactivities, video, lecture notes, and the *ExamView®* QuickTake assessment tool.
- To introduce this chapter by using PresentationExpress, ask students with which of the following statements they most agree: **A) If the overwhelming majority of people in a nation practice the same religion, there is nothing wrong with making that religion the nation's official faith. B) No nation should ever have an official state religion. C) A state religion unifies a nation and is, therefore, a good idea.** Take a class poll or record students' answers by using the QuickTake feature, and discuss their responses. Tell them that in this chapter, they will read how questions about faith and other issues arose in the nineteenth century. Continue introducing the chapter by using the chapter opener slide show and Witness History audio.

Technology Resources

- StudentEXPRESS CD-ROM
- Teacher Resource Library DVD
- PresentationEXPRESS PREMIUM DVD
- *ExamView®* Test Bank CD-ROM English and Spanish
- **Guided Reading Audio,** Spanish
- **Student Edition on Audio**

THE ESSENTIAL ? VIDEO By Students For Students
For videos on Amercian Issues, go to *www.pearsonschool.com/ushist*

CHAPTER 2 Manifest Destiny, Civil War, and Reconstruction 1800–1877

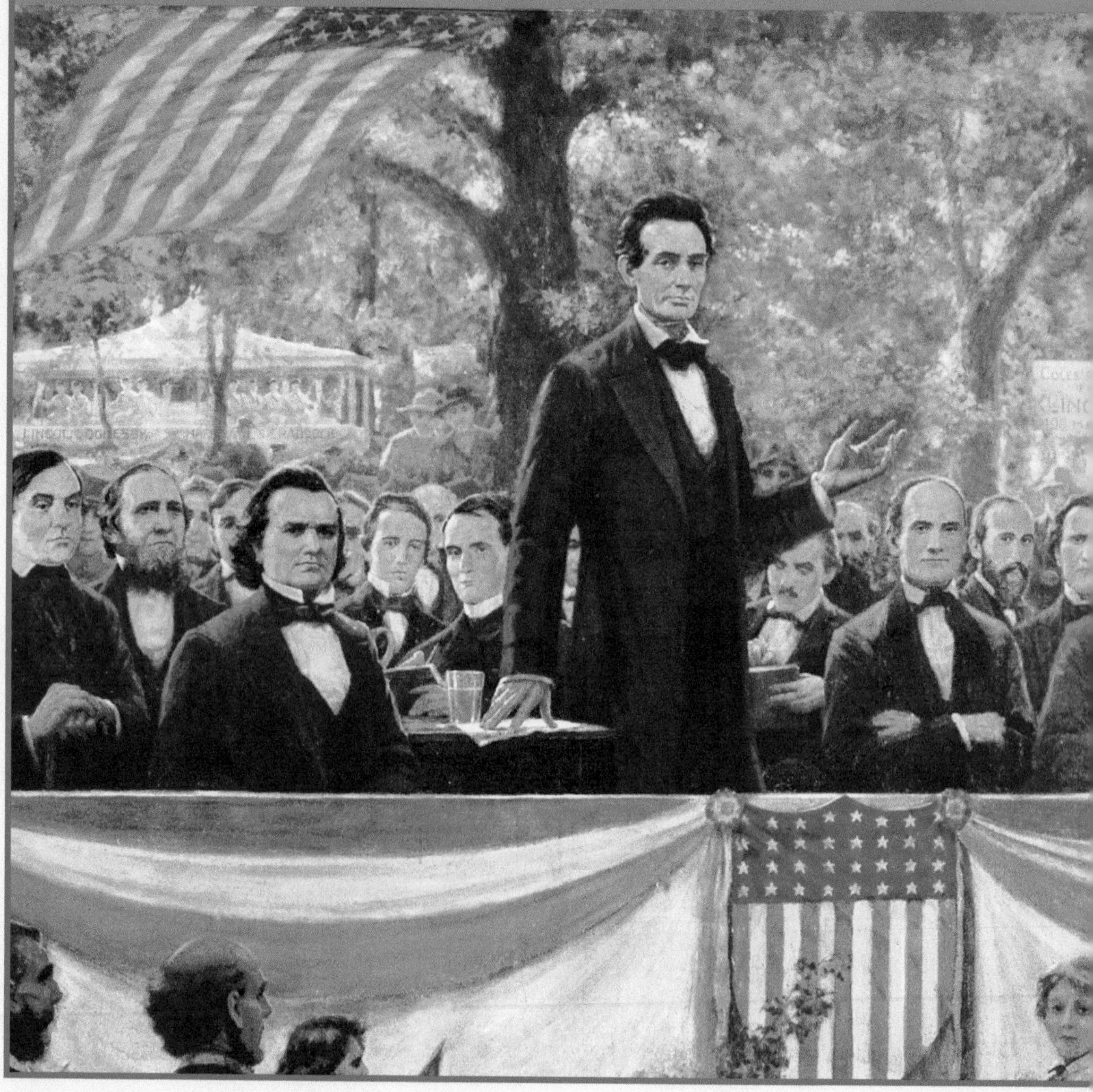

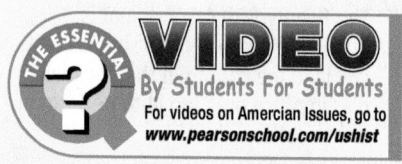

Bibliography

For the Teacher

Cover, Robert. *Justice Accused: Antislavery and the Judicial Process.* Yale University Press, 1984.

McPherson, James M. *Battle Cry of Freedom: The Era of the Civil War.* Oxford University Press, 1988.

Wilentz, Sean. *Andrew Jackson.* Times Books, 2005.

For the Student

L2 Burns, Ken and Geoffrey C. Ward. *Not For Ourselves Alone: The Story of Elizabeth Cady Stanton and Susan B. Anthony.* Knopf, 2001.

L3 Woodward, C. Vann and William S. McFeely. *The Strange Career of Jim Crow.* Oxford University Press, 2001.

L4 Donald, David Herbert. *Lincoln.* Simon and Schuster, 1996.

WITNESS HISTORY

A House Divided

In 1858, thousands of people from all over Illinois traveled for miles just to stand in the hot sun and listen to two candidates for the Senate talk. Stephen Douglas, known as the Little Giant, had a commanding presence and voice. Abraham Lincoln was tall and gangly and spoke in a hesitant manner. For three hours at a stretch, these longtime rivals debated the most troubling issue of the day: slavery.

Douglas proclaimed that each state should decide the issue for itself. But Lincoln said, "A house divided against itself cannot stand. I believe this government cannot endure, permanently half slave and half free."

Antislavery newspaper

◄ Abraham Lincoln addresses the crowd at one of his debates with Stephen Douglas.

Gold miner's pan with gold

Chapter Preview

Chapter Focus Question: What challenges did the United States face as a result of expansion, regional differences, and slavery?

Section 1
Reform and Westward Expansion

Section 2
The Union in Crisis

Section 3
The Civil War

Section 4
The Reconstruction Era

Civil War caps from South (left) and North

Use the ☑ **Quick Study Timeline** at the end of this chapter to preview chapter events.

Note Taking Study Guide *Online*
For: Note Taking and American Issues Connector
www.pearsonschool.com/ushist

Differentiated Instruction Solutions for All Learners

The following Teacher's Edition strategies are suitable for students of varying abilities.

L1 Special Needs Students, pp. 36, 40, 43, 45, 49, 52, 56 SN

L2 English Language Learners, pp. 36, 40, 43, 45, 49, 52, 56 ELL

L2 Less Proficient Readers, pp. 36, 40, 43, 45, 49, 52, 56 LPR

L4 Advanced Readers, pp. 39, 46, 51, 58 AR

L4 Gifted and Talented Students, pp. 39, 46, 51, 58 GT

Previewing the Chapter

- **WITNESS HISTORY** Read the Witness History selection aloud. Tell students that Lincoln and Douglas debated seven times between August and October of 1858. Ask students to summarize the differences between Douglas's and Lincoln's views on the politics of slavery. Point out to students that the discussion was not about the immorality of slavery so much as the balance of power between free and slave states.

- **Analyzing the Visuals** Ask students to study the visuals on these two pages. **What do these images indicate about events in the United States between 1800 and 1877?** *(Possible answer: The discovery of gold in California caused people to move west, and political tensions over the issue of slavery led to war.)*

- **Focus** Write the Chapter Focus Question on the board. Tell students to keep this question in mind as they read the chapter. Then, have students preview the section titles in this chapter.

- **Preread** Have students complete the chapter's Preread the Chapter Worksheet. Teaching Resources, pp. 8–9

Have students access **www.pearsonschool.com/ushist** for the Note Taking Study Guide *Online* as an alternative to the *Reading and Note Taking Study Guide* booklet.

Objectives

As you teach this section, keep students focused on the following objectives to help them answer the Section Focus Question and master core content.

- Analyze growing democratization, as well as limits on democracy, in the early 1800s.
- Discuss the importance of the Second Great Awakening and the rise of various reform movements.
- Explain how the nation expanded westward.

Prepare to Read

Background Knowledge L3

Ask students what they know about voting rights in the United States during the first half of the nineteenth century. Ask them to predict how the right to vote might change in the coming decades.

Set a Purpose L3

- **WITNESS HISTORY** Read the selection aloud.

  Ask **Why was there such disorder at the White House?** (*Sample answer: Jackson's supporters celebrated his inauguration and it got out of control.*) **What is Smith's attitude toward "the People"?** (*great disdain*)

- **Focus** Point out the Section Focus Question, and write it on the board. Tell students to refer to this question as they read. (*Answer appears with Section 1 Assessment answers.*)

- **Preview** Have students preview the Section Objectives and the list of Terms and People.

- **NoteTaking** Using the Guided Questioning strategy (TE, p. T20), have students read this section. As they read, have students outline the main ideas of the section. Reading and Note Taking Study Guide

WITNESS HISTORY

A "Mob" at the White House

Washington, D.C., March 4, 1829. Andrew Jackson, a popular war hero from the Tennessee frontier, had been sworn in as President. The aristocratic Margaret Bayard Smith was horrified to see the White House overrun by what she called "a rabble, a mob":

❝Cut glass and china to the amount of several thousand dollars had been broken in the struggle to get the refreshments. . . . Ladies fainted, men were seen with bloody noses and such a scene of confusion took place as is impossible to describe. . . . But it was the People's day, and the People's President and the People would rule.❞

—Margaret Bayard Smith, *The First Forty Years of Washington Society*

▲ Andrew Jackson, known as the "People's President"

Reform and Westward Expansion

Objectives

- Analyze growing democratization, as well as limits on democracy, in the early 1800s.
- Discuss the importance of the Second Great Awakening and the rise of various reform movements.
- Explain how the nation expanded westward.

Terms and People

Andrew Jackson	Missouri Compromise
tariff	Frederick Douglass
Second Great Awakening	Underground Railroad
civil disobedience	Elizabeth Cady Stanton
abolitionist	Susan B. Anthony
	Manifest Destiny

NoteTaking

Reading Skill: Identify Main Ideas As you read, outline the main ideas.

> I. Democracy and the Age of Jackson
>   A. More Americans can vote
>   1. Suffrage grows in West
>   2.

Why It Matters The Constitution established the framework for a democratic government based on principles of liberty and justice. In the mid-1800s, as the nation expanded westward, some Americans also called for an expansion of democratic rights. Today, issues raised by reformers in such areas as women's rights continue to stir debate. **Section Focus Question: What trends in democratization and reform were taking shape in the United States by 1850?**

Democracy and the Age of Jackson

In the first years of the Republic, political power was concentrated. Congressional caucuses nominated presidential candidates, and state legislatures chose the electors who cast votes for President. In general, only adult white men who owned property and paid taxes could vote.

More Americans Can Vote A major political shift began on the western frontier, where suffrage laws gave the vote to any white man over 21. Gradually, most eastern states also ended property requirements. Voting remained restricted—free African American men could vote in only a handful of northern states; women and Native Americans could not vote at all. Still, by 1828, more white men could vote than ever before.

Jackson Becomes President This new generation of voters made **Andrew Jackson** the overwhelming winner of the presidential election of 1828. Seen as a representative of the "common man," Jackson had a background quite different from earlier Presidents.

Vocabulary Builder

Use the information below and the following resource to teach students the high-use words from this section. Teaching Resources, Vocabulary Builder, p. 11

High-Use Word	Definition and Sample Sentence
compel	*v.* to force The government had no choice but to **compel** the rebels to pay the new tax.
manifest	*adj.* obvious; clear; plain The Revolutionary War made **manifest** to Europeans that Americans were determined to have their own government and nation.

Born to poor Irish immigrant parents, he had little early education. He had made a name for himself as a military hero in the War of 1812. By the time he became President, he had acquired wealth and a plantation, but he never lost his appeal to ordinary voters.

Although the Jackson era saw increased rights for some, Jackson's policies restricted the rights of Native Americans. He supported Georgia's efforts to reverse earlier treaties that had guaranteed lands to the Cherokees. When the Supreme Court upheld the Cherokees' rights, Jackson refused to enforce the decision. Instead, he ordered the relocation of Indians across the Mississippi to the West. Beginning in 1831, tens of thousands of Indians were <u>compelled</u> to leave their homes in Florida, Mississippi, and Alabama and march to what is now Oklahoma. The forced march of the Cherokees from Georgia in 1838 caused so much suffering and death that it became known as the Trail of Tears.

Vocabulary Builder
compel–(kuhm PEHL) *v.* to force

Tariffs Threaten National Unity Another issue during Jackson's presidency highlighted a growing conflict between state and federal power. The federal government had imposed high **tariffs,** or taxes on imported products. These tariffs protected northern manufacturers by raising the prices of foreign-made goods. But southerners resented paying higher prices for imports. John Calhoun of South Carolina argued that the tariff gave too much authority to the federal government—and that states had the right to nullify, or cancel, any federal law that went against their interests.

When South Carolina passed a law nullifying a federal tariff, Jackson responded strongly to the Nullification Crisis. He asked Congress for the authority to use federal troops if necessary. Congress eased tensions by lowering the tariff. Though the immediate crisis passed, southern distrust of federal authority continued to fester.

✔ **Checkpoint** How did tariffs lead to a conflict between federal and state authority?

Religion and Social Reform

Even while strife divided diverse groups, many American men and women supported religious, political, or social experiments to create a better society. Reformers came from many backgrounds and all regions of the country.

Religious Revival Sweeps the Nation Starting in the 1820s, a religious movement swept across America that become known as the **Second Great Awakening.** Marked by outdoor camp meetings that might last as long as a week, this movement attracted thousands of religious converts. The Second Great Awakening encouraged the belief that people could and should work to achieve a state of moral perfection. The Second Great Awakening helped bring religious fervor to social reform.

The Second Great Awakening fueled the rapid growth of several Christian denominations, especially the Baptists and Methodists. Other denominations also expanded during this period, including the African

The Growing Electorate
Before 1824, presidential election results did not even include a popular vote count. By 1840, the number of voters had skyrocketed. *Which Americans were not represented on the table below?*

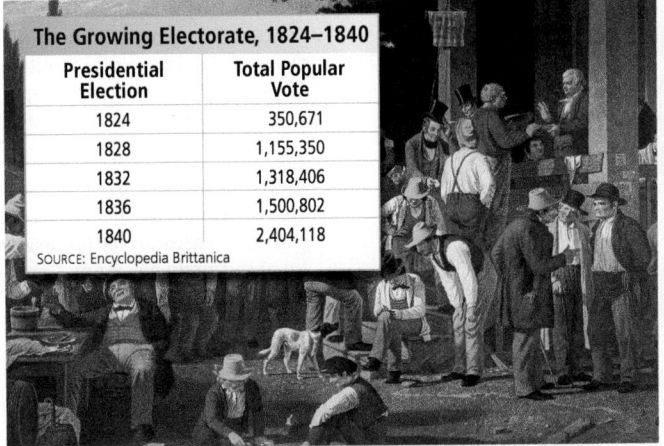

The Growing Electorate, 1824–1840	
Presidential Election	**Total Popular Vote**
1824	350,671
1828	1,155,350
1832	1,318,406
1836	1,500,802
1840	2,404,118

SOURCE: Encyclopedia Brittanica

Federal Revenue In order for the federal government to carry out its functions, it must have a source of revenue, or income. For that reason, Article I, Section 8, Clause 1 of the U.S. Constitution states that, "Congress shall have Power To lay and collect Taxes, Duties, Imposts and Excises, to pay the Debts and provide for the common Defence and general Welfare of the United States." Today, the federal government's main source of revenue is income tax; however, until the Civil War, it was tariffs. A tariff is a duty, or tax, levied on imported (and sometimes exported) goods.

During the Civil War, the federal government's need for additional revenue led it to impose the nation's first income tax. The government repealed the Civil War income tax in 1872. More than 40 years would pass before federal efforts to impose another income tax were successful. In 1913, the states ratified the Sixteenth Amendment, which stated that, "Congress shall have power to lay and collect taxes on incomes, from whatever source derived, without apportionment among the several States, and without regard to any census or enumeration."

Instruct

- **Introduce: Key Terms** Direct students' attention to the key terms **abolitionists, Missouri Compromise,** and **Underground Railroad** (in bold) in the text. Ask **How are these terms related?** (*They can all be related to slavery.*)

- **Teach** Ask **What was the Second Great Awakening?** (*a religious movement in the 1820s*) **How did Transcendentalists become involved in social reform?** (*They encouraged people to follow their conscience and introduced the concept of civil disobedience.*) **Why did slavery become such an important political issue?** (*Possible response: The North, which had gradually abolished slavery, became politically separated from the slave states in the South; the two regions began to struggle for political control at the federal level.*)

- **Quick Activity** Display Color Transparency: *The Second Great Awakening.* Use the lesson in the transparency book to guide a discussion of this important religious movement. Color Transparencies **A-69**

Independent Practice

- Have students write paragraphs describing the efforts of African Americans to resist slavery.

- Have students access **www.pearsonschool.com/ushist** to experience the History Interactive. Then, ask them to read and complete *Link to Literature: Narrative of the Life of Frederick Douglass, an American Slave.* Teaching Resources, **p. 27**

Monitor Progress

As students complete their paragraphs, circulate to make sure that they understand the scope of African American resistance to slavery.

Answer

✔ It encouraged people to work for moral perfection. Many believers took up such causes as the end of alcohol abuse and the improvement of public schools.

Methodist Episcopal Church. One of the most dramatic developments was the founding of the Church of Jesus Christ of Latter-day Saints, or Mormon Church, in 1830.

Religious Conflicts Surface From the earliest days of the Republic, Americans debated the relationship between church and government. While some favored what Thomas Jefferson called a "wall of separation" between church and state, others felt that the government should encourage public morality by supporting religion. In the 1830s, reformers known as Sabbatarians urged the federal government to officially observe Sunday, the Christian day of rest and worship. While the post office did end Sunday mail delivery, Congress rejected petitions to ban commerce on Sundays.

Members of minority religious groups, such as Roman Catholics and Jews, often faced discrimination. Most state constitutions forbade non-Christians from holding public office. Anti-Catholic rioting broke out in Philadelphia and Boston. In Illinois, Mormon leader Joseph Smith was murdered by an angry mob. As you will read, the murder of Smith spurred the Mormons to seek a safe haven in Utah.

Reformers Work to Improve Society The link between religious zeal and social reform was especially clear in the temperance movement, which worked to end alcohol abuse. But social reform took many other shapes. Dorothea Dix worked to improve the treatment of prisoners and the mentally ill. Horace Mann fought for the improvement of public schools.

A group of thinkers known as Transcendentalists also became involved in social reform. They included Ralph Waldo Emerson and Margaret Fuller, who taught that it was important to follow one's conscience. Henry David Thoreau went even further, arguing that people should peacefully refuse to obey laws they considered to be immoral. He called this concept **civil disobedience.** Thoreau himself once went to jail for refusing to pay a tax to support a war that he felt encouraged the spread of slavery.

✔ **Checkpoint** How did the Second Great Awakening encourage reform?

The Antislavery Movement

Thoreau was one of a small but fervent number of reformers, known as **abolitionists,** who sought a gradual or immediate end to slavery. They insisted that owning another human being was morally wrong, harming both slaves and slaveholders. Still, abolitionists faced an uphill struggle because many Americans believed their prosperity rested on the institution of slavery. Cotton produced by slave labor in the agrarian South supplied the textile mills of the industrial North.

Slavery Causes Suffering Some 2 million African Americans were unfairly treated by law as human property. Most labored at backbreaking tasks—picking tobacco or cotton, loading freight onto ships, or preparing meals in scorching kitchens. At any time, enslaved people could be whipped or sold away from their families.

Historians estimate that nearly 200 significant slave revolts took place in the first half of the 1800s. In 1831, Nat Turner led a rebellion in which more than 60 white Virginians were killed. Turner was later captured, tried, and executed. Fear of slave revolts led slave states to impose even harsher treatment. New laws made it a crime to teach a slave to read and write.

Differentiated Instruction   Solutions for All Learners

L1 Special Needs Students   **L2 English Language Learners**   **L2 Less Proficient Readers**

Some students may have difficulty following the discussion of Christian denominations in the passage about the Second Great Awakening. For these students, provide an outline on the board of the major branches of Protestantism. Explain that Protestantism emerged from Roman Catholicism during the Reformation, which began in the early 1500s in Europe. Ask

students to recall that many of the people who settled in what became the United States belonged to Protestant churches. Point out that the denominations, or religious groups, mentioned in the passages about the Second Great Awakening—including the Baptist, Methodist, and African Methodist Episcopal churches—are Protestant denominations.

Church and State

TRACK THE ISSUE

What is the proper relationship between government and religion?

The First Amendment says that government may not establish an official church or interfere with the free exercise of religion. But Americans differ over whether "separation of church and state" is meant to keep government out of religion or religion out of government. Use the timeline below to explore this enduring issue.

● **1791 Bill of Rights**
First Amendment bars government involvement in religion.

● **1840s Sabbatarian Controversy**
Congress debates whether to ban commerce and mail delivery on Sundays.

● **1947 *Everson* v. *Board of Education***
Supreme Court affirms separation of government and religion.

● **1984 Federal Equal Access Act**
Law allows students to form religious clubs at public high schools.

● **2000 *Mitchell* v. *Helms***
Ruling allows private schools to receive federal funds for educational materials.

A church of the early 1800s

Students pray around a flagpole outside their school.

DEBATE THE ISSUE

Should prayer be allowed in public schools? One controversial topic in the church-state debate is the issue of prayer in public schools. Current law prohibits public-school-sponsored prayers. Some Christians believe this ban violates their right to practice their beliefs.

"We're deeply religious. . . . And we believe that prayer in school is a necessity because, although yes, my children say blessings at home and pray at home and they learn to do that at church, most of their waking hours are spent in school. So why shouldn't they be able to pray, on the intercom, anywhere."
—Pat Mounce, high school parent, Pontotoc, Mississippi

"I'm a Catholic and I hope a devout one, but I think that the public school classroom is no place for me to try and impose my world formula for prayer on children who don't share it, and for that very reason, I don't want my children in a public school classroom to be exposed to someone else's religion or formula."
—Senator Phillip A. Hart, Michigan

? TRANSFER Activities

1. **Compare** What views do Mounce and Hart share? On what point do they differ?

2. **Analyze** How do you think each of these two speakers would have reacted to the issue of outlawing commerce on Sunday?

3. **Transfer** Use the following Web site to see a video, try a WebQuest, and write in your journal. www.pearsonschool.com/ushist

Objectives

● Examine the First Amendment's language on religion.

● Explain how different interpretations of the First Amendment's language have led to disagreements regarding the separation of church and state.

● Discuss how these disagreements still persist today.

Background Knowledge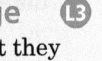

Ask students to reflect on what they know about the historical role of religion in states and societies. Have students explain the role of religion today.

Instruct

Point out that the timeline shows how the debate over the separation of church and state has developed from the nation's founding to the present. Ask **Why might the Supreme Court be involved repeatedly in church-state issues?** (*Possible answer: Citizens who believe that religious practice is very important apply pressure for legislation that supports their beliefs, and the Supreme Court is often called on to ensure that such legislation is not a violation of the First Amendment.*) **Why might the founders have thought it important to separate the church and state?** (*They believed that it was necessary to protect individual freedoms.*)

Monitor Progress

■ Have students complete the Issues Connector Worksheet, *Church and State*. Check student work to make sure that they fully understand the issue. Teaching Resources, **pp. 15–18**

■ Remind students to complete their American Issues Connector Journal worksheets notes. Review their work for accuracy. Reading and Note Taking Study Guide

Answers

Transfer Activities

1. Both share a belief in the value of religion, but they disagree on the role of religion in public schools.

2. Mounce would have supported the proposal and Hart would have opposed it.

3. For more information about the arguments for and against prayer in public schools, have students access **www.pearsonschool.com/ushist**.

History Background

Virginia Statute for Religious Freedom Many of the Founders knew from their extensive study of history and political science that government participation in religious affairs was a potential source of social conflict. In 1786, future President Thomas Jefferson drafted the *Virginia Statute for Religious Freedom*. The statute prohibited the state government from forcing citizens to support any religion, and confirmed that the civil rights of Virginia's citizens would in no way be diminished because of their beliefs.

In an essay in which he discusses the importance of guarding the separation of religion and government, James Madison observed that for American political and civil institutions, "the danger of encroachment by Ecclesiastical Bodies may be illustrated by precedents already furnished in their short history." For this reason, Madison and others took measures to separate these bodies from the government—and vice versa—by including Jefferson's ideas from the Virginia Statute in the First Amendment to the U.S. Constitution.

Instruct

- **Introduce** Ask students to find the names *Elizabeth Cady Stanton* and *Susan B. Anthony* (in bold) in the text and identify them. Ask students to predict when the United States might grant women the right to vote.

- **Teach** Using the Idea Wave strategy (TE p. T22), discuss the issues that arose in this period around women's rights. Ask **When did women in the United States begin working in factories?** *(during the early 1800s)* **How did the abolitionist movement influence the women's rights movement?** *(Possible response: Women reformers who had been involved in the abolitionist movement began to seek their own rights.)* **Why did the activists who gathered at Seneca Falls draw up a statement of purpose based on the Declaration of Independence?** *(Sample answer: They believed that the comparison would compel people to see how the principles described in the Declaration of Independence should also apply to women.)*

Answer

Thinking Critically

Tubman helped transport enslaved Africans to freedom, while Douglass and Garrison relied on speaking and on the printed word in their efforts to abolish slavery.

● **INFOGRAPHIC**

Three Antislavery Heroes

Today, we take for granted that slavery is wrong. But in the mid-1800s, it took courage to oppose slavery. These three abolitionists took great risks to stand up for their beliefs.

Harriet Tubman
As a conductor on the Underground Railroad, Harriet Tubman risked enslavement and death every time she returned to the South. Called the Black Moses, Tubman helped so many fugitives escape that slave-owners offered a $40,000 reward for her capture.

William Lloyd Garrison
William Lloyd Garrison published The Liberator, the most influential abolitionist newspaper. In October 1835, a proslavery mob put a rope around his neck and dragged him through the streets of Boston.

Frederick Douglass
When Frederick Douglass revealed at a public meeting that he had escaped from slavery, he knowingly ran the risk of being recaptured. Here, police break up an antislavery rally where Douglass is speaking.

Thinking Critically

Contrast How did Tubman's method of opposing slavery differ from those of Garrison and Douglass?

History *Interactive* ✱

For: More about the Underground Railroad
www.pearsonschool.com/ushist

Slavery Becomes a Political Issue Slavery became one of many issues separating the slaveholding South and the northern states, which had gradually done away with slavery. American leaders sought to keep a balance of power between North and South in Congress. The **Missouri Compromise** of 1820 allowed Missouri to enter the Union as a slave state, so long as a free state—Maine—was admitted at the same time. It also set 36°30′N latitude as the dividing line between slave territory and free territory. This compromise worked until the 1840s. But by then, abolitionists had begun to increase the outcry against slavery.

Connect to Your World

Modern Slavery Many people consider slavery something that happened in the past. However, according to a recent investigative report in *National Geographic Magazine*, "There are more slaves today than were seized from Africa in four centuries of the trans-Atlantic slave trade." The magazine's September 2003 article "21st-Century Slaves" stated that "an estimated 27 million men, women, and children in the world . . . are enslaved—physically confined or restrained and forced to work, or controlled through violence, or in some way treated as property." *National Geographic* also suggested that there might be as many as 150,000 enslaved people in the United States. Many of these people fled wars and natural disasters in Central America and bought their passage to the United States from people called "coyotes," who force them into slave labor. Some people, such as those at the Coalition of Immokalee Workers and the Coalition to Abolish Slavery and Trafficking, work with the United States government to end slavery.

Abolitionists Call For Freedom Some leading abolitionists had firsthand knowledge of slavery: they themselves had been born into slavery and ran away to seek freedom in the North. In 1838, **Frederick Douglass** struck out for the North from Maryland. In time, he started an antislavery newspaper and became a powerful speaker at abolitionist meetings. His booming voice filled lecture halls as he recounted the harrowing stories of his cruel master and his daring escape.

Like Douglass, Harriet Tubman had fled from slavery in Maryland. But Tubman returned to the South many times to help others escape. For this she earned the nickname Black Moses, after the biblical figure who led the Jewish people out of bondage. Tubman was one of the many "conductors" on the **Underground Railroad,** a network of abolitionists—white and black—who led enslaved people to freedom in the North or in Canada.

Douglass and Tubman added their efforts to those of a small but increasing number of white abolitionists. In January 1831, Bostonian William Lloyd Garrison began publishing *The Liberator,* which became the most influential abolitionist newspaper. Garrison proclaimed his mission: "I will be as harsh as Truth, and as uncompromising as justice. I am in earnest. I will not equivocate, I will not excuse, I will not retreat a single inch, and I WILL BE HEARD." Unlike most white abolitionists, Garrison called not only for the immediate emancipation of all people held in slavery, but also for full political and social rights for African Americans.

In several northern states, abolitionists faced violent attacks. In Alton, Illinois, an irate crowd killed abolitionist newspaper editor Elijah Lovejoy. Such violence only increased the determination of abolitionists.

✓ **Checkpoint** How did the goals of the abolitionist movement change over time?

The Women's Rights Movement

While the abolitionist movement was gaining strength, another reform movement was just beginning. The focus of this movement was the political and legal rights of women.

Women Have Limited Rights Under the law, women could not hold office or vote. Married women could not own property in their own name. In the rare instances of divorce, husbands usually gained custody of children. When women began working in factories in the early 1800s, their wages went to their fathers or husbands. In addition, colleges and most professions were closed to women.

Slowly, some restrictions loosened. By the 1840s, a few women's labor unions asked for higher wages and more control over their own wages for women. Some women worked for educational reform. Emma Willard opened the Troy Female Academy in New York to offer women a chance at higher education.

Women Begin to Organize Real progress began when women began to take a leading role in the abolitionist movement. In the 1830s, the Philadelphia Female Anti-Slavery Society, an organization of middle-class white and black women, led the movement to gain economic and political rights for both women and African Americans.

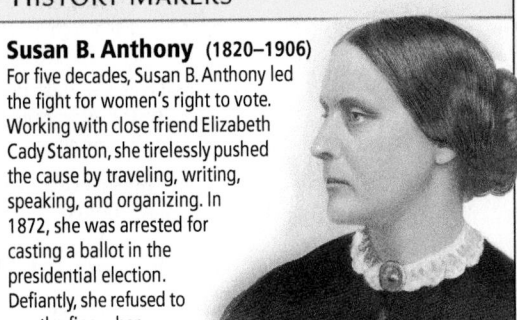

HISTORY MAKERS

Susan B. Anthony (1820–1906)
For five decades, Susan B. Anthony led the fight for women's right to vote. Working with close friend Elizabeth Cady Stanton, she tirelessly pushed the cause by traveling, writing, speaking, and organizing. In 1872, she was arrested for casting a ballot in the presidential election. Defiantly, she refused to pay the fine when found guilty.

Manifest Destiny L3

Instruct

- **Introduce: Key Term** Ask students to find the key term *Manifest Destiny* (in bold) in the text and explain its meaning. Ask them to predict whether some people might disagree with O'Sullivan's vision.

- **Teach** Ask **Where did many migrants begin their trek westward after the 1850s?** *(St. Louis, Missouri)* **What was the name of the new country established in North America in 1836? Why did it only last until 1845?** *(The Republic of Texas; the United States annexed it in that year.)* **Why might people in slave states have been enthusiastic about the Mexican-American War?** *(Sample response: They believed that if the war was successful, then it would mean additional territory in which slave states could be established, which in turn would augment their power at the federal level of government.)*

- **Analyzing the Visuals** Ask students to study the map on this page. Ask **What U.S. states today include territory that once belonged to Mexico?** *(California, Nevada, New Mexico, Colorado, Utah, Arizona, Wyoming, Texas, Oklahoma, and Kansas)*

Independent Practice

Have students access **www.pearson-school.com/ushist** to use the Geography Interactive map and answer the map skills questions in the text.

Monitor Progress

Circulate to make sure that students answer the map skills questions accurately.

Answers

✓ She helped organize the nation's first women's rights convention in 1848 and helped to draft the Declaration of Sentiments.

Map Skills

1. Review locations with students.
2. the eastern United States, Florida, the Southwest, the West
3. Students' answers will vary, depending on the state in which they live.

Growth of the United States

Map Skills By 1853, the United States had extended its borders to the Pacific Ocean, achieving the goal of Manifest Destiny.

1. **Locate:** (a) Oregon, (b) Texas, (c) the Mexican Cession, (d) the Pacific Ocean

2. **Regions** What areas did the United States gain as a result of war?

3. **Link Past to Present** Was the state in which you live part of the United States by 1803? By 1853? If so, how was it acquired?

Geography *Interactive*
For: Interactive map
www.pearsonschool.com/ushist

Then, in 1848, **Elizabeth Cady Stanton** and Lucretia Mott helped organize the nation's first women's rights convention. Several hundred men and women, black and white, attended this gathering at Seneca Falls, New York. There they drew up a Declaration of Sentiments, modeled after the Declaration of Independence, beginning with the lines, "We hold these truths to be self-evident: that all men and women are created equal." The document goes on to charge:

> **Primary Source** "The history of mankind is a history of repeated injuries and usurpations on the part of man toward woman, having in direct object the establishment of an absolute tyranny over her. . . . He has taken from her all right in property, even to the wages she earns. . . . He has denied her the facilities for obtaining a thorough education."
>
> —Elizabeth Cady Stanton, Declaration of Sentiments

Over the next decades, women's rights leaders such as Stanton and **Susan B. Anthony** worked to achieve greater rights for women. But their ultimate goal—suffrage, or the right to vote—would not be attained in their lifetimes.

✓ **Checkpoint** How did Elizabeth Cady Stanton try to promote women's rights?

Manifest Destiny

As in colonial times, Americans continued to expand westward. Seeking good farmland, gold, or animal furs—or just to satisfy a sense of adventure—some men crossed the Great Plains to explore the West. They marked out trails that crossed the Rocky Mountains and the Sierra Nevadas. By 1850, St. Louis, Mis-

---

Differentiated Instruction   Solutions for All Learners

 **Special Needs Students**  **English Language Learners**  **Less Proficient Readers**

To help students master vocabulary, have them list this section's high-use words, key terms, and people. Encourage students to include in the list additional terms that may be new to them, such as *fester, fervor, denominations, equivocate,* and *providence.* Then, have students create flashcards with the term on one side and its definition (or, in the case of a key person, an identifying statement) on the other. For English Language Learners, you may wish to have students add explanations in their first language to go with the flashcards. Pair students, and have them use their flashcards to quiz each other.

souri, had become the launching point from which settlers traveled west along the Santa Fe Trail, the Oregon Trail, the Mormon Trail, or the California Trail.

In 1845, journalist John O'Sullivan predicted that it was the nation's "manifest destiny . . . to overspread the continent allotted by Providence for the free development of our yearly multiplying millions." The term **Manifest Destiny** came to stand for the idea that the United States was intended by God to stretch from the Atlantic Ocean all the way to the Pacific Ocean.

Conflict Erupts With Mexico Westward expansion brought the United States into conflict with Mexico. In the 1820s, the Mexican government encouraged Americans to move into Texas. Many did so, especially southerners with slaves. By the 1830s, these American Texans sought independence from Mexico. In 1836, after a short war against Mexico, they won their independence, and Texas became the Republic of Texas. Suddenly, without having moved, many Mexicans lived in a new country—one in which they often were treated as second-class citizens.

The United States annexed Texas as a state in 1845. The following year, a dispute over the boundary between Texas and Mexico led to the outbreak of war. Some northerners opposed the Mexican-American War, viewing it as an attempt to extend slavery. Still, the United States won a quick victory. In 1848, the Treaty of Guadalupe Hidalgo set the Rio Grande as the southern boundary of Texas. Mexico also agreed to cede an immense expanse of land to the United States, including California and parts of other southwest states.

Gold Brings Settlers to California In 1848, gold was discovered in California. Within months, easterners were streaming into California in search of quick riches. These "forty-niners" set up campsites and hastily constructed towns as they staked a claim to a plot of land that they hoped would make them wealthy. The gold rush also attracted emigrants from as far away as China.

In 1850, enough American citizens lived in California that it was able to apply for statehood as a free state. This request would inflame the growing national conflict over slavery.

✔ **Checkpoint** What were the causes and effects of the Mexican-American War?

Vocabulary Builder
manifest–(MAN uh fehst) *adj.* obvious; clear; plain

Gold Rush
News about the discovery of gold brought thousands of "forty-niners" like these rushing to California.

SECTION 1 Assessment

Comprehension

1. **Terms and People** Write a sentence explaining how each of the following was connected with reform or the growth of democracy.
   - Andrew Jackson
   - Second Great Awakening
   - civil disobedience
   - abolitionist
   - Frederick Douglass
   - Underground Railroad
   - Elizabeth Cady Stanton
   - Susan B. Anthony

2. **NoteTaking Reading Skill: Identify Main Ideas** Use your outline to answer the Section Focus Question: What trends in democratization and reform were taking shape in the United States by 1850?

Writing About History

3. **Quick Write: Identify a Viewpoint** Write a paragraph describing one of the two viewpoints on the Nullification Crisis discussed in this section. Be sure to identify the underlying attitude about the nature of federal versus state authority.

Critical Thinking

4. **Evaluate Information** To what extent did the presidency of Andrew Jackson represent a move toward democratization? How was this trend limited?

5. **Analyze Effects** Describe one direct and one indirect effect of the Second Great Awakening.

6. **Compare and Contrast** How were the abolitionist movement and the women's rights movement similar? How were they different?

Assess and Reteach

Assess Progress L3

- Have students complete the Section Assessment.

- Administer the Section Quiz. Teaching Resources, **p. 33**

- To further assess student understanding, use Progress Monitoring Transparencies, **14**.

Reteach

If students need more instruction, have them read the section summary.

Reading and Note Taking Study Guide L3

Adapted Reading and Note Taking Study Guide L1 L2

Spanish Reading and Note Taking Study Guide L2

Extend L4

In 1829, David Walker wrote, "America is more our country than it is the whites—, we have enriched it with our blood and tears." Have students use the Internet or library resources to find and read David Walker's *Appeal*. Then, have them give a class presentation comparing Walker's views with those of other abolitionists.

Answer

✔ a boundary dispute between the United States and Mexico; the Rio Grande became the southern boundary of the U.S. state of Texas.

Section 1 Assessment

1. Students' sentences should reflect an understanding of how each term or person is connected with reform or the growth of democracy.

2. Democratization was reflected in widening suffrage for white males, and the spirit of reform was evident in efforts to reduce alcohol consumption; to improve prisons, public schools, and public health; and to abolish slavery.

3. Encourage students to carefully consider opposing viewpoints as they compose their paragraphs.

4. Viewed as a man of the people, Jackson also expanded voting rights; at the same time, he restricted the rights of Native Americans in the South.

5. The movement directly fueled the growth of several Christian denominations and indirectly inspired reform efforts such as the temperance movement.

6. Both movements fought for groups deprived of important rights. The focus of abolitionists was on ending slavery, and advocates for women sought the expansion of existing rights.

For additional assessment, have students access **Progress Monitoring Online** at www.pearsonschool.com/ushist.

Objectives

As you teach this section, keep students focused on the following objectives to help them answer the Section Focus Question and master core content.

- Trace the growing conflict over the issue of slavery in the western territories.
- Analyze the importance of the Dred Scott decision.
- Explain how the election of Abraham Lincoln in 1860 led to secession.

Prepare to Read

Background Knowledge **L3**

Remind students of the fast pace of westward expansion during the 1800s, and ask them to predict how this growth might affect the political situation in the United States.

Set a Purpose **L3**

- **WITNESS HISTORY** Read the selection aloud.

  Ask **Do you think the observers in the courtroom were worried about being punished for helping Louis? Why?** (*Possible response: No; they believed that helping Louis was the right thing to do.*)

- **Focus** Point out the Section Focus Question, and write it on the board. Tell students to refer to this question as they read. (*Answer appears with Section 2 Assessment answers.*)

- **Preview** Have students preview the Section Objectives and the list of Terms and People.

- **Reading Skill** Have students use the *Reading Strategy: Recognize Sequence* worksheet. Teaching Resources, **p. 12**

- **NoteTaking** Using the Paragraph Shrinking strategy (TE, p. T20), have students read this section. As they read, have students sequence the events that divided the Union. Reading and Note Taking Study Guide

CAUTION!!
COLORED PEOPLE
OF BOSTON, ONE & ALL,
You are hereby respectfully CAUTIONED and
advised, to avoid conversing with the
Watchmen and Police Officers
of Boston,
For since the recent ORDER OF THE MAYOR &
ALDERMEN, they are empowered to act as
KIDNAPPERS
AND
Slave Catchers,

▲ This poster warns African Americans in Boston about the arrival of "slave catchers" like the ones shown at left.

WITNESS HISTORY

A Fugitive Escapes

The Fugitive Slave Law of 1850 made it a crime to help African Americans escape slavery. But that did not stop Levi Coffin and his fellow abolitionists from taking action when slave catchers in Indiana arrested a fugitive named Louis. Coffin described how Louis escaped from a public courtroom in broad daylight:

❝[Louis] slipped his chair back a little way. Neither his master nor the marshal noticed the movement, as they were intently listening to the judge, and he slipped his chair again, until he was back of them. . . . Next he rose quietly to his feet and took a step backward. Some abolitionist friendly to his cause gave him an encouraging touch on the foot, and he stepped farther back. Then a good hat was placed on his head by some one behind, and he quietly and cautiously made his way . . . toward the door.❞
—*Reminiscences of Levi Coffin*

The Union in Crisis

Objectives

- Trace the growing conflict over the issue of slavery in the western territories.
- Analyze the importance of the Dred Scott decision.
- Explain how the election of Abraham Lincoln in 1860 led to secession.

Terms and People

Wilmot Proviso	Kansas-Nebraska Act
Free-Soil Party	*Dred Scott* v. *Sandford*
Compromise of 1850	Abraham Lincoln
popular sovereignty	John Brown
Harriet Beecher Stowe	secede

NoteTaking

Reading Skill: Recognize Sequence As you read, trace the sequence of events that led to the division of the Union.

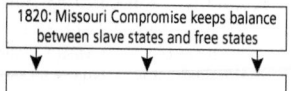

1820: Missouri Compromise keeps balance between slave states and free states

Why It Matters Regional differences between the North and South had existed since colonial times. These differences widened in the 1800s as the North developed an industrial economy while the South continued to depend on plantation agriculture and slavery. In time, conflict over the issue of slavery led to an armed struggle that would forever change the nation: the Civil War. **Section Focus Question: How did the issue of slavery divide the Union?**

Slavery and Western Expansion

After the Mexican-American War, the question of slavery in the West emerged as a major issue. A Pennsylvania congressman proposed the **Wilmot Proviso,** which stated that, though slavery would continue in the South, it would be banned in the territory won from Mexico. The proposal passed the House of Representatives, where northern members held a majority, but was defeated in the Senate, where some northern Democrats opposed the measure.

New Parties Oppose Slavery The Wilmot Proviso helped spur the rise of antislavery political parties. In 1848, the **Free-Soil Party** nominated former President Martin Van Buren for President. Although Van Buren did not win, he and other Free-Soil candidates garnered enough votes to show that the party's motto of "free soil, free speech, free labor, and free men" would not easily be silenced.

Vocabulary Builder

Use the information below and the following resource to teach students the high-use word from this section. Teaching Resources, Vocabulary Builder, p. 11

High-Use Word	Definition and Sample Sentence
intense	*adj.* very strong; violent; extreme Many immigrants came to the United States because of their **intense** desire to escape religious persecution.

Congress Tries to Compromise In 1850, California applied to enter the Union as a free state, thus threatening the balance between slave and free states in Congress. To ease southern concerns, Congress passed what became known as the **Compromise of 1850.** According to this measure, California was admitted as a free state. In the rest of the territory acquired from Mexico, voters would decide for themselves whether or not to allow slavery. This approach became known as **popular sovereignty.** By permitting slavery north of 36°30′N latitude, the Compromise of 1850 undid the Missouri Compromise.

Another provision of the Compromise of 1850, the Fugitive Slave Act, required citizens to help apprehend runaway slaves. Northern opponents of the law mounted an <u>intense</u> and disruptive resistance. In 1851, at Christiana, Pennsylvania, a small band of African Americans gathered to protect several runaways from southern slave catchers. Local white bystanders not only refused to help the slave-hunting party but, when the slave owner died in the scuffle, a white jury refused to convict the killers. In other northern cities, white and black opponents found nonviolent ways to defy the hated law.

✓ **Checkpoint** How did the Compromise of 1850 lead to conflict between the North and South?

Vocabulary Builder
<u>intense</u>–(ihn TEHNS) *adj.* very strong; violent; extreme

The Road to Disunion

Resentment against the Fugitive Slave Act spurred **Harriet Beecher Stowe** to write the antislavery novel *Uncle Tom's Cabin.* Southerners argued that Stowe presented a false picture of slavery and the South. But the novel became a best-seller in the North, increasing opposition to slavery.

Violence Erupts in Kansas In 1854, Congress again tried to settle the issue of slavery in the West by passing the **Kansas-Nebraska Act,** which divided the Nebraska Territory into Kansas and Nebraska. Voters in each territory would decide the issue of slavery by popular sovereignty. Many northerners complained that this plan allowed slavery in areas where it had been banned by the Missouri Compromise.

Soon, both proslavery and antislavery settlers were flocking to Kansas, each hoping to outnumber the other when the time came to vote on slavery. By 1856, Kansas had two governments, one proslavery, the other antislavery. For several months there was so much violence between the two sides that the territory became known as "Bleeding Kansas." Finally, in 1861, Kansas entered the Union as a free state.

The Republican Party Emerges The election of 1856 pitted Democrat James Buchanan against John C. Frémont, candidate of the new Republican Party. Like the earlier Free-Soil Party, the Republican Party opposed the extension of slavery into the western territories. Republicans included abolitionists who believed slavery was immoral, business leaders who felt that slavery stifled industry, and northerners who argued that the Fugitive Slave Act intruded into state politics.

Bleeding Kansas
In the dispute over slavery in Kansas, both sides turned to violence. Below, proslavery raiders attack settlers who oppose slavery.

L1 Special Needs Students   **L2 English Language Learners**   **L2 Less Proficient Readers**

Students who are having a difficult time with vocabulary may benefit from an exercise that asks them to utilize new terms in sentences and paragraphs of their own creation. Have students list the key terms under the first two blue headings, "Slavery and Western Expansion" and "The Road to Disunion": *Wilmot Proviso, Compromise of 1850, popular sovereignty, Harriet Beecher Stowe, Kansas-Nebraska Act,* Dred Scott *v.* Sandford, *Abraham Lincoln,* and *John Brown.*

Have them list any other words with which they might be unfamiliar, such as *garnered, mounted, scuffle, flocking, championing, pitted, stifled, underscored, crystallized, arsenal,* and *martyr.* After students have compiled their lists and familiarized themselves with the words' definitions, have them write sentences or paragraphs that use a specified number of terms. Encourage students to be creative, and invite volunteers to read their sentences aloud to the class.

Slavery and Western Expansion/The Road to Disunion   L3

Instruct

- **Introduce: Key Terms** Have students find the key terms *Compromise of 1850* and *Kansas-Nebraska Act* (in bold) and define them. Remind students of the Missouri Compromise, and then ask how the U.S. representational system of government made such compromises necessary.

- **Teach** Using the Think-Write-Pair-Share strategy (TE p. T23), have students discuss how western expansion led to conflicts over slavery, which began to threaten the Union. Ask **What was the Fugitive Slave Act?** *(part of the Compromise of 1850 that required citizens to help apprehend runaway slaves)* **How did the act affect writer Harriet Beecher Stowe?** *(It inspired her to write the novel* Uncle Tom's Cabin.*)* **Why were northerners outraged by the *Dred Scott* decision?** *(Sample answer: The Supreme Court ruled that the Missouri Compromise was unconstitutional and supported the notion that slaves were considered property.)* Display Color Transparency: *The Struggle Against Slavery.* Use the lesson suggested in the transparency book to guide a discussion about how the issue of slavery divided Americans. Color Transparencies A-70

- **Analyzing the Visuals** Have students study the image "Bleeding Kansas." Ask **Do you think that people were right to use violence to stop the spread of slavery?** *(Possible answer: No; then pro-slavery supporters could use similar logic to justify violent behavior in situations for which it was not called.)*

Answer

✓ by threatening the congressional balance between free and slave states

Objectives

- Review the system of government established by the U.S. Constitution.
- Explain the concept of states' rights.
- Analyze the role of the Supreme Court in issues of states' rights.

Background Knowledge **L3**

Ask students to think about the factors that have influenced the shifting distribution of power between the states and the federal government. Do they think the trend has been increasing power for the states or for the federal government? Explain.

Instruct **L3**

Explain that the timeline shows significant controversies over states' rights that emerged after the ratification of the Bill of Rights. **Ask How did the court battle between California and the EPA reflect the issue of states' rights?** *(California felt it had the right, by federal law, to set its own emission standards.)*

Monitor Progress

- Have students complete the Issues Connector Worksheet, *Federal Power and States' Rights.* Check students' work to make sure they that grasp the aspects of the issue. Teaching Resources, **pp. 19–22**

- Remind students to complete their American Issues Connector Journal worksheets notes. Review their work for accuracy. Reading and Note Taking Study Guide

Answers

Transfer Activities

1. Schwarzenegger argues the Supreme Court and a federal court in California granted California the right to determine the emissions standards but the EPA did not honor that decision.

2. Johnson feels the standard set by the federal government is sufficient and should not be challenged.

3. For more information about federal power and states' rights, have students access **www.pearsonschool.com/ushist.**

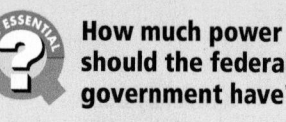

TRACK THE ISSUE

How much power should the federal government have?

Under the Constitution, all powers not granted to the federal government belong to the states. Over time, however, the federal government has expanded its scope, especially in the area of social programs. Use the timeline below to explore this enduring issue.

1791 Bill of Rights
Tenth Amendment reserves most powers to the states

1798 Kentucky and Virginia Resolutions
States argue that they can void federal legislation.

1831 Nullification Crisis
John C. Calhoun declares that states may overturn federal laws.

1857 Dred Scott v. Sandford
Supreme Court rules that federal government does not have power to outlaw slavery within territories.

1930s New Deal
Government expands power over economy and social services.

1965 Voting Rights Act
Law allows federal officers to register voters.

Dred Scott

Exhaust and waste gases from cars are just one of the many issues in the center of the continuing national debate about the environment.

DEBATE THE ISSUE

The Environment and States' Rights Since 1967, the Environmental Protection Agency (EPA) has allowed California to make its own emissions rules. California is exempt from the Clean Air Acts as long as its rules are stricter than those of the federal government and it obtains a waiver from the federal government. In November 2007, Governor Arnold Schwarzenegger sued the federal government because the EPA denied California a waiver.

> "The authority of the States to address greenhouse gas emissions from motor vehicles has been supported—by the Supreme Court [and] by a federal court here in California. On this issue, the ... EPA ... has failed to follow the States' lead ... we are prepared to force it out of the way ... to protect the environment."
>
> —Governor Arnold Schwarzenegger, April 2, 2008

> "I believe that Congress by passing a ... federal standard of 35 mpg (miles per gallon) delivers significant reductions that are more effective than a state-by-state approach. This applies to all 50 states. ... and that's great for the economy, for national security, and for the environment."
>
> —Stephen L. Johnson, EPA Administrator

 TRANSFER Activities

1. **Compare** Why does Governor Schwarzenegger feel California should oppose the federal government? Why does Stephen Johnson disagree?

1. **Analyze** Should a state have the right to determine its own environmental standards?

1. **Transfer** Use the following Web site to see a video, try a WebQuest, and write in your journal. www.pearsonschool.com/ushist

---

History Background

A Complicated Issue The balancing of federal power with states' rights has absorbed the United States since its founding. There are few better places to start to better understand this complex issue than with the *Federalist Papers*, written in 1787 and 1788, that argue for a strong central government as described in the new Constitution. Alexander Hamilton, author of most of the *Federalist Papers*, recognized the obstacles. In "Federalist No. 15," Hamilton wrote: "If the road over which you will still have to pass should in some places appear to you tedious or irksome, you will recollect that you are in quest of information on a subject the most momentous which can engage the attention of a free people, that the field through which you have to travel is in itself spacious, and that the difficulties of the journey have been unnecessarily increased by the mazes with which sophistry has beset the way."

Buchanan won the election. But Frémont's strong showing underscored the importance of the slavery issue and the growing appeal of the new party.

The Dred Scott Decision Inflames the Nation In 1857, a Supreme Court decision widened the growing divisions over slavery. Dred Scott, an enslaved African American from Missouri, had sued for his freedom, based on the fact that he had traveled with his master into free territory.

In **Dred Scott v. Sandford,** the Court made a sweeping ruling that went far beyond the particulars of Scott's case. The Court declared that African Americans were not citizens, and therefore were not entitled to sue in the courts. Furthermore, the Court ruled that the federal government did not have the power to ban slavery in any territory and that the Missouri Compromise was unconstitutional, since it could deprive citizens of their property without due process of law. Southerners were delighted with the Dred Scott decision, but northerners were outraged.

Lincoln Debates Douglas The 1858 Senate race in Illinois crystallized the slavery issue for many Americans. At a series of debates, Republican **Abraham Lincoln** challenged Democrat Stephen Douglas, architect of the Kansas-Nebraska Act. Lincoln did not call for the immediate abolition of slavery, nor for political equality for African Americans. Still, he argued:

> **Primary Source** ❝There is no reason in the world why the negro is not entitled to all the natural rights enumerated in the Declaration of Independence, the right to life, liberty and the pursuit of happiness. . . . In the right to eat the bread, without leave of anybody else, which his own hand earns, he is my equal and the equal of Judge Douglas, and the equal of every living man.❞
> —Abraham Lincoln, debate at Ottawa, Illinois

Douglas continued to champion popular sovereignty. "This Union was established on the right of each State to do as it pleased on the question of slavery, and every other question," he insisted. Douglas won the senate race, but the debates helped Lincoln win national attention.

John Brown Plans a Revolt In 1859, a violent attack on slavery occurred in northern Virginia. In the fall of 1859, white abolitionist **John Brown** led a small band of white and black followers in an attempt to seize a federal arsenal in Harpers Ferry, Virginia (now in West Virginia). He hoped to inspire local enslaved African Americans to join a revolution that would destroy slavery in the South. Brown's plan failed.

Put on trial for treason, Brown proclaimed his willingness to "mingle my blood . . . with the blood of millions in this slave country whose rights are disregarded by wicked, cruel, and unjust enactments." In the eyes of many abolitionists, Brown's defense of his actions and the dignified calm with which he faced execution made him a heroic martyr to the antislavery cause. Northern support for Brown further inflamed southern anger.

✓ **Checkpoint** How did northerners and southerners react to the Dred Scott decision?

HISTORY MAKERS

Abraham Lincoln (1809–1865)
Born in a log cabin to a struggling farmer, Abraham Lincoln had little formal education. "When I came of age I did not know much," he later wrote. "I could read, write, and cipher . . . but that was all. I have not been to school since." Still, he developed a thirst for learning, eventually gaining enough knowledge to practice law and enter politics. He was elected to the Illinois state legislature four times and, in 1846, was elected to the U.S. House of Representatives. While in Congress, he spoke out against the Mexican-American War—an unpopular position that cost him reelection. Ten years later, he joined the newly formed Republican Party.

Independent Practice

- Tell students to reflect on how a democratic concept, such as popular sovereignty, might result in a decidedly undemocratic outcome. Ask them to create a political cartoon that is based on this idea.

- Have students read and complete *Viewpoints: Douglas and Lincoln.* Teaching Resources, **p. 30**

- Have students read the HISTORY MAKERS feature about Abraham Lincoln and the Primary Source quotation from the Ottawa debate. Ask students to write a newspaper editorial explaining why Lincoln would or would not support today's Republican Party.

- Ask students to reread the passages about John Brown and then write a paragraph about his role as a martyr in the abolitionist movement.

Monitor Progress

As students fill in their flowcharts, circulate to make sure that they understand the sequence of events that led to the division of the Union. For a completed version of the flowchart, see Note Taking Transparencies, **B-79**.

Differentiated Instruction Solutions for All Learners

L1 Special Needs Students **L2 English Language Learners** **L2 Less Proficient Readers**

To help students analyze the similarities and differences between Abraham Lincoln's and Stephen Douglas's views on slavery, ask them to create two-column charts comparing and contrasting the views on both sides of the issue. As they read the chapter, have students record relevant information on their charts. After they have completed their charts, have partners work together to write summary paragraphs of each candidate's views. Tell students to use their charts and summaries to complete *View Points: The Illinois Senate Campaign of 1858*. Teaching Resources, **pp. 28–29**

Answer

✓ Many southerners were delighted with the decision, but most northerners were outraged.

Lincoln, Secession, and War

Instruct

- **Introduce: Key Term** Ask students to find the key term *secede* (in bold) in the text and explain its meaning. Ask students to predict how the federal government may react to the secession of slave states.

- **Teach** Ask **Who won the 1860 election?** (*Republican candidate Abraham Lincoln*) **How did the southern states react to Lincoln's victory?** (*Several decided to secede from the Union.*) **Why might Lincoln have postponed declaring war until a Confederate attack?** (*Possible response: He did not want the Union to appear to be the aggressor, and the outrage caused among northerners meant that Lincoln was likely to have more public support.*)

- **Analyzing the Visuals** Have students examine the political cartoon on this page. Ask **Which candidate do you think the cartoonist preferred?** (*Sample answer: The cartoon appears to be nonpartisan; it is a parody of all the candidates.*) **What do you think of the artist's decision to portray the candidates as caricatures?** *Sample response: The artist may have wanted to show that the candidates were acting foolishly as they fought to gain support from Americans.*)

Independent Practice

Have students analyze the Infographic and answer the questions that accompany it.

Monitor Progress

Circulate to make sure that students understand the full range of views of the American public at the time of the 1860 election.

Answers

Thinking Critically

1. the Republican Party
2. No; in the cartoon, Lincoln and Douglas tear at the western part of the country, while Breckinridge attacks the South. Bell is trying to repair the Northeast. On the map Lincoln won the North and West, and Douglas won the South.

● **INFOGRAPHIC**

The Election of 1860

"**W**e believe that this election is a turning-point in our history." So wrote poet James Russell Lowell a month before the presidential election of 1860. In fact, he was right. The victory of Abraham Lincoln literally split the nation in two.

▲ This 1860 cartoon shows Lincoln and Douglas (left) fighting over slavery in the West. While Breckinridge (center) tears off the South, Bell (right) vainly tries to glue the Union back together.

Lincoln campaign banner ▼

The issue of slavery was so divisive in 1860 that the Democratic Party nominated different candidates in the North and South. As the map and chart show, each of the four presidential candidates won support in a different region. ▼

FOR PRESIDENT,
ABRAHAM LINCOLN
VICE PRESIDENT,
HANNIBAL HAMLI

Candidate (Party)	Electoral Vote	Popular Vote	% Electoral Vote	% Popular Vote
☐ Abraham Lincoln (Republican)	180	1,866,452	59	40
☐ John C. Breckinridge (Southern-Democratic)	72	847,953	24	18
☐ Stephen A. Douglas (Democratic)	12	1,380,202	4	29
☐ John Bell (Constitutional Union)	39	590,901	13	13

Thinking Critically
1. **Analyze a Map** Which party won nearly all the northern states?
1. **Synthesize Information** Does the cartoon accurately reflect the information given on the map? Explain.

Lincoln, Secession, and War

Brown's execution and the Dred Scott decision were still fresh in voters' minds as the 1860 presidential elections approached. Meeting in Chicago, the Republican Party adopted a platform that affirmed the Wilmot Proviso and the authority of Congress to ban slavery in the territories.

The Election Fragments the Nation Republicans saw Abraham Lincoln, with his reputation for integrity, as the ideal candidate to carry their platform to victory. Around the country, newspapers had publicized Lincoln's positions—his objections to slavery, and his defense of the West as a land of opportunity for

---

Differentiated Instruction Solutions for All Learners

L4 Advanced Readers L4 Gifted and Talented Students

Have students do further research on one of the Lincoln-Douglas debates. Ask partners to choose a specific debate and then conduct a mock debate presenting accurate views of either man. Remind students that they need to choose a debate from the 1858 race for the Illinois Senate. After partners have completed their research and chosen a viewpoint, ask them to present their debates to the class. Follow up the debates with a class discussion about each candidate's views.

free white men. Meanwhile, the Democratic Party fractured over the slavery issue. Northern Democrats nominated Stephen Douglas, while Southern Democrats nominated John Breckinridge. A fourth candidate, John Bell, represented a small moderate coalition who wanted to keep the Union together.

Benefiting from the Democrat split, Lincoln easily won the election, carrying 18 northern and western free states. He ended up with only 40 percent of the popular vote but almost 60 percent of the electoral vote, even though he did not receive a single southern electoral vote.

The South Secedes To southerners, the election was a clear sign that the more populous free states were now in a position to control national politics. On December 20, 1860, a convention in South Carolina declared that "the union now subsisting between South Carolina and the other States . . . is hereby dissolved." South Carolina thus became the first state to **secede,** or break away, from the Union.

Six other states soon joined South Carolina to establish the Confederate States of America. They framed a constitution modeled on the U.S. Constitution but with some important differences. First, the Confederate constitution stressed the independence of each state, implying that states had the right to secede. Second, the new constitution guaranteed the protection of slavery. In time, four additional states joined the Confederacy.

War Begins at Fort Sumter At first, Lincoln insisted he had no authority to force Confederate states to return to the Union. Then, the Confederacy began to seize federal military bases in southern states. When Fort Sumter, in the harbor of Charleston, South Carolina, ran short of supplies, Lincoln notified the Confederacy that he was sending food but no armaments. Confederates decided to try to seize the fort before provisions could arrive.

On April 11, 1861, Confederate troops demanded that Union troops give up Fort Sumter. When the commander refused, the Confederates fired on the fort. After heavy bombardment, the federal troops surrendered. The fall of Fort Sumter marked the start of the Civil War, a four-year struggle that threatened to bring the Union to a bloody end.

Fort Sumter Flag
The tattered Union flag shown below was flying over Fort Sumter when Confederate troops fired on the fort.

✔ **Checkpoint** How did the election of 1860 split the nation in two?

Assess and Reteach

Assess Progress L3
- Have students complete the Section Assessment.
- Administer the Section Quiz. Teaching Resources, **p. 34**
- To further assess student understanding, use Progress Monitoring Transparencies, **15**.

Reteach L3
If students need more instruction, have them read the section summary.

Reading and Note Taking Study Guide L3

Adapted Reading and Note Taking Study Guide L1 L2

Spanish Reading and Note Taking Study Guide L2

Extend L4
Remind students of John Brown's actions at Harpers Ferry. Tell students that Brown also took part in antislavery raids in "Bleeding Kansas." Ask students to conduct research on Brown and to use their research to create an annotated and illustrated timeline of Brown's life.

SECTION 2 Assessment

Progress Monitoring Online
For: Self-test with vocabulary practice
www.pearsonschool.com/ushist

Comprehension

1. **Terms and People** Write a sentence explaining how each of the following was connected with the growing rift between North and South.
   - Wilmot Proviso
   - Free-Soil Party
   - Compromise of 1850
   - popular sovereignty
   - Kansas-Nebraska Act
   - *Dred Scott* v. *Sandford*
   - Abraham Lincoln
   - John Brown
   - secede

2. **NoteTaking Reading Skill: Recognize Sequence** Use your flowchart to answer the Section Focus Question: How did the issue of slavery divide the Union?

Writing About History

3. **Quick Write: State a Point of View** Write a paragraph defining a viewpoint on the following issue: Should states have the right to secede from the Union? Give one argument someone might use to support that viewpoint.

Critical Thinking

4. **Draw Inferences** Why do you think southerners in Congress insisted on the passage of a Fugitive Slave Act? Why did many northerners oppose it?

5. **Analyze Information** Why was the *Dred Scott* decision a blow to those who opposed the extension of slavery?

6. **Draw Conclusions** Do you think the issue of slavery could have been settled without war? Why or why not?

Answer

✔ Viewing Lincoln's election in 1860 as a sign that free states would dominate national politics, many slave states seceded from the Union.

Section 2 Assessment

1. Students' sentences should reflect an understanding of how each term or person was connected with the growing rift between the North and the South.

2. As the nation grew, more states entered the Union, and the question of whether these states should allow or prohibit slavery caused political problems that eventually divided the nation and led to civil war.

3. Encourage students to support their arguments by citing passages from the U.S. Constitution.

4. Possible answers: Many southerners saw slaves as property and believed that the government should defend their property rights; many northerners thought slavery was evil or immoral, and since slavery was illegal in these states the act was seen as an intrusion.

5. because it held that the federal government did not have the authority to ban slavery in any territory

6. Possible response: No; the South's economy was too deeply rooted in the institution of slavery for southerners to end slavery voluntarily.

For additional assessment, have students access **Progress Monitoring Online** at **www.pearsonschool.com/ushist.**

Objectives

As you teach this section, keep students focused on the following objectives to help them answer the Section Focus Question and master core content.

- Evaluate the advantages the North enjoyed in the Civil War.
- Analyze the impact of the Civil War on the North and South, especially the impact of the Emancipation Proclamation.
- Explore the outcome and aftermath of the Civil War.

Background Knowledge L3

Ask students to recall that the Confederate attack on Fort Sumter in April 1861 started the Civil War. Have them predict how long the war will last and the toll that it will take.

Set a Purpose L3

- **WITNESS HISTORY** Read the selection aloud.

  Ask **What is Farley's attitude toward the battle scene he describes?** *(He seems to be impressed by the dramatic and chaotic scene and at the same time determined to do his duty as a soldier.)*

- **Focus** Point out the Section Focus Question, and write it on the board. Tell students to refer to this question as they read. *(Answer appears with Section 3 Assessment answers.)*

- **Preview** Have students preview the Section Objectives and the list of Terms and People.

- **NoteTaking** Using the Structured Read Aloud strategy (TE, p. T20), have students read this section. As they read, have students identify events that led to Union victory in the Civil War. Reading and Note Taking Study Guide

▲ Civil War soldier and gear

WITNESS HISTORY

The Battle of Gettysburg: A Soldier's Story

On July 1, 1863, the Battle of Gettysburg began. The Union victory on July 3 ended General Lee's invasion of the North and was a turning point in the Civil War. A 22-year-old lieutenant from New York described the Battle of Little Round Top:

❝As we reached the crest a never to be forgotten scene burst upon us. A great basin lay before us full of smoke and fire, and literally swarming with riderless horses and fighting, fleeing and pursuing men. The air was saturated with the sulphurous fumes of battle and was ringing with the shouts and groans of the combatants. The wild cries of charging lines, the rattle of musketry, the booming of artillery and the shrieks of the wounded were the orchestral accompaniments of a scene like very hell itself. . . . But fascinating as was this terrible scene we had no time to spend upon it. Bloody work was ready for us at our very feet.❞

—Lieutenant Porter Farley, 140th New York Infantry, Weed's Brigade

The Civil War

Objectives

- Evaluate the advantages the North enjoyed in the Civil War.
- Analyze the impact of the Civil War on the North and South, especially the impact of the Emancipation Proclamation.
- Explore the outcome and aftermath of the Civil War.

Terms and People

Robert E. Lee	Ulysses S. Grant
Anaconda Plan	Battle of Gettysburg
Emancipation Proclamation	Gettysburg Address
	William T. Sherman
habeas corpus	total war
inflation	

NoteTaking

Reading Skill: Recognize Sequence As you read, identify the events and developments that led to the final Union victory in the Civil War.

Civil War
begins

1861   1862   1863   1864   1865

Why It Matters With the election of Lincoln, the slavery issue that had long divided North from South finally split the nation in two. From April 1861 to April 1865, the United States of America and the Confederate States of America faced each other in the bloody Civil War. At stake was the future not only of slavery but of the Union itself. **Section Focus Question: What factors and events led to the Union victory in the Civil War?**

Resources, Strategies, and Early Battles

As the Civil War began, each side had a clear goal. The North was determined to preserve the Union, arguing that no state had the right to secede. The southern states who formed the Confederacy aimed to gain their independence from a Union that they felt had become hostile to their interests, especially slavery.

Advantages and Disadvantages Although each side faced challenges, a variety of factors favored the Union. In the Northeast, growing urban populations supported a wide range of manufacturing. Replenished by a continuing influx of immigrant workers from Europe, northern factories were able to increase production of the supplies needed to wage war: ammunition, arms, uniforms, medical supplies, food, ships, and railroad cars.

Across the North, the railroad network was well developed, as were systems for farming, mining, and processing raw materials. Banking, insurance, and financing industries were also clustered in the urbanized North. The federal government had a well-organized navy. By the end of 1861, the Union navy had outfitted and launched

Use the information below and the following resource to teach students the high-use words from this section. Teaching Resources, Vocabulary Builder, p. 11

High-Use Word	Definition and Sample Sentence
anticipate	*v.* to expect; to look forward to Some of the convention's members did not **anticipate** the need for a bill of rights.
emphasize	*v.* to stress; to give special attention or importance Because women could not vote, election day only served to **emphasize** their lack of civil rights in the United States.

more than 250 warships and was constructing dozens more. Naval superiority allowed the Union to blockade the South's few vital ports.

Given such advantages, northerners <u>anticipated</u> a quick victory. But the North had distinct disadvantages as well. When the war began, the Union army consisted of only about 16,000 men. Although the South had an even smaller army, its troops at the outset of the war were generally more highly committed to the fight. In addition, some of the nation's finest military leaders were from the South. The experienced and inspiring **Robert E. Lee** had originally been offered command of Union forces but chose instead to remain loyal to his native Virginia. Throughout the war, General Lee provided the Confederacy with expert military leadership. The North struggled for much of the war to find a commander of comparable skill and daring.

North and South Develop Their Strategies Each side had a clear military goal. Here, again, the South enjoyed an advantage. The Confederacy simply had to survive, keeping their armies in the field until northerners became tired of fighting. The Union, however, had to crush and conquer the Confederacy.

The North adopted a strategy designed to starve the South into submission. It was called the **Anaconda Plan** after the snake that slowly squeezes its prey to death. The plan involved seizing the Mississippi River and the Gulf of Mexico so that the South could not send or receive shipments. By the middle of 1862, with victories in Mississippi and New Orleans, the North had captured the Mississippi Valley. Union soldiers also seized the strategic railroad juncture at Chattanooga, Tennessee, and scored victories in battles as far west as New Mexico.

A Confederate Victory
Two major Civil War battles took place at Bull Run, a creek in Virginia. Both were Confederate victories. The painting below depicts the Second Battle of Bull Run (known in the South as the Second Battle of Manassas.) *What advantages might the Confederates have had at Bull Run?*

Teach

Resources, Strategies, and Early Battles

Instruct

- **Introduce: Key Term** Ask students to find the name **Robert E. Lee** (in bold) in the text, and tell students that Lee was a Virginian to whom the command of the Union forces was initially offered. Ask students to predict Lee's response.

- **Teach** Ask **Which side, the North or the South, had more economic advantages at the beginning of the Civil War?** *(the North)* **What was the North's military strategy?** *(to starve the South into submission by setting up a blockade of southern seaports and seizing control of the Mississippi River)* **Do you think that the number of casualties during the Civil War was unusually high? Explain.** *(Possible answer: yes, because of new and deadlier weapons and limited medical care)*

- **Analyzing the Visuals** Have students examine the illustration of the Battle of Bull Run. Ask them to list at least five sensory words or action verbs that could be applied to the scene. Challenge them to list ten words, and then use them all in a short narrative describing what is happening.

Independent Practice

To help students understand the advantages and disadvantages of the North and the South, have them create a two-column chart comparing and contrasting the resources of each side. Ask students to write sentences summarizing the information in their charts.

Monitor Progress

As students fill in their timelines, circulate to make sure that they understand the events and developments that led to the final major Union victory in the Civil War. For a completed version of the timeline, see Note Taking Transparencies, **B-80a.**

Differentiated Instruction Solutions for All Learners

L1 Special Needs Students   **L2 English Language Learners**   **L2 Less Proficient Readers**

Discuss with students the concept of the "graphic novel." Explain that there is not a strict definition of the graphic novel, but that they are generally understood to be books in the form of a comic strip that have a more mature or literary quality than traditional comics. One early example of the graphic novel is Art Spiegelman's series *Maus,* which won a Pulitzer Prize in 1992 for its exploration of Spiegelman's parents'

survival of the Holocaust. Find other examples of this genre at the library or on the Internet to share with students if they are unfamiliar with the genre. Then, have partners create a "graphic story" about one of the following topics: the First Battle of Bull Run, General Ulysses S. Grant's Siege of Vicksburg, or medical care during the Civil War.

Answer

Caption They were fighting the enemy on their own territory.

Lincoln Proclaims Emancipation

Instruct

- **Introduce: Key Term** Ask students to find the key term *Emancipation Proclamation* (in bold) in the text and define it. Ask them to explain why Lincoln might have waited nearly two years to make the proclamation.

- **Teach** Ask **What was Lincoln's primary goal at the beginning of the Civil War?** *(to preserve the Union)* **Did Lincoln have strategic reasons for not opposing slavery immediately? Explain.** *(Yes; such a position might have alienated slave states that had remained loyal to the Union.)* **Why did the Emancipation Proclamation free slaves only in states that were at war with the Union?** *(Possible response: Lincoln did not want to interfere with states' rights in those states that had not seceded from the Union.)*

- **Analyzing the Visuals** Have students study the Infographic on the next page. Ask **What effect do you think the Emancipation Proclamation had on African American soldiers fighting for the Union?** *(Sample answer: They probably became formidable opponents because they were dedicated to the cause for which they were fighting.)* **Would African American troops face unique dangers in the South?** *(Possible answer: Yes; it was likely that, if captured, they would face dangers that white troops would not.)*

Independent Practice

Have students write paragraphs explaining the strategic reasons for Lincoln's issuing the Emancipation Proclamation. Ask them to predict how the Emancipation Proclamation might change the outcome of the Civil War.

Monitor Progress

Circulate to make sure that students understand why Lincoln issued the Emancipation Proclamation.

Answers

- ✓ industrial and financial strength; better transportation; naval superiority

- ✓ The proclamation freed slaves in rebellious states while at the same time symbolically redefining the war as being "about slavery."

Vocabulary Builder

emphasize–(EHM fuh sīz) *v.* to stress; to give special attention or importance

NoteTaking

Reading Skills: Compare and Contrast As you read, note effects of the war on the North and South.

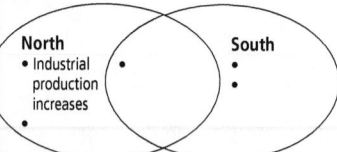

A Stalemate Develops On the east coast, though both sides won battles, neither side could gain a clear and decisive victory in the early part of the war. Union armies hoped to capture the Confederate capital of Richmond, Virginia. But troops outside Washington, D.C., could not seem to make progress toward that goal. Confederate troops were equally unsuccessful in pushing the war north toward Washington, D.C.

Thanks to efficient new weapons—especially more accurate rifles and deadlier bullets—a single day's battle might produce more than 10,000 casualties. This new lethal warfare stung the public consciousness. Battle sites such as Bull Run (July 1861), Shiloh (April 1862), Antietam (September 1862), and Fredericksburg (December 1862) are still remembered as the scenes of some of the deadliest encounters in American history. Limited medical care ensured that many of the wounded died of infection rather than of the wounds themselves.

✓ **Checkpoint** What advantages did the Union enjoy as the Civil War began?

Lincoln Proclaims Emancipation

Early in the war, President Lincoln insisted that he did not have the authority to end slavery. In his public statements, he emphasized the fact that his chief goal was to preserve the Union. Although Lincoln personally opposed slavery, he did not want to lose the support of the four slave states—Maryland, Delaware, Kentucky, and Missouri—that had remained loyal to the Union.

However, by the autumn of 1862, Lincoln decided that he did, indeed, have the authority to proclaim the end of slavery, and that as a "practical war measure" he wished to do so. In January 1863, he issued the **Emancipation Proclamation.** This presidential decree declared that "all persons held as slaves within any State or designated part of a State, the people whereof shall then be in rebellion against the United States, shall be then, thenceforward, and forever free."

The Emancipation Proclamation did not apply to the loyal slave states or to those areas of the South already under Union control. As a result, it did not immediately free a single slave. Nevertheless, it was an important turning point because it encouraged enslaved African Americans in the South to run away to Union army encampments and to aid the Union cause. It also symbolically redefined the war as being "about slavery."

African Americans had always believed that the war should be about slavery, and they had volunteered to fight as soon as the war began. But at first they were turned away and told "this is a white man's war." After the Emancipation Proclamation, however, the Union began to actively recruit both free blacks from the North and newly freed African Americans from the South. Eventually, some 180,000 African American men served in the Union Army.

✓ **Checkpoint** What was the impact of the Emancipation Proclamation?

War Affects Daily Life

The Civil War transformed the nation's civilian life. In the North, mines and factories stepped up production to supply military needs such as ships, railroads, weapons, uniforms, provisions, and fuel. To pay for the war, the federal government raised tariffs, imposed income taxes, and printed money. Congress also encouraged western settlement and offered free land to soldiers who would give two years of military service. Such land grants sparked agricultural growth, which helped feed Union troops.

History Background

Rifles Among the technological advances that made the Civil War's death toll so high were improvements in rifles. The interior of a gun barrel can be smooth or "rifled"—channeled with spiral grooves that make a bullet spin as it travels down the barrel. Spinning projectiles go farther with greater accuracy. Rifled weapons had existed for centuries, but they were not widely used until the 1800s. Because breech-loading weapons were still uncommon, one of the problems faced by nineteenth-century manufacturers was designing bullets that would fit easily into the rifled barrels of muzzle-loading weapons. A few years before the Civil War, a French army officer named Claude-Étienne Minié designed a new bullet called the Minié ball. It was a cylinder with a conical point that fit easily into rifled bores. The Minié ball, however, had an iron cup inserted into its hollow base that expanded on firing to make the bullet engage as it traveled down the barrel. The new technology made it possible for soldiers to hit targets accurately at a range of about 250 yards. Military leaders had to adjust their strategies and tactics to take into account the new technology.

Emancipation is Proclaimed

Issued January 1, 1863, the Emancipation Proclamation did not free a single slave. It applied only to those areas still "in rebellion against the United States." Yet Lincoln's bold declaration changed the nature of the war, offered hope to enslaved persons, and led to the complete abolition of slavery.

◀ Lincoln's hand-written copy of the Emancipation Proclamation

From Slave to Soldier ▶
The Emancipation Proclamation paved the way for African Americans to serve in the U.S. military. *The Recruit*, an 1866 painting by Thomas Waterman Wood, depicts a newly freed African American who has become a proud Union soldier.

"... thenceforward, and forever free ..."

The Promise of Freedom
This 1863 drawing, *The Sanctuary*, shows an enslaved family heading toward a Union camp—toward freedom. Though greatly idealized, the picture does express the hope enslaved people felt when they heard of the Emancipation Proclamation.

Thinking Critically
1. **Apply Information** Why did the family in the drawing need to reach the army camp in order to become free?
1. **Identify Effects** How did the Emancipation Proclamation aid the Union cause?

The North Faces Problems As the war dragged on, the Union army experienced a shortage of volunteers. When Congress passed a draft law in 1863, requiring all able-bodied men between the ages of 20 and 45 to serve in the military if called, riots broke out in several northern cities. The most severe rioting took place in New York City in July 1863. White workers attacked free African Americans as well as wealthy New Yorkers who were able to pay a fee to avoid military service.

Some Northerners opposed Lincoln's conduct of the war and demanded immediate peace. To deal with dissent, Lincoln suspended the Constitutional right of **habeas corpus,** which guarantees that no one can be held in prison without specific charges being filed. Union troops arrested many people suspected of

---

Differentiated Instruction   Solutions for All Learners

L4 Advanced Readers   L4 Gifted and Talented Students

Tell students that not long after the beginning of the war in Iraq (March 2003), the United States was considering a military draft. The United States had not had a draft for three decades, having discontinued the policy in 1973. Ask students who oppose a draft to raise their hands. Organize these students in groups of four. Then, organize the remaining students in groups of four. Have each group write a letter to the editor, explaining why the United States should or should not reinstate the draft. Introduce

the subject by mentioning one or two historical and contemporary issues associated with this policy. For example, you may point out that compulsory drafts can cause social unrest and remind them of the draft riots that took place in New York City during the Civil War. After introducing the topic, have groups discuss other issues pertinent to military drafts. Then, have them use the results of their discussion to create arguments in their letters to the editor.

War Affects Daily Life   **L3**

Instruct

- **Introduce** Explain that during the Civil War, Congress enacted the first income tax law. Tell students that it was a progressive tax, and explain briefly what that means.

- **Teach** Using the Numbered Heads strategy (TE, p. T23), discuss with students the ways in which the Civil War affected daily life in both the North and South. Ask **How did the North address the shortage of volunteer soldiers?** *(by imposing a draft)* **Why did the Civil War cause more damage in the South than in the North?** *(because the majority of the battles took place in the South)* **How did the war affect social roles?** *(Because so many men were fighting, women took on new roles that had not been available to them in the past, such as nursing and teaching.)*

- **Quick Activity** Write the following sentence on the board: *President Lincoln violated the U.S. Constitution when he suspended habeas corpus during the war.* Have students write a paragraph explaining why they agree or disagree with this statement.

Independent Practice

- Have students read and complete *Reading a Chart: The Northern Economy During the Civil War.* Teaching Resources, **p. 31**

- NoteTaking Have students complete the Venn diagram to compare and contrast the war's effects on the North and South. Reading and Note Taking Study Guide

Monitor Progress

As they complete the diagram, circulate to make sure that students understand how the war affected both sides. For a completed version of the Venn diagram, see Note Taking Transparencies, **B-80b.**

Answers

Thinking Critically
1. Without the protection of Union troops, they risked capture and re-enslavement.
2. It paved the way for African Americans to serve in the military, giving the Union more troops.

Instruct

- **Introduce: Key Term** Ask students to find the name *William T. Sherman* (in bold) and identify him. Ask them to think about how the strategies of today's military leaders are different from or the same as those practiced by Sherman.

- **Teach** Display Color Transparency: *The Civil War Ends.* Use the lesson suggested in the transparency book to guide a discussion about significant battles that helped end the Civil War. Ask **What battle marked the last time that Confederate troops invaded the North?** *(the Battle of Gettysburg in July 1863)* **Why did Lee surrender to Grant at Appomattox Court House?** *(Possible answer: The Confederate army was exhausted, and the Union had captured the Confederate capital.)* **What impact did the Civil War have on Americans' political identity?** *(Americans began to see themselves as citizens not just of states but of a united nation.)* Color Transparencies A-71

- **Quick Activity** Ask students to read the HISTORY MAKERS feature about Ulysses S. Grant and Robert E. Lee. Ask **What was Grant's goal in May 1864?** *(to capture the Confederate capital, Richmond)* **What does this phase of the war indicate about Lee's and Grant's abilities as generals?** *(Sample response: that they were evenly matched)*

Answer

✓ The war helped the North modernize its economy, but it devastated the South's economy.

---

disloyalty. Although Lincoln felt such measures were necessary to preserve the Union, others criticized his actions as unconstitutional.

The South Suffers Hardships Almost all of the battles took place on southern soil. The fighting destroyed some of the South's traditional strengths, such as large-scale agriculture, and stripped the Confederacy of the resources it might have used to rebuild. By 1863, the Union plan to starve the South into submission seemed to be on the verge of succeeding.

The South seized every opportunity to ease its economic problems. As Lincoln had done, Confederate President Jefferson Davis authorized the Confederacy to issue paper money, backed only by the government's promise to pay. Doubts about the true value of Confederate money led to severe **inflation,** or price increases. The combination of rising prices and food shortages sparked food riots in some parts of the South.

War Leads to Social Change On both sides, the war gave women new tasks. Women set up field hospitals and nursed wounded soldiers. Many Confederate women took to the fields to harvest crops. White and black teachers from the North went south to become teachers of newly freed slaves.

Churches in both the North and South supported the war effort. Confederate soldiers often held revival meetings near the field of battle. One Virginia chaplain claimed that many southern men "have come out of this war Christian soldiers."

✓ **Checkpoint** How did the Civil War affect the economies of the North and South?

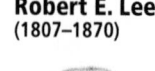

HISTORY MAKERS

In May 1864, Robert E. Lee's Army of Northern Virginia beat back Ulysses S. Grant's Army of the Potomac in several fierce battles between Washington and Richmond. After each fight, Grant sidestepped Lee to march closer to the southern capital. However, as the Union army moved, Lee followed and set up strong defensive positions, which forced Grant to attack. In a month's time, the two armies suffered nearly 70,000 combined casualties. By late summer, the bloody contest between Grant and Lee had settled into a siege at Petersburg, south of Richmond. In April 1865, Lee abandoned the city and eventually surrendered to Grant.

Ulysses S. Grant
(1822–1885)

Robert E. Lee
(1807–1870)

The Union Prevails

In the summer of 1863, the Union succeeded in capturing Vicksburg, Mississippi. Advancing from the Louisiana side of the Mississippi River, Union General **Ulysses S. Grant** scored five victories in three weeks, ending with the surrender of 30,000 Confederate troops. The Anaconda Plan had achieved one of its major goals: Confederate territory was split apart.

The Union Wins a Victory at Gettysburg Meanwhile, in the East, General Lee marched into Pennsylvania. He hoped to win a surprise victory, then swing south to Washington, D.C. But in July 1863, Union troops defeated Lee at the town of Gettysburg. The **Battle of Gettysburg** destroyed one third of Lee's forces and marked the last major Confederate attempt to invade the North.

A few months later, the President went to Gettysburg to help dedicate a battle cemetery. In a speech known as the **Gettysburg Address,** Lincoln used the occasion to reaffirm the ideas for which the Union was fighting:

> **Primary Source** "We here highly resolve that these dead shall not have died in vain—that this nation, under God, shall have a new birth of freedom—and that government of the people, by the people, for the people, shall not perish from the earth."
>
> —Abraham Lincoln, *Gettysburg Address,* November 19, 1863

Differentiated Instruction Solutions for All Learners

L1 Special Needs Students **L2 English Language Learners** **L2 Less Proficient Readers**

Organize students in groups of four, taking care that each group has a mixture of less proficient and more proficient readers. Provide each group with its own copy of the Gettysburg Address. Tell students that many people consider Lincoln's Gettysburg Address a "masterpiece of prose poetry" and among the greatest speeches of all time.

Have students rewrite a section of the address in their own words. Encourage them to use language and imagery that they think would inspire their peers. After students have completed their translations, have each group select one member to read aloud its version of the address to the class. After all the groups have delivered their addresses, lead a class discussion about the effect the Gettysburg Address may have had on the Union.

Geography *Interactive*
For: Interactive map
www.pearsonschool.com/ushist

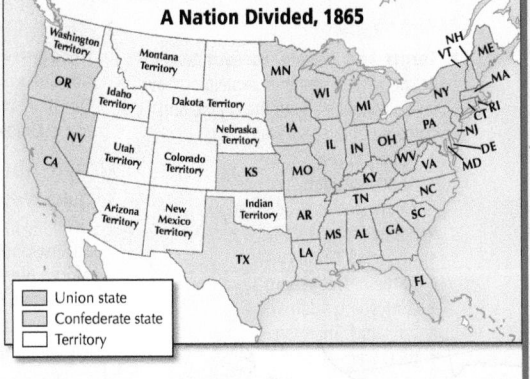

Map Legend
- ★ Union victory
- ★ Confederate victory
- 🏰 Union naval blockade
- → Sherman's March

A Nation Divided, 1865

- ☐ Union state
- ☐ Confederate state
- ☐ Territory

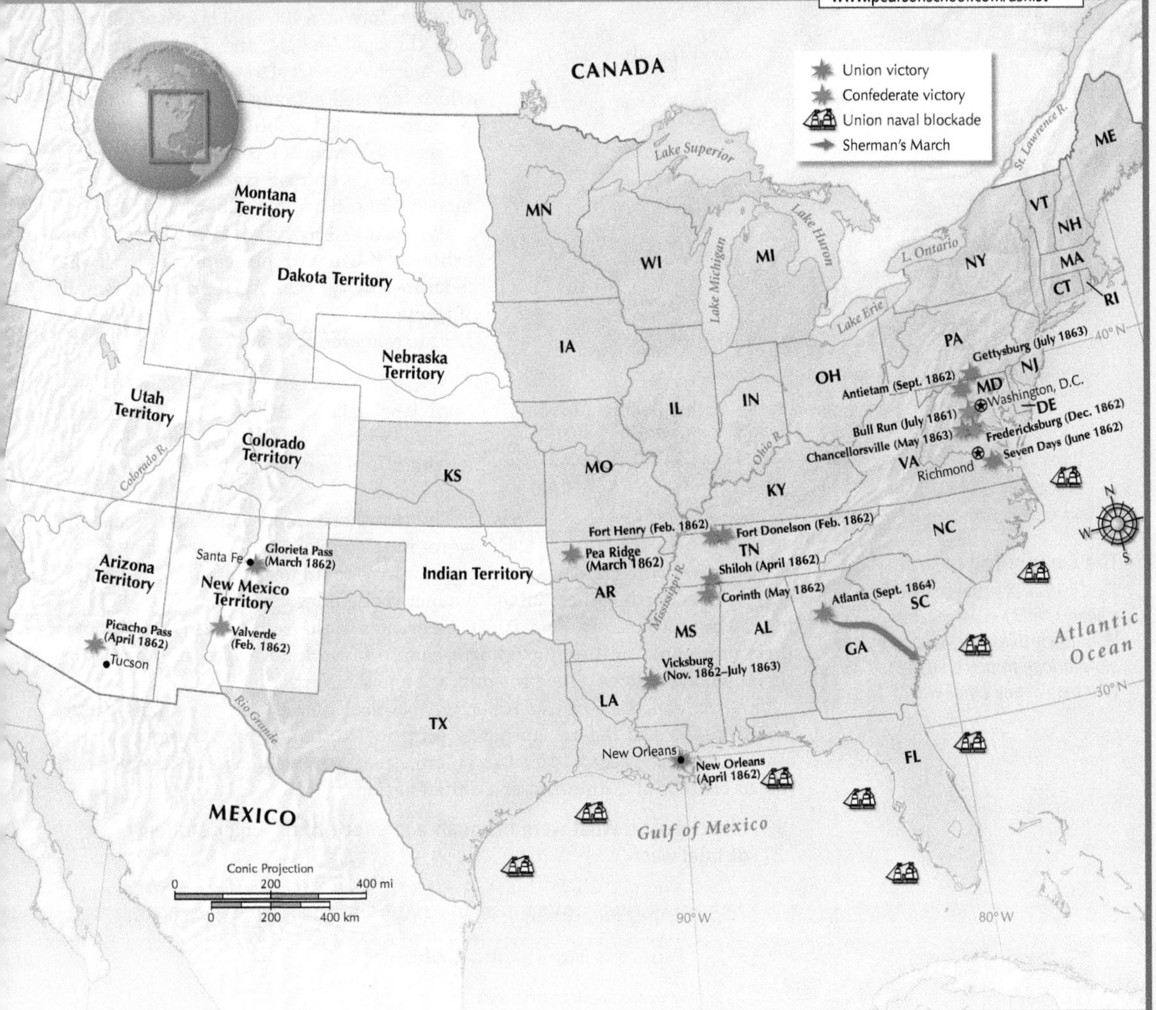

Map Skills The Civil War split the nation into two opposing countries. Although most of the fighting took place on Confederate land, some fighting extended north into Pennsylvania or as far west as Arizona.

1. **Locate:** (a) Gettysburg, (b) Vicksburg, (c) Richmond, (d) Washington, D.C.

2. **Regions** How would northern control of the Mississippi River affect the Confederacy?

3. **Draw Conclusions** Describe the Union naval blockade. What do you think was its goal?

Independent Practice

- Have students access **www.pearsonschool.com/ushist** to use the **Geography Interactive map,** and then have them answer the map skills questions in the text.

- Remind students that Native American nations were forcibly moved to Indian Territory. Ask students to write a paragraph predicting how Native Americans reacted to the war. Tell students to explain the logic behind their predictions.

Monitor Progress

Circulate to make sure that students are answering the map skills questions accurately.

Connect to Your World

Civil War Tours Because many people thought that the Civil War would be a quick war, it was originally funded with loans. As the war continued, the Northern states needed more money. The Revenue Act of 1862 created the first federal income tax as well as the organization that would become the Internal Revenue Service. Although the Civil War ended up costing the federal government about $3 billion, the Civil War now makes money for many states in the form of "heritage tourism." States with Civil War battle sites have turned historic battlefields and locations into sources of revenue. Tourists flock to these sites to feel close to history. In Virginia, history tourism represents 78.9 percent of travel, with Civil War sites making up 11 percent of that number. A study found that at just seven historic Civil War sites in the nation, visitors spent almost $157 million in 2003, bringing state and local governments about $22.4 million. The federal government has also preserved historic Civil War sites, such as Appomattox Courthouse, Virginia, which has become a 1,743-acre national historic park with tours of the house and its surrounding buildings and land.

Answers

Map Skills

1. Review locations with students.

2. Possible answer: It would cut them off from shipping in the Gulf and prevent resources from arriving from the West.

3. The Union positioned its navy along the Atlantic and Gulf coasts to prevent the South from exporting its goods and receiving war supplies.

Assess Progress L3

- Have students complete the Section Assessment.

- Administer the Section Quiz. Teaching Resources, **p. 35**

- To further assess student understanding, use Progress Monitoring Transparencies, **16.**

Reteach

If students need more instruction, have them read the section summary.

Reading and Note Taking L3
Study Guide

Adapted Reading and L1 L2
Note Taking Study Guide

Spanish Reading and L2
Note Taking Study Guide

Extend L4

Have students read and complete the Enrichment Worksheet: *Build a Model: The Battle of Gettysburg.* Teaching Resources, **pp. 13–14**

Answers

Caption because of a combination of advanced weaponry and inadequate medical resources; it was also fought bitterly by Americans on both sides.

✔ The goal of targeting not only troops but all the resources needed to sustain them exhausted and demoralized the South and helped lead to the Union victory.

The War Ends In the fall of 1864, Union General **William T. Sherman** led more than 60,000 troops on a 400-mile march of destruction through Georgia and South Carolina. The march was part of a strategy of **total war,** which targeted not only troops but all of the resources needed to feed, clothe, and support an army. Sherman's troops burned crops in fields, tore up railroad tracks, and destroyed homes, plantations, and public buildings.

By spring 1865, the Confederacy was exhausted. Union troops captured the Confederate capital. On April 9, in the small Virginia town of Appomattox Court House, Lee surrendered to Grant.

The Civil War Has Lasting Impact The Civil War ushered in the harsh reality of modern warfare. More than one third of northern and southern soldiers were killed or disabled.

The southern landscape and economy were in shambles. Millions of dislocated southerners drifted north in search of new lives in Illinois, Indiana, Missouri, or other points north. Others joined the increasing migration to the West, becoming cowboys or farmers. For African Americans in the South, freedom promised them new opportunities, including a chance to work for wages and to control their own lives. Some joined the migration to the North and West.

The war ended an era in American political life. Although debates about states' rights and federal authority continue to this day, never again would states attempt to secede. More and more, Americans would see themselves not just as citizens of a state, but of a united nation.

✔ **Checkpoint** What were the goals and effects of the Union strategy of total war?

Civil War Casualties, 1861–1865

	Total Forces	Wounded	Battle Deaths	Other Deaths in Service	Total Deaths
Union	2,213,363	280,040	140,414	224,097	364,511
Confederate	1,050,000	226,000	94,000	166,000	260,000

SOURCES: U.S. Department of Veterans Affairs; *Encyclopedia of the Confederacy*

The Deadly Toll of War
The Civil War was the deadliest military conflict in American history. *Why do you think a higher percentage of American troops died in the Civil War than in any other war?*

SECTION **3** Assessment

Progress Monitoring Online
For: Self-test with vocabulary practice
www.pearsonschool.com/ushist

Comprehension

1. **Terms and People** For each item below, write a sentence explaining how it was connected with the course and outcome of the Civil War.
   - Robert E. Lee
   - Anaconda Plan
   - Emancipation Proclamation
   - habeas corpus
   - Ulysses S. Grant
   - Battle of Gettysburg
   - Gettysburg Address
   - William T. Sherman
   - total war

2. **NoteTaking Reading Skill: Recognize Sequence** Use your timeline to answer the Section Focus Question: What factors and events led to the Union victory in the Civil War?

Writing About History

3. **Quick Write: Prioritize Arguments** List three arguments in favor of or against Lincoln freeing all enslaved African Americans as soon as the war began. Then, order the three arguments from most important to least important.

Critical Thinking

4. **Recognize Causes and Effects** What impact did the economic differences between the North and South have on the course of the Civil War?

5. **Draw Inferences** How do you think the Anaconda Plan and Sherman's march affected southerners psychologically?

6. **Predict Consequences** List three challenges that African Americans in the South might face after emancipation from slavery.

For additional assessment, have students access **Progress Monitoring Online** at **www.pearsonschool.com/ushist.**

WITNESS HISTORY

The Devastated South

Mary Chesnut was the wife of a wealthy and respected South Carolina planter and politician. Now, at war's end, the family was penniless. The world they had known was gone. Chesnut described the devastation:

❝Mrs. Bartow drove me to our house at Mulberry. On one side of the house, every window was broken, every bell torn down, every piece of furniture destroyed, every door smashed in. . . . [The Yankee soldiers] carried off sacks of our books and our papers, our letters were strewed along the Charleston road. Potter's raid ruined us. He burned our mills and gins, and a hundred bales of cotton. Indeed nothing is left now but the bare land.❞

—Mary Boykin Chesnut, *A Diary From Dixie*

▲ A southerner sits amid the postwar ruins of Charleston, Virginia.

The Reconstruction Era

Objectives
- Explore how Congress and the President clashed over Reconstruction.
- Describe the impact of Reconstruction on the South.
- Explain how Reconstruction came to an end.

Terms and People

Reconstruction	impeachment
Freedmen's Bureau	Fourteenth Amendment
Andrew Johnson	Fifteenth Amendment
Thirteenth Amendment	Ku Klux Klan
Radical Republican	de jure segregation

NoteTaking

Reading Skill: Categorize As you read, identify the political, social, and economic aspects of Reconstruction.

Political	Social	Economic
• Radical Republicans clash with President •	• •	• Sharecropping develops

Why It Matters The Civil War ended in April 1865 with the Union victorious. Now, North and South faced the challenge of reunion. Political decisions made in the next decades helped shape the modern South. And constitutional amendments passed during this period redefined American notions of citizenship and civil rights. **Section Focus Question: What were the immediate and long-term effects of Reconstruction?**

The Nation Moves Toward Reunion

Even while the war was in progress, Union politicians had been debating ways to achieve **Reconstruction,** bringing the South back into the Union. For President Lincoln, the major goal was to reunify the nation—in the words of his Second Inaugural Address, to "bind up the nation's wounds." But some congressional leaders favored a harsh Reconstruction plan designed to punish the South.

The Freedmen's Bureau Aids Southerners Shortly before the war ended, Lincoln and Congress did agree on the creation of the **Freedmen's Bureau,** a federal agency designed to aid freed slaves and relieve the South's immediate needs. The black and white agents of the Bureau delivered food and healthcare and began to develop a public school system for both black and white southerners. It also helped to reunite families separated by slavery and to negotiate fair labor contracts between formerly enslaved African Americans and white landowners.

Vocabulary Builder

Use the information below and the following resource to teach students the high-use words from this section. Teaching Resources, Vocabulary Builder, p. 11

High-Use Word	Definition and Sample Sentence
status	*n.* standing or position, especially with regard to the law Social **status** was important in Europe, where the traditions of the aristocracy were much stronger.
withdrawn	*v.* removed; pulled back from The soldier had **withdrawn** from the skirmish after having been wounded a second time.

The Nation Moves Toward Reunion/The Reconstruction South Ⓛ3

Instruct

- **Introduce: Vocabulary Builder** Have students locate the vocabulary term *status* and its definition. Tell students that they will learn how the Civil War radically transformed the *status* of African Americans.

- **Teach** Ask **When was Lincoln assassinated?** *(April 14, 1865)* **What constitutional amendments were passed as a result of the war? What did each stipulate?** *(Thirteenth Amendment ended slavery; Fourteenth Amendment guaranteed full citizenship and rights to all persons born in the United States; Fifteenth Amendment guaranteed that no male citizen could be denied the right to vote)* **Do you think that the Fourteenth Amendment was effective? Explain.** *(Sample answer: In the short term, it had modest results, but African Americans would later use it to win equal rights.)* Discuss the work of the Freedmen's Bureau and discuss which activities of the bureau were most important.

- **Quick Activity** Display Color Transparency: *Reconstruction and the New South*. Use the lesson in the transparency book to discuss how the South dealt with Reconstruction. Color Transparencies **A-72**

Independent Practice

To help students understand why Andrew Johnson was impeached and the impact of the impeachment, have them examine *History Comics: Johnson's Impeachment,* and complete the worksheet. Teaching Resources, **p. 32**

Monitor Progress

As students fill in their charts, circulate to make sure that they understand the various aspects of Reconstruction. For a completed version of the chart, see Note Taking Transparencies, **B-81**.

Answer

✔ to bring the South back into the Union through punitive reorganization

Vocabulary Builder
status—(STAT uhs) *n.* standing or position, especially with regard to the law

---

President and Congress Clash Meanwhile, debate over Reconstruction continued. Before he could gain support for his moderate plan, Abraham Lincoln was assassinated on April 14, 1865. As the nation mourned, Vice President **Andrew Johnson** became President.

Johnson favored a plan that restored political power to southerners if they merely swore allegiance to the United States. Under Johnson's plan, the South also had to accept the **Thirteenth Amendment,** which ended slavery in 1865. In return, the new President promised to uphold states' rights, with the laws of individual states taking precedence over federal regulations.

Many congressmen disagreed. Arguing that southerners had caused the war, these **Radical Republicans** favored punishment and harsh reorganization for the South. Radicals also advocated full citizens' rights for African Americans and wanted states' authority to be subordinate to federal power. When southern legislatures passed laws to restrict the activities of African Americans, Radicals became even more determined to impose a harsh Reconstruction policy on the South.

Johnson and the Radicals in Congress clashed repeatedly. In 1868, Congress voted to impeach Johnson. **Impeachment** is the act of bringing charges against an official in order to determine whether he or she should be removed from office. The Senate narrowly voted not to remove Johnson from office, but by that time he had lost control of Reconstruction. A few months later, Civil War hero Ulysses S. Grant was elected President.

✔ **Checkpoint** What were the Reconstruction goals of the Radical Republicans?

The Reconstruction South

With Congress firmly under their control, Radical Republicans designed a sweeping Reconstruction plan. They divided the South into five military districts under the command of Union generals. As a condition of readmission to the Union, all southern states were required to grant the vote to African American men. Perhaps most important, Radicals passed the **Fourteenth Amendment,** which guaranteed full citizenship status and rights to every person born in the United States, including African Americans. The Amendment was ratified in 1868.

African Americans Gain Political Rights Under Radical Reconstruction, many white southerners were not eligible to vote or chose to stay away from the polls. African American men, on the other hand, eagerly signed up to exercise their new right of suffrage. Thus, by 1868, many southern states had black elected officials and were dominated by a strong Republican Party. South Carolina—the first state to secede—became the only state where, for a short time, an African American majority dominated the legislature.

At this time, no laws guaranteed the vote to African Americans in the North. To remedy this imbalance, Congress passed the **Fifteenth Amendment,** which guaranteed that no male citizen could be denied the right to vote on the basis of "race, color, or previous condition of servitude." It was ratified in 1870.

Freedmen Rebuild Their Lives In the South, formerly enslaved African Americans worked to carve out new lives. Some struck out for the North or West. But many more stayed in the South. They assembled their scattered families and built strong churches that also served as community centers, employment agencies, schoolhouses, and—in later years—centers of protest.

For the first time, many African American men and women could legalize and celebrate their marriages, set up housekeeping with their families and make

---

Differentiated Instruction Solutions for All Learners

Ⓛ1 **Special Needs Students** Ⓛ2 **English Language Learners** Ⓛ2 **Less Proficient Readers**

To help students understand and remember the three Civil War amendments to the U.S. Constitution, ask them to design a poster about them. Tell them that the poster's content must include a title, such as "Civil War Amendments to the U.S. Constitution," a brief explanatory paragraph describing the historical circumstances that led to the amendments, and the text of each of the amendments, as well as their dates of ratification. Explain to students that they are to use their imagination and creative abilities to incorporate these elements into a design that will best communicate the subject matter. Encourage students to include additional text commentary, as well as images and any other visual elements that they think are appropriate.

TRACK THE ISSUE

Does any branch of the government have too much power?

Our system of checks and balances is meant to prevent any branch of government from becoming too powerful. Yet at times the balance of power between the executive, legislative, and judicial branches has shifted. Use the timeline below to explore this enduring issue.

1803 *Marbury* v. *Madison*
John Marshall affirms Supreme Court's right of judicial review.

1830s Jackson Presidency
Andrew Jackson increases executive power.

1868 Johnson Impeachment
Congress tries to remove President Andrew Johnson from office.

1930s New Deal
Franklin D. Roosevelt boosts presidential power to fight the depression.

1960s Warren Court
Supreme Court under Earl Warren becomes a force for social reform.

1973 War Powers Act
Congress limits the President's power to wage war.

2000s War on Terrorism
Congress increases executive branch powers to combat terrorism.

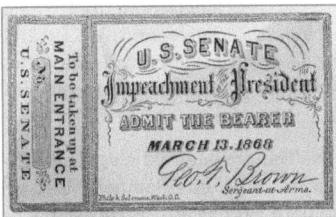

Ticket to Andrew Johnson's trial

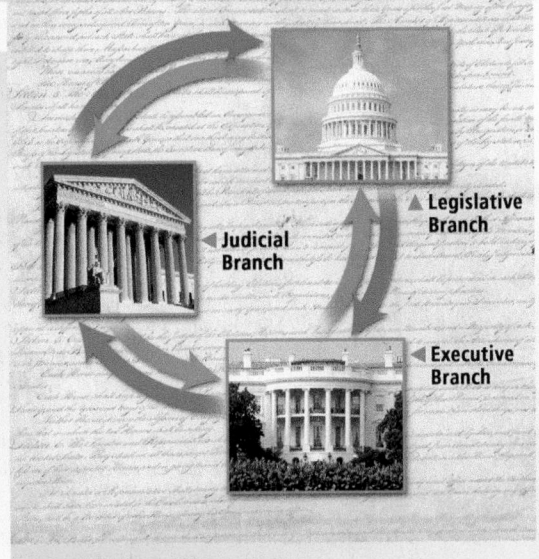

▲ Legislative Branch

◄ Judicial Branch

► Executive Branch

DEBATE THE ISSUE

Imbalance of Power? During the administration of President George W. Bush, much debate focused on the relative powers of the President and Congress.

"I do have the view that over the years there had been an erosion of presidential power. . . . I served in the Congress for 10 years. I've got enormous regard for the other body, Title I of the Constitution, but . . . the President of the United States needs to have his constitutional powers unimpaired, if you will, in terms of the conduct of national security policy."
—Vice President Richard Cheney, December 20, 2005

"During the early years of the post–World War II era, power was relatively well-balanced . . . but major shifts, particularly those in the last two decades of the 20th century, have made Congress much weaker and the President dangerously stronger. . . . The Bush presidency has attained a level of power over Congress that undermines sound democratic governance."
—Walter Williams, *Seattle Times*, May 2004

? *TRANSFER* Activities

1. **Compare** When does Vice President Cheney feel the President should have more power? Why would Walter Williams disagree?

2. **Analyze** How did the administration of President Andrew Johnson reflect a similar power struggle?

3. **Transfer** Use the following Web site to see a video, try a WebQuest, and write in your journal. www.pearsonschool.com/ushist

Objectives

- Review the system of checks and balances established by the U.S. Constitution.
- Examine historical shifts in the balance of power among the three branches of the federal government.

Background Knowledge

Ask students to recall the functions of the three branches of the federal government. Ask **Which branch of the federal government seemed most powerful in the early years of the republic and which branch seems the most powerful now?** (*Possible response: the legislative branch; the executive branch*)

Instruct

Point out that the timeline shows examples of how different branches have used their Constitutional powers to check the power of the other. Ask **What is judicial review?** (*the power of the Supreme Court to determine the constitutionality of a law or official act of government*) **In recent decades, why has Congress limited the President's power?** (*Possible answer: to prevent the President from declaring war without its approval*)

Monitor Progress

- Have students complete the Issues Connector Worksheet, *Checks and Balances*. Monitor students' work to make sure that they grasp the aspects of the issue. Teaching Resources, pp. 23–26

- Remind students to complete their American Issues Connector Journal worksheets notes. Review their work for accuracy. Reading and Note Taking Study Guide

Answers

Transfer Activities

1. They have opposing views of how much power the executive branch should have.

2. Johnson clashed repeatedly with the legislative branch over the authority to determine Reconstruction policies.

3. For more information about the clashes between the executive and legislative branches, have students access www.pearsonschool.com/ushist.

History Background

Madison's Notes The notes that James Madison took during the 1787 Constitutional Convention are important in understanding the principles of the U.S. Constitution. For example, in his notes for Tuesday, May 29, Madison records that Virginian Edmund Randolph proposed (per Madison's "Virginia Plan") that "the Executive and a convenient number of the National Judiciary, ought to compose a Council of revision with the authority to examine every act of the National Legislature before it shall operate." The delegates took up the idea of a "Council of Revision"

again on June 4, when Massachusetts delegate Elbridge Gerry expressed his doubts that "the Judiciary ought to form a part of [a Council of revision], as they will have a sufficient check [against] encroachments on their own department by their exposition of the laws, which involved the power of deciding on their Constitutionality." Gerry finally proposed "'that the National Executive shall have a right to negative any Legislative act which shall not be afterwards passed by [left blank] parts of each branch of the national Legislature.'"

Instruct

- **Introduce: Key Term** Ask students to find the key term *segregation* (in bold) in the text and explain its meaning. Ask them whether *segregation* exists in the United States today.

- **Teach** Using the Idea Wave strategy (TE, p. T22), discuss whether or not students think that Reconstruction was a success, and why or why not. Ask **When did the federal government begin to withdraw troops from the South, and when was the Freedman's Bureau dissolved?** *(1871; 1872)* **What event and year signaled the official end of Reconstruction? Why?** *(The presidential election of 1876; President Hayes withdrew all federal troops from the South in 1877.)* Have students examine the cause-and-effect chart on the following page. Ask **Was segregation an inevitable outcome of the Civil War?** *(Possible response: No; this development resulted from a failure of the federal government to create and enforce policies to eradicate racism and defend the rights of its citizens.)*

Independent Practice

Point out that the South was overwhelmingly Democratic after the end of Reconstruction. Ask students whether or not the Democratic party is still dominant in the South today. Have them write a paragraph explaining why or why not.

Monitor Progress

To review this section, ask students to summarize the prospects for African Americans at the end of Reconstruction.

Answer

✓ They became full citizens with the attendant rights, including, for adult males, the right to vote.

The Ku Klux Klan
Ku Klux Klan members wore hoods, like those shown above, to hide their identities and terrorize their victims.

Vocabulary Builder
withdraw–(wihth DRAW) *v.* to remove; to pull back from

---

choices about where they would reside. Freed women could care for their families and leave field labor. Freed people also realized the importance of learning to read and to count their money. So the Freedmen's Bureau schools quickly filled. By 1869, as many as 300,000 African American adults and children were acquiring basic literacy.

The Ku Klux Klan Uses Terror Tactics Even though the South remained under military occupation, organized secret societies, such as the **Ku Klux Klan,** used terror and violence against African Americans and their white supporters. A federal grand jury concluded that the chief goal of the Klan attacks was to keep African Americans from voting:

> **Primary Source** "The Klan . . . inflicted summary vengeance on the colored citizens of these counties by breaking into their houses at the dead of night, dragging them from their beds, torturing them in the most inhuman manner, and in many instances murdering them; and this, mainly, on account of their political affiliations."
> —42nd Congress, House Report No. 22, 1871

Congress passed federal laws making it a crime to use violence to prevent people from voting. Although Klan activities lessened somewhat, the threat of violence persisted, keeping many southern African Americans from the polls.

✓ **Checkpoint** What political gains did African Americans make in the early phases of Reconstruction?

Reconstruction Comes to an End

After a decade of Reconstruction, northerners began to lose interest in remaking the South and to focus on other social, political, and economic issues. In the fall of 1873, a series of bank failures sparked a severe economic downturn. At the same time, a series of political scandals in the Grant administration damaged the Radical Republicans. Under these circumstances, Reconstruction began to fade. Gradually and quietly, beginning in 1871, troops were withdrawn from the South. In 1872, Congress dissolved the Freedmen's Bureau.

Southern Democrats Regain Power Meanwhile, southern white Democrats patiently devised a strategy for regaining political control of the South. They argued that Republican programs for public schools and road building resulted in higher taxes. Most white southerners shunned anyone who supported Radical Republicans. Southern Democrats grasped every opportunity to discredit African American politicians as corrupt and incompetent. At the same time, the ever-present threat of violence kept African Americans from voting, thus depriving the Republicans of a large segment of their political base.

One by one, southern states reinstated wealthy white southern men as governors and sent former Confederate leaders to the U.S. Congress. In the 1874 elections, the Republicans lost control of the House of Representatives. By 1876, only South Carolina, Florida, and Louisiana—three states with large African American populations—still had Reconstruction governments and remained under military occupation.

Election of 1876 Ends Reconstruction The presidential election of 1876 signaled the end of Reconstruction. Democratic candidate Samuel Tilden won more popular votes than Republican candidate Rutherford B. Hayes, but the

---

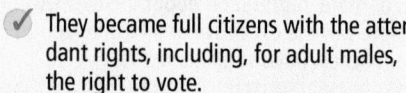

Differentiated Instruction Solutions for All Learners

L4 Advanced Readers **L4 Gifted and Talented Students**

Remind students that it is often helpful to think like a historian when studying historical events, such as those that took place before and after Reconstruction. One way to think like a historian is to examine primary and secondary sources. Ask students to review the last blue heading in this section. Have them answer the question "Was Reconstruction successful?" by doing additional Internet or library research and writing a position paper in which they present an argument and support it with specific examples. Have students present their position papers orally, and then conduct a class discussion on the main points of each paper.

electoral vote was in dispute. The disputed votes were those of Florida, South Carolina, and Louisiana, the three southern states still controlled by Republican Reconstruction governments.

In an informal compromise, a congressional committee declared Hayes the winner. In return, he promised to pull all remaining federal troops from the South. In effect, the election of Hayes ended Reconstruction.

Historians Evaluate Reconstruction
Was Reconstruction a success or a failure? Southerners and northerners, black and white, then and now would give different answers. All will agree, however, that some things were changed forever by those dozen years during which the victorious North tried to remake the vanquished South.

Certainly, Radical Reconstruction failed in most of its aims. By the end of the century, the political rights of African Americans in the South had eroded. Southern states slowly took away the voting rights of African Americans. **De jure segregation,** or legal separation of the races, became the law in all southern states.

Still, Reconstruction did mark the beginning of the physical and economic rebuilding of the South. Despite continuing conflicts and resentments, the nation was permanently reunited. And the constitutional amendments passed during Reconstruction, especially the Fourteenth Amendment, would eventually form the basis for a revived civil rights movement that sought political equality for all citizens.

✓ **Checkpoint** How did the influence of Radical Reconstruction in the South erode?

Cause and Effect

Causes
- Civil War destroys South's economy and infrastructure.
- Freed slaves and war victims need help.
- Black codes discriminate against African Americans.
- Radical Republicans want to restructure the South.
- Southern states need to rejoin Union.

Reconstruction

Effects
- South is divided into military districts.
- African Americans gain citizenship and voting rights.
- Union is restored.
- Sharecropping becomes the new farming system.
- White backlash leads to Ku Klux Klan and segregation.

Connections to Today
- Constitutional amendments protect civil rights.
- Debate over states' rights and the federal government continues.

Analyze Cause and Effect
Although it failed in some of its major goals, Reconstruction had a lasting impact, especially on the South. *Which of the effects of Reconstruction were temporary?*

Assess and Reteach

Assess Progress
- Have students complete the Section Assessment.
- Administer the Section Quiz. **Teaching Resources, p. 35**
- To further assess student understanding, use **Progress Monitoring Transparencies, 17.**

Reteach
If students need more instruction, have them read the section summary.

Reading and Note Taking Study Guide

Adapted Reading and Note Taking Study Guide

Spanish Reading and Note Taking Study Guide

Extend
See this chapter's Professional Development pages for the Extend Online activity on Reconstruction.

Answers

✓ The North's waning interest in Reconstruction, a national economic downturn, political scandal in the Grant administration, and the emergence of white Democratic power in the South all contributed to the erosion of Radical Reconstruction programs.

Caption The South is divided into military districts; sharecropping becomes the new farming system.

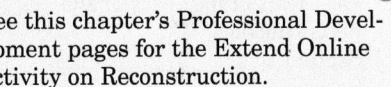
SECTION 4 Assessment

Progress Monitoring Online
For: Self-test with vocabulary practice
www.pearsonschool.com/ushist

Comprehension
1. **Terms and People** For each item below, write a sentence explaining how it was connected with the reshaping of the South after the Civil War.
   - Reconstruction
   - Freedmen's Bureau
   - Andrew Johnson
   - Thirteenth Amendment
   - Radical Republican
   - impeachment
   - Fourteenth Amendment
   - Fifteenth Amendment
   - Ku Klux Klan
   - du jure segregation

2. **NoteTaking Reading Skill: Categorize** Use your table to answer the Section Focus Question: What were the immediate and long-term effects of Reconstruction?

Writing About History
3. **Quick Write: Chart Conflicting Arguments** Make a table with two columns. In one column, list two arguments in favor of a harsh Reconstruction policy toward the South. In the other column, list two arguments in favor of a lenient Reconstruction policy.

Critical Thinking
4. **Recognize Ideologies** How did the clash between President Johnson and Congress reflect a difference in attitudes about the role of the federal government?
5. **Evaluate Information** How did the Fifteenth Amendment guarantee the voting rights of some Americans but not others?
6. **Contrast Viewpoints** How do you think a northern Radical Republican and a southern Democrat would evaluate the long-term impact of Reconstruction?

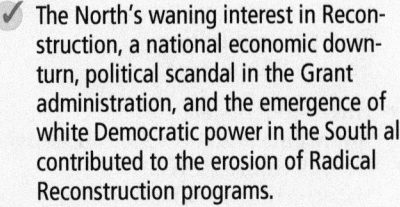
Section 4 Assessment

1. Sentences should reflect an understanding of how each term or person was connected to the reshaping of the South after the Civil War.
2. Immediate: reunited the nation and initiated the physical and economic rebuilding of the South; Long-term: laid the foundation, through constitutional amendments, for the eventual extension of political equality to all citizens
3. Sample answer: Column 1: a) Only a harsh program would bring immediate

relief to the formerly enslaved African Americans. b) Racism would vanish more quickly if southern whites knew that the federal government would use force to protect African Americans. Column 2: a) A lenient policy would attract moderate whites and accelerate reunification. b) It was less likely to cause an outbreak of hostility and violence toward formerly enslaved African Americans.
4. The Radical Republicans' preference for federal power, compared with Johnson's inclination to defer to the states, points out the tensions in the federal system.

5. by extending suffrage to all male citizens, but not to females
6. Possible answer: A Radical Republican might be saddened by the missed opportunity to achieve genuine change, and a southern Democrat might be satisfied that the South's social structure would survive for several decades.

For additional assessment, have students access **Progress Monitoring Online** at **www.pearsonschool.com.ushist.**

Quick Study Guide

Progress Monitoring *Online*
For: Self-test with vocabulary practice
www.pearsonschool.com/ushist

Quick Study Guide

- Have students use the Quick Study Guide to prepare for the chapter test. Students may wish to refer to the following sections as they review:

Reform Movements
Section 1

Civil War Amendments to the Constitution
Section 4

Cause and Effect: The Civil War
Section 2
Section 3
Section 4

Key Events of the Civil War and Reconstruction
Section 2
Section 3
Section 4

- For additional review, remind students to refer to the Reading and Note Taking Study Guide
Section Note Taking
Section Summaries

- Have students access **www.pearsonschool.com/ushist** for this chapter's History Interactive timeline, which includes expanded entries and additional events.

- If students need more instruction on analyzing graphic data, have them read the Skills Handbook, **p. SH21.**

For **Progress Monitoring *Online*,** refer students to the Self-test with vocabulary practice at **www.pearsonschool.com/ushist.**

■ Reform Movements

■ Civil War Amendments to the Constitution

Amendment	Ratified	Provisions
Thirteenth Amendment	1865	Abolishes slavery throughout United States
Fourteenth Amendment	1868	Defines citizenship; guarantees all citizens "equal protection of the laws"
Fifteenth Amendment	1870	Guarantees that right to vote cannot be denied on basis of race

■ Cause and Effect: The Civil War

Cause and Effect
Causes
• Economic differences divide agrarian South and industrial North.
• Abolitionist movement grows in North
• Compromise of 1850, *Uncle Tom's Cabin*, violence in Kansas, and Dred Scott decision increase tensions
• Election of Lincoln leads to secession of southern states
• Confederate troops fire on Fort Sumter.

▼

The Civil War

Effects
• Confederacy is defeated; Union is restored
• Much of South lies in ruins
• Thirteenth Amendment abolishes slavery
• Radical Reconstruction puts South under military rule
• African Americans in South temporarily gain political rights

☑ Quick Study Timeline

Jackson Forever!
The Hero of Two Wars and of Orleans!
The Man of the People!
PRESIDENCY!
BECAUSE
It should be derived from the
PEOPLE!
KNOCK DOWN
OLD HICKORY

In America

1820	1828		1848
Missouri Compromise	Election of Jackson marks widening of suffrage		Seneca Falls women's rights conference

Presidential Terms	Monroe 1817–1825	Adams 1825–1829	Jackson 1829–1837	Van Buren 1837–1841	Harrison 1841 Tyler 1841–1845	Polk 1845–1849

1820   **1830**   **1840**

Around the World

1822	1832	1840	1848
Liberia founded as colony for freed slaves	Reform Act in Britain expands suffrage	World Anti-Slavery Convention	Democratic revolutions sweep Europe

Differentiated Instruction   Solutions for All Learners

L1 Special Needs Students   **L2 English Language Learners**   **L2 Less Proficient Readers**

Use the following study guide resources to help students acquiring basic skills:
Adapted Reading and Note Taking Study Guide
- Section Note Taking
- Section Summaries

Use the following study guide resources to help Spanish-speaking students:
Spanish Reading and Note Taking Study Guide
- Section Note Taking
- Section Summaries

American Issues
•—•—•—• Connector

By connecting prior knowledge with what you have learned in this chapter, you can gradually build your understanding of enduring questions that still affect America today. Answer the questions below. Then, use your American Issues Connector study guide (or go online: www.pearsonschool.com/ushist).

Issues You Learned About

● **Checks and Balances** Each of the three branches of the federal government has the ability to check the powers of the others.

1. How can the executive branch check the power of the legislative branch? How can the Supreme Court check both?

2. Was President Jackson's refusal to uphold the Supreme Court's decision in the debate over Cherokee rights a legitimate usage of the system of checks and balances? Explain.

3. How did Congress check the power of the President during Reconstruction? Was this effort successful?

● **Federal Power and States' Rights** Conflicting ideas about federal and state authority under the Constitution have persisted for more than 200 years.

4. According to southern leaders during the tariff crisis in the early 1800s, what could states do if the federal government passed a law that went against their interests?

5. How did the system of popular sovereignty favor state power over federal power?

● **Church and State** The United States follows a policy of keeping religion separate from matters of government.

6. What guarantees the American people the right to freedom of religion?

7. Describe the debate about the relationship between church and state that emerged during the Second Great Awakening.

8. Some communities and states have passed "blue laws" banning the sale of certain goods on Sundays. Do you think such laws violate the separation of church and state?

Connect to Your World	Activity

Voting Rights As you have learned, the Fifteenth Amendment promised full voting rights to African American men. Today African Americans enjoy equal voting rights, but do they have equal political power? Conduct research online or go to the local library to investigate this question. Consider the percentage of the population that is African American as it compares to the percentage of African American elected officials and to the percentage of voters who are African American. Write a paragraph analyzing the political power of African Americans in this country and share your thoughts on what the future holds.

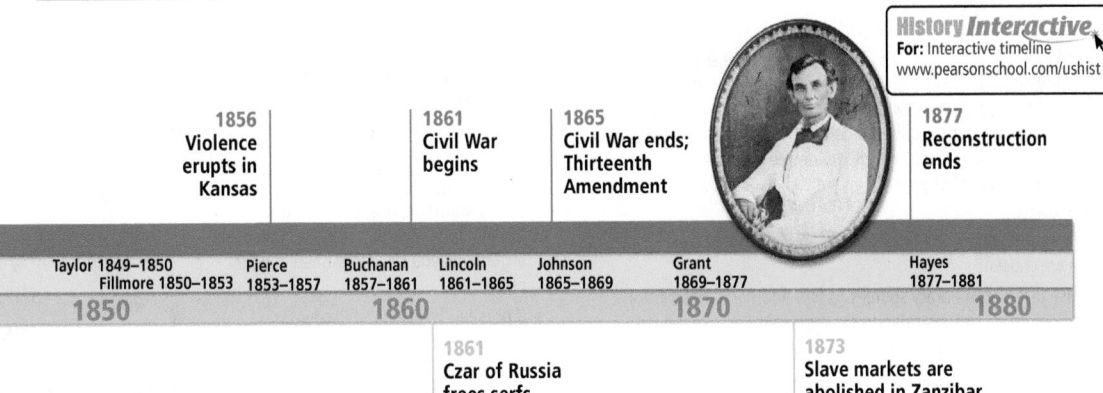

History Interactive
For: Interactive timeline
www.pearsonschool.com/ushist

| 1856 Violence erupts in Kansas | 1861 Civil War begins | 1865 Civil War ends; Thirteenth Amendment | 1877 Reconstruction ends |

Taylor 1849–1850
Fillmore 1850–1853 Pierce 1853–1857 Buchanan 1857–1861 Lincoln 1861–1865 Johnson 1865–1869 Grant 1869–1877 Hayes 1877–1881

1850   1860   1870   1880

1861 Czar of Russia frees serfs

1873 Slave markets are abolished in Zanzibar

American Issues
•—•—•—• Connector

Tell students that the main issues for this chapter are Checks and Balances, Federal Power and States' Rights, and Church and State. Then, ask students to answer the Issues You Learned About questions on this page. Discuss the Connect to Your World topic(s), and ask students to complete the project that follows.

American Issues Connector

1. The executive branch can check the power of the legislative branch with the President's veto. The Supreme Court can check the power of the other two branches by deciding on the constitutionality of executive acts and laws passed by Congress.

2. No; he broke the law.

3. The House initiated impeachment proceedings against President Johnson. The impeachment was not successful because the Senate voted not to convict the President.

4. nullify the laws

5. It shifted the balance of power to the states by allowing each state to decide for itself how to respond to certain issues such as slavery.

6. the First Amendment

7. Motivated by the Second Great Awakening, citizens debated the meaning of the First Amendment and argued that the government should encourage public morality by supporting religion.

8. Possible answer: Yes; such laws favor the Christian sabbath over the holy days of other religions.

Connect to Your World

Paragraphs should include statistical data that supports students' analyses of the political power of African Americans.

For additional review of this chapter's enduring issues, remind students to refer to the Reading and Note Taking Study Guide American Issues Journal.

Terms and People

1. Stanton was a leading figure in the early women's rights movement, whose main goal was to see that women won the right to vote.

2. The citizens of each state would vote to decide whether their state would allow slavery.

3. The Supreme Court ruled that slaves were property, not citizens, and that the government did not have the power to ban slavery; it was condemned by people who believed in human rights and by northerners whose political interests were endangered by the threat to the Missouri Compromise.

4. In April 1865 at Appomattox Court House in Virginia, General Robert E. Lee, leader of the Confederate Army, surrendered to General Ulysses S. Grant, leader of the Union Army, bringing an end to the Civil War.

5. During the Reconstruction, Radical Republicans favored punishment and reorganization for the South. They also advocated full citizens' rights for African Americans and federal power over states' authority.

6. The Fifteenth Amendment, ratified in 1870, guaranteed male citizens the right to vote.

Focus Questions

7. Democratization was reflected in widening suffrage for white males, and the spirit of reform was evident in efforts to reduce alcohol consumption, to improve prisons, public schools, and public health; and to abolish slavery.

8. As the nation grew, more states entered the Union, and the question of whether these states should allow or prohibit slavery caused political problems that eventually contributed to the secession of many slave states.

9. the North's industrial, financial, and naval superiority; the Emancipation Proclamation; important victories such as those at Gettysburg and Vicksburg; the total war waged by General Sherman

Chapter Assessment

Terms and People

1. Who was **Elizabeth Cady Stanton**? What was her main goal?

2. How would decisions about slavery be made under **popular sovereignty**?

3. What did the Supreme Court decide in the case of **Dred Scott v. Sandford?** Which Americans condemned this decision?

4. Who were **Robert E. Lee** and **Ulysses S. Grant**? What happened to these men in April 1865?

5. Who were the **Radical Republicans**? What were their goals?

6. What was the **Fifteenth Amendment**? To whom did it apply?

Focus Questions

The focus question for this chapter is **What challenges did the United States face as a result of expansion, regional differences, and slavery?** Build answers to this big question by answering the focus questions for Sections 1 through 4 and the Critical Thinking questions that follow.

Section 1
7. What trends in democratization and reform were taking shape in the United States by 1850?

Section 2
8. How did the issue of slavery divide the Union?

Section 3
9. What factors and events led to the Union victory in the Civil War?

Section 4
10. What were the immediate and long-term effects of Reconstruction?

Writing About History

Writing a Persuasive Essay In a persuasive essay, you try to identify an issue and present arguments that will persuade the readers to support a particular viewpoint. Choose one of the reform movements described in Section 1 of this chapter. Write a three-paragraph essay in which you define the issue and give reasons in support of your viewpoint.

Prewriting
• Read the text in this chapter relating to the topic you have chosen.
• Use Internet or library sources to find additional descriptions and primary sources relating to your topic.
• Decide what viewpoint you wish to support.
• Make a list of arguments that might be used to support that viewpoint. Identify the two strongest arguments.

10. Immediate: reunited the nation and initiated the physical and economic rebuilding of the South; Long-term: laid the foundation, through constitutional amendments, for the eventual extension of political equality to all citizens

Critical Thinking

11. Possible answer: Jackson did come from a less privileged background than his predecessors; however, his treatment of Native Americans proves that he was not a "People's President" in the modern sense.

Critical Thinking

11. **Draw Conclusions** Andrew Jackson has been called the "People's President." How accurate do you think this nickname is? Explain your answer.

12. **Draw Conclusions** Why do you think many preachers of the Second Great Awakening supported the temperance and abolitionist movements?

13. **Solve Problems** What issue did the Missouri Compromise settle? How long did this compromise last, and why did it come to an end?

14. **Analyze Graphs** Describe the information shown on this pie graph. What impact do you think this data had on the outcome of the Civil War?

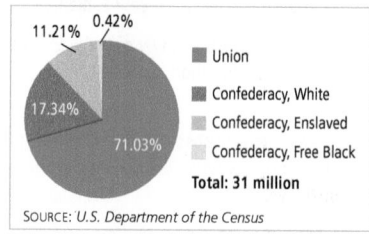

Population of North and South, 1860

11.21% 0.42%
17.34%
71.03%

■ Union
■ Confederacy, White
■ Confederacy, Enslaved
■ Confederacy, Free Black

Total: 31 million

SOURCE: *U.S. Department of the Census*

15. **Analyze Information** How did Lincoln's and the Union's attitude toward African Americans change as the Civil War progressed?

16. **Draw Inferences** Why did southern states develop a strong Republican Party?

Drafting
• Make an outline identifying what aspects of your topic you want to describe.
• Write an opening paragraph in which you describe the issue and explain why it is important. Include a thesis statement.
• Write two persuasive paragraphs. In each paragraph, use reasoned but forceful language that explains one of the arguments you have identified in your prewriting.
• If possible, anticipate and counter possible objections to your arguments.

Revising
• Use the guidelines on page SH16 of the Writing Handbook to revise your writing.

12. Their interpretation of the Bible led them to believe that slavery and the abuse of alcohol were wrong.

13. The compromise settled balance-of-power issues related to the admission of Missouri to the Union as a slave state, but it lasted only until 1854, when the federal government passed the Kansas-Nebraska Act.

14. It shows a Civil War population distribution, and the data indicates that the North had an advantage, not only in that it had far more people than the South, but also in that about 40 percent of the South's population was made up of enslaved

Document-Based Assessment

American Democracy in the Age of Jackson

Historians have often used the term *Jacksonian democracy* to describe the expansion of democratic government during the era of President Andrew Jackson. But how democratic was Jacksonian democracy? Use your knowledge of the chapter material and Documents A, B, C, D, and E to answer questions 1 through 4.

Document A

"In America the people name those who make the law and those who execute it; they themselves form the jury that punishes infractions of the law. Not only are the institutions democratic in their principle, but also in all their developments; thus the people name their representatives directly and generally choose them every year in order to keep them more completely under their dependence. It is therefore really the people who direct."

— *Alexis de Tocqueville,* Democracy in America, *1835*

Document B

The Trail of Tears, 1838

Document C

"Jacksonians believed that there was a deep-rooted conflict in society between the 'producing' and 'non-producing' classes— the farmers and laborers, on the one hand, and the business community on the other. . . . Jacksonian democracy was [one] phase of that enduring struggle between the business community and the rest of society which is the guarantee of freedom in a liberal capitalist state."

— *Arthur M. Schlesinger, Jr.,* The Age of Jackson, *1945*

Document D

"The Jacksonian period, our Jacksonian democracy: Arthur Schlesinger writes this glowing book about Andrew Jackson and Jacksonian democracy. What else was going on? And then I find out that Jackson is responsible for the brutal treatment of the Indians in the Southeast, driving them across the Mississippi, thousands of them dying. Jackson is a racist. Jackson is a slave owner. Under Jackson, the industrial system begins with the mill girls going to work at the age of 12 and dying at the age of 25."

— *Howard Zinn, interview, 2001*

Document E

"These Americans . . . were champions of equality—that is, of course, for those who were white and male. . . . Women, blacks, and Indians just didn't enter the thinking of these people when they argued for equality.

To fault Americans of this period for failing to understand what the modern world means by equality is a pointless and futile exercise. But if they are examined on their own terms, with all their faults and limitations, they make an exciting bunch to watch as they changed their world and shaped so many things that became basic to the American system."

— *Robert V. Remini,* The Revolutionary Age of Andrew Jackson, *1976*

---

1. According to Document A, what was the most important feature of American democracy in the 1830s?
   A Americans had the right to trial by jury.
   B Americans considered all people equal.
   C The people were the source of political authority.
   D All Americans had the right to vote.

2. Document B best illustrates one of the main points made in
   A Document A.
   B Document C.
   C Documents C and E.
   D Documents D and E.

3. According to Document C, which of the following groups benefited most from Jacksonian Democracy?
   A Factory workers
   B Bankers
   C Westerners
   D Slaveholders

4. **Writing Task** Was Jacksonian democracy democratic by modern standards? By the standards of the time? Use your knowledge of the chapter content and specific evidence from the primary sources above to support your opinion.

African Americans, who were likely to impede the South's cause.

15. At first, the North's stated goal was to preserve the Union, but as the war progressed, the opposition to slavery—as evidenced by the Emancipation Proclamation—became a more important factor.

16. The South developed a strong Republican party because under Radical Reconstruction, African American men had the right and the ability to vote, while many white Southerners were no longer eligible or chose not to vote.

Writing About History

As students begin the assignment, refer them to page SH15 of the Writing Handbook for help in writing a persuasive essay. Remind them of the steps they should take to complete their assignment, including prewriting, drafting, and revising.

The opening paragraph of students' persuasive essays should reveal a clear thesis. The body of each essay should support the thesis and discount opposing arguments, and it should flow logically to a valid conclusion. For scoring rubrics, see Assessment Rubrics.

Document-Based Assessment

- To help students understand the documents, give them the following **TIP Analyze each of the points made in the documents arguing for and against the subject by writing the main fact that each author presents and judging how important and persuasive you think it is.**

- To provide students with further practice in answering document-based questions, go to Test Prep With Document-Based Assessment.

- If students need more instruction on analyzing graphic data, have them read the Skills Handbook, **p. SH21.**

Answers

1. C   2. D   3. A

4. In formulating their opinions, students should try to anticipate counterarguments and be prepared to answer them.

CHAPTER **3**

The Development of Industrial America
1870–1914

Teach With Technology
Presentation**EXPRESS**™
PREMIUM DVD

- Teach this chapter's core content by using **PresentationExpress,** which includes interactivities, video, lecture notes, and the *ExamView*® QuickTake assessment tool.

- To introduce this chapter by using **PresentationExpress,** ask students with which of the following statements they most agree:
  A) The industrial development of the United States brought only positive social changes.
  B) The industrial development of the United States brought only negative social changes.
  C) The industrial development of the United States brought some positive social changes and some negative social changes. Take a class poll or record students' answers by using the QuickTake feature, and discuss their responses. Point out that in this chapter, students will read about how the nation dealt with changes brought on by immigration, industrial development, and urbanization at the end of the nineteenth century.

Technology Resources

- Student**EXPRESS** CD-ROM

- Teacher Resource Library DVD

- Presentation**EXPRESS**
  PREMIUM DVD

- *ExamView*® **Test Bank CD-ROM**
  English and Spanish

- **Guided Reading Audio,** Spanish

- **Student Edition on Audio**

VIDEO
THE ESSENTIAL ?
By Students For Students
For videos on Amercian Issues, go to
www.pearsonschool.com/ushist

Bibliography

For the Teacher
Brown, Dee A. *Bury My Heart at Wounded Knee: An Indian History of the American West.* Henry Holt, 2001.

Meyer, David R. *The Roots of American Industrialization.* Johns Hopkins University Press, 2003.

Takaki, Ronald T. *Strangers from a Distant Shore: A History of Asian Americans.* Little, Brown, 1998.

For the Student
L2 Coan, Peter M. *Ellis Island Interviews: Immigrants Tell Their Stories in Their Own Words.* Barnes & Noble Books, 2004.

L3 Nazario, Sonia. *Enrique's Journey: The Story of a Boy's Dangerous Odyssey to Reunite with His Mother.* Random House, 2006.

L4 Ambrose, Stephen E. *Nothing Like It in the World: The Men Who Built the Transcontinental Railroad, 1863–1869.* Simon & Schuster, 2001.

WITNESS HISTORY

Exciting Times

At the turn of the twentieth century, a new period of industrialization began to sweep across the United States. As waves of immigrants came into America's cities, urban areas such as New York City, Chicago, and San Francisco rapidly grew into cosmopolitan centers that offered exciting new experiences and opportunities. One such exciting experience was the opening of Coney Island in New York.

"They took the lid off Coney Island May 15, 1904, and a quarter of a million men and women got a glimpse of a swaying, rocking, glittering magic city by the sea. It was Coney Island's opening day, . . . there were more dazzling, wriggling, spectacular amusements offered than had ever before been collected together at any one place at any time."
—from "Review of Opening Night at Coney Island," *The New York Times,* May 16, 1904

Brooklyn Bridge newspaper ad

Pin from 1896 presidential campaign

◄ Workers build one of the first skyscrapers in New York City.

Chapter Preview

Chapter Focus Question: How did industrialization affect the United States?

Section 1
The Triumph of Industry

Section 2
Immigration and Urbanization

Section 3
The South and West Transformed

Section 4
Issues of the Gilded Age

Sears, Roebuck and Company catalog

Use the ☑ **Quick Study Timeline** at the end of this chapter to preview chapter events.

Note Taking Study Guide *Online*
For: Note Taking and American Issues Connector
www.pearsonschool.com/ushist

Chapter-Level Resources

All in One Letter Home (English and Spanish), Preread the Chapter, Vocabulary Builder, Reading Strategy, Social Studies Skills Practice, Enrichment, Issues Connector, Chapter Tests

- Test Prep With Document-Based Assessments
- AYP Monitoring Assessments
- *ExamView*® Test Bank CD-ROM
- Guided Reading Audio (Spanish)
- Student Edition Audio

Previewing the Chapter

- **WITNESS HISTORY** Ask students whether they prefer when things are familiar or when things are quickly changing around them. Then, have them discuss how they would feel in a new environment where nothing was familiar. Tell students that in this chapter, they will learn about a period of U.S. history in which many changes occurred. Read the Witness History selection aloud.

- **Analyzing the Visuals** Have students look at the photograph that opens the chapter. Ask **What do you think the point of this photograph was when it was taken?** *(Sample answer: It dramatically illustrated the new technology of skyscrapers and the expertise that made their construction possible.)*

- **Focus** Write the Chapter Focus Question on the board. Tell students to keep this question in mind as they read the chapter. Then, have students preview the section titles in this chapter.

- **Preread** Have students complete the chapter's Preread the Chapter Worksheet Teaching Resources, pp. 8–9.

Have students access **www.pearsonschool.com/ushist** for the Note Taking Study Guide *Online* as an alternative to the *Reading and Note Taking Study Guide* booklet.

Step-by-Step Instruction

Objectives

As you teach this section, keep students focused on the following objectives to help them answer the Section Focus Question and master core content.

- Analyze the growth of the United States as an industrial power.
- Summarize the rise of big business.
- Understand the plight of the industrial worker and how workers tried to improve their condition.
- Identify reasons that workers and big business clashed.

Prepare to Read

Background Knowledge L3

Remind students that at this time, the nation had only recently emerged from the turmoil of the Civil War and Reconstruction. Have students predict the types of changes that might occur as the nation enters a new period of expansion and development.

Set a Purpose L3

- **WITNESS HISTORY** Read the selection aloud.

  Ask **What did the bridge symbolize about the United States?** *(It symbolized the new industrial era.)*

- **Focus** Point out the Section Focus Question, and write it on the board. Tell students to refer to this question as they read. *(Answer appears with Section 1 Assessment answers.)*

- **Preview** Have students preview the Section Objectives and the list of Terms and People.

- **Reading Skill** Have students use the *Reading Strategy: Identify Causes and Effects* worksheet. **Teaching Resources, p. 12**

- **NoteTaking** Using the Paragraph Shrinking strategy (TE, p. T20), have students read this section. As they read, have students list the causes and effects of industrialization in America. Reading and Note Taking Study Guide

▼ Brooklyn Bridge under construction

Building the Brooklyn Bridge

At the time of its dedication, in 1883, some hailed the Brooklyn Bridge as the "Eighth Wonder of the World." The bridge, which linked Manhattan to Brooklyn, towered over New York City. Built largely of steel, it symbolized the new industrial era and still stands as a landmark achievement in the history of engineering.

"It is distinctly an American triumph. American genius designed it, American skill built it, and American workshops made it."

—New York City Mayor Seth Low, "Dedication remarks," 1883

The Triumph of Industry

Objectives
- Analyze the growth of the United States as an industrial power.
- Summarize the rise of big business.
- Understand the plight of the industrial worker and how workers tried to improve their condition.
- Identify reasons that workers and big business clashed.

Terms and People

Thomas Alva Edison	Gospel of Wealth
Andrew Carnegie	monopoly
John D. Rockefeller	Knights of Labor
trust	AFL
Social Darwinism	anarchist

NoteTaking

Reading Skill: Identify Causes and Effects
Fill in a table like the one below with the causes and effects of industrialization.

The Industrialization of America	
Causes	**Effects**
• Natural resources	• Growth of cities
•	•

Why It Matters Although manufacturing and factory towns had sprung up in the Northeast before the Civil War, an even greater period of industrial growth occurred at the end of the century. Industrial towns soon dominated the landscape throughout much of the North and had established a presence in the South. Industrialization rapidly transformed the United States into one of the most powerful nations in the world and dramatically altered how Americans lived. **Section Focus Question: What factors led to the industrialization of America, and what impact did industrialization have on society?**

Industry and Technology Advance Rapidly

The numbers alone display the nation's emergence as an industrial power. Between the end of the Civil War and the beginning of the twentieth century, coal production skyrocketed 800 percent and steel production increased even more. The nation built tens of thousands of miles of railroads and sprouted brand-new industries, including the production of petroleum and electricity. When the Civil War began, the majority of Americans worked as farmers. By 1900, those who made a living from farming were outnumbered by nearly three to one.

Causes of Industrial Expansion There were many reasons for rapid industrial expansion in the United States. First, the nation's physical geography provided an abundance of natural resources— including lumber, coal, and oil—that manufacturers relied on to power their factories and lubricate their machines. Second, as

Vocabulary Builder

Use the information below and the following resource to teach students the high-use word from this section. Teaching Resources, Vocabulary Builder, p. 11

High-Use Word	Definition and Sample Sentence
doctrine	*n.* teachings, principles, or beliefs
	Each religion is based on a specific **doctrine** that believers follow.

industries expanded, millions of immigrants from Southern and Eastern Europe, as well as from Asia, poured into the United States to fill the demand for labor. Third, government policies encouraged the success of businesses in the late 1800s. Finally, the nation's cultural climate, with its favorable view of entrepreneurs, contributed to the growth of industry.

New Technologies Transform the Economy The combination of factors just described contributed to an outbreak of creative inventions, many of which had a profound impact on the economy. No one better symbolizes this inventiveness than **Thomas Alva Edison,** who designed the electric light bulb and the phonograph, in addition to numerous other inventions. Large utility companies soon formed to power his light bulbs and machines. New and better railroads, improvements in the telegraph, and the invention of the telephone all made communication and transportation less costly and more efficient.

The Impact of Industrialization Industrialization had a broad and long-lasting impact on American society, including a rise in most people's standard of living. The nation's cities grew upward and outward. New and more efficient production techniques, as well as improvements in transportation and communication, paved the way for the rise of mass consumerism. For example, rather than making their own clothes, Americans increasingly bought ready-made garments.

✓ **Checkpoint** What factors contributed to the industrialization of America?

The Rise of Big Business

Before the Civil War, most businesses were small and family-owned. By the end of the nineteenth century, large corporations dominated the American scene. The owners of these firms amassed enormous fortunes and power over the lives of hundreds of thousands of workers and related small businesses. As they did, the nation grappled with the costs and benefits of big business.

Corporations Amass Huge Fortunes In 1901, **Andrew Carnegie** sold his steel business to the newly formed United States Steel Corporation. At the time, investors valued U.S. Steel at $1.5 billion, making it the richest corporation in the world. It also made Carnegie one of the wealthiest men in the world—but he was not alone. During the latter decades of the nineteenth century, **John D. Rockefeller** gained control of the oil industry through his company Standard Oil, while Gustavus Swift and Philip Armour came to dominate meatpacking. Other powerful industrialists dominated the sale and production of tobacco, farm machinery, and sewing machines. These industrialists and financiers were often called robber barons, implying they "stole" their fortunes by paying their workers low wages. Others considered these men to be "captains of industry"—steering the country in the direction of economic prosperity.

Part of the success of these corporations lay in the development of new forms of business arrangements, such as cartels, or associations of producers that coordinate prices and production. Industrialists also established trusts. In a

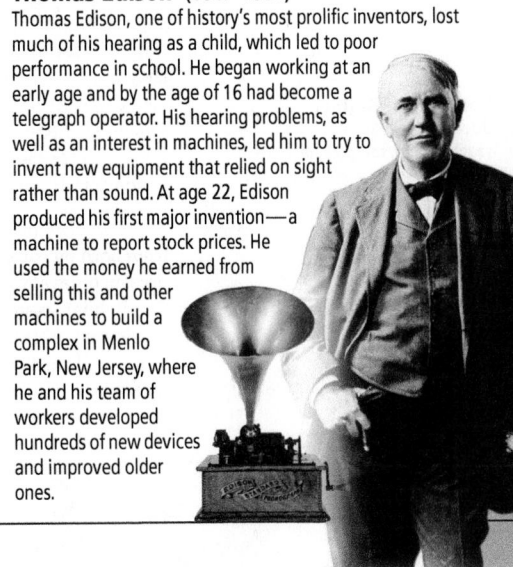

HISTORY MAKERS

Thomas Edison (1847–1931)
Thomas Edison, one of history's most prolific inventors, lost much of his hearing as a child, which led to poor performance in school. He began working at an early age and by the age of 16 had become a telegraph operator. His hearing problems, as well as an interest in machines, led him to try to invent new equipment that relied on sight rather than sound. At age 22, Edison produced his first major invention—a machine to report stock prices. He used the money he earned from selling this and other machines to build a complex in Menlo Park, New Jersey, where he and his team of workers developed hundreds of new devices and improved older ones.

Differentiated Instruction   Solutions for All Learners

🄻🄴 **Advanced Readers**   🄻🄴 **Gifted and Talented Students**

Remind students that new technologies can have huge effects on society. One invention can dramatically change the way that people live and work or can affect the environment. For example, the invention of the elevator was one factor that made the building of skyscrapers possible. Air conditioners made it possible for large numbers of people to live

and work comfortably in hot climates, such as in California or Florida. Challenge students to use school-approved Internet sources and library research to find an invention from this era that had multiple effects on society, culture, or the environment. Have students work in pairs and present their findings to the class in the form of an informational flowchart.

Instruct

- **Introduce: Key Term** Have students locate the name ***Thomas Alva Edison*** (in bold) in the text. Tell students to read to find out more about technological advances in this period and in what ways Edison contributed to U.S. industrialization.

- **Teach** Direct students' attention to the red heading "Causes of Industrial Expansion." Have students debate which cause discussed in the paragraph is the most important. Using the Idea Wave strategy (TE, p. T22), discuss the types of technological advances that became important in the late nineteenth and early twentieth centuries. Ask **How might industrialization have raised the standard of living for many Americans?** (*Growing businesses in cities paid higher wages than did work on farms and in rural areas.*) Have students discuss how industrialization paved the way for consumerism in the United States.

- **Quick Activity** Refer students to the HISTORY MAKERS biography of Thomas Edison on this page. Ask students to write a paragraph explaining in what ways Edison typifies this era of industrial growth and technological advancement.

Independent Practice

Have students begin to fill in the Note Taking table for this section by recording the causes and effects of industrialization.

Monitor Progress

As students fill in their tables, circulate to make sure that they correctly identify the causes and the effects of industrialization. For a completed version of the table, see Note Taking Transparencies, **B-82a.**

Answer

✓ an abundance of natural resources, a large labor pool provided by immigration, government policies that encouraged business, and the nation's favorable view of entrepreneurs

Instruct

- **Introduce: Key Terms** Point out the key terms *Social Darwinism* and *Gospel of Wealth* (in bold) in the text. Explain that business owners used these two concepts to justify their business methods and accumulation of wealth. Ask students to discuss whether these two concepts can be applied to today's business practices and, if so, in what ways.

- **Teach** Ask **What are cartels, trusts, and monopolies?** *(types of business organizations in which companies coordinate prices and production [or join with other companies involved in different aspects of the same industry] to form giant corporations that may control most aspects of production and distribution)* **How did federal regulations seek to control these types of businesses?** *(Laws were passed to decrease their power and influence. The Interstate Commerce Commission was created to control railroad monopolies, and the Sherman Antitrust Act outlawed mergers and monopolies.)* **Why do you think these regulations had little effect on big business?** *(Some government officials were closely allied with the businesses and did not push for enforcement.)*

- **Quick Activity** To enrich and extend the lesson, have students access the **History Interactive** at **www.pearsonschool.com/ushist.** After students experience the History Interactive, ask them to share their reactions by posing questions like these: **What was it like to work in a steel mill during this period? What were the dangers of this type of work?**

Independent Practice

Display Color Transparency: *The Robber Barons.* Then, have students create Venn diagrams to compare and contrast the activities and interests of Andrew Carnegie and John D. Rockefeller. Tell them to consider whether each man was a "captain of industry" or a "robber baron" and write a few sentences to explain their reasoning. Color Transparencies **A-73**

Monitor Progress

As students create their diagrams, circulate to be sure that they support their opinions with details.

---

trust, companies assign their stock to a board of trustees, who combine the stocks into a new organization. The trustees then run the organization, paying the shareholders dividends on profits. To form cartels and trusts, corporations often bought out or merged with smaller firms. By joining with firms involved in different aspects of the steel industry, such as the mining of iron, Carnegie gained an edge on his competitors. In a similar manner, by taking advantage of special deals he had arranged with the railroads, Rockefeller compelled his competitors to join his firm or risk bankruptcy.

Vocabulary Builder
doctrine–(DAHK trihn) *n.*
teachings, principles, or beliefs

Carnegie and the Gospel of Wealth Carnegie and others developed sophisticated explanations to defend their business methods and the accumulation of massive sums of money. Borrowing from Darwin's theory of evolution, they applied the principle of natural selection to society, arguing that life consisted of a struggle in which only the fittest survived. This view of the world was known as **Social Darwinism.** Carnegie added to this a <u>doctrine</u> that came to be known as the **Gospel of Wealth,** which called on those who accumulated wealth to share their riches for the betterment of society.

Federal Regulations Target Corporate Abuses Even though politicians from both political parties tended to agree with the Social Darwinist view of life, pressure developed to combat the growing power of the biggest corporations. Small businessmen complained about the dangers of **monopolies,** whereby single corporations came to control entire industries. As George Rice, the owner of a small oil firm put it, John D. Rockefeller had "ruined" him by using his "great power and wealth" to run him out of business.

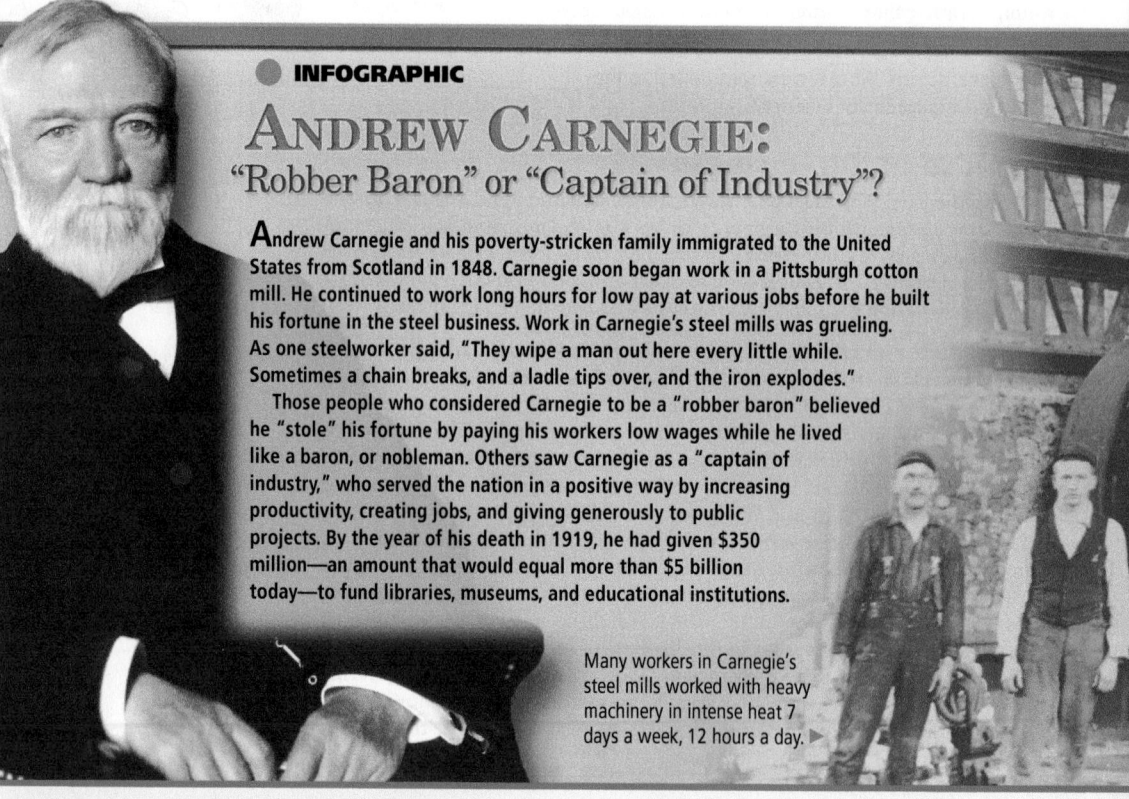

● **INFOGRAPHIC**

ANDREW CARNEGIE:
"Robber Baron" or "Captain of Industry"?

Andrew Carnegie and his poverty-stricken family immigrated to the United States from Scotland in 1848. Carnegie soon began work in a Pittsburgh cotton mill. He continued to work long hours for low pay at various jobs before he built his fortune in the steel business. Work in Carnegie's steel mills was grueling. As one steelworker said, "They wipe a man out here every little while. Sometimes a chain breaks, and a ladle tips over, and the iron explodes."

Those people who considered Carnegie to be a "robber baron" believed he "stole" his fortune by paying his workers low wages while he lived like a baron, or nobleman. Others saw Carnegie as a "captain of industry," who served the nation in a positive way by increasing productivity, creating jobs, and giving generously to public projects. By the year of his death in 1919, he had given $350 million—an amount that would equal more than $5 billion today—to fund libraries, museums, and educational institutions.

Many workers in Carnegie's steel mills worked with heavy machinery in intense heat 7 days a week, 12 hours a day. ▶

History Background

William Graham Sumner, Social Darwinist
One of the major proponents of Social Darwinism was William Graham Sumner. After graduating from Yale University, Sumner received additional training in Europe and later was ordained as an Episcopal priest. In 1872, Sumner returned to Yale, where he taught political and social science and became influenced by Charles Darwin's theory of evolution. Sumner ardently extolled the merits of individual liberty, the laissez-faire policy, and the intrinsic inequalities of humans, believing that each of these elements greatly benefited society. He judged that economic competition between individuals and businesses would only make society stronger because the fittest would survive by earning wealth and the ill-adapted would be eliminated. Therefore, he opposed any law that allowed the government to intervene socially or economically. He reasoned that by helping those people who were unable to adapt, the government would hurt the "forgotten people" who had adjusted to social and economic conditions—the middle class.

Partly in response to the complaints of small businesses, the federal government created the Interstate Commerce Commission in 1887 to oversee railroad operations. Railroad owners were often considered the worst abusers of their monopoly status. The federal government then became involved in regulating trusts and enacted the Sherman Antitrust Act in 1890, which outlawed mergers and monopolies. Initially, these reforms had little impact, in part because the nation's leaders chose not to strongly enforce them. In the spirit of Social Darwinism, leading economists such as William Graham Sumner promoted a policy of laissez faire, in which businesses operate with little or no government interference.

✓ **Checkpoint** What factors explained the emergence of large corporations, and what did Americans think of them?

Workers Organize

The United States had been created as a land of opportunity, free from the corruption and exploitation that had existed in Europe. But as the nation industrialized, the extremes of wealth and poverty so apparent in industrial England began to appear in the United States as well.

Workers Endure Hardships Most industrial workers endured long days in poor conditions for low pay. Whereas Carnegie amassed a fortune, steelworkers in his plants labored 10 to 12 hours a day, six days a week, for about 15 cents an hour. They received no health benefits, no vacation time, and suffered from

▼ Carnegie devoted himself to philanthropic endeavors after his retirement. Today, people across the country enjoy the more than 2,800 libraries (top) and many museums (bottom) that he funded.

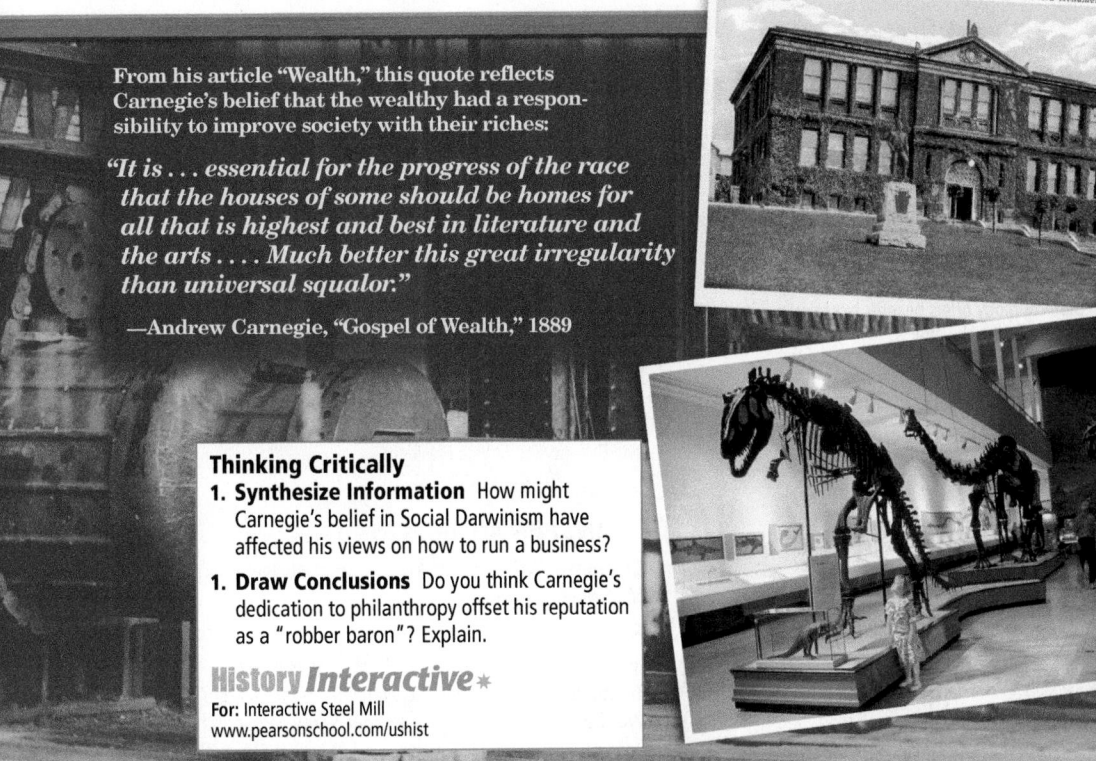

From his article "Wealth," this quote reflects Carnegie's belief that the wealthy had a responsibility to improve society with their riches:

"It is . . . essential for the progress of the race that the houses of some should be homes for all that is highest and best in literature and the arts . . . . Much better this great irregularity than universal squalor."

—Andrew Carnegie, "Gospel of Wealth," 1889

Thinking Critically
1. **Synthesize Information** How might Carnegie's belief in Social Darwinism have affected his views on how to run a business?
1. **Draw Conclusions** Do you think Carnegie's dedication to philanthropy offset his reputation as a "robber baron"? Explain.

History *Interactive* ✶
For: Interactive Steel Mill
www.pearsonschool.com/ushist

Differentiated Instruction Solutions for All Learners

L1 Special Needs Students **L2 English Language Learners** **L2 Less Proficient Readers**

Have students examine the Infographic about Andrew Carnegie. Ask them to discuss whether the pictures depict Carnegie as a robber baron or as a philanthropist—a person who gives to others and to the community. Ask students to think of adjectives to describe the way that Carnegie appears in the images. Have students suggest other images that could give a different impression of Carnegie. Discuss

how these images can influence one's point of view.
To help students better comprehend the role of Eugene V. Debs in American politics, have them complete the worksheet *Biography: Eugene V. Debs*. Teaching Resources, **p. 31**

Instruct

- **Introduce: Key Terms** Have students locate the key terms *Knights of Labor* and *American Federation of Labor* (in bold). Tell students to read to find out about the history and goals of both organizations.

- **Teach** Ask **What was mill or mine work like at this time?** *(Workers put in long hours, often in dangerous conditions, received low pay, and did not have health benefits or vacation time.)* **How did the goals of the AFL differ from those of the Knights of Labor?** *(The AFL was a loose organization of skilled workers focused on specific labor issues, such as wages and working hours. The Knights included both skilled and unskilled workers and sought broad social reforms.)* Discuss the reasons for socialism's growth in the United States during the late nineteenth century and for its inability to gain the following that it had in Europe.

- **Quick Activity** Have students read and complete the *Biography: American Socialists* worksheet. Teaching Resources, **p. 32**

Independent Practice

NoteTaking Tell students to record main ideas about the growth of organized labor. Reading and Note Taking Study Guide

Monitor Progress

As students fill in their concept webs, circulate to make sure that they understand the rise of organized labor. For a completed version of the concept web, see Note Taking Transparencies, **B-82b**.

Answers

✓ New business arrangements emerged, such as cartels and trusts. These worked together to control prices and production within their industries and to buy or merge with competing firms. Many people were uneasy about the growing power of these corporations.

Thinking Critically
1. Carnegie may have believed that anything was fair while competing in business because businesses that could not stand up to competition were unfit to survive.
2. Sample answer: These contributions do offset Carnegie's "robber baron" activities. His legacy consists of the libraries and museums that he built.

American Issues Connector

Objectives

- Draw conclusions about the benefits and the costs of new technology.
- Identify arguments for and against the use of nuclear power plants for the production of electricity.

Background Knowledge L3

Explain that all technologies also have drawbacks or costs. Ask students to name one modern technology that they use, and explain a benefit and a cost involved in using that technology.

Instruct L3

Have students study the timeline of technological advances. Point out that a new technology is usually accepted when the benefits far exceed the costs—or the perceived costs. Ask **Why do you think that many Americans debate the use of nuclear energy?** *(because the benefits are not much greater, at least at this time, than the costs)*

Monitor Progress

- Have students complete the Issues Connector Worksheet, *Technology and Society.* Check students' work to make sure that they grasp the issue. Teaching Resources, **pp. 15–18**
- Remind students to complete their American Issues Connector Journal worksheets notes. Review their work for accuracy. Reading and Note Taking Study Guide

Answers

Transfer Activities

1. According to Kane, nuclear energy is clean, reliable, affordable, safe, and does not produce the emissions of other major fuels used today. Sweeney states that the use of nuclear energy generates toxic substances that threaten people and the environment.
2. Sweeney
3. For more information about the use of nuclear power, have students access **www.pearsonschool.com/ushist**.

American Issues Connector — Technology and Society

TRACK THE ISSUE

What are the benefits and costs of technology?

Technology has had a great impact on American life. It has produced economic and social benefits for the nation, yet has also had some negative effects. What are the benefits and costs of technological change? Use the timeline below to explore this enduring issue.

Late 1700s Factory System
Water-powered mills boost production but worsen conditions for workers.

1859 Oil Refining
Oil fuels industrial growth and raises standard of living but encourages American dependence on a single resource and worsens pollution.

1930s Polymers
Manufactured materials like plastics have many uses but also increase pollution.

1940s Nuclear Reactor
Nuclear energy holds promise but carries the threat of radioactive meltdown and nuclear waste.

2000s Genetic Engineering
Biotechnology offers benefits but may also have harmful effects.

Factory workers circa 1900

Nuclear power plant, Illinois

DEBATE THE ISSUE

Nuclear Energy Building more nuclear plants would help meet our energy needs and limit fossil-fuel emissions that contribute to global warming. But the radioactive material used may pose grave risks to human health and safety.

"Nuclear energy supplies clean, reliable, affordable and safe electricity and is the only emission-free source that can be readily expanded to meet our nation's growing energy needs. . . . Nuclear power plants produce electricity that otherwise would be supplied by oil-, gas-, or coal-fired generating capacity, and thus *prevent* the emissions associated with that fossil-fueled capacity."
—John E. Kane, Senior Vice President, Nuclear Energy Institute

"There is strong skepticism . . . [about] the promises of the nuclear industry. . . . This is an industry that on a daily basis, as a direct result of its work, generates the most toxic and long-lived substances known to humans. It is an industry that poses a grievous threat to the health of humans and to the wider biosphere."
—Dave Sweeney, nuclear campaign, Australian Conservation Foundation

TRANSFER Activities

1. **Compare** Why does Mr. Kane support nuclear energy? Why does Mr. Sweeney oppose it?
2. **Analyze** Which of the authors cited above would be more likely to question the factory system's impact on workers?
3. **Transfer** Use the following Web site to see a video, try a WebQuest, and write in your journal. www.pearsonschool.com/ushist

History Background

Atoms for Electricity On December 2, 1942, Enrico Fermi and a group of scientists at the University of Chicago created the first self-sustaining nuclear fission chain reaction. It was the dawn of the nuclear age. The fission of uranium atoms produced a great deal of energy—much of it heat. Nuclear power was first put to military use. Still, scientists searched for a way to use nuclear fission for civilian purposes.

In the 1950s, scientists moved closer to finding a way to split atoms to generate electric power. Conventional electric power plants that use fossil fuels burn the fuels to heat water. The water produces steam that, under pressure, can turn a turbine that spins a generator. That generator produces electricity. Scientists merely substituted heat from splitting atoms for heat from burning coal or oil.

The first commercial nuclear power plant attained full power in Shippingport, Pennsylvania, in 1957. Nuclear power grew as an electricity producer in the United States in the 1960s. However, accidents and concerns about safety and waste disposal caused further development to stall. No new nuclear power plants have been commissioned in this country for more than 30 years.

periodic layoffs because of downturns in the business cycle. In addition, workers took little pride in what they did and often performed the same repetitive task day after day.

Women and children toiled in the nation's factories alongside the men. Mines hired young boys, known as breaker boys, to separate coal needed for fuel from slate and other rocks. Textile mills employed young girls to help operate their power looms around the clock. Women worked in textile mills, as well as in many light industries, such as manufacturing light bulbs. Nearly all women and child laborers were paid even less than men.

Labor Unions Promote Workers' Rights To improve their conditions, workers formed unions. The **Knights of Labor,** which sought to organize all workers—male and female, black and white, skilled and unskilled—grew rapidly in the early 1880s. Reaching a peak membership of about 700,000 in 1885, the Knights sought broad social reforms, such as transcending the wage labor system by creating cooperatives in which workers would own the factories where they labored.

In the mid-1880s, the Knights rallied tens of thousands of workers around obtaining an eight-hour workday. "Eight hours of work, eight hours of sleep, eight hours for what we will," supporters of the Knights would chant at mass rallies. For a variety of reasons, including the Haymarket Riot that you will soon read about, the Knights of Labor fell apart in the late 1880s, leaving it to others to forge a successful labor movement.

No sooner had the Knights collapsed than the **American Federation of Labor (AFL)** emerged. Unlike the Knights, the AFL did not aim for larger social gains for workers. Instead, it focused on very specific workers' issues such as wages, working hours, and working conditions. Led by Samuel Gompers, the AFL operated like a business. It was a loose organization of skilled workers from some 100 local craft unions, each devoted to a specific craft or trade.

Workers and Socialism In addition to unions, some workers became attracted to socialism as a means to improve their condition and place in society. They considered the Social Darwinist rationalization of cutthroat business practices inhumane and antidemocratic. Eugene V. Debs, who ran for President on the Socialist Party ticket five times, demanded government ownership of the railroads and called for workers to organize industrial unions to counter the power of big business. Although socialists enjoyed some success in local politics, they never attained nearly as large a following as did Socialist parties in Europe.

 Checkpoint How did workers respond to the rise of industrialization?

Workers and Big Business Clash

Workers and big business often clashed violently in the latter decades of the nineteenth century. On May 4, 1886, an event known as the Haymarket Riot erupted during a labor rally in Haymarket Square, in Chicago. It began when someone threw a bomb that killed a police officer. More police officers and civilians died in the bloody fight that followed. Government authorities reacted by rounding up eight **anarchists,** political radicals opposed to any form of government, and convicted them of conspiracy to commit murder.

The following excerpt is from the Preamble of the Knights of Labor's Constitution. *What "power" do the Knights of Labor want to place limits on?*

Primary Source "The recent alarming development and aggression of aggregated wealth, which, unless checked, will inevitably lead to the pauperization and hopeless degradation of the toiling masses, render it imperative, if we desire to enjoy the blessings of life, that a check should be placed upon its power and upon unjust accumulation."

—Preamble to the Constitution of the Knights of Labor, 1878

NoteTaking

Reading Skill: Identify Main Ideas Record the main ideas about the rise of organized labor in a concept web like the one below.

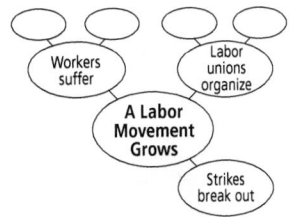

Connect to Your World

Workers' Rights The Haymarket Riot is part of the history of the standard workday's development. During the latter part of the nineteenth century, people worked much longer hours than they do today. This was partly because, in previous eras, most people had worked on farms. In the new industrial jobs, the work environment frequently required workers to operate dangerous machinery in poorly-ventilated spaces—far different from agricultural work, which was regulated by hours of sunlight with tasks done out-of-doors. In

factories, people had trouble staying alert, and therefore safe, for more than eight hours at a time.

During the early 1900s, some large corporations finally adopted the eight-hour day. Ford started an eight-hour workday for its employees in 1914. Federal law gave railroad workers a 48-hour workweek in 1916. Then in 1938, under the New Deal, the Fair Labor Standards Act made the 44-hour workweek law in the United States. Congress amended the law to provide a 40-hour workweek in 1940. By the 1950s, the eight-hour workday was common.

Instruct

- **Introduce: Key Term** Explain that when there is widespread political or cultural oppression, radical ideas flourish. As students have read, socialism appealed to many people in the late 1800s. Another group, *anarchists,* or people who are opposed to all forms of government, also gained followers at this time. Have students predict how *anarchists* would become involved in American labor disputes.

- **Teach** During the late nineteenth century, labor disputes often broke into violence, such as the Pullman Strike shown on the next page. Have students discuss the causes and effects of specific labor disputes, such as the Haymarket Riot, the Homestead Strike, and the Pullman Strike. To facilitate the discussion, make a two-column chart, and list the major labor disputes in the first column. In the second column, invite volunteers to provide information from the text on the results of each action.

- **Quick Activity** Ask a volunteer to read aloud the Primary Source quotation on this page. Ask **Is this a realistic or an unrealistic goal for a labor organization in any time? Why or why not?** *(Sample answer: It is an unrealistic goal because it is so broad and would be counter to the capitalist system.)*

Independent Practice

Have students compare and contrast the labor disputes of this period by writing newspaper articles. Articles should be written in the standard informative style of newspapers, including headlines and answering the questions who, what, where, when, how, and why.

Monitor Progress

As students write their articles, circulate to make sure that they understand the major labor disputes of the time.

Answers

 They organized unions to improve their pay and working conditions.

Caption the accumulation of vast wealth and the power that stems from it

Assess Progress L3

- Have students complete the Section Assessment.

- Administer the Section Quiz. Teaching Resources, **p. 36**

- To further assess student understanding, use Progress Monitoring Transparencies, **18.**

Reteach

If students need more instruction, have them read the section summary.

Reading and Note Taking L3
Study Guide

Adapted Reading and L1 L2
Note Taking Study Guide

Spanish Reading and L2
Note Taking Study Guide

Extend L4

To extend the lesson content about technological advances of this period, have students complete the Enrichment Worksheet, *Research: Inventions in the Hall of Fame.* Teaching Resources, **pp. 13–14**

Answer

✓ Organized labor experienced several setbacks when unions held strikes against large corporations; some of these strikes became violent and brought about government intervention.

In 1892, fighting broke out between steelworkers and Andrew Carnegie's business partner, Henry Frick, in Homestead, Pennsylvania. With the help of strikebreakers, or those sent to break up the strike, and members of the National Guard, Frick and Carnegie crushed the Homestead Strike and broke apart a union that represented skilled workers in the plant. As a result, steelworkers went without a union for decades.

Two years later, in 1894, a nationwide strike erupted against the railroad companies. The Pullman Strike began with a walkout in the Illinois town where the famous Pullman passenger cars were manufactured when an economic downturn led the Pullman company to cut hours and wages. The American Railway Union, led by Eugene V. Debs (who was fired by George Pullman for protesting pay cuts and layoffs), came to the Pullman workers' aid. In turn, other railroad companies joined forces with Pullman. By the time the strike ended, President Cleveland had sent federal troops to Chicago to protect the railroads and the U.S. Attorney General had thrown Debs in jail for violating an injunction against leading the strike.

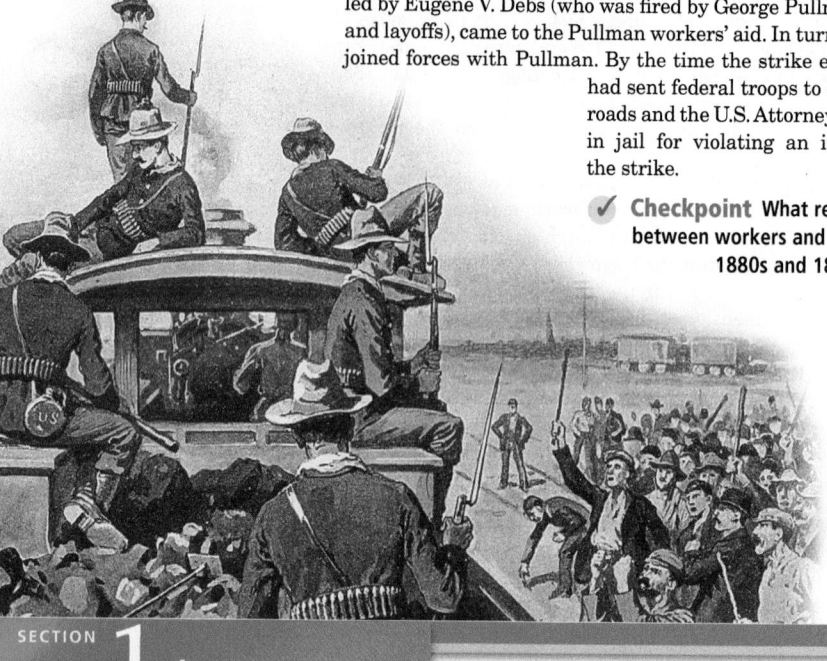

▼ Soldiers guard a mail train against rioters during the Pullman Strike, 1894.

✓ **Checkpoint** What resulted from the clashes between workers and big business during the 1880s and 1890s?

SECTION 1 Assessment

Progress Monitoring Online
For: Self-test with vocabulary practice
www.pearsonschool.com/ushist

Comprehension

1. **Terms and People** For each item below, write a sentence explaining how it related to the rise of big business.
   - Andrew Carnegie
   - John D. Rockefeller
   - trust
   - Social Darwinism
   - Gospel of Wealth
   - monopoly

2. **NoteTaking Reading Skill: Identify Causes and Effects** Use your table to answer the Section Focus Question: What factors led to the industrialization of America, and what impact did industrialization have on society?

Writing About History

3. **Quick Write: Select a Topic** Choose a topic from this section that interests you, such as America's industrial growth or the rise of big business. To prepare for an oral presentation, write what you already know about the topic in one or two paragraphs.

Critical Thinking

4. **Determine Relevance** How did technology impact the growth of the United States?

5. **Draw Inferences** How did the rise of big business lead to the formation of labor unions?

6. **Summarize** What occurred during the Pullman Strike?

Section 1 Assessment

1. Sentences should demonstrate students' understanding of how each term or person helped big business grow.

2. abundant natural resources, a growing labor force, the public's positive view of entrepreneurship, and government support of business; Industrialization raised the standard of living for many Americans, improved transportation and communication, and spurred urban growth. However, the growth of a wealthy business class helped widen the gap between rich and poor.

3. Paragraphs should demonstrate students' understanding of the subject, based on their reading.

4. Sample answer: Technology increased productivity, created new industries, strengthened the economy, and raised the standard of living for many people in the United States.

5. As corporations became more powerful, workers were often exploited, and they formed unions to receive decent wages, improve conditions, and obtain fair treatment in the workplace.

6. The conflict between Pullman and its workers grew as pro-labor forces joined strikers, and other companies sided with Pullman. The workers eventually lost when federal troops were sent to protect the railroads and a major union leader, Eugene V. Debs, was jailed.

For additional assessment, have students access **Progress Monitoring Online** at **www.pearsonschool.com/ushist**.

▲ Workers in Armour's meatpacking house, Chicago, Illinois

WITNESS HISTORY

The New Urban America

Chicago—with its enormous stockyards and packinghouses, railroad depots, and machine-making plants—symbolized the new urban America perhaps more than any other city. Chicago attracted waves of immigrants who filtered into the city's ever-expanding ethnic neighborhoods. The poet Carl Sandburg describes the city:

❝Hog Butcher for the World,
    Tool Maker, Stacker of Wheat,
    Player with Railroads and the Nation's
      Freight Handler;
    Stormy, husky, brawling,
    City of the Big Shoulders. . . .
    Come and show me another city with lifted head
      singing so proud to be alive and coarse and strong
      and cunning.❞

—Carl Sandburg, "Chicago,"
from *Chicago Poems,* 1916

Immigration and Urbanization

Objectives
- Understand the reasons that immigrants came to America.
- Explain the immigrants' experience upon arriving in the United States.
- Identify the changes that took place in cities of the late nineteenth century.
- Describe the urban middle class.

Terms and People
Ellis Island   suburb
Angel Island   tenement

NoteTaking
Reading Skill: Understand Effects As you read the section, use a concept web to record the various effects of immigrants on American society.

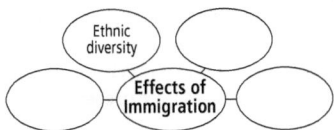

Why It Matters "Give me your tired, your poor, your huddled masses yearning to breathe free," Emma Lazarus wrote in the poem *The New Colossus* in 1883. But many Americans did not share her sentiments that the United States should welcome all newcomers. Instead, they feared that the waves of immigrants from Southern and Eastern Europe, as well as from Asia, posed a threat to their American way of life. They feared immigrants would take their jobs and undermine their culture. Today, however, nearly all acknowledge that these immigrants helped build America into one of the most powerful nations in the world. Lazarus's poem now appears at the main entrance to the Statue of Liberty, reflecting the nation's vision of itself as a refuge for the immigrants of the world. **Section Focus Question: Why did immigrants come to the United States, and how did they impact society?**

New Immigrants Come to America

Immigration is central to American history. In the 1840s and 1850s, millions of Europeans came to America, especially from Ireland and Germany. Between 1880 and 1920, the United States experienced a second, even larger, wave of immigration. From afar, these immigrants saw America in biblical terms, as a "land of milk and honey." Yet upon arrival, some, because of the hardships they had to endure, cursed their new homeland as a place of tears.

Vocabulary Builder

Use the information below and the following resource to teach students the high-use word from this section. Teaching Resources, Vocabulary Builder, p. 11

High-Use Word	Definition and Sample Sentence
urban	*adj.* of, relating to, or characteristic of a city The **urban** roadways in our state are congested with traffic during rush hour.

SECTION 2

Step-by-Step Instruction

Objectives
As you teach this section, keep students focused on the following objectives to help them answer the Section Focus Question and master core content.

- Understand the reasons that immigrants came to America.
- Explain the immigrants' experience upon arriving in the United States.
- Identify the changes that took place in cities of the late nineteenth century.
- Describe the urban middle class.

Prepare to Read

Background Knowledge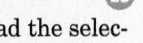
Ask students to recall the growth of U.S. industry in the late 1800s. Ask them to predict how this growth might encourage immigration.

Set a Purpose L3
- **WITNESS HISTORY** Read the selection aloud.

  Ask **In what terms does Sandburg describe Chicago?** (*He describes Chicago in terms of the types of jobs its citizens do.*) **What is the tone of this excerpt?** (*Sample answer: The tone is celebratory because it commemorates the diversity and strength of a growing city.*)

- **Focus** Point out the Section Focus Question, and write it on the board. Tell students to refer to this question as they read. (*Answer appears with Section 2 Assessment answers.*)

- **Preview** Have students preview the Section Objectives and the list of Terms and People.

- **NoteTaking** Using the Guided Questioning strategy (TE, p. T20), have students read this section. As they read, have students record the various effects of immigrants on American society. Reading and Note Taking Study Guide

New Immigrants Come to America ⓛ₃

Instruct

- **Introduce** Review with students the "push-and-pull" theory of immigration. Have students offer reasons that might *pull* people to a new country or might *push* them away from the country in which they live.

- **Teach** Ask **Why did this new wave of immigrants seem more threatening to many Americans than had earlier immigrants?** *(The newer immigrants' home countries were not those of most of the earlier immigrants. Many new immigrants did not speak English, and many practiced different religions.)* **Do you think "push" factors or "pull" factors were more important to immigrants at this time?** *(Sample answers: Pull factors were more important because the United States was relatively prosperous, and many people came here for jobs and to improve their standard of living. Push factors were more important because Jews, for example, were being murdered in Eastern Europe and fled for their lives.)*

- **Quick Activity** Display Color Transparency: *New Immigrants.* Use the lesson suggested in the transparency book to lead a discussion about the countries of origin of the immigrants who came to America between 1880 and 1910. Color Transparencies **A-74**

Independent Practice

Have students study the *Reading a Chart: Immigration, 1880–1920* worksheet, and tell them to answer the questions. Teaching Resources, **p. 33**

Monitor Progress

As students fill in their concept webs, circulate to make sure that they record effects, not causes. For a completed version of the concept web, see Note Taking Transparencies, **B-83**.

Answer

✓ Pre–Civil War immigrants came mostly from northern and western European countries. They were primarily Protestant, and most spoke English. Between 1880 and 1920, immigrants came primarily from Southern and Eastern Europe, were Catholic or Jewish, and often did not speak English.

New Immigrants Arrive From Many Lands Between 1880 and 1920, more than 18 million European immigrants poured into the United States. Another quarter million immigrants came from Asia, especially from China. Unlike most who had preceded them, the European newcomers came from Southern and Eastern Europe. Most were Catholic or Jewish (instead of Protestant), which changed the religious makeup of the nation. They also did not speak English, had few skills, and had little experience living in cities.

Push-and-Pull Factors Much like those who came from Northern and Western Europe, the new wave of immigrants left their homelands for a variety of "push-and-pull" reasons. Religious persecution and mandatory military service were among the "push" factors. They were "pulled" to the United States by the prospect of finding work in the expanding industrial economy, as well as by the promise of greater political and religious freedom. Like earlier generations of immigrants, they hoped to provide a better future for their children.

✓ **Checkpoint** How did pre–Civil War immigrants differ from those who entered America between 1880 and 1920?

▲ Chinese immigrants on Angel Island, San Francisco Bay

Vocabulary Builder
urban–(ER buhn) *adj.* of, relating to, or characteristic of a city

The Immigrant Experience

Although no two immigrants had exactly the same experience, all of them had to endure the long journey to America and then find a job and a place to live. In addition to very difficult living and working conditions, they had to overcome prejudice, both from those who had been in the United States for generations and, in many cases, from their own assimilated countrymen who derided them as "greenhorns," meaning they looked green, or new, to the American way of life.

Arriving in a New Land After a journey that could range from a week to several months, the immigrants would arrive in New York City, Boston, Philadelphia, Galveston, or another American port. Starting in 1892, the vast majority first stepped on American soil at **Ellis Island** in New York Harbor. Government clerks asked the immigrants a series of questions at these entry points. If authorities believed the newcomers posed a risk to public health, perhaps because they had polio or another disease, they would send them back to Europe.

From the early 1850s to 1882, hundreds of thousands of Chinese immigrants came to the West Coast, mostly to work on the new railroads that were being built. Between 1910 and 1940, most Asian immigrants disembarked at **Angel Island** in San Francisco Bay, where they experienced much harsher conditions than those at Ellis Island. Some waited months or even years before processing and questioning came to an end.

Opportunities and Challenges Some immigrants received help from fraternal organizations, such as the Irish Hibernian Association, the Hebrew Immigrant Aid Society, and the Italian Knights of Columbus. Most had some kin or contacts from the old country who helped them find work and a place to live. Still, adjusting to urban industrial life could prove extremely difficult. Neighborhoods and living quarters were overcrowded; work was long, dangerous, and poorly paid; and the threat of disease, such as tuberculosis, was ever present.

Differentiated Instruction Solutions for All Learners

ⓛ₄ Advanced Readers ⓛ₄ Gifted and Talented Students

Remind students that the immigrants who reached the United States in the pre–Civil War years were different from those who came in the late nineteenth century and early twentieth century. Have students do research to create a graphic organizer that compares the two groups. For example, the organizer might be in the form of a two-column chart. Tell students to label the first column "Immigration, 1820–1860" and the second column "Immigration, 1880–1920." Explain that organizers should include such facts as the number of immigrants, major countries of origin, destinations within the United States, religion, skills, marital status, and so on.

ELLIS ISLAND

On a typical day in the early 1900s, thousands of immigrants steamed past the Statue of Liberty in New York Harbor and landed at Ellis Island. As soon as immigrants arrived, they checked their baggage and then walked up to the Great Hall on the second floor. Doctors watched closely, looking for signs of illness. About one tenth of the immigrants were marked with chalk and sent for a closer medical examination. In the Great Hall, immigrants waited in long lines for an interview with a customs officer who checked their paperwork and determined whether they would be able to support themselves. If approved and admitted to the United States, immigrants would meet up with family members, whom they may not have seen in years. By 1924, an estimated 17 million immigrants had passed through this process at Ellis Island.

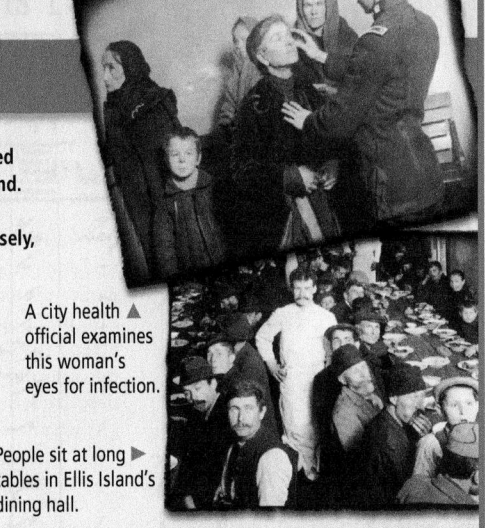

▲ A city health official examines this woman's eyes for infection.

► People sit at long tables in Ellis Island's dining hall.

◄ Immigrants land at Ellis Island, New York. Some carry a piece of paper in their mouth that they hope to exchange for a visa.

A ship's log contains passengers' names and information, such as who paid for their tickets and where they are going. ▼

Thinking Critically
1. **Identify Point of View** What did immigrants experience upon their arrival at Ellis Island?
1. **Draw Conclusions** How might the culture of the United States be different if immigrants were not an integral part of its history? Explain.

▲ Aerial view of Ellis Island

The new immigrants contributed to the American economy and culture in countless ways. They built churches and synagogues, established foreign-language newspapers, and established cultural institutions, such as Yiddish theaters. Irving Berlin, who immigrated to the United States in 1893, composed "God Bless America" and "White Christmas," two of the most popular songs in American history. Still, some Americans did not recognize the new immigrants' contributions for many years.

✓ **Checkpoint** What experiences were common to most immigrants who came to America?

Connect to Your World

Angel Island Between 1910 and 1940, about 175,000 Chinese immigrants passed through the Angel Island immigration entry point, located on a small island in the middle of San Francisco Bay. However, the purpose of Angel Island was to keep out immigrants.

Chinese immigrants had been coming to the United States at least since the California Gold Rush days of the mid-1800s. Many Chinese also came in the 1860s to help build the railroads in the west. The resent-ment of American workers, who thought that the Chinese were taking jobs away from them, resulted in the passage of the Chinese Exclusion Act of 1882. The act was not repealed until 1943. Until then, the Chinese who attempted to enter the United States through California often met a barrier at Angel Island.

Today, the Angel Island immigration station is a historic site. Like Ellis Island, it is a reminder—although not necessarily a pleasant one—of an important part of this country's immigrant history.

The Immigrant Experience Ⓛ3

Instruct

- **Introduce: Key Terms** and **Vocabulary Builder** Point out to students the key terms *Ellis Island* and *Angel Island* (in bold) in the text, as well as the vocabulary term *urban.* Ask students why immigration stations were located outside *urban* areas.

- **Teach** Using the Think-Write-Pair-Share strategy (TE, p. T23), have students discuss what the immigrant experience at this time must have been like. Ask **What difficulties did new immigrants face?** *(They had to adjust to a new culture, and many had to deal with widespread prejudice.)* **How did many immigrants bring their cultures with them?** *(They built their own churches and synagogues, started foreign-language newspapers, and reestablished cultural traditions.)*

- **Analyzing the Visuals** Draw students' attention to the images included in the Infographic on Ellis Island. Ask **What kinds of people passed through Ellis Island?** *(They seem to be mostly white and not wealthy.)*

Independent Practice

Tell students to imagine that they are immigrants and that their ship has just entered New York Harbor in 1900. Have students write a letter to a family member at home, expressing how they felt about a new life in the United States.

Monitor Progress

As students write their letters, circulate to make sure that they understand the feelings that new immigrants might have had at such a time.

Answers

Thinking Critically
1. They had to pass a medical examination and then complete an interview with a customs official.
2. Sample answer: The culture of the United States would not have absorbed the diverse elements of many cultures—music, food, language, religion.

✓ Immigrants often arrived after a difficult journey. Finding work and a place to live was challenging, especially because of discrimination.

Instruct

- **Introduce: Key Terms** Have students locate the key terms *suburbs* and *tenements* (in bold) in the text. As a class, create a brief Venn diagram to compare life in the *suburbs* with life in the *tenements.*

- **Teach** Have students read the Primary Source quotation on this page. Ask **Why did cities grow during the late nineteenth and early twentieth centuries?** *(Many American-born farmers and foreign immigrants flocked to cities for jobs or to experience a more interesting and cosmopolitan lifestyle.)* **How did technology improve urban life?** *(Electric streetlights increased safety, new modes of transportation helped people move around and away from the city, and improvements in sewer and water systems improved sanitation and public health.)* **How did the rapid rise in population in some cities create problems?** *(A shortage of decent, affordable housing existed for lower income immigrants; these people were often forced to live in dirty, crowded, and dangerous tenements.)*

- **Analyzing the Visuals** Have students examine the photos of cities on this page and on the page following the American Issues Connector feature. Have students offer adjectives to describe the scenes. Ask students how they think cities are similar or different today.

Independent Practice

Instruct students to create a newspaper advertisement that announces the availability of new homes in a suburb. The advertisement should attempt to attract people to suburban living by mentioning its advantages.

Monitor Progress

As students write their advertisements, circulate to make sure that they understand the features that might have attracted people to move from cities to suburbs.

Answer

Caption Many cities were overcrowded because of a lack of housing; many people were forced to live in cramped, unhealthy, and dingy tenements.

Cities Experience Growth and Change

Throughout most of U.S. history, the vast majority of Americans lived in rural areas. In the latter half of the nineteenth century, however, cities grew so rapidly that it became clear that urban Americans would soon make up the majority. At the same time, cities themselves changed. They grew larger, more complex, and much more diverse in terms of the ethnic heritage of their residents.

Immigrants and Farmers Move to Cities Both foreign-born immigrants and American-born farmers moved to cities for a variety of reasons. Foremost, as the centers of industry and commerce, cities offered newcomers jobs. They also promised a more cosmopolitan lifestyle than rural areas. Residents could attend the theater and sporting events; socialize at neighborhood bars, coffee-houses, and dance halls; and shop at department stores. Theodore Dreiser described the allure of a department store in *Sister Carrie,* a novel about a farm girl who moves to the big city.

Urban Life
New electric streetlights (top) line the streets in St. Louis, Missouri. Mulberry Street (bottom) in New York City is filled with life as the streets teem with people. *What was the impact of the rapid growth that occurred in cities during this time?*

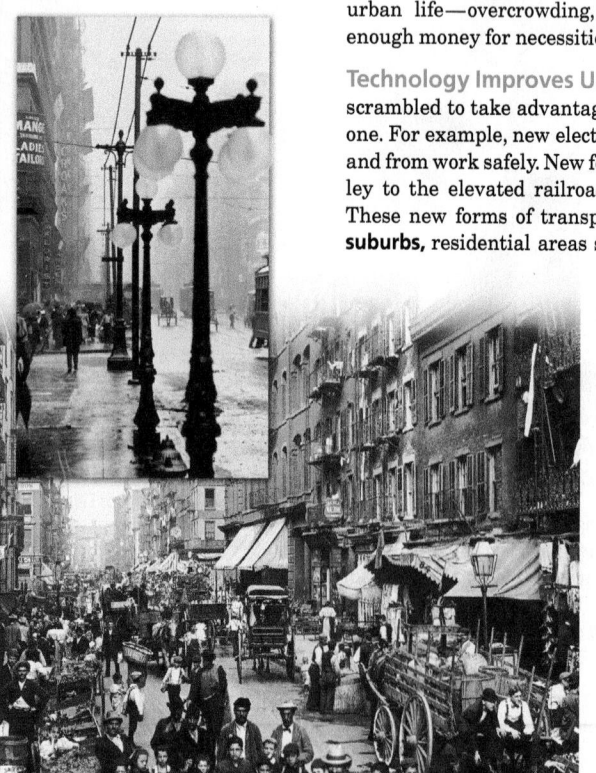

> **Primary Source** "Carrie passed along the busy aisles, much affected by the remarkable display of trinkets, dress goods, station[e]ry, and jewelry. Each separate counter was a show place of dazzling interest and attraction. . . . There was nothing there, which she could not have used—nothing which she did not long to own. The dainty slippers and stockings, the delicately frilled skirts and petticoats, the laces, ribbons, hair combs, purses, all touched her with individual desire."
> —Theodore Dreiser, *Sister Carrie,* 1900

Of course, as Sister Carrie soon discovered, she could not afford the items in the store. Like most immigrant workers, she had to adjust to the difficulties of urban life—overcrowding, vice, and crime. Most newcomers barely made enough money for necessities in their new neighborhoods.

Technology Improves Urban Life As cities grew, city planners and workers scrambled to take advantage of new technologies to make life better for everyone. For example, new electric streetlights allowed factory workers to travel to and from work safely. New forms of transportation—from the horse-drawn trolley to the elevated railroad and electric trolleys—allowed cities to expand. These new forms of transportation eased travel and made possible the first **suburbs,** residential areas surrounding the cities. Those who could not afford the new suburbs lived in densely populated urban ghettos, or areas where one ethnic or racial group dominates.

Although urban boosters celebrated the construction of the first skyscrapers and subways as symbols of technological advancement, perhaps the most important progress took place in the innards of the nation's cities. Public-works departments constructed miles of sewers and massive reservoirs, along with intricate systems of underground pipes to carry fresh water to residents and wastewater away from their homes. The ability of America's cities to quickly create the infrastructure necessary to support such a huge influx of residents remains one of the nation's greatest industrial accomplishments.

Urban Life Creates Problems Despite some of the technological advances, urban dwellers faced

Differentiated Instruction Solutions for All Learners

L1 Special Needs Students L2 English Language Learners L2 Less Proficient Readers

Note that a series of events led to the growth of cities and suburbs. The following list contains major stages in that process:

- Industries grow and new jobs open.
- People move to cities for jobs in industry.
- Cities begin to grow as more people move in.
- Cities become overcrowded.

- Transportation improvements allow people to move to suburbs from overcrowded cities.
- Suburbs grow.

On the board, write the events out of sequence, and have each student write them on a separate sheet of paper. Next, tell students to cut the paper into strips, one for each sentence. Then, have partners rearrange the strips of paper to put the sentences into the proper sequence.

TRACK THE ISSUE

How does migration affect patterns of settlement in America?

Several migration trends have shaped settlement patterns in the United States. One is the movement of people to the West and to the southern "Sunbelt." Another is the movement from rural to urban areas, which then developed suburbs. These migrations have had a great influence on American life. Use the timeline below to explore this enduring issue.

1862 Homestead Act
Offer of free land brings settlers to the Great Plains

1880-1920 Urban Migration
Millions of Americans leave farms for the city. By 1920, urban population exceeds rural population.

1910–1930 Great Migration
Southern blacks move north, giving rise to the first large African American neighborhoods in northern cities.

1950s Suburban Flight
Mass movement begins from central cities to suburbs.

1970s Present Sunbelt Growth
Sunbelt states grow rapidly as Americans move to the warmer, southern half of the country.

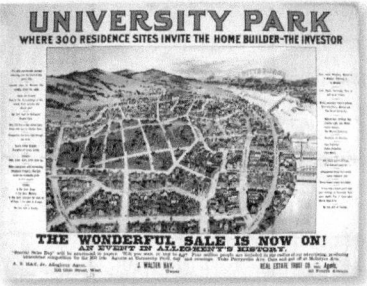

A poster advertising a new suburb

A modern suburb of Las Vegas, Nevada

DEBATE THE ISSUE

Expanding Suburbs American suburbs began in the 1800s but mushroomed after World War II. By 1990, nearly half of all Americans lived in suburbs. These communities offered many benefits. But critics say they have contributed to urban sprawl, traffic congestion, and other problems.

"Suburbanization represents a significant improvement in the quality of life for people who settle there. Most people who move out of their older homes do so because their needs have changed. Suburban and rural areas often meet these new needs better than older, more densely populated central cities."
—Samuel Stanley, Reason Public Policy Institute

"Sprawling patterns of growth are an inefficient use of land that scatters jobs, houses, schools and shopping across the landscape. . . . It leaves people little choice but to use their auto for any trip. . . . It fragments the ecosystems that protect our drinking water and wildlife habitat and that provide recreational opportunities that we all enjoy."
—Robert J. Pirani, Regional Plan Association, New York

TRANSFER Activities

1. **Compare** How do the two quotations differ in their perspective on suburbs?

2. **Analyze** How did the growth of the suburbs affect urban life and growth?

3. **Transfer** Use the following Web site to see a video, try a WebQuest, and write in your journal. www.pearsonschool.com/ushist

History Background

Early Suburbs In the late 1800s, the first suburbs were built for the wealthy. The idea was to create a healthy and pleasant natural environment in which upper-class or upper middle-class families could live in tasteful homes in parklike surroundings, removed from the congestion and filth of cities. Places such as Llewellyn Park, New Jersey, were among the earliest suburbs. The stately homes of the residents were surrounded by landscaped gardens, open green space, and roads that looked like curved country lanes.

When the middle class expanded and transportation improved in the late 1800s and early 1900s, suburbs expanded too. Suburbs remained the domain of the wealthy and the upper-middle class until the post-World War II period, when the ability to build cheap homes and the means to finance them through the GI Bill made ownership of suburban homes possible for ordinary Americans. This was the era of huge developments such as Levittown, New York, which came to epitomize the suburbs in the mid-twentieth century.

Instruct

- **Introduce** Have students read the introductory sentences and the three red headings under "Social and Cultural Trends." Have them predict what they will learn under each red heading. Then, have students read to find out whether their predictions were accurate.

- **Teach** Using the Idea Wave strategy (TE, p. T22), have students discuss the ways that industrialization and urbanization changed American society. Ask **Why did a new middle class rise during the late 1800s and early 1900s?** *(Industries had become more sophisticated, creating more white-collar jobs.)* **How did the expansion of higher education, which included more women, affect the U.S. economy?** *(A more highly educated workforce provided a more skilled workforce. People were able to earn more money and spend more on consumer goods, which boosted the economy.)* **How did the American lifestyle during the late 1800s and early 1900s change?** *(Disposable income and leisure time increased for many people. People began to spend more time and money on mass entertainment, such as sporting events and amusement parks.)*

- **Analyzing the Visuals** Ask students to study the photograph on the next page and describe factors that allowed more people to purchase goods from department stores and catalogs.

Independent Practice

Have students review the blue heading "Social and Cultural Trends" by making an outline of the content.

Monitor Progress

As students work on their outlines, make sure that they are including only the most important ideas. If necessary, review the outline format.

Answer

✔ Cities were noisy, crowded, and dirty; many of the less well-to-do residents lived in small, cramped, and unhealthy tenements. With few parks, poor or immigrant children had to play in the city streets.

▲ A traffic jam of people, horse-drawn trolleys, and electric trolleys in Chicago, Illinois

the problem of overcrowding. Rapid growth led to a shortage of housing, and unscrupulous landlords often took advantage of the newcomers' desperate need for a place to live. Immigrants crowded into subdivided homes called **tenements**. These tenements often housed twenty families, each in a virtually airless, tiny, cramped space where parents and children slept, ate, and often worked together. With few windows and little sanitation, tenements were unhealthy and dangerous. To make matters worse, few parks or public squares existed, leaving children only the streets as play areas. There, they encountered heaps of garbage, thieves, and rival street gangs.

✔ **Checkpoint** What was urban life like for most city residents?

Social and Cultural Trends

Even with its problems, industrialization and urbanization created the foundation for the emergence of a more modern society. Instead of providing just basic needs for survival, the economy began to generate a wide variety of consumer goods and leisure activities. Besides the wealthy elite, a growing middle class had the ability to take advantage of many of these new goods and services. The working classes also occasionally had the opportunity to attend a ballgame or visit an amusement park.

A New Middle Class Emerges As industries grew larger and more sophisticated, they generated a demand for skilled white-collar workers—engineers, accountants, and attorneys. Big businesses hired salesclerks to sell their goods and managers to supervise their workers. In turn, these workers (mostly men) and their families had enough money to purchase items that historically only the elite could afford. Advances in technology and greater business efficiency and productivity further expanded the variety of goods and services within their reach.

One place where the middle class could find the things they desired was at the modern department store. New York shoppers flocked to Macy's, and Philadelphians flooded Wanamaker's. To boost sales, these department stores advertised in local newspapers and magazines, creating an atmosphere that made shopping fun.

Culture and Entertainment Abound The growing middle class also supported an expansion of higher education. At the same time, colleges and universities began to transform their curriculums. Some even began to focus on training graduate students. An increasing number of women went to college. Overall, illiteracy declined and a high school diploma came within reach for more and more people.

Alongside the expansion of education, the arts thrived. Some of the nation's greatest authors wrote during this time period. Among them were Edith Wharton and Mark Twain. Ironically, Twain considered the era crass and often satirized

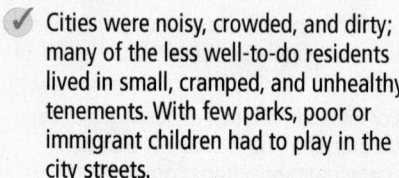

Differentiated Instruction Solutions for All Learners

L1 Special Needs Students **L2 English Language Learners** **L1 Less Proficient Readers**

Have partners use library and Internet resources to find photographs of Americans during the late 1800s and early 1900s. Ask students to select photos of people who are enjoying and participating in a leisure activity, such as attending a sporting event or visiting an amusement park. Have them print out or photocopy the images they find. Then, have students write a few sentences or words that describe the activity and compare it to similar activities today. Remind students to consider what the people in the photograph are doing, how they are dressed, what their mood might be, what the facilities look like, and so on.

it. Other well-known authors included the poet Emily Dickinson and the novelist Henry James.

Perhaps one of the most important cultural developments of the era was the rise of mass entertainment, from collegiate and professional sports to amusement parks. Major league baseball, with teams in many of the nation's largest cities and in stadiums that charged admission, led the way. Mark Twain touted baseball as "the very symbol, the outward and visible expression of the drive and push and rush and struggle of the raging, tearing, booming nineteenth century." Daily newspapers advanced the fortunes of professional sports by establishing sports pages dedicated to covering the games.

Religion Attracts Urban Masses As America's cities grew, religious leaders appealed to the urban masses. Liberal theologians stressed the importance and value of each individual person. Building on this idea, Walter Rauschenbusch and others developed the Social Gospel movement, which promoted better working conditions and decent wages.

Dwight L. Moody and other evangelical Protestants traveled from city to city with their religious revival meetings. Moody used preaching, inspirational prayer, and gospel songs to spread a message of Christian love and compassion. After Moody left town, local congregations would swell with new members.

✓ **Checkpoint** How did religious leaders appeal to city residents?

The Department Store
Pedestrians peer into a Marshall Field's department store (below). Even people in rural areas had access to department-store items from a Sears, Roebuck and Company catalog (below left).

Assess and Reteach

Assess Progress (L3)

- Have students complete the Section Assessment.

- Administer the Section Quiz.
  Teaching Resources, **p. 37**

- To further assess student understanding, use Progress Monitoring Transparencies, **19**.

Reteach

If students need more instruction, have them read the section summary.

Reading and Note Taking (L3)
Study Guide

Adapted Reading and (L1) (L2)
Note Taking Study Guide

Spanish Reading and (L2)
Note Taking Study Guide

Extend (L4)

See this chapter's Professional Development pages for the Extend Online activity on immigration.

Answer

✓ They developed the Social Gospel movement, which promoted better working conditions and decent wages. They also used preaching, inspirational prayer, and gospel songs to spread their message.

SECTION 2 Assessment

Progress Monitoring *Online*
For: Self-test with vocabulary practice
www.pearsonschool.com/ushist

Comprehension

1. Terms and People For each term below, write a sentence explaining how it relates to either immigration or urbanization.
- Ellis Island
- Angel Island
- suburb
- tenement

2. NoteTaking Reading Skill: Understand Effects Use your completed concept web to answer the Section Focus Question: Why did immigrants come to the United States, and how did they impact society?

Writing About History

3. Quick Write: Gather Evidence In order to prepare for an oral presentation, you should gather information on your selected topic. Research to gather evidence on the growth and development of cities as discussed in this section. List several sources and image ideas after your preliminary research.

Critical Thinking

4. Identify Point of View What challenges did immigrants face upon their arrival in America?

5. Recognize Cause and Effect (a) How did technology affect the growth of cities? **(b)** How did the growth of cities affect housing within them?

6. Identify Central Issues How did industrialization and urbanization lead to the rise of the middle class?

Section 2 Assessment

1. Sentences should demonstrate an understanding of the terms listed.

2. Immigrants came to the United States to escape religious persecution and military service. They hoped to find work, a better life, and greater freedom. Immigrants helped build the United States with their labor, and they contributed to the diversity of American culture.

3. Lists should demonstrate students' ability to locate sources and images on the growth and development of cities.

4. Sample answer: Immigrants had to find jobs to support themselves. Many had to learn English and face discrimination.

5. (a) New forms of transportation, such as electric trolleys and subways, helped cities grow. Electric streetlights made cities safer. New water and sewer systems provided healthier drinking water and better sanitation to residents. (b) Rapid population growth in some cities caused housing shortages that forced many immigrants and poor people into crowded tenements.

6. Industrialization and urbanization increased the number of white collar jobs, which paid better than jobs for laborers. More people had more money to spend, so they were able to afford an education, consumer goods, and homes.

For additional assessment, have students access **Progress Monitoring *Online*** at **www.pearsonschool.com/ushist.**

Objectives

As you teach this section, keep students focused on the following objectives to help them answer the Section Focus Question and master core content.

- Explain the development of the New South

- Understand the impact on Native Americans as settlers moved to the West.

- Identify who moved to the West and their reasons for doing so.

Background Knowledge ⒀

Review the ways that industrialization, urbanization, and immigration changed the Northeast and Midwest. Ask students to predict the effects that these changes will have on the less developed South and West.

Set a Purpose ⒀

- **WITNESS HISTORY** Read the selection aloud.

    Ask **As workers sang this song, how did their work affect the future growth of the country?** *(The railroads that they were building expanded into the South and the West, helping those regions develop.)*

- **Focus** Point out the Section Focus Question, and write it on the board. Tell students to refer to this question as they read. *(Answer appears with Section 3 Assessment answers.)*

- **Preview** Have students preview the Section Objectives and the list of Terms and People.

- **NoteTaking** Using the Guided Questioning strategy (TE, p. T20), have students read this section. As they read, have students summarize the main events that occurred in the New South and in the West. Reading and Note Taking Study Guide

◀ Workers lay railroad track in Nebraska, 1866.

▲ Golden spike that joined Central Pacific and Union railroads, Promontory, Utah, 1869

Working on the Railroad

Railroad construction boomed in the latter half of the nineteenth century. The railroads opened the West to a rush of settlers and played a key role in the rise of a number of southern cities. Hundreds of thousands of workers constructed about a quarter of a million miles of railroad tracks. Thousands more worked for the railroads after the tracks had been completed. As they toiled, many sang one of America's most popular folk tunes:

❝I've been working on the railroad,
All the livelong day.
I've been working on the railroad,
Just to pass the time away.
Don't you hear the whistle blowing?
Rise up so early in the morn.
Don't you hear the captain shouting,
'Dinah, blow your horn'?❞
—from "I've Been Working on the Railroad,"
Unknown

The South and West Transformed

Objectives

- Explain the development of the New South.

- Understand the impact on Native Americans as settlers moved to the West.

- Identify who moved to the West and their reasons for doing so.

Terms and People

sharecropping	assimilate
Dawes Act	open range

NoteTaking

Reading Skill: Summarize Prepare an outline to summarize the main events of the section.

I. The South and West Transformed
  A. The New South
    1. Industries and Cities Grow
      a. Railroad construction
      b.

Why It Matters In the wake of the Civil War, southerners sought to rebuild their economy, knowing they could not simply revive the old system of plantation agriculture based on slave labor. The end of the war also unleashed a massive wave of migration to the West, which led to a boom in ranching, mining, and farming. This migration would cause the end to a way of life for most American Plains Indians. These developments transformed the way people in the South and the West lived. **Section Focus Question: What were the most important developments in the South and the West?**

The New South

After Reconstruction came to an end, some of the South's leading citizens hoped to create a new economy. Henry Grady, the editor of the *Atlanta Constitution,* touted what he called a "New South." Unlike the Old South, the New South would have a mixed economy. Rather than shipping its raw products, namely cotton, to northern textile mills, it would develop its own manufacturing firms.

Industries and Cities Grow To an extent, Grady's vision took hold. Textile mills cropped up in the Carolina hill country, and the

Use the information below and the following resource to teach students the high-use word from this section. Teaching Resources, Vocabulary Builder, p. 11

High-Use Word	Definition and Sample Sentence
decade	*n.* ten-year period The construction project should have taken nine years to complete, but it was a full **decade** before it was finished.

timber industry expanded in the Gulf States. Making use of nearby iron deposits, Birmingham, Alabama, developed into a steel-producing center. In the years following Reconstruction, railway construction boomed. Taking note of these developments, Wilbur Fisk Tillett of Vanderbilt University concluded that few if any parts of the country had made "such a marvelous advance" in such a short period of time.

Yet, such optimistic assessments glossed over persistent problems that beset the region. While the southern economy grew, it did not grow as rapidly as the economies of the North and the Midwest. Shortages of capital compelled southern industrialists to borrow from northern financiers, to the benefit of New York bankers. High illiteracy rates, persistent discrimination against African Americans, and a distrust of foreign immigrants weighed down the South.

Southern Farmers Face Difficult Times Hard times especially hit southern farmers. Overly dependent on a single product—cotton—southern farmers, white and black, suffered from declining prices for their crops. Also, beginning in 1890, farmers faced a new pest called the boll weevil. This beetle could completely destroy an entire planting, leaving farmers with little choice but to move north for jobs.

The **sharecropping** system also contributed to the hardships that southern farmers faced. Under this system, landowners dictated the crop and provided the sharecropper with a place to live, as well as seeds and tools, in exchange for a share of the harvested crop. Landowners and merchants often cheated sharecroppers at harvest time and discouraged them from diversifying their crops. Often, sharecroppers had to forfeit their entire crop just to pay off their previous debt and then had to take on further debt to survive.

African Americans Suffer Setbacks Although some African Americans managed to buy land and gain a higher education, overall the post-Reconstruction

The Sharecropping System

In theory, sharecropping provided an opportunity for poor, landless freedmen and white southerners to save money to purchase their own land. However, as the chart at right illustrates, sharecropping proved to be an endless cycle of debt and poverty that southern farmers could rarely escape. As agriculture was key to the southern economy, the sharecropping system remained a major source of labor until mechanized farming reduced the need for human laborers by the 1940s.

Why was the sharecropping system considered an endless cycle for southern farmers?

◄ Cotton was the primary crop of sharecroppers.

Sharecropping Cycle of Poverty

1 Landowner provides land, seed, and tools to sharecropper in exchange for a large share of the harvested crop.

2 Sharecropper purchases supplies from landowner's store on credit, often at high interest rates.

3 Sharecropper plants and harvests the crop.

4 Landowner sells the crop and takes the predetermined share. The sharecropper's portion of the crop is worth less than the amount owed to the landowner.

5 Sharecropper must promise the landowner a larger share of the next year's crop and becomes trapped in a cycle of debt.

Differentiated Instruction Solutions for All Learners

L4 Advanced Readers **L4 Gifted and Talented Students**

The infestation of boll weevils that descended on the cotton crop in the South during this era decimated agriculture across large areas. Crops were destroyed and farm families were ruined. Have students research the boll weevil problem and its impact on the farms and people of one area of the South. Then, have each student take the part of a farmer affected by the blight, writing a journal entry about what he or she is experiencing.

Encourage students to include descriptive language, details, and facts about daily life during that period to make their writing more interesting and vivid. Invite volunteers to share their journal entries with the class.

The New South **L3**

Instruct

- **Introduce: Key Term** Write the key term *sharecropping* (in bold) on the board. Explain that it is a compound word formed from the words *share* and *cropping.* Have students consider the meaning of the two words that form *sharecropping,* and ask them to predict the term's meaning.

- **Teach** Remind students that the South had little industry before the Civil War and that the conflict devastated the region. Ask **What was Grady's vision of the "New South"?** *(a mixed economy that would develop its own industries and businesses)* **Why did development fall short of Grady's vision?** *(There was a shortage of investment capital; many workers were illiterate and unskilled; immigrants were not as welcome in the South as in the North; discrimination against African Americans marginalized a large part of the population; and cotton was largely destroyed by a boll weevil infestation in the South.)*

- **Analyzing the Visuals** Have students study the chart on this page. Then, have them describe the standard of living for farmers or farm workers in the South at this time. Ask **How did the boll weevil make farmers' lives even more difficult?** *(It killed cotton plants, destroying crops and forcing many farmers to move away.)*

Independent Practice

Have students begin to fill in the Note Taking outline summarizing the advances and setbacks in the New South.

Monitor Progress

As students fill in their outlines, circulate to make sure that they understand events that occurred in the South and the West. For a completed version of the outline, see Note Taking Transparencies, **B-84.**

Answer

Often, sharecroppers did not raise enough crops to pay off debts and were forced to continue borrowing money, leading to even more debt.

Instruct

- **Introduce: Key Terms** Draw a concept web on the board, with "Native American Policy" in the center oval and the key terms *assimilation* and *Dawes Act* in subordinate ovals. Use the concept web to preview the terms, providing definitions and explaining how each element was part of the federal government's approach to Native Americans at this time.

- **Teach** Using the Idea Wave strategy (TE, p. T22), discuss the causes and effects of the conflict between Native Americans and white Americans in the West. Ask **Why did Native Americans and white Americans clash in the West?** *(Both groups wanted to live on, take resources from, and control the same land.)* **How did the Dawes Act affect Native Americans?** *(This attempt to subdivide reservations and force Native Americans to assimilate into American society was a failure; Native Americans lost much of their culture and their land, falling further into poverty.)*

- **Quick Activity** Have students read the HISTORY MAKERS biography of Chief Joseph. Ask students to write a few sentences explaining why the speech is so emotionally powerful, even today.

Independent Practice

To learn more about Native American struggles to keep their lands, have students read the *Link to Literature: Chief Joseph Surrenders* and then answer the questions on the worksheet. Teaching Resources, **p. 34**

Monitor Progress

To check students' understanding, have them write one cause-and-effect statement for each of the red headings in their text.

Answer

✔ Advances: Industries grew and the railroad system expanded, leading to the growth of urban areas. Setbacks: There was a lack of capital, and because the South's economy was still dependent on cotton, many farmers were wiped out by the boll weevil.

---

era was a bleak one. Undeterred by northern military forces, which the federal government withdrew from the South after the election of 1876, the white southern majority slowly stripped African Americans of the political and civil rights they had gained following the Civil War. Groups like the Ku Klux Klan terrorized African Americans who sought to exercise their new political rights.

✔ **Checkpoint** What were the advances and setbacks in the development of the New South?

Cultures Clash in the West

For centuries, European settlers and their descendants had pressed westward, pushing Native Americans off their lands. Although Native Americans were lumped together in the minds of most Americans as "Indians," they embraced many different belief systems, languages, and ways of life. In the 1830s, Congress enacted the Indian Removal Act and forced tribes in the Southeast to move beyond the Mississippi River to Indian Territory in present-day Oklahoma.

Plains Indians Under Pressure After the Civil War and a brief period of Indian wars, the federal government compelled Plains Indians to move to reservations, or public land specifically reserved for them. "All who cling to their old hunting-grounds," declared one federal army commander, "will be killed off." The Indians fell into a cycle of poverty and despair. Even when they sought to revive their traditional customs and religious practices, they encountered resistance and persecution.

Approximately 250,000 Plains Indians lived west of the Mississippi River at the end of the Civil War. Their livelihoods were based on hunting buffalo and other wild game. Even before large numbers of farmers and ranchers migrated west, hunters had already started to undermine their culture by decimating the great buffalo herds that roamed the Plains. Killing the animals for their hides and for sport, hunters nearly drove them into extinction and with them, the Native Americans' traditional way of life.

Native Americans Resist Although some Native Americans moved to the reservations without a fight, others decided to defend land they believed was rightfully theirs. In the middle of the Civil War, following a conflict between the Dakota tribe and settlers in Minnesota, the U.S. military captured 300 Dakota warriors and sentenced them to death. Ultimately, the army executed 39 of them, the largest public hanging in American history.

In a reversal of fortune, the Sioux crushed American troops commanded by General George Custer at the Battle of Little Bighorn in 1876. Not a single American soldier survived the famous fight. Custer's Last Stand, as the battle became known, however, proved to be the exception, not the rule.

HISTORY MAKERS

Chief Joseph
(1840?–1904)
For almost three months, starting in June 1877, Chief Joseph led about 700 of his people on a 1,000-mile retreat toward Canada. Despite being outnumbered by at least ten to one, the Nez Percés won several battles and outmaneuvered the army through the month of September. When troops surrounded the Nez Percés, however, Chief Joseph surrendered with this famous speech:

"I am tired of fighting. Our chiefs are killed. . . . The little children are freezing to death. . . . Hear me, my chiefs! I am tired. My heart is sick and sad. From where the sun now stands I will fight no more forever."

—Chief Joseph, "I Will Fight No More Forever," 1877

Chief Joseph's retreat is considered one of the great military actions in American history, despite the fact that he and his people were eventually taken to a reservation.

Differentiated Instruction Solutions for All Learners

L1 Special Needs Students **L2 English Language Learners** **L2 Less Proficient Readers**

To aid students in mastering vocabulary, have them list the key terms and people as well as any high-use words in this section. Tell students that they can also list any other words or phrases that are new to them, such as *ancestral* and *unscrupulous*. Then, have students make flashcards with the term on one side and its definition (or in the case of a person, an identify-ing statement) on the other. For English language learners, you may want to allow students to add explanations in their first language to the flashcards. Pair students, and have partners use the cards to test each other. You may wish to pair English language learners with fluent speakers of English.

American Indian Policy

TRACK THE ISSUE

How should the federal government deal with Indian nations?

From its earliest days, the federal government has grappled with the issue of relations with Native Americans. Since Indians in the West were forced to move onto reservations, government policy has shifted several times. Use the timeline below to explore this enduring issue.

1787 U.S. Constitution
Federal government given power to regulate trade with Native Americans

1824 Bureau of Indian Affairs
Agency created to handle relations with Native Americans

1887 Dawes Act
Government divides reservations into individual land holdings.

1934 Indian Reorganization Act
Tribal governments gain more control over their own affairs.

1975 Indian Self-Determination and Educational Assistance Act
Indians win control over reservation schools and government services.

Comanche girls, 1892

Native Americans in traditional garb press for Indian rights in Washington, D.C.

DEBATE THE ISSUE

Native American Land Claims Today, several Native American nations have made claims to their original lands, arguing that old treaties were illegal. Opponents say that to recognize these claims after so many years would lead to injustice of a different kind to the people now living on those lands.

"For over 200 years, we have endured hardship and indignities from the unjust taking of our ancestral land. We have been confined to a small reservation. We have suffered the painful loss of our traditional way of life.... There will be no actions to evict our neighbors from their homes as we know all too well the pain and suffering displacement causes."
—Tadodaho (Sidney Hill) of the Onondaga Nation, March 10, 2005

"Employing a unique body of laws, today's courts have decided to hear cases based on alleged violations of federal law that occurred over 200 years ago. Even more incredible than the ability and willingness of our judicial system to resurrect these ancient claims, is its [tendency] to apply modern legal interpretations to ancient events and blatantly disregard the historical record."
—Scott Peterman, May 25, 2002

TRANSFER Activities

1. **Compare** How do Tadodaho and Peterman differ on the subject of land claims?
2. **Analyze** How do you think Tadodaho would view the Dawes Act?
3. **Transfer** Use the following Web site to see a video, try a WebQuest, and write in your journal. www.pearsonschool.com/ushist

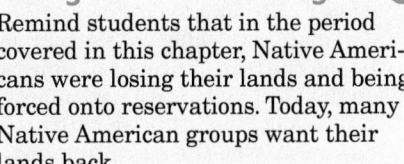

Objectives

- Describe the ways in which federal policy toward Native Americans has shifted since the origins of the nation.
- Identify arguments for and against Native American claims on lands that they inhabited before white settlement of North America.

Background Knowledge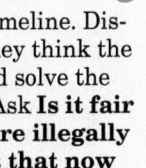

Remind students that in the period covered in this chapter, Native Americans were losing their lands and being forced onto reservations. Today, many Native American groups want their lands back.

Instruct

Review the items in the timeline. Discuss with students how they think the federal government should solve the issues over Indian lands. Ask **Is it fair to return lands that were illegally or immorally taken but that now belong to others?** *(Answers will vary but should be supported by logical reasoning.)*

Monitor Progress

- Have students complete the Issues Connector Worksheet, *American Indian Policy.* Check student work to make sure they grasp the aspects of the issue. Teaching Resources, **pp. 23–26**

- Remind students to complete their American Issues Connector Journal worksheets notes. Review their work for accuracy. Reading and Note Taking Study Guide

History Background

Reservations Native American reservations are recognized by treaties and other agreements. Between 270 and 300 reservations exist in the United States, mostly in the West. The largest is the Navajo Reservation, which covers about 16 million acres in Arizona, New Mexico, and Utah. The smaller reservations consist of less than 100 acres and many of these are located in California.

More than 550 Native American groups exist in the United States; not every group has a reservation, and not every Native American lives on one. Many of the nation's more than one million Native Americans live in towns and cities around the country.

Today's reservations are the legacy of a land policy that sought to confine Native Americans to smaller areas. After Native Americans were pushed west of the Mississippi River, a series of treaties in the mid-1800s limited tribes to progressively smaller areas reserved for them. As a result of the Dawes Act, the federal government took about 60 million additional acres of Native American land.

Answers

Transfer Activities

1. Tadodaho believes that the land claims are legitimate because the lands were taken unjustly. Peterman believes that the claims are questionable and too old to be heard in courts today.
2. Tadodaho would probably find it harmful and unjust.
3. For more information about American Indian Policy, have students access **www.pearsonschool.com/ushist**.

Instruct

- **Introduce: Vocabulary Builder**
Write the vocabulary term *decade* on the board. Explain to students that it means "ten-year period." Point out the word part *deca-* and explain that it comes from a Greek word meaning "ten." Ask students how many *decades* are in a century.

- **Teach** Discuss the fact that the transformation of the West was achieved by the end of the 1800s, especially by the expansion of the railroads. Display Color Transparency: *Driving the Golden Spike*, and discuss the effect of the completion of the transcontinental railroad on the West and on the nation as a whole. Ask **How did the railroads contribute to the development of the West?** *(They opened new areas and brought many settlers to the region. They also linked the West with the cities in the East, allowing farmers to get their crops to market, and brought machinery and other manufactured goods to the region for people to buy.)* **What was the significance of cattle to the western economy?** *(The vast areas of open range and the desire for beef in the eastern cities made cattle one of the main industries in the West and caused the development of the cowboy culture.)* Color Transparencies **A-75**

Vocabulary Builder
<u>decade</u>–(DEHK ayd) *n.* ten-year period

The story of the Nez Percé tribe better depicted the fate of Native Americans. The leaders of the peaceful Nez Percé tribe did not want to desert their ancestral homelands in the Northwest. When General Oliver Otis Howard threatened to force them onto the reservation, however, they realized they could not match the firepower of the United States Army. Therefore, the chief of the Nez Percés, Chief Joseph, reluctantly agreed to lead his people toward a reservation in Idaho. Soon after, however, about 20 young warriors, unhappy about losing their homeland, attacked nearby white settlements. The army immediately began a pursuit of the Nez Percés. With little choice left, Chief Joseph led a fighting retreat toward Canada that is remembered to this day for its skill and audacity. Within 40 miles of the Canadian border, American troops surrounded the Nez Percés. Finally, Chief Joseph surrendered.

The Government Promotes Assimilation Only after the federal government crushed most of the resistance and placed the remaining Indians on reservations did expressions of regret about the nation's Native American policy appear. In 1881, Helen Hunt Jackson wrote *A Century of Dishonor*. As the title of her book suggests, Jackson contended that the United States had pursued a dishonorable policy toward Native Americans since its founding.

Partly in response to her work, which became a bestseller, the United States enacted the **Dawes Act** in 1887. This act sought to destroy the Native American way of life by urging Native Americans to **assimilate,** or to be absorbed into the main culture of American society. The act gave the federal government the authority to divide the reservations into 160-acre privately owned plots of land and to give Native Americans the opportunity to become citizens. However, the act utterly failed to achieve its goal. Indians lost more than 50 percent of their land over the next 50 years, largely to unscrupulous investors, and fell further into poverty.

Yet another tragic chapter in the history of Native Americans took place in 1890. In the northern plains, many Indians looked to their traditions as a way to regain their spirit. Following the advice of some of their shamans, or religious leaders, they took part in the Ghost Dance, an ancient religious ritual. Fearing that the Ghost Dances would lead to an armed insurrection, federal officials banned them. Ultimately, this led to the massacre at Wounded Knee, in which the federal cavalry killed 250 Native Americans, mostly women and children. Black Elk, a Sioux Chief, later wrote about the massacre in *Black Elk Speaks,* one of the most widely read books written by a Native American.

✓ **Checkpoint** What impact did U.S. policies have on Native Americans?

The Transformation of the West

Millions of American citizens poured into the West in the latter half of the nineteenth century. They came searching for gold and silver, to establish farms and ranches, and to work in the cities that sprang up along the railroad lines that stretched as far west as San Francisco. This mass migration would eventually transform the West into a mainstay of the American economy.

Miners and Railroaders The discovery of gold and silver—first in California and later in Nevada, Colorado, Montana, Idaho, and the Black Hills of South Dakota—attracted hordes of prospectors in the middle <u>decades</u> of the 1800s. These prospectors gathered in mining towns, many of which quickly became ghost towns when the gold and silver ran out.

Answer

✓ Initially, U.S. policies forced Native Americans off their lands and onto reservations and also interfered with the practice of cultural traditions. Many Native Americans were killed in clashes with federal troops during this period. Later, laws such as the Dawes Act stripped Native Americans of much of their reservation land and increased their poverty.

Connect to Your World

Impact of Railroads When Leland Stanford drove the last spike to complete the nation's first transcontinental railroad, he joined the Union Pacific Railroad from the East with the Central Pacific Railroad from the West.

The building of the Central Pacific was an amazing feat of engineering and of human courage, perseverance, and strength. The railroad started at Sacramento, California, and headed east. Workers had to dig, blast, and tunnel their way over and through the rock of the most rugged mountain range in the continental United States, the Sierra Nevada. The heavy, gasoline-driven machinery used today for such projects was not available. Most of the work was done with shovels, picks, and other hand tools.

The route of the Central Pacific, completed primarily by thousands of Chinese immigrants, is still part of the nation's transportation system. One of Amtrak's transcontinental lines, the California Zephyr, follows part of this route between Chicago and San Francisco. When a train snakes through the Sierra Nevada passes and rolls across the desert of northern Nevada, it is riding on a rail bed that was constructed more than a century ago.

Economic Development of the West

Geography *Interactive*
For: Interactive map
www.pearsonschool.com/ushist

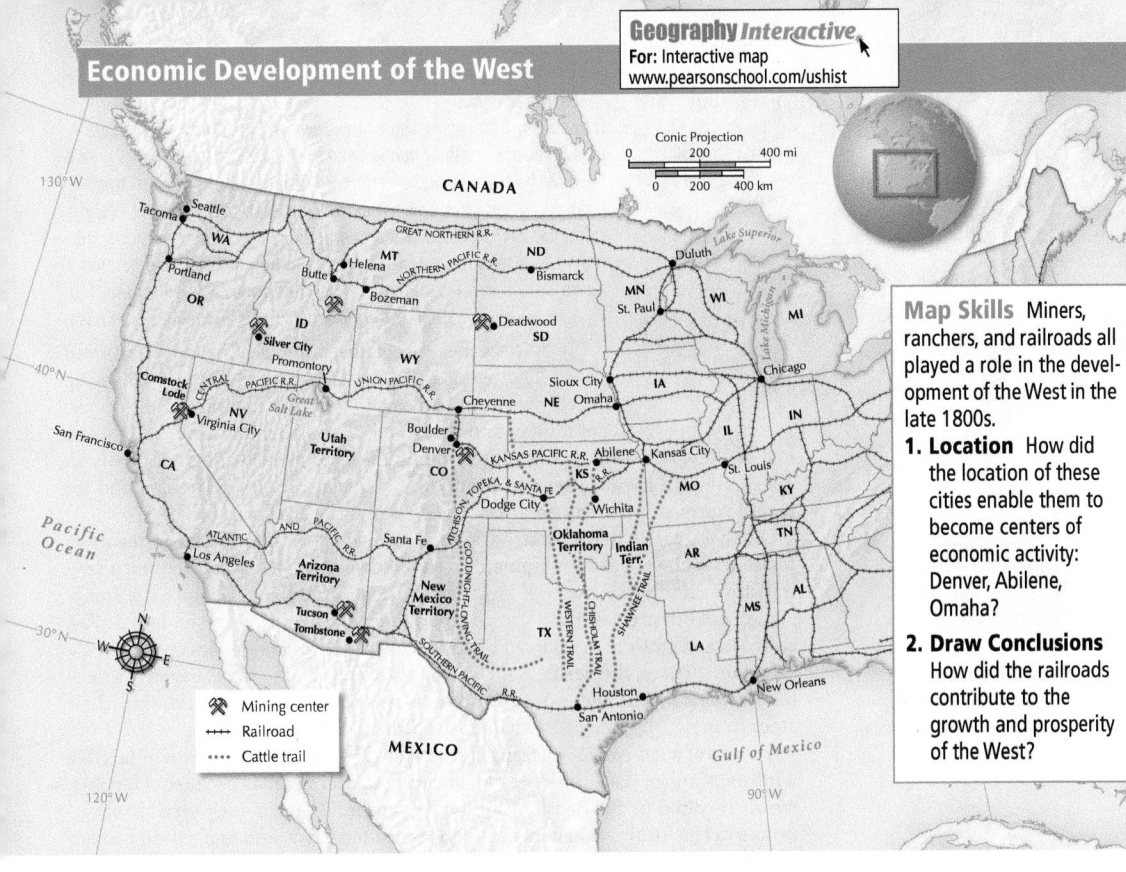

Map Skills Miners, ranchers, and railroads all played a role in the development of the West in the late 1800s.

1. Location How did the location of these cities enable them to become centers of economic activity: Denver, Abilene, Omaha?

2. Draw Conclusions How did the railroads contribute to the growth and prosperity of the West?

While gold and silver provided the first impetus for the migration westward, the transcontinental railroad opened the West to long-term economic development. The construction of the railroads was a massive undertaking. To encourage private corporations to lay the tracks, the federal government granted them nearly 200 million acres of land. In May 1869, the first transcontinental railroad was completed when Leland Stanford drove the final golden spike into the ground at Promontory, Utah.

By the turn of the century, railroads had transformed a country of isolated communities into an interconnected nation of towns and cities. Without the railroads, farmers and ranchers would have found it difficult to get their products to market. In turn, they could not have acquired the farm machinery and home amenities that they wanted. Over time, however, tensions increased between the owners of the railroads, who charged high rates for carrying freight, and the farmers who had no other way to ship their crops to the East.

Ranchers and Farmers Americans from the East who migrated west encountered a strange land. The Great Plains had few trees, very little rainfall, and the land from Missouri to the Rocky Mountains stretched on that way for miles. To heat their homes—initially constructed of sod—they had to burn dried buffalo chips, or dung. They relied on barbed wire for fencing. Moreover, spread out over vast expanses of land, they often lived in social isolation. Ida Lindgren's letter to her mother reflected these difficulties:

- **Analyzing the Visuals** Have students access **www.pearsonschool.com/ushist** to use the Geography Interactive map and then answer the map skills questions in the text. Have students locate each city listed in question 1 on the map. Ask students why most of the economic centers are in the Midwest.

Independent Practice

Ask students to write a sentence explaining how each of the following helped transform the West: ranchers, railroad builders, and miners.

Monitor Progress

Circulate to make sure that students' sentences explain how each group contributed to western development.

Differentiated Instruction Solutions for All Learners

L1 Special Needs Students **L2 English Language Learners** **L2 Less Proficient Readers**

Have students read the Primary Source letter of Ida Lindgren and the paragraph introducing it. Tell students to make an illustration that expresses some aspect of Ida Lindgren's life. Note that students can use material that Lindgren states directly, but they can also read between the lines to draw additional conclusions about her daily life, the way she feels about living on the Great Plains, and what her hopes are. Invite volunteers to present their drawings to the class, along with brief descriptions. Use the drawings as a basis for the discussion of the lives of nineteenth-century American settlers of the Great Plains.

Answers

Map Skills

1. Denver: located near both mines and railroads that could transport ore; Reno: located near a mining center and a transcontinental railroad line; Abilene: located at the head of a cattle trail and near an important east-west railroad line; Omaha: located at the point where east-west and north-south rail lines met

2. As the railroad network grew, it helped expand areas of settlement, transported raw materials to eastern industrial centers, and carried finished goods back to towns in the West.

Assess and Reteach

Assess Progress L3

- Have students complete the Section Assessment.
- Administer the Section Quiz. Teaching Resources, p. 38
- To further assess student understanding, use Progress Monitoring Transparencies, 20.

Reteach

If students need more instruction, have them read the section summary.

Reading and Note Taking Study Guide L3

Adapted Reading and Note Taking Study Guide L1 L2

Spanish Reading and Note Taking Study Guide L2

Extend L4

Have students search in current newspapers and magazines for stories related to the section content. Have them write a summary of the article, explaining how it relates to a topic in this section, and share the summary with the class.

Answer

✓ Many Americans moved west to acquire and work their own farms and ranches. Others came west to strike it rich in the gold and silver mines or in the cattle business. Some went west to work on the railroads.

Era of the Cowboy
Cold Morning on the Range by Frederic Remington (top); American cowboy, c. 1885 (bottom)

Primary Source

❝Beloved Mamma,
It has been a long time since I have written, hasn't it? . . . [W]hen one never has anything fun to write about, it is not fun to write. . . . We have not had rain since the beginning of June, and then with this heat and often strong winds as well, you can imagine how everything has dried out. . . . Then one fine day there came millions, trillions of grasshoppers in great clouds, hiding the sun, and coming down onto the fields, eating up everything that was still there.❞
—Ida Lindgren, Letters, August 25, 1874, Manhattan, Kansas

In spite of these obstacles, millions of Americans moved west. They came to realize the American dream of owning their own land and working for themselves or, in the case of miners and the first cowboys, to make a fortune. At the end of the Civil War, approximately 5 million head of cattle roamed freely in Texas under a herding system created by Mexican ranchers. The demand for meat back east led to the great cattle drives and the era of the cowboy.

On these cattle drives, entrepreneurs herded cattle from Texas to towns in Missouri and Kansas for shipment to the Midwest and the East. Immortalized in fiction and the movies, the long drives ended in Abilene, Dodge City, Tombstone, and other cities that had railroad depots. Beginning in the late 1870s, cowboys and cattlemen realized it made more sense to raise steers on the northern plains. There, the herds could feed on the **open range**—a vast area of grassland owned by the federal government—and then cowboys could ship their steer from nearby railroads without the difficulty of the long drive.

The era of open-range ranching came to an abrupt end with a series of terrible winters. Many of the animals could not get to sheltered areas because of fencing, which resulted in the death of millions of cattle. To avoid such terrible occurrences in the future, ranchers built fences around their land and raised enough feed for their herds.

✓ **Checkpoint** Who moved west in the latter half of the nineteenth century and why?

SECTION 3 Assessment

Progress Monitoring Online
For: Self-test with vocabulary practice
www.pearsonschool.com/ushist

Comprehension

1. Terms and People For each term below, write a sentence explaining its significance to the South or the West.
- sharecropping
- Dawes Act
- open range

2. NoteTaking Reading Skill: Summarize Use your completed outline to answer the Section Focus Question: What were the most important developments in the South and the West?

Writing About History

3. Quick Write: Prepare an Outline Make an outline for an oral presentation on the development of the New South. This will help you structure the information in a logical way. Identify main ideas with Roman numerals and supporting details with capital letters.

Critical Thinking

4. Synthesize Information What factors led to the rise of the New South, and what resulted?

5. Make Generalizations How did the United States change as settlers moved westward?

6. Make Comparisons What were the similarities and differences between the economic development of the South and that of the West?

Section 3 Assessment

1. Students' responses should demonstrate their understanding of each term's significance.

2. Sample response: South: the end of Reconstruction; expansion of railroads and industry; growth of cities; boll weevil infestation; discrimination against African Americans and rise of groups such as the KKK. West: removal of Native Americans from lands; the Dawes Act; gold and silver strikes that lured settlers; expansion of railroads; cattle and cowboy culture.

3. Students should demonstrate their ability to identify and organize main ideas and details in a correct outline format.

4. The South diversified its economy, created more industry, and improved its transportation system. The economy expanded and cities grew.

5. The white and black populations of the West grew as the Native American population declined. New mines and expanding railroads led to an influx of settlers in the region and the growth of towns as mining and transportation centers.

6. The populations of both regions grew with the expansion of railroads. Economic development in the West was based largely on mining and ranching, but the South's development depended primarily on single-crop agriculture, with some local manufacturing.

For additional assessment, have students access **Progress Monitoring Online** at **www.pearsonschool.com/ushist**.

"Gold Bug" from the 1896 McKinley-Bryan presidential campaign ▶

WITNESS HISTORY

The Populist Platform

By the 1890s, numerous Americans felt that the United States lay on the verge of ruin. In reaction, they joined various political movements, such as the Populist, or People's, Party. Made up largely of farmers, the Populists met in Omaha, Nebraska, in 1892, to draft a party platform. The preamble of this platform reflected the angry mood that had set in across much of the nation:

❝The conditions which surround us best justify our cooperation; we meet in the midst of a nation brought to the verge of moral, political, and material ruin. Corruption dominates the ballot-box, the legislatures, the Congress, and touches even the ermine [weasels] of the bench. The people are demoralized. . . .❞

—The Preamble of the Platform of the Populist Party, 1892

▲ Members of the Populist Party, 1890

Issues of the Gilded Age

Objectives

- Understand the segregation and social tensions that troubled the nation during the late 1800s.
- Identify the political and economic challenges that existed during the Gilded Age.
- Analyze the effects of the Populists' programs and activities.

Terms and People

Gilded Age
Jim Crow laws
graft
Pendleton Act

gold standard
Populist Party
William Jennings Bryan

<u>NoteTaking</u>

Reading Skill: Recognize Multiple Causes
Create a chart in which you record key events and developments that led to the Populist movement.

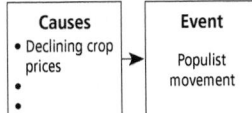

Causes	Event
• Declining crop prices • •	Populist movement

Why It Matters The pace of industrialization and westward expansion in the latter part of the nineteenth century suggested that the United States had reached a new golden age. Yet the nation still faced many troubles, including the distance between people's dreams of wealth and the reality of their sometimes difficult lives. This period during the late nineteenth century is often referred to as the **Gilded Age,** implying that under the glittery, or gilded, surface of prosperity lurked troubling issues, including poverty, unemployment, and corruption. **Section Focus Question: What challenges arose for the nation during the Gilded Age?**

Segregation and Social Tensions

One issue that troubled the nation was the persistence of racial inequality. During the last decades of the nineteenth century, African Americans, other minorities, and women found themselves fighting a losing battle to gain equality.

Separate but Equal During the decades after Reconstruction, southern states passed laws that separated blacks and whites. These laws were known as **Jim Crow laws.** In the 1896 case *Plessy* v. *Ferguson*, the Supreme Court upheld segregation as long as states maintained "separate but equal" facilities for both races. Yet facilities for blacks almost always were inferior. During the same time period, southern states enacted laws such as poll taxes and literacy tests that stripped blacks of the vote. As W.E.B. Du Bois, a leading

Objectives

As you teach this section, keep students focused on the following objectives to help them answer the Section Focus Question and master core content.

- Understand the segregation and social tensions that troubled the nation during the late 1800s.
- Identify the political and economic challenges that existed during the Gilded Age.
- Analyze the effects of the Populists' programs and activities.

Prepare to Read

Background Knowledge L3

Ask students to recall the economic and social changes of this era.

Set a Purpose L3

- **WITNESS HISTORY** Read the selection aloud.

  Ask **What did the Populists think was the most serious problem facing the United States?** *(political corruption at all levels of government)* **How did the Populists want to solve this problem?** *(Sample answer: They wanted people to come together to vote corrupt politicians out of office.)*

- **Focus** Point out the Section Focus Question, and write it on the board. Tell students to refer to this question as they read. *(Answer appears with Section 4 Assessment answers.)*

- **Preview** Have students preview the Section Objectives and the list of Terms and People.

- **NoteTaking** Using the Read Aloud strategy (TE, p. T20), have students read this section. As they read, have students record key events and developments that led to the Populist movement. Reading and Note Taking Study Guide

Vocabulary Builder

Use the information below and the following resource to teach students the high-use word from this section. Teaching Resources, Vocabulary Builder, p. 11

High-Use Word	Definition and Sample Sentence
trend	*n.* general course of events In the late 1800s, a new settlement **trend** developed in which many Americans moved from rural areas to cities.

Segregation and Social Tensions/Political Challenges L3

Instruct

- **Introduce: Key Term** Have students read the section's introductory paragraph. Ask students to decide whether the key term *Gilded Age* (in bold) is appropriate for this era.

- **Teach** Ask **What were Jim Crow laws?** *(laws passed by southern states after Reconstruction to deny civil rights and equality to African Americans)* **Why did some Mexican Americans in the Southwest fight to retain the title to certain lands?** *(Whites prodded the federal government to take away lands pledged to Mexican Americans before those lands became part of the United States.)* **What was the significance of the Pendleton Act?** *(The act attempted to decrease government corruption by creating a civil service system, so that people would obtain government jobs based on merit, not political favors.)*

- **Analyzing the Visuals** Refer students to the political cartoon on this page. Have them explain the main idea of the cartoon. Ask **What is the cartoonist's point about the Senate?** *(that it is controlled by big business)*

Independent Practice

Have students complete *Interpreting a Political Cartoon: The Gilded Age* and answer the questions on the worksheet. Teaching Resources, **p. 35**

Monitor Progress

As students answer the questions on the worksheet, circulate to make sure that they have correctly interpreted the cartoon.

Answers

✓ Jim Crow laws limited African American advancement in the South. Mexican Americans struggled to preserve their lands in the Southwest. Asian immigrants faced discrimination. Women did not have the right to vote nationally.

Analyzing Political Cartoons

1. Large corporations had a lot of influence on the government.

2. Large corporations

---

civil rights activist, observed: "The freedman has not yet found in freedom his promised land."

In spite of these setbacks, some hope for a brighter future emerged. Booker T. Washington, who had been born a slave, built the Tuskegee Institute in Alabama into an important symbol of black self-help. In the same time period, Ida B. Wells's brave crusade against lynching gained some traction, especially among northern blacks who began to organize into clubs and civil rights organizations to demand full equality.

Mexican Americans and Chinese Immigrants Face Discrimination
During the same period, Mexican Americans struggled against long odds to maintain their lands in the Southwest. Prominent whites prodded the federal government to grant them title over property pledged to Mexicans who lived in the Southwest before it became part of the United States. Federal courts tended to side with the whites when Mexican Americans pressed their legal case for the land. Some Mexican Americans resorted to warlike tactics to protect their lands. For instance, masked men known as *Las Gorras Blancas,* or the White Caps, sabotaged railroad lines and cut holes in fences to protest the displacement of Mexican Americans.

Asian immigrants, especially the Chinese, faced persistent discrimination, too. Western states enacted laws that prohibited the Chinese from working at certain jobs. Mobs of white workers terrorized Chinese migrants, claiming the migrants were taking the white workers' jobs. In 1882, the federal government temporarily banned further immigration from China for 10 years under the Chinese Exclusion Act. In 1902, the government made the ban permanent.

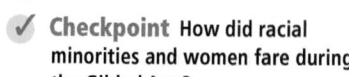

Analyzing Political Cartoons

This nineteenth-century political cartoon titled "The Bosses of the Senate" shows the influence that large corporations exerted on government.
1. How does the cartoonist illustrate the corruption of the time?
2. What do the men towering over the senators represent?

Women's Suffrage Makes Gains
Women experienced both gains and setbacks during the Gilded Age. In spite of tireless efforts by Susan B. Anthony and Elizabeth Cady Stanton, the fight to gain a women's suffrage amendment stalled, although a few western states granted women the vote. At the same time, educational opportunities for women grew. By 1900, women made up one third of all college students.

✓ **Checkpoint** How did racial minorities and women fare during the Gilded Age?

Political Challenges

As future President Woodrow Wilson lamented in 1885, "the conditions of public life in this country are not what they were in the early years of the Republic. We . . . are perplexed at finding ourselves denied a new order of statesmanship to suit the altered conditions." As a result, many of the nation's problems went unresolved.

Differentiated Instruction Solutions for All Learners

L1 Special Needs Students **L2 English Language Learners** **L2 Less Proficient Readers**

As students read the first blue head, "Segregation and Social Tensions," have them search for facts about the problems that African Americans faced in the South during this era. Tell students to make a bulleted list of the information that they find. Then,

have each student use the list to write a one-sentence summary of the material under the blue head. Instruct students to repeat these steps for each of the other blue heads in the section.

Corruption Plagues Government As cities grew, politicians gained power by providing jobs or patronage and services in exchange for political support. **Graft,** or bribery and corruption, touched nearly all aspects of public life. Some politicians, such as George Washington Plunkitt of New York City's Tammany Hall political club, even defended their actions.

Tariffs, Civil Service, and Monetary Policy On the national level, few issues divided the major political parties as much as the tariff, with the Republicans supporting high protective tariffs and the Democrats favoring lower duties, or taxes, on imported goods. Following the assassination of President James Garfield by a disgruntled former federal employee, the Democrats supported the **Pendleton Act,** which created a civil service system for the federal government. This meant that individuals who wanted to work for the government were required to take an exam. They were then given a job based on their performance on the exam, instead of on who they knew. Both Republican and Democratic Presidents also favored a hard monetary policy, the **gold standard,** much to the chagrin of many farmers who felt that this hurt them by keeping prices low.

✓ **Checkpoint** What issues plagued the government during the Gilded Age?

Farmers and Populism

In the late 1880s and early 1890s, a massive political insurgency developed called populism. It grew out of the frustration that many Americans felt toward the federal government. Farmers in particular displayed their anger.

Farmers Face Complex Problems Farmers migrated to the West knowing that they would have to toil long hours in difficult conditions. But they expected that their circumstances would improve and that their children would be better off. Instead, as the nineteenth century drew to a close, many farmers felt that they were losing ground.

Several interrelated problems beset American farmers during this era. The prices paid for the main crops—corn, wheat, and cotton—declined significantly between the end of the Civil War and the early 1890s. At the same time, farmers accumulated growing debts that they found harder and harder to repay. Government monetary policies contributed to both of these <u>trends</u>.

Farmers Organize and Demand Reforms Immediately following the Civil War, farmers came together to address their problems. First, farmers in the Midwest banded together in the Grange movement. Their counterparts in the South and the Plains states established the Farmers' Alliance. These organizations sought to lower shipping and storage rates, either through government regulation of the railroads or use of grain elevators, or both.

Members of the Farmers' Alliance, in both the South and the West, soon formed the People's Party, or the **Populist Party,** and met in Omaha, Nebraska, to spell out its views. They endorsed General James Weaver for the presidency in 1892, as well as slates of candidates for state and local offices. They did well in several

Farmers' Alliance Seeks Lower Storage Rates
Farmers waiting to unload wheat at a grain elevator, 1879

Vocabulary Builder
trend–(trehnd) *n.* general course of events

Instruct

- **Introduce: Key Term** and **Vocabulary Builder** Point out to students the key term *Populist Party* (in bold) and the vocabulary word *trend(s)* in the text on this page. Tell students to read to find out what *trends* led to the rise of the *Populist Party.*

- **Teach** Using the Idea Wave strategy (TE, p. T22), discuss with students the political and economic issues in the United States that led to the development of populism and the Populist Party. Ask **What problems did farmers face?** (*Crop prices were low, and many farmers were sinking into debt.*) **What was the significance of the fight over "free silver"?** (*The Populists wanted the nation to go off the gold standard and mint silver coins, which would make money cheaper and, therefore, more available.*) Have students discuss the Primary Source quotation on the following page. Ask **Were the Populists successful? Why or why not?** (*Sample answers: The Populists ultimately failed because their candidates were not elected, and few of their initiatives became law. They were successful because William Jennings Bryan's campaign style of appealing directly to the people became the norm, and reforms, such as the secret ballot, direct election of senators, and the graduated income tax, became law.*)

- **Quick Activity** Display Color Transparency: *The Election of 1896.* Have students analyze the map showing voting patterns in the presidential election of 1896, in which William McKinley opposed Populist candidate William Jennings Bryan. Color Transparencies **A-76**

Independent Practice

Ask students to complete the Note Taking charts for this section.

Monitor Progress

As students fill in their charts, circulate to make sure that they understand the events that led to the Populist movement. Note Taking Transparencies, **B-85**.

Answer

✓ government corruption, whether or not to have a tariff, civil service reform, and conflict over monetary policy

Assess and Reteach

Assess Progress   L3

- Have students complete the Section Assessment.

- Administer the Section Quiz. Teaching Resources, p. 39

- To further assess student understanding, use Progress Monitoring Transparencies, 21.

Reteach

If students need more instruction, have them read the section summary.

Reading and Note Taking   L3
Study Guide

Adapted Reading and   L1 L2
Note Taking Study Guide

Spanish Reading and   L2
Note Taking Study Guide

Extend   L4

Have students conduct research to create an annotated timeline of William Jennings Bryan's life, including important personal milestones as well as public events or achievements.

Answers

 The rise of the Populists grew out of the frustration that many Americans, especially farmers, felt toward the federal government. Farmers believed that government policies contributed to their economic problems.

Plains states, leading some to believe that they could challenge the two major political parties on the national level.

The Populists favored reforms that addressed their main problems. To lower the cost of transportation, they sought regulation or ownership of the railroads. In order to make it easier for farmers to borrow money and pay off their debts, they called for the creation of subtreasury banks and the coinage of silver or "free silver." **William Jennings Bryan,** the Democratic and Populist candidate for the presidency in 1896, made the call for free silver the centerpiece of his campaign. The Populists also sought political and economic reforms, such as the secret ballot, the direct election of senators, and a graduated income tax.

Economic Crisis and Populism's Decline During the election of 1896, the Populists hoped to gain the support of many industrial workers whose situations had taken a turn for the worse because of an economic depression. In one of the hardest fought campaigns in American history, Bryan crisscrossed the country, championing the cause of the American farmer and denouncing the monetary policies of the Republicans, namely the gold standard.

▲ William J. Bryan, during a speech made in the 1896 presidential campaign

> **Primary Source** "If they [the Republicans] dare to come out in the open field and defend the gold standard as a good thing, we will fight them to the uttermost. Having behind us the producing masses of this nation . . . we will answer their demand for a gold standard by saying to them: You shall not press down upon the brow of labor this crown of thorns, you shall not crucify mankind upon a cross of gold."
>
> —William J. Bryan, "Cross of Gold" Speech, 1896

In part because he failed to convince industrial workers that the policy of free silver would benefit them, Bryan failed to win a state outside of the South and the West. As a result, William McKinley, the Republican candidate, won the presidency. The Populist Party never recovered from its defeat in 1896. Yet, even in defeat, the Populist movement had an impact upon the political system. Bryan's style of appealing directly to the people became the norm rather than the exception. In addition, a number of the Populist's specific proposals, such as the graduated income tax, became law during the Progressive Era.

✓ **Checkpoint** What factors led to the rise of the Populists?

SECTION

4 Assessment

Progress Monitoring Online
For: Self-test with vocabulary practice
www.pearsonschool.com/ushist

Comprehension

1. Terms and People For each term below, write a sentence explaining its significance.
- Gilded Age
- Pendleton Act
- gold standard
- Populist Party

2. NoteTaking Reading Skill: Recognize Multiple Causes Use your completed chart to answer the Section Focus Question: What challenges arose for the nation during the Gilded Age?

Writing About History

3. Quick Write: Use Numbered Note Cards It is helpful to use numbered note cards to organize the main points for an oral presentation. On note cards, write the main ideas about the rise of populism. Determine the order in which you will likely deliver your speech on this topic, and number each card accordingly.

Critical Thinking

4. Identify Main Ideas Describe several factors that caused the public to feel demoralized during the late 1800s.

5. Predict Consequences What additional actions might the government have taken to address the political corruption of the Gilded Age?

6. Determine Relevance What impact did the Populists have on society?

Section 4 Assessment

1. Sentences should demonstrate students' understanding of the significance of each term.

2. Injustice against minorities and women continued, government corruption was rampant, disagreements about monetary policy flared, and farmers faced economic hardship.

3. Students should demonstrate their ability to organize and briefly record main ideas for an oral presentation in the form of numbered note cards.

4. evidence of government corruption, racial and gender inequality, the assassination of a President, and the economic difficulties that hard-working people faced

5. Sample answer: The government might have made examples of corrupt politicians by sending them to jail; it might also have allowed the public to vote on more political issues to remove the possibility of exchanging favors for political support.

6. The Populists popularized the campaign style of appealing directly to the people. Some of their proposals, such as the graduated income tax, became law during the Progressive Era.

For additional assessment, have students access **Progress Monitoring Online** at
www.pearsonschool.com/ushist.

Women in American Society

TRACK THE ISSUE

Why do Americans disagree over women's rights?

In early America, women had few legal rights. They could not vote, hold office, or work at most jobs. Married women could not own property and were under the legal authority of their husbands. The women's movement helped change this, but Americans are still divided over women's rights. Use the timeline below to explore this enduring issue.

1848 Seneca Falls Convention
Women meet in upstate New York to declare support for women's rights.

1869 The National Woman Suffrage Association
Anthony and Stanton form organization to fight for women's suffrage

1920 Nineteeth Amendment
Women gain right to vote

1964 Title VII of the Civil Rights Act
Law protects women against job discrimination.

1972 Title IX of the Education Codes
Law bans sex discrimination in schools.

Supporters of women's suffrage gather in protest.

While many women today have successful careers, some still feel limited in their efforts to land higher positions in their chosen fields.

DEBATE THE ISSUE

Women in the Workplace On average, women earn less than men in the workplace. This wage gap has led to charges of sex discrimination. Feminists also argue that a "glass ceiling" keeps many women from rising to the top of their profession. But other factors may be involved, too.

❝The wage gap is the result of a number of factors in addition to discrimination, such as the differences in women's education, their shorter time in the workforce, and their concentration in a narrow range of jobs that are underpaid because women are in them. Nonetheless, a significant portion is attributable to discrimination.❞

—Sonia Pressman Fuentes, founding member, National Organization for Women

❝[Feminists] often portray working women as victims of rampant discrimination . . . [which] renders women powerless in the face of an impenetrable glass ceiling. While discrimination does exist in the workplace, levels of education . . . and time spent in the workforce play a far greater role in determining women's pay and promotion.❞

—Naomi Lopez, Director, Center for Enterprise and Opportunity

❓ *TRANSFER* Activities

1. **Compare** How do the two writers agree? How do they disagree?

2. **Analyze** Affirmative action makes it possible for women and minorities to compete in the workplace. Which of the two women quoted above might support this?

3. **Transfer** Use the following Web site to see a video, try a WebQuest, and write in your journal. www.pearsonschool.com/ushist

History Background

The Seneca Falls Convention On July 19 and 20, 1848, about 260 women and 40 men gathered in a church in Seneca Falls, New York, for the first women's rights convention in the United States.

Organizers Lucretia Mott and Elizabeth Cady Stanton had met several years earlier at an antislavery convention in London. When the organizers of the convention refused to seat them and others because they were women, Mott and Stanton decided to work for both abolition and women's rights.

Attendees at the Seneca Falls Convention voted on a set of resolutions calling for equality for women in

several areas. However, a demand to allow women the vote was considered too radical. Then, Frederick Douglass rose and spoke in defense of the resolution. Douglass was persuasive, and the call for women's suffrage was made part of the convention's final declaration.

In 1920, the Nineteenth Amendment finally granted women throughout the nation the right to vote. However, only one woman who attended the Seneca Falls Convention, Charlotte Woodward, lived to see that happen.

Objectives

- Describe how the legal situation for women spurred the women's rights movement in the 1800s.
- Identify major milestones in the struggle for women's rights in the United States.
- Explain opposing viewpoints for the wage gap that exists today between men and women.

Background Knowledge L3

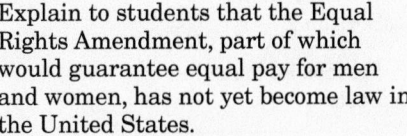

Explain to students that the Equal Rights Amendment, part of which would guarantee equal pay for men and women, has not yet become law in the United States.

Instruct L3

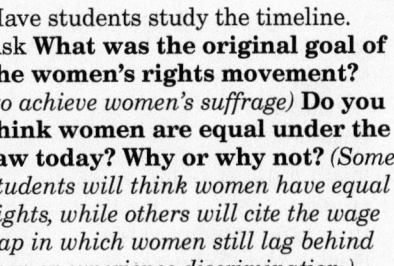

Have students study the timeline. Ask **What was the original goal of the women's rights movement?** *(to achieve women's suffrage)* **Do you think women are equal under the law today? Why or why not?** *(Some students will think women have equal rights, while others will cite the wage gap in which women still lag behind men or experience discrimination.)*

Monitor Progress

- Have students complete the Issues Connector Worksheet, *Women in American Society.* Check their work to make sure that students grasp all aspects of the issue. Teaching Resources, **pp. 27–30**

- Remind students to complete their American Issues Connector Journal worksheets notes. Review their work for accuracy. Reading and Note Taking Study Guide

Answers

Transfer Activities

1. Both agree that level of education, experience in the workforce, and career choices affect lower pay for women. Only Fuentes thinks that discrimination is a major factor in pay disparity.

2. Fuentes

3. For more information about Women in American Society, have students access **www.pearsonschool.com/ushist**.

Quick Study Guide

Quick Study Guide

- Have students use the Quick Study Guide to prepare for the chapter test. Students may wish to refer to the following sections as they review:

Causes of Industrialization
Section 1
Section 2
Section 3

The "New South"
Section 2

Reasons for Immigrating
Section 3

The Populist Party Platform
Section 4

Key Events of Industrial America
Section 1
Section 2
Section 3
Section 4

- For additional review, remind students to refer to the Reading and Note Taking Study Guide
Section Note Taking
Section Summaries

- Have students access **www.pearsonschool.com/ushist** for this chapter's History Interactive timeline, which includes expanded entries and additional events.

- If students need more instruction on analyzing graphic data, have them read the Skills Handbook, **p. SH21.**

For **Progress Monitoring Online,** refer students to the Self-test with vocabulary practice at **www.pearsonschool.com/ushist.**

Quick Study Guide

Progress Monitoring Online
For: Self-test with vocabulary practice
www.pearsonschool.com/ushist

■ Causes of Industrialization

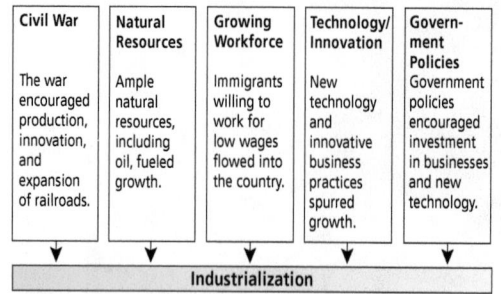

Civil War	Natural Resources	Growing Workforce	Technology/ Innovation	Government Policies
The war encouraged production, innovation, and expansion of railroads.	Ample natural resources, including oil, fueled growth.	Immigrants willing to work for low wages flowed into the country.	New technology and innovative business practices spurred growth.	Government policies encouraged investment in businesses and new technology.

↓ ↓ ↓ ↓ ↓

Industrialization

■ Reasons For Immigrating

Push and Pull Factors	
Push Factors	**Pull Factors**
• Religious persecution	• Religious freedom
• War and mandatory military service	• Political freedom
• Economic hardship	• Affordable land
• Lack of jobs	• Factory jobs

■ The "New South"

Economic Growth	Limits to Growth
• Development of new industries such as textiles, lumber, iron, steel	• Shortage of skilled workers
• Expansion of rail lines	• Wealth concentrated in hands of a few
• Some agricultural diversification to reduce dependence on cotton	• Few banks to finance business expansion

■ The Populist Party Platform

- Increase in money supply
- Graduated income tax
- Federal loan program for farmers
- Election of U.S. senators by popular vote
- Eight-hour workday
- Restriction on immigration
- Government ownership of railroads

☑ Quick Study Timeline

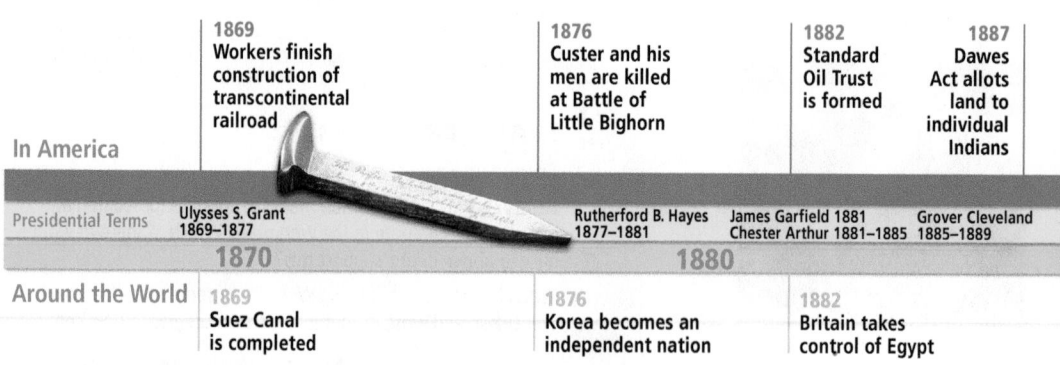

In America

| 1869 Workers finish construction of transcontinental railroad | 1876 Custer and his men are killed at Battle of Little Bighorn | 1882 Standard Oil Trust is formed | 1887 Dawes Act allots land to individual Indians |

Presidential Terms Ulysses S. Grant 1869–1877 | Rutherford B. Hayes 1877–1881 | James Garfield 1881 Chester Arthur 1881–1885 | Grover Cleveland 1885–1889

1870 | **1880**

Around the World

| 1869 Suez Canal is completed | 1876 Korea becomes an independent nation | 1882 Britain takes control of Egypt |

Differentiated Instruction Solutions for All Learners

L1 Special Needs Students   **L2 English Language Learners**   **L2 Less Proficient Readers**

Use the following study guide resources to help students acquiring basic skills:
Adapted Reading and Note Taking Study Guide
- Section Note Taking
- Section Summaries

Use the following study guide resources to help Spanish-speaking students:
Spanish Reading and Note Taking Study Guide
- Section Note Taking
- Section Summaries

American Issues
•—•—• **Connector**

By connecting prior knowledge with what you have learned in this chapter, you can gradually build your understanding of enduring questions that still affect America today. Answer the questions below. Then, use your American Issues Connector study guide (or go online: www.pearsonschool.com/ushist).

Issues You Learned About

● **Migration and Urbanization** Immigrants have overcome many obstacles in their quest to improve their lives in the United States.

1. The Immigrant Experience Millions of immigrants moved to American cities in the late 1800s and early 1900s. Write a short narrative describing the life of one of these immigrants. Consider the following:
  • reasons for immigration
  • working conditions
  • life in the cities
  • the process of adapting to American culture

● **Technology and Society** New technology can bring both positive and negative changes to society.

2. List the three main causes of industrial expansion in the United States.

3. What positive effects did industrialization have on American society? What negative effects did it have?

4. Identify and describe one invention that impacted the lives of industrial workers.

● **American Indian Policy** During the 1800s, Native Americans lost their native lands to white settlers.

5. In the post–Civil War years, what policy did the federal government impose on Native Americans? How did they respond?

6. Why did Chief Joseph surrender to federal troops?

7. What were the causes and effects of the Dawes Act?

Connect to Your World	Activity

Poverty and Prosperity: Wealthy Companies and Individuals In this chapter, you learned about the leading companies and entrepreneurs from the age of big business. Study the list of companies here, and choose one. Then, go online or to your local library to learn more about your choice. Find out the company's main business, revenue, size, area of operation, and its contributions to society, including charitable work. Write one or two paragraphs to have a profile of the company.

Top Ten Private U.S. Companies by Revenue, 2004

1. Cargill
2. Koch Industries
3. Mars
4. Publix Super Markets
5. Bechtel
6. PricewaterhouseCoopers
7. Ernst & Young
8. C&S Wholesale
9. Meijer
10. HE Butt Grocery

1890 **Congress passes Sherman Antitrust Act**	1894 **Pullman Strike occurs**	1907 **Immigration to United States reaches all-time high**

Benjamin Harrison 1889–1893 Grover Cleveland 1893–1897 William McKinley 1897–1901 Theodore Roosevelt 1901–1909

1890   **1900**   **1910**

1889 **Eiffel Tower is completed in Paris**	1893 **New Zealand grants women the right to vote**	1899 **Boer War breaks out in southern Africa**	**History Interactive** For: Interactive timeline www.pearsonschool.com/ushist

American Issues
•—•—• **Connector**

Tell students that the main issues for this chapter are Migration and Urbanization, Technology and Society, and American Indian Policy. Then, ask students to answer the Issues You Learned About questions on this page. Discuss the Connect to Your World topic(s), and ask students to complete the project that follows.

American Issues Connector

1. Narratives should demonstrate students' comprehension of the way each of the factors affected immigrants.

2. the nation's wealth of natural resources, a growing labor pool, and pro-business policies

3. Positive: rise in the standard of living for many people; new and more efficient production techniques; improvements in transportation and communication; Negative: misuse of power by corporations; the widening gap between rich and poor; union clashes with large corporations

4. Sample answer: Electric streetlights made traveling to and from work in cities safer for workers.

5. Sample answer: Native Americans were forced to live on reservations. Some accepted this, but others fought to retain their lands.

6. Chief Joseph surrendered because he realized that they could neither continue their flight nor win if they fought.

Connect to Your World

Paragraphs should demonstrate students' ability to research a subject and organize information.

For additional review of this chapter's enduring issues, remind students to refer to the Reading and Note Taking Study Guide American Issues Journal.

Chapter Assessment

Terms and People

1. a single corporation that controls an entire industry; it passed the Sherman Antitrust Act.

2. Social Darwinism is a philosophy that views life as a struggle in which only the fittest survive.

3. Ellis Island and Angel Island were immigration stations and the entry points for millions of immigrants coming to the United States in the late 1800s and early 1900s. Immigrants had medical exams and interviews to determine whether they could stay.

4. Sharecropping was a system in which farmers received a place to live, seeds, and tools to produce crops on another person's land. In return, they gave the landowner a share of the crop. Often, sharecroppers had to turn over almost an entire crop to pay their debts, limiting their chances of getting ahead.

5. laws passed in southern states to separate blacks and whites

Focus Questions

6. abundant natural resources, a growing labor force, the public's positive view of entrepreneurship, and government support of business; Industrialization raised the standard of living for many Americans, improved transportation and communication, and spurred urban growth. However, corporations became extremely powerful, widening the gap between rich and poor.

7. to escape religious persecution, military service at home, and to find work; they helped build the United States with their labor and contributed to the diversity of American culture.

8. Sample response: South—the end of Reconstruction; expansion of railroads and industry; growth of cities; West—gold and silver strikes that lured settlers; expansion of railroads; cattle and cowboy culture

9. Injustice against minorities and women continued, government corruption was rampant, disagreements about monetary policy flared, and farmers faced economic hardship.

Terms and People

1. Define **monopoly**. How did the federal government attempt to prevent the formation of monopolies?

2. What was **Social Darwinism**?

3. What were **Ellis Island** and **Angel Island**? What happened at these locations?

4. Explain how **sharecropping** worked. Did sharecroppers have a fair chance to get ahead economically?

5. What were the **Jim Crow laws**?

Focus Questions

The focus question for this chapter is **How did industrialization affect the United States?** Build an answer to this big question by answering the focus questions for Sections 1 through 4 and the Critical Thinking questions that follow.

Section 1
6. What factors led to the industrialization of America, and what impact did industrialization have on society?

Section 2
7. Why did immigrants come to the United States, and how did they impact society?

Section 3
8. What were the most important developments in the South and the West?

Section 4
9. What challenges arose for the nation during the Gilded Age?

Writing About History

Preparing for an Oral Presentation The late 1800s were a time of growth and great change in the United States. As industrialization took hold, immigrants arrived, businesses boomed, and cities expanded as people moved there to live and to work. Soon, industrialization also spread to the South and led to the development of the West. Write an oral presentation that you might deliver to a private corporation during this time to encourage it to play a role in the development of the West.

Prewriting
• Gather information on why corporations might have been interested in the development of the West in the late 1800s.
• Make a graphic organizer to arrange the information you find. In a two-column chart, for example, one column could be entitled "Why People Are Moving West" and the other "Why Businesses Should Move West."

Critical Thinking

10. **Explain Effects** How did the rise of industrialization change the nature of American businesses?

11. **Predict Consequences** What would a modern-day entrepreneur who believed in the Gospel of Wealth do with his or her fortune?

12. **Determine Relevance** Explain the relationship between the growth of the middle class, the changes in the economy, and new forms of mass entertainment.

13. **Analyze Information** According to Henry Grady, what would characterize the "New South"? Did the society he envisioned develop? What was the "New South" like for African Americans?

14. **Draw Conclusions** Would farmers and ranchers have settled in the West without the construction of the transcontinental railroad?

15. **Explain Causes** Why was the Pendleton Act passed?

16. **Evaluate Credibility of Sources** The editor of a farmers' paper wrote in 1890, "There are three great crops raised in Nebraska. One is the crop of corn, one a crop of freight rates, and one a crop of interest." Do you think this statement should be taken at face value? Explain your reasoning.

Drafting
• Develop a working thesis in which you clearly state the purpose of your speech.
• Write an introduction that will hook your listeners with the top three reasons they should agree with your position and take action.
• Make an outline for your presentation, and fill in facts and examples that support your position.

Revising
• Use the guidelines on page SH31 of the Writing Handbook to revise your presentation.

Critical Thinking

10. Businesses changed from mostly small, family-owned operations to large corporations with great wealth and power.

11. The entrepreneur would use a portion of his or her wealth to do good works that would benefit the public or would establish or contribute to charities.

12. The growing middle class had more money to spend and more leisure time, and it increasingly spent that money and time on forms of mass entertainment.

13. Grady envisioned a New South that would develop a mixed economy in which southern factories would make products with southern resources. Some aspects of this notion were realized, but much of the South remained dependent on agriculture, and the region as a whole lagged behind the Northeast and Midwest economically. African Americans continued to face discrimination because of Jim Crow laws.

14. Sample answer: Farmers and ranchers would have settled the West, but not in such high numbers or as quickly.

Document-Based Assessment

Attitudes of business and government toward organized labor

Were labor unions successful in working out their disputes with big-business owners? What roles did the federal government and the courts play in settling these disputes? Use your knowledge of the organized labor movement and Documents A, B, C, and D to answer questions 1 through 4.

Document A

"The workers at the blast furnaces in our steel-rail works once sent in a 'round-robin' stating that unless the firm gave them an advance of wages by Monday afternoon at four o'clock they would leave the furnaces. . . . Gentlemen of the Blast Furnace Committee, you have threatened our firm that you will break your agreement and that you will leave these blast furnaces . . . unless you get a favorable answer to your threat by four o'clock today. It is not three but your answer is ready. You may leave the blast furnaces. . . . The worst day that labor has ever seen in this world is that day in which it dishonors itself by breaking its agreement. You have your answer."
— The Autobiography of Andrew Carnegie, *August 1920*

Document B

THE CHIVALRY OF MODERN KNIGHTS.

Document C

"There was a time when workmen were denied the right of leaving their employers, when they were part of the soil, owned by their employers. . . . Not many years ago, when workmen counseled with each other for the purpose of resisting a reduction in their wages or making an effort to secure an increase, it was held to be a conspiracy punishable by imprisonment. Through the effort of organized labor, an enlightened public sentiment changed all this until to-day the right to unite for material, moral, and social improvement on the part of workers is accepted by all."
— *Samuel Gompers to Editor,* Washington Evening Star, *May 15, 1900*

Document D

"In the winter of 1893–1894 the employees of the Pullman Palace Car Company . . . were greatly disturbed because of a wage reduction. . . . They joined the new American Railway Union . . . attempting to organize all workers connected with the railways. . . . The [Pullman] company refused to consider arbitration and the boycott went into effect. . . . Indictments charging Debs [president of the American Railway Union] and others of violations of the Sherman Act were secured. . . . As a result of the various injunctions, indictments, and the activities of federal troops which reached Chicago, following directions from President Cleveland, the strike and the consequent violence were practically at an end by the middle of July."
— *Labor and the Sherman Act by Edward Berman, 1930*

1. In Document A, what view does Andrew Carnegie take toward organized labor?
   A He believes that businesses should bargain with employees.
   B He believes that workers should be paid fair wages.
   C He believes that employees should honor their original work agreement.
   D He believes that business owners should take workers' threats seriously.

2. Which document is a secondary source that describes how the Sherman Act was used as a legal tool to end a strike?
   A Document A
   B Document B
   C Document C
   D Document D

3. Who does the cartoonist make fun of in Document B?
   A The government
   B The Knights of Labor
   C The Sherman Antitrust Act
   D George Pullman

4. **Writing Task** What were the goals of the labor movement? How did big business, the government, and the courts respond to labor unions? Use your knowledge of the chapter content and specific evidence from the primary sources above to support your opinion.

Document-Based Assessment

- To help students understand the documents, give them the following **TIP When researching on the Internet, use only recent documents from reputable sources.**

- To provide students with further practice in answering document-based questions, go to Test Prep With Document-Based Assessment.

- If students need more instruction on analyzing primary sources, have them read the Skills Handbook, **p. SH24.**

Answers

1. C   2. D   3. B
4. Essays should demonstrate students' knowledge of chapter content on organized labor and their ability to construct distinct and convincing arguments based on supporting details from the documents on this page.

15. The Pendleton Act was passed in reaction to the assassination of President Garfield. It created a civil service system that required people to take exams to qualify for government jobs.

16. Sample answer: No, the statement is sarcastic. The editor is expressing the view that the railroads and banks in Nebraska are making as much, if not more, money than farmers—and the editor probably means that the railroads and banks are taking profits away from farmers.

Writing About History

As students begin the assignment, refer them to page SH31 of the Writing Handbook for help in preparing an oral presentation. Remind students of the steps they should take to complete their assignment, including outlining, making numbered note cards, and rehearsing.

Remind students that an oral presentation must hold their listeners' interest. Encourage students to make their presentations interesting and lively by including visuals, such as photographs, illustrations, graphs, or charts. For scoring rubrics, see Assessment Rubrics.

Reflections: Little Bighorn

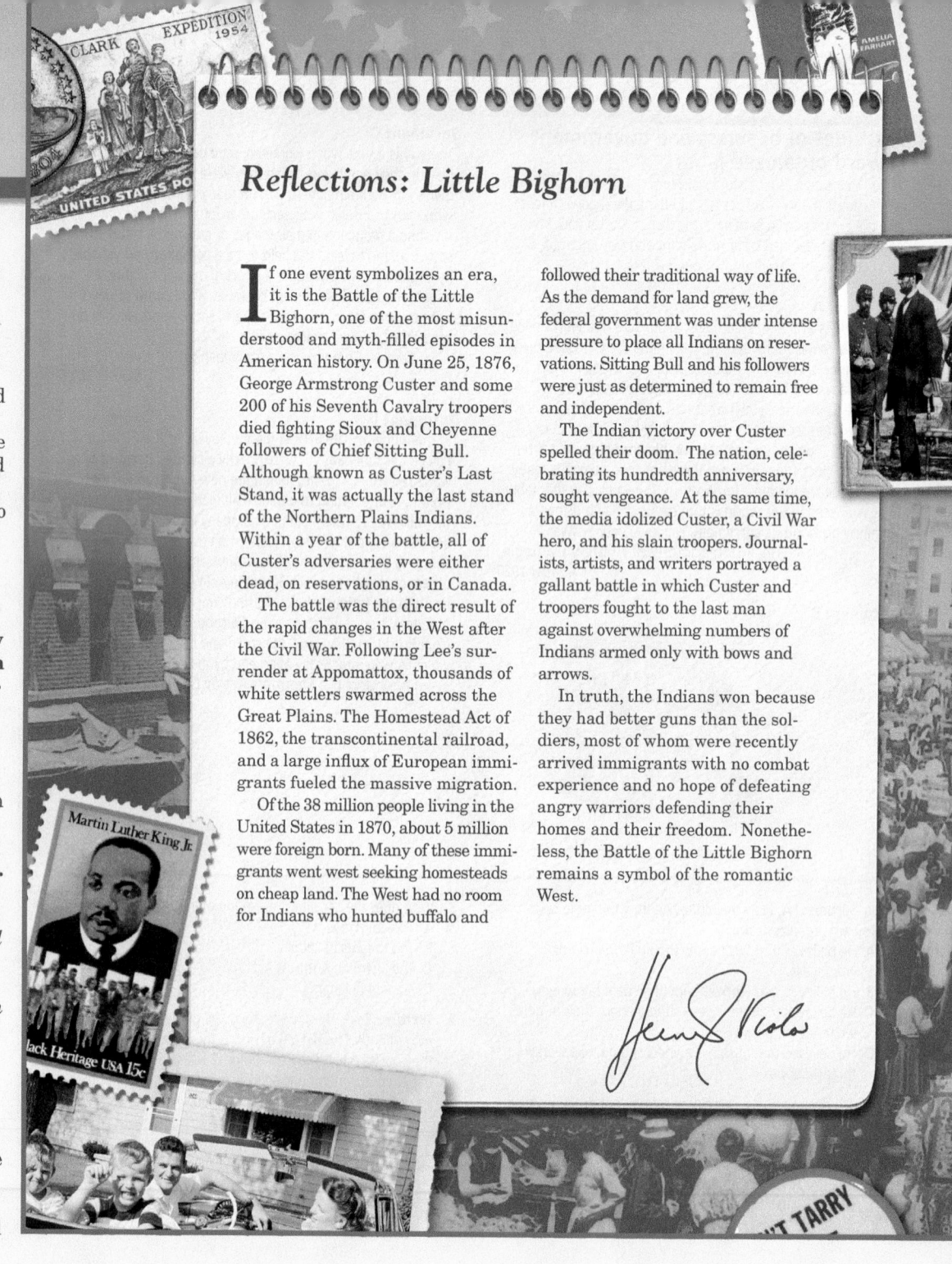

Background Knowledge

Display a large map of the United States, and ask students to locate the Great Plains and Montana, the site of the Battle of the Little Bighorn. Then, point out the eastern part of the United States, and note that about 150 to 200 years before the Battle of the Little Bighorn, many Native Americans lived there. During the late 1800s, Native Americans made a desperate attempt to retain some remnants of their land on the Plains.

Instruct

Have students read the essay. Ask **How did the amount of Native American land change between the first contact with European explorers and the late 1800s?** (*The amount of land held by Native Americans steadily decreased.*) Lead a class discussion about why the amount of land on which Native Americans lived continued to decrease. Ask **Was the conflict between Native Americans and U.S. troops and settlers inevitable? Could conflict have been avoided?** (*Possible answer: Native Americans and U.S. settlers wanted to live on the same land. The conflict could have been avoided if the U.S. government had been more willing to share the land with Native Americans.*)

Looking Ahead

The removal of the Native Americans from their land paved the way for white settlement in the West. It also set the stage for exploitation of the region's resources, and this activity contributed to the rapid economic development of the United States around the turn of the twentieth century.

If one event symbolizes an era, it is the Battle of the Little Bighorn, one of the most misunderstood and myth-filled episodes in American history. On June 25, 1876, George Armstrong Custer and some 200 of his Seventh Cavalry troopers died fighting Sioux and Cheyenne followers of Chief Sitting Bull. Although known as Custer's Last Stand, it was actually the last stand of the Northern Plains Indians. Within a year of the battle, all of Custer's adversaries were either dead, on reservations, or in Canada.

The battle was the direct result of the rapid changes in the West after the Civil War. Following Lee's surrender at Appomattox, thousands of white settlers swarmed across the Great Plains. The Homestead Act of 1862, the transcontinental railroad, and a large influx of European immigrants fueled the massive migration.

Of the 38 million people living in the United States in 1870, about 5 million were foreign born. Many of these immigrants went west seeking homesteads on cheap land. The West had no room for Indians who hunted buffalo and followed their traditional way of life. As the demand for land grew, the federal government was under intense pressure to place all Indians on reservations. Sitting Bull and his followers were just as determined to remain free and independent.

The Indian victory over Custer spelled their doom. The nation, celebrating its hundredth anniversary, sought vengeance. At the same time, the media idolized Custer, a Civil War hero, and his slain troopers. Journalists, artists, and writers portrayed a gallant battle in which Custer and troopers fought to the last man against overwhelming numbers of Indians armed only with bows and arrows.

In truth, the Indians won because they had better guns than the soldiers, most of whom were recently arrived immigrants with no combat experience and no hope of defeating angry warriors defending their homes and their freedom. Nonetheless, the Battle of the Little Bighorn remains a symbol of the romantic West.

EMERGENCE OF THE MODERN UNITED STATES

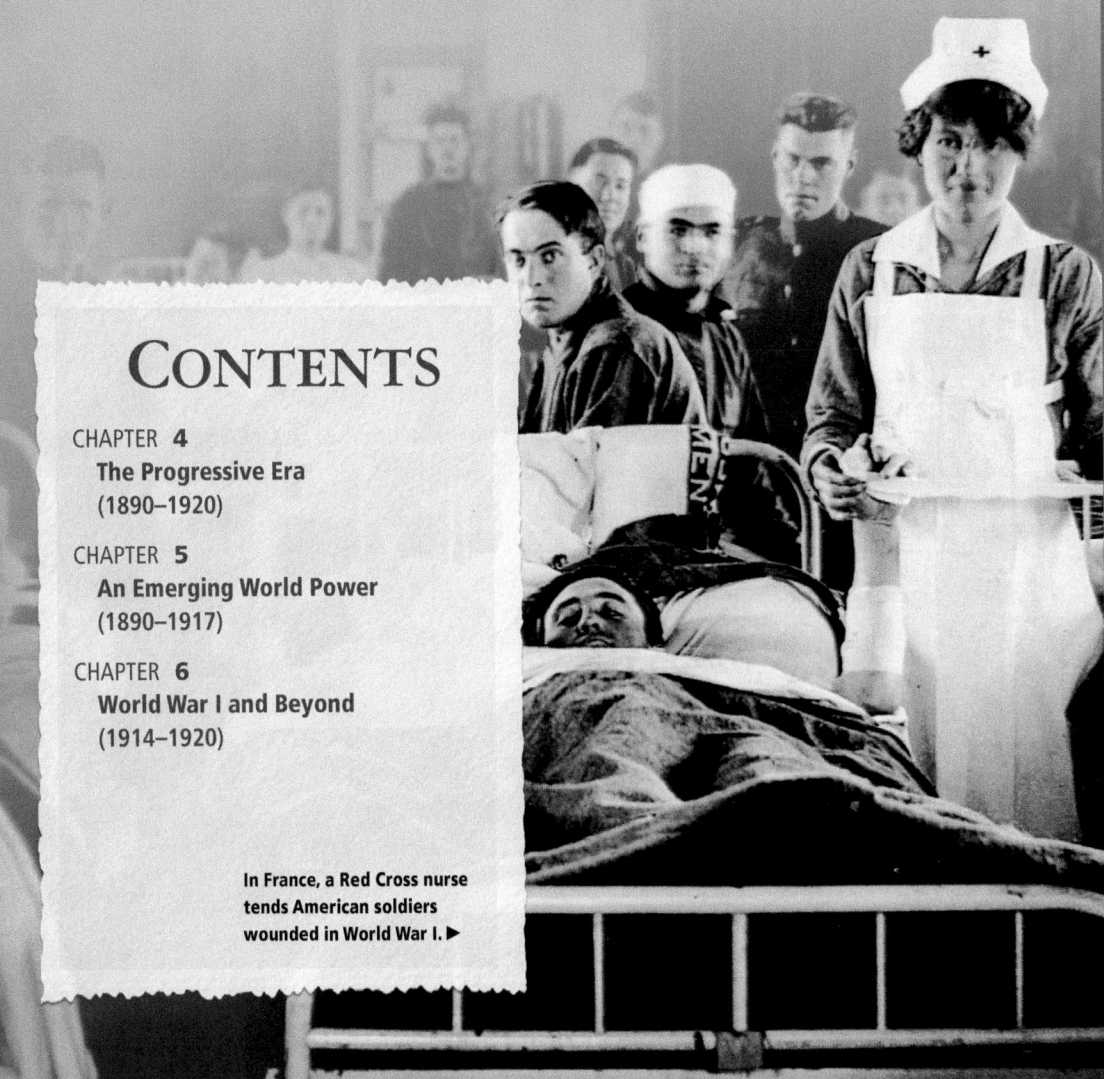

CONTENTS

In France, a Red Cross nurse tends American soldiers wounded in World War I. ▶

Emergence of the Modern United States

Era Overview

Emergence of the Modern United States presents the United States as it first began to look outward, forming its role as an important leader among nations of the world and contending with domestic issues and global conflicts.

Chapter 4 describes how early twentieth-century Progressives strove for social and political reforms on issues including the urban poor, women's suffrage, discrimination, and civil rights. **Issues:** Social Problems and Reforms, Voting Rights, Government's Role in the Economy

Chapter 5 focuses on America's emergence as a new imperialist powerhouse, whose economic interests and foreign policies led to the Spanish-American War, tensions with East Asia, and resentment and conflict in Latin America. **Issues:** Territorial Expansion of the United States, America and the World, America Goes to War

Chapter 6 examines the causes of World War I, the inevitable involvement of the United States on both the European front and the home front, the subsequent peace, and the effects of the war both domestically and internationally. **Issues:** America Goes to War, Civil Liberties and National Security, Checks and Balances

CHAPTER 4 The Progressive Era
1890–1920

Teach With Technology

Presentation**EXPRESS**™
PREMIUM DVD

- Teach this chapter's core content by using **PresentationExpress**, which includes interactivities, video, lecture notes, and the *ExamView*® QuickTake assessment tool.

- To introduce this chapter by using **PresentationExpress**, ask students with which of the following statements they most agree: **A) It is the role of government to ensure the health and welfare of all citizens. B) It is the role of private organizations and charities to ensure the health and welfare of all citizens. C) It is the role of both government and private organizations to ensure the health and welfare of all citizens.** Take a class poll or record students' answers by using the Quick-Take feature, and discuss their responses. Point out that in this chapter, they will read about the Progressive Movement, which sought to improve society through legislation or government regulation.

Technology Resources

- Student**EXPRESS** CD-ROM
- Teacher Resource Library **DVD**
- Presentation**EXPRESS** PREMIUM DVD
- *ExamView*® **Test Bank CD-ROM** English and Spanish
- **Guided Reading Audio,** Spanish
- **Student Edition on Audio**

THE ESSENTIAL
VIDEO
By Students For Students
For videos on Amercian Issues, go to
www.pearsonschool.com/ushist

Bibliography

For the Teacher

Chambers II, John Whiteclay. *The Tyranny of Change: America in the Progressive Era, 1890–1920, 2nd Edition.* Rutgers University Press, 2000.

McGerr, Michael. *A Fierce Discontent: The Rise and Fall of the Progressive Movement in America, 1870–1920.* Free Press, 2003.

Sadovnik, Alan R. and Susan F. Semel. *Founding Mothers and Others: Women Educational Leaders During the Progressive Era.* Palgrave Macmillan, 2002.

For the Student

(L2) Lukes, Bonnie L. *Woodrow Wilson* and *the Progressive Era.* Morgan Reynolds Publishing, 2005.

(L3) Addams, Jane. *Twenty Years at Hull-House.* Signet Classics, 1999.

(L4) Fink, Leon. *Major Problems in the Gilded Age and the Progressive Era: Documents and Essays.* Houghton Mifflin Company, 2000.

WITNESS HISTORY

Slum Sisters

In 1865, Methodist minister William Booth opened a street-corner mission in the slums of London. This was the beginning of the Salvation Army. By 1889, the Salvation Army had taken root in New York City. The Army sent pairs of women, known as "slum sisters," to visit tenement dwellers. Carrying mops and buckets along with religious pamphlets, these volunteers scrubbed floors, cooked meals, and cared for the sick. As cities grew and industry boomed, the slum sisters of the Salvation Army were just a few of the reformers who dedicated themselves to the needs of the poorest of the poor.

◄ A Salvation Army volunteer delivers Christmas dinner to the poor in New York City.

THE JUNGLE

UPTON SINCLAIR

The Jungle exposed the abuses of the meatpacking industry

Chapter Preview

Chapter Focus Question: What were the causes and effects of the Progressive Movement?

Section 1
The Drive for Reform

Section 2
Women Make Progress

Section 3
The Struggle Against Discrimination

Section 4
Roosevelt's Square Deal

Section 5
Wilson's New Freedom

PROGRESSIVE

1912 Progressive Party presidential campaign button

VOTES FOR WOMEN

Women's suffrage statuette

Use the ☑ **Quick Study Timeline** at the end of this chapter to preview chapter events.

Note Taking Study Guide *Online*
For: Note Taking and American Issues Connector
www.pearsonschool.com/ushist

Chapter-Level Resources

All in One Letter Home (English and Spanish), Preread the Chapter, Vocabulary Builder, Reading Strategy, Social Studies Skills Practice, Enrichment, Issues Connector, Chapter Tests

- Test Prep With Document-Based Assessment
- AYP Monitoring Assessments
- *ExamView®* Test Bank CD-ROM
- Guided Reading Audio (Spanish)
- Student Edition Audio

Previewing the Chapter

- **WITNESS HISTORY** Explain that the Salvation Army was one of several reform groups that were begun to provide social services in response to the problems caused by rapid industrialization, urbanization, and immigration in the 1800s. Point out that during this time, the government generally did not provide services for the needy. Read the Witness History selection aloud. Ask students to consider why private citizens and organizations began to work for social reform.

- **Analyzing the Visuals** Ask students to study the images on these two pages. Ask **What do you think *progressive* means? How do you think these images are connected to that word?** (*Progressive means "moving forward or improving." The images seem to connect to improvements and reforms.*)

- **Focus** Write the Chapter Focus Question on the board. Tell students to keep this question in mind as they read the chapter. Then, have students preview the section titles in this chapter.

- **Preread** Have students complete the chapter's Preread the Chapter worksheet. Teaching Resources, pp. 9–10

Have students access **www.pearsonschool.com/ushist** for the Note Taking Study Guide *Online* as an alternative to the *Reading and Note Taking Study Guide* booklet.

Differentiated Instruction Solutions for All Learners

The following Teacher's Edition strategies are suitable for students of varying abilities.

L1 Special Needs Students, pp. 101, 110, 118, 125, 126, 129 SN

L2 English Language Learners, pp. 101, 110, 118, 125, 129 ELL

L2 Less Proficient Readers, pp. 101, 105, 110, 118, 125, 126, 129 LPR

L4 Advanced Readers, pp. 103, 106, 113, 117, 122 AR

L4 Gifted and Talented Students, pp. 103, 106, 113, 122 GT

Objectives

As you teach this section, keep students focused on the following objectives to help them answer the Section Focus Question and master core content.

- Identify the causes of Progressivism and compare it to Populism.
- Analyze the role that journalists played in the Progressive Movement.
- Evaluate some of the social reforms that Progressives tackled.
- Explain what Progressives hoped to achieve through political reforms.

Background Knowledge **L3**

Discuss how industrialization changed society during the Gilded Age. Have students predict what types of problems industrialization may have caused.

Set a Purpose **L3**

- **WITNESS HISTORY** Read the selection aloud.

  Ask **Why were children allowed to work at dangerous jobs, such as mining?** *(There were no child labor laws, there was a need for unskilled labor, and their families probably needed the income.)*

- **Focus** Point out the Section Focus Question, and write it on the board. Tell students to refer to this question as they read. *(Answer appears with Section 1 Assessment answers.)*

- **Preview** Have students preview the Section Objectives and the list of Terms and People.

- **Reading Skill** Have students use the *Reading Strategy: Main Ideas and Details* worksheet. Teaching Resources, **p. 13**

- **NoteTaking** Using the Guided Questioning strategy (TE, p. T20), have students read this section. As they read, have students record details about Progressivism. Reading and Note Taking Study Guide

WITNESS HISTORY

Children in the Coal Mines

Progressive reformers were appalled by the child labor that was common in coal mines, textile mills, and other industries. John Spargo, a union organizer and socialist, sadly described the terrible conditions endured by boys working in the coal mines.

"The coal is hard, and accidents to the hands, such as cut, broken, or crushed fingers, are common among the boys. Sometimes there is a worse accident: a terrified shriek is heard, and a boy is mangled and torn in the machinery, or disappears in the chute to be picked out later smothered and dead. Clouds of dust fill the breakers and are inhaled by the boys, laying the foundations for asthma and miners' consumption. "

—John Spargo, *The Bitter Cry of the Children*, 1906

▲ These boys toiled in a West Virginia coal mine.

The Drive for Reform

Objectives

- Identify the causes of Progressivism and compare it to Populism.
- Analyze the role that journalists played in the Progressive Movement.
- Evaluate some of the social reforms that Progressives tackled.
- Explain what Progressives hoped to achieve through political reforms.

Terms and People

Progressivism	Jane Addams
muckraker	direct primary
Lincoln Steffens	initiative
Jacob Riis	referendum
Social Gospel	recall
settlement house	

NoteTaking

Reading Skill: Identify Details Fill in a chart like this one with details about Progressivism.

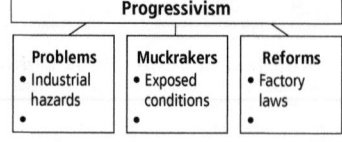

Progressivism		
Problems	**Muckrakers**	**Reforms**
• Industrial hazards	• Exposed conditions	• Factory laws
•	•	•

Why It Matters Industrialization, urbanization, and immigration brought many benefits to America, but they also produced challenging social problems. In response, a movement called **Progressivism** emerged in the 1890s. Progressives believed that new ideas and honest, efficient government could bring about social justice. Progressive ideas brought lasting reforms that still affect society today. **Section Focus Question: What areas did Progressives think were in need of the greatest reform?**

Origins of Progressivism

The people who made up the Progressive Movement came from many walks of life. They came from all political parties, social classes, ethnic groups, and religions. Many Progressive leaders emerged from the growing middle class, whose power and influence was rapidly spreading. Dissatisfied industrial workers also joined the Progressive Movement. So did a few wealthy Americans driven by a desire to act for the good of society.

Progressives Share Common Beliefs What the Progressives shared in common was a belief that industrialization and urbanization had created troubling social and political problems. Progressives wanted to bring about reforms that would correct these problems and injustices. They encouraged their state legislatures and the federal government to enact laws to address the issues faced by the poor. Progressives wanted to use logic and reason to make society work in a more efficient and orderly way. Many, motivated by religious faith, sought social justice.

Vocabulary Builder

Use the information below and the following resource to teach students the high-use word from this section. Teaching Resources, Vocabulary Builder, p. 12

High-Use Word	Definition and Sample Sentence
dynamic	*adj.* energetic; relating to change or productive activity Many leaders have **dynamic** personalities that enable them to inspire others.

Progressivism was similar to the Populist Movement of the late 1800s. Both were reform movements that wanted to get rid of corrupt government officials and make government more responsive to people's needs. Both sought to eliminate the abuses of big business. Still, the two movements differed. At the forefront of Progressivism were middle-class people. They believed that highly educated leaders should use modern ideas and scientific techniques to improve society. Leaders of the Populist Movement, on the other hand, consisted mostly of farmers and workers.

Progressives Target a Variety of Problems Some Progressives thought that political reform was the most urgent need. For many women, the number one goal was winning the right to vote. Other Progressives considered honest government to be the most important goal. Reformers targeted city officials who built corrupt organizations, called political machines. The bosses of these political machines used bribery and violence to influence voters and win elections. They counted on the loyalty of city workers who looked the other way when they took public money for themselves. Bosses also helped people solve personal problems, which often kept voters loyal.

Corrupt and ineffective government combined with the booming growth of cities produced other problems. The people living in America's crowded cities needed paved streets, safe drinking water, decent housing, and adequate municipal services. The lack of adequate services led to wretched living conditions for the urban poor. Too often, dishonest business owners and politicians controlled municipal services. Bribes and shady deals made them rich while conditions for urban residents remained unsafe and little changed.

While some Progressives focused on government, others were worried about big business. As you have learned, wealthy industrialists took over businesses and built huge trusts that limited competition and raised prices. Middle-class Progressives wanted the government to "bust the trusts" and so create more economic opportunities for smaller businesses. Progressives complained that the Sherman Antitrust Act of 1890 was inadequate and ineffective in limiting the abuses of big business.

Other Progressive reformers focused on the class system. Often motivated by religious faith, they sought to reduce the growing gap between the rich and the poor. They attacked the harsh conditions endured by miners, factory workers, and other laborers. They wanted to improve conditions in city slums. They wanted social welfare laws to help children, as well as government regulations to aid workers and consumers.

✓ **Checkpoint** What problems did Progressive reformers hope to solve?

THE SHARP METHOD.—IT WORKS WITH ANY BOARD OF ALDERMEN.

Analyzing Political Cartoons

Business and Government Corruption In the 1880s, Jacob Sharp expanded his streetcar business by bribing New York City aldermen and other government officials.
1. What symbols represent the corruption of city government?
2. According to the cartoonist, what is the effect of the street railroad monopoly on the taxpayer?

Teach

Origins of Progressivism L3

Instruct

- **Introduce: Key Term** Ask students to find the key term **Progressivism** (in bold) in the text. Ask **How do you think the Progressive Movement got its name?** (*It probably came from the word* progress, *meaning "to move forward." People in this movement wanted to apply new ideas to improve society and move it forward.*) Have students predict what types of reforms the Progressives might want to make.

- **Teach** Using the Idea Wave strategy (TE p. T22), have students list problems Progressives targeted for reform. As you discuss each problem, ask students to identify which groups of people specifically wanted the reforms and give reasons why each problem was a focus for Progressives. Then, ask students to compare and contrast Populists and Progressives.

- **Analyzing the Visuals** Ask **How does the political cartoon illustrate the problems with many city governments at the time?** (*It shows how corrupt leaders cheated citizens out of services and tax money.*)

Independent Practice

Ask students to suppose that they are living in the United States during the late 1800s. Have them write a paragraph explaining whether they believe that political reform or business reform is needed more.

Monitor Progress

As students fill in their flowcharts, circulate to make sure that they understand the problems that Progressives wanted to address. For a completed version of the flowchart, see Note Taking Transparencies, **B-86**.

Differentiated Instruction   Solutions for All Learners

L1 Special Needs Students   L2 English Language Learners   L2 Less Proficient Readers

To help students master vocabulary, have them make a list of this section's key terms and people and high-use words. Encourage students to list additional terms that may be new to them, such as *origins, journalists, moderation, formation, fascination, policy, regulation,* and *massacre.* Then have them create flashcards with the term on one side and its definition—or in the case of key people, an identification—on the other side. For English Language Learners, you may wish to have them add explanations in their first language along with the English definitions and identifications. Pair students, and have them use the flashcards to quiz each other.

Answers

Analyzing Political Cartoons
1. the bags of money and the aldermen's notes to the railroad companies
2. The taxpayer does not have a choice over which form of transportation to use.

✓ problems in the areas of politics and government, business, social welfare, and labor conditions

Instruct

- **Introduce: Key Term** Ask students to find the key term ***muckraker*** (in bold) in the text. Have students discuss the origin of the term and explain why Roosevelt used it to describe Progressive journalists. Explain that one of the most important catalysts for change during the Progressive Era was the work of journalists known as ***muckrakers.***

- **Teach** Ask students to read the Primary Source quotation on this page. Invite volunteers to explain the topic and main idea of the quotation and how it illustrates ideas of the Progressive Movement. Ask **Why was the work of the muckrakers so effective in bringing about reform?** *(Their work was so effective because their sensational accounts were published in magazines and newspapers that were read by millions of Americans.)*

Muckrakers Reveal the Need for Reform

Socially conscious journalists and other writers dramatized the need for reform. Their sensational investigative reports uncovered a wide range of ills afflicting America in the early 1900s. Even though Theodore Roosevelt agreed with much of what they said, he called these writers **muckrakers** because he thought them too fascinated with the ugliest side of things. (A muckrake is a tool used to clean manure and hay out of animals' stables.) The writers were angry at first but in time took up Roosevelt's taunting name as a badge of honor. The muckrakers' articles appeared in magazines and newspapers that entered millions of American homes. People across the nation were horrified by the conditions that were revealed to them.

Journalists Uncover Injustices One leading muckraker was **Lincoln Steffens,** managing editor at *McClure's,* a magazine known for uncovering social problems. In 1903, Steffens published *The Shame of the Cities,* a collection of articles on political corruption. His reports exposed how the government of Philadelphia let utility companies charge their customers excessively high fees. He showed how corrupt politicians won elections by bribing and threatening voters, and revealed how political corruption affected all aspects of life in a city.

Jacob Riis ▼

Primary Source "The visitor [to St. Louis] is told of the wealth of the residents, of the financial strength of the banks, and of the growing importance of the industries; yet he sees poorly paved, refuse-burdened streets, and dusty or mud-covered alleys; he passes a ramshackle firetrap crowded with the sick and learns that it is the City Hospital. . . . Finally, he turns a tap in the hotel to see liquid mud flow into [the] wash basin or bathtub."

—Lincoln Steffens and Claude Wetmore, "Corruption and Reform in St. Louis," *McClure's Magazine,* October 1902

● **INFOGRAPHIC**

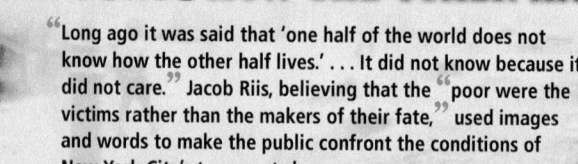

EXPOSING HOW THE OTHER HALF LIVES

"Long ago it was said that 'one half of the world does not know how the other half lives.' . . . It did not know because it did not care." Jacob Riis, believing that the "poor were the victims rather than the makers of their fate," used images and words to make the public confront the conditions of New York City's tenement slums.

Riis's 1890 book ▼

▲ A horse lies dead in a New York City street as children play nearby. A lack of city services forced slum-dwellers to live in unsanitary conditions.

□HOW THE OTHER HALF LIVES STVDIES AMONG THE TENEMENTS OF NEW YORK

Another influential muckraker was **Jacob Riis,** a photographer for the *New York Evening Sun.* Riis turned his camera on the crowded, unsafe, rat-infested tenement buildings where the urban poor lived. Between 1890 and 1903, he published several works, including *How the Other Half Lives* (see Infographic below), that shocked the nation's conscience and led to reforms.

Other outraged writers joined Riis and Steffens. In *The History of Standard Oil,* Ida Tarbell reported that John D. Rockefeller used ruthless methods to ruin his competitors, charge higher prices, and thereby reap huge profits. Others proclaimed the need to improve schools or warned of the breakdown of family life because mothers had to work long hours in factories. John Spargo focused attention on the dangerous and difficult lives of child workers. (See the Witness History at the beginning of this section.)

Novelists Defend the Downtrodden Fiction writers put a human face on social problems. They developed a new genre—the naturalist novel—that honestly portrayed human misery and the struggles of common people. Theodore Dreiser, a midwesterner raised in poverty, published *Sister Carrie* in 1900. His provocative novel traces the fate of a small-town girl drawn into the brutal urban worlds of Chicago and New York.

Naturalist novels became very popular. Frank Norris's *The Octopus* fascinated readers by dramatizing the Southern Pacific Railroad's stranglehold on struggling California farmers. In *The Jungle,* Upton Sinclair related the despair of immigrants working in Chicago's stockyards and revealed the unsanitary conditions in the industry. (See an excerpt from the novel at the end of this section.) African American author Frances Ellen Watkins portrayed some of the struggles of black Americans in her 1892 novel *Iola Leroy.*

✔ **Checkpoint** What role did journalists and other writers play in the Progressive Movement?

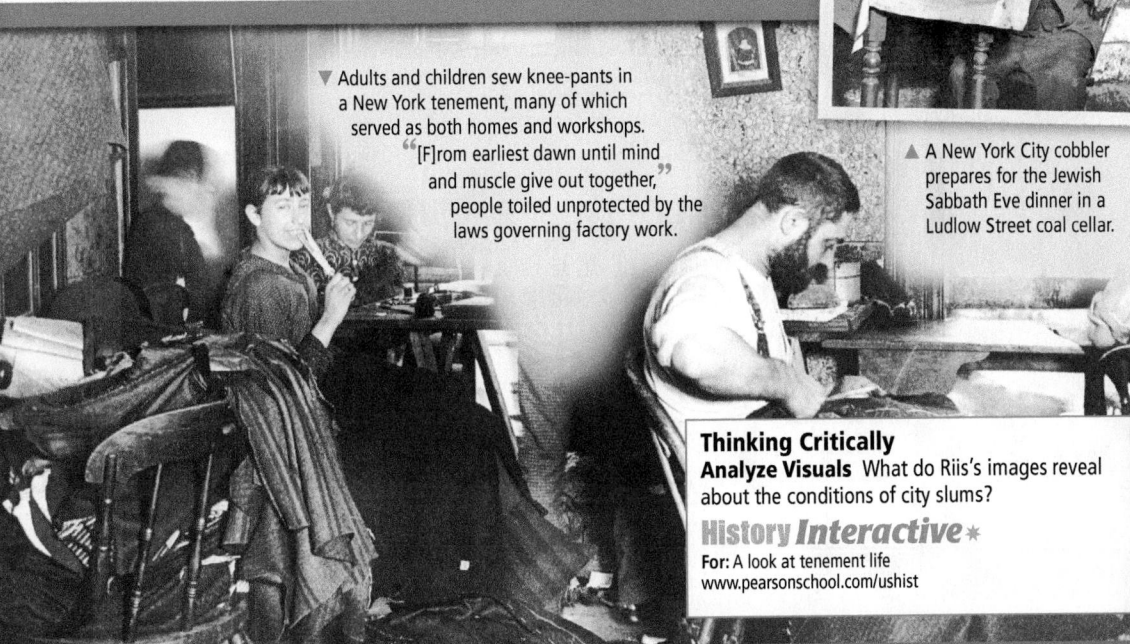

▼ Adults and children sew knee-pants in a New York tenement, many of which served as both homes and workshops. "[F]rom earliest dawn until mind and muscle give out together," people toiled unprotected by the laws governing factory work.

▲ A New York City cobbler prepares for the Jewish Sabbath Eve dinner in a Ludlow Street coal cellar.

Thinking Critically
Analyze Visuals What do Riis's images reveal about the conditions of city slums?

History *Interactive* *
For: A look at tenement life
www.pearsonschool.com/ushist

Independent Practice

- To enrich and extend the lesson, have students access the History Interactive at **www.pearson-school.com/ushist.** After students have experienced the History Interactive, ask them to write paragraphs describing tenement life during the early 1900s and explaining how the tenements might have changed after Riis published his photographs.

- To help students further understand the work of muckrakers, have them complete the worksheet *Link to Literature: The Octopus.* Teaching Resources, **p. 20**

- Ask students to fill in the second part of the flowchart for this section under "Muckrackers."

Monitor Progress

As students write their paragraphs, complete their worksheets, and fill in their flowcharts, circulate to make sure that they understand the role and significance of the muckrakers in this period.

Differentiated Instruction Solutions for All Learners

L4 Advanced Readers   L4 Gifted and Talented Students

Explain that Jacob Riis was a pioneer of photojournalism, or the art of visual reporting. Over the last century, gifted photographers, such as Margaret Bourke-White and Robert Capa, provided stunning images of major world events that have highlighted social problems. Many images, such as Joe Rosenthal's Pulitzer Prize–winning photograph of the flag raising on Iwo Jima during World War II, have become iconic. Have students conduct more research about the development of photojournalism and collect some of the iconic photographs that were taken during the twentieth century. Tell students to create posters displaying the images they have collected. For each photograph, have students write a caption that explains the photograph's significance and tells how it influenced American society. Invite volunteers to present their posters to the class.

Answers

✔ They wrote sensational reports on a variety of serious problems facing the United States in the late 1800s and early 1900s. Their works were published in newspapers, magazines, and books that were read by millions of Americans. Their works sparked outrage and motivated people to demand reforms.

Thinking Critically
The images graphically reveal the terrible poverty, made worse by a lack of adequate services, in the city slums.

Instruct

- **Introduce: Key Term** Ask students to find the key term *Social Gospel* (in bold) in the text. Then, write the term on the board and provide the definition. Explain that *gospel* refers to the teaching of Jesus as described in the four Gospels of the Christian New Testament. Have students recall the information in the Witness History quotation in the chapter opener about the Salvation Army. Discuss how and why religious beliefs were and continue to be a powerful motivator for many reformers.

- **Teach** Remind students that rapid industrialization, massive immigration, and urbanization at the end of the nineteenth century caused many major problems. Discuss how Progressives worked to improve life in the cities and their successes and failures in the areas of aid to the urban poor, children, and education, labor laws, and workplace conditions.

- **Analyzing the Visuals** Have students study the images relating to the Triangle Shirtwaist Factory fire. Discuss the event and how these images and the newspaper headlines helped motivate reformers. Ask **Are tragic events still motivators for reform? Why or why not?** (*Sample answer: Yes, they are. For example, the events of September 11, 2001, demonstrated a need to reform airline security.*)

Answer

Caption It helped Progressives in their efforts because the reports of the fire created outrage and graphically illustrated the need for workplace reform.

Progressives Reform Society

The work of the muckrakers increased popular support for Progressivism. Progressive activists promoted laws to improve living conditions, public health, and schools. They urged government to regulate businesses. They believed that careful social planning would make American life better.

The Social Gospel Guides Reform Efforts Many reformers, like Walter Rauschenbusch, thought that Christianity should be the basis of social reform. A child of German immigrants, Rauschenbusch had become a Baptist minister. He blended ideas from German socialism and American Progressivism to form what he called the **Social Gospel**. By following Bible teachings about charity and justice, he explained, people could make society "the kingdom of God."

Many Protestant leaders followed Rauschenbusch's program. They began to urge the end of child labor and a shorter workweek. They also pushed for the federal government to limit the power of corporations and trusts.

Settlement House Workers Aid the Urban Poor An important goal of many Progressives was to improve the lives of poor people in the cities. One approach was the **settlement house,** a community center that provided social services to the urban poor. Before settlement houses, there were private charities that helped poor people. Settlement house workers gave mothers classes in child care and taught English to immigrants. They ran nursery schools and kindergartens. They also provided theater, art, and dance programs for adults.

A woman named **Jane Addams** became a leading figure in the settlement house movement. While visiting Europe, she was inspired by the work at Toynbee Hall, a settlement house in London. In 1889, Addams opened Hull House, a settlement house in Chicago. Over the years, Hull House grew to include 13 buildings. Its success inspired other college-educated, middle-class women to become social workers. By 1911, the country had more than 400 settlement houses.

Religious organizations such as the Young Men's Christian Association (YMCA) also provided services to the urban poor. In addition to its goal of promoting Christian values, the YMCA offered classes, dances, and sports.

The 1911 Triangle Shirtwaist Factory Fire
A firefighter overcome by fumes from the Triangle Shirtwaist Factory fire recovers on the sidewalk. *How did the fire help or hurt Progressives' efforts to reform workplace conditions?*

History Background

Jane Addams Reformer, feminist, and international peace advocate Jane Addams was born in Cedarville, Illinois, in 1860. After graduating from Rockford Female Seminary (now Rockford College), she studied medicine. It was not until she was 27 and on a tour of Europe that she found her true calling. While in London, Addams and her friend Ellen Starr visited Toynbee House, a settlement house in the city's slums. This inspired her and Starr to establish a similar settlement in a poor, immigrant neighborhood in Chicago called Hull House. Addams also became an active supporter of other issues, such as women's suffrage, workers' rights, child welfare, and racial equality. In 1910, she was named president of the National Conference of Social Work. A dedicated pacifist, Addams also became president of the Women's International League for Peace and Freedom in 1919. One year later, she helped found the American Civil Liberties Union, or ACLU. In 1931, she was awarded the Nobel Peace Prize for her leadership of the Women's International League for Peace and Freedom—the first American woman to win a Nobel Prize.

Protecting Children and Improving Education Progressives also tried to help children. Leading the effort was a lawyer named Florence Kelley. Kelley helped convince the state of Illinois to ban child labor, and other states soon passed similar laws. In 1902, Kelley helped form the National Child Labor Committee, which successfully lobbied the federal government to create the U.S. Children's Bureau in 1912. This new agency examined any issue that affected the health and welfare of children. The agency still works to protect children today.

But progress in children's rights had a long way to go. In 1916, Congress passed the Keating-Owens Act, which banned child labor. However, two years later, the Supreme Court ruled the law unconstitutional. It was not until 1938 that Congress would end child labor for good.

Progressives also tried to better children's lives by improving education. A number of states passed laws that required children to attend school until a certain age. However, there were heated debates about what children should learn and how they should learn. Some argued that they should be taught only work skills. Others said they should learn to appreciate literature and music. Most educators agreed that girls should learn different things from boys.

Educator John Dewey criticized American schools for teaching children to memorize facts but not to think creatively. Dewey wanted schools to teach new subjects such as history and geography, as well as practical skills like cooking and carpentry. His ideas were not adopted at once, but in later years, many states put them into effect.

Progressives Help Industrial Workers In the early 1900s, the United States had the highest rate of industrial accidents in the world. Long hours, poor ventilation, hazardous fumes, and unsafe machinery threatened not only workers' health but also their lives. Each year some thirty thousand workers died on the job, while another half a million were injured.

In March 1911, a fire at the Triangle Shirtwaist Factory in New York City shocked Americans and focused attention on the need to protect workers. Workers in the factory had little chance to escape the raging fire because managers had locked most of the exits. The fire killed 146 workers, most of them young Jewish women. Many jumped from the windows in desperation. Inside the smoldering ruins, firefighters found many more victims, "skeletons bending over sewing machines."

After the blaze, outraged Progressives intensified their calls for reform. New York passed laws to make workplaces safer, and other cities and states followed suit. Many states also adopted workers' compensation laws, which set up funds to pay workers who were hurt on the job.

Progressives also persuaded some states to pass laws limiting the workday to 10 hours. However, their efforts suffered a blow in 1905 when the Supreme Court ruled in *Lochner* v. *New York* that such laws were unconstitutional.

✓ **Checkpoint** How did Progressives work to help the urban poor?

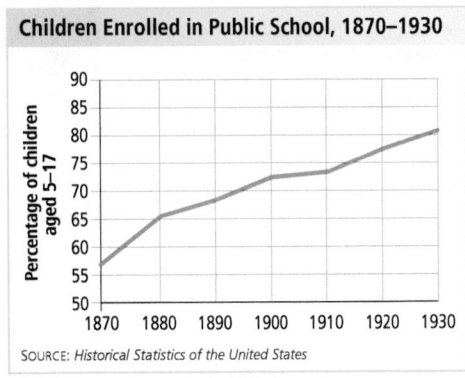

Children Enrolled in Public School, 1870–1930

SOURCE: *Historical Statistics of the United States*

Children Employed, 1870–1930

SOURCE: U.S. Census Bureau

Graph Skills During the Progressive Era, child labor declined sharply while school enrollment increased. *According to the graphs, how did the percentage of children employed change from 1890 to 1920? How did school enrollment change during the same period?*

Independent Practice
Have students study the two graphs on this page and write a paragraph that explains how the change in one set of data may have caused the change in the other.

Monitor Progress
Have students compare paragraphs with a partner to check their reasoning. Circulate as they discuss their ideas to make sure that they understand correctly the relationship between the two graphs.

Answers

✓ Progressives helped the urban poor by establishing settlement houses that provided crucial services. Progressives also worked to end child labor, improve education, and improve workplace conditions.

Graph Skills Between 1890 and 1900, the percentage of children employed increased slightly; from 1900 to 1920 it dropped from more than 18 percent to about 11 percent. During the same period, school enrollment increased from about 68 percent to about 77 percent.

Instruct

- **Introduce: Vocabulary Builder**
Have students locate the vocabulary term **dynamic** and its definition. Tell students that they will learn how **dynamic** leaders helped to further Progressive goals in the area of government reform.

- **Teach** Make a three-column chart on the board. Label the columns "initiative," "referendum," and "recall" and include the definition of each. Discuss the importance of these reforms. Using the Idea Wave strategy (TE, p. T22), ask students to brainstorm a list of initiatives they would like to see on the ballot in the next elections in their city or state.

- Display Color Transparency: *City Commission*. Discuss with students the advantages and disadvantages of the commission form of government compared with those of the mayoral form of government. Ask them what form of government their own city or town has. Color Transparencies A-77

- **Analyzing the Visuals** Direct students' attention to the photograph on this page. Ask **How have present-day disasters demonstrated a need for government reform?** (Sample answer: The events after Hurricane Katrina in 2005 demonstrated that local, state, and federal governments needed to improve their abilities to respond to large-scale disasters.)

Independent Practice

Instruct students to complete the flowchart for this section by filling in the information under "Reforms."

Monitor Progress

As students complete their flowcharts, circulate to make sure that they have identified key information.

Post-Hurricane Reforms in Galveston

- Galveston adopts a new commission form of government that spreads to other reform-minded cities.
- New city government builds a 17-foot-high seawall as protection against future storms.
- City government uses landfill to raise low-lying neighborhoods above sea level.

Devastated Galveston

After the coastal city of Galveston, Texas, was hit by a powerful hurricane, it adopted the commission form of government to lead the rebuilding effort. *What features would a city government need to handle a reconstruction job of the scale seen here?*

Reforming Government

Progressive reformers realized that they needed to reform the political process in order to reform society. They would have to free government from the control of political bosses and powerful business interests. They wanted to give people more control over their government and make government more effective and efficient in serving the public.

Reformers Improve City Government Just as the Triangle Shirtwaist Factory fire spurred reformers to action, so did another disaster. In 1900, a massive hurricane left the city of Galveston, Texas, in ruins. The greatest national calamity in American history, the hurricane killed more than 8,000 people. As an emergency measure, Galveston replaced its mayor and board of aldermen with a five-person commission. The commission form of government proved very efficient as the city carried out a tremendous rebuilding effort. The following year, Galveston decided to permanently adopt the commission form of government.

Known as the Galveston plan, many other cities decided to take up the commission form of government. By 1918, nearly 500 cities had adopted some form of the Galveston plan. Dayton, Ohio, and other cities modified the plan by adding a city manager to head the commission. The new city governments curbed the power of bosses and their political machines. The reform governments purchased public utilities so that electric, gas, and water companies could not charge city residents unfairly high rates.

Progressives Reform Election Rules Progressives also pushed for election reforms, taking up some Populist ideas. Traditionally, it was the party leaders who picked candidates for state and local offices. But in Wisconsin, reform governor Robert M. La Follette established a **direct primary**, an election in which citizens themselves vote to select nominees for upcoming elections. By 1916, all but four states had direct primaries.

Differentiated Instruction   Solutions for All Learners

L4 Advanced Readers   **L4 Gifted and Talented Students**

Have students conduct research to write a report about a Progressive law that still affects people today. In their reports, students should include the purpose of the legislation, the major figures involved in its passage, the immediate results, how effective it has been, and how people may or may not benefit from this law today.

Answer

Caption Sample answer: strong managers, good communication, and access to experts

Progressives also wanted to make sure that elected officials would follow citizens' wishes. To achieve this goal, they worked for three other political reforms: the initiative, the referendum, and the recall. The **initiative** gave people the power to put a proposed new law directly on the ballot in the next election by collecting citizens' signatures on a petition. This meant that voters themselves could pass laws instead of waiting for elected officials to act. The **referendum** allowed citizens to approve or reject laws passed by a legislature. The **recall** gave voters the power to remove public servants from office before their terms ended.

Progressives won yet another political reform: They adopted the Populist call for the direct election of senators by voters, not state legislators. That reform became law in 1913 when the Seventeenth Amendment to the Constitution was approved.

Progressive Governors Take Charge <u>Dynamic</u> Progressives became the leaders of several states, and chief among them was Robert La Follette of Wisconsin. Elected governor in 1900, "Fighting Bob" won the passage of many reform laws. Under his leadership, the Wisconsin state government forced railroads to charge lower fees and pay higher taxes. La Follette helped his state to improve education, make factories safer, and adopt the direct primary. Progressives called Wisconsin the "laboratory of democracy."

Hiram Johnson, governor of California, shattered the Southern Pacific Railroad's stranglehold on state government. He put in place the direct primary, initiative, referendum, and recall. He also pushed for another goal of some Progressives—planning for the careful use of natural resources such as water, forests, and wildlife.

Other Progressive governors included Theodore Roosevelt of New York and Woodrow Wilson of New Jersey. Roosevelt worked to develop a fair system for hiring state workers and made some corporations pay taxes. Wilson reduced the railroads' power and pushed for a direct primary law. Both Roosevelt and Wilson later became President and brought reforms to the White House.

✔ **Checkpoint** How did Progressive reformers change local and state governments?

Vocabulary Builder
<u>dynamic</u>–(dī NAM ihk) *adj.* energetic; relating to change or productive activity

---

SECTION 1 Assessment

Progress Monitoring *Online*
For: Self-test with vocabulary practice
www.pearsonschool.com/ushist

Comprehension

1. **Terms** Explain how each of the following terms is an example of a social or political reform.
   - settlement house
   - direct primary
   - initiative
   - referendum
   - recall

2. **NoteTaking Reading Skill: Identify Details** Use your flowchart to answer the Section Focus Question: What areas did Progressives think were in need of the greatest reform?

Writing About History

3. **Quick Write: Compare and Contrast Points of View** In a narrative essay, you may compare and contrast points of view on an issue through the opinions of various individuals. Compare and contrast Social Darwinism with Social Gospel through the personalities of William Graham Sumner, Billy Sunday, and Dwight L. Moody. Use library or Internet resources to complete this assignment.

Critical Thinking

4. **Recognize Cause and Effect** What problems did muckrakers expose and what effects did their work have on Progressive reform?

5. **Summarize** Describe Walter Rauschenbusch's ideas about Social Gospel and the Progressive Movement.

6. **Identify Points of View** Which groups in American society might have opposed Progressive reform? Explain.

American LITERATURE

The Jungle by Upton Sinclair

Objectives

- Understand an excerpt from an important book published during the Progressive Era.

- Describe the impact of Sinclair's style on readers of the time.

- Evaluate the work as an example of muckraking journalism.

Background Knowledge L3

Remind students that public reaction to *The Jungle* led to quick legislation. Have students predict their own reaction to what they are about to read.

Instruct L3

Ask **How would you react if you were reading *The Jungle* when it was first published?** *(Most students will say that they would be outraged or sickened.)* **If it were published today, do you think it would lead to reform? Why?** *(Most students will agree that it would lead to reform because of its graphic and detailed descriptions.)* **How does the term *muckraker* apply to Sinclair?** *(He "raked" through the "muck" of the stockyards to expose the dangerous and unsanitary conditions.)*

Monitor Progress

Refer students back to their predictions from the Background Knowledge exercise. Have them write a short paragraph reacting to the excerpt. Have students include parts of the excerpts in their writing.

When Upton Sinclair published *The Jungle* in 1906, he meant to open America's eyes to the plight of workers in the filthy, dangerous Chicago stockyards. Instead, popular outrage focused on the wider-reaching threat of spoiled meat. Congress quickly passed the nation's first legislation regulating the meat, food, and drug industries. Sinclair, disappointed by his failure to provoke more sympathy for the overworked, underpaid workers, noted "I aimed at the public's heart, and by accident I hit it in the stomach."

There was never the least attention paid to what was cut up for sausage.... There would be meat that had tumbled out on the floor, in the dirt and sawdust, where the workers had tramped and spit uncounted billions of consumption [tuberculosis] germs. There would be meat stored in great piles in rooms; and the water from leaky roofs would drip over it, and thousands of rats would race about on it. It was too dark in these storage places to see well, but a man could run his hand over these piles of meat and sweep off handfuls of the dried dung of rats. These rats were nuisances, and the packers would put poisoned bread out for them; they would die, and then rats, bread, and meat would go into the hoppers together. This is no fairy story and no joke; the meat would be shoveled into carts, and the man who did the shoveling would not trouble to lift out a rat even when he saw one—there were things that went into the sausage in comparison with which a poisoned rat was a tidbit. There was no place for the men to wash their hands before they ate their dinner, and so they made a practice of washing them in the water that was to be ladled into the sausage. There were the butt-ends of smoked meat, and the scraps of corned beef, and all the odds and ends of the waste of the plants, that would be dumped into old barrels in the cellar and left there. Under the system of rigid economy which the packers enforced, there were some jobs that it only paid to do once in a long time, and among these was the cleaning out of the waste barrels. Every spring they did it; and in the barrels would be dirt and rust and old nails and stale water—and cartload after cartload of it would be taken up and dumped into the hoppers with fresh meat, and sent out to the public's breakfast.

Thinking Critically

1. **Analyze Literature** Describe the author's style in this excerpt.

2. **Evaluate Literature** How does Sinclair's way of writing boost his credibility?

History Background

Upton Sinclair Perhaps the most famous of the muckrakers, Upton Sinclair was born in Baltimore, Maryland, in 1878. His family was poor, but his mother had wealthy relatives, and Sinclair was exposed early to issues of class disparity. Sinclair graduated from the College of the City of New York in 1897, attended graduate school at Columbia University, and then worked as a journalist. After he was sent to Chicago by the socialist newspaper Appeal to Reason to write an investigative report on the working conditions in the Chicago stockyards, Sinclair wrote *The Jungle.* The often-disturbing work led to major reforms in food purity regulation and is still in print today. Sinclair eventually published more than 80 books, including his 11-book cycle of contemporary historical novels featuring antifascist hero Lanny Budd. One of these novels, *Dragon's Teeth,* won the Pulitzer Prize for fiction in 1943. Sinclair continued to write both fiction and nonfiction works of social criticism throughout his life. He died in Bound Brook, New Jersey, in 1968.

Answers

Thinking Critically

1. unemotional, factual, journalistic
2. He gives only facts, not personal opinions.

◀ A woman working at a Pittsburgh cigar factory in 1909

WITNESS HISTORY

Women at Work

As the Progressive Movement wore on, many reformers took up causes that affected women. Although women spearheaded a number of Progressive reforms, they did not have the right to vote in national elections. In workplaces like the Triangle Shirtwaist Factory, women endured the awful conditions described by one worker:

❝It was a world of greed; the human being didn't mean anything. The hours were from 7:30 in the morning to 6:30 at night when it wasn't busy. When the season was on we worked until 9:00. No overtime pay, not even supper money. . . . When you were told Saturday afternoon, through a sign on the elevator, 'If you don't come in on Sunday, you needn't come in on Monday,' what choice did you have? You had no choice.❞

—Pauline Newman, organizer of the International Ladies Garment Workers Union

▲ A week's wages—only $1.50!

Objectives

As you teach this section, keep students focused on the following objectives to help them answer the Section Focus Question and master core content.

- Analyze the impact of changes in women's education on women's roles in society.
- Explain what women did to win workers' rights and to improve family life.
- Evaluate the tactics women used to win passage of the Nineteenth Amendment.

Women Make Progress

Objectives

- Analyze the impact of changes in women's education on women's roles in society.
- Explain what women did to win workers' rights and to improve family life.
- Evaluate the tactics women used to win passage of the Nineteenth Amendment.

Terms and People

Florence Kelley
NCL
temperance movement
Margaret Sanger
Ida B. Wells

suffrage
Carrie Chapman Catt
NAWSA
Alice Paul
Nineteenth Amendment

NoteTaking

Reading Skill: Identify Main Ideas As you read this section, complete an outline like the one below to capture the main ideas.

> I. Women Expand Reforms
>   A. Hardships for women
>   1.
>   2.
>   B.

Why It Matters In the early 1900s, a growing number of women were no longer content to have a limited role in society. Women activists helped bring about Progressive reforms and won the right to vote. In the years ahead, women would continue the struggle to expand their roles and rights. **Section Focus Question: How did women of the Progressive Era make progress and win the right to vote?**

Progressive Women Expand Reforms

In the early 1900s, a growing number of women wanted to do more than fulfill their roles as wives and mothers. They were ready to move beyond raising children, cooking meals, keeping the home tidy, and caring for family members. They wanted to expand their role in the community.

Education helped women achieve their goals. By the 1890s, a growing number of women's colleges prepared them for careers as teachers or nurses. Some, such as Bryn Mawr College in Pennsylvania and the School of Social Work in New York, trained them to lead the new organizations working for social reform. Armed with education and modern ideas, many middle-class white women began to tackle problems they saw in society.

Working Women Face Hardships For most women, however, working outside the home meant difficult jobs, with long hours and dangerous conditions. And these women were usually expected to

Prepare to Read

Background Knowledge L3

Remind students that the Progressives wanted to reform the political process. Ask students to predict what obstacles women might have had to overcome to achieve the right to vote.

Set a Purpose L3

- **WITNESS HISTORY** Read the selection aloud.

  Ask **How would voting help women change the conditions in which they worked?** *(It would give them more political power so that they could vote for lawmakers who would pass labor reform laws.)*

- **Focus** Point out the Section Focus Question, and write it on the board. Tell students to refer to this question as they read. *(Answer appears with Section 2 Assessment answers.)*

- **Preview** Have students preview the Section Objectives and the list of Terms and People.

- **NoteTaking** Using the Paragraph Shrinking strategy (TE, p. T20), have students read this section. As they read, have students outline the section's main ideas. Reading and Note Taking Study Guide

Vocabulary Builder

Use the information below and the following resource to teach students the high-use word from this section. Teaching Resources, Vocabulary Builder, p. 12

High-Use Word	Definition and Sample Sentence
strategy	*n.* a plan or an action based on a plan The citizens developed a **strategy** to help them achieve certain basic rights.

Progressive Women Expand Reforms

Instruct

- **Introduce: Key Term** Ask students to find the key term **temperance movement** (in bold) in the text. Then, write the term on the board and provide the definition. Ask students to read to find out how the **temperance movement** became a focus of Progressive women.

- **Teach** Ask **What hardships did women face at this time? Why did they want the right to vote?** *(Women could not vote, most had little or no education, and if they worked outside the home, they had difficult, low-paying jobs. Women wanted the right to vote so they would gain political power to improve their lives.)* **With what other areas of life were women reformers concerned?** *(labor conditions, product safety, family issues, temperance)* Discuss with students why these issues were tackled by women. Then, make a table on the board showing some key accomplishments and the women responsible for them.

- **Analyzing the Visuals** Have students examine the photograph on this page. Explain that *dry* describes a place where it is illegal to sell or consume alcohol. Ask students to explain why the women might be wearing white dresses and stars and stripes.

Independent Practice

Instruct students to begin recording the main ideas in the outline for this section.

Monitor Progress

As students fill in their outlines, circulate to make sure that they understand the main ideas of the section. For a completed version of the outline, see Note Taking Transparencies, **B-87.**

---

hand over their wages to their husbands, fathers, or brothers. Many women labored in factories that made cigars or clothing. Others toiled as laundresses or servants. Immigrants, African Americans, and women from rural areas filled these jobs, and most of them had little or no education. As a result, they could easily be cheated or bullied by their employers. Without being able to vote, women had little influence on the politicians who could expand their rights and look after their interests.

Reformers Champion Working Women's Rights A key goal of women reformers was to limit the number of work hours. They succeeded in several states. For example, a 1903 Oregon law capped women's workdays at ten hours. Five years later, in *Muller* v. *Oregon*, the Supreme Court reviewed that law. Lawyer Louis D. Brandeis argued that long working hours harmed working women and their families.

The Supreme Court agreed with Brandeis. Based on their role as mothers, it said, women could be "properly placed in a class" by themselves. As a result, laws could limit their work hours, even if similar laws would not be allowed for men. At the time, Progressives viewed this decision as a victory for women workers. In later years, however, this ruling was used to justify paying women less than men for the same job.

Florence Kelley believed that women were hurt by the unfair prices of goods they had to buy to run their homes. In 1899, she helped found the **National Consumers League (NCL),** which is still active today. The NCL gave special labels to "goods produced under fair, safe, and healthy working conditions" and urged women to buy them and avoid products that did not have these labels. The NCL pushed for other reforms as well. It backed laws calling for the government to inspect meatpacking plants, to make workplaces safer, and to make payments to the unemployed.

Florence Kelley also helped form the Women's Trade Union League (WTUL), another group that tried to improve conditions for female factory workers. It was one of the few groups in which upper-class and working-class women served together as leaders. The WTUL pushed for federal laws that set a minimum wage and an eight-hour workday. It also created the first workers' strike fund, which could be used to help support families who refused to work in unsafe or unfair conditions.

Women Work for Changes in Family Life A main goal of Progressive women was to improve family life. They pushed for laws that could help mothers keep families healthy and safe. One focus of this effort was the **temperance movement** led by the Women's Christian Temperance Union (WCTU). This group promoted temperance, the practice of never drinking alcohol. Members felt that alcohol often led men to spend their earnings on liquor, neglect their families, and abuse their wives. Formed in the 1870s, the WCTU gained strength during the Progressive Era. Their work led to the passage of the Eighteenth Amendment, which outlawed the production and sale of alcohol.

Nurse **Margaret Sanger** thought that family life and women's health would improve if mothers had fewer children. In 1916, Sanger, herself one of 11 children, opened the country's first birth-control clinic. Sanger was jailed several times as a "public nuisance." But federal courts eventually said doctors could give out information about family planning. In 1921, Sanger founded the American Birth Control League to make this information available to more women.

Women Campaign for Temperance

Minnesota women march to ban alcohol. The temperance movement gained a victory when Congress passed the 18th Amendment in 1917.

Differentiated Instruction   Solutions for All Learners

L1 Special Needs Students   **L2 English Language Learners**   **L2 Less Proficient Readers**

Have students review all images in this section. Then, on the basis of those images, have each student create a cartoon, poster, collage, or other visual work that expresses the main goals and achievements of women reformers in this period. For example, students might make a poster for the National Consumers League. Ask students to include a brief caption or a title for their work.

African American women also worked for social change. In 1896, **Ida B. Wells,** a black teacher, helped form the National Association of Colored Women (NACW). The group aimed to help families strive for success and to assist those who were less fortunate. With money raised from educated black women, the NACW set up day-care centers to protect and educate black children while their parents went to work.

✓ **Checkpoint** What steps did women take to win workers' rights?

Women Fight for the Right to Vote

One of the boldest goals of Progressive women was **suffrage**—the right to vote. They argued that this was the only way to make sure that the government would protect children, foster education, and support family life. As Jane Addams explained, women needed the vote because political issues reached inside people's homes.

> **Primary Source** "If the street is not cleaned by the city authorities no amount of private sweeping will keep the tenement free from grime; if the garbage is not properly collected and destroyed a tenement-house mother may see her children sicken and die of diseases from which she alone is powerless to shield them, although her tenderness and devotion are unbounded. She cannot even secure untainted meat for her household, . . . unless the meat has been inspected by city officials."
> —Jane Addams, *Ladies Home Journal,* 1910

Since the 1860s, reformers such as Susan B. Anthony and Elizabeth Cady Stanton had tirelessly struggled for the right for women to have a voice in political issues. They failed at the federal level, but by the end of the 1890s, women in western states such as Wyoming and Colorado had won the right to vote.

Catt Takes Charge of the Movement In the 1890s, the national suffrage effort was reenergized by **Carrie Chapman Catt.** Catt had studied law and worked as one of the country's first female school superintendents. A captivating speaker, Catt traveled around the country urging women to join the **National American Woman Suffrage Association (NAWSA).** In 1900, she became the president of the NAWSA. Catt promoted what became known as her "winning plan," which called for action on two fronts. Some teams of women lobbied Congress to pass a constitutional amendment giving women the right to vote. Meanwhile, other teams used the new referendum process to try to pass state suffrage laws. By 1918, this <u>strategy</u> had helped women win the right to vote in New York, Michigan, and Oklahoma.

Catt introduced a "society plan" to recruit wealthy, well-educated women. She and her army of workers signed on women from all levels of society, including African Americans, Mexican Americans, and Jewish immigrants. All these women, called "suffragettes," helped promote suffrage in their own areas.

While the suffrage movement gained ground, some women worked against it. The National Association Opposed to Woman Suffrage (NAOWS) believed that the effort to win the vote would take women's attention away from family and volunteer work that benefited society in many ways. But as the pressure for women's suffrage grew stronger, the NAOWS faded away.

HISTORY MAKERS

Ida B. Wells (1862–1931)
Wells had gained fame for her campaign against the lynching of African Americans. But she was also a tireless worker for women's suffrage and joined in the famous 1913 march for universal suffrage that took place in Washington, D.C. Not able to tolerate injustice of any kind, Ida B. Wells, along with Jane Addams, successfully blocked the establishment of segregated schools in Chicago. In 1930, she ran for the Illinois State legislature, which made her one of the first black women to run for public office in the United States.

Ida B. Wells
25
Black Heritage USA

Vocabulary Builder
strategy—(STRAT uh jee) *n.* plan or an action based on a plan

Women Fight for the Right to Vote

Instruct

■ **Introduce: Key Term** Ask students to find the key term *suffrage* (in bold) in the text. Then, write the term on the board and provide the definition. Discuss with students the different strategies that Carrie Chapman Catt and Alice Paul used to achieve *suffrage.*

■ **Teach** Display Color Transparency: *Women's Suffrage.* Discuss the subject and tone of the cartoon. Ask **Why was there so much resistance to women receiving the right to vote?** *(Men might have thought that because many women at the time had little or no education, they were not educated enough to vote.)* Have students read the HISTORY MAKERS biography of Ida B. Wells on this page. Ask **What did universal suffrage and school desegregation have in common?** *(Both addressed injustice.)* Have students discuss the individuals and organizations that fought for women's suffrage and the events that led to the passage and ratification of the Nineteenth Amendment. Refer students to the map at the end of this section. Ask **Why do you think women's suffrage was legal in western states before becoming legal in much of the rest of the country?** *(Sample answer: These were new states, and many people who lived there were very independent and open to new ideas. Also, those people may have needed women's votes to achieve statehood.)* Color Transparencies **A-78**

History Background

The United States v. Susan B. Anthony Although it was illegal for women to vote in federal elections until 1920, some challenged the law. Basing their actions on a section of the Fourteenth Amendment that states that "No state shall make or enforce any law which shall abridge the privileges or immunities of citizens of the United States," suffragists Susan B. Anthony and Elizabeth Cady Stanton urged women to vote in federal elections. In the 1872 national election, Anthony and 14 other women cast ballots for President and for representatives to Congress from New York. The women were arrested a few weeks later. Anthony refused twice to pay her bail, but both times her lawyer, Henry Selden, arranged her release, explaining that he did not want to "see a lady I respected put in jail." At Anthony's trial in a New York federal district court, Judge Ward Hunt fined Anthony $100, which she refused to pay, but Hunt blocked her attempt to keep the case going by, paradoxically, refusing to jail her until she paid the fine. Anthony never did pay the fine.

Answer

✓ Women Progressives succeeded in several states to reduce the number of work hours for women. Florence Kelley formed the Women's Trade Union League, which worked for a minimum wage and an eight-hour workday, and created the first workers' strike fund.

- **Quick Activity** Refer students to the Events That Changed America feature "Suffragists Win the Vote." Have a volunteer read aloud the text of the large banner titled "To the Russian Envoys." Discuss the reasons why Paul and her fellow activists chose to hold their protest when they did and why it evoked such a strong reaction. Ask students whether they think the protest was appropriate, and have them explain their reasoning.

Activists Carry on the Struggle Some women, known as social activists, grew more daring in their strategies to win the vote. **Alice Paul,** their best-known leader, was raised in a Quaker home where she was encouraged to be independent. Paul attended a Quaker college and the New York School of Social Work before earning a Ph.D. from the University of Pennsylvania in 1912. She believed that drastic steps were needed to win the vote. By 1913, she was organizing women to recruit others across the nation. They drew in women of many backgrounds, from Maud Younger, known as the "millionaire waitress" because she organized California's first waitresses' union, to Nina Otero-Warren, a Hispanic who headed New Mexico's State Board of Health.

By 1917, Paul formed the National Woman's Party (NWP), which used public protest marches. The NWP became the first group to march with picket signs

INTERACTIVE
Whiteboard

Events That Changed America

SUFFRAGISTS WIN THE VOTE

The National Woman's Party began picketing the White House, urging President Wilson to back the woman's suffrage amendment. Susan B. Anthony had introduced the amendment nearly 40 years earlier, but the Senate had rejected it twice. So when America entered World War I, and Wilson proclaimed, "The world must be made safe for democracy," the weary suffragists were astounded. They wondered how could America be a democracy if women could not vote?

Then, when envoys from Russia visited Wilson in June, Alice Paul and her activists saw a golden opportunity. The Russians had just overthrown the czar, established a republic, and granted women the right to vote. As the envoys neared the White House, the suffragists stunned and embarrassed Wilson by unveiling a new banner that claimed America was not a democracy. The women set in motion a series of events that would change America.

▲ **"America is Not a Democracy"**
An angry mob shredded protestors' banners. The police warned the women not to return.

Suffrage Poster ▶
In marches on Washington, D.C., women urged Congress to vote for suffrage.

Connect to Your World

Equal Rights Amendment Drafted to eliminate federal and state laws that discriminated on the basis of gender, the Equal Rights Amendment (ERA) was first proposed to Congress in 1923. Finally approved by the Senate in 1972, the amendment was then submitted for ratification to the states. Although the seven-year deadline for ratification was extended to 1982, the amendment fell 3 states short of the 38-state majority needed to become the Twenty-seventh Amendment. Since then, it has been reintroduced in each new Congress; in 2005, the amendment moved as far as the House Subcommittee on the Constitution.

outside the White House. Hundreds of women were arrested in these protests. Some went on hunger strikes, refusing to eat until they could vote. The NWP methods angered many people, including women in other suffrage groups. Nevertheless, they did help win women the right to vote, because the NWP's actions made less-radical groups like the NAWSA look tame by comparison.

The Nineteenth Amendment Becomes Law When the United States entered World War I in 1917, Carrie Catt and Florence Kelley led the NAWSA to support the war effort. Their actions and those of the NWP convinced a growing number of legislators to support a women's suffrage amendment. In June 1919, Congress approved the **Nineteenth Amendment,** which stated that the right to vote "shall not be denied or abridged on account of sex." On August 18, 1920, the

Independent Practice
- For additional information on Carrie Chapman Catt, assign the *Biography: Carrie Chapman Catt* worksheet and have students answer the questions. Teaching Resources, **p. 21**
- Have students complete the outlines for this section.

Monitor Progress
As students complete their outlines, circulate to make sure that they have listed the main ideas. Remind students that the blue headings coincide with the Roman numerals and the red headings coincide with the capital letters.

▲ **Civil Disobedience and Arrests**
Alice Paul continued to lead protests in front of the White House. She and 168 others were arrested and jailed.

Suffering for the Cause ▶
The jailed women went on hunger strikes. They endured forced-feedings, beatings, disease, and poor medical treatment.

◀ **Spreading the Word**
The suffragists traveled the country, telling their story. They kept attention focused on women's suffrage when the issue might otherwise have been eclipsed by World War I.

Why It Matters
The efforts of these women swayed public opinion and helped the Susan B. Anthony Amendment become law. The House passed the amendment in 1918. Then the Senate passed it by one vote in 1919. Finally, in 1920, Tennessee became the 36th state to ratify the 19th Amendment. At long last, women in every state of the nation could vote. America had changed.

Thinking Critically
Why was the banner that was unveiled when the Russians visited Wilson so effective in stirring public opinion?

Differentiated Instruction   **Solutions for All Learners**

L4 Advanced Readers   **L4 Gifted and Talented Students**

Invite students to research the Progressive Era changes to the U.S. Constitution. Have them explain how the Progressive Movement led to the reforms embodied by the Sixteenth, Seventeenth, Eighteenth, and Nineteenth amendments. Have them report their findings to the class.

Answer

Thinking Critically
Sample answer: Because it was addressed to foreigners and was so critical of the United States, the banner probably embarrassed many Americans.

Assess Progress L3

- Have students complete the Section Assessment.
- Administer the Section Quiz. Teaching Resources, **p. 27**
- To further assess student understanding, use **Progress Monitoring Transparencies, 83.**

Reteach

If students need more instruction, have them read the section summary.

Reading and Note Taking L3
Study Guide

Adapted Reading and L1 L2
Note Taking Study Guide

Spanish Reading and L2
Note Taking Study Guide

Extend L4

Have students find the year in which women achieved the vote in as many countries as possible and create a map similar to the suffrage map of the United States on this page.

Answers

Caption Overall, most of the midwestern and western states granted suffrage to women earlier than did the eastern states.

✔ They lobbied Congress to pass a constitutional amendment; used the referendum process to pass state suffrage laws; recruited wealthy, well-educated women to work for suffrage; and held protest marches and hunger strikes.

Passage of Women's Suffrage

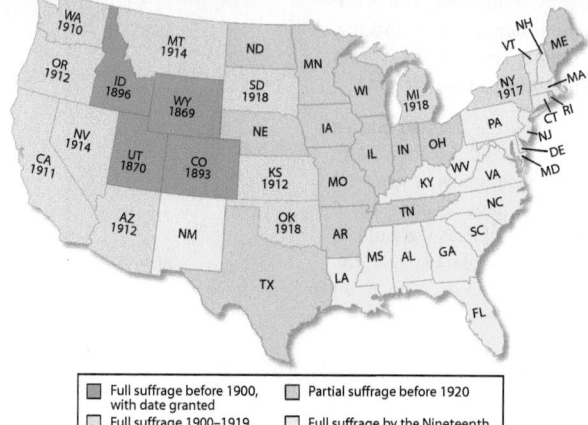

- Full suffrage before 1900, with date granted
- Full suffrage 1900–1919, with date granted
- Partial suffrage before 1920
- Full suffrage by the Nineteenth Amendment, 1920

Women's Suffrage

What pattern do you see in the passage of suffrage at the state level?

Tennessee State House of Representatives passed the amendment by one vote. With Tennessee's ratification, enough states had passed the amendment that it became official.

Alice Paul and Carrie Catt both claimed responsibility for the victory. In fact, according to historian Nancy Cott, "neither the shocking militancy of the National Women's Party nor the ladylike moderation of NAWSA was so solely responsible for victory as each group publicly claimed." The rival groups both contributed to the triumph of the women's suffrage movement. As a result, on November 2, 1920, Catt, Paul, and millions of other American women voted for the first time in a U.S. presidential election.

✔ **Checkpoint** What tactics did Progressive women use to win the right to vote?

SECTION 2 Assessment

Progress Monitoring *Online*
For: Self-test with vocabulary practice
www.pearsonschool.com/ushist

Comprehension

1. **People** Explain how each of the following people changed the lives of women.
   - Florence Kelley
   - Margaret Sanger
   - Ida B. Wells
   - Carrie Chapman Catt
   - Alice Paul

2. **NoteTaking Reading Skill: Identify Main Idea** Use your outline to answer the Section Focus Question: How did women of the Progressive Era make progress and win the right to vote?

Writing About History

3. **Quick Write: Communicate Perspective** Look at the map on the passage of women's suffrage in this section. In one paragraph, describe the map from the perspective of a supporter of suffrage for women. In a second paragraph, describe the map as viewed by a suffrage opponent.

Critical Thinking

4. **Draw Conclusions** Why would education have led middle-class women to address societal problems?

5. **Solve Problems** Choose one specific social problem and explain how Progressive women reformers proposed to solve that problem.

6. **Analyze Effects** How did suffragists' efforts at the state level affect their effort to win the right to vote at the national level?

Section 2 Assessment

1. Answers should reflect an understanding of each woman's role in the reform movement and the results of her work.

2. Possible answers: by lobbying Congress to pass a constitutional amendment giving women the right to vote; by using the referendum process to pass state suffrage laws; by holding protest marches and hunger strikes

3. Sample answer: Supporters might emphasize states that had suffrage before 1900 and the fact that all states

had suffrage by 1920. Opponents might point to how long it took to achieve full suffrage.

4. Through education, middle-class women may have been more socially aware. Also, women with an education tended to be financially well off and so had the time and money to spend on reform work.

5. Sample response: Worker's rights— Reformer Florence Kelley formed the Women's Trade Union League (WTUL), which combined the efforts of upper-class and working women to push for federal

laws that set a minimum wage, set an eight-hour workday, and created the first strike fund.

6. By achieving the vote at the state level, women could elect leaders who would support national women's suffrage and would ratify the Nineteenth Amendment.

> For additional assessment, have students access **Progress Monitoring *Online*** at **www.pearsonschool.com/ushist.**

Social Problems and Reforms

TRACK THE ISSUE

What are the most pressing problems, and how can we solve them?

There have been many movements for social reform in the United States. But Americans do not always agree on the need for reform or on the best way to achieve it. In fact, some reform ideas face strong opposition. Why do some reform movements win support, while others do not? Use the timeline below to explore this enduring issue.

1790s–1820s
Second Great Awakening
Revival of Christian faith sparks moral and spiritual reform.

1830s–1850s Abolitionism
Antislavery forces demand an end to the slave system.

1890–1920 Progressivism
Reformers urge a broad range of social and political changes.

1950s–1960s Civil Rights
African Americans lead movement for racial equality.

1990s–2000s
Healthcare Reform
Reformers combat the spiraling costs of healthcare and insurance.

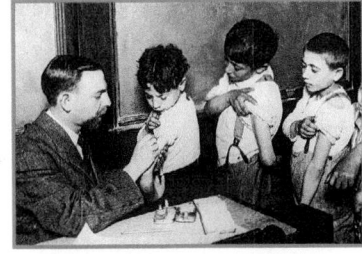

Young children line up to receive vaccinations in a school clinic.

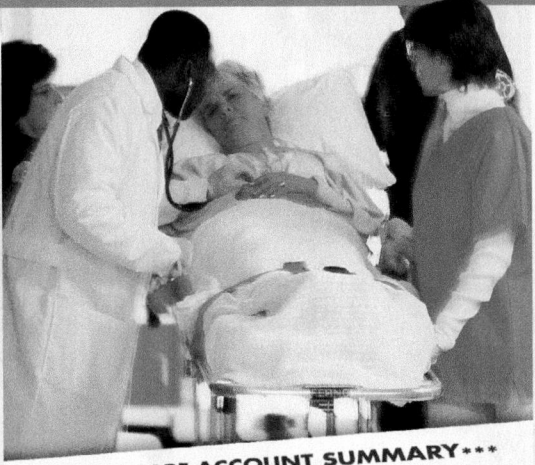

···HEALTH CARE ACCOUNT SUMMARY···

01/11/05	MRI LUMBAR W/O CONTRAST	$1,874.00
01/12/05	INSURANCE/PAYMENTS	$250.00
	AMOUNT DUE FROM PATIENT	$1,624.00

Healthcare costs are a major issue.

DEBATE THE ISSUE

Health Insurance Medical costs are soaring. Many Americans lack health insurance and cannot pay their bills. Some reformers want the government to provide universal health insurance, also known as a single-payer system. Others say this approach will cause more harm than good.

" . . . Everybody has . . . to be covered. There's only three ways of doing it. You can have a single-payer system, you can require employers, or you can have individual responsibility. My plan combines employers and individual responsibility, while maintaining Medicare and Medicaid. The whole idea of universal health care is . . . a core Democratic principle . . . "

—Senator Hillary Clinton, 2008

" A single-payer system promotes higher taxes, limits technology, produces waiting lists, rations care, and prolongs suffering. . . . A universal healthcare system run by government will reduce the quality and access to health care for all Americans. It's a prescription for disaster. "

—Sally Pipes, President, Pacific Research Institute

? TRANSFER Activities

1. **Compare** Why does Hillary Clinton support universal health care? Why does Sally Pipes oppose it?

2. **Analyze** Do you think Sally Pipes would support the efforts of some Progressive Era city governments to purchase public utilities? Explain.

3. **Transfer** Use the following Web site to see a video, try a WebQuest, and write in your journal. www.pearsonschool.com/ushist

History Background

Medicare and Medicaid In a 1945 address to Congress, President Harry Truman proposed a government program of comprehensive health insurance for all Americans, to be administered through the Social Security Administration. Congress did not respond. By the late 1950s, however, the elderly made up a growing percentage of the population, and a national survey showed that only 56 percent of people over 65 had health insurance. President John F. Kennedy put pressure on Congress during his administration to provide health insurance for at least the elderly. However, it was not until 1965 that Congress passed the Medicare and Medicaid Bill as part of President Lyndon Johnson's Great Society program. Medicare provides affordable, comprehensive health insurance for retirees, as well as for certain other groups, such as the disabled. Medicaid provides health insurance for those who are unable to afford their own. To honor the President who had started it all, Johnson signed the Medicare and Medicaid Bill in Independence, Missouri, at the Truman Library. Harry Truman was presented with the first Medicare card at the event.

Objectives

As you teach this section, keep students focused on the following objectives to help them answer the Section Focus Question and master core content.

- Analyze Progressives' attitudes toward minority rights.
- Explain why African Americans organized.
- Examine the strategies used by members of other minority groups to defend their rights.

Prepare to Read

Background Knowledge L3

Remind students that during the Progressive Era, women struggled for the right to vote. Explain that minorities also faced discrimination and injustice during this time. Ask students to predict how these groups will work to overcome inequality.

Set a Purpose L3

- **WITNESS HISTORY** Read the selection aloud.
  Ask **What situation is Bryan describing?** *(wage discrimination against Mexican Americans)* **What is his attitude toward this problem?** *(He admits that they are being paid unfairly.)* Explore why Progressives might have failed to help or excluded some groups.

- **Focus** Point out the Section Focus Question, and write it on the board. Tell students to refer to this question as they read. *(Answer appears with Section 3 Assessment answers.)*

- **Preview** Have students preview the Section Objectives and the list of Terms and People.

- NoteTaking Using the Structured Read Aloud strategy (TE, p. T20), have students read this section. As they read, have students outline the section's main ideas and details.
  Reading and Note Taking Study Guide

▲ Cuero family, Warner Springs, California, 1904

WITNESS HISTORY

Voices of Protest

The sympathy that reformers felt for the plight of the poor did not often extend to minorities. In 1912, Progressive journalist Samuel Bryan wrote an investigative article about Mexican immigrants. Displaying a common bias, Bryan concluded that the immigrants did not work hard enough. Yet, he was forced to admit that Mexican Americans faced discrimination. He wrote:

❝[Mexican Americans] are now employed to a considerable extent in the coal mines of Colorado and New Mexico, in the ore mines of Colorado and Arizona, in the smelters of Arizona, in the cement factories of Colorado and California, . . . and in fruit growing and canning in California. . . . Where they are employed in other industries, the same wage discrimination against them as was noted in the case of railroad employees is generally apparent.❞

—Samuel Bryan, *The Survey,* September 1912

The Struggle Against Discrimination

Objectives

- Analyze Progressives' attitudes toward minority rights.
- Explain why African Americans organized.
- Examine the strategies used by members of other minority groups to defend their rights.

Terms and People

Americanization	NAACP
Booker T. Washington	Urban League
W.E.B. Du Bois	Anti-Defamation League
Niagara Movement	mutualistas

NoteTaking

Reading Skill: Main Idea and Details
Outline the section's main ideas and details.

> I. The Struggle Against Discrimination
> A.

Why It Matters Prejudice and discrimination against minorities continued even as the Progressive Movement got underway. But in the spirit of Progressivism, African Americans, Latinos, Catholics, Jews, and new immigrant groups worked to help themselves. Their efforts paved the way for the era of civil rights that would follow decades later. **Section Focus Question: What steps did minorities take to combat social problems and discrimination?**

Progressivism Presents Contradictions

The Progressive Era was not so progressive for nonwhite and immigrant Americans. Most Progressives were white Anglo-Saxon Protestant reformers who were indifferent or actively hostile to minorities. They tried to make the United States a model society by encouraging everyone to follow white, middle-class ways of life.

Social Reform or Social Control? Settlement houses and other civic groups played a prominent role in the **Americanization** efforts of many Progressives. While they taught immigrants English, their programs also tried to change how immigrants lived. They advised immigrants how to dress like white middle-class Americans and pushed them to replace the foods and customs of their homelands with

Vocabulary Builder

Use the information below and the following resource to teach students the high-use words from this section. Teaching Resources, Vocabulary Builder, p. 12

High-Use Words	Definitions and Sample Sentences
so-called	*adj.* commonly named; falsely or improperly named The **so-called** cease-fire did not really bring an end to the fighting.
acknowledge	*v.* to admit to be true In June 1919, Congress **acknowledged** women's right to vote when it approved the Nineteenth Amendment.

Protestant practices and values. These reformers believed that assimilating immigrants into American society would make them more loyal and moral citizens.

Many Progressives found the immigrants' use of alcohol especially alarming. In many European countries, it was customary for families to serve wine or beer with meals. Many reformers, however, believed that these practices showed moral faults. As a result, prejudice against immigrants was one of the forces behind the temperance movement.

Racism Limits the Goals of Progressivism Many Progressives shared the same prejudice against nonwhites held by other white Americans of the time. They believed that some people were more fit than others to play a leading role in society. They agreed with <u>so-called</u> scientific theories that said that dark-skinned peoples had less intelligence than whites. In the late 1800s, southern Progressives used these misguided theories to justify the passage of laws that kept African Americans from voting. Some southern Progressives urged an end to the violence and terrorism waged against African Americans. Edgar Gardner Murphy, an Episcopal minister and a leading Alabama Progressive, advised that African Americans "will accept in the white man's country the place assigned him by the white man, . . . not by stress of rivalry, but by genial cooperation with the white man's interests."

After the Supreme Court issued its *Plessy* v. *Ferguson* decision, states across the North and the South had passed segregation laws. By 1910, segregation was the norm across the nation. After 1914, even the offices of the federal

Vocabulary Builder
so-called–(SOH kawld) *adj.* commonly named; falsely or improperly named

---

Progressivism Presents Contradictions L3

Instruct

- **Introduce: Key Term** Ask students to find the key term *Americanization* (in bold) in the text. Ask what they think it means, and then, if necessary, clarify the definition. Tell students that they will learn how *Americanization* played a role in limiting the effectiveness of the Progressive Movement.

- **Teach** Remind students that Progressivism was mainly a white, middle-class, Protestant movement. Explain that although Progressives did enormous good, sometimes their viewpoints and beliefs led to prejudice and discrimination against nonwhites and people of different religious and economic backgrounds. Ask **What was the result of Progressive attitudes toward nonwhites?** (*Segregation became widespread and the norm.*)

- **Quick Activity** Have students write a paragraph comparing the Americanization movement of the Progressive Era with the debate over immigration into the United States today.

Independent Practice

Instruct students to fill in the outline for this section by recording main ideas and details about Progressivism and discrimination.

Monitor Progress

As students fill in their outlines, circulate to make sure that they understand how different groups struggled against discrimination. For a completed version of the flowchart, see Note Taking Transparencies, **B-88.**

Answers

Compare

1. Washington believed that African Americans should work to achieve economic independence first and that civil rights would follow. Du Bois believed that African Americans should demand and work actively for civil rights.

2. Sample answers: They were living before the civil rights movement, which made it clear that conflict would be necessary to effect change. Leaders today would probably not urge patience, but may differ on whether it is better to effect change through protest or through legal action.

How should we respond to discrimination?

African Americans were freed from slavery, but discriminatory laws and racist attitudes kept them oppressed and threatened. African Americans debated how they should respond to this discrimination.

BOOKER T. WASHINGTON

Washington (1856–1915) believed that African Americans had to achieve economic independence before civil rights. Black people must tolerate discrimination while they proved themselves equal to white people. Slowly, civil rights would come.

Primary Source

❝[The Negro must] live peaceably with his white neighbors . . . the Negro [must] deport himself modestly . . . depending upon the slow but sure influences that proceed from the possessions of property, intelligence, and high character for the full recognition of his political rights.❞

W.E.B. DU BOIS

Du Bois (1868–1963) believed that black Americans had to demand their social and civil rights or else become permanent victims of racism. African Americans must fight every day for the rights given to them in the Constitution.

Primary Source

❝We claim for ourselves every single right that belongs to a freeborn American . . . and until we get these rights we will never cease to protest. . . . How shall we get them? By voting where we may vote, by persistent, unceasing agitation, by hammering at the truth, by sacrifice and work.❞

Compare

1. How did the views of Washington and Du Bois about the nature of civil rights differ?

2. How do these leaders' opinions reflect the era in which they lived? Would leaders today make similar arguments? Explain.

Differentiated Instruction Solutions for All Learners

L4 Advanced Readers **L4 Gifted and Talented Students**

Explain that the debate between Booker T. Washington and W.E.B. Du Bois was of great importance to the African American community at this time. Have students locate a copy of the poem "Booker T. and W.E.B." by Dudley Randall, published in 1966. Then, in small groups, have them discuss the work by analyzing its tone and point of view. Encourage students to consider the accuracy of Randall's presentation of the subjects' views and whether he had more sympathy with one man over the other. If so, ask why they think this is and whether they agree or disagree with the author's viewpoint.

African Americans Demand Reform

Instruct

- **Introduce** Ask students to find the key people **Booker T. Washington** and **W.E.B. Du Bois** (in bold) in the text. Then, write their names on the board and clarify the pronunciation of Du Bois (doo BOYZ). Tell students that these two African American leaders had very different ideas about how to attain equality.

- **Teach** Using the Idea Wave strategy (TE, p. T22), have students review the ideas of Booker T. Washington and W.E.B. Du Bois in the Comparing Viewpoints feature. Using the feature's questions as a basis for discussion, explore the differences in the theories of these two leaders and record students' responses on the board under either *Washington* or *Du Bois*. Then, display Color Transparency: *Organizing for Civil Rights*. Have students compare and contrast the organizations that began the struggle for civil rights.
  Color Transparencies **A-79**

- **Analyzing the Visuals** Refer students to the photograph from the Springfield riot. Explain that this was one of 89 recorded lynchings of African Americans in that year. Ask students to describe how the image represents the degree of racism in the United States during the early 1900s.

Independent Practice

To help students further analyze the ideas of Washington and Du Bois, have students read the *Viewpoints: Washington and Du Bois* worksheet and answer the questions. Teaching Resources, **p. 22**

Monitor Progress

Have students reread the blue heading "African Americans Demand Reform" and write the main idea of each paragraph in their own words.

Answer

✔ Most Progressives were prejudiced against those who were nonwhite, non-Protestant, and non-middle class, and they often worked to assimilate immigrants through Americanization.

government in Washington, D.C., were segregated as a result of policies approved by President Woodrow Wilson, a Progressive.

✔ **Checkpoint** What attitudes did most Progressives hold about minorities and immigrant groups?

African Americans Demand Reform

In the face of these injustices, the nation's most visible African American leader urged patience. **Booker T. Washington** told blacks to move slowly toward racial progress. By working hard and waiting patiently, he believed, African Americans would gradually win white Americans' respect and eventually would be able to exercise their full voting and citizenship rights.

Other African Americans rejected this view. The most outspoken among them were **W.E.B. Du Bois** and William Monroe Trotter. Both men had been raised in New England and educated at Harvard University. Both urged African Americans to demand immediately all the rights guaranteed by the Constitution.

African Americans Form the Niagara Movement Du Bois and Trotter were especially concerned that all across the South, black men were being denied the right to vote. In the summer of 1905, they and other leading African American thinkers met at Niagara Falls. They had to meet in Canada because no hotel on the New York side of the border would give them rooms.

The **Niagara Movement**, as the group called itself, denounced the idea of gradual progress. Washington, they said, was too willing to compromise African Americans' basic rights. They also condemned his notion of teaching only trade skills. This kind of education, Du Bois said, "can create workers, but it cannot make *men*." Talented blacks should be taught history, literature, and philosophy, so they could think for themselves.

Despite its bold ideas, the Niagara Movement never grew to more than a few hundred strong. To make a difference, African Americans needed a more powerful voice.

Riots Lead to Formation of NAACP In the summer of 1908, a white mob in Springfield, Illinois, attempted to lynch two African American prisoners in the city jail. Upon learning that the prisoners had been removed to safety, the rioters turned their anger against the city's black residents, killing two people and burning 40 homes. The Niagara Movement members were outraged that such an attack could happen in Abraham Lincoln's hometown.

Niagara Movement
The original leaders of the Niagara Movement met in response to W.E.B. Du Bois's call to "organize thoroughly the intelligent honest Negroes throughout the United States."

This lynching occurred during the 1908 Springfield, Illinois, riot.

Differentiated Instruction — Solutions for All Learners

L1 Special Needs Students   **L2 English Language Learners**   **L2 Less Proficient Readers**

Explain to students that the NAACP was formed in reaction to the injustices of the time. To help them better understand the events that led to that organization's formation, have students create a flowchart that summarizes visually the key events under the heading *African Americans Demand Reform*. Have students work in pairs to compare their flowcharts and revise them as needed.

The Springfield riot also got the attention of a number of white reformers. They now <u>acknowledged</u> the need to help African Americans protect their lives, win the right to vote, and secure their civil rights. In 1909, they joined with leaders of the Niagara Movement to form the **National Association for the Advancement of Colored People (NAACP).** The NAACP aimed to help African Americans be "physically free from peonage [forced, low-paid labor], mentally free from ignorance, politically free from disfranchisement, and socially free from insult."

NAACP leaders included white and black Progressives who had worked in other areas of social reform. Among them were Jane Addams, Ray Stannard Baker, and Florence Kelley. Ida B. Wells, owner of a Tennessee newspaper, used her publication to make clear the horror of lynching. She and the others planned the group's strategy—to use the courts to challenge unfair laws. In the early 1900s, the NAACP focused on the battle for equal access to decent housing and professional careers like teaching.

African Americans Form the Urban League Across the country, African Americans were migrating from rural to urban areas during this period. Local black clubs and churches set up employment agencies and relief efforts to help African Americans get settled and find work. In 1911, more than 100 of these groups in many cities joined into a network called the **Urban League.** While the NAACP helped middle-class blacks struggle for political and social justice, the Urban League focused on poorer workers. It helped families buy clothes and books and send children to school. It helped factory workers and maids find jobs. Both the NAACP and the Urban League still aid African Americans today.

✔ **Checkpoint** Why did African Americans and others decide it was time to organize against discrimination?

Reducing Prejudice and Protecting Rights

African Americans were not alone in seeking their rights. Individuals and organizations of diverse ethnic groups spoke out against unfair treatment and took action by creating self-help agencies. For example, in northern cities, Catholic parishes offered a variety of social services to immigrants. In Chicago, a network of Polish Catholic groups grew so strong that it earned the nickname American Warsaw.

The Anti-Defamation League Aids Jews Jews in New York had formed the B'nai B'rith in 1843 to provide religious education and to help Jewish families. In response to growing anti-Semitism, the group founded the **Anti-Defamation League** in 1913. Its goal was—and still is—to defend Jews and others against physical and verbal attacks, false statements, and "to secure justice and fair treatment to all citizens alike. . . ."

Mexican Americans Organize Mexican Americans also organized to help themselves. Those living in Arizona formed the Partido Liberal Mexicano (PLM), which offered Mexican Americans many of the same services that the Urban League gave to African Americans. In several states, Mexican Americans formed **mutualistas,** groups that made loans and provided legal assistance. The mutualistas also had insurance programs to help members if they were too sick to work.

Vocabulary Builder

<u>acknowledge</u>–(ak NAHL ihj) *v.* to admit to be true

HISTORY MAKERS

Octaviano Larrazolo (1859–1930)

Larrazolo was a Progressive governor in New Mexico who worked for many reforms. He helped make sure that New Mexico's first state constitution protected Latinos from discrimination. Elected governor in 1918, he pushed for laws aimed at helping children and improving public health. He also favored bilingual education and voting rights for women. That last stand cost him the support of his Republican Party, and he served only one term as governor.

Reducing Prejudice and Protecting Rights

Instruct

- **Introduce: Key Term** Ask students to find the key term **Anti-Defamation League** (in bold) in the text. Then, write the term on the board and provide the definition. On the basis of the definition, have students explain how the **Anti-Defamation League** is similar to and different from the Urban League.

- **Teach** Create a four-column chart on the board, labeling the columns as follows: "Jewish Americans," "Mexican Americans," "Native Americans," and "Asian Americans." Use this chart to record the goals, reforms, and achievements of these different groups of people as the class reads. Discuss with students why these groups had to organize to help themselves and what they had in common with one another.

- **Quick Activity** Have students read the HISTORY MAKERS biography of Octaviano Larrazolo on this page. Ask them to list ways in which Larrazolo's goals were Progressive, but at the same time worked against Americanization.

Independent Practice

Ask students to reread the text under the blue heading "Reducing Prejudice and Protecting Rights." Have students create outlines summarizing the information in several key points.

Monitor Progress

As students create their outlines, circulate to make sure that they have not missed important facts and details.

Connect to Your World

The Urban League The Urban League is one of the oldest and largest community-based organizations working in the United States for the empowerment of African Americans. In 1911, the League was formed from the merger of three different groups: the Committee for the Improvement of Industrial Conditions Among Negroes in New York, the National League for the Protection of Colored Women, and the Committee on Urban Conditions Among Negroes. Today, the League works through its more than 100 affiliates in 35 states and in Washington, D.C., to provide support and assistance in areas such as job training, education, health, public policy, and civil rights.

Answer

✔ Public acknowledgment of the need for civil rights reform drew attention to African Americans' situation. Becoming organized not only took advantage of the greater number of people now living in urban areas, it also served to give the reformers the strategic strength they needed to gain nationwide attention and support for their cause.

Assess and Reteach

Assess Progress

- Have students complete the Section Assessment.

- Administer the Section Quiz. **Teaching Resources, p. 28**

- To further assess student understanding, use **Progress Monitoring Transparencies, 84.**

Reteach

If students need more instruction, have them read the section summary.

Reading and Note Taking Study Guide L3

Adapted Reading and Note Taking Study Guide L1 L2

Spanish Reading and Note Taking Study Guide L2

Extend L4

See this Chapter's Professional Development pages for the Extend Online activity on African American leaders during the Progressive Era.

Answer

✓ These groups formed self-help agencies and social justice organizations. Some groups took legal action.

Japanese Field Workers
Japanese immigrants, like those above, often found work tending the fruit orchards of California. Through hard work, many were later able to buy land and orchards of their own.

Many Mexican Americans were forced to sign unfair labor contracts that kept them in debt to people whose land they worked. In 1911, the Supreme Court struck down a law that enforced that system.

Native Americans Take Action Progressives did little to help Native Americans. The Dawes Act, passed in 1887, had divided reservations into plots for individuals to farm. But the law also said that lands not given to individual Indians could be sold to the general public. By 1932, nearly two thirds of the lands held by tribes in 1887 were in the hands of whites.

Carlos Montezuma, a Native American from Arizona, helped establish the Society of American Indians in 1911, the first organization for Indian rights to protest federal Indian policy. A doctor, Montezuma treated Native Americans living on reservations. He urged Native Americans to preserve their cultures and avoid being dependent on the government.

Asian Americans Fight Unfair Laws Asian Americans also had to protect themselves. A 1913 California law said that only American citizens could own land. Because Japanese immigrants could not become citizens, the law forced them to sell their land. Japanese Americans found a way around this, however, by putting the land in their children's names. Because their children had been born in the United States, they were American citizens.

Takao Ozawa fought the law in court that blocked Asian Americans from becoming citizens. In 1922, however, the Supreme Court ruled against him. A newspaper read by Japanese Americans commented, "The slim hope that we had entertained . . . has been shattered completely."

✓ **Checkpoint** What strategies did other minority groups use to defend their rights?

SECTION **3** Assessment

Progress Monitoring *Online*
For: Self-test with vocabulary practice
www.pearsonschool.com/ushist

Comprehension

1. Terms and People For each item below, write a sentence explaining its significance.
- Booker T. Washington
- W.E.B. Du Bois
- Niagara Movement
- NAACP
- Urban League
- Anti-Defamation League
- mutualistas

2. NoteTaking Reading Skill: Main Ideas and Details Use your outline to answer the Section Focus Question: What steps did minorities take to combat social problems and discrimination?

Writing About History

3. Quick Write: Gather Details Suppose you want to write a narrative about the effect of the Urban League's work in the Progressive Era. Conduct research to find descriptions and images of African American life before and during this period.

Critical Thinking

4. Analyze Information How did Progressives' views about race and values foster prejudice?

5. Draw Inferences What do the differing approaches of Booker T. Washington and W.E.B. Du Bois suggest about their views of American society?

6. Compare Were the goals and actions of the mutualistas more similar to those of the Urban League or to those of the Anti-Defamation League? Explain.

Section 3 Assessment

1. Sentences should reflect an understanding of each term or person listed.

2. Minorities united, formed social justice and self-help agencies, took legal action, spoke out publicly, and ran for public office.

3. Students should collect and organize materials and information on the lives of African Americans before and during the Progressive Era.

4. Most Progressives were white, Protestant, and middle-class. Their views on what the ideal American society should look and be like led many Progressives to work for the Americanization of immigrants and to look down on, disapprove of, or be prejudiced against people who were different from themselves.

5. Washington's views reflected a desire to avoid confrontation and a belief that whites would respond justly to African Americans as they climbed the economic ladder. Du Bois's views reflected a belief that white Americans would never act justly or extend equality without being forced to do so.

6. The mutualistas' goals were similar to those of the Urban League in that the mutualistas provided grass-roots services to the needy in the Mexican American community, such as loans, disability programs, and legal assistance.

For additional assessment, have students access **Progress Monitoring *Online*** at **www.pearsonschool.com/ushist.**

"Teddy" bear ▶

WITNESS HISTORY

A Bold Leader Takes Control

When Theodore Roosevelt entered the White House, never before had the country had so young a leader. He brought to the presidency tremendous energy, vision, and a willingness to expand presidential power in order to improve American lives. In a rousing speech, he urged some young supporters:

❝The principles for which we stand are the principles of fair play and a square deal for every man and every woman in the United States. . . . I wish to see you boys join the Progressive Party, and act in that part and as good citizens in the same way I'd expect any one of you to act in a football game. In other words, don't flinch, don't fold, and hit the line hard.❞

—Theodore Roosevelt, Address to Boy's Progressive League, 1913

▲ Theodore Roosevelt speaking in New York City

Objectives

As you teach this section, keep students focused on the following objectives to help them answer the Section Focus Question and master core content.

- Discuss Theodore Roosevelt's ideas on the role of government.
- Analyze how Roosevelt changed the government's role in the economy.
- Explain the impact of Roosevelt's actions on natural resources.
- Compare and contrast Taft's policies with Roosevelt's.

Roosevelt's Square Deal

Objectives

- Discuss Theodore Roosevelt's ideas on the role of government.
- Analyze how Roosevelt changed the government's role in the economy.
- Explain the impact of Roosevelt's actions on natural resources.
- Compare and contrast Taft's policies with Roosevelt's.

Terms and People

Theodore Roosevelt	Gifford Pinchot
Square Deal	National Reclamation
Hepburn Act	Act
Meat Inspection Act	New Nationalism
Pure Food and Drug Act	Progressive Party
John Muir	

NoteTaking

Reading Skill: Identify Main Ideas As you read this section, use a concept web like the one below to record the main ideas.

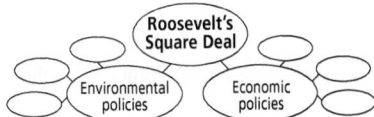

Why It Matters In the late 1800s, the United States had several weak and ineffective Presidents. The arrival of Theodore Roosevelt, a charismatic figure who embraced Progressive ideals, ushered in a new era. Roosevelt passed Progressive reforms and expanded the powers of the presidency. He changed the way Americans viewed the roles of the President and the government. **Section Focus Question: What did Roosevelt think government should do for citizens?**

Roosevelt Shapes the Modern Presidency

In 1901, when **Theodore Roosevelt** became President of the United States, he was only 43 years old. However, Roosevelt had packed quite a lot into those years, gaining a reputation for being smart, energetic, and opinionated. The sickly child of wealthy parents, he had used his family's resources to develop both his strength and his mind. Observers said he generated so much energy that if you met him, you left the event with bits of his personality "stuck to your clothes."

Roosevelt Rises to the Presidency Roosevelt had graduated with honors from Harvard University in 1880. He spent only a few months studying law at Columbia University before being elected to the New York State Assembly. After three years' service there, and after the deaths of both his mother and his wife, Alice, Roosevelt retired to a ranch in the West. There he developed a love of the wilderness.

Prepare to Read

Background Knowledge L3

Explain to students that Theodore Roosevelt was a Progressive President. Have students preview the section headings and then write a sentence to describe what they think Roosevelt's presidency was like.

Set a Purpose L3

- **WITNESS HISTORY** Read the selection aloud.

  Ask **To what does Roosevelt compare the work of the Progressive Party?** *(a football game)* **What does this quotation tell you about Roosevelt's personality?** *(He was bold, strong, forceful, enthusiastic, aggressive, and he liked sports.)*

- **Focus** Point out the Section Focus Question, and write it on the board. Tell students to refer to this question as they read. *(Answer appears with Section 4 Assessment answers.)*

- **Preview** Have students preview the Section Objectives and the list of Terms and People.

- **NoteTaking** Using the Guided Questioning strategy (TE, p. T20), have students read this section. As they read, have students complete the concept web by recording this section's main ideas. Reading and Note Taking Study Guide

Vocabulary Builder

Use the information below and the following resource to teach students the high-use words from this section. Teaching Resources, Vocabulary Builder, p. 12

High-Use Words	Definitions and Sample Sentences
dominate	*v.* to have a commanding place or position in Muckraker journalists **dominated** the news media of the early 1900s and introduced Progressive ideals to the American public.
rational	*adj.* relating to or based on reason; reasonable Thomas Jefferson was influenced by the **rational** philosophies of Enlightenment thinkers.

Roosevelt Shapes the Modern Presidency L3

Instruct

- **Introduce: Key Term** Ask students to find the key term **Square Deal** (in bold) in the text. Then, write it on the board and provide the definition. Have students read to find out how the **Square Deal** reflected Progressive ideas.

- **Teach** Have a volunteer read aloud the Primary Source quotation on this page. Using the Think-Write-Pair-Share strategy (TE, p. T23), have students restate the quotation to explain Roosevelt's theory of government in their own words. Use students' responses as a basis for discussion of Roosevelt's view of his role as President and the government's role in the lives of citizens. Ask **How were Roosevelt's beliefs representative of Progressive ideals?** *(Roosevelt believed that it was the job of the President and of the government to use the power of regulation and legislation to create a fair and just environment for all Americans.)*

Independent Practice

Have students select a current issue, such as global warming or healthcare, and have them write a paragraph explaining what they think Theodore Roosevelt might have thought the federal government's role ought to be in addressing the issue.

Monitor Progress

As students fill in their concept webs, circulate to make sure they are recording the most relevant details about Roosevelt's Square Deal. For a completed version of the concept web, see Note Taking Transparencies, B-89a.

Answer

✔ He wanted it to create a fair, honest, and just society in which everyone had an equal chance to succeed.

INFOGRAPHIC

A Rough Rider in the White House

Theodore Roosevelt's energetic leadership style enabled him to redefine the presidency. He took on industry and tackled tough issues. Roosevelt used his presidential power to bust illegal monopolies, reduce abusive business practices, and make a symbolic statement against segregation.

This 1909 cartoon shows ▶ Roosevelt's differing approaches to "good" and "bad" trusts.

Vocabulary Builder
dominate – (DAHM ih nayt) *v.* to have a commanding place or position in

Roosevelt could not remain long out of the spotlight, however. By 1889, he had returned to politics. As president of New York City's Board of Police Commissioners, he gained fame by fighting corruption. President William McKinley noticed him and named him Assistant Secretary of the Navy. When the Spanish-American War broke out in 1898, Roosevelt resigned the post to form the Rough Riders, a volunteer cavalry unit that became famous during the war.

After the end of the conflict, the young war hero was elected governor of New York, where he pushed for Progressive reforms. His reform efforts annoyed Republican leaders in the state, though. They convinced McKinley to choose Roosevelt as his running mate so Roosevelt would leave New York—and them—alone. McKinley was reelected President in 1900, but within a few months he was assassinated, and Roosevelt became President. Roosevelt soon dominated public attention. Journalists vied for interviews with him and children begged their parents for a teddy bear, the new stuffed animal named for him.

Roosevelt greatly expanded the power of the President. He used his office and its powers to convince Americans of the need for change and to push through his reform proposals. He called his program the **Square Deal,** and its goals were to keep the wealthy and powerful from taking advantage of small business owners and the poor. His idea of fair government did not mean that everyone would get rich or that the government should take care of the lazy. He compared his Square Deal to a hand of cards.

> **Primary Source** "When I say I believe in a square deal, I do not mean to give every man the best hand. If good cards do not come to any man, or if they do come, and he has not got the power to play them, that is his affair. All I mean is that there shall be no crookedness in the dealing."
>
> —Theodore Roosevelt, 1905

✔ **Checkpoint** What did Roosevelt want his Square Deal program to achieve?

Differentiated Instruction Solutions for All Learners

L4 Advanced Readers   L4 Gifted and Talented Students

Have students reread the quotation in the first paragraph under the blue heading "Roosevelt Shapes the Modern Presidency." Invite students to use that quotation as the inspiration for writing a realistic, yet obviously fictional, first-person account in which the narrator meets Roosevelt in person. Encourage students to be detailed in their descriptions of Roosevelt's personality and behavior. Stories do not have to be political in nature—for example, students could write about going on a hunt with the President. Have students share their stories with the class.

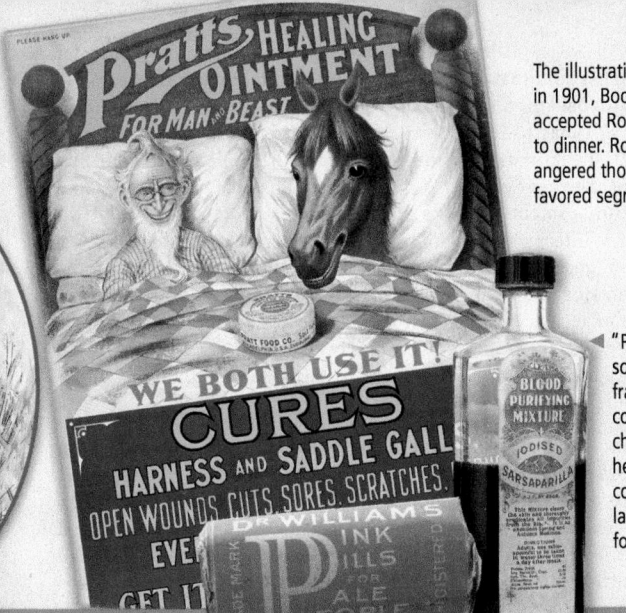

The illustration shows that ▶ in 1901, Booker T. Washington accepted Roosevelt's invitation to dinner. Roosevelt's actions angered those who favored segregation.

EQUALITY

◀ "Patent medications" sometimes made fraudulent claims or contained harmful chemicals. Roosevelt helped restore consumer confidence by supporting laws that regulated the food and drug industries.

Thinking Critically

1. **Analyze Visuals** Look at the image of Roosevelt's dinner with Washington. Why would the artist have placed a painting of Abraham Lincoln in the background?

2. **Make Generalizations** Using the information in these visuals, make one generalization about Theodore Roosevelt as President.

Instruct

- **Introduce: Key Terms** Ask students to find the key terms *Hepburn Act, Meat Inspection Act,* and *Pure Food and Drug Act* (in bold) in the text. Then, write them on the board, and briefly explain the purpose of each law. Ask students what these pieces of legislation have in common.

- **Teach** Explain that Theodore Roosevelt, along with Progressives in Congress, greatly extended the federal government's role in the economy. Ask **Why did Roosevelt work to establish the Department of Commerce and Labor?** *(to monitor businesses engaged in interstate commerce and to keep capitalists from abusing their power)* Explore the other major acts passed during Roosevelt's presidency and how these acts expressed Progressive ideals and fulfilled Roosevelt's Square Deal program.

Independent Practice

Have students study the Infographic and write paragraphs describing how each image shows that Roosevelt supported Progressive ideals.

Monitor Progress

As students write their paragraphs, circulate to make sure that they understand Roosevelt's policies toward big business, the food and drug industries, and segregation.

Trustbusting and Regulating Industry

Roosevelt often stepped in with the authority and power of the federal government. One example was in 1902, when Pennsylvania coal miners went on strike. The miners wanted a pay raise and a shorter workday. Roosevelt sympathized with the overworked miners, but he knew that a steady supply of coal was needed to keep factories running and homes warm. He wanted the strike ended quickly.

First, Roosevelt tried to get mine owners to listen to workers' concerns. When this failed, he threatened to send federal troops to take control of the mines and to run them with federal employees. His threat forced the mine owners to give the miners a small pay raise and a nine-hour workday. For the first time, the federal government had stepped in to help workers in a labor dispute.

The coal strike was one of many steps Roosevelt took to control the power of corporations. Within a year, Roosevelt convinced Congress to establish the Department of Commerce and Labor to monitor businesses engaged in interstate commerce and to keep capitalists from abusing their power.

Roosevelt Takes on the Railroads The cost of shipping freight on railroads had been an issue since the 1870s. Railroad companies could charge whatever they wanted. The railroads' power was especially troublesome for western farmers. They had no other way to move their products to eastern markets.

In 1887, Congress had created the Interstate Commerce Commission (ICC) to oversee rail charges for shipments that passed through more than one state. The ICC was supposed to make sure that all shippers were charged the same amounts. By 1900, though, the Supreme Court had stripped away most of the ICC's power. So Roosevelt pushed Congress to pass the Elkins Act in 1903, which imposed fines on railroads that gave special rates to favored shippers. In 1906, he got Congress to pass the **Hepburn Act,** which gave the ICC strong enforcement powers. This law gave the government the authority to set and limit shipping costs. The act also set maximum prices for ferries, bridge tolls, and oil pipelines.

History Background

The Teddy Bear Theodore Roosevelt was an enthusiastic hunter as well as a conservationist. In November 1902, the President went on a bear hunt in Mississippi, but his group found it difficult to locate any game. Eventually a black bear was cornered and subdued so that the President could kill it. When Roosevelt surveyed the situation, however, he refused to shoot the animal on the grounds that it was unsporting. Hearing of this episode, artist Clifford K. Berryman of the *Washington Post* created a humorous cartoon with the caption "Drawing the line in Mississippi." Americans were delighted by both the cartoon and their President's sense of fair play. The popularity of the cartoon prompted the owners of what would become the Ideal Toy Company to market stuffed bears as "Teddy's bears." The teddy bear became an immediate hit and is still one of the world's most beloved toys. One of the original "Teddy's bears" was donated to the Smithsonian Institution by Roosevelt's son Kermit and is on display at the National Museum of American History in Washington, D.C.

Answers

Thinking Critically

1. Sample answer: Abraham Lincoln was a great hero to African Americans and a role model for Presidents; the painting may be there to imply that Lincoln would have approved of the dinner.

2. Sample answer: Roosevelt was devoted to reform and favored government regulation.

The Government Manages the Environment

- **Introduce: Vocabulary Builder**
Have students locate the vocabulary term *rational* and its definition. Tell students that they will learn how Roosevelt's environmental legislation, such as the National Reclamation Act, was based on the theory of *rational use*. Ask them to predict what *rational use* might mean in this context.

- **Teach** Explain to students that because Roosevelt was a passionate hunter and outdoorsman, he worked hard to conserve America's vast natural resources. Discuss the difference between preserving and conserving the environment and ask students to give examples of each approach. Ask **What was the difference between the philosophies of John Muir and Gifford Pinchot on how to treat America's wild areas?** *(Muir thought that all wild areas should be preserved, untouched. Pinchot believed in* rational use—*the idea that public wild lands should be used and managed to the benefit of citizens.)* **Who do you think had the greater influence on Roosevelt's environmental policy?** *(Although Roosevelt admired Muir and agreed to preserve more than 100 million acres of forestland, he based his major policies on Pinchot's* rational use *ideas for conservation and the practical use of wild lands.)*

Vocabulary Builder
<u>rational</u>—(RASH uhn uhl) *adj.*
relating to or based on reason;
reasonable

Roosevelt Enforces the Sherman Antitrust Act It did not take long for the President and his administration to earn a reputation as "trustbusters." In response to an antitrust suit filed by Roosevelt's attorney general, the Supreme Court ruled in 1904 that the Northern Securities Company—a big railroad company—was an illegal trust. The decision forced the company to split into smaller companies. The next year, the Court found that a beef trust and several powerful agricultural companies broke antitrust laws.

Roosevelt was not interested in bringing down all large companies. He saw a difference between "good trusts" and "bad trusts." Big businesses could often be more efficient than small ones, he believed. Big business was bad, he said, only if it bullied smaller outfits or cheated consumers. So he supported powerful corporations as long as they did business fairly. His supporters called him a "trust-tamer," but some wealthy Progressives criticized his trustbusting.

Regulating Food and Drug Industries In 1906, Upton Sinclair published his novel *The Jungle*. His descriptions of the filthy, unhealthy conditions in meatpacking plants revolted the public and infuriated the President. Roosevelt urged Congress to pass the **Meat Inspection Act** that same year. It provided federal agents to inspect any meat sold across state lines and required federal inspection of meat-processing plants. Today, when we eat lunchmeat or grilled chicken, we trust that federal inspectors have monitored the plant where it is produced. If there is a serious problem, the government can force the meatpacker to pull the product off the shelves before many people become sick. This regulation is one lasting result of Progressives' insistence that the government take responsibility for food safety.

The **Pure Food and Drug Act** placed the same controls on other foods and on medicines. It also banned the interstate shipment of impure food and the mislabeling of food and drugs. Today, the Food and Drug Administration (FDA) still enforces this law and others. The FDA monitors companies to make sure people are not hurt by dangerous substances or dishonest labels. For example, before a drug can be sold, it must be tested and approved by the FDA.

 Checkpoint What impact did Roosevelt's actions have on the government's role in the economy?

The Government Manages the Environment

Roosevelt's deep reverence for nature also shaped his policies. The books he published on hunting and the rugged West reflected his fascination with the competition between humans and the wilderness. He was pleased that the federal government had established Yellowstone National Park in 1872 to protect wildlife, and he admired California naturalist **John Muir,** whose efforts had led Congress to create Yosemite National Park in 1890.

Should National Forests Be Conserved or Preserved? In 1891, Congress had given the President the power to protect timberlands by setting aside land as federal forests. Following Muir's advice, Roosevelt closed off more than 100 million acres of forestland. However, the President did not agree with Muir that all wild areas should be preserved, or left untouched. Some wild lands held valuable resources, and Roosevelt thought those resources were meant to be used. This view became clear in his forest policy. In typical Progressive style, he called on experts to draw up plans for both conserving and using the forests.

Roosevelt drew on the "<u>rational</u> use" ideas of **Gifford Pinchot,** who led the Division of Forestry in the U.S. Department of Agriculture. Pinchot recommended a different approach—that forests be preserved for public use. By this, he meant

---

Answer

 Roosevelt's actions greatly increased the role of the federal government in regulating and monitoring the economy and labor issues.

Managing the Environment Today The issue of whether and how public lands are used is still an extremely hot topic. The Arctic National Wildlife Refuge (ANWR) is one major modern-day battleground between those who believe in rational use and those who believe in protecting wild areas. Today, the 19.2-million-acre refuge is actively "managed" by the U.S. government, but activities are limited to environmental maintenance and periodic biological studies. However, as Americans have begun to worry more about their dependency on foreign oil, some have suggested that the area should be opened up to allow drilling for what could be as much as 16 billion barrels of recoverable oil. Many government leaders, oil companies, and energy policy analysts argue that the United States needs to use every resource it has for the good of the economy and the nation's security. Environmentalists argue that drilling for oil could destroy irreplaceable, pristine ecological systems. Government impact studies continue in Area 1002, the 1.5-million-acre area along the coast, where experts say that drilling would cause the least damage.

Geography *Interactive*
For: Interactive map
www.pearsonschool.com/ushist

National Parks and Forests
- Established before Roosevelt's presidency
- Established during Roosevelt's presidency
- Established after Roosevelt's presidency

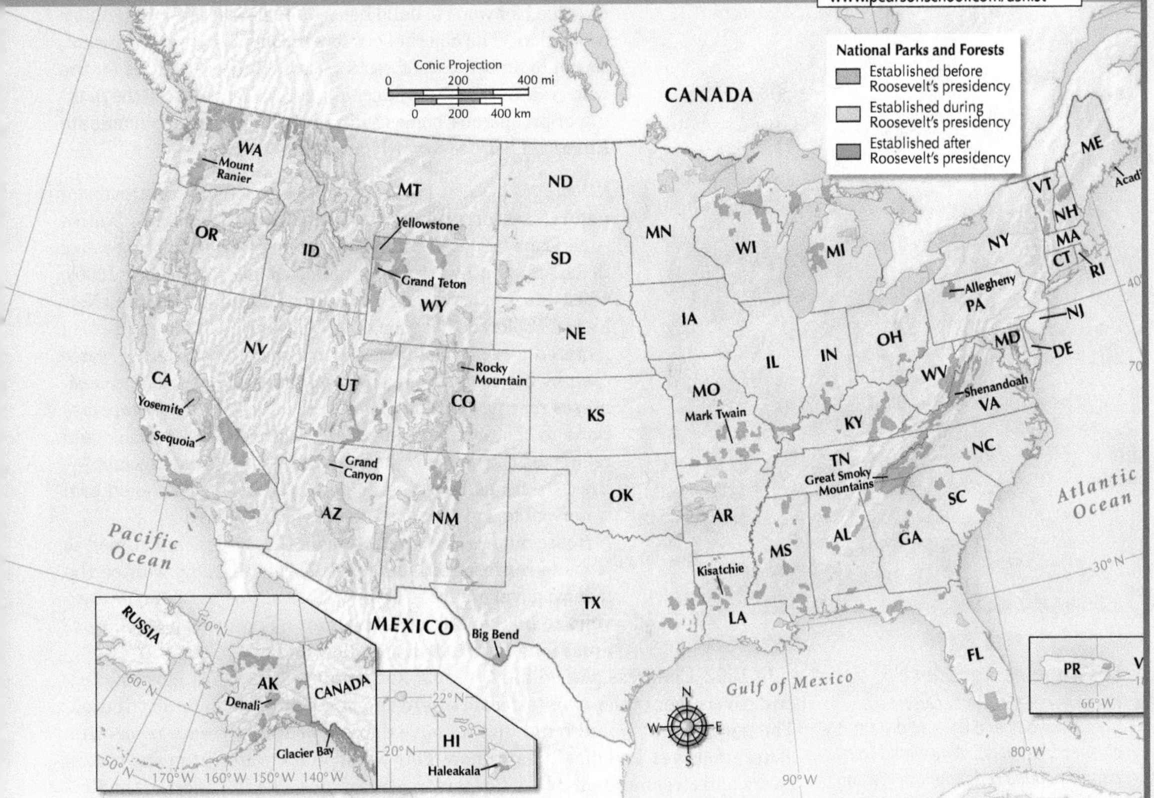

In 1892, John Muir helped found the Sierra Club to help people enjoy California's wild places and to lobby for protection of natural resources.

Primary Source "Climb the mountains and get their good tidings, Nature's peace will flow into you as sunshine flows into trees. The winds will blow their own freshness into you and the storms their energy, while cares will drop off like autumn leaves. As age comes on, one source of enjoyment after another is closed, but nature's sources never fail."

—John Muir, *Our National Parks*, 1901

Map Skills The land conservation movement of the Progressive Era led to the conservation of millions of acres of United States land.

1. **Human-Environment Interaction** How does preserving land for national parks and forests benefit people?

2. **Regions** What region of the country has the greatest area of conservation lands? Why do you think this is so?

President Theodore Roosevelt and conservationist John Muir at California's Yosemite National Park in 1903

Independent Practice

- Have students access **www.pearsonschool.com/ushist** to launch the Geography Interactive map. Have students complete the activity and then answer the map skills questions in the textbook.

- Have students complete the *Outline Map: The National Parks System* worksheet and answer the questions. Teaching Resources, **p. 24**

- Ask students to read the Primary Source quotation on this page and study the photograph of Roosevelt and Muir. Have students make a Venn diagram to compare and contrast the actions and ideas of these two men.

Monitor Progress

Circulate to make sure that students are completing their *Outline Map* worksheets accurately.

Answers

Map Skills

1. Preserving land for national parks and forests allows people to enjoy nature and helps protect natural resources.

2. The West has the greatest area of conservation lands because at the time, it was the least-populous area in the country, so it had more open wilderness.

Instruct

- **Introduce: Key Term** Have students locate the key term **Progressive Party** (in bold) in the text. Tell students that they will learn how Roosevelt's annoyance with his successor's independence led Progressives to establish their own party with Roosevelt as their presidential candidate.

- **Teach** Ask **How was Taft's administration different from Roosevelt's?** *(Taft did not lower tariffs as much as Roosevelt wished. He encouraged the proposal of an income tax, and, most importantly, he did not distinguish between good and bad trusts. Some of Roosevelt's decisions were reversed.)* **How did Roosevelt react to this?** *(He was very angry, split with Taft and the Republican Party, declared a program of New Nationalism, and became the presidential candidate for the Progressive Party.)*

- **Analyzing the Visuals** Have students study the political cartoon on the next page and answer the questions.

Independent Practice

NoteTaking Have students complete a Venn diagram that compares and contrasts Roosevelt and Taft.
Reading and Note Taking Study Guide

Monitor Progress

As students fill in their Venn diagrams, circulate to make sure they understand how Taft's administration diverged from Roosevelt's. For a completed version of the Venn diagram, see Note Taking Transparencies, **B-89b.**

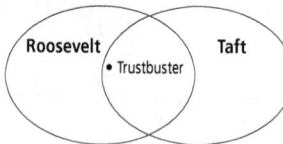

Los Angeles Aqueduct
Massive water projects carry water from reservoirs and lakes to distant cities and farmland. *Why would some people oppose redirecting water in such ways?*

NoteTaking

Reading Skill: Compare and Contrast As you read, fill in the Venn diagram with similarities and differences between Roosevelt and Taft.

Roosevelt — • Trustbuster — Taft

---

that forests should be protected so that trees would have time to mature into good lumber. Then, the protected areas should be logged for wood to build houses and new areas placed under protection. "The object of our forest policy," explained Pinchot, "is not to preserve the forests because they are refuges for the wild creatures of the wilderness, but rather they are the making of prosperous homes." Pinchot's views came to dominate American policies toward natural resources.

Roosevelt Changes Water Policy A highly controversial natural resource issue was water. Over centuries, Native Americans had used various irrigation methods to bring water to the arid Southwest. The situation changed in the late 1800s, when prospectors began mining and farming in Utah, New Mexico, Colorado, Nevada, and California. Mining machinery required a great deal of water, and systems of sharing water used by Mexican Americans were fought by people and businesses moving into these states. Private irrigation companies came to the area, staked claims to sections of riverbeds and redirected the water so farmers could revive—or "reclaim"— dried-up fields. Bitter fights developed over who should own water rights and how the water should be shared.

Roosevelt sprang into action on this issue. He listened to Nevada representative Francis Newlands, who wanted the federal government to help western states build huge reservoirs to hold and to conserve water. Roosevelt pushed Congress for a law that would allow it.

In 1902, Congress passed the **National Reclamation Act,** which gave the federal government the power to decide where and how water would be distributed. The government would build and manage dams that would create reservoirs, generate power, and direct water flow. This would make water from one state's rivers and streams available to farmers in other states. The full effect of the Reclamation Act was felt over the next few decades, as water management projects created huge reservoirs and lakes where there had been dry canyons. Examples include the Salt Valley Project in Arizona and the Roosevelt Dam and Hoover Dam on the Colorado River.

✓ **Checkpoint** How did Roosevelt's policies affect the environment?

Roosevelt and Taft Differ

Roosevelt left the presidency after two terms in office, saying he wished to enjoy private life. He was still a powerful force in the Republican Party, however, and he used that power to help Secretary of War William Howard Taft win the presidency in 1908. Roosevelt expected Taft to continue his programs of managing business and natural resources. Political cartoonists made caricatures of Roosevelt handing over what he called "my policies" to Taft, who seemed to have no ideas of his own.

Taft Takes His Own Course But Taft soon set his own agenda. He approved the Payne-Aldrich Act (1909), which did not lower tariffs as much as Roosevelt had wanted. He also pushed Congress to pass the Mann-Elkins Act (1910), which gave the government control over telephone and telegraph rates. He encouraged Congress to propose an income tax. Perhaps, most importantly,

---

Answers

Caption Sample answer: Dams destroy habitats and can also flood whole communities. Also, a dam or an irrigation project can deplete the water to which people downstream previously had access.

✓ Because of Roosevelt's policies, national wild lands would now be managed for their natural resources, and water reclamation projects would irrigate much desert land in the Southwest. The Roosevelt administration also preserved 100 million acres of national wild lands.

L1 Special Needs Students   **L2 Less Proficient Readers**

Have students reread the blue headings and red headings in this section and write a paraphrase of the main idea under each one. Remind students that paraphrasing is explaining something in their own words. Check to make sure that students understand the difference between *preserve* and *conserve* in the context of Roosevelt's public land policies.

he dropped Roosevelt's distinction between good trusts and bad trusts.

Taft's Justice Department brought lawsuits against twice as many corporations as Roosevelt's had done. As a result, in 1911, the Supreme Court "busted" the trust built by the Standard Oil Company. But Taft also supported what the Court called its "rule of reason," which relaxed the hard line set by the Sherman Antitrust Act. The rule of reason allowed big monopolies so long as they did not "unreasonably" squeeze out smaller companies. Roosevelt publicly criticized these decisions. Then, Taft's attorney general sued to force U.S. Steel to sell a coal company it had bought. Roosevelt, who had approved the purchase of the company, fumed.

Taft further infuriated Roosevelt and other Progressives in the Republican Party when he fired Gifford Pinchot for publicly criticizing Secretary of the Interior Richard Ballinger. Pinchot charged that Ballinger, who opposed Roosevelt's conservation policies, had worked with business interests to sell federal land rich in coal deposits in Alaska.

Roosevelt Strikes Back Roosevelt began traveling the country speaking about what he called the **New Nationalism**—a program to restore the government's trustbusting power. (See an excerpt from Roosevelt's New Nationalism speech at the end of this book.) Declaring himself as "strong as a bull moose," Roosevelt vowed to tackle the trusts in a third presidential term. The Taft-Roosevelt battle split the Republican Party as an election neared. Progressives bolted from the Republican party and set up the **Progressive Party**. Reformer Jane Addams nominated Roosevelt as the Progressive Party's candidate for the 1912 presidential election. The Republicans nominated Taft. A bitter election loomed.

✓ **Checkpoint** How did William Howard Taft's policies compare with Theodore Roosevelt's?

Analyzing Political Cartoons

Taft in the White House Theodore Roosevelt looks on as President Taft is entangled in troubles.
1. What details illustrate Taft's troubles?
2. What does the cartoon suggest about Roosevelt's reaction to Taft's situation?

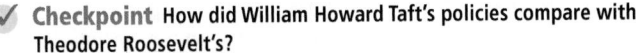

SECTION 4 Assessment

Progress Monitoring Online
For: Self-test with vocabulary practice
www.pearsonschool.com/ushist

Comprehension
1. **Terms** Explain how each of the following acts and policies reflects Progressivism's influence.
   - Square Deal
   - Hepburn Act
   - Meat Inspection Act
   - Pure Food and Drug Act
   - National Reclamation Act
   - New Nationalism

2. **NoteTaking Reading Skill: Identify Main Ideas** Use your concept web to answer the Section Focus Question: What did Roosevelt think government should do for citizens?

Writing About History
3. **Quick Write: Present a Point of View** Choose one of the industries that President Roosevelt regulated. Imagine that you are a worker or business owner in the industry. In one or two paragraphs, describe your reaction to the President's actions. Use details to relate the effect of the government's actions on your work.

Critical Thinking
4. **Recognize Causes** Why might Theodore Roosevelt's push for reforms have angered some political leaders?
5. **Apply Information** How did Roosevelt's use of presidential and federal power differ from that of earlier Presidents? Give two examples.
6. **Analyze** How did Theodore Roosevelt's national forest policy reflect his ideas about conservation and preservation?
7. **Draw Conclusions** Do you think Roosevelt's public criticisms of Taft were justified? Why or why not?

Objectives

As you teach this section, keep students focused on the following objectives to help them answer the Section Focus Question and master core content.

- Evaluate what Wilson hoped to do with his "New Freedom" program.
- Describe Wilson's efforts to regulate the economy.
- Assess the legacy of the Progressive Era.

Background Knowledge L3

In the previous section, students learned about the Progressive presidencies of Roosevelt and Taft. Have students explain how the Progressive policies of Roosevelt and Taft affect the United States today.

Set a Purpose L3

- **WITNESS HISTORY** Read the selection aloud.

  Ask **How did Wilson's desire to end the eating clubs at Princeton reflect the ideas of Progressivism?** (*It was an attempt at reform to end a perceived injustice.*)

- **Focus** Point out the Section Focus Question, and write it on the board. Tell students to refer to this question as they read. (*Answer appears with Section 5 Assessment answers.*)

- **Preview** Have students preview the Section Objectives and the list of Terms and People.

- **NoteTaking** Using the Paragraph Shrinking strategy (TE, p. T20), have students read this section. As they read, have students complete the concept web by recording details about Wilson's New Freedom plan. Reading and Note Taking Study Guide

---

◀ Woodrow Wilson, 1919

▲ Wilson campaign button

WITNESS HISTORY

A History of Reform

Before becoming President of the United States, Woodrow Wilson was president of Princeton University in New Jersey. At the time, most Princeton students were sons of wealthy families. These students joined "eating clubs" that excluded poor students and other outsiders.

Wilson objected. The eating clubs, he said, made social life more important than learning. Furthermore, he said, the clubs were unfair and damaging to those students who were excluded. Wilson lost his fight to do away with the eating clubs. But he won a reputation as a high-minded reformer who would speak out against social injustice. Wilson's reform efforts would continue in his role as President of the United States.

Wilson's New Freedom

Objectives

- Evaluate what Wilson hoped to do with his "New Freedom" program.
- Describe Wilson's efforts to regulate the economy.
- Assess the legacy of the Progressive Era.

Terms and People

Woodrow Wilson	Federal Trade
New Freedom	Commission
Sixteenth Amendment	Clayton Antitrust Act
Federal Reserve Act	

NoteTaking

Reading Skill: Identify Details As you read this section, fill in a concept web like the one below to record details from the section.

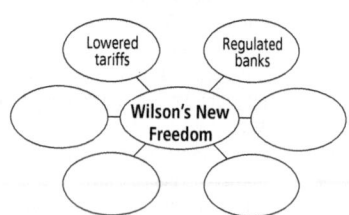

Why It Matters Republicans Theodore Roosevelt and William Howard Taft introduced the country to forceful Progressive Presidents. Democrat Woodrow Wilson used the expanded power of the presidency to promote a far-reaching reform agenda. Some of Wilson's economic and antitrust measures are still important in American life today. **Section Focus Question: What steps did Wilson take to increase the government's role in the economy?**

Wilson and the Democrats Prevail

In 1912, the Republican Party split over the issue of reform. Those who wanted a more active government formed the Progressive Party and chose Theodore Roosevelt as their candidate for President. Loyal Republicans gave the nod to President William Howard Taft.

The split created an opportunity for the Democrats and their candidate, **Woodrow Wilson,** to win the White House. Wilson's ideas had caught the attention of William Jennings Bryan, who helped Wilson win the Democratic nomination. As a student and later as a professor, Wilson had thought a great deal about good government. His doctoral thesis, *Congressional Government,* had launched him on a career teaching in college before he became the reforming governor of New Jersey.

Wilson shaped his ideas into a program he called the **New Freedom.** His plan looked much like Roosevelt's New Nationalism. It, too, would place strict government controls on corporations.

Vocabulary Builder

Use the information below and the following resource to teach students the high-use word from this section. Teaching Resources, Vocabulary Builder, p. 12

High-Use Word	Definition and Sample Sentence
intellectual	*adj.* guided by thought; possessing great power of thought and reason The professor's **intellectual** approach made him popular with his students.

In a speech on the New Freedom, Wilson outlined his aim to provide more opportunities—more freedom—for small businesses.

Primary Source "The man with only a little capital is finding it harder and harder to get into the field, more and more impossible to compete with the big fellow. Why? Because the laws of this country do not prevent the strong from crushing the weak."

—Woodrow Wilson, "The New Freedom," 1913

Though he did not win the majority of the popular vote, Wilson received more than four times the number of Electoral College votes that went to Roosevelt or to Taft. The pious and <u>intellectual</u> son of a Virginia minister, Wilson was the first man born in the South to win the presidency in almost 60 years.

☑ **Checkpoint** How did Republican divisions help Wilson win the presidency?

Wilson Regulates the Economy

President Wilson attacked what he called the "triple wall of privilege"—the tariffs, the banks, and the trusts—that blocked businesses from being free. Early in his first term, he pushed for new laws that would bring down those three walls and give the government more control over the economy.

Congress Lowers Tariffs and Raises Taxes First, Wilson aimed to prevent big manufacturers from unfairly charging high prices to their customers. One way to do this was to lower the tariffs on goods imported from foreign countries so, if American companies' prices were too high, consumers could buy foreign goods. Wilson called a special session of Congress and convinced its members to pass the Underwood Tariff Bill, which cut tariffs.

The Underwood Tariff Act of 1913 included a provision to create a graduated income tax, which the recently passed **Sixteenth Amendment** gave Congress the power to do. A graduated income tax means that wealthy people pay a higher percentage of their income than do poor people. The revenue from the income tax more than made up for the money the government lost by lowering tariffs on imports.

Federal Reserve Act Next, Wilson tried to reform the banking system. At the time, the country had no central authority to supervise banks. As a result, interest rates for loans could fluctuate wildly, and a few wealthy bankers had a great deal of control over the national, state, and local banks' reserve funds. This meant that a bank might not have full access to its reserves when customers needed to withdraw or borrow money.

Wilson pushed Congress to pass the **Federal Reserve Act** (1913). This law placed national banks under the control of a Federal Reserve Board, which set up regional banks to hold the reserve funds from commercial banks. This system, still in place today, helps protect the American economy from having too much

Vocabulary Builder
intellectual–(ihn tuh LEHK choo uhl) *adj.* guided by thought; possessing great power of thought and reason

Progressive Party button

Presidential Election of 1912

Candidate (Party)	Electoral Vote	Popular Vote	% Electoral Vote	% Popular Vote
☐ Woodrow Wilson (Democrat)	435	6,296,547	82	42
☐ Theodore Roosevelt (Progressive)	88	4,118,571	17	27
☐ William H. Taft (Republican)	8	3,486,720	1	23

*Two of California's electors voted for Wilson

Differentiated Instruction Solutions for All Learners

L1 Special Needs Students **L2 English Language Learners** **L2 Less Proficient Readers**

Explain to students that Wilson's "triple wall of privilege" is a metaphor—a way to describe something by likening it to something else. Clarify that these were not actual walls, but areas in the economy that Wilson believed blocked the success of small businesses. Pair students and have them draw three large boxes labeled "Tariffs," "Banks," and "Trusts." Direct students to review the section and to copy in the appropriate box each act, law, or amendment that Wilson worked to pass. For example, the Underwood Tariff Act and the Sixteenth Amendment go in the "Tariff" box.

Teach

Wilson and the Democrats Prevail/Wilson Regulates the Economy **L3**

Instruct

- **Introduce: Key Term** Have students locate the key term **New Freedom** (in bold) in the text and discuss the policies it established. Then, have students compare and contrast Wilson's **New Freedom** with New Nationalism and the Square Deal.

- **Teach** Display Color Transparency: *The Election of 1912.* Have students discuss the political party and platform of each candidate. Then, write the expression "the triple wall of privilege" on the board. Ask **What were the three walls?** *(tariffs, banks, and trusts)* Discuss how Wilson went about weakening these barriers. Ask **How did Wilson's agenda further expand the government's role in the economy?** *(He convinced Congress to pass the Underwood Tariff Bill, which cut tariffs and created the income tax, pushed for passage of the Federal Reserve Act, and strengthened antitrust regulation, which also protected labor unions.)* Color Transparencies A-80

- **Quick Activity** Read aloud the Primary Source selection. Ask students to discuss how owners of large businesses might have felt about Wilson's New Freedom program.

Independent Practice

- Assign students the *Interpreting a Political Cartoon: Progressive Era Legislation* worksheet. Teaching Resources, p. 25

- Have students fill in the concept web for this section to record details about Wilson's New Freedom plan.

Monitor Progress

As students complete their concept webs, circulate to make sure that they understand the provisions of the plan. For a completed version of the concept web, see Note Taking Transparencies, B-90.

Answer

☑ The formation of the Progressive Party and its nomination of Theodore Roosevelt as its presidential candidate caused a split among Republican voters and helped the Democratic candidate, Wilson, win the election.

Instruct

- **Introduce** Refer students to the Progressive Era Legislation and Constitutional Amendments chart on this page. Have students identify the legislation in the chart that directly affects their lives. For example, some students may pay federal income tax, so they are directly affected by the Sixteenth Amendment.

- **Teach** Using the Idea Wave strategy (TE, p. T22), discuss whether students think that Progressivism was ultimately a successful movement or a movement that failed. Draw a Successful/Failed chart on the board, and elicit and record students' opinions about this question. Remind students that answers should be reasoned and supported by details.

- **Quick Activity** Have students use the chart on this page to make a timeline from 1890 to 1920 and list each date of key legislation from the chart. Then, have students review the whole chapter to add any other important dates, such as the founding of the Urban League in 1911.

Independent Practice

After the class discussion, have each student write a sentence summing up his or her opinion of the legacy of Progressivism.

Monitor Progress

As students write their sentences, circulate to make sure that they understand the legacy of Progressivism.

money end up in the hands of one person, bank, or region. The Federal Reserve Board also sets the interest rate that banks pay to borrow money from other banks, and it supervises banks to make sure they are well run. Historians have called the Federal Reserve Act the most important piece of economic legislation before the 1930s.

Wilson Strengthens Antitrust Regulation Like Presidents before him, Wilson focused on trusts. Wilson agreed with Roosevelt that trusts were not dangerous as long as they did not engage in unfair practices. In 1914, he persuaded Congress to create the **Federal Trade Commission (FTC).** Members of this group were named by the President to monitor business practices that might lead to monopoly. The FTC was also charged with watching out for false advertising or dishonest labeling. Congress also passed the **Clayton Antitrust Act (1914),** which strengthened earlier antitrust laws by spelling out those activities in which businesses could not engage.

These laws are still in effect today, protecting both businesses and consumers from abusive business activities. In recent years, the FTC has prosecuted companies that traded stocks dishonestly and fined companies that published false ads. The FTC also regulates buying on the Internet.

Workers' Rights Protected The Clayton Antitrust Act also ushered in a new era for workers by protecting labor unions from being attacked as trusts. Now, workers could organize more freely. Samuel Gompers of the American Federation of Labor (AFL) praised the new law as the "Magna Carta" of labor.

On the heels of these protections came the Workingman's Compensation Act (1916), which gave wages to temporarily disabled civil service employees. That same year, Wilson pushed for the Adamson Act to prevent a nationwide railroad strike, which would have stopped the movement of coal and food, leaving millions of Americans cold and hungry. Railroad union leaders insisted on the eight-hour day, but railroad managers would not accept it. Wilson called many company leaders to the White House, pleading with them to change their minds and avert a strike. When those efforts failed, he worked with Congress to pass the Adamson Act, which limited railroad employees' workdays to eight hours.

However, Wilson did not always support organized labor, as a tragic incident known as the Ludlow Massacre showed. In the fall of 1913, coal miners in Ludlow, Colorado, demanded safer conditions, higher pay, and the right to form a union. When the coal company refused, they walked off the job. Evicted from company housing, the miners and their families set up in a tent city near

Progressive Era Legislation and Constitutional Amendments

Legislation/Amendment	Effect
Sherman Antitrust Act (1890)	Outlawed monopolies and practices that restrained trade, such as price fixing
National Reclamation Act (1902)	Provided for federal irrigation projects by using money from the sale of public lands
Elkins Act (1903)	Imposed fines on railroads that gave special rates to favored shippers
Hepburn Act (1906)	Authorized the federal government to regulate railroad rates and set maximum prices for ferries, bridge tolls, and oil pipelines
Meat Inspection Act (1906)	Allowed the federal government to inspect meat sold across state lines and required inspection of meat-processing plants
Pure Food and Drug Act (1906)	Allowed federal inspection of food and medicine and banned the shipment and sale of impure food and the mislabeling of food and medicine
Sixteenth Amendment (1913)	Gave Congress the power to collect taxes on people's income
Seventeenth Amendment (1913)	Instituted the direct election of senators by the people of each state
Underwood Tariff Act (1913)	Lowered tariffs on imported goods and established a graduated income tax
Federal Reserve Act (1913)	Created the Federal Reserve Board to oversee banks and manage reserve funds
Federal Trade Commission Act (1914)	Established the Federal Trade Commission to monitor business practices, false advertising, and dishonest labeling
Clayton Antitrust Act (1914)	Strengthened the Sherman Antitrust Act by spelling out specific activities businesses could not do
Eighteenth Amendment (1919)	Banned the making, selling, and transporting of alcoholic beverages in the United States
Nineteenth Amendment (1920)	Gave women the right to vote in all elections

History Background

The Adamson Act The Adamson Act of 1916 was an important step forward in the struggle by organized labor for the eight-hour workday. The movement had been active globally since the start of the Industrial Revolution. In 1866, the National Labor Union made a failed effort to lobby Congress for the eight-hour workday, and later the Knights of Labor continued the fight but also failed. "Eight hours for work, eight hours for rest, and eight hours for what you will," was a popular slogan of organized labor at this time.

The Adamson Act was the first piece of federal legislation regulating the work period in a private company. However, because of labor needs during World War I, little progress was made to limit the workday or at least to pay overtime. In 1933, however, Congress passed the National Industrial Recovery Act, which established a limit to work hours, set a minimum wage, and guaranteed the right of unions to bargain collectively. By the 1950s, most workers had an eight-hour workday.

the mines. The strike continued through the winter. Then, on April 20, 1914, the Colorado National Guard opened fire on the tent city and set fire to the tents, killing some 26 men, women, and children. In the end, Wilson sent federal troops to restore order and break up the strike. The miners' attempt to form a union had failed.

 Checkpoint What policies did Wilson pursue in support of his New Freedom program?

Progressivism Leaves a Lasting Legacy

The political reforms of the Progressives had a lasting effect on the American political system. The initiative, referendum, and recall and the Nineteenth Amendment expanded voters' influence. Progressive reforms also paved the way for future trends. Starting in this period, the federal government grew to offer more protection to Americans' private lives while at the same time, gaining more control over peoples' lives.

The American economy today showcases the strength of the Progressives' legacy. Antitrust laws, the Federal Reserve Board, and the other federal agencies watch closely over the economy. The controls that Roosevelt and Wilson put in place continue to provide consumer protections. In later years, the government built on those actions to extend regulation over other aspects of business.

The Progressive years also greatly expanded the government's role in managing natural resources. Especially in the West, federal action on dams, national parks, and resource use remain major areas of debate. Those debates and decisions affect people in other regions as well. For example, while farmers in California, Arizona, or New Mexico worry about getting enough water to grow crops, the rest of the nation awaits the delivery of the food they grow.

It is true that many of the problems identified by the Progressives still plague us today. There are still dishonest sellers, unfair employment practices, and problems in schools, cities, the environment, and public health. However, the Progressive reformers passed on the idea that government can take action to help people fix those problems.

 Checkpoint What was the long-term impact of the Progressive Era on American life?

Assess and Reteach

Assess Progress

- Have students complete the Section Assessment.

- Administer the Section Quiz. *Teaching Resources*, **p. 30**

- To further assess student understanding, use **Progress Monitoring Transparencies, 86.**

Reteach
If students need more instruction, have them read the section summary.

Reading and Note Taking
Study Guide

Adapted Reading and
Note Taking Study Guide

Spanish Reading and
Note Taking Study Guide

Extend
Have students write a newspaper report on the results of the 1912 election and explain why Wilson won. Students should include details, such as the actual vote in your state during the election, in their reports. Encourage students to read authentic election reports as a prelude to writing.

SECTION 5 Assessment

Progress Monitoring *Online*
For: Self-test with vocabulary practice
www.pearsonschool.com/ushist

Comprehension
1. **Terms and People** For each item below, write a sentence explaining its significance.
   - Woodrow Wilson
   - New Freedom
   - Sixteenth Amendment
   - Federal Reserve Act
   - Federal Trade Commission
   - Clayton Antitrust Act

2. **NoteTaking Reading Skill: Identify Details** Use your concept web to answer the Section Focus Question: What steps did Wilson take to increase the government's role in the economy?

Writing About History
3. **Quick Write: Use Vivid Language** Choose an event discussed in this section. In one or two paragraphs, retell a portion of the event. Be sure to use vivid language and include details. Do additional research if needed.

Critical Thinking
4. **Compare and Contrast** How were the goals and actions of Wilson's New Freedom similar to Roosevelt's New Nationalism? How were they different?

5. **Draw Conclusions** Describe how each of the following met Progressive goals: the Sixteenth Amendment; the Clayton Antitrust Act; the FTC.

6. **Demonstrate Reasoned Judgment** In which area do you think government reforms had the greatest impact? Why?

Answers

 Wilson pushed for laws that would give the federal government more power over tariffs, banks, and trusts.

 The Progressives established the idea that government can take action to help solve problems in society and the economy.

---

1. Sentences should reflect an understanding of each term or person listed.

2. He worked to reform tariffs, banking, and trusts.

3. Students' paragraphs should focus on an event from this section, such as the Election of 1912 or the Ludlow Massacre, and apply vivid language and details in the writing.

4. Like Roosevelt's New Nationalism, Wilson's New Freedom plan focused on trusts. Unlike Roosevelt's New National-

ism plan, Wilson's New Freedom plan also focused on tariffs and banks.

5. The Sixteenth Amendment helped lower prices and increase economic competition by allowing Congress to create an income tax, which allowed the government to lower tariffs. The Clayton Antitrust Act helped "bust the trusts" by strengthening existing antitrust legislation. The FTC regulated big business by watching for false advertising and labeling.

6. Sample answer: The greatest impact was in the area of politics. The referendum, initiative, and recall put legislative power directly into the hands of the voters, and the extension of suffrage to women increased enormously the level of democracy in the country.

For additional assessment, have students access **Progress Monitoring *Online*** at **www.pearsonschool.com/ushist.**

Quick Study Guide

Progress Monitoring Online
For: Self-test with vocabulary practice
www.pearsonschool.com/ushist

Quick Study Guide

- Have students use the Quick Study Guide to prepare for the chapter test. Students may wish to refer to the following sections as they review:

Effects of Social Progressivism
Section 1
Section 2
Section 3
Section 4
Section 5

Progressive Organizations That Worked for Rights
Section 2
Section 3

Municipal Reforms
Section 1

Key Events of the Progressive Movement
Section 1
Section 2
Section 3
Section 4
Section 5

- For additional review, remind students to refer to the Reading and Note Taking Study Guide.
  Section Note Taking
  Section Summaries

- Have students access **www.pearsonschool.com/ushist** for this chapter's History Interactive timeline, which includes expanded entries and additional events.

- If students need more instruction on analyzing graphic data, have them read the Skills Handbook, **p. SH21.**

For **Progress Monitoring Online,** refer students to the Self-test with vocabulary practice at **www.pearsonschool.com/ushist.**

Effects of Social Progressivism

Living Conditions	• Immigrants gain access to child care and English classes. • Municipal governments are pressured to improve sanitation and tenement safety. • Minority groups organize, create self-help agencies, and fight discrimination. • Immigrants are encouraged to become "Americanized." • Laws regulate safety of foods and medicine.
Working Conditions	• City and state laws improve workplace safety. • Workers' compensation laws provide for payments to injured workers. • Laws limit workday hours; Supreme Court upholds limits for women but not for men. • State and federal governments were urged to adopt minimum wage and make other reforms. • Strike fund aids workers who reject unsafe working conditions. • Minority job seekers gain access to more jobs.
Children	• State and federal laws ban child labor; Supreme Court overturns federal ban. • Compulsory-education laws require children to attend school. • Poor children gain access to nursery schools and kindergartens.

Progressive Organizations That Worked for Rights

Municipal Reforms

Government Reforms	Election Reforms
• Commission form of government • City managers • Trained administrators • City-owned public utilities	• Direct primary • Initiative • Referendum • Recall

✓ Quick Study Timeline

In America					
	1892 John Muir helps found Sierra Club	**1899** Florence Kelley helps found National Consumers League	**1900** Hurricane devastates Galveston, Texas	**1902** President Roosevelt signs the National Reclamation Act

Presidential Terms	Grover Cleveland 1893–1897	William McKinley 1897–1901	Theodore Roosevelt 1901–1909

1895   **1900**

Around the World	**1893** New Zealand becomes first nation to grant women the right to vote	**1900** Boxer Rebellion erupts in China	**1901** Britain outlaws employing children under the age of 12 in factories or workshops

Differentiated Instruction   Solutions for All Learners

L1 Special Needs Students   **L2 English Language Learners**   **L2 Less Proficient Readers**

Use the following study guide resources to help students acquiring basic skills:
Adapted Reading and Note Taking Study Guide
- Section Note Taking
- Section Summaries

Use the following study guide resources to help Spanish-speaking students:
Spanish Reading and Note Taking Study Guide
- Section Note Taking
- Section Summaries

American Issues
•—•—•—• Connector

By connecting prior knowledge with what you have learned in this chapter, you can gradually build your understanding of enduring questions that still affect America today. Answer the questions below. Then, use your American Issues Connector study guide (or go online: www.pearsonschool.com/ushist).

Issues You Learned About

● **Social Problems and Reforms** Again and again, Americans have worked to reform problems that afflict society.

1. Think about the social problems that you have read about in this chapter. Identify the five problems that you think posed the biggest threat to society or to groups of Americans. Create a chart showing the following:
   • social problems
   • reform efforts
   • reformers involved
   • results of reform efforts

● **Voting Rights** Over the years, Americans have gradually expanded the democratic right to vote.

2. Who were some of the nineteenth-century leaders of the women's suffrage movement?

3. What methods did Carrie Chapman Catt use to help women win voting rights?

4. How did Alice Paul's methods differ from Catt's?

● **Government's Role in the Economy** Americans often debate the proper balance between free enterprise and government regulation of the economy.

5. What is a trust?

6. How did Roosevelt's and Taft's attitudes toward trusts differ?

7. What effect did Wilson have on trusts?

Connect to Your World	Activity

Interaction With the Environment Today, the National Park System includes about 80 million acres of land. Since the creation of the first national park in 1872, politicians, business leaders, and citizens have debated how to use this land. Some Americans feel that national parks need to be kept untouched. Other Americans support developments, such as logging and oil drilling, in these areas. Still others believe that the parks' natural resources should be used on a limited basis. What do you think? Go online or to your local library to research different points of view about land usage at America's national parks. Decide your own opinion on the best way to use this valuable land. Then, write an oral presentation to share your ideas with the class.

1906	1909	1913	1920
Congress passes the Meat Inspection and Pure Food and Drug acts	NAACP is formed	Congress passes the Federal Reserve Act	Nineteenth Amendment is ratified

William H. Taft 1909–1913   Woodrow Wilson 1913–1921

| 1905 | 1910 | 1915 | 1920 |

| | 1910 | 1914 | |
| | Mexican Revolution begins | World War I begins in Europe | |

History _Interactive_
For: Interactive timeline
www.pearsonschool.com/ushist

Differentiated Instruction   Solutions for All Learners

L1 Special Needs Students   **L2 English Language Learners**   **L2 Less Proficient Readers**

Use the following study guide resource to help students acquiring basic skills:
Adapted Reading and Note Taking Study Guide
• American Issues Journal

Use the following study guide resource to help Spanish-speaking students:
Spanish Reading and Note Taking Study Guide
• American Issues Journal

American Issues
•—•—•—• Connector

Tell students that the main issues for this chapter are Social Problems and Reforms, Voting Rights, and Government's Role in the Economy. Then, ask them to answer the Issues You Learned About questions on this page. Discuss the Connect to Your World topic and ask students to complete the project that follows.

American Issues Connector

1. Students should use information from the text to create their charts.

2. Susan B. Anthony and Elizabeth Cady Stanton

3. Catt led women to lobby Congress to pass a constitutional amendment, used the referendum process to pass state suffrage laws, and recruited wealthy, well-educated women to work for suffrage.

4. Alice Paul's methods were more radical and more dramatically public than Catt's. Paul established the NWP, which used protest marches to try to bring about women's suffrage.

5. A trust is a business monopoly that can limit competition and cause a rise in prices.

6. Roosevelt believed that there are good trusts and bad trusts, whereas Taft did not think there was a distinction between the two.

7. Under Wilson, Congress passed legislation that strengthened antitrust regulations.

Connect to Your World

Students' presentations should reflect a clear understanding of the different points of view regarding the use of national park lands.

For additional review of this chapter's enduring issues, remind students to refer to the Reading and Note Taking Study Guide American Issues Journal.

Terms and People

1. socially conscious writers who dramatized the need for reform; their work brought widespread attention to some of the serious problems of the Progressive Era.

2. the right to vote; to ensure that government would protect their rights and the rights of their families

3. Washington and Du Bois were African American civil rights reformers. Washington believed that racial equality should be achieved through patience and hard work and by economic success. Du Bois believed that African Americans should demand immediately the rights guaranteed to them by the Constitution.

4. This act places restrictions on what foods and medicines can be sold and ensures the quality and safety of products. The FDA enforces the act by monitoring the production of foods and medicines and label content.

5. This amendment gave Congress the power to implement a federal income tax. It provided the federal government with revenue to offset the losses caused by the lowering of tariffs.

Focus Questions

6. the government, urban poor, labor, and education

7. Possible answers: by lobbying Congress to pass a constitutional amendment giving women the right to vote; by using the referendum process to pass state suffrage laws; by holding protest marches and hunger strikes

8. Minorities united, formed social justice and self-help agencies, took legal action, spoke out publicly, and ran for public office.

9. He believed that government's role was to keep the powerful from taking advantage of smaller businesses and the poor so that everyone got a "square deal."

10. Wilson encouraged Congress to lower tariffs, reformed the banking system, and persuaded Congress to establish the FTC and Clayton Antitrust Act, both of which monitor business practices.

Chapter Assessment

Terms and People

1. Who were the **muckrakers**? Explain the effect the muckrakers had on American life.

2. Define **suffrage**. Why did Progressive women demand suffrage?

3. Who were **Booker T. Washington** and **W.E.B. Du Bois**? What different ideas did they hold?

4. What was the **Pure Food and Drug Act**? Which government agency enforces this act, and how does it do so?

5. Define the **Sixteenth Amendment**. How did it help the government?

Focus Questions

The focus question for this chapter is **What were the causes and effects of the Progressive Movement?** Build an answer to this big question by answering the focus questions for Sections 1 through 5 and the Critical Thinking questions that follow.

Section 1

6. What areas did Progressives think were in need of the greatest reform?

Section 2

7. How did women of the Progressive Era make progress and win the right to vote?

Section 3

8. What steps did minorities take to combat social problems and discrimination?

Section 4

9. What did Roosevelt think government should do for citizens?

Section 5

10. What steps did Wilson take to increase the government's role in the economy?

Critical Thinking

11. **Analyze Visuals** Study the photograph of the child coal miners on the opening page of Section 1. What does this image tell you about the life of young laborers?

12. **Identify Point of View** Explain the different points of view Progressives held on the education of children. What point of view did John Dewey hold?

13. **Draw Inferences** In what way did the Court ruling in *Muller* v. *Oregon* contradict the ideas behind the women's rights movement?

14. **Draw Inferences** What factors may have pushed African Americans to migrate from rural areas to urban areas?

15. **Make Generalizations** How did nonwhites and minority groups seek to better themselves during the Progressive Era?

16. **Determine Relevance** How important was Upton Sinclair's *The Jungle* to passage of the Meat Inspection Act? Explain.

17. **Explain Effects** How did the Progressive Party affect the presidential election of 1912?

18. **Analyze Information** Why do historians believe that the Federal Reserve Act was the most important piece of economic legislation before the 1930s?

19. **Analyze Ideas and Effects** Compare the Social Gospel Movement and its results with Social Darwinism, which you read about earlier.

20. **Predict Consequences** Do you think that either the NAWSA or the NWP could have succeeded in gaining suffrage for women on its own? Explain.

Writing About History

Writing a Narrative Essay Write a narrative essay that tells a story about one of the reform efforts of the Progressive Era in the United States. Tell the story from the point of view of a historical individual or a fictional character of the period.

Prewriting
• Choose a reform effort that interests you most. Take notes about the people and locations involved.

• Choose a purpose for your essay. For example, you may want to highlight a certain event or result that you think deserves attention.

• Gather the facts and details you will need to tell your story, including any historic background.

Drafting
• Identify the climax, or most important part, of your story. Then, decide what will happen in the beginning, middle, and end of the essay.

• Write an opening for the essay that will grab a reader's interest and make sure to include sensory details.

• Use many details to make the story vivid. Include dialogue when possible to convey the thoughts of your character.

• Write a conclusion that summarizes the significance of the experience to the character.

Revising
• Use the guidelines on page SH11 of the Writing Handbook to revise your narrative essay.

Critical Thinking

11. Sample answer: Very young children were expected to work under dangerous conditions, such as in coal mines.

12. Some Progressives thought that children should be taught work skills; others thought that they should be taught literature and music. Most agreed that girls should be taught different subjects from boys. Dewey believed that children should learn academic subjects as well as practical subjects.

13. This ruling stated that it was legal to consider women in a separate class from men, and so it was fair to limit their work hours. Later, however, this ruling was used to justify paying women less than men for the same work.

14. Sample answer: African Americans may have moved from rural areas to urban areas because more jobs were available in urban areas. Also, networks such as the Urban League helped African American families buy clothing and books and send children to school.

Document-Based Assessment

Regulation of the Economy

During the Progressive Era, Presidents such as Theodore Roosevelt and Woodrow Wilson called for the federal government to take on a greater role in regulating the economy. But not all Americans approved of the expansion of federal power. Use your knowledge of the Progressive Era and Documents A, B, C, and D to answer questions 1 through 4.

Document A

"This country belongs to the people who inhabit it. Its resources, its businesses, its institutions, and its laws should be utilized, maintained, or altered in whatever manner will best promote the general interest. It is time to set the public welfare in the first place. . . .

We demand . . . that those who profit by control of business affairs shall justify that profit and that control by sharing with the public the fruits thereof. We therefore demand a strong national regulation of interstate corporations. . . .

We pledge our party to establish a Department of Labor, with a seat in the Cabinet, and with wide jurisdiction over matters affecting the conditions of labor and living."
—*Progressive "Bull Moose" Party Platform, 1912*

Document B

Federal Reserve System

Board of Governors	• Appointed by the President; confirmed by the Senate • Sets cash-reserve requirements for member banks • Reviews the short-term rates set by reserve banks

↓

12 Federal Reserve Banks	• Each serves one of 12 regional districts • Set short-term interest rates for member banks

↓

All nationally chartered banks required to be members

Document C

"What effect is what you may do here going to have upon the future welfare, productiveness, and value of the greatest single industrial interest of the country?. . . . Gentlemen, you may pass an act that will so compromise the value of the property and the prosperity of the communities of this country that it will bring widespread disaster. . . .

What I say, gentlemen, is that [it] is a very, very serious moment when an Anglo-Saxon government undertakes the charge of the people's money and says how much they shall earn by the exercise of their constitutional rights of liberty and property. And it should be recognized that possibly we are at the parting of the ways, and that if this be done it will go on until those constitutional guarantees have but little value, and the only profession worth exercising in the country will be that of holding office in some administrative board."
—*David Wilcox, President of Delaware and Hudson Railroad, testimony to Congress, 1905*

Document D

"We have studied, as perhaps no other nation has, the most effective means of production, but we have not studied cost or economy as we should either as organizers of industry, as statesmen, or as individuals. Nor have we studied and perfected the means by which government may be put to the service of humanity, in safeguarding the health of the nation, the health of its men and its women and its children, as well as their rights in the struggle for existence. . . .

The first duty of law is to keep sound the society it serves. Sanitary laws, pure-food laws, and laws determining conditions of labor, which individuals are powerless to determine for themselves, are intimate parts of the very business of justice and legal efficiency."
—*Woodrow Wilson, First Inaugural Address, 1913*

1. Which of the documents above most closely reflects a belief in laissez-faire economics?
   A Document A
   B Document B
   C Document C
   D Document D

2. Why does the Progressive Party platform favor the creation of a federal Department of Labor?
   A It would increase the profits of corporations.
   B It would promote the good of the people.
   C It would lead to the regulation of interstate commerce.
   D It would limit the growing power of the federal government.

3. Based on Document B, how did the Federal Reserve Act increase the role of the federal government?
   A It gave a federal board greater power to regulate interest rates.
   B It increased the number of commercial banks.
   C It made the Board of Governors independent of the President and Senate.
   D It gave the people the right to elect the Board of Governors of the Federal Reserve.

4. **Writing Task** Should the federal government have broad power over the economy and people's lives? Use your knowledge of the Progressive Era and specific evidence from the primary sources above to support your opinion.

15. Minority groups formed self-help agencies and political organizations. They published their writings about social injustice and worked for legal reforms in the courts.

16. Sinclair's *The Jungle* was the main reason why the Meat Inspection Act was passed. When the novel was published in 1906, the public and President Roosevelt were outraged, and Roosevelt urged Congress to pass the act.

17. The Progressive Party caused a split among Republicans, some of whom voted for Taft and some of whom voted for Roosevelt, and helped Democratic candidate Woodrow Wilson win the White House.

18. The system set up by the Federal Reserve Act still brings stability to the U.S. economy by preventing too much money from ending up in the hands of one person, bank, or region.

19. Unlike Social Darwinism, which applied the concept of "survival of the fittest" to society, the Social Gospel Movement applied the Bible's teachings on charity and justice to improve society.

20. Yes; both groups used effective methods that swayed public support for women's suffrage.

CHAPTER 5

Teach With Technology

PresentationEXPRESS™ PREMIUM DVD

- Teach this chapter's core content by using PresentationExpress, which includes interactivities, video, lecture notes, and the *ExamView®* QuickTake assessment tool.
- To introduce this chapter by using PresentationExpress, ask students with which of the following statements they most agree: **A) Strong nations should be able to control the trade of weaker nations. B) Imperialism most benefits weaker nations because it increases trade. C) Nations with sufficient military and trade powers should take territories to benefit themselves. D) Countries controlled by imperialist nations welcomed colonial ties to the stronger nations.** Take a class poll or record students' answers by using the QuickTake feature and discuss their responses. Point out that in this chapter, they will read about the expansion of the United States as it acquires territories and emerges as a world power. Continue introducing the chapter by using the chapter opener slide show.

Technology Resources

- StudentEXPRESS CD-ROM
- Teacher Resource Library DVD
- PresentationEXPRESS PREMIUM DVD
- *ExamView®* **Test Bank** CD-ROM English and Spanish
- **Guided Reading Audio,** Spanish
- **Student Edition on Audio**

THE ESSENTIAL ? VIDEO By Students For Students
For videos on Amercian Issues, go to ***www.pearsonschool.com/ushist***

CHAPTER 5 An Emerging World Power 1890–1917

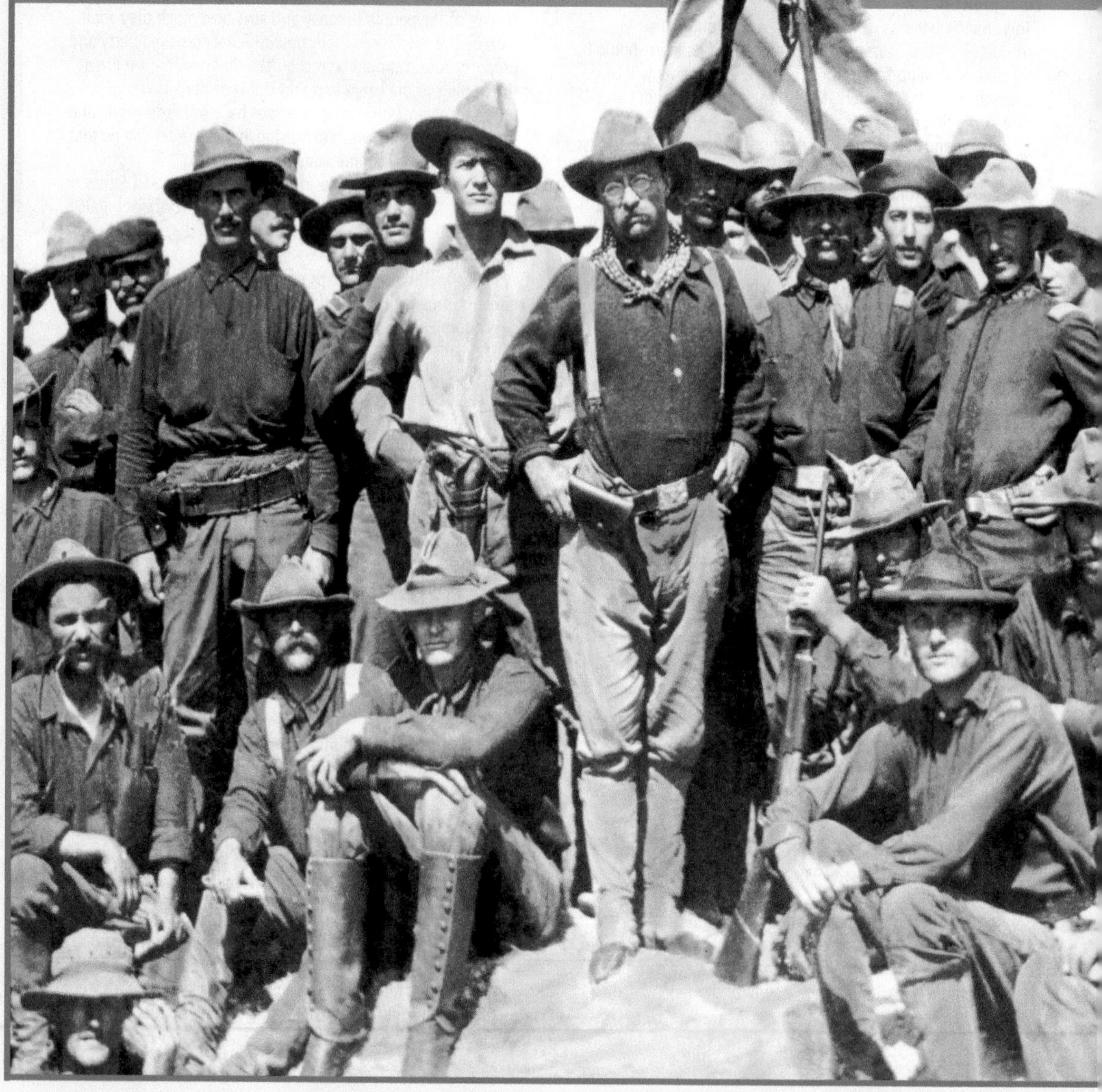

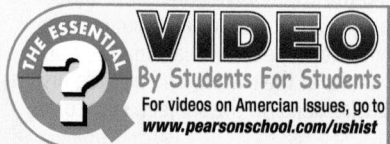

Bibliography

For the Teacher

Langellier, John Phillip. *Uncle Sam's Little Wars: The Spanish-American War, Philippine Insurrection and Boxer Rebellion, 1898–1902.* Stackpole Press, 1999.

McCullough, David. *The Path Between the Seas: The Creation of the Panama Canal, 1870–1914.* Simon and Schuster, 2004.

Trask, David F. *The War with Spain in 1898.* University of Nebraska Press, 1997.

For the Student

L1 Kent, Zachary. *William Seward: The Mastermind of the Alaska Purchase.* Enslow, 2001.

L2 Linnea, Sharon. *Princess Ka'lulani: Hope of a Nation, Heart of a People.* Eerdman's, 1999.

L3 Roosevelt, Theodore, *The Rough Riders.* Modern Library, 1999. First published in 1899.

L4 Ninkovich, Frank. *The United States and Imperialism.* Blackwell Publishers, 2000.

WITNESS HISTORY

Americans Charge to Victory

When Theodore Roosevelt assumed command of the First U.S. Regiment of Volunteer Cavalry, the press nicknamed his new unit "Roosevelt's Rough Riders." On July 1, 1898, the Rough Riders, together with other units—including African American troops from the U.S. Ninth and Tenth Cavalries—stormed into battle outside Santiago, Cuba. A junior officer who would later become a decorated general remembered the unity of his fellow soldiers as the Americans charged up Spanish-held San Juan Hill:

Carving of Commodore Matthew Perry on an animal tusk

“White regiments, black regiments, regulars and Rough Riders, representing the young manhood of the North and South, fought shoulder to shoulder, unmindful of race or color . . . mindful only of their common duty as Americans.”

—Lieutenant John J. Pershing

◄ Future President Theodore Roosevelt poses with his victorious Rough Riders atop San Juan Hill.

Chapter Preview

Chapter Focus Question: How did the United States become a global power?

Section 1
The Roots of Imperialism

Section 2
The Spanish-American War

Section 3
The United States and East Asia

Section 4
The United States and Latin America

Poster from the Spanish-American War

Medal won by African American soldier in Spanish-American War

Use the ☑ **Quick Study Timeline** at the end of this chapter to preview chapter events.

Note Taking Study Guide Online
For: Note Taking and American Issues Connector
www.pearsonschool.com/ushist

Chapter-Level Resources

All in One Letter Home (English and Spanish), Preread the Chapter, Vocabulary Builder, Reading Strategy, Social Studies Skills Practice, Enrichment, Issues Connector, Chapter Tests

- Test Prep With Document-Based Assessment
- AYP Monitoring Assessments
- *ExamView®* Test Bank CD-ROM
- Guided Reading Audio (Spanish)
- Student Edition Audio

Previewing the Chapter

- **WITNESS HISTORY** Remind students that racial segregation and discrimination were common in the United States in the late 1800s and early 1900s. Then, read the Witness History selection aloud. Ask students to discuss what the quotation suggests about the ability of soldiers to work together against a common foe.

- **Analyzing the Visuals** Ask students to examine the soldiers depicted in the photo on these pages. **What does the image tell you about the experiences of the soldiers?** (*The soldiers look hot, tired, and grim, as if they have worked hard.*) The caption says that the soldiers are "victorious." **What about the image tells you that they have won?** (*The American flag in the background indicates that the men have succeeded.*)

- **Focus** Write the Chapter Focus Question on the board. Tell students to keep this question in mind as they read the chapter. Then, have students preview the section titles in this chapter.

- **Preread** Have students complete the chapter's Preread the Chapter worksheet. Teaching Resources, pp. 8–9

Differentiated Instruction   Solutions for All Learners

The following Teacher's Edition strategies are suitable for students of varying abilities.

L1 Special Needs Students, pp. 139, 141, 145, 149, 152, 153, 154, 160, 162, 164, 165 SN

L2 English Language Learners, pp. 139, 141, 149, 152, 153, 154, 160, 162, 164, 165 ELL

L2 Less Proficient Readers, pp. 139, 145, 149, 152, 153, 154, 161, 162, 164, 165 LPR

L4 Advanced Readers, pp. 147, 158 AR

L4 Gifted and Talented Students, pp. 147,158 GT

Have students access **www.pearsonschool. com/ushist** for the Note Taking Study Guide *Online* as an alternative to the *Reading and Note Taking Study Guide* booklet.

Step-by-Step Instruction

Objectives

As you teach this section, keep students focused on the following objectives to help them answer the Section Focus Question and master core content.

- Identify the key factors that prodded America to expand.
- Explain how the United States took its first steps toward increased global power.
- Summarize the chain of events leading up to the U.S. annexation of Hawaii.

Prepare to Read

Background Knowledge ⓛ③

Ask students to recall the relationship between Britain and its American colonies. Have them predict the types of conflict that might arise between the United States and its own colonies.

Set a Purpose ⓛ③

- **WITNESS HISTORY** Read the selection aloud.

  Ask **What does the description of Hawaii as a "pear" indicate about the way that the United States views the islands?** *(The United States sees Hawaii as a resource to be harvested.)*

- **Focus** Point out the Section Focus Question, and write it on the board. Tell students to refer to this question as they read. *(Answer appears with Section 1 Assessment answers.)*

- **Preview** Have students preview the Section Objectives and the list of Terms and People.

- **Reading Skill** Have students use the *Reading Strategy: Main Ideas and Details* worksheet. Teaching Resources, **p. 12**

- **NoteTaking** Using the Structured Read Aloud strategy (TE, p. T20), have students read this section. As they read, have students fill in the concept web with key events that marked America's first steps toward world power. Reading and Note Taking Study Guide

---

▼ A grove of coconut trees in Hawaii in the 1890s

SECTION 1

America Eyes Hawaii

"The Hawaiian pear is now fully ripe and this is the golden hour for the United States to pluck it." John Stevens, U.S. minister to Hawaii, was not talking about fruit when he sent this note to the Secretary of State in 1893. He was talking about the United States taking over the Hawaiian Islands—along with their rich fields of sugar cane and pineapples. And Stevens did more than just talk. He ordered the United States Marines to aid in a revolt against the queen of Hawaii.

Five years later, the Senate finally agreed to annex Hawaii. The "Hawaiian pear" became part of the United States.

The Roots of Imperialism

Objectives

- Identify the key factors that prodded America to expand.
- Explain how the United States took its first steps toward increased global power.
- Summarize the chain of events leading up to the U.S. annexation of Hawaii.

Terms and People

imperialism	Frederick J. Turner
extractive economy	Matthew Perry
Alfred T. Mahan	Queen Liliuokalani
Social Darwinism	

NoteTaking

Reading Skill: Identify Main Ideas As you read, fill in a concept web like the one below with the key events that marked America's first steps toward world power.

Why It Matters For most of its early history, America played a small role in world affairs. But in the late 1800s, this began to change. With leading spokesmen calling for the United States to join the ranks of the world's major powers, the United States began to acquire influence and territories outside its continental borders. The United States was abandoning isolationism and emerging as a new power on the global stage. **Section Focus Question: How and why did the United States take a more active role in world affairs?**

The Causes of Imperialism

During the Age of Imperialism, from the mid-1800s through the early 1900s, powerful nations engaged in a mad dash to extend their influence across much of the world. European nations added to colonies they had established during the Age of Exploration by acquiring new colonies in Africa and Asia. Following European success, Japan and the United States also began to consider the benefits of **imperialism,** the policy by which strong nations extend their political, military, and economic control over weaker territories.

Imperialists Seek Economic Benefits One reason for the rush to grab colonies was the desire for raw materials and natural resources. This was especially true for European nations and Japan. They sought colonies to provide tea, rubber, iron, petroleum, and other materials for their industries at home. These colonial economies were examples of **extractive economies.** The imperial country extracted, or removed, raw materials from the colony and

---

Vocabulary Builder

Use the information below and the following resource to teach students the high-use words from this section. Teaching Resources, Vocabulary Builder, p. 11

High-Use Words	Definitions and Sample Sentences
commodity	*n.* anything bought or sold; any article of commerce The producer of a U.S. **commodity,** such as a crop or factory good, would benefit from developing markets overseas.
successor	*n.* person or thing that succeeds, or follows, another Queen Liliuokalani was King Kalakaua's **successor,** and she ruled after the death of her brother.

shipped them to the home country. Possession of colonies gave nations an edge in the competition for global resources. In contrast to other world powers, the resource-rich United States had fewer concerns about shortages of raw materials in the nineteenth century.

For Americans, the problem was not a shortage of materials, but a surplus of goods. The booming U.S. economy of the late 1800s was producing more goods than Americans could consume. Farmers complained that excess production resulted in declining crop prices and profits. Industrialists urged expanding trade into new overseas markets where American <u>commodities</u> could be sold. Otherwise, they warned, American factories would close and unemployment would rise. Senator Albert J. Beveridge, a Progressive and friend of Theodore Roosevelt, explained why the United States needed to become a world power:

Vocabulary Builder
<u>commodity</u>–(kuh MAHD uh tee) *n.* anything bought or sold; any article of commerce

Primary Source ❝Today we are raising more [crops] than we can consume. Today we are making more than we can use. . . . Therefore we must find new markets for our produce, new occupation for our capital, new work for our labor.❞
—Senator Albert J. Beveridge, "The March of the Flag," 1898

Imperialists Stress Military Strength To expand and protect their interests around the world, imperialist nations built up their military strength. **Alfred T. Mahan,** a military historian and an officer in the United States Navy, played a key role in transforming America into a naval power. In *The Influence of Sea Power Upon History*, Mahan asserted that since ancient times, many great nations had owed their greatness to powerful navies. He called upon America to build a modern fleet. Mahan also argued that the United States would need to acquire foreign bases where American ships could refuel and gather fresh supplies. Influenced by the ideas of Mahan and others, the United States expanded and modernized its navy by building new steel-plated, steam-powered battleships such as the USS *Maine*. By 1900, the United States had the third largest navy in the world.

A Strong Navy
Prominent imperialists like Alfred T. Mahan called for a strong American navy to protect U.S. interests overseas. *How could a strong navy benefit American exporters?*

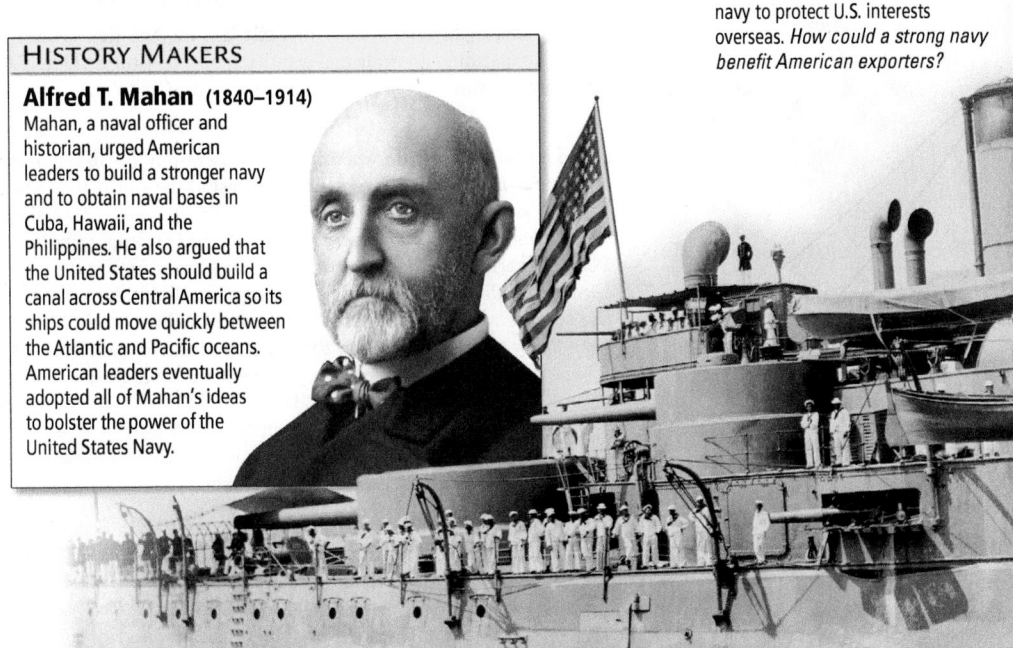

HISTORY MAKERS

Alfred T. Mahan (1840–1914)
Mahan, a naval officer and historian, urged American leaders to build a stronger navy and to obtain naval bases in Cuba, Hawaii, and the Philippines. He also argued that the United States should build a canal across Central America so its ships could move quickly between the Atlantic and Pacific oceans. American leaders eventually adopted all of Mahan's ideas to bolster the power of the United States Navy.

Teach

The Causes of Imperialism

Instruct

- **Introduce: Key Term** Ask students to find the key term *imperialism* (in bold) in the text. Then, write the term on the board, say it aloud, have students say it with you, and provide the definition. Help students recall the relationship between Britain and the American colonies. Ask them to predict the relationship that the United States will have with the colonies that it will acquire in the nineteenth and twentieth centuries.

- **Teach** Using the Idea Wave strategy (TE, p. T22), ask students to list the similarities and differences between imperial nations and colonies. Then, ask students to discuss how a country might become an imperial nation, and what events might cause a sovereign country to lose power and become a colony.

- **Analyzing the Visuals** Direct students to the photo of the U.S. ship on this page. Then, have students read the HISTORY MAKERS about Alfred T. Mahan. Discuss how a strong navy would help the United States acquire and control colonies.

Independent Practice

Ask students to suppose that they are living in the United States in 1900. Have them write paragraphs explaining whether they support the United States in acquiring colonies and giving reasons for their positions.

Monitor Progress

As students fill in their concept webs, circulate to make sure that they understand America's first steps toward world power. For a completed version of the concept web, see Note Taking Transparencies, **B-91**.

Differentiated Instruction Solutions for All Learners

L1 Special Needs Students **L2 English Language Learners** **L2 Less Proficient Readers**

To help students understand the key details about the rise of U.S. imperialism, have them make two-column charts to summarize the causes of imperialism. Ask students to label the first column "Economic Conditions" and list ways that colonies helped nations and businesses earn more money. Have students label the second column "Beliefs of Superiority" and list the ideas that imperialists used to justify colonizing other territories. Then, have students work together to write a summary of the causes of imperialism.

Answer

Caption A strong navy would ensure an uninterrupted flow of materials from the colony back to American businesses.

Instruct

- **Introduce** Have students preview the map on the next page. Ask them to estimate the distance from the United States to both Japan and Alaska. Ask students why they think the United States would be interested in trading with nations that are so far away.

- **Teach** Ask **Why was Perry's arrival in Japan important?** *(He opened the country to trade with the United States.)* Refer students to the map on the next page. Ask **How could the acquisition of Alaska contribute to U.S. trade with Japan?** *(The United States could sell Japan raw materials from Alaska. U.S. merchants might refuel in Alaska on their way to Japan.)*

- **Quick Activity** Have students access **www.pearsonschool.com/ushist** to use the Geography Interactive map and answer the map skills questions in the textbook.

Independent Practice

- To ensure that students understand the importance of Seward's purchase of Alaska, have them read Seward's biography and answer the questions that follow. Teaching Resources, **p. 19**

- Ask students to suppose that they are business people who are attending the first International Pan-American Conference in 1889. Have them write paragraphs describing the experience and why the meeting is important to their business.

Monitor Progress

To review this section, ask students to explain why Japan, Alaska, and Latin America were strategically important to the United States.

Answers

Caption Many Americans believed that the United States was superior to other countries and that it should rule over those nations.

✔ Americans had surplus goods and wanted to find other markets for them. In addition, imperialists embraced Social Darwinism and believed in America's Manifest Destiny.

Nationalism Fuels Pursuit of Empire

In the late nineteenth century, patriotic songs by composers such as John Philip Sousa reinforced Americans' widespread belief in the national superiority of the United States. *How did nationalism contribute to the rise of American imperialism?*

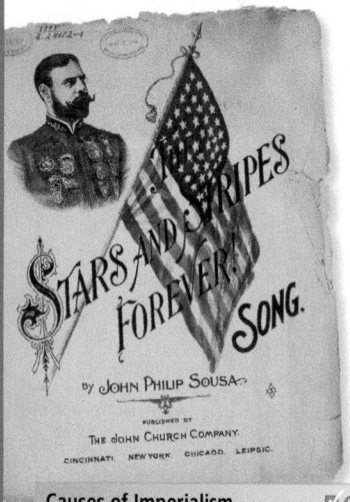

STARS AND STRIPES FOREVER SONG.

BY JOHN PHILIP SOUSA

PUBLISHED BY
THE JOHN CHURCH COMPANY.
CINCINNATI   NEW YORK   CHICAGO   LEIPSIC

Causes of Imperialism	☑ Quick Study
Economic gain	• Industrialists want raw materials for industries in their home countries. • Entrepreneurs want to sell their goods and invest in new overseas markets.
Militarism	Colonial powers seek bases for naval forces that protect their global trade networks.
Nationalism and Social Darwinism	Imperialists feel a moral duty to spread their culture to peoples they consider inferior.

Imperialists Believe in National Superiority Imperialists around the world used ideas of racial, national, and cultural superiority to justify imperialism. One of these ideas was **Social Darwinism,** the belief that life consists of competitive struggles in which only the fittest survive. Social Darwinists felt that certain nations and races were superior to others and therefore were destined to rule over inferior peoples and cultures. Prominent Americans worried that if the United States remained isolated while European nations gobbled up the rest of the world, America would not survive.

One reason that these Americans embraced Social Darwinism was that they had long believed that God had granted them the right and responsibility to settle the frontier. They spoke of America's "Manifest Destiny" to expand all the way to the Pacific Ocean. In a best-selling work titled *Our Country,* Josiah Strong picked up on this theme. A religious missionary, Strong argued that Americans had a responsibility to spread their Western values. "God is training the Anglo-Saxon race," he asserted, "for its mission [to civilize] weaker races." American missionaries who shared Strong's belief journeyed to foreign lands to gain converts to Christianity.

In *The Significance of the Frontier in American History,* historian **Frederick Jackson Turner** noted that the frontier had been closed by gradual settlement in the nineteenth century. Throughout American history, he continued, the frontier had traditionally supplied an arena where ambitious Americans could pursue their fortunes and secure a fresh start. It had thus served as a "safety valve," siphoning off potential discontent. Now that America had spanned the continent, advocates of Turner's thesis urged overseas expansion as a way to keep the "safety valve" open and avoid internal conflict.

✔ **Checkpoint** What factors influenced Americans to play a more active role in the world?

America's First Steps Toward World Power

Beginning in the mid-1800s, with little fanfare, America focused more and more on expanding its trade and acquiring new territories. One of America's first moves toward world power came before the Civil War.

U.S. Power Grows in the Pacific In 1853, Commodore **Matthew Perry** sailed a fleet of American warships into present-day Tokyo Bay, Japan. Prior to Perry's arrival, Japan had denied the rest of the world access to its ports. In fact, because most Japanese people had never seen steamships before, they thought the ships in Perry's fleet were "giant dragons puffing smoke." Perry cleverly won the Japanese emperor's favor by showering him with lavish gifts. Japanese leaders also realized that by closing off their nation to the outside world, they had fallen behind in military technology. Within a year, Perry negotiated a treaty that opened Japan to trade with America.

Perry's journey set a precedent for further expansion across the Pacific Ocean. In 1867, the United States took possession of the Midway Islands. Treaties in 1875 and 1887 increased trade with the Hawaiian Islands and gave the United States the right to build a naval base at Pearl Harbor.

Seward Purchases Alaska In 1867, Secretary of State William Seward bought Alaska from Russia for $7.2 million. Journalists scoffed at the purchase and referred to Alaska as "Seward's Folly" and "Seward's Icebox." They wondered why the United States would want a vast tundra of snow and ice 1,000 miles north

Connect to Your World

Japan: Then and Now Matthew Perry's expedition brought many immediate and far-reaching changes to Japan. His arrival forced the Japanese to abandon their country's isolationist policy or risk attack from the United States Navy. Perry negotiated a treaty that promised better treatment for sailors shipwrecked in Japan, allowed U.S. ships to purchase fuel from the Japanese, and opened Japanese ports to U.S. trade. Soon, European countries demanded and signed similar treaties. Many Japanese felt humiliated by abandoning isolationism. Pressure by foreign governments deepened social and economic concerns in Japan, leading to the upheaval of its government and sparking the Meiji Restoration. The Meiji Restoration modernized Japan and led to the adoption of Western technology, sciences, and laws. Following World War II, Japan experienced rapid economic growth and became one of the world's financial leaders. Today, Japan has become one of the most technologically and economically advanced societies in the world.

U.S. Acquisitions in the Pacific

Geography *Interactive*
For: Interactive map
www.pearsonschool.com/ushist

Map Skills Between 1853 and 1898, the United States opened Japan to American trade and gained valuable possessions across the Pacific Ocean.
1. **Locate:** (a) Japan, (b) Alaska, (c) Hawaiian Islands
2. **Place** Which islands lie about halfway between the United States and Japan?
3. **Analyze** Why were the Hawaiian Islands important to U.S. naval and merchant ships?

Engraving of Matthew Perry on an animal tusk

of its border. But Seward's purchase almost doubled the country's size, and the "icebox" turned out to be rich in timber, oil, and other natural resources. Alaska also greatly expanded America's reach across the Pacific. Scholars today see Seward's purchase as a key milestone on America's road to power.

U.S. Influence in Latin America Grows U.S. businessmen saw Latin America as a natural place to expand their trade and investments. Secretary of State James Blaine helped them by sponsoring the First International Pan-American Conference in 1889. Blaine preached the benefits of economic cooperation to delegates of 17 Latin American countries. The conference also paved the way for the construction of the Pan-American Highway system, which linked the United States to Central and South America.

In 1895, tensions rose between America and Great Britain because of a border dispute between British Guiana and Venezuela. Claiming that Britain was violating the Monroe Doctrine, President Cleveland threatened U.S. intervention. After some international saber-rattling, the British accepted a growing U.S. sphere of influence in Latin America. Relations between Britain and the United States soon improved.

✔ **Checkpoint** Why did journalists criticize Seward for his purchase of Alaska?

The United States Acquires Hawaii

The Hawaiian Islands had been economically linked to the United States for almost a century. Since the 1790s, American merchant ships had stopped at Hawaii on their way to East Asia. Missionaries had established Christian churches and schools on the islands. Americans had also established sugar cane

The United States Acquires Hawaii ⓵⓷

Instruct
- **Introduce: Vocabulary Builder** Have students locate the vocabulary term **successor** and its definition. Tell students that each ruler of Hawaii had a **successor** who continued the work of governing the country.
- **Teach** Ask **How did Queen Liliuokalani respond to the attempts of U.S. planters to control Hawaii?** (She abolished the constitution that favored the rights of white planters.) **Why did sugar growers want the United States to annex Hawaii?** (If the United States annexed Hawaii, sugar growers would avoid paying a high tax on exported sugar.) **Why were sugar growers able to change the government of Hawaii?** (Sugar growers were wealthy and powerful. They had connections to the leaders of the U.S. government.)
- **Quick Activity** Display Color Transparency: American Imperialism. Use the lesson suggested in the transparency book to guide a discussion about the territories that the United States acquired in the late 1800s and early 1900s. Color Transparencies **A-81**

Independent Practice
Have students make a timeline that traces Hawaiian history from King Kalakaua's reign to Hawaii's annexation by the United States in 1898. Direct students to use the timeline on the next page as a model.

Monitor Progress
Circulate to make sure that students complete their timelines in chronological order and understand the issues of Hawaiian annexation.

Differentiated Instruction Solutions for All Learners

L1 Special Needs Students **L2 English Language Learners**

Use the map on this page to illustrate the expansion of the United States into territories bordering the Pacific Ocean. Have each student use a sheet of paper to measure the distance from the western border of the United States to Alaska, Japan, and the Hawaiian Islands. Have students plot the route that merchants transporting Alaskan timber and Hawaiian sugar to Japan might take. Ask **How might U.S.** merchants benefit from having Alaska and Hawaii under U.S. control? (U.S. merchants might have easier access to ports or lower tariffs on goods.) **How do you think the acquisition of Alaska and Hawaii affected ports on the Pacific coast of the United States?** (Goods from Alaska and Hawaii probably were shipped to the nearest U.S. ports, which are on the country's Pacific coast.)

Answers

✔ Journalists criticized Seward's purchase because of the distance between Alaska and the United States and because they believed that the area lacked natural resources.

Map Skills
1. Review locations with students.
2. the Hawaiian Islands
3. The base protected U.S. trade ships that used the Hawaiian Islands as a stopping place.

Chapter 5 Section 1   **141**

Objectives

- Describe how the U.S. has expanded its territory.
- Analyze the political, economic, and social ramifications of the U.S. territorial expansion into Hawaii.

Background Knowledge ⓛ₃

Ask students to name U.S. territories, such as Guam and Puerto Rico. Have students discuss the challenges of governing a widespread area that includes people of different backgrounds.

Instruct ⓛ₃

Point out that the timeline shows how the United States expanded. Ask **How did different territories become part of the United States?** *(Some areas were purchased, and some were acquired after war or rebellion.)*

Monitor Progress

- Have students complete the Issues Connector Worksheet, *Territorial Expansion of the United States.* Check their work to make sure that students grasp the aspects of the issue. Teaching Resources, pp. 15–18

- Remind students to complete their American Issues Journal worksheets. Review their work for accuracy. Reading and Note Taking Study Guide

Answers

Transfer Activities

1. Hee favors political recognition of native Hawaiians. Senator Kyl argues that self-rule would lead to racial conflict.
2. With sovereignty, native Hawaiians could form their own government. They might pass laws that emphasize Hawaiian customs and interests and de-emphasize U.S. trade interests.
3. For more information about Hawaiian sovereignty, have students access **www.pearsonschool.com/ushist.**

TRACK THE ISSUE

Should the United States expand its territory?

The United States has expanded its territory many times. It has done so through various means, including negotiation, treaty, annexation, and war. But territorial expansion has often aroused strong debate among Americans. Use the timeline below to explore this enduring issue.

1803 Louisiana Purchase
Jefferson buys Louisiana Territory despite doubts about constitutionality.

1845 Texas Annexation
Texas joins the Union despite opposition from Mexico and nonslave states.

1848 Mexican Cession
United States gains vast lands in the Southwest as a result of war with Mexico.

1867 Alaska Purchase
Critics say Alaska is an icebox and call the deal "Seward's Folly."

1893 Hawaiian Revolt
American planters overthrow Queen Liliuokalani and pave way to annexation in 1898.

1898 Spanish-American War
Victory over Spain puts Cuba, Puerto Rico, the Philippines, and Guam under U.S. control.

Queen Liliuokalani

Protesters want to restore the native sovereignty of the Hawaiian Islands.

DEBATE THE ISSUE

Native Hawaiian Sovereignty In 1898, the United States annexed Hawaii without the consent of native Hawaiians. In recent years, some Hawaiians have called for the return of native sovereignty. One possible solution is the establishment of some form of self-rule for natives, much like the "nation within a nation" status of Native Americans.

"For the overwhelming majority of Hawaiians, justice means political status and federal recognition, the restoration of our inherent sovereignty and redress from the United States for the illegal overthrow of the Kingdom of Hawaii. . . . Although there are more Hawaiians than . . . any other native peoples in the United States, Hawaiians have remained without recognition of our right to self-govern."

—Clayton Hee, Office of Hawaiian Affairs

"Would the citizens of [a] Native Hawaiian government—like reservation Indians—be immune from state laws, regulations and taxes? . . . If Congress were to create a separate tribal government for Native Hawaiians, it would be imposing just such a system on the people of Hawaii. Persons of different races, who live together in the same society, would be subject to different legal codes. This . . . is a recipe for permanent racial conflict."

—John Kyl, senator from Arizona

TRANSFER Activities

1. **Compare** How do the two speakers differ on the issue of self-rule for Hawaiians?

2. **Analyze** If Native Hawaiians gain sovereignty, how would their lives change?

3. **Transfer** Use the following Web site to see a video, try a WebQuest, and write in your journal. www.pearsonschool.com/ushist

History Background

The Republic of Hawaii The plans of the United States to take control of Hawaii were delayed when President Grover Cleveland refused to annex the islands. At the same time, the islands were declared the Republic of Hawaii, and Sanford Ballard Dole was declared its president in 1894. In 1895, protesters who supported Queen Liliuokalani staged a revolt, but the uprising was promptly quelled. The former queen was arrested and charged with treason. Dole, who was born in Hawaii to missionary parents, served as president until 1898, when he was appointed Hawaii's first territorial governor. As Hawaii's last queen, Liliuokalani renounced her claims to the throne, but she never accepted the annexation of Hawaii by the United States. In her retirement, she wrote her autobiography, as well as many songs. One of her best-known songs is "Aloha Oe," a farewell to Hawaii.

plantations there. In 1887, American planters convinced King Kalakaua (kah LAH kah oo ah) to amend Hawaii's constitution so that voting rights were limited to only wealthy landowners, who were, of course, the white planters.

American Planters Increase Their Power In the early 1890s, American planters in Hawaii faced two crises. First, a new U.S. tariff law imposed duties on previously duty-free Hawaiian sugar. This made Hawaiian sugar more expensive than sugar produced in the United States. The sugar-growers in Hawaii therefore feared that they would suffer decreasing sales and profits.

The other problem was that in 1891, Kalakaua died and his sister Lili-uokalani (lih lee oo oh kah LAH nee) was his successor. A determined Hawaiian nationalist, **Queen Liliuokalani** resented the increasing power of the white planters, who owned much of the Hawaiian land. She abolished the constitution that had given political power to the white minority.

With the backing of U.S. officials, the American planters responded quickly and forcefully. In 1893, they overthrew the queen. John Stevens, U.S. minister to Hawaii, ordered United States Marines to help the rebels seize power. The new government, led by wealthy planter Sanford B. Dole, asked President Benjamin Harrison to annex Hawaii into the United States.

The United States Annexes Hawaii President Harrison signed the treaty of annexation but could not get the required Senate approval before Grover Cleveland became President. Cleveland ordered a full investigation, which revealed that the majority of the Hawaiian people did not approve of the treaty. Cleveland refused to sign the agreement and apologized for the "flagrant wrong" done by the "reprehensible conduct of the American minister."

However, American sentiment for annexation remained strong, especially on the West Coast, where California business interests had close ties with the planters in Hawaii. In 1897, a new President entered the White House. William McKinley's administration favored annexation, and in 1898, after the outbreak of the Spanish-American War, Congress proclaimed Hawaii an official U.S. territory.

 Checkpoint How did American planters react to Queen Liliuokalani's actions when she gained power?

Vocabulary Builder
successor–(suhk SEHS uhr) *n.* person or thing that succeeds, or follows, another

---

Progress Monitoring *Online*
For: Self-test with vocabulary practice
www.pearsonschool.com/ushist

Comprehension

1. Terms and People For each person listed below, write a sentence explaining his or her significance to American imperialism.
- Alfred T. Mahan
- Frederick J. Turner
- Matthew Perry
- Queen Liliuokalani

2. NoteTaking Reading Skill: Identify Main Ideas Use your concept web to answer the Section Focus Question: How and why did the United States take a more active role in world affairs?

Writing About History

3. Quick Write: Choose a Topic To write a narrative essay, start by choosing a topic. Suppose that you want to write a narrative from the perspective of the American imperialist Alfred T. Mahan. Make a list of topics that interest you, such as the construction of new battleships for the United States Navy or an account of a U.S. exploration for unclaimed territory in the Pacific Ocean. You may want to do research in books and on the Internet before you decide on a topic.

Critical Thinking

4. Evaluate Information Which of the motives for American imperialism do you think was the most important? Why?

5. Compare Points of View How did public opinion about the purchase of Alaska in 1867 differ from the view of historians today?

6. Make Decisions If you had been President in 1894, would you have supported or opposed the annexation of Hawaii? Give reasons for your answer.

Objectives

As you teach this section, keep students focused on the following objectives to help them answer the Section Focus Question and master core content.

- Explain the causes of the Spanish-American War.
- Identify the major battles of the war.
- Describe the consequences of the war, including the debate over imperialism.

Prepare to Read

Background Knowledge L3

Ask students to recall conflicts that have led the United States into war. Ask students to predict the types of conflict that might lead the United States to war with Spain.

Set a Purpose L3

- **WITNESS HISTORY** Read the selection aloud.

  Ask **What does H. W. Petrie want people to think caused the *Maine*'s destruction?** (*Spain deliberately wrecked the* Maine.) **How do you think Petrie wants the United States to "teach a lesson" to Spain?** (*Petrie wants the U.S. to go to war to defeat Spain.*)

- **Focus** Point out the Section Focus Question, and write it on the board. Tell students to refer to this question as they read. (*Answer appears with Section 2 Assessment answers.*)

- **Preview** Have students preview the Section Objectives and the list of Terms and People.

- **NoteTaking** Using the Guided Questioning strategy (TE, p. T20), have students read this section. As they read, have students note the causes, key events, and effects of the Spanish-American War. Reading and Note Taking Study Guide

1898 recruiting poster ▶

▲ Nameplate from the *Maine's* wreckage

WITNESS HISTORY

Remember the *Maine*!

On February 15, 1898, an explosion ripped through the hull of the USS *Maine* in Havana harbor, in the Spanish colony of Cuba. More than 250 American sailors died. The incident ignited a furor as Americans clamored for war with Spain. In newspapers, speeches, and songs, patriots implored their fellow citizens to remember the *Maine*:

❝And shall our country let it pass, this deed of foul intent?
And shall our country dare believe it was an accident? . . .
Come arm, we all, and let us teach a lesson to bold Spain.
We will avenge, by more than speech the destruction of the *Maine*!❞

—H. W. Petrie, lyrics from "The Wreck
of the *Maine*," 1898

The Spanish-American War

Objectives

- Explain the causes of the Spanish-American War.
- Identify the major battles of the war.
- Describe the consequences of the war, including the debate over imperialism.

Terms and People

José Martí	George Dewey
William Randolph Hearst	Emilio Aguinaldo
Yellow Press	Rough Riders
jingoism	Treaty of Paris

NoteTaking

Reading Skill: Identify Causes and Effects
Note the causes, key events, and effects of the Spanish-American War.

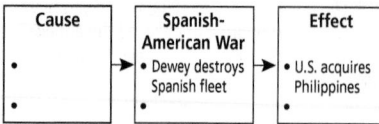

Cause	Spanish-American War	Effect
•	• Dewey destroys Spanish fleet	• U.S. acquires Philippines
•	•	•

Why It Matters American power and economic interests around the world were growing. Still, the United States remained reluctant to risk war with other powers to acquire colonies. That changed, however, in 1898, when America went to war against Spain. The United States acquired colonies and became a world power. **Section Focus Question: What were the causes and effects of the Spanish-American War?**

Causes of the War

At the end of the nineteenth century, Spain was an imperial nation in decline. Its formerly vast empire had dwindled to a small number of possessions, including the Philippine Islands in the Pacific and the Caribbean islands of Puerto Rico and Cuba.

Cubans Rebel Against Spanish Rule By 1897, American entrepreneurs had invested $50 million in sugar cane plantations and other ventures in Cuba, which lay just 90 miles off the Florida coast. These businessmen saw Cuba as a growing market for American products. However, the island was very unstable. Yearning for freedom, the Cubans repeatedly rebelled against Spanish rule.

In 1895, Cuban patriot **José Martí** launched a war for independence from Spain. With cries of *"Cuba Libre!"* ("Free Cuba!"), rebel fighters used guerrilla tactics of hit-and-run raids against Spanish forces. In response, Spanish General Valeriano Weyler devised a

Vocabulary Builder

Use the information below and the following resource to teach students the high-use words from this section. Teaching Resources, Vocabulary Builder, p. 11

High-Use Words	Definitions and Sample Sentences
stipulate	*v.* to include specifically in the terms of an agreement A treaty between the United States and the Hawaiian Islands **stipulated** that the United States could build a naval base at Pearl Harbor.
obsolete	*adj.* no longer in use or practice; out-of-date When the United States began to embrace imperialism, the idea of isolationism became **obsolete**.

Rebellion in Cuba

Spain sent 150,000 troops and one of its best generals, Valeriano Weyler, to smash the uprising. Here, rebel cavalry forces charge into battle. *What attitude do you think the artist had toward the rebels? How can you tell?*

plan to deprive the rebels of food and recruits. He herded the rural population into reconcentration camps, where tens of thousands died from disease and starvation. Meanwhile, the Cubans and Spanish destroyed American property.

Many Americans favored the Cubans, whose struggle for freedom and democracy reminded Americans of their own revolutionary heritage. The brutality of Spanish tactics intensified American affection and sympathy for the rebels. But other Americans, especially business people, were worried about U.S. economic interests in Cuba and hoped that Spain would quickly put down the rebellion.

The Yellow Press Inflames Opinion Rival newspaper publishers Joseph Pulitzer and **William Randolph Hearst** heightened the public's dislike of the Spanish government. Their publications were called the **Yellow Press** because they featured a popular comic-strip character called The Yellow Kid. To boost readership, Pulitzer's *New York World,* Hearst's *New York Journal,* and similar newspapers pasted sensational headlines and pictures on their front pages. Their stories exaggerated Spanish atrocities and compared Cuban rebels to the patriots of the American Revolution.

President William McKinley warned the Spanish to quickly establish peace, or the United States would take whatever steps it "should deem necessary to procure this result." Spain recalled General Weyler and offered the Cuban rebels some reforms. But the rebels insisted on independence, which Spain refused to grant. McKinley ordered the battleship *Maine* to Havana harbor to protect American citizens in Cuba.

Then, in February 1898, the *Journal* published a private letter written by Enrique Dupuy de Lôme, Spain's ambassador to Washington, D.C. The letter, stolen by Cuban rebels and leaked to Hearst, called McKinley a weak and stupid politician. Hearst published the letter under the sensational headline, "Worst Insult to the United States in Its History." The letter fueled American **jingoism,** or aggressive nationalism, and inflamed relations with Spain.

Differentiated Instruction   Solutions for All Learners

L1 Special Needs Students   L2 Less Proficient Readers

Direct visual learners and less proficient readers to the Infographic. Invite volunteers to describe the emotions the artists wanted to elicit from the audience who would have seen the picture of the *Maine* and the political cartoon. Have students identify the details that provide drama and excitement or evoke a particular feeling. Remind students that newspapers would have used illustrations such as these to persuade read-

ers to view Cuba's conflict with Spain in a particular way. Ask students to consider how the artists wanted the audience to feel about Cuba's conflict with Spain. With the class, discuss the use of images in persuasive arguments. Have students use evidence from the illustrations to explain why these scenes in Cuba might have persuaded readers of the time more effectively than would written arguments.

Teach

Causes of the War   L3

Instruct

- **Introduce** Draw students' attention to the painting on this page depicting the Cuban rebels charging into battle. Ask students to tell what they know about Cuba. Tell students that the Cuban rebels and the American soldiers during the Revolutionary War were similar in that both groups fought against other nations to win independence. Ask students to predict the outcome of the rebellion in Cuba.

- **Teach** Help students understand the causes of the Spanish-American War. Ask **Why did many Americans favor the Cubans in their struggle for independence from the Spanish?** *(The Cuban struggle for independence reminded many Americans of their own revolutionary heritage.)* **Why did many business people support Spain?** *(Business people worried that rebels would destroy American property and hurt U.S. economic interests in the country.)* **How did the *New York World* and *New York Journal* encourage U.S. citizens to support a war against Spain?** *(The newspapers made war seem justified and exciting.)* **What are some circumstances that can prevent the news media from presenting ideas objectively?** *(Possible responses: an emotional environment, a desire to affect the outcome of events, or a reporter's wish to "improve" the story)*

- **Quick Activity** Ask students to suppose that they are living in the United States in 1898. Have them write letters to the editor of either the *New York World* or the *New York Journal* that explain why they think the United States should or should not go to war against Spain.

Answer

Caption The artist probably supported the rebels since he depicted them as determined and brave in the face of battle.

Have students analyze the Infographic. Ask them to write sentences that explain how each image illustrates one or more of the circumstances that led to the Spanish-American War.

Monitor Progress

As students fill in their cause-and-effect charts, circulate to make sure that they understand the causes, key events, and effects of the Spanish-American War. For a completed version of the cause-and-effect chart, see Note Taking Transparencies, **B-92**.

Vocabulary Builder
stipulate – (STIHP yuh layt) v. to include specifically in the terms of an agreement

Spanish misrule of Cuba and the sinking of the USS *Maine* moved the nation toward war with Spain. ▼

The *Maine* Blows Up Soon after the *Journal* published de Lôme's letter, the *Maine* exploded in Havana harbor. Of the 350 officers and crew on board at the time, 266 died. The Yellow Press promptly accused Spain of blowing up the battleship. One *Journal* headline even declared: "War? Sure!"

But President McKinley did not ask Congress to declare war just yet. Instead, he ordered a special naval board of inquiry to investigate the cause of the explosion. On March 28, 1898, the board concluded that a mine had destroyed the battleship. Years later, follow-up investigations raised doubts about the naval board's findings, but, at the time, most people blamed Spain.

The Nation Goes to War War fever gripped the nation. In newspapers, speeches, and songs, patriotic Americans implored their fellow citizens to "Remember the *Maine*!" In response to American demands, Spain agreed to abolish the reconcentration camps and make other concessions, but it was too little too late. On April 11, 1898, McKinley asked Congress for the authority to use force against Spain to end the fighting in Cuba "in the name of humanity, in the name of civilization, in behalf of endangered American interests."

Eight days later, Congress enacted four resolutions that amounted to a declaration of war on Spain. The fourth resolution—the Teller Amendment—stipulated that the United States had no intention of annexing Cuba. The navy quickly blockaded Cuban ports, and McKinley called for more than 100,000 volunteers to join the army. In response, Spain declared war on the United States.

✓ **Checkpoint** Why did Americans object to Spanish actions in Cuba?

● **INFOGRAPHIC**

To War!

THE COMING OF THE SPANISH-AMERICAN WAR

Three circumstances came together to sweep the United States into war in 1898: Two New York newspapers, *The New York World* and the *New York Journal*, were competing for bigger readership. Cubans were rebelling against Spain, and the United States was immersed in the spirit of imperialism.

When Cuban rebels burned plantations and blew up trains, Spain responded with brutal measures. The *Journal* and the *World* inflamed American public opinion—and increased their sales—by printing tabloid headlines about Spanish atrocities. Then, shortly after the U.S. government dispatched the USS *Maine* to Cuba to protect American interests, the ship exploded in Havana harbor. Americans clamored for war.

History Background

The Sinking of the *Maine* Why did the *Maine* explode in Havana harbor? The Spanish government claimed that the explosion originated inside the battleship, not, as Americans claimed, from contact with a mine. Investigators from the U.S. Navy investigated the wreck in 1898, and divers claimed that evidence pointed toward the mine theory. In 1910, the U.S. Corps of Engineers built a cofferdam around the wreck where it lay in the harbor. Construction of this ring allowed investigators to pump out the ocean water and look at the remains of the Spanish-American War icon. In 1911, the Navy ruled that a mine had sunk the *Maine*.

An investigation in the 1970s, however, reached a different conclusion. Admiral Hyman Rickover gathered a group of engineers to review data from previous studies. This new investigation determined that the explosion that ripped apart the *Maine* could have started in the ship's own coal bunker. The heat from this fire could have ignited the ship's ammunition supply. Rickover's engineers speculated that the *Maine* might have been sunk by its own gunpowder.

Answer

✓ Americans believed that Spain had treated Cuban rebels brutally, and they wanted to support the Cuban fight for freedom. Americans also believed that Spain had destroyed the U.S. battleship *Maine*.

American Troops Battle the Spanish

Americans responded enthusiastically to the war. About 200,000 men enlisted in the army, up from the 25,000 that enlisted at the beginning of 1898. In early May, as the United States Army prepared to attack, Americans heard news of a great naval victory over Spain. But, surprisingly, the victory was not in Cuba. Rather, it was in the Pacific Ocean, on the opposite side of the world.

Dewey Takes the Philippines On May 1, 1898, Commodore **George Dewey** steamed his squadron of vessels into Manila Bay, in the Spanish-held Philippines. The Americans completely surprised the Spanish fleet that was stationed in the bay. Upon issuing the order to "fire when ready," Dewey watched his ships quickly destroy the Spanish force. While no American died during the naval battle, nearly 400 Spanish sailors lost their lives. Americans gleefully received news of the victory and proclaimed Dewey a hero.

While Dewey was winning an astounding victory over the Spanish navy, Filipino nationalists led by **Emilio Aguinaldo** (ahg ee NAHL doh) were defeating the Spanish army. Like the Cubans, the Filipinos were fighting for freedom from Spain. In August, after some 15,000 U.S. soldiers had landed on the islands, Spanish troops surrendered to the United States.

U.S. Forces Win in Cuba Meanwhile, American troops landed in Cuba in June 1898. U.S. Marines captured Guantánamo Bay, and a force of 17,000 soldiers under U.S. Army General William Shafter stormed ashore east of Santiago.

In spite of their excitement for the war, the troops faced deplorable conditions. They were poorly trained and supplied. As they assembled for duty around

With each new headline, the Yellow Press sold more papers to Americans angry with Spain. ▼

New York Journal Sales

Number of subscriptions: 1,000,000 / 800,000 / 600,000 / 400,000 / 200,000 / 0

1895 1897 1898

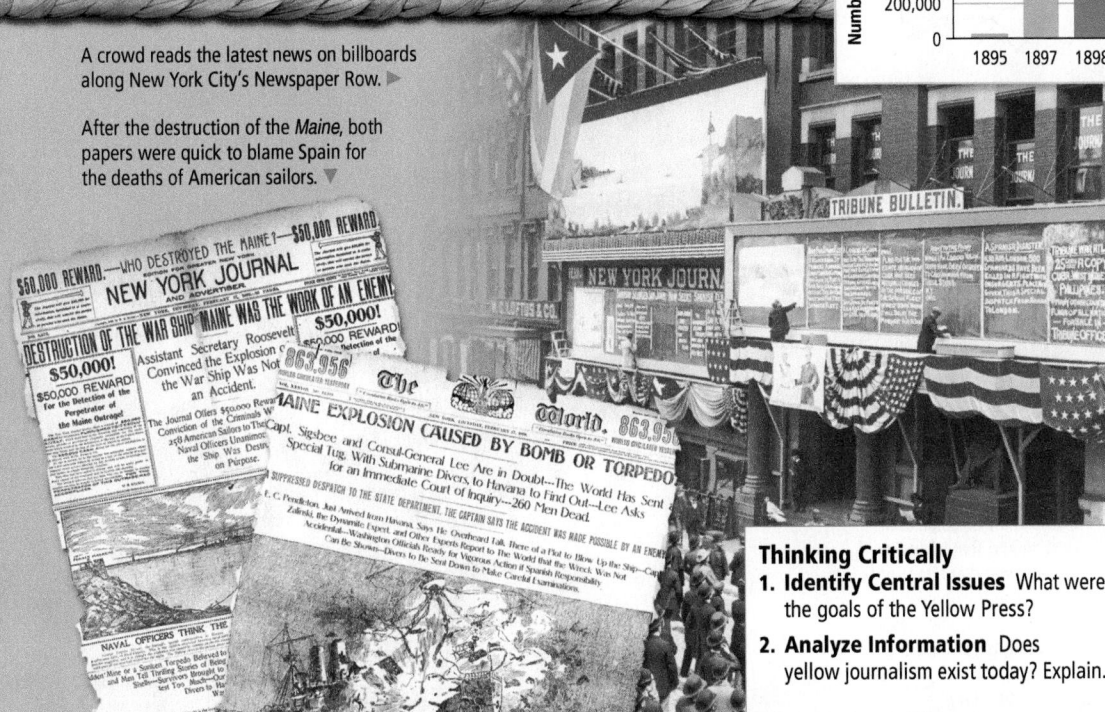

A crowd reads the latest news on billboards along New York City's Newspaper Row. ▶

After the destruction of the *Maine*, both papers were quick to blame Spain for the deaths of American sailors. ▼

Thinking Critically
1. **Identify Central Issues** What were the goals of the Yellow Press?
2. **Analyze Information** Does yellow journalism exist today? Explain.

American Troops Battle the Spanish L3

Instruct

- **Introduce** Have students read the Primary Source quotation on the next page. Ask **What does the war correspondent report about the U.S. forces in Cuba?** *(The soldiers fought bravely and confidently, and they decisively defeated the Spanish.)* Ask students to predict the outcome of the war.

- **Teach** Help students understand key events during the Spanish-American War. Ask **How did the United States defeat the Spanish in the Philippines?** *(Commodore Dewey's squadron surprised the Spanish fleet stationed in Manila Bay and quickly destroyed the Spanish ships.)* Display Color Transparency: *Charge of the Rough Riders at San Juan Hill.* **What role did the Rough Riders play in Cuba?** *(The Rough Riders helped secure the high ground of the Kettle and San Juan hills and helped bring about the Spanish surrender of Santiago.)* Direct students' attention to the circle graph on the following pages near the Spanish-American War map. Ask students to consider why few American soldiers died during battle. Color Transparencies **A-82**

- **Analyzing the Visuals** Draw students' attention to the photograph of African American soldiers on the next page. Ask **How are the soldiers depicted in this photograph?** *(They are standing at attention in a long line; they appear to be in dress uniform with white gloves as if participating in a ceremony rather than awaiting orders on the battlefield.)* Then, direct students to the photographs of the medals. Ask students to discuss what these medals suggest about the African American soldiers who served in Cuba.

Differentiated Instruction   Solutions for All Learners

L4 Advanced Readers   L4 Gifted and Talented Students

After Christopher Columbus arrived in the Western Hemisphere, Spain claimed much of the land in the Americas and amassed a large empire. Have students research the extent of the Spanish Empire and trace its rise and decline up to the time of the Spanish-American War. Challenge students to look for any evidence of Spain's influence that remains in its former colonies, including the language and customs of the former colonial power. Have students record their findings on an annotated world map that illustrates the different periods of Spanish rule in the Americas.

Answers

Thinking Critically

1. The Yellow Press wanted the United States to go to war with Spain to free Cuba. It also wanted to increase sales of newspapers.

2. Students may say that yellow journalism exists today in the form of newspapers and Web sites that distort information in an attempt to persuade or shock readers.

Tampa, Florida, the soldiers were issued obsolete weapons and heavy wool uniforms that were unsuitable for Cuba's tropical climate. Corrupt and inefficient officials provided the men with rotting and contaminated food.

General Shafter's army consisted of state National Guard units and regular army units, including the African American Ninth and Tenth Cavalry regiments from the western frontier. Another cavalry unit was organized and commanded by the future President Theodore Roosevelt. His **Rough Riders** consisted of rugged westerners and upper-class easterners who relished what Roosevelt called the "strenuous life."

The Rough Riders and Roosevelt gained fame for the role they played in the battles for Kettle and San Juan hills outside Santiago, Cuba. Joined by African American soldiers from the Ninth and Tenth Cavalries, the Riders stormed up those hills to secure high ground surrounding Santiago. One war correspondent described a charge of the African American soldiers:

Primary Source "[T]hey followed their leader up the terrible hill from whose crest the desperate Spaniards poured down a deadly fire of shell and musketry. They never faltered. . . . [T]heir aim was splendid, their coolness was superb. . . . The war had not shown greater heroism."

—War correspondent, 1898

Two days after the battle of San Juan Hill, the Spanish navy made a desperate attempt to escape from Santiago's harbor. U.S. forces, which had blockaded the harbor, destroyed the Spanish fleet as it tried to break out. Surrounded, outnumbered, and dispirited, Spanish forces in Santiago surrendered. Although a few battles followed when U.S. forces occupied the island of Puerto Rico, another Spanish

African Americans Serve Their Country
African American soldiers of the Ninth and Tenth Cavalry regiments stand at attention after fighting the Spanish in Cuba. The medals above were won by Augustus L. Reed, an African American officer in the United States Navy.

History Background

The First United States Volunteer Cavalry
When the United States declared war on Spain, Theodore Roosevelt was Assistant Secretary of the Navy. He resigned his post to lead a volunteer cavalry unit originally intended to consist of men from the southwest territories of New Mexico, Arizona, Oklahoma, and the Indian Territory. This unit, the First United States Volunteer Cavalry, became known as the Rough Riders. In his autobiography, Roosevelt recalls the outpouring of volunteers. "The difficulty in organizing was not in selecting, but in rejecting men. Within a day or two after it was announced that we were to raise the regiment, we were literally deluged with applications from every quarter of the Union. Without the slightest trouble, so far as men went, we could have raised a brigade or even a division. The difficulty lay in arming, equipping, mounting, and disciplining the men we selected."

Evidence of the patriotism inspired by the Rough Riders can be seen in Spanish-American War monuments. The monument to volunteer Roy V. Cashion in Hennessey, Oklahoma, for example, is one of the state's oldest outdoor sculptures.

The Spanish-American War, 1898

Geography *Interactive*
For: Interactive map
www.pearsonschool.com/ushist

CHINA

UNITED STATES

Hong Kong (Br.)

Formosa (Japan)

Pacific Ocean

South China Sea

Manila

Manila Bay

Miller Projection
0   50   100 mi
0   50 100 km

Philippines

Tampa

Key West

February 1898
USS *Maine* sunk

Havana

Cuba

Atlantic Ocean

Bahamas (Br.)

Miller Projection
0   100   200 mi
0   100 200 km

San Juan Hill

Santiago

HAITI   DOMINICAN REPUBLIC

San Juan

Puerto Rico

Jamaica (Br.)

From Spain

Caribbean Sea

Spanish colonies
→ U.S. forces
✦ U.S. victory

Spanish colonies
→ U.S. forces
→ Spanish forces
U.S. naval blockade
✦ U.S. victory

Map Skills The Spanish-American War was fought on two fronts on opposite sides of the world. The United States won a quick victory over Spain.
1. **Locate:** (a) Havana, (b) Puerto Rico, (c) Hong Kong, (d) the Philippines

2. **Regions** Identify the two different regions of the world in which the war was fought.

3. **Draw Conclusions** Why do you think more Americans died from sickness and disease than in battle?

Causes of American Deaths in the Spanish-American War

385 Death in battle

2,061 Death from sickness and disease

SOURCE: *Historical Statistics of the United States*

possession, the fighting had come to an end. Although almost 3,000 Americans died during the war, only around 380 died in combat. Disease, especially malaria and yellow fever, caused most of the deaths.

 **Checkpoint** How did the Rough Riders and African American cavalry units contribute to the war effort?

Effects of the War

Secretary of State John Hay referred to the conflict with Spain as a "splendid little war" because of the ease and thoroughness of America's victory. Although the war may have been "splendid," it created a new dilemma for Americans: What should the United States do with Spain's former possessions?

The Treaty of Paris Signed by Spain and the United States in December 1898, the **Treaty of Paris** officially ended the war. Spain gave up control of Cuba, Puerto Rico, and the Pacific island of Guam. It also sold the Philippines to the United States for $20 million.

Differentiated Instruction   Solutions for All Learners

L1 Special Needs Students   **L2 English Language Learners**   **L2 Less Proficient Readers**

Pair struggling readers with more proficient readers. Have each pair scan the text under the heading "Effects of the War." Then, have the pairs list the terms of the Treaty of Paris agreed upon by the United States and Spain and discuss potential disagreements that could arise from the treaty. Ask each pair to a create two-column chart. Ask students to label the first column "Imperialists" and list the main arguments for the U.S. control of the Philip-

pines. Have students label the second column "Anti-Imperialists" and list the main arguments against U.S. control of the Philippines. Have students use their charts to debate whether the United States should take control of the Philippines. On the basis of their discussion, ask students to predict whether they think the United States will choose to extend its control over the Philippines or allow the Philippines to become an independent nation.

Assess Progress

- Have students complete the Section Assessment.

- Administer the Section Quiz. Teaching Resources, **p. 26**

- To further assess student understanding, use Progress Monitoring Transparencies, **88**.

Reteach

If students need more instruction, have them read the section summary.

Reading and Note Taking Study Guide

Adapted Reading and Note Taking Study Guide ①②

Spanish Reading and Note Taking Study Guide ②

Extend ④

Have students read *History Challenges: The Spanish-American War— The War We Wanted to Fight?* and complete the worksheet. Teaching Resources, **pp. 13–14**

Answer

 Some American leaders believed that a presence in the Philippines would be valuable in increasing U.S. trade with China.

The Teller Amendment, passed by Congress when it declared war on Spain, prevented the United States from taking possession of Cuba. The amendment did not, however, apply to the Philippines. Americans disagreed over whether to grant the Philippines independence or take full control of the Pacific nation.

Americans Debate Imperialism In an 1899 interview, President McKinley explained, "We could not give [the Philippines] back to Spain—that would be cowardly and dishonorable." He believed that America had no choice but to "take them all, and to educate the Filipinos, and uplift and civilize . . . them." McKinley's imperialist supporters presented similar reasons for maintaining control of the Philippines. They argued that the United States had a responsibility to govern the Filipinos. They reasoned that the islands represented a valuable stepping stone to trade in China. They warned that if the United States gave up the Philippines, other nations would take control of them.

Anti-imperialists, including William Jennings Bryan and Mark Twain, rejected these arguments. In 1899, a large group of anti-imperialists formed the American Anti-Imperialist League. The league condemned imperialism as a crime and attacked it as "open disloyalty to the distinctive principles of our government."

The debate between imperialists and anti-imperialists reached its climax in the U.S. Senate, where senators had to consider ratifying the Treaty of Paris. In February 1899, the Senate voted 57 to 27 in favor of the treaty. By a single "yes" ballot, the vote met the two-thirds majority necessary to ratify the treaty.

America Assumes a New Role in the World In 1900, William Jennings Bryan ran against William McKinley for the presidency. To bolster his chances of winning reelection, the Republican McKinley named Theodore Roosevelt, the "hero of San Juan Hill," as his vice-presidential running mate. Emphasizing the overwhelming U.S. victory over Spain, McKinley soundly defeated Bryan. The President's reelection signaled America's continuing faith in his imperialist policies.

As a result of the Spanish-American War, the United States had an empire and a new stature in world affairs. The war marked a turning point in the history of American foreign policy.

 Checkpoint Why did American leaders think it was important to keep the Philippines?

SECTION **2** **Assessment**

Progress Monitoring *Online*
For: Self-test with vocabulary practice
www.pearsonschool.com/ushist

Comprehension

1. Terms and People What do the following terms and people have in common?
- José Martí
- William Randolph Hearst
- Yellow Press
- jingoism

2. NoteTaking Reading Skill: Identify Causes and Effects Use your cause-and-effect chart to answer the Section Focus Question: What were the causes and effects of the Spanish-American War?

Writing About History

3. Quick Write: Gather Details When you write a narrative essay, you often need to gather details about your topic. Suppose that you want to write a narrative diary entry as a witness to the destruction of the USS *Maine*. Conduct research to find descriptions of the explosion and illustrations of the event from newspapers of the time. You may want to research particular newspapers such as the *New York World* and the *New York Journal*.

Critical Thinking

4. Draw Conclusions Do you think the United States would have gone to war with Spain without the explosion of the *Maine*? Why or why not?

5. Identify Points of View Who might agree with John Hay's opinion that the Spanish-American War was a "splendid little war"? Who might disagree? Why?

6. Summarize What were the principal issues dividing imperialists and anti-imperialists?

Section 2 Assessment

1. José Martí, William Randolph Hearst, the Yellow Press, and jingoism each played a role in causing the Spanish-American War.

2. The Spanish-American War was caused by American sympathy for the Cuban rebels, sensational reports by the Yellow Press about Spanish atrocities in Cuba, and the explosion of the USS *Maine*. As a result of the war, the United States acquired Puerto Rico, Guam, the Philippines, and control of Cuba.

3. Responses should show an understanding of the kinds of primary source details needed to write a narrative essay.

4. Possible answer: The United States would have gone to war with Spain because Americans felt sympathy for the Cubans and because newspapers continued to exaggerate Spanish atrocities, inflaming public opinion.

5. Imperialist supporters would agree because of the ease and thoroughness of America's victory; however, the Filipinos,

for example, disagreed because they fell under U.S. control.

6. Imperialists wanted the United States to control the Philippines. Anti-imperialists believed that acquiring colonies violated the principles on which the United States was founded.

For additional assessment, have students access **Progress Monitoring** *Online* at **www.pearsonschool.com/ushist.**

▲ An American soldier and two Filipino women

A Plea for Peace

Sixto Lopez, a leading Filipino spokesman, wrote to President McKinley to express his disapproval of America's decision to keep control of the Philippines. When he wrote the letter, many Filipinos had already taken up arms against the U.S. military.

"I only know that the Filipino people are asking for [what] the American people have enjoyed for more than a hundred years. . . . At this season of peace I plead for peace. I plead on behalf of the wife and mother whose cheeks are coursing the silent tears . . . on behalf of the sad little faces, too young to realize what has happened. . . ."

—Sixto Lopez, 1900

The United States and East Asia

Objectives
- Examine the causes and consequences of the Philippine insurrection.
- Analyze the effects of the Open Door Policy.
- Describe how the United States dealt with the rising power of Japan.

Terms and People

insurrection
guerrilla warfare
William Howard Taft
sphere of influence
John Hay
Boxer Rebellion

Open Door Policy
Russo-Japanese War
"Gentlemen's Agreement"
Great White Fleet

NoteTaking

Reading Skill: Recognize Sequence As you read, use a timeline to trace events and developments in East Asia that tested America's new global power.

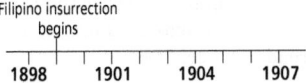

Filipino insurrection begins

1898   1901   1904   1907

Why It Matters America's decision to keep the Philippines reflected a desire to expand its influence, compete with European colonial powers, and gain new trade in Asia. American leaders devised policies to open China and other Asian markets to U.S. producers. They also wanted to extend the benefits of American culture to the people of the region. Imperialism in East Asia brought greater power and wealth to Americans, but it also increased international tensions in Asia. **Section Focus Question: How did the United States extend its influence in Asia?**

Filipinos Rebel Against U.S. Rule

The Filipino nationalist leader Emilio Aguinaldo had thought that the United States was an ally in the Filipino struggle for independence. His forces had fought side by side with the Americans against the Spanish. However, after the United States decided to maintain possession of the Philippines, Aguinaldo grew disillusioned with America. He helped organize an **insurrection,** or rebellion, against U.S. rule. The rebels believed they were fighting for the same principle of self-rule that had inspired America's colonial patriots during the American Revolution.

Guerrilla War Erupts in the Philippines Outgunned by American troops, Filipino insurgents relied on **guerrilla warfare,** a form of nontraditional warfare generally involving small bands of fighters

---

As you teach this section, keep students focused on the following objectives to help them answer the Section Focus Question and master core content.
- Examine the causes and consequences of the Philippine insurrection.
- Analyze the effects of the Open Door Policy.
- Describe how the United States dealt with the rising power of Japan.

Prepare to Read

Background Knowledge ⓛ³

Remind students that in the late 1800s and early 1900s, the United States acquired Alaska, Hawaii, and the Philippines. Ask students to predict how countries in the Pacific and East Asia will respond to the presence of the United States.

Set a Purpose ⓛ³

- **WITNESS HISTORY** Read the selection aloud.

  Ask **In what way is this time period both a "season of peace" and the beginning of conflict for the speaker?** *(It is Christmas and war has ended between Spain and the United States, but Filipinos are preparing to resist U.S. involvement in the Philippines.)*

- **Focus** Point out the Section Focus Question, and write it on the board. Tell students to refer to this question as they read. *(Answer appears with Section 3 Assessment answers.)*

- **Preview** Have students preview the Section Objectives and the list of Terms and People.

- **NoteTaking** Using the Guided Questioning strategy (TE, p. T20), have students read this section. As they read, have students use a timeline to trace events and developments in East Asia that tested America's new global power.
  Reading and Note Taking Study Guide

Vocabulary Builder

Use the information below and the following resource to teach students the high-use word from this section. Teaching Resources, Vocabulary Builder, p. 11

High-Use Word	Definition and Sample Sentence
rigor	*n.* extreme hardship or difficulty Despite the **rigors** of fighting the Spanish in Cuba with outdated weapons, the United States won the Spanish-American War.

Filipinos Rebel Against U.S. Rule

Instruct

- **Introduce** Ask students to recall why the Filipinos rebelled against Spanish rule. Point out that the United States helped the Filipinos defeat the Spanish. Ask **How do you think the Filipinos felt when the United States joined the fight against Spain?** *(Sample answer: The Filipinos welcomed U.S. support because they thought the United States would help them win independence.)* Ask students to predict how the Filipinos will respond to American rule.

- **Teach** Ask students to read the Primary Source quotation on this page. Using the Think-Write-Pair-Share strategy (TE, p. T23), have students discuss how the United States viewed the Philippines. Then, ask **Why did the capture of Emilio Aguinaldo mark the beginning of the end of the insurrection?** *(Aguinaldo was the leader of the insurrection, and his capture lowered the morale of the other insurgents.)* **What did the Jones Act do?** *(The Jones Act pledged that the United States would leave so that the Philippines could become an independent nation.)* Ask students to discuss why Congress passed the Jones Act.

- **Analyzing the Visuals** Have students analyze the Infographic. Ask students to use the photographs to compare and contrast the cultures of the United States and the Philippines.

Independent Practice

Have students access **www.pearson-school.com/ushist** to take the History Interactive Audio Guided Tour. Then, ask them to write a paragraph describing whether the American experience in the Philippines was positive or negative.

Monitor Progress

As students fill in their timelines, circulate to make sure that they understand the events and developments in East Asia that tested America's new global power. For a completed version of the timeline, see Note Taking Transparencies, **B-93**.

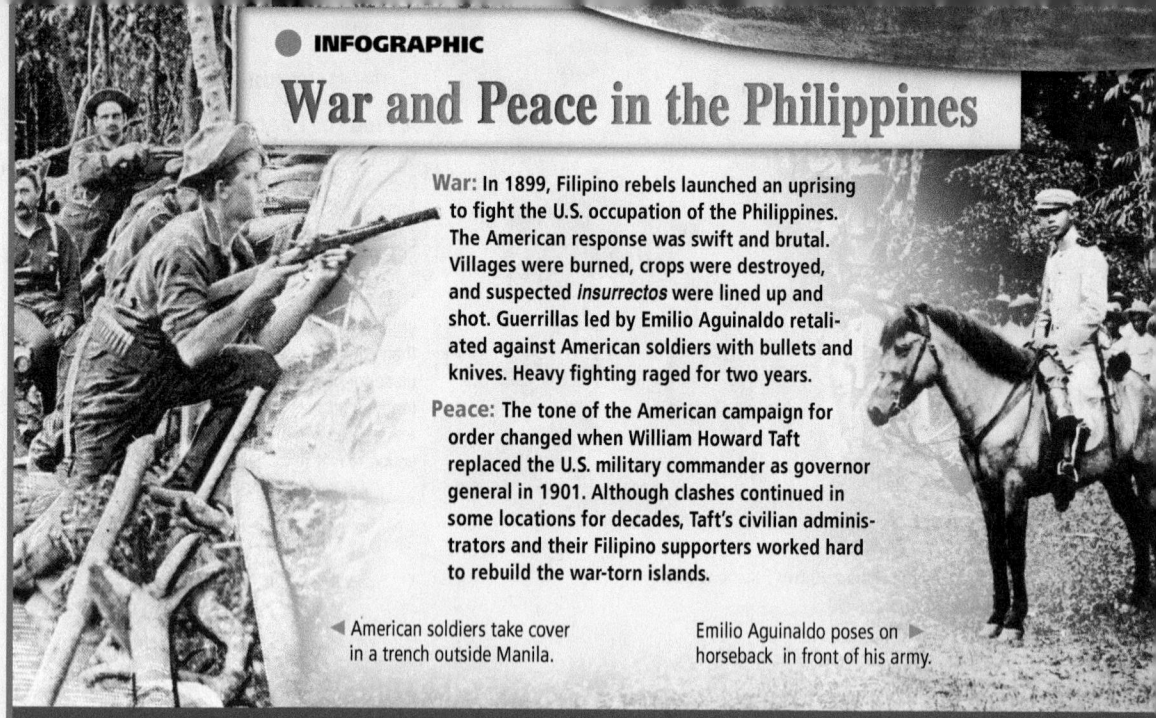

INFOGRAPHIC
War and Peace in the Philippines

War: In 1899, Filipino rebels launched an uprising to fight the U.S. occupation of the Philippines. The American response was swift and brutal. Villages were burned, crops were destroyed, and suspected *insurrectos* were lined up and shot. Guerrillas led by Emilio Aguinaldo retaliated against American soldiers with bullets and knives. Heavy fighting raged for two years.

Peace: The tone of the American campaign for order changed when William Howard Taft replaced the U.S. military commander as governor general in 1901. Although clashes continued in some locations for decades, Taft's civilian administrators and their Filipino supporters worked hard to rebuild the war-torn islands.

◀ American soldiers take cover in a trench outside Manila.

Emilio Aguinaldo poses on ▶ horseback in front of his army.

to attack behind American lines. In turn, the American military used extraordinary measures to crush the rebellion. Like the Spanish in Cuba, U.S. soldiers gathered civilians into overcrowded concentration camps. General Jacob Smith ordered his soldiers not to take prisoners. "I wish you to kill and burn, the more you kill and burn the better you will please me," he commented. A California newspaper defended such actions:

> **Primary Source** "Let us all be frank. WE DO NOT WANT THE FILIPINOS. WE DO WANT THE PHILIPPINES. All of our troubles in this annexation matter have been caused by the presence in the Philippine Islands of the Filipinos. . . . The more of them killed the better. It seems harsh. But they must yield before the superior race."
> —San Francisco *Argonaut,* 1902

In the spring of 1901, the Americans captured Aguinaldo. Although the fighting did not end immediately, his capture marked the beginning of the end of the insurrection. The war in the Philippines took more lives than the Spanish-American War. Nearly 5,000 Americans and 200,000 Filipinos died in the fighting. The U.S. government sent more than 100,000 troops to fight in the war and spent upwards of $400 million to defeat the insurgency. The conflict highlighted the <u>rigors</u> of fighting against guerrilla insurgents.

Vocabulary Builder
<u>rigor</u> – (RIHG uhr) *n.* extreme hardship or difficulty

Reforms Lead to Promise of Self-Rule In 1901, **William Howard Taft**—a future President of the United States—became governor of the Philippines. Taft had large ambitions for helping the islands recover from the rebellion. He censored the press and placed dissidents in jail to maintain order and to win the support of the Filipino people. At the same time, he extended limited self-rule and ordered the construction of schools, roads, and bridges.

Differentiated Instruction   Solutions for All Learners

L1 Special Needs Students   **L2 English Language Learners**   **L2 Less Proficient Readers**

To help students master vocabulary, have them list in their notebooks the section's high-use vocabulary word and terms and people. Encourage students to include in their lists the terms *disillusioned, dissidents, commerce, indemnity,* and *emigration.* Then, have them create flashcards with the term (or the person's name) on one side and its definition (or, in the case of key people, a one-sentence identifying statement) on the other side. For English Language Learners, you may wish to have students add explanations in their first language to go with the flashcards. Pair students and have partners use the flashcards to quiz each other.

▲ Filipino rebels often used bolo knives in addition to rifles to fight American soldiers.

The American presence in the Philippines provided several benefits for Filipinos:

- **Political reform:** After 1901, Taft's civilian government extended limited self-rule to Filipinos. The Philippine Assembly (shown above) convened in Manila in 1907.
- **Healthcare:** U.S. administrators established a public health system to care for Filipinos. At right, American doctors aid a Filipino woman wounded during the insurrection.
- **Education:** The American commission also built new schools for Filipino children and staffed them with teachers from the United States. (See photo at far right.)

In 1916, Congress passed the Jones Act, which pledged that the Philippines would ultimately gain their independence. Thirty years later, after U.S. forces liberated the islands from Japanese occupation at the end of World War II, the Philippines finally became an independent nation.

✔ **Checkpoint** Why did hostilities erupt in the Philippines after the Spanish-American War?

The United States Pursues Interests in China

By 1899, once-mighty China had fallen into political, economic, and military disarray. Its huge population, however, was a tempting target for other nations' imported goods. Rather than compete for Chinese trade, Britain, France, Germany, and Russia carved China into distinct **spheres of influence**. Within its zone, each power had privileged access to Chinese ports and markets. Japan also expanded its regional influence, grabbing territory in China and Korea. Since the United States did not have a zone, this system of "special privileges" threatened to limit American trade in China.

America Declares Equal Trade in China In order to overcome these barriers, U.S. Secretary of State **John Hay** issued the first of a series of notes to foreign diplomats in 1899. He notified the leaders of imperialist nations that the United States expected "perfect equality of treatment for commerce" in China. Hay's note had little immediate impact on the actions of European nations or Japan. However, it served as a guiding principle of American foreign policy in Asia for years to come.

Thinking Critically
1. **Make Generalizations** How did the Filipino uprising present a new challenge to American soldiers?
2. **Explain Effects** What two things happened in 1901 that signaled a shift in the rebellion?

History Interactive

For: To discover more about the Filipino insurrection
www.pearsonschool.com/ushist

Instruct

- **Introduce: Key Term** Ask students to find the key term *"Gentlemen's Agreement"* (in bold) in the text. Ask **Does a "Gentlemen's Agreement" sound more formal or less formal than a law?** *(less formal)* **What might be the benefits or difficulties of a "Gentlemen's Agreement" between two countries?** *(A "Gentlemen's Agreement" might be a way to bypass technicalities to solve a problem. However, it might also be an understanding that is not clearly explained and that could be perceived as secretive.)*

- **Teach** Help students understand that tensions with Japan arose from Japan's own colonial interests. Ask **Why did Japan begin a conflict with Russia?** *(Japan wanted to protect its interests in China without competition from Russia.)* **Why would Japan's territorial expansion concern other countries, such as China, Korea, and Russia?** *(Japan's expansion might make other countries fear that they would lose their trading rights. Weaker countries might fear that Japan would seize some of their territory.)*

- **Analyzing the Visuals** Direct students to the illustration of the American fleet. Ask them to discuss the impact that the sight of these battleships might have had at ports around the world, and tell them to consider the effect of the color of the battleships.

Independent Practice

Have students use details from the text to create political cartoons or news articles about the Russo-Japanese War, Roosevelt's "Gentlemen's Agreement" with Japan, or the Great White Fleet.

Monitor Progress

Ask students to examine how the foreign policy actions of Japan and China resulted in anti-Asian sentiment toward people of Japanese, Chinese, and Korean origin living in the United States.

Answer

✓ The United States protected its commercial interests in China with the Open Door Policy, asserting its right to trade on the same footing as European countries.

The U.S. Intervenes in the Boxer Rebellion In response to the growing influence of outsiders in their country, some Chinese joined secret societies. One such society, the Righteous and Harmonious Fists, won the nickname "Boxers" from Europeans because its members trained in martial arts. The secret societies celebrated traditional Chinese customs and criticized Western ways. They also condemned Chinese converts to Christianity. Over time, simmering anger exploded into an outright rebellion against the "foreign devils."

In May 1900, the Boxers killed foreign missionaries and besieged the foreign diplomats' district in Beijing. A multinational force of European, American, and Japanese troops was sent to the Chinese capital to quash the **Boxer Rebellion.** An initial force of 2,100 soldiers grew to more than 20,000, including 2,000 Americans. After putting down the rebellion, European powers compelled China's imperial government to pay an indemnity, or money to repair damage caused by the rebellion. This poured more fuel onto the nationalist fire. Chinese nationalists would eventually revolt and overthrow the emperor in 1911.

Hay Reaffirms the Open Door Policy As the Boxer Rebellion engulfed China, Secretary of State Hay reasserted America's **Open Door Policy.** In a second note to European powers, Hay stated that the United States wanted to "preserve Chinese territorial and administrative entity." In other words, America did not want colonies in China; it just wanted free trade there. As an act of goodwill, the United States used some of the indemnity money it received from China to fund scholarships for Chinese students to study in America.

✓ **Checkpoint** How did the United States protect its commercial interests in China?

American Soldiers Rescue Diplomats in China
U.S. troops went into the Chinese capital of Beijing in 1900 to help put an end to the Boxer Rebellion. Below, the troops march through the Forbidden City in close ranks.

Tensions Rise Between America and Japan

Like the United States, Japan wanted to expand its influence in China. Japan also disapproved of the European "carve-up" of the region. Furthermore, the Japanese took offense to the presence of Russian troops in Manchuria, a region of China that bordered Russia. In February 1904, without a declaration of war, Japan attacked and bottled up Russia's Pacific fleet stationed at Port Arthur, China. The Japanese followed up on this victory with a series of major land engagements in Manchuria that caused more than 100,000 Russian casualties. However, Japan also suffered heavy losses in the fighting.

Connect to Your World

Chinese Uprisings The Boxer Rebellion of 1900 was quelled, but it had a lasting impact on Chinese politics. The country's dowager empress, Ci Xi, had supported the Boxers, hoping that they could help rid the country of foreign influence. The Boxers' defeat, in addition to the reparations debt owed to foreigners, led to the overthrow of the Qing Dynasty, which had ruled China since 1644.

Another such expression of public dissatisfaction was the Tiananmen Square uprising of 1989. The pro-democracy protest was begun by students, who were joined by many other demonstrators in the large public square in Beijing. These protesters, arguing for government reforms, occupied the square from April to June. On the nights of June 3 and 4, the Chinese government sent troops to disband the crowd. Many people were killed in the conflict.

Since the Tiananmen Square uprising, international agencies such as Amnesty International and Human Rights Watch have urged the Chinese government to reexamine its policies on human rights.

Roosevelt Settles the Russo-Japanese War In 1905, representatives from Russia and Japan met in Portsmouth, New Hampshire, to negotiate an end to the **Russo-Japanese War.** When the talks stalled, President Theodore Roosevelt intervened and convinced the two sides to sign a peace treaty. (Roosevelt had become President when McKinley was assassinated in 1901.) For his efforts, Roosevelt won the Nobel Peace Prize. The President's intervention—and his receipt of the famous award—prominently displayed America's growing role in world affairs.

Anti-Asian Prejudice Troubles Relations Despite Roosevelt's achievement, America entered troubled waters in its relations with Japan. A root cause of this trouble was anti-Asian sentiment on the West Coast of the United States. In the fall of 1906, the San Francisco School Board banned Japanese, Chinese, and Korean children from attending public schools with white children. The incident drew Japan's immediate wrath. One Tokyo journal demanded that Japan retaliate. "Stand up Japanese nation! Our countrymen have been HUMILIATED on the other side of the Pacific," the newspaper cried out.

Roosevelt disapproved of the decision to segregate Asian children in the San Francisco schools. He understood Japan's anger with America. To calm tensions, he negotiated a **"Gentlemen's Agreement"** with Japan. According to the pact, the school board pledged to end its segregation policy. In return, Japan agreed to limit the emigration of its citizens to the United States.

The Great White Fleet Sets Sail While Roosevelt used diplomacy to ease tensions with Japan, he also promoted military preparedness to protect U.S. interests in Asia. Expressing rising concerns about Japan's territorial expansion at the expense of China, Korea, and Russia—the President won congressional support for a new force of navy ships, known as the **Great White Fleet.** In 1907, Roosevelt sent this armada of 16 white battleships on a "good will cruise" around the world. The voyage of the Great White Fleet demonstrated America's increased military power to the world.

✓ **Checkpoint** What were some of the difficulties America faced in maintaining good relations with Japan?

A Mighty American Fleet
After stopping at several Latin American ports, the Great White Fleet moved on to Asia and made a friendly visit to the Japanese port city of Yokohama. *How do you think the Japanese felt about the U.S. warships' visit?*

Progress Monitoring *Online*
For: Self-test with vocabulary practice
www.pearsonschool.com/ushist

SECTION 3 Assessment

Comprehension

1. **Terms and People** For each item below, write a sentence explaining its significance.
   - insurrection
   - guerrilla warfare
   - William Howard Taft
   - Boxer Rebellion
   - Open Door Policy

2. **NoteTaking Reading Skill: Recognize Sequence** Use your timeline to answer the Section Focus Question: How did the United States extend its influence in Asia?

Writing About History

3. **Quick Write: Write an Introduction** A narrative essay needs an introduction that "hooks" a reader and draws him or her into your story. Suppose that you want to write a narrative from the perspective of an American sailor aboard a battleship in the Great White Fleet. Draft an introduction that captures the excitement and purpose of the fleet's departure from America.

Critical Thinking

4. **Recognize Bias** Based on what you have read, what role do you think racial attitudes played in U.S. policy in the Philippines?

5. **Analyze Information** Identify two threats to U.S. interests in China, and describe how the U.S. government responded to those threats.

6. **Apply Information** How do President Roosevelt's actions toward Japan illustrate the use of diplomacy and compromise?

Objectives

As you teach this section, keep students focused on the following objectives to help them answer the Section Focus Question and master core content.

- Examine what happened to Puerto Rico and Cuba after the Spanish-American War.
- Analyze the effects of Roosevelt's "big stick" diplomacy.
- Compare Wilson's "moral diplomacy" with the foreign policies of his predecessors.

Prepare to Read

Background Knowledge L3

Ask students to recall the challenges that the United States encountered in Asia. Ask them to predict the challenges that may arise between the United States and Latin America.

Set a Purpose L3

- **WITNESS HISTORY** Read the selection aloud.

  Ask **According to Taft, what foreign interests will the United States support?** *(legitimate interests and those that benefit U.S. businesses)* **How will U.S. foreign policy change?** *(The United States will support its interests through business instead of through conflict.)*

- **Focus** Point out the Section Focus Question, and write it on the board. Tell students to refer to this question as they read. *(Answer appears with Section 4 Assessment answers.)*

- **Preview** Have students preview the Section Objectives and the list of Terms and People.

- **NoteTaking** Using the Structured Read Aloud strategy (TE, p. T20), have students read this section. As they read, have students note how the U.S. dealt with Puerto Rico and Cuba. Reading and Note Taking Study Guide

▲ William Howard Taft

WITNESS HISTORY

Dollars for Bullets

Like President Roosevelt, President William Howard Taft stressed the need to assert American power around the world. Taft's "dollar diplomacy" aimed to expand American investments abroad:

❝The diplomacy of the present administration . . . has been characterized as substituting dollars for bullets. . . . It is [a policy] frankly directed to the increase of American trade upon the axiomatic principle that the government of the United States shall extend all proper support to every legitimate and beneficial American enterprise abroad.❞

—President William Howard Taft, 1912

The United States and Latin America

Objectives

- Examine what happened to Puerto Rico and Cuba after the Spanish-American War.
- Analyze the effects of Roosevelt's "big stick" diplomacy.
- Compare Wilson's "moral diplomacy" with the foreign policies of his predecessors.

Terms and People

Foraker Act	Roosevelt Corollary
Platt Amendment	"dollar diplomacy"
"big stick" diplomacy	"moral diplomacy"
Panama Canal	Francisco "Pancho" Villa

NoteTaking

Reading Skill: Identify Supporting Details Complete a table like the one below to note how the U.S. dealt with Puerto Rico and Cuba.

American Policy After Spanish-American War	
Puerto Rico	**Cuba**
• Foraker Act establishes civil government in 1900	•
	•

Why It Matters As the United States tentatively asserted its interests in East Asia, Americans called for a more aggressive role in Latin America. American entrepreneurs and government leaders viewed the region as the nation's backyard and as a sphere of influence from which other great powers should be excluded. American influence in Latin America brought obvious benefits to the United States, but it also contributed to anti-American hostility and instability in the region. **Section Focus Question: What actions did the United States take to achieve its goals in Latin America?**

U.S. Policy in Puerto Rico and Cuba

America's victory over Spain liberated the Puerto Rican and Cuban people from Spanish rule. But victory left the fates of these islands unresolved. Would Puerto Rico and Cuba become independent nations? Or would they become colonies of the United States? As questions lingered in the aftermath of war, the United States assumed control in Puerto Rico and Cuba.

Civil Government in Puerto Rico As the smoke from the Spanish-American War cleared, Puerto Rico remained under direct U.S. military rule. In 1900, Congress passed the **Foraker Act,** which established a civil government in Puerto Rico. The act authorized the President of the United States to appoint a governor and part of the Puerto Rican legislature. Puerto Ricans could fill the rest of the legislature in a general election.

Vocabulary Builder

Use the information below and the following resource to teach students the high-use words from this section. Teaching Resources, Vocabulary Builder, p. 11

High-Use Words	Definitions and Sample Sentences
assess	*v.* to impose a fine, tax, or special payment on a person or property The U.S. government can **assess** taxes on foreign goods sold in this country.
nevertheless	*adv.* in spite of that; however The United States defeated the Filipino insurgents in 1901 and gained control of the Philippines; **nevertheless,** the Philippines eventually became an independent nation.

Whether Puerto Ricans could enjoy citizenship rights in the United States, however, remained unclear. This unusual situation led to a series of court cases, known as Insular Cases, in which the Supreme Court determined the rights of Puerto Ricans. One case examined whether the U.S. government could <u>assess</u> taxes on Puerto Rican goods sold in the United States. The Supreme Court ruled the taxes legal and determined that Puerto Ricans did not enjoy the same rights as U.S. citizens.

In 1917, President Woodrow Wilson signed the Jones-Shafroth Act. It granted Puerto Ricans more citizenship rights and gave the islanders greater control over their own legislature. Still, many Puerto Ricans expressed their discontent because they did not enjoy all of the same rights as Americans.

United States Establishes Cuban Protectorate Although the Treaty of Paris granted Cuban independence, the United States Army did not withdraw from the island until 1902. But before the U.S. military left, Congress obliged Cuba to add to its constitution the **Platt Amendment.** The amendment restricted the rights of newly independent Cubans and effectively brought the island within the U.S. sphere. It prevented Cuba from signing a treaty with another nation without American approval. It also required Cuba to lease naval stations to the United States. Additionally, the Platt Amendment granted the United States the "right to intervene" to preserve order in Cuba.

Many Cubans strongly disliked the Platt Amendment but soon realized that America would not otherwise end its military government of the island. The United States, for its part, was unwilling to risk Cuba's becoming a base for a potentially hostile great power. Cuba thus added the Platt Amendment to its constitution as part of a treaty with the United States. The treaty made Cuba a protectorate of the United States and governed their relationship for decades.

✓ **Checkpoint** Why did Cubans dislike the Platt Amendment?

Roosevelt Pursues "Big Stick" Diplomacy

Upon assuming the presidency after McKinley's assassination, Theodore Roosevelt promoted a new kind of diplomacy based on America's success in the Spanish-American War. Beyond determining what would happen to Puerto Rico and Cuba, Roosevelt developed a broader policy for U.S. action in Latin America. Historians have called this Roosevelt's **"big stick" diplomacy** since it depended on a strong military to achieve America's goals. "Big stick" stemmed from the President's admiration for an old African saying, "Speak softly and carry a big stick; you will go far."

Roosevelt's view that America needed to carry a big stick during the Age of Imperialism flowed from his adherence to balance-of-power principles and from his view of the United States as a special nation with a moral responsibility to "civilize," or uplift, weaker nations. In this sense, the new President held beliefs similar to those of other imperial powers in Europe and Asia. Roosevelt also felt that America's elite—its statesmen and captains of industry—had to accept the challenge of international leadership.

HISTORY MAKERS

Theodore Roosevelt (1858–1919)
As a boy, Theodore Roosevelt suffered from asthma and poor eyesight. Determined not to be held back by physical limitations, he took on an active program of exercise that included boxing and horseback riding.

In 1898, when Roosevelt was Assistant Secretary of the Navy, he again showcased his determination. Two months before the United States declared war on Spain, he secretly ordered Commodore George Dewey to sail for Hong Kong, within striking distance of the Philippines. Thus, when the war began, U.S. ships were instantly ready to attack the Spanish fleet in Manila Bay. Soon after Dewey's victory, Roosevelt resigned from his post and organized the Rough Riders.

Teach

U.S. Policy in Puerto Rico and Cuba ⓵③

Instruct

- **Introduce: Vocabulary Builder** Have students locate the vocabulary term *assess* and its definition. Ask **Why does a government assess taxes?** *(to raise money to pay for government services)* Have students discuss why the U.S. government might want to *assess* taxes on Puerto Rican goods sold in the United States.

- **Teach** Ask **What did the Foraker Act do?** *(It established civil government in Puerto Rico. It also allowed the U.S. President to appoint the Puerto Rican governor and part of the Puerto Rican legislature.)* **Why did Cuba add the Platt Amendment to its constitution?** *(The United States would not end military government in Cuba unless the amendment was included.)* Using the Idea Wave strategy (TE, p. T22), have students discuss the advantages and disadvantages Puerto Rico and Cuba may have experienced under U.S. policies.

- **Quick Activity** Using the Numbered Head strategy (TE, p. T23), have students debate whether the United States was right or wrong to pass the Foraker Act and require Cuba to add the Platt Amendment to its constitution.

Independent Practice

Have students make Venn diagrams to compare and contrast U.S. involvement in Puerto Rico and Cuba.

Monitor Progress

As students fill in their tables, circulate to make sure that they understand how the U.S. dealt with Puerto Rico and Cuba. For a completed version of the table, see Note Taking Transparencies, B-94a.

Vocabulary Builder

assess–(uh SEHS) *v.* to impose a fine, tax, or special payment on a person or property

Answer

✓ The Platt Amendment brought Cuba under U.S. control, restricted Cubans' rights, and allowed the United States to intervene in Cuban affairs.

Roosevelt Pursues "Big Stick" Diplomacy ⓛ₃

Instruct

- **Introduce: Key Term** Ask students to find the key term **"big stick" diplomacy** (in bold) in the text. Then, write the term on the board, and provide the definition. Direct students to the HISTORY MAKERS feature about Theodore Roosevelt. Have students discuss how Roosevelt's actions during the Spanish-American War foreshadowed his use of **"big stick" diplomacy.** Then, have students debate the advantages and disadvantages of adopting Roosevelt's **"big stick"** policy in the United States.

- **Teach** Ask **What role did Roosevelt play in the history of the Panama Canal?** *(Roosevelt sent the United States Navy to support the Panamanian rebellion against Colombia. After winning independence, Panama granted the United States control of the Canal Zone.)* **According to the Roosevelt Corollary, how did the United States justify continued military intervention in Latin America?** *(The United States intervened in Latin American affairs in order to keep European powers from using force in the region.)* **Why might Latin American countries object to Roosevelt's policies?** *(They might see his policies as unwanted interventions in their affairs.)* **How did Taft shift U.S. foreign policy?** *(Taft relied less on "big stick" diplomacy and adopted "dollar diplomacy," which emphasized increasing American investments in Central American and Caribbean banks and businesses.)*

- **Quick Activity** Display Color Transparency: *Building the Panama Canal.* Use the lesson suggestions in the transparency book to guide a discussion about the challenges of building this important shipping route.
Color Transparencies **A-84**

Focus On Geography

The Panama Canal

The construction of the Panama Canal was a monumental engineering feat. It fulfilled a vision of shortening the travel distance between the Atlantic and Pacific oceans that traced back to when the Spanish first began shipping gold and silver from the Americas in the 1500s. To complete the canal, workers built a series of locks to raise ships to the level of Gatún Lake, 85 feet above sea level, to cross the isthmus. (See the diagram below.) From 1904 to 1913, tens of thousands of laborers worked on the canal. In the end, the challenge of the landscape was overshadowed by the threat of the deadly mosquito, which spread yellow fever and malaria. "If we do not control malaria, our mortality is going to be heavy," warned Dr. William Gorgas, a United States Army surgeon. He convinced the chief engineer that fighting the mosquito was vital to keeping American steam shovels in action.

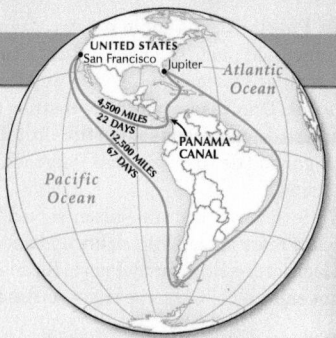

▲ In 1898, the U.S. battleship *Oregon* raced around South America to fight the Spanish in Cuba. Without a Central American canal to shorten its voyage to Florida, the *Oregon* spent more than two months at sea.

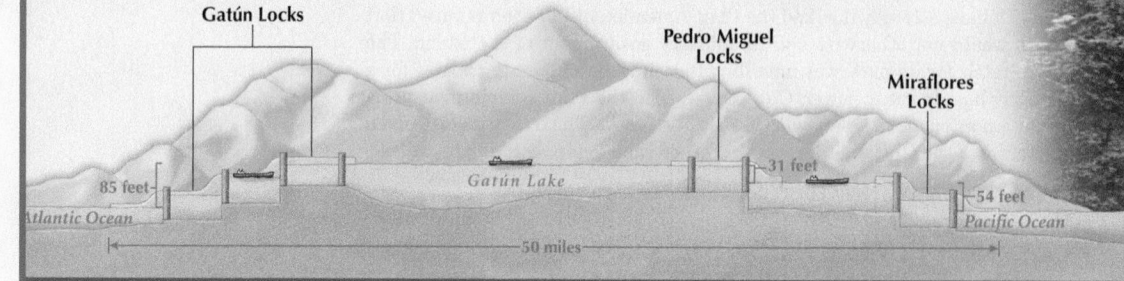

Gatún Locks
Pedro Miguel Locks
Miraflores Locks
85 feet
Gatún Lake
31 feet
54 feet
Atlantic Ocean
Pacific Ocean
50 miles

Vocabulary Builder
nevertheless–(nehv er thuh LEHS) *adv.* in spite of that; however

America Builds the Panama Canal Although the plan to dig a canal across Central America did not originate with Roosevelt, he <u>nevertheless</u> played a crucial role in its history. In the late 1800s, a French company had tried to link the Atlantic to the Pacific across the Isthmus of Panama but failed. Afterward, some suggested building a canal through Nicaragua. However, those plans came to nothing. Eventually, an agent from the French company that had abandoned its canal attempt convinced the United States to buy the company's claim. In 1903, the U.S. government bought the Panama route for $40 million.

Before it could build a canal through Panama, however, the United States needed the consent of the Colombian government. At that time, Panama was part of independent Colombia. American efforts to negotiate a purchase of land across the isthmus stalled when Colombia demanded more than the United States was willing to provide.

So Roosevelt stepped in. The President dispatched U.S. warships to the waters off Panama to support a Panamanian rebellion against Colombia. The appearance of the United States Navy convinced the Colombians not to suppress the uprising. Panama soon declared its independence from Colombia. The new nation immediately granted America control over the "Canal Zone." To secure this land for its vital trade link, America agreed to pay Panama $10 million and an annual rent of $250,000.

Differentiated Instruction   Solutions for All Learners

ⓛ₄ Advanced Readers   ⓛ₄ Gifted and Talented Students

Students may enjoy reading about the conflicts of imperialism as depicted in Joseph Conrad's novel *Nostromo* (1904). Set in the fictitious country of Costaguana, the novel describes how rich natural resources draw Europeans to Latin America during a time of revolution. Ask students to look for parallels between Conrad's fiction and the events in Latin America during the early 1900s.

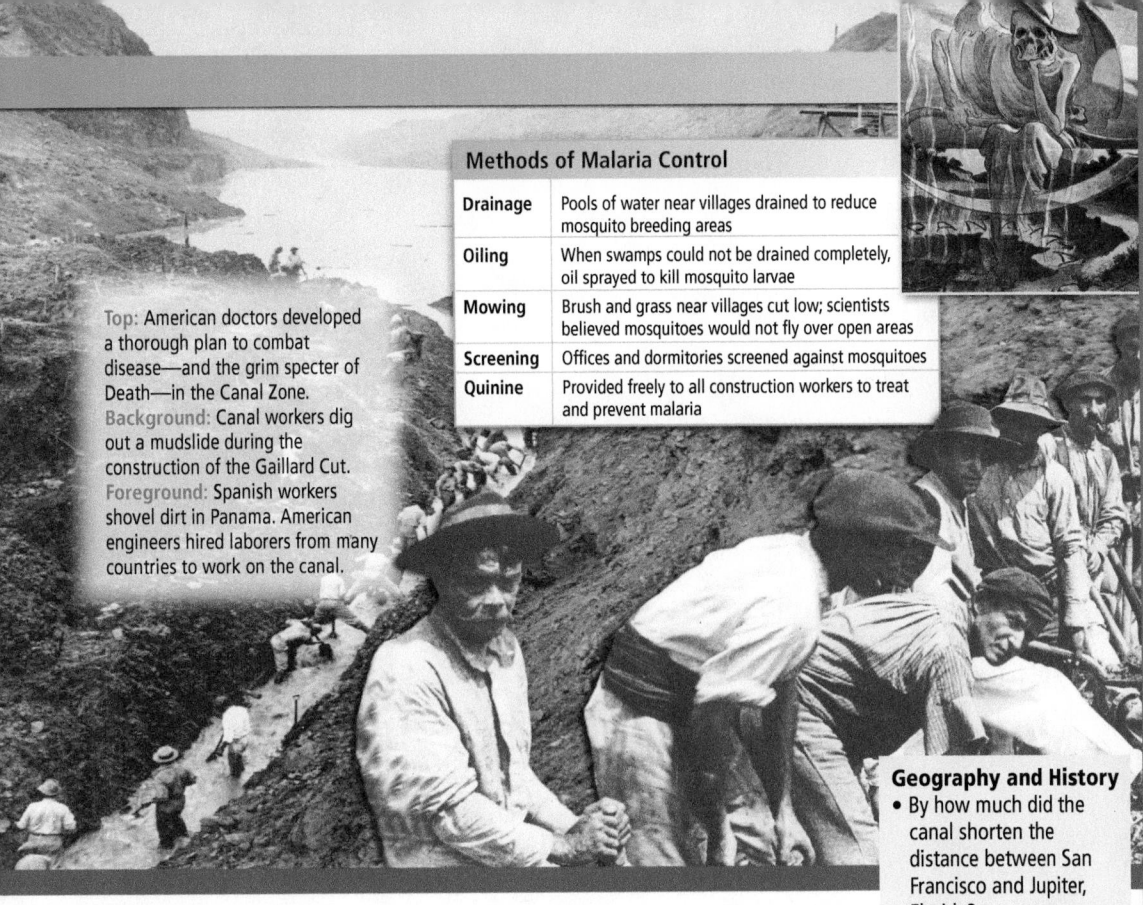

Top: American doctors developed a thorough plan to combat disease—and the grim specter of Death—in the Canal Zone. Background: Canal workers dig out a mudslide during the construction of the Gaillard Cut. Foreground: Spanish workers shovel dirt in Panama. American engineers hired laborers from many countries to work on the canal.

Methods of Malaria Control

Drainage	Pools of water near villages drained to reduce mosquito breeding areas
Oiling	When swamps could not be drained completely, oil sprayed to kill mosquito larvae
Mowing	Brush and grass near villages cut low; scientists believed mosquitoes would not fly over open areas
Screening	Offices and dormitories screened against mosquitoes
Quinine	Provided freely to all construction workers to treat and prevent malaria

Independent Practice
- Have students read the Focus on Geography feature and answer the questions that accompany the feature.
- Have students read the *Geography and History: The Panama Canal* worksheet and answer the questions that follow. Teaching Resources, pp. 23–24

More than 35,000 workers helped dig the **Panama Canal,** often in very difficult conditions. Completion of the canal depended on scientific breakthroughs by doctors as they learned how to combat tropical diseases. Still, more than 5,000 canal workers died from disease or accidents while building the canal. When the finished waterway opened in 1914, it cut some 8,000 nautical miles off the trip from the west coast to the east coast of the United States.

Roosevelt Updates the Monroe Doctrine In the early 1900s, the inability of Latin American nations to pay their debts to foreign investors raised the possibility of European intervention. In 1903, for example, Germany and Britain blockaded Venezuelan ports to ensure that debts to European bankers were repaid. Roosevelt concluded: "If we intend to say hands off to the powers of Europe, then sooner or later we must keep order ourselves." So in a 1904 message to Congress, he announced a new Latin American policy.

The President's **Roosevelt Corollary** updated the Monroe Doctrine for an age of economic imperialism. In the case of "chronic wrongdoing" by a Latin American nation—the kind that Europeans might use to justify military intervention—the United States would assume the role of police power, restoring order and depriving other creditors of the excuse to intervene. This change, Roosevelt argued, merely reasserted America's long-standing policy of keeping the Western Hemisphere free from European intervention.

Geography and History
- By how much did the canal shorten the distance between San Francisco and Jupiter, Florida?
- Which methods of malaria control involved direct changes to the physical environment of the Canal Zone?

History Background

Panama Canal Treaty The presence of the canal was a contentious issue to Panamanians. The territory encompassing the Canal Zone was, in effect, a foreign colony under foreign control. In 1977, leaders of the United States and Panama, U.S. President Jimmy Carter and General Omar Torrijos Herrera, signed the Panama Canal Treaty. The treaty nullified all previous treaties that had allowed the United States to build, operate, and occupy the Canal Zone, including those dating back to the time of Theodore Roosevelt. As if in answer to the Roosevelt Corollary, Torrijos declared at the treaty signing that "The Republic of Panama will reject, in unity and with decisiveness and firmness, any attempt by any country to intervene in its internal or external affairs." From 1979 to 1999, Panama and the United States operated the canal jointly as ownership of the canal transitioned from the United States to Panama. During a ceremony on December 14, 1999, the United States transferred full control of the canal to Panama.

Answers

Geography and History
- The canal shortened the distance between Jupiter, Florida, and San Francisco by 45 days or 8,000 miles.
- draining pools of water, spraying swamps with oil, and mowing brush and grass

- Have students access **www.pearsonschool.com/ushist** to use the Geography Interactive map and then answer the map skills questions in the text.

Monitor Progress

To review this section, have students discuss the advantages and disadvantages of "big stick" diplomacy and "dollar diplomacy." Ask students to use details from the text to support their answers.

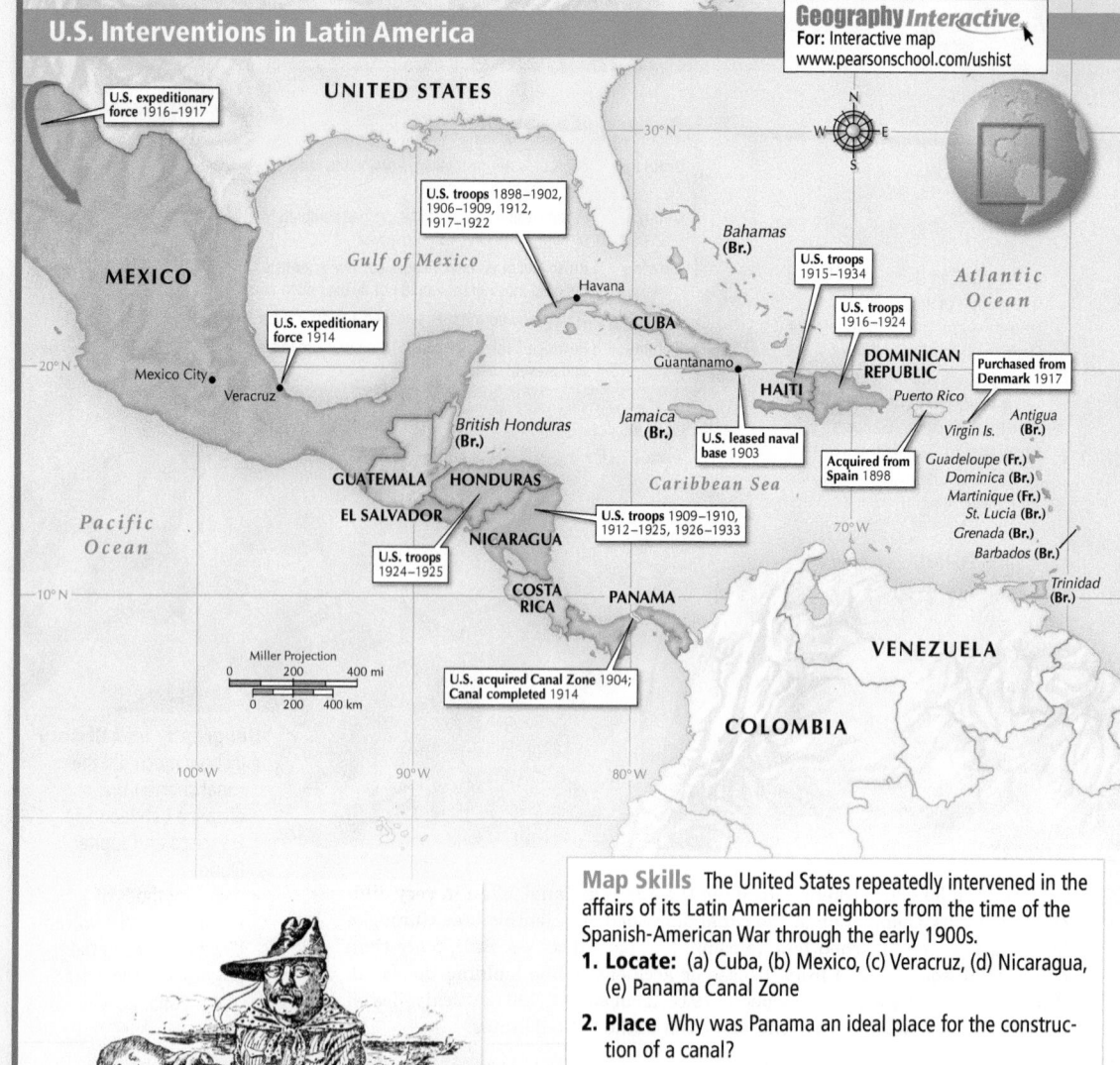

U.S. Interventions in Latin America

Geography *Interactive*
For: Interactive map
www.pearsonschool.com/ushist

UNITED STATES

U.S. expeditionary force 1916–1917

30°N

Gulf of Mexico

MEXICO

Bahamas **(Br.)**

U.S. troops 1898–1902, 1906–1909, 1912, 1917–1922

Atlantic Ocean

U.S. troops 1915–1934

20°N

Mexico City •

Havana

CUBA

U.S. troops 1916–1924

U.S. expeditionary force 1914

Veracruz •

Guantanamo

HAITI

DOMINICAN REPUBLIC

Puerto Rico

Purchased from Denmark 1917

Jamaica **(Br.)**

U.S. leased naval base 1903

Virgin Is.

Antigua **(Br.)**

British Honduras **(Br.)**

Acquired from Spain 1898

Guadeloupe **(Fr.)**
Dominica **(Br.)**
Martinique **(Fr.)**
St. Lucia **(Br.)**
Grenada **(Br.)**
Barbados **(Br.)**

GUATEMALA   HONDURAS

Caribbean Sea

EL SALVADOR

U.S. troops 1909–1910, 1912–1925, 1926–1933

70°W

Pacific Ocean

NICARAGUA

10°N

U.S. troops 1924–1925

COSTA RICA

PANAMA

Trinidad **(Br.)**

Miller Projection
0   200   400 mi
0   200   400 km

U.S. acquired Canal Zone 1904; Canal completed 1914

VENEZUELA

COLOMBIA

100°W   90°W   80°W

Map Skills The United States repeatedly intervened in the affairs of its Latin American neighbors from the time of the Spanish-American War through the early 1900s.

1. Locate: (a) Cuba, (b) Mexico, (c) Veracruz, (d) Nicaragua, (e) Panama Canal Zone

2. Place Why was Panama an ideal place for the construction of a canal?

3. Analyze Why was Cuba vital to U.S. operations in Central America and the Caribbean?

◄ **Wielding the Big Stick**
With his update to the Monroe Doctrine, Roosevelt wanted only "to see neighboring countries stable, orderly, and prosperous." But if those governments were to collapse, the United States stood ready to restore order and prevent European intervention.

Differentiated Instruction   Solutions for All Learners

L1 Special Needs Students   L2 English Language Learners

Have students use the map on this page to locate the names of islands and Central American countries. Have them identify the names that are followed by parentheses, such as **(Br.)** for Great Britain or **(Fr.)** for France. Tell students that countries with this designation are colonies of the countries in parentheses. Have students list the countries that were colonized, the countries in which the United States intervened, and the countries that show no foreign interference. Ask **Which countries on the map do not show**

ties to European countries? *(Mexico, Guatemala, El Salvador, Honduras, Nicaragua, Costa Rica, Panama, Cuba, Puerto Rico, Haiti, and the Dominican Republic)* **Which of those countries did not have U.S. troops sent there in the early 1900s?** *(Guatemala, El Salvador, and Costa Rica)* Have students draw conclusions about attitudes toward foreign intervention in Latin America, and ask them how Latin Americans might have responded to foreign intervention.

Answers

Map Skills

1. Review locations with students.

2. Panama's isthmus was narrow and offered the shortest distance between the two oceans.

3. Cuba is centrally located in the Caribbean and would provide an important base of operations.

Latin Americans React to the Roosevelt Corollary Many Latin Americans resented America's role as the hemisphere's police force. They disagreed with Roosevelt's belief that Latin Americans could not police themselves. Francisco García Calderón, a Peruvian diplomat, contended that the Monroe Doctrine had taken on an "aggressive form with Mr. Roosevelt." Like Calderón, Nicaraguan spokesman Augusto Sandino felt that the United States threatened the "sovereignty and liberty" of his people. Sandino eventually led an army of guerrillas against U.S. Marines in Nicaragua in the 1920s.

Taft Switches to Dollar Diplomacy Roosevelt handpicked William Howard Taft to succeed him as the Republican candidate for President in 1908. Taft shared Roosevelt's basic foreign policy objectives. After defeating William Jennings Bryan in the general election, Taft wanted to maintain the Open Door Policy in Asia and ensure ongoing stability in Latin America. The new President pursued both goals with the aim of expanding American trade.

Taft hoped to achieve these ends by relying less on the "big stick" and more on **"dollar diplomacy."** As Taft commented in 1912, he looked to substitute "dollars for bullets." The policy aimed to increase American investments in businesses and banks throughout Central America and the Caribbean. Americans busily invested in plantations, mines, oil wells, railways, and other ventures in those regions. Of course, "dollar diplomacy" sometimes required a return to the "big stick" and military intervention. Such was the case when President Taft dispatched troops to Nicaragua in 1909—and again in 1912—to protect the formation of a pro-American government there.

✓ **Checkpoint** What were Roosevelt's most important foreign-policy initiatives in Latin America?

Wilson Pursues Moral Diplomacy

During the 1912 presidential election campaign, Democratic candidate Woodrow Wilson criticized the foreign policies of his Republican predecessors Theodore Roosevelt and William Howard Taft. After his election victory, Wilson appointed the anti-imperialist William Jennings Bryan as Secretary of State, which sent a strong message to the American people.

The U.S. Supports Honest Government in Latin America The new President intended to take U.S. foreign policy in a different direction. He promised that the United States would "never again seek one additional foot of territory by conquest" but would instead work to promote "human rights, national integrity, and opportunity." Wilson spelled out his new **"moral diplomacy"** in a message to the American people:

> **Primary Source** ❝We must prove ourselves [Latin America's] friends and champions upon terms of equality and honor. . . . We must show ourselves friends by comprehending their interest, whether it squares with our own interest or not. . . . Comprehension must be the soil in which shall grow all the fruits of friendship. . . . I mean the development of constitutional liberty in the world.❞
> —Woodrow Wilson, October 27, 1913

In spite of his stated preference for "moral diplomacy" over "big stick" or "dollar diplomacy," Wilson used the military on a number of occasions to guide Latin Americans in the directions that he thought proper. In 1915, Wilson sent marines to Haiti to protect American investments and to guard against the potential of German or French aggression in the nation. Wilson prodded the government of Haiti to sign an agreement that essentially gave the United

NoteTaking

Reading Skill: Compare As you read, compare Wilson's moral diplomacy with the foreign policies of Roosevelt and Taft by completing a flowchart like the one below.

United States Foreign Policy		
Roosevelt	**Taft**	**Wilson**
•	•	• "Moral diplomacy"
• Supported rebellion in Panama	•	

Instruct

- **Introduce: Key Term** Ask students to find the key term **"moral diplomacy"** (in bold) in the text. Then, write the term on the board, and provide the definition. Have students read the Primary Source quotation of Wilson's speech on this page. Ask **According to Wilson, what is the main goal of "moral diplomacy"?** (*The main goal is for the United States to become friends with Latin American countries by treating them as equals and understanding their interests, a process that will cultivate constitutional liberty.*)

- **Teach** Help students understand the emphasis of Woodrow Wilson's foreign policies. Ask **What "morals" did Wilson support in creating a new foreign policy?** (*Wilson supported honor and respect. He pledged not to take advantage of Latin American countries, but to honor their sovereignty.*) **How did events in Mexico present a challenge to Wilson's "moral diplomacy"?** (*Victoriano Huerta executed Francisco Madero to take control of Mexico. Wilson refused to accept Huerta as Mexico's rightful leader and worked to support a "moral" leader, Venustiano Carranza.*) **How did Wilson respond to Huerta's rule?** (*Wilson sent marines to Mexico, causing the collapse of Huerta's government and allowing Wilson-supported Venustiano Carranza to take control of Mexico.*) Have students use information from the text to evaluate the success of Wilson's "moral diplomacy."

- **Quick Activity** As they read, have students fill in the flowchart comparing Wilson's "moral diplomacy" with the foreign policies of Roosevelt and Taft. For a completed version of the flowchart, see Note Taking Transparencies, **B-94b**.

Answer

✓ Roosevelt's most important foreign-policy initiatives in Latin America were his Corollary, which claimed the U.S. right to intervene in the affairs of Latin America, and his "big stick" diplomacy, which emphasized a strong U.S. military.

- Have students analyze the Infographic, read the text that accompanies it, and answer the questions that follow in the text.

- Ask students to use what they know about Roosevelt's and Taft's foreign policies to write paragraphs describing how each President might have dealt with the Mexican Revolution.

Monitor Progress

To review this section, ask students to summarize the events that tested Wilson's "moral diplomacy." Ask them to categorize each event as aligning with or deviating from "moral diplomacy." Have students explain their reasons for their method of categorizing the events.

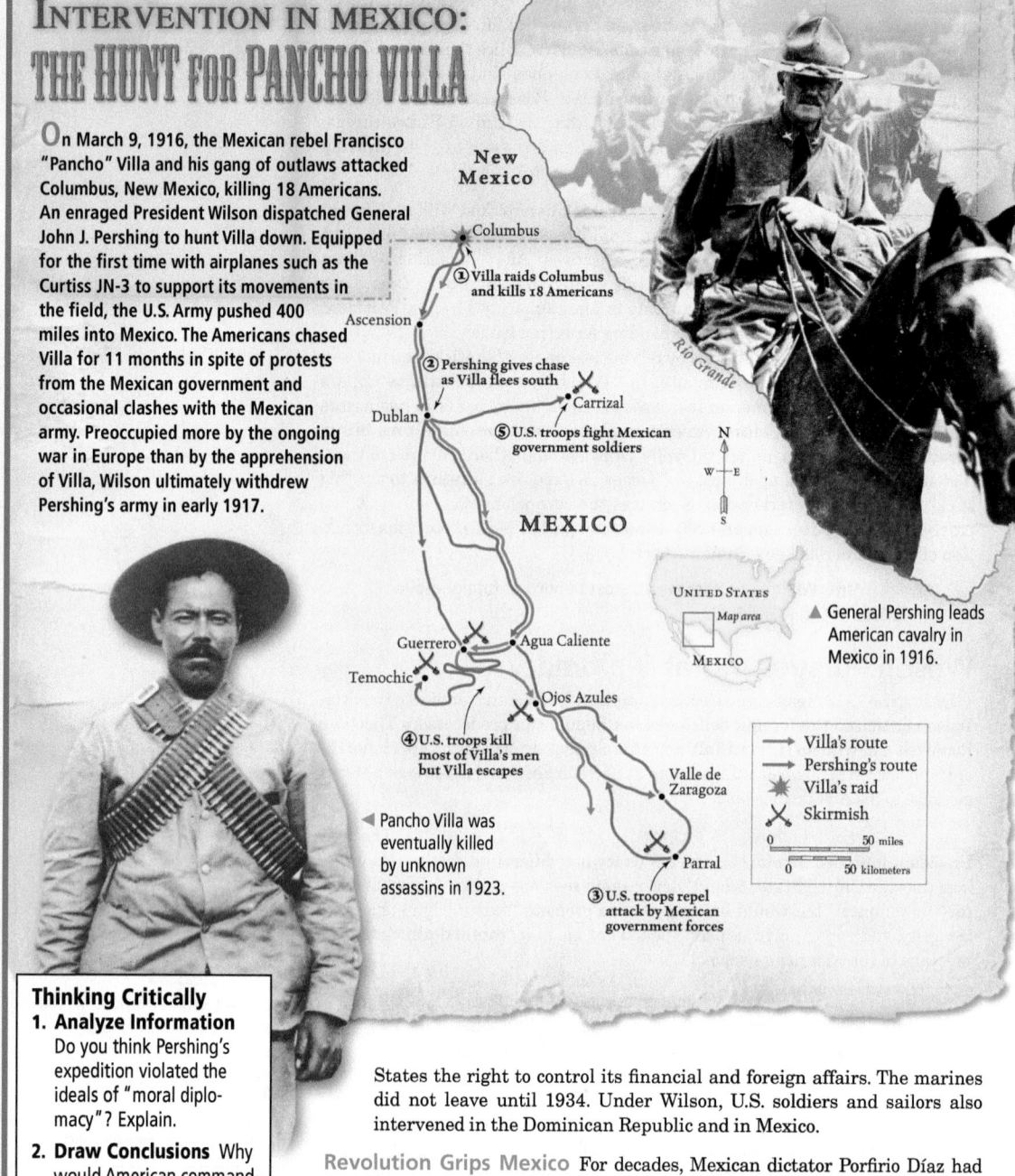

● **INFOGRAPHIC**

INTERVENTION IN MEXICO: THE HUNT FOR PANCHO VILLA

On March 9, 1916, the Mexican rebel Francisco "Pancho" Villa and his gang of outlaws attacked Columbus, New Mexico, killing 18 Americans. An enraged President Wilson dispatched General John J. Pershing to hunt Villa down. Equipped for the first time with airplanes such as the Curtiss JN-3 to support its movements in the field, the U.S. Army pushed 400 miles into Mexico. The Americans chased Villa for 11 months in spite of protests from the Mexican government and occasional clashes with the Mexican army. Preoccupied more by the ongoing war in Europe than by the apprehension of Villa, Wilson ultimately withdrew Pershing's army in early 1917.

New Mexico

Columbus

① Villa raids Columbus and kills 18 Americans

Ascension

② Pershing gives chase as Villa flees south

Carrizal

Dublan

⑤ U.S. troops fight Mexican government soldiers

Rio Grande

MEXICO

UNITED STATES
Map area

MEXICO

▲ General Pershing leads American cavalry in Mexico in 1916.

Guerrero · Agua Caliente

Temochic

Ojos Azules

④ U.S. troops kill most of Villa's men but Villa escapes

Valle de Zaragoza

◄ Pancho Villa was eventually killed by unknown assassins in 1923.

Parral

③ U.S. troops repel attack by Mexican government forces

→ Villa's route
→ Pershing's route
✳ Villa's raid
✕ Skirmish

0   50 miles
0   50 kilometers

Thinking Critically

1. **Analyze Information** Do you think Pershing's expedition violated the ideals of "moral diplomacy"? Explain.

2. **Draw Conclusions** Why would American commanders be eager to test new military technology in the field against Villa?

States the right to control its financial and foreign affairs. The marines did not leave until 1934. Under Wilson, U.S. soldiers and sailors also intervened in the Dominican Republic and in Mexico.

Revolution Grips Mexico For decades, Mexican dictator Porfirio Díaz had benefited his country's small upper class of wealthy landowners, clerics, and military men. With Díaz's encouragement, foreign investments in Mexico grew. As a result, American business people owned large portions of Mexico's industries. While foreign investors and Mexico's aristocracy grew rich, Mexico's large population of farmers struggled in poverty.

Answers

Thinking Critically

1. No; Pershing's expedition balanced the imperative of "moral diplomacy" to respect the sovereignty of other nations with the U.S. right to protect its own citizens from attack.

2. The new technology would give the military an advantage in hunting down Villa. In addition, American commanders would want to test airplanes in Mexico, in a limited campaign, before taking them to the larger conflict in Europe.

Differentiated Instruction   **Solutions for All Learners**

L1 Special Needs Students   **L2 English Language Learners**   **L2 Less Proficient Readers**

For visual learners and students who need help with basic skills, direct attention to the Infographic on this page. Remind students that this visual shows the scope of Pancho Villa's raid into the United States and the intensity of the U.S. military's response. Ask volunteers to identify the symbols in the map key and to find them on the map. With the class, discuss why President Wilson focused on punishing Villa's raid and pursued the rebel so far into Mexico.

In 1911, Francisco Madero led the Mexican Revolution that toppled Díaz. Madero was committed to reforms but was a weak administrator. In 1913, General Victoriano Huerta seized power and executed Madero. Under "dollar diplomacy," Taft probably would have recognized Huerta as the leader of Mexico because Huerta pledged to protect American investments. But under "moral diplomacy," Wilson refused to do so, declaring that he would not accept a "government of butchers." Instead, Wilson favored Venustiano Carranza, another reformer, who had organized anti-Huerta forces.

Wilson Sends U.S. Troops Into Mexico In 1914, the President used the Mexican arrest of American sailors as an opportunity to help Carranza attain power. Wilson sent marines to occupy the Mexican port of Veracruz. The action caused Huerta's government to collapse, and Carranza assumed the presidency.

Huerta's fall from power cheered many Mexicans and appeared to validate Wilson's "moral diplomacy." However, Wilson soon discovered that he faced more trouble in Mexico. The new Carranza government was slow in bringing about reforms, and rebels again rose up, this time under the leadership of **Francisco "Pancho" Villa.** For a while, Wilson courted Villa. After American support disappeared in 1916, Villa's forces crossed into New Mexico and raided the town of Columbus, leaving 18 Americans dead. President Wilson responded by sending General John J. Pershing and more than 10,000 troops on a "punitive expedition" to Mexico.

Pershing's forces chased Villa for several months but failed to capture the rebel leader. Wilson eventually withdrew American troops from Mexico in 1917, mostly because of his concerns about World War I raging in Europe. Not long afterward, the United States declared war on Germany. Free from hunting Villa, Pershing took command of the American Expeditionary Force in France.

A generation earlier, few would have believed it possible that more than one million American troops would engage in a large-scale war in Europe. But the triumph over Spain and U.S. actions in Asia and Latin America demonstrated that America had emerged as a world power. Now, World War I would test that new global strength.

✓ **Checkpoint** What was "moral diplomacy"?

Assess Progress

- Have students complete the Section Assessment.

- Administer the Section Quiz. Teaching Resources, **p. 28**

- To further assess student understanding, use Progress Monitoring Transparencies, **90.**

Reteach

If students need more instruction, have them read the section summary.

Reading and Note Taking   L3
Study Guide

Adapted Reading and   L1 L2
Note Taking Study Guide

Spanish Reading and   L2
Note Taking Study Guide

Extend   L4

See this chapter's Professional Development pages for the Extend Online activity on the Panama Canal.

Answer

✓ "Moral diplomacy" was a policy that stressed respecting the rights of other nations to govern and not using force to impose U.S. policies on other sovereign governments.

SECTION
4 Assessment

Progress Monitoring *Online*
For: Self-test with vocabulary practice
www.pearsonschool.com/ushist

Comprehension

1. **Terms and People** Define each term below. How are they similar? How are they different?
   - "big stick" diplomacy
   - "dollar diplomacy"
   - "moral diplomacy"

2. **NoteTaking Reading Skill: Identify Supporting Details** Use your table to answer the Section Focus Question: What actions did the United States take to achieve its goals in Latin America?

Writing About History

3. **Quick Write: Write a Conclusion** A narrative essay should include a conclusion that wraps up the events described in your story. Suppose that you want to write a narrative from the perspective of United States Army General John J. Pershing as he pursued "Pancho" Villa through northern Mexico. Write a conclusion to the story Pershing would tell of the pursuit.

Critical Thinking

4. **Analyze Geography** What impact did the building of the Panama Canal have on American trade?

5. **Identify Assumptions** How do the Platt Amendment and the Roosevelt Corollary reflect similar assumptions about the governments of Latin American nations?

6. **Draw Conclusions** Do you think Woodrow Wilson succeeded in carrying out the principle of "moral diplomacy" in Latin America? Explain.

Section 4 Assessment

1. Sentences should reflect an understanding of each term and tell how they are both similar and different.

2. The United States passed the Foraker Act, obliged Cuba to add the Platt Amendment to its constitution, negotiated with Panama to build and operate a canal, intervened with its military to protect U.S. interests abroad, and increased U.S. investments in Latin American businesses and banks.

3. Responses should show students' ability to effectively wrap up events in a narrative essay with an effective conclusion.

4. The Panama Canal increased trade by decreasing the shipping time required to move goods between the Atlantic and Pacific oceans.

5. Both the Platt Amendment and the Roosevelt Corollary assumed that Latin American countries were not skilled or powerful enough to govern themselves. The Platt Amendment reflected this idea by restricting Cuban rights, even though the country was newly independent. The

Roosevelt Corollary reflected this by assuming that the United States should intervene militarily in any Latin American conflict that threatened to disrupt trade.

6. Possible response: Wilson succeeded because he honored Mexico's status as a sovereign nation and did not immediately send U.S. troops to quell its revolution.

For additional assessment, have students access **Progress Monitoring *Online*** at **www.pearsonschool.com/ushist.**

5

Quick Study Guide

Quick Study Guide

- Have students use the Quick Study Guide to prepare for the chapter test. Students may wish to refer to the following sections as they review:

Cause and Effect: American Imperialism
Section 1
Section 2
Section 3
Section 4

The Panama Canal
Section 4

U.S. Interventions in Latin America
Section 1
Section 2
Section 4

Key Events of U.S. Imperialism
Section 1
Section 2
Section 3
Section 4

- For additional review, remind students to refer to the Reading and Note Taking Study Guide.
Section Note Taking
Section Summaries

- Have students access **www.pearsonschool.com/ ushist** for this chapter's History Interactive timeline, which includes expanded entries and additional events.

- If students need more instruction on analyzing graphic data, have them read the Skills Handbook, **p. SH21.**

■ Cause and Effect: American Imperialism

Causes
- Industrialized nations compete for raw materials and markets.
- Nations seek overseas bases to support naval and commercial interests.
- Imperialists believe in a superior American culture.

↓

American Imperialism

Effects
- The United States purchases Alaska from Russia in 1867.
- American planters, supported by U.S. Marines, overthrow Hawaii's Queen Liliuokalani in 1893; the United States annexes Hawaii in 1898.
- The United States wins the Spanish-American War and acquires colonies in the Caribbean Sea and in the Pacific.
- In 1899, U.S. Secretary of State John Hay establishes the Open Door Policy to protect American trading rights in China.
- Panama rebels against Colombian rule; President Roosevelt acquires land for the construction of the Panama Canal.
- President Wilson sends U.S. troops on a "punitive expedition" into Mexico to hunt and capture the rebel Pancho Villa.

☑ Quick Study Timeline

■ The Panama Canal

(map of Panama Canal area)

Caribbean Sea
Colón
Gatún Locks
Gatún Lake
PANAMA
Gaillard Cut
PANAMA
Pedro Miguel Locks
Miraflores Locks
Panama City
Continental Divide
Pacific Ocean
79°30'W
80°W

UNITED STATES
Gulf of Mexico
Caribbean Sea
Pacific Ocean
Area enlarged

Canal Zone (1903–1979)
Canal route
Locks
Capital

■ U.S. Interventions in Latin America

Country	Type of Intervention	Year
Cuba	Occupation	1898–1902, 1906–1909, 1912, 1917–1922
Dominican Republic	Military intervention Occupation	1905–1907 1916–1924
Haiti	Occupation	1915–1934
Mexico	Military intervention	1914, 1916–1917
Nicaragua	Occupation	1912–1925, 1927–1933
Panama	Acquisition of Canal Zone	1904
Puerto Rico	Military invasion and territorial acquisition	1898

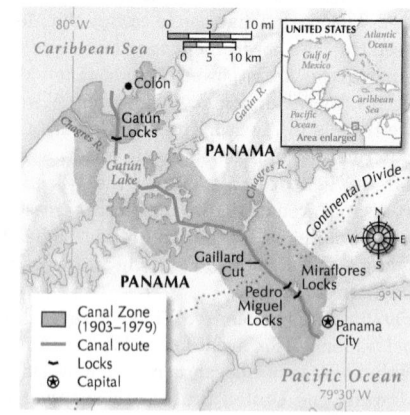

1890
Mahan publishes *The Influence of Sea Power Upon History*

1898
United States annexes Hawaii; Spanish-American War

In America

| Presidential Terms | Benjamin Harrison 1889–1893 | Grover Cleveland 1893–1897 | William McKinley 1897–1901 |

1890 — **1895** — **1900**

Around the World

1893
Americans overthrow Queen Liliuokalani in Hawaii

1899
Filipino insurrection

1900
Boxer Rebellion

Differentiated Instruction — Solutions for All Learners

L1 Special Needs Students   L2 English Language Learners   L2 Less Proficient Readers

Use the following study guide resources to help students acquiring basic skills:
Adapted Reading and Note Taking Study Guide
- Section Note Taking
- Section Summaries

Use the following study guide resources to help Spanish-speaking students:
Spanish Reading and Note Taking Study Guide
- Section Note Taking
- Section Summaries

American Issues
•─•─•─• Connector

By connecting prior knowledge with what you have learned in this chapter, you can gradually build your understanding of enduring questions that still affect America today. Answer the questions below. Then, use your American Issues Connector study guide (or go online: www.pearsonschool.com/ushist).

Issues You Learned About

● **Territorial Expansion of the United States** The United States has acquired land inside and outside of the continental United States.

1. Think about the events that led to the annexation of Hawaii. Write a paragraph explaining whether you think the United States had the right to take control of Hawaii. Consider the following:
   • the initial status of the Hawaiian Islands
   • changes made to the Hawaiian constitution by the monarchy
   • the role of American planters in Hawaii's government and society
   • the reasons that some Americans sought annexation
   • the Senate's initial response to the treaty of annexation

● **America and the World** At times, the United States chooses to get involved in the affairs of other countries.

2. Who proclaimed the Monroe Doctrine, and why?

3. How did the Roosevelt Corollary demonstrate Roosevelt's belief in "big stick" diplomacy?

4. What policies did Taft and Wilson develop for their involvement in Latin American affairs?

● **America Goes to War** The United States sometimes becomes involved in regional conflicts in other parts of the world.

5. Why did many Americans favor the Cuban revolutionaries in their struggle for freedom from Spain?

6. What event caused President McKinley and Congress to prepare for war with Spain?

Connect to Your World   Activity

U.S. Exports, 1990–2005

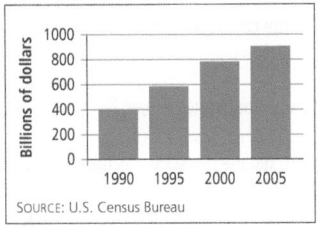

SOURCE: U.S. Census Bureau

Global Interdependence The United States continues to conduct a great deal of trade with other nations. Go online or to your local library to research American exports. Create a table that shows the 10 countries that receive the most American goods, the types of those goods, and their total value over the past 10 years.

| 1907 Great White Fleet | 1908 President Taft embraces "dollar diplomacy" | | 1916 Pershing hunts Pancho Villa in Mexico |

Theodore Roosevelt 1901–1909   William H. Taft 1909–1913   Woodrow Wilson 1913–1921

1905   **1910**   **1915**   **1920**

| 1904 U.S. gains control of Canal Zone in Panama | 1910 Mexican Revolution begins | 1914 World War I breaks out in Europe |

History *Interactive*
For: Interactive timeline
www.pearsonschool.com/ushist

American Issues
•─•─•─• Connector

Tell students that the main issues for this chapter are Territorial Expansion of the United States, America and the World, and America Goes to War. Then, ask them to answer the Issues You Learned About questions on this page. Discuss the Connect to Your World topic and ask students to complete the project that follows.

American Issues Connector

1. Students should use information from the text to support their answers.

2. President James Monroe proclaimed the Monroe Doctrine in 1823 in order to prohibit further European colonization in the Western hemisphere.

3. The Corollary asserted the right of the United States to use a "big stick," or military force, to police the Western Hemisphere.

4. Taft's "dollar diplomacy" encouraged the use of economic, rather than military, incentives to build relationships with Latin America. Wilson's "moral diplomacy" policy rejected U.S. intervention in Latin American affairs.

5. Many Americans were horrified by news of Spanish atrocities; in addition, the Cuban fight for independence echoed the American colonies' rebellion against the British.

6. the explosion of the USS *Maine*

Connect to Your World

Students' tables should reflect sound research and a clear understanding of U.S. trade with other nations.

For additional review of this chapter's enduring issues, remind students to refer to the Reading and Note Taking Study Guide American Issues Journal.

Chapter Assessment

Terms and People

1. The belief that some nations and races are superior to others; imperialists used this idea as justification for controlling other countries.

2. The last queen of Hawaii; she abolished the Hawaiian constitution that had relinquished the political power of the Hawaiians to the white minority.

3. An agreement between the United States and Spain to end the Spanish-American War; Spain gave up control of Cuba, Puerto Rico, and Guam and sold the Philippines to the United States.

4. A non-traditional military tactic that relies on surprise raids; Filipinos relied on it in their uprising against U.S. forces.

5. The Foraker Act established a government in Puerto Rico; the Platt Amendment altered the Cuban constitution to bring the country's government under U.S. control; neither fully settled the debate over U.S. policies in those countries.

Focus Questions

6. The U.S. government asserted its right to trade in Japan and acquired territories in Alaska and Hawaii to increase its opportunity for trade.

7. The Spanish-American War was caused by American sympathy for the Cuban rebels, sensational reports by the Yellow Press about Spanish atrocities in Cuba, and the explosion of the USS *Maine*. As a result of the war, the United States acquired Puerto Rico, Guam, the Philippines, and control of Cuba.

8. The United States maintained control of the Philippines after the Spanish-American War. The Open Door Policy also asserted the U.S. right to trade with China. Roosevelt showed his influence as he helped end the war between Russia and Japan.

9. The United States asserted its right to police Latin America in order to prevent European intervention. Its "dollar diplomacy" used economic incentives to assert the U.S. right to trade with Latin American countries.

Terms and People

1. Define **Social Darwinism.** How did some imperialists make use of this concept?

2. Who was **Queen Liliuokalani**? What changes did she bring to her country?

3. What was the **Treaty of Paris**? What were its terms?

4. Define **guerrilla warfare.** Who relied on guerrilla warfare?

5. Define the **Foraker Act** and **Platt Amendment.** Did they settle the debate over U.S. policy in Puerto Rico and Cuba?

Focus Questions

The focus question for this chapter is **How did the United States become a global power?** Build an answer to this big question by answering the focus questions for Sections 1 through 4 and the Critical Thinking questions that follow.

Section 1
6. How and why did the United States take a more active role in world affairs?

Section 2
7. What were the causes and effects of the Spanish-American War?

Section 3
8. How did the United States extend its influence in Asia?

Section 4
9. What actions did the United States take to achieve its goals in Latin America?

Critical Thinking

10. **Recognize Ideologies** How did U.S. expansion in the late nineteenth century extend and change the principle of Manifest Destiny?

11. **Make Comparisons** Choose two of the following: Commodore Perry's mission to Japan; the revolt in Hawaii; the Open Door Policy; the building of the Panama Canal. Explain how the two were similar yet different in terms of U.S. goals and actions.

12. **Recognize Propaganda** How did the Yellow Press contribute to U.S. actions against Spain?

13. **Compare Points of View** Explain the different opinions held by imperialists and anti-imperialists in the debate over the Philippines.

14. **Analyze Line Graphs** How were growing tensions with Japan linked to the trend shown on the graph below?

U.S. Navy Yearly Federal Budget, 1898–1908

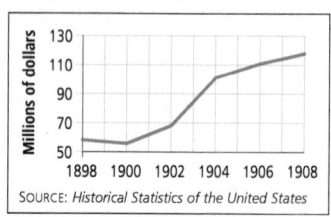

SOURCE: *Historical Statistics of the United States*

15. **Draw Conclusions** What was the goal of U.S. policy toward China? Why do you think Hay did not favor establishing colonies in China?

16. **Predict Consequences** If Wilson had been President when the United States was seeking to build the Panama Canal, do you think he would have supported Panama's rebellion against Colombia? Justify your answer.

Writing About History

Write a Narrative Essay Write a narrative essay telling a story about America's emergence as a global power in the late 1800s and early 1900s. Write your essay from the point of view of an imperialist or an anti-imperialist. Consult page SH11 of the Writing Handbook for additional help.

Prewriting
• Choose a chapter event that interests you most to write about.
• Choose a purpose for your essay. You might highlight a certain aspect of the event that you think deserves attention.
• Gather details related to your essay topic.

Drafting
• Identify the climax, or the most important part, of your story. Then, decide what will happen in the beginning, middle, and end of the essay.

• Write an introduction for the essay that will grab a reader's interest.

• Use many details to make the story vivid. When possible, include dialogue to convey the thoughts of the character.

• Write a conclusion that summarizes the significance of the experience to the character.

Revising
• Use the guidelines on page SH11 of the Writing Handbook to revise your essay.

Critical Thinking

10. Manifest Destiny justified U.S. expansion west to the Pacific coast. U.S. expansion in the late nineteenth century extended this principle, asserting that the United States had the right to compete with European nations for trade and territories.

11. Sample answer: Commodore Perry's mission to Japan opened Japanese markets to U.S. trade. The Open Door Policy asserted the U.S. right to trade with China. The United States used intimidation to get trade concessions from Japan. With the

Open Door Policy, the United States did not negotiate with China's weak government. Instead, it advised European nations that it would expect equal trading rights in Chinese territories.

12. The Yellow Press inflamed public opinion with sensational stories and encouraged the United States to enter into war.

13. Imperialists thought that Filipinos were not capable of governing their own country. Anti-imperialists thought that Filipinos should be given their independence.

Document-Based Assessment

American Imperialism

Should the United States annex territories in order to establish a global empire? Or should it honor American roots by granting self-rule to the native peoples of those lands? Use your knowledge of the debate over American imperialism and the following documents to answer questions 1 through 4.

Document A

Uncle Sam Wrestles With Filipino Insurgency

Document B

The taking of the Philippines does not violate the principles of the Declaration of Independence, but will spread them among a people who have never known liberty and who in a few years will be unwilling to leave the shelter of the American flag. . . . The form of government natural to the Asiatic has always been despotism. . . . [T]o abandon those islands is to leave them to anarchy, [and] to short-lived military dictatorships. . . .

Senator Henry Cabot Lodge, March 1900

Document C

I wanted the American eagle to go screaming into the Pacific. It seemed tiresome and tame for it to content itself with the Rockies. Why not spread its wings over the Philippines, I asked myself? And I thought it would be a real good thing to do. . . . But I have thought some more, since then, and I have read carefully the treaty of Paris, and I have seen that we do not intend to free, but to subjugate the people of the Philippines. We have gone there to conquer, not to redeem. . . . And so I am an anti-imperialist. I am opposed to having the eagle put its talons on any other land.

Mark Twain, October 1900

Document D

WELL, I HARDLY KNOW WHICH TO TAKE FIRST!

1. Which of the documents is a primary source that supports the maintenance of American control over the Philippines to ensure a stable government there?
   A Document A
   B Document B
   C Document C
   D Document D

2. According to Document A, how did the cartoonist choose to portray the Filipino population?
   A Filipinos are resisting the American presence in the Philippines.
   B Filipinos are cooperating with American officials to maintain U.S. control.
   C Filipinos are fleeing their homes in fear of American soldiers.
   D Filipinos are celebrating their independence from Spain.

3. Mark Twain most closely agrees with which of the other documents?
   A Documents A and D
   B Documents A and B
   C Document B
   D Document D

4. **Writing Task** How did the principles of the American Revolution influence the debate over American imperialism in the Philippines? Use your knowledge of the aftermath of the Spanish-American War and specific evidence from the primary sources above to support your opinion.

---

14. Tensions with Japan caused the United States to increase its military strength by expanding its navy.

15. U.S. policy in China was to claim access to Chinese markets. Hay may have objected to establishing colonies in China because doing so might have led to conflict with the European nations already trading there.

16. If the rebellion seemed to be a legitimate expression of grievances, Wilson might have supported it, but not to the extent that he would have sent troops to ensure its success.

Writing About History

As students begin the assignment, refer them to page SH7 of the Writing Handbook for help in writing a narrative essay. Remind them of the steps they should take to complete their assignment, including prewriting, drafting, and revising.

Students' narrative essays should open strongly, use sensory details, and consider audience and purpose. Their papers should show evidence of thoughtful and thorough research if appropriate, include a clear and dramatic climax, and be free of grammatical and spelling errors. For scoring rubrics, see Assessment Rubrics.

Document-Based Assessment

- To help students understand the documents, give them the following **TIP List metaphors and symbols as you encounter them. Review the list when you finish reading to decipher what each metaphor or symbol represents.**

- To provide students with further practice in answering document-based questions, go to Test Prep With Document-Based Assessment.

- If students need more instruction on analyzing primary sources, have them read the Skills Handbook, p. SH24.

Answers

1. B   2. A   3. D
4. Responses should show a clear understanding of the American Revolution's anti-imperialist stance and the way that people who opposed imperialism, such as Mark Twain, drew parallels between the American colonies and the Philippines' fight for independence.

CHAPTER 6

Teach With Technology

PresentationEXPRESS™ PREMIUM DVD

- Teach this chapter's core content by using PresentationExpress, which includes interactivities, video, lecture notes, and the *ExamView®* QuickTake assessment tool.
- To introduce this chapter by using PresentationExpress, ask students with which of the following statements they most agree: **A) War should be avoided at all costs. B) War should be fought only to save innocent lives. C) War is a noble pursuit. D) War should be used to gain territory and increase power.** Take a class poll or record students' answers by using the QuickTake feature, and discuss their responses. Point out that in this chapter, students will read about the reasons the United States entered World War I and the effects the war had on the home front. Continue introducing the chapter by using the chapter opener slide show.

Technology Resources

- Student**EXPRESS** CD-ROM
- Teacher Resource Library **DVD**
- Presentation**EXPRESS** PREMIUM DVD
- *ExamView®* **Test Bank** CD-ROM English and Spanish
- **Guided Reading Audio,** Spanish
- **Student Edition on Audio**

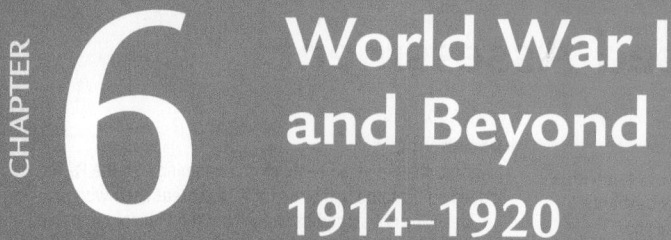

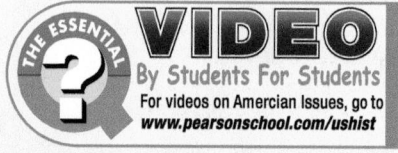

THE ESSENTIAL ? VIDEO By Students For Students
For videos on Amercian Issues, go to *www.pearsonschool.com/ushist*

CHAPTER 6 World War I and Beyond

1914–1920

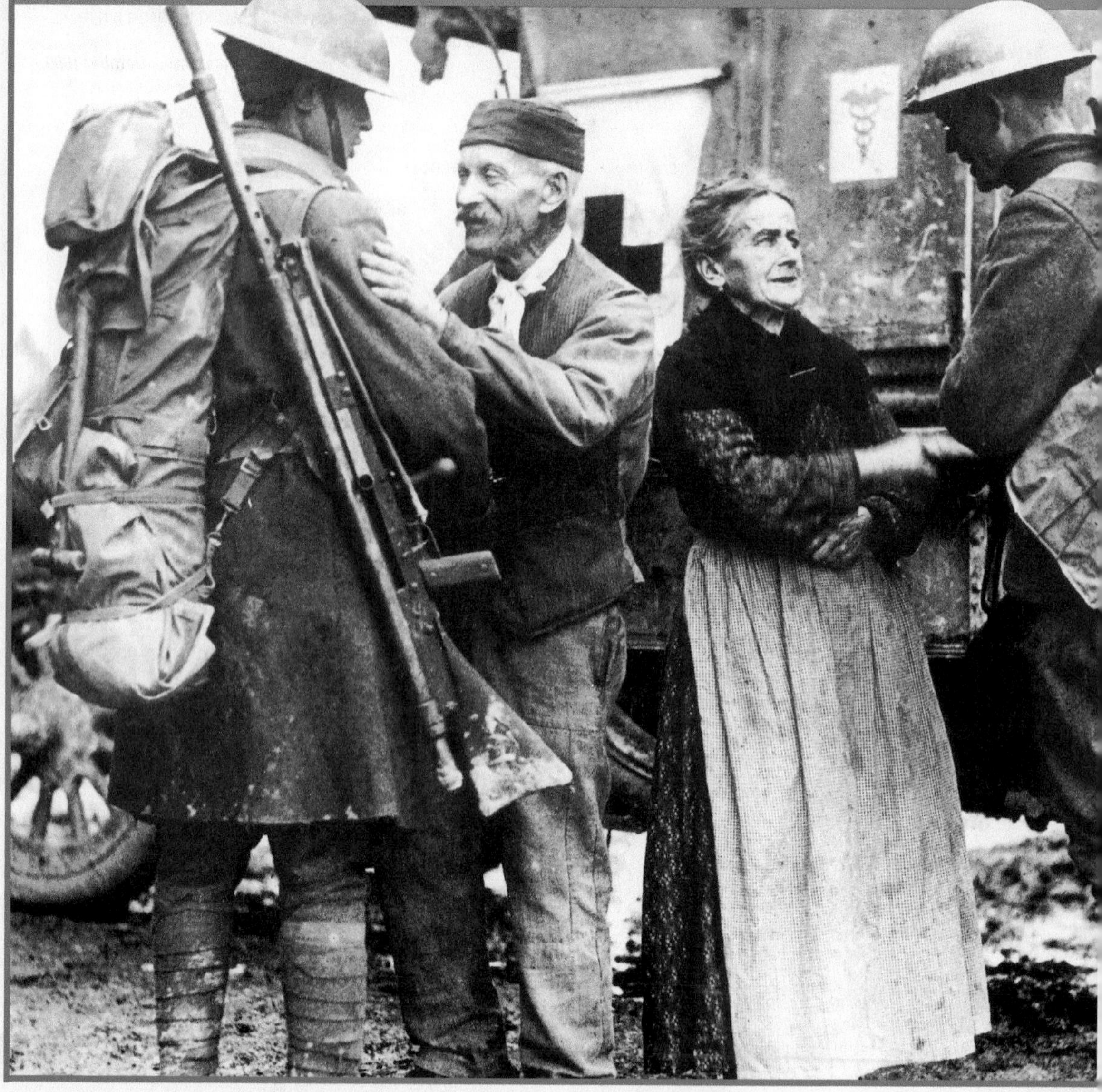

Bibliography

For the Teacher

Cowley, Robert. *The Great War: Perspectives on the First World War.* Random House, 2004.

Ellis, John. *Eye-Deep in Hell: Trench Warfare in World War I.* Johns Hopkins, 1976.

Keegan, John. *The First World War.* Vintage Books, 2000.

Travers, Tim. *How the War Was Won.* Pen & Sword Books, 2005.

For the Student

L2 Cooper, Michael L. *Hell Fighters: African American Soldiers in World War I.* Lodestar Books, 1997.

L3 Wallas, Sarah and Svetlana Palmer, eds. *Intimate Voices from the First World War.* William Morrow, 2004.

L4 Reed, John. *Ten Days That Shook the World.* Penguin, 1990. First published 1919.

American Soldiers Arrive "Over There"

During World War I, nearly 4 million American soldiers went "over there"—to France—to help the Allies win the war. A British volunteer nurse working near the front in France described the arrival of the new American troops:

"I pressed forward with the others to watch the United States physically entering the War, so god-like, so magnificent, so splendidly unimpaired in comparison with the tired, nerve-racked men of the British Army. So these were our deliverers at last, marching up the road to Camiers in the spring sunshine!"

—Vera Brittain, *Testament of Youth*

American soldier's helmet

◄ A French couple greets American soldiers in France in 1918.

I WANT YOU FOR U.S. ARMY
NEAREST RECRUITING STATION

American recruitment poster

Chapter Preview

Chapter Focus Question: What caused the United States to become involved in World War I, and how did the United States change as a result of its involvement?

Section 1
From Neutrality to War

Section 2
The Home Front

Section 3
Wilson, War, and Peace

Section 4
Effects of the War

World War I–era airplane

Use the ☑ **Quick Study Timeline** at the end of this chapter to preview chapter events.

Note Taking Study Guide *Online*
For: Note Taking and American Issues Connector
www.pearsonschool.com/ushist

Chapter-Level Resources

All in One Letter Home (English and Spanish), Preread the Chapter, Vocabulary Builder, Reading Strategy, Social Studies Skills Practice, Enrichment, Issues Connector, Chapter Tests

- Test Prep With Document-Based Assessment
- AYP Monitoring Assessments
- *ExamView®* Test Bank CD-ROM
- Guided Reading Audio (Spanish)
- Student Edition Audio

Previewing the Chapter

- **WITNESS HISTORY** Explain that World War I was fought mostly in Europe. The war had been raging for over two years before the United States entered the conflict. The United States fought alongside the Allies' weary troops. Ask students to describe how the arrival of American troops boosted Allied morale. Read the selection aloud.

- **Analyzing the Visuals** Have students study the photo of the American soldiers arriving in France. Ask **What does the image tell you about the mood of the World War I era?** *(The French were grateful for help from the United States.)*

- **Focus** Write the Chapter Focus question on the board. Tell students to keep this question in mind as they read the chapter. Then, have students preview the section titles in this chapter.

- **Preread** Have students complete the chapter's Preread the Chapter Worksheets. Teaching Resources, pp. 8–9

Differentiated Instruction   Solutions for All Learners

The following Teacher's Edition strategies are suitable for students of varying abilities.

L1 Special Needs Students, pp. 171, 172, 175, 176, 183, 184, 186, 191, 193, 194, 200, 204, 205 SN

L2 English Language Learners, pp. 171, 172, 176, 183, 184, 186, 191, 193, 194, 204, 205 ELL

L2 Less Proficient Readers, pp. 171, 172, 175, 176, 183, 184, 186, 191, 193, 194, 200, 204, 205 LPR

L4 Advanced Readers, pp. 177, 182, 190, 196, 202 AR

L4 Gifted and Talented Students, pp. 177, 182, 190, 196, 202 GT

Have students access **www.pearsonschool. com/ushist** for the Note Taking Study Guide *Online* as an alternative to the *Reading and Note Taking Study Guide* booklet.

Step-by-Step Instruction

Objectives

As you teach this section, keep students focused on the following objectives to help them answer the Section Focus Question and master core content.

- Identify the causes of World War I.
- Describe the course and character of the war.
- Explain why the United States entered the conflict on the side of the Allies.

Prepare to Read

Background Knowledge **L3**

Remind students of the conflict leading up to the Civil War and how the war was fought. Have them predict what might cause a world war and how the causes may be different.

Set a Purpose **L3**

- **WITNESS HISTORY** Read the selection aloud. Ask **Why did the United States shift its position from neutrality to involvement?** *(Americans were angered at ruthless acts of injustice.)* **Why might the Germans have destroyed Louvain?** *(Possible answer: to demonstrate their power)*

- **Focus** Point out the Section Focus Question, and write it on the board. Tell students to refer to this question as they read. *(Answer appears with Section 1 Assessment answers.)*

- **Preview** Have students preview the Section Objectives and the list of Terms and People.

- **NoteTaking** Using the Paragraph Shrinking strategy (TE, p. T20), have students read this section. As they read, have students identify the causes of World War I, the conditions facing soldiers, and the reasons for U.S. involvement. Reading and Note Taking Study Guide

A 1917 cartoon shows the German leader William II considering the U.S. flag looming on the horizon. ▶

Objectives

- Identify the causes of World War I.
- Describe the course and character of the war.
- Explain why the United States entered the conflict on the side of the Allies.

Terms and People

Alsace-Lorraine	casualty
militarism	contraband
Francis Ferdinand	U-boat
William II	*Lusitania*
Western Front	Zimmermann note

NoteTaking

Reading Skill: Identify Causes As you read, identify the causes of World War I, the conditions facing soldiers, and the reasons for U.S. involvement.

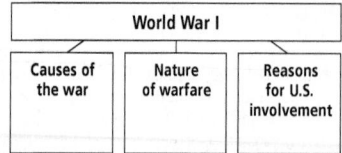

WITNESS HISTORY

To Fight or Not to Fight?

When war broke out in Europe in 1914, the United States decided to stay neutral. However, incidents like the senseless destruction of Louvain, a medieval university town in Belgium, by German troops turned American opinion against Germany.

❝For two hours on Thursday night I was in what for six hundred years had been the city of Louvain. The Germans were burning it . . . the story . . . was told to us by German soldiers incoherent with excesses; and we could read it in the faces of the women and children being led to concentration camps and of the citizens on their way to be shot.❞

—American journalist Richard Harding Davis, August 1914

From Neutrality to War

Why It Matters In 1914, nationalism, militarism, imperialism, and entangling alliances combined with other factors to lead the nations of Europe into a brutal war. The war quickly stretched around the globe. The United States remained neutral at first but ended up abandoning its long tradition of staying out of European conflicts. **Section Focus Question: What caused World War I, and why did the United States enter the war?**

What Caused World War I?

Until 1914, there had not been a large-scale European conflict for nearly one hundred years. However, bitter, deep-rooted problems simmered beneath the surface of polite diplomacy. Europe was sitting on a powder keg of nationalism, regional tensions, economic rivalries, imperial ambitions, and militarism.

Nationalism and Competition Heighten Tension Nationalism, or devotion to one's nation, kick-started international and domestic tension. In the late 1800s, many Europeans began to reject the earlier idea of a nation as a collection of different ethnic groups. Instead, they believed that a nation should express the nationalism of a single ethnic group. This belief evolved into an intense form of nationalism that heightened international rivalries. For example, France longed to avenge its humiliating defeat by a collection of German states in 1871 and regain **Alsace-Lorraine,** the territory it lost during that conflict. Nationalism also threatened minority groups within nation-states. If a country existed as the expression of "its people," the majority ethnic group, where did ethnic minorities fit in?

Vocabulary Builder

Use the information below and the following resource to teach students the high-use word from this section. Teaching Resources, Vocabulary Builder, p. 11

High-Use Word	Definition and Sample Sentence
ally	*n.* person, nation, or group joined with another for a common purpose With his Open Door Policy, John Hay hoped to make an **ally** of China by protecting the two countries' mutual trade interests.

The spread of the theory of Social Darwinism did not help soothe the competitive instinct. Social Darwinism applied biologist Charles Darwin's ideas of natural selection and "survival of the fittest" to human society. Social Darwinists believed that the best nation would come out ahead in the constant competition among countries.

Nationalism also destabilized old multinational empires such as Austria-Hungary and the Ottoman Empire. This was particularly true in the Balkan region of southeastern Europe. For example, when Serbia emerged as an independent nation in 1878, it challenged the nearby empire of Austria-Hungary in two ways: by trying to gain territory controlled by the empire, where Serbs lived, and by the example it offered to Austria-Hungary's diverse peoples.

The nationalist sentiments of the period sometimes spilled over into the economic goals of each nation. Industrial output, trade, and the possession of an overseas empire were the yardsticks of wealth and greatness. The leading industrial nations competed for lands rich in raw materials as well as for places to build military bases to protect their empires. Britain already had a large empire, and France commanded a smaller one. But Germany, Italy, Belgium, Japan, and the United States also rushed to join the imperial race. Together, industrialized nations jostled among themselves as they carved colonies out of Africa, claimed islands in the Pacific, and began to nibble away at China.

Militarism Produces an Arms Race For some European leaders, the question was not so much *if* a great war would start but *when*. To prepare, leaders increased the size of their armies and stockpiles of weapons. No nation readied its war machinery more than Germany. By 1914, it had a huge standing army and the largest, deadliest collection of guns in the world. It also built up its navy enough to rival Britain's, the world's strongest at that time. To keep up, Britain, too, increased the size of its navy. A spirit of **militarism,** or glorification of the military, grew in the competing countries and fueled this arms race even more.

The contest between Germany and Britain at sea and between Germany, France, and Russia on land guaranteed one important thing: The next major war would involve more troops and more technologically advanced weapons than ever before. Machine guns, mobile artillery, tanks, submarines, and airplanes would change the nature of warfare.

Building the War Machine
In the early 1900s, European countries raced to keep up with one another's military might. Below, workers build artillery in Essen, a German city, in 1904. *According to the chart, which country had the largest army in 1914? Which had the largest navy?*

Military Strength, 1914

Germany	
Austria-Hungary	
Russia	
France	
Britain	
United States	

👤 200,000 troops   ⚓ 2 large warships

SOURCE: *Encyclopædia Britannica Online*, 2005; *The Pity of War*, Niall Ferguson

Teach

What Caused World War I? 🅛🄳

Instruct

- **Introduce: Key Term** Ask students to find the key term *militarism* (in bold) in the text. Then, write it on the board, say it aloud, have students say it with you, and provide them with the definition. Ask **Why did *militarism* make it more difficult to avoid the outbreak of war?** (*Militarism made it more tempting to resort to violence and to use weapons that had been stockpiled in the arms race.*)

- **Teach** Explain that there were multiple causes of World War I. Ask **How did many Europeans' idea of nationalism change in the late 1800s?** (*They began to reject the idea of a nation with different ethnic groups and turn toward the idea of a nation representing a single ethnic group.*) **How did France's loss of Alsace-Lorraine add to tension in Europe?** (*France wanted to reclaim the land from Germany.*) **What predictors of war were in place before fighting began?** (*European countries increased the size of their armies, navies, and weaponry. They also made alliances.*) **Why did European countries form so many alliances?** (*Possible responses: to protect themselves; to strengthen their defense because a country is stronger fighting with an ally than alone; to deter other countries from entering into war with them because the aggressor would be fighting not just one nation, but also its allies*)

- **Analyzing the Visuals** Have students study the graph on this page. Ask them to summarize the information presented and predict the effect of the relative sizes of the armies and navies on the outcome of the war.

Differentiated Instruction   Solutions for All Learners

🄛① Special Needs Students   **🄛② English Language Learners**   **🄛② Less Proficient Readers**

This section introduces and reviews several social studies terms. To help students master these terms, write the following in a column on the board: *nationalism, militarism,* and *imperialism*. Discuss each root word and how the suffix -ism changes the meaning of the root words.

Have students create flashcards with the term on one side and its definition on the other. Then, pair students and have them quiz each other, using the flashcards. Students can add other terms that are new to them. Have students incorporate the terms into sentences explaining the causes of World War I.

Answer

Caption Germany; Britain

Have students use **www.pearson-school.com/ushist** to access the Geography Interactive map and then answer the map skills questions.

Monitor Progress

As students fill in their organizers, circulate to make sure that they understand the causes of World War I. For a completed version of the graphic organizer, see Note Taking Transparencies, **B-95**.

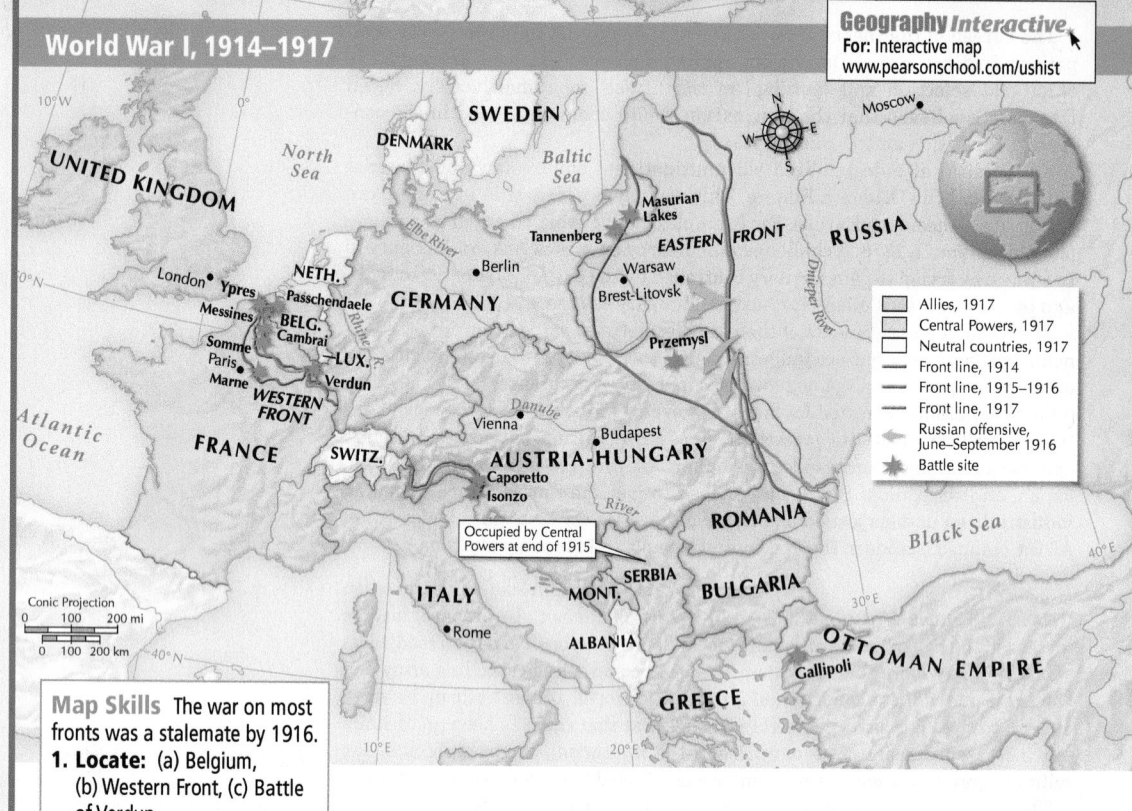

World War I, 1914–1917

Geography *Interactive*
For: Interactive map
www.pearsonschool.com/ushist

Legend:
- Allies, 1917
- Central Powers, 1917
- Neutral countries, 1917
- Front line, 1914
- Front line, 1915–1916
- Front line, 1917
- Russian offensive, June–September 1916
- Battle site

Occupied by Central Powers at end of 1915

Conic Projection
0   100   200 mi
0   100 200 km

Map Skills The war on most fronts was a stalemate by 1916.

1. **Locate:** (a) Belgium, (b) Western Front, (c) Battle of Verdun

2. **Location** What challenge did Germany's location present to its pursuit of victory in the war?

3. **Synthesize Information** Describe the movement of the opposing lines of the Western Front between 1914 and 1917.

Vocabulary Builder

ally–(AL ī) *n.* person, nation, or group joined with another for a common purpose

Alliances Make Nations Overconfident and Reckless European leaders also prepared for war by forming alliances. Before 1914, two major ones emerged. Germany, Austria-Hungary, and Italy joined together in the Triple Alliance (although Italy never fought with it). Opposed to the Triple Alliance was the Triple Entente, made up of France, Russia, and Great Britain. Alliances emboldened leaders to act recklessly. They knew that if they did declare war, powerful <u>allies</u> were obligated to fight along with them. No country wanted to be seen as an unreliable partner. As years passed, European leaders thought less of the advantages of peace and more of the possible benefits of war. Some also hoped that a foreign war would help to smooth over domestic problems.

Assassination Hurtles Europe Toward World War On June 28, 1914, Archduke **Francis Ferdinand**, heir to the throne of Austria-Hungary, and his wife Sophie left for what they thought would be a routine visit to Sarajevo (sar uh YAY voh), the capital city of the Austro-Hungarian province of Bosnia. But a handful of young Bosnians had other plans for the archduke and his wife. These men were ethnic Serbs who believed that Bosnia rightfully belonged to Serbia, and they saw Francis Ferdinand as a tyrant. After the archduke's driver made a wrong turn, Gavrilo Princip, one of the conspirators, noticed the couple in the car, pulled a pistol from his pocket, and fired it twice. First Sophie and then Francis Ferdinand died. People around the world were shocked by the senseless murders. But no one expected that they would lead to a great world war.

✓ **Checkpoint** How did nationalism and militarism both work to push Europe toward war?

Answers

Map Skills

1. Review locations with students.

2. The Allies were located both east and west of Germany. As a result, Germany had to divide its armies to protect both borders. Germany had only indirect access to the Atlantic Ocean, which made shipping supplies more difficult.

3. The front moved eastward from France into Belgium.

✓ Nationalism heightened tensions among ethnic groups, exacerbated territorial disputes, and increased economic competition. Militarism led to new weapons technology and created an arms race. Overall, these two factors increased competition among nations and aggravated existing tensions.

Differentiated Instruction Solutions for All Learners

L1 Special Needs Students   **L2 English Language Learners**   **L2 Less Proficient Readers**

To reinforce the concept of alliances, ask students to suppose that they came across two groups of classmates involved in a fight and each group asks them to join their side. Ask students to determine good points and bad points of staying out of the fight or getting involved. Have them explain how they would decide whom to help.

The Fighting Begins

Everything was in place for a great conflict—nationalist ambitions, large armies, stockpiles of weapons, alliances, and military plans. The nations of Europe were hurtling like giant trains toward a great collision. Archduke Francis Ferdinand's assassination was the incident that triggered this conflict.

Alliances Cause a Chain Reaction Soon after the assassination, Kaiser **William II,** the German emperor, assured Austria-Hungary that Germany would stand by its ally if war came. Confident in Germany's support, Austria-Hungary then sent a harsh ultimatum to Serbia demanding Serbia's total cooperation in an investigation into the assassination. When Serbia did not agree to all of the demands, Austria-Hungary declared war on July 28, 1914.

Because of the alliance system, what otherwise might have been a localized quarrel quickly spread. In early August, Russia mobilized for war to help its ally Serbia against Austria. This caused Germany to declare war against Russia. France, Russia's ally, promptly declared war against Germany. The very next day, Germany declared war against neutral Belgium, so that it could launch an invasion of France through that small country. Great Britain, which had treaties with France and Belgium, immediately declared war against Germany. In less than one week, the Central Powers of Germany and Austria-Hungary were at war against the Allied Powers of Britain, France, Russia, and Serbia. The Ottoman Empire later joined the Central Powers.

German soldiers fought through Belgium and moved southwest into France, toward Paris. Then in September, with the German advance only 30 miles from Paris, the French and the British counterattacked and stopped the German forces near the Marne River.

Deadly Technology Leads to Stalemate After the Battle of the Marne, the Germans settled onto high ground, dug trenches, and fortified their position. When the French and British attacked, the German troops used machine guns and artillery to kill thousands of them. The French and British then dug their own trenches and used the same weapons to kill thousands of counterattacking Germans. Soon, 450 miles of trenches stretched like a huge scar from the coast of Belgium to the border of Switzerland. Although fighting went on in Eastern Europe, the Middle East, and in other parts of the world, this **Western Front** in France became the critical battle front. The side that won there would win the war.

The war dragged on for years, and it was hideously deadly—much more so than anyone had expected. The primary reason for the length of the war and its deadly nature was the simple fact that the defensive weapons of the time were better and more devastating than the offensive ones. Generals on each side threw their soldiers into assaults against the enemy without fully considering the new technology. Charging toward trenches that were defended by artillery, machine guns, and rifles was futile. In virtually every battle on the Western Front, the attacking force suffered terribly. Even the use of poison gas did nothing to benefit the offense, despite its horrifying effects. Ineffective offensives and effective defensives produced only a deadly stalemate.

War in the Trenches

German soldiers hunker down in a shallow trench that stretches into the distance to protect themselves from enemy fire. *How did new technology make defenses such as trenches necessary?*

Instruct

- **Introduce** Ask students to preview the Primary Source quotation and Quick Study chart on the next page. Explain that the new technology of warfare required soldiers to respond in ways that they had not needed to in previous wars. Ask students why armies might have wanted to use chemical weapons in trench warfare.

- **Teach** Have students explain what is meant by the red heading "Alliances Cause a Chain Reaction." Ask pairs of students to create a series of cause-and-effect charts explaining this chain reaction, which led to the involvement of multiple European countries in World War I. Have students examine the photograph on this page and its caption. Ask **What does an army sacrifice when it commits to the protection provided by a trench?** *(mobility)* **What is a stalemate?** *(a situation in which neither side can make any further worthwhile action; a tie)* **Why was the war on the Western Front at a stalemate?** *(Trench warfare and the use of new defensive weapons, such as machine guns, resulted in massive yet roughly equal numbers of casualties from attacking armies.)*

Connect to Your World

Chemical Warfare Modern chemical warfare was first introduced in World War I in the form of poison gas. The use of the gas did not have a significant effect on the course of the war, mainly because protective measures such as gas masks were quickly developed. Still, poison gas inspired terror.

The Geneva Protocol of 1925 banned the use of chemical weapons, but not their production. As a result, these weapons continued to be used in war.

The Nazis used Zyklon-B gas in World War II to kill millions in extermination camps. The United States used herbicides, such as Agent Orange, in Vietnam. In 1992, an international treaty called for the complete ban of production, stockpiling, and use of chemical weapons by 2007. The international community is still refining this agreement to rid the world of chemical weapons.

Answer

Caption The development of machine guns and more powerful artillery made circumstances deadly for infantry soldiers on the ground. From a trench, soldiers had protection from shells and the spray of machine gun bullets.

Independent Practice

Have students continue to fill in the graphic organizer from the beginning of the section, adding a description of the nature of war.

Monitor Progress

As students fill in their graphic organizers, circulate to make sure that they understand the nature of warfare in World War I. For a completed version of the graphic organizer, see Note Taking Transparencies, **B-95**.

The Reality of Trench Warfare The stalemate led to gruesome conditions for the men in the trenches of the Western Front. The soldiers battled the harsh conditions of life often as fiercely as they attacked the enemy. They developed "trench foot" from standing for hours in wet, muddy trenches. They contracted lice from the millions of rats that infested the trenches. Dug into the ground, the soldiers lived in constant fear, afraid to pop their heads out of their holes and always aware that the next offensive might be their last.

Even on a quiet day, soldiers could be killed by snipers or a surprise gas attack, like the one described by French officer Paul Truffaut at Verdun:

> **Primary Source** "The special shells the men call "shells on wheels" [shells filled with poison gas] are whizzing by continuously. They explode silently and have no smell but can be deadly. They killed several men yesterday. One of my men refused to put his mask on because he couldn't smell anything. All of a sudden, he was dizzy, foaming at the mouth and his skin went black, then he went rigid and died."
> —Paul Truffaut, March 5, 1917

In between enemy lines was an area known as "no man's land." Artillery barrages had blasted no man's land until any fields, trees, or homes, that had once existed there, were charred beyond recognition. Soldiers went "over the top" of their trenches into this muddy, nearly impassable wasteland when they attempted to attack the entrenched enemy.

Horror of Modern Warfare
Although gas masks were soon developed to counter poison gas, gas attacks were still particularly horrifying to soldiers. *According to the chart, which type of weapon caused the most casualties?*

Casualties—or soldiers killed, wounded, and missing—mounted first in thousands, then hundreds of thousands, and finally in millions. Almost one million French soldiers were killed or wounded in just the first three months of the war. The Germans lost only slightly fewer. In two battles in 1916—Verdun (ver DUHN) and the Somme (suhm)—the British, French, and Germans sustained more than 2 million casualties. The British suffered 60,000 casualties on the first day alone at the Somme and achieved virtually nothing. And still the stalemate dragged on.

✓ **Checkpoint** Why did both sides embrace trench warfare as a strategy to win the war?

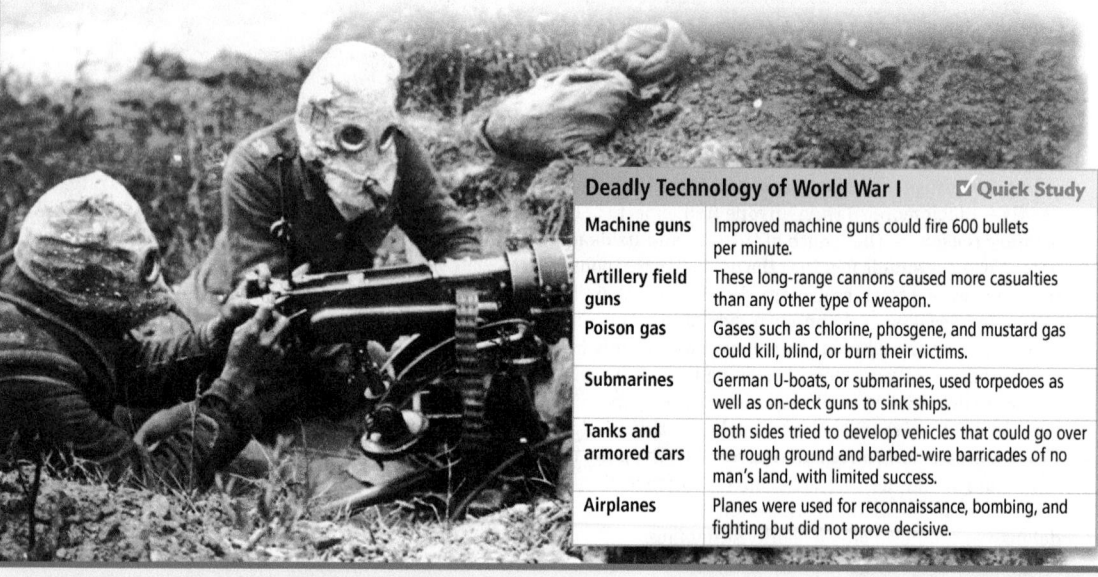

Deadly Technology of World War I	☑ Quick Study
Machine guns	Improved machine guns could fire 600 bullets per minute.
Artillery field guns	These long-range cannons caused more casualties than any other type of weapon.
Poison gas	Gases such as chlorine, phosgene, and mustard gas could kill, blind, or burn their victims.
Submarines	German U-boats, or submarines, used torpedoes as well as on-deck guns to sink ships.
Tanks and armored cars	Both sides tried to develop vehicles that could go over the rough ground and barbed-wire barricades of no man's land, with limited success.
Airplanes	Planes were used for reconnaissance, bombing, and fighting but did not prove decisive.

History Background

Communication in the Trenches Although some trenches had a system of wires or cables to provide telephone service, both sides also used messenger dogs or carrier pigeons to communicate. Although well trained, both dogs and pigeons could be injured while carrying messages or arrive too late to make a difference. However, in 1918, a pigeon saved the American 77th Division from almost certain destruction. The Americans were caught behind enemy lines and under heavy bombardment from their own artillery units. They released a pigeon with their location and this frantic message: "For heaven's sake, stop it." Although missing an eye and a leg, the pigeon reached the Allied lines. It delivered the message, and the shelling was stopped. The bird was later awarded a Distinguished Service Cross.

Answers

Caption artillery field guns

✓ Both sides embraced trench warfare as a response to the change in military technology. The trenches offered protective defenses.

Wilson Urges Neutrality

As the war spread in Europe, President Woodrow Wilson called for Americans to be "impartial in thought as well as action." In a "melting pot" nation that tried to make Americans of peoples from diverse origins, Wilson did not want to see the war set Americans against one another. At first, most Americans viewed the conflict as a distant European quarrel for land and influence. Unless the nation's interests were directly threatened, Americans wanted no part of it. They preferred to maintain what they viewed as traditional American isolation from European disputes. Still, many Americans felt the war's effects and few were truly impartial in thought. Most held a preference for one or another combatant, and many businesses benefited from the increased demand by warring nations for American goods.

Americans Have Divided Loyalties In 1914, one third of Americans were foreign-born. Many still thought of themselves in terms of their former homelands—as German Americans, Irish Americans, Polish Americans, and so on. With relatives in Europe, many people supported the nation in which they were born.

Some German Americans in the Midwest and some Irish Americans along the East Coast felt strongly that the Central Powers were justified in their actions. Many Americans had emigrated from Germany or Austria-Hungary. Millions of Irish Americans harbored intense grudges over the centuries of Great Britain's domination of their homeland. They hoped that Ireland would gain its independence as Britain became entangled in the war. Many Jewish Americans who had fled Russia to escape the Czarist regimes' murderous pogroms against Jews hoped for Russia's defeat.

Most Americans, however, sided with Britain and France, both of which had strong historic ties with the United States. America's national language was English, its cultural heritage was largely British, and its leading trading partner was Britain. France had aided the American cause during the Revolutionary War.

American Opinion Crystallizes No event at the beginning of the war swayed American opinion more than the vicious German invasion of neutral Belgium. German soldiers marching through Belgium committed numerous atrocities, killing unarmed civilians and destroying entire towns. British journalists and propagandists stressed, and sometimes exaggerated, the brutality of the Germans' actions. Americans might have only dimly understood the causes of the war, but they clearly perceived the human cost of the war for Belgium.

Eventually, three distinct positions on the war crystallized among Americans. One group, the isolationists, believed that the war was none of America's business and that the nation should isolate itself from the hostilities. A second group, the interventionists, felt that the war did affect American interests and that the United States should intervene in the conflict on the side of the Allies. A third group, the internationalists, occupied the middle ground. Internationalists believed that the United States should play an active role in world affairs and work toward achieving a just peace but not enter the war.

✓ **Checkpoint** Why did President Wilson fear that the war would set Americans against one another?

Stop!

Analyzing Political Cartoons

The Question of Neutrality In this 1916 cartoon, President Wilson tries to neutralize German Kaiser William II's bloody sword (representing Germany's policy of unrestricted submarine warfare) by pointing it toward the ground.
1. How does the cartoonist portray Kaiser William II?
2. What position do you think the cartoonist holds on American involvement in the war?

Wilson Urges Neutrality L3

Instruct

- **Introduce** Remind students of the ways militarism and nationalism affected Europeans. Discuss with students the extent to which militarism and nationalism affected Americans' positions on the war.

- **Teach** Ask **Why did some Americans not want to enter the war in Europe?** (*They believed in isolationism, did not think that their interests were directly threatened, and believed that it would be costly.*) Create a two-column chart on the board, labeling one column "American Positions" and the other "Goals." Ask volunteers to fill in the chart with the three main positions held by Americans and their main goals. Then, have students use the chart to summarize the shift in Americans' perspectives of the war from 1914 to 1915.

- **Analyzing the Visuals** Direct students' attention to the political cartoon. Ask **How is President Wilson portrayed?** (*He is portrayed as the distinguished gentleman trying to calmly, but sternly, resolve a dispute.*)

Independent Practice

Have groups of three students each take on the role of an isolationist, an interventionist, and an internationalist. Ask each student to write a statement in support of his or her position. Tell them to be prepared to share their position statements with the class.

Monitor Progress

Ask students to share their position statements without identifying their position, and have the class explain which one it is.

Differentiated Instruction Solutions for All Learners

L1 Special Needs Students L2 Less Proficient Readers

This section introduces several social studies terms. To help students master these vocabulary terms, write the following terms in a column on the board: *isolationist, interventionist,* and *internationalist.* Discuss each word part, focusing on meaning. Discuss how the suffix *-ist* changes the meaning of the roots.

Word Part Definitions:
isolate: to separate
intervene: to get involved
national: relating to or belonging to a nation
inter-: among, between
-tion: state or quality of
-ist: one who practices

Answers

✓ Wilson feared that if the United States entered the war, Americans of different national backgrounds would be angry or might turn against one another.

Analyzing Political Cartoons
1. brutal, ruthless
2. Possible response: The cartoonist favors the internationalist view: play an active role in working toward peace, but do not enter the war.

Instruct

- **Introduce: Key Terms** Ask students to find the key terms **contra-band** and **U-boats** (in bold) on this page. Write both terms on the board. Direct students' attention to the map in the Infographic on the page. Ask **How might a *U-boat* be able to stop the delivery of *contra-band* from one country to another?** (*U-boats could sink the ship carrying* **contraband**.)

- **Teach** Use the Numbered Heads strategy (TE, p. T23) to discuss the reasons why the United States entered the war. Ask **Why did Germany violate its promise to spare unarmed ships even at the risk of drawing the United States into the war?** (*Students may mention Germany's desperate situation and its resulting desperate acts. Students may also state that Germany believed that it could win the war before the United States became fully involved.*) **What do you think might have happened if the Germans had kept their pledge not to sink another unarmed ship?** (*Students may argue that the United States would not have entered the war. They may speculate that Britain still would have defeated Germany.*) Direct students' attention to the Infographic on this page. Ask a volunteer to read the paragraph and map caption aloud. Ask students to use the timeline to summarize the shift in Americans' attitudes toward entering the war.

- **Quick Activity** Display Color Transparency: *German U-Boat.* Use the lesson suggested in the transparency book to guide a discussion about the importance of the new submarine technology in warfare.
Color Transparencies **A-85**

Neutrality Gives Way to War

An internationalist, President Wilson sincerely desired peace in his country and around the world. Between the start of the war in 1914 and America's entry into it in 1917, Wilson attempted to use his influence to end the conflict among the warring countries. He failed in this great effort. Ultimately, he also failed to keep the United States out of the war.

Britain Blockades Germany Early in the war, British leaders decided to use their navy to blockade Germany to keep essential goods from reaching the other country. International law generally allowed **contraband** goods, usually defined as weapons and other articles used to fight a war, to be confiscated legally by any belligerent nation. Noncontraband goods, such as food, medical supplies, and other nonmilitary items, could not be confiscated. Britain, however, contested the definition of noncontraband articles. As the war continued, Britain expanded its definition of contraband until it encompassed virtually every product, including gasoline, cotton, and even food—in spite of international law.

German Submarines Violate Neutral Rights Germany responded by attempting to blockade Britain—even though it lacked the conventional naval forces to do so. Instead, in February 1915, Germany began sinking Allied ships using its **U-boats,** or submarines. The reality of the German blockade struck America on May 7, 1915, when a German U-boat sank the British passenger liner *Lusitania* off the coast of Ireland. German officials correctly claimed that

● INFOGRAPHIC

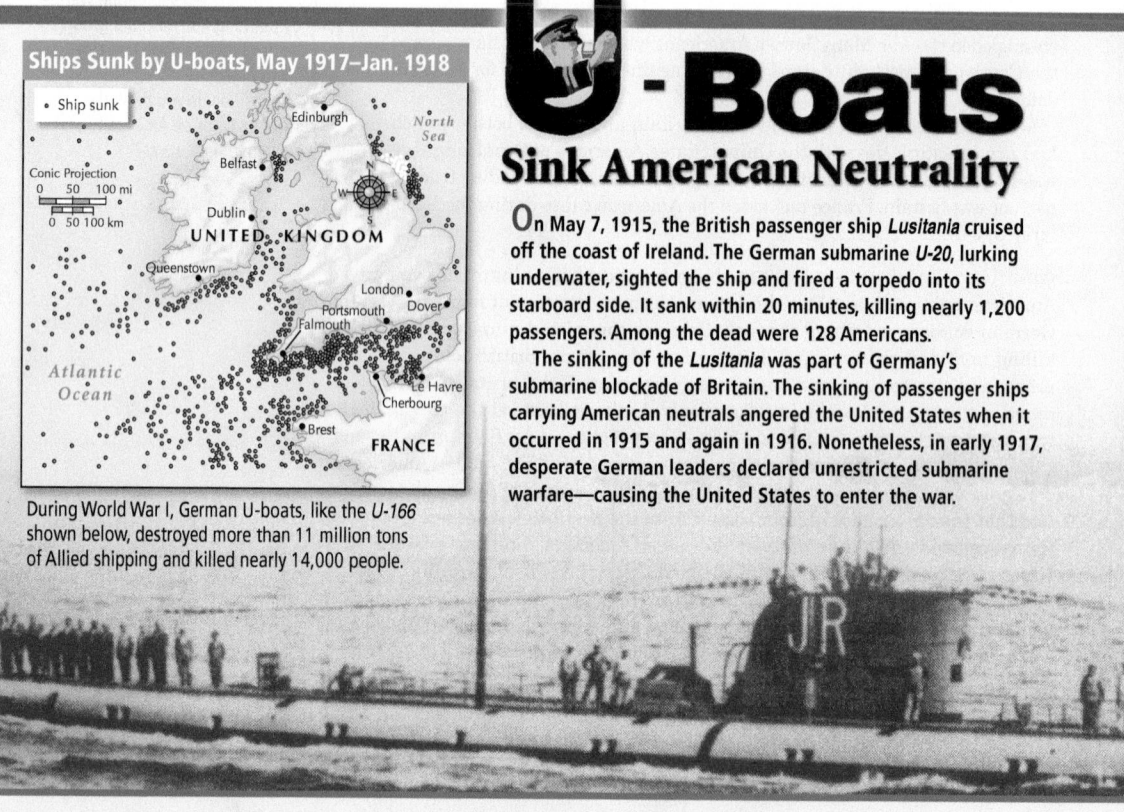

Ships Sunk by U-boats, May 1917–Jan. 1918

- Ship sunk

Conic Projection
0 50 100 mi
0 50 100 km

North Sea
Edinburgh
Belfast
Dublin
UNITED KINGDOM
Queenstown
London
Portsmouth
Falmouth
Dover
Le Havre
Cherbourg
Brest
FRANCE
Atlantic Ocean

During World War I, German U-boats, like the *U-166* shown below, destroyed more than 11 million tons of Allied shipping and killed nearly 14,000 people.

U-Boats
Sink American Neutrality

On May 7, 1915, the British passenger ship *Lusitania* cruised off the coast of Ireland. The German submarine *U-20*, lurking underwater, sighted the ship and fired a torpedo into its starboard side. It sank within 20 minutes, killing nearly 1,200 passengers. Among the dead were 128 Americans.

The sinking of the *Lusitania* was part of Germany's submarine blockade of Britain. The sinking of passenger ships carrying American neutrals angered the United States when it occurred in 1915 and again in 1916. Nonetheless, in early 1917, desperate German leaders declared unrestricted submarine warfare—causing the United States to enter the war.

Differentiated Instruction Solutions for All Learners

Ⓛ¹ **Special Needs Students** Ⓛ² **English Language Learners** Ⓛ² **Less Proficient Readers**

Organize students into groups of four. Have each group work together to review the text under one of the following red headings: "Britain Blockades Germany," "German Submarines Violate Neutral Rights," "Wilson Prepares for War," and "America Enters the War." Have each group write a one- or two-sentence summary of their subsection. Ask groups to share their summaries. Then, ask questions that require stu-

dents to use their knowledge of the section content. For example, ask **What are two reasons why the United States decided to enter the war?** (*German submarines were sinking passenger ships that carried Americans. Germany attempted to entice Mexico into entering the war on the Central Powers' side by promising in the Zimmermann note to return Texas to Mexico after the war.*)

the ship was carrying ammunition and other contraband. Americans protested that an unarmed and unresisting ship should not be sunk without first being warned and provided with safety for its passengers. President Wilson was stunned but still wanted peace. "There is such a thing as a man being too proud to fight," he told his fellow citizens. "There is such a thing as a nation being so right that it does not need to convince others by force that it is right."

Germany helped to keep the United States out of the war by eventually promising not to sink any more passenger ships. But in 1916, Germany violated that promise by sinking the unarmed French passenger ship *Sussex*. Another storm of protest erupted in America. Again, Germany pledged not to sink unarmed ships. This promise, called the Sussex Pledge, would not last long.

Wilson Prepares for War President Wilson wanted to remain at peace, but even he must have realized the futility of that hope. At the end of 1915, Wilson began to prepare the nation for war. Many believed that "preparedness" was a dangerous course that could actually provoke war. Even so, Congress passed two pieces of legislation in 1916 to prepare for the possibility of U.S. involvement. The National Defense Act expanded the size of the army, and the Naval Construction Act ordered the building of more warships.

Still, Wilson hoped to avoid the conflict. In 1916, he ran for reelection with the slogan, "He kept us out of war." It was a close election, but Wilson won a narrow victory over Republican Charles Evans Hughes.

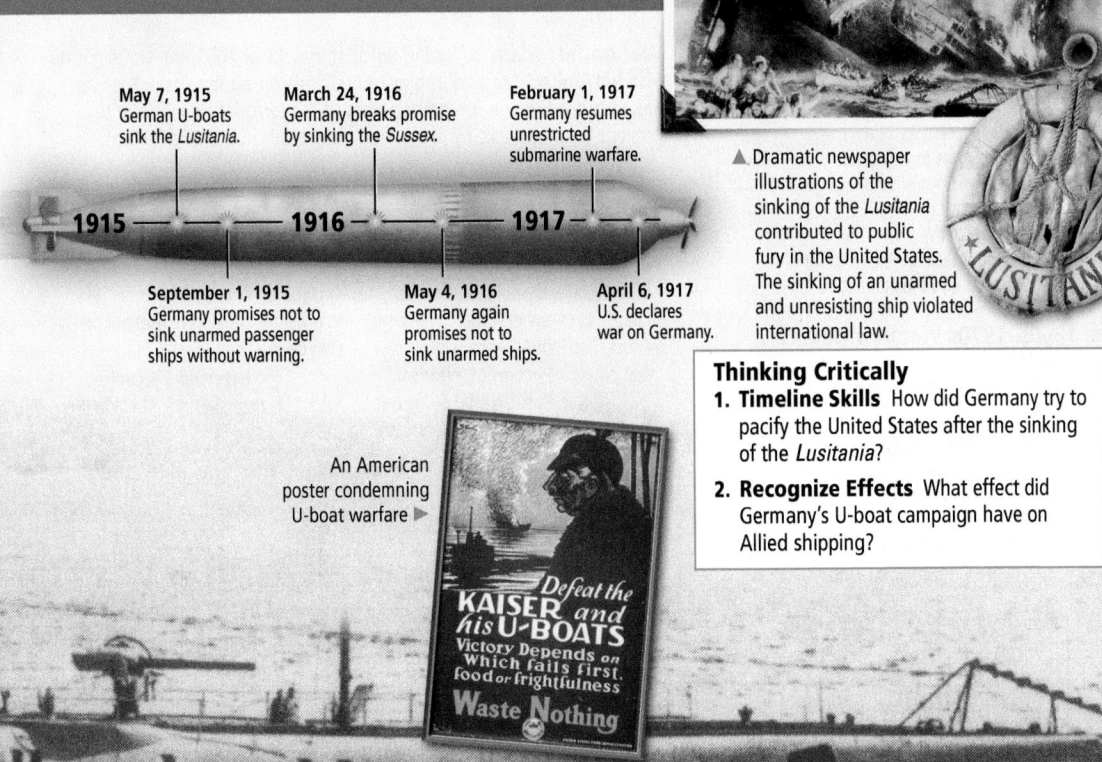

May 7, 1915
German U-boats sink the *Lusitania*.

March 24, 1916
Germany breaks promise by sinking the *Sussex*.

February 1, 1917
Germany resumes unrestricted submarine warfare.

1915 — 1916 — 1917 —

September 1, 1915
Germany promises not to sink unarmed passenger ships without warning.

May 4, 1916
Germany again promises not to sink unarmed ships.

April 6, 1917
U.S. declares war on Germany.

▲ Dramatic newspaper illustrations of the sinking of the *Lusitania* contributed to public fury in the United States. The sinking of an unarmed and unresisting ship violated international law.

An American poster condemning U-boat warfare ▶

Defeat the KAISER and his U-BOATS
Victory Depends on Which fails first, food or frightfulness
Waste Nothing

Thinking Critically
1. **Timeline Skills** How did Germany try to pacify the United States after the sinking of the *Lusitania*?
2. **Recognize Effects** What effect did Germany's U-boat campaign have on Allied shipping?

Independent Practice

- To help students understand a political cartoon and analyze the reasons why the United States entered World War I, have them complete the worksheet *Interpreting a Political Cartoon: World War I*. Teaching Resources, **p. 19**

- Direct students to the HISTORY MAKERS feature on Jeannette Rankin at the end of this section. Have students write a letter responding either positively or negatively to Rankin's decision to vote against the war. Students' letters should explain clearly why they support or oppose Rankin's decision.

- Have students read the Primary Source quotation by Woodrow Wilson on the last page of this section. Pair students and have those pairs make a two-column chart comparing Wilson's approach to war in 1914 and his approach in 1917.

- Have students complete the graphic organizer from the beginning of the section by adding the reasons for U.S. involvement in the war.

Monitor Progress

As students fill in their graphic organizer and worksheet, circulate to make sure that they understand the reasons for U.S. entrance into World War I. For a completed version of the graphic organizer, see Note Taking Transparencies, **B-95**.

Differentiated Instruction   Solutions for All Learners

L4 Advanced Readers   **L4 Gifted and Talented Students**

Organize students into groups of three or four. Assign each group to create a talk show discussing whether America should join World War I. Have one student in each group assume the role of the talk-show host, while the other two students act as guests. Guests should have opposing viewpoints regarding the U.S. position on the war. Students should prepare for their roles by developing pertinent questions and answers based on information in the text. Then, ask each group to present their show to the classroom audience.

Answers

Thinking Critically

1. Germany promised not to sink another unarmed passenger ship without warning.
2. Ships often were unable to deliver their cargo because they were torpedoed and sunk by German U-boats.

Objectives

- Identify reasons for entering a war.
- Debate the considerations involved in deciding to enter a war.

Background Knowledge (L3)

Ask students to identify the reasons why the United States entered into World War I. Remind them that at first, the country remained neutral. Then, ask students about the War on Terrorism that followed the terrorist attacks in 2001. Do students think that the United States was justified in beginning that war?

Instruct (L3)

- Point out that the timeline shows previous wars and the reason why the United States entered each. Ask **In general, why has the United States entered into past wars?** *(because Americans' rights, freedoms, or safety were threatened)* **Do you think the United States could enter a war in which the entire population supported its decision?** *(No; some people will always oppose war.)*

Monitor Progress

- Have students complete the Issues Connector Worksheet, *America Goes to War.* Check students' work to make sure that they grasp the aspects of the issue. Teaching Resources, **pp. 15–18**
- Remind students to complete their American Issues Journal worksheets. Review their work for accuracy. Reading and Note Taking Study Guide

Answers

Transfer Activities

1. George believes that the government should do whatever is necessary to protect Americans from terrorism. Hehir believes that war should be a last resort in extreme cases when there is no other solution.

2. Hehir might not have supported the decision to enter World War I because innocent American civilians had been killed.

3. Have students access **www.pearsonschool.com/ushist** for information while writing their arguments.

American Issues Connector — America Goes to War

TRACK THE ISSUE

When should America go to war?

Over the years, the United States has had many motives for going to war. The nation has gone to war to protect itself, gain economic benefits, aid its allies, expand its borders, or increase its power and influence. Under what circumstances is war justified? Americans debate this issue each time the country fights. Use the timeline below to explore this enduring issue.

1812 War of 1812
Americans fight to stop Britain from seizing American ships and sailors.

1860s Civil War
North and South fight over slavery, states' rights, and preservation of the Union.

1917–1918 World War I
United States goes to war after Germany violates American neutrality.

1940s World War II
The Japanese attack on Pearl Harbor draws America into the conflict.

1960s–1970s Vietnam War
United States fights to halt spread of communism in Southeast Asia.

A newspaper announces America's entry into World War I on April 6, 1917.

U.S. soldiers patrol the streets in Baghdad, Iraq.

DEBATE THE ISSUE

War on Terrorism After the terrorist attacks of 2001, the United States invaded Afghanistan and Iraq as part of the War on Terrorism. The war aimed to track down the perpetrators of the terrorist attacks and to prevent future attacks by promoting democracy in the Middle East.

"The use of military force against terrorist networks and regimes abetting their crimes is certainly justifiable. . . . Our leaders are, in my judgment, morally obligated to use as much force as necessary . . . to protect innocent Americans and other potential victims of terrorism."
—Robert P. George, professor, Princeton University

"When you make the argument that there is a 'just war,' what you are saying is that there is an aggression, a major offense is being committed and you do not have any other way to protect people from that aggression except to use force."
—Reverend J. Brian Hehir, Catholic theologian

TRANSFER Activities

1. **Compare** Why does Professor George support the War on Terrorism? Why does Reverend Hehir oppose it?

2. **Analyze** Do you think Hehir would have supported the decision to enter World War I? Explain.

3. **Transfer** Use the following Web site to see a video, try a WebQuest, and write in your journal. www.pearsonschool.com/ushist

History Background

The War on Terrorism Following the attacks on September 11, 2001, the United States made fighting terrorism and ensuring homeland security top priorities. The government strengthened and reorganized its intelligence services and passed the Patriot Act as part of the increased security measures. Among the act's most hotly debated provisions were new laws allowing the federal government easier access to private records.

President George W. Bush declared war against terrorism in general and against al Qaeda (also spelled al-Qaida) in particular. President Bush outlined strategies to fight the war. These included preventing terrorist attacks before they occur, denying weapons of mass destruction to outlaw regimes and their terrorist allies, and bringing democracy to nations in the Middle East.

America Enters the War Wilson did not have much time to enjoy his victory. In early 1917, two events occurred that helped to push the United States into the war. American trade with the Allies had sustained Britain and France in the war, while the British blockade of Germany had stopped the flow of American goods to the Central Powers. As far as Germany was concerned, desperate times demanded desperate measures.

In January 1917, suffering severe supply shortages due to the blockade, Germany took action. First, German Foreign Minister Arthur Zimmermann sent a telegram to Mexico. The **Zimmermann note** proposed an alliance with Mexico, stating that if the United States declared war on Germany, Mexico should declare war on the United States. In return, after a German victory, Mexico would get back the states of Texas, New Mexico, and Arizona, which it had lost in 1848 after its defeat in the Mexican-American War. The telegram was intercepted by the British, who gave it to American authorities. Next, Germany once again announced unrestricted submarine warfare against Britain.

Although most leaders knew Mexico had no intention of attacking the United States, Americans were shocked by the publication of the Zimmermann note. Even Wilson no longer called for peace. On April 2, 1917, he asked Congress for a declaration of war against Germany:

Primary Source "The world must be made safe for democracy. Its peace must be planted upon the tested foundations of political liberty. . . . We are but one of the champions of the rights of mankind. We shall be satisfied when those rights have been made as secure as the faith and the freedom of nations can make them."
—Woodrow Wilson, April 2, 1917

Congress responded on April 6, 1917, with a declaration of war. Wilson's long struggle to keep America at peace was over.

✔ **Checkpoint** What German actions led the United States to enter World War I?

HISTORY MAKERS

Jeannette Rankin (1880–1973)
In 1916, Jeannette Rankin became the first woman elected to Congress. Committed to women's rights, she was also a dedicated pacifist. She and 49 other members of Congress voted against declaring war on Germany in 1917. Twenty-four years later, in 1941, she was the only member of Congress to vote against the declaration of war against Japan. "As a woman," Rankin said, "I can't go to war, and I refuse to send anyone else." She lost her bid for reelection in the election years that followed both votes.

SECTION 1 Assessment

Progress Monitoring Online
For: Self-test with vocabulary practice
www.pearsonschool.com/ushist

Comprehension

1. **Terms and People** For each item below, write a sentence explaining its significance to the outbreak and course of World War I.
   • militarism
   • Francis Ferdinand
   • William II
   • casualty
   • U-boat
   • *Lusitania*

2. **NoteTaking** **Reading Skill: Identify Causes** Use your chart to answer the Section Focus Question: What caused World War I, and why did the United States enter the war?

Writing About History

3. **Quick Write: Identify Causes** List each cause of U.S. entry into World War I, and then organize them in order of importance. Finally, turn your list into a paragraph describing the causes of U.S. involvement in the war.

Critical Thinking

4. **Draw Conclusions** Why did a stalemate develop on the Western Front?

5. **Compare Points of View** Compare the three positions Americans took on the issue of whether or not the United States should enter the war.

6. **Synthesize Information** Why did the United States decide to enter the war and fight on the side of the Allies?

Objectives

As you teach this section, keep students focused on the following objectives to help them answer the Section Focus Question and master core content.

- Analyze how the American government mobilized the public to support the war effort.
- Describe opposition to the war.
- Outline significant social changes that occurred during the war.

Background Knowledge L3

Remind students of the causes of the U.S. entrance into World War I. Ask them to predict the effect that the country's entrance into the war might have on politics, the economy, and people's attitudes at home.

Set a Purpose L3

- **WITNESS HISTORY** Read the selection aloud. Ask **Why would the government want citizens to support the war effort?** (*A war requires citizens to make sacrifices. Without their support, conducting the war would be more difficult.*)

- **Focus** Point out the Section Focus Question, and write it on the board. Tell students to refer to this question as they read. (*Answer appears with Section 2 Assessment answers.*)

- **Preview** Have students preview the Section Objectives and the list of Terms and People.

- **NoteTaking** Using the Paragraph Shrinking strategy (TE, p. T20), have students read this section. As they read, have students summarize the impact of the war on the home front. Reading and Note Taking Study Guide

WITNESS HISTORY

Supporting the War

While soldiers trained to fight in the war, Americans on the home front supported the war by working in war industries, lending money to the government, and conserving food to feed the troops abroad.

"Perhaps it will not be long before we will read each day long lists of American boys killed or wounded in the trenches of France. There will be boys in those lists that you know, boys that I know. And as our eyes film over with tears it will be at least some comfort to us to be able to say, 'I am helping too. I am saving food for the boys who are fighting.'"

—Committee on Public Information bulletin,
July 1917

▲ Girl Scouts collect peach pits to be used in gas-mask filters.

The Home Front

Objectives

- Analyze how the American government mobilized the public to support the war effort.
- Describe opposition to the war.
- Outline significant social changes that occurred during the war.

Terms and People

Selective Service Act
Bernard Baruch
CPI
George Creel
conscientious objector
Espionage Act
Great Migration

NoteTaking

Reading Skill: Summarize As you read, summarize the key points made in the section in a chart like the one below.

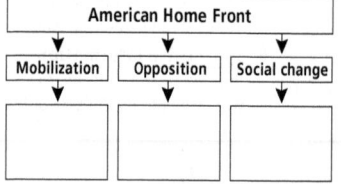

Why It Matters Before the war, the federal government played a minor role in the daily lives of most Americans. But during World War I, the government assumed new powers. It regulated industrial and agricultural production, worked to shape public opinion, and established a new military draft. While war required sacrifice, it also brought new economic opportunities, and many Americans migrated to other parts of the country in search of these opportunities. The war permanently changed Americans' relationship with their government. **Section Focus Question: How did the war affect Americans at home?**

America Mobilizes for War

War affects many things, but its greatest impact is on the lives of ordinary people. People fight, sacrifice, and sometimes die in war. People work to produce the food that soldiers eat and the guns that soldiers fire. People shape the information that others receive about the war. War may be the result of conflicts between nations, but it touches the lives of millions of individuals.

Building an Army When the United States entered World War I, the United States Army was only a fraction of the size of European armies. To build the army, President Wilson encouraged Americans to volunteer for service and pushed Congress to pass the **Selective Service Act.** The act, which Congress passed in May 1917, authorized a draft of young men for military service in Europe. On the

Use the information below and the following resource to teach students the high-use words from this section. Teaching Resources, Vocabulary Builder, p. 11

High-Use Word	Definition and Sample Sentence
conserve	*v.* to keep from wasting We are encouraged to **conserve** our natural resources.
objective	*n.* something worked toward; goal The Allies' **objective** was to win the war.

first day of its enactment, June 5, 1917, more than 9.6 million Americans registered for the draft and were assigned a number. The government held a "great national lottery" in July to decide the order in which the first draftees would be called into service. Blindfolded, Secretary of War Newton D. Baker pulled number 258 out of a jar. The group of men assigned that number became the very first draftees.

Over the course of the war, more than 24 million Americans registered for the draft. Of these, about 2.8 million were actually drafted into the armed forces. Including volunteers, the total number of American men in uniform during World War I reached nearly 4.8 million. More than 4 million of these were sent to help the Allies in France.

Constructing a War Economy While the Selective Service Commission raised an army, President Wilson worked to shift the national economy from peacetime to wartime production. This process proved slow and frustrating. First, the Council of National Defense, which was formed in August 1916, created an array of new federal administrative agencies to oversee different phases of the war effort. Individual agencies regulated food production, coal and petroleum distribution, and railway use. In practical terms, this meant that the government determined what crops farmers grew, what products industries produced, and how supplies moved around on the nation's trains.

Problems and administrative overlap soon led to the creation of the War Industries Board (WIB). The WIB eventually became independent of the Council of National Defense. Headed by **Bernard Baruch** (buh ROOK), an influential Wall Street investment broker who reported directly to the President, the WIB regulated all industries engaged in the war effort. Baruch's agency determined what products industries would make, where those products went, and how much they would cost. The system of free enterprise was curtailed to fulfill the nation's acute need for war materials. Americans realized that they had to cooperate rather than compete in order to defeat the Central Powers.

What Baruch did for industry, future U.S. president Herbert Hoover achieved for agriculture. As head of the Food Administration, he set prices high for wheat and other foodstuffs to encourage farmers to increase production. He also asked

Wartime Production
These women worked during the war inspecting bullets for rifles. *According to the graph, by what percentage did manufacturing increase between 1915 and 1918?*

Rising U.S. Production, 1915–1918

Percentage of increase over 1914 production levels

Textiles   Manufacturing   Agriculture

* In 1916, agricultural output did not increase above the 1914 levels.
SOURCE: *The American Home Front*, James L. Abrahamson

America Mobilizes for War

Instruct

- **Introduce: Key Term** Ask students to find the key term *Selective Service Act* (in bold) in the text. Analyze the meaning of each word of the term. Ask **Why might the government institute a draft?** *(to increase the size of its army)*

- **Teach** Draw a three-column chart on the board with the headings "Military," "Economy," and "Public Opinion." Discuss and record the changes to each brought about by the U.S. entrance into the war. Draw students' attention to the image and bar graph on this page. Ask **How did industry change during the war?** *(The government took a more active role, identifying war goods to be produced and their price.)* **Why did Hoover encourage food conservation?** *(so that more food would be available for the troops)* **Why did the government establish the Committee on Public Information?** *(to develop and maintain support for the war)*

- **Quick Activity** Display Color Transparency: *Supporting the War.* Use the lesson in the transparency book to guide a discussion about the use of propaganda during World War I. Color Transparencies **A-86**

Independent Practice

Have students suppose that they live in the United States in 1917. Have them write letters to the editor explaining how people on the home front can support the war effort and why it is important. Students' letters should be logically presented and include information from the section.

Monitor Progress

- As students work on their letters, circulate to ensure they understand the impact of mobilization on Americans on the home front.

- As students complete their charts, circulate to make sure that they understand how the war affected the American home front. For a completed version of the chart, see Note Taking Transparencies, **B-96**.

Answer

Caption by 20 percent

Opposition and Its Consequences

Instruct

- **Introduce: Key Term** Point out the term **conscientious objectors** (in bold) in the text. Examine each word in the term. Explain that **conscientious objectors** are people who cannot fight in a war because of their moral or religious beliefs. Then, have students read the Vocabulary Builder term and definition. Have students compare and contrast the terms **objectors** and **objective**.

- **Teach** Discuss with students the ways the government encouraged public support for the war, such as using patriotic postcards similar to the one on this page. Draw a two-column chart on the board with the headings "Opposition" and "Consequences." Have volunteers suggest forms of opposition from the text. Then, ask students to identify resulting consequences of opposition to the war. Record their suggestions in the chart. Ask **How did some men evade the draft?** (They refused to cooperate with the Selective Service process, or claimed to be conscientious objectors.) **What happened to those men?** (They were often court-martialed and imprisoned or treated badly.) **Why do you think NAWSA decided to support the war?** (Possible answer: They thought that it would be considered more responsible and patriotic if they supported the soldiers, government, and America by dropping their peace initiatives. They also might have hoped that an increase in membership would further the cause of suffrage once the war ended.) **Why did some people fear that the Espionage Act would erode Americans' civil liberties?** (The Espionage Act restricted individual rights by limiting freedom of speech and press.)

Answer

✓ The U.S. government instituted the draft to build its military, dictated a change in industry and agriculture to meet the needs of wartime, and also began the Committee on Public Information to convince Americans that the war effort was worthwhile and just.

Vocabulary Builder
conserve–(kuhn SERV) *v.* to keep from wasting

Americans to <u>conserve</u> food as a patriotic gesture. If the American people ate less, then more food could be shipped to American and other Allied soldiers fighting the war overseas. To this end, Hoover instituted wheatless Mondays and Wednesdays, meatless Tuesdays, and porkless Thursdays and Saturdays.

Shaping Public Opinion Hoover's efforts would have been fruitless if the American people did not believe in supporting the war. Most Americans did not understand the reasons for the war in 1914, and many questioned why the United States became involved in 1917. It was the job of the **Committee on Public Information (CPI)** to educate the public about the causes and nature of the war. The CPI had to convince Americans that the war effort was a just cause.

Wilson appointed **George Creel** as the director of the CPI. A former journalist and a passionate admirer of American institutions, Creel combined education and a widespread advertising campaign to "sell America." The CPI distributed 75 million pamphlets and 6,000 press releases, and it assembled an army of 75,000 speakers who gave lectures and brief speeches on America's war aims and the nature of the enemy. In addition, the CPI designed, printed, and distributed millions of posters that dramatized the needs of America and its allies. The CPI also stressed the cruelty and wickedness of the enemy, particularly Germany, which in some cases aggravated resentment toward German Americans. Still, using these methods, Creel and the CPI earned widespread support for the American war effort.

✓ **Checkpoint** How did the United States ready its military, economy, and people for war?

Opposition and Its Consequences

The CPI's work was important because Americans did not always peacefully agree with one another about the war. Members of two large ethnic groups, German Americans and Irish Americans, tended to oppose the Allies for different reasons. Swept up in patriotic fervor, some people treated German Americans with prejudice, or intolerance. Other Americans were pacifists who opposed war for any reason. To quiet dissent, or differing opinions, the government acted in ways that sometimes trespassed on individual liberties.

Resistance to the Draft Without a doubt, the draft created controversy. Some Americans believed it was an illegal intrusion of the federal government into their private lives. Some men refused to cooperate with the Selective Service process. They were often court-martialed and imprisoned. Others simply tried to avoid the draft. Perhaps as many as 12 percent of men who received draft notices never responded to them.

Another group resisted the draft by becoming **conscientious objectors,** people whose moral or religious beliefs forbid them to fight in wars. In theory, the Selective Service Act exempted from combat service members of "any well recognized religious sect or organization . . . whose existing creed or principles forbid its members to participate in war." In practice, this policy was widely ignored. Some conscientious objectors were treated badly by their local draft boards, and others were humiliated in training camps. As America's participation in the war increased, however, the government improved its treatment of conscientious objectors.

Noble Goals
Postcards like this one emphasized Wilson's goal of making the world "safe for democracy."

Differentiated Instruction   **Solutions for All Learners**

L4 Advanced Readers   **L4 Gifted and Talented Students**

Remind students that President Wilson instituted the draft with the signing of the Selective Service Act. Although the draft ended after World War I, it was reinstated during World War II, and remained in place until the 1970s. Today, male citizens age 18 to 25 are still required to register, although the military is all voluntary.

Have students research opinions on the draft, including the issue of requiring women to register. Have them prepare a brief but thorough argument supporting or opposing reinstatement of the draft or the inclusion of women in the registration and draft process.

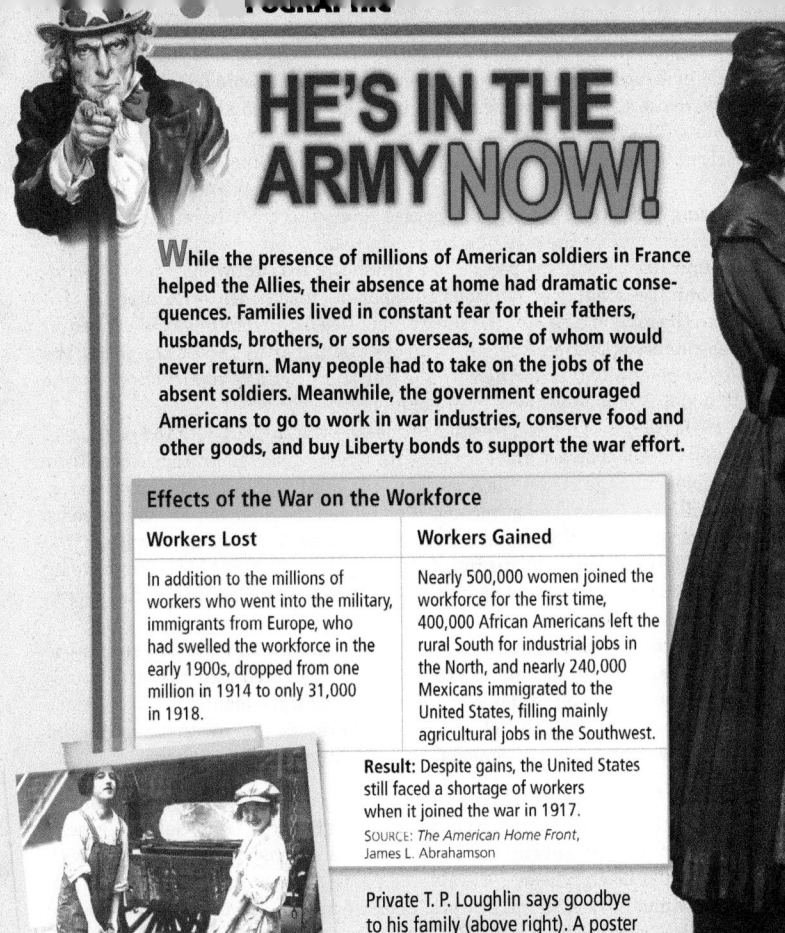

HE'S IN THE ARMY NOW!

While the presence of millions of American soldiers in France helped the Allies, their absence at home had dramatic consequences. Families lived in constant fear for their fathers, husbands, brothers, or sons overseas, some of whom would never return. Many people had to take on the jobs of the absent soldiers. Meanwhile, the government encouraged Americans to go to work in war industries, conserve food and other goods, and buy Liberty bonds to support the war effort.

Effects of the War on the Workforce

Workers Lost	Workers Gained
In addition to the millions of workers who went into the military, immigrants from Europe, who had swelled the workforce in the early 1900s, dropped from one million in 1914 to only 31,000 in 1918.	Nearly 500,000 women joined the workforce for the first time, 400,000 African Americans left the rural South for industrial jobs in the North, and nearly 240,000 Mexicans immigrated to the United States, filling mainly agricultural jobs in the Southwest.

Result: Despite gains, the United States still faced a shortage of workers when it joined the war in 1917.

SOURCE: *The American Home Front*, James L. Abrahamson

Private T. P. Loughlin says goodbye to his family (above right). A poster with a stirring message urges Americans to buy Liberty bonds (far right). Two women deliver ice, a job formerly done by men (left).

OVER THE
FOR YOU

Buy U.S. Gov't Bon
THIRD LIBERTY L[

Women Work for Peace Some American women also opposed the war. Before the war, a number of leading American feminists, including reformer Jane Addams, formed the Women's Peace Party and, with pacifist women from other countries, the Women's International League for Peace and Freedom. Jeannette Rankin, the first woman to serve in the U.S. House of Representatives, voted against the declaration of war. After America joined the Allies, some women continued to oppose the war, but most supported American war efforts. For example, the influential National American Woman Suffrage Association (NAWSA) dropped its initial peace initiatives and supported America's war objectives. After adopting this new policy, NAWSA doubled in size.

Thinking Critically

1. **Draw Conclusions** How did conserving food on the home front help the war effort?

2. **Predict Consequences** What do you think will happen to the women and African Americans who took new jobs during the war when the war ends?

Vocabulary Builder
objective–(uhb JEHK tihv) *n.*
something worked toward; goal

Have students complete the middle portion of the chart summarizing war opposition and ensuing consequences.

Monitor Progress

As students complete the second part of their charts, circulate to make sure that students understand the opposition to World War I that citizens expressed on the home front. For a completed version of the summary chart, see Note Taking Transparencies, **B-96.**

The Government Cracks Down on Dissent The work of the CPI created a mood in America that did not welcome open debate. Some felt the CPI stifled the free expression of controversial opinions and worried about the impact of a rigorous military campaign on democracy. They did not want the freedoms that Americans held most dear to become victims of the conflict. As in previous and future wars, the government navigated a difficult path between respecting and restricting individual rights. Authorities tended to treat harshly individuals who worked against the goal of winning the war.

In June 1917, Congress passed the **Espionage Act,** allowing postal authorities to ban treasonable or seditious newspapers, magazines, or printed materials from the mail. It also enacted severe penalties for anyone engaged in disloyal or treasonable activities. Anyone found obstructing army recruiters, aiding the enemy, or generally interfering with the war effort could be punished with up to a $10,000 fine and 20 years of imprisonment.

In 1918, Congress limited freedom of speech even further with the passage of the Sedition Act. The act made it unlawful to use "disloyal, profane, scurrilous, or abusive language" about the American form of government, the Constitution, or the military forces. The government employed the Sedition Act to prosecute socialists, political radicals, and pacifists. Eugene V. Debs, the leader of the Socialist Party in America, was imprisoned under the act. For his crime—giving a mildly antiwar speech to a convention of socialists in Canton, Ohio—he was sentenced to a 10-year term in a federal prison.

The Supreme Court upheld the constitutionality of the Sedition Act in the case of *Schenck* v. *United States* (1919). The Court ruled that there are times when the need for public order is so pressing that First Amendment protections of speech do not apply. The Debs case and others like it show that the war did lead to some suppression of personal freedoms and individual rights.

Prejudice Against German Americans Sometimes, the war enthusiasm created by the CPI and other groups took an ugly turn. Some German Americans were treated harshly during the war. Americans regarded Germany—with its arrogant kaiser, ruthless generals, and spike-helmeted soldiers—as the primary foe among the Central Powers. Popular movies, such as *The Kaiser, the Beast of Berlin,* as well as some CPI posters and speeches intensified this feeling by portraying Germany as a cruel enemy. Some Americans wrongly generalized that if Germany was cruel, then all German people were cruel.

Eugene V. Debs Protests

In June 1918, Socialist leader Eugene V. Debs was arrested for making an antiwar speech in Canton, Ohio (below). While in prison, Debs accepted the Socialist Party's nomination for President and won more than 900,000 votes in the 1920 election.

As a result, Americans stopped teaching German in public schools and discontinued playing the music of Beethoven and Brahms. They renamed German measles "liberty measles," cooked "liberty steaks" instead of hamburgers, and walked their "liberty pups" instead of dachshunds. German Americans were pressured to prove their loyalty to America by condemning the German government, giving up speaking German and reading German-language newspapers, and participating enthusiastically in any patriotic drive. Occasionally, hatred of the German enemy boiled over into violence against German Americans. Some German Americans were harassed, others were beaten, and a few were killed for no other reason than they were born in Germany or spoke with a German accent.

✔ **Checkpoint** Compare and contrast the reasons some Americans did not support the war.

Answer

✔ Most Americans came to support the war. However, some continued to oppose it. Some opposed the draft and refused to cooperate with the Selective Service process. Some opposed the war because it gave rise to government action that limited individual rights. Some women opposed the war and worked for peace. Some immigrants, especially from Germany, opposed the war because they supported the Central Powers' cause.

Differentiated Instruction   Solutions for All Learners

L1 Special Needs Students   **L2 English Language Learners**   **L2 Less Proficient Readers**

Pair struggling readers with more advanced learners. As a way to help students understand the relationships presented in the text, have each pair create a cause-and-effect chart for each red heading ("Resistance to the Draft," "Women Work for Peace," "The Government Cracks Down on Dissent," and "Prejudice Against German Americans").

Remind students that there can be more than one cause that produces a single effect. Similarly, there can be more than one effect produced by a single cause. Have pairs of students discuss their charts with other pairs.

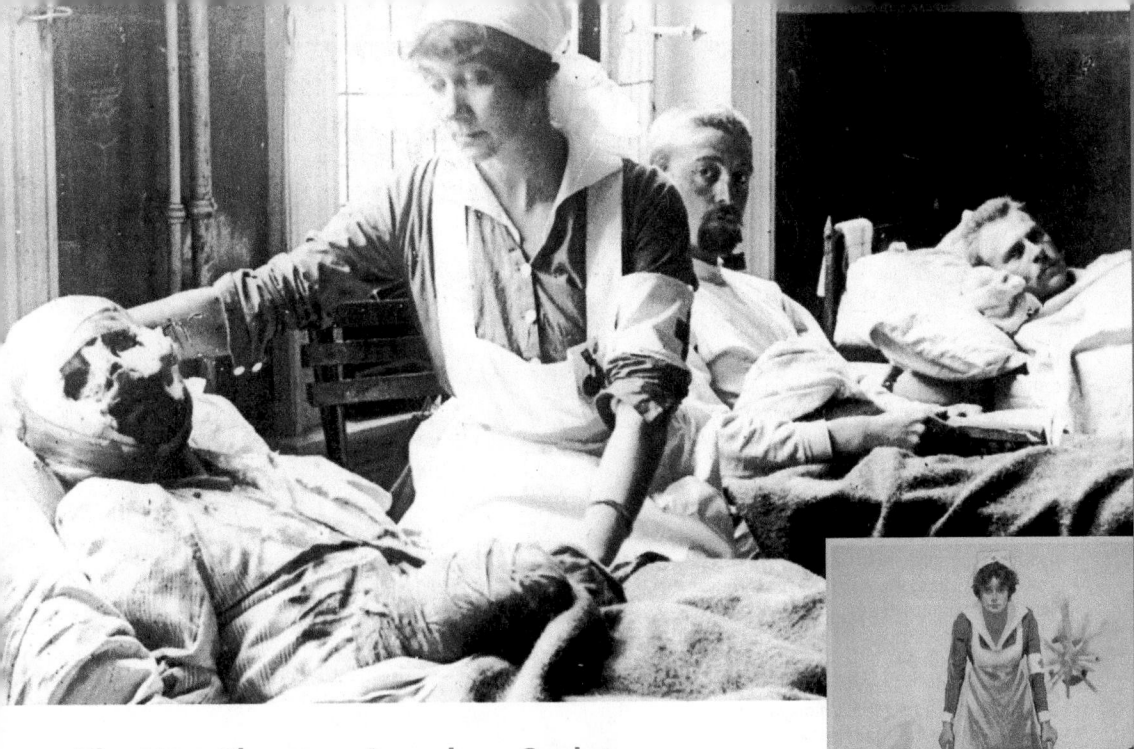

The War Changes American Society

The war not only changed the economic and political lives of Americans, but it also brought substantial social changes. New opportunities opened up for women, African Americans, and Mexican Americans. Some left their homes to seek new ones where they could take advantage of these opportunities.

Women Embrace New Opportunities Before the war, some American women campaigned for women's suffrage. They won the vote in several western states and still hoped to gain the franchise nationally. Many feared that the war would draw attention away from their efforts. In fact, the war gave women new chances and won them the right to vote.

As men entered the armed forces, many women moved into the workforce for the first time. Women filled jobs that were vacated by men who had gone to fight. They worked in munitions factories, on the railroads, as telegraph operators and trolley conductors, and in other jobs that were previously open only to men. Others labored on farms. Some joined the Red Cross or the American Women's Hospital Service and went overseas. They worked as doctors, nurses, ambulance drivers, and clerks. Thousands enlisted when the Army Corps of Nurses was created in 1918. Women proved that they could succeed in any type of job, regardless of difficulty or risk.

By their efforts and sacrifices during the war, women convinced President Wilson to support their suffrage demands. He contended that granting the vote to women was "vital to winning the war." If women could do the work of men, they certainly deserved the same voting privileges as men. Finally, in 1919, Congress passed the Nineteenth Amendment giving the vote to women. The required two thirds of states ratified the amendment in the summer of 1920, a victory more than 70 years in the making.

Nursing the Wounded

About 18,000 American Red Cross nurses cared for wounded soldiers and civilians during World War I. Their job was difficult and often dangerous—nearly 300 nurses lost their lives. The poster above urges civilians to do their part to support the Red Cross.

Connect to Your World

Nursing Nurses played an important role in caring for the sick and wounded during World War I. Today, nurses work to prevent disease, promote health, and help patients cope with illness. With today's aging population and changing healthcare system, nursing is a continually expanding field. Nurses work in a variety of environments, including hospitals, nursing homes, schools, and rehabilitation centers.

In addition to treating patients, nurses also work in administration, management, and research. A registered nurse must first pass state or national licensing exams and should have an associate's degree or bachelor's degree in nursing. Nursing is a good career option for those who enjoy working with people and are caring, sympathetic, responsible, and detail-oriented.

The War Changes American Society 🔵

Instruct

- **Introduce: Key Term** Write the term *Great Migration* on the board. Ask students to predict the meaning of the term. Explain that the *Great Migration* was a movement, during World War I, of a large number of African Americans from the agricultural South to the industrial North. Direct students' attention to the Primary Source quotation from the *Chicago Defender* on the last page of this section. Ask **Why might African Americans want to migrate from the South to the North?** *(to escape prejudice, to find better jobs and earn higher wages, to reconnect with family already living in the North)*

- **Teach** Use the images on this page to begin a discussion with students about how the entrance of the United States into the war created new opportunities for women. Using the Idea Wave strategy (TE, p. T22), discuss the causes and effects of these social changes among women, African Americans, and Mexican Americans. Ask **What circumstances allowed these social changes to take place?** *(Many men left their jobs to fight in the war. The number of available jobs also rose because industrial production for war supplies increased. The need for agricultural products also increased, leading to a need for more farmworkers.)* Then, display Color Transparency: *The Great Migration.* Use the lesson in the transparency book to guide a discussion about the Great Migration. Color Transparencies A-87

- **Analyzing the Visuals** Direct students' attention to the Focus On Geography Feature on the next page. After they read the feature, have students close their books. Read one of the push or pull factors, and have students identify whether it was a reason for leaving the South or a reason to go to the North.

Independent Practice

- To make sure that students understand the migration of African Americans to the North, have students complete the worksheet *Geography and History: The Great Migration.* Teaching Resources, **p. 20**

- Have students complete the note-taking chart they started at the beginning of the section by summarizing the social changes brought about by the U.S. entrance into World War I.

Monitor Progress

- To review this section, ask students to summarize the social changes, including the Great Migration, that occurred on the home front during World War I.

- As students fill in their charts, circulate to make sure that they understand the social effects the war had on the home front. For a completed version of the summary chart, see Note Taking Transparencies, **B-96.**

Answer

Geography and History World War I created a labor shortage in two ways. Thousands of men left their jobs to fight in the war. In addition, new jobs were created as industrial and agricultural demands increased to meet the military's war needs. These increased demands led to economic prosperity in northern cities.

186 World War I and Beyond

Focus On Geography

The Great Migration During World War I and after, several push factors caused thousands of African Americans to decide to move away from their homes in the South. A handful of pull factors drew them to new homes in the North.

Pushed from the South by...
- Jim Crow segregation laws
- Lynchings and other racial violence
- Low-paying jobs as sharecroppers or servants
- Ruined cotton crops due to boll weevil infestation

Pulled to the North by...
- Economic prosperity in northern cities
- Job openings due to reduced immigration
- Aid from African Americans in the North

Geography and History How did World War I contribute to the prosperity and labor shortage that caused migration?

African Americans Follow Opportunity North The war similarly presented new opportunities to African Americans. From the outset, most African American leaders supported the war. "If this is our country, then this is our war," wrote African American leader W.E.B. Du Bois. He viewed the struggle as an excellent opportunity to show all Americans the loyalty and patriotism of African Americans. Thousands of them enlisted or were drafted into the army and sailed for the battlefields of France. On the battlefield, they fought in segregated units under the command of white officers. Altogether, 367,000 African Americans served in the military. Hundreds died for their country.

Meanwhile, a great movement of African Americans from the rural South to the industrial North was taking place. This movement to the "Land of Hope," as many African Americans referred to the North at that time, is called the **Great Migration.** African Americans left their homes in the South for many reasons. Some hoped to escape the violent racism of the South. Others desired better jobs and a chance for economic advancement, which wartime industry in the North offered. Still others dreamed of a better future for their children. Between 1910 and 1920, more than 1.2 million African Americans moved to the North.

Some whites in the South tried to get blacks to stay in the region of their birth, using methods that ranged from persuasion to violence. Meanwhile, African

---

Differentiated Instruction Solutions for All Learners

L1 Special Needs Students **L2 English Language Learners** **L2 Less Proficient Readers**

Use Color Transparency: *The Great Migration* to help students understand the impact of World War I on African Americans. Use the map to help them trace the movement and ask them to describe the migration from the South to the North.

Pair students, and have them quiz each other about the Great Migration using the Color Transparency and the Focus on Geography feature to complement their lesson.

Americans who already lived in the North encouraged migration. Newspapers in the North, such as the Chicago *Defender*, an African American newspaper that was widely read in the South, pushed home this point:

Primary Source "I beg you, my brother, to leave the benighted land.... Get out of the South.... Come north then, all you folks, both good and bad.... The *Defender* says come."

— *Chicago Defender*

African Americans moved to Chicago, as the *Defender* encouraged, where they found work in meatpacking plants. They migrated to Detroit, where they obtained jobs in auto factories. They traveled to smaller industrial towns in the Midwest and to the giant cities of the Northeast. Millions eventually made the exodus, and although they did not entirely escape discrimination, many did forge better futures. The Great Migration was one of the most important episodes in African American history.

Mexican Americans Move North Some of the same reasons that led African Americans to move north caused Mexicans to cross the border into the United States. Many Mexicans also faced violence and desperate poverty, and they also wanted better lives for themselves and their children. Most immigrated to the American West, where they sought work on large ranches and farms in Texas and along the Pacific Coast. Increased demands for food and a decrease in American farmworkers created jobs that Mexican migrants filled.

Some of the Mexican migration was seasonal. Many workers crossed the border to harvest fruits or grains or to pick cotton while each crop was in season, then crossed back into Mexico. But others stayed and made the United States their home. Some Mexican workers migrated first to the Southwest and then to the northern states in search of factory jobs, but a large population stayed in California. They formed *barrios* (BAHR ee ohz), or Hispanic neighborhoods, in Los Angeles and in smaller cities in California's Imperial Valley. California had always had a rich Hispanic heritage, but these new immigrants added an important economic dimension to that heritage.

✓ **Checkpoint** How did the war provide new opportunities for women, African Americans, and Mexican Americans?

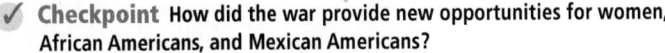

SECTION 2 Assessment

Progress Monitoring Online
For: Self-test with vocabulary practice
www.pearsonschool.com/ushist

Comprehension

1. **Terms and People** For each item below, write a sentence explaining how it affected the American home front during World War I.
   - Selective Service Act
   - Bernard Baruch
   - CPI
   - George Creel
   - conscientious objector
   - Espionage Act
   - Great Migration

2. **NoteTaking** **Reading Skill Summarize** Use your chart to answer the Section Focus Question: How did the war affect Americans at home?

Writing About History

3. **Quick Write: Identify Multiple Effects** Write a paragraph describing three effects that World War I had on the American home front. Think about economic and social changes caused by the war. Be sure to include at least one example of each effect to support your statements.

Critical Thinking

4. **Categorize** In what ways did Americans support the war effort?

5. **Identify Point of View** How did the Supreme Court justify the restrictions of the Sedition Act?

6. **Predict Consequences** How do you think returning soldiers reacted to changes at home when the war ended?

Assess and Reteach

Assess Progress L3

- Have students complete the Section Assessment.

- Administer the Section Quiz. Teaching Resources, **p. 27**

- To further assess student understanding, use Progress Monitoring Transparencies, **92.**

Reteach

If students need more instruction, have them read the section summary.

Reading and Note Taking Study Guide L3

Adapted Reading and Note Taking Study Guide L1 L2

Spanish Reading and Note Taking Study Guide L2

Extend L4

See this chapter's Professional Development pages for the Extend Online activity on propaganda.

Answer

✓ Women successfully performed jobs that had once been done only by men. Their efforts contributed to the passage of the Nineteenth Amendment. War enlistment opened up employment opportunities for African Americans who moved North in the Great Migration. The war also created an increased need for food supplies and a decrease in the number of American farmworkers, which attracted Mexican workers to the United States to fill these jobs.

Section 2 Assessment

1. Sentences should reflect an understanding of each listed term.

2. Even though the war was fought in Europe, Americans at home were affected. Men were drafted. There was an economic shift toward the production of war goods. Civil liberties were curtailed. New job opportunities became available to women, African Americans, and Mexican Americans.

3. Paragraphs should describe three effects that are supported by examples from the text.

4. Americans supported the war effort by volunteering to fight, taking jobs vacated by men who had gone to war, conserving food, and buying war bonds.

5. The Supreme Court ruled that during extreme times, such as wartime, the need for public order was so pressing that the First Amendment protections on speech should be set aside in favor of national security.

6. Possible response: Returning soldiers will go back to their jobs, displacing women and African Americans. The soldiers probably will also have trouble readjusting to life in the United States after fighting in the war.

For additional assessment, have students access **Progress Monitoring Online** at **www.pearsonschool.com/ushist**

Landmark Decisions of the Supreme Court

What Are the Limits of Free Speech?

What Are the Limits of Free Speech?

Objectives

- Describe First Amendment protections of free speech and the different forms that free speech may take.

- Understand that there are limits to free speech.

- Analyze Supreme Court decisions regarding free speech.

Background Knowledge ⬛L3

Discuss the First Amendment and its protection of the right of free speech. Then review the circumstances of *Schenck* v. *United States*. Examine how public opinion in 1917 might have differed from opinion during the 1960s.

Instruct ⬛L3

- Ask students to describe different forms of public speech (verbal speech, signs, pamphlets, letters, advertisements, newspapers, or television broadcasts). Ask **How do these forms of public speech constitute free speech as described in the First Amendment?** (*These examples constitute free speech in that they are public expressions.*)

- **Connect to Your World** Refer students to the Key Supreme Court Cases section for summaries of this case. You may also wish students to conduct additional research using **www.pearsonschool.com/ushist**. Responses should show a clear understanding of the case chosen and specific reasons why students agree or disagree with the decision.

- Have students complete the *Landmark Decisions of the Supreme Court: What Are the Limits of Free Speech?* worksheet. Teaching Resources, **p. 21**

Monitor Progress

Review the concept of "clear and present danger" and ask students to write a short paragraph on how this idea can affect national security or individual rights.

What Are the Limits of Free Speech?

The First Amendment guarantees that each person has the right to free speech, both spoken and written. It protects the right of people to have their say and to hear what others have to say. But can the government limit freedom of speech in order to protect the rights or safety of individuals and the nation?

Schenck v. *United States* (1919)

The Facts	The Issue	The Decision
• During World War I, Charles Schenck was convicted of violating the Espionage Act of 1917, which made it a crime to cause refusal of duty in the military. • Schenck had distributed pamphlets urging men to resist the military draft.	Schenck's appeal to the Supreme Court argued that his actions were protected by the First Amendment.	The Court unanimously upheld Schenck's conviction and said that in times of war the government may place reasonable limitations on freedom of speech.

Why It Matters

The Supreme Court reasoned that there are limits to freedom of speech. Justice Oliver Wendell Holmes pointed out that one does not have the right to falsely shout "Fire!" in a crowded theater and cause a panic. He then set his famous "clear and present danger" test for determining the limits of the First Amendment protection of speech.

> "The question in every case is whether the words used are used in such circumstances and are of such a nature as to create a clear and present danger that they will bring about the substantive evils that Congress has a right to prevent."

The Supreme Court has protected the right to express unpopular ideas. But the Court has also said that free speech is limited. There are laws against making false and damaging statements about others, either written (libel) or spoken (slander). Other restrictions include obscenities, words that incite violence, and words that pose an immediate threat to individuals or to national security.

▲ A World War I–era poster

Connect to Your World

What are the limits of free speech in schools? Select one of the cases below. Research and summarize the facts of the case, the Court's decision, and the reasoning behind the decision. Explain why you agree or disagree with the decision.

- *Tinker* v. *Des Moines School District* (1969)
- *Hazelwood School District* v. *Kuhlmeier* (1988)

For: Supreme Court cases
www.pearsonschool.com/ushist

◄ **Free Speech in School**
In 1969, Mary Beth Tinker went to the Supreme Court to test her right to protest the Vietnam War in school.

History Background

Taking on the Supreme Court Mary Beth Tinker was a 13-year-old student when she arrived at school wearing a black armband. It was 1965, America was fighting the Vietnam War, and Mary Beth used the armband to show her support for a Christmas truce in Vietnam. Since she and her brother had been old enough to hold picket signs, they had accompanied their parents on civil rights demonstrations. As Quakers, the Tinkers were also pacifists, or opposed to war. The school board viewed the armband as a "disturbing influence" and ordered Mary Beth, her brother, and a friend not to wear them. The students refused and were suspended. The Tinker family hired an attorney, who eventually presented the case to the Supreme Court. Justice Abe Fortas's 1969 ruling in favor of Mary Beth established an important milestone in the history of the First Amendment. Today, Mary Beth Tinker works as a nurse and still follows free speech cases closely, especially if they involve the rights of young people.

WITNESS HISTORY

War Enthusiasm

Although the first American troops arrived in France in 1917, American soldiers did not reach France in great numbers until 1918. George M. Cohan's song "Over There" was used effectively to recruit troops and raise morale.

❝Over there, over there.
Send the word, send the word over there,
That the Yanks are coming,
The Yanks are coming . . .
So prepare, say a pray'r,
Send the word, send the word to beware.
We'll be over, we're coming over,
and we won't come back till it's over
Over there.❞

—From the song "Over There," written by George M. Cohan in 1917

▲ "Over There" sheet music

▲ American troops disembark in France.

Wilson, War, and Peace

Objectives

- Understand how the United States military contributed to the Allied victory in the war.
- Describe the aims of the Fourteen Points.
- Analyze the decisions made at the Paris Peace Conference.
- Explain why the United States Senate refused to ratify the treaty ending World War I.

Terms and People

convoy	League of Nations
Vladimir Lenin	Henry Cabot Lodge
John J. Pershing	reparations
Fourteen Points	"irreconcilables"
self-determination	"reservationists"

NoteTaking

Reading Skill: Sequence As you read, sequence the events leading to the end of World War I in a timeline.

U-boat war intensifies.		Armistice ends war.
March 1917		Nov. 1918

Why It Matters When the United States entered World War I in the spring of 1917, the conflict had become a deadly, bloody stalemate. The war would be won or lost on the Western Front in France. Since 1914, both sides had tried desperately to break the stalemate there—and failed. The American entry into the war would play a key role in the Allied victory. **Section Focus Question: How did Americans affect the end of World War I and its peace settlements?**

America Gives the Allies the Edge

To European leaders, the United States was a great unknown. Ethnic divisions in America raised questions about how committed American troops would be in combat. Some doubted that the United States could raise, train, equip, and transport an army fast enough to influence the outcome of the war. Desperate German military leaders renewed unrestricted submarine warfare, hoping to end the conflict before the Americans could make a difference.

Allied Convoys Protect Shipping The Allies immediately felt the impact of the renewed unrestricted submarine warfare. German U-boats sank merchant ships in alarming numbers, faster than replacements could be built. As one merchant ship after another sank to the bottom of the sea, the Allies lost crucial supplies.

Together, the Allies addressed the problem of submarine warfare by adopting an old naval tactic: convoying. In a **convoy**, groups of

Prepare to Read

Background Knowledge L3

Ask students to predict what will happen to the strength and confidence of the Allies when American soldiers join World War I.

Set a Purpose L3

- **WITNESS HISTORY** Read the selection aloud. Ask **What do you think was the purpose of this song?** *(to motivate troops)* **Do you think it fulfills its purpose?** *(Possible answer: Yes, it fills listeners with pride in their country and a desire to volunteer.)*

- **Focus** Point out the Section Focus Question, and write it on the board. Tell students to refer to this question as they read. *(Answer appears with Section 3 Assessment answers.)*

- **Preview** Have students preview the Section Objectives and the list of Terms and People.

- **Reading Skill** Have students use the *Reading Strategy: Sequence* worksheet. Teaching Resources, **p. 12**

- **NoteTaking** Using the Guided Questioning strategy (TE, p. T20), have students read this section. As they read, have students fill in the timeline to sequence the events that led to the end of the war. Reading and Note Taking Study Guide

Vocabulary Builder

Use the information below and the following resource to teach students the high-use words from this section. Teaching Resources, Vocabulary Builder, p. 11

High-Use Words	Definitions and Sample Sentences
mutual	*adj.* shared The countries had a **mutual** agreement to end the war.
contradict	*v.* to go against The Supreme Court overturns laws that **contradict** the U.S. Constitution.

America Gives the Allies the Edge Ⓛ3

Instruct

- **Introduce: Key Term and Vocabulary Builder** Have students locate the key term *convoy* and the vocabulary term *mutual* in the text. Explain that the Allies devised a strategy to protect their ships from German U-boats. Use the illustration of the *convoy* on the map to aid your explanation. Tell students that merchant ships and warships traveled together in a *convoy*, which provided the merchant ships and the warships *mutual* protection from the U-boats.

- **Teach** Discuss how the U.S. military presence changed the outcome of the war. Ask **What was the goal of the Allies' convoys?** *(to provide mutual protection to warships and merchant ships from German U-boats)* **Was the strategy successful?** *(Yes; fewer ships were sunk by U-boats.)* **Describe how the entrance of America led to the end of the war.** *(The German military weakened with each battle, and the Allies' hope for victory increased. Eventually, the Central Powers were forced to surrender because their troops refused to fight any longer.)* Have students discuss the results of World War I and predict the outcome of the peace talks that followed the war. Have students read the HISTORY MAKERS biography of Pershing on this page. Ask students to summarize the importance of Pershing's role in the war.

Vocabulary Builder
mutual–(MYOO choo uhl) *adj.* shared

merchant ships sailed together, protected by warships. The arrangement was designed to provide <u>mutual</u> safety at sea. Convoys made up of British and American ships proved to be an instant success. Shipping losses from U-boat attacks fell as sharply as they had risen. Germany's gamble had failed.

The Allies Struggle Meanwhile, the situation on land began to swing in favor of the Central Powers. The Allies were exhausted by years of combat. Russia was torn by revolutions. In March 1917, a moderate, democratic revolution overthrew Czar Nicholas II but kept Russia in the war. In November 1917, radical communists led by **Vladimir Lenin** (LEHN ihn) staged a revolution and gained control of Russia. Russia stopped fighting in mid-December, and on March 3, 1918, the Treaty of Brest-Litovsk ended the war between Russia (soon to become the Soviet Union) and Germany. The end of the war on the Eastern Front allowed Germany to send more soldiers to the Western Front.

In the spring of 1918, Germany launched an all-out offensive on the Western Front. The fierce attacks threatened to break through Allied defenses and open a path to Paris. The hard-pressed Allies organized a joint command under French General Ferdinand Foch (fawsh).

American Troops Join the Fight General **John J. Pershing,** the commander of American forces in Europe, arrived in France in June 1917, with a small American force. However, it was not until early 1918 that American troops began arriving in larger numbers. At about the same time, the German offensive began to stall. By the end of March 1918, Allied counterattacks and German exhaustion ended the great German offensive.

More fighting followed, and with each passing week, American troops assumed more of the burden on the battlefield. Germany launched several more offensives. Allied defenses buckled and stretched but did not break. Each failed offensive weakened Germany a bit more and raised Allied hopes.

American Troops Distinguish Themselves American troops called "doughboys," saw significant action in the late spring and summer of 1918. Americans fought on the defensive along with the French at the Second Battle of the Marne and on the offensive at the Battle of Cantigny (kahn tee NYEE), where they dislodged a large German force from fortified positions. They battled valiantly at Château-Thierry (sha TOH tir EE) and Belleau (beh LOH) Wood, Meuse-Argonne (myooz ahr GAHN) and Saint-Mihiel (mee YEHL). Although it took some time, American troops learned quickly and fought bravely.

HISTORY MAKERS

John J. Pershing (1860–1948)
John J. Pershing was an experienced soldier and leader who had fought in several wars before the beginning of American involvement in World War I. After the U.S. declaration of war, Pershing guided the creation of the American Expeditionary Force. He faced the difficult task of turning millions of untrained men into an effective fighting force. He then led this force in France. His skill in doing so helped the Allies win the war.

One of America's greatest war heroes was Alvin York of Tennessee. On October 8, 1918, York was one of thousands of Americans fighting in the Meuse-Argonne region of northeastern France. Trapped behind enemy lines, York and 16 other Americans took cover from blistering machine-gun fire. As half of the American force fell to German bullets, York took aim with his rifle and silenced a nearby German machine-gun nest. He then dodged a flurry of bullets to attack several other machine gunners and even charged one German position with only a pistol! When the firefight died down, York and the surviving Americans had taken the German position against amazing odds. York's battlefield heroics earned him a Congressional Medal of Honor.

Differentiated Instruction   Solutions for All Learners

Ⓛ4 Advanced Readers   Ⓛ4 Gifted and Talented Students

Explain that convoys were first used to protect merchant ships from pirates. During World War I, the Allies effectively used convoys to protect their merchant ships and ensure that necessary supplies were delivered. In order for a German U-boat to strike a merchant ship in a convoy, it would first come under attack by the British warships, which contained heavy artillery, torpedoes, and depth charges.

Tell students that convoys were also used in World War II. Have them conduct research to determine how convoys changed from World War I to World War II, and whether the World War II convoys were more, less, or equally effective. Students should write a summation essay and include details about the changes in convoy strategy (sonar, air escorts, voice radio communications, and so on) and the changes in German U-boat warfare ("wolf packs" of 8 to 20 submarines attacking a convoy).

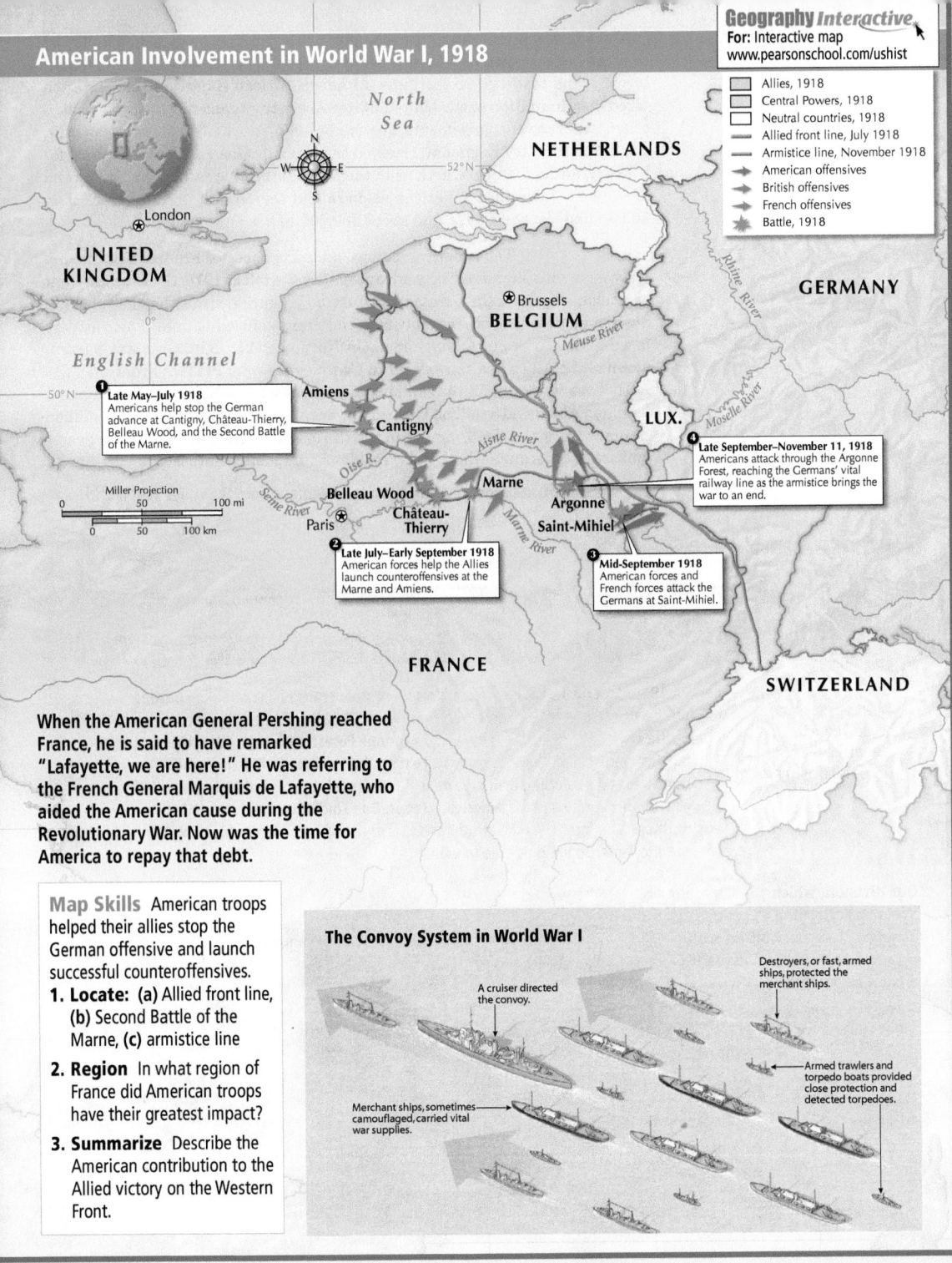

American Involvement in World War I, 1918

Geography *Interactive*
For: Interactive map
www.pearsonschool.com/ushist

Key

- Allies, 1918
- Central Powers, 1918
- Neutral countries, 1918
- Allied front line, July 1918
- Armistice line, November 1918
- American offensives
- British offensives
- French offensives
- Battle, 1918

North Sea

NETHERLANDS

52°N

London

UNITED KINGDOM

English Channel

50°N

Brussels

BELGIUM

Meuse River

Rhine River

GERMANY

LUX.

Moselle River

Amiens

❶ Late May–July 1918
Americans help stop the German advance at Cantigny, Château-Thierry, Belleau Wood, and the Second Battle of the Marne.

Cantigny

Aisne River

Oise R.

❹ Late September–November 11, 1918
Americans attack through the Argonne Forest, reaching the Germans' vital railway line as the armistice brings the war to an end.

Miller Projection
0   50   100 mi
0   50   100 km

Belleau Wood

Seine River

Paris

Château-Thierry

Marne

Argonne

Saint-Mihiel

Marne River

❷ Late July–Early September 1918
American forces help the Allies launch counteroffensives at the Marne and Amiens.

❸ Mid-September 1918
American forces and French forces attack the Germans at Saint-Mihiel.

FRANCE

SWITZERLAND

When the American General Pershing reached France, he is said to have remarked "Lafayette, we are here!" He was referring to the French General Marquis de Lafayette, who aided the American cause during the Revolutionary War. Now was the time for America to repay that debt.

Map Skills American troops helped their allies stop the German offensive and launch successful counteroffensives.

1. **Locate:** (a) Allied front line, (b) Second Battle of the Marne, (c) armistice line

2. **Region** In what region of France did American troops have their greatest impact?

3. **Summarize** Describe the American contribution to the Allied victory on the Western Front.

The Convoy System in World War I

A cruiser directed the convoy.

Destroyers, or fast, armed ships, protected the merchant ships.

Armed trawlers and torpedo boats provided close protection and detected torpedoes.

Merchant ships, sometimes camouflaged, carried vital war supplies.

Differentiated Instruction   Solutions for All Learners

L1 Special Needs Students   **L2 English Language Learners**   **L2 Less Proficient Readers**

For students who need help with basic skills, direct their attention to the map. Remind students that the map shows how the arrival of the United States troops helped lead the Allies to victory. Ask volunteers to explain which part of the world is depicted on the map. With students, point out and discuss the map key and its contents. Have students trace the movement of the offensives and describe the progression. Point out the sequence of callouts and read them aloud. Help students understand that at the same time the troops were fighting on land, merchant ships and warships were traveling across the Atlantic to deliver needed supplies to the Allies.

Answers

Map Skills

1. Review locations with students.

2. in northeastern France, especially the Argonne Forest

3. Upon their arrival, American troops helped stop the German advance into France. They then helped launch counteroffensives against the Central Powers. They participated in direct attacks against the Germans. The result was a breakdown in the German army and victory for the Allies.

- Have students assume the role of speechwriters for the Committee on Public Information (CPI). Have them write brief speeches outlining the progress of the war, addressed to Americans on the home front. The speeches should use information from the text to describe the successful use of ground troops and convoys and the morale of the Allies and the Central Powers. Remind students to consider the tone a CPI writer would use when writing a speech for Americans.

- Have students access the History Interactive at **www.pearson-school.com/ushist.** After students experience the History Interactive, ask them to share their reactions by posing questions such as: What was it like to fight in World War I? What were some of the emotional effects? Why did soldiers keep journals during the war? Would you?

- NoteTaking Have students complete the timeline to sequence the events that led to the end of World War I.

Monitor Progress

- Have students present their CPI speeches to the class.

- As students fill in their timelines, circulate to make sure that they understand the sequence of events leading to the end of the war. For a completed version of the timeline, see Note Taking Transparencies, **B-97a.**

Alvin York was only one of thousands of heroes, many of whom died and most of whom were never recognized for their deeds. They followed orders, fought bravely, and made great sacrifices. Although African American soldiers often faced discrimination in the United States Army, they demonstrated their patriotism in dozens of engagements. For example, an entire African American unit, the 369th Infantry Regiment, received the *Croix de Guerre*, a French award for bravery, for its members' actions in the Meuse-Argonne campaign. By the end of the war, 1.3 million American soldiers had served on the front, more than 50,000 had lost their lives, and about 230,000 had been wounded.

The War Ends The American troops, added to those of France, Britain, and Italy, gave the Allies a military advantage. By the fall of 1918, the German front was collapsing. Both the German and Austro-Hungarian armies had had enough. Some men deserted, others mutinied, and many refused to fight. Their leaders faced little choice but to surrender. On November 11, 1918, Germany surrendered to the Allies in a railway car in Compiegne (kohn PYEHN), France.

The war was over. Of the millions of soldiers who mobilized to fight, almost 5 million Allied and 8 million Central Power troops were dead. Nearly 6.5 million civilians were also dead, victims of the terrible conflict. It was left to the peacemakers to determine whether the results would justify the costs.

✓ **Checkpoint** How did American involvement help the Allies win World War I?

● **INFOGRAPHIC**

American Voices From the Western Front

▲ American doughboy helmet, worn by a member of the first U.S. division in France

In 1918, Americans fought alongside other Allied troops in several key battles on the Western Front, including Belleau Wood, Château-Thierry, the Second Battle of the Marne, Saint-Mihiel, and Argonne Forest. Although all of these battles were Allied victories, they were nonetheless deadly. Machine-gun barrages and exploding artillery shells filled with shrapnel or deadly gas killed or wounded thousands of American troops. One soldier wrote home to his mother: "Don't worry. I am alright and it is worthwhile...we are blocking the road to Paris. So we don't die in vain."

"Our division, which went into action yesterday morning at practically full strength, has lost half its men. ...I am just beginning to realize what war really is."

—John Clark, fighting in the Second Battle of the Marne, July 19, 1918

American machine-gunners at Belleau Wood

History Background

Versailles Treaty In 1919 the Allies held a peace conference at Versailles, France. President Wilson promoted "peace without victory," but the other Allied leaders were not motivated by Wilson's idealism. The Allies blamed Germany for the war, and under the treaty, the Germans were forced to pay high reparations. Germany's economy suffered dramatically as payments were made to the Allies. The treaty had a negative impact on the country. The German people felt bitter and betrayed, and some wanted revenge. The radical right-wing German Workers' Party formed. Adolf Hitler joined this party, and rose to leadership of what would eventually become the Nazi Party.

Answer

✓ U.S. troops helped reverse the German advance and boosted Allied morale. U.S. ships assisted in protecting convoys.

Wilson Promotes Peace Without Victory

Vladimir Lenin, leader of the communist revolution in Russia, maintained that the entire war was nothing more than an imperialistic land-grab. Once in power, he exposed secret treaties that Russia had made with the other Allies in which they agreed to divide among themselves the empires of their enemies. These revelations undercut the morality of the Allied cause in the war.

For President Woodrow Wilson, however, the war was not about acquisitions and imperialism—it was about peace and freedom. In January 1917, Wilson had introduced the idea of a "peace without victory" in an address to Congress:

Primary Source "Only a tranquil Europe can be a stable Europe. . . . [There] must be a peace without victory. . . . Victory would mean peace forced upon the loser, a victor's terms imposed upon the vanquished. It would be accepted in humiliation . . . and would leave a sting, a resentment, a bitter memory upon which terms of peace would rest, not permanently, but only as upon quicksand."
—Woodrow Wilson, "Peace Without Victory" speech, January 22, 1917

In another address to Congress in January 1918, Wilson answered Lenin's charges about the nature of the conflict by outlining America's war aims in what became known as the **Fourteen Points.** At the heart of the Fourteen Points was his idea of "peace without victory." Wilson proposed a peace inspired by noble ideals, not greed and vengeance.

Military Casualties of World War I

Troops (in millions) — Russia, British Empire, France, Italy, United States (Allies); Germany, Austria-Hungary (Central Powers)

☐ Troops mobilized
▨ Troops killed, wounded, or missing

SOURCE: *Encyclopædia Britannica Online*

"Sept 29 at 5.50 A.M. Several men were gassed before we went over. Advanced to top of ridge. Capt. Smith killed. 1st Lt. McKory and 2nd Lt. Kerr killed later. No officers left. Piece of shrapnel hit helmet and went through canister of my gas mask."
—Corporal Wilfred H. Allen, fighting in late September 1918

Private Martin P. Coogan
75th Field Artillery

Gas mask ▶

American soldiers bandaged after a gas attack ▼

Devastated battlefield near Ypres

Thinking Critically
Why do you think American casualties were relatively few compared with the casualties of the other combatants?

History *Interactive* ✴

For: Interactive content
www.pearsonschool.com/ushist

Wilson at the Paris Peace Conference L3

Instruct

- **Introduce: Key Term** Have students find the key term *reparations* (in bold) in the text and explain its definition. Ask them to predict the problems with making the defeated countries pay the victors for war damage.

- **Teach** Tell students that Germany was not a part of the negotiations at the Paris Peace Conference. Using the Numbered Heads strategy (TE, p. T23), have students discuss the difference between Wilson's goals and those of the other Allied leaders at the peace conference. Ask **Why might Clemenceau have been more concerned than Wilson with making Germany unable to fight another war?** *(France borders Germany; the United States does not. France lost many more people than did the United States during the war.)* **What was the outcome of the Paris Peace Conference?** *(The Allies drafted a treaty for Germany that was quite different from Wilson's Fourteen Points. The treaty did not include freedom of the seas, free trade, colonial liberation, or disarmament. It did include a League of Nations.)*

NoteTaking

Reading Skill: Summarize As you read, summarize Wilson's goals for peace and whether or not each goal was fulfilled.

Wilson's Ideas for Peace	Decision Made at Paris Peace Conference
Peace without victory	Great Britain and France make Germany pay reparations.
Open diplomacy	
Freedom of seas and free trade	
Move toward ending colonialism	
Self-determination	
League of Nations	

The Fourteen Points sought to fundamentally change the world by promoting openness, encouraging independence, and supporting freedom. Critical of all secret treaties, Wilson called for open diplomacy. He insisted on freedom of the seas, free trade, a move toward ending colonialism, and a general reduction of armaments. He also championed national **self-determination,** or the right of people to choose their own form of government. This would lead to the creation of several new, independent states but also raised many questions of which populations would achieve statehood and under what circumstances. Finally, he asked for a **League of Nations** to secure "mutual guarantees of political independence and territorial integrity to great and small states alike."

In early 1919, the victorious Allies held a peace conference in Versailles (ver Sī), a suburb of Paris, in the former palace of Louis XIV. President Wilson believed that the peace conference was too important to be left to career diplomats and lesser politicians, so he crossed the Atlantic Ocean himself to represent the United States at the conference, something no President had ever done.

Wilson did not invite any leading Republicans to join him in his peace delegation. Senator **Henry Cabot Lodge,** a Republican foreign policy expert, was left behind because Wilson disliked him intensely. Wilson's decision angered Republicans, who had won control of Congress in the 1918 elections. However, when the American President arrived in France, adoring crowds greeted him. "Never has a king, never has an emperor received such a welcome," wrote one journalist.

✓ **Checkpoint** Why did Wilson believe that a "peace without victory" would help avoid future wars?

Wilson at the Paris Peace Conference

Wilson's idealism did not inspire the other Allied leaders at the peace conference. They blamed Germany for starting the war, reminded Wilson that they had suffered more in the war than the United States, and insisted that Germany make **reparations,** or payment for war damages. They wanted to weaken Germany so that it would never threaten Europe again.

HISTORY MAKERS

Woodrow Wilson (1856–1924)
Before entering politics, Woodrow Wilson was first a professor and then the president of Princeton University. He brought his intellect and his idealism to the presidency. Wilson believed that relations between nations should be based on the principles of collective security and the common good. During the Paris Peace Conference, he urged other nations to form an international organization that could be used to promote peace. Although the League of Nations was ultimately unable to ensure peace in Europe, it laid the groundwork for the United Nations, which the United States took an active role in creating after World War II.

Allied Leaders Reject Wilson's Ideas British prime minister David Lloyd-George and French premier Georges Clemenceau (klay mahn SOH) knew that the citizens of their countries expected both peace and victory. Lloyd-George insisted on protecting the existing colonial status quo and punishing Germany. Clemenceau wanted to make Germany pay dearly for what it had done to France. In addition to reparations, he demanded the return of Alsace-Lorraine and several key German colonies. Besides Britain and France, other Allies also had goals of their own and were skeptical of Wilson's grand vision.

Allies Create a League of Nations Once the Versailles conference began, Clemenceau, Lloyd-George, Italian Premier Vittorio Orlando, and other Allied leaders started to chip away at Wilson's Fourteen Points. Onto the scrap heap of failed proposals they piled freedom of the seas, free trade, the liberation of colonial empires, a general disarmament, and several other ideas.

Differentiated Instruction Solutions for All Learners

L1 Special Needs Students   **L2 English Language Learners**   **L2 Less Proficient Readers**

Pair struggling readers with more advanced learners. Have each pair scan the information under the blue headings "Wilson Promotes Peace Without Victory," and "Wilson at the Paris Peace Conference." Have student pairs make a two-column chart. In the first column, students should list Wilson's goals for the conference. In the second column, students should list any of the remainder of the Allies' goals for the conference. Encourage pairs to determine which goals Wilson was willing to sacrifice. Have students

discuss why Wilson agreed to give up some of his principles and why he was unwilling to abandon the idea of the League of Nations. Also, have them discuss why Wilson and other Allied leaders disagreed about what provisions the treaties should contain.

To help students understand Wilson's peace proposals, have them complete the worksheet *Primary Source: The Fourteen Points.* Teaching Resources, **p. 23**

Answer

✓ Wilson believed that if the terms of the treaty were not punitive, but encouraged self-determination, future wars might be avoided. He believed that if victors punished losers, there would be resentment in Europe and future wars could result. He considered his proposal a way to achieve peace without victory.

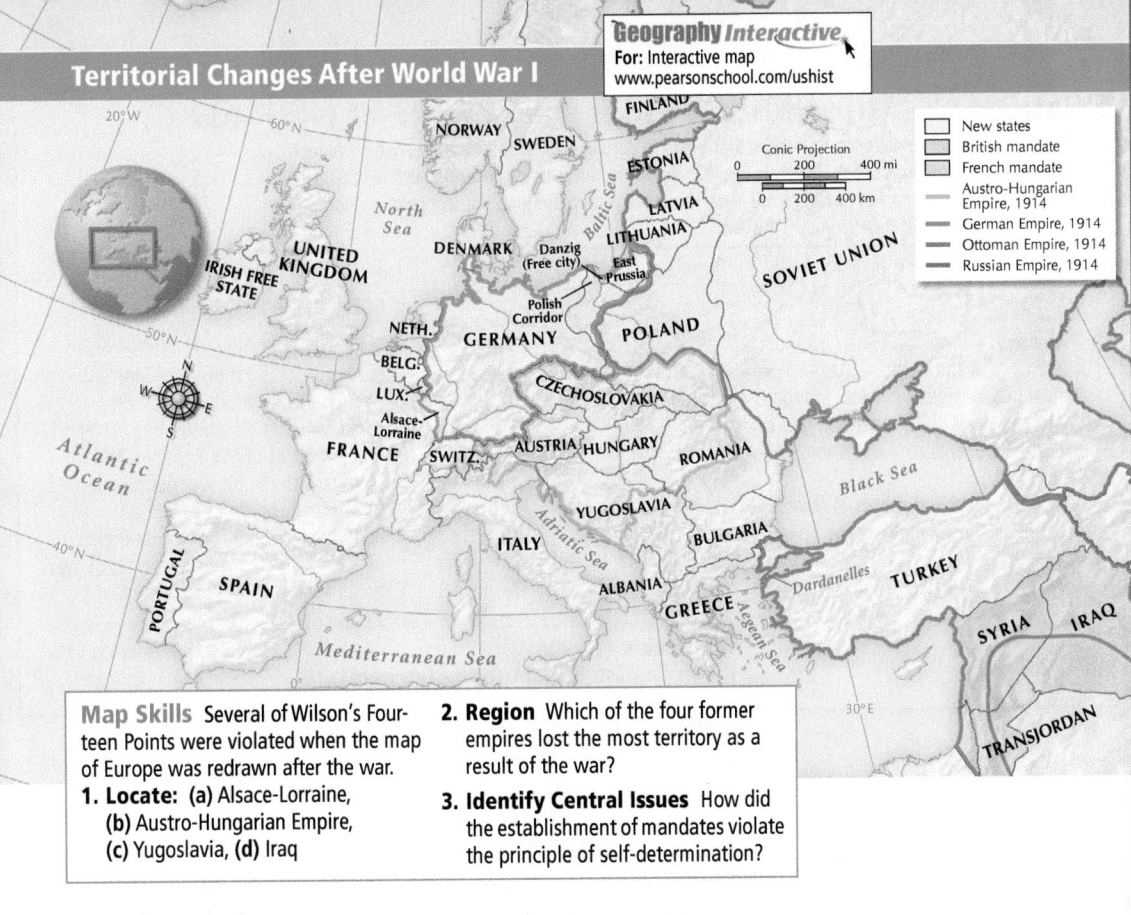

Territorial Changes After World War I

Geography *Interactive*
For: Interactive map
www.pearsonschool.com/ushist

Conic Projection

0   200   400 mi

0   200   400 km

New states
British mandate
French mandate
Austro-Hungarian Empire, 1914
German Empire, 1914
Ottoman Empire, 1914
Russian Empire, 1914

Map Skills Several of Wilson's Fourteen Points were violated when the map of Europe was redrawn after the war.
1. Locate: (a) Alsace-Lorraine, **(b)** Austro-Hungarian Empire, **(c)** Yugoslavia, **(d)** Iraq

2. Region Which of the four former empires lost the most territory as a result of the war?

3. Identify Central Issues How did the establishment of mandates violate the principle of self-determination?

Wilson lost a number of battles but kept fighting to salvage a League of Nations, a world organization where countries could gather and peacefully resolve their quarrels. On this point, Wilson refused to compromise. The other delegates finally voted to make the League of Nations part of the treaty.

Problems With the Peace In the end, the various peace treaties created almost as many problems as they solved. In the new map that emerged from the conference, national self-determination was violated almost as often as it was confirmed. In Europe, several populations of Germans found themselves attached to non-German nations. The same was true of several Austrian populations.

Furthermore, in the Middle East, the breakup of the Ottoman Empire led to new states in which ethnic groups were clustered together randomly. To form Iraq, for example, the Versailles peacemakers threw together three provinces of the defeated Ottoman Empire—Basra, Baghdad, and Mosul. But Basra had natural links to the Persian Gulf and India, Baghdad to Persia, and Mosul to Turkey and Syria. The various regions had no sense of Iraqi nationalism. In addition, Iraq, like other holdings in the Middle East, Asia, and Africa, was not allowed to practice self-determination. It was attached to Britain as a mandate, or territory overseen by another nation.

✔ **Checkpoint** How did the decisions at the Paris Peace Conference violate the Fourteen Points?

Connect to Your World

The Middle East Arabs were outraged by the European-controlled mandates set up at the Paris Peace Conference. During the war, Arabs had helped the Allies against the Central Powers, especially the Ottoman Empire. The Allies led the Arabs to believe that following the war, they would gain independence. However, at the war's end, the Allies divided the Ottoman lands, giving France mandates in Syria and Lebanon and Britain mandates in Palestine and Iraq. Later, Trans-Jordan was separated from the British Palestine Mandate. The Balfour Declaration of 1917 promised the Jewish people a national home in the Palestine Mandate. Arabs felt betrayed by the West—a feeling that has endured to this day.

■ **Analyzing the Visuals** Ask students to study the map. Tell them to trace the outlines of the empires and describe their changes as a result of the Paris Peace Conference. Have students access **www.pearsonschool.com/ushist** to use the Geography Interactive map and then answer the map skills questions in the text.

Independent Practice

■ Have students read the HISTORY MAKERS biography of Woodrow Wilson. Ask them to explain the terms *collective security* and *common good* and describe how Wilson worked to achieve these goals.

■ NoteTaking Have students complete the Note Taking chart by filling in the second column.

Monitor Progress

■ Have students describe how President Wilson demonstrated his belief in and commitment to collective security and the common good.

■ For a completed version of the summarizing graphic organizer, see Note Taking Transparencies, **B-97b**.

Answers

Map Skills
1. Review locations with students.
2. Austro-Hungarian Empire
3. These new states were not allowed to practice self-determination. They became territories ruled by other nations.

✔ The decisions ignored the principle of self-determination, harshly punished the former Central Powers, and failed to include other ideas from the Fourteen Points, such as freedom of the seas, free trade, the liberation of colonial empires, and disarmament.

America Rejects the Treaty ⓛ³

Instruct

- **Introduce: Vocabulary Builder**
Have students read the Vocabulary Builder term and definition. Ask them to consider how the treaty *contradicted* the Fourteen Points. Ask students to predict how this might lead to problems in Germany and on the home front.

- **Teach** Ask **What were the different views in Congress regarding the treaty?** *(Some supported the treaty as it was written. Irreconcilables were isolationists who did not want the United States to be involved in world politics. They wanted the League of Nations removed from the treaty. Reservationists were in favor of parts of the treaty, but they wanted parts of it changed.)* **What was the result of the conflicting views?** *(The United States did not ratify the treaty.)*

- **Quick Activity** Have two volunteers read the quotations in the Decision Point feature. Then, have the class discuss them. Take a vote to determine whether the majority of students would have joined the League of Nations.

Independent Practice

- Assign students *Interpreting a Political Cartoon: The League of Nations* and answer the questions on the worksheet. Teaching Resources, **p. 22**

- Ask students to write a short argument from the viewpoint of a Wilson supporter, an irreconcilable, or a reservationist persuading other members of Congress to share their viewpoint regarding the treaty.

Monitor Progress

Circulate to ensure that students have constructed a clear central argument.

Answers

You Decide

1. He believed that granting both strong and weak countries voices in a world organization was essential for peace.

2. He believed that it violated sovereignty and democracy because being a member of the League of Nations would have bound the United States to decisions made partly by foreign powers.

3. Answers will vary but should reflect logical reasoning.

Should the United States Join the League of Nations?

After the Paris Peace Conference, the United States had to decide whether to join the League of Nations. The League's purpose was to help maintain peace in the world. In the political cartoon below, Wilson overloads a dove, a symbol of peace, with a large, heavy branch representing the League of Nations. Read the options below. Then you make the call.

President Wilson Favors Joining

Primary Source

❝A general association of nations must be formed . . . for the purpose of affording mutual guarantees of political independence and territorial integrity to great and small states alike. . . . It is the principle of justice to all peoples . . . and their right to live on equal terms . . . with one another, whether they be strong or weak.❞

—President Woodrow Wilson, January 8, 1918

Senator Borah Opposes Joining

Primary Source

❝Mr. President, there is another reason . . . why I shall record my vote against this treaty. It imperils what I conceive to be the underlying, the very first principles of this Republic. It is in conflict with the right of our people to govern themselves free from all restraint, legal or moral, of foreign powers. It challenges every tenet of my political faith.❞

—Senator William Borah, November 19, 1919

You Decide

1. Why did Wilson favor joining the League of Nations?
2. Why did Borah oppose joining?
3. What decision would you have made? Why?

America Rejects the Treaty

When Wilson left Versailles to return to the United States, he knew the treaty was not perfect. But he believed that over time the League could correct its problems. He still thought that a lasting peace could emerge.

Wilson Faces Troubles at Home Wilson did not leave his problems in France when he boarded a ship bound for the United States. German Americans thought the treaty was too harsh toward Germany, especially the "war guilt clause" that suggested that Germany had caused the war. Irish Americans criticized the failure to create an independent Ireland. Most importantly, however, the treaty would need to be submitted to the Republican-controlled Senate Foreign Relations Committee and then ratified, or approved, by the Republican-controlled Senate. In both bodies, as well as in his own Democratic Party, Wilson faced stiff opposition.

A handful of senators believed that the United States should not get entangled in world politics or involved in world organizations. Known as **"irreconcilables,"** these isolationist senators opposed any treaty that had a League of Nations folded into it. They particularly disliked Article 10 of the League covenant. Article 10 called for mutual defense by the signers of the treaty, a pledge that each nation would "respect and preserve . . . the territorial integrity and existing political independence of all the Members of the League."

A larger group of senators, led by Henry Cabot Lodge and known as **"reservationists,"** were opposed to the treaty as it was written. Some wanted only small changes, while others demanded larger ones. For example, many felt

---

Differentiated Instruction   Solutions for All Learners

ⓛ⁴ **Advanced Readers**   ⓛ⁴ **Gifted and Talented Students**

Have students use information from the section to write four diary entries, assuming the role of President Wilson or one of his supporters. The entries should be written for each of the following periods: (1) after writing and presenting the Fourteen Points; (2) on the way from the United States to Paris for the Paris Peace Conference; (3) on the way back to the United States after the peace conference ended; and (4) after presenting the treaty to Congress. Entries should include facts presented in the text, as well as expressions of the author's beliefs and feelings.

Article 10 could lead the United States into a war without the consent of Congress, which was unconstitutional. Reservationists believed that the language of the article was too vague and demanded that it not <u>contradict</u> the power of Congress to declare war. But with some changes, the reservationists were prepared to vote for the Treaty of Versailles. They knew that polls indicated that the American people favored the League of Nations.

Wilson had compromised in Versailles, but he was not ready to compromise in Washington, D.C. When the Senate delayed its ratification vote, Wilson took his case directly to the people. The League of Nations had become his personal crusade. Even though he was ill and weak, he set himself the grueling task of crossing the country and giving 32 addresses in 33 days. But his health failed on September 25, 1919, in Pueblo, Colorado. He was rushed back to Washington, D.C., but suffered a debilitating stroke a few days later. As the Senate prepared to vote on the treaty, Wilson lay close to death, barely able to speak.

The Senate Rejects the Versailles Treaty In November 1919, one year after the war ended, a treaty revised to eliminate the complaints of the reservationists reached the Senate for a vote. Wilson would not compromise and told his Democratic supporters to vote with the irreconcilables against it. They did, and it was defeated. Next, the Senate voted on the treaty without any changes. The Democrats voted for it, but the combined strength of the irreconcilables and reservationists defeated it. Once more it was voted on, this time with only modest changes. Again, Wilson told his followers to vote against it. Although some Democrats voted for it, the combination of Wilson Democrats and irreconcilables defeated the treaty.

The problem was not that most of the Senate was isolationist. Except for the irreconcilables, most senators wanted the United States to participate in world affairs. They differed slightly on what form that participation would take. However, at a moment that demanded compromise, Wilson and his opponents refused to put aside personal and political differences for the good of the country. The tragedy of the failed votes was that without full American support, the League of Nations proved unable to maintain peace among nations.

✓ **Checkpoint** What reservations did Henry Cabot Lodge and his followers have about the peace treaty?

Vocabulary Builder
<u>contradict</u>–(kahn truh DIHKT) v. to go against

Assess Progress

- Have students complete the Section Assessment.

- Administer the Section Quiz. Teaching Resources, **p. 28**

- To further assess student understanding, use Progress Monitoring Transparencies, **93.**

Reteach

If students need more instruction, have them read the section summary.

Reading and Note Taking Study Guide   **L3**

Adapted Reading and Note Taking Study Guide   **L1 L2**

Spanish Reading and Note Taking Study Guide   **L2**

Extend   **L4**

Have students research and write an essay comparing the League of Nations with the United Nations, and discussing ways in which Wilson's idea for the League of Nations may be reflected in the UN today.

Answer

✓ Many reservationists feared that as written, the treaty could lead the United States into a war without the consent of Congress, which was unconstitutional. They wanted the treaty revised to ensure that it would not contradict the power of Congress to declare war.

SECTION

3 Assessment

Progress Monitoring Online
For: Self-test with vocabulary practice
www.pearsonschool.com/ushist

Comprehension

1. **Terms and People** For each item below, write a sentence explaining why it is significant to the end of World War I.
   - convoy
   - Fourteen Points
   - self-determination
   - League of Nations
   - Henry Cabot Lodge
   - reparations
   - "irreconcilables"
   - "reservationists"

2. **NoteTaking Reading Skill: Sequence** Use your timeline and chart to answer the Section Focus Question: How did Americans affect the end of World War I and its peace settlements?

Writing About History

3. **Quick Write: Create an Effects Diagram** Predict at least three problems that could stem from the Treaty of Versailles. Create a diagram showing these effects.

Critical Thinking

4. **Summarize** Describe America's contributions to the Allied war effort.

5. **Express Problems Clearly** What problems did the peace treaties solve? What problems did they create?

6. **Draw Conclusions** Why did the United States Senate ultimately reject the peace treaty and the League of Nations?

Section 3 Assessment

1. Sentences should reflect an understanding of each term or person listed.

2. The Allies were strengthened when the United States joined the war. The Allies were then able to demoralize the Central Powers and win. The Fourteen Points further encouraged Germany to end the war, but the European Allies did not accept Wilson's plan.

3. Diagrams should make logical predictions about at least three problems that could stem from the Treaty of Versailles.

4. America contributed ships, supplies, and troops to the war effort. America's involvement boosted Allied morale. On the home front, Americans conserved food, produced war goods, and bought Liberty Bonds to help fund the war.

5. The peace treaties ended the war, but fostered resentments and hostilities between Germany and the Allies. They also created controversy at home about the peace terms.

6. The Senate ultimately rejected the peace treaty and the League of Nations because some senators and Wilson were unable to overcome personal and political differences.

For additional assessment, have students access **Progress Monitoring Online** at **www.pearsonschool.com/ushist.**

Objectives

- Analyze the main ideas presented in Woodrow Wilson's Fourteen Points.
- Understand Wilson's idea of "moral diplomacy" as expressed in his Fourteen Points.

Background Knowledge ⓛ

Remind students of Woodrow Wilson's commitment to "peace without victory." Have students recall the main ideas of the Fourteen Points and the controversy they created.

Instruct ⓛ

Direct students' attention to the "Summary of the Fourteen Points" chart. Ask **Which of the Fourteen Points refer to self-determination?** *(5–13)* **What do you think Wilson may have feared would happen should the Fourteen Points not be implemented?** *(another world war)* **Would the Central Powers have agreed to the Armistice without Wilson's plan? Explain.** *(They probably would not have agreed because they would have feared punishment by the European Allies.)*

Monitor Progress

Have students work in pairs to choose what they consider to be the most important of the Fourteen Points. Volunteers can share their opinions with the class. Each student should be prepared to explain why the chosen point is the most important.

Answers

Thinking Critically

1. He believes that if the Fourteen Points are not followed, long-lasting peace cannot be achieved.

2. 14

Woodrow Wilson: *The Fourteen Points*

In a speech to Congress on January 8, 1918, President Wilson laid out America's war aims and his vision for peace after the war. His speech included fourteen key points upon which he believed the peace following the war must be based. However, not all of Wilson's ideas were adopted at the Paris Peace Conference.

What we demand in this war, therefore, is nothing peculiar to ourselves. It is that the world be made fit and safe to live in; and particularly that it be made safe for every peace-loving nation which, like our own, wishes to live its own life, [and] determine its own institutions.... The program of the world's peace, therefore, is our only program; and that program, the only possible program as we see it, is this:

1. Open covenants[1] of peace, openly arrived at, after which there shall be no private international understandings of any kind but diplomacy shall proceed always frankly and in the public view.

2. Absolute freedom of navigation upon the seas, outside territorial waters, alike in peace and in war, except as the seas may be closed in whole or in part by international action for the enforcement of international covenants.

3. The removal, so far as possible, of all economic barriers and the establishment of an equality of trade conditions among all the nations consenting to the peace and associating themselves for its maintenance.

4. Adequate guarantees given and taken that national armaments will be reduced to the lowest point consistent with domestic safety.

5. A free, open-minded, and absolutely impartial adjustment of all colonial claims, based upon a strict observance of the principle that in determining all such questions of sovereignty the interests of the populations concerned must have equal weight with the equitable claims of the government whose title is to be determined....

14. A general association of nations must be formed under specific covenants for the purpose of affording mutual guarantees of political independence and territorial integrity to great and small states alike.

Thinking Critically

1. **Make Inferences** Why does President Wilson think that the Fourteen Points are "the only possible program" for the world's peace?

2. **Synthesize Information** Which of the Fourteen Points introduced the idea of the League of Nations?

1. **covenant** (KUHV uh nuhnt) *n.* formal agreement.

Summary of the Fourteen Points

1.	Make no secret diplomatic agreements.
2.	Allow freedom of the seas in peace and war.
3.	Remove as many economic trade barriers as possible between countries.
4.	Reduce stockpiles of military armaments to lowest point needed for domestic safety.
5.	Adjust colonial claims, giving more weight to the views of the colonized peoples.
6.	Evacuate and restore Russian territories seized during the war.
7.	Restore and protect Belgium's sovereignty.
8.	Restore French territory and settle the debate over Alsace-Lorraine.
9.	Adjust Italy's boundaries according to the nationalities of populations living there.
10.	Allow the peoples of the former Austro-Hungarian Empire to choose their own governments.
11.	Redraw boundaries of Balkan states based on nationalities and historical allegiances.
12.	Separate the Ottoman Empire into independent countries according to nationality; guarantee all nations access to the Dardanelles.
13.	Restore and protect Poland as a sovereign state with access to the sea.
14.	Establish an association of nations to provide collective security and to ensure peace.

▼ President Wilson giving a speech in support of the League of Nations in 1919

History Background

A Presidency of Challenges President Woodrow Wilson asserted his concern for the people and determination to work for peace throughout his presidency. Although Wilson won the presidency with only 42 percent of the popular vote, he saw himself as a representative and protector of the American people.

During his first term, he signed three pieces of legislation that provided for a lower tariff, increased the nation's money supply, and prohibited unfair business tactics. Despite the popularity of this legislation, Wilson won his second term by only a narrow margin.

President Wilson's desire for peace can be traced to his childhood in the Civil War–torn South. Still, he realized that the Allies needed the United States. When it came time to gain support for the Treaty of Versailles, Wilson ignored his doctor's wishes and began a national tour that caused him to have a near-fatal stroke. Despite his efforts, the treaty was defeated in the Senate by just seven votes.

A Difficult Transition

The service of African Americans during the war renewed hopes for equal rights for African Americans. However, the reality changed little.

"It is necessary now as never before that the black man press his claims as an American citizen. . . . The Government laid claim to him, both body and soul, and used him as freely as if he were the equal of any other man behind the guns. . . . The path he had to walk was just as rough, the load he had to carry was just as heavy, and the life he gave just as sweet, as that of any other man who laid his all upon the altar. He should contend, therefore, for every privilege, every comfort, every right which other men enjoy."

—Dr. A. A. Graham, African American leader

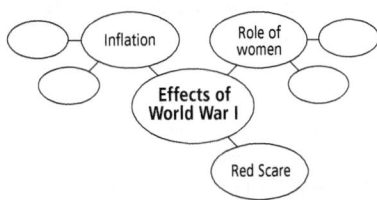

▲ Members of the famous 369th Infantry Regiment are welcomed home in New York City, 1919.

Effects of the War

Objectives

- Describe the problems Americans faced immediately after the war.
- Analyze how these problems contributed to the Red Scare.
- Understand how the war changed America's role in world affairs.

Terms and People

influenza	Nicola Sacco
inflation	Bartolomeo Vanzetti
Red Scare	Warren G. Harding
Palmer Raids	creditor nation

NoteTaking

Reading Skill: Identify Main Ideas As you read, identify and record the main ideas of this section in a concept web like the one below.

Why It Matters The end of World War I produced an unstable international order. The loss of territory and the harsh reparations imposed by the Allies encouraged a strong desire for revenge in Germany. Meanwhile, Lenin's Soviet Russia threatened revolution throughout the industrial world. In the United States, the horrors of the war along with widespread fear of communists and radicals led Americans to question their political, if not their economic, role in the world. **Section Focus Question: What political, economic, and social effects did World War I have on the United States?**

America Adjusts to Peace

World War I produced significant economic, social, political, and cultural changes in America and throughout the world. This led to important, occasionally painful, adjustments.

Flu Epidemic Grips the Nation The movement from war to peace would have been difficult even in the best of times. But the end of 1918 and 1919 were not the best of times. In September 1918, an unusually deadly form of the **influenza,** or flu, virus appeared. Research in recent years shows that the 1918 influenza virus was originally a bird flu that mutated to spread to humans. Many historians now believe that the virus originated in the United States, then traveled around the world. Once the virus began, it spread like a wildfire and killed millions worldwide like a predator feasting on its prey. The great influenza pandemic, coming on the heels of the Great War, gave a sense of doom and dread to people around the globe.

Prepare to Read

Background Knowledge

Ask students to recall World War I's effects on Europe. Then, review the struggle in Congress over the Treaty of Versailles. Ask students to predict how Americans might have reacted to the end of the war.

Set a Purpose

- **WITNESS HISTORY** Read the selection aloud.

  Ask **What is Dr. Graham's reaction to the treatment of African Americans after the war?** *(He is discouraged because African Americans are not treated equally with whites. He makes the point that African Americans fought equally in the war. Therefore, they should have equality after the war.)*

- **Focus** Point out the Section Focus Question, and write it on the board. Tell students to refer to this question as they read. *(Answer appears with Section 4 Assessment answers.)*

- **Preview** Have students preview the Section Objectives and the list of Terms and People.

- **NoteTaking** Using the Structured Read Aloud strategy (TE, p. T20), have students read this section. As they read, have students outline the section's main ideas in a concept web. Reading and Note Taking Study Guide

Vocabulary Builder

Use the information below and the following resource to teach students the high-use word from this section. Teaching Resources, Vocabulary Builder, p. 11

High-Use Word	Definition and Sample Sentence
emergence	*n.* rise or development The **emergence** of nationalism in Europe during the late 1800s gave rise to the tensions that led to World War I.

America Adjusts to Peace L3

Instruct

- **Introduce: Key Term** Remind students that during the war the economy was strong. Women, African Americans, and Mexican Americans were working and earning money. After the war, there was a shift from wartime production to peacetime production. Ask students to locate the word *inflation* (in bold) in the text and give the definition. Ask **What impact might inflation have on people's spending power?** *(They might not be able to buy as much because items would cost more.)*

- **Teach** Explain that there were multiple causes of hardship following the war. Have students discuss the images and map on this page. Ask **What made the influenza that spread in 1918 into a pandemic?** *(It spread quickly around the country and the world, causing many deaths.)* **Why was there a decrease in the number of women and African Americans in the workforce following the war?** *(Their jobs were given to returning white soldiers.)* **What caused the sharp rise in inflation after the war?** *(People stopped buying war bonds and began buying consumer goods. Fewer of these goods were produced during the war, leading to a shortage. That, coupled with high demand, led to skyrocketing prices.)*

Independent Practice

Organize students in three groups. Assign each group a separate red heading describing problems that plagued Americans following the war. Have each group summarize their red headings. Then, have students share their summaries.

Monitor Progress

As students fill in their main idea concept webs, circulate to make sure that they understand the effects of World War I on Americans. For a completed version of the main idea concept web, see Note Taking Transparencies, **B-98**.

The Influenza Pandemic Hits the United States

The influenza attack of 1918 was a pandemic, an epidemic that affects many people all over the world. Oddly, the virus hit men and women in their twenties and thirties the hardest, rather than children and the elderly. The flu pandemic killed 550,000 Americans, including 50,000 soldiers. Worldwide, it probably claimed between 50 and 100 million lives. **Describe how the influenza virus spread in the United States.**

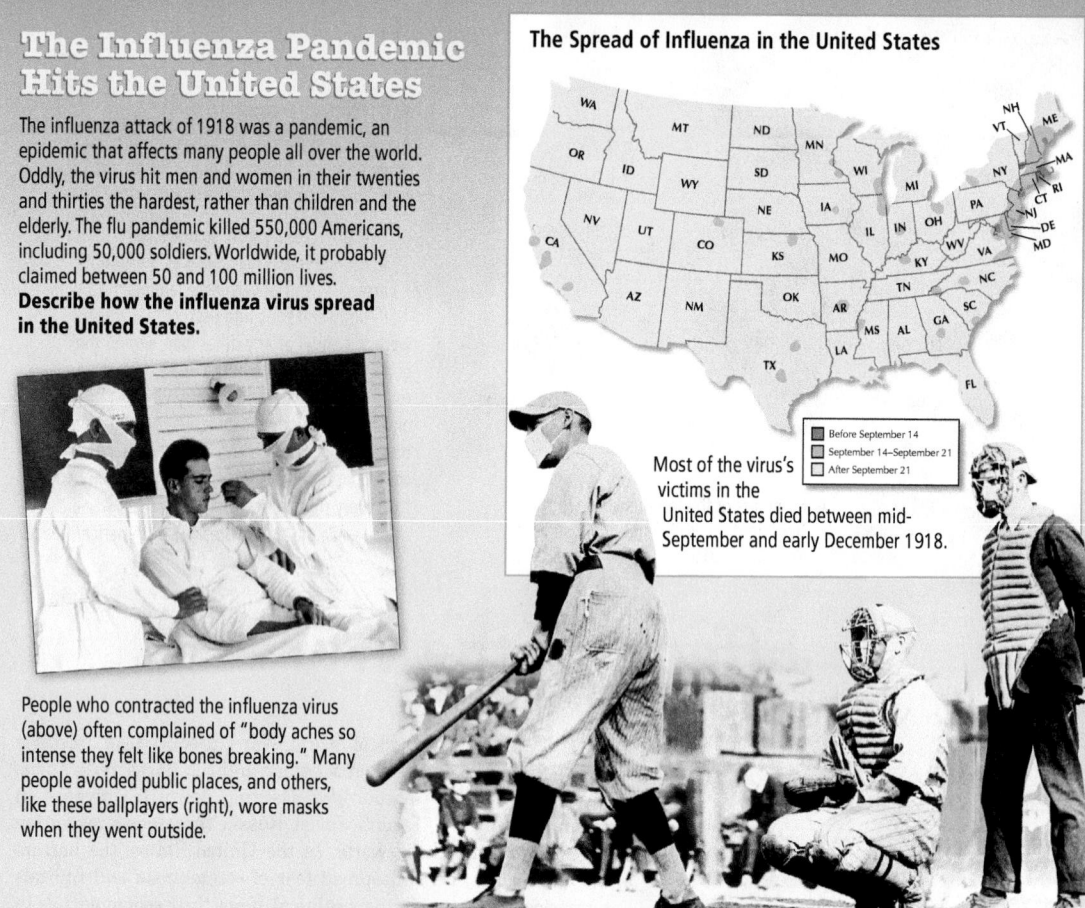

The Spread of Influenza in the United States

- Before September 14
- September 14–September 21
- After September 21

Most of the virus's victims in the United States died between mid-September and early December 1918.

People who contracted the influenza virus (above) often complained of "body aches so intense they felt like bones breaking." Many people avoided public places, and others, like these ballplayers (right), wore masks when they went outside.

Women and African Americans Confront New Realities Women and African Americans made significant advances during the war. However, the end of the war also spelled the end of wartime economic opportunities for both groups. A postwar recession, or economic slowdown, created a competitive job market. By 1920, there were fewer women in the workforce than there had been in 1910.

In northern industrial cities, African American workers vied with returning soldiers for jobs and housing. During the hot summer of 1919, race riots erupted in cities throughout the country. The worst, in Chicago, was triggered by the drowning of a young black man by whites, and went on for 13 days. In 1921, violence erupted in Tulsa, Oklahoma, when armed African American men—many of them returning veterans—tried to protect a young black man from lynching. By the time the Tulsa race riots were over, at least 10 whites and 26 African Americans were dead. In one African American neighborhood, white rioters burned 35 city blocks to the ground.

Inflation Leads to Labor Unrest During the war, **inflation,** or rising prices, had been held in check. After the conflict, Americans rushed to buy consumer goods rather than war bonds. The scarcity of these goods, coupled with widespread demand, caused inflation. During the war, the price of corn, wheat, cotton,

Differentiated Instruction   Solutions for All Learners

L1 Special Needs Students L2 Less Proficient Readers

Remind students that they can use text headings to get an idea of what a section is about. Have them read the section title and all the headings in the section. Ask students to use the headings to answer this question: What problems did Americans face after World War I? Have students refer to the headings to explain their answer.

cattle, and other agricultural goods had risen, with help from Hoover's policies. After the war, prices fell sharply, making it difficult for farmers to pay their mortgages or buy what they needed for the next growing season. This began a long period of tough times for farmers.

Industrial workers also felt the pain of inflation when their wages did not buy as much as they had during the war. In 1919, more than 4 million workers, or 20 percent of the workforce, went on strike at one time or another. Demanding rewards for their wartime patriotism, workers struck for higher wages and shorter workdays. In Boston, even the police force struck. The workers won some of the strikes, but they lost far more. When some strikes turned violent, the pro-management press blamed the presence of radicals among the strike leaders.

✓ **Checkpoint** How did the economic situation after the war lead to labor unrest?

The Red Scare

The reaction against labor was partly spurred by a wave of fear of radicals and communists. The <u>emergence</u> of the Soviet Union as a communist nation, which began in 1917, fed these fears. Communist ideology called for an international workers' revolution as a prelude to the death of capitalism. To this end, Soviet leader Vladimir Lenin encouraged and supported revolutions outside of his country. In Central and Eastern Europe, a series of communist revolts did break out, making it seem like the worldwide revolution was starting.

Fear of Communism Starts the Red Scare This revolutionary activity abroad, coupled with strikes across the United States, prompted the first American **Red Scare**, a wave of widespread fear of suspected communists and radicals thought to be plotting revolution within the United States. Real revolutionary activity inside America gave substance to the scare. Authorities discovered bombs mailed to important industrialists and government officials, including Attorney General A. Mitchell Palmer. Suspected anarchists, members of a radical political movement, exploded bombs in cities across America.

As the leading law-enforcement official, Palmer mounted a broad offensive against radicals in the United States in 1919 and 1920. In a series of raids in early 1920, known as the **Palmer Raids,** police arrested thousands of people, some who were radicals and some who were simply immigrants from southern or Eastern Europe. Most were never charged or tried for a crime. The government then deported hundreds of radicals.

To many, these actions seemed to attack the liberties that Americans held most dear. A group of people in New York City formed the American Civil Liberties Union (ACLU) in 1920 to protect these liberties. The ACLU tried to do this by becoming involved in important court cases. To this end, the ACLU became involved in one of America's most controversial court cases: the trial of Nicola Sacco and Bartolomeo Vanzetti.

Sacco and Vanzetti Are Executed **Nicola Sacco** (SAH koh) and **Bartolomeo Vanzetti** (van ZEHT ee) were Italian immigrants and known anarchists. They were charged with shooting and killing two men during a holdup at a shoe factory in a town

Vocabulary Builder
emergence–(ee MER juhns) *n.* rise or development

Guilty or Innocent?
Rosina Sacco visits her husband, Nicola Sacco, and Bartolomeo Vanzetti as the two men wait in the prisoners' dock during their famous trial. Debate whether both were truly guilty still continues.

History Background

Red Scare At the end of the war, Americans had a general feeling of distrust toward immigrants, foreigners, and radicals. This distrust turned to paranoia as Americans witnessed a wave of strikes, the Chicago race riot, and a series of bombings by suspected anarchists. During the Red Scare, civil liberties were frequently violated or ignored. Often, people were suspected merely because of their ethnic backgrounds. When a clothing salesman stated that Lenin was smart, he was sentenced to six months in jail. Hysteria similar to the Red Scare took place after World War II, when Senator Joseph McCarthy accused unnamed high government officials and military officials of being communists.

Instruct

- **Introduce: Key Term** Have students find the key term **Red Scare** (in bold) in the text and explain its meaning. Tell students that communists were often called "reds."

- **Teach** Explain to students that while Americans were battling the influenza epidemic, labor unrest, and rising inflation, they harbored a fear of a political unrest. Ask **What caused the Red Scare?** (*Vladimir Lenin encouraged and supported revolutions outside his country. Revolutions occurred in some European nations. Violent radicals exploded bombs in cities across America.*) **How did the government attempt to stop the Red Scare?** (*They arrested people who were radicals or who they thought might be radicals.*) **Why was the ACLU formed?** (*Its founders feared that the government's attempts to respond to the Red Scare threatened Americans' liberties. The ACLU was formed to protect civil liberties.*)

- **Quick Activity** Display Color Transparency: *Reaction to Radicals.* Use the lesson suggested in the transparency book to guide a discussion about the driving force behind the Red Scare. Color Transparencies A-88

Independent Practice

Have students complete the worksheet *Viewpoints: The Red Scare* to understand how the fear of communism led to the Red Scare and the resulting protests of the ACLU and other groups. Teaching Resources, **p. 25**

Monitor Progress

To check students' understanding, point out the picture of the Wall Street bombing. Ask students to describe how such an incident could lead to an elevated fear of radical political activity.

Answer

✓ After the war, the economy slowed and inflation rose. The recession caused a competitive job market, just as soldiers were returning from the war and seeking jobs. People fought for their jobs and for their rights as workers.

Instruct

- **Introduce** Have students read the blue and red headings in this section. Ask them to use the headings to predict how America changed after the Red Scare. Then, have them read to evaluate their predictions.

- **Teach** Ask **Why did Warren Harding win the presidential election?** *(Americans were tired of Wilson's progressive reforms and foreign involvement. They wanted to return to what they believed had been simpler times, before World War I.)* Using the Think-Write-Pair-Share strategy (TE, p. T23), have students discuss the shift in the U.S. role in international affairs. Ask **Why was it unlikely that Americans' lives would return to pre-war state of "normalcy"?** *(The United States emerged as an economic world leader. It would be impossible for it to stay out of international affairs.)*

Independent Practice

NoteTaking Have students identify main ideas by completing the concept web from the beginning of the section.

Monitor Progress

As students fill in their concept webs, circulate to make sure that they understand the effects of the end of World War I on Americans. For a completed version of the concept web, see Note Taking Transparencies, **B-98**.

The Wall Street Bombing
On September 16, 1920, just days after Sacco and Vanzetti's murder indictment, a horsecart filled with dynamite exploded in the financial heart of New York City. The explosion and flying debris killed about 40 people and caused the New York Stock Exchange to close early that day. Investigators suspected that anarchists had staged the bombing, but the culprits were never found.

near Boston. Eyewitnesses of the event said the robbers "looked Italian." Sacco and Vanzetti were arrested and charged with the crime. Even though the ACLU provided defense counsel, the two men were found guilty in a swift and decisive trial, despite the fact that there was little hard evidence against them. Some prominent legal scholars, intellectuals, and liberal politicians charged that the convictions were based more on Sacco and Vanzetti's ethnicity and political beliefs than on the facts of the crime. Nevertheless, on August 23, 1927, the two men were put to death in the electric chair.

At its worst, hysteria accompanied by violence characterized the Red Scare. Mobs attacked suspected radicals, abused immigrants, and committed crimes in the name of justice. But eventually, the great fear ended. Americans saw that democracy and capitalism were more powerful in the United States than Lenin's call for worldwide revolution. By the summer of 1920, the Red Scare hysteria, like the great influenza, had run its course.

 Checkpoint How did the rise of communism in the Soviet Union contribute to the Red Scare?

Americans Embrace Normalcy

Woodrow Wilson hoped that the presidential election of 1920 would prove that Americans supported both the League of Nations and his vision of the role the United States should play in the world. He suggested that electing Democratic presidential candidate James M. Cox of Ohio would show support for the League. The election of Republican candidate **Warren G. Harding** of Ohio would serve as a final rejection of the League.

Harding had a different view of the presidential race. He knew that national elections seldom turned on a single issue. Harding campaigned for a rejection of Wilsonian idealism. He was tired of progressive reforms and foreign crusades. Harding called for a return to "normalcy," by which he meant the "normality" of

Answer

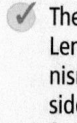 The Soviet Union's leader, Vladimir Lenin, supported the spread of communism. He encouraged revolutions outside the Soviet Union. Many Americans feared that there would be a revolution in the United States.

what he believed had been a simpler time before Wilson took office in 1913. Harding won in a landslide, and Republicans won control of Congress, as well. Americans had decisively rejected Wilson's ideas.

A Quiet American Giant Despite Harding's election and all it implied, the United States did not plan to totally withdraw from world affairs. By 1920, the United States was an economic giant. It was the richest, most industrialized country in the world. Even before the war, America led all other nations in industrial output. Now, British and French demands for American goods created an immense trade imbalance. Europeans had to borrow money from American bankers and obtain lines of credit with American business firms to pay for the goods.

This situation fundamentally changed America's economic standing in the world. The United States was now the largest **creditor nation** in the world, meaning that other countries owed the United States more money than the United States owed them. World War I shifted the economic center of the world from London to New York City. The United States embraced its new role as a quiet giant. A world without America playing a major economic role had become simply impossible to conceive.

The World Adjusts to a New Order World War I had caused sweeping changes around the globe. German and Russian monarchies toppled, and new forms of government were created. The Austro-Hungarian and Ottoman empires ceased to exist. Britain and France emerged from the war victorious but economically and politically weakened. In contrast, the victorious United States came out of the war strong, confident, and prosperous.

An old order five hundred years in the making had collapsed in just a few years. It was as if the world's compass was out of whack and no one knew where to turn for directions. The United States was unsure of the requirements of its new status. Could America retreat into isolationism in political but not economic affairs? After rejecting the League of Nations, how could it exert its moral authority in the world? Americans would wrestle with these questions—and many others—in the decades ahead.

✓ **Checkpoint** Why did the United States become the leading economic power after World War I?

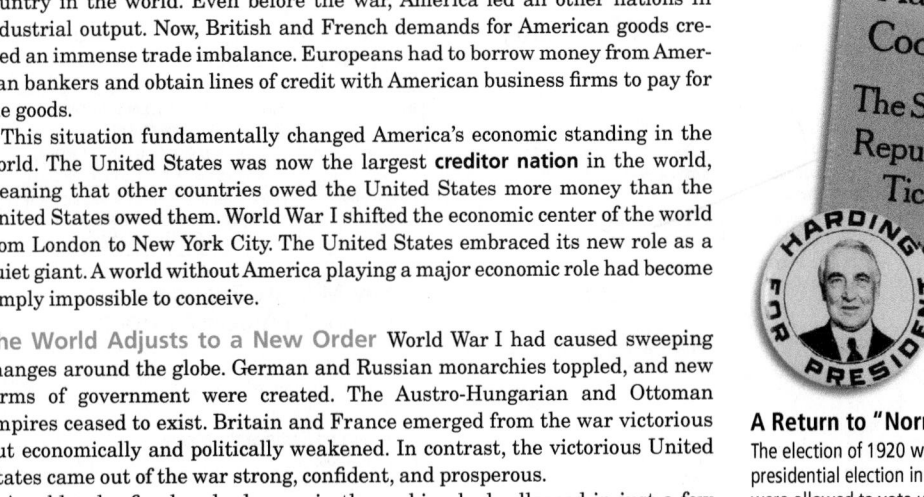

A Return to "Normalcy"
The election of 1920 was the first presidential election in which women were allowed to vote under the Nineteenth Amendment. American voters overwhelmingly elected Warren G. Harding, who promised a return to simpler days.

Assess and Reteach

Assess Progress L3
- Have students complete the Section Assessment.
- Administer the Section Quiz. Teaching Resources, **p. 29**
- To further assess student understanding, use Progress Monitoring Transparencies, **94**.

Reteach
If students need more instruction, have them read the section summary.

Reading and Note Taking L3
Study Guide

Adapted Reading and L1 L2
Note Taking Study Guide

Spanish Reading and L2
Note Taking Study Guide

Extend L4
Ask students to suppose that they are living during World War I. Have them write a news article about one particular aspect of the impact of the war on Americans in the postwar period. Have volunteers read their articles to the class.

Answer

✓ After World War I, Britain and France bought many American goods. They had to borrow money from American bankers to pay for the goods. The United States became the largest creditor nation in the world.

SECTION 4 Assessment

Progress Monitoring *Online*
For: Self-test with vocabulary practice
www.pearsonschool.com/ushist

Comprehension
1. **Terms and People** For each item below, write a sentence explaining its significance to events in the United States after World War I.
   - influenza
   - inflation
   - Red Scare
   - Palmer Raids
   - Nicola Sacco
   - Bartolomeo Vanzetti
   - Warren G. Harding

2. **NoteTaking Reading Skill: Summarize** Use your concept web to answer the Section Focus Question: What political, economic, and social effects did World War I have on the United States?

Writing About History
3. **Quick Write: Write a Thesis Statement** Write a thesis statement for a cause-and-effect essay on the effects of World War I on the United States. Your thesis statement should state a point you will argue.

Critical Thinking
4. **Analyze Information** How did the influenza pandemic make the transition from war to peace more difficult?
5. **Determine Relevance** How does the Sacco and Vanzetti case demonstrate the mindset of the Red Scare?
6. **Draw Inferences** How did Americans both reject and embrace the new global influence of the United States?

Section 4 Assessment

1. Sentences should reflect an understanding of each term or person listed.
2. The United States changed after World War I. Politically, Americans tired of Wilson's foreign policy and elected a new President who promised a "return to normalcy." The nation was gripped by the Red Scare and repressive reactions to it. Economically, Americans endured rising inflation and a competitive job market. Socially, Americans faced the deadly influenza pandemic, confronted questions about the rights of women and African Americans, and dealt with fears about a communist revolution.
3. Students' thesis statements should pertain to an effect of World War I on the United States and should state a viewpoint about that effect.
4. The influenza pandemic killed many people and created a sense of doom and dread.
5. The Sacco and Vanzetti case shows how much Americans feared radicals. The two men were convicted largely because of circumstantial evidence and suspicion based on their ethnicity and past actions.
6. Americans rejected the country's new global influence by returning to political isolationism. They embraced it by becoming the largest creditor nation.

For additional assessment, have students access **Progress Monitoring *Online*** at **www.pearsonschool.com/ushist**.

Chapter 6 Section 4   **203**

Quick Study Guide

Progress Monitoring *Online*
For: Self-test with vocabulary practice
www.pearsonschool.com/ushist

Quick Study Guide

- Have students use the Quick Study Guide to prepare for the chapter test. Students may wish to refer to the following sections as they review:

Causes and Effects of America's Entry into World War I
Section 1
Section 2
Section 3
Section 4

Views on America's Decision to Fight or Not to Fight
Section 1

Key Military Engagements Involving American Troops
Section 3

Key Events During and After World War I
Section 1
Section 2
Section 3
Section 4

- For additional review, remind students to refer to the Reading and Note Taking Study Guide.
Section Note Taking
Section Summaries

- Have students access
www.pearsonschool.com/ushist
for this chapter's History Interactive timeline, which includes expanded entries and additional events.

- If students need more instruction on analyzing graphic data, have them read the Skills Handbook, **p. SH21.**

■ Causes and Effects of America's Entry into World War I

Causes
- Many Americans have cultural ties with Britain and France.
- Reports of German atrocities in Belgium outrage Americans.
- Germany continues its policy of unrestricted submarine warfare, despite promises to stop.
- In the Zimmermann note, Germany offers Mexico the chance to regain lost U.S. territory.

↓

America's Entry Into World War I

↓

Effects
- The Allies defeat the Central Powers.
- The government's role in daily life increases.
- African Americans and Mexican Americans migrate north.
- More women enter the workforce.
- The United States refuses to join the League of Nations.
- The United States becomes a leading economic power.

■ Views on America's Decision to Fight or Not to Fight

Isolationists	Believed the United States should isolate itself from all foreign conflicts
Internationalists	Believed the United States should actively work for peace but not enter the war
Interventionists	Believed the United States should intervene in the war on the side of the Allies, protect U.S. interests, and fulfill U.S. obligations

■ Key Military Engagements Involving American Troops

- Cantigny
- Château-Thierry
- Belleau Wood
- Second Battle of the Marne
- Amiens
- Saint-Mihiel
- Meuse-Argonne Offensive

☑ Quick Study Timeline

In America

| 1914 President Wilson announces American neutrality in World War I | 1915 Sinking of the *Lusitania* angers Americans |

Presidential Terms — Woodrow Wilson 1913–1921

Around the World

| 1914 Assassination of Austrian archduke triggers World War I | 1915 Poison gas first used on Western Front | 1916 More than 2 million casualties suffered in battle of Verdun and battle of the Somme on Western Front |

Differentiated Instruction   Solutions for All Learners

L1 Special Needs Students   **L2 English Language Learners**   **L2 Less Proficient Readers**

Use the following study guide resources to help students acquiring basic skills:
Adapted Reading and Note Taking Study Guide
- Section Note Taking
- Section Summaries

Use the following study guide resources to help Spanish-speaking students:
Spanish Reading and Note Taking Study Guide
- Section Note Taking
- Section Summaries

American Issues
●—●—●—● Connector

By connecting prior knowledge with what you have learned in this chapter, you can gradually build your understanding of enduring questions that still affect America today. Answer the questions below. Then, use your American Issues Connector study guide (or go online: www.pearsonschool.com/ushist).

Issues You Learned About

● **America Goes to War** The United States has been involved in two global conflicts.

1. How has the United States made the decision to declare war in past conflicts?

2. In 1916, Wilson won reelection using the campaign slogan "He kept us out of war," but less than a year later, the United States joined World War I. What happened to change Wilson's mind?

3. Why did some Americans oppose American involvement in World War I?

● **Civil Liberties and National Security** At times, Americans' civil liberties are curtailed, resulting in major debates over constitutional rights and powers.

4. How does the Constitution guarantee that accused criminals will receive fair trials?

5. Why did some people protest the execution of Sacco and Vanzetti?

6. Describe another event during the Red Scare that seemed to curtail civil liberties.

● **Checks and Balances** Responsibilities are shared among the three branches of the federal government.

7. Which branch of the government has the power to make treaties?

8. How did the battle over the Treaty of Versailles demonstrate the ways in which the different branches of the federal government may void one another's decisions?

Connect to Your World	Activity

Technology and Society World War I witnessed the first widespread use of chemical weapons, including chlorine gas, mustard gas, and phosgene. Despite efforts to ban their use and development, chemical weapons continue to pose a threat today. Go online or use library resources to learn more about the Chemical Weapons Convention (CWC) and the Organization for the Prohibition of Chemical Weapons. Write two paragraphs summarizing the scope and purpose of the CWC and the actions taken by the organization to prohibit the spread and use of chemical weapons.

1917
United States declares war on Germany

1919
United States Senate rejects membership in League of Nations

History *Interactive*
For: Interactive timeline
www.pearsonschool.com/ushist

| 1917 | 1918 | 1919 | 1920 |

1918
Armistice with Germany ends war

1918–1919
Deadly influenza pandemic sweeps across the world

Terms and People

1. The Western Front was a critical series of battle lines in France and Belgium; it was characterized by stalemate and trench warfare.

2. Creel was the director of the Committee on Public Information; he gave speeches and distributed pamphlets and posters that both dramatized the needs of America and its allies and highlighted the cruelty of the enemy.

3. The League of Nations was an organization of nations established at the end of World War I. Its goal was to prevent war by providing a forum for peace discussions and negotiations. It was unsuccessful in large part because the United States did not become a member.

4. Reparations are payments for the repair of war damages. Britain and France wanted Germany to pay reparations.

5. Influenza is the flu virus. After World War I, it decreased the world's population in an epidemic that killed millions.

Focus Questions

6. World War I was caused by a military buildup among European countries, a heightened sense of militarism and nationalism, and a series of alliances that caused the war to expand throughout Europe. The United States entered the war because Germany began infringing on Americans' rights and safety.

7. Men on the home front left their jobs to fight in the war. Women and African Americans went to work to fill those jobs. Mexican Americans migrated to take agricultural jobs. People conserved food and bought Liberty Bonds to support the war effort.

8. Americans provided needed reinforcement to the Allies. They were able to help push back the Germans. Germany agreed to peace talks because of Wilson's Fourteen Points.

9. The United States changed after World War I. Socially, Americans endured the deadly influenza pandemic and encountered fears about a

Chapter Assessment

Terms and People

1. Define **Western Front.** What characterized this region during World War I?

2. Who was **George Creel**? What methods did he introduce to "sell America"?

3. What was the **League of Nations**? How successful was the League of Nations?

4. Define **reparations.** What stance did Britain and France take on reparations?

5. Define **influenza.** What effect did it have on the world's population immediately after World War I?

Focus Questions

The focus question for this chapter is **What caused the United States to become involved in World War I, and how did the United States change as a result of its involvement?** Build an answer to this big question by answering the focus questions for Sections 1 through 4 and the Critical Thinking questions that follow.

Section 1
6. What caused World War I, and why did the United States enter the war?

Section 2
7. How did the war affect Americans at home?

Section 3
8. How did Americans affect the end of World War I and its peace settlements?

Section 4
9. What political, economic, and social effects did World War I have on the United States?

Critical Thinking

10. **Recognize Causes** Identify and explain the causes of World War I.

11. **Analyze Credibility** How do you know the Zimmermann note was a reliable source? Explain.

12. **Distinguish False From Accurate Images** Is the image to the right an accurate or inaccurate image of Germans during World War I? Why do you think the artist chose this representation?

13. **Draw Conclusions** How did Wilson arrive at the decision that women deserved the right to vote?

14. **Summarize** What was the main goal that Wilson wanted to accomplish with the Fourteen Points?

15. **Categorize** Who were the main groups of senators opposed to the Versailles Treaty, and what positions did they hold? Who supported the treaty?

16. **Express Problems Clearly** What problems led to a weak postwar economy?

17. **Determine Relevance** How did the presidential election of 1920 show Americans' rejection of Wilson's ideas?

Writing About History

Write a Cause-and-Effect Essay World War I both caused and affected many different events around the world. Write an essay in which you explain how several different causes led to an event or trend that occurred during World War I. Consider one of the following topics: the stalemate on the Western Front, the increased role of women in the war effort, or the defeat of the Treaty of Versailles in the United States.

Prewriting
• Choose the topic above that interests you the most. Consider what caused the event in question.
• List the multiple causes. Conduct research if necessary to gather more information.

Drafting
• Develop a thesis that clearly states the causal relationship between your event and its main causes.
• Choose an organizational structure for your essay.
• Write an introduction, several body paragraphs, and a conclusion.

Revising
• Use the guidelines on page SH11 of the Writing Handbook to revise your essay.

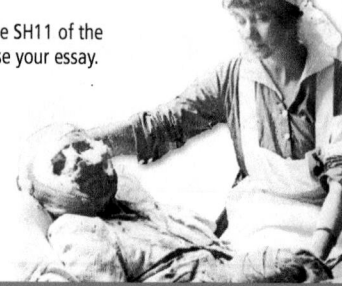

communist revolution. Economically, they faced rising inflation and a competitive job market. Politically, they tired of Wilson's foreign policy and elected a new President who promised a "return to normalcy."

Critical Thinking

10. World War I broke out because of rising international tensions, heightened militarism and nationalism, and the European alliance system.

11. It was intercepted by the British, an ally of the United States, and the German response was belligerent.

12. Sample answer: Inaccurate; during the war, the government wanted to convince Americans that the war was just. It overemphasized the cruelty of the Germans to appeal to Americans' emotions.

13. Wilson took note that women had successfully performed jobs once reserved for men. He reasoned that if they were able to do equal work, they deserved an equal voice in politics.

Document-Based Assessment

Americans for and Against the War

Both before and after the U.S. entry into World War I, Americans differed in their opinions about the war. While most Americans demonstrated their patriotism with enthusiasm by buying war bonds, conserving food, and enlisting in the army, others, including Quakers and pacifists, continued to oppose the war. Use your knowledge of Americans' opinions on World War I and the following documents to answer questions 1 through 4.

Document A

"I find myself a soldier among millions of others in the great Allied Armies, fighting for all I believe to be right and civilized and humane against a power which is evil and which threatens the existence of all the rights we prize and the freedom we enjoy, although some of you in California as yet fail to realize it. It may seem to you that for me this is all quite uncalled for, that it can only mean the supreme sacrifice for nothing or some of the best years of my life wasted, but I tell you that not only am I willing to give my life to this enterprise . . . but that I firmly believe if I live through it to spend a useful lifetime with you, that never will I have an opportunity to gain so much honorable advancement for my own soul, or to do so much for the cause of the world's progress. . . ."

—*Harry Butters, an American volunteering with the Allies in 1915*

Document B

"I could not look at those long lines of fine looking men, marching so gaily along, and with so little realization of what it all means, without a fresh outburst of tears. How little they realized that they were endorsing a system which means that great armies of splendid manhood shall go forth and slay other great armies. And why? Because stupid diplomats were too avaricious [greedy], too selfish, too ambitious to sanely handle the affairs entrusted to their care. . . . And yet we, blind and stupid as we are, are rushing into the same horrible cataclysm [disaster]."

—*Lella Secor*

Document C

"It was quite black out there on the Atlantic and in the blackness the [*Lusitania's*] life-boats alternately rose on the crests of the waves and sank into the black valley between. The boats carried women and children whose hair hung in icicles over their shoulders. . . . Now and then a half-dead passenger uttered a shriek of pain or of anguish as she realized that a friend or relative had died in her arms. . . . Meanwhile, in the dark hull of the German submarine, the captain watching through the periscope finally turned his head away. Even this man, agent of Prussian cruelty, had witnessed a scene upon which he did not care to gaze."

—*Wesley Frost, giving a speech sponsored by the Committee on Public Information*

Document D

MAY THE SPARKS NEVER REACH IT!

---

1. Which of the documents above reflects the views of a pacifist opposed to the war?
   A Document A
   B Document B
   C Document C
   D Document D

2. The speech in Document C is designed to promote
   A sympathy for the sailors on the German U-boats.
   B sympathy for the innocent victims of a U-boat attack.
   C support for pacifists.
   D support for the British.

3. What point of view does Document D express?
   A Interventionist
   B Internationalist
   C Isolationist
   D Pacifist

4. Writing Task Why did some Americans support the war effort while others opposed it? Use your knowledge of World War I and specific evidence from the documents to support your answer.

---

14. Wilson wanted to establish lasting peace.

15. The irreconcilables opposed any treaty with mention of a League of Nations. They wanted America to remain isolationist. The reservationists, including Henry Cabot Lodge, wanted the treaty to be modified. In particular, they feared that the treaty superseded the power of Congress to decide to declare war. Some fellow Democrats did support the treaty but voted against it when Wilson asked them to.

16. There was a shift from the production of war goods to consumer goods. There was a simultaneous increase in demand for consumer goods. Limited supply led to inflation. In addition, as the soldiers returned and wanted their jobs back, the job market became very competitive.

17. Americans elected Warren G. Harding, who proposed a "return to normalcy," which did not include involvement in foreign affairs. This showed their rejection of Wilson's ideas.

Background Knowledge

Discuss the stark contrast between the United States of the mid-1800s and the nation that took shape between 1890 and 1920. Write the following topics on the board: *transportation, communication, size of the United States, settlement patterns, Indian lands,* and *rights for women and minorities.* Have students discuss the changes in each of these areas between 1890 and 1920.

Instruct

Have students read the essay. Ask **What changes within the United States characterized the Progressive Era?** *(Many reforms were put in place, such as giving women the right to vote, ending child labor, guaranteeing fairer wages and shorter hours for workers, and controlling some of the most harmful business practices.)* **Why do you think the changes came at this time?** *(Sample response: As the level of education and income rose for many Americans, people looked for ways to improve conditions in the country.)* Lead a class discussion about conditions that contributed to the growing involvement of the United States in world affairs.

Looking Ahead

By the end of the Progressive Era, Americans were enjoying unprecedented prosperity and would continue to thrive during the 1920s. However, the good times were about to end, testing both the nation's institutions and the resolve of the American people.

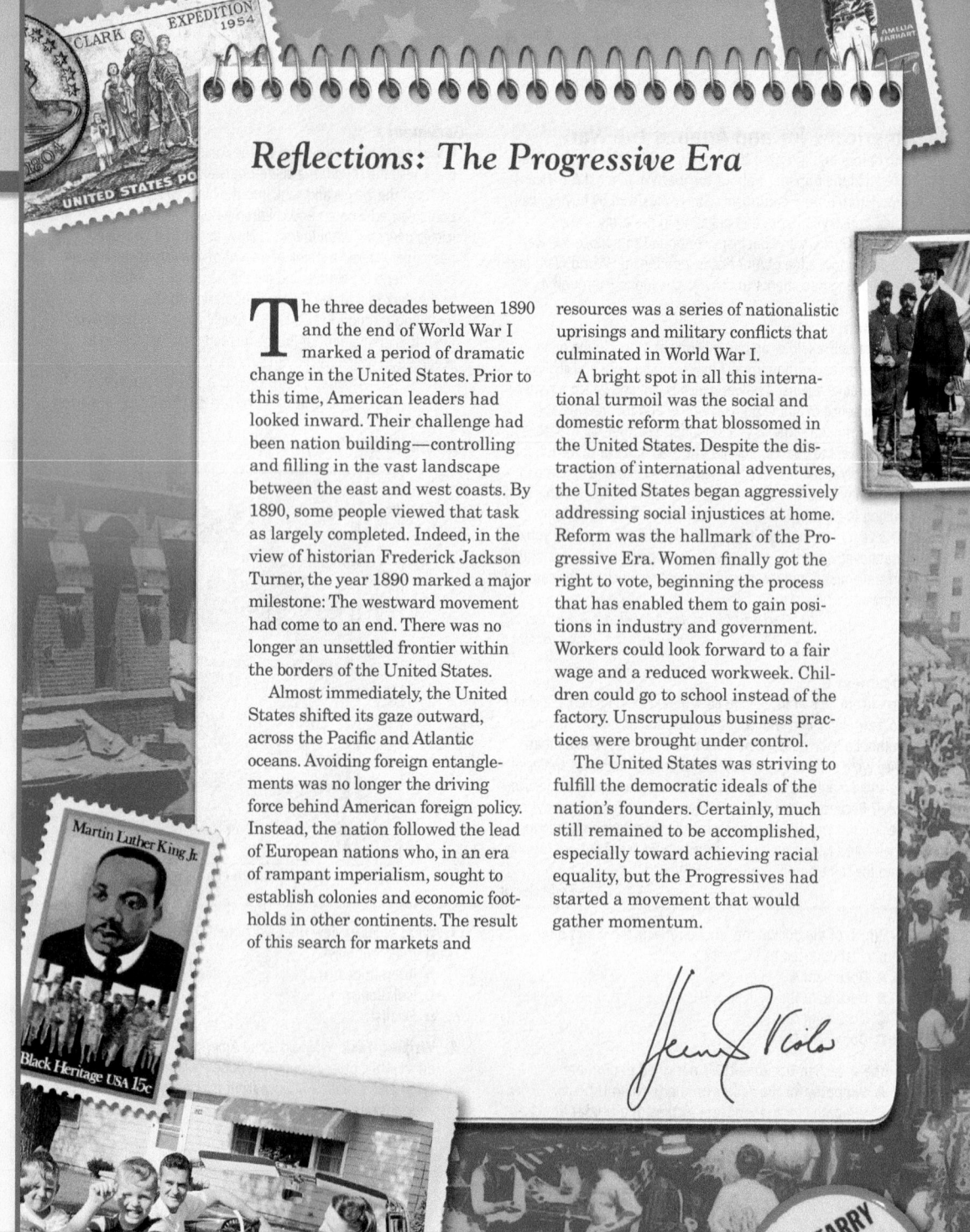

Reflections: The Progressive Era

The three decades between 1890 and the end of World War I marked a period of dramatic change in the United States. Prior to this time, American leaders had looked inward. Their challenge had been nation building—controlling and filling in the vast landscape between the east and west coasts. By 1890, some people viewed that task as largely completed. Indeed, in the view of historian Frederick Jackson Turner, the year 1890 marked a major milestone: The westward movement had come to an end. There was no longer an unsettled frontier within the borders of the United States.

Almost immediately, the United States shifted its gaze outward, across the Pacific and Atlantic oceans. Avoiding foreign entanglements was no longer the driving force behind American foreign policy. Instead, the nation followed the lead of European nations who, in an era of rampant imperialism, sought to establish colonies and economic footholds in other continents. The result of this search for markets and resources was a series of nationalistic uprisings and military conflicts that culminated in World War I.

A bright spot in all this international turmoil was the social and domestic reform that blossomed in the United States. Despite the distraction of international adventures, the United States began aggressively addressing social injustices at home. Reform was the hallmark of the Progressive Era. Women finally got the right to vote, beginning the process that has enabled them to gain positions in industry and government. Workers could look forward to a fair wage and a reduced workweek. Children could go to school instead of the factory. Unscrupulous business practices were brought under control.

The United States was striving to fulfill the democratic ideals of the nation's founders. Certainly, much still remained to be accomplished, especially toward achieving racial equality, but the Progressives had started a movement that would gather momentum.

PROSPERITY AND DEPRESSION

CONTENTS

Construction of the Dam,
by William Gropper,
celebrates American
workers who struggled
through hard times. ▶

Prosperity and Depression

Era Overview

Prosperity and Depression discusses the growth of American affluence after World War I, analyzes the factors that contributed to the 1929 stock market crash and the Great Depression, and describes the New Deal programs enacted by the Roosevelt administration to bring relief to U.S. citizens during the Depression.

Chapter 7 describes the United States during the 1920s, including the booming American economy, the political landscape forged by the Harding and Coolidge administrations, the cultural and social divisions that arose, the introduction of new trends in popular culture, and the Harlem Renaissance.
Issues: U.S. Immigration Policy, Women in American Society, Technology and Society

Chapter 8 examines the causes of the Great Depression, its impact on American citizens and institutions, and the actions taken by American leaders to address the crisis. **Issues:** Government's Role in the Economy, Migration and Urbanization, Global Interdependence

Chapter 9 explores the major programs initiated by President Franklin D. Roosevelt's New Deal and evaluates the economic, social, and political effects of these programs on the United States. **Issues:** Government's Role in the Economy, American Indian Policy, Federal Power and States' Rights

CHAPTER **7** The Twenties
1919–1929

Teach With Technology
Presentation**EXPRESS**™
PREMIUM DVD

- Teach this chapter's core content by using **PresentationExpress,** which includes interactivities, video, lecture notes, and the *ExamView®* QuickTake assessment tool.

- To introduce this chapter by using **PresentationExpress,** ask students with which of the following statements they most agree: **A) The 1920s were a time of great prosperity. B) The 1920s were a time of great tension. C) The 1920s were a time of great creativity. D) The 1920s were a time of great inequality.** Take a class poll or record students' answers by using the QuickTake feature, and discuss their responses. Point out that in this chapter, they will read about the 1920s. Continue introducing the chapter by using the chapter opener slide show.

Technology Resources

- Student**EXPRESS** CD-ROM

- Teacher Resource Library DVD

- Presentation**EXPRESS** PREMIUM DVD

- *ExamView®* **Test Bank CD-ROM** English and Spanish

- **Guided Reading Audio,** Spanish

- **Student Edition on Audio**

THE ESSENTIAL **VIDEO**
By Students For Students
For videos on Amercian Issues, go to
www.pearsonschool.com/ushist

Bibliography

For the Teacher
Bierman, Jr., Harold. *The Great Myths of 1929 and the Lessons to Be Learned.* Greenwood Press, 1991.

Dumenil, Lynn and Eric Foner. *The Modern Temper: American Culture and Society in the 1920s.* Hill & Wang, 1995.

Rhodes, Chip. *Structures of the Jazz Age: Mass Culture, Progressive Education, and Racial Discourse in American Modernism.* Verso, 1998.

For the Student
L2 Hill, Laban Carrick. *Harlem Stomp! A Cultural History of the Harlem Renaissance.* Megan Tingley, 2004.

L3 Blumenthal, Karen. *Six Days in October: The Stock Market Crash of 1929.* Atheneum, 2002.

L4 Kyvig, David E. *Daily Life in the United States, 1920–1939: Decades of Promise and Pain.* Greenwood Press, 2002.

WITNESS HISTORY

Kings of Jazz

When he was 14 years old, Louis Armstrong began to haunt the jazz clubs of New Orleans, Louisiana. King Oliver, an experienced musician, took the boy under his wing and bought him his first cornet. Before long, young Armstrong—nicknamed Satchmo—was making a name for himself playing in clubs and on riverboats.

Then, he got a telegram from King Oliver asking him to come to Chicago to join his Creole Jazz Band. Armstrong was scared, but he made the move north. Satchmo would become America's ambassador of jazz, and jazz would become the music that made the "Roaring Twenties" roar.

◄ King Oliver's Creole Jazz Band, left, helped create the jazz sound.

Dancing the Charleston

Chapter Preview

Chapter Focus Question: How did the United States experience both economic growth and social change in the decade after World War I?

Section 1
A Booming Economy

Section 2
The Business of Government

Section 3
Social and Cultural Tensions

Section 4
A New Mass Culture

Section 5
The Harlem Renaissance

Campaign button for Warren G. Harding

FOR PRESIDENT
WARREN G. HARDING

Ford Model T

Use the ☑ **Quick Study Timeline** at the end of this chapter to preview chapter events.

Note Taking Study Guide *Online*
For: Note Taking and American Issues Connector
www.pearsonschool.com/ushist

Previewing the Chapter

- **WITNESS HISTORY** Read the Witness History selection aloud. Tell students that jazz seemed to symbolize America itself at the time: it was fast, loud, and modern, and it broke all the rules. Some Americans loved jazz for these reasons; others hated it. Discuss the fact that jazz was created mostly by African Americans and that although American society promoted jazz, many discriminated against the African-American musicians who created it.

- **Analyzing the Visuals** Ask students to study the photos on these pages. Have students describe the different musicians and how they are sitting or standing. Ask **How does their clothing contrast with their posture?** *(Their clothing is formal yet they are not standing rigidly; the man at the far right is even seated on the piano.)*

- **Focus** Write the Chapter Focus question on the board. Tell students to keep this question in mind as they read the chapter. Then, have students preview the section titles in this chapter.

- **Preread** Have students complete the chapter's Preread the Chapter Worksheet. Teaching Resources, pp. 8–9

Differentiated Instruction Solutions for All Learners

The following Teacher's Edition strategies are suitable for students of varying abilities.

- **L1** Special Needs Students, pp. 213, 219, 220, 224, 227, 232, 237, 243 SN

- **L2** English Language Learners, pp. 213, 219, 220, 224, 232, 237 ELL

- **L2** Less Proficient Readers, pp. 213, 219, 220, 224, 227, 232, 237, 243 LPR

- **L4** Advanced Readers, pp. 214, 225, 233, 236, 238, 245 AR

- **L4** Gifted and Talented Students, pp. 214, 225, 233, 236, 238, 245 GT

Have students access **www.pearsonschool. com/ushist** for the Note Taking Study Guide *Online* as an alternative to the *Reading and Note Taking Study Guide* booklet.

Objectives

As you teach this section, keep students focused on the following objectives to help them answer the Section Focus Question and master core content.

- Explain the impact of Henry Ford and the automobile.
- Analyze the consumer revolution and the bull market of the 1920s.
- Compare the different effects of the economic boom on urban and rural America.

Prepare to Read

Background Knowledge L3

Remind students that the United States emerged from World War I as a world power. Ask students to predict how this new status will affect the U.S. economy in the 1920s.

Set a Purpose L3

- **WITNESS HISTORY** Read the selection aloud.

  Ask **What did Will Rogers see as the problem with buying goods on credit?** *(People are tempted to spend too much because they don't think about having to pay back the borrowed money.)*

- **Focus** Point out the Section Focus Question, and write it on the board. Tell students to refer to this question as they read. *(Answer appears with Section 1 Assessment answers.)*

- **Preview** Have students preview the Section Objectives and the list of Terms and People.

- NoteTaking Using the Paragraph Shrinking strategy (TE, p. T20), have students read this section. As they read, have students fill in the concept web by noting examples of economic changes during the 1920s. Reading and Note Taking Study Guide

---

◀ 1920s magazine ad

The gift that simplifies housekeeping ...and safeguards health

GENERAL ELECTRIC Refrigerator

▲ Will Rogers

WITNESS HISTORY

Paying for It?

Folksy comedian Will Rogers was one of the most beloved entertainers of his day. Whether standing onstage twirling a rope or chatting on the radio, he could always be counted on to deliver good-natured, amusing comments on the American scene. In the 1920s—with the nation in the midst of a giant economic boom—Rogers turned his keen eye on Americans' passion for buying things:

❝No nation in the history of the world was ever sitting as pretty. If we want anything, all we have to do is go and buy it on credit. So that leaves us without any economic problems whatsoever, except perhaps some day having to pay for them. But we are certainly not thinking of that this early.❞
—Will Rogers, radio commentary, 1928

A Booming Economy

Objectives

- Explain the impact of Henry Ford and the automobile.

- Analyze the consumer revolution and the bull market of the 1920s.

- Compare the different effects of the economic boom on urban and rural America.

Terms and People

Henry Ford	consumer revolution
mass production	installment buying
Model T	bull market
scientific management	buying on margin
assembly line	

NoteTaking

Reading Skill: Identify Supporting Details Note specific economic changes of the 1920s.

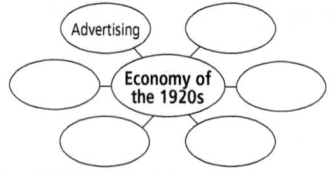

Why It Matters In the decade after World War I, the American economy experienced tremendous growth. Using revolutionary mass-production techniques, American workers produced more goods in less time than ever before. The boom fundamentally changed the lives of millions of people and helped create the modern consumer economy. **Section Focus Question: How did the booming economy of the 1920s lead to changes in American life?**

The Automobile Drives Prosperity

Rarely, if ever, has the nation enjoyed such an economic boom as it did in the 1920s. The recession that had followed World War I quickly ended. All signs pointed to economic growth. Stock prices rose rapidly. Factories produced more and more goods and, with wages on the rise, more and more people could afford to buy them.

Much of this explosive growth was sparked by a single business: the automobile industry. Carmaker **Henry Ford** introduced a series of methods and ideas that revolutionized production, wages, working conditions, and daily life.

Ford Pioneers Mass Production Ford did not originate the idea of **mass production,** the rapid manufacture of large numbers of identical products. It had been used, for example, to make sewing machines and typewriters. But such products involved only hundreds of parts—not the thousands that go into the production of cars. Ford brought mass production to new heights.

Vocabulary Builder

Use the information below and the following resource to teach students the high-use words from this section. Teaching Resources, Vocabulary Builder, p. 11

High-Use Words	Definitions and Sample Sentences
innovation	*n.* change in the way of doing something; act of introducing such a change Ford's use of the assembly line was an **innovation** that allowed cars to be made much more quickly.
stimulate	*v.* to excite to action; to cause to grow or act Buying items on credit **stimulated** manufacturing by increasing demand, which meant that manufacturers hired more people and produced more goods to meet that demand.

Early in the century, only wealthy city dwellers could afford cars. The automobile was often seen as a symbol of the class divisions in the country. City drivers who ventured out onto country roads frightened horses and cows, coated crops with dust, and rutted dirt roads. "To the countryman," said Woodrow Wilson in 1906, cars "are a picture of the arrogance of wealth."

Ransom Olds had introduced a less expensive car, the Oldsmobile in 1901. But it was Henry Ford who truly brought the automobile to the people. In 1908, he introduced the **Model T,** a reliable car the average American could afford. The first Model T sold for $850. Soon after, Ford opened a new plant on the Detroit River. The Detroit location gave Ford easy access to steel, glass, oil, and rubber manufactured in Pennsylvania, Ohio, Indiana, and Illinois.

Ford hired **scientific management** experts to improve his mass-production techniques. Scientific management was a relatively new method of improving efficiency, in which experts looked at every step of a manufacturing process to find ways to reduce time, effort, and expense. Ford also studied the techniques of Chicago meatpacking houses, where beef carcasses were moved on chains past a series of meat cutters, each of whom cut off a specific part of the carcass. Ford reversed the process. He put his cars on moving **assembly lines.** At each step, a worker added something to construct the automobile. In two years, assembly line techniques reduced the time it took to manufacture a Model T—from more than 12 hours to just 90 minutes.

The assembly-line allowed Ford to keep dropping the sale price. The cost of a Model T fell to $350 by 1916 and to $290 by 1927. It was slow, dull, and available only in black. But the Model T was the first car that ordinary people could afford. In 1919, only 10 percent of American families owned an automobile. By 1927, 56 percent did.

Graph Skills The economic boom of the 1920s was reflected in many aspects of the economy, from wages to industrial production to stock prices. *By how much did wages increase between 1910 and 1925? During what years did stock prices soar the most?*

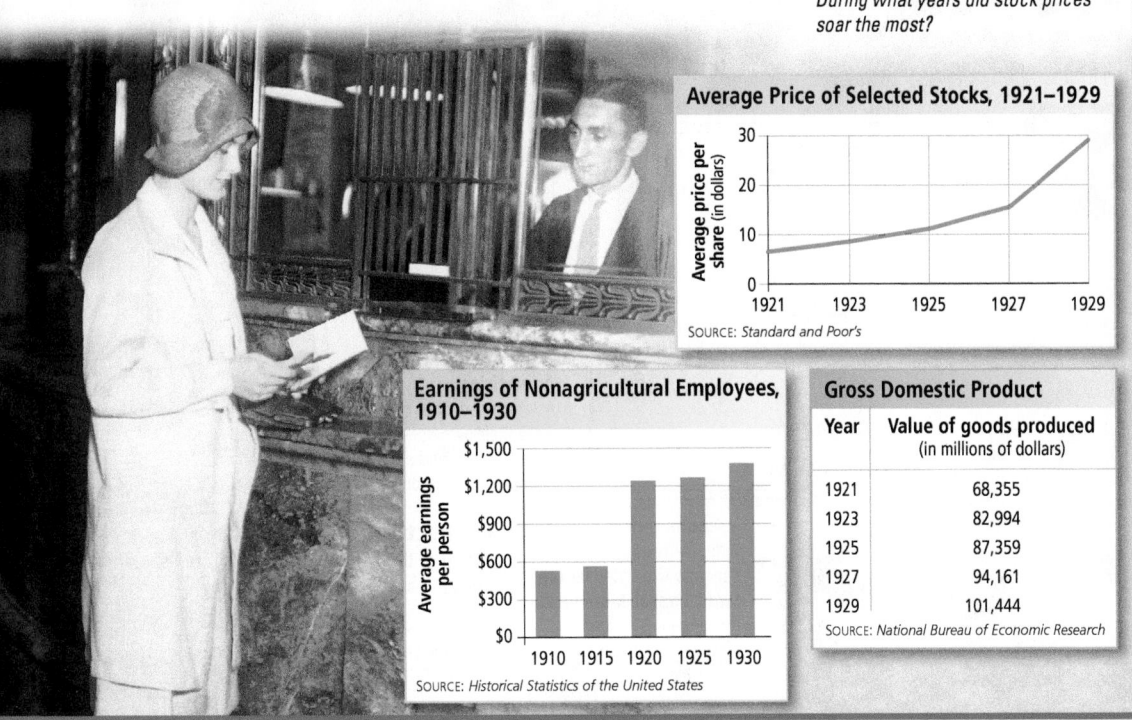

Average Price of Selected Stocks, 1921–1929

SOURCE: *Standard and Poor's*

Earnings of Nonagricultural Employees, 1910–1930

SOURCE: *Historical Statistics of the United States*

Gross Domestic Product

Year	Value of goods produced (in millions of dollars)
1921	68,355
1923	82,994
1925	87,359
1927	94,161
1929	101,444

SOURCE: *National Bureau of Economic Research*

Independent Practice

■ Organize students in pairs, and ask them to write one or two sentences summarizing the importance of Henry Ford to manufacturing processes in America. Have students share their statements. Then, lead a discussion about the impact of the assembly line on labor and manufacturing in America.

■ Ask students to suppose that they were living in America in the 1920s. Have them write journal entries about the ways in which the automobile changed their lives.

Monitor Progress

As students fill in their concept webs, circulate to make sure they note specific examples that support the idea that the economy changed during the 1920s. For a completed version of the concept web, see Note Taking Transparencies, **B-99.**

INFOGRAPHIC

◄ The automobile gave Americans new freedom to enjoy picnics, camping, and Sunday drives.

YELLOWSTONE PARK

Impact of the *Automobile*

Henry Ford made the automobile affordable for the average American. By the 1920s, the growing "car culture" was changing the nation in deeper ways than even Ford might have imagined.

STANDARD

The Gas Station ►
Automobiles encouraged the growth of related industries—especially the oil industry. The gas station—and gas fumes—became a permanent feature of the U.S. landscape.

US 66

U.S. HIGHWAY SYSTEM
1926

Pacific Ocean

Atlantic Ocean

— Major U.S. highway

◄ The Highway System
By 1925, states had built hundreds of highways, and the federal government organized them into a numbered system. One of the first federal highways was Route 66, which ran from Illinois to California.

Advertising ►
Ads stressed what cars gave their owners—speed, status, and a new sense of freedom.

CADILLAC

Enjoy our Southern Hospitality
HARBIN'S TOURIST COURT

◄ Vacation Industry
Americans used their new cars and expanded leisure time to travel. Motels and motor camps sprung up all over the nation.

Connect to Your World
Which of the features of "car culture" shown here are still part of American life today?

History *Interactive* ✳
For: More on the automobile
www.pearsonschool.com/ushist

Differentiated Instruction   Solutions for All Learners

L4 Advanced Readers   L4 Gifted and Talented Students

To reinforce the effect that Henry Ford and the automobile had on the United States, have students make concept maps summarizing key details about Ford's use of mass production and the changes the automobile industry brought to the United States. Ask students use their concept maps to discuss the importance of Henry Ford and the automobile industry to the modern United States. Then, challenge students to write alternative histories, speculating about the ways in which the United States might be different today if Henry Ford had not revolutionized the use of mass production and the automobile industry had not grown as quickly as it did.

Answer

Connect to Your World Gas stations, highways, and car ads are still part of American life today.

When it came to managing the men who worked along his assembly lines, Ford also proved that he was not afraid of <u>innovation</u>. In 1914, he more than doubled the wages of a large number of his workers, from $2.35 to $5 a day. He also reduced their workday from 9 hours to 8 hours. In 1926, he became the first major industrialist to give his workers Saturday and Sunday off. Before Ford, the idea of a "weekend" hardly existed. Ford shrewdly realized that if workers made more money and had more leisure time, they would become potential customers for his automobiles. The combination of the Model T and the "five-dollar day, forty-hour week" made Ford not only a very rich man but also one of the shapers of the modern world.

The Automobile Changes America The boom in the automotive industry <u>stimulated</u> growth in other industries related to car manufacture or use. The steel, glass, rubber, asphalt, wood, gasoline, insurance, and road-construction industries all benefited. For example, one seventh of all steel output was used to make automobiles. The need for gasoline prompted a nationwide search for oil deposits. Oil discoveries in California, Texas, New Mexico, and Oklahoma brought workers and money to the Southwest.

Road construction boomed, especially when the federal government introduced the system of numbered highways in 1926. The millions of cars on American roads led to the rapid appearance of thousands of service stations, diners, and motor hotels (a term later shortened to *motels*). The growth in all these industries created new and often better-paying jobs, spurring national prosperity.

The automobile caused additional economic effects. Other forms of ground transportation, such as railroads and trolleys, suffered a decline in use. With cars, people could go where they wanted, when they wanted. They did not have to travel along set tracks on set schedules.

The automobile prompted a new sense of freedom and prosperity. Never had Americans been so mobile. Entire families crowded into their cars for cross-country vacations or Sunday drives to the country. Ownership of an automobile came to symbolize participation in the American dream of success.

Finally, automobiles altered residential patterns. The ability to drive to work permitted people to live farther from their places of employment. This led to the development of suburban communities linked to cities by arteries of highways and roads. Los Angeles, one of the first cities whose growth was influenced by the automobile, developed in a sprawling, haphazard fashion. It became, according to one observer, "a series of suburbs in search of a city."

✓ **Checkpoint** How did Henry Ford increase the production and sale of automobiles?

A Bustling Economy

The 1920s saw what has been called a **consumer revolution,** in which a flood of new, affordable goods became available to the public. The widespread availability of electrical power supported the consumer revolution. Electric washing machines, vacuum cleaners, and irons made housekeeping easier and less time-consuming. Accessible electricity also contributed to radio and refrigerator sales.

Advertising and Credit Build a Consumer Culture The growing advertising industry also played its part. Using new "scientific" techniques and psychological research, advertisers were able to sell more products to more Americans than ever before. Magazine and newspaper ads often focused on the desires and fears of Americans more than on what people really needed.

Vocabulary Builder
innovation–(ihn uh VAY shuhn) *n.* change in the way of doing something; act of introducing such a change

Vocabulary Builder
stimulate–(STIHM yuh layt) *v.* to excite to action; to cause to grow or act

History Background

Advertising Tactics Advertisers in the 1920s tried to scare consumers into making purchases. A good example of this is the advertising of kitchen appliances.

These ads claimed that only with modern electrical stoves and refrigerators could a mother protect her family. Advertisements claimed that electric stoves cooked food more thoroughly and evenly, killing germs, and that refrigerators kept food from spoiling—a common problem before electricity. General Electric sold its new refrigerator in 1929 with advertisements that focused on safety: "Faithfully,

quietly, automatically, the General Electric gives you the perfect refrigeration that safeguards health."

In one ad, a little boy is shown smiling as he looks into a well-stocked refrigerator, while his mother is told: "What will he be like when he grows up? Will he be tall and strong? Will he be—happy? So much of his future depends on the food he eats. . . . Nothing can give you greater assurance that his food will be wholesome and healthful than a General Electric Refrigerator."

Instruct

- **Introduce** Have students look at the chart on this page. Ask them to suggest, given what they know about increased manufacturing, reasons that cities grew so much during the 1920s. (*Factories were located in cities; people moved to cities to work in the factories.*)

- **Teach** Help students understand what the "other America" was. Ask **How did the "other America" develop?** (*As people moved to the cities to work in factories, workers' wages grew very slowly, while owners and managers grew rich. People who worked in agriculture experienced increasing debt, falling farm prices, and reduced incomes.*) Display Color Transparency: *New York City Skyline.* Ask **How does New York City's skyline indicate prosperity?** (*The skyscrapers indicate a high population density, and construction and growth symbolize economic power.*) Color Transparencies **A-89**

- **Quick Activity** Direct students to the line graph on the next page, and have them read the Primary Source quotation on the same page as well. Ask **How does the line graph show the lack of economic gains that are described in the song by Bob Miller and Emma Dermer?** (*Farmers experienced reduced earnings and poor markets in the 1920s.*)

Independent Practice

Ask students to write a short essay describing the uneven economic picture in America in the 1920s. Ask them to suggest ways in which prosperity could have been more far-reaching in society at the time.

Monitor Progress

To review this section, ask students to summarize the economic extremes of the United States during the 1920s.

Answers

 Buying on margin allowed more people to invest in the stock market because even if they could afford only 10 percent of the stock price, the buyers could make the purchase, hoping to repay the other 90 percent from future profits.

Caption Detroit grew quickly because the new auto industry was located there.

Urban Growth
Built by automaker Walter P. Chrysler in 1928, New York's Chrysler Building (below) was the world's tallest skyscraper—but only for a short time. *Look at the table below. Why do you think Detroit grew so fast after 1910?*

Population of Selected U.S. Cities, 1910–1930			
City	1910	1920	1930
New York	4,766,883	5,620,048	6,930,446
Chicago	2,185,283	2,701,705	3,376,478
St. Louis	687,029	772,897	821,960
Los Angeles	319,198	576,673	1,238,048
Detroit	465,766	993,078	1,568,662

SOURCE: U.S. Census Bureau

Advertisers celebrated consumption as an end in itself, convincing people that they could be the person they wanted to be just by buying the right products. From Kleenex to Listerine, Americans bought products that years earlier they could never have imagined they needed.

Finally, new ways of buying fueled the consumer revolution. People who did not have enough ready cash could buy what they wanted on credit. **Installment buying,** in which a consumer would make a small down payment and then pay off the rest of the debt in regular monthly payments, allowed Americans to own products they might otherwise have had to save up for years in order to buy.

The Big Bull Market Makes Fortunes Consumers were not the only Americans buying and selling in a big way. During the 1920s, the stock market enjoyed a dizzying **bull market,** a period of rising stock prices. More and more Americans put their money into stocks in an effort to get rich quick. By 1929, around 4 million Americans owned stocks.

The pounding desire to strike it rich often led investors to ignore financial risks. As the market soared, people began **buying on margin**—another form of buying on credit. By purchasing stock on margin, a buyer paid as little as 10 percent of the stock price upfront to a broker. The buyer then paid the broker for the rest of the stock over a period of months. The stock served as collateral, or security, for the broker's loan. As long as the price of the stock rose, the buyer had no trouble paying off the loan and making a profit. But if the price fell, the buyer still had to pay off the loan. Buyers gambled that they would be able to sell the stock at a profit long before the loan came due.

In truth, the big bull market stood on very shaky ground. But most people ignored the dangers. By the middle of 1929, economic authorities proclaimed that America and the stock market had entered a "new era." Stock prices would continue their march upward, they said, while boom-and-bust economics would become a thing of the past.

✓ **Checkpoint** How did buying on margin allow more people to invest in the stock market?

Cities, Suburbs, and Country

The economic boom did not affect all parts of the nation equally. While urban and suburban areas prospered, rural Americans faced hardships.

People Flock to Cities In the 1920s, the movement of people was toward cities. Immigrants settled in cities. Farmers left their fields for cities. The direction of the African American Great Migration was toward northern cities. Mexican Americans crossing the border relocated to southwestern cities.

As in the late nineteenth century, cities grew and changed shape. In addition, the adoption of skyscraper technology caused cities to stretch skyward. Steel-framed skyscrapers with light coverings of masonry and glass began to dominate the skylines of the nation's cities. New York's Empire State Building, finished in 1931, symbolized the power and majesty of the United States.

The Suburbs Grow Improved mass transportation and the widespread use of automobiles caused cities to expand outward. More urban workers moved to the suburbs. Western and southern cities, developed after the automobile revolution, encompassed suburban areas as well as inner cities. Suburbs mushroomed, growing much faster than inner cities.

Connect to Your World

The Spread of Urban and Suburban Areas In the 1920s, America's population quickly shifted from mostly rural to more urban and suburban. America had always been a nation of farmers and small towns. But in the 1920s, many people left the farms for higher paying manufacturing jobs.

In the year 2000, the U.S. Census found that about 80 percent of Americans were urban. Almost half of those urban Americans lived in suburbs. The spread of suburbs has created urbanized areas, cities ringed by suburbs that are connected by complex interstate and local highway systems. In the 1920s, people traveled through miles of countryside to reach a city. Today, suburban roads and local highways extend for miles before travelers reach the countryside.

Slowly at first, but more rapidly as the century progressed, suburbs drained people and resources from the cities. Catering to middle- and upper-class residents, suburbs tended to be more conservative and Republican. Meanwhile, the inner cities at the heart of older urban areas began a slow but steady decline.

Many Americans Face Hardship In the cities and suburbs, Americans enjoyed prosperity and the fruits of growth. They participated in the consumer economy and in the joys of automobile ownership. The wealthiest urban residents—owners and managers of businesses—reaped fabulous rewards, which they often pumped back into the bull market. But there were problems looming ahead. America's wealth was poorly distributed. Industrial wages rose at a much slower rate than corporate salaries.

Even worse, farm incomes declined during the decade. Many people living in the country did not participate in the consumer benefits and economic gains of the decade. They formed part of another America—poorer and outside the economic boom. In particular, farmers suffered from growing debt and falling farm prices. A protest song of 1928 expressed their frustration:

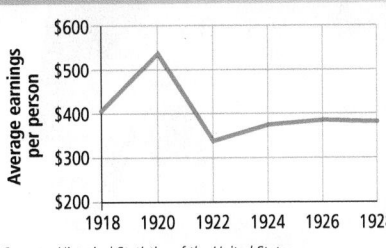

Earnings of Agricultural Employees, 1918–1928

SOURCE: *Historical Statistics of the United States*

Rural Struggles
American farmers did not share in the prosperity of the 1920s. *Compare this graph to the economic graphs at the beginning of this section and make a generalization about farm wages versus nonfarm wages in the 1920s.*

Primary Source

❝'Leven-cent cotton, forty-cent meat,
How in the world can a poor man eat?
Mule's in the barn, no crop's laid by,
Corncrib empty and the cow's gone dry.❞
—Bob Miller and Emma Dermer,
"Eleven Cent Cotton"

If the wealthy believed that the country had entered an age of permanent prosperity, the "other Americans" saw things differently.

✓ **Checkpoint** What impact did the development of suburbs have on American society?

SECTION **1** Assessment

Progress Monitoring *Online*
For: Self-test with vocabulary practice
www.pearsonschool.com/ushist

Comprehension

1. **Terms and People** For each of the following, write a sentence explaining how that person or item was connected with the changing economy of the 1920s.
   - Henry Ford
   - mass production
   - assembly line
   - consumer revolution
   - installment buying
   - bull market
   - buying on margin

2. NoteTaking **Reading Skill: Identify Supporting Details** Use your concept web to answer the Section Focus Question: How did the booming economy of the 1920s lead to changes in American life?

Writing About History

3. **Summarize a Historical Interpretation** Using information from the text, write a paragraph summarizing the reasons for the historical viewpoint that Henry Ford was one of the chief makers of the modern world.

Critical Thinking

4. **Analyze Effects** How is the rise of the automobile an example of technology affecting attitudes or values?

5. **Draw Conclusions** Why do you think many advertisers began to focus on the benefits of their products rather than on the products themselves?

6. **Predict Consequences** Identify two potential signs of weakness in the economy of the 1920s, and predict what might happen if those problems are not solved.

Objectives

As you teach this section, keep students focused on the following objectives to help them answer the Section Focus Question and master core content.

- Analyze how the policies of Presidents Harding and Coolidge favored business growth.
- Discuss the most significant scandals during Harding's presidency.
- Explain the role that the United States played in the world during the 1920s.

Prepare to Read

Background Knowledge L3

Remind students that after World War I, the U.S. government was anxious to boost the economy. Ask students to predict how this may have influenced the regulation of big business.

Set a Purpose L3

- **WITNESS HISTORY** Read the selection aloud.

  Ask **How did Harding's personality symbolize the Jazz Age?** *(He was friendly, fun, and loved music.)*

- **Focus** Point out the Section Focus Question, and write it on the board. Tell students to refer to this question as they read. *(Answer appears with Section 2 Assessment answers.)*

- **Preview** Have students preview the Section Objectives and the list of Terms and People.

- **Reading Skill** Have students use the *Reading Strategy: Compare and Contrast* worksheet. Teaching Resources, **p. 12**

- **NoteTaking** Using the Guided Questioning/Silent Reading strategy (TE, p. T20), have students read this section. As they read, have students note similarities and differences between Presidents Harding and Coolidge. Reading and Note Taking Study Guide

▲ President Harding joins a parade.

WITNESS HISTORY

A Fun-Loving President

In 1920, voters turned from the intellectualism and rigid idealism of Woodrow Wilson to someone who presented himself as an average American, Warren G. Harding. "I am a man of limited talents from a small town," Harding admitted. "I don't seem to grasp that I am President." The genial politician from Marion, Ohio, enjoyed golf, poker, and music. He once claimed that he could play every band instrument "but the slide trombone and the e-flat cornet." But what Harding loved most was shaking hands with tourists who visited the White House:

❝I love to meet people. It is the most pleasant thing I do; it is really the only fun I have. It does not tax me, and it seems to be a very great pleasure to them.❞
—Warren G. Harding, U.S. President

The Business of Government

Objectives

- Analyze how the policies of Presidents Harding and Coolidge favored business growth.
- Discuss the most significant scandals during Harding's presidency.
- Explain the role that the United States played in the world during the 1920s.

Terms and People

Andrew Mellon
Herbert Hoover
Teapot Dome scandal
Calvin Coolidge

Washington Naval Disarmament Conference
Kellogg-Briand Pact
Dawes Plan

NoteTaking

Reading Skill: Compare and Contrast
Note similarities and differences between Presidents Harding and Coolidge.

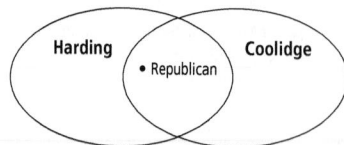

Harding — Republican — Coolidge

Why It Matters In 1920, Warren G. Harding was elected President on a pledge of a "return to normalcy." Rather than pursue reform, as the Progressives had done, Harding and his successor, Calvin Coolidge, favored more conservative policies that aided the growth of business. This pattern—a period of activism followed by a more laissez-faire approach—would repeat itself in the 1950s and 1980s. **Section Focus Question: How did domestic and foreign policy change direction under Harding and Coolidge?**

The Harding Administration

What exactly did a "return to normalcy" mean? Different voters saw different things in the vague phrase. Some saw it as a retreat from involvement in world affairs, others as a rejection of Progressive reform efforts or a swing back to laissez-faire economics. Once in office, however, Harding had to give substance to his promise.

New Policies Favor Big Business Harding signaled the economic direction of his administration by naming wealthy banker **Andrew Mellon** Secretary of the Treasury. Mellon's idea of prudent economic policy was to support legislation that advanced business interests. He disliked the relatively new income tax, favoring instead low taxes on individuals and corporations. Mellon also cut the fat from the budget. By 1925, Congress had reduced spending from a wartime high of $18 billion to $3 billion. Instead of sinking deeper into debt, the Treasury actually showed a surplus.

Vocabulary Builder

Use the information below and the following resource to teach students the high-use words from this section. Teaching Resources, Vocabulary Builder, p. 11

High-Use Words	Definitions and Sample Sentences
incentive	*n.* something intended to encourage someone to take action or work harder Lowering taxes for businesses was an **incentive** for expansion because businesses could use the money they would have paid in taxes to open up new stores and factories.
mediate	*v.* to bring about the settlement of a dispute between two parties Leaders in the 1920s who hoped to avoid another war tried to **mediate** conflicts between nations.

Harding signed a bill raising protective tariff rates by about 25 percent. The tax on imports made it easier for American producers to sell goods at home. However, in retaliation, European nations also hiked tariffs, making American goods harder to sell overseas. This tariff war weakened the world economy.

Under the Progressive leadership of Roosevelt and Wilson, the federal government had passed laws to break up monopolies, protect workers, and restrict the absolute freedom of business leaders. By contrast, Harding favored a return to a more traditional laissez-faire approach. He and Mellon worked to reduce government regulation of business.

Still, the Harding administration did not abandon social goals. Harding's thoughtful and energetic Secretary of Commerce, **Herbert Hoover,** worked with business and labor leaders to achieve voluntary advancements. What the Progressives hoped to achieve through legislation, Hoover attempted to attain with the cooperation of interest groups. He enjoyed great successes at getting people to work together instead of battling one another.

The Ohio Gang Cashes In Harding was a kind, likable man, but he was not especially intelligent. Perhaps no President was friendlier, and few had less sense of what was expected of a President. Faced with a tax issue, Harding lamented, "I listen to one side and they seem right . . . I talk to the other side, and they seem just as right, and here I am where I started. . . . What a job!"

Rather than struggle to master the complexities of the job, Harding trusted others to make decisions. Many were his close friends, men he enjoyed relaxing and gambling with at late-night poker games. Known as the Ohio Gang, they were not honest public servants like Mellon and Hoover. They were mostly greedy, small-minded men who saw government service as a chance to get rich at the expense of the very citizens they were supposed to serve.

Charles Forbes, head of the Veterans' Bureau, practiced graft on an immense scale and wasted hundreds of millions of taxpayers' dollars. For example, his department bought $70,000 worth of floor cleaner—enough to last 100 years—at more than 24 times the fair price. Another Harding pal, Attorney General Harry Daugherty, used his position to accept money from criminals.

The Teapot Dome Scandal Explodes The worst scandal involved Secretary of the Interior Albert Fall. In 1921, Fall arranged to transfer oil reserves in Elk Hills, California, and Teapot Dome, Wyoming, from the Navy Department to the Interior Department. The oil reserves were intended for the navy's use in time of emergency. Harding signed the transfer.

Once Fall had control of the oil, he forgot about the needs of the navy. He leased the properties to private oilmen in return for "loans"—which were actually bribes. Rumors of the deal led to a Senate investigation, and, by 1924, the entire

Analyzing Political Cartoons

The Teapot Dome Scandal This cartoon comments on the most notorious scandal of the Harding administration.
1. What object is used to represent the scandal? Why?
2. According to the cartoon, what is the impact of the scandal?

Coolidge Prosperity

Instruct

- **Introduce** Have students read the red headings only and then compare the section about Coolidge that they are about to read with the section they just read on Harding. Ask **What similarities do the two men share?** *(Both supported big business, and both faced troubles in their administrations.)*

- **Teach** Using the Idea Wave strategy (TE, p. T22), have students discuss Coolidge's economic policy. Point out that although Coolidge, like Harding, believed that government should use legislation to help big business achieve economic change, he did not believe that government should use legislation to achieve social change. Discuss the Primary Source quotation on this page. Ask **Why do you think Coolidge thought the government should legislate economic change but not social change?** *(Responses could include that Coolidge's approach allowed American business to grow without government control, which led to the economic boom of the 1920s; legislating social change might lead to unintended results and people's over-dependence on government.)*

Independent Practice

To help students understand the growth of the economy during the Coolidge presidency, display Color Transparency: *A Booming Economy.* Have students write sentences summarizing the information shown in the chart.
Color Transparencies **A-90**

Monitor Progress

Read aloud the red headings in this section, and ask students to summarize the content under each.

Answer

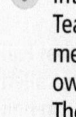 Interior Secretary Albert Fall caused the Teapot Dome Scandal by selling government oil reserves to private oil business owners and then keeping the money. The oil reserves were supposed to be used for the Navy. As a result, Fall went to jail, the business owners lost the reserves, and Harding began to suspect that his Ohio Gang was corrupt.

220 The Twenties

Inauguration
In 1923, Calvin Coolidge was sworn in at his father's farm in Vermont. After winning the election the next year, he had a full inauguration ceremony in Washington, D.C.

sordid affair was revealed to the public. Later, the oil reserves were returned to the government. Fall was sentenced to a year in prison.

Harding himself never saw the full extent of the **Teapot Dome scandal.** In fact, he only had a growing suspicion that his friends were up to no good. But that was enough, as he said, to keep him "walking the floor nights." In July 1923, he visited Alaska during a speaking tour. On his return voyage, he suffered a heart attack and died on August 2. Americans mourned Harding as they had mourned no other President since Lincoln. When the full extent of the scandals emerged, however, the public formed a different opinion of him.

 Checkpoint What were the causes and effects of the Teapot Dome scandal?

Coolidge Prosperity

News of Harding's death reached Vice President **Calvin Coolidge** during a visit to his father's Vermont farm. Almost immediately, the elder Coolidge, a justice of the peace, used the family Bible to swear in his son as President.

In personality, Coolidge was far different from the outgoing, back-slapping Harding. Known as Silent Cal, he was quiet, honest, and frugal—a man who measured his words carefully. He placed his trust in business and put his administration in the hands of men who held to the simple virtues of an older America. Political sharpies out to make a quick buck had no place in the Coolidge administration. Neither did Progressives who believed in an activist government bent on sweeping reforms.

Silent Cal Supports Big Business Coolidge admired productive business leaders. "The man who builds a factory," Coolidge once said, "builds a temple." He believed that the creation of wealth benefited the nation as a whole. In 1925, he expressed this view in his best-known speech:

> **Primary Source** "The chief business of the American people is business. They are profoundly concerned with producing, buying, selling, investing, and prospering in the world. . . . We make no concealment of the fact that we want wealth, but there are many other things that we want very much more. We want peace and honor, and that charity which is so strong an element of all civilization. The chief ideal of the American people is idealism."
> —Calvin Coolidge, speech to the American Society of Newspaper Editors

---

Differentiated Instruction   Solutions for All Learners

 **Special Needs Students**    **English Language Learners**    **Less Proficient Readers**

Help students understand the term "big business" by writing it on the board and then writing descriptions below it, such as *large corporations, companies that have many factories, companies whose leaders influence government policy.* Explain that President Harding and President Coolidge believed that businesses and their investors made the economy grow and helped the country prosper. Because of this belief, they favored policies that supported big business.
Ask students to look for examples of this support as they read the text under the red heading "Silent Cal Supports Big Business."

Coolidge's statement of values and principles has often been oversimplified as "the business of America is business."

In his approach to the economy, Coolidge continued to follow the goals of Secretary of the Treasury Mellon by reducing the national debt, trimming the federal budget, and lowering taxes to give <u>incentives</u> for businesses. Coolidge thus oversaw a spectacular boom in the national economy. For almost six years, the economy soared, generating industrial profits, spectacular growth in the stock market, and general prosperity, especially for urban Americans.

Vocabulary Builder

<u>incentive</u>—(ihn SEHNT ihv) *n.* something intended to encourage someone to take action or work harder

Troubles Brew Beneath the Surface Yet, there were grave problems breeding in the nation. Farmers struggled to keep their land as the prices of their goods fell. Labor unions demanded higher wages and better working conditions. African Americans faced severe discrimination, especially in the South, where Jim Crow laws made enforced segregation a way of life. African American leaders urged Congress to pass an antilynching law. In the Southwest, Mexican Americans confronted shamefully low wages and efforts to force them to return to Mexico.

To all of these concerns, Silent Cal remained silent. Like Harding, he mistrusted the use of legislation to achieve social change. Unlike Progressive Presidents, he believed that it was not the business of the federal government to help create an ideal nation.

✓ **Checkpoint** What policies did Calvin Coolidge favor to support economic growth?

America's Role in the World

Under both Harding and Coolidge, America continued to play an increasingly important role in world business and trade. Beyond that, U.S. foreign policy was largely shaped by reaction to World War I. No previous war had been as deadly. Citizens of all nations agreed: It must never happen again. But how could this goal be achieved?

Seeking an End to War One solution was to avoid another arms race, such as the naval rivalry between Germany and Britain that had contributed to the outbreak of the war. In 1921 and 1922, diplomats gathered in Washington, D.C., to halt another naval arms race before it got out of control. World leaders agreed to limit construction of large warships and hammered out a settlement on several problems between Japan and the West. This **Washington Naval Disarmament Conference** did not end the world's naval problems, but it raised hopes that nations could solve disagreements without resorting to war.

A later attempt to prevent war was the **Kellogg-Briand Pact** of 1928. Secretary of State Frank B. Kellogg and French Foreign Minister Aristide Briand (bree

The United States in International Affairs, 1920–1929		✓ Quick Study
	Goal	**U.S. Action**
League of Nations	To prevent war and settle disputes between nations	U.S. membership favored by Wilson; rejected by Senate
World Court	To make judgments in international disputes voluntarily submitted by nations	U.S. participation favored by Harding; rejected by Senate
Washington Naval Conference	To reduce arms race and size of navies of major powers	U.S. agreed with leading naval powers to limit construction of warships.
Kellogg-Briand Pact	To "outlaw war … as an instrument of national policy"	U.S. agreed with many other nations to renounce war as a means of settling international disputes.

History Background

The Washington Naval Disarmament Conference In 1921, the United States called an international conference to slow the naval arms race and agree about the way to handle conflicts in the Pacific. As a result of the conference, the United States signed several treaties. The Four-Power Pact specified that the United States, Britain, Japan, and France would work together to resolve any conflict that arose between them regarding their interests in the Pacific. These countries also signed the Five-Power Naval Limitation Treaty with Italy. This treaty was drafted from U.S. Secretary of State Charles

Evans Hughes's proposal that the victors of World War I and Japan dispose of almost 1,900,000 tons of warships. Although the treaty did not call for such drastic measures, it helped reverse the rapid production of warships that occurred after World War I. The Nine-Power Pact signed by the United States, Britain, France, Japan, Italy, the Netherlands, Portugal, Belgium, and China affirmed that China was an independent and sovereign nation. It also provided equal terms for all of the signatories when doing business with China.

America's Role in the World

Instruct

- **Introduce: Vocabulary Builder** Have students read the Vocabulary Builder term *mediate* and its definition on the following page. Ask them to predict why the United States and other countries would want an international body to help *mediate* disputes.

- **Teach** Point out to students that because the United States had emerged victorious from World War I, it was expected to play a bigger role in world politics in the 1920s. But the United States refused that role, retreating into isolationism. Ask **Which two international political bodies did the United States refuse to join?** *(the World Court and the League of Nations)* **Why do you think the United States sponsored the Kellogg-Briand Pact of 1928?** *(The United States hoped that by outlawing war, it would never again be involved in a foreign war.)* **What are the potential consequences of isolationism?** *(Possible response: Another war could start without the United States realizing it was brewing, and if the United States refused to get involved early on, it could turn into another world war.)*

- **Analyzing the Visuals** Refer students to the chart on international affairs. Ask them to predict how U.S. actions affected international relations.

Independent Practice

Ask students to write paragraphs summarizing U.S. foreign policy under Coolidge and explain how collecting the war debt hurt America's reputation.

Monitor Progress

Circulate to make sure that students are identifying the most important details of Coolidge's foreign policy.

Answer

✓ Coolidge favored reducing the national debt, trimming the federal budget, and lowering taxes to provide incentives for businesses.

Assess Progress **L3**

- Have students complete the Section Assessment.

- Administer the Section Quiz.
  Teaching Resources, **p. 26**

- To further assess student understanding, use Progress Monitoring Transparencies, **96.**

Reteach

If students need more instruction, have them read the section summary.

Reading and Note Taking **L3**
Study Guide

Adapted Reading and **L1** **L2**
Note Taking Study Guide

Spanish Reading and **L2**
Note Taking Study Guide

Extend **L4**

Have students research the creation of the United Nations after World War II and write a short essay about a recent United Nations news story.

Answer

 The United States supported world peace efforts in the 1920s by hosting the Washington Naval Conference and supporting the Kellogg-Briand Pact.

AHN) drew up a treaty to "outlaw" war "as an instrument of national policy." Eventually, 62 nations ratified the pact. But, in reality, the pact was unenforceable. Kellogg knew it, Briand knew it, and so did the rest of the diplomats. No sooner was the ink dry than everyone involved forgot about it.

Although Congress applauded the useless Kellogg-Briand Pact, it refused to join the World Court, an international body which at least promised to help <u>mediate</u> international disputes. As much as possible, most American leaders in the 1920s hoped to avoid another war by keeping the rest of the world at arm's length.

Collecting War Debts Money issues were another matter. The United States insisted that Britain and France repay their huge war debts to the United States. For this to happen, though, Germany had to make the reparation payments to Britain and France imposed by the Treaty of Versailles. The complex financial issue threatened to undermine the international economy. Some statesmen suggested reducing or even canceling both war debts and reparations. But the frugal Coolidge insisted that a debt was a debt and had to be paid.

In 1924, an agreement known as the **Dawes Plan** arranged U.S. loans to Germany. By enabling Germany to make reparation payments to Britain and France, the Dawes Plan helped Britain and France to repay their debts to the United States. Of course, the entire scheme was financed by U.S. money. After the stock market crash of 1929, however, the well of U.S. money went dry. Germany stopped reparation payments, and Britain and France ended war-debt payments to the United States.

In the end, the war-debt situation damaged America's reputation in the eyes of the world. People from England and France thought that it was heartless for American bankers and politicians to insist on repayment of debts and not to take into account the human costs of the war. In the next war, the United States would take a more flexible approach to war loans.

 Checkpoint How did the United States support world peace efforts during the 1920s?

Vocabulary Builder
<u>mediate</u>–(MEE dee ayt) *v.* to bring about the settlement of a dispute between two parties

---

SECTION **2** Assessment

Progress Monitoring *Online*
For: Self-test with vocabulary practice
www.pearsonschool.com/ushist

Comprehension

1. **Terms and People** For each of the following, write a sentence explaining its importance to national politics of the 1920s.
   - Teapot Dome scandal
   - Washington Naval Disarmament Conference
   - Kellogg-Briand Pact
   - Dawes Plan

2. **NoteTaking Reading Skill: Compare and Contrast** Use your Venn diagram to answer the Section Focus Question: How did domestic and foreign policy change direction under Harding and Coolidge?

Writing About History

3. **Comparing Historical Interpretations** Some people view Coolidge as a moral, idealistic President who restored integrity to government and promoted prosperity. Others see him as a stiff, unimaginative President who retreated from the idealism of the Progressive Era and cared only for the interests of business. Make a Venn diagram comparing these differing historical interpretations.

Critical Thinking

4. **Make Comparisons** How did the approach to government of Harding and Coolidge differ from that of the Progressives?

5. **Draw Conclusions** Do you think that Harding should be held responsible for the scandals in his administration? Why or why not?

6. **Evaluate Information** Many Americans in the 1920s seemed to support both isolationism and an active role in international affairs. Do you agree?

---

1. Sentences should reflect an understanding of how each term or person was important to national politics of the 1920s.

2. Domestic and foreign policy changed direction under Harding and Coolidge in two ways: the United States returned to isolationism, refusing to join the League of Nations; and the United States became focused on collecting war debts from England and France even though this was percieved as heartless by European nations devastated by World War I.

3. Students' diagrams should include Coolidge's honesty, commitment to getting the nation out of debt, and policies that grew the economy. Diagrams also should include Coolidge's hands-off approach to social issues.

4. Unlike the Progressives, Harding and Coolidge did not believe government should try to solve social problems.

5. Possible answer: Harding should not be held responsible for the scandals because he had a trusting personality and he struggled to understand and perform his duties as President.

6. Yes, Americans wanted to avoid future international entanglements by supporting disarmament and foreign policy treaties. The United States also pursued war debt collection from Britain and France and loaned Germany funds to help that nation meet its obligations under the Treaty of Versailles.

For additional assessment, have students access **Progress Monitoring *Online*** at **www.pearsonschool.com/ushist.**

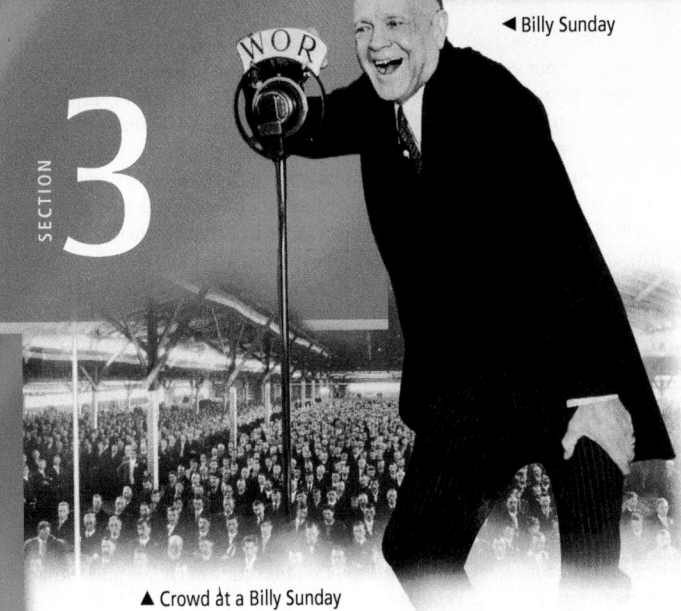

◄ Billy Sunday

▲ Crowd at a Billy Sunday revival meeting

WITNESS HISTORY

Kicking, Fighting, Butting, and Biting

In a time of rapid social change, with a deadly war behind them, many Americans sought a return to more traditional values. They found comfort and strength in the words of preachers such as Billy Sunday. A former pro baseball player, Sunday never lost the dynamic energy of an athlete. Arms flailing, fists punching the air, he railed against the evils of greed, card playing, dancing, and, especially, drinking. He liked to tell audiences:

❝I'm against sin. I'll kick it as long as I've got a foot, and I'll fight it as long as I've got a fist. I'll butt it as long as I've got a head. I'll bite it as long as I've got a tooth. And when I'm old and fistless and footless and toothless, I'll gum it 'till I go home to Glory.❞

—Billy Sunday, sermon

Social and Cultural Tensions

Objectives

- Compare economic and cultural life in rural America to that in urban America.
- Discuss the changes in U.S. immigration policy in the 1920s.
- Analyze the goals and motives of the Ku Klux Klan in the 1920s.
- Discuss the successes and failures of the Eighteenth Amendment.

Terms and People

modernism	Ku Klux Klan
fundamentalism	Prohibition
Scopes Trial	Eighteenth Amendment
Clarence Darrow	Volstead Act
quota system	bootlegger

NoteTaking

Reading Skill: Contrast As you read, look for issues that divided Americans in the 1920s.

Differing Viewpoints	
Education	• Viewpoint 1 • Viewpoint 2
Evolution	

Why It Matters In the 1920s, while many city dwellers enjoyed a rising standard of living, most farmers suffered through hard times. Conflicting visions of what the nation should be heightened the urban-rural division. Some of these issues, such as immigration policy and teaching the theory of evolution, still divide Americans today. **Section Focus Question: How did Americans differ on major social and cultural issues?**

Traditionalism and Modernism Clash

The 1920 census reported that, for the first time in American history, more people lived in urban areas than in rural regions. This simple fact had profound consequences. The nation had been divided before, but usually along north-south or east-west lines. In the 1920s, however, the split was between urban America and rural America. On virtually every important social and cultural issue, the two groups were divided.

Urban Americans enjoyed new consumer products and a wide array of leisure activities. They generally showed an openness toward social change and the new discoveries of science. The growing trend to emphasize science and secular values over traditional ideas about religion became known as **modernism.**

By contrast, rural Americans did not participate fully in the consumer bonanzas, and they missed out on many of the new forms of leisure. People in the country generally embraced a more traditional view of religion, science, and culture.

Objectives

As you teach this section, keep students focused on the following objectives to help them answer the Section Focus Question and master core content.

- Compare economic and cultural life in rural America to that in urban America.
- Discuss the changes in U.S. immigration policy in the 1920s.
- Analyze the goals and motives of the Ku Klux Klan in the 1920s.
- Discuss the successes and failures of the Eighteenth Amendment.

Prepare to Read

Background Knowledge

Remind students that the 1920s were a time of great disparity between rich and poor, urban and rural. Ask students to predict how this discrepancy might affect people's lives in the coming years.

Set a Purpose ⑬

- **WITNESS HISTORY** Read the selection aloud.

  Ask **Who wouldn't agree with Sunday's message?** *(younger, urban workers who wanted to take advantage of the new pleasures the Jazz Age offered)*

- **Focus** Point out the Section Focus Question, and write it on the board. Tell students to refer to this question as they read. *(Answer appears with Section 3 Assessment answers.)*

- **Preview** Have students preview the Section Objectives and the list of Terms and People.

- **NoteTaking** Using the Structured Read Aloud strategy (TE, p. T20), have students read this section. As they read, have students look for issues that divided Americans in the 1920s. Reading and Note Taking Study Guide

Vocabulary Builder

Use the information below and the following resource to teach students the high-use words from this section. Teaching Resources, Vocabulary Builder, p. 11

High-Use Words	Definitions and Sample Sentences
imperial	*adj.* relating to an empire or emperor; having supreme authority Advertisers might use a word such as **imperial** to suggest the superiority or prestige of their product.
advocate	*n.* supporter; one who argues in favor of something **Advocates** of Prohibition believed that illegal alcohol sales contributed to a variety of social problems.

Traditionalism and Modernism Clash ⓛ₃

Instruct

- **Introduce: Key Terms** Ask students to find the key terms *modernism* and *fundamentalism* (in bold) in the text. Ask **What is the difference between *fundamentalism* and *modernism*?** (*Fundamentalism emphasized Protestant teachings and the belief that every word in the Bible was literal truth.* **Modernism** *stressed science and secular ideas.*)

- **Teach** Draw students' attention to the graph on this page and the Comparing Viewpoints feature on the next page. Have students answer the questions. Discuss the Scopes Trial and why it drew nationwide attention. Use the Idea Wave strategy (TE, p. T22) and ask **Why do you think the trial was emotionally charged?** (*People might have felt as if the theory of evolution and the Bible itself were on trial.*) **Why do you think the conflict over evolution continues today?** (*Sample answer: The conflict continues because people still debate the merits of the theory of evolution and the description of creation in the Bible.*)

Independent Practice

Have students complete the *Biography: John Scopes* worksheet. Teaching Resources, **p. 22**

Monitor Progress

As students fill in their tables, circulate to make sure they understand the issues that divided Americans in the 1920s. For a completed version of the table, see Note Taking Transparencies, **B-101.**

High School Education, 1900–1930	
Year	High School Graduates (percentage of 17-year-olds)
1900	6.3
1910	8.6
1920	16.3
1930	28.8
SOURCE: U.S. Census Bureau	

Americans Go to School
Although school attendance grew steadily, fewer than half of American children graduated from high school by 1930. *How much did the high school graduation rate increase during the 1920s?*

Education Becomes More Important Rural and urban Americans differed in their attitudes toward formal education. In rural America, prolonged formal education had not seemed vital. Farmers expected their children to master the "Three R's"—reading, writing, and arithmetic. But beyond that, education collided with the many farm tasks that needed to be done. Muscle, endurance, and knowledge of crops and animals seemed more important to farmers than "book learning."

Formal education took on more importance in urban America. Mental ability, not muscular fitness, was seen as the essential ingredient for success. Mastery of mathematics and language could spell the difference between a low-paying, unskilled job and a higher-paying position as an office worker. By 1930, more American teens were graduating from high school, and more Americans than ever before went to college.

Religious Fundamentalism Grows In the 1920s, many devout Americans believed that Christianity was under siege throughout the world. They pointed to Soviet communist attacks on the Orthodox Church in Russia and to the Mexican revolutionary assaults on the Roman Catholic Church in Mexico.

At home, a growing number of Christians were upset by what they saw as secular trends in religion and culture. They reaffirmed their belief in the fundamental, or basic, truths of their religion. This approach, often called **fundamentalism,** emphasized Protestant teachings and the belief that every word in the Bible was literal truth. Fundamentalists believed that the answer to every important moral and scientific question was in their holy book. Their ideas took root all over the country but were especially strong in rural America.

Americans Clash Over Evolution Fundamentalism and modernism clashed head-on in the **Scopes Trial** of 1925. At issue was the theory of evolution, developed by English scientist Charles Darwin. Darwin believed that complex forms of life, such as human beings, had developed gradually from simpler forms of life. This theory clashed with the description of creation in the Bible.

In 1925, Tennessee passed a law making it illegal to teach Darwin's theory in the state's public schools. The American Civil Liberties Union convinced John Scopes, a high school biology teacher in Dayton, Tennessee, to challenge the law. When Scopes taught evolution in his classroom, he was promptly arrested.

The Scopes Trial drew nationwide attention. Journalists flocked to Dayton to cover the emotionally charged event, which many dubbed the "Monkey Trial" because of the mistaken belief that Darwin claimed that human beings descended from monkeys. **Clarence Darrow,** the most celebrated defense attorney in America, traveled from his home in Chicago to defend Scopes. Three-time presidential candidate William Jennings Bryan, a long-time defender of rural values, served as an expert for the prosecution.

The highlight of the trial came when Darrow called Bryan to the stand as an expert on the Bible. Bryan affirmed that the Bible stated the literal truth. He testified that he believed that God created Adam and Eve and that Joshua made the sun stand still. Darrow tried to use science to cast doubt on such beliefs, but Bryan firmly stated, "I accept the Bible absolutely."

Scopes was found guilty of breaking the law—a fact that was never in question—and fined $100. While the Scopes Trial showcased a major cultural and religious division, it did not heal the conflict or answer its central questions. When the trial was over, each side still believed in the truth of its position. The conflict over evolution continues today.

✓ **Checkpoint** How did the Scopes Trial illustrate the urban-rural split in the 1920s?

Answers

Caption by just over 12 percent

✓ The Scopes Trial illustrated the urban-rural split in the 1920s by demonstrating the difference in attitudes toward science and religion. Religious fundamentalism was especially strong in rural areas, where many people did not want Darwin's theory of evolution to be taught in public schools.

Differentiated Instruction   Solutions for All Learners

ⓛ₁ Special Needs Students   ⓛ₂ English Language Learners   ⓛ₂ Less Proficient Readers

Have students write explanations of key terms by illustrating the words, writing a definition, and using the word in context. Students can make flashcards by writing a term and an illustration on one side of each card and a definition and context sentence on the reverse side.

Restricting Immigration

Another cultural clash involved the ongoing boom in immigration. As in the past, Americans known as nativists argued that the new arrivals took jobs away from native-born workers and threatened American religious, political, and cultural traditions.

Nativists Oppose Immigration Although nativist politicians had been able to restrict immigration from China in 1882, they had failed to push through laws to restrict immigration from southern and eastern Europe. On the eve of World War I, however, Congress did pass a law requiring immigrants to take a literacy test. Immigrants who could not read or write their own language were prohibited from entering the United States. President Wilson vetoed the law, but Congress overrode Wilson's veto.

During the postwar Red Scare, fear that communists and socialists from eastern Europe were traveling to the United States with their revolutionary doctrines added an emotional edge to the debate. The problem that confronted nativists was traditional immigration policy. All Americans who could trace their ancestry back far enough discovered foreign origins. Many viewed the immigration experience as part of what made an American an American.

Quota Laws Limit Newcomers World War I, the Russian Revolution, and the Red Scare strengthened the nativist position. Two important laws—the Emergency Quota Act of 1921 and the National Origins Act of 1924—established a **quota system** to govern immigration from specific countries.

Comparing Viewpoints

Should a State Ban Teaching of Darwin's Theory of Evolution?

The Scopes Trial of 1925 revolved around a Tennessee law that banned the teaching of Darwin's theory of evolution. The deeper issue involved a clash between traditional religious beliefs and modern science.

THE PROSECUTION

William Jennings Bryan believed that Tennessee had a right to protect its children from ideas that violated biblical teachings.

Primary Source

"Science is a magnificent force, but it is not a teacher of morals. . . . In war, science has proven itself an evil genius; it has made war more terrible than it ever was before."

"It is for the jury to determine whether this attack upon the Christian religion shall be permitted in the public schools of Tennessee by teachers employed by the state."

"When Shall We Three Meet Again?"

Compare

1. How does Bryan's view of science differ from that of Malone?

2. What does each man feel should happen when science clashes with religion?

THE DEFENSE

Dudley Field Malone, who joined Clarence Darrow in the defense of Scopes, argued against a state determining what should be taught.

Primary Source

"We feel we stand with progress. We feel we stand with science. We feel we stand with intelligence. We feel we stand with fundamental freedom in America."

"Let the children have their minds kept open. Close no doors to their knowledge. Shut no door from them. Make the distinction between theology and science. Let them have both. Let them be taught both. Let them both live."

- **Introduce: Key Term** Ask students to find the key term *quota system* (in bold) in the text, then write it on the board, say it aloud, have the students say it with you, and provide them with the definition. Ask **What events strengthened the nativist position and eventually led to the establishment of an immigration *quota system*?** (*World War I, the Russian Revolution, and the Red Scare*)

- **Teach** Ask **Why were nativists worried by the boom in immigration?** (*They argued that the new arrivals took jobs away from native-born workers and threatened American religious, political, and cultural traditions.*) **What was the problem that confronted nativists?** (*Traditional immigration policy was a problem for nativists as the immigrant experience was one that almost all Americans shared.*)

- **Quick Activity** Ask students to name, if possible, one of the countries from which their ancestors immigrated.

Independent Practice

Have students suppose that they are living in 1924. Have them write a newspaper editorial about the passing of the National Origins Act.

Monitor Progress

To review this section, ask students to summarize the point of view of the nativists. Then ask them to consider how immigrants from southern and Eastern Europe might have felt about the nativist point of view.

Answers

Compare

1. Bryan believes that science can be used for good or evil. He argues that the jury should decide whether attacks on religion should be taught in schools that are supported with public money. He mentions military technology as an example of the evil use of science. Malone counters that no doors should be closed to children, that both religion and science should be available to them.

2. Bryan believes that religion should overrule science. Malone thinks that both should be given equal consideration.

American Issues Connector

Objectives

- Analyze previous policies used by the government to limit immigration to the United States.

- Understand that U.S. immigration policy continues to be debated today.

Background Knowledge ⑬

Tell students that U.S. immigration has always been controversial. Americans have always worried that there would not be enough resources or jobs if immigration were unlimited. Those who oppose immigration have often been criticized for being the descendants of immigrants themselves. Ask students how much immigration is too much.

Instruct

Ask **What characteristics have been identified as barriers to immigration over the years?** *(ethnicity, political beliefs, the number of immigrants already in the United States from each country, legal status, and work status)* **What U.S. immigration issue is being debated today?** *(whether to allow illegal immigrants to stay in America)*

Monitor Progress

- Have students complete the Issues Connector Worksheet, *U.S. Immigration Policy.* Check student work to make sure they grasp the aspects of the issue. Teaching Resources, **pp. 15–18.**

- Remind students to complete their American Issues Journal worksheets. Review their work for accuracy. Reading and Note Taking Study Guide

Answers

Transfer Activities

1. Head feels it will help to end the flow of illegal immigrants coming to look for work and all the problems associated with hiring illegal immigrant workers. Erler argues that illegal actions should not be rewarded.

2. They are different because in 1924 the issue was not about illegal immigrants, but about whether some countries were too dangerous for the United States to welcome their citizens; they are similar because both debates are about whether immigrants will hurt or help America.

3. For more information about U.S. Immigration Policy, have students access **www.pearsonschool.com/ushist.**

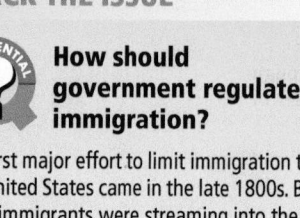

American Issues Connector | U.S. Immigration Policy

Immigrants and foreign visitors go through a careful check before they are allowed to enter the country.

TRACK THE ISSUE

How should government regulate immigration?

The first major effort to limit immigration to the United States came in the late 1800s. By then, immigrants were streaming into the country. Many Americans worried about losing their jobs or their sense of national identity. Since then, immigration and immigration policy have remained controversial issues. Use the timeline below to explore this enduring issue.

1882 Chinese Exclusion Act
Federal government makes first law to exclude a specific national group.

1924 National Origins Act
Law sets quotas on numbers of immigrants from each country.

1952 McCarran-Walter Act
Law establishes political beliefs as criteria for exclusion.

1965 Immigration Act Amended
Congress abolishes national quotas but sets ceiling for each hemisphere.

1986 Immigration Reform and Control Act
Law offers amnesty to some illegal aliens.

2004 Guest Worker Program
President Bush proposes law allowing temporary foreign workers.

Immigrants enter New York's Ellis Island in the 1920s.

DEBATE THE ISSUE

Amnesty for Illegal Immigrants In recent years, Americans have hotly debated the question of amnesty for illegal immigrants. Some Americans favor laws providing a legal route to citizenship. Critics say that laws curbing further illegal immigration would be more effective.

"Amnesty combined with serious penalties for employers that hire undocumented workers . . . is the only real way out of [this] situation. . . . It . . . is . . . the option most likely to secure the border and end the system of undocumented worker exploitation—which is precisely why our well-funded leaders in Washington have no intention of pursuing it."
—Tom Head, author

"Amnesty for illegal aliens is simply a reward for law-breaking. No system depending on a strict regard for the rule of law can treat law-breaking so casually. Amnesty will be a magnet for further illegal immigrants, who hope to be future recipients of the nation's compassion."
—Edward J. Erler, Senior Fellow, Claremont Institute

 TRANSFER Activities

1. **Compare** Why does Tom Head support amnesty? Why does Erler oppose it?

2. **Analyze** How does the issue debated today differ from the issues that led to the passage of the National Origins Act?

3. **Transfer** Use the following Web site to see a video, try a WebQuest, and write in your journal. www.pearsonschool.com/ushist

Connect to Your World

Changing U.S. Immigration Policies Until the early twentieth century, the United States placed few restrictions on immigration from Europe, though immigrants from Asia faced obstacles. Beginning in the 1920s, the United States sharply limited immigration. In the 1960s, the United States again opened the way for expanded immigration. However, regulations still limited the number of legal immigrants. To get around those limits, many immigrants crossed the border between Mexico and the United States illegally. Latin American immigrants became an important part of the workforce in some states. When President Bush took office in 2001, he hoped to make it easier for Latin Americans to work in the United States legally. However, terrorist attacks in 2001 created great concern about the safety of the U.S. borders. New security measures have made it more difficult to cross over the Mexican border into the U.S.

The National Origins Act set up a simple formula: The number of immigrants of a given nationality each year could not exceed 2 percent of the number of people of that nationality living in the United States in 1890. The year 1890 was chosen because it was before the great wave of immigration from southern and eastern Europe. For example, the act permitted about 65,721 immigrants from England and Northern Ireland to come to America every year, but it allowed only about 5,802 immigrants from Italy. The act also continued to exclude most Asian immigrants. America had closed its "golden door" to many of the people trying to enter.

More Mexicans Come North The quota system did not apply to Mexico, which was still reeling from the 1910 revolution. Settling in sparsely populated regions of the Southwest, Mexican immigrants made major contributions to the local economies. Most found work harvesting crops in California and Texas. A smaller number sought jobs in the factories and farms of the North or Midwest.

Many Mexican immigrants faced discrimination and hostility in their new homes. They often competed with native-born Americans for jobs and were frequently subjected to brutality and violence.

✓ **Checkpoint** How did new laws change U.S. immigration policy in the 1920s?

The New Ku Klux Klan

Immigration restriction was an attempt to turn back the clock to what many saw as a simpler, better time. Rural Americans saw the country become increasingly urban and their own position in the nation slip in relative importance. Many lashed out against symbols of change. Some even turned to organizations that supported doctrines of hate and employed violence and terror to achieve their ends.

The Klan Rises Again In 1915, on Stone Mountain in Georgia, a group of angry men revived the **Ku Klux Klan.** The original Klan had been formed in the South during Reconstruction largely to terrorize African Americans who sought to vote. Although the new Klan continued to promote hatred of African Americans, it was also aimed at the new America taking shape in the cities. It targeted Jews, Catholics, and immigrants. In the wake of postwar labor unrest, the Klan opposed labor unions—especially because many union members were immigrants or political radicals. The Klan also claimed to stand against lawbreaking and immorality.

At its height, the Klan's "Invisible Empire" had perhaps 4 to 5 million members. Most were in the South, but there were also branches in the Midwest, Northeast, and West—in both rural areas and in small industrial cities. One center of Klan strength was Indiana, where Klan leader David Stephenson ruled with an iron fist and controlled numerous politicians. There were special women's branches of the Klan as well. However, some male Klan leaders were strongly opposed to women taking an active role in politics.

Klan members boycotted businesses owned by anyone who was Jewish, Catholic, or African American. The Klan terrorized citizens in the night, often by

The New Ku Klux Klan
In 1925, thousands of Klansmen (below) staged a huge march in Washington, D.C.

Instruct

- **Introduce: Vocabulary Builder** Have students locate the term *imperial,* then write it on the board, say it aloud, have the students say it with you, and read the definition. Tell students that an *Imperial* Wizard was a leader with great authority in the Ku Klux Klan.

- **Teach** Have students understand the difference between the original Ku Klux Klan and the new Klan that emerged in 1915. Then, ask **Why do you think the new Klan eventually had millions of members?** *(Many Americans were prejudiced against African Americans, Jews, and Catholics.)* **Why did the Klan eventually decrease in importance?** *(Many groups opposed it. Also, it was corrupt. Its leaders bribed politicians, stole from its members' dues, and lied to its members.)*

- **Analyzing the Visuals** Direct students to the photograph of Klansmen marching in Washington, D.C. Discuss how the beliefs of the Ku Klux Klan contrast with the ideals on which the United States was founded.

Differentiated Instruction Solutions for All Learners

L1 Special Needs Students L2 Less Proficient Readers

To help students practice previewing, ask them to skim the following before they read the section: headings, images, bold key terms. Tell them that the subject of the section shifts from one topic (the emergence of the new Ku Klux Klan) to another, related topic (opposition to the Klan) part way through. Based on their previewing, ask them to pinpoint when this shift occurs.

Answer

✓ New laws changed U.S. immigration policy in the 1920s by setting quotas for certain countries. No Asians were allowed in, and most countries could send very few people (except for northwestern European countries).

Have students read the Primary Source quotation from the William Allen White letter. Using the Think-Write-Pair-Share strategy (TE, p. T23), have students write paragraphs explaining why Americans such as White opposed the Ku Klux Klan and how Americans can promote diversity in the United States.

Monitor Progress

As students write their paragraphs, circulate to make sure that they understand why many Americans opposed the Ku Klux Klan and its values, focusing instead on the positive elements of the "melting pot" aspect of American heritage.

Vocabulary Builder

imperial—(ihm PIR ee uhl) adj. relating to an empire or emperor; having supreme authority

burning crosses outside their homes. Klansmen usually wore masks to conceal their identities, met to wave flags and preach hate, and followed leaders with such titles as Grand Dragon and Imperial Wizard. But behind the Klan's confident facade were Americans fearful of change.

Americans Oppose the Klan Individuals, as well as organizations such as the NAACP and the Jewish Anti-Defamation League, battled against the Klan and its values. They embraced the idea of racial, ethnic, religious, and cultural diversity. For them, the notion of the "melting pot" was as old as America itself, and they drew strength from American traditions and saw hope in the American future. Journalist William Allen White noted:

> **Primary Source** "To make a case against a birthplace, a religion, or a race is wickedly un-American and cowardly. The whole trouble with the Ku Klux Klan is that it is based upon such deep foolishness that it is bound to be a menace to good government in any community."
>
> —William Allen White, letter to the editor of the *New York World,* 1921

The Klan itself became thoroughly corrupt. Its leaders bribed politicians, stole from its members' dues, and lied to its members. Stephenson ended up going to prison for assault and second-degree murder. By the late 1920s, the Klan stood exposed. Although it never disappeared, it withered in importance.

✓ **Checkpoint** How did the goals of the new Ku Klux Klan differ from those of the old Klan?

● **INFOGRAPHIC**

PROHIBITION AND CRIME

Supporters of Prohibition rightly pointed out that alcohol was at the root of many social ills, from child abuse to lost productivity on the job. Sadly, the attempt to ban alcohol opened the door to a new set of social problems.

During Prohibition, many ordinary Americans—rich and poor—became lawbreakers. Ignoring the Volstead Act, they found creative ways to hide alcohol. This woman has a flask hidden in her boot. ▼

Federal agents destroy a still used to manufacture illegal alcohol. Although these "feds" worked tirelessly, there were not enough of them to enforce Prohibition effectively. ▼

History Background

Revival of the Ku Klux Klan The Ku Klux Klan was fading into a memory by 1915, when Colonel William J. Simmons organized its revival. Simmons, a preacher from Georgia, was inspired to reorganize the Klan by a book written by Thomas Dixon in 1905 called *The Clansman* and the 1915 movie *Birth of a Nation,* directed by D. W. Griffith. The book and the movie told the story of the South before and after the Civil War, and claimed that only the efforts of the heroic Klan saved the South from depraved white northerners and freed black slaves.

Few joined Simmons's group until Edward Y. Clark and Mrs. Elizabeth Tyler helped publicize the revival and raise additional funds. People favored the Klan for several reasons. Some viewed joining the new Klan as an expression of their patriotism, while others felt it was a link to the post–Civil War South. Most important to the growth of the revived Klan was that many people felt threatened by the Bolshevik revolution in Russia and by the large volume of immigrants to the United States. They wanted to stop the changing ethnic character of American society.

Answer

✓ The new Klan was different from the old one because it targeted not only African Americans but Jews, Catholics, and immigrants as well.

Prohibition and Crime

Another divisive issue was **Prohibition,** the banning of alcohol use. Since the early 1800s, temperance reformers had crusaded against alcohol. By 1917, some 75 percent of Americans lived in "dry" counties that had banned liquor. World War I increased support for temperance. It seemed unpatriotic to use corn, wheat, and barley to make alcohol when soldiers overseas needed bread.

Government Bans Alcoholic Beverages In 1919, the states ratified the **Eighteenth Amendment** to the Constitution. It forbade the manufacture, distribution, and sale of alcohol anywhere in the United States. The amendment had been passed largely on the strength of rural votes. Congress then passed the **Volstead Act,** a law that officially enforced the amendment.

Advocates of Prohibition, known as "drys," called it a "noble experiment." They argued that Prohibition improved individuals, strengthened families, and created better societies. In fact, drinking—as well as alcoholism and liver disease caused by drinking—did decline during Prohibition.

Opponents of Prohibition, dubbed "wets," countered that the ban on alcohol did not stop people from drinking. Instead, they argued, Prohibition helped create an atmosphere of hypocrisy and increased organized crime.

Americans Break the Law As the wets noted, the Volstead Act did not stop Americans from drinking, but it did prevent them from purchasing drinks

Vocabulary Builder
advocate—(AD vuh kiht) *n.* supporter; one who argues in favor of something

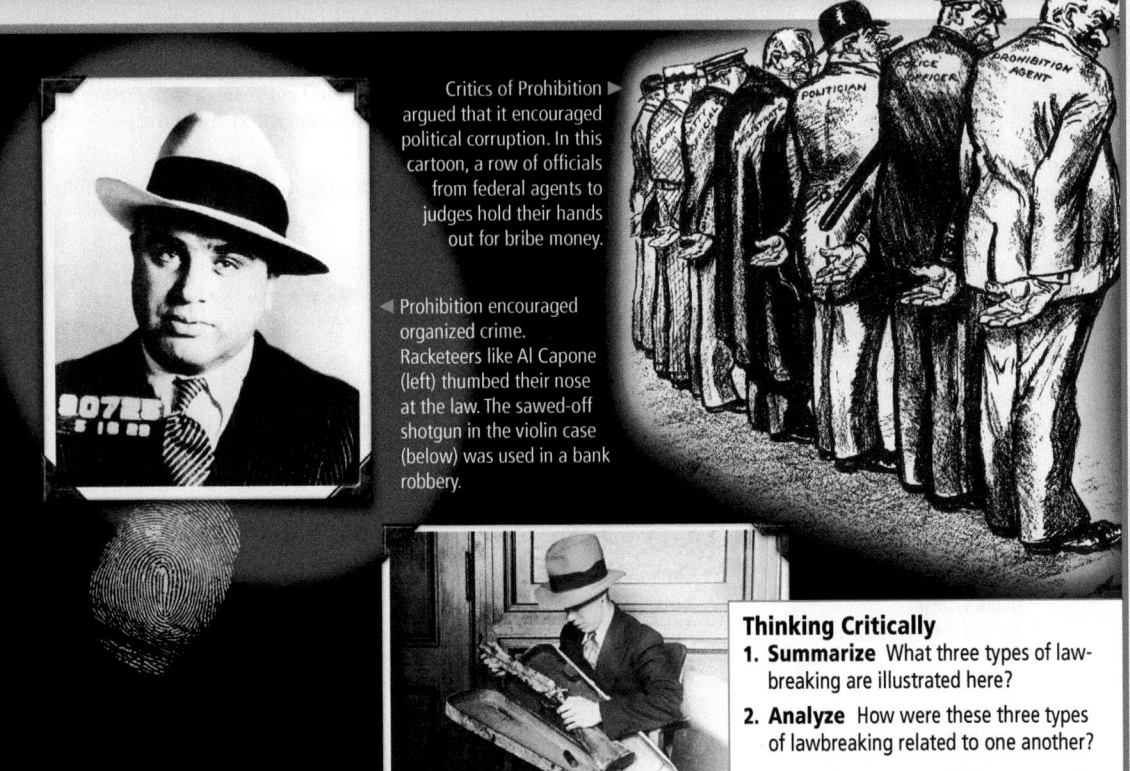

Critics of Prohibition ▶ argued that it encouraged political corruption. In this cartoon, a row of officials from federal agents to judges hold their hands out for bribe money.

◀ Prohibition encouraged organized crime. Racketeers like Al Capone (left) thumbed their nose at the law. The sawed-off shotgun in the violin case (below) was used in a bank robbery.

Thinking Critically
1. **Summarize** What three types of law-breaking are illustrated here?
2. **Analyze** How were these three types of lawbreaking related to one another?

Connect to Your World

Dry Counties Today Following the repeal of the Eighteenth Amendment, ending nationally sponsored Prohibition, many U.S. citizens continued to oppose the sale and consumption of alcohol. Because of this opposition, some states continued to prohibit alcohol while other states permitted county governments to decide whether to allow alcohol to be bought and sold within their borders. A county that passes a law prohibiting the sale and use of alcohol within its limits is called a dry county. Dry counties can be found in states such as Alabama, Arkansas, Florida, Kansas, Kentucky, Mississippi, Texas, and Virginia. Today, the United States has hundreds of dry counties consisting of about 18,000,000 people and covering about 10 percent of the nation's land area.

Assess and Reteach

Assess Progress L3

- Have students complete the Section Assessment.

- Administer the Section Quiz. **Teaching Resources, p. 27**

- To further assess student understanding, use **Progress Monitoring Transparencies, 97.**

Reteach

If students need more instruction, have them read the section summary.

Reading and Note Taking Study Guide L3

Adapted Reading and Note Taking Study Guide L1 L2

Spanish Reading and Note Taking Study Guide L2

Extend L4

Have students research the aftermath of Prohibition, including public attitudes toward drinking and the effect of organized crime on American society. Ask students to present their findings in an essay.

Answer

 The effects of the Eighteenth Amendment and the Volstead Act include an increase in the bootlegging of illegal alcohol and in organized crime.

THEIR SECURITY DEMANDS YOU VOTE REPEAL

WOMEN'S ORGANIZATION FOR NATIONAL PROHIBITION REFORM

Wets Seek Repeal
Supporters of the Eighteenth Amendment had often used images of mothers and children to press for a ban on alcohol. This propaganda poster uses similar images to press for the repeal.

---

legally. The gap between the law and individual desires was filled by a large illegal network. People made alcohol in homemade stills or smuggled it in from other countries. **Bootleggers** sold illegal alcohol to consumers. In cities, secret drinking establishments, known as speakeasies, attracted eager customers.

Government agents worked tirelessly to stop the flow of illegal liquor. However, they were short-handed, and the demand for alcohol was too great. There were millions of dollars to be made by both organized and unorganized criminals. Particularly in cities, policemen and politicians tended to look the other way when liquor was involved. They rationalized their actions by saying that if people wanted to drink, they would drink.

Al Capone, a Chicago gang leader, was the most famous criminal of the Prohibition era. He defended his illegal actions:

> **Primary Source** "I make my money from supplying a public demand. If I break the law, my customers, who number hundreds of the best people in Chicago, are as guilty as I am. The only difference between us is that I sell and they buy. Everybody calls me a racketeer. I call myself a businessman."
> —Al Capone, quoted in *Era of Excess* (Sinclair)

The problem was that under the guise of providing a glass of beer or scotch, organized crime spread into other areas of society. Capone's other "businesses" included prostitution, drugs, robbery, and murder. Thus, Prohibition contributed to the growth of organized crime in America.

Prohibition Divides the Nation By the mid-1920s, most city politicians clamored for the repeal of the Eighteenth Amendment. But to many rural Americans, liquor and crime were tied to other divisive cultural issues of the day. Thus, like immigration and evolution, the debate over Prohibition became part of a battle over the future of America.

In the culturally divided 1920s, Americans could not reach a satisfactory settlement on the issue. Not until 1933 did the Twenty-first Amendment finally repeal Prohibition.

✔ **Checkpoint** What were the effects of the Eighteenth Amendment and the Volstead Act?

SECTION **3** Assessment

Progress Monitoring Online
For: Self-test with vocabulary practice
www.pearsonschool.com/ushist

Comprehension

1. **Terms and People** For each of the following, write a sentence explaining its importance to the social and cultural clashes of the 1920s.
   - modernism
   - fundamentalism
   - Scopes Trial
   - quota system
   - Ku Klux Klan
   - Prohibition
   - Eighteenth Amendment
   - Volstead Act
   - bootlegger

2. **NoteTaking Reading Skill: Contrast** Use your table to answer the Section Focus Question: How did Americans differ on major social and cultural issues?

Writing About History

3. **Compare and Contrast** Write the opening paragraph for an essay comparing supporters and opponents of Prohibition. Use the information in this section as well as your own thoughts. Consider the goals and values that wets and drys might have had in common as well as the ways in which they differed.

Critical Thinking

4. **Recognize Ideologies** How did the two sides in the Scopes Trial represent conflicting value systems? What did each side value most?

5. **Identify Points of View** Why did both supporters and opponents of immigration quotas believe they were defending American traditions and values?

6. **Draw Conclusions** Why do you think the revived Ku Klux Klan was able to spread beyond the South and even into some urban areas?

Section 3 Assessment

1. Sentences should reflect an understanding of the significance of each term to the social and cultural clashes of the 1920s.

2. Rural and urban Americans differed on major social issues including prohibition, the value of education, and the roles of science and religion. Rural Americans were not involved in many of the changes that city dwellers experienced; they were alarmed by modern changes and reacted against modern ideas. Many urban Americans embraced modern life and rejected the traditional values that rural people held.

3. Paragraphs should include the concern of prohibition supporters for family safety and the belief of prohibition opponents that drinking could not be banned successfully.

4. William Jennings Bryan, an expert for the prosecution, favored traditional Christian values rather than evolution. The defense, led by Clarence Darrow, represented science as the source of facts and rejected the supremacy of faith over science.

5. Supporters of quotas thought that they were preserving traditional American values, language, and customs. Opponents believed they were living up to America's offer of freedom for all.

6. The Ku Klux Klan may have appealed to some urban workers who feared that they would have to compete with immigrants and African Americans for jobs.

For additional assessment, have students access **Progress Monitoring Online** at **www.pearsonschool.com/ushist.**

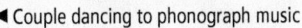

◀ Couple dancing to phonograph music

WITNESS HISTORY

"Ain't We Got Fun?"

The phonograph had come a long way from that day in 1877 when inventor Thomas Edison recorded himself reciting "Mary Had a Little Lamb." By the 1920s, Americans were buying thousands of phonographs and millions of shiny phonograph records. In the comfort of their living rooms, they listened and danced to popular songs that reflected the carefree spirit of the age. One hit tune of 1921 told of a young couple who were determined to enjoy themselves even though they didn't have much money:

❝Night or daytime, it's all playtime,
   Ain't we got fun?
   Hot or cold days, any old days,
   Ain't we got fun?
   If wifie wishes to go to a play,
   Don't wash the dishes, just throw them away!❞

—Gus Kahn and Raymond B. Egan,
   "Ain't We Got Fun?"

A New Mass Culture

Objectives

- Trace the reasons that leisure time increased during the 1920s.
- Analyze how the development of popular culture united Americans and created new activities and heroes.
- Discuss the advancements of women in the 1920s.
- Analyze the concept of modernism and its impact on writers and painters in the 1920s.

Terms and People

Charlie Chaplin
The Jazz Singer
Babe Ruth
Charles Lindbergh
flapper

Sigmund Freud
"Lost Generation"
F. Scott Fitzgerald
Ernest Hemingway

NoteTaking

Reading Skill: Summarize Look for ways in which culture changed during the 1920s.

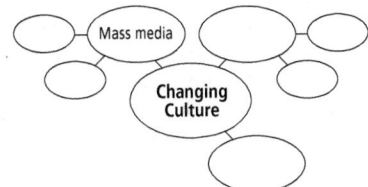

Why It Matters The automobile reshaped American culture, creating new forms of recreation and making it easier for people to travel. Other factors also contributed to changing ways of daily life. Americans listened to the radio, went to the movies, and followed the exploits of sports heroes. In the process, a new mass culture emerged—one whose shape and character closely resemble our own. **Section Focus Question: How did the new mass culture reflect technological and social changes?**

New Trends in Popular Culture

The 1920s was in many respects the first decade of our modern era. Even as cultural issues divided Americans from different regions or economic levels, technology was beginning to break down other barriers. Nowhere is this more evident than in the leisure interests of the American people.

Americans Enjoy More Leisure Time The growth of cities changed leisure patterns. On farms, people worked from dawn to dusk, with little time to spare. In the evenings, a farm family might play games, read, or sing together around the piano. Occasionally, they joined other farm families and townsfolk for picnics or a game of baseball. They did not have the time or the money for more extensive leisure pursuits.

City life was different. The average workweek in all industries fell from 70 hours in 1850 to 55 in 1910 to 45 by 1930. The workweek itself also changed from seven days a week to six and at last to five. At the same time, salaries and wages were on the rise.

Vocabulary Builder

Use the information below and the following resource to teach students the high-use words from this section. Teaching Resources, Vocabulary Builder, p. 11

High-Use Words	Definitions and Sample Sentences
sociological	*adj.* having to do with the study of human society and social relations In the 1920s, the popularity of **sociological** research increased because people believed that the rules for human social life were changing.
psychologist	*n.* scientist who studies the human mind and the process of thought and emotion Many people consult **psychologists** to help them explore their own thoughts and feelings.

Step-by-Step Instruction

SECTION 4

Objectives

As you teach this section, keep students focused on the following objectives to help them answer the Section Focus Question and master core content.

- Trace the reasons that leisure time increased during the 1920s.
- Analyze how the development of popular culture united Americans and created new activities and heroes.
- Discuss the advancements of women in the 1920s.
- Analyze the concept of modernism and its impact on writers and painters in the 1920s.

Prepare to Read

Background Knowledge L3

Ask students to recall that the United States experienced great economic growth during the 1920s. Ask them to predict how the strong economy might affect mass culture in America.

Set a Purpose L3

- **WITNESS HISTORY** Read the selection aloud.

   Ask **What do the lyrics to "Ain't We Got Fun?" reveal about the changing U.S. culture in the 1920s?** *(Americans had more time to pursue recreational activities.)* Ask students to discuss the role that phonograph records might play in changing U.S. culture.

- **Focus** Point out the Section Focus Question, and write it on the board. Tell students to refer to this question as they read. *(Answer appears with Section 4 Assessment answers.)*

- **Preview** Have students preview the Section Objectives and the list of Terms and People.

- **NoteTaking** Have students read this section using the Paragraph Shrinking strategy (TE, p. T20). As they read, have students fill in the concept web by finding examples of the ways in which U.S. culture changed during the 1920s. Reading and Note Taking Study Guide

▼ Charlie Chaplin, the comic "common man"

► Lon Chaney, star of horror films like *The Phantom of the Opera*

▲ Douglas Fairbanks, athletic star of adventure movies

▲ Mary Pickford, known as America's Sweetheart

Teach

New Trends in Popular Culture ⒧3

Instruct

- **Introduce** Draw students' attention to the photos of movie stars during the 1920s. Explain that during most of the 1920s movies were silent as filmmakers had not yet perfected the technology for sound accompaniment. Ask students to discuss why these actors may have been so popular during the 1920s.

- **Teach** Discuss the ways that movies, radios, and phonographs united Americans during the 1920s. Ask **Why did movies appeal to so many people?** (*Movies offered universal stories that almost anyone could enjoy; in addition, movies without spoken dialogue appealed to audiences whether or not they understood English. Movies also cost less money than other forms of entertainment.*) **How did radios help standardize culture in the United States?** (*Radios allowed Americans who lived in all parts of the country to listen to the same songs and share popular culture.*)

- **Quick Activity** Have students discuss how the United States might have been different today without radios, phonographs, and movies.

Independent Practice

Ask students to research the birth of the Hollywood movie industry and find out why movie studios moved from New York to California. Have students write paragraphs summarizing their research. Their research should reveal that the California climate was better suited to filming outdoors so filmmakers were not dependent on expensive studio space.

Monitor Progress

As students fill in their concept webs, circulate to make sure they understand ways in which American culture changed during the 1920s. For a completed version of the concept web, see Note Taking Transparencies, **B-102a.**

Silent Movie Stars
Each silent movie star had his or her own special appeal. The four shown above were among the most popular not only in the United States but around the world.

Americans Flock to the Movies With more free time and disposable income, urban and suburban Americans looked to new sources of entertainment. Motion pictures helped supply that demand.

The technology to make motion pictures had been around for a generation, but the movie industry rose to new heights in the 1920s. A handful of huge studios in Hollywood, California, established monopolies that controlled the production, distribution, and exhibition of movies. During the 1920s, from 60 to 100 million Americans went to the movies each week. Ornate movie palaces or small local theaters became America's cultural classrooms.

For most of the decade, the studios made silent pictures. They were an ideal entertainment at a time when millions of immigrants spoke little English. Motion pictures transcended languages and even literacy, treating universal themes in familiar ways that allowed any viewer to follow the stories. Motion pictures became America's democratic art. Unlike theatrical productions or classical concerts, movies were available to anyone with a few cents to spare. In addition, the fact that movies were silent made it easier for them to cut across geographic boundaries. Hollywood's biggest movies and stars became nearly as popular in far corners of the world as they were at home.

Many stars of the silent era portrayed ordinary folks. Comedian **Charlie Chaplin,** the most popular silent film star, played the Little Tramp. The character was equal parts hobo, dreamer, and poet but an eternal optimist in his ability to charm his audience and continually reinvent himself. Other stars played more romantic types. Handsome Rudolph Valentino was the sheik, as exotic to ordinary Americans as the deserts of Arabia. William S. Hart was a steely-eyed cowboy who came into town to restore law and order.

In 1927, film history changed, suddenly and forever, with the release of *The Jazz Singer,* the first movie with sound synchronized to the action. Audiences were amazed when Al Jolson said—not pantomimed—"You ain't heard nothin' yet" and then launched into a song. Silent pictures quickly faded out, replaced by "talkies." But whether silent or with sound, movies spoke directly to the desires, needs, fears, and fantasies of millions of people in the United States and around the world.

Differentiated Instruction   Solutions for All Learners

⒧1 Special Needs Students   ⒧2 English Language Learners   ⒧2 Less Proficient Readers

To help students understand the importance of movies, radios, and phonographs to the cultural development of the United States during the 1920s, have students make three-column charts summarizing the ways that these forms of entertainment changed the lives of Americans. In the first column, ask students to list the reasons that movies appealed to many people. In the second column, have students explain how radio helped standardize the popular culture of the United States. In the third column, ask students to describe how phonographs helped spread local music to the rest of the country. Then, ask students to use their charts to write paragraphs summarizing this section.

The Radio and Phonograph Break Barriers Like the movies, the phonograph and the radio also became powerful instruments of mass popular culture. Each was the result of both technological advances and business enterprise. Millions of radios and phonographs (as well as phonograph records) were marketed in the 1920s. On a deeper level, the phonograph and radio helped produce a standardized culture. Americans in the East and West and North and South listened to the same songs, learned the same dances, and shared the same popular culture as they never had before.

The radio, or wireless, was developed in the 1890s by Italian inventor Guglielmo Marconi. Before the 1920s, the radio was an innovation used by a small group of military technicians, telephone operators, and amateur "wireless" operators. Then, in 1920, an executive of the Westinghouse company started radio station KDKA in Pittsburgh, Pennsylvania. It was an immediate success. Within three years, there were almost 600 licensed stations broadcasting to more than 600,000 radio sets. Americans listened to music, educational lectures and religious sermons, and news and weather reports. They also heard commercials for a wide variety of consumer products.

Radios brought distant events into millions of homes in a way unmatched by newspapers or magazines. In 1927, much of America listened to a championship boxing match between Gene Tunney and Jack Dempsey. That night, theaters and movie houses played to empty seats as Americans huddled next to their sets. Even the men on death row at Sing Sing prison listened to the broadcast. Before the 1920s, such coverage of an event had been impossible.

The phonograph allowed people to listen to the same music they heard on the radio, but whenever they wanted. Early phonographs employed difficult-to-use wax cylinders and suffered from poor sound quality. In the 1920s, grooved disc recordings and superior sound reproduction improved the sound of the earlier machines. Recordings helped spread country and western music from the South and West to the North and East, while pop tunes from New York City's Tin Pan Alley traveled in the other direction. As they listened to the same songs, Americans also learned the same fashionable dances, from the fox trot to the Charleston.

✓ **Checkpoint** How did movies and the radio cut across geographic barriers?

An Age of Heroes

Hollywood's chief rivals for the creation of heroes were the nation's baseball parks, football fields, and boxing rings. Before the 1920s, there were relatively few nationally famous athletes, such as boxer John L. Sullivan and all-around athlete Jim Thorpe. Most sports stars were local heroes. This changed by the 1920s, often called the Golden Age of Sports.

Sports Heroes Win Fans Thanks to increased newspaper readership and the rise of radio coverage, every major sport boasted nationally famous performers. Perhaps the leading sports hero was baseball home-run king **Babe Ruth.** Others included Red Grange in football, Jack Dempsey in boxing, Bobby Jones in golf, and Bill Tilden in tennis. Women athletes, too, gained fame, from tennis player Helen Wills to Gertrude Ederle, the first woman to swim the English Channel.

HISTORY MAKERS

Babe Ruth (1895–1948)
Babe Ruth—also known as the Bambino and the Sultan of Swat—towered over major league baseball, not only while he was playing but for decades after. Originally a standout pitcher for the Boston Red Sox, Ruth gained fame as a slugging outfielder for the New York Yankees. In 1920, baseball was suffering from a gambling scandal. Ruth's amazing home runs and great appeal helped the sport win back fans. His record for most home runs in a season stood for more than 30 years, and his record for most home runs in a career lasted even longer.

Instruct

- **Introduce** Direct students to the HISTORY MAKERS feature about Babe Ruth. Ask **Why was Babe Ruth a hero to so many Americans during the 1920s?** (*Ruth's outstanding performance as an athlete brought many fans back to the game of baseball.*) Then, have students discuss the qualities they believe all heroes should possess.

- **Teach** Have students discuss the importance of heroes to American society during the 1920s. Ask **How did World War I affect the world-view of Americans and increase the popularity of athletes?** (*After World War I, many Americans lost faith in progress and viewed the world as flawed. Athletes helped restore Americans' optimism and sense of hope.*) **Why was Charles Lindbergh a hero for many Americans during the 1920s?** (*His bravery and mastery of the airplane, along with the intense media coverage of his flight, excited millions.*) Have students discuss why Lindbergh received the nickname "Lucky Lindy."

- **Analyzing the Visuals** Draw students' attention to the photo of Charles Lindbergh on the next page. Ask students to discuss why Lindbergh's flight across the Atlantic Ocean was so monumental.

Independent Practice

Have students write short essays explaining why Americans needed heroes during the 1920s and evaluating the need for heroes in today's society. Ask students to provide evidence to support their responses.

Monitor Progress

As students write their responses, circulate to ensure that they are expressing their opinions clearly and supporting them with evidence.

Answer

✓ Unlike newspapers and magazines which generally reached only local audiences, the nationwide distribution of movies and radio broadcasts created a shared culture among Americans from coast-to-coast.

Instruct

- **Introduce: Key Term** Ask students to find the key term *flapper* in the text. Then, give students the definition. Ask **How did *flappers* represent a shift in the attitude women had toward their roles in society?** (*Flappers represented an attitude of rebellion against social norms and women's traditional roles in society. They expected to be socially and politically equal to men.*)

- **Teach** Discuss ways in which women's roles changed during the 1920s. Ask **What were some characteristics of the New Woman in the 1920s?** (*The New Woman was more liberated than women had been during the Victorian Age. She wore makeup and dresses with shorter hemlines. She also believed that she had the same political and social rights as any man.*) **How did family life change for women during the 1920s?** (*Compared with women of earlier times, women during the 1920s lived longer, married later, had fewer children, and pursued broader interests. Women also benefited from better technology as electric appliances enabled them to do household chores in less time.*) Have students compare and contrast the ways of life for women who lived in urban areas and women who lived in rural areas.

- **Quick Activity** Ask students to complete the *Viewpoints: The "New Woman"* worksheet. Teaching Resources, p. 23

Answer

✓ The new mass media contributed to the popularity of heroes by capturing the excitement of sports events or Lindbergh's solo crossing in newspaper articles, and radio broadcasts throughout the country.

The New York Times.

LINDBERGH DOES IT! TO PARIS IN 33½ HOURS; FLIES 1,000 MILES THROUGH SNOW AND SLEET; CHEERING FRENCH CARRY HIM OFF FIELD

Lucky Lindy Crosses the Atlantic

"Well, I made it," Charles Lindbergh said simply as he landed his airplane, the *Spirit of St. Louis*, in Paris. Moments later, soldiers had to rescue him from the thousands of well-wishers who crowded the airfield.

NoteTaking

Reading Skill: Summarize As you read, classify the various types of changes that took place in women's lives in the 1920s.

Women in the 1920s		
Social Changes	Political Changes	Economic Changes

Why did athletes reach such heights of popularity? Part of the answer is that the Golden Age of Sports was also the Golden Age of the Sportswriter. Such journalists as Damon Runyon and Grantland Rice captured the excitement of sports events in their colorful prose. Turning the finest athletes into seemingly immortal gods, the sportswriters nicknamed Babe Ruth the Sultan of Swat and dubbed Notre Dame's football backfield the Four Horsemen.

The other part of the answer is that the decade needed heroes. World War I had shattered many Americans' faith in progress, making the world seem cheap and flawed. Athletic heroes reassured Americans that people were capable of great feats and lofty dreams. If in our heroes we see our idealized selves, the sports heroes of the 1920s gave Americans a sense of hope.

Lucky Lindy Crosses the Atlantic Even the biggest sports stars could not match the adoration given aviator **Charles Lindbergh**. In the 1920s, the airline industry was in its infancy. Flying aces had played a role in World War I, and a few small domestic airlines carried mail and passengers. But airplanes were still a novel sight to most Americans. The pilot became a new breed of hero, a romantic daredevil who risked death with every flight.

Lindbergh outdid them all. In May 1927, he took off from Long Island, New York, in his tiny single-engine plane, the *Spirit of St. Louis*, and headed east—to Paris, France. Other pilots had flown across the Atlantic Ocean before, but Lindbergh was the first to do it solo and non-stop. The flight took more than 33 hours, and the lone pilot had to stay awake the entire time. He also recalled, "In the daytime I knew where I was going, but in the evening and at night it was largely a matter of guesswork."

When Lindbergh landed in Paris, he became an instant media celebrity, dubbed Lucky Lindy and the Lone Eagle. The radio reported on his landing, and movie newsreels showed his triumphant return home. The modest young man from the Midwest became the greatest hero of his time.

✓ **Checkpoint** How did the new mass media contribute to the popularity of heroes?

Women Assume New Roles

In a 1931 book, *Only Yesterday*, journalist Frederick Lewis Allen attempted to make sense of the fads, heroes, and problems of the 1920s. Featured prominently was the New Woman. During the decade, many women challenged political, economic, social, and educational boundaries, to prove that their role was as vital outside the home as inside it.

Flappers Challenge Older Limits During the Victorian Age of the late 1800s and early 1900s, women had been expected to center their lives on the home and family. The New Woman of the 1920s, noted Allen, was more liberated. She wore dresses with shorter hemlines, put on more makeup, danced to the latest crazes, and generally assumed that she had the same political and social rights as any man.

History Background

Amelia Earhart America went wild when Charles Lindbergh crossed the Atlantic solo in 1927. A year later, another aviator made history.

Amelia Earhart was a pilot in the 1920s. She set the women's altitude record (14,000 feet) in 1922, just a year after she started flying. After Lindbergh's feat, Earhart received a phone call asking whether she wanted to be the first woman to fly across the Atlantic. She wouldn't be flying the plane—just helping out the male pilot. At first, Earhart wasn't excited. She didn't want to just be "extra weight." But the chance to cross the Atlantic was tempting, and Earhart accepted. In June 1928, just a year after Lindbergh, Earhart and two male pilots crossed the Atlantic.

When Earhart returned home, she got a tickertape parade and a phone call of congratulations from President Coolidge. The press called her "Lady Lindy."

Earhart wasn't satisfied. In 1932, she became the first female pilot to cross the Atlantic, and she did it solo. Earhart was a famous example of the "New Woman" of the 1920s, and she inspired girls and women to be bold and adventurous.

THE NEW Woman?

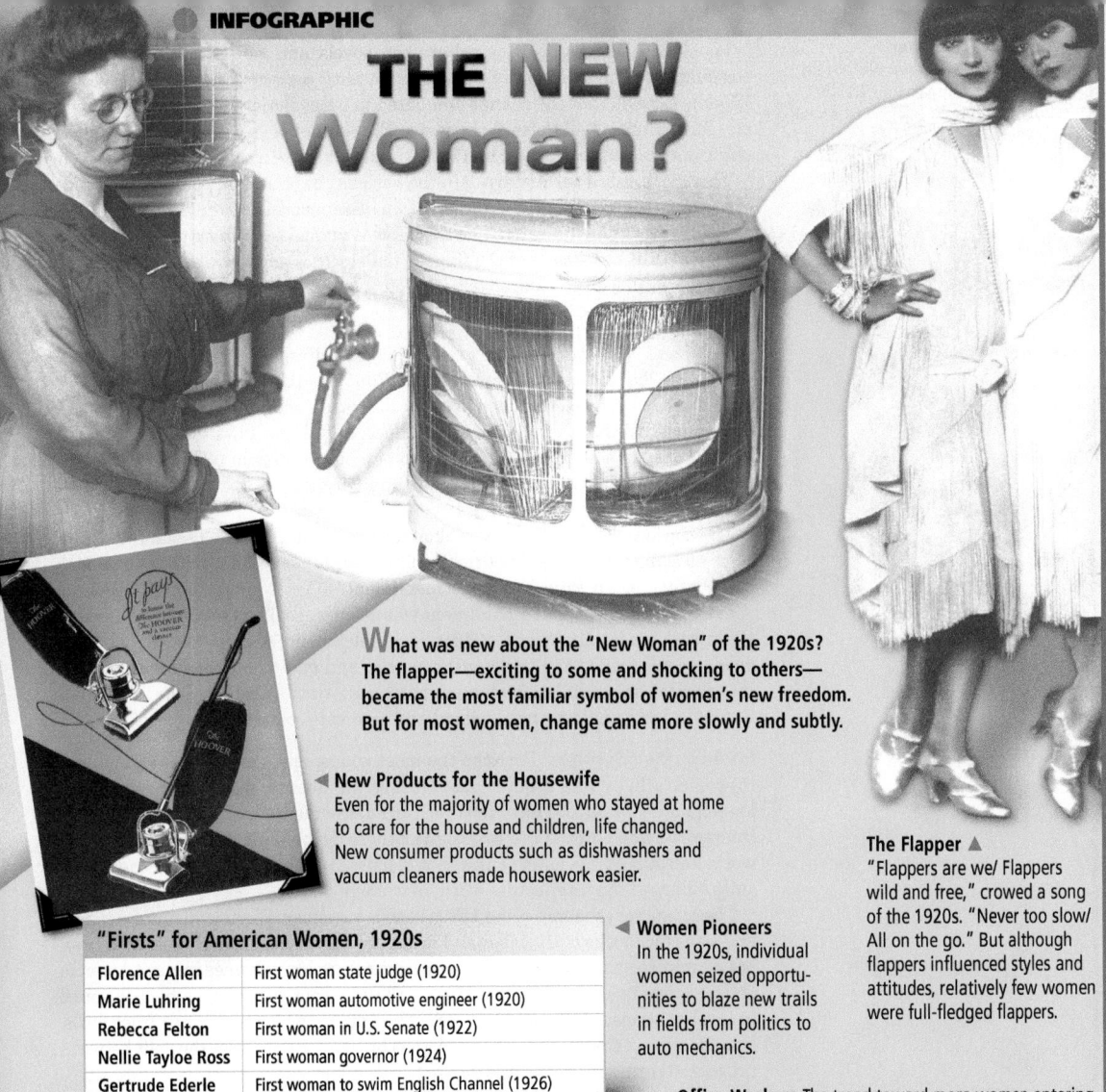

What was new about the "New Woman" of the 1920s? The flapper—exciting to some and shocking to others—became the most familiar symbol of women's new freedom. But for most women, change came more slowly and subtly.

◄ **New Products for the Housewife**
Even for the majority of women who stayed at home to care for the house and children, life changed. New consumer products such as dishwashers and vacuum cleaners made housework easier.

The Flapper ▲
"Flappers are we/ Flappers wild and free," crowed a song of the 1920s. "Never too slow/ All on the go." But although flappers influenced styles and attitudes, relatively few women were full-fledged flappers.

◄ **Women Pioneers**
In the 1920s, individual women seized opportunities to blaze new trails in fields from politics to auto mechanics.

"Firsts" for American Women, 1920s

Florence Allen	First woman state judge (1920)
Marie Luhring	First woman automotive engineer (1920)
Rebecca Felton	First woman in U.S. Senate (1922)
Nellie Tayloe Ross	First woman governor (1924)
Gertrude Ederle	First woman to swim English Channel (1926)
Dorothy Arzner	First woman to direct a talking movie (1927)
Phoebe Omlie	First woman to earn a federal pilot's license (1927)

Office Workers The trend toward more women entering the workforce continued throughout the decade. Some white-collar jobs, such as stenographers and telephone ◄ operators, became predominantly female.

Thinking Critically

1. **Evaluate Information** Why were the "Firsts" shown on the table at left important?

2. **Draw Conclusions** Why do you think the flapper became a major symbol even though relatively few women were flappers?

Connect to Your World

Women in Power Since the 1920s, women have continued to earn positions of power that had previously been available only to men. Here are a few examples:

Sandra Day O'Connor graduated from law school in 1952, turned to politics, and became the nation's first female senate majority leader in Arizona. In 1981, President Reagan chose O'Connor to become the first female justice of the Supreme Court.

In 1983, NASA astronaut Sally Ride became the first American woman to go into space. She was one of the shuttle's flight engineers and operated its robot arm.

In 1997, Madeleine Albright became the first female U.S. Secretary of State. As Jews in Czechoslovakia, Albright and her family fled the country at the start of World War II. As secretary of state, her achievements included ratification of the Chemical Weapons Convention.

Condoleezza Rice, the first woman to be appointed national security advisor, helped construct and recommend the Bush administration's foreign policy. As the first African American female secretary of state, Rice met routinely with foreign leaders and was a persistent defender of the U.S. war on terror.

Instruct

- **Introduce: Vocabulary Builder** Have students find the term ***psychologist.*** Then, write the word on the board, say it aloud, have the students say it with you, and give them the definition. Explain that Sigmund Freud was a ***psychologist*** who studied how the mind works and treated mental disorders. Ask **How did Freud's work affect art and literature?** *(Freud's theories led writers and artists to explore the subconscious mind.)*

- **Teach** Discuss the effect that World War I had on art and literature produced during the 1920s. Ask **What was the difference between modernist paintings and traditionalist paintings?** *(Modernist paintings experimented with abstract styles, and traditionalist paintings represented real life.)* **What did the "Lost Generation" try to find in its writing?** *(a new set of rules to live by—created by each individual for himself or herself alone)* Have students read the Primary Sources quotations by F. Scott Fitzgerald and Ernest Hemingway. Ask students to discuss how these quotations reflect the attitudes of the "Lost Generation."

- **Analyzing the Visuals** Direct students to the images on the next page. Have students discuss whether people during the 1920s would have accepted each painting as high art or considered each to be part of the "lunatic fringe."

Answer

✓ After the Nineteenth Amendment was ratified, women became more politically active. During the 1920s, women were elected as governors of the states of Texas and Wyoming.

Vocabulary Builder
sociological–(soh see uh LAH jih kuhl) *adj.* having to do with the study of human society and social relations

Popular magazines, sociological studies, novels, and movies all echoed Allen's observations. The rejection of Victorian morality seemed so total and the New Woman so novel that the change amounted to a "revolution in manners and morals." The symbol of all these changes was the **flapper,** a young woman with short skirts and rouged cheeks who had her hair cropped close in a style known as a bob.

There was only a germ of truth in the various observations. The Victorian code of separate spheres for men and women was disappearing but not as rapidly or as completely as Allen indicated. The flapper was undoubtedly more publicized than imitated. Still, the image of the flapper underscores an important aspect of the decade. Not all women aspired to be flappers, but many wanted more control over their lives—and got it.

Women Make Strides The great fight for suffrage had been won with the passage of the Nineteenth Amendment. What was the next step? Some groups, such as the National American Woman Suffrage Association, called on women to work in reform movements, run for office, or fight for laws to protect women and children in the workplace. Some women had success in public life. In 1925, Nellie Tayloe Ross of Wyoming and Miriam Ferguson of Texas became the first women elected as state governors.

The National Women's Party took a more militant position, demanding complete economic, social, and political equality with men. Their primary goal was the passage of an Equal Rights Amendment. Most women, though, believed that a new constitutional amendment was premature. They set more achievable goals and made significant strides in employment. Although most working women continued to toil in domestic service and manufacturing, others moved into clerical, sales, and management positions. Women also won jobs in journalism, aviation, banking, and the legal and medical professions.

Family Life Changes Perhaps the most widespread revolution taking place in women's lives was a quiet one. During the decade, women tended to live longer, marry later, and have fewer children, freeing their time to pursue other interests. Some entered the workforce, others devoted more time to charitable work, and still others joined clubs that discussed books and ideas. All these pursuits enlarged the intellectual world of women.

The consumer economy of the 1920s benefited women. Electric vacuum cleaners and irons took some of the labor and drudgery out of household chores. Of course, not all women shared in the blessings of technology. Many homes in rural America had no access to electricity. For women in these regions, household labor continued to involve intense, even painful, work. They drew and carried water from wells, heated irons on stoves, and washed clothes by hand. Here again, the split between urban and rural Americans was distinct.

✓ **Checkpoint** What political gains did American women make during the 1920s?

Modernism in Art and Literature

No area of American life, however, reflected the impact of World War I more than literature and the arts. The war altered the way writers and artists viewed the world, changed the way they approached their craft, and inspired them to experiment with new forms and fresh ideas.

The Arts Reflect a Mood of Uncertainty During the Victorian era, most poets and novelists had expressed a belief in progress, placing boundless faith in human potential. But World War I called the notion of progress into question.

How could a society ruled by the idea of progress embark on a war that killed millions of people, destroyed monuments of civilization, and left survivors hungry, homeless, and hopeless? This was not an action of a rational people, a new generation of writers argued, but the irrational exploits of civilization without a sense of direction. This pessimistic, skeptical worldview sparked an artistic movement known as modernism.

The theories of Austrian <u>psychologist</u> **Sigmund Freud** (SIHG muhnd froid) also contributed to literary and artistic modernism. Freud argued that much of human behavior is driven not by rational thought but by unconscious desires. To live in society, people learn to suppress these desires. But the tension between outward behavior and the subconscious, said Freud, could lead to mental and even physical illness. Freud's theories led writers and artists to explore the subconscious mind.

Modern Painting Challenges Tradition Modernism clashed head-on with traditionalism most dramatically in the field of modern art. Since the late 1800s, European painters had led the way in seeking a fresh visual idiom, or language. They moved away from representational paintings that simply reproduced real life and experimented with more abstract styles.

Modern Art

By the 1920s, many artists had broken away from purely representational styles. The two American artists shown here used vastly different methods in their work. *How do these paintings reflect the changing world of the 1920s? How do they express differing moods?*

Edward Hopper: *Automat*
Basically realistic, Edward Hopper's works often reflect the loneliness and anonymity of urban life. In this 1927 painting, a woman dressed in flapper style eats in a restaurant where even the food is dispensed by machine.

Joseph Stella: *Brooklyn Bridge*
Joseph Stella was one of the few American painters to follow a European style called futurism, which celebrated change and technology. This 1920 painting is more abstract than Hopper's, but the subject matter is still recognizable.

Independent Practice

- As they read, have students use the table on the next page to understand the main themes of American postwar novelists: social changes, some good, some bad; the constraints of traditional society; and the emptiness of everyday life.

- Ask students to read the HISTORY MAKERS feature on Gertrude Stein. Have students answer the question "How did Stein help change American literature?" by writing a personal response paragraph. (*In two ways: With her own work and through the encouragement she gave other writers, helping them break free of tradition and create a new kind of American literature.*)

- Have students reread the paragraph on Freud at the top of this page. Ask students to describe in a short essay the ways in which people in 1920s America tried to shake off the traditional rules of behavior and become less inhibited.

Differentiated Instruction Solutions for All Learners

L1 Special Needs Students **L2 English Language Learners** **L2 Less Proficient Readers**

Ask students to describe the two paintings on this page to a partner. Students can start out by talking about the realism in the Hopper painting and the emotions they feel when they look at it. Then, they can talk about the Stella painting's abstract image, and whether they can see a bridge in it. Remind students that abstract art does not reproduce an object exactly the way it looks. The abstract artist tries to show the subject, in this case a bridge, of the painting in a new way.

Have students play a game in which they work in pairs. One student sketches a person or an object on notebook paper and then shows it to his or her partner. The partner has to guess what the drawing represents. Have students make both abstract and realistic sketches. When the partners describe the sketches, encourage them to use these two terms and explain why they think a sketch is realistic or abstract.

Answer

Caption The paintings reflect the changing world of the 1920s by showing even familiar things as somehow strange and unknowable. In addition, the viewer is encouraged to interpret the paintings in his or her own way. No one single interpretation is correct, and interpretations are open to change depending on the viewer's mood or circumstances.

Monitor Progress

Ask students to choose one of the authors mentioned in this section and conduct research on that writer's life and work. Ask them to read one short story by that author and then describe and respond to it in a personal response essay.

▲ The cover of *Main Street* on display in the Sinclair Lewis Interpretive Center in Sauk Centre, Minnesota, Lewis's home town.

Novelist	Major Themes	Representative Work
American Postwar Novelists		☑ Quick Study
Willa Cather (1873–1947)	Frontier life on the Great Plains	***My Ántonia*** (1918) depicts the passing of the American frontier through the life of an immigrant girl in Nebraska.
William Faulkner (1897–1962)	Life in the South; inner workings of mind	***The Sound and the Fury*** (1929) uses different narrators to tell the story of the complex inner workings of a Southern family.
F. Scott Fitzgerald (1896–1940)	The Jazz Age	***The Great Gatsby*** (1925) shows the emptiness of the Jazz-Age world of flappers and bootleggers.
Ernest Hemingway (1899–1961)	Disillusionment of postwar generation	***A Farewell to Arms*** (1929) tells the story of doomed love between a cynical American ambulance driver and a nurse during World War I.
Sinclair Lewis (1885–1951)	Small-town life in the Midwest	***Main Street*** (1920) paints a satirical portrait of small-minded people in an American town.
Edith Wharton (1862–1937)	Life among the rich in New York	***The Age of Innocence*** (1920) depicts a wealthy young man prevented by social conventions from marrying the woman he loves.

Most Americans got their first real glimpse of the new European approach at a major art show at New York's 69th Infantry Regimental Armory in 1913. Traditionalists were outraged by the Armory Show, and Theodore Roosevelt said that most of it represented the "lunatic fringe" of the art world. But many American painters were inspired by the bold new styles. They began their own search for artistic honesty in abstract patterns. In the 1920s, paintings by Edward Hopper, Man Ray, Joseph Stella, and Georgia O'Keeffe demonstrated the richness and varied styles of American artists. At the same time, the works of artists such as Archibald Motley and William H. Johnson portrayed African American perspectives on modern life.

Postwar American Literature Flowers American writers of the 1920s are often referred to as the **"Lost Generation"** because they no longer had faith in the cultural guideposts of the Victorian era. But many were inspired by their "lost" condition to search for new truths and fresh ways of expressing those truths. Never in American history had one decade seen the emergence of so many great literary talents. A list of writers who rose to distinction in the 1920s includes F. Scott Fitzgerald, Ernest Hemingway, Edith Wharton, Sinclair Lewis, William Faulkner, Gertrude Stein, Eugene O'Neill, and T. S. Eliot. Each of these writers remains today on any list of distinguished American authors.

Novelist **F. Scott Fitzgerald** explored the reality of the American dream of wealth, success, and emotional fulfillment. In *This Side of Paradise*, he wrote that his generation had "grown up to find all Gods dead, all wars fought, and all faiths in man shaken." In *The Great Gatsby* (1925), his most accomplished work, Fitzgerald showed the American dream ending in nightmare. In the novel, through hard work and careful planning, James Gatz re-creates himself as Jay Gatsby, a successful tycoon. Gatsby fills his home with wild parties, dancing, bootleg liquor, and endless activity:

Primary Source   ❝In the main hall a bar with a real brass rail was set up, and stocked with gins and liquors and with cordials so long forgotten that most of his female guests were too young to know one from another. By seven o'clock the orchestra had arrived, no thin five-piece affair, but a whole pitful of oboes and trombones and saxophones. . . . People were not invited—they went there. They got into automobiles which bore them out to Long Island, and somehow they ended up at Gatsby's door.❞
—F. Scott Fitzgerald, *The Great Gatsby*

But in the end, Gatsby is destroyed by the very things he hoped to achieve. His lofty dreams end in a violent, meaningless death.

Fitzgerald's fellow novelist and good friend **Ernest Hemingway** explored similar themes but in a new idiom. Hemingway felt betrayed, not only by the American dream, but also by literary language itself. In *A Farewell to Arms*, his 1929 novel about World War I, Hemingway's narrator says:

> **Primary Source** "I was always embarrassed by the words sacred, glorious, and sacrifice. . . . I had seen nothing sacred, and the things that were glorious had no glory and the sacrifices were like the stockyards at Chicago if nothing was done with the meat except to bury it. . . . Abstract words such as glory, honor, courage, or hallow were obscene beside the concrete names of villages, the numbers of roads, the names of rivers, the numbers of regiments and the dates."
> —Ernest Hemingway, *A Farewell to Arms*

In his short stories and novels, Hemingway worked to develop a writing style that reflected his insights. He wrote in unadorned sentences, stripped of vague adjectives and adverbs. He created a style that was as concrete and as powerful as a rifle shot.

Influenced by Freud, other writers explored the subconscious mind. Playwright Eugene O'Neill experimented with techniques that put the subconscious right on stage. In *The Emperor Jones*, the title character gets lost in a jungle and is attacked by imaginary beings called Little Formless Fears. In *Strange Interlude*, characters turn away from their conversations with other people on stage and speak their thoughts directly to the audience.

Certainly, many poets and novelists of the decade were disillusioned. Like Hemingway and Fitzgerald, they wrestled with the meaning of the war and life itself. But in the end, their efforts resulted in the creation of literary masterpieces, not worthless products of aimless despair.

✔ **Checkpoint** What impact did World War I have on postwar American literature?

HISTORY MAKERS

Gertrude Stein (1874–1946)
Gertrude Stein lived for a while in Europe as a child and returned there after college. A poet and writer, her poetry was highly experimental and often difficult to understand. But her Paris home became a gathering place for writers and artists. She supported new styles and encouraged several American writers, including Ernest Hemingway and F. Scott Fitzgerald. It was Stein who called this group the "Lost Generation."

SECTION 4 Assessment

Progress Monitoring Online
For: Self-test with vocabulary practice
www.pearsonschool.com/ushist

Comprehension

1. **Terms and People** For each of the following, write a sentence explaining the importance of that person or item to American culture of the 1920s.
   - Charlie Chaplin
   - *The Jazz Singer*
   - flapper
   - Sigmund Freud
   - "Lost Generation"
   - F. Scott Fitzgerald
   - Ernest Hemingway

2. **NoteTaking Reading Skill: Summarize** Use your concept web to answer the Section Focus Question: How did the new mass culture reflect technological and social changes?

Writing About History

3. **Compare** Write a paragraph comparing the mass culture of today with the mass culture of the 1920s. Consider: What technologies form part of the mass culture? What role do they play in our lives?

Critical Thinking

4. **Analyze Information** How did the increased popularity of sports heroes and the disillusionment of the "Lost Generation" writers represent different responses to the same events?

5. **Identify Main Ideas** How did the political role of American women change in the years after World War I?

6. **Analyze Literature** Reread the selection from *The Great Gatsby*, on the previous page. How does it reflect other information you have learned about the society of the 1920s?

Assess and Reteach

Assess Progress

- Have students complete the Section Assessment.

- Administer the Section Quiz. Teaching Resources, **p. 28**

- To further assess student understanding, use Progress Monitoring Transparencies, **98**.

Reteach

If students need more instruction, have them read the section summary.

Reading and Note Taking Study Guide ⓛ3

Adapted Reading and Note Taking Study Guide ⓛ1 ⓛ2

Spanish Reading and Note Taking Study Guide ⓛ2

Extend ⓛ4

See this chapter's Professional Development pages for the Extend Online activity on the Gold and Glory Sweepstakes.

Answer

✔ Writers of postwar American literature had lost faith in traditional ideas and values after witnessing the devastation of war. They searched for new ways to express modern life and its new influences and ideas.

Section 4 Assessment

1. Sentences should reflect an understanding of the significance of each term or person to American culture of the 1920s.

2. New electric appliances made work easier and provided entertainment. Mass culture emphasized leisure, sports, and celebrities, and provided examples that helped expand women's horizons.

3. Similarities: movies, radio, sports, and movie stars, and the use of machines to make life easier. Differences: greatly increased exposure to mass media, more diverse cultural life, fewer restrictions on career choices for women, and less distinction between information and entertainment.

4. After World War I, many Americans felt that the world was flawed. Sports heroes provided a sense of hope. The "Lost Generation" writers explored their disillusionment through new literary themes and ideas.

5. After World War I, women could vote; they entered politics knowing that other women might vote for them. Many women who did not seek careers in politics still expected to play a role in local politics.

6. Gatsby's liquor stock violates Prohibition, his female guests are liberated enough to attend an unchaperoned party where alcohol will be consumed, and all the guests have cars to convey them to Gatsby's house.

For additional assessment, have students access **Progress Monitoring Online** at **www.pearsonschool.com/ushist**.

Objectives

- Discuss the various forms of entertainment that became popular during the 1920s.
- Describe how technology affected leisure activities.
- Explain how technology helped spread popular culture during the 1920s.

Background Knowledge ⓛ

Remind students that popular culture was more readily available to Americans in the 1920s, when new technologies and electricity brought movies, radio, and phonograph records to the people. Actors, dances, music, and ideas could reach more Americans and reach them more quickly. Americans could see and hear their favorite actors and music every day, instead of only when they went to the theater.

Instruct

- Have students read the introduction and review the pictures and captions in the feature. Ask **Why do you think Americans went to the movies so often?** *(Movies offered cheap entertainment in a fun atmosphere made glamorous by elaborate theaters filled with electric lights and people dressed up for a night out.)* **What things did movies, radio, and records offer consumers that musical theaters or concerts could not?** *(Movies, radio, and phonograph music offered a variety of entertainment at affordable prices. In addition, this entertainment often could be enjoyed on demand, even at home.)*

- Ask students to study the graph "Households With Radios 1922–1930" and the photo and caption below the graph. Using the Numbered Heads strategy (TE, p. T23), have students explain how radio made baseball even more popular and why it could especially reach out to children. *(Children who couldn't go to games, either because they were expensive or there was no major league team in their town, could listen to baseball on the radio.)*

EXPERIENCE THE ROARING TWENTIES

Turn on the radio! Let's go to the movies! In the 1920s, Americans were having fun in ways that hadn't even been invented half a century earlier. And, with new forms of mass communication, fads and entertainment were spreading faster and wider than ever before. For a few pennies, a farmer in Indiana could go to the movies and enjoy the same laughs and thrills as a factory worker in New York or a businessman in San Francisco. Practically every American knew ballplayer Ty Cobb, actress Mary Pickford, and singer Rudy Vallee.

Today, the technology and the fads have changed. But the age of mass culture has never left us.

◀ **The Charleston**
No fad symbolizes the Roaring Twenties more than the Charleston. Here, two young people demonstrate the wild, loose-limbed dance that swept the nation.

Saturday Night at the Movies ▼
By the 1920s, Americans were going to the movies so often that attendance at other forms of public entertainment, such as theater, suffered. Decades later, the rise of television would have the same effect on movie attendance.

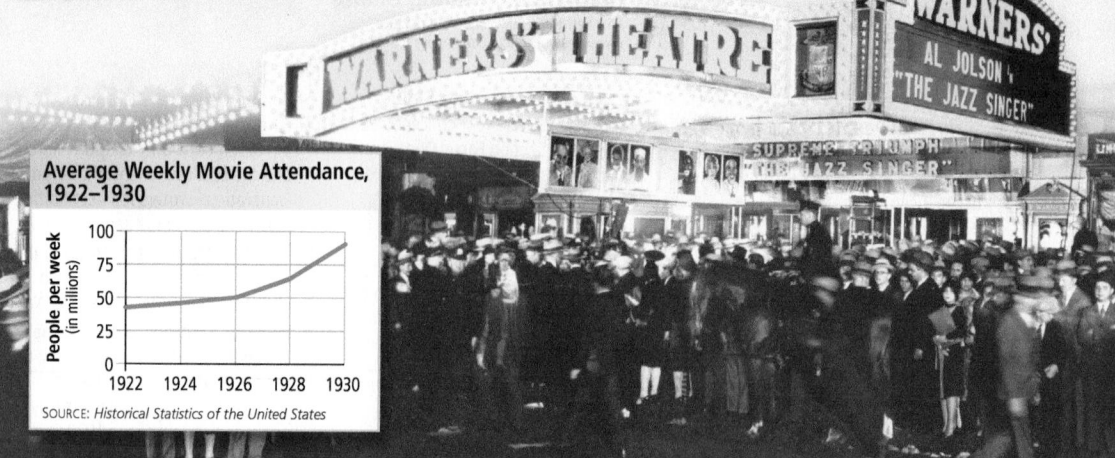

Average Weekly Movie Attendance, 1922–1930

[Line graph: People per week (in millions) on vertical axis, ranging 0 to 100; years 1922 to 1930 on horizontal axis. Attendance rises from about 40 million in 1922 to about 90 million in 1930.]

SOURCE: *Historical Statistics of the United States*

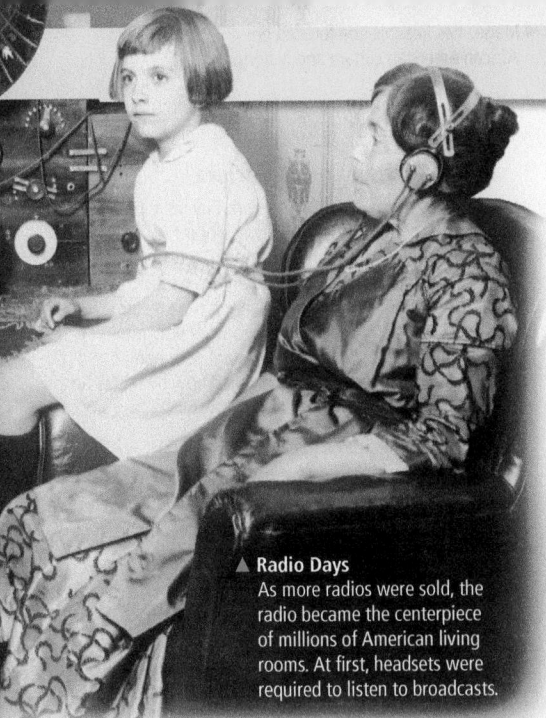

▲ **Radio Days**
As more radios were sold, the radio became the centerpiece of millions of American living rooms. At first, headsets were required to listen to broadcasts.

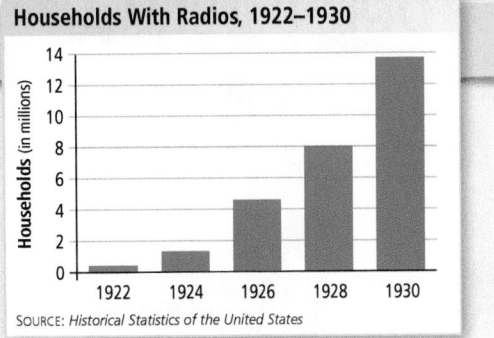

Households With Radios, 1922–1930

SOURCE: *Historical Statistics of the United States*

The Great American Pastime
Baseball remained America's favorite sport, but mass media brought it to an entirely new audience. Here, veteran superstar Ty Cobb (below) of the Detroit Tigers greets some young fans. ▼

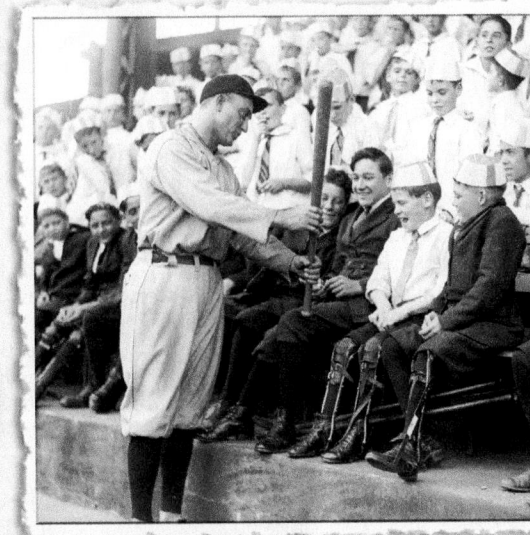

▲ **Casual Reading**
Mass-market magazines with eye-catching covers were more popular than ever. This *Life* magazine cover (left) highlights the growing popularity of golf among both men and women. *Amazing Stories* (right) was the first "pulp" magazine devoted exclusively to science fiction.

Thinking Critically
1. **Analyze Visuals** Identify two ways that technology affected leisure activities.
2. **Draw Conclusions** Do you think mass entertainment, such as movies and radio, promoted greater understanding and unity among Americans? Explain.

Connect to Today Many people worry that some of today's leisure activities, such as video games and the Internet, have a negative impact on family togetherness. Do you agree or disagree? Give reasons for your answer.

History *Interactive* ✱
For: Experience the Mass Culture of the 20s video, audio, and analysis
www.pearsonschool.com/ushist

Independent Practice
To enrich and extend the lesson, have students access the History Interactive at **www.pearsonschool.com/ushist.** After students experience the History Interactive, ask them to share their reactions by posing questions such as: What would it be like if you lived in the 1920s, when entertainment was not available online and on television, but you went to the movies two or three times a week? How would your family's purchase of a radio have changed your life in the 1920s? What would it be like to listen to radio soap operas, mysteries, or detective shows for which the only visuals were in your own head?

Answers

Thinking Critically
1. Sample answers: Radios and phonographs allowed people to bring music, sports, and other leisure pastimes into their homes; movies showed models of modern behavior and style that people could admire and copy; cars allowed people to travel easily and more often.
2. Answers will vary; students should mention that by making the same people, programs, or items popular all over the nation at the same time, technology gave Americans of all different classes and locations something in common with one another. At the same time, it did not erase class and financial differences and, in fact, might have reinforced some differences.

Connect to Today Students may argue that the same criticisms were made about older technologies. They may suggest that parents' careers are more threatening to the family than leisure activities.

OPPORTUNITY
A JOURNAL OF NEGRO LIFE

JUNE 1926

◀ Magazines like this one focused on African American culture and history.

Objectives

As you teach this section, keep students focused on the following objectives to help them answer the Section Focus Question and master core content.

- Analyze the racial and economic philosophies of Marcus Garvey.
- Trace the development and impact of jazz.
- Discuss the themes explored by writers of the Harlem Renaissance.

Prepare to Read

Background Knowledge L3

Remind students that during the 1920s, African Americans faced racism and discrimination. Have students predict what methods African Americans might use to convey their experiences to others.

Set a Purpose L3

- **WITNESS HISTORY** Read the selection aloud.

  Ask **Why might a young African American male from the South feel "happy again" in Harlem?** *(Many African Americans lived in Harlem, so he would be less burdened by racism and would have more opportunities to succeed in life.)*

- **Focus** Point out the Section Focus Question and write it on the board. Tell students to refer to this question as they read. *(Answer appears with Section 5 Assessment answers.)*

- **Preview** Have students preview the Section Objectives and the list of Terms and People.

- NoteTaking Using the Structured Read Aloud strategy (TE, p. T20), have students read this section. As they read, have students outline the section's main ideas and supporting details. Reading and Note Taking Study Guide

WITNESS HISTORY

The Excitement of Harlem

In the early 1920s, the New York City neighborhood known as Harlem was the most vibrant African American community in the nation. Teeming with people and teeming with activity, it was also, as one observer noted, "a great magnet for the Negro intellectual." Among those who were drawn to Harlem was a young Missouri-born poet named Langston Hughes. He later recalled how he felt as he stepped off the subway:

❝I can never put on paper the thrill of the underground ride to Harlem. I went up the steps and out into the bright September sunlight. Harlem! I stood there, dropped my bags, took a deep breath and felt happy again.❞

—Langston Hughes, *The Big Sea*

The Harlem Renaissance

Objectives

- Analyze the racial and economic philosophies of Marcus Garvey.
- Trace the development and impact of jazz.
- Discuss the themes explored by writers of the Harlem Renaissance.

Terms and People

Marcus Garvey	Harlem Renaissance
jazz	Claude McKay
Louis Armstrong	Langston Hughes
Bessie Smith	Zora Neale Hurston

NoteTaking

Reading Skill: Identify Main Ideas As you read, identify the main ideas.

```
I. New "Black Consciousness"
   A. New Chances, New Challenges
      1. Migration to North continues
      2.
   B.
II.
```

Why It Matters As a result of World War I and the Great Migration, millions of African Americans relocated from the rural South to the urban North. This mass migration continued through the 1920s and contributed to a flowering of music and literature. Jazz and the Harlem Renaissance made a lasting impact, not only on African Americans but on the culture all Americans share. **Section Focus Question: How did African Americans express a new sense of hope and pride?**

A New "Black Consciousness"

Like the immigrants who traveled from Europe and Asia, African Americans who left the South dreamed of a better future. They had heard stories of economic opportunity, social advancement, and greater political rights. The South, they reasoned, was a dead end. Locked into low-paying rural jobs, barred from decent schools, faced with the reality of Jim Crow oppression and the threat of lynching, they pointed their compasses north.

Migrants Face Chances and Challenges Most African American migrants to the north probably found a better life. Wages in a Detroit auto plant or a Pittsburgh steel mill were far better than what a sharecropper earned in the South. In such cities as New York, Chicago, Pittsburgh, and Cleveland, African Americans had a growing political voice. In those towns, there also existed black middle and upper classes. African American ministers, physicians, lawyers, teachers, and journalists practiced their professions and served as role models to the younger generation.

Vocabulary Builder

Use the information below and the following resource to teach students the high-use word from this section. Teaching Resources, Vocabulary Builder, p. 11

High-Use Word	Definition and Sample Sentence
indigenous	*adj.* native to; growing out of a particular region or country Critics of U.S. imperialism feared that the influence of American culture would change the **indigenous** culture of the Philippines.

But in coming North, African Americans had certainly not escaped racism and oppression. On average, they were forced to live in the worst housing and labor in the lowest paying jobs. In addition, as the race riots of the summer of 1919 demonstrated, violence was a threat to African Americans north as well as south of the Mason-Dixon line. After World War I, African Americans increased their demand for a real solution to the country's racial problems.

New York City's Harlem became the focal point for the aspirations of hundreds of thousands of African Americans. Some 200,000 blacks settled in Harlem. Migrants from the South mixed with recently arrived immigrants from Caribbean islands, such as Jamaica. This dynamic blend of different cultures and traditions bred new ideas.

Garvey Calls for Racial Pride The most prominent new African American leader to emerge in the 1920s was **Marcus Garvey.** Born in Jamaica, Garvey traveled widely before immigrating to Harlem in 1916. From his travels, Garvey drew one important conclusion: Blacks were exploited everywhere. To combat the problem, he promoted the idea of universal black nationalism and organized a "Back to Africa" movement. Unlike Booker T. Washington or W.E.B. Du Bois, Garvey did not call for blacks and whites to work together to improve America. Instead, Garvey advocated the separation of the races.

Garvey's message found willing converts in American cities. By the mid-1920s, his Universal Negro Improvement Association boasted almost 2.5 million members and sympathizers. His advocacy of black pride and black support of black-run businesses won considerable support.

Garvey's movement fell apart in the second half of the decade. The federal government sent him to prison for mail fraud and then deported him to Jamaica. Without his powerful leadership, the Universal Negro Improvement Association lost its focus and appeal.

Although Garvey's movement died, his ideas did not fade. The nationalist and separatist aspects of the Nation of Islam and the Black Power movement in the 1960s owed much to Garvey. So, too, did later appeals to black pride, self-reliance, and cultural ties to Africa. Harlem's major newspaper, the *Amsterdam News*, later wrote, "In a world where black is despised, he taught [African Americans] to admire and praise black things and black people."

✓ **Checkpoint** How did Marcus Garvey encourage African American pride?

The Jazz Age

It was F. Scott Fitzgerald who called the 1920s the "Jazz Age." However, it was African Americans who gave the age its jazz. A truly <u>indigenous</u> American musical form, **jazz** is a musical form based on improvisation. Jazz musicians creatively recombine different forms of music, including African American blues and ragtime, and European-based popular music.

A Unique American Music Emerges Jazz emerged in the South and Midwest, particularly New Orleans, where different cultures and traditions came together and influenced each other. Early jazz artists won fame playing in

Marcus Garvey
Dressed in a ceremonial uniform, Marcus Garvey rides in a New York City parade on the opening day of a 1922 convention of a group called Negro Peoples of the World.

Vocabulary Builder
<u>indigenous</u>–(ihn DIHJ uh nuhs) *adj.* native to; growing out of a particular region or country

Teach

A New "Black Consciousness" ⓛ³

Instruct

- **Introduce** Remind students that during the Great Migration, many African Americans moved from the South to northern cities, such as New York. Tell students that Harlem is a district in New York City that in particular attracted thousands of African Americans.

- **Teach** Ask **What is consciousness?** *(awareness of something)* **What is racial consciousness?** *(awareness of people being identified primarily by their race)* Explain that in the 1920s, a new "Black Consciousness" arose. African Americans took pride in their racial identity and tried to increase awareness of it. Then, have students discuss the role that Marcus Garvey played in raising the new "Black Consciousness" during the 1920s and the effect his ideas had on future African American movements.

- **Analyzing the Visuals** Have students look at the photo of Garvey on this page. Ask **What emotions might this image of Garvey inspire in African Americans in the 1920s?** *(pride, hope, confidence)*

Independent Practice

Ask students to make a list summarizing Marcus Garvey's achievements and historical importance.

Monitor Progress

As students fill in their section outlines, circulate to make sure that they understand the main ideas relating to the flowering of African American culture in the 1920s. For a completed version of the outline, see Note Taking Transparencies, **B-103.**

Differentiated Instruction **Solutions for All Learners**

ⓛ¹ Special Needs Students **ⓛ² Less Proficient Readers**

Write the following questions on the board: *What did I read about in this subsection? What did I learn from the reading? What do I still not understand? What conclusions can I draw from this reading?* Have students apply these questions to the red heading "A New 'Black Consciousness.'" Encourage them to use the same questions with the other subsections in Section 5.

Answer

✓ Marcus Garvey promoted the idea of universal black nationalism and organized a "Back to Africa" movement.

The Jazz Age

Instruct

- **Introduce: Key Term** Ask students to find the key term *jazz* (in bold) in the text. Ask **Where did jazz originate?** *(Jazz originated in the South and Midwest, particularly in New Orleans.)* **How did jazz spread north?** *(It spread north with the Great Migration of African Americans.)*

- **Teach** Discuss the famous jazz artists of the time shown on this page. Using the Numbered Heads strategy (TE, p. T23), have students discuss the ways that jazz symbolized the Roaring Twenties. Ask **How did jazz quickly bridge the races?** *(White musicians contributed to the styles and popularity of jazz, and jazz influenced white songwriters and composers.)* **How do you think African Americans felt about the popularity of jazz among whites?** *(Some African Americans might have been proud that whites had embraced an African American art form. Some African Americans might have felt that whites were simply using an African American art form for their own popularity and benefit.)*

- **Quick Activity** Organize a quick debate on whether or not jazz is truly a unique American musical form, since it has some European influences.

Independent Practice

Ask students to write a paragraph answering this question: **Why do you think jazz is important to American culture?** *(Sample answer: Jazz is a uniquely American form of music. Jazz music reflects the diversity of American society. It has affected the development of popular music.)*

Monitor Progress

As students work on their paragraphs, circulate to make sure that they understand that jazz is still popular around the world and is not just a "historical" music form.

Storyville, a section of New Orleans known for its night life. From the South, it spread north with the Great Migration of African Americans.

Trumpet player **Louis Armstrong** became the unofficial ambassador of jazz. After playing with King Oliver's band in New Orleans and Chicago and with Fletcher Henderson's orchestra in New York, Armstrong began to organize his own groups. His ability to play the trumpet and his subtle sense of improvisation made him a legend and influenced the development of jazz. After Armstrong, all jazz bands featured soloists. Many also began to feature vocal soloists, such as **Bessie Smith,** the "Empress of the Blues."

Jazz Wins Worldwide Popularity Jazz was more than a musical style. It was also a symbol of the Roaring Twenties. It was part of the Prohibition era, played in speakeasies and nightspots in New York, Chicago, St. Louis, and Los Angeles. It was the sound of the Cotton Club, one of Harlem's most famous attractions, where African Americans played African American music to all-white audiences. Phonograph records and radio spread the influence of jazz across the country and beyond. By the end of the decade, the popularity of jazz had spread to Europe as well.

But jazz was still more. It was a demonstration of the depth and richness of African American culture. Gerald Early, a modern scholar of English and African American studies, predicted that, in the future, America will be best remembered for three great contributions—the Constitution, baseball, and jazz. All three enriched lives, opened windows to new possibilities, and lifted the human spirit. Jazz announced that the United States was a land of shared cultures and traditions, a place where people came together and created something greater than their parts.

Jazz quickly bridged the races. Trumpeter Bix Beiderbecke (Bī der behk) became the first white musician to contribute to the styles and popularity of jazz. Jazz sounds influenced such white songwriters and composers as Cole

Stars of the Jazz Age
Not only was Louis Armstrong (below left) an influential trumpeter, he also pioneered "scat," a style in which the singer improvises meaningless syllables that mimic the sounds of musical instruments. The recordings and concerts of blues singer Bessie Smith (below right) made her the highest-paid African American entertainer of the 1920s.

History Background

Notable Records In the 1920s, records and phonograph players were not new. Yet during this decade, record sales soared. Record companies adopted the small disc format for recordings, making record production easy and records themselves convenient for consumers. Double-sided records offered music fans a relatively inexpensive way to hear many of their favorite bands. In 1927 alone, Americans bought more than 100 million jazz records. Recordings by acts such as Louis Armstrong's Hot Five brought jazz to remote areas that rarely saw live bands. These phonograph records made the rapid spread of jazz music possible, and for the first time turned music and music production into a major industry.

Porter, Irving Berlin, and George Gershwin, whose jazz-inspired orchestral work *Rhapsody in Blue* premiered in 1924. The title of a song by African American band leader Duke Ellington best captures how jazz changed popular music: "It Don't Mean a Thing If It Ain't Got That Swing."

✔ **Checkpoint** How did jazz spread from its roots in the South to the North in the 1920s?

The Harlem Renaissance

Jazz and blues were expressions of the African American experience. The pain of the African American experience can be heard in the blues, and the joy of that experience in the soaring notes of jazz. The range of such African American musicians as Duke Ellington and Cab Calloway speaks to the varieties of African American life. But in the 1920s, there were other expressions of African American culture. Novelists, poets, and artists celebrated their culture and explored questions of race in America. This flowering of African American culture became known as the **Harlem Renaissance**. The Harlem Renaissance helped give a new vocabulary and dynamic to race relations in the United States.

African American Literature Flowers In the 1920s, the term the "New Negro" entered the American vocabulary. It suggested a radical break with the past. No longer would African Americans silently endure the old ways of exploitation and discrimination. The new mood was most vividly expressed in Harlem, which attracted African American novelists, essayists, poets, and journalists from all over the country and beyond. In their work, these writers explored the pains and joys of being black in America, leaving a literary legacy that spoke to all Americans of all times.

Jean Toomer's *Cane* (1923) set the tone for the Harlem Renaissance. A collection of short stories, poems, and sketches, *Cane* presented African American life and folk culture in all its richness. It was not a blueprint for where African Americans needed to move politically in the future, but a plea to remember and preserve the past.

Soon, other African American writers joined Toomer at the forefront of the Harlem Renaissance. Jamaican immigrant **Claude McKay** was the most militant of these writers. In his novels and poems, McKay showed ordinary African Americans struggling for dignity and advancement in the face of discrimination and economic hardships. A poem that McKay wrote after Chicago was stricken by violent race riots captured his sense of anger and militancy:

Primary Source

"If we must die—let it not be like hogs,
Hunted and penned in an inglorious spot.
While round us bark the mad and hungry dogs,
Marking their mark at our accursed lot. . . .
What though before us lies the open grave?
Like men we will face the murderous, cowardly pack,
Pressed to the wall, dying but fighting back!"
—Claude McKay, "If We Must Die"

The Harlem Renaissance ⓑ

Instruct

- **Introduce: Key Term** Ask students to find the key term *Harlem Renaissance* (in bold) in the text. Point out that the word "renaissance" means rebirth. Ask **Why was the work of black artists and writers in the 1920s called the Harlem Renaissance?** *(It was a rebirth or flowering of African American culture.)*

- **Teach** Discuss the different Harlem Renaissance writers and the works of literature that they published. Then, display Color Transparency: *The Harlem Renaissance*. Use the lesson suggested in the transparency book to discuss the art that was created during the Harlem Renaissance. Ask **What was one lasting impact of the Harlem Renaissance?** *(It altered the way that many white Americans viewed African American culture and even the way that African Americans viewed themselves.)* Color Transparencies **A-92**

- **Quick Activity** Have students reread the quotation from Claude McKay's poem "If We Must Die." Ask them how they think the ideas presented in this poem summarize the ideas of the Harlem Renaissance.

Independent Practice

Have students read and complete the *Link to Literature*: *Their Eyes Were Watching God* worksheet. Teaching Resources, **p. 24**

Monitor Progress

As students complete their worksheets, circulate to make sure that they understand that African American literature flourished during the Harlem Renaissance.

Differentiated Instruction   Solutions for All Learners

ⓛ Advanced Readers   ⓛ Gifted and Talented Students

Have students research Harlem today. Ask them to answer the following questions: In what ways has Harlem changed since the Harlem Renaissance? In what ways has Harlem not changed? Do students think that there could be another Harlem Renaissance in the future? Have them explain why this could or could not happen.

Answer

✔ Jazz spread from its roots in the South to the North with the Great Migration of southern workers who left for the North during and after World War I, looking for new opportunities.

Assess and Reteach

Assess Progress

- Have students complete the Section Assessment.

- Administer the Section Quiz. Teaching Resources, **p. 29**

- To further assess student understanding, use Progress Monitoring Transparencies, **99.**

Reteach

If students need more instruction, have them read the section summary.

Reading and Note Taking
Study Guide

Adapted Reading and
Note Taking Study Guide

Spanish Reading and
Note Taking Study Guide

Extend

Have students select an author or poet of the Harlem Renaissance to research. Ask students to use their findings to write a short story or poem in the style of their selected writer.

Answer

 Hughes captured the remarkable diversity of everyday African American life. Hurston expressed the new longing for independence felt by so many women, black and white.

McKay represented the political and ideological left wing of the Harlem Renaissance. More in the center was **Langston Hughes,** probably the most powerful African American literary voice of his time. For Hughes, the force of the movement was not politics but a celebration of African American culture and life. (See the American Literature feature on the next page.) In more than 50 works of fiction, poetry, journalism, and criticism, he captured the remarkable diversity of everyday African American life. In the last line of his autobiography *The Big Sea*, Hughes wrote, "Literature is a big sea full of many fish. I let down my nets and pulled. I'm still pulling."

Another powerful voice was **Zora Neale Hurston.** Hurston traveled the rural back roads of her native Florida, collecting folk tales in books such as *Mules and Men.* But Hurston also looked to the future. Her 1937 novel *Their Eyes Were Watching God* expressed the new longing for independence felt by many women, black and white.

The Harlem Renaissance Has Lasting Impact The Harlem Renaissance gave a voice to African American culture, just as jazz and blues gave it a tune. It altered the way many white Americans viewed African American culture, and even the way African Americans viewed themselves. James Weldon Johnson, poet and secretary of the NAACP, noted:

> **Primary Source** ❝A great deal has been accomplished in this decade of 'renaissance.' . . . Today, one may see undesirable stories, but one may also read stories about Negro singers, Negro actors, Negro authors, Negro poets. The connotations of the very word *Negro* have changed. A generation ago many Negroes were half or wholly ashamed of the term. Today, they have every reason to be proud of it.❞
> —James Weldon Johnson, article in *Harper's* magazine, 1928

The Harlem Renaissance ended with the national financial collapse that also ended the nation's decade of prosperity. But the sense of group identity and African American solidarity that it created would become part of the bedrock on which the later civil rights movement would be constructed.

✓ **Checkpoint** What themes did Langston Hughes and Zora Neale Hurston explore?

▲ Zora Neale Hurston

SECTION 5 Assessment

Progress Monitoring *Online*
For: Self-test with vocabulary practice
www.pearsonschool.com/ushist

Comprehension

1. **Terms and People** For each of the following, write a sentence explaining the importance of that person or item to the development of African American culture.
   - Marcus Garvey
   - jazz
   - Louis Armstrong
   - Bessie Smith
   - Harlem Renaissance
   - Claude McKay
   - Langston Hughes
   - Zora Neale Hurston

2. **NoteTaking Identify Main Ideas** Use your section outline to answer the Section Focus Question: How did African Americans express a new sense of hope and pride?

Writing About History

3. **Compare and Contrast** Write a thesis statement and introductory paragraph for an essay in which you compare the influence of jazz to the influence of the Harlem Renaissance. Consider both the similarities and differences in the two cultural developments.

Critical Thinking

4. **Identify Points of View** Why do you think Marcus Garvey rejected the goals of earlier African American leaders such as Washington and Du Bois?

5. **Analyze Information** How did jazz blend cultural influences and cross-cultural divides?

6. **Identify Main Ideas** Paraphrase the main idea of Claude McKay's poem "If We Must Die" in your own words.

Section 5 Assessment

1. Sentences should reflect an understanding of the importance of each term or person to the development of African American culture.

2. African Americans expressed a new sense of hope and pride by moving north to find new opportunities. They created jazz, which grew popular across the nation, and provided a cultural common ground for Americans. They celebrated their culture and identity and stood up for their rights.

3. Thesis statements and paragraphs should mention that both jazz and the Harlem Renaissance were started and led by African Americans, both influenced the entire nation, and both were sources of pride for African Americans.

4. Garvey rejected the goals of earlier African American leaders because in his travels he saw that blacks were exploited everywhere. He advocated separation of the races because he did not think that blacks and whites could work together to improve America.

5. Jazz emerged in the South and Midwest, particularly in New Orleans, where different cultures and traditions came together and influenced one another. Also, white musicians contributed to the styles and popularity of jazz.

6. Possible answer: If African Americans must die because of white violence, they should resist with pride and self-respect.

For additional assessment, have students access **Progress Monitoring *Online*** at **www.pearsonschool.com/ushist.**

Two Poems by Langston Hughes

Langston Hughes wrote about how it felt to be African American, from the pain of racial prejudice to his deep pride in his culture and heritage. The two poems below are among his most famous.

The Negro Speaks of Rivers
> I've known rivers:
> I've known rivers ancient as the world and older than the flow of human
> blood in human veins.
>
> My soul has grown deep like the rivers.
>
> I bathed in the Euphrates when dawns were young.[1]
> I built my hut near the Congo and it lulled me to sleep.
> I looked upon the Nile and raised the pyramids above it.
> I heard the singing of the Mississippi when Abe Lincoln went down to
> New Orleans, and I've seen its muddy bosom turn all golden in the
> sunset.
>
> I've known rivers:
> Ancient, dusky rivers.
>
> My soul has grown deep like the rivers.

My People
> The night is beautiful,
> So the faces of my people.
>
> The stars are beautiful,
> So the eyes of my people.
>
> Beautiful, also, is the sun.
> Beautiful, also, are the souls of my people.

▲ Langston Hughes

Harlem street scene, 1920s ►

Thinking Critically
1. **Analyze Literature** In "The Negro Speaks of Rivers," what point do you think Hughes is making when he names four rivers at four different periods of history?
2. **Make Inferences** How would you describe the speaker's attitude toward being African American in these poems?

---

1. The Euphrates is a river in the Middle East. The Nile and the Congo are rivers in Africa.

History Background

John Mercer Langston Langston Hughes was named for his distinguished great-uncle, John Mercer Langston (1829–1897). Langston was born free in Virginia, the son of a white planter and an emancipated slave. After his parents died, Langston received a sizable inheritance and moved to Ohio where he enrolled at age 14 in Oberlin College, graduating in 1849. He passed the bar in 1854 and became the first black lawyer in Ohio; his election to township clerk made him the first African American to hold elected office in the United States. An outspoken advocate of abolition and women's rights, Langston believed that only

through public service could these goals be achieved. He briefly considered a more radical approach and conspired with John Brown on the Harpers Ferry raid, but he did not participate. Langston led suffrage campaigns in Ohio, Kansas, and Missouri, worked for the Freedmen's Bureau, and organized the law department at Howard University. For eight years, he served as consul-general in Haiti and returned to the United States for a short term in the House of Representatives, the first African American from Virginia elected to Congress. Langston chronicled his life in an autobiography published in 1894.

American Literature

Two Poems
by Langston Hughes

Objectives
- Understand a key piece of literature written during the Harlem Renaissance.
- Describe how the poetry of Langston Hughes expresses pride in African American culture and heritage.

Background Knowledge **L3**
Review what students have already learned about Langston Hughes. Tell students that Hughes was born in Missouri in 1902 and moved to New York City after finishing high school to go to Columbia University. He left Columbia after one year, and in 1923 he traveled through Africa and Europe, exploring the different cultures he encountered.

Instruct **L3**
Read each poem aloud. Make sure students understand the references to specific places in the poems, such as the Euphrates, Congo, and Nile rivers. Encourage students to look for underlying themes, or main ideas, in the two poems.

Monitor Progress
Have students answer the Thinking Critically questions. Then, have students summarize the themes of each poem in their own words.

Answers

Thinking Critically
1. African Americans have had a long important history, and they have lived in different parts of the world.
2. The speaker wants to remind African Americans of their ancient heritage and instill a sense of pride.

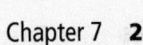

7 Quick Study Guide

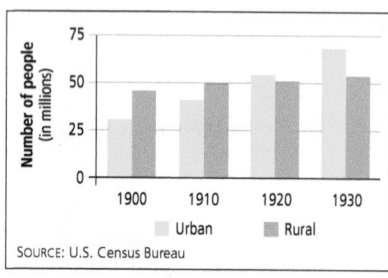

Progress Monitoring Online
For: Self-test with vocabulary practice
www.pearsonschool.com/ushist

Quick Study Guide

- Have students use the Quick Study Guide to prepare for the chapter test. Students may wish to refer to the following sections as they review:

Rise of the Automobile
Section 1
Section 4

Urban and Rural Population, 1900–1930
Section 1
Section 4

Economic Policies of Harding and Coolidge
Section 1
Section 2

New Cultural Trends
Section 3
Section 4
Section 5

Key Events of the Twenties
Section 1
Section 2
Section 3
Section 4
Section 5

- For additional review, remind students to refer to the Reading and Note Taking Study Guide.
Section Note Taking
Section Summaries

- Have students access **www.pearsonschool.com/ ushist** for this chapter's History Interactive timeline, which includes expanded entries and additional events.

- If students need more instruction on analyzing graphic data, have them read the Skills Handbook, **p. SH21.**

For **Progress Monitoring Online,** refer students to the Self-test with vocabulary practice at **www.pearsonschool.com/ushist.**

■ Rise of the Automobile

- Decline of railroads, trolleys
- Higher wages for auto workers
- Mass production; lower prices
- **Rise of the Automobile**
- Greater freedom
- Growth of suburbs
- Highway system
- Growth in related industries

■ Urban and Rural Population, 1900–1930

Number of people (in millions)

Year	Urban	Rural
1900	~30	~46
1910	~42	~50
1920	~53	~50
1930	~68	~52

■ Urban ■ Rural

SOURCE: U.S. Census Bureau

☑ Quick Study Timeline

In America

1919 Eighteenth Amendment is ratified

1920 Warren Harding elected President

1922 Investigations into Teapot Dome scandal begin

Presidential Terms: Woodrow Wilson 1913–1921 | Warren Harding 1921–1923

1919 | **1921** | **1923**

Around the World

1919 Paris peace conference meets

1921 World Court is founded in the Netherlands

1923 Reparations contribute to inflation in Germany

■ Economic Policies of Harding and Coolidge

Goal: Support Economic Growth

Policy: Raise Tariffs	Policy: Cut Government Spending	Policy: Support Business
• Increased sales of domestic goods • Led to tariff war with foreign nations	• Cut national debt • Created federal budget surplus	• Encouraged business growth through tax incentives and reduced regulations • Caused organized labor to lose ground

■ New Cultural Trends

Mass culture	Radio and movies unite people of different regions.
Prohibition	Crime rises as people find ways to avoid the ban on alcohol.
Fundamentalism	Many Christians promote a literal interpretation of the Bible and return to traditional values.
Modernism	Literature and art depict postwar disillusionment and the influence of the subconscious on human behavior.
Jazz	Musical style blends elements of African American and European forms.
Harlem Renaissance	Literature and art express pride and aspirations of African Americans.

Differentiated Instruction Solutions for All Learners

L1 Special Needs Students **L2 English Language Learners** **L2 Less Proficient Readers**

Use the following study guide resources to help students acquiring basic skills:
Adapted Reading and Note Taking Study Guide
- Section Note Taking
- Section Summaries

Use the following study guide resources to help Spanish-speaking students:
Spanish Reading and Note Taking Study Guide
- Section Note Taking
- Section Summaries

American Issues
Connector

By connecting prior knowledge with what you have learned in this chapter, you can gradually build your understanding of enduring questions that still affect America today. Answer the questions below. Then, use your American Issues Connector study guide (or go online: www.pearsonschool.com/ushist).

Issues You Learned About

● **U.S. Immigration Policy** The U.S. government makes decisions about how many immigrants to allow into the country.

1. In the mid-1800s, the United States experienced a wave of immigration. From which countries did the majority of these immigrants come?

2. What measures had been taken to restrict immigration before the 1920s?

3. Was the National Origins Act biased? Explain.

● **Women in American Society** Women's roles in society continue to change and evolve, allowing women greater opportunities.

4. What amendment gave women the right to vote, and when was it ratified?

5. What immediate changes were the result of women's winning the right to vote?

6. How did the role of women in society change in the 1920s?

● **Technology and Society** New technological developments continually change the way Americans work and play.

7. Prior to the automobile, what inventions in transportation transformed the way people and goods traveled in the United States?

8. What social changes did the automobile bring to America?

9. What other technological changes affected American culture in the 1920s?

Connect to Your World | Activity

Migration and Urbanization In the 1920s, the migration of Americans throughout the country formed new urban centers. Over the decades, American population centers have continued to shift. For instance, in 1920 only one western city—Los Angeles—had a population greater than 500,000. Conduct research to find out which American cities have a population greater than one million. Then, create a map that shows your findings. Write a summary statement explaining how population centers have shifted since 1920.

History *Interactive*
For: Interactive timeline
www.pearsonschool.com/ushist

| 1924 National Origins Act sets up quota system for immigration | 1925 Scopes trial begins in Tennessee | 1927 *The Jazz Singer,* first talking movie, opens | 1929 Stock market crash marks end of 1920s prosperity |

Calvin Coolidge 1923–1929   Herbert Hoover 1929–1933

1925   **1927**   **1929**

| 1924 Stalin comes to power in the Soviet Union | 1927 Civil war begins in China | 1928 Major nations sign Kellogg-Briand Pact to ban war |

American Issues
Connector

Tell students that the main issues for this chapter are U.S. Immigration Policy, Women in American Society, and Technology and Society, and then ask them to answer the Issues You Learned About questions on this page. Discuss the Connect to Your World topics, and ask students to complete the project that follows.

American Issues Connector

1. northern and western Europe, especially Germany

2. Immigrants who could not read or write their own language were prohibited from entering the United States.

3. Yes; it established a quota system that limited the number of immigrants from southern and eastern Europe. The Act also prevented many Asians from immigrating.

4. the Nineteenth Amendment, ratified in 1920

5. Women worked in reform movements, ran for office, and fought for laws to protect women and children in the workplace.

6. Technology gave women more time in which to work outside the home. Women married later and had fewer children.

7. steamboats and trains

8. It brought about car culture, led to the growth of suburbs, and allowed people to travel whenever and wherever they wanted.

9. Radio, movies, movies with sound, electricity (for appliances), and phonographs

Connect to Your World

Students' maps and statements should conclude that there has been a shift in population toward the West and the South.

For additional review of this chapter's enduring issues, remind students to refer to the Reading and Note Taking Study Guide American Issues Journal.

Terms and People

1. a period of rising stock prices; The bull market of the 1920s led more Americans to buy stock on credit, which put them in debt and artificially increased stock values.

2. Secretary of the Treasury under President Harding; he reduced government spending and created a Treasury surplus.

3. It forbade the manufacture, distribution, and sale of alcoholic beverages anywhere in the United States. Lawmakers who represented mostly rural constituencies supported the amendment.

4. Modernism was a perspective that challenged traditional values. Modern writers created characters who did not follow outdated values but rather made their own rules.

5. Sample answer: The Harlem Renaissance was the flowering of African American music, art, and literature in the 1920s. Claude McKay was a poet who depicted African Americans struggling for dignity and advancement in the face of discrimination and economic hardship. Zora Neale Hurston was a novelist who wrote about modern African American women who wanted independence and freedom.

Focus Questions

6. The workweek shortened to 40 hours and allowed people extra leisure time. People used credit to buy new machines and stocks. Many prosperous Americans relied on cars for transportation and moved to the suburbs where they could enjoy more space.

7. Both men refused to use legislation to make social changes. Unlike the Progressives, their economic policies favored big business. Both Presidents also maintained isolationist stances in world affairs.

8. Many rural Americans were more religious and traditional, and many urban Americans were more interested in science and modernity. Rural Americans often opposed evolution and new roles for women, and supported Prohibition.

Chapter Assessment

Terms and People

1. Define **bull market.** How did it affect the investment activities of Americans?

2. Who was **Andrew Mellon**? What economic goals did he achieve?

3. What was the **Eighteenth Amendment**? Which lawmakers supported it?

4. Define **modernism.** Explain how modernist ideas could be viewed in literature.

5. What was the **Harlem Renaissance**? Name and describe the accomplishments of two people who took part in it.

Focus Questions

The focus question for this chapter is **How did the United States experience both economic growth and social change in the decade after World War I?** Build an answer to this big question by answering the focus questions for Sections 1 through 5 and the Critical Thinking questions that follow.

Section 1
6. How did the booming economy of the 1920s lead to changes in American life?

Section 2
7. How did domestic and foreign policy change direction under Harding and Coolidge?

Section 3
8. How did Americans differ on major social and cultural issues?

Section 4
9. How did the new mass culture reflect technological and social changes?

Section 5
10. How did African Americans express a new sense of hope and pride?

Critical Thinking

11. **Analyze Evidence** What evidence supports the conclusion that Henry Ford cared about the quality of life of his workers?

12. **Predict Consequences** What likely happened in the 1930s to people who, in the 1920s, bought goods they could not afford on the installment plan?

13. **Analyze Information** Did Harding show good leadership of the country? Explain.

14. **Draw Inferences** Why did Congress support the Kellogg-Briand Pact even when lawmakers knew that its provision could not be enforced?

15. **Summarize** How could you describe the cultural differences between rural and urban Americans in the 1920s? What issues led to cultural clashes between the two groups?

16. **Analyze Information** What did athletes represent for Americans in the 1920s?

17. **Evaluate Information** List four changes that affected women in the 1920s. Which of these do you think had the most immediate effect? Which do you think was most important in the long term?

18. **Identify Central Issues** What did southern African Americans hope to find by moving north? Did they achieve their goals?

Writing About History

Writing a Comparison-and-Contrast Essay Evaluations and interpretations of historical eras often change over time or differ from historian to historian. Write the introductory paragraph and outline for an essay comparing two historical views on one of the following topics: the prosperity of the 1920s; the presidency of Calvin Coolidge; the role of the United States in world affairs after World War I; the "New Woman."

Prewriting
• Use Internet or library sources to find two different interpretations or descriptions of one of the topics above. You may use this textbook as one of your sources.

• Make a Venn diagram to identify similarities and differences in the two articles.

Drafting
• Develop a working thesis in which you define the differences between the two historical interpretations.

• Write an opening paragraph in which you introduce the topic and summarize the major differences between your two sources.

• Make an outline organizing your supporting details.

Revising
• Use the guidelines on page SH11 of the Writing Handbook to revise your writing.

9. Movies, radio, and records all reached a national audience, and created celebrities and trends at the same time across the country. The new American society was reflected in action movies and radio shows, and fast dance music on records.

10. African Americans created art that reflected their own experiences and presented it to the world with pride. Jazz and African American literature were known around the world, and African Americans demanded recognition for their cultural contributions.

Critical Thinking

11. He doubled their wages and shortened the workday and the workweek, creating weekends of leisure time.

12. They probably lost everything because when they could not make the payments, their goods probably were repossessed.

13. Possible response: No; he left governing to his friends without making sure they were honest. This led to scandals and mismanagement.

Document-Based Assessment

Scientific Management and Mass Production

The legacy of Henry Ford included not only the popularly priced automobile but techniques of mass production. What were his goals in introducing these techniques, and what impact did they have? Use your knowledge of the chapter material and Documents A, B, C, and D to answer questions 1 through 4.

Document A

"If you and your workman have become so skillful that you and he together are making two pairs of shoes in a day, while your competitor and his workman are making only one pair, it is clear that after selling your two pairs of shoes you can pay your workman much higher wages than your competitor who produces only one pair of shoes is able to pay his man, and that there will still be enough money left over for you to have a larger profit than your competitor.... The greatest permanent prosperity for the workman, coupled with the greatest prosperity for the employer, can be brought about only when the work of the establishment is done with the smallest combined expenditure of human effort, plus nature's resources, plus the cost for the use of capital in the shape of machines, buildings."

—*Frederick Taylor*, Principles of Scientific Management, *1911*

Document B

"[In 1914], Ford announced that he would nearly double the minimum salary paid to his 13,600 workers to $5 a day, and reduce the workday from nine hours to eight. In a stroke, he transformed the people who manufacture automobiles into the people who buy them.... The reaction from business thinkers was generally negative. 'He's crazy, isn't he?' asked Adolph Ochs, publisher of the *New York Times*.... The *Wall Street Journal* went even further, accusing Ford of having 'committed economic blunders, if not crimes' and applying 'spiritual' principles where they don't belong.'"

—*Kevin Baker*, "Ford's Paradox," *2000*

Document C

Assembly line at Ford auto plant, 1928

Document D

"We have decided upon and at once put into effect through all the branches of our industries the five day week. Hereafter there will be no more work with us on Saturdays and Sundays. These will be free days, but the men, according to merit, will receive the same pay equivalent as for a full six day week.... It does not pay to put men at work, excepting in continuous operations, from midnight until morning. As a part of low cost production— and only low cost production can pay high wages—one must have a big investment in machinery and power plants. Expensive tools cannot remain idle. They ought to work twenty-four hours a day, but here the human element comes in, for although many men like to work all night and have part of their day free, they do not work so well and hence it is not economical, or at least that is our experience, to go through the full twenty-four hours."

—*Henry Ford*, "Why I Favor Five Days' Work With Six Days' Pay," *1926*

---

1. Documents C and D provide evidence that Henry Ford
   A applied the principles described in Document A.
   B disagreed with the principles described in Document A.
   C had influenced the writer of Document A.
   D had listened to the criticisms of the business leaders quoted in Document B.

2. According to Document B, why did many business leaders disapprove of Ford's wage plan?
   A It did not take the well-being of his workers into account.
   B It was not based on accepted business principles.
   C It violated antitrust laws.
   D It would give Ford an unfair advantage over his competitors.

3. According to Document D, why did Ford institute the five-day workweek?
   A If his machinery was not used over the weekend, it would last longer.
   B His company would save money if he could pay his workers for only five days' work instead of six.
   C He was giving in to the demands of labor unions for a shorter workweek.
   D The five-day workweek would allow maximum productivity and efficiency.

4. **Writing Task** Who was right: Henry Ford or his critics? Use your knowledge of the chapter content and specific evidence from the primary sources above to support your opinion.

CHAPTER 8 The Great Depression
1928–1932

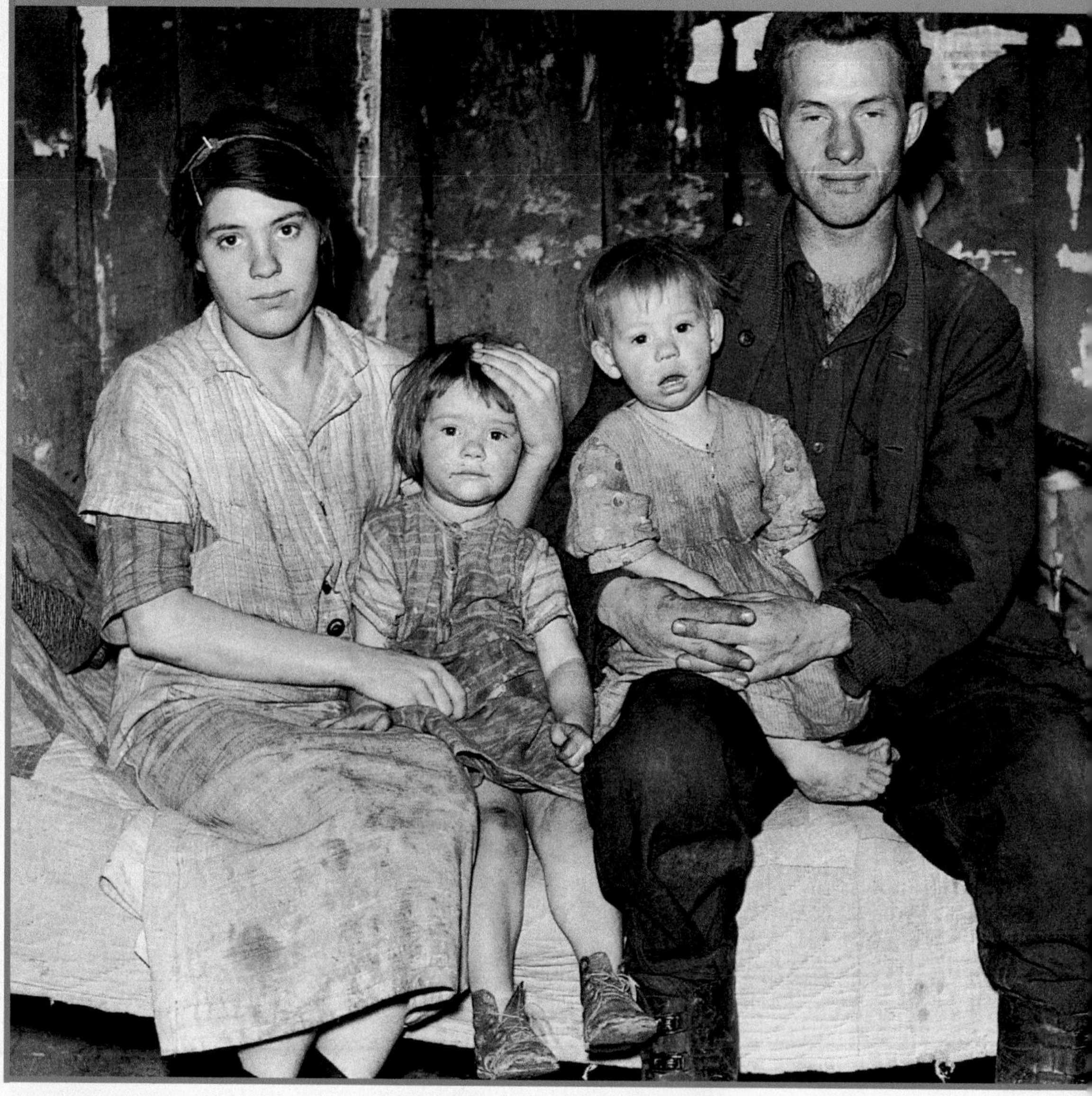

Teach With Technology

PresentationEXPRESS™
PREMIUM DVD

- Teach this chapter's core content by using PresentationExpress, which includes interactivities, video, lecture notes, and the *ExamView®* QuickTake assessment tool.

- To introduce this chapter by using PresentationExpress, ask students with which of the following statements they most agree: **A) The U.S. government should intervene in the economy during a depression. B) The U.S. government should intervene in the economy during a boom. C) The U.S. government should never intervene in the economy.** Take a class poll or record students' answers by using the QuickTake feature, and discuss their responses. Point out that in this chapter, students will read about the Great Depression and see how this crisis forced people to consider such issues in new ways. Continue introducing the chapter by using the chapter opener slide show.

Technology Resources

- Student**EXPRESS** CD-ROM

- Teacher Resource Library **DVD**

- Presentation**EXPRESS** **PREMIUM DVD**

- *ExamView®* **Test Bank CD-ROM** English and Spanish

- **Guided Reading Audio,** Spanish

- **Student Edition on Audio**

For videos on Amercian Issues, go to
www.pearsonschool.com/ushist

Bibliography

For the Teacher
Bernanke, Ben S. *Essays on the Great Depression.* Princeton University Press, 2000.

Fausold, Martin L. *The Presidency of Herbert C. Hoover.* University Press of Kansas, 1985.

Terkel, Studs. *Hard Times: An Oral History of the Great Depression.* Pantheon Books, 1970.

For the Student
L2 Smiley, Gene. *Rethinking the Great Depression.* Ivan R. Dee, Publisher, 2003.

L3 Egan, Timothy. *The Worst Hard Time: The Untold Story of Those Who Survived the Great American Dust Bowl.* Houghton Mifflin, 2006.

L4 Agee, James. *Let Us Now Praise Famous Men.* Mariner Books, 2001.

The Depression Descends on America

No one who lived through the Great Depression ever forgot it. Panicked investors watched their fortunes dwindle to nothing overnight. Jobless men trudged anywhere and everywhere looking for work. The hungry lined up for handouts from churches and charitable organizations. Misery stalked Americans at virtually every turn. One survivor of the Depression remembered:

❝There were many beggars, who would come to your back door, and they would say they were hungry. I wouldn't give them money because I didn't have it. But I did take them in and put them in my kitchen and give them something to eat.❞
—Kitty McCulloch

◀ A poor family from rural Maryland poses for a photograph.

Stock ticker machine

Variety headline from October 1929

World War I victory medal worn by Bonus Army veteran

Chapter Preview

Chapter Focus Question: How did the Great Depression happen, and how did Americans respond to it?

Section 1
Causes of the Depression

Section 2
Americans Face Hard Times

Section 3
Hoover's Response Fails

Use the ☑ **Quick Study Timeline** at the end of this chapter to preview chapter events.

Note Taking Study Guide *Online*
For: Note Taking and American Issues Connector
www.pearsonschool.com/ushist

Chapter-Level Resources

All In One Letter Home (English and Spanish), Preread the Chapter, Vocabulary Builder, Reading Strategy, Social Studies Skills Practice, Enrichment, Issues Connector, Chapter Tests

- Test Prep With Document-Based Assessment
- AYP Monitoring Assessments
- *ExamView®* Test Bank CD-ROM
- Guided Reading Audio (Spanish)
- Student Edition Audio

Previewing the Chapter

- **WITNESS HISTORY** Explain that the Great Depression dramatically increased the number of Americans who faced severe economic hardship. Read the Witness History selection aloud. Then, ask students to imagine the impact that such widespread poverty and despair had on the people who lived through this era.

- **Analyzing the Visuals** Ask students to study the photo of the family and the images on the right side of the page. Ask **What does the photo of the family tell you about life during the Great Depression?** *(Sample response: Many people struggled financially during the Great Depression.)* **What do you think stock prices had to do with the Great Depression?** *(Possible answer: Stock prices reflect the value of businesses, so a serious economic crisis would probably be reflected in falling stock prices.)*

- **Focus** Write the Chapter Focus question on the board. Tell students to keep this question in mind as they read the chapter. Then, have students preview the section titles in this chapter.

- **Preread** Have students complete the chapter's Preread the Chapter Worksheet. Teaching Resources, pp. 7–8

Have students access **www.pearsonschool.com/ushist** for the Note Taking Study Guide *Online* as an alternative to the *Reading and Note Taking Study Guide* booklet.

Differentiated Instruction   Solutions for All Learners

The following Teacher's Edition strategies are suitable for students of varying abilities.

L1 Special Needs Students, pp. 255, 256, 259, 262, 263, 267, 273 SN

L2 English Language Learners, pp. 255, 256, 259, 262, 263, 273 ELL

L2 Less Proficient Readers, pp. 255, 256, 259, 262, 263, 267, 273 LPR

L4 Advanced Readers, pp. 259, 265, 275 AR

L4 Gifted and Talented Students, pp. 259, 265, 275 GT

Objectives

As you teach this section, keep students focused on the following objectives to help them answer the Section Focus Question and master core content.

- Discuss the weaknesses in the economy of the 1920s.
- Explain how the stock market crash contributed to the coming of the Great Depression.
- Describe how the Depression spread overseas.

Prepare to Read

Background Knowledge L3

Remind students that the United States experienced great prosperity during the 1920s. Ask students to predict what might have caused this prosperity to end in the next decade.

Set a Purpose L3

- **WITNESS HISTORY** Read the selection aloud.

  Ask **Why might Americans have invested their money in stocks instead of putting it into savings accounts?** *(They believed that the return on their investment would be far greater if they put their money into stocks.)*

- **Focus** Point out the Section Focus Question, and write it on the board. Tell students to refer to this question as they read. *(Answer appears with Section 1 Assessment answers.)*

- **Preview** Have students preview the Section Objectives and the list of Terms and People.

- **Reading Skill** Have students use the *Reading Strategy: Recognize Multiple Causes* worksheet. Teaching Resources, p. 11

◄ An affluent middle-class family, 1924

SECTION

1

WITNESS HISTORY

Stock Market Prosperity

As the 1920s roared along, millions of Americans poured their savings into the soaring "bull" market. Excited investors bought and sold stocks based on "tips" from friends or brokers. Many investors amassed huge fortunes on the strength of rising stock prices. Families who had to scrimp and save at the beginning of the decade found themselves fabulously wealthy by its end. George Mehales described how he was caught up in the Wall Street fever:

❝One day, one of my customers showed me how much money he was making in the market.... I bit with what you folks call 'hook, line and sinker.' All the money I took in, I put into stocks. The first day of October in 1929 made me feel like I was rich. The stocks I bought had gone up and up.❞

— From American Life Histories: *Manuscripts from the Federal Writers Projects, 1936–1940*

▲ Stock ticker tape

Causes of the Depression

Objectives

- Discuss the weaknesses in the economy of the 1920s.
- Explain how the stock market crash contributed to the coming of the Great Depression.
- Describe how the Depression spread overseas.

Terms and People

Herbert Hoover	business cycle
speculation	Great Depression
Black Tuesday	Hawley-Smoot Tariff

NoteTaking

Reading Skill: Recognize Multiple Causes
Identify the causes of the Great Depression.

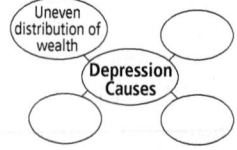

Why It Matters During the Roaring Twenties, many Americans enjoyed what seemed like an endless era of prosperity. Then, in October 1929, the mighty bull market crashed. As production fell and unemployment rose, the U.S. economy lurched into a period of dramatic decline. Years after the Great Depression began, many Americans came to see this contraction as a regular feature of the nation's business cycle. **Section Focus Question: How did the prosperity of the 1920s give way to the Great Depression?**

Prosperity Hides Troubles

In 1928, Republican leaders exuded confidence about both their party and their country. The Roaring Twenties had been a Republican decade. In 1920, Americans sent Warren G. Harding to the White House, and four years after that they sent Calvin Coolidge. Neither election had been close.

Once in office, both Presidents watched the country grow increasingly prosperous. As the decade passed, consumption went up, the gross national product went up, and the stock market went up. No matter what index an economist chose to consult, the conclusion was always the same: Times were good in America—and they were getting better. Republicans took credit for the bullish economy, and Americans heartily agreed.

Vocabulary Builder

Use the information below and the following resource to teach students the high-use word from this section. Teaching Resources, Vocabulary Builder, p. 10

High-Use Word	Definition and Sample Sentence
converge	*v.* to move or be directed toward the same purpose or result Republican leaders **converged** on Kansas City to participate in their nominating convention.

Optimism Sweeps Hoover to Victory When the Republicans met at their 1928 nominating convention, they chose **Herbert Hoover**—an accomplished public servant—to run for the White House. Born in Iowa, Hoover was orphaned as a child. But he overcame this personal tragedy and eventually graduated from Stanford University with a degree in geology. He became a mining engineer and worked all over the world. By 1914, after amassing a vast fortune, he retired from engineering and devoted himself to public service.

Herbert Hoover came to the attention of Americans during World War I, first as the brilliant coordinator of the Belgium relief program and then as head of the Food Administration. During the Harding and Coolidge administrations, Hoover served as Secretary of Commerce. His philosophy was simple but effective. He stressed the importance of competition, but he also believed in voluntary cooperation between labor and management. American greatness showed itself, Hoover maintained, when owners, workers, and government officials <u>converged</u> on common goals.

With a solid record of accomplishments behind him and seemingly endless prosperity in front of him, Hoover was a formidable presidential candidate in 1928. While his campaign ads noted how Republicans had "put the proverbial 'chicken in every pot,'" Hoover spoke glowingly of ending poverty in America:

> **Primary Source** "By adherence to the principles of decentralized self-government, ordered liberty, equal opportunity, and freedom to the individual, our American experiment in human welfare has yielded a degree of well-being unparalleled in all the world. It has come nearer to the abolition of poverty, to the abolition of fear of want, than humanity has ever reached before."
>
> —Herbert Hoover, campaign speech, 1928

Hoover's contest with Democratic nominee Alfred E. Smith of New York was, in the end, no contest at all. Americans voted overwhelmingly for Hoover, prosperity, and the continuation of Republican government. When the new President took office in March 1929, America was awash in a sea of confidence. Few imagined that an economic disaster lay just seven months in the future.

But even as Hoover delivered his victory speeches, economic troubles were beginning to worry some Americans. The prosperity of the 1920s was not as deep or as sturdy as Hoover claimed. Throughout the U.S. economy, there were troubling signs.

Problems Plague the Agricultural Sector American farmers faced difficult times during the 1920s. Farmers made up one fourth of the American workforce during the decade. To meet the unprecedented crop demands created by World War I, they had increased harvest yields and bought more land to put under the plow. They also bought costly tractors and other mechanized farm equipment. Farmers contracted huge debts doing this, and the additional mortgage payments followed them into the 1920s.

After the war, the demand for American crops fell sharply. Despite this drop, postwar production remained high because of increasingly mechanized farm equipment and more intensive farming methods. Farms were getting bigger and yielding bumper crops at harvest. However, farmers were failing to sell off their huge crop surpluses and to pay the debts they owed banks and other institutions.

The result was a rural depression that affected millions of Americans. Hard-pressed to pay their debts, forced to sell in a glutted and competitive world market, and confronted by several natural disasters, farmers did not share in the boom times of the 1920s. They did not have the cash to buy the new consumer goods produced by

Vocabulary Builder
<u>converge</u>—(kuhn VERJ) v. to move or be directed toward the same purpose or result

Farmers Struggle to Get By
Farmers who could not meet their debts faced bank foreclosures on their land, equipment, and livestock. Here, a horse is paraded in front of prospective buyers at a Missouri farm sale.

■ **NoteTaking** Using the Paragraph Shrinking strategy (TE, p. T20), have students read this section. As they read, have students use a concept web to identify the causes of the Great Depression. *Reading and Note Taking Study Guide*

Teach

Prosperity Hides Troubles ⒧⒊

Instruct

■ **Introduce: Vocabulary Builder** Have students locate the vocabulary term ***converge***. Then, write the word on the board, say it aloud, have students say it with you, and read the definition. Tell students that they will learn that several kinds of economic troubles in the United States ***converged*** during the 1920s to threaten the nation's prosperity.

■ **Teach** Using the Idea Wave strategy (TE, p. T22), ask students to review the Primary Source quotation from Herbert Hoover's campaign speech. Ask **To what did Hoover attribute the economic prosperity of the United States?** *(Hoover believed that the decentralization of the national government and the assurance that all U.S. citizens have liberty, equal opportunity, and individual freedom caused the economic prosperity in the United States.)* Then, have students discuss some of the signs of trouble for the U.S. economy. Ask **Why did many farmers face economic difficulties during the 1920s?** *(During World War I, farmers accumulated debt by buying more land and new equipment to meet increased demand. After the war ended, demand for crops fell. Farmers continued to produce large amounts of crops that they could not sell to pay off their debts.)* **Why did the uneven distribution of wealth contribute to the economic troubles of the United States?** *(U.S. factories produced more goods than the average industrial worker could afford to buy.)* **What problem did the availability of easy credit create?** *(debt)* Ask students to predict how these economic trends would affect the prosperity of the United States.

Differentiated Instruction Solutions for All Learners

⒧⒈ **Special Needs Students** ⒧⒉ **English Language Learners** ⒧⒉ **Less Proficient Readers**

Explain that many people who want to buy a home do not have enough money to pay for a property all at once. To buy property, they have to borrow money—usually from a bank—and then gradually pay back the money. When banks make such loans, they have borrowers sign a contract called a *mortgage*. This contract allows the bank to take possession of the property if the borrower does not pay back the loan. When a bank takes possession of a

property for such reasons, it is called a *foreclosure*. Encourage students to list any additional terms that may be new to them, such as *index, disposable income,* and *credit*. Then, have them create flashcards with the term on one side and its definition on the other. For English Language Learners, you may wish to have students add explanations in their first language on the flashcards. Pair students, and have them quiz each other, using the flashcards.

- Have students imagine that they are farmers living in the United States during the 1920s. Ask them to write paragraphs explaining their economic situations and providing possible solutions for how they can pay off their debts.

- Have students analyze the Infographic and answer the questions that accompany it. Then, ask students to use the images on this page and the next to draw a political cartoon showing the differences between the rich and the poor during the 1920s.

- Ask students to write short essays describing how the distribution of wealth might affect a nation's economy, politics, and culture.

● **INFOGRAPHIC**

Causes of the Great Depression

Lured by luxury and easy credit, many Americans bought expensive new cars during the 1920s. ▼

History remembers the 1920s as a decade of bull markets and new fortunes. However, by 1929, the surging American economy was on the brink of financial collapse. Soaring stock prices made rich people richer and concentrated more wealth into fewer hands. Excited by a stream of new products and buyer-friendly payment plans, consumers piled up huge debts as they purchased goods on credit. Everywhere, the economy expanded, soaring toward its peak in the summer of 1929 and then pausing on the verge of contraction—and economic chaos. (See the diagram below.)

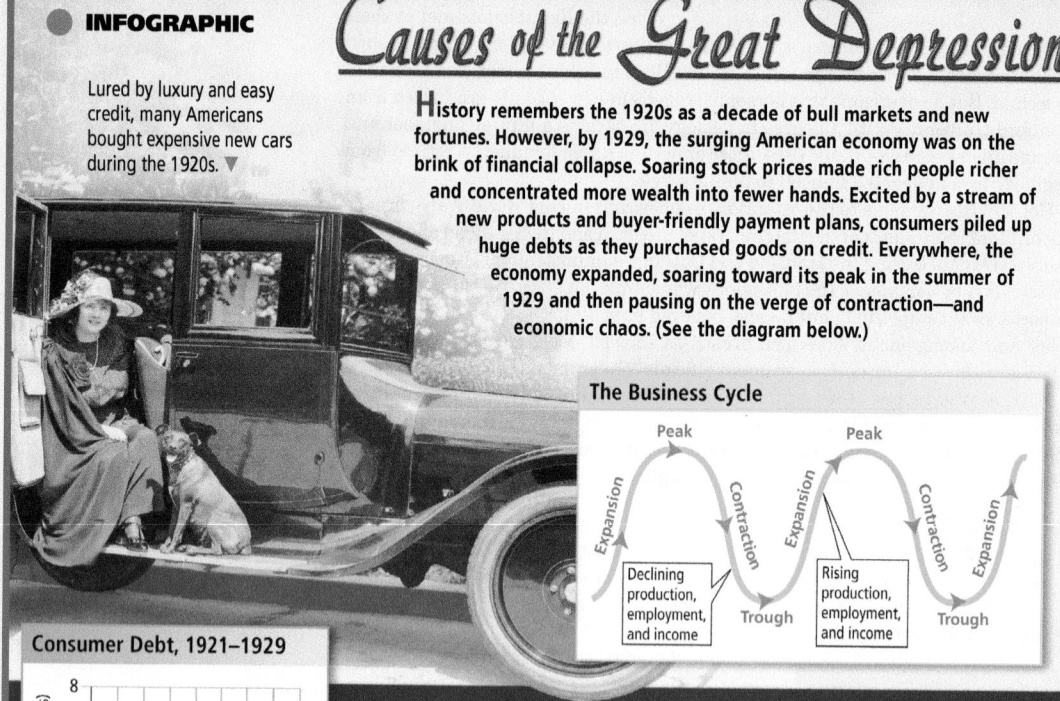

The Business Cycle

Peak — Peak

Expansion — Contraction — Expansion — Contraction — Expansion

Declining production, employment, and income — Trough — Rising production, employment, and income — Trough

Consumer Debt, 1921–1929

Dollars (in billions): 8, 6, 4, 2, 0

1921 1923 1925 1927 1929

SOURCE: *Historical Statistics of the United States*

▲ American consumers racked up more than $6 billion of debt by 1929—more than double what they owed at the beginning of the decade.

American industries. They lived largely on credit from month to month, often teetering on the brink of financial ruin. Any downward slide in the economy was likely to hit America's struggling farmers first and hardest.

Wealth Is Distributed Unevenly Unlike farmers, industrial workers participated in the great national success story. During the 1920s, their wages rose steadily, as did their disposable income. Many purchased Model T Fords along with a variety of other consumer products. Though they were certainly not wealthy, industrial laborers were in a better financial position than their fathers had been a generation before.

But the problem was that while wages rose gradually, worker productivity increased astronomically. Between 1923 and 1929, output per person-hour jumped 32 percent, but workers' wages inched up only 8 percent. During that same period, corporate profits from worker output skyrocketed 65 percent. All these figures pointed to the fact that during the 1920s, the rich became much, much richer, while industrial workers simply became less poor. In few periods of the country's history have so small a number of rich Americans dominated such a large percentage of the country's total wealth. In 1929, for example, the wealthiest 1 percent of the population earned about the same amount of money as the bottom 42 percent.

This uneven distribution of the nation's wealth created economic problems. More than 60 percent of all American families had yearly incomes of less than $2,000 per year. Twenty-four thousand of the country's wealthiest families enjoyed annual incomes of more than $100,000, which was 50 times more than what most families were earning. But these wealthy families did not eat 50 times more food than lower-income families. The wealthiest households did not

As the pie chart below shows, income was distributed unevenly among Americans in the 1920s. The wealthiest 1 percent of the population, like the women at right, could afford luxurious homes and expensive clothing. But most Americans earned considerably less. The poorest segment of the population was sometimes reduced to begging for money, like the man below.

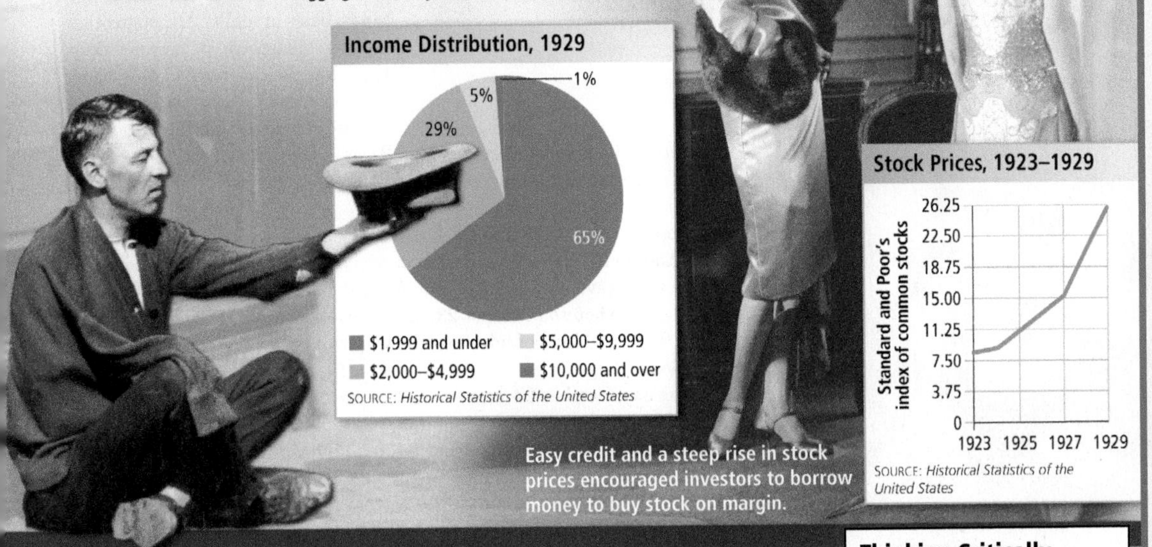

Income Distribution, 1929

- 1%
- 5%
- 29%
- 65%

■ $1,999 and under   □ $5,000–$9,999
■ $2,000–$4,999   ■ $10,000 and over

SOURCE: *Historical Statistics of the United States*

Stock Prices, 1923–1929

Standard and Poor's index of common stocks

26.25, 22.50, 18.75, 15.00, 11.25, 7.50, 3.75, 0

1923 1925 1927 1929

SOURCE: *Historical Statistics of the United States*

Easy credit and a steep rise in stock prices encouraged investors to borrow money to buy stock on margin.

Monitor Progress

As students fill in their concept webs, circulate to make sure that they understand the multiple causes of the Great Depression. For a completed version of the concept web, see Note Taking Transparencies, B-104a.

purchase 50 times more automobiles or radios or ovens. The rich undoubtedly spent a lot on consumer products. The problem was that the wealthiest few did not buy enough to keep the economy booming.

A healthy economy needs more people to buy more products, which in turn creates even more wealth. In this way, a healthy economy avoids underconsumption that can limit economic growth. The uneven distribution of wealth in the 1920s pointed to an uncertain future for the American economy.

From the overproduction of the struggling farmer to the underconsumption of the lower-income industrial worker, deep-seated problems created economic instability. Too many Americans did not have enough money to buy what they needed or wanted.

Easy Credit Hides Problems For a time, the expansion of credit partially hid this problem. Americans bought automobiles, appliances, radios, and other goods on credit. Using the installment plan, they paid a small percentage down and the rest over a period of months or years. By the end of the decade, 80 percent of radios and 60 percent of cars were purchased on installment credit. Americans even bought stock on credit, making such stock purchases on margin. Every year, Americans accumulated more debt. In the past, they had feared debt and put off buying goods until they had the cash to pay for those items. However, easy credit changed this behavior during the 1920s. The growing credit burden could mask the problem of Americans living beyond their means for only so long before the economy imploded.

✔ **Checkpoint** What economic problems lurked beneath the general prosperity of the 1920s?

Thinking Critically

1. **Make Generalizations** Is it fair to suggest that the American economy stood "on thin ice" in 1929? Why or why not?

2. **Analyze Costs and Benefits** How did easy credit and buying stock on margin provide both costs and benefits to the U.S. economy?

Connect to Your World

Consumer Debt Today Consumer debt did not vanish after the Great Depression. Americans continued to borrow large sums of money. Borrowing became much easier with the advent of the credit card. Lenders first issued credit cards in the 1950s, although real growth came with the innovation of the standardized magnetic strip in the 1970s.

Credit card debt is a type of revolving debt. A lender allows customers to borrow against a certain amount of credit when purchasing goods and services. The lender then bills the borrower for that amount plus interest.

The revolving debt of U.S. consumers increased from around $124 billion in 1985 to about $900 billion in 2007. By 2005, the average credit card debt among American households was more than $8,000.

With such convenience, it is hardly surprising that many Americans are mired in debt. In 2005, Americans spent more money than they earned. For the first time since the height of the Great Depression, the United States experienced a negative personal savings rate.

Answers

Thinking Critically

1. Possible answer: Yes; unsustainable practices in finance, agriculture, and industry had been fueling economic expansion for too long.

2. Possible answer: Easy credit and buying on margin allowed people to purchase goods, services, and stocks they otherwise would not have been able to afford, but this practice led to increasing debt. While the overall economic picture appeared prosperous, it was also dangerous.

✔ Economic problems included agricultural overproduction, the uneven distribution of wealth, underconsumption, and the growing credit burden.

The Stock Market Crashes

Instruct

- **Introduce: Key Terms** Ask students to find the key terms *speculation, Black Tuesday,* and *business cycle* (in bold) in the text. Then, write them on the board and provide the definitions. Have students discuss the ways that these terms are related to the economic troubles of the United States.

- **Teach** Discuss with students the ways in which stock market speculation is similar to gambling. Ask **What was the basis for the soaring stock prices during the 1920s?** *(the confidence of investors)* **What happened when investors in 1929 lost confidence in the stock market?** *(Investors sold their stock, and the stock market crashed.)* Display Color Transparency: *Stock Market Crash.* Then, have students discuss how investment practices during the 1920s led the stock market to crash. Color Transparencies A-93

- **Analyzing the Visuals** Draw students' attention to the photo of the newspaper and the political cartoon on this page. Ask students to discuss how the newspaper headline captures the feelings of many Americans after the stock market crashed.

Independent Practice

Ask students to consider the rewards and risks that investors encountered during the 1920s. Have them write paragraphs telling whether or not they would have invested in the stock market during the 1920s and why.

Monitor Progress

Circulate to make sure that students understand why Americans invested heavily in the stock market during the 1920s.

Answer

✓ The U.S. stock market collapsed in the Great Crash, leading to billions of dollars in losses and signaling the beginning of the Great Depression.

BROOKLYN DAILY EAGLE
And Complete Long Island News

WALL ST. IN PANIC AS STOCKS CRASH

Attempt Made to Kill Italy's Crown Prince

The Panic Spreads
The sudden collapse of stock prices sent brokers and investors into a panic throughout New York's financial district and across the country. A cartoonist for the *New York World* captured the feelings of many Americans in the aftermath of the Great Crash.

The Stock Market Crashes

By 1929, some economists observed that soaring stock prices were based on little more than confidence. Prices had no basis in reality. Although other experts disagreed, it became clear that too much money was being poured into stock **speculation**. Investors were gambling, often with money they did not even have, on stock increases to turn quick profits. If the market's upward climb suddenly reversed course, many investors would face economic devastation.

On September 3, 1929, the stock market began to sputter and fall. Prices peaked and then slid downward in an uneven way. At the end of October, however, the slide gave way to a free fall. After the Dow Jones average dropped 21 points in one hour on October 23, many investors concluded that the boom was over. They had lost confidence—the very thing that had kept the market up for so long.

The next day, October 24, came to be known as Black Thursday. With confidence in the stock market failing, nervous investors started to sell. Stock in General Electric that once sold at $400 a share plunged to $283. Across the United States, investors raced to pull their money out of the stock market. On October 29, **Black Tuesday**, the bottom fell out. More than 16 million shares were sold as the stock market collapsed in the Great Crash. Billions of dollars were lost. Whole fortunes were wiped out in hours. Many speculators who had bought stock on margin lost everything they had. President Hoover tried to soothe Americans by insisting that the "business of the country is on a sound and prosperous basis." But by November 13, the Dow Jones average had dropped like a brick from its September high of 381 to 198.7. The Great Crash represented another hallmark of the nation's **business cycle,** which explained the periodic growth and contraction of the economy.

✓ **Checkpoint** What happened on October 29, 1929?

The Great Depression Begins

The stock market crash marked the beginning of the **Great Depression,** a period lasting from 1929 to 1941 in which the economy faltered and unemployment soared. Though it did not start the depression by itself, the crash sparked a chain of events that quickened the collapse of the U.S. economy.

The Banks Collapse One of the first institutions to feel the effects of the stock market crash was the country's banking system. The crisis in confidence continued as frightened depositors feared for their money and tried to withdraw it from their banks. Few banks could survive a sustained "run" of requests by depositors for their money. In 1929, 641 commercial banks failed. A year later, 1,350 failed. And a year after that, 1,700 went under. By 1932, many Americans believed that no banks would be left standing.

Another cause of many bank failures was misguided monetary policy. During the 1920s, the Federal Reserve, which regulates the amount of money in circulation, cut interest rates to stimulate economic growth. But in 1929, worried about investor overspeculation, the "Fed" limited the money supply to discourage lending. As a

History Background

The Federal Reserve System The Federal Reserve System, or the Fed, is the central banking system of the United States. The system began after the 1913 passage of the Federal Reserve Act. The act established a hierarchical system, at the top of which sits the Federal Reserve Board. The board is made up of seven members nominated by the president and confirmed by the Senate. The board oversees the operations of 12 Federal Reserve Banks, each of which is located in one of 12 Federal Reserve Districts. These regional Reserve Banks, in turn, serve member banks in their district.

The government created the Federal Reserve to provide the nation with a more flexible and stable economy. The Fed works to fulfill this mission by setting monetary policy. Monetary policy refers to actions taken by the Fed to influence the supply of money and rates of interest. Monetary policy is not an exact science, however. As the Great Depression shows, the Fed's policies have not always been successful.

result, there was too little money in circulation to help the economy after the stock market crash. When plummeting stock prices sent investors to the banks to secure whatever hard money they had left, the banks were cleaned out of currency and forced to close.

Businesses Close and Unemployment Rises Banks were not the only institutions to face the harsh financial realities of the depression. The collapse of stock prices, combined with reduced consumer spending, spelled trouble for American businesses. Business leaders believed that the survival of their companies depended on production cutbacks, to maintain price levels, and layoffs, to reduce payroll. While their stocks were still falling, companies began closing plants and forcing workers onto the growing lists of the unemployed. In August 1931, Henry Ford closed several of his Detroit automobile factories, putting nearly 75,000 people out of work.

Like a snowball rolling down a hill, the problem of production cuts kept getting bigger and bigger. As businesses closed plants and fired workers to save money, more Americans lost their jobs. As unemployment grew and incomes shrank, consumers spent less money. So businesses cut production even more, closing more plants and firing more workers. By 1933, nearly 25 percent of all American workers had lost their jobs.

Tariffs Add to the Woes Hoping to reverse the downward slide, the government moved to protect American products from foreign competition. In June 1930, Congress passed the **Hawley-Smoot Tariff,** which raised prices on foreign imports to such a level that they could not compete in the American market. The tariff inspired European countries to retaliate and enact protective tariffs of their own.

Far from solving the problems of the depression, the Hawley-Smoot Tariff added to them. At a time when American manufacturers and farms had a glut of unsold products, the international move toward high protective tariffs closed markets. This closure was not just harmful to American producers. It was equally disastrous to the global economy. The ripple effect caused by the Hawley-Smoot Tariff helped to destroy international trade.

The Depression Goes Global The Hawley-Smoot Tariff was only one of the causes of a depression spreading across the globe. As we saw earlier, the European problems of reparation payments, war debt payments, and international imbalance of trade had already created a shaky economic structure. In the early 1930s, the structure collapsed. Germany ceased their reparation payments, and the United States agreed to suspend France and Britain's war debt payments. The international economy had largely been funded by American loans to Europe, but the crisis in the United States drastically curtailed those loans. As a result, European nations

NoteTaking

Reading Skill: Recognize Sequence Use a flowchart to note what happened in the wake of the stock market crash.

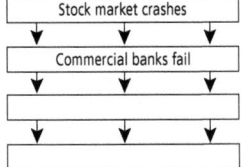

Banks Fail

In 1931, more than 1,500 banks ran out of money and closed their doors. Depositors lost untold savings. Here, a crowd gathers outside the closed doors of a bank in New York City. *How might Americans react today if hundreds of banks failed?*

The Great Depression Begins/What Caused the Great Depression? L3

Instruct

- **Introduce: Key Term** Ask students to find the key term ***Great Depression*** (in bold) in the text. Have students predict how long the ***Great Depression*** lasted.

- **Teach** Ask **How were the stock market crash and the collapse of the banking system related?** *(Investors and depositors tried to withdraw their money after losing confidence in both institutions.)* **How did these events affect the nation's workers and businesses?** *(Plummeting stock prices and reduced spending led businesses to cut production and lay-off workers, and the resulting unemployment further reduced spending, which led to even more business closings and layoffs.)* Direct students' attention to the diagram on the following page. Have students debate the effectiveness of the Hawley-Smoot Tariff. Then, ask them to compare the theories of Milton Friedman and John Maynard Keynes.

- **Quick Activity** Have students read and complete the worksheet *Reading a Chart: Rising Unemployment and Business Closings.* Teaching Resources, **p. 15**

Independent Practice

NoteTaking Have students complete the flowchart to track what happened to the U.S. economy in the wake of the stock market crash. For a completed version of the flowchart, see Note Taking Transparencies, **B-104b.**

Monitor Progress

Circulate to make sure that students are completing their flowcharts accurately and understand the events that occurred after the stock market crash.

Differentiated Instruction Solutions for All Learners

L1 **Special Needs Students**
L2 **English Language Learners**
L2 **Less Proficient Readers**
To help students understand the levels of unemployment during the Great Depression, have them read and complete the worksheet *Reading a Chart: Unemployment.* Teaching Resources, **p. 14**

L4 **Advanced Readers**
L4 **Gifted and Talented Students**
Explain that during the 1980s, a wave of failures swept the savings and loans industry, leading to a collapse of U.S. financial institutions. More than 1,000 thrifts failed, costing taxpayers about $124 billion. Ask students to do further research about the collapse of banks during the Great Depression and the savings and loan crisis of the 1980s. Then, have them write essays that compare and contrast the two episodes.

Answer

Caption Sample response: Americans might react with great anger because such a failure would mean that the banking industry and its regulators did not learn the lessons taught by the failures of the Great Depression.

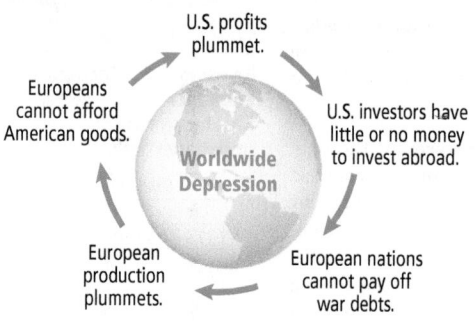

Diagram Skills The diagram above shows how the stock market collapse contributed to a global economic crisis. *How did European war debts affect the U.S. economy?*

experienced the same cycle of business failures, bank collapses, and high unemployment as the United States. The depression had become a global nightmare.

✓ **Checkpoint** How did the stock market crash contribute to the onset of the depression?

What Caused the Great Depression?

Historians and economists disagree on the exact causes of the Great Depression. Some have stressed a single root cause in their explanations of the financial crisis. Milton Friedman, one economist, believed that the depression resulted from a contraction in the money supply. The twin events of the stock market crash in 1929 and the run of bank failures in 1930 left too little money in circulation for the nation's economic needs.

John Maynard Keynes was one of the most influential economists of the depression. He argued that the lack of government interference in the economy led to the depression. Critical problems in money supply, distribution of wealth, stock speculation, consumer spending, productivity, and employment could have been controlled, he said, by proactive government policies. Keynes's work points to a fundamental difference between many economists regarding the depression. While Keynes recommended that governments spend more money to keep people employed when the economy slows, other noted economists like Ludwig von Mises and Friedrich von Hayek criticized centralized economic planning and management.

There will never be a fully accepted answer to the question of what caused the Great Depression. But clearly, problems in consumption contributed heavily to it. Economic hardships before 1929 in Europe and rural America, coupled with an uneven distribution of wealth and overspeculation in the stock market, created dangerous economic conditions. When this was combined with poor or misinformed economic decisions by Congress and President Hoover, the Great Depression resulted.

✓ **Checkpoint** What were the primary causes of the Great Depression?

Comprehension

1. Terms For each term below, write a sentence explaining its significance.
- speculation
- business cycle
- Great Depression
- Hawley-Smoot Tariff

2. NoteTaking Reading Skill: Recognize Causes Use your concept web to answer the Section Focus Question: How did the prosperity of the 1920s give way to the Great Depression?

Writing About History

3. Quick Write: Define a Problem Choose one topic from this section that you could use to write a problem-solution essay. For example, you could write about the weaknesses in the agricultural sector of the economy. Make a list of details, facts, and examples that define the problems that this weakness poses to a stable economy.

Critical Thinking

4. Explain Causes How did the uneven distribution of the nation's wealth weaken the American economy?

5. Analyze Information Why was recovery so difficult after the stock market crash?

6. Draw Conclusions Do you think the nation would have experienced an economic depression even if the stock market had not crashed? Why or why not?

For additional assessment, have students access **Progress Monitoring *Online*** at **www.pearsonschool.com/ushist.**

WITNESS HISTORY

Riding the Rails

As the country plunged deeper into the Great Depression, many young people left home, either out of necessity or to follow their dreams of a better life. Nearly a quarter million teenagers hit the road during the early 1930s, jumping freight trains to ride from town to town. Some looked for work, others thirsted for adventure, but all faced the dangers of the hobo life. Charley Bull, who left his California home at 18, recalled:

❝You could ride on top of a freight car and then you just had to be careful. If a train is going sixty or seventy miles an hour and hits a curve and you're walking and your back's to the turn and you don't see it coming—a little tiny turn can throw you right off the train. A lot of people have been killed like that.❞

—Charley Bull, from a PBS presentation "The American Experience—Riding the Rails"

Americans Face Hard Times

Objectives

- Examine the spread of unemployment in America's cities.
- Discuss the impact of the Great Depression on rural America.
- Explain the human and geographical factors that created the Dust Bowl.

Terms and People

bread line	Dust Bowl
Hooverville	Okies
tenant farmer	repatriation

NoteTaking

Reading Skill: Categorize As you read, use a Venn diagram to note how the Great Depression affected both urban and rural America.

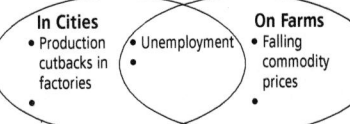

In Cities
- Production cutbacks in factories
- •Unemployment•

On Farms
- Falling commodity prices

Why It Matters The stock market crash signaled the end of boom times and the beginning of hard times. As investors mourned their losses, Americans watched the economy stagger into the Great Depression. In the cities and on the farms, desperate poverty gripped the nation. Even after prosperity returned, those who lived through the crisis would remember the pain and worries of the depression. Tested by extreme hardship, this generation of Americans forged a character and will strong enough to overcome economic ruin and restore prosperity. **Section Focus Question: How did the Great Depression affect the lives of urban and rural Americans?**

Misery and Despair Grip America's Cities

The Great Depression had a deep and lasting impact on the lives of the people who lived through it. Few Americans grasped the underlying problems of the 1920s economy or the subtle reasons for the stock market crash. Fewer still comprehended how the crash led to the Great Depression. But they did understand the *impact* of the economic crisis. Workers understood having a job one day and being unemployed the next. Whole families knew the shame and fear of losing their homes.

The Great Depression touched every American because every American either experienced or knew someone who experienced the hardships and loss caused by the economic catastrophe. For many, their lives were never the same again.

Vocabulary Builder

Use the information below and the following resource to teach students the high-use word from this section. Teaching Resources, Vocabulary Builder, p. 10

High-Use Word	Definition and Sample Sentence
drastic	*adj.* harsh or severe Critics of the 1918 Sedition Act viewed its enforcement methods as **drastic** and excessive.

Misery and Despair Grip America's Cities L3

Instruct

- **Introduce: Key Terms** Ask students to find the key terms **bread line** and **Hoovervilles** (in bold) in the text and explain their meanings. Remind students that the Great Depression brought poverty to a large number of families, many of whom became so poor that they could not afford food and faced homelessness. Ask students to consider the range of feelings experienced by families who had to depend on charity and faced the loss of their homes.

- **Teach** Ask **What impact did the Great Depression have on employment rates?** *(By 1933, the unemployment rate was nearly 25 percent, up from a 1920s high of 3.7 percent.)* Read aloud the Primary Source quotation on this page, and then ask **To whom does the "They" in Harburg's song refer?** *(Possible answers: employers, the government, powerful people and institutions)* **What are the social implications of Harburg's song?** *(Harburg suggests strongly that the government and big business have a responsibility for the economic welfare of hard-working citizens.)* Have students describe the circumstances that led people to build Hoovervilles. Ask students to discuss the origin of Hoovervilles and why some groups, such as the Taxpayer Protection League, tried to thwart evictions.

- **Analyzing the Visuals** Have students study the bar and line graphs on this page. Ask students to discuss what these graphs show about the way that the Great Depression affected U.S. families.

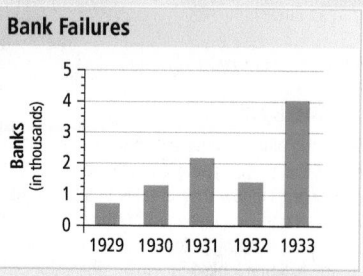

Bank Failures

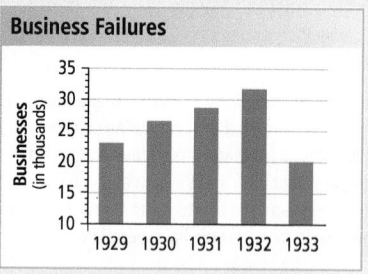

Business Failures

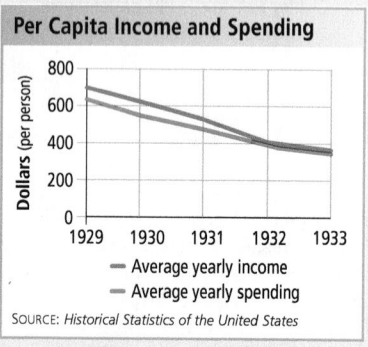

Per Capita Income and Spending

- Average yearly income
- Average yearly spending

SOURCE: *Historical Statistics of the United States*

Graph Skills The year 1929 marked the start of a pronounced downturn in the American economy. *In what year did the largest number of banks fail? By roughly how much did Americans' average yearly income decrease between 1929 and 1933?*

Searching for a Job and a Meal The threat of unemployment and destitution haunted workers in cities and towns across the United States. Between 1921 and 1929, annual average unemployment rates had never risen above 3.7 percent. But then the depression hit, and the rate shot up. By 1933, it had climbed to a shocking 24.9 percent.

Despite this high rate, millions of workers were able to keep their jobs. However, most had their wages or hours cut. Many workers brought home paychecks that were 10, 20, sometimes 30 percent less than their pre-depression checks.

Yet statistics tell only part of the story. The human drama of unemployment unfolded over and over again, in city after city across the nation. For a man employed as a factory worker, the 1920s had promised a chance at upward economic mobility. He had been able to provide for his family, enjoy a decent standard of living, and save something for retirement. Then the depression hit. The man saw his hours cut and his workweek shortened. Eventually, he was laid off. Looking for another job, he trudged from one factory to the next. "No help wanted here" or "We don't need nobody" greeted him at every turn. The man's clothes began to look worn. His collars and cuffs became frayed, and his pants became shiny at the knees. He said less, stared more, moved slower.

Maybe his wife was able to find work washing and ironing clothes or laboring as a maid. But those jobs were hard to find, too. At home, children ate smaller meals. Water replaced milk. Meat disappeared from the table. Hunger lurked about the home like an unwanted guest. Sometimes the parents and children received free meals in public soup kitchens. Often the only place for the family to get a free scrap of food was in a **bread line**, where people lined up for handouts from charities or public agencies.

Descending Into Poverty Men like the factory worker just described moved from unemployed to unemployable. Whole families descended into hunger and homelessness. Their dreams of success and prosperity turned into nightmares of failure and poverty.

This feeling of loss—this sense of the "American Dream" betrayed—wove through the cultural fabric of the Great Depression. The widespread despair found expression in an early-1930s song by E. Y. Harburg. It tells the story of an American "Everyman," a worker who labored to build the country and a citizen soldier who fought to defend it. However, the depression has left him out of work, out of money, and out of dreams:

Primary Source

"They used to tell me I was building a dream
And so I followed the mob.
When there was earth to plow or guns to bear,
I was always there, right on the job.
They used to tell me I was building a dream
With peace and glory ahead—
Why should I be standing in line,
Just waiting for bread?
Once I built a railroad, I made it run,
Made it run against time.
Once I built a railroad, now it's done—
Brother can you spare a dime?"
—song lyrics, "Brother Can You Spare a Dime?"

Differentiated Instruction Solutions for All Learners

L1 Special Needs Students **L2 English Language Learners** **L2 Less Proficient Readers**

Read and explain to students the Primary Source quotation at the bottom of this page. Tell students that popular culture, as expressed in songs, can often provide a unique perspective on social, political, or economic events. Organize the class in groups and ask students to brainstorm songs with which they are familiar that say something about the times in which they live. Have each group choose a member to keep a list, which should include the songs' titles, the individual artists or groups who sang them, the lyric or theme that they find relevant, and a brief explanation of the songs' meanings. Then, ask students to discuss whether any songs they listed might also apply to life during the Great Depression.

Answer

Graph Skills 1933; by about $300

Effects of the
Great Depression

After the stock market crash, the American economy slowed to a crawl in the face of a devastating global Depression. Bank failures more than quadrupled from 1929 to 1933. Companies fired thousands of workers to keep from going out of business. As a result, unemployment soared, condemning a quarter of the American workforce to poverty. (See the line graph below.) Jobless people crowded outside employment offices, clamoring for work to put food on their tables. Life became a daily struggle for many Americans during these lean times.

Unemployed men wait for a chance to register for municipal jobs in New York City in 1933. ▼

Top: Women and children wait in a bread line set up by a religious mission.
Center: This 1932 cartoon summarized the feelings of many depositors when their banks failed.
Bottom right: Unable to support their families, some men gave in to despair.

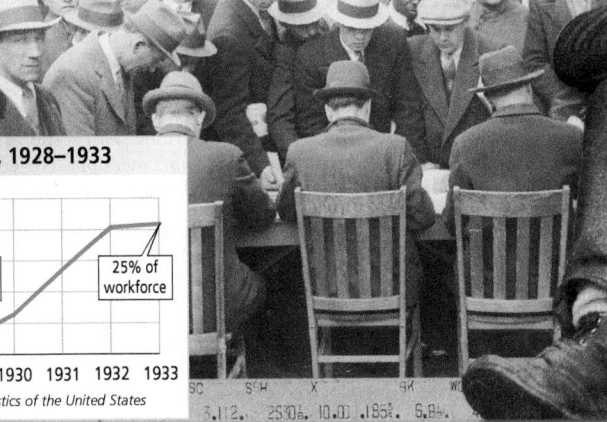

Unemployment, 1928–1933

3% of workforce

25% of workforce

SOURCE: *Historical Statistics of the United States*

Harburg said the song asked a simple question about the nature of the depression. "This is a man who says: I built the railroads.... I fought your wars.... [Why] should I be standing in line now? What happened to all this wealth I created?"

Looking for a Place to Live As Americans lost their jobs and ran through their savings, they had to scrounge wherever they could to keep from going hungry. They sold furniture, pawned jewelry, and moved to cheaper lodgings—anything to keep their pantries stocked and rents paid. In many cities, they ran out of money, were evicted from their homes, and ended up on the streets.

Thinking Critically

1. **Analyze Information**
   How did the shrinking economy lead to increased layoffs of workers?

2. **Draw Conclusions** What effect might a high unemployment rate have on the wages of Americans who still had jobs?

Independent Practice

- Have students analyze the Infographic. Ask students to write sentences describing how each image depicts an effect of the Great Depression. Then, have students answer the questions that accompany the Infographic.

- Tell students to read the paragraphs under the red heading "Looking for a Place to Live." Then, ask students to use the passage to write a short essay reflecting on the ways in which economic problems might become political problems.

Monitor Progress

As students fill in their Venn diagrams, circulate to make sure that they understand how the Great Depression affected both urban and rural America. For a completed version of the Venn diagram, see Note Taking Transparencies, **B-105**.

Differentiated Instruction   Solutions for All Learners

L1 Special Needs Students   **L2 English Language Learners**   **L2 Less Proficient Readers**

Ask students who need extra reading practice to look at the visuals and skim the red and blue headings in the section. Help them make outlines that explain what they predict they will learn from the section.

Then, ask students to revise their outlines as they read. After they have finished reading the section and revising their outlines, ask students to use their outlines to write paragraphs summarizing the section.

Answers

Thinking Critically

1. Because Americans had less and less money to spend on goods and services, scores of businesses had to cut production or close altogether, leading to massive layoffs.

2. Because the demand for jobs was very high and the supply was very low, employers were in a position to offer lower wages.

A field-worker's home in California

Poverty Devastates Rural America ⓛ³

Instruct

- **Introduce: Key Terms** Ask students to find the key terms *tenant farmers, Dust Bowl,* and *Okies* (in bold) in the text. Then, write them on the board and provide the definitions. Prompt students to recall what they read about agricultural problems in the previous section. Then, display Color Transparency: *The Great Depression.* Ask students to discuss the types of problems farmers faced during the Great Depression. Color Transparencies **A-96**

- **Teach** Ask **How did Depression-era crop and livestock prices affect farmers?** (*During the 1930s, prices were so low that a large number of family farms could not survive.*) **What other disaster caused the collapse of many farms?** (*the Dust Bowl*) **What happened to families who lost their livelihoods in these ways?** (*Some remained on their land as tenant farmers, and others migrated to search for work elsewhere.*) Using the Numbered Heads strategy (TE, p. T23), ask students to consider the impact the Great Depression and the Dust Bowl had on rural America. **How did these calamities affect the agricultural industry?** (*Because large farming operations were the most likely to survive the Great Depression, the upheaval probably increased the average farm size. In addition, the government began to initiate large-scale irrigation projects.*) Display Color Transparency: *The Dust Bowl.* Use the transparency book to guide a discussion about the displacement of farmers because of the Dust Bowl. Color Transparencies **A-94**

family in Alabama

Americans Face Hard Times
Photographs of the 1930s conveyed the gritty realism of daily life under the boot heels of hunger, homelessness, and destitution. Cartoonists of the time criticized political leaders, President Hoover foremost among them, for the parts they played in bringing about, or failing to prevent, the depression. *Judging from these images, what would it have been like to live in a Hooverville?*

Homeless people slept on park benches, in empty railway cars, or in cardboard boxes. Many grouped together in **Hoovervilles,** makeshift shantytowns of tents and shacks built on public land or vacant lots. Homeless people, some of whom had worked as skilled carpenters before the crisis, cobbled houses together out of lumber scraps, tar paper, tin, and glass. One of the largest Hoovervilles in the country sprang up in the middle of Central Park in New York City. There, the homeless covered themselves with newspapers, called Hoover blankets, to stay warm at night. They walked around looking for jobs with their empty pants pockets turned inside out, a sign of poverty known as Hoover flags.

Despite the difficulties of life during the depression, many Americans did what they could to boost morale and help their neighbors. During a New York City newspaper strike, Mayor Fiorello LaGuardia read comic strips to children over the radio. In Reading, Pennsylvania, members of the Taxpayers Protection League staged nonviolent protests to thwart evictions. Nevertheless, thousands of other Americans found no such escapes from their misery.

✔ **Checkpoint** How did the Great Depression affect American cities in the early 1930s?

Poverty Devastates Rural America

In cities and towns across the nation, Americans faced a terrible plight. The numbers of the unemployed, homeless, and hopeless increased like a casualty list in some great war. In rural America, people fared no better. In fact, sometimes their condition was even worse. Farmers had been suffering even before the Great Depression. Falling commodity prices and accumulating debt had made it a struggle for farmers to keep their heads above water. Many failed to stay afloat and sank so deep that they lost their farms.

Commodity Prices Plunge But then the bottom fell out of the economy and the depression added more woes. Crop prices fell even further, and new debts were added to old debts. To make matters even worse, the Great Plains was suffering through a choking drought, an ecological disaster that lasted for years. As a result, many more farmers lost their farms and moved. They traveled about the country, looking for work and fighting for survival.

Answers

✔ The Great Depression caused massive unemployment, which led to widespread poverty and homelessness in many American cities.

Caption A Hooverville would have been drafty, unprotected from the elements, lacking in plumbing, and generally uncomfortable.

A sprawling Hooverville in Seattle, Washington

The basic reality of farm life was the low prices paid to farmers for crops they grew for market. In 1919, a bushel of wheat sold for $2.16; in 1932, it sold for 38 cents. A pound of cotton fetched 35.34 cents in 1919; the same pound fetched 6.52 cents in 1932. The sharp fall in prices was evident with other farm products—corn and beans, cattle and hogs. The income farmers generated was not enough to allow them to continue farming. They could not pay their debts, purchase more seed, repair equipment, and buy what their families needed to survive. Overburdened by the diminishing returns for their labor, some farmers buckled under the stress.

In Sioux City, Iowa, in 1932, the Sioux City Milk Producers Association threatened to strike if its members did not see higher profits for their milk. When the association's threats were ignored by local storeowners, farmers dumped 1,000 gallons of milk on a road outside the city. Despite such a <u>drastic</u>—and for many Americans unthinkable—action, farmers everywhere feared losing everything.

Vocabulary Builder
<u>drastic</u>–(DRAS tihk) *adj.* harsh or severe

Farmers Lose Their Farms Between 1930 and 1934, nearly one million farmers failed to pay their mortgages and lost their farms. Banks foreclosed on their lands and houses and repossessed their farming equipment. The bankers sold what they could at public auctions. Some farmers remained on the land as **tenant farmers,** working for bigger landowners rather than for themselves. Others drifted away from their communities, looking for some other kind of work.

Cesar Chavez, who later became a well-known labor organizer, recalled the troubles his proud father had during the depression. A California bank repossessed his father's small ranch, and the family was evicted from their house. Chavez remembered how it felt to lose his home:

> **Primary Source** "We had been poor, but we knew every night there was a bed *there*, and *this* was our room. . . . But that all of a sudden changed. When you're small, you can't figure these things out. You know something's not right and you don't like it, but you don't . . . let that get you down. You sort of just continue to move."
> —Cesar Chavez

Like the Chavez family, other farmers moved on after their losses. But for those who remained, Mother Nature dealt a cruel blow to already cruel times.

Differentiated Instruction Solutions for All Learners

L4 Advanced Readers **L4 Gifted and Talented Students**

Ask students to conduct research to uncover specific details about family life in the United States before the Great Depression, the hardships people faced during the depression, and descriptions of daily life in Hoovervilles in cities such as Bakersfield, California, or Portland, Oregon. Then, have students suppose that they and their families are living before and during the Great Depression. Students should use their research to write autobiographical essays describing their lives in middle class surroundings before the Great Depression and explaining what it was like to lose everything and find themselves living in Hoovervilles. Invite volunteers to present their essays to the class.

Focus On Geography

History Interactive
For: To learn more about the Dust Bowl
www.pearsonschool.com/ushist

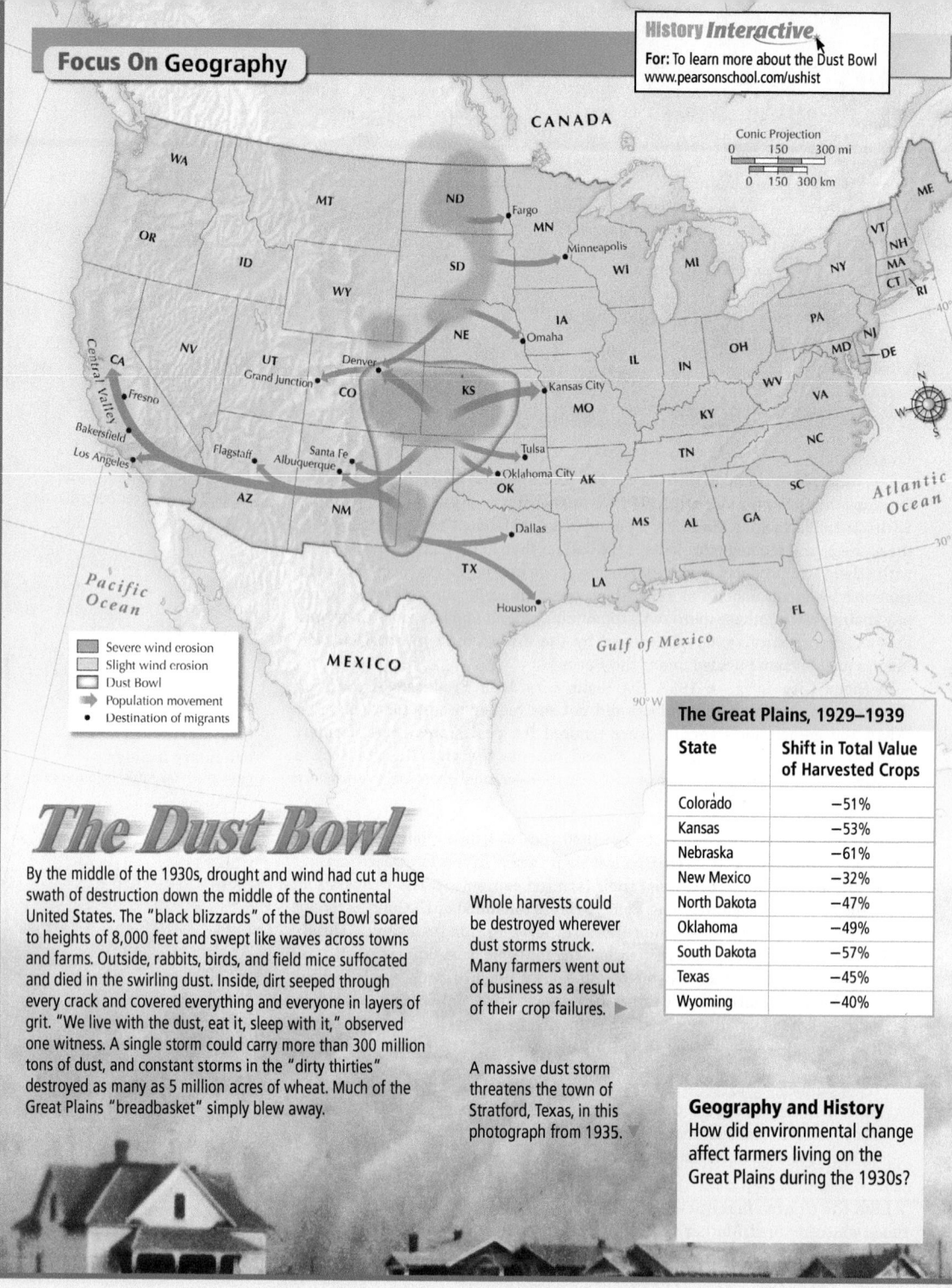

State	Shift in Total Value of Harvested Crops
Colorado	−51%
Kansas	−53%
Nebraska	−61%
New Mexico	−32%
North Dakota	−47%
Oklahoma	−49%
South Dakota	−57%
Texas	−45%
Wyoming	−40%

The Great Plains, 1929–1939

Legend:
- Severe wind erosion
- Slight wind erosion
- Dust Bowl
- Population movement
- Destination of migrants

The Dust Bowl

By the middle of the 1930s, drought and wind had cut a huge swath of destruction down the middle of the continental United States. The "black blizzards" of the Dust Bowl soared to heights of 8,000 feet and swept like waves across towns and farms. Outside, rabbits, birds, and field mice suffocated and died in the swirling dust. Inside, dirt seeped through every crack and covered everything and everyone in layers of grit. "We live with the dust, eat it, sleep with it," observed one witness. A single storm could carry more than 300 million tons of dust, and constant storms in the "dirty thirties" destroyed as many as 5 million acres of wheat. Much of the Great Plains "breadbasket" simply blew away.

Whole harvests could be destroyed wherever dust storms struck. Many farmers went out of business as a result of their crop failures. ▶

A massive dust storm threatens the town of Stratford, Texas, in this photograph from 1935. ▶

Geography and History
How did environmental change affect farmers living on the Great Plains during the 1930s?

Connect to Your World

Natural Disasters In August 2005, Hurricane Katrina wreaked havoc along America's Gulf Coast. Katrina cut a swath of destruction more than 100 miles from its center, doing horrendous damage to the coastal communities of Alabama, Louisiana, and Mississippi. In Louisiana, Katrina caused the breach of levees in New Orleans, leading to the flooding of nearly 80 percent of the low-lying city. The storm caused billions of dollars in damage and resulted in the deaths of more than 1,300 people. Hurricane Katrina, like the Dust Bowl, provoked questions about the role that humans play in natural disasters. Coastal scientists, for example, have pointed out that the construction of embankments, levees, and shipping channels in and around New Orleans has caused significant loss of wetlands, making the city far more vulnerable to hurricane storm surges. Even more controversially, a number of climatologists have asserted that the destruction caused by Katrina is partly due to global warming, which, they argue, has led to more hurricanes developing at greater intensities.

The Great Plains Becomes a Dust Bowl Farmers who survived the tumble in prices were still not safe. Through the mid-1930s, a drought in the Great Plains added to their problems. Water was a constant problem in the region. Normal rainfall seldom exceeded the 20 inches a year that traditional American agricultural practices demanded. As a result, droughts on the Great Plains were often more devastating than those in the East and Midwest. In the years before America's western rivers were dammed and irrigation practices became widespread, there were few answers to the drought threat.

New farming methods made drought conditions worse. Intensive farming came to prominence throughout the region in the late nineteenth and early twentieth centuries. Farmers then had moved onto the plains and plowed under much of the natural grasses in order to plant oceans of winter wheat. The landscape shift tipped the ecological balance of the region. In the past, plains grasses prevented the topsoil from blowing away during periods of drought. By the early 1930s, that dwindling grassy safety net could no longer do the job.

By 1932, the combination of drought, loose topsoil, and high winds resulted in disaster on the Great Plains. The winds kicked up towering dust storms that began to blow east. These gigantic clouds of dust and dirt could rise from ground level to a height of 8,000 feet. The dust storms moved as fast as 100 miles per hour and blotted out the sun, plunging daylight into darkness.

Most of the dust storms started in the southern Great Plains, especially the high plains regions of Texas, Oklahoma, Kansas, New Mexico, and Colorado. This swath of parched earth became known as the **Dust Bowl.** For people living in these hardest hit regions, depression and dust storms defined the misery of the "dirty thirties."

Those unfortunate enough to be caught in a dust storm were temporarily choked and blinded by the swirling dirt. The storms killed cattle and birds, blanketed rivers, and suffocated fish. Dirt seeped into houses, covering everything with a thick coat of grime. Some dust clouds blew east as far as the Atlantic coast, dumping acres of dirt on Boston, New York, and Washington. Altogether, dust storms displaced twice as much dirt as Americans had scooped out to build the Panama Canal.

Desperation Causes Migration Many farm families trapped in the Dust Bowl had no choice but to migrate out of the region. They had lost their farms to the banks. Dust storms had destroyed most remaining opportunities. They were low on everything except despair. Although only some came from Oklahoma, Dust Bowl refugees were generally referred to as **Okies,** regardless of their states of origin.

Okie families packed onto rickety trucks and headed toward California or Oregon or Washington, any place where a job might be found. Before the pace slowed, 800,000 people migrated out of Missouri, Arkansas, Oklahoma, and Texas alone.

Agricultural collapse and the Great Plains Dust Bowl forced millions of Americans to leave the midwestern and southern regions where they were born. Many moved to California, lured by the promise of jobs, but were crushed when that promise too often proved empty. Others headed to the cities of the Northeast and Midwest, again looking for jobs, shelter, and relief. As a result of the migration, rural states lost population while states with large cities gained population.

Okies Flee the Dust Bowl
The Okie exodus from the Great Plains carried thousands of Americans west to the rich farmlands of California. Okies also packed up and headed east to great industrial centers like Chicago, Pittsburgh, and New York. Here, a migrant family arrives in California.

- To help students understand why farmers left the Great Plains during the Great Depression, have them read and complete the worksheet *Geography and History: The Dust Bowl. Teaching Resources,* **p. 16**

- Have students write paragraphs that analyze how the Dust Bowl exacerbated urban problems during the Great Depression.

Monitor Progress

Circulate to make sure that students understand the Primary Source quotation and the ways that the Dust Bowl affected farmers. Also, ensure that students are filling in their Geography and History worksheets accurately.

Differentiated Instruction   Solutions for All Learners

L1 Special Needs Students   **L2 Less Proficient Readers**

To help visual learners understand the causes and effects of the Dust Bowl, have them look at the map on the previous page. Ask them to create a two-column chart. Have them label one column "States Abandoned by Dust Bowl Migrants." Have them label the second column "Destinations of Dust Bowl Migrants." Then, ask students to fill in the chart, using information on the map. Finally, ask students to imagine that they were to read a history of each of the cities they listed in the second column. Ask them what they would expect to find in passages about the 1930s. Have them make a list of their expectations.

- **Introduce: Key Term** Ask students to find the key term *repatriation* (in bold) in the text. Tell students that the issue of Mexican immigration to the United States is still a prominent feature of the nation's politics.

- **Teach** Discuss the ways that the Great Depression affected family life. Ask **How did the Great Depression affect unemployed men?** *(The Great Depression had great psychological effects on unemployed men. Many believed that they betrayed their families because they could not provide for them.)* Compare the effects of the Great Depression on unemployed men with its effects on those men who still had jobs. Then, discuss how it affected women, children, and minorities. Ask **How did the Dust Bowl affect many Mexican Americans?** *(Dust Bowl migrants not only competed with Mexican Americans for jobs, but these mostly white farmhands also exacerbated existing discrimination. Some white Americans even encouraged the repatriation of Mexican Americans.)*

Independent Practice

- Ask students to write paragraphs predicting how the anxiety experienced by Americans in the Great Depression might affect their behavior after the nation's recovery.

- Have students read the Primary Source quotation on the next page. Ask students to write short paragraphs reacting to Clifford Burke's opinion that the Great Depression "only became official when it hit the white man."

Monitor Progress

Circulate to make sure that students understand that different groups of people experienced the Great Depression differently.

Answers

✓ After they had already lost their farms, the Dust Bowl forced many families to abandon their communities as well.

Caption A migrant farm worker's job is labor intensive and seasonal and migrant farm workers actually help raise crops, not just harvest them.

Fierce Job Competition in California
As Okies flowed into California, Mexican and Mexican American migrants already there faced stiff new competition for scarce jobs. Here, a Mexican migrant worker tends to a cantaloupe crop in California's Imperial Valley. *What does the photograph suggest about the life of a migrant worker?*

There were other effects of the Dust Bowl. The farmers best able to survive the Great Depression were the ones with the biggest operations. They often bought repossessed land at rock-bottom prices and expanded their holdings into large commercial farms. The Dust Bowl also motivated the government to help Great Plains farmers. After the initial crisis, immense federal projects dammed western rivers. Dams eventually provided irrigation that made farm profits possible on the Great Plains.

✓ **Checkpoint** How did the Dust Bowl make life even more difficult for farmers on the Great Plains?

Few Americans Escape Hard Times

One of the ironies of the depression was the word itself. In the nineteenth and early twentieth centuries, an economic slump was called a "panic" or a "crisis." President Hoover used the word *depression* to describe the state of affairs because he thought it sounded less severe than the other terms. But before long, Hoover's "depression" gave way to the "Depression" and then the "Great Depression." The term described not only a state of mind, but also an economic reality. It showed a despondent America, filled with people overwhelmed by seemingly inescapable poverty. Not only did the depression make victims of the men and women who lost jobs, it also was an economic and emotional crisis that profoundly affected Americans in all walks of life.

The Depression Attacks Family Life For millions of Americans, the depression was an intensely personal affair. Men who lost their jobs and could not find other work often felt that they had betrayed their families. They had been the "breadwinners," the providers, the ones whose paychecks fed and clothed the family and kept a roof over everyone's head. The loss of a job meant a reduction in status. Different men reacted differently to unemployment. Many labored tirelessly to find a new job, while others sank into shame and despair. Some even deserted their families.

The unemployed were not the only ones who suffered. Men lucky enough to have jobs lived in constant fear that the next paycheck would be their last. They often felt guilty for being employed while so many of their relatives and friends were suffering. Few Americans were spared from the crisis.

Wives and children experienced the pain of their husbands and fathers. Birthrates plummeted to the lowest marks in American history—a sure sign of family distress. Mothers worked constantly to stretch meager family incomes. They sewed clothes, searched for odd jobs, and valiantly tried to meet their families' needs. With both parents preoccupied with making something out of nothing, family discipline often declined. Some children quit school. Others ran away from home. Families coped with the depression as best they could. Some huddled together, working to survive the hard times. Others broke apart, making those times even harder and lonelier.

History Background

Repatriation of Mexican Americans Although the Great Depression caused extreme economic hardships for all Americans, Mexican Americans faced the additional threats of harassment and deportation. The economic turmoil caused many Americans to fear that illegal immigrants were taking the few available jobs. The U.S. government responded by tightening the rules to obtain a visa for legal residency and targeting Mexican Americans, many of whom were born here, in the country legally, or were naturalized citizens, in an anti-immigrant campaign. Government officials raided public squares, restaurants, and boarding houses, searching for illegal immigrants. During a raid of a Mexican American family's home in Montana, the family was not allowed to take any of their possessions with them, even the children's birth certificates proving that they were American citizens. The climate of fear and anxiety caused many Mexican Americans to leave voluntarily. Although no precise figures exist, it is estimated that more than 300,000 Mexicans and Mexican Americans were coerced into leaving the United States between 1930 and 1935.

Minorities Suffer Hardships The depression affected everyone, but it did not affect them equally. Americans on the bottom rung of the economic ladder—the poorest of the poor, often minorities with no financial resources—felt the sting of the depression the keenest. A Howard University sociologist noted early in the crisis that African Americans were "the last to be hired and the first to be fired." In the South, landowners threw African American sharecroppers off the plots they had been farming. Many of these workers migrated to northern cities, but there were no jobs waiting there. Only more poverty greeted them. In 1932, unemployment among African Americans hovered around 50 percent, nearly double the national rate.

However, African Americans had long stood firm against the challenges of poverty. They relied on the emotional resources of family and religion to cope with grim times. During his interview with a depression historian, an African American man explained what the depression meant to African Americans:

> **Primary Source** "The Negro was born in depression. It didn't mean too much to him, The Great American Depression, as you call it. There was no such thing. The best he could be was a janitor or a porter or shoeshine boy. It only became official when it hit the white man."
>
> —Clifford Burke, quoted in *Hard Times*, 1970

Hard times came upon Mexican Americans as well. As more Okies headed west out of the Dust Bowl, the competition for jobs between those migrants and Mexican American farmworkers in states like California heated up. A flood tide of workers struggled to find and keep farm jobs. Often, Mexican Americans faced the additional burden of discrimination when competing with white farmhands for those jobs. In the Southwest, many white Americans clamored for Mexican American **repatriation**. Repatriation involved efforts by local, state, and federal governments to encourage or coerce Mexican immigrants and their naturalized children to return to Mexico. Hundreds of thousands of people of Mexican ancestry—many of them U.S. citizens—were pushed out of the United States. Even so, many more remained. By the end of the 1930s, Mexican Americans were working in most industries of the Southwest, including farming, ranching, and industry.

✓ **Checkpoint** How did the depression take a toll on women, children, and minorities in America?

Poverty in the South
African Americans who had long faced discrimination and segregation were especially hard-hit by the depression. Many moved from the South to seek jobs in the North. Here, a man sits forlornly outside his home in Atlanta, Georgia.

Assess and Reteach

Assess Progress L3

- Have students complete the Section Assessment.
- Administer the Section Quiz. Teaching Resources, **p. 19**
- To further assess student understanding, use Progress Monitoring Transparencies, **101**.

Reteach
If students need more instruction, have them read the section summary.

Reading and Note Taking Study Guide L3

Adapted Reading and Note Taking Study Guide L1 L2

Spanish Reading and Note Taking Study Guide L2

Extend L4
Have students read and complete the Enrichment Worksheet, *Cover Story: Let Us Now Praise Famous Men.* Teaching Resources, **pp. 12–13**

Answer

✓ Possible answer: Women shared in the anxiety and stress of the Depression and often had to take work to supplement their family's income. Some children ran away from home, and others quit school. Minorities had to endure racism, which magnified their communities' economic hardships.

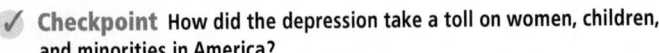

SECTION 2 Assessment

Progress Monitoring *Online*
For: Self-test with vocabulary practice
www.pearsonschool.com/ushist

Comprehension

1. **Terms and People** What do each of the following terms have in common? Explain.
   - bread line
   - Hooverville
   - tenant farmer
   - Okies

2. **NoteTaking Reading Skill: Categorize** Use your Venn diagram to answer the Section Focus Question: How did the Great Depression affect the lives of urban and rural Americans?

Writing About History

3. **Quick Write: Brainstorm for Possible Solutions** Choose one topic from this section, such as skyrocketing unemployment in American cities, about which you could write a problem-solution essay. Use the text and your own knowledge to list possible solutions to the problem. Next, organize your list by ranking the solutions from most effective to least effective.

Critical Thinking

4. **Compare and Contrast** How were the experiences of the urban unemployed and the rural poor similar? How were they different?

5. **Recognize Effects** How do you think the arrival of so many Okies affected native Californians?

6. **Draw Inferences** Where might Americans have laid the blame for their difficulties during the early 1930s?

Section 2 Assessment

1. All are related to the economic hardship of the Great Depression.

2. The Great Depression caused economic turmoil in both areas. In urban areas, production cutbacks in factories caused many people to lose their jobs and their homes. Homeless communities called Hoovervilles sprang up in many American cities. In rural areas, many farmers were already experiencing economic troubles. The Great Depression caused

crop prices to plummet and many farmers to lose their farms and homes.

3. Students' choices should reflect an understanding of the suitability of the topics to the problem-solution format.

4. The general economic upheaval of the Great Depression caused loss of jobs, income, and often homes for both urban and rural communities. Their experiences were different in that the two groups had different kinds of skills which might affect how they weathered these years.

5. Possible answer: The arrival of Dust Bowl refugees increased the demand for jobs, which lowered wages and made it harder for less-favored workers, such as migrant workers from Mexico, to get work.

6. New terms such as *Hooverville* and *Hoover blanket* suggest that many Americans blamed the government for their difficulties.

For additional assessment, have students access **Progress Monitoring *Online*** at **www.pearsonschool.com/ushist.**

Objectives

- Discuss the variety of individual responses to the hardships of the Great Depression.
- Explore the ways in which the business cycle has changed since the Great Depression.

Background Knowledge ⓛ

Remind students that though times were hard during the Great Depression, people found ways to cope, some positive, some negative. The Great Depression showed American resilience and inventiveness in the midst of instability and uncertainty.

Instruct ⓛ

- Have students read the introduction and review the pictures and captions in the feature. Ask **What were some of the ways Americans responded to the Great Depression?** *(Some Americans responded to the Great Depression by selling apples on sidewalks to make money, helping at soup kitchens and bread lines, or seeing movies.)* **Why would people spend money on the cinema during the Great Depression rather than save it for necessities?** *(Possible answer: By putting their troubles out of their minds, however briefly, movies may have reinvigorated people and helped them tackle their daily burdens with renewed vigor and optimism.)*

- Have students reread the quotation from the mayor of Youngstown, Ohio. Ask them to write short essays explaining whether positive changes might have occurred during the Great Depression because of the "equality of misery."

EXPERIENCE THE GREAT DEPRESSION

Moviegoers cheered as Shirley Temple sang "Prosperity Is Just Around the Corner." Salvation Army volunteers handed out clothing and food to the needy. While some of the unemployed sold apples on sidewalks, others rioted in the streets.

There were many reactions to the Great Depression, some hopeful and some desperate, but everywhere Americans struggled to ease the daily burden of their poverty. The mayor of Youngstown, Ohio, captured the universality of the Depression when he described its victims laid low in his city: "These were old men gnarled by heavy labor, young mechanics tasting the first bitterness of defeat, clerks and white-collar workers learning the equality of misery, derelicts who fared no worse in bad times than in good, Negroes who only a short time before had come from Southern cotton fields, immigrants who had been lured to [the] 'land of youth and freedom'—each one a personal tragedy, and all together an overwhelming catastrophe for the nation. . . ."

As unemployment soared, the jobless often demonstrated against their former employers. A protest at a Ford Motor Company plant in March 1931 erupted in violence that left four workers dead. Here, a man is carried off during a demonstration in New York City. ▼

To enrich and extend the lesson, have students access the **History Interactive** at **www.pearson-school.com/ushist.** After students experience the History Interactive, ask them to share their reactions by posing questions such as these: How would you have felt if you had lost your job and your home during the Great Depression? Why do you think that some people chose to help others despite their own hardships? How do you think that an American today would respond to a similar situation?

Monitor Progress

Have students complete the Thinking Critically questions. Have them share their answers with the class.

◄ Fred Bell, like his cartoon counterpart above, lost millions of dollars in the stock market crash and then sold apples on the street.

Despite their own hardships, ► many Americans volunteered in soup kitchens and at bread lines. Here, relief-agency workers help hand out potatoes to the hungry.

During the Depression, trips to the movies helped people forget their troubles. Shirley Temple cheered crowds, as did the Marx Brothers and the Three Stooges. ►

SHIRLEY TEMP

IN

"Bright Eyes"

with

JAMES DUNN

▲ As the Depression worsened, many sharecroppers like the Arkansas family shown here were evicted by landowners across the South.

Thinking Critically

1. **Analyze Visuals** What were some of the positive ways in which people responded to the Depression? What were some of the negative responses?

2. **Draw Conclusions** How did apple selling and riding the rails help men cope with losing their jobs?

Connect to Today Do research to learn about the nation's business cycle. How are the peaks and valleys of the modern American economy different from those of the late 1920s and early 1930s?

History *Interactive* ✳

For: To discover more about the Great Depression
www.pearsonschool.com/ushist

Answers

Thinking Critically

1. Possible response: Some people responded positively by providing entertainment so that others could forget about their troubles. Other people set aside their own problems to help others in soup kitchens and bread lines, for example. Some people responded negatively by rioting in the streets or evicting families from their homes.

2. Possible answers: Selling apples took vendors' minds off their problems and at the same time made them feel as if they were doing something constructive. Riding the rails may have been, for some, a way of turning a loss into an opportunity for discovery and adventure.

Connect to Today Have students share their findings with the class, which probably will include information about competing business cycle theories. Students' reports may also discuss the effect of government policies that are made to offset the regularity of fluctuations in the business cycle.

Objectives

As you teach this section, keep students focused on the following objectives to help them answer the Section Focus Question and master core content.

- Discuss how Hoover's initial conservative response to the Depression failed.
- Explain the changes in the President's policies as the crisis continued.
- Describe how Americans reacted to Hoover's relief programs.

Background Knowledge ⓛ⓷

Remind students about the anxiety and despair that many Americans felt as the national economy collapsed. Ask students to predict how U.S. political leaders responded to the crisis.

Set a Purpose ⓛ⓷

- **WITNESS HISTORY** Read the selection aloud.

    Ask **Why did Gray depict Annie as determined and self-reliant?** *(Possible response: Gray wanted to depict Annie as a symbol of hope and resilience. Annie provided an example for the way that Gray believed Americans should act during these difficult times.)*

- **Focus** Point out the Section Focus Question, and write it on the board. Tell students to refer to this question as they read. *(Answer appears with Section 3 Assessment answers.)*

- **Preview** Have students preview the Section Objectives and the list of Terms and People.

- **NoteTaking** Using the Structured Read Aloud strategy (TE, p. T20), have students read this section. As they read, have students fill in the outline with details about President Hoover's response to the Depression.
    Reading and Note Taking Study Guide

◄ Two young residents of a Hooverville, 1932

HOOVER'S POOR FARM FUND

HARD TIMES ARE STILL HOOVER ING OVER US

Little Orphan Annie comic book ►

Hoover's Response Fails

Objectives

- Discuss how Hoover's initial conservative response to the depression failed.
- Explain the changes in the President's policies as the crisis continued.
- Describe how Americans reacted to Hoover's relief programs.

Terms and People

localism	Hoover Dam
Reconstruction Finance Corporation	Bonus Army
	Douglas MacArthur
trickle-down economics	

NoteTaking

Reading Skill: Identify Supporting Details As you read, fill in the outline with details about President Hoover's response to the depression.

> I. Cautious Response to Depression Fails
>   A. Hoover Turns to Volunteerism
>   1. Calls on business leaders to maintain employment, wages, prices
>   2.
>   B. Volunteerism Fails to Bring Relief
>   1.
> II. Hoover Adopts More Activist Policies

Why It Matters From big cities to small towns, the Great Depression spread misery far and wide across America. The unemployed and the homeless crowded into shantytowns. Giant dust storms swallowed the Great Plains. Yet as the crisis deepened, Herbert Hoover struggled to respond to the nation's problems. As a result of Hoover's failed response, in 1932 Americans would turn to a new leader and increased government intervention to stop the depression. **Section Focus Question: Why did Herbert Hoover's policies fail to solve the country's economic crisis?**

Cautious Response to Depression Fails

Herbert Hoover did not cause the Great Depression. But Americans looked to him as their President to solve the crisis. He tried. Hoover was an intelligent man, familiar with business methods and economic theory. He labored long hours, consulted a wide range of experts, and tried to marshal the resources of the country to solve the problems of the depression. As the economic situation worsened, he tried several different approaches. In the end, he failed to discover the right formula, but it was not because of a lack of effort.

Hoover Turns to Volunteerism At the start of the economic downturn, Hoover followed a hands-off policy. Like most economists of the day, Hoover viewed the upswings and downswings of business cycles as natural occurrences. He felt that government should not

Vocabulary Builder

Use the information below and the following resource to teach students the high-use word from this section. Teaching Resources, Vocabulary Builder, p. 10

High-Use Word	Definition and Sample Sentence
simultaneously	*adv.* done at the same time Women suffragists pursued strategies **simultaneously** at the federal and the state level to win the right to vote.

interfere with such events. Periodic depressions were like storms. They could not be avoided, but strong businesses could weather them without the support of the government.

A policy of doing nothing, however, was no policy at all. Hoover soon recognized this fact and turned to a policy he had used in the past. As Secretary of Commerce during the 1920s, Hoover had encouraged business and labor to voluntarily work toward common goals. To address the current crisis, he asked business and industrial leaders to keep employment, wages, and prices at current levels. He <u>simultaneously</u> called for the government to reduce taxes, lower interest rates, and create public-works programs. The plan was to put more money into the hands of businesses and individuals to encourage more production and consumption. This, Hoover said, would reverse the cycle that led to the depression.

Lastly, Hoover requested that wealthier individuals give more money to charity. Millions of Americans gave money, clothing, and food to private and religious charities, which in turn distributed the goods to those in need. The idea was for all Americans to voluntarily join forces to combat the depression.

Volunteerism Fails to Bring Relief Although the ideas behind the plan were sound, Hoover's program relied too much on voluntary cooperation. The President believed he could persuade Americans to act not in their own best interests but in those of the country as a whole. He was cautious to encourage, not legislate, America's recovery. But volunteerism did not work. Businesses cut wages and laid off workers because it was in their own best interests. Farmers boosted production because it was in the best interests of their families. Most Americans followed individual, not cooperative, courses.

Hoover had also asked state and local governments to provide more jobs and relief measures. He had faith in **localism,** the policy whereby problems could best be solved at local and state levels. However, towns and states simply did not have the financial or human resources to successfully combat the crisis. Making matters worse, the President strongly resisted using federal resources to provide direct relief to individuals. Believing it to be unconstitutional, Hoover opposed public assistance and instead favored "rugged individualism" so that people could better themselves through their own efforts. Yet as the months wore on, unemployment increased, charities ran low on money, and local and state governments could no longer plug the leaks in the economy. The crisis demanded decisive federal action.

✓ **Checkpoint** Why was Hoover reluctant to have the federal government interfere with the economy?

Hoover Adopts More Activist Policies

With Hoovervilles and homelessness on the rise, the President's failed policies were laid bare. Poor Americans called trucks pulled by horse or mule "Hoover wagons," campfires "Hoover heaters," and cardboard boxes "Hoover houses." The association of the President's name with suffering and want indicated Americans' negative feelings about their leader.

Vocabulary Builder
<u>simultaneously</u>—(sī muhl TAY nee uhs lee) *adv.* done at the same time

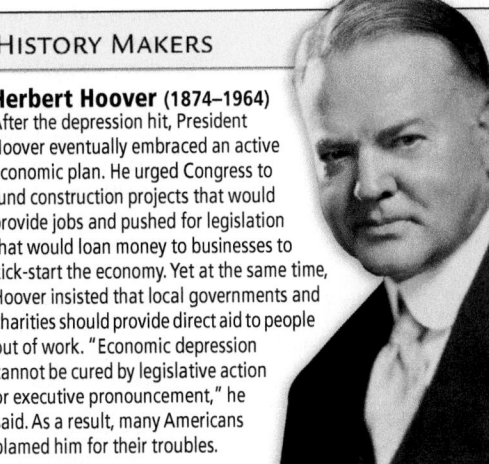

HISTORY MAKERS

Herbert Hoover (1874–1964)
After the depression hit, President Hoover eventually embraced an active economic plan. He urged Congress to fund construction projects that would provide jobs and pushed for legislation that would loan money to businesses to kick-start the economy. Yet at the same time, Hoover insisted that local governments and charities should provide direct aid to people out of work. "Economic depression cannot be cured by legislative action or executive pronouncement," he said. As a result, many Americans blamed him for their troubles.

Hoover Adopts More Activist Policies

Instruct

- **Introduce: Key Terms** Ask students to find the key terms *Reconstruction Finance Corporation (RFC)* and *trickle-down economics* (in bold) in the text. Ask **How was Hoover's *RFC* an example of *trickle-down economics*?** *(The government expected the **RFC** loans it distributed to banks and large business to **trickle down** to the middle and lower classes.)*

- **Teach** Have students read the HISTORY MAKERS about Herbert Hoover on the previous page and discuss Hoover's activist policies. Ask **Were the RFC loans distributed by Hoover's government successful in combating the Great Depression? Explain.** *(No; bankers did not increase loans to businesses, nor did businesses hire more workers.)* **Did the government originally propose to dam the Colorado River as a Depression-era project? Explain.** *(No; the proposal came during the 1920s, when Hoover was Secretary of Commerce.)* Using the Think-Write-Pair-Share strategy (TE, p. T23), have students discuss why the construction of the Boulder Dam might have been such a successful project.

- **Quick Activity** Display Color Transparency: *Building the Hoover Dam.* Use the lesson suggested in the transparency book to guide a discussion about the ways that the construction of the dam helped stimulate the economy of the Southwest. **Color Transparencies A-95**

Independent Practice

Have students analyze the energy use graph on this page. Ask them to write a paragraph explaining why California might consume such a large percentage of the energy generated by the dam.

Monitor Progress

To help students understand the idea of trickle-down economics, have them design a flowchart that is based on the theory.

Answer

✓ He urged Congress to create the Reconstruction Finance Corporation, hoping to see good effects from trickle-down economics.

Hoover Dam Energy Use

Arizona 19%

Nevada 24%

California 57%

SOURCE: U.S. Bureau of Reclamation

Hoover Dam Powers the West

Hoover Dam contains 325 million cubic yards of concrete—enough to pave a highway 16 feet wide from New York City to San Francisco—and provides power to more than a million people each year. It also irrigates millions of acres of farmland in western states.

Hoover decided to reverse course and use federal resources to battle the depression. Believing the economy suffered from a lack of credit, Hoover urged Congress to create the **Reconstruction Finance Corporation (RFC).** Passed in 1932, the RFC gave more than a billion dollars of government loans to railroads and large businesses. The act also lent money to banks so that they could extend more loans to struggling businesses. Hoover believed that if the government lent money to bankers, they would lend it in turn to businesses. Companies would then hire workers, production and consumption would increase, and the depression would end. This theory, known as **trickle-down economics,** held that money poured into the top of the economic pyramid will trickle down to the base.

Although the RFC put the federal government at the center of economic life, it did not work well under Hoover's guidance. The RFC lent out billions, but all too often bankers did not increase their loans to businesses. Additionally, businesses often did not use the loans they received to hire more workers. In the end, the money did not trickle down to the people who needed it the most.

Despite the failings of the RFC, Hoover succeeded with one project that made a difference. During the 1920s, Secretary of Commerce Hoover had called for the construction of a dam on the Colorado River. By the time Hoover became President in 1929, Congress had approved the project as part of a massive public-works program. Workers broke ground on Boulder Dam (later renamed **Hoover Dam**) in 1930. Construction brought much-needed employment to the Southwest during the early 1930s.

 Checkpoint What actions did Herbert Hoover take to fight the effects of the depression?

Americans Protest Hoover's Failures

From the Oval Office, Hoover worked hard to end the depression. But to many out-of-work Americans, the President became a symbol of failure. Some people blamed capitalism, while others questioned the responsiveness of democracy. Many believed the American system was due for an overhaul.

Some Urge Radical Change Some Americans thought the answer to the country's problems was the rejection of capitalism and the acceptance of socialism or communism. They argued that capitalism created great inequities of wealth and an unhealthy atmosphere of competition in society. In fact, they saw the depression as a sign that capitalism was about to collapse. Looking at the Soviet Union, they maintained that a state-run economy was the only avenue out of the depression. Even during the worst of the crisis, though, communist calls for revolution proved no match for American dreams of progress, opportunity, and individual freedom.

Fascist appeals from the political right also failed to hold any attraction. Economic troubles in Europe contributed to the rise to power of fascist leaders like Benito Mussolini in Italy and Adolf Hitler in Germany. Despite this political shift abroad, no fascist gained power in the United States. Although some questioned the ability of America's capitalistic and democratic institutions to overcome the crisis, most Americans never lost faith in their country.

History Background

Other Federal Programs Herbert Hoover has a reputation as a President who did too little for the nation in one of its darkest hours. But Hoover felt deeply for his fellow Americans. His dedication is reflected in the many policies and programs he pursued as President. For example, the President's awareness of the plight of farmers compelled him to persuade a special session of Congress to establish a Federal Farm Board to buttress farm prices. Hoover also supported tax cuts that favored low-income Americans and oversaw a 100 percent increase in healthcare spending. Hoover's passion for fairness also can be seen in the antitrust division he founded to prosecute unfair business practices and in the reforms he initiated at the Bureau of Indian Affairs to protect Native Americans. In spite of the President's perceived role in the Bonus Army incident, it was Hoover who created the Veterans Administration and presided over a dramatic increase in the number of veterans' medical facilities. Herbert Hoover failed to lift the nation out of the Great Depression, though it was not through lack of effort.

The Bonus Army Marches on Washington Most Americans did not want a revolution, but many did desire substantial changes. In 1932, one such group arrived in Washington, D.C., demanding a solution to their particular problem. From across the country came World War I veterans seeking the bonus Congress had promised them. They became known as the **Bonus Army.** In 1924, Congress had passed the Adjusted Compensation Act, which provided for a lump-sum payment to the veterans in 1945. But in 1931, many veteran groups began to call for an early payment of the bonus, arguing that out-of-work vets needed the money to support themselves. The House of Representatives agreed and passed a bill to provide early payment of the bonuses. However, the bill was defeated in the Senate.

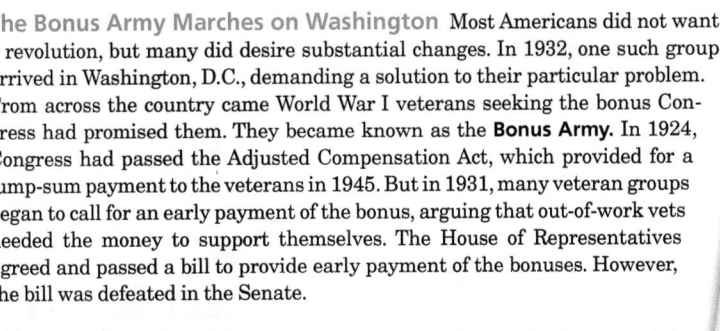
▼ The Bonus Army gathers on Capitol Hill.

● **INFOGRAPHIC**

THE BONUS ARMY

During the economic boom of the 1920s, Congress promised a bonus to World War I veterans to be paid out in 1945. In the summer of 1932, as the nation struggled in the grasp of the Depression, the "Bonus Expeditionary Force" of veterans converged on Washington, D.C., seeking immediate payment. When the Senate rejected their demands, President Hoover called upon the army to keep order. General Douglas MacArthur brought in troops to drive the protesters out of the city. Evalyn McLean, a Washington, D.C., resident, remembered the federal action: "I saw in a news reel the tanks, the cavalry, and the gas-bomb throwers running those wretched Americans out of our capital. I was so raging mad . . . ." Memories of the event influenced the next presidential election.

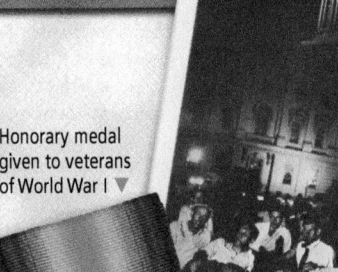
Honorary medal given to veterans of World War I ▼

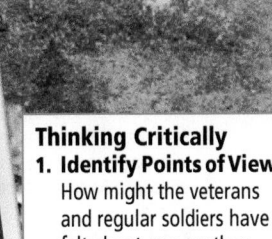
U.S. troops set fire to the Bonus Army camps after driving out the protesters.

General MacArthur (left) and his aide, ▲ Colonel Dwight Eisenhower (right), supervise the removal of the Bonus Army.

Thinking Critically
1. **Identify Points of View** How might the veterans and regular soldiers have felt about one another during the standoff?
2. **Make Generalizations** Was the Bonus Army justified in its protest? Why or why not?

Differentiated Instruction   Solutions for All Learners

🔵 **Advanced Readers**   🔵 **Gifted and Talented Students**

Remind students that the communist revolution had succeeded in Russia during World War I and that communist ideology had begun to exert a powerful influence around the world. Ask students to research the influence of communist ideas in the United States during the Great Depression. As students carry out their research, ask each student to choose one individual who was in some way affected, either positively or negatively, by this ideology. Then, have students use their research to write biographies of their chosen individuals. Encourage students to choose people about whom they feel strongly.

Instruct

- **Introduce: Key Term** Ask students to find the key term **Bonus Army** (in bold) in the text. Ask students to discuss why the **Bonus Army** was formed and how it illustrates the failures of Hoover's presidency.

- **Teach** Discuss the reasons why, during the Great Depression, some Americans questioned capitalism. Ask **Is the competition fostered by capitalism a positive force in societies? Explain.** *(Possible answer: Yes; when properly guided, capitalist competition can be a positive social force because it makes use of the powerful incentives of wealth and power.)* Have students read the Primary Source quotation from Douglas MacArthur on the next page. Ask students to use evidence from the text to debate whether MacArthur used excessive force to disperse the Bonus Army.

- **Quick Activity** Have students analyze the Infographic and answer the questions that accompany it.

Independent Practice

Have students write paragraphs describing the factors that Hoover had to consider before vetoing the Congressional bill authorizing early payment of veterans' bonuses.

Monitor Progress

To check their understanding of radical appeals for change from both the left and the right, help students create a chart that compares and contrasts the aspirations of communists and fascists during the Great Depression.

Answers

Thinking Critically
1. Possible answer: Because of the camaraderie bred in the army, a great deal of sympathy probably existed between the two sides.
2. Possible answer: Yes; without such concrete and visible actions, leaders in Washington, D.C., would have remained unaware of the genuine and serious problems faced by veterans.

In protest, veteran groups marched on Washington. In the summer of 1932, almost twenty thousand veterans arrived in the capital, setting up camps and occupying empty government buildings. A riot broke out in July when police tried to evict the marchers from their makeshift settlements.

Hoover Orders the Bonus Army Out Although President Hoover sympathized with the marchers, he called for General **Douglas MacArthur** and federal troops to "[s]urround the affected area and clear it without delay." MacArthur exceeded his order, deciding to move the marchers out of the city altogether. He ordered his troops to ready tear gas and fix bayonets.

The Army force that pushed the marchers out included not only MacArthur but also the future World War II generals Dwight Eisenhower and George Patton. While Eisenhower regretted the use of the Army to solve a political problem, Patton ordered his troops to brandish their sabers in a show of force. Force, perhaps excessive, was exactly what MacArthur used. More than one thousand marchers were tear-gassed, and many were injured, some very badly.

After the removal, MacArthur said that the marchers were a gang of revolutionaries bent on taking over the government:

> **Primary Source** "They had come to the conclusion, beyond a shadow of a doubt, that they were about to take over . . . direct control of the government. . . . It is my opinion that had the president let it go on another week the institutions of our government would have been very severely threatened."
>
> —Douglas MacArthur, 1932

The Aftermath Dooms Hoover Hoover had not ordered the use of such force against the veterans. Nevertheless, photographs of American troops marching with fixed bayonets against ragged veterans shocked the nation. Any chance that Hoover had for winning reelection in November ended after the summer of 1932. With unemployment nearing 25 percent, stomachs grumbling from hunger, and the number of homeless people increasing every day, Hoover's policies had failed completely. Americans were ready for a change.

✔ **Checkpoint** Why did Hoover order the removal of the Bonus Army from its camps?

SECTION **3** Assessment

Progress Monitoring *Online*
For: Self-test with vocabulary practice
www.pearsonschool.com/ushist

Comprehension

1. **Terms and People** For each of the following terms, write a sentence explaining its significance.
   - localism
   - RFC
   - Hoover Dam
   - Bonus Army

2. NoteTaking **Reading Skill: Identify Supporting Details** Use your outline to answer the Section Focus Question: Why did Herbert Hoover's policies fail to solve the country's economic crisis?

Writing About History

3. **Quick Write: Analyze Solutions** Based on what you have read, list supporting information—such as details, data, and facts—for the following thesis statement of a problem-solution essay: Although President Hoover responded to the developing economic crisis, he ultimately failed to stop it.

Critical Thinking

4. **Recognize Ideologies** How did Hoover's views on government influence his response to the depression? Give two examples.

5. **Analyze Evidence** What facts show that Hoover's policies to reverse the depression failed?

6. **Recognize Effects** How did MacArthur's tactics in removing the Bonus Army affect Hoover's political future?

The Grapes of Wrath by John Steinbeck

Published during the depths of the depression, *The Grapes of Wrath* won its author the Pulitzer Prize in 1940. Steinbeck's sympathetic portrayal of dispossessed Okies, along with his searing criticism of the rich and powerful who profited from their plight, caused an immediate sensation. The novel tells the story of the Joad family, hardy Dust Bowl farmers who are forced off their land by the bank. The Joads join the mass migration west, to the "promised land" of California. There, instead of opportunity, they find low wages, harsh conditions, discrimination—and finally, after years of drought, the cruel irony of a killing flood.

▲ First edition cover of the novel

I n the barns, the people sat huddled together; and the terror came over them, and their faces were gray with terror. The children cried with hunger, and there was no food.

Then the sickness came, pneumonia, and measles that went to the eyes and to the mastoids.[1]

And the rain fell steadily, and the water flowed over the highways, for the culverts[2] could not carry the water.

Then from the tents, from the crowded barns, groups of sodden men went out, their clothes slopping rags, their shoes muddy pulp. They splashed out through the water, to the towns, to the country stores, to the relief offices, to beg for food, to cringe and beg for food, to beg for relief, to try to steal, to lie. And under the begging, and under the cringing, a hopeless anger began to smolder. And in the little towns pity for the sodden men changed to anger, and anger at the hungry people changed to fear of them. Then sheriffs swore in deputies in droves, and orders were rushed for rifles, for tear gas, for ammunition. Then the hungry men crowded the alleys behind the stores to beg for bread, to beg for rotting vegetables, to steal when they could.

Frantic men pounded on the doors of the doctors; and the doctors were busy. And sad men left word at country stores for the coroner to send a car. The coroners were not too busy. The coroners' wagons backed up through the mud and took out the dead.

And the rain pattered relentlessly down, and the streams broke their banks and spread out over the country.

▲ The Joads, from the 1940 film *The Grapes of Wrath,* starring Henry Fonda

1. **mastoids** (MAS toidz) *n.* infection-prone areas of the skull behind the ears.
2. **culverts** (KUHL vertz) *n.* drainage ditches crossing under roads.

Thinking Critically
1. **Draw Inferences** Why did the townspeople's pity for the hungry migrant workers change to anger and then to fear?

2. **Analyze Literature** Notice the words Steinbeck uses to describe the rain and flooding. What might the flood symbolize in the story?

History Background

The Grapes of Wrath and Migrant Workers The troubles faced by migrant workers angered Steinbeck enough to write about them. His first attempt was a story called "The Oklahomans," which he did not publish. As Steinbeck reworked the structure of the novel, his wife, Carol, typed the manuscript and chose the title *The Grapes of Wrath.* The title is a reference to the following passage from "The Battle Hymn of the Republic": "Mine eyes have seen the glory of the coming of the Lord; He is trampling out the vintage where the grapes of wrath are

stored . . ." When the first edition was published, Steinbeck insisted that it include all of the verses of the song to avoid people's identifying the book with communism and fascism. The novel still drew controversy. Some critics asserted that the novel exaggerated the conditions of migrant camps. Others believed that Steinbeck sympathized with communists. The controversies drew the attention of Eleanor Roosevelt, who defended Steinbeck. Eventually, Congress held hearings about the conditions of the migrant camps, which led to changes in labor laws.

American Literature

The Grapes of Wrath by John Steinbeck

Objectives
- Understand a key piece of literature that describes the Great Depression.
- Describe the characters and themes of *The Grapes of Wrath.*

Background Knowledge Ⓛ3
Ask students to recall what they know about the Dust Bowl and the massive migration it caused. Remind them that the promise of jobs drew many migrants to California but that, on their arrival, that promise too often proved empty.

Instruct Ⓛ3
Point out the use of water imagery in the passage. Ask **Why might Steinbeck have chosen water as a motif of his story?** *(Possible answer: Water is a particularly poignant motif because of its centrality to the life of farmers and their crops. Its pervasiveness and abundance in this passage contrasts with the terrible scarcity of water that drove families like the Joads from their homes in the Midwest.)*

Monitor Progress
Circulate to make sure that students are imaginatively interpreting Steinbeck's use of symbolism and that they use details to support their interpretations of the passage.

Answers

Thinking Critically
1. Possible answer: The migrants' misery and needs may have begun to represent a threat to their own livelihoods and safety.
2. Possible answer: Steinbeck's description of how "the streams broke their banks and spread out over the country" might symbolize the flood of families and individuals who migrated westward from the Great Plains because of the Dust Bowl.

Quick Study Guide

- Have students use the Quick Study Guide to prepare for the chapter test. Students may wish to refer to the following sections as they review:

The Cycle of Production Cutbacks
Section 1
Section 2

Causes of the Dust Bowl
Section 2

Cause and Effect: The Great Depression
Section 1
Section 2
Section 3

Key Events of the Great Depression
Section 1
Section 2
Section 3

- For additional review, remind students to refer to the Reading and Note Taking Study Guide.
Section Note Taking
Section Summaries

- Have students access **www.pearsonschool.com/ushist** for this chapter's History Interactive timeline, which includes expanded entries and additional events.

- If students need more instruction on analyzing graphic data, have them read the Skills Handbook, **p. SH21.**

For **Progress Monitoring *Online*,** refer students to the Self-test with vocabulary practice at **www.pearsonschool.com/ushist.**

Quick Study Guide

Progress Monitoring *Online*
For: Self-test with vocabulary practice
www.pearsonschool.com/ushist

■ The Cycle of Production Cutbacks

The stock market crashes and companies' stock prices plummet.

Companies' sales fall and revenue declines.

Companies cut production and lay off workers to reduce expenses and stabilize stock prices.

Consumers spend less money and buy fewer goods.

More workers lose their jobs and collect less income.

■ Causes of the Dust Bowl

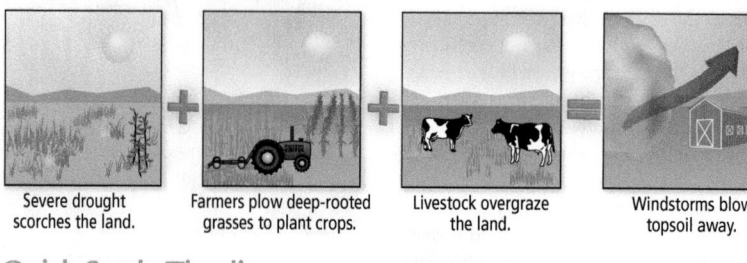

Severe drought scorches the land. + Farmers plow deep-rooted grasses to plant crops. + Livestock overgraze the land. = Windstorms blow topsoil away.

■ Cause and Effect: The Great Depression

Causes
- Overproduction and underconsumption of agricultural crops
- Uneven distribution of income
- Gradual accumulation of consumer debt
- Widespread stock market speculation

↓

The Great Depression

↓

Effects
- Banks and businesses fail.
- Unemployment soars.
- Personal incomes shrink.
- Countries enact high tariffs to protect their products from foreign competition; world trade declines.
- American loans to Europe dry up.

☑ Quick Study Timeline

In America

| 1928 Hoover elected President | October 1929 Stock market crashes | June 1930 Hawley-Smoot Tariff |

Presidential Terms Calvin Coolidge 1923–1929   Herbert Hoover 1929–1933

| 1928 | 1929 | 1930 |

Around the World

1928 Stalin launches first Five-Year Plan in the Soviet Union

1930 Haile Selassie becomes emperor of Ethiopia

Differentiated Instruction   Solutions for All Learners

L1 Special Needs Students   **L2 English Language Learners**   **L2 Less Proficient Readers**

Use the following study guide resources to help students acquiring basic skills:
Adapted Reading and Note Taking Study Guide
- Section Note Taking
- Section Summaries

Use the following study guide resources to help Spanish-speaking students:
Spanish Reading and Note Taking Study Guide
- Section Note Taking
- Section Summaries

American Issues
Connector

By connecting prior knowledge with what you have learned in this chapter, you can gradually build your understanding of enduring questions that still affect America today. Answer the questions below. Then, use your American Issues Connector study guide (or go online: www.pearsonschool.com/ushist).

Issues You Learned About

● **Government's Role in the Economy** Like other Presidents, Hoover sought the right balance between free enterprise and government intervention in the economy.

1. Think about the problems that emerged in society during the Great Depression and Hoover's response to them. Write a paragraph suggesting what Hoover might have done to improve the nation's economic situation and morale. Consider the following:
   - the depression's impact on families, businesses, industries, agriculture, and the banking system
   - the rising unemployment rate
   - the falling prices for farm products
   - Hoover's belief in volunteerism
   - responses to Hoover's policies

● **Migration and Urbanization** Economic changes often lead to migration around the country.

2. Why did thousands of people who lived in the Great Plains leave the region in the 1930s?

3. How did the drought on the Great Plains change population distribution in the country?

4. What other migrations took place as a result of the Great Depression?

● **Global Interdependence** The economies of nations around the world are impacted by distant events.

5. What economic practice of the 1920s contributed to the weakening of European economies?

6. What happened to European economies as a result of the Great Depression in the United States?

Connect to Your World	Activity

Poverty and Prosperity The 1920s was a period in which wealth was concentrated among the richest Americans. Conduct research to find out how wealth is distributed in the United States today. When you have completed your research, create a pie graph similar to the income-distribution graph in the Section 1 Infographic "Causes of the the Great Depression". How does income distribution today compare with income distribution in 1929?

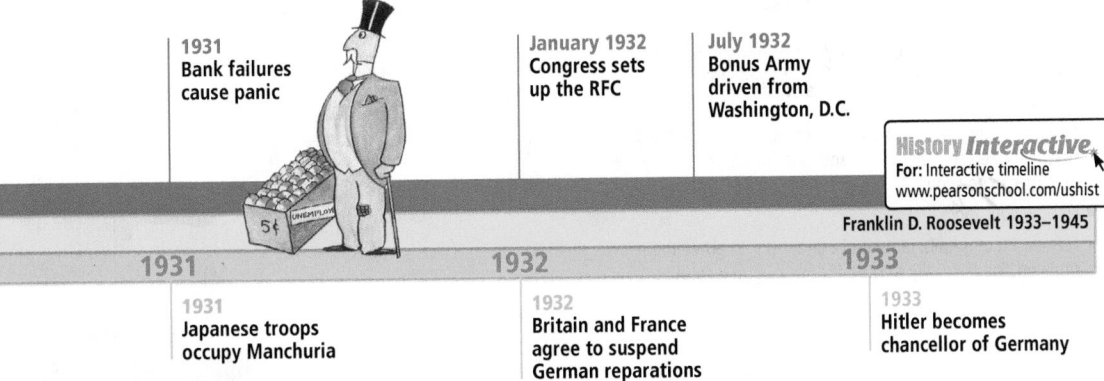

1931
Bank failures cause panic

January 1932
Congress sets up the RFC

July 1932
Bonus Army driven from Washington, D.C.

History Interactive
For: Interactive timeline
www.pearsonschool.com/ushist

Franklin D. Roosevelt 1933–1945

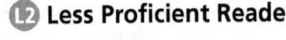

1931
1932
1933

1931
Japanese troops occupy Manchuria

1932
Britain and France agree to suspend German reparations

1933
Hitler becomes chancellor of Germany

Differentiated Instruction   Solutions for All Learners

L1 Special Needs Students   **L2 English Language Learners**   **L2 Less Proficient Readers**

Use the following study guide resource to help students acquiring basic skills:
Adapted Reading and Note Taking Study Guide
- American Issues Journal

Use the following study guide resource to help Spanish-speaking students:
Spanish Reading and Note Taking Study Guide
- American Issues Journal

American Issues
Connector

Tell students that the main issues for this chapter are Government's Role in the Economy, Migration and Urbanization, and Global Interdependence. Then, ask them to answer the Issues You Learned About questions on this page. Discuss the Connect to Your World topic, and ask students to complete the project that follows.

American Issues Connector

1. Paragraphs should reflect an understanding of Hoover's policies during the Great Depression and offer alternative policies that might have improved the nation.

2. Drought, high winds, and unstable topsoil combined to transform much of the Great Plains into a Dust Bowl, causing the land to be unusable for growing crops.

3. The Dust Bowl forced approximately 800,000 people to migrate out of the Great Plains to other regions.

4. Many African Americans migrated from rural areas to cities to find work. Some Mexican Americans returned to Mexico as a result of the increased migration of people from the Great Plains.

5. The repayment of British and French war debts to the United States and the German reparation payments to Britain and France contributed to the weak economies in Europe.

6. The Great Depression in the United States caused Europe to experience the same cycle of business failures, bank collapses, and high unemployment.

Connect to Your World

Students should collect data from a number of reliable sources and draw graphs that reflect this data as accurately as possible.

For additional review of this chapter's enduring issues, remind students to refer to the Reading and Note Taking Study Guide American Issues Journal.

Terms and People

1. a seasoned political and business leader who represented the promise of continued prosperity to Americans, who elected him as their thirty-first President (1929–1933)

2. a model for explaining periodic economic growth and contraction; as a plunge into a cyclical trough

3. a place where people lined up to receive free food from charities or public agencies

4. a movement among white Americans in the Southwest to encourage or coerce Mexican immigrants to return to Mexico; although many Mexicans were frightened into leaving, many remained

5. a theory that the money poured into the top of the economic pyramid will trickle down to the base; Hoover administration programs based on this model, such as the RFC, proved unsuccessful

Focus Questions

6. Unsustainable practices in finance, agriculture, consumption, and industry, which fueled economic expansion during the 1920s, contributed to the collapse that brought on the Great Depression.

7. The Great Depression caused economic turmoil in both areas. In urban areas, production cutbacks in factories caused many people to lose their jobs and their homes. Homeless communities called Hoovervilles sprang up in many American cities. In rural areas, many farmers were already experiencing economic troubles. The Great Depression caused crop prices to plummet and many farmers to lose their farms and homes.

8. Reluctant to impose legislation, he relied on volunteerism and on trickle-down economics, both of which were inadequate to meet the crisis.

Chapter Assessment

Terms and People

1. Who was **Herbert Hoover**? What did he represent to the American people in 1928?

2. What is the **business cycle**? If you were to chart the business cycle of 1929, how would you represent the period from mid-October through mid-November?

3. Define **bread line.** Who ran bread lines during the depression?

4. What was Mexican American **repatriation**? How did Mexican Americans respond to this effort?

5. Define **trickle-down economics.** Explain how the depression proved whether or not this theory worked.

Focus Questions

The focus question for this chapter is **How did the Great Depression happen, and how did Americans respond to it?** Build an answer to this big question by answering the focus questions for Sections 1 through 3 and the Critical Thinking questions that follow.

Section 1
6. How did the prosperity of the 1920s give way to the Great Depression?

Section 2
7. How did the Great Depression affect the lives of urban and rural Americans?

Section 3
8. Why did Herbert Hoover's policies fail to solve the country's economic crisis?

Critical Thinking

9. **Identify Central Issues** What weaknesses existed in the U.S. economy before the stock market crash?

10. **Recognize Causes** How did the Dust Bowl cause Okies to prefer life in California over life on the Great Plains?

11. **Analyze Line Graphs** Based on the graph below, between which two years did unemployment rise the most? Based on your reading, explain why the increase was especially great during this period.

U.S. Unemployment Rate, 1925–1933

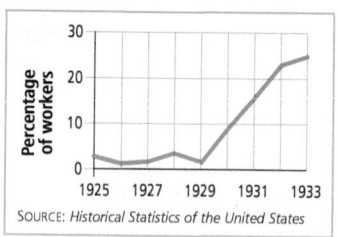

SOURCE: *Historical Statistics of the United States*

12. **Synthesize Information** Why did some men find their role in the family diminished during the depression? What were some of the different ways these men reacted?

13. **Identify Central Issues** Do you think the depression changed people's goals and expectations? Why or why not?

14. **Draw Conclusions** Why did Hoover turn from volunteerism and localism to more activist policies to fight the depression?

15. **Identify Fact Versus Opinion** What demands did the Bonus Army make? What did General MacArthur think about the Bonus Army?

Writing About History

Writing a Problem-Solution Essay Throughout its history, the United States has experienced periods of economic decline. However, not all these downturns ended in a general depression. In 1929, underlying problems surfaced to sink the American economy in the wake of the stock market crash. Write a problem-solution essay about one of these causes of the depression or choose your own topic relating to the content in this chapter.

Prewriting
• Choose the topic that interests you the most. If you have a personal interest in a problem and its solution, your essay will be easier to develop.

• Narrow your topic.

• Make a list of details, facts, and examples that prove there is a problem. Then, identify the specific parts of your solution.

Drafting
• Develop a working thesis and choose information to support it.

• Organize the paragraphs in a logical order so that readers can understand the solution you propose.

Revising
• Use the guidelines on page SH16 of the Writing Handbook to revise your essay.

Critical Thinking

9. a collapse in unsustainable trends in consumption, finance, agriculture, and industry, which had been fueling economic expansion

10. The Dust Bowl led Okies to look elsewhere for jobs and homes, leaving devastated farms for possible jobs in other areas of the country, such as California.

11. The vicious circle of business cutbacks and layoffs that began in the 1930s caused unemployment to increase most precipitously between 1930 and 1932.

12. Many men who lost their jobs felt a loss of status because they could no longer act in their traditional role as family "breadwinner." Some men tried to find new jobs, and others sank into despair.

13. Yes; a large percentage of people discovered that their lives could suddenly be turned upside down and that they were powerless to do anything about it.

Document-Based Assessment

Worldwide Depression

In 1929, the stock market crash echoed across the Atlantic Ocean to a European continent still suffering the aftereffects of war. Use your knowledge of the Great Depression and the following documents to answer questions 1 through 4.

Document A

"Values decreased, prices fell, production lessened. The American faith began its decline as extremely as had its illusions been created. Simultaneously, with the misfortunes of business in America came the catastrophes of Europe. . . . The [American] government made unheard-of efforts in the last three years to contain the avalanche. . . . But they made the big mistake of believing they could save the nation in isolation."

—El Sol, Madrid newspaper, March 7, 1933

Document B

Nations indebted to the United States, 1914–1925
Loans given by the United States, 1914–1918
Loans given by the United States for reconstruction, 1919–1925
$160 Total debt (in millions of dollars)
*Debt repudiated in 1918

Document C

"The Hawley-Smoot Tariff went into effect in June 1930, in the full blast of the depression. Under the circumstances there was great indignation and resentment on the part of the majority of the countries of the world, but that of the debtor countries of Europe was extreme. This intense indignation, coupled with the absolute necessity of securing a favorable trade balance, could result in but one course of action: retaliatory tariff increases against the United States."

—Joseph M. Jones, Jr., Tariff Retaliation: Repercussions of the Hawley-Smoot Bill

Document D

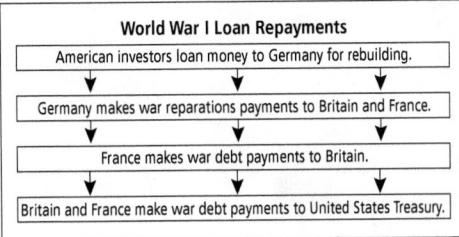

World War I Loan Repayments

American investors loan money to Germany for rebuilding.

Germany makes war reparations payments to Britain and France.

France makes war debt payments to Britain.

Britain and France make war debt payments to United States Treasury.

---

1. Which of the documents is a primary source that explains how the stock market crash snowballed into an international economic crisis?
   A Document A
   B Document B
   C Document C
   D Document D

2. Which conclusion is best supported by Document D?
   A The U.S. government helped Germany make reparation payments.
   B Britain owed a large war debt to France.
   C Funds from U.S. investors ended up in the hands of the U.S. government.
   D Germany made reparations payments to the United States.

3. According to Joseph Jones, which of the following statements is an accurate assessment of the Hawley-Smoot Tariff?
   A It caused European countries to pass their own protective tariffs.
   B It opened international markets and stimulated world trade.
   C It put limits on Allied war debts.
   D It established the funds for the Reconstruction Finance Corporation.

4. **Writing Task** How did the structure of loans to rebuild Europe after World War I collapse under the weight of economic depression? Use your knowledge of the war, the Great Depression, and specific evidence from the primary sources above to support your opinion.

14. Volunteerism and localism were not ending the Depression, and Americans were becoming angry at his failure to alleviate the crisis.

15. The Bonus Army sought early payment of the veterans' bonuses; MacArthur thought that the Bonus Army was an imminent threat to the U.S. government.

Writing About History

As students begin the assignment, refer them to page SH15 of the Writing Handbook for help in writing a problem-solution essay. Remind them of the steps they should take to complete their assignment, including prewriting, drafting, and revising.

Students' essays should focus on a narrow topic that they can address effectively. They should develop a solution through a thesis with specific details and examples to support it. Students should show evidence of thoughtful organization, and their essays should be free of grammatical and spelling errors. For scoring rubrics, see Assessment Rubrics.

CHAPTER 9 The New Deal
1932–1941

Teach With Technology
Presentation**EXPRESS**™
PREMIUM DVD

- Teach this chapter's core content by using PresentationExpress, which includes interactivities, video, lecture notes, and the *ExamView®* QuickTake assessment tool.

- To introduce this chapter by using PresentationExpress, ask students with which of the following statements they most agree: **A) When the nation is in crisis, it is wise to give far-reaching powers to a leader who can solve the problems. B) Giving a leader too much power can be dangerous because the leader may abuse that power.** Take a class poll or record students' answers by using the QuickTake feature, and discuss their responses. Point out that in this chapter, students will read about the way in which Americans dealt with this question and others as they tried to lift the nation out of the depression. Continue introducing the chapter by using the chapter opener slide show.

Technology Resources

- Student**EXPRESS** CD-ROM

- Teacher Resource Library **DVD**

- Presentation**EXPRESS** **PREMIUM** DVD

- *ExamView®* **Test Bank CD-ROM** English and Spanish

- **Guided Reading Audio,** Spanish

- **Student Edition on Audio**

THE ESSENTIAL
VIDEO
By Students For Students
For videos on Amercian Issues, go to
www.pearsonschool.com/ushist

Bibliography

For the Teacher
Buhite, Russell D. and Levy, David W., eds. *FDR's Fireside Chats*. University of Oklahoma Press, 1992.

Cook, Blanche W. *Eleanor Roosevelt: The Defining Years, 1933–1938. Vol. 2*. Penguin Group, 2000.

Kennedy, David M. *Freedom from Fear: The American People in Depression and War, 1929–1945*. Oxford University Press, 1999.

For the Student
L2 Freedman, Russsell. *Children of the Great Depression*. Clarion, 2005.

L3 Kyvig, David E. *Daily Life in the United States, 1920–1940: How Americans Lived Through the Roaring Twenties and the Great Depression*. Dee, Ivan R. Publisher, 2004.

L4 Terkel, Studs. *Hard Times: An Oral History of the Great Depression*. Pantheon, 1986.

WITNESS HISTORY

A New Beginning

Still suffering through the worst economic crisis in the nation's history, depression-weary Americans anxiously awaited Franklin D. Roosevelt's Inaugural Address.

"Saturday, March 4, 1933.

Turn on the radio. It's time for the inauguration.

There is a tension in the air today—a sense of momentousness and of expectation. When you went downtown this morning you found the banks shut. . . . But what next? . . . The one thing you want to hear, that everybody wants to hear, is the Inaugural Address. All over the country people are huddled round their radios, wondering what Roosevelt's answer to disaster will be."

—Frederick Lewis Allen, *Since Yesterday: The 1930s In America*

◀ On the campaign trail in West Virginia, Governor Roosevelt greets a coal miner.

Movie poster for *King Kong*

1932 presidential campaign button

Chapter Preview

Chapter Focus Question: How did the New Deal respond to the ravages of the depression and change the role of the federal government?

Section 1
FDR Offers Relief and Recovery

Section 2
The Second New Deal

Section 3
Effects of the New Deal

Section 4
Culture of the 1930s

The CCC provided government jobs for unemployed young men.

Use the ✓ **Quick Study Timeline** at the end of this chapter to preview chapter events.

Note Taking Study Guide *Online*
For: Note Taking and American Issues Connector
www.pearsonschool.com/ushist

Chapter-Level Resources

All In One Letter Home (English and Spanish), Preread the Chapter, Vocabulary Builder, Reading Strategy, Social Studies Skills Practice, Enrichment, Issues Connector, Chapter Tests

- Test Prep With Document-Based Assessment
- AYP Monitoring Assessments
- *ExamView®* Test Bank CD-ROM
- Guided Reading Audio (Spanish)
- Student Edition Audio

Previewing the Chapter

- **WITNESS HISTORY** Have students recall the hardships that most Americans faced during the depression. Read the Witness History selection aloud. Ask students to discuss how they might feel sitting in front of the radio awaiting the new President's address.

- **Analyzing the Visuals** Tell students to look at the photo of Franklin D. Roosevelt during the presidential campaign of 1932. When he could, Roosevelt liked to meet ordinary working people. Ask **How does this photo show Roosevelt as "a man of the people?"** *(He is shown shaking hands with a coal miner.)* **Why would it be important for Roosevelt to project this image?** *(The image of Roosevelt in contact with ordinary men and women was likely to gain him their votes.)*

- **Focus** Write the Chapter Focus Question on the board. Tell students to keep this question in mind as they read the chapter. Then, have students preview the section titles in this chapter.

- **Preread** Have students complete the chapter's Preread the Chapter Worksheet. Teaching Resources, pp. 8–9

Differentiated Instruction   Solutions for All Learners

The following Teacher's Edition strategies are suitable for students of varying abilities.

L1 Special Needs Students, pp. 286, 289, 290, 295, 297, 304, 306, 307, 311 SN

L2 English Language Learners, pp. 286, 289, 290, 295, 297, 306, 311 ELL

L2 Less Proficient Readers, pp. 286, 289, 290, 295, 297, 304, 306, 307, 311 LPR

L4 Advanced Readers, pp. 287, 294, 302, 313 AR

L4 Gifted and Talented Students, pp. 287, 294, 302, 313 GT

Have students access **www.pearsonschool.com/ushist** for the Note Taking Study Guide *Online* as an alternative to the *Reading and Note Taking Study Guide* booklet.

Objectives

As you teach this section, keep students focused on the following objectives to help them answer the Section Focus Question and master core content.

- Analyze the impact Franklin D. Roosevelt had on the American people after becoming President.
- Describe the programs that were part of the first New Deal and their immediate impact.
- Identify critical responses to the New Deal.

Prepare to Read

Background Knowledge L3

Remind students that Americans faced huge problems during the Great Depression. Then, ask them to predict the actions FDR might take to help the nation.

Set a Purpose L3

- **WITNESS HISTORY** Read the selection aloud.

  Ask **What was the main goal of Roosevelt's speech?** *(to assure the nation that it could overcome its difficulties)*

- **Focus** Point out the Section Focus Question, and write it on the board. Tell students to refer to this question as they read. *(Answer appears with Section 1 Assessment answers.)*

- **Preview** Have students preview the Section Objectives and the list of Terms and People.

- **Reading Skill** Have students use the *Reading Strategy: Connect Ideas* worksheet. Teaching Resources, **p. 12**

- **NoteTaking** Using the Paragraph Shrinking strategy (TE, p. T20), have students read this section. As they read, have students list problems FDR faced and the steps he took to solve them. Reading and Note Taking Study Guide

▼ Franklin Delano Roosevelt

▼ Roosevelt campaign banner

FDR Offers Relief and Recovery

Objectives
- Analyze the impact Franklin D. Roosevelt had on the American people after becoming President.
- Describe the programs that were part of the first New Deal and their immediate impact.
- Identify critical responses to the New Deal.

Terms and People

Franklin D. Roosevelt	CCC
Eleanor Roosevelt	NRA
New Deal	PWA
fireside chat	Charles Coughlin
FDIC	Huey Long
TVA	

NoteTaking

Reading Skill: Connect Ideas Fill in a chart like the one below with the problems that FDR faced and the steps he took to overcome them.

FDR Tackles Tough Problems	
Problem	FDR's Policy
Failing banks	

Why It Matters The Great Depression challenged the faith of Americans that democracy could handle the crisis. Faced with similar circumstances, people in Germany, Italy, and Japan had turned to dictators to deliver them from despair. The New Deal had great significance because America's response to the Great Depression proved that a democratic society could overcome the challenges presented by the severe economic crisis. **Section Focus Question: How did the New Deal attempt to address the problems of the depression?**

Roosevelt Takes Charge

In 1928, Herbert Hoover had almost no chance of losing his bid for the presidency. In 1932 however, Hoover had almost no chance of winning reelection. The depression had taken its toll. About 25 percent of the population was unemployed. Bank failures had wiped out peoples' savings. The hungry waited on long lines at soup kitchens.

Americans were ready for a change. In July of 1932, the relatively unknown governor of New York, **Franklin D. Roosevelt,** accepted the Democratic Party's nomination for President.

Roosevelt Overcame Obstacles Strangely enough, Americans had chosen a presidential candidate who had never known economic hardship. As a child, Franklin Delano Roosevelt had enjoyed all the privileges of an upper-class upbringing, including education at elite schools and colleges. From his parents and teachers, FDR gained a great deal of self-confidence and a belief that public service was a noble calling.

Vocabulary Builder

Use the information below and the following resource to teach students the high-use word from this section. Teaching Resources, Vocabulary Builder, p. 11

High-Use Word	Definition and Sample Sentence
ensure	*v.* to make safe; guarantee Many Americans worked in government programs that could **ensure** them an income.

In 1905, Franklin married his distant cousin **Eleanor Roosevelt.** President Theodore Roosevelt, Eleanor's uncle and Franklin's fifth cousin gave the bride away. In time, Eleanor would become deeply involved in public affairs.

Like Teddy Roosevelt, Franklin rose quickly through the political ranks. After election to the New York State Senate, he served as Woodrow Wilson's Assistant Secretary of the Navy. In 1920, Roosevelt was the Democratic Party's vice presidential nominee. Although the Democrats lost the election, many considered him the rising star of the party.

Then, in the summer of 1921, tragedy struck. While vacationing, FDR slipped off his boat into the chilly waters of the North Atlantic. That evening, he awoke with a high fever and severe pains in his back and legs. Two weeks later, Roosevelt was diagnosed with polio, a dreaded disease that at the time had no treatment. He never fully recovered the use of his legs.

FDR did not allow his physical disability to break his spirit. With Eleanor's encouragement, Roosevelt made a political comeback. In 1928, he was elected governor of New York and earned a reputation as a reformer. In 1932, he became the Democrats' presidential candidate, pledging "a new deal for the American people."

Voters Elect a New President When FDR pledged a **"New Deal,"** he had only a vague idea of how he intended to combat the depression. Convinced that the federal government needed to play an active role in promoting recovery and providing relief to Americans, he experimented with different approaches to see which one worked best.

> **Primary Source** ❝The country needs and, unless I mistake its temper, the country demands bold, persistent experimentation. It is common sense to take a method and to try it. If it fails, admit it frankly and try another. But above all, try something!❞
> —Franklin D. Roosevelt, speech at Oglethorpe University, May 22, 1932

The 1932 election campaign pitted Roosevelt against President Herbert Hoover. The two men advocated very different approaches to the problems of the Great Depression. Hoover believed that depression relief should come from state and local governments and private agencies. Roosevelt believed that the depression required strong action and leadership by the federal government. As Hoover noted, "This campaign is more than a contest between two men. . . . It is a contest between two philosophies of government."

Hoover's popularity declined as the Great Depression worsened. Even longtime Republicans deserted him. FDR—with the support of those who embraced his ideas as well as those who opposed Hoover's approach—won a landslide presidential victory, defeating Hoover by more than 7 million votes.

Americans had to wait four long months between Roosevelt's election, in November 1932, and his inauguration, in March 1933. Meanwhile, they watched helplessly as thousands of banks collapsed and unemployment soared. What would Roosevelt do to combat the depression? Even the experts did not know what to expect.

Putting Together a Winning Team To help him plan the New Deal, FDR sought the advice of a diverse group of men and women. Among the most influential was a group of professionals and academics whom the press nicknamed the

FDR Not Slowed by Polio
Despite the debilitating effects of polio, FDR continued to serve in public office. *How do you think FDR's earlier jobs and experiences prepared him to serve as President?*

- 1903 Earned BA in history from Harvard University
- 1910 Elected to the New York State Senate
- 1913 Appointed Assistant Secretary of the Navy
- 1920 Campaigned as Democratic nominee for Vice President
- 1921 Contracted polio, which paralyzed his legs
- 1928 Elected governor of New York State
- 1933 Inaugurated as President of the United States

Instruct

- **Introduce: Key Term** Have students find the key term **New Deal** in the text. Ask students to discuss why the **New Deal** would appeal to many U.S. voters.

- **Teach** Have students study the timeline and photograph on this page. Ask **What obstacle did FDR overcome to return to politics?** *(the loss of the use of his legs caused by polio)* Using the Idea Wave strategy (TE, p. T22), have students compare and contrast FDR's approach to stimulating the U.S. economy with President Hoover's approach. **How did FDR's Cabinet nominations show his willingness to experiment with new ideas to solve the nation's problems?** *(Although FDR was a Democrat, he chose Republicans to serve in his Cabinet. He also appointed the first woman Cabinet member.)*

- **Quick Activity** Have students read the Primary Source quotation from Roosevelt's campaign speech. Ask **What does Roosevelt suggest the nation needs to end the Great Depression?** *(bold experimentation)*

Independent Practice

Ask students to suppose that they are living in the United States during the Great Depression. Tell them to consider the main problems and fears of people living during that time. Have students write a short letter to President Roosevelt expressing their concerns and stating what they hope he will accomplish.

Monitor Progress

As students fill in their charts, circulate to make sure that they understand the steps FDR took to overcome the nation's problems. For a completed version of the chart, see Note Taking Transparencies, **B-107.**

Answer

Caption He gained military knowledge as Assistant Secretary of the Navy. As governor of New York, FDR ran a large executive department, where he could experiment with reforms.

Instruct

- **Introduce: Key Term** Have students find the key term *fireside chats* (in bold) in the text. Ask **Why do you think the President's *fireside chats* inspired confidence in the American people?** *(The informal nature of the radio broadcasts made it seem as if the President were speaking to Americans as friends to whom he was offering sound advice, rather than as an impersonal leader describing public policy.)*

- **Teach** Ask **What was the purpose of the New Deal?** *(to provide immediate relief to Americans in greatest need, help the nation's recovery, and reform institutions to make future depressions less likely)* **How did FDR attempt to restore the nation's confidence in banks?** *(He closed banks temporarily to stop panic withdrawals and to allow banks to organize their accounts. He created the FDIC to assure people that they would not lose the money they deposited in banks. He also used fireside chats.)* **Why was restoring confidence in the banking system important?** *(Sample answer: The collapse of the banking system would have destroyed the American economy and could have undermined any confidence Americans had left in their government and the capitalist system.)* Display Color Transparency: *Civilian Conservation Corps.* Briefly discuss the table showing what the CCC did as part of the New Deal. Color Transparencies **A-97**

Answer

✔ Roosevelt's sense of self-confidence, nurtured from childhood by his parents and teachers, made him appear strong and capable to the public. Unlike Hoover, Roosevelt believed strongly in the federal government's ability and duty to help people.

"Brain Trust." Roosevelt, a Democrat, displayed his openness by nominating two Republicans, Henry Wallace and Harold Ickes (IHK uhs), to serve as his Secretary of Agriculture and Secretary of Interior. Roosevelt also nominated Frances Perkins, a social worker, to serve as his Secretary of Labor. She became the first woman Cabinet member in U.S. history.

Throughout his presidency, FDR depended heavily on his wife, Eleanor. She traveled widely, interacting with the American people and serving as FDR's "eyes and ears." For example, in 1933, the Bonus Army, which had marched on Washington, D.C., in 1932, returned to the capital, seeking an early payment of its bonus for World War I service. Like Hoover, FDR informed the marchers that the government could not afford to pay them their bonus. But unlike Hoover, who had sent the army to evict the Bonus Army, FDR sent Eleanor. She sang songs with the veterans and made them feel that the government cared.

✔ **Checkpoint** How did FDR's background and actions help build confidence among the American people?

The First Hundred Days Provide Instant Action

During his first hundred days in office, Roosevelt proposed and Congress passed 15 bills. These measures, known as the First New Deal, had three goals: relief, recovery, and reform. Roosevelt wanted to provide relief from the immediate hardships of the depression and achieve a long-term economic recovery. He also instituted reforms to prevent future depressions.

FDR Swiftly Restores the Nation's Confidence Roosevelt wasted no time dealing with the nation's number one crisis. Late in 1932, banks had begun to

---

⬤ INFOGRAPHIC

RELIEF, RECOVERY, AND REFORM
THE FIRST 100 DAYS

Working together, President Roosevelt and Congress quickly passed many new laws to provide job relief, speed economic recovery, and reform business practices. These New Deal programs marked the beginning of the federal government's increasingly active role in shaping the economy and society.

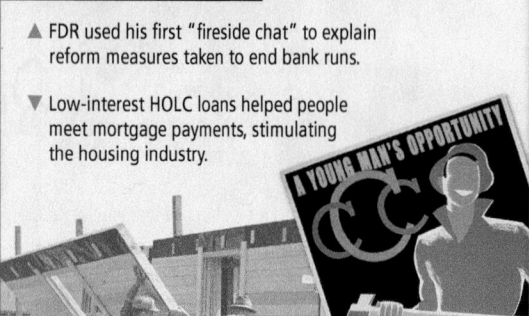

▲ FDR used his first "fireside chat" to explain reform measures taken to end bank runs.

▼ Low-interest HOLC loans helped people meet mortgage payments, stimulating the housing industry.

Achievements of the First Hundred Days
Federal Deposit Insurance Corporation (FDIC)
National Recovery Administration (NRA)
Civilian Conservation Corps (CCC)
Public Works Administration (PWA)
Agricultural Adjustment Act (AAA)
Tennessee Valley Authority (TVA)
Home Owners' Loan Corporation (HOLC)

Differentiated Instruction   Solutions for All Learners

L1 Special Needs Students   **L2 English Language Learners**   **L2 Less Proficient Readers**

To help visual learners summarize the various programs that were part of FDR's New Deal, have them create an illustrated graphic organizer. Each graphic organizer should show the major programs discussed in the text. For each program, instruct students to write the name of the program in one column and either to write a description of the program or draw a simple sketch illustrating something about the program in the other column. Then, tell students to use their graphic organizers to write paragraphs summarizing FDR's New Deal programs.

fail in great numbers. A banking panic gripped the nation as frightened depositors lined up outside banks, trying to withdraw their savings.

The day after his inauguration, Roosevelt called Congress into a special session and convinced them to pass laws to shore up the nation's banking system. The Emergency Banking Bill gave the President broad powers—including the power to declare a four-day bank "holiday." Banks all over the country were ordered to close. The closings gave banks time to get their accounts in order before they reopened for business.

Eight days after becoming President, Roosevelt delivered an informal radio speech to the American people. This was the first of many presidential **fireside chats.** They became an important way for Roosevelt to communicate with the American people. In the first fireside chat, FDR explained the measures he had taken to stem the run on banks. His calming words reassured the American people. When the bank holiday ended, Americans did not rush to their banks to withdraw their funds. Roosevelt had convinced them that the banks were a safe place to keep their money.

Reforming the Financial System A number of Roosevelt's proposals sought to reform the nation's financial institutions. One act created the **Federal Deposit Insurance Corporation (FDIC),** which insured bank deposits up to $5,000. In the following year, Congress established the Securities and Exchange Commission (SEC) to regulate the stock market and make it a safer place for investments.

These financial reforms helped restore confidence in the economy. Runs on banks ended, largely because Americans now had confidence that they would not lose their lifetime savings if a bank failed. The stock markets also stabilized as regulated trading practices reassured investors.

Independent Practice

- Have students analyze the Infographic and answer the questions in the text.

- Organize the class into two groups, identifying half of the class as wage earners and half as owners of businesses that employ such workers. Have students research whether wage earners and business owners supported or opposed the minimum wage. Then, have them formulate their positions for or against a minimum wage, depending on the group of which they are members. Ask students to list reasons for supporting or opposing a minimum wage. Then, have students use their findings to debate whether the U.S. government should mandate a minimum wage.

The Tennessee Valley Authority

Conic Projection
0   50 mi
0   50 km

Region served by TVA
— Dam
Power plant

▲ The TVA built dams and power plants, providing electricity and improving living conditions in the Southeast.

◀ CCC workers like these young men labored on environmental conservation projects.

▼ PWA projects provided construction jobs on roads, bridges, and public buildings.

Thinking Critically

1. **Analyze Maps** Name the states that were affected by TVA projects.

2. **Analyze Information** How did the programs of the first 100 days benefit both the economy and the environment?

Differentiated Instruction   Solutions for All Learners

L4 Advanced Readers   **L4 Gifted and Talented Students**

Draw this "vicious cycle" graphic organizer on the board for students to analyze: Banks fail. → People lose confidence in banks. → People withdraw their money from banks. → More banks fail. Ask students to work in groups and answer the following questions: (1) Where would the government have to intervene to stop this vicious cycle? For example, would passing a law that prohibits people from taking their money out of personal bank accounts solve the problem, or would it make people panic and lose even more confidence in the system? (2) Where did Roosevelt initially intervene in this cycle and why? Why did Roosevelt's approach work?

Answers

Thinking Critically

1. Alabama, Georgia, Kentucky, Mississippi, North Carolina, Tennessee, Virginia
2. The programs provided jobs for the unemployed, giving them money to spend on the goods that U.S. companies produced. TVA power plants and other infrastructure improvements helped industrial growth. CCC workers completed conservation projects that helped the environment.

Monitor Progress

Tell students to make an outline of information under the blue heading "The First Hundred Days Provide Instant Action." Instruct them to use the red headings as the basic framework. Have students then include at least two details found under each red heading to build the outline.

Government Puts People to Work

The Works Progress Administration poster (above) promoted the benefits of putting people to work. These TVA workers (right) assembled generators at the Cherokee Dam in Tennessee. *If you had been out of work during the depression, what effect might these images have had on you? Why?*

Helping Farmers A number of New Deal programs aimed at easing the desperate plight of American farmers. For years, the supply of crops grown by American farmers had far exceeded demand. Prices dropped to the point where it was no longer profitable to grow some crops. To counter this, Congress passed the Agricultural Adjustment Act (AAA), which sought to end overproduction and raise crop prices. To accomplish these goals, the AAA provided financial aid, paying farmers subsidies not to plant part of their land and to kill off excess livestock. Many Americans believed it was immoral to kill livestock or destroy crops while people went hungry. However, by 1934, farm prices began to rise.

The TVA Aids Rural Southerners Americans living in the Tennessee River valley were among the poorest in the nation. Few had electricity, running water, or proper sewage systems. In 1933, Congress responded by creating a government agency called the **Tennessee Valley Authority (TVA)**. The TVA built a series of dams in the Tennessee River valley to control floods and to generate electric power. The agency also replanted forests, built fertilizer plants, created jobs, and attracted industry with the promise of cheap power.

Despite its accomplishments, the TVA attracted a host of critics. Some called the TVA "socialist," because it gave government direct control of a business. Private power companies complained that they could not compete with the TVA, because the agency paid no taxes. However, the TVA's successes in improving life in the Tennessee Valley have ensured its survival to the present.

Providing Relief and Promoting Industrial Recovery During his first hundred days as President, Roosevelt proposed and Congress enacted numerous other relief measures. To counter the depression's devastating impact on young men, FDR created the **Civilian Conservation Corps (CCC)**. The CCC provided jobs for more than 2 million young men. They replanted forests, built trails, dug irrigation ditches, and fought fires. As time went on, programs such as the CCC became more inclusive, extending work and training to Mexican American and other minority youth, as well as to whites. FDR called the CCC his favorite New Deal program.

Congress passed a number of other relief acts. The Federal Emergency Relief Act (FERA) granted federal funds to state and local agencies to help the unemployed. The short-lived Civil Works Administration (CWA) provided jobs on public-works projects. On another front, Congress created the Home Owners Loan Corporation (HOLC), which loaned money at low interest rates to homeowners who could not meet mortgage payments. The Federal Housing Administration (FHA) insured bank loans used for building and repairing homes.

History Background

The Green Towns The architects of the New Deal not only built dams, roads, bridges, and water tunnels. They also built towns. In the mid-1930s, FDR's New Deal planners came up with the idea of building several planned communities. The towns would provide years of work for the unemployed and low-cost housing for low-income families in healthy, green environments.

In 1935, the government broke ground for the first of the government-owned garden towns, Greenbelt, Maryland. Homes were built in clusters with walkways in between. A buffer of park or woodland surrounded the whole community. Labor-saving machinery was not used, so that the construction crews could work and collect needed paychecks for as long as possible. Even an artificial lake was dug with shovels instead of heavy machinery. The first residents of Greenbelt moved into the town in 1937. The plan to build green towns throughout the country was never realized. However, two other green towns were completed: at Greenhills, Ohio, and Greendale, Wisconsin. The three green towns still exist today, although the federal government gave up its control of them decades ago.

Answer

Caption The images of ordinary people working for the WPA would have been encouraging and would have given unemployed people hope that they might also get a job working on a government project.

These New Deal measures marked a clear break from the policies of the Hoover administration, which had disapproved of direct relief to individuals. The $500 million appropriated for FERA represented the largest peacetime expenditure by the federal government to that time.

The centerpiece of the early New Deal's recovery program was the National Industrial Recovery Act, which established the **National Recovery Administration (NRA).** Roosevelt called the NRA "the most important and far-reaching legislation ever enacted by the American Congress." Working with business and labor leaders, the NRA developed codes of fair competition to govern whole industries. These codes established minimum wages for workers and minimum prices for the goods that businesses sold. The idea behind these codes was to increase the wages of workers so they could buy more goods and raise prices so companies could make a profit.

Another New Deal legislative achievement was the **Public Works Administration (PWA),** which built bridges, dams, power plants, and government buildings. The PWA was responsible for building many important projects still in use today, such as New York City's Triborough Bridge, the Overseas Highway linking Miami and Key West, and the Bonneville Dam on the Columbia River in the Pacific Northwest. These public-works projects improved the nation's infrastructure and created millions of new jobs for workers.

✓ **Checkpoint** What actions did Roosevelt take during his first hundred days in office?

Opposition to the New Deal Emerges

While Roosevelt had little difficulty gaining support from Congress for his proposals, a minority of Americans expressed their opposition to the New Deal. Some thought the changes it brought were too radical. Others thought that the New Deal was not radical enough. Several of FDR's critics attracted mass followings and made plans to challenge him for the presidency in 1936.

The Right Says "Too Much" The chief complaint against the New Deal was that it made the government too powerful. Critics contended that the government was telling business how to operate, spending large sums of money, and piling up a huge national debt.

To many conservatives, the New Deal was destroying free enterprise and undermining individualism. In a 1934 book entitled *The Challenge to Liberty*, former President Herbert Hoover described the New Deal as "the most stupendous invasion of the whole spirit of liberty" in the nation's history. Robert Taft, the son of former President William Howard Taft and a leading Republican in Congress, claimed Roosevelt's programs threatened individual freedom.

In 1934, these critics formed the American Liberty League. Supporters included prominent business leaders, such as Alfred Sloan and William Knudsen of General Motors. Leading Democrats, such as John W. Davis, the Democrats' presidential nominee in 1924, and Al Smith, the nominee in 1928, joined the Liberty League because they felt Roosevelt had deserted the Democratic Party's principles of a limited federal government.

Analyzing Political Cartoons

The Galloping Snail This cartoon represents the relationship between President Roosevelt and Congress during FDR's first hundred days in office.

Ⓐ President Roosevelt

Ⓑ Congress

Ⓒ Roosevelt's New Deal agenda

1. Why did the cartoonist use a snail to represent Congress?
2. What is the cartoonist saying about the relationship between the President and Congress?

- Have students analyze the Comparing Viewpoints feature on this page and answer the questions in the text.

- Have students read and complete the worksheet *Interpreting a Political Cartoon: FDR and the New Deal*. Teaching Resources, **p. 20**

- Have pairs of students draw posters that might have been displayed at a rally either supporting or opposing the New Deal. Encourage them to be creative in the use of both text and graphics. Students may use arguments found in the text as well as humor to express their point of view.

Monitor Progress

Circulate to make sure that students understand the major issues that caused people to support or oppose the New Deal.

The New Deal: Too Much—or Not Enough?

Franklin Roosevelt's New Deal raised the issue of how involved the government should be in the economy and in the lives of its citizens. This question divided many Americans.

ALFRED E. SMITH

Smith (1873–1944) served as governor of New York and ran for President in 1928. He believed the New Deal made the government too powerful and described it as a "trend toward Fascist control" and "the end of democracy."

Primary Source

"Something has taken place in this country—there is a certain kind of foreign 'ism' crawling over [it]. . . . There can be only one Capitol, Washington or Moscow! There can be only one atmosphere of government, [the] clear, pure, fresh air of free America, or the foul breath of Communistic Russia."

FRANCIS TOWNSEND

Townsend (1867–1960) was a medical doctor who felt the New Deal did not do enough to help older Americans devastated by the depression. He proposed a pension plan funded by a national sales tax.

Primary Source

THE TOWNSEND PLAN
$200. PER MONTH FOR THOSE OVER
60 YRS OF AGE THE SPENDING OF THIS
MONEY WILL PUT THE CONTROL
OF CREDIT IN THE HANDS OF
THE PEOPLE – PREVENTING
ECONOMIC CHAOS

Compare

1. Which man thought that the New Deal went too far? Which man thought that the New Deal did not go far enough?

2. Why does each oppose the New Deal?

Vocabulary Builder

ensure–(ehn SHUR) *v.* to make safe; guarantee

The Left Says "Not Enough" While conservatives accused FDR of supporting socialism, some leading socialists charged that the New Deal did not do enough to end the depression. Norman Thomas, the Socialist Party's presidential candidate, claimed that FDR's only concern was saving the banking system and <u>ensuring</u> profits for big business. The American Communist Party described the New Deal as a "capitalist ruse."

Populist Critics Challenge FDR The most significant criticism of FDR came from a cluster of figures whose roots were in the Populist movement. They saw themselves as spokesmen for poor Americans, challenging the power of the elite. Roosevelt's strongest critics were Francis Townsend, Father Charles Coughlin, and Huey Long.

Townsend, a doctor from California, had a simple program. It called for the federal government to provide $200 a month to all citizens over the age of 60. These funds, he argued, would filter out to the rest of society and produce an economic recovery. To promote this plan, he established "Townsend Clubs" and held meetings that resembled old-time church revivals.

Father **Charles Coughlin** presented an even bigger challenge to FDR. Coughlin, a Roman Catholic priest, had attracted millions of listeners to his weekly radio show. At first, Coughlin supported the New Deal, but in time he broke with FDR, accusing him of not doing enough to fight the depression. Coughlin

---

Differentiated Instruction — Solutions for All Learners

L1 Special Needs Students **L2 English Language Learners** **L2 Less Proficient Readers**

To help students master vocabulary, have them list this section's high-use words and key terms and people. Then, have students create flashcards with a term on one side and its definition (or in the case of key people, one-sentence identifying statements) on the other. For English Language Learners, you may wish to have students add explanations in their first language to go with the flashcards. Pair students and have them quiz each other using the flashcards.

Answers

Compare

1. Smith thought it went too far. Townsend thought it did not go far enough.

2. Smith thought the New Deal concentrated too much power over people's lives in government. Townsend thought the New Deal did not go far enough in helping elderly people hit hard by the Great Depression.

said that Roosevelt had "out-Hoovered Hoover" and called the New Deal "the raw deal."

Coughlin mixed calls for the nationalization of industry with anti-Semitic remarks and attacks on "communists" who, he charged, were running the country. By the early 1940s, Coughlin's views became so extreme that Roman Catholic officials forced him to end his broadcasts.

Canadian by birth, Coughlin could not run against FDR in the 1936 election. However, he threatened to throw his support behind an even more popular New Deal critic, Senator **Huey Long** of Louisiana. Long was an expert performer whose folksy speeches delighted audiences. Long's solution to the depression was his "Share Our Wealth" program that proposed high taxes on the wealthy and large corporations, and the redistribution of their income to poor Americans.

> **Primary Source** "God invited us all to come and eat and drink all we wanted. He smiled on our land and we grew crops of plenty to eat and wear. . . . [But then] Rockefeller, Morgan, and their crowd stepped up and took enough for 120,000,000 people and left only enough for 5,000,000 for all the other 125,000,000 to eat. And so the millions must go hungry and without those good things God gave us unless we call on them to put some of it back."
>
> —Huey Long radio broadcast, 1934

Roosevelt viewed Long as a serious political threat. But unlike Roosevelt, Long did not have a deep faith in democracy. Ruling Louisiana as if he owned the state, he made many enemies. In 1935, a political enemy assassinated Long, ending the most serious threat to Roosevelt's presidency.

✓ **Checkpoint** What were the two major criticisms of FDR's New Deal economic policies?

Huey Long Challenges the Roosevelt Administration
Huey Long used his Share Our Wealth Society to promote the redistribution of wealth in the country. *How might Long's efforts have influenced FDR's policies?*

Comprehension

1. **Terms and People** For each item below, write a sentence explaining how it affected the lives of people during the New Deal.
   - Eleanor Roosevelt
   - fireside chat
   - TVA
   - PWA
   - Charles Coughlin
   - Huey Long

2. **NoteTaking Reading Skill: Connect Ideas** Use your problem-solution table to answer the Section Focus Question: How did the New Deal attempt to address the problems of the depression?

Writing About History

3. **Quick Write: Identify Main Ideas** Before you can synthesize, you must understand the main idea, or thesis, of each source. Study the political cartoon in this section and write a sentence summarizing its main idea about FDR. Then, review the Alfred E. Smith primary source quote. Write a sentence paraphrasing Smith's view of FDR.

Critical Thinking

4. **Draw Inferences** Why did President Roosevelt need his wife, Eleanor, to serve as his "eyes and ears"?

5. **Make Comparisons** How did FDR's economic policies differ from those of Herbert Hoover?

6. **Identify Central Issues** Why do you think the depression led to the development of some extreme proposals?

Answers

✓ Some critics said the New Deal made the government so powerful that it threatened free enterprise and individual freedom. Others said it was overly concerned with helping banks and businesses and was not doing enough for the poor.

Caption FDR might have given more attention to helping the poor in order to decrease Long's influence with the public and to blunt his criticism of the New Deal.

Section 1 Assessment

1. Sentences should demonstrate students' comprehension of the way that each person, event, or program affected Americans during the New Deal era.

2. In general, the New Deal put programs in place to give quick relief to people suffering the effects of the Great Depression, such as creating jobs. It created programs to help the nation recover over the long term, such as building dams to bring electricity and attract industry to poorly developed regions. It also reformed the banking system, the stock market, and the relationship between business and labor to help prevent future depressions.

3. Responses should show students' ability to synthesize the main idea conveyed by a political cartoon or a quotation.

4. It is often difficult for a President to make frequent trips to talk to people personally. It was easier for Eleanor Roosevelt to do this and tell the President what she had learned.

5. Hoover believed that state and local governments and private institutions should provide relief during the Great Depression.

FDR believed that the problems were so widespread that the federal government should intervene to help solve them.

6. During the Great Depression, Americans faced hardships on a massive scale. Because the problems were so overwhelming and people were so desperate, many of the solutions proposed were extreme by previous standards.

Objectives

As you teach this section, keep students focused on the following objectives to help them answer the Section Focus Question and master core content.

- Discuss the programs of social and economic reform in the Second New Deal.
- Explain how New Deal legislation affected the growth of organized labor.
- Describe the impact of Roosevelt's court-packing plan on the course of the New Deal.

Prepare to Read

Background Knowledge L3

Remind students that even with the unveiling of the New Deal, there were still problems to solve. Ask students to predict the types of measures that FDR might take to solve these problems.

Set a Purpose L3

- **WITNESS HISTORY** Read the selection aloud.

  Ask **Why did the child write a letter to Roosevelt?** *(The boy wanted Roosevelt to help his family because his father and sister could not find jobs to pay for food, electricity, and gas.)*

- **Focus** Point out the Section Focus Question, and write it on the board. Tell students to refer to this question as they read. *(Answer appears with Section 2 Assessment answers.)*

- **Preview** Have students preview the Section Objectives and the list of Terms and People.

- **NoteTaking** Using the Structured Read Aloud strategy (TE, p. T20), have students read this section. As they read, have students record programs of the Second New Deal and the problems each addressed. Reading and Note Taking Study Guide

Children picket for the Workers' Alliance during the Great Depression. ▶

WITNESS HISTORY

Trying to Survive

During the Great Depression, people found themselves desperate for work. Daily visits to the unemployment office and workplaces often turned up nothing. Some of the jobless lost their homes. Others could not feed their children. One 12-year-old boy wrote to President Roosevelt to ask for help for his family.

❝My father hasn't worked for 5 months. . . . Please you do something. . . . We haven't paid the gas bill, and the electric bill, haven't paid grocery bill. . . . I have a sister she's twenty years, she can't find work. My father he staying home. All the time he's crying because he can't find work.❞

—Anonymous 12-year-old boy, Chicago, 1936

The Second New Deal

Objectives

- Discuss the programs of social and economic reform in the second New Deal.
- Explain how New Deal legislation affected the growth of organized labor.
- Describe the impact of Roosevelt's court-packing plan on the course of the New Deal.

Terms and People

Second New Deal	collective bargaining
WPA	Fair Labor Standards Act
John Maynard Keynes	CIO
pump priming	sit-down strikes
Social Security Act	court packing
Wagner Act	

NoteTaking

Reading Skill: Connect Ideas Complete a table like the one below to record problems and the second New Deal's solutions.

The Second New Deal	
Problem	Solution
Unemployment	

Why It Matters FDR's goals for the first New Deal were relief, recovery, and reform. Progress had been made, but there was still much work that needed to be done. Beginning in early 1935, Roosevelt launched an aggressive campaign to find solutions to the ongoing problems caused by the Great Depression. This campaign, known as the Second New Deal, created Social Security and other programs that continue to have a profound impact on the everyday lives of Americans. **Section Focus Question: What major issues did the Second New Deal address?**

Extending Social and Economic Reform

In his fireside chats, press conferences, and major addresses, Roosevelt explained the challenges facing the nation. He said that the complexities of the modern world compelled the federal government to "promote the general welfare" and to intervene to protect citizens' rights. Roosevelt used legislation passed during the **Second New Deal** to accomplish these goals. The Second New Deal addressed the problems of the elderly, the poor, and the unemployed; created new public-works projects; helped farmers; and enacted measures to protect workers' rights. It was during this period that the first serious challenges to the New Deal emerged.

New Programs Provide Jobs In the spring of 1935, Congress appropriated $5 billion for new jobs and created the **Works Progress Administration (WPA)** to administer the program. Roosevelt placed his longtime associate Harry Hopkins in charge. The WPA built or improved a good part of the nation's highways, dredged rivers and

Vocabulary Builder

Use the information below and the following resource to teach students the high-use word from this section. Teaching Resources, Vocabulary Builder, p. 11

High-Use Word	Definition and Sample Sentence
upsurge	*n.* a sudden rapid increase FDR's recovery programs during the first 100 days created an **upsurge** in public confidence.

harbors, and promoted soil and water conservation. The WPA even provided programs in the arts for displaced artists. As Hopkins explained, artists "have to eat just like other people."

By 1943, the WPA had employed more than 8 million people and spent about $11 billion. Its workers built more than 650,000 miles of highways and 125,000 public buildings. Among the most famous projects funded by the WPA were the San Antonio River Walk and parts of the Appalachian Trail.

All of these programs were expensive, and the government paid for them by spending money it did not have. The federal deficit—$461 million in 1932—grew to $4.4 billion in 1936. The enormous expenditures and growing debt led many to criticize the government's public-works projects as wasteful. Some economists disagreed. British economist **John Maynard Keynes** argued that deficit spending was needed to end the depression. According to Keynes, putting people to work on public projects put money into the hands of consumers who would buy more goods, stimulating the economy. Keynes called this theory **pump priming.**

Social Security Eases the Burden on Older Americans The United States was one of the few industrialized nations in the world that did not have some form of pension system for the elderly. During the depression, many elderly people had lost their homes and their life savings and were living in poverty. On January 17, 1935, President Roosevelt unveiled his plans for Social Security.

In addition to creating a pension system for retirees, the **Social Security Act** that Congress enacted established unemployment insurance for workers who lost their jobs. The law also created insurance for victims of work-related accidents and provided aid for poverty-stricken mothers and children, the blind, and the disabled.

The Social Security Act had many flaws. At first, it did not apply to domestics or farmworkers. Since African Americans were disproportionately employed in these fields, they were not eligible for many of the benefits of Social Security. Widows received smaller benefits than widowers, because people presumed that elderly women could manage on less money than elderly men. Despite these shortcomings, Social Security proved the most popular and significant of the New Deal programs.

More Aid Goes to Farmers The Second New Deal included further help for farmers. When the depression began, only 10 percent of all farms had electricity, largely because utility companies did not find it profitable to run electric lines to communities with small populations. To bring farmers into the light, Congress established the Rural Electrification Administration (REA). The REA loaned money to electric utilities to build power lines, bringing electricity to isolated rural areas. The program was so successful that by 1950, more than 80 percent of American farms had electricity.

New Deal programs changed the relationship of the federal government to the American farmer. The government was now committed to providing price supports, or subsidies, for agriculture. Critics attacked price supports for undermining the free market. Others observed that large

Electricity Comes to Rural Farms

The success of the REA allowed farm families to light their homes, pump water, and run radios, refrigerators, and washing machines.

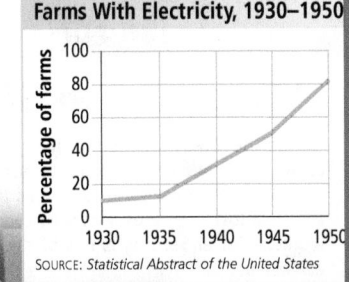

Farms With Electricity, 1930–1950

SOURCE: *Statistical Abstract of the United States*

History Background

John Maynard Keynes Keynes, a British economist, is best remembered for what is known as "Keynesian" economic theory. It supports government intervention to spur employment and consumer spending when economies stumble.

Early in his career, Keynes did not challenge the prevailing economic wisdom—largely adhered to by Herbert Hoover in the opening years of the Great Depression—of laissez faire, or allowing the free market to correct itself. In Britain, however, Keynes saw that this policy resulted in misery for people who lost their jobs during periodic recessions. He

advocated the use of government deficit spending to create public works jobs to stimulate a sluggish economy.

Keynes's theories were not well-known when he first proposed them, but many people, including FDR, came around to this economist's way of thinking. Having government employ the jobless in an attempt to end the Great Depression was groundbreaking in the United States—and Keynes's economic theories were influential in the United States for many decades.

Extending Social and Economic Reform

Instruct

- **Introduce: Key Terms** Have students find the key terms *Second New Deal, WPA, pump priming,* and *Social Security Act* in the text. Have students discuss how these terms might be related to extending social and economic reform in the United States.

- **Teach** Display Color Transparency: *Critics of the New Deal.* Have students review some of the programs the New Deal established and discuss their goals. Note that these programs caused the government to spend massive amounts of money it did not have. Ask **Why did economists such as Keynes say that deficit spending was beneficial?** *(Keynes's pump-priming theory stated that putting money into consumers' pockets would stimulate the economy because they would buy more goods.)* **What did the Social Security Act establish?** *(It provided a pension for elderly Americans, as well as money for the unemployed, the disabled, poor mothers with children, and people injured on the job.)* **Did Social Security cover all workers equally?** *(Not at first. Domestics and farm workers were not covered initially. Widows also received lower death benefits than widowers.)* Draw students' attention to the line graph on this page. Ask **How did the REA change the percentage of farm families with electricity during the 1930s?** *(There was a steady increase in the 1930s, especially between 1935 and 1940.)* **Why did African American farmers often not share equally in the benefits received from the New Deal?** *(As sharecroppers and tenant farmers, African Americans were itinerant or short-term workers and did not share fully in these programs.)* **Why were New Deal water projects so important to the development of parts of the West?** *(They provided irrigation for the spread of agriculture; they also provided cheap hydroelectric power that helped the growth of cities and industry.)* Color Transparencies A-98

■ **Quick Activity** Have students read the Primary Source quotation from Woody Guthrie's song "Roll on, Columbia" on the next page. Ask students to discuss the benefits of the Columbia River water projects described in the lyrics.

Independent Practice

■ To extend lesson content, have students access the History Interactive at **www.pearsonschool.com/ushist.** After viewing the History Interactive, have them write essays about the changes Social Security has experienced since its creation in 1935. As students write their essays, they may want to keep in mind the following questions: Before Social Security, how did retired people without savings or people who suddenly lost their jobs get along? How did Social Security affect the occurrence of poverty among older Americans? Would you have supported Social Security when FDR first proposed it?

■ Have students read and complete the worksheet *Reading a Chart: New Deal Programs.* Teaching Resources, **p. 21**

farms, not small farmers, benefited most from federal farm programs. Even during the 1930s, many noticed that tenant farmers and sharecroppers, often African Americans, did not fully share in the federal programs. Yet farm prices stabilized, and agriculture remained a productive sector of the economy.

Water Projects Change the Face of the West Many of the New Deal public-works water projects had an enormous impact on the development of the American West. The government funded the complex Central Valley irrigation system in California. The massive Bonneville Dam in the Pacific Northwest controlled flooding and provided electricity to a vast number of citizens. In 1941, the Department of the Interior's Bonneville Power Administration (BPA) hired folk singer Woody Guthrie for one month to write songs for a movie they had made

INTERACTIVE Whiteboard

Events That Changed America

Milestones in SOCIAL SECURITY

During the Great Depression, many elderly Americans had lost their life savings and were struggling to survive. The 1935 Social Security Act created a pension system as well as unemployment insurance for workers who had lost their jobs. Financed through a payroll tax on employers and workers, Social Security is one of the country's most important legislative achievements.

1935–1950 The Social Security program was expanded in 1939 to pay benefits to the widows and young children of deceased workers. In 1950, amendments to the Social Security Act increased benefit payments and extended coverage to more workers. As a result, almost all working Americans now contribute to Social Security and are eligible for benefits.

◄ Since 1940, senior citizens have depended on their monthly Social Security retirement checks.

Social Security benefits ► helped widows feed their children.

Differentiated Instruction Solutions for All Learners

L4 Advanced Readers L4 Gifted and Talented Students

Beginning during the Great Depression, more than a dozen large dams were built to harness the power of the Columbia River for hydroelectricity. Have students draw a map of the Columbia River, locating the major dams built along it between the 1930s and 1950s. The availability of large amounts of cheap electricity contributed to the growth of towns and industries—especially the energy-intensive aluminum industry—in the Pacific Northwest. Then, ask students to draw on the map major towns and industrial and government facilities that grew up along the Columbia because of the availability of cheap energy.

Have students prepare a short oral presentation in which they display the map and explain how federal programs of the New Deal contributed to development in this region.

promoting the benefits of electricity. Guthrie's song, "Roll on, Columbia," pays tribute to the projects that harnessed the power of the Columbia River.

Monitor Progress

As students fill in their tables, circulate to make sure that they understand the programs that were part of the second New Deal and the problems each was meant to address. For a completed version of the table, see Note Taking Transparencies, **B-108**.

Primary Source

"Your power is turning our darkness to dawn,
And on up the river is the Grand Coulee Dam,
The Mightiest thing ever built by a man,
To run the great factories and water the land."

—Woody Guthrie, "Roll On, Columbia," 1941

✔ **Checkpoint** Why did the onset of the depression make it essential to have some form of Social Security?

▲ Medicaid makes healthcare more available to low-income families.

1950–1970 During the 1950s and 1960s, Social Security expanded to provide benefits to people with disabilities. In 1965, two new Social Security programs, Medicare and Medicaid, were introduced. Medicare is a health-insurance program for Americans age 65 and older, and Medicaid provides health insurance to needy persons of any age.

The Elderly and Poverty, 1940–2000

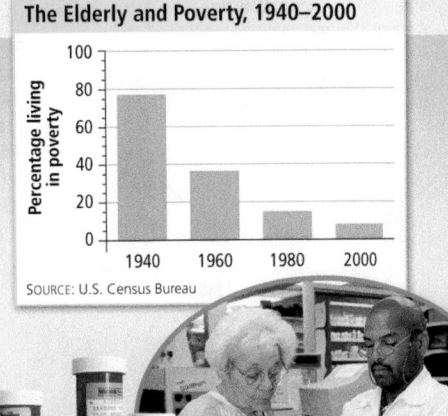

SOURCE: U.S. Census Bureau

1970–Today The Supplemental Social Security Income (SSI) program, begun in 1974, provides monthly payments to the needy elderly and to people who are blind or who have a disability. The Medicare Prescription Drug program, passed in 2003, provides Medicare recipients with voluntary prescription-drug coverage and discounts. President George W. Bush's proposal to allow younger workers to invest Social Security tax money in personal retirement accounts was rejected by the public in 2005.

▼ Supplemental Security Income benefits help people who are blind.

The Medicare Prescription ▶ Drug program helps seniors manage rising drug costs.

Why It Matters

For more than 70 years, Social Security has provided basic economic security to millions of Americans. Social Security programs act as a safety net for senior citizens, the poor, and others in financial need. Popular support for Social Security continues, although concern mounts over the program's long-term funding.

Thinking Critically

Describe four different kinds of benefits that the Social Security system provides today.

History *Interactive*

For: More about Social Security
www.pearsonschool.com/ushist

Differentiated Instruction Solutions for All Learners

L1 Special Needs Students **L2 English Language Learners** **L2 Less Proficient Readers**

Have students reread the heading "Extending Social and Economic Reform." Remind students that the term *economic* refers to business and finance, while *social* refers to all interactions between people. Have partners make a chart and list in one column the economic changes brought about by the New Deal and

in a second column the social changes that resulted. Review the charts as a class. Then, lead a class discussion concerning how these two terms can influence each other. Discuss how economic changes can cause social changes, and vice versa.

Answers

✔ When the Great Depression hit, there was no pension system for the elderly. Many elderly people lost their homes and savings and lived in poverty. The Social Security system provides a safety net for the elderly as well as for people who are disabled, injured on the job, or unemployed.

Thinking Critically

Any four of the following: a monthly check to retired senior citizens; money to widows and children of deceased workers; benefits to the blind; benefits that help seniors pay for medications; benefits for the disabled; healthcare benefits to low-income families

Labor Unions Find a New Energy

Instruct

- **Introduce: Key Terms** Have students find the key terms *collective bargaining* and *sit-down strike* (in bold) in the text. Discuss how *collective bargaining* and *sit-down strikes* affected the relationship between workers and employers during the Great Depression.

- **Teach** Ask **Why did FDR believe that strengthening the position of industrial workers was important?** *(He believed that raising their standard of living would help improve the whole economy.)* **How did the Wagner Act and the Fair Labor Standards Act strengthen workers in the 1930s?** *(The Wagner Act allowed workers to join unions and to bargain collectively with employers. The Fair Labor Standards Act established minimum wages and a maximum workweek, and outlawed child labor.)* Have students read the Primary Source quotation on the next page. Ask **Why did the autoworkers sit-down committee issue this statement?** *(It wanted to show that it would not use violence unless provoked. It also wanted to win public sympathy if the government used force to remove them.)*

- **Analyzing the Visuals** Direct students to the photo of striking autoworkers on this page. Ask **Why do these workers want to present a peaceful image of the strike?** *(Example: to get public support and to persuade their employer to negotiate with them)*

Independent Practice

Organize the class into groups. Have each group write a script for an interview that a reporter might have had with workers in the sit-down strike. Tell students to consider why the workers were striking and what their goals and fears were.

Monitor Progress

As students write their scripts, circulate to make sure that they understand the opposing points of view of the striking autoworkers and the employers.

Answer

Caption The success of union strikes led to increased membership as workers gained better wages and working conditions.

Vocabulary Builder
upsurge–(UHP serj) *n.* a sudden, rapid increase

Sit-Down Strikes Lead to Union Gains

The success of the UAW's sit-down strike against General Motors led the U.S. Steel Company to recognize the steelworkers' union. *How do you think strikes affected union membership?*

Labor Union Membership, 1920–1960

SOURCE: *Historical Statistics of the United States*

Labor Unions Find a New Energy

Even before the Great Depression, most industrial workers labored long hours for little pay. Few belonged to labor unions. However, during the Great Depression, there was an <u>upsurge</u> in union activity. New unions enlisted millions of workers from the mining and automobile industries.

Granting New Rights to Workers Roosevelt believed that the success of the New Deal depended on raising the standard of living for American industrial workers. This, he believed, would improve the entire economy. The National Labor Relations Act was the most important piece of New Deal labor legislation. Called the **Wagner Act,** it recognized the right of employees to join labor unions and gave workers the right to **collective bargaining.** Collective bargaining meant that employers had to negotiate with unions about hours, wages, and other working conditions. The law created the National Labor Relations Board (NLRB) to look into workers' complaints.

The **Fair Labor Standards Act** of 1938 provided workers with additional rights. It established a minimum wage, initially at 25 cents per hour, and a maximum workweek of 44 hours. It also outlawed child labor. The minimum wage remains one of the New Deal's most controversial legacies. In the years ahead, the minimum wage would be gradually raised. Today, whenever a raise in the minimum wage is proposed, economists and political leaders debate the wisdom of such an increase.

Workers Use Their Newfound Rights The upsurge in union activity came at the same time as a bitter feud within the major labor federation, the American Federation of Labor (AFL). The AFL represented skilled workers—such as plumbers, carpenters, and electricians—who joined trade or craft unions. Few workers in the major industries belonged to the AFL, and the union made little effort to organize them.

Fed up with the AFL's reluctance to organize, John L. Lewis, the president of the United Mine Workers, and a number of other labor leaders established the **Congress of Industrial Organizations (CIO).** The workers targeted by the CIO-organizing campaigns tended to be lower paid and ethnically more diverse than those workers represented by the AFL.

Connect to Your World

Labor Unions The strength of labor unions increased in the 1930s under the New Deal. Union membership continued to climb throughout the 1940s and into the start of the 1960s, along with the clout of organized labor.

Since that time, membership in unions has dropped off considerably in the United States. Today, union workers represent between 12 and 13 percent of the American workforce—only about one third of the percentage of workers in the mid-1950s. Reasons include massive layoffs, plant closings, and the outsourcing of jobs in industries that have been heavily unionized.

Roosevelt's pro-union policies were meant to raise the wages and standard of living of industrial workers—whose higher earnings would then be used for consumer spending that would help the entire economy. Because union members have traditionally earned higher wages than unorganized industrial workers, the decline in union membership could have a negative effect on the economy as spending on consumer goods falls.

The Second New Deal

Program	Year	Effects
Social Security Act (SSA)	1935	Established a pension system and unemployment insurance; provided payments to workers injured on the job, the poor, and people with disabilities
Works Progress Administration (WPA)	1935	Employed millions of people on government projects ranging from highway construction to arts programs
Rural Electrification Administration (REA)	1935	Provided loans to electric companies to build power lines, bringing electricity to isolated rural areas
National Labor Relations Act (Wagner Act)	1935	Outlawed unfair labor practices; granted workers the right to organize unions and to bargain collectively; created the National Labor Relations Board
National Youth Administration (NYA)	1935	Trained and provided jobs and counseling for unemployed youth between the ages of 16 and 25
Banking Act of 1935	1935	Finalized the creation of the FDIC and made insurance for bank deposits permanent; created a board to regulate the nation's money supply and interest rates on loans
United States Housing Authority (USHA)	1937	Subsidized construction of low-cost public housing by providing federal loans
Fair Labor Standards Act	1938	Banned child labor, established a minimum hourly wage, and set the workweek at 44 hours
Food, Drug, and Cosmetic Act	1938	Prohibited the mislabeling of food, drugs, and cosmetics, and ensured the safety and purity of these products

This 1934 cartoon pokes fun at the many programs of FDR's New Deal. Critics mocked the abbreviated titles, or acronyms, of the New Deal programs as "alphabet soup." *Use the chart to identify five programs from the second New Deal that helped workers.*

In December 1936, members of the CIO's newly formed United Automobile Workers Union (UAW) staged a **sit-down strike,** occupying one of General Motors' most important plants in Flint, Michigan. In a sit-down strike, workers refuse to leave the workplace until a settlement is reached. When the police and state militia threatened to remove them by force, the workers informed Michigan governor Frank Murphy that they would not leave.

Primary Source "We fully expect that if a violent effort is made to oust us many of us will be killed and we take this means of making it known to our wives, to our children, to the people of the State of Michigan and the country, that if this result follows from the attempt to eject us, you are the one who must be held responsible for our deaths!"
—Auto workers sit-down committee, Flint, Michigan, January 1936

The strike lasted for 44 days until General Motors, then the largest company in the world, agreed to recognize the UAW. This union success led to others. By 1940, 9 million workers belonged to unions, twice the number of members in 1930. Just as important, union members gained better wages and working conditions.

✓ **Checkpoint** How did the New Deal affect trade unions?

Challenges to the New Deal

Franklin Roosevelt won an overwhelming victory in the presidential election of 1936. He received 61 percent of the vote, compared to just 37 percent for his Republican challenger, Alfred M. Landon. Roosevelt carried every state but Maine and Vermont. FDR entered his second term determined to challenge the group that he considered the main enemy of the New Deal—a Supreme Court that had struck down many of his programs.

- Have students analyze the political cartoon on this page and answer the questions in the text.

- Ask students to read the Primary Source quotation by Dorothy Thompson. Have them write a paragraph explaining whether they agree with Thompson and whether they would have supported or opposed FDR's plan to change the Supreme Court to help support the New Deal.

Monitor Progress

As students work on their paragraphs, circulate to ensure that they understand the reasons that FDR proposed his court-packing scheme and why many people opposed it.

The Supreme Court Opposes the New Deal A year before the 1936 election, the Supreme Court had overturned one of the key laws of Roosevelt's first hundred days. In the case of *Schechter Poultry* v. *United States,* the Supreme Court unanimously ruled that since the President has no power to regulate interstate commerce, the National Industrial Recovery Act was unconstitutional. One pro–New Deal newspaper captured the mood of many Democrats: "AMERICA STUNNED; ROOSEVELT'S TWO YEARS' WORK KILLED IN TWENTY MINUTES."

Not long afterward, the Court ruled a key part of the Agricultural Adjustment Act unconstitutional. Roosevelt charged that the Court had taken the nation back to "horse-and-buggy" days. He expected the Court to strike down other New Deal measures, limiting his ability to enact new reforms.

FDR Proposes "Packing" the Court On February 5, 1937, in a special address to Congress, FDR unveiled a plan that would dilute the power of the sitting Justices of the Supreme Court. He called for adding up to six new Justices to the nine-member Court. He justified his proposal by noting that the Constitution did not specify the number of judges on the Court. He added that many of the Justices were elderly and overworked. Critics, recognizing that Roosevelt's new appointees would most likely be New Deal supporters, called his plan **court packing.** They accused him of trying to increase presidential power and upsetting the delicate balance between the three branches of the federal government. Some critics urged Americans to speak out.

Primary Source "If the American people accept this last audacity of the President without letting out a yell to high heaven, they have ceased to be jealous of their liberties and are ripe for ruin."

—Dorothy Thompson, newspaper columnist, 1937

Given Roosevelt's enormous popularity, he might have convinced Congress to enact his plan but he did not have to because the Court began to turn his way. On March 29, 1937, the Court ruled 5 to 4 in favor of a minimum wage law. Two weeks later, again by a vote of 5 to 4, the Supreme Court upheld the constitutionality of the Wagner Act. In both cases, Justice Owen J. Roberts provided the deciding vote. Pundits called it the "switch in time to save nine," because Roberts had previously voted against several New Deal programs. Roberts's two votes in support of the New Deal removed FDR's main reason for packing the Court.

Shortly after this switch, Judge Willis Van Devanter, who had helped strike down several New Deal programs, resigned from the Court. This enabled FDR to nominate a Justice friendlier to the New Deal. With more retirements, Roosevelt nominated a number of other new Justices, including Felix Frankfurter, one of his top advisers.

Indeed, 1937 marked a turning point in the history of the Court. For years to come, the Court more willingly accepted a larger role for the federal government. Yet the court-packing incident weakened FDR politically. Before the court-packing plan, FDR's popularity prevented critics from challenging him. Now that Roosevelt had lost momentum, critics felt free to take him on. And even though the Court did not strike down any more laws, after 1937 Roosevelt found the public much less willing to support further New Deal legislation.

THE INGENIOUS QUARTERBACK!

Analyzing Political Cartoons

The Ingenious Quarterback! This 1937 cartoon makes fun of FDR's court-packing plan.
1. Why did the cartoonist make FDR the quarterback and Congress the referee?
2. What is the cartoonist's message?

History Background

Schechter Poultry* v. *United States The Supreme Court decision in this case struck down one of the most important pieces of New Deal legislation, the National Industrial Recovery Act (NIRA).

The case began in New York, with a lawsuit brought against a Brooklyn poultry slaughterhouse. The suit claimed the Schechter Company sold sick chickens, failed to pay workers the minimum wage (at least 50 cents per hour), and did not adhere to the maximum work hours rules (no more than 40 hours per week). These regulations were mandated by the NIRA's

Live Poultry Code. The Court declared the NIRA unconstitutional on several grounds, ruling that the federal government could regulate interstate commerce but could not set rules for a business operating within a state. In addition, the power to make such rules for industry belonged to Congress and could not be delegated to the President.

The Court then struck down other New Deal legislation, causing FDR to worry that the Court would ultimately revoke his whole New Deal program. "Court packing" became his solution.

Answers

Analyzing Political Cartoons

1. because FDR was taking the lead in trying to remake the Court and persuade Congress to change the rules of the game in terms of the number of members of the Court

2. The cartoon shows the way that FDR was plotting to bring in additional pro-New Deal justices without removing the present justices from the Court, with the goal of ending the power of the present Court to wreck the New Deal.

A New Downturn Spurs Conservative Gains The turmoil over the Supreme Court had barely faded when the Roosevelt administration faced another crisis. During 1935 and 1936, economic conditions had begun to improve. Unemployment had fallen 10 percent in four years. With the economy doing better, FDR cut back on federal spending in order to reduce the rising deficit. But he miscalculated.

While Roosevelt reduced federal spending, the Federal Reserve Board raised interest rates, making it more difficult for businesses to expand and for consumers to borrow to buy new goods. Suddenly, the economy was in another tailspin. Unemployment soared to more than 20 percent. Nearly all of the gains in employment and production were wiped out.

Largely because of the downturn, the Democrats suffered a setback in the 1938 congressional elections. Republicans picked up 7 Senate and 75 House seats. Although Democrats still maintained a majority in both houses of Congress, Roosevelt's power base was shaken because many southern Democrats were lukewarm supporters of the New Deal. Needing their support for his foreign policies, FDR chose not to try to force more reforms through Congress.

✔ **Checkpoint** What setbacks did Roosevelt face during his second term as President?

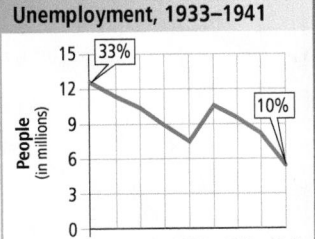

Unemployment, 1933–1941

SOURCE: *Historical Statistics of the United States*

Millions Look for Jobs
While New Deal programs employed many Americans, millions of others continued to search for work. *What happened to the unemployment rate in 1937?*

Assess Progress ⓛ③
- Have students complete the Section Assessment.
- Administer the Section Quiz. Teaching Resources, **p. 25**
- To further assess student understanding, use Progress Monitoring Transparencies, **104**.

Reteach
If students need more instruction, have them read the section summary.

Reading and Note ⓛ③
Taking Study Guide

Adapted Reading and ⓛ① ⓛ②
Note Taking Study Guide

Spanish Reading and ⓛ②
Note Taking Study Guide

Extend ⓛ④
Have students write four newspaper headlines that summarize the major New Deal programs.

SECTION
2 Assessment

Progress Monitoring Online
For: Self-test with vocabulary practice
www.pearsonschool.com/ushist

Comprehension
1. **Terms** For each act or New Deal agency below, explain how it eased conditions during the depression.
   - WPA
   - Social Security Act
   - Wagner Act
   - Fair Labor Standards Act

2. **NoteTaking Reading Skill: Connect Ideas** Use your table to answer the Section Focus Question: What major issues did the second New Deal address?

Writing About History
3. **Quick Write: Compare and Contrast** In order to synthesize, you need to compare and contrast different sources. List some emotions expressed by the photos on the first and last pages of this section. Do these images convey the same idea as the graph above? Explain in one or two sentences.

Critical Thinking
4. **Identify Central Issues** What were the most important reforms of the Second New Deal?

5. **Make Comparisons** Why did American labor make greater progress during the 1930s than during the prosperous 1920s?

6. **Demonstrate Reasoned Judgment** Do you think that FDR's court-packing plan was justified? Explain your answer.

Answers

✔ The Supreme Court ruled that certain key provisions of the New Deal were unconstitutional. FDR lost political support when he proposed expanding the Court to help himself politically. Also, an economic downturn in his second term cost the Democrats seats in Congress.

Caption After a steady decline for several years, the unemployment rate began to climb again in 1937.

Section 2 Assessment

1. Statements should demonstrate students' understanding of each term.

2. The Second New Deal addressed problems of the elderly, the poor, and the unemployed. It created new public-works projects, helped farmers, and enacted legislation to protect workers' rights.

3. Responses should demonstrate students' ability to both analyze the graph and interpret the photos.

4. Samples: the Social Security system for providing pensions for the first time to the elderly and guaranteeing an income for the disabled, the unemployed, and those injured at work; the Fair Labor Standards Act and Wagner Act for giving more power to workers to improve their wages and working conditions

5. Several pieces of New Deal legislation strengthened unions, mandated minimum wages, limited normal work hours,

and outlawed child labor. In the 1920s, most industrial workers worked long hours for low pay and did not benefit from union membership.

6. Accept either point of view. Some students will think FDR wanted to protect the New Deal. Others will think he wanted to increase his presidential powers.

For additional assessment, have students access **Progress Monitoring Online** at **www.pearsonschool.com/ushist**.

Objectives

As you teach this section, keep students focused on the following objectives to help them answer the Section Focus Question and master core content.

- Describe how the New Deal affected different groups in American society.
- Analyze how the New Deal changed the shape of American party politics.
- Discuss the impact of Franklin D. Roosevelt on the presidency.

Prepare to Read

Background Knowledge L3

Tell students that the New Deal affected America in the 1930s and still affects the nation today.

Set a Purpose L3

- **WITNESS HISTORY** Read the selection aloud.

  Ask **How did Eleanor Roosevelt help support FDR's administration?** *(She traveled the United States, keeping FDR informed about what people needed and expected of him.)* **How did Eleanor Roosevelt's work affect FDR's popularity and programs?** *(Many Americans appreciated Eleanor Roosevelt's efforts to help ordinary people, so her popularity helped gain support for him and his programs.)*

- **Focus** Point out the Section Focus Question, and write it on the board. Tell students to refer to this question as they read. *(Answer appears with Section 3 Assessment answers.)*

- **Preview** Have students preview the Section Objectives and the list of Terms and People.

- **NoteTaking** Using the Guided Questioning strategy (TE, p. T20), have students read this section. As they read, have students identify the effects of the New Deal. Reading and Note Taking Study Guide

▲ Eleanor Roosevelt serves food to unemployed women and their children.

WITNESS HISTORY

The Caring First Lady

Eleanor Roosevelt played a crucial role in the New Deal. She traveled to places FDR could not, advised her husband, and served as an inspiration to millions of Americans. Mrs. Roosevelt also corresponded with thousands of citizens. The following letter reflects the affection that many citizens felt for the first lady.

❝Ridley Park, Pennsylvania
 Dear Mrs. Roosevelt:
. . . Just to look at your picture and that of our President seems to me like looking at the picture of a saint. So when you answered my letter and promised to have some one help me it only proved that you are our own Mrs. Roosevelt. I have told everyone what you have done for me. I want them to know you are not too busy to answer our letters and give us what help and advice you can. You hold the highest place any woman can hold still you are not to[o] proud to befriend the poor. . . . Thank you and God bless you both.❞
—Letter to Eleanor Roosevelt, September 1, 1935

Effects of the New Deal

Objectives

- Describe how the New Deal affected different groups in American society.
- Analyze how the New Deal changed the shape of American party politics.
- Discuss the impact of Franklin D. Roosevelt on the presidency.

Terms and People

Black Cabinet	New Deal coalition
Mary McLeod Bethune	welfare state
Indian New Deal	

NoteTaking

Reading Skill: Identify Main Ideas As you read, identify the lasting effects of the New Deal upon American society.

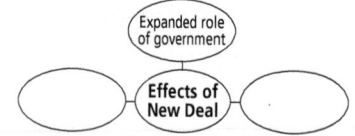

Expanded role of government

Effects of New Deal

Why It Matters The New Deal provided desperately needed relief from the depression and enacted reforms that guarded against economic catastrophe. It did not end the depression. World War II, with its massive military spending, would do that. Yet, the New Deal mattered enormously because it brought fundamental changes to the nation. It changed the role of the federal government in the economy, the power of the presidency, and the relationship of the American people to their government. **Section Focus Question: How did the New Deal change the social, economic, and political landscape of the United States for future generations?**

Women Help Lead the New Deal

The New Deal provided some women with the opportunity to increase their political influence and to promote women's rights. Foremost among them was Eleanor Roosevelt, who transformed the office of First Lady from a largely ceremonial role to a position of action and deep involvement in the political process. Representing the President, she toured the nation. She visited farms and Indian reservations and traveled deep into a coal mine. She helped FDR on his campaigns and offered advice on policy issues. In her newspaper column, "My Day," she called on Americans to live up to the goal of equal justice for all.

Vocabulary Builder

Use the information below and the following resource to teach students the high-use words from this section. Teaching Resources, Vocabulary Builder, p. 11

High-Use Words	Definitions and Sample Sentences
gender	*n.* a person's sex Before 1920, the absence of women's suffrage was one kind of **gender** discrimination.
ethnic	*adj.* relating to groups of people with a common national, racial, religious, or cultural heritage Because of immigration, the people of the United States belong to many **ethnic** groups.

"Eleanor Roosevelt is the First Lady of Main Street," explained magazine writer Margaret Marshall. "She occupies the highest social position in the land. Yet she makes friends on a plane or a train even as you and I." Mrs. Roosevelt's causes included advancing public health and education, promoting the arts in rural areas, and even addressing flood control. She exhibited boundless energy, traveling more than 60,000 miles in two years.

Molly Dewson, head of the Women's Division of the Democratic Party, observed that Eleanor Roosevelt provided women with an unprecedented access to the President. "When I wanted help on some definite point, Mrs. Roosevelt gave [me] the opportunity to sit by the President at dinner and the matter was settled before we finished our soup."

The Roosevelt Administration included the first female Cabinet member, Secretary of Labor Frances Perkins. She played a leading role in establishing Social Security. Perkins also helped win approval of the Fair Labor Standards Act, which ended child labor and established a minimum wage.

However, the New Deal did not fight to end gender discrimination in the workplace. Indeed, some historians have argued that a number of New Deal programs reinforced traditional <u>gender</u> differences. The WPA and other relief programs employed women but made a much greater effort to provide work to men first. For example, women were not eligible to work for the CCC. However, the increased homeownership and insured savings accounts brought by the New Deal were of special benefit to the widows of men who were covered.

Vocabulary Builder
<u>gender</u>–(JEHN der) *n.* a person's sex

✓ **Checkpoint** What impact did the New Deal have on women?

African Americans Make Advances and Face Challenges

When the depression hit, African American workers were often the first to lose their jobs. By 1934, the unemployment rate for African Americans was almost 50 percent, more than twice the national average. Eleanor Roosevelt and others urged the President to improve the situation of African Americans.

As the New Deal progressed, Eleanor Roosevelt increasingly used her position to protest against racial discrimination. At a meeting held by the Southern Conference on Human Welfare, a biracial group that sought to promote racial reforms, the first lady sat with the black delegates—a daring move in segregated Birmingham, Alabama. When a white police officer told her that she was violating local segregation laws, Mrs. Roosevelt moved her chair to the space between the black and white sides. She then delivered a rousing and provocative keynote address in favor of racial reform.

Primary Source "We are the leading democracy of the world and as such must prove to the world that democracy is possible and capable of living up to the principles upon which it was founded. The eyes of the world are upon us, and often we find they are not too friendly eyes."
—Eleanor Roosevelt, November 22, 1938

HISTORY MAKERS

Frances Perkins (1882–1965)
After graduating from college, Frances Perkins earned her master's degree in economics. From 1912, until being named Secretary of Labor, she held various jobs in New York State government. She was a strong voice for consumers and workers, especially working women and children.

Mary McLeod Bethune (1875–1955)
Mary McLeod Bethune was a teacher who worked to improve educational opportunities for African Americans. Bethune served as FDR's special adviser on minority affairs. As the director of Negro Affairs of the National Youth Administration, Bethune was the first black woman to head a federal agency.

Instruct

- **Introduce: Key Term** Have students locate the key term *Black Cabinet* in the text and explain its meaning. Ask them what influence a *Black Cabinet* might have had on policy.

- **Teach** Ask **What did the Black Cabinet do?** *(Its members advised the President on issues that related to African Americans.)* **Was the Black Cabinet effective in influencing Roosevelt on issues that were important to African Americans?** *(It had access to the President and influence on some issues. However, Roosevelt went against the advice of the Black Cabinet and did not back anti-lynching legislation for fear of losing support in the South.)*

- **Analyzing the Visuals** Have students look at the bar graph on the next page. Ask **Why did African American voting patterns change between 1932 and 1940?** *(African Americans switched from voting primarily Republican to voting primarily Democratic largely because of support for FDR and the New Deal.)*

Independent Practice

Have students continue to fill in the concept web from the beginning of the section, describing the lasting effects of the New Deal on American society.

Monitor Progress

Reread the title of this section. To monitor student's understanding, instruct them to summarize the advances made by African Americans during the New Deal. Make sure that students understand that there were setbacks as well.

Answers

✓ The New Deal did not greatly reduce racial injustice in the United States. For example, FDR refused to support anti-lynching legislation for fear of losing support for the New Deal in the South; and some New Deal programs, such as the WPA, paid African Americans less than they paid white workers.

Caption Part of this program provided funding for the construction of new hospitals.

The President invited many African American leaders to advise him. These unofficial advisers became known as the **Black Cabinet.** They included Robert Weaver and William Hastie, Harvard University graduates who rose to high positions within the Department of the Interior. Hastie later became a federal judge, and Weaver was the first African American Cabinet member.

Mary McLeod Bethune was another member of the Black Cabinet. The founder of what came to be known as Bethune Cookman College, she was a powerful champion of racial equality. In her view, the New Deal had created a "new day" for African Americans. She noted that African Americans gained unprecedented access to the White House and positions within the government during Roosevelt's presidency.

Nevertheless, Roosevelt did not always follow the advice of his Black Cabinet. Racial discrimination and injustice continued to plague African Americans. When the NAACP launched an energetic campaign in favor of a federal antilynching law, the President refused to support it. FDR told black leaders that he could not support an antilynching law, because if he did, southern Democrats "would block every bill I ask Congress to pass." Hence, no civil rights reforms became law during the 1930s.

Several New Deal measures also unintentionally hurt African Americans. Federal payments to farmers to produce fewer crops led white landowners to evict unneeded black sharecroppers from their farms. Even though they benefited from the WPA and other relief measures, African Americans often did not receive equal wages. Social Security and the Fair Labor Standards Act exempted domestic workers and farm laborers, two occupations in which African Americans were employed in great numbers.

✓ **Checkpoint** How did the New Deal affect African Americans?

Native Americans Benefit From Building Projects
Navajo medicine men attend the opening of a new hospital in Fort Defiance, Arizona, in 1938. *How was this project part of the Indian New Deal?*

The New Deal Affects Native Americans

Attempting to improve the lives of Native Americans, the Roosevelt administration made major changes in long-standing policies. The 1887 Dawes Act had divided tribal lands into smaller plots. By the early 1930s, it was clear that the

act had worsened the condition of the people it was designed to help. Of the original 138 million acres American Indians had owned in 1887, only 48 million remained in American Indian hands, and much of it was too arid to farm. John Collier, the New Deal's Commissioner of Indian Affairs, warned that the Dawes Act was resulting in "total landlessness for the Indians."

To prevent further loss of land and improve living conditions for Native Americans, Collier developed the **Indian New Deal,** a program that gave Indians economic assistance and greater control over their own affairs. Collier got funding from New Deal agencies for the construction of new schools and hospitals and to create an Indian Civilian Conservation Corps. In addition, the Bureau of Indian Affairs, in a reversal of previous policies, encouraged the practice of Indian religions, native languages, and traditional customs. Collier also convinced Congress to pass the Indian Reorganization Act of 1934, considered the centerpiece of the Indian New Deal. This law restored tribal control over Native American land.

Although it did not immediately improve their standard of living, the Indian Reorganization Act gave Native Americans greater control over their destiny. But some New Deal measures actually hurt Native Americans. For example, federal authorities determined that large herds of sheep tended by the Navajos were causing soil erosion on the Colorado Plateau. As a result, the federal government enacted a Navajo Livestock Reduction program, which mandated that the Navajo sell or kill thousands of sheep. The Navajo deeply resented this act. They did not believe that their sheep threatened the soil and they did not trust the motives of government agents.

✓ **Checkpoint** In what ways did the New Deal alter the U.S. policies toward Native Americans?

The New Deal Creates a New Political Coalition

By the time he died in 1945, Roosevelt had been elected to four terms as President. His legendary political skills had united an unlikely group of Americans into a strong political force called the **New Deal coalition.** This coalition brought together southern whites, northern blue-collar workers—especially those with immigrant roots—poor midwestern farmers, and African Americans.

African American voting patterns show the importance of the New Deal coalition. Before the New Deal, most African Americans voted Republican, the party of Abraham Lincoln. Responding to the efforts of Franklin and Eleanor Roosevelt, African Americans began to vote Democratic during the 1930s. This trend was strongest in the West and the North. For example, in 1934, Arthur W. Mitchell, an African American Democrat, defeated Oscar De Priest, an African American Republican, to represent the largely black south side of Chicago. Mitchell became the first African American Democrat elected to Congress.

The New Deal coalition gave the Democratic Party a sizable majority in both houses of Congress. Before FDR's election, the Democrats had been the minority party in the House of Representatives for all but eight years since 1895. But from 1932 to 1995, the Democrats controlled the majority of seats in the House of Representatives for all but four years. The coalition that elected Roosevelt in 1932 went on to secure the White House for the Democrats in six of the next eight presidential elections.

African Americans Join New Deal Coalition
In Atlanta, African Americans register to vote in a Democratic primary election. *What percentage of African American voters voted Democratic in 1932? What was the percentage in 2004?*

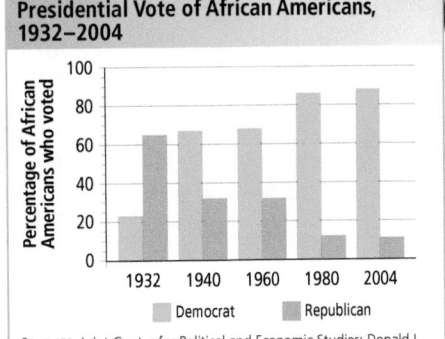

Presidential Vote of African Americans, 1932–2004

Percentage of African Americans who voted (vertical axis: 0, 20, 40, 60, 80, 100)

Years: 1932, 1940, 1960, 1980, 2004

Legend: ☐ Democrat ☐ Republican

SOURCES: Joint Center for Political and Economic Studies; Donald L. Grant, *The Way It Was in the South: The Black Experience in Georgia;* Sean J. Savage, *Roosevelt: The Party Leader, 1932–1945;* CNN.com

History Background

The Dawes Act The Dawes Act, the brainchild of Rep. Henry Dawes of Massachusetts, was passed in 1887. Its goal was to break up Native American groups and force Native American people to assimilate into white American culture.

Rep. Dawes laid out his goals plainly when he said that he was hopeful the law would have the effect of making the Native Americans ". . . be civilized . . . [and] wear civilized clothes . . . cultivate the ground, live in houses, ride in Studebaker [chuck] wagons, send children to school, drink whiskey [and] own property."

The Act provided for 160 acres of farmland or 320 acres of pasture land for grazing for each head of an Indian household. The Native Americans had to give up any remaining land, and it was offered to white settlers. Within a couple of decades of the passage of the Dawes Act, much of the land that had belonged to Native Americans was gone.

The Dawes Act remained a main feature of the relationship between the federal government and Native American nations until the 1930s, when John Collier, as head of the Bureau of Indian Affairs, changed the policy.

The New Deal Creates a New Political Coalition

Instruct

- **Introduce** Draw students' attention to the blue heading on the previous page. Ask students to define the word *coalition*, if they can. (*A unit formed from several individuals or groups that work together for a common goal.*)

- **Teach** Ask **Which groups formed the New Deal Coalition?** (*It included southern whites, northern blue collar workers, poor Midwestern farmers, and African Americans.*) **How did the New Deal coalition change the balance of power in Washington?** (*It gave the Democratic party large majorities in both houses of Congress, elected FDR to four terms in office, and kept the Democrats in power in both Congress and the White House for many decades.*)

- **Quick Activity** Have students read the Primary Source quotation on this page. Discuss why a New Deal program such as the CCC would bring people of different ethnic and racial groups together for the first time and how such a program might change prejudices about others.

Independent Practice

Have students work in groups using the Internet or library resources to research the demographic pattern of Democrats and Republicans to see whether the New Deal coalition groups still affect today's voting patterns. Have them present and discuss their findings.

Monitor Progress

To review the section, ask students to briefly explain what the New Deal coalition was and how it developed.

Answer

✔ Ethnic and social divisions decreased somewhat during the 1930s because of the New Deal. Programs such as the WPA and CCC brought people of various backgrounds together as co-workers for the first time, breaking down prejudices. Immigrants also felt more a part of mainstream America as the result of working in New Deal programs.

Vocabulary Builder
ethnic–(EHTH nĭhk) *adj.* relating to groups of people with a common national, racial, religious, or cultural heritage

Besides forging a powerful political coalition, Roosevelt and the New Deal helped to unify the nation. Social and ethnic divisions, so much a part of the 1920s, diminished significantly during the 1930s. Immigrant communities, in particular, gained a greater sense of belonging to the mainstream. Programs such as the CCC and WPA allowed individuals of varied backgrounds to get to know one another, breaking down regional and ethnic prejudices. As one CCC worker observed:

Primary Source "The Civilian Conservation Corps is a smaller melting pot within the big one. We are thrown together in such a way that we have to get acquainted whether or not we want to. . . . Different races and nationalities look each other in the face, work and eat together for the first time. And it is a safe bet, we think, that this process many times results in the elimination of traditional prejudices based on ignorance and misinformation."

—C. W. Kirkpatrick, CCC worker

✔ **Checkpoint** How did New Deal policies affect ethnic and social divisions?

The Role of Government Expands

New Deal programs greatly increased the size and scope of the federal government. "For the first time for many Americans," writes historian William Leuchtenburg, "the federal government became an institution that was directly experienced. More than the state and local governments, it came to be *the* government." Moreover, the government began to do things it had never done before, from withdrawing taxes directly from workers' paychecks to distributing benefits to the elderly.

Though the New Deal did not end the depression, it did help restore the American economy. It created the foundation for sustained and stable growth. According to Pulitzer Prize–winning historian David Kennedy, "the unparalleled economic vitality of the post-1940 decades was attributable to many factors. But the [economic expansion] . . . owed much to the New Deal."

Playing a Larger Role in the Economy With the New Deal, the federal government broke from the tradition of laissez faire, or leaving the economy alone, which had characterized most of American history. Now the federal government accepted responsibility for spurring economic growth, or pump priming. For the first time, the government had acted as an employer of the unemployed and a sponsor of work projects. FDR accepted the idea that the federal government had to do something to get the economy going again, and Democrats and many Republicans agreed.

FDR's rejection of laissez-faire policies led a number of New Deal critics to accuse him of promoting socialism. However, many New Deal measures actually strengthened capitalism and helped make possible the economic boom of the post–World War II era. The FDIC and SEC restored Americans' trust in banks and the stock market. The Federal Housing Authority (FHA) provided low-interest loans, increasing homeownership.

The New Deal affected millions of workers and their families. The Wagner Act boosted union membership, which continued to grow after World War II. Minimum wage increases improved the purchasing power of minorities and those at the bottom rung of the economic ladder. New Deal legislation created child labor laws, workers' compensation laws, and unemployment insurance, programs that had important and enduring impacts on the U.S. economy.

Differentiated Instruction **Solutions for All Learners**

L1 Special Needs Students   **L2 Less Proficient Readers**

To help students understand the extent of U.S. government growth during the Great Depression, have each student create a three-column chart summarizing the New Deal programs. Tell students to write the names of each New Deal program in the first column. In the second column, have students note the reason why each program was enacted.

Point out that programs designed to help businesses and the economy are economic programs. Also, explain that programs designed to give aid directly to people, such as Social Security, were social programs. In the third column, ask students to categorize each program as either economic or social.

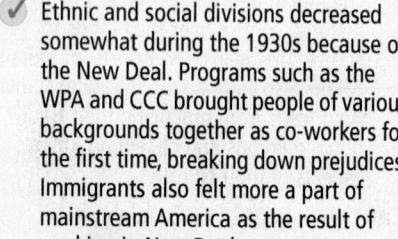

TRACK THE ISSUE

What is the proper balance between free enterprise and government regulation of the economy?

In theory, a free-enterprise system should function with little government interference. In practice, though, our government often plays a strong economic role. How much government regulation of the economy is appropriate? Use the timeline below to explore this enduring issue.

1890 Sherman Antitrust Act
Congress tries to curb the power of monopolies.

1906 Pure Food and Drug Act
Progressive law regulates the safety of food and medicine.

1913 Federal Reserve Act
Federal Reserve system is established to control the money supply.

1933 Agricultural Adjustment Act
New Deal law pays farmers to reduce production, causing higher crop prices and farm profits.

2001 Tax Cuts
Government lowers taxes in an effort to promote economic growth.

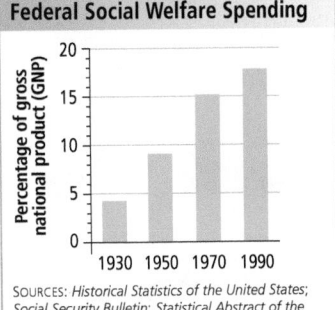

Federal Social Welfare Spending

Percentage of gross national product (GNP)

| 1930 | 1950 | 1970 | 1990 |

SOURCES: *Historical Statistics of the United States; Social Security Bulletin; Statistical Abstract of the United States*

Activists protest plans to privatize Social Security.

DEBATE THE ISSUE

Social Security's Effectiveness The government manages retirement accounts for millions of Americans through the Social Security system. But with the coming retirement of millions of baby boomers, some people believe that Social Security can no longer achieve its original goals.

"Well, the system is facing serious financial problems, but more than that it has become an increasingly bad deal for today's workers. Workers are paying 12 1/2 percent of their income into a system that is providing a poorer and poorer return. It's a system in which workers don't own their assets, have no legal rights to their benefits, don't control their money, and a system that penalizes groups like African Americans and working women."
—Michael Tanner, Cato Institute

"Social Security is one of the most successful government programs. It has consistently provided a safety net for seniors so that retirees are able to support themselves through their retirement and pay for food, housing, and medical costs. By helping to support the elderly and vulnerable among us, Social Security provides Americans with the guarantee of security for life."
—Center for American Progress

? TRANSFER Activities

1. **Compare** Do you think that today's Center for American Progress would support or oppose New Deal laws like the AAA?
2. **Analyze Costs and Benefits** Compare the data on this page to the data in the Section 2 Social Security feature. Do you think that the costs of Social Security outweigh the benefits?
3. **Transfer** Use the following Web site to see a video, try a WebQuest, and write in your journal. www.pearsonschool.com/ushist

History Background

Agricultural Adjustment Act When FDR took office, many farmers were in desperate circumstances. The Agricultural Adjustment Act (AAA), passed in May 1933, had the goal of raising farm income by increasing the value of dairy products, hogs, and crops such as corn, wheat, cotton, and rice. Farmers were paid government subsidies to take certain amounts of their cropland out of production. The smaller supply of crops would then cause their prices to rise, thus gradually increasing farm incomes. In the case of hog farmers, the aim was the same—to decrease the supply. Therefore, hog farmers were paid to send thousands of hogs to slaughter. Some people complained that the program caused a shameful waste of food. But the government made the pork available to food programs. The AAA did cause prices to rise. However, the Supreme Court declared it unconstitutional in 1936. The subsequent passage of the Soil Conservation Act made up somewhat for the loss of the original AAA. Under this law, the federal government paid farmers to grow crops that conserved the soil. A slightly revised version of the AAA was passed two years later.

Objectives

- Analyze the tension between government regulation and free enterprise in the U.S. economy.
- Evaluate the effectiveness of Social Security now and in the future.

Background Knowledge

Have students recall how the role of the federal government changed under the New Deal. (*The federal government took a much more active and central role in the U.S. economy and the regulation of business and financial institutions.*)

Instruct

Have students look at the timeline that shows several federal regulations. Discuss the reason for each regulation and whether or not it was helpful to the public. Ask **Is the trend of the federal government toward more or less regulations?** (*toward more*)

Monitor Progress

- Have students complete the American Issues Journal worksheet, *Government's Role in the Economy.* Check students' work to make sure that they grasp the aspects of the issue. Teaching Resources, **pp. 15–18**

- Remind students to complete their American Issues Journal worksheets. Review their work for accuracy. Reading and Note Taking Study Guide

Answers

Transfer Activities

1. Today's Center for American Progress would probably support New Deal laws such as the AAA because they provide a safety net for Americans and help secure a decent standard of living.

2. Possible response: Yes; although the United States is spending more on social welfare, fewer elderly Americans are living in poverty.

3. Students should conduct library or Internet research to learn more about the government's role in the economy. For more information about the government's economic role, have students access **www.pearsonschool.com/ushist.**

The Role of Government Expands (L3)

Instruct

- **Introduce** Remind students that the New Deal expanded the role of government in the lives of ordinary Americans. Ask them to recall one way in which the New Deal did this. Write a list of reasons on the board as students discuss.

- **Teach** Using the Idea Wave strategy (TE, p. T22), have students discuss how the New Deal expanded the role of the federal government. Ask **How did the New Deal increase the role of government in the lives of American workers?** *(Sample responses: It made the government a large-scale employer and sponsor of public works projects. It helped the growth of unions, established minimum wage and maximum work-hour laws, eliminated child labor, and began payments to people who were unemployed.)* **How did the government increase its connection to American farmers in the New Deal era?** *(Government projects built dams that provided electricity in rural areas, reduced flooding, and provided water for irrigation. The government also provided subsidies to farmers.* **What is the welfare state?** *(a government that assumes responsibility for the welfare of its citizens)* **Why was this a radical change for the United States?** *(Until the New Deal era, the federal government had not taken direct responsibility for the day-to-day welfare of citizens. Help generally came from state and local governments or from private organizations.)*

Answer

Thinking Critically

Sample response: New PWA and WPA construction projects such as schools, libraries, and hospitals would bring new jobs to the communities in which these buildings had been built. Infrastructure improvements such as roads, bridges, and power plants would help both businesses and individuals.

The New Deal had a great impact on rural Americans. Regional public-works projects, such as the TVA and Bonneville Dam, reduced flooding and provided water for irrigation. Along with the Rural Electrification Administration, these dams brought electricity to farmers in the Southeast and the Northwest. Rose Dudley Scearce of Shelby, Kentucky, recalled what the REA meant to her farm family:

Primary Source "The first benefit we received from the REA was light, and aren't lights grand? My little boy expressed my sentiments when he said, 'Mother, I didn't realize how dark our house was until we got electric lights.' . . . Like the rest of the people, we changed our storage-battery radio into an electric radio. . . . Next we bought an electric refrigerator. . . . The next benefit we received from the current was our electric stove. . . . Now with a vacuum cleaner, I can even dust the furniture before I clean the carpet, the carpet gets clean, and I stay in good humor."
—Rose Dudley Scearce, "What the REA Service Means to Our Farm House"

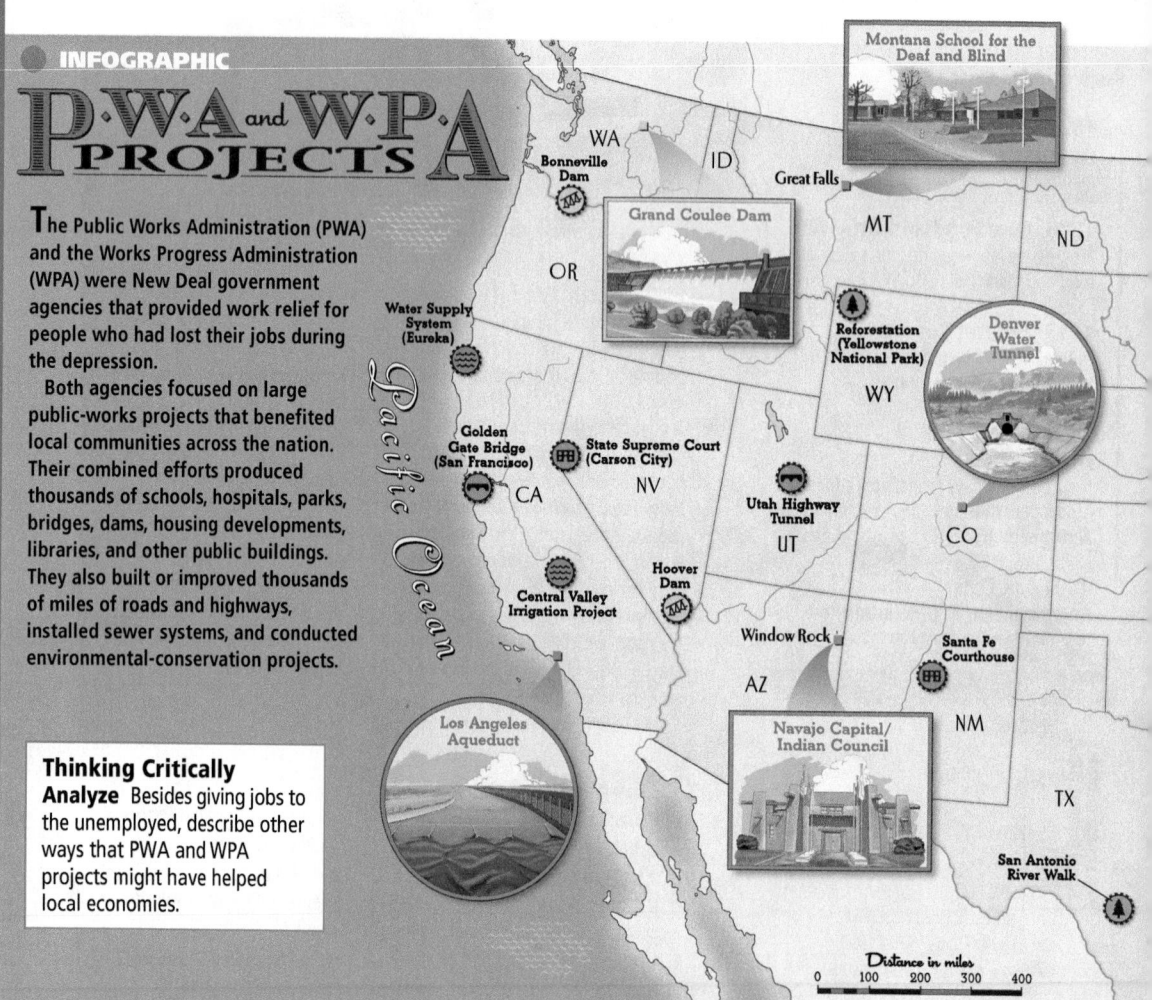

INFOGRAPHIC

P·W·A and W·P·A PROJECTS

The Public Works Administration (PWA) and the Works Progress Administration (WPA) were New Deal government agencies that provided work relief for people who had lost their jobs during the depression.

Both agencies focused on large public-works projects that benefited local communities across the nation. Their combined efforts produced thousands of schools, hospitals, parks, bridges, dams, housing developments, libraries, and other public buildings. They also built or improved thousands of miles of roads and highways, installed sewer systems, and conducted environmental-conservation projects.

Thinking Critically
Analyze Besides giving jobs to the unemployed, describe other ways that PWA and WPA projects might have helped local economies.

Map labels: Montana School for the Deaf and Blind; Bonneville Dam; Grand Coulee Dam; Great Falls; WA; ID; MT; ND; OR; Reforestation (Yellowstone National Park); Denver Water Tunnel; WY; Water Supply System (Eureka); Golden Gate Bridge (San Francisco); State Supreme Court (Carson City); CA; NV; Utah Highway Tunnel; UT; CO; Central Valley Irrigation Project; Hoover Dam; Window Rock; Santa Fe Courthouse; AZ; Navajo Capital/Indian Council; NM; Los Angeles Aqueduct; TX; San Antonio River Walk; Pacific Ocean; Distance in miles 0 100 200 300 400

Differentiated Instruction — Solutions for All Learners

(L1) Special Needs Students (L2) English Language Learners (L2) Less Proficient Readers

Have students look at the map on these pages. Ask them to work in pairs and list the types of projects shown on the map. Ask **What type of project is most common on the map?** *(structures such as government buildings, museums, public housing, airports)* **What other type of public works project was common?** *(dams, bridges, forest projects)* Have students discuss reasons why these types of projects were common. *(They were expensive projects that local governments could not afford; they would benefit many people; and they would employ many people for a long time.)*

Creating a Welfare State "We are going to make a country in which no one is left out," Franklin Roosevelt once told Frances Perkins. The many programs he enacted to realize this goal led to the rise of a **welfare state** in the United States, a government that assumes responsibility for providing for the welfare of children and the poor, elderly, sick, disabled, and unemployed.

The creation of the American welfare state was a major change in government policy. With the exception of military veterans, most Americans had never received any direct benefits from the federal government. State and local governments, private charities, and families had long served as the safety net for needy Americans. True, the New Deal did not achieve FDR's goal of "a country in which no one is left out," because it exempted many Americans from Social Security and other programs. Still, the New Deal established the principle that the federal government was responsible for the welfare of all Americans. In the latter half of the twentieth century, the reach of government programs would grow greatly.

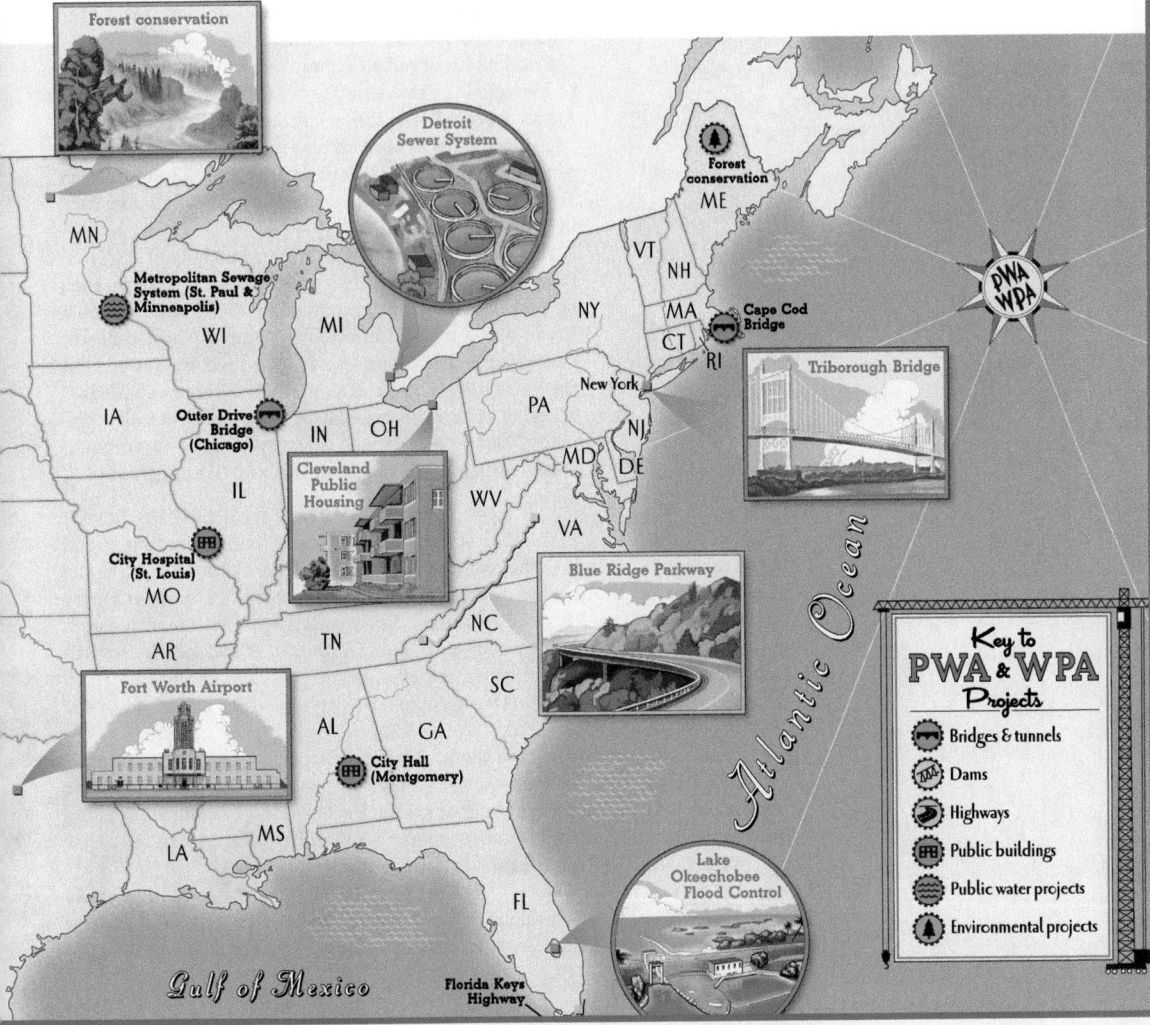

Key to PWA & WPA Projects

- Bridges & tunnels
- Dams
- Highways
- Public buildings
- Public water projects
- Environmental projects

- Have students study the Infographic on this spread. Discuss the benefits of PWA and WPA projects. Then, ask **How did New Deal programs help the environment?** *(The CCC completed reforestation projects; some programs focused on soil conservation; land was set aside for several new national parks.)* **Did New Deal programs have any negative effects on the environment?** *(Yes; the large dams built in the West displaced some people and upset the natural habitats of some aquatic life.)* **How did FDR change the nature of the presidency?** *(With the growth in power of the federal government, the power of the presidency also increased. Some called it the imperial presidency because they said FDR had powers similar to those of past rulers of empires.)* **What law was passed to limit presidential power after Roosevelt's death?** *(The Twenty-second Amendment to the U.S. Constitution, which limited Presidents to two consecutive terms.)* **Why did some people think this law was needed?** *(Roosevelt had served four terms, unlike Presidents before him who had served just two. Some people believed that a President who stayed in office too long would amass too much power.)*

- **Quick Activity** Display Color Transparency: *The New Deal Provides Jobs.* Have students think about the values of a government that includes funding for art in a nationwide relief program. Ask why so much of the art was displayed in public areas such as post offices. Color Transparencies **A-99**

- Have students analyze the cause-and-effect chart on this page and answer the question that accompanies it. Then, ask students to write paragraphs that describe current events that illustrate how the New Deal still affects the United States today.

- Ask students to suppose they are members of the Senate at the time when the Twenty-second Amendment to the Constitution is being considered. Each of them must make a brief speech—no more than one minute long—either supporting or opposing the passage of the amendment. Then, after hearing the speech of each "senator," have the class vote on whether or not to approve the amendment.

Monitor Progress

To confirm students' understanding, have them briefly summarize the way that Roosevelt changed the presidency.

Cause and Effect

Causes

- Stock market crash
- Failure of farms and businesses
- Sharp decline in prices and production
- Failure of banks
- Massive unemployment and low wages
- Homelessness and Hoovervilles
- Drought, crop failures, and Dust Bowl

The New Deal

Effects

- Millions employed in new government programs
- Banking system is stabilized
- Regulated stock market restores confidence
- Social-insurance programs aid elderly and poor
- Agricultural subsidies help farmers
- Government takes more active role in economy

Connections to Today

- Social Security and other New Deal programs still exist
- Size and role of federal government still debated
- Costs and benefits of social welfare programs still debated

Analyze Cause and Effect The New Deal brought dramatic changes to the United States. *Identify one economic and one political effect of the New Deal.*

New Deal reforms provided the framework for the debate over the proper role of the federal government in the private lives of Americans. It energized liberals who would push for an even greater role for the federal government in future years. But it troubled conservatives who would argue that the expansion of the federal government limited American rights. Indeed, this very debate divides liberals and conservatives to this day.

Restoring the Environment Reared in New York State's beautiful Hudson River valley, Franklin Roosevelt had a great love of nature. As a child, FDR also loved outdoor sports and became an expert swimmer and sailor. A number of his New Deal programs, such as the CCC, aimed at restoring forests and preserving the environment. Other federal agencies started soil conservation efforts. Perhaps most visibly, New Dealers worked hard to end the Dust Bowl, a symbol of the degraded state of the land at the beginning of the depression.

Franklin Roosevelt also continued the conservation work of his cousin, President Theodore Roosevelt. Although funds were short, the government set aside about 12 million acres of land for new national parks, including Shenandoah National Park in Virginia, Kings Canyon National Park in California, and Olympic National Park in Washington State.

However, not all New Deal programs helped the environment. Several of the large public-works projects, such as the TVA and the string of dams along the Columbia River, had a mixed impact. The dams controlled floods, generated electric power, and provided irrigation, but they also upset the natural habitats of some aquatic life. Massive reservoirs created by these projects also displaced some people and destroyed some traditional Native American burial, hunting, and fishing grounds.

Changing the Nature of the Presidency In no area did FDR have a greater impact than on the office of the President itself. The expanding role of the government, including the creation of many new federal agencies, gave the executive branch much more power. New Deal administrators, such as Harry Hopkins, head of the WPA, commanded large bureaucracies with massive budgets and little supervision by Congress. Their authority increased Roosevelt's influence. Indeed, some commentators even began to speak of the rise of an imperial presidency, an unflattering comparison to the power exercised in the past by rulers of great empires.

FDR also affected the style of the presidency. His mastery of the radio captivated Americans. His close relations with the press assured a generally popular response to his projects from the major media. Because he served for such a long time and was such an outstanding communicator, FDR set a standard that future Presidents had a hard time fulfilling.

Later, during World War II, FDR's presidential power grew even greater. As commander in chief of the nation's armed forces, he exercised enormous authority over many aspects of life. Most Americans accepted the President's increased

History Background

The Twenty-second Amendment Before the Twenty-second Amendment, the U.S. Congress had never passed a law limiting the number of terms that a President could serve. George Washington established a precedent, which all Presidents respected for more than 100 years.

Franklin Roosevelt stands out as the only President to serve more than two terms in office. Roosevelt was first elected in 1932. He won re-election three times, although he died in office after serving only about one year of his fourth term.

Many of Roosevelt's political opponents were troubled by the length of time he remained in office. The Twenty-second Amendment, ratified in February 1951, would ensure that no future President would follow Roosevelt's example.

Some people have criticized the Twenty-second Amendment, saying that it limits the American public's freedom to elect someone as President for as many years as the public wants the person to serve. Others believe that the Amendment is a safeguard against a popular leader becoming a President for life.

Answer

Analyze Cause and Effect Possible responses: Economic—The economy improved as the government employed people in public works jobs. Political—The role of government in national economy matters increased.

FDR's Effect on the Presidency ☑ Quick Study

- Increased power of the President and the executive branch
- Made mass media, such as radio, an essential tool in advertising and promoting policies
- Expanded role of the President in managing the economy
- Expanded role of the President in developing social policy
- Won third and fourth terms, leading to passage of Twenty-second Amendment, which limited Presidents to two consecutive terms

authority as a necessary condition of wartime. But after the war, they sought to protect the delicate balance between the different branches of government and between the federal and state governments.

One way that Americans sought to guard against the growing power of the President was by amending the Constitution. When Roosevelt ran for an unprecedented third term in 1940, he knew that he had broken an unwritten rule, established by George Washington, that Presidents should serve only two terms. He won that election and then ran and won again in 1944. But after Roosevelt's death in 1945, there was a growing call for limiting a President's term in office. In 1951, the Twenty-second Amendment was ratified, limiting the President to two consecutive terms.

✓ **Checkpoint** In what ways did the role of the federal government grow during Franklin Roosevelt's presidency?

The Presidency After Roosevelt

Franklin Roosevelt had a dramatic impact on the role of the presidency. *Was FDR's impact positive or negative?*

SECTION **3** Assessment

Progress Monitoring Online
For: Self-test with vocabulary practice
www.pearsonschool.com/ushist

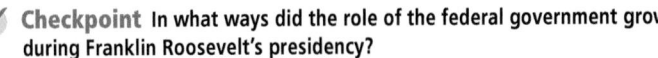

Comprehension

1. Terms and People What is the relationship between each of the following terms or people and the enduring significance of the New Deal?
- Black Cabinet
- Mary McLeod Bethune
- Indian New Deal
- New Deal coalition
- welfare state

2. NoteTaking Reading Skill: Identify Main Ideas Use your concept web to answer the Section Focus Question: How did the New Deal change the social, economic, and political landscape of the United States for future generations?

Writing About History

3. Quick Write: Draw Conclusions After comparing information from different sources, the next step in synthesizing is to draw conclusions. Compare the photograph of Eleanor Roosevelt with the primary source on the section's opening page. Write a paragraph that describes Mrs. Roosevelt's personality.

Critical Thinking

4. Recognize Cause and Effect Why do you think African Americans suffered more extensive discrimination during the depression than during more prosperous times?

5. Determine Relevance Has the New Deal coalition affected politics in your community today? Explain your answer.

6. Synthesize Information Did the growth in the powers of the federal government during the New Deal benefit the nation? Explain your answer.

Section 3 Assessment

1. Answers should demonstrate students' understanding of the relationship between each term and person and the enduring significance of the New Deal.

2. The New Deal expanded the role of government; increased the power of the presidency; put government in control of the economy as never before; gave rise to the welfare state; created a coalition of groups that strengthened the Democratic Party; had a great impact on rural America through public works projects, electri-

fication, and subsidies to farmers; and affected groups such as Native Americans.

3. Responses should demonstrate students' abilities to analyze photos and text.

4. African Americans were often first to lose their jobs when unemployment increased, so their unemployment rates grew during the Depression. During difficult times, conflict between groups competing for limited resources also increases, causing heightened discrimination against less powerful groups.

5. Students might say that their community has a history of voting Democratic

because of the influence of groups that were part of the New Deal coalition.

6. Some will think it did because it helped many people and restored the economy. Others will disagree saying the government became too powerful and took over functions that should have been left to local and state government or private institutions.

Objectives

As you teach this section, keep students focused on the following objectives to help them answer the Section Focus Question and master core content.

- Trace the growth of radio and the movies in the 1930s and the changes in popular culture.
- Describe the major themes of literature of the New Deal era.

Prepare to Read

Background Knowledge L3

Review some of the difficulties that Americans faced during the Great Depression. Discuss what people in the 1930s might have done to find relief from their hardships.

Set a Purpose L3

- **WITNESS HISTORY** Read the selection aloud.

  Ask **Why did the song "Over the Rainbow" appeal to people during the Depression?** *(It describes a happy place where there are no troubles and dreams come true.)*

- **Focus** Point out the Section Focus Question, and write it on the board. Tell students to refer to this question as they read. *(Answer appears with Section 4 Assessment answers.)*

- **Preview** Have students preview the Section Objectives and the list of Terms and People.

- **NoteTaking** Using the Paragraph Shrinking strategy (TE, p. T20), have students read this section. As they read, have students record examples of the cultural or popular media of the 1930s. Reading and Note Taking Study Guide

▲ *The Wizard of Oz's* Dorothy, Tin Man, and Scarecrow

"Somewhere Over the Rainbow"

Americans eager to escape the gloom of the depression regularly sought refuge in the fantasy world presented by the movies. One of their favorites was *The Wizard of Oz*, which opened in 1939. In an early scene, the farm girl Dorothy sings of better times:

❝Somewhere over the rainbow
Way up high,
There's a land that I've heard of
Once in a lullaby.

Somewhere over the rainbow
Skies are blue,
And the dreams that you dare to dream
Really do come true.

Some day I'll wish upon a star
And wake up where the clouds are far behind me.
Where troubles melt like lemon drops
Away above the chimney tops
That's where you'll find me.❞

— "Over the Rainbow," E. Y. Harburg, 1939

Culture of the 1930s

Objectives

- Trace the growth of radio and the movies in the 1930s and the changes in popular culture.
- Describe the major themes of literature in the New Deal era.

Terms and People

Frank Capra
Federal Art Project
mural

Dorothea Lange
John Steinbeck
Lillian Hellman

NoteTaking

Reading Skill: Identify Main Ideas and Details Complete a table like the one below to record examples of cultural or popular media.

Cultural or Popular Media	Example
Movies	

Why It Matters Mass entertainment, such as *The Wizard of Oz*, flourished during the New Deal years as Americans sought escape from the worries of the depression. And, for the first time, the government played an active role in the arts, creating programs that put artists to work. It was a golden age for entertainment, and the movies, music, and works of literature produced during this era hold a unique place in American culture. **Section Focus Question: How did the men and women of the depression find relief from their hardships in the popular culture?**

Movies and Radio Captivate Americans

Entertainment became big business during the 1930s. Large radio networks, such as NBC and CBS, were broadcasting giants while a cluster of film companies—including MGM, Warner Brothers, Twentieth Century Fox, and Paramount—dominated the silver screen. By 1935, two in three homes owned a radio; by the end of the decade, about nine in ten did. In 1939, nearly two thirds of all Americans attended at least one movie a week. Stars in both industries made fortunes and attracted loyal followings. Glossy fan magazines tracked the stars' personal and professional lives.

Vocabulary Builder

Use the information below and the following resource to teach students the high-use word from this section. Teaching Resources, Vocabulary Builder, p. 11

High-Use Word	Definition and Sample Sentence
episode	*n.* television or radio program that is one of a series of programs telling one story Everyone was eager to watch the next **episode** of the hit television series.

Enjoying Escapism Above all, when Americans went to the movies during the Great Depression, they did so as a means of escapism. They sought relief from their concerns through a good laugh, a good cry, a lyrical song, or by seeing good triumph over evil. *The Wizard of Oz,* one of the most memorable depression-era films, delivered all four. It promised weary audiences that their dreams really would come true.

The big movie studios churned out musicals, romantic comedies, and gangster films. Children marveled at the colorful animation of Walt Disney's *Snow White and the Seven Dwarfs.* For a good scare, teens and young adults flocked to *Frankenstein.* Adults watched dancers Fred Astaire and Ginger Rogers glide effortlessly across the ballroom floor in *Top Hat.* And millions wept as they watched the stormy love affair between Clark Gable and Vivien Leigh in the Civil War epic *Gone With the Wind.*

Providing Social Commentary In the early 1930s, many films reflected the public's distrust of big business and government. Gangster movies, such as *Public Enemy* starring James Cagney, were very popular. These films showed a declining faith in government and law enforcement, with characters turning to crime to survive the depression. But as the New Deal restored confidence, the government regained its glow, and movies began portraying government officials as heroes. In 1935, Cagney portrayed an FBI agent who captured the bad guys in *G-Men.*

Other films focused on the strength of average Americans. Director **Frank Capra** was a leader of this genre. The characters in his films were everyday people struggling with the hardships of the time. In Capra's *Mr. Smith Goes to Washington,* actor James Stewart plays a junior senator who fights against the greed and corruption he finds in the nation's capital. Depression-era audiences cheered Capra's films, which celebrate American idealism and the triumph of the common man over the forces of adversity.

Radio's Golden Age The success of the movie industry was matched by that of radio. The national radio networks broadcast popular shows starring comedians such as Bob Hope and Jack Benny. Americans avidly followed soap operas,

Radio Captures the Nation
Americans united in their love for the radio and its stars, including mainstays George Burns and Gracie Allen (below).

Movies and Radio Captivate Americans

Instruct

- **Introduce** Display Color Transparency: *Big Bands Swing,* showing a swing band performing in a club. Discuss the feeling conveyed by the photo, and ask students to describe how people would have felt listening to this band. Color Transparencies **A-100**

- **Teach** Ask **What was the main reason for the popularity of bands, movies, and radio programs during the 1930s?** *(They provided an escape for people whose everyday lives were often difficult; provided commentary on social and political issues of the time; and inspired Americans with tales of common people overcoming adversity.)* **How did FDR use the radio?** *(He used it to provide information and encouragement to the American people through his fireside chats.)*

- **Analyzing the Visuals** Tell students to look at the photos at the bottom of the page. Ask students what the photos tell them about the place of radio in terms of family entertainment in the New Deal era. Ask **Which form of household entertainment would they compare it to today?** *(television)*

Independent Practice

Have students read and complete *Link to Literature: Roll on, Columbia.* Discuss how Guthrie's lyrics reflected the times in which he lived and wrote. Teaching Resources, **p. 23**

Monitor Progress

As students complete their tables, circulate to make sure that they record examples of cultural or popular media during the 1930s. For a completed version of the table, see Note Taking Transparencies, **B-110.**

Differentiated Instruction   Solutions for All Learners

L1 Special Needs Students   **L2 English Language Learners**   **L2 Less Proficient Readers**

Pair an L1 or L2 student with an advanced student to research and report on a radio program or film that was popular in the 1930s or early 1940s. Students should give the program or film's name, explain what it was about, and discuss its appeal and popularity. Reports should list the characters and actors of the program or film. Students may also

prepare an excerpt from a script that they can read aloud. Have students classify the work as a drama, a comedy, or a thriller. After the presentation, have students discuss the appeal of such entertainment during the Great Depression, and whether it would have appeal today.

Instruct

- **Introduce** Discuss the role of art—music, painting, drama, dance, writing—in society. Ask students whether they believe that art is essential and to explain their answer. Then, discuss the role of artists in the New Deal.

- **Teach** Ask **Why did New Deal programs pay unemployed artists, just as it paid unemployed carpenters and truck drivers?** *(Artists were also facing hard times and needed help just as did people in other professions.)* **How did the WPA help actors, musicians, and writers?** *(Actors and musicians were paid to perform for the public, while writers were paid to write a series of books about American history and folklore.)* **Why did Congressional support for the program decrease at the end of the 1930s?** *(Some members of Congress thought the views expressed by some of the artists were too radical and should not get government support.)*

- **Analyzing the Visuals** Have students study the murals on this page and the next page. Discuss how this artwork celebrates the people who helped build this nation.

Independent Practice

In groups, have students stage a debate about whether the New Deal arts benefited the United States, with one side defending these programs and the other criticizing them.

Monitor Progress

As students write their paragraphs, circulate to make sure that they understand that during the New Deal, the U.S. government provided funding for the arts for the first time.

Answer

✓ Trends included movies that featured escapist themes and social commentary, as well as radio comedies, soap operas, detective serials, and dramas. Americans also enjoyed swing, blues, and folk music.

Vocabulary Builder
episode–(EHP uh sohd) *n.* television or radio program that is one of a series of programs telling one story

Funding the Arts
The Federal Art Project poster (below) promotes an exhibition of works by WPA artists. William Gropper's mural, *Construction of a Dam,* was a tribute to the strength and dignity of labor inspired by the construction of two western dams.

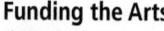

---

variety shows, and humorists, such as Will Rogers. Dramatic shows were also popular. *The Lone Ranger* started its run in 1933 and ran for more than 20 years. The detective serial *The Shadow* began each thrilling <u>episode</u> with the haunting line, "Who knows what evil lurks in the hearts of men?"

In addition to providing entertainment, the family radio provided information. FDR used his fireside chats to explain and promote his New Deal programs. Newscasters delivered the daily news and political commentary.

On at least one occasion, radio listeners had a hard time recognizing the difference between news and entertainment. It happened on the night of October 30, 1938, when millions of Americans tuned in to a drama called *War of the Worlds*, directed by Orson Welles. The Mercury Theatre broadcast was so realistic that many people believed that Martians were actually invading. Panic gripped areas of the country until announcers insisted that it was all make-believe.

Swinging to the Sounds of the Era Like films and radio shows, music provided a diversion from hard times. Whether listening to the radio at home or dancing in nightclubs, Americans enjoyed the popular music of the day. "Swing" music played by "big bands" topped the charts. Duke Ellington, Benny Goodman, Artie Shaw, Glenn Miller, and Jimmy and Tommy Dorsey were some of the top swing musicians, a term probably derived from Ellington's tune "It Don't Mean a Thing If It Ain't Got That Swing." *Your Hit Parade* and *Make Believe Ballroom*—the program that introduced disc jockeys—were just two of the radio shows that brought the latest tunes to listeners. The most popular vocalist of the era was Bing Crosby.

Latin music was very popular. The rhythms of the rumba and the samba had a special appeal for dancers, and Latin bands were prominently featured in films and on the radio. Folk and ethnic music also gained a following during the 1930s. Black singers focused on the harsh conditions faced by African Americans. Huddie Ledbetter, a folk singer known as Leadbelly, described experiences of African Americans with the songs "Cotton Fields" and "The Midnight Special." Woody Guthrie wrote ballads about the Okies, farmers who fled Dust Bowl states and headed to California. Guthrie's song "Dust Bowl Refugee" helped listeners understand the Okies' plight.

✓ **Checkpoint** What were some of the most important popular cultural trends of the 1930s?

History Background

Big Bands Swing The 1930s and early 1940s formed the era of "swing" music, a type of jazz. Swing was played by large groups of musicians, commonly called "big bands." Some of the major big bands were those of Duke Ellington, Count Basie, and Benny Goodman.

A big band usually had a section of trumpets, trombones, and saxophones, as well as a rhythm section containing drums, a piano, an acoustic guitar, and a bass. Vocalists sometimes sang with the bands and became famous in their own right.

Radio was important in spreading the popularity of big band swing music, especially for black bands that had been playing swing, but did not have wide public exposure. The first well-known national broadcast featuring big band swing featured Benny Goodman on his *Let's Dance* broadcasts, starting in 1934. As swing music grew in popularity and recording technology advanced, disc jockeys playing swing records joined broadcasts of live performances on the radio. The swing music of the big bands became the soundtrack of the New Deal era.

The New Deal and the Arts

During the New Deal, the federal government provided funding for the arts for the first time in American history. Recognizing that many artists and writers faced dire circumstances, WPA administrator Harry Hopkins established a special branch of the WPA to provide artists with work. Programs such as the **Federal Art Project,** the Federal Writers' Project, and the Federal Theater Project offered a variety of job opportunities to artists.

In federally funded theaters, musicians and actors staged performances that were often free to the public. In a series of new state guidebooks, WPA writers recorded the history and folklore of the nation. Artists painted huge, dramatic **murals** on public buildings across the nation. These paintings celebrated the accomplishments of the workers who helped build the nation. Many of the murals can still be seen in public buildings today.

Photographers also benefited from federal arts programs. The Resettlement and Farm Security Administration (FSA) sought to document the plight of America's farmers. Roosevelt's top aide, Rexford Tugwell, told the head of the FSA, "Show the city people what it's like to live on the farm." Walker Evans and **Dorothea Lange** were among the FSA photographers who created powerful images of impoverished farmers and migrant workers, including Lange's famous photo "Migrant Mother."

> **Primary Source** "When Dorothea took that picture that was the ultimate. She never surpassed it. . . . She has all the suffering of mankind in her but all the perseverance too. A restraint and a strange courage."
> —Roy Stryker, FSA, on Dorothea Lange's "Migrant Mother"

Some members of Congress attacked the Federal Art programs for promoting radical values. Congressman J. Parnell Thomas described the Federal Writers' and Theater projects as "a hotbed for Communists." Eleanor Roosevelt and others defended the Federal Art programs on the grounds that they did not "believe in censoring anything." Nonetheless, congressional support for the programs declined. Although the Federal Art programs ceased to exist in the early 1940s, they set a precedent for further federal funding of the arts and humanities in the 1960s.

✓ **Checkpoint** In what ways did the New Deal support American arts?

California
One of several WPA murals in San Francisco's Coit Tower, *California* was painted by Maxine Albro, an artist who painted many scenes of Mexican life after studying with noted Mexican muralist Diego Rivera.

Native Son

Richard Wright's novel about the
psychological pressures that lead a
young black man to commit murder
sold more than 200,000 copies in one
month. During the 1930s, the author
worked as a writer and editor for the
Federal Writers' Project in Chicago.

The Literature of the Depression

The literature of the 1920s, from authors such as F. Scott Fitzgerald and Ernest Hemingway, sometimes overshadowed the literature of the 1930s. Still, the depression era produced some memorable works.

During the depression, many writers drifted to the left and crafted novels featuring working-class heroes. They believed that the American economic system no longer worked and they blamed this failure on political and business leaders. Many artists of the 1930s saw "ordinary Americans" as the best hope for a better day.

The most famous novel of the 1930s was **John Steinbeck's** *The Grapes of Wrath.* Steinbeck follows the fictional Joad family from their home in Oklahoma, which has been ravaged by Dust Bowl conditions, to California, where they hope to build a better life. But instead of the Promised Land, the Joads encounter exploitation, disease, hunger, and political corruption.

African American writers captured the special plight of blacks, facing both the depression and continuing prejudice. Richard Wright's *Native Son* explored racial prejudice in a northern urban setting. Wright was an outspoken critic of racial discrimination.

In New York, some important playwrights had their first successes during the New Deal period. **Lillian Hellman,** a New Orleans native, wrote several plays featuring strong roles for women. Hellman's plays *The Children's Hour, The Little Foxes,* and *Watch on the Rhine* are also notable for their socially conscious subject matter. Clifford Odets was another dramatist who achieved prominence in the 1930s. His plays *Waiting for Lefty* and *Awake and Sing!* chronicle the struggles of the working class during the Great Depression.

On a lighter note, many Americans devoured comic strips and comic books during the 1930s. Among the most popular comic strips were *Flash Gordon,* a science-fiction saga; *Dick Tracy,* a detective story; and *Superman,* the first great "superhero" comic. The success of *Superman,* which began in 1938, quickly led to a radio show and later to a popular television series and several feature films. *Superman* reassured Americans that ordinary citizens, like mild-mannered Clark Kent, could overcome evil.

✓ **Checkpoint** Describe the most notable works of literature of the 1930s.

SECTION

4 Assessment

Progress Monitoring *Online*
For: Self-test with vocabulary practice
www.pearsonschool.com/ushist

Comprehension

1. **Terms and People** For each item below, write a sentence explaining how it affected the people of the era.
   - *The Wizard of Oz*
   - Frank Capra
   - *War of the Worlds*
   - Federal Art Project

2. **NoteTaking Reading Skill: Identify Main Ideas and Details** Use your table to answer the Section Focus Question: How did the men and women of the depression find relief from their hardships in the popular culture?

Writing About History

3. **Quick Write: Make Generalizations** Compare *The Wizard of Oz* and *War of the Worlds.* Write a few sentences describing how both were escapist fare that helped people forget their troubles.

Critical Thinking

4. **Make Generalizations** What values did the movies and other popular entertainment of the depression reinforce for Americans?

5. **Identify Effects** How did federal support of the arts benefit both artists and the public?

6. **Identify Point of View** How did the work of New Deal era artists and writers contribute to our appreciation today of the New Deal?

The Golden Age of Hollywood

The 1930s were a Golden Age for Hollywood—and for moviegoers. Depression-era audiences watched the latest Hollywood spectacles in beautiful theaters that were a far cry from today's multiplexes. Advancements in color and sound added more realism to movies that depicted lives of glamour and adventure unknown to most Americans. But it was the outstanding quality of the films that made the 1930s Hollywood's Golden Age.

▲ **King Kong** (1933)
King Kong was the thrilling adventure tale of a giant ape and the woman he loved. The film's innovative special effects helped make it a huge box-office hit.

◀ **Gone With the Wind** (1939)
Clark Gable was Rhett Butler, and Vivien Leigh was Scarlett O'Hara in the Civil War saga adapted from Margaret Mitchell's Pulitzer Prize–winning novel.

▼ **Dead End** (1937)
A gritty social drama about life in a Manhattan slum, *Dead End* starred Humphrey Bogart and introduced the Dead End Kids.

▲ **Swing Time** (1936)
Fred Astaire and Ginger Rogers became one of the silver screen's legendary teams as they danced their way through a series of popular musicals.

Thinking Critically
1. **Make Inferences** Why would people who were struggling just to get by enjoy films portraying extravagant upper-class lifestyles?
2. **Connect to Today** Do you think Hollywood movies give an accurate picture of contemporary American life? Explain.

History Background

Hollywood American movie-making did not start in Hollywood, but by the 1920s, it was firmly established there. Today, although American movies are no longer made exclusively in Hollywood, the name still stands for the American motion picture industry.

The name "Hollywood" was first recorded in 1887, when Horace Wilcox filed a map of his land with county authorities. Wilcox had come from Kansas to southern California to begin a religious community, but Hollywood developed much differently.

Lured by the sunshine and warm weather, the pleasant landscape, and a large labor force, movie studios gradually left the New York City area for Hollywood in the first decade of the 1900s. The trickle became a flood by 1920, with many companies building movie-making facilities and crews shooting constantly in and around Hollywood.

During the 1920s, millions of Americans went to the movies each week. By the New Deal era of the 1930s, motion pictures became one of America's most successful industries.

American Art

The Golden Age of Hollywood

Objectives
- Explain the growth in popularity of movies in the 1930s.
- Describe the types of movies most frequently produced in Hollywood.

Background Knowledge ⓛ₃
Ask students to think about why they go to the movies. Do they go to learn something new, escape into a fantasy world, or enjoy the performance of a favorite actor? Have students compare the types of movies of today with those of the 1930s and the motivations of fans then and now.

Instruct ⓛ₃
Draw students' attention to the variety of movies represented by the photos on this page. Discuss what type of movie each photo shows. **Was it possible for movies to fulfill any of the goals of the New Deal? Explain.** *(Yes. Movie production employed many people and helped local economies; depending on its subject matter, a movie could lift American spirits or even inspire patriotism and support for the government.)*

Monitor Progress
Have students write a sentence that expresses the main idea of this American Art feature. Tell students to exchange their work with a partner and discuss what each has written.

Answers

Thinking Critically
1. This was a way for them to escape into an opulent fantasy world that was far removed from the difficulties of their everyday lives.
2. Some students will think that they are not realistic and do not show the lives of Americans accurately. Others will think that some aspects of contemporary American life, especially some of today's problems, are shown fairly accurately.

Quick Study Guide

Progress Monitoring Online
For: Self-test with vocabulary practice
www.pearsonschool.com/ushist

Quick Study Guide

- Have students use the Quick Study Guide to prepare for the chapter test. Students may wish to refer to the following sections as they review:

New Deal Legislation
Section 1
Section 2
Section 3
Section 4

Effects of the New Deal
Section 3

Opposition to the New Deal
Section 1
Section 2

Key Events of the New Deal
Section 1
Section 2
Section 3
Section 4

- For additional review, remind students to refer to the Reading and Note Taking Study Guide.
Section Note Taking
Section Summaries

- Have students access **www.pearsonschool.com/ushist** for this chapter's History Interactive timeline, which includes expanded entries and additional events.

- If students need more instruction on analyzing graphic data, have them read the Skills Handbook, **p. SH21.**

For **Progress Monitoring Online,** refer students to the Self-test with vocabulary practice at **www.pearsonschool.com/ushist.**

New Deal Legislation

New Deal Program	Effects
Federal Deposit Insurance Corporation (FDIC), 1933	Guaranteed bank deposits up to $5,000 to ease banking crisis
National Recovery Administration (NRA), 1933	Established codes to regulate wages and prices, stimulate consumer activity, and promote fair competition
Securities and Exchange Commission (SEC), 1934	Regulated the stock market and restored investor confidence
Civilian Conservation Corps (CCC), 1933	Provided jobs for millions of young, single men on conservation projects
Public Works Administration (PWA), 1933	Sponsored large-scale government construction projects to create new jobs and improve the nation's infrastructure
Agricultural Adjustment Act (AAA), 1933	Paid subsidies to lower production on farms and raise crop prices
Tennessee Valley Authority (TVA), 1933	Built dams and hydroelectric plants in the Tennessee River valley to control flooding, generate power, and attract industry to the South
Home Owners' Loan Corporation (HOLC), 1933	Provided low-interest loans to homeowners who were unable to make mortgage payments

Effects of the New Deal

Immediate Effects
• Banking system is stabilized.
• Federal payments help farmers.
• Work-relief programs provide jobs.
• Social Security provides safety net.
• New Deal helps to unify the nation.

Long-term Effects
• Power of the presidency increases.
• Government takes active role in economy.
• New Deal coalition is powerful political force.
• Wagner Act protects workers and raises standard of living.
• Minorities and women gain positions in government.

Opposition to the New Deal

On the Left	On the Right
• New Deal does not do enough to end the depression.	• New Deal makes government too powerful.
• FDR's only concern is saving banks and big business.	• Increased government role in economy equals socialism.
• New Deal does not address redistribution of wealth.	• New Deal destroys free enterprise and individual freedom.
• New Deal does not help the elderly.	• New Deal creates huge national debt.

☑ Quick Study Timeline

In America

1932	1933	1934	1935
More than 5,000 banks close	FDR begins New Deal	Dust Bowl worsens	Social Security Act passed

Presidential Terms Herbert Hoover 1929–1933   Franklin D. Roosevelt 1933–1945

1932   1935

Around the World

1932	1933	1935
Aldous Huxley's *Brave New World* is published	Nazis begin burning of books	Italy invades Ethiopia

American Issues
●──●──● Connector

By connecting prior knowledge with what you have learned in this chapter, you can gradually build your understanding of enduring questions that still affect America today. Answer the questions below. Then, use your American Issues Connector study guide (or go online: www.pearsonschool.com/ushist).

Issues You Learned About

● **Government's Role in the Economy** Political leaders disagree on how much control the government should have over the national economy.

1. Do you agree with the statement that many Americans probably thought that Herbert Hoover should have let his administration take a greater role in the economy? Explain.

2. Following the tradition of laissez faire, how did the federal government respond to the downturn of the economy under Hoover? How did it respond under Roosevelt?

● **American Indian Policy** The U.S. government has followed different policies toward Native Americans.

3. What did the Indian Removal Act demand? What action did some Indian tribes, that did not want to follow the Indian Removal Act, take?

4. What was the Dawes Act? Did it achieve its goals?

5. How did John Collier bring changes to American Indian life and culture?

● **Federal Power and States' Rights** At times, the national government may seem to go beyond its constitutional rights.

6. According to the Constitution, what powers does the national government have over trade? What powers does each state government have?

7. In response to the Supreme Court ruling in *Schechter Poultry v. United States,* one newspaper proclaimed this headline: "ROOSEVELT'S TWO YEARS' WORK KILLED IN TWENTY MINUTES." What did the headline mean?

Connect to Your World	Activity

Interaction With the Environment The Bureau of Reclamation, founded in 1902, has constructed dams, power plants, and canals in the western states, including the Hoover Dam and the Grand Coulee Dam. However, the job does not end with the completion of water systems. Conduct research to find out about the bureau's work today. Create a fact sheet about the Bureau of Reclamation, explaining its key roles in water management, presenting important statistics and describing its current programs and activities.

1936 UAW stages sit-down strike

1939 *Gone With the Wind* breaks box-office records

1940 FDR reelected to third term

History *Interactive*
For: Interactive timeline
www.pearsonschool.com/ushist

1938

1936 Spanish Civil War begins

1937 Pablo Picasso paints *Guernica*

1939 Radio broadcasts WWII events

1941

1941 Japanese attack Pearl Harbor

Differentiated Instruction Solutions for All Learners

L1 Special Needs Students   **L2 English Language Learners**   **L2 Less Proficient Readers**

Use the following study guide resource to help students acquiring basic skills:
Adapted Reading and Note Taking Study Guide
• American Issues Journal

Use the following study guide resource to help Spanish-speaking students:
Spanish Reading and Note Taking Study Guide
• American Issues Journal

American Issues
●──●──● Connector

Tell students that the main issues for this chapter are Government's Role in the Economy, American Indian Policy, and Federal Power and States' Rights. Then, ask them to answer the Issues You Learned About questions on this page. Discuss the Connect to Your World topics, and ask students to complete the project that follows.

American Issues Connector

1. Yes; economic conditions worsened during Hoover's term, probably resulting in his loss to Roosevelt.

2. Under Hoover, the federal government had a mainly hands-off approach. Under Roosevelt, it provided relief and recovery.

3. It mandated that eastern groups move west of the Mississippi so that their lands could be opened to white settlement. Some Native Americans resisted removal through warfare, while others opposed the policy in court.

4. It was a law passed in 1887 to break up Native American tribes and force them to assimilate into U.S. society. It succeeded in breaking up some tribal groups and resulted in the loss of a great deal of Native American land.

5. He won passage of the Indian Reorganization Act in 1934, which gave Native Americans control of their own lands again. He also allowed Native Americans to practice their own religions and cultural traditions.

6. The federal government can regulate interstate commerce. A state can regulate trade within its own boundaries.

7. It meant that two years of progress under the New Deal were undone with a ruling from the Court that took just a few minutes to decide.

Connect to Your World

Fact sheets should reflect students' understanding of the Bureau of Reclamation and its effects on the economy and the environment.

For additional review of this chapter's enduring issues, remind students to refer to the *Reading and Note Taking Study Guide American Issues Journal.*

Terms and People

1. The Civilian Conservation Corps, or CCC, was a New Deal program. It employed millions of young men to do public service jobs that helped the environment.

2. Pump priming is using government spending to stimulate the economy; the WPA employed millions of people who then spent their pay to buy consumer goods, which boosted the economy.

3. In collective bargaining, employers negotiate with unions representing employee interests in matters such as work hours, wages, and other working conditions. In a sit-down strike, workers cease working and occupy the workplace until a settlement is reached. Both methods were very effective.

4. She was an African American woman who supported the New Deal and advised FDR on issues affecting blacks; she later founded a college.

5. They were New Deal projects that employed actors, writers, and artists during the Depression. They ended in the 1940s as a result of complaints from some members of Congress that the artists were spreading radical values.

Focus Questions

6. It created several government programs that gave immediate relief to Americans, often through public works projects that provided jobs.

7. The Second New Deal addressed the needs of the elderly, the poor, the unemployed, and the disabled with the passage of the Social Security Act. The Wagner Act gave workers to right to join unions and engage in collective bargaining. Other legislation assisted farmers and created new public works projects.

8. It forged a New Deal coalition that still influences politics today. It set the economy back on track and made the federal government the major force in the economic system. It also brought about the rise of the welfare state.

Chapter Assessment

Terms and People

1. What was the **CCC**? How did it help individual Americans as well as the country?

2. Define **pump priming.** Give an example of pump priming in the second New Deal.

3. Define **collective bargaining** and **sit-down strikes.** How effective did workers find these methods?

4. Who was **Mary McLeod Bethune**? How did she feel about the New Deal?

5. What were the Federal Theater Project, the Federal Writers' Project, and the **Federal Art Project**? When and why did they come to an end?

Focus Questions

The focus question for this chapter is **How did the New Deal respond to the ravages of the depression and change the role of the federal government?** Build an answer to this big question by answering the focus questions for Sections 1 through 4 and the Critical Thinking questions that follow.

Section 1
6. How did the New Deal attempt to address the problems of the depression?

Section 2
7. What major issues did the second New Deal address?

Section 3
8. How did the New Deal change the social, economic, and political landscape of the United States for future generations?

Section 4
9. How did the men and women of the depression find relief from their hardships in the popular culture?

Writing About History

Synthesize Information In this chapter there are different images of President Roosevelt. One photograph might present FDR as weak, while another shows him as strong and confident. A cartoon might praise or criticize him. Write a few paragraphs in which you compare several different viewpoints on FDR, and then draw your own conclusion about him.

Prewriting
• Find four different images of Roosevelt that you will compare and contrast.
• Identify the main idea or viewpoint that is conveyed by each photograph or cartoon.

Drafting
• For each image, write a brief paragraph describing the main idea of the image.

Critical Thinking

10. **Analyze Information** The first New Deal had three goals: relief, recovery, and reform. Choose one of the laws or programs created by the first New Deal and explain how the program met one, two, or all of these goals.

11. **Compare Points of View** Why did both the right and the left protest the New Deal?

12. **Summarize** What impact did New Deal programs and legislation have on the lives of industrial workers?

13. **Analyze Graphs** Study the graph below.

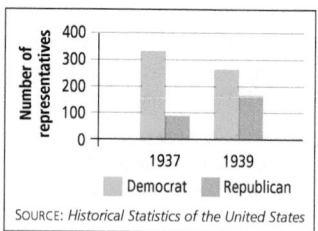

SOURCE: *Historical Statistics of the United States*

What political shift does this graph show? What caused this change?

14. **Draw Inferences** Why did New Deal work programs place a greater emphasis on employing men than women?

15. **Determine Relevance** What does the creation of a welfare state say about the changing priorities of the United States? Does this principle still hold today? Give examples to support your answer.

16. **Identify Point of View** Why might filmmakers have chosen to produce movies that drew on America's historical past?

17. **Evaluate Credibility of Sources** Do you think the work of depression-era writers can be read for historical value? Explain.

• Then, write a paragraph in which you point out how the portrayals of FDR are similar and different.
• Finally, write a concluding paragraph in which you draw your own conclusions and make some generalizations about the nature of FDR.

Revising
• Use the guidelines on page SH11 of the Writing Handbook to revise your essay.

9. They enjoyed escapist activities such as going to the movies, listening to radio shows, and dancing to the music of swing bands.

Critical Thinking

10. Sample answer: The Agricultural Adjustment Act: relief by paying subsidies to farmers; recovery by stopping the loss of family farms; reform by changing the system, and taking cropland out of production to allow crop prices to rise.

11. The right thought that it gave too much power to the federal government, threatening individual freedom and free enterprise. The left thought that it concentrated too heavily on helping banks and businesses and not enough on reforming the system to help the poor.

12. Industrial workers benefited by getting the right to join unions and use collective bargaining. They also gained a minimum wage, maximum work-hour mandates, and the promise of a check if they were unemployed or were injured on the job and unable to work.

Document-Based Assessment

The Tennessee Valley Authority

Was the Tennessee Valley Authority (TVA) a federal program that would bring jobs and electricity to rural towns in the region? Or was it an expensive, poorly planned federal program that taxpayers would have to shoulder and that would also cause many environmental problems? Use your knowledge of the TVA and Documents A, B, C, and D to answer questions 1 through 4.

Document A

"... The continued idleness of a great national investment in the Tennessee Valley leads me to ask Congress for legislation necessary to enlist this project in the service of the people. It is clear that the Muscle Shoals development is but a small part of the potential public usefulness of the entire Tennessee River. Such use, if envisioned in its entirety, transcends mere power development; it enters the wide fields of flood control, soil erosion, afforestation, elimination from agricultural use of marginal lands, and distribution and diversification of industry."

—President Franklin D. Roosevelt, April 10, 1933

Document B

Document C

"... The TVA has.therefore appeared to be on the side of the angels in the controversy between it and the utilities. But the conservation program of the TVA is only a masquerade. It has no functional connection with the power program of the Authority, and the amount spent on it is only an insignificant portion of the Authority's total expenditures. Other departments of government, both state and national, are charged with the duty of caring for soil erosion and are doing such work effectively without the building of dams and power facilities.... The American people are paying more than half a billion dollars for eleven dams, chiefly designed to supply power to one area. But this power is to be supplied to this area at less than cost.... [The] TVA will operate annually at a deficit, and these deficits must ... be paid for out of the pockets of the taxpayers."

—From "Political Power" by Wendell L. Willkie from *Atlantic Monthly* 160 (August 1937) pp. 211–214

Document D

"One of TVA's original missions was to manage the region's natural resources, but the agency has long invoked the ire of environmentalists. TVA ... was the leading promoter of destructive coal strip-mining.... TVA still remains the nation's worst violator of the Clean Air Act. The agency, in fact, is the largest emitter among eastern utilities of nitrogen oxide (NOx), which causes smog. It is the third largest emitter of sulfur dioxide (SO_2) and carbon dioxide (CO_2), which has been identified as the leading cause of global warming. TVA's nuclear program has been so plagued with safety and economic problems that consumer activist Ralph Nader in 1998 declared: 'The TVA ... has the most expensive set of nuclear reactors, has a debt of $29 billion, has the poorest safety record with TVA reactors spending more time on the Nuclear Regulatory Commission's watch list than any other utility.'"

—"Restructure TVA: Why the Tennessee Valley Authority Must Be Reformed" by Richard Munson (September 17, 2001)

1. Which document is a secondary source that criticizes the environmental impact of the Tennessee Valley Authority?
   A Document A
   B Document B
   C Document C
   D Document D

2. According to Documents B and C, why were taxpayers concerned about the Tennessee Valley Authority?
   A It provided cheap electricity only to people in Tennessee.
   B Taxpayers demanded an investigation because it operated at a deficit.
   C Taxpayers in Tennessee wanted the government to promise better flood control.
   D It did not build enough dams to provide adequate electricity.

3. In Document A, what message is President Roosevelt trying to convey to Congress?
   A He wanted Congress to view the TVA as a way to control the region's environmental problems.
   B He wanted Congress to build the TVA only to provide electricity.
   C He wanted Congress to provide money to the region's farmers.
   D He wanted Congress to plan many additional watershed projects throughout the country.

4. **Writing Task** Who was right about the impact of the Tennessee Valley Authority: President Roosevelt or his critics? Use your knowledge of the chapter and evidence from the primary sources above to support your opinion.

13. It shows the Democratic Party losing seats, while the Republican Party is gaining them. The loss could have been caused by opposition to the New Deal.

14. In the 1930s, men made up the majority of the workforce and were usually the sole household breadwinners.

15. Americans began to believe that the government had a duty to help provide for the welfare of citizens. Many Americans still believe this. For example, the government still provides Social Security and unemployment benefits to those Americans who qualify to receive them. It also provides subsidized housing and healthcare for the poor.

16. Films that highlighted important, positive events in American history probably restored pride and confidence in Americans.

17. Sample response: Yes; they witnessed important events in American history, which are bound to influence or be reflected in their work.

Background Knowledge

Have students discuss the effects of the Great Depression on the United States. Point out that many people were unemployed during this period. Through New Deal programs, the federal government provided jobs for millions of people during the Depression, including artists. Have students study the PWA and WPA Projects map (in The New Deal chapter), and ask them to discuss how these New Deal programs affected the United States.

Instruct

Have students read the essay. Ask **How did the federal government support the arts during the Depression?** *(It paid painters, writers, actors, musicians, and dancers to use their talents to perform and create new art.)* **Why was it important to include artists in a program such as the WPA?** *(Sample response: Like other Americans, artists were unemployed and needed help to support themselves. Also, officials may have believed that art was especially important to lift the spirits of Americans during this difficult period.)* Lead a class discussion about the way that the WPA changed the arts in the United States.

Looking Ahead

The United States stumbled during the Great Depression, but the country developed a new sense of confidence during that period and World War II. In the years that followed, that confidence, along with increasing economic and military might, helped America become a world power.

Reflections: Art in the New Deal

In reflecting back over 200 years of our nation's history, I am struck by the American capacity to triumph over adversity. The reaction to the economic depression that followed the 1929 stock market crash is a striking example. For many people, it appeared that America had screeched to a stop. Yet, the common suffering of the Great Depression brought the nation together as nothing else—short of the attacks on Pearl Harbor and the Twin Towers—has ever done.

Much of the credit for rallying the country must go to President Franklin Roosevelt and his advisers. Their challenge was to ease unemployment while preserving the skills and self-esteem of the unemployed. Often lost in the "alphabet soup" of Roosevelt's New Deal programs is the Works Progress Administration Arts Project, popularly known as the WPA.

Unlike most depression era projects, the WPA sought to help unemployed artists, actors, and musicians. Today, the arts in this country receive financial support from a variety of sources, including the federal government. In the 1930s, the idea of using tax dollars to pay people to paint, act, write, play music, or dance seemed a waste to many wealthy Americans. In the view of some people, even worse was that many of the artists began producing socially conscious art. In other words, it seemed that the government was using the taxes paid by successful business people to pay other people to criticize these same taxpayers.

Despite widespread opposition at the time, the WPA is now regarded as one of the most successful and important of Roosevelt's New Deal projects. In the graphic arts alone, it accounted for somewhere in the neighborhood of 2,500 murals, 17,000 sculptures, 100,000 paintings, and 240,000 prints and posters.

For their efforts, most of the artists received a weekly paycheck of $23—a princely sum at the time. An unexpected benefit was that the artists had to stand in line each week to receive their checks and, in so doing, they met other artists, thereby forming lifelong friendships and contacts in the art world. The remarkable success of American literature and visual arts today are legacies, in part, of that pioneering federal program.

WORLD WAR II AND POSTWAR AMERICA

CONTENTS

This famous photo, taken in New York City's Times Square, captured the nation's joy at the end of World War II. ▶

Era Overview

World War II and Postwar America traces the causes of the Second World War, the role the United States played in the outcome of the war, and how the disagreements between the United States and the Soviet Union after the war led to the start of the Cold War.

Chapter 10 explains how the rise of totalitarian governments in Europe and Asia contributed to the beginning of World War II and the factors that led the United States to abandon its isolationist policies to join the Allies' struggle against the Axis Powers. **Issues:** America and the World, Global Interdependence, America Goes to War

Chapter 11 examines the contributions of the United States in Europe and in the Pacific during World War II, describes the ways that Americans aided the war effort at home, examines the major Allied victories that ended the war, discusses the mistreatment of Jewish prisoners during the Holocaust, and analyzes the domestic and international effects of the war. **Issues:** Protecting and Expanding Civil Rights, Civil Liberties and National Security, Technology and Society

Chapter 12 discusses the Cold War between the United States and the Soviet Union and how this tension led to the Korean War, the expansion of U.S. and Soviet nuclear programs, and the growing anxiety of Americans at home. **Issues:** Civil Liberties and National Security, Balance of Power in Government, America Goes to War

Chapter 13 describes the United States during the 1950s, including its economic growth, the migration of Americans to the Sunbelt region, the evolution of mass culture and family life, and discusses the reasons why some Americans criticized the culture that had developed during this time. **Issues:** Poverty and Prosperity, Technology and Society, Migration and Urbanization

CHAPTER 10

Teach With Technology

PresentationEXPRESS™ PREMIUM DVD

- Teach this chapter's core content by using PresentationExpress, which includes interactivities, video, lecture notes, and the *ExamView®* QuickTake assessment tool.
- To introduce this chapter by using PresentationExpress, ask students with which of the following statements they most agree: **A) The United States should avoid conflict with other countries at any cost. B) The United States should object to the policies of other countries to protect others, even when our own security is not at risk. C) The United States should object to the policies of other countries only if our own security is at risk.** Take a class poll or record students' answers by using the QuickTake feature and discuss their responses. Point out that in this chapter, they will read about how the nation became involved in World War II. Continue introducing the chapter by using the chapter opener slide show.

Technology Resources

- Student**EXPRESS** CD-ROM
- Teacher Resource Library **DVD**
- Presentation**EXPRESS** PREMIUM DVD
- *ExamView®* **Test Bank CD-ROM** English and Spanish
- **Guided Reading Audio,** Spanish
- **Student Edition on Audio**

THE ESSENTIAL ? VIDEO By Students For Students

For videos on Amercian Issues, go to **www.pearsonschool.com/ushist**

CHAPTER 10

The Coming of War 1931–1942

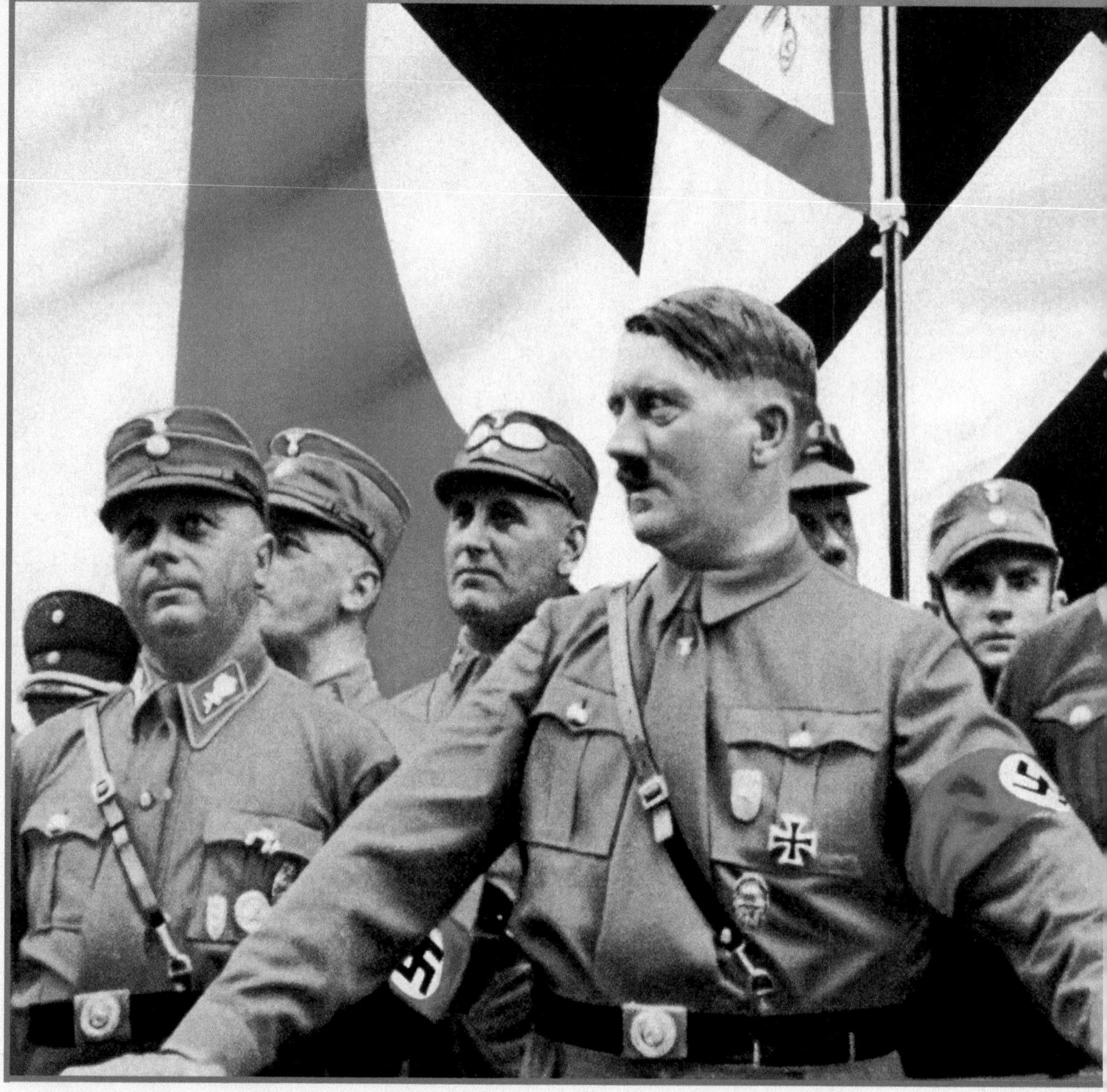

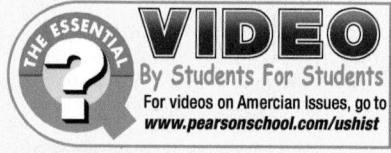

Bibliography

For the Teacher

Kennedy, David M. *The American People in World War II: Freedom from Fear, Part Two.* Oxford University Press, 2003.

Simmons, Thomas E. *Forgotten Heroes of World War II: Personal Accounts of Ordinary Soldiers.* Cumberland House Publishing, 2002.

Story, Ronald. *Concise Historical Atlas of World War Two: The Geography of Conflict.* Oxford University Press, 2005.

For the Student

L2 Corbridge, Fiona. *Going to War in World War Two.* Franklin Watts Ltd., 2006.

L3 Addison, Paul. *Churchill: The Unexpected Hero.* Oxford University Press, 2005.

L4 Martin, Simon. *Football and Fascism: The National Game Under Mussolini.* Berg Publishers, 2004.

German dictator Adolf Hitler at a Nazi Party rally in the 1930s

WITNESS HISTORY

A Rendezvous With Destiny

In the 1930s, Adolf Hitler, a ruthless dictator, rose to power in Germany. Early in 1939, American President Franklin Roosevelt contrasted American life with life under a dictatorship like Hitler's:

“Dictatorship, however, involves costs which the American people will never pay: The cost of our spiritual values. . . . The cost of having our children brought up, not as free and dignified human beings, but as pawns molded and enslaved by a machine. . . . Once I prophesied that this generation of Americans had a rendezvous with destiny. That prophecy comes true. To us much is given; more is expected.”
—Franklin Roosevelt, State of the Union Address, January 4, 1939

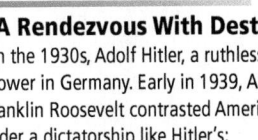

Button for the America First Committee, an isolationist group

Headline from the *Honolulu Star-Bulletin*

Hitler's manifesto, *Mein Kampf*

Chapter Preview

Chapter Focus Question: What events caused World War II, and how did the United States become involved?

Section 1
Dictators and War

Section 2
From Isolation to Involvement

Section 3
America Enters the War

Use the ☑ **Quick Study Timeline** at the end of this chapter to preview chapter events.

Note Taking Study Guide *Online*
For: Note Taking and American Issues Connector
www.pearsonschool.com/ushist

Chapter-Level Resources

All In One Letter Home (English and Spanish), Preread the Chapter, Vocabulary Builder, Reading Strategy, Social Studies Skills Practice, Enrichment, Issues Connector, Chapter Tests

- Test Prep With Document-Based Assessment
- AYP Monitoring Assessments
- *ExamView*® Test Bank CD-ROM
- Guided Reading Audio (Spanish)
- Student Edition Audio

Previewing the Chapter

- **WITNESS HISTORY** Explain that after Hitler came to power, the United States and many European nations disagreed with the way that he governed Germany. Read aloud the Witness History selection. Then, ask students to paraphrase Roosevelt's 1939 State of the Union Address and predict what problems will arise between Germany and the United States.

- **Analyzing the Visuals** Have students study the photo of Hitler at a Nazi Party rally in the 1930s and the images on this page. Ask **What questions do the images and the Witness History selection bring to mind?** (*Sample responses: How did Hitler come to power? Will differences in values cause the United States and Germany to clash? Will the United States end its isolationist policies to fight Germany?*)

- **Focus** Write the Chapter Focus question on the board. Tell students to keep this question in mind as they read the chapter. Then, have students preview the section titles in this chapter.

- **Preread** Have students complete the chapter's Preread the Chapter Worksheet. Teaching Resources, pp. 7–8

Have students access **www.pearsonschool. com/ushist** for the Note Taking Study Guide *Online* as an alternative to the *Reading and Note Taking Study Guide* booklet.

Step-by-Step Instruction

Objectives

As you teach this section, keep students focused on the following objectives to help them answer the Section Focus Question and master core content.

- Explain how dictators and militaristic regimes arose in several countries in the 1930s.
- Summarize the actions taken by aggressive regimes in Europe and Asia.
- Analyze the responses of Britain, France, and the United States to the aggressive regimes.

Prepare to Read

Background Knowledge **L3**

Ask students to think about how the Great Depression affected the way the U.S. government worked. Ask them to predict how the Depression might have affected the governments of other countries.

Set a Purpose **L3**

- **WITNESS HISTORY** Read the selection aloud.

  Ask **What role do you think morality and ethics played in Hitler's government?** *(very little, as the only thing that mattered was winning through military strength)*

- **Focus** Point out the Section Focus Question and write it on the board. Tell students to refer to this question as they read. *(Answer appears with Section 1 Assessment answers.)*

- **Preview** Have students preview the Section Objectives and the list of Terms and People.

- **Reading Skill** Have students use the *Reading Strategy: Summarizing* worksheet. Teaching Resources, **p. 11**

- **NoteTaking** Using the Structured Reading Aloud strategy (TE, p. T20), have students read this section. As they read, have students summarize the actions in the 1930s of each country listed in the table. Reading and Note Taking Study Guide

Hitler's Brutal Determination

For the German dictator Adolf Hitler, war was an ennobling experience. War united a nation, demanded righteous sacrifices, and culminated in territorial acquisitions. Hitler believed that there was no morality in war, just victory and defeat. He instructed his generals:

❝The victor will not be asked afterwards whether he told the truth or not. When starting and waging a war it is not right that matters, but victory. Close your hearts to pity. Act brutally. Eighty million people [Germans] must obtain what is their right. Their existence must be made secure. The stronger man is right.❞
—Adolf Hitler, August 1939

◄ Hitler speaks to the German people.

Dictators and War

Objectives

- Explain how dictators and militarist regimes arose in several countries in the 1930s.
- Summarize the actions taken by aggressive regimes in Europe and Asia.
- Analyze the responses of Britain, France, and the United States to the aggressive regimes.

Terms and People

totalitarianism	Spanish Civil War
Joseph Stalin	appeasement
Benito Mussolini	Anschluss
Adolf Hitler	Munich Pact
anti-Semitic	

NoteTaking

Reading Skill: Summarize As you read, summarize the actions in the 1930s of each of the countries listed in the table below.

Soviet Union	Italy	Germany	Japan

Why It Matters The effects of World War I and the Great Depression touched almost every corner of the world. In some countries, these upheavals led to the rise of a new kind of brutal dictatorship—the totalitarian state. Led by aggressive dictators, these states would destroy the peace established after World War I and spark a new, even deadlier, global conflict. **Section Focus Question: Why did totalitarian states rise after World War I, and what did they do?**

A Bitter Peace Unravels

In November 1918, World War I ended when Germany surrendered to the Allies. In 1919, delegates from 27 nations met in Versailles to hammer out a peace agreement, but only Britain, France, and the United States had a real say in most of the important decisions. Germany and Russia were not even present. From the first, many Germans resented the resulting Treaty of Versailles. Other nations also grumbled over the peace settlements. Italy and Japan, both Allies, had expected far more land for their sacrifices. The war that American President Woodrow Wilson had called "a war to end all wars" had left behind a mountain of bitterness, anger, frustration, and despair, often capped by a burning desire for revenge.

During the 1920s many nations, new and old, moved steadily toward democracy and freedom. Others, however, took the opposite direction, embracing repressive dictatorships and **totalitarianism,** a theory of government in which a single party or leader controls the economic, social, and cultural lives of its people. Throughout history

Vocabulary Builder

Use the information below and the following resource to teach students the high-use word from this section. Teaching Resources, Vocabulary Builder, p. 10

High-Use Word	Definition and Sample Sentence
ideology	*n.* a system of ideas that guides an individual, movement, or political program Hitler built his political career on an **ideology** of militarism and anti-Semitism.

there have been dictatorships, countries ruled by one person or small groups of people. But totalitarianism was a twentieth-century phenomenon. It was more extreme than a simple dictatorship, as the chart below shows. Why were totalitarian regimes able to take hold in the years leading up to World War II? As you will read, historians lay much of the blame on the destruction and bitterness left behind by World War I and the desperation caused by the Great Depression.

✓ **Checkpoint** What legacy did World War I leave behind?

Repression in the Soviet Union and Italy

The 1917 communist revolution in Russia inaugurated the first totalitarian state. The communist leader Vladimir Lenin created the beginnings of a totalitarian system of control to maintain power. His programs resulted in civil war, starvation, famine, and the death of millions of Russians.

Stalin's Grip on the Soviet Union After Lenin's death in 1924, **Joseph Stalin** took Lenin's place as the head of the Communist Party. In Russian, *Stalin* means "man of steel," and it is an apt description of the dictator's personality. Stalin was suspicious, cruel, ruthless, and tyrannical. He did not think twice about killing rivals or sentencing innocent people to death. His efforts to transform the Soviet Union into an industrial power and form state-run collective farms resulted in the deaths of at least 10 million people. In what became known as the Great Terror, Stalin purged the Communist Party of real or suspected traitors in the 1930s, ordering the deaths or imprisonment of up to a million people. The purge also included most of the higher officers of the Red Army, among many others. A combination of fear and massive propaganda kept Stalin in power.

Mussolini's Fascist Party Controls Italy Italian totalitarianism was in many ways a direct result of the war and the peace treaties. Although Italy was on the winning side, it did not get the land along the Adriatic coast it had hoped to obtain from the division of Austria-Hungary. Added to this frustration, the postwar economic depression made it difficult for returning veterans to find jobs, a communist movement was growing, and the government seemed weak and inept.

It was during this period that **Benito Mussolini** entered the world stage. In 1919, Mussolini founded the *Fasci di Combattimento* (FAH shee dee kohm ba tee MEHN toh), or Fascist Party, a right-wing organization that trumpeted nationalism and promised to make Italy great again. Followers of Mussolini, known as Black Shirts, fought in the streets against socialists and communists. Fearing revolution, in 1922, Italian King Victor Emmanuel III asked Mussolini to form a government. Calling himself *Il Duce* (ihl DOO chay), or "the leader," Mussolini consolidated his control over the government and the army within a few years. He outlawed political parties, took over the press, created a secret police, organized youth groups to indoctrinate the young, and suppressed strikes. He opposed liberalism and socialism. Still, his hold over Italy was never as powerful as Stalin's grip on the Soviet Union.

✓ **Checkpoint** How did Stalin and Mussolini maintain their power?

Stalin: A Gentle Father?

In this staged photo, a fatherly Stalin poses with a young girl, Galia Markifova. Years later, Stalin's government sent Galia to the dreaded Gulag, a chain of labor camps where millions of Soviets were imprisoned during Stalin's rule. *How is this photo an example of propaganda?*

Characteristics of a Totalitarian State

- Single-party dictatorship exerting control over all aspects of life
- Strong, charismatic leader often at head of government
- State control of the economy
- Use of police, spies, and terror to enforce the will of the state
- Government control of the media and use of propaganda to indoctrinate citizens
- Use of schools and youth organizations to spread ideology to children
- Strict censorship of artists, intellectuals, and political rivals with dissenting opinions

Teach

A Bitter Peace Unravels

Instruct

- **Introduce: Key Term** Ask students to find the key term *totalitarianism* (in bold) in the text. Ask **How does a totalitarian government differ from a democratic one?** (*one person or party rules, rather than the people*) Then, discuss the kinds of rights that might be limited in a totalitarian government. (*Examples: freedom of speech; right to vote*)

- **Teach** Have students point out some of the feelings that the German people experienced after the Treaty of Versailles. (*bitterness, anger, frustration, despair, and a desire for revenge*) Then, ask **How might these feelings have led to their supporting a totalitarian government?** (*The people were looking for a government that would take revenge on their enemies, even if it meant giving up their own freedoms.*)

- **Analyzing the Visuals** Direct students to the photo of Hitler on the previous page. Ask students to use the photograph to discuss what type of leader they think Hitler will be.

Independent Practice

Ask students to discuss the feelings of people who lived in Germany during and after World War I. Have them write a letter to the editor of a newspaper explaining why some Germans were upset with the outcome of the Treaty of Versailles.

Monitor Progress

As students fill in their tables, circulate to make sure that they understand the actions of the Soviet Union, Italy, Germany, and Japan in the 1930s. For a completed version of the table, see Note Taking Transparencies, **B-111a**.

Answers

✓ It left behind anger and resentment, especially in Germany.

Caption It promotes the idea that though his name suggests a steely personality, Stalin is also kind and loved by children.

✓ Stalin killed or terrorized his political enemies. Mussolini used censorship and fear tactics to keep signs of dissent to a minimum.

Repression in the Soviet Union and Italy 🄻🄳

Instruct

- **Introduce** Have students examine the chart "Characteristics of a Totalitarian State" on the previous page. Ask students to discuss which characteristics in the chart describe Stalin's Soviet Union and which describe Mussolini's Italy.

- **Teach** Ask **What was the result of some of Stalin's domestic policies?** *(the deaths of more than 10 million people)* **How did the failures of the Italian government contribute to the rise of fascism?** *(The government was weak and unable to deal with the country's problems, especially unemployment.)* **How did Stalin and Mussolini compare with one another?** *(Both were dictators who outlawed opposition and tried to control the press; Stalin relied heavily on the use of terror and had total control over his country.)*

Independent Practice

Have students examine the image of Stalin in the photo on the previous page. Ask them to consider their impressions of Stalin from the photo and write paragraphs about how control of the media can influence public perceptions of political leaders.

Monitor Progress

Circulate to make sure that students understand the possible effects of propaganda and why Stalin used it to maintain control of the Soviet Union.

Aggressive Leaders in Germany and Japan

After World War I, Germany became a democracy. The Weimar (VĪ mahr) Republic (named after the town of Weimar where the government was created) struggled throughout the 1920s to establish a functional democracy. However, Germany was beset by severe economic troubles in the 1920s, including runaway inflation. Anger over the Treaty of Versailles and internal disunity also plagued the young government. The Weimar Republic's ship of state was slowly sinking.

The Nazis Rise In the early 1930s, the worldwide Great Depression hit the Weimar Republic hard, worsening the problems that already existed. Increasingly, antidemocratic parties on the right, especially the National Socialist German Workers' Party, or Nazi (NAHT see) Party, threatened the republic. Regardless of the party's name, Nazis were not socialists. They bitterly opposed socialism, communism, or any other *ism* that promoted class interests or workers' rights above German ethnic solidarity. **Adolf Hitler** led the Nazi Party. The son of a minor Austrian civil servant, Hitler was a failed artist, a wounded and decorated World War I soldier, and a person who teetered on the brink of madness.

Hitler joined the small Nazi Party after the war and soon gained control of it. While in prison after the party attempted a rebellion, Hitler dictated the book *Mein Kampf* ("My Struggle"), in which he stated his explanations for the problems facing Germany. He criticized many people, political programs, and

INFOGRAPHIC

HITLER'S STRANGLEHOLD ON GERMANY

When Adolf Hitler came to power, he promised that Germany would rise again from the quagmire of reparations and the economic Depression that it had floundered in since World War I. For many, those promises seemed to come true in the 1930s. "[O]nce Hitler came to power, it was wonderful. Everybody had a job and there weren't any more unemployed people," remembers one German citizen. But from the beginning, Hitler's promises had dark undertones of oppression, based on extreme antisemitism and the rejection of democracy. Hitler maintained his power by alternately brainwashing the public with lies and propaganda drives or terrifying them into silence through ruthless violence. His rule led ultimately to genocide and the devastation of World War II.

Propaganda images like this presented Hitler as Germany's savior. Medals (above right) rewarded German mothers who bore several children.

German soldiers humiliate a Jewish boy and his father by forcing the boy to cut off his father's beard in 1933.

Differentiated Instruction   Solutions for All Learners

🄻🄸 Special Needs Students   **🄻🄶 Less Proficient Readers**

Direct visual learners and students who need help with basic skills to the Infographic on this page. Organize the class into groups, and ask each group to study the pictures in the Infographic and describe what they show. Remind students that one of Hitler's most powerful weapons was a skillful manipulation of propaganda, especially his use of the media to promote his ideas and to publish idealized images of himself. Have students compare these images with how Stalin was portrayed in the Soviet Union. Then, ask volunteers to explain how such propaganda might help a dictator increase his political power.

ideologies, but his sharpest assaults were against communists and Jews. Hitler was violently **anti-Semitic,** or prejudiced against Jewish people. Anti-Semitism had troubled Europe for centuries, mainly motivated by religious intolerance and economic resentment. In the late nineteenth century, new pseudo-scientific theories about Jews as a race, along with the rise of nationalism, caused Jews to be marginalized as ethnic outsiders. Hitler believed and spread this type of thinking. He preached that the greatest threat confronting Germany was the Jewish people who lived there. In *Mein Kampf,* which quickly became a national bestseller, Hitler presented a blueprint of his hatreds and plans for world domination.

Hitler Seizes Power The shattered German economy—the widespread unemployment, homelessness, and hunger—played into the Nazis' hands. Recognizing the power of Hitler's party, in January 1933, the president of the Weimar Republic appointed Hitler chancellor of Germany. Over the next two years, Hitler became president as well as chancellor, consolidated his power, and ruled unchecked by the Reichstag (RĪKS tahg), or the German parliament. By 1935, the democratic institutions of the Weimar Republic were silenced, and Hitler spoke alone as the voice of Germany.

Like Stalin and Mussolini, Hitler was the symbol of his totalitarian regime. Aided by a secret police that crushed all opposition, a state-controlled press that praised his accomplishments, and a state-controlled educational system that

Vocabulary Builder

ideology–(ī dee AHL uh jee) *n.* a system of ideas that guides an individual, movement, or political program

- **Introduce: Key Term** and **Vocabulary Builder** Have students identify the key term ***anti-Semitic*** and the vocabulary builder term ***ideology.*** Explain that ***anti-Semitism*** was an ***ideology*** supported by Adolf Hitler.

- **Teach** Ask **How did Germany's economic problems contribute to the rise of the Nazi Party?** *(The government was weak and turned to the Nazi Party for help.)* Have students view Color Transparency: *The Nazi Party.* Ask students to discuss how this cartoon reflects the concern people felt about the rise of the Nazi Party. Then, ask **How did economics influence the rise of militarism in Japan?** *(Japanese leaders saw military expansion as the key to easing their economic problems.)* **Would leaders such as those in Germany and Japan have successfully gained power in countries such as Britain? Why or why not?** *(Sample response: No; the British government was not weak.)* Color Transparencies A-101

- **Quick Activity** Have students analyze the Infographic and answer the questions that accompany it. Then, ask students to read the Primary Source quotation on the next page. Discuss how Hitler developed a "cult-like" following.

Independent Practice

Have students access **www.pearsonschool.com/ushist** to use the Geography Interactive map and then answer the map skills question in the text.

Monitor Progress

Circulate to make sure that students understand the expansion of Japanese influence during the 1930s.

Answers

Thinking Critically

1. a strong, charismatic leader, often the head of the government; government control of the media and use of propaganda to indoctrinate citizens; use of schools and youth organizations to spread ideology; censorship of dissenting artists and intellectuals and political rivals
2. They wanted to teach children to be loyal to the state above all else.

Through organizations such as the Hitler Youth for boys and the League of German Girls, young people were indoctrinated with Nazi ideas. ►

Young Nazis confiscate books that they consider "un-German" to be burned in a huge demonstration in Berlin in May 1933.

◄ A 1932 voting slip for Adolf Hitler offers the public a government of "freedom and peace."

Thinking Critically
1. **Synthesize** Which of the characteristics listed in the chart earlier in this section are illustrated here?
2. **Draw Inferences** Why did the Nazi government try to win the loyalty of young Germans?

History Background

Hitler's Youth Groups The Nazi Party ensured participation in the Hitler Youth and League of German Girls by outlawing all other youth organizations. By 1935, nearly 60 percent of all German boys belonged to the Hitler Youth. Typically, a child was registered in one of the groups at the age of 10 and spent most of his or her teenage years in training. The goal of both organizations was to ensure complete dedication to the Nazi cause. Children were taught to be loyal to the state above all else—even their parents. Boys practiced military training to prepare them for their required military service to the state. Girls were encouraged to participate in athletics in order to maintain good health so that they could be mothers to many "Aryan" children. Hitler taught that one way to combat "racial impurity" was to encourage higher birthrates among "Aryans." Enthusiasm for the programs apparently waned over time. Although membership in the groups was required, by 1939 participation was so low that the government passed new laws making attendance at meetings mandatory.

Instruct

- **Introduce: Key Term** Ask students to find the key term *Spanish Civil War* in the text. Ask **What was the *Spanish Civil War*?** *(a conflict between Spain's democratic Republican government and Nationalist forces led by General Francisco Franco)* **Why did other nations become involved in the conflict?** *(Germany and Italy did not want a democratic government to be in power in Spain; the Soviet Union wanted the Republicans to stay in power.)*

- **Teach** Point out to students that the League of Nations was weak largely because it had no real power to enforce its policies. Ask **Which countries suffered from the League's refusal to get involved in military conflicts?** *(Ethiopia, Spain)* **Why did Hitler defy the League of Nations?** *(because he wanted to build up his military and conquer more lands)* Have students read the HISTORY MAKERS feature about Mussolini and Hitler. Using the Idea Wave strategy (TE, p. T22), ask students to discuss why the two leaders supported each other in their efforts to control Europe.

- **Quick Activity** Have students color in the *Outline Map: German Aggression* to show how far Germany had expanded by 1938 and list the year in which Germany occupied new land. Teaching Resources, p. 14

Independent Practice

Have students use the notes from their tables to write a brief summary sentence for each country stating how it changed in the 1930s.

Monitor Progress

As students write their sentences, circulate to make sure that they understand the ways that the Soviet Union, Germany, Italy, and Japan changed during the 1930s.

Answers

☑ It led to the rise of the Nazi Party in Germany and militaristic leaders in Japan.

Map Skills

1. Much of it was separated from the main island by water and bordered hostile countries.

---

indoctrinated the young, Hitler assumed a godlike aura. One German described the emotions of seeing Hitler address a crowd:

Primary Source "There stood Hitler in a simple black coat and looked over the crowd. . . . How many look up to him with a touching faith! As their helper, their savior, their deliverer from unbearable distress—to him who rescues . . . the scholar, the clergyman, the farmer, the worker, the unemployed, who leads them from the [jumbled political] parties back into the nation."

—Louise Solmitz, a schoolteacher who observed an early Nazi rally

By the late 1930s, Hitler's economic policies, including rearmament and massive public-works projects, had ended the depression in Germany. Many Germans followed his lead and cheered for him at Nazi rallies. Meanwhile, his political initiatives restricted freedom. He openly attacked Jewish people, communists, and socialists.

Militarists Gain Power in Japan In Japan, as in Germany, the 1920s was a period of increased democracy and peaceful change. The Japanese government reduced the power of the military, passed laws to give all men the right to vote, legalized trade unions, and allowed several diverse political parties to be established. This period ended when the Great Depression discredited Japan's civilian leaders in the 1930s.

Reasserting their traditional powers, military leaders argued that expansion throughout Asia would solve Japan's economic troubles and guarantee future security. Throughout the 1930s, the military played a significant role in shaping Japanese civilian and military policy.

Japan, however, did not become a totalitarian dictatorship. No charismatic leader like Stalin or Hitler emerged. Instead, Japan continued as a constitutional monarchy headed by a mainly aloof emperor.

The Japanese Expand Their Empire As the power shifted toward military control, Japan started on a course of aggressive military expansion. In 1931, Japan attacked Manchuria (man CHUR ee uh), a region in northeastern China, and established a puppet state. The new nation was named Manchukuo (man choo kwoh). Japan controlled its domestic and foreign policies, as well as its abundant natural resources. In 1937, Japan moved against China, gaining control over major Chinese railroad links and coastal areas. In the then-capital city of Nanjing, Japanese soldiers acted with such brutality—murdering more than 200,000 residents and burning a large section of the city—that the incident became known as the "Rape of Nanjing."

☑ **Checkpoint** How did the Great Depression affect political life in Germany and Japan?

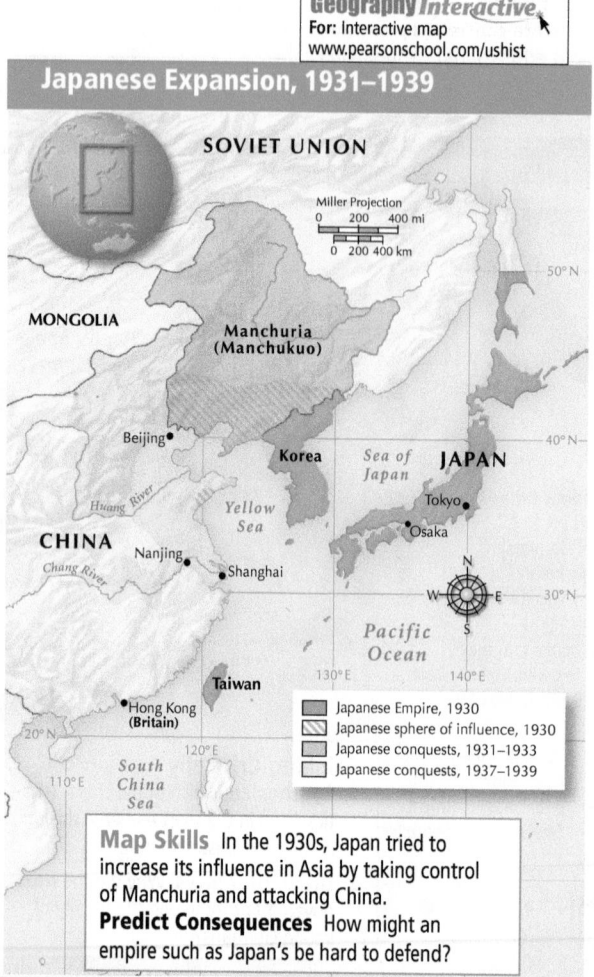

Geography *Interactive*
For: Interactive map
www.pearsonschool.com/ushist

Japanese Expansion, 1931–1939

SOVIET UNION

Miller Projection
0   200   400 mi
0   200 400 km

MONGOLIA

Manchuria (Manchukuo)

Beijing

Korea

Sea of Japan

JAPAN

Tokyo

Osaka

Huang River

Yellow Sea

CHINA

Nanjing

Shanghai

Chang River

Pacific Ocean

Taiwan

Hong Kong (Britain)

South China Sea

☐ Japanese Empire, 1930
▨ Japanese sphere of influence, 1930
☐ Japanese conquests, 1931–1933
☐ Japanese conquests, 1937–1939

Map Skills In the 1930s, Japan tried to increase its influence in Asia by taking control of Manchuria and attacking China.
Predict Consequences How might an empire such as Japan's be hard to defend?

Differentiated Instruction **Solutions for All Learners**

L4 Advanced Readers **L4 Gifted and Talented Students**

Explain to students that one of the reasons why Japan never became a dictatorship was because of the special role the emperor had in Japanese history and culture. Although military leaders increased their influence over the country, they never dared to threaten the emperor, who was considered almost godlike. On the surface, Japan and Germany seemed to share many similarities, including the desire for military conquest, strong racial pride, and a godlike leader. Yet the two cultures were very different, and the roles of the emperor and Hitler were quite different. Have students conduct further research on the government of Japan in the early twentieth century. Then have them create an illustrated compare-and-contrast chart explaining why Japan did not take the same political route as Germany, even though Japan supported a somewhat similar militaristic ideology.

Dictators Turn to Aggression

In the 1930s, Italy and Germany resorted to acts of aggression similar to those of Japan in Asia. Throughout the decade, neither the League of Nations nor democratic nations succeeded in stopping the aggression. It was a time that recalled a line from Irish poet William Butler Yeats: "The best lack all conviction and the worst are full of passionate intensity."

Weakness of the League of Nations In many ways, the League of Nations never recovered from America's refusal to join it. The League was also handicapped by its own charter. It had no standing army and no real power to enforce its decrees. It was only as strong as its members' resolve, and during the worldwide depression of the 1930s, those members lacked resolve. When aggressive nations began to test the League, they discovered that the organization was long on words and short on action.

Hitler and Mussolini Threaten the Peace From the first, Hitler focused on restoring Germany's strength and nullifying the provisions of the Treaty of Versailles. From 1933 to 1936, he rebuilt the German economy and dramatically enlarged the army, navy, and air force in direct defiance of the Treaty of Versailles. In the mid-1930s, Hitler began to move toward his goal of reunifying all Germanic people into one Reich, or state. He spoke often of the need for Germany to expand to gain *Lebensraum* (LAY buhns rowm), or living space, for its people. In 1935, he reclaimed the Saar (sahr) region from French control. In 1936, in a direct challenge to the League, he sent German troops into the Rhineland. The League failed to respond.

Meanwhile, Mussolini commenced his own imperial plans. In 1935, Italy invaded Ethiopia, an independent country in east Africa. Its emperor, Haile Selassie (HĪ luh suh lah SEE), appealed to the League of Nations for support. The organization did almost nothing, and Ethiopia fell.

Fighting Breaks Out in Spain Fascists were also victorious in the **Spanish Civil War,** a bloody conflict that raged from 1936 until 1939. The Nationalists, who had fascist tendencies, rebelled against Spain's democratic Republican government. Both Hitler and Mussolini sent military and economic aid to the Nationalist leader, General Francisco Franco, using the conflict to test some of their new military technology. Though the Soviet Union provided some support for the Republican side, France, Britain, and the United States remained largely on the sidelines, deploring the bloodshed but refusing to provide weapons to the Republican forces.

✓ **Checkpoint** Why did the League of Nations fail to halt German and Italian aggression?

Aggression Goes Unchecked

The policy that France and Britain pursued against aggressive nations during the 1930s is known as **appeasement.** It is a policy of granting concessions to a potential enemy in the hope that it will maintain peace. Unfortunately,

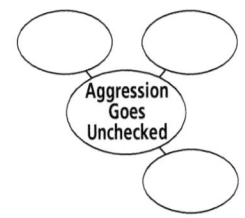

HISTORY MAKERS

Benito Mussolini (1883–1945)
Adolf Hitler (1889–1945)
Benito Mussolini's involvement in radical politics began when he was a young man. In 1919, he formed the Fascist Party and quickly gained followers with his powerful speaking style and by terrorizing opponents. Other world leaders criticized him when he sent Italian armies to invade Ethiopia in 1935. Only Germany's Adolf Hitler supported the move, and the two leaders became allies.

Before World War I, Adolf Hitler lived in Vienna and tried to make his living as an artist. During the war, he fought for Germany and was wounded several times. In 1933, Hitler became head of the German government. He quickly took absolute power using propaganda and violence. Though never close, he and Benito Mussolini supported each other in their efforts to control Europe.

NoteTaking

Reading Skill: Identify Main Ideas Use a concept web like the one below to record the main ideas about the policies of Great Britain, France, and the United States toward aggressive nations.

Aggression Goes Unchecked

Instruct

- **Introduce: Key Term** Ask students to find the key term *appeasement* (in bold) in the text. Ask them to think about a time when they have observed *appeasement* in action in daily life. Have student volunteers share their observations.

- **Teach** Point out to students that memories of World War I made some people want to avoid war at any cost. Ask **What country did some Western nations view as a greater threat than Germany? Why?** *(the Soviet Union because some Western nations feared the spread of communism)* **What effect did the United States policy of isolationism have on the British and French policy of appeasement toward Germany?** *(Since the United States was otherwise occupied with its economic troubles in the early years of the war, Britain and France had to determine the best course of action toward Germany, namely a policy of appeasement.)* **How did Hitler take advantage of appeasement?** *(He took over Austria and Sudetenland in Czechoslovakia.)*

- **Analyzing the Visuals** Draw students' attention to the photograph of Chamberlain and Hitler on the next page. Ask **Why are the two leaders shaking hands?** *(The two leaders are meeting at the Munich Conference, where they will discuss ways to maintain peace in Europe.)* Have students discuss why the Munich Conference did not preserve peace in Europe.

Independent Practice

Have students complete the concept web to record the main ideas about the policies of Great Britain, France, and the United States toward aggressive nations. For a completed version of the concept web, see Note Taking Transparencies, **B-111b.**

Monitor Progress

Circulate to make sure that students are filling in their concept webs correctly and that they understand the policies that these nations had toward aggressive nations.

Answer

✓ The League had no enforcement power.

Assess Progress **L3**

- Have students complete the Section Assessment.

- Administer the Section Quiz.
  Teaching Resources, **p. 19**

- To further assess student understanding, use Progress Monitoring Transparencies, **107**.

Reteach

If students need more instruction, have them read the section summary.

Reading and Note Taking **L3**
Study Guide

Adapted Reading and **L1** **L2**
Note Taking Study Guide

Spanish Reading and **L2**
Note Taking Study Guide

Extend **L4**

Organize students into two teams. Have students research the subject of appeasement and conduct a debate between the teams representing the supporters and opponents of the policy.

Answer

 They wanted to avoid another conflict like World War I. They also wanted a strong Germany to act as a buffer between the Soviet Union and Europe.

---

appeasement only spurred the fascist leaders to become more bold, adventurous, and aggressive.

Why did France and Britain appease the fascist powers? There were a number of reasons. World War I was so horrible that some leaders vowed never to allow another such war to break out. Other leaders believed that the Soviet Union posed a greater threat than Nazi Germany. They maintained that a strong Germany would provide a buffer against the Soviet menace. Still other leaders questioned the resolve of their own people and their allies—particularly the United States.

The United States played an important role in this appeasement policy. Although, in the 1930s, President Franklin Roosevelt pursued a Good Neighbor policy with Latin America and improved relations with the Soviet Union, he did not take a forceful line against German aggression. Instead, the country concerned itself with its own economic troubles and embraced a policy of isolationism.

Hitler took advantage of the lack of commitment and unity among France, Britain, and the United States. In the spring of 1938, he brought Austria into his Reich. Austria was given little choice but to accept this union, called the **Anschluss** (AHN shloos). In the fall, Hitler turned toward the Sudetenland, a portion of western Czechoslovakia that was largely populated by ethnic Germans.

Many people expected the conflict over the Sudetenland to lead to a general war. But once again, Britain and France appeased Germany. At the Munich Conference with Hitler, British prime minister Neville Chamberlain and French premier Edouard Daladier sacrificed the Sudetenland to preserve the peace. On his return to London, Chamberlain told a cheering crowd that the **Munich** (MYOO nihk) **Pact,** the agreement reached at the conference, had preserved "peace for our time." He was wrong. It merely postponed the war for 11 months.

✓ **Checkpoint** Why did Britain, France, and the United States not stop fascist aggression in the 1930s?

Appeasement at Munich
British prime minister Neville Chamberlain greets Hitler at the Munich Conference in 1938. Historians still debate why Britain and France pursued the policy of appeasement leading up to World War II.

SECTION **1** Assessment

Progress Monitoring Online
For: Self-test with vocabulary practice
www.pearsonschool.com/ushist

Comprehension

1. **Terms and People** Write several sentences describing what the items listed below have in common.
   - totalitarianism
   - Joseph Stalin
   - Benito Mussolini
   - Adolf Hitler
   - anti-Semitic
   - Anschluss

2. **NoteTaking Reading Skill: Summarize** Use your table and concept web to answer the Section Focus Question: Why did totalitarian states rise after World War I, and what did they do?

Writing About History

3. **Quick Write: Analyze Primary Sources** Reread the Primary Source in this section describing the crowd at one of Hitler's speeches. Write one paragraph analyzing the source. Consider the following questions: What key words are used to describe Hitler? What do these words suggest about how the crowd viewed Hitler?

Critical Thinking

4. **Recognize Effects** How did World War I contribute to the rise of dictators in Europe?

5. **Make Comparisons** How were Germany and Japan similar in the 1930s? How were they different?

6. **Express Problems Clearly** How did the policy of appeasement encourage aggression?

Section 1 Assessment

1. Example: Joseph Stalin, Benito Mussolini, and Adolf Hitler were all leaders of totalitarian governments that controlled all aspects of daily life. Hitler rose to power by preaching anti-Semitism, or hatred against Jews, and promising to expand Germany through military conquest. The forced union between Germany and Austria, called the Anschluss, was a major goal on his path toward expanding the German empire.

2. Weak governments in countries such as Germany and Italy were unable to relieve the suffering of people during the Great Depression. Strong fascist leaders such as Hitler and Mussolini promised to solve their countries' economic problems through militarism and nationalism.

3. Students' paragraphs should note some of the words such as *helper, savior,* and *deliverer,* which suggests that the crowd sees him as a godlike rescuer from their pain.

4. The Treaty of Versailles left bitter feelings among Germans. The inability of the League of Nations to enforce its laws led some dictators to build powerful new armies.

5. Both became militaristic and started expanding their empires. However, Japan never developed a totalitarian dictatorship like Germany did.

6. The policy of appeasement made Hitler more confident, and he pushed for additional lands. Rather than avoid war, appeasement merely delayed it for a few months.

For additional assessment, have students access **Progress Monitoring Online** at **www.pearsonschool.com/ushist.**

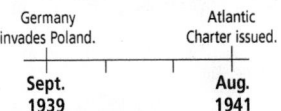

▲ Women protesting the Lend-Lease Act

WITNESS HISTORY

An Isolationist Voice

As war erupted in Europe, Americans debated what stance the United States should take on the global conflict. Charles A. Lindbergh, the popular aviation hero, felt strongly that it would be a mistake for the United States to enter the new war in Europe:

❝We must band together to prevent the loss of more American lives in these internal struggles of Europe. . . . Modern war with all its consequences is too tragic and too devastating to be approached from anything but a purely American standpoint. We should never enter a war unless it is absolutely essential to the future welfare of our nation. . . . Our safety does not lie in fighting European wars. It lies in our own internal strength, in the character of the American people and of American institutions.❞

—Charles Lindbergh, radio address, September 15, 1939

Objectives

As you teach this section, keep students focused on the following objectives to help them answer the Section Focus Question and master core content.

- Understand the course of the early years of World War II in Europe.
- Describe Franklin Roosevelt's foreign policy in the mid-1930s and the great debate between interventionists and isolationists.
- Explain how the United States became more involved in the conflict.

From Isolation to Involvement

Objectives

- Understand the course of the early years of World War II in Europe.
- Describe Franklin Roosevelt's foreign policy in the mid-1930s and the great debate between interventionists and isolationists.
- Explain how the United States became more involved in the conflict.

Terms and People

blitzkrieg	Neutrality Act of 1939
Axis Powers	Tripartite Pact
Allies	Lend-Lease Act
Winston Churchill	Atlantic Charter

NoteTaking

Reading Skill: Sequence Sequence the major events described in the section in a timeline.

Germany invades Poland.	Atlantic Charter issued.
Sept. 1939	**Aug. 1941**

Why It Matters While Britain and France appeased the dictator in Germany at Munich, American President Franklin Roosevelt condemned aggression in Asia but did little to stop it. As war exploded in Europe, it became increasingly difficult for the United States to maintain its neutrality. Once again, Americans would have to decide what role they were willing to play in shaping world events. **Section Focus Question: How did Americans react to events in Europe and Asia in the early years of World War II?**

Roosevelt Opposes Aggression

The unrestrained violence of the 1937 Japanese attack on China shocked Americans, even before the notorious Rape of Nanjing in December 1937. Japan attacked without a declaration of war. Its planes rained terror on Chinese cities, especially Shanghai and Nanjing. The Japanese had even killed three American sailors when Japanese warplanes sank the United States gunboat *Panay* on the Chang River.

In the midst of these bloody events, President Franklin Roosevelt criticized Japan's aggression in a speech in Chicago on October 5, 1937. He lamented the "reign of terror and international lawlessness," the bombing of civilian populations, and the horrible acts of cruelty. Speaking in a city where American isolationist sentiments

Prepare to Read

Background Knowledge L3

Remind students that the United States favored the policies of appeasement and isolationism. Ask students to think about what might cause the United States to abandon these policies.

Set a Purpose L3

- **WITNESS HISTORY** Read the selection aloud.

  Ask **Why did Lindbergh think that European wars had little to do with the safety of the United States?** *(Sample response: There is a great distance between the United States and Europe. Joining a war that poses no immediate threat to the nation may jeopardize the safety of the United States.)*

- **Focus** Point out the Section Focus Question, and write it on the board. Tell students to refer to this question as they read. *(Answer appears with Section 2 Assessment answers.)*

- **Preview** Have students preview the Section Objectives and the list of Terms and People.

- **NoteTaking** Using the Guided Reading strategy (TE, p. T20), have students read this section. As they read, have students sequence events that happened in the first two years of the war. Reading and Note Taking Study Guide

---

Vocabulary Builder

Use the information below and the following resource to teach students the high-use words from this section. Teaching Resources, Vocabulary Builder, p. 10

High-Use Words	Definitions and Sample Sentences
coordinate	*v.* to place in order or harmonize German forces **coordinated** the use of planes and tanks to break through the Polish defenses.
evaluate	*v.* to judge or find the value of France, Britain, and the United States **evaluated** the threat posed by Germany and Italy and chose to pursue a policy of appeasement.

Roosevelt Opposes Aggression

Instruct

- **Introduce** Have students read the Primary Source quotation from Roosevelt's Quarantine speech on this page. Ask **To what does Roosevelt compare war?** *(a disease)* Have students discuss whether they think this comparison is valid.

- **Teach** Ask **What was so shocking about Japan's attack on China?** *(It was extremely violent and was done without declaring war.)* **Why did Roosevelt propose that peaceful nations try to isolate aggressive ones?** *(Students may answer that he hoped to stop the spread of aggression and show aggressors that peaceful nations would not tolerate their behavior without going to war.)* Using the Idea Wave strategy (TE, p. T22), have students discuss why some people criticized Roosevelt's Quarantine speech.

- **Analyzing the Visuals** Direct students to the photograph of the two women on the previous page. Ask **Would these women be more likely to support Lindbergh's or Roosevelt's point of view? Explain.** *(Lindbergh; they are holding signs that oppose sending American soldiers to fight in a war.)*

Independent Practice

Have each student write one sentence explaining how a supporter might respond to Roosevelt's Quarantine speech and another sentence explaining how an opponent of the speech might respond.

Monitor Progress

As students fill in their timelines, circulate to make sure that they understand the sequence of the major events described in this section. For a completed version of the timeline, see Note Taking Transparencies, B-112.

Answer

✓ He called for isolating Japan, but did not specify how.

---

were strong, Roosevelt suggested that no part of the world was truly isolated from the rest of the world. He warned:

> **Primary Source** "When an epidemic of physical disease starts to spread, the community approves and joins in a quarantine of the patients in order to protect the health of the community against the spread of the disease. . . . War is a contagion, whether it be declared or undeclared. It can engulf states and peoples remote from the original scene of hostilities. We are determined to keep out of war, yet we cannot insure ourselves against the disastrous effects of war and the dangers of involvement."
> —President Franklin Roosevelt, Quarantine speech, October 5, 1937

Roosevelt's solution for stopping aggression involved an informal alliance of the peace-loving nations, but he did not suggest what steps the peaceful nations should take in quarantining the aggressive ones. Roosevelt's speech was widely criticized, and for a time, the President backed away from his more interventionist stance. The speech did, however, alert some Americans to the threat Japan posed to the United States.

✓ **Checkpoint** How did President Roosevelt react to Japan's aggression in China in the late 1930s?

War Erupts in Europe

Roosevelt's words failed to prevent Japan from extending its control over much of China. Similarly, France and Britain's efforts to appease Hitler in Europe failed to limit the dictator's expansionist plans. By the end of 1938, even the leaders of France and Britain realized that Hitler's armed aggression could only be halted by a firm, armed defense. The urgency of the situation grew in the spring of 1939 when Hitler violated the Munich Pact by absorbing the remainder of Czechoslovakia into his German Reich.

Hitler Launches a Blitzkrieg Against Poland Finally, British and French leaders saw the need to take action. They vowed not to let Hitler take over another country without consequences. Realizing that Hitler's next move would be against Poland, Britain and France signed an alliance with Poland, guaranteeing aid if Hitler attacked. Hitler, however, was more concerned about war with the Soviet Union than with Britain and France. Not wanting to fight a war on two fronts, Germany signed the Nazi-Soviet Nonaggression Pact with the Soviets on August 23, 1939. The two former rivals publicly promised not to

The German Juggernaut Rolls Through Europe

As the map on the next page shows, the Nazi war machine rampaged through Europe from 1939 through 1941. Below, victorious German troops parade through the Arc de Triomphe in Paris, France (left), after Nazi tanks had rolled through Belgium (right).

Differentiated Instruction   Solutions for All Learners

L1 Special Needs Students   **L2 English Language Learners**   **L2 Less Proficient Readers**

For students who are visual learners or who have trouble mastering concepts, have them view the images of the women at the top of the previous page. Ask them to describe what they see. Explain that these women are expressing isolationist viewpoints by opposing a bill to help democratic countries that were fighting against fascist governments. Have students explain, in their own words, why the women oppose the bill. Then, have them explain how those feelings relate to the concept of isolationism.

attack one another. Secretly, they agreed to invade and divide Poland and recognize each other's territorial ambitions. The public agreement alone shocked the West and guaranteed a German offensive against Poland.

War came to Europe in the early hours of September 1, 1939, when a massive German **blitzkrieg** (BLIHTS kreeg), or sudden attack, hit Poland from three directions. *Blitzkrieg* means "lightning war." It was a relatively new style of warfare that emphasized the use of speed and firepower to penetrate deep into the enemy's territory. The newest military technologies made it devastatingly effective. Using a coordinated assault by tanks and planes, followed by motorized vehicles and infantry, Germany broke through Poland's defenses and destroyed its air force. The situation became even more hopeless on September 17 when the Soviet Union invaded Poland from the east. Although France and Britain declared war against Germany, they did nothing to help save Poland. By the end of the month, a devastated Poland fell in defeat.

France Falls to the Axis Powers Europe was at war, just as it had been 21 years earlier. The **Axis Powers** eventually included Germany, Italy, Japan, and several other nations. The **Allies** included Britain, France, and eventually many other nations, including the Soviet Union, the United States, and China. But after the Polish campaign, the war entered an eight-month period of relative quiet, known in Britain as the "phony war." Things would not remain quiet for long, however.

The next storm erupted with raging fury in the spring of 1940. Germany's nonaggression pact with the Soviet Union freed Hitler to send his army west. On April 9, 1940, Germany attacked Denmark and Norway. The two countries fell almost immediately. On May 10, he sent his blitzkrieg forces into the

A woman weeps as she salutes her new rulers.

German Aggression, 1936–1941

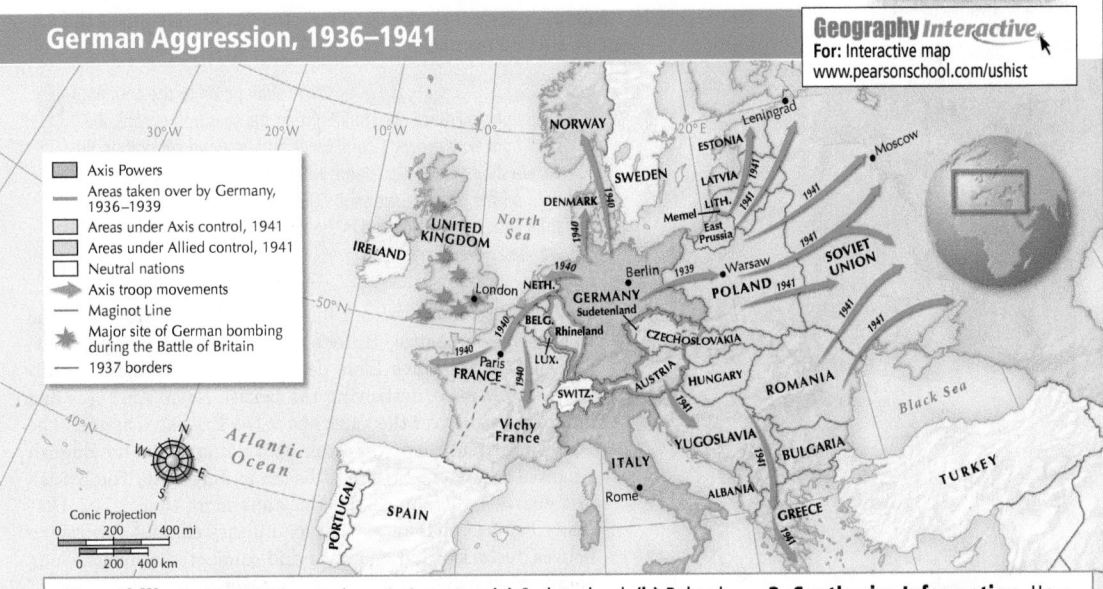

Geography *Interactive*
For: Interactive map
www.pearsonschool.com/ushist

Legend:
- Axis Powers
- Areas taken over by Germany, 1936–1939
- Areas under Axis control, 1941
- Areas under Allied control, 1941
- Neutral nations
- Axis troop movements
- Maginot Line
- Major site of German bombing during the Battle of Britain
- 1937 borders

Conic Projection
0   200   400 mi
0   200   400 km

Map Skills In 1939, Hitler used force, rather than diplomatic gymnastics to add territory to the German Reich.

1. **Locate:** (a) Sudetenland, (b) Poland, (c) Vichy France

2. **Location** What made Poland a difficult ally for France and Britain to protect?

3. **Synthesize Information** How does this map illustrate the dire situation of the Allies in 1941?

War Erupts in Europe ⓭

Instruct

- **Introduce: Key Term** Ask students to find the key term ***blitzkrieg*** (in bold) in the text. Then, write the term on the board, say it aloud, have the students say it with you, and provide them with a definition. Have students analyze the photos of German troops in Paris and Belgium on the previous page. Ask them to discuss how these photos illustrate ***blitzkrieg.*** Then, show them Color Transparency: *German Blitzkrieg.* Ask **Why was *blitzkrieg* such a devastating form of warfare?** (*It used new technology to quickly strike deep within enemy lines and with great force.*) Ask students to think about how ***blitzkrieg*** differs from forms of fighting they have read about in previous wars. Color Transparencies **A-102**

- **Teach** Explain that Hitler had a very clear plan for conquering Europe. Ask **Why was it important for Germany to ensure Soviet cooperation before attacking Poland?** (*Hitler did not want to fight a two-front war.*) Have students read the Primary Source quotation from Winston Churchill's 1940 speech on the next page. Ask **What effect do you think Churchill's speech had on the British people at this point in the war?** (*It lifted them up and inspired them at a time when Germany seemed unstoppable.*)

- **Quick Activity** Have students access **www.pearsonschool.com/ushist** to use the Geography Interactive map and then answer the map skills questions in the text.

Differentiated Instruction   Solutions for All Learners

ⓛ **Special Needs Students** ⓛ **English Language Learners** ⓛ **Less Proficient Readers**

To help students understand Hitler's plan for victory, ask them to read the text under the blue heading "War Erupts in Europe." Have students outline the text as they read, and model the first few entries on the board for them. Tell students that their outlines should note why Germany signed a treaty with the Soviet Union, how blitzkrieg gave the Nazi army the military advantage over the rest of Europe, and how Hitler planned to deal with France and Britain. Then, ask students to use their outlines to write paragraphs summarizing Hitler's strategy for conquering Europe.

Answers

Map Skills

1. Review locations with students.
2. It was on the other side of Germany.
3. The map shows that German troops were advancing very quickly throughout Europe.

Netherlands, Belgium, and Luxembourg. The small nations fell like tumbling dominoes. Hitler seemed invincible; his army unstoppable.

Hitler next set his sights on France. France had prepared for Germany's invasion by constructing an interconnected series of fortresses known as the Maginot Line along its border with Germany. Additionally, France had stationed its finest armies along its border with Belgium—the route that Germany had used to attack France in 1914. In between the Maginot Line and Belgium lay the Ardennes, a hilly, forested area that military experts considered invasion proof.

But once again the military experts were wrong. In early May 1940, German tanks rolled through the Ardennes, ripped a hole in the thin French line there, and raced north toward the English Channel. The German plan involved attacking the French and British forces from the front and the rear and trapping them against the channel. It almost worked. Only a few tactical German mistakes gave Britain enough time to evacuate its forces from the French port of Dunkirk. Some 338,000 British and French troops escaped, to Britain. Had they not escaped, it is doubtful if Britain could have remained in the war.

The Miracle of Dunkirk was a proud moment for Britain, but as the new prime minister **Winston Churchill** cautioned Parliament, "wars are not won by evacuations." Although the British army escaped, the Germans took Paris and forced the French to surrender in the same railway car that the French had used for the German surrender in 1918. France was then divided into two sections: a larger northern section controlled by the Germans and known as Occupied France, and a smaller southern section administered by the French and known as Unoccupied France, or Vichy France, after its capital city. Although Vichy France was officially neutral, it collaborated with the Nazis.

The Battle of Britain Is Fought in the Air France had fallen to Hitler in just 35 days. Hitler next turned his fury on Britain. After the evacuation at Dunkirk, Churchill made it clear that he had no intention of continuing the policy of appeasement. He told his nation:

Primary Source "We shall go on to the end. We shall fight in France, we shall fight on the seas and oceans, we shall fight with growing confidence and growing strength in the air, we shall defend our island, whatever the cost may be, we shall fight on the beaches, we shall fight on the landing grounds, we shall fight in the fields and in the streets, we shall fight in the hills; we shall never surrender."

—Winston Churchill, June 4, 1940

Churchill's words stirred his nation as the British readied themselves for battle. Hitler's plan to invade Britain, code-named Operation Sea Lion, depended upon Germany's Luftwaffe, or air force, destroying the British Royal Air Force and gaining control over the skies above the English Channel. The Battle of Britain, then, was an air battle, fought over the English Channel and Great Britain. It began in July 1940. The British lost nearly 1,000 planes, the Germans more than 1,700. Germany bombed civilian as well as military targets, destroying houses, factories, and churches and conducted a months-long bombing campaign against London itself, known as "the blitz." But the British held on and, sensing failure, Hitler made a tactical decision to postpone the invasion of Britain indefinitely.

✔ **Checkpoint** Which side seemed to be winning the war at the end of 1940?

The Miracle of Dunkirk
Almost cut off from escape by the German army, British and French troops evacuated from Dunkirk using almost any sailing vessel available, including private yachts and fishing boats as small as 14 feet long! Some of the small boats were used to get close to shore to pick up men and then ferry them to larger naval vessels waiting in deeper waters. *Why do you think the evacuation from Dunkirk raised morale in Britain?*

Independent Practice
Have students examine the image on this page and answer the accompanying question. Then, have them write a newspaper article describing the reactions of British citizens to the speech that Winston Churchill gave after the evacuation of Dunkirk.

Monitor Progress
To review this section, ask **What event caused Britain and France to form an alliance with Poland?** *(Hitler violated the Munich Pact and took control of what remained of Czechoslovakia.)* **What guaranteed a German offensive against Poland?** *(the Nazi-Soviet Nonaggression Pact)*

History Background

Arguing Against Appeasement Throughout the 1930s, Churchill was critical of British foreign policies. While most British political leaders were supporting appeasement, Churchill was almost a lone voice in warning the world about the dangers of increasing German aggression. In fact, Churchill correctly predicted every move that Hitler would make to seize more land, while the British government tried unsuccessfully to appease Germany. In time, his astute observations and outspokenness won him many new supporters. On the day that Britain declared war on Germany, Prime Minister Chamberlain appointed Churchill to lead the British navy. As the Nazi army plowed through Europe, it became increasingly obvious that Britain needed a strong leader. When Chamberlain resigned in May 1940, the major political parties put aside most of their differences to form a united front. The members of Parliament agreed that Churchill should lead the country. In an unusual move, Churchill served not only as prime minister but also as the minister of defense.

Answers

Caption It showed that the British troops could survive even in the face of seeming defeat.

✔ the Axis Powers

Edward R. Murrow Reports on the Blitz

American news correspondent Edward R. Murrow (above) broadcast live from London as the Luftwaffe bombed the city. He described the purpose of his reports: "I have an old-fashioned belief that Americans like to make up their own minds on the basis of all available information."

How do you think Murrow's reports influenced Americans?

A milkman (above) delivers milk as usual in October 1940 amid the devastation of an air raid. Londoners (left) take refuge in an underground train station converted into an air-raid shelter.

Americans Debate Involvement

Winston Churchill referred to the United States in many of his speeches during the crisis in France and the Battle of Britain. The fight against Hitler, Churchill implied, was more than simply a European struggle. Nazi aggression threatened the freedoms and rights cherished by democratic nations everywhere. The contest was between ideologies as well as nations.

America Favors Isolation President Roosevelt shared Churchill's concerns, but at the beginning of the war in Europe he understood that the majority of Americans opposed U.S. intervention. The severe economic crisis of the Great Depression had served to pin the nation's attention firmly on domestic affairs throughout the 1930s. In addition, many believed that U.S. involvement in World War I had been a deadly, expensive mistake. The rise of fascism in Europe made the sacrifices of World War I seem even more pointless.

In the 1930s, numerous books and articles presented a new theory about why the United States had become involved in World War I that disturbed many Americans. The theory held that big business had conspired to enter the war in order to make huge fortunes selling weapons. In 1934, a senate committee chaired by Gerald Nye of South Dakota looked into the question. Although the Nye Committee discovered little hard evidence, its findings suggested that "merchants of death"—American bankers and arms manufacturers—had indeed pulled the United States into World War I. The committee's findings further reinforced isolationist sentiments.

In order to avoid making the "mistakes" that had led to U.S. involvement in World War I, Congress passed the Neutrality Acts of 1935, 1936, and 1937.

Americans Debate Involvement L3

Instruct

- **Introduce: Vocabulary Builder** Have students locate the vocabulary term *evaluate* and its definition. Point out to students that the "value" part of the word reflects its meaning, in that when people *evaluate* something, they determine its value, or how good it is. Explain that the United States needed to *evaluate* its stance about whether to enter the war in Europe.

- **Teach** Discuss the widespread feelings of isolationism in the United States in the 1930s. Ask **How did Congress try to ensure that the United States stayed out of foreign conflicts?** *(by passing the Neutrality Acts)* **What were some of the arguments of the interventionists and the isolationists?** *(Interventionists argued that Great Britain needed U.S. help to defend democracy; Isolationists argued that the greatest dangers were from Japan and the Soviet Union and that the only way to avoid war was through neutrality)* Ask **What do you think was the most important step that the United States took in preparing for the possibility of war?** *(Answers will vary, but students will probably say the Selective Service Act.)*

- **Analyzing the Visuals** Have students examine the images on this page. Ask them to write paragraphs explaining how seeing such images might make people change their minds about neutrality.

Answer

Caption Murrow's reports probably caused many Americans to consider U.S. involvement in Europe.

- To help students understand why many Americans favored neutrality, ask students to read and complete the worksheet *Interpreting a Political Cartoon: Neutrality.* Teaching Resources, **p. 15**

- Have students examine the Analyzing Political Cartoons activity and answer the questions in the text.

- To reinforce understanding of the argument between isolationists and interventionists in the United States, ask students to use the table on the next page to write a brief paragraph summarizing each viewpoint.

Monitor Progress

Circulate to make sure that students understand the debate between isolationists and interventionists.

The acts imposed certain restrictions on Americans during times of war. For example, Americans were prohibited from sailing on ships owned by belligerents or nations at war. The acts also prevented Americans from making loans to belligerents or selling them arms and munitions. The acts did not distinguish between aggressors like Germany and Italy and victims like Poland, or their allies, France and Britain.

Interventionists Urge Support for the Allies Once war began in Europe, Roosevelt felt confined by the limitations of the Neutrality Acts. Though he issued a proclamation of American neutrality, he was firmly anti-Nazi and wanted to aid the democracies of Europe. In the end, Congress agreed and passed the **Neutrality Act of 1939,** which included a cash-and-carry provision. This provision allowed belligerent nations to buy goods and arms in the United States if they paid cash and carried the merchandise on their own ships. Since the British navy controlled the seas, cash-and-carry in effect aided the Allies.

Many Americans disagreed with Roosevelt's openly pro-Allies position. They argued that FDR's policies violated American neutrality and threatened to push the United States into the war. Between early 1940 and late 1941, a great debate raged in America between isolationists and interventionists. The debate became particularly heated after the fall of France left Britain standing by itself in Europe against Germany. Interventionist organizations such as the Committee to Defend America by Aiding the Allies claimed that Britain was fighting for free countries everywhere. Sending aid to Britain was a way for America to stay out of the conflict.

Isolationists Argue for Neutrality Isolationists countered by claiming that giving aid to the Allies was automatically harming the Axis and would culminate with the United States entering the conflict. They argued that the only way to keep America safe was to follow a policy of complete neutrality. The America First Committee, an isolationist group, held rallies and sponsored speeches that criticized Roosevelt's openly pro-British policies. Charles Lindbergh became the leading isolationist voice. Lindbergh believed that the real threats to America were the Soviet Union and Japan, and he did not want to see his country weaken itself fighting in Western Europe to save Britain. Lindbergh's addresses were measured and clear. He appealed to Americans' minds but not their hearts.

Roosevelt Inches Toward Involvement Events in Europe shocked Americans out of strict neutrality. Reports by Edward R. Murrow, a CBS reporter stationed in London, during the blitz brought the war into American living rooms. His frequent live radio reports, which began with the words "This is London," emphasized that the Germans were bombing not armies or military sites but civilians—grandparents, parents, and children.

These reports and the turn of events in Europe against the Allies convinced many Americans that the United States needed to at least prepare to defend itself. Shortly after the fall of France in September 1940, Germany, Italy, and Japan signed the **Tripartite Pact** and became

The Only Way We Can Save Her

"STAY OUT! STAY OUT FOR MY SAKE, AS WELL AS YOUR OWN!"

AMERICA: THE LAST REFUGE OF DEMOCRACY

Analyzing Political Cartoons

The Only Way to Save Democracy? In this cartoon, a figure symbolizing democracy begs Uncle Sam to stay out of the war in Europe.
1. What does this cartoonist think has happened to democracy in Europe?
2. According to this cartoonist's vision, how will the United States be able to save democracy?

Connect to Your World

Debating Foreign Involvement The debate between isolationists and interventionists has existed since the founding of the republic. As President George Washington left office, he cautioned the country against becoming involved in foreign "entanglements." For many years most U.S. presidents followed this advice. In general, most Americans have preferred to avoid war unless directly threatened. That sentiment still seems to be true. For example, after terrorists attacked the United States on September 11, 2001, the U.S. government sent forces into Afghanistan to weed out the terrorists who were responsible and to oust the Taliban government, which had aided them. Polls showed that the majority of Americans supported these efforts. Less than two years later, the United States invaded Iraq to overthrow its dictator Saddam Hussein. At first, the many Americans who supported this effort did so because they believed that Hussein was building powerful weapons to use against the United States. When these weapons of mass destruction were not found, public support for the war waned.

Answers

Analyzing Political Cartoons
1. It has been destroyed.
2. by staying out of Europe's fight

Should the United States Enter World War II?	☑ Quick Study
Isolationist Viewpoint	**Interventionist Viewpoint**
• The United States should avoid alliances with other nations.	• The United States should work with other nations to promote collective security.
• Americans should focus on issues at home, such as the Depression.	• Axis aggressions were wrong and threatened American interests.
• Complete neutrality was the way to keep the United States safe.	• The United States should aid the Allies, who were fighting for democracy and freedom.
• Intervention in a foreign war would be a mistake, just as World War I was.	• The United States should put pressure on the Axis Powers and prepare for war.

allies. In that same month, after a heated debate between isolationists and interventionists, Congress passed a Selective Service Act—a peacetime draft—providing for the military training of 1.2 million troops and 800,000 reserve troops each year.

At the same time, President Roosevelt took an additional step to strengthen Britain. He gave Britain fifty World War I–era battleships in exchange for eight British defense bases. Britain needed the ships to convoy goods across the Atlantic. Believing the act to be an emergency measure, Roosevelt made the transfer without the consent of Congress.

The American people <u>evaluated</u> FDR's leadership the next month in the presidential election. Roosevelt ran for an unprecedented third term against Republican nominee Wendell L. Willkie of Indiana. Willkie was critical of FDR's handling of both the economy and foreign affairs but not of the President's basic positions on either. Given such little differences between candidates, Americans voted overwhelmingly not to change leaders in the middle of a crisis.

 Checkpoint According to interventionists, how would aiding the Allies actually keep the United States out of the war?

America Takes Steps Toward War

Once safely reelected, President Roosevelt increased his support of Britain. When Britain began to run short on funds to purchase cash-and-carry goods in the United States, FDR took the opportunity to address Congress. On January 6, 1941, he spoke about "four freedoms"—freedom of speech, freedom of worship, freedom from want, and freedom from fear—that were threatened by Nazi and Japanese militarism. Roosevelt believed that the best way to stay out of the conflict with Germany was to aid Britain.

Lend-Lease Gives Aid to the Allies Roosevelt compared America's situation to the scenario of a fire in a neighbor's home. If a neighbor asked to borrow your fire hose to put out the fire, you would not debate the issue or try to sell the hose. Extending help was both being a good neighbor and acting to keep the fire from spreading to your own home.

Britain, Roosevelt said, needed American aid, and it had run out of money to pay for it. The President called for America to become "the great arsenal for democracy." Once again, America answered Britain's plea for help. In March 1941, Congress approved the **Lend-Lease Act,** symbolically numbered 1776, after another heated debate between isolationists and interventionists. The act authorized Roosevelt to

Aid to Britain
The president of Bundles for Britain (above) collects money for her organization, which sent food and clothing to help British people suffering from the effects of the war. *Is Bundles for Britain an example of the interventionist or isolationist viewpoint?*

Vocabulary Builder
<u>evaluate</u>–(ee VAL yoo ayt) *v.* to judge or find the value of

America Takes Steps Toward War 🄻🄳

Instruct

- **Introduce: Key Terms** Ask students to find the key terms **Lend-Lease Act** and **Atlantic Charter** (in bold) in the text. Ask **How did the *Lend-Lease Act* and the *Atlantic Charter* move the United States away from neutrality in different ways?** *(The Lend-Lease Act increased economic aid to Britain; the **Atlantic Charter** signaled a deeper alliance between the United States and Great Britain.)*

- **Teach** Ask **What did Roosevelt think was the best way to avoid war with Germany?** *(by aiding Britain)* **How did Germany react to U.S. support of the Allies?** *(Germany ordered attacks on U.S. ships that were assisting the Allies.)* Have students study the image on the following page and answer the question that accompanies it.

- **Analyzing the Visuals** Have students examine the image of the Bundles for Britain leader. Have them brainstorm some "sales pitches" that the group might use to persuade people to support the cause.

Independent Practice

- Have students read and complete *Primary Source: The "Four Freedoms" Speech and George W. Bush's Address to a Joint Session of Congress.* Teaching Resources, **p. 17**

- Have students select a current issue, such as the war in Iraq, and then write a paragraph explaining whether Franklin Roosevelt might have taken an isolationist or interventionist position if he were living today.

Monitor Progress

To review this section, ask students to look over their timelines and evaluate which of the events that took place between September 1939 and August 1941 were the most significant.

Answers

✓ They argued that Britain was fighting for free countries everywhere, including the United States.

Caption interventionist viewpoint

Assess and Reteach

Assess Progress   L3

- Have students complete the Section Assessment.

- Administer the Section Quiz. Teaching Resources, **p. 20**

- To further assess student understanding, use Progress Monitoring Transparencies, **108**.

Reteach

If students need more instruction, have them read the section summary.

Reading and Note Taking   L3
Study Guide

Adapted Reading and   L1 L2
Note Taking Study Guide

Spanish Reading and   L2
Note Taking Study Guide

Extend   L4

Have students read and complete the Enrichment Worksheet: *Oral History: FDR's Fireside Chats.* Teaching Resources, **pp. 12–13**

Answers

✓ It increased economic aid and provided naval support to Britain.

Caption by showing that he saw the United States and Britain as long-term allies

Roosevelt and Churchill
President Roosevelt (left) met with British prime minister Winston Churchill (right) in August 1941. Although the United States was still not at war with Germany, the two leaders set out some common goals in the Atlantic Charter. *How did President Roosevelt's actions reveal his interventionist stance?*

"sell, transfer title to, exchange, lease, lend, or otherwise dispose of, to any such government any defense article" whenever he thought it was "necessary in the interests of the defense of the United States." By 1945, the United States had sent more than $40 billion of Lend-Lease aid to the Allies, including the Soviet Union. The Lend-Lease Act was nothing less than an economic declaration of war against Germany and the Axis Powers.

The Atlantic Charter Reinforces America's Support of Britain In August 1941, President Roosevelt and prime minister Churchill met secretly on a warship off the misty coast of Newfoundland. They talked not only about Britain's problems in the war but also about their hopes for the world after Hitler's defeat. On board the ship they signed the **Atlantic Charter,** a document that endorsed national self-determination and an international system of "general security." The signing of the Atlantic Charter signaled the deepening alliance between the two nations.

U.S. Navy Battles German U-Boats Hitler was not blind to America's actions in support of the Allies. Nor did he fail to notice the fact that the United States had begun to escort arms shipments to Iceland, where the British picked them up and transported them to England.

In the fall of 1941, he ordered his German U-boats, or submarines, to attack American ships. The U-boats shot at the USS *Greer,* hit the USS *Kearny,* and sunk the USS *Reuben James,* killing more than a hundred sailors. The attacks shocked and angered Americans, moving them closer to declaring war on Germany. Though the United States was still officially a neutral nation, Roosevelt gave orders to the navy to attack German U-boats on sight. In June 1941, Germany had gone to war against the Soviet Union, and by November, war against the United States seemed inevitable.

✓ **Checkpoint** How did the United States support the Allies after Roosevelt's reelection?

SECTION **2** Assessment

Progress Monitoring *Online*
For: Self-test with vocabulary practice
www.pearsonschool.com/ushist

Comprehension

1. **Terms and People** For each item below, write a sentence explaining its significance.
   - blitzkrieg
   - Axis Powers
   - Allies
   - Winston Churchill
   - Neutrality Act of 1939
   - Tripartite Pact
   - Lend-Lease Act
   - Atlantic Charter

2. **NoteTaking Reading Skill: Sequence** Use your timeline to answer the Section Focus Question: How did Americans react to events in Europe and Asia in the early years of World War II?

Writing About History

3. **Quick Write: Compare Points of View** Compare the image of the women protesting the Lend-Lease Act to the excerpt from Roosevelt's Quarantine speech in this section. Write a paragraph summarizing the two different points of view presented by these two documents.

Critical Thinking

4. **Summarize** Describe the course of World War II in Europe until the end of 1940.

5. **Identify Point of View** Why did members of the America First Committee believe that the United States should avoid war with Germany?

6. **Recognize Causes** Why did the United States give more and more help to the Allies?

Section 2 Assessment

1. Sentences should reflect an understanding of each term or person listed.

2. Americans were alarmed but wanted to try to avoid war. They gradually began to accept the idea of preparing for war and aiding the Allies.

3. Paragraphs should note that the women felt that any involvement in the conflict, even economic, would draw the United

States into war. Roosevelt argued that the United States could avoid war by helping to isolate aggressive nations.

4. Germany seemed to be winning the war because it had won most of the battles and had taken over several countries in Western Europe.

5. They believed that the Soviet Union and Japan were greater threats to U.S. security than Germany was.

6. Without economic aid, the Allies might have lost the war, and the United States did not want that to happen.

For additional assessment, have students access **Progress Monitoring *Online*** at **www.pearsonschool.com/ushist.**

Franklin Delano Roosevelt: The "Four Freedoms" Speech

In his State of the Union address to Congress on January 6, 1941, President Roosevelt stressed the danger that aggressive fascist powers presented to the United States. He urged the American people to support those "who are resisting aggression and are thereby keeping war away from our Hemisphere"—namely the Allies. Congress passed the Lend-Lease Act three months later to do just that. Finally, Roosevelt set out the ideals that he believed Americans should fight for: the Four Freedoms.

I address you, the Members of the Seventy-Seventh Congress, at a moment unprecedented[1] in the history of the Union. I use the word "unprecedented" because at no previous time has American security been as seriously threatened from without as it is today. . . .

In the future days, which we seek to make secure, we look forward to a world founded upon four essential human freedoms.

The first is freedom of speech and expression—everywhere in the world.

The second is freedom of every person to worship God in his own way—everywhere in the world.

The third is freedom from want—which, translated into world terms, means economic understandings which will secure to every nation a healthy peace time life for its inhabitants—everywhere in the world.

The fourth is freedom from fear—which, translated into world terms, means a worldwide reduction of armaments to such a point and in such a thorough fashion that no nation will be in a position to commit an act of physical aggression against any neighbor—anywhere in the world.

That is no vision of a distant millennium. It is a definite basis for a kind of world attainable in our own time and generation. That kind of world is the very antithesis[2] of the so-called new order of tyranny which the dictators seek to create with the crash of a bomb. . . . The world order which we seek is the cooperation of free countries, working together in a friendly, civilized society.

This nation has placed its destiny in the hands and heads and hearts of its millions of free men and women; and its faith in freedom under the guidance of God. Freedom means the supremacy of human rights everywhere. Our support goes to those who struggle to gain those rights and keep them. Our strength is our unity of purpose.

To that high concept there can be no end save victory.

1. **unprecedented** (uhn PREHS uh dehn tihd) *adj.* new, having no previous example.
2. **antithesis** (an TIHTH uh sihs) *n.* exact opposite.

SAVE FREEDOM OF SPEECH

BUY WAR BONDS

Inspired by Roosevelt's speech, the illustrator Norman Rockwell created four paintings, each illustrating one of the Four Freedoms. In *Freedom of Speech*, Rockwell shows a man speaking at his town meeting.

Thinking Critically

1. **Summarize** What are the Four Freedoms?

2. **Predict Consequences** How do you think an isolationist would respond to Roosevelt's speech?

History Background

Rockwell's *Four Freedoms* After the United States joined the war, artist Norman Rockwell lent his talents to the war effort. Inspired by Roosevelt's speech, Rockwell spent six months in 1942 producing four paintings. Each one represented his vision of what Roosevelt meant by each of the four freedoms. The paintings depicted ordinary Americans in scenes that could have taken place in daily life anywhere in the United States.

Prints of the paintings were published widely in *The Saturday Evening Post*, a popular magazine that often used Rockwell paintings for its covers. With each

painting was a moving essay by a famous writer expounding on the meaning of that freedom. The response was so overwhelming that soon a national tour of the original paintings was organized. The U.S. government used the paintings to increase financial support for the war effort. It is estimated that the paintings helped raise some $130 million in war bonds. Throughout the war Rockwell continued to produce popular images that reflected daily life in America.

Objectives

- Analyze documents from primary and secondary sources.
- Summarize points of view.
- Identify main ideas and details.

Background Knowledge L3

Remind students that Roosevelt made this speech when the United States was still officially neutral in the war. Point out that the first two freedoms he mentions refer to specific rights granted to all Americans in the Bill of Rights.

Instruct L3

After students read the speech, conduct a class discussion on these questions: **What was the main theme of the speech?** *(that the Allies, as democratic nations, were fighting for freedoms shared by the United States)* **What was Roosevelt's main political objective in making the speech?** *(to convince Americans to support aid to the Allies)* **Do you think he was persuasive?** *(Most students will probably say "yes" because he uses simple, forthright language and appeals to universal needs.)*

Monitor Progress

Organize students into four groups, each representing a different freedom. Have groups suggest examples of such freedoms in the world today. Have a representative from each group share the group's ideas with the rest of the class.

Answers

Thinking Critically

1. freedom of speech, freedom of religion, freedom from want, freedom from fear

2. Example: An isolationist would argue that the best way to protect American freedoms is to remain neutral.

Objectives

As you teach this section, keep students focused on the following objectives to help them answer the Section Focus Question and master core content.

- Explain why Japan decided to attack Pearl Harbor, and describe the attack itself.
- Outline how the United States mobilized for war after the attack on Pearl Harbor.
- Summarize the course of the war in the Pacific through the summer of 1942.

Prepare to Read

Background Knowledge L3

Have students recall under what conditions even strict isolationists thought the United States would be justified in going to war. Ask students to predict what might cause the United States to enter World War II.

Set a Purpose L3

- **WITNESS HISTORY** Read the selection aloud.

  Ask **Why did Roosevelt refer to the date of the Japanese attack on the United States as one that would "live in infamy?"** (It would forever be recalled as the date of an evil act.) **What might people infer from Roosevelt's comments about the length of the war?** (It might take a long time to win the war.)

- **Focus** Point out the Section Focus Question, and write it on the board. Tell students to refer to this question as they read. (Answer appears with Section 3 Assessment answers.)

- **Preview** Have students preview the Section Objectives and the list of Terms and People.

- **NoteTaking** Using the Guided Reading strategy (TE, p. T20), have students read this section. As they read, have students note the causes and effects of the attack on Pearl Harbor. Reading and Note Taking Study Guide

WITNESS HISTORY

A Date Which Will Live in Infamy

In December 1941, the Japanese mounted a surprise attack on the U.S. naval base at Pearl Harbor, Hawaii. The next day Franklin Delano Roosevelt spoke to the shocked American public:

❝Yesterday, December 7, 1941—a date which will live in infamy—the United States of America was suddenly and deliberately attacked by naval and air forces of the Empire of Japan. . . . The facts of yesterday speak for themselves. The people of the United States have already formed their opinions and well understand the implications to the very life and safety of our nation. . . . No matter how long it may take us to overcome this premeditated invasion, the American people in their righteous might will win through to absolute victory.❞

—Franklin Roosevelt, Message Asking for War Against Japan, December 8, 1941

▲ President Roosevelt addresses Americans after the attack on Pearl Harbor

America Enters the War

Objectives

- Explain why Japan decided to attack Pearl Harbor, and describe the attack itself.
- Outline how the United States mobilized for war after the attack on Pearl Harbor.
- Summarize the course of the war in the Pacific through the summer of 1942.

Terms and People

Hideki Tojo	Douglas MacArthur
Pearl Harbor	Bataan Death March
WAC	Battle of Coral Sea

NoteTaking

Reading Skill: Identify Causes and Effects
As you read, record the causes and effects of the attack on Pearl Harbor, as well as details about the attack itself, in a chart like the one below.

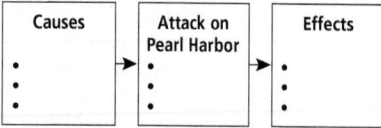

Causes	Attack on Pearl Harbor	Effects
•	•	•
•	•	•
•	•	•

Why It Matters In the beginning of December 1941, the United States had engaged in warlike activity but had yet to commit itself. A surprise attack on Pearl Harbor, an American naval base in Hawaii, ended all debate and brought the United States into the war. The participation of the United States in this war, as in World War I, would decide the struggle's conclusion. **Section Focus Question: How did the United States react to the Japanese attack on Pearl Harbor?**

Japan Attacks the United States

Although Japan and the United States had been allies in World War I, conflict over power in Asia and the Pacific had been brewing between the two nations for decades prior to 1941. Japan, as the area's industrial and economic leader, resented any threats to its authority in the region. America's presence in Guam and the Philippines and its support of China posed such a threat. Yet Japan relied on trade with the United States to supply much-needed natural resources.

Trouble in the Pacific As war broke out in Europe, the Japanese Empire continued to grow in China and began to move into Indochina. President Roosevelt tried to stop this expansion, in July of 1940, by placing an embargo on important naval and aviation supplies to Japan, such as oil, iron ore, fuel, steel, and rubber. After Japan signed the Tripartite Pact in 1940 with Germany and Italy, FDR instituted a more extensive embargo. The embargo slowed, but did not stop, Japanese expansion as the Japanese were able to secure the resources they needed within their new possessions.

Vocabulary Builder

Use the information below and the following resource to teach students the high-use words from this section. Teaching Resources, Vocabulary Builder, p. 10

High-Use Words	Definitions and Sample Sentences
allocate	*v.* to distribute according to a plan During World War II, the United States effectively **allocated** its resources to quickly build the war industry.
minimal	*adj.* smallest or least amount possible The troops hoped to take the hill with **minimal** casualties.

In 1941, General **Hideki Tojo** (hī DEHK ee TOH joh) became the Japanese prime minister. Known as "the Razor" for his sharp mind, he focused intently on military expansion but sought to keep the United States neutral. Throughout the summer of 1941, Japan and the United States attempted to negotiate an end to their disagreement, but with little success. Japan was bent on further expansion, and the United States was firmly against it. Finally, in late November 1941, Cordell Hull, the U.S. Secretary of State, rejected Japan's latest demands. Formal diplomatic relations continued for the next week, but Tojo had given up on peace. By the beginning of December he had made the decision to deliver a decisive first blow against the United States.

The Japanese Attack Pearl Harbor As Japanese diplomats wrangled in the U.S. capital, Japan's navy sailed for **Pearl Harbor,** Hawaii, the site of the United States Navy's main Pacific base. The forces that Tojo sent from Japan under the command of Vice Admiral Chuichi Nagumo (joo EE chee nah GOO moh) included 6 aircraft carriers, 360 airplanes, an assortment of battleships and cruisers, and a number of submarines. Their mission was to eradicate the American naval and air presence in the Pacific with a surprise attack. Such a blow would prevent Americans from mounting a strong resistance to Japanese expansion.

The attackers struck with devastating power, taking the American forces completely by surprise. A sailor aboard the hospital ship USS *Solace* recalled the destruction of the USS *Arizona:*

> **Primary Source** "I saw more planes coming in, passing over Battleship Row dropping bombs. I remember very clearly what looked like a dive-bomber coming in over the *Arizona* and dropping a bomb. I saw that bomb go down through what looked like a stack, and almost instantly it cracked the bottom of the *Arizona,* blowing the whole bow loose. It rose out of the water and settled. I could see flames, fire, and smoke coming out of that ship, and I saw two men fling through the air and the fire, screaming as they went."
> —Corpsman James F. Anderson, aboard the USS *Solace* in Pearl Harbor

Results of the Attack The Americans suffered heavy losses: nearly 2,500 people killed, 8 battleships severely damaged, 3 destroyers left unusable, 3 light cruisers damaged, and 160 aircraft destroyed and 128 more damaged. The U.S. battlefleet was knocked out of commission for nearly six months, allowing the Japanese to freely access the needed raw materials of their newly conquered territories, just as they had planned.

Despite these losses, the situation was not as bad as it could have been. The most important ships—aircraft carriers—were out at sea at the time of the attack and survived untouched. In addition, seven heavy cruisers were out at sea and also avoided detection by the Japanese. Of the battleships in Pearl Harbor, only three—the USS *Arizona,* the USS *Oklahoma,* and the USS *Utah*—suffered irreparable damage. American submarine bases also survived the morning, as did important fuel supplies and maintenance facilities. In the final analysis, Nagumo proved too conservative. He canceled a third wave of bombers, refused to seek out the aircraft carriers, and turned back toward home because he feared an American counterstrike. The American Pacific Fleet survived.

America Declares War As the news about Pearl Harbor spread across the nation and FDR prepared to address Congress, Americans rallied together. Many did not know what to expect, but they anticipated monumental changes. Journalist Marquis Child recalled thinking, "Nothing will ever be the same," and added, "it never was the same."

Japanese Ambitions
In late 1941, General Hideki Tojo (below) decided to stage a surprise attack on American forces. Items like this matchbook (below left) glorified Japan's military might. On the matchbook, planes emerge from a Japanese flag and fly in the direction of the flags of Britain and the United States.

Japan Attacks the United States

Instruct

- **Introduce: Key Term** Ask students to find the key term *Pearl Harbor* (in bold) in the text. Explain that the term has become synonymous with the attack that signaled the entrance of the United States into World War II.

- **Teach** Ask **What was the relationship between the United States and Japan prior to 1941?** *(Through trade, the United States supplied Japan with much needed natural resources.)* Explain that the United States placed an embargo on naval and aviation supplies that were traded to Japan. **What was the root of the conflict between the United States and Japan?** *(Japan's desire to expand its control over Asia and U.S. resistance to this expansion)* Have students read the Primary Source quotation from Corpsman James F. Anderson. Using the Numbered Heads strategy (TE, p. T23), have students discuss why the Japanese attacked Pearl Harbor and how the attack affected the United States.

- **Quick Activity** Have students access the History Interactive at **www.pearsonschool.com/ushist**. After students experience the History Interactive, ask them to share their reactions and think about how they would have been affected if they had lived in the United States at the time of the attack.

Connect to Your World

Reporting National Tragedy While Japan's assault on Pearl Harbor was the worst military attack on American soil, the attacks on September 11, 2001 were the worst terrorist attacks in American history. Both resulted in similar numbers of casualties, but the media covered each event very differently. Most Americans learned about Pearl Harbor through radio and newspaper reports. On September 11, most Americans watched the events unfold live on television starting soon after the first airplane hit the World Trade Center. The ability of modern media to bring events into people's homes made many Americans eyewitnesses to the event.

Independent Practice

Remind students that many Americans were reluctant to enter World War II. Then, review the images of the attack on Pearl Harbor on this page and the facing one. Have students suppose that they are living in the United States in 1941. Ask them to write journal entries explaining why the attack on Pearl Harbor so sharply changed the American attitude toward entering the war.

Monitor Progress

As students fill in their charts, circulate to make sure that they understand the causes and effects of the attack on Pearl Harbor, as well as details about the attack itself. For a completed version of the chart, see Note Taking Transparencies, B-113a.

The attack on Pearl Harbor left little doubt about declaring war on Japan. The Soviet Union's conversion to the Allied side, following Germany's invasion in June 1941, made some Americans doubt the wisdom of supporting the Allies. The attack on Pearl Harbor changed that. It made the necessity of declaring war on Japan clear and ended any continuing political divisions between isolationists and interventionists. After President Roosevelt's speech, the House voted 388 to 1 to declare war, and the Senate joined them unanimously. True to their military commitments with Japan, Germany and Italy declared war on America. Both Democrats and Republicans put aside their political differences to unify the nation in facing the task of winning a global war.

✔ **Checkpoint** What did the Japanese military leaders hope to achieve by attacking Pearl Harbor? Were they successful in this goal?

INTERACTIVE Whiteboard

Events That Changed America

SURPRISE ATTACK! PEARL HARBOR

December 7, 1941, dawned an overcast day in Pearl Harbor, Hawaii. The members of the U.S. military stationed there went about their usual Sunday activities. About half of the United States Navy's Pacific Fleet, including eight huge battleships, sat clustered in the harbor. At nearby Hickam Field and other airfields, American planes sat quietly wing-to-wing in perfect rows.

Just before 8 A.M., the Japanese attack on the unsuspecting Americans below had begun. Over the next several hours, Japanese bombers torpedoed the moored ships, while fighters and dive-bombers machine-gunned and bombed ship decks and airfields. American military forces, caught completely by surprise, attempted to ward off the attackers with little effect. The scene was one of utter destruction.

Sailors at Ford Island Naval Air Station are stunned by the wreckage around them. ▼

◀ The USS *Arizona* sank during the attack. Nearly 1,200 sailors and marines died on this ship alone.

Differentiated Instruction   Solutions for All Learners

L4 Gifted and Talented Students

Have students work in small groups to develop a radio program about the attack on Pearl Harbor. Students should work together to develop a script for the program. Remind them that it should include perspectives from many different people, including the reporters, eyewitnesses, U.S. sailors who were attacked, doctors who treated casualties, experts on East Asia, and so on. Also remind students that for a radio program, they cannot rely on visual images to get their story across but that they can use sound effects, music, and other audio techniques.

After students have developed their scripts, ask them to perform the radio program for the rest of the class. Have the students listening to the performance close their eyes so that they can better experience how Americans might have felt listening to such a program in 1941.

Answer

✔ Their goal was to wipe out the U.S. fleet and prevent the United States from halting Japanese expansion in Asia. The Japanese were not successful because the U.S. fleet survived and the United States entered World War II.

Mobilizing for War

Following the Japanese attack, a spirit of patriotism and service swept across the country. Americans looked for ways to contribute to the war effort. They joined the military, volunteered with the Red Cross and other organizations, and moved into new jobs to help.

Responding to the Call During the course of the war, more than 16 million Americans served in the military. From 1941 to 1942 alone, the army grew from about 1.4 million to more than 3 million, the navy increased from under 300,000 to more than 600,000, and the marines expanded from only about 54,000 to almost 150,000. Americans from all ethnic and racial backgrounds joined the fight. Approximately 300,000 Mexican Americans and 25,000 Native Americans

Damage at Pearl Harbor

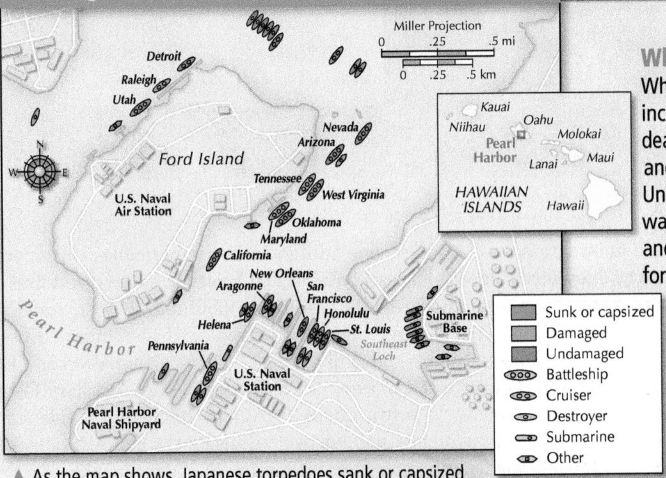

Miller Projection
0   .25   .5 mi
0   .25   .5 km

Detroit
Raleigh
Utah
Ford Island
Nevada
Arizona
U.S. Naval Air Station
Tennessee
West Virginia
Oklahoma
Maryland
California
New Orleans
Aragonne
San Francisco
Honolulu
Helena
St. Louis
Pennsylvania
Southeast Loch
U.S. Naval Station
Pearl Harbor Naval Shipyard
Submarine Base

HAWAIIAN ISLANDS
Kauai
Niihau
Oahu
Pearl Harbor
Molokai
Lanai
Maui
Hawaii

Sunk or capsized
Damaged
Undamaged
Battleship
Cruiser
Destroyer
Submarine
Other

▲ As the map shows, Japanese torpedoes sank or capsized eight huge battleships and several smaller ships at Pearl Harbor. Most of the damaged ships were eventually repaired.

Soon, newspapers such as the *Honolulu Star-Bulletin* (below) spread grief and outrage around the country. Pearl Harbor inspired motivation for the U.S. war effort.

Why It Matters

When the smoke cleared, nearly 2,500 people, including military personnel and civilians, were dead. The Pacific Fleet had taken a big hit— and there was no longer any question that the United States would enter World War II. The war would change the lives of all Americans, and its effects would ripple across the globe for decades after the last shot was fired.

Female firefighters try to douse fires after the attack. ▼

Thinking Critically
How did Pearl Harbor change American opinion about the war?

History *Interactive*

For: More information about Pearl Harbor
www.pearsonschool.com/ushist

Honolulu Star-Bulletin 1st EXTRA
SAN FRANCISCO, Dec. 7.—President Roosevelt announced this morning that Japanese planes had attacked Manila and Pearl Harbor.

WAR!
OAHU BOMBED BY JAPANESE PLANES

SIX KNOWN DEAD, 21 INJURED, AT EMERGENCY HOSPITAL
Attack Made On Island's Defense Areas
Hundreds See City Bombed

AVENGE December 7

History Background

The Airline Industry World War II helped boost the airline business. U.S. aircraft companies were able to produce large numbers of planes in short amounts of time and at lower costs. Near the end of the war, aviation industry leaders worried that they would experience an economic downturn. However, after the airplanes and airfields used in battle were converted for commercial air travel, many airline companies flourished. At the end of the war, the United States and Great Britain were among the few countries with strong airline industries. Along with the conversion of military planes, another reason these countries' airline industries remained strong was the relocation of German industry after the war. The United States and Great Britain worked out agreements to allow for greater expansion of postwar commercial flights. Better, less expensive planes, coupled with an economic boom and greater familiarity with airplanes among veterans increased people's willingness to use airlines for personal travel. By 1957, more people were crossing the Atlantic Ocean by plane than by ship.

Independent Practice

Have students read and complete the worksheet *Reading a Chart: Industry During World War II.* Teaching Resources, p. 18

Monitor Progress

Circulate to make sure that students understand the effect of World War II on the U.S. economy.

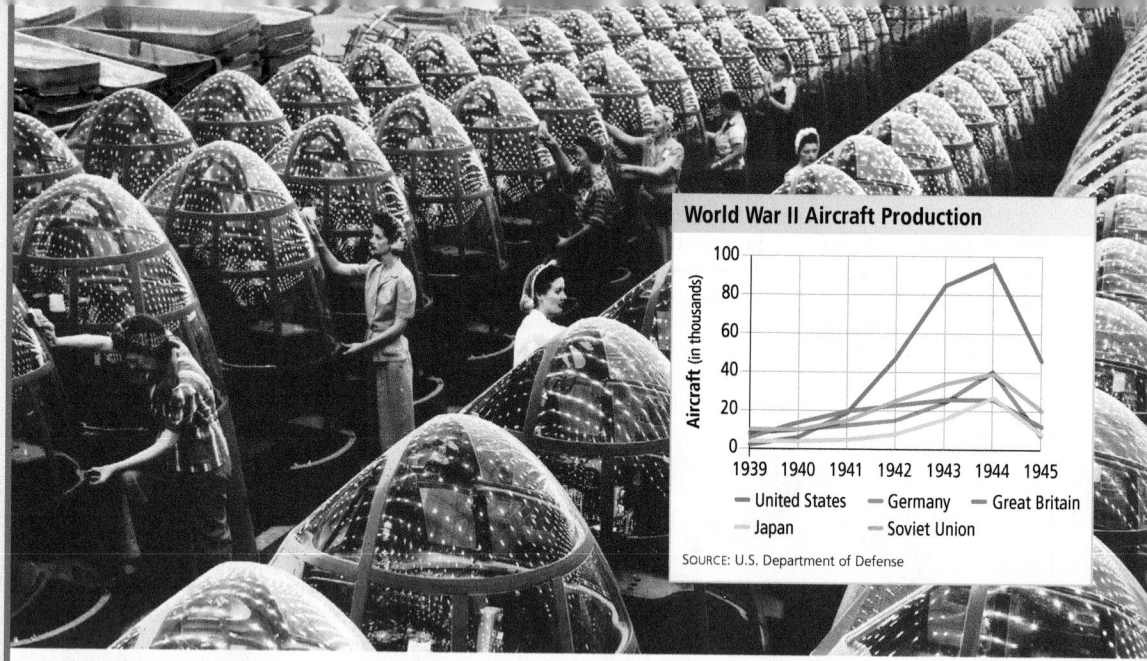

World War II Aircraft Production

SOURCE: U.S. Department of Defense

The Production Miracle

America's productive capability proved to be one of the Allies' main advantages in World War II. Above, female workers inspect the noses of A-20 attack bomber aircraft. *By how much did U.S. aircraft production increase between 1941 and 1944?*

Vocabulary Builder
allocate–(AL oh kayt) *v.* to distribute according to a plan

served in integrated units. Nearly one million African Americans also joined the military. They served mostly in segregated units, however, and were at first limited to supporting roles. However, as casualties mounted, African Americans saw more active combat, and some eventually served in white combat units.

Over 350,000 women also responded to the call. In 1941, Congresswoman Edith Nourse Rogers introduced a bill to establish a Women's Army Auxiliary Corps—which became the **Women's Army Corps (WAC)** in 1943—to provide clerical workers, truck drivers, instructors, and lab technicians for the United States Army. More than 150,000 women volunteered for the service; 15,000 served abroad over the course of the war and over 600 received medals for their service. More than 57,000 nurses served in the Army Nurse Corps, putting themselves in danger to care for the wounded in Europe and the Pacific. Tens of thousands more American women joined similar navy and Coast Guard auxiliaries.

Mobilizing Industry From the start, Roosevelt and the other Allied leaders knew that American production would play a key role in helping the Allies win the war. Although America's industry had started to mobilize in response to the Lend-Lease Act, American production still needed to increase the rate at which it churned out war materials. In January 1942, the government set up the War Production Board (WPB) to oversee the conversion of peacetime industry to war industry. Later, the government created a host of other agencies that worked together to <u>allocate</u> scarce materials into the proper industries, regulate the production of civilian goods, establish production contracts, negotiate with organized labor, and control inflation, with the Office of War Mobilization (OWM) to supervise all of these efforts.

Under the direction of the government, Americans worked to create a "production miracle." The massive defense spending finally ended the Great Depression; for the first time in more than a decade there was a job for every worker. Each year of the war, the United States raised its production goals for military

Answer

Caption from about 20,000 to about 95,000

materials, and each year it met these goals. The Ford Motor Company poured all of its resources into war production, building over 8,000 B-24 Liberator bombers. Henry J. Kaiser's shipyards produced large merchant "Liberty Ships" in as little as four and a half days. In 1944, American production levels were double those of all the Axis nations put together, giving the Allies a crucial advantage. In a toast at a wartime conference, even Joseph Stalin, an Allied leader, praised American production: "To American production, without which the war would have been lost."

✓ **Checkpoint** What were the first actions taken by the United States once war was declared?

Fierce Fighting in the Pacific

With Pearl Harbor smoldering, the Japanese knew they had to move fast to gain important footholds in Asia and the Pacific. Although Japan's population was smaller than America's, the Japanese did have military advantages, including technologically advanced weapons and a well-trained and highly motivated military. At the start of the Pacific war the outlook was grim for America.

Japanese Forces Take the Philippines In December 1941, General **Douglas MacArthur,** commander of United States Army forces in Asia, struggled to hold the U.S. positions in the Philippines with little support. This task grew even more daunting when the Japanese destroyed half of the army's fighter planes in the region and rapidly took Guam (gwahm), Wake Island, and Hong Kong. The main land attack came on December 22. MacArthur positioned his forces to repel the Japanese invasion, but he badly miscalculated the strength of the enemy and was forced to retreat. U.S. forces fell back from Manila to the Bataan (buh TAN) Peninsula and a fortification on Corregidor (kuh REHG uh dor) Island, where they dug in for a long siege. Trapped in Corregidor, Americans suffered, lacking necessary military and medical supplies and living on half and quarter rations.

Although MacArthur was ordered to evacuate to Australia, the other Americans remained behind. They held out until early May 1942, when 75,000 Allied soldiers surrendered. Japanese troops forced the sick and malnourished prisoners of war, or POWs, to march 55 miles up the Bataan Peninsula to reach a railway that took them inland where they were forced to march 8 more miles. More than 7,000 American and Filipino troops died during the grueling journey, which is known as the **Bataan Death March.**

Japanese Forces Advance Throughout the Pacific, Japanese forces attacked and conquered. These advances secured important oil and rubber supplies for Japan, and brought Southeast Asia and the western Pacific securely under Japanese control. By the summer of 1942, Japan appeared ready to dominate the Indian Ocean, Australia, New Zealand, and the central Pacific. If the Allies did not regroup quickly, they would have little hope of victory in the Pacific.

NoteTaking

Reading Skill: Sequence
Sequence the fighting that followed Pearl Harbor in a table like the one below.

Early War in the Pacific	
May 1942	The Philippines fall to the Japanese.

America Mobilizes
These young men train to fight abroad. Training went on for months before soldiers were considered ready for combat.

Instruct

- **Introduce: Vocabulary Builder** Ask students to locate the vocabulary term *minimal* and its definition. Tell students that one U.S. strategic goal in the Pacific was to preserve forces by engaging in a *minimal* number of battles. To achieve this, the United States focused on taking key strategic targets in order to isolate Japanese forces rather than trying to take large amounts of land. Ask **How can taking *minimal* amounts of land maximize benefits in the long run?** (*By targeting key locations, one can gain a greater victory over time.*)

- **Teach** Ask **How did the war in the Pacific progress in the first six months of fighting?** (*The Japanese had the advantage, and they drove U.S. forces out of the Philippines and advanced farther into Southeast Asia and the Western Pacific.*) **What was the main effect of Doolittle's Raid?** (*It boosted American morale.*) **Why was the Battle of the Coral Sea important?** (*The U.S. victory prevented Japan from attacking New Guinea and threatening Australia.*)

- **Quick Activity** Have students complete the timetable to sequence the fighting that followed Pearl Harbor. Reading and Note Taking Study Guide

Answer

✓ Americans joined organizations that supported the war effort and they volunteered for the military. The U.S. government increased defense spending and set up agencies to oversee the war industry, which was increasing production goals and meeting those goals.

Have students access **www.pearsonschool.com/ushist** to use the Geography Interactive map and then answer the map skills questions in the text.

Monitor Progress

Circulate to make sure that students complete the sequence timetable correctly and understand the fighting that followed Pearl Harbor. For a completed version of the timetable, see Note Taking Transparencies, **B-113b.**

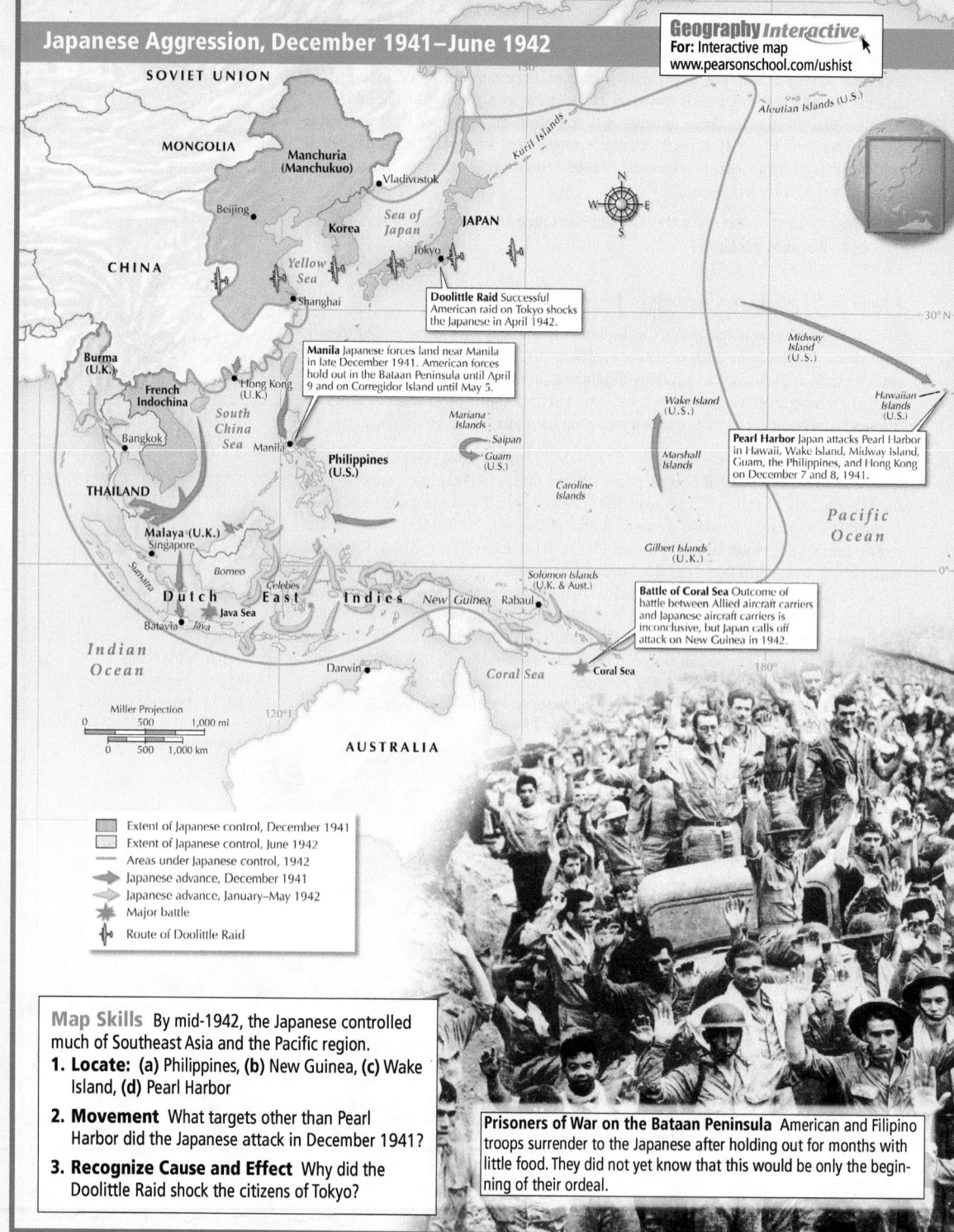

Japanese Aggression, December 1941–June 1942

Geography *Interactive*
For: Interactive map
www.pearsonschool.com/ushist

Doolittle Raid Successful American raid on Tokyo shocks the Japanese in April 1942.

Manila Japanese forces land near Manila in late December 1941. American forces hold out in the Bataan Peninsula until April 9 and on Corregidor Island until May 5.

Pearl Harbor Japan attacks Pearl Harbor in Hawaii, Wake Island, Midway Island, Guam, the Philippines, and Hong Kong on December 7 and 8, 1941.

Battle of Coral Sea Outcome of battle between Allied aircraft carriers and Japanese aircraft carriers is inconclusive, but Japan calls off attack on New Guinea in 1942.

Miller Projection
0 500 1,000 mi
0 500 1,000 km

Extent of Japanese control, December 1941
Extent of Japanese control, June 1942
Areas under Japanese control, 1942
Japanese advance, December 1941
Japanese advance, January–May 1942
Major battle
Route of Doolittle Raid

Map Skills By mid-1942, the Japanese controlled much of Southeast Asia and the Pacific region.
1. **Locate:** (a) Philippines, (b) New Guinea, (c) Wake Island, (d) Pearl Harbor
2. **Movement** What targets other than Pearl Harbor did the Japanese attack in December 1941?
3. **Recognize Cause and Effect** Why did the Doolittle Raid shock the citizens of Tokyo?

Prisoners of War on the Bataan Peninsula American and Filipino troops surrender to the Japanese after holding out for months with little food. They did not yet know that this would be only the beginning of their ordeal.

Differentiated Instruction Solutions for All Learners

L4 Advanced Readers   L4 Gifted and Talented Students

Have students conduct further research on the U.S. war strategy between December 1941 and May 1942. Then, have them construct a three-dimensional war strategy map, using small toy or model ships and planes. Have them develop an oral presentation using their maps to illustrate the U.S. war strategy at the beginning of the war.

Answers

Map Skills

1. Students should correctly identify the location of each place.
2. Manila, in the Philippines
3. Sample response: Japan did not expect the United States to be capable of carrying out such an attack so soon after Pearl Harbor.

America Strikes Back With the Doolittle Raid After Pearl Harbor, FDR wanted America to retaliate against Japan. American military leaders devised a plan for a nighttime bombing raid from the deck of the aircraft carrier USS *Hornet,* led by Colonel James Doolittle. While still 800 miles away from mainland Japan, the *Hornet* was detected, so rather than wait for night, Doolittle led a force of 16 B-25 bombers against Tokyo. They delivered their payload on the Japanese capital just after noon.

The raid killed 50 Japanese people and damaged 100 buildings. The pilots then flew to China, where they crash-landed. Doolittle's Raid proved a <u>minimal</u> military gain, but it bolstered American morale for the long fight ahead.

The Battle of Coral Sea Gives Hope A second event, the **Battle of Coral Sea,** also helped to kindle hope for the American military in the Pacific. In early May 1942, the Japanese moved to take Port Moresby in New Guinea. From that position they could threaten Australia and protect their important military bases at Rabaul (also in New Guinea). To counter Japan's move, the United States sent two aircraft carriers, the USS *Lexington* and USS *Yorktown*, along with support vessels.

On May 7 and 8, in the middle of a Pacific storm, Japanese and U.S. aircraft carriers engaged in battle. It was the first sea fight in which enemy warships never sighted one another. Instead, U.S. airplanes attacked Japanese ships and vice versa. Although technically the Battle of Coral Sea proved a draw, strategically it was a victory for the United States because it forced the Japanese to call off their attack on New Guinea. It marked a shift in momentum toward the Americans. From that day on, the Pacific theater of battle would be won or lost on the strength of aircraft carriers and planes—and here, America's productive capacity gave Americans a marked advantage over their adversaries.

The Battle of Coral Sea and the Doolittle Raid gave the United States a renewed sense of confidence. The war would last three more years, but the dark days of early 1942 were over.

✔ **Checkpoint** What military advantages did the United States have over Japan?

Vocabulary Builder
<u>minimal</u>–(MIHN uh muhl) *adj.* smallest or least amount possible

---

SECTION

3 Assessment

Progress Monitoring *Online*
For: Self-test with vocabulary practice
www.pearsonschool.com/ushist

Comprehension

1. **Terms and People** For each item below, write a sentence explaining how it related to the entry of the United States into World War II.
   - Hideki Tojo
   - Pearl Harbor
   - WAC
   - Douglas MacArthur
   - Bataan Death March
   - Battle of Coral Sea

2. **NoteTaking Reading Skill: Identify Causes and Effects** Use your chart and table to answer the Section Focus Question: How did the United States react to the Japanese attack on Pearl Harbor?

Writing About History

3. **Quick Write: Compare Primary Sources** Compare the primary source describing the attack on Pearl Harbor to the images of the attack in this section. Write one paragraph paraphrasing the information that both sources convey about the event.

Critical Thinking

4. **Identify Points of View** Was the Japanese attack on Pearl Harbor a success or failure from the Japanese point of view? Explain.

5. **Predict Consequences** What role do you think the productive capacity of the United States played in World War II?

6. **Draw Conclusions** Why was the Battle of Coral Sea a turning point for the Allies?

Assess and Reteach

Assess Progress L3

- Have students complete the Section Assessment.

- Administer the Section Quiz. Teaching Resources, **p. 21**

- To further assess student understanding, use Progress Monitoring Transparencies, **109**.

Reteach

If students need more instruction, have them read the section summary.

Reading and Note Taking L3
Study Guide

Adapted Reading and L1 L2
Note Taking Study Guide

Spanish Reading and L2
Note Taking Study Guide

Extend L4

See this chapter's Professional Development pages for the Extend Online activity on reactions to Pearl Harbor.

Answer

✔ It had a greater capacity to produce aircraft carriers and planes.

Section 3 Assessment

1. Examples: The United States entered the war after the Japanese attacked U.S. forces at Pearl Harbor. Japanese Prime Minister Hideki Tojo planned the attack against the United States to prevent it from stopping Japanese expansion in the Pacific.

2. The United States declared war on Japan and quickly mobilized its armed forces and industries to fight.

3. Paragraphs should note the shocking and horrifying nature of the attacks.

4. Sample response: The Japanese attack on Pearl Harbor was not a success. It increased U.S. opposition to Japanese expansion. The United States mobilized to fight back faster than Japan had anticipated.

5. Sample response: The huge capacity of U.S. industries allowed the nation to organize and prepare for war quickly.

6. It prevented Japan from expanding farther into mainland Asia and boosted American confidence.

For additional assessment, have students access **Progress Monitoring *Online*** at **www.pearsonschool.com/ushist.**

10

Quick Study Guide

Quick Study Guide

- Have students use the Quick Study Guide to prepare for the chapter test. Students may wish to refer to the following sections as they review:

Key Causes of World War II
Section 1
Section 2

Key Allied Powers and Axis Powers and Their Leaders
Section 1
Section 2
Section 3

Steps Toward American Entry Into World War II
Section 1
Section 2
Section 3

Key Events Leading to World War II
Section 1
Section 2
Section 3

- For additional review, remind students to refer to the Reading and Note Taking Study Guide.
Section Note Taking
Section Summaries

- Have students access **www.pearsonschool.com/ushist** for this chapter's History Interactive timeline, which includes expanded entries and additional events.

- If students need more instruction on analyzing graphic data, have them read the Skills Handbook, p. SH21.

■ Key Causes of World War II

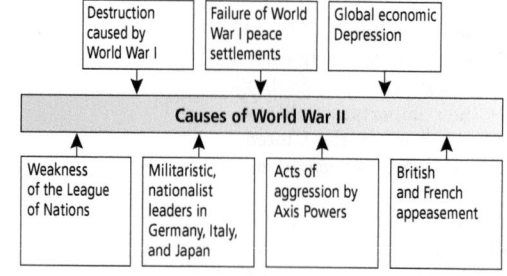

Destruction caused by World War I → Failure of World War I peace settlements → Global economic Depression → **Causes of World War II** ← Weakness of the League of Nations ← Militaristic, nationalist leaders in Germany, Italy, and Japan ← Acts of aggression by Axis Powers ← British and French appeasement

■ Key Allied Powers and Axis Powers and Their Leaders

Allies	Leaders
Great Britain	Winston Churchill, prime minister
France	Charles de Gaulle, leader of French not under German control
Soviet Union	Joseph Stalin, communist dictator
United States	Franklin D. Roosevelt, President

Axis Powers	Leaders
Germany	Adolf Hitler, Nazi dictator
Italy	Benito Mussolini, fascist dictator
Japan	Hideki Tojo, army general and prime minister; Hirohito, emperor

■ Steps Toward American Entry Into World War II

1935–1937	Congress passes Neutrality Acts to help prevent the United States from being drawn into any foreign wars.
1939	The Neutrality Act of 1939 allows belligerent nations to buy supplies from the United States on a cash-and-carry basis; The act favors the Allies.
September 1940	Roosevelt tightens trade embargo against Japan; Congress passes Selective Service Act, instituting a peacetime draft.
March 1941	Congress passes the Lend-Lease Act, allowing the United States to give aid to the Allies.
August 1941	Roosevelt and Churchill issue the Atlantic Charter.
Summer 1941	Japanese and American diplomats try to resolve differences.
October–November 1941	German U-boats sink United States Navy ships; U.S. merchant ships are armed and given permission to sink U-boats.
December 1941	Japan attacks Pearl Harbor; the United States declares war on Japan and later on Germany and Italy.

☑ Quick Study Timeline

In America

1933	1934–1936	1935
Nearly one in four American workers is unemployed	Nye Committee scrutinizes reasons for U.S. involvement in World War I	Congress bans the sale of arms to countries at war

Presidential Terms — Franklin D. Roosevelt 1933–1945

1931 **1933** **1935**

Around the World

1931	1933	1935
Japanese army overruns Manchuria	Hitler becomes chancellor of Germany	Italy invades Ethiopia

---

American Issues
•—•—•—• Connector

By connecting prior knowledge with what you have learned in this chapter, you can gradually build your understanding of enduring questions that still affect America today. Answer the questions below. Then, use your American Issues Connector study guide (or go online: www.pearsonschool.com/ushist).

Issues You Learned About

● **America and the World** Americans debated involvement in World War II.

1. What viewpoint on the war did isolationists hold? What viewpoint did interventionists hold?

2. Write a speech as if you were a member of Congress who is either an isolationist or an interventionist. In your speech, you should express your view and attempt to persuade others to believe as you do. Consider the following:
- the spread of fascist governments
- the aggression of Japan, Italy, and Germany
- the lessons of World War I
- the Neutrality Acts
- the Tripartite Pact

● **Global Interdependence** Countries develop specific policies about ways to deal with other countries' aggressive acts.

3. What was decided at the Munich Conference?

4. What happened after Hitler absorbed Czechoslovakia into the German Reich in the spring of 1939?

5. Did the appeasement policies of Britain and France prove to be effective? Explain.

● **America Goes to War** The United States became involved in World War II after an attack on its own soil.

6. What earlier global conflict had the United States been involved in? Why did the country get involved in that conflict?

7. How did the attack on Pearl Harbor draw the United States into war with Germany and Italy?

Connect to Your World	Activity

Women in American Society: Women in the Military As you have learned, more than 350,000 women enlisted in the military during World War II, but they were restricted to certain jobs. For instance, they were not allowed to take part in combat. Today, however, women take much more active roles in the military. Conduct research to find out the gradual introduction of women into more and more aspects of military life. Then, create a timeline that shows how women became integrated into the military. Make sure your timeline continues to the present day and includes information about how many women are currently enlisted in the U.S. military and what roles they fulfill.

1937
Roosevelt condemns aggression in Quarantine speech

1940
Roosevelt wins third term

1941
Pearl Harbor is attacked

WAR! OAHU BOMBED BY JAPANESE PLANES

1937

1939

1941

1938
Germany annexes Austria

1939
Germany invades Poland, beginning World War II

1941
Germany invades the Soviet Union

History Interactive
For: Interactive timeline
www.pearsonschool.com/ushist

American Issues
•—•—•—• Connector

Tell students that the main issues for this chapter are America and the World, Global Interdependence, and America Goes to War. Then, ask them to answer the Issues You Learned About questions on this page. Discuss the Connect to Your World topic, and ask students to complete the project that follows.

American Issues Connector

1. Isolationists believed that the war was a European problem that the United States should avoid. Interventionists believed that the United States should help the Allies protect democracy.

2. Speeches should contain persuasive language that accurately reflects the viewpoint of the chosen side.

3. Germany was allowed to take the Sudetenland.

4. Britain and France signed a pact promising to protect Poland if it was attacked by Germany. When Germany did attack, the Allies declared war.

5. No; Hitler's armies continued their aggression.

6. World War I; to protect U.S. interests and democratic allies

7. When the United States declared war on Japan, Germany and Italy declared war on the United States to protect their ally.

Connect to Your World

Timelines should include key events in the history of women in the military, including current figures for enlistment.

For additional review of this chapter's enduring issues, remind students to refer to the Reading and Note Taking Study Guide American Issues Journal.

Terms and People

1. Hitler was the leader of Germany during World War II. He blamed Germany's problems on the outcome of World War I and Jews and promised to return the country to glory.

2. The Spanish Civil War was a fight between the democratic Republic government and Nationalists led by Francisco Franco. Germany and Italy aided the Nationalists, and the Soviet Union gave some aid to the Republicans, but most powers remained neutral.

3. It was an act passed in 1941 that allowed the United States to give great economic aid to the Allies; it clearly showed that the United States supported the Allies.

4. The United States officially entered the war.

5. MacArthur was the head of U.S. forces driven from the Philippines by the Japanese. He fled to Australia with many of his troops, but captured U.S. soldiers suffered in the Bataan Death March.

Focus Questions

6. Weak democratic governments were not able to ease the severe economic problems caused by the Great Depression, and people turned to stronger types of governments that promised them relief.

7. They were shocked, but most Americans wanted to avoid involvement in war if at all possible.

8. The United States declared war on Japan and began to mobilize its armed forces and industry to fight.

Critical Thinking

9. They were fascist totalitarian dictatorships.

10. Some students may conclude that it did, since aggression continued; others may note that the League opposed the aggression but had no power to enforce its policies, so its opposition was ineffective.

11. Germany wanted to avoid having to fight a two-front war with both the Soviet Union and the Western European powers.

Chapter Assessment

Terms and People

1. Who was **Adolf Hitler**? How did he rise to power?

2. What was the **Spanish Civil War**? Describe other European countries' involvement in that war.

3. What was the **Lend-Lease Act**? How did it involve the United States in World War II?

4. What happened as a result of Japan's attack on **Pearl Harbor**?

5. Who was General **Douglas MacArthur**? What happened to him and his soldiers in the Philippines?

Focus Questions

The focus question for this chapter is **What events caused World War II, and how did the United States become involved?** Build an answer to this big question by answering the focus questions for Sections 1 through 3 and the Critical Thinking questions that follow.

Section 1

6. Why did totalitarian states rise after World War I, and what did they do?

Section 2

7. How did Americans react to events in Europe and Asia in the early years of World War II?

Section 3

8. How did the United States react to the Japanese attack on Pearl Harbor?

Writing About History

Analyzing Point of View Between early 1940 and late 1941, a great debate raged in America between isolationists and interventionists. Go online to **www.pearsonschool.com/ushist** to read a series of primary sources on the Lend-Lease Act, each reflecting a different point of view. Then, write an essay comparing and contrasting the different viewpoints on the act.

Prewriting

• On note cards, paraphrase each of the primary sources in your own words focusing on the writer's particular argument(s) in support of or opposed to the Lend-Lease Act.

• Organize your summaries into two piles: those supporting and those opposing the Lend-Lease Act.

Critical Thinking

9. **Make Comparisons** What did the governments in Italy and Germany in the 1930s have in common?

10. **Draw Conclusions** Do you think the League of Nations followed a policy of appeasement toward aggressors? Explain.

11. **Recognize Causes** Why do you think Germany wanted to sign a nonaggression pact with the Soviet Union?

12. **Draw Inferences** Why did Hitler decide to call off Operation Sea Lion?

13. **Determine Relevance** When did the United States declare war on Japan? How much Lend-Lease aid had the United States provided to Allies by this time?

Lend-Lease Aid Given by the United States

Year	To British Empire	To Soviet Union
1941 (March–December)	$1.1 billion	$20.0 million
1942	$4.8 billion	$1.4 billion
1943	$9.0 billion	$2.4 billion
1944	$10.8 billion	$4.1 billion
1945 (January–August)	$4.4 billion	$2.8 billion
Total	$30.1 billion	$10.7 billion

SOURCE: *British War Economy*, W. K. Hancock and M. M. Gowing

14. **Predict Consequences** Do you think the United States would have eventually joined World War II if the Japanese had not attacked Pearl Harbor?

15. **Identify Central Issues** What was Japan's primary goal in taking part in World War II?

16. **Summarize** Describe the war in the Pacific from December 1941 through May 1942.

Drafting

• Develop a working thesis and choose information to support the thesis.

• Make an outline organizing your essay.

• Write an introduction in which you point out what you think were the strongest arguments of both sides of the debate.

• Write a body and a conclusion. Be sure to include and cite quotes from the primary sources to support your main points.

Revising

• Use the guidelines on page SH11 of the Writing Handbook to revise your essay.

12. Hitler probably sensed that he might lose the battle, so he withdrew his forces before that could happen.

13. December 1941; more than $1 billion

14. Sample answer: The United States probably would have entered World War II without the Japanese attack on Pearl Harbor because the United States continued to increase its aid to the Allies.

15. to expand its Asian empire

16. Japan dominated the fighting and expanded its territory; a U.S. victory at the Battle of the Coral Sea finally stopped Japanese expansion.

Document-Based Assessment

American Contributions to the War Effort

Both prior to and during World War II, Americans mobilized to produce the material needed to win the war. Factories quickly converted from producing consumer goods to military goods, and each year the country increased and met its production goals. The following documents illustrate the role of American industrial output during the war. Use your knowledge of American production during World War II and Documents A, B, C, and D to answer questions 1 through 4.

Document A

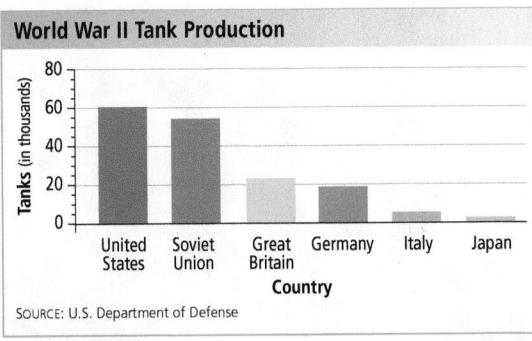

World War II Tank Production

Tanks (in thousands), by Country: United States (~61), Soviet Union (~55), Great Britain (~24), Germany (~20), Italy (~7), Japan (~3)

SOURCE: U.S. Department of Defense

Document B

"The superiority of the United Nations [Allies] in munitions and ships must be overwhelming—so overwhelming that the Axis nations can never hope to catch up with it. In order to attain this overwhelming superiority the United Nations must build planes and tanks and guns and ships to the utmost limit of our national capacity. . . . This production of ours in the United States must be raised far above its present levels. . . . Let no man say it cannot be done. It must be done—and we have undertaken to do it."

President Franklin D. Roosevelt, Annual Message to Congress, January 6, 1942

Document C

The Liberty Ship Robert E. Peary *was built in a matter of days.*

Document D

"The reliance on American aid indicates just how much the Allied war effort owed to the exceptional material and logistical strength of the United States.

The ability of the world's largest industrial economy to convert to the mass production of weapons and war equipment is usually taken for granted. Yet the transition from peace to war was so rapid and effective that the USA was able to make up for the lag in building up effectively trained armed forces by exerting a massive material superiority.

This success owed . . . a great deal to the character of American industrial capitalism, with its 'can-do' ethos, high levels of engineering skill and tough-minded entrepreneurs. After a decade of recession the manufacturing community had a good deal of spare, unemployed capacity to absorb. . . ."

From World War Two: How the Allies Won, *Professor Richard Overy*

---

1. According to Document A, which of the following countries produced the most tanks during World War II?
   A Germany and Italy
   B Italy and Japan
   C the United States and the Soviet Union
   D the Soviet Union and the Great Britain

2. In Document B, President Roosevelt is calling for
   A the immediate recruitment of troops.
   B a dramatic increase in the production of armaments.
   C a dramatic increase in the workforce.
   D production levels to match those of the Axis Powers.

3. According to the author of Document D,
   A the Allied victory is often taken for granted.
   B America's transition to war production was slow but effective.
   C Allied success was partly a result of American know-how and effort.
   D the training of American troops was superior to that of the enemies' troops.

4. **Writing Task** Do you agree that America's role in the war was crucial to the Allies eventual success? Why? Use your knowledge from the chapter and specific evidence from the documents to support your view.

Document-Based Assessment

- To help students understand the documents, give them the following **TIP** **Write down the main idea of each document as you study it.**

- To provide students with further practice in answering document-based questions, go to Test Prep With Document-Based Assessment.

- If students need more instruction on analyzing primary sources, have them read the Skills Handbook, **p. SH24.**

Answers

1. C   2. B   3. C
4. Responses should show that students understand the major role that the United States played in the Allied war effort.

Writing About History

As students begin the assignment, refer them to page SH12 of the Writing Handbook for help in writing an essay. Remind them of the steps they should take to complete their assignment, including prewriting, drafting, and revising.

Students' essays should focus on one of the points of view on the Lend-Lease Act. They should be well organized and contain an introduction, a body, and a conclusion. They should be free of grammatical and spelling errors. For scoring rubrics, see Assessment Rubrics.

Teach With Technology

Presentation**EXPRESS**™
PREMIUM DVD

- Teach this chapter's core content by using PresentationExpress, which includes interactivities, video, lecture notes, and the *ExamView®* QuickTake assessment tool.

- To introduce this chapter by using PresentationExpress, ask students with which of the following statements they most agree: **A) The United States should never become involved in foreign wars under any circumstances. B) The United States should become involved in foreign wars whenever an ally is attacked. C) The United States should fight in wars only after it has been directly attacked.** Take a class poll or record students' answers by using the Quick-Take feature, and discuss their responses. Point out that in this chapter, students will read about the role of the United States in the major conflict known as World War II.

Technology Resources

- Student**EXPRESS** CD-ROM

- Teacher Resource Library **DVD**

- Presentation**EXPRESS**
PREMIUM DVD

- *ExamView®* **Test Bank CD-ROM**
English and Spanish

- **Guided Reading Audio,** Spanish

- **Student Edition on Audio**

VIDEO
By Students For Students
For videos on Amercian Issues, go to
www.pearsonschool.com/ushist

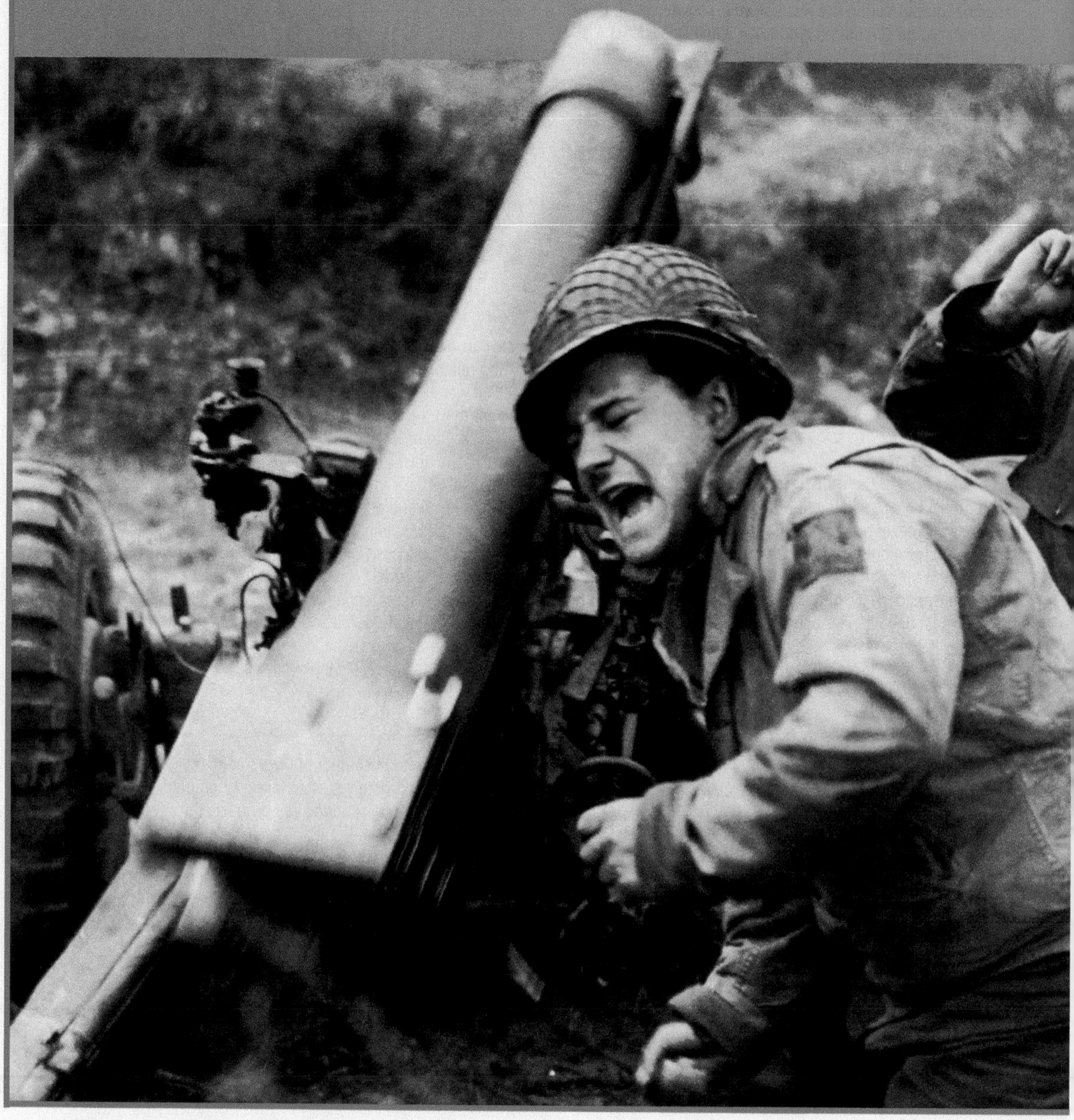

Bibliography

For the Teacher

Dear, I.C.B. and M.R.D. Foot. *The Oxford Companion to World War II.* Oxford University Press, USA, 2005.

Kirk, Tim and Anthony McElligott, eds. *Opposing Fascism: Community, Authority, and Resistance in Europe.* Cambridge University Press, 1999.

Yellin, Emily. *Our Mothers' War: American Women at Home and at the Front During World War II.* Free Press, 2005.

For the Student

L2 Gottfried, Ted. *Children of the Slaughter: Young People of the Holocaust.* Twenty-First Century Books, 2001.

L3 Bernstein, Mark, et al. *World War II on the Air: Edward R. Morrow and the Broadcasts That Riveted a Nation.* Sourcebooks Mediafusion, 2005.

L4 Hersey, John. *Hiroshima.* Vintage, 1989. First published in 1946.

WITNESS HISTORY

The Slow March to Victory

In June 1944, Allied troops landed in German-held France and began their push toward the defeat of Hitler. An American soldier later described his memories:

"Trying to stay clean, trying to rest when possible, eating when possible. . . . Feeling very thankful that one of the guys just looking upwards into a tree observed a German and without hesitation fired his rifle from the hip—Hollywood fashion—killing the German, who no doubt was waiting for the last GI in the platoon to pass by and would then open fire from the rear. . . . On the move constantly, pushing inland, small villages with buildings burning."

—Dick Biehl, quoted in *June 6, 1944: The Voices of D-Day*

◀ Near a French village, an American soldier fires a cannon at retreating German soldiers in 1944.

Chapter Preview

Chapter Focus Question: What impact did World War II have on America and the world?

Section 1
The Allies Turn the Tide

Section 2
The Home Front

Section 3
Victory in Europe and the Pacific

Section 4
The Holocaust

Section 5
Effects of the War

Use the ☑ **Quick Study Timeline** at the end of this chapter to preview chapter events.

Navajos in the United States Marines sent coded messages in their native language.

Patch commemorating the Battle of Guadalcanal

American tank

Note Taking Study Guide *Online*
For: Note Taking and American Issues Connector
www.pearsonschool.com/ushist

Chapter-Level Resources

All in One Letter Home (English and Spanish), Preread the Chapter, Vocabulary Builder, Reading Strategy, Social Studies Skills Practice, Enrichment, Issues Connector, Chapter Tests

- Test Prep With Document-Based Assessment
- AYP Monitoring Assessments
- *ExamView®* Test Bank CD-ROM
- Guided Reading Audio (Spanish)
- Student Edition Audio

Previewing the Chapter

- **WITNESS HISTORY** Read the Witness History selection aloud. Ask **What do you think the invasion was like for those who took part in it?** (*Sample response: It must have been frightening, although the soldiers may also have felt proud to be fighting to push the Germans out of France.*) **Why did the French people greet U.S. soldiers with cider?** (*The French people wanted to celebrate and thank the Americans.*) Tell students that in the chapter they will learn more about the U.S. role in the war and its growing power.

- **Analyzing the Visuals** Ask students to study the images on these two pages. Explain that often people refer to World War II as the last "good war." Discuss what this expression means. Ask students to predict how each image relates to the war and the U.S. role in it.

- **Focus** Write the Chapter Focus Question on the board. Tell students to keep this question in mind as they read the chapter. Then, have students preview the section titles in this chapter.

- **Preread** Have students complete the chapter's Preread the Chapter Worksheet. Teaching Resources, pp. 9–10

Differentiated Instruction   Solutions for All Learners

The following Teacher's Edition strategies are suitable for students of varying abilities.

L1 Special Needs Students, pp. 355, 356, 362, 364, 371, 373, 376, 381, 382, 389 SN

L2 English Language Learners, pp. 355, 356, 362, 364, 371, 373, 376, 381, 382, 389 ELL

L2 Less Proficient Readers, pp. 355, 356, 362, 364, 371, 373, 376, 381, 382, 389 LPR

L4 Advanced Readers, pp. 357, 364, 374, 375, 378, 381, 388 AR

L4 Gifted and Talented Students, pp. 357, 364, 374, 378, 381, 388 GT

Have students access **www.pearsonschool. com/ushist** for the Note Taking Study Guide *Online* as an alternative to the *Reading and Note Taking Study Guide* booklet.

Objectives

As you teach this section, keep students focused on the following objectives to help them answer the Section Focus Question and master core content.

- Analyze the reasons for and impact of the Allies' "Europe First" strategy.
- Explain why the battles of Stalingrad and Midway were major turning points in the war.
- Discuss how the Allies put increasing pressure on the Axis in North Africa and Europe.

Background Knowledge L3

Have students recall the situation in Europe and the Pacific when the United States entered World War II. Using a world map, point out the areas of fighting at this stage of the war. Ask students to predict how the United States would change the course of the war.

Set a Purpose L3

- **WITNESS HISTORY** Read the selection aloud.

  Ask **According to Robert Leckie, what dangers did soldiers in the Pacific face?** *(mud, muck, and bad air; crocodiles, scorpions, and other dangerous creatures)*

- **Focus** Point out the Section Focus Question, and write it on the board. Tell students to refer to this question as they read. *(Answer appears with Section 1 Assessment answers.)*

- **Preview** Have students preview the Section Objectives and the list of Terms and People.

- **NoteTaking** Using the Guided Questioning strategy (TE, p. T20), have students read this section. As they read, have students list the steps in which the Allies turned back the Axis advance. Reading and Note Taking Study Guide

Guadalcanal patch ▶

WITNESS HISTORY

Spiders as Big as Your Fist

World War II placed U.S. soldiers in a variety of settings, from mountains to deserts to forests to tropical isles. One marine described the ordeal of fighting on a Pacific island:

❝It was beautiful, but beneath the loveliness ... Guadalcanal was a mass of slops and stinks and pestilence; of scum-crusted lagoons and vile swamps inhabited by giant crocodiles; a place of spiders as big as your fist and wasps as long as your finger ... of ants that bite like fire, of tree leeches that fall, fasten and suck; of scorpions, of centipedes whose foul scurrying across human skin leaves a track of inflamed flesh, of snakes and land crabs, rats and bats and carrion birds and of a myriad of stinging insects.❞

—Robert Leckie, *Delivered From Evil: The Saga of World War II*

▲ American marines on Guadalcanal

The Allies Turn the Tide

Objectives

- Analyze the reasons for and impact of the Allies' "Europe First" strategy.
- Explain why the battles of Stalingrad and Midway were major turning points in the war.
- Discuss how the Allies put increasing pressure on the Axis in North Africa and Europe.

Terms and People

Dwight Eisenhower	strategic bombing
George S. Patton, Jr.	Tuskegee Airmen
unconditional surrender	Chester Nimitz
saturation bombing	Battle of Midway

NoteTaking

Reading Skill: Summarize List the ways in which the Allies turned back the Axis advance.

Turning Back the Axis	
In Europe	In the Pacific
• Battle against U-boats in Atlantic	•
•	•

Why It Matters The attack on Pearl Harbor brought America into World War II on the Allied side. In 1942, the Allies began to stop the seemingly unstoppable Axis onslaught. Though years of fighting lay ahead, the most aggressive threat to world peace and democracy in modern times had been halted. **Section Focus Question: How did the Allies turn the tide against the Axis?**

Axis and Allies Plan Strategy

By June 1942, the Allies were battered but still fighting. As you have read, British pilots had fought off a Nazi invasion of their island, while at the Battle of Coral Sea, the U.S. Navy had frustrated Japanese plans to extend their domination in the Pacific. Although the war was not close to being over, the Allies spied signs of hope.

The Axis Powers never had a coordinated strategy to defeat the Allies. Germany, Italy, and Japan shared common enemies but nurtured individual dreams. Hitler wanted to dominate Europe and eliminate "inferior" peoples. Mussolini harbored dreams of an Italian empire stretching from the eastern Adriatic to East Africa. Tojo sought Japanese control of the Western Pacific and Asia.

The Allies shared more unified goals. Roosevelt, Churchill, and Stalin considered Germany the most dangerous enemy. None felt Japan or Italy posed a serious long-term threat. Only Germany had the resources to bomb Britain, fight U.S. and British navies on the

Atlantic, and invade the Soviet Union across a 1,200-mile front. Thus, although their <u>ultimate</u> goal was to fight and win a two-front war, the Allies agreed to pursue a "Europe First" strategy. Until Hitler was defeated, the Pacific would be a secondary theater of war.

✓ **Checkpoint** Why did the Allies decide to concentrate first on the war in Europe?

Turning the Tide in Europe

The first blow America struck against the Axis was by fulfilling FDR's promise to be the "arsenal of democracy." American industries turned out millions of tons of guns, tanks, and other supplies—enough to keep the Soviets and British battling Germany for years. The problem was delivering the supplies.

Allies Battle U-Boats in the Atlantic Hitler was determined to cut the sea lines between the United States and Europe before American aid could make a difference. "Wolf packs" of German U-boats patrolled the Atlantic and Caribbean, sinking more than 3,500 merchant ships and killing tens of thousands of Allied seamen. "The only thing that ever really frightened me during the war was the U-boat peril," Churchill later wrote.

Finally, in mid-1943, the Allies began to win the war in the North Atlantic. As in World War I, convoys of escort carriers protected Allied shipping. A new invention, radar, helped Allied vessels locate U-boats on the surface at night. Long-range aerial bombers and underwater depth charges allowed Allied forces to sink U-boats faster than Germany could manufacture them.

Soviets Turn Back Nazis at Stalingrad Germany had attacked Russia in June 1941, sending one army north toward Leningrad, a second east toward Moscow, and a third south toward Stalingrad. Although Hitler's forces penetrated deep into Soviet territory, killing or capturing millions of soldiers and civilians, they did not achieve their main objective of conquering the Soviet Union. Soviet resistance and a brutal Russia winter stopped the German advance.

In 1942, Hitler narrowed his sights and concentrated his armies in southern Russia. His goal this time was to control the rich Caucasus oil fields. To achieve this objective, he would have to capture the city of Stalingrad.

The struggle for Stalingrad was especially ferocious. German troops advanced slowly, fighting bitter block-by-block, house-by-house battles in the bombed-out buildings and rubble. Soviet troops then counterattacked, trapping the German forces. Yet Hitler refused to allow his army to retreat. Starving, sick, and suffering from frostbite, the surviving German troops finally surrendered on January 31, 1943.

The battle of Stalingrad was the true turning point of the war in Europe. It ended any realistic plans Hitler had of dominating Europe. Nazi armies were forced to retreat westward back toward Germany. Instead, it was the Soviet Union that now went on the offensive.

Surrender at Stalingrad
The long Battle of Stalingrad ended in January 1943 with the surrender of German troops like these. Of the 91,000 prisoners taken by the Soviets, only about 5,000 eventually survived and returned to Germany.

Instruct

- **Introduce** Have students find the names **Dwight Eisenhower** and **George S. Patton, Jr.,** (in bold) in the text. Ask students to discuss each man's role in defeating the Germans in North Africa.

- **Teach** Discuss with students the steps the Allies took to contain or push back Hitler in Europe and in North Africa. Ask **Why was the Battle of Stalingrad a major turning point in the war in Europe?** *(The Soviet victory ended Hitler's plans for dominating Europe.)* **How might the outcome of World War II have been different had the Germans captured Stalingrad?** *(Hitler might have gained control of Europe because his army would have had to fight only on the western front.)* Direct students' attention to the Focus on Geography feature. Ask **What about North Africa's location made control of the region so strategically important in the war?** *(Whoever controlled North Africa could control much of the Mediterranean Sea; the region was also a launching area for the invasion of Italy.)*

- **Quick Activity** Direct students to read the Primary Source quotation on the next page. Have students paraphrase Patton's remarks. Ask **How does this quotation illustrate Patton's nickname "Blood and Guts"?** *(Patton was focused on winning at all costs and suggests that even relatively "minor" injuries should not stop the advance.)*

Independent Practice

Help students understand the geography of North Africa and the battles fought there by having them complete *Geography and History: North Africa* and answer the questions on the worksheet. Teaching Resources, **p. 16**

Monitor Progress

As students complete their worksheets, circulate to make sure that they understand the importance of the Allies' winning control of North Africa from the Germans.

Answer

Geography and History

The Allied ships had to travel near areas that were controlled by the Axis in order to reach the Allied troops.

Focus On Geography

Desert Warfare American soldiers had to fight in many unfamiliar types of terrain. But the Sahara of North Africa—the world's largest desert—presented special challenges:

- In hot, dry weather, sandstorms choked and blinded troops.
- In wet weather, mud halted machinery.
- The high visibility of the desert terrain made it difficult for troops to move without being seen.
- Poisonous reptiles, ants, and scorpions added to the problems.

Brilliant tank strategists like Patton and Rommel were able to overcome such challenges. But the tanks themselves caused other problems, such as kicking up enormous dust clouds that could be seen miles away.

WIN TANK BATTLES IN AFRICA

OUR BULLETS WILL DO IT!

Geography and History Most supplies for Allied troops in North Africa had to be brought by sea. According to the map, why would this have posed a problem?

Allies Drive Germans Out of North Africa Meanwhile, another important campaign was taking place in the deserts and mountains of North Africa, where the British had been fighting the Germans and Italians since 1940. Several goals motivated the Allied campaign in North Africa. Stalin had wanted America and Britain to relieve the Soviet Union by establishing a second front in France. However, FDR and Churchill felt they needed more time to prepare for an invasion across the English Channel. An invasion of North Africa, however, required less planning and fewer supplies. In addition, forcing Germany out of North Africa would pave the way for an invasion of Italy.

In October 1942, the British won a major victory at El Alamein (ehl al uh MAYN) in Egypt and began to push westward. The next month, Allied troops landed in Morocco and Algeria and began to move east toward key German positions. An energetic American officer, General **Dwight Eisenhower**—known as Ike—commanded the Allied invasion of North Africa.

In February 1943, German general Erwin Rommel (known as the Desert Fox) led his Afrika Korps against the Americans at the Kasserine Pass in Tunisia. Rommel broke through the American lines in an attempt to reach the Allied supply base at Tebessa in Algeria. Finally, American soldiers stopped the assault. Lack of supplies then forced Rommel to retreat.

Differentiated Instruction   Solutions for All Learners

L1 Special Needs Students   L2 English Language Learners   L2 Less Proficient Readers

To help students understand the sequence of events in the Allied strategy early in the war, have students create flowcharts to record the steps taken by the Allies to stop the Axis offensives in Europe and the Pacific. Have students begin by writing a title for the flowchart and write a sentence about the Allied offensive against the U-boats in the Atlantic. Tell students that they will end their flowcharts with the battle on Guadalcanal discussed at the end of the section. Students may either annotate or illustrate their flowcharts. Have each student use the completed flowchart to explain the sequence of events to a partner.

The fighting at the Kasserine Pass taught American leaders valuable lessons. They needed aggressive officers and troops better trained for desert fighting. To that end, Eisenhower put American forces in North Africa under the command of **George S. Patton, Jr.,** an innovative tank commander. A single-minded general known as Blood and Guts, Patton told his junior officers:

Primary Source "You usually will know where the front is by the sound of gunfire, and that's the direction you should proceed. Now, suppose you lose a hand or an ear is shot off, or perhaps a piece of your nose, and you think you should walk back to get first aid. If I see you, it will be the last . . . walk you'll ever take."
—George S. Patton, Jr., 1943

Patton's forces advanced east with heightened confidence. Simultaneously, the British pressed westward from Egypt, trapping Axis forces in a continually shrinking pocket in Tunisia. Rommel escaped, but his army did not. In May 1943, German and Italian forces—some 240,000 troops—surrendered.

✔ **Checkpoint** Why was the Battle of Stalingrad a turning point in World War II?

Increasing the Pressure on Germany

Germany was now on the defensive, and the Allies planned to keep it that way. In January 1943, Roosevelt and Churchill met in Casablanca, Morocco, to plan their next move. The conference resulted in two important decisions. First, the Allies decided to increase bombing of Germany and invade Italy. Second, FDR announced that the Allies would accept only **unconditional surrender,** or giving up completely without any concessions. Hitler, Mussolini, and Tojo could not hope to stay in power through a negotiated peace.

Allies Invade Italy The Allies next eyed Italy. Situated across the Mediterranean from Tunisia and 2 miles from the Italian mainland, Sicily was the obvious target for an invasion. The Allies could invade Sicily without great risk from U-boats and under the protection of air superiority. In July 1943, British and American armies made separate landings in Sicily and began to advance across the island before joining forces in the north. Once again, Eisenhower commanded the joint American-British forces.

Ike hoped to trap Axis forces on Sicily, but they escaped to the Italian mainland. Still, the 38-day campaign achieved important results: It gave the Allies complete control of the western Mediterranean, paved the way for an invasion of Italy, and ended the rule of Benito Mussolini. On September 3, 1943, Italy surrendered to the Allies and five weeks later declared war on Germany.

But Hitler was not through with Italy. After a small German airborne force rescued Mussolini from a mountaintop fortress, Hitler installed him as head of a puppet state in northern Italy. In the south, German military forces continued the fight against the Allies.

On the Beach at Sicily
Using only a small foldable shovel, an American soldier digs himself a foxhole on the beach at Sicily.

Turning the Tide in the Pacific ⓛ

Instruct

- **Introduce: Vocabulary Builder** Ask students to find the vocabulary term *momentum* in the text. Have students read the first paragraph under this heading. Ask **Who had momentum in the Pacific at this time?** *(Japan)*

- **Teach** Using the Think-Write-Pair-Share strategy (TE, p. T23) and the Color Transparency: *The Battle of Midway,* have students discuss the significance of the Battle of Midway. Ask **How did the U.S. victory at the Battle of Midway change the course of the war in the Pacific?** *(Victory at the Battle of Midway halted the Japanese advance in the Pacific, prevented Japan from threatening Hawaii and attaining Pacific domination, and provided the United States with a launching point for their own Pacific offensive.)* **Why did the United States want to force Japan to fight a two-front war?** *(The United States wanted to split Japanese forces to make them easier to defeat.)* Have students predict the ways that U.S. victory in the Pacific might affect the war in Europe.
  Color Transparencies **A-104**

- **Analyzing the Visuals** Direct students' attention to the photograph taken during the Battle of Midway on the next spread. Discuss the innovation of the aircraft carrier. Ask **How was Midway a new type of naval battle?** *(Instead of direct ship-to-ship attacks, the Battle of Midway featured attacks by planes stationed on aircraft carriers.)*

The invasion of Italy was a slow, grinding slog. Italy was crisscrossed with mountains and rivers. Heavy rains and mountain snows made combat difficult and painful. Men fought in ankle-deep mud. In the mountains, where tanks and heavy artillery were useless, Allied forces depended on mules to haul supplies up slippery and steep roads. To make matters worse, the Germans occupied the best defensive positions. Fighting continued into 1945. The Allies won battles, but none were important enough to alter the basic German defensive policy.

Bombers Batter Germany Stalin continued his demand that Roosevelt and Churchill open a second front in France. While the Allies did not launch a massive invasion of France until 1944, they did open a second front of another kind in early 1942. From bases in England, Allied bombers launched nonstop attacks against Germany. Flying by night in order to avoid being shot down in large numbers, British planes dropped massive amounts of bombs on German cities. The goal of this **saturation bombing** was to inflict maximum damage.

By day, American bombers targeted Germany's key political and industrial centers. The goal of this campaign of **strategic bombing** was to destroy Germany's capacity to make war. A Nazi official later commented that "the fleets of bombers might appear at any time over any large German city or important factory."

An African American fighter squadron known as the **Tuskegee Airmen** played a key role in the campaign, escorting bombers and protecting them from enemy fighter pilots. In more than 1,500 missions over enemy territory in Europe, the Tuskegee Airmen did not lose a single bomber.

Overall, though, the bombing missions cost the Allies dearly. Bomber crews suffered an incredibly high 20 percent casualty rate. But they successfully

Air War Over Europe

INFOGRAPHIC

During World War II, the B-24 *Liberator* was the king of American bombers, faster than previous planes and with a greater long-range flight capacity. The B-24s and the men who flew them played a critical and demanding role in the air war over Europe.

◀ Hollywood hero Jimmy Stewart (seated) became a real hero: He emerged from the Air Force as a Brigadier General.

▼ Silver Air Force Gunner Wings pin

U.S. Air War in Europe

Flight crew members killed	30,099
Flight crew members wounded	13,360
Combat missions	1,693,565
Tons of bombs dropped	1,554,463
Planes lost in combat	18,418
Enemy aircraft destroyed	29,916

SOURCE: Army Air Force Statistical Digests

Connect to Your World

The United States Air Force The United States Air Force has developed steadily in each conflict involving the nation since World War I. At the end of World War I, the U.S. Air Service consisted of only a few hundred squadrons. By World War II, planes were used for spying, combat, strategic bombing missions, as cargo and paratrooper transporters, and as support for ground operations. The National Security Act of 1947 made the United States Air Force an independent service with its own Cabinet secretary. During the Cold War, the Air Force was central to America's nuclear defense. In the last two decades, Air Force jet fighters have been instrumental in both conflicts in Iraq. During the attacks on September 11, 2001, F-15 fighter jets stayed on patrol for weeks. Aeronautic technology has put the Air Force at the center of major modern U.S. offensive action, and its units continue to fly patrol, transport, and combat missions around the world.

carried the war into Germany, day after day and night after night. This second front in the sky did indeed relieve some of the pressure on the Soviet armies on the Eastern Front and helped pave the way for an all-out Allied offensive.

✓ **Checkpoint** What were the goals of British and American bombing runs over Germany?

Turning the Tide in the Pacific

While the Allies pursued their "Europe First" strategy, they did not ignore the Pacific. Through May 1942, Japanese forces continued to advance with seemingly unstoppable <u>momentum</u>. They had attacked American, British, and Dutch colonies, winning control of the Philippines, Malaya, Dutch East Indies, Hong Kong, Wake Island, Guam, and Burma. Then, the United States struck back. As you have read in the last chapter, the Battle of Coral Sea served as a warning that America might be down in the Pacific, but it was not out.

Vocabulary Builder
<u>momentum</u>–(moh MEHN tuhm)
n. forward motion; push

Turning Point: Americans Triumph at Midway Admiral Yamamoto, commander of Japanese forces in the Pacific, knew that the United States Navy was still a powerful threat. Before the Americans could retaliate for Pearl Harbor, Yamamoto sought to destroy American aircraft carriers in the Pacific. He turned his attention to Midway, an American naval base in the Central Pacific that was vital to the defense of Hawaii. Losing Midway would force American defenses back to the California coast. Yamamoto's ambitious plan entailed taking Midway and establishing a military presence in the Aleutians, a string of islands off the coast of Alaska.

The B-24 took more crew members to operate than any flying machine ever built. Each member of the 10-man crew had a vital job. (1, 2, 3, 4, 5, 10) **Gunners:** defend the B-24 from attacking enemy planes coming from any direction (5) **Flight Engineer:** handles any mechanical problems; doubles as gunner (6) **Radio Operator:** communicates with ground, other planes (7) **Pilot:** responsible for entire mission (8) **Co-pilot:** assists pilot in flying plane (9) **Navigator:** plots course of plane; also doubles as Bombardier in charge of aiming and dropping bomb

Tuskegee Airmen Rather than carrying bombs, some planes escorted and protected the planes that did. The most celebrated of these escort crews were the Tuskegee Airmen, a special unit of African American pilots. In more than 1,500 missions over Europe, the Tuskegee Airmen did not lose a single bomber.

Thinking Critically
1. **Draw Inferences** Which members of the flight crew carried out the main objective of the mission? What was the chief job of the other members?
2. **Synthesize Information** How did the Tuskegee Airmen affect the casualty figures listed in the chart at left?

History Background

The Enigma Code The intelligence work that helped produce the American victory at Midway owed part of its success to a Polish mathematician. In the 1930s, the Germans developed a machine called Enigma that allowed them to put military communications into code. Polish mathematician Marian Rejewski led a team that cracked that code. The Polish team gave the information to the British, who developed a new device that decoded messages created by an updated version of Enigma. The Germans had given an Enigma machine to the Japanese, and the United States created its own machine to decode Japanese messages. As a result, U.S. naval intelligence officers were able to intercept the Japanese plans to attack Midway. Knowing the Japanese plans, Admiral Nimitz positioned U.S. aircraft carriers to beat back the Japanese attack and achieved an important victory.

Independent Practice
Ask students to suppose that they are newspaper reporters living in 1942. Have students write news articles describing the Battle of Midway, its outcome, and how it changed the U.S. war in the Pacific.

Monitor Progress
As students write their news articles, circulate to make sure that students understand the significance of the Battle of Midway to the U.S. war in the Pacific.

Answers

✓ to destroy Germany's capacity to make war

Thinking Critically
1. All crew members were important, but for bombing missions, the bombardier dropped the bombs while gunners defended the plane. The flight engineer addressed mechanical problems, the radio operator handled communication, the pilot and copilot flew the plane, and the navigator plotted the plane's course. Some crew members handled two roles.
2. The Tuskegee Airmen protected U.S. bombers from enemy fighter planes so that the bombers could attack their targets; their efforts helped keep casualty numbers low.

Assess Progress　L3

- Have students complete the Section Assessment.

- Administer the Section Quiz.
  Teaching Resources, p. 23

- To further assess student understanding, use Progress Monitoring Transparencies, 110.

Reteach

If students need more instruction, have them read the section summary.

Reading and Note Taking　L3
Study Guide

Adapted Reading and　L1　L2
Note Taking Study Guide

Spanish Reading and　L2
Note Taking Study Guide

Extend　L4

Have students research one of the major Allied victories discussed in this section. Ask students to present their findings in reports that describe the specific role of the U.S. forces in the battle, explain the overall significance of the victory to the war effort, and consider what might have happened had the Allies lost the battle.

Answer

 The Battle of Midway halted the Japanese from expanding their control in the Pacific, and prevented their ever dominating the region again.

The Battle of Midway
Midway was a new kind of naval battle. Instead of armed ships facing each other directly, the fighting was carried on by swift airplanes that took off from the decks of aircraft carriers to bomb vessels many miles away.

What Yamamoto did not realize was that Admiral **Chester Nimitz,** commander of the United States Navy in the Pacific, knew the Japanese plans. Navy code breakers had intercepted Japanese messages. To meet the expected assault, Nimitz sent his only available aircraft carriers to Midway. The Japanese navy was stretched out across more than a thousand miles, from the Aleutians to well west of Midway. American forces were all concentrated near Midway.

The Japanese commenced their attack on June 4, 1942. In the most important naval battle of World War II, the United States dealt Japan a decisive defeat. Torpedo planes and dive bombers sank 4 Japanese aircraft carriers, along with all 250 aircraft on board and many of Japan's most experienced pilots. America lost only one aircraft carrier.

The **Battle of Midway** was the turning point of the war in the Pacific, ending the seemingly unstoppable Japanese advance. Japan still had a powerful navy, committed troops, and fortified positions. But Japanese forces would never again threaten Hawaii or dominate the Pacific. Japan was now on the defensive.

Americans Take the Offensive The first American offensive in the Pacific took place in August 1942, with an assault on Guadalcanal in the Solomon Islands. (See the Witness History at the beginning of this section.) After three months of intense fighting, the United States Marines drove the Japanese off the island.

Guadalcanal was the first leg in a strategy to approach Japan from both the southwest Pacific and the central Pacific, using combined U.S. Marine, Navy, and Army forces. The logic behind the dual offensives was to force Japan to fight a two-front war and to capture bases from which to bomb the Japanese home islands. In jungles and coral reefs, under torrential monsoons and the blistering sun, fighting for every new piece of territory, American servicemen began their slow, painful trek toward Japan.

 Checkpoint What impact did the Battle of Midway have on Japanese expansion in the Pacific?

SECTION **1** **Assessment**

Progress Monitoring Online
For: Self-test with vocabulary practice
www.pearsonschool.com/ushist

Comprehension

1. Terms and People Write a sentence explaining how each of the following was connected with the Allied effort to turn back the Axis offensive.
- Dwight Eisenhower
- George S. Patton, Jr.
- unconditional surrender
- saturation bombing
- strategic bombing
- Tuskegee Airmen
- Chester Nimitz
- Battle of Midway

2. NoteTaking Reading Skill: Summarize Use your table to answer the Section Focus Question: How did the Allies turn the tide against the Axis?

Writing About History

3. Quick Write: Describe a Photograph Look at the photograph from Stalingrad in this section. Write a two-sentence factual description of what is happening in the picture. Use at least one descriptive adjective and one action verb.

Critical Thinking

4. Analyze Causes Why did Roosevelt support a "Europe First" strategy even though it was Japan that had first attacked the United States?

5. Evaluate Information Was the Allied invasion of Italy a success? Give reasons for your answer.

6. Apply Information How does the Battle of Midway illustrate the importance of intelligence gathering and espionage in modern warfare?

Section 1 Assessment

1. Sentences should reflect an understanding of each term, person, or group listed.

2. In Europe, the Allies stopped German progress at Stalingrad, in the Atlantic, and in North Africa, and put Germany on the defensive. In the Pacific, the Americans defeated the Japanese at the Battle of Midway, putting Japan on the defensive.

3. Sample answer: The dispirited German troops withdrew from Stalingrad across the frozen ground. In these miserable conditions, the prisoners watched many of their countrymen die from starvation and frostbite.

4. Roosevelt believed that Hitler and Germany were the more dangerous enemy and so had to be defeated first.

5. The invasion of Italy was a mixed success. The initial drive into Sicily gave the Allies complete control of the western Mediterranean and ended the rule of Mussolini. However, the invasion of the mainland was not a success. German troops occupied the best positions and forced the fighting to continue as late as 1945.

6. U.S. Navy code breakers intercepted and decoded messages about Japan's intention to take Midway. Because the U.S. Navy was forewarned by these messages, it was able to win the Battle of Midway and halt the Japanese offensive.

For additional assessment, have students access **Progress Monitoring Online** at **www.pearsonschool.com/ushist**.

◄ Workers in an aircraft plant

WITNESS HISTORY

Rosie the Riveter

Who was Rosie the Riveter? The image of a strong, determined worker, hair tucked under a kerchief, graced countless magazines and posters. The name was first used in a 1942 song, and several real-life Rosies won national publicity. But "Rosie" was really a symbol for an army of women who made artillery shells, sewed uniforms, and welded planes. Years later, one of them spoke about the contribution that women had made:

❝Our war effort … it was a good success and a good thing that we did it. It's a good thing that the women went in. It's a good thing that they showed the world that they can do things too. 'Oh, it's dirty work.' Well, making a pie can be dirty work.❞
—Meda Montana Hallyburton Brendall, Veterans History Project, Library of Congress

◄ "Rosie the Riveter" poster

The Home Front

Objectives

- Explain how World War II increased opportunities for women and minorities.
- Analyze the effects of the war on civil liberties for Japanese Americans and others.
- Examine how the need to support the war effort changed American lives.

Terms and People

A. Philip Randolph
Executive Order 8802
bracero program
internment

442nd Regimental
  Combat Team
rationing
OWI

NoteTaking

Reading Skill: Identify Main Ideas As you read, identify the major effects of World War II on the home front.

The Home Front, World War II		
Economy	Effects on Women	Effects on Minorities
• War bonds • Wage controls	• •	• •

Why It Matters World War II engaged the peoples and resources of the countries involved. The war effort stirred patriotism and promoted economic recovery. And, while wartime fears and tensions tested civil liberties, new opportunities for women and minorities would spur stronger efforts to ensure equal rights after the war was over. **Section Focus Question: How did the war change America at home?**

New Economic Opportunities

American industry quickly converted to war production to meet the nation's military needs. Once industry exhausted the available men, women found more jobs for the taking. Government and industry launched an all-out publicity campaign urging women to do their part to meet wartime production quotas. In time, women made up one third of the wartime workforce.

Women Work for Victory A woman working outside the home was nothing new, but wartime pressures created two sharp breaks from the past. Many women found jobs, especially in heavy industry, that fell outside the traditional realm of women's work. The need for labor also weakened the common practice that a woman quit her job once she married. Three fourths of women working in war industries were married, and 60 percent were older than 35 years.

The image of Rosie the Riveter's rolled up sleeves, red kerchief, and rivet gun gave Americans an enduring image of women in wartime production. Still, women labored in both blue-collar and white-collar jobs. Most factory owners expected women to step aside

Vocabulary Builder

Use the information below and the following resource to teach students the high-use words from this section. Teaching Resources, Vocabulary Builder, p. 12

High-Use Words	Definitions and Sample Sentences
initiate	*v.* to begin or originate The United States **initiated** strategic bombings of key political and industrial centers in Germany to limit the nation's capacity to make war.
comprise	*v.* to include; to make up During World War II, women would **comprise** a surprisingly high percentage of the industrial workforce.

Objectives

As you teach this section, keep students focused on the following objectives to help them answer the Section Focus Question and master core content.

- Explain how World War II increased opportunities for women and minorities.
- Analyze the effects of the war on civil liberties for Japanese Americans and others.
- Examine how the need to support the war effort changed American lives.

Prepare to Read

Background Knowledge

Remind students of the ways that U.S. citizens on the home front contributed to the war effort during World War I. Ask students to predict the ways in which the U.S. citizens at home would respond during World War II.

Set a Purpose L3

- **WITNESS HISTORY** Read the selection aloud.

  Ask students to explain the meaning of "It's Our Fight Too!" Ask **How were women making history?** (*Women were taking jobs that traditionally were held by men and were changing the way that they were perceived in the workplace.*)

- **Focus** Point out the Section Focus Question, and write it on the board. Tell students to refer to this question as they read. (*Answer appears with Section 2 Assessment answers.*)

- **Preview** Have students preview the Section Objectives and the list of Terms and People.

- **NoteTaking** Using the Paragraph Shrinking strategy (TE, p. T20), have students read this section. As they read, have students complete the outline identifying the major effects of World War II on the home front. Reading and Note Taking Study Guide

New Economic Opportunities

Instruct

- **Introduce: Key Term** Ask students to find the key term **Executive Order 8802** (in bold) in the text. Explain that an executive order is a proclamation from the President, not a law passed by Congress. Ask students to discuss why a President would issue an executive order.

- **Teach** Refer students to the HISTORY MAKERS feature on this page. Ask **How did Randolph achieve economic improvements for African Americans during the war?** *(He forced the Pullman Company to sign a contract with the Brotherhood of Sleeping Car Porters, and he pressured FDR to issue Executive Order 8802, which guaranteed fair hiring practices in any job funded by the government.)* Have students predict the challenges that women and African Americans would face after the war ended.

Independent Practice

Have each student write a summary statement explaining why FDR issued Executive Order 8802 and the short- and long-term results of this law.

Monitor Progress

As students fill in their outlines, circulate to make sure that they identify the major effects of World War II on the home front. For a completed version of the outline, see Note Taking Transparencies, **B-115**.

Answer

 African American leaders initiated the "Double V" campaign to defeat fascism abroad and discrimination at home; labor leaders such as A. Philip Randolph fought for fair treatment; and FDR issued Executive Order 8802, which assured fair hiring practices in government-funded jobs.

---

once men returned home at war's end. In white-collar settings, however, the war accelerated long-term trends toward increased employment. During the 1940s, the number of women employed in secretarial and clerical work increased fivefold.

The benefits that women gained from wartime work cannot be underestimated. They earned paychecks, formed new and different relationships, and gained organizational experience. "I decided that if I could learn to weld like a man," noted one laborer, "I could do anything it took to make a living." The confidence and knowledge women developed enriched their postwar experiences and helped create opportunities for their daughters in the years ahead.

With fathers in the military and mothers in the workplace, children's lives began to change. The federal government spent $50 million building day-care centers for children of working mothers. Still, only about 130,000 kids ended up in day-care centers. Many women preferred to leave their children in the care of neighbors or relatives.

African Americans Demand Fair Employment Many African American leaders hoped the war might provide jobs and alleviate their dismal economic situations. However, few found meaningful employment with national defense employers. Out of 100,000 Americans working in the aircraft industry in 1940, for example, only 240 were African Americans. Even jobs provided by the government and military remained segregated.

African American leaders stressed the need for a "Double V" campaign—victory against fascism abroad and victory against discrimination at home. The charismatic and savvy labor leader **A. Philip Randolph** asserted that African Americans would no longer accept second-class citizenship. "We loyal Negro American citizens demand the right to work and fight for our country," he proclaimed. Randolph presented President Roosevelt a list of demands, including the end of discriminatory practices in government-funded training, employment, and the armed services. He also took steps to organize a massive protest march on Washington, D.C.

FDR had hoped to put civil rights reform on the back burner while fighting the Axis Powers. But Randolph persisted in his plans. Roosevelt feared that the sight of a huge protest march on the nation's capital would undermine wartime unity and provide ammunition for enemy propaganda. So, under pressure, he issued **Executive Order 8802.** This measure assured fair hiring practices in any job funded with government money and established the Fair Employment Practices Committee to enforce these requirements.

Such victories encouraged African Americans to join organizations dedicated to promoting equal rights. The NAACP grew to 500,000 members. In 1942, civil rights leaders founded the Congress of Racial Equality (CORE), an organization that sought to apply nonviolent protest as a means of fighting segregation. Although segregation still prevailed in the military, the South, and other parts of the nation, wartime developments helped set the agenda for the civil rights struggles of the coming decades.

✓ **Checkpoint** How did the war create new opportunities for African Americans?

HISTORY MAKERS

A. Philip Randolph (1889–1979)

In 1925, A. Philip Randolph became head of the Brotherhood of Sleeping Car Porters. At the time, virtually all the nation's porters were African American. The Pullman Corporation, which employed them, refused to deal with labor unions. In fact, the Brotherhood had to be organized in secret. For 12 years, the company fired or threatened union members and attacked Randolph as a dangerous radical. But Randolph refused to give up. Finally, in 1937, the Pullman company gave in and signed the first contract in history between a major company and an African American labor union.

 **Special Needs Students**  **English Language Learners** **L2 Less Proficient Readers**

Discuss with students the meaning of the term *irony.* Explain that it means using words to convey a meaning that is the opposite of the literal meaning. Use an example such as saying "Beautiful weather, isn't it?" on a stormy day. Then, work with students to be sure they understand the central irony of the situation facing minority groups during World War II. Point out

the explanation of the "Double V" campaign on this page, and clarify for students how ironic it was that America was fighting for freedom and justice in Europe when freedom and justice were still not available to everyone at home. To check comprehension, have students write a one- or two-sentence summary of this ironic situation.

Workers on the Move

Wartime needs encouraged migration. California alone gained 2 million new residents seeking work in shipyards and other war industries. The South lost residents in its rural areas, but grew by a million new people as a whole. Older industrial cities in the North, such as Detroit and Chicago, also boomed.

Populations Start to Shift Movement of people fostered long-term changes. After receiving billions of dollars to fund industry, the South and Southwest became a growing economic and political force. This trend continues to this day.

Population shifts affected Native Americans, too. As Native Americans left reservations to work in defense industries, they had the opportunity to learn new skills and had greater contacts with non-Indians. Many of these people, as well as Native American veterans, never returned to the reservations after the war.

To alleviate the rural population drain, especially in the West, the United States partnered with Mexico to operate the **bracero program,** bringing laborers from Mexico to work on American farms. During the war years, several hundred thousand braceros migrated to the United States. In the long term, the bracero program initiated decades of migratory labor in the West.

Migration Triggers Conflict In the summer of 1943, migration led to racial violence in some cities. The worst occurred in Detroit, where conflict rose over the construction of housing for black workers drawn north to defense plants. Some 100,000 whites and blacks broke into scattered fights at a city park. By the next morning, full-scale riots erupted in which 34 people were killed. Federal troops ended the violence, but the city's problems were never resolved.

Mexican Americans had long dealt with similar tensions. Few had mastered the English language, and many languished in slums while struggling to find work. A violent incident highlighted the problems. In the Los Angeles area, many Mexican and Mexican American youths dressed in stylish "zoot suits" with baggy pants and long jackets. In June 1943, mobs of off-duty sailors roamed through the Mexican sections of Los Angeles, attacking "zooters." When the fighting ended, police arrested the zoot-suited victims, not their attackers.

Vocabulary Builder
initiate—(ih NIHSH ee ayt) *v.* to begin or originate

After the Zoot Suit Riots
Los Angeles police arrest a group of young Mexican Americans after a spate of violence in June 1943. Some, like the second prisoner from the right, wear the flashy, baggy zoot suits that gave the incident its name.

Instruct

- **Introduce: Key Term** Ask students to find the key term ***bracero program*** (in bold) in the text. Then write the term on the board, say it aloud, have the students say it with you, and provide the definition. Tell students that ***bracero*** is Spanish for "laborer." Ask students to discuss why the United States and Mexico operated this program.

- **Teach** Have students discuss how wartime production needs created racial tensions on the U.S. home front. Tell students to create Venn diagrams comparing and contrasting the racial tensions in Detroit and Los Angeles during the war. Using the Idea Wave strategy (TE, p. T22), have students discuss the causes of the riots in Detroit and Los Angeles. Ask students to propose ways that these riots could have been avoided.

- **Analyzing the Visuals** Have students study the photograph on this page. Ask students to draw conclusions as to why only zoot-suited victims were arrested and write paragraphs explaining their conclusions.

Independent Practice

Have students outline information under the blue heading "Workers on the Move." Then, ask students to use their outlines to write paragraphs summarizing how World War II caused the U.S. population to shift.

Monitor Progress

As students fill in their outlines, circulate to make sure that they understand how the availability of jobs during World War II caused a shift in the U.S. population.

History Background

1943 Detroit Race Riots Because of its importance to war production, Detroit was known as the "Arsenal of Democracy"—it was also an area of racial tension and a bastion of the Ku Klux Klan. In order to fill defense jobs, recruiters had encouraged Southern African Americans and whites to migrate north to the Michigan city. The large influx of people created a shortage of services and housing, adding to the existing racial friction. By 1943, there were incidents involving white workers angry at having to share workspace and restrooms with black workers. In addition, discontent spread due to exhaustion from long working hours and general war anxiety to create a volatile atmosphere in the city. On June 20, 1943, a series of skirmishes exploded into a race riot, with groups of African Americans and whites burning and overturning cars, looting, and fighting as they went. City police were overwhelmed, but federal troops finally restored peace. The riot lasted for 36 hours, during which 9 whites and 25 African Americans were killed—17 of the latter by white police officers. More than 1,800 people—mostly blacks—were arrested.

A Challenge to Civil Liberties

Instruct

- **Introduce: Key Term** Have students find the key term *internment* (in bold) in the text. Have students discuss why the U.S. government built *internment* camps during World War II.

- **Teach** Remind students that in the United States during World War I, some groups were targets of discrimination. Ask **Whose civil liberties did the U.S. government violate during World War II, and in what ways?** *(German and Italian immigrants and citizens were held in camps or faced curfews and travel restrictions, and they had to leave the West Coast temporarily. Japanese immigrants and Japanese Americans were forced to sell their property and were relocated to internment camps for the duration of the war.)* Explore the justifications for Executive Order 9066, and read the Primary Source quotation on the next page. Ask students to debate whether the government is ever justified in incarcerating an entire group of people on the basis of national security concerns. Then, ask students to discuss the contributions of the 442nd Regimental Combat Team to the war effort.

- **Analyzing the Visuals** Have students examine the photographs from Japanese internment camps. Ask students to discuss the conditions under which many Japanese Americans lived in these camps.

Independent Practice

To help them learn more about the contributions of minority groups during World War II, assign students *Biography: Navaho Code Talkers,* and have them answer the questions on the worksheet. Teaching Resources, **p. 17**

Monitor Progress

As students complete the worksheet, circulate to ensure that they are able to answer the questions.

Answers

✔ People flocked to cities that offered industrial jobs and had built up industries for war production. The South and Southwest, in particular, saw a huge growth in population.

Caption California, Arizona, Idaho, Wyoming, Utah, Colorado

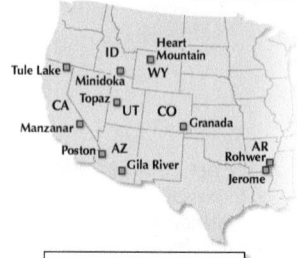

▪ Japanese internment camp

Manzanar Internment Camp
At the Manzanar internment camp in California's Owens Valley (above, right), Japanese Americans lived in bleak barracks, subject to heat and dust storms. Above, a mother and her children await relocation. *Which western states housed internment camps?*

After the riots, an indignant Governor Earl Warren formed a committee to investigate the causes of the outbreak and demanded that the guilty parties be punished. Although the committee blamed the lack of sufficient recreation for the violence, long-brewing racial tensions acted as the true spark.

✔ **Checkpoint** How did the war affect the location of industries and workers in the United States?

A Challenge to Civil Liberties

The attack on Pearl Harbor spread fear across America. The federal government began drafting policies toward immigrants and aliens from the Axis nations. All resident "enemy aliens" were required to register with the government, submit to fingerprinting, and list their organizational affiliations.

Aliens Face Restrictions Originally, laws made no distinction among nationalities. German, Italian, and Japanese aliens were subject to arrest or deportation if deemed dangerous to national security. Some 11,000 German immigrants and hundreds of Italian immigrants were held in camps; others faced curfews or travel restrictions. Federal orders also forced all three groups to vacate the West Coast temporarily in the winter of 1942. Once public fears subsided, FDR removed Germans and Italians from the enemy aliens list.

Japanese aliens and Japanese American citizens received no such respite. Believing Japanese Americans to be inherently disloyal, West Coast leaders pressed FDR to address the "threat." In February 1942, the President issued Executive Order 9066, designating certain areas as war zones from which anyone might be removed for any reason. By September, the government evacuated more than 100,000 Japanese Americans on the West Coast. Evacuees—including both Issei, Japanese immigrants, and Nisei, native-born American citizens of Japanese descent—were forced to sell their property at a loss and allowed to take only necessary items.

Why did Japanese Americans generally face harsher treatment than Italian or German Americans? Several factors help explain the difference: racism, the smaller numbers of Japanese Americans, their lack of political clout, and their

---

Differentiated Instruction   Solutions for All Learners

L1 Special Needs Students
L2 English Language Learners
L2 Less Proficient Readers

To support comprehension of the section, have students review the text and list unfamiliar or challenging terms, such as *discriminatory, aliens, evacuees,* and *stereotypical.* Then, have students work in pairs and use context clues to determine the meanings of the words on their lists. Ask students to write a sentence for each word in their lists.

L4 Advanced Readers
L4 Gifted and Talented Students

As students have learned in this section, many minority groups who were denied equal rights or experienced a loss of civil liberties at home, including women, made important contributions to the war effort. Have students select a group mentioned in this section and do research to prepare an oral report that describes the challenges, experiences, and contributions of that group during World War II.

relative isolation from other Americans. In Hawaii, where Japanese Americans <u>comprised</u> one third of a multiracial society, they escaped a similar fate.

Vocabulary Builder
comprise—(kuhm PRĬZ) *v.* to include; to make up

Japanese Americans Are Interned The first orders stipulated only that Japanese Americans must leave designated military zones, but leaders in interior states objected. The governor of Arizona insisted his state did not want to become a "dumping ground for enemy aliens." The War Department then initiated a policy of **internment,** or temporary imprisonment of members of a specific group. Japanese American men, women, and children were transported to camps in isolated locations such as Poston, Arizona, and the Gila River Indian Reservation. With few exceptions, Nisei and Issei remained in the camps for the duration of the war.

Families huddled into stark one-room shacks, while single people were herded into drafty bunkhouses. Camp schools were hopelessly underfunded. Internees often suffered from food shortages and substandard medical care. The psychological effects could be just as severe. One internee reported:

Primary Source "The resettlement center is actually a jail—armed guards in towers with spotlights and deadly tommy guns, fifteen feet of barbed-wire fences, everyone confined to quarters at nine. . . . What really hurts [is being called] 'Japs.' 'Japs' are the guys we are fighting."
—Ted Nakashima, *The New Republic*, June 5, 1942

Some Japanese Americans went to court to seek their rights. In the 1944 case of Korematsu v. United States, the Supreme Court upheld the government's wartime internment policy. (See Landmark Decisions of the Supreme Court at the end of this section.) Not until 1988 did the government offer an apology and $20,000 payments to surviving internees.

Japanese Americans also faced another form of discrimination. At first, they were not accepted into the armed forces. But after the government lifted the ban in early 1943, many eagerly enlisted. The all-Nisei **442nd Regimental Combat Team** fought in the Italian campaign and became the most decorated military unit in American history. The 442nd helped counter the notion that Japanese Americans were not loyal citizens.

✔ **Checkpoint** Why were Japanese Americans interned during World War II?

Supporting the War Effort

The war eventually cost Americans $330 billion, which was double the total amount of federal expenditures since the founding of the nation. In six years, the national debt skyrocketed from $42 billion to $269 billion. To help raise funds, Congress levied a 5 percent tax on all working Americans. In addition, millions of Americans bought war bonds to save income and invest in the war effort. The government reminded Americans that every dollar spent on war bonds meant another bullet or bomb and another step closer to victory. (See the American Experience feature at the end of this section.)

The Government Manages the Economy Increased production of war goods created a scarcity of consumer products. As shortages led to price increases, many feared that inflation

The Cost of Waging War
The cost of building arms and paying and equipping military personnel caused the federal budget to skyrocket. *Based on the combined information on the two graphs, approximately how much was spent on national defense in 1945?*

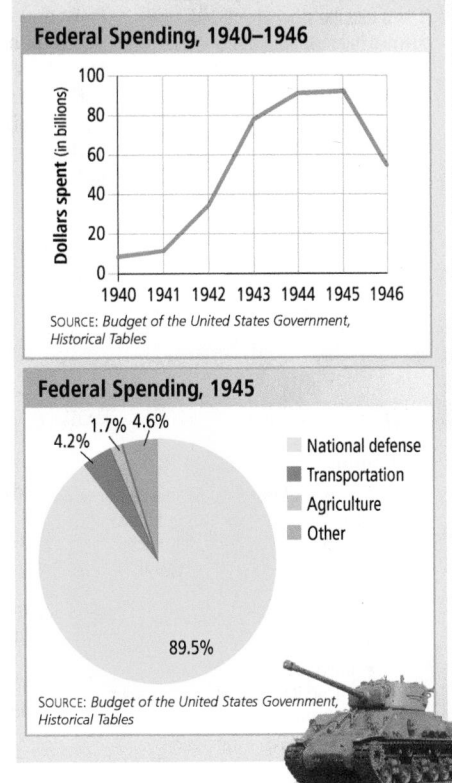

Federal Spending, 1940–1946

Dollars spent (in billions) — 1940: ~7, 1941: ~12, 1942: ~35, 1943: ~78, 1944: ~90, 1945: ~92, 1946: ~55 (years 1940 1941 1942 1943 1944 1945 1946)

SOURCE: *Budget of the United States Government, Historical Tables*

Federal Spending, 1945
- 4.2% — 1.7% — 4.6%
- National defense 89.5%
- Transportation
- Agriculture
- Other

SOURCE: *Budget of the United States Government, Historical Tables*

Sherman tank ▶

Supporting the War Effort ⑬

Instruct

- **Introduce: Key Term** Have students find the key term *rationing* (in bold) in the text, and provide the definition. Have students discuss how rationing helped the U.S. war effort.

- **Teach** Ask **Why did the United States ration consumer goods during World War II?** *(to ensure a continuing supply of certain materials for war production)* In what other way did the U.S. government control the economy during the war? *(Through the Office of Price Administration, the government controlled wages and set maximum prices.)* Display Color Transparency: *Victory Gardens.* Have students discuss how planting victory gardens contributed to the war efforts.
Color Transparencies **A-105**

- **Analyzing the Visuals** Have students study the two graphs on this page. Ask **What effect do you think the end of the war, which concluded in 1945, had on the U.S. economy? Why?** *(The end of the war had a negative effect on the U.S. economy because of the enormous drop in federal spending on war production.)*

Independent Practice

Have students choose one aspect of home-front support during World War II and write a government radio promotion encouraging Americans to support that effort. Example topics include working in war production, buying war bonds, rationing, reducing waste, recycling, or planting a victory garden.

Monitor Progress

As students write their radio promotions, circulate to make sure they understand the different ways that Americans contributed to the war effort.

Answers

Graph Skills almost 85 billion dollars

✔ Some political and military leaders believed that Japanese immigrants or Japanese Americans would be disloyal to the United States. The internment was based on factors of war hysteria, racism, the Japanese people's lack of political power, and their isolation from other Americans.

Connect to Your World

Association of Patriotic Arab Americans
Today, Muslim or Arab immigrants and citizens are in a situation similar to that of German, Italian, and Japanese Americans during World War II. Although Muslims and Arabs in America have not experienced a widespread abridgment of their civil rights since September 11, 2001, they sometimes have been the undeserving targets of attacks and suspicion, as well as possible racial profiling. Currently, however, some are proving their loyalty to the United States by serving in the military, just as the Japanese American 442nd Regimental Combat Team did in

World War II. Four-star U.S. General John Abizaid is head of Central Command, which is responsible for conducting the U.S. military operations in Iraq and elsewhere in Southwest and Central Asia, North Africa, and the Seychelles. Marine Gunnery Sergeant Jamal Baadani emigrated from Egypt to the United States when he was a child and joined the Marine Corps at age 17. Shortly after September 11, he established the Association of Patriotic Arab Americans (APAAM) to give voice to the approximately 3,500 people of Arab descent and 10,000 Muslims serving in the U.S. military.

Hollywood Goes to War
The two films above dealt with the fall of the Philippines. *Back to Bataan* (1945) told the story of anti-Japanese guerrilla fighters. *So Proudly We Hail* (1943) paid tribute to the courage of army nurses.

would run wild. To manage this problem, FDR created the Office of Price Administration, which had the authority to control wages and set maximum prices. Another form of economic control was **rationing**. Americans were issued coupon books that limited the amount of certain goods, such as butter and tires, that they could buy. Rationing ensured that raw materials such as rubber and oil found their way into war production.

Although most Americans accepted the need for wartime controls, others resented the restrictions. Unscrupulous profiteers manipulated the ration coupon system to create a "black market," an illegal underground network for the sale of restricted goods. Because the government restricted job mobility to ensure constant production and because wages lagged behind rising prices and profits, some workers accused their employers of unfair practices. Still, Americans created a powerful industrial network that contributed to victory and carried long-term consequences.

Media Boosts Morale Sacrifices on the home front took a toll on morale. The federal **Office of War Information (OWI)** worked closely with the media to encourage support of the war effort. The OWI tried to spotlight common needs, minimize racial and economic divisions, and downplay problems of poverty and crime. The radio, print, and film industries reminded Americans that they were in a struggle between dictatorship and democracy.

Hollywood proved a capable and willing ally in this cause. Documentaries like Frank Capra's *Why We Fight* series highlighted the need to defeat fascism. Fiction films showed patriotic Americans pitching in overseas or on the home front and stirred hatred of the enemy with stereotypical portrayals of treacherous Japanese and brutal Germans. Movie stars and popular singers volunteered their time to sell war bonds and entertain the troops.

Encouraged by government and media, Americans voluntarily contributed to the war effort in dozens of large and small ways. They planted victory gardens and collected paper, scrap metal, and fat. Instead of buying new, many people followed the motto "Use it up, wear it out, make it do, and do without."

✓ **Checkpoint** How did the federal government control resources needed for the war effort?

Comprehension

1. **Terms and People** Write a sentence explaining how each of the following was connected with the American home front during World War II.
   - A. Philip Randolph
   - Executive Order 8802
   - bracero program
   - internment
   - 442nd Regimental Combat Team
   - rationing
   - Office of War Information

2. **NoteTaking Reading Skill: Identify Main Ideas** Use your table to answer the Section Focus Question: How did the war change America at home?

Writing About History

3. **Quick Write: Describe a Scene** Review the text relating to Japanese American internment during World War II. Write a two-sentence factual description of what you might witness as a family is being sent to a camp. Use at least one descriptive adjective and one action verb.

Critical Thinking

4. **Predict Consequences** Predict two possible consequences for wartime women factory workers when men began to return from overseas after the war.

5. **Compare** How were the causes of the Detroit race riots and the Los Angeles Zoot Suit Riots similar?

6. **Draw Conclusions** Do you think the federal government was justified in limiting individual freedom by imposing wage and price controls and by rationing during wartime? Why or why not?

Can government limit a group's liberties during wartime?

Because some leaders feared that some Japanese Americans might be disloyal, the government took action against the whole group. How should national security be balanced against civil rights?

Korematsu v. United States (1944)

The Facts	The Issue	The Decision
• In 1942, President Roosevelt ordered that select people could be banned from war zones. • The army relocated Japanese Americans on the West Coast to internment camps. • Fred Korematsu was arrested for resisting the army's order.	Korematsu argued that he was denied equal protection under the law simply because he was a Japanese American.	The Court held that the military order was justified for security reasons. Three judges dissented. Justice Frank Murphy wrote that internment "falls into the ugly abyss of racism."

Why It Matters

Most experts today agree with Murphy that the *Korematsu* case was a triumph of prejudice over justice. In recent years, the war on terrorism has revived talk of *Korematsu* in discussions of "racial profiling." Racial profiling is a law enforcement technique in which police or federal investigators single out members of a particular racial or ethnic group for questioning. Defenders of profiling argue that, because several deadly terrorist attacks were carried out by radical Muslims, it is only logical for law enforcement officials to pay special attention to Muslims. Critics insist that racial profiling is a form of prejudice that violates the civil rights of individuals.

▲ A Japanese American is arrested in 1943.

Connect to Your World

Discussing racial profiling in 2004, Fred Korematsu warned, "No one should ever be locked away simply because they share the same race, ethnicity, or religion as a spy or terrorist. If that principle was not learned from the internment of Japanese Americans, then these are very dangerous times for our democracy." Write an editorial agreeing or disagreeing with Fred Korematsu's position.

For: Supreme Court cases
www.pearsonschool.com/ushist

◄ Americans today protest against racial profiling by law enforcement officials.

History Background

Civil Liberties and the War on Terrorism Less than two months after the September 11 attacks in 2001, Congress rushed to pass the Patriot Act, reflecting an urgent desire to protect the nation, but at the cost of certain freedoms. Among the act's most hotly debated provisions were new laws allowing the federal government easier access to private records, including personal financial, library, travel, telephone, and medical records that had previously been inaccessible to the government without a court-issued warrant. It also became easier for the government to conduct phone taps and other surveillance. Civil liberties advocates argued that fighting terrorism did not justify eroding the rights of American citizens, although some of these concerns were addressed in a revised version of the act that passed in 2006. Proponents of the law countered that the government needs expanded powers to protect the nation. They argue that wiretaps in the United States are necessary to prevent terrorist activity and monitor suspected terrorists.

Landmark Decisions of the Supreme Court

Can government limit a group's liberties during wartime?

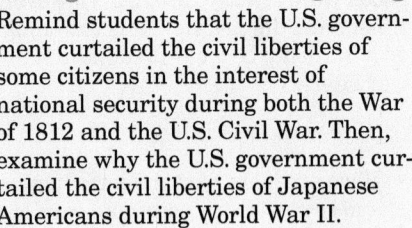

Objectives

▪ Understand the ways in which the balance between national security and civil rights may be adjusted during national emergencies.

▪ Examine past and current examples of government limits on civil liberties during wartime.

▪ Analyze a Supreme Court decision regarding wartime curtailment of civil liberties.

Background Knowledge L3

Remind students that the U.S. government curtailed the civil liberties of some citizens in the interest of national security during both the War of 1812 and the U.S. Civil War. Then, examine why the U.S. government curtailed the civil liberties of Japanese Americans during World War II.

Instruct L3

▪ Have students discuss recent civil liberties issues such as racial profiling or possibly illegal wire-tapping. Ask students to debate whether limiting the civil liberties of a specific group makes the country safer. Have students offer reasons for or against the curtailment of civil liberties in wartime.

▪ For further analysis of this Supreme Court case and the resulting decision, have students complete the worksheet *Landmark Decisions: Can government limit a group's liberties during wartime? Teaching Resources*, p. 18

▪ **Connect to Your World** Refer students to the Key Supreme Court Cases section. You may also want students to do additional research. Responses should show a clear understanding of Korematsu's statement and offer specific reasons why students agree or disagree with it.

Monitor Progress

Conduct a class discussion about the question posed in the lesson title.

EXPERIENCE THE WORLD WAR II HOME FRONT

Objectives

- Examine the contributions and sacrifices that Americans on the home front made during World War II.
- Understand how the efforts of Americans on the home front helped the Allies win the war.

Background Knowledge L3

Remind students of the situation on the American home front during World War II. Because of the needs of war production, all Americans had to do without many common items and materials. Food, gasoline, and other goods were strictly rationed. However, Americans did not view this rationing as a hardship because it supported the war effort.

Instruct L3

- Have students read the introduction and review the pictures and captions in the feature. Point out that the victory garden in the picture is being planted in an empty city lot. Ask **Why did Americans grow "victory gardens"?** (*to grow produce for personal use on the home front*) **Why do you think people called these personal gardens "victory gardens"?** (*When Americans grew their own produce, they needed to buy less, which helped redirect food to American troops and aid the Allies in winning the war.*)

- Tell students that the USO still exists today. Ask **How did Hollywood and the USO contribute to the war effort?** (*They kept up soldiers' morale by providing entertainment and moments of fun and glamor.*)

- Ask students to study the rationing system poster and make a flowchart to summarize the steps in using the stamps. Tell students to analyze the photograph of children collecting scrap for the war. Using the Idea Wave strategy (TE, p. T22), have students identify the types of scrap items collected for the war effort.

While fathers, sons, husbands, and brothers were serving overseas, their families served on the home front. Every American was expected to help boost morale and make sacrifices to shoulder the cost of the war.

Since World War II, the United States has not experienced a war that required so much of Americans on the home front. However, soldiers today continue to face combat, homesickness, and occasional boredom. That is why the USO and ordinary citizens still work to provide support for America's troops.

▲ **Collecting Scrap**
Here, children collect junk metal that might be turned into bullets or old clothes that could be recycled into blankets and uniforms.

▼ **Victory Gardens**
With so much farm produce going to feed the troops, people planted "victory gardens" in vacant lots (below) or in their backyards.

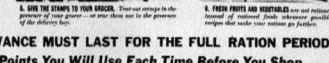

▲ **Rationing**
Households were issued ration books and stamps, which told them how much of certain items, such as sugar or butter, they were allowed to buy. The above poster explains how the rationing system worked.

▼ USO
Through the United Service Organizations (USO), volunteers boosted the morale of those who were fighting the war. At the USO's Hollywood Canteen in Los Angeles, a soldier could get a hot meal served by a celebrity or dance with their favorite movie star. Here, servicemen pose with glamorous actress Hedy Lamarr.

War Bonds Poster ▶

They're fighting harder than ever

are you buying MORE WAR BONDS THAN EVER?

Thinking Critically

1. **Analyze Visuals** Choose one of the posters shown on this spread and describe what message it gave to people.

2. **Draw Conclusions** Do you think the effort on the home front helped to win the war? Explain.

Connect to Today How do Americans today give support and encouragement to people serving in the military?

History *Interactive* *

For: More about the home front in World War II
www.pearsonschool.com/ushist

Independent Practice L3

To enrich and extend the lesson, have students access the History Interactive at **www.pearson-school.com/ushist.** After students experience the History Interactive, ask them to share their reactions by posing questions such as these: **How would you feel if the government started a program of gasoline rationing? How would that program affect you or your family's daily life? How is recycling today different from recycling during World War II? What types of materials do you recycle? What materials does your family or school recycle?**

Monitor Progress

Have students complete the Thinking Critically questions. Then, have them share their answers with the class.

Answers

Thinking Critically

1. Sample answer: The war bonds poster is designed to encourage people to keep buying war bonds, even if they have already purchased bonds. The soldiers on the poster are meant to remind civilians that buying bonds helps American soldiers.

2. Sample answer: Yes; it helped because it freed materials for the war effort. If people had refused to recycle or had resisted in the rationing system, it would have been much more difficult to supply war machinery and food to the troops. The result would have been great difficulty in fighting the war.

Connect to Today Have students share their responses, which may include these: USO shows in which celebrities entertain the troops, pen-pal programs in which Americans at home volunteer to write to a U.S. soldier, displaying American flags or patriotic bumper stickers, hanging yellow ribbons, and posting supportive signs on bridges or in other public places.

Objectives

As you read this section, keep students focused on the following objectives to help them answer the Section Focus Question and master core content.

- Analyze the planning and impact of the D-Day invasion of France.
- Understand how the Allies achieved final victory in Europe.
- Explore the reasons President Truman decided to use the atomic bomb against Japan.

Prepare to Read

Background Knowledge Ⓛ③

Remind students that Allied victories in Stalingrad, North Africa, Sicily, and Midway put the Axis Powers on the defensive. Have students predict the steps Allied forces would take to win the war.

Set a Purpose Ⓛ③

- **WITNESS HISTORY** Read the selection aloud.

  Ask **According to the Medal of Honor Citation, what was heroic about Murphy's actions?** *(Despite being injured, Murphy bravely held off German troops until he could organize a counterattack.)*

- **Focus** Point out the Section Focus Question, and write it on the board. Tell students to refer to this question as they read. *(Answer appears with Section 3 Assessment answers.)*

- **Preview** Have students preview the Section Objectives and the list of Terms and People.

- **Reading Skill** Have students use the *Reading Strategy: Recognize Sequence* worksheet. Teaching Resources, **p. 13**

Lieutenant Audie Murphy ▶

SECTION 3

WITNESS HISTORY

Audie Murphy, American Hero

Audie Murphy received more medals than any other American in World War II. In January 1945, his squad was set upon by German troops near Holtzwihr, France. Ordering his men to withdraw, Murphy climbed atop a burning tank that was in danger of exploding. For an hour, the young lieutenant used the tank's machine gun to hold off the enemy on three sides:

"Germans reached as close as 10 yards, only to be mowed down by his fire. He received a leg wound, but ignored it and continued the single-handed fight until his ammunition was exhausted. He then made his way to his company, refused medical attention, and organized the company in a counterattack."

—Medal of Honor Citation for Audie Murphy

Victory in Europe and the Pacific

Objectives

- Analyze the planning and impact of the D-Day invasion of France.
- Understand how the Allies achieved final victory in Europe.
- Explore the reasons that President Truman decided to use the atomic bomb against Japan.

Terms and People

D-Day	kamikaze
Battle of the Bulge	Albert Einstein
Harry S. Truman	Manhattan Project
island hopping	J. Robert Oppenheimer

NoteTaking

Reading Skill: Recognize Sequence
Identify the steps that led to the Allied victory.

Europe	The Pacific
• Allies land at Normandy on D-Day	•
	•

↓ ↓

Allies Win World War II

Why It Matters In 1942 and 1943, the Allies turned back the Axis advances. In the last two years of the war, 1944 and 1945, they delivered the final, crushing blow. They attacked Germany from the west and east, and the United States advanced across the Pacific to the doorstep of Japan. In the process, Americans created a new form of weapon that would change both warfare and global politics. **Section Focus Question: How did the Allies defeat the Axis Powers?**

Planning Germany's Defeat

Throughout 1943, Roosevelt, Churchill, and Stalin squabbled over when they would start a second front in France. Up to that point, Soviet troops had done most of the fighting in Europe. Stalin insisted that Britain and the United States carry more of the military burden by attacking Germany in the west, thereby forcing Germany to divide its troops.

Roosevelt sympathized with Stalin's position, but Churchill hesitated and delayed. Recalling the slaughter of British troops on the Western Front in World War I, he was not anxious to see history repeat itself. He argued that the German U-boat presence was too great in the English Channel and that the Allies needed more landing craft, more equipment, and better-trained soldiers.

In November 1943, Roosevelt and Churchill traveled to Teheran, Iran, for their first face-to-face meeting with Stalin. Churchill continued to voice reservations about a cross-channel invasion, but

---

Vocabulary Builder

Use the information below and the following resource to teach students the high-use words from this section. Teaching Resources, Vocabulary Builder, p. 12

High-Use Words	Definitions and Sample Sentences
scenario	*n.* outline for a proposed series of events; script By following the proposed **scenario**, the United States could not possibly lose the war.
priority	*n.* degree of importance or urgency For the Big Three, winning the war against Hitler became the highest **priority**.

FDR sided with Stalin. Reluctantly, Churchill agreed. After years of war, British and American soldiers would invade France and begin their march toward Germany. At the end of the Teheran Conference, the Big Three issued a joint statement that gave no hint of their earlier disagreements:

Primary Source "We have reached complete agreement as to the scope and timing of the operations to be undertaken from the east, west and south. The common understanding which we have here reached guarantees that victory will be ours. . . . No power on earth can prevent our destroying the German armies by land, their U Boats by sea, and their war planes from the air."
—Declaration of the Three Powers, December 1, 1943

Six months after the Teheran Conference, the plan to open a second front in France became reality. The massive Allied invasion of France was given the code name Operation Overlord.

✓ **Checkpoint** On what issues did Stalin, Roosevelt, and Churchill disagree?

D-Day Invasion of Normandy

Overlord involved the most experienced Allied officers in Europe. American General Dwight D. Eisenhower again served as Supreme Commander. British General Bernard Montgomery served as commander of the ground forces, while General Omar Bradley led the United States First Army.

Eisenhower Plans the Invasion Overlord involved landing 21 American divisions and 26 British, Canadian, and Polish divisions on a 50-mile stretch of beaches in Normandy. The fleet was the largest ever assembled, comprising more than 4,400 ships and landing crafts.

The plan dictated striking five beaches in Normandy (code-named Utah, Omaha, Gold, Juno, and Sword), but it also involved an elaborate deception. The Allies created a fictional army under General Patton. Although the army existed only on paper, the Allies set up fake headquarters in southeast England across the English Channel from Calais, equipped with wood and cardboard tanks, useless ships, and detectable radio traffic. The Allies hoped to convince the Germans that the Allied attack would come at Calais, not farther west in Normandy. In the end, the deception worked. Hitler ordered his top tank division to Calais.

Heroes Storm the Beaches On June 6, 1944—known as **D-Day**—the Allies hit German forces. More than 11,000 planes prepared the way, attempting to destroy German communication and transportation networks and soften Nazi beach defenses. At 6:30 A.M., after a rough crossing of the English Channel, the first troops landed.

On four of the beaches, the landings were only lightly opposed and casualties relatively low. But at Omaha, one of the two beaches assigned to American forces, the Germans offered stiff opposition. On the cliffs overlooking the beach, the Germans had dug trenches and built small concrete pillbox structures from which heavy artillery could be fired. They had the beach covered with

HISTORY MAKERS

Dwight D. Eisenhower (1890–1969)

As a young man, Dwight Eisenhower had not been considered a brilliant student at the U.S. Military Academy at West Point. During the 1930s, though, his career rose due to his organizational skill and ability to work with others. In 1942, Ike was given command of all American forces in Europe—even though more than 350 other generals had more seniority. After strong performances in North Africa and Italy, he was made Supreme Commander of Allied Forces. His skillful handling of the D-Day invasion and the drive to Germany won wide respect. Eisenhower went on to serve two terms as President before retiring.

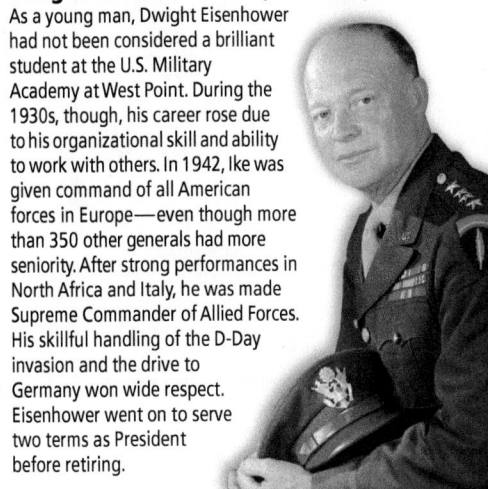

■ **NoteTaking** Using the Structured Read Aloud strategy (TE, p. T20), have students read this section. As they read, have students identify the steps that led to victory in Europe and the Pacific. Reading and Note Taking Study Guide

Teach

Planning Germany's Defeat/D-Day Invasion of Normandy 🔵³

Instruct

■ **Introduce: Key Term** Ask students to find the phrase *Operation Overlord* and key term **D-Day** (in bold) in the text. Tell students that although the Allies had agreed to a "Europe First" plan, by 1943 only the Soviet Union had actively engaged the Germans. Have students discuss how these two terms are related to the Allied victory in Europe.

■ **Teach** Have students discuss why Stalin wanted the United States and Britain to attack Germany from the west. Using the Think-Write-Pair-Share strategy (TE, p. T23), have students discuss the events surrounding the D-Day invasion of France. Ask **Why did the Americans and British wait until 1944 to invade France?** (*They believed that they were not ready; Churchill was concerned about the high casualties if the Allies did not wait until they had more equipment and landing craft and better-trained soldiers.*) **Where did the D-Day invasion take place?** (*on the beaches of Normandy, in northwestern France*) **What made the invasion at Omaha beach so dangerous and difficult?** (*Germans with heavy artillery were stationed on cliffs overlooking the beaches.*) **Why was it important for Operation Overlord to succeed?** (*If U.S. and British forces failed to reclaim France, Germany would have had to fight on only one front and could have won the war.*)

■ **Quick Activity** Have students read the HISTORY MAKERS feature about Dwight Eisenhower. Then, ask students to write paragraphs explaining why the ability to work with others was an important character trait, and may have helped the Allies win the conflict.

Answer

✓ They disagreed on when to start a second European front in France.

Have students access **www.pearson-school.com/ushist** to complete the History Interactive, and then answer the Thinking Critically question in the text. Then, ask students to write paragraphs that answer one of the following questions: **What actions have you seen and heard about that required impressive courage and sacrifice from the Allied soldiers on D-Day? What might it have been like to be part of the force invading France?**

Monitor Progress

As students fill in their sequence charts, circulate to make sure that they identify the steps that led to victory in Europe and the Pacific. For a completed version of the sequence chart, see Note Taking Transparencies, **B-116.**

a wide variety of deadly guns. They had also heavily mined the beaches. When the first American soldiers landed, they stepped out of their landing crafts into a rainstorm of bullets, shells, and death. Some crafts dumped their occupants too far from the beach; soldiers, weighted down by heavy packs, drowned.

One writer called D-Day "the longest day." For many Americans, it was a very short day—and their last on Earth. Some fought bravely and died. Others fought bravely and survived. By the end of the day, the Allies had gained a toehold in France. Within a month, more than one million Allied troops had landed at Normandy. Berlin, the capital of Germany, was still a long road ahead, but the Allies had taken the first, and most important, step on that road.

✓ **Checkpoint** What was the primary objective of the D-Day invasion at Normandy?

INTERACTIVE
Whiteboard

Events That Changed America

THE ALLIES LAND ON D-DAY

"You are about to embark upon the Great Crusade, toward which we have striven these many months." General Eisenhower gave this message to Allied troops on the morning of June 6, 1944. "You will bring about the destruction of the German war machine, the elimination of Nazi tyranny over oppressed peoples of Europe, and security for ourselves in a free world." That day, Allied troops stormed the beaches of Normandy, paving the way for the liberation of France and the final defeat of the Nazis. But victory came at a tremendous cost. Wave after wave of soldiers were mowed down by German fire. One American later recalled, "As our boat touched sand and the ramp went down, I became a visitor to hell."

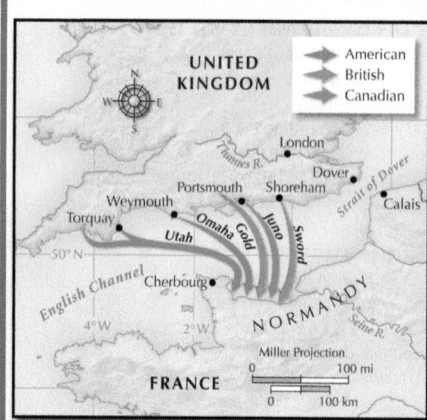

" *The carnage on the beach was indescribable.... Although many wounded men were crying for help, aid-men were scarce and others could not help because they had an assigned task to accomplish.* "
—Thomas E. Herring, C Company

▲ The invasion of Normandy was truly a massive international effort. U.S., Canadian, and British forces were assigned to different beaches. Members of the French Underground were waiting to offer aid and support.

Connect to Your World

World War II Memorial It was not until 2004 that those Americans who served and sacrificed during World War II were honored with a national memorial. (The statue of the Marines raising the flag on Iwo Jima was dedicated in 1954; however, it is specifically a Marine Corps memorial.) Perhaps it was characteristic of the "Greatest Generation" that its members did not build a monument to themselves; but in 1993, a veteran did ask Ohio Representative Marcy Kaptur why a memorial did not exist, and the idea took root. Kaptur sponsored a bill that was signed into law by President Bill Clinton in 1993, authorizing a commission to plan, fund, and build a national World War II memorial. The commission was chaired by World War II veteran Senator Robert Dole and Federal Express Corporation founder, and former U.S. Marine Frederick Smith. Ground breaking took place in 2001. The memorial, which was dedicated in May 2004, the sixtieth anniversary of D-Day, not only honors the Americans who died in the war, but also those who served and survived, as well as the many millions of Americans who worked for the war effort on the home front.

Liberation of Europe

After D-Day, Germany faced a hopeless two-front war. Soviet soldiers were advancing steadily from the east, forcing German armies out of Latvia, Romania, Slovakia, and Hungary. Mile by mile, Germany lost the lands it had once dominated and the natural resources it had once plundered.

Allies Advance Allied armies were also on the move in the west. In August 1944, the Allies liberated Paris. Hitler had ordered his generals to destroy the French capital, but they disobeyed him, leaving the "City of Lights" as beautiful as ever. As Parisians celebrated, Allied troops kept advancing.

As a mood of hopelessness fell over Germany, Rommel and other leading generals plotted to overthrow Hitler. On July 20, 1944, an officer planted a bomb at Hitler's headquarters. The explosion killed or wounded 20 people, but Hitler

I remember the bullets flying over our craft and seeing the ricochets of the bullets hitting the water. The landing craft's door fell open and we ran into the surf. We were in very deep water and I thought I was either going to drown or be shot before getting to land. By the grace of God, I made it ashore and started running through the deep water toward the seawall.
—Jack Fox, combat medic

Sixty years after D-Day, an American veteran revisits the cemetery in Normandy where so many of his comrades are buried.

Why It Matters

Six decades later, Americans still take pride in the young heroes who secured Omaha Beach. Whether they died on the blood-soaked sands or survived against impossible odds, the D-Day invaders helped create an enduring standard of courage, sacrifice, and patriotism. Books like Tom Brokaw's *The Greatest Generation* and movies like Steven Spielberg's *Saving Private Ryan* honor their memory.

Thinking Critically

Why do you think a veteran of D-Day would choose to return to a place where so many people died?

History *Interactive* *

For: Eyewitness accounts of D-Day
www.pearsonschool.com/ushist

Differentiated Instruction Solutions for All Learners

L1 Special Needs Students   **L2 English Language Learners**   **L2 Less Proficient Readers**

To help students understand what happened in World War II Europe after D-Day, pair an L1 or L2 student with an advanced student to research and make an illustrated timeline covering the German counterattacks and the Allied push for victory. Images could include small maps, photographs of important areas, or photographs of soldiers. Have each pair exchange their timeline with another pair and add any missing information. Then, ask partners to use their timelines to write paragraphs summarizing the events that led to the Allied victory in Europe.

Instruct

- **Introduce: Vocabulary Builder** Have students find the vocabulary term *scenario* and its definition in the text. Tell students that the Allied success in Normandy changed the *scenario* of the war in Europe. Have students look at the map labeled "World War II in Europe, 1942–1945." Ask **How did the scenario change for Germany in 1944 and 1945?** (*In 1944 and 1945, Germany lost much of the land it had conquered, and Allied forces were advancing toward Germany from the east, west, and south.*)

- **Teach** Remind students that the Germans had feared a two-front war, which after D-Day, they were forced to fight. Discuss the events that ended the war in Europe. Ask **What was significant about the Battle of the Bulge?** (*It was the last German offensive. With enormous difficulty, American forces held the Germans in place long enough to enable Allied air attacks. After this battle, German forces were steadily pushed back into Germany.*) **How did Germany's location contribute to its defeat?** (*Germany lay between the Soviet Union and the invading Allies in the West, so was surrounded.*)

- **Quick Activity** Have students write a series of three to five newspaper headlines that summarize the course of the war after D-Day. Remind students that newspaper headlines should be short but informative.

Answer

Thinking Critically

Sample answer: Often, people want to return to the scene of a dramatic happening to relive the event. In the case of Normandy, a veteran might return there to celebrate having survived, to pay tribute to fallen friends, or to celebrate what the invasion accomplished.

Independent Practice

Have students access **www.pearson-school.com/ushist** to use the **Geography Interactive map,** and then answer the map skills questions in the text.

Monitor Progress

As students answer the map skills questions, circulate to make sure that they are interpreting the map key correctly.

World War II in Europe, 1942–1945

Geography *Interactive*
For: Interactive map
www.pearsonschool.com/ushist

- Axis Powers, 1942
- Greatest extent of Axis control, 1942
- Allied territory, 1942
- Neutral nations, 1942
- Allied advance
- Major battle

Winston Churchill gave U.S. forces full credit for the Allied victory at the Battle of the Bulge:

Primary Source "The United States troops have done almost all the fighting and have suffered almost all the losses. They have suffered losses almost equal to those of both sides at the Battle of Gettysburg. . . . [The Battle of the Bulge] will, I believe, be regarded as an ever-famous American victory."

—Winston Churchill, Address to the House of Commons, January 18, 1945

Map Skills In the final phases of the war in Europe, the Allies hemmed in Germany from the east, west, and south.
1. **Locate:** (a) Stalingrad, (b) Sicily, (c) Normandy, (d) Berlin

2. **Movement** Describe American and German troop movements at the Battle of the Bulge.

3. **Draw Conclusions** Why do you think there was no Allied attempt to approach Germany from the north?

Battle of the Bulge

- Axis control, Dec. 15, 1944
- Allied control, Dec. 15, 1944
- German offensive
- Allied counterattack
- Front line, Dec. 16, 1944
- Front line, Dec. 25, 1944
- Front line, Jan. 16, 1945

Battle of the Bulge ▲
The Battle of the Bulge was the last Nazi offensive of the war. After its failure, the German armies were in constant retreat.

Answers

Map Skills

1. Review locations with students.

2. In late 1944, German forces punched through the front line of the U.S. forces, forming a "bulge" that reached into Belgium. Bad weather prevented Allied air attacks. However, Allied forces held the lines around the bulge for weeks until the skies cleared and bombers could attack the German positions. Then, with reinforcements and air support, the Allies steadily pushed the Germans back into Germany.

3. Possible answer: Because it was winter, the conditions in the seas north of Germany would have made it difficult to land there. Also, Sweden was a neutral nation and might not have supported an invasion from its shores.

Differentiated Instruction Solutions for All Learners

L4 Advanced Readers L4 Gifted and Talented Students

Challenge students to interview a family member, neighbor, or community member who was alive during World War II. Students may interview someone who fought in the war or who experienced the war at home. Have students list questions that they would like to ask. Tell students to bring a tape or video recorder to the interview or be prepared to take good notes. Remind students using recording devices to obtain the interviewee's permission to do so. Have stu-dents write their interviews in a question-and-answer format. Remind them to quote their subjects exactly because they are creating a primary source document. Point out that, as a courtesy, students should give the finished interview to the subject for approval. Then, have students make any necessary revisions. Collect and bind the interviews to create a World War II primary source volume for the classroom or for the school library.

survived. Rommel took poison to escape being put on trial. Claiming that fate was on his side, Hitler refused to surrender to the advancing troops.

Germany Counterattacks In December 1944, Hitler ordered a counterattack. With Allied troops strung out between the English Channel and the Alps, German forces massed near the Ardennes. Hitler's <u>scenario</u> called for English-speaking German soldiers in U.S. uniforms to cut telephone lines, change road signs, and spread confusion. German tanks would then secure communication and transportation hubs.

The counterattack, known as the **Battle of the Bulge,** almost succeeded. The Germans caught the Allies by surprise, created a bulge in the American line, and captured several key towns. Snowy, cloudy skies prevented the Allies from exploiting their air superiority. But at the Belgian town of Bastogne (bas TOHN), American forces held despite frostbite and brutal German assaults. Then, on December 23, the skies cleared and Allied bombers attacked German positions. After reinforcements arrived, the Allies went back on the offensive, steadily pushing the Germans out of France.

The Battle of the Bulge was a desperate attempt to drive a wedge between American and British forces. Instead, it crippled Germany by using its reserves and demoralizing its troops. Ultimately, it shortened the time Hitler had left.

Allies Push to Victory By January, the Soviet Army had reached the Oder River outside Berlin. The Allies also advanced northward in Italy. In April 1945, Mussolini tried to flee to Switzerland but was captured and executed. By this time, American and British troops had crossed the Rhine River into Germany. In April, a U.S. army reached the Elbe River, 50 miles west of Berlin. Allied forces were now in position for an all-out assault against Hitler's capital.

Hitler was by now a physical wreck: shaken by tremors, paranoid from drugs, and kept alive by mad dreams of a final victory. He gave orders that no one followed and planned campaigns that no one would ever fight. Finally, on April 30, he and a few of his closest associates committed suicide. His "Thousand Year Reich" had lasted only a dozen years.

On May 7, in a little French schoolhouse that had served as Eisenhower's headquarters, Germany surrendered. Americans celebrated V-E (Victory in Europe) Day. Sadly, FDR did not see the momentous day. He had died a few weeks earlier. It would be up to the new President, **Harry S. Truman,** to see the nation through to final victory.

✔ **Checkpoint** What were the results of the Battle of the Bulge?

Advancing in the Pacific

While war still raged in Europe, American forces in the Pacific had been advancing in giant leaps. They followed an **island-hopping** strategy, capturing some Japanese-held islands and ignoring others in a steady path toward Japan. From Tarawa and Makin in the Gilbert Islands, American forces jumped ahead to Eniwetok and Kwajalein in the Marshall Islands. Then, they took another leap to Saipan, Tinian, and Guam in the Mariana Islands.

Japanese Troops Fight to the Death American forces took each island only after a nearly unbelievable life-and-death struggle. Time and again, Japanese defenders fought

Vocabulary Builder
<u>scenario</u>–(suh NAIR ee oh) *n.* outline for a proposed series of events; script

Navajo Code Talkers
Navajo troops played a vital role in the Pacific island-hopping campaign. Using a code based on their own language—which was a mystery to the Japanese—Navajo radio operators sent critical messages from island to island. *What other special ethnic units played a role in the American war effort?*

Advancing in the Pacific

Instruct

- **Introduce: Key Term** Ask students to find the key term *island-hopping* (in bold) in the text. Then, write the term on the board and provide the definition. Have students predict reasons that explain why *island-hopping* would be an important part of the U.S. strategy to defeat Japan.

- **Teach** Remind students that victory at the Battle of Midway allowed the United States to take the offensive in the Pacific war. Ask **What strategy did the Japanese use to fight U.S. forces?** *(The Japanese fought to the last man, and kamikaze pilots deliberately crashed their planes into U.S. ships.)* **Why was it important for the United States to control Okinawa and other Pacific islands?** *(From these islands, U.S. pilots could bomb the Japanese home islands.)* Ask students to evaluate the effectiveness of the Japanese and U.S. strategies in the Pacific.

- **Quick Activity** To help students learn more about the sacrifices made in the battle for Iwo Jima, have them read *Biography: The Marines at Iwo Jima,* and complete the worksheet. Teaching Resources, p. 20

Differentiated Instruction   Solutions for All Learners

L4 Advanced Readers

Have students do research on a member of one of the minority or female American military units active during World War II. Students may choose members of the Navajo code talkers, the Tuskegee Airmen, the 442nd Regimental Combat Team, the Women's Army Corps (WACs), or the Women Air Force Service Pilots (WASPs). Have each student use the findings to write a narrative essay about the selected individual. Tell students to explain the origins of the group, how the selected individual joined the group, and the particular challenges that the individual faced. Students should also list any special achievements of the subject individual.

Answers

Caption Examples include the Japanese American 442nd Regimental Combat Team and the African American Tuskegee Airmen.

✔ It crippled Germany and demoralized its troops; they were pushed back into Germany and never went on the offensive again.

Independent Practice

Have students access **www.pearson-school.com/ushist** to use the Geography Interactive map and then answer the map skills questions in the text.

Monitor Progress

As students answer the map skills questions, circulate to make sure that they are able to locate the places listed in Question 1.

World War II in the Pacific, 1942–1945

Legend:
- Areas under Japanese control, 1942
- Extent of Japanese control, June 1942
- Extent of Japanese control, June 1944
- Allied advance
- Atomic bomb target
- Major battle

Map Skills The island-hopping strategy brought U.S. forces closer and closer to the Japanese home islands, but it took even more drastic measures to bring the war in the Pacific to an end.

1. Locate: (a) Guadalcanal, (b) Okinawa, (c) Iwo Jima, (d) Hiroshima, (e) Nagasaki

2. Movement Describe the two separate island-hopping paths that brought American marines to Okinawa.

3. Predict Consequences What might have happened in the Pacific if Japan had been able to take Midway and Hawaii early in the war?

Answers

Map Skills

1. Review locations with students.

2. One group of U.S. Marines traveled from Hawaii to the Marshall Islands, then to Saipan and Guam, and then toward the Japanese home islands. The second group of Marines traveled from the Coral Sea to Guadalcanal, then to the Solomon Islands, then to New Guinea and the Philippines, and finally to the Japanese home islands.

3. The United States would have had no launching point for the island-hopping strategy, and Japan might have conquered and held the entire Pacific area, creating a constant threat to the U.S. west coast.

Differentiated Instruction Solutions for All Learners

L1 Special Needs Students **L2 English Language Learners** **L2 Less Proficient Readers**

To help students track Allied advances, have them turn the information from the map on this page into a chart. Tell students to create four-column charts with the following headings: China and Korea, Southeast Asia, Pacific Islands, and Japan. Then, have students use the information from the map and text to fill in the chart with the dates of Allied advances in each region and the areas taken in those attacks. Ask students to use the information in their charts to write paragraphs summarizing the events that took place as the United States battled Japan in the Pacific.

Then, have students read and complete the worksheet Biography: Ira Hayes. Teaching Resources, p. 19

virtually to the last man. Rather than surrender, many Japanese troops readily killed themselves. At the same time, Japanese **kamikaze** (kah muh KAH zee) pilots deliberately crashed their planes into American ships. By the end of the war, more than 3,000 Japanese pilots had died in kamikaze missions. Their deaths, however, did not prevent General Douglas MacArthur from retaking the Philippines or the United States Navy from sinking Japanese ships.

American Forces Near Japan One of the fiercest battles in the island-hopping campaign took place in February and March 1945. On Iwo Jima (EE woh JEE muh), a 5-mile-long island 650 miles southeast of Tokyo, United States Marines faced a dug-in, determined enemy. In 36 days of fighting, more than 23,000 marines became casualties. But they took the island. The famous photograph of six marines (including Native American Ira Hayes) planting the American flag on Iwo Jima symbolized the heroic sacrifice of American soldiers.

The fight for Okinawa (oh kuh NAH wuh) in April 1945 was even deadlier. Only 340 miles from Japan, Okinawa contained a vital air base, necessary for the planned invasion of Japan. Taking Okinawa was the most complex and costly operation in the Pacific campaign, involving half a million troops and 1,213 warships. U.S. forces finally took Okinawa but at a cost of roughly 50,000 casualties.

From Okinawa and other Pacific bases, American pilots could bomb the Japanese home islands. Short on pilots and aircraft, low on fuel and ammunition, Japan was virtually defenseless. American bombers hit factories, military bases, and cities. In a single night in March 1945, B-29 bombers destroyed 16 square miles of Tokyo. The raid killed over 83,000 Japanese—more than either of the later atomic bombs—and injured 100,000 more.

✓ **Checkpoint** Why was the island-hopping campaign in the Pacific so deadly to both sides?

The Atomic Bomb Ends the War

Advances in technology, as well as the troops, helped determine the outcome of World War II. (See the Quick Study chart.) Allied and Axis scientists labored to make planes faster, bombs deadlier, and weapons more accurate. The most crucial scientific development of all was the atomic bomb.

▼ A soldier reading a radar screen

The Manhattan Project Develops the A-Bomb The atomic bomb began with an idea. In the early 1930s, scientists learned how to split the nuclei of certain elements. They also discovered that this process of nuclear fission released tremendous energy. Over the next decade, they learned more about the nature of the atom, the effect of a chain reaction, and the military uses of uranium.

Science and Technology of World War II		☑ Quick Study
Advance	**Military Use in WWII**	**Civilian Applications**
Radar	Detected objects such as bombs, incoming gunfire, or enemy ships	Used to track weather systems and monitor automobile speed
Calculating machines	Allowed cryptographers to break enemy codes by detecting letter patterns and frequencies	Developed into small personal computers
Jet engines	Enabled planes to fly much faster than non-jet-powered planes	Used in commercial airplanes
Penicillin	Cured soldiers' infected wounds, saving many lives	Used to treat bacterial infections

History Background

The Brain Drain Among the thousands of people who escaped Nazi control before and during World War II were gifted artists, scholars, and scientists, many of whom were Jewish. Among the scientists were specialists who played a vital role in the Manhattan Project. After learning that Germans might develop an atomic weapon, Albert Einstein wrote a letter to President Roosevelt, which led to the American development of atomic weapons. Einstein's leftist political views caused the government to regard him as a potential security risk and to ban him from working on the Manhattan Project. In 1945, Einstein again wrote to Roosevelt urging him to meet with fellow escapee and Manhattan Project scientist, Leo Szilard, about their opposition to the bomb. One Jewish scientist who left Nazi Germany, Edward Teller, supported the U.S. creation of atomic weapons and worked with other scientists to continue developing atomic weapons. Hitler showed little concern about the negative effect that the departure of these brilliant minds would have on German science. He once said, "If the dismissal of Jewish scientists means the annihilation of contemporary German science, then we shall do without science for a few years."

Instruct

- **Introduce: Key Term** and **Vocabulary Builder** Ask students to find the key term *Manhattan Project* (in bold) and the vocabulary term *priority* in the text. Then, write the terms on the board, and provide the definitions. Using the Idea Wave strategy (TE, p. T22), have students predict the reasons that explain why the *Manhattan Project* would be a *priority* for the United States.

- **Teach** Ask **Why did Manhattan Project scientists need to work quickly to develop an atomic bomb?** *(Axis Powers scientists were also working on developing an atomic bomb.)* **How did the way that the Japanese fought in the Pacific affect the decision to use the atomic bomb against Japan?** *(Truman's military advisors were sure that the number of American casualties resulting from an invasion of the Japanese home islands would be very high.)* **Why did the United States drop a second atomic bomb on Japan?** *(Japan refused to surrender after the bombing of Hiroshima and the Soviet invasion of Manchuria.)*

- **Quick Activity** Display Color Transparency: *The Manhattan Project.* Use the lesson suggested in the transparency book to lead a discussion about the making of the atomic bomb. Color Transparencies A-106

Answer

✓ American forces took control of islands only after life-and-death struggles against Japanese troops who fought fiercely to the last man; kamikaze pilots also crashed into American ships.

- Have students examine the Quick Study chart on the previous page. Ask them to write paragraphs identifying the technology that they think has been most valuable since World War II and explaining their reasoning.

- Have students read the Decision Point feature and answer the questions in the text.

- Display Color Transparency: *The Allies Win the War.* Have students use the headline on the front page of the newspaper to write articles describing the Allied victory. Color Transparencies **A-107**

Monitor Progress

Circulate to make sure that students understand the types of technology that were developed during World War II and how they are used today. Also, ensure that students understand the ethical dilemma caused by the creation and the use of the atomic bomb.

Vocabulary Builder
priority–(prī AHR uh tee) *n.* degree of importance or urgency

Early in the war, **Albert Einstein,** the world's most famous scientist, signed a letter that alerted President Roosevelt about the need to proceed with atomic development. In 1942, FDR gave the highest national priority to the development of an atomic bomb. The program, code-named the **Manhattan Project,** cost several billion dollars and employed tens of thousands of people.

The two primary leaders of the project were General Leslie Groves and physicist **J. Robert Oppenheimer.** Groves was responsible for building facilities, acquiring the necessary materials, recruiting scientists, and providing security. Oppenheimer ran the scientific aspect of the project from the construction site in Los Alamos, New Mexico. Scientists working on the project included many refugees from Europe, including Enrico Fermi, developer of the first atomic reactor. Security on the Manhattan Project was tight. People worked on small parts of the puzzle, little realizing the whole picture.

On the morning of July 16, 1945, in a barren area outside of Alamogordo, New Mexico, the first atomic bomb was tested. The flash of light was clearly visible 180 miles away, and the sound was heard at a distance of 100 miles. Watching the blast, Oppenheimer recalled the following line from a Hindu poem: "Now I am become Death, the destroyer of Worlds."

The general's thoughts were less poetic. Turning to an aide, Groves said, "The war's over. One or two of those things and Japan will be finished."

Truman Makes His Decision The decision to use the bomb fell directly on the shoulders of Harry Truman. The new President fully understood the ethical issues presented by using the bomb, especially against civilians. At the same time, he also knew that the Axis Powers had nuclear scientists, and there was no way to tell how close they were to developing their own bomb. Ultimately, Truman's chief priority was to save American lives. His military advisers predicted that, in light of the ferocious defense waged by Japanese soldiers during

Decision ○ Point

Should the United States Drop the Atomic Bomb?

President Truman had to decide whether to drop the bomb on Japan. Read the options below. Then, you decide.

Truman Favors Using the Bomb

Primary Source

"I asked Gen. Marshall what it would cost in lives to land . . . in Japan. It was his opinion that 1/4 million casualties would be the minimum cost. . . . I asked Sec. Stimson which cities in Japan were devoted exclusively to war production. He . . . named Hiroshima and Nagasaki. We sent an ultimatum to Japan. It was ignored. I ordered atomic bombs dropped on the two cities. . . . Dropping the bombs ended the war, saved lives and gave the free nations a chance to face the facts."

—President Harry S. Truman

Scientists Advise Caution

Primary Source

"We the undersigned scientists . . . believe that the United States ought not resort to the use of atomic bombs in the present phase of the war, at least not unless . . . Japan is given an opportunity to surrender. . . . A nation which sets the precedent of using these newly liberated forces of nature for purposes of destruction may have to bear the responsibility of opening the door to an era of devastation on an unimaginable scale."

—Scientist Leo Szilard

You Decide
1. Why did Truman decide to drop the bomb?
2. What course of action did Szilard favor?
3. What decision would you have made? Why?

Differentiated Instruction   Solutions for All Learners

L4 Advanced Readers   L4 Gifted and Talented Students

Have students research the long-term social, political, and economic effects of the atomic bomb on the cities of Hiroshima and Nagasaki and on the country of Japan as a whole. Students also may research present-day articles that describe how Japanese people and other members of the international community feel about the bombings today. Ask students to use their findings to prepare oral presentations describing the long-term effects of the atomic bomb on Japan and explaining how world leaders are working together to avoid the use of nuclear weapons.

Answers

You Decide

1. He believed that it would save about a quarter of a million American lives.

2. He thought that the terms for Japan's surrender should be made public and that Japan should be told about the bomb and given the chance to surrender.

3. Answers will vary, but should demonstrate an understanding of the facets of the issue and be supported by logical reasoning.

the island-hopping campaign, an invasion of Japan might cost as many as 1,000,000 American casualties.

In truth, Truman did not agonize over the decision to use the atomic bomb against Japan. For the President, abstract ethical issues did not outweigh very real American lives and an opportunity to end the war. Later, some critics would condemn Truman's decision. But in the late summer of 1945, no one close to him did so.

Hiroshima and Nagasaki Are Destroyed On August 6, 1945, U.S. pilots dropped an atomic bomb on Hiroshima. It exploded at 8:15 A.M. One survivor of the blast later recalled the first moments:

> **Primary Source** "After I noticed the flash, white clouds spread over the blue sky. It was amazing. It was as if blue morning-glories had suddenly bloomed up in the sky. . . . Then came the heat wave. It was very, very hot. Even though there was a window glass in front of me, I felt really hot. It was as if I was looking directly into a kitchen oven."
> —Isao Kita, *Hiroshima Witness*

Within two minutes, more than 60,000 of Hiroshima's 344,000 residents were dead or missing.

Over the next three days, Japanese leaders debated whether to surrender or continue to fight. Then, on August 9, two events rocked Japan. First, the Soviet Union declared war against Japan and invaded Manchuria. Next, the United States dropped a second atomic bomb on Nagasaki, killing 35,000 residents.

Debate continued at the highest levels of Japanese government. Finally, Emperor Hirohito made the decision to surrender. On August 15, the Allies celebrated V-J (Victory in Japan) Day. Japan officially surrendered on September 2 aboard the USS *Missouri*. The most costly war in history was over. As many as 60,000,000 people, mostly civilians, had died in the conflict.

✔ **Checkpoint** What were the consequences of the decision to bomb Hiroshima and Nagasaki?

Hiroshima
This 1945 photograph shows the effects of just one atomic bomb on the city of Hiroshima. The heat was so intense that it melted this bottle (right).

Assess and Reteach

Assess Progress L3

- Have students complete the Section Assessment.

- Administer the Section Quiz. **Teaching Resources, p. 25**

- To further assess student understanding, use **Progress Monitoring Transparencies, 112**.

Reteach

If students need more instruction, have them read the section summary.

Reading and Note Taking Study Guide L3

Adapted Reading and Note Taking Study Guide L1 L2

Spanish Reading and Note Taking Study Guide L2

Extend L4

See this Chapter's Professional Development pages for the Extend Online activity on the events that led to Truman's decision to drop atomic bombs on Hiroshima and Nagasaki.

Answer

✔ Ninety-five thousand Japanese residents of Hiroshima and Nagasaki were instantly killed or missing, but Japan surrendered, ending the war.

Progress Monitoring Online
For: Self-test with vocabulary practice
www.pearsonschool.com/ushist

Comprehension

1. **Terms and People** Write a sentence explaining how each of the following was connected with the Allies' final push toward victory in World War II.
   - D-Day
   - Battle of the Bulge
   - Harry S. Truman
   - island hopping
   - kamikaze
   - Manhattan Project
   - J. Robert Oppenheimer

2. **NoteTaking Reading Skill: Recognize Sequence** Use your table to answer the Section Focus Question: How did the Allies defeat the Axis Powers?

Writing About History

3. **Quick Write: Identify Impressions** Review the text description of the D-Day landings, including the Events That Changed America feature. Then, make a list of sights, sounds, and smells associated with the event.

Critical Thinking

4. **Summarize** Summarize the arguments for and against an Allied invasion of France before 1944.

5. **Compare and Contrast** How were the final phases of the war in Europe similar to the final phases of the war in the Pacific? How were they different?

6. **Predict Consequences** What effect do you think possession of the atomic bomb will have on the role of the United States in the postwar world?

Section 3 Assessment

1. Sentences should reflect an understanding of each term or person listed.

2. In Europe, the Germans were defeated by Allied armies pushing from both the west and the east. In the Pacific, the United States dropped two atomic bombs on Japan, an act that forced the Japanese to surrender.

3. Sights: 11,000 planes, casualties, cliffs, pillbox structures, rainstorm of bullets, carnage, ricochets hitting the water, blood-soaked; Sounds: wounded men crying for help, bullets, shells; Smells: surf, blood, gun powder

4. For: The Soviet Union needed support in its fight against Hitler. Against: Churchill remembered the slaughter on the western front during World War I and did not want it repeated.

5. Same: Both Japan and Germany were pushed back to their homelands. Different: Hitler committed suicide and Germany surrendered. Japanese leaders would not give up until the United States destroyed two Japanese cities with atomic bombs.

6. Sample answer: Possession of the atomic bomb will make the United States powerful in the postwar world, but it will cause other countries to work hard to acquire the same capability, launching an atomic arms race.

For additional assessment, have students access **Progress Monitoring Online** at **www.pearsonschool.com/ushist**.

4 Step-by-Step Instruction

Objectives

As you teach this section, keep students focused on the following objectives to help them answer the Section Focus Question and master core content.

- Trace the roots and progress of Hitler's campaign against the Jews.
- Explore the goals of Hitler's "final solution" and the nature of the Nazi death camps.
- Examine how the United States responded to the Holocaust.

Prepare to Read

Background Knowledge **L3**

Remind students that after Hitler was appointed chancellor in 1933, he became increasingly aggressive. Finally, in 1939, he attacked Poland, starting World War II. Also remind students that Hitler was virulently anti-Semitic. Ask students to predict how Hitler's hatred would affect European Jews during the war.

Set a Purpose **L3**

- **WITNESS HISTORY** Read the selection aloud.

  Ask **Why does Murrow call the survivors at Buchenwald "the living dead"?** (*They were so abused, starved, and sick that they were essentially dead while still breathing.*)

- **Focus** Point out the Section Focus Question, and write it on the board. Tell students to refer to this question as they read. (*Answer appears with Section 4 Assessment answers.*)

- **Preview** Have students preview the Section Objectives and the list of Terms and People.

- **NoteTaking** Using the Guided Questioning strategy (TE, p. T20), have students read this section. As they read, have students list the steps that led to Hitler's attempt to exterminate European Jews.
  Reading and Note Taking Study Guide

▲ These starving prisoners at the Ebensee death camp in Austria were liberated by American soldiers.

WITNESS HISTORY

"I Have No Words"

On April 15, 1945, American radio listeners sat stunned as newsman Edward R. Murrow told of a horror beyond belief. Murrow was reporting about his visit to the Nazi concentration camp at Buchenwald. He described the emaciated, hollow-eyed prisoners, the stink which was "beyond all description," the children with identification numbers tattooed on their arms, and the hundreds of "bodies stacked up like cordwood." Toward the end of his report, Murrow said:

❝I pray you to believe what I have said about Buchenwald. I have reported what I saw and heard, but only part of it. For most of it I have no words. Dead men are plentiful in war, but the living dead, more than twenty thousand of them in one camp.... If I've offended you by this rather mild account of Buchenwald, I'm not in the least sorry.❞

—Edward R. Murrow, CBS Radio Broadcast, April 15, 1945

The Holocaust

Objectives

- Trace the roots and progress of Hitler's campaign against the Jews.
- Explore the goals of Hitler's "final solution" and the nature of the Nazi death camps.
- Examine how the United States responded to the Holocaust.

Terms and People

Holocaust	genocide
anti-Semitism	concentration camp
Nuremberg Laws	death camp
Kristallnacht	War Refugee Board

NoteTaking

Reading Skill: Recognize Sequence As you read, identify the steps that led to Hitler's attempt to exterminate European Jews.

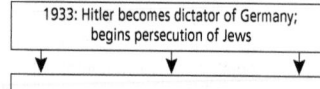

1933: Hitler becomes dictator of Germany; begins persecution of Jews

Why It Matters From the time he came to power, Adolf Hitler had targeted Jews for persecution. By the end of the war, the Nazis had murdered 6 million Jews and 5 million other people they considered inferior. Today, we continue to remember this tragedy and seek ways to prevent anything like it from ever happening again. **Section Focus Question: How did the Holocaust develop and what were its results?**

Roots of the Holocaust

What Edward R. Murrow saw at Buchenwald was just a fragment of the most horrific chapter of the Nazi era. In 1945, there was no word for it. Today, it is called the **Holocaust,** the Nazi attempt to kill all Jews under their control. The mass murders of Jews, as well as other "undesirables," were a direct result of a racist Nazi ideology that considered Aryans (white gentiles, especially those of Germanic, Nordic, and Anglo-Saxon blood) superior to other people.

Hitler Preaches Hate From the start, the Nazi movement trafficked in hatred and **anti-Semitism.** Hitler blamed Jews for all the ills of Germany, from communism to inflation to abstract painting—and, especially, for the defeat of Germany in World War I.

Other extremists influenced Hitler's ideas and shared his prejudices. In the 1920s, his was just another angry voice in the Weimar Republic, advancing simplistic answers for the nation's grave economic, political, and social troubles. In 1933, however, Hitler became chancellor of Germany.

Vocabulary Builder

Use the information below and the following resource to teach students the high-use words from this section. Teaching Resources, Vocabulary Builder, p. 12

High-Use Words	Definitions and Sample Sentences
restraint	*n.* control; something that holds someone back from action The veteran showed great dignity and **restraint,** holding back tears as he visited the cemetery in Normandy where many of his friends are buried.
arbitrary	*adj.* not following any fixed rule or plan; random The success of the D-Day invasion was due to its extensive planning and organization—nothing about its execution was **arbitrary.**

Nazis Begin the Persecution Hitler's persecution of the Jews began as soon as he came to power. At first, his focus was economic. He urged Germans to boycott Jewish-owned businesses, and he barred Jews from jobs in civil service, banking, the stock exchange, law, journalism, and medicine. In 1935, Hitler moved to a broader legal persecution. The **Nuremberg Laws,** named for the city that served as the spiritual center of Nazism, denied German citizenship to Jews, banned marriage between Jews and non-Jews, and segregated Jews at every level of society. Yet even these measures were not enough for Hitler. He hinted that, in the future, there might be what he called the "Final Solution to the Jewish question."

Hitler employed the full power of the state in his anti-Semitic campaigns. Newspapers printed scandalous attacks against Jews. Children in schools and the Hitler Youth movement were taught that Jews were "polluting" German society and culture. Comic books contained vile caricatures of Jews.

Violence Erupts on Kristallnacht Acts of violence against Jews were common. The most serious attack occurred on November 9, 1938, and is known as **Kristallnacht** (KRIHS tahl nahkt), or the "Night of the Broken Glass." After a Jewish refugee killed a German diplomat in Paris, Nazi officials ordered attacks on Jews in Germany, Austria and the Sudetenland. Secret police and military units destroyed more than 1,500 synagogues and 7,500 Jewish-owned businesses, killed more than 200 Jews, and injured more than 600 others. The Nazis arrested thousands of Jews.

Jewish Refugees Face Obstacles Between 1933 and 1937, about 129,000 Jews fled Germany and Nazi-controlled Austria. They included some of the most notable figures in the scientific and artistic world, including physicist Albert Einstein.

More Jews would have left, but they were not generally welcomed into other countries. During the Great Depression, with jobs scarce, the United States and other countries barred their doors to many Jews. In 1939, the ocean liner *St. Louis* departed Germany for Cuba with more than 900 Jewish refugees on board. Only 22 of the passengers received permission to stay in Cuba. U.S. officials refused to accept any of the refugees. The ship returned to Germany. Almost 600 of the Jews aboard the *St. Louis* later died in Nazi concentration camps.

✓ **Checkpoint** How did Hitler enforce anti-Semitism as chancellor of Germany?

German Jews Face Persecution
In Nazi Germany, Jews were forced to wear yellow stars (below right) with the word *Jude* ("Jew"). By the time of Kristallnacht (below left), Hitler's policy of anti-Semitism had progressed from discrimination to organized violence—but there was even worse to come.

Independent Practice

Ask students to analyze the Infographic and answer the questions in
the text. Have students reread the
motto that appeared above the gate
at Auschwitz. Ask them to write a
paragraph explaining what the motto
implies and describing what really
occurred at the death camp.

Monitor Progress

As students fill in their flowcharts, circulate to make sure that they identify
the steps that led to Hitler's attempt to
exterminate European Jews. For a completed version of the flowchart, see
Note Taking Transparencies, B-117a.

● INFOGRAPHIC

CONCENTRATION CAMP

Auschwitz . . . Buchenwald . . . Dachau . . . The names of
these and other concentration camps are a roll call of
horror. Above, the motto over the gate at Auschwitz reads
"Work makes you free." It gave no hint of what prisoners
faced inside. Whether they died of disease or starvation,
survived, or were murdered, all were dehumanized by a
regime that treated them as less than human.

Prisoners are shipped to a
camp in railroad cattle cars.

The youngest
"enemies of the state"

Inside the barracks, jammed onto bunks

Wedding rings stolen
from Holocaust victims

The crematorium, where
human bodies were burned

Prisoners were identified by
the triangular, color-coded
patches they wore.
Yellow: Jew
Purple: Jehovah's Witness
Pink: homosexual
Red: political prisoner
Blue: immigrant
Green: criminal
Black: "antisocial"

Thinking Critically
1. **Identify Central Issues**
   How did Nazi Germany use
   concentration camps to
   carry out genocide?

2. **Predict Consequences**
   After the war, what do you
   think will happen to the
   Nazi officials who ran the
   camps?

Differentiated Instruction Solutions for All Learners

L1 **Special Needs Students** L2 **English Language Learners** L2 **Less Proficient Readers**

To help students interpret and understand the Infographic, have them read the introductory paragraph
and discuss its meaning. Ask **What is the main idea
of the paragraph?** (Concentration camps were
places of dehumanization and horror.) Ask students
to analyze each image and its caption. Have students
consider how each image relates to the introductory

paragraph. **How does the chart of patches relate
to the introductory paragraph?** (The chart shows
the system that was used to categorize people in the
concentration camps. The patches were based on the
different types of people brought to concentration
camps. These patches dehumanize prisoners because
their names were erased in favor of symbols.)

Answers

Thinking Critically

1. The annihilation began when Jews were
   rounded up and transported like animals
   to the camps. If they survived transport,
   they were starved or worked to death in
   the camps. Those not working were gassed
   and burned in the camp crematoria.

2. After the war, when the full horror of the
   Holocaust emerged, there would be investigations and some of those responsible
   tried and punished.

Nazis Adopt the "Final Solution"

Since 1933, the Nazis had denied Jews the rights of citizenship and committed acts of brutality against them. These acts of persecution were steps toward Hitler's "Final Solution to the Jewish question": nothing short of the systematic extermination of all Jews living in the regions controlled by the Third Reich. Today, we call such willful annihilation of a racial, political, or cultural group **genocide**.

Nazis Build Concentration Camps In 1933, the year he became chancellor, Hitler opened the first Nazi **concentration camps,** where members of specially designated groups were confined. The earliest camps included Dachau, Sachsenhausen, and Buchenwald. Later, Ravensbruck, not far from Berlin, was opened for female prisoners.

In theory, the camps were designed not to kill prisoners, but to turn them into "useful members" of the Third Reich. The Nazis imprisoned political opponents such as labor leaders, socialists, and communists, as well as anyone—journalists or novelists, ministers or priests—who spoke out against Hitler. Many Jews as well as Aryans who had intimate relations with Jews were sent to camps. Other groups targeted as "undesirable" included Gypsies, Jehovah's Witnesses, homosexuals, beggars, drunkards, conscientious objectors, the physically disabled, and people with mental illness.

Camp administrators tattooed numbers on the arms of prisoners and dressed them in vertically striped uniforms with triangular insignias. For example, political prisoners wore red insignias, homosexuals pink, Jews yellow, and Jehovah's Witnesses purple. Inside the walls of the concentration camps, there were no real <u>restraints</u> on sadistic guards. They tortured and even killed prisoners with no fear of reprisals from their superiors.

Death by starvation and disease was an everyday occurrence. In addition, doctors at camps such as Dachau conducted horrible medical experiments that either killed inmates or left them deformed. Prisoners were made subjects of bogus experiments on oxygen deprivation, hypothermia, and the effects of altitude. Bodies were mutilated without anesthesia. Thousands of prisoners died in agonizing pain, including some 5,000 mentally or physically disabled children.

Millions Are Murdered in Death Camps When Germany invaded Poland and the Soviet Union, the Nazis gained control of large territories that were home to millions of Jews. Under Nazi rule, Jews in Warsaw, Lodz, and other Polish cities were forced to live in crowded, walled ghettos. Nazis also constructed additional concentration camps in Poland and Eastern Europe.

At first, the murder of Jews and other prisoners tended to be more <u>arbitrary</u> than systematic. But at the Wannsee Conference in January 1942, Nazi leaders made the decision to move toward Hitler's "Final Solution." Reinhard Heydrich, an SS leader known as "the man with an iron heart," outlined a plan to exterminate about 11,000,000 Jews. Although the minutes of the meeting do not use the word "kill," everyone there understood that killing was their goal.

Many concentration camps, especially in Poland, were designated as **death camps,** where prisoners were systematically exterminated. The largest death camp was Auschwitz in southern Poland. Others included Treblinka, Maidenek, Sobibor, Belsec, and Chelmno. Prisoners from various parts of the Reich were transported by trains to the death camps and murdered. Nazis forced

Nazi Concentration Camps

The Nazi system of concentration and slave labor camps extended over several countries. The six death camps in Poland were designed specifically for the extermination of Jewish prisoners.

Concentration Camps in Europe

- ■ Death camp
- ■ Major concentration or forced-labor camp

Vocabulary Builder

<u>restraint</u>–(rih STRAYNT) *n.* control; something that holds someone back from action

Vocabulary Builder

<u>arbitrary</u>–(AR buh trer ee) *adj.* not following any fixed rule or plan; random

Instruct

- **Introduce: Key Terms** Have students find the key terms **genocide, concentration camps,** and **death camps** (in bold). Ask students to discuss how these terms are related to the Nazis' "Final Solution."

- **Teach** Ask **How did the Nazis originally intend to use the concentration camps?** *(as prisons for political opponents, anyone who spoke out against Hitler, and people who belonged to "undesirable" groups)* Have students discuss why Nazi leaders chose to move toward Hitler's "Final Solution" and how the Nazis implemented this decision. **How do you think measures such as the Nuremberg Laws and Kristallnacht contributed to the Nazis' ability to implement the "Final Solution"?** *(Sample answer: These measures created a sense of "otherness" about Jewish people in the minds of non-Jewish Germans. When people feel that a group is alien to themselves, it becomes easier to persecute that group.)*

- **Analyzing the Visuals** Have students examine the map showing the locations of concentration camps in Europe. Ask students to note the locations of the death camps and discuss why they think all of the death camps were located east of Germany.

Independent Practice

To help students develop a deeper understanding of the gruesome reality of the Holocaust, have them read the excerpt from *Link to Literature: Liberation,* and answer the questions on the worksheet. Teaching Resources, **p. 21**

Monitor Progress

As students complete the worksheet, circulate to discuss issues or questions that students have and to make sure that they are able to answer the questions.

History Background

Resisting the Final Solution Across Europe, ordinary citizens resisted Nazi control by hiding Jewish people or helping them escape. In Denmark, where few German troops were stationed, Danish people successfully smuggled almost all of the country's Jews to neutral Sweden. Another pocket of resistance was found in Le Chambon, in Vichy, France. There, villagers provided a safe haven for 5,000 Jews. Even in the death camps, some Jews fought back. In the summer of 1944, a young Jewish Polish woman, Rosa

Robota, was approached by a member of the Jewish underground to help in a plot to smuggle gunpowder into Auschwitz. She and her group succeeded in exploding Crematorium IV in October 1944. Rosa was captured and tortured horribly, but she would not give her interrogators any information. Just before she and three of her collaborators were hanged, she smuggled out of her prison cell a note that read "Be strong and brave."

The Allies and the Holocaust

---

prisoners into death chambers and pumped in carbon monoxide or crammed the prisoners into showerlike facilities and released the insecticide Zyklon B.

Some concentration camps that the Nazis converted into death camps did not have gassing equipment. In these camps, Nazi guards shot hundreds of thousands of prisoners. Nazi "Action Groups" that followed the army into Eastern Europe also shot several million Jews and buried them in ditches.

In fully functioning death camps, the bodies of murdered prisoners were further desecrated. Human fat was turned into soap; human hair was woven into wigs, slippers, and mattresses; cash, gold fillings, wedding rings, and other valuables were stripped off the victims. After the Nazis had taken what they wanted, they burned the bodies in crematoriums.

By 1945, about 6 million European Jews had been murdered. But Jews were not the only victims. As many as 5 million others lay dead, including nearly 2 million non-Jewish Poles. While many survivors lived with constant nightmares of the experience, or with the sorrow and guilt of being the last members of their families, many others determined to rebuild their lives and families in the United States, Israel, or elsewhere and continue to be productive citizens.

✓ **Checkpoint** What actions did the Nazis take to carry out Hitler's "Final Solution"?

The Allies and the Holocaust

The inevitable question about the Holocaust is: Could it have been prevented? Could the nations in the democratic West—especially Britain, France, and the United States—have intervened at some point and stopped the slaughter of millions of innocent people? There are no simple answers to these questions. However, many people today believe that the West could have done more than it did.

Early Response Was Weak Before the war, the United States (as well as other countries) could have done more if it had relaxed its immigration policy. It could have accepted more Jewish refugees and saved the lives of many German and Austrian Jews. However, the State Department at first made a conscious effort to block Jewish immigration. Later commentators have blamed this failure to help European Jews on a variety of factors: anti-Semitism, apathy, preoccupation with the problems of the Great Depression, and a tendency to underestimate Hitler's genocidal plans.

American Government Takes Action Once the war started, news of the mass killings filtered to the West. By the end of 1942, the allies issued a statement acknowledging that Jews were being taken to Poland and killed there. In April 1943, British and American officials hosted the Bermuda Conference to discuss the possibility of rescuing the surviving Jewish refugees from Europe. However, no concrete action was taken.

By early 1944, however, FDR began to respond to the reports. He established the **War Refugee Board,** which worked with the Red Cross to save thousands of Eastern European Jews, especially in Romania and Hungary.

Tragically, too few were saved. Of the Allies, the Soviet Union was closest to the death camps, but Stalin showed no concern. Britain and the United States expressed sympathy, but their resources and strategy were focused on defeating Hitler not on stopping his genocidal campaign. They might have bombed railway lines to the death camps, but the camps were not military targets. A War Department official told the Refugee Board that bombing the railway lines "could be executed only by the diversion of considerable air support essential to

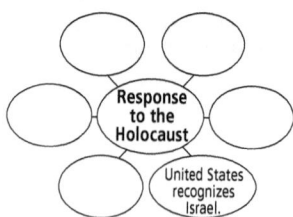

Connect to Your World

Yom HaShoah The term *Holocaust* was not the first one used to describe the genocide of the Jews in Nazi Germany during World War II. Although the common noun *holocaust,* which comes from the Greek for "wholly burnt," was used to describe those events in a general sense, the term was not used as a proper noun until the late 1950s. After World War II, Jews referred to the genocide as *Shoah,* Hebrew for "catastrophe." In 1951, after the State of Israel was established as a homeland for the Jews, the Israeli parliament declared an annual day of remembrance to commemorate those who died or who resisted during the *Shoah, Yom HaShoah,* or Holocaust Remembrance Day, is held each spring, on the twenty-seventh day of the Jewish month of Nissan. The commemoration also coincides with the anniversary of the Warsaw Ghetto Uprising of 1943. Today, *Yom HaShoah* is observed in Israel, the United States, and elsewhere around the world with prayer, the lighting of candles or torches to signify the 6 million Jews killed, and by the reading of the names of the victims.

the success of our forces now engaged in decisive operations elsewhere." The Allies also refused to pressure countries within the Nazi sphere of influence to stop the transportation of Jews to Germany.

Allied Soldiers Liberate the Camps For most Americans, the enormity of the Nazi crime became real only when soldiers began to liberate the concentration camps that dotted the map of Germany. When they saw it all—the piles of dead bodies, the warehouses full of human hair and jewelry, the ashes in crematoriums, the half-dead emaciated survivors—they realized as never before that evil was more than an abstraction.

Hardened by war, accustomed to the sight and smell of death, the soldiers who liberated the camps were nevertheless unprepared for what they saw. Major Richard Winters—who had parachuted behind enemy lines on D-Day, defended Bastogne at the Battle of the Bulge, and risked his life in a number of other engagements—was stunned almost beyond belief:

> **Primary Source** "The memory of starved, dazed men, who dropped their eyes and heads when we looked at them through the chain-link fence, in the same manner that a beaten, mistreated dog would cringe, leaves feelings that cannot be described and will never be forgotten. The impact of seeing those people behind that fence left me saying, only to myself, 'Now I know why I'm here.'"
> —Richard Winters, quoted in *Band of Brothers* (Ambrose)

The liberation of the camps led to an outpouring of American sympathy and sincere longing to aid the victims. Many survivors found temporary or permanent homes in the United States.

The revelation of the Holocaust also increased demand and support for an independent Jewish homeland. In 1948, when the Jewish community in Palestine proclaimed the State of Israel, President Truman immediately recognized the new nation. The United States became perhaps the staunchest ally of the new Jewish State.

✓ **Checkpoint** How did the U.S. government respond to the German campaign against European Jews?

A Survivor Bears Witness
This 90-year-old Holocaust survivor continues to speak to young Germans about his time in the Auschwitz death camp. He still bears a physical reminder of his suffering: the identification number tattooed on his arm.

SECTION 4 Assessment

Progress Monitoring *Online*
For: Self-test with vocabulary practice
www.pearsonschool.com/ushist

Comprehension

1. **Terms and People** For each term below, write a sentence explaining how it was connected with the Nazi campaign against the Jews and the U.S. reaction.
   - Holocaust
   - anti-Semitism
   - Nuremberg Laws
   - Kristallnacht
   - genocide
   - concentration camp
   - death camp
   - War Refugee Board

2. **NoteTaking Reading Skill: Recognize Sequence** Use your flowchart to answer the Section Focus Question: How did the Holocaust develop and what were its results?

Writing About History

3. **Quick Write: Describe Emotions** Write three sentences describing the emotions of an American soldier liberating a concentration camp in Germany. Be sure to use adjectives and nouns that express specific inner feelings.

Critical Thinking

4. **Identify Ideologies** How were Hitler's racial ideas and policies connected to his concept of extreme nationalism?

5. **Analyze Information** One historian has said that the Holocaust began on "the day that the Jews started to be treated differently." Explain what this statement means and what evidence supports it.

6. **Make Decisions** Do you think that the U.S. military should have decided to bomb railway lines leading to the death camps? Why or why not?

5 Step-by-Step Instruction

Objectives

As you teach this section, keep students focused on the following objectives to help them answer the Section Focus Question and master core content.

- Evaluate the goals that Allied leaders set for the postwar world.
- Describe the steps that the United States and other nations took toward international cooperation.
- Explain the impact of World War II on the postwar United States.

Prepare to Read

Background Knowledge ⬛

Discuss the relationship between the United States and the Soviet Union during World War II. Have students predict how the relationship might change after the war, and both nations emerge as world powers.

Set a Purpose ⬛

- **WITNESS HISTORY** Read the selection aloud.

  Ask **According to Robert Jackson, what might happen if people do not learn from the cruelties of the Holocaust?** *(If the atrocities and inhumanities of the Holocaust are repeated, human civilization is doomed.)*

- **Focus** Point out the Section Focus Question, and write it on the board. Tell students to refer to this question as they read. *(Answer appears with Section 5 Assessment answers.)*

- **Preview** Have students preview the Section Objectives and the list of Terms and People.

- **NoteTaking** Using the Paragraph Shrinking strategy (TE, p. T20), have students read this section. As they read, have students record various developments in the postwar world that resulted from World War II.
  Reading and Note Taking Study Guide

Nazism on Trial

In October 1945, a historic trial unlike any other began. The 21 defendants were the cream of the Third Reich, leaders of Hitler's war machine and architects of the Holocaust. Robert Jackson, the American prosecutor, scoffed as men like Hermann Goering, Hitler's handpicked successor, claimed to be tools of Hitler, unaware of his true plans. In his closing speech, Jackson turned the spotlight not on the defendants alone, but on the future of humanity:

❝No half-century ever witnessed slaughter on such a scale, such cruelties and inhumanities. . . . If we cannot eliminate the causes and prevent the repetition of these barbaric events, it is not an irresponsible prophecy to say that this twentieth century may yet succeed in bringing the doom of civilization.❞

—Robert Jackson, closing speech, Nuremberg War Crimes Trials, 1946

▲ Defendant Hermann Goering (right) at the Nuremberg Trials

Effects of the War

Objectives

- Evaluate the goals that Allied leaders set for the postwar world.
- Describe the steps that United States and other nations took toward international cooperation.
- Explain the impact of World War II on the postwar United States.

Terms and People

Yalta Conference
superpower
GATT
United Nations

Universal Declaration of Human Rights
Geneva Convention
Nuremberg Trials

NoteTaking

Reading Skill: Understand Effects As you read, look for various developments in the postwar world that resulted from World War II.

Why It Matters World War II changed the nation in profound ways. Many Americans came home determined to extend the ideals of democracy and freedom at home as well as abroad. In addition, the United States emerged from the war prepared to take on the complex and vital role in world affairs that it still holds today. **Section Focus Question: What were the major immediate and long-term effects of World War II?**

Allies Set Postwar Goals

World War II differed from World War I in several ways. One major difference was that it was fought to the bitter end. In 1918, the Kaiser surrendered before the Allies could invade Germany. By contrast, in World War II, Japan and Germany kept fighting long after their defeat was certain. In the last year of the war, they lost battle after battle, retreated from the lands they had conquered, and saw the slow destruction of their military forces. Allied bombing devastated their cities and industries. Yet Germany fought on until Hitler committed suicide, and Japan refused to surrender until after the bombing of Hiroshima and Nagasaki.

Allies Make Plans at Yalta The protracted fighting gave the Allies time to make plans for a postwar world. Roosevelt, Churchill, and Stalin met at Yalta on the Black Sea in February 1945 to discuss final strategy and crucial questions concerning postwar Germany, Eastern Europe, and Asia. At the **Yalta Conference,** the Big Three agreed that Poland, Bulgaria, and Romania would hold free elections. However, Stalin later reneged on this promise.

Vocabulary Builder

Use the information below and the following resource to teach students the high-use word from this section. Teaching Resources, Vocabulary Builder, p. 12

High-Use Word	Definition and Sample Sentence
predominant	*adj.* having the greatest amount of authority or dominance The **predominant** struggle during World War II was between the Allies and the Axis Powers.

Roosevelt and Churchill were not in a good position to press Stalin too hard. The Red Army already occupied much of Eastern Europe, and Roosevelt wanted Soviet help in the war against Japan. Vague promises were about as much as Stalin would give.

Truman Faces Stalin at Potsdam A dramatically altered Big Three met in July 1945 in the Berlin suburb of Potsdam. Although Stalin remained in power in the Soviet Union, Harry S. Truman had become U.S. President upon the death of FDR. After the start of the conference, Clement Atlee replaced Churchill as prime minister of Britain.

While in Potsdam, Truman learned of the successful test of the atomic bomb. But he was more focused on Europe and the Soviet Union than on Asia. At the meeting, the Big Three formalized the decision to divide Germany into four zones of occupation: Soviet, American, British, and French. They agreed to new borders and free elections for Poland, and they recognized the Soviets' right to claim reparations for war damages from the German sector they controlled. Stalin also reaffirmed his Yalta pledge to enter the war against Japan.

✔ **Checkpoint** What goals did the Allies set for Eastern Europe at the Yalta Conference?

A New World Takes Shape

After the war ended in August 1945, plans for the postwar world had to be turned into realities. However, the changes that took place were not often what the Allies had envisioned at Yalta and Potsdam.

The World Map Changes World War II altered the political realities of the world. The borders of Poland, for example, shifted slightly to the west. In time, as you will read in the next chapter, differences between the Soviet Union and its former Allies led to the division of Germany into two countries: communist East Germany and noncommunist West Germany. Nearly all the nations of Eastern Europe became communist states under Soviet control.

Other countries experienced profound political changes. Communist and non-communist interests clashed in Eastern Europe. In China, a long-standing civil war between Nationalists and communists resumed.

In Japan, General Douglas MacArthur headed an American military occupation and supervised the writing of a new constitution. It abolished the armed forces except for purposes of defense, gave women the right to vote, enacted democratic reforms, and established the groundwork for full economic recovery.

Imperialism Goes Into Decline The war also marked the end of Western European domination of the world.

The Big Three at Yalta
This famous photo shows (left to right) Churchill, Roosevelt, and Stalin at the Yalta Conference. Their glum looks seem to say: Here are not victors, but potential enemies. In addition, FDR looks ill and tired—he died only months after this picture was taken.

Independent Practice

- To help students understand what occurred at the Yalta Conference, have them complete the worksheet *History Comics: Postwar Goals.* **Teaching Resources, p. 22**

- Have students access **www.pearsonschool.com/ushist** to use the Geography Interactive map and answer the map skills questions in the text. Then, have students write a summary of the information presented in the map.

Monitor Progress

As students complete their concept webs, circulate to make sure that they identify various developments that resulted from World War II. For a completed version of the concept web, see Note Taking Transparencies, **B-118.**

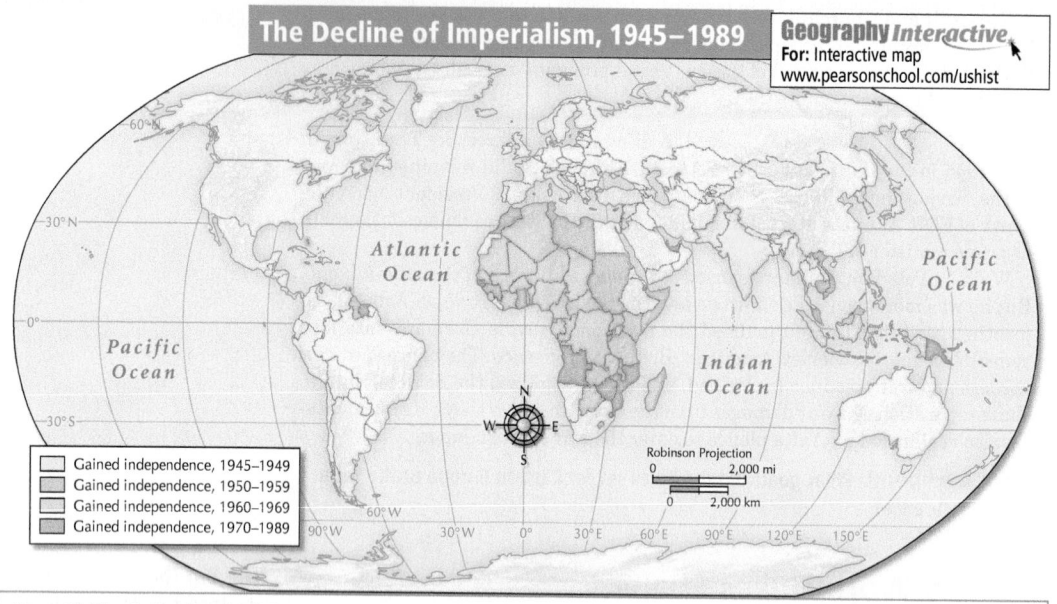

The Decline of Imperialism, 1945–1989

Geography *Interactive*
For: Interactive map
www.pearsonschool.com/ushist

Gained independence, 1945–1949
Gained independence, 1950–1959
Gained independence, 1960–1969
Gained independence, 1970–1989

Robinson Projection

Map Skills In the decades following World War II, the Age of Imperialism ended as colony after colony won independence.

1. **Locate:** (a) Europe, (b) Africa, (c) Asia, (d) the Soviet Union

2. **Regions** On what continent did the largest number of nations win independence?

3. **Predict Consequences** How might the appearance of so many new nations affect the balance of power in the postwar world?

Since the 1500s, nations such as Britain, France, and Spain had exerted paramount influence on global developments. They colonized much of Africa, the Middle East, Asia, and the Americas. They had controlled world trade and finance, led the industrial revolution, and stood at the forefront of world military power.

The aggressive acquisition of territories by Japan and Germany underscored the abuses of imperialism. After World War II, colonial peoples renewed their drive for independence from European powers. Freed from Japanese domination, the East Indies had no interest in returning to Dutch colonial status. Nor did Indochina want to see the return of French rule. India, Burma, colonies in the Middle East and Africa—all had their sights set on independence.

By the end of the war, it was clear that the Age of Imperialism was in the twilight of its existence. The British Empire, the predominant power of the nineteenth century, came out of the war suffering severe economic shortages and, within decades, would see the loss of most of its colonies.

Vocabulary Builder
predominant–(pree DAHM uh nuhnt) *adj.* having the greatest amount of authority or dominance

The Balance of Power Shifts Into the power vacuum stepped the United States and the Soviet Union. They had played the most decisive roles in defeating the Axis Powers, and they emerged from the war confident and strong. Indeed, they so dominated the postwar world that they became known as **superpowers.**

Of the two superpowers, the United States was clearly the stronger. Except for the attack on Pearl Harbor, no major battle had been fought on U.S. soil. In addition, American industry had boomed during the war. By 1945, America was wealthy, militarily powerful, and confident. By contrast, much of the war had

---

Differentiated Instruction   Solutions for All Learners

L4 Advanced Readers   L4 Gifted and Talented Students

Have each student select one of the men who represented the Big Three at Yalta or Potsdam—FDR, Truman, Churchill, Atlee, or Stalin—and do research to learn more about the political and diplomatic role of the chosen leader during those meetings. Have students use their findings to write three to five journal entries from the perspective of their chosen leaders. Students' journal entries may describe what their chosen leaders hoped to accomplish at each meeting, how their chosen leaders may have responded to the decisions made at each of the meetings, why their chosen leaders supported or opposed these decisions, and so on.

Answers

Map Skills

1. Review locations with students.

2. Africa

3. Possible answer: Former colonial powers would become weaker, and new nations could form blocs of their own or ally with either of the superpowers.

been fought on Soviet soil. Its industries, cities, and peoples had suffered terribly. Still, the Red Army controlled most of Eastern Europe and threatened to move farther west. Militarily, although the Americans had the atomic bomb, the Soviets had the Red Army, the world's largest military force.

✓ **Checkpoint** What impact did World War II have on the relative roles of the United States and Britain in the world?

International Cooperation

Americans were quick to recognize that their nation had taken on a new position in the world. After World War I, the Senate had rejected the Treaty of Versailles and refused to join the League of Nations. Many Americans now viewed these decisions as mistakes that contributed to the rise of fascism and the outbreak of another war. As World War II drew to a close, Americans were ready to embrace the idea of world organizations.

A New World Economy Takes Shape The United States took on major responsibilities in shaping the postwar world economy. After meeting in 1944 with the Allies in Bretton Woods, New Hampshire, the U.S. government pushed for establishment of the International Monetary Fund and the World Bank. The United States provided most of the working capital for these new organizations, which worked to foster global economic and financial stability. The United States also signed the **General Agreement on Tariffs and Trade (GATT)**, a 1948 treaty designed to expand world trade by reducing tariffs.

The United Nations Is Formed Even more importantly, the United States led the charge for the establishment of the **United Nations (UN)**, an organization that, many hoped, would succeed where the League of Nations had failed. In April 1945, delegates from 50 nations met in San Francisco to write the charter for the UN. The Senate overwhelmingly ratified the charter, and the UN later set up its permanent home in New York City.

The United Nations was organized on the basis of cooperation between the Great Powers, not on the absolute equality of all nations. All member nations sat on the General Assembly. However, the five major World War II Allies—the United States, the Soviet Union, Britain, France, and China—were assigned permanent seats on the most powerful arm of the UN, the Security Council.

Over the next decades, the UN aided the move away from colonialism, helped to create the Jewish state of Israel, mediated regional conflicts, and provided food and other aid to much of the world. The UN also issued the **Universal Declaration of Human Rights** in 1948. This idealistic document states:

Primary Source "Recognition of the inherent dignity and of the equal and inalienable rights of all members of the human family is the foundation of freedom, justice and peace in the world. . . . All human beings are born free and equal in dignity and rights. They are endowed with reason and conscience and should act toward one another in a spirit of brotherhood."
—Universal Declaration of Human Rights

HISTORY MAKERS

Eleanor Roosevelt (1884–1962)
As First Lady, Eleanor Roosevelt had been a valuable, if unofficial, part of her husband's presidential administration. After FDR's death, President Truman named her to represent the United States at the United Nations. As elected chair of the Commission on Human Rights, she guided the drafting of the Universal Declaration of Human Rights, which she hoped would "become the international Magna Carta for all men everywhere." Her work on behalf of human rights won Roosevelt the nickname First Lady of the World. Shortly before her death, President John F. Kennedy named Roosevelt to head his Commission on the Status of Women.

A New American Identity

The Declaration condemns slavery and torture, upholds freedom of speech and religion, and affirms that "everyone has the right to a standard of living adequate for the health and well-being of himself and his family." Though the document sets lofty goals it has proved difficult to enforce.

War Criminals Go on Trial In the effort to create a better world, the Allies did not forget to punish the people who had caused so much destruction and death. During the war, the Axis Powers had repeatedly violated the **Geneva Convention,** an international agreement governing the humane treatment of wounded soldiers and prisoners of war.

The Allies tried more than a thousand Japanese citizens for committing atrocities in China, Korea, and Southeast Asia and brutally mistreating prisoners of war. Hundreds were condemned to death, including Prime Minister Hideki Tojo and the general responsible for the Bataan Death March.

Americans more closely followed the **Nuremberg Trials,** in which the Allies prosecuted Nazis for war crimes. The trials turned a glaring spotlight on the evils of the Third Reich. The first of the Nuremberg Trials involved key leaders of Nazi Germany, such as Hermann Goring. Day by day, prosecutors described their crimes, detailing especially the horrors of the Holocaust. Most of the defendants pleaded that they were just following orders, that Hitler was the source of all the crimes. The judges at Nuremberg did not accept their excuses. Some of the Nazis were hanged; others received long prison terms.

In the following decades, Allied or Israeli authorities captured and tried such other Nazis as Adolf Eichmann, a leading architect of the "Final Solution." The periodic trials kept alive the memory of the Nazi crimes against humanity.

 Checkpoint What steps did the United States take to increase its role in the postwar world?

A New American Identity

A new American identity rose from the ashes of World War II, one formed as the antithesis of the Nazi ideal. Americans regarded the Nazis as totalitarian, racist, and warlike. They defined themselves as democratic, tolerant, and peaceful. During the war, U.S. leaders and American popular culture had emphasized these positive themes, repeating constantly that the Allies were fighting a "people's war" for tolerance, freedom, democracy, and peace. Although many Americans felt that their country had not always lived up to that ideal, they hoped that the postwar period would usher in significant changes.

The United States Assumes Global Leadership Millions of Americans had spent several years closely following the war. They had attached world maps to their walls and traced the paths of U.S. troops in the deserts of North Africa, the forests of Europe, and the coral islands of the Pacific. For this generation of Americans, the world had somehow become a smaller, more interconnected place. They had learned to think in global terms.

Few Americans called for a return to a policy of isolationism or retreat from their global responsibilities. They recognized that what happened in the far reaches of the globe affected them, that the economic and political health of

America was tied to world peace and economic development. They knew that America's national security involved world security.

Commitment to Civil Rights Grows African American soldiers in World War II had clearly believed they were fighting two foes: dictatorship overseas and racism in the United States. As the great African American poet Langston Hughes put it:

Primary Source

"You tell me that Hitler
Is a mighty bad man.
I guess he took lessons
From the Ku Klux Klan."
—Langston Hughes, quoted in *The Fight of the Century* (Hietala)

World War II gave renewed vigor to the fight for civil rights. In this battle, African Americans were not alone. A growing number of white Americans also called for the nation to fully live up to its promise as a beacon of freedom, democracy, and justice.

The Nation Prospers World War II ended the Great Depression and ushered in decades of economic growth. It also redistributed wealth across the country. Defense industries and military bases in the South and West spurred people to move to these regions, which in turn created more wealth and encouraged further migration.

The driving force for all the jobs and prosperity was the federal government. Like other wars, World War II led to a greater governmental influence in economic affairs. From the collection of raw materials to attempts to control inflation, the government had made the important decisions to guide the economy. In the process, it established the expanded economic role that government would play in postwar America.

✓ **Checkpoint** How did World War II foster support for civil rights?

A Hero Comes Home
For millions of Americans, World War II was not truly over until their loved ones came home from overseas. Here, a wounded G.I. embraces his parents.

SECTION 5 Assessment

Progress Monitoring *Online*
For: Self-test with vocabulary practice
www.pearsonschool.com/ushist

Comprehension

1. Terms and People For each term below, write a sentence explaining how it was connected with the building of the postwar world.
- Yalta Conference
- superpower
- GATT
- United Nations
- Universal Declaration of Human Rights
- Geneva Convention
- Nuremberg Trials

2. NoteTaking Reading Skill: Understand Effects Use your concept web to answer the Section Focus Question: What were the major immediate and long-term effects of World War II?

Writing About History

3. Quick Write: Write a Descriptive Paragraph Write a paragraph describing the look and feel of the Nuremberg Trials. Describe both what you might see and the emotional mood in the room.

Critical Thinking

4. Predict Consequences Identify one possible postwar consequence of the Allied disagreements at Yalta and Potsdam.

5. Recognize Causes and Effects Why do you think Americans supported participation in the UN after World War II when they had opposed participation in the League of Nations after World War I?

6. Compare In what way were both the Universal Declaration of Human Rights and the postwar push for civil rights reactions to the war?

Quick Study Guide

Progress Monitoring *Online*
For: Self-test with vocabulary practice
www.pearsonschool.com/ushist

Quick Study Guide

- Have students use the Quick Study Guide to prepare for the chapter test. Students may wish to refer to the following sections as they review:

Allied Leaders, World War II
Section 1
Section 3
Section 5

World War II Home Front
Section 2

Five Turning Points of World War II
Section 1
Section 3

World War II Deaths, Selected Nations
Section 1
Section 3
Section 4

Key Events of World War II
Section 1
Section 2
Section 3
Section 4
Section 5

- For additional review, remind students to refer to the Reading and Note Taking Study Guide.
  Section Note Taking
  Section Summaries

- Have students access **www.pearsonschool.com/ ushist** for this chapter's History Interactive timeline, which includes expanded entries and additional events.

- If students need more instruction on analyzing graphic data, have them read the Skills Handbook, **p. SH21.**

For **Progress Monitoring** *Online,* refer students to the Self-test with vocabulary practice at **www.pearsonschool.com/ushist.**

■ Allied Leaders, World War II

World Political	U.S. Military
• Winston Churchill, Britain • Joseph Stalin, Soviet Union • Franklin D. Roosevelt, United States • Harry S. Truman, United States	**In Europe** • Dwight Eisenhower • George S. Patton • Omar Bradley **In the Pacific** • Douglas MacArthur • Chester Nimitz

■ World War II Home Front

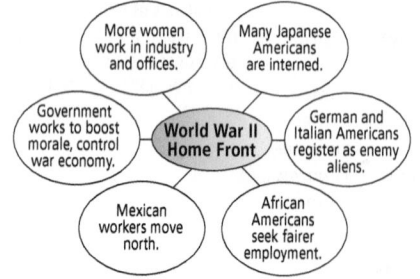

- More women work in industry and offices.
- Many Japanese Americans are interned.
- Government works to boost morale, control war economy.
- **World War II Home Front**
- German and Italian Americans register as enemy aliens.
- Mexican workers move north.
- African Americans seek fairer employment.

■ Five Turning Points of World War II

1942	**Battle of Midway** halts Japanese expansion in Pacific.
1942–1943	**Battle of Stalingrad** ends Nazi advances in Europe.
1942	**Battle of El Alamein** begins Allied offensive against Axis Powers in North Africa.
1944	**D-Day** invasion opens second front in Europe, paving way for final defeat of Germany.
1945	**Manhattan Project** develops atomic bomb, used to end war in Pacific.

■ World War II Deaths, Selected Nations

Country	Military Deaths	Civilian Deaths
Axis		
Germany	3,500,000	780,000
Italy	242,000	153,000
Japan	1,300,000	672,000
Allies		
France	213,000	350,000
Britain	264,000	93,000
China	1,310,000	1,000,000
Soviet Union	7,500,000	15,000,000
United States	292,000	6,000

SOURCES: Henri Michel, *Encyclopaedia Britannica; Harper Encyclopedia of Military History*
All figures are estimates.

☑ Quick Study Timeline

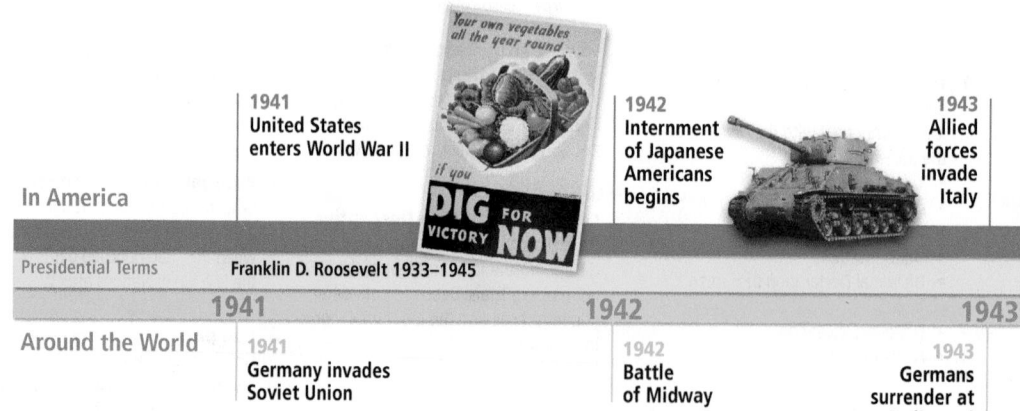

In America

1941
United States enters World War II

1942
Internment of Japanese Americans begins

1943
Allied forces invade Italy

Presidential Terms   Franklin D. Roosevelt 1933–1945

1941   1942   1943

Around the World

1941
Germany invades Soviet Union

1942
Battle of Midway

1943
Germans surrender at Stalingrad

Differentiated Instruction   Solutions for All Learners

L1 Special Needs Students   **L2 English Language Learners**   **L2 Less Proficient Readers**

Use the following study guide resources to help students acquiring basic skills:
Adapted Reading and Note Taking Study Guide
- Section Note Taking
- Section Summaries

Use the following study guide resources to help Spanish-speaking students:
Spanish Reading and Note Taking Study Guide
- Section Note Taking
- Section Summaries

American Issues
•—•—•—• Connector

By connecting prior knowledge with what you have learned in this chapter, you can gradually build your understanding of enduring questions that still affect America today. Answer the questions below. Then, use your American Issues Connector study guide (or go online: www.pearsonschool.com/ushist).

Issues You Learned About

● **Protecting and Expanding Civil Rights** Americans may organize to demand fair treatment and civil rights.

1. Why did Roosevelt decide to issue an executive order assuring fair hiring practices in any job funded by the government?

2. What was the NAACP, when was it founded, and why did its membership grow during the war years?

3. How did World War II motivate African Americans' fight for civil rights? What do you think African Americans did after the war ended to win more civil rights?

● **Civil Liberties and National Security** During wartime, the government has often taken steps to suspend civil liberties.

4. During World War II, which groups of people suffered from persecution? Did the U.S. government violate these groups' civil liberties? Explain.

5. How did the United States defend its internment of Japanese Americans? How did some Japanese Americans respond?

6. Was there any evidence that Japanese Americans threatened national security? Present evidence that supports or weakens this claim.

● **Technology and Society** New technological developments can hurt society as well as help it.

7. What new technology contributed to the high casualties of World War II?

8. What was the atomic bomb? How powerful was the first one that was tested?

9. What effect did the dropping of atomic bombs on Hiroshima and Nagasaki have on the progress of World War II?

Connect to Your World | Activity

Global Interdependence What role should the United States play in the United Nations? In recent years, the relationship between the United States and the UN has sometimes been tense. Some Americans believe that the UN should provide more backing to the United States, which is the organization's largest financial contributor. Other Americans believe that the United States does not pay enough attention to the opinions of the UN when taking steps that affect world security. What do you think? Go online or to your local library to research current American involvement with the UN. Pay special attention to differences of opinion between the United States and the global organization. Then, write a summary sharing what you learned and expressing your own thoughts about American involvement in the UN.

1944
D-Day landing in France

1945
World War II ends

History *Interactive.*
For: Interactive timeline
www.pearsonschool.com/ushist

Harry S. Truman 1945–1953

1944   **1945**   **1946**

1945
Nazi death camps liberated

1946
Nuremberg war crimes trials

Differentiated Instruction   Solutions for All Learners

L1 Special Needs Students   **L2 English Language Learners**   **L2 Less Proficient Readers**

Use the following study guide resource to help students acquiring basic skills:
Adapted Reading and Note Taking Study Guide
• American Issues Journal

Use the following study guide resource to help Spanish-speaking students:
Spanish Reading and Note Taking Study Guide
• American Issues Journal

American Issues
•—•—• Connector

Tell students that the main issues for this chapter are Protecting and Expanding Civil Rights, Civil Liberties and National Security, and Technology and Society. Then, ask students to answer the Issues You Learned About questions on this page. Discuss the Connect to Your World topic(s), and ask students to complete the project that follows.

American Issues Connector

1. FDR feared that marches would undermine national unity.

2. an organization founded in 1909 to fight segregation; victories such as Executive Order 8802 encouraged African Americans to join the NAACP.

3. African American leaders argued that while the United States was fighting fascism abroad, it also should fight discrimination at home. After the war, many fought for equality by demonstrating and using the courts to dispute discrimination.

4. Socialists, political radicals, pacifists, and those against the war were treated harshly. Yes; by passing and enforcing the Espionage Act and the Sedition Act.

5. Some leaders believed that they were inherently disloyal. Some went to court to demand their rights.

6. No; the all-Nisei 442nd Regimental Combat Team fought with distinction in Europe and became the most decorated military unit in U.S. history.

7. the machine gun, the submarine, and poison gases, such as mustard gas

8. a device that uses a fission reaction to produce an explosion; it was strong enough to be seen 180 miles away and heard 100 miles away.

9. Japan surrendered and ended World War II.

Connect to Your World

Summaries should express a clear point of view about the U.S. involvement in the UN and make reasoned arguments of support.

For additional review of this chapter's enduring issues, remind students to refer to the **Reading and Note Taking Study Guide** American Issues Journal.

Terms and People

1. Eisenhower and Patton were U.S. generals during World War II. Both were involved in the Allied invasion of North Africa.

2. Japanese Americans; families in one-room shacks; single people in drafty bunkhouses; food shortages; substandard medical care

3. Operation Overlord was the code name for the Allied invasion of France. D-Day was the first day of the invasion, June 6, 1944. The successful invasion gave the Allies a foothold in France.

4. to develop an atomic bomb

5. the willful annihilation of a racial, political, or cultural group; Hitler's "Final Solution" involved the systematic gathering and imprisoning of Jewish people in concentration camps where they were tortured, experimented on, worked to death, starved, or gassed.

6. to prosecute Nazi leaders for war crimes

Focus Questions

7. In Europe, the Allies stopped German progress at Stalingrad, in the Atlantic, and in North Africa, and put Germany on the defensive. In the Pacific, the Americans defeated the Japanese at the Battle of Midway, putting Japan on the defensive.

8. Women and minorities found new opportunities in the workplace. African Americans achieved some improvements in civil rights. However, injustices occurred. The U.S. government also helped manage the economy.

9. In Europe, the Germans were defeated by Allied armies pushing from both the west and the east. In the Pacific, the U.S. atomic bombs and Russia's declaration of war persuaded the Japanese emperor to surrender.

10. When Hitler became chancellor of Germany, he institutionalized anti-Semitism. In 1935, the Nuremberg Laws denied Jews their German citizenship. Many Jews were put into concentration camps. Later, Nazi leaders adopted Hitler's

Chapter Assessment

Terms and People

1. Who were **Dwight D. Eisenhower** and **George S. Patton, Jr.**? How were the two men linked?

2. What Americans were sent to **internment camps**? What were conditions like in these camps?

3. Define **D-Day**. What was the result of this strategy?

4. What was the goal of the **Manhattan Project**?

5. Define **genocide**. How did Hitler attempt to accomplish genocide?

6. What was the purpose of the **Nuremberg Trials**?

Focus Questions

The focus question for this chapter is **What impact did World War II have on America and the world?** Build an answer to this big question by answering the focus questions for Sections 1 through 5 and the Critical Thinking questions that follow.

Section 1
7. How did the Allies turn the tide against the Axis?

Section 2
8. How did the war change America at home?

Section 3
9. How did the Allies defeat the Axis Powers?

Section 4
10. How did the Holocaust develop and what were its results?

Section 5
11. What were the major immediate and long-term effects of World War II?

Critical Thinking

12. **Recognize Effects** Explain the significance of Allied victories at Stalingrad and in North Africa.

13. **Evaluate Information** The Americans who fought in World War II have been called the "Greatest Generation." What do you think this means? What evidence supports this claim?

14. **Summarize** Summarize the contributions of two of these groups to the war effort: women, Mexican Americans, African Americans, Navajos.

15. **Interpreting a Political Cartoon** What is the main point of the cartoon below? How do you think American soldiers reacted to this cartoon?

"America is a myth, the superiority of her war potential is a legend, and the arsenal of democracy is a bogey for scared Europeans."
DR. OTTO DIETRICH, OCT. 29, 1942

16. **Make Decisions** Do you think Truman's decision to drop the atomic bomb was justified at the time? Was it justified in light of future events?

17. **Recognize Propaganda** How did Hitler use propaganda in his campaign against German Jews?

18. **Synthesize Information** **(a)** How do the meetings at Yalta and Potsdam reflect a new balance of global power? **(b)** What type of relationship do you think the United States and the Soviet Union will have in the post–World War II years?

Writing About History

Writing a Descriptive Essay In a descriptive essay, you try to convey in words the look, sound, and mood of an event. Write a three-paragraph descriptive essay on one of the following topics: an American flight crew making a bombing run over Germany; women going to work in defense industries during World War II; soldiers walking on Omaha Beach after D-Day; American soldiers liberating a concentration camp.

Prewriting
• Look at the pictures and read the text in this chapter relating to the topic you have chosen.
• Use Internet or library sources to find additional pictures and descriptions relating to your topic.
• Make a list of sights, sounds, impressions, and connections to your topic.

Drafting
• Make an outline identifying what aspects of your topic you want to describe.
• Write an opening paragraph in which you introduce the topic and identify the setting.
• Write descriptions using precise adjectives and specific action verbs. Avoid generalizations that are too broad or too vague.

Revising
• Use the guidelines on page SH8 of the Writing Handbook to revise your writing.

"Final Solution," which resulted in millions of murders.

11. The United States became a prosperous world power. Americans viewed the world in global terms and stopped favoring isolationism.

Critical Thinking

12. Both victories put Germany on the defensive.

13. Sample answer: Through their hard work, courage, and selflessness, Americans survived the depression, fought World War II, and made the United States a global

leader. The fact that Americans worked hard and made sacrifices is evidence that supports the claim.

14. Sample answer: Women worked in factories, fed and clothed their families on war rations, and kept up morale. Through the bracero program, Mexicans worked on farms while American men were fighting overseas.

15. The cartoon depicts the German view that America's military reputation is false; however, the giant Uncle Sam says otherwise. American soldiers may have been proud and scoffed at Germany's delusion.

Document-Based Assessment

The Battle of Midway
The Battle of Midway is considered a major turning point of World War II. But why was it so important? How was it viewed by the participants? Use your knowledge of the chapter material and Documents A, B, C, and D to answer questions 1 through 4.

Document A

War in Asia and the Pacific, December 1941–August 1942	
December 7, 1941	Japan bombs Pearl Harbor.
December 23, 1941	Japan captures Wake Island.
December 25, 1941	Japan captures Hong Kong.
February 15, 1942	Japan captures Singapore.
April 8, 1942	Japan captures Bataan, Philippines.
May 4, 1942	Japanese offensive stalls at Battle of the Coral Sea.
May 20, 1942	Japan drives British out of Burma.
June 4–7, 1942	United States Navy wins Battle of Midway.
August 7, 1942	Americans begin assault on Guadalcanal.

Document B
"In numerous and widespread engagements lasting from the 3rd to 6th of June, with carrier based planes as the spearhead of the attack, combined forces of the Navy, Marine Corps and Army in the Hawaiian Area defeated a large part of the Japanese fleet and frustrated the enemy's powerful move against Midway that was undoubtedly the keystone of larger plans. All participating personnel, without exception, displayed unhesitating devotion to duty, loyalty and courage. This superb spirit in all three services made possible the application of the destructive power that routed the enemy. . . . These results were achieved at the cost of the *Yorktown* and *Hamman* sunk and about 150 planes lost in action or damaged beyond repair. Our total personnel losses were about ninety-two (92) officers and two hundred and fifteen (215) men."
— *Admiral Chester A. Nimitz, official report of the Battle of Midway, filed June 28, 1942*

Document C
"Had Yamamoto fulfilled his projects of taking Midway and destroying Nimitz's carriers, the next program on his agenda was to turn to the Australian campaign. And with the aerial striking power of the U.S. Pacific Fleet out of the running, there would have been precious little to stop him. . . . And in the meantime, possession of Midway would have given Japan the means to harass at least the Hawaiian Islands and even the West Coast. . . . At Midway, the United States laid aside the shield and picked up the sword, and through all the engagements to follow, never again yielded the strategic offensive."
— *Gordon W. Prange,* Miracle at Midway, *1982*

Document D
"It was Japan that had attacked the United States, and it was Japan on which the anger of the American people had focused. . . . Had it not been for Midway, Roosevelt could not have persevered with a Europe-first policy. Public opinion would not have allowed it. . . . Through an extraordinary combination of the skill and courage of our pilots, splendid intelligence, prudent risk-taking by our commanders that paid off, and sheer good luck, the apparently inferior American forces were victorious. This victory occurred despite the inferiority of our aircraft, the ineffectiveness of our torpedoes, the substantial absence of backup surface ships, and our overall numerical inferiority. You know the rest! Four Japanese carriers had been sunk. . . . The Japanese offensive had now been blunted. The Japanese fleet turned back toward the Home Islands and the opportunity for victory had been lost forever. . . . After Midway, the United States could, to the chagrin of Douglas MacArthur, turn its primary attention back to the European theatre."
— *Former Secretary of Defense James R. Schlesinger, June 5, 2003*

1. Which conclusion is best supported by Document A?
   A Japan lost the war as a direct result of the Battle of Midway.
   B Before the Battle of Midway, Japan had been on the offensive.
   C The Japanese invasion of Burma led to the Battle of Bataan.
   D The Battle of Midway was the last Japanese victory in the Pacific.

2. On what point do Document B and Document C agree?
   A The Battle of Midway was a setback for Japan.
   B The Battle of Midway was a setback for the United States.
   C The Battle of Midway was equally damaging to both sides.
   D U.S. forces were undamaged at the Battle of Midway.

3. According to Document D, how did the Battle of Midway make it easier for Roosevelt to pursue a "Europe First" strategy?
   A It convinced Americans that Japan was no longer a threat.
   B It roused public anger against Germany.
   C It satisfied immediate public demand for action against Japan.
   D It showed that the United States could not win in the Pacific unless it conquered Germany first.

4. **Writing Task** What might have happened if Japanese forces had won the Battle of Midway? Use your knowledge of the chapter content and specific evidence from the primary sources above to support your opinion.

16. Sample answer: Yes; Truman's decision was practical because dropping the bomb saved countless American lives and ended the war quickly. Despite the ethical issues surrounding it, Truman's duty was to the United States, not to Japan. His decision also was justified in light of future events because the United States led the Soviet Union in the nuclear arms race, and so maintained a military balance against the power of the Red Army.

17. Hitler used newspapers to print scandalous attacks on Jewish people, schools taught children that Jews were polluting German society and culture, and comic books contained vile caricatures of Jews.

18. (a) The main struggles were between Roosevelt and Stalin at Yalta and between Truman and Stalin at Potsdam indicating that the United States and the Soviet Union were now the most powerful nations. (b) The Soviet Union and the United States will probably experience a great deal of tension and competition.

CHAPTER 12

CHAPTER 12 The Cold War 1945–1960

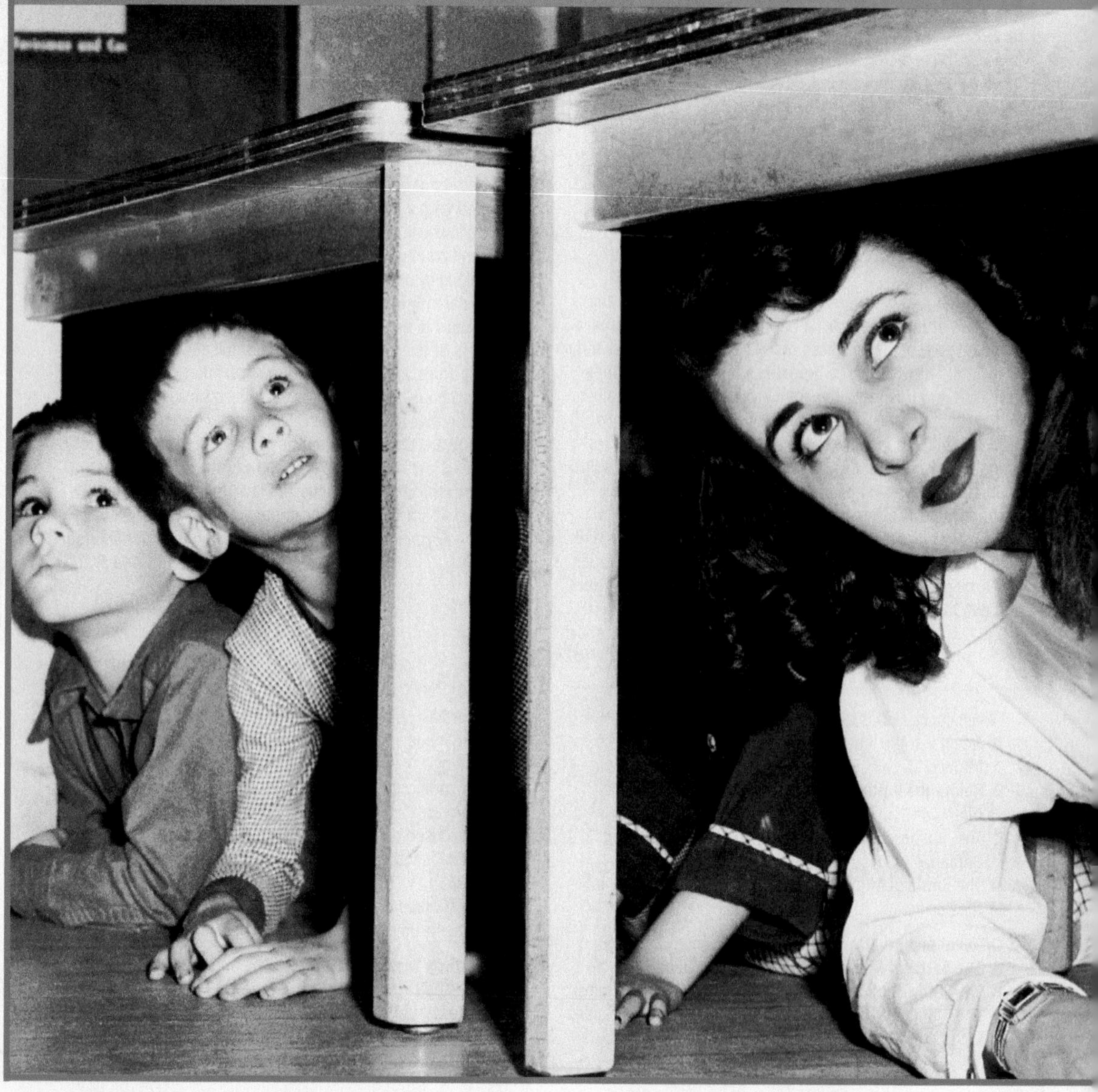

Teach With Technology

Presentation**EXPRESS™**
PREMIUM DVD

- Teach this chapter's core content by using PresentationExpress, which includes interactivities, video, lecture notes, and the *ExamView*® QuickTake assessment tool.
- To introduce this chapter by using PresentationExpress, ask students with which of the following statements they most agree: **A) When the nation is threatened, it is acceptable to arrest people who might be part of the threat, even if there is less evidence against them than is usually required. B) Even when the nation is threatened, the rights of accused people must be protected.** Take a class poll or record students' answers by using the QuickTake feature, and discuss their responses. Point out that in this chapter, they will read about the ways the nation dealt with these questions during the Cold War. Continue introducing the chapter by using the chapter opener slide show.

Technology Resources

- Student**EXPRESS** CD-ROM
- Teacher Resource Library **DVD**
- Presentation**EXPRESS** **PREMIUM DVD**
- *ExamView*® **Test Bank CD-ROM** English and Spanish
- **Guided Reading Audio,** Spanish
- **Student Edition on Audio**

THE ESSENTIAL VIDEO By Students For Students
For videos on Amercian Issues, go to **www.pearsonschool.com/ushist**

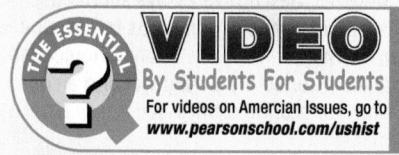

Bibliography

For the Teacher

Fried, Richard M. *Nightmare in Red: The McCarthy Era in Perspective.* Oxford University Press, 1990.

Gladdis, John Lewis. *The United States and the Origins of the Cold War.* Columbia University Press, 2000.

Peters, Richard and Xiaobing Li. *Voices From the Korean War.* The University Press of Kentucky, 2004.

For the Student

L2 Gimpel, Lee. *Fighting Wars, Planning for Peace: The Story of George C. Marshall.* Morgan Reynolds Publishing, 2005.

L3 Varhola, Michael J. *Fire and Ice: The Korean War, 1950–1953.* Savas Publishing Company, 2000.

L4 Doherty, Thomas Patrick. *Cold War, Cool Medium: Television, McCarthyism, and American Culture.* Columbia University Press, 2003.

WITNESS HISTORY

Preparing for Attack

June 15, 1955—Wailing sirens announce that Soviet nuclear weapons are on the way. Their targets are New York, Los Angeles, and dozens of other U.S. cities. Schoolchildren duck for cover under their desks. People flee their homes and offices and rush to underground shelters. President Eisenhower is whisked away to a secret mountain location. Millions of casualties are expected. . . .

But this was only a drill. Called Operation Alert, it was one of numerous drills that took place during the Cold War, when the United States was locked in a desperate worldwide struggle against communism and the Soviet Union.

Korean War medal

◄ Schoolchildren try to stay calm during a "duck and cover" nuclear air-raid drill.

Sign marking a nuclear bomb fallout shelter

Chapter Preview

Chapter Focus Question: What were the causes, main events, and effects of the early Cold War?

Section 1
The Cold War Begins

Section 2
The Korean War

Section 3
The Cold War Expands

Section 4
The Cold War at Home

Comic book warning about the threat of communism

Use the ☑ Quick Study Timeline at the end of this chapter to preview chapter events.

> **Note Taking Study Guide** *Online*
> **For:** Note Taking and American Issues Connector
> www.pearsonschool.com/ushist

Chapter-Level Resources

All in One Letter Home (English and Spanish), Preread the Chapter, Vocabulary Builder, Reading Strategy, Social Studies Skills Practice, Enrichment, Issues Connector, Chapter Tests

- Test Prep With Document-Based Assessment
- AYP Monitoring Assessments
- *ExamView®* Test Bank CD-ROM
- Guided Reading Audio (Spanish)
- Student Edition Audio

Previewing the Chapter

- **WITNESS HISTORY** Point out that although it now seems naïve to think that hiding under a desk would protect people in a nuclear attack, the fact that children did so can help us appreciate the fear that gripped the nation during the Cold War. Read the Witness History selection aloud. Then, ask students to describe images that came to mind as they listened. Tell them they will learn more about Operation Alert and other aspects of the Cold War in this chapter.

- **Analyzing the Visuals** Ask students to study the images on the right side of the page. **What do the images have in common? What do they tell you about the mood of the era?** (*All relate to war or fear of war.*) Tell students to read this chapter to understand the events connected to these images.

- **Focus** Write the Chapter Focus Question on the board. Tell students to keep this question in mind as they read the chapter. Then, have students preview the section titles in this chapter.

- **Preread** Have students complete the chapter's Preread the Chapter Worksheet. Teaching Resources, pp. 8–9

Differentiated Instruction Solutions for All Learners

The following Teacher's Edition strategies are suitable for students of varying abilities.

L1 Special Needs Students, pp. 511, 513, 520, 526, 528, 534, 538 SN

L2 English Language Learners, pp. 511, 513, 520, 526, 528, 534 ELL

L2 Less Proficient Readers, pp. 511, 512, 513, 520, 526, 528, 534, 538 LPR

L4 Advanced Readers, pp. 514, 522, 527, 533, 537 AR

L4 Gifted and Talented Students, pp. 514, 522, 527, 533, 537 GT

> Have students access **www.pearsonschool.com/ushist** for the Note Taking Study Guide *Online* as an alternative to the *Reading and Note Taking Study Guide* booklet.

◄ General George Patton

Objectives
As you teach this section, keep students focused on the following objectives to help them answer the Section Focus Question and master core content.

- Trace the reasons that the wartime alliance between the United States and the Soviet Union unraveled.
- Explain how President Truman responded to Soviet domination of Eastern Europe.
- Describe the causes and results of Stalin's blockade of Berlin.

A New Enemy

After World War II, U.S. General George Patton administered western Germany, while Soviet officials governed eastern Germany. Patton looked to the east and proclaimed:

❝Russia knows what she wants. World domination! . . . Let's keep our boots polished, bayonets sharpened, and present a picture of force and strength to the Russians. This is the only language that they understand and respect. If we fail to do this, then I would like to say that we have had a victory over the Germans and have disarmed them, but we have lost the war.❞
—General George S. Patton, October 1945

▲ U.S. and Soviet soldiers celebrate the Allied victory.

The Cold War Begins

Prepare to Read

Background Knowledge ⑬

Ask students to recall some of the conflicts that remained at the end of World War II. Have them predict ways that the Soviet Union and United States might clash in the postwar years.

Set a Purpose ⑬

- **WITNESS HISTORY** Read the selection aloud.

  Ask **According to Patton, what is the goal of the Soviet Union?** *(to control the world)* **If Patton was correct, how does the photo at left capture the irony of recent events?** *(It shows that, not long before, American and Soviet forces considered themselves allies.)*

- **Focus** Point out the Section Focus Question, and write it on the board. Tell students to refer to this question as they read. *(Answer appears with Section 1 Assessment answers.)*

- **Preview** Have students preview the Section Objectives and the list of Terms and People.

- **Reading Skill** Have students use the *Reading Strategy: Contrast* worksheet. Teaching Resources, **p. 12**

Objectives
- Trace the reasons that the wartime alliance between the United States and the Soviet Union unraveled.
- Explain how President Truman responded to Soviet domination of Eastern Europe.
- Describe the causes and results of Stalin's blockade of Berlin.

Terms and People

satellite state	containment
Cold War	Marshall Plan
iron curtain	Berlin airlift
Truman Doctrine	NATO
George F. Kennan	Warsaw Pact

NoteTaking

Reading Skill: Contrast As you read, contrast the conflicting goals of the United States and the Soviet Union.

American Goals	Soviet Goals

Why It Matters In the 1930s, the policies of isolationism and appeasement had contributed to the rise of dictatorships and the outbreak of global war. After World War II, U.S. leaders viewed these past policies as mistakes. They sought new ways to keep the United States safe and to protect its interests around the world. **Section Focus Question: How did U.S. leaders respond to the threat of Soviet expansion in Europe?**

Roots of the Cold War

When Franklin Roosevelt died in April 1945, the nation was at a critical point. The United States was still at war. In addition, relations with the Soviet Union—one of the most important wartime allies—were beginning to break down.

American and Soviet Systems Differ The United States and the Soviet Union had been united only in their opposition to Nazi Germany. Beyond that, they had little in common. The United States was a capitalist democracy. Its citizens believed in free elections, economic and religious freedom, private property, and respect for individual differences. The Soviet Union was a dictatorship. Under Joseph Stalin, the Communist Party made all key economic, political, and military decisions. The Soviet people could not worship as they pleased, own private property, or express their views freely. Those who opposed or questioned Stalin risked imprisonment and death.

Vocabulary Builder

Use the information below and the following resource to teach students the high-use words from this section. Teaching Resources, Vocabulary Builder, p. 11

High-Use Words	Definitions and Sample Sentences
aspiration	*n.* ambition; strong desire to achieve a particular goal Truman's **aspiration** was to complete a successful presidency.
acknowledge	*v.* to admit or recognize It took many years for the U.S. government to **acknowledge** the contributions of the Navajo Code Talkers in winning the Pacific War.

Allies Disagree on Future of Eastern Europe By the time Roosevelt, Stalin, and Churchill met at Yalta in February 1945, it was clear that the Allies would defeat Germany. But it was unclear how Germany and the nations of Eastern Europe would be governed after the war. Soviet troops already occupied much of Eastern Europe and some of Germany.

Stalin wanted to keep Germany weak and divided. He also wanted Eastern Europe to remain under the control of the Soviet Union. The United States and Great Britain sought a stronger, united Germany and independent nations in Eastern Europe. At the conference, Stalin agreed to establish "broadly representative" governments and free elections in Eastern Europe and to divide Germany only temporarily into zones of occupation.

Despite Stalin's promises, nearly all of the lands occupied by the Soviet Red Army in the spring of 1945 remained under Soviet control after the war. The Eastern European countries of Poland, Czechoslovakia, Hungary, Romania, and Bulgaria, as well as the eastern portion of Germany, became **satellite states** controlled by the Soviet Union.

Truman and Stalin Clash at Potsdam By the time Soviet, British, and U.S. leaders met at Potsdam in the summer of 1945, Harry Truman had succeeded Roosevelt as President. Truman and Clement Attlee, the new British prime minister, hoped that Stalin would confirm the decisions made at Yalta. However, Stalin refused to make a commitment to allow free elections in Eastern Europe.

Comparing Viewpoints

What Will Happen to Postwar Europe?

The Soviet Union and United States disagreed on what should happen to Europe after World War II. The disagreement had much to do with the conflicting values of the two countries and their leaders.

JOSEPH STALIN

Stalin was a dictator who ruled the Soviet Union from the 1920s to the 1950s. His policy of collectivizing land led to famine and to the death of millions. He also ordered the execution of thousands of communist officials.

Primary Source

"To choose one's victims, to prepare one's plan minutely, to slake [satisfy] an implacable vengeance, and then to go to bed . . . there is nothing sweeter in the world."

"This war is different from all earlier ones; the conqueror of a region imposes his own social system on it."

HARRY S. TRUMAN

As President from 1945 until 1953, Truman tried to stop the spread of communism. He promoted a "Fair Deal" program that included more social security benefits, public health insurance, and an end to racial discrimination.

Primary Source

"I would rather have peace in the world than be President."

"The American people desire, and are determined to work for, a world in which all nations and all peoples are free to govern themselves as they see fit, and to achieve a decent and satisfying life."

Compare
1. How did Truman's views on power differ from those of Stalin?
2. How did the two leaders disagree on the issue of self-government in Eastern Europe?

- **NoteTaking** Using the Paragraph Shrinking strategy (TE, p. T20), have students read the section. As they read, have students compare and contrast the conflicting goals of the United States and Soviet Union. *Reading and Note Taking Study Guide*

Teach

Roots of the Cold War

Instruct

- **Introduce** Ask students to read the introductory paragraphs and the three red headings under "Roots of the Cold War" and predict how people will react to the Cold War. Then, have them read to find out whether their predictions were accurate.

- **Teach** Using the Idea Wave strategy (TE, p. T22), ask students to review the quotations from Stalin and Truman in the Comparing Viewpoints feature. Have volunteers restate the quotations in their own words. Then, discuss the Compare questions together.

Independent Practice

To help students better understand the roots of the Cold War, have them complete the worksheet *Reading a Chart: Causes and Effects of the Cold War.* Tell them to explain what they consider to be the most important cause. *Teaching Resources,* **p. 19**

Monitor Progress

As students fill in their tables, circulate to make sure that they understand the conflicting goals of the United States and Soviet Union. For a completed version of the table, see *Note Taking Transparencies,* **B-119a.**

Answers

Compare
1. Truman believed in using power to promote peace and well-being; Stalin believed in wielding power to impose his will and his nation's ideology on others.
2. They each favored policies like those in their own countries. Stalin wanted to impose Soviet ways on the satellite states; Truman wanted the people in those countries to make decisions for themselves.

- **Introduce: Key Term** Point out the key term ***Truman Doctrine*** (in bold) in the text. Ask students to recall what they know about the Monroe Doctrine. Remind them that this was an official statement of U.S. policy toward other nations. *(It stated the U.S. policy to keep European nations from interfering in the affairs of Latin American nations.)* Ask students to predict the topic or ideas of the ***Truman Doctrine.*** After reading the text, students should review their predictions.

- **Teach** Have students look at the map on the next page and trace the course of the iron curtain. Ask **Where might the Cold War have been most likely to erupt into a hot war?** *(Students may point out that the borders between communist and noncommunist nations were most likely to experience conflict.)* **According to Churchill's speech, did communists make up the majority in Eastern European countries?** *(No, Churchill states that the communist parties were small, but they had a degree of influence beyond their numbers because of Soviet support.)*

- **Quick Activity** Have students read the Primary Source excerpt from the "Iron Curtain" speech on the next page. Ask students to review what they know about the iron curtain by comparing the information in this quotation with the text following the key term ***iron curtain*** (in bold) on this page. Have students explain the term ***iron curtain*** in their own words.

Vocabulary Builder

<u>aspiration</u>—(as pih RAY shuhn) *n.* ambition; strong desire to achieve a particular goal

NoteTaking

Reading Skill: Recognize Sequence As you read, trace events and developments in Europe that contributed to the growth of Cold War tensions.

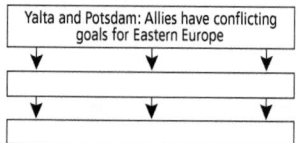

Yalta and Potsdam: Allies have conflicting goals for Eastern Europe

Truman left Potsdam believing that the Soviet Union was "planning world conquest" and that the alliance with the Soviet Union was falling apart. With the Soviet Red Army at his command, Stalin seemed to present a real threat. Thus, the stage was set for a worldwide rivalry between the United States and the Soviet Union. The 46-year struggle became known as the **Cold War** because the two superpowers never faced each other directly in a "hot" military conflict.

✓ **Checkpoint** How did the goals of U.S. and Soviet foreign policy differ after World War II?

Meeting the Soviet Challenge

President Truman was not the only world leader who believed that Stalin had <u>aspirations</u> toward world domination. Winston Churchill also spoke out forcefully against the Soviet Union. On March 5, 1946, he gave an important speech at Fulton College in Missouri, Truman's home state. Referring to a map of Europe, Churchill noted that "an **iron curtain** has descended across the Continent." (See the Primary Source on the opposite page.) East of that iron curtain, the Soviet Union was gaining more control by installing communist governments and police states and by crushing political and religious dissent. In addition, Churchill feared, the Soviets were attempting to spread communism to Western Europe and East Asia. The only solution, Churchill said, was for the United States and other democratic countries to stand firm.

Truman Faces a Crisis Truman shared Churchill's beliefs. Born in a small town in Missouri, Truman had been too poor to attend college. He was the only president in the twentieth century with no college education. Instead, he worked the family farm, fought in France during World War I, and eventually began a political career. His life was a testament to honesty, integrity, hard work, and a willingness to make difficult decisions. "The buck stops here," was his motto as President. It meant that the person sitting in the Oval Office had the obligation to face problems head-on and make hard decisions.

In 1947, no issue was more weighty than the growing crisis between the United States and the Soviet Union. After the war, a number of European and Asian countries were struggling against communist movements supported by the Soviets. In particular, the governments of Greece and Turkey were battling communist forces seeking to gain control. Greece and Turkey needed aid, and in 1947 the United States was the only country with the resources to help them.

The Truman Doctrine Opposes Communist Expansion On March 12, 1947, President Truman addressed both houses of Congress. With emotion in his voice, Truman described the plight of the Greek and Turkish people. The fight they were waging, he said, was the fight that all free people had to confront. Truman requested money from Congress "to support free peoples who are resisting attempted subjugation [conquest] by armed minorities or by outside pressures." If the United States retreated into isolationism, he warned, the peace of the world and the welfare of the nation would be in danger.

Congress responded by voting to give $400 million in aid for Greece and Turkey. President Truman's promise to aid nations struggling against communist movements became known as the **Truman Doctrine,** and it set a new course for American foreign policy.

✓ **Checkpoint** What events caused President Truman to propose what became known as the Truman Doctrine?

Answers

✓ The Soviet Union sought to increase its influence and extend communism. The U.S. wanted to limit communism and rebuild the defeated nations in Europe.

✓ The Greek and Turkish governments were trying to keep communists from taking over. Truman wanted the U.S. to send money to support the anticommunist efforts.

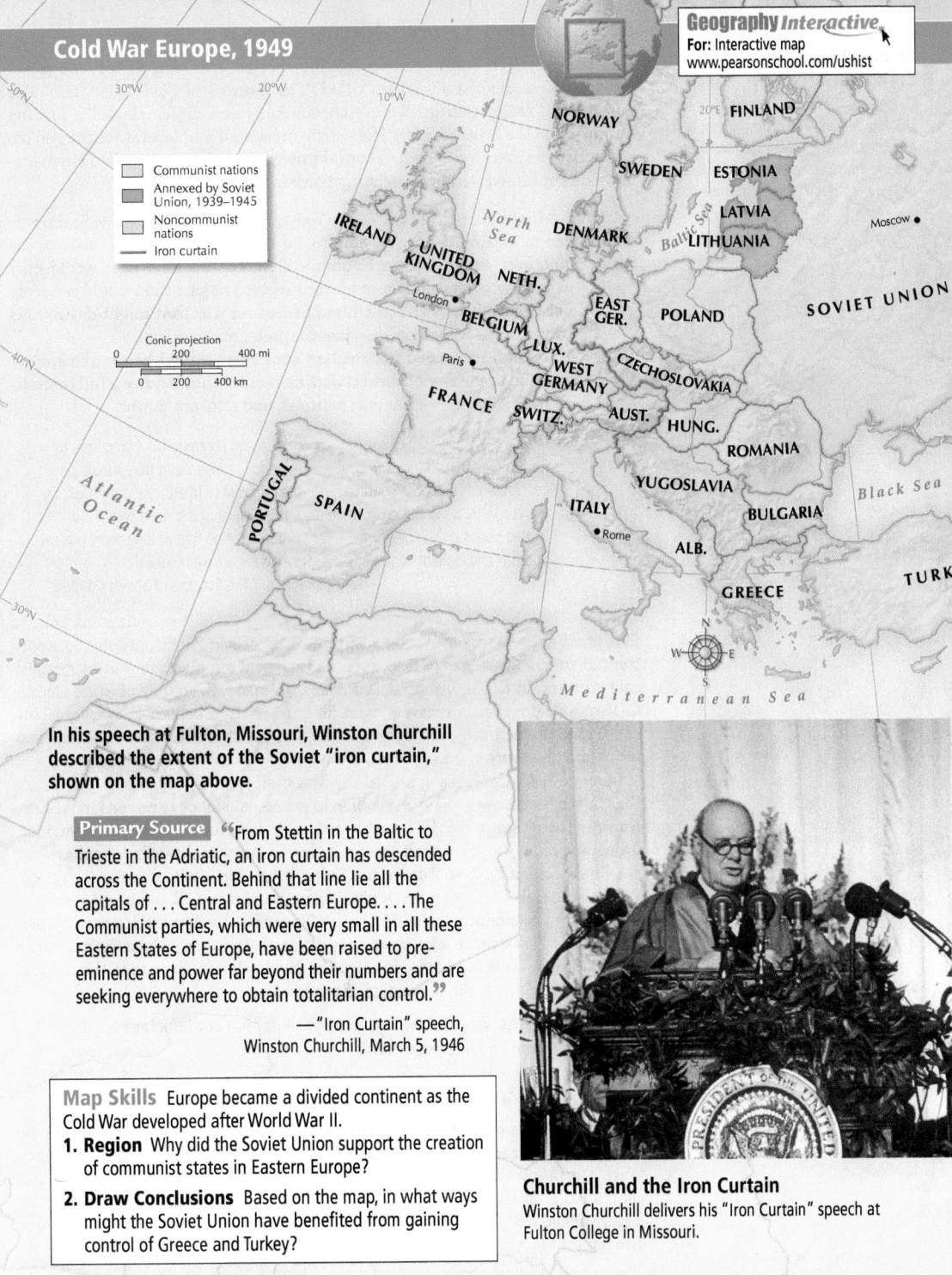

Cold War Europe, 1949

Geography *Interactive*
For: Interactive map
www.pearsonschool.com/ushist

Legend:
- Communist nations
- Annexed by Soviet Union, 1939–1945
- Noncommunist nations
- Iron curtain

Conic projection
0   200   400 mi
0   200   400 km

(Map labels: NORWAY, FINLAND, SWEDEN, ESTONIA, LATVIA, LITHUANIA, IRELAND, UNITED KINGDOM, DENMARK, NETH., EAST GER., POLAND, SOVIET UNION, Moscow, BELGIUM, LUX., WEST GERMANY, CZECHOSLOVAKIA, FRANCE, SWITZ., AUST., HUNG., ROMANIA, PORTUGAL, SPAIN, ITALY, YUGOSLAVIA, BULGARIA, Black Sea, ALB., GREECE, TURK., London, Paris, Rome, North Sea, Baltic Sea, Atlantic Ocean, Mediterranean Sea)

In his speech at Fulton, Missouri, Winston Churchill described the extent of the Soviet "iron curtain," shown on the map above.

Primary Source "From Stettin in the Baltic to Trieste in the Adriatic, an iron curtain has descended across the Continent. Behind that line lie all the capitals of . . . Central and Eastern Europe. . . . The Communist parties, which were very small in all these Eastern States of Europe, have been raised to pre-eminence and power far beyond their numbers and are seeking everywhere to obtain totalitarian control."

—"Iron Curtain" speech,
Winston Churchill, March 5, 1946

Map Skills Europe became a divided continent as the Cold War developed after World War II.

1. **Region** Why did the Soviet Union support the creation of communist states in Eastern Europe?

2. **Draw Conclusions** Based on the map, in what ways might the Soviet Union have benefited from gaining control of Greece and Turkey?

Churchill and the Iron Curtain
Winston Churchill delivers his "Iron Curtain" speech at Fulton College in Missouri.

Independent Practice

- **NoteTaking** Have students complete the notetaking flowchart to trace the events that added to Cold War tensions. Reading and Note Taking Study Guide

- Have students read and complete *Primary Sources: The Truman Doctrine and American Foreign Policy.* Teaching Resources, **p. 21**

- Have students access **www.pearsonschool.com/ushist** to use the Geography Interactive map and then answer the map skills questions found in their textbook.

Monitor Progress

As students complete their notetaking flowcharts, circulate to make sure that they trace the events that added to Cold War tensions. For a completed version of the notetaking flowchart, see Note Taking Transparencies, **B-119b**.

Differentiated Instruction   Solutions for All Learners

L1 Special Needs Students   L2 English Language Learners   L2 Less Proficient Readers

Use the map on this page to reinforce the idea of an "iron curtain" dividing Europe. Have students use their fingers to follow the line that divided Europe. Ask students to locate the Soviet Union and identify the nations that were behind the iron curtain. Ask **What does the term *iron* imply about the division?** *(Possible answers: It was strong; it prevented things from entering or leaving; it was permanent.)* **Why**

do you think Churchill used the phrase? *(Possible answer: The Soviet Union was forcing satellite states to stay under communism and would not allow free movement of people or ideas.)* Then, ask students to think about why Truman promised to aid nations struggling against communism. Have students read and complete *Primary Sources:* The Truman Doctrine. Teaching Resources, **p. 20**

Answers

Map Skills

1. These states would act as a buffer between the Soviet Union and the West, and they would be the beginning of the spread of communism throughout Europe.

2. It would make it easier for them to trade through the Black Sea to the Mediterranean.

Containing Soviet Expansion L3

Instruct

- **Introduce** Have students look again at the map of the iron curtain. Ask them to propose policies that the United States could follow in response to the iron curtain. (*Students might suggest policies such as stationing troops along the border; giving financial support to the non-communist countries to keep them from becoming communist.*)

- **Teach** Tell students that in 1948 the United States began helping Europe rebuild through a program called the Marshall Plan. Direct their attention to the circle graph on this page. Ask **What were the goals of the Marshall Plan?** (*to rebuild the economies of war-torn Europe*) **How could achieving these goals help the United States?** (*The United States wanted to form political and economic alliances with vital, democratic nations.*) Color Transparencies **A-109**

- **Quick Activity** Display Color Transparency: *The Cost of Containment.* Use the transparency to help students analyze the aid provided by the Marshall Plan.

Independent Practice

Have students read the Primary Source quotation on this page. Ask them to write paragraphs explaining whether they agree with Kennan's containment policy. Tell them to provide reasons to support their answers.

Monitor Progress

As students write their paragraphs, circulate to make sure that they understand Kennan's containment policy and provide reasons to support their answers.

Answers

Caption Thirty-two percent of aid went directly to providing food to reduce famine; the other aid might also have helped reduce famine by making it easier to reestablish farms and food processing.

✓ Kennan did not believe that the Soviets would go so far as to put their own country in danger of war, so if the United States was patient in containing Soviet expansion, it would win in the end.

402 The Cold War

Marshall Plan Aids European Recovery

These Greek children benefited from U.S. aid designed to promote stable democracies in Europe. *According to the pie chart, what portion of U.S. aid was devoted to reducing famine?*

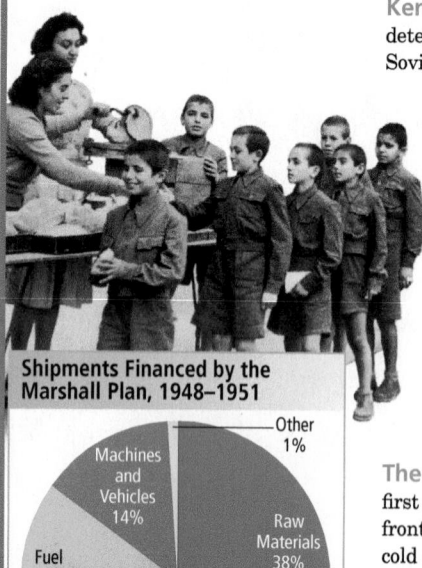

Shipments Financed by the Marshall Plan, 1948–1951

- Raw Materials 38%
- Food and Other Produce 32%
- Fuel 16%
- Machines and Vehicles 14%
- Other 1%

Containing Soviet Expansion

In the July 1947 issue of the magazine *Foreign Affairs*, a writer who called himself "X" published an article titled "The Sources of Soviet Conduct." The author was really **George F. Kennan,** an American diplomat and a leading authority on the Soviet Union. His article presented a blueprint for the American policy that became known as **containment** because its goal was to keep communism contained within its existing borders.

Kennan Argues for Containment Kennan contended that while Stalin was determined to expand the Soviet empire, he would not risk the security of the Soviet Union for expansion. In Kennan's view, the Soviet Union would only expand when it could do so without serious risks. Stalin would certainly not chance war with the United States—a war that might destroy his power in the Soviet Union—just to spread communism.

Kennan cautioned his readers that there would be no quick, easy solution to the Soviet threat. Containment would require a full commitment of American economic, political, and military power:

> **Primary Source** "We are going to continue for a long time to find the Russians difficult to deal with. It does not mean that they should be considered as embarked upon a do-or-die program to overthrow our society by a given date. . . . In these circumstances, it is clear that the main element of any United States policy toward the Soviet Union must be that of long-term, patient but firm and vigilant containment of Russian expansive tendencies."
> —George Kennan, "The Sources of Soviet Conduct"

The Marshall Plan Aids Europe's Economies The containment policy's first great success was in Western Europe. After World War II, people there confronted severe shortages of food, fuel, and medical supplies, as well as brutally cold winters. In this environment of desperate need, Secretary of State George C. Marshall unveiled a recovery plan for Europe. In a speech at Harvard University, he warned that without economic health, "there can be no political stability and no assured peace."

In early 1948, Congress approved the **Marshall Plan.** Over the next four years, the United States gave about $13 billion in grants and loans to nations in Western Europe. The program provided food to reduce famine, fuel to heat houses and factories, and money to jump-start economic growth. Aid was also offered to the Soviet satellite states in Eastern Europe, but Stalin refused to let them accept it.

The Marshall Plan provided a vivid example of how U.S. aid could serve the ends of both economic and foreign policy. The aid helped countries that desperately needed assistance. The prosperity it stimulated then helped the American economy by increasing trade. Finally, the good relationships that the aid created worked against the expansion of communism.

✓ **Checkpoint** Why did George Kennan think that containment would work against Soviet expansion?

The Cold War Heats Up

The front lines of the Cold War were located in Germany. The zones that were controlled by France, Britain, and the United States were combined to form West Germany. West Germany was bordered on the east by the Soviet-controlled East Germany. The Allies also controlled the western part of Berlin, a city tucked deep inside communist East Germany. (See the map on the opposite page.)

Differentiated Instruction Solutions for All Learners

L4 Advanced Readers **L4 Gifted and Talented Students**

The Marshall Plan committed the United States to help rebuild Europe. The United States invited Soviet and Eastern European participation, but under terms that would have reduced Moscow's control over its satellite economies. The Soviets refused and organized their Eastern European satellites into their own association for Mutual Economic Assistance, or Comecon, in 1949. Have students research both of these programs and compare the successes or failures of each. Have them write a paragraph summarizing their findings to share with the class.

Berlin Airlift Saves West Berlin West Berlin was, as one Soviet leader later described it, "a bone in the throat" of the Soviet Union. Its relative prosperity and freedom stood in contrast to the bleak life of East Berliners. Stalin was determined to capture West Berlin or win other concessions from the Western allies. In June 1948, he stopped all highway, railway, and waterway traffic from western Germany into West Berlin. Without any means of receiving aid, West Berlin would fall to the communists.

Stalin was able to close roads, stop barges, and block railways, but he could not blockade the sky. For almost a year, the United States and Britain supplied West Berlin through a massive airlift. Food, fuel, medical supplies, clothing, toys—everything the residents of West Berlin needed was flown into the city.

INFOGRAPHIC

Airlift Saves Blockaded Berlin

The Soviet blockade caused more than 2 million West Berliners to face severe shortages of food and other vital supplies. For more than a year, American and British pilots flew round-the-clock deliveries into the city—sometimes at the rate of a plane per minute. Each flight brought food, fuel, and occasionally candy to the desperate population.

Divided Germany

West Berlin lay deep inside the communist country of East Germany.

0 50 100 mi
0 50 100 km

DENMARK

North Sea

NETH.

POL.

Berlin

WEST GERMANY

EAST GERMANY

LUX.

CZECH.

FRANCE

SWITZ.

AUSTRIA

West Berlin

East Berlin

Divided City of Berlin

◄ Children cheer as a plane delivers much needed supplies.

Thinking Critically
1. **Analyze Maps** Why could the Allies not use land routes to supply West Berlin?
2. **Analyze Visuals** How did the airlift affect West German attitudes toward the United States and Britain?

History Interactive *

For: More about the Berlin Airlift
www.pearsonschool.com/ushist

History Background

Soviet Siege In June 1948, the Soviets blockaded Berlin in the hopes of pushing the Americans and their allies out of the city. Emmet Hughes filed an eyewitness account of conditions in the city, which was published in *Life* magazine: " . . . East and West were locked in their direst test of strength since they shared their fragile victory. The Soviet siege of Berlin is tight—dangerously tight. Not the smallest detail has been overlooked: the Soviets have prohibited even the supply of horsemeat and dog food to 70 dogs 'traitorously' helping the blind in Berlin's Western sector. . . .

" . . . Somehow Mark Twain and canned beef also got dragged into the fray. The beef (990 tons) came in with an American food shipment. Its labels innocently showed a picture of a horse and rider, so Military Government soon had to quash Russian rumors that it was feeding horsemeat to Berliners. And American officials had to stop a sly Russian attempt to have Berlin's children read a special edition of *Tom Sawyer* with a preface lauding the author as a sarcastic writer who exposed the 'whole mendacity of the capitalist class. . . .'"

Instruct

- **Introduce: Key Term** Ask students to find the key term **Berlin Airlift** (in bold), and read the sentence. Have students read the title of the Infographic on the facing page and look at the map. Ask students to predict why the **Berlin Airlift** might have been so important to the people of West Berlin. Then, have students read the Infographic and review their predictions.

- **Teach** Using the Numbered Heads strategy (TE, p. T23), have the class quickly name the countries that belonged to each alliance. Ask **What was the purpose of each organization?** *(to support its members against the other side)* **How does this system of alliances compare to the alliances before World War I?** *(In both cases, the countries promised to defend one another militarily, if necessary. However, before World War I, the United States did not participate in the alliance system.)* **What risks did the two sides take in forming these alliances?** *(They risked another world war.)*

- **Analyzing the Visuals** Have students analyze the Infographic. Then, ask a volunteer to read the eyewitness account on the following page. Discuss with students how the quotation supports the visuals in the Infographic. Then, have students access **www.pearsonschool.com/ushist** to experience the History Interactive.

Independent Practice

Remind students of the Witness History at the beginning of the section. Have them write a short paragraph explaining how Patton might have reacted to the formation of NATO.

Monitor Progress

Have students create an outline of this section, using the blue and red headings to get started. Students should add at least two details in the outline to support each heading.

Answers

Thinking Critically
1. because the East Germans and Soviets controlled all the land routes
2. They were thankful to the United States and Britain for helping them through this difficult period.

Assess and Reteach

Assess Progress · L3

- Have students complete the Section Assessment.

- Administer the Section Quiz.
  Teaching Resources, **p. 25**

- To further assess student understanding, use Progress Monitoring Transparencies, **115**.

Reteach

If students need more instruction, have them read the section summary.

Reading and Note Taking · L3
Study Guide

Adapted Reading and · L1 · L2
Note Taking Study Guide

Spanish Reading and · L2
Note Taking Study Guide

Extend · L4

Have students write a short argument for or against global military expansion during the early Cold War years. They can use information from the section or other information and independent reasoning for support.

Answer

✓ America supported governments that resisted communism, and it formed NATO, whose goal was to counter Soviet expansion.

Even through rain and snow, goods arrived regularly. The **Berlin airlift** demonstrated to West Berlin, the Soviet Union, and the world how far the United States would go to protect noncommunist parts of Europe and contain communism.

Cold War Rivals Form Alliances In May 1949, Stalin was forced to acknowledge that his attempt to blockade Berlin had failed. The Berlin airlift was a proud moment for Americans and Berliners and a major success for the policy of containment. One Berlin resident later recalled her feelings when the blockade was finally lifted:

Vocabulary Builder
acknowledge–(ak NAHL ihj) *v.* to admit or recognize

> **Primary Source** ❝Sheer joy—nothing else. Nothing else. Joy, and [the feeling that], 'We have done it! And it works!' . . . That was so very important. The West has won! I say this quite deliberately in such a crass way because you wanted to know how I felt emotionally. The West—well, we have succeeded. And the West has won and the others have not!❞
>
> —Ella Barowsky, CNN interview, 1996

The Berlin airlift demonstrated that Stalin could be contained if Western nations were prepared to take forceful action. The **North Atlantic Treaty Organization (NATO),** formed in 1949, provided the military alliance to counter Soviet expansion. Twelve Western European and North American nations agreed to act together in the defense of Western Europe. Member nations agreed that "an armed attack against one or more of them . . . shall be considered an attack against all of them." This principle of mutual military assistance is called collective security.

In 1955, West Germany became a member of NATO. In response, the Soviet Union and its satellite states formed a rival military alliance, called the **Warsaw Pact.** All the communist states of Eastern Europe except Yugoslavia were members. Like members of NATO, nations of the Warsaw Pact pledged to defend one another if attacked. Although members agreed on paper not to interfere in one another's internal affairs, the Soviet Union continued to exert firm control over its Warsaw Pact allies.

✓ **Checkpoint** How did the United States and its allies apply the containment policy in Europe?

SECTION **1** Assessment

Progress Monitoring *Online*
For: Self-test with vocabulary practice
www.pearsonschool.com/ushist

Comprehension

1. **Terms** For each term below, write a sentence explaining how it changed the lives of people living in post-World War II Europe.
   - satellite state
   - iron curtain
   - Truman Doctrine
   - Marshall Plan
   - Berlin airlift
   - NATO

2. **NoteTaking Reading Skill: Contrast** Use your chart to answer the Section Focus Question: How did U.S. leaders respond to the threat of Soviet expansion in Europe?

Writing About History

3. **Quick Write: Frame Research Questions** Choose one event from this section. Write three questions that you could use as the basis for a research paper. For example, if you chose the Berlin airlift, you might ask, "How much food was flown into Berlin?"

Critical Thinking

4. **Draw Conclusions** How would having control over satellite states benefit the Soviet Union if it became involved in a European war?

5. **Contrast** How did U.S. foreign policy after World War II differ from U.S. foreign policy after World War I?

6. **Identify Alternatives** What options besides containment might Truman have considered in response to Soviet expansion?

Section 1 Assessment

1. Sentences should reflect an understanding of each term or person listed.

2. The United States sought to rebuild Europe and to prevent the expansion of communism into more territories. The United States instituted the Marshall Plan and formed NATO to accomplish these goals. The Soviet Union sought to bolster its strength in Europe and expand its influence. It used military crackdowns and the formation of the Warsaw Pact to accomplish its goals.

3. Responses should show an understanding of how questions can be used to direct research on a specific topic in the section.

4. The Soviet Union could recruit soldiers and obtain raw materials or finished goods from those countries. It might be possible to confine battles to the satellite states and thus avoid physical damage to the Soviet Union itself.

5. After World War I, the U.S. declined to join the League of Nations and tried to become less entangled in foreign affairs. After World War II, the U.S. stayed engaged in foreign affairs, helping to rebuild and form alliances with other countries.

6. Possible answers: outright war or nuclear attack; appeasement; retreat into neutrality

> For additional assessment, have students access **Progress Monitoring *Online*** at **www.pearsonschool.com/ushist.**

Harry S. Truman:
The Truman Doctrine

In this address to Congress, President Truman stressed the duty of the United States to combat totalitarian regimes worldwide. His March 12, 1947, speech called for $400 million in aid to Greece and Turkey, both of which he said were threatened by communism. Congress approved the financial aid as well as the commitment of U.S. troops to administer postwar reconstruction.

▲ President Truman delivering a speech

The peoples of a number of countries of the world have recently had totalitarian regimes forced upon them against their will. The government of the United States has made frequent protests against coercion[1] and intimidation, in violation of the Yalta agreement, in Poland, Romania, and Bulgaria. I must also state that in a number of other countries there have been similar developments.

At the present moment in world history nearly every nation must choose between alternative ways of life. The choice is too often not a free one. One way of life is based upon the will of the majority, and is distinguished by free institutions, representative government, free elections, guarantees of individual liberty, freedom of speech and religion, and freedom from political oppression. The second way of life is based upon the will of a minority forcibly imposed upon the majority. It relies upon terror and oppression, a controlled press and radio, fixed elections and the suppression of personal freedoms.

I believe that it must be the policy of the United States to support free peoples who are resisting attempted subjugation[2] by armed minorities or by outside pressures.

I believe that we must assist free peoples to work out their own destinies in their own way.

I believe that our help should be primarily through economic and financial aid which is essential to economic stability and orderly political processes. . . .

The seeds of totalitarian regimes are nurtured by misery and want. They spread and grow in the evil soil of poverty and strife. They reach their full growth when the hope of a people for a better life has died. We must keep that hope alive.

The free peoples of the world look to us for support in maintaining their freedoms. If we falter in our leadership, we may endanger the peace of the world—and we shall surely endanger the welfare of our own nation.

---

1. **coercion** (koh ER zhuhn) *n.* government by force.
2. **subjugation** (suhb juh GAY shuhn) *n.* condition of being under the control of a conqueror.

Thinking Critically
1. **Make Inferences** What is President Truman referring to when he mentions the two "alternative ways of life"?
2. **Recognize Causes and Effects** According to Truman, how would economic aid support freedom in Greece and Turkey?

Objectives
- Understand the nature of the Truman Doctrine and why the president called for it.
- Describe the kind of commitments the United States was willing to make to those nations threatened by totalitarian governments.
- Analyze the language Truman uses to compare the two forms of government described in his speech.

Background Knowledge L3
Remind students that Truman issued his doctrine in response to communist pressure in Greece and Turkey. Have students refresh their mental maps by locating Greece, Turkey, and the Soviet Union on the map in the section.

Instruct L3
After students read the speech, conduct a class discussion by using these questions: **What was Truman's goal in speaking to Congress?** *(to get money to help Greece and Turkey)* **Identify three arguments he used to convince Congress.** *(People are being subjugated; the United States has a responsibility to help people win self-determination; people may turn to communism if they are poor and miserable; people of the world expect the United States to help them.)*

Monitor Progress
Have students work in pairs to choose what they consider to be the most important paragraph of the speech. Volunteers can deliver that paragraph to the class. Each student should be prepared to explain why the chosen paragraph is most important.

Answers

Thinking Critically
1. the American way, based on the will of the majority, and the Soviet way, based on the subjugation of the minority
2. He states that people might turn to communism if they are in "misery and want." Therefore, if the United States helps people improve their lives, it will be harder for communism to take hold.

History Background

Iranian Crisis At first, it seemed that Iran, an oil-rich country located along the southern border of the Soviet Union, would be the center of the first showdown of the Cold War. During World War II, the United States had become increasingly interested in the region, and after the war, the Soviets failed to remove their troops, despite a promise to do so. In March 1946, the U.S. Secretary of State went to the UN, looking for support to force the Soviets to withdraw. Before the debate could be waged, however, the Soviets reached an agreement with Iran to pull out their troops. Thus, control of Greece and Turkey became the first real contest of the Cold War.

Step-by-Step Instruction

Objectives

As you teach this section, keep students focused on the following objectives to help them answer the Section Focus Question and master core content.

- Explain how Mao Zedong and the communists gained power in China.
- Describe the causes and progress of the war in Korea.
- Identify the long-term effects of the Korean War.

Prepare to Read

Background Knowledge ⓛ3

Remind students that U.S. policy in Europe after World War II focused on containment of Soviet expansion. Have them predict how the U.S. will respond to the efforts of communists to control nations in East Asia.

Set a Purpose ⓛ3

- **WITNESS HISTORY** Read the selection aloud.

  Ask **Why did General Puller joke about the peril of being surrounded by the enemy?** *(to give his troops courage to fight back under such terrible circumstances)*

- **Focus** Point out the Section Focus Question, and write it on the board. Tell students to refer to this question as they read. *(Answer appears with Section 2 Assessment answers.)*

- **Preview** Have students preview the Section Objectives and the list of Terms and People.

- **NoteTaking** Using the Paragraph Shrinking strategy (TE, p. T20), have students read the section. As they read, have students note the problems in East Asia and the steps that President Truman took to solve them. Reading and Note Taking Study Guide

Korean War Medal of Honor ▶

▲ American machine-gunners in Korea

The Korean War

Objectives

- Explain how Mao Zedong and the communists gained power in China.
- Describe the causes and progress of the war in Korea.
- Identify the long-term effects of the Korean War.

Terms and People

Jiang Jieshi	Douglas MacArthur
Mao Zedong	limited war
38th parallel	SEATO

NoteTaking

Reading Skill: Categorize As you read, note problems and the steps that President Truman took to solve them. Use a problem-solution table like the one below.

Problem	Solution
Communists threaten takeover of China	

Why It Matters Europe had been the first focus of the Cold War. But in the early 1950s, U.S. involvement in the Korean War made East Asia the prime battleground in the long, hard Cold War struggle. The division between North and South Korea remains a source of international tension today. **Section Focus Question: How did President Truman use the power of the presidency to limit the spread of communism in East Asia?**

Communists Gain Control of China

Since the time of the Russian Revolution in 1917, the Soviets had hoped to spread communism to every corner of the world, training foreigners in Marxist theory and revolutionary strategy. The Soviets were confident that communism would reach worldwide influence. In 1949, events in China seemed to justify their confidence.

Civil War Divides China Before Japan invaded China in 1937, Nationalist leader **Jiang Jieshi** (zhee AHNG zhǐ SHEE), known in the United States as Chiang Kai-shek, had been fighting a civil war against communists led by **Mao Zedong** (mow zeh DUHNG). Although Jiang and Mao temporarily joined forces in an uneasy alliance to fight Japan, the civil war resumed with a new fury after the war ended.

The Soviet Union supported Mao, while the United States sent several billion dollars in aid to Jiang. American leaders feared that Jiang's defeat would create a communist superpower spanning most of Asia.

Jiang's regime proved unequal to the task. Nationalist generals were reluctant to fight. And, while masses of Chinese people faced starvation, corrupt officials diverted U.S. aid dollars into their own pockets. By promising to feed the people, Mao won increased support.

Vocabulary Builder

Use the information below and the following resource to teach students the high-use words from this section. Teaching Resources, Vocabulary Builder, p. 11

High-Use Words	Definitions and Sample Sentences
intervene	*v.* to become involved in; to take action to settle a dispute or influence a course of action During the Spanish-American War, the United States **intervened** in the Philippines to defeat the Spanish.
confront	*v.* to face An accused person has the right to **confront** his or her accuser in court.

Communists Win in China In 1948, Mao's forces dominated the war. Jiang appealed for American military intervention. However, the U.S. government had no intention of sending American troops to support the corrupt Jiang. In 1949, Jiang fled the Chinese mainland, taking control of the large offshore island of Taiwan. Mao's communists then took control of the world's most populous country, renaming it the People's Republic of China.

Mao's victory was an immense shock to Americans. Not only was China under the control of sworn enemies of the United States, but communist regimes controlled about one fourth of the world's landmass and one third of its population. "Who lost China?" Americans asked. Many critics blamed the Truman administration, saying that the United States had failed to give enough support to Jiang. But Secretary of State Dean Acheson argued:

Communist Victory in China
Carrying hundreds of pictures of their leader, Mao Zedong, these Chinese communists celebrate the defeat of Jiang Jieshi in 1949.

Primary Source ❝The unfortunate but inescapable fact is that the ominous result of the civil war in China was beyond the control of the government of the United States. Nothing that this country did or could have done within the reasonable limits of its capabilities could have changed the result.❞
—Secretary of State Dean Acheson, "White Paper on China," August 1949

✔ **Checkpoint** Why were the communists able to win the Chinese Civil War?

Americans Fight in Korea

The focus of attention turned to the peninsula of Korea, separated from northeast China by the Yalu River. Once controlled by Japan, Korea had been divided into two independent countries by the United States and the Soviet Union after World War II. The dividing line was set at the **38th parallel** of latitude. In North Korea, the Soviets installed a communist government and equipped its armed forces. The United States provided smaller amounts of aid to noncommunist South Korea.

North Korea Invades South Korea American occupation troops remained in South Korea until June 1949. Their departure coincided with the communist victory in China. Soon after, North Korea began a major military buildup.

On June 25, 1950, North Korean forces attacked across the 38th parallel. The 90,000 North Korean troops were armed with powerful tanks and other Soviet weapons. Within days, the northerners overtook the South Korean capital city of Seoul and set out after the retreating South Korean army.

U.S. Forces Defend South Korea President Truman remembered how the policy of appeasement had failed to check the German aggression that sparked World War II. Determined that history would not repeat itself, he announced that the United States would aid South Korea.

Within days, the UN Security Council unanimously voted to follow Truman's lead, recommending that "the Members of the United Nations furnish such assistance to the Republic of Korea as may be necessary to repel the armed attack and to restore international peace and security in the area." Undoubtedly, the Soviet Union would have used its veto power to block the UN resolution if it had been present for the vote. However, it had been boycotting Security Council sessions because the UN had refused to seat Mao's People's Republic of China.

History Background

The Cult of Mao As chairman of the People's Republic of China, Mao Zedong (1893–1976) was a harsh authoritarian; however, he was also much beloved by his people. Under Mao, China experienced modernization, mainly through large-scale industrialization, widespread literacy, and an increase in population. Mao positioned himself as the people's hero, and his followers enthusiastically supported him, considering his *Little Red Book of Quotations* a source of infallible truth. Propaganda posters extolled him as a "red sun at the center of our hearts" and "the savior of the people." Mao became the center of a cult of personality, a phenomenon in which a political institution uses mass media to give its leader a larger-than-life public image. Mao's leadership did not go unchallenged, but by the time he proposed the Cultural Revolution of 1966, he had the support of millions, especially among Chinese youth who had grown up learning to love their leader.

Americans Fight in Korea

Instruct

- **Introduce: Vocabulary Builder**
  Have students read the Vocabulary Builder terms and definitions. Then, ask them to read the introductory sentences and the four red headings under "Americans Fight in Korea." Have them predict what they will learn under each red heading. Then, have them read to find out whether their predictions were accurate.

- **Teach** Explain how the Korean conflict began, why Truman sent troops to aid South Korea, and how he gained the support of the United Nations. Ask **What happened when General MacArthur counterattacked the North Koreans?** *(He surprised the North Koreans at Inch'on and the communist forces fled to North Korea.)* Display Color Transparency: *The Korean War.* Use the lesson suggested in the transparency book to guide a discussion about the different opinions regarding the limits of UN forces in Korea. **Why did MacArthur's forces advance into North Korea instead of stopping at the 38th parallel?** *(MacArthur convinced Truman that the Chinese would not intervene, and the United States hoped to establish a democratic, unified Korea.)*
  Color Transparencies **A-110**

Truman did not ask Congress for a formal declaration of war, as required by the Constitution. However, supported by the UN resolution, Truman ordered American troops who were stationed in Japan to move to South Korea. The soldiers were mainly occupation troops who had not been trained for forced marches in monsoon rains or heavy combat in rice paddies, nor did they have the military equipment needed to stop the invasion. Soon, they joined their South Korean allies in retreating to the southeast corner of the peninsula near the city of Pusan. There, the allies held fast. As fresh supplies and troops arrived from Japan, soldiers from other UN countries joined the American and South Korean forces.

MacArthur Drives Back the North Koreans By September 1950, the UN forces were ready to counterattack. General **Douglas MacArthur,** the World War II hero, had a bold plan to drive the invaders from South Korea. He suspected that the rapid advance of North Korean troops had left North Korea with limited supply lines. He decided to strike at this weakness by launching a surprise attack on the port city of Inchon, well behind enemy lines. Because Inchon was such a poor landing site, with swift currents and treacherous tides, MacArthur knew that the enemy would not expect an attack there.

The Korean War

Geography *Interactive*
For: Interactive map
www.pearsonschool.com/ushist

North Korea Invades

▲ American GIs advance as South Korean civilians retreat from the North Korean onslaught.

① **June 1950** North Korea invades South Korea.

② **July 1950** U.S. and South Korean forces halt their retreat near Pusan.

Differentiated Instruction   Solutions for All Learners

L1 Special Needs Students   **L2 English Language Learners**   **L2 Less Proficient Readers**

For visual learners and students who need help with basic skills, direct attention to the Infographic on the Korean War. Remind students that these maps show the struggle over Korea as the communists advanced and retreated. Ask a volunteer to describe what is happening in the photograph on the left. Then, ask four volunteers to explain what information is shown on each of the maps. *(For example, the image shows troops entering a Korean town. The first map shows that it took North Korea about one month to conquer nearly all of Korea when it first invaded.)*

MacArthur's bold gamble paid off handsomely. On the morning of September 15, 1950, U.S. Marines landed at Inchon and launched an attack into the rear guard of the North Koreans. Communist forces began fleeing for the North Korean border. By October 1950, the North Koreans had been driven north of the 38th parallel.

With the retreat of North Korean forces, U.S. officials had to decide what to do next. Should they declare their UN mandate accomplished and end the war? Or should they send their forces north of the 38th parallel and punish the communists for the invasion? Truman was concerned about the action China would take if the United States carried the war into North Korea. Chinese leaders publicly warned the Americans not to advance near its borders. But MacArthur did not take this warning seriously. He assured Truman that China would not intervene in the war. Based on this advice, the United States pushed a resolution through the UN, calling for a "unified, independent, and democratic" Korea.

China Forces a Stalemate Highly confident, MacArthur attacked north of the 38th parallel. Despite mountainous terrain and freezing temperatures, by Thanksgiving the Allied advance had reached the Chinese border at the Yalu River. Then, on November 25, 1950, some 300,000 Chinese soldiers attacked

Vocabulary Builder
intervene–(ihn ter VEEN) *v.* to become involved in; to take action to settle a dispute or influence a course of action

Independent Practice
- Have students access **www.pearsonschool.com/ushist** to use the Geography Interactive map and then answer the map skills questions in the text.

- Organize students into groups and assign each group one of the following nations: China, South Korea, North Korea, the United States, the Soviet Union. Ask each group to write a few paragraphs on the position of their country during the Korean War. Then, have the groups present their positions to the class.

- To help students understand the conflict between MacArthur and Truman and how it affected the Korean War, have students read and complete *Viewpoints: MacArthur and Truman.* Teaching Resources, p. 22

Monitor Progress
Make sure that students understand the position of their country. If a group is having difficulty, direct them to the portion of the text that explains it.

Map Skills During the Korean War, UN troops supported South Korea, while China backed North Korea. Advantage seesawed between the two sides.
1. **Locate:** (a) 38th parallel, (b) Pusan, (c) Inchon, (d) Yalu River

2. **Movement** Describe the movement of communist troops after November 1950.

3. **Compare** How does the first map differ from the last one?

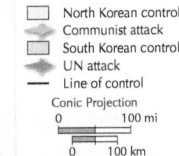
☐ North Korean control
▨ Communist attack
☐ South Korean control
➤ UN attack
— Line of control
Conic Projection
0   100 mi
0   100 km

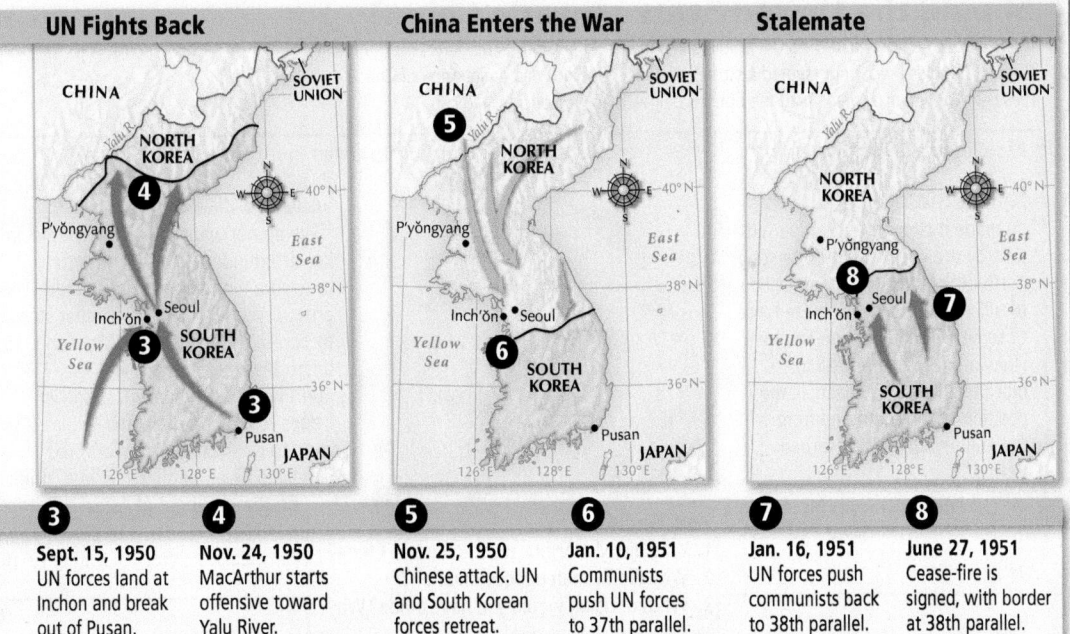

UN Fights Back | **China Enters the War** | **Stalemate**

❸ Sept. 15, 1950 UN forces land at Inchon and break out of Pusan.

❹ Nov. 24, 1950 MacArthur starts offensive toward Yalu River.

❺ Nov. 25, 1950 Chinese attack. UN and South Korean forces retreat.

❻ Jan. 10, 1951 Communists push UN forces to 37th parallel.

❼ Jan. 16, 1951 UN forces push communists back to 38th parallel.

❽ June 27, 1951 Cease-fire is signed, with border at 38th parallel.

Connect to Your World

North Korea For about 20 years after the war, North Korea's resource-rich economy fared better than South Korea's economy. However, years of harsh communist dictatorship, lack of support from the Soviets, and droughts and floods brought shortages and near starvation to hundreds of thousands of North Koreans. During the same period, democratic South Korea became the twelfth largest economy in the world.

In 2005, talk of the unification of the two Koreas was tied to North Korea's nuclear disarmament. South Korea offered millions of dollars if this were to happen. It did not. The Korean Summit in 2007 began with hopes for achieving peace. The talks resulted in plans for economic opportunity, for North Korea's nuclear disarmament, and for working to sign a peace treaty ending the Korean War.

Answers

Map Skills

1. Review locations with students.

2. After November 1950, communist troops advanced south to the 37th parallel, but at the end of the war they had retreated to about the 38th parallel.

3. South Korea increased in size; North Korea decreased in size.

The Korean War Has Lasting Effects

Instruct

- **Introduce** Tell students that even though neither side won the Korean War, it affected U.S. policy. Ask students to predict in what ways the war changed the United States.

- **Teach** Discuss the lasting effects of the Korean War. Ask **What two circumstances convinced the communists to end the war?** (*the death of Stalin and President Eisenhower's threat to use atomic weapons*) **In what way did Truman enlarge the powers of the presidency?** (*He committed troops to war without a debate in or the approval of Congress, although Congress eventually funded the war.*)

- **Quick Activity** Have students read and complete the Decision Point feature. Hold a whole-class discussion about the debate between MacArthur and Truman. Ask **What might the short-term and long-term effects have been if MacArthur had prevailed?** (*In the short term, the war might have broadened to include more of the region, or the North Koreans might have been defeated, with the dividing line between the two nations being farther north. Possible long-term effects might have been reunification between the two Koreas or another war.*)

Independent Practice

Tell students that the U.S. Constitution assigns the power to declare war to Congress. Americans disagree about whether the President should be able to commit troops to war on his own. Ask students to write a short argument for or against a U.S. President's right to send troops to war.

Monitor Progress

Circulate to ensure that students have constructed a logical and clear central argument.

Answers

 He ordered U.S. troops to South Korea and obtained the support of the United Nations for a counterattack.

You Decide

1. He wanted to win the war, which he believed required destroying bases in China.

2. He wanted to prevent a world war.

3. Answers will vary but should reflect logical reasoning.

South Korean and U.S. positions. Badly outnumbered, the UN troops were forced back.

With China now in the war, the United States <u>confronted</u> a major land war in Asia. It was possible that this war could not be won without huge commitments of troops and even atomic weapons. Truman steadfastly ruled out both of these options. MacArthur, who favored an invasion of China, was enraged. He distrusted Truman's policy of a **limited war** fought to achieve only specific goals. As a soldier, MacArthur favored total victory.

Unable to sway Truman, the general sent a letter to the House Republican leader attacking the President's policies. After the letter became public, Truman fired MacArthur for insubordination. There was a huge outcry in the United States, and MacArthur returned home a national hero.

✓ **Checkpoint** How did President Truman react to the North Korean invasion of South Korea?

The Korean War Has Lasting Effects

By the spring of 1951, Allied forces had regrouped and stabilized their position near the 38th parallel. The stalemate lasted until 1953. During that time, the two sides fought small, bloody battles with limited results. At the same time, diplomats tried to devise an acceptable peace agreement.

The War Becomes a Political Issue The stalemate was a key issue in the presidential election of 1952. Republican candidate Dwight D. Eisenhower promised that if elected he would end the war. Upon his election, he visited Korea, spoke with the troops, and studied the enemy's fortifications.

Decision Point

Should the United States Invade China?

China's troops advanced, driving U.S. soldiers and marines back into South Korea. General Douglas MacArthur favored a strong response that included an invasion of China. President Truman disagreed. Read the options below. Then, you decide.

MacArthur Favors Invasion

Primary Source

"I made it clear that if not permitted to destroy the enemy built-up bases north of the Yalu, if not permitted to utilize the friendly Chinese force of some 600,000 men on Formosa [Taiwan], if not permitted to blockade the China coast . . . the position of the command from the military standpoint forbade victory."

—General Douglas MacArthur, April 19, 1951

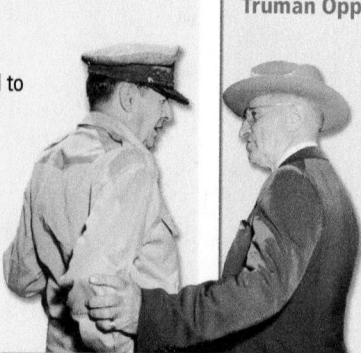

Truman Opposes Invasion

Primary Source

"We do not want to see the conflict in Korea extended. We are trying to prevent a world war—not to start one. . . . Why can't we take other steps to punish the aggressor? Why don't we bomb Manchuria and China itself? Why don't we assist Chinese Nationalist troops to land on mainland China? If we were to do these things we would . . . become entangled in a vast conflict on the continent of Asia. . . ."

—President Truman, April 11, 1951

You Decide
1. Why did MacArthur want to invade China?
2. Why did Truman oppose invasion?
3. What decision would you have made? Why?

Differentiated Instruction
Solutions for All Learners

L4 Advanced Readers
L4 Gifted and Talented Students

Remind students that in the 1950s, the United States organized a new alliance, SEATO, to prevent communist aggression. Tell them that the organization has since disbanded. Ask them to research SEATO and find out whether or not it was effective and why.

Korean War's Impact on America	☑ Quick Study
Immediate Effects	**Long-Term Effects**
• 37,000 Americans killed • 103,000 Americans wounded • Relations with China worsen • Armed forces racially integrated	• Military spending increases • Military commitments increase worldwide • Relations with Japan improve • Future presidents send military into combat without Congressional approval

Eisenhower became convinced that only strong action would break the stalemate. When peace talks threatened to fail, he hinted that he might introduce nuclear weapons into the conflict. That warning, along with the death of Joseph Stalin, convinced the communists to settle the conflict. On July 27, 1953, after slightly more than three years of fighting, the two sides signed a cease-fire. That cease-fire is still in effect today.

Examining the Lessons of the Korean War There was no victory in the Korean War. North Korea remained a communist country allied to China and the Soviet Union, and South Korea stayed a noncommunist country allied to the United States and the major democracies. The two Koreas remained divided at about the 38th parallel.

Yet, the war had an important long-term result. Truman had committed U.S. troops to battle without a congressional declaration of war. This set a precedent that future Presidents would follow. The Korean War also led to increased military spending. By 1960, military spending accounted for nearly half of the federal budget. More than a million U.S. soldiers were stationed around the world.

A new alliance underscored U.S. interest in Asia. Like NATO, the **Southeast Asia Treaty Organization (SEATO)** was a defensive alliance aimed at preventing the spread of communism. Its members included Pakistan, Thailand, the Philippines, Australia, New Zealand, France, Britain, and the United States.

✔ **Checkpoint** What were the most important results of U.S. participation in the Korean War?

U.S. Troops Remain in Korea
American soldiers have stayed in Korea since the war. They patrol the border between the Koreas to prevent another North Korean invasion of South Korea.

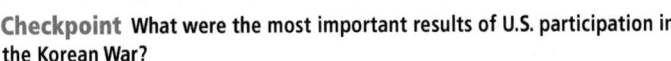

SECTION 2 Assessment

Progress Monitoring Online
For: Self-test with vocabulary practice
www.pearsonschool.com/ushist

Comprehension

1. **Terms and People** What is the relationship between each of the following items and American policy in East Asia?
   - Jiang Jieshi
   - Mao Zedong
   - 38th parallel
   - limited war
   - SEATO

2. **NoteTaking Reading Skill: Categorize** Use your problem-solution table to answer the Section Focus Question: How did President Truman use the power of the presidency to limit the spread of communism in East Asia?

Writing About History

3. **Quick Write: Plan an Interview** Suppose that you were going to interview some American veterans of the Korean War. Write five questions that you might ask about their experiences and their views of the war.

Critical Thinking

4. **Identify Central Issues** Why did American aid to Jiang's Nationalists fail to prevent Mao's communists from taking control of China?

5. **Demonstrate Reasoned Judgment** How did General MacArthur's decision to advance toward the Yalu River change the course of the Korean War?

6. **Identify Central Issues** How did the way in which Truman handled the Korean crisis affect the powers of the presidency?

Section 2 Assessment

1. The terms *Jiang Jieshi, Mao Zedong, 38th parallel, limited war,* and *SEATO* have in common the fact that they affected American policy in East Asia. Mao won the Chinese civil war when the United States refused to commit troops to help Jiang. The United States had agreed to the division of Korea at the 38th parallel but conducted a limited war for fear of starting a third world war. SEATO was started in an effort to further contain communism in East Asia.

2. President Truman committed troops without authorization by Congress, gained support from the United Nations, and fired General MacArthur.

3. Students' questions should reflect a basic understanding of events of the war. They might include both policy questions and questions about personal experiences.

4. Nationalists used American aid poorly and even corruptly. Some administrators took the money for themselves, and some generals were reluctant to fight.

5. China had warned the United States not to advance beyond the 38th parallel. If

MacArthur had not taken his forces all the way to the Yalu River, China would probably not have attacked and the war might have ended years earlier with the same stalemate.

6. Presidential powers increased when Truman sent troops into combat without congressional approval.

Objectives

As you teach this section, keep students focused on the following objectives to help them answer the Section Focus Question and master core content.

- Describe the causes and results of the arms race between the United States and the Soviet Union.

- Explain how Eisenhower's response to communism differed from that of Truman.

- Analyze worldwide Cold War conflicts that erupted in Eastern Europe, the Middle East, and other places.

- Discuss the effects of Soviet efforts in space exploration.

Background Knowledge L3

Ask students to recall the conflicts fueling the Cold War and how these conflicts affected the nations of China and Korea. Ask them to predict how the proliferation of nuclear warheads will change the global Cold War picture.

Set a Purpose L3

- **WITNESS HISTORY** Read the selection aloud.

  Ask **How did President Truman and the U.S. public feel about the threat of war?** *(Truman and the public feared that the Soviets might use nuclear weapons against the United States.)*

- **Focus** Point out the Section Focus Question, and write it on the board. Tell students to refer to this question as they read. *(Answer appears with Section 3 Assessment answers.)*

- **Preview** Have students preview the Section Objectives and the list of Terms and People.

- **NoteTaking** Using the Paragraph Shrinking strategy (TE, p. T20) have students read this section. As they read, have students fill in the graphic organizer identifying the details that support the main idea about Cold War tactics. Reading and Note Taking Study Guide

Civil defense poster ▶

Nuclear fallout shelter sign ▶

WITNESS HISTORY

The Threat of War

After the Soviet Union tested an atomic bomb in 1949, President Truman reported to the nation that the nature of war had forever changed:

❝[W]ar has undergone a technological change which makes it a very different thing from what it used to be. War today between the Soviet empire and the free nations might dig the grave not only of our Stalinist opponents, but of our own society. . . . Such a war is not a possible policy for rational men.❞

—President Harry S. Truman

The Cold War Expands

Objectives

- Describe the causes and results of the arms race between the United States and the Soviet Union.

- Explain how Eisenhower's response to communism differed from that of Truman.

- Analyze worldwide Cold War conflicts that erupted in Eastern Europe, the Middle East, and other places.

- Discuss the effects of Soviet efforts in space exploration.

Terms and People

arms race	Nikita Khrushchev
mutually assured destruction	nationalize
	Suez crisis
John Foster Dulles	Eisenhower Doctrine
massive retaliation	CIA
brinkmanship	NASA

NoteTaking

Reading Skill: Identify Main Ideas Identify the tactics used to wage the Cold War.

Cold War tactics

Why It Matters By 1950, the United States and the Soviet Union were the two most powerful nations in the world. The conflicting ideologies and goals of these rival nations led to a worldwide struggle for influence. The policies followed by the two superpowers helped shape the modern history of much of the world, from Latin America to the Middle East. **Section Focus Question: What methods did the United States use in its global struggle against the Soviet Union?**

The Arms Race Heightens Tensions

A change in the balance of world power is usually gradual, taking place over decades or even centuries. But sometimes, the shift happens in a blink of an eye. Such a major shift in the balance of power in the Cold War took place on September 2, 1949. Instruments in an American B-29 aircraft flying over Alaska detected unusual atmospheric radiation. The radiation cloud was drifting eastward from the direction of Siberia.

American nuclear scientists analyzed the data that the aircraft had gathered. They then reached an inescapable conclusion: The Soviet Union had set off an atomic bomb.

Communist Advances Shock the Nation The news shook U.S. leaders. They had believed that the Soviet Union was years away from developing an atomic bomb. Now, the Americans no longer had a monopoly on atomic weaponry.

The news that the Soviets had the bomb was followed the next month by news of the communist takeover of China. In a very short time, Americans sensed that the world was a much more dangerous and threatening place.

Vocabulary Builder

Use the information below and the following resource to teach students the high-use word from this section. Teaching Resources, Vocabulary Builder, p. 11

High-Use Word	Definition and Sample Sentence
perpetual	*adj.* constant; continuing without interruption Some citizens do not believe that the **perpetual** threat of severe punishment helps to prevent crime.

Nuclear Arsenals Expand Three months later, Truman ordered the Atomic Energy Commission to produce a hydrogen bomb. Developers predicted that the H-Bomb would be 1,000 times as powerful as an atomic bomb. They hoped it would restore the United States advantage over the Soviets.

Some scientists, such as J. Robert Oppenheimer and Albert Einstein, opposed developing the H-Bomb, claiming it would only lead to a perpetual arms race. Others argued that Stalin would continue to develop more powerful weapons no matter what the United States did.

In 1952, the United States tested the first hydrogen bomb. The next year, the Soviets tested one of their own. More bombs and tests followed. Most of these tests were conducted aboveground, spewing radioactive waste into the atmosphere. Atomic testing in the American west, at sites such as the Nevada desert, led to increased atmospheric radiation and long-range health problems for people living downwind of the test sites.

During the next four decades, the United States and the Soviet Union developed and stockpiled increasingly powerful nuclear weapons. They armed planes, submarines, and missiles with nuclear warheads powerful enough to destroy each other many times over. Both sides hoped that this program of **mutually assured destruction** would prevent either country from actually using a nuclear device against the other. Still, the threat of nuclear destruction seemed to hang over the world like a dark cloud.

✓ **Checkpoint** Why did the United States government decide to build a hydrogen bomb?

Eisenhower Introduces New Policies

President Dwight Eisenhower knew firsthand the horrors of war and the need to defend democracy. He had led the World War II Allied invasions of North Africa, Italy, and Normandy. Having worked with top military and political leaders during the war, he was capable of speaking the language of both.

Eisenhower accepted much of Truman's foreign policy. He believed strongly in a policy to actively contain communism. Eisenhower's secretary of state, **John Foster Dulles,** was an experienced diplomat who had helped organize the United Nations after World War II. Dulles endorsed the President's vision of the role the United States should play in the world.

In their approach toward foreign policy, Eisenhower and Dulles differed significantly from Truman and his Secretary of State, Dean Acheson. Both teams of men considered the spread of communism the greatest threat to the free world. But Eisenhower believed that Truman's approach to foreign policy had dragged the United States into an endless series of conflicts begun by the Soviet Union. These limited, regional conflicts threatened to drain the country's resources.

Eisenhower Favors Massive Retaliation Eisenhower opposed spending billions of dollars on conventional forces, such as troops, ships, tanks, and artillery. Instead, he focused on stockpiling nuclear weapons and building the planes, missiles, and submarines needed to deliver them. He assumed that if there were a major war, it would be nuclear.

Ike's new policy drew some criticism: Conservatives felt that downgrading conventional forces would weaken American defense, while liberals feared that preparing for nuclear

The Arms Race

Nuclear Warhead Proliferation

Year	U.S.	USSR	Britain	France	China
1945	6	0	0	0	0
1950	369	5	0	0	0
1955	3,057	200	10	0	0
1960	20,434	1,605	30	0	0
1965	31,642	6,129	310	4	1

Chart Skills The chart above shows effects of the arms race. *How did the Soviet Union's development of nuclear weapons affect U.S. defense spending? How did Eisenhower's policies affect defense spending? Explain.*

SOURCE: *Bulletin of the Atomic Scientists*

History Background

On Thermonuclear War In 1960, Princeton University published a seminal work of this title by Herman Kahn. It caused something of an uproar among both critics and supporters of mutually assured destruction because of its scientific analysis of the possible results of nuclear war. Many had concluded that nuclear war would result in total annihilation. Kahn showed that there were many levels of devastation that might occur. His analysis examined deterrence and defense; attack conditions; fallout; survival; restoring the economy; and medical and genetic problems. Although many of his findings were grim, Kahn and his colleagues came reluctantly to believe that many people might survive a nuclear war and that those who did might live relatively normal lives.

Instruct

- **Introduce** Ask students to read the Primary Source quotation on this page. Have volunteers explain in their own words what John Foster Dulles meant.

- **Teach** Describe Eisenhower's policies of massive retaliation and brinkmanship. Ask **Why did Eisenhower oppose spending on conventional forces and instead stockpile a nuclear arsenal and delivery systems?** *(He assumed that the next major war would be a nuclear one.)* **In what ways was Dulles's policy of brinkmanship different from Truman's Cold War policies?** *(Dulles believed that the nation should take chances and go to the brink of nuclear war to protect allies and discourage communist aggression. Truman had been willing to wage conventional war to stop communists.)* Using the Idea Wave strategy (TE, p. T22), have students discuss how technology developed during the Cold War continues to influence their lives.

- **Analyzing the Visuals** Direct students to the chart The Arms Race on the previous page. Have volunteers read aloud the number of warheads each nation had in 1945, 1955, and 1965. Then, ask students to use the information in the chart to create a line graph showing nuclear warhead proliferation for the United States and Soviet Union.

Independent Practice

- Have students study the Infographic and answer the question that accompanies it.

- Ask students to list the key terms and people in this section and write an explanation or description of each.

Monitor Progress

Circulate to make sure that students are creating accurate definitions and descriptions based on the information in this section.

Answer

Connect to Your World Military technology spun off new inventions that were useful in households, from microwave ovens to smoke detectors.

---

war made such a war more likely. Still, Eisenhower's approach did save money by providing a "bigger bang for the buck." In 1953, the defense budget was $50.5 billion; in 1955, it dropped down to $35.8 billion.

In 1954, Dulles announced the policy of **massive retaliation**. The United States would respond to communist threats to its allies by threatening to use crushing, overwhelming force, perhaps even nuclear weapons.

Primary Source "A potential aggressor must know that he cannot always prescribe battle conditions to suit him. . . . The way to deter aggression is for the free community to be willing and able to respond vigorously at places and with means of his choosing."

—John Foster Dulles, 1954

Dulles believed that only by going to the brink of war could the United States protect its allies, discourage communist aggression, and prevent war. "You have to take some chances for peace, just as you must take chances in war," he said in 1956. Dulles's approach became known as **brinkmanship**.

INFOGRAPHIC

Domestic Uses Of COLD WAR Technology

To give their nations a military advantage, Cold War scientists rushed to invent advanced weaponry, transportation, and communication. Inventions whose origins go back to the Cold War include space travel, satellites, the Internet, and more.

Military Technology Led to These Inventions

1946	Microwave oven
1946	Computer
1948	Hang glider
1958	Nuclear energy plant
1960	Communications satellite
1970s	Smoke detector
1980s	Global Positioning System

▲ **MONSTER COMPUTERS!** This 1946 computer calculated artillery trajectories and other military computations. Unlike today's laptop, it filled an entire room, required extensive wiring, and weighed about 30 tons.

▲ **5-FOOT-TALL MICROWAVE!** In 1946, a scientist working on radar-related military research noticed that the candy bar in his pocket had melted. Knowing a good thing when he saw it, he eventually invented the "Radarange." The early model above was about 5 feet tall.

Connect to Your World How did military technology indirectly affect the way of life in American homes?

Differentiated Instruction   Solutions for All Learners

L1 Special Needs Students   **L2 English Language Learners**   **L2 Less Proficient Readers**

For visual learners and students who need help with basic skills, direct attention to the Infographic on this page. Remind students that this visual shows how inventors used the military technology from the Cold War to make products useful to citizens on a daily basis. Ask volunteers to explain in what way the two images show how Cold War technology was put to civilian use. Ask another volunteer to read the chart aloud. Ask students to think of other inventions that might have spun off from military technology.

Stalin's Death Eases Tensions On March 5, 1953, Joseph Stalin died, setting off a short power struggle. **Nikita Khrushchev** soon emerged as the new head of the Soviet Union. Although a communist and a determined opponent of the United States, Khrushchev was not as suspicious or as cruel as Stalin. He condemned the excesses of the Stalin regime and inched toward more peaceful relations with the democratic West.

In July 1955, Khrushchev met with Eisenhower at a conference in Geneva, Switzerland. Although the meeting yielded few significant results, it did seem to be a small move toward "peaceful co-existence" of the two powers.

✓ **Checkpoint** How was Eisenhower's approach to foreign affairs different from that of Truman?

The Cold War Goes Global

Peaceful co-existence was easier to imagine than it was to practice. The United States and the Soviet Union remained deeply divided. The Soviet Union would not allow free elections in the areas it controlled, and it continued to attempt to spread communism around the world. Dulles talked about "rolling back" communism and liberating the countries under Soviet rule.

Unrest Explodes Behind the Iron Curtain American talk of "rolling back" communist borders and Khrushchev's talk of "peaceful co-existence" were taken seriously by people in Soviet-dominated countries behind the iron curtain. People in Poland, Hungary, and Czechoslovakia resented the control exerted by the Soviet Union. Many hungered for more political and economic freedom.

In 1956, two uprisings shook Eastern Europe. First, workers in Poland rioted against Soviet rule and won greater control of their government. Since the Polish government did not attempt to leave the Warsaw Pact, Soviet leaders permitted the actions.

Then, encouraged by Khrushchev's words and Poland's example, Hungarian students and workers organized huge demonstrations. They demanded that pro-Soviet Hungarian officials be replaced, that Soviet troops be withdrawn, and that noncommunist political parties be organized. Khrushchev responded brutally, sending Soviet soldiers and tanks to crush the Hungarian revolution. The Soviets executed many of the revolution's leaders, killed hundreds of other Hungarians, and restored hard-line communists to power.

Americans could only watch these events in horror. Eisenhower's massive retaliation approach was powerless. The United States would not use nuclear weapons—or any other weapons—to guarantee Hungarian independence from the Soviet Union.

The Hungarian revolt added a new level of hostility to international relations. At the 1956 Olympic Games, held that November in Melbourne, Australia, the bitter feelings surfaced. A water-polo match between the Soviet Union and Hungary turned violent. Sportswriters called it the "blood in the water" match.

The U.S. Defuses the Suez Crisis The United States found itself involved in another world conflict, this time in the Middle East. As Cold War tensions increased, Egypt's president Gamal Abdel Nasser tried to use the U.S.–Soviet rivalry to his advantage.

Nasser wanted to construct a dam on the Nile River at Aswan. The United States and Britain initially offered to fund the project, but when Nasser recognized the People's Republic of China and

Revolt in Hungary
Protesters burn government propaganda in Budapest, Hungary, in 1956. Americans admired the brave men and women who sacrificed their lives fighting against Soviet domination in Hungary.

- Have students complete the note-taking chart that traces the main tactics of the Cold War.

- Have students access **www.pearsonschool.com/ushist** to use the Geography Interactive map and then answer the map skills question in their text.

- To make sure that students understand the global impact of the Cold War, have them work in pairs or small groups to complete the *Outline Map: Europe During the Cold War.* Teaching Resources, **p. 23**

Monitor Progress

As students complete their notetaking chart, circulate to make sure that they understand the main tactics used in the Cold War. For a completed version of the graphic organizer, see Note Taking Transparencies, **B-121.**

opened talks with the Soviet Union, the Eisenhower administration withdrew its offer. In response, Nasser **nationalized** the Suez Canal, placing it under government control. The canal, which connects the Mediterranean Sea with the Red Sea, had originally been managed by a British-French company and was protected by British armed forces.

Nasser's action threatened the flow of Middle Eastern oil to Europe. Without consulting with Eisenhower, Britain and France plotted to get the canal back into Western hands. They joined forces with Israel, a young nation that had long suffered from raids along its border with Egypt. Britain and France used the **Suez crisis** as an excuse to seize control of the Suez Canal.

President Eisenhower was outraged by these actions. Rather than support his Western allies, Ike criticized them and refused to supply them with U.S. oil. The three nations had counted on Eisenhower's support, and when it did not come, they were forced to withdraw their troops from Egypt.

Eisenhower Promises Strong Action In response to Soviet influence in the Middle East and elsewhere, the President made a statement in January 1957 that became known as the **Eisenhower Doctrine.** Eisenhower announced that the United States would use force to help any Middle Eastern nation threatened by communism. Eisenhower used his doctrine in 1958 to justify

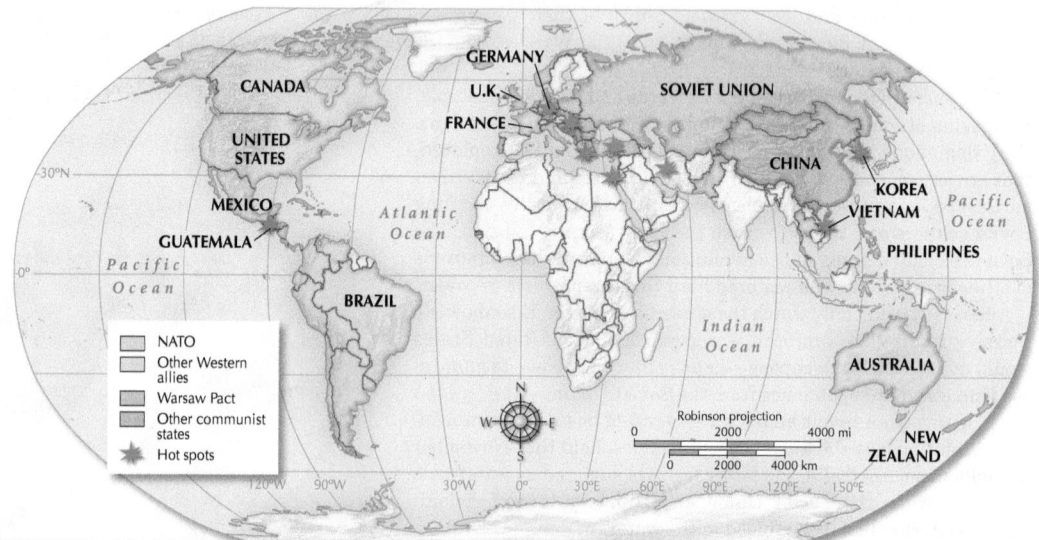

Geography Interactive
For: Interactive map
www.pearsonschool.com/ushist

Global Cold War, 1946–1956

Map Skills The Cold War spread globally as the United States and the Soviet Union formed alliances and competed for power around the world. NATO and the Warsaw Pact were the two strongest alliances.

1. **Region** Identify a region where there were many Cold War hot spots. Why do you think there were so many conflicts in that region?

2. **Compare** How was Latin America important to the United States in the same way that Eastern Europe was important to the Soviet Union?

Differentiated Instruction Solutions for All Learners

L1 Special Needs Students **L2 English Language Learners** **L2 Less Proficient Readers**

Organize students into pairs. Have each pair construct a concept map to show the events and ideas that raised tensions and caused the Cold War to become global. Students should note the main idea—the

Cold War goes global—and determine the supporting events or ideas. Then, have them use their concept maps to discuss in what ways each event or idea added to the tension of the Cold War.

Answers

Map Skills

1. There are hot spots from Eastern Europe to the Mediterranean. All these places are in close proximity to the Soviet Union, which sought to increase its power.

2. Latin America was allied with the United States and balanced the alliances between Eastern Europe and the Soviet Union.

sending troops to Lebanon to put down a revolt against its pro-American government.

The Eisenhower administration also used the **Central Intelligence Agency (CIA)** in its struggle against communism. Congress had created the CIA in 1947 as an intelligence-gathering organization. Eisenhower gave it a new task. He approved covert, or secret, CIA operations to protect American interests. In 1953, the CIA aided a coup that installed a new government in Iran. In 1954, it accomplished a similar mission in Guatemala. While both operations helped to place anticommunist leaders in power, they also created long-term resentment against the United States.

The Cold War Blasts Off Into Space Although the United States successfully contained the spread of communism on the ground, it did suffer a setback in outer space. On October 4, 1957, the Soviet Union launched a 184-pound steel ball containing a small transmitter into an orbit of Earth. The Soviets named the tiny satellite *Sputnik 1*. The following month they launched a much larger satellite. It carried a dog, named Laika, to see how a living creature would react to life in outer space. Since there was no way to return the satellite to Earth, Laika died in orbit.

The launches shocked many Americans, who had long believed that superior technology would keep the United States ahead of the Soviet Union. Would Soviet space technology give them the rocket power to launch missiles onto American cities?

In a state of crisis, Congress quickly approved the National Defense Education Act, a $1 billion program intended to produce more scientists and teachers of science. The act authorized money for loans to enable high school and college graduates to continue their education in science. In addition, Congress created the **National Aeronautics and Space Administration (NASA)** to coordinate the space-related efforts of American scientists and the military.

✔️ **Checkpoint** How did the Hungarian and Suez crises of 1956 raise Cold War tensions?

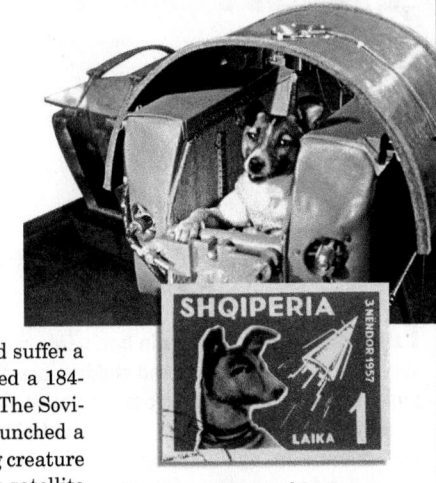

Russians Succeed in Space
The dog Laika, aboard *Sputnik 2*, was the first living creature to orbit Earth. He was hailed as a Soviet hero.

Assess and Reteach

Assess Progress

- Have students complete the Section Assessment.
- Administer the Section Quiz. Teaching Resources, **p. 27**
- To further assess student understanding, use Progress Monitoring Transparencies, **117.**

Reteach

If students need more instruction, have them read the section summary.

Reading and Note Taking Study Guide   L3

Adapted Reading and Note Taking Study Guide   L1 L2

Spanish Reading and Note Taking Study Guide   L2

Extend   L4

See this chapter's Professional Development pages for the Extend Online activity about Cold War crises.

Answer

✔️ Americans and their allies were horrified by Soviet brutality toward the Hungarians, and Egypt's nationalization of the Suez canal and its recognition of communist China provoked fears about losing oil supplies.

SECTION

3 **Assessment**

Progress Monitoring *Online*
For: Self-test with vocabulary practice
www.pearsonschool.com/ushist

Comprehension

1. Terms For each term below, write a sentence explaining its importance to the United States during the Cold War.
- arms race
- mutually assured destruction
- massive retaliation
- brinkmanship
- Eisenhower Doctrine

2. NoteTaking Reading Skill: Identify Main Ideas Use your completed concept web to answer the Section Focus Question: What methods did the United States use in its global struggle against the Soviet Union?

Writing About History

3. Quick Write: Identify Sources Identify two sources you might use to find answers to research questions about the arms race. One source should be a book from your school or public library. The other should be a reliable site on the Internet.

Critical Thinking

4. Identify Point of View Do you think that the massive retaliation policy favored by John Foster Dulles successfully deterred the Soviet Union? Explain your answer.

5. Contrast How were the covert operations of the CIA in Guatemala and Iran different from the military operations of the United States Army in Korea?

6. Demonstrate Reasoned Judgment Were Americans justified in being alarmed when the Soviets launched *Sputnik 1*? Explain.

Section 3 Assessment

1. Sentences should reflect an understanding of each listed term.

2. During the Cold War, the United States agreed with the policy of mutually assured destruction, in which it promised to retaliate fully if attacked by nuclear weapons. It used the policy of brinkmanship to protect allies and discourage communist aggression. Under the Eisenhower Doctrine, the United States agreed to use force to help any nation threatened by communism.

3. Students' sources should meet the criteria set in the assignment. Review with students how to choose reliable Internet sites.

4. Answers should include logical reasons, evidence, and/or examples.

5. The covert operations were conducted in secrecy and without debate among U.S. citizens. Military operations in Korea were undertaken openly and in the full view of public disclosure and discussion.

6. Sample response: Probably. Citizens feared that the Soviets would arm orbiting missiles with nuclear warheads that would be able to destroy U.S. targets more quickly. If they had first-strike capability, they might use it, and the doctrine of mutually assured destruction would be null.

For additional assessment, have students access **Progress Monitoring *Online*** at **www.pearsonschool.com/ushist.**

Objectives

- Describe Cold War preparations for nuclear attack.
- Analyze the ways printed materials were used to encourage preparedness and safety for families during the Cold War.
- Examine how civil defense practices of the 1950s and 1960s have been incorporated into present-day homeland security.

Background Knowledge   L3

Remind students that Americans who had lived through World War II knew about the devastating effects of the nuclear bombs dropped on Japan, and they were aware of the presence of nuclear weapons in the Soviet Union. As distrust grew, many Americans felt they had to be prepared for the worst.

Instruct   L3

- Have students read the introduction and review the pictures and captions in the feature. Ask **What were people supposed to do in the case of an emergency?** (*People were supposed to go underground; schoolchildren were supposed to crawl under their desks; people were supposed to store food and water and be prepared to spend time in a fallout shelter.*) **How did people seem to react to the aspects of the civil defense system? Explain.** (*The pictures make it seem as if people were concerned but cooperative.*)

- Ask students to study the picture of the family in the fallout shelter. Using the Idea Wave strategy (TE, T22), have them identify details in the picture that show the types of preparations the family has made. Then, ask each student to write a letter that one member of the family might have written to a friend while participating in a drill in the shelter. The letter should touch on why the family is there, what it feels like to be there, and other reactions to the situation.

EXPERIENCE THE COLD WAR

Fathers built bomb shelters in backyards, mothers stocked survival kits in basements, and children practiced ducking under their school desks. Across the nation, Americans prepared for the possibility that the Soviet Union might launch nuclear weapons against American cities. This was all part of the civil defense system of the early Cold War.

Throughout the 1950s and early 1960s, the civil defense system shaped American attitudes about their country and the Cold War. As the Cold War ended, civil defense became less important. But since 2001 and the rise of terrorism, it reemerged in a new form known as homeland security.

▼ **Stay Tuned!**
Emergency information would be broadcast on AM radio stations.

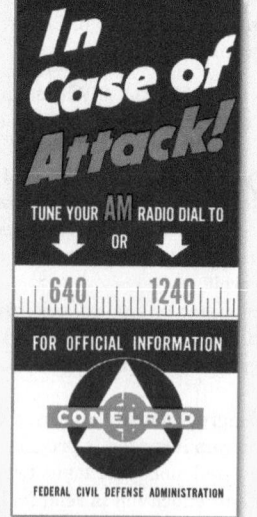

Duck and Cover! ▶
Schoolchildren were taught to "duck and cover" under their desks during nuclear air-raid drills.

▲ **Evacuate!**
In 1955, wailing sirens signaled a simulated nuclear attack and sent New Yorkers scurrying into underground fallout shelters. Similar drills took place across the nation.

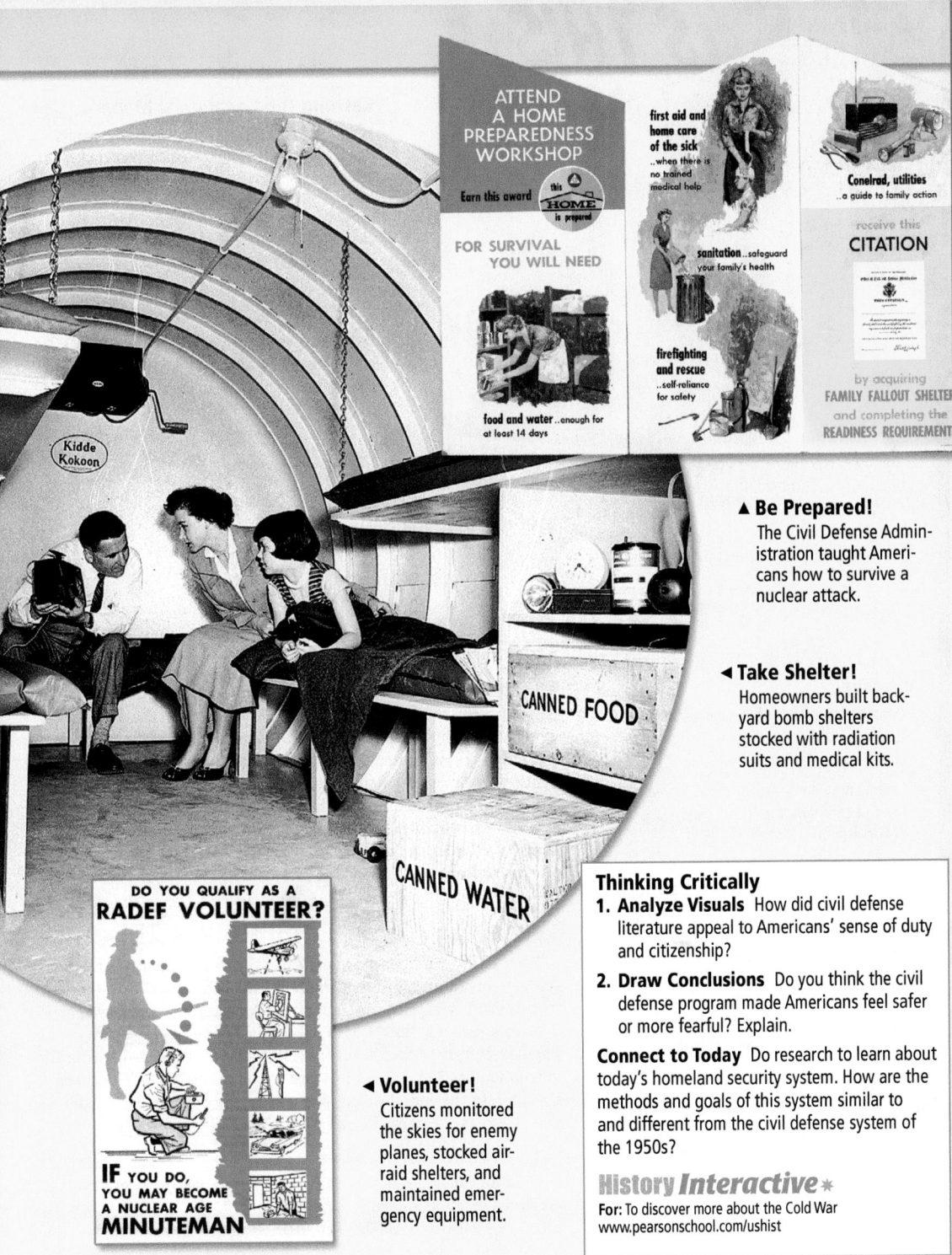

ATTEND A HOME PREPAREDNESS WORKSHOP

Earn this award

this HOME is prepared

FOR SURVIVAL YOU WILL NEED

food and water ..enough for at least 14 days

first aid and home care of the sick ..when there is no trained medical help

sanitation..safeguard your family's health

firefighting and rescue ..self-reliance for safety

Conelrad, utilities ..a guide to family action

receive this CITATION

by acquiring FAMILY FALLOUT SHELTER and completing the READINESS REQUIREMENT

Kidde Kokoon

CANNED FOOD

CANNED WATER

▲ Be Prepared!
The Civil Defense Administration taught Americans how to survive a nuclear attack.

◄ Take Shelter!
Homeowners built backyard bomb shelters stocked with radiation suits and medical kits.

DO YOU QUALIFY AS A RADEF VOLUNTEER?

IF YOU DO, YOU MAY BECOME A NUCLEAR AGE MINUTEMAN

◄ Volunteer!
Citizens monitored the skies for enemy planes, stocked air-raid shelters, and maintained emergency equipment.

Thinking Critically
1. **Analyze Visuals** How did civil defense literature appeal to Americans' sense of duty and citizenship?
2. **Draw Conclusions** Do you think the civil defense program made Americans feel safer or more fearful? Explain.

Connect to Today Do research to learn about today's homeland security system. How are the methods and goals of this system similar to and different from the civil defense system of the 1950s?

History *Interactive* ✳
For: To discover more about the Cold War
www.pearsonschool.com/ushist

Independent Practice
To enrich and extend the lesson, have students access the History Interactive at **www.pearson-school.com/ushist.** After students experience the History Interactive, ask them to share their reactions by posing questions such as: How would you have felt if you had heard the wailing civil defense sirens? What would you have done? How would you react today if you learned that your community was on orange or red alert? Why are things today the same as or different from the 1950s?

Monitor Progress
Have students complete the Thinking Critically questions. Have them share their answers with the class.

Answers

Thinking Critically
1. Possible answers: The RADEF volunteer poster promised that people could become a "nuclear age minuteman." This was intended to liken volunteers to patriots of the American Revolution. If people attended the preparedness workshops, they would receive a citation, another way of rewarding people for cooperating with the program.
2. Students who think it made people feel safer may mention that by taking action people would feel they were doing something to protect themselves instead of simply waiting for an attack. Others might think that the preparations would make people more anxious about the dangers and thus feel less safe.

Connect to Today Have students share their findings with the class, which may include information such as: There are still degrees of emergency (today, represented by colors), and there are still radio warnings. People are still asked to restrict their activities, for example by not carrying certain items on airplanes. However, people are no longer asked to go underground or build shelters as a form of protection.

Objectives

As you teach this section, keep students focused on the following objectives to help them answer the Section Focus Question and master core content.

- Describe the efforts of President Truman and the House of Representatives to fight communism at home.
- Explain how domestic spy cases increased fears of communist influence in the U.S. government.
- Analyze the rise and fall of Senator Joseph McCarthy and the methods of McCarthyism.

Prepare to Read

Background Knowledge L3

Ask students to recall what they know about U.S. treatment of Japanese Americans at the start of World War II. What do they think might happen to all U.S. citizens' rights and freedoms during the Cold War?

Set a Purpose L3

- **WITNESS HISTORY** Read the selection aloud.

  Ask **What does the comic-book character believe is threatening young people?** *(that communists are secretly working to convert young people to communism)*

- **Focus** Point out the Section Focus Question, and write it on the board. Tell students to refer to this question as they read. *(Answer appears with Section 4 Assessment answers.)*

- **Preview** Have students preview the Section Objectives and the list of Terms and People.

- **NoteTaking** Using the Paragraph Shrinking strategy (TE, p. T20), have students read the section. As they read, have students list anticommunist policies and describe how these policies affected the rights of U.S. citizens. Reading and Note Taking Study Guide

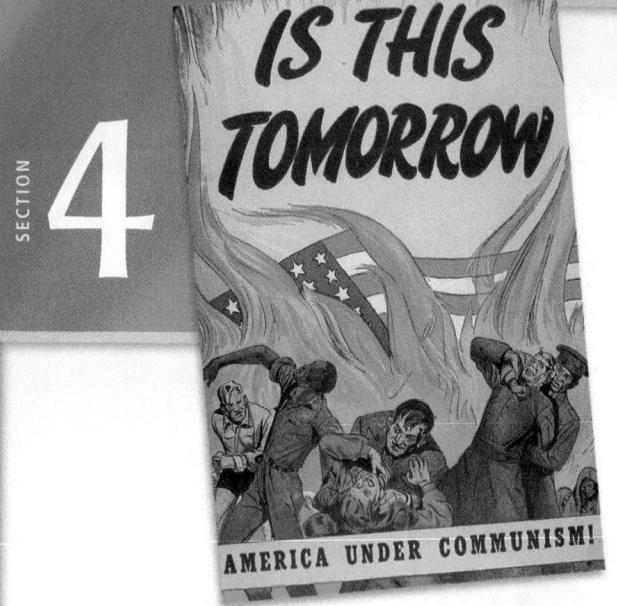

IS THIS TOMORROW

AMERICA UNDER COMMUNISM!

▲ Anticommunist comic

WITNESS HISTORY

Battling the Communist Menace

In the 1950s, Americans were alarmed by charges that communists had infiltrated their government and other institutions. Cold War themes made their way into movies, television shows, and novels. Even comic-book heroes like Superman battled the communist menace. In a 1952 comic book, a character states the concerns of many Americans:

❝Today's headlines shout of battles with Communist hordes in Korea—of Red riots in Rome and Paris and Berlin! But there's another secret battle taking place—right here, right now! A [secret] underground fight between Communism and democracy for the youth of America.❞

— "Backyard Battleground," in
Daring Confessions, 1953

The Cold War at Home

Objectives

- Describe the efforts of President Truman and the House of Representatives to fight communism at home.
- Explain how domestic spy cases increased fears of communist influence in the U.S. government.
- Analyze the rise and fall of Senator Joseph McCarthy and the methods of McCarthyism.

Terms and People

Red Scare	Alger Hiss
Smith Act	Julius and Ethel
HUAC	Rosenberg
Hollywood Ten	Joseph R. McCarthy
blacklist	McCarthyism

NoteTaking

Reading Skill: Identify Causes and Effects
List efforts taken to protect Americans from communism and how these policies affected rights.

Anticommunist Policy	Effect on Rights

Why It Matters Americans have often faced the difficult task of balancing the need to provide national security with the need to protect people's rights and freedoms. In times of crisis, rights have sometimes been limited. Beginning in the late 1940s, the Cold War dominated American life. For some of those years, the nation was in the grip of a new Red Scare. The hunt for communists netted some spies, but it also disrupted the lives of thousands of innocent Americans. **Section Focus Question: How did fear of domestic communism affect American society during the Cold War?**

Worrying About Communists at Home

The Cold War influenced many aspects of American life. American soldiers fought and died in Korea. Industries hummed with activity, turning out weapons and supplies. Americans read newspaper articles about who "lost" China or who was winning the "space race." Popular culture reflected an us-versus-them attitude—democrats versus totalitarians, capitalists versus communists, the West versus the East. In the end, the Cold War was turning out to be every bit as global and as encompassing as World War II had been.

Truman Roots Out Communists The fear that communists both outside and inside America were working to destroy American life created a reaction known as a **Red Scare**. This fear was not unique to the late 1940s and 1950s. The 1917 Russian Revolution and the

Vocabulary Builder

Use the information below and the following resource to teach students the high-use words from this section. Teaching Resources, Vocabulary Builder, p. 11

High-Use Words	Definitions and Sample Sentences
academic	*adj.* related to education Support for education is essential to people in the **academic** community.
tangible	*adj.* solid; definite; capable of being felt or understood That Eisenhower won the election was a **tangible** expression of support for his ideas.

communists' call for worldwide revolution had led to a similar Red Scare in 1919 and 1920. However, the Red Scare that followed World War II went deeper and wider—and lasted far longer—than the earlier Red Scare. Truman's Attorney General, J. Howard McGrath, expressed the widespread fear of communist influence when he warned that communists "are everywhere—in factories, offices, butcher stores, on street corners, and private businesses. And each carries in himself the death of our society."

The spread of communism into Eastern Europe and Asia raised concerns that American communists, some in influential government positions, were working for the enemy. In truth, some American communists were agents of the Soviet Union, and a handful of them held high-ranking positions in government. However, overwhelmingly, government officials were loyal to the United States.

Recognizing public concern about domestic communism, President Truman created a Federal Employee Loyalty Program in March 1947. The order permitted the FBI and other government security agencies to screen federal employees for signs of political disloyalty. About 3,000 federal employees either were dismissed or resigned after the investigation. The order also empowered the Attorney General to compile a list of "totalitarian, fascist, or subversive organizations" in the United States. Americans who belonged to or supported organizations on the Attorney General's list were singled out for more intense scrutiny. Many were labeled "security risks" and dismissed from their jobs.

The Truman administration also used the 1940 **Smith Act** to cripple the Communist Party in the United States. This act made it unlawful to teach or advocate the violent overthrow of the U.S. government. In 1949, a New York jury found 11 communists guilty of violating the Smith Act and sent them to prison.

Congress Hunts Communists Congress joined in the search for communists. In 1938, the House of Representatives had created the **House Un-American Activities Committee (HUAC)** to investigate possible subversive activities by fascists, Nazis, or communists. After the war, the committee conducted several highly publicized hearings on communist activities in the United States. HUAC investigators probed the government, armed forces, unions, education, science, newspapers, and other aspects of American life.

The best-known HUAC hearings targeted the movie industry in 1947. The HUAC investigations uncovered people who were, or had been, communists during the 1930s and 1940s. A group of left-wing writers, directors, and producers known as the **Hollywood Ten** refused to answer questions, asserting their Fifth Amendment rights against self-incrimination. The hearings turned into a war of attacks and counterattacks as committee members and witnesses yelled at each other and pointed accusatory fingers.

Analyzing Political Cartoons

Red Scare or Red Smear This American cartoon appeared in 1949, when government officials were prosecuting communists and others for subversive activities.

1. What is the cartoonist's attitude toward the attempt to uncover communists?
2. How do you think President Truman might have responded to this cartoon?

Have students study the Infographic and answer the questions that accompany it. Ask students to write sentences describing how each image illustrates Red Scare culture.

Monitor Progress

As students complete their tables, circulate to make sure that they list efforts taken to protect Americans from communism and how these policies affected rights. For a completed version of the table, see Note Taking Transparencies, **B-122a.**

After the hearings, the Hollywood Ten were cited for contempt of Congress and were tried, convicted, and sent to prison. Movie executives circulated a **blacklist** of entertainment figures who should not be hired because of their suspected communist ties. The careers of those on the list were shattered. Not until the case of *Watkins* v. *United States* (1957) did the Supreme Court decide that witnesses before HUAC could not be forced to name radicals they knew.

The HUAC investigation had a powerful impact on filmmaking. In the past, Hollywood had been willing to make movies about controversial subjects such as racism and anti-Semitism. Now, most producers concentrated only on entertainment and avoided addressing sensitive social issues.

Freedom of Speech Takes a Hit The case of the Hollywood Ten demonstrated that in the mood of fear created by Soviet aggression, freedom of speech was not guaranteed. Americans lost their jobs because they had belonged to or contributed to an organization on the Attorney General's list. Others were fired for associating with people who were known communists or for making remarks that were considered disloyal. Teachers and librarians, mail carriers and longshoremen, electricians and construction workers—people from all walks of life—might be accused and dismissed from their jobs.

The effort to root out communist influence from American life cut across many levels of society. Communists were exposed and blacklisted in the country's <u>academic</u> institutions, labor unions, scientific laboratories, and city halls.

Government Investigates Oppenheimer The case of J. Robert Oppenheimer illustrates the difficulty of distinguishing loyalty from disloyalty. During World War II, Oppenheimer had led the Manhattan Project, which developed the atomic bomb. After the war, he became chairman of the General Advisory Committee of the U.S. Atomic Energy Commission (AEC). However, Oppenheimer

Vocabulary Builder
<u>academic</u>–(ak uh DEHM ihk) *adj.*
related to education

INFOGRAPHIC

RED SCARE CULTURE

Pop culture reflected the fears of the time. Some books and films bordered on hysteria. Audiences were shocked by the 1950 film *I Married a Communist,* but they cheered when John Wayne starred as Big Jim McClain, a two-fisted HUAC investigator chasing communists in Hawaii.

▲ This comic book enlisted a popular hero in the fight against communism.

THEY PUSH A BUTTON AND VAST CITIES VANISH BEFORE YOUR VERY EYES!

INVASION U.S.A.

GERALD MOHR · PEGGIE CASTLE · DAN O'HERLIHY

▲ Some novels and movies predicted a devastating atomic war between the United States and the Soviet Union.

Differentiated Instruction   Solutions for All Learners

L1 Special Needs Students   **L2 English Language Learners**   **L2 Less Proficient Readers**

For visual learners and students who need help with basic skills, direct attention to the Infographic on these pages. Remind students that this visual shows how pop culture reflected Americans' fears of communism during the Red Scare. Ask volunteers to explain how each image relates to the Red Scare.

had ties to people who belonged to the Communist Party, including his wife and brother.

In 1954, the AEC denied Oppenheimer access to classified information. Although the AEC had no evidence that Oppenheimer himself had ever been disloyal to the United States, it questioned whether his communist ties disqualified him from holding this position.

✓ **Checkpoint** What steps did Truman and Congress take to investigate communist influence in the United States?

Spy Cases Worry Americans

Two sensational spy trials drew the nation's attention to the threat posed by communist agents working to subvert the United States. The accused in the two cases could not have been more different. **Alger Hiss** had been educated at Johns Hopkins University and Harvard Law School. **Julius and Ethel Rosenberg** were from the poor, lower east side of Manhattan. Although Hiss and the Rosenbergs never met, their crimes and their trials have linked them in the public's imagination.

Whittaker Chambers Accuses Alger Hiss Until 1948, Alger Hiss's career seemed flawless. A seemingly dedicated government servant, Hiss had worked on several important New Deal agencies and helped to organize the United Nations. But a man named Whittaker Chambers disrupted Hiss's image.

As a young man, Chambers had become a communist espionage agent. But Chambers later turned against communism because of the brutality of Stalin's rule. Chambers began writing compellingly about the evils of communism. In 1948, he testified before HUAC about his

NoteTaking

Reading Skill: Compare and Contrast As you read, identify similarities and differences between the Hiss case and the Rosenberg case. Consider both the facts and the impact of the two spy cases.

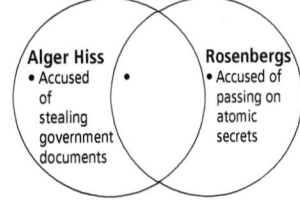

Alger Hiss
• Accused of stealing government documents

Rosenbergs
• Accused of passing on atomic secrets

THE SATURDAY EVENING POST SERIAL THAT JOLTED MILLIONS!

I WAS A COMMUNIST FOR THE F.B.I.
FRANK LOVEJOY

I Was a Communist for the F.B.I. thrilled movie-goers in 1951.

In this science-fiction classic, aliens invade Earth and take over people's minds. Many viewed this as a warning about communist influence. ▶

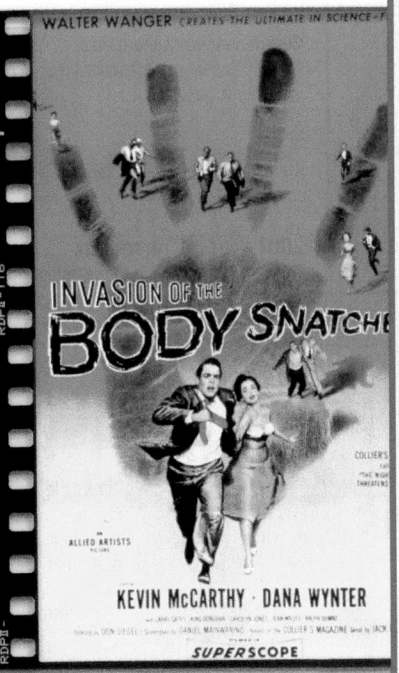

WALTER WANGER CREATES THE ULTIMATE IN SCIENCE-F

INVASION OF THE BODY SNATCHERS

ALLIED ARTISTS

KEVIN McCARTHY · DANA WYNTER

SUPERSCOPE

Thinking Critically
1. **Draw Conclusions** Do you think the investigations of the HUAC influenced the nature of pop culture? Explain.
2. **Recognize Cause and Effect** Do you think the culture of the 1950s made Americans feel safe? Explain.

History Background

Whittaker Chambers J. Vivian (Whittaker) Chambers (1901–1961) was born in Philadelphia, Pennsylvania, but spent most of his youth in New York City. He studied briefly at Columbia University, where he first learned about communism. In 1925, he joined the Communist Party and wrote for its periodicals *The New Masses* and *The Daily Worker.* Chambers joined the communist underground in 1932, where he met Alger Hiss a State department official who helped create the United Nations. The next year, he went to Moscow for training as a spy. From 1934 to 1938, Chambers worked as a Party organizer and courier.

He left the Party in 1938, becoming disillusioned by Stalin's Great Purges. The next year, he went to work as an editor at *Time* magazine, and his politics shifted to the right. He then became known as a strong anticommunist. In 1948, Chambers accused Hiss of being a communist spy. The resulting "trial of the century" was one of unprecedented publicity although Hiss was convicted of only one count of perjury. Chambers's 1952 autobiography *Witness* was a bestseller, and many observers credit him with changing the political climate of the Cold War. Hiss's guilt is still debated.

Objectives

- Summarize historical situations in the United States in which civil liberties have been curtailed and why.

- Understand the nature of the debate surrounding civil liberties and national security.

- Identify additional viewpoints on the Patriot Act through further research.

Background Knowledge **L3**

Ask students to think about the ways in which life in the United States has changed since the terrorist attacks of September 11, 2001. Do they think citizens' rights have been expanded or limited since then? Explain.

Instruct **L3**

Point out that the timeline shows that certain civil liberties of U.S. citizens have been curtailed at various times in the past. Ask **In what ways is the reduction of civil liberties under the Patriot Act similar to and different from the internment of Japanese Americans during World War II?** *(Similar: Both curtail individual liberties and target people of certain ethnic background. Different: The Patriot Act does not generally deprive people of their right to live where they choose, unless they are arrested.)*

Monitor Progress

- Have students complete the American Issues Journal worksheet, *Civil Liberties and National Security*. Check student work to make sure that they grasp the aspects of the issue. Teaching Resources, **pp. 15–18**

- Remind students to complete their American Issues Journal worksheets. Review their work for accuracy. Reading and Note Taking Study Guide

Answers

Transfer Activities

1. Cole believes that governments should not spy on their citizens without probable cause. Dinh believes that his duty to prevent another attack overrides certain civil rights.

2. Cole; he opposes the Patriot Act because it lets the government spy on its citizens, which is what HUAC sometimes did.

3. For more information about civil liberties and the war on terrorism, have students access **www.pearsonschool.com/ushist**.

TRACK THE ISSUE

What is the proper balance between national security and civil liberties?

The Constitution guarantees rights and freedoms to all American citizens. But during war and other crises, government leaders have limited such civil liberties in order to protect citizens' lives. Should they? Use the timeline below to explore this enduring issue.

1790s Undeclared War With France
Alien Act allows President to imprison or deport resident aliens. Sedition Act limits freedoms of speech and press.

1860s Civil War
Lincoln suspends the right of habeas corpus.

1940s World War II
Government sends more than 100,000 Japanese Americans into internment camps.

1950s Cold War
Anticommunist investigations violate some people's rights.

2001 War on Terrorism
Patriot Act helps catch terrorists but may reduce privacy rights.

The World Trade Center towers in New York City burn after the September 11, 2001, terrorist attacks.

A traveler has his baggage searched at an airport security checkpoint.

DEBATE THE ISSUE

Terrorism and the Patriot Act After the devastating terrorist attacks of September 11, 2001, the United States declared a "War on Terrorism." Congress passed the Patriot Act to help law enforcement agencies prevent future terrorist attacks. The Act was to expire in 2005. In spite of controversy regarding it, Congress voted to extend provisions of the Patriot Act in 2011.

"I have a lot of problems with the Patriot Act. . . . It gives the government the ability to spy on its citizens and on foreign nationals without probable cause of a crime, to get wiretaps and warrants. It gives them the ability to get records from libraries and bookstores on people who are not targets of any criminal investigation."

—David Cole, professor, Center for Constitutional Rights

"Right after 9-11, the President turned to the Attorney General and said very simply, "John, you make sure this does not happen again." Preventing another catastrophic attack on the American homeland would have been extremely difficult if not impossibly so without the tools that Congress provided in the USA Patriot Act."

—Viet Dinh, Assistant U.S. Attorney General

 TRANSFER Activities

1. **Compare** Why does Professor Cole oppose the Patriot Act? Why does the Assistant Attorney General support it?

2. **Analyze** Which of the two people above would have been more likely to oppose the work of HUAC during the Cold War? Why?

3. **Transfer** Use the following Web site to see a video, try a WebQuest, and write in your journal. www.pearsonschool.com/ushist

---

History Background

The Patriot Act The Patriot Act again raised the American issue of how to balance people's civil liberties with the nation's need to maintain security. Some of the most controversial issues raised by the Patriot Act included information sharing (should information from criminal investigations be shared with the intelligence and other areas of the government?); wire-taps (should approval of one wiretap be allowed to cover all of a person's communications devices, such as cell phones, land lines, and computers?); searches (should police be allowed to search a person's home or business without immediately informing the person that he or she was being investigated?).

communist past and named Alger Hiss as one of his contacts in the federal government.

Hiss soon appeared before HUAC. He denied that he was a communist and an espionage agent, and he denied that he even knew Whittaker Chambers. But Richard Nixon, a young member of Congress from California, convinced the other committee members to press the case. Slowly, Hiss's story began to unravel. Chambers proved that he did know Hiss and that Hiss had given him confidential government documents. Chambers had even kept a microfilm copy of some of those documents, storing them in a hollowed-out pumpkin on his Maryland farm.

Hiss was tried for perjury. The first trial ended in a hung jury. At his second trial, he was found guilty and sentenced to five years in prison. Even after his conviction, many Americans continued to believe that Hiss was innocent. However, as years passed, the evidence grew overwhelmingly against him. The fact that someone as influential as Hiss was a communist agent raised serious concerns. The Hiss case had another unexpected effect. The congressional hearings thrust Richard Nixon into the national spotlight. In 1952, he was named Eisenhower's running mate and would later become President.

The Rosenbergs Are Executed Nothing created more concern about internal security than the charge that some Americans had helped the Soviets build an atomic bomb. The case began when a scientist named Klaus Fuchs was charged with sending atomic secrets to the Soviet Union. The investigation against Fuchs ultimately led to the arrest of Ethel and Julius Rosenberg in 1950. The Rosenbergs were charged with conspiring to pass secret information about nuclear science to Soviet agents.

The trial of the Rosenbergs generated intense controversy in America and around the world. The case against them was based largely on the word of one confessed spy. Pleading innocent, the Rosenbergs claimed that they were being persecuted for being Jewish and for holding unpopular beliefs. In the end, both were found guilty and sentenced to death. Many believed that the harsh sentence was intended as a lever to force them to identify other members of the alleged spy ring. But the Rosenbergs claimed they had no such information.

After 26 months on death row, the Rosenbergs were electrocuted in 1953. Years of debate followed the executions. Some believe that anti-Semitic sentiment did influence the outcome. In the 1990s, <u>tangible</u> evidence emerged indicating that Julius Rosenberg was guilty. Ethel Rosenberg appears to have played only a minor role in the espionage. Many people continue to believe that the death penalty was too severe for the little involvement she may have had.

✔ **Checkpoint** Why did the Rosenberg case attract nationwide attention and controversy?

McCarthy Uses Ruthless Tactics

The early Cold War years saw one ominous event after another. The fall of China, Soviet nuclear bombs, and the exposure of Soviet agents in the United States all undermined American confidence. At that time, as Americans worried about the nation's security, a clever and unscrupulous man began to take

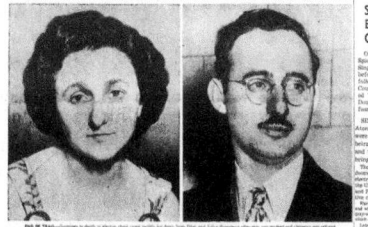

Rosenbergs Executed
Julius and Ethel Rosenberg were executed after being found guilty of spying for the Soviet Union.

Vocabulary Builder
tangible–(TAN juh buhl) adj.
solid; definite; capable of being felt or understood

 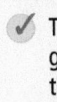

Independent Practice

- Have students read and complete *Interpreting a Political Cartoon: McCarthyism.* Teaching Resources, p. 24

- Have students reread the HISTORY MAKERS biography of Margaret Chase Smith on this page. Ask them to define character assassination. Challenge them to summarize her stand against McCarthyism.

Monitor Progress

Have students read their summaries to one another in small groups. Circulate and listen to the readings, making sure that students have summarized accurately.

advantage of this sense of fear and helplessness. He suggested that these setbacks were really caused by the work of traitors inside the United States.

McCarthy Makes Accusations In February 1950, a little-known senator from Wisconsin made a speech in Wheeling, West Virginia. The senator, **Joseph R. McCarthy,** charged that the State Department was infested with communist agents. He waved a piece of paper, which, he said, contained the names of State Department employees who were secretly communists.

> **Primary Source** "The reason why we find ourselves in a position of [weakness] is not because the enemy has sent men to invade our shores, but rather because of the traitorous actions of those who have had all the benefits that the wealthiest nation on earth has had to offer—the finest homes, the finest college educations, and the finest jobs in Government we can give. . . . I have here in my hand a list of 205 [individuals] that were known to the Secretary of State as being members of the Communist Party and who nevertheless are still working and shaping the policy of the State Department."
>
> —Joseph McCarthy, February 9, 1950

The charge provoked a furor. When challenged to give specific names, McCarthy said he had meant that there were "205 bad security risks" in the department. Then, he claimed that 57 employees were communists. Over the next months, the numbers on his list changed. McCarthy never did produce the list of communists. Still, with the outbreak of the Korean War in June 1950, McCarthy's accusations grabbed the attention of the American public.

At the time of the above speech, McCarthy was finishing his first term in the Senate. He had accomplished very little in that term and was looking for a popular issue on which to focus his 1952 reelection campaign. Anticommunism seemed to be just the issue. McCarthy was easily reelected to a second term.

McCarthy's Power Increases In the following four years, McCarthy put forward his own brand of anticommunism—so much so that the term **McCarthyism** became a catchword for extreme, reckless charges. By making irresponsible allegations, McCarthy did more to discredit legitimate concerns about domestic communism than any other single American.

Between 1950 and 1954, McCarthy was perhaps the most powerful politician in the United States. Piling baseless accusations on top of charges that could not be proved, McCarthy became chairman of an investigations subcommittee. Merely being accused by McCarthy caused people to lose their jobs and destroyed their reputations. He attacked ruthlessly. When caught in a lie, he told another. When one case faded, he introduced a new one.

Confident because of his increasing power, McCarthy took on larger targets. He attacked former Secretary of State George Marshall, a national hero and author of the Marshall Plan. Even other senators came to fear McCarthy. They worried that he would brand them as communist sympathizers.

McCarthy Falls From Power In 1954, McCarthy went after the United States Army, claiming that it, too, was full of communists. Army leaders responded that McCarthy's attacks were personally motivated.

HISTORY MAKERS

Margaret Chase Smith (1897–1995)

In 1950, Margaret Chase Smith of Maine was the only woman in the U.S. Senate. Like McCarthy, Smith was a Republican, but she strongly opposed her colleague's tactics. In June 1950, she spoke out, delivering what she called her "Declaration of Conscience" on the Senate floor. "Those of us who shout the loudest about Americanism in making character assassinations," she said, "are all too frequently those who . . . ignore some of the basic principles of Americanism: the right to criticize, the right to hold unpopular beliefs, the right to protest.

Her stand against McCarthyism won Smith nationwide attention. In 1964, she ran for president— the first woman nominated for that office at the convention of a major party. She finally retired in 1972 after 32 years in the Senate.

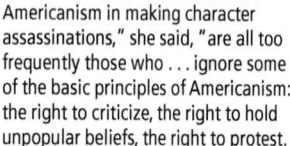

Differentiated Instruction   Solutions for All Learners

L1 Special Needs   L2 Less Proficient Readers

Direct students to choose three key events discussed in this section and create illustrations for a newspaper reporting on these events *(Hollywood blacklists entertainers, McCarthy accuses State Department communists).* Then, write the blue headings on a bulletin board. Ask students to display their drawings underneath the appropriate heading. To review this content, discuss the events illustrated under each heading.

Finally, the Senate decided to hold televised hearings to sort out the allegations. For weeks, Americans were riveted to their television sets. Most were horrified by McCarthy's bullying tactics. For the first time, the public saw McCarthy badger witnesses, twist the truth, and snicker at the suffering of others. It was an upsetting sight for many Americans.

By the time the hearings ended in mid-June, the senator had lost many of his strongest supporters. The Senate formally censured, or condemned, him for his reckless accusations. Although McCarthy continued to serve in the Senate, he had lost virtually all of his power and influence.

The end of the Korean War in 1953 and McCarthy's downfall in 1954 signaled the decline of the Red Scare. The nation had been damaged by the suppression of free speech and by the lack of open, honest debate. However, Americans had come to realize how important their democratic institutions were and how critical it was to preserve them.

✓ **Checkpoint** What events led to Senator McCarthy being censured by the U.S. Senate?

McCarthy Accuses
Day after day, from April to June 1954, Americans watched the Army-McCarthy hearings on TV. Here, the senator displays a piece of evidence. *How can TV coverage influence government and court proceedings?*

SECTION 4 Assessment

Progress Monitoring *Online*
For: Self-test with vocabulary practice
www.pearsonschool.com/ushist

Comprehension

1. **Terms and People** For each of the following items, write a sentence explaining its significance.
   • HUAC
   • blacklist
   • Alger Hiss
   • Julius and Ethel Rosenberg
   • McCarthyism

2. **NoteTaking Reading Skill: Identify Causes and Effects** How did fear of domestic communism affect American society during the Cold War?

Writing About History

3. **Quick Write: Plan Research** Choose one specific topic from this section as the basis for a possible research paper. Write a paragraph describing how you would begin doing research on this topic. Identify one question you would like to answer. Then, describe how you would try to find the information. Be specific about the steps you would take in your research.

Critical Thinking

4. **Identify Central Issues** Were Americans correct in worrying that domestic communists endangered their security?

5. **Draw Conclusions** How effective was McCarthy's campaign against communists in government?

6. **Identify Points of View** How do movies reflect the values of a society?

12

Quick Study Guide

Quick Study Guide

Progress Monitoring *Online*
For: Self-test with vocabulary practice
www.pearsonschool.com/ushist

Quick Study Guide

- Have students use the Quick Study Guide to prepare for the chapter test. Students may wish to refer to the following sections as they review:

Early Cold War Flashpoints
Section 1
Section 2
Section 3

Divided Europe
Section 1

Cold War at Home
Section 4

Cold War Alliances, 1955
Section 1

Key Events of the Cold War
Section 1
Section 2
Section 3
Section 4

- For additional review, remind students to refer to the Reading and Note Taking Study Guide.
  Section Note Taking
  Section Summaries

- Have students access **www.pearsonschool.com/ushist** for this chapter's History Interactive timeline, which includes expanded entries and additional events.

- If students need more instruction on analyzing graphic data, have them read the Skills Handbook, **p. SH21.**

For **Progress Monitoring *Online*,** refer students to the Self-test with vocabulary practice at **www.pearsonschool.com/ushist.**

■ Early Cold War Flashpoints

Flashpoint	Action and Reaction
Poland	• U.S. urges democratic elections. • USSR installs communist government.
Turkey	• USSR demands territory from Turkey and communist rebels threaten Greece. • U.S. approves Truman doctrine to aid Turkey, Greece, and other states resisting communism.
Berlin	• USSR blockades West Berlin. • U.S., Britain, and France airlift supplies to the city.
Korea	• North Korea invades South Korea. • U.S. and UN enter war on South Korean side. • China enters war on North Korean side.
Europe	• U.S. forms NATO for mutual defense. • USSR forms Warsaw Pact for mutual defense.

■ Cold War at Home

Loyalty Review Board — Smith Act — Hollywood blacklists — **Cold War at Home** — Oppenheimer case — Senator McCarthy — Spy cases

■ Divided Europe

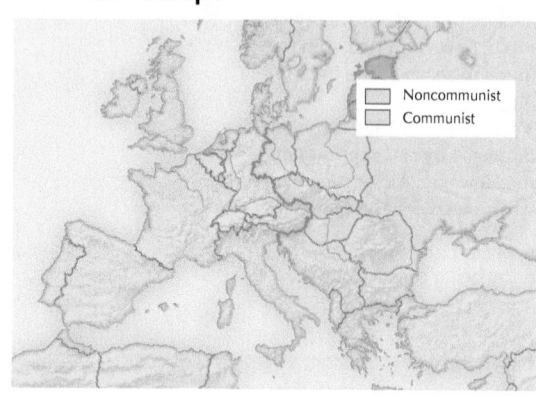

☐ Noncommunist
☐ Communist

■ Cold War Alliances, 1955

NATO		Warsaw Pact
Belgium	Netherlands	Albania
Canada	Norway	Bulgaria
Denmark	Portugal	Czechoslovakia
France	Turkey	East Germany
Greece	United Kingdom	Hungary
Iceland	United States	Poland
Italy	West Germany	Romania
Luxembourg		Soviet Union

☑ Quick Study Timeline

In America

1947 Truman proposes the Truman Doctrine to fight communism

1948 Marshall Plan brings relief to Europe

1949 United States joins NATO

Presidential Terms — Harry S. Truman 1945–1953

1945   1947   1949

Around the World

1945 United Nations is established

1948 State of Israel is established

1949 China becomes a communist nation

Soviet Union tests an atomic bomb

Differentiated Instruction   Solutions for All Learners

L1 Special Needs Students   **L2 English Language Learners**   **L2 Less Proficient Readers**

Use the following study guide resource to help students acquiring basic skills:
Adapted Reading and Note Taking Study Guide
- Section Note Taking
- Section Summaries

Use the following study guide resource to help Spanish-speaking students:
Spanish Reading and Note Taking Study Guide
- Section Note Taking
- Section Summaries

American Issues
Connector

By connecting prior knowledge with what you have learned in this chapter, you can gradually build your understanding of enduring questions that still affect America today. Answer the questions below. Then, use your American Issues Connector study guide (or go online: www.pearsonschool.com/ushist).

Issues You Learned About

● **Civil Liberties and National Security** From the beginning of the American republic, Americans have debated to what extent individual freedom should be limited when the safety of the nation is at stake.

1. How does the Bill of Rights guarantee the rights of people accused of crimes?

2. During the Civil War, what action did President Lincoln take that limited these guaranteed rights? Why?

3. During the Cold War, what effect did the actions of HUAC and Senator McCarthy have on individual rights?

● **Balance of Power in Government** The balance of power in American government changes over time.

4. According to the Constitution, which branch of government has the power to declare war?

5. How did U.S. soldiers fight in Korea without a declaration of war?

6. How did Truman's actions affect the balance of power between the executive and legislative branches of the government?

● **America Goes to War** During times of conflict, Americans debate whether U.S. entry into war is justified.

7. What were arguments in favor of the United States going to war against North Korea?

8. What were arguments against U.S. entry into the Korean War?

Connect to Your World	Activity

America and the World What is America's best course of action when dealing with threats to regional stability throughout the world? During the Cold War, Presidents Truman and Eisenhower believed the primary role of the United States was to contain or reverse the spread of communism. Today, many Americans feel that it is in the nation's best interests to support the growth of democracy around the globe. Other Americans feel that the burden of military intervention should be shared among the countries of the United Nations. Still, more Americans feel that the United States should get involved only when the situation poses an immediate threat to the country. What do you think? Go online or to your local library to research recent U.S. actions abroad. Create a table to detail the different opinions surrounding each action.

1950
Senator McCarthy starts an anticommunist campaign

1954
Senate censures McCarthy

1957
Eisenhower Doctrine combats Soviet influence in the Middle East

Dwight D. Eisenhower 1953–1961

1951   **1953**   **1955**

1950
United States and China clash in Korea

1954
CIA helps overthrow Guatemala's government

1956
Soviets crush the Hungarian uprising

History Interactive
For: Interactive timeline
www.pearsonschool.com/ushist

American Issues
Connector

Tell students that the main issues for this chapter are Civil Liberties and National Security, Balance of Power in Government, and America Goes to War. Then, ask them to answer the Issues You Learned About questions on this page. Discuss the Connect to Your World topic and ask students to complete the project that follows.

American Issues Connector

1. The Fifth and Sixth Amendments entitle them to certain rights, such as the right to a speedy trial and to an attorney.

2. During the Civil War, Lincoln suspended habeas corpus, which means that people could be arrested without charges being brought against them. He did this to keep people from disrupting the war effort.

3. Individual rights were curtailed, and people became fearful of speaking out for fear of being accused of being a communist.

4. the legislative branch (Congress)

5. President Truman ordered them into battle, and they did so under the auspices of the UN.

6. Presidential power increased; Congressional power decreased.

7. Arguments in favor included: containing communism, which had recently spread to China; appeasement had not worked before World War II and it was unlikely to work in Korea.

8. Arguments against included: American troops in the area were not adequately prepared or supplied; protecting South Korea was not in the national interest.

Connect to Your World

Students' tables should reflect sound research and clear understanding of the opinions surrounding recent U.S. actions abroad.

For additional review of this chapter's enduring issues, remind students to refer to the Reading and Note Taking Study Guide American Issues Journal.

Terms and People

1. a country controlled by another nation; in order to expand communism worldwide and to create a buffer between the Soviet Union and the West

2. Truman's policy to aid with military force nations struggling against communism; the United States and Britain airlifted supplies to the people of Berlin.

3. Jiang led the Chinese Nationalists, and Mao led the Chinese communists during the Chinese Civil War. The United States supplied aid but not troops to the Nationalists.

4. a competition between nations to develop more powerful weapons than their enemies; Americans feared that the Soviets would drop a nuclear bomb on the United States, which drove the movement to rid the nation of communists who, some feared, would help the Soviet Union.

5. The House Un-American Activities Committee; it conducted highly publicized hearings on communist activities in the United States, as McCarthy later did, as well.

Focus Questions

6. U.S. leaders developed new policies and alliances to actively contain the advance of communism around the world.

7. Truman expanded the power of the presidency by committing troops to fight the North Koreans without congressional approval and by gaining United Nations support for his decision.

8. The United States expanded its nuclear arsenal, practiced brinkmanship, used the CIA to gather information, and sent troops under the Eisenhower Doctrine.

9. Fear of communism made Americans willing to limit certain civil liberties in the effort to protect the nation from communist espionage.

Chapter Assessment

Terms and People

1. Define **satellite state.** Why did the Soviets want satellite states?

2. Define the **Truman Doctrine.** How was it implemented in Berlin?

3. Who were **Jiang** and **Mao?** What role did the United States play in their conflict?

4. Define **arms race.** How did the nuclear arms race promote the Red Scare in the United States?

5. What was the **HUAC?** How did its tactics help lead to McCarthyism?

Focus Questions

The focus question for this chapter is **What were the causes, main events, and effects of the early Cold War?** Build an answer to this big question by answering the focus questions for Sections 1 through 4 and the Critical Thinking questions that follow.

Section 1
6. How did U.S. leaders respond to the threat of Soviet expansion in Europe?

Section 2
7. How did President Truman use the power of the presidency to limit the spread of communism in East Asia?

Section 3
8. What methods did the United States use in its global struggle against the Soviet Union?

Section 4
9. How did fear of domestic communism affect American society during the Cold War?

Critical Thinking

10. **Explain Causes** What were the causes of the Cold War?

11. **Problem Solving** What problem did the Marshall Plan help solve?

12. **Compare and Contrast** How were Soviet activities in Berlin and Hungary similar? How were they different?

13. **Decision Making** Identify two key decisions made by President Truman regarding the Korean War. Explain the reasons that Truman had for his decisions. Explain the significant effects of each decision.

14. **Analyzing Tables** The table below shows Korean war casualties. Did communists or non-communists suffer more casualties? What are some possible reasons for the difference between communist and noncommunist losses?

Country or Organization	Total Killed and Wounded
China	900,000
South Korea	843,572
North Korea	520,000
United States	157,530
United Nations	15,465

SOURCE: U.S. Department of Defense

15. **Explain Effects** How did the arms race affect the United States economy?

16. **Compare** How was the Eisenhower Doctrine similar to the Truman Doctrine?

17. **Explain Effects** How did the Cold War affect freedom of speech and freedom of the press in the United States?

Writing About History

Writing a Research Report The early Cold War includes many stories of great courage and personal sacrifice. Write a research report that describes the actions of the person or group and explains why their actions were heroic. Write your report on one of the following topics: Pilots in the Berlin airlift, U.S. troops at Inchon, Senator Margaret Chase Smith opposing Senator McCarthy.

Prewriting
• Choose the topic that most interests you, and create a set of questions about the topic.
• Take notes about the people involved and the personal risks they took.
• Gather additional resources.

Drafting
• Develop a working thesis, and choose supporting information to support the thesis.
• Make an outline to organize the report.
• Write an introduction that explains why the topic is interesting, and then write a body and a conclusion.

Revising
• Use the guidelines on page SH14 of the Writing Handbook to revise your report.

Critical Thinking

10. The Cold War was caused by the great gulf between the beliefs, values, and goals of democratic nations and their fear and distrust of communist nations.

11. The Marshall Plan helped restore the economies of Europe.

12. In both cases, the Soviets used force to gain its ends. In the case of West Berlin, the Soviets were unable to cut off the city from the Allies. In the case of Hungary, it was already a satellite state and there was nothing the United States could do.

13. Sample answer: 1) Truman committed troops to fight in Korea without congressional approval. From the lessons learned in World War II, Truman believed that only action, not appeasement, would work. His action had significance far beyond the Korean War since it increased the power of the presidency. 2) Truman believed MacArthur that the Chinese would not intervene in the Korean War. MacArthur was an experienced, respected military general. Because MacArthur was wrong, the United States faced the enormous human resources of China in a war that

Document-Based Assessment

Analysis of Senator McCarthy

Was Senator McCarthy a power-hungry politician who deliberately misled and manipulated people? Or was he a product of the time, working like other officials to defend the American people against the threat of communism? Use your knowledge of the Cold War and Documents A, B, C, and D to answer questions 1 through 4.

Document A

In my opinion the State Department, which is one of the most important government departments, is thoroughly infested with communists. I have in my hand 57 cases of individuals who would appear to be either card-carrying members or certainly loyal to the Communist Party, but who nevertheless are still helping to shape our foreign policy.

Senator Joseph McCarthy, February 1950

Document B

Document C

[He] was in many ways the most gifted demagogue ever bred on these shores. No bolder seditionist ever moved among us—nor any politician with a surer, swifter access to the dark places of the American mind. The major phase of McCarthy's career was mercifully short. It began in 1950, three years after he had taken his seat in the Senate, where he had seemed a dim and inconsiderable figure. . . . If he was anything at all in the realm of ideas, principles, doctrines, he was a species of nihilist; he was an essentially destructive force, a revolutionist without any revolutionary vision, a rebel without a cause.

Richard H. Rovere, Senator Joe McCarthy

Document D

Emotions ran very, very high about how to conduct the Cold War, about how to deal with the threat of Stalinism, both abroad but also at home. You had American soldiers dying in Korea. The Korean War formed the vivid backdrop for all of McCarthy's career. There was a bitter, bitter partisan battle in which people were prepared to say almost anything to blacken the reputations and to smear their political opponents. McCarthy did it, and his Republican allies did it. You also have to remember that the Democrats were quite prepared to do the same thing, and often did against McCarthy, calling him a Nazi sympathizer, talking about his investigations as posing a threat to American democracy and so on, charges which really don't, in the light of historical evidence and historical perspective, hold any kind of water.

Arthur Herman, The Rise and Fall of Joseph McCarthy

1. Which of the documents is a secondary source that claims that McCarthy was like other politicians of his time and not a significant threat to the American political system?
   A Document A
   B Document B
   C Document C
   D Document D

2. According to Richard Rovere, which of the following statements is the most accurate assessment of McCarthy?
   A He was a power-hungry politician who destroyed people without good reason.
   B He was a gifted politician who protected Americans from destructive forces.
   C He was a man with high ideals whose career in politics was too short.
   D He was evil, but he helped defeat communism.

3. The political cartoon most closely agrees with which of the other documents?
   A Documents A and D
   B Documents C and D
   C Document C
   D Document D

4. **Writing Task** With which of the historians quoted in the documents above do you most strongly agree? Use your knowledge of the Cold War, the Red Scare, and specific evidence from the primary sources above to support your opinion.

---

ended in a stalemate when the U.S. refused to use atomic weapons.

14. The communists had more casualties. The communists may not have been as well-armed or as well-defended as the noncommunists.

15. The United States spent billions of dollars stockpiling nuclear weapons and delivery systems, which boosted the economy.

16. Both doctrines stated that the United States would help nations threatened by communism, although Eisenhower resorted to both covert and military operations.

17. The Cold War and the fears it created had a chilling effect on freedom of speech and freedom of the press. As people found themselves accused of being anti-American or communist sympathizers, they began to watch how they spoke and behaved.

CHAPTER 13

Teach With Technology

PresentationEXPRESS™ PREMIUM DVD

- Teach this chapter's core content by using PresentationExpress, which includes interactivities, video, lecture notes, and the *ExamView*® QuickTake assessment tool.
- To introduce this chapter by using PresentationExpress, ask students with which of the following statements they most agree: **A) After victory in World War II, it was natural for Americans to feel extremely confident and optimistic about their nation's future. B) After the trauma of World War II and recent experience of the depression, it was natural for Americans to feel anxious and uncertain about their nation's future.** Take a class poll or record students' answers by using the QuickTake feature, and discuss their responses. Point out that in this chapter, they will read about the political, economic, and social changes that shaped life in the United States in the late 1940s and 1950s. Continue introducing the chapter by using the chapter opener slide show.

Technology Resources

- StudentEXPRESS CD-ROM
- Teacher Resource Library DVD
- PresentationEXPRESS PREMIUM DVD
- *ExamView*® Test Bank CD-ROM English and Spanish
- **Guided Reading Audio,** Spanish
- **Student Edition on Audio**

THE ESSENTIAL ? VIDEO By Students For Students
For videos on Amercian Issues, go to **www.pearsonschool.com/ushist**

CHAPTER 13 Postwar Confidence and Anxiety

1945–1960

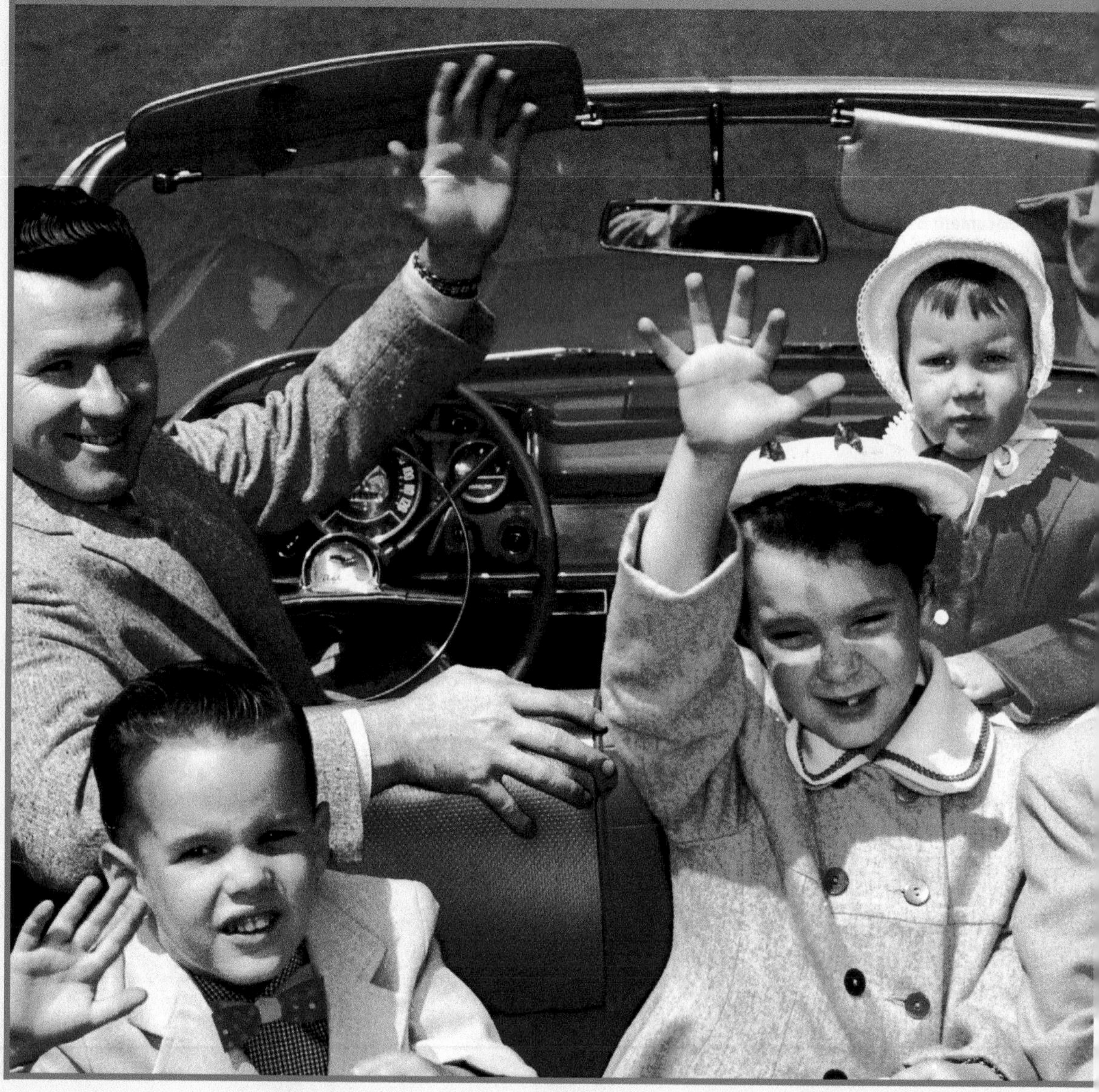

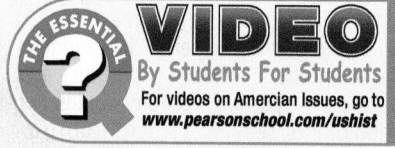

Bibliography

For the Teacher

Hayden, Dolores. *Building Suburbia: Green Fields and Urban Growth, 1820–2000.* Knopf Publishing, 2004.

Miller, Merle. *Plain Speaking: An Oral Biography of Harry S. Truman.* Black Dog & Leventhal Publishers, Inc. (revised), 2005.

Wicker, Tom. *Dwight D. Eisenhower.* Henry Holt & Company, 2002.

For the Student

L2 Kallen, Stuart A., ed. *The 1950s (America's Decades).* Greenhaven Press, 2000.

L3 Wilson, Sloan. *The Man in the Gray Flannel Suit.* Avalon Publishing, 2002.

L4 Harrington, Michael. *The Other America: Poverty in the United States.* Simon & Schuster, 1997.

1950s car ad

WITNESS HISTORY

Postwar Prosperity

World War II was over, and Americans wanted nothing more than to put it and all its horrors behind them. Government spending helped new families make ends meet and helped change the economy from making bombs and warplanes to making cars and refrigerators. Americans were eager to buy these newly available items. They bought houses in the suburbs, cars, washing machines, automatic mixers, radios, and cameras. The future seemed rosy.

◀ A favorite family pastime was taking a long afternoon drive in the family car.

A cosmetic container served as an Eisenhower campaign item.

Elvis Presley

Chapter Preview

Chapter Focus Question: How did social and economic changes after World War II affect Americans?

Section 1
An Economic Boom

Section 2
A Society on the Move

Section 3
Mass Culture and Family Life

Section 4
Dissent and Discontent

Use the ☑ **Quick Study Timeline** at the end of this chapter to preview chapter events.

Note Taking Study Guide *Online*
For: Note Taking and American Issues Connector
www.pearsonschool.com/ushist

Previewing the Chapter

- **WITNESS HISTORY** Remind students that at the end of World War II, the United States was a global superpower for the first time. However, Americans feared the spread of communism around the world and a return to the problems of the Great Depression. Read the Witness History selection aloud. Ask students what images come to mind as they listen to the selection.

- **Analyzing the Visuals** Tell students to look at the image of the family on these pages. Ask **How would you describe the family in this photograph?** (*Sample answer: They seem happy and prosperous.*) **How does the image of this family contrast with images of Americans during the previous years of the depression and World War II?** (*Sample response: This image projects confidence, optimism, happiness, and prosperity, as opposed to images of want, despair, hardship, and fear in photos from the 1930s and early 1940s.*)

- **Focus** Write the Chapter Focus Question on the board. Tell students to keep this question in mind as they read the chapter. Then, have students preview the section titles in this chapter.

- **Preread** Have students complete the chapter's Preread the Chapter Worksheet. Teaching Resources, pp. 8–9

Have students access **www.pearsonschool.com/ushist** for the Note Taking Study Guide *Online* as an alternative to the *Reading and Note Taking Study Guide* booklet.

Differentiated Instruction Solutions for All Learners

The following Teacher's Edition strategies are suitable for students of varying abilities.

L1 Special Needs Students, pp. 549, 554, 558, 561, 564, 569 SN

L2 English Language Learners, pp. 548, 549, 554, 558, 561, 564 ELL

L2 Less Proficient Readers, pp. 548, 549, 554, 558, 561, 564, 569 LPR

L4 Advanced Readers, pp. 550, 555, 557, 562, 568 AR

L4 Gifted and Talented Students, pp. 550, 555, 557, 562, 568 GT

Objectives

As you teach this section, keep students focused on the following objectives to help them answer the Section Focus Question and master core content.

- Describe how the United States made the transformation to a peacetime economy.
- Discuss the accomplishments of Presidents Harry Truman and Dwight Eisenhower.
- Analyze the 1950s economic boom.

Prepare to Read

Background Knowledge **L3**

Note that during World War II, many Americans served in the military or worked for industries that supported the war effort. Ask students to predict the effects of the return of millions of GIs and the shift from wartime to peacetime.

Set a Purpose **L3**

- **WITNESS HISTORY** Read the selection aloud.

  Ask **How did the GI Bill change America?** (*Sample answer: The bill created a more educated population and allowed people to move up to the middle class through education.*)

- **Focus** Point out the Section Focus Question, and write it on the board. Tell students to refer to this question as they read. (*Answer appears with Section 1 Assessment answers.*)

- **Preview** Have students preview the Section Objectives and the list of Terms and People.

- **NoteTaking** Using the Structured Read Aloud strategy (TE, p. T20), have students read this section. As they read, have students complete the table showing problems and solutions. Reading and Note Taking Study Guide

WITNESS HISTORY

The GI Bill of Rights

Passed in 1944, the Serviceman's Readjustment Act, known as the GI Bill of Rights, was intended to ease the soldier's transition from wartime to peacetime. One veteran remembers how the GI Bill affected his life:

❝You were able to go to any school that accepted you . . . So I . . . found the best school that I [could] go to, regardless of tuition, which was Columbia in New York, and they accepted me. I graduated [with] a Bachelor of Science in Business Administration and they accepted me into the Master's program in business at Columbia and I was amazed that [the government] paid the entire tuition. . . . [It] was a revolution that all these people, who never would go to college, went to college because of the GI Bill.❞
—Interview with Harvey S. Lowy, Rutgers Oral History Archives of World War II

An Economic Boom

Objectives

- Describe how the United States made the transformation to a peacetime economy.
- Discuss the accomplishments of Presidents Harry Truman and Dwight Eisenhower.
- Analyze the 1950s economic boom.

Terms and People

demobilization
GI Bill of Rights
baby boom

productivity
Taft-Hartley Act
Fair Deal

NoteTaking

Reading Skill: Understand Effects List the problems raised by the shift to a peacetime economy and the steps taken to solve them.

United States After WWII	
Problem	**Solution**
• Returning soldiers need jobs	• GI Bill

Why It Matters After World War II, many Americans worried that the war's end would bring renewed economic depression. Numerous economists shared this pessimistic view of the future, predicting that the American economy could not produce enough jobs to employ all those who were returning from the military. Yet, instead of a depression, Americans experienced the longest period of economic growth in American history, a boom that enabled millions of Americans to enter the middle class. This era of sustained growth fostered a widespread sense of optimism about the nation's future. **Section Focus Question: How did the nation experience recovery and economic prosperity after World War II?**

The Nation Recovers From War

At the end of the war in August 1945, more than 12 million Americans were in the military. Thousands of American factories were churning out ships, planes, tanks, and all the materials required to help fight the war in the Pacific. Virtually overnight, both the need for such a huge military machine and the focus on war production came to an end. Orders went out from Washington, D.C., canceling defense contracts, causing millions of defense workers to lose their jobs. Wartime industries had to be converted to meet peacetime needs.

Vocabulary Builder

Use the information below and the following resource to teach students the high-use words from this section. Teaching Resources, Vocabulary Builder, p. 11

High-Use Words	Definitions and Sample Sentences
upsurge	*n.* sudden increase There was an **upsurge** in nonmilitary jobs after the war.
initiate	*v.* to arrange for something to start The federal government **initiated** many changes after World War II.

As Americans set about enjoying the fruits of peace, President Harry Truman responded to calls to "bring the boys home for Christmas" by starting the **demobilization**, or sending home members, of the army. By July 1946, only 3 million remained in the military.

Americans were happy that the war was over, but they retained some sense of unease about the future. One poll taken in the fall of 1945 showed that 60 percent of Americans expected their earnings to fall with the return of a peacetime economy. "The American soldier is . . . worried sick about postwar joblessness," *Fortune* magazine observed.

The GI Bill Aids Returning Soldiers To help deal with this anxiety, the federal government enacted a law popularly known as the **GI Bill of Rights**. It granted veterans a variety of benefits. It provided a year of unemployment payments to veterans who were unable to find work. Those who attended college after the war received financial aid. The act also entitled veterans to government loans for building homes and starting businesses.

The GI bill had an enormous impact on American society. Home loans to veterans fueled an <u>upsurge</u> in home construction, which led to explosive growth in suburban areas. Perhaps the greatest contribution of the GI bill came in education. The average soldier was inducted into the armed forces at the time when he or she would have been finishing high school. The bill encouraged veterans to enter or return to college. Each veteran was eligible to receive $500 a year for college tuition. The bill also provided $50 a month for living expenses and $75 a month for married veterans. Eight million veterans eventually took advantage of the education benefits.

A Baby Boom Fills Classrooms Upon their return, soldiers quickly made up for lost time by marrying and having children. Americans had put off having children because of the depression and war. Now, confident that the bad times were behind them, many married couples started families. This led to what population experts termed a **baby boom**. In 1957, at the peak of the baby boom, one American baby was born every 7 seconds, a grand total of 4.3 million for the year. One newspaper columnist commented, "Just imagine how much these extra people . . . will absorb—in food, in clothing, in gadgets, in housing, in services. . . ." Between 1940 and 1955, the U.S. population experienced its greatest increase, growing 27 percent from about 130 to about 165 million.

Converting From a Wartime Economy Fortunately, unemployment did not materialize, nor did a depression return. However, Americans experienced some serious economic problems. The most painful was skyrocketing prices. With war's end, the federal government ended rationing and price controls, both of which had helped keep inflation in check during the war. A postwar rush to buy goods created severe inflationary pressures. There was just too much money to spend on too few goods. Overall, prices rose about 18 percent in 1946. The price of some products, such as beef, nearly doubled within a year.

Vocabulary Builder
upsurge–(UHP suhrj) *n.* sudden increase

New Families
Marriage rates soared as soldiers returned home. Confident that the bad times were behind them, newly wed couples bought new homes and started families. The increase in the birthrate began in 1946 and slowed by 1964.

Birthrate, 1940–1960

SOURCE: *Historical Statistics of the United States*

Teach

The Nation Recovers From War

Instruct

- **Introduce** Note that World War II ended in 1945. Ask **How many years had passed since the Great Depression?** *(only about five years)* **Do you think memories of the hardships suffered during the Depression were still strong?** *(yes)* In light of this, discuss with students why an end to the war might have made Americans uneasy about the economic future of the nation.

- **Teach** Tell students that the end of the war brought great change to the United States—some of which was very different from what many people expected. Ask **What did many people fear as millions of soldiers returned from the war?** *(They feared another period of hard times when jobs would be scarce.)* **How does this fear contrast with what really happened?** *(The fears were unfounded. The United States entered a long period of economic growth.)* **How did the GI Bill contribute to economic expansion?** *(Sample responses: It provided 1) money for unemployed veterans to spend on consumer goods, 2) loans that enabled many veterans to buy homes and boost the construction industry, and 3) money for college educations that allowed veterans to earn more, increasing their buying power and standard of living.)* **What economic problem did Americans face in the postwar years? Why did it occur?** *(Americans faced inflation. Inflation occurred because the government ended wartime price controls and there were too few goods for the number of people who wanted to buy them.)* **How did purchasing new cars or appliances help create more jobs?** *(As people bought more goods, more workers were needed to produce those goods.)* **How did federal spending help create more jobs?** *(The federal government funded projects that required new workers.)*

■ **Analyzing the Visuals** Have students analyze the graph showing birthrates in the United States between 1940 and 1960 on the previous page. Ask **Why do you think the number of births spiked between 1945 and 1950?** *(Many soldiers were returning home from the war, getting married, and beginning families.)* **How might the prosperity of the postwar economy have influenced U.S. marriage and birth rates?** *(Postwar prosperity meant that people had more money, so they were less worried about being able to provide for their families.)*

Independent Practice

■ Have students analyze the Infographic on this page. Ask them to determine the ways the people in the photographs illustrate the booming U.S. economy. Then, have students write answers to the Thinking Critically questions on the next page.

■ Tell students to take the part of a veteran writing a letter of thanks to President Truman for the help received because of the GI Bill. Have students share their letters with the class.

Monitor Progress

As students fill in their tables, circulate to make sure that they understand the problems created by the need to shift from wartime to a peacetime economy and the steps taken to address those problems. For a completed version of the table, see Note Taking Transparencies, B-123.

The U.S. Dominates the World Economy During the depression, Americans could not buy the goods they desired. The economy improved during the war, but wartime restrictions kept spending down and limited economic growth. The end of wartime restrictions finally opened the floodgates to consumer purchases. As demand soared, businesses employed more people to produce goods. This created a cycle in which people bought new goods, leading businesses to hire more workers, who in turn bought more goods.

At the end of World War II, the United States was the only developed nation untouched by the devastation. Although it had only 6 percent of the world's population, the United States produced about 50 percent of the world's total output. This allowed Americans to enjoy a higher standard of living than any other nation in the world.

Technological Progress Boosts Productivity The American economy benefited from numerous technological advances during the postwar period. Some developments, such as the use of atomic energy, were the result of war research. The use of computers increased, and businesses gradually began to depend on them. Worker **productivity**—the rate at which goods are produced or services performed—continued to improve, largely because of new technology.

Government Spending Supports Growth Increased government spending boosted the economy, too. With the outbreak of the Korean War, the United States once again committed a significant part of its budget to defense spending. Military spending led to the development of new technologies and new materials, such as plastics and new light metal alloys, that found widespread use outside the military. Other large federal spending programs, such as the Marshall Plan, initiated foreign demand for goods made in the United States.

Vocabulary Builder
initiate—(ih NIHSH ee ayt) *v.* to arrange for something to start

✓ **Checkpoint** What did many Americans expect to happen to the American economy after World War II?

INFOGRAPHIC

AMERICA Returns to WORK

When World War II ended, nearly everyone feared hard times. However, the postwar years ushered in a period of domestic prosperity that lasted nearly 20 years. The United States became the richest country in the world. Many Americans found that they had greater buying power than ever before.

◄ By 1950, 3 out of 10 women were in the workforce.

The rise in the GNP signaled ► the nation's economic success. Between 1945 and 1960, the GNP more than doubled.

U.S. GNP, 1945–1960

SOURCE: USInfo.State.Gov

Differentiated Instruction Solutions for All Learners

L2 English Language Learners   L2 Less Proficient Readers

Pair struggling readers and readers learning English with advanced readers to complete an illustrated timeline featuring some of the major events that appear in this section. Students should use other sources, such as encyclopedias or the Internet, to look up some of the dates. Have students go through the chapter first to choose events for the timeline. Then, have them determine the date of each event. Students should then draw the timeline on a sheet of paper and place each event on the timeline with a hashmark and label. Either above or below each hashmark, have students make a simple drawing that illustrates the event. Students might choose events from the section such as the end of World War II, the start and end dates of the Korean War, the dates of passage of the GI Bill and the Taft-Hartley Act, and the dates on which Presidents Truman and Eisenhower were elected.

Answer

✓ Many expected a downturn in the U.S. economy and a loss of jobs.

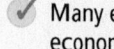

Truman Overcomes Huge Obstacles

On April 12, 1945, when Franklin Roosevelt died, Harry S. Truman had been Vice President for only 4 months. When Eleanor Roosevelt told him that her husband had died, Truman responded "Is there anything I can do for you?" She replied, "Is there anything we can do for you? For you are the one in trouble now."

Eleanor Roosevelt's remark captured Harry Truman's predicament. He had to preside over one of the more difficult times in American history. The postwar years saw the beginning of the Cold War and communist takeovers in Europe and Asia. At home, there was inflation and labor unrest. Communist advances and a troubled domestic economy created a sense of deep unrest in the American public during the Truman years.

Grappling With Congress and Labor From the first days of his presidency, Truman faced a double-barreled challenge: a restless labor movement and a combative Republican Party. Trade unionists demanded pay increases to keep up with inflation. When employers refused to meet labor's demands, millions of steel, coal, railroad, and automotive workers went on strike.

The wave of strikes was one of the largest in American history. It prompted Congress to enact the **Taft-Hartley Act,** a law that outlawed the closed shop—a workplace in which only union members can be hired. Taft-Hartley rolled back some of the rights that labor unions had gained during the New Deal. Although Truman vetoed the Taft-Hartley Act, Congress overrode his veto.

Angering Segregationists Unlike FDR, who feared challenging the power of white southern senators and representatives, Truman refused to remain passive. He established a special committee on civil rights to investigate race relations. The committee made several recommendations for civil rights reforms. However, Congress rejected the recommendations

American families wanted their own homes. Home construction contributed to the booming economy. ▼

As the demand for consumer goods soared, manufacturers turned out an increasing number of products. Here, a worker assembles a television set. ▼

Thinking Critically

1. **Analyze Graphs** How much did the GNP increase between 1945 and 1960?

2. **Analyze Information** Why was the postwar period a time of prosperity for most Americans?

Truman Overcomes Huge Obstacles/Eisenhower Charts a Middle Path L3

Instruct

- **Introduce** Tell students that even during the U.S. economic boom, there were still problems that had to be solved. Using the Idea Wave strategy (TE, p. T22), have students list problems that a nation might have even in a time of economic growth.

- **Teach** Remind students that labor unions gained strength during the New Deal era of the 1930s. Ask **What caused union workers to go on strike in the early part of Truman's term?** *(They did not receive raises to keep pace with inflation.)* Note that the strikes caused Congress to pass the Taft-Hartley Act. Ask **Did Truman succeed in fighting discrimination?** *(Truman desegregated the military, but Congress did not pass any meaningful civil rights laws during his term.)* **Why was Truman unsuccessful in instituting much of his Fair Deal program?** *(He was not able to get Congress to pass it.)* Have students use the Think-Write-Pair-Share strategy (TE, p. T23) to evaluate the political situation during Eisenhower's term. Ask **Why did both Democrats and Republicans support Eisenhower?** *(Sample response: Eisenhower believed that the federal government had grown too strong, but he did not dismantle New Deal programs. He increased federal spending for education as well as for the building of interstate highways. Economic prosperity also bolstered his popularity.)*

Differentiated Instruction Solutions for All Learners

L1 Special Needs Students L2 English Language Learners L2 Less Proficient Readers

Have students reread the section under the blue heading "Truman Overcomes Huge Obstacles," with the goal of creating a series of cause-and-effect graphic organizers for each red heading within it. Tell students to look for something that happens in each section and the event or person that caused it. Review with students how to make a simple cause-and-effect graphic organizer—two identical boxes

side-by-side, with an arrow between them pointing from the box on the left toward the box on the right. Then, have students draw the graphic organizers. Have each student exchange and compare graphic organizers with that of a partner when the activity is completed. Have students use their graphic organizers to help them complete the worksheet *Viewpoints: Labor Strikes.* Teaching Resources, **p. 15**

Answers

Thinking Critically

1. It increased by about $300 billion.

2. Americans had more money than in previous years. This money allowed people to buy homes and goods that were unavailable before.

Independent Practice

Have students consider Truman's proposal for national health insurance and write an editorial either supporting or opposing the program. Remind students that many people at the time did not have health insurance.

Monitor Progress

As students compose their letters to the editor, circulate to ensure that they understand what health insurance provides and the problems faced by families who do not have it.

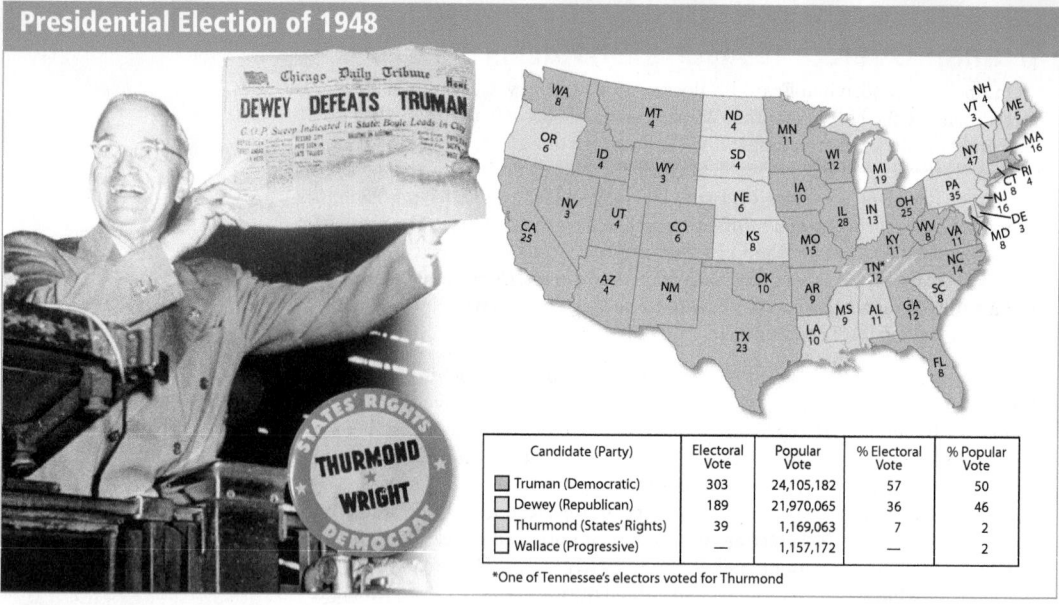

Presidential Election of 1948

Candidate (Party)	Electoral Vote	Popular Vote	% Electoral Vote	% Popular Vote
☐ Truman (Democratic)	303	24,105,182	57	50
☐ Dewey (Republican)	189	21,970,065	36	46
☐ Thurmond (States' Rights)	39	1,169,063	7	2
☐ Wallace (Progressive)	—	1,157,172	—	2

*One of Tennessee's electors voted for Thurmond

A Truman Victory

Despite the mistaken headline, Truman defeated Dewey in a close election. The Democrats won with a popular vote of 24 million to the Republicans' popular vote of nearly 22 million. The campaign button promoted Truman's opponents, Thurmond and Wright from the States' Rights Party. *What role should the media have in elections?*

and did not pass any meaningful civil rights reforms until the late 1950s. Truman also issued an executive order desegregating the military. This was more successful. By 1951, most units had been integrated.

Truman Upsets Dewey By the spring of 1948, Truman's standing had sunk so low that he faced challenges from both the right and the left in his own Democratic Party. Southern Democrats, angry at Truman's support for civil rights, left the party and established the States' Rights Party. They named South Carolina governor Strom Thurmond as their candidate for President. At the other end of the political spectrum, Henry Wallace, who had been Vice President during FDR's third term, broke with Truman over foreign policy issues. Wallace became the candidate of a new Progressive Party.

The breakaway of two large blocs of Democrats was accompanied by the Republican Party's nomination of Thomas Dewey, the well-known governor of New York, for President. Few people thought that Truman had any chance of winning the 1948 election. Truman, however, did not see it that way. He staged an energetic "whistle stop" train tour of the nation, delivering over 300 speeches and traveling 31,000 miles in a matter of weeks. At train stops in small towns, Truman attacked the current Congress as "do nothing" and the worst in history. "Give 'em hell, Harry!" some in the crowd would cry out during his speeches. Although every political poll predicted that Dewey would win easily, Truman won by a narrow victory. He had managed the political upset of the century.

Truman Proposes a Fair Deal Shortly after the election, Truman announced a far-ranging legislative program, which he called the **Fair Deal.** The Fair Deal, he explained, would strengthen existing New Deal reforms and establish new programs, such as national health insurance. But Congress was not in a reforming mood, and Truman failed to win approval for most of his Fair Deal proposals.

Legislative failure and a stalled war in Korea contributed to Truman's loss of popularity. He chose not to seek the 1952 Democratic nomination. His reputation, however, has improved through the years. Today, many historians applaud

Differentiated Instruction **Solutions for All Learners**

L4 Advanced Readers **L4 Gifted and Talented Students**

Have students study the map on this page and then write an analysis of the election results based on it. Each analysis should include the answers to questions such as the following: Who won the election, and to which political party did he belong? How did the Democratic and Republican parties split the electoral and popular vote? In which parts of the country was each political party strong? How did third-party

candidates do, and how did they affect the race? Where were third-party candidates the strongest?

Students should explain the results and trends, referring to the text and additional information located through research. Have students present their reviews in the form of an analysis that a political reporter would give as returns are coming in after an election.

Answer

Caption Sample answer: The media should accurately and fairly report the candidates' positions on issues to help the public make decisions about the candidate they want to support.

him for his common-sense approach, as the first President to challenge public discrimination and as a determined opponent of communist expansion.

✓ **Checkpoint** Why were workers dissatisfied during the postwar period?

Eisenhower Charts a Middle Path

The 1952 election was hardly a contest. The Republican candidate, Dwight Eisenhower, was so popular that both the Democratic and Republican parties had wanted him as their presidential candidate. Eisenhower, whose nickname was Ike, charmed the public with his friendly smile, reassuring personality, and record of service and honesty. The Democratic candidate, Adlai Stevenson, a senator from Illinois, failed to catch the popular imagination the way Eisenhower did.

Dwight Eisenhower had spent nearly his entire adult life in the military and had never held a political office before 1952. Thus, Americans could not know for certain which way he would guide the nation upon taking office. However, most Americans believed that Eisenhower's calm personality mirrored his political views and that he would keep to the "middle road," achieving a balance between liberal and conservative positions.

Eisenhower charted a middle course as President. While he shared the conservative view that the federal government had grown too strong, he did not repeal existing New Deal programs, such as Social Security and the minimum wage. Federal spending actually increased during his presidency. Eisenhower even introduced several large new programs. For example, he created an interstate highway system and began to spend federal dollars for education, specifically to train more scientists.

One reason for Eisenhower's popularity was the strength of the American economy during the 1950s. His presidency was one of the most prosperous, peaceful, and politically tranquil in the twentieth century.

Dwight Eisenhower

✓ **Checkpoint** Why did federal spending increase during Eisenhower's presidency?

Assess and Reteach

Assess Progress L3

- Have students complete the Section Assessment.

- Administer the Section Quiz. Teaching Resources, **p. 20**

- To further assess student understanding, use Progress Monitoring Transparencies, **119**.

Reteach

If students need more instruction, have them read the section summary.

Reading and Note Taking L3
Study Guide

Adapted Reading and L1 L2
Note Taking Study Guide

Spanish Reading and L2
Note Taking Study Guide

Extend L4

Ask students to write a paragraph drawing conclusions about why Congress was less cooperative with Truman after his election in 1948 than it had been with Roosevelt during the beginning of his presidency.

Answers

✓ Many workers worried that their wages were not keeping pace with inflation.

✓ Eisenhower introduced several large and expensive federal initiatives, such as building the interstate highway system and funding education programs to train students in science.

SECTION 1 Assessment

Progress Monitoring Online
For: Self-test with vocabulary practice
www.pearsonschool.com/ushist

Comprehension

1. **Terms and People** Explain how each of the following changed the lives of Americans during the postwar years.
   - GI Bill of Rights
   - baby boom
   - productivity
   - Fair Deal

2. **NoteTaking Reading Skill: Understand Effects** Use your problem-and-solution chart to answer the Section Focus Question: How did the nation experience recovery and economic prosperity after World War II?

Writing About History

3. **Quick Write: Gather Information** Use the library and reliable Internet sources to find information about the Taft-Hartley Act. Use the words *Taft-Hartley Act* as key words to begin a search. Once you have found several sites, create note cards to gather the information you have found.

Critical Thinking

4. **Identify Assumptions** Why was the government willing to give billions of dollars in assistance to returning World War II veterans?

5. **Draw Conclusions** After the war, Truman faced challenges with labor unions. Would you consider Truman as working for or against organized labor? Explain.

6. **Synthesize Information** How did the baby boom impact the postwar economy?

Section 1 Assessment

1. Students' responses should demonstrate their understanding of each term's relationship to changes in American life in the postwar period.

2. The nation initially experienced postwar inflation, but a postwar boom in manufacturing and productivity boosted industrial output and employment. Increased federal spending also helped strengthen the economy.

3. Students' results should demonstrate their ability to complete an Internet search.

4. Sample answer: The government believed that it owed a debt to Americans who had served in the military.

5. Sample response: Truman worked more for labor than against it. He did not roll back any of the pro-labor New Deal legislation. He also vetoed the anti-labor Taft-Hartley Act, although it became law when Congress overrode his veto.

6. The baby boom caused the U.S. economy to grow. New homes and schools were built and people bought more goods for their children.

For additional assessment, have students access **Progress Monitoring Online** at **www.pearsonschool.com/ushist**.

Objectives

As you teach this section, keep students focused on the following objectives to help them answer the Section Focus Question and master core content.

- Examine the rise of the suburbs and the growth of the Sunbelt.
- Describe changes in the U.S. economy and education in the postwar period.

Prepare to Read

Background Knowledge ⬛

Students have just analyzed the economic changes of the postwar years. Ask students to predict the way those changes affected the everyday lives of Americans.

Set a Purpose ⬛

- **WITNESS HISTORY** Read the selection aloud.

  Ask **How did Levitt make it possible for many people to become homeowners?** *(He constructed homes in a way that allowed him to sell them fairly cheaply.)*

- **Focus** Point out the Section Focus Question, and write it on the board. Tell students to refer to this question as they read. *(Answer appears with Section 2 Assessment answers.)*

- **Preview** Have students preview the Section Objectives and the list of Terms and People.

- **Reading Skill** Have students use the *Reading Strategy: Identify Main Ideas and Supporting Details* worksheet. Teaching Resources, **p. 12**

-  Using the Paragraph Shrinking strategy (TE, p. T20), have students read this section. As they read, have students record the section's main ideas. Reading and Note Taking Study Guide

---

▲ Moving vans line the street of a new suburban neighborhood.

WITNESS HISTORY 🔊

Homes for Veterans

In 1949, developer William Levitt purchased thousands of acres of farmland in Hempstead, on Long Island, New York. Drawing on modern production techniques, he constructed thousands of homes that he sold for just under $8,000 each. Advertisements for Levittown captured the mood of the country as it stood poised to begin an era of unprecedented prosperity.

❝This is Levittown! All yours for $58 [a month]. You're a lucky fellow, Mr. Veteran. Uncle Sam and the world's largest builder have made [it] possible for you to live in a charming house in a delightful community without having to pay for them with your eyeteeth.❞

—Advertisement for Levittown homes,
The New York Times, March 1949

A Society on the Move

Objectives

- Examine the rise of the suburbs and the growth of the Sunbelt.
- Describe changes in the U.S. economy and education in the postwar period.

Terms and People

Interstate Highway Act	multinational
Sunbelt	corporation
service sector	AFL-CIO
information industry	California Master Plan
franchise business	

NoteTaking

Reading Skill: Identify Main Ideas
Complete a chart like the one below to capture the main ideas.

Postwar Changes		
Society	Economy	Education
• Growth of suburbs	• Service economy	•

Why It Matters Since the first colonists arrived in Jamestown, Virginia, Americans have been on the move. In the years following World War II, mobility became especially important. People moved to the suburbs and to the Sunbelt. They also moved into white-collar jobs. At the same time, the American economy was changing. The impact of these changes still affects us today. **Section Focus Question: What social and economic factors changed American life during the 1950s?**

Americans Move to the Suburbs

Between 1940 and 1960, more than 40 million Americans moved to the suburbs, one of the largest mass migrations in history. Rural regions suffered the most dramatic decline in population, but people also came by the thousands from older industrial cities, seeking, as one father put it, a place where "a kid could grow up with grass stains on his pants." During the same time period, many older industrial cities lost population.

Suburbs Attract Young Americans People flocked to the suburbs in part because the nation suffered from a severe shortage of urban housing. During the depression and World War II, new housing construction had come to a near standstill. At war's end, as Americans married and formed families, they went in search of a place they could call their own.

Vocabulary Builder

Use the information below and the following resource to teach students the high-use words from this section. Teaching Resources, Vocabulary Builder, p. 11

High-Use Words	Definitions and Sample Sentences
undertake	*v.* to take upon oneself; agree to do The nation prepared to **undertake** the building of a new highway system.
frustrate	*v.* to annoy; disappoint Skyrocketing prices after World War II **frustrated** many Americans.

Fortunately, at this time of peak demand, developers figured out how to build affordable housing in a hurry. William Levitt became a leader in mass producing suburban homes. Entire rows of houses in Levittown were built using the same plan. This method enabled workers to build houses in weeks rather than in months. On the installment plan, buyers could pay $58 a month toward the cost of a home. Demand for the homes was so great that Levitt built two other Levittowns—one outside Philadelphia, Pennsylvania, and the other in New Jersey. These houses were ideal for young couples starting out because they were affordable and comfortable. Other developers adopted Levitt's techniques, and suburbs were soon springing up across the country.

Suburban development depended on help from the government. State and federal governments constructed thousands of miles of highways that linked the suburbs to cities. New home buyers benefited from the GI bill and the Federal Housing Administration (FHA), which provided low-interest loans. FHA-backed loans allowed home buyers to pay as little as 5 to 10 percent of the purchase price and to pay off their mortgages over 30 years.

Residents of new suburbs faced the challenge of establishing new towns with churches and schools and police and fire departments. Through these institutions, the suburbanites forged a sense of community. During the 1950s, the suburbs became increasingly self-contained. While suburban residents of earlier generations had depended on the city for entertainment and shopping, the postwar suburban dweller could find a vast array of goods and services in nearby shopping centers.

The "Car Culture" Takes Over During the 1920s, automobile ownership had soared in the United States. With the explosion of suburban growth in the 1950s, Americans grew even more dependent upon their cars. The number of registered automobiles jumped from 26 million in 1945 to 60 million in 1960.

The Car Culture

The automobile industry thrived and, as a result, led to new businesses. As shown here, Americans were happy to spend leisure time in their cars and watch a movie at the local drive-in theater. The number of families that owned cars increased drastically between 1950 and 1960. *Do you think increased car ownership may have had negative effects?*

Car Ownership, 1950–1965

SOURCE: *Historical Statistics of the United States*

History Background

Levittown Levittown was built to fill a need—the need of returning World War II veterans for decent, affordable housing. Levitt and Sons, the company started by William Levitt's father, perfected techniques for mass-producing housing when it got a Navy contract to quickly build homes for shipyard workers at the start of World War II. The assembly-line houses were built on slabs, using precut lumber.

The first Levittown was built on former potato fields in Long Island, New York. Levitt and Sons initially planned 2,000 rental houses. The company announced this plan, and within two days, the eager public had rented half of the homes.

In 1949, Levitt and Sons turned to building larger homes that families could buy for about $8,000. The terms were generous—only about $100 down and a monthly payments of just $58.00.

By 1951, Levitt and Sons had built more than 17,000 homes on Long Island. Other Levittowns also were built during the postwar years—one in Pennsylvania and the other in New Jersey.

Chapter 13 Section 2 **441**

Independent Practice
Display Color Transparency: *Levittown.* Tell students to take the role of a developer trying to sell new suburban houses to city dwellers. Have students create a print ad that would run in a daily newspaper. Color Transparencies **A-113**

Monitor Progress
As students fill in their charts, circulate to make sure that they understand the main ideas of the section. For a completed version of the table, see Note Taking Transparencies, **B-124a.**

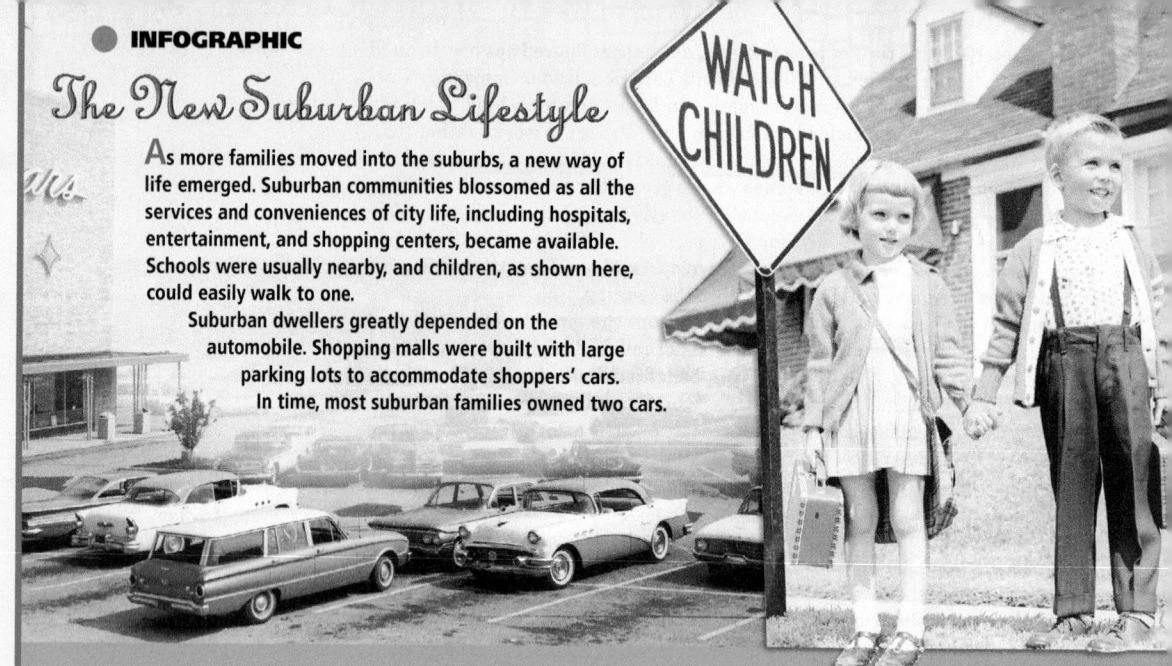

● **INFOGRAPHIC**

The New Suburban Lifestyle

As more families moved into the suburbs, a new way of life emerged. Suburban communities blossomed as all the services and conveniences of city life, including hospitals, entertainment, and shopping centers, became available. Schools were usually nearby, and children, as shown here, could easily walk to one.

Suburban dwellers greatly depended on the automobile. Shopping malls were built with large parking lots to accommodate shoppers' cars. In time, most suburban families owned two cars.

These new automobiles tended to have big engines and enormous horsepower. They came with the newest technology, such as power steering and brakes and automatic transmission. Harley Earl of the Ford Motor Company captured the mood of the 1950s by designing cars with lots of chrome that reminded people of jet planes.

While some suburbanites rode the train or other forms of mass transportation, Americans increasingly depended upon their cars to commute to work. Suburbanites also needed their cars to shop at suburban shopping malls. Entrepreneurs opened fast-food restaurants and drive-in movie theaters, both of which catered to the car culture. While these businesses flourished, many older businesses, often located in older city neighborhoods, struggled to survive.

✔ **Checkpoint** How did Americans living in the suburbs benefit from the "car culture"?

Eisenhower Interstate Highway System

The scale of suburban growth would not have been remotely possible without a massive federal program of highway building. Committed to the idea of easing automobile travel, President Eisenhower authorized the first funding of the interstate system in 1953. Further legislation passed by Congress in 1956 resulted in the **Interstate Highway Act,** which authorized funds to build 41,000 miles of highway consisting of multilane expressways that would connect the nation's major cities. This represented the biggest expenditure on public works in history, bigger by far than any project <u>undertaken</u> during the New Deal. In 1990, further recognition of President Eisenhower's role in establishing the massive highway system led to a renaming of the highways. It became the Dwight D. Eisenhower System of Interstate and Defense Highways.

Vocabulary Builder
<u>undertake</u>–(uhn der TAYK) *v.* to take upon oneself; agree to do

---

Differentiated Instruction Solutions for All Learners

L1 Special Needs Students **L2 English Language Learners** **L2 Less Proficient Readers**

Students see newspaper headlines every day. Ask **Do newspaper headlines ever express a point of view, or do they just tell what happened?** *(They sometimes express a point of view.)* **How do you know whether a headline is expressing a point of view?** *(You can tell by the kind of language it uses and what it says.)* Then, write these two "headlines" on the board. "New Shopping Mall Opens on Oak Street," and "New Mall Kills Hometown

Businesses." Ask **Which headline expresses the writer's point of view? Why?** *(The second one; it says that the mall "kills" businesses.)* **How does the writer of the second headline feel about the new shopping mall?** *(The writer probably does not support the new mall.)* Now, have each student write a headline for the Interstate Highway Act on the board. Have the class determine whether each headline states facts or expresses a certain bias.

Answer

✔ Many new businesses opened in the suburbs—shopping malls, fast-food restaurants, drive-in movie theaters—that people could reach easily only by car.

Suburban dwellers began to spend more time taking ▶ care of their lawns and gardens. As a result, lawn mowers became increasingly popular. The young man here is using his new lawn mower.

◀ Families tended to spend more time together. Backyard cookouts were popular pastimes. Usually, hamburgers or frankfurters were prepared on outdoor grills.

Thinking Critically

1. **Recognize Cause and Effect** How did the growth of the suburbs affect Americans?

2. **Draw Conclusions** One author described suburban living as "a life of dreariness." Do you agree? Explain.

History *Interactive* ∗

For: More about suburban life in the 1950s
www.pearsonschool.com/ushist

Besides easing commutes from suburbs to cities, highways boosted the travel and vacation industries. Vacationers drove to national parks, to beaches, and to new destinations, such as Las Vegas. With more money and more children, families sought leisure activity. Walt Disney met this demand by building an extraordinary amusement park in California. Disneyland excited the imagination with visions of the future, including make-believe rides in space.

✓ **Checkpoint** How did the Interstate Highway System spur the growth of the suburbs?

Migrating to the Sunbelt

In 1958, two New York baseball teams—the Dodgers and the Giants—moved to California. Their move reflected another crucial trend of the postwar era, the growth of the **Sunbelt,** the name given to the southern and western states. By the mid-1960s, California passed New York as the state with the largest population. The migration to Sunbelt cities, such as Houston, Texas, and Los Angeles, California, continued for the rest of the twentieth century.

Reasons for Migration Many factors played a role in attracting people to the Sunbelt. California, which added more than 5 million new residents in the 1940s and 1950s, had both an appealing climate and a large number of jobs in defense industries. The explosive growth of the aerospace and electronics industries also attracted newcomers to the Sunbelt.

The development of air conditioning also played a major role. Invented in 1902, air conditioners were at first used only in public buildings, such as movie theaters and courthouses. But after World War II, the development of window units made it possible to cool homes. Northerners who had visited states like Florida, Texas, or Arizona only in winter could now live in hotter climates all year round.

NoteTaking

Reading Skill: Identify Causes and Effects As you read, identify the effects of the population shift to the Sunbelt.

Moving to the Sunbelt	
Causes	**Effects**
• Jobs	•
•	•

Eisenhower Interstate Highway System ⑬

Instruct

- **Introduce** Display Color Transparency: *The Interstate Highway System.* Then, have students analyze the photograph. Ask students to discuss the image of America that the photograph conveys. Color Transparencies **A-114**

- **Teach** Ask **What was the Interstate Highway Act?** *(It was legislation that authorized the spending of billions of dollars to build a system of thousands of miles of interstate highways in the United States.)* **How did the new highways affect the economy?** *(They allowed people and goods to travel more easily between cities and suburbs, and they aided the growth of the travel and tourism industries.)* **Would political leaders from cities or suburbs have been more supportive of the new highways? Why?** *(Leaders from the suburbs would have been more supportive because the new highways benefited their constituents.)*

Independent Practice

Instruct students to complete the worksheet *Outline Map: Interstate Highways.* Teaching Resources, **p. 17**

Monitor Progress

As students complete their worksheets, circulate to make sure that they are completing the map properly.

Differentiated Instruction   Solutions for All Learners

ⓛ Advanced Readers   ⓛ Gifted and Talented Students

Migration to the Sunbelt was a feature of the postwar years in the United States. Have students research the migration routes—who went south and west, what their main destinations were, and why they went. Have each student choose a migration route and destination and think of himself or herself as a person who moved to the Sunbelt along that route in the 1950s. Instruct students to write a letter home to a friend explaining and describing where and how they traveled, where they intend to live, and what they hope their life will be like in their new home. Invite volunteers to read their letters to the class.

Answers

✓ The new highways made it easier for people to live in the suburbs but still use cars to commute to jobs in the cities.

Thinking Critically

1. Possible response: As the population increased, city-life services became available in the suburbs. Also, people depended more on their cars.

2. Possible response: No, because suburbs have more open space in which to enjoy outdoor activities.

Migrating to the Sunbelt

Instruct

- **Introduce: Key Term** Ask students to locate the key term *Sunbelt* (in bold) in the text and define it. Discuss why the southern and western states would have been given the name *"Sunbelt."*

- **Teach** Ask **Why did many people migrate to the Sunbelt during the postwar years?** *(There were many jobs available and the climate also appealed to many people.)* **Where in the Sunbelt did various groups of Latino immigrants live?** *(Many Cubans went to Miami, and most Mexicans and Mexican Americans lived in cities such as Los Angeles, El Paso, and Phoenix.)* **How did migration to the Sunbelt affect the balance of political power in the United States?** *(Urban areas of the Northeast and Midwest suffered losses of political power, and areas in the Sunbelt gained political power.)*

Independent Practice

- Have students access **www.pearsonschool.com/ushist** to use the Geography Interactive map and then answer the map skills questions in the text.

- **NoteTaking** Have students complete the graphic organizer identifying the causes of the migration to the Sunbelt and the effects of the population shift. Reading and Note Taking Study Guide

Monitor Progress

As students complete their graphic organizers, circulate to make sure that they understand the causes and the effects of the population shift. For a completed version of the graphic organizer, see Note Taking Transparencies, B-124b.

Answers

Map Skills

1. Review locations with students.
2. Possible response: Nevada, California, Arizona
3. Sample answer: Population probably decreased because people were moving to the suburbs and to Sunbelt states.

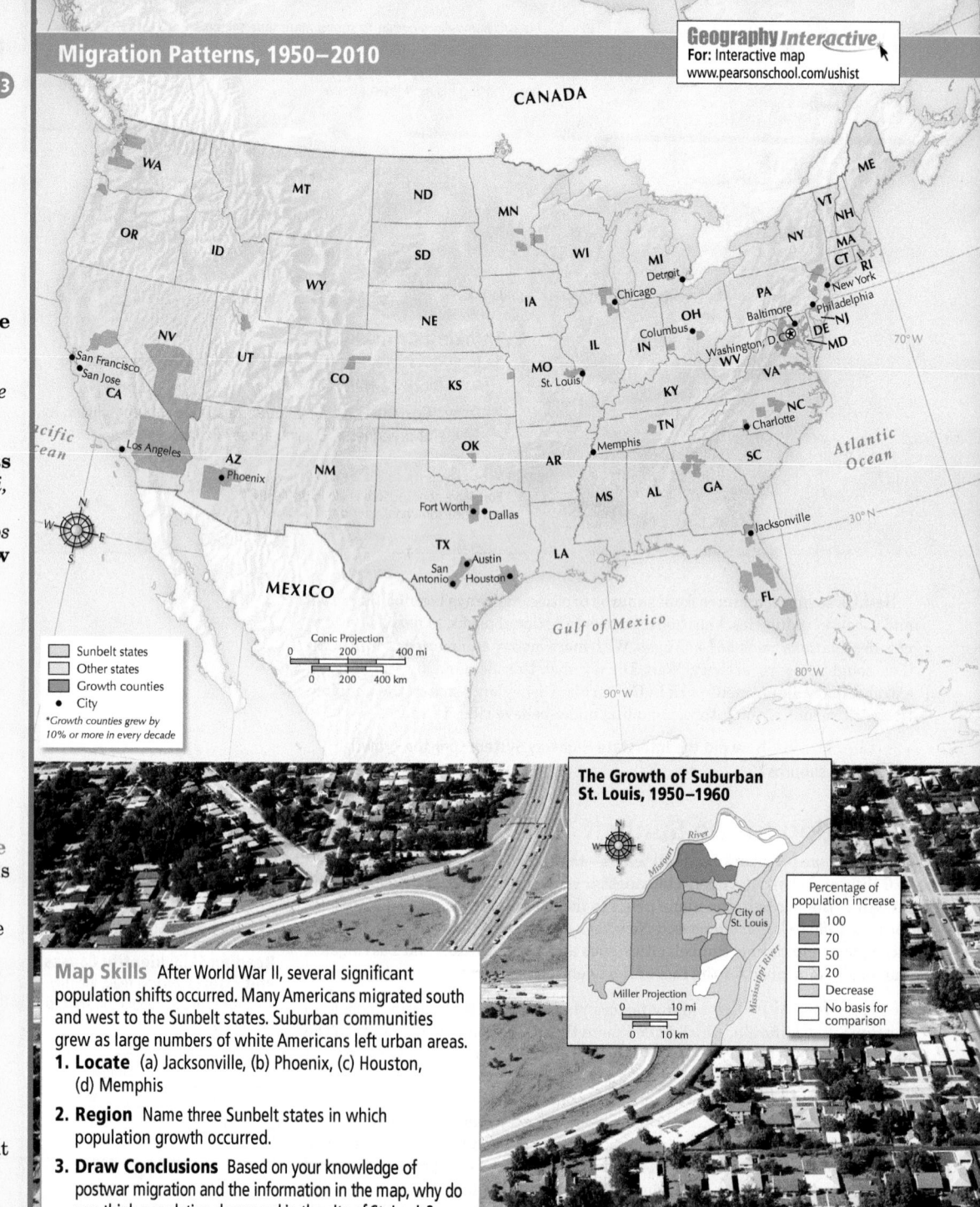

Migration Patterns, 1950–2010

Geography *Interactive*
For: Interactive map
www.pearsonschool.com/ushist

Legend:
- Sunbelt states
- Other states
- Growth counties
- • City

*Growth counties grew by 10% or more in every decade

Conic Projection
0   200   400 mi
0   200   400 km

The Growth of Suburban St. Louis, 1950–1960

Percentage of population increase
- 100
- 70
- 50
- 20
- Decrease
- No basis for comparison

Miller Projection
0   10 mi
0   10 km

Map Skills After World War II, several significant population shifts occurred. Many Americans migrated south and west to the Sunbelt states. Suburban communities grew as large numbers of white Americans left urban areas.

1. **Locate** (a) Jacksonville, (b) Phoenix, (c) Houston, (d) Memphis

2. **Region** Name three Sunbelt states in which population growth occurred.

3. **Draw Conclusions** Based on your knowledge of postwar migration and the information in the map, why do you think population decreased in the city of St. Louis?

Connect to Your World

Sunbelt Migration Warm weather attracted large numbers of people to the Sunbelt states. Still, there is a good chance that the population of this area would not have grown as large or as quickly as it did without help from the federal government and one important invention.

The growth of cities and farms in the West is dependent on the availability of water. A system of dams, aqueducts, water tunnels, and other infrastructure brings water to this region, much of which is desert. Many of these projects were built with federal funds. For example, federal and state money paid for a system to bring water to the Central Valley and Los Angeles. The federally funded Hoover Dam provides electricity and a reliable water supply to Las Vegas—a city located in a dry region that is among the fastest-growing areas in the nation.

Also contributing to Sunbelt growth, the window air conditioner became largely affordable in the 1950s. As a result, life in the deserts of the Southwest or the summer heat of Florida became possible for people who otherwise would not have considered Sunbelt homes.

Latinos contributed to the growth of the Sunbelt. In the late 1950s and early 1960s, many Cubans, who were escaping the new regime of Fidel Castro, made Miami, Florida, their new home. Prior to World War II, most Mexican Americans lived in rural areas. However, by the 1960s, the majority of them migrated to urban areas, such as Los Angeles, El Paso, and Phoenix.

Impact of Migration The shift to the suburbs and the Sunbelt had a momentous impact on American society. As people moved, their political power went with them. Thus, suburbs and the Sunbelt gained representation. Urbanites in the Northeast and Midwest lost political power. California's representation in the House of Representatives, for example, more than doubled between 1948 and 1998.

Urban and suburban growth created environmental concerns, ranging from traffic jams and smog to water shortages. In the 1960s and 1970s, environmental groups would begin to grapple with some of the byproducts of this growth.

✓ **Checkpoint** What motivated so many Americans to migrate to the Sunbelt?

The American Economy Changes Focus

These important postwar population shifts were matched by equally groundbreaking structural changes in the American economy. For the first time in American history, more people found employment in the **service sector,** businesses that provide services, such as healthcare, law, retail, banking, or insurance, than in the manufacturing sector. These shifts led some to describe the United States as a postindustrial society.

The Service Sector Grows Between 1947 and 1957, the percentage of the American workforce employed in industrial or blue-collar jobs declined 4 percent. During the same time period, employment in the service sector, or white-collar jobs, rapidly grew. The new workforce included many who worked in **information industries,** including those who built or operated the first computers. These computers were enormous. One of the first, named ENIAC, short for Electronic Numerical Integrator and Computer, took up roughly 18,000 square feet, or the size of three basketball courts! Despite its size, it was less powerful than today's desktop computer.

Still, ENIAC was a remarkable advance. By the 1960s, the government and private industry had found many uses for the computer. Hotels used computers to help make reservations, and banks used them to keep track of accounts. Industries started using computers to automate work or perform jobs once done by people.

Meanwhile, the number of women in the labor force continued to grow, doubling between 1940 and 1960. Many of these women worked part time. Few pursued long-term careers and most remained underpaid. Yet, without their paychecks, their families would have found it difficult to remain in the middle class.

While the service sector grew rapidly, both the number and percentage of Americans who made a living by farming continued to decline. In 1935, one fourth of the nation's families lived on farms. By 1960, less than one in ten families did. At the same

White-Collar Jobs
The number of white-collar workers, such as the office workers shown here, greatly increased in the 1950s.

The American Economy Changes Focus Ⓦ

Instruct

- **Introduce: Key Term** Have students find the key term *service sector* (in bold) in the text and define it. Tell students that, for the first time, more people found jobs in the *service sector* than in manufacturing. Have students list some *service sector* businesses. Discuss why these businesses grew in the 1950s.

- **Teach** Direct students to look at the image on the bottom of this page. Ask **Do you think these people work in the service sector or in manufacturing? Why?** *(The service sector; they are in an office, which probably provides a service such as insurance or accounting, rather than in a factory, which manufactures goods.)* **How did the introduction of computers increase productivity?** *(Computers could quickly do the work once done by people.)* **How did new technology affect farmers?** *(It allowed them to grow more food per acre but also resulted in fewer family farms.)* **Why would the new AFL-CIO have had more power than the two unions did separately?** *(Sample response: With more members, the union would have had more power because of its ability to call strikes that could disrupt more industries.)*

- **Quick Activity** Have each student write a question about the U.S. economy on one side of a note card and the answer on the other. Have students exchange note cards with a partner and write the answer. Students should check their answers.

Independent Practice

Have students write paragraphs explaining why the United States emerged as a world economic power following World War II.

Monitor Progress

As students write their responses, circulate to make sure that they understand the factors that led to U.S. economic dominance after the war.

Answer

✓ Appealing climate, new highways, and jobs in industries such as electronics and petrochemicals. Air conditioning also made it easier for people to live in the Sunbelt.

Educational Opportunities Expand

Instruct

- **Introduce** Note that the number of people graduating from high school and college soared in the postwar years. Have students discuss why many people believed that this was important for continued improvement of the U.S. economy.

- **Teach** Ask **Why was the National Defense Education Act passed?** *(Its goal was to produce more scientists and science teachers.)* **Why was this an important national goal?** *(The U.S. government felt threatened by Soviet advances in space and did not want to fall behind.)* **Why did the U.S. government try to make education more accessible in the postwar years?** *(Sample answer: Higher education increased productivity. It also allowed workers to increase their standard of living, which helped the economy.)*

- **Analyzing the Visuals** Have students look at the image on the next page. Ask **What do you notice about this classroom?** *(Sample response: Classes were full, desks are in rows and look different from desks used today.)* **Why did the U.S. government greatly increase education funds to states during this decade?** *(to meet the demands of growing classrooms and to stay in the space race with the Soviet Union)*

Independent Practice

The postwar period was a time of growth for organized labor. Ask students to form small groups and create a brochure either encouraging people to join a union or discouraging people from joining.

Monitor Progress

As students complete their brochures, circulate to make sure that they understand the benefits and issues surrounding unions in the 1950s.

Answer

✔ More people began to find jobs in the service sector of the economy rather than in manufacturing or farming. Information industries grew, as did franchises. Many companies also became multinational, doing business throughout the world instead of only in the United States.

---

time, improvements in technology, ranging from mechanical cotton pickers to chemical pesticides, made agriculture much more productive. This allowed fewer workers to grow even more food. New irrigation systems helped transform much of the land in the Southwest from arid to fertile fields.

Entrepreneurs Start Businesses At home, the postwar era saw the rise of **franchise businesses.** A franchise business allows a company to distribute its products or services through retail outlets owned by independent operators. Franchises were attractive to consumers because they stressed quality and sameness, no matter where one was in the United States. The Holiday Inn franchise came into existence following a trip that home builder Kemmons Wilson took to Washington, D.C., with his family of five children. <u>Frustrated</u>, Wilson found hotels difficult to locate, overpriced, and lacking adequate parking facilities. As he traveled, according to author David Halberstam, "Wilson became more irritated until he turned to his wife and announced that he was going into the hotel business. Everyone in this country, he thought, had a car and a family, and sooner or later everyone had to go somewhere." Today, there are tens of thousands of Holiday Inn hotels all over the world.

Many postwar critics lamented the growth of franchise businesses. For them, the franchises represented a growing lack of originality, evidence that the United States was becoming a "bland" nation in which people ate bland food, lived in bland look-a-like houses, and watched bland television shows that followed the same plot line.

American Corporations Go Multinational As the postwar economy expanded, so did **multinational corporations,** companies that produced and sold their goods and services all over the world and established branches abroad. General Motors, General Electric, and IBM, produced a larger and larger share of all of the goods sold. Many of these corporations earned large portions of their profits abroad. Coca Cola, for instance, sold its soft drinks all over the globe. Hollywood movies found eager audiences in Tokyo, Mexico City, and Germany.

Unions Consolidate Their Gains The prosperity of the 1950s was reflected in generally good times for the labor movement. In 1955, the AFL and the CIO, which had split in the mid-1930s, united to form the **AFL-CIO.** The new organization enjoyed a good deal of political clout, especially within the Democratic Party. Yet, trade unions also lost some momentum during the late 1940s and early 1950s. Most of the new white-collar workers did not join unions, and labor's image was tarnished by a corruption scandal involving the Teamsters Union. Government investigators accused the Teamsters, who represented truck drivers, of illegally using their members' funds.

✔ **Checkpoint** In what ways did American businesses change during the postwar period?

Educational Opportunities Expand

As the economy grew, so too did opportunities for Americans to attain higher education. A more educated workforce boosted economic productivity. In 1940, only about 15 percent of college-age Americans attended college. By the early 1960s, however, close to 40 percent did. The percentage of Americans who completed high school also rose sharply. "The astonishing growth of education in the late

Vocabulary Builder
<u>frustrate</u>–(FRUHS trayt) *v.* to annoy; disappoint

Labor Leader
George Meany served as the first president of the AFL-CIO.

Differentiated Instruction — Solutions for All Learners

L1 Special Needs Students   **L2 English Language Learners**   **L2 Less Proficient Readers**

Have students choose one person, event, or trend featured in this section. Then have them create an illustration of that person, event, or trend. Students should then write a caption under the illustration to clearly explain it. Illustrations can be anything from descriptive drawings to political cartoons.

Encourage students to use creativity as well as humor. Ask English-speaking students to help students learning English with composing simple captions for their illustrations.

1940s (and thereafter)," wrote historian James Patterson, "seemed yet another sign that the American Dream was well and alive."

Government Provides Funding for Education Large sums of money were needed to meet the education needs of the baby-boom generation. In the 1950s and early 1960s, California opened a new school about once a week. Most of the funding for education came from local and state governments, but after the Soviet Union launched *Sputnik 1* in 1957, many Americans called for more federal funds for education.

In a mood of crisis, Congress quickly approved the National Defense Education Act. Its $1 billion program was aimed at producing more scientists and science teachers. The act authorized money for loans to high school and college graduates to continue their scientific education.

Education Is "Democratized" The postwar era saw the stirrings of a movement to make education more accessible. Many states poured funds into their public universities, making it easier for ordinary Americans to attend college. California, for example, established a **California Master Plan,** which called for three tiers of higher education: research universities, state colleges, and community colleges. All of them were to be accessible to all of the state's citizens. Other states also built or expanded their college systems. On another front, in 1954, the Supreme Court ruled in *Brown* v. *Board of Education of Topeka* that segregated schools were unconstitutional. However, it would be years before many schools were actually integrated.

✔ **Checkpoint** How did American education change in the years following World War II?

Growing Classrooms
Class sizes increased as baby-boom children reached school age. The number of high school and college graduates soared.

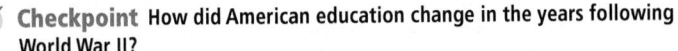

SECTION

2 **Assessment**

Progress Monitoring *Online*
For: Self-test with vocabulary practice
www.pearsonschool.com/ushist

Comprehension

1. **Terms and People** What is the relationship between each of the following terms and the social and economic changes that took place in the postwar period?
   - Interstate Highway Act
   - Sunbelt
   - service sector
   - information industries
   - franchise business

2. NoteTaking **Reading Skill: Identify Main Ideas** Use your chart to answer the Section Focus Question: What social and economic factors changed American life during the 1950s?

Writing About History

3. **Quick Write: Evaluate Sources** Choose a topic from this section for further research. Use the Internet or the library to find one source that provides information about your selected topic. Determine the reliability of the source. Consider the following:
   - Is it a primary or secondary source?
   - Is the information supported by the evidence?
   - Is the information mostly facts or mostly opinions?
   - If you are using the Internet, is the information from a Web site that is known for being reliable?

Critical Thinking

4. **Draw Conclusions** What were the benefits of the Interstate Highway Act? What were the disadvantages?

5. **Demonstrate Reasoned Judgment** Do you think it was easy for people in declining manufacturing industries to switch into the service sector? Explain your answer.

6. **Synthesize Information** How did the Sunbelt states benefit from the growth of the automobile and air conditioning industries?

Objectives

As you teach this section, keep students focused on the following objectives to help them answer the Section Focus Question and master core content.

- Explain why consumer spending increased.
- Discuss postwar changes in family life.
- Describe the rise of new forms of mass culture.

Prepare to Read

Background Knowledge L3

Refer students to the images on this page, and have them describe these fads of the 1950s. Have them identify the types of things that usually generate fads—popular TV shows, movies, music, and so on.

Set a Purpose L3

- **WITNESS HISTORY** Read the selection aloud.

  Ask **What was the source of the Davy Crockett fad?** (*a popular TV show*) **What does the Spielberg quotation suggest about the power of such fads?** (*Sample answer: that most people were swept up in them, and those who were not often felt like outsiders or were treated that way*)

- **Focus** Point out the Section Focus Question, and write it on the board. Tell students to refer to this question as they read. (*Answer appears with Section 3 Assessment answers.*)

- **Preview** Have students preview the Section Objectives and the list of Terms and People.

- NoteTaking Using the Guided Questioning strategy (TE, p. T20), have students read this section. As they read, have students complete the outline by identifying changes during the postwar years. Reading and Note Taking Study Guide

◀ Baby-boomer fads were often based on popular television shows.

WITNESS HISTORY

The Latest Fad

As baby boomers went to school, new fads came and went with amazing speed. One such fad revolved around a popular television show about the American folk hero Davy Crockett. Steven Spielberg, who later would become one of Hollywood's most successful movie directors, recalled the craze.

❝I was in third grade at the time. Suddenly, the next day, everybody in my class but me was Davy Crockett. And because I didn't have my coonskin cap and my powder horn, or Old Betsy, my rifle, and my chaps, I was deemed the Mexican leader, Santa Anna. And they chased me home from school until I got my parents to buy me a coonskin cap.❞

—Steven Spielberg, recalling the Davy Crockett craze of 1955

Mass Culture and Family Life

Objectives
- Explain why consumer spending increased.
- Discuss postwar changes in family life.
- Describe the rise of new forms of mass culture.

Terms and People

consumerism
median family income
nuclear family

Benjamin Spock
rock-and-roll
Elvis Presley

NoteTaking

Reading Skill: Identify Main Ideas Identify postwar changes in daily life and popular culture.

> I. The Culture of Consumerism
>   A. Americans spend more
>   1. Increased family income
>   2.

Why It Matters During the 1950s, the ideal family was one in which men worked and supported their families and women stayed home and reared their children. Television and other forms of mass culture suggested that this ideal was the norm. Whether most American families actually lived like the ones they saw on prime-time television, however, remains unclear. The family values of the 1950s still affect who we are and who we want to be. **Section Focus Question: How did popular culture and family life change during the 1950s?**

The Culture of Consumerism

For much of our history, Americans had been taught to save their money. "A penny saved is a penny earned," advised Benjamin Franklin. However, as the U.S. economy began to boom in the postwar era, Americans were caught up in a wave of **consumerism,** buying as much as they could, much of it on credit. What accounted for this spending spree?

Spending Is Easy One reason Americans spent more was that they had more money to spend. During the 1950s, **median family income,** or average family income, rose from $3,319 to $5,417. The average American family now had twice as much real income as the average family had during the prosperous years of the 1920s. Consumer-oriented companies found new and innovative ways to encourage buying on credit. For example, General Motors advertised

Vocabulary Builder

Use the information below and the following resource to teach students the high-use words from this section. Teaching Resources, Vocabulary Builder, p. 11

High-Use Words	Definitions and Sample Sentences
nevertheless	*adv.* in spite of that; however Many children seemed to have everything they needed; **nevertheless,** parents continued to indulge them.
recur	*v.* to happen or occur again, especially after some lapse of time After the industrial expansion of World War II ended, many people thought the hard times of the depression might **recur.**

its cars with the slogan "Buy Now, Pay Later." The Diner's Club introduced the first credit card.

Buying New Conveniences Home appliances topped the list of the goods that Americans bought. Families purchased electric washing machines and dryers, refrigerators and ranges. These labor-saving appliances helped transform housework, lessening the physical demands of everything from washing clothes to preserving foods.

With money to spend, easy credit, and new goods to buy, shopping became a new pastime for Americans. Supermarkets, where customers could buy everything from milk to mops, appeared. Shopping centers sprouted all over suburbia.

One product that Americans bought in record numbers was a television. In 1946, manufacturers produced fewer than 6,000 TV sets. Seven years later, Americans purchased 7 million sets and by the end of the decade, 90 percent of all households owned a television.

✓ **Checkpoint** What were some reasons why consumer spending skyrocketed in the postwar era?

Family Life in the Fifties

During World War II, many women—including married women with children—had gone off to work in factories. In 1943, women made up 25 percent of the workers in the wartime auto industry. With the war's end, however, most of the women who had entered the workforce returned to being homemakers. Now, a more traditional image of the family took hold, one in which women stayed home and men served as "breadwinners." Women who wanted a career outside the home faced social pressures to rethink their decisions.

Portraying the "Ideal" Family In the popular magazines of the postwar era, social scientists and other opinion makers described the **nuclear family,** or a household consisting of a mother and father and their children, as the backbone of American society. For the nuclear family to function smoothly, experts claimed, women had to accept their role as homemakers. Television shows and movies made similar assertions. For example, in the 1955 Hollywood movie *The Tender Trap,* actress Debbie Reynolds declared, "A woman isn't a woman unless she's been married and had children."

As the 1950s progressed, however, more women were willing to challenge the view that a woman could not have a career outside the home. By 1960, women held one third of the nation's jobs. Approximately half of these women workers were married.

Children Are the Focus More so than in the past, family life revolved around children. Not surprisingly, the best-selling book of the era was Dr. **Benjamin Spock**'s *Common Sense Book of Baby and Child Care.* Parents bought and read his book because they wanted expert advice on how to raise their children. Spock emphasized the importance of nurturing children, from their earliest days as infants through their teen years. Mothers, Spock suggested, should not

The Homemaker
The ideal housewife stayed at home and raised the children. She used the latest appliances, dressed well, and took advantage of faster ways to prepare meals. The ad is for a convenience food—rice that can be prepared in a few minutes.

Teach

The Culture of Consumerism 🅛

Instruct

- **Introduce: Key Term** Direct students' attention to the key term *consumerism* (in bold), and discuss the values it suggests were important in 1950s America. Ask students to determine what a "culture of *consumerism*" might be.

- **Teach** Using the Numbered Heads strategy (TE, p. T23), have students analyze the effects of consumerism. Ask **How do you think buying on credit changed the habits of American consumers in the 1950s?** *(Sample answer: It led people of ordinary means to buy expensive items that they probably could not have afforded otherwise.)* **How did this affect the American economy?** *(It led to growth as the purchase of more goods caused factories to hire more people to make the goods.)*

- **Quick Activity** Tell students to choose a product and write the script for a radio ad that would promote it. Instruct students to pay attention to the benefits of owning or using the product. If possible, have students record their ads. Play the ads in class, and have students evaluate their effectiveness.

Independent Practice

Have students debate the effects of consumerism on American society in the 1950s. Include effects on businesses, workers, and family finances in the discussion.

Monitor Progress

As students complete their outlines, circulate to make sure that they understand the ways in which daily life and popular culture changed during the postwar years. For a completed version of the outline, see Note Taking Transparencies, B-125.

Answer

✓ Incomes rose, and Americans had more money to spend. People wanted to buy new labor-saving appliances, cars, and other goods, which were increasingly available to buy on credit.

Instruct

- **Introduce** Discuss what "family life" means to students. Ask them whether they think family life changes from one period in history to another.

- **Teach** Ask **What was the ideal family of the 1950s like?** *(a married couple with children, in which the man worked and the woman stayed at home caring for the home and the children)* **How does the ideal family of the 1950s compare with the family of today?** *(Answers should contain the idea that people have many types of families today.)* Discuss with students the HISTORY MAKERS feature on this page and the effects of improved health care. **How did the emphasis on children contribute to the growth of the American economy in the 1950s?** *(Parents indulged their children, spending a great deal of money on them for goods and services, which boosted the economy.)* **Was indulging children positive for their development?** *(Accept either point of view. Some students will say it spoiled children, and others will say it nurtured them.)*

- **Quick Activity** Tell students to recall the WITNESS HISTORY at the start of the section. Also, have students examine the Primary Source quotation on this page. Have them write a brief paragraph identifying a fad they once were (or are) part of and what attracted them to the fashion, activity, food, or other thing that had gained popularity.

Independent Practice

Have students look at the Infographic on the next page and answer the Thinking Critically questions.

Monitor Progress

As students write their paragraphs, circulate to make sure that they understand what a fad is and what contributes to creating one.

Answer

✓ American families spent a great deal of money on children and were advised by child-rearing experts to indulge children as much as possible. Women were encouraged to stay at home to take care of the house and raise the children.

Vocabulary Builder
nevertheless–(nehv er thuh LEHS) *adv.* in spite of that; however

Vocabulary Builder
recur–(rih KUHR) *v.* to happen or occur again, especially after some lapse of time

worry about spoiling their children because children could not get too much comfort and love. Some criticized Spock for promoting what they called "a permissive culture." Nevertheless, Spock's book remained extremely popular for several decades.

Another sign of the degree to which family life revolved around children was the amount of money parents spent on their children. Some parents even defended their spending by arguing that such spending guaranteed against the recurrence of another depression.

As baby boomers became teens, their impact on the economy and American culture became even more noticeable. While as children they received toys, such as Davy Crockett caps and Barbie dolls, as teens they purchased very expensive items. As *LIFE* magazine observed:

> **Primary Source** "The time is past when a boy's chief possession was his bike and a girl's party wardrobe consisted of a fancy dress worn with a string of dime-store pearls. . . . Today's teenagers surround themselves with a fantastic array of garish and often expensive baubles and amusements. They own 10 million phonographs, over a million TV sets, 13 million cameras."
>
> —*LIFE*, August 31, 1959

Celebrating a Religious Revival The 1950s also witnessed a revival of religion in the United States. Organized religious groups became more powerful and more church buildings were built. Regular church attendance rose from about 50 million in 1940 to about 80 million in 1958. The increased number of churches in suburban communities across the country helped to strengthen community ties. The evangelist Billy Graham attracted millions to religious revivals that he held around the nation. Roman Catholic bishop Fulton Sheen effectively used television to reach audiences estimated at 10 million a week. During the 1950s, Congress added the words "In God We Trust" to the dollar bill and "under God," to the Pledge of Allegiance. These additions were aimed at making clear the contrast between the centrality of religion in American society and the atheist basis of communist societies.

Improved Healthcare Benefits Baby Boomers During the 1950s, American families benefited from numerous advances in medicine. In 1954, Dr. Jonas Salk developed a vaccine against polio, the disease that had struck down Franklin Roosevelt and that, in 1952 alone, had crippled tens of thousands and killed 1,400, mostly children. By 1960, the widespread distribution of Salk's new vaccine and an oral vaccine developed by Albert Sabin had nearly eliminated the disease.

At the same time, antibiotics, such as penicillin, came into widespread use. The antibiotics helped control numerous infectious diseases caused by bacteria, such as whooping cough and tuberculosis. As a result of these medical advances and a better understanding of the importance of diet, children born after 1946 had a longer life expectancy than those born before 1946.

✓ **Checkpoint** In what ways did family life revolve around children during the 1950s?

HISTORY MAKERS

Jonas Salk (1914–1995)
As a doctor, Salk showed early interest in developing vaccines. In the late 1940s, he turned his attention to polio, which was becoming an alarmingly serious problem. Some researchers thought a polio vaccine would have to use live virus cells, which carried risks. Salk believed dead cells could be used and succeeded in 1952 in developing such a vaccine. When tests proved it successful, the vaccine was ordered for all American children. Eventually, it was used around the world and contributed to eliminating polio.

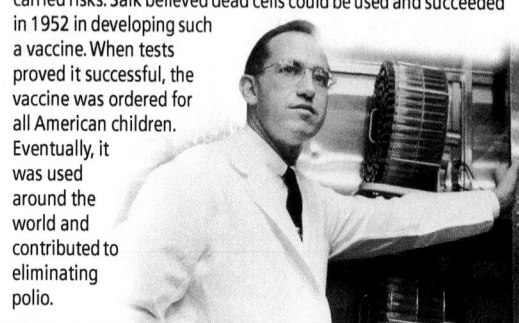

Television Takes Center Stage

In 1938, when television was still just a curiosity, E. B. White, author of *Charlotte's Web*, wrote that it "is going to be the test of the modern world.... We shall stand or fall by the television." While White's view may have been exaggerated, clearly television has had an enormous impact on American society.

Between 1945 and 1960, Americans purchased television sets at a faster pace than they had bought either radios or cars during the 1920s. The popularity of this new technology threatened the movie industry because families stayed home to watch TV rather than go out to watch movies at the theater.

● **INFOGRAPHIC**

BABY-BOOM KIDS

Unlike families in past generations where children were supposed to be seen but not heard, many baby-boom families centered around the children. Dr. Benjamin Spock advised parents to "trust themselves" and not to spank or scold their children. The economy responded to the needs of growing families for housing, clothing, food, and child-friendly entertainment.

▼ *Captain Kangaroo* was a popular children's television program, while a vacation at Disneyland was a treat for the whole family.

First published in ▶ 1946, Dr. Spock's book on child care is still available.

THE CENTURY'S GREATEST BESTSELLER
THE ONE ESSENTIAL PARENTING BOOK

DR. SPOCK'S BABY AND CHILD CARE
BENJAMIN SPOCK, M.D., and MICHAEL B. ROTHENBERG, M.D

▲ These parents happily cater to the needs of their child.

▼ Toy sales rose during the 1950s.

Thinking Critically
1. **Analyze Information** Why do you think the book by Dr. Spock was a bestseller in the 1950s?
2. **Draw Conclusions** How did the baby boom affect American society and economy?

Connect to Your World

African Americans on Television Although African Americans were an important part of American society in the 1950s, images of African American families were rare on TV. Most shows featured all-white casts living in cities or suburban neighborhoods with a lack of racial or ethnic diversity.

The first nationally broadcast show with an African American lead was "Beulah," which ran from 1950–1953. The sitcom centered on the life of an African American maid working for a white family. "Beulah" was joined in 1951 by "Amos 'n' Andy," another sit-com. Some African Americans widely criticized both shows for portraying them in a negative light. "Amos 'n' Andy" ended its short run in 1953.

Fifteen years later, another show with an African American lead finally hit the airwaves. "Julia," a half-hour comedy about a widowed nurse and her young son, ran from 1968 to 1971.

Today, weekly comedies with mainly African American casts are common. However, there are few African American drama series.

Instruct

- **Introduce** Have students read the blue heading "Television Takes Center Stage." Discuss what this meant for family life in the 1950s. Compare and contrast the role of TV today.

- **Teach** Ask **How did television affect other mass media, such as radio and movies?** (*It outpaced both of them during the postwar period.*) **How do you think television shows affected the values and behavior of Americans?** (*Sample answer: Popular television shows influenced the way people behaved and dressed, as well as the products they bought.*) **Why did TV erode regional differences in the United States?** (*With people all over the United States seeing the same programs and ads, tastes and behavior became more similar across the country.*)

- **Quick Activity** Display Color Transparency: *Television and the American Family* and have students look at the images on the next page. Discuss the place that TV had in American life. Color Transparencies A-115

Independent Practice

Have students take the part of an educator giving a speech on the growing influence television is having on children in the 1950s. Have them write a brief speech either praising television's influence and potential for good or denouncing the new medium for its negative impact. Have students share their speeches in class.

Monitor Progress

As students write their speeches, circulate to make sure that they understand the possible positive and negative aspects of television in the 1950s.

Answers

Thinking Critically
1. Because many families centered around children, parents wanted expert advice on raising them.
2. The baby boom benefited the economy because parents spent a lot of money on their children. Society changed because it became more centered on families and children.

Rock-and-Roll Shakes the Nation

L3

Instruct

- **Introduce** Tell students that often teens like and listen to music that some people of older generations do not accept as readily. In the 1950s, it was rock-and-roll. Have students identify types of music today that are accepted more by younger people than by their parents.

- **Teach** Ask **What is the origin of rock music?** *(African American musical traditions such as gospel and rhythm and blues.)* **Why were the earliest forms of rock-and-roll known more to African Americans than to whites?** *(Jim Crow laws kept the races separate, and many whites were not exposed to the music that many African Americans listened to.)* **How did Elvis Presley's music make white teens aware of African American-influenced rock-and-roll?** *(Presley was a white performer who incorporated African American musical traditions into his music. Because he was white, Presley's music had the type of exposure to a white audience that the music of African American performers did not.)*

- **Quick Activity** Families all across America sat down together to watch Ed Sullivan every Sunday night. Have students write an introduction that Ed Sullivan might have used when introducing Presley on stage for the first time. Tell students that the introduction has to capture who Presley was, why his music was important, and why Sullivan wanted to present him to the American public.

Independent Practice

Have students read the worksheet, *Biography: Rock-and-Roll Musicians* and answer the questions. Teaching Resources, **p. 18**

Monitor Progress

To ensure comprehension of the material in this section, have students write one sentence that summarizes the main idea of each blue heading within it.

Answer

✓ TV sitcoms often portrayed idealized families living in the suburbs. Seeing these images reinforced this idea of the nuclear family in the minds of Americans.

A New Entertainment

Each week, families gathered to watch their favorite television shows. Viewers followed the adventures of a masked Lone Ranger and his Indian companion Tonto. The beloved sitcom *I Love Lucy*, starring Lucille Ball, ran for nearly six years. *Beat the Clock*, a popular game show, challenged participants to engage in unusual stunts. Ads such as the one below urged Americans to keep buying televisions.

◄ Lucille Ball

◄ The Lone Ranger and Tonto

▲ Beat The Clock

Although television attracted viewers of all ages, it had a special influence on children. Baby-boom children rushed home from school to watch the *Howdy Doody Show* or the *Mickey Mouse Club*. Children also watched hours of cartoons and shows featuring their favorite superheroes, such as the Lone Ranger. Westerns were especially popular during the 1950s and early 1960s.

Among the most memorable shows were sitcoms about families. Fifty million Americans tuned in each week to watch the *I Love Lucy* show, starring the comedic actress Lucille Ball. Other popular family sitcoms included *Leave It to Beaver*, *The Adventures of Ozzie and Harriet*, and *Father Knows Best*.

These shows reflected and reinforced the ideal of the 1950s family. None of the family sitcoms had important African American characters. None of the major characters got divorced. Major real-life problems, such as mental illness, alcoholism, and personal depression, rarely, if ever, appeared. Writes David Halberstam, "No family problem was so great that it could not be cleared up within the allotted twenty-two minutes."

Even before television emerged in the 1950s, a mass national culture had begun to develop in the United States. Nationally broadcast radio programs, Hollywood films, and other forms of popular culture had helped erode distinct regional and ethnic cultures. Television sped up and reinforced this process. Americans in every region of the country watched the same shows and bought the same goods they saw advertised.

Television changed political campaigns. During the 1952 presidential campaign, Americans could see the candidates in action. Usually, candidates with more money could buy more advertising time. The impact of television on elections continues today.

✓ **Checkpoint** How did television reflect and reinforce the ideal of the nuclear family in the postwar period?

Differentiated Instruction Solutions for All Learners

L1 Special Needs Students **L2 English Language Learners** **L2 Less Proficient Readers**

Instruct students to make a web diagram that shows information about rock-and-roll. Have them start by rereading the text under the blue heading "Rock-and-Roll Shakes the Nation." Students can then write the word "rock-and-roll" in the middle of a circle and start to connect details to it, such as "gospel and blues origins." Tell students to take as much detail about rock-and-roll out of the text as they can to flesh out their web diagrams. Have them share and compare their web diagrams with a partner when they are finished.

Give your family a new thrill this Christmas morning
Motorola TV

VITAMEATAVEGAMIN FOR HEALTH

Rock-and-Roll Shakes the Nation

In the summer of 1951, a relatively unknown white disc jockey named Alan Freed began broadcasting what commonly had been called "race" music to listeners across the Midwest. Renaming the music **rock-and-roll,** Freed planted the seed for a cultural revolution that would blossom in the mid-1950s.

Drawing on African American Roots Rock music originated in the rhythm and blues traditions of African Americans. As African Americans began to move north, they brought their musical traditions with them. Independent recording companies began recording rhythm and blues (R&B) music. Rock-and-roll borrowed heavily from rhythm and blues. As Chuck Berry, known as the pioneer of rock-and-roll, put it, "It used to be called boogie-woogie, it used to be called blues, used to be called rhythm and blues. . . . It's called rock now."

Attracting a Wider Audience Live performances of rhythm and blues music was long kept separate from whites by Jim Crow laws in the South or by more subtle forms of segregation in the North. Through the radio, it began to attract a wider white audience in the postwar era. For example, a young **Elvis Presley** listened to a Memphis radio station that played African American gospel tunes. He began to integrate those tunes into the music he played. Meanwhile, in the early 1950s, Sam Phillips set up a recording studio in Memphis to record and play the music of some of Memphis's best African American blues performers, such as B. B. King. One day Phillips heard Presley and almost immediately recognized that he had found the person he had been looking for.

Presley's arrival set off the new rock craze. His first hit, "Heartbreak Hotel," sold in the millions and his success sparked popularity for rock music.

Yet, not everyone liked Elvis or the new rock craze. When Ed Sullivan, the host of a famous TV variety show, invited Elvis to sing on his show, he directed cameramen to show Elvis only from the waist up, because many parents objected to Elvis's gyrating hips and tight pants. Ministers complained about the passions that rock music seemed to unleash among so many youngsters. Congress held hearings on the subversive nature of rock music. Nonetheless, it became a symbol of the emerging youth culture and of the growing power of youth on mass culture.

✔ **Checkpoint** How did rock-and-roll gain popularity?

Popular Music
The record business boomed during the 1950s. Phonograph records, such as the one shown here, were made from vinyl, a plastic material. Listeners could enjoy nearly 30 minutes of music on each side.

Comprehension

1. **Terms and People** For each item below, write two or three sentences explaining its significance.
   • consumerism
   • median family income
   • Benjamin Spock
   • Elvis Presley

2. NoteTaking **Reading Skill: Identify Main Ideas** Use your outline about changes in daily life and popular culture to answer the Section Focus Question: How did popular culture and family life change during the 1950s?

Writing About History

3. **Quick Write: Create an Annotated Bibliography** Choose one topic from this section, such as family life in the 1950s or the impact of suburban growth on the nation. Using the library or the Internet, find three or more sources on your chosen topic. Use these sources to prepare an annotated bibliography in which you record the information each source provides.

Critical Thinking

4. **Make Comparisons** In what ways was the mood of the 1950s different from the mood of the 1930s?

5. **Identify Point of View** Why do you think the nuclear family became more important during the 1950s?

6. **Identify Central Issues** Why was television a better medium than radio for consumerism?

American Music

Rock-and-Roll

Objectives

- Describe the origins of rock-and-roll.
- Explain the importance of rock-and-roll in the popular culture of the 1950s.

Background Knowledge ⒧

Have students discuss what they have learned about the postwar period of the 1950s. Tell students to use that knowledge to draw conclusions about why rock-and-roll was popular at the time.

Instruct ⒧

- Ask **Why do you think rock-and-roll became so popular with teens?** *(Sample answer: The music was upbeat and easy to dance to.)* **Rock-and-roll is still popular today, but with people of all ages. Why has this change come about?** *(Sample response: The music is more mainstream, plus many of the teens who listened to it still enjoy it today as adults.)*

- To enrich and extend the feature content, have students access the **History Interactive** material at **www.pearsonschool.com/ushist.**

Monitor Progress

Play a rock-and-roll song of the period for students, possibly a tune by Elvis Presley. Have students write a brief essay on how this music reflected the times they have been learning about.

Answers

Thinking Critically

1. During a time when African Americans experienced a great deal of discrimination, a white singer would have been accepted more readily, even if he were playing the same music as an African American performer.
2. Sample answer: There are some types of music today that are popular with teens (such as hip-hop) but are generally rejected by parents.

Rock-and-Roll

Rock-and-roll music burst on the scene in the 1950s, thrilling teenagers and horrifying their parents. A faster version of the rhythm and blues played by B. B. King and other Memphis musicians, rock-and-roll made stars of singers such as Little Richard and Chuck Berry. The biggest rock-and-roll idol was Elvis Presley. Girls screamed and fainted at the sight of Elvis, and his concerts were mobbed. He sold 40 million records in two years. Critics said the new music was just a fad, but disc jockeys and TV hosts such as Dick Clark, whose *American Bandstand* got 45,000 fan letters a week, knew rock-and-roll was here to stay.

Elvis Presley and fans

On his hit television show, Dick Clark (above) played the records of Little Richard, Chuck Berry (top), and other rock-and-roll stars.

Thinking Critically

1. **Make Inferences** Why would Elvis Presley have achieved greater success than African American musicians in the 1950s?

2. **Connect to Today** How do reactions to current music resemble the early responses to rock-and-roll?

History Background

Teens and Rock-and-Roll The music teens listened to in the 1950s was different from the music of earlier decades, but the teens of the 1950s were different as well.

Teens of the depression and war years had adult responsibilities. Teen boys were expected to prepare to go to work or join the military. Teen girls were to get married and have children. Few teens went to college. Most had little of their own money. Furthermore, parents controlled many decisions about family life, including entertainment.

With the hard times of depression and war in the past, many parents indulged their teenage children. Teenagers of this decade had more leisure time and were given money to spend on items they wanted.

With radios of their own, teens began to listen to music that was different from the music that their parents listened to. They were attracted to the energy of rock-and-roll, and an increasing number of stations began to play it. The fact that most parents did not like rock music only increased its appeal to teens.

▼ Claude Brown, author of *Manchild in the Promised Land*

WITNESS HISTORY

Troubles in the Promised Land

In the twentieth century, millions of African Americans left the rural South and migrated to cities in the North and West. Yet, many of these migrants were disappointed. Claude Brown, who grew up in Harlem, wrote about their disillusionment in his novel *Manchild in the Promised Land*.

❝The children of these disillusioned colored pioneers inherited the total lot of their parents—their disappointments, the anger. To add to their misery, they had little hope of deliverance. For where does one run to when he's already in the Promised Land?❞

—Claude Brown, *Manchild in the Promised Land*
Manchild in the Promised Land/
Claude Brown/Touchstone Books
(Simon & Schuster)/1965

Dissent and Discontent

Objectives

- Summarize the arguments made by critics who rejected the culture of the fifties.
- Describe the causes and effects of urban and rural poverty.
- Explain the problems that many minority group members faced in the postwar era.

Terms and People

beatnik
inner city
urban renewal
termination policy

NoteTaking

Reading Skill: Identify Main Ideas Record the main ideas and supporting details.

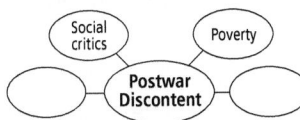

Social critics — Postwar Discontent — Poverty

Why It Matters Despite the prosperity of the 1950s, not all people benefited. Some, such as Claude Brown, were left out and had little hope of deliverance. Others, who had benefited, wondered whether all of the material things they acquired had actually led to a better life. The discontents of the 1950s would manifest the first signs of the dissent that would dominate the 1960s. **Section Focus Question: Why were some groups of Americans dissatisfied with conditions in postwar America?**

Critics Reject the Fifties Culture

The failure of society to provide equal opportunities to minorities was one source of discontent during the postwar era. Another was the belief that while material conditions were better in the 1950s, the *quality* of life had not improved. Many intellectuals and artists did not consider homes in the suburbs, shopping centers, and an unending supply of new gadgets as representing a better life.

Objecting to Conformity Many social critics complained about an emphasis on conformity. In a book called *The Lonely Crowd*, sociologists David Riesman and Nathan Glazer lamented that Americans had sacrificed their individualism in order to fit into the larger community. They also criticized the power of advertising to mold public tastes. The theme of alienation, or the feeling of being cut off from mainstream society, dominated a number of the most popular novels of the era. The bestseller *The Man in the Gray Flannel Suit*, by Sloan

Objectives

As you teach this section, keep students focused on the following objectives to help them answer the Section Focus Question and master core content.

- Summarize the arguments made by critics who rejected the culture of the fifties.
- Describe the causes and effects of urban and rural poverty.
- Explain the problems that many minority group members faced in the postwar era.

Prepare to Read

Background Knowledge

Have students recall that the 1950s was a time of prosperity and contentment for many people. Have them predict sources of discontent in American society.

Set a Purpose

- **WITNESS HISTORY** Read the selection aloud.

  Ask **Why were many African Americans discontented?** *(Many had moved from the rural cities in the West and South to the North, expecting a better life, but they found that they still faced many of the same problems.)*

- **Focus** Point out the Section Focus Question, and write it on the board. Tell students to refer to this question as they read. *(Answer appears with Section 4 Assessment answers.)*

- **Preview** Have students preview the Section Objectives and the list of Terms and People.

- **NoteTaking** Using the Structured Read Aloud strategy (TE, p. T20), have students read this section. As they read, have students record the section's main ideas and supporting details. Reading and Note Taking Study Guide

Vocabulary Builder

Use the information below and the following resource to teach students the high-use words from this section. Teaching Resources, Vocabulary Builder, p. 11

High-Use Words	Definitions and Sample Sentences
affluence	*n.* abundance or riches; wealth The **affluence** of the 1950s differed from the hard times of the depression.
trend	*n.* general or prevailing course, as of events, a discussion, etc. The **trend** of more middle class people owning homes continued throughout the 1950s.

Critics Reject the Fifties Culture

Instruct

- **Introduce** Tell students that some Americans rejected 1950s culture. Have students predict the way in which someone who rejects the norms of a culture might show his or her discontent.

- **Teach** Ask **What were the main arguments of groups who rejected the culture of the 1950s?** *(They rejected what they saw as conformity and lack of individualism and run-away materialism.)* **Why was J. D. Salinger's *Catcher in the Rye* so popular with teens?** *(It mocked the phoniness of adult society.)* **How did the actions of the beats show their contempt for mainstream culture?** *(The way that they dressed, spoke, acted, and thought was not acceptable to mainstream society.)*

- **Analyzing the Visuals** Tell students to look at the movie poster on this page. Have them read the title of the movie. Discuss with students what a movie called "Rebel Without a Cause" might be about, and why this idea would be attractive to some people.

Independent Practice

Challenge students to identify a group that questions the norms of American society today. Ask students to write a paragraph that explains how the group shows its discontent and compare that with the actions of the beats and other social critics in the 1950s.

Monitor Progress

As students fill in their concept webs, circulate to make sure that they understand the main ideas and supporting details in Section 4. For a completed version of the concept web, see Note Taking Transparencies, **B-126**.

The Rebel
James Dean starred in the movie *Rebel Without a Cause*, which seemed to symbolize the way many young people felt at the time.

Vocabulary Builder
affluence—(AF loo uhns) *n.* abundance or riches; wealth

Wilson, followed a World War II veteran who could not find real meaning in life after the war. Holden Caulfield, the main character in J. D. Salinger's *Catcher in the Rye*, a favorite among many teens, mocked what Salinger saw as the phoniness of adult society.

Although not published until 1963, Betty Friedan's *The Feminine Mystique* described the plight of the suburban housewife during the 1950s. By the 1960s, Friedan would be at the forefront of a movement to change the social and political status of women in American society.

The Beats Reject Middle-Class Life An additional critique of American society came from a small group of writers and artists called **beatniks,** or the beats. The beats refused to conform to accepted ways of dressing, thinking, and acting. Conformity, they insisted, stifled individualism. They displayed their dislike of American society by careless dress and colorful jargon.

In their poems, such as Allen Ginsberg's "Howl," and novels, such as Jack Kerouac's *On the Road,* the beats lambasted what they saw as crass materialism and conformity of the American middle class. Many Americans, in turn, were outraged by their behavior.

✓ **Checkpoint** Why did many intellectuals and artists criticize American culture during the 1950s?

Rural and Urban Poverty

Hidden behind the new household appliances, the spreading suburbs, the burgeoning shopping malls, and the ribbons of highways was a very different United States. It was a nation of urban slums, desperate rural poverty, and discrimination. People who were poor and dispossessed were well hidden.

In an influential 1962 book entitled *The Other America,* Michael Harrington shocked many Americans by arguing that poverty was widespread in the United States. Harrington claimed that 50 million Americans, one fourth of the nation, lived in poverty. Despite American affluence, Harrington said, poverty plagued African Americans in the inner cities, rural whites in areas such as Appalachia, and Hispanics in migrant farm labor camps and urban barrios. Harrington argued that Americans could not afford to ignore the existence of the poor:

> **Primary Source** "The poor live in a culture of poverty. [They] get sick more than anyone else in the society. . . . Because they are sick more often and longer than anyone else, they lose wages and work and find it difficult to hold a steady job. And because of this, . . . their prospect is to move to an even lower level . . . toward even more suffering."
>
> —Michael Harrington, *The Other America,* 1962

Cities Suffer a Decline During the decades that followed World War II, African Americans and other nonwhite minorities moved in great numbers from rural areas to cities. Most migrated in search of better economic opportunities. In the same period, however, American cities were suffering a severe decline as middle-class white families moved to the suburbs.

The loss of the middle class hurt cities economically because the middle class paid a large share of the taxes. It hurt them politically, as well, because as the suburbs gained population, they also gained representation in state legislatures and the national government. This combination of declining economic and political power put a serious strain on cities, leading to a deterioration of services, such as garbage removal and street repair. In turn, as the conditions

Differentiated Instruction   Solons for All Learners

L4 Advanced Readers   L4 Gifted and Talented Students

Ask students who would like an extra challenge and have an interest in literature to read one of the postwar-era books listed in the text, such as *Catcher in the Rye* or *The Man in the Gray Flannel Suit,* if they are available in the school library. Students can also choose other books from this era that appeal to

them. After reading his or her book selection, have each student write a book review as it might have appeared in a daily newspaper of the time. Ask students to share their reviews with the class. Encourage other students who are interested in these books to read them on their own.

Answer

✓ They saw an overemphasis on conformity and loss of individualism.

worsened and crime increased in what was now called the **inner city,** more of the middle class decided to move to the suburbs. Inner city refers to the older, central part of a city with crowded neighborhoods in which low-income, usually minority, groups live. Inner cities are often plagued with problems such as inadequate housing and schools, as well as crime.

Federal, state, and local governments tried to reverse the downward <u>trend</u> in American cities by developing **urban renewal** projects. With these projects, the government cleared large tracts of older housing and built freeways and developments which, it was hoped, would "revitalize" downtown areas. Unfortunately, the projects often backfired. Urban renewal drove people from their homes to make room for the new projects and highways. The poor were forced to seek housing in neighborhoods that were already overcrowded and overburdened. One resident of East Harlem, New York, who lost his home to an urban renewal project observed:

Primary Source "Nobody cared what we wanted when they built this place. They threw our houses down and pushed us there and pushed our friends somewhere else. We don't have a place around here to get a cup of coffee or a newspaper even, or borrow fifty cents."

—*America's History Since 1865*

The federal government tried to ease the shortage of affordable housing by constructing public housing. At the time, these housing projects seemed a godsend to those who lived there. Rent was cheap and the residents often enjoyed certain services, like hot running water, for the first time in their lives. Yet, since the public housing was often built in poor neighborhoods, the projects led to an even greater concentration of poverty. This, in turn led to other problems, such as crime.

The Rural Poor Also Suffer The plight of the rural poor was just as bad if not worse than that of the urban poor. Mississippi Delta sharecroppers, coal

The Faces of Poverty
As revealed in Michael Harrington's *The Other America,* poverty existed in urban and rural America. Crowded city tenements, such as the one shown at left below, were usually homes to large numbers of poor African Americans. In rural areas, poor whites and blacks endured lives of hardship. Below, a mother and her children stand in the doorway of a ragged shack.

Instruct

- **Introduce** Ask students to preview the visuals in this section. In a class discussion, have them describe the content of the images and graphs. Ask them how this information contrasts with the America they learned about in previous sections of the chapter.

- **Teach** Ask **Why was Michael Harrington's book *The Other America* such a shock to many Americans?** *(It opened the eyes of many Americans for the first time to the poverty that still existed in the United States.)* **What transformation occurred in cities during the 1950s?** *(African Americans and other minorities moved to cities; many middle class whites moved to the suburbs.)* Using the Idea Wave strategy (TE, p. T22), have students analyze the impact of public housing. Ask **How did federally subsidized housing for low-income people both help and hurt urban areas?** *(Sample responses: It provided good, affordable housing for people with low incomes, but it also concentrated the poor and all the problems associated with poverty in some urban areas.)* Discuss how rural poverty compared with urban poverty.

- **Quick Activity** Have students review the Primary Source quotations on this spread and discuss the ways they illustrate the effects of urban poverty.

Independent Practice

Have students read the worksheet *Reading a Chart: Suburban Growth and Urban Decline.* Have students analyze the *graph* and write a brief paragraph that explains how suburban growth and urban decline were linked.
Teaching Resources, **p. 19**

Monitor Progress

As students work on their paragraphs, circulate to make sure that they have properly interpreted the graph.

Differentiated Instruction   Solutions for All Learners

① Special Needs Students   ② Less Proficient Readers

Urban renewal was a double-edged sword for many urban areas. Although it cleared out blighted neighborhoods, it often also displaced people and destroyed communities. As a class, briefly review what urban renewal was and what it did. Then, have students think about the issue and take either the position that it was good for cities or that it was ultimately bad for cities. Have students take part in a classroom debate. Moderate the debate to make sure

that it stays on subject. To stimulate discussion when it starts to lag, prompt students with questions such as these: Did the government go too far in destroying homes because they were rundown? Why were the people who lost their homes in some areas not happy to leave their rundown neighborhoods? Why did the people in these neighborhoods not just move to the suburbs?

Instruct

- **Introduce** Have students brainstorm the types of things that would be an injustice to someone. Ask students to predict whether any of the injustices listed would have been common in the United States in the 1950s.

- **Teach** Note that groups such as Puerto Ricans, Mexicans, and Native Americans faced many of the same problems of poverty and discrimination that African Americans faced. Ask **Why do you think the government did little to deal with the problems of these groups?** *(Sample answer: These groups had little political power, so their problems were not a priority.)* Display Color Transparency: *Native American Relocation.* Discuss the images. Ask students how Native Americans may have felt about this program. Color Transparencies A-116

- **Quick Activity** Have students read the HISTORY MAKERS feature about Ernesto Galarza on the next page. Ask them to write short obituaries for Galarza, in their own words, about who he was, what he did, and why his work was important.

Independent Practice

Have students work with a partner to create a graphic organizer that shows the types of injustices faced by each of the groups highlighted in this subsection. When they have finished, have students share and compare their work.

Monitor Progress

As students create their graphic organizers, circulate to make sure that they understand the injustices many groups faced.

Answers

Caption about 20%; Sample answer: Because minorities probably faced discrimination at work and in schools, they were prevented from being as successful as many whites.

✔ It developed urban renewal projects and built new developments and highways. The government also built public housing.

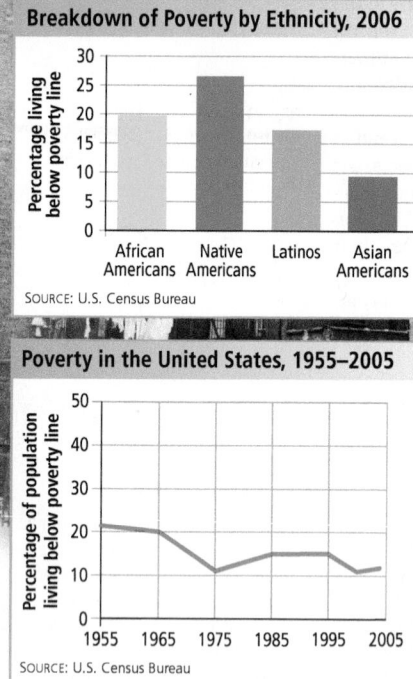

Breakdown of Poverty by Ethnicity, 2006

(bar graph: Percentage living below poverty line)
- African Americans: ~20
- Native Americans: ~26
- Latinos: ~17
- Asian Americans: ~9
- Whites: ~7

SOURCE: U.S. Census Bureau

Poverty in the United States, 1955–2005

(line graph: Percentage of population living below poverty line, from 1955 to 2005)

SOURCE: U.S. Census Bureau

Graph Skills The number of people living below the poverty line decreased between 1955 and 2005. However, many Americans continue to struggle to find the steady jobs and decent housing that will help them break through the poverty cycle. *What percentage of Americans lived below the poverty line in 1965? Why do you think the poverty rate remains higher among minorities?*

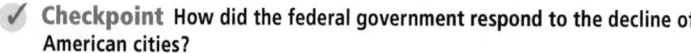

miners in Appalachia, and farmers in remote areas were left behind as others prospered, and often their economic situation got worse as time passed. A major transformation in farming was taking place. Corporations and large-farm owners came to dominate farm production. Many independent small-farm owners found it difficult to compete with the large farms and slipped into poverty.

Many farmers responded by leaving their rural communities behind, joining the waves of the poor who relocated to the city. Others remained behind, wondering if they would ever get to enjoy the benefits of the new economy.

✔ **Checkpoint** How did the federal government respond to the decline of American cities?

"Other Americans" Face Injustice

During the postwar years, the battle for civil rights in the South began to gain headlines. Yet, in the same time period, African Americans and other minorities also fought for equality in the urban north and west. Central to their struggles were efforts to overcome housing and employment discrimination.

Puerto Ricans Latinos from Puerto Rico and Mexico and Native Americans faced many of the same problems that African Americans encountered in the years following World War II. Puerto Rican migrants to New York City, for example, often found themselves clustered together in many of the poorest inner city neighborhoods with employment opportunities limited by both formal and informal forms of discrimination. As newcomers whose native language was not English, they enjoyed little political power. Thus, they received little help from city governments in getting better services, education, or an end to discriminatory practices.

Connect to Your World

Native Americans Today According to the 2004 estimates, approximately 4.4 million Native Americans make up 1.5 percent of the U.S. population. California has the greatest Native American population, with 687,400 people. The state with the largest percentage of Native American population is Alaska, where one in five people is of Native American or Alaska Native ancestry.

Some 381,000 Native Americans speak a Native American language at home. Of those, nearly half speak Navajo. While more than three fourths of Native Americans have at least a high school diploma and about 14 percent have at least a college degree, these numbers are still less than the national percentages.

Native American families also battle poverty. This poverty is due in part to many reservations' rural locations and insufficient resources to encourage economic development. The poverty rate for the nation's people as a whole is about 12.7 percent, but it is twice as high among Native Americans. However, this situation is improving. The median income for Native American households is about $33,000, and about six in ten Native Americans own their own homes.

Mexicans Both Mexicans and Mexican Americans faced a similar situation in the United States. During World War II, the U.S. government had established the bracero program as a means to address the shortage of agricultural workers. *Braceros* was a term for Mexican migrant farmworkers in the United States. The program gave temporary visas to Mexican immigrants. By 1964, 3 million Mexicans had worked in the United States under the program, most of them as farm laborers. Many were exploited and cheated by their employers. Mexican workers followed crops from state to state. Often, children worked alongside their parents. The migrants had little power to oppose the exploitation, for if they complained about conditions, employers threatened to deport them back to Mexico. One U.S. Department of Labor official called the program "legalized slavery."

One champion of the rights of Mexican migrant workers, Ernesto Galarza, joined the effort to organize unions for Mexican farm laborers.

Native Americans In 1953, the federal government enacted the **termination policy,** a major change in the rules governing Native Americans. The law sought to end tribal government and to relocate Native Americans to the nation's cities. It also terminated federal responsibility for the health and welfare of Native Americans. Proponents of the policy argued that it would free American Indians to assimilate, or merge, into American society. While some Native Americans praised the intent of the program, most came to agree with Senator Mark Hatfield of Oregon who argued that it made things worse for them. "[T]he social and economic devastation which these policies have wrought upon many groups has been tremendous. . . . While these problems were already severe among Indian societies generally, they have become epidemic among terminated Indians."

✔ **Checkpoint** What were some of the problems that minorities had to overcome in the postwar era?

HISTORY MAKERS

Ernesto Galarza
(1905–1984)
Born in Mexico, Galarza came with his family to Sacramento, California, at age six. For a time, he worked as a farm laborer. More fortunate than most Mexican American children, he succeeded in school and eventually received a Ph.D. He began to help migrant farmworkers—many of them Mexican Americans—organize unions. His book, *Merchants of Labor,* exposed the poor working conditions of the braceros.

SECTION
4 Assessment

Progress Monitoring *Online*
For: Self-test with vocabulary practice
www.pearsonschool.com/ushist

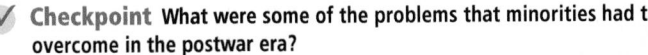

Comprehension

1. **Terms and People** Explain how each term below relates to problems or issues in the 1950s.
   - beatnik
   - urban renewal
   - termination policy

2. **NoteTaking Reading Skill: Identify Main Ideas** Use your concept web to answer the Section Focus Question: Why were some groups of Americans dissatisfied with conditions in postwar America?

Writing About History

3. **Quick Write: Credit Sources** When you use quotes or ideas from sources in your research paper, you must provide proper credit. One way to do this is to list the author and page number of the material you have used in parentheses following the statement. If you have used the Internet, list the Web site. Research a topic from this section and write a paragraph using two sources. Credit the sources where appropriate and list them at the end.

Critical Thinking

4. **Summarize** Summarize the arguments made by critics who rejected the culture of the fifties.

5. **Synthesize Information** During the 1950s, many middle-class Americans were unaware of poverty. Are poor people invisible today? Explain.

6. **Draw Conclusions** Why would the bracero program attract Mexican workers? What disadvantages did these workers face compared with other workers in the United States?

Section 4 Assessment

1. Students' responses should show that they understand how these terms are related to issues of the 1950s.

2. Social critics complained about the emphasis on conformity. Latinos, African Americans, and Native Americans faced discrimination.

3. Responses should demonstrate students' ability to find Internet sources, extract data from them, and properly cite the sources in a bibliography.

4. Sample response: Many critics believed that society had been taken over by consumerism and conformity. They also thought that many of society's serious problems, such as the plight of the poor, were being overlooked by the majority, who enjoyed good times.

5. Sample response: Poor people are perhaps less invisible because of television, but they still struggle to survive.

6. It allowed Mexican workers to come to the United States legally to work for a period of time. Because they were not citizens and had few rights, employers often threatened to deport workers who complained about conditions.

Assess and Reteach

Assess Progress   L3
- Have students complete the Section Assessment.
- Administer the Section Quiz. Teaching Resources, **p. 23**
- To further assess student understanding, use **Progress Monitoring Transparencies, 122.**

Reteach
If students need more instruction, have them read the section summary.

Reading and Note Taking   L3
Study Guide

Adapted Reading and   L1 L2
Note Taking Study Guide

Spanish Reading and   L2
Note Taking Study Guide

Extend   L4
Have students read and complete the Enrichment worksheet *Urban Renewal: Connection to Economics.* Teaching Resources, **pp. 13–14**

Answer

✔ Many African Americans and Latinos faced employment discrimination and segregation. Mexican migrant farm laborers were often exploited and lived in substandard conditions. U.S. government policy sought to destroy Native American tribal governments and cut off aid for healthcare and other services.

For additional assessment, have students access **Progress Monitoring *Online*** at **www.pearsonschool.com/ushist**

Quick Study Guide

Progress Monitoring *Online*
For: Self-test with vocabulary practice
www.pearsonschool.com/ushist

Quick Study Guide

- Have students use the Quick Study Guide to prepare for the chapter test. Students may wish to refer to the following sections as they review:

The Postwar Years
Section 1
Section 2
Section 3

Population Shifts, 1950–1970
Section 2

Life in America, 1950s
Section 1
Section 2
Section 3
Section 4

Causes of Discontent
Section 4

Key Events of Postwar America
Section 1
Section 2
Section 3
Section 4

- For additional review, remind students to refer to the Reading and Note Taking Study Guide
Section Note Taking
Section Summaries

- Have students access **www.pearsonschool.com/ushist** for this chapter's History Interactive timeline, which includes expanded entries and additional events.

- If students need more instruction on analyzing graphic data, have them read the Skills Handbook, **p. SH21.**

■ The Postwar Years

Worker productivity improves.
Wages increase.
Consumerism rises.
Baby boom boosts population.
GI Bill helps veterans.
Government spending increases.

■ Population Shifts, 1950–1970

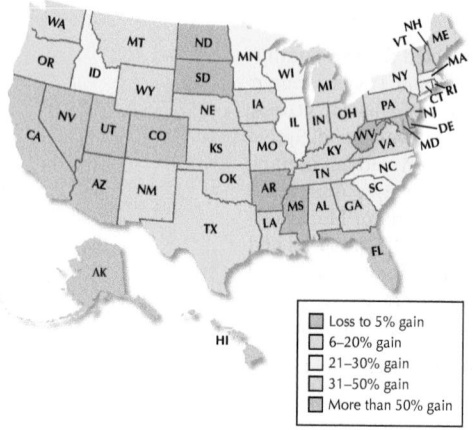

- Loss to 5% gain
- 6–20% gain
- 21–30% gain
- 31–50% gain
- More than 50% gain

■ Life in America, 1950s

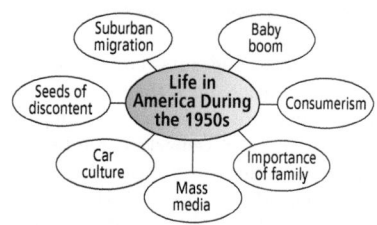

Life in America During the 1950s
- Suburban migration
- Baby boom
- Seeds of discontent
- Consumerism
- Car culture
- Importance of family
- Mass media

■ Causes of Discontent

Farmers suffer hardships and begin to migrate to cities.
Cities experience political and economic decline.
African Americans, Latinos, and Native Americans continue to suffer discrimination.
Poverty is widespread among Americans in urban and rural areas.
Writers and artists protest values of life in the 1950s.

☑ Quick Study Timeline

In America	1944 GI Bill helps returning veterans	1947 Taft-Hartley Act limits power of unions	1951 Levittown, the first postwar suburb, is built on Long Island
Presidential Terms		Harry S. Truman 1945–1953	
	1945		**1950**
Around the World	1945 World War II ends		1950 Korean War begins

---

Differentiated Instruction   Solutions for All Learners

L1 Special Needs Students   **L2 Less Proficient Readers**   **L2 English Language Learners**

Use the following study guide resources to help students acquiring basic skills:
Adapted Reading and Note Taking Study Guide
- Section Note Taking
- Section Summaries

Use the following study guide resources to help Spanish-speaking students:
Spanish Reading and Note Taking Study Guide
- Section Note Taking
- Section Summaries

For **Progress Monitoring *Online*,** refer students to the Self-test with vocabulary practice at **www.pearsonschool.com/ushist.**

American Issues
●──●──● Connector

By connecting prior knowledge with what you have learned in this chapter, you can gradually build your understanding of enduring questions that still affect America today. Answer the questions below. Then, use your American Issues Connector study guide (or go online: www.pearsonschool.com/ushist).

Issues You Learned About

● **Poverty and Prosperity** Not all Americans have shared in the nation's more prosperous times.

1. In the postwar decades, some Americans enjoyed new prosperity while others sank deeper into poverty. Write a paragraph contrasting the haves and have nots in American postwar society.

● **Technology and Society** New technological advances impact American cultural life.

2. How did technology change American society in the 1950s? What were the effects of these inventions?

3. What view of American society did television programs of the 1950s present? How accurate was this view?

4. How did Elvis Presley's appearance on Ed Sullivan's TV variety show reflect the clash of values among Americans in the 1950s?

● **Migration and Urbanization** Americans are constantly moving, leading to the rise and fall of populations in cities, states, and regions.

5. In the 1950s and 1960s, more and more Americans moved to the Sunbelt. Describe another specific migration movement in the United States.

6. Why might the Brooklyn Dodgers have made the decision to relocate to Los Angeles in 1958?

Connect to Your World	Activity

Education and American Society Today, Americans are debating how public education in the United States can best provide a solid academic background for all students. Some feel that our education system is doing a great job already. Some say more money is needed. Other Americans believe that public education needs a complete overhaul and that spending more on the existing system is useless. Still others bypass the public education system and do not want their tax dollars supporting a system they do not use. Go online or to your local library and find out more about the debate over public education in the United States today. Write a few paragraphs explaining the different views.

History *Interactive*
For: Interactive timeline
www.pearsonschool.com/ushist

1954	1956		1962
Salk develops polio vaccine	Interstate Highway Act expands highway construction		Michael Harrington's *The Other America* defines poverty in America

Dwight D. Eisenhower 1953–1961 | John F. Kennedy 1961–1963

1955 | **1960** | **1965**

1955	1959	1963
Soviet Union establishes Warsaw Pact	Fidel Castro gains power in Cuba	Military coup ends Diem government in South Vietnam

---

Differentiated Instruction — Solutions for All Learners

L1 Special Needs Students   **L2 English Language Learners**   **L2 Less Proficient Readers**

Use the following study guide resource to help students acquiring basic skills:
Adapted Reading and Note Taking Study Guide
• American Issues Journal

Use the following study guide resource to help Spanish-speaking students:
Spanish Reading and Note Taking Study Guide
• American Issues Journal

American Issues
●──●──● Connector

Tell students that the main issues for this chapter are Poverty and Prosperity, Technology and Society, and Migration and Urbanization, and then ask them to answer the Issues You Learned About questions on this page. Discuss the Connect to Your World topic(s), and ask students to complete the project that follows.

American Issues Connector

1. Paragraphs should demonstrate an understanding of the way in which the lives of suburban Americans contrasted with the lives of Americans living in urban and rural poverty.

2. Sample answer: Advances such as computers, automobiles, and television led to better productivity, the development of suburbs, and a rise in consumerism.

3. Television showed prosperous, suburban families. Although many people lived this way, the society shown on television did not include non-white families, nor did it touch on family or societal problems.

4. Elvis Presley's appearance showed that many people enjoyed rock-and-roll music. However, Sullivan's direction that Elvis only be shown from the waist up shows that society also worried over his possible "subversive" influence.

5. Sample response: African Americans and members of other nonwhite groups moved from rural areas to cities after World War II.

6. Sample answers: The team probably thought that it could develop a large fan base among the people who were pouring into the sunbelt.

Connect to Your World

Paragraphs should demonstrate comprehensive research on the issue as well as students' understanding of the position taken by each side.

For additional review of this chapter's enduring issues, remind students to refer to the Reading and Note Taking Study Guide American Issues Journal.

Terms and People

1. The baby boom was a huge increase in the number of births in postwar America. Baby boom children were often placed at the center of suburban family life.

2. The Act authorized the spending of billions of dollars to build thousands of miles of new highways throughout the nation. The highways decreased commuting time between cities and suburbs and also boosted the travel and vacation industries.

3. Spock was the author of a popular book on child rearing. Spock encouraged parents to nurture their children with all the love and material comforts they could muster, without concern about spoiling them.

4. Beatniks, or beats, were artists and writers who refused to conform to the norms of society in the 1950s. They were dissatisfied with what they saw as the materialism and conformity of the middle class.

Focus Questions

5. The nation initially experienced postwar inflation, but a postwar boom in manufacturing and productivity boosted industrial output and employment. Increased federal spending also helped strengthen the economy.

6. Factors included the growth of suburbs and "car culture," migration to the Sunbelt, the growth of the service sector in industry, the decline of industrial and farming jobs, the increase in employment and incomes, expanded opportunities in education, the growth of consumerism, and the baby boom.

7. Nationally broadcast TV and radio shows, as well as movies seen nationwide, helped erode regional and ethnic differences. Television programs influenced American values and resulted in many Americans' buying the same products. Rock-and-roll also became the music of the younger generation all over the country. Families became more child-centered and church-going.

8. They saw that many Americans living in poverty and suffering dis-

Chapter Assessment

Terms and People

1. Define **baby boom.** Explain the effect of the baby boom on American life.

2. What was the **Interstate Highway Act**? How did it help boost the postwar economy?

3. Who was **Benjamin Spock**? What different ideas did he have that changed people's views?

4. Define **beatnik.** Why was such a person dissatisfied?

Focus Questions

The focus question for this chapter is **How did social and economic changes after World War II affect Americans?** Build an answer to this big question by answering the focus questions for Sections 1 through 4 and the Critical Thinking questions that follow.

Section 1
5. How did the nation experience recovery and economic prosperity after World War II?

Section 2
6. What social and economic factors changed American life during the 1950s?

Section 3
7. How did popular culture and family life change during the 1950s?

Section 4
8. Why were some groups of Americans dissatisfied with conditions in postwar America?

Writing About History

Writing a Research Report Musicians were not the only artists who responded to the changing culture of the postwar years. Painters experimented and began to record their vision of the postwar culture. Write a research report in which you choose two artists and explain the significance of their works. Here are some possible choices: Jackson Pollock, Romare Bearden, Willem de Kooning, Mark Rothko, Robert Rauschenberg, John T. Biggers.

Prewriting
• Do online research to read about the artists.

• Choose two artists. Gather information about the artists and their works.

• Create a set of questions about the artists you have chosen. Gather any additional information you need.

Critical Thinking

9. **Analyze Information** How did the development of the interstate highway contribute to postwar prosperity?

10. **Synthesize Information** What measures did the government take to spark the economy after the war?

11. **Explain Effects** How did automobile production affect the economy?

12. **Draw Conclusions** How did technology both help and harm the farming industry?

13. **Analyzing Visuals** Study the visual below. In which election was this campaign button used? What voters would have supported these candidates and political party? Why?

14. **Identify Point of View** When describing company workers during the 1950s, one sociologist said, "When white-collar people get jobs, they sell not only their time and energy but their personalities as well." Why do you think some people agreed with this point of view?

15. **Analyze Information** Do you think life in the suburbs became the model for the American dream? Explain.

Drafting
• Develop a working thesis, and choose supporting information to support the thesis.

• Make an outline to organize the report.

• Write an introduction that explains why the topic is interesting, and then write a body and a conclusion.

Revising
• Use the guidelines on page SH14 of the Writing Handbook to revise your report.

crimination had been left out of the economic boom enjoyed by many people in the middle class. In addition, they objected to conformity and consumerism.

Critical Thinking

9. Highways allowed the faster growth of suburbs and also helped some industries, such as those involved in travel and vacations, grow and prosper.

10. Sample response: The government spent money to boost the growth of some industries and the development of technology, funded home loans to boost construction,

increased funding for the education of GIs and of scientists, and built highways to improve transportation.

11. Sample answer: The auto industry provided many jobs that provided good incomes. The money earned in this industry was then spent on homes and consumer goods that helped the American economy.

Document-Based Assessment

Impact of the Suburbs

During the postwar era, the population began to shift from the cities to the suburbs. What impact did this population shift have on American life? What impact did it have on the economy? Use your knowledge of the postwar era and Documents A, B, C, and D to answer questions 1 through 4.

Document A

Document B

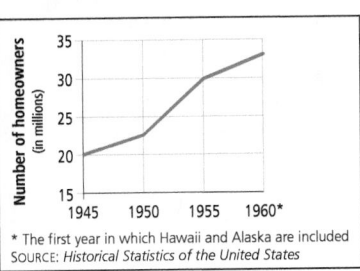

* The first year in which Hawaii and Alaska are included
SOURCE: *Historical Statistics of the United States*

Document C

This is the way you live at LEVITTOWN

Document D

"William Levitt . . . looked upon a green expanse of woods . . . in . . . Bucks County, Pa., and dreamed of instant suburbia. . . . When he marketed his mass-produced homes in beautiful color brochures, thousands of young families wanted to buy. . . . They came to escape crowded cities like Trenton . . . or Philadelphia. . . . They came to own their own home, cook with their own appliances, mow their own lawn. They had GI loans in hand, babies on the way, and a '50s brand of pioneering spirit. . . . 'We were young, all of us who moved to Levittown, and we thought Bill Levitt was the greatest man in the world. Imagine it—$10 deposit, $90 at settlement, and you had a house of your own!' . . . Levittown was a fresh marvel of modern planning to a Northeast corridor bursting at its seams in the early 1950s. . . . It took only $100 . . . to make a down payment on a Levittown home. Levitt, . . . said . . . 'that every family in the United States is entitled to decent shelter.'"

"1951: American dream houses, all in a row"
—by Jon Blackwell, *The Trentonian,* June 20, 1999

1. According to Document D, what caused the shift of population from the cities to the suburbs?
   A The availability of affordable housing.
   B Fewer apartment buildings were built.
   C People saved more money to buy a home.
   D Cities provided good public transportation.

2. Which document most clearly explains the impact of housing on the natural environment?
   A Document D
   B Document A
   C Document C
   D Document B

3. What can you conclude about life in the postwar era from Documents A and C?
   A Most people wanted homes close to the city.
   B People looked at cheap houses as a way to escape crowded cities.
   C Most Americans could not afford new houses.
   D Cities were attractive and affordable places to live.

4. **Writing Task** What role did home ownership play in the population shift from cities to suburbs? What impact did it have on the economy? Use your knowledge of the chapter content and specific evidence from the primary sources above to support your opinion.

---

12. Technology made agriculture more productive so that fewer farmers and farm workers could grow more food. However, the number of family farms continued to decline during this time, with many farm families forced off their land.

13. 1948 Presidential election; Southern Democrats; They were angry at Truman's support for civil rights.

14. Sample response: Some people complained that America was becoming a nation of people who conformed to the values spread by mass media and corporations.

15. Sample response: Yes; having a well-paying job, a house in the suburbs, modern conveniences, income to spend on luxuries and vacations, and a nuclear family seemed to be realized in the suburban life that became popular in America in the 1950s. This is, in large part, the American dream.

Background Knowledge

Have students describe the United States as it was immediately after World War II. Explain that many of the aspects that define American popular culture today emerged during this postwar era. Ask partners to discuss products, ideas, or characteristics that were developed during the 1950s and 1960s and that define American culture today. Have students share their ideas. Then, challenge each pair to draw a graphic organizer that traces the people, events, inventions, or laws that contributed to the emergence of this part of American culture.

Instruct

Have students read the essay. Ask **According to the author, what icon of the American way of life developed quickly after World War II?** *(fast food)* Lead a class discussion about the factors that contributed to the launch of the fast-food industry. Ask **How did the automobile and the highway system contribute to the popularity of fast food in the United States?** *(Possible answer: As more Americans bought automobiles, the federal government built the highway system, enabling Americans to drive longer distances. Because Americans spent more time driving from place to place, they needed quicker eating options, and this situation led to the growth of the fast-food industry.)* Have students evaluate whether fast food defines the American culture and character.

Looking Ahead

Despite the prosperity of the postwar years, many groups in the United States continued to struggle for equality. During the years that followed the postwar era, such groups demanded that the rest of the United States hear their calls for equal treatment and protection under the law.

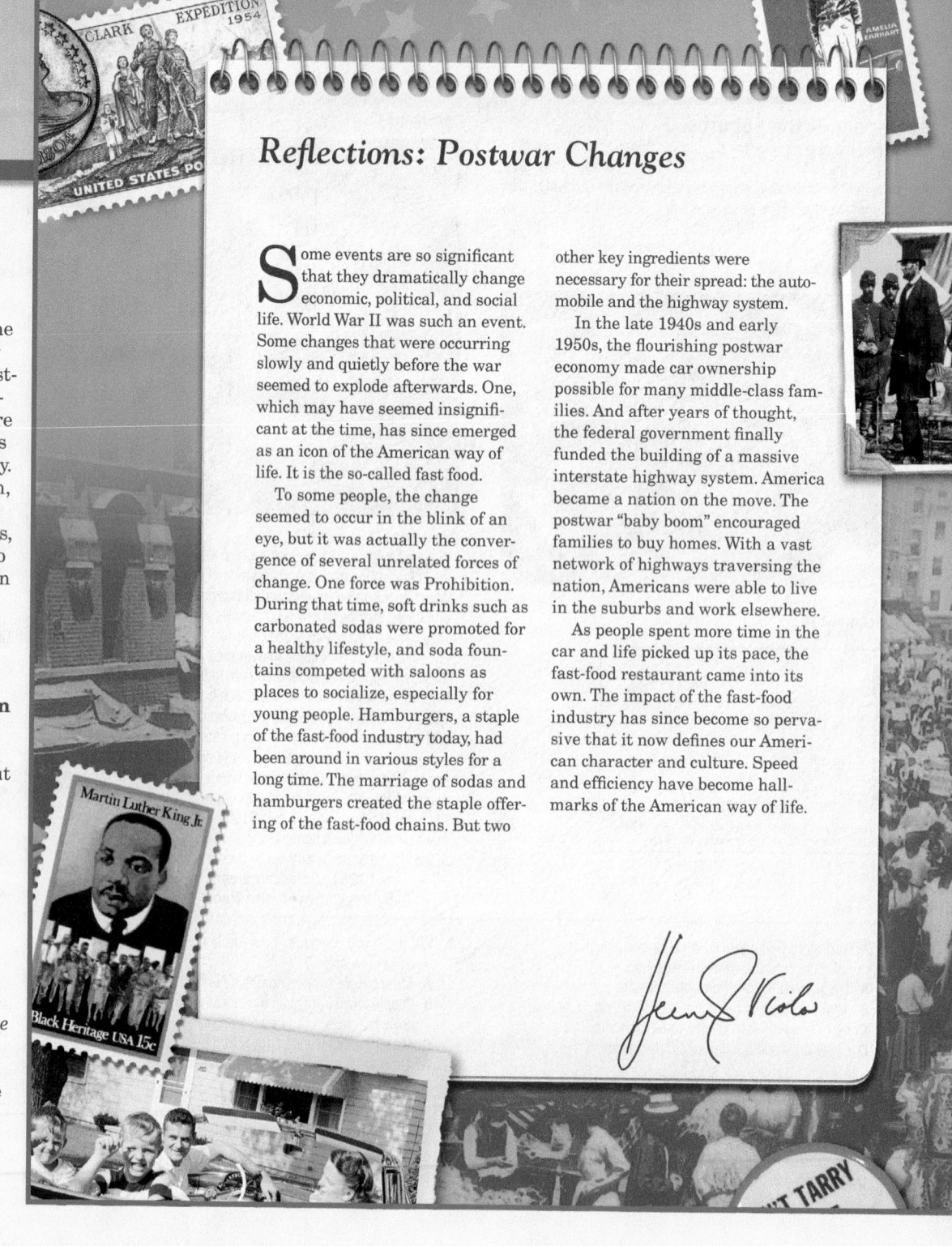

Reflections: Postwar Changes

Some events are so significant that they dramatically change economic, political, and social life. World War II was such an event. Some changes that were occurring slowly and quietly before the war seemed to explode afterwards. One, which may have seemed insignificant at the time, has since emerged as an icon of the American way of life. It is the so-called fast food.

To some people, the change seemed to occur in the blink of an eye, but it was actually the convergence of several unrelated forces of change. One force was Prohibition. During that time, soft drinks such as carbonated sodas were promoted for a healthy lifestyle, and soda fountains competed with saloons as places to socialize, especially for young people. Hamburgers, a staple of the fast-food industry today, had been around in various styles for a long time. The marriage of sodas and hamburgers created the staple offering of the fast-food chains. But two other key ingredients were necessary for their spread: the automobile and the highway system.

In the late 1940s and early 1950s, the flourishing postwar economy made car ownership possible for many middle-class families. And after years of thought, the federal government finally funded the building of a massive interstate highway system. America became a nation on the move. The postwar "baby boom" encouraged families to buy homes. With a vast network of highways traversing the nation, Americans were able to live in the suburbs and work elsewhere.

As people spent more time in the car and life picked up its pace, the fast-food restaurant came into its own. The impact of the fast-food industry has since become so pervasive that it now defines our American character and culture. Speed and efficiency have become hallmarks of the American way of life.

CHALLENGES AND CHANGE

CONTENTS

Cesar Chavez leads a United
Farm Workers rally in 1966. ▶

Challenges and Change

Era Overview

Challenges and Change investigates the issues that caused turbulence within the United States after World War II and in what ways these issues changed the social, political, and economic landscape of the nation.

Chapter 14 describes the civil rights movement from the 1940s through the 1970s, the challenges it faced, and the significant gains it made securing the rights of African Americans. **Issues:** Voting Rights, Federal Power and States' Rights, Sectionalism and National Politics

Chapter 15 focuses on the policies of the Kennedy and Johnson administrations, including Kennedy's response to the Cold War, his New Frontier program, and Johnson's Great Society program. **Issues:** Poverty and Prosperity, America and the World, Social Problems and Reform

Chapter 16 examines the causes of the Vietnam War, the increasing domestic tensions as a result of the war, the effects of the war both domestically and internationally, and Nixon's new approach to American foreign policy. **Issues:** America and the World, America Goes to War, Global Interdependence

Chapter 17 discusses the rise of the counterculture and describes different protest movements that grew during the 1960s and the 1970s, such as the women's rights movement, the Chicano movement, and the environmental movement. **Issues:** Interaction With the Environment, Women in American Society, U.S. Immigration Policy

Chapter 18 analyzes the causes and effects of the Watergate scandal and compares and contrasts the foreign and domestic policies of the Ford and Carter administrations. **Issues:** Checks and Balances, Church and State, Sectionalism and National Politics

CHAPTER 14

Teach With Technology

PresentationEXPRESS™ PREMIUM DVD

- Teach this chapter's core content by using PresentationExpress, which includes interactivities, video, lecture notes, and the *ExamView®* QuickTake assessment tool.
- To introduce this chapter by using PresentationExpress, ask students with which of the following statements they most agree: **A) The years 1945–1975 were a time of positive change in American society. B) The years 1945–1975 were a time of anger and violence in American society. C) The years 1945–1975 were a time of injustice in American society. D) The years 1945–1975 were a time when injustice ended in American society.** Take a class poll or record students' answers by using the QuickTake feature, and discuss their responses. Point out that in this chapter, students will read about the civil rights movement. Continue introducing the chapter by using the chapter opener slide show.

Technology Resources

- Student**EXPRESS** CD-ROM
- Teacher Resource Library **DVD**
- Presentation**EXPRESS** PREMIUM DVD
- *ExamView®* **Test Bank CD-ROM** English and Spanish
- **Guided Reading Audio,** Spanish
- **Student Edition on Audio**

THE ESSENTIAL ? VIDEO By Students For Students
For videos on Amercian Issues, go to **www.pearsonschool.com/ushist**

CHAPTER

14 The Civil Rights Movement 1945–1975

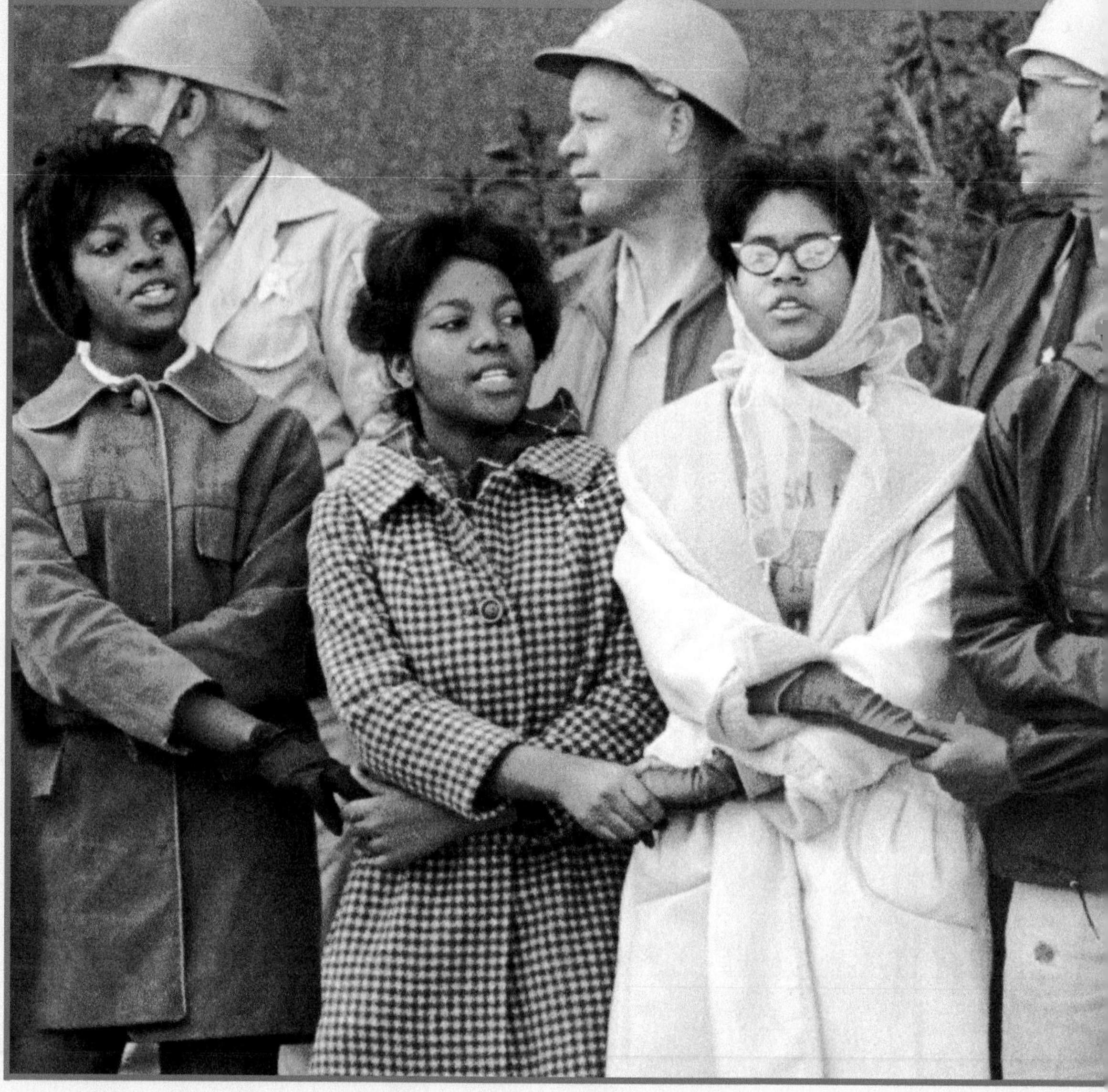

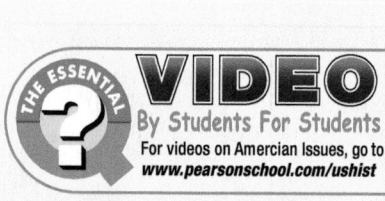

Bibliography

For the Teacher

King, Martin Luther, Jr. *The Autobiography of Martin Luther King, Jr.* Warner Books, Inc., 2001.

Levy, Peter B. *The Civil Rights Movement.* Greenwood Press, 1998.

Raffel, Jeffrey A. *Historical Dictionary of School Segregation and Desegregation: The American Experience.* Greenwood Press, 1998.

For the Student

L2 Kasher, Steven, and Myrlie Evers-Williams. *The Civil Rights Movement: A Photographic History, 1954–68.* Abbeville Press, 1998.

L3 Karson, Jill, et al. *Leaders of the Civil Rights Movement.* Greenhaven Press, 2004.

L4 Malcolm X. *By Any Means Necessary.* Pathfinder Press, 1992.

WITNESS HISTORY

Human Chain of Freedom

In the 1950s and 1960s, African Americans intensified their efforts to gain equal rights. During civil rights marches, peaceful protesters had to find the strength to face taunts and violence. Often, they found that strength in music. Hand in hand, they would face their opponents and sing. In the stirring civil rights anthem "Eyes on the Prize," they proclaimed:

"Freedom's name is mighty sweet,
Soon one day we're gonna meet. . . .
The only thing we did wrong,
Stayed in the wilderness a day too long.
But the one thing we did right,
Was the day we started to fight."
—Alice Wine, "Eyes on the Prize"

Sign protesting segregated restaurants

◄ Protesters hold hands and sing during a 1965 civil rights march in Selma, Alabama.

James Meredith, first black student at the University of Mississippi

Button of a militant African American organization

Chapter Preview

Chapter Focus Question: What were the causes, main events, and effects of the civil rights movement?

Section 1
Early Demands for Equality

Section 2
The Movement Gains Ground

Section 3
New Successes and Challenges

Use the ☑ **Quick Study Timeline** at the end of this chapter to preview chapter events.

Note Taking Study Guide *Online*
For: Note Taking and American Issues Connector
www.pearsonschool.com/ushist

Previewing the Chapter

- **WITNESS HISTORY** Read the Witness History selection aloud. Point out the themes on which the selection focuses, including the frustrations of African Americans who wished to participate fully in the life of the nation. Explain that these frustrations led to the rise of the civil rights movement.

- **Analyzing the Visuals** Ask **What can you tell about the protestors by their expressions?** *(They seem optimistic, dignified, and calm.)* **Why do you think the police officers are looking away from the protestors?** *(Sample response: Perhaps the police officers do not want to recognize certain individuals or interact with the protestors.)* Have students discuss how the photograph of the protestors and the images on the right side of the page might be related.

- **Focus** Write the Chapter Focus Question on the board. Tell students to keep this question in mind as they read the chapter. Then, have students preview the section titles in this chapter.

- **Preread** Have students complete the chapter's Preread the Chapter Worksheet. Teaching Resources, pp. 7–8

Differentiated Instruction Solutions for All Learners

The following Teacher's Edition strategies are suitable for students of varying abilities.

L1 Special Needs Students, pp. 469, 473, 478, 482, 489, 493, 494 SN

L2 English Language Learners, pp. 469, 473, 478, 482, 483, 489, 493, 494 ELL

L2 Less Proficient Readers, pp. 469, 473, 478, 482, 483, 489, 493, 494 LPR

L4 Advanced Readers, pp. 472, 480, 481, 492 LPR AR

L4 Gifted and Talented Students, pp. 472, 480, 481, 492 LPR GT

Have students access **www.pearsonschool.com/ushist** for the Note Taking Study Guide *Online* as an alternative to the *Reading and Note Taking Study Guide* booklet.

Objectives

As you teach this section, keep students focused on the following objectives to help them answer the Section Focus Question and master core content.

- Describe efforts to end segregation in the 1940s and 1950s.
- Explain the importance of *Brown* v. *Board of Education.*
- Describe the controversy over school desegregation in Little Rock, Arkansas.
- Discuss the Montgomery bus boycott and its impact.

Prepare to Read

Background Knowledge ⓛ3

Remind students that after World War II the United States was prosperous, but access to prosperity was not equally available to all Americans. Ask students to predict what social changes some Americans might demand in the decades after the war.

Set a Purpose ⓛ3

- **WITNESS HISTORY** Read the selection aloud.

  Ask **Why was Medgar Evers unable to live as an ordinary U.S. citizen?** *(Institutional racism prevented African Americans from exercising basic rights.)*

- **Focus** Point out the Section Focus Question, and write it on the board. Tell students to refer to this question as they read. *(Answer appears with Section 1 Assessment answers.)*

- **Preview** Have students preview the Section Objectives and the list of Terms and People.

- **Reading Skill** Have students use the *Reading Strategy: Summarize* worksheet. Teaching Resources, **p. 11**

- **NoteTaking** Using the Paragraph Shrinking strategy (TE, p. T20), have students read this section. As they read, have students fill in the timeline with ways that African Americans challenged segregation. Reading and Note Taking Study Guide

◄ Medgar Evers

A Different Kind of Enemy

After serving in the army in Europe in World War II, Medgar Evers returned home to the South, where he faced a different kind of enemy: discrimination. When he and some other African American veterans tried to register to vote, a mob of armed whites blocked their way. "All we wanted to be was ordinary citizens," Evers later said, frustrated to find his life at risk in his own country. "We fought during the war for America, Mississippi included." Evers retreated that day, but he did not give up on his goal. He became an active member of the NAACP and a leader in the fight for civil rights.

◄ Sign at a segregated bus station

Early Demands for Equality

Objectives

- Describe efforts to end segregation in the 1940s and 1950s.
- Explain the importance of *Brown* v. *Board of Education.*
- Describe the controversy over school desegregation in Little Rock, Arkansas.
- Discuss the Montgomery bus boycott and its impact.

Terms and People

de jure segregation
de facto segregation
Thurgood Marshall
Earl Warren
Brown v. *Board of Education*

Civil Rights Act of 1957
Rosa Parks
Montgomery bus boycott
Martin Luther King, Jr.

NoteTaking

Reading Skill: Summarize Copy the timeline below and fill it in with events of the early civil rights movement. When you finish, write two sentences that summarize the information in your timeline.

```
                    Montgomery
                    bus boycott

    1945    1950    1955    1960
```

Why It Matters The postwar period brought prosperity to many, but most African Americans were still treated as second-class citizens. The civil rights movement, a broad and diverse effort to attain racial equality, compelled the nation to live up to its ideal that all are created equal. The movement also demonstrated that ordinary men and women could perform extraordinary acts of courage and sacrifice to achieve social justice, a lesson that continues to inspire people around the world today. **Section Focus Question: How did African Americans challenge segregation after World War II?**

Segregation Divides America

African Americans had a long history of fighting for their rights. After World War II, the struggle intensified, as African Americans grew increasingly dissatisfied with their second-class status.

Jim Crow Laws Limit African Americans In the South, Jim Crow laws enforced strict separation of the races. Segregation that is imposed by law is known as **de jure segregation.** In 1896, in *Plessy* v. *Ferguson,* the Supreme Court had ruled that such segregation was constitutional as long as the facilities for blacks and whites were "separate but equal." But this was seldom the case. The facilities for African Americans were rarely, if ever, equal.

In the South and elsewhere, segregation extended to most areas of public life. Officials enforced segregation of schools, hospitals, transportation, restaurants, cemeteries, and beaches. One city even forbade blacks and whites from playing checkers together.

Segregation Prevails Around the Nation In the North, too, African Americans faced segregation and discrimination. Even where there were no explicit laws, **de facto segregation,** or segregation by

Vocabulary Builder

Use the information below and the following resource to teach students the high-use word from this section. Teaching Resources, Vocabulary Builder, p. 10

High-Use Word	Definition and Sample Sentence
compliance	*n.* the act of obeying a rule or law The factory that employed children was not in **compliance** with the law.

unwritten custom or tradition, was a fact of life. African Americans in the North were denied housing in many neighborhoods. They faced discrimination in employment and often could get only low-paying jobs.

Jim Crow laws and more subtle forms of discrimination had a widespread and severe impact on African Americans. Black Americans occupied the bottom rungs of the economic ladder. Compared to white Americans, they had significantly higher rates of poverty and illiteracy, as well as lower rates of homeownership and life expectancy. Although African Americans living in the North could vote, most who lived in the South could not. Very few African Americans held public office.

In the West and Southwest, Asian Americans and Mexican Americans, too, faced de facto segregation and, in some cases, legal restrictions. (Their struggle for equality will be discussed in a later chapter.)

The Civil Rights Movement Grows In many ways, World War II set the stage for the rise of the modern civil rights movement. President Roosevelt banned discrimination in defense industries in 1941. Gunnar Myrdal's publication in 1944 of *An American Dilemma* brought the issue of American prejudice to the forefront of public consciousness. Lastly, after risking their lives defending freedom abroad, African Americans were unwilling to accept discrimination at home.

In the 1940s, new efforts arose to try to bring an end to racial injustice. James Farmer and several others founded the Congress of Racial Equality (CORE). Its members were deeply influenced by Henry David Thoreau and Mohandas Gandhi. They became convinced that African Americans could apply direct nonviolent methods to gain civil rights. CORE organized protests against segregation in Chicago, Detroit, Denver, and other northern cities.

Success was limited, but one highly visible break in the wall of segregation did take place in 1947. Jackie Robinson joined the Brooklyn Dodgers, becoming the first African American to play major league baseball. Robinson braved death threats and rough treatment, but throughout his career he won the hearts of millions and paved the way for integration of other sports.

Nevertheless, African Americans continued to face discrimination and felt that racial equality was long overdue.

African Americans Are Segregated

In some parts of the country, even drinking fountains were segregated (below, left). On public buses, African Americans had to sit in the back. *Were the separate facilities for African Americans shown here "equal"?*

Segregation Divides America 🄻3

Instruct

- **Introduce: Key Terms** Ask students to find the key terms *de jure segregation* and *de facto segregation* (in bold) in the text. Explain the difference between the two kinds of segregation. Have students predict why the fight for equal rights might be different in states with *de jure segregation* than in states with *de facto segregation.*

- **Teach** Ask **What did the Supreme Court rule in *Plessy* v. *Ferguson*?** (*that de jure segregation was legal as long as separate-but-equal facilities were provided for both African Americans and whites*) Using the Idea Wave strategy (TE, p. T22) and the images on this page, discuss ways in which Jim Crow laws hurt African Americans. Ask **Why were African Americans less willing to accept Jim Crow laws after World War II?** (*African Americans had served in the U.S. military during World War II, and they wanted the U.S. government to recognize their equality and guarantee equal rights.*)

- **Quick Activity** Display Color Transparency: *Working Toward Equal Rights.* Use the lesson suggested in the transparency book to guide a discussion about efforts to achieve equal rights during the civil rights movement. Color Transparencies **A-117**

Independent Practice

Have students read the worksheet *Biography: Jackie Robinson* and answer the questions that follow. Teaching Resources, **p. 18**

Monitor Progress

As students fill in their timelines, circulate to make sure that they understand the events of the early civil rights movement. For a completed version of the timeline, see Note Taking Transparencies, **B-127**.

Differentiated Instruction   Solutions for All Learners

🄛1 Special Needs Students   🄛2 English Language Learners   🄛2 Less Proficient Readers

Before they read, have students write down these terms and names: Plessy *v.* Ferguson, *separate but equal, discrimination, CORE, Jackie Robinson,* and *Committee on Civil Rights.* As they read, have students write definitions or descriptions for each of these terms or names.

Tell students that the main idea of the reading is that African Americans faced many kinds of discrimination. Ask students to read a paragraph of the section aloud and list details from the paragraph that support the main idea.

Answer

Caption No; the water fountain for whites is larger and cleaner. African Americans had to squeeze into the back of the bus.

Brown v. Board of Education ⓛ₃

Instruct

- **Introduce** Ask students to read the HISTORY MAKERS feature on the next page about Thurgood Marshall. Point out that as an attorney for the NAACP, Marshall represented Linda Brown in the Supreme Court case *Brown v. Board of Education*. Ask students to predict ways in which the case might still affect the United States today.

- **Teach** Trace the steps the NAACP took to desegregate schools. Ask **What decision did the Supreme Court make in *Sweatt v. Painter*?** *(The state of Texas had violated the Fourteenth Amendment by establishing a separate African American law school that was not equal to white law schools in the state.)* Have students discuss ways in which the *McLaurin* case was similar to the *Sweatt* case. **What main argument did the NAACP make in *Brown v. Board of Education*?** *(that segregated public education and "separate but equal" laws were unconstitutional)* Have students discuss the effectiveness of the NAACP strategy of using the courts to challenge the legality of segregation.

- **Analyzing the Visuals** Have students access **www.pearsonschool.com/ushist** to use the Geography Interactive map and answer the map skills questions in the text. Have students use this information to predict where the resistance to desegregation would be most intense.

Public School Segregation, 1954

Segregation required
Segregation allowed
Segregation prohibited
No specific legislation

Map Skills Before the *Brown* decision, many states had laws mandating segregation in public schools. Even in states that had no laws regarding segregation, there was de facto segregation in schools. The photograph shows Linda Brown, the student at the center of the *Brown* case, in her classroom in Topeka, Kansas.

1. Region Which states had laws requiring school segregation? What was the status of segregation in the state where Linda Brown lived?

2. Draw Conclusions Why did school segregation exist even where it was not mandated by law?

However, the vast majority of white Americans took the opposite view. Racial violence erupted in the South, sometimes against veterans who were just trying to register to vote.

In the wake of this violence, President Truman appointed a Committee on Civil Rights to investigate race relations. In its report, the committee recommended a number of measures to ensure equal opportunity for all Americans, including an antilynching law and federal protection of voting rights. Unfortunately, Truman was unable to win congressional support for these initiatives. However, in 1948, he did use his executive power to order the desegregation of the military. Over time, the U.S. armed forces would become one of the most integrated institutions in the United States.

 **Checkpoint** How did segregation affect the lives of African Americans?

Brown v. Board of Education

Although the civil rights movement had made some gains in the 1940s, it stalled in the early 1950s. Feeling that the executive and legislative branches of government were unwilling to promote additional reforms, the NAACP decided to turn to the federal courts to attain its goals.

The NAACP Challenges Segregation By the end of World War II, the NAACP had become the largest and most powerful civil rights organization in the nation. It attracted a wide array of individuals, both black and white, including a

---

Answers

Map Skills

1. the southern states, and Missouri, Maryland, and Delaware; Segregation was allowed but not required.

2. Segregation was a longstanding, unwritten custom in many places in the North.

✓ Facilities for African Americans were seldom equal to those provided for white people and were often allowed to become run-down. African Americans did not experience the economic prosperity that white Americans did.

History Background

Precedent for *Brown* Many people believe that *Brown v. Board of Education* was the first case to challenge the constitutionality of school segregation. It was not, but it was the first successful challenge.

In 1849, Benjamin Roberts sued the city of Boston on behalf of his daughter Sarah. Boston had separate schools for African American students, and Roberts filed a lawsuit as part of a continuing effort to desegregate Boston schools. He took his daughter to the nearest public school and tried to enroll her, but Sarah was forcibly removed from the school.

Roberts's attorney was Charles Sumner, the abolitionist and later U.S. senator. However, the Boston judge ruled against Roberts, stating that the Boston school committee had the right to set whatever education policies it saw fit. The case of *Roberts* v. *City of Boston, Massachusetts,* shocked black northerners, who saw the country giving in more and more to the interests of southern slaveholders. It would be more than 100 years later before American schools were required to desegregate.

---

number of lawyers. In the 1940s, a team of NAACP attorneys pursued a strategy to challenge in the courts the legality of segregation. **Thurgood Marshall,** an African American lawyer from Baltimore, Maryland, headed the legal team that mounted this challenge.

In 1950, the NAACP won a number of key cases. In *Sweatt* v. *Painter*, the Supreme Court ruled that the state of Texas had violated the Fourteenth Amendment by establishing a separate, but unequal, all-black law school. Similarly, in the *McLaurin* v. *Oklahoma State Regents*, the Court ruled that the state of Oklahoma had violated George McLaurin's constitutional rights. Even though McLaurin had been admitted to the graduate school of the University of Oklahoma, he was denied equal access to the library, dining hall, and classrooms. According to the Supreme Court, a truly equal education involved more than simply admitting African Americans to previously all-white universities.

The Court Strikes Down Segregated Schools Not long after it won these cases, the NAACP mounted a much broader challenge to segregated public education at all grade levels. This challenge became known as *Brown* v. *Board of Education, Topeka, Kansas*. In the *Sweatt* and *McLaurin* cases, the NAACP asserted that Texas and Oklahoma had failed to provide equal educational experiences. In the *Brown* case, however, the NAACP challenged the "separate but equal" principle itself, which had been established in the 1896 *Plessy* v. *Ferguson* case.

The Supreme Court agreed with the NAACP's argument that segregated public education violated the U.S. Constitution. All nine of the Court's Justices supported the *Brown* decision, which was written by newly appointed Chief Justice **Earl Warren.** "Does segregation of children in public schools solely on the basis of race . . . deprive the children of the minority group equal education opportunities?" Warren asked in his decision. "We believe that it does." The Chief Justice and the Court declared, "in the field of public education the doctrine of 'separate but equal' has no place."

In the same month as the *Brown* decision, the Supreme Court decided another civil rights case, this time involving Mexican Americans. In *Hernandez* v. *Texas*, the Court ended the exclusion of Mexican Americans from trial juries. The *Hernandez* decision was the first Supreme Court ruling against discrimination targeting a group other than African Americans.

Reaction to *Brown* The *Brown* decision was one of the most significant and controversial in American history. Because public education touched so many Americans, it had a much greater impact than cases involving only professional and graduate schools. Moreover, by overturning the principle of "separate but equal," the Court lent its support to the views of many civil rights advocates that all forms of segregation are wrong.

In a separate ruling, known as *Brown II*, the Court called for the implementation of its decision "with all deliberate speed" across the nation. However, most southerners had no intention of desegregating their schools without a fight. In 1956, about 100 southern members of Congress endorsed "The Southern Manifesto." They pledged to oppose the *Brown* ruling through all "lawful means," on the grounds that the Court had misinterpreted the Constitution.

More ominously, the Ku Klux Klan staged a revival. Many prominent white southerners and businessmen

HISTORY MAKERS

Thurgood Marshall (1908–1993)
An excellent student, Thurgood Marshall applied to the University of Maryland Law School but was turned down because he was an African American. He went to the law school at Howard University, an historically all-black school. The law school dean, Charles Hamilton Houston, trained the students to use the law to fight segregation, and in 1936, Marshall joined the NAACP legal team. *Brown* v. *Board of Education* was just one victory among many that he won. From 1965 until 1991, Marshall was a Justice on the Supreme Court.

Independent Practice
Have students review each court case mentioned under this blue heading by writing a brief summary describing the case and the Supreme Court decision.

Monitor Progress
As students write their summaries, circulate to ensure that they understand the main ideas and decision for each case.

Connect to Your World

E-Rate In the mid-1990s, the Internet was becoming widely available. Well-funded public schools were able to provide Internet access for their students, but less well-funded schools could not. In 1996, Congress passed legislation mandating that all schools have access to advanced telecommunications services, including the Internet.

To help enforce this law, the U.S. Department of Education established the E-rate program. E-rate offered Internet access at a discounted rate, based on the income level of the school's community. In 1994, only 35 percent of public schools provided Internet access to students. By 2000, 98 percent of schools were connected. The federal E-rate program helped schools compete equally and prevented the creation of a disparity based on school-district income levels.

Instruct

- **Introduce: Key Term** Ask students to find the key term *Civil Rights Act of 1957* (in bold) in the text. Explain that it was the first civil rights act that Congress had passed since Reconstruction. Ask students to predict the effect on American society of this new civil rights legislation.

- **Teach** Have students discuss the Primary Source quotation on the following page. Ask **Why do you think Eisenhower made this speech?** *(He probably wanted to stress that though a state might not agree with a law, it had to respect the power of the federal government.)* **Why did Governor Faubus send the Arkansas National Guard to Central High School in Little Rock?** *(to stop nine African American students from entering the school)* Discuss how the events in Little Rock affected the passage of the Civil Rights Act of 1957.

- **Analyzing the Visuals** Have students study the photograph with Elizabeth Eckford. Tell them that the white woman shouting is named Hazel Bryan. Explain that Bryan came to regret her actions, called Eckford to apologize, and has since devoted her time to fighting racism. Ask students to discuss why people might change their opinion about desegregation.

Independent Practice

Ask students to work in pairs to write a script of what might have been said during the reconciliation phone call between Bryan and Eckford.

Monitor Progress

As students write their scripts, circulate to make sure that the scripts reflect positive changes.

Answers

 It overturned the principle of "separate but equal" and touched the lives of most Americans because it affected schools.

Caption Eckford is walking purposefully toward the school and ignoring the taunts and threats of the angry crowd.

---

organized "White Citizens Councils" that declared that the South would not be integrated. The Citizens Councils imposed economic and political pressure against those who favored compliance with the Supreme Court's decision.

✓ **Checkpoint** Why was the *Brown* v. *Board of Education* decision important?

Federal and State Governments Clash

Historically, education had been a state matter. States and local school boards ran the schools, and the federal government had little involvement. Local and state officials resisted the *Brown* decision's order to desegregate, and clashes with the federal government resulted. The most famous battle took place in 1957 in Little Rock, Arkansas.

A Conflict Erupts in Little Rock The Little Rock school board had established a plan to gradually desegregate its schools, beginning with Central High School. Nine young African American students volunteered to enroll. But Arkansas Governor Orval Faubus announced his opposition to integration and called out the Arkansas state National Guard. When the nine students arrived at Central High, the soldiers blocked their way.

One of the nine, Elizabeth Eckford, has described the scene. An angry white mob began to approach her, with some screaming, "Lynch her! Lynch her!" Eckford sought out a friendly face, someone who might help. "I looked into the face of an old woman and it seemed a kind face," she recalled, "but when I looked at her again she spat on me." Fortunately, another white woman whisked Eckford away on a public bus before the mob could have its way. None of the Little Rock Nine gained entrance to the school that day.

Up until the Little Rock crisis, President Eisenhower had provided little leadership on the civil rights front. Following the *Brown* decision, he did not urge the nation to rapidly desegregate its schools. Privately, he expressed his misgivings

Integrating Little Rock Schools

Angry white students surrounded Elizabeth Eckford (below, right) as she tried to enter Central High in Little Rock. *How is Eckford responding to the white students?*

Differentiated Instruction   Solutions for All Learners

Advanced Readers   Gifted and Talented Students

The nine African American students who volunteered to desegregate Central High School in Little Rock, Arkansas, were brave. They faced danger every day to acquire an education and to challenge racism. Many people are aware of the events that took place during the desegregation of Central High School, but few can name the nine students who helped desegregate the high school, the details of those students' experiences, or say what the nine did after they graduated. Have students research the Little Rock Nine and write a brief biography of each. Then, have students write a newspaper article about one of the students whose story proved particularly moving or inspiring.

about the ruling. But when Governor Faubus resisted the will of the federal courts, Eisenhower realized he had to act. He sent federal troops to Little Rock to protect the students and to enforce the Court's decision. Eisenhower explained this action in a nationally televised address:

Primary Source "It is important that the reasons for my action be understood by all our citizens. . . . A foundation of our American way of life is our national respect for law. . . . If resistance to the federal court orders ceases at once, the further presence of federal troops will be unnecessary and the City of Little Rock will return to its normal habits of peace and order and a blot upon the fair name and high honor of our nation in the world will be removed."
—President Dwight D. Eisenhower, "Address on Little Rock," 1957

For the entire school year, federal troops stayed in Little Rock, escorting the nine students to and from Central High and guarding them on the school grounds. On the last day of class, Ernest Green, the one senior of the nine, became the first African American to graduate from Central High School. The showdown demonstrated that the President would not tolerate open defiance of the law. Still, most southern states found ways to resist full compliance with the Court's decision. Many years would pass before black and white children went to school together.

Vocabulary Builder
compliance–(kuhm PLĪ uhns) *n.* the act of obeying a rule or law

Congress Passes a Civil Rights Law Civil rights forces enjoyed a small victory when Congress passed the **Civil Rights Act of 1957** and President Eisenhower signed it into law. This law established the United States Civil Rights Commission, which had the power to investigate violations of civil rights. The law also gave the U.S. Attorney General greater power to protect the voting rights of African Americans. But overall, the law lacked teeth. Its main significance was that it was the first civil rights bill passed by Congress since Reconstruction.

 Checkpoint Why did President Eisenhower send federal troops to Little Rock?

The Montgomery Bus Boycott

In addition to legal efforts during this era, some civil rights activists took direct action to end segregation. On December 1, 1955, **Rosa Parks,** an African American seamstress, boarded a bus in Montgomery, Alabama, and sat down in an empty seat. Several stops later, the bus driver requested that she give up her seat to a white passenger. Montgomery law required African American passengers to give up their seats to whites. After Rosa Parks refused to obey the law, she was arrested. "The [policemen] asked if the driver had asked me to stand up, and I said yes, and they wanted to know why I didn't," Parks later recalled. "I told them I didn't think I should have to stand up. After I had paid my fare and occupied a seat, I didn't think I should have to give it up."

Rosa Parks Launches a Movement Parks's action set in motion a chain of events that transformed the civil rights movement. Over the next few days, a core of civil rights activists in Montgomery organized a one-day bus boycott. They called upon the black community

HISTORY MAKERS

Rosa Parks (1913–2005)
On December 1, 1955, in Montgomery, Alabama, Rosa Parks was arrested for refusing to give up her bus seat to a white passenger. African Americans responded with a boycott of city buses that lasted more than a year. Parks later moved to Detroit and worked for many years for Representative John Conyers, an African American member of Congress. She founded a nonprofit institute whose goal was to help young people improve their school, work, and interpersonal skills. When she died in 2005, her body was laid in honor at the Capitol in Washington, D.C., making her the first woman ever to be recognized in this way.

For a long while, many people thought that Parks had refused to give up her seat simply because she was tired after a long day of work. But, in reality, Parks had a record of fighting for civil rights. She had been active in the Montgomery chapter of the NAACP for years. This does not mean that she set out to get arrested and spark a movement. But Parks and other activists welcomed the chance to use the incident to protest bus segregation.

- **Analyzing the Visuals** Draw students' attention to the Infographic on this page. Ask students to summarize the information provided in the quotations. Then, have them use this information to predict how King might motivate African Americans to maintain nonviolent protest when confronting physical violence.

Independent Practice

Write the following red headings from the text on the board: Rosa Parks Launches a Movement and Martin Luther King, Jr., Urges Nonviolence. Ask students to work in pairs to list supporting details from the text for each red heading.

Monitor Progress

Circulate to make sure that students' lists include pertinent details about the Montgomery bus boycott and responses to it.

● **INFOGRAPHIC**

King's Philosophy of
NONVIOLENT PROTEST

For Martin Luther King, Jr., the strategy of nonviolent protest had diverse roots. As the son and grandson of Baptist preachers, King absorbed the teachings of Jesus at an early age. Later, a deep interest in philosophy led him to explore the writings of the American author Henry David Thoreau, who advocated civil disobedience, or refusing to obey unjust government or laws. Mohandas Gandhi was another critical influence on King. During India's struggle for independence from British rule, Gandhi expanded on Thoreau's approach, preaching nonviolence as the only way to achieve victory against much stronger foes.

King read Thoreau's *Essay on Civil Disobedience.* ▶

"*Fascinated by the idea of refusing to cooperate with an evil system, I was so deeply moved that I reread the work several times. This was my first intellectual contact with the theory of nonviolent resistance.*"

Gandhi's tactics inspired King. ▶

"*It was in this Gandhian emphasis on love and nonviolence that I discovered the method for social reform that I had been seeking.*"

King was a Baptist preacher with a deep faith in God and in the teachings of Jesus. ▼

"*In the midst of … dangers I have felt an inner calm and known resources of strength that only God could give…. I have felt the power of God transforming the fatigue of despair into the buoyancy of hope.*"

Thinking Critically

1. **Apply Information** How did King put his belief in nonviolence into practice in the Montgomery bus boycott?

2. **Draw Conclusions** What are the advantages and disadvantages of nonviolent protest?

History Background

Gandhi and the Civil Rights Movement The civil rights movement in the United States was heavily influenced by the ideas of Mohandas Gandhi. The Indian leader's nonviolent protests, which helped free India from British rule in the 1940s, set a standard for peaceful civil disobedience that many civil rights activists, including Martin Luther King, Jr., emulated. Gandhi's ideas also inspired James Farmer, who helped found the Congress of Racial Equality (CORE) in 1942. Farmer and other CORE members believed that using the nonviolent methods proposed by Gandhi would help African Americans in the United States win their civil rights.

Answers

Thinking Critically

1. King persuaded African Americans to channel their anger and eagerness for change into committed nonviolent protest.

2. An advantage is that nonviolent protesters always have the moral high ground; they reveal the brutality of their violent opponents. The disadvantages are that nonviolent protesters can be abused, or even killed, by violent opponents.

Martin Luther King Urges Nonviolence On the evening following the boycott, the Montgomery Improvement Association (MIA), the organization that sponsored the bus boycott, held a meeting. Dr. **Martin Luther King, Jr.,** a Baptist minister, addressed the group. Though he had had little time to prepare, King delivered an inspirational speech that brought the audience to its feet. Noting that African Americans were tired of segregation and oppression, King declared that there was no alternative but to protest. However, he called for the protest to be nonviolent. He urged them not to become resentful, which would lead to hatred toward whites, but rather to follow Christian doctrine and love them.

After King spoke, the MIA vowed to continue the boycott and chose King as its leader. For more than a year, African Americans in Montgomery maintained their boycott of the buses. They did so despite economic pressures from their employers and threats of violence by the Ku Klux Klan. King himself survived a bombing of his house. Fortunately, his wife and baby daughter were not home at the time. Finally, in 1956, the Supreme Court ruled that the Montgomery city law that segregated buses was unconstitutional. After more than a year, the MIA ended its boycott, and African Americans began to ride the buses again.

Ministers Form the SCLC The bus boycott represented a tremendous victory for African Americans in Montgomery and across the nation. The boycott revealed the power that African Americans could have if they joined together. The protest also elevated King and his philosophy of nonviolence into a prominent position within the civil rights movement.

After the boycott, King and another Montgomery minister, Ralph Abernathy, established the Southern Christian Leadership Conference (SCLC) to continue the struggle for civil rights. Made up largely of southern African American ministers, the SCLC advocated nonviolent resistance to fight injustice. The SCLC went on to organize a series of protests, including a Prayer Pilgrimage in Washington, D.C., in 1957, which helped convince Congress to pass civil rights legislation. Still, discrimination and segregation remained widespread.

✔ **Checkpoint** What role did Rosa Parks and Martin Luther King, Jr., play in the Montgomery bus boycott?

SECTION **1** Assessment

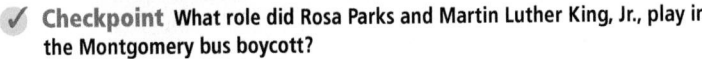

Progress Monitoring *Online*
For: Self-test with vocabulary practice
www.pearsonschool.com/ushist

Comprehension

1. **Terms and People** For each item below, write a sentence explaining its significance:
   • de jure segregation
   • de facto segregation
   • Thurgood Marshall
   • *Brown* v. *Board of Education*
   • Earl Warren
   • Civil Rights Act of 1957
   • Rosa Parks
   • Montgomery bus boycott
   • Martin Luther King, Jr.

2. **NoteTaking Reading Skill: Summarize** Use your timeline to answer the Section Focus Question: How did African Americans challenge segregation after World War II?

Writing About History

3. **Quick Write: Identify Questions** Historical research begins with identifying unanswered questions. Such questions often relate to the causes of an event or development. Reread this section and identify two events or developments that raise unanswered questions in your mind. Try to write questions that begin with *Why* or *How.*

Critical Thinking

4. **Recognize Cause and Effect** Why did the struggle for equal rights intensify after World War II?

5. **Analyze Information** How did the *Brown* decision lead to conflict between federal and state governments?

6. **Synthesize Information** Why is the Montgomery bus boycott considered a turning point in the civil rights movement?

Landmark Decisions of the Supreme Court

How Does Segregation Affect Education?

Objectives

- Explain the importance of *Brown* v. *Board of Education.*
- Describe trends in desegregation since 1968.

Background Knowledge ⓛ

Discuss the *Plessy* v. *Ferguson* ruling of 1896 and how "separate but equal" affected African Americans in the decades after the ruling.

Instruct ⓛ

- Ask students to describe what "separate but equal" facilities were like by the time Linda Brown was going to school. Ask **What do you suppose the school that Brown was expected to attend was like?** *(It may have been in poor condition with fewer textbooks and other supplies than white schools.)* Ask **What did Brown want to do?** *(She wanted to go to the school near where she lived, one that had the supplies and resources that a school should have.)*

- Have students complete the *Landmark Decisions of the Supreme Court: How Does Segregation Affect Education?* worksheet. **Teaching Resources, p. 19**

- **Connect to Your World** Refer students to the Key Supreme Court Cases section for summaries of this case. You may also wish students to do additional research. Students' graphs should accurately reflect the data provided. Students' research should indicate trends since 2001 and offer plausible explanations for any changes.

Monitor Progress

Circulate to make sure that students correctly interpret the political cartoon and answer the questions on the worksheet.

How Does Segregation Affect Education?

Until the 1950s, public schools throughout the United States were segregated by race. This separation of students was legal because of the 1896 *Plessy* v. *Ferguson* decision, in which the Supreme Court ruled that "separate but equal" facilities did not violate the Constitution. However, many believed that segregated schools could never provide an equal education.

▼ Linda Brown

Brown v. *Board of Education* (1954)

The Facts	The Issue	The Decision
• Linda Brown was an African American student in the segregated school district of Topeka, Kansas. • Linda's parents tried to enroll her in an all-white school closer to home, but school officials denied the application on the basis of race. • The NAACP filed a lawsuit against the Board of Education on behalf of the Browns and several other black families.	The NAACP argued that segregated schools deprived African American students the equal protection of the law required by the Fourteenth Amendment.	The Supreme Court ruled unanimously that segregated schools were inherently unequal and violated the Fourteenth Amendment.

Why It Matters

Brown v. *Board of Education* was a major legal victory in the civil rights movement. This landmark decision brought America one step closer to securing equal rights for all. Chief Justice Earl Warren declared that segregation in education was unconstitutional because it prevented an equal education for all races:

"In these days, it is doubtful that any child may reasonably be expected to succeed in life if he is denied the opportunity of an education. Such an opportunity . . . is a right which must be made available to all on equal terms. . . . To separate them [children in grade and high schools] from others of similar age and qualifications solely because of their race generates a feeling of inferiority . . . that may affect their hearts and minds in a way unlikely to ever be undone. . . ."

▼ Students at a high school in Texas

Connect to Your World

Use the data in the table to create a graph, and describe the trend that you see. Then, research school segregation today. Have schools become more or less segregated since 2001? What might explain this change?

School Desegregation After *Brown*			
(Percentage of African American students in 90 percent minority schools)			
	1968	1988	1991	2001
---	---	---	---	---
South	78	24	26	31
Northeast	43	48	50	51
Midwest	58	42	40	47
West	51	29	27	30

SOURCE: *National Center for Education Statistics Common Core of Data*

History Background

The *Plessy* Decision Chief Justice Warren's decision in *Brown* v. *Board of Education* was a response to Justice Billings Brown's language in *Plessy* v. *Ferguson* in 1896. Brown had written that although the Fourteenth Amendment established the equality of the two races before the law, ". . . in the nature of things it could not have been intended to abolish distinctions based upon color, or to enforce social, as distinguished from political, equality . . . Laws [requiring] their separation in [public] places do not necessarily imply the inferiority of either race . . . We consider the underlying fallacy of [the plaintiff's] argument to [be] that the enforced separation of the two races stamps the colored race with a badge of inferiority. If this be so, it is not by reason of anything found in the act, but solely because the colored race chooses to put that construction upon it. . . . The argument [assumes] that social prejudices may be overcome by legislation, and that equal rights cannot be secured to the negro except by an enforced commingling of the two races. We cannot accept this proposition."

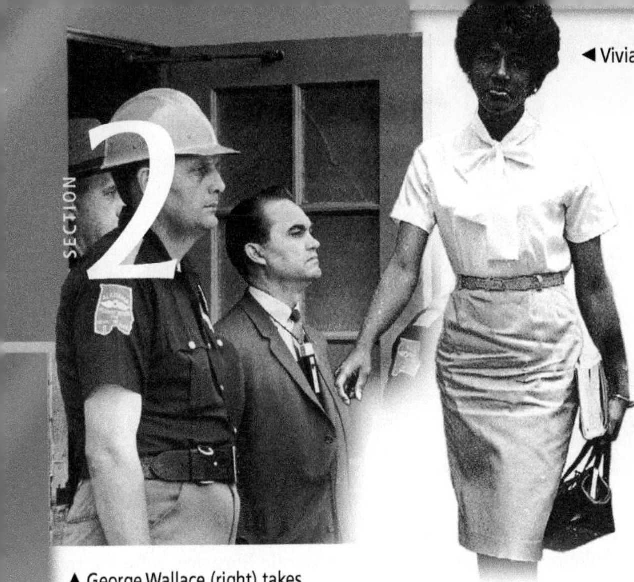

◄ Vivian Malone

▲ George Wallace (right) takes a stand against integration.

WITNESS HISTORY

Blocking the Schoolhouse Door

Alabama Governor George Wallace made it clear where he stood on civil rights: "I say segregation now! Segregation tomorrow! Segregation forever!" Wallace vowed to stand "in the schoolhouse door" and personally block any attempt to integrate Alabama schools. On June 11, 1963, he got his chance. As federal marshals escorted two African American students to register at the University of Alabama, Wallace stood on the steps of the school. He proclaimed the right of states to regulate their own schools. One of the students later recalled:

> "I didn't feel I should sneak in. I didn't feel I should go around the back door. If [Wallace] were standing in the door, I had every right in the world to face him and to go to school."
>
> —Vivian Malone Jones, 2003

The Movement Gains Ground

Objectives

- Describe the sit-ins, freedom rides, and the actions of James Meredith in the early 1960s.
- Explain how the protests at Birmingham and the March on Washington were linked to the Civil Rights Act of 1964.
- Summarize the provisions of the Civil Rights Act of 1964.

Terms and People

sit-in	Medgar Evers
SNCC	March on Washington
freedom ride	filibuster
James Meredith	Civil Rights Act of 1964

NoteTaking

Reading Skill: Summarize Use a concept web like the one below to record information about the civil rights protests of the 1960s.

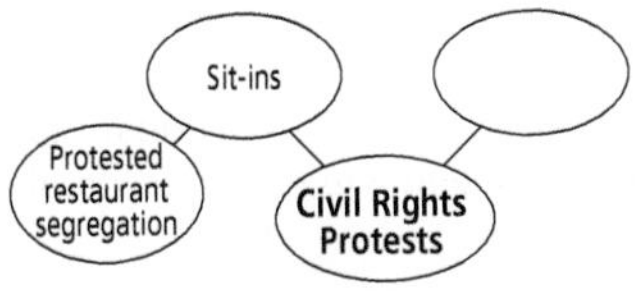

Why It Matters Despite the *Brown* decision and other civil rights victories, little changed in the everyday lives of most African Americans. Nonetheless, activists continued to struggle for civil rights. In the early 1960s, the movement experienced a groundswell of support. This surge produced a dramatic shift in race relations, led to the passage of landmark civil rights legislation in 1964, and set the stage for future reforms. **Section Focus Question: How did the civil rights movement gain ground in the 1960s?**

Student Activists Make a Difference

After the *Brown* decision, many black youths expected that their schools would integrate quickly and that other racial reforms would follow. Change was not quick to come, however. Disappointed by the lack of progress, young African Americans began to challenge segregation with new vigor and determination.

Sit-ins Challenge Segregation On February 1, 1960, four African American college students ordered doughnuts and coffee at a Woolworth's lunch counter in Greensboro, North Carolina. As they expected, the white waitress refused to serve them. In the South, nearly all restaurants that served whites refused to serve blacks. To protest this discrimination, the four students sat down on the stools at the lunch counter, where they stayed until closing time.

Word of the Greensboro **sit-in** spread rapidly, sparking a wave of similar protests across the nation. In Nashville, Tennessee, for instance, students led by the Reverend James Lawson staged sit-ins

Vocabulary Builder

Use the information below and the following resource to teach students the high-use word from this section. Teaching Resources, Vocabulary Builder, p. 10

High-Use Word	Definition and Sample Sentence
tolerate	*v.* to allow or put up with The Allies refused to **tolerate** Hitler's aggression.

SECTION 2 Step-by-Step Instruction

Objectives

As you teach this section, keep students focused on the following objectives to help them answer the Section Focus Question and master core content.

- Describe the sit-ins, freedom rides, and the actions of James Meredith in the early 1960s.
- Explain how the protests at Birmingham and the March on Washington were linked to the Civil Rights Act of 1964.
- Summarize the provisions of the Civil Rights Act of 1964.

Prepare to Read

Background Knowledge (L3)

Remind students about the successes of the civil rights movement in the 1950s. Ask students to predict what challenges the civil rights movement might face in the 1960s.

Set a Purpose (L3)

- **WITNESS HISTORY** Read the selection aloud.

  Ask **Why did Vivian Malone not enter the school from the back door?** *(She believed that she had the right to enter by its main door.)*
- **Focus** Point out the Section Focus Question, and write it on the board. Tell students to refer to this question as they read. *(Answer appears with Section 2 Assessment answers.)*
- **Preview** Have students preview the Section Objectives and the list of Terms and People.
- **NoteTaking** Using the Guided Questioning strategy (TE, p. T20), have students read this section. As they read, have students record information about the civil rights protests of the 1960s. Reading and Note Taking Study Guide

Student Activists Make a Difference L3

Instruct

- **Introduce: Key Terms** Ask students to find the key terms ***sit-in*** and ***SNCC*** (in bold) in the text and provide definitions. Have students predict the effect that *sit-ins* and the *SNCC* will have on the civil rights movement.

- **Teach** Ask **What did the people who participated in sit-ins hope to accomplish?** *(They wanted to force public places to desegregate.)* Have a student read the Primary Source quotation on this page aloud. Ask **On what strategy did protestors at sit-ins rely?** *(the power of nonviolent civil disobedience to reveal the injustice of segregation)* **What was the goal of the SNCC?** *(to unite all African Americans in the fight against racial discrimination)* Discuss how the goals of sit-ins and the SNCC were linked.

- **Analyzing the Visuals** Draw students' attention to the photograph of the sit-in. Ask students to identify those participating in the sit-in and those who are there to threaten the participants. Discuss the dangers that sit-in participants faced.

Independent Practice

Have students write journal entries from the viewpoint of a sit-in participant, describing their experiences and emotions.

Monitor Progress

As students fill in their concept webs, circulate to make sure that they accurately connect information about the civil rights protests of the 1960s. For a completed version of the concept web, see Note Taking Transparencies, **B-128**.

Answers

Caption The atmosphere is tense and threatening.

✓ Young people brought an attitude of urgency to the movement. They wanted change to come quickly, not in decades. They organized sit-ins and other activities to speed change and build on the momentum of the 1950s.

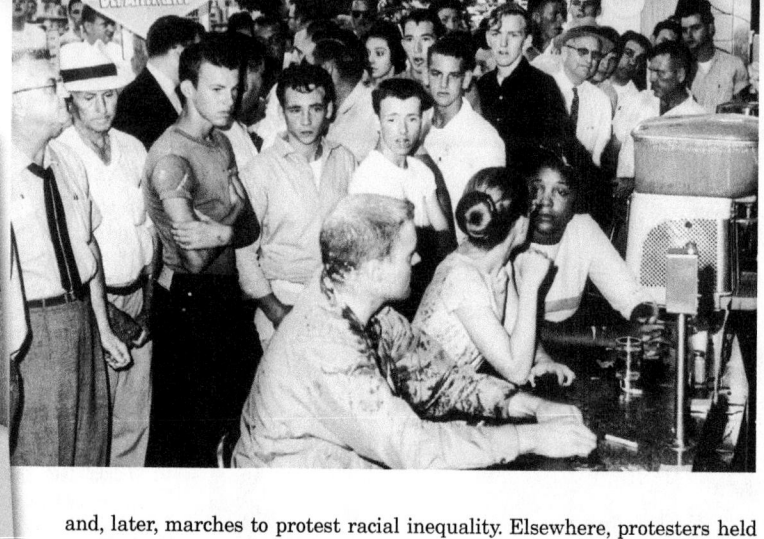

Protesting Segregation
Protesters challenged segregation at lunch counters by picketing (above, left). Later activists held sit-ins, like the one (above, right) in Jackson, Mississippi. Sit-in participants were trained not to react, even when hostile onlookers dumped food on them. *How would you describe the atmosphere at this lunch counter?*

and, later, marches to protest racial inequality. Elsewhere, protesters held "wade-ins" at public beaches and "read-ins" at public libraries, refusing to leave beaches or libraries reserved for whites only. Other activists carried picket signs in demonstrations and wrote letters to newspapers and government officials to express their support of the protests in the South.

SNCC Promotes Nonviolent Protest The sit-ins marked the birth of a new militancy, especially among young African Americans. To build on the momentum they had gained, about 175 students from 30 states met at Shaw University, in Raleigh, North Carolina. There, on Easter weekend in 1960, they listened to James Lawson deliver an inspiring address:

> **Primary Source** "We who are demonstrators are trying to raise what we call the 'moral issue.' That is, we are pointing to the viciousness of racial segregation and prejudice and calling it evil or sin. . . . [We are also] asserting, 'get moving.' The pace of change is too slow. At this rate it will be another generation before the major forms of segregation disappear. . . . Most of us will be grandparents before we can live normal human lives."
>
> —James Lawson, "From a Lunch Counter Stool," 1960

Ella Baker, a veteran of the struggle for civil rights, had organized the meeting. The granddaughter of enslaved African Americans, Baker had been active in the NAACP and SCLC. She helped the young activists to establish a new civil rights organization, the **Student Nonviolent Coordinating Committee**, or **SNCC**. Its goal was to create a grass-roots movement that involved all classes of African Americans in the struggle to defeat white racism and to obtain equality.

✓ **Checkpoint** How did young people energize the civil rights movement in the 1960s?

Riding for Freedom

The next battleground was interstate transportation. Activists targeted this industry because they knew that travel between states was subject to federal rather than state regulation. In fact, the Supreme Court had recently ruled in *Boynton* v. *Virginia* (1960) that segregation on interstate buses and in waiting rooms was illegal. Civil rights activists were now going to test the federal government's willingness to enforce the law.

Differentiated Instruction Solutions for All Learners

L1 Special Needs Students **L2 English Language Learners** **L2 Less Proficient Readers**

Direct each student to choose three key events discussed in this section and create illustrations for a newspaper reporting on these events. For example, students may wish to illustrate the sit-in at Woolworth's in Greensboro, North Carolina, or Martin Luther King, Jr., giving his "I Have a Dream" speech in Washington, D.C. Then, write the red headings for this section on the board. Ask students to explain the significance of the events they illustrated and tell under which red heading each illustration should appear. After students have categorized all their illustrations under the section red headings, have students confirm that each illustration appears under the appropriate red heading.

Freedom Riders Face Angry Mobs In the spring of 1961, CORE staged a **"freedom ride"** through the Deep South. Riders set off in two separate buses from Washington, D.C., bound for New Orleans. En route, they defied segregationist codes. African Americans sat in the front of the bus and used "white" restrooms in bus stations.

In Alabama, the trip took a dangerous turn. After departing from Anniston, prosegregationists firebombed one of the buses. When the second bus arrived in Birmingham, a white mob attacked the riders.

INFOGRAPHIC

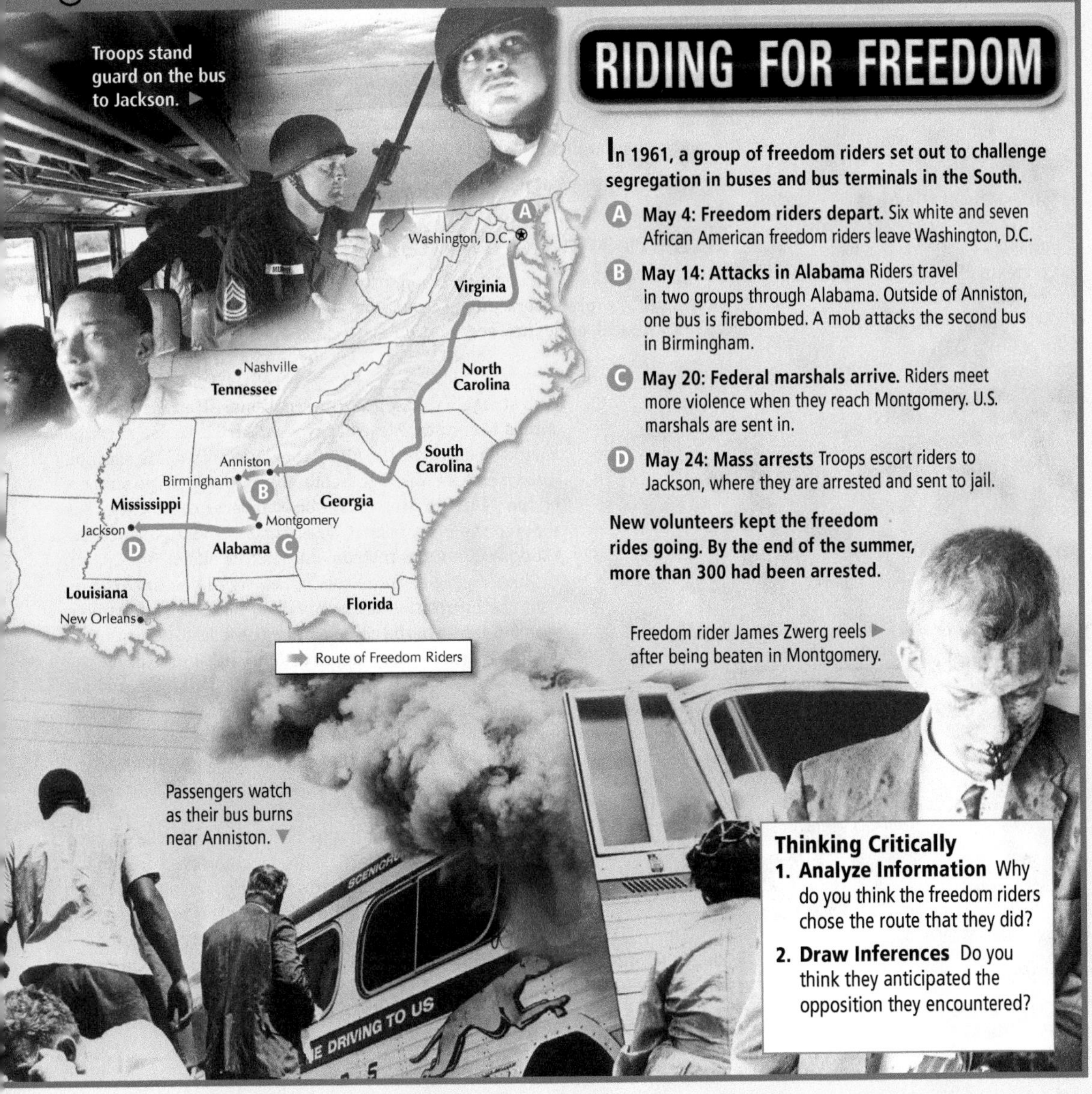

RIDING FOR FREEDOM

◄ Troops stand guard on the bus to Jackson.

In 1961, a group of freedom riders set out to challenge segregation in buses and bus terminals in the South.

A **May 4: Freedom riders depart.** Six white and seven African American freedom riders leave Washington, D.C.

B **May 14: Attacks in Alabama** Riders travel in two groups through Alabama. Outside of Anniston, one bus is firebombed. A mob attacks the second bus in Birmingham.

C **May 20: Federal marshals arrive.** Riders meet more violence when they reach Montgomery. U.S. marshals are sent in.

D **May 24: Mass arrests** Troops escort riders to Jackson, where they are arrested and sent to jail.

New volunteers kept the freedom rides going. By the end of the summer, more than 300 had been arrested.

Washington, D.C.
Virginia
Nashville
Tennessee
North Carolina
South Carolina
Anniston
Birmingham
Mississippi
Georgia
Jackson
Montgomery
Alabama
Louisiana
New Orleans
Florida

Route of Freedom Riders

► Freedom rider James Zwerg reels after being beaten in Montgomery.

▼ Passengers watch as their bus burns near Anniston.

Thinking Critically
1. **Analyze Information** Why do you think the freedom riders chose the route that they did?
2. **Draw Inferences** Do you think they anticipated the opposition they encountered?

Connect to Your World

Freedom Riders The freedom riders in 1961 worked to integrate public transportation in the South. In 2003, a new group of freedom riders boarded buses to support the Immigrant Workers Freedom Ride.

About 800 immigrant workers rode buses to New York City and Washington, D.C., stopping in more than 100 cities on the way to urge Americans to recognize the civil rights of immigrant workers. The freedom riders of 2003 wanted to persuade the U.S.

government to make citizenship easier for immigrant workers to attain and to protect these workers from unsafe workplaces.

One of the leaders of the 2003 freedom riders was Representative John Lewis of Georgia, who participated in the 1961 freedom rides. Lewis said: "Like the Freedom Rides of 1961, Freedom Ride 2003 calls on ordinary people to do extraordinary things . . . to stand up for the rights of others . . . and to challenge the federal government to act. . . ."

Protests and Confrontations Intensify

Instruct

- **Introduce: Vocabulary Builder**
  Have students locate the vocabulary term *tolerate* and its definition. Then, write the word on the board, say it aloud, have students say it with you, and read the definition. Have students discuss the ways in which African Americans refused to *tolerate* discrimination in the 1950s and the early 1960s.

- **Teach** Have students examine the photographs of James Meredith on this page. Ask **Why did federal marshals accompany Meredith to the University of Mississippi?** *(They were assigned to protect Meredith from white protestors.)* **How did President Kennedy respond to the University of Mississippi rioters?** *(In a televised address to the nation, he said that the rioters were free to disagree with desegregation laws, but not to disobey them.)* To help students understand the differences of opinion between President Kennedy and Governor Wallace over segregation, have students read and complete *Viewpoints: Kennedy and Wallace*. Then, have students read the Primary Source quotation on the next page. Ask **Why did Martin Luther King, Jr., say that African Americans could no longer wait for reform?** *(He believed that the longer African Americans waited for reform, the longer the national and state governments would procrastinate in enacting it.)* Teaching Resources, p. 20

Integrating Ole Miss

Accompanied by federal marshals, James Meredith arrived at the University of Mississippi in 1962. He went on to graduate from the university in 1963.

President Kennedy Takes Action Photographs of the bombed-out bus and the injured riders appeared in newspapers and on television screens around the world, prodding President John F. Kennedy to intervene. Kennedy had intervened before. The previous year, when he was running for the presidency, Kennedy had helped to win Martin Luther King's release from a Georgia prison after state officials had sentenced King to 6 months in jail for a traffic violation. King was freed and Kennedy, with the help of African American voters, went on to win the presidential election of 1960.

Kennedy now took action to stem the violence against the freedom riders. His administration worked out a deal with Mississippi's leaders. Police and state troopers agreed to protect the riders. The Federal Transportation Commission also issued an order mandating the desegregation of interstate transportation. In exchange, the Kennedy administration agreed not to intervene when Mississippi authorities arrested the activists and sentenced them to jail for disturbing the peace.

The freedom riders achieved their immediate goal. They compelled a reluctant federal government to act. By refusing to allow violent mobs to deter them, the riders also displayed that intimidation would not defeat the movement.

✔ **Checkpoint** What did the freedom rides accomplish?

Protests and Confrontations Intensify

In the fall of 1962 and spring of 1963, protests against racial discrimination intensified. The protesters put pressure on the federal government to help break down legal, or de jure, segregation.

Meredith Integrates the University of Mississippi
One struggle that gained international attention involved **James Meredith**. Meredith was an Air Force veteran who sought to enroll at the all-white University of Mississippi, known as "Ole Miss." In September 1962, with the support of the NAACP, Meredith won a federal court case that ordered the university to desegregate. Civil rights activist **Medgar Evers** was instrumental in this effort.

Mississippi governor Ross Barnett was determined to prevent the integration of the university. The issue became a standoff between the governor and the federal government.

On September 30, rumors of Meredith's arrival on the university's campus began to spread. Federal marshals had been assigned to protect him. Over the course of the night, a full-scale riot erupted, with federal marshals battling white protesters intent on scaring Meredith away.

As the rioting took place, President Kennedy addressed the nation on television. "Americans are free . . . to disagree with the law but not to disobey it," he declared. "For any government of laws . . . , no man, however prominent and powerful . . . is entitled to defy a court of law." The rioting went on throughout the night. By the time it ended, 160 people had been injured and 2 men had been killed.

The following morning, Meredith registered as a student and took his first class. He graduated from Ole Miss in 1963 and went on to obtain his law degree from Columbia University in New York City. Tragically, Medgar Evers was assassi-

Answer

✔ The freedom rides led to desegregation of interstate public transportation and related facilities in the South.

nated, on his front doorstep, in June 1963. Three years later, Meredith was shot and nearly killed. Both shootings stand as historical reminders of the high costs of fighting racial discrimination.

King Campaigns in Birmingham In the spring of 1963, Martin Luther King, Jr., and the SCLC targeted Birmingham, Alabama, for a major civil rights campaign. They chose Birmingham because of its reputation as the most segregated city in the South.

The campaign began nonviolently at first with protest marches and sit-ins. City officials got a court order prohibiting the demonstrations. On Good Friday, April 12, 1963, King decided to violate the order and join the demonstration personally, even though he knew it would lead to his arrest. From his jail cell, King wrote a letter explaining why he and other civil rights activists were tired of waiting for reform: "For years now I have heard the word 'wait!' It rings in the ear of every Negro with piercing familiarity. This 'Wait!' has almost always meant 'Never.'"

One of the most poignant passages of the letter describes King's concern about the impact of discrimination on his children:

Clash in Birmingham
Police in Birmingham, Alabama, used police dogs to break up civil rights marches in 1963. *How do you think Americans reacted when they saw images like these on television and in newspapers?*

> **Primary Source** "Perhaps it is easy for those who have never felt the stinging darts of segregation to say, 'Wait.' But . . . when you suddenly find your tongue twisted and your speech stammering as you seek to explain to your six-year-old daughter why she can't go to the public amusement park that has just been advertised on television, and see tears welling up in her eyes when she is told that Funtown is closed to colored children. . . . Then you will understand why we find it difficult to wait."
> —Martin Luther King, Jr., "Letter From Birmingham Jail," 1963

After King was released from jail, the SCLC increased the frequency of the demonstrations. For the first time, schoolchildren joined the "freedom marches." Finally, Birmingham's Public Safety Commissioner, T. Eugene "Bull" Connor, would not <u>tolerate</u> the demonstrations any longer. He used police dogs and fire hoses on the protesters. Many Americans were shocked by photographs and news coverage of nonviolent protesters set upon by dogs and overwhelmed by the powerful jets of water from fire hoses. They sent telegrams and letters by the thousands to the White House, calling on the President to act.

Vocabulary Builder
tolerate–(TAHL er ayt) *v.* to allow or put up with

Kennedy Backs Civil Rights In addition to the conflict in Birmingham, civil rights protests were taking place in cities from Jackson, Mississippi, to Cambridge, Maryland. President Kennedy became convinced that he had to take a more active role in promoting civil rights.

On June 11, 1963, Kennedy delivered a moving televised address. Calling civil rights a "moral issue," he declared that the nation had an obligation to "fulfill its promise" of giving all Americans "equal rights and equal opportunities." President Kennedy sent to Congress a proposal for sweeping civil rights legislation. His brother, Attorney General Robert F. Kennedy, led the charge for passage of the bill.

✓ **Checkpoint** How did James Meredith and Martin Luther King, Jr., prompt President Kennedy to promote civil rights?

Differentiated Instruction   Solutions for All Learners

L4 Advanced Readers   L4 Gifted and Talented Students

Have students conduct research on one of the following topics from the civil rights movement: the role of African American churches in the civil rights movement; the impact of television coverage on American attitudes toward the movement; or the struggle to register southern African Americans to vote.

Ask students to use their findings to write newspaper articles that may have been written during the 1960s about their chosen topics. Ensure that students' newspaper articles answer the *Who, What, Where, When, Why,* and *How* of their topics.

- **Analyzing the Visuals** Direct students to the photograph of the African American protestor. Ask **What role did the media play in the civil rights movement?** *(Many Americans were shocked when they saw photographs and news covering the violence against peaceful protesters and called on President Kennedy to act in favor of the protestors.)*

Independent Practice
Ask students to write a paragraph describing the events that occurred at the University of Mississippi in September 1962. Then, have them write another paragraph describing the federal government's actions in response to those events.

Monitor Progress
As students write their paragraphs, circulate to make sure that they understand what happened at the University of Mississippi and the response to it. Also, make sure that students know how to organize the information in their paragraphs.

Answers

Caption Americans were shocked and angered to see police and violent mobs savagely beating peaceful protestors (often young people). Many people came to support the protestors and the civil rights movement because of images such as this one.

✓ The violent reaction to Meredith's enrollment at the University of Mississippi led President Kennedy to address the nation and insist that desegregation laws be obeyed. Martin Luther King, Jr.'s, "Letter From Birmingham Jail," helped persuade Kennedy to send civil rights legislation to Congress.

The Movement Marches on Washington L3

Instruct

- **Introduce: Key Term** Ask students to find the key term **March on Washington** (in bold) in the text. Then display Color Transparency: *The March on Washington.* Use the lesson suggested in the transparency book to introduce information about the **March on Washington.** Color Transparencies **A-118**

- **Teach** Ask **What was the purpose of the March on Washington?** *(to put pressure on Congress to pass a new civil rights bill)* **Why were SNCC leaders dissatisfied with the march?** *(They had wanted a more militant event that would precipitate faster action in Congress.)* Have students debate the effectiveness of the March on Washington.

- **Quick Activity** To help students gain a greater understanding of the impact of this famous speech, assign students "*Interpreting President Kennedy's Report on Civil Rights Speech*", and have them answer the questions on the worksheet. Teaching Resources, **p. 22**

Independent Practice

To enrich and extend the lesson, have students access the History Interactive at **www.pearsonschool.com/ushist**. After students experience the History Interactive, have them write paragraphs explaining why the March on Washington had such a profound effect on the nation.

Monitor Progress

Have students complete the Thinking Critically question on the next page and share their answers with the class.

The Movement Marches on Washington

To put pressure on Congress to pass the new civil rights bill, supporters made plans for a massive demonstration in Washington, D.C. The event brought together the major civil rights groups—including the NAACP, SCLC, and SNCC—as well as labor unions and religious groups.

The **March on Washington** took place on August 28, 1963. Organizers had hoped for 100,000 demonstrators. More than double that number showed up, having made the journey to the capital from around the country. Before the march, there had been some concern about maintaining order at such a huge demonstration. Yet despite the massive numbers, the day was peaceful and even festive. Popular celebrities and entertainers were on hand to perform for the crowd.

The main rally took place in front of the Lincoln Memorial, where a distinguished roster of speakers addressed the crowd. The highlight of the day came

Events That Changed America

INTERACTIVE Whiteboard

THE MARCH ON WASHINGTON

The March on Washington drew more than 200,000 people to Washington, D.C. The demonstrators were a diverse group from all parts of the country. They were young and old and came from various classes and religious backgrounds. More than a quarter of them were white.

The Washington Monument was the starting point for the day's events. Prominent singers performed songs, including the civil rights movement's unofficial anthem, "We Shall Overcome." Then, the throng marched to the Lincoln Memorial for the main rally. A. Philip Randolph, the elder statesman of the civil rights movement, gave the opening remarks, followed by representatives of various religious and labor groups. The final speaker was Martin Luther King, Jr., whose moving speech enthralled the crowd—and the millions more watching on television.

▼ King addresses the crowd around the reflecting pool between the Lincoln Memorial and the Washington Monument.

Differentiated Instruction
Solutions for All Learners

- L1 **Special Needs Students**
- L2 **English Language Learners**
- L2 **Less Proficient Readers**

To help students increase their comprehension of this important speech, assign them *Primary Source: I Have a Dream,* and have them answer the questions on the worksheet. Have students work in pairs to check their responses. Teaching Resources, **p. 21**

---

when Martin Luther King, Jr., took the podium. King held the audience spell-bound as he described his dream of a colorblind society "when all God's children" would be free and equal. Millions more watched King's address live on television. This powerful and eloquent speech has come to be known as the "I Have a Dream" speech. (You will read an excerpt from the "I Have a Dream" speech later in this chapter.)

Behind the scenes, there was some tension between the organizations that had planned the March. SNCC, in particular, had wanted to stage a more militant protest to show its dissatisfaction with the pace of change. Yet for the public at large and for most who took part, the March on Washington represented a magical moment in American history.

✔ **Checkpoint** What is considered the highlight of the March on Washington?

▲ Button from the march urging interracial cooperation

Why It Matters

The March on Washington was one of the largest political demonstrations in U.S. history. Widely covered in the media, the march increased awareness of the movement and built momentum for the passage of civil rights legislation. Despite the huge numbers and the emotional intensity of the day, the march remained orderly and is considered a model for peaceful protest. The March on Washington has come to symbolize the civil rights movement.

▼ The crowd erupts in cheers after hearing King's speech.

Thinking Critically
Why was the March on Washington a symbolic and appropriate choice for a civil rights demonstration?

History *Interactive*

For: More on the March on Washington
www.pearsonschool.com/ushist

Assess Progress

- Have students complete the Section Assessment.

- Administer the Section Quiz. Teaching Resources, **p. 25**

- To further assess student understanding, use Progress Monitoring Transparencies, **124.**

Reteach

If students need more instruction, have them read the section summary.

Reading and Note Taking
Study Guide

Adapted Reading and
Note Taking Study Guide

Spanish Reading and
Note Taking Study Guide

Extend

See this chapter's Professional Development pages for the Extend Online activity on SNCC.

Answer

 The Civil Rights Act of 1964 outlawed segregation in public places and in the workplace and gave the federal government power to require that state and local school boards desegregate their schools. The act also gave the Justice Department power to prosecute people who violated the civil rights of others.

Congress Passes the Civil Rights Act of 1964

On September 15, 1963, less than three weeks after the march, a bomb exploded in the Sixteenth Street Baptist Church in Birmingham. The church had been the SCLC's headquarters earlier that spring. Four young African American girls, all dressed in their Sunday best, were killed in the bombing.

Two months later, on November 22, 1963, President John F. Kennedy was assassinated in Dallas, Texas. Vice President Lyndon B. Johnson assumed the presidency.

Johnson was a southerner with an undistinguished record on racial matters. However, he surprised many Americans by immediately throwing his support behind the cause of civil rights. "No eulogy could more eloquently honor President Kennedy's memory," Johnson told Congress and the nation, "[than the] earliest passage of the civil rights bill for which he fought so long."

The civil rights bill faced strong opposition in Congress, but Johnson put his considerable political skills to work for its passage. The bill passed in the House of Representatives, but it faced a more difficult fight in the Senate, where a group of southern senators attempted to block it by means of a **filibuster.** This is a tactic by which senators give long speeches to hold up legislative business. The filibuster went on for more than 80 days until supporters finally put together enough votes to overcome it. In the end, the measure passed in the Senate, and President Johnson signed the **Civil Rights Act of 1964** into law in July.

The act banned segregation in public accommodations and gave the federal government the ability to compel state and local school boards to desegregate their schools. The act also allowed the Justice Department to prosecute individuals who violated people's civil rights and outlawed discrimination in employment on account of race, color, sex, or national origin. It also established the Equal Employment Opportunity Commission (EEOC), which is responsible for enforcing these provisions and investigating charges of job discrimination.

✓ **Checkpoint** How did the Civil Rights Act of 1964 try to end discrimination?

SECTION **2** Assessment

Progress Monitoring Online
For: Self-test with vocabulary practice
www.pearsonschool.com/ushist

Comprehension

1. Terms and People For each item below, write a sentence explaining its significance:
- sit-in
- SNCC
- freedom ride
- James Meredith
- Medgar Evers
- March on Washington
- filibuster
- Civil Rights Act of 1964

2. NoteTaking Reading Skill: Summarize Use your concept web to answer the Section Focus Question: How did the civil rights movement gain ground in the 1960s?

Writing About History

3. Quick Write: Construct a Hypothesis After identifying an unanswered question, a historian might form a hypothesis, an unproven answer to that question. Write a one-sentence hypothesis to answer the following question: Why was Johnson more successful than Truman in getting civil rights legislation passed? Remem-

ber, your statement is not a fact but a theory that might or might not be supported by further research. The sentence you write could later become the thesis statement for a research paper.

Critical Thinking

4. Draw Conclusions Why were sit-ins often a successful tactic?

5. Analyze Information Why did the freedom rides lead to violence?

6. Recognize Cause and Effect What events led to passage of the Civil Rights Act of 1964?

For additional assessment, have students access
Progress Monitoring Online at
www.pearsonschool.com/ushist.

Martin Luther King, Jr.:
I Have a Dream

Martin Luther King, Jr., delivered the closing address at the March on Washington. For approximately 20 minutes, he mesmerized the crowd with one of the most powerful speeches ever delivered. In this excerpt, King speaks of his dream for America:

I say to you today, my friends, that in spite of the difficulties and frustrations of the moment I still have a dream. It is a dream deeply rooted in the American dream.

I have a dream that one day this nation will rise up and live out the true meaning of its creed[1]: "We hold these truths to be self-evident; that all men are created equal."

I have a dream that one day on the red hills of Georgia the sons of former slaves and the sons of former slaveowners will be able to sit down together at the table of brotherhood.

I have a dream that one day even the state of Mississippi . . . will be transformed into an oasis of freedom and justice.

I have a dream that my four little children will one day live in a nation where they will not be judged by the color of their skin but by the content of their character.

I have a dream today.

I have a dream that one day the state of Alabama . . . will be transformed into a situation where little black boys and black girls will be able to join hands with little white boys and girls and walk together as sisters and brothers. . . .

This is our hope. This is the faith with which I return to the South. With this faith we will be able to hew[2] out of the mountain of despair a stone of hope. With this faith we will be able to transform the jangling discords of our nation into a beautiful symphony of brotherhood. . . .

This will be the day when all of God's children will be able to sing with new meaning, "My country 'tis of thee, sweet land of liberty, of thee I sing. Land where my father died, land of the Pilgrims' pride, from every mountainside, let freedom ring." . . .

When we let freedom ring, when we let it ring from every village and every hamlet, from every state and every city, we will be able to speed up that day when all of God's children, black men and white men, Jews and Gentiles[3], Protestants and Catholics, will be able to join hands and sing in the words of the old Negro spiritual, "Free at last! Free at last! Thank God Almighty, we are free at last!"

1. **creed** (kreed) *n.* beliefs or principles
2. **hew** (hyoo) *v.* carve
3. **Gentiles** (JEHN tilz) *n.* non-Jews

▲ Martin Luther King, Jr., at the March on Washington

Thinking Critically
1. **Identify Central Issues** What is the "American dream" to which King refers?
2. **Draw Inferences** How well does King think the nation has lived up to its promises?

History Background

Asa Philip Randolph The director of the 1963 March on Washington was Asa Philip Randolph. This was Randolph's first march on Washington, but it was not the first time Randolph had made an impact.

In 1925, Randolph founded the Brotherhood of Sleeping Car Porters, a union that organized African American railroad porters. Randolph had to fight to get railroad companies to recognize this union, but he succeeded.

In 1941, Randolph told President Franklin D. Roosevelt of his intention to lead a mass march on Washington to protest that African Americans were

being kept out of jobs in the all-important defense industries. To stop the march, Roosevelt created the Fair Employment Practices Committee, which made discrimination in the defense industries illegal. Randolph also encouraged President Truman to desegregate the U.S. military, and Truman did so in 1948.

When leaders of the civil rights movement were looking for someone to organize a new march on Washington, they asked Randolph for help. Randolph oversaw the march. He died in 1979.

Objectives

- View and interpret photographs of non-violent protest by students and other civil rights activists.

- Identify the symbolic, economic, and social effects of nonviolent direct action during the civil rights movement.

Background Knowledge L3

Public protests against segregation became more frequent in the 1960s, especially as SNCC organized sit-ins, wade-ins, and other events at which African Americans tried to use "whites only" facilities. Have students offer specific examples from their reading of nonviolent protests.

Instruct L3

- Have students read the introduction and review the photographs and captions in the feature. Ask **What does the young woman's sign mean?** *(Like whites, African Americans should be allowed equal access to services in public places, such as in restaurants and on buses.)* Explain that the African American civil rights movement encouraged other groups, such as people who have physical disabilities, to work for their own civil rights. **What might keep people with physical disabilities out of public buildings?** *(stairs, narrow doorways, curbs, doors that open outward)*

- Using the Idea Wave strategy (TE, p. T22), have students discuss the types of non-violent protests they see on this spread and describe the emotions the protesters in each photograph might have felt.

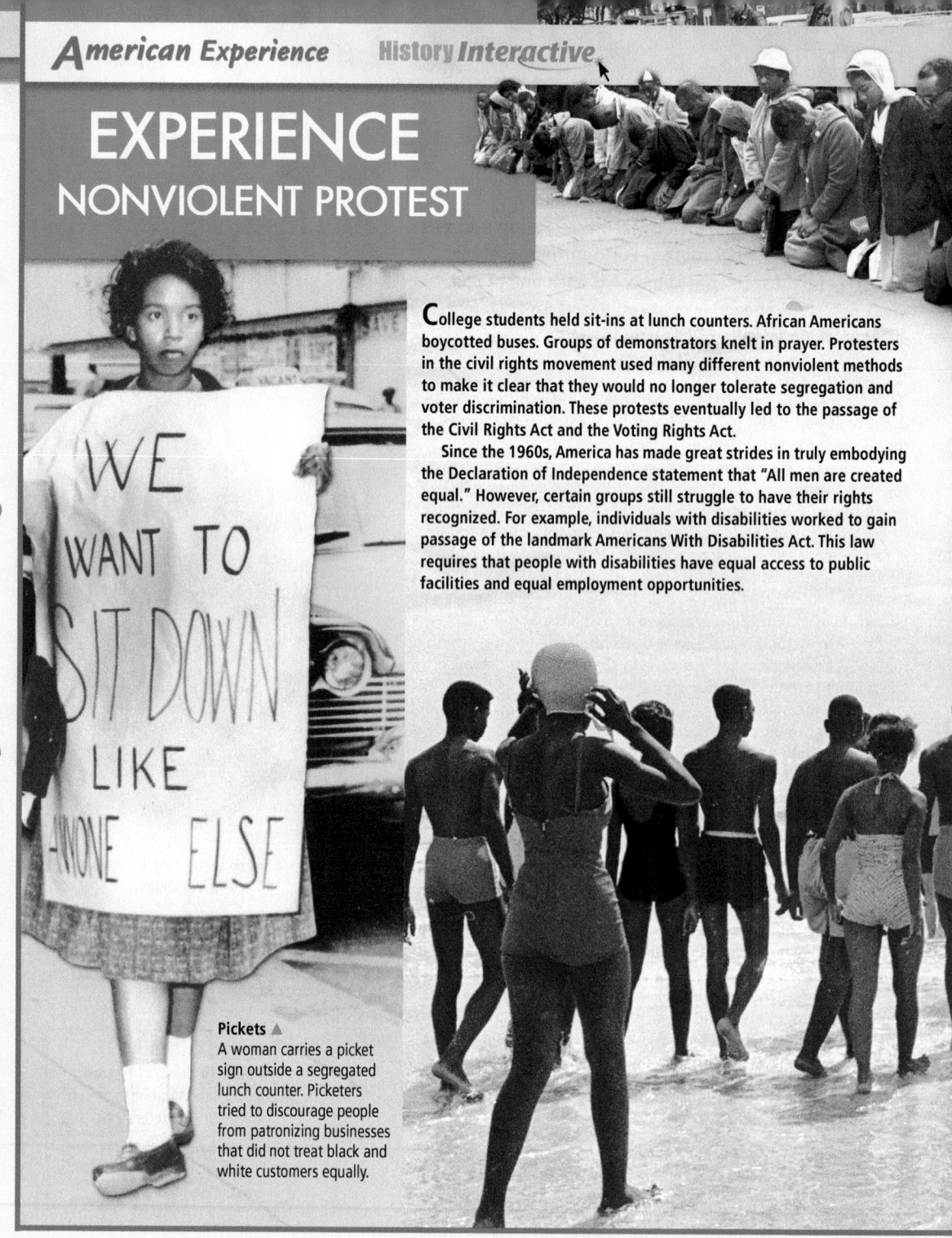

EXPERIENCE
NONVIOLENT PROTEST

College students held sit-ins at lunch counters. African Americans boycotted buses. Groups of demonstrators knelt in prayer. Protesters in the civil rights movement used many different nonviolent methods to make it clear that they would no longer tolerate segregation and voter discrimination. These protests eventually led to the passage of the Civil Rights Act and the Voting Rights Act.

Since the 1960s, America has made great strides in truly embodying the Declaration of Independence statement that "All men are created equal." However, certain groups still struggle to have their rights recognized. For example, individuals with disabilities worked to gain passage of the landmark Americans With Disabilities Act. This law requires that people with disabilities have equal access to public facilities and equal employment opportunities.

Pickets ▲
A woman carries a picket sign outside a segregated lunch counter. Picketers tried to discourage people from patronizing businesses that did not treat black and white customers equally.

WE WANT TO SIT DOWN LIKE ANYONE ELSE

Prayerful Protests ▲
A group of demonstrators kneel in prayer during a hearing for arrested freedom riders in Albany, Georgia, in 1961. Nonviolent protests often took the form of prayer vigils like this.

Wade-ins ▼
Black protesters march onto a "whites only" public beach, ready to swim. Whites who did not want the beach desegregated face off against them as police stand guard.

Boycotts ▲
African American students at Florida A&M College jeer at a nearly empty city bus as it passes through the campus. Protesters in Tallahassee were boycotting the buses to protest segregation on the bus lines.

Thinking Critically
1. **Analyze Visuals** How did whites support or oppose black protesters?
2. **Draw Conclusions** Do you think the civil rights movement would have been as effective if protesters had not used peaceful protest methods?

Connect to Today Do research to learn about the passage of the Americans With Disabilities Act. How were the methods and goals of that movement similar to and different from the movement for racial equality in the 1960s? Did the bill succeed in gaining equal rights and opportunities for people with disabilities?

History *Interactive* ✳
For: Learn more about civil rights tactics
www.pearsonschool.com/ushist

Independent Practice
To enrich and extend the lesson, have students access the History Interactive at **www.pearson-school.com/ushist.** After students experience the History Interactive, ask them to share their reactions by posing questions such as: **How would you have felt if you were walking past the kneeling and praying protesters? If you believed in a particular cause today, would you demonstrate on a public street? Have you ever protested something publicly or seen someone protesting publicly? What reactions did you experience? Do you believe that nonviolent protest is a useful way to effect change? What are other peaceful ways to effect change?**

Monitor Progress
Have students complete the Thinking Critically questions, and share their answers with the class.

Answers

Thinking Critically
1. Some whites supported African Americans by joining in protests. Others opposed them by confronting protesters with taunts and threats, by violently attacking them, and by arresting and jailing them.
2. Sample answer: The movement might have accomplished less if it had been violent. If civil rights protesters had attacked racists, then racists would have been able to justify violence against protesters. Also, the cause itself would have seemed less moral or righteous if protesters had used violence.

Connect to Today Possible findings: The differences include that those working for the passage of the ADA did not get as much media attention and there was no violence against them. Similarities include that both groups focused attention on problems most other Americans had not considered and that each group used public protests to effect change. The bill was mostly successful; all public buildings today must be wheelchair accessible.

Objectives

As you teach this section, keep students focused on the following objectives to help them answer the Section Focus Question and master core content.

- Explain the significance of Freedom Summer, the march on Selma, and why violence erupted in some American cities in the 1960s.
- Compare the goals and methods of African American leaders.
- Describe the social and economic situation of African Americans by 1975.

Prepare to Read

Background Knowledge **L3**

Explain to students that although the Civil Rights Act of 1964 was an important piece of legislation, African Americans still faced racial injustice. Ask students to read the section title and predict what successes and challenges might lie ahead.

Set a Purpose **L3**

- **WITNESS HISTORY** Read the selection aloud.

  Ask **How do you think other African Americans felt about Malcolm X's message?** *(Possible answer: Some may have preferred to remain nonviolent, but others probably shared Malcolm X's frustration and advocated using self-defense.)*

- **Focus** Point out the Section Focus Question, and write it on the board. Tell students to refer to this question as they read. *(Answer appears with Section 3 Assessment answers.)*

- **Preview** Have students preview the Section Objectives and the list of Terms and People.

- **NoteTaking** Using the Structured Read Aloud strategy (TE, p. T20), have students read this section. As they read, have students complete an outline summarizing the section. **Reading and Note Taking Study Guide**

◄ Malcolm X

▲ Button honoring Malcolm X

WITNESS HISTORY

Entering a New Era

Although the civil rights movement was making headway, many black activists were impatient with King's nonviolent methods and his emphasis on integration. Some believed that integration was not the solution. Others felt that more needed to be done to remove what they saw as oppression by white society.

Malcolm X (also known by his religious name, el-Hajj Malik el-Shabazz) became one of the most prominent voices for this faction. As a minister of the Nation of Islam, he preached a message of self-reliance and self-protection. He called for black pride and spread the idea of black nationalism, a belief in the separate identity and racial unity of the African American community. Malcolm was a "charismatic speaker who could play an audience as great musicians play instruments." His dynamic speeches won many adherents to his cause. The civil rights movement had entered a new era.

New Successes and Challenges

Objectives

- Explain the significance of Freedom Summer, the march on Selma, and why violence erupted in some American cities in the 1960s.
- Compare the goals and methods of African American leaders.
- Describe the social and economic situation of African Americans by 1975.

Terms and People

Freedom Summer	Kerner Commission
Fannie Lou Hamer	Malcolm X
Voting Rights Act	Nation of Islam
Twenty-fourth Amendment	black power
	Black Panthers

NoteTaking

Reading Skill: Summarize Complete an outline to summarize the contents of this section.

> I. Push for Voting Rights
>   A. Freedom Summer
>   1.
>   2.

Why It Matters During the 1950s and 1960s, the civil rights movement made great strides forward. Yet racial injustice was not fully eradicated. Frustration with this situation led some African Americans to turn to more radical and sometimes violent methods. African Americans achieved further successes, but for some the radicalism of the times left a bitter legacy. **Section Focus Question: What successes and challenges faced the civil rights movement after 1964?**

The Push for Voting Rights

None of the federal court decisions or civil rights measures passed through 1964 fundamentally affected the right to vote. The problem was a southern political system that used literacy tests, poll taxes, and intimidation to keep blacks from voting. In Mississippi, in 1964, for instance, not a single African American person was registered to vote in five counties that had African American majorities. All of the major civil rights organizations sought to overcome these political injustices.

SNCC Stages Freedom Summer SNCC had spent several years organizing voter education projects in Mississippi. It met with little success and a great deal of violent opposition. But in 1964, it called for a major campaign, known as **Freedom Summer**. About 1,000 volunteers, mostly black and white students, were to flood Mississippi. They would focus on registering African Americans to

Vocabulary Builder

Use the information below and the following resource to teach students the high-use word from this section. Teaching Resources, Vocabulary Builder, p. 10

High-Use Word	Definition and Sample Sentence
confrontation	*n.* situation in which there is angry disagreement between opposing people or groups Different opinions about civil rights led to a violent **confrontation**.

vote. They would also form the Mississippi Freedom Democratic Party (MFDP), an alternative to the state's all-white regular Democratic Party.

Even before most of the volunteers had arrived, three civil rights workers—Michael Schwerner, James Chaney, and Andrew Goodman—disappeared. SNCC claimed that they were murdered; state authorities denied these charges. President Johnson ordered a massive search for the three, which ended when their bodies were found buried in an earthen dam. All had been shot at point-blank range. Yet, despite the obvious dangers, almost all of the other volunteers remained in the state.

After Freedom Summer ended in August 1964, an MFDP delegation traveled to the Democratic Convention in New Jersey, seeking to be recognized as Mississippi's only Democratic Party. At the convention, **Fannie Lou Hamer,** one of the MFDP's leaders, gave powerful testimony. She described how she and other activists had been beaten, fired from their jobs, and displaced from their homes all because, as she put it, they wanted "to register" and "live as decent human beings."

Despite Hamer's testimony, the Democrats refused to seat the MFDP. Instead, party officials offered a compromise: They would seat two MFDP members as "at-large delegates" and reform the nomination rules to guarantee greater minority representation in the future. The MFDP rejected this offer. Ironically, Mississippi's regular Democratic delegation left the convention in protest because the national party had made the offer to the MFDP.

Marching on Selma Early in 1965, Martin Luther King, Jr., and the SCLC organized a major campaign in Selma, Alabama, to pressure the federal government to enact voting rights legislation. The protests climaxed in a series of confrontations on the Edmund Pettus Bridge, on the main route from Selma to Montgomery. The first of these confrontations took place on March 7, 1965, a day that became known as "Bloody Sunday." Heavily armed state troopers and other authorities attacked the marchers as they tried to cross the bridge. Sheyann Webb, a six-year-old girl at the time, recalled the scene:

Vocabulary Builder
confrontation–(kahn fruhn TAY shuhn) *n.* situation in which there is angry disagreement between opposing people or groups

> **Primary Source** "I heard all of this screaming and . . . somebody yelled, 'Oh God, they're killing us!' . . . And I looked and I saw the troopers charging us . . . swinging their arms and throwing canisters of tear gas. . . . Some of them had clubs and others had ropes and whips. . . . It was like a nightmare. . . . I just knew then that I was going to die."
>
> —Sheyann Webb, *Selma, Lord, Selma*

Standoff in Selma
Police officers block the path of protesters attempting to march to Selma, Alabama.

Teach

The Push for Voting Rights L3

Instruct

- **Introduce: Vocabulary Builder** Have students locate the vocabulary term *confrontation* and its definition in the text. Tell students that they will learn about the types of *confrontation* that occurred during protests for voting rights.

- **Teach** Ask **What was the goal of Freedom Summer?** *(to register African Americans in Mississippi to vote)* **What happened on "Bloody Sunday"?** *(Heavily armed state troopers and other authorities attacked protest marchers as they tried to cross a bridge in Selma, Alabama.)* **What was the result of "Bloody Sunday"?** *(The nation was outraged; President Johnson called for a strong federal voting rights law.)* **How did the Voting Rights Act of 1965 protect voting rights?** *(It banned literacy tests for voter registration and gave the federal government power to oversee state voting registration and elections in states that had discriminated against minorities).* Using the graph on the next page, discuss the impact of voting rights legislation.

- **Analyzing the Visuals** Direct students' attention to the image of the march on Selma, Alabama. Ask students to contrast the marchers and the police officers. *(Sample answer: Unlike the police officers, the marchers are diverse in race and gender. They are also peacefully resisting the police actions.)*

Independent Practice

Organize students into four groups. Assign one of the following topics to each group: Freedom Summer, the March on Selma, the Voting Rights Act, and the Twenty-fourth Amendment. Then, have each group create a poster illustrating the importance of their assigned event or legislation.

Monitor Progress

As students fill in their outlines, circulate to make sure that they understand the successes and challenges that faced the civil rights movement after 1964. For a completed version of the outline, see Note Taking Transparencies, **B-129.**

Differentiated Instruction Solutions for All Learners

L1 Special Needs Students   **L2 English Language Learners**   **L2 Less Proficient Readers**

Ask students to read aloud the red headings under "The Push for Voting Rights." As students read, write each red heading on the board. Explain that these red headings are main ideas. Then, have volunteers come to the board and list supporting details under each main idea. When the activity is complete, there should be from two to five supporting details under each red heading.

■ **Introduce: Key Term** Ask students to find the key term **Kerner Commission** in the text. Explain that the **Kerner Commission** determined the causes of riots in American cities during the 1960s. Have students predict what the **Kerner Commission** concluded, then read to find out if their predictions are accurate.

■ **Teach** Ask **In which two cities did the worst violence occur in the summer of 1967?** (Newark, New Jersey, and Detroit, Michigan) **What did the Kerner Commission conclude?** (that long-standing racial discrimination was the single most important cause of the violence) **Why were the Kerner Commission's findings controversial?** (The commission recommended giving money to federal programs to help urban African Americans, and some people believed that doing so meant rewarding the rioters.)

Independent Practice

Display Color Transparency: *Urban Riots.* Lead a discussion about the riots that took place in American cities in the mid-1960s. Color Transparencies A-119

Monitor Progress

Reread the red heading "Racial Violence Plagues Cities." Ask students to summarize the events related to the race riots.

African American Voter Registration		
(Percentage of voting-age African Americans)		
State	**1964**	**1968**
Alabama	23.0	56.7
Louisiana	32.0	59.3
Mississippi	6.7	59.4
Texas	57.7	83.1
Virginia	45.7	58.4

SOURCE: Stanley, Harold W. *Voter Mobilization and the Politics of Race: The South and Universal Suffrage, 1952–1984*

Voting Rights Legislation Takes Effect

The table shows voter registration rates in some southern states before and after the Voting Rights Act of 1965. The women shown above are learning how to mark the ballot at a voter education class in Alabama in 1966. *Which state listed in the table had the greatest increase in voter registration between 1964 and 1968?*

Webb survived, but the rampage continued. Television coverage of the violence outraged the nation. On March 15, President Johnson went on national television and called for a strong federal voting rights law. Historically, regulation of voting rights had been left to the states, but Johnson argued that "it is wrong to deny any of your fellow citizens the right to vote." He added, "Their cause is our cause too, because it is not just Negroes, but really it is all of us, who must overcome the crippling legacy of bigotry and injustice. And, *we shall overcome.*"

New Legislation Guarantees Voting Rights Spurred by the actions of protesters and the words of the President, Congress passed the **Voting Rights Act** of 1965. The act banned literacy tests and empowered the federal government to oversee voting registration and elections in states that had discriminated against minorities. In 1975, Congress extended coverage to Hispanic voters in the Southwest.

Another legal landmark was the **Twenty-fourth Amendment** to the Constitution, ratified in 1964. It banned the poll tax, which had been used to keep poor African Americans from voting. In addition, the federal courts handed down several important decisions. *Baker* v. *Carr* and *Reynolds* v. *Simms* limited racial gerrymandering, the practice of drawing election districts in such a way as to dilute the African American vote, and established the legal principle of "one man, one vote."

These laws and decisions had a profound impact. Particularly in the Deep South, African American participation in politics skyrocketed. In Mississippi, the percentage of African Americans registered to vote jumped from just under 7 percent in 1964 to about 70 percent in 1986. Nationwide, the number of African American elected officials rose from fewer than 100 to more than 6,000 by the mid-1980s.

✓ **Checkpoint** What impact did the protests in Selma, Alabama, have on the nation?

Frustration Explodes Into Violence

Many celebrated the passage of the Voting Rights Act of 1965. Yet for some African Americans, things had not changed much. In many urban areas, there was anger and frustration over continuing discrimination and poverty. That anger exploded into violence in several cities.

Racial Violence Plagues Cities Less than a week after Johnson signed the Voting Rights Act, one of the worst race riots in American history erupted in the predominantly African American neighborhood of Watts in Los Angeles. Violence, looting, and arson spread for several days before National Guard troops restored order.

Watts was one of many race riots that erupted in the 1960s. The worst violence occurred in Newark, New Jersey, and Detroit, Michigan, in the summer of 1967. In Detroit, 43 people died, and property damage reached $50 million. The outbursts frightened many white Americans. In most previous race riots, whites had used violence to keep African Americans "in their place." But now, blacks were using violence against police and white business owners in black neighborhoods.

The Kerner Commission The Kerner Commission's 1968 report concluded that racial discrimination was deeply rooted in cities and that addressing it effectively would be a long and complex process. The Kerner Commission Report stated that poverty among African Americans had resulted in isolation from the mainstream of American society. The report urged Congress to create jobs, job training programs, and housing programs for African Americans in cities. President Johnson did not attempt to implement commission's findings.

In 1992, rioting broke out in Los Angeles, California, after police officers were videotaped brutally beating an African American named Rodney King. The 1992 Los Angeles riot was among the worst in U.S. history. Congressional representative Maxine Waters of California concluded that the Kerner Commission's prediction had come true: that failure to act to help urban African Americans would result in continued violence. The problems of poverty, inadequate social services, and poorly funded public schools that the Kerner Report had said made conditions in American cities "separate and unequal" in 1968 remained unsolved in 1992.

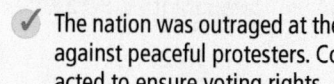

Answers

Caption Mississippi, at 52.7 percent

✓ The nation was outraged at the violence against peaceful protesters. Congress acted to ensure voting rights.

TRACK THE ISSUE

What should the government do to promote voting rights?

Although the right to vote is a corner-stone of American democracy, many restrictions have been placed on voting rights over the years. As the history of the civil rights movement shows, gaining full electoral rights has been a struggle. How can the government ensure fair and free suffrage in America? Use the timeline below to explore this enduring question.

1820s–1830s Age of Jackson
States move toward universal white male suffrage.

1870 Fifteenth Amendment
Vote is extended to African American men, but this right is often violated.

1920 Nineteenth Amendment
Women's suffrage becomes law.

1965 Voting Rights Act
Law strengthens African American voting rights.

1971 Twenty-sixth Amendment
Voting age is lowered from 21 to 18.

2000 Presidential Election
Polling-place irregularities lead some states to reform voting process.

A voter registration drive for ex-felons

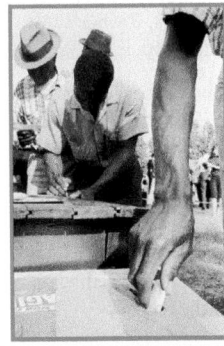

African Americans in Alabama voting for the first time after passage of the Voting Rights Act

DEBATE THE ISSUE

Voting Rights for Convicted Felons Most states do not allow felons to vote while they are in prison. In some states, this ban continues even after they are released. Should ex-convicts have their voting rights restored?

"About 4.7 million Americans, more than 2 percent of the adult population, are barred from voting because of a felony conviction. Denying the vote to ex-offenders is antidemocratic and undermines the nation's commitment to rehabilitating people who have paid their debt to society."
— *The New York Times*, editorial

"Individuals who have shown they are unwilling to follow the law cannot claim the right to make laws for the rest of us. We don't let everyone vote—not children, for instance, or noncitizens. . . . We have . . . standards of trustworthiness before we let people participate in the serious business of self-government, and people who commit serious crimes don't meet those standards."
—Roger Clegg, General Counsel, Center for Economic Opportunity

? TRANSFER Activities

1. **Compare** How do these two views of felon voting rights differ?

2. **Contrast** How does the issue of voting rights for felons differ from the issue of voting rights in the 1960s?

3. **Transfer** Use the following Web site to see a video, try a WebQuest, and write in your journal. www.pearsonschool.com/ushist

History Background

The Fight for the Fifteenth Amendment In 1870, the Reconstruction Congress passed the Fifteenth Amendment, which guaranteed voting rights to African American men. However, starting in 1895, states that resisted allowing African American men to vote created temporary laws that permitted anyone who had been registered to vote by January 1, 1867, or that person's descendents, to register without taking a literacy test. All others had to be able to pass a test. Of course, few African Ameri-

cans had been registered to vote in 1867, so these "grandfather" laws kept most African Americans away from the polls. However, illiterate white people were allowed to vote without taking a literacy test because they had "grandfathers" who had voted in 1867.

It wasn't until the passage of the Voting Rights Act of 1965, which strengthened African American voting rights by abolishing literacy tests, that the Fifteenth Amendment finally went into full effect.

Objectives

- Explain how the right to vote in the United States was extended to more people over time.

- Understand that the issue of voting rights in the United States continues to be debated today.

Background Knowledge

Ask students to think about the right to vote. **Why is voting a critically important right?** *(Voting is one of the main ways people can effect change. If a group cannot vote, government may not address its interests.)*

Instruct

Point out that the timeline shows that the U.S. government has changed voting restrictions several times to widen the definition of eligibility. Ask **When were African Americans given the right to vote?** *(African American men were given the right to vote in 1870, and African American women were given the right to vote in 1920. However, many states prevented African Americans from voting until passage of the Voting Rights Act of 1965.)*

Monitor Progress

- Have students complete the American Issues Journal worksheet, *Voting Rights.* Check their work for accuracy. Teaching Resources, **pp. 14–17**

- Remind students to complete their American Issues Journal work-sheets. Review their work for accuracy. Reading and Note Taking Study Guide

Answers

Transfer Activities

1. *The New York Times* editorial states that people convicted of felonies should be allowed to vote because they have been rehabilitated and have paid their debt to society. Roger Clegg says that voting is a privilege for the law-abiding, not a right for criminals.

2. One could argue that people convicted of felonies are not trustworthy enough to vote, or have forfeited the privilege. However, African Americans as a group were being denied the vote because of race, not because of any wrongdoing. There was no valid reason to keep them from voting.

3. For more information, have students access www.pearsonschool.com/ushist.

New Voices for African Americans ⑬

Instruct

- **Introduce: Key Term** Ask students to find the key term **black power** in the text and provide the definition. Have students use the Numbered Heads strategy (TE, p. T23) to discuss the different approaches that might be advocated by the new voices in the African American community.

- **Teach** Ask **Why did Malcolm X call for an end to integration?** *(He was a member of the Nation of Islam, which demanded a separation of the races.)* **How did the concept of black power differ from Martin Luther King, Jr.'s, approach to civil rights?** *(Black power advocates believed that African Americans should use their economic and political resources collectively to become self-reliant and independent of white influence, instead of trying to gain acceptance from whites.)* **Why were many Americans afraid of black power?** *(They thought it was a call for violence.)* **How did the Black Panthers influence African American culture?** *(They changed hairstyles, language, clothing styles, attitudes, and the ways in which black people celebrated their African heritage.)*

- **Analyzing the Visuals** Draw students' attention to the photograph on this page. Ask them to contrast the stance and attitude of the protesters in this image with that of the protesters in the images in Section 2.

Increasing Militancy
Black Panthers (above) demonstrated outside the courthouse where Huey Newton was on trial, charged with killing a police officer.

The Kerner Commission Seeks the Cause To determine the causes of the riots, President Johnson established the National Advisory Commission on Civil Disorders, known as the **Kerner Commission.** It concluded that long-term racial discrimination stood as the single most important cause of violence. The commission also recommended establishing and expanding federal programs aimed at overcoming the problems of America's urban ghettos.

> **Primary Source** "Our nation is moving toward two societies, one black, one white, separate and unequal. . . . Segregation and poverty have created the racial ghetto and a destructive environment totally unknown to most Americans."
> —National Advisory Commission on Civil Disorders, *Report,* 1967

The Kerner Commission's findings proved highly controversial. A number of conservative commentators argued against expanding federal spending. They said that this amounted to rewarding the rioters. Others noted that the black-white split that the report described ignored other minorities.

President Johnson did not follow up on the commission's recommendations, largely because the Vietnam War was consuming enormous sums of federal money. The riots also fueled a white backlash. Many whites opposed further reforms.

✔ **Checkpoint** Why was the Kerner Commission formed?

New Voices for African Americans

The racial rioting of the mid-1960s coincided with the radicalization of many African Americans, particularly young urban African Americans. Rather than advocating nonviolence and integration, they called for another approach.

Malcolm X Offers a Different Vision The most well-known African American radical was **Malcolm X,** who was born Malcolm Little in Omaha, Nebraska, in 1925. He adopted the *X* to represent his lost African name. Little, he argued, was his slave name. Malcolm had a difficult childhood. In his teens, Malcolm moved to Boston and then to New York City, where he became involved in drugs and crime and landed in prison on burglary charges at age 21.

While in prison, Malcolm became a convert to the **Nation of Islam,** a religious sect headed by Elijah Muhammad. The group prescribed strict rules of behavior, including no drugs or alcohol, and demanded a separation of the races.

Differentiated Instruction Solutions for All Learners

L4 Advanced Readers   L4 Gifted and Talented Students

Ask students to conduct research about the life and influence of one of the African American leaders they have learned about in this section. Ask them to write a short but thorough biography and create an accompanying illustration such as a poster, photo collage, or electronic multimedia presentation. Ask students to read their biographies to the class. Remind them to use their visuals to enrich their presentations.

Answer

 The Kerner Commission was formed to determine the causes of the riots in American cities.

Independent Practice
Have students read the Primary Source quotation and complete the worksheet *Viewpoints: Carmichael and M. L. King, Jr. Teaching Resources*, **p. 23**

Monitor Progress
Reread the information below the red heading "Militants Form the Black Panthers," and ask students to compare the militant approach with the nonviolent approach of Martin Luther King, Jr.

After his release from prison, Malcolm became the Nation of Islam's most prominent minister. In 1964, however, he broke away from the Nation of Islam and formed his own organization. He then made a pilgrimage to Mecca, the holy city of Islam. Returning to the United States, he seemed willing to consider limited acceptance of whites. In February 1965, however, Malcolm X was shot and killed. Three members of the Nation of Islam were convicted of the murder.

Young Leaders Call for Black Power Many young African Americans saw themselves as heirs of the radical Malcolm X. They began to move away from the principle of nonviolence. They also began to question the goal of integration. As SNCC leader Stokely Carmichael put it:

> **Primary Source** "Integration . . . has been based on complete acceptance of the fact that in order to have a decent house or education, blacks must move into a white neighborhood or send their children to a white school. This reinforces the notion . . . that 'white' is automatically better and 'black' is by definition inferior."
> — "What We Want," 1966

Carmichael first used the term **"black power"** in 1966. In that year, James Meredith had set off on a "March Against Fear" across the state of Mississippi to encourage African Americans to register and vote. Meredith traveled only 20 miles before he was shot and left for dead by a white supremacist. SNCC, CORE, and SCLC members vowed to continue the march.

When they reached Greenwood, Mississippi, Carmichael and some other marchers were arrested. After his release, Carmichael told a crowd that African Americans needed "black power." He later said that black power meant African Americans should collectively use their economic and political muscle to gain equality. Yet, many white Americans felt threatened. They believed that black power meant black violence.

Militants Form the Black Panthers Not long after Carmichael's "black power" speech, Huey Newton and Bobby Seale formed the Black Panther Party in Oakland, California. Almost overnight, the **Black Panthers** became the symbol of young militant African Americans. The Black Panthers organized armed patrols of urban neighborhoods to protect people from police abuse. They also created antipoverty programs, such as free breakfasts for poor African American children. The Black Panthers gained national attention when they entered the state

Olympic Protest
At the 1968 Summer Olympics, U.S. athletes Tommie Smith and John Carlos raised gloved fists in protest against discrimination.

Differentiated Instruction Solutions for All Learners

L1 Special Needs Students **L2 English Language Learners** **L2 Less Proficient Readers**

Have students make definition flashcards for any unfamiliar words they find in the section. Such words may include *pilgrimage, convert, supremacist, militant,* and *collective*. Have students work in pairs and use the flashcards to quiz each other.

To help students understand unfamiliar words such as *supremacist, militant,* and *collective,* model the process of identifying word families, prefixes, suffixes, and roots. When students understand the words, ask them to find a synonym and antonym for each one.

Martin Luther King's Final Days L3

Instruct

- **Introduce** Have students locate the timeline "Long, Hot Summers" in the Infographic. Ask students to predict the focus of Martin Luther King, Jr.'s, work in the last part of his life.

- **Teach** Tell students that the progress against segregation in the south had been dramatic, but it had not changed the economic conditions that African Americans in northern cities experienced. Martin Luther King, Jr., began to address the social and economic issues of the urban poor and northern African Americans during the last years of his life. Ask **What was the goal of the Poor People's Campaign?** *(The goal was to pressure the government to do more to help the poor.)* **What was King's response to the black power movement?** *(He sympathized with the anger of its members, but disagreed with their call for violent protest.)*

- **Analyzing the Visuals** Draw students' attention to the Infographic "Turbulent Times." Ask students to write a paragraph contrasting King's, funeral with the riots that had occurred before and after his death.

Independent Practice

Discuss the history of martyrdom, the impact of martyrs in general, and specifically of the individuals involved in the civil rights movement.

Monitor Progress

To review understanding, ask students to explain the ways in which King expanded the scope of his civil rights work toward the end of his life.

Answers

Thinking Critically

1. Long-term poverty and racism, along with impatience at the slow pace of change and anger at racist violence contributed to the riots.

2. Sample response: The violence probably weakened the civil rights movement because the movement had gained sympathy and respect by adhering to a nonviolent strategy. In addition, with King's death, the civil rights movement lost one of its main leaders.

494   The Civil Rights Movement

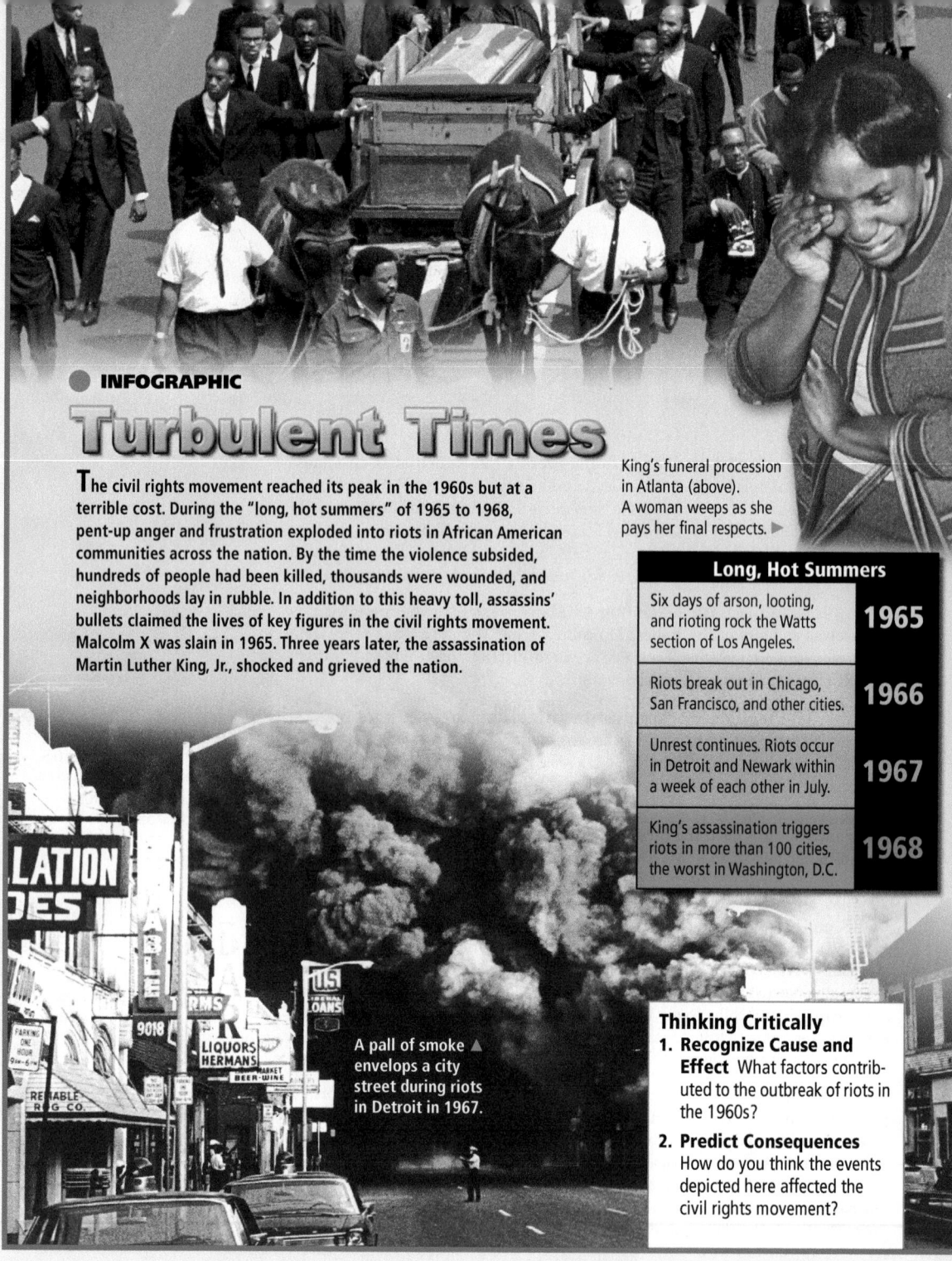

● **INFOGRAPHIC**

Turbulent Times

The civil rights movement reached its peak in the 1960s but at a terrible cost. During the "long, hot summers" of 1965 to 1968, pent-up anger and frustration exploded into riots in African American communities across the nation. By the time the violence subsided, hundreds of people had been killed, thousands were wounded, and neighborhoods lay in rubble. In addition to this heavy toll, assassins' bullets claimed the lives of key figures in the civil rights movement. Malcolm X was slain in 1965. Three years later, the assassination of Martin Luther King, Jr., shocked and grieved the nation.

King's funeral procession in Atlanta (above). A woman weeps as she pays her final respects. ▶

Long, Hot Summers	
Six days of arson, looting, and rioting rock the Watts section of Los Angeles.	**1965**
Riots break out in Chicago, San Francisco, and other cities.	**1966**
Unrest continues. Riots occur in Detroit and Newark within a week of each other in July.	**1967**
King's assassination triggers riots in more than 100 cities, the worst in Washington, D.C.	**1968**

A pall of smoke ▲ envelops a city street during riots in Detroit in 1967.

Thinking Critically

1. **Recognize Cause and Effect** What factors contributed to the outbreak of riots in the 1960s?

2. **Predict Consequences** How do you think the events depicted here affected the civil rights movement?

Differentiated Instruction   **Solutions for All Learners**

L1 **Special Needs Students**   L2 **English Language Learners**   L2 **Less Proficient Readers**

Lead students through the Infographic, dividing it into its component parts (narrative and timeline) and asking comprehension questions about its images. For example, be sure that students understand the meaning of the word *turbulent*. Ask students to explain each image in the photo collage. Invite students to choose the image they think is most important and to give a short explanation of that choice.

capitol in Sacramento carrying shotguns and wearing black leather jackets and berets to protest attempts to restrict their right to bear arms.

The Panthers' style appealed to many young African Americans, who began to wear their hair in "Afros" and to refer to themselves as "black" rather than "Negro" or "colored." Some, following the lead of Malcolm X, changed their name and celebrated their African heritage. At the same time, the Panthers' militancy often led to violent confrontations with police. Each side accused the other of instigating the violence.

✔ **Checkpoint** What impact did Malcolm X have on the civil rights movement?

Martin Luther King's Final Days

Martin Luther King understood the anger and frustration of many urban African Americans whose lives had changed little despite the civil rights reforms of the 1960s. However, he disagreed with the call for "black power" and sought a nonviolent alternative to combat economic injustice. After spending about a year in Chicago's slums to protest conditions there, King made plans for a massive "Poor People's Campaign." The campaign's goal was to pressure the nation to do more to address the needs of the poor.

As part of this effort, King journeyed to Memphis, Tennessee, in early April 1968. There, he offered his assistance to sanitation workers who were striking for better wages and working conditions.

On April 3, King addressed his followers. He referred to threats that had been made against his life. "Like anybody, I would like to live a long life," King declared. "But I'm not concerned about that now. I just want to do God's will."

The following day, as King stood on the balcony outside his motel room, he was struck by a shot from a high-powered rifle. He died at a hospital shortly afterward, at the age of 39. James Earl Ray, a white ex-convict, was later charged with King's murder.

Robert F. Kennedy was campaigning for the presidency in Indianapolis when he heard of King's death. RFK stopped his campaign speech to give the audience the sad news. He reminded them that he had lost his own brother to an assassin's bullet. Kennedy asked those assembled to honor King's memory by replacing their anger and desire for revenge "with an effort to understand with compassion and love." Despite Kennedy's plea, riots broke out in hundreds of cities after King's assassination. Two months later, Robert Kennedy's life, too, was cut short by an assassin.

✔ **Checkpoint** Why did King go to Memphis in 1968?

Significant Gains and Controversial Issues

King's assassination marked an important turning point. The protests for black freedom and racial equality that began in the mid-1950s crested in the late 1960s around the time of King's death. By then, the civil rights movement had made significant gains. Yet, white racism and the social and economic gap between many blacks and whites remained. New measures aimed at closing this gap tended to provoke more controversy than consensus in America.

Civil Rights Are Advanced The civil rights movement of the 1950s and 1960s succeeded in eliminating legal, or de jure, segregation and knocking down barriers to African American voting and political participation. During the same period, African American poverty rates fell and the median income of African American men and women rose rapidly, as did the number of African

Significant Gains and Controversial Issues

Instruct

- **Introduce:** Draw students' attention to the red headings "Civil Rights Are Advanced" and "Controversial Issues Remain." Ask students to predict what advances will be made and what issues will remain unresolved.

- **Teach:** Ask **What was the Fair Housing Act of 1965?** *(It was a law that banned discrimination in housing.)* **What did the Nixon administration do to advance civil rights?** *(It created the affirmative action plan.)* **Why was affirmative action controversial?** *(Supporters believed that it addressed unequal conditions caused by centuries of oppression, but opponents believed that it was another kind of unfairness and racism, and that it prevented the development of a society that does not use race to evaluate people.)*

- **Quick Activity** Display Color Transparency: *The Lamp*. Use the lesson suggested in the transparency book to guide a discussion of the artwork. Color Transparencies A-120

Independent Practice

Have students use the Quick Study chart on the next page and work in groups to create a list of the achievements of the civil rights movement in the 1960s. Then have each group choose one or two achievements that have the greatest effect on their own lives.

Monitor Progress

As students create their lists, circulate through the room to make sure they include all the important achievements studied in this chapter.

History Background

Violent Protests After King's Death Martin Luther King, Jr.'s, assassination on April 4, 1968, set off a wave of riots in dozens of American cities. Washington, D.C., where King had delivered the "I Have a Dream" speech, experienced some of the worst rioting. Three thousand people were arrested and 12,000 National Guard soldiers were brought in to help keep order in the city and protect fire fighters battling fires that rioters had set.

King's friend and the new leader of the SCLC, the Reverend Ralph Abernathy, appealed for calm, urging

Americans to honor King's non-violent legacy. But Lincoln Lynch, the head of the United Black Front, a militant organization, stated that "It is imperative to abandon the unconditional non-violent concept expounded by Dr. King. . . ."

King was buried on April 9, 1968, and after his funeral, most of the rioting ended. On April 11, President Johnson signed the Civil Rights Bill to protect the rights for which King had worked so tirelessly.

Answers

✔ Malcolm X proposed that African Americans abandon the goal of integration and instead create an independent African American community within the United States. He also advocated self-defense.

✔ He went to Memphis to support a strike by sanitation workers seeking better wages and working conditions.

Effects of the Civil Rights Movement ☑ Quick Study

- End of legal segregation
- Passage of federal laws to protect civil rights
- End of legal barriers to African American voting and political participation
- Creation of affirmative action programs

Americans who graduated from high school. One symbol of the progress that had been made was the appointment of Thurgood Marshall as the first African American Supreme Court Justice in 1967. The following year, in the wake of King's murder, Congress passed one final civil rights measure, the Fair Housing Act, which banned discrimination in housing.

Controversial Issues Remain Attempts to increase the economic opportunities for African Americans and to integrate neighborhoods and schools encountered more difficulties. To achieve desegregated schools, the federal courts had ordered the use of forced busing. Richard Nixon, who succeeded Lyndon Johnson as president, criticized busing as a means of attaining racial balance.

At the same time, the Nixon administration formally established affirmative action as a means of closing the economic gap between blacks and whites. In a short period of time, colleges and universities, businesses, and local and state governments followed the federal government's lead and implemented their own affirmative action plans to increase African American representation in schools and the workforce.

Affirmative action proved controversial almost from the start. Some whites argued that it constituted reverse discrimination and violated the goal of creating a colorblind society. Justice Thurgood Marshall disagreed. "Three hundred and fifty years ago, the Negro was dragged to this country in chains to be sold into slavery," Marshall wrote. "The position of the Negro today in America is the tragic but inevitable consequence of centuries of unequal treatment."

Until the nation addressed the legacy of this unequal treatment, Marshall asserted, it would not fulfill its promise of providing equal rights and opportunities to all. This debate or controversy, as you will see in future chapters, remained unresolved.

✔ **Checkpoint** What gains did the civil rights movement make by the early 1970s?

SECTION **3** Assessment

Progress Monitoring Online
For: Self-test with vocabulary practice
www.pearsonschool.com/ushist

Comprehension

1. Terms and People For each of the items below, write a sentence explaining its significance:
- Freedom Summer
- Fannie Lou Hamer
- Voting Rights Act
- Twenty-fourth Amendment
- Kerner Commission
- Malcolm X
- Nation of Islam
- black power
- Black Panthers

2. NoteTaking Reading Skill: Summarize Use your outline to answer the Section Focus Question: What successes and challenges faced the civil rights movement after 1964?

Writing About History

3. Quick Write: Identify Sources After constructing a hypothesis, historians look for evidence that might either prove or disprove the hypothesis. List three sources of information that you might use to test the following hypothesis: The drive for voting rights in the South could have succeeded without the involvement of the federal government.

Critical Thinking

4. Recognize Cause and Effect How did the Selma march help lead to the passage of civil rights legislation?

5. Make Comparisons How did Malcolm X's views differ from Martin Luther King, Jr.'s views?

6. Identify Points of View Why did Justice Thurgood Marshall support affirmative action?

A Raisin in the Sun
by Lorraine Hansberry

The 1940s and 1950s brought an explosion of literature that exposed the harsh discrimination African Americans faced. One of the most powerful writers of the period was the playwright Lorraine Hansberry. Her most famous work, *A Raisin in the Sun*, focuses on the struggles of a black family living in the South Side of Chicago.

In this excerpt, Lindner—a white man—tries to dissuade the family from moving into his neighborhood.

LINDNER: I am sure you people must be aware of some of the incidents which have happened in various parts of the city when colored people have moved into certain areas—Well—because we have what I think is going to be a unique type of organization in American community life—not only do we deplore that kind of thing—but we are trying to do something about it. We feel—we feel that most of the trouble in this world, . . . exists because people just don't sit down and talk to each other.

RUTH: You can say that again, mister.

LINDNER: That we don't try hard enough in this world to understand the other fellow's problems. The other guy's point of view.

RUTH: Now that's right.

LINDNER: Yes—that's the way we feel out in Clybourne Park. And that's why I was elected to come here this afternoon and talk to you people. Friendly like, you know, the way people should talk to each other. . . . As I say, the whole business is a matter of *caring* about the other fellow. Anybody can see that you are a nice family of folks, hard working and honest I'm sure. Today everybody knows what it means to be on the outside of *something*. And of course, there is always somebody who is out to take the advantage of people who don't always understand."

WALTER: What do you mean?

LINDNER: Well—you see our community is made up of people who've worked hard as the dickens for years to build up that little community. They're not rich and fancy people; just hard-working, honest people who don't really have much but those little homes and a dream of the kind of community they want to raise their children in. Now I don't say we are perfect and there is a lot wrong in some of the things they want. But you've got to admit that a man, right or wrong, has the right to want to have the neighborhood he lives in a certain kind of way. And at the moment the overwhelming majority of our people out there feel that people get along better, take more of a common interest in the life of the community, when they share a common background. I want you to believe me when I tell you that race prejudice simply doesn't enter into it. It is a matter of the people of Clybourne Park believing, rightly or wrongly, as I say, that for the happiness of all concerned that our Negro families are happier when they live in their *own* communities.

BENETHEA: This, friends, is the Welcoming Committee!

▲ Scene from a production of *A Raisin in the Sun*

Thinking Critically
1. **Synthesize Information** What reasons did Lindner give for not wanting the family to move into his neighborhood?

2. **Make Inferences** What obstacles did African Americans face in gaining social equality in the 1950s?

History Background

Lorraine Hansberry When *A Raisin in the Sun* opened on Broadway in 1959, Hansberry was only 29 years old. The play's honest treatment of the different ways that racism can dash the hopes of African Americans won the New York Drama Critics' Circle Award. Hansberry was the youngest American and the first African American to win this award.

Hansberry was inspired to deal with racism by her father, who filed suit against the U.S government to overturn laws that banned African Americans from white neighborhoods in Chicago, where Hansberry grew up. Her father, Carl Hansberry, won his case before the Supreme Court in 1940.

Lorraine Hansberry died of cancer in 1965 at the age of 34. Her writings were collected and published in 1969 with the title *To Be Young, Gifted, and Black*.

Quick Study Guide

- Have students use the Quick Study Guide to prepare for the chapter test. Students may wish to refer to the following sections as they review:

Struggle for Equality
Section 1
Section 2
Section 3

Civil Rights Legislation
Section 1
Section 2
Section 3

Civil Rights Organizations
Section 1
Section 2
Section 3

Key Events in the Civil Rights Movement
Section 1
Section 2
Section 3

- For additional review, remind students to refer to the Reading and Note Taking Study Guide.
Section Note Taking
Section Summaries

- Have students access **www.pearsonschool.com/ushist** for this chapter's History Interactive timeline, which includes expanded entries and additional events.

- If students need more instruction on analyzing graphic data, have them read the Skills Handbook, **p. SH21.**

■ Struggle for Equality

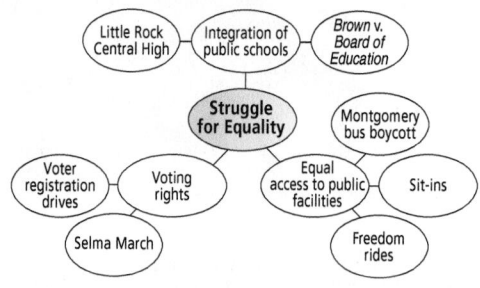

Little Rock Central High — Integration of public schools — Brown v. Board of Education — Struggle for Equality — Montgomery bus boycott — Voter registration drives — Voting rights — Equal access to public facilities — Sit-ins — Selma March — Freedom rides

■ Civil Rights Legislation

Civil Rights Act of 1964	• Banned segregation in public accommodations • Increased federal authority to enforce school desegregation • Outlawed discrimination in employment on basis of race, color, and sex
Twenty-fourth Amendment (1964)	• Eliminated poll tax as voting requirement
Voting Rights Act of 1965	• Banned literacy tests as voting requirement • Empowered the federal government to supervise voter registration and elections
Fair Housing Act of 1968	• Banned discrimination in housing

■ Civil Rights Organizations

Organization and Date Founded	Key People	Key Features
National Association for the Advancement of Colored People (NAACP) 1909	Thurgood Marshall	Focused on legal cases to end segregation and gain legal equality
Nation of Islam 1930	Elijah Muhammad; Malcolm X	Advocated separation of the races
Congress of Racial Equality (CORE) 1942	James Farmer	Organized peaceful protests to gain civil rights
Southern Christian Leadership Conference (SCLC) 1957	Martin Luther King, Jr.; Ralph Abernathy	Church-based group dedicated to nonviolent resistance; organized demonstrations and protest campaigns
Student Nonviolent Coordinating Committee (SNCC) 1960	James Lawson; Ella Baker; Stokely Carmichael	Grass-roots movement of young activists; organized voter education projects in the South
Black Panther Party 1966	Huey Newton; Bobby Seale	Militant group advocating armed confrontation; organized antipoverty programs

☑ Quick Study Timeline

In America

1954 Supreme Court rules school segregation unconstitutional

1955 Bus boycott begins in Montgomery, Alabama

1957 Desegregation of Central High in Little Rock, Arkansas

Presidential Terms Harry Truman 1945–1953   Dwight D. Eisenhower 1953–1961

1953   1956   1959

Around the World

1956 Crisis over Suez Canal

1959 Castro comes to power in Cuba

Differentiated Instruction   Solutions for All Learners

L1 Special Needs Students   L2 English Language Learners   L2 Less Proficient Readers

Use the following study guide resources to help students acquiring basic skills:
Adapted Reading and Note Taking Study Guide
- Section Note Taking
- Section Summaries

Use the following study guide resources to help Spanish-speaking students:
Spanish Reading and Note Taking Study Guide
- Section Note Taking
- Section Summaries

American Issues
•—•—• Connector

By connecting prior knowledge with what you have learned in this chapter, you can gradually build your understanding of enduring questions that still affect America today. Answer the questions below. Then, use your American Issues Connector study guide (or go online: www.pearsonschool.com/ushist).

Issues You Learned About

● **Voting Rights** Minority groups in America sometimes have had to fight for their political rights.

1. Do you think the Voting Rights Act of 1965 did enough to ensure that African Americans would be allowed to exercise their voting rights? Consider the following:
   • the results of Freedom Summer
   • the number of African American elected officials before and after 1965
   • the percentage of southern African Americans registered to vote before and after 1965
   • the black power movement

● **Federal Power and States' Rights** The national government and the state governments sometimes disagree over the delegation of power.

2. *Brown* v. *Board of Education* sparked a clash between the federal government and several southern state governments. Describe an earlier incident in which the federal government and state government disagreed over the authority of the federal government.

3. How did Arkansas governor Orval Faubus attempt to assert his authority over that of the Supreme Court? How did President Eisenhower respond on behalf of the federal government?

● **Sectionalism and National Politics** Different regions of the country often respond to events in contradictory ways.

4. Why was the civil rights movement centered in the South?

5. How do you think the South and the North responded to the Voting Rights Act of 1965? Explain.

Connect to Your World	Activity

Expanding and Protecting Civil Rights As you have read, many people were injured or even lost their lives during the civil rights era, including some who were the victims of violent crimes. During the times these crimes were committed, few people were brought to justice for their actions. However, as the political climate changed over the decades, more people have been made to stand at a fair, unbiased trial. Go online or to your local library and find out about the efforts to convict those responsible for the murders of Medgar Evers, the three freedom riders, and the four young girls killed in the Birmingham Church bombing. Create a chart that contrasts the original law enforcement efforts with more recent ones.

History *Interactive*
For: Interactive timeline
www.pearsonschool.com/ushist

1960
Greensboro sit-ins

1963
King speaks at March on Washington

1965
Riots break out in Watts section of Los Angeles

1968
Martin Luther King, Jr., is assassinated

John F. Kennedy 1961–1963   Lyndon B. Johnson 1963–1969

1962   **1965**   **1968**

1961
East Germany builds the Berlin Wall

1962
Mandela is jailed in South Africa

1966
Cultural Revolution in China

Differentiated Instruction   Solutions for All Learners

L1 Special Needs Students   **L2 English Language Learners**   **L2 Less Proficient Readers**

Use the following study guide resource to help students acquiring basic skills:
Adapted Reading and Note Taking Study Guide
• American Issues Journal

Use the following study guide resource to help Spanish-speaking students:
Spanish Reading and Note Taking Study Guide
• American Issues Journal

American Issues
•—•—• Connector

Tell students that the main issues for this chapter are Voting Rights, Federal Power and States' Rights, and Sectionalism and National Politics, and then ask them to answer the Issues You Learned About questions on this page. Discuss the Connect to Your World topic, and ask students to complete the project that follows.

American Issues Connector

1. Sample answer: No; it did erase barriers to voting, and the percentage of southern African Americans who registered to vote after 1965 rose, and more African Americans were elected. However, the level of violence against African Americans during Freedom Summer showed that many white officials, especially in the South, would not protect African Americans.

2. Sample answer: In 1950, the NAACP won the case of *Sweatt* v. *Painter*. The Supreme Court ruled that the state of Texas violated the Fourteenth Amendment by establishing an all-black law school.

3. Faubus tried to stop the desegregation of Central High School. Eisenhower sent federal soldiers to Little Rock to make sure that the African American students were allowed to attend the school.

4. The South had the most de jure segregation laws and the largest African American population.

5. The North probably had less violence, because it had a lower African American population and no Jim Crow laws. The South, with its large African American population and de jure segregation, experienced more violence.

Connect to Your World

Students' charts should examine the reasons that these crimes were not adequately investigated or prosecuted and why that systemic injustice changed in later years.

For additional review of this chapter's enduring issues, remind students to refer to the Reading and Note Taking Study Guide American Issues Journal.

Chapter Assessment

Terms and People

1. the most visible major civil rights leader from 1955 to 1968; King led the Montgomery bus boycott in 1955, helped found the SCLC, led marches for equality, and gave the "I Have A Dream" speech at the March on Washington. King made the idea of nonviolent protest the key to the civil rights movement.

2. a form of protest in which protesters sat at restaurant tables or counters reserved for whites; The first sit-in provoked an angry response from racists, but inspired others.

3. It banned segregation in public accommodations; gave the federal government authority to compel state and local school boards to desegregate their schools; allowed the Justice Department to prosecute individuals who violated people's civil rights; outlawed discrimination in employment; Lyndon B. Johnson

4. banned the poll tax; It kept states from using the tax to prevent poor African Americans from voting.

5. Created by President Johnson to find the causes of African American rioting in American cities, it recommended establishing and expanding federal programs to address the poverty that perpetuated racial injustice.

Focus Questions

6. They tried to end discrimination, founded CORE, and organized protests against segregation in northern cities. The NAACP successfully argued in *Brown* that school segregation was unconstitutional.

7. Sit-ins, Freedom Rides, and other nonviolent protests received press attention, which caused Americans to favor the movement. Martin Luther King, Jr., led the movement in a nonviolent strategy that showed the morality of its position and pressured the President to introduce civil rights legislation. The March on Washington in 1963 was a turning point.

8. Legislation continued to be passed, but violence against civil rights

Terms and People

1. Who was **Martin Luther King, Jr.**? What did he achieve in his lifetime?

2. Define **sit-ins.** What response did the first sit-in of the civil rights movement—at a Woolworth's lunch counter in 1960—provoke throughout the South?

3. What did the **Civil Rights Act of 1964** accomplish? Who worked to push this bill through Congress?

4. What did the **Twenty-fourth Amendment** do? How did it help African Americans?

5. What was the **Kerner Commission**? What recommendations did it make?

Focus Questions

The focus question for this chapter is **What were the causes, main events, and effects of the civil rights movement?** Build an answer to this big question by answering the focus questions for Sections 1 through 3 and the Critical Thinking questions that follow.

Section 1
6. How did African Americans challenge segregation after World War II?

Section 2
7. How did the civil rights movement gain ground in the 1960s?

Section 3
8. What successes and challenges faced the civil rights movement after 1964?

Critical Thinking

9. **Decision Making** What reasoning did the Supreme Court apply in the *Brown* v. *Board of Education* ruling?

10. **Analyze Maps** Study the map below. What civil rights campaign does this map show? Was this campaign successful?

11. **Categorize** In what general areas did civil rights activists focus their efforts? List at least three general categories along with their key victories.

12. **Analyze Information** What role did television play in the civil rights movement of the 1950s and early 1960s? Do you think television contributed to the success of the movement? Explain.

13. **Comparing Points of View** How did Stokely Carmichael's and Martin Luther King, Jr.'s attitudes toward the civil rights movement differ?

14. **Express Problems Clearly** Why was affirmative action begun? Explain the controversy surrounding it.

Writing About History

Writing a Research Paper Write a hypothesis about one of the following aspects of the civil rights movement: the growth of de facto segregation in the North; the Montgomery bus boycott; the role of northern volunteers in the southern civil rights movement; the urban riots of the 1960s; the conflict between Malcolm X and Martin Luther King, Jr. Use your hypothesis as the basis of an essay that tests the hypothesis.

Prewriting
• Identify an unanswered question about the topic you have chosen.
• Write a one-sentence hypothesis that provides a possible answer to the question.
• Use the library or Internet to find three different sources of information that can be used to support or disprove your hypothesis.

Drafting
• Write an introductory paragraph in which you identify the question you are trying to answer and propose one hypothesis. Use your hypothesis as a thesis statement for the paragraph.
• In separate paragraphs, explain how each piece of evidence you have found either supports or disproves your hypothesis.
• Write a concluding paragraph in which you restate, modify, or reject your original hypothesis.

Revising
• Use the guidelines on page SH14 of the Writing Handbook to revise your writing.

workers in the South led some African Americans to believe that nonviolence was not working. Riots took place in many American cities, and the Black Panthers, Malcolm X, and the Nation of Islam advocated violent tactics. When King was assassinated in 1968, the movement lost some momentum.

Critical Thinking

9. that separate was inherently unequal

10. the Freedom Ride campaign; yes

11. Students' answers should include at least three areas of civil rights activities and the main victories in each.

12. It showed Americans the brutality of the racist attacks on young, peaceful protesters. Many came to believe that the protesters were right and that their racist attackers were wrong. Television contributed to the success of the movement by showing people the reality of racism in the United States.

Document-Based Assessment

Civil Disobedience

During the 1960s, Martin Luther King, Jr., advocated the use of civil disobedience to end segregation in the South. What forms of civil disobedience were effective tools in ending segregation? Was nonviolence more effective than violence in achieving civil rights for African Americans? Use your knowledge of the civil rights movement and Documents A, B, C, and D to answer questions 1 through 4.

Document A

"... Unjust laws exist; shall we be content to obey them, or shall we endeavor to amend them, and obey them until we have succeeded, or shall we transgress them at once? Men generally, under such a government as this, think that they ought to wait until they have persuaded the majority to alter them. They think that, if they should resist, the remedy would be worse than the evil. But it is the fault of the government itself that the remedy is worse than the evil. It makes it worse. Why is it not more apt to anticipate and provide for reform? Why does it not cherish its wise minority? Why does it cry and resist before it is hurt? Why does it not encourage its citizens to be on the alert to point out its faults, and do better than it would have them?"

—*Henry David Thoreau*, Civil Disobedience, *1849*

Document B

"[Young African Americans] are developing attitudes which seem to say: 'That if this is such that I cannot attain gainful employment, then I am inclined to pursue that course of action which, in my opinion, will contribute to a downfall, a deterioration . . . of that society that denies me the opportunity of employment. I think we find that expressed in a number of areas in increasing numbers. We note the formation of various and numerous black nationalist oriented organizations and I think that is a reflection, an outgrowth of the frustration that the young people face today."

—Clifton Jeffers, quoted in *a time to listen. . . . a time to act, Voices from the ghettos of the Nation's cities* U.S. Commission on Civil Rights, November 1967

Document C
Birmingham, 1963

Document D

"Oppressed people cannot remain oppressed forever. The yearning for freedom eventually manifests itself, and that is what has happened to the American Negro. . . . If one recognizes this vital urge that has engulfed the Negro community, one should readily understand why public demonstrations are taking place. The Negro has many pent-up resentments and latent frustrations, and he must release them. So let him march; let him make prayer pilgrimages to the city hall; let him go on freedom rides—and try to understand why he must do so. If his repressed emotions are not released in nonviolent ways, they will seek expression through violence; this is not a threat but a fact of history. So I have not said to my people: 'Get rid of your discontent.' Rather, I have tried to say that this normal and healthy discontent can be channeled into the creative outlet of nonviolent direct action."

—*Martin Luther King, Jr.*, "Letter From Birmingham Jail," *1963*

---

1. Which document suggests that violence may be used if racism against African Americans is not ended?
   A Document A
   B Document B
   C Document C
   D Document D

2. According to Document D, how does Martin Luther King, Jr., describe demonstrations such as freedom rides?
   A unjust laws
   B expression through violence
   C nonviolent direct action
   D discrimination

3. According to Document A, what does Thoreau think about the role of government in addressing unjust laws?
   A The government should listen only to the majority viewpoint.
   B The government should listen to the minority viewpoint.
   C Violence should be used as an option to end oppression.
   D The public should be content with the laws.

4. Writing Task What do you think about the role of government depicted in Document C? How does that image contrast with the ideas of King and Thoreau? Use your knowledge of the chapter content and evidence from the primary sources above to support your opinion.

Document-Based Assessment

- To help students understand the documents, give them the following **TIP** **Study each document to assess its purpose. Look at the attribution line to help determine who created it, when, and why.**

- To provide students with further practice in answering document-based questions, go to Test Prep With Document-Based Assessment.

- If students need more instruction on analyzing primary sources, have them read the Skills Handbook, p. SH24.

Answers

1. B	**2.** C	**3.** B

4. Responses should point out that the photograph shows the government violently suppressing public protest and examine how the opinions of King, Thoreau, and Carmichael are similar and different.

---

13. Carmichael argued that advocates of integration assumed that the only good life was in white neighborhoods and white schools and that black meant inferior. Conversely, King said that there could not be two Americas, one white and one African American.

14. to close the economic and employment gaps between blacks and whites; Affirmative action was controversial because some whites perceived it as reverse discrimination and believed that it violated the goal of creating a colorblind society.

Writing About History

As students begin the assignment, refer them to page SH12 of the Writing Handbook for help in writing a research paper. Remind them of the steps they should take to complete their assignment, including prewriting, drafting, and revising.

Students' research papers should test a hypothesis about one aspect of the civil rights movement and explain its significance. They should each contain an introduction, a body, and a conclusion. For scoring rubrics, see Assessment Rubrics.

CHAPTER 15
The Kennedy and Johnson Years
1960–1968

Teach With Technology

Presentation**EXPRESS**™
PREMIUM DVD

- Teach this chapter's core content by using **PresentationExpress**, which includes the *ExamView*® QuickTake assessment tool.

- To introduce this chapter by using **PresentationExpress**, ask students with which of the following statements they most agree: **A) The U.S. government has the responsibility to oust other nations' leaders if those leaders are doing harm to their own people. B) It is not the responsibility of the U.S. government to oust the leaders of another nation, unless that nation's citizens ask for aid. C) It is never the responsibility or the right of one nation's government to oust the leaders of another nation's government.** Using the QuickTake feature, take a class poll or record students' answers, and then discuss their responses. Point out that in this chapter, students will read about the ways that the nation dealt with these questions during the Cold War.

Technology Resources

- Student**EXPRESS** CD-ROM
- Teacher Resource Library **DVD**
- Presentation**EXPRESS** **PREMIUM** DVD
- *ExamView*® **Test Bank** CD-ROM English and Spanish
- **Guided Reading Audio,** Spanish
- **Student Edition on Audio**

THE ESSENTIAL **VIDEO**
By Students For Students
For videos on American Issues, go to
www.pearsonschool.com/ushist

Bibliography

For the Teacher
Caro, Robert A. *The Years of Lyndon Johnson: Master of the Senate.* Knopf, 2002.

Halberstam, David. *The Best and the Brightest.* Ballantine, 1993.

Harrington, Michael. *The Other America.* Scribner, 1997.

Kornbluh, Peter, ed. *Bay of Pigs Declassified: The Secret CIA Report on the Invasion of Cuba.* New Press, 1998.

For the Student
L2 Kuhn, Betsy. *The Race for Space: The United States and the Soviet Union Compete for the New Frontier (People's History).* Twenty-First Century Books, 2006.

L3 Schmemann, Serge. *When the Wall Came Down: The Berlin Wall and the Fall of Soviet Communism.* Kingfisher, 2006.

L4 Horwitz, Morton J. *The Warren Court and the Pursuit of Justice.* Hill and Wang, 1999.

WITNESS HISTORY

The Trumpet Summons Us

On January 20, 1961, John F. Kennedy was sworn in as President of the United States. His stirring Inaugural Address announced the dawn of a new era and rallied the nation to battle against the common enemies of man.

"Now the trumpet summons us again—not as a call to bear arms, though arms we need—not as a call to battle, though embattled we are—but a call to bear the burden of a long twilight struggle, year in and year out, 'rejoicing in hope; patient in tribulation,' a struggle against the common enemies of man: tyranny, poverty, disease, and war itself. . . .

And so, my fellow Americans, ask not what your country can do for you; ask what you can do for your country."

—John F. Kennedy, Inaugural Address

The challenge of fulfilling these goals would inspire the agenda of President Kennedy and that of his successor, Lyndon B. Johnson.

Kennedy campaign button

Peace Corps logo

◄ Senator John F. Kennedy, the 1960 Democratic presidential candidate, is greeted by his supporters.

The space rocket *Saturn V*

Chapter Preview

Chapter Focus Question: How did the policies of Presidents Kennedy and Johnson affect the nation?

Section 1
Kennedy and the Cold War

Section 2
Kennedy's New Frontier

Section 3
Johnson's Great Society

Use the ☑ **Quick Study Timeline** at the end of this chapter to preview chapter events.

Note Taking Study Guide *Online*
For: Note Taking and American Issues Connector
www.pearsonschool.com/ushist

Differentiated Instruction Solutions for All Learners

The following Teacher's Edition strategies are suitable for students of varying abilities.

L1 Special Needs Students, pp. 507, 508, 509, 514, 520, 521, 523 SN

L2 English Language Learners, pp. 507, 508, 509, 514, 520, 521, 523 ELL

L2 Less Proficient Readers, pp. 507, 508, 509, 514, 520, 521, 523 LPR

L4 Advanced Readers, pp. 505, 513, 522 AR

L4 Gifted and Talented Students, pp. 505, 513, 522 GT

Chapter-Level Resources

All in One Letter Home (English and Spanish), Preread the Chapter, Vocabulary Builder, Reading Strategy, Social Studies Skills Practice, Enrichment, Issues Connector, Chapter Tests

- Test Prep With Document-Based Assessment
- AYP Monitoring Assessments
- *ExamView*® Test Bank CD-ROM
- Guided Reading Audio (Spanish)
- Student Edition Audio

Previewing the Chapter

- **WITNESS HISTORY** Point out that it is the custom of each newly elected President, or newly elected incumbent President to give an inaugural address. This speech traditionally outlines the administration's agenda for the coming term. Read aloud the Witness History selection. Then, ask students to predict the goals of Kennedy's administration.

- **Analyzing the Visuals** Ask students to study the visuals. **What clues do these images offer about the tone of the coming Kennedy administration?** (*Possible answer: Kennedy seems to be a charismatic figure with broad appeal, especially to youth, who will support the goals of space exploration and the Peace Corps.*)

- **Focus** Write the Chapter Focus Question on the board. Tell students to keep this question in mind as they read the chapter. Then, have students preview the section titles in this chapter.

- **Preread** Have students complete the chapter's Preread the Chapter Worksheet. Teaching Resources, pp. 7–8

Have students access **www.pearsonschool.com/ushist** for the Note Taking Study Guide *Online* as an alternative to the *Reading and Note Taking Study Guide* booklet.

Step-by-Step Instruction

Objectives

As you teach this section, keep students focused on the following objectives to help them answer the Section Focus Question and master core content.

- Explain the steps Kennedy took to change American foreign policy.

- Analyze the causes and effects of the Bay of Pigs invasion and the Cuban Missile Crisis.

- Assess the results of the Berlin Crisis and other foreign-policy events of the 1960s.

Prepare to Read

Background Knowledge L3

Ask students to recall how Truman and Eisenhower confronted the challenges of the Cold War. Tell them to predict whether subsequent Presidents will follow earlier policies or work out new approaches to the conflict.

Set a Purpose L3

- **WITNESS HISTORY** Read the selection aloud.

  Ask **Why might Kennedy's faith have concerned voters?** *(Possible answer: All previous Presidents had been Protestants. The Catholic Church has a strong central authority—the papacy—and voters may have been anxious about how Kennedy might be influenced by the pope.)*

- **Focus** Point out the Section Focus Question, and write it on the board. Tell students to refer to this question as they read. *(Answer appears with Section 1 Assessment answers.)*

- **Preview** Have students preview the Section Objectives and the list of Terms and People.

- **NoteTaking** Using the Structured Read Aloud strategy (TE, p. T20), have students read this section. As they read, have students list the results of the Cold War crises. Reading and Note Taking Study Guide

SECTION 1

A NEW LEADER FOR THE 60's

FACTS FOR NEW YORK VOTERS:

KENNEDY JOHNSON
FOR VICE PRESIDENT
N. Y. Democratic State Campaign Committee
Biltmore Hotel, N.Y. 17, N.Y.

KENNEDY FOR PRESIDENT

A TIME FOR GREATNESS

U. S. SENATOR JOHN F. KENNEDY FOR PRESIDENT

◀ Kennedy campaign posters

WITNESS HISTORY

The Democratic Candidate

During the election of 1960, John F. Kennedy's Catholicism became an important issue. Some Americans openly questioned whether a Catholic was independent enough from his church to serve as President. Kennedy dismissed such questions, insisting that a candidate's religion should not be a factor in running for office:

❝I am not the Catholic candidate for President. I am the Democratic Party's candidate for President, who happens also to be a Catholic.❞

—John F. Kennedy, address to Southern Baptist Leaders, 1960

Kennedy and the Cold War

Objectives

- Explain the steps Kennedy took to change American foreign policy.

- Analyze the causes and effects of the Bay of Pigs invasion and the Cuban Missile Crisis.

- Assess the results of the Berlin Crisis and other foreign-policy events of the 1960s.

Terms and People

John F. Kennedy	Bay of Pigs invasion
Richard M. Nixon	Cuban missile crisis
Fidel Castro	Nikita Khrushchev
flexible response	hot line
Peace Corps	Nuclear Test Ban Treaty
Alliance for Progress	Berlin Wall

NoteTaking

Reading Skill: Understand Effects As you read, list the Cold War crises Kennedy faced and the effects of each event.

Cold War Crisis	Result
Bay of Pigs Invasion	

Why It Matters As the Cold War continued into the 1960s, Kennedy took office facing the spread of communism abroad and the threat of nuclear war. Determined to succeed where he felt Eisenhower had failed, Kennedy's enthusiasm and commitment to change offered the hope that with hard work and persistence the United States could win the Cold War. **Section Focus Question: How did Kennedy respond to the continuing challenges of the Cold War?**

Kennedy Defeats Nixon in 1960

For eight years, President Dwight Eisenhower had presided over a nation that had generally enjoyed peace and prosperity. But even so, there were a number of issues that caused Americans grave concern. The launch of *Sputnik 1* showed that the rivalry between the United States and the Soviet Union was still intense. The U-2 spy plane incident demonstrated that the Cold War might heat up at a moment's notice. The Montgomery bus boycott provided clear evidence that the *Brown* decision had not ended racial discrimination in the land. Deep, unsettled problems remained—problems for a new decade and a new generation of political leadership.

The Candidates In the presidential election of 1960, Democrat **John F. Kennedy** and Republican **Richard M. Nixon** were quite similar in a variety of ways. For the first time in U.S. history, both candidates had been born in the twentieth century, Nixon in 1913 and Kennedy in 1917. Both had served in the navy during World War II.

Vocabulary Builder

Use the information below and the following resource to teach students the high-use words from this section. Teaching Resources, Vocabulary Builder, p. 10

High-Use Words	Definitions and Sample Sentences
align	*v.* to decide to publicly support or not support a political group or country After the Japanese bombed Pearl Harbor, the United States **aligned** with the Allies fighting in Europe.
regime	*n.* a particular administration or government During World War II, the Allies removed the **regime** of Adolf Hitler and the Nazi Party.

Both had been elected to Congress in 1946 and to the Senate in the early 1950s. Both were passionate about foreign affairs and supported the Cold War fight against communism. Young and energetic, intelligent and hard-working, both wanted to be the first of their generation to lead the country.

Their differences, however, were as significant as their similarities. Kennedy was the son of a wealthy Boston businessman. His grandfather had been a state senator, and his father had served as the ambassador to Great Britain. Kennedy attended Harvard University. Although he was a Catholic and his religion was an issue in the election, he insisted that what church he attended should not be a factor.

Nixon, born in California, did not enjoy the advantages of a wealthy upbringing. His father struggled to make a living. As a young man, Nixon had to balance his time between his school studies and work to help support the family. Many voters, however, respected him for his experiences as Vice President under Eisenhower.

Televised Debates Make the Difference The 1960 election highlighted the growing power and influence of television. The candidates agreed to four televised debates. During the campaign, Nixon was hospitalized with a knee infection. After getting out of the hospital, he committed himself to a grueling schedule of public appearances. By the time of the first debate, held in late September in Chicago and watched by about 70 million people, Nixon looked pale and exhausted. Nixon arrived at the television studio an hour early, but he refused the offer to have makeup applied to hide his newly-growing beard. By contrast, Kennedy, tanned from open-air campaigning in California, looked healthy and confident. His relaxed manner, easy charm, and quick sense of humor added to his appeal.

In many ways, the debate boiled down to how the candidates looked and spoke, rather than what they said. Most Americans who listened to the debate on radio believed that Nixon had won. But the larger audience who watched the debate on television concluded that Kennedy was the clear victor. Although Nixon tried to change his image in the later debates, he was unable to significantly alter the country's initial impression of him. Kennedy's "victory" in the Chicago debate proved crucial in the election.

Kennedy Wins a Close Election Kennedy not only looked better on television, he also demonstrated an ability to react more quickly to unexpected events. For example, several weeks before the election, civil rights leader Martin Luther King, Jr., and a group of African American students were imprisoned during a protest in Atlanta, Georgia. Nixon said nothing publicly about the episode. Kennedy, however, telephoned King's wife, Coretta Scott King, to express his concern. He also worked behind the scenes to obtain King's release on bail. Kennedy's actions attracted the strong support of African Americans in the election.

The election of 1960 was the tightest presidential election since 1888.

Televised Debate

Richard Nixon (left) and John Kennedy (right) face each other in a televised debate. Kennedy won the election by a slim margin. *How did TV change political campaigns?*

The Presidential Election of 1960				
Candidate	Electoral Vote	Popular Vote	% Electoral Vote	% Popular Vote
John Kennedy (Democrat)	303	34,227,096	56.4	49.7
Richard Nixon (Republican)	219	34,107,646	40.8	49.6

In an election that witnessed the largest voter turnout in the country's history, Kennedy won by less than 120,000 of the 68 million popular votes cast. Had a few thousand people voted differently in Illinois and Texas, the election would have gone to Nixon. Kennedy's electoral victory was more convincing. He carried enough states to give him 303 electoral votes to Nixon's 219.

 Checkpoint How did the television debates affect the 1960 presidential election?

Kennedy Launches New Cold War Strategies

John Kennedy's 1960 campaign stressed the need for the United States to move forward with vigor and determination. Kennedy argued that during the Eisenhower years America had lost ground in the Cold War struggle against communism. He pointed to the new communist regime under **Fidel Castro** in Cuba and charged that there was now a "missile gap" that left the U.S. nuclear missile force inferior to that of the Soviet Union. The first goal of the Kennedy administration would be to build up the nation's armed forces.

Nowhere was the difference between Eisenhower and Kennedy more evident than in two important 1961 addresses. In his Farewell Address, Eisenhower counseled caution in foreign affairs. "The potential for the disastrous rise of misplaced power exists and will persist," he said.

Comparing Viewpoints

How Should the United States Fight the Cold War?

Both Presidents Eisenhower and Kennedy were strongly committed to containing communism. Their differences lay in their beliefs about the amount of military spending needed to carry out their goals.

DWIGHT D. EISENHOWER
In spite of numerous Cold War challenges, Eisenhower prided himself on having maintained peace. In his Farewell Address, he warned Americans about the effects of heavy defense spending.

Primary Source

"We annually spend on military security more than the net income of all United States corporations.... This ... immense military establishment ... is new in the American experience. We recognize the ... need for this development. Yet we must not fail to comprehend its grave implications. Our toil, resources and livelihood are all involved."

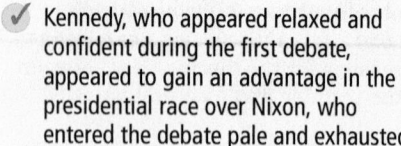

JOHN F. KENNEDY
Determined to prepare the United States against nuclear attack, Kennedy supported programs that resulted in a $6 billion increase in defense spending. He defends his action in a State of the Union address:

Primary Source

"Our moral and physical strength begins at home.... But it includes our military strength as well.... [W]e must arm to deter others from aggression. We have increased the previous defense budget ... not in the expectation of war but for the preservation of peace."

Compare
1. How does Eisenhower's plan for containing communism differ from Kennedy's?
2. Which plan may have prevented an attack on the United States? Explain.

History Background

The Second Vatican Council In four sessions held between 1962 and 1965, leaders of the Catholic Church convened the Second Vatican Council. At that time, they reconsidered the Church's position in the modern world and agreed on several significant changes. First, the Council redefined how the Church related to the rest of the world by deemphasizing the separation between the secular and the religious and proclaiming unity with the rest of the world. Next, the Council took a more positive view of non-Catholic and non-Christian religions and helped forge opportunities to discuss and debate different doctrines. The Council affirmed the connection between Judaism and Christianity, repudiated the charge of deicide against the Jews, and deplored all displays of anti-Semitism. Then, the Council revised the way that the liturgy was celebrated by allowing the priest to perform the mass in the vernacular instead of in Latin. The Council also redefined the role of the laity by encouraging them to participate more in the liturgy. Finally, the Council affirmed that people should be free to choose their religion and acknowledged that the Church had not always adhered to this belief in the past.

As the first President born in this century, Kennedy proclaimed that a "new generation of Americans" was ready to meet any challenge. In his Inaugural Address, Kennedy warned his country's enemies:

Primary Source "Let every nation know, whether it wishes us well or ill, that we shall pay any price, bear any burden, meet any hardship, support any friend, oppose any foe to assure the survival and the success of liberty."
—John F. Kennedy, Inaugural Address, January 20, 1961

Kennedy issued a challenge to Americans: "Ask not what your country can do for you; ask what you can do for your country."

Building the Nation's Military Eisenhower's defense policy of "massive retaliation" had emphasized the construction of nuclear weapons. Although Kennedy did not ignore the possibility of a nuclear war, he wanted to make sure that the United States was prepared to fight both conventional wars and conflicts against guerrilla forces. Kennedy therefore gave increased funding to conventional United States Army and Navy forces as well as to Army Special Forces, such as the Green Berets. He wanted a **"flexible response"** defense policy, one that prepared the United States to fight any type of conflict.

Pursuing New Initiatives in the "Third World" The "Third World," as it was known at the time, was the developing nations in Africa, Asia, and Latin America that did not <u>align</u> with the United States or the Soviet Union. According to Soviet propaganda, Western capitalism created poverty and inequalities in the Third World, whereas communism promoted equality.

Like previous American leaders, Kennedy believed that democracy combined with prosperity would contain or limit the spread of communism. Therefore, he initiated programs to economically and politically strengthen the Third World. The **Peace Corps,** created in 1961, sent American volunteers around the world on "missions of freedom" to assist developing countries. They worked to provide technical, educational, and health services. Other programs stressed purely economic development. The **Alliance for Progress** promised to resurrect America's Good Neighbor policy toward Latin America. During the 1950s, many Latin Americans had grown increasingly resentful of the United States, claiming that it had too much influence in their region. Kennedy hoped to change that view with this program. It promoted economic assistance to Latin America. Unlike the Peace Corps, the Alliance for Progress was not successful.

✔ **Checkpoint** What strategies did Kennedy use to improve relations between the United States and developing countries?

Kennedy's Plan

Special fighting forces (left), such as the Green Berets, were ready at all times for any attack. But Kennedy's Cold War strategy also involved creating goodwill among nations. The establishment of the Peace Corps (right) fulfilled that goal. *How could the Peace Corps help America win the Cold War?*

Vocabulary Builder
<u>align</u>–(uh LĪN) *v.* to decide to publicly support or not support a political group or country

Confronting Communism in Cuba

L3

Instruct

- **Introduce: Key Term** Ask students to find the key term **Bay of Pigs invasion** (in bold) in the text and define it. Ask **With all the might of the United States, why did the *Bay of Pigs invasion* fail?** *(Possible answer: The invasion was inadequately planned and poorly executed.)*

- **Teach** Remind students that Castro threatened to nationalize land held by private U.S. citizens. Ask **Why was the U.S. government concerned about private overseas investments?** *(Possible answers: because of a concern for international law and order; because many of the same citizens had close ties to government officials)* Display Color Transparency: *The Cuban Missile Crisis.* Ask students to consider Kennedy's protective actions as he keeps Khrushchev from falling over the cliff symbolizing the brink of nuclear war. **Why would Kennedy want to keep Khrushchev from falling?** *(Sample: Because nuclear war would be a disaster, and Kennedy hopes that saving Khrushchev would make the Soviet premier more reasonable.).* Color Transparencies A-121

- **Analyzing the Visuals** Have students study the chart on this page. Ask **With which of these effects were many Americans unfamiliar?** *(the removal of U.S. missiles from Turkey)*

Independent Practice

- Have students access **www.pearsonschool.com/ushist** to use the Geography Interactive map and then answer the map skills questions in the text.

Monitor Progress

Have students reread the introductory paragraph under the blue heading "Confronting Communism in Cuba," and ask them to predict the impact that Cuban exiles will have on the United States.

Vocabulary Builder
regime–(ruh ZHEEM) *n.* particular administration or government

Confronting Communism in Cuba

In 1959, Cuban revolutionary Fidel Castro succeeded in overthrowing the regime of Fulgencio Batista. Initially, the United States attempted to cultivate good relations with Castro. However, it soon became clear that the Cuban leader was determined to nationalize land held by private U.S. citizens, enforce radical reform measures, and accept Soviet economic and military aid. Thousands of wealthy and middle-class Cubans fled their country, many settling in Miami and southern Florida. Proud of their heritage and deeply anticommunist, they made new lives for themselves and their families in the United States.

Bay of Pigs Invasion After breaking diplomatic relations with Cuba in 1961, the Eisenhower administration authorized the Central Intelligence Agency (CIA) to plan an invasion of Cuba to overthrow Castro. The CIA recruited Cuban exiles and trained them in Guatemala. But when Eisenhower left office, the invasion plan was still that—an unexecuted, untried plan.

Pressured by members of the CIA and his own aides, Kennedy decided to implement the plan. On April 17, 1961, a CIA-led force of Cuban exiles attacked Cuba in the **Bay of Pigs invasion.** The invasion was badly mismanaged. The poorly equipped forces landed at the site with no protective cover. All but 300 of the 1,400 invaders were killed or captured. Not only did the Bay of Pigs invasion fail, it probably strengthened Castro's position in Cuba. It also turned many Cuban Americans against Kennedy.

Kennedy took personal responsibility for the failed invasion. However, he emphasized that the United States would continue to resist "communist penetration" in the Western Hemisphere.

Effects of the Cuban Missile Crisis ☑ Quick Study

- The Soviet Union removes missiles from Cuba.
- The United States removes missiles from Turkey.
- The United States and the Soviet Union avoid nuclear war.
- Kennedy and Khrushchev establish a "hot line" telephone system to keep communications open.
- In 1963, the United States, Great Britain, and the Soviet Union sign the Nuclear Test Ban Treaty.

The Cuban Missile Crisis Kennedy's efforts to contain communism were severely threatened during the **Cuban missile crisis.** In August and September of 1962 U.S. intelligence discovered that the Soviets were building nuclear missile sites in Cuba, apparently to protect Castro from another American invasion. When the sites were completed, major East Coast cities and the Panama Canal would be in range of the missiles.

Kennedy demanded the removal of the missiles. In a dramatic television address on October 22, 1962, he blamed **Nikita Khrushchev,** the Soviet premier, for causing a "reckless and provocative threat to world peace." He also announced that he had approved a naval quarantine (blockade) of Cuba to prevent the Soviets from completing the bases. Behind the scenes, however, Kennedy worked toward a diplomatic settlement. He indicated that he would remove U.S. missiles in Turkey and Italy if the Soviets removed their missiles in Cuba.

After six tense days when nuclear war seemed a real possibility, Khrushchev agreed to honor the blockade and remove the missiles. As Secretary of State Dean Rusk later told a reporter, "Remember, when you report this, that, eyeball to eyeball, they blinked first."

The Results of the Crisis During the Cuban missile crisis, Kennedy and Khrushchev stood on the edge of a nuclear war and then slowly backed away. In the Soviet Union, Khrushchev lost prestige and more hard-line leaders chipped away at his power. In the United States, Kennedy emerged as a more mature and thoughtful leader, one who had faced a frightening test and had remained calm and resolute. The crisis prompted both leaders to move toward détente. They installed a **"hot line"** telephone system between Moscow and Washington, D.C.,

Differentiated Instruction   Solutions for All Learners

L1 Special Needs Students   **L2 English Language Learners**   **L2 Less Proficient Readers**

Organize students in groups of four, and ask each group to take the role of the directors of a large and profitable business operating in Cuba. Inform students that they have begun to hear announcements from the Castro regime suggesting that their businesses will be taken over and nationalized. Tell students that they have gathered today to begin discussing the different actions that they should take to save the businesses. Before students begin, make sure that each group chooses one member to record ideas. After five to ten minutes, ask each group to refine the idea lists. Each group's members should focus on two or three effective ideas and then work together to write a proposal that details how they will proceed. As they develop their proposals, encourage students to consider what might go wrong and to include contingency plans designed to address such circumstances.

Geography *Interactive*
For: Interactive map
www.pearsonschool.com/ushist

Soviet missile base
U.S. naval blockade
U.S. naval base

Gulf of Mexico

Havana

San Cristobal

Isle of Pines

Bay of Pigs site

Santa Clara

Trinidad

CUBA

Caribbean Sea

Guantanamo Bay

Miller Projection
0   50   100 mi
0   50   100 km

Aerial photographs such as the one below, taken by an American U-2 spy plane, revealed the presence of Soviet missile bases in Cuba.

MRBM LAUNCH SITE 1
SAN CRISTOBAL, CUBA
23 OCTOBER 1962

Cuban Missile Bases

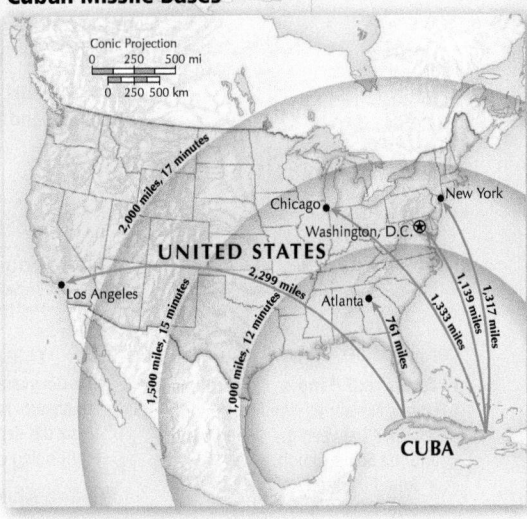

Conic Projection
0   250   500 mi
0   250   500 km

2,000 miles, 17 minutes

Chicago

New York

Washington, D.C.

UNITED STATES

Los Angeles

2,299 miles

Atlanta

1,500 miles, 15 minutes

1,000 miles, 12 minutes

761 miles

1,533 miles

1,139 miles

1,317 miles

CUBA

The location of missile bases in Cuba posed an immediate threat to several major American cities.

Map Skills Kennedy, aware of the Soviet arms buildup in Cuba, faced a difficult crisis.

1. **Place** Which U.S. city shown on the map was in the greatest danger from a nuclear attack? How long would it take a missile to reach that city?

2. **Draw Conclusions** How did the crisis affect U.S. relations with Cuba and the Soviet Union?

The Berlin Crisis L3

Instruct

- **Introduce: Key Term** Have students find the key term **Berlin Wall** (in bold), and ask them to share what they know about this structure.

- **Teach** Ask **In what year did Khrushchev demand that the United States end its military presence in Berlin?** *(1961)* **Why was Khrushchev so determined that the United States leave West Berlin?** *(because it lay within East Germany)* Ask students to consider the short- and long-term effects that the construction of the Berlin Wall might have on German citizens. Ask **What are some of the variables that might affect the development of the divided city?** *(Possible answers: military and financial resources devoted to the city; communication links with the rest of the world)*

Independent Practice

Have students write a paraphrase of the information below the blue heading "The Berlin Crisis."

Monitor Progress

As students fill in their charts, circulate to make sure that they understand the Cold War challenges faced by Kennedy and the results of each event. For a completed version of the graphic organizer, see Note Taking Transparencies, B-130.

Differentiated Instruction Solutions for All Learners

L1 Special Needs Students **L2 English Language Learners** **L2 Less Proficient Readers**

Use the map on this page to reinforce the idea of the proximity of Cuba's Soviet missile bases to major population centers in the United States. Have students locate Cuba on the small map, and then have them use their fingers to trace the missile trajectories from Cuba to major U.S. cities. Ask **Where is Cuba?** *(south of Florida, in the Caribbean Sea)* **What major cities could be struck within 15 minutes of a missile launch from Cuba?** *(Atlanta, New York,*

Washington, D.C., Chicago) Have students examine the photograph in the lower left-hand corner of the page. Explain that MRBM stands for "Medium-Range Ballistic Missile" and that San Cristobal is a city southwest of Havana. Ask **How might U.S. intelligence agencies have acquired such a detailed photograph of the San Cristobal site?** *(Possible answer: from a spy plane)*

Answers

Map Skills

1. Atlanta; A missile would take less than 12 minutes to reach Atlanta, the city closest to Cuba on the map.

2. The crisis made a tense situation worse, leading to deteriorating relations between the US and Cuba and the US and the Soviet Union.

Assess Progress L3

- Have students complete the Section Assessment.
- Administer the Section Quiz. Teaching Resources, p. 24
- To further assess student understanding, use Progress Monitoring Transparencies, 126.

Reteach

If students need more instruction, have them read the section summary.

Reading and Note Taking Study Guide L3

Adapted Reading and Note Taking Study Guide L1 L2

Spanish Reading and Note Taking Study Guide L2

Extend L4

See this chapter's Professional Development pages for the Extend Online activity on the Peace Corps.

Answers

 because major East Coast cities and the Panama Canal would be vulnerable to attack from the sites

 It exacerbated tensions between the two leaders.

---

to improve communication. In 1963, the year after the crisis, the United States, Great Britain, and the Soviet Union signed the **Nuclear Test Ban Treaty,** the first nuclear-weapons agreement, which ended aboveground nuclear tests. Thirty-six other nations soon signed the agreement.

 Checkpoint Why was the United States concerned about the missile sites in Cuba?

The Berlin Crisis

Since 1958, Khrushchev wanted to sign a peace treaty that would put the western zones of Berlin under control of East Germany. His actions were motivated by the steady flow of skilled East German workers into West Berlin. Desiring to show his strength, Kennedy stood firm on America's commitment to defending the rights of West Berliners and West Germans. At a conference in Vienna in June 1961, Kennedy and Khrushchev focused on Berlin as the key issue. Khrushchev called the present situation "intolerable." He demanded that the United States recognize the formal division of Germany and end its military presence in West Berlin. Kennedy refused. He did not want to give up occupation rights he considered critical to defending Western Europe. In a tense atmosphere, Khrushchev said, "I want peace, but if you want war, that is your problem." Kennedy answered, "It is you, not I who wants to force a change." The meeting ended abruptly. The conference, meant to relax Cold War tensions, only increased them.

After returning home, both world leaders made moves that threatened the peace. Kennedy asked Congress to dramatically increase military spending. Khrushchev ordered the construction of a wall between East and West Berlin. The **Berlin Wall** became a visible symbol of the reality of the two Germanys and the gulf between the communist East and democratic West. Kennedy responded by sending 1,500 U.S. troops to West Berlin. For a time, Russian and American tanks moved within sight of each other. Yet, neither side could fully claim a victory.

✓ **Checkpoint** How did the meeting in Vienna affect relations between Kennedy and Khrushchev?

Progress Monitoring Online
For: Self-test with vocabulary practice
www.pearsonschool.com/ushist

Comprehension

1. **Terms and People** For each item below, explain its significance to the relations between the United States and the Soviet Union.
   - John F. Kennedy
   - Fidel Castro
   - Bay of Pigs invasion
   - Cuban missile crisis
   - Nikita Khrushchev
   - Berlin Wall

2. **NoteTaking Reading Skill: Understand Effects** Use your chart to answer the Section Focus Question: How did Kennedy respond to the continuing challenges of the Cold War?

Writing About History

3. **Quick Write: Support a Point of View** Identify one point of view regarding President Kennedy's actions in starting the Peace Corps. List three arguments in favor of this point of view. Then, prioritize them by identifying the most persuasive argument.

Critical Thinking

4. **Draw Conclusions** Television played an important role in the 1960 presidential election. How influential is television in presidential elections today? Explain.

5. **Synthesize Information** The flexible response policy increased the military budget. How do you think this affected the nuclear arms race?

6. **Identify Point of View** How did the Cuban missile crisis affect public opinion about President Kennedy?

---

1. Sentences should reflect students' understanding of how each of these terms and people is related to the Cold War relations between the United States and the Soviet Union.

2. Kennedy responded to these challenges calmly and with resolve, gaining prestige as a thoughtful leader capable of handling crises. However, the Bay of Pigs Invasion was viewed as a huge setback for the President.

3. Encourage students to consider contrary points of view in deciding which argument is most persuasive.

4. Possible answer: Because most Americans today rely on television for news and current events, this medium is even more influential now than it was in the 1960s.

5. It escalated the nuclear arms race because military spending increased generally.

6. The resolution of the crisis boosted Kennedy's status because Kennedy had forced the Soviets to yield to U.S. pressure.

> For additional assessment, have students access **Progress Monitoring Online** at **www.pearsonschool.com/ushist.**

WITNESS HISTORY

Civil Rights

Although Kennedy did not have a strong civil rights record while in the Senate, he did portray himself as a crusader for African American rights during his campaign. Toward the end of his presidency, he abandoned his cautious approach. In a special report to the American people on civil rights, he talked about the racial inequality that had long endured in the nation:

❝It ought to be possible for American students of any color to attend any public institution. . . . It ought to be possible for American consumers of any color to receive equal service in places of public accommodation . . . and it ought to be possible for American citizens of any color to register and to vote in a free election. . . . We preach freedom around the world, and we mean it, and we cherish it here at home, but are we to say to the world and, much more importantly, to each other that this is the land of the free except for the Negroes . . .?❞

—John F. Kennedy, June 11, 1963

▲ President Kennedy with prominent civil rights and labor leaders in 1963. Dr. Martin Luther King, Jr., is at the far left.

Kennedy's New Frontier

Objectives
- Evaluate Kennedy's domestic policies.
- Assess the impact of the Kennedy assassination.

Terms and People

New Frontier
Equal Pay Act
deficit spending
space race
Warren Commission

Why It Matters Kennedy's determination to change life at home resulted in his domestic agenda called the New Frontier. Faced with a conservative Congress, Kennedy met with opposition as he fought to turn his vision into a reality. Still, he had some success in making changes in Social Security benefits, dealing with poverty and racial discrimination, and spurring new interest and expectations for the space program. **Section Focus Question: What were the goals of Kennedy's New Frontier?**

The Kennedy Style

As John Kennedy showed in his 1960 campaign and in his Inaugural Address, he had a special quality—or charisma—that separated him from other politicians. With his exquisitely tailored clothes, quick smile, and sense of humor, he seemed closer to a movie star than to a run-of-the-mill politician. Although he suffered many health problems, he projected youthful health and energy.

He surrounded himself with other distinguished men. Reporters dubbed them "the best and the brightest." They came from some of the country's most prestigious businesses and universities. Robert McNamara, president of Ford Motor Company, agreed to serve as Secretary of Defense. Dean Rusk, president of the Rockefeller

NoteTaking

Reading Skill: Identify Main Ideas List the characteristics of John F. Kennedy's style that appealed to the American people.

The Kennedy Image
• Youthful
•
•

Objectives

As you teach this section, keep students focused on the following objectives to help them answer the Section Focus Question and master core content.
- Evaluate Kennedy's domestic policies.
- Assess the impact of the Kennedy assassination.

Prepare to Read

Background Knowledge L3

Remind students about the domestic programs of previous Presidents. Ask them to predict the kinds of domestic programs Kennedy will enact.

Set a Purpose L3

- **WITNESS HISTORY** Read the selection aloud.

  Ask **To what events does Kennedy refer when he says that students of any color should be able to attend public institutions?** *(Possible answer: to events in 1957 at Arkansas's Little Rock Central High School)*

- **Focus** Point out the Section Focus Question, and write it on the board. Tell students to refer to this question as they read. *(Answer appears with Section 2 Assessment answers.)*

- **Preview** Have students preview the Section Objectives and the list of Terms and People.

- **Reading Skill** Have students use the *Reading Strategy: Identify Main Ideas* worksheet. Teaching Resources, p. 11

- **NoteTaking** Using the Guided Questioning strategy (TE, p. T20), have students read this section. As they read, have students list the characteristics of Kennedy that appealed to Americans. Reading and Note Taking Study Guide

Vocabulary Builder

Use the information below and the following resource to teach students the high-use words from this section. Teaching Resources, Vocabulary Builder, p. 10

High-Use Words	Definitions and Sample Sentences
crucial	*adj.* of vital importance The televised debates were **crucial** to Kennedy's successful election in 1960.
advocate	*v.* to speak or write in support of, be in favor of Civil rights leaders such as Martin Luther King, Jr., strongly **advocated** the use of nonviolent protest.

The Kennedy Style ⓛ³

Instruct

- **Introduce: Key Term** Have students locate the key term **New Frontier** (in bold) in the text. Ask them to think about the appeal that the idea of "frontier" has had in U.S. history.

- **Teach** Ask **Who did Americans think was the more charismatic leader—Kennedy or Nixon?** *(Kennedy)* **Should voters consider charisma in their choice of elected officials?** *(Possible answers: Yes—charismatic leaders will be more effective in establishing their policy goals. No—voters should focus on the candidates' substantive attributes, such as their intelligence and wisdom and their policy statements.)*

- **Quick Activity** Read aloud the Primary Source quotation on this page. Ask students to make a six-column chart with headings made up of words that Kennedy uses to describe what lies ahead on America's frontier (problems, battles, opportunities, perils, hopes, and threats). Then, ask students to fill in their charts with specifics that Kennedy might have placed in these categories.

Independent Practice

- Have students fill in the list of JFK's character traits that appealed to the American people.

- Ask students to think about the benefits and the costs to a leader seeking "the best and the brightest" advisers.

Monitor Progress

As students complete their lists, check to be sure that they are including character traits and not political or other information about Kennedy. For a completed version of this list, see Note Taking Transparencies, B-131a.

Answer

✓ Compared with other leaders, Kennedy appeared youthful, energetic, and charismatic.

The Kennedy Family
The new First Family charmed Americans with their youth and energy. Often, the President's children, Caroline and John, Jr., visited their father in the Oval Office.

Foundation, signed on as Secretary of State. Arthur Schlesinger, Jr., a Pulitzer Prize-winning historian, worked at the White House as a spokesperson for liberal causes and was a source of ideas for the President.

President Kennedy promised Americans that his administration would blaze a **"New Frontier."** The term described Kennedy's proposals to improve the economy, education, healthcare, and civil rights. He also hoped to jump-start the space program. In his presidential acceptance speech on July 15, 1960, in Los Angeles, California, Kennedy said,

> **Primary Source** "I stand tonight facing west on what was once the last frontier. . . . From the lands that stretch three thousand miles behind me, the pioneers of old gave up their safety, their comforts and sometimes their lives to build a new world here in the West. . . . But the problems are not all solved and the battles are not all won, and we stand today on the edge of a new frontier—the frontier of the 1960s—the frontier of unknown opportunities and perils—a frontier of unfulfilled hopes and threats."
>
> —John F. Kennedy, July 15, 1960

✓ **Checkpoint** Why did people feel that Kennedy was a different kind of politician?

Kennedy's Domestic Program

Early in his presidency, occupied by events in Cuba and Berlin, Kennedy devoted most of his attention to foreign affairs. But by 1963 he had become more concerned about pressing problems at home.

Kennedy—like millions of other Americans—was troubled by the high levels of poverty in the United States. *The Other America*, Michael Harrington's best-selling and influential 1962 exposé of poverty in America, shocked Kennedy and many other Americans.

While Kennedy failed to get Congress to accept his more ambitious social programs, he did push through an increase in the minimum wage, an extension in Social Security benefits, and improvements in the welfare system.

In addition, in 1962 Kennedy established the President's Commission on the Status of Women, a blue-ribbon panel that studied how poverty and

NoteTaking

Reading Skill: Identify Main Ideas As you read, identify details of Kennedy's domestic program.

- Space Program
- Domestic Program

History Background

The "Frontier Thesis" John F. Kennedy's reference to the frontier in his 1960 inaugural address was rooted firmly in the American historical tradition. The idea that the frontier had played an important role in the development of the United States had for decades been an important focus of academics—at least since 1893, when Frederick Jackson Turner delivered his famous speech, "The Significance of the Frontier in American History." In his speech, he developed his "frontier thesis," in which he argued that the United States was historically exceptional because of the frontier's significance in forging the democratic character of Americans and their institutions. "The frontier individualism," said Turner, "has from the beginning promoted democracy." Turner argued that "the peculiarity of American institutions is the fact that they have been compelled to adapt themselves to the changes of an expanding people—to the changes involved in crossing a continent, in winning a wilderness." Though historians today debate the extent of the frontier's impact on the United States, few question its general significance.

discrimination affected women. The difference in wages received by men and women for the same work was an especially glaring problem. The **Equal Pay Act** (1963) required equal wages for "equal work" in industries engaged in commerce or producing goods for commerce. Although it contained various loopholes, the law was a _crucial_ step on the road to fair and equal employment practices. The next year Congress would prohibit discrimination by employers on the basis of race, color, religion, national origin, or sex.

Stimulating a Sluggish Economy Kennedy believed that increased prosperity would help to eliminate some of the nation's social problems. When he became President, the country was suffering from a high unemployment rate and a sluggish economy. To help the sagging economy, Kennedy proposed tax credits to encourage business investment in new factory equipment. At the same time, increased military spending created new jobs and boosted the economy. Finally, Kennedy accepted the "new economics" of theorist John Maynard Keynes that _advocated_ **deficit spending** to stimulate the economy. Deficit spending is the government practice of borrowing money in order to spend more than is received from taxes. In 1963, Kennedy called for dramatic tax cuts for middle-class Americans as a way to put more money in the pockets of more people. At the same time, he increased the tax burden on wealthier citizens. Kennedy's economic initiatives jump-started the tremendous economic growth of the late 1960s.

Moving Cautiously on Civil Rights Kennedy pursued a timid approach toward civil rights. He had narrowly won the 1960 election, and he had little real influence in Congress or even complete partisan support. He did not want to anger conservative, white southern members of Congress in his own party. They stood ready to block any civil rights legislation.

While Kennedy remained largely passive on civil rights issues, African Americans and their white allies challenged segregation in the South. In 1961, they took "freedom rides" to desegregate interstate bus travel. In 1963, Martin Luther King, Jr., took the civil rights struggle to Birmingham, Alabama. Such actions took courage and were met by angry, oftentimes violent, responses by white southerners.

In early 1963, Kennedy introduced a civil rights bill that demanded prosecution for voting-rights violations and federal money to aid school desegregation. Further violence in the South prompted Kennedy to introduce stronger civil rights legislation.

Racing Into Space The launching of the satellite _Sputnik 1_ by the Soviet Union in 1957 called into question American technological superiority. Although Congress created the National Aeronautics and Space Administration (NASA) in 1958, the Soviets' space program remained several steps ahead of the American program. In April 1961, for example, the Soviet cosmonaut Yuri Gagarin became the first human to orbit Earth.

Kennedy recognized that the United States and the Soviet Union were locked in a **"space race."** _Space race_ was the term used to describe the competition between the Soviet Union and the United States to develop technology to successfully land on the moon. In May 1961, NASA put astronaut Alan Shepard into a suborbital space flight aboard the Project Mercury space capsule _Freedom 7_. Encouraged by the success of Project Mercury, Kennedy committed the United States to landing a man on the moon by 1970.

Vocabulary Builder
crucial–(KROO shuhl) _adj._ of vital importance

Vocabulary Builder
advocate–(AD vuh kayt) _v._ to speak or write in support of; to be in favor of

—from Straight Herblock
(Simon & Schuster, 1964)

Analyzing Political Cartoons

Civil Rights This cartoon, titled "Eclipse," appeared in 1963, at a time when the civil rights struggle reached national prominence.
1. Define _eclipse_. Why do you think the cartoonist chose this title?
2. Do you think all Americans responded the same way to this cartoon? Explain.

Kennedy's Domestic Program

Instruct

- **Introduce: Key Term** Ask students to find the key term _**deficit spending**_ (in bold) in the text. Ask them to predict how _**deficit spending**_ might affect the U.S. economy during the Kennedy and Johnson administrations.

- **Teach** Using the Numbered Heads strategy (TE, p. T23), have students discuss the main aspects of Kennedy's domestic program. Ask **What effect might an increase in the minimum wage have on the U.S. economy?** (_Possible answer: It might increase consumption, stimulate the economy, and expand the buying power of lower-income families._) Have students study the Infographic. Ask **How important was the "space race"?** (_Possible answer: very important, because it was a symbol of the nation's scientific ability and progress_)

- **Quick Activity** Display Color Transparency: _The Kennedy Years._ Use the lesson suggested in the transparency book to guide a discussion about initiatives of the Kennedy administration and the goals of each program. Color Transparencies **A-122**

Independent Practice

- NoteTaking Have students complete the concept web to identify details of Kennedy's New Frontier program. Reading and Note Taking Study Guide

- Assign _Reading a Chart: Kennedy's Programs,_ and have students answer the questions on the worksheet. Teaching Resources, **p. 20**

Monitor Progress

As students fill in their concept webs, circulate to make sure that they identify details of Kennedy's New Frontier program. For a completed version of the concept web, see Note Taking Transparencies, **B-131b**.

Differentiated Instruction Solutions for All Learners

L4 Advanced Readers **L4 Gifted and Talented Students**

Have students examine the political cartoon on this page. Ask them to discuss what the cartoonist's views of the civil rights crisis in the United States might be. Tell students to provide evidence from the cartoon that supports their conclusions. Then, have students draw political cartoons analyzing one of the domestic policies of the Kennedy administration discussed in this section. Have each student write a paragraph that describes the policy illustrated by the cartoon, tells whether the cartoon praises or criticizes it, and explains why he or she chose to draw a cartoon that supports or opposes the policy. Encourage volunteers to share their cartoons with the class.

Answers

Analyzing Political Cartoons
1. An eclipse is when the moon blocks the sun casting a shadow on Earth; because civil rights were eclipsing, or blocking, progress on everything else.
2. Possible answer: No; some may not have felt that civil rights were that important.

The President Is Assassinated

L3

Instruct

- **Introduce: Key Term** Have students locate the key term **Warren Commission** (in bold) in the text. Ask **What was the *Warren Commission*?** *(The Warren Commission was a group of government officials who investigated Kennedy's assassination.)*

- **Teach** Have students reread the introductory paragraph of "The President Is Assassinated." Ask **Do you think that a President should change while in office or should he or she come to the office with firm values, opinions, and beliefs and stick by them?** *(Possible answer: The President must come to the office with some firm values and opinions because citizens need to know what the President stands for and what his beliefs and values are; however, the President must also be flexible, open-minded, and capable of compromise.)* **Does the assassination of a national leader cause problems in the presidential succession in the United States?** *(No, the United States has firm and established rules regarding the order of succession as outlined in the Constitution.)*

Independent Practice

Have students write paragraphs assessing the contributions of the Kennedy administration and how it affected the United States.

Monitor Progress

Review this section by discussing how the United States might have been different had President Kennedy survived to win and complete a second term.

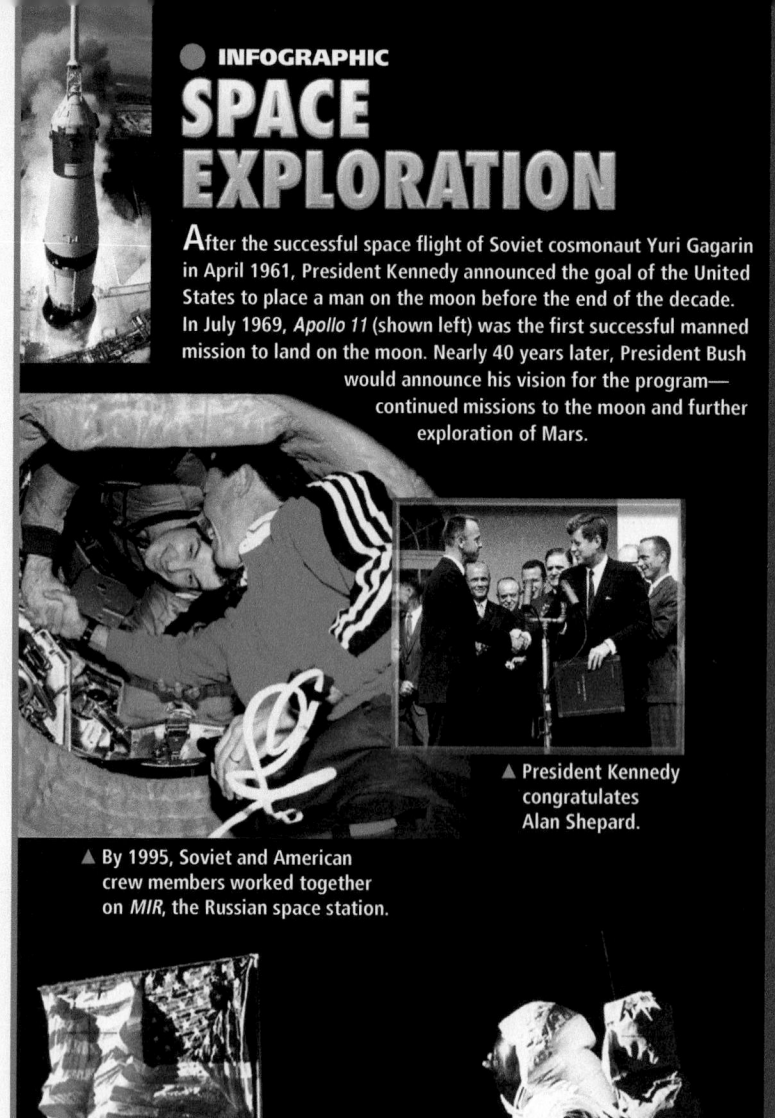

● **INFOGRAPHIC**

SPACE EXPLORATION

After the successful space flight of Soviet cosmonaut Yuri Gagarin in April 1961, President Kennedy announced the goal of the United States to place a man on the moon before the end of the decade. In July 1969, *Apollo 11* (shown left) was the first successful manned mission to land on the moon. Nearly 40 years later, President Bush would announce his vision for the program—continued missions to the moon and further exploration of Mars.

Ed White ► floats outside *Gemini 4* during a mission in 1965.

▲ President Kennedy congratulates Alan Shepard.

▲ By 1995, Soviet and American crew members worked together on *MIR*, the Russian space station.

Edwin Aldrin stands ► on the surface of the moon next to the American flag in 1969.

October 1958 NASA is created.

May 1961 Alan Shepard becomes the first American to make a space flight.

February 1962 John Glenn is the first American to orbit Earth.

January 1967 Fire kills *Apollo* astronauts Roger Chaffee, Virgil Grissom, and Edward White.

July 1969 *Apollo 11* astronauts successfully land on the moon.

June 1976 *Viking 1* transmits the first close-up images of Mars.

January 1986 Spacecraft *Challenger* explodes 73 seconds after takeoff. Seven astronauts are killed.

April 1990 *Hubble Space Telescope* is launched.

April 1997 *Pathfinder* lands on Mars.

November 1998 Construction of the *International Space Station* begins.

November 2000 The first crew takes residence in the *International Space Station*.

Thinking Critically
1. **Identify Causes** How did international competition lead to space exploration?
2. **Identify Central Issues** How did the loss of *Challenger* lead Americans to reexamine the costs and benefits of the space program?

Differentiated Instruction Solutions for All Learners

L1 Special Needs Students   **L2 English Language Learners**   **L2 Less Proficient Readers**

For visual learners and students who need help with basic skills, direct attention to the Infographic on this page. Remind students that this visual shows the development of American space exploration. Ask volunteers to examine the photographs and point out aspects of the images that indicate the kinds of chal-

lenges scientists faced in planning space voyages. Ask others volunteers to take turns reading the timeline aloud. Have students discuss how scientists today continue to build on scientific achievements of the Kennedy years to further space exploration.

Answers

Thinking Critically

1. Competition with the Soviet Union in many aspects of science and technology, such as space exploration, pushed the United States to develop its own program.

2. It made people question if the gains or goals of the space program were worth the dangers and failures.

America's quest to reach the moon was punctuated by enormous successes and heartbreaking failures. Astronaut John Glenn became the first American to orbit Earth in February 1962. But astronauts Virgil Grissom, Edward White, and Roger Chaffee burned to death when their docked capsule exploded in fire during a routine test. Finally, in July of 1969, astronaut Neil Armstrong left his spacecraft *Columbia*'s landing vehicle and became the first man to step on the moon. The mission was a successful completion of Kennedy's bold dream.

✓ **Checkpoint** Why did Kennedy change the way in which he addressed civil rights issues?

The President Is Assassinated

During his first two and a half years in office, Kennedy made the transition from politician to national leader. In foreign affairs he confronted Soviet challenges, made hard decisions, and won the respect of Soviet leaders and American citizens. He also spoke eloquently about the need to move toward a peaceful future. In domestic affairs he finally came to the conclusion that the federal government had to lead the struggle for civil rights. Added to his new maturity was his ability to inspire Americans to dream noble dreams and work toward lofty ends.

In November 1963, Kennedy traveled to Dallas, Texas, to mend political fences for his 1964 reelection bid. He never lived to see 1964. While his motorcade moved through the city, assassin Lee Harvey Oswald, perched by a window on the sixth floor of the Texas School Book Depository, fired three shots at the President. The third shot hit Kennedy in the back of his head. A half hour later, doctors at Parkland Memorial Hospital pronounced him dead. Texan Lyndon B. Johnson, Kennedy's Vice President, was sworn in as the new President. Although many people would later question whether Oswald acted alone, the **Warren Commission,** which conducted the official investigation of the assassination, described Oswald as the "lone killer."

The senseless murder deeply saddened Americans across the nation. Millions of people watched Kennedy's funeral procession on television, and many reacted as if they had lost a family member. It seemed as if part of America's innocence had died with him.

✓ **Checkpoint** What was the purpose of the Warren Commission?

A Son's Farewell
John F. Kennedy, Jr., salutes his father's casket as it passes by in the funeral procession.

Assess and Reteach

Assess Progress ⒧3

- Have students complete the Section Assessment.
- Administer the Section Quiz. Teaching Resources, p. 25
- To further assess student understanding, use Progress Monitoring Transparencies, 127.

Reteach

If students need more instruction, have them read the section summary.

Reading and Note Taking ⒧3
Study Guide

Adapted Reading and ⒧1 ⒧2
Note Taking Study Guide

Spanish Reading and ⒧2
Note Taking Study Guide

Extend ⒧4

To help students familiarize themselves with the issues of the Cold War "space race," have them read and complete the Enrichment worksheet, *Create a Board Game: The Space Race.* Teaching Resources, pp. 12–13

Answers

✓ The strong reactions of many white southerners to the civil rights movement made it clear to Kennedy that he would have to put more pressure on southern authorities who were reluctant to protect their citizens' civil rights.

✓ to conduct an official investigation into the assassination of President Kennedy

---

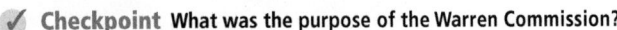

SECTION 2 Assessment

Progress Monitoring *Online*
For: Self-test with vocabulary practice
www.pearsonschool.com/ushist

Comprehension

1. **Terms and People** Discuss how each of the following terms met a goal of Kennedy's domestic program.
   - New Frontier
   - Equal Pay Act
   - deficit spending

2. NoteTaking **Reading Skill: Identify Main Ideas** Use your concept web to answer the Section Focus Question: What were the goals of Kennedy's domestic program?

Writing About History

3. **Quick Write: Identify Counterarguments** Identify one point of view regarding President Kennedy's decision to move cautiously on civil rights. Then, identify one argument that someone might use *against* this point of view. Remember, an effective counterargument does not simply state that the original argument was wrong but gives specific reasons for the opposing point of view.

Critical Thinking

4. **Analyze Information** Why did Kennedy consider foreign policy to be the most important issue of his administration?

5. **Draw Inferences** Why do you think Kennedy called his domestic program the New Frontier?

6. **Draw Conclusions** Was Kennedy's commitment to the space program an extension of the Cold War? Explain.

Section 2 Assessment

1. Kennedy used the phrase *New Frontier* to describe his domestic program. He intended to remedy social problems by using all available tools, including new legislation (such as the *Equal Pay Act*) and *deficit spending*—a relatively new fiscal tool that allowed Kennedy to acquire more funds for social programs.

2. the reduction of poverty and gender discrimination, increased employment, enforcement of civil rights, and more support for science and space exploration

3. Possible answers: Kennedy would not win popular or political support if he moved too quickly; the potential for problems is not sufficient reason for failing to do what is right.

4. Possible answer: He believed that Cuba's communist government and the missile gap showed that the United States had lost ground in the Cold War struggle.

5. because of the powerful influence that the frontier exerted over American history

6. Possible answer: Yes; he did not want the Soviet Union to dominate the United States in any way, so he advocated the space program to ensure U.S. superiority in all areas.

For additional assessment, have students access **Progress Monitoring *Online*** at **www.pearsonschool.com/ushist.**

Can a Poor Person Get a Fair Trial?

Objectives
- Analyze the Sixth Amendment regarding the right to "the assistance of counsel."
- Understand both the facts and arguments in the case of *Gideon* v. *Wainwright*.
- Investigate the impact of the court's decision on criminal defendants who cannot afford an attorney.

Background Knowledge L3
Ask students to offer their own answer to the title question, and offer facts and reasoning to support it.

Instruct L3
- Lead a class discussion about the due process clause of the Fourteenth Amendment and *Gideon* v. *Wainwright*. Ask **Should American taxpayers pay for the defense of criminal defendants who cannot afford an attorney?** *(Possible answer: Yes; it is warranted to ensure that a person's right to justice does not depend on personal finances.)*

- Have students complete the worksheet *Landmark Decisions of the Supreme Court: Can a Poor Person Get a Fair Trial?* Teaching Resources, p. 21

- **Connect to Your World** Refer students to the Key Supreme Court Cases section for summaries of this case. Responses should show a clear understanding of the case and provide specific details that support students' explanations.

Monitor Progress
To review, write the statistic: "In four out of five criminal cases today, the accused person is too poor to afford an attorney" on the board. Lead a class discussion on the relationship between poverty and crime.

Can a Poor Person Get a Fair Trial?

The Sixth Amendment gives a person accused of a crime the right to "the assistance of counsel." But what about poor defendants? They don't have the money to pay for a lawyer. If a poor person goes to trial without a lawyer and is convicted, was justice done?

Gideon v. *Wainwright* (1963)

The Facts	The Issue	The Decision
• Clarence Gideon was tried in a Florida court for breaking into a building. • Gideon said he was too poor to afford a lawyer and asked the court to appoint one. • After the judge refused, Gideon defended himself and was found guilty.	Gideon claimed he had been denied his rights to an attorney and to due process.	The Supreme Court ruled unanimously that Florida should have provided an attorney for Gideon.

Why It Matters
The Court's ruling in *Gideon* was forceful. All nine justices agreed that Florida should have given Gideon an attorney. They clearly stated why having an attorney is so important:

> "Any person hauled into court, who is too poor to hire a lawyer, cannot be assured a fair trial unless counsel is provided for him. This seems to us to be an obvious truth."

The decision had a tremendous impact on the country's legal system. Public defenders are state-paid officials who defend people who are too poor to hire their own lawyers.

But has the promise of *Gideon* been fulfilled? Critics say problems still remain. Many states do not fully fund the public defenders' offices that furnish lawyers for poor defendants. These defenders are overworked and underpaid, making it harder for them to do their job well. They lack the resources to hire experts to evaluate evidence. Many public defenders are not brought into a case as soon as a charge is made. This prevents them from properly advising their clients. Finally, public defenders do not have the time or resources to effectively carry out appeals to higher courts.

▲ Clarence Gideon

Connect to Your World
Research the use of public defenders in your state or community. Then, write an essay titled "*Gideon Today*," in which you explain whether you think the justice system is fair for poor people.

For: Supreme Court cases
www.pearsonschool.com/ushist

◄ A public defender and his client face the judge during a court hearing.

History Background

Betts* v. *Brady Until the U.S. Supreme Court agreed to hear Gideon's case in 1963, the lower courts had depended on the 1942 decision in *Betts* v. *Brady* for guidance. In that case, Smith Betts, who was accused of robbery, asked a judge to appoint a lawyer for him because he could not afford one. The refusal of the judge led Betts to pursue his case on the grounds that his right to due process, guaranteed by the Fourteenth Amendment, had been violated. When Betts's case reached the Supreme Court, the justices decided that his case was not a denial of due process. But in the

decades intervening between *Betts* and *Gideon*, new justices had joined the court, and some questioned the fairness of that decision, and the court decided to hear Gideon's case. The justices appointed Abe Fortas (a future Supreme Court justice) to represent Gideon and argue with opposing counsel the question of whether *Betts* v. *Brady* should be reconsidered. Their arguments led the court to rule that the Sixth Amendment right to counsel was applicable to the states through the Fourteenth Amendment's due process clause, overturning the *Betts* v. *Brady* decision.

President Johnson's Hopes for America

In 1965, President Lyndon B. Johnson addressed a joint session of Congress. In the speech he talked about some of his hopes for America and how he wished to be remembered by history. He explained,

❝I do not want to be the President who built empires, or sought grandeur, or extended dominion. I want to be the President who educated young children . . . who helped to feed the hungry . . . who helped the poor to find their own way. . . .❞
— President Johnson, speech before Congress, March 15, 1965

◄ Lyndon Johnson is sworn in as President, in 1963, after Kennedy's assassination.

Objectives

As you teach this section, keep students focused on the following objectives to help them answer the Section Focus Question and master core content.

- Evaluate Johnson's policies up to his victory in the 1964 presidential election.
- Analyze Johnson's goals and actions as seen in his Great Society programs.
- Assess the achievements of the Great Society.

Johnson's Great Society

Objectives

- Evaluate Johnson's policies up to his victory in the 1964 presidential election.
- Analyze Johnson's goals and actions as seen in his Great Society programs.
- Assess the achievements of the Great Society.

Terms and People

Lyndon B. Johnson	Medicare
Civil Rights Act	Medicaid
War on Poverty	Immigration and
Economic Opportunity	Nationality Act of
Act	1965
Great Society	Warren Court

NoteTaking

Reading Skill: Identify Main Ideas Identify Great Society programs.

The Great Society			
Education	Healthcare	Immigration	Poverty
•	• Medicare	•	•

Why It Matters Lyndon B. Johnson, who became President after Kennedy's assassination, shared the same goals as his predecessor. These goals shaped the purpose of Johnson's Great Society program. A seasoned politician, Johnson successfully pushed through significant domestic legislation that he hoped would become the first step to achieving the quality of life he thought all Americans should enjoy. **Section Focus Question: How did Johnson's Great Society programs change life for most Americans?**

Johnson's Rise to Leadership

Born in Stonewall, Texas, Lyndon B. Johnson was raised in the Hill Country town of Johnson City. He attended Southwest Texas State College and then taught for several years in Cotulla, Texas. There, at a tiny segregated school for Mexican Americans, he confronted firsthand the challenges faced by poverty-stricken minority students, and the lessons he learned remained with him for the rest of his life.

A Determined Texan After teaching for several years, Johnson entered politics—first as a Texas congressman's secretary and then as the head of the Texas National Youth Administration.

In 1937, Johnson was elected to Congress, and during the next several decades he became the most powerful person on Capitol Hill. Elected to the Senate in 1948, Johnson proved himself a master of party politics and rose to the position of Senate majority

Prepare to Read

Background Knowledge

Students have studied the domestic policy initiatives of the Kennedy administration. Ask them to predict the ways in which Johnson may follow, add to, or depart from the initiatives of his predecessor.

Set a Purpose

- **WITNESS HISTORY** Read the selection aloud.

  Ask **How might U.S. policies change during the Johnson administration?** *(There might be a greater focus on domestic policy, especially on education and poverty.)*

- **Focus** Point out the Section Focus Question, and write it on the board. Tell students to refer to this question as they read. *(Answer appears with Section 3 Assessment answers.)*

- **Preview** Have students preview the Section Objectives and the list of Terms and People.

- **NoteTaking** Using the Paragraph Shrinking strategy (TE, p. T20), have students read this section. As they read, have students identify details about the Great Society programs. Reading and Note Taking Study Guide

Vocabulary Builder

Use the information below and the following resource to teach students the high-use words from this section. Teaching Resources, Vocabulary Builder, p. 10

High-Use Words	Definitions and Sample Sentences
outcome	*n.* final result of a meeting, process, or series of events The **outcome** of the 1960 presidential election was one of the closest in U.S. history.
overall	*adj.* including or considering everything The **overall** failure of the Bay of Pigs invasion helped turn many Cuban Americans against Kennedy.

Johnson's Rise to Leadership ⓛ

Instruct

- **Introduce: Key Terms** Ask students to find the key terms *Civil Rights Act* and *War on Poverty* (in bold). Ask **How are these terms related?** (*Possible answer: They were important components of Johnson's domestic policy.*) Have students examine the complex relationship between class and race in the United States.

- **Teach** Ask **Why might Johnson have been so concerned about poverty?** (*Possible answer: because of his experiences as a teacher*) **How does the design of the Head Start program reflect Johnson's experiences?** (*The program operates on the idea that a child's success in school is directly linked to his or her family's socio-economic circumstances —something Johnson observed during his time as a teacher.*) **Do you think the sentiments expressed by Johnson in the Primary Source quotation on this page are genuine or calculated to achieve his policy goals? Explain.** (*Possible answer: Johnson's sentiments were genuine. He shared the same goals as Kennedy did and wanted Congress to pass the Civil Rights Bill.*)

- **Analyzing the Visuals** Have students examine the bar graph on this page. Ask **What is the change in percentage of Americans living below the poverty line from 1960 to 1970?** (*10 percent decrease*)

Independent Practice

To review the 1964 presidential election, ask students to reread the red heading "Johnson Defeats Goldwater." Ask students to discuss why Goldwater's economic and social views were referred to as "extremist" and why Johnson used this to gain votes.

Monitor Progress

Have students write a sentence to explain the main characteristics of each Key Term under this blue heading.

leader in 1955. In the Senate, he was adept at avoiding conflict, building political coalitions, and working out compromises. His skill was instrumental in pushing the 1957 Civil Rights Act through Congress.

In 1960, he hoped to be chosen by the Democratic Party to run for President, but when Kennedy got the nomination Johnson agreed to join him on the ticket as the vice presidential nominee. A New Englander and a Catholic, Kennedy needed Johnson to help carry the heavily Protestant South. Johnson was also popular both with Mexican American voters and in the Southwest. He was an important part of Kennedy's victory in 1960.

The Kennedy Legacy On becoming President after Kennedy's assassination, Johnson radiated reassurance and strength. His every action indicated that he was ready for the job and that the government was in good hands. Less than a week after the assassination, Johnson addressed a joint session of Congress.

Job Training
President Johnson visits a job training center in Texas. The success of Johnson's antipoverty programs is reflected in the declining numbers of Americans living below the poverty line.

Primary Source " . . . [N]o memorial oration or eulogy could more eloquently honor President Kennedy's memory than the earliest possible passage of the Civil Rights Bill for which he fought so long."
—President Johnson, speech before a Joint Session of Congress, 1963

With Johnson's ability to build consensus, or agreement on an issue by a group, the **Civil Rights Act** became law in the summer of 1964. It outlawed discrimination in voting, education, and public accommodations. The act demanded an end to discrimination in hospitals, restaurants, theaters, and other places open to the public. It also created the Equal Employment Opportunity Commission to fight discrimination in hiring. African Americans and Mexican Americans who faced almost daily discrimination benefited immeasurably from the legislation. Finally, Title VII of the 1964 Civil Rights Act prohibited discrimination on the basis of sex.

Johnson Declares a War on Poverty Johnson made his intentions clear in his first State of the Union address when he said it was time to "declare an unconditional war on poverty." The new President planned to fuse his own dreams for America onto Kennedy's legislative agenda. Although Kennedy had failed to get Congress to approve his tax bill calling for dramatic tax cuts for middle-class Americans, Johnson was able to maneuver it through. In addition, he had added a billion-dollar **War on Poverty** to the bill.

Johnson's War on Poverty introduced measures to train the jobless, educate the uneducated, and provide healthcare for those in need. The 1964 **Economic Opportunity Act** created the Job Corps to train young men and women between the ages of 16 and 21 in the work skills they needed to acquire better jobs and move out of poverty. The act also established Volunteers in Service to America, or VISTA, patterned after Kennedy's Peace Corps, which sent American volunteers into poverty-stricken American communities in an effort to solve the country's pressing economic, educational, and medical problems. The volunteers served in inner-city schools and on Indian reservations. They worked in rural health clinics and urban hospitals.

War on Poverty

(bar graph)
Percentage of Americans living below poverty line
1960: approximately 22
1970: approximately 12
SOURCE: U.S. Census Bureau

Connect to Your World

VISTA and AmeriCorps The Volunteers in Service to America (VISTA) program created by President Johnson in 1964 still exists. Today, the program is part of AmeriCorps, a network of national service programs that was organized after President Bill Clinton signed the National and Community Service Trust Act in 1993. U.S. citizens who are at least 17 years of age are eligible to join AmeriCorps. After joining, members work full- or part-time over a 10 to 12 month period. They participate in programs designed "to meet the nation's critical needs in education, public safety, health, and the environment." In the past, AmeriCorps members have worked with nonprofit groups, such as the American Red Cross, as well as with smaller community organizations. In exchange for their service, AmeriCorps members receive an education award that can be used to pay for college or student loans. Since 1994, hundreds of thousands of Americans have served in AmeriCorps programs.

Poverty and Prosperity

TRACK THE ISSUE

How should Americans deal with the gap between rich and poor?

Over the years, Americans have tried to balance the extremes of wealth and poverty in society. Some have favored private charity to help the poor, while others have backed government policies to distribute wealth. Still, the gap remains. Use the timeline below to explore this enduring issue.

1800s Community Aid
Private charities provide aid for the poor.

1900 Poverty Level
An estimated 40 percent of Americans live in poverty.

1933 New Deal
Federal government provides aid for the poor.

1964 War on Poverty
President Johnson expands programs to reduce poverty.

1980s Reaganomics
President Reagan promotes business growth to reduce poverty.

1996 Welfare Reform
Government limits welfare programs.

Migrant farm family in Virginia

Many workers, such as the grocery clerk shown here, hold minimum-wage jobs.

DEBATE THE ISSUE

The Minimum Wage The government has tried to reduce poverty for working people by setting a minimum wage. Supporters say this wage is too low to provide a decent living. Critics say an increase would hurt employers and make it harder for them to provide low-level jobs.

"We all lose when American workers are underpaid. It's a myth that small businesses can't pay a higher minimum wage. . . . When businesses don't pay a living wage, all society pays. We pay through poverty . . . [and] needless disease. . . . We pay as businesses and communities suffer economic decline."
—Margot Dorfman, CEO, U.S. Women's Chamber of Commerce

"Decades of economic research confirm that increasing the minimum wage destroys jobs for low-skilled workers while doing little to address poverty. When faced with higher labor costs, employers tend to hire fewer, more highly-skilled and experienced employees. That leaves unskilled or low-skilled workers . . . out in the cold."
—from The Economics Policy Institute

? TRANSFER Activities

1. **Compare** Why does Margot Dorfman support the minimum wage? Why does the Economic Policy Institute oppose it?

2. **Analyze** Does a minimum wage help reduce poverty? Explain.

3. **Transfer** Use the following Web site to see a video, try a WebQuest, and write in your journal. www.pearsonschool.com/ushist

Objectives

- Explain the scope of poverty in the United States.
- Analyze the costs and benefits of public and private efforts to alleviate poverty.

Background Knowledge

Ask students to consider the differences between the use of private charity and public policy to address poverty issues. Make a two-column chart on the board, and list the advantages and disadvantages that students associate with each.

Instruct ⓛ

- Have students examine the timeline. Ask **When did a major policy change regarding poverty in the United States first take place?** *(in 1933)* **What might have triggered this?** *(the Great Depression)* **How did Reagan's poverty-reduction strategies differ from those used in New Deal and War on Poverty programs?** *(Possible answer: Reagan relied on business growth instead of direct aid to the poor.)*

Monitor Progress

- Have students complete the Issues Connector worksheet, *Prosperity and Poverty*. Check their work to make sure that students understand the aspects of the issue. Teaching Resources, **pp. 14–17**

- Remind students to complete their American Issues Connector notes. Review their work for accuracy. Reading and Note Taking Study Guide

History Background

Minimum Wages The U.S. government first established a federal minimum wage in 1938 with the Fair Labor Standards Act (FLSA). Congress passed the law because it found that wages that do not allow a standard of living necessary for health, efficiency, and general well being of workers were detrimental to the nation's economic interests. The original legislation mandated a wage of 25 cents per hour. Since then, Congress has raised the minimum wage many times. In 2006, the federal minimum wage was $5.15 per hour—a rate established in 1997. The cost of living may rise from year to year, but the minimum wage does not automatically increase. Congress must pass a bill, which the President must sign into law. Although there is a federal minimum wage, many states have passed their own minimum wage laws. In 2008, the state of Washington had the highest minimum wage—$8.08 per hour. If a state's minimum wage is lower than the federal rate, employers must pay the higher rate covered by the federal law.

Answers

Transfer Activities

1. because it helps fulltime workers meet basic needs; because it reduces job prospects for unskilled youth and burdens taxpayers

2. Sample answer: Yes; because a minimum wage enables a fulltime worker to meet basic needs.

3. For more information, have students access **www.pearsonschool.com/ushist**.

Instruct

- **Introduce: Key Term** Ask students to find the key term *Great Society* (in bold) in the text. Ask them to examine the Primary Source quotation on the next page and discuss the way in which Johnson distinguishes a great society from a rich and powerful society.

- **Teach** Using the Think-Write-Pair-Share strategy (TE, p. T23), discuss with students the major legislation and goals of the Great Society. Ask **On what aspects of American life did Johnson focus his reforms in order to achieve what he called the "Great Society?"** *(poverty, healthcare, education, environmental and consumer protection, and immigration)* Have students study the Infographic. Then, display Color Transparency: *Head Start*. Use the lesson suggested in the transparency book to guide a discussion about the Head Start program and how it attempted to meet the goals of the Great Society. Then, ask **How might the interests of private-property owners come into conflict with environmental legislation passed under Johnson?** *(Possible answer: It is likely that the owners of factories and coal plants, for example, would need to spend money on improvements in order to meet the new clean air standards.)* **Does a relationship exist between immigration and poverty? Explain.** *(Possible answer: Yes; some immigrants are poor and have come to the United States in search of economic opportunities.)*
Color Transparencies **A-124**

Perhaps the most successful element of the Economic Opportunity Act was the Head Start program. Funds were provided for play groups, day care, and activities designed to help underprivileged children get ready for elementary school. Head Start enjoyed bipartisan support for decades.

Johnson Defeats Goldwater If Johnson was to continue his War on Poverty and other social goals, he needed to win the 1964 presidential election. In that year, the Republicans nominated Arizona senator Barry Goldwater, whose economic and social views were directly opposed to Johnson's. Whereas Johnson believed the federal government could best regulate the economy and promote social justice, Goldwater maintained that the federal government was the problem, not the solution. According to Goldwater, social and economic issues, such as racism and poverty, should not be addressed by the federal government.

If elected, Goldwater would rein in the federal government by reducing its size and restricting its activities. He favored significant tax cuts and right-to-work laws, and he opposed social welfare legislation and government spending on educational, public housing, and urban renewal programs.

In 1964, most Americans were not ready either for Goldwater's belligerent tone or his conservative message. Johnson's campaign played up Goldwater's extremism, suggesting that his election would ensure the repeal of civil rights legislation and economic ruin.

Johnson had prosperity on his side, as well as his own impressive legislative record and the legacy of Kennedy. In the November election, he won a landslide

▲ President Johnson signs the Higher Education Act on November 8, 1965, at the one-room schoolhouse near Stonewall, Texas, where his own education began.

History Interactive
For: To discover more about the Great Society programs
www.pearsonschool.com/ushist

● **INFOGRAPHIC**

The Great Society
Arts and Education

At a 1965 news conference, President Johnson declared, "When I was young, poverty was so common that we didn't know it had a name. And education was something you had to fight for . . . ." Seemingly inspired by his own upbringing, Johnson set out to create the Great Society. The program included support for education and the arts.

▼ Project Head Start and the Elementary and Secondary Education Act committed the federal government to providing resources for individuals and schools. At left, a teacher works with students at a preschool program. Below, students work together in a school library.

Differentiated Instruction Solutions for All Learners

L1 Special Needs Students **L2 English Language Learners** **L2 Less Proficient Readers**

Organize students in pairs. Have each pair construct a concept map to show the programs and policies that Johnson initiated to address the hardships of America's poor. Students should note the main idea—the Great Society—and identify the programs under it. Then, have them use their concept maps to discuss in what ways each program or policy helped alleviate poverty in the United States.

victory, capturing more than 60 percent of the popular vote and carrying all but six states. Goldwater carried only Arizona and five southern states—Louisiana, Mississippi, Alabama, Georgia, and South Carolina. Furthermore, the outcome of the election was significant. The South was no longer solidly Democrat. Not only had Johnson won a ringing victory, but Democrats had captured both houses of Congress.

Vocabulary Builder
outcome–(OWT kuhm) *n.* final result of a meeting, process, or series of events

✔ **Checkpoint** How did Johnson continue Kennedy's plan to eliminate poverty in the United States?

The Great Society

In the spring of 1964, in a speech at the University of Michigan, Johnson outlined his vision for America, calling it the **Great Society.** He said that during the previous several centuries, Americans had spread across the continent, developed industrially, and created great wealth. But the work of America was not complete. He added,

Primary Source "The challenge of the next half century is whether we have the wisdom to use that wealth to enrich and elevate our national life, and to advance the quality of our American civilization. . . . [W]e have the opportunity to move not only toward the rich society and the powerful society, but upward to the Great Society."
—President Johnson, University of Michigan, May 22, 1964

For Johnson, the Great Society demanded "an end to poverty and racial injustice" and opportunity for every child.

▶ Public radio and television gained support through the sponsorship of the Corporation for Public Broadcasting. *Sesame Street,* featuring Big Bird and the Muppets, combines education and entertainment for children.

▲ The National Endowment for the Arts financially assists artists, arts education, and arts organizations. Wynton Marsalis (above) and Helen Frankenthaler (left) each won the National Medal of Honor.

Thinking Critically
1. **Draw Inferences** How might education programs be used to create a great society?
2. **Identify Point of View** Should the government provide funds to support the arts? Explain.

■ **Quick Activity** To enrich and extend the lesson, have students access the **History Interactive** at **www.pearsonschool.com/ushist.** After students experience the History Interactive, ask them to share their reactions by posing questions such as: How does public television benefit American society? Have you or your family benefited from it? In what ways? Do you think the federal government should legislate public education or should education be controlled locally? Explain.

Independent Practice

To help students understand the various programs of the Great Society, have them analyze *Reading a Chart: The Great Society,* and complete the worksheet. Teaching Resources, **p. 22**

Monitor Progress

As students fill in their graphic organizers, circulate to make sure they are identifying important details related to Johnson's Great Society programs. For a completed version of the graphic organizer, see Note Taking Transparencies, **B-132.**

Answers

✔ by pushing Kennedy's tax bill through Congress after adding a billion-dollar "War on Poverty" program

Thinking Critically
1. Education programs give children knowledge, encouragement to learn, and opportunities for advancement. Children who have benefited from the programs generally enjoy greater success as adults.
2. Sample answers: No—government funding for the arts should be limited because the government may decide not to fund controversial art forms and some critics consider this a kind of censorship; Yes—many worthwhile works are not commercially successful but valuable nonetheless. They could not be produced without government funds.

Differentiated Instruction **Solutions for All Learners**

L1 Special Needs Students **L2 English Language Learners** **L2 Less Proficient Readers**

Ask students to consider the ways in which the visuals in the Infographic help illustrate President Johnson's pursuit of the "Great Society." Ask **How do these photographs relate to the idea of a Great Society?** *(Possible Answer: Johnson believed that a Great Society did its best to elevate the nation, and to this end he supported programs to improve education in America. He also supported the arts to enrich life through encouraging creativity and inno-*

vation.) Tell students that when Johnson signed legislation for the Public Broadcasting Act of 1967, he said that "our Nation wants more than just material wealth; our Nation wants more than a chicken in every pot." Encourage students to explain the meaning of this quotation. Tell them that many people in the United States not only work to produce goods and create wealth, but also to enrich the human spirit.

Instruct

- **Introduce** Ask students to preview the HISTORY MAKERS feature on Earl Warren on the next page. Explain that Warren was Chief Justice during a period in which the Supreme Court issued decisions, such as *Brown* v. *Board of Education,* that were met with disapproval by many conservatives. Ask students what they know about the views of the Supreme Court today.

- **Teach** Ask **How do states usually determine the apportionment of seats in their legislatures?** *(through a census)* **Why might people be upset if seats are not periodically reapportioned?** *(because population growth and movement might bring about changes that give an unfair advantage to certain districts—an advantage that could then be exploited by those in power)* **Did the Warren Court go too far in protecting the rights of the accused? Why or why not?** *(Possible answers: No. The way we treat the accused is a sign of a just and democratic society. Yes. The Warren Court's decisions created precedents in which the rights of lawbreakers could be given more protection than those of law-abiding citizens.)*

- **Quick Activity** Display Color Transparency: *The Warren Court.* Use the lesson suggested in the transparency book to guide a discussion about important cases decided by the Warren Court, including *Brown* v. *Board of Education, Miranda* v. *Arizona,* and *Engel* v. *Vitale.* Color Transparencies **A-123**

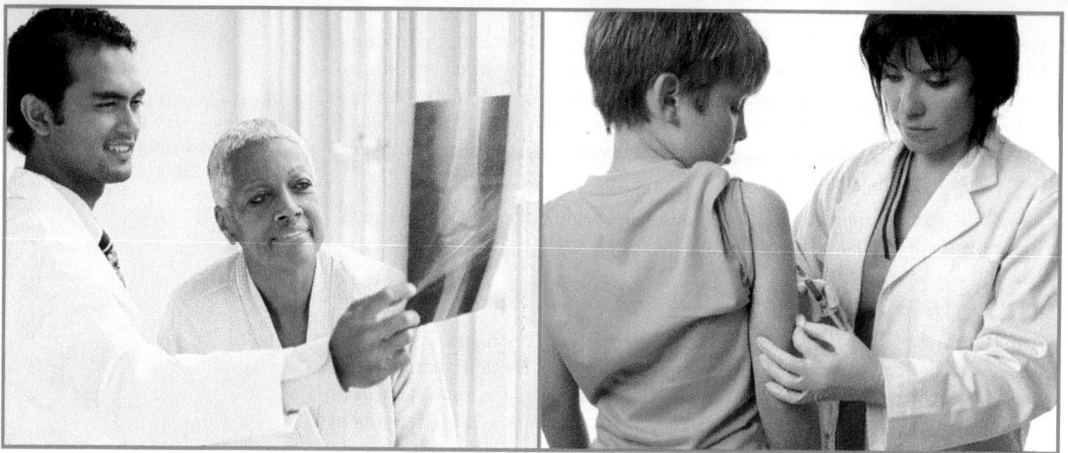

Healthier Citizens
President Johnson gave healthcare special attention. With Medicare and Medicaid, more Americans could receive basic healthcare.

Vocabulary Builder
overall—(OH ver awl) *adj.* including or considering everything

Healthcare Insurance In the first half of 1965, Congress passed parts of Johnson's Great Society legislation. Kennedy had supported similar legislation that failed to win congressional support. Johnson's agenda amended the Social Security Act by adding the Medical Care for the Aged Program, or **Medicare** as it was more popularly called. Medicare provided basic hospital insurance for Americans in the Social Security system who were age 65 and older. It also included a **Medicaid** feature that provided basic medical services to poor and disabled Americans who were not part of the Social Security system.

Johnson signed the bill into law in Independence, Missouri, home of former President Harry Truman, who had called for a national health insurance program almost 20 years earlier.

Education Along with health, education was one of the centerpieces of the Great Society program. Improved healthcare and education were necessary steps toward the goal of ending poverty. The 1965 Elementary and Secondary Education Act was designed to aid schools in poorer communities. It provided federal funds to improve school libraries, learning centers, language laboratories, and services in impoverished school districts. The act dramatically increased funding for Indian, inner city, and Mexican American schools.

Protecting the Environment and the Consumer The Great Society program extended to improving the overall quality of American life. In the early 1960s, several best-selling books raised Americans' awareness about environmental and consumer problems. Rachel Carson's *Silent Spring* (1962) detailed how chemical fertilizers and pesticides were damaging the fragile ecosystem. Ralph Nader's *Unsafe at Any Speed* (1965) attacked the automotive industry for its lack of concern for passenger safety.

Both these books helped to foster environmental and consumer activity and led to several important pieces of legislation. The Water Quality Act (1965) and the Clean Water Restoration Act (1966) aimed at improving water and air standards in the country. The National Traffic and Motor Vehicle Safety Act (1966) established safety standards for automotive vehicles.

New Immigration Policies Meanwhile, the civil rights movement was raising questions about America's long-standing immigration policy. The National Origins Acts of 1921 and 1924 had established a quota system that favored Western European immigrants and limited immigrants from other parts of the

Differentiated Instruction Solutions for All Learners

L4 Advanced Readers L4 Gifted and Talented Students

Tell students that healthcare insurance is still a major issue in the United States. According to the U.S. Census Bureau, 47 million Americans (15.8 percent of the population) in 2008 were uninsured. Of those uninsured, 8.7 million were children. As was the case during the Johnson administration, health insurance is still closely related to poverty issues. Children living in poverty are more likely to be uninsured, and a recent study has shown that personal bankruptcies are often related to the high cost of medical care. Explain that the United States is one of a few industrialized nations without a system of universal healthcare. Have students study the positions of advocates of universal healthcare as well as the arguments of those who oppose such a system. Tell students to evaluate the different positions and develop a presentation in which they attempt to persuade others of their opinions.

world. Such a discriminatory policy was clearly out of touch with the mood of the country in the early 1960s.

The **Immigration and Nationality Act of 1965** altered America's quota system. Nearly 170,000 immigrants from the Eastern Hemisphere were allowed into the country. Nearly 120,000 immigrants from the Western Hemisphere were welcomed. Immigrants from Latin America, Central America, the Caribbean, and Asia soon began to pour into the United States, providing the country with a pool of ideas, talent, and skills. During the 1960s and 1970s, millions of immigrants would arrive on American shores. Once again, the doors of America were open to immigrants from around the world. As in the late nineteenth and early twentieth centuries, New York and the urban East and West coasts attracted many of the country's newest immigrants.

The Legacy While the Great Society programs did not completely alter America, they did improve the lives of millions of individual Americans. Poverty and infant mortality rates declined. Medicare and Medicaid delivered needed healthcare to millions of elderly and poor Americans. Head Start and other anti-poverty programs provided the educational tools many underprivileged Americans needed to escape poverty. Furthermore, Congress also provided artists and scholars with assistance through the National Endowment for the Arts and Humanities, created in 1965. The Great Society victories may not have been as grandiose as Johnson predicted, but they were victories. The simple fact that 22.2 percent of all Americans lived below the poverty line in 1960 and 12.6 percent lived below the poverty line in 1970 says something about the triumphs of the Great Society.

✓ **Checkpoint** Which immigrant groups were affected by the Immigration and Nationality Act of 1965?

The Supreme Court and Reform

During the 1960s, the Supreme Court demonstrated a willingness to take the lead on controversial social, religious, and political issues. Led by Chief Justice Earl Warren, the Supreme Court at this time—often called the **Warren Court**—became the most liberal in American history. Its decisions supported civil rights, civil liberties, voting rights, and personal privacy.

Congressional Districts and Voters' Rights In several decisions the Supreme Court ruled in favor of the "one man, one vote" principle. The problem was one of apportionment of seats in state legislatures. During the twentieth century, large numbers of voters moved from rural to urban areas, but many state governments had not changed, or reapportioned, electoral districts to reflect the new conditions. This led to an electoral imbalance. In many states, rural areas had more power and urban areas had less power than their populations actually mandated.

In *Baker* v. *Carr* (1962), the Supreme Court ruled in favor of reapportionment on the basis of "one man, one vote." Electoral districts, it said, had to reflect the numbers of people in those districts. In *Reynolds* v. *Sims* (1964), the Court reaffirmed its decision, adding that any arrangement other than "one man, one vote" violated the equal protection clause of the Fourteenth Amendment.

HISTORY MAKERS

Earl Warren (1891–1974)
One of the country's most influential Chief Justices, Earl Warren was governor of California before being named to head the Supreme Court. As Chief Justice, he guided the Court to a unanimous ruling outlawing school segregation in *Brown* v. *Board of Education*. The Warren Court issued many landmark rulings in the areas of civil rights, criminal justice, First Amendment issues, and legislative districting. These decisions led many Americans to call for Warren's removal, though he remained on the Court until retiring in 1969.

Independent Practice

- Have students consider the ramifications of the exclusionary rule and ask them to formulate arguments both for and against the rule. Have students list the arguments in a two-column chart.

- Organize students in groups, and have them discuss the separation of church and state, particularly as it pertains to the Supreme Court's decision in *Engel* v. *Vitale*.

Monitor Progress

Circulate to make sure that students have an understanding of the arguments both for and against the exclusionary rule.

Differentiated Instruction Solutions for All Learners

L1 Special Needs Students **L2 English Language Learners** **L2 Less Proficient Readers**

Have students review the red headings below the blue heading "The Supreme Court and Reform." Then, create a three-column chart on the board. Label each column with a red heading from this subsection. Invite volunteers to list the Supreme

Court cases mentioned under this blue heading in the correct columns of the chart. Then, organize students in pairs. Have partners write a one-sentence summary for each Supreme Court decision listed in the chart.

Answer

✓ those previously excluded by immigration laws passed during the 1920s, which favored Western Europeans

Assess Progress

- Have students complete the Section Assessment.
- Administer the Section Quiz. Teaching Resources, **p. 26**
- To further assess student understanding, use Progress Monitoring Transparencies, **128**.

Reteach

If students need more instruction, have them read the section summary.

Reading and Note Taking
Study Guide

Adapted Reading and
Note Taking Study Guide

Spanish Reading and
Note Taking Study Guide

Extend

Ask students to do more research on immigration issues, particularly issues that relate to culture, such as notions of acculturation and assimilation. Have each student write an essay explaining his or her view of how framers of immigration policy should take such processes into consideration.

Answer

 Gideon v. *Wainwright* (1963)

Rights of the Accused The Warren Court also showed a heightened concern for the constitutional rights of accused lawbreakers. In four landmark cases, the Court broadened the individual rights of accused criminals and narrowed those of federal, state, and local government officials. In *Mapp* v. *Ohio* (1961), the Court ruled that evidence obtained illegally violated the Fourth Amendment and had to be excluded from federal and state trials. In *Gideon* v. *Wainwright* (1963), the Court decided that all accused criminals had the right to a lawyer whether or not they could pay for one. In *Escobedo* v. *Illinois* (1964), the Warren Court expanded on *Gideon* v. *Wainwright* by adding that every accused lawbreaker had to be offered access to a lawyer before questioning, and all evidence obtained from a suspect who had not been informed of his or her right to a lawyer could not be used in court. Finally, in *Miranda* v. *Arizona* (1966), the Court ruled that an accused criminal had to be informed of his or her Fifth and Sixth Amendment rights before being questioned.

Critics of these decisions argued that the Warren Court had tipped the balance of justice in favor of the rights of accused criminals. Today, many conservative justices still side with this opinion. The majority of the members of the Warren Court, however, have countered that the rights of individuals had to be protected, especially when freedom hung in the balance.

Separation of Church and State The Warren Court addressed the separation of church and state in the case of *Engel* v. *Vitale* (1962). The case involved whether or not a public school could require students to recite a state-sanctioned prayer. The Court ruled that school prayer was a violation of the First Amendment and an attempt by a governmental body to promote religion. The next year, the Court ruled in *Abington* v. *Schempp* that Bible reading in public schools also violated the First Amendment. The two decisions divided religious groups and the American people. Some welcomed the rulings, saying the government should have no say in personal religious matters. Others insisted the decisions were hostile to religion. The two decisions ignited, and continue to ignite, controversy. For more than 40 years, various religious groups have railed against these decisions.

✓ **Checkpoint** What major court ruling gave a person accused of a crime the right to have a lawyer?

SECTION **3** **Assessment**

Progress Monitoring Online
For: Self-test with vocabulary practice
www.pearsonschool.com/ushist

Comprehension

1. **Terms and People** Explain the relationship of the following terms to social reform.
   - War on Poverty
   - Great Society
   - Medicare
   - Medicaid

2. **NoteTaking Reading Skill: Identify Main Ideas** Use your chart to answer the Section Focus Question: How did Johnson's Great Society programs change life for most Americans?

Writing About History

3. **Quick Write: Chart Arguments and Counterarguments** Identify one point of view regarding the use of government funds to support massive social programs. Then, make a chart with two columns. In the first column, list two arguments in favor of that point of view. In the second column, list two arguments against that point of view.

Critical Thinking

4. **Make Comparisons** Were there differences in the goals of the New Frontier and the Great Society? Explain.

5. **Recognize Cause and Effect** How do you think the Immigration and Nationality Act of 1965 changed political activity in the nation?

6. **Identify Point of View** Why did some Americans feel that Supreme Court decisions during the 1960s considered only the rights of the poor?

1. Students should provide pertinent details to support their explanations.

2. They provided more opportunities for people at the bottom of the socio-economic ladder and helped reduce significantly the number of Americans living below the poverty line. They also increased environmental and consumer protections and supported the arts, public radio, and public television.

3. Remind students that their arguments and counterarguments must be logically defensible.

4. Possible answer: Yes; Great Society programs attacked poverty more aggressively than did those of the New Frontier. The New Frontier also focused on developing a U.S. space program, whereas the Great Society focused on improving arts and education.

5. Possible answer: The policies created new constituencies to which politicians had to respond.

6. Possible answer: People probably felt this way because the media focused attention on landmark decisions that addressed injustices being done to lower-income Americans and minorities.

For additional assessment, have students access **Progress Monitoring Online** at **www.pearsonschool.com/ushist.**

What Rights Should an Accused Person Have?

Police officers try to obtain confessions from suspects. Yet, the Fifth Amendment protects people from self-incrimination—stating facts that will result in their being accused of a crime. The Sixth Amendment gives them the right to an attorney. How do those guaranteed rights come into play when a person is being questioned by police?

Miranda v. *Arizona* (1966)

The Facts	The Issue	The Decision
• Ernesto Miranda, under questioning by police, confessed that he had kidnapped and assaulted a woman. • Miranda was convicted in state court of the crimes in part because of the confession.	Miranda claimed the confession should not be used because police had not warned him of his right to avoid self-incrimination or to have a lawyer present.	A 5:4 majority ruled that the conviction should be thrown out because police had violated Miranda's rights when it obtained the confession.

▲ A suspect is advised of his Miranda rights.

Why It Matters

The majority based its reasoning on "the necessity for procedures which assure" the protection of Fifth Amendment rights. It spelled out those procedures:

> "Prior to any questioning, the person must be warned that he has a right to remain silent, that any statement he does make may be used as evidence against him, and that he has a right to the presence of an attorney."

That statement is familiar to many Americans from hearing it on television crime dramas. The majority also ruled that people who request a lawyer must be provided with one, even if they are too poor to pay for one themselves.

The decision has had a profound effect on the criminal justice system. Police officers must inform suspects of their rights. Only then can statements made by the suspect be used in a trial.

Connect to Your World
The Court addressed the issue of confessions by minors in *Yarborough* v. *Alvarado* (2004). Research the case. Write a summary that explains the facts, the Court's decision, Justice Sandra Day O'Connor's concerns about the rights of minors, and the views of the dissent.

For: Supreme Court Cases
www.pearsonschool.com/ushist

◄ A police officer holds the Miranda Warning card.

History Background

Different Kinds of Force In its decision in *Miranda* v. *Arizona,* the Supreme Court noted that "We sometimes forget how long it has taken to establish the privilege against self-incrimination, the sources from which it came and the fervor with which it was defended." In *Miranda,* the court had to decide how far that privilege could go. That is, was it "fully applicable during a period of custodial interrogation," in which no physical force was used? In rendering their decision, the justices observed that "the modern practice of in-custody interrogation is psychologically rather than physically oriented. As we have stated before . . . this Court has recognized that coercion can be mental as well as physical, and that the blood of the accused is not the only hallmark of an unconstitutional inquisition."

What Rights Should an Accused Person Have?

Objectives
- Explain how the Fifth Amendment protects the rights of people suspected of committing a crime.
- Analyze the facts and arguments made in *Miranda* v. *Arizona.*
- Understand how the court's decision affected law enforcement practices.

Background Knowledge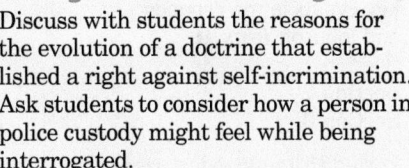
Discuss with students the reasons for the evolution of a doctrine that established a right against self-incrimination. Ask students to consider how a person in police custody might feel while being interrogated.

Instruct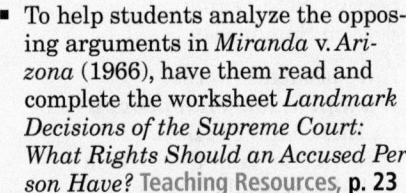
- To help students analyze the opposing arguments in *Miranda* v. *Arizona* (1966), have them read and complete the worksheet *Landmark Decisions of the Supreme Court: What Rights Should an Accused Person Have? Teaching Resources,* **p. 23**

- **Connect to Your World** Refer students to the Key Supreme Court Cases section for summaries of this case. You may wish to have students do additional research. Responses should show a clear understanding of the case and explain the facts, the Court's decision, Justice O'Connor's concerns, and the views of the dissent.

Monitor Progress
As students complete their worksheets, circulate to make sure they understand the background and reasons behind the Fifth Amendment and *Miranda* protections against self-incrimination.

Quick Study Guide

Progress Monitoring Online
For: Self-test with vocabulary practice
www.pearsonschool.com/ushist

Quick Study Guide

- Have students use the Quick Study Guide to prepare for the chapter test. Students may wish to refer to the following sections as they review:

The New Frontier Paves the Way
Section 2

The Warren Court
Section 3

NASA Spending
Section 2

Cold War Challenges
Section 1

Key Events in the Kennedy and Johnson Years
Section 1
Section 2
Section 3

- For additional review, remind students to refer to the Reading and Note Taking Study Guide
Section Note Taking
Section Summaries

- Have students access **www.pearsonschool.com/ushist** for this chapter's History Interactive timeline, which includes expanded entries and additional events.

- If students need more instruction on analyzing graphic data, have them read the Skills Handbook, **p. SH21.**

For **Progress Monitoring Online,** refer students to the Self-test with vocabulary practice at **www.pearsonschool.com/ushist.**

■ The New Frontier Paves the Way

New Frontier	Great Society
• Anti-poverty legislation • Peace Corps, Alliance for Progress • Education legislation • Healthcare legislation • Civil rights goals	• Economic Opportunity Act • Volunteers in Service to America • Head Start • Medicare, Medicaid • Civil Rights Act, 1964

■ NASA Spending 1950–1965

SOURCE: *Historical Statistics of the United States*

■ The Warren Court

- Baker v. Carr
- Mapp v. Ohio
- Engel v. Vitale
- Miranda v. Arizona
- **The Warren Court**
- Gideon v. Wainwright
- Escobedo v. Illinois
- Reynolds v. Sims
- Abington v. Schempp

■ Cold War Challenges

Bay of Pigs	Berlin	Cuban Missile Crisis
• American CIA arms and trains anti-Castro forces. • Bay of Pigs invasion fails. • Soviets suspect weakness in Kennedy.	• Kennedy meets with Khrushchev in Vienna. • East Germans and Soviets build Berlin Wall. • In West Berlin, Kennedy delivers speech assuring West Germans of continued U.S. support.	• United States discovers Soviet missile sites in Cuba. • Kennedy imposes blockade of Cuba. • Khrushchev removes missiles from Cuba.

☑ Quick Study Timeline

In America

| | 1961
Peace Corps established | 1962
Cuban missile crisis | 1963
President Kennedy assassinated |

Presidential Terms — John F. Kennedy 1961–1963 — Lyndon B. Johnson 1963–1969

1960 — **1963**

Around the World

| | 1961
Berlin Wall is built | | 1963
Civil War breaks out in Cyprus between Greeks and Turks |

Differentiated Instruction   Solutions for All Learners

L1 Special Needs Students   **L2 English Language Learners**   **L2 Less Proficient Readers**

Use the following study guide resources to help students acquiring basic skills:
Adapted Reading and Note Taking Study Guide
- Section Note Taking
- Section Summaries

Use the following study guide resources to help Spanish-speaking students:
Spanish Reading and Note Taking Study Guide
- Section Note Taking
- Section Summaries

American Issues
Connector

By connecting prior knowledge with what you have learned in this chapter, you can gradually build your understanding of enduring questions that still affect America today. Answer the questions below. Then, use your American Issues Connector study guide (or go online: www.pearsonschool.com/ushist).

Issues You Learned About

● **Poverty and Prosperity** While some people find America to be a true "land of opportunity," others face a daily struggle to make ends meet.

1. What was revealed in Michael Harrington's book *The Other America*? How did Kennedy respond to this book?

2. Did Kennedy's new tax policies benefit upper-class Americans? Explain.

3. What did Johnson hope to accomplish with his War on Poverty? Describe one new program that was part of this effort.

● **America and the World** As part of the Cold War, the United States combated communism in Latin America.

4. What was the Cold War, and when and why did it begin?

5. Did the Peace Corps serve as a tool for promoting democracy or for helping developing nations? Explain.

6. Why do you think the U.S. government was willing to invade communist Cuba in hopes of overthrowing its leader but was not willing to invade other communist countries?

● **Social Problems and Reforms** In the 1960s, the government grew concerned with social problems and made efforts to fix them.

7. In 1963, Kennedy told the nation in a televised address that civil rights was a "moral issue . . . as clear as the American Constitution." Did Kennedy always hold this belief about civil rights? Explain.

8. List at least five different areas in which reform legislation was passed in the 1960s. Which was the most significant? Explain your choice.

Connect to Your World   Activity

Technology and Society The television broadcast of the first presidential debate between Kennedy and Nixon strongly influenced the outcome of the election. Choose an important event from a print or online newspaper. Then, locate coverage of that same story on a reputable television news program. Write a paragraph explaining how coverage of the event differed between the sources. Did your perception of the events change after you saw the newscast? Explain.

1965
Immigration and Nationality Act

1966
***Miranda v. Arizona* protects rights of the accused**

History *Interactive*
For: Interactive timeline
www.pearsonschool.com/ushist

1966　　　　　　　　　　　　　　　**1969**

1965
India and Pakistan fight over control of Kashmir

1968
Fighting breaks out between Catholics and Protestants in Northern Ireland

---

American Issues
Connector

Tell students that the main issues for this chapter are Poverty and Prosperity, America and the World, and Social Problems and Reform. Then, ask students to answer the Issues You Learned About questions on this page. Discuss the Connect to Your World topic(s), and ask students to complete the project that follows.

American Issues Connector

1. the scope of poverty in the United States; by urging Congress to take actions that reduced poverty

2. No; he increased the tax burden on wealthier citizens.

3. to reduce poverty through job training, education, and healthcare; the Job Corps trained people to help them acquire better jobs.

4. political antagonism between the U.S.-led Western nations and the Soviet bloc countries; it began after World War II because of ideological disagreements between the United States and the Soviet Union.

5. The Peace Corps, while providing developing nations with services, was also intended to lay the groundwork for strong democracies.

6. Possible answer: Cuba was in this country's "backyard," and U.S. leaders believed that the potential costs would not be excessive.

7. No. Kennedy had been passive on civil rights, but the behavior of many white southerners altered his views.

8. discrimination, poverty, education, healthcare, immigration; programs to assist the poor were the most effective because they helped to reduce the number of poor people.

Connect to Your World

Encourage students to familiarize themselves with the political orientation of the print and television news sources they have chosen before they make their analyses.

For additional review of this chapter's enduring issues, remind students to refer to the Reading and Note Taking Study Guide American Issues Journal.

Chapter Assessment

Terms and People

1. Unlike Eisenhower, Kennedy chose a policy of flexible response—one that prepared the U.S. to meet any type of conflict—that in addition to preparing the military for nuclear conflict, also aimed to equip U.S. forces for conventional and counter-insurgency conflicts.

2. The treaty, whose signatories agreed to end above-ground nuclear testing, was important because it took a small step toward reducing the danger of nuclear annihilation.

3. The Warren Commission, which convened to conduct an official investigation into the Kennedy assassination, determined that Lee Harvey Oswald acted alone in committing the crime.

4. Medicare provides basic hospital insurance for Americans age 65 and over who receive Social Security. Medicaid provides basic medical services to the poor and disabled who are not eligible for Social Security. President Johnson led the campaign for these programs as part of the Social Security Act.

5. The act overturned the quota system established in the 1920s, which favored Western Europeans; most of the new immigrants came from Asia and from Latin America.

Focus Questions

6. Kennedy initially adopted a bold stance against the Soviet Union, and though he remained resolute, his approach became more tempered and thoughtful as he gained experience.

7. to tackle issues of poverty, gender, and racial discrimination and to make sure that the Soviet Union did not outperform the United States in terms of scientific achievements

8. by reducing poverty and by reforming healthcare, environmental, immigration, and education policies; by passing legislation to protect consumers; by supporting the arts, public radio, and public television

Terms and People

1. Define a **"flexible response"** defense policy. How did this defense policy differ from Eisenhower's defense policy?

2. What was the **Nuclear Test Ban Treaty**? Why was it so important?

3. What was the **Warren Commission**? What were its findings?

4. What was the purpose of **Medicare** and **Medicaid**? Who led the campaign for this legislation, and which legislation were they part of?

5. What was the **Immigration and Nationality Act of 1965**? Where did most of the new immigrants come from?

Focus Questions

The focus question for this chapter is **How did the policies of Presidents Kennedy and Johnson affect the nation?** Build an answer to this big question by answering the focus questions for Sections 1 through 3 and the Critical Thinking questions that follow.

Section 1
6. How did Kennedy respond to the continuing challenges of the Cold War?

Section 2
7. What were the goals of Kennedy's New Frontier?

Section 3
8. How did Johnson's Great Society programs change life for most Americans?

Critical Thinking

9. **Identify Central Issues** How did the education legislation passed during the Great Society build upon the War on Poverty's education program?

10. **Investigate Problems** How did the issues surrounding East and West Germany contribute to Cold War tensions between the United States and the Soviet Union?

11. **Analyze Information** The Equal Pay Act of 1963 required that women be paid the same wages as men for "equal work." Do you think this legislation had an effect on the passage of the Civil Rights Act of 1964? Explain.

12. **Analyze Charts** The chart below shows successful space launches. Use the chart, as well as your reading of the chapter, to describe the progress of the space race for the years shown. According to one source, the space program is a way to "unite" all nations. Do you agree or disagree? Explain.

Country	1957–1964	1965–1969	1970–1974
Soviet Union	82	302	405
United States	207	279	139
Japan			5
China			2
France			3
United Kingdom			1
Total	**289**	**581**	**555**

13. **Analyze Information** In what ways might Johnson's career as a teacher have made him aware that the nation faced serious social problems that needed to be addressed and reformed?

Writing About History

Writing a Persuasive Essay An effective persuasive essay does not simply argue its own point of view. It also anticipates and counters arguments that might be used by the other side. Write a three-paragraph persuasive essay on the subject of the Warren Court and its decisions regarding the rights of the accused.

Prewriting
• Identify the point of view that you will take in your essay.
• List any arguments you can think of in favor of your point of view. Prioritize them from the most persuasive to the least persuasive.
• Make a chart listing the two most persuasive arguments in one column and a possible counterargument to each argument in the other.

Drafting
• Write an introductory paragraph in which you define the issue and state your viewpoint.
• In the first paragraph, state your most persuasive argument.
• In the second paragraph, identify a counterargument to your argument. Give specific reasons why you disagree with the counterargument.
• Throughout your essay, use clear, direct language that makes your argument sound both reasonable and forceful. Remember, overly emotional language and name-calling can sometimes make your argument seem less persuasive, not more persuasive.

Revising
• Use the guidelines on page SH22 of the Writing Handbook to revise your writing.

Critical Thinking

9. Legislators used the success of the War on Poverty's education program as a basis for continued education legislation and passed the 1965 Elementary and Secondary Education Act to aid schools in poorer communities.

10. U.S. determination to retain influence over West Berlin, which lay entirely within Soviet-controlled East Germany, angered Russian leaders, who responded by building the Berlin Wall.

11. Possible answer: Yes; passing the Equal Pay Act of 1963, which affirmed women's equality with men, probably made it easier to pass the Civil Rights Act of 1964, which protected the rights of minorities who were discriminated against by people who believed themselves to be racially superior.

12. No; the space race set some nations against each other in an attempt to demonstrate technological superiority, and many nations could not compete in the race at all, further distancing themselves from those nations that could.

Document-Based Assessment

The Effectiveness of President Johnson's Great Society Programs

In 1964, President Johnson proposed his vision for the United States called the Great Society. Johnson's goal was to end poverty and racial injustice and to give every child an opportunity to receive a good education. Would President Johnson's Great Society programs meet his goals or would they become a burden to taxpayers? Use your knowledge of Johnson's Great Society legislation and Documents A, B, and C to answer questions 1 through 4.

Document A

"Project Head Start was created during the heady, idealistic days of the mid-1960s. President Lyndon Johnson believed that it was the nation's duty to provide not just legal equality but also equality of opportunity. In his 1965 commencement address at Howard University, he called for the 'next and the more profound stage' in the civil rights struggle. 'We seek not just freedom but opportunity.' . . . Johnson's War on Poverty would include a host of initiatives designed to bring blacks and other disadvantaged Americans to what he called 'the starting line' of American life with the skills and abilities necessary to compete on a level playing field. The War on Poverty focused on education as a tool for upward mobility, and Head Start was to become one of the cornerstones of the federal effort."

—"Competing Visions," Ron Haskins, 2004

Document B

Head Start Budget, 1965–2005

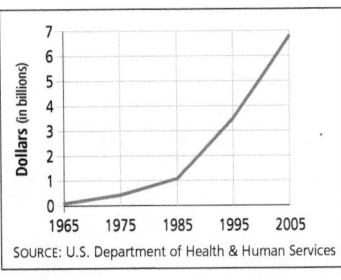

SOURCE: U.S. Department of Health & Human Services

Document C

"On many domestic issues, [Senator] Dirksen continued the balancing act so central to his effectiveness, as he saw it: maintain a constructive relationship with the opposition and the loyalty of the Republican troops. He took issue with Medicare, for example: 'I would be eligible,' he said indignantly. 'Why should I be allowed to use dollars the government is taking from some young factory worker in Cleveland in the promise of providing for his old age?' The accumulation of Great Society spending programs appalled Dirksen. The taxpayers would have to come up with nearly $160 billion to fund them. Moreover, the programs brought with them an expanding federal bureaucracy and increasing centralization. To Dirksen, the Great Society was a misguided attempt at creating an immediate, utopian 'blueprint for paradise.'"

—*The Education of a Senator*, Frank H. Mackaman, 1998

---

1. According to Document A, why did President Johnson use Head Start as part of his War on Poverty?
   A He wanted to use Head Start to provide legal equality for disadvantaged Americans.
   B He wanted to create Head Start for Americans with exceptional abilities.
   C He wanted to use Head Start as a tool to help people achieve upward mobility.
   D He wanted to use Head Start to maintain a constructive relationship with the Republicans.

2. Which documents imply that the Great Society had a positive effect on the lives of Americans?
   A Documents A and C
   B Documents B and C
   C Documents A and B
   D Documents A, B, and C

3. In Document C, what viewpoint does Senator Dirksen take toward the Great Society programs?
   A He believed that Medicare would not help him.
   B He opposed the Republican view of the Great Society programs.
   C He proposed his own Great Society programs.
   D He believed that the Great Society programs would lead to an expanding federal government.

4. **Writing Task** Would President Johnson's Great Society programs meet his goals, or would they become a burden to taxpayers? Use your knowledge of the chapter content and specific evidence from the primary sources above to support your opinion.

13. Possible answer: As a former teacher, Johnson came face-to-face with socioeconomic problems in schools. With his prior knowledge and experience, he pushed effectively for such reforms during his presidency.

Writing About History

As students begin the assignment, refer them to page SH15 of the Writing Handbook for help in writing a persuasive essay. Remind them of the steps they should take to complete their assignment, including prewriting, drafting, and revising.

Students' essays should define the issue under discussion, advance a clearly stated position, and support that position with specific reasons and evidence. The essays should contain an introduction, a body, and a conclusion. They should show evidence of reflection and be free of grammatical and spelling errors. For scoring rubrics, see Assessment Rubrics.

The Vietnam War Era
1954–1975

Teach With Technology
Presentation**EXPRESS**™
PREMIUM DVD

- Teach this chapter's core content by using **PresentationExpress,** which includes interactivities, video, lecture notes, and the *ExamView®* QuickTake assessment tool.

- To introduce this chapter by using **PresentationExpress,** ask students with which of the following statements they most agree: **A) Nations should give moral support to governments they favor. B) Nations should supply money to governments they favor. C) Nations should give military aid to governments they favor in other nations. D) Nations should send troops to support governments they favor in other nations.** Take a class poll, or record students' answers by using the QuickTake feature, and discuss their responses. Point out that in this chapter, they will read about American military involvement in Vietnam and its impact in both the United States and Southeast Asia.

Technology Resources

- Student**EXPRESS** CD-ROM
- Teacher Resource Library **DVD**
- Presentation**EXPRESS** PREMIUM DVD
- *ExamView®* **Test Bank CD-ROM** English and Spanish
- **Guided Reading Audio,** Spanish
- **Student Edition on Audio**

THE ESSENTIAL
VIDEO
By Students For Students
For videos on Amercian Issues, go to
www.pearsonschool.com/ushist

Bibliography

For the Teacher
Appy, Christian G. *Patriots: The Vietnam War Remembered from All Sides.* Penguin, 2004.

Kissinger, Henry. *Ending the Vietnam War: A History of America's Involvement in and Extrication from the Vietnam War.* Simon & Schuster, 2003.

Logevall, Fredrik. *The Origins of the Vietnam War.* Longman, 2001.

For the Student
L2 McNab, Chris, and Andy Wiest. *The Illustrated History of the Vietnam War.* Advantage Publishers, 2000.

L3 Edelman, Bernard, ed. *Dear America: Letters Home from Vietnam.* W.W. Norton, 2002.

L4 Newman, Rick and Don Shepperd. *Bury Us Upside Down: The Misty Pilots and the Secret Battle for the Ho Chi Minh Trail.* Presidio Press, 2006.

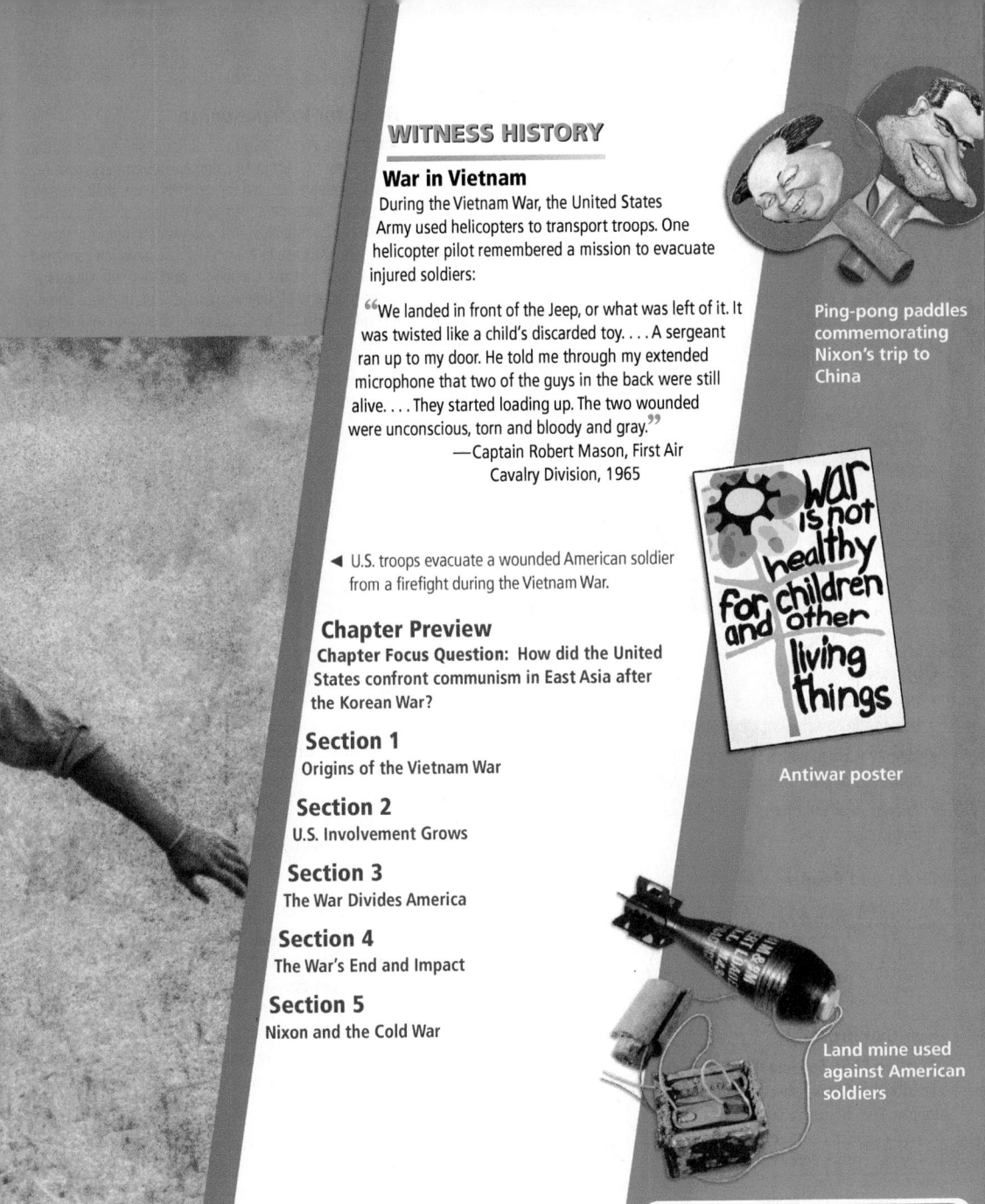

WITNESS HISTORY

War in Vietnam

During the Vietnam War, the United States Army used helicopters to transport troops. One helicopter pilot remembered a mission to evacuate injured soldiers:

❝We landed in front of the Jeep, or what was left of it. It was twisted like a child's discarded toy. . . . A sergeant ran up to my door. He told me through my extended microphone that two of the guys in the back were still alive. . . . They started loading up. The two wounded were unconscious, torn and bloody and gray.❞
—Captain Robert Mason, First Air Cavalry Division, 1965

◀ U.S. troops evacuate a wounded American soldier from a firefight during the Vietnam War.

Ping-pong paddles commemorating Nixon's trip to China

Antiwar poster

Land mine used against American soldiers

Chapter Preview

Chapter Focus Question: How did the United States confront communism in East Asia after the Korean War?

Section 1
Origins of the Vietnam War

Section 2
U.S. Involvement Grows

Section 3
The War Divides America

Section 4
The War's End and Impact

Section 5
Nixon and the Cold War

Use the ✓ Quick Study Timeline at the end of this chapter to preview chapter events.

Note Taking Study Guide Online
For: Note Taking and American Issues Connector
www.pearsonschool.com/ushist

Chapter-Level Resources

All in One Letter Home (English and Spanish), Preread the Chapter, Vocabulary Builder, Reading Strategy, Social Studies Skills Practice, Enrichment, Issues Connector, Chapter Tests

- Test Prep With Document-Based Assessment
- AYP Monitoring Assessments
- *ExamView®* Test Bank CD-ROM
- Guided Reading Audio (Spanish)
- Student Edition Audio

Previewing the Chapter

- **WITNESS HISTORY** Point out that while the U.S. military had more developed technology, the enemy's tactics and Vietnam's terrain frustrated U.S. troops. Read the Witness History selection aloud. Ask **How does this selection illustrate American technology?** *(The soldier mentions the helicopters and trucks used in the war.)* Discuss how the soldier might have felt when his helicopter landed in Vietnam.

- **Analyzing the Visuals** Ask students to study the photo of U.S. troops evacuating a wounded soldier. Ask **What questions do the photo and the Witness History selection bring to mind?** *(Sample answers: How many soldiers were wounded or died during the Vietnam War? How many are missing in action?)*

- **Focus** Write the Chapter Focus question on the board. Tell students to keep this question in mind as they read the chapter. Then, have students preview the section titles in this chapter.

- **Preread** Have students complete the chapter's Preread the Chapter Worksheet. Teaching Resources, pp. 8–9

Have students access **www.pearsonschool.com/ushist** for the Note Taking Study Guide *Online* as an alternative to the *Reading and Note Taking Study Guide* booklet.

Differentiated Instruction Solutions for All Learners

The following Teacher's Edition strategies are suitable for students of varying abilities.

L1 Special Needs Students, pp. 533, 540, 541, 546, 549, 557, 561 SN

L2 English Language Learners, pp. 533, 540, 541, 546, 549, 553, 561 ELL

L2 Less Proficient Readers, pp. 533, 540, 541, 546, 549, 553, 557, 561 LPR

L4 Advanced Readers, pp. 535, 538, 545, 550, 554, 562 AR

L4 Gifted and Talented Students, pp. 535, 538, 545, 550, 554, 562 GT

Objectives

As you teach this section, keep students focused on the following objectives to help them answer the Section Focus Question and master core content.

- Describe the reasons that the United States helped the French fight the Vietnamese.
- Identify ways in which the United States opposed communism in Southeast Asia.
- Analyze how the United States increased its involvement in Vietnam.

Prepare to Read

Background Knowledge Ⓛ₃

Ask students to recall what they know about the Cold War policies of Presidents Truman, Eisenhower, Kennedy, and Johnson. Ask students to predict how the United States might react to a call for Vietnamese independence from a leader who embraced communism.

Set a Purpose Ⓛ₃

- **WITNESS HISTORY** Read the selection aloud.

  Ask **What does Ho Chi Minh suggest that the people of Vietnam have in common with other peoples who want independence?** *(They are kept down by a power that does not want them to be free.)*

- **Focus** Point out the Section Focus Question, and write it on the board. Tell students to refer to this question as they read. *(Answer appears with Section 1 Assessment answers.)*

- **Preview** Have students preview the Section Objectives and the list of Terms and People.

- **NoteTaking** Using the Paragraph Shrinking strategy (TE, p. T20), have students read this section. As they read, have students fill in the chart summarizing the Presidents' Vietnam policies Reading and Note Taking Study Guide

WITNESS HISTORY

Hope for Independence

After World War II, a spirit of nationalism and revolution spread among European colonies around the world. As colonial peoples strived for independence, their struggles sometimes became mixed up with the Cold War conflict between communist states and western democracies. Such was the case in French Indochina, which consisted of the lands of Laos, Cambodia, and Vietnam. Unaware of the long and bloody war ahead, a Vietnamese communist named Ho Chi Minh dreamed of a Vietnam free from French rule:

❝The oppressed the world over are wresting back their independence. We should not lag behind. . . . Under the Vietminh banner, let us valiantly march forward!❞
—Ho Chi Minh, 1945

▲ Ho Chi Minh depicted in a Vietnamese propaganda poster

Origins of the Vietnam War

Objectives

- Describe the reasons that the United States helped the French fight the Vietnamese.
- Identify ways in which the United States opposed communism in Southeast Asia.
- Analyze how the United States increased its involvement in Vietnam.

Terms and People

Ho Chi Minh
domino theory
SEATO

Vietcong
Gulf of Tonkin Resolution

NoteTaking

Reading Skill: Summarize As you read, describe the Vietnam policies of Presidents Truman, Eisenhower, Kennedy, and Johnson.

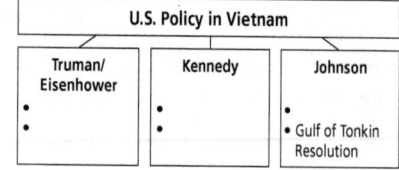

U.S. Policy in Vietnam		
Truman/Eisenhower	Kennedy	Johnson
• •	• •	• • Gulf of Tonkin Resolution

Why It Matters Presidents Kennedy and Johnson shared a vision for a better America in the 1960s. They also shared a vision for a better world in which America would emerge victorious from its Cold War struggle against global communism. As part of this strategic and ideological battle, the United States established a new line of defense against communism in Vietnam. The conflict in Southeast Asia would grow to be one of the costliest wars in American history. **Section Focus Question: Why did the United States become involved in Vietnam?**

America and the War in Indochina

Situated far away in Southeast Asia, Vietnam did not attract significant American attention until the 1960s. Television news shows rarely mentioned it, and most Americans could not locate it on a map. But over a span of more than ten years, the United States sent several million soldiers to fight in Vietnam. America's involvement in Vietnam had roots in European colonialism, Cold War politics, and Vietnamese calls for national independence.

France Rules Indochina in Southeast Asia In the 1800s, French military forces established control over Indochina, a peninsula in Southeast Asia that includes the modern countries of Vietnam, Cambodia, and Laos. Slightly larger than the state of Texas, Indochina included almost 27 million people by the end of World War II. French colonial officials ruled Vietnam with an iron fist. They transplanted French laws into Vietnam and imposed high taxes. French business people acquired large rice and rubber

Vocabulary Builder

Use the information below and the following resource to teach students the high-use words from this section. Teaching Resources, Vocabulary Builder, p. 11

High-Use Words	Definitions and Sample Sentences
ensure	*v.* to guarantee; secure The United States wanted to **ensure** that communism did not spread.
auspices	*n.* approval and support Food was delivered to Berlin under the **auspices** of the United States and other Western powers.

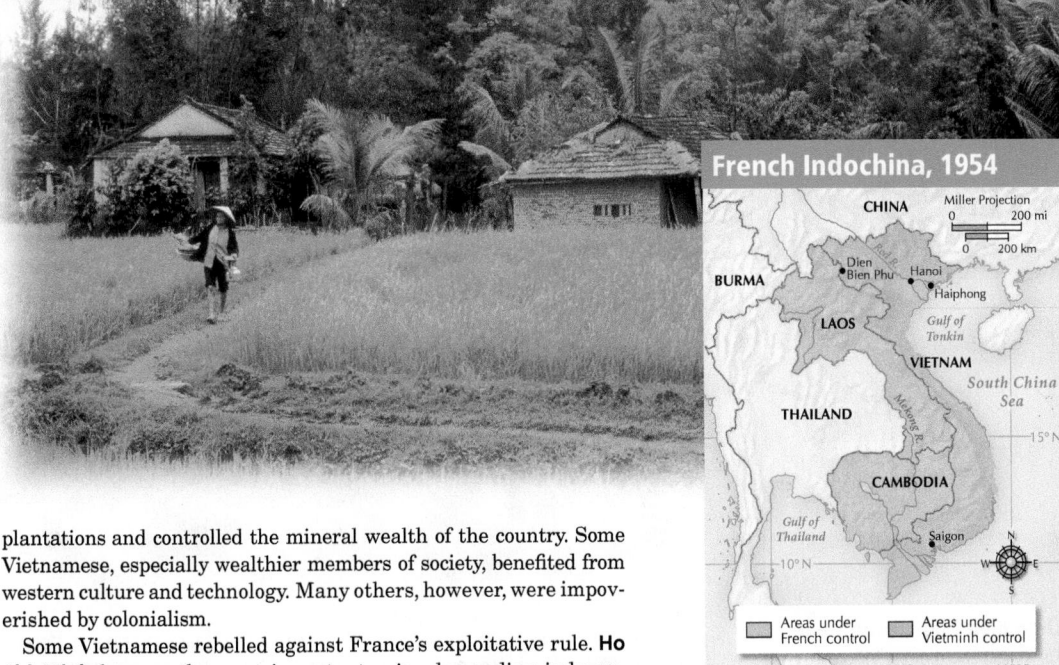

French Indochina, 1954

plantations and controlled the mineral wealth of the country. Some Vietnamese, especially wealthier members of society, benefited from western culture and technology. Many others, however, were impoverished by colonialism.

Some Vietnamese rebelled against France's exploitative rule. **Ho Chi Minh** became the most important voice demanding independence for Vietnam. Born in 1890, Ho became involved in anti-French organizations as a young man and fled Vietnam in 1912. He traveled the world, visiting American ports and living periodically in London, Paris, and Moscow. During his 30-year absence, Ho constantly thought and wrote about Vietnam, and he searched for westerners who would support his plans for Vietnamese independence. Ho embraced communism, and eventually Soviet communists rallied to his cause.

The French Battle Nationalism and Communism During World War II, Japan had undermined French control over Vietnam. But when the conflict ended, France reasserted its colonial aims there. France's problem, however, was that colonialism was a dying institution. World War II had strengthened nationalist movements while weakening the economic and military positions of traditional European powers. In Vietnam, Ho Chi Minh clamored for independence as France struggled to maintain its dwindling global power.

Meanwhile, the United States faced a difficult decision. On the one hand, it supported decolonization. On the other hand, America wanted France as an ally in its Cold War effort to contain the Soviet Union. President Harry S. Truman believed that if he supported Vietnamese independence, he would weaken anticommunist forces in France. So, to ensure a strong, anticommunist Western Europe, Truman sacrificed his own anticolonial sentiments.

Vietnam thus became a pawn in Cold War politics. To <u>ensure</u> French support in the Cold War, Truman agreed to aid France's efforts to regain control over Vietnam. After communist forces won the civil war in China in 1949, America increased its aid to the French in Vietnam. Truman did not want to see another communist victory in Asia. Between 1950 and 1954, the United States contributed $2.6 billion to France's war efforts. Containing Ho Chi Minh's communist Vietminh—an abbreviation of the League for the Independence of Vietnam— became a national priority.

Vietnam Under French Rule
During the French colonial era, rural villagers failed to see the same profits as French plantation owners. Ho Chi Minh found many supporters for his anticolonial efforts in villages like the one above. *In 1954, what regions of Indochina were under communist control?*

Vocabulary Builder
ensure–(en SHOR) *v.* to guarantee; secure

Independent Practice

- Ask students to examine the photographs on this page. Tell students to use the photographs to write brief paragraphs describing what the fighting between the French and the Vietminh might have been like.

- Have students fill in the *Outline Map: Spread of Communism in Asia* to grasp the global reach of the Cold War. Teaching Resources, **p. 20**

Monitor Progress

As students fill in their charts, circulate to make sure that they understand the Vietnam policies of Presidents Truman, Eisenhower, Kennedy, and Johnson. For a completed version of the chart, see Note Taking Transparencies, **B-133**.

Dien Bien Phu Under Siege

For almost two months, Vietminh soldiers hammered at French military positions around Dien Bien Phu. At left, Vietnamese communists take cover in a trench during the siege. At right, French troops guard Vietminh soldiers taken captive during the fighting.

The Domino Theory and Dien Bien Phu When President Dwight D. Eisenhower took office in early 1953, he continued Truman's policies toward Vietnam. He sent monetary aid to the French, arguing that by battling Ho Chi Minh, they were containing the spread of communism. Eisenhower told a journalist that the fight in Vietnam involved more than the future of just one country:

> **Primary Source** "You have a row of dominos set up, you knock over the first one, and what will happen to the last one is the certainty that it will go over very quickly. So you could have a beginning of a disintegration that would have the most profound influences."
>
> —Dwight D. Eisenhower, 1954

The **domino theory** was the idea that if Vietnam fell to communism, its closest neighbors would follow. This in turn would threaten Japan, the Philippines, and Australia. In short, stopping the communists in Vietnam was important to the protection of the entire region.

In 1954, however, the French lost their eight-year struggle to regain Vietnam. The Vietminh trapped a large French garrison at Dien Bien Phu, a military base in northwest Vietnam, and laid siege to it for 55 days. During the siege, which one Frenchman described as "hell in a very small place," Vietminh troops destroyed the French airstrip, cut French supply lines, and dug trenches to attack key French positions. Finally, on May 7, 1954, after suffering some 15,000 casualties, the French surrendered.

The very next day at an international peace conference in Geneva, Switzerland, France sued for peace. According to the Geneva Accords, France granted independence to Vietnam, Laos, and Cambodia. The accords also divided Vietnam at the seventeenth parallel into two countries, North Vietnam and South Vietnam. Ho Chi Minh's communist forces ruled in North Vietnam, and an anticommunist government, supported by the United States, assumed power in South Vietnam. The accords also called for free elections in 1956 to unify Vietnam.

 Checkpoint Why did Presidents Truman and Eisenhower support French efforts against Ho Chi Minh?

History Background

The Domino Theory President Eisenhower explained the domino theory, also known as the domino effect, at a press conference on April 7, 1954, during the Battle of Dien Bien Phu. Eisenhower referred to the idea as the "falling domino" principle. The metaphor was first used in the 1940s by the Truman administration to rationalize sending military aid to Greece and Turkey and became popular in the 1950s after its use by Eisenhower as applied to Southeast Asia. Presidents Kennedy and Johnson continued to use the concept to justify ramping up U.S. involvement in Vietnam in the 1960s.

Answer

✓ Presidents Truman and Eisenhower supported French efforts against Ho Chi Minh because they wanted to contain the spread of communism in Asia and to ensure a strong anti-communist Western Europe.

America Opposes Communism in Vietnam

During the Battle of Dien Bien Phu, France appealed to the United States for military support. President Eisenhower was willing to supply money but not soldiers. Ike would not commit American troops to defend colonialism in Asia. Nevertheless, the President firmly supported the new anticommunist government of South Vietnam.

The United States Aids South Vietnam America channeled aid to South Vietnam in different ways. In 1954, the United States and seven other countries formed the **Southeast Asia Treaty Organization (SEATO)**. Similar to NATO, SEATO's goal was to contain the spread of communism in Southeast Asia.

The United States provided economic and military aid to the South Vietnamese government led by Ngo Dinh Diem. Diem was an ardent nationalist and anticommunist. Although he lacked popular appeal, his anticommunism guaranteed American support. When it came time for the 1956 unification elections, American intelligence analysts predicted that Diem would lose to the more popular Ho Chi Minh. Rather than risk losing, Diem refused to participate in the elections, a move made under the <u>auspices</u> of the United States government.

Communist Opposition Grows By 1957, a communist rebel group in the South, known as the National Liberation Front (NLF), had committed themselves to undermining the Diem government and uniting Vietnam under a communist flag. NLF guerrilla fighters, called **Vietcong**, launched an insurgency in which they assassinated government officials and destroyed roads and bridges. Supplied by communists in North Vietnam, the Vietcong employed surprise hit-and-run tactics to weaken Diem's hold on South Vietnam.

Diem's own policies also weakened his position in South Vietnam. A devout Roman Catholic in an overwhelmingly Buddhist nation, Diem did little to build a broad political base. Instead, he signed anti-Buddhist legislation and refused to enact significant land reforms. His lack of popular support hurt him in the civil war against North Vietnam. Only the support of the United States kept the unpopular leader in power.

Kennedy Sends U.S. Troops to Vietnam After his election in 1960, President John F. Kennedy took a more aggressive stand against the communists in Vietnam. Beginning in 1961, he sent Special Forces troops to South Vietnam to advise the Army of the Republic of Vietnam (ARVN) on more effective ways to fight the communist forces. By 1963, more than 15,000 American "advisers" were fighting in Vietnam.

Although U.S. advisers fought bravely and achieved some success, Diem continued to alienate South Vietnamese citizens. By late 1963, his regime was in shambles. Buddhists protested his restrictive policies, occasionally by setting themselves on fire. The Kennedy administration eventually concluded that South Vietnam needed new leadership. Working behind the scenes, Americans plotted with anti-Diem generals to overthrow Diem's government. On November 1, 1963, Diem was removed from power and later assassinated.

✓ **Checkpoint** How did the United States help the South Vietnamese government resist communism?

Vocabulary Builder
<u>auspices</u>—(AWS puh sihz) *n.* approval and support

▼ A Buddhist monk sets himself on fire in Saigon to protest the Diem regime.

America Opposes Communism in Vietnam/ Johnson Leads the Nation Into War 🔢 L3

Instruct

- **Introduce: Key Term** Ask students to find the key term *Gulf of Tonkin Resolution* (in bold) in the text. Point out that the *Gulf of Tonkin Resolution* marked a turning point in American involvement in the conflict in Vietnam.

- **Teach** Ask **What groups posed a serious threat to the South Vietnamese government?** *(a communist rebel group known as the NLF and their guerrilla fighters, the Vietcong)* **How did U.S. aid to South Vietnam change under President Kennedy?** *(Kennedy sent Special Forces troops to advise and fight alongside the South Vietnamese.)* **What led President Johnson to go to war against North Vietnam?** *(the North Vietnamese attack on the USS* Maddox *and increasing aggression against South Vietnam)*

- **Quick Activity** Display Color Transparency: *Rising U.S. Involvement in Vietnam.* Use the lesson suggested in the transparency book to guide a discussion of the escalating contribution of the United States to the war effort in Vietnam between 1950 and 1964. Color Transparencies A-125

Independent Practice

Have students study the political cartoon on the next page and write a short paragraph interpreting it.

Monitor Progress

Circulate to make sure that students accurately interpret the political cartoon.

Differentiated Instruction   Solutions for All Learners

L4 Advanced Readers   L4 Gifted and Talented Students

Have each student choose three key events discussed in this section and create headlines for a newspaper reporting on these events. Examples of events include the Battle of Dien Bien Phu, the 1954 Geneva peace conference, the attack on the USS *Maddox*, and the Gulf of Tonkin Resolution.

Ask each student to choose one of the headlines he or she wrote and use it to write a newspaper article that may have been written soon after the event occurred. Students may wish to conduct further research about the events discussed in this section. Have students assemble their articles and publish a class newspaper.

Answer

✓ It formed SEATO with seven other countries, provided economic and military aid to the anticommunist government of Diem, and sent Special Forces troops to advise and fight alongside the army of South Vietnam.

Assess Progress

- Have students complete the Section Assessment.

- Administer the Section Quiz. Teaching Resources, **p. 25**

- To further assess student understanding, use Progress Monitoring Transparencies, **129.**

Reteach

If students need more instruction, have them read the section summary.

Reading and Note Taking Study Guide

Adapted Reading and Note Taking Study Guide (L1) (L2)

Spanish Reading and Note Taking Study Guide (L2)

Extend (L4)

Have students write a paragraph about the effect of the Gulf of Tonkin Resolution on checks and balances as set forth in the Constitution.

Answer

 The Gulf of Tonkin Resolution gave President Johnson the authority to send troops to South Vietnam without congressional approval.

Johnson Leads the Nation Into War

Three weeks after Diem's fall, an assassin's bullet struck down President Kennedy. Vice President Lyndon B. Johnson was sworn in as the new President. Johnson was a Cold War traditionalist who held a monolithic view of communism. For this "Cold Warrior," communism in the Soviet Union, China, and Vietnam were all the same. He did not recognize subtle differences. He also knew that the American people expected victory in Vietnam.

North Vietnamese and U.S. Forces Clash In 1964, President Johnson faced his first crisis in Vietnam. On August 2, North Vietnamese torpedo boats fired on the American destroyer USS *Maddox* as it patrolled the Gulf of Tonkin off the coast of North Vietnam. The *Maddox* was not hit, and it returned fire on the North Vietnamese boat. Johnson promptly responded to the attack and to other North Vietnamese provocations. He announced that "aggression by terror against peaceful villages of South Vietnam has now been joined by open aggression on the high seas against the United States of America." Troubled by increasing strikes against an American ally, Johnson ordered an airstrike against North Vietnam.

Congress Gives Johnson Broad Military Powers The President next asked Congress to authorize the use of force to defend American troops. With little debate and only two senators voting against it, Congress agreed to Johnson's request and passed the **Gulf of Tonkin Resolution.** The resolution authorized the President "to take all necessary measures to repel any armed attack against the forces of the United States and to prevent further aggression." The resolution gave Johnson tremendous war powers. It allowed him to commit U.S. troops to South Vietnam and fight a war against North Vietnam without ever going back to Congress to ask for a declaration of war.

✓ **Checkpoint** What was the significance of the Gulf of Tonkin Resolution?

SECTION **1** Assessment

Progress Monitoring *Online*
For: Self-test with vocabulary practice
www.pearsonschool.com/ushist

Comprehension

1. Terms and People For each item below, write a sentence explaining its significance.
- Ho Chi Minh
- domino theory
- Vietcong
- Gulf of Tonkin Resolution

2. NoteTaking Reading Skill: Summarize Use your flowchart to answer the Section Focus Question: Why did the United States become involved in Vietnam?

Writing About History

3. Quick Write: Generate an Argument Choose a topic from this section that could be the subject of a persuasive essay. For example, you might choose the domino theory. Then, write a thesis statement arguing in favor of or against U.S. intervention in Southeast Asia. Make sure that the argument clearly explains your opinion on the topic.

Critical Thinking

4. Identify Central Issues Identify one argument for and one argument against Truman's decision to support the French rather than the Vietnamese nationalists.

5. Make Decisions What goals motivated President Kennedy's policy decisions regarding Vietnam?

6. Recognize Cause and Effect How did the *Maddox* incident contribute to the outbreak of war? How did it lead to a change in the balance of power in the American government?

---

1. Sentences should reflect an understanding of each item listed.

2. The United States initially became involved in Vietnam to aid the French. Then, the United States gradually committed more and more troops to prevent communism from spreading in Southeast Asia.

3. Students' thesis statements should clearly state a point of view on the topic they have chosen.

4. One argument for Truman's decision to support the French instead of the Vietnamese nationalists is that it helped contain the spread of communism in the region; one argument against his decision is that it supported colonialism in the region.

5. Kennedy wanted to make the South Vietnamese army more effective and the government of South Vietnam stronger against the communists.

6. It was seen as open aggression against the United States by North Vietnam. The attack led Congress to give President Johnson the power to send U.S. troops to Vietnam and to go to war without a formal declaration of war from Congress.

For additional assessment, have students access **Progress Monitoring *Online*** at **www.pearsonschool.com/ushist**.

◀ A young American soldier in Vietnam

WITNESS HISTORY

American Soldiers on Patrol

The war in Vietnam was different from previous wars. There were no front lines—the enemy was everywhere. The terrain was difficult and littered with mines and booby traps. Drenched in sweat, the men waded through flooded rice paddies and along tangled paths, stopping occasionally to pick leeches out of their boots. One soldier recalled the difficulties of maneuvering in the overgrown and disorienting jungle during the war:

❝You carried 50 to 70 pounds of equipment, and it was tough going, particularly in forested areas. Often you'd have to pull yourself along from one tree branch to the next, or we'd have to help each other by gripping hands. And you couldn't see anything, so you didn't know what was there around you.❞

—Sergeant William Ehrhart,
United States Marines

▲ Vietcong land mine used against American soldiers

U.S. Involvement Grows

Objectives

- Identify the factors that caused President Johnson to increase American troop strength in Vietnam.

- Assess the nature of the war in Vietnam and the difficulties faced by both sides.

- Evaluate the effects of low morale on American troops and on the home front.

Terms and People

William Westmoreland	hawk
napalm	dove

NoteTaking

Reading Skill: Identify Supporting Details
As you read, fill in the outline with details about the escalation of the American war effort.

> I. "Americanizing" the War
>   A.
>   1.
>   2.

Why It Matters After the Gulf of Tonkin Resolution, President Johnson began to shift U.S. military efforts in Vietnam into high gear. But America's leaders and soldiers soon found themselves stuck in a deadly quagmire with no quick victory in sight. The war began to weaken the economy, divide the American people, and erode the nation's morale. **Section Focus Question: What were the causes and effects of America's growing involvement in the Vietnam War?**

"Americanizing" the War

In February 1965, President Johnson dramatically altered the U.S. role in the Vietnam War. In response to a Vietcong attack that killed American troops at Pleiku, Johnson ordered the start of Operation Rolling Thunder, the first sustained bombing campaign against North Vietnam. Johnson hoped that this new strategy of intensive bombing would convince North Vietnam to stop reinforcing the Vietcong in South Vietnam.

The bombs rained down destruction, but they failed to convince North Vietnam to make peace. As the communist forces continued to fight, the United States committed more troops to battle them on the ground. American soldiers moved beyond their adviser roles and assumed greater military responsibilities, while South Vietnamese

Vocabulary Builder

Use the information below and the following resource to teach students the high-use words from this section. Teaching Resources, Vocabulary Builder, p. 11

High-Use Words	Definitions and Sample Sentences
doctrine	*n.* teachings The Truman **Doctrine** stated that the United States would support people around the world fighting for freedom.
assert	*v.* to state positively; declare The President **asserted** that the United States would help its allies.

SECTION **2** **Step-by-Step Instruction**

Objectives

As you teach this section, keep students focused on the following objectives to help them answer the Section Focus Question and master core content.

- Identify the factors that caused President Johnson to increase American troop strength in Vietnam.

- Assess the nature of the war in Vietnam and the difficulties faced by both sides.

- Evaluate the effects of low morale on American troops and on the home front.

Prepare to Read

Background Knowledge L3

Remind students that U.S. involvement in the conflict in Vietnam was limited until Congress passed the Gulf of Tonkin Resolution. Ask students to predict how the conflict changed when more U.S. troops were involved.

Set a Purpose L3

- **WITNESS HISTORY** Read the selection aloud.

  Ask **What thoughts and feelings might a soldier have had in the conditions described by Sergeant Ehrhart?** *(Sample responses: how far from home he was or what new dangers he would encounter; tension, uncertainty, disorientation, fear)*

- **Focus** Point out the Section Focus Question, and write it on the board. Tell students to refer to this question as they read. *(Answer appears with Section 2 Assessment answers.)*

- **Preview** Have students preview the Section Objectives and the list of Terms and People.

- **NoteTaking** Using the Structured Read Aloud strategy (TE, p. T20), have students read this section. As they read, have students outline details about the escalation of the American war effort. Reading and Note Taking Study Guide

"Americanizing" the War **L3**

Instruct

- **Introduce: Vocabulary Builder**
Have students locate the vocabulary term *doctrine* and its definition. Tell students that they will learn how Ho Chi Minh's *doctrine* of never fighting on the enemy's terms gave the Vietcong an advantage over U.S. troops.

- **Teach** Review the assumptions, strategies, and effects of Operation Rolling Thunder. Ask **What did Defense Secretary McNamara and General Westmoreland advise President Johnson to do to win the war in Vietnam?** *(increase the military presence of the United States in Vietnam and have U.S. troops do more of the fighting)* **How did the Vietcong wear down U.S. troops?** *(They ambushed the Americans and fought at night; they used explosives and booby traps.)* **How did the United States respond to the limited results of the first stage of the war?** *(It committed more troops and resources to the conflict.)* **How might the corruption of the South Vietnamese government have undermined the U.S. military presence in Vietnam?** *(The South Vietnamese government did not have much support outside the cities. The Vietnamese living in villages may not have helped U.S. troops fight the Vietcong because they knew that the United States supported a government that they opposed.)*

- **Quick Activity** Draw students' attention to the troop and casualty statistics provided under the red heading "A Costly and Frustrating War." Have students use the data to draw a line graph illustrating the increase in troops and casualties between 1965 and 1968.

---

troops accepted a secondary, more limited role in the war. U.S. military and civilian leaders hoped that American airstrikes, along with the troops on the ground, would eventually force the communists to the peace table.

American Assumptions and Strategies Johnson's change in strategy in 1965 stemmed primarily from the counsel of Secretary of Defense Robert McNamara and General **William Westmoreland,** the American commander in South Vietnam. These two advisers believed that the United States needed to increase its military presence in Vietnam and do more of the fighting in order to win the war. Operation Rolling Thunder and increased troop commitments fulfilled this need to "Americanize" the war effort.

Beginning in March 1965, U.S. airstrikes hammered North Vietnam and Vietcong strong points in South Vietnam. Between 1965 and 1973, American pilots dropped more than 6 million tons of bombs on enemy positions—almost three times the tonnage dropped by all the combatants during World War II. In addition to conventional bombs, American pilots dropped napalm and sprayed Agent Orange. **Napalm** is a jellied gasoline which was dropped in large canisters that exploded on impact, covering large areas in flames. It clung to anything it touched and was difficult to extinguish. Agent Orange is an herbicide meant to kill plant life. Almost half of South Vietnam's forested areas were sprayed at least once, and the ecological impact was devastating. U.S. forces used it to defoliate the countryside and disrupt the enemy's food supply. Many scientists believe that Agent Orange causes cancers and other physical problems.

As airstrikes intensified, American ground troops landed in South Vietnam. On March 8, 1965, U.S. Marines arrived to defend the airbase at Da Nang. They were soon followed by other troops. The soldiers accepted a wide range of missions. Some guarded bases. Others conducted search-and-destroy missions to kill as many Vietcong guerrillas as they could. Helicopters ferried commandos to and from remote locations for quick strikes against enemy positions.

An Elusive and Determined Enemy Large-scale battles against Vietcong or North Vietnamese Army units were not typical of America's strategy in Vietnam. American soldiers generally fought lightly armed Vietcong guerrillas in small engagements. Ho Chi Minh's military <u>doctrine</u> hinged on fighting only when victory was assured, which meant never fighting on his opponents' terms. He compared his troops to a tiger, while the Americans were like an elephant. If the tiger stands still, the elephant will crush it. But if the tiger keeps moving and occasionally jumps on the elephant to take a bite out of it, the elephant will slowly bleed to death.

During the war, the Vietcong behaved like Ho's tiger. They traveled light, often carrying just a rifle and a few handfuls of rice. They dug tunnels to hide in during the day and emerged at night to ambush American patrols. They infiltrated American bases and set off explosives. They set booby traps that maimed and crippled American troops. Their strategy was to wear the American elephant down. The leaders of North Vietnam and the Vietcong remained convinced that if they could avoid losing the war, the Americans would eventually leave.

A Costly and Frustrating War American strategy during this stage of the war yielded limited results. U.S. bombers did disrupt North Vietnamese industry and slow the movement of supplies to the Vietcong. But when the communists did not sue for peace, American troop commitments and battlefield deaths escalated rapidly. By the end of 1965, there were 184,300 U.S. troops in Vietnam and only 636 American soldiers had died in the war. Three years later, there were more than half a million U.S. troops in Vietnam and the number of American dead had risen to more than 30,000.

Vocabulary Builder
<u>doctrine</u>–(DAHK trihn) *n.* teachings

Differentiated Instruction Solutions for All Learners

L4 Advanced Readers   **L4** Gifted and Talented Students

Have students create political cartoons based on Ho Chi Minh's imagery of the tiger and the elephant, his doctrine of never fighting on the enemy's terms, and details in the section about the Vietcong's strategies. Tell students to use words and images in their cartoons to express a point of view about the fighting in Vietnam. Have students share their cartoons with their classmates, and invite their classmates to interpret the cartoons. Students also may research political cartoons from the Vietnam War era and share their findings and their interpretations of the cartoons with their classmates.

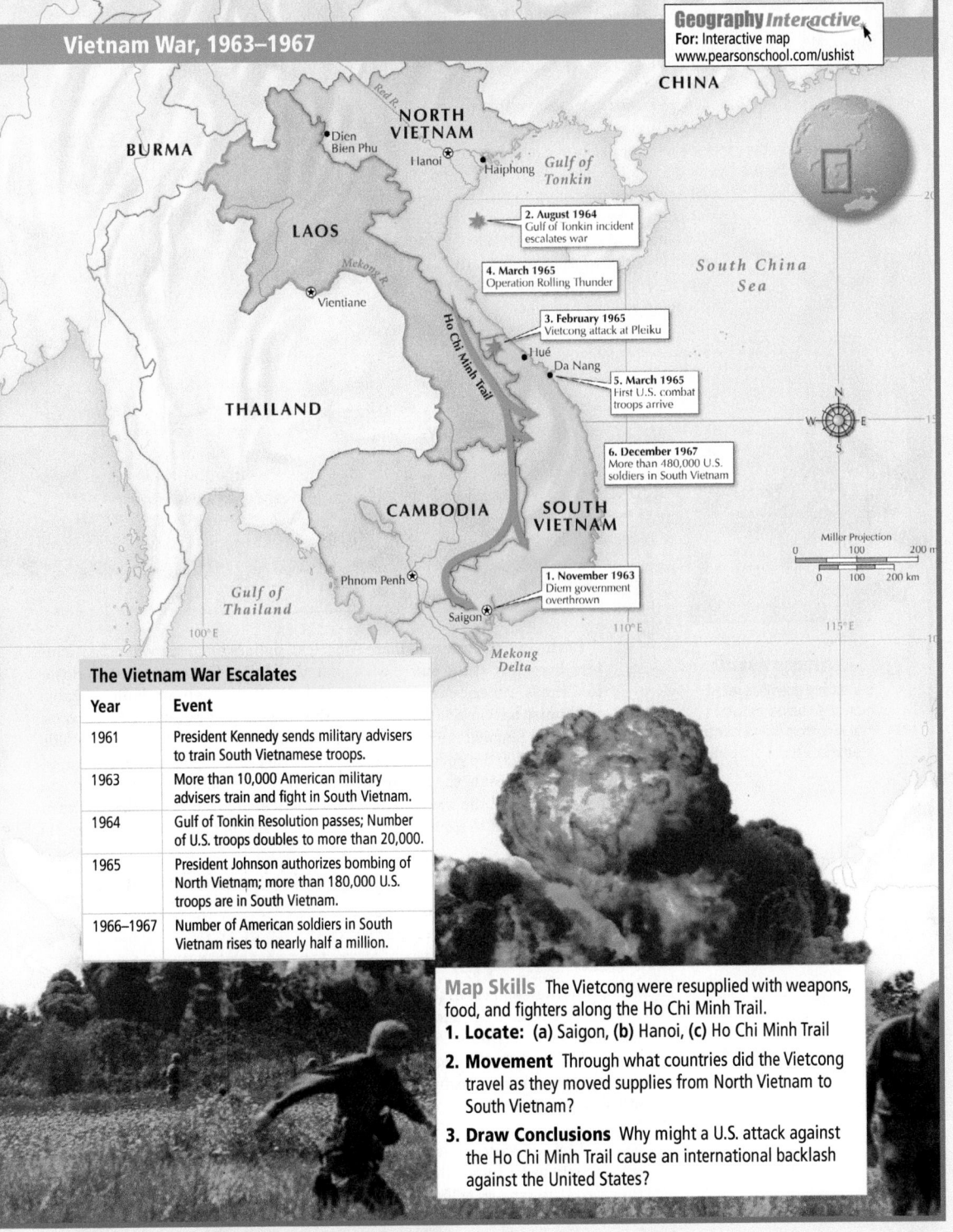

Geography *Interactive*
For: Interactive map
www.pearsonschool.com/ushist

2. August 1964
Gulf of Tonkin incident
escalates war

4. March 1965
Operation Rolling Thunder

3. February 1965
Vietcong attack at Pleiku

5. March 1965
First U.S. combat
troops arrive

6. December 1967
More than 480,000 U.S.
soldiers in South Vietnam

1. November 1963
Diem government
overthrown

Miller Projection

| 0 | 100 | 200 mi |

| 0 | 100 | 200 km |

The Vietnam War Escalates

Year	Event
1961	President Kennedy sends military advisers to train South Vietnamese troops.
1963	More than 10,000 American military advisers train and fight in South Vietnam.
1964	Gulf of Tonkin Resolution passes; Number of U.S. troops doubles to more than 20,000.
1965	President Johnson authorizes bombing of North Vietnam; more than 180,000 U.S. troops are in South Vietnam.
1966–1967	Number of American soldiers in South Vietnam rises to nearly half a million.

Map Skills The Vietcong were resupplied with weapons, food, and fighters along the Ho Chi Minh Trail.

1. **Locate:** (a) Saigon, (b) Hanoi, (c) Ho Chi Minh Trail

2. **Movement** Through what countries did the Vietcong travel as they moved supplies from North Vietnam to South Vietnam?

3. **Draw Conclusions** Why might a U.S. attack against the Ho Chi Minh Trail cause an international backlash against the United States?

History Background

The Ho Chi Minh Trail An intricate network of paths, tracks, and roads through the jungles and mountains of Laos and Cambodia, the Ho Chi Minh Trail was a crucial supply route for North Vietnamese forces in South Vietnam during the Vietnam War. The American media named the supply highway after the communist leader Ho Chi Minh. The North Vietnamese called the trail Truong-Son after the mountain chain along the Vietnam-Laos border. Covering thousands of miles, the trail helped soldiers, weapons, ammunition, and food reach their destinations in the south by foot, bike, and truck. During the war, parts of the trail were paved and widened to make travel and transportation easier.

The United States made bombing raids on the trail, but damage was quickly repaired and traffic was hardly disrupted. Today, the Ho Chi Minh Trail is a tourist destination. Parts of the old trail have been integrated into the road networks of Laos and Cambodia and into Vietnam's Ho Chi Minh National Highway, which runs from Hanoi to Ho Chi Minh City (formerly Saigon).

Independent Practice

Have students access **www.pearsonschool.com/ushist** to use the Geography Interactive map and answer the map skills questions in the text. Direct students' attention to the photograph below the map. Ask students to discuss the conditions that soldiers faced while serving in Vietnam.

Monitor Progress

As students fill in their outlines, circulate to make sure that they understand the escalation of the American war effort. For a completed version of the outline, see Note Taking Transparencies, **B-134**.

Answers

Map Skills

1. Review locations with students.
2. Laos, Cambodia
3. The trail ran largely through Laos and Cambodia, two countries that were not fighting in the war.

Instruct

- **Introduce** Write the word *quagmire* on the board, and review its meaning as it is explained at the end of the first paragraph on this page. Ask **Why did some people compare the Vietnam War to a quagmire?** *(Sample answer: No headway was being made in winning the war; the United States seemed stuck in Vietnam.)* **In such a situation, how might U.S. soldiers fighting in Vietnam have felt?** *(Possible responses: that they could not give up; that they were losing more than they were gaining)*

- **Teach** Using the Idea Wave strategy (TE, p. T22), have students discuss the challenges American soldiers faced. Ask **What made fighting the Vietcong and North Vietnamese difficult?** *(They avoided significant engagements and fought in smaller skirmishes; they knew the landscape and used its natural cover for surprise attacks and to escape; most of the fighting took place at night.)* **What helped American soldiers fulfill their duty in the difficult conditions?** *(They believed in the cause for which they were fighting.)* **What might have raised morale for many American soldiers in Vietnam?** *(Sample response: decisively defeating the Vietcong in small skirmishes and large battles; knowing that the South Vietnamese appreciated the involvement of the United States in Vietnam)*

- **Quick Activity** Have students read the Primary Source quotation on the next page. Then, organize the students in groups, and have them discuss whether they agree or disagree with the point of view expressed.

Answer

 The strategic aim of Operation Rolling Thunder was to persuade North Vietnam to stop reinforcing the Vietcong in South Vietnam.

INFOGRAPHIC

THE HARDSHIPS OF WAR IN VIETNAM

By 1968, the morale of American troops in Vietnam was on the wane. Units would fight to drive the Vietcong out of a village only to return weeks later to do the same job all over again. In a land where anyone could be the enemy, U.S. soldiers lived in a state of constant tension. Survival demanded remaining on the lookout for snipers, ambushes, and booby traps. The amount of rice cooking in a pot could be a clue to an impending attack. Was there just enough food for the people in view, or had others disappeared as the Americans approached? A moment of inattention could spell disaster.

Concealed entrance under cooking pot

Upper trench

Vent

Lower tunnel and hiding place

▲ Vietcong guerrillas relied on large tunnel networks to hide from—and launch surprise attacks against—American forces.

Each year, the war cost more American dollars and claimed more American lives. But at the end of each year, the United States seemed no closer to success. America's mission was to help South Vietnam build a stable noncommunist nation and thereby win the "hearts and minds" of its citizens. But corruption plagued the South Vietnamese administrative structure. Outside of the major cities, the government enjoyed little real support. Although American forces won most of the larger battles, they did not achieve a successful end to the war. By 1967, the war had devolved into a stalemate. Some U.S. critics of the war compared it to a quagmire—muddy terrain that sinks underfoot and is difficult to exit.

✓ **Checkpoint** What was the strategic aim of Operation Rolling Thunder?

Patriotism, Heroism, and Sinking Morale

For American soldiers in the field, the Vietnam War presented difficult challenges that demanded courage and patience. Unlike World War II, the Vietnam War did not emphasize territorial acquisition. The United States and its allies did not invade North Vietnam, march on Ho Chi Minh's capital of Hanoi, or attempt to destroy the communist regime. As in the Korean War, the United States was fearful of triggering both Chinese and Soviet entry into the conflict. Instead, American forces supported the survival and development of South Vietnam, which was besieged by the Vietcong and their North Vietnamese allies. In this fight, U.S. troops could never fully tell their friends from their enemies. Yet from the outset, they faced the dangers of Vietnam's battlefields with dedication and bravery.

Differentiated Instruction   Solutions for All Learners

⑴ Special Needs Students   ⑵ English Language Learners   ⑵ Less Proficient Readers

Lead students through the Infographic on this spread. Invite a volunteer to read the title aloud. Then, direct students' attention to the soldier on the left. Ask **On what side was the soldier on the left fighting? How can you tell?** *(the communist or North Vietnamese side; his hat and black pajamas)* Next, have students look at the cutaway diagram. Ask a volunteer to read the labels aloud. Ask **How did the Vietcong get into the upper trench?** *(by moving the* *cooking pot and climbing down)* **Why did the lower tunnel have a vent?** *(to ensure that people could breathe)* Have students read the caption and describe the scene in the middle picture. Then, invite a volunteer to read the postcard and its caption aloud. Discuss why soldiers might try to reassure their families. Finally, have students focus on the helicopters and troops at the right. Discuss why the U.S. military relied on helicopters.

▲ Despite the dangers they faced in combat, many American troops wrote reassuring letters to their worried families at home.

◄ A tank is used to evacuate wounded American soldiers from battle.

▲ U.S. soldiers from the 173rd Airborne Brigade exit their helicopter transports in South Vietnam.

Independent Practice

- To enhance understanding of the dangers American soldiers faced, have students access the History Interactive at **www.pearsonschool.com/ushist**. After students experience the History Interactive, ask them to share their reactions by posing questions such as these: What hardships did American soldiers experience in the war? How did technology such as helicopters help U.S. troops? How might helicopters have had a negative impact?

Monitor Progress

To help students review the section so far, ask them to describe American expectations in the war. Have them discuss whether American expectations for the war have been met and explain why or why not.

Danger on a New Battlefield Although American troops won numerous battles, they could not win the war outright. The problem was that the Vietcong and North Vietnamese avoided significant engagements. Rather than expose themselves to superior American firepower, the communists fought smaller skirmishes where their small-unit abilities and their knowledge of the landscape bettered their chances for victory.

U.S. forces often had no alternative but to fight indecisive battles in the jungles, rice paddies, and mountains of Vietnam. Most of these battlefields abounded with natural cover. Clad in black pajamas, Vietcong gunmen would spring out of the dense foliage, attack with automatic rifles and grenades, and disappear back into the landscape. Much of this fighting took place at night, which reduced the effectiveness of American planes, artillery, and troop tactics.

American Soldiers Fulfill Their Duty Despite the trials of war, American soldiers adapted to adverse conditions in Vietnam and fought with the same intensity that U.S. forces had shown in World Wars I and II. Many fought to prevent the spread of communism. Some fought to protect villagers in South Vietnam and win their trust and respect. Others fought because their country was at war, and they felt it was their duty. A medic in the First Infantry Division explained his reason for going to Vietnam:

> **Primary Source** "I volunteered. . . . Ever since the American Revolution my family had people in all the different wars, and that was always the thing—when your country needs you, you go. You don't ask a lot of questions. . . . "
> —David Ross, United States Army medic

Thinking Critically

1. **Compare** How were communist combat tactics different from those of American troops?

2. **Draw Conclusions** How did images such as these, shown on television news shows, affect the home front?

History Interactive ✶
For: To learn more about the hardships of the Vietnam War
www.pearsonschool.com/ushist

Differentiated Instruction Solutions for All Learners

L1 Special Needs Students   **L2 English Language Learners**   **L2 Less Proficient Readers**

Read aloud selections from *Dear America: Letters Home from Vietnam,* edited by Bernard Edelman. Ask students to respond orally to each selection, telling what insights it gives them into the war and the hardships soldiers experienced. Then, organize students in pairs, and ask them to apply what they have learned from the text and the discussion to write letters responding to one of the selections that was read aloud. Invite volunteers to read their letters to the class.

Answers

Thinking Critically

1. The communist fighters used the natural cover of the landscape, darkness, secret tunnels, and surprise tactics; American troops were equipped for larger engagements during the day and in the open; American troops used helicopters, which could be easily spotted by the enemy, to get in and out quickly.

2. Images of U.S. tanks and helicopters would give people at home a sense of the technological superiority of the United States, but images of wounded soldiers would emphasize the losses the United States was suffering in spite of its technological advances.

Doubt Grows on the Home Front

Instruct

- **Introduce: Key Terms** Ask students to find the key terms *hawk* and *dove* (in bold) in the text. Point out the qualities traditionally associated with each type of bird and how those qualities can illustrate opposing viewpoints regarding war.

- **Teach** Help students understand how Americans' views of the war changed and why. Ask **What effect did spending for the war have on the U.S. economy?** (*Spending for the war led to inflation, higher taxes, and cutbacks in the Great Society programs.*) **What do you think people who saw the Vietnam conflict as a localized civil war wanted the United States to do?** (*to bring U.S. troops home and let the Vietnamese fight the war themselves*)

Independent Practice

- To help students understand how massive spending on the war affected the economy, have students read and complete *Reading a Chart: War Weakens the Economy.* Teaching Resources, **p. 21**

- Have students examine the political cartoon on the next page. Ask students to discuss the meaning of the political cartoon with a partner and write paragraphs summarizing their discussion.

Monitor Progress

Circulate to make sure that students are filling out their worksheets accurately and understand the effects of the Vietnam War on the U.S. economy.

Nurses in Vietnam
U.S. Army nurses Capt. Gladys E. Sepulveda, left, of Puerto Rico, and 2nd Lt. Lois Ferrari, of Pittsburgh, rest on sandbags at Cam Ranh Bay in South Vietnam on July 14, 1965. They were awaiting transportation to Nha Trang, where they were set to work in the 8th field hospital.

Vocabulary Builder
assert–(uh SERT) *v.* to state positively; declare

Later, many did ask questions about America's involvement in the war, but overwhelmingly while they were in Vietnam, the soldiers met their duties with courage. More than 58,000 of them gave their lives for their country.

Women also displayed courage and valor. About 10,000 American military women served in Vietnam during the war. Most female military personnel were nurses. Not only did they face danger working close to the front, but they also had to cope with the emotional toll of constantly working with injured and dying soldiers and civilians.

Lynda Van Devanter volunteered to go to Vietnam and spent a year there as a nurse. Like other nurses, she confronted war and death on a daily basis. However, on one occasion she had to deliver a baby. She later recalled:

> **Primary Source** "It was creation of life in the midst of all that destruction. And creation of life restored your sanity.... Those were the things that kept you going. That there was life coming. There was still hope."
> —Lynda Van Devanter, United States Army nurse

Morale Declines as War Wears On As the war lengthened, many Americans began to question U.S. involvement. The earliest soldiers in Vietnam had been volunteers, men committed to the fight against communism. But by the end of 1965, most American soldiers in Vietnam had been drafted into military service, and they were not as certain that preserving the government in South Vietnam was crucial to American interests. They sensed that many South Vietnamese people were indifferent—if not openly hostile—to their own nation. Increasingly, it seemed that Americans were dying to defend a nation whose people were unwilling to die to defend themselves.

✓ **Checkpoint** Why did the morale of American troops decline as the war continued?

Doubt Grows on the Home Front

The lack of progress toward victory in Vietnam also led to doubt in the United States. When President Johnson had begun to send troops to war, Americans had expected a relatively quick victory. After all, the United States was a militarily powerful, technologically advanced country, and North Vietnam was a poor country with comparatively little technology. Over the next few years, the Johnson administration kept <u>asserting</u> that an American victory was close at hand. But when that did not come, many began to question the President's foreign policy.

The War Weakens the Economy The war strained government finances. President Johnson's Great Society plan called for enormous domestic spending to eliminate poverty, improve education and medical care, and fight racial discrimination. The costs of fighting a war on the other side of the world were just as mammoth. Although massive government spending lowered the unemployment rate, it also led to rising prices and inflation. The combination of heavy government spending, rising prices, and inflation forced Johnson to raise taxes.

Connect to Your World

Domino Theory in the Middle East The domino theory has a new application in the twenty-first century. Since before the war in Iraq, officials in the Bush administration have spoken of a possible democratic domino effect in the Middle East. Their theory, which can be seen as the reverse of the old idea that if Vietnam fell to communism, its neighbors in Southeast Asia would too, is that the fall of Saddam Hussein in Iraq is likely to be followed by the collapse of other totalitarian regimes in the Middle East and their replacement by democratic governments. That is, the democratization of Iraq could be followed by a shift toward democracy in Syria, Iran, and even perhaps beyond the Middle East, in North Korea. Others, however, doubt whether this will happen, noting that Southeast Asia did not collapse into communism after communist North Vietnam's victory in the Vietnam War as proponents of the domino theory predicted that it would.

Answer

✓ Many U.S. troops questioned whether preserving the government in South Vietnam was crucial to American interests.

Ultimately, Johnson had to cut back on his Great Society reform initiatives to help pay for the war.

Antiwar Movement Begins to Emerge As long as America's involvement in Vietnam had been small and relatively inexpensive, few politicians voiced serious opposition. Despite its bipartisan support for the Vietnam policies of Johnson's predecessors, after the Gulf of Tonkin Resolution, Congress soon split over the President's escalation of the war.

Beginning in 1967, Congress—and eventually most of America—divided into two camps: hawks and doves. The mostly conservative **hawks** supported Johnson's war policy. Believing strongly in the containment of communism and the domino theory, they accepted rising troop levels, escalating costs, and increasing numbers of battlefield deaths. For the hawks, Vietnam was a crucial front in the Cold War. **Doves,** however, broke with Johnson's war policy. A diverse group of liberal politicians, pacifists, student radicals, and civil rights leaders, doves questioned the war on both moral and strategic grounds. For them, the conflict was a localized civil war, not a vital Cold War battleground.

Senator J. William Fulbright, chairman of the Senate Foreign Relations Committee, emerged as the early leader of the doves in Congress. A Democrat who had supported the Gulf of Tonkin Resolution, Fulbright soon came to believe that the war in Vietnam was a national civil war, not a Cold War conflict whose shots were called in Moscow or Beijing. In 1967 and 1968, Fulbright held public hearings on the war, providing a platform for critics of the conflict.

✓ **Checkpoint** What were the opposing viewpoints of hawks and doves?

Onward And Upward And Onward And—

JUST ONE MORE STEP-UP IN THE BOMBING

INCREASED BOMBING WILL BREAK HANOI'S MORALE

INCREASED BOMBING WILL STOP THE INFILTRATION

INCREASED BOMBING WILL WIN THE WAR

© 1967 HERBLOCK
THE WASHINGTON POST

Analyzing Political Cartoons

The Bombing Campaign U.S. officials promised that increased bombing would bring America closer to victory.
1. Does the emotion on the person's face suggest that the plan is working? Explain.
2. Do you think the cartoonist was a hawk or a dove? Explain.

Progress Monitoring *Online*
For: Self-test with vocabulary practice
www.pearsonschool.com/ushist

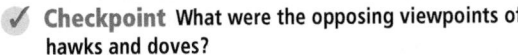

SECTION 2 Assessment

Comprehension
1. **Terms and People** For each item below, write a sentence explaining its significance.
   - William Westmoreland
   - napalm
   - dove
2. **NoteTaking Reading Skill: Identify Supporting Details** Use your outline to answer the Section Focus Question: What were the causes and effects of America's growing involvement in the Vietnam War?

Writing About History
3. **Quick Write: Support an Opinion With Evidence** Consider the following topic from the section: America's escalation of the war in Vietnam. Gather and present evidence from the text that supports the Americanization of the war effort.

Critical Thinking
4. **Evaluate Information** What military strategies did the United States employ in Vietnam? How successful were these strategies?
5. **Summarize** What difficulties did American soldiers face in Vietnam? What effect did these difficulties have?
6. **Contrast** How did the disagreements between hawks and doves reflect different views about war and world politics?

Assess and Reteach

Assess Progress L3
- Have students complete the Section Assessment.
- Administer the Section Quiz. Teaching Resources, **p. 26**
- To further assess student understanding, use Progress Monitoring Transparencies, **130.**

Reteach
If students need more instruction, have them read the section summary.

Reading and Note Taking Study Guide L3

Adapted Reading and Note Taking Study Guide L1 L2

Spanish Reading and Note Taking Study Guide L2

Extend L4
See this Chapter's Professional Development pages for the Extend Online activity on the ways that war affected people who lived and fought in Vietnam.

Answers

✓ Hawks believed that American involvement in the war was helping contain communism. Doves believed that the conflict was a localized civil war in which U.S. troops should not be involved.

Analyzing Political Cartoons
1. No; the person has a desperate and exhausted, rather than a confident, look.
2. a dove; the cartoon suggests that no amount of bombing will end the war.

Section 2 Assessment

1. Sentences should reflect an understanding of each item listed.
2. Lack of progress toward victory led to the commitment of more U.S. troops and resources; the commitment of more troops and resources without progress toward victory weakened the U.S. economy, divided Americans, and caused a decline in military morale.
3. Students should support the opinion with reasons, examples, and other details from the text.

4. The United States used intensive bombing, including napalm and Agent Orange, to defoliate the landscape and disrupt supply routes, and it used helicopters for quick strikes in remote places. These strategies were not very successful overall.
5. U.S. soldiers had to fight indecisive small battles, often at night, in a landscape with which they were not familiar. These difficulties reduced the effectiveness of American tactics, planes, and artillery.
6. Hawks believed that war and the rising troop levels, escalating costs, and

increasing casualties it required were justified in containing communism. Doves believed that war was morally wrong and that the war in Vietnam was a localized civil war that did not require others' involvement.

For additional assessment, have students access **Progress Monitoring** *Online* at **www.pearsonschool.com/ushist**.

Objectives

As you teach this section, keep students focused on the following objectives to help them answer the Section Focus Question and master core content.

- Describe the divisions within American society over the Vietnam War.
- Analyze the Tet Offensive and the American reaction to it.
- Summarize the factors that influenced the outcome of the 1968 presidential election.

Background Knowledge L3

Remind students that the Vietnam War was weakening the U.S. economy and dividing Americans. Ask students to predict how the Vietnam War would cause further rifts in American society.

Set a Purpose L3

- **WITNESS HISTORY** Read the selection aloud.

  Ask **What is Cronkite's criticism of American leaders' optimism?** *(It is not based on what is really going on Vietnam.)* **What is the basis of his view of the war?** *(his own visit to Vietnam)*

- **Focus** Point out the Section Focus Question, and write it on the board. Tell students to refer to this question as they read. *(Answer appears with Section 3 Assessment answers.)*

- **Preview** Have students preview the Section Objectives and the list of Terms and People.

- **Reading Skill** Have students use the *Reading Strategy: Recognize Sequence* worksheet. Teaching Resources, **p. 12**

- **NoteTaking** Using the Paragraph Shrinking strategy (TE, p. T20), have students read this section. As they read, have students fill in the flowchart sequencing the events leading up to the 1968 election. Reading and Note Taking Study Guide

◄ A Vietnam veteran protests the war in 1970.

WITNESS HISTORY

The "Living-Room War"

Walter Cronkite, the anchor of the CBS Evening News, was the most respected television journalist of the 1960s. His many reports on the Vietnam War were models of balanced journalism and inspired the confidence of viewers across the United States. But during the Tet Offensive, Cronkite was shocked by the disconnect between Johnson's optimistic statements and the gritty reality of the fighting. After visiting Vietnam in February of 1968, he told his viewers:

"We have been too often disappointed by the optimism of the American leaders, both in Vietnam and Washington, to have faith any longer in the silver linings they find in the darkest clouds. . . . [I]t seems now more certain than ever that the bloody experience of Vietnam is to end in stalemate."

—Walter Cronkite, 1968

▲ Walter Cronkite

The War Divides America

Objectives

- Describe the divisions within American society over the Vietnam War.
- Analyze the Tet Offensive and the American reaction to it.
- Summarize the factors that influenced the outcome of the 1968 presidential election.

Terms and People

draftee	Tet Offensive
SDS	Eugene McCarthy
"credibility gap"	Robert Kennedy

NoteTaking

Reading Skill: Recognize Sequence Note the events leading up to the 1968 election.

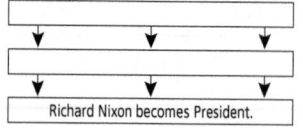

Richard Nixon becomes President.

Why It Matters President Johnson sent more American troops to Vietnam in order to win the war. But with each passing year, casualty lists got longer and victory seemed further away. As soldiers died abroad and hawks and doves argued at home, the Vietnam War opened up a deep emotional rift in American society. After the war ended, it would take years for the country to heal itself. **Section Focus Question: How did the American war effort in Vietnam lead to rising protests and social divisions back home?**

Antiwar Protests Increase

The war in Vietnam divided Americans more deeply than any conflict since the Civil War. Although most Americans initially supported President Johnson's bombings and troop deployments, by 1966 critics began speaking out. Senator Fulbright's opposition to the war hurt Johnson in Congress, and the senator was soon joined by like-minded activists who believed that American soldiers were dying in a war that had little to do with American interests.

The Draft Becomes Increasingly Unpopular By 1965, most of the troops sent to Vietnam were no longer volunteers who had enlisted in the army. Instead, they were **draftees**—young men drafted into military service—who had been assigned a tour in Vietnam. In accordance with the Selective Service Act of 1948, the government drafted more than 1.5 million men into military service during the Vietnam War. All males had to register for the draft when they turned 18, and the Selective Service System called up draftees based on projected military needs.

Vocabulary Builder

Use the information below and the following resource to teach students the high-use words from this section. Teaching Resources, Vocabulary Builder, p. 11

High-Use Words	Definitions and Sample Sentences
deferment	*n.* postponement The **deferment** of aid left many people without needed supplies.
inevitable	*adj.* certain to happen Casualties are **inevitable** in war.

Critics of the Selective Service System argued that the draft was not fair. The system gave local draft boards considerable influence in selecting men for service, and it also granted <u>deferments</u> to college students and men who worked in certain designated occupations. Most of the 2.5 million men who served in Vietnam came from working-class and poor backgrounds.

During the Johnson presidency, the number of African American troops fighting and dying in Vietnam was also disproportionately high. At the beginning of the war, African Americans suffered more than 20 percent of the total combat deaths, roughly twice their percentage of the U.S. population. Additionally, African American soldiers were more likely to serve in combat positions and less likely to become commissioned officers.

Civil rights leader Martin Luther King, Jr., spoke out against the added war burden shouldered by African American soldiers. Speaking at a New York church in 1967, King said that the war was hurting both poor blacks and whites. Vietnam was drawing human and economic resources away from America's other wars on poverty and discrimination. He added that it hindered poor Americans in other more direct ways:

Vocabulary Builder
deferment–(dee FER muhnt) *n.*
postponement

Primary Source ❝It was sending their sons and their brothers and their husbands to fight and to die in extraordinary high proportions relative to the rest of the population. . . . [W]e have been repeatedly faced with the cruel irony of watching Negro and white boys on TV screens as they kill and die together for a nation that has been unable to seat them together in the same schools.❞

—Martin Luther King, Jr., 1967

Perceived inequities in the draft led to widespread resistance. Antiwar advocates sponsored a Stop-the-Draft week in October 1967, and some draft-eligible males burned their draft cards in protest. Finally, in 1969, the Selective Service System adopted a lottery that was designed to eliminate deferment abuses and create a more diverse army of draftees.

African American Soldiers in Battle
The Vietnam War witnessed the highest proportion of African Americans ever to serve in an American war. Here, an African American Marine ducks behind a wall for cover while firing on an enemy position. *Based on the line graph, why might African American recruits be unhappy with the draft?*

African Americans and the Vietnam War

Percentage of African Americans

25
20
15
10
5
0

1961–1964 1965 1966 1967 1968

— African American combat deaths (U.S. Army)
— African Americans in U.S. population

SOURCES: Department of Defense; *Historical Statistics of the United States*

- Have students read the Primary Source quotation from Martin Luther King, Jr., and examine the photograph of the African American soldier and the graph on the previous page. Ask students to write brief paragraphs describing what King found ironic about U.S. combat in Vietnam and how the photograph and the graph support King's opinion.

- Ask students to examine the photograph of the Vietnam War supporters on this page. Have students use information from the text to write letters to the editor telling whether they support or oppose the union members in the photograph and explaining their reasons for their support or opposition.

Monitor Progress

As students fill in their flowcharts, circulate to make sure that they understand the events that led to the 1968 election. For a completed version of the flowchart, see Note Taking Transparencies, **B-135.**

Activism Spreads on College Campuses Across America, college campuses became centers of antiwar sentiment. Professors and students criticized the war for a variety of reasons, ranging from pacifism and the war's effects on the economy to a personal desire to avoid military service. Antiwar activity on college campuses did not, however, reflect the attitudes of all Americans. In fact, many professors remained vocal in their defense of the war effort during lectures and at protest rallies. For the most part, though, colleges and universities represented the strongest antiwar opinion.

Antiwar activities were part of more significant changes taking place on college campuses. Never before the 1960s had so many Americans entered colleges and universities. Between 1946 and 1970, the number of students enrolled in institutions of higher education increased from 2 million to 8 million. Many college students became a class unto themselves—segregated from the workforce, free from many adult responsibilities, and encouraged by their professors to think critically. Many of the students who embraced the antiwar cause came from middle-class families. Students from working-class families were less likely to protest against the war.

The University of Michigan and the University of California at Berkeley became important hubs of the antiwar movement. The **Students for a Democratic Society (SDS)** was founded in 1960 at the University of Michigan. Originally formed to campaign against racism and poverty, the SDS soon began campaigning to end the war in Vietnam. By 1964, SDS had organized campus "teach-ins" and demonstrations against the war and encouraged draft-age males to sign "We Won't Go" petitions.

Students Clash With Authorities Student activism led to a clash with administrators and police in 1964. Students at the University of California at Berkeley protested against the school's decision not to allow them to use university grounds to organize off-campus political activities. The students formed the Free Speech Movement to contest the decision. When protesters occupied a university building, the police arrested them. In response, students cut classes to march in support of the FSM. University officials eventually relented and allowed students to engage in free speech activities on school grounds. The victory by students at Berkeley led to challenges at other colleges and universities.

More and More Americans Oppose the War Outside college campuses, other Americans soon enlisted in the antiwar cause. The war in Vietnam was the first "living-room war." Americans watched the progress—or lack of it—in their living rooms on nightly newscasts. The intimacy of television made news of the war unavoidable. But unlike World War II, there was no march to victory. Americans could not put maps of Vietnam on their walls and trace the routes the troops were taking to Hanoi.

Hawks and doves drifted farther apart. More groups organized against the war, their names corresponding with whom they represented—Vietnam Veterans Against the War, Catholic Peace Fellowship, Another Mother for Peace. Antiwar Americans—rich and poor, black and white—read reports from war correspondents who questioned U.S. progress in Vietnam. They watched government officials issue optimistic statement after optimistic statement. Soon, a **"credibility gap"** emerged between what the Johnson administration said and what many journalists reported. This gap referred to the American public's growing distrust of statements made by the government.

Hawks Respond to Protests
Despite doves' vocal opposition to the war, hawks organized their own demonstrations to support U.S. policy in Vietnam. Below, New York City union members rally behind the American war effort in 1967.

✓ **Checkpoint** Why did the antiwar movement grow across the nation?

Differentiated Instruction — Solutions for All Learners

① Special Needs Students   ② English Language Learners   ② Less Proficient Readers

Pair struggling readers with more advanced learners. Have each pair scan the text under the blue heading "Antiwar Protests Increase" and list reasons that many Americans opposed the Vietnam War. Then, have pairs scan the text and list ways that Americans showed their opposition to the war. Have partners use their lists to write three to five newspaper headlines that summarize how and why antiwar protests

increased *(Sample answers: Selective Service System Unfair, Lottery Will Decide Who Goes to War).*
Remind students that newspaper headlines should be short but informative. Then, have students read their headlines to the class and explain how the headline relates to the increase in antiwar protests in the United States.

Answer

✓ Numbers of casualties continued to increase as victory seemed farther away. Many people no longer believed that the government was telling the truth about progress in the war.

Tet Offensive Is the Turning Point

In November 1967, President Johnson brought General Westmoreland home from Vietnam to address the nation's concerns about the war. Westmoreland said that the Vietcong were declining in strength and could no longer mount a major offensive. As Westmoreland made his claims, however, the North Vietnamese and Vietcong were planning just such an attack.

Communist Assault Shocks Americans

In early 1968, U.S. officials anticipated a communist offensive. As expected, on January 21, the North Vietnamese Army hit Khe Sanh in northwest South Vietnam. However, nine days later, the communists expanded their attack by hitting U.S. and ARVN positions throughout South Vietnam. The **Tet Offensive**—named after the Vietnamese lunar new year—was a coordinated assault on 36 provincial capitals and 5 major cities, as well as the U.S. embassy in Saigon.

The communists planned to take and hold the cities until the urban population took up arms in their support. They thought the Tet Offensive had a good chance of ending the war. The fighting was fierce, but in the end, American and South Vietnamese forces repelled the offensive, and there was no popular uprising against the government of South Vietnam. Although U.S. forces won a tactical victory by preventing the Vietcong and North Vietnamese Army from achieving their primary objectives, the Tet Offensive was a strategic blow to the Americans. It demonstrated that the communists had not lost the will or the ability to fight on.

War's End Is Nowhere in Sight

After the Tet Offensive, American military leaders seemed less confident of a quick end to the war. When Westmoreland requested more troops, President Johnson asked his new Secretary of Defense Clark Clifford to take an objective look at the military and political situation in Vietnam. The deeper Clifford delved into the matter, the more pessimistic he became. Sending more troops would <u>inevitably</u> require raising taxes, increasing draft rolls, and calling up reserves. It would lead to increased casualties in the field and dissent at home. And it still might not lead to victory. Clifford concluded that the President should radically shift U.S. policy from one that pursued victory to one that pursued a negotiated peace.

Johnson Steps Down

While Clifford deliberated, many Americans began to turn dramatically against the war. Some marched in protest and engaged in antiwar activities. Others registered their disapproval at the polls. In early

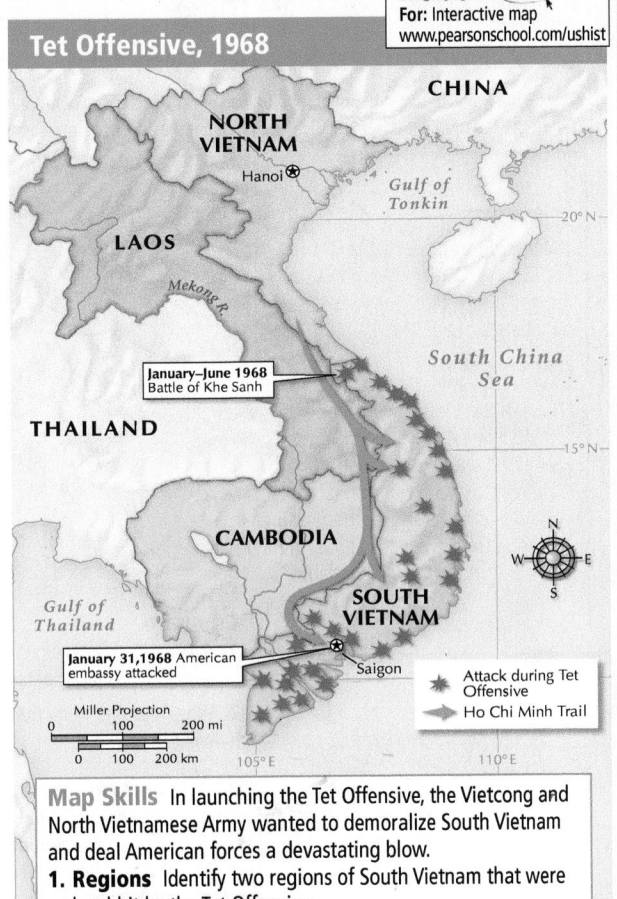

Geography *Interactive*
For: Interactive map
www.pearsonschool.com/ushist

Tet Offensive, 1968

CHINA

NORTH VIETNAM
Hanoi ⊛

Gulf of Tonkin

20° N

LAOS

Mekong R.

THAILAND

South China Sea

January–June 1968
Battle of Khe Sanh

15° N

CAMBODIA

Gulf of Thailand

SOUTH VIETNAM

January 31, 1968 American embassy attacked

Saigon ⊛

★ Attack during Tet Offensive
➤ Ho Chi Minh Trail

Miller Projection
0   100   200 mi
0   100   200 km

105° E   110° E

Map Skills In launching the Tet Offensive, the Vietcong and North Vietnamese Army wanted to demoralize South Vietnam and deal American forces a devastating blow.

1. Regions Identify two regions of South Vietnam that were hard-hit by the Tet Offensive.

2. Draw Conclusions How do you think the Tet Offensive affected the morale of North Vietnam? Explain.

Vocabulary Builder
<u>inevitable</u>–(ihn EHV ih tuh buhl) *adj.* certain to happen

---

Tet Offensive Is the Turning Point

L3

Instruct

- **Introduce: Key Term** Ask students to find the key term **Tet Offensive** (in bold) in the text. Note that General Westmoreland reported to President Johnson in late 1967 that the Vietcong did not have the strength to launch a major attack. The **Tet Offensive** proved Westmoreland wrong. Ask students to predict how the offensive would affect U.S. goals in the war.

- **Teach** Using the Think-Write-Pair-Share strategy (TE, p. T23), have students discuss how the communists carried out the Tet Offensive in 1968 and why the attacks shocked U.S. officials. Ask **What did Defense Secretary Clifford recommend after the Tet Offensive?** *(pursuing a negotiated peace instead of victory)* **How was the Tet Offensive a turning point in the war?** *(The Tet Offensive demonstrated that the Vietcong were capable of mounting a large-scale attack and that they had not lost the will to fight. It also caused the United States to change its strategy to end the war from fighting for victory to pursuing a negotiated peace. Many Americans began to dramatically oppose the war.)* **How did the Tet Offensive influence the political process in the United States?** *(It led to Johnson's decision not to run for a second term.)*

- **Quick Activity** Have students access **www.pearsonschool.com/ushist** to use the Geography Interactive map and then answer the map skills questions in the text.

History Background

A Turning Point Despite huge casualties, the Tet Offensive turned the tide for North Vietnam. Communist forces attacked some 100 cities and military bases, including the embassy in Saigon. The battle convinced the American public that the war could not continue at current levels. Soon after, President Johnson announced that he would not run for reelection. When General Westmoreland requested 206,000 additional troops, Johnson refused and declared that bombing north of the 20th parallel would cease. This decision opened the way for negotiations with Hanoi. By October 1968, peace talks were underway, although it would be five more years before a cease-fire would be achieved.

Answers

Map Skills

1. the northeastern coast and the extreme south in and around Saigon

2. The morale of North Vietnam may have declined right after the offensive because the communist forces were repelled, and no popular uprising against the government of South Vietnam took place; however, when the North Vietnamese learned that the United States was not going to pursue victory but negotiate for peace, their morale may have improved.

Independent Practice

- Have students read Comparing Viewpoints feature and answer the questions that accompany it.

- To increase understanding of the differences of opinion concerning U.S. involvement in Vietnam, have students read *Viewpoints: Can the United States Win the War in Vietnam?* and complete the worksheet. Teaching Resources, **p. 22**

Monitor Progress

Circulate to make sure that students are not having difficulty completing their Viewpoints worksheets, and that they understand the points of view expressed about whether to continue the war in Vietnam.

Answers

Compare

1. when North Vietnam stops its campaign to destroy the Republic of Vietnam in the south

2. The conflict is a both a guerrilla war and a civil war, and the local population does not want to cooperate.

✔ The Tet Offensive was a victory for the United States because American and South Vietnamese troops kept the Vietcong and North Vietnamese from achieving their goals. It was a defeat because it showed that there was no end to the war in sight, forcing the United States to shift its policy from fighting for victory to pursuing a negotiated peace.

548 The Vietnam War Era

Can the United States Win the War in Vietnam?

Despite the war's growing unpopularity, Johnson was reluctant to withdraw from Vietnam. Some urged him to get out of "Kennedy's war." His own Cabinet was divided on the issue.

DEAN RUSK

Citing Chamberlain and Hitler as an example, Secretary of State Rusk opposed appeasement. He supported increased bombing and troops to force North Vietnam to negotiate a peace.

Primary Source

"If . . . North Vietnam will stop [its] campaign to destroy the Republic of Vietnam, the measures we are taking to assist South Vietnam . . . will no longer be necessary. . . . We see no necessity for international negotiations. . . . [W]e cannot [think of] any points that would be negotiable."
—Dean Rusk, 1963

GEORGE BALL

Undersecretary of State Ball urged President Johnson in 1965 to stop sending U.S. soldiers to Vietnam.

Primary Source

"No one can assure you that we can beat the Viet Cong . . . no matter how many . . . troops we deploy. No [ground forces] of whatever size can win a guerrilla war—which is at the same time a civil war . . . in jungle terrain in the midst of a population that refuses cooperation. . . ."
—George Ball, 1965

Compare

1. According to Rusk, when should the United States end its participation in the war?

2. Why does Ball think that Rusk's strategy will not work?

1968, Minnesota senator **Eugene McCarthy**, the antiwar candidate for the Democratic Party nomination, made a surprisingly strong showing in the New Hampshire primary. Sensing that Johnson was in a politically weakened position, New York's Democratic senator **Robert Kennedy** announced his candidacy for the presidency. Both McCarthy and Kennedy believed that the war had divided America and drained resources away from the fights against poverty and discrimination. What Johnson feared most was happening: The war was undermining his presidency.

On March 31, 1968, two months after the Tet Offensive, the President addressed the nation on television. He announced that America would limit its bombing of North Vietnam and seek a negotiated settlement to the war. Johnson then shocked the nation by announcing that he would not run for another term as President. The speech marked another turning point in the war. The fight for victory was over. Peace was now the official government policy.

✔ **Checkpoint** How was the Tet Offensive both a victory and a defeat for the United States?

Violence Rocks 1968 Presidential Race

Johnson's decision not to seek reelection in 1968 threw the presidential race wide open. Many Americans believed it provided an opportunity to enact fundamental political and social changes. They argued that the future of the country was at stake. It was a time of new ideas and new plans. But the optimism and high hopes of the early campaign would soon die amidst political infighting, violence, and assassination.

Connect to Your World

Decreasing Public Support In 1964, when the U.S. Congress overwhelmingly passed the Gulf of Tonkin Resolution, American public opinion was largely supportive. Americans saw the Vietnam War as a part of the larger Cold War struggle against communism. But the Tet Offensive in 1968 inflamed the fears of many that the government was not forthcoming about conditions in Vietnam. As the war continued, public support continued to decline. Five years later, when the U.S. military involvement ended, many believed that the United States should have withdrawn sooner.

Today, comparisons have been drawn between the Vietnam War and the war in Iraq. Public support for the war in Iraq started out high, just as it did for the Vietnam War. However, as the war progressed and casualties mounted, support began to decline. The decline in support for the war in Iraq was faster than it was during the Vietnam War. One reason for this may be that some Americans do not consider the war in Iraq to be part of a larger principled conflict, like the Vietnam War.

Chicago 1968:
Politics and Protest

HUMPHREY *Unity* **RESPONSIBLE LEADERSHIP** for **PRESIDENT** in '68

A breath of fresh air.
Gene McCarthy

As Democrats prepared to select a new presidential candidate at their convention in Chicago (see campaign artifacts at left), antiwar activists converged on the city in August 1968. Inside the main hall, dissension between hawks and doves in the party sparked angry outbursts. On the streets outside, violent clashes broke out between antiwar protesters and the Chicago police. The crowds chanted, "The whole world is watching! The whole world is watching!" And indeed it was. Television viewers saw a vivid display of the political strife and social unrest besieging America.

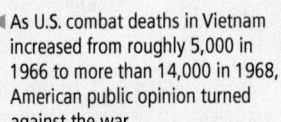

Opposition to the Vietnam War

In view of the developments since we entered the fighting in Vietnam, do you think the United States made a mistake sending troops to fight in Vietnam?

	March 1966	April 1967	April 1968
Yes	26%	37%	48%
No	59%	50%	40%
Don't Know	16%	13%	12%

SOURCE: American Institute of Public Opinion (Gallup Poll)

◄ As U.S. combat deaths in Vietnam increased from roughly 5,000 in 1966 to more than 14,000 in 1968, American public opinion turned against the war.

▲ Chicago mayor Richard J. Daley shouts insults at Senator Abraham Ribicoff during the senator's speech criticizing the tactics of the Chicago police.

Many protesters sought only ► to exercise their right to free speech. Others, aware of the ever-present television cameras, attracted a police response. Here, a melee erupts outside a hotel where delegates are gathered.

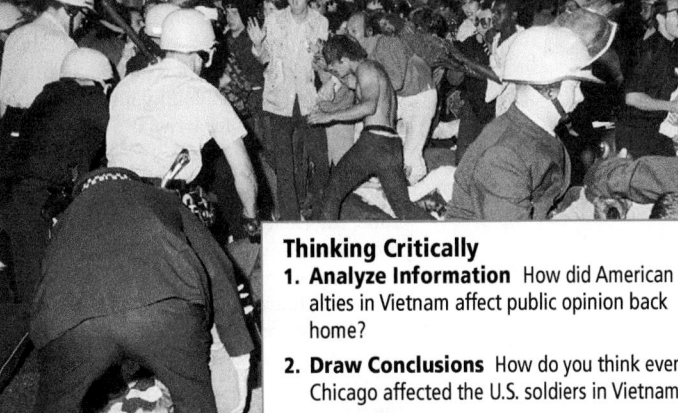

Thinking Critically

1. **Analyze Information** How did American casualties in Vietnam affect public opinion back home?

2. **Draw Conclusions** How do you think events in Chicago affected the U.S. soldiers in Vietnam?

Violence Rocks 1968 Presidential Race **L3**

Instruct

- **Introduce** Write the names Eugene McCarthy and Robert Kennedy on the board. Have students create charts to list the facts that they recall about each person and how he relates to the 1968 presidential race. Then, ask students to skim this blue heading for other people linked with the 1968 presidential race to add to the chart.

- **Teach** Using the Idea Wave strategy (TE, p. T22), have students review important events before, during, and after the 1968 election and discuss their significance. Ask **What tragic events occurred in the spring and summer of 1968?** *(the assassinations of civil rights leader Martin Luther King, Jr., and Democratic presidential candidate Robert Kennedy)* Direct students to the Infographic on this page. Review the images, and read the captions. Have students read the chart and describe what it shows about opposition to the war. Ask **How did the Democratic Convention compare with the Republican Convention?** *(Violent protests took place outside the Democratic Convention. By contrast, the Republican Convention was peaceful.)* **Why do you think antiwar protesters attended the Democratic Convention in Chicago?** *(President Johnson was a Democrat who led the United States into the Vietnam War. The protesters wanted to ensure that the next Democratic candidate knew that there was major opposition to the war.)*

- **Analyzing the Visuals** Have students examine the photographs of the campaign artifacts on this page. Ask **Why did Nixon call his supporters the "silent majority"?** *(Sample response: Nixon called his supporters the "silent majority" because they were middle class, conservative Americans who supported Nixon and who did not oppose the war.)*

Differentiated Instruction **Solutions for All Learners**

L1 Special Needs Students **L2 English Language Learners** **L2 Less Proficient Readers**

To help students understand the 1968 presidential election and its outcome, have pairs of students work together to create three-column charts summarizing information about each candidate. In each column, have students list the name of the candidate, his political party, and describe who might have voted

for him and give reasons why. Then, ask students to use their charts to write paragraphs summarizing the 1968 presidential election. Students should name the candidate who won the election and examine why that candidate won. Invite volunteers to read their paragraphs to the class.

Answers

Thinking Critically

1. Public opinion turned against the war.

2. Possible response: Some soldiers may have questioned why they were fighting in Vietnam.

Have students access **www.pearsonschool.com/ushist** to use the Geography Interactive map and then answer the map skills questions in the text. Direct students' attention to the map. Ask **Why does New York, a relatively small state, have more electoral votes than Texas, a much larger state?** *(Electoral votes are based on population, not land size. New York has a larger population than Texas does.)*

Monitor Progress

Circulate to make sure that students understand that the map shows how U.S. citizens voted in the 1968 election.

Presidential Election of 1968

Geography *Interactive*
For: Interactive map
www.pearsonschool.com/ushist

Candidate (Party)	Electoral Vote	Popular Vote	% Electoral Vote	% Popular Vote**
☐ Richard M. Nixon (Republican)	301	31,710,470	56	43.6
☐ Hubert H. Humphrey (Democratic)	191	30,898,055	36	42.5
☐ George C. Wallace (American Independent)	46	9,906,473	8	13.6

*One Nixon elector voted outside the party's endorsement
**Minor parties received 0.3% of the popular vote

Map Skills In 1968, Richard Nixon defeated Vice President Hubert Humphrey and third-party candidate George Wallace, who had split from the Democratic Party.

1. **Regions** From where did Wallace draw most of his support?

2. **Draw Conclusions** What might have happened if Wallace had renounced his candidacy and rejoined the Democratic ranks?

Two Leaders Fall In the spring and summer of the campaign season, bullets struck down two Americans who spoke out eloquently for peace in Vietnam and peaceful change in American society. Martin Luther King, Jr., the most prominent leader of the civil rights movement, had publicly turned against the war in 1967. He contributed compelling social and moral reasons to the argument for peace. But his voice was tragically silenced on April 4, 1968, when a racist assassin shot and killed him in Memphis, Tennessee.

Robert Kennedy was the next leader to fall. He had based his campaign for the presidency on compassion and idealism, and millions of Americans rallied to his camp. On June 5, 1968, at a rally celebrating his victory in the California primary, Kennedy asserted that "we are a great country, an unselfish country, a compassionate country," and that he intended "to make that the basis of my running." Minutes later, a Palestinian immigrant named Sirhan Sirhan shot Kennedy in the head, killing him instantly. Sirhan may have wanted revenge for America's support for Israel in that country's war with Egypt the year before.

Protesters Disrupt Chicago Democratic Convention The murders of King and Kennedy cast a dark shadow over the election campaigns. In August 1968, the Democrats convened in Chicago to choose a presidential candidate to represent their party in the November election. As the delegates arrived, so too did antiwar protesters. Chicago's mayor deployed police and members of the National Guard to prevent any outbreaks of violence.

Inside the convention, the Democrats angrily debated placing an antiwar plank in the party platform. They chose Hubert Humphrey, Johnson's Vice President, over Eugene McCarthy, who had garnered support from many antiwar groups. As the delegates cast their votes, violence erupted outside the convention between police and protesters. After police beat activists with nightsticks, some protesters retaliated by throwing rocks and bottles at the onrushing tide of police.

Differentiated Instruction Solutions for All Learners

L4 Advanced Readers   L4 Gifted and Talented Students

Have students form small groups to create election-night newscasts, using information from the visual on this page and from the information presented under the blue heading "Violence Rocks 1968 Presidential Race." Students should include commentary on the events of 1968 in addition to election results in their coverage of election night. Groups should divide up tasks for the newscast: writing copy, creating visuals, and reading copy. Have students rehearse their broadcast and then perform it for the class.

Answers

Map Skills

1. the South

2. Sample responses: The Democratic candidate, Hubert Humphrey, might have become President; Nixon might have won by a greater margin because more conservative Democrats from the South might have voted Republican in the election.

The television coverage of the fierce fighting in the streets and bitter arguments on the convention floor shocked Americans. Chaos and civil disorder appeared to have replaced civil debate in the political arena. The divisions and violence in Chicago mirrored the deep divisions in American politics and the heartbreaking violence on the front lines in Vietnam.

Richard Nixon Wins the Presidency At a much more peaceful convention in Miami, Republicans nominated Richard M. Nixon, who promised if elected he would deliver "peace with honor." He wanted the United States out of Vietnam, but he also demanded honorable peace terms. He promised to listen to "the great, quiet forgotten majority—the nonshouters and the nondemonstrators." This large group of Americans, described by one commentator as "the young, the unblack, and the unpoor," was dubbed the "silent majority." Throughout his campaign, Nixon used a "southern strategy" of courting more conservative southern voters with appeals to law and order, striving to pull them away from their traditional support of the Democratic Party.

Alabama governor George Wallace also ran for the presidency on a third-party ticket. A lifelong Democrat prior to his entry into the race, Wallace said that neither of the traditional political parties represented southern voters who were unsettled by the cultural and social changes in the country. He had no sympathy for the demands of antiwar radicals, counterculture hippies, or African American militants. He represented the "white backlash" against the civil rights movement and the desire to press forward to victory in Vietnam.

The combination of Nixon's "southern strategy" and Wallace's third-party candidacy siphoned traditionally Democratic votes away from Humphrey. In a close election, Nixon captured victory by winning 43.6 percent of the popular vote and 301 electoral votes. Humphrey received 42.5 percent of the popular vote and Wallace 13.6 percent. The election marked the end of the Democratic "Solid South" and signaled significant changes in the nation's political landscape. Richard Nixon's ascendancy marked a new Republican domination of the American presidency.

✔️ **Checkpoint** What happened at the 1968 Democratic Convention in Chicago?

"Silent" Supporters
In 1969, President Nixon called his supporters the "silent majority." Especially strong in the South and West, the silent majority consisted of patriotic veterans of World War II and the Korean War, middle class blue-collar workers, conservative young Americans, and many others.

SECTION 3 Assessment

Progress Monitoring Online
For: Self-test with vocabulary practice
www.pearsonschool.com/ushist

Comprehension

1. **Terms and People** For each item below, write a sentence explaining its significance.
   - draftee
   - "credibility gap"
   - Tet Offensive
   - Eugene McCarthy

2. **NoteTaking Reading Skill: Recognize Sequence** Use your flowchart to answer the Section Focus Question: How did the American war effort in Vietnam lead to rising protests and social divisions back home?

Writing About History

3. **Quick Write: Answer Opposing Arguments** To write a strong persuasive essay, you need to address arguments that could be raised to refute your own position. Choose a topic from this section, such as whether Johnson made the right decision by withdrawing from the 1968 presidential race. Then, create a chart listing arguments on both sides of the debate.

Critical Thinking

4. **Evaluate Information** Identify three factors that led to the growth of the antiwar movement. Which do you think was the most important?

5. **Identify Effects** How did the military outcome of the Tet Offensive differ from its impact on the American people?

6. **Draw Conclusions** What were the chief weaknesses of the Democrats in the 1968 election? How did these weaknesses aid the election of Richard Nixon?

SECTION

4

Objectives

As you teach this section, keep students focused on the following objectives to help them answer the Section Focus Question and master core content.

- Assess Nixon's new approach to the war, and explain why protests continued.
- Explain what led to the Paris Peace Accords and why South Vietnam eventually fell to the communists.
- Evaluate the impact of the Vietnam War on the United States.

▲ Antiwar demonstrators march in Washington, D.C.

Antiwar Protests Spread

As Richard Nixon entered the White House in January 1969, students across the country continued to protest the war. And their words were starting to reach ordinary Americans, not just "long-haired radicals." In late 1969, antiwar protesters organized a series of peaceful demonstrations called "moratoriums." On October 15, the mayor of New York City addressed a crowd of these protesters:

❝We cannot [accept] the charge from Washington that this peaceful protest is unpatriotic. We heard that charge five years ago and three years ago. . . . The fact is that this dissent is the highest form of patriotism. It is the peaceful American way to turn the nation away from a self-defeating course.❞
—New York mayor John Lindsay, 1969

The War's End and Impact

Prepare to Read

Background Knowledge ⓛ

Remind students that the United States decided to pursue a negotiated peace in Vietnam rather than victory. Ask students to predict the effects of a war that ends without victory.

Set a Purpose ⓛ

- **WITNESS HISTORY** Read the selection aloud.

  Ask **What does Mayor Lindsay consider the highest form of patriotism?** (*peaceful protest of a government's policies*) **Why does he call it the highest form?** (*because its goal is to turn government away from a wrong decision or course of action*)

- **Focus** Point out the Section Focus Question, and write it on the board. Tell students to refer to this question as they read. (*Answer appears with Section 4 Assessment answers.*)

- **Preview** Have students preview the Section Objectives and the list of Terms and People.

- **NoteTaking** Using the Guided Questioning strategy (TE, p. T20), have students read this section. As they read, have students compare and contrast the Vietnam policies of Nixon and Johnson. Reading and Note Taking Study Guide

Objectives

- Assess Nixon's new approach to the war, and explain why protests continued.
- Explain what led to the Paris Peace Accords and why South Vietnam eventually fell to the communists.
- Evaluate the impact of the Vietnam War on the United States.

Terms and People

Vietnamization	Paris Peace Accords
My Lai	War Powers Act
Pentagon Papers	

NoteTaking

Reading Skill: Compare and Contrast
Note the similarities and differences between Nixon's Vietnam policy and that of Lyndon Johnson.

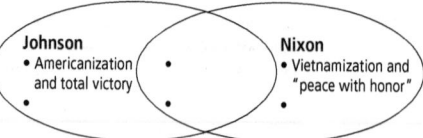

Johnson
- Americanization and total victory
- •

Nixon
- Vietnamization and "peace with honor"

Why It Matters As a presidential candidate, Richard Nixon promised "peace with honor" and an end to a war that had fractured American society. Nixon did indeed withdraw American troops, and the Vietnam War finally ended. But the impact of the war endured. As the nation recovered from war, Americans reexamined the struggle against communism, the power of the presidency, and America's role in the world. **Section Focus Question: How did the Vietnam War end, and what were its lasting effects?**

Nixon Starts the Pullout

Nixon's defenders argued that he was a hard-working patriot with a new vision for America. His critics charged that he was a deceitful politician bent on acquiring power and punishing his enemies. There were elements of truth to both views. But defenders and critics alike agreed that Richard Nixon was a determined man with abundant political talent. From his first day in office, the new President realized that ending the Vietnam War was the key to everything else he hoped to achieve.

Peace Talks Stall Though formal peace talks between the warring parties had begun in May 1968, they were bogged down from the outset by disagreements and a lack of compromise. When Richard Nixon took office in January 1969, his peace delegation firmly believed they could break the impasse. The Americans and South Vietnamese wanted all communist troops out of South Vietnam.

Vocabulary Builder

Use the information below and the following resource to teach students the high-use word from this section. Teaching Resources, Vocabulary Builder, p. 11

High-Use Word	Definition and Sample Sentence
induce	*v.* to bring about; cause
	The bombing of Pearl Harbor **induced** President Roosevelt to ask Congress to declare war.

They also wanted prisoners of war (POWs) returned. Meanwhile, the North Vietnamese demanded an immediate American withdrawal from Vietnam and the formation of a coalition government in South Vietnam that would include representatives from the Vietcong. Still hoping to win the war in the field, North Vietnam refused to budge from its initial position. And South Vietnam refused to sign any agreement that compromised its security.

Nixon's Plan: Vietnamization and Peace With Honor President Nixon refused to accept the North Vietnamese peace terms. He was committed to a policy of "peace with honor" and believed that there were still military options. He continued a gradual pullout of American troops, and expressed faith in the ability of the Army of the Republic of Vietnam to assume the burden of war. He called his approach **Vietnamization**—U.S. forces would withdraw as ARVN troops assumed more combat duties. The hope was that with continued American aid behind the front lines, the ARVN would fight its own battles to secure South Vietnam.

To reduce the flow of communist supplies to the Vietcong, Nixon ordered the secret bombing of the Ho Chi Minh Trail in Cambodia. This was a controversial move because it widened the scope of the war and helped to undermine the neutral government in Cambodia. In the end, neither Vietnamization nor secret bombings dramatically improved South Vietnam's chances of winning a war against the communists.

✔ **Checkpoint** How did Vietnamization differ from the war policies of Nixon's predecessors?

Troubles on the Home Front Intensify

Nixon inherited two things from Lyndon Johnson: an unpopular war and a vocal American opposition to it. The new President wanted "peace with honor," security for America's ally South Vietnam, and international respect for U.S. foreign policy. Antiwar activists wanted the war ended and American troops out of Vietnam—on any terms. Nixon found it increasingly difficult to achieve his goals and satisfy the snowballing antiwar movement.

American Troops in Cambodia More than a year into office, Nixon had grown impatient with the snail's pace of the peace negotiations. In 1970, he attempted to break the stalemate by ordering a ground attack on North Vietnamese Army and Vietcong bases in Cambodia. Nixon also hoped to aid the pro-American Cambodian government in its fight against the Khmer Rouge, a communist movement supported by North Vietnam.

On the evening of April 30, Nixon addressed the American people, informing them of his decision to carry the war into Cambodia. He stressed that the war had become a measure of how committed the United States was to preserving freedom around the world:

Primary Source "If, when the chips are down, the world's most powerful nation, the United States of America, acts like a pitiful, helpless giant, the forces of totalitarianism and anarchy will threaten free nations . . . throughout the world."
—President Richard Nixon, 1970

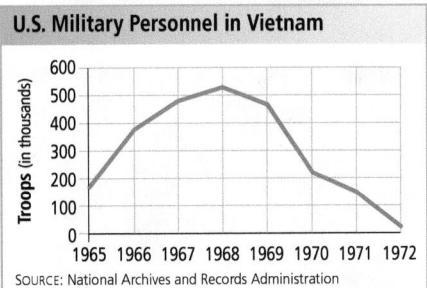

U.S. Military Personnel in Vietnam

Troops (in thousands)

SOURCE: National Archives and Records Administration

Vietnamizing the War
The United States scaled back its commitment of ground troops to Vietnam after 1968. However, while more American troops left for home, U.S. air forces dropped more bombs on communist targets in North Vietnam and along the Ho Chi Minh Trail. *How did the shift in American tactics ensure Nixon's "peace with honor"?*

Nixon Starts the Pullout Ⓛ3

Instruct

- **Introduce: Key Term** Ask students to find the key term *Vietnamization* (in bold) in the text. Then, write the term on the board, say it aloud, have students say it with you, and provide the definition. Have students contrast Nixon's plan for Vietnamization with President Johnson's Americanization of the war.

- **Teach** Using the Numbered Heads strategy (TE, p. T23), have students discuss the steps Nixon took to end the war in Vietnam. Ask **What was the status of the Paris Peace talks when Nixon took office?** *(They had reached an impasse.)* **What did the secret bombing of the Ho Chi Minh Trail indicate about Nixon's plan for peace?** *(He had not given up military options for ending the war, and he did not want the communists to take over South Vietnam.)*

- **Analyzing the Visuals** Have students examine the photograph of the U.S. bomber. Ask **Why was the U.S. strategy to bomb the Ho Chi Minh Trail risky?** *(It brought the war to Cambodia and forced the Cambodian government to choose sides in the war.)*

Independent Practice

Have students make a chart listing the contrasting demands of North Vietnam and South Vietnam at the peace talks.

Monitor Progress

As students fill in their Venn diagrams, circulate to make sure that they understand the similarities and differences between the Vietnam policies of the two Presidents. For a completed version of the Venn diagram, see Note Taking Transparencies, **B-136a.**

Answers

✔ Instead of sending more troops to Vietnam, Vietnamization pulled U.S. troops out of the country and gave more combat duties to the South Vietnamese.

Caption It brought U.S. troops home but did not ease military pressure on the Vietcong or allow the communists to take over South Vietnam.

Troubles on the Home Front Intensify

Instruct

- **Introduce: Key Term** Ask students to find the term Kent State University in the text. Ask students to predict why Kent State University is discussed in this subsection. *(Possible answer: Students there protested against the war.)* Tell students that they will learn how an antiwar demonstration at Kent State ended in tragedy.

- **Teach** Use a concept map to organize main ideas of the text under the blue heading "Troubles on the Home Front Intensify." Write "Troubles on the Home Front" in the center of the map and "Cambodia," "Kent State University," "Jackson State University," "My Lai," and "Pentagon Papers" in ovals connected to the center. Have students write a sentence describing the importance of each subtopic. Then, add these descriptions to the map. Ask students to discuss how these troubles intensified opposition in the United States to the Vietnam War.

- **Quick Activity** Display Color Transparency: *Protesting the Vietnam War.* Use the lesson suggested in the transparency book to guide a discussion of American participation in demonstrations against the war.
Color Transparencies **A-127**

The next morning, U.S. and ARVN forces crossed the border into Cambodia. These soldiers captured large stockpiles of weapons and supplies, but they did not break the stalemate. North Vietnam remained determined to have peace on its terms or no peace at all.

Violence Erupts at Kent State The Cambodian incursion had a profound impact on the peace movement at home. It stirred antiwar activists, who argued that Nixon had widened the war and made the world a more dangerous place. Throughout the country, college campuses erupted with protests. Several demonstrations prompted the police and National Guard to step in to preserve order.

On two campuses, confrontations between students and armed authorities led to deaths. Four days after Nixon's speech, demonstrators at Kent State University in Ohio threw rocks and bottles at members of the National Guard. When one guardsman thought he heard a sniper's shot, he fired his rifle. The shot prompted other National Guardsmen to discharge a volley of gunfire into a group of protesters, killing four youths. The Kent State killings led to demonstrations on other campuses. At Jackson State University, a traditionally African American college in Mississippi, a confrontation between students and police ended with two students dead.

College demonstrations against the war sometimes prompted counterprotests by Americans who supported the President. In response to a May 8, 1970, antiwar rally in downtown New York City, construction workers decided to demonstrate, carrying American flags and chanting "All the Way USA." Believing that some anti-

Protest and Death in Ohio

A student photographer at Kent State snapped this photograph moments after the Ohio National Guard opened fire on student protesters on May 4, 1970. *How do you think people reacted to seeing this photograph in the newspaper?*

L4 Advanced Learners   L4 Gifted and Talented Students

Soon after the Kent State shootings, the musician Neil Young composed the song "Ohio," which was recorded by the rock group Crosby, Stills, Nash, and Young. Its lyrics captured the shock many Americans felt after the shootings. Over the course of the Vietnam War, some songs supported the war effort; others opposed it. Many songs told the stories of the soldiers who fought in the war. Long after the war had ended, artists such as Bruce Springsteen and

Billy Joel continued to write and sing about it. The Vietnam War compelled many people to think and talk about the causes and consequences of warfare.

Have students find recordings of songs written about the Vietnam War and related events of the 1960s and 1970s. Suggest that students locate a sampling that presents different views. Have students play the songs for the class. Invite students to share ideas about the feelings expressed in the songs.

Answer

Caption Sample answer: They were shocked that college students protesting the war were killed.

war demonstrators had spit on the American flag, they pushed into the crowd and started hitting protesters. The clash drew national attention. Days later, thousands of construction workers, businessmen, secretaries, and housewives marched peacefully through Manhattan's streets in support of Nixon and the war effort. One man expressed his feelings about the march:

Primary Source "I'm very proud to be an American, and I know my boy that was killed in Vietnam would be here today if he was alive, marching with us. . . . I know he died for the right cause, because in his letters he wrote to me he knew what he was fighting for: to keep America free. . . ."
—Robert Geary, May 20, 1970

As the fighting continued in Vietnam, the American home front became its own physical and emotional battlefield.

American Soldiers Kill Civilians at My Lai In 1971, two events increased the pressure on Nixon to pull U.S. troops out of Vietnam. The first event had roots in a U.S. action in South Vietnam three years earlier. On March 16, 1968, American forces searching for enemy troops in an area with a strong Vietcong presence came upon the village of **My Lai.** By this point in the war, many American troops had been injured and killed by Vietcong fighters posing as civilians. It was a recipe for disaster at My Lai, where Lieutenant William Calley's unit began shooting and killing unarmed civilians. During the assault, U.S. soldiers killed between four and five hundred Vietnamese.

Lt. Calley later maintained that he was following orders, but many of the soldiers present did not participate in the massacre. At least one risked his own life to stop it. The tragedy was made even worse by an inadequate military investigation of the incident. *Life* magazine eventually published photos taken during the event, and in March 1971, a military court convicted Lt. Calley of his participation in the attack. News of the My Lai massacre, the coverup, and Calley's trial shocked many Americans and added fuel to the burning antiwar fire.

Pentagon Papers Undermine Public Trust On the heels of My Lai came the 1971 publication of the **Pentagon Papers** in *The New York Times.* The term referred to a classified government history of America's involvement in Vietnam. The study was leaked to *The Times* by one of its coauthors, Daniel Ellsberg. Nixon tried to block the full publication, but in *New York Times* v. *United States,* the Supreme Court ruled against the administration. The study revealed that American leaders involved the U.S. in Vietnam without fully informing the American people and occasionally even lied to Congress.

✓ **Checkpoint** What happened at Kent State and Jackson State universities in 1970?

The War Finally Ends

The failings of Vietnamization and growing dissent at home forced President Nixon to search for some final way out of the conflict. A 1971 public-opinion poll revealed that two thirds of Americans favored withdrawing American troops, even if it meant a communist takeover of South Vietnam. Sensitive to the public mood, Congress pressed Nixon to bring the troops home. Many believed that to win reelection in 1972, he had to end the war.

Slaughter and Coverup in South Vietnam
A photographer captured the terror in the village of My Lai as American troops were killing hundreds of civilians. The massacre was followed by a military investigation, but only Lt. William Calley was convicted. *Why were many Americans dissatisfied with the result of the military investigation?*

History Background

The Pentagon Papers The Pentagon Papers comprised a 47-volume study of U.S. involvement in Vietnam. The study was commissioned in 1967 by Robert McNamara and completed in 1969 by a team of analysts that included Daniel Ellsberg. Ellsberg, who came to oppose the war while working on the project, leaked portions of the papers to *The New York Times* reporter Neil Sheehan. The documents traced U.S. decision-making regarding Vietnam from the Truman years through the Johnson administration. The documents revealed that President Johnson had been sending troops to Vietnam and had plans for waging war there long before the incident that led to the Gulf of Tonkin Resolution, and that the resolution itself had been drafted prior to the incident. Although the papers did not implicate the Nixon administration, it took steps to block publication of the classified documents, citing national security concerns, and was briefly successful. On June 30, 1971, however, the Supreme Court ruled that free speech superseded other concerns and allowed the newspapers to continue making the material public.

Independent Practice
- Ask students to read the Primary Source quotation from Robert Geary. Have them write paragraphs responding to Geary's comments and explaining whether they agree or disagree with his point of view.
- Have students examine the photographs on this and the previous page. Ask each student to choose one of the photos and write a paragraph describing the emotions of the people shown, as well as his or her own reaction to the image.

Monitor Progress
Circulate to make sure that students understand why Americans supported and opposed the Vietnam War.

Answers

✓ Students who were protesting the war were killed during confrontations with the National Guard and police.

Caption The military investigation was thought to be inadequate.

The War Finally Ends L3

Instruct

- **Introduce** Draw a cause-and-effect diagram that has boxes for four causes, with arrows pointing to this single effect: President Nixon looks for a way to end the Vietnam War. Have students read the introductory paragraph under the blue heading "The War Finally Ends" and identify four causes of the effect in the diagram.

- **Teach** Discuss the Paris Peace Accords and their aftermath. Ask **What did the United States have to do under the terms of the agreement?** *(withdraw its troops from South Vietnam)* **What was the ultimate effect of the withdrawal of American troops?** *(South Vietnam fell to the communists and was unified with North Vietnam.)* Have students predict how the terms of the Paris Peace Accords might have affected domestic issues in the United States.

- **Analyzing the Visuals** Draw students' attention to the Infographic. Ask them to describe each image and explain what it tells them about the experiences of Vietnam veterans.

Independent Practice

To enhance appreciation of the experiences of American soldiers during and shortly after the Vietnam War, have students read *Link to Literature: Night Patrol* and complete the worksheet. Teaching Resources, **p. 23**

Monitor Progress

To confirm students' understanding, ask them to summarize how the war ended.

Answer

✓ The United States agreed to withdraw its troops from South Vietnam and to exchange POWs. The North Vietnamese would be allowed to stay in South Vietnam, and the NLF would become a legitimate political party there. The noncommunist government in South Vietnam would stay in power until there was a political settlement.

Vocabulary Builder
induce–(ihn DOOS) *v.* to bring about; cause

American Troops Leave Vietnam In October 1972, the United States and North Vietnam came to terms on a peace settlement. One month later, with lasting peace almost at hand, Nixon easily defeated the antiwar Democrat George McGovern for reelection. But Nixon's triumph was short-lived. The Vietnamese peace fell apart when North Vietnam refused to sign the agreement. Talks broke off, but renewed American bombing in North Vietnam finally induced the North Vietnamese to resume negotiations.

At last, in January 1973, the United States, South Vietnam, North Vietnam, and the Vietcong signed the **Paris Peace Accords.** The parties agreed to a cease-fire and a U.S. troop withdrawal from South Vietnam. POWs would be exchanged, but North Vietnamese troops would remain in South Vietnam. The National Liberation Front would become a legitimate political party in South Vietnam, and South Vietnam's noncommunist government would remain in power pending a political settlement. With the war ended, the last American troops came home. Among the returning soldiers were more than 550 POWs, most of whom were pilots shot down during the war.

Saigon Falls For the United States, the war in Vietnam was over. For the Vietnamese, however, it continued. Neither North nor South Vietnam honored the cease-fire or worked toward a diplomatic settlement of their differences. In the spring of 1975, minor fighting escalated when North Vietnam launched an offensive against the South. Without American aid and ground support, the ARVN was no match for the Soviet-supplied North Vietnamese Army. By the end of April, the communists had taken Saigon. After decades of fighting and millions of deaths, Vietnam was unified under one flag.

✓ **Checkpoint** What did the signing parties agree to in the Paris Peace Accords?

◄ A Purple Heart is awarded to members of the U.S. armed forces who are wounded or killed by an enemy in combat.

● **INFOGRAPHIC**

America's Veterans Return From Vietnam

In April 1973, a plane carrying the last American prisoners of war from Vietnam touched down in Hawaii. The flight marked the end of an era that had seen hundreds of thousands of American troops deployed to fight in the Vietnam War. The homecoming for many of these soldiers had been bittersweet. While some came home to exuberant family reunions and community parades, many Vietnam veterans received little or no public acknowledgment of their sacrifices. It was not until nearly a decade later that the nation dedicated the Vietnam Veterans Memorial (see photo at far right) to honor these brave Americans.

◄ A Vietnam veteran takes part in a 1973 parade in New York City to honor those who served in the war.

Some veterans, like this ► man in San Francisco in 1994, faced hard times after they reentered American society.

Connect to Your World

Modern Vietnam Vietnam's official name today is the Socialist Republic of Vietnam. In 1976, the two Vietnams—South and North—unified and became one nation under communist rule. That same year, Saigon, the former capital of South Vietnam, was renamed Ho Chi Minh City. After a period of isolation, especially from the West but also from China as a result of Vietnam's occupation of neighboring Cambodia, Vietnam was accepted as a member of the Association of Southeast Asian Nations (ASEAN) in 1995. In the same year the nation established diplomatic relations with its old enemy, the United States. Vietnam hoped for economic benefits from its new relationship with the United States, which had lifted an economic embargo against Vietnam in 1994. The United States hoped that its new relationship with Vietnam would help resolve the fate of more than 2,000 American soldiers who were still considered missing in action in Vietnam. Economically, the future is encouraging for Vietnam: poverty is declining and regulations have recently changed allowing greater export of clothing and textiles, one of the country's growth industries.

The Vietnam War Has a Lasting Impact

More than 58,000 American soldiers gave their lives serving their country in Vietnam; another 300,000 were wounded. Although figures are not exact, the Vietnamese death toll most likely exceeded 2 million. Peace, however, did not mean the end of pain and hardship. The end of the war created other problems in Southeast Asia. The war also affected American attitudes toward world affairs.

Southeast Asia Suffers Further Turmoil Many foreign-policy experts in the United States had predicted that if North Vietnam won the Vietnamese civil war, communism would spread to other nations in Southeast Asia. In a limited sense, they were right. Communist regimes eventually came to power in both Laos and Cambodia. In Cambodia, the ruling Khmer Rouge unleashed a genocide on the populace, killing everyone who had ties to the West or previous Cambodian governments. Between 1975 and 1979, upwards of 2 million Cambodians were executed or died in labor camps.

In an expanded sense, however, many American foreign-policy strategists misjudged the spread of communism. They concluded it was a monolithic global movement controlled by Moscow and Beijing. However, as the war's aftermath would attest, communist movements in Southeast Asia were nationalistic and intolerant of outside influences. In 1978, Vietnam invaded Cambodia and installed a pro-Vietnamese government. China supported the ousted Khmer Rouge. For more than ten years, the U.S. supported a coalition of anti-communist Cambodian opposition groups that included the Khmer Rouge.

Veterans Return Home to Mixed Reactions The war and the peace divided Americans. Some argued that the United States should never have entered the war and that their leaders had lied to them. Others countered that the war was part of an ongoing struggle against communism and that in the

The families of Americans still missing after the Vietnam War hope that those prisoners and missing will one day be returned to them. ▼

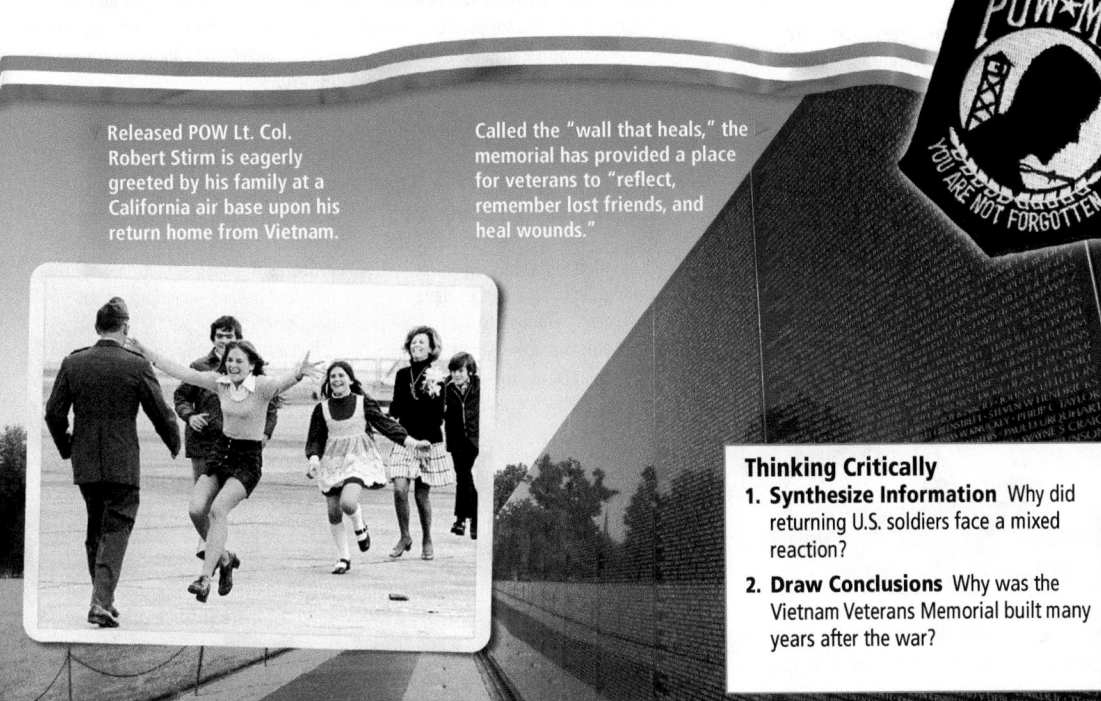

Released POW Lt. Col. Robert Stirm is eagerly greeted by his family at a California air base upon his return home from Vietnam.

Called the "wall that heals," the memorial has provided a place for veterans to "reflect, remember lost friends, and heal wounds."

Thinking Critically
1. **Synthesize Information** Why did returning U.S. soldiers face a mixed reaction?
2. **Draw Conclusions** Why was the Vietnam Veterans Memorial built many years after the war?

The Vietnam War Has a Lasting Impact

Instruct

- **Introduce: Key Term** Have students locate the key term *War Powers Act* (in bold). Tell students that they will learn about how the *War Powers Act* restricted the power of the President.

- **Teach** Use the Numbered Heads strategy (TE, p. T23) to review the impact of the Vietnam War. Ask **Where did communism spread in Southeast Asia after the Vietnam War?** *(Vietnam, Laos, and Cambodia)* **What ideas about the war might some veterans have found hurtful on their return?** *(that the United States should never have entered the war; that the United States betrayed South Vietnam by withdrawing)* **What effect did the Vietnam War have on the power of the President?** *(It led Congress to pass the War Powers Act, which restricted the President's power to take unilateral military action.)* Ask students to discuss whether the United States betrayed South Vietnam in the struggle against communism.

- **Quick Activity** Display Color Transparency: *The Vietnam Veterans Memorial*. Use the lesson suggested in the transparency book to guide a discussion of the memorial wall. Color Transparencies **A-128**

Independent Practice

NoteTaking Have students complete the concept web identifying the effects of the Vietnam War. Reading and Note Taking Study Guide

Monitor Progress

As students fill in their concept webs, circulate to make sure that they accurately identify the effects of the Vietnam War. For a completed version of the concept web, see Note Taking Transparencies, **B-136b**.

Answers

Thinking Critically
1. U.S. soldiers faced a mixed reaction because of the opposition to the war at home and because there had been no real victory for the United States in Vietnam.
2. The nation needed to heal, and Americans had not yet fully honored the service and memory of those who fought in Vietnam.

Objectives

- Trace America's involvement in world affairs throughout its history.
- Evaluate the effects of U.S. intervention in Afghanistan.

Background Knowledge L3

Ask students to name actual examples of American intervention in other countries. Then, have students discuss under what circumstances they think the United States should be involved in the affairs of other countries.

Instruct L3

Point out the timeline. Ask **In what way have Americans changed their view of the role of the United States in the world over the past 200 years?** *(In 1796, George Washington warned against joining foreign alliances. Today, the United States works with other countries to fight global terrorism.)*

Monitor Progress

- Have students complete the American Issues Journal worksheet, *America and the World.* Check students' work to make sure that they grasp the aspects of the issue. Teaching Resources, **pp. 15–18**

- Remind students to complete their American Issues Journal notes. Review their work for accuracy. Reading and Note Taking Study Guide

Answers

Transfer Activities

1. The first quotation suggests that intervention has created a more stable country. The second quotation says that the intervention did not change much in the country and that much of Afghanistan is not stable.

2. Possible answer: educating the people about democracy and adapting democracy to ways of life in Afghanistan

3. For more information about U.S. action in Afghanistan, have students access **www.pearsonschool.com/ushist**.

TRACK THE ISSUE

What is America's role in the world?

At times throughout its history, the United States has tried to avoid getting involved in other countries' affairs. At other times, it has played an active part in world affairs. Today, America is deeply involved around the world. But what should its role be? Use the timeline below to explore this enduring issue.

1796 Washington's Farewell Address
President Washington warns against foreign alliances.

1823 Monroe Doctrine
President Monroe tells Europe to stay out of the Americas.

1898 Spanish-American War
The United States defeats Spain and expands overseas.

1940s–1980s Cold War
The United States tries to stop the spread of communism around the world.

2000s War on Terrorism
The United States works with other countries to fight global terrorism.

Since 2001, Afghanistan has labored to remake its government into a stable democracy.

American soldiers fought in Vietnam during the Cold War.

DEBATE THE ISSUE

Intervention and Democracy In 2001, the United States invaded Afghanistan and toppled the Taliban government, ending Taliban support for terrorism. Since then, the United States has helped to rebuild Afghanistan. Can intervention bring progress to a country?

"The United States and Afghanistan have made great progress. . . . Together we have . . . worked to ensure that Afghanistan will never again be a safe haven for terrorists. The United States has supported the Afghan people as they have established a moderate, representative government."

—Joint Declaration of the United States-Afghanistan Strategic Partnership

"The [George W.] Bush administration has consistently labeled the invasion of [Afghanistan] a success. But reports from humanitarian organizations, United Nations officials and Afghanis themselves paint a very different picture—warlords dominate much of the country, the Taliban is still a force in many parts, and the illegal drug trade is flourishing."

—Seymour Hersh, journalist for *The New Yorker*

 TRANSFER Activities

1. **Compare** What does the first quotation say about the results of intervention? What does the second quotation say?

2. **Analyze** What kinds of challenges might leaders from both countries face as they work to create a functioning democratic government?

3. **Transfer** Use the following Web site to see a video, try a WebQuest, and write in your journal. www.pearsonschool.com/ushist

---

History Background

Afghanistan in the Twenty-first Century The Taliban regime, which controlled most of Afghanistan by the late 1990s, consisted of ultraconservative Islamic fundamentalists. The Taliban offered protection to Muslim extremists from all over the world, including Osama bin Laden, the mastermind of the September 11, 2001, attacks on the United States, and other members of al-Qaeda. When the Taliban refused to surrender bin Laden after the attacks, the United States and Great Britain launched bombing attacks, later supported by ground troops, and eventually toppled the Taliban. Under United Nations auspices, four Afghan factions formed an interim government, with the Pashtun leader Hamid Karzai as head. By 2004, Afghanistan had a constitution that set up a government with a president, a two-house legislature, and independent courts. Afghanistan held its first presidential election in 2004 and its first parliamentary election in 2005. Today, NATO troops and nearly 100,000 U.S. soldiers are stationed in Afghanistan to defend the Karzai government against Taliban and guerrilla forces.

end, the United States betrayed South Vietnam. An unfortunate result of the controversy was that the nation never fully expressed its appreciation to the returning veterans.

Overwhelmingly, the 2.5 million enlisted men who served in Vietnam did so with honor and distinction. Yet, unlike the soldiers that returned to the United States after World Wars I and II—the famed Doughboys and G.I. Joes—few Vietnam vets enjoyed the warmth and adulation of victory parades. In addition to the indifference that some veterans encountered, some also suffered from physical and psychological ailments for years when they returned home.

Not until almost a decade after the end of the war did Americans begin to fully honor the courage and sacrifice of these veterans. The Vietnam Veterans Memorial, dedicated in Washington, D.C., in 1982, stands as an eloquent testament to the men and women who served and died in Vietnam.

Vietnam Changes American Policies The war was costly both monetarily and in the human toll of shattered lives. The war also altered American domestic and foreign policies. Lyndon Johnson's Great Society campaign against poverty and racism fell victim to the conflict. Increasingly, between 1964 and 1968, Johnson could not pay for both the Vietnam War and the Great Society. Paying for more guns left less money to pay for textbooks, school lunches, and prenatal care.

Additionally, the war undermined Americans' trust in their leaders and fragmented the Cold War consensus on foreign affairs. In 1973, Congress passed the **War Powers Act.** The act restricted the President's war-making powers by requiring him to consult with Congress within 48 hours of committing American forces to a foreign conflict. The act was a congressional attempt to check the unilateral formation of American foreign policy and stop the growth of the "imperial presidency."

Finally, the Vietnam War made Americans more suspicious of foreign commitments and less likely to intervene in the affairs of other countries. For the next 30 years, many Americans would view conflicts in Central America, Africa, the Balkans, and the Middle East through a lens tinted by the Vietnamese quagmire. The fear of "another Vietnam" had profound effects on American foreign policy in the postwar world.

✔ **Checkpoint** What did the War Powers Act do?

NoteTaking

Reading Skill: Recognize Effects As you read, use a concept web to identify the effects of the Vietnam War.

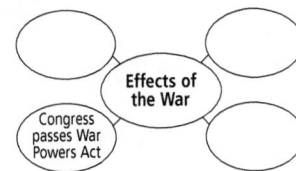

Effects of the War

Congress passes War Powers Act

SECTION 4 Assessment

Progress Monitoring Online
For: Self-test with vocabulary practice
www.pearsonschool.com/ushist

Comprehension

1. **Terms and People** For each term below, write a sentence explaining its significance.
   • Vietnamization
   • Paris Peace Accords
   • War Powers Act

2. **NoteTaking Reading Skill: Compare and Contrast** Use your Venn diagram to answer the Section Focus Question: How did the Vietnam War end, and what were its lasting effects?

Writing About History

3. **Quick Write: Choose Strongest Argument** Consider this thesis statement: Richard Nixon won the Vietnam War. List possible arguments for a persuasive essay that supports this thesis. Review each argument and choose the strongest one. Make sure that factual points from the text support your argument.

Critical Thinking

4. **Synthesize Information** How did Nixon redirect the peace process when he became President? Did his plan have the desired result?

5. **Explain Effects** What impact did the events of 1970 and 1971 have on Nixon's actions in Vietnam?

6. **Draw Conclusions** Which two effects of the Vietnam War do you think had the biggest long-term impact? Explain.

Assess and Reteach

Assess Progress L3

- Have students complete the Section Assessment.

- Administer the Section Quiz. Teaching Resources, p. 28

- To further assess student understanding, use Progress Monitoring Transparencies, 132.

Reteach

If students need more instruction, have them read the section summary.

Reading and Note Taking L3
Study Guide

Adapted Reading and L1 L2
Note Taking Study Guide

Spanish Reading and L2
Note Taking Study Guide

Extend L4

Have students read and complete the Enrichment worksheet, *Build a Model: The Vietnam Veterans Memorial.* Teaching Resources, pp. 13–14

Answer

✔ It restricted the President's war-making powers by requiring him to consult with Congress within 48 hours of committing U.S. troops to a foreign conflict.

Section 4 Assessment

1. Sentences should reflect an understanding of each item listed.

2. The Vietnam War ended with the United States withdrawing its troops from South Vietnam. The war's lasting effects included the communist takeover of South Vietnam, lack of recognition for Vietnam veterans, a long period of healing for the nation, restriction of the President's war-making powers, and distrust of leaders and hesitancy on the part of

the American public about intervening in the affairs of other countries.

3. Students' arguments should support the thesis with facts from the text.

4. Nixon pursued peace with honor by gradually pulling out troops and handing over more combat duties to the South Vietnamese. However, he did not rule out military options, and secretly bombed Cambodia. The plan was not successful in stopping the communists.

5. The events of 1970 and 1971 forced Nixon to find a way out of the war and

ultimately to agree to a complete withdrawal of U.S. troops.

6. Sample answer: Two effects of the Vietnam War that had the biggest long-term impact were the lack of recognition for Vietnam veterans and the long period of healing for the nation. Neither has been entirely resolved, even more than 30 years later.

For additional assessment, have students access **Progress Monitoring Online** at **www.pearsonschool.com/ushist**.

Chinese and American flags ▶

Objectives

As you teach this section, keep students focused on the following objectives to help them answer the Section Focus Question and master core content.

- Explain the thinking behind Richard Nixon's foreign policy.
- Define Nixon's foreign policy toward China and the Soviet Union.

Prepare to Read

Background Knowledge L3

Discuss how many Americans felt about the Cold War policy of containing communism after the Vietnam War. Have students predict how the Cold War policy of the United States might change after the Vietnam War.

Set a Purpose L3

- **WITNESS HISTORY** Read the selection aloud.

  Ask **What did Dulles want to show Zhou Enlai by not shaking his hand at Geneva?** *(that the United States did not approve of the communist regime in China)* **What did Nixon want to show by extending his hand to Zhou?** *(that the United States had a new approach toward China)*

- **Focus** Point out the Section Focus Question, and write it on the board. Tell students to refer to this question as they read. *(Answer appears with Section 5 Assessment answers.)*

- **Preview** Have students preview the Section Objectives and the list of Terms and People.

- **NoteTaking** Using the Paragraph Shrinking strategy (TE, p. T20), have students read this section. As they read, have students describe how Nixon dealt with China and the Soviet Union. Reading and Note Taking Study Guide

WITNESS HISTORY

A New Era Begins

When Richard Nixon visited the People's Republic of China in February of 1972, Premier Zhou Enlai greeted the President as he landed in Beijing. Once on the wind-swept tarmac, Nixon walked toward his host with his arm outstretched. Recalling John Foster Dulles's refusal to shake Zhou's hand at the Geneva Conference in 1954, Nixon made certain not to repeat the insult to the Chinese leader. Nixon remembered the occasion in his memoir:

❝When I reached the bottom step, therefore, I made a point of extending my hand as I walked toward him. When our hands met, one era ended and another began.❞

—Richard Nixon

▲Nixon and Zhou shake hands in China in 1972.

Nixon and the Cold War

Objectives

- Explain the thinking behind Richard Nixon's foreign policy.
- Define Nixon's foreign policy toward China and the Soviet Union.

Terms and People

Henry Kissinger
realpolitik
Zhou Enlai

Strategic Arms Limitation Treaty
détente

NoteTaking

Reading Skill: Categorize As you read, describe Nixon's Cold War foreign policies in dealing with China and the Soviet Union.

Nixon's Cold War Policies	
China	Soviet Union
• Normalization of relations will drive wedge between China and Soviet Union. • •	• Diplomacy with China will create Soviet fear of isolation. • •

Why It Matters As a presidential candidate, Richard Nixon had promised to end U.S. military involvement in the Vietnam War. Recognizing the potency of Soviet power and the increasing unwillingness of many Americans to pay the costs of containing communism everywhere, Nixon developed a new approach to the Cold War. His bold program redefined America's relations with the two titans of global communism, China and the Soviet Union. **Section Focus Question: How did Richard Nixon change Cold War diplomacy during his presidency?**

Nixon Redefines American Foreign Policy

During his years in office, Richard Nixon fundamentally reshaped the way the United States approached the world. Before Nixon took office, most American leaders shared a common Cold War ideology. They stressed that there existed a basic conflict between democratic, capitalist countries and totalitarian, communist ones. They divided the world into "us" and "them," and they established policies based on an assumption commonly held that "the enemy of my enemy is my friend." Therefore, a country opposed to communism was, by this definition, a friend of the United States. Nixon and **Henry Kissinger,** his leading adviser on national security and international affairs, altered this Cold War policy approach.

At first glance, Richard Nixon's partnership with Henry Kissinger seemed improbable. Nixon was a conservative California Republican, suspicious of the more liberal East Coast Republicans and exhausted with the political and strategic theories of Ivy League intellectuals. Kissinger was a Harvard-educated Jewish émigré from Germany and

Vocabulary Builder

Use the information below and the following resource to teach students the high-use word from this section. Teaching Resources, Vocabulary Builder, p. 11

High-Use Word	Definition and Sample Sentence
pragmatic	*adj.* practical; having to do with real actions and results rather than ideas and theories President Roosevelt's **pragmatic** approach to unemployment helped put many Americans back to work.

a prominent figure in East Coast intellectual circles. In several prior presidential campaigns, Kissinger had actually worked against Nixon. However, both men were outsiders, equipped with an outsider's readiness to question accepted orthodoxy.

In foreign affairs, Nixon and Kissinger embraced the idea of **realpolitik,** a German word meaning "real politics." According to realpolitik, political goals should be defined by concrete national interests instead of abstract ideologies. The two statesmen argued that if Americans would put aside their Cold War biases and look at the world with fresh eyes, U.S. global interests could be surveyed not in black and white but in shades of gray. For example, China and the Soviet Union—America's ideological enemies—could actually become excellent trading partners. At the same time, West Germany and Japan—America's ideological friends—were fast developing into economic rivals.

Nixon and Kissinger also questioned some lingering Cold War assumptions. For instance, they concluded that there was no united worldwide communist movement, as Lyndon Johnson and other Presidents had believed. There were important differences between the unique ideologies of the Soviet Union and China and other communist countries, such as Yugoslavia, North Korea, and North Vietnam, which often behaved quite independently. As President, Nixon insisted on a flexible, <u>pragmatic</u> foreign policy that avoided ideological absolutes.

> **Vocabulary Builder**
> <u>pragmatic</u>—(prag MAT ihk) *adj.* practical; having to do with real actions and results rather than ideas and theories

✓ **Checkpoint** How did Nixon and Kissinger reshape America's approach to foreign affairs?

Playing the China Card

From his first days in office, Nixon seemed determined to leave his mark on the nation's international affairs. Lyndon Johnson focused primarily on domestic affairs—the nuts and bolts of legislation and political deal-making. Nixon was more a man of the world, fascinated by global politics and shifting alliances. Johnson believed his Great Society would solidify his reputation as a great President. In stark contrast, Nixon thought his reorientation of American foreign policy would cement his legacy in the annals of United States history.

Reasons for Reaching Out to China "You're not going to believe this," a Nixon aide told a journalist in 1969, "but Nixon wants to recognize China." It was an odd, almost unbelievable, statement. At the time, the communist People's Republic of China was the most populous country in the world, but it was not officially recognized by the United States. Nor had it been admitted to the United Nations. The China that the United States recognized as the official representative body of the Chinese people was the Nationalist Chinese government exiled on the island of Taiwan. Nixon built his impressive career as a hard-line "Cold Warrior," a vigilant opponent of communism. He was the last politician Americans could imagine to extend the olive branch of recognition—and thus peace—to the communists.

Ever the political realist, Nixon knew that the People's Republic of China could not be ignored forever. He recognized that establishing diplomatic relations with the Chinese communists would benefit the United States. From an economic standpoint, improved relations would

HISTORY MAKERS

Henry Kissinger (b. 1923)

Born in Germany, Henry Kissinger came to the United States in 1938 when his family decided to flee the Nazis' growing persecution of Jews. After serving in the United States Army during World War II, he went to college. A brilliant student, Kissinger earned his bachelor's degree with highest honors and gained a Ph.D. at Harvard in just four years. Kissinger became a noted expert on national security and defense issues and soon impressed Richard Nixon with his foreign-policy analysis. When Nixon became President, he named Kissinger as his top national security adviser. The two worked closely together to end the Vietnam War, open relations with communist China, and shape the new diplomacy of détente with the Soviet Union. Nixon eventually named Kissinger his Secretary of State in 1973.

Playing the China Card/ Détente With the Soviet Union ⑬

Instruct

- **Introduce: Key Term** Ask students to find the key term *détente* (in bold) in the text. Explain that the term comes from French and means "calm" or "relaxation." Ask **How does the meaning of the word in French connect to Nixon's new Cold War strategies?** *(An aim of Nixon's policies was the relaxation of tensions between the United States and old Cold War adversaries.)*

- **Teach** Using the Think-Write-Pair-Share strategy (TE, p. T23), have students analyze the outcome of changes in U.S. policy toward China and the Soviet Union. Ask **What were the concrete results of Nixon's visits to China and the Soviet Union?** *(normalization of relations with China and trade; the signing of SALT I with the Soviet Union)* Ask students to predict how Nixon's new foreign policy toward China and the Soviet Union helped bring the world closer to ending the Cold War.

- **Analyzing the Visuals** Ask students to examine the photographs on this and the next page. Discuss how these images show the renewed U.S. relationships with China and the Soviet Union.

Independent Practice

- To increase understanding of Nixon's visit to China, have students read and complete *History Comics: Nixon Goes to China.* Teaching Resources, **p. 24**

- Have students review the Primary Source quotation on this page and list other areas in which the Soviet Union and the United States agreed to work together.

Monitor Progress

Circulate to make sure that students understand the reasons why Nixon worked to restore the U.S. relationship with China and the Soviet Union and how Nixon's efforts helped bring the world closer to ending the Cold War.

Answer

✓ for trade agreements; to create more tension between China and the Soviet Union; for help persuading North Vietnam to accept a peace agreement

562 The Vietnam War Era

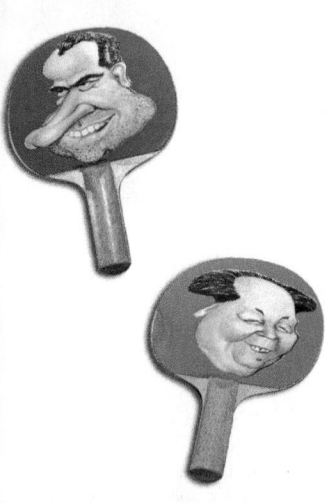

Ping-Pong Diplomacy
Nine American table-tennis players journeyed to China in 1971 to play matches against Chinese competitors. Americans commemorated the event with special ping-pong paddles fashioned after Nixon and Chinese leader Mao Zedong.

bring significant trade agreements, especially benefiting California and the Pacific Coast. Politically, U.S. normalization would drive a wedge between China and the Soviet Union, who had strayed from their traditional alliance and become rivals for territory and diplomatic influence. Finally, if the United States forged stronger relations with the Chinese, they might pressure North Vietnam to accept a negotiated peace to end the conflict still raging at the time.

Nixon Normalizes Relations With China With so much to gain and so little to lose, Nixon quietly pushed ahead with his plans. In public, the Chinese made symbolic overtures toward a meeting. In April 1971, China invited an American table-tennis team to play against its athletes. This small action demonstrated China's willingness to talk. Henry Kissinger worked behind the scenes, talking with Chinese leaders and ironing out sensitive issues with Premier **Zhou Enlai.** Then, in July 1971, Nixon announced that he would make an official state visit to China.

In February 1972, the President made the trip and toured the Great Wall, the Imperial Palace, and other historic sites. Nixon sat down for lengthy talks with Zhou Enlai and Communist Party Chairman Mao Zedong. He even learned enough Chinese to make a toast in the language of his host country. The visit was a great success and an important step toward normalizing diplomatic relations with China. The following year, American tourists started visiting and American companies set up a thriving trade with China. Nixon's China trip was the high point of his presidency. It bridged, as Zhou Enlai said, "the vastest ocean in the world, twenty-five years of no communication." In 1979, the United States and China established full diplomatic relations.

✓ **Checkpoint** Why did Nixon reach out to China?

Détente With the Soviet Union

Nixon's trip to the People's Republic of China prompted an immediate reaction from the Soviet Union, which had strained relations with both countries. Soviet leader Leonid Brezhnev feared that improved U.S.-Chinese relations would isolate Russia. Therefore, he invited Nixon to visit Moscow. Nixon made the trip in May 1972. Afterward, the President reported to Congress that he and Brezhnev had reached agreements in a wide variety of areas:

> **Primary Source** "Recognizing the responsibility of the advanced industrial nations to set an example in combating mankind's common enemies, the United States and the Soviet Union have agreed to cooperate in efforts to reduce pollution and enhance environmental quality. We have agreed to work together in the . . . conquest of cancer and heart disease."
>
> —Richard Nixon, speech to Congress, June 1, 1972

Nixon also announced plans to conduct a joint U.S.-Soviet space mission.

However, by far the high point of the summit was the signing of the first **Strategic Arms Limitation Treaty.** Otherwise known as SALT I, the treaty froze the deployment of intercontinental ballistic missiles (ICBMs) and placed limits on antiballistic missiles (ABMs), but it did not alter the stockpiling of the more dangerous multiple independent reentry vehicles (MIRVs). SALT I did not end the arms race between the United States and the Soviet Union. But it was a giant step toward that goal.

The importance of SALT I stemmed first and foremost from U.S. and Soviet efforts to reduce tensions between them. A policy aimed at easing Cold War tensions, **détente** had replaced previous diplomatic efforts based on suspicion and

---

Differentiated Instruction Solutions for All Learners

⑭ Advanced Readers   ⑭ Gifted and Talented Students

Tell students that Mao's regime gave the first public sign of improved relations between the People's Republic of China and the United States when it invited the U.S. Ping-Pong team to visit China. The team toured the Great Wall and the Summer Palace and played exhibition games against their host. The trip became known as Ping-Pong Diplomacy. Have students use the example of Ping-Pong Diplomacy as a springboard to write an essay about how sports and other human interests bring people of different cultures together and help them understand one another better.

Nuclear Arms Treaty
As Leonid Brezhnev (seated, right) looks on, President Nixon signs the SALT I treaty during his historic visit to Moscow.

distrust. With his visits to China and the Soviet Union, coming within six months of each other, Richard Nixon dramatically altered America's global strategy. He relaxed the nation's inflexible stance toward communism and applied a more pragmatic approach to foreign policy. In the short term, the new relationships he forged helped the United States to end the Vietnam War. In the long term, Nixon's foreign-policy breakthroughs moved the world a step closer to the end of the Cold War.

✓ **Checkpoint** How did SALT I support Nixon's new policy for dealing with the Soviet Union?

SECTION 5 Assessment

Progress Monitoring Online
For: Self-test with vocabulary practice
www.pearsonschool.com/ushist

Comprehension

1. **Terms and People** For each item below, write a sentence explaining its significance.
   - Henry Kissinger
   - realpolitik
   - Zhou Enlai
   - détente

2. **NoteTaking Reading Skill: Categorize** Use your table to answer the Section Focus Question: How did Richard Nixon change Cold War diplomacy during his presidency?

Writing About History

3. **Quick Write: Write the Essay Body** Choose a topic from the section on which you might write a persuasive essay. For example, you might discuss whether Nixon was a better Cold War President than his predecessors. Write the body of your essay, using a list of points you have made to guide you. Remember to open and close the body of the essay with strong arguments.

Critical Thinking

4. **Apply Information** How did Nixon's policy toward China reflect the philosophy of realpolitik?

5. **Draw Conclusions** Why did Nixon and Kissinger believe détente was a beneficial foreign policy?

6. **Predict Consequences** Did Richard Nixon position the United States to win the Cold War? Why or why not?

Quick Study Guide

- Have students use the Quick Study Guide to prepare for the chapter test. Students may wish to refer to the following sections as they review:

Roots of the U.S. Action in Vietnam
Section 1

Arms Control Agreements
Section 5

The Vietnam War, 1969–1972
Section 4

Key Events of 1950–1975
Section 1
Section 2
Section 3
Section 4
Section 5

- For additional review, remind students to refer to the Reading and Note Taking Study Guide.
Section Note Taking
Section Summaries

- Have students access **www.pearsonschool.com/ushist** for this chapter's History Interactive timeline, which includes expanded entries and additional events.

- If students need more instruction on analyzing graphic data, have them read the Skills Handbook, **p. SH21.**

For **Progress Monitoring Online,** refer students to the Self-test with vocabulary practice at **www.pearsonschool.com/ushist.**

Quick Study Guide

Progress Monitoring *Online*
For: Self-test with vocabulary practice
www.pearsonschool.com/ushist

■ Roots of the U.S. Action in Vietnam

French Surrender at Dien Bien Phu	
Before	**After**
• **French-Indochinese War:** French forces battle Vietnamese communists under Ho Chi Minh.	• **Geneva Accords:** France grants independence to former colonies; Vietnam divided.
• **Cold War:** Truman helps France in order to maintain Cold War alliance against the Soviets.	• **SEATO:** U.S. assembles coalition to oppose spread of communism in Southeast Asia.
• **Domino Theory:** Eisenhower continues aid to French to prevent communist victory.	• **U.S. Intervention:** U.S. supports anticommunist Diem regime and sends troops to Vietnam.

■ Arms Control Agreements

Year	Agreement	Effect
1963	Nuclear Test Ban Treaty	Banned testing of nuclear weapons in the atmosphere
1972	SALT I Interim Agreement	Froze existing number of weapons held by each side
1972	SALT I Anti-Ballistic Missile Treaty	Set strict limits on missiles that could shoot down missiles from the other side
1979	SALT II Treaty	Set absolute limit on number of weapons each side could hold

■ The Vietnam War, 1969–1972

3. December 1972 United States launches bombing of Hanoi region.

2. May 1972 United States mines Haiphong harbor.

1. April 1970 United States and South Vietnam attack communist bases in Cambodia.

4. March 1973 Last remaining U.S. troops withdraw from South Vietnam.

Major U.S. bombing targets
⊛ National capital

Miller Projection
0   100   200 mi
0   100 200 km

☑ Quick Study Timeline

	1950–1954	1954	1963
In America	United States aids French war effort in Indochina	United States supports South Vietnam; SEATO forms	American involvement in South Vietnam increases; Kennedy assassinated
Presidential Terms	Harry S. Truman 1945–1953	Dwight D. Eisenhower 1953–1961	John F. Kennedy 1961–1963
	1950	**1955**	**1960**
Around the World	1950–1953 Korean War	1954 Dien Bien Phu falls; Geneva Accords	1963 South Vietnamese citizens protest Diem regime

Differentiated Instruction   Solutions for All Learners

L1 Special Needs Students   **L2 English Language Learners**   **L2 Less Proficient Readers**

Use the following study guide resources to help students acquiring basic skills:
Adapted Reading and Note Taking Study Guide
- Section Note Taking
- Section Summaries

Use the following study guide resources to help Spanish-speaking students:
Spanish Reading and Note Taking Study Guide
- Section Note Taking
- Section Summaries

American Issues
•—•—• Connector

By connecting prior knowledge with what you have learned in this chapter, you can gradually build your understanding of enduring questions that still affect America today. Answer the questions below. Then, use your American Issues Connector study guide (or go online: www.pearsonschool.com/ushist).

Issues You Learned About

● **America and the World** During the Cold War, the United States tried to spread democracy, increase American power around the world, and limit the expansion of communism.

1. Think about the reasons for U.S. involvement in the Vietnam War and the reasons for opposition to America's role in the war. Then, write your own evaluation of whether the United States made the best decision in taking an active role in the Vietnam War. Consider the following:
   • domino theory and its validity
   • Gulf of Tonkin incident
   • implementation of the draft
   • conflict between hawks and doves
   • total of American casualties

● **America Goes to War** Again and again, Americans have faced the tough decision of whether or not to go to war.

2. What steps are usually followed before committing U.S. forces to war? Was this process followed in the Vietnam War? Explain.

3. Why did Johnson follow a policy of "Americanizing" the war effort? How did the war escalate under Johnson?

4. Why did President Nixon order bombing attacks on neighboring Cambodia? Why was this move controversial?

● **Global Interdependence** U.S. leaders often use diplomacy to improve relations with our friends and to reduce tensions with our rivals.

5. How did Nixon's China policy affect relations between the United States and the Soviet Union?

6. Explain the importance of SALT I.

Connect to Your World	Activity

Sectionalism and National Politics Over the years, different regions of the country have traditionally supported one political party or the other. However, these support bases are open to change. For example, the traditionally Democratic South voted Republican or Independent in 1968. Compare the 1968 electoral map on page 550 with the electoral map below. Then, write a summary explaining the current political landscape of the country.

Election of 2004
Candidate (Party)
☐ George W. Bush (Republican)
■ John Kerry (Democratic)

1964 Gulf of Tonkin Resolution	1968 Violence erupts at Democratic National Convention	1972 Nixon visits China

Lyndon B. Johnson 1963–1969   Richard M. Nixon 1969–1974

1965   **1970**   **1975**

1965 Operation Rolling Thunder	1968 Tet Offensive	1973 Paris Peace Accords

History Interactive
For: Interactive timeline
www.pearsonschool.com/ushist

American Issues
•—•—• Connector

Tell students that the main issues for this chapter are America and the World, America Goes to War, and Global Interdependence. Then, ask them to answer the Issues You Learned About questions on this page. Discuss the Connect to Your World topic(s), and ask students to complete the project that follows.

American Issues Connector

1. Students' evaluations of the decision should reflect sound reasoning and a clear understanding of the events and ideologies listed.

2. The President asks Congress to declare war and then commits troops. No; instead, President Johnson ordered an attack on the North Vietnamese, and Congress gave him the power to commit troops to war without asking for a declaration of war.

3. Johnson and his advisers believed that the United States had to increase its military presence in Vietnam. Troop commitments and casualties escalated under Johnson.

4. Nixon wanted to reduce the flow of supplies that ran through Laos and Cambodia. It was controversial because these neighboring countries were drawn into war.

5. His China policy prompted the Soviet Union, fearful of isolation, to invite Nixon to Moscow; to reach agreements on many issues; and to sign the SALT I treaty.

6. SALT I represented a giant step toward ending the arms race.

Connect to Your World

Sample answer: "The Democratic party has made gains in the West and Midwest and continues to have a firm hold on the Northeast, and the Republican party has established a hold on the Deep South and held onto its traditional regions."

For additional review of this chapter's enduring issues, remind students to refer to the Reading and Note Taking Study Guide American Issues Connector.

Chapter Assessment

Terms and People

1. Ho Chi Minh was the communist leader of North Vietnam who was the first to call for Vietnam's independence from France.

2. Hawks supported the U.S. involvement in Vietnam, and doves opposed it. Hawks subscribed to the idea of containment of communism and the domino theory. Most were conservative. Doves questioned the war on moral and strategic grounds and held that it was a localized civil war. Doves included liberal politicians, pacifists, student radicals, and civil rights leaders.

3. The Tet Offensive was a campaign by the North Vietnamese and the Vietcong to attack American and ARVN positions in South Vietnam. It was a tactical victory for the Americans because they and the ARVN kept the communists from achieving their goals, but it was a strategic victory for the communists because it convinced the United States that the war was not going to end quickly.

4. The Gulf of Tonkin Resolution gave President Johnson wide-ranging war powers that allowed him to commit troops without asking Congress to declare war. The War Powers Act restricted the President so that he could not take unilateral action to enter a foreign conflict, as the Gulf of Tonkin Resolution allowed President Johnson to do, without consulting Congress within 48 hours.

5. Realpolitik is the idea that political goals should be defined by practical goals and national interests. Nixon and Kissinger used realpolitik to approach the Soviet Union and China.

Focus Questions

6. to stop the spread of communism in Southeast Asia

7. Lack of progress toward victory led to the commitment of more U.S. resources; the commitment of more resources weakened the U.S. economy, divided Americans, and caused a decline in military morale.

8. Little progress was being made in the war; there were many casualties; most soldiers were from poor and working-class backgrounds, and a large number were African Americans; and the government issued optimistic statements despite increasing news reports showing the contrary.

9. The Vietnam War ended with the United States withdrawing its troops from South Vietnam. The war's lasting effects included the communist takeover of South Vietnam, lack of recognition for Vietnam veterans, a long period of healing for the nation, restriction of the President's war-making powers, and distrust of leaders and hesitancy on the part of the American public about intervening in the affairs of other countries.

10. He worked to reduce tensions between the United States, China, and the Soviet Union.

Critical Thinking

11. Presidents Truman and Eisenhower gave monetary aid to the French and South Vietnamese, Kennedy sent Special Forces to advise the South Vietnamese army and to fight alongside them, Johnson committed large numbers of American troops and went to war with North Vietnam, and

---

Terms and People

1. Who was **Ho Chi Minh**? What role did he play in Vietnam's history?

2. Define **hawks** and **doves**. What generalizations can you make about each group?

3. What was the **Tet Offensive**? Why was it a tactical victory for the Americans but a strategic victory for the communists?

4. Define the **Gulf of Tonkin Resolution** and the **War Powers Act**. What was the relationship between them?

5. Define **realpolitik**. Give an example of realpolitik in the 1970s.

Focus Questions

The focus question for this chapter is **How did the United States confront communism in East Asia after the Korean War?** Build an answer to this big question by answering the focus questions for Sections 1 through 5 and the Critical Thinking questions that follow.

Section 1
6. Why did the United States become involved in Vietnam?

Section 2
7. What were the causes and effects of America's growing involvement in the Vietnam War?

Section 3
8. How did the American war effort in Vietnam lead to rising protests and social divisions back home?

Section 4
9. How did the Vietnam War end and what were its lasting effects?

Section 5
10. How did Richard Nixon change Cold War diplomacy during his presidency?

Writing About History

Writing a Persuasive Essay From 1954 to 1975, the United States supported South Vietnam in an ultimately losing battle against communist forces from North Vietnam. Write a persuasive essay in which you argue for or against the following thesis: The Vietnam War could have been won by the United States and South Vietnam. Consult page SH16 of the Writing Handbook for additional help.

Prewriting
• Choose a side of the argument.
• Collect evidence, using a graphic organizer to list points on both sides of the issue.
• Research Internet or print sources to find materials that analyze your position from both sides. Take notes on relevant details, events, and people.

Critical Thinking

11. **Compare** Compare the involvement of Presidents Truman, Eisenhower, Kennedy, Johnson, and Nixon in Vietnam.

12. **Explain Effects** What impact did the Vietnam War have on the United States domestic economy?

13. **Evaluate Credibility of Sources** In February 1968, a television journalist reported to his viewers that there was a "credibility gap" between Johnson's statements about the war and the reality of the fighting. Why did Americans come to doubt the word of their President?

14. **Analyze Charts** Study the chart below. Why were casualties the highest between 1967 and 1969? Why were casualties much lower in 1972?

American Casualties in Vietnam

Year	Killed in Action	Wounded in Action	Missing in Action
1961–1965	1,864	7,337	18
1966	5,008	29,992	61
1967	9,378	56,013	113
1968	14,594	87,388	176
1969	9,414	55,390	112
1970	4,221	24,835	101
1971	1,380	18,109	16
1972	300	3,936	11

SOURCE: National Archives and Records Administration

15. **Categorize** In his efforts to end the Vietnam War, Nixon followed some policies that seemed to lessen U.S. involvement and some that seemed to increase U.S. involvement. Give examples of each type of policy.

16. **Identify Assumptions** Before Nixon took office, what did Cold War foreign-policy strategists believe about the spread of communism? What assumptions did Nixon and Kissinger make when it came to foreign affairs?

Drafting
• Clearly state the position that you will argue in a thesis statement. Use the rest of your introduction to provide necessary context about the issue.
• Make an outline to organize your argument and its supporting details. Then, choose information from your research that supports each part of your outline.

Revising
• Use the guidelines on page SH16 of the Writing Handbook to revise your essay.

Document-Based Assessment

The 1968 Presidential Race

After the Tet Offensive showed the United States sinking deeper into a stalemate in Vietnam, the antiwar movement took center stage during the race for the White House. Use your knowledge of the election and the following documents to answer questions 1 through 4.

Document A

"The feud that helped define the public lives of LBJ and RFK also helped shape the two greatest national undertakings of their times—the war on poverty and the war in Vietnam. Consumed by contempt for Kennedy, Johnson transformed a potential ally into an archenemy. . . . As Johnson and Kennedy became ever more bitter enemies, they divided constituencies they once shared, weakening their party by forcing its members to choose between them. They exposed and exacerbated the growing divide within the Democratic Party and American politics in general."

—*Jeff Shesol,* Mutual Contempt

Document B

"[I]t is true that a house divided against itself by the spirit of faction, of party, of region, of religion, of race, is a house that cannot stand. There is division in the American house now. . . . I should not permit the Presidency to become involved in the partisan divisions that are developing in this political year. With America's sons in the fields far away, with America's future under challenge right here at home, with our hopes and the world's hopes for peace in the balance every day, I do not believe that I should devote an hour or a day of my time to any personal partisan causes or to any duties other than the awesome duties of this office—the Presidency of your country. Accordingly, I shall not seek, and I will not accept, the nomination of my party for another term as your President."

—*President Lyndon B. Johnson, March 31, 1968*

Document C

Chicago police remove an antiwar protester from a demonstration during the 1968 Democratic National Convention.

Document D

"For four years America's fighting men have set a record for courage and sacrifice unsurpassed in our history. . . . Never has so much military and economic and diplomatic power been used so ineffectively. . . . I say the time has come for the American people to turn to new leadership not tied to the mistakes and policies of the past. That is what we offer to America. And I pledge to you tonight that the first priority foreign policy objective of our next Administration will be to bring an honorable end to the war in Vietnam. We shall not stop there. We need a policy to prevent more Vietnams."

—*Republican Presidential Nominee Richard M. Nixon, August 8, 1968*

---

1. According to Document B, Johnson has chosen not to run for reelection because he
   A does not believe he can win.
   B is tired of trying to lead a divided nation.
   C has more vital duties to perform.
   D thinks the nation needs new leadership.

2. Which of the documents focus primarily on the causes of divisions within the Democratic Party?
   A Documents B and D
   B Documents A and D
   C Documents C and D
   D Documents A and C

3. The speakers in Documents B and D would most likely agree that
   A ending the Vietnam War is a top priority for the President.
   B the Vietnam War has been badly managed.
   C the United States is on the verge of winning in Vietnam.
   D the United States should pull its troops out of Vietnam immediately.

4. **Writing Task** What were the most important factors that led to the defeat of the Democrats in 1968? Write a paragraph answering this question, using your knowledge of the chapter content and specific evidence from the primary sources above.

Nixon ended the war by handing over combat duties to the South Vietnamese and secretly bombing the Ho Chi Minh Trail.

12. Although the unemployment rate fell, the war led to rising prices and inflation and strained government finances.

13. The news Americans heard of casualties and developments in the war and the images they saw did not match the optimistic picture the President gave them.

14. Casualties were highest between 1967 and 1969 because troop levels were higher and there was more fighting in Vietnam; they were lower in 1972 because peace talks were underway and a gradual pullout of U.S. troops had begun.

15. The pullout of U.S. troops and handing over of combat duties to the South Vietnamese seemed to lessen U.S. involvement; secret bombing and attacks in Cambodia seemed to increase U.S. involvement.

16. Before Nixon took office, Cold War foreign-policy strategists believed that there was a united worldwide communist movement. Nixon and Kissinger believed that there were important differences among communist countries and that they could be approached individually.

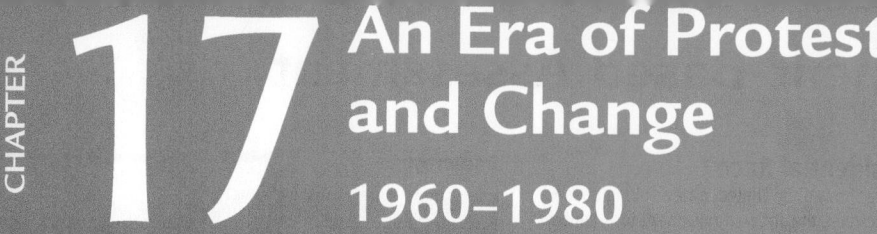

Teach With Technology

Presentation EXPRESS™
PREMIUM DVD

- Teach this chapter's core content by using **PresentationExpress,** which includes interactivities, video, lecture notes, and the *ExamView®* QuickTake assessment tool.

- To introduce this chapter by using **PresentationExpress,** ask students with which of the following statements they most agree: **A) The United States is strengthened by its popular culture and diversity of values. B) Popular culture and diversity of personal values have led to moral decay in the United States.** Take a class poll or record students' answers by using the QuickTake feature, and discuss their responses. Point out that in this chapter, they will read about changes in American society during the 1960s. Continue introducing the chapter by using the chapter opener slide show.

Technology Resources

- Student**EXPRESS** CD-ROM

- Teacher Resource Library **DVD**

- Presentation**EXPRESS**
  PREMIUM DVD
- *ExamView®* **Test Bank CD-ROM** English and Spanish

- **Guided Reading Audio,** Spanish

- **Student Edition on Audio**

VIDEO
? THE ESSENTIAL
By Students For Students
For videos on Amercian Issues, go to
www.pearsonschool.com/ushist

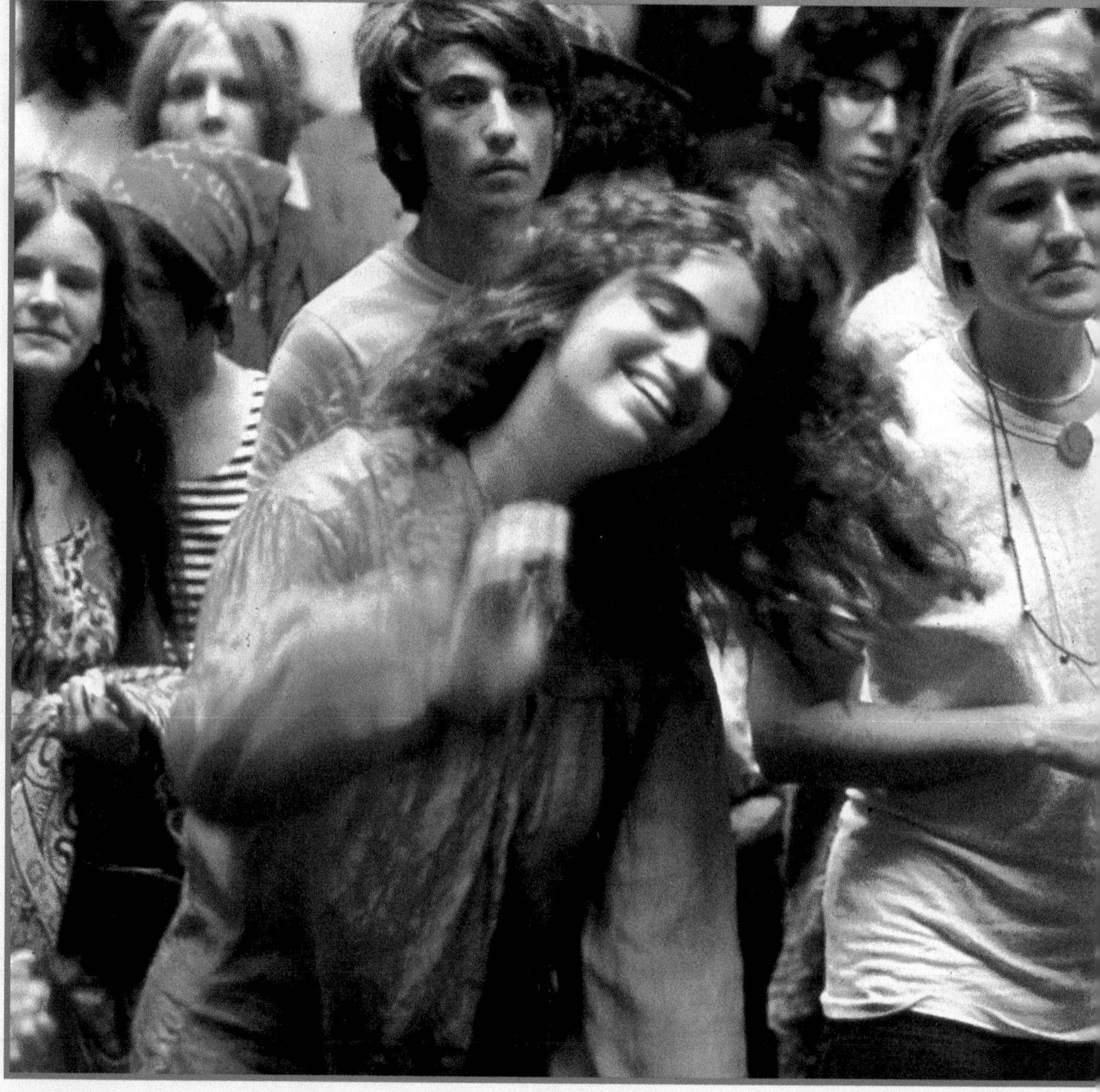

Bibliography

For the Teacher

Gitlin, Todd. *The Sixties: Years of Hope, Days of Rage.* Bantam, 1993 (Revised Edition).

Nader, Ralph. *The Ralph Nader Reader.* Seven Stories Press, 2001.

Rosen, Ruth. *The World Split Open: How the Modern Women's Movement Changed America.* Viking Adult, 2000.

For the Student

L2 Soto, Gary. *Jesse de la Cruz: A Profile of a United Farm Worker.* Persea Books., 2002.

L3 Glassman, Bruce, et al. *The Counterculture Movement of the 1960s.* Greenhaven Press, 2004.

L4 Switzer, Jacqueline Vaughn. *Disabled Rights: American Disability Policy and the Struggle for Equality.* Georgetown University Press, 2003.

WITNESS HISTORY

The Hippie Experience

Many young Americans in the 1960s identified with a cultural movement that rejected the social conventions of their parents' generation. Their long hair and flowing clothes set them apart from mainstream America. So did their name—hippies. A magazine article described the attitude of the hippie movement:

“If there were a hippie code, it would include these flexible guidelines: Do your own thing, wherever you have to do it and whenever you want. Drop out. Leave society as you have known it. Leave it utterly.”

— "Youth: The Hippies,"
Time Magazine, July 7, 1967

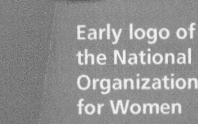

Early logo of the National Organization for Women

◄ A hippie woman dances at the Woodstock music festival in New York, 1969.

Chapter Preview

Chapter Focus Question: How did the counterculture and the expanding rights revolution of the 1960s and 1970s influence American society?

Section 1
The Counterculture

Section 2
The Women's Rights Movement

Section 3
The Rights Revolution Expands

Section 4
The Environmental Movement

The Beatles

Protesters holding up a peace sign

Use the ☑ **Quick Study Timeline** at the end of this chapter to preview chapter events.

Note Taking Study Guide *Online*
For: Note Taking and American Issues Connector
www.pearsonschool.com/ushist

Chapter-Level Resources

All in One Letter Home (English and Spanish), Preread the Chapter, Vocabulary Builder, Reading Strategy, Social Studies Skills Practice, Enrichment, Issues Connector, Chapter Tests

- Test Prep With Document-Based Assessment
- AYP Monitoring Assessments
- *ExamView*® Test Bank CD-ROM
- Guided Reading Audio (Spanish)
- Student Edition Audio

Previewing the Chapter

- **WITNESS HISTORY** Read the Witness History selection aloud. Ask **Why are "hippie guidelines" flexible?** (*Hippies rejected society's values and didn't want to set any rules.*) Then, tell students to think about the United States during the 1950s and the early 1960s. Have students discuss reasons why hippies rejected the social conventions of their parents' generation.

- **Analyzing the Visuals** Have students study the images on these pages. Ask them to compare the clothing and hairstyles of people in the large image to images they have seen of people in the 1950s (revisit Chapter 13 if needed). Ask **How do you think changes in clothing and hairstyles reflected larger changes in American society?** (*Possible responses: more experimentation, greater diversity*)

- **Focus** Write the Chapter Focus question on the board. Tell students to keep this question in mind as they read the chapter. Then, have students preview the section titles in this chapter.

- **Preread** Have students complete the chapter's Preread the Chapter Worksheet. Teaching Resources, pp. 8–9

Differentiated Instruction   Solutions for All Learners

The following Teacher's Edition strategies are suitable for students of varying abilities.

- **L1** Special Needs Students, pp. 575, 582, 587 SN
- **L2** English Language Learners, pp. 571, 575, 582, 587 ELL

- **L2** Less Proficient Readers, pp. 571, 575, 582 LPR
- **L4** Advanced Readers, pp. 577, 583, 588, 590 AR
- **L4** Gifted and Talented Students, pp. 577, 583, 588, 590 GT

Have students access **www.pearsonschool. com/ushist** for the Note Taking Study Guide *Online* as an alternative to the *Reading and Note Taking Study Guide* booklet.

Step-by-Step Instruction

Objectives

As you teach this section, keep students focused on the following objectives to help them answer the Section Focus Question and master core content.

- Describe the rise of the counterculture.
- List the major characteristics of the counterculture.
- Evaluate the impact of the counterculture on American values and society.

Prepare to Read

Background Knowledge L3

Ask students to think about how the civil rights movement and Vietnam antiwar protests challenged American society. Ask students to predict other ways that people might challenge society's assumptions.

Set a Purpose L3

- **WITNESS HISTORY** Read the selection aloud.

  Ask **Judging from this quote, what do you think was the overall focus of the counterculture?** *(to enjoy freedom of expression, reexamine social values, and promote the ideals of peace and love)*

- **Focus** Point out the Section Focus Question, and write it on the board. Tell students to refer to this question as they read. *(Answer appears with Section 1 Assessment answers.)*

- **Preview** Have students preview the Section Objectives and the list of Terms and People.

- **NoteTaking** Using the Structured Reading Aloud strategy (TE, p. T20), have students read this section. As they read, have students identify the main ideas of the counterculture.
  Reading and Note Taking Study Guide

◄ Some audience members make their own music.

◄ A 1969 poster promises "3 days of peace & music" at the Woodstock concert.

Remembering Woodstock

In the summer of 1969, hundreds of thousands of people gathered for a rock concert in Bethel, New York. Most of the media criticized the three-day event because of the concertgoers' widespread use of drugs and open displays of "free love." The people who went to Woodstock felt differently. For them, Woodstock showed that close to half a million people could come together peacefully. Twenty-five years later, many who attended Woodstock still remember their experiences vividly.

❝Woodstock was a time of social changes in human freedom and expression. . . . We learned not to be ashamed of our bodies. . . . We spent time with our kids. . . . That festival set the standards for peace, music, people and expression and showed to the world that all was not just violence and hatred . . . it was LIFE!❞

—Juan C. Morales

The Counterculture

Objectives

- Describe the rise of the counterculture.
- List the major characteristics of the counterculture.
- Evaluate the impact of the counterculture on American values and society.

Terms and People

counterculture	commune
generation gap	Timothy Leary
Beatles	

NoteTaking

Reading Skill: Identify Main Ideas As you read, use a concept web like the one below to record main ideas about the counterculture.

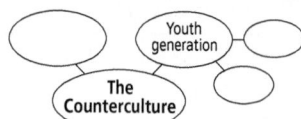

Why It Matters Woodstock was a dynamic expression of a **counterculture** that arose in the 1960s. Members of the counterculture adopted values that ran counter to mainstream culture. They rebelled against long-standing customs in dress, music, and personal behavior. The counterculture both challenged the values of mainstream American society and unleashed a movement to reassert traditional values. **Section Focus Question: What was the counterculture, and what impact did it have on American society?**

The Counterculture Rises

The counterculture was rooted in the social and political events of the 1950s. The Beat movement had emphasized freedom from materialism and the importance of personal experience. The civil rights movement introduced the idea of social and political protest, which stimulated the Vietnam antiwar movement. Both movements prompted many people to question traditional boundaries, whether restrictions on rights or cultural norms in dress or hairstyles. It also heightened distrust of authority, leading some in the counterculture to declare, "Don't trust anyone over 30."

Members of the counterculture valued youth, spontaneity, and freedom of expression. Also called hippies, these young people promoted peace, love, and freedom. They experimented with new styles of dress and music, freer attitudes toward sexual relationships, and

Vocabulary Builder

Use the information below and the following resource to teach students the high-use word from this section. Teaching Resources, Vocabulary Builder, p. 11

High-Use Word	Definition and Sample Sentence
contradict	*v.* to go against expressed views The peace activists held a press conference to **contradict** the statements of those who supported the war.

the recreational use of drugs. Their values were so different from traditional ones that many social analysts described the resulting situation as a **generation gap,** in which there was a lack of understanding and communication between the older and younger generations. Jerry Rubin, a political activist, described how long hair divided parents from their children:

Primary Source "Young kids identify short hair with authority, discipline. . . . Wherever we go, our hair tells people where we stand on Vietnam, Wallace, campus disruption, dope. . . . Yesterday I was walking down the street. A car passed by, parents in the front seat and a young kid, about eight, in the back seat. The kid flashed me the clenched fist sign. [Meaning: He identified with Rubin's long hair.]"
—Jerry Rubin, *America in the Sixties*

The baby boom that followed World War II resulted in a huge student population in the 1960s. By sheer numbers, the baby boomers became a force for social change. The music industry rushed to produce the music they liked; clothing designers copied the styles they introduced; universities were forced to change college courses and rules to accommodate them.

✔ **Checkpoint** What factors influenced the rise of the counterculture?

Defining the Counterculture

Many people have used the so-called trinity of the counterculture—sex, drugs, and rock-and-roll—to define the youth generation. But the counterculture was also marked by an interest in spirituality.

Music and Art Shape Youth Culture By the 1960s, rock-and-roll had become a defining characteristic of the baby-boom generation. When the **Beatles** made a triumphant visit to the United States in 1964, more than 70 million Americans watched the English rock band perform on Ed Sullivan's television show. The Beatles also had an impact on folk musicians like Bob Dylan, whose protest songs highlighted the civil rights and peace movements. As radical musician John Sinclair put it, rock became "a weapon of cultural revolution," urging listeners to reject conventions and, in many cases, the political policies of the government. Even after the counterculture had declined in significance, rock music remained popular among baby-boomers as well as their children.

The art and literature of the 1960s and 1970s also displayed a rebellious side. Andy Warhol's realistic paintings of common items of American culture, such as Campbell soup cans, questioned satirically what was "real." In literature, the novels of Tom Wolfe and Hunter S. Thompson blurred the lines between reporting and political activism.

The Sexual Revolution Members of the counterculture rejected many traditional restrictions on sexual behavior in what became known as the "sexual revolution." They called for the separation of sex from traditional family life and often advocated new living patterns. For example, many hippies lived together in **communes,** or small communities in which the people have common interests and share resources. The sexual revolution was one of the strongest indicators of the generation gap. One poll showed that nearly two-thirds of all Americans over the age of 30 opposed premarital sex, whereas a majority of those under age 29 did not. Eventually, however, the sexual revolution led to a more open discussion of sex in the mainstream media.

Rock Art
The pop art that decorated concert posters, such as this one from the late 1960s, often challenged tradition.

PRESENTED IN SAN FRANCISCO BY BILL GRAHAM

TICKETS

Instruct

- **Introduce:** Key Term Ask students to find the key term *commune* (in bold) in the text. Ask **How did *communes* differ from other forms of community?** *(People in communes lived together in small groups, held the same values, and shared common resources, while communities are generally more diverse.)* Ask students to discuss what might be the advantages and disadvantages of such living arrangements.

- **Teach** Ask **In what other art forms, aside from music, did the counterculture find expression?** *(the satirical paintings of Andy Warhol and the writings of Tom Wolfe and Hunter S. Thompson)* **Why might John Sinclair have said that rock music became a "weapon of cultural revolution"?** *(Rock music was played mostly by baby boomers who expressed the values of the counterculture. The music urged listeners to reject conventional mores and political policies.)*

- **Quick Activity** Have students read the worksheet *Link to Literature: "Santa Barbara Declaration of Environmental Rights"* and answer the questions that follow. Teaching Resources, **p. 19**

Independent Practice

Have students complete the History Interactive at **www.pearsonschool.com/ushist.** Then, ask students to write brief paragraphs describing the major differences between the boomer generation and the silent generation.

Monitor Progress

Circulate to make sure that students understand the key ideas of the counterculture and the generation gap.

Answer

Thinking Critically

The silent generation did not draw attention to themselves with radical music, dress, or reading matter. Their conformity gave the impression of silence.

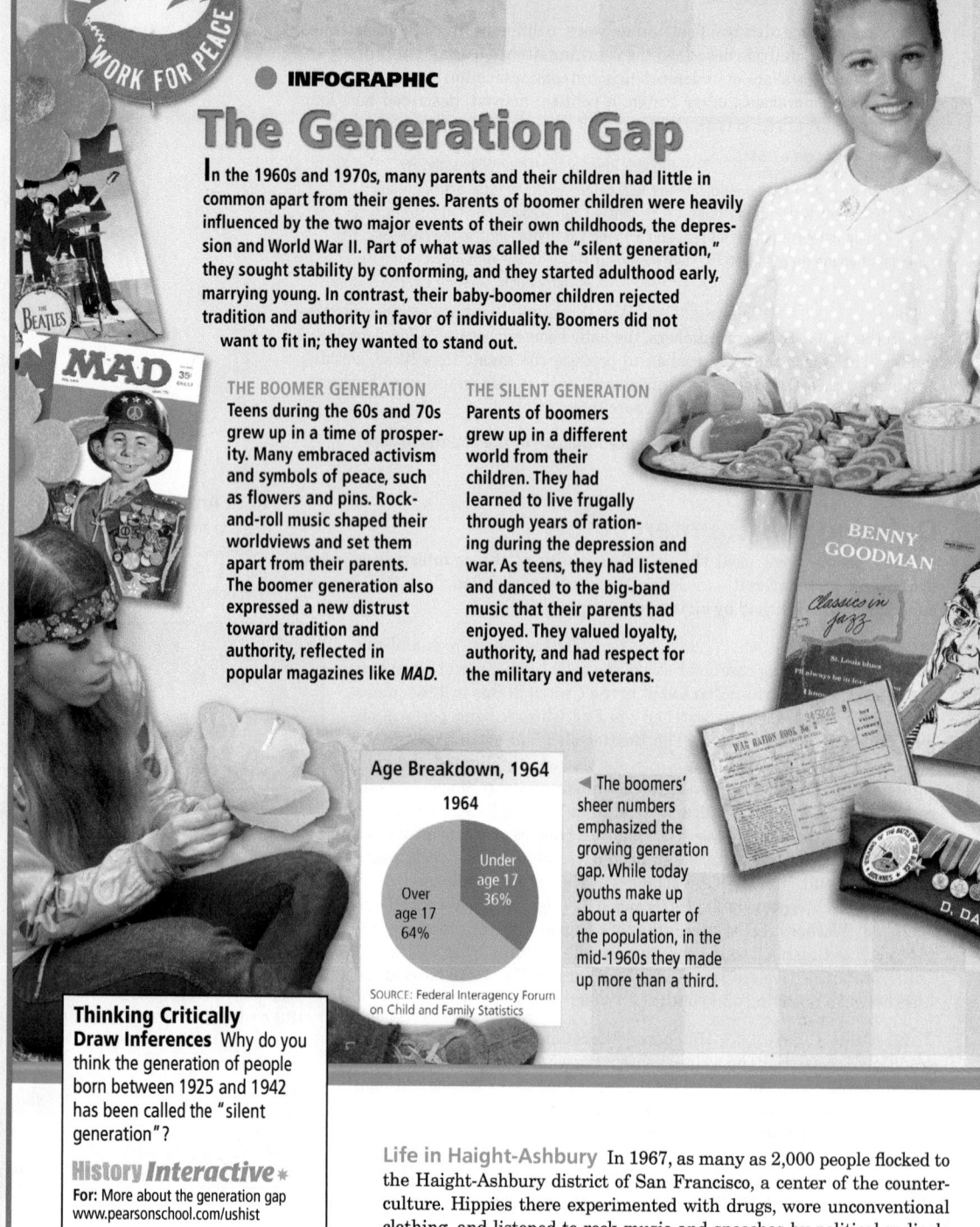

● **INFOGRAPHIC**

The Generation Gap

In the 1960s and 1970s, many parents and their children had little in common apart from their genes. Parents of boomer children were heavily influenced by the two major events of their own childhoods, the depression and World War II. Part of what was called the "silent generation," they sought stability by conforming, and they started adulthood early, marrying young. In contrast, their baby-boomer children rejected tradition and authority in favor of individuality. Boomers did not want to fit in; they wanted to stand out.

THE BOOMER GENERATION
Teens during the 60s and 70s grew up in a time of prosperity. Many embraced activism and symbols of peace, such as flowers and pins. Rock-and-roll music shaped their worldviews and set them apart from their parents. The boomer generation also expressed a new distrust toward tradition and authority, reflected in popular magazines like *MAD*.

THE SILENT GENERATION
Parents of boomers grew up in a different world from their children. They had learned to live frugally through years of rationing during the depression and war. As teens, they had listened and danced to the big-band music that their parents had enjoyed. They valued loyalty, authority, and had respect for the military and veterans.

Age Breakdown, 1964

1964

- Under age 17 36%
- Over age 17 64%

SOURCE: Federal Interagency Forum on Child and Family Statistics

◄ The boomers' sheer numbers emphasized the growing generation gap. While today youths make up about a quarter of the population, in the mid-1960s they made up more than a third.

Thinking Critically
Draw Inferences Why do you think the generation of people born between 1925 and 1942 has been called the "silent generation"?

History *Interactive* ✱
For: More about the generation gap
www.pearsonschool.com/ushist

Life in Haight-Ashbury In 1967, as many as 2,000 people flocked to the Haight-Ashbury district of San Francisco, a center of the counterculture. Hippies there experimented with drugs, wore unconventional clothing, and listened to rock music and speeches by political radicals like Timothy Leary, a one-time Harvard researcher. He preached that drugs could free the mind, and he encouraged American youths to "tune

Connect to Your World

Aging Baby Boomers In 2006, the first of the baby boomers began to turn 60, inching ever closer to retirement age. The huge population of aging baby boomers had led to concerns over how the country will handle their medical and financial needs. Some experts have predicted that the costs of covering Social Security and Medicare benefits for the boomers will place such a drain on resources that there will not be enough left for the system to support the next generation. These concerns sparked political debates about reforming the Social Security and Medicare systems. Some experts have argued that boomers' spontaneous attitudes kept them from planning and investing their money wisely when they were young. This contributed to a dramatic decrease in family savings during their lifetimes. Others claim that the boomers were not as thrifty as they should have been or did not anticipate that many employers would stop contributing to employee pension plans. Whatever the cause, many predict that in the early 2000s, the government will face tough choices concerning the retirement of aging boomers and future generations.

in," "turn on" to drugs, and "drop out" of mainstream society. The hippies of San Francisco attracted a great deal of media attention, much of it critical of the life-styles they advocated. Life in Haight-Ashbury did prove to have unwanted effects. As in other enclaves of hippie culture, it experienced high rates of drug abuse which led to increased crime.

Exploring Different Routes to Spirituality Some members of the counter-culture sought spiritual enlightenment outside of the Judeo-Christian traditions in which they had been raised. Many explored Buddhism and other Eastern religions, while others sought spirituality by living in harmony with nature. Particularly in the late 1960s and early 1970s, some hippies established rural communes, seeking to live off the land as Native Americans had in the past. These beliefs had a lasting impact on the budding environmental movement.

✓ **Checkpoint** What characteristics define the counterculture?

The Counterculture Ends

By the end of the 1960s, many people, even those within the counterculture, had become disillusioned with some of its excesses. The utopian urge to discover a more authentic way of living had an unfortunate underside. Drug addictions and deaths from overdoses rose. A number of rock musicians, most famously Jimi Hendrix and Janis Joplin, died of drug overdoses while only in their twenties. The downward spiral continued in 1969 with a tragedy at a music festival sponsored in Altamont, California. While the Rolling Stones played, members of the Hells Angels, a motorcycle gang that had been hired to provide security, stabbed to death a black man who had approached the stage. The ugly violence <u>contradicted</u> the values of "peace and love" that many hippies embraced.

At the same time, the movement's values were becoming increasingly shallow and self-centered. When the counterculture fell apart, most hippies abandoned their social experiments and melted right back into the mainstream. Still, the seeds of protest they had sown would influence the growing "rights revolution."

✓ **Checkpoint** Why did the counterculture fall apart?

Vocabulary Builder
contradict–(kahn truh DIHKT) *v.*
to go against expressed views

SECTION **1** Assessment

Progress Monitoring Online
For: Self-test with vocabulary practice
www.pearsonschool.com/ushist

Comprehension

1. **Terms and People** For each item below, write a sentence explaining how it influenced the counterculture.
   - generation gap
   - Beatles
   - commune
   - Timothy Leary

2. **NoteTaking Reading Skill: Identify Main Ideas** Use your concept web to answer the Section Focus Question: What was the counterculture, and what impact did it have on American society?

Writing About History

3. **Quick Write: Identify Issues** You are a teenager in the 1960s, and you have been invited to your father's club to give a speech about the values of the youth generation. Identify the issues that you will address, keeping your audience in mind.

Critical Thinking

4. **Identify Assumptions** What assumptions about mainstream culture were made by the counterculture?

5. **Analyze Information** Explain whether you agree with the following statement: "The counterculture was a form of protest."

6. **Recognize Cause and Effect** How did trends within the counterculture movement contribute to its downfall?

Objectives

As you teach this section, keep students focused on the following objectives to help them answer the Section Focus Question and master core content.

- Analyze how a movement for women's rights arose in the 1960s.
- Explain the goals and tactics of the women's movement.
- Assess the impact of the women's movement on American society.

Prepare to Read

Background Knowledge L3

Have students consider how the counterculture affected young people's ideas about traditional social arrangements. Ask students to predict the ways that the counterculture might have challenged ideas about gender.

Set a Purpose L3

- **WITNESS HISTORY** Read the selection aloud.

  Ask **Is Chisholm's assessment of attitudes towards gender still true today? Explain.** *(Example: Yes, although women have accomplished much since the late 1960s, they still struggle against stereotypes and discrimination.)*

- **Focus** Point out the Section Focus Question, and write it on the board. Tell students to refer to this question as they read. *(Answer appears with Section 2 Assessment answers.)*

- **Preview** Have students preview the Section Objectives and the list of Terms and People.

- **Reading Skill** Have students use the *Reading Strategy: Identify Causes and Effects* worksheet. Teaching Resources, **p. 12**

SECTION

2

▲ National Organization for Women button

▲ Civil rights leader Coretta Scott King speaks to a group of feminists at a National Women's Conference.

Challenging a Stereotype

"The unspoken assumption is that women are different. They do not have executive ability, orderly minds, stability, leadership skills, and they are too emotional. It has been observed before, that society for a long time discriminated against another minority, the blacks, on the same basis—that they were different and inferior. The happy little homemaker and the contented "old darkey" on the plantation were both produced by prejudice. As a black person, I am no stranger to race prejudice. But the truth is that in the political world I have been far oftener discriminated against because I am a woman than because I am black."

—Shirley Chisholm, Address to the United States House of Representatives, May 21, 1969

The Women's Rights Movement

Objectives

- Analyze how a movement for women's rights arose in the 1960s.
- Explain the goals and tactics of the women's movement.
- Assess the impact of the women's movement on American society.

Terms and People

feminism	ERA
Betty Friedan	Gloria Steinem
NOW	Phyllis Schlafly

NoteTaking

Reading Skill: Identify Causes and Effects Record the causes, effects, and main figures of the women's movement in a chart like this one.

```
        The Women's Movement
    ┌───────────┬──────────────┬───────────┐
    │  Causes   │ Proponents/  │  Effects  │
    │           │  Opponents   │           │
    └───────────┴──────────────┴───────────┘
       • •          • •            • •
```

Why It Matters After World War II, most women gave up their jobs to returning servicemen and went back to their homes to take care of their families. Social analysts and popular culture portrayed women, especially suburban housewives, as the personification of America's achievement of the good life. By the end of the 1960s, however, a broad-based movement to attain sexual equality had arisen. The women's movement fundamentally changed American life—from family and education to careers and political issues. **Section Focus Question: What led to the rise of the women's movement, and what impact did it have on American society?**

A Women's Movement Arises

Historians often refer to the women's movement of the 1960s and 1970s as the second wave of **feminism,** or the theory of political, social, and economic equality of men and women. The struggle for women's rights has had a long history, going back at least to the 1840s, when women drafted the Declaration of Sentiments at Seneca Falls, New York. The phrase *second wave of feminism* also reminds us that the first wave, which culminated with women winning the right to vote in 1920, ended well before the nation addressed the call for full equality. In the decades that followed, women made little legal or social headway in the battle for equal rights. Several factors influenced the rebirth of the women's movement in the 1960s and 1970s.

Vocabulary Builder

Use the information below and the following resource to teach students the high-use word from this section. Teaching Resources, Vocabulary Builder, p. 11

High-Use Word	Definition and Sample Sentence
gender	*n.* a person's sex The Nineteenth Amendment ended **gender** discrimination in voting.

Seeking to Redefine Traditional Roles The civil rights struggle prompted women to look at the ways in which society judged and discriminated against them as a group. As Casey Hayden and Mary King, two veterans of that movement, put it: "Sex and caste. There seem to be many parallels that can be drawn between the treatment of Negroes and the treatment of women in society as a whole." The civil rights movement both inspired women to demand <u>gender</u> equality and taught them ways to get it. It also brought black and white women together, strengthening their shared cause.

Women also wanted to redefine how they were viewed. Many women objected to the inaccuracy of the housewife stereotype. Some needed to work to support themselves or their families. Others wanted more opportunities than their lives as housewives could offer. **Betty Friedan** powerfully articulated this message in her groundbreaking book *The Feminine Mystique.*

Vocabulary Builder
gender–(JEHN der) *n.* a person's sex

Primary Source "The problem lay buried, unspoken, for many years in the minds of American women. It was a strange stirring, a sense of dissatisfaction. . . . Each suburban wife struggled with it alone. As she made the beds, shopped for groceries, matched slipcover material, ate peanut butter sandwiches with her children, chauffeured Cub Scouts and Brownies, lay beside her husband at night—she was afraid to ask even of herself the silent question—'Is this all?'"
—Betty Friedan, *The Feminine Mystique,* 1963

Looking for Better Work Despite the stereotypes, the number of women in the workforce grew throughout the 1950s and 1960s. Yet working women often found themselves in deadend jobs. Even those with training and education had their access to careers or advancement blocked, in many cases, by blatantly discriminatory employers. Sandra Day O'Connor, who ultimately became the first female Supreme Court Justice, graduated near the top of her class at Stanford Law School in the early 1950s. Yet while she found few employment opportunities upon graduation, her male counterparts won job offers at prestigious law firms. Facing such restrictions, women increasingly demanded equal treatment in the workplace.

✓ **Checkpoint** How did the women's movement of the 1960s begin?

Women Find Their Voices

Several years after she wrote *The Feminine Mystique,* Betty Friedan helped establish the **National Organization for Women (NOW).** The organization—which dedicated itself to winning "true equality for all women" and to attaining a "full and equal partnership of the sexes"—galvanized the women's movement.

NOW's Goals and Tactics NOW set out to break down barriers of discrimination in the workplace and in education. It attacked stereotypes of women in the media and called for more balance in roles in marriages. It had two major priorities. The first was to bring about passage of the **Equal Rights Amendment (ERA),** an amendment to the Constitution that would guarantee gender equality under the law. The ERA initially had been proposed in the early 1920s but had never passed. The second was to protect reproductive rights,

HISTORY MAKERS

Betty Friedan (1921–2006)
Educated at Smith College, where she edited the school newspaper, Betty Friedan did graduate work in psychology before becoming a journalist. She married in 1947 and was fired from her job when she became pregnant with her second child. Friedan raised three children and occasionally wrote articles for magazines. As she was working on one article, she realized that many educated women who had become housewives shared the uneasiness she felt about her life. This led her to write *The Feminine Mystique* in 1963, which helped launch the women's movement by inspiring women to join in the struggle for equal rights. In a later book, *The Second Stage* (1981), she criticized the direction of the women's movement, arguing that it had become too hostile to families.

■ **NoteTaking** Using the Guided Reading strategy (TE, p. T20), have students note the causes, effects, and main figures of the women's movement. Reading and Note Taking Study Guide

Teach

A Women's Movement Arises

Instruct

- **Introduce: Key Term** Ask students to find the key term *feminism* (in bold) in the text. Ask **What was the main goal of *feminism*?** *(political, social, and economic equality between men and women)*

- **Teach** Ask **How did the civil rights movement influence the women's movement?** *(It inspired women to look at how society judged women, provided examples of ways to work for equal rights and an end to workplace discrimination, and united African American and white women in a common cause.)* Using the Think-Write-Pair-Share strategy (TE, p. T23), ask students to discuss how the stereotype of the "happy housewife" was false. **Why might women in the 1960s have been dissatisfied with traditional gender roles?** *(They might have believed that traditional roles kept them from exploring greater opportunities.)*

- **Quick Activity** Have students list female political and business leaders of today. Then, have them read the HISTORY MAKERS biography of Betty Friedan. Ask students to discuss whether the women on their lists could have achieved their success without her work.

Independent Practice

Have students begin filling in their cause-and-effect flowcharts by noting the causes and some main figures of the women's movement.

Monitor Progress

Circulate to make sure that students record the causes and main figures of the women's movement. For a completed version, see Note Taking Transparencies, **B-139.**

Answer

✓ The women's movement was inspired by earlier feminist movements, dissatisfaction with limited social roles, and the civil rights movement.

Differentiated Instruction   Solutions for All Learners

 Special Needs Students **English Language Learners** **Less Proficient Readers**

Reread the Primary Source quotation from Betty Friedan's *The Feminine Mystique* with students. Then, have students read and complete the Teaching Resource worksheet *Biography: Gloria Steinem.* Create two columns on the board, labeled "Women's Lives Before the Women's Movement" and "Women's Lives After the Women's Movement." Invite students to volunteer information comparing and contrasting the traditional social and economic roles of women with the new options women could pursue more easily after the second wave of feminism. Then, ask students to use this chart to help them understand the importance and accomplishments of the women's movement. Teaching Resources, **p. 20**

Women Find Their Voices

Instruct

- **Introduce: Key Terms** Ask students to find the key terms *NOW* and *ERA* (in bold) in the text. Ask **Why might members of *NOW* have wanted to see the *ERA* become part of the Constitution?** *(They believed that it would end gender discrimination in the law and that it would give women relief from workplace discrimination.)* Ask students to speculate about how society might be different if the *ERA* had been ratified.

- **Teach** Point out that NOW worked for political change by lobbying for reform and preparing court cases to enforce existing laws against discrimination. Ask **In what other ways did feminists challenge society?** *(Others engaged in protests to challenge society's ideas about women.)* Ask **Why do you think some women opposed the movement?** *(Possible responses: Some feared that they would lose the option of remaining in traditional women's roles. Some may have identified the women's movement with other movements with which they disagreed.)*

- **Quick Activity** Display Color Transparency: *The Equal Rights Amendment.* Have students examine the map and discuss what geographic patterns they notice about support for the ERA. Color Transparencies A–130

Independent Practice

Ask students to choose which proponent or opponent of women's rights had the most significant effect on women's rights. Have students write a short statement supporting their choice.

Monitor Progress

As students write their statements, circulate to make sure that they support their choices with information from the section.

Answers

Caption Issues of workplace protection and equality of opportunity might have been important.

✔ NOW wanted the ERA and reproductive rights; others wanted to challenge social ideas about women.

A Diverse Movement
Women take part in a NOW rally in Washington, D.C., in 1970. A *Ms.* magazine cover from 1972 shows that women from all different backgrounds participated in the women's movement. *What women's issues might have been especially important to women in the military?*

especially the right to an abortion. NOW worked within the existing political system, lobbying for political reforms and readying court cases to compel the government to enforce existing legislation that banned discrimination. For some women, NOW seemed too extreme; for others, it was not extreme enough. Still, NOW served as a rallying point to promote equality for all women.

Raising Society's Awareness Finding NOW too tame, radical feminists sought a more fundamental restructuring of society. Rather than seeking legislative change, these protesters sought to show the way society trapped women into adopting restrictive roles. In addition to public protests of the Miss America Pageant, radical feminists engaged in small-scale consciousness-raising efforts. Other feminists sought to raise public awareness by making personal issues political. Charlotte Bunch, for example, wrote that "there is no private domain of a person's life that is not political and there is no political issue that is not ultimately personal."

Some feminists, like **Gloria Steinem,** tried to change awareness through the mass media. After graduating from college, Steinem worked as a freelance writer, including a stint of undercover work at a club run by *Playboy* magazine. While society tended to view Playboy bunnies in glamorous terms, Steinem revealed how much humiliation they had to endure to make a living. In 1972, she helped co-found *Ms.*, a feminist magazine. Its title meant to protest the social custom of identifying women by their marital status rather than as individuals.

Opposing the Women's Movement Some Americans—both men and women—openly challenged the women's movement. **Phyllis Schlafly,** for example, is a conservative political activist who denounced women's liberation as "a total assault on the family, on marriage, and on children." She worked hard to defeat the ERA, arguing that the act would compel women to fight in the military, end sex-segregated bathrooms, and hurt the family. Her argument resonated with many conservatives. Due to conservative opposition, the ERA fell three states short of becoming a constitutional amendment.

✔ **Checkpoint** What were the goals of the women's movement?

History Background

Phyllis Stewart Schlafly It might seem odd that Phyllis Schlafly became the leader of the "antifeminist" movement. In many ways, she was very much like feminists such as Betty Friedan. Schlafly was valedictorian of her high school class and a top student in college. She earned a law degree at Washington University and a master's degree in political science at Harvard. Although she married and had six children, she continued to write professionally and took an active role in Republican Party politics.

Despite her own success and ambition, Schlafly opposed many ideas of modern feminists, especially the ERA. She thought that the ERA would lead to inappropriate intrusions by the federal government into issues that she believed should be addressed by state or local governments or by individuals. Also, Schlafly believed that modern feminists harmed women by portraying them mainly as victims. She encouraged women to find success within existing circumstances, rather than relying on the government to defend their rights or protect them from discrimination. Schlafly continues to be active in her pro-family movement as an author, commentator, and public speaker.

Lasting Effects of the Women's Movement

The women's movement affected all aspects of American society. Women's roles and opportunities expanded. Women gained legal rights that had been denied them. And feminists sparked an important debate about equality that continues today. Yet the issues they raised continue to divide Americans. Some say that women haven't made enough gains. Others fear that the movement has actually harmed society.

Making Legal Headway Before the 1960s, there were no federal laws prohibiting gender discrimination. The Civil Rights Act of 1964, however, gave feminists a legal tool. It included a clause, called Title VII, that outlawed discrimination on the basis of sex. The clause was actually inserted by civil rights opponents, who thought it was so outlandish that it would make the entire bill look ridiculous. When the bill actually passed, however, women used Title VII to challenge discrimination. The bill also set up the Equal Employment Opportunity Commission (EEOC) to enforce the federal prohibition on job discrimination.

Enforcing Title VII, even with the EEOC, was often difficult. Still, NOW and other feminist organizations tirelessly filed suits against employers who refused to hire women or to pay them fairly, compelling the federal government to act. President Kennedy established the Commission on the Status of Women in 1961 to examine workplace discrimination. Title IX of the Higher Education Act of 1972 banned discrimination in education. The Equal Credit Opportunity Act, passed in 1974, made it illegal to deny credit to a woman just because of her gender.

Comparing Viewpoints

Do Women Need to Fight for Equal Rights?

Inspired by the successes of the civil rights movement, many American women in the late 1960s renewed their own demand for equal rights. Other women, however, argued that their demand was destructive.

PHYLLIS SCHLAFLY

Schlafly (born 1924) is a lawyer and political organizer who first became famous for her anticommunist views. She became an opponent of feminism.

Primary Source

"Feminism is doomed . . . because it [attempts] to repeal and restructure human nature."

"Women have babies and men provide support. If you don't like the way we're made you've got to take it up with God."

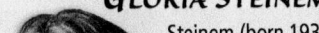

GLORIA STEINEM

Steinem (born 1934) is a journalist who founded political organizations to help women lobby for equal rights. She became the most famous feminist leader of the 1970s.

Primary Source

"Sex and race, because they are easily visible differences, have been the primary ways of organizing human beings into superior and inferior groups, and into the cheap labor on which this system still depends."

Compare

1. What do you think each woman would say about the role that biology plays in women's lives?

2. What is unusual about Schlafly's insistence that women should devote themselves to staying home and raising a family?

Differentiated Instruction   Solutions for All Learners

L4 Advanced Readers   **L4 Gifted and Talented Students**

Ask students who need an extra challenge to conduct more research on economic changes for women since the feminist movement. Organize students in two teams to debate this question: Has feminism benefited women economically? Before the debate, have each team develop a list of arguments and facts to support those arguments.

Assess and Reteach

Assess Progress L3

- Have students complete the Section Assessment.

- Administer the Section Quiz.
  Teaching Resources, **p. 25**

- To further assess student understanding, use Progress Monitoring Transparencies, **135.**

Reteach

If students need more instruction, have them read the section summary.

Reading and Note Taking Study Guide **L3**

Adapted Reading and Note Taking Study Guide **L1 L2**

Spanish Reading and Note Taking Study Guide **L2**

Extend **L4**

Ask students to research information on women's participation in politics, education, and the military. Then, have them use the data they find to create illustrated charts showing how feminism changed life in the United States.

Answers

Graph Skills In 1970, more women in the 25–34 age group probably left the workforce to have children. By 2002, more of these women were continuing to work.

✓ Women have greater protection from discrimination and greater reproductive rights.

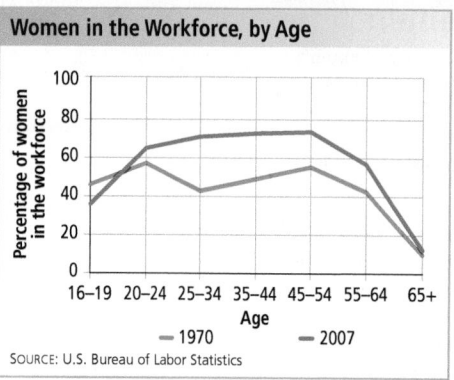

Women in the Workforce, by Age

Percentage of women in the workforce (y-axis: 0, 20, 40, 60, 80, 100)

Age (x-axis: 16–19, 20–24, 25–34, 35–44, 45–54, 55–64, 65+)

— 1970   — 2007

SOURCE: U.S. Bureau of Labor Statistics

Graph Skills Compare the lines for 1970 and 2007 on the graph. Notice that the 1970 line makes the shape of a letter *m. What factors explain this? Why is the 2007 line different?*

Some feminists considered their most important legal victory to be the 1973 Supreme Court decision in *Roe* v. *Wade,* which assured women the right to legal abortions. Prior to *Roe,* most states outlawed or severely restricted abortion. Some women turned to illegal and often dangerous ways to end their pregnancies. The case and its decision was highly controversial at the time and still is today.

The Workplace Slowly Changes The women's movement fostered a shift in attitudes among both men and women, and the American workplace today reflects this change. The percentage of women in the workforce has grown, from about 30 percent in 1950 to more than 60 percent in 2000. So, too, has the number of married female workers. Fields long closed or severely limited to women—such as medicine, law, and accounting—have opened up as well. The general shift in attitudes symbolized by these changes has created a world of possibilities for many young women who never knew a time when women were not allowed to do these things.

Despite these gains, the average woman still earns less than the average man, partly because many women continue to work in fields that pay less. Some people have referred to this situation as a "pink collar ghetto." Whether this is because of discrimination, or because women who shoulder family responsibilities often have limited job choices, remains a matter of debate. Many studies suggest that a "glass ceiling" exists, limiting the advancement of even the most highly educated and skilled women workers.

Most troubling, the United States has witnessed a feminization of poverty over the past 30 years. This means that the majority of the nation's poor people are single women. These are the women in the lowest-paying jobs, with the fewest benefits. Many of these poor women are single mothers, who must bear the costs and responsibilities of raising children alone while also working.

✓ **Checkpoint** What legal and social gains have the women's movement made?

SECTION **2** Assessment

Progress Monitoring Online
For: Self-test with vocabulary practice
www.pearsonschool.com/ushist

Comprehension

1. **Terms and People** What is the relationship between each of the following items and the women's movement?
   - feminism
   - Betty Friedan
   - NOW
   - ERA
   - Gloria Steinem
   - Phyllis Schlafly

2. **NoteTaking Reading Skill: Identify Causes and Effects** Use your cause-and-effect chart to answer the Section Focus Question: What led to the rise of the women's movement, and what impact did it have on American society?

Writing About History

3. **Quick Write: Identify Arguments** Suppose that you are either Betty Friedan or Phyllis Schlafly and you are giving a speech about women's roles in society. Identify and list the main arguments that would support your position.

Critical Thinking

4. **Draw Inferences** Why did so much time elapse between the first and second waves of feminism?

5. **Identify Assumptions** What beliefs led women to support the women's movement? What beliefs led women to oppose it?

6. **Formulating Questions** Make up two or three questions that will help you decide whether American women have made significant strides toward equality.

Section 2 Assessment

1. Sentences should reflect an understanding of the relationship each person or term had to the women's movement.

2. The civil rights movement and the earlier women's suffrage movement inspired the women's movement. The movement gave women greater political and social equality.

3. Speeches should accurately reflect the main ideas of the person selected.

4. After women won the right to vote, there was little activity or progress toward social equality because the limits of suffrage were not yet clear. Also, during the middle decades of the century, people were preoccupied with the Great Depression and World War II.

5. The belief that women should have the same rights and opportunities as men led some to support the movement; the belief that men and women are fundamentally different led others to oppose it.

6. Questions should help students determine how much women have gained or lost. Possible questions: What career opportunities were available to women because of the movement? What effect did the movement have on family support systems?

> For additional assessment, have students access **Progress Monitoring Online** at **www.pearsonschool.com/ushist.**

Esmeralda Santiago: *Almost a Woman*

Esmeralda Santiago

As more Latinos arrived in America, their experiences as immigrants drew them together despite their different nationalities. As Latinos, they faced discrimination, lack of opportunity, and a mainstream society in which their voices were often unheard. In this excerpt from her memoir *Almost a Woman*, Esmeralda Santiago tells what happened to her the first day after her family moved from Puerto Rico to New York.

There was no horizon in Brooklyn. Everywhere I looked, my eyes met a vertical maze of gray and brown straight-edged buildings with sharp corners and deep shadows. Every few blocks there was a cement playground surrounded by [a] chain-link fence. And in between, weedy lots mounded with garbage and rusting cars.

A girl came out of the building next door, a jump rope in her hand. She appraised me shyly. I pretended to ignore her. She stepped on the rope, stretched the ends overhead as if to measure their length, and then began to skip, slowly, grunting each time she came down on the sidewalk. Swish splat grunt swish, she turned her back to me; swish splat grunt swish, she faced me again and smiled. I smiled back, and she hopped over.

"*¿Tú eres hispana?*" she asked, as she whirled the rope in lazy arcs.

"No, I'm Puerto Rican."

"Same thing. Puerto Rican, Hispanic. That's what we are here." She skipped a tight circle, stopped abruptly, and shoved the rope in my direction. "Want a turn?"

"Sure." I hopped on one leg, then the other. "So, if you're Puerto Rican, they call you Hispanic?"

"Yeah. Anybody who speaks Spanish."

I jumped a circle, as she had done, but faster. "You mean, if you speak Spanish, you're Hispanic?"

"Well, yeah. No . . . I mean your parents have to be Puerto Rican or Cuban or something."

I whirled the rope to the right, then the left, like a boxer. "Okay, your parents are Cuban, let's say, and you're born here, but you don't speak Spanish. Are you Hispanic?"

She bit her lower lip. "I guess so," she finally said. "It has to do with being from a Spanish country. I mean, you or your parents, like, even if you don't speak Spanish, you're Hispanic, you know?" She looked at me uncertainly. I nodded and returned her rope.

But I didn't know. I'd always been Puerto Rican, and it hadn't occurred to me that in Brooklyn I'd be someone else.

Girls skip rope in a city playground.

Thinking Critically

1. **Make Inferences** Reread the first paragraph. How does Esmeralda feel about her new surroundings?

2. **Interpret the Literature** What would it mean to come to a new country and be "someone else"?

American Literature

Objectives

- Analyze documents from primary and secondary sources.
- Summarize points of view.
- Identify main ideas and details.

Background Knowledge

Ask students to recall what they know about the civil rights movement and the women's movement. Remind them that other groups in the United States faced discrimination.

Instruct ⓛ³

After students read the excerpt, conduct a class discussion based on the following questions: **What was the main point of the story?** *(to show how people can be evaluated on the basis of ethnic stereotypes and how people feel about being stereotyped)* **What does the story reflect about American society?** *(People's impressions of others are often influenced by existing ideas and misconceptions about ethnic groups.)*

Monitor Progress ⓛ³

As a class, write a short paragraph summarizing Santiago's experience. Discuss how being Puerto Rican would be different from being "Hispanic" in Santiago's new home.

History Background

Puerto Rican Migration In contrast to other Latinos in the United States, Puerto Ricans have unique legal circumstances. Puerto Ricans are American citizens because Puerto Rico is a commonwealth of the United States. The percentage of Puerto Ricans migrating to the mainland United States increased dramatically after World War II. During that era, the island experienced severe economic difficulties as the mainland United States was experiencing a booming economy. The island was also experiencing a population boom, partially because of longer life expectancy resulting from improved health care after the U.S. occupation. Many major American businesses began recruiting workers from Puerto Rico who flocked to major U.S. cities seeking jobs. Between 1945 and 1946, the Puerto Rican population of New York City alone jumped from 13,000 to more than 50,000. Many of these Puerto Ricans live in neighborhoods known as barrios.

Answers

Thinking Critically

1. She feels confined and trapped by the buildings and fences of the city.

2. In a new country, a person might be perceived differently because of ethnic or cultural background.

Objectives

As you teach this section, keep students focused on the following objectives to help them answer the Section Focus Question and master core content.

- Explain how the Latino population grew after World War I.
- Analyze the Latino and Native American rights movements of the 1960s and 1970s.
- Describe the expansion of rights for consumers and the disabled.

Background Knowledge L3

Ask students to think about the discrimination African Americans faced before the civil rights movement. Explain that in many places, Hispanic Americans faced similar discrimination.

Set a Purpose L3

- **WITNESS HISTORY** Read the selection aloud.

  Ask **How did Judith Baca try to redirect her students' negative behavior into something positive?** *(She helped her students use their talents to create murals rather than graffiti.)* **What do the students document in the murals?** *(Latino culture and history)*

- **Focus** Point out the Section Focus Question, and write it on the board. Tell students to refer to this question as they read. *(Answer appears with Section 3 Assessment answers.)*

- **Preview** Have students preview the Section Objectives and the list of Terms and People.

- **NoteTaking** Using the Guided Reading strategy (TE, p. T20), have students read this section. As they read, have students complete the Venn diagram to compare and contrast the Latino and Native American rights movements.
  Reading and Note Taking Study Guide

WITNESS HISTORY

From Graffiti to Art

Judith Baca, the daughter of Mexican immigrants, taught art in public schools in a rough Los Angeles neighborhood in the early 1970s. Between her classes, she watched young Latinos hanging out in parks and writing graffiti on the walls. Intrigued by the kids' graffiti, she developed the idea of channeling their creative energy into painting murals. Her idea spread to other U.S. cities, where kids used murals to document and celebrate Latino culture and history. Their work was just one part of a growing movement that sought to educate, respect, and politically organize American Latinos.

◄ A mural from the Philadelphia Mural Arts Program, begun in 1984, honors the great Mexican muralist, Diego Rivera (seated at center).

The Rights Revolution Expands

Objectives

- Explain how the Latino population grew after World War I.
- Analyze the Latino and Native American rights movements of the 1960s and 1970s.
- Describe the expansion of rights for consumers and the disabled.

Terms and People

Cesar Chavez	AIM
migrant farmworker	Japanese American
UFW	Citizens League
Chicano movement	Ralph Nader

NoteTaking

Reading Skill: Compare and Contrast
Create a Venn diagram to compare and contrast the Latino and Native American rights movements.

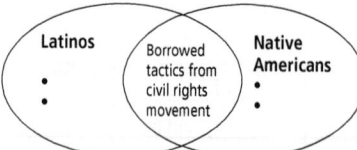

Why It Matters Successes in the civil rights and women's movements signaled a growing rights revolution in the United States. Latinos, Native Americans, and Asian Americans engaged in their own struggles for equality during the 1960s and 1970s, fighting to influence laws and government. Meanwhile, activists worked to expand rights for two broad groups: consumers and people with disabilities. **Section Focus Question: How did the rights movements of the 1960s and 1970s expand rights for diverse groups of Americans?**

The Latino Population Grows

After World War I, the United States passed legislation limiting European immigration. Yet during and after World War II, the country faced a growing demand for cheap labor. At the same time, the populations of Mexico and other Latin American nations grew steadily while job opportunities there declined. The combination of these factors created a steady stream of new immigrants to the United States.

A Spanish-Speaking Population People whose family origins are in Spanish-speaking Latin America are called Latinos or Hispanics. They come from many different places, but they share the same language and some elements of culture. Spanish-speaking people lived in many parts of western North America before settlers from the United States arrived, and their numbers have grown steadily. Mexican Americans, known as Chicanos, have always made up the largest group of U.S. Latinos.

Mexican Americans Farm the Land Beginning in 1942, Mexican immigrants came to the United States under the *bracero*, or farmhand, program. This program granted Mexican migrants temporary guest worker status, and over a period of 25 years, more than 4 million entered the U.S. The *braceros* played a crucial role in sustaining American agriculture during and after World War II.

Along with Mexicans who had migrated to the U.S. illegally in search of work, *braceros* who had outstayed their permits were targeted for deportation in the 1950s. In 1965, however, the government passed the Immigration and Nationality Act Amendments, eliminating national-origin quotas for immigrants. In the decades that followed, the number of legal Mexican and Asian immigrants surged. More than 400,000 Mexicans arrived during the 1960s, another 630,000 in the 1970s, and more than 1.5 million in the 1980s.

Emerging Latino Communities on the East Coast After World War II, large numbers of Puerto Ricans, Dominicans, and Cubans migrated to the United States. As citizens of a United States territory, Puerto Ricans came legally, leaving their homeland in search of better-paying jobs. In contrast, most Cuban and Dominican immigrants came to America as political refugees, fleeing their countries to escape the harsh rule of dictators. Most Puerto Rican, Cuban, and Dominican immigrants settled in urban areas, especially in New York City and Miami, Florida.

✔ **Checkpoint** Why did Mexicans and immigrants from other Latin American countries migrate to the United States?

Pressing for Equal Rights

Like other minorities, Latinos had long faced discrimination. After World War II, Latino veterans began agitating for equal treatment. Veteran Hector Garcia, for example, formed the American G.I. Forum to battle discrimination. In the 1960s and 1970s, influenced by the growing civil rights movement, Latinos increasingly fought for equal rights. They demanded better working conditions, salaries, and educational opportunities. Like African Americans, they sought federal protection of their right to vote and campaigned to elect politicians who represented their interests.

Cesar Chavez Organizes Farmworkers The most influential Latino activist was **Cesar Chavez.** Chavez fought for rights for farm laborers, who were among the most exploited workers in the nation. Because they migrated from farm to farm—and often from state to state—to pick fruits and vegetables, they were known as **migrant farmworkers.** They labored for long hours in deplorable conditions, with no benefits.

In 1962, Chavez organized a farmworkers' union in Delano, California. In the late 1960s, he merged his union with a separate union of Filipino farm laborers to form what became the **United Farm Workers (UFW).**

United States Latino Population

Bar graph showing Latino population (in millions):
- 1970: 4.5%
- 1980: 6.4%
- 1990: 8.8%
- 2000: 12.5%
- 2010*: 15.4%
- 2020*: 18.0%

* Projected growth
Percentages indicate proportion of total U.S. population that is Latino.
SOURCE: U.S. Census Bureau; Pew Hispanic Center

Graph Skills Describe the growth of the Latino population from 1970 to 2020.

HISTORY MAKERS

Cesar Chavez (1927–1993)
Cesar Chavez spent his childhood and youth toiling, like his parents, as a migrant farmworker. In the 1950s, he trained to be a community organizer. His skills led him to be named chief of the group doing the training. In 1962, he formed the National Farm Workers Association. Migrant workers had tried to form unions before and failed; Chavez made the effort succeed. In an impassioned letter to the grape industry, he expressed the workers' suffering and determination. "We are men and women who have suffered and endured much," he wrote. "Generation after generation have sought to demoralize us, to break our human spirit. But God knows that we are not beasts of burden, agricultural implements or rented slaves; we are men."

DON'T BUY CALIFORNIA GRAPES!

Connect to Your World

A Day Without Immigrants By 2006, it was estimated that some 11 million illegal immigrants lived in the United States, the majority of them from Mexico. With increased concerns about national security, some legislators argued for tightening enforcement of immigration laws. The House of Representatives passed a bill that would make it a felony to immigrate illegally. The bill also called for building a 700-mile wall along the border between the United States and Mexico. Opponents of the bill argued for less harsh measures, pointing out that about 5 percent of the labor force was made up of illegal immigrants.

They represented 24 percent of farmworkers and 14 percent of construction workers. To illustrate the contributions of immigrants to the U.S. economy, on May 1, 2006, activists organized "A Day Without Immigrants," which urged immigrants to stay home from work and boycott all consumer goods.

The boycotts were not unanimously supported by Hispanics across the nation. Some groups concerned about a negative political backlash stated that while they supported the rallies, they did not agree with boycotting.

Teach

The Latino Population Grows   L3

Instruct

- **Introduce** Discuss the relationship between the United States and Latin America through the 1950s. Ask them to predict how U.S. involvement in Latin America might have affected immigration trends.

- **Teach** Ask **What did the Immigration and Nationality Act Amendments do?** *(They made Latino immigration to the United States easier.)* **What were some reasons that Latinos immigrated to the United States?** *(to seek jobs, to escape dictators)* **Why do you think the United States did not limit immigration from Latin America the way it did from other parts of the world?** *(Sample response: As close neighbors, Americans may have been more familiar and comfortable with people from Latin American countries.)* Using the Numbered Heads strategy (TE, p. T23), have students discuss the ways in which different reasons for coming to the United States may have shaped different Latino communities.

- **Analyzing the Visuals** Have students examine the mural on the previous page. Ask students to write paragraphs describing the ways that the mural illustrates cultural values.

Independent Practice

Have students create outlines summarizing the information below the blue heading "The Latino Population Grows."

Monitor Progress

As students complete their Venn diagrams, circulate to make sure that they compare and contrast the Latino and Native American rights movements. For a completed version of the Venn diagram, see Note Taking Transparencies, B-140a.

Answers

Graph Skills The graph shows a projected increase of more than 500 percent.

✔ Most wanted better jobs. Some were fleeing political persecution.

Pressing for Equal Rights

Instruct

- **Introduce: Key Terms** Ask students to find the key terms *migrant farmworkers* and *UFW* (in bold) in the text. Point out that the *UFW* represented farmworkers of all backgrounds, a large number of whom were Latinos. Ask **From whom might the *UFW* have drawn inspiration?** (*the civil rights movement*)

- **Teach** Ask **What tactics from the civil rights movement did the UFW employ?** (*nonviolence, organizing large group protests, boycotts*) **How was the focus of the Chicano movement different from the goals of the UFW?** (*The Chicano movement focused more on cultural recognition and political gains, rather than concentrating on labor rights.*) **How did the Chicano movement focus its political efforts?** (*It concentrated on reducing poverty and discrimination and on creating opportunities.*) Have students read the HISTORY MAKERS biography of Cesar Chavez on the previous page. Ask **How did Chavez's experiences affect his activism?** (*As a child of migrant farmworkers, he understood the hardships they faced.*)

- **Quick Activity** Display Color Transparency: *The Latino Movement.* Use the lesson suggested in the transparency book to guide a discussion about the role of Cesar Chavez in the Latino movement.
  Color Transparencies **A-131**

Independent Practice

- Have students read *History Comics: Cesar Chavez and the UFW* and answer the questions that follow. Teaching Resources, **p. 22**

- Ask students to examine the Infographic on these two pages. Have students write paragraphs describing the conditions many migrant workers experienced.

Monitor Progress

Circulate to make sure that students complete their worksheets and understand that migrant farmworkers experienced unsafe working conditions.

Answer

✔ better wages and working conditions, recognition of culture in schools, greater political representation

582   An Era of Protest and Change

Vocabulary Builder
implement – (IHM pluh mehnt) *v.* to bring about

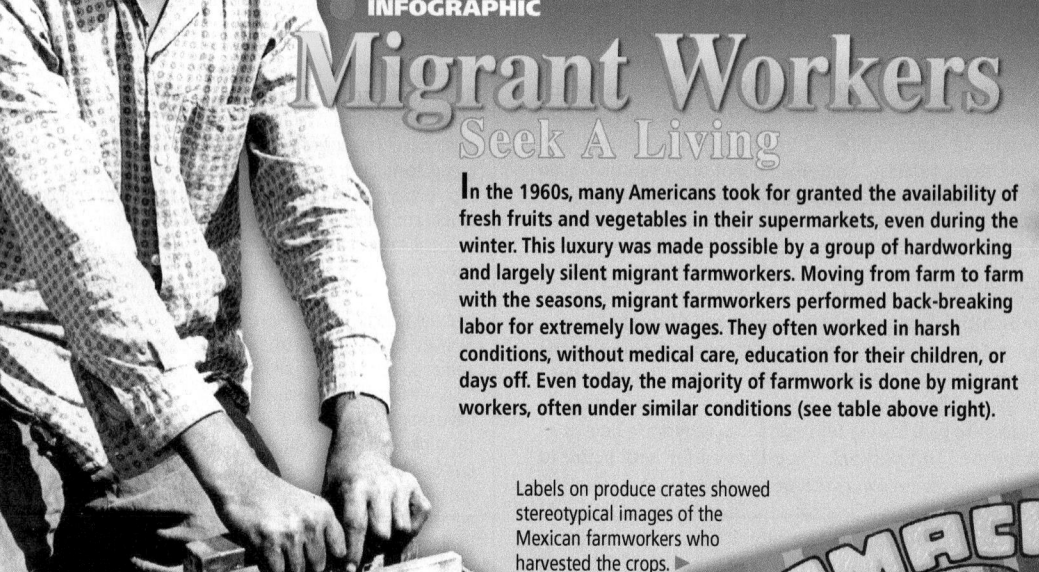

A worker picks strawberries at a California farm in 1963. ▼

Committed to nonviolent tactics, the UFW <u>implemented</u> a workers' strike and consumer boycott of table grapes. With the help of Dolores Huerta, Chavez's top aide, the UFW urged people across the nation to boycott California grapes in order to win recognition from the growers. In 1975, California passed a law requiring collective bargaining between growers and union representatives. Farmworkers finally had a legal basis to ask for better working conditions.

The Chicano Movement Grows While Chavez focused on farmworkers' rights, a broader Mexican American social and political effort grew, which came to be known as the **Chicano movement.** Part of it was dedicated to increasing Latinos' awareness of their history and culture. At California colleges and high schools, and in other states with a Mexican American population, Chicano students demanded that educators teach more about their heritage. Others in the movement focused on quality-of-life issues. For example, the National Council of La Raza was founded in 1968 with the goal of reducing poverty and discrimination and providing better opportunities for Latinos.

Much of the movement's energy was concentrated on attaining political strength for Latinos, or what some called "brown power." José Angel Gutiérrez organized the political party La Raza Unida in Texas. The party worked for better housing and jobs, and it successfully supported Latino political candidates. By 1980, six Hispanics sat in Congress, representing districts from New York to California. Moreover, Hispanics gained greater representation in state, county, and city governments.

✔ **Checkpoint** What were some of the demands of Latino groups in the 1960s and 1970s?

INFOGRAPHIC

Migrant Workers
Seek A Living

In the 1960s, many Americans took for granted the availability of fresh fruits and vegetables in their supermarkets, even during the winter. This luxury was made possible by a group of hardworking and largely silent migrant farmworkers. Moving from farm to farm with the seasons, migrant farmworkers performed back-breaking labor for extremely low wages. They often worked in harsh conditions, without medical care, education for their children, or days off. Even today, the majority of farmwork is done by migrant workers, often under similar conditions (see table above right).

Labels on produce crates showed stereotypical images of the Mexican farmworkers who harvested the crops. ▶

Differentiated Instruction   Solutions for All Learners

L1 Special Needs Students   L2 English Language Learners   L2 Less Proficient Readers

Lead students through the Infographic. First, read the text on the left aloud to students. Then, read the captions of each image. Ask **Why might produce companies choose to use a stereotypical drawing on the label instead of a photo of an actual farmworker, such as the man pictured here?** (*A picture of an actual farmworker could remind customers of the realities of fruit harvesting.*) **If workers** became sick from exposure to pesticides, who would pay for their medical care? (*They would have to pay themselves, if they could afford to get care. Most had no medical care at all.*) **Why is strawberry picking more difficult than picking some other fruits?** (*Strawberries grow near the ground, requiring workers to remain bent over as they find and pick the fruit.*)

Native Americans and Asian Americans Battle Discrimination

Native Americans had a long history of discrimination and suffered high rates of poverty, unemployment, and suicide. Inspired by the struggle for civil rights, they forged their own protest movements in the 1960s and 1970s. At the same time, Asian Americans fought long-standing discrimination.

Activist Groups Form As with the civil rights movement, the young took the lead in demanding change for American Indians. In 1961, the National Indian Youth Council (NIYC) formed, with the goal of preserving native fishing rights in the Northwest. Over time, the group expanded its aims to include broad civil rights for Native Americans. In 1968, the Chippewa activists Dennis Banks and George Mitchell founded the **American Indian Movement (AIM)**. At first, AIM focused on helping Indians living in urban ghettos. Before long, however, AIM was addressing all civil rights issues, particularly the securing of land, legal rights, and self-government for Native Americans.

Confronting the Government As Indians' dissatisfaction with the government grew, their activism became more militant. In late 1969, a group of American Indians occupied the island of Alcatraz, the site of a federal prison in San Francisco Bay that had closed in 1963. Members of the Sioux tribe asserted that the island belonged to them under a treaty provision granting them unused federal land. About 100 American Indians representing 50 tribes joined the occupation. In spite of efforts by the Coast Guard and other federal authorities to evict them, the Indians maintained control of the island until mid-1971.

The 1970s saw another series of confrontations. Led by Dennis Banks and Russell Means, AIM orchestrated a "long march" from San Francisco to Washington, D.C., in 1972. Upon arriving in the capital, they took control

Migrant Farmworkers Today

- 81 percent are foreign-born; of these, 77 percent are Mexican.
- 52 percent are illegal immigrants.
- The average migrant farmworker is a 31-year-old Spanish-speaking male.
- Half of all migrant farmworkers live far below the poverty level.
- The life expectancy for a migrant farmworker is 49 years.

SOURCE: U.S. Department of Labor; ERIC Digest

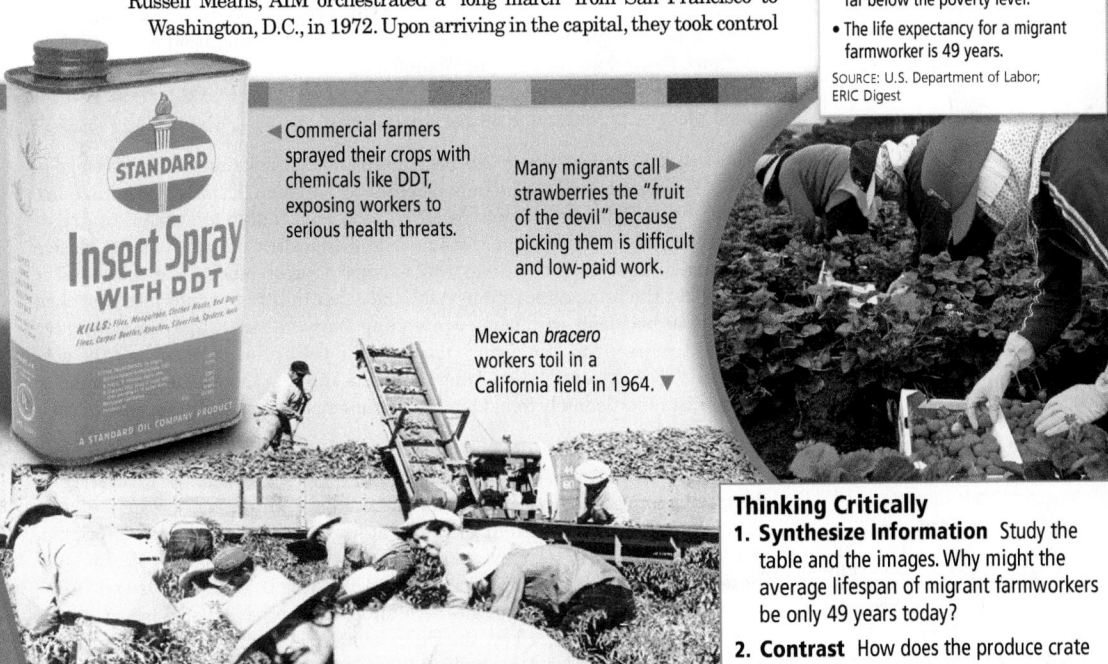

◄ Commercial farmers sprayed their crops with chemicals like DDT, exposing workers to serious health threats.

Many migrants call ► strawberries the "fruit of the devil" because picking them is difficult and low-paid work.

Mexican *bracero* workers toil in a California field in 1964. ▼

Thinking Critically

1. **Synthesize Information** Study the table and the images. Why might the average lifespan of migrant farmworkers be only 49 years today?

2. **Contrast** How does the produce crate label contrast with the actual conditions of migrant farmworkers?

Instruct

- **Introduce** Explain that Ralph Nader was an advocate for consumer rights and protection before he was a presidential candidate. Discuss the reasons that a consumer advocate might choose to run for public office.

- **Teach** Ask **What consumer products were first revealed to be unsafe by Ralph Nader?** *(certain models of automobiles)* **Why do you think the Nixon administration created a government agency to oversee workplace safety?** *(to make sure that employers' workplace practices were not hazardous to workers)* **How did their sister's experience influence John Kennedy and Eunice Shriver's actions on behalf of people with disabilities?** *(Possible response: They wanted to bring the issue to the public's attention so that people with disabilities would be given consideration and respect.)*

- **Quick Activity** Have students list some product defects that might prompt producers to recall those products. Discuss the legal liability that manufacturers might be subject to if they fail to recall unsafe products. Invite students to read product defects from their lists and explain what might affect the decision to recall those products.

Independent Practice

NoteTaking Have students fill in the chart identifying causes of the movements for Asian Americans, consumer rights, and the rights of people with disabilities. Reading and Note Taking Study Guide

Monitor Progress

As students complete their charts, circulate to make sure that they understand the causes of these two movements. For a completed version of the chart, see Note Taking Transparencies, **B-140b.**

Answer

 They wanted to secure land and legal rights.

HISTORY MAKERS

Daniel Inouye (born 1924)
When Hawaii became a state in 1959, Daniel Inouye was elected its first representative to Congress. Three years later, he became the Senate's first Asian American. The son of Japanese immigrants, Inouye entered the army after the bombing of Pearl Harbor. He lost an arm in combat and received the Medal of Honor. Inouye graduated from law school before entering public office.
In more than forty years in the Senate, Inouye, a Democrat, has championed the interests of Hawaiians as well as healthcare and education for all children.

Ben Nighthorse Campbell (born 1933)
The son of a Portuguese immigrant mother and a Cheyenne Indian father, Ben Nighthorse Campbell joined the Air Force and served in the Korean War before entering college. In 1982, he was elected to the Colorado State Legislature. He went on to careers as a U.S. representative and then a senator. He did not run for reelection in 2005. Throughout his years in Congress, he worked for Native American rights and on policy relating to natural resources. Originally a Democrat, Campbell became a Republican in 1995.

NoteTaking

Reading Skill: Identify Causes
Identify causes of expanding rights for Asian Americans, consumers, and those with disabilities.

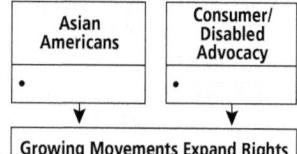

---

of the Bureau of Indian Affairs building. They temporarily renamed it the Native American Embassy, suggesting Native Americans are treated as foreigners.

Siege at Wounded Knee In 1970, Dee Brown published *Bury My Heart at Wounded Knee,* about the 1890 massacre of Sioux at Wounded Knee, South Dakota. Brown noted that in all the history of the American West,

> **Primary Source** "Only occasionally was the voice of an Indian heard, and then more often than not it was recorded by the pen of a white man. The Indian was the dark menace of the myths, and even if he had known how to write in English, where would he have found a printer or a publisher?"

The best-selling book raised public consciousness about the historic mistreatment of Native Americans. Building on this momentum, AIM planned a dramatic confrontation at Wounded Knee. In late February of 1973, AIM took over the village and refused to leave until the government agreed to investigate the condition of reservation Indians. Federal authorities put Wounded Knee under siege, and two AIM members died in the resulting gunfire. The standoff ended in May when the government pledged to reexamine native treaty rights.

Making Legal Headway Native American activism spurred the passage of several laws in the 1970s. The Indian Self-Determination Act of 1975, for instance, fulfilled one of the main demands of the American Indian movement by granting tribes greater control over resources and education on reservations. Native Americans also continued to win legal battles to regain land, mineral, and water rights. Yet the protests staged by AIM and other militant groups also provoked a political backlash with some contending that the federal government gave special treatment to American Indians. While politicians debated how the government should treat Native Americans, the Indians themselves continued to suffer disproportionately from high rates of unemployment and other social ills.

Asian Americans Fight Discrimination Prejudice against people of Japanese and Chinese ancestry, who had come to the United States as laborers, had long been part of the American social and economic climate. The **Japanese American Citizens League**, founded in 1929 to protect Japanese Americans' civil rights, worked for decades to receive government compensation for property lost by Japanese Americans interned in camps during World War II. In the 1960s and 1970s, in the wake of the expanding rights revolution, many other groups formed to combat discrimination and protect the rights of all Asian Americans. The Immigration and Nationality Act Amendments (1965) also aided Asian immigrants.

✔ **Checkpoint** Why did Native Americans work to expand their rights?

History Background

Asian American Movement It was not until the late 1960s that people of Asian descent in the United States began to develop a common racial identity. During this time, a majority of the Asian population in the United States were citizens by birth; however, they were not treated as such and, as a result of a long history of legal discrimination they were the victims of racism. Their experiences with racism helped Asians identify with the African American civil rights movement, which showed them how to assert their own racial identities and combat institutional racism. In 1968, Yuji Ichioka, a graduate student at U.C.

Berkeley, coined the term "Asian American" and helped found the Asian American Political Alliance. His goal was to unite Asian Americans and use their numbers to gain more political power. At the same time, other Asian American students joined together in opposition to the Vietnam War, spurring the Asian American movement. In addition to opposing the Vietnam War, the Asian American movement worked to obtain Asian American courses in colleges and universities and fair treatment when applying for a job, purchasing a home, or receiving medical treatment.

New Rights for Consumers and the Disabled

In the same way that many activists worked to extend rights to women and minorities and to protect the environment, others worked to protect the rights of consumers and Americans with disabilities.

During the Progressive Era, reformers had pushed for measures to protect consumers, ranging from the Pure Food and Drug Act to the Meat Inspection Act. The consumer rights movement reemerged during the 1960s and 1970s. It was led by **Ralph Nader,** a lawyer who began to investigate whether flawed car designs led to increased traffic accidents and deaths. His book, *Unsafe at Any Speed* (1965), attacked automakers whose thirst for profits produced unsafe vehicles that endangered the public. Nader's best-selling book stirred the nation and prompted Congress to pass the National Traffic and Motor Vehicle Safety Act in 1966. Among other things, the act made safety belts standard equipment in all cars. Nader went on to form several consumer advocacy groups. Under his influence, consumer advocacy adopted many of the practices that shape it today, including research and government lobbying. Advocacy for workers began to gain more prominence as well. The Nixon administration proposed the idea for the Occupational Safety and Health Administration (OSHA), which mandated workplace safety regulations.

Historically, the nation had treated people with disabilities as defective. FDR hid the fact that he could not walk because he did not want society to assume he was incapable of serving as President. Yet by the 1970s, Americans with disabilities were making great strides toward expanding their rights. Disabled veterans from the Korean and Vietnam wars took part in this activism. The Kennedy administration called for change by establishing the Panel on Mental Retardation in 1961 to explore ways for the government to help people with intellectual disabilities. The next year, Eunice Shriver, Kennedy's sister, began an athletic camp for young people with disabilities that eventually became the Special Olympics. Over the next few years, the government passed several laws guaranteeing equal access to education for people with disabilities.

A Winner
A girl shows her sister the gold medal she won at a 2003 Special Olympics event in South Carolina.

 Checkpoint How did rights for consumers and people with disabilities expand during the 1960s and 1970s?

Progress Monitoring *Online*
For: Self-test with vocabulary practice
www.pearsonschool.com/ushist

SECTION 3 Assessment

Comprehension

1. Terms and People What is the relationship of each of the items below to Latino, Native American, and Asian American movements for equality?
- Cesar Chavez
- migrant farmworker
- UFW
- Chicano movement
- AIM
- Japanese American Citizens League

2. NoteTaking Reading Skill: Compare and Contrast Use your completed Venn diagram to answer the Section Focus Question: How did the rights movements of the 1960s and 1970s expand rights for diverse groups of Americans?

Writing About History

3. Quick Write: Anticipate Opposing Arguments Suppose that you are going to give a speech in support of making migrant farmworkers legal citizens with full benefits. Anticipate any opposing arguments, and note ways to address them in your speech.

Critical Thinking

4. Draw Inferences How did the government make immigration for Latinos and Asians easier in the 1960s?

5. Identify Central Issues Why was it particularly important to Latino activists to gain political rights?

6. Draw Comparisons How and why was the Native American struggle for equality different from that of Latinos?

7. Predict Consequences Do you think rights for people with disabilities would have been achieved earlier if FDR had openly shown his disability? Explain.

Objectives

As you teach this section, keep students focused on the following objectives to help them answer the Section Focus Question and master core content.

- Assess the causes and effects of the environmental movement.
- Analyze why environmental protection became a controversial issue.

Prepare to Read

Background Knowledge L3

Remind students that many activists of the 1960s fought against injustice to improve the world around them. Ask students to predict how some came to believe that this improvement needed to include protection of Earth's ability to support life.

Set a Purpose L3

- **WITNESS HISTORY** Read the selection aloud.

  Ask **What do you think Carson was implying in her last sentence?** *(She was implying that pollution produced by humans was responsible for the deaths of the animals.)*

- **Focus** Point out the Section Focus Question, and write it on the board. Tell students to refer to this question as they read. *(Answer appears with Section 4 Assessment answers.)*

- **Preview** Have students preview the Section Objectives and the list of Terms and People.

- **NoteTaking** Using the Guided Reading strategy (TE, p. T20), have students read this section. As they read, have students record major events in the environmental movement. Reading and Note Taking Study Guide

▲ Rachel Carson

A 1962 cartoon shows a man choking on fumes from a pesticide he uses to kill a fly. ▶

WITNESS HISTORY

An Environmental Wake-up Call

"There once was a town in the heart of America where all life seemed to live in harmony with its surroundings. . . . Then a strange blight crept over the area and everything began to change. Mysterious maladies swept across the flocks of chickens; the cattle and sheep sickened and died. . . . There was a strange stillness. The birds, for example—where had they gone? . . . On the mornings that had once throbbed with the dawn chorus of robins, catbirds, doves, jays, wrens, and scores of other bird voices there was now no sound; only silence lay over the fields and woods and marsh. . . . No witchcraft, no enemy action had silenced the rebirth of new life in this stricken world. The people had done it to themselves."

—Rachel Carson, *Silent Spring*, 1962

The Environmental Movement

Objectives

- Assess the causes and effects of the environmental movement.
- Analyze why environmental protection became a controversial issue.

Terms and People

Rachel Carson	Clean Air Act
toxic waste	Clean Water Act
Earth Day	Endangered Species
EPA	Act

NoteTaking

Reading Skill: Recognize Sequence As you read, record major events in the environmental movement in a flowchart like the one below.

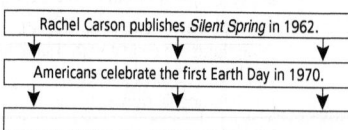

Rachel Carson publishes *Silent Spring* in 1962.

Americans celebrate the first Earth Day in 1970.

Why It Matters The "rights revolution" of the 1960s and 1970s eventually influenced all aspects of American life—including people's right to a clean and safe environment. The story told by **Rachel Carson** pointed out that human actions were harming not only the environment but people themselves. Public awareness of environmental issues prompted an important debate about the government's role in environmental regulations. **Section Focus Question: What forces gave rise to the environmental movement, and what impact did it have?**

Vocabulary Builder

Use the information below and the following resource to teach students the high-use word from this section. Teaching Resources, Vocabulary Builder, p. 11

High-Use Word	Definition and Sample Sentence
compel	*v.* to force someone to do something The progressive movement encouraged Congress to **compel** food producers to make food safe.

Environmental Activists Speak Out

In the 1920s, Progressives had worked to conserve public lands and parks. But no one thought to worry much about the ill effects of industrialization. In 1952, however, a blanket of deadly smog, caused by coal fires, engulfed the city of London, killing some 12,000 people. Ten years after the London smog, a book sparked the modern environmental movement.

Silent Spring Sparks a Movement Coal smog is just one kind of **toxic waste,** or poisonous byproduct of human activity. Another is acid rain, or moisture in the air caused by the mixing of water with chemicals produced by the burning of fossil fuels. Toxic wastes are also produced when nuclear power is generated. Throughout the 1960s and 1970s, scientists learned more about toxic wastes and other environmental threats.

In 1962, biologist Rachel Carson's book *Silent Spring* described the deadly impact that pesticides were having on birds and other animals. Her book caused a sensation. Though the chemical industry fought back, the public was convinced by her argument. Carson did more than point to the dangers of chemicals and toxic waste. She also insisted that human activity drastically altered the environment and that humans had a responsibility to protect it. Her work eventually <u>compelled</u> Congress to restrict the use of the pesticide DDT. It also spurred widespread environmental activism among Americans.

When a fire erupted on the Cuyahoga River in Cleveland, Ohio, in 1969, activists instantly spoke out. The fire occurred when a spark ignited floating oil and debris—byproducts of industrialization—on the river's surface. *Time* magazine reported that the river "oozes, rather than flows." Even more luridly, the magazine remarked that in the Cuyahoga, a person "does not drown but decays."

Inaugurating Earth Day Events like the Cuyahoga fire seemed to confirm the dire predictions of *Silent Spring*. One response to growing environmental concerns was a nationwide protest called **Earth Day.** Wisconsin senator Gaylord Nelson, who played the leading role in organizing the protest, wanted "to shake up the political establishment and force this issue [environment] onto the national agenda." On April 22, 1970, close to 20 million Americans took part in Earth Day events across the nation. The yearly event attracted the support of many of the same people who had advocated civil and women's rights. It was also backed by a number of grassroots groups, including the Sierra Club, founded by John Muir in 1892, and the Wilderness Society, established in 1935. Historically, these groups had focused on conservation. With the rise of the environmental movement, however, they called for broader environmental protections.

Vocabulary Builder
compel–(kuhm PEHL) *v.* to force someone to do something

Earth Day, Then and Now
Students march through the streets of St. Louis on the first Earth Day to protest pollution caused by cars (left); students on Earth Day in 2005 rush to break a world record for the most trees planted in an hour.

Independent Practice

Have students fill in additional boxes in their Recognize Sequence flowcharts to show events in the environmental movement that happened after Earth Day 1970.

Monitor Progress

As students complete their flowcharts, circulate to make sure that they record the entries in chronological order and that they understand the effect of Rachel Carson's book *Silent Spring*. For a completed version of the flowchart, see Note Taking Transparencies, **B-141**.

Superfund Sites, 2008

Geography *Interactive*
For: Interactive map
www.pearsonschool.com/ushist

• EPA Superfund site

▲ **Love Canal, New York:** The first designated Superfund site in 1983, Love Canal was successfully cleaned up and removed from the high-priority list in 2004.

Map Skills In 1980, Congress established Superfund, a program financed by taxes on oil and certain chemicals, to clean up sites that had extreme environmental pollution. Today, more than 1,500 sites remain on the high-priority list.

1. **Identify** In general, where are most Superfund sites located? Why do you think this is so?

2. **Draw Inferences** Do sites in urban areas pose greater risks than sites in rural areas? Explain.

3. **Synthesize Information** Study the bar graph. What varied benefits does repurposing Superfund sites bring that would not be accomplished by just cleaning up the sites?

A President Turns Environmentalist In 1969, President Nixon declared that the 1970s "must be the years when America pays its debts to the past by reclaiming the purity of its air, its water and our living environment." Nixon had not come into office as an environmental activist. But the public's increasing concern with protecting the environment convinced him to support environmental reforms.

Under Nixon's leadership, Congress created the **Environmental Protection Agency (EPA)** in 1970. This federal agency's mission was to protect the "entire ecological chain." In addition to cleaning up and protecting the environment, the EPA sought to limit or to eliminate pollutants that posed a risk to the public's health, such as toxic substances that cause cancer. Nixon also signed a number of environmental laws. The **Clean Air Act** (1970) combated air pollution by, among other things, limiting the emissions from factories and automobiles. The **Clean Water Act** (1973) sought to limit the pollution of water by industry and agriculture. The **Endangered Species Act** (1973) promoted the protection of endangered plants and animals.

President Gerald Ford continued in Nixon's footsteps. In 1974, he created the Nuclear Regulatory Commission to make sure nuclear materials would be handled safely without harmful impacts on people or the environment.

✓ **Checkpoint** How did the modern environmental movement grow?

Answers

Map Skills

1. In the east, especially the Northeast; more industrial cities are located there.

2. Urban areas have larger populations, which mean more people who could be harmed by environmental pollution.

3. The new uses might be safer and more economically beneficial for the communities.

✓ Alarmed by *Silent Spring*, people organized gatherings such as Earth Day to draw attention to environmental issues. When people expressed this concern, the government responded by passing environmental protection laws.

Differentiated Instruction Solutions for All Learners

L4 Advanced Readers L4 Gifted and Talented Students

In the years since the Environmental Protection Agency (EPA) was established, opinions of its effectiveness have varied. Some people argue that it does not do enough to protect the environment and that it has often been weakened by politicians who are opposed to environmental protection laws. Others, especially corporate leaders, argue that it goes too far, harms businesses and acts on the basis of scientific ideas that are not sufficiently proven. Have students imagine that they are government analysts charged with deciding whether the EPA should continue to function. Have them research the history and activities of the EPA and make presentations to the class as though the class were a group of government officials. The presentation should explain whether the EPA is effective and necessary. If students recommend against keeping the EPA, they should propose and explain alternate solutions to environmental issues.

Bowers Landfill, Before Cleanup: Bowers Landfill in Ohio was a municipal dump for garbage and hazardous chemical and industrial waste for several decades starting in the 1960s.

Bowers Landfill, 1991: After removing all of the contaminated soil, this site was completely restored for use as a wetland.

Bowers Landfill, Today: Wetlands provide a safe habitat for a variety of plants and wildlife, and they also protect the surrounding ecosystem by preventing flooding.

Superfund Cleanup, 2004

Superfund sites

1,750
1,500
1,250
1,000 (900)
750
500
250 (248)
0

☐ Site cleanups completed   ■ Sites restored for new uses

One of Superfund's goals is to restore sites in ways that provide economic or environmental benefits to communities.

Environmental Setbacks

As the 1970s drew to a close, a series of environmental crises made the headlines. They reinforced the public's concern about the environment and produced calls for even more far-reaching actions. Yet, at the same time, a number of people began to wonder if the government had enacted too many regulations. Rather than calling for more federal action, they tried to limit the government's role in environmental protection.

The EPA Investigates Love Canal In 1978, a resident of Love Canal, a community near Niagara Falls in upstate New York, hung a sign from his home that read: "Give me Liberty. I've Already Got Death." This sign referred to the fact that residents of the community had exceptionally high rates of birth defects and cancer. Newspaper reporters and EPA investigators determined that these illnesses were caused by thousands of tons of toxic chemicals, which industries had been dumping in the ground for decades. One EPA administrator recalled the scene he witnessed following a heavy rain that sent toxic chemicals percolating up through the ground.

> **Primary Source** "I visited the canal area at that time. Corroding waste-disposal drums could be seen breaking up through the grounds of backyards. Trees and gardens were turning black and dying. . . . Puddles of noxious substances were pointed out to me by the residents. Some of these puddles were in their yards, some were in their basements, others yet were on the school grounds. Everywhere the air had a faint, choking smell. Children returned from play with burns on their hands and faces."
> —Eckhardt Beck, *EPA Journal*, 1979

The Love Canal contamination, along with other events involving hazardous waste, prompted Congress to establish Superfund (see feature at top) in 1980.

History Background

China Syndrome Twelve days before the Three Mile Island meltdown, Columbia Studios released *The China Syndrome,* a fictional story of an accident at a nuclear power plant that was covered up by plant officials. The term "China Syndrome" referred to people's fears that there could be a nuclear accident so bad it would melt a hole through Earth all the way to China. Few Americans had seriously considered such an idea. The accident, coupled with the movie, suddenly made the phrase "China Syndrome" a national phenomenon. Many scientists and engineers argued that the film contained flaws that misrepresented the nuclear power industry. Others pointed out that some elements in the film were based on real plant operating errors that had received no publicity. For example, in the film the nuclear accident almost happens because of a malfunctioning temperature gauge. A similar event really had happened at a nuclear plant near Chicago, Illinois. *The China Syndrome* became a symbol of the antinuclear movement and compelled many people to call for greater regulation of the nuclear power industry.

Environmental Setbacks

Instruct

- **Introduce** Explain that for many people in the 1970s "Love Canal" became synonymous with toxic waste and "Three Mile Island" with the dangers of nuclear power plants. Ask **Why did these places become so memorable to people?** *(Heightened public awareness of environmental issues and increasing media coverage, including presidential visits, kept these sites in the public mind.)*

- **Teach** Ask **How did toxic waste that had been dumped at Love Canal harm the people who lived there?** *(The waste caused increased rates of birth defects and cancer, killed plants, injured children, and ruined property.)* Display Color Transparency: *Three Mile Island.* Ask **Why did the governor of Pennsylvania order that the Three Mile Island nuclear plant be shut down?** *(to prevent the malfunctioning reactor from releasing radioactive gas into the air as it melted down)* Using the Numbered Heads strategy (TE, p. T23), ask students to list environmental concerns that arose in the 1970s. Students should mention threats from environmental pollution to people, the contamination of food and water, and the effects of air and water pollution on species and the ecosystem as a whole. To help them draw conclusions, ask **How did environmental disasters highlight the dangers to the environment?** *(They showed that dangers existed, even in residential areas.)* Color Transparencies, **A-132**

- **Quick Activity** Ask students to complete *Reading a Chart: Nuclear Energy.* Then, have them use the chart to conduct a debate on whether the country should expand the use of nuclear energy. Teaching Resources, **p. 23**

Independent Practice

Have students access the **Geography Interactive map** at **www.pearsonschool.com/ushist.** Have students complete the web activity and answer the map skills questions.

Monitor Progress

Circulate to make sure that students understand the significance of Superfund.

Objectives

- Understand how economic concerns can affect environmental policies.
- Understand the concept of balancing economic, social, and political concerns.

Background Knowledge   **L3**

Have students recall why the national parks system was created. Ask students to consider why some people and corporations advocate using National Parks and Forests for industry.

Instruct   **L3**

Point out that the timeline shows events related to protection of the environment. Ask **How does failing to ratify the Kyoto Protocol reflect American uncertainty about protecting the global environment?** *(It shows that not everyone agrees about how to prioritize the protection of the global environment.)* **Why do some people support oil exploration in the Arctic Refuge?** *(It would allow America to be less dependent on foreign oil reserves; supporters also say the drilling would be environmentally responsible.)* **What are the dangers of drilling in the Arctic Refuge?** *(damage to wildlife habitats; smaller oil reserves than anticipated)*

Monitor Progress

- Have students complete the American Issues Journal Worksheet, *Interaction with the Environment*. Check students' work to make sure that they grasp the aspects of the issue. Teaching Resources, **pp. 15–18**

- Remind students to complete their American Issues Journal notes. Review their work for accuracy. Reading and Note Taking Study Guide

Answers

Transfer Activities

1. It would not be harmful to the environment and it would lead to a huge amount of new jobs. Those opposed say that it is harmful to the environment and in addition would not yield enough oil.

2. The first source would have been supportive.

3. For more information, have students access **www.pearsonschool.com/ushist.**

TRACK THE ISSUE

How can we balance economic development and environmental protection?

The goals of economic growth and environmental protection are often in conflict. For example, power plants provide energy, but they pollute the air. Dams supply water, but they destroy natural habitats. Finding a balance between growth and conservation may involve trade-offs. Use the timeline below to explore this enduring issue.

1872 Yellowstone
First national park is established.

1916 National Park Service
Congress creates the National Park System.

1962 *Silent Spring*
Rachel Carson's book exposes dangers of pesticides.

1970 Clean Air Act
Congress establishes air quality standards.

1973 Endangered Species Act
Law offers protection for threatened species.

1997 Kyoto Protocol
United States signs international agreement on CO_2 emissions, but Congress fails to ratify it.

A view of Yellowstone's Grand Canyon painted in 1872

A caribou grazes on a plain near an oil-drilling facility in Alaska.

DEBATE THE ISSUE

The Search for Oil   Alaska's Arctic National Wildlife Refuge (ANWR) is a large nature preserve with an abundance of wildlife. It may also contain large deposits of crude oil. Some people want to drill for this oil, while others believe oil drilling would ruin the pristine wilderness.

> "There are good reasons . . . to permit ANWR drilling. . . . It could be done without wrecking the environment. . . . Only 2,000 acres of the 19 million-acre ANWR refuge would be subject to drilling. . . . Drilling could create 250,000 to 735,000 jobs nationwide. . . . [Drilling] in an environmentally sensitive fashion is important insurance against future energy shocks."
>
> —Editorial, *USA Today*, 2005

> "Drilling in the Arctic Refuge is not a path to energy independence or lower prices at the pump. The United States Geological Survey estimates that the Refuge has less than a single year's supply of oil that would not reach the market for at least 10 years. Meanwhile, the harm to wildlife and to our greatest wildlife refuge would be irreparable."
>
> —Defenders of Wildlife

 TRANSFER Activities

1. **Compare** Why does the first source support drilling in the arctic refuge? Why does Defenders of Wildlife oppose it?

2. **Analyze** How might the first source have responded to the creation of the National Park Service in 1916? Explain.

3. **Transfer** Use the following Web site to see a video, try a WebQuest, and write in your journal. www.pearsonschool.com/ushist

---

History Background

The Kyoto Protocol In December 1997, representatives from more than 170 nations met in Kyoto, Japan, to develop a treaty that was intended to slow global climate change by reducing greenhouse gas emissions. The Kyoto Protocol specified a goal of slightly more than 5 percent emissions reduction by 2012. The treaty specified that the developed industrial nations that had historically emitted the most greenhouse gases would take the lead in reducing emissions. Less was expected of developing countries such as those in Africa and, notably, of India and China. Although President Clinton signed the treaty, Congress refused to ratify it. When the Kyoto Treaty Protocol went into force after its ratification by Russia in 2005, the United States still had not ratified it. Some U.S. leaders consider the provisions of the treaty to place an unfair economic burden on the United States and believe that the treaty allows China, which has a trade surplus with the United States, to avoid responsibility for the pollution it produces.

Meltdown at Three Mile Island Shortly after the investigation at Love Canal, an accident occurred in the nuclear energy industry. On March 28, 1979, the core of the nuclear reactor at Three Mile Island outside Harrisburg, Pennsylvania, began to melt after the reactor malfunctioned. When the plant threatened to release radioactive gas, the governor declared a state of emergency and shut it down. To reassure the public that plant managers had contained the accident, President Jimmy Carter and his wife traveled to Three Mile Island and toured the reactor.

Even though the incident was contained and there proved to be no health risks, it had profound effects on America's energy policy. In the wake of the accident, Americans opposed nuclear energy, fearful of possible disasters. The government temporarily stopped building new nuclear power plants. Even though it later lifted the ban, no new American nuclear plants were ordered for more than a quarter of a century. In the 2000s, with energy shortages, many Americans began to call for building new nuclear plants.

Questioning Environmental Regulation As more environmental regulations were passed, opposition to them grew. Conservatives complained that they stripped individuals of their property rights by restricting what they could or could not do with their land. Some argued that private property owners would do a better job of protecting the environment than the government because the owners had an interest in preserving the profitability of their land. Many people—and especially industry leaders—also worried that too much environmental regulation would hamper business and jobs by diverting funds to cleaning up the air and water. Therefore, as the 1970s came to a close, Americans remained divided about what role the government should play in regulating industry and protecting the environment.

 Checkpoint Why did some people oppose the environmental movement?

SECTION 4 Assessment

Progress Monitoring Online
For: Self-test with vocabulary practice
www.pearsonschool.com/ushist

Comprehension

1. **Terms and People** For each item below, write a sentence explaining how it helped expand a right or provide a protection.
   - Rachel Carson
   - Earth Day
   - EPA
   - Clean Air Act
   - Clean Water Act
   - Endangered Species Act

2. **NoteTaking Reading Skill: Recognize Sequence** Use your completed flowchart to answer the Section Focus Question: What forces gave rise to the environmental movement, and what impact did it have?

Writing About History

3. **Quick Write: Organize the Material** You need to give a speech describing environmental problems in your region and how they could affect the local economy. Outline topics and arguments, remembering to begin with a strong argument or a personal story and to end with your most compelling argument.

Critical Thinking

4. **Recognize Cause and Effect** How did Rachel Carson's concern about DDT spark the environmental movement?

5. **Make Comparisons** How did the goals and tactics of the environmental movement compare with those of the women's movement?

6. **Identify Assumptions** What basic assumptions about the environment did opponents to environmental regulation have?

Section 4 Assessment

1. Sentences should reflect an understanding of the way that each person or term helped expand a right or provide a protection.

2. Research published in *Silent Spring*, accidents caused by environmental problems, and awareness events such as Earth Day gave rise to the environmental movement and led to widespread popular support for protecting the environment.

3. Students' speeches should accurately reflect environmental and economic issues in the region or community.

4. Carson's research showed a connection between chemicals and animal health, leading many people to act to protect the environment and human health.

5. Although the focus of their efforts was different, both the environmental and women's movements acted to achieve their goals through political protests and legal reforms.

6. They did not believe that the damage to the environment was significant. They assumed that the environment was meant to be used for financial gain.

Quick Study Guide

Progress Monitoring Online
For: Self-test with vocabulary practice
www.pearsonschool.com/ushist

Quick Study Guide

- Have students use the Quick Study Guide to prepare for the chapter test. Students may wish to refer to the following sections as they review:

Rights-Expanding Legislation
Section 2
Section 3
Section 4

Major Activists and Groups
Section 1
Section 2
Section 3
Section 4

Influence of the Civil Rights Movement
Section 1
Section 2
Section 3
Section 4

Key Events of the Era of Protest and Change
Section 1
Section 2
Section 3
Section 4

- For additional review, remind students to refer to the Reading and Note Taking Study Guide.
Section Note Taking
Section Summaries

- Have students access **www.pearsonschool.com/ushist** for this chapter's History Interactive timeline, which includes expanded entries and additional events.

- If students need more instruction on analyzing graphic data, have them read the Skills Handbook, **p. SH21.**

For **Progress Monitoring Online**, refer students to the Self-test with vocabulary practice at **www.pearsonschool.com/ushist.**

■ Rights-Expanding Legislation

Equal Rights Amendment (ERA) (First proposed 1921; never passed)	Proposed constitutional amendment to guarantee gender equality
Panel on Mental Retardation (1961)	Explored ways the government could help people with disabilities
Title VII of the Civil Rights Act (1964)	Outlawed sex-based discrimination
Immigration and Nationality Act (1965)	Eased restrictions, making immigration easier for Latinos and Asians
National Traffic and Motor Vehicle Safety Act (1966)	Mandated safety equipment in cars
Environmental Protection Agency (1970)	Established to clean up degraded environments and to prevent further contamination
Clean Air Act (1970)	Limited emissions from factories and cars
Clean Water Act (1973)	Limited pollution of water by industry and agriculture
Endangered Species Act (1973)	Protected endangered plants and animals
Indian Self-Determination Act (1975)	Gave Native Americans control over resources on reservations

■ Major Activists and Groups

Activist/Group	Goal
Betty Friedan/National Organization of Women (NOW)	Win true equality for all women; pass ERA; make abortion legal
Phyllis Schlafly	Defeat the ERA
Cesar Chavez/United Farm Workers	Obtain better working conditions for migrant farmworkers
National Council of La Raza	Reduce Latino discrimination
La Raza Unida	Support Latino political candidates; obtain better jobs and housing for Latinos
Dennis Banks/American Indian Movement (AIM)	Secure legal rights and self-government for Native Americans
Rachel Carson	Publicize dangers of chemicals to environment
Ralph Nader	Enact legislation and regulations to protect consumers
Japanese American Citizens League	Secure civil rights for Japanese Americans

■ Influence of the Civil Rights Movement

The Civil Rights Movement	The Civil Rights Movement Influences Other Protest Movements
• African Americans push for legal and social equality. • Groups use different tactics, including protesting, raising social consciousness, and working for political and legal change. • Important legislation is passed, including the Civil Rights Act of 1964.	**Goals** • Women, Latinos, Native Americans, Asian Americans, and people with disabilities push for legal and social equality. • Environmental and consumer groups demand legal changes. **Tactics** • Women, Latinos, Native Americans, and environmentalists use civil rights protest tactics to support their own causes.

☑ Quick Study Timeline

In America

1962	1963	1966	1969
Rachel Carson's *Silent Spring* launches environmental movement	Betty Friedan publishes *The Feminine Mystique*	United Farm Workers union is formed	Woodstock festival celebrates the counterculture

Presidential Terms   John F. Kennedy 1961–1963   Lyndon B. Johnson 1963–1969

1960	1964	1968

Around the World

1960	1963	1966
Ceylon (now Sri Lanka) elects world's first female prime minister	Soviet cosmonaut Valentina Tereshkova becomes first woman in space	Indira Gandhi becomes India's first female prime minister

Differentiated Instruction   Solutions for All Learners

L1 Special Needs Students   L2 English Language Learners   L2 Less Proficient Readers

Use the following study guide resources to help students acquiring basic skills:
Adapted Reading and Note Taking Study Guide
- Section Note Taking
- Section Summaries

Use the following study guide resources to help Spanish-speaking students:
Spanish Reading and Note Taking Study Guide
- Section Note Taking
- Section Summaries

American Issues
Connector

By connecting prior knowledge with what you have learned in this chapter, you can gradually build your understanding of enduring questions that still affect America today. Answer the questions below. Then, use your American Issues Connector study guide (or go online: www.pearsonschool.com/ushist).

Issues You Learned About

● **Interaction With the Environment** The federal government seeks to balance environmental conservation with development.

1. How did John Muir and Theodore Roosevelt contribute to the early conservation movement in the United States?

2. Give three examples of human activities that have harmed the environment.

3. Give three examples of the way individuals or the government have tried to protect the environment.

● **Women in American Society** Women's movements have organized to demand greater equality in American society.

4. Describe the first wave of feminism, including its leaders and its goals.

5. Explain the goals of the second wave of feminism.

6. What are some reasons that the average woman continues to earn less than the average man?

● **U.S. Immigration Policy** The country's immigration laws change over time, often in response to outside influences.

7. In the past, Congress has passed laws preventing people from certain countries from immigrating to the United States. Identify one of these laws, its provisions, and the people against whom it was directed.

8. Why was the *bracero* program initiated in 1942?

9. What happened as a result of the Immigration and Nationality Acts Amendments?

Connect to Your World	Activity

American Indian Policy The United States considers federally recognized Native American tribes to be sovereign political bodies. These tribes have the right to form their own government, enforce laws, and raise taxes. They also possess the right to operate casinos and other gaming facilities free of state regulation and taxation. Today, gaming is a leading industry among tribal bodies. However, Indian casinos have caused a great deal of controversy. Conduct research online or at your local library to learn about some of the controversies surrounding Native American casinos. Create a list of pros and cons of these casinos. Then, based upon your findings, write a statement explaining your opinion on Indian gaming.

1970 EPA is established	1973 Supreme Court legalizes abortion in *Roe v. Wade*; AIM confronts government at Wounded Knee	1979 Nuclear disaster occurs at Three Mile Island

Richard M. Nixon 1969–1974	Gerald R. Ford 1974–1977	Jimmy Carter 1977–1981
1972	**1976**	**1980**

1971 Environmental group Greenpeace founded in Vancouver, Canada	1973 American involvement in Vietnam War ends

History *Interactive*
For: Interactive timeline
www.pearsonschool.com/ushist

Differentiated Instruction   Solutions for All Learners

L1 Special Needs Students   **L2** English Language Learners   **L2** Less Proficient Readers

Use the following study guide resource to help students acquiring basic skills:
Adapted Reading and Note Taking Study Guide
• American Issues Journal

Use the following study guide resource to help Spanish-speaking students:
Spanish Reading and Note Taking Study Guide
• American Issues Journal

American Issues
Connector

Tell students that the main issues for this chapter are Interaction With the Environment, Women in American Society, and U.S. Immigration Policy. Then, ask them to answer the Issues You Learned About questions on this page. Discuss the Connect to Your World topic, and ask students to complete the project that follows.

American Issues Connector

1. They supported setting aside land for the creation of national parks.

2. Examples: manufacturing steel, burning trash, dumping industrial waste in rivers

3. Examples: Rachel Carson's book, the EPA, clean air and water acts

4. The first wave was led by suffragists such as Susan B. Anthony and Elizabeth Cady Stanton and focused on gaining the vote for women and progressive reforms.

5. The second wave sought more complete legal and economic equality for women.

6. Examples: In some cases, discrimination still exists; fields in which more women work tend to be lower paying; and more women work part time.

7. Possible answer: The Chinese Exclusion Act, passed in 1882, almost completely prohibited legal immigration by Chinese people.

8. It was created to address the shortage of agricultural workers during World War II.

9. These acts established new guidelines for which immigrants would be allowed in the United States, giving preference to skilled workers.

Connect to Your World

Students' analyses should include reasonable arguments for and against casino gambling.

For additional review of this chapter's enduring issues, remind students to refer to the Reading and Note Taking Study Guide American Issues Journal.

Terms and People

1. Chicano movement
2. counterculture
3. toxic waste
4. generation gap
5. feminism
6. migrant farmworkers

Focus Questions

7. The counterculture was a movement among young people that challenged the traditional ideas and customs of society. It changed social and political boundaries and cultural values.

8. The civil rights movement and the earlier women's suffrage movement inspired the women's movement. Women gained legal rights and more rights and protections in the workplace.

9. Migrant farmworkers won collective bargaining rights in some states; Latinos worked to gain better political representation; Native Americans fought to secure legal rights and regain land; Asian Americans sought to correct long-standing discrimination; and most Americans learned to change their perceptions of people with disabilities.

10. Research published in *Silent Spring,* accidents caused by environmental problems, and awareness events such as Earth Day gave rise to the environmental movement and led to widespread popular support for protecting the environment.

Critical Thinking

11. The sound of the music was different from anything that had preceded it. The subject matter of the music often expressed the social or political ideas of the counterculture thus promoting change.

12. They all addressed economic, legal, and social inequality.

13. The counterculture was focused less on political issues and more on allowing people to express their individuality. It left a lasting impression, making society more accepting of differences, but also aggravated problems such as drug

Chapter Assessment

Terms and People

Match the following definitions with the items below.

counterculture	migrant farmworker
generation gap	Chicano movement
feminism	toxic waste

1. The _____ sought to raise cultural awareness among Latinos.
2. Members of the _____ promoted the sexual revolution.
3. Acid rain and the byproducts of nuclear power are examples of _____.
4. The baby boomers' rejection of traditional values set them apart from the older generation, creating a _____.
5. Phyllis Schlafly opposed _____ because she believed it hurt families.
6. Cesar Chavez led a movement to improve working conditions for the _____.

Focus Questions

The focus question for this chapter is **How did the counterculture and the expanding rights revolution of the 1960s and 1970s influence American society?** Build an answer to this big question by answering the focus questions for Sections 1 through 4 and the Critical Thinking questions that follow.

Section 1
7. What was the counterculture, and what impact did it have on American society?

Section 2
8. What led to the rise of the women's movement, and what impact did it have on American society?

Section 3
9. How did the rights movements of the 1960s and 1970s expand rights for diverse groups of Americans?

Section 4
10. What forces gave rise to the environmental movement, and what impact did it have?

Critical Thinking

11. **Recognize Ideologies** How did rock and folk music become, in the words of the musician John Sinclair, "a weapon of cultural revolution"?

12. **Synthesize Information** What underlying problem in American society did the rights movements of the 1960s and 1970s address?

13. **Make Comparisons** How were the lasting effects of the counterculture similar to and different from those of the other rights movements discussed in this chapter?

14. **Analyzing Visuals** Use information from the chapter to explain the data on the graph below.

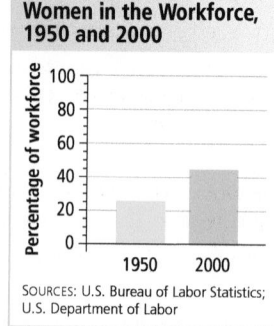

Women in the Workforce, 1950 and 2000

Percentage of workforce (0–100)

1950, 2000

SOURCES: U.S. Bureau of Labor Statistics; U.S. Department of Labor

15. **Predict Consequences** Would the rights movements of the 1960s and 1970s have been as successful without the examples of civil rights activists? Explain.

16. **Geography and History** Why was geography a central issue of the Native American movement but not of the other rights movements?

Writing About History

Writing a Persuasive Speech During the 1960s, many people used speeches to draw attention to their causes. Write a persuasive speech from the point of view of one of these people discussed in the chapter: Betty Friedan, Phyllis Schlafly, Cesar Chavez, Dennis Banks, Ralph Nader, or Rachel Carson. Deliver your completed speech to a classmate or to the entire class.

Prewriting
- Choose the person who most interests you. Take notes about the person's motivations and methods.
- Identify the venue where the speech will be delivered, as well as its audience.

Drafting
- Develop a thesis, and choose information to support it.
- List arguments that support your thesis, and answer opposing arguments.
- Write the speech, remembering to open with an attention-grabbing statement and to end with your strongest argument.

Revising
- Use the guidelines on page SH16 of the Writing Handbook to revise your speech.

---

abuse. Conversely, the rights movements each made political progress, although some accomplished more than others.

14. Feminism pushed for more opportunities for woman and equal treatment in the workplace. As a result, it became more acceptable for women to work and today more of the workforce is made up of women.

15. Possible response: The rights movements of the 1960s and 1970s probably would have been less successful without the example of the civil rights movement, because those

movements learned many of their tactics from the civil rights movement.

16. Native Americans had been pushed off their land and forced into certain geographic areas. Regaining control of their land was a major concern. Identifying with the land provides a sense of historical connectedness for Native Americans.

Document-Based Assessment

The Voting Rights Act

In 1965, Congress passed the Voting Rights Act, removing the barriers that had kept African Americans disenfranchised. In 1975, Congress amended the act to address voting barriers related to Latino and Native American voters. Section 203 of the law required that voting materials be published in languages other than English in certain areas. Section 5 required that certain counties with a history of discrimination pre-clear any voting changes with the U.S. Department of Justice. Use your knowledge of the civil rights movement and Documents A, B, C, and D to answer questions 1 through 4.

Document A

Citizens of language minorities have been effectively excluded from participation in the electoral process. Among other factors, the denial of the right to vote of such minority group citizens is ordinarily directly related to the unequal educational opportunities afforded them resulting in high illiteracy and low voting participation. . . . The requirements of the law are straightforward: all election information that is available in English must also be available in the minority language so that all citizens will have an effective opportunity to register, learn the details of the elections, and cast a free and effective ballot.

—*From Section 203 of the Voting Rights Act, 1975*

Document B

I'm a naturalized citizen now, born in the Philippines and it just put a smile to my face as well as the rest of the people in our household when we get those ballots in Tagalog. We DON'T even have those in the country I came from so the more I appreciate all the efforts of you guys put into making sure every eligible citizen [is] able to understand and get informed with regards to all the candidates and all the measures by sending them tools in their native languages. America is truly the best country in the world to live in. . . . Proud to be a U.S. Citizen. . . . Thanks to all of you and keep up the good work.

—*A voter from San Diego County, California*

Document C

This nation is still subject to the problem that Section 5 was developed to address. Even today, many jurisdictions still respond to growth in minority political power by restricting minority political opportunity. In Texas and Arizona, for example, the Justice Department continues to interpose a significant number of objections; the deterrent effect of Section 5 stops many discriminatory election changes before they are enacted by covered jurisdictions. Despite what you may hear from opponents of the Voting Rights Act, the emergency that led to the adoption of Section 5 has not passed. Latino voters have not yet closed the gap in voter registration and turnout in the Southwest. . . . I urge you today to reauthorize Section 5 with language clarifying congressional intent to prohibit intentional discrimination and to restore ability to elect. . . .

—*Nina Perales, counsel to the Mexican American Legal Defense and Education Fund, 2005*

Document D

1. Document B supports the purpose and outcome of which other document?
   A Document A
   B Document C
   C Document D
   D none of the documents

2. In Document C, a lawyer testifies before Congress, urging it to
   A change key provisions of the Voting Rights Act.
   B disallow the Voting Rights Act.
   C reauthorize the Voting Rights Act.
   D amend the Voting Rights Act so that it applies to only Native Americans.

3. In Document D, what is the cartoonist's opinion about American political parties and Latino voting rights?
   A The Democrats alone are concerned about Latino voting rights.
   B The Republicans alone are concerned about Latino voting rights.
   C Both parties are concerned about Latino voting rights.
   D Neither party is concerned about Latino voting rights.

4. **Writing Task** Explain why Latinos have focused on expanding voter participation, the obstacles they have faced, and the successes they have had. Use the documents on this page, along with material from the chapter, to support your assessment.

Teach With Technology

Presentation**EXPRESS**™
PREMIUM DVD

- Teach this chapter's core content by using PresentationExpress, which includes interactivities, video, lecture notes, and the *ExamView*® QuickTake assessment tool.

- To introduce this chapter by using PresentationExpress, ask students with which of the following statements they most agree: **A) To accomplish the government's goals efficiently, the executive branch should be the most powerful branch of the federal government. B) Congress, as direct representatives of the people, should be the most powerful branch. C) The current system of government works well; no branch of the federal government should be more powerful than the others.** Take a class poll or record students' answers by using the QuickTake feature, and discuss their responses. Point out that in this chapter, students will read about major events, issues, and policies during the 1970s that shaped the way that people viewed the United States.

Technology Resources

- Student**EXPRESS** CD-ROM
- Teacher Resource Library DVD
- Presentation**EXPRESS** PREMIUM DVD
- *ExamView*® **Test Bank** CD-ROM English and Spanish
- **Guided Reading Audio,** Spanish
- **Student Edition on Audio**

VIDEO
By Students For Students
For videos on American Issues, go to
www.pearsonschool.com/ushist

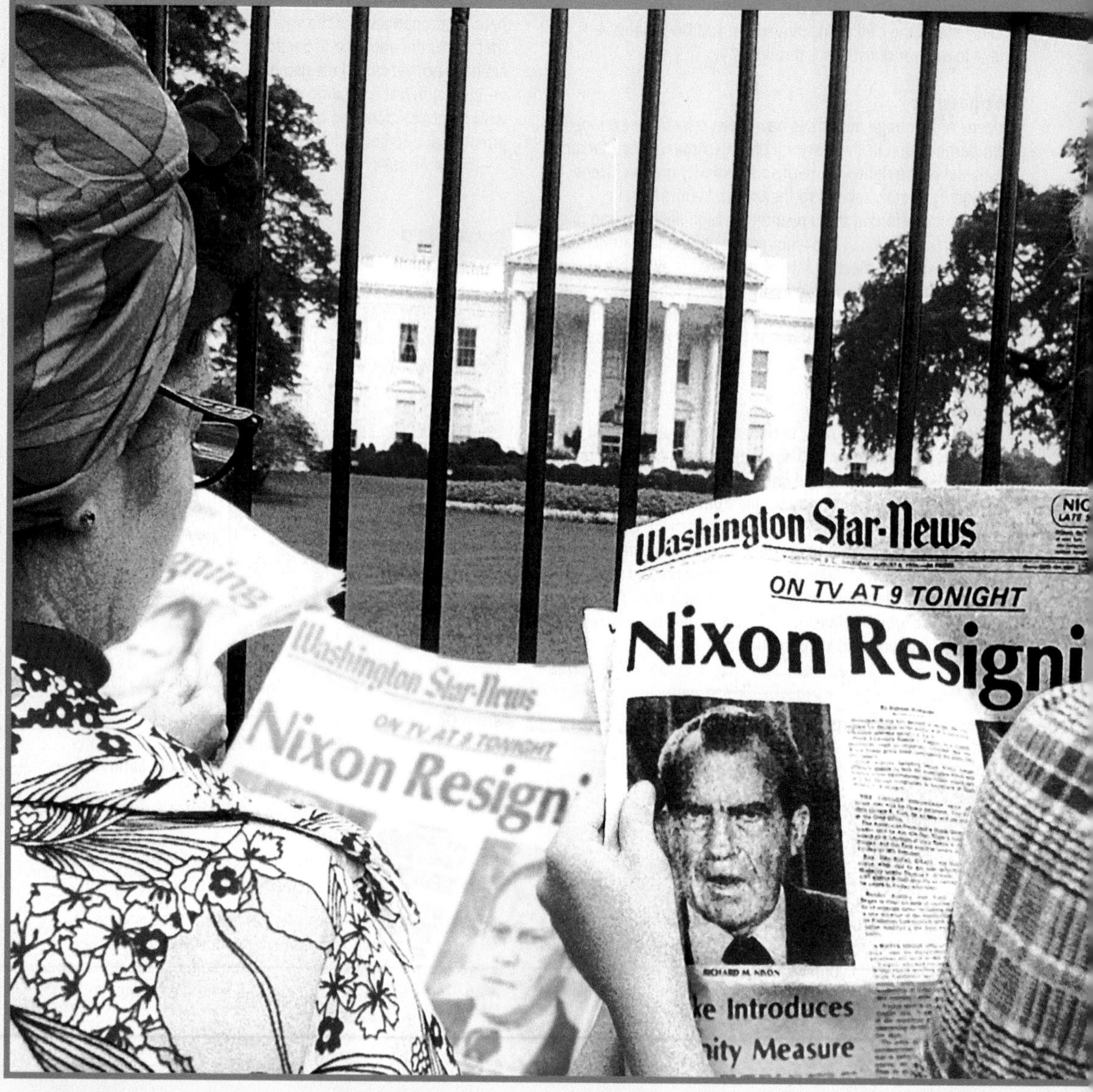

Bibliography

For the Teacher

Farber, David. *Taken Hostage: The Iran Hostage Crisis and America's First Encounter with Radical Islam.* Princeton University Press, 2004.

Mieczkowski, Yanek. *Gerald Ford and the Challenges of the 1970s.* University Press of Kentucky, 2005.

Woodward, Bob and Carl Bernstein. *All the President's Men, 2nd Edition.* Simon & Schuster, 1994.

For the Student

L2 Fremon, Daniel. *The Watergate Scandal in American History.* Enslow Publishers, 1998.

L3 Horowitz, Daniel, ed. *Jimmy Carter and the Energy Crisis of the 1970s: The "Crisis of Confidence" Speech of July 15, 1979 (The Bedford Series in History and Culture).* Bedford/St. Martin's, 2004.

L4 Bailey, Beth L. and Dave Farber, eds. *America in the Seventies.* University Press of Kansas, 2004.

WITNESS HISTORY

A Long National Nightmare

In the late summer of 1974, President Richard Nixon's resignation ended the drawn-out Watergate scandal. However, the nation still reeled from the shadow that Watergate had cast on its President. New President Gerald Ford attempted to set a new tone for the troubled nation:

"My fellow Americans, our long national nightmare is over. Our Constitution works; our great Republic is a government of laws and not of men. . . . As we bind up the internal wounds of Watergate, more painful and more poisonous than those of foreign wars, let us restore the golden rule to our political process, and let brotherly love purge our hearts of suspicion and of hate."

—President Gerald Ford, August 9, 1974

◀ Two tourists in front of the White House read headlines announcing Nixon's intention to resign on August 8, 1974.

Yellow ribbon symbolizing the hope that hostages held in Iran would return home safely

Tape recorder used by President Nixon in the Oval Office

Chapter Preview

Chapter Focus Question: What caused Americans to suffer a crisis of confidence during the 1970s?

Section 1
Nixon and the Watergate Scandal

Section 2
The Ford and Carter Years

Section 3
Foreign Policy Troubles

SORRY NO GAS

Sign on a Volkswagen Beetle announces a gas shortage

Use the ☑ **Quick Study Timeline** at the end of this chapter to preview chapter events.

Note Taking Study Guide *Online*
For: Note Taking and American Issues Connector
www.pearsonschool.com/ushist

Chapter-Level Resources

All in One Letter Home (English and Spanish), Preread the Chapter, Vocabulary Builder; Reading Strategy, Social Studies Skills Practice, Enrichment, Chapter Tests

- Test Prep With Document-Based Assessment
- AYP Monitoring Assessments
- *ExamView*® Test Bank CD-ROM
- Guided Reading Audio (Spanish)
- Student Edition Audio

Previewing the Chapter

- **WITNESS HISTORY** Explain that the 1970s was a turbulent decade in U.S. history. One of the central events of the era—and a test of the American system of government—was the Watergate scandal. Read the Witness History selection aloud. Ask **Why does Ford describe the Watergate scandal as a "national nightmare"?** *(Possible response: The Watergate scandal caused many Americans to question the credibility of the government and the foundations on which it was built.)* Tell students that they will learn more about Richard Nixon, Watergate, and the events of the era in this chapter.

- **Analyzing the Visuals** Ask students to study the images on this page. Ask **What do these images have in common?** *(Sample response: All represent some serious crisis from the period.)*

- **Focus** Write the Chapter Focus question on the board. Tell students to keep this question in mind as they read the chapter. Then, have students preview the section titles in this chapter.

- **Preread** Have students complete the chapter's Preread the Chapter Worksheet.

Differentiated Instruction   Solutions for All Learners

The following Teacher's Edition strategies are suitable for students of varying abilities.

L1 Special Needs Students, pp. 599, 600, 603, 609, 611, 612, 618 SN

L2 English Language Learners, pp. 599, 600, 603, 611, 612, 616, 618 ELL

L2 Less Proficient Readers, pp. 599, 600, 603, 609, 611, 616, 618 LPR

L4 Advanced Readers, pp. 601, 609, 612, 616 AR

L4 Gifted and Talented Students, pp. 601, 609, 612, 616 GT

Have students access **www.pearsonschool. com/ushist** for the Note Taking Study Guide *Online* as an alternative to the *Reading and Note Taking Study Guide* booklet.

Objectives

As you teach this section, keep students focused on the following objectives to help them answer the Section Focus Question and master core content.

- Describe Richard Nixon's attitude toward "big" government.
- Analyze Nixon's southern strategy.
- Explain the Watergate incident and its consequences.

Background Knowledge

Ask students to recall some of the major issues and movements of the 1970s, such as civil rights and the women's movement. Ask students to read the section title and predict what will happen to Richard Nixon.

Set a Purpose

- **WITNESS HISTORY** Read the selection aloud.

  Ask **What does Haldeman mean when he says that the FBI is not under control?** *(The FBI will not easily be kept from investigating this crime without pressure from the White House.)*

- **Focus** Point out the Section Focus Question, and write it on the board. Tell students to refer to this question as they read. *(Answer appears with Section 1 Assessment answers.)*

- **Preview** Have students preview the Section Objectives and the list of Terms and People.

- **Reading Skill** Have students use the *Reading Strategy: Identify Main Ideas* worksheet. Teaching Resources, **p. 10**

- **NoteTaking** Using the Guided Questioning strategy (TE, p. T20), have students read this section. As they read, have students record details about Nixon's major domestic policies and goals. Reading and Note Taking Study Guide

▲ Nixon and aide H. R. Haldeman

WITNESS HISTORY

The Watergate Tapes

Not long after President Nixon's 1972 reelection, the huge Watergate scandal began to unfold. The root of the scandal was a break-in at the Democratic Party's headquarters in Washington, D.C. Tapes of White House conversations later revealed that Richard Nixon and his top aides had tried to cover up the break-in:

❝ **H. R. Haldeman [assistant to the President]:** Now, on the investigation, you know, the Democratic break-in thing, we're back to the—in the problem area because the FBI is not under control, because [FBI Director L. Patrick] Gray doesn't exactly know how to control them [his agents]. . . . [The] way to handle this now is for us to have [Deputy CIA Director] Walters call Pat Gray and just say, 'Stay . . . out of this.' . . . **President Nixon:** You call them in. . . . Play it tough. That's the way they play it and that's the way we are going to play it. ❞

—Taped conversation, Oval Office, White House, June 23, 1972

Nixon and the Watergate Scandal

Objectives

- Describe Richard Nixon's attitude toward "big" government.
- Analyze Nixon's southern strategy.
- Explain the Watergate incident and its consequences.

Terms and People

silent majority	affirmative action
stagflation	Watergate
OPEC	Twenty-fifth Amendment
southern strategy	executive privilege

NoteTaking

Reading Skill: Identify Main Ideas Record Nixon's major domestic policies and goals in a chart like the one below.

Nixon's Domestic Policies and Strategies	
New Federalism	Southern Strategy

Why It Matters President Richard Nixon stood at the summit of his long government career when he was reelected President in a landslide in November 1972. Yet, less than two years later, Nixon left office in disgrace, the first time a President of the United States had resigned. The Watergate scandal gripped the nation and shaped the values and attitudes toward government that many Americans hold today. **Section Focus Question: What events led to Richard Nixon's resignation as President in 1974?**

Nixon's Policies Target Middle America

Richard Nixon's political career had more ups and downs than a roller coaster ride. Brought up in hard times, he worked his way through college and law school. After service in the navy during World War II, Nixon was elected to the House of Representatives in 1946 and then to the Senate in 1950. As Dwight Eisenhower's running mate in 1952, he became Vice President with Eisenhower's victory. Nixon was not yet 40 years old.

Then came the defeats. In 1960, Nixon narrowly lost to John F. Kennedy in the race for the White House. Two years later, Nixon's career hit bottom when he lost an election to become governor of California. In 1968, however, Nixon made a dramatic comeback, narrowly defeating Democrat Hubert Humphrey to win the presidency.

Vocabulary Builder

Use the information below and the following resource to teach students the high-use words from this section. Teaching Resources, Vocabulary Builder, p. 9

High-Use Words	Definitions and Sample Sentences
pollution	*n.* environmental contamination Since the 1970s, many laws have been passed to reduce **pollution** in the United States.
crucial	*adj.* of vital importance The Allies' successful invasion of France was **crucial** to Germany's defeat.

Nixon Calls for a "New Federalism" During the campaign for President, Nixon cast himself as the spokesperson for those he called Middle Americans, or the **silent majority.** As Nixon put it at the 1968 Republican convention, he sought to speak for the "non-shouters, the non-demonstrators," the men and women who "work in America's factories . . . run America's businesses . . . serve in the Government . . . provide most of the soldiers . . . [and] give life to the American dream."

Winning the support of Middle America proved a tricky task. Nixon believed that Americans had tired of the "big" government of Lyndon Johnson's Great Society. However, he also believed that the American people still wanted the government to address various social ills, ranging from crime to pollution.

Nixon's solution was to call for the establishment of a "new federalism." As he explained in his 1971 State of the Union address, the nation needed "to reverse the flow of power and resources from the States and communities to Washington and start power and resources flowing back from Washington to the States and communities." Nixon proposed revenue sharing with the states. Under revenue sharing, the federal government gave the states the money to fund social programs. The states then controlled the operations of these programs.

Nixon Expands the Government's Role However, while returning power and money to the states, Nixon also sponsored many programs that increased the size and role of the federal government. During his presidency, a number of powerful new federal agencies and laws came into existence. The Occupational Safety and Health Administration (OSHA) regulates workplaces to make them safer for workers. The DEA, or Drug Enforcement Administration, administers the federal war against illegal drugs. The Environmental Protection Agency (EPA) enforces federal environmental standards. The Clean Air Act, signed into law in 1970, gives the EPA the power to set air quality standards.

Nixon's welfare policies also reflected his complicated domestic strategy. To decrease the power of the federal government, Nixon began to dismantle the Office of Economic Opportunity, the cornerstone of Lyndon Johnson's "war on poverty." Yet, Nixon also proposed creating a Family Assistance Plan (FAP), which called for providing a guaranteed or minimum income to every American family. Although the FAP did not become law, federal spending on other social welfare programs, such as Medicare and public housing, grew steadily, especially during Nixon's early years.

The Economy Struggles As his presidency progressed, Nixon grappled with an increasingly troublesome economy. After decades of strong growth and low inflation, the U.S. economy experienced both recession and inflation at the same time. These symptoms began during the Johnson administration, but they grew stronger during the Nixon years. The combination of recession and inflation baffled economists and led them to coin a new term, **stagflation,** to describe the dual conditions of a stagnating economy and inflationary pressures.

Stagflation had several causes. Expanding federal budget deficits caused by the Vietnam War produced inflation. Another cause was rising foreign competition, which cost thousands of Americans their jobs. Heavy industries such as steel and auto production, which had enjoyed a dominant position since World War II, proved especially vulnerable to foreign competition. Yet

Vocabulary Builder
pollution–(puh LOO shuhn) *n.* environmental contamination

Inflation on the Rise
Protesters in California greet President Nixon in 1970. While inflation drove prices up, most workers' wages stayed the same. *How would high unemployment make the situation even worse?*

Inflation and Unemployment Rates, 1970–1980

Percent (vertical axis: 0, 2, 4, 6, 8, 10, 12, 14)
Years (horizontal axis: 1970, 1972, 1974, 1976, 1978, 1980)

— Inflation   — Unemployment

SOURCE: U.S. Bureau of Labor Statistics

LESS TALK MORE JOBS!
WE NEED JOBS NOT WORDS!
YOU SPEAK SO LOUD WE CAN'T HEAR WHAT YOU SAY
NIXON BEAR MARKET

Instruct

- **Introduce: Key Term** Ask students to find the key term *affirmative action* (in bold) in the text and explain its meaning. Then, have students examine the photographs showing the conflict over court-ordered busing in the 1970s. Ask students to discuss whether busing students from one neighborhood to attend a school in another neighborhood is a form of *affirmative action.*

- **Teach** Explain to students that after his losses in the late 1960s, Nixon placed much importance on his reelection. Ask **What was Nixon's southern strategy?** *(targeting southern whites' votes in the 1972 election)* Direct students to the images on this page. Discuss the question in the caption. Ask **How did his request for a moratorium on court-ordered busing help Nixon appeal to more voters?** *(Nixon became more appealing to southern whites and white blue-collar workers in other regions who resisted busing.)* **Did the Philadelphia Plan and his speech against busing represent a contradiction in Nixon's views on civil rights? Why or why not?** *(Because the Philadelphia Plan dates from the first year of Nixon's first term, before he took his stand on busing, it is possible to infer that the antibusing speech was made purely for political reasons; in any case, Nixon's actions were contradictory.)*

Turmoil Over Busing
Court-ordered busing continued to be a controversial issue in the 1970s. A police escort (left) protects a school bus carrying African American students into a white neighborhood as part of the busing. Anti-busing demonstrations (right) went on around the country. *Why do you think that busing provoked such a strong reaction?*

the factor that caused most Americans pain was the rapid increase in the price of oil.

During the 1973 Arab war against Israel, the **Organization of Petroleum Exporting Countries (OPEC),** a group of mostly Arab countries that sells oil to other nations and cooperates to regulate the price and supply of oil, placed an embargo on Israel's allies, including the United States. Dependent on imports for nearly one-third of their energy, Americans soon felt the sting of this embargo as oil prices skyrocketed 400 percent in a single year. The embargo lasted until the spring of 1974 and resulted in gas lines at the pumps that stretched for blocks. With the end of the embargo, gas prices remained high.

Nixon fought stagflation in a variety of ways. Most dramatically, in August 1971, he placed a 90-day freeze on all wages and prices. The controls worked for a short time, causing a spurt of economic growth. However, price controls do not work well in a free economy, and the economy went into a tailspin in the mid-1970s.

✓ **Checkpoint** What was the goal of President Nixon's "new federalism"?

Nixon Follows a Southern Strategy

Having narrowly won the presidency in 1968, Richard Nixon set out to expand his base of support. He targeted blue-collar workers and southern whites, both of whom had traditionally voted for Democrats. By winning the support of southern whites, Nixon hoped to make the Republican Party a powerful force in the South. Commentators called this Nixon's **southern strategy.**

Controversy Rages Over Busing As part of his southern strategy, Nixon tried to place a number of conservative southerners as judges in federal courts. Most prominently, he nominated Clement Haynsworth and G. Harrold Carswell to serve on the U.S. Supreme Court. Both men failed to win Senate confirmation, in part because both had supported segregation in the past.

Criticizing court-ordered busing of children to schools outside their neighborhood was another way Nixon reached out to southern whites and urban blue-collar workers. For years, many school districts in both the South and the North had resisted desegregation. In 1971, federal courts ordered school districts to bus students to achieve greater racial balance. Recognizing the unpopularity of busing, Nixon made a nationally televised address in which he called for a moratorium, or freeze, on court-ordered busing. By speaking forcefully, Nixon won the support of many busing opponents.

Nixon Proposes New Civil Rights Initiatives Yet, as with much else that he did, Nixon's stance on civil rights was mixed. In 1969, the Nixon administration initiated the Philadelphia Plan, a program

Answers

✓ Nixon wanted to transfer more power to the state governments.

Caption Sample answer: The strong reaction could have been due to lingering racial attitudes, to parents' concerns about educational quality and personal safety, and to their objections that busing distances to other school districts placed a burden on their children and limited options for extracurricular activities.

that required labor unions and federal contractors to submit goals and timetables for the hiring of minorities. It was a type of **affirmative action**, a policy that gives special consideration to women and minorities in the fields of education and employment, in order to make up for past discrimination. Nixon's Assistant Secretary of Labor, Arthur Fletcher, who designed the Philadelphia Plan, argued:

> **Primary Source** "The Federal Government has an obligation to see that every citizen has an equal chance at the most basic freedom of all—the right to succeed.... Segregation didn't occur naturally—it was imposed.... The gap ... between black and white ... was growing wider and wider.... Visible, measurable goals to correct [these] imbalances are essential."
> —Arthur Fletcher, Assistant Secretary of Labor, speech on affirmative action, 1969

Nixon's Strategy Succeeds By the 1972 election, Nixon enjoyed high approval ratings. Some of this popularity was based on his trips to the Soviet Union and China. Some was based on his domestic policies.

Nixon ran a masterful political campaign in 1972, positioning himself as a moderate. He portrayed his opponents—George McGovern, an antiwar senator from South Dakota, and Alabama governor George Wallace—as extremists. (Wallace's campaign was cut short when he was shot and left paralyzed by a would-be assassin.) Nixon and his Vice President, Spiro Agnew, successfully cast themselves as spokespersons for the silent majority. On election day, Nixon won almost 61 percent of the popular vote and nearly all of the electoral votes. He became the first Republican presidential candidate to sweep the entire South.

> ✓ **Checkpoint** In what ways did Nixon appear to send mixed messages about civil rights?

The Watergate Scandal Brings Nixon Down

As a triumphant Richard Nixon stood before the cameras on election night 1972, he had no idea that the seeds of his downfall had already begun to sprout. The botched burglary of Democratic Party headquarters at the Watergate complex in June 1972 received little attention at first. But as investigators began to unravel the connections between the burglars and the White House, **Watergate**, as the scandal become known, came to dominate the national news.

The Watergate burglars were tried in 1973. After the trial, one of them, James McCord, charged that administration officials had been involved in the break-in. This led to a Senate investigation and to televised hearings, where numerous witnesses charged that the President and his top aides had taken part in a coverup. From the first news of the break-in, President Nixon denied any wrongdoing. Yet, as time went on, investigators discovered important links between the burglars and top Nixon administration officials.

Watergate Goes Public Two young *Washington Post* journalists, Bob Woodward and Carl Bernstein, played a <u>crucial</u> role in lifting the veil of secrecy from

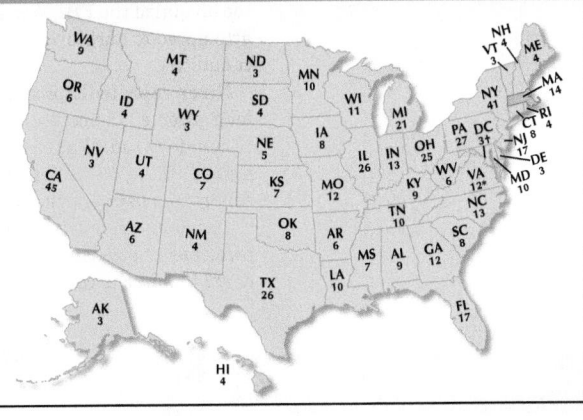

Presidential Election of 1972

Candidate (Party)	Electoral Vote	Popular Vote	% Electoral Vote	% Popular Vote
☐ Richard M. Nixon (Republican)	520	46,740,323	96.7	60.7
☐ George S. McGovern (Democratic)	17	28,901,598	3.1	37.5
☐ Other	1	1,341,502	0.2	1.7

*One elector from Virginia voted for John Hospers (Libertarian)
†McGovern received 3 electoral votes from Washington, D.C.

NoteTaking

Reading Skill: Identify Causes and Effects Use a chart like the one below to record the causes and effects of the Watergate crisis.

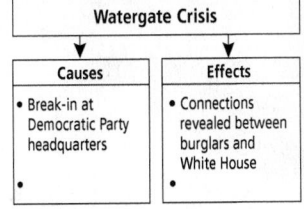

Vocabulary Builder
crucial–(KROO shuhl) *adj.* of vital importance

Instruct

- **Introduce: Key Term** Ask students to find the key term *Watergate* (in bold) in the text. Explain that a botched burglary of Democratic Party headquarters at the *Watergate* complex and the subsequent cover-up caused Nixon to resign the presidency. Ask students to predict how the *Watergate* scandal would affect the trust Americans had in the government.

- **Teach** Remind students of the efforts Nixon made to win the 1972 election. Using the Think-Write-Pair-Share technique (TE p. T23), discuss the origins and results of the Watergate scandal. Ask **What was the origin of the Watergate scandal?** *(a break-in at Democratic Party headquarters in the Watergate Hotel)* **How was the break-in connected to Nixon?** *(The men who attempted the burglary had close ties to Nixon's reelection committee.)* Have students discuss the circumstances that led to the clash between the three branches of government. Ask **Why did Congress want Nixon to turn over taped conversations from the Oval Office?** *(Members of Congress believed that the tapes might reveal that Nixon had played a role in covering up the Watergate break-in.)* **What did the Supreme Court rule in *United States v. Nixon?*** *(Nixon could not use the principle of executive privilege to justify withholding the Oval Office tapes from Congress.)* **How did the Watergate scandal force Nixon to resign?** *(Regardless of his role in the break-in, Nixon was caught in tape recordings ordering a cover-up of the crime.)* **Why did Gerald Ford become President after Nixon, instead of Vice President Spiro Agnew?** *(Agnew had resigned in the face of an unrelated legal scandal, so, as stipulated by the Twenty-fifth Amendment, Nixon nominated Ford, who was confirmed by a vote of Congress.)* Have students discuss whether or not the Watergate scandal still affects the way that the government works today.

the Watergate scandal. The two reporters followed tips provided by a secret government informant known as "Deep Throat," who was later revealed to be a top official of the FBI. Woodward and Bernstein reported that the men, who had attempted to burglarize the Watergate hotel, had close ties to Nixon's reelection committee.

Nixon repeatedly proclaimed his innocence. For example, in November 1973, long after evidence had implicated his top aides and forced them to resign, Nixon declared, "I am not a crook." Yet the polls indicated that the public disagreed. One poll, taken the next month, showed that fewer than one in five Americans believed that he was being honest about the Watergate affair.

The Watergate scandal created a historic showdown between the three branches of government. How far would Congress go to investigate the President? Would the courts demand that the President turn over information that

---

Events That Changed America

WATERGATE FORCES NIXON FROM OFFICE

One of the biggest political scandals in American history, Watergate has become synonymous with corruption and abuse of power. It began when President Nixon's reelection committee tried to record the conversations of political opponents, led to a string of coverups at the highest levels of the U.S. government, and ultimately forced Nixon from office. Nixon's role in the coverup shocked the nation.

The public might never have learned of the President's actions without the investigative reporting of journalists Bob Woodward and Carl Bernstein of the *Washington Post,* who broke the story in a series of articles. Their revelations, and those of other reporters, may have left the American people's faith in government shaken, but the aftermath reinforced the public's trust in the constitutional system.

June 1972
Five men linked to President Nixon's reelection campaign are arrested for trying to bug the offices of the Democratic National Committee in the Watergate complex (shown here) in Washington, D.C.

April 1973 Nixon denies knowledge of the Watergate break-in or any coverup.

May 1973 Archibald Cox is named as the Justice Department's special prosecutor for Watergate. The Senate Watergate Committee begins nationally televised hearings.

June 1973
Former White House counsel John Dean (right) tells investigators that Nixon authorized a coverup.

◀ Members of Congress hold a news conference about the scandal in May 1974.

Connect to Your World

Mystery Solved In 2005, Bob Woodward and Carl Bernstein's anonymous contact in the Nixon administration, known as Deep Throat, came forward in a *Vanity Fair* magazine article. The 30-year-old mystery ended when the shadowy figure turned out to be former high-level FBI official, Mark Felt. During the investigations, Felt had guided the reporters and confirmed, but did not provide, information that they needed for their Pulitzer Prize-winning reports for the *Washington Post.*

Everyone from Nixon himself to a group of college students had tried to discover Deep Throat's identity, but the secret remained intact until Felt's confession. Felt, motivated to help the reporters by Nixon's attempts to control and manipulate the FBI, devised various ways to meet the reporters including the use of signals, such as a clock printed on Woodward's daily articles in *The New York Times.* Although surprised by Felt's action, the reporters confirmed that the mystery had been solved.

might implicate him? And if the courts sided with Congress, would the President comply with its decisions?

Revealing the White House Tapes The Watergate scandal came to a climax with a dizzying array of developments. In the fall of 1973, Vice President Spiro Agnew resigned in the face of an unrelated corruption scandal. According to the procedures established by the **Twenty-fifth Amendment,** which deals with presidential succession, Nixon nominated Gerald Ford to become his new Vice President. Nixon's troubles multiplied when, in the summer of 1973, it was revealed that he had been secretly taping Oval Office conversations for many years. Many commentators speculated that these tapes would show that the President had played a leading role in trying to cover up the break-in.

■ **Quick Activity** To enrich and extend the lesson, have students access the **History Interactive** at **www.pearsonschool.com/ushist.** After students experience the History Interactive, ask them to share their reactions by posing questions such as these: **Did Nixon deserve the treatment he received? Why or why not? Do you think the Supreme Court and Congress fulfilled their proper roles? How did Watergate test the American system of government? What were the positive and negative results of Watergate for the nation as a whole?**

▼ James McCord demonstrates a phone wiretap.

July 1973 Nixon, claiming executive privilege, refuses to release the tapes of secretly recorded Oval Office conversations.

October 1973 Nixon offers investigators summaries of tapes, which Special Prosecutor Cox refuses. Nixon fires Cox. This triggers other firings and resignations in what becomes known as the Saturday Night Massacre.

March 1974 Former Nixon administration officials are indicted on charges of conspiracy in the Watergate break-in. Richard Nixon is named as an "unindicted co-conspirator."

July 1974 The Supreme Court rules unanimously that Nixon must surrender all of the White House recordings requested by the new special prosecutor. The House Judiciary Committee recommends impeachment.

August 1974 Transcripts of tapes show that Nixon ordered a coverup of the Watergate break-in. On August 9, Nixon becomes first U.S. President to resign.

Why It Matters
While Watergate damaged the public's trust of government officials, the U.S. government's system of checks and balances withstood the crisis. Lawmakers passed laws to prevent similar abuses from happening. The role of the press in bringing the scandal to light reminded the public of the importance of a free press in a democratic society.

Journalists Bernstein ▶ (left) and Woodward (right) with *Washington Post* publisher Katharine Graham

Thinking Critically
How did Congress and the Supreme Court balance the role of the executive branch during the Watergate crisis?

History *Interactive* ★
For: More information about Watergate
www.pearsonschool.com/ushist

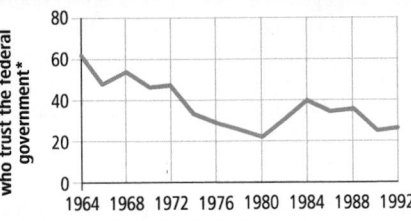

Public Trust in the Federal Government, 1964–1992

Percentage of Americans who trust the federal government*

80
60
40
20
0
1964 1968 1972 1976 1980 1984 1988 1992

SOURCE: The American National Election Studies
*Most of the time

Differentiated Instruction **Solutions for All Learners**

L1 Special Needs Students **L2 English Language Learners** **L2 Less Proficient Readers**

Refer students to the Infographic on Watergate. Have them preview the images and record any questions they have. Read aloud the introductory paragraph, and then examine each event, starting with June 1972, the break-in. Be sure that students understand special terminology, such as *bug, special prosecutor, counsel,* and *transcript,* and clarify the pronunciation of *indicted.* Ask students questions like these: **Who was John Dean, and what was his**

role in the scandal? What did people think when Nixon refused to turn over the tapes? Why did the special prosecutor refuse to accept a transcript of the tapes? According to the graph, how likely is it that Watergate affected public trust? Work with students to answer these and any other questions they may have about the text and images.

Answer

Thinking Critically
The Supreme Court curbed Nixon's power by denying his right to withhold the secret tapes under executive privilege; Congress balanced the executive's power by investigating the Watergate break-in and advising that impeachment proceedings begin.

- Display Color Transparency: *The Watergate Scandal.* Have each student write a paragraph summarizing what this cartoon indicates about the public opinion of Nixon and the events surrounding Watergate. Color Transparencies A-133

- **NoteTaking** Using the Paragraph Shrinking strategy (TE, p. T20), have students read the text under the red heading "The Watergate Scandal Brings Nixon Down." As they read, have students record the causes and effects of the Watergate crisis. Reading and Note Taking Study Guide

- Have students study the chart on the next page. Have each student write a paragraph telling which post-Watergate government reform was most important and explaining why.

- To find out more about the role of a key member of Congress in the Watergate crisis, assign students *Biography: Barbara Jordan,* and have them answer the questions on the worksheet. Teaching Resources, p. 13

- Have students examine the images on this page. Ask **In what way do these images show the strength of the federal government?** Have each student write a paragraph answering the question and explaining why.

Monitor Progress

Circulate to make sure that students understand the causes and effects of the Watergate scandal and the role that Barbara Jordan played during the Watergate hearings. For a completed version of the cause-and-effect chart, see Note Taking Transparencies, B-142b.

Nixon Quits
After his historic resignation, Nixon boards the helicopter that will fly him and his family away from the White House.

Nixon refused to turn over these tapes to the special prosecutor investigating the scandal. The President justified withholding the tapes by claiming **executive privilege.** Executive privilege is the principle that the President has the right to keep certain information confidential. It took almost a year for the courts to sort out the matter. On July 24, 1974, in the case of *United States* v. *Nixon,* the Supreme Court disagreed that the tapes fell under the principle of executive privilege and ordered Nixon to turn them over. Chief Justice Warren Burger made it clear that the Court rejected Nixon's claim of executive privilege in this instance:

> **Primary Source** "The expectation of a President to the confidentiality of his conversations and correspondence . . . has all the values to which we accord deference for the privacy of all citizens. . . . But this presumptive privilege must be considered in light of our historic commitment to the rule of law [the principle that all citizens are bound by the same laws]. . . . The very integrity of the judicial system and public confidence in the system depend on full disclosure of all the facts, within the framework of the rules of evidence."
> —U.S. Supreme Court, *United States* v. *Nixon,* 1974

Nixon Resigns When investigators listened to the tapes, they found that crucial parts of the conversations were missing. Nixon claimed his secretary had mistakenly erased them. Still, the tapes provided enough evidence of Nixon's involvement in the coverup to lead the Judiciary Committee of the House of Representatives to vote to impeach the President. The committee charged Nixon with obstructing justice in the coverup of the Watergate break-in, misuse of power, and refusing to comply with House subpoenas. A number of Republican committee members joined the Democrats in voting for impeachment.

Recognizing that the full House of Representatives would vote in favor of impeachment and that many Republicans would vote to convict him in a trial in the Senate, Nixon decided to resign. In a speech to the American public on August 8, 1974, Nixon informed the nation that he would step down the following day in the hope that he "will have hastened the start of that process of healing which is so desperately needed in America." The long ordeal of Watergate had finally come to an end. With it, Nixon became the first and only President to resign the presidency.

Historians disagree about whether Nixon knew beforehand of the decision to burglarize Democratic Party headquarters. However, few doubt that he took part in the coverup. Testimony by his top aides, the Watergate tapes, and evidence gathered in the prosecution of the burglars all show that the President sought to quash the investigation.

Moreover, investigations revealed that Nixon had committed other abuses of presidential power. His reelection team had engaged in dirty tricks to secure his election. He had developed an "enemies list" and used federal agencies to go after his enemies. The President had ordered the FBI to place wiretaps on the telephones of those government employees and reporters he suspected of leaking information unfavorable to the administration.

Watergate Has a Lasting Impact In pursuit of personal power, Richard Nixon damaged the reputation of the

History Background

Presidential Impeachment Article II, Section 4 of the U.S. Constitution states the following: "The President, Vice President and all civil officers of the United States, shall be removed from office on impeachment for, and conviction of, treason, bribery, or other high crimes and misdemeanors." Impeachment is the sole responsibility of the House of Representatives, and is the act of bringing charges. The Senate carries out the actual trial. There have been only two impeachments involving the President. In 1868, President Andrew Johnson was impeached under 11 articles, or charges, stemming mostly from

his illegal attempt to remove the Secretary of War, to force an Army general to violate an act of Congress, and for being in contempt of Congress. The Senate acquitted Johnson by one vote. In 1998, Bill Clinton was impeached under two articles—for perjury and for obstruction of justice. He was found not guilty by a Senate vote of 55 to 45 on the perjury charge. The vote was 50 to 50 on the obstruction of justice charge. If found guilty in an impeachment proceeding, the person is removed from office; no other punishment applies to impeachment.

presidency and shook the public's confidence in government. One conservative commentator, formerly a supporter of Nixon, echoed the disillusionment of many Americans:

Primary Source "The lies, the lies, the lies! . . . What a pity, what a pity! Here was a President who got us out of Vietnam, ended the draft . . . and by his bold overtures to Red China opened new avenues toward world peace. Now the good vanishes in the wreckage of the bad. The swearing-in of Gerald Ford can't come one hour too soon."

—James J. Kilpatrick, *National Review,* August 30, 1974

Polls revealed that from the late 1950s to the mid-1970s, the percentage of Americans who believed in the truth of government statements plummeted from 80 percent to 33 percent.

In the wake of Watergate, Congress enacted numerous reforms to try to restore the public's confidence in government and to prevent abuses of power in the future. It established a procedure for naming an independent counsel to investigate charges against the White House. The Federal Election Campaign Act of 1974 sought to limit the amount of money that individuals could give candidates, in order to prevent the corruption of the political process.

Yet, the Watergate affair also demonstrated that the nation could weather such a crisis. It showed the strength of the system of checks and balances. Both Congress and the Supreme Court had successfully checked the power of the President. According to *Time* magazine, Nixon's resignation represented an "extraordinary triumph of the American system." Watergate demonstrated that no person, not even a President, is above the law. As Gerald Ford said when he became President: "Our great republic is a government of laws and not of men."

✔ **Checkpoint** What role did Richard Nixon and his top aides play in the Watergate scandal?

Post-Watergate Government Reforms

Federal Election Campaign Act Amendments (1974)	Set limit on campaign contributions, provided partial federal funding for presidential campaigns, created the Federal Election Commission to enforce these laws
Freedom of Information Act Amendments (1974)	Penalized government officials who withheld documents illegally
Government in the Sunshine Act (1976)	Opened meetings of many government agencies to the public. By 1977, all states had passed sunshine laws.
Ethics in Government Act of 1978	Required financial disclosure forms from public officials, restricted government officials' ability to lobby, created the office of special prosecutor

A Breach of Faith
The laws and measures listed above were passed after Watergate to make government more transparent. *Do you think these laws helped to restore the public's faith in government? Explain.*

Progress Monitoring Online
For: Self-test with vocabulary practice
www.pearsonschool.com/ushist

Comprehension

1. Terms and People For each term below, write a sentence explaining its relationship to the domestic policy record of the Nixon administration.
- silent majority
- stagflation
- affirmative action
- Watergate
- executive privilege

2. NoteTaking Reading Skill: Identify Main Ideas Use your chart to answer the Section Focus Question: What events led to Richard Nixon's resignation as President in 1974?

Writing About History

3. Quick Write: Write a Résumé Conduct research on Richard Nixon's life and career, and then create a résumé for the former President that lists his educational background, work experience, and any awards he received.

Critical Thinking

4. Summarize How did Nixon respond to the economic problems he faced as President?

5. Synthesize Information In the long run, how successful was Richard Nixon's southern strategy?

6. Draw Inferences Opinion polls taken before and after Watergate showed a sharp drop in people's confidence in government. List two other results of the scandal.

Assess Progress (L3)

- Have students complete the Section Assessment.

- Administer the Section Quiz. Teaching Resources, **p. 19**

- To further assess student understanding, use Progress Monitoring Transparencies, **138.**

Reteach

If students need more instruction, have them read the section summary.

Reading and Note Taking Study Guide (L3)

Adapted Reading and Note Taking Study Guide (L1) (L2)

Spanish Reading and Note Taking Study Guide (L2)

Extend (L4)

Have students review the Primary Source quotation on the previous page. Have each student write a paragraph that discusses how this decision affects the role of any future President.

Answers

Caption Sample response: In time, these laws helped restore people's faith in the government, but people probably were angry with the government for quite a while.

✔ Nixon and his aides may or may not have ordered or had knowledge of the break-in, but they did take part in the attempted cover-up.

Section 1 Assessment

1. Sentences should reflect an understanding of how each term is related to the domestic policy record of the Nixon administration.

2. Burglars who broke into Democratic Party headquarters in the Watergate Hotel had connections to Nixon's reelection committee. President Nixon tried to cover up the crime. Congress investigated and was about to start impeachment proceedings, when Nixon chose to resign instead.

3. Students' résumés should include highlights from Nixon's life and career, his educational background, and his special achievements and awards and be done in résumé format.

4. Nixon tried several solutions, but the most dramatic was a 90-day freeze on prices and wages.

5. The strategy was successful in that it helped reelect Nixon. However, it may have driven African Americans away from the Republican Party, to which many had been loyal since Reconstruction.

6. Sample answer: Congress enacted many reforms to restore public confidence in the government. Watergate also proved that the American system of government worked and could withstand such a serious crisis.

For additional assessment, have students access **Progress Monitoring Online** at **www.pearsonschool.com/ushist**.

What Are the Limits of Executive Privilege?

Objectives

- Understand aspects of the concept of executive privilege.
- Examine historic examples of the application of executive privilege.
- Analyze a Supreme Court decision regarding the application of executive privilege.

Background Knowledge L3

Explain that certain traditions or powers relating to governing the nation are not explicitly stated in the Constitution, and that *executive privilege* is one of them. Write the term on the board, and remind students of its meaning. Ask students to consider the types of information the President should, or should not be allowed to keep secret.

Instruct L3

- Review the circumstances of *United States* v. *Nixon,* and discuss recent issues that involve executive privilege. Give students at least three real or hypothetical examples of when a President has or might invoke executive privilege, and have students rate each example on a scale of 1 to 10, with 10 being "most applicable." Have students provide reasons to support their ratings.

- For further analysis of this Supreme Court case and the resulting decision, have students complete the worksheet *Landmark Decisions of the Supreme Court: What Are the Limits of Executive Privilege?* Teaching Resources, **p. 14**

- **Connect to Your World** Refer students to the Key Supreme Court Cases section for summaries of this case. Responses should show a clear understanding of the concept of executive privilege and offer specific reasons why students are defending or arguing against this particular use.

Monitor Progress

Direct students to use the class discussion and the rating exercise to write paragraphs answering the following question: What are the limits of executive privilege?

What Are the Limits of Executive Privilege?

The President's power to keep certain communications with his advisers confidential is called executive privilege. This power is based on the idea that members of the executive branch should be able to advise the President without worrying that their opinions will be revealed to other branches of government or to the public.

United States v. Nixon (1974)

The Facts	The Issue	The Decision
• Congressional investigation revealed that President Richard Nixon and his aides may have committed illegal acts. • Taped Oval Office conversations between President Nixon and his aides were sought as evidence. • President Nixon refused to surrender the tapes to the Department of Justice.	President Nixon argued that executive privilege gave him the absolute right to withhold the tapes from the Department of Justice.	The Supreme Court ruled that executive privilege has limits. They said that executive privilege could not protect the President from the judicial process. Nixon must surrender the tapes to prosecutors.

Why It Matters

Although not specifically granted by the Constitution, Presidents have long assumed that executive privilege is implied by the constitutional separation of powers. *United States* v. *Nixon* was the test case that allowed the Supreme Court to define executive privilege and to set limits on its use.

In his written opinion, Chief Justice Burger recognized that there is a need for confidentiality in the executive branch, particularly when "military, diplomatic or sensitive national security secrets" must be protected. Under those conditions, the President has the absolute right to keep communications confidential. However, communications between the President and his advisers often concern policy that has nothing to do with national security. In those cases, Burger said, executive privilege is limited. A judge can decide that there is overwhelming government interest in obtaining the President's privileged communications. The due process of law in a criminal case is one example of overwhelming government interest.

A few days after the decision in *United States* v. *Nixon*, President Nixon resigned from office. The Court's ruling had proved that the President is not above the law.

▲ President Nixon secretly recorded Oval Office conversations.

Connect to Your World

Consider the limits of executive privilege outlined in *United States* v. *Nixon*. During their respective terms in office, recent Presidents Bill Clinton and George W. Bush have applied executive privilege in controversial situations. Research one example and then write a paragraph either defending or arguing against this use of executive privilege.

For: Supreme Court cases
www.pearsonschool.com/ushist

History Background

Founding Fathers and Executive Privilege

Many U.S. Presidents have believed that they could claim the right of executive privilege. Washington, as he did in so many other areas, set this precedent when he refused to give to the House of Representatives papers it had requested that were related to the Jay Treaty. Washington claimed that as it was the Senate that ratified treaties, the House had no right to those documents, and that his position as chief executive allowed him to make this decision. The first legal event involving executive privilege occurred during Aaron Burr's trial for treason in 1807. The judge in the case was John Marshall, Chief Justice of the Supreme Court. On the basis of the Sixth Amendment right of due process, with which he believed even the President could not interfere, Marshall issued a subpoena to force President Thomas Jefferson, an enemy of Burr's, to produce a letter that the defense thought would help Burr's case. Eventually, Jefferson complied—voluntarily, he said—while explicitly denying that the judiciary had the power or the authority to compel him, as President, to do so.

▲ This man expresses the flagging spirit of many Americans during the late 1970s.

WITNESS HISTORY

A Crisis of Confidence

On July 4, 1976, the United States celebrated its bicentennial, or two hundredth anniversary. By the end of the decade, however, the celebratory mood had evaporated in the face of a series of crises that tested the nation's spirit. President Jimmy Carter took note of what he called the nation's crisis of confidence.

❝The symptoms of this crisis of the American spirit are all around us. For the first time in the history of our country a majority of our people believe that the next five years will be worse than the past five years. Two thirds of the people do not even vote. The productivity of workers is actually dropping. . . . There is a growing disrespect for government and for churches and for schools. . . . This is not a message of happiness or reassurance, but it is the truth and it is a warning.❞

—President Jimmy Carter, "Crisis of Confidence" speech, 1979

Objectives

As you teach this section, keep students focused on the following objectives to help them answer the Section Focus Question and master core content.

• Evaluate the presidency of Gerald Ford.

• Assess the domestic policies of Jimmy Carter.

• Analyze how American society changed in the 1970s.

The Ford and Carter Years

Objectives

• Evaluate the presidency of Gerald Ford.

• Assess the domestic policies of Jimmy Carter.

• Analyze how American society changed in the 1970s.

Terms and People

Gerald Ford
pardon
Jimmy Carter

Christian fundamentalist
amnesty
televangelist

NoteTaking

Reading Skill: Identify Main Ideas Create an outline like the one below to record the political, economic, and social problems of the era and their impact on American society.

    I. Gerald Ford's Presidency
      A. Major Domestic Issues
        1.
        2.
      B.

Why It Matters In 1982, historian Peter Carroll published a history of the 1970s entitled *It Seemed Like Nothing Happened*. Compared to the turbulent 1960s, indeed, the 1970s appeared mostly uneventful. Yet, the decade witnessed significant social, economic, and cultural changes. These changes contributed to a growing sense among Americans that something had gone wrong, that the nation had gotten off the right track. This sense of disquiet is even now a part of the nation's political dialogue. **Section Focus Question: What accounted for the changes in American attitudes during the 1970s?**

Ford Faces Political and Economic Woes

Gerald Ford brought a long record of public service to the presidency. A star football player at the University of Michigan, Ford enlisted in the United States Navy and fought in World War II. Following the war, Ford successfully ran for a seat in the U.S. Congress, where he served for 25 years, rising to the position of House Minority Leader in 1965. Democrats as well as Republicans supported Ford's nomination for Vice President because he had a stellar reputation for hard work, integrity, and dependability.

Ford stepped into a delicate situation when he became President after Richard Nixon's resignation. Watergate had scarred the public's faith in government. Furthermore, the nation struggled with the

Prepare to Read

Background Knowledge L3

Remind students that the Watergate scandal took place during a period of great change. Have students preview the section and predict the challenges to come during the Ford and Carter administrations.

Set a Purpose L3

▪ **WITNESS HISTORY** Read the selection aloud.

  Ask **According to Carter, what was one symptom of America's crisis of confidence?** *(Sample: For the first time, people believed that the next five years would be worse than the last five.)* Ask students whether they think this crisis continues today.

▪ **Focus** Point out the Section Focus Question, and write it on the board. Tell students to refer to this question as they read. *(Answer appears with Section 2 Assessment answers.)*

▪ **Preview** Have students preview the Section Objectives and the list of Terms and People.

▪ **NoteTaking** Using the Paragraph Shrinking strategy (TE, p. T20), have students read this section and create outlines recording the problems of the era and their impact. Reading and Note Taking Study Guide

Vocabulary Builder

Use the information below and the following resource to teach students the high-use word from this section. Teaching Resources, Vocabulary Builder, p. 9

High-Use Word	Definition and Sample Sentence
contend	*v.* to fight In the 1960s, the nation had to **contend** with the social and political issues brought on by the war in Vietnam.

Ford Faces Political and Economic Woes

Instruct

- **Introduce: Key Term** Ask students to find the key term ***pardoned*** (in bold) in the text. Then, write the term on the board and provide the definition. Have students predict why Gerald Ford ***pardoned*** Richard Nixon and how the ***pardon*** affected Ford's credibility as U.S. President.

- **Teach** Discuss the national mood and state of the economy when Ford became President. Ask **What problems of the Nixon administration did Ford inherit?** *(the public's lack of faith in the government as a result of the Watergate scandal; stagflation)* **How did Ford attempt to solve these problems?** *(He pardoned Nixon to put an end to the Watergate scandal and put forward his ill-fated WIN program.)* Point out that Ford's unpopularity caused the Republican Party to lose power in Congress. Have students discuss the way that the popularity of the President can affect the outcome of elections for other offices.

- **Analyzing the Visuals** Direct students' attention to the previous page's photograph of the man holding the sign. Ask students to review the problems that divided Americans during the mid-1970s and to discuss solutions that could bring Americans together.

Independent Practice

Instruct students to begin recording the main ideas in the Note Taking outline for this section.

Monitor Progress

As students fill in their outlines, circulate to make sure that they understand the political, economic, and social problems of the 1970s and the impact of these problems on American society. For a completed version of the outline, see Note Taking Transparencies, **B-143.**

Answer

✔ The WIN program tried to address inflation through voluntary measures, and it was a clear failure.

608 A Crisis in Confidence

WIN Fails
Despite enthusiastic campaigning by Ford, his WIN plan failed to tame inflation.

most severe economic problems it had faced since the depression. Ford wrestled with these problems but not very successfully. He left office with the economy still suffering and the public's distrust of government still high.

Ford Pardons Nixon Ford moved quickly to try to restore confidence in government. He selected Nelson Rockefeller, a former governor of New York State, to serve as his Vice President. He also promised to continue the foreign policy approaches of the Nixon administration.

Whatever support he gained from these steps was lost when Ford announced that he had **pardoned,** or officially forgiven, Richard Nixon for any crimes he may have committed as President. Though the pardon was meant to heal the nation's wounds, in some ways it achieved just the opposite effect. Ford's critics accused him of having made a secret deal, promising Nixon the pardon in exchange for the vice presidential nomination. Though Ford strongly denied this, his popularity declined dramatically.

The congressional election results of 1974 indicated the public's disapproval of the pardon and the impact of Watergate in general. The Republicans lost 48 seats in the House of Representatives, including Ford's longtime district in Grand Rapids, Michigan.

Stagflation Plagues the Nation President Ford might have overcome this backlash if not for the troubled economy. Inflation hit double digits in 1974 and early 1975. To fight skyrocketing prices, Ford promoted a mostly voluntary plan known as WIN, or Whip Inflation Now. Unfortunately, WIN was a clear failure. Instead of improving, the economy took a turn for the worse. Factories closed down, consumer demand for goods dropped sharply, and the rate of unemployment rose steadily. Ford's popularity plummeted.

✔ **Checkpoint** How did President Ford's WIN program try to address inflation, and how successful was it?

A Washington "Outsider" Becomes President

Prior to the mid-1970s, few Americans outside Georgia had ever heard of **Jimmy Carter,** a one-time governor of that state. But on election day 1976, Americans elected Carter President of the United States. He won a slim popular majority, receiving slightly more than 50 percent of the vote to Ford's 48 percent. In the electoral college, Carter won 297 votes compared to 240 for Ford.

Carter's rise was the result of several factors. Most important was the turmoil of the 1960s and Watergate, which created a backlash against professional politicians. Carter seized this opportunity by casting himself as a fresh face, with no ties to Washington, D.C. A born-again Christian who taught Sunday school, Carter won the support of many **Christian fundamentalists,** people who believe in a strict, literal interpretation of the Bible as the foundation of the Christian faith. This group became increasingly involved in politics in the 1970s.

Carter Pays a Price for Inexperience From the beginning of his presidency, Jimmy Carter sought to portray himself as a "citizens' President." He became the first President since William Henry Harrison to walk all the way from the Capitol to the White House during the inaugural parade. He held town meetings, wore casual clothes, and carried his own suitcase.

History Background

Whip Inflation Now Whip Inflation Now (WIN) attempted to combat the psychology of inflation without applying a program to solve the actual effects of inflation. Developed by Ford's advisers, including then White House Chief of Staff Dick Cheney and Alan Greenspan, later Chairman of the Federal Reserve Board from 1987 until 2006, WIN was introduced in a 1974 televised speech to Congress. Ford suggested, among other ideas, that American farmers increase production, a new energy board be established to lower domestic consumption of oil, and Congress

extend unemployment benefits and pass tax increases. The speech also asked Americans to join the program by wearing buttons and signing an "enlistment form" that would appear in many major newspapers. Members were to conserve energy by walking, carpooling, and bicycling; producing more and wasting less food; and shopping more efficiently. The campaign was widely ridiculed and many people wore their WIN buttons upside down so that they read NIM—No Instant Miracles. What Ford envisioned as an economic transformation ended in dismal failure.

However, Carter's inexperience, which helped him get elected, hurt him during the early days of his presidency. As an outsider, he did not have close ties with the Democratic leadership in Congress. He submitted numerous bills to Congress, but few of them passed without major changes by his own party.

Just one day after his inauguration, Carter fulfilled one of his campaign pledges by granting **amnesty,** or political pardons, to Americans who had evaded the draft during the Vietnam War. Carter hoped this act would help the nation move beyond the divisions caused by that war. Yet the war remained an emotional issue, and many Americans criticized the President for forgiving those who had refused to fight. Republican senator Barry Goldwater called the amnesty "the most disgraceful thing that a President has ever done."

Problems Sap the Nation's Confidence Like Ford, Carter <u>contended</u> with the energy crisis and severe inflation. Inflation ate away at people's savings, raised the prices of necessities, and made American goods more costly abroad. The U.S. automobile industry, long a symbol of the nation's economic power, became a symbol of its ills. Japanese car companies vastly expanded their sales in the United States by selling better-built and more fuel-efficient cars at reasonable prices. The situation grew so bad that Chrysler, one of the three major American automobile companies, needed a federal loan to survive.

At the center of the nation's economic ills lay the ongoing energy crisis. In 1973, a gallon of gas cost about 40 cents. By the end of the decade, it cost close to $1.20. To make matters worse, the winter of 1976 to 1977 was an especially bitter one in parts of the United States, increasing the need for heating oil. Fuel shortages caused factory closings and business losses.

Vocabulary Builder
<u>contend</u>–(kuhn TEHND) v. to fight

In 1974, gas stations all over the country ran out of gas to sell motorists.

RUNNING OUT OF GAS

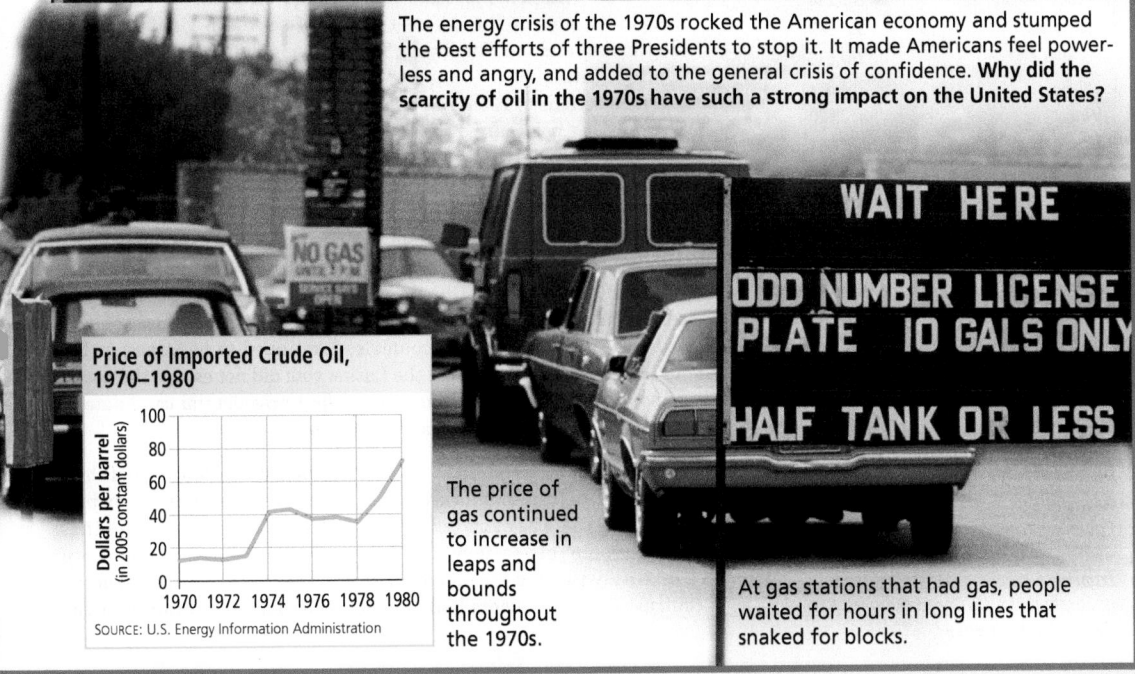

The energy crisis of the 1970s rocked the American economy and stumped the best efforts of three Presidents to stop it. It made Americans feel powerless and angry, and added to the general crisis of confidence. **Why did the scarcity of oil in the 1970s have such a strong impact on the United States?**

WAIT HERE
ODD NUMBER LICENSE PLATE   10 GALS ONLY
HALF TANK OR LESS

Price of Imported Crude Oil, 1970–1980

Dollars per barrel (in 2005 constant dollars): 0, 20, 40, 60, 80, 100
Years: 1970 1972 1974 1976 1978 1980

SOURCE: U.S. Energy Information Administration

The price of gas continued to increase in leaps and bounds throughout the 1970s.

At gas stations that had gas, people waited for hours in long lines that snaked for blocks.

Immigration to the United States, 1971–1980	
Country of Origin	Number of Immigrants
Mexico	640,294
Philippines	354,987
Korea	267,638
Cuba	264,863
Vietnam	172,820
India	164,134
Dominican Republic	148,135
Jamaica	137,577
United Kingdom	137,374
Italy	129,368
China	124,326
Hong Kong	113,467

SOURCE: U.S. Office of Immigration Statistics

Immigration Changes America

In the 1970s, immigration continued from Southeast Asia and Latin America. Girls from families of Cuban refugees (above) attend a Catholic school in Miami, Florida. *From which region did more people emigrate in the 1970s—Southeast Asia or Latin America?*

Carter responded to the oil crisis by calling on Americans to conserve and by asking Congress to raise taxes on crude oil, which he hoped would encourage conservation. However, the bill that finally passed in the Senate had few of the President's ideas in it. Critics saw this as one more example of Carter's poor leadership skills.

Carter did implement several domestic policies that his successors would build on during the 1980s. To fight inflation, Carter nominated Paul Volcker to head the Federal Reserve Board. Under Volcker's lead, the Federal Reserve began raising interest rates. In the long term, this policy helped to bring an end to the inflation that had plagued the nation for so long.

✓ **Checkpoint** What challenges did President Carter face?

Changing Values Stir Unease

Social and cultural changes that had begun in the 1950s and 1960s continued unabated in the 1970s. As a result, by the end of the decade, the United States was a very different society from the one it had been a generation earlier. These differences gave rise to an ongoing debate about the nation's values.

Demography Affects Politics The migration of Americans to the Sunbelt and the continued growth of the suburbs, both of which had begun in the post–World War II years, continued during the 1970s. As northern industries suffered, many blue-collar workers and their families moved from the Rust Belt states of the Northeast and Midwest to the Sunbelt of the South and West. They sought work in the oil fields of Texas and Oklahoma and in the defense plants of southern California, the Southwest, and the Northwest. These trends changed the face of the United States.

The elections of Richard Nixon and Jimmy Carter demonstrated the growing political power of the Sunbelt. Earlier in the century, Presidents tended to come from the large northern industrial states, such as New York and Ohio. In the latter decades of the twentieth century, Presidents tended to come from the Sunbelt.

The influx of immigrants from Latin America and Asia represented a different kind of demographic change. Even before the 1970s, hundreds of thousands of Cubans, Puerto Ricans, and Mexicans had migrated to the United States. This migration, especially from Mexico and other Latin American countries, continued to be strong in the 1970s. The growing power of the Latino vote did not escape the notice of politicians. Richard Nixon was the first presidential candidate to seriously court the Spanish-speaking vote.

The "Me Generation" Comes of Age During the 1960s, radicals had challenged many of society's traditional values. They questioned restrictions on premarital sex and drug use. They sported casual clothing and long hairstyles that many of their parents' generation found improper. Yet the counterculture remained a relatively isolated phenomenon during the 1960s. By the end of the 1970s, in contrast, these behaviors had become more common. Nationwide, the

Connect to Your World

U.S. Immigration Until the early twentieth century, the United States had placed few restrictions on immigration from Europe, although immigrants from Asia faced obstacles. Beginning in the 1920s, the United States sharply limited immigration. In the 1960s, the United States again opened the way for expanded immigration. However, regulations still limited the number of legal immigrants. To circumvent those limits, many immigrants crossed the border between Mexico and the United States illegally. When President George W. Bush took office in 2001, he hoped to make it easier for Latin Americans to work in the United States legally. However, terrorist attacks in 2001 created concern about the security of U.S. borders. Recently, debate has raged over U.S. immigration policy, with some citizens and members of Congress arguing that illegal immigrants should be deported, while others want to work for a general amnesty or some set of guidelines that would move illegal immigrants currently in the United States toward legal status and citizenship.

Focus On Geography

Sunbelt Migration During the 1970s, large numbers of Americans began to migrate from the North to the South. Manufacturers relocated because they could produce goods more cheaply in the South and West, or Sunbelt. Businesses and individuals were also drawn south and west because of the warm climate and lower cost of living. The northern states, known both as the Rust Belt and the Frostbelt, lost people, jobs, and political influence. The Sunbelt, on the other hand, was soon faced with the need for more roads, water, and other services for its growing population.

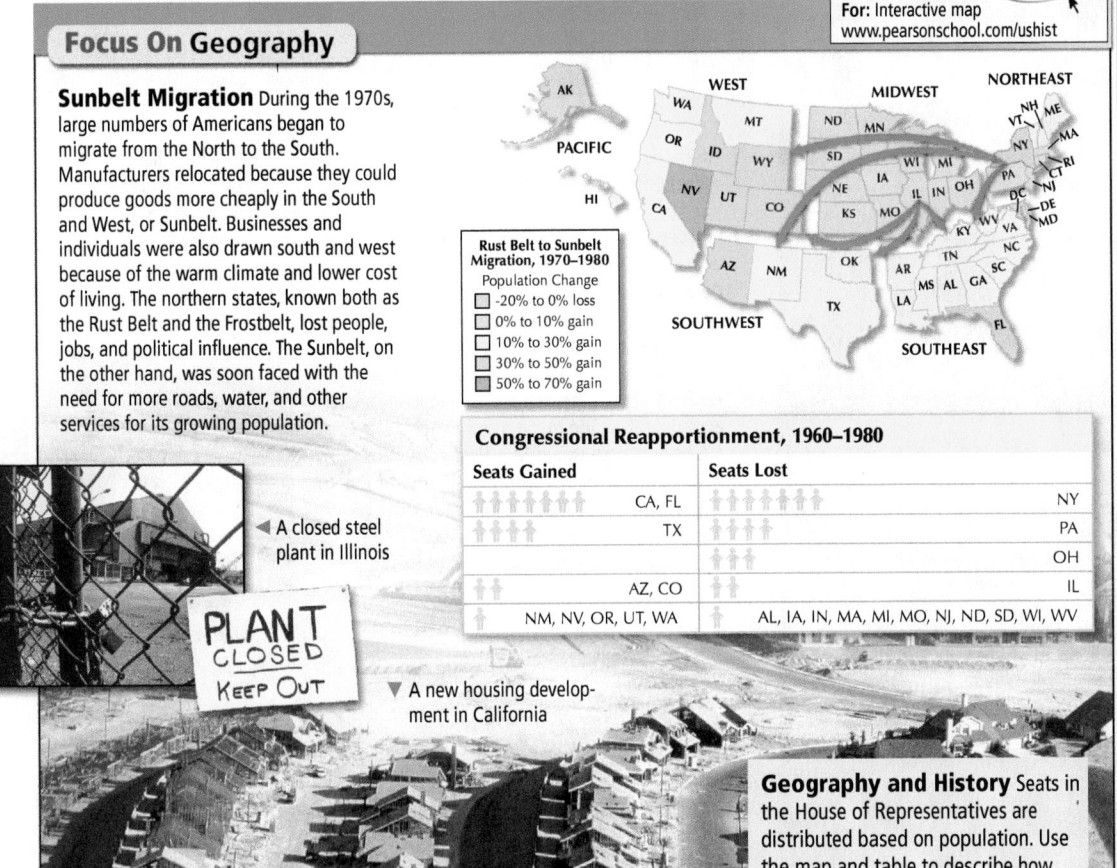

Rust Belt to Sunbelt Migration, 1970–1980
Population Change
- ☐ -20% to 0% loss
- ☐ 0% to 10% gain
- ☐ 10% to 30% gain
- ☐ 30% to 50% gain
- ☐ 50% to 70% gain

◄ A closed steel plant in Illinois

PLANT CLOSED KEEP OUT

▼ A new housing development in California

Congressional Reapportionment, 1960–1980

Seats Gained	Seats Lost
CA, FL	NY
TX	PA
	OH
AZ, CO	IL
NM, NV, OR, UT, WA	AL, IA, IN, MA, MI, MO, NJ, ND, SD, WI, WV

Geography and History Seats in the House of Representatives are distributed based on population. Use the map and table to describe how political power shifted in the 1970s.

divorce rate had more than doubled between 1965 and 1979, and twice as many children were born out of wedlock. To some Americans, the new ways were a sign of troubled times.

Some critics called the 1970s the "me decade" because many Americans appeared to be absorbed with improving themselves. This trend was reflected in the rise of movements like Transcendental Meditation (TM), a practice based in Eastern religious ideas. Those who practiced TM sought to find inner relaxation and vitality by chanting their personal mantras for about half an hour twice a day.

The seventies also witnessed an increasing interest in personal fitness and health. Millions began to jog for exercise and to eat natural, or less processed, foods. In 1970, just over 100 men and women ran in the New York City Marathon. Ten years later, more than 14,000 ran in the race. Body building took off, too, largely due to the influence of Arnold Schwarzenegger. A charismatic personality, Schwarzenegger went on to become one of Hollywood's most popular actors and, later, governor of California.

Differentiated Instruction   Solutions for All Learners

L1 Special Needs Students   L2 English Language Learners   L2 Less Proficient Readers

To help students learn more about the population shift in the 1970s, have them study the Focus on Geography feature on this page. Read the introductory paragraph aloud. Then, tell students to examine the pictures and the map and read the captions. Ask **Why do the photographs of the steel plant in Illinois and the housing development in California appear together?** *(The photographs appear together to show the way that migration affected different states. As people moved away from Illinois,*

businesses closed. However, as people moved to California, more housing developments were built.) **How does the map support what is shown in the photographs?** *(The map shows that many people are moving away from states in the Northeast and moving to states in the West.)* To help students understand the region known as the Sunbelt, have them read *Geography and History: The Sunbelt,* and complete the worksheet. Teaching Resources, **p. 15**

Changing Values Stir Unease   L3

Instruct

- **Introduce: Key Term** Ask students to find the key term *televangelists* (in bold) in the text. Tell students that the word was formed from *tele-*, from *television*, and *evangelists*, who are people who preach religion. Ask students to predict how fundamentalist Christian *televangelists* and their followers would affect politics in the 1970s.

- **Teach** Discuss reasons for some of the societal changes that took place in the 1970s. Ask **What kinds of changes in demographics occurred during this period?** *(There was a large influx of immigrants from Latin America and Southeast Asia and a population shift from the North and Northeast to the South and West.)* Have students study the chart on the previous page. Ask **Why did some critics call the 1970s the "me decade"?** *(because so many people were focused on themselves and their own needs)* Point out that many conservatives tended to distrust rapid change and idealized an earlier way of life. Ask **Why would major changes in society bring about a rise in fundamentalist Christianity and other conservative movements?** *(In the 1970s, many people feared or disliked the ways in which society was changing or viewed these developments as evidence of the nation's moral decay. Historically in times of great turmoil or change, fundamentalist or politically conservative beliefs often become popular.)*

- **Quick Activity** Have students access **www.pearsonschool.com/ushist** to use the Geography Interactive map and then answer the question in the text. Then, display Color Transparency: *Moving to the Sunbelt.* Use the lesson suggested in the transparency book to lead a discussion about how the 1970s population shifts affected the United States. Color Transparencies **A-136**

Answer

Geography and History

As people migrated from states in the Northeast and near the Great Lakes to states in the South and the West, those northern and midwestern states lost seats in the House of Representatives while southern and western states gained seats.

Independent Practice

- Have students study the images and text in the Infographic on this page and then answer the questions.

- To help students understand why people left the region known as the Rustbelt for the Sunbelt, have them complete the worksheet *Geography and History: From Rust Belt to Sunbelt.* Teaching Resources, **pp. 15–16**

Monitor Progress

Circulate to make sure that students understand why many people migrated from the Rustbelt to the Sunbelt and how television has been used to comment on the political, social, and economic issues of the day.

● **INFOGRAPHIC**

TV Breaks New Ground

In the early 1970s, the face of television began to change. Shows based on escapist fantasy or nostalgia gave way to shows that focused on current, hot-button issues and featured more minorities. The show that most typified this trend was the situation comedy, or sitcom, *All in the Family,* which remained the number one television show from 1971 through 1976. Conflicts between the central character—blue-collar bigot Archie Bunker— and his liberal, hippie son-in-law Michael (below left) brought debates over national issues onto the TV screen.

Toward the end of the decade, perhaps as a result of Watergate and the defeat in Vietnam, escapist television made a comeback with 1950s nostalgia shows like *Happy Days* and *Laverne & Shirley.* The rising popularity of the newsmagazine *60 Minutes,* however, showed that Americans were still interested in tuning in to learn about relevant issues.

M*A*S*H ❶ , a comedy about a mobile hospital unit during the Korean War, resonated with viewers who were used to watching news reports on the Vietnam War. Shows like *Sanford and Son* ❷ and *Chico and the Man* ❸ proved that viewers would tune in to shows featuring minority characters. *60 Minutes* ❹ was the first television newsmagazine. *Roots* ❺, a graphic historical miniseries that followed the life of a slave and his descendants, fascinated more than 100 million viewers.

Happy Days (top) was about a teenager growing up in the 1950s, while its spin-off, *Laverne & Shirley* (bottom), followed two lifelong friends living and working together in Milwaukee.

Thinking Critically
1. **Identify Central Issues** How did television change in the 1970s?
2. **Determine Relevance** How did these changes reflect broader changes taking place in American culture?

Differentiated Instruction   Solutions for All Learners

L1 Special Needs Students
L2 English Language Learners

Refer students to the television programs listed in the Infographic on this page. Have students locate a video of an episode in the local library or plan to watch one on television. (Many of these programs still play regularly.) Have students write brief essays in which they summarize the content of the episode and explain how the program and this particular episode reflect the time in which it aired.

L4 Advanced Readers
L4 Gifted and Talented Students

Have students gather images from old newspapers, magazines, or the Internet that track cultural trends or changes in American society in the 1970s. Students should focus their research on one trend such as the rise of the situation comedy or the development of the fitness craze. Students should assemble these images into a visual timeline and present it to the class in an oral presentation that follows how their chosen topic evolved.

Answers

Thinking Critically
1. Television became more open, political, and realistic. Later, escapist television also regained popularity.
2. These changes reflected the interest of the American public in issues such as civil rights, women's rights, the Vietnam War, family and fundamentalist Christian values, and, later, a desire to return to a seemingly happier time.

Conservatives Reassert Traditional Values The 1970s witnessed a resurgence of fundamental Christianity, partly as a response to the shift in values. To some commentators, it seemed as if the nation was experiencing another Great Awakening, like the great religious movements of the eighteenth and nineteenth centuries. Although the total number of Americans who attended church on a regular basis did not change much, the number of men and women who belonged to evangelical churches rose rapidly. One in five Americans considered himself or herself a religious fundamentalist by 1980.

Evangelical ministers used the media to gain a broader audience. Those who preached on television—known as **televangelists**—such as Jerry Falwell, Oral Roberts, and Marion "Pat" Robertson, reached millions of viewers. Falwell's daily radio broadcasts were carried by 280 radio stations, and his weekly television show was broadcast to 1.5 million viewers.

Religious conservatives firmly opposed many of the social changes begun in the 1960s that had gone mainstream in the 1970s. They opposed the Supreme Court's rulings that legalized abortion and restricted prayer in school. Falwell formed a prominent Christian conservative organization known as the Moral Majority in 1979. He voiced the concerns of many fundamentalists:

Primary Source "We must reverse the trend America finds herself in today. Young people . . . have been born and reared in a different world than Americans of past worlds. . . . They have learned to disrespect the family as God has established it. . . . They have been taught that the Bible is just another book of literature. . . . They have been introduced to the drug culture."
—Reverend Jerry Falwell, *Listen America,* 1980

During the 1970s, religious conservatives began forming alliances with other conservatives. They worked with economic conservatives, who sought to cut taxes and government spending, as well as with supporters of a stronger foreign policy, who favored increasing defense spending. Together, they began forging a new political majority. By 1980, Ronald Reagan, another political outsider, would use this alliance to win election to the White House.

✔ **Checkpoint** In what ways did the United States change socially and culturally during the 1970s?

SECTION **2** Assessment

Progress Monitoring *Online*
For: Self-test with vocabulary practice
www.pearsonschool.com/ushist

Comprehension

1. **Terms and People** For each item below, write a sentence explaining its effect on social and economic conditions in the 1970s.
   - Gerald Ford
   - pardon
   - Jimmy Carter
   - Christian fundamentalist
   - amnesty
   - televangelist

2. **NoteTaking Reading Skill: Identify Main Ideas** Use your outline to answer the Section Focus Question: What accounted for the changes in American attitudes during the 1970s?

Writing About History

3. **Quick Write: List Qualifications** Suppose that you are Gerald Ford applying for the position of Vice President in the mid-1970s. Research Ford's background and skills. Then, list the qualifications that you would highlight to try to get the position.

Critical Thinking

4. **Demonstrate Reasoned Judgment** Should Gerald Ford have pardoned Richard Nixon?

5. **Identify Point of View** What arguments would you expect people to give for and against President Carter's decision to grant amnesty to Americans who had evaded the draft?

6. **Draw Inferences** How do you think Watergate affected social trends in the 1970s?

Landmark Decisions of the Supreme Court

Are Affirmative Action Programs Fair?

Objectives

- Understand the ways in which civil rights have been addressed through the judicial system.

- Examine past and contemporary examples of affirmative action programs.

- Analyze a Supreme Court decision regarding affirmative action.

Background Knowledge ⓛ

Explain that affirmative action programs began as an effort to make hiring and school enrollment more fair. However, problems arose when, to enroll or hire a minority group member or a woman, a more qualified white male might lose the job or place in the school. Ask students what they think and whether affirmative action programs are fair.

Instruct ⓛ

- Review *Regents of the University of California v. Bakke.* Explain that a quota system holds open positions for minority or female candidates. A "plus factor" system takes race and gender into account while maintaining fair hiring or enrollment practices. Discuss why the Court found quotas objectionable, but not the idea of race or female gender as a "plus factor." Have students offer their ideas in support of or against using race or gender as factors in hiring or enrollment. Have students discuss whether affirmative action is necessary today.

- For further analysis of this Supreme Court case and the resulting decision, have students complete the worksheet *Landmark Decisions of the Supreme Court: Are Affirmative Action Programs Fair? Teaching Resources,* p. 17

- **Connect to Your World** Refer students to the Key Supreme Court Cases section. Students may do additional research. Responses should show understanding of the case and offer specific reasons why students agree or disagree with the ruling.

Monitor Progress

Have students write an opinion essay that answers the question posed in the lesson title.

Are Affirmative Action Programs Fair?

In the 1970s, the government urged employers and schools to adopt affirmative action programs. These programs aimed to increase the number of women and minority group members in college, postgraduate schools, and higher-paying jobs. The goal was to make up for past discrimination against these groups. Did those programs now discriminate against white males?

Regents of the University of California v. Bakke (1978)

The Facts	The Issue	The Decision
• Allan Bakke, a white man, was twice denied admission to a University of California medical school. • Bakke had a stronger academic record than 16 minority group applicants that the school had accepted under a special program.	Bakke claimed that his rights under the equal protection clause of the Fourteenth Amendment had been violated.	• Five Justices agreed that racial quotas violated Bakke's rights. • One of those Justices and four others agreed that race could be a factor in admissions decisions.

Why It Matters

Some people predicted that *Bakke* would end affirmative action. That did not happen, however. Justice Lewis Powell was the key figure in the Court's complex statements on the issue. He agreed with four Justices that quotas were not acceptable, but he also agreed with the other four that using race as a factor in admissions was acceptable. Powell favored using race as a "plus factor," just like artistic or musical ability, athletic talent, or other factors.

After the Court's decision, universities dropped quota systems. Many also followed Powell's opinion by setting up programs that consider a person's race as one factor among many.

▲ Protesters in Michigan support the University of California.

Connect to Your World

In 2003, the Court visited the issue again. In *Grutter* v. *Bollinger,* a 5-to-4 majority ruled that a law school's admissions policy met the standards of *Bakke* by using race as part of the process but not as a deciding factor. Read more about the case, then take the role of a newspaper editor and write an editorial agreeing or disagreeing with the Court's decision.

For: Supreme Court cases
www.pearsonschool.com/ushist

◀ Today's college classrooms reflect a greater gender and ethnic diversity in part because of affirmative action policies.

History Background

Supreme Court Indecision Public opinion on affirmative action continues to change. In more recent cases, the Supreme Court's decisions on affirmative action could be seen as contradictory.

In 1996, the California Civil Rights Initiative, also known as Proposition 209, eliminated affirmative action programs from both state and local government. One year later, the Supreme Court refused to hear a challenge to the execution of the law, effectively upholding it. Proposition 209 was a victory for critics of affirmative action and other states began proposing similar legislation.

In 2003, the U.S. Supreme Court seemed to change its position. Barbara Grutter, after being denied admission to the University of Michigan Law School, brought a lawsuit against the college based on the decision of *Regents of the University of California* v. *Bakke.* In *Grutter* v. *Bollinger,* the Supreme Court decided by a 5–4 split that the law school's affirmative action policy was constitutional. While voting to uphold the school's policy, Justice Sandra Day O'Connor did write that she hoped that affirmative action policies would become unnecessary in the future.

▲ President Carter and Panama's leader General Omar Torrijos in 1978

WITNESS HISTORY

Human Rights and American Foreign Policy

As President, Jimmy Carter sought to center America's foreign policy on human rights rather than on anticommunism. Carter outlined his views in 1977:

"For too many years, we've been willing to adopt the flawed and erroneous principles and tactics of our adversaries, sometimes abandoning our own values for theirs. We've fought fire with fire, never thinking that fire is better quenched with water. . . . [I] believe that it is a mistake to under-value the power of words and of the ideas that words embody."

—President Jimmy Carter, Commencement Address at Notre Dame University, 1977

Foreign Policy Troubles

Objectives

- Compare the policies of Gerald Ford and Jimmy Carter toward the Soviet Union.
- Discuss changing U.S. foreign policy in the developing world.
- Identify the successes and failures of Carter's foreign policy in the Middle East.

Terms and People

Helsinki Accords	sanctions
human rights	developing world
SALT II	Camp David Accords
boat people	Ayatollah Khomeini

NoteTaking

Reading Skill: Identify Supporting Details
Use a concept web like the one below to record the main ideas and details about the foreign policies of presidents Ford and Carter.

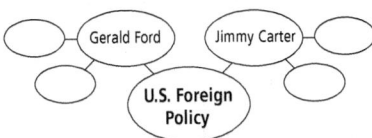

Why It Matters The ordeal of the Vietnam War led many to question the direction of American foreign policy. They asked: Why was the United States so concerned with fighting communism that it ended up supporting oppressive anticommunist governments? Should the United States continue to pursue détente with the Soviets? Or should it instead demand that the Soviet government grant its people more freedoms? The echoes of these debates continue to be heard today. **Section Focus Question: What were the goals of American foreign policy during the Ford and Carter years, and how successful were Ford's and Carter's policies?**

Ford Continues Nixon's Foreign Policies

Relations with the Soviet Union remained central to U.S. foreign policy during the Ford and Carter administrations. Upon assuming the presidency, Gerald Ford made clear that his foreign policy would differ little from that of Richard Nixon's. Ford retained Henry Kissinger as his Secretary of State and continued to pursue détente with the Soviet Union and China.

Pursuing Détente Ford and Soviet leader Leonid Brezhnev met in late 1974 and again the next year, when the two leaders endorsed the **Helsinki Accords.** This document put the nations of Europe on record in favor of **human rights,** or the basic rights that every human being is entitled to have. Some thought that President Ford

Objectives

As you teach this section, keep students focused on the following objectives to help them answer the Section Focus Question and master core content.

- Compare the policies of Gerald Ford and Jimmy Carter toward the Soviet Union.
- Discuss changing U.S. foreign policy in the developing world.
- Identify the successes and failures of Carter's foreign policy in the Middle East.

Prepare to Read

Background Knowledge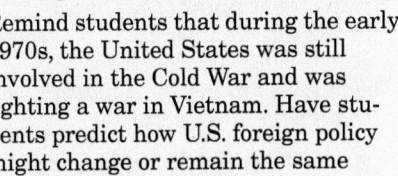

Remind students that during the early 1970s, the United States was still involved in the Cold War and was fighting a war in Vietnam. Have students predict how U.S. foreign policy might change or remain the same under Ford and Carter.

Set a Purpose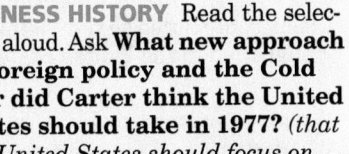

- **WITNESS HISTORY** Read the selection aloud. Ask **What new approach to foreign policy and the Cold War did Carter think the United States should take in 1977?** (*that the United States should focus on ideas and human rights to fight communism*)

- **Focus** Point out the Section Focus Question, and write it on the board. Tell students to refer to this question as they read. (*Answer appears with Section 3 Assessment answers.*)

- **Preview** Have students preview the Section Objectives and the list of Terms and People.

- **NoteTaking** Using the Structured Read Aloud strategy (TE, p. T20), have students read this section. As they read, have students record supporting details about the foreign policies of Ford and Carter. Reading and Note Taking Study Guide

Vocabulary Builder

Use the information below and the following resource to teach students the high-use words from this section. Teaching Resources, Vocabulary Builder, p. 9

High-Use Word	Definition and Sample Sentence
repression	*n.* the act of suppressing or keeping down It is the goal of human rights activists to fight hatred and **repression** around the world.
emphasis	*n.* special attention In her report on the war, the student put greater **emphasis** on the diplomacy of the time than on military actions.

Ford Continues Nixon's Foreign Policies L3

Instruct

- **Introduce: Key Terms** Ask students to find the key terms *Helsinki Accords* and *human rights* (in bold) in the text. Have students predict how the two terms are related. Ask **How are these terms related to the foreign policies of Ford and Carter?** *(Both terms represent a shift in U.S. foreign policy from fighting communism exclusively to working to improve the status of human rights.)*

- **Teach** Using the Numbered Heads strategy (TE, p. T23), have students discuss Ford's approach to U.S. foreign policy. Ask **How did Ford continue to follow Nixon's foreign policy?** *(He kept Kissinger as Secretary of State and continued to pursue détente.)* **How had U.S. foreign policy changed with regard to Southeast Asia?** *(The United States did not interfere in the region, even during the Khmer Rouge genocide, except to free the American merchant ship* Mayaguez.*)*

- **Analyzing the Visuals** Direct students to the photograph of Vietnamese boat people on this page. Ask students to discuss how Ford's foreign policy regarding Southeast Asia contributed to the Vietnamese migration to the United States.

Independent Practice

Ask students to fill in the concept web for this section by recording the approaches of Ford and Carter to U.S. foreign policy.

Monitor Progress

As students complete their concept webs, circulate to make sure that they are recording main ideas and details about the foreign policies of Ford and Carter. For a completed version of the concept web, see Note Taking Transparencies, B-144.

Answer

✔ Ford continued pursuing détente with the Soviet Union through the Helsinki Accords and SALT II. He did not interfere in Southeast Asia after the Vietnam War ended, except to free an American merchant ship.

Vietnamese Boat People

These Vietnamese refugees wait in their rickety boat in Hong Kong's harbor in September 1979, having survived the voyage from Vietnam.

Vocabulary Builder

repression–(rih PREHSH uhn) *n.* the act of suppressing or keeping down

would try to compel the Soviet Union to allow more political freedoms, but Ford decided to put arms control ahead of human rights. At his direction, the United States continued disarmament talks with the Soviets. These talks led to an agreement known as **SALT II,** in which the two nations pledged to limit nuclear arms production.

Trouble in Southeast Asia Under Ford, the United States sought to put the turmoil of the Vietnam War behind it. When the communist Khmer Rouge government of Cambodia began a genocidal slaughter of civilians, killing about 1.5 million people between 1975 and 1979, the United States did not intervene. The main exception to this policy of noninvolvement came in May 1975, when the Khmer Rouge seized an American merchant ship, the *Mayaguez*, which had been steaming just outside Cambodian waters. Ford responded by sending in some United States Marines, who freed the ship.

During Ford's presidency, South Vietnam fell to North Vietnam. As the communists took over, hundreds of thousands of Vietnamese, many of whom had worked with the United States, tried to escape. Many refugees took to the seas in rickety, unseaworthy boats. These **boat people** represented the largest mass migration of humanity by sea in modern history. Over a 20-year period, more than one million men, women, and children braved storms, pirates, and starvation in search of refuge abroad. Their immediate destinations were in other nations of Southeast Asia, but many eventually found that refuge in the United States and Canada.

✔ **Checkpoint** How did Ford approach foreign policy challenges during his presidency?

Carter Changes Course

Early in his presidency, Jimmy Carter proclaimed that as much as possible, American foreign policy would be guided by a concern for human rights. Carter hoped to make his foreign policy into a tool to end acts of political repression such as torture, murder, and imprisonment without trial. This policy direction helped reaffirm the position of the United States as a nation of freedom and justice. However, it undercut the goal of better relations with the Soviet Union.

Relations With the Soviet Union Cool At first, Carter continued Nixon's and Ford's policies toward the Soviet Union. He worked to achieve détente. He continued efforts at arms control, meeting with Leonid Brezhnev in June 1979 and signing the SALT II treaty.

However, relations between the two superpowers soon took a decidedly frosty turn. The SALT II treaty was bitterly debated in the United States Senate, where its opponents argued that it put the national security of the United States in jeopardy. Then, in December 1979, the Soviet Union invaded the neighboring country of Afghanistan to prop up a tottering communist government. Carter responded by withdrawing the SALT II treaty from Senate consideration and by imposing **sanctions,** or penalties, on the Soviets. The sanctions included a U.S. boycott of the 1980 Summer Olympic Games held in Moscow as well as a suspension of grain sales to the Soviet Union.

Differentiated Instruction   Solutions for All Learners

L2 English Language Learners
L2 Less Proficient Readers

Have students create their own Panama Canal Infographic. Have them use the Index in this textbook to locate information about the Canal's origins, the people and events involved, and its eventual return to Panamanian control. Provide students with blank outline maps to fill in and use as locator maps. Students should study the Infographics in the textbook for design and layout ideas. Encourage students to include captions where necessary and to select a title.

L4 Advanced Readers
L4 Gifted and Talented Students

Have students research and write a biography of one of the key international figures of this period. Examples many may include, Henry Kissinger, Richard Nixon, Shah Mohammed Reza Pahlavi of Iran, Menachem Begin and Anwar el-Sadat. Biographies should focus on the figure as a leader, and include information on the subject's origins, rise to power, major achievements or failures, and current status. Have students present their biographies to the class.

Carter Supports Human Rights in the Developing World Since the end of World War II, American Presidents had tended to see the **developing world**—the poor nations of Asia, Africa, and Latin America—as another stage for the Cold War. Carter broke with that approach and insisted that foreign policy toward the developing world should revolve around the expansion of human rights. Carter believed that U.S. relations with foreign countries should be determined by how a country treated its citizens.

Carter's <u>emphasis</u> on human rights led him to alter the U.S. relationship with a number of dictators. In Nicaragua, the Somoza family had ruled the country with an iron grip since the mid-1930s, most of the time with the support of the United States. In 1978, a leftist group known as the Sandinistas began a rebellion against the country's ruler, General Anastasio Somoza. His brutal response to the rebellion helped convince Carter to withdraw U.S. support. Without U.S. aid, General Somoza had to flee Nicaragua, and the Sandinistas came to power.

Carter's Policies Get Mixed Results in Latin America The Carter administration briefly sought to improve relations with Cuba, ruled by communist Fidel Castro since 1959. However, U.S.-Cuban relations soured in 1980 when Castro announced that any Cuban could leave the island from the port of Mariel for the United States. However, Castro insisted that any boats headed to the United States would also have to take criminals from the island's prisons. Because of this condition, the Mariel boatlift developed a bad reputation in the eyes of many Americans. Fewer than 20 percent of the people transported had spent time in prison, and many of those were political prisoners. Still, Americans were repelled by Castro's lack of concern for the welfare of the emigrants and by the idea that he would send criminals to the United States.

Carter's most controversial foreign policy move involved his decision to return the Panama Canal Zone to Panama. You will recall that Panama had given the United States control of a wide strip of land across the middle of the country in 1903 that later became the site of the Panama Canal. In 1977, Carter negotiated a set of treaties to return the Canal Zone to Panama by 1999. Many Americans worried that the loss of control over the canal would threaten American shipping and security. Nonetheless, the United States Senate narrowly ratified the treaties in 1978, and all control of the canal was ultimately turned over to Panama.

✓ **Checkpoint** In what ways did President Carter's policies differ from those of Ford?

Success and Setback in the Middle East

Carter's greatest achievement in foreign policy came in the region that also saw his greatest setback. He helped negotiate a historic peace agreement between Israel and Egypt, but he failed to win the release of Americans held hostage by Iranian radicals.

Israel and Egypt Agree to Peace Egypt had opposed Israel's existence since Israel's founding in 1948. As recently as 1973, Egypt and Syria had attacked Israel. By 1977, eager to improve relations, Egyptian President Anwar el-Sadat and Israeli prime minister Menachem Begin met in Jerusalem to negotiate a peace agreement. To help continue the negotiations, Carter invited the two leaders to Camp David, the presidential retreat. For

Vocabulary Builder
emphasis–(EHM fuh sihs) n. special attention

HISTORY MAKERS

Jimmy Carter (born 1924)
A former navy officer and peanut farmer, Jimmy Carter's presidency began with high hopes and calls for a new emphasis on human rights. Carter lost his bid for reelection but continued to work to promote human rights and democracy around the world. He set up an organization called the Carter Center that promotes peace and human rights, and he has helped several countries' efforts to hold free and fair elections. He even joined Habitat for Humanity to help poor people build and afford new homes.

Connect to Your World

Iranian Nuclear Development Despite a brief, hopeful period in which Iranians elected less conservative leaders who were friendlier toward western nations, relations between Iran and the United States had soured by the early 2000s. Perhaps the most disturbing conflict between the two nations has been over Iran's nuclear development. In 1968, over 60 countries, including Iran, signed the Nuclear Nonproliferation Treaty (NPT). Nevertheless, Iran has been working on nuclear development for several years while claiming that its goal is energy production only. However, the International Atomic Energy Agency (IAEA), which has the task of monitoring signatory nations, announced that Iran had not fully disclosed the true progress of its nuclear program and was intending to open a uranium enrichment facility for use in nuclear weapons. Representatives of the European Union tried to negotiate with Iran, but they failed to reach any binding agreements. Many speculate that either Israel or the United States will make pre-emptive strikes on Iranian nuclear sites because Iran's president has vowed to destroy Israel, attack Saudi Arabia, cut off Western supplies of oil and otherwise destabilize the Middle East.

Instruct

- **Introduce: Key Terms** Ask students to find the key terms **sanctions** and **developing world** (in bold) in the text and discuss what each word means. Have students predict how **sanctions** and the **developing world** are related to Carter's foreign policy.

- **Teach** Remind students that since the end of World War II, the United States had been focused mainly on fighting communist regimes or movements around the world as part of the larger struggle of the Cold War. Ask **How did Carter's foreign policy goals affect U.S.-Soviet relations?** *(When the Soviets invaded Afghanistan, Carter imposed sanctions that included a boycott of the Summer Olympics and the suspension of grain sales. These tactics angered the Soviets, and relations between the two nations cooled.)* **What was controversial about Carter's negotiations to return control of the Panama Canal to Panama?** *(Many Americans feared that losing control of the Canal would threaten U.S. shipping and security.)*

- **Quick Activity** Have students read the HISTORY MAKERS biography of Jimmy Carter. Discuss with students the factors that may contribute to an unsuccessful presidency. Ask students to consider if Carter's difficulties as President were caused by his personality or by the events of the time.

Independent Practice

Have students create timelines of the major foreign policy events of the Ford and Carter terms.

Monitor Progress

As students create their timelines, circulate to make sure that they list events in chronological order.

Answer

✓ Carter believed that the focus of U.S. foreign policy should shift from fighting communism to supporting the struggle for human rights. He stopped pursuing détente with the Soviets and imposed sanctions on them. He also changed U.S. relations with some dictators by withdrawing U.S. support.

Instruct

- **Introduce: Key Term** Have students find the key term *Camp David Accords* (in bold) in the text. Then, write the term on the board and explain its significance. Ask students to discuss in what way the *Camp David Accords* were consistent with Carter's foreign policy goals.

- **Teach** Display Color Transparency, *Camp David Accords*. Ask **Who were the main participants in negotiating the Camp David Accords?** *(U.S. President Jimmy Carter, Egyptian President Anwar el-Sadat, and Israeli Prime Minister Menachem Begin)* **Why were the Accords so significant?** *(Egypt had opposed Israel's existence since Israel's founding in 1948. The Camp David Accords were a huge step forward to ending the conflict in the Middle East.)* **How were the Accords an example of the change in U.S. foreign policy?** *(They had nothing to do with fighting communism; the goal was to create peace and stability.)* Discuss the hostage crisis in Iran. Have students explain why this event represented a foreign policy failure, and how it changed American views about what threatened national security. Color Transparencies **A-135**

- **Quick Activity** Have students study the images and chart in the Infographic on this spread and write a paragraph summarizing the events in the Iranian hostage crisis.

Independent Practice

To find out more about the hostages who were held in Iran, have students complete the worksheet *Biography: The American Hostages.* Teaching Resources, **p. 18**

Monitor Progress

As students complete their worksheets, circulate to make sure that they understand why the American hostages were in Iran and how these people coped with their ordeal.

● INFOGRAPHIC

IRAN HOSTAGE CRISIS

The Iranian Revolution, which toppled the Shah and brought the Ayatollah Khomeini to power in 1979, had a strong anti-American component. The United States had supported Mohammad Reza Shah Pahlavi, Iran's Shah, to secure a firm ally against communism in the region. However, the Shah's rule grew more oppressive after 1953, when the CIA had helped him control a challenge to his power. Resentment over political interference and foreign involvement in Iran's oil industry boiled over when the deposed Shah entered the United States for medical treatment. Outraged Iranians seized 66 American hostages and held 52 of them for 444 days.

▲ The Ayatollah Khomeini

◀ A blindfolded American hostage is shown to the press.

The Crisis Unfolds

- **January 1979** The Iranian Revolution forces the Shah into exile.
- **February 1979** Ayatollah Khomeini returns to Iran after 15 years in exile.
- **April 1979** Khomeini takes power.
- **October 1979** The Shah enters the United States.
- **November 1979** Militant students take 66 Americans hostage. Carter halts oil imports and freezes Iranian assets in the United States.
- **April 1980** Carter severs diplomatic relations with Iran and imposes an economic embargo. A military mission to free the hostages ends in disaster.
- **January 1981** On the day of Reagan's inauguration, the hostages are released for $8 billion in frozen assets and a promise to lift trade sanctions against Iran.

nearly two weeks, the three leaders carried on the difficult negotiations that produced what is known as the **Camp David Accords.** These agreements provided the framework for a peace treaty in which Egypt formally recognized the nation of Israel, becoming the first Arab nation to do so. In return, Israel withdrew its troops from the Sinai Peninsula, which it had controlled since the 1967 war. The preamble to the Accords states:

> **Primary Source** "After four wars during 30 years, despite intensive human efforts, the Middle East, which is the cradle of civilization and the birthplace of three great religions, does not enjoy the blessings of peace. . . . [Israel and Egypt] recognize that for peace to endure, it must involve all those who have been most deeply affected by the conflict. They therefore agree that this framework, as appropriate, is intended by them to constitute a basis for peace not only between Egypt and Israel, but also between Israel and each of its other neighbors. . . . "
> —Camp David Accords, September 19, 1978

Iran Seizes American Hostages Carter hoped that the Camp David Accords would usher in a new era of cooperation in the Middle East. Yet, events in Iran showed that troubles in the region were far from over. Since the 1950s, the United States had supported the rule of the Shah, or emperor, of Iran. In the 1970s, however, opposition to the Shah began to grow within Iran.

Dying of cancer, the Shah fled from Iran in January 1979. Fundamentalist Islamic clerics, led by the **Ayatollah Khomeini** (ī yuh TOH luh koh MAYN ee), took power. Carter allowed the Shah to enter the United States to seek medical treatment. Enraged Iranian radical students invaded the U.S. Embassy and took 66 Americans as hostages. The Khomeini government then took control of both the embassy and the hostages to defy the United States.

The hostage crisis consumed the attention of Carter during the last year of his presidency. To many Americans, Carter's failure to win all of the hostages' release was evidence of American weakness. As Peter Bourne put it in his biography of

---

Differentiated Instruction   Solutions for All Learners

L1 Special Needs Students   **L2 English Language Learners**   **L2 Less Proficient Readers**

To help students practice geography skills, provide them with blank outline maps of the world. Have students review the section and list any locations mentioned in the text, such as Cuba, Camp David, Egypt, Israel, Iran, or Cambodia. Then, ask students to locate and label each place on their maps. Tell students that each location should include a label and a brief caption. Have students use one symbol to represent places related to Ford's foreign policy, another symbol to represent places related to Carter's foreign policy, and a third symbol to represent locations related to both. Tell students to include the symbols in a simple map key.

◄ Iranian students burn an American flag at the U.S. embassy in Tehran; protesters call for the CIA to stop interfering in Iran (right).

▲ The freed hostages arrive in the United States after their ordeal finally ends in January 1981.

Assess and Reteach

Assess Progress   L3

- Have students complete the Section Assessment.
- Administer the Section Quiz. Teaching Resources, **p. 21**
- To further assess student understanding, use Progress Monitoring Transparencies, **140**.

Reteach

If students need more instruction, have them read the section summary.

Reading and Note Taking   L3
Study Guide

Adapted Reading and   L1 L2
Note Taking Study Guide

Spanish Reading and Note   L2
Taking Study Guide

Extend   L4

Have students complete *Newspaper Year in Review: 1979* to learn more about this year. Teaching Resources, **pp. 11–12**

Thinking Critically

1. **Recognize Causes** What event triggered the seizure of the American hostages in Iran?
2. **Synthesize Information** What actions did Carter take to try to get the hostages released?

Jimmy Carter, "Because people felt that Carter had not been tough enough in foreign policy . . . some bunch of students could seize American diplomatic officials and hold them prisoner and thumb their nose at the United States."

The hostage crisis began to change the way Americans viewed the world outside their borders. Nuclear war between the two superpowers was no longer the only threat to the United States. Although the Cold War still concerned Americans, the threats posed by conflicts in the Middle East threatened to become the greatest foreign policy challenge of the United States.

✓ **Checkpoint** How did the seizure of the U.S. Embassy by Iranian students affect Americans' view of the world?

SECTION **3** Assessment

Progress Monitoring *Online*
For: Self-test with vocabulary practice
www.pearsonschool.com/ushist

Comprehension

1. **Terms and People** For each item below, write a sentence explaining the way it affected U.S. foreign policy.
   - human rights
   - SALT II
   - boat people
   - sanctions
   - developing world
   - Camp David Accords
   - Ayatollah Khomeini

2. **NoteTaking Reading Skill: Identify Supporting Details** Use your concept web to answer the Section Focus Question: What were the goals of American foreign policy during the Ford and Carter years, and how successful were Ford's and Carter's policies?

Writing About History

3. **Quick Write: Present Skills** Put yourself in the place of someone applying to be the U.S. Ambassador to Panama in the mid-1970s. Write a paragraph describing the key qualities needed for the job.

Critical Thinking

4. **Draw Conclusions** What do you think were the most important foreign policy accomplishments of Gerald Ford and Jimmy Carter?

5. **Draw Inferences** What did Carter's inability to secure the release of the hostages in Iran symbolize to many Americans?

Answers

Thinking Critically

1. Carter allowed the Shah of Iran to enter the United States for medical treatment.

2. halted oil imports, froze Iranian assets, severed diplomatic ties, imposed sanctions, and tried a military operation

✓ Americans realized their vulnerability and became aware that Islamic fundamentalism and Middle East conflicts presented serious foreign policy challenges.

Section 3 Assessment

1. Sentences should reflect an understanding of how each person or term affected U.S. foreign policy.

2. Ford's foreign policy was to continue pursuing détente with the Soviet Union and China. Ford also pursued non-involvement in Southeast Asia. Carter's foreign policy was guided by a concern for human rights, instead of on Cold War competition. Ford was probably more successful in fulfilling his foreign policy goals than was Carter, who, in taking a stand on human rights, brought about a negative turn in U.S.-Soviet relations. Carter also experienced mixed results in Latin America. In the Middle East, Carter saw his greatest achievement and worst setback: he brokered the Camp David Accords, but then had to face the Iranian hostage crisis.

3. Student answers should include the education, qualities, and experiences that a diplomat to a Latin American nation during the mid-1970s should have possessed.

4. Sample response: I think the Helsinki Accords were Ford's greatest foreign policy accomplishment and the Camp David Accords were Carter's.

5. that the United States was weaker and held less international power than many Americans had believed

For additional assessment, have students access **Progress Monitoring *Online*** at **www.pearsonschool.com/ushist**.

Quick Study Guide

Progress Monitoring Online
For: Self-test with vocabulary practice
www.pearsonschool.com/ushist

Quick Study Guide

- Have students use the Quick Study Guide to prepare for the chapter test. Students may wish to refer to the following sections as they review:

Watergate in Review
Section 1

Economic Problems of the 1970s
Section 1
Section 2

International Relations in the 1970s
Section 3

Domestic Controversies in the 1970s
Section 1
Section 2

Key Events of 1968–1981
Section 1
Section 2
Section 3

- For additional review, remind students to refer to the Reading and Note Taking Study Guide.
Section Note Taking
Section Summaries

- Have students access **www.pearsonschool.com/ushist** for this chapter's History Interactive timeline, which includes expanded entries and additional events.

- If students need more instruction on analyzing graphic data, have them read the Skills Handbook, **p. SH21.**

For **Progress Monitoring Online,** refer students to the Self-test with vocabulary practice at **www.pearsonschool.com/ushist.**

Watergate in Review

Issues	Consequences
• Presidential abuse of power (FBI wiretaps of "enemies") • Limits of executive privilege • Supreme Court's power to rule on presidential actions • Willingness of Congress to confront presidential power	• Shook public confidence in government • Damaged the reputation of the presidency • Confirmed the independent power of legislative and judicial branches • Demonstrated strength of checks and balances system • Prompted laws to govern independent counsel investigations and reform election finance practices

Economic Problems of the 1970s

Slow economic growth
Inflation
Energy crisis
Foreign competition

International Relations in the 1970s

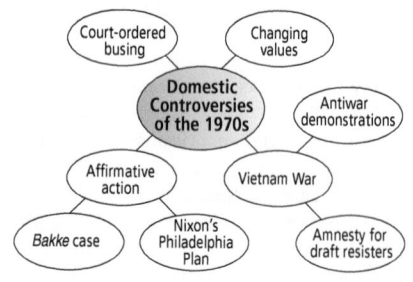

International Relations in the 1970s		
Hot Spots	**Disputes**	**Improvements**
• Vietnam • Cambodia • Afghanistan	• Soviet Union • Cuba • OPEC countries • Iran	• China • Panama • Israel • Egypt • Nicaragua

Domestic Controversies in the 1970s

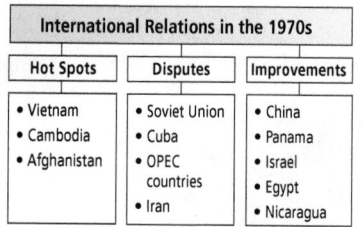

Court-ordered busing — Changing values — Domestic Controversies of the 1970s — Antiwar demonstrations — Affirmative action — Vietnam War — Bakke case — Nixon's Philadelphia Plan — Amnesty for draft resisters

✓ Quick Study Timeline

In America

1970
Clean Air Act becomes law

1973
OPEC oil embargo causes U.S. energy prices to soar

1974
Nixon resigns in wake of Watergate scandal; Ford becomes President

Presidential Terms   Richard M. Nixon 1969–1974   Gerald R. Ford 1974–1977

1970   1972   1974

Around the World

1970
United States invades Cambodia

1971
Idi Amin takes power in Uganda

1972
Terrorists kill Israeli athletes at Munich Olympics

1975
South Vietnam surrenders to North Vietnam

Differentiated Instruction   Solutions for All Learners

L1 Special Needs Students   L2 Less Proficient Readers   L2 English Language Learners

Use the following study guide resources to help students acquiring basic skills:
Adapted Reading and Note Taking Study Guide
- Section Note Taking
- Section Summaries

Use the following study guide resources to help Spanish-speaking students:
Spanish Reading and Note Taking Study Guide
- Section Note Taking
- Section Summaries

American Issues
•—•—•— Connector

By connecting prior knowledge with what you have learned in this chapter, you can gradually build your understanding of enduring questions that still affect America today. Answer the questions below. Then, use your American Issues Connector study guide (or go online: www.pearsonschool.com/ushist).

Issues You Learned About

● **Checks and Balances** Political leaders disagree on how much authority each branch can exert over the others.

1. Why is the principle of checks and balances important to the U.S. government? Give an example of checks and balances at work.

2. Describe the role of the judicial branch and the legislative branch in the move to impeach President Nixon. What did *Time* magazine mean when it called Nixon's resignation an "extraordinary triumph of the American system"?

● **Church and State** The First Amendment of the United States Constitution, known as the Establishment Clause, calls for the separation of church and state.

3. Read the 1787 Virginia Statute for Religious Freedom, which appears in the documents section at the end of this book. What was the importance of this document?

4. Since the 1960s, the Supreme Court has made a number of rulings limiting prayers and religious readings in public schools. Why do you think that the Supreme Court banned prayer in public schools?

● **Sectionalism and National Politics** Different regions of the country often can be defined by their political beliefs.

5. Why did southern states traditionally vote for Democrats? What was remarkable about Nixon's presidential victory in 1972?

6. How did Nixon expand his base of support from the 1968 election? What was this strategy called?

7. Why did the Sunbelt gain political power in the 1970s?

Connect to Your World	Activity

America and the World As you have read, in 1973 the United States experienced an oil shortage due to an embargo by OPEC. In one year, oil prices shot up 400 percent. Today, the United States remains dependent on foreign oil, and the country's import needs are expected to rise in the future. Many Americans believe that this reliance on foreign oil compromises the independence and security of the United States. Conduct research online, or go to the local library, to find out about the current debate over America's reliance on foreign oil. Create a chart that shows some of the different options that people have proposed to lessen this reliance.

1976 America celebrates Bicentennial	1977 President Carter pardons Vietnam War draft evaders	1979 Protesters seize U.S. embassy and hostages in Tehran	**History** *Interactive* For: Interactive timeline www.pearsonschool.com/ushist

Jimmy Carter 1977–1981 .... Ronald Reagan 1981–1989

1976	1978	1980

1978 Egypt and Israel sign Camp David Accords	1979 Soviet Union invades Afghanistan	1980 Iraq invades Iran	1981 Egyptian President Anwar Sadat is assassinated

American Issues
•—•—•— Connector

Tell students that the main issues for this chapter are Checks and Balances, Church and State, and Sectionalism and National Politics. Then, ask them to answer the Issues You Learned About questions on this page. Discuss the Connect to Your World topic, and ask students to complete the project that follows.

American Issues Connector

1. because it ensures that no one branch will have total control of the government; the Supreme Court strikes down a law because the law is found to be unconstitutional

2. Senate investigated Watergate break-in; Supreme Court ruled Nixon must turn over tape recordings; House of Representatives Judiciary Committee recommended impeachment proceedings. Watergate was a test of the checks-and-balances system, which worked well.

3. led to the inclusion of religion clauses in First Amendment of U.S. Constitution; was important reference for Supreme Court when interpreting First Amendment in later times

4. Public schools are under the jurisdiction of the government, and prayer is a religious activity.

5. because the Democratic Party supported segregation; Nixon persuaded many Democrats to vote for him, a Republican.

6. He targeted white blue-collar workers and southern whites; the southern strategy

7. Millions of people—and their votes—moved to the Sunbelt states.

Connect to Your World

Students' charts should reflect sound research and a thoughtful consideration of the question. They should include at least three alternative fuel options.

For additional review of this chapter's enduring issues, remind students to refer to the Reading and Note Taking Study Guide American Issues Journal.

Chapter Assessment

Terms and People

1. a dual condition of a stagnating economy and inflationary pressures; expanding federal deficits, rising foreign competition, and the rapid increase in the price of oil

2. the principle that the President has the right to keep certain information confidential; that Nixon's tape recordings were not protected by executive privilege

3. political pardon; many were angry that those who had refused to fight would escape punishment.

4. the poor nations of Asia, Africa, and Latin America; Carter moved policy from treating them as arenas for fighting the Cold War to areas where human rights should be protected.

5. leader of the fundamentalist Islamic clerics who overthrew the Shah of Iran in 1979; in retaliation for allowing the Shah to enter the United States for medical treatment, Iranians under Khomeini's rule took over the U.S. embassy in Iran and held 52 American hostages for more than a year.

Focus Questions

6. Burglars who broke into Democratic headquarters in the Watergate Hotel had connections to Nixon's reelection committee. Nixon tried to cover up the crime. Congress investigated and was about to start impeachment proceedings, when Nixon chose to resign instead.

7. migration of Americans to the Sunbelt; influx of immigrants from Latin America and Southeast Asia; coming of age of the "Me Generation"; events such as Watergate; strengthening of conservative fundamentalist Christianity

8. Ford: continue pursuing détente with the Soviet Union and China and pursue non-involvement in Southeast Asia. Carter was guided by concern for human rights, instead of Cold War competition. Ford was probably more successful than was Carter, who, in taking a stand on human rights, negatively affected U.S.-Soviet relations. Carter also experienced mixed results in Latin

Terms and People

1. Define **stagflation.** What were the causes of stagflation in the early 1970s?

2. Define **executive privilege.** How did the Supreme Court rule on executive privilege in *United States* v. *Nixon*?

3. What is **amnesty**? Why did Carter's granting of amnesty to draft evaders anger some Americans?

4. What is the **developing world**? How did Carter change U.S. foreign policy toward the developing world?

5. Who was the **Ayatollah Khomeini**? How did his actions affect the Carter presidency?

Focus Questions

The focus question for this chapter is **What caused Americans to suffer a crisis of confidence during the 1970s?** Build an answer to this big question by answering the focus questions for Sections 1 through 3 and the Critical Thinking questions that follow.

Section 1
6. What events led to Richard Nixon's resignation as President in 1974?

Section 2
7. What accounted for the changes in American attitudes during the 1970s?

Section 3
8. What were the goals of American foreign policy during the Ford and Carter years, and how successful were Ford's and Carter's policies?

Critical Thinking

9. **Synthesize Information** Think about Nixon's approach to new programs and policies designed to ease racial inequality. Would you call him a supporter or an opponent of civil rights? Explain.

10. **Analyze Political Cartoons** Study the political cartoon in the Landmark Decisions of the Supreme Court feature about executive privilege that appears earlier in this chapter. Explain the political issue depicted in the cartoon and the cartoonist's view of it.

11. **Recognize Cause and Effect** Why did Ford pardon Nixon for any crimes he may have committed as President? What effect did this pardon have on American politics over the next few years?

12. **Analyze Information** How did Carter's role as a political outsider both help and hinder him in Washington, D.C.?

13. **Summarize** Summarize the responses of Nixon, Ford, and Carter to the downturn of the American economy, and explain what impact these measures had.

14. **Compare Points of View** Compare Ford's and Carter's foreign policy toward the Soviet Union.

15. **Identify Central Issues** Identify and describe two regions in the world in which Carter's policies had a major impact.

Writing About History

Applying for a Job Throughout American history, many talented individuals have worked in the federal government to try to address the energy and economic problems that have troubled the nation. Write an essay from the point of view of a college graduate in 1977 trying to get a job in the newly established Department of Energy. Explain what your qualifications are and how they are a good fit with the job's needs.

Prewriting
• Research the skills needed to fill a job in the Department of Energy in 1977.
• Develop the character of a 1977 college graduate based on those skills.

Drafting
• Write a thesis statement that expresses the key qualifications, skills, and qualities that you (as the college graduate) possess that suit the Department of Energy job.
• Expand upon these positive factors in the body of your essay.
• Close with an effective and well-worded conclusion.

Revising
• Use the guidelines on page SH16 of the Writing Handbook to revise your essay.

America. In the Middle East, he brokered the Camp David Accords, but then had to face the Iranian hostage crisis.

Critical Thinking

9. Sample response: Neither; he opposed court-ordered busing but his administration initiated the Philadelphia Plan, which required labor unions and federal contractors to submit plans for hiring minorities.

10. Sample answer: It represents the constitutional struggle during Watergate between the executive branch and the legislative

branch. The cartoonist's view is that the struggle between Nixon and Congress represents a larger struggle for control between two government branches.

11. Ford said that he did it to heal the nation's wounds. This pardon made people angry and cynical, which caused Ford's popularity to fall sharply, and lost the Republicans 48 seats in the House of Representatives. Along with the worsening economy, the pardon led to the election of Washington outsiders.

Document-Based Assessment

Anatomy of a Scandal

President Richard Nixon's administration was marred by a political scandal, called Watergate, that led to his resignation. What were the roles of the Congress, the press, and the courts in investigating President Nixon's unchecked presidential power? Use your knowledge of the Watergate scandal and Documents A, B, and C to answer questions 1 through 4.

Document A

Document B

"If the president, for example, approves something because of the national security, or in this case because of a threat to internal peace and order of significant magnitude, then the president's decision in that instance is one that enables those who carry it out, to carry it out without violating a law. Otherwise they're in an impossible position. . . . [It] has been however argued that as far as a president is concerned, that in war time, a president does have certain extraordinary powers which would make acts that would otherwise be unlawful, lawful if undertaken for the purpose of preserving the nation and the Constitution, which is essential for the rights we're all talking about."

— *President Nixon, from an interview with British TV host, David Frost, May 19, 1977*

Document C

"The Constitution charges the president with the task of taking care that the laws be faithfully executed, and yet the president has counseled his aides to commit perjury, willfully disregard the secrecy of grand jury proceedings, conceal surreptitious entry, attempt to compromise a federal judge, while publicly displaying his cooperation with the processes of criminal justice. . . . Has the president committed offenses, and planned, and directed, and acquiesced in a course of conduct which the Constitution will not tolerate? That's the question. It is reason, and not passion, which must guide our deliberations, guide our debate, and guide our decision."

— *Barbara Jordan, statement at the U.S. House Judiciary Committee Impeachment Hearings, Washington, D.C., July 25, 1974*

1. What point of view does Document A present?
   A The judicial viewpoint
   B The executive viewpoint
   C The viewpoint of Congress
   D The viewpoint of the press

2. Document B shows the role of the press in the Watergate scandal because it shows
   A that Nixon was accountable to the press.
   B how reporters began to investigate the story.
   C how Nixon was forced to confess his role in the scandal.
   D Nixon's willingness to accuse others of committing minor crimes.

3. In Document C, what was the purpose of Barbara Jordan's statement?
   A It defended the actions of the President.
   B It tried to determine the grounds for impeachment.
   C It clarified Congress's role in the Watergate scandal.
   D It explained that the Constitution tolerated the President's conduct.

4. **Writing Task** Did Congress, the press, and the courts successfully do their jobs in investigating the Watergate scandal that led to President Richard Nixon's resignation? Use your knowledge of the chapter content and specific evidence from the primary sources above to support your opinion.

Document-Based Assessment

- To help students understand the documents, give them the following **TIP Determine who wrote the document before reading it so that you can evaluate author bias and whether he or she is likely to distort the facts.**

- To provide students with further practice in answering document-based questions, go to Document-Based Assessments.

- If students need more instruction on analyzing graphic data, have them read the Skills Handbook, p. SH21.

Answers

1. D   2. C   3. B
4. Most students will probably say that Congress, the press, and the courts were successful in their roles during the Watergate scandal. Students' responses should be well reasoned and include supporting details from the documents on this page, as well as from the chapter.

---

12. Carter had new ideas, and people welcomed his honesty. However, Carter was also uninformed, unconnected, and sometimes naïve, and these circumstances made it difficult for him to lead effectively.

13. Nixon pushed through wage and price controls, which made problems worse. Ford tried to establish the Whip Inflation Now program, but it also failed. Carter urged people to conserve fuel and tried to pass a tax on crude oil, which was weak. However, Carter did appoint Paul Volker to the Federal Reserve Board, who stopped inflation.

14. Ford continued pursuing détente; Carter began by working for détente and arms control, but later took a more forceful approach and also pushed the Soviets on human rights.

15. Sample answer: Middle East: he brokered the Camp David Accords between Egypt and Israel. Latin America: he worked to return the Panama Canal to Panamanian control.

Writing About History

As students begin the assignment, refer them to page SH7 of the Writing Handbook for help in writing a job application essay. Remind them of the steps they should take to complete their assignment, including pre-writing, drafting, and revising.

Students' essays should include the key qualifications, skills, and qualities that qualify them for the position. The essays should also contain an introduction, a body, and a conclusion and be free of grammatical and spelling errors. For scoring rubrics, see Assessment Rubrics.

Reflections: The Civil Rights Struggle

Background Knowledge

Have students discuss the student population of U.S. schools before, during, and immediately after World War II. Then, direct students to the Public School Segregation map (in The Civil Rights Movement chapter) and have them list the states that supported segregation and the states that opposed it. Explain that *Brown* v. *Board of Education of Topeka* led to the eventual desegregation of schools in the United States.

Instruct

Have students read the essay. Ask **How did World War II contribute to the start of the civil rights era?** *(The African American and Native American soldiers who fought in World War II experienced unprecedented freedoms while they were stationed in Europe. When they returned to the United States, they refused to accept racial inequality.)* **What problems did the African American students in Virginia face?** *(They attended a rundown and inadequate school, and they wanted school facilities comparable to those provided for white students.)* **Why do you think that the students were willing to use such extreme measures to make their point?** *(Sample answer: They were determined to achieve their goal and probably believed that they would be ignored if they did not try something extreme.)* Lead a class discussion about the inequalities that minorities in the United States faced during the 1950s, 1960s, and 1970s. Elicit from students the ways that each group used to win more civil rights.

Looking Ahead

The struggles and triumphs of the civil rights era improved conditions for people of all races in the United States. However, additional challenges that would test the nation emerged in the following decades.

Reflections: The Civil Rights Struggle

World War II was the seedbed of the social unrest that marked the civil rights era. During the war, thousands of African American soldiers and Native American soldiers had proudly fought to defend freedom and democracy. They had experienced social freedoms overseas unheard of at home. When they returned to their own country after the war, they were no longer willing to accept its racial inequality.

The civil rights movement was carried out by many people who decided to take action either individually or collectively. One striking example was a group of African American students who launched a project to improve the wretched conditions at their segregated high school in Virginia. In 1951, the concern of the students, which included several army veterans now trying to get their high school diplomas, was not segregation but frustration. How could they get an equal education in the three tarpaper shacks that passed for classrooms? "Each shack had a potbelly stove that roasted students near it while leaving those in the back chilled," remembers John Stokes, senior class president and one of the planners.

When county officials insisted they lacked funds to build a new school for the black students, the students decided upon a bold and daring plot to bring attention to their cause. The organizers asked students gathered at an assembly to go out on strike to demand better educational facilities. All together, they marched from the school to bring attention to their plight.

Later, 115 of the students and their parents signed a petition protesting the inadequate classrooms at their school. The Supreme Court eventually heard the petition as part of the *Brown* v. *Board of Education of Topeka* (1954) case, the landmark decision that ended segregated classrooms across the country. Stokes and his fellow conspirators had not been seeking an end to segregation. They just wanted better classrooms, like those of the white students. It was an exciting yet terrifying time for the young activists. "Today I wonder how we ever pulled it off," marvels Stokes, who went on to become a high school principal in Baltimore, Maryland.

CHANGING AND ENDURING ISSUES

CONTENTS

In classrooms across the country, today's students prepare to be tomorrow's leaders. ▶

Era Overview

Changing and Enduring Issues examines the political, social, and economic landscape of the United States from the 1980s to the early 2000s.

Chapter 19 analyzes the political divisions between liberals and conservatives, describes the growth of the conservative movement, examines the domestic and foreign policies of the Reagan administration, and explains the causes and effects of the end of the Cold War. **Issues:** America and the World, Sectionalism and National Politics, Government's Role in the Economy

Chapter 20 describes the growth of the computer and technology industries in the United States, explains the domestic and foreign policies of Bill Clinton and George W. Bush, and examines issues that have affected the United States in the twenty-first century. **Issues:** Education and American Society, Technology and Society, Global Interdependence

CHAPTER **19** The Conservative Resurgence
1980–1993

Teach With Technology
Presentation**EXPRESS**™
PREMIUM DVD

- Teach this chapter's core content by using **PresentationExpress,** which includes interactivities, video, lecture notes, and the *ExamView®* QuickTake assessment tool.

- To introduce this chapter by using **PresentationExpress,** ask students with which of the following statements they most agree: **A) The best way to ensure lasting change is when voters of a nation elect new officials B) The best way to ensure lasting change is when foreign powers intervene in the nation's government. C) The best way to ensure lasting change is when large numbers of people in a nation demand reforms.** Take a class poll or record students' answers by using the QuickTake feature, and discuss their responses. Point out that in this chapter, students will read about the change in leadership in the United States to a conservative political party. Continue introducing the chapter by using the chapter opener slide show.

Technology Resources

- Student**EXPRESS** CD-ROM

- Teacher Resource Library **DVD**

- Presentation**EXPRESS** **PREMIUM** DVD

- *ExamView®* **Test Bank** CD-ROM English and Spanish

- **Guided Reading Audio,** Spanish

- **Student Edition on Audio**

VIDEO
THE ESSENTIAL **?**
By Students For Students
For videos on Amercian Issues, go to
www.pearsonschool.com/ushist

Bibliography

For the Teacher
Nathan, Andrew. *Children of the Dragon: The Story of Tiananmen Square.* Macmillan, 1990.

Rosenberg, Tina. *The Haunted Land: Facing Europe's Ghosts After Communism.* Random House, 1995.

Tygiel, Jules. *Ronald Reagan and the Triumph of American Conservatism.* Pearson, 2006.

For the Student
L2 Young, Jeff. *Great Communicator: The Story of Ronald Reagan.* Morgan Reynolds, 2003.

L3 Schmemann, Serge. *When the Wall Came Down: The Berlin Wall and the Fall of Soviet Communism.* New York: Houghton Mifflin, 2006.

L4 Remnick, David. *Lenin's Tomb: The Last Days of the Soviet Empire.* Knopf, 1994.

WITNESS HISTORY

A New Agenda

Americans were tired of the prolonged economic and foreign policy problems of the 1970s. Many looked to Ronald Reagan, the Republican candidate for President in 1980:

“I cannot and will not stand by and see this great country destroy itself. . . . I don't agree that our nation must resign itself to inevitable decline, yielding its proud position to other hands. . . . The crisis we face is not the result of any failure of the American spirit; it is the failure of our leaders to establish rational goals and give our people something to order their lives by. If I am elected, I shall regard my election as proof that the people of the United States have decided to set a new agenda. . . .”

—Ronald Reagan, November 13, 1979

◀ Reagan on the campaign trail in 1980

Chapter Preview

Chapter Focus Question: What was the conservative resurgence, and how did it affect the domestic and foreign policies of the United States?

Section 1
The Conservative Movement Grows

Section 2
The Reagan Revolution

Section 3
The End of the Cold War

Section 4
Foreign Policy After the Cold War

Use the ☑ **Quick Study Timeline** at the end of this chapter to preview chapter events.

1980 campaign pin

Piece of the Berlin Wall after its fall

Linda Evans and John Forsythe, stars of television's *Dynasty*

Note Taking Study Guide *Online*
For: Note Taking and American Issues Connector
www.pearsonschool.com/ushist

Objectives

As you teach this section, keep students focused on the following objectives to help them answer the Section Focus Question and master core content.

- Describe the differences between liberal and conservative viewpoints.
- Analyze the reasons behind the rise of conservatism in the early 1980s.
- Explain why Ronald Reagan won the presidency in 1980.

Prepare to Read

Background Knowledge L3

Ask students if they have heard the terms "conservative" or "liberal." Ask them to predict how the two terms might differ.

Set a Purpose L3

- **WITNESS HISTORY** Read the selection aloud.

  Ask **According to Charles Murray, what was the difference between "elite wisdom" and "popular wisdom?"** (*"Elite wisdom" shaped social policy, while "popular wisdom" explained why things were falling apart.*)

- **Focus** Point out the Section Focus Question, and write it on the board. Tell students to refer to this question as they read. (*Answer appears with Section 1 Assessment answers.*)

- **Preview** Have students preview the Section Objectives and the list of Terms and People.

- **Reading Skill** Have students use the *Reading Strategy: Summarize* worksheet. Teaching Resources, **p. 12**

Frustration over ▶ controversial issues in the 1970s, such as the busing battle, lingered into the 1980s.

WITNESS HISTORY

Backlash Against Liberal Programs

By 1980, public discontent with liberal programs, from welfare to school busing, had grown considerably. Many middle- and working-class Americans, in particular, felt that the reforms enacted during the 1960s and carried out in the 1970s threatened the American dream.

"If, during the 1960s and 1970s, there was an elite wisdom that shaped the directions of social policy, there was also a popular wisdom that explained why things were falling apart. . . . The popular wisdom is characterized by hostility toward welfare (it makes people lazy), toward lenient judges (they encourage crime), and toward socially conscious schools (too busy busing kids to teach them to read)."

—Charles Murray, *Losing Ground,* 1984

The Conservative Movement Grows

Objectives

- Describe the differences between liberal and conservative viewpoints.
- Analyze the reasons behind the rise of conservatism in the early 1980s.
- Explain why Ronald Reagan won the presidency in 1980.

Terms and People

liberal	unfunded mandate
conservative	Moral Majority
New Right	Ronald Reagan

NoteTaking

Reading Skill: Summarize As you read, summarize the rise of the conservative movement in an outline. Use the one below as a starting point.

> I. Two Views: Liberal and Conservative
>   A. Liberal ideas and goals
>   1.
>   2.

Why It Matters The 1964 election marked a low point for conservatives in the post–World War II era. Barry Goldwater, favorite of the conservative movement, lost the election in a landslide. Nonetheless, conservatives were not defeated by this loss at the polls. On the contrary, they set out to build an organization and to put forth a clear vision of their goals and values that would enable them to win in the future. By 1980, their plan had worked: Ronald Reagan, the new hero of the conservatives, was elected President. The modern conservative movement spearheaded by Ronald Reagan deeply affected the nation's policies for decades. **Section Focus Question: What spurred the rise of conservatism in the late 1970s and early 1980s?**

Two Views: Liberal and Conservative

The two major political parties in the United States in the late twentieth century were the Democrats, many of whom were "liberals," and the Republicans, who were often labeled "conservatives." **Liberals** generally favored government intervention to help the needy, whereas **conservatives** generally favored allowing the free market, private organizations, and individuals to do that. Although the two parties did agree on many basic issues, including core American values such as freedom and equality, they diverged on many others. In addition, individual members within both parties did not always conform to their party's majority.

Vocabulary Builder

Use the information below and the following resource to teach students the high-use word from this section. Teaching Resources, Vocabulary Builder, p. 11

High-Use Word	Definition and Sample Sentence
degeneration	*n.* declining in quality The environmental movement grew as citizens tried to stop air and water **degeneration**.

The Ideas and Goals of Liberalism In the late 1970s, liberals tended to believe that the federal government should play a significant role in improving the lives of all Americans. They valued social programs that helped the poor, unemployed, elderly, and others. They also sponsored laws that protected the rights of minorities and women, especially in the post–World War II period. They supported greater government regulation of industry. In the foreign policy realm, liberals tended to favor cooperating with international organizations like the United Nations.

The Ideas and Goals of Conservatism In contrast, some conservatives felt that a large central government endangered economic growth and individual choice. They felt the liberal policies of the 1960s amd 1970s left a legacy of rising inflation and enormous waste. Futhermore, some conservatives criticized the liberal solution of "throwing money" at social problems. They sought to reduce taxes and limit government regulation of industry in order to promote economic growth. As conservative economist Milton Friedman and his wife Rose Friedman wrote in their book *Free to Choose*, "The story of the United States is the story of an economic miracle. . . . What produced this miracle? Clearly not central direction by government."

Other conservatives, neoconservatives or traditionalists, warned about the dangers posed to society by abandoning traditional values in favor of the new freedoms exemplified by the counterculture and advertised by the mass media. This concern with the perceived <u>degeneration</u> of modern youth dovetailed with many conservatives' religious beliefs.

Anticommunism formed the third leg of modern conservatism. Most anticommunists focused on the dangers posed to the United States by the Soviet Union. They questioned the wisdom of the détente policy followed by Presidents Nixon, Ford, and Carter. They also fought against the SALT II treaty in the Senate.

✓ **Checkpoint** How was conservatism different from liberalism in the early 1980s?

The Conservative Movement Gains Strength

During the 1940s and 1950s, the lines separating Republicans and Democrats had blurred. The two parties had developed a bipartisan foreign policy aimed at containing communism. Both favored a relatively significant role for the government in domestic affairs. However, during the 1960s and 1970s, many Republicans became increasingly critical of the liberal policies of the Democrats. They advanced a new conservative agenda. The differences between the two major parties grew more pronounced. The **New Right,** as the resurgent conservative movement was called, grew rapidly and was a coalition of several different groups with varying ideas and goals.

Vocabulary Builder
<u>degeneration</u>–(dee jehn er AY shuhn) *n.* declining in quality

Two Viewpoints: Liberal and Conservative		☑ Quick Study
Issue	**Liberal Viewpoint**	**Conservative Viewpoint**
Role of government in the economy	Favored more government involvement to lessen extreme economic inequalities through • social programs (often leading to higher taxes) • government regulation of industry	Favored limited government involvement in order to stimulate economic growth by • reducing taxes • decreasing regulation of industry
Foreign policy	Favored international diplomacy to combat communism in other countries	Favored relying on our own national defense and actively fighting against communism in other countries

History Background

An American Original The grandson of Polish Jewish immigrants, Barry Goldwater (1909–1998) came from a family that made its fortune operating department stores in Arizona. Running these stores, Goldwater instituted progressive policies such as higher wages, profit sharing, health insurance, and a 40-hour work week. During World War II, Goldwater served as an air force reserve pilot. He entered politics as a conservative Republican in predominantly Democrat Arizona and became a senator in 1952.

The senator's abrasive personality and unyielding politics caused supporters and detractors alike to label him a right-wing extremist. Johnson's victory over Goldwater in the 1964 presidential election showed that America had indeed been wary of Goldwater and his anti-civil rights and pro-Vietnam War voting record.

In spite of his loss, Goldwater did not leave politics. He was a five-term senator and even played a crucial role in the Watergate scandal. Today, he is remembered as a "true American original" and noted for paving the way for the 1980s conservative resurgence.

■ **NoteTaking** Using the Paragraph Shrinking strategy (TE, p. T20), have students read this section. As they read, have students summarize the rise of the conservative movement. Reading and Note Taking Study Guide

Teach

Two Views: Liberal and Conservative

Instruct

■ **Introduce: Key Terms** Ask students to find the key terms *liberals* and *conservatives* (in bold) in the text. Ask **What is the difference between what *liberals* and *conservatives* expect from their government?** (*Liberals* expect intervention, but *conservatives* do not.)

■ **Teach** Have students describe the different political parties' approaches to social problems. Ask **How might liberals and conservatives use different approaches to help the poor or unemployed?** (*Sample response: Liberals might give them money or work through a government program. Conservatives might lower taxes to promote economic growth so that businesses will have more money to hire people.*)

■ **Quick Activity** To help students better understand the difference between liberal and conservative viewpoints, have them complete the worksheet *Viewpoints: Liberals and Conservatives.* Teaching Resources, **p. 15**

Independent Practice

Have students use their outlines to begin summarizing information about the conservative movement.

Monitor Progress

As students fill in their outlines, circulate to make sure that they understand the differences between liberal and conservative opinions. For a completed version of the graphic organizer, see Note Taking Transparencies, **B-145**.

Answer

✓ Liberalism supported government programs and intervention to help the poor and needy. Conservatism supported less government intervention and a smaller central government.

The Conservative Movement Gains Strength

Instruct

- **Introduce: Key Term** Ask students to find the key term **Moral Majority** (in bold). Guide students in understanding how religious organizations such as the **Moral Majority** might increase the political activism of a previously less-prominent voting group. Point out that these religious groups opposed many liberal policies, and have students predict how the **Moral Majority** will affect the Republican Party.

- **Teach** Using the Quick Study chart on the previous page, review the differences between liberals and conservatives with students. Point out that many cultural and demographic factors contributed to the rise of the New Right. Create a two-column chart on the board, labeling one column "Cultural Changes" and the other "Effect on Political Parties." Ask volunteers to first fill in the chart with information relating to cultural and social events of the 1960s and 1970s. Then, have the class work together to fill in the second column, describing how the changes helped or hindered the two major political parties.

- **Quick Activity** Display Color Transparency: *Winning the South.* Use the lesson suggested in the transparency book to guide a discussion about Republican gains in the Sunbelt states. Color Transparencies A-137

Independent Practice

Group students in pairs, and ask them to explore the growth of the New Right. Ask partners to create a cause-and-effect chart explaining the reasons that a particular event or change encouraged the New Right at the expense of liberalism.

Monitor Progress

To check student understanding, point out the image of Jerry Falwell. Ask students to draw connections between his increasingly active role in politics and the rise of the conservative movement.

Answer

Caption Unlike traditional religious groups, the Moral Majority billed itself as a political organization and took specific political stands on issues.

Liberalism Loses Its Appeal One reason for the revival of the Republican Party was the unraveling of the Democratic Party. The Vietnam War and urban riots of the 1960s divided the same people who had rallied around President Johnson's vision of the Great Society. The rise of the counterculture alienated many midwestern Americans and white conservative Christians in the South. Watergate, the oil crises of the 1970s, and the Iran hostage crisis further weakened the public's faith in the federal government.

Just as importantly, the shifts in the economy of the 1970s, including the decline in northern industries, dampened America's optimism about the future. America had supported the Great Society, in part, because Johnson had suggested that the war on poverty and other new programs would not demand higher taxes. When the economy stagnated, liberal ideas lost their pull and conservative beliefs became more attractive.

The New Right Criticizes Liberal Programs Many conservatives believed that liberal policies were responsible for stagflation and other economic problems of the late 1970s. They believed that the government taxed citizens and businesses too heavily and spent too much on the wrong programs. They complained about **unfunded mandates,** programs required but not paid for by the federal government.

Some conservatives also criticized federal welfare programs, arguing that they rewarded lack of effort. Furthermore, they thought that the Great Society had made the problem of poverty worse, not better. They believed that welfare contributed to the rise in the number of children born out of wedlock and therefore encouraged the decline of the traditional family, consisting of a married father and mother and their children. They also felt that affirmative action programs went too far and contributed to reverse discrimination.

Another group that supported the conservative platform was the "sagebrush rebels." Sagebrush rebels were activists who believed that the federal government controlled too much land in the western states. They thought the federal government should give control of this land to the states, to be used to their best economic advantage. Most environmentalists opposed the movement, not wanting to expose preserved lands to possible development.

Religious Participation Rises At the same time, concern with cultural change caused more religious groups to become actively involved in politics. The **Moral Majority,** founded by Reverend Jerry Falwell in 1979, was a political organization working to fulfill religious goals. It also worried about the decline of the traditional family. The Moral Majority opposed the 1962 Supreme Court decision *Engel* v. *Vitale,* which forbade religious teaching in schools, as well as the historic 1973 *Roe* v. *Wade* decision, which legalized abortion. It condemned the Equal Rights Amendment and homosexuality.

The Moral Majority boosted the Republican Party's chances of winning the presidency by reaching out to Americans who had traditionally not participated in the political process. With other groups like it, the Moral Majority registered at least 2 million new voters before the 1980 presidential election. One of their tactics was to distribute Moral Majority "report cards" on candidates, which almost always favored Republicans.

Politics and Religion Meet
Reverend Jerry Falwell, founder of the Moral Majority, stands in front of his home church in Lynchburg, Virginia, in August 1980. A banner on top of the church's sign encourages members to register to vote. *How was the Moral Majority different from traditional religious groups?*

Differentiated Instruction   Solutions for All Learners

L1 Special Needs Students   **L2 English Language Learners**   **L2 Less Proficient Readers**

Explain that the words *liberal* and *conservative* can have different meanings in different contexts. Have students find different definitions of the words in dictionaries and then make a chart with two columns. In the left column, have them list the terms' positive connotations. In the right column, have them list the terms' negative connotations. After students explore the different meanings of the terms, have them discuss what aspects of these terms the Republican and Democratic parties used to describe their policies. Then, ask how the opposition used the negative connotations of these terms as a criticism of the other party's policies.

Population Trends Boost Conservatism Demographic, or population, trends also strengthened the conservative movement. Historically, northern cities stood as the stronghold of liberal Democrats. When an increasing number of Americans moved to the suburbs, their attachment to liberalism waned as they struggled financially during the tough economic days of the late 1970s. At the same time, Republicans emphasized issues that they believed would convince moderate liberals to switch their party allegiance. For instance, Republicans attacked school busing as a form of social engineering that threatened the long-cherished ideal of neighborhood schools.

Republicans also benefited from the migration from the Rust Belt to the Sunbelt, which took place in the 1970s, and a historical realignment of white voters in the Deep South. Since the Civil War, most white southerners had voted for the Democratic Party. Following the enactment of civil rights legislation in the mid-1960s, however, many white southerners began to shift their party allegiance. By the 1980s, the Republicans had become the dominant political party in the region.

✓ **Checkpoint** What were some of the forces that helped the Republican Party grow during the 1970s?

Reagan Wins the Presidency

The growing conservative movement swept the Republican presidential candidate, a man named **Ronald Reagan,** to victory in the 1980 election. Much more charismatic and polished than Goldwater, Reagan made clear his opposition to big government, his support for a strong military, and his faith in traditional values. Just as importantly, he radiated optimism, convincing Americans that he would usher in a new era of prosperity and patriotism.

Reagan's Path to the White House Born in Tampico, Illinois, in 1911, Reagan suffered the hardships of the Great Depression as a young adult before landing a job in Hollywood as a movie actor. Never a big star, Reagan appeared in many "B" or low-budget films. His most famous starring role was in *Knute Rockne,* a film based on the life of Notre Dame's legendary football coach.

When his acting career began to wane, Reagan became a spokesperson for General Electric and toured the nation giving speeches. Although once a staunch New Dealer, Reagan had become a Goldwater conservative. In these speeches he began to criticize big government and high taxes and warned of the dangers of communism. In 1964, near the end of Goldwater's presidential campaign, Reagan delivered a nationally televised address in which he spelled out these views:

> **Primary Source** "This is the issue of this election, whether we believe in our capacity for self-government or whether we abandon the American Revolution and confess that a little intellectual elite in a far-distant capital can plan our lives for us better than we can plan them ourselves."
> —Ronald Reagan, "A Time for Choosing," 1964

HISTORY MAKERS

Ronald Reagan (1911–2004)
Ronald Reagan's easy communication style, which appealed so much to his supporters, was rooted in his background as an entertainer. After graduating from college, he worked as a radio sports announcer until, in 1937, he signed a contract with a movie studio. In 1954, he began hosting a television show sponsored by General Electric. Soon, he was touring the country for the company, giving speeches that promoted traditional values and American business. As Reagan's views became more conservative, he switched from the Democratic to the Republican Party. He gained political fame in 1964 with a speech supporting conservative senator Barry Goldwater's run for the presidency.

Connect to Your World

Iran Hostage Crisis On November 4, 1979, a group of Iranian university students overran the U.S. embassy in Tehran, taking 52 Americans hostage. Iran had just overthrown its shah, Mohammad Reza Pahlavi, whose dictatorship was supported by the United States. The new government, led by the religious leader Ayatollah Khomeini, was hostile to the United States. President Jimmy Carter responded to the assault by halting oil imports from Iran and freezing Iranian assets held in the United States. Efforts at freeing the Americans failed. For 444 days, militants held the hostages within the embassy, releasing them 20 minutes after Ronald Reagan took office.

One of the Iranian instigators was engineering student Ebrahim Asgharzadeh. Today, he is a reform politician who has been critical of the current Iranian government led by President Mahmoud Ahmad, another hostage-taker. The former embassy is now an anti-American museum, called by Iranians the "den of spies." Artifacts from the former embassy are on permanent display in "The Great Aban 13th Exhibition," the date on the Persian calendar that corresponds with November 4.

Reagan Wins the Presidency

Instruct

- **Introduce** Ask students to preview the HISTORY MAKERS feature about Ronald Reagan on this page. Explain that Reagan's communication skills contributed greatly to his success both before and after his presidency. Ask students to consider how an entertainment background could help or hinder a politician's career.

- **Teach** Ask **What events weakened Carter's position as an incumbent?** *(inflation, the hostage crisis, the Soviet invasion of Afghanistan)* **How would Reagan's background have helped him to succeed in the presidential debate?** *(Reagan's background as an actor would help him appear comfortable and confident before an audience.)*

- **Quick Activity** Direct students to the Presidential Election map on the next page. Ask them to summarize the results of the popular and electoral votes. Using the Think-Write-Pair-Share strategy (TE, p. T23), have them analyze why the popular vote was so much closer than the electoral vote.

Independent Practice

To make sure that students understand the main issues of the growing conservative movement, have them analyze the Primary Source quotation from "A Time for Choosing." Ask them to complete these sentences: "Reagan wants Americans to reject *(being governed by a small, distant group.)*" and "Reagan wants Americans to support *(self-government).*"

Monitor Progress

To review this section, ask students to trace Reagan's path from Hollywood to Washington, D.C. Remind them to list the personal qualities, as well as the world events, that helped Reagan win the election.

Answer

✓ a stagnant economy, the rise of religious groups such as the Moral Majority, a decline in cities, and a movement from cities to suburbs

Assess Progress **L3**

- Have students complete the Section Assessment.

- Administer the Section Quiz. Teaching Resources, **p. 21**

- To further assess student understanding, use Progress Monitoring Transparencies, **141**.

Reteach

If students need more instruction, have them read the section summary.

Reading and Note Taking Study Guide **L3**

Adapted Reading and Note Taking Study Guide **L1 L2**

Spanish Reading and Note Taking Study Guide **L2**

Extend **L4**

Have students use a "conservative" or a "liberal" approach in writing a short argument that addresses a particular problem. Students should use information that describes Republican and Democratic responses to issues such as healthcare, poverty, or foreign affairs.

Answer

 Reagan promised to restore prosperity and patriotism to the United States.

While the speech failed to bolster Goldwater's campaign, it won the admiration of many conservatives. Two years later, Reagan won the governorship of California. He served for two terms as governor and nearly won the Republican presidential nomination in 1976. In 1980, he won the nomination by a landslide. His opponent was Jimmy Carter, the Democratic incumbent.

Reagan Wins a Close Election As the election approached, Carter looked like a lame duck. Persistent inflation, the Iran hostage crisis, and the Soviet invasion of Afghanistan made it easy for Reagan to cast the Carter presidency in a negative light. "Are you better off than you were four years ago?" Reagan asked audiences on the campaign trail, knowing that most Americans would say, "No."

The race remained relatively close until about one week before the election, when Reagan and Carter held their only presidential debate. In this debate, Reagan's gifts as a communicator shone. He appeared friendly and even-tempered and calmed fears that he did not have enough experience to serve as President. On Election Day, Reagan won 50.6 percent of the popular vote. Because most states award electoral votes on a "winner-takes-all" basis, Reagan won an overwhelming majority of electoral college votes despite the narrow margin by which he won the popular vote. Even though the Democrats maintained control of the House of Representatives, Republicans captured the U.S. Senate for the first time since 1955. The conservatives were back.

The Presidential Election of 1980

Candidate (Party)	Electoral Vote	Popular Vote	% Electoral Vote	% Popular Vote
Ronald Reagan (Republican)	489	43,642,639	90.9	50.6
James Carter (Democratic)	49	35,480,948	9.1	41.2
John Anderson (Independent)	—	5,719,437	—	6.6

✔ **Checkpoint** What did Ronald Reagan promise to do if elected to the presidency?

Progress Monitoring Online
For: Self-test with vocabulary practice
www.pearsonschool.com/ushist

SECTION 1 Assessment

Comprehension

1. Terms and People For each item below, write a sentence explaining how it related to the rise of conservatism in the late 1970s.
- liberal
- conservative
- New Right
- unfunded mandate
- Moral Majority
- Ronald Reagan

2. NoteTaking Reading Skill: Summarize Use your outline to answer the Section Focus Question: What spurred the rise of conservatism in the late 1970s and early 1980s?

Writing About History

3. Quick Write: Choose a Topic Choose a topic from this section, such as Ronald Reagan's path to the White House, that would suit the creation of a multimedia presentation. Keep in mind that a multimedia presentation is an oral report that is enhanced with artwork, charts, music, videos, and so on.

Critical Thinking

4. Compare Points of View Describe one major difference between liberals and conservatives in the early 1980s.

5. Identify Central Issues What policies did members of the New Right criticize?

6. Summarize How did the Moral Majority help strengthen the Republican Party?

7. Draw Conclusions Why did Americans elect Ronald Reagan to the presidency in 1980?

Section 1 Assessment

1. Sentences should reflect an understanding of how each term or person is related to the rise of conservatism in the 1970s.

2. Conservatives valued most the ideas of individualism, patriotism, and self-determination. The social and economic declines of the 1970s showed the failure of the liberal response to these problems and led to the rise of conservatism.

3. Responses should show the ability to highlight historical incidents that can be easily illustrated through the use of multimedia devices.

4. Possible response: Liberals believed that the government should provide programs for the poor or disadvantaged. Conservatives believed that private charities or tax incentives would provide aid and produce jobs for those in need.

5. Members of the New Right criticized policies, such as welfare, which they believed were too expensive, failed to provide adequate results, and encouraged the decline of the traditional family.

6. The Moral Majority increased participation in elections, encouraging Republican-minded voters to participate.

7. Americans elected Reagan because the economy was suffering and American foreign policy was not going well. Voters thought Reagan would bring positive changes.

For additional assessment, have students access **Progress Monitoring Online** at **www.pearsonschool.com/ushist**.

▲ Ronald Reagan and his wife Nancy after his victory in the 1980 election. Above, a campaign button for Reagan.

WITNESS HISTORY

Reagan's Vision

During his eight years as President, Ronald Reagan earned a reputation as the "Great Communicator" because of his speaking abilities. In his farewell speech, he expressed his satisfaction with what he had accomplished:

❝After 200 years, two centuries, . . . [America is] still a beacon, still a magnet for all who must have freedom. . . . We've done our part. And as I walk off into the city streets, a final word to the men and women of the Reagan revolution, the men and women across America who for eight years did the work that brought America back. My friends: We did it.❞

—Ronald Reagan, Farewell Address, January 11, 1989

The Reagan Revolution

Objectives

- Analyze Reagan's economic policies as President.
- Summarize how Reagan strengthened the conservative movement.
- Evaluate the steps taken to address various problems in the 1980s and early 1990s.

Terms and People

supply-side economics   Savings and Loan crisis
deregulation   voucher
budget deficit   AIDS
national debt

NoteTaking

Reading Skill: Identify Main Ideas Identify the main ideas behind Reagan's policies.

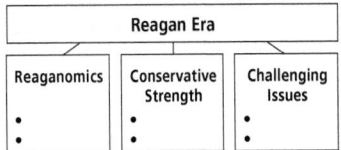

Why It Matters Conservatives celebrated Ronald Reagan's election as the fulfillment of their dreams. Some even referred to his coming to power as the "Reagan Revolution." The Reagan Revolution would bring a significant shift in the political direction of the nation. **Section Focus Question: What were the major characteristics of the conservative Reagan Revolution?**

Reaganomics Guides the Economy

Reagan and his advisers based their economic policies on the theory of "supply-side economics," sometimes called "Reaganomics." The theory of **supply-side economics** rests on the assumption that if taxes are reduced, people will work more and have more money to spend, causing the economy to grow. The government will then collect more in taxes. To cut taxes while still balancing the federal budget, however, Reagan also needed to reduce federal spending on programs favored by both Democrats and Republicans.

New Policies to Boost the Economy Congress approved most of Reagan's plan to institute supply-side economics by passing the Economic Recovery Act of 1981, which reduced taxes by 25 percent over three years. The richest Americans received the largest tax cuts. Reagan justified this move by saying that the wealthy would use the money they saved to invest in new businesses, which would

Prepare to Read

Background Knowledge L3

Remind students that conservatives believe that the role of the federal government should be limited in order to encourage individual choice and economic growth. Then, ask them to predict if the Reagan administration will recommend an increase or a decrease in the federal budget.

Set a Purpose L3

- **WITNESS HISTORY** Read the selection aloud

  Ask **What two time periods does Reagan's statement compare?** (He compares the "Reagan Revolution" and the American Revolution.)

- **Focus** Point out the Section Focus Question, and write it on the board. Tell students to refer to this question as they read. (Answer appears with Section 2 Assessment answers.)

- **Preview** Have students preview the Section Objectives and the list of Terms and People.

- **NoteTaking** Using the Guided Questioning/Silent Reading strategy (TE, p. T20), have students read this section. As they read, have students identify the main ideas behind Reagan's policies. Reading and Note Taking Study Guide

Vocabulary Builder

Use the information below and the following resource to teach students the high-use word from this section. Teaching Resources, Vocabulary Builder, p. 11

High-Use Word	Definition and Sample Sentence
momentum	*n.* forward motion; push In spite of Barry Goldwater's defeat, conservatives gained **momentum** for the election of Ronald Reagan.

Reaganomics Guides the Economy L3

Instruct

- **Introduce: Key Term** Ask students to find the key term *supply-side economics* (in bold) in the text. Write the term on the board and define it. Help students understand how *supply-side economics* reflected a change in government policy. Ask students to predict which response will make the nation's economy grow: an increase in government spending or a decrease in taxes.

- **Teach** Use the Idea Wave strategy (TE, p. T22) to help students understand the period of economic downturn and recovery during the Reagan administration. Ask **Who benefited most from Reagan's tax cuts?** *(The wealthy received the largest tax cuts.)* **What caused the budget shortfall to skyrocket under Reagan?** *(Increased defense spending along with the failure to win huge spending cuts)*

- **Quick Activity** Have students use the comparison diagram on this page to debate which response better combats an economic recession.

Independent Practice

Have students complete the note-taking chart to identify the main ideas of Reagan's policies.

Monitor Progress

As students fill in their note-taking graphic organizers, circulate to make sure that they understand the main ideas of Reagan's policies. For a completed version of the graphic organizer, see Note Taking Transparencies, **B-146**.

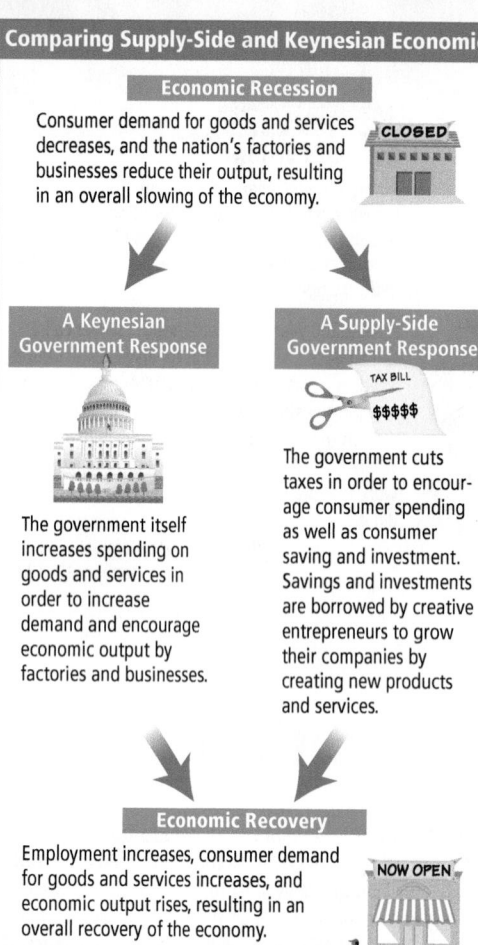

Comparing Supply-Side and Keynesian Economics

Economic Recession

Consumer demand for goods and services decreases, and the nation's factories and businesses reduce their output, resulting in an overall slowing of the economy.

A Keynesian Government Response

The government itself increases spending on goods and services in order to increase demand and encourage economic output by factories and businesses.

A Supply-Side Government Response

The government cuts taxes in order to encourage consumer spending as well as consumer saving and investment. Savings and investments are borrowed by creative entrepreneurs to grow their companies by creating new products and services.

Economic Recovery

Employment increases, consumer demand for goods and services increases, and economic output rises, resulting in an overall recovery of the economy.

Diagram Skills Can you predict what might be the upsides and downsides of both of the responses shown above?

help everyone. Reagan also convinced Congress to cut about $40 billion from the federal budget, mostly by cutting spending for social programs.

In addition to cutting taxes, Reagan also reduced the government's role in the economy by calling for **deregulation,** or the removal of government control over industry. By the mid-1980s, Congress had deregulated the airline, telecommunications, and banking industries. The Reagan administration also cut funding for federal agencies that oversaw many other industries.

Recession and Recovery Despite Reagan's economic policies, the economy experienced a severe recession from 1980 to 1982. Unemployment rose to more than 10 percent in 1982. The recession hit blue-collar workers particularly hard. Many farmers, facing overseas competition, lost their farms. The policies that Paul Volcker, as head of the Federal Reserve Board, had introduced to tame the great inflation of the 1970s contributed to the recession in the early 1980s. Beginning in early 1983, however, the economy began to turn around. Inflation fell dramatically. The Gross National Product, or the annual income earned by Americans and American businesses, expanded at a healthy pace. America's economy seemed revitalized.

Despite this, the number of poor people, including the working poor, actually increased. In addition, immigrants from Latin America and Asia continued to pour into the United States. More than 7.3 million legal immigrants and hundreds of thousands of undocumented immigrants entered the country in the 1980s. Many of these newcomers worked in low-paying jobs and struggled to make ends meet. Meanwhile, the richest Americans grew richer.

Problems With Budget Deficits Reagan increased defense spending but failed to win huge cuts in government spending in other areas. This caused the federal **budget deficit,** or the shortfall between the amount of money spent and the amount taken in by the government, to skyrocket from about $79 billion in 1981 to more than $221 billion in 1986. The **national debt,** the amount of money the federal government owes to owners of government bonds, rose to $2.5 trillion.

In response to persistent budget deficits, Congress passed the Gramm Rudman-Hollings Act in 1985. The act sought to balance the budget by 1990 by requiring automatic cuts in federal spending if the deficit exceeded a certain amount. However, the federal budget deficit set new records into the early 1990s.

The **Savings and Loan, or S&L, crisis** in 1989 exacerbated deficit problems. In the late 1980s, about 1,000 Savings and Loan banks failed, some because of fraudulent behavior and others because they made too many risky loans. Critics blamed Reagan's deregulation policies for encouraging the banks to invest in riskier propositions. To prevent a broader panic, the federal government spent upwards of $200 billion to bail out depositors at the failed banks.

✔ **Checkpoint** What is supply-side economics?

Answers

Diagram Skills Possible response: Upside: the Keynesian approach may lead to economic growth as it did in the late 1960s; the supply-side response may lead to more manufacturing jobs as spending on machinery increases. Downside: both approaches may cause huge deficits because the government spends more money than it collects.

✔ Supply-side economics was a policy that cut taxes to encourage job growth and consumer spending.

Differentiated Instruction Solutions for All Learners

L4 Advanced Readers L4 Gifted and Talented Students

The deregulation of industries during the Reagan administration had lasting effects. For example, the airline industry has experienced the benefits of greater competition and increased productivity, while travellers have enjoyed lower airfares and safer planes. Such massive deregulation is not without a price, however, and deregulated industries have encountered labor difficulties, market gluts, and price discrimination. Have students research the positive and negative effects of deregulation on the airline, telecommunications, or banking industries. Ask them to write a paragraph analyzing the reasons for deregulating the industry and whether the change in government control had the desired result. Have students share their findings in oral presentations.

Conservative Strength Grows

Despite budget and debt problems, the economic recovery improved the national mood and helped Ronald Reagan's popularity. Reagan used his time in office to strengthen the conservative cause.

Reagan Wins Reelection in 1984 During the 1984 presidential campaign, Reagan used the phrase "It is morning in America" as a campaign slogan:

> **Primary Source** "It's morning again in America. In a town not too far from where you live, a young family has just moved into a new home. . . . Right down the street one of the neighbors has just bought himself a new car, with all the options. The factory down the river is working again. . . . Life is better, America is back. And people have a sense of pride they never felt they'd feel again."
> —Campaign commercial for the reelection of Ronald Reagan, 1984

This theme dovetailed nicely with Reagan's upbeat spirit, which he displayed even in his darkest moments. For example, on March 30, 1981, a disturbed man named John Hinckley, Jr., tried to assassinate the President. One bullet from Hinckley's gun lodged in Reagan's chest. According to one account, Reagan joked to his doctors, "I hope you are all Republicans."

Americans voted overwhelmingly to reelect Reagan in 1984. He easily defeated Walter Mondale, the Democratic presidential nominee, and his running mate, Geraldine Ferraro, the first woman to be nominated for Vice President by a major political party. However, Reagan's <u>momentum</u> did not lead to a total triumph for conservatives, as Democrats retained control of the House of Representatives.

Vocabulary Builder
<u>momentum</u>–(moh MEHN tuhm)
n. forward motion; push

Conservative Supreme Court Justices and the Equal Access Act
During his two terms, Reagan appointed judges who he hoped would reverse the liberal drift of the federal courts. He appointed three new Justices—Sandra Day O'Connor, Antonin Scalia, and Anthony Kennedy—to the Supreme Court and elevated William Rehnquist, a well-known conservative, to the position of Chief Justice in 1986. Sandra Day O'Connor, nominated in 1981, was the first female Justice and a moderate conservative. Although she voted with other conservatives on many issues, she consistently voted to uphold *Roe* v. *Wade,* which Reagan opposed.

Near the end of Reagan's first term, Congress passed the Equal Access Act. This act required public secondary schools to allow any group equal access to school facilities. Conservative Christian groups supported the act's passage because many public schools did not allow religious groups to meet on school property. The Supreme Court confirmed the constitutionality of the Equal Access Act in 1990 in *Board of Education of Westside Community Schools* v. *Mergens.*

George H.W. Bush Becomes President Reagan used his personal popularity to promote George H.W. Bush, his Vice President for eight years, as Bush campaigned for the presidency against Massachusetts governor Michael Dukakis in 1988. Bush called for a "kinder, gentler nation," yet both candidates attacked the other using negative campaign ads. Bush cemented his support among conservatives by promising not to raise taxes and by casting himself as a defender of

HISTORY MAKERS

Sandra Day O'Connor (born 1930)
After getting her law degree in 1952, Sandra Day O'Connor served as a lawyer for many years before becoming involved in Arizona state politics in the late 1960s. She was serving as a judge on the Arizona Court of Appeals when she was nominated to the Supreme Court in 1981.

O'Connor sat on the Supreme Court for nearly 25 years. Her vote was the tiebreaker on several influential court cases, causing her to be called one of the most powerful women in the United States.

Connect to Your World

Supreme Court Appointees Sandra Day O'Connor broke new ground when she was appointed the first woman justice to the Supreme Court. Though attitudes have since changed, when she graduated from Stanford Law School in 1952, she could not find a position since California law firms did not hire women. When O'Connor decided to step down in 2005, President George W. Bush nominated another woman to replace her, White House counsel Harriet Miers. Miers, however, withdrew her nomination after criticism that she was too close to Bush and lacked experience with constitutional law.

After Miers's withdrawal, Bush moved quickly to nominate Samuel Alito, a judge serving on the U.S. Court of Appeals. Alito was quickly confirmed by the U.S. Senate. His appointment raised questions about how his rulings would differ from those of his predecessor. O'Connor was viewed as a moderate, and her rulings included maintaining abortion rights. In contrast, Alito's philosophy is considered much more conservative, and his rulings have favored limitations on abortion.

Instruct

- **Introduce: Vocabulary Builder** Have students locate the vocabulary term *momentum* and its definition. Tell students that one of Reagan's achievements was to create *momentum* and enthusiasm for the Republican Party. Ask **How can one successful event lead to another?** *(People can build on the enthusiasm of an event to create another success.)*

- **Teach** Review with students the Primary Source quotation on this page. Point out that the success of Republicans in the executive branch led to conservative influence in other areas of government. Ask **How did Reagan's election influence the Supreme Court?** *(Reagan appointed three conservative Supreme Court justices and elevated a conservative to Chief Justice.)* **How did Congress's actions reflect Reagan's conservative agenda?** *(Congress passed an Equal Access Act that allowed religious groups to meet on school property.)*

- **Analyzing the Visuals** Have students view the Infographic on the next page. Then, have them discuss the headlines. Have them explain how each is related or unrelated to Reagan's conservative policies.

Independent Practice

Organize students in groups and assign each group one of the following branches of government: executive, judicial, and legislative. Ask each group to write a paragraph explaining how the "Reagan Revolution" affected their branch of the government.

Monitor Progress

To check student understanding, point out the HISTORY MAKERS feature on Sandra Day O'Connor. Ask students to discuss the importance of her appointment to the Supreme Court for both conservatives and women.

Confronting Challenging Issues L3

Instruct

- **Introduce: Key Term** Ask students to find the key term *Acquired Immunodeficiency Syndrome (AIDS)* (in bold) in the text. Help students recognize that in the 1980s *AIDS* was not well understood.

- **Teach** Ask **How did Reagan's response to Social Security challenges reflect his conservative values?** *(Reagan raised the retirement age and increased money taken from payrolls, following the conservative idea of trying to effect improvement by encouraging change at the level of individuals rather than legislation on the nation at large.)* Have students discuss the possible advantages and disadvantages of a voucher system.

- **Quick Activity** Have students complete the *Reading a Chart: Social Security* worksheet. Teaching Resources, p. 16

Independent Practice

Have students make a chart proposing two different responses for controlling three different challenges of the Reagan era: funding Social Security, improving education, and coping with AIDS. Have them mark the points that would make their responses attractive to either liberals or conservatives.

Monitor Progress

Reread the information in the paragraphs under the blue heading "Confronting Challenging Issues." Ask students to summarize the challenges that the Reagan administration faced.

Answers

Thinking Critically
1. The trade imbalance must have added to the national debt, since the United States was buying more goods than it was selling.
2. Video technology allowed people to learn about many different kinds of exercise programs and watch them in their own homes.

✓ Reagan added to conservative gains by appointing conservative judges to the Supreme Court. Also, through his own popularity, Reagan helped promote his Vice President George H.W. Bush who would win the presidential election in 1988.

INFOGRAPHIC

TV Review:
**Dynasty:
Living large and
behaving badly**
Fans love the Wednesday night favorite, *Dynasty*, featuring Linda Evans as Krystle Carrington and John Forsythe as Blake Carrington. ■ See p. B6

TIMES of the Eighties
A SNAPSHOT OF THE REAGAN YEARS

Personal Computers: Hot item. ■ See p. A12

Are you a Yuppie?
If you're under 30, live in a city, and work in an office, then *yes*—you're a Young Urban Professional, or Yuppie.
■ See p. A7

In the Economy

Trade Imbalance With Japan Deepens
Japan's import restrictions are keeping American goods off of Japanese store shelves.

U.S. Trade Deficit With Japan, 1980–1990

U.S. Exports to Japan →
← Japanese Imports to U.S.

Dollars (in billions): 0, 20, 40, 60, 80, 100
1980 1982 1984 1986 1988 1990
SOURCE: *Statistical Abstract of the United States*

Trend Spotting

VCRs Bring Fitness Craze Home

Videotapes of popular exercise programs, such as Judi Missett's Jazzercise fitness plan, are flying off the shelves.

Thinking Critically
1. **Draw Conclusions** How do you think the trade imbalance with Japan affected the American economy?
2. **Summarize** How did new technologies help advance the personal fitness craze?

ADA Passed!

- The Americans With Disabilities Act (ADA) was passed by Congress and signed into law by President George H.W. Bush in July 1990.
- The act will ensure that Americans with disabilities will receive the same opportunities in employment and access to public transportation and public places as other Americans.
- The act benefits more than 43 million people and is another stride forward in the quest to protect the rights of all Americans.

Space Shuttle *Challenger* Explodes
Reagan Comforts the Nation

CAPE CANAVERAL, FLORIDA On January 28, 1986, the long-awaited launch of the space shuttle *Challenger* ended in tragedy when the shuttle exploded 73 seconds after take-off. The shuttle carried seven astronauts, including New Hampshire schoolteacher Christa McAuliffe. Her flight would have been the first time a private citizen entered space.

President Reagan spoke to the nation following the tragedy:

Primary Source "For the families of the seven [astronauts], we cannot bear, as you do, the full impact of this tragedy. But we feel the loss, and we're thinking about you so very much. Your loved ones were daring and brave, and they had that special grace, that special spirit that says, 'Give me a challenge and I'll meet it with joy.' They had a hunger to explore the universe and discover its truths. They wished to serve, and they did. They served all of us."

The space shuttle *Challenger* exploded shortly after lifting off from Kennedy Space Center. Inset: Schoolteacher Christa McAuliffe (far left) and six career astronauts died aboard the shuttle.

---

traditional values. However, Democrats won a majority of seats in both houses of Congress.

President Bush sought to control federal spending by encouraging Americans to volunteer. Government, he asserted, could take a smaller role in daily life if, "like a thousand points of light," community organizations and volunteers provided more help to the disabled, illiterate, and poor.

✓ **Checkpoint** How did Reagan try to build upon conservative gains during his presidency?

Differentiated Instruction Solutions for All Learners

L1 **Special Needs Students** L2 **English Language Learners** L2 **Less Proficient Readers**

Use the Infographic on this page to reinforce the idea of Ronald Reagan's communication skills and popularity in the face of challenges. Ask **What items on this page show difficulties facing the nation?** *(the trade deficit charts and the article on the explosion of the space shuttle)* Ask **What do you think a nation wants from its leaders in times of a** national crisis? *(Possible answer: words of comfort; evidence of competence and strength)* Read aloud the excerpt from Reagan's speech following the *Challenger* explosion. Ask students to describe how the speech makes them feel and to select words or phrases that they think would have comforted listeners.

Confronting Challenging Issues

Despite Reagan and Bush's successes, the nation continued to face a number of pressing problems. In 1981 when thousands of air-traffic controllers went on strike, Reagan refused to negotiate with the Professional Air Traffic Controllers Organization (PATCO) and fired the striking workers because they were violating a law forbidding federal employees from striking. Many Americans admired Reagan's strong, decisive stance. Some union supporters, however, claimed that Reagan's action represented an assault on the labor movement.

In the 1980s, the rising cost of Social Security caused concern. As the number of elderly people in America grew, the Social Security system began to collect less money than it paid out. In 1983, Reagan signed the Social Security Reform Act, which raised the minimum retirement age and increased payroll taxes for Social Security. It provided a temporary fix but did not solve the long-term problems of the Social Security program.

Many Americans also worried about the state of America's public education system. In 1983, the Department of Education issued *A Nation at Risk*. This study showed that students were consistently scoring lower on standardized tests as time passed. The report argued that America's schools failed to prepare students adequately to compete with students around the globe.

Even before the report appeared, conservatives called for providing **vouchers,** or government checks, that could be used by parents to pay tuition at private schools. Conservatives argued that vouchers would force public schools to improve in order to attract and retain students. Liberals in Congress argued that vouchers would take much-needed money away from public schools.

In addition, the nation faced the threat of a new disease, **Acquired Immunodeficiency Syndrome (AIDS),** which first appeared in 1981. AIDS is the last stage of the Human Immunodeficiency Virus (HIV), which attacks the immune system of its victims. There is no known cure. At first, AIDS spread mainly among homosexual men and intravenous drug users. Later, the virus infected different groups of people. By 1994, AIDS had killed more than 250,000 Americans. President Reagan responded slowly to the AIDS epidemic. During George H.W. Bush's presidency, funding for research on the disease rose substantially.

The AIDS Quilt

When the AIDS Quilt was displayed in Washington, D.C., in October 1988, it consisted of 8,288 panels, each created in the memory of a person who had died of AIDS. Today, the quilt has more than 44,000 memorial panels.

✔ **Checkpoint** What were some of the challenges that the nation faced during the 1980s and early 1990s?

SECTION

2 Assessment

Progress Monitoring *Online*
For: Self-test with vocabulary practice
www.pearsonschool.com/ushist

Comprehension

1. Terms and People For each term below, write a sentence explaining its significance to the Reagan era.
- supply-side economics
- deregulation
- budget deficit
- national debt
- Savings and Loan crisis
- AIDS

2. NoteTaking Reading Skill: Identify Main Ideas Use your chart to answer the Section Focus Question: What were the major characteristics of the conservative Reagan Revolution?

Writing About History

3. Quick Write: Create a Storyboard Create a storyboard that illustrates one of the challenges facing Americans during this period. Use a combination of words and images to express your points.

Critical Thinking

4. Summarize In what ways did Reagan try to fulfill the goal of less government involvement in the economy?

5. Draw Conclusions How did Reagan strengthen the conservative cause?

6. Identify Central Issues How did Reagan address problems with Social Security?

Section 2 Assessment

1. Sentences should reflect an understanding of the significance of each term to the Reagan or Bush presidencies.

2. The Reagan Revolution focused on reducing the size and influence of government. It lowered taxes and limited government intervention in Social Security, health-care, and education.

3. Responses should show an understanding of how to incorporate visual aids to enhance a story.

4. Reagan reduced government involvement in the economy by reducing taxes and by deregulating industries such as airlines and banking.

5. Reagan strengthened the conservative cause by appointing conservative judges to the Supreme Court. His personal popularity helped George H.W. Bush win the presidency in 1988.

6. He raised the minimum retirement age and increased payroll taxes.

Objectives

- Identify the symbols of the Cold War and the reforms that ended it.
- Analyze the role of the Reagan administration in the victory of the West in the Cold War.
- Discuss the significant foreign policy speeches of Ronald Reagan with regard to communism and the Cold War.

Background Knowledge ③

Remind students that the problems of the Berlin Wall arose from the division of Eastern Europe after World War II. Have students review a map of Europe before the fall of the Soviet Union to see West Berlin's location in relation to East Germany and to the Soviet Union.

Instruct ③

- After students read the speech, conduct a class discussion on the following questions: **Why does Reagan want the wall to come down?** *(He believes that removing the wall will bring better relations between the Soviet Union and the West.)* **Why does Reagan associate peace with prosperity?** *(Possible answer: He may believe that prosperity is the incentive that will make Soviet leaders bring freedoms to the people of the Soviet bloc.)*

- Have students read and complete *Primary Source: Understanding Reagan's "Tear Down This Wall" Speech.* Teaching Resources, **p. 18**

Monitor Progress

To confirm students' understanding, ask them to list Reagan's criticisms of the Soviet Union and his suggestions for changes to the Soviet government.

Answers

Thinking Critically

1. He argues that freedom leads to peace and prosperity. He claims that the Soviets' policy of restrictions has led to failures of healthcare, technology, and agriculture.

2. Reagan challenges Gorbachev to open the Brandenburg Gate and tear down the Berlin Wall.

Ronald Reagan: *Tear Down This Wall*

On June 12, 1987, President Reagan spoke at the Brandenburg Gate, near the Berlin Wall, in West Berlin, Germany. His speech acknowledged the new Soviet leader Mikhail Gorbachev's efforts at reform in the Soviet Union. However, Reagan was not satisfied with Gorbachev's limited measures. He challenged the Soviet leader to show a real commitment to reform by tearing down the Berlin Wall that had stood between East and West Berlin since 1961. This wall symbolized the division between communism and democracy.

In the 1950s, Khrushchev predicted: "We will bury you." But in the West today, we see a free world that has achieved a level of prosperity and well-being unprecedented in all human history. In the Communist world, we see failure, technological backwardness, declining standards of health, even want of the most basic kind—too little food. Even today, the Soviet Union still cannot feed itself. After these four decades, then, there stands before the entire world one great and inescapable conclusion: Freedom leads to prosperity. Freedom replaces the ancient hatreds among the nations with comity [courtesy] and peace. Freedom is the victor.

And now the Soviets themselves may, in a limited way, be coming to understand the importance of freedom. We hear much from Moscow about a new policy of reform and openness. Some political prisoners have been released. Certain foreign news broadcasts are no longer being jammed. Some economic enterprises have been permitted to operate with greater freedom from state control.

Are these the beginnings of profound changes in the Soviet state? Or are they token gestures, intended to raise false hopes in the West, or to strengthen the Soviet system without changing it? We welcome change and openness; for we believe that freedom and security go together, that the advance of human liberty can only strengthen the cause of world peace. There is one sign the Soviets can make that would be unmistakable, that would advance dramatically the cause of freedom and peace.

General Secretary Gorbachev, if you seek peace, if you seek prosperity for the Soviet Union and Eastern Europe, if you seek liberalization: Come here to this gate! Mr. Gorbachev, open this gate! Mr. Gorbachev, tear down this wall!

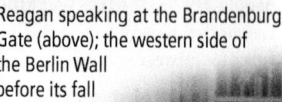

Reagan speaking at the Brandenburg Gate (above); the western side of the Berlin Wall before its fall (below)

Thinking Critically

1. **Demonstrate Reasoned Judgment** How does Reagan support his statement "Freedom is the victor"?

2. **Identify Central Issues** How does Reagan challenge Gorbachev to prove that his reforms are not "token gestures"?

Differentiated Instruction Solutions for All Learners

L1 Special Needs Students **L2 English Language Learners** **L2 Less Proficient Readers**

To help students understand the role that the United States played in the fall of communism, help them analyze Ronald Reagan's speech at the Brandenburg Gate in Berlin. Provide them with *Primary Source: Tear Down This Wall.* Begin by writing two headings on the board: "Statements About Freedom" and "Calls for Action." Then, ask students to look for words and phrases that include this information, such as "freedom leads to prosperity" or "Come here to this gate!" Have volunteers write the statements they find under the headings on the board. When students have completed their lists, have them summarize Ronald Reagan's argument for the need for change in the Soviet Union. Ask students how they think the audience at the Berlin Wall might have responded to Reagan's argument. Teaching Resources, **p. 17**

▲ A soldier trains at Fort Dix in New Jersey in the 1980s.

A Strong Approach to Communism

During the first term of his presidency, Ronald Reagan challenged the Soviet Union by building up America's military and casting the Cold War as a struggle between good and evil:

"But if history teaches anything, it teaches that simpleminded appeasement or wishful thinking about our adversaries is folly. . . . I urge you to speak against those who would place the United States in a position of military and moral inferiority . . . beware the temptation . . . to ignore the facts of history and the aggressive impulses of an evil empire, to simply call the arms race a giant misunderstanding and thereby remove yourself from the struggle between right and wrong and good and evil."

—President Ronald Reagan, March 8, 1983

The End of the Cold War

Objectives
- Analyze the ways that Ronald Reagan challenged communism and the Soviet Union.
- Explain why communism collapsed in Europe and in the Soviet Union.
- Describe other foreign policy challenges that faced the United States in the 1980s.

Terms and People

Strategic Defense Initiative
Contras
Mikhail Gorbachev
glasnost
perestroika
Iran-Contra affair

NoteTaking

Reading Skill: Sequence As you read this section, use a flowchart like the one below to sequence major events related to the fall of communism in Europe and the Soviet Union.

Reagan supports buildup of United States military.
▼   ▼   ▼

Why It Matters President Ronald Reagan believed that the United States had lost its way in the wake of the Vietnam War. Rather than détente, he felt the United States should seek to roll back Soviet rule in Eastern Europe and elsewhere. Reagan believed that peace would come through strength. Although Reagan's foreign policies initially increased tension between the two superpowers, they contributed to the end of the Cold War. **Section Focus Question: What were Reagan's foreign policies, and how did they contribute to the fall of communism in Europe?**

Reagan Challenges Communism

President Reagan believed that the United States needed to weaken communism by challenging it as much as possible without provoking war. To this end, he devised policies aimed at toppling communist nations, ranging from building new nuclear missile systems to funding covert operations against Soviet troops and allies around the globe.

Reagan Builds Up the U.S. Military Under Reagan, the United States committed itself to the largest peacetime military buildup in its history. Reagan dedicated billions of dollars to the development and production of B-1 and B-2 bombers, MX missile systems, and other projects. In spite of massive protests by the nuclear freeze movement in the United States and abroad, the Reagan administration placed a new generation of nuclear missiles in Europe.

Reagan supported this massive military buildup, in part, because he did not believe that the Soviet Union could afford to spend as much on defense as the United States could. Reagan felt this

Reagan Challenges Communism [L3]

Instruct

- **Introduce: Key Terms** Ask students to find the key terms *glasnost* and *perestroika* (in bold) in the text. Ask **How could *glasnost* and *perestroika* affect Soviet foreign policy?** *(These policies would permit a new exchange of ideas with Western nations.)*

- **Teach** Write on the board *Afghanistan, El Salvador, Grenada,* and the *Soviet Union.* Have students locate each on a map, describe the impact of communism in each, and discuss the U.S. response to each. Also, have students discuss how the chart and photograph on this page illustrate foreign policy issues during Reagan's administration.

- **Analyzing the Visuals** Refer students to the political cartoon on the following page and Color Transparency: *Reagan's Foreign Policy.* Have students discuss their meaning with a partner. Then, discuss the visuals as a class. Color Transparencies **A-138**

Independent Practice

- Ask students to write a paragraph comparing the excerpt of President Reagan's "evil empire" speech with the Primary Source quotation on the next page.

- To make sure students understand the extent of increased defense spending, have them view the chart showing military spending during Reagan's administration on *Reading a Chart: Military Spending* and answer the questions that follow. Teaching Resources, **p. 19**

Monitor Progress

As students fill in their flowcharts, circulate to make sure that they understand the fall of communism in both places. For a completed version of the flowchart, see Note Taking Transparencies, **B-147a.**

Answers

Chart Skills Defense spending increased about $200 billion.

Caption U.S. officials were probably alarmed by a socialist government so close to the United States, especially one that was funded by the Soviet Union.

Federal Defense Spending, 1978–1990

Dollars (in billions): 0, 50, 100, 150, 200, 250, 300, 350

Years: 1978, 1980, 1982, 1984, 1986, 1988, 1990

SOURCE: *Statistical Abstract of the United States*

Graph Skills Reagan's foreign policy stance caused defense spending to increase dramatically. *How much did defense spending increase between 1978 and 1988?*

The Contras in Nicaragua

After coming to power in 1939, Nicaragua's socialist Sandinista government accepted aid from Cuba and the Soviet Union, alarming the United States. Below, a group of Contras review a map at a base camp along the San Juan River. Contras opposed the Sandinista government. *How did a socialist government in Nicaragua alarm foreign policy officials in the United States?*

---

applied particularly to the **Strategic Defense Initiative (SDI),** a proposed program in which land- and space-based lasers would destroy any missiles aimed at the United States before they could reach their targets. Some dubbed the missile program "Star Wars," after the popular science-fiction movie trilogy, and claimed that it was unrealistic.

Reagan Aids Anticommunists Reagan also sought to weaken the Soviet Union by supporting anticommunist rebellions around the globe. To this end, the United States funded and trained the mujahedeen (moo jah huh DEEN), anti-Soviet rebels in Afghanistan. Reagan's advisers believed that with U.S. help, these guerrillas could drive the Soviets out of Afghanistan. In 1988, Soviet forces finally began to withdraw after years of fierce Afghan resistance.

Closer to home, Secretary of State Alexander Haig feared that the newly formed Sandinista government in Nicaragua provided the Soviets with a "safe house" in America's backyard. To counter this threat, the administration backed a group of anticommunist counterrevolutionaries, known as the **Contras.** At the same time, the United States supported a right-wing government in El Salvador as it battled leftist rebels. Many human rights activists strongly objected to this policy; even U.S. Ambassador Robert White described the legal system in El Salvador as "rotten" and called for the United States to suspend aid to the nation. Instead, Congress made funding for El Salvador's government dependent on the nation making progress on human rights.

In 1983, Reagan acted to counter another perceived threat in the Western Hemisphere. Members of a radical leftist movement, with some help from Cuba, had violently ousted the Grenadian prime minister. On October 25, 1983, U.S. troops invaded Grenada to prevent the island nation from becoming a communist outpost and to protect the lives of American medical students. Even though the legal grounds for this invasion proved questionable, most Americans approved of Reagan's decision.

Gorbachev Pursues Reform In 1985, **Mikhail Gorbachev** (mee kah EEL GOR buh chawf) became the President of the Soviet Union. Gorbachev ushered in a new Soviet era by pursuing the twin policies of *glasnost* and *perestroika.* **Glasnost** means "a new openness," and **perestroika** refers to reforming the Soviet system—for instance, by moving away from a socialist or state-controlled economy. Gorbachev's reforms created an opening for a shift in relations between the two superpowers.

Gorbachev started these reforms mostly because the Soviet Union's economy lay in shambles. The nation faced regular shortages of food. Its factories and workers could not compete with their Western counterparts. A huge chunk of the Soviet economy's money went toward paying for the military. The war in Afghanistan had drained Soviet resources. Gorbachev realized that his nation could not match the military buildup initiated by the Reagan administration.

History Background

Mikhail Gorbachev Mikhail Gorbachev was a leader who could make changes happen fast. When elected general secretary of the Communist Party of the Soviet Union in 1985, he was the youngest member of the Politburo, the government's policy-making body. For the changes he brought about through his reforms, Gorbachev received the Nobel Prize for Peace five years later. Though he moved his country away from totalitarianism, Gorbachev was unable to forge a democratic state. On December 25, 1991, he resigned as president of the Soviet Union, a country that had just a few months earlier ceased to exist. Then, Gorbachev became head of a think tank, the Foundation for Social, Economic and Political Research.

The Two Leaders Meet Gorbachev's policies and personality helped soften the Soviet Union's international image. Reagan responded to this change by moderating his own stance toward the Soviet Union. While the two nations had held no summits during Reagan's first four years in office, their leaders met four times between 1985 and 1989. During their final meeting in Moscow, Reagan and Gorbachev toasted each other at a state dinner, toured the sights like old friends, and held a joint press conference. At the press conference, a reporter asked Reagan about his description of the Soviet Union as an "evil empire." Reagan responded, "I was talking about another era." Then, Gorbachev allowed President Reagan to address students at Moscow State University on the benefits of the free-enterprise system and democracy:

Instruct

- **Introduce** Point out to students the photograph of Reagan and Gorbachev on the following page. Ask them to describe the leaders' expressions and to predict what their friendship could reflect about the relationship between their countries.

- **Teach** Read aloud the quotation from *Time* magazine on this page. Ask **What is the "historic shift" that the passage describes?** *(the shift in Eastern Europe and the Soviet Union from communism to democracy)* **How did this shift affect people living in the former Soviet Union?** *(People in the former Soviet Union were allowed more freedoms and were able to participate more freely in their government.)* **Why did the fall of communism affect the way the United States allocated its spending?** *(With the fall of communism, the United States no longer faced a threatening adversary and no longer needed to spend as much money on defense.)*

- **Quick Activity** Display Color Transparency: *The End of Communism.* Use the lesson suggested in the transparency book to guide a discussion about the end of communism in Eastern Europe and the Soviet Union.
  Color Transparencies **A-139**

> **Primary Source** "Your generation is living in one of the most exciting times in Soviet history. It is a time when the first breath of freedom stirs the air and the heart beats to the accelerated rhythm of hope, when the accumulated spiritual energies of a long silence yearn to break free.... We do not know what the conclusion of this journey will be, but we're hopeful that the promise of reform will be fulfilled ... leading to a new world of reconciliation, friendship, and peace."
> —Ronald Reagan, May 31, 1988

Analyzing Political Cartoons

Breaking Up In this cartoon, Soviet leader Mikhail Gorbachev looks at a crossed hammer and sickle, the official symbols of the Soviet Union.

1. Read the first paragraph on the next page. Why does the cartoonist show the hammer and sickle broken into 15 pieces?
2. How does Gorbachev seem to feel about what has happened? Why do you think he feels this way?

Even before this summit, the two nations had signed a historic nuclear arms pact and had begun negotiations on the START I Treaty, which would reduce the number of nuclear weapons in the world.

✓ **Checkpoint** What policies toward communism did President Reagan pursue?

The Cold War Ends

In a little over three years' time after Reagan's speech in Moscow, the Cold War had come to an end. The Berlin Wall came down; Poland, Czechoslovakia, and Hungary held democratic elections; and the Soviet Union disintegrated into numerous separate republics. *Time* magazine observed: "It was one of those rare times when the tectonic plates of history shift beneath men's feet, and nothing after is quite the same."

Communism Ends in Eastern Europe More so than any other event, the fall of the Berlin Wall symbolized the end of communism in Europe. For decades, the wall had blocked travel from communist East Berlin to democratic West Berlin. Guards shot those who attempted to escape over the wall to West Berlin. Then, in November 1989, following the fall of East Germany's communist government, East German authorities opened the wall's gates. Thousands climbed atop the wall; some even took sledgehammers and chipped away at the barricade. Within a year, East and West Germany would reunite as one single nation. Communists also lost power in Poland, Hungary, Czechoslovakia, Bulgaria, and Romania in 1989; in Albania in 1990; and in Yugoslavia in 1991.

Answers

Analyzing Political Cartoons
1. The Soviet Union broke apart into 15 separate republics.
2. Gorbachev is upset. He had hoped that his reforms would strengthen the Soviet Union, but instead the nation fell apart.

✓ Reagan built up the U.S. military to challenge communism. He also supported anticommunist rebellions against communism.

Connect to Your World

The Russian Federation The largest of the former Soviet republics is now known as the Russian Federation. With the collapse of the U.S.S.R. came many challenges. For example, Chechnya, an area with an ethnic minority, declared its independence in 1991. Struggles with Chechnya led to terrorist attacks in Russian cities and ongoing guerilla warfare.

President Vladimir Putin created seven administrative districts in the Russian Federation, a move designed to increase central control of the country. He moved to control rich business tycoons, called oligarchs, who had used their wealth to influence the government. Putin maintained friendlier ties with the West than some of his Soviet predecessors and supported the U.S. "war on terrorism." The Russian Federation experienced a financial crisis in 1998, but Putin's reforms worked to stabilize the country and help it recover both economically and politically. Observers have noted with some concern that Putin's most recent policies seem to be bringing Russia's government closer to its highly-centralized predecessors rather than to democratic models.

■ Have students analyze the Events That Changed America feature on this spread. Ask them to write sentences that explain how each image illustrates the fall of communism. Then, have students access **www.pearsonschool.com/ushist**, and use the History Interactive feature and then answer the question in the text.

Monitor Progress

To review this section, ask students to explain whether they think it was inevitable that the Soviet Union would fall. Ask them to list what the Soviet leaders might have done to maintain their government.

America's buildup of weapons, such as long-range nuclear missiles, threatens the Soviet Union.

The Soviet Union Breaks Apart In August 1991, hard-liners in the Soviet Union attempted to stage a coup in a last-gasp attempt to maintain communist rule. But when millions of Russians, led by Boris Yeltsin, rallied in the streets of Moscow in support of Gorbachev, the coup fell apart. Not long afterward, the Communist Party lost power, and the Soviet Union separated into 15 independent republics. Boris Yeltsin became the new leader of the largest new republic, the Russian Federation.

Historians do not totally agree on what caused the Soviet Union to collapse. Most acknowledge that Gorbachev's policy of *glasnost* opened the floodgates to rebellions against Soviet domination of Eastern Europe. Likewise, they note that his policy of *perestroika* fostered a challenge to communist rule within the Soviet Union. Yet, a number of scholars give Reagan credit for bringing an end

INTERACTIVE
Whiteboard

Events That Changed America

THE FALL OF COMMUNISM IN EUROPE

In the early 1980s, Ronald Reagan began to build up the American military. Knowing that the struggling Soviet economy could not match this buildup, Mikhail Gorbachev began reforms in the Soviet Union and sought a better relationship with the United States.

Then came 1989, the "year of the miracle." In that year, the nations of Eastern Europe experienced a series of bloodless revolutions. In June 1989, Solidarity, Poland's anticommunist reform party, swept into power. Its leader, Lech Walesa, was elected President in 1990. In November 1989, the Berlin Wall fell. People were allowed to travel freely from East to West Berlin for the first time in nearly 40 years. Next, massive demonstrations by university students in Czechoslovakia ended communist rule there. Finally, in August 1991, following a failed coup against Gorbachev, millions of Russians led by Boris Yeltsin protested against the central Soviet government, breaking its power. Not long afterward, the Soviet Union ceased to exist. President George H.W. Bush and Boris Yeltsin, the President of the new Russian Federation, established a friendly relationship between their nations.

▲ An American game about the Soviet policy of *glasnost*

▼ Reagan shares a friendly moment with Soviet leader Mikhail Gorbachev.

Lech Walesa, head of Poland's Solidarity movement, takes his oath as President. ▼

Differentiated Instruction   Solutions for All Learners

L4 Advanced Readers   L4 Gifted and Talented Students

Remind students that the fall of communism affected many countries around the globe. Have students find out more about one of those nations. Ask students to choose one country that was communist during the Cold War, conduct research in the library or online, and write a three-paragraph report on the country today. Have students answer the following questions: How have daily conditions changed for most people? How has the country's relationship with the United States changed? How has the United States supported or invested in the country's government or businesses?

to the Cold War. By dedicating America to a massive arms buildup, they argue, he hastened the collapse of the Soviet economy. In turn, this compelled Gorbachev to promote reform at home and relinquish control of Eastern Europe.

The key rival, competitor, and enemy of the United States for so many years had suddenly disappeared. President George H.W. Bush met and signed agreements with first Gorbachev and then Yeltsin to scale down and even eliminate certain types of nuclear weapons. Bush and Yeltsin issued a joint statement in 1992 pledging friendship and cooperation. The long Cold War, which had absorbed so much of the energy and resources of the Soviet Union and the United States since 1945, was finally over.

✔ **Checkpoint** What key actions and events brought about the end of the Cold War?

Why It Matters

Although communism survived in China, Cuba, and a few other nations, the fall of communism in Eastern Europe and the Soviet Union ended the Cold War. American leaders now faced new challenges and daunting questions: Should military spending be decreased? What new direction should American foreign policy take in the post–Cold War world?

◄ Thousands of Czechs hold peaceful protests and candlelight vigils to protest Czechoslovakia's communist regime.

A child plays on a statue of Stalin that has been knocked down in Gorky Park in Moscow. ▼

◄ West Germans celebrate the fall of the Berlin Wall and the reunification of Berlin.

▲ Bush and Yeltsin meet at Camp David to discuss joint foreign-policy proposals.

Thinking Critically
How did Reagan end up influencing Soviet policy in the mid-1980s?

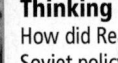

For: More images from the fall of communism in Eastern Europe and the Soviet Union
www.pearsonschool.com/ushist

Trouble Persists in the Middle East L3

Instruct

- **Introduce: Key Term** Ask students to find the key term *Iran-Contra affair* (in bold) in the text. Ask **If giving money to the Contras helped fight communism, why did Reagan keep his actions secret?** (*Congress had banned giving money to the Contras.*)

- **Teach** Using the Think-Write-Pair-Share strategy (TE, p. T23), have students describe the U.S. role in Middle Eastern affairs. Ask **In what way did the United States intervene in the Middle East?** (*The United States sent peacekeepers to Lebanon, opposed the leader of Libya, and sold weapons to Iran.*) **What were the benefits that U.S. leaders hoped to gain from these actions?** (*a more stable region*)

- **Quick Activity** Assign three groups to study the role of the United States in Lebanon, Libya, and Iran. Then organize a quick debate on the effectiveness of U.S. policy in each of these countries.

Independent Practice

NoteTaking Have students record main ideas related to events in the Middle East during Reagan's presidency. Reading and Note Taking Study Guide

Monitor Progress

As students fill in their concept webs, circulate to make sure that they understand the troubles in the Middle East. For a completed version of the concept web, see Note Taking Transparencies, **B-147b.**

Answers

✔ The U.S. buildup of arms may have contributed to Gorbachev's reform policies. The openness of *glasnost* and *perestroika* contributed to the rebellions in Eastern Europe.

Thinking Critically
Reagan influenced Soviet policy by building up the U.S. military. Because the Soviets did not have enough money to build up their own military in return, they had to alter their responses to the United States and were no longer able to repress continued calls for reform.

Differentiated Instruction Solutions for All Learners

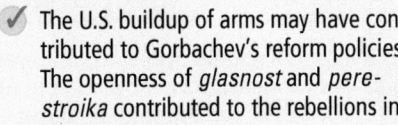

L1 Special Needs Students **L2 English Language Learners** **L2 Less Proficient Readers**

To help students master vocabulary, have them list this section's high-use words and key terms and people. Encourage them to include additional terms and phrases that may be new to them, such as *superpowers, provoking, covert, "safe house," summit, hardliners, terrorist,* and *scandal.* Then have them create flashcards with the term on one side and its definition

(or, in the case of key people, an identifying statement) on the other. For English Language Learners, you may wish to have students add explanations in their home language to go with the flashcards. Pair students and have them use the flashcards to quiz each other.

Assess Progress L3

- Have students complete the Section Assessment.

- Administer the Section Quiz. Teaching Resources, **p. 23**

- To further assess student understanding, use Progress Monitoring Transparencies, **143**.

Reteach

If students need more instruction, have them read the section summary.

Reading and Note Taking L3
Study Guide

Adapted Reading and L1 L2
Note Taking Study Guide

Spanish Reading and L2
Note Taking Study Guide

Extend L4

See this chapter's Professional Development pages for the Extend Online activity on the Berlin Wall.

Answer

✔ The Iran-Contra scandal arose when the Reagan administration negotiated with terrorist groups and sold arms to Iran. The administration gave the proceeds from arms sales to the Nicaraguan Contras, despite a Congressional ban on giving funds to this group.

NoteTaking

Identify Main Ideas Record the main ideas related to events in the Middle East during Reagan's presidency in a concept web like the one below.

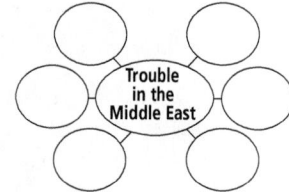

Vocabulary Builder
contradict–(kahn truh DIHKT) *v.*
to go against

Trouble Persists in the Middle East

Even as the Soviet Union collapsed, the United States continued to confront problems in the Middle East. In 1982, Reagan sent a group of 800 United States Marines to Lebanon as part of an international force trying to bring peace to a nation torn by civil war. On October 23, 1983, a truck loaded with thousands of pounds of explosives smashed through barriers at the headquarters of the United States Marines in Beirut (bay ROOT), Lebanon's capital, and into a four-story building that housed hundreds of military personnel. The explosion killed 241 marines. Reagan withdrew the remaining marines in February 1984. The incident illustrated, once again, the complicated nature of Middle Eastern politics.

During the 1980s, the United States often clashed with Libya. Led by Muammar al-Qaddafi (MOO uh mahr al kuh DAH fee), whom Reagan described as "the mad dog of the Middle East," Libya supported terrorist groups. In 1986, following a terrorist attack on a Berlin nightclub, which Reagan blamed on Qaddafi, U.S. warplanes bombed Libya. The air raid killed one of Qaddafi's daughters. Even though Qaddafi was unharmed, his criticism of the United States dwindled.

Reagan's presidency started with a breakthrough in the Middle East. Twenty minutes after he took the oath of office on January 20, 1981, Iran released all 52 Americans it had held hostage since 1979. But during his second term, the Iran-Contra affair badly tarnished Reagan's reputation.

The **Iran-Contra affair** began when the United States sold weapons to Iran in 1985 in exchange for Iran's promise to pressure terrorist groups in Lebanon to release some American hostages. The plan didn't work, and it contradicted the administration's policy of refusing to negotiate with terrorists. Then, the administration used the money from the sale to fund the Contras in Nicaragua, despite the fact that in 1983 Congress had banned sending funds to the Contras. News of these deals came out in 1986. Although President Reagan accepted responsibility for the actions of his administration, he never admitted to ordering his aides to support the Contras. Ultimately, several leading administration officials and a top aide, Oliver North, were convicted on charges stemming from the scandal, although many of the convictions were later overturned on technical grounds. In spite of this, Reagan left office with extremely high approval ratings.

✔ **Checkpoint** What was the Iran-Contra scandal?

SECTION **3 Assessment**

Progress Monitoring Online
For: Self-test with vocabulary practice
www.pearsonschool.com/ushist

Comprehension

1. **Terms and People** For each item below, write a sentence explaining how the term or person is related to the fall of communism in Europe and the Soviet Union in the late 1980s and early 1990s.
   - Strategic Defense Initiative
   - Mikhail Gorbachev
   - *glasnost*
   - *perestroika*

2. **NoteTaking Reading Skill: Sequence** Use your flowchart to answer the Section Focus Question: What were Reagan's foreign policies, and how did they contribute to the fall of communism in Europe?

Writing About History

3. **Quick Write: Choose Images** Using library books or approved Internet sources, select images and write captions to create a multimedia presentation about the fall of the Berlin Wall.

Critical Thinking

4. **Draw Inferences** How did Reagan's foreign policy differ from that of Carter?

5. **Identify Point of View** During his first term, Reagan called the Soviet Union an "evil empire," but in his second term, he developed a working relationship with Gorbachev. What accounts for this change in strategy?

6. **Synthesize Information** Why did Reagan order an air raid on Libya?

Section 3 Assessment

1. Sentences should reflect an understanding of how each term or person is related to the fall of communism in Europe in the late 1980s and early 1990s.

2. Reagan sought to confront communism, and he greatly expanded the U.S. military budget on programs such as the Strategic Defense Initiative. The Soviets could not match the U.S. arms buildup, and their military disadvantage contributed to the fall of communism.

3. Responses should show the ability to find images that show the fall of the Berlin Wall.

4. Carter had reduced defense spending, and Reagan greatly increased it.

5. After Gorbachev indicated that he wanted to achieve significant reforms in the Soviet Union, Reagan showed his commitment toward working with the Soviet leader in a positive way.

6. Reagan ordered an air raid on Libya because its leader, Muammar al-Qaddafi, supported terrorist groups.

For additional assessment, have students access **Progress Monitoring Online** at **www.pearsonschool.com/ushist.**

WITNESS HISTORY

A New World Order

Less than two years after the Berlin Wall fell, the United States found itself involved in another war after Iraq invaded its neighbor Kuwait. President George H.W. Bush spoke about his vision for this war:

❝We stand today at a unique and extraordinary moment. The crisis in the Persian Gulf, as grave as it is, also offers a rare opportunity to move toward a historic period of cooperation. Out of these troubled times . . . a new world order can emerge; a new era—freer from the threat of terror, stronger in the pursuit of justice; and more secure in the quest of peace, an era in which the nations of the world, East and West, North and South, can prosper and live in harmony.❞

—George Herbert Walker Bush, Address to Congress, September 11, 1990

▲ President Bush and his wife, Barbara, visiting troops in Saudi Arabia during the Persian Gulf War

Objectives

As you teach this section, keep students focused on the following objectives to help them answer the Section Focus Question and master core content.

- Analyze why George H.W. Bush decided to use force in some foreign disputes and not in others.
- Summarize the Persian Gulf War and its results.

Foreign Policy After the Cold War

Objectives

- Analyze why George H.W. Bush decided to use force in some foreign disputes and not in others.
- Summarize the Persian Gulf War and its results.

Terms and People

Manuel Noriega	divest
Tiananmen Square	Saddam Hussein
apartheid	Operation Desert Storm
Nelson Mandela	

NoteTaking

Reading Skill: Summarize Use a chart like the one below to summarize Bush's major foreign-policy decisions.

Post-Cold War Foreign Policy	
America's new role in the world	Persian Gulf War
•	•
•	•

Why It Matters When the Cold War came to an end, many Americans hoped that a new era of peace would dawn. Yet, America's foreign policy during the Bush years demonstrated that the end of the Cold War would not lead to a new era of peace, but instead to a dangerous era of regional conflicts. **Section Focus Question: What actions did the United States take abroad during George H.W. Bush's presidency?**

A New Role in the World

When the Soviet Union collapsed, the United States became the only unopposed superpower poised to take a leading role in world affairs under the leadership of President George H.W. Bush. Few leaders entered the White House with as much foreign policy experience as Bush. A graduate of Yale and a veteran of World War II, Bush had served as the U.S. Ambassador to the United Nations, as director of the CIA, and as Ronald Reagan's Vice President. His experience would be put to the test as America faced a series of difficult international crises during the late 1980s and early 1990s.

Latin America and the War on Drugs In the late 1980s and early 1990s, Latin America experienced a wave of democracy. In Central America, a peace plan devised by Costa Rican leader Oscar Arias (AH ree uhs) brought free elections in Nicaragua and the end of a long civil war in El Salvador. In Chile, the notorious military dictator Augusto Pinochet (ah GOO stoh pee noh SHAY) gave up power.

Prepare to Read

Background Knowledge   L3

Ask students to recall the reasons for the fall of the Soviet Union. Ask them to predict how U.S. foreign policy might respond to its fall.

Set a Purpose   L3

- **WITNESS HISTORY** Read the selection aloud.

  Ask **How did President Bush see this crisis as an opportunity?** (*He thought that the crisis would cause nations to cooperate and work together for peace.*)

- **Focus** Point out the Section Focus Question, and write it on the board. Tell students to refer to this question as they read. (*Answer appears with Section 4 Assessment answers.*)

- **Preview** Have students preview the Section Objectives and the list of Terms and People.

- **NoteTaking** Using the Paragraph Shrinking strategy (TE, p. T20), have students read this section. As they read, have students summarize Bush's foreign policy decisions.
  Reading and Note Taking Study Guide

Vocabulary Builder

Use the information below and the following resource to teach students the high-use word from this section. Teaching Resources, Vocabulary Builder, p. 11

High-Use Word	Definition and Sample Sentence
tolerate	*v.* to put up with In the 1990s, the Soviet people decided they could no longer **tolerate** the communist system of government.

A New Role in the World ⑬

Instruct

- **Introduce: Key Terms** Ask students to find the key terms *apartheid* and *divest* in the text. Ask **Why did the South African government change its racial policy after private firms *divested* from South Africa?** *(The country's economy suffered; regaining foreign investment was an incentive for change.)*

- **Teach** Ask **How was the crisis in Yugoslavia tied directly to the fall of the Soviet Union?** *(Yugoslavia was a communist country and experienced civil war when the Soviet Union collapsed.)* Have students examine the photographs on this spread and the map on this page and answer the accompanying question. Ask **Why would the U.S. response to changes in Latin America, China, or South Africa be affected by the end of the Cold War?** *(The United States would no longer have to consider the Soviet response to its foreign policy.)*

- **Quick Activity** Display Color Transparency: *Tiananmen Square Protests.* Use the lesson suggested in the transparency book to guide a discussion about the protests at Tiananmen Square. Color Transparencies A-140

Independent Practice

Have students make a timeline of events titled *Government Changes After the Cold War.* Direct them to list the countries and events described in this section.

Monitor Progress

As students fill in their summary charts, circulate to make sure that they understand Bush's foreign policy decisions. For a completed version of the summary chart, see Note Taking Transparencies, B-148.

Answer

Caption The purpose of Bush's invasion of Panama was to arrest the dictator Manuel Noriega for drug-related crimes. Bush's policy in Somalia was a humanitarian effort to bring peace and vital supplies to people suffering from a conflict between rival warlords.

Foreign Policy Under Bush

President Bush faced several foreign-policy challenges. He adjusted his policy depending on each situation. **How did Bush's approach in Somalia differ from his approach in Panama?**

▲ **Promoting Democracy in South Africa**
Bush greets South African leader Nelson Mandela soon after Mandela's release from prison in 1990.

Not all developments in Latin America, however, pleased the Bush administration. Since the Nixon administration, the government had been waging a "war on drugs," or an attempt to stop illegal drug use by going after both sellers and users. Groups of racketeers in Latin America supplied a significant amount of the illegal drugs in the United States. The Bush administration arrested and tried several international drug figures, including Eduardo Martinez Romero, the reputed financier of a Colombian drug cartel. Even more spectacularly, in December 1989, Bush sent more than 12,000 U.S. troops to invade Panama and arrest Panama's dictator **Manuel Noriega.** Brought to the United States for trial, Noriega was convicted of several charges of drug trafficking and sentenced to 40 years in prison.

China Cracks Down on Critics Meanwhile, in the spring of 1989, Chinese students captured the world's attention by staging prodemocracy protests in **Tiananmen Square** in the heart of Beijing. Many Americans hoped that these protests might result in the fall of communism in China. Instead, on June 4, Chinese tanks rolled into Beijing, killed hundreds of protesters, crushed the demonstrations, and imprisoned many prodemocracy activists.

The Bush administration condemned this action and suspended arms sales to China. However, Bush did not believe that stiffer penalties would influence Chinese leaders. He made the pragmatic choice to remain engaged with China economically and diplomatically, rather than cut off ties with the country.

Change Comes to South Africa While China resisted changes, long overdue ones were taking place in South Africa. For years, the South African government, controlled by whites, had maintained an oppressive system of rigid segregation known as **apartheid.** The leader of the antiapartheid movement, **Nelson Mandela** (man DEHL uh), had been imprisoned since 1962. In the late 1980s, protests against apartheid within South Africa and around the globe grew. In the United States, many private firms **divested,** or withdrew investments, from South Africa. Congress imposed economic sanctions instead of fully divesting, not wanting to destabilize the struggling nation. President Bush met with Mandela after his release from jail in 1990 and endorsed the drive to bring democracy to South Africa. Soon after, apartheid began to be dismantled, and South Africans elected Mandela as their leader in 1994 in their first free elections.

Connect to Your World

Civic Responsibility South Africans who opposed apartheid wrote articles or speeches describing apartheid's injustices, led demonstrations against the government, or worked for opposition parties. These actions were risky because the government often cracked down on critics.

Point out to students that Americans, whose rights of free speech, petition, and assembly are guaranteed by the Constitution, have many ways to voice their opinions and work to promote changes in their laws.

Voting is one of the most important tools for change that citizens have.

In 1989, there were only 3.1 million registered voters in South Africa. That changed before the first free elections in 1994 when more than 22 million people registered and almost 88 percent of those actually cast ballots.

Not all Americans take advantage of their voting privileges. In 2006, while more than 220 million people were eligible to vote, 81 million people actually cast ballots.

▲ **Fighting Drug Trafficking in Panama** The U.S. Justice Department takes a mug shot of Panamanian dictator Manuel Noriega after his removal from Panama.

▲ **Providing Aid in Somalia** An American soldier receives a warm welcome from a Somalian child.

▲ **Being Careful With China** Bush reacted cautiously when the Chinese government suppressed prodemocracy protests in Tiananmen Square.

Peacekeeping and Police Actions With the fall of communism in 1991, the nation of Yugoslavia disintegrated into a bloody civil war. Bush chose not to send troops because he feared that the tangled conflict could embroil the United States in another Vietnam. Not until 1992, however, did he back a modest UN plan to restore peace in Bosnia, one of the new republics carved out of Yugoslavia. By then, more than 150,000 civilians had died.

The Bush administration acted more swiftly to protect human rights in Somalia. As part of "Operation Restore Hope," United States Marines landed in this East African nation in December 1992 to help establish a cease-fire between rival warlords and to deliver food to hundreds of thousands of starving people. The American humanitarian mission reinforced UN efforts at peacekeeping and relief. Even some of Bush's most persistent critics applauded his decision to intervene in Somalia.

✓ **Checkpoint** What domestic problems caused President Bush to order the invasion of Panama?

The Persian Gulf War

The most important foreign-policy challenge faced by the Bush administration took place in the Persian Gulf. On August 2, 1990, Iraq invaded its tiny neighbor Kuwait. Nearly 150,000 Iraqi troops quickly overran Kuwaiti forces.

Causes of the War **Saddam Hussein,** Iraq's ruthless dictator, had run the Middle Eastern nation with an iron fist since 1979. By invading Kuwait, Hussein sought to take over Kuwait's rich oil deposits. With Kuwait in his power, Hussein would control nearly 20 percent of the oil produced around the world. The United States feared how Hussein would use the influence that controlling such a large amount of oil would give him. In addition, nearby Saudi Arabia possessed even more massive oil reserves. The United States did not want Hussein to seek to gain control of those reserves next. President Bush made it clear that he would not <u>tolerate</u> Iraq's aggression against its neighbor. He worked to build an international coalition and backed a UN resolution demanding that Iraqi troops withdraw.

Vocabulary Builder
<u>tolerate</u>—(TAHL er ayt) *v.* to put up with

Instruct

- **Introduce: Key Term** Ask students to find the key term *Operation Desert Storm* (in bold) in the text. Then, write the term on the board and provide the definition. Tell students to view the map on the following page. Ask **What act of aggression did Saddam Hussein commit upon a neighboring country?** *(He ordered the invasion Kuwait.)* **What does the coalition of countries involved in *Operation Desert Storm* indicate about how the world viewed Hussein's actions?** *(Many countries around the world objected to the invasion.)*

- **Teach** Discuss the response to Saddam Hussein's invasion of Kuwait. Ask **Why was Kuwait an appealing target for Iraq?** *(Kuwait is rich in oil.)* **What was one strength and one weaknesses of fighting Operation Desert Storm with a coalition of many countries?** *(Strength: The coalition showed that countries were united in their opposition to Iraq's actions. Weakness: Making decisions involving so many countries would have been difficult.)* **In what way did Operation Desert Storm end the "Vietnam syndrome" of warfare?** *(Operation Desert Storm was fought quickly and with little loss of U.S. troops. Unlike the Vietnam War, this engagement was not prolonged and it met its goals.)*

- **Quick Activity** Have students access **www.pearsonschool.com/ushist** to use the Geography Interactive map and answer the map skills questions in the text.

L4 Advanced Readers **L4 Gifted and Talented Students**

Have students conduct library and Internet research to learn more about one of the conflicts discussed in this section, for example, the breakup of Yugoslavia, the conflict in Somalia, or apartheid in South Africa. Ask students to find out about the conflict's historical roots and key events. Have them present their findings either in a timeline that highlights key developments or a poster that uses images and maps to summarize the conflict. Ask students to present their finished products to the class.

Answer

✓ Bush ordered the invasion of Panama to arrest its leader, Manuel Noriega, on charges of drug trafficking. He wanted to stop illegal drug sales in the United States.

- Have students fill in the *Outline Map: World Oil Reserves* worksheet with the names of countries that have significant oil resources. Teaching Resources, **p. 20**

- Have students review the HISTORY MAKERS feature on the next page. Discuss Colin Powell's continuing involvement in foreign affairs.

Monitor Progress

Circulate to make sure that students are filling in their outline maps accurately and understand the location of the world's oil reserves.

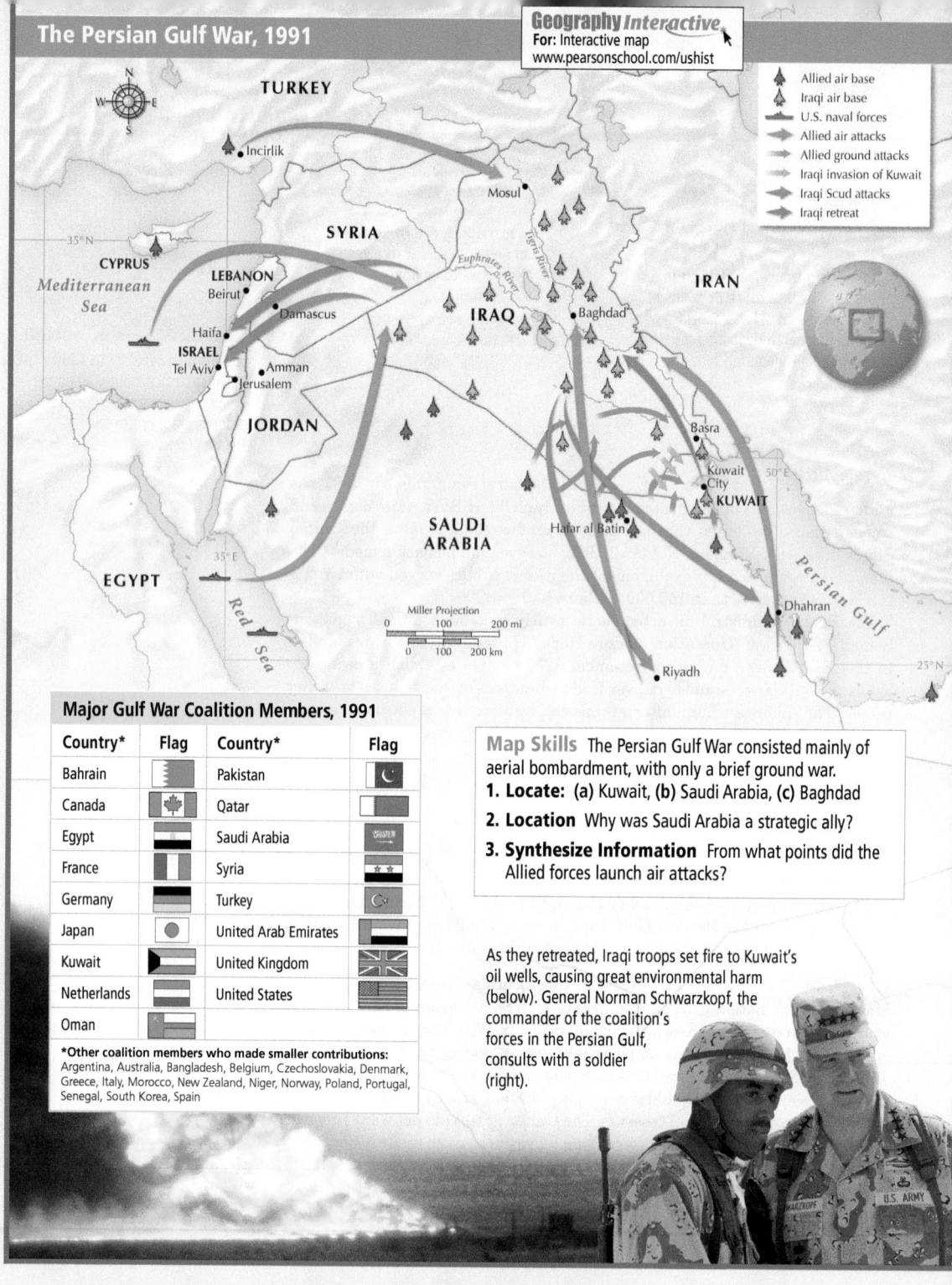

The Persian Gulf War, 1991

Geography *Interactive*
For: Interactive map
www.pearsonschool.com/ushist

- ▲ Allied air base
- ▲ Iraqi air base
- ⬥ U.S. naval forces
- ➡ Allied air attacks
- ➡ Allied ground attacks
- ➡ Iraqi invasion of Kuwait
- ➡ Iraqi Scud attacks
- ➡ Iraqi retreat

Major Gulf War Coalition Members, 1991

Country*	Flag	Country*	Flag
Bahrain		Pakistan	
Canada		Qatar	
Egypt		Saudi Arabia	
France		Syria	
Germany		Turkey	
Japan		United Arab Emirates	
Kuwait		United Kingdom	
Netherlands		United States	
Oman			

***Other coalition members who made smaller contributions:**
Argentina, Australia, Bangladesh, Belgium, Czechoslovakia, Denmark, Greece, Italy, Morocco, New Zealand, Niger, Norway, Poland, Portugal, Senegal, South Korea, Spain

Map Skills The Persian Gulf War consisted mainly of aerial bombardment, with only a brief ground war.
1. **Locate:** (a) Kuwait, (b) Saudi Arabia, (c) Baghdad
2. **Location** Why was Saudi Arabia a strategic ally?
3. **Synthesize Information** From what points did the Allied forces launch air attacks?

As they retreated, Iraqi troops set fire to Kuwait's oil wells, causing great environmental harm (below). General Norman Schwarzkopf, the commander of the coalition's forces in the Persian Gulf, consults with a soldier (right).

Differentiated Instruction   Solutions for All Learners

L1 Special Needs Students   L2 English Language Learners   L2 Less Proficient Readers

To help students distill significant facts about Middle Eastern countries, ask them to modify and annotate a map of the Middle East. To begin, have them take out their outline maps of World Oil Reserves (see Teaching Resources, p. 20). Then, have them identify the countries pictured on the map that were members of the Gulf War Coalition. Explain that maps sometimes include labels, or callouts, that provide additional information about an area on the map. Have students use the information in this section to create

callouts for countries pictured on the map. Callouts should be enclosed in a box on the map near the appropriate country with a line from the box to the country. Callouts should be short: "150,000 Iraqi troops invaded Kuwait" or "Iraq attacked Israel, although Israel was not part of the coalition." When students have finished their maps, have them discuss how their modifications help clarify the events of the Gulf War.

Answers

Map Skills

1. Review locations with students.
2. Saudi Arabia borders Iraq and provides an important site for U.S. air bases.
3. Possible answer: The Allied forces launched air and ground attacks from coalition-friendly points outside of Iraq.

Operation Desert Storm By late fall, about 700,000 troops had assembled in Saudi Arabia, including nearly 500,000 American forces. Britain, France, Egypt, and Saudi Arabia, among others, also sent troops. Other nations, for example Japan, agreed to help pay for the costs of the operation. Initially, Bush hoped that the presence of these troops, along with the economic sanctions against Iraq, would convince Hussein to withdraw his soldiers. At the same time, the President asked for and received from Congress the authority to use force, if necessary, to back up the UN's resolution that Iraq leave Kuwait.

Operation Desert Storm, the name given to the American-led attack on Iraqi forces, began on January 16, 1991. General Colin Powell, the Chairman of the Joint Chiefs of Staff, and General Norman Schwarzkopf devised and executed a strategy that began with five weeks of devastating aerial bombardment on Iraqi forces. Iraq countered by launching Scud missiles on both coalition forces and Israel. Although these missiles did little serious damage, they struck terror in the hearts of many who feared they were armed with chemical warheads.

On February 23, coalition troops stormed into Kuwait. Easily overmatched, Iraqi troops surrendered or fled, setting fire to Kuwaiti oil rigs along the way. Less than five days after the ground war began, Iraq agreed to a UN cease-fire. It had lost an estimated 25,000 soldiers. American deaths totaled 148. "We've kicked the Vietnam syndrome once and for all," proclaimed Bush. He then chose to limit American actions to enforcing the UN resolution. The coalition's forces would compel Iraq to leave Kuwait but would not continue on to Baghdad, Iraq's capital, to topple Saddam Hussein. As a result, Hussein and his regime survived the war. Bush's public approval rating skyrocketed.

✔ **Checkpoint** What strategic political and economic interests caused the United States to become involved in the Persian Gulf War?

HISTORY MAKERS

Colin Powell (born 1937)
The son of Jamaican immigrants, Colin Powell joined the army after college and served two tours of duty in Vietnam. He held several jobs in the army and in the government during the 1970s and 1980s. In 1989, President George H.W. Bush named General Powell Chairman of the Joint Chiefs of Staff. From that post, he guided the American victories in Panama and the Persian Gulf War. Powell later served as Secretary of State under President George W. Bush.

Assess and Reteach

Assess Progress ⓁⒹ

- Have students complete the Section Assessment.
- Administer the Section Quiz. Teaching Resources, **p. 24**
- To further assess student understanding, use Progress Monitoring Transparencies, **144.**

Reteach

If students need more instruction, have them read the section summary.

Reading and Note Taking Study Guide ⓁⒹ

Adapted Reading and Note Taking Study Guide Ⓛ①Ⓛ②

Spanish Reading and Note Taking Study Guide Ⓛ②

Extend Ⓛ④

Organize students in three groups and assign each group a topic: democratic protests in China, the end of apartheid in South Africa, or the disintegration of Yugoslavia. Have each group research and present to the class the changes that occurred in each country, how they were carried out, and their legacies.

Answers

✔ The United States became involved in the Persian Gulf War because Saddam Hussein's invasion of Kuwait was unprovoked and because his actions enabled him to gain control over a significant portion of the world's oil deposits.

SECTION 4 Assessment

Progress Monitoring Online
For: Self-test with vocabulary practice
www.pearsonschool.com/ushist

Comprehension

1. **Terms and People** For each item below, write a sentence explaining how the term or person demonstrated the new role of the United States after the end of the Cold War.
   - Manuel Noriega
   - Tiananmen Square
   - apartheid
   - Nelson Mandela
   - divest
   - Saddam Hussein
   - Operation Desert Storm

2. **NoteTaking Reading Skill: Summarize** Use your chart to answer the Section Focus Question: What actions did the United States take abroad during George H.W. Bush's presidency?

Writing About History

3. **Quick Write: Create a Timeline** Plan, draft, and create a multimedia timeline featuring American foreign policy after the Cold War. Consider using a slideshow computer application to present your timeline.

Critical Thinking

4. **Draw Inferences** Why did President Bush respond differently to the crisis in Somalia than he did to the crisis in China?

5. **Compare** How was the Persian Gulf War fought differently from the Vietnam War?

6. **Draw Conclusions** Why did the U.S.-led coalition decide not to invade Baghdad or try to oust Hussein after driving Iraq out of Kuwait?

Section 4 Assessment

1. Students' sentences should reflect an understanding of each term or person.

2. George H.W. Bush took action to control the flow of drugs from Panama, sent peacekeeping forces to Bosnia and Somalia, suspended arms sales to China to protest its human rights violations, and initiated Operation Desert Storm to free Kuwait from the Iraqis.

3. Timelines should present ideas sequentially and should include images to illustrate important elements of post–Cold War foreign policies.

4. Bush protested human rights violations in both China and Somalia; however, he maintained ties with China, an important trading partner, while his intervention in Somalia involved mainly peacekeeping and humanitarian efforts.

5. The Persian Gulf War involved few troops on the ground, and the engagement lasted only a short time.

6. The coalition may not have had support to extend its attack. The coalition may have determined that its goal was to liberate Kuwait, not to attack Iraq.

For additional assessment, have students access **Progress Monitoring Online** at **www.pearsonschool.com/ushist.**

Quick Study Guide

Progress Monitoring *Online*
For: Self-test with vocabulary practice
www.pearsonschool.com/ushist

Quick Study Guide

- Have students use the Quick Study Guide to prepare for the chapter test. Students may wish to refer to the following sections as they review:

  Key Policies and Actions of Ronald Reagan
  Section 1
  Section 2

  Key Events in George H.W. Bush's Presidency
  Section 4

  The Fall of Communism in Eastern Europe and the Soviet Union
  Section 2
  Section 3

  Key Events of the Conservative Resurgence
  Section 1
  Section 2
  Section 3
  Section 4

- For additional review, remind students to refer to the Reading and Note Taking Study Guide
  Section Note Taking
  Section Summaries

- Have students access **www.pearsonschool.com/ushist** for this chapter's History Interactive timeline, which includes expanded entries and additional events.

- If students need more instruction on analyzing graphic data, have them read the Skills Handbook, **p. SH21.**

For **Progress Monitoring *Online*,** refer students to the Self-test with vocabulary practice at **www.pearsonschool.com/ushist.**

Key Policies and Actions of Ronald Reagan

Domestic
Supported tax cuts and deregulation to stimulate demand under the theory of supply-side economics
Took a strong stance on air-traffic controllers' strike
Appointed conservative Justices to the Supreme Court
Reformed Social Security
Increased defense spending

Foreign
Pressured the Soviet Union by building up the American military, including the Strategic Defense Initiative program
Aided anticommunist forces in several countries, including Afghanistan and Grenada
Signed arms control agreements with Soviet leader Mikhail Gorbachev
Sent peacekeeping force to Lebanon
Ordered an air raid on Libya because of Libyan leader Muammar al-Qaddafi's involvement in terrorist attacks

Key Events in George H.W. Bush's Presidency

- Signed Americans With Disabilities Act into law
- Forged friendly relationship between the United States and the new Russian Federation
- Continued the war on drugs by invading Panama and arresting Panamanian dictator Manuel Noriega on drug-trafficking charges
- Sent humanitarian mission to Somalia
- Headed an international coalition of forces in the Persian Gulf War

The Fall of Communism in Eastern Europe and the Soviet Union

✔ Quick Study Timeline

In America

1981	1983
Hostages in Iran released on first day of Reagan's presidency	Economy starts to recover from recession

Presidential Terms — Ronald Reagan 1981–1989

1980   1982   1984

Around the World

1982	1984
Argentina and Great Britain battle for control of Falkland Islands	Indira Gandhi, prime minister of India, is assassinated

Differentiated Instruction   Solutions for All Learners

L1 Special Needs Students   **L2 English Language Learners**   **L2 Less Proficient Readers**

Use the following study guide resources to help students acquiring basic skills:
Adapted Reading and Note Taking Study Guide
- Section Note Taking
- Section Summaries

Use the following study guide resources to help Spanish-speaking students:
Spanish Reading and Note Taking Study Guide
- Section Note Taking
- Section Summaries

American Issues
●—●—● Connector

By connecting prior knowledge with what you have learned in this chapter, you can gradually build your understanding of enduring questions that still affect America today. Answer the questions below. Then, use your American Issues Connector study guide (or go online: www.pearsonschool.com/ushist).

Issues You Learned About

● **America and the World** The Cold War dominated American foreign policy for half a century, starting in the 1940s.

1. When and why was the Berlin Wall constructed? How did the United States respond at the time?

2. Why did Reagan's attitude toward Soviet leader Gorbachev change? What events and policies demonstrated this change?

3. What role do some historians believe the United States played in the fall of the Soviet Union?

● **Sectionalism and National Politics** Most politicians in the United States are members of a political party.

4. What were the first two major political parties in the United States, and what policies did they generally favor? In the late twentieth century, what were the country's two major political parties, and what policies did they generally favor?

5. What complaints did Republicans lodge against Democratic economic policies in the late 1970s?

6. Why had many white southerners changed their historical allegiance from the Democratic Party to the Republican Party by the 1980s?

● **Government's Role in the Economy** Different administrations back their own economic policies, such as raising or lowering taxes and increasing or decreasing funds for government programs.

7. What is supply-side economics? What changes did Reagan's application of supply-side economics bring to taxpayers?

8. What steps did Reagan take to lessen the federal government's role in the economy?

Connect to Your World — Activity

America Goes to War: War in Iraq On March 20, 2003, the United States and allied forces became involved in another conflict with Iraq. Conduct research online or go to your local library to learn more about this conflict. Use your findings to create a timeline of the Iraq War similar to the one below.

Iraq occupies Kuwait.	UN sets Jan.15, 1991, as the deadline for Iraqi withdrawal.	U.S.-led coalition begins aerial bombardment of Iraq.	Coalition troops storm into Kuwait and southern Iraq.	Iraqi resistance crumbles.
Aug. 2, 1990	Nov. 29, 1990	Jan. 16, 1991	Feb. 23, 1991	Feb. 28, 1991

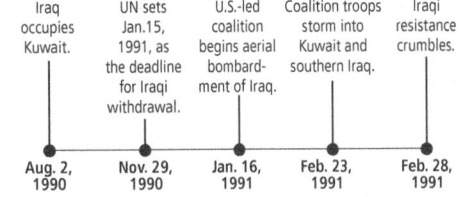

1987
Reagan and Gorbachev sign treaty agreeing to eliminate some nuclear missiles

1991
United States leads coalition of forces in Persian Gulf War

George H. W. Bush 1989–1993

1986   1988   1990   1992

1988
Soviet forces begin to pull out of Afghanistan

1989
Berlin Wall falls

1991
Soviet Union breaks up; Cold War ends

History *Interactive*
For: Interactive timeline
www.pearsonschool.com/ushist

American Issues
●—●—● Connector

Tell students that the main issues for this chapter are America and the World, Sectionalism and National Politics, and the Government's Role in the Economy. Then, ask students to answer the Issues You Learned About questions on this page. Discuss the Connect to Your World topic(s), and ask students to complete the project that follows.

American Issues Connector

1. in 1961 to prevent travel between East and West Berlin; The United States helped West Berlin by airlifting food and supplies.

2. After Gorbachev began reforming his government, Reagan signed a nuclear arms agreement with the Soviets.

3. Some believe the U.S. buildup of weapons caused the communist government to collapse.

4. the Federalists, who favored a strong central government, and the Republicans, who favored states' rights; the Democrats, who favored expanding the role of federal government, and the Republicans, who called for reducing government activism

5. that liberals were expanding the role of government with social programs and industry regulation that were not performing adequately, hampering economic growth

6. because of the enactment of civil rights legislation under the Democrats in the 1960s

7. It argues that spending will increase if taxes are reduced. Reagan reduced taxes by 25 percent, with the largest cuts going to the wealthy.

8. deregulating banking, telecommunications, and airlines

Connect to Your World
Students' timelines should show events during the war in Iraq.

For additional review, remind students to refer to the Reading and Note Taking Study Guide American Issues Journal.

Chapter Assessment

Terms and People

1. What was the **New Right**? Give two reasons for the rise of the New Right.

2. What was the **Savings and Loan crisis**? How did the federal government respond to this crisis?

3. What is **AIDS**? How did Reagan and Bush react to the increase of AIDS in the United States?

4. What were *glasnost* and *perestroika*? What effect did they have on the Soviet Union?

5. Define **apartheid.** What actions did the United States take to end apartheid?

Focus Questions

The focus question for this chapter is **What was the conservative resurgence, and how did it affect the domestic and foreign policies of the United States?** Build an answer to this big question by answering the focus questions for Sections 1 through 4 and the Critical Thinking questions that follow.

Section 1
6. What spurred the rise of conservatism in the late 1970s and early 1980s?

Section 2
7. What were the major characteristics of the conservative Reagan Revolution?

Section 3
8. What were Reagan's foreign policies, and how did they contribute to the fall of communism in Europe?

Section 4
9. What actions did the United States take abroad during George H.W. Bush's presidency?

Critical Thinking

10. **Categorize** Identify the goals of the conservative movement in the early 1980s.

11. **Analyze Charts** Study the chart below. Use it, along with your reading of this chapter, to explain how the conservative movement affected Congress.

Composition of Congress, 1979–1983

Year	House of Representatives			Senate		
	Dem.	Rep.	Ind.	Dem.	Rep.	Ind.
1979	276	157	0	58	41	1
1981	243	192	0	46	53	1
1983	269	165	0	46	54	0

12. **Recognize Effects** Think about the economic policies that Reagan followed. Then, identify and describe one positive and one negative effect that his policies had on the economy.

13. **Identify Central Issues** In the Iran-Contra affair, what actions of several members of Reagan's administration went against the policies of the federal government?

14. **Make Generalizations** Describe the political policies that led to U.S. involvement in Afghanistan, Nicaragua, El Salvador, and Grenada.

15. **Synthesize Information** Reagan's foreign policy was directed at stopping communism. What was the basis of Bush's foreign policy? Give one specific example of this foreign policy.

16. **Draw Inferences** How did George H.W. Bush approach the war against Iraq in 1991?

Writing About History

Create a Multimedia Presentation In the late 1980s and early 1990s, sweeping changes happened in Europe and other places around the world. These changes affected the United States in subtler but still significant ways. Choose one of these changes, and create a multimedia presentation showing what happened and how it affected the United States.

Prewriting
• Go online to www.pearsonschool.com/ushist to review several presentations that use different types of media to make their points.
• Brainstorm topics and choose the one that you think lends itself best to a multimedia format.
• Outline the main points you would like to make and choose the type of media you will use to make each point.

Drafting
• Write a draft of your presentation.
• Search for or create images and artwork to enhance your presentation.
• Create storyboards showing how you will blend the text and images in your presentation.
• Consider using a computer application to put together the final presentation.

Revising
• Use the guidelines on page SH31 of the Writing Handbook to revise your work.

Terms and People

1. The New Right was a growing conservative movement in the 1960s and 1970s that supported a conservative agenda. It developed as people became disillusioned with the liberal policies of the Great Society and conservative religious groups became more politicized.

2. The Savings and Loan crisis developed as these institutions failed because of fraud and risky loans. The government bailed out many depositors who lost money in this crisis.

3. AIDS is a disease that develops from a virus that attacks the immune system. Reagan responded slowly to the spread of the disease; Bush provided increased funding for research.

4. *Glasnost* and *perestroika* were policies of openness and reform for the Soviet Union. Gorbachev's introduction of these policies helped improve relations between the United States and the Soviets.

5. Apartheid was a policy of racial segregation in South Africa. In the United States, many private firms divested themselves of South African holdings to pressure the country to reform its policies.

Focus Questions

6. Conservatives valued most the ideas of individualism, patriotism, and self-determination. The social and economic declines of the 1970s showed the failure of the liberal response to these problems and spurred the rise of conservatism.

7. The Reagan Revolution focused on reducing the size and influence of government. It lowered taxes and limited government intervention in Social Security, healthcare, and education.

8. Reagan sought to confront communism, and he greatly expanded the U.S. military budget on programs such as the Strategic Defense Initiative. The Soviets could not match the U.S. arms buildup, and their military disadvantage contributed to the fall of communism.

9. George H.W. Bush took action to control the flow of drugs from Panama, sent peacekeeping forces to Bosnia and Somalia, suspended arms sales to China to protest its human rights violations, and initiated Operation Desert Storm to free Kuwait from the Iraqis.

Critical Thinking

10. The goals of the conservative movement were to limit government regulation and reduce taxes, support traditional values and religious beliefs, and oppose communism.

11. Students should note that the Republicans gained a number of House seats in the 1981 election, but many of those seats were lost in the 1983 election. In the Senate, Republicans made gains in the 1981 election and maintained their seats in the 1983 election.

12. Reagan's policy of supply-side economics lowered taxes. However, his policy, combined with increased spending on defense, led to a large budget deficit and increased the national debt to $2.5 trillion.

Document-Based Assessment

Is the National Debt a Problem?

During the 1980s, the Reagan administration lowered tax rates, hoping to pull the economy out of a recession. At the same time, defense spending increased. These factors, in part, led to annual budget deficits that added substantially to the national debt. There remains considerable debate about the costs and benefits of national debt. Use your knowledge of Ronald Reagan's economic policies and Documents A, B, and C to answer questions 1 through 4.

Document A
Budget Surpluses and Deficits, 1950–2006

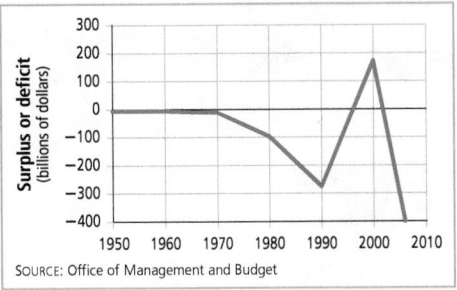

SOURCE: Office of Management and Budget

Document B
National Debt as a Percentage of GDP, 1940–2010

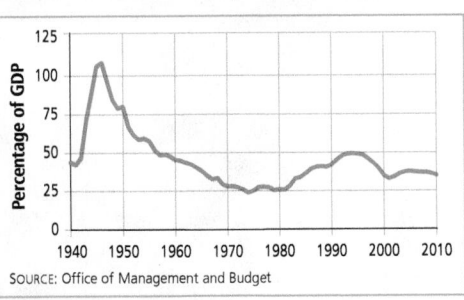

SOURCE: Office of Management and Budget

Document C

"Large deficits and rising federal debt constrain future economic growth and living standards by reducing the amount of saving in the United States available for private investment. Federal borrowing to finance deficits may also put upward pressure on interest rates, which increases household borrowing costs for such things as homes, cars, and college loans.

In addition to these economic consequences, the budgetary effects of deficits and growing debt reduce the federal government's flexibility in funding various programs and activities. . . . In fiscal year 2003, net interest spending was the sixth largest item in the federal budget—about 7 percent of total federal spending was primarily used to pay interest on debt held by the public rather than to finance other public priorities. . . .

Federal borrowing has both advantages and disadvantages. . . . Borrowing, in lieu of higher taxes or lower government spending, may be viewed as appropriate during times of economic recession, war, and other temporary challenges. . . . Borrowing for such short-term circumstances can permit the government to hold tax rates relatively stable and avoid economic disruptions. Federal borrowing might also be viewed as appropriate for federal investment, such as building roads, training workers, and conducting scientific research, contributing to the nation's capital stock and productivity. . . . In concept, federal spending that is well chosen . . . could ultimately contribute to producing a larger economy from which to pay the interest and principal on the borrowed funds. However, in practice, [the Congressional Budget Office] concluded that many federal investments might not significantly increase economic growth because some are selected for political or other noneconomic reasons and others displace more productive investments by the private sector or state and local governments."

—*from* Federal Debt: Answers to Frequently Asked Questions, *U.S. Government Accountability Office, 2004*

1. According to Document A, annual budget deficits
   A remained relatively low during the 1980s.
   B increased dramatically during the 1980s.
   C decreased dramatically during the 1980s.
   D disappeared during the 1980s.

2. According to Document B, national debt
   A was at its lowest point ever during the 1980s.
   B was at its highest point ever during the 1980s.
   C increased during the 1980s.
   D decreased during the 1980s.

3. According to Document C, federal debt
   A makes it easier for individual citizens and companies to borrow money.
   B makes it more difficult for the government to fund other public priorities.
   C is never desirable.
   D always increases economic growth.

4. **Writing Task** Do you think benefits of the increased national debt during the 1980s and 1990s outweighed the costs? Why or why not? Use evidence from the documents and the chapter to support your answer.

13. Several members of Reagan's administration went against the administration's policy of refusing to negotiate with terrorists when they sold weapons to Iran. In addition, the administration gave money from the arm sales to the Contras in Nicaragua, a policy that violated a congressional ban on aid to the anticommunist group.

14. In general, the United States opposed communism abroad by funding anticommunist rebellions and sending troops to protect U.S. citizens from communist aggression.

15. The basis of Bush's foreign policy was to protect the interests of U.S. companies and citizens. The Persian Gulf War, fought to protect Kuwait's oil fields, is an example of protecting U.S. energy interests.

16. Bush approached the war by creating a coalition of many nations that opposed the Iraqi invasion of Kuwait. He created a limited military action that could be carried out in a short time.

Teach With Technology
Presentation**EXPRESS**™
PREMIUM DVD

- Teach this chapter's core content by using PresentationExpress, which includes interactivities, video, lecture notes, and the *ExamView®* QuickTake assessment tool.

- To introduce this chapter by using PresentationExpress, ask students with which of the following statements they most agree: **A) The best way to deal with global challenges is for each nation to protect its own interests. B) Nations should cooperate only with other nations that share their points of view. C) Cooperation among all nations is necessary to address global challenges. D) National interests have less importance in the face of global challenges, which need to be addressed through international bodies such as the United Nations.** Take a class poll or record students' answers by using the QuickTake feature, and discuss their responses. Point out that in this chapter, they will read about issues that have shaped the United States in recent years.

Technology Resources

- Student**EXPRESS** CD-ROM
- Teacher Resource Library **DVD**
- Presentation**EXPRESS** **PREMIUM** DVD
- *ExamView®* **Test Bank CD-ROM** English and Spanish
- **Guided Reading Audio,** Spanish
- **Student Edition on Audio**

THE ESSENTIAL **VIDEO** By Students For Students
For videos on Amercian Issues, go to
www.pearsonschool.com/ushist

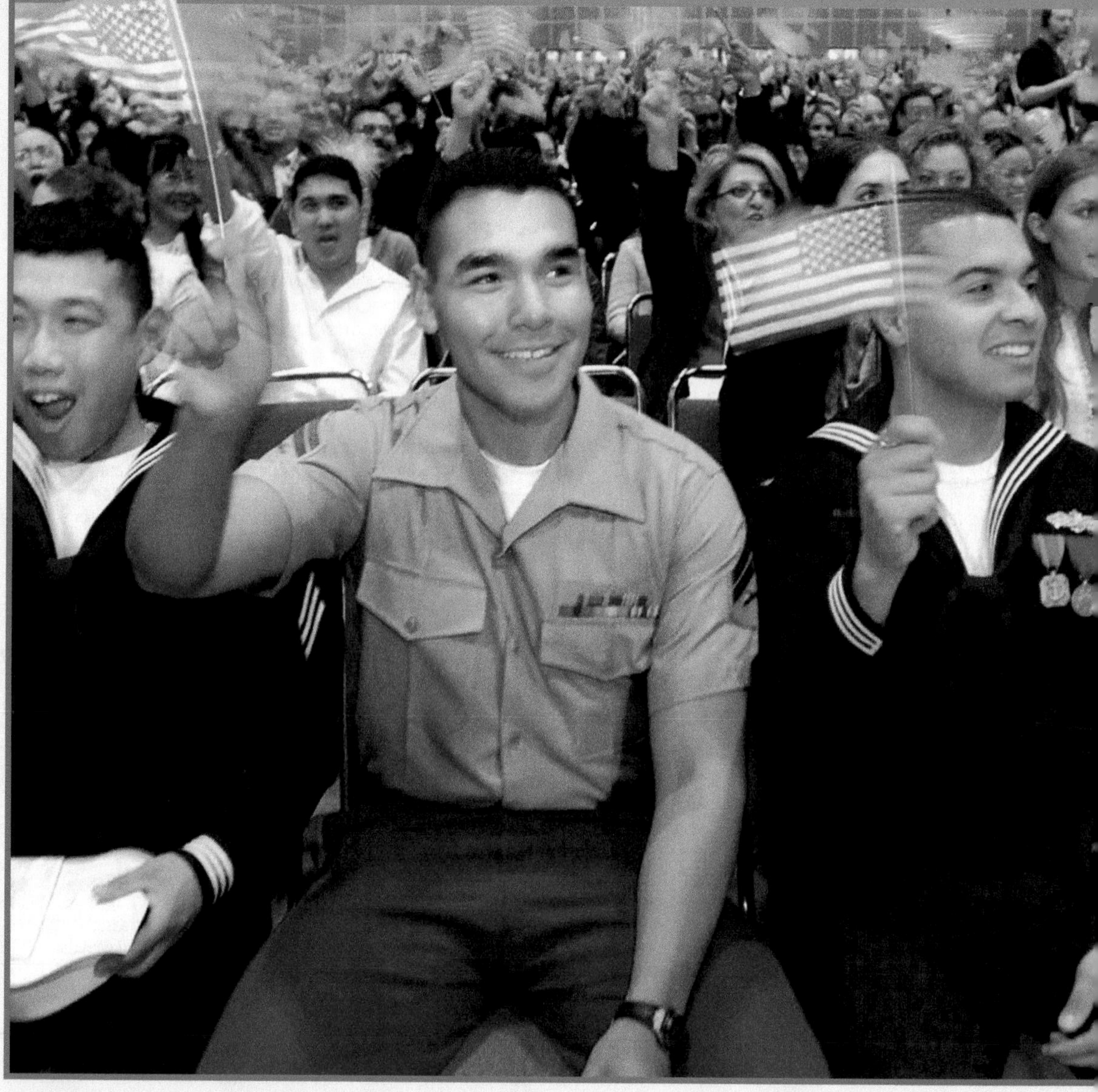

Bibliography

For the Teacher

Friedman, Thomas L. *The World Is Flat [Updated and Expanded]: A Brief History of the Twenty-First Century.* Farrar, Straus & Giroux, 2006.

Lewis, Bernard. *What Went Wrong? The Clash Between Islam and Modernity in the Middle East.* HarperCollins Publishers, 2003.

Mandelbaum, Michael. *The Case for Goliath: How America Acts as the World's Government in the Twenty-First Century.* Perseus Publishing, 2005.

For the Student

L2 Frank, Mitch. *Understanding September 11th: Answering Questions About the Attacks on America.* Viking, 2002.

L3 Clinton, Bill. *My Life: The Presidential Years.* Vintage, 2005.

L4 Egendorf, Laura, ed. *Terrorism.* Greenhaven Press, 2004.

WITNESS HISTORY

Becoming American Citizens

Every year, hundreds of thousands of immigrants change their lives by taking part in naturalization ceremonies to become U.S. citizens. After declaring their commitment to this nation and renouncing allegiance to their home countries, they join other Americans in lending their talents, skills, and dreams to their new country. President George W. Bush has described citizenship in this way:

❝America has never been united by blood or birth or soil, we are bound by ideals that move us beyond our backgrounds. . . . Every immigrant by embracing these ideals makes our country more, not less, American.**❞**

◄ Immigrants wait to be sworn in as U.S. citizens during a ceremony in Los Angeles, California, in February 2005.

Saddam Hussein's statue being toppled in Iraq

A simple "W '04" declares Bush's reelection campaign

Chapter Preview

Chapter Focus Question: What political, social, technological, and economic trends have shaped American life since 1990?

Section 1
The Computer and Technology Revolutions

Section 2
The Clinton Presidency

Section 3
Global Politics and Economics

Section 4
The Bush and Obama Presidencies

Section 5
Americans Look to the Future

NASA rover exploring Mars

Use the ☑ **Quick Study Timeline** at the end of this chapter to preview chapter events.

Note Taking Study Guide Online
For: Note Taking and American Issues Connector
www.pearsonschool.com/ushist

Chapter-Level Resources

All in One Letter Home (English and Spanish), Preread the Chapter, Vocabulary Builder, Reading Strategy, Social Studies Skills Practice, Enrichment, Issues Connector, Chapter Tests

- Test Prep With Document-Based Assessment
- AYP Monitoring Assessments
- *ExamView*® Test Bank CD-ROM
- Guided Reading Audio (Spanish)
- Student Edition Audio

Previewing the Chapter

- **WITNESS HISTORY** Read the Witness History selection aloud. Ask **What is the main idea of Bush's statement?** (*America is a nation of immigrants. Americans are defined by the belief in certain ideals, such as freedom.*) Then, ask students why an immigrant would want to become an American citizen. Tell students that in this chapter, they will learn more about immigration today and the debate that surrounds it.

- **Analyzing the Visuals** Have a volunteer read the title of each section in the chapter. Then, ask students to study the images on this page. Ask **Which images do you think are related to which sections?** (*Image 1 to Section 3 and Section 4; Image 2 to Section 4; Image 3 to Section 1*) Ask students to read ahead to check their matches.

- **Focus** Write the Chapter Focus question on the board. Tell students to keep this question in mind as they read the chapter. Then, have students preview the section titles in this chapter.

- **Preread** Have students complete the chapter's Preread the Chapter Worksheet. Teaching Resources, pp. 8–9

Differentiated Instruction Solutions for All Learners

The following Teacher's Edition strategies are suitable for students of varying abilities.

L1 Special Needs Students, pp. 659, 662, 667, 672, 676, 681 SN

L2 English Language Learners, pp. 659, 662, 667, 672, 676, 681 ELL

L2 Less Proficient Readers, pp. 659, 662, 667, 672, 676 LPR

L4 Advanced Readers, pp. 657, 663, 668, 673, 674, 681 AR

L4 Gifted and Talented Students, pp. 657, 663, 668, 673, 674, 681 GT

Have students access **www.pearsonschool.com/ushist** for the Note Taking Study Guide *Online* as an alternative to the *Reading and Note Taking Study Guide* booklet.

Step-by-Step Instruction

Objectives

As you teach this section, keep students focused on the following objectives to help them answer the Section Focus Question and master core content.

- Describe the development of the computer and its impact on business and industry.

- Analyze the impact of new technology on communications.

- Explain how globalization and the rise of the service sector affected the American economy.

Prepare to Read

Background Knowledge ⓛ³

Ask students to recall the changes that came after World War II. Have students predict technology's role in the years after the Cold War.

Set a Purpose ⓛ³

- **WITNESS HISTORY** Read the selection aloud.

  Ask **How did Michael Dell develop his global corporation?** *(He learned by experimenting and making mistakes.)*

- **Focus** Point out the Section Focus Question, and write it on the board. Tell students to refer to this question as they read. *(Answer appears with Section 1 Assessment answers.)*

- **Preview** Have students preview the Section Objectives and the list of Terms.

- **Reading Skill** Have students use the *Reading Strategy: Categorize* worksheet. Teaching Resources, **p. 12**

- NoteTaking Using the Paragraph Shrinking strategy (TE, p. T20), have students read this section. As they read, have students categorize technological changes and their impact. Reading and Note Taking Study Guide

◄ Michael Dell with one of his computers

WITNESS HISTORY

A Young Entrepreneur

In 1980, a Texas teenager named Michael Dell bought his first computer. He immediately took the computer apart to see if he could rebuild it. Though Dell entered college intending to become a doctor, his real interest lay in the computer company he started from his college dorm room. By 2003, that small company had grown into a global corporation called Dell Inc.—the most profitable company in the computer industry.

❝There were obviously no classes on learning how to start and run a business in my high school, so I clearly had a lot to learn. And learn I did, mostly by experimenting and making a bunch of mistakes.❞
—Michael Dell, 1999

The Computer and Technology Revolutions

Objectives

- Describe the development of the computer and its impact on business and industry.

- Analyze the impact of new technology on communications.

- Explain how globalization and the rise of the service sector affected the American economy.

Terms

personal computer
biotechnology
satellite
Internet

globalization
multinational corporation
service economy

NoteTaking

Reading Skill: Categorize As you read, fill in a flowchart like this one to help you categorize technological changes and their impact.

Technology Revolution		
Computers	Communications	Globalization
•	•	•
•	•	•

Why It Matters During the twentieth century, the rate of technological change sped up dramatically. New technology touched every aspect of life, including how Americans worked, played, and communicated. At the same time, globalization transformed the American economy, bringing both new challenges and new opportunities. **Section Focus Question: How have technological changes and globalization transformed the American economy?**

Technology Changes American Life

The 1900s was a century of unparalleled change. In 1903, Orville Wright flew the first airplane. Less than 70 years later, astronaut Neil Armstrong walked on the moon. During that same span of time, television went from a novelty at a World's Fair to a standard household possession, and sophisticated microscopes and telescopes unveiled previously hidden worlds. One of the most important innovations was the development of the computer.

Developing the Modern Computer Intense rivalry between enemies during World War II brought about a life-and-death race to develop new technologies, such as the computer. The U.S. government funded research that led to the creation of the first modern computer in 1946. This huge machine occupied the entire basement of the research lab. It calculated artillery ranges and performed computations for the atomic bomb.

Vocabulary Builder

Use the information below and the following resource to teach students the high-use word from this section. Teaching Resources, Vocabulary Builder, p. 11

High-Use Word	Definition and Sample Sentence
access	*n.* means of getting or using During the Cold War, several countries gained **access** to nuclear weapons.

Soon after World War II, universities and corporations joined government agencies to develop smaller, faster, more powerful computers that could perform a range of functions. The IBM company developed one of the first commercially successful computers in 1954. In the 1960s, a few companies located south of San Francisco, California, focused on developing improved technology for running the computer. Their efforts led to the microchip, a tiny fragment of silicon containing complex circuits, and the microprocessor, a silicon chip that held a central processing unit. These chips made possible the development of small computers, called **personal computers.**

Transforming Business and Industry At first, personal computers were a novelty item, used mainly by hobbyists. But by the 1980s, computers were transforming industries, research labs, and businesses. Personal computers could perform many different tasks but were small and simple enough for the average person to use. The technology that created them eventually spread to many other industries. Video games, cellular telephones, and other electronics all depended on microchips and microprocessors. Entrepreneurs played a large role in accelerating the use of personal computers. Steve Jobs's Apple Computers and Bill Gates's Microsoft made computers and software affordable for millions of Americans. Jeff Bezos's Amazon.com ushered in buying and selling products by computer. Like Andrew Carnegie and John D. Rockefeller a century before, these men amassed great fortunes by pioneering new technologies.

Revolutions in Science and Agriculture Medical science also moved ahead by gigantic leaps in the twentieth century, often aided by computer technology. Scientists developed drugs that extended patients' lives, reduced pain, and battled a huge number of diseases. They made artificial hearts and learned how to successfully transplant body organs. Such advancements, along with **biotechnology,** or the use of living organisms in the development of new products, have produced a level of healthcare unknown to any previous generation.

Advances in agricultural technology, including improved machinery, irrigation techniques, and growing methods, have brought profound changes to American society. While farms have grown larger and more productive, fewer people are needed to work them. In 1900, 50 percent of the labor force worked on farms. At the end of the century, only 2 percent did.

✓ **Checkpoint** What was the impact of the personal computer?

A Communications Revolution

Late in the twentieth century, commentators began to describe their times as the "information age." Access to information, they claimed, was access to power. Computers, cellphones, e-mails, and instant messaging became the tools of the information age. Entrepreneurs who could control these tools became wealthy—and powerful. For example, media executives who decide what gets on television can exert influence on political elections and controversial topics. But computer and communication technologies also have a democratic leveling effect. Anyone with access to a computer can acquire information that was once available only to a few, well-connected leaders.

A New Form of I.D.
A vet implants a tiny microchip (inset) into a puppy. If the dog is lost, a simple scan of the chip will reveal its name and its owner's address.

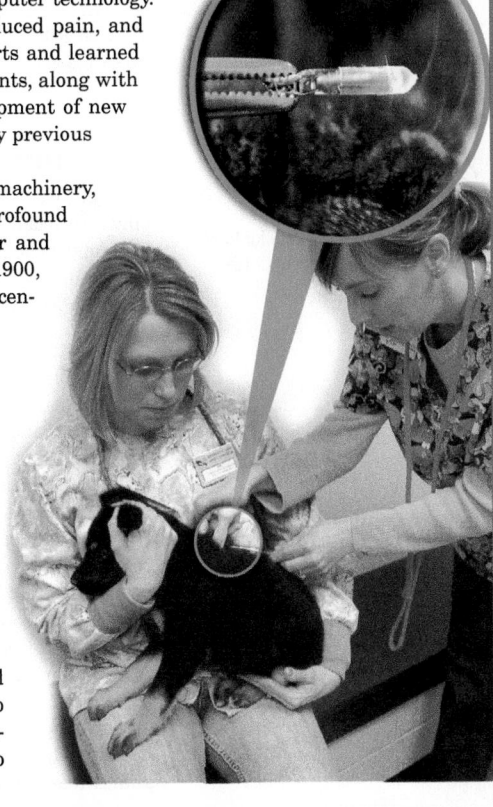

A Communications Revolution

Instruct

- **Introduce: Key Terms and Vocabulary Builder** Have students locate the key terms *satellites* and *Internet* (in bold) on this page. Discuss the definitions. Then, have students read the definition for the vocabulary builder term *access*. Ask **How do *satellites* help people gain *access* to information, including data on the *Internet*? (*Satellites receive and send information-filled signals. These signals are then sent to computers. People can access the information through the Internet.*)

- **Teach** Ask **How does the Internet play a role in modern life?** (*Sample response: It allows people to access information and to communicate instantly.*) **How do you think the Internet has led to greater interdependence among nations?** (*People in nations around the world use the Internet to communicate with one another and for commerce.*)

- **Analyzing the Visuals** Draw students' attention to the graph on this page. Ask them to summarize the information provided. Then, have them predict the future of the trend of computer ownership and Internet access and explain their predictions.

Independent Practice

Have students choose one of the advances in communications technology they read about under this blue heading and write a sentence to explain its significance.

Monitor Progress

As students continue to complete their categorize charts, circulate to make sure that they have sorted the information into the correct categories.

Answers

Graph Skills Widespread ownership of personal computers began in the 1980s and surged in the 1990s. Until the mid-1990s, the Internet was not used by the general public.

✓ The Internet and the use of satellites made communication global and almost instantaneous.

Vocabulary Builder

access – (AK sehs) *n.* means of getting or using

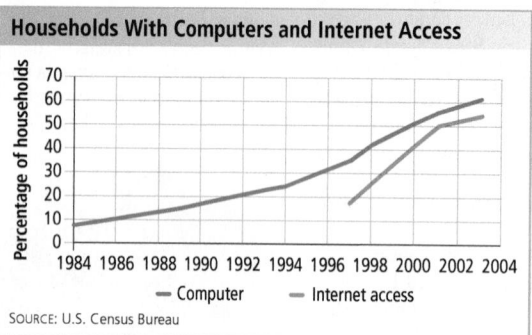

Households With Computers and Internet Access

SOURCE: U.S. Census Bureau

Graph Skills The graph shows how Americans' access to computers and the Internet has changed over the past two decades. Describe the change. Note that the data for Internet access do not begin until 1997. Why might this be so?

Satellite Technology Satellite technology increased the speed of global communications. **Satellites** are mechanical devices that orbit Earth in space, receiving and sending information-filled signals that are then relayed to televisions, telephones, and computers. Originally developed for military purposes during the Cold War, satellite technology was used in the 1970s by businessman Ted Turner to run the first "superstation," broadcasting into cable-equipped households across the country. In 1980, Turner began the 24-hour-per-day, all-news Cable News Network (CNN). Cellular telephones used similar satellite technology, allowing people to communicate away from their homes.

The Internet Is Born In the 1970s, various branches of the U.S. government along with groups in several American universities led efforts to link computer systems together via cables and satellites. By the 1980s, the **Internet**, or World Wide Web, had been born, reaching the general public in the 1990s. The Web made communication and access to information almost instantaneous. This breakthrough completely and profoundly transformed commerce, education, research, and entertainment. E-mail provided great advantages over the delays of postal mail and the expense of telephones. The impact has been especially great on people living in rural areas. The Internet's immense storage capacity also changed the world of research. In the 1980s, scientists and scholars primarily used the Internet to share information. By the early 1990s, they were using it as a research tool and an online database.

✓ **Checkpoint** How did new technology revolutionize communications?

A Changing American Economy

All of these technological changes had a dramatic effect on the American economy. New technology influenced how and where people did their jobs. In this changing economy, one sector—the service industry—grew rapidly. A lower percentage of Americans than ever before worked on assembly lines or on farms. Instead, they provided services.

The Impact of Globalization New communications infrastructures—especially satellites and computers—have made it easier for companies to do global business. This has increased **globalization**, or the process by which national economies, politics, cultures, and societies become integrated with those of other nations around the world. **Multinational corporations** are one example. Such a corporation might have its financial headquarters in one country and manufacturing plants in several others, and may obtain its raw materials from many different places. The company then sells the products it makes to a worldwide market.

Globalization has made more products and services available to greater numbers of people, often at lower prices. It has hastened the development of some nations. But it has also had some drawbacks. Industrial nations have seen their manufacturing jobs flow out to less developed nations. Steel that was once manufactured in Pittsburgh, for example, might now be made in South Korea. In less developed nations, workers often do not enjoy the protections that workers have in industrial nations. Finally, the interconnection of world economies almost guarantees that economic problems in one region will be felt in others.

Connect to Your World

The Internet Brings Change When the Internet was first invented, pundits announced that it would change the way people live. In the United States, the Internet has changed people's ways of getting information and news, ways of shopping, and even ways of meeting socially. In many foreign countries, computers and the Internet have also brought significant change. For instance, in Peru, farmers have been able to increase their profits by selling their products online—some farmers report earning five times their former profits. In Africa, the Internet has helped farmers prepare for droughts and fend off potential famine. In China, Internet outrage after a prisoner died in police custody led the government to change laws on how it detains prisoners. Worldwide, the Internet has allowed people with severe physical handicaps to enjoy greater access to communications and work opportunities.

Computers Transform Workplaces Computer technology has also changed the nature of the American economy. Many workers have found that they need computer skills to get jobs. Banking, stockbroking, programming, and the many other occupations dependent on information and computers have added millions of jobs to the service economy. Many white-collar workers in the information economy have seen their jobs radically change. Professional workers are

---

● **INFOGRAPHIC**

The Global Reach of E-commerce

Global communications, especially the Internet, have reshaped ways of doing business. Just 15 years ago, shoppers bought almost everything they needed at local stores, and most things they bought were made in the country where they lived. The Internet and e-commerce—electronic commerce, or business conducted over the Internet—have helped to change that. This illustration shows an example of e-commerce in progress.

1 A woman in Minneapolis, MN, shops for a pair of snowshoes online. She has questions about a model she likes and requests to speak with customer service on the Web site.

2 A customer-service representative in Bangalore, India, types answers to her questions in real-time.

3 The customer's order is received and processed by a computer at the sporting-goods company in Stockholm, Sweden. The computer sends messages to two locations.

4 A message to the Swedish company's U.S. warehouse in Los Angeles, CA, tells workers there to ship the shopper a pair of snowshoes.

5 Another message to a factory in Shanghai, China, tells workers there to produce more snowshoes and ship them to Los Angeles, CA.

Thinking Critically
Synthesize Information Use the illustration above to describe the impact of globalization.

History Interactive ∗
For: More about e-commerce
www.pearsonschool.com/ushist

A Changing American Economy L3

Instruct

- **Introduce: Key Term** Have students find the key term **globalization** in the text, (in bold). Ask students to predict the ways that they think **globalization** may have changed the American economy.

- **Teach** Draw a line with a midpoint on the board. Label one end "positive" and the other "negative." Using the Think-Write-Pair-Share strategy (TE, p. T23), have students suggest ways in which globalization has been both positive and negative for the United States. Discuss the shift in America's economy from an industry-based economy to a service-based economy. **How can the service industry provide both the highest- and lowest-paying jobs?** *(Some service industry jobs require advanced education and skills and some are entry-level.)* **How has the shift to a service economy affected organized labor?** *(It has led to fewer blue-collar jobs and a decline of the political power of unions.)*

- **Quick Activity** Have students examine the Infographic on this page and access the History Interactive at **www.pearsonschool.com/ushist.** Then, have students answer the Thinking Critically question.

Independent Practice

To help students better understand the growth of America's service economy, have them answer the chart skills question on the following page and complete *Reading a Chart: A Service Economy.* Teaching Resources, **p. 19**

Monitor Progress

As students complete their worksheets, circulate to make sure that students understand the growth of America's service industry.

Answer

Thinking Critically
Through globalization, businesses now make and sell their products around the world. It has changed the way corporations are structured and how people shop. They can buy a product on the Internet and have it shipped from another country. Globalization also means that workers and consumers need to learn how to communicate with people from other nations.

Differentiated Instruction   Solutions for All Learners

L1 Special Needs Students   L2 English Language Learners   L2 Less Proficient Readers

To check understanding of the Infographic "The Global Reach of E-Commerce," have students reiterate the steps in the purchase of snowshoes in the form of a flowchart. Then, have students work in pairs to check their work to ensure that they included each step in the correct order.

To help students connect their flowcharts to current events, have them browse the Internet, newspapers,

or magazines to find one image or story related to globalization. Students might find articles related to the rising cost of oil, competition, or multinational corporations. Students should study their image or article and summarize its main idea. Then, have students explain their selected piece in a small group and clarify how it relates to the Infographic.

Assess Progress

- Have students complete the Section Assessment.

- Administer the Section Quiz.
  Teaching Resources, **p. 25**

- To further assess student understanding, use Progress Monitoring Transparencies, **145**.

Reteach

If students need more instruction, have them read the section summary.

Reading and Note Taking
Study Guide

Adapted Reading and
Note Taking Study Guide

Spanish Reading and
Note Taking Study Guide

Extend

Have pairs of students write an exchange of letters between family members or friends. One person should live in the United States and the other in a developing or less-developed nation. The letters should address an aspect of globalization, tell how it is affecting the writer's life, and express a view for or against globalization.

Answers

Chart Skills occupations in medical fields and computer technology

It has fostered entrepreneurship, created new jobs in the service industry, and led to a decrease in manufacturing jobs.

Occupations Predicted to Grow the Fastest, 2004–2014

- Home health aides
- Network systems analysts
- Medical assistants
- Computer software engineers
- Physical therapist assistants
- Dental hygienists

SOURCE: U.S. Department of Labor

Chart Skills Americans' occupations in the next few years will be dramatically different from what they were 100 years ago. *Which two fields are projected to grow the fastest in the next few years?*

---

linked by a network of computers, fax machines, television screens, and cell phones. They often telecommunicate, holding meetings that involve participants sitting in offices around the world.

The Service Sector Expands With the production of services increasing faster than the production of goods, some economists say that America now has a **service economy.** Jobs in the service sector vary widely. Lawyers, teachers, doctors, research analysts, police officers, professional athletes, and movie stars are all service workers, as are salespeople and the people behind fast-food counters. Service workers are among the lowest paid and the highest paid people in the United States.

The transition from an industry-based economy to a service-based one has created opportunities for entrepreneurs. For example, Californians Richard and Maurice McDonald opened their new restaurant in 1948. The brothers emphasized efficiency, low prices, high volume, and quick service. They did away with anything that slowed down the process, including plates, glasses, dishwashing, and tipping. In 1955, Ray Kroc began to franchise the McDonald's system and name. By the end of the century, McDonald's had become the most successful food service organization in history, and the name McDonald's came to stand for low-priced, standardized-quality food.

Other entrepreneurs' names also came to symbolize their businesses. For example, Wal-Mart, a discount merchandising business founded by Sam Walton, became one of the most successful businesses in the late twentieth century.

Organized Labor Declines The rise of the service economy and the decline in American coal mining, steelmaking, and automobile manufacturing has had a strong impact on organized labor. At its peak in 1945, about 35 percent of all American workers belonged to unions. In 2000, less than 15 percent of workers did. Blue-collar jobs, once the mainstay of American labor, declined dramatically in the second half of the twentieth century. As a result, the political power of labor unions, as well as farm organizations, has fallen. At the same time, workers' average wages—especially those of nonprofessional workers—have fallen.

✓ **Checkpoint** How has globalization affected the American economy?

SECTION 1 Assessment

Progress Monitoring *Online*
For: Self-test with vocabulary practice
www.pearsonschool.com/ushist

Comprehension

1. **Terms and People** For each term below, write a sentence explaining its effect on American society or the economy.
   - personal computer
   - biotechnology
   - satellite
   - Internet
   - globalization
   - multinational corporation
   - service economy

2. **NoteTaking Reading Skill: Categorize** Use your flowchart to answer the Section Focus Question: How have technological changes and globalization transformed the American economy?

Writing About History

3. **Quick Write: Choose a Topic** Recall all the American issues you have studied in this course. Identify an issue that comes into play in this section, and explain how.

Critical Thinking

4. **Draw Inferences** Why are new technologies often developed as a result of waging war?

5. **Recognize Cause and Effect** How has the computer sped up the pace of globalization?

6. **Test Conclusions** Cite evidence to support or refute this statement: A service economy provides more opportunities to entrepreneurs than does an industrial economy.

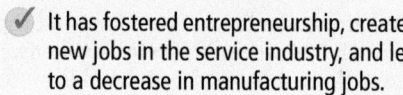

1. Sentences should reflect an understanding of how each term is related to the American economy or society.

2. Technological changes and globalization have changed the American economy into a service economy. The nation is more connected to economies and societies around the world. A large number of new service jobs continue to be created in the United States, while the number of manufacturing jobs declines.

3. Responses should show an understanding of how previous content relates to this chapter's content. Responses may focus on aspects such as interdependence, the role of the United States in a world economy, or the shift from an industrial economy to a service economy.

4. Nations involved in a war often put much of their resources into advancing technology in an attempt to win the war.

5. The computer revolution has brought nations into closer contact by facilitating access to global information and the ability to communicate and trade globally.

6. Sample response: I think that a service economy provides more opportunities for entrepreneurs because, with globalization and the Internet, people can find niches for small service businesses that do not need huge amounts of resources or large numbers of employees to start.

> For additional assessment, have students access **Progress Monitoring *Online*** at **www.pearsonschool.com/ushist.**

▲ Sixteen-year-old Bill Clinton meets President Kennedy on July 26, 1963. A campaign button proclaims his own presidential bid nearly 30 years later.

WITNESS HISTORY

Becoming President

In 1963, a high school student named Bill Clinton from Hope, Arkansas, went to the White House as part of a youth leadership conference. He was first in line to shake President Kennedy's hand. Thirty years later, Clinton was sworn in as President of the United States.

❝Thomas Jefferson believed that to preserve the very foundation of our nation, we would need dramatic change from time to time. Well, my fellow citizens, this is our time. . . . And so today, we pledge an end to the era of deadlock and drift—a new season of American renewal has begun.❞

—Bill Clinton, First Inaugural Address, 1993

The Clinton Presidency

Objectives

- Explain why Bill Clinton won the presidency in 1992.
- Assess the success of Clinton's domestic policies.
- Describe the Contract With America and its impact.
- Analyze the Clinton impeachment.

Terms and People

William Jefferson Clinton
H. Ross Perot
Family Medical Leave Act
Brady Bill
Newt Gingrich
Contract With America
Kenneth Starr
impeachment

NoteTaking

Reading Skill: Summarize As you read, create an outline like the one below to summarize information about the Clinton presidency.

```
I. The 1992 Election
   A. Bush's popularity plummets
   B. Clinton runs as "New Democrat"
   C. Clinton carries the election
II. Clinton's Domestic Policies
   A.
```

Why It Matters The conservative revolution of the 1980s had kept Republicans in the White House for 12 straight years and influenced every branch of government. The election of Bill Clinton to the presidency in 1992 signaled that Americans were ready for a change. Clinton's position as a moderate, practical Democrat had broad appeal for a wide range of voters. **Section Focus Question: What were the successes and failures of the Clinton presidency?**

The 1992 Election

After the 1991 Persian Gulf War ended, President George H.W. Bush's approval rating reached 91 percent. In less than one year, however, public opinion had changed. Saddam Hussein had stayed in power, continuing to threaten peace in the Middle East. The American economy had gone into recession and the federal deficit had risen. People were angered by Bush's betrayal of his 1988 campaign pledge not to raise taxes. Bush's sinking popularity opened up the way for the Democratic challenge.

Clinton Raises the Challenge The Democrats nominated **William Jefferson Clinton,** governor of Arkansas, as their presidential candidate. Clinton was born in 1946 into a humble home and had worked his way through college and law school before being elected governor of Arkansas in 1978. To widen his appeal and distance himself from traditional "tax and spend" liberals, Clinton promoted himself as a "New Democrat." New Democrats were centrists who sought to

Objectives

As you teach this section, keep students focused on the following objectives to help them answer the Section Focus Question and master core content.

- Explain why Bill Clinton won the presidency in 1992.
- Assess the success of Clinton's domestic policies.
- Describe the Contract With America and its impact.
- Analyze the Clinton impeachment.

Vocabulary Builder

Use the information below and the following resource to teach students the high-use word from this section. Teaching Resources, Vocabulary Builder, p. 11

High-Use Word	Definition and Sample Sentence
ultimately	*adv.* in the end; finally The personal computer **ultimately** changed lives around the world.

Celebrating Victory
Newly elected President Bill Clinton, Vice President Al Gore, and their families greet supporters in Arkansas on November 3, 1992.

Teach

The 1992 Election/ Clinton's Domestic Policies ⬤

Instruct

- **Introduce: Key Term** Point out the key term *Family Medical Leave Act* (in bold) in the text. Ask students to predict what the act might provide. Explain that this was one of Clinton's changes to domestic policy.

- **Teach** Remind students that Republicans Ronald Reagan and George H. W. Bush had led the country for 12 years. Ask **What problems caused the majority of Americans to vote for Democrat Bill Clinton in the 1992 election?** *(Saddam Hussein remained in power, threatening peace in the Middle East; the American economy had entered a recession; the federal deficit had risen; President Bush had raised taxes despite his pledge not to do so.)* **Why was Clinton unable to reform the system of healthcare in the United States?** *(His proposed reform, which was based on a new federal bureaucracy, was not supported by the majority of Americans, who were against enlarging the federal government in this way.)*

- **Quick Activity** Have students select the domestic policy legislation passed during Clinton's presidency that they believe was the most important. Have them explain it to a partner and tell why they believe that it is the most important.

Independent Practice

Ask students to write a short paragraph explaining how Clinton's views made him a centrist. Then, have them analyze whether his policies confirmed his centrist stance.

Monitor Progress

As students fill in their outlines, circulate to make sure that they understand Clinton's domestic policies. For a completed version of the outline, see Note Taking Transparencies, **B-150.**

Answer

✓ Clinton's stance appealed to a wide range of voters, including conservative and liberal Democrats and moderate Republicans.

reconcile liberal and conservative ideals. They believed in strong national defense, tough stands on crime, free trade, welfare reform, and closer ties with corporations. They believed that government was necessary and important but that it had grown large and inefficient. Clinton's centrist position attracted conservative and liberal Democrats as well as moderate Republicans.

Winning the White House By 1992, Clinton was poised to capitalize on Bush's political problems. He entered the presidential race along with Texas billionaire **H. Ross Perot,** who led a self-funded independent party and promised to govern by sound business principles. Clinton's campaign focused on economic and social opportunity. Clinton charged that Bush's economic policies had made the rich richer. He also pointed out that, unlike Bush, he came from a family that had struggled through hard times and knew what it was like to worry about paying bills. Bush responded by attacking Clinton's character. Republicans accused the governor of draft-dodging, marital infidelity, and other moral laxities. Bush also suggested that Clinton and his vice presidential candidate Al Gore were too inexperienced to lead the nation.

In the end, Clinton's message carried the election. In the largest voter turnout since 1960, more than one hundred million Americans turned out at the polls. Clinton received 43 percent of the popular vote to Bush's 37 percent and Perot's 19 percent. Democrats also retained control of the House of Representatives and the Senate.

✓ **Checkpoint** How did Clinton use his stance as a moderate to attract voters?

Clinton's Domestic Policies

When Bill Clinton took the presidential oath of office on January 20, 1993, he faced a great challenge. Since 1968, Americans had chosen Republican Presidents in five out of six elections. The Republican argument that government was the problem, not the solution, resonated with many Americans. Clinton therefore needed to chart a middle course between the limited role for government advocated by Republicans and the traditional Democratic reliance on government programs to address social problems.

Signing New Laws Early in his presidency, Clinton signed the **Family Medical Leave Act,** which had been vetoed by President Bush despite having bipartisan support. The act guaranteed most full-time employees 12 workweeks of unpaid leave each year for the birth and care of a newborn child, to recover

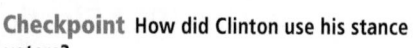

Differentiated Instruction **Solutions for All Learners**

⬤ Special Needs Students **⬤ English Language Learners** **⬤ Less Proficient Readers**

Direct students' attention to the blue heading "Clinton's Domestic Policies." Explain that *domestic policy* refers to laws and programs that are directly related to issues within the United States. These policies often relate to taxes, the economy, Social Security, welfare, and the environment.

Have pairs of students work together to make a chart identifying Clinton's domestic policies described in the section. As a class, review the meaning of each policy and how it has affected American society.

from a serious illness, or to care for an immediate family member with one. The Clinton administration also raised the minimum wage, increased access to college loans, and expanded tax credits for higher education.

Healthcare Reform Fails Healthcare reform headed Clinton's list of priorities. The United States was the only developed country without national healthcare. Though Clinton did not advocate socialized medicine, he wanted a program that would guarantee care for all Americans. His wife, Hillary Clinton, was appointed to head a healthcare task force to investigate the issue. The task force conducted highly publicized hearings and produced a long, detailed proposal that attracted immediate criticism from diverse interest groups. The bill never won congressional support and was <u>ultimately</u> dropped after about a year of debate.

Clinton had miscalculated Americans' faith in the federal government to solve the country's social problems. Millions of Americans simply did not feel that enlarging the federal bureaucracy and allowing the government to run healthcare was a good idea.

Dealing With Violence Clinton also tried to address the issue of violence in American society. In 1993, he signed the **Brady Bill,** a gun-control act named for presidential aide James Brady, who had been wounded in the 1981 assassination attempt on Ronald Reagan. Under Clinton, Congress also passed a $30 billion anticrime bill that increased funding for police and banned several kinds of assault weapons.

Still, violence continued to haunt the nation. In 1995, Americans were horrified by the bombing of a government building in Oklahoma City that killed 168 people and injured more than 800 others. The mass murder was committed, not by foreign terrorists, but by home-grown anti-government extremists. To deal with the threat of terrorism, federal buildings in major cities were surrounded with barriers to ward off similar attacks. New laws were passed to deter terrorism and impose stiffer penalties.

In 1999, yet another act of senseless violence stirred nationwide debate. At Colorado's Columbine High School, two heavily armed students killed 12 fellow students and a teacher, as well as wounding 24 others. In the aftermath of this tragedy, schools across the nation installed metal detectors and other security measures. Many schools instituted new anti-bully policies and "zero tolerance" approaches to school violence.

✓ **Checkpoint** What were Clinton's legislative successes and failures?

The Republicans Galvanize

After two years in office, Clinton had achieved a few lasting legislative victories. Yet the failure of his healthcare initiative signaled that his popularity, and his control of Congress, was waning. With the 1994 midterm elections approaching, congressional Republicans seized the opportunity to advance their own ideas.

Vocabulary Builder
ultimately – (UHL tuh miht lee)
adv. in the end; finally

Oklahoma City Bombing
The Oklahoma City bombing of April 1995 was the worst act of domestic terrorism in American history. The victims included a number of children in a day care center.

The Republicans Galvanize

Instruct

- **Introduce: Key Term** Have students locate the key term *Contract With America* (in bold) in the text. Ask **What would you expect to be the nature of this *Contract With America*?** *(a promise between Americans and the government)* **Why might Republicans have developed such a contract?** *(to convince Americans that Republicans would change the government)*

- **Teach** Explain that *galvanize* means "to stimulate someone into great activity." Ask **How did Newt Gingrich *galvanize* American voters?** *(He presented Americans with the Contract With America, which attacked big government and emphasized patriotism and traditional values.)* **What was significant about the 1994 election?** *(Republicans took control of both the House and the Senate for the first time in 40 years.)* **Why do you think the voters brought about such a considerable change?** *(They were unhappy with a Democrat-led government.)*

- **Quick Activity** Use the images on this page, the Primary Source quotation, and Color Transparency: *Republicans Take Over Congress* to discuss the political issues of Clinton's presidency. Color Transparencies **A-142**

Independent Practice

To help students better understand the political differences between Clinton and Gingrich, have them complete the worksheet *Viewpoints: Clinton and Gingrich.* Teaching Resources, **p. 20**

Monitor Progress

To check understanding, ask students to identify one difference between the views of Clinton and Gingrich that they learned about from the worksheet.

Differentiated Instruction   Solutions for All Learners

L4 Advanced Readers   L4 Gifted and Talented Students

Have students compare and contrast the goals of the Contract With America with Clinton's domestic policies. Then, students should assume the role of either a Clinton supporter or a Gingrich supporter. The Clinton supporters should write position statements regarding Clinton's domestic policy and the Contract With America. Similarly, Gingrich supporters should write position statements about the ineffectiveness of the President's domestic policies and the goals of the Contract With America. Students should then use their position statements to hold a debate on the two approaches to domestic policy.

Answer

✓ Clinton successfully enacted the Family Medical Leave Act, raised the minimum wage, expanded tax credits, and passed anticrime bills. He failed in reforming healthcare.

Scandals, Impeachment, and Trial ⓛ

Instruct

- **Introduce: Key Term** Write the word ***impeachment*** on the board. Explain that *impeach* means "to charge a public official with improper conduct." ***Impeachment*** is not a synonym for ousting a public official from office. However, it is often used to describe the entire process from accusation to removal from office.

- **Teach** Ask **What scandals plagued Clinton's presidency?** *(sexual harassment accusations, unlawful Whitewater investments, and an affair with a White House intern)* **What effect do you think the trial had on Clinton's presidency?** *(People around the world were focused on the scandal rather than on domestic or foreign policy.)* **How might the trial have affected the 2000 presidential election?** *(Americans may have distrusted Democrats, prompting them to elect a Republican president.)*

Independent Practice

Have students suppose that they are television news reporters covering the Clinton trial. Have them prepare a news report that summarizes the events under this blue heading.

Monitor Progress

As students work on their news reports, circulate to ensure that they are mentioning specific and important details related to the origins of the scandal, the impeachment process, and the results of the trial.

Goals of the Contract With America
- Balanced federal budget
- Welfare reform
- Tax cuts for middle-income families
- Decreased federal bureaucracy
- Term limits for members of Congress

The "Gingrich Revolution"
Gingrich explains his Contract with America at a press conference in January 1994. *How did his goals attract voters who were opposed to "big government"?*

Gingrich's Contract With America Georgia congressman **Newt Gingrich** led the opposition to Clinton. Gingrich was bold and aggressive and not interested in compromising with the Democrats: "We will cooperate, but we won't compromise." Many people thought that Gingrich's goal of the Republicans gaining control of the House of Representatives in 1994 was a nearly impossible task. After all, the Democrats had controlled the House for 58 of the previous 62 years.

Gingrich, however, galvanized Republicans around his **Contract With America,** a plan that attacked big government and emphasized patriotism and traditional values. The Contract With America called for congressional term limits, reduction of the federal bureaucracy, a balanced budget amendment to the Constitution, and large tax cuts, as well as increased defense spending, significant welfare reform, and tough anticrime legislation. The idea was to capture the votes of Americans who felt the federal government was too big, too wasteful, and too liberal.

Capturing the 1994 Elections Although most eligible voters did not vote in 1994, there was a strong turnout among Republicans. For the first time in 40 years, the Republicans won control of the House. They also captured the Senate and most of the governorships. *Newsweek* magazine observed:

> **Primary Source** "Last week in one of the most profound electoral routs in American history, Republicans won the right to occupy the Capitol and mount what their . . . commanders think of as a counter-revolution: a full-scale attack on the notion that a central government should play a central role in the life of the nation."

Once in office, Republicans passed most of Gingrich's program, but their attempts to slash Medicare and other government programs proved unpopular. Many Americans were also upset when the government shut down in 1995 because Congress would not pass Clinton's budget. Meanwhile, Clinton incorporated some of the conservative agenda into his own 1996 reelection bid. He signed a bill to reform welfare, passed legislation that appropriated more money for law enforcement, and called for stiffer sentencing for criminals. Finally, he made balancing the budget and reducing the federal deficit a priority.

Clinton Wins Reelection Beginning in the mid-1990s, the American economy broke out of recession and began to soar, starting the longest period of sustained growth in the country's history. Americans benefited from low unemployment, low inflation levels, and the government's efforts to balance the budget and reduce the deficit. In 1994, Clinton's disapproval rating had exceeded 60 percent, and few expected him to win a second term. As the 1996 election approached, however, the booming economy meant that few Americans had a compelling reason to change leadership.

The Republicans nominated Senate Majority Leader Robert Dole, a World War II hero and a moderate Republican. H. Ross Perot entered the race as the Reform Party candidate. Clinton skillfully captured the middle ground, labeling Dole as an out-of-touch conservative and Perot as a political quack. On election day, Americans chose Clinton by a wide margin. The House of Representatives and Senate, however, retained their Republican majorities.

✔ **Checkpoint** How did the Republicans take control of Congress?

Answers

Caption Gingrich's plan called for reducing the federal bureaucracy and making tax cuts, which appealed to discontented voters who saw the government as bloated, wasteful, and too liberal.

✔ There was a strong turnout among Republican voters. They elected Republican men and women to Congress, which resulted in a majority of Republicans in the House and Senate.

History Background

Impeachment History To date, the House has begun to assemble impeachment charges against nine Presidents: John Tyler, Andrew Johnson, Grover Cleveland, Herbert Hoover, Harry S Truman, Richard M. Nixon, Ronald Reagan, George H. W. Bush, and Bill Clinton. However, only Andrew Johnson and Bill Clinton were actually impeached by the House. In 1868, the House voted to pass 11 articles of impeachment against Andrew Johnson. The Senate voted 35 to 19 to acquit him. If one additional senator had voted against Johnson, he would have been removed from office. In 1974, Richard Nixon resigned after the House Judiciary Committee approved the articles of impeachment but before the entire House could vote on it. Most observers believe that had he not resigned, Nixon would have been impeached by the House and faced trial in the Senate, and he would have been removed from office.

Scandals, Impeachment, and Trial

President Clinton had dodged scandals from his first days in office. One, a sexual harassment suit, had stemmed from his years as governor of Arkansas. Another concerned investments that Bill and Hillary Clinton had made in the Whitewater Development Corporation, an Arkansas real estate company, in the 1970s and 1980s.

Prosecuting Clinton A special prosecutor appointed by Attorney General Janet Reno investigated the Whitewater investment case and recommended that no criminal charges be filed. However, in July, Congress passed a new law requiring that special prosecutors be selected by a three-judge panel from the U.S. Court of Appeals. As a result, in August of 1994, special prosecutor **Kenneth Starr** was appointed to investigate the case again. In seven years of investigation, Starr failed to uncover any conclusive evidence of the Clintons' guilt, though some of their associates were convicted.

In the process of prosecuting Whitewater, Starr began investigating Clinton's relationship with a White House intern. Clinton had denied under oath that the two had an affair. Eventually, Clinton admitted that he had lied. The Whitewater case was quickly overshadowed by the new scandal. In 1998, Starr recommended **impeachment** proceedings on a number of counts, all related to the intern scandal rather than to Whitewater.

Impeaching the President Most Americans condemned Clinton's actions but opposed impeachment. Congressional Democrats, similarly, did not believe his behavior met the standard of "Treason, Bribery, or other high Crimes and Misdemeanors" required by the Constitution for the impeachment and removal of a President. Nevertheless, the House of Representatives, led by the Republican majority, impeached Clinton on the charges of perjury and obstruction of justice.

In January 1999, the Senate tried the President. The removal of a President requires a two-thirds majority of senators, and from the beginning, it was clear that Clinton's opposition did not have the necessary votes. After a short trial, the President was acquitted on both counts on February 12.

✓ **Checkpoint** What was the outcome of the Clinton impeachment?

SECTION 2 Assessment

Progress Monitoring *Online*
For: Self-test with vocabulary practice
www.pearsonschool.com/ushist

Comprehension

1. Terms and People For each item below, write a sentence explaining how it relates to Clinton's presidency.
- H. Ross Perot
- Family Medical Leave Act
- Brady Bill
- Newt Gingrich
- Contract With America
- Kenneth Starr
- impeachment

2. NoteTaking **Reading Skill: Summarize** Use your completed outline to answer the Section Focus Question: What were the successes and failures of the Clinton presidency?

Writing About History

3. Quick Write: Form a Main Idea This section touches on the American issue of social problems and reforms. Compare the scandals surrounding Clinton to historical scandals you have read about. Write down a main idea that you will present in your response.

Critical Thinking

4. Identify Central Issues How did Clinton position himself ideologically in order to win over both Democrats and Republicans in the 1992 election?

5. Recognize Ideologies On what domestic issues did Democrats and Republicans differ during Clinton's presidency?

6. Synthesize Information Why did Clinton win reelection?

7. Summarize Summarize the events surrounding Clinton's impeachment.

Section 2 Assessment

1. Sentences should reflect an understanding of how each listed person or term relates to the Clinton presidency.

2. President Clinton succeeded in implementing several domestic policies. However, he failed to get one of his largest programs—healthcare reform—passed, and his presidency was overshadowed by scandal.

3. Students' main idea statements should compare the Clinton scandal with an earlier presidential scandal, such as Teapot Dome or Watergate.

4. as a moderate Democrat

5. on government spending and taxation, federal bureaucracy, and the level of government involvement in Americans' everyday lives

6. He captured the middle ground, appealing to moderate Democrats and Republicans.

7. Special prosecutor Kenneth Starr investigated Clinton's involvement in the Whitewater case and, in the process, exposed Clinton's affair with an intern. Clinton lied under oath about the affair. These events led to his impeachment on charges of perjury and obstruction of justice.

For additional assessment, have students access **Progress Monitoring *Online*** at **www.pearsonschool.com/ushist.**

Step-by-Step Instruction

Objectives

As you teach this section, keep students focused on the following objectives to help them answer the Section Focus Question and master core content.

- Analyze how the United States responded to changes in the global economy.
- Assess the foreign policy goals and actions of the Clinton administration.
- Describe U.S. relations with various Middle Eastern countries and groups.

Prepare to Read

Background Knowledge ⓛ

Ask students to recall the movement toward globalization after the end of the Cold War. Then, ask them to predict the impact of globalization on free trade and American foreign policy.

Set a Purpose ⓛ

- **WITNESS HISTORY** Read the selection aloud.

  Ask **In the title of this feature, to what does the phrase "shared future" refer?** *(Nations should work together to make globalization a benefit to all.)*

- **Focus** Point out the Section Focus Question, and write it on the board. Tell students to refer to this question as they read. *(Answer appears with Section 3 Assessment answers.)*

- **Preview** Have students preview the Section Objectives and the list of Terms.

- **NoteTaking** Using the Guided Questioning strategy (TE, p. T20), have students read this section. As they read, have students identify the main ideas about global politics and economics. Reading and Note Taking Study Guide

---

▲ Former White House official John Sununu meets with Saudi Arabian government leaders at a dinner during the Millennium Summit in New York City in 2000.

Global Politics and Economics

Objectives

- Analyze how the United States responded to changes in the global economy.
- Assess the foreign policy goals and actions of the Clinton administration.
- Describe U.S. relations with various Middle Eastern countries and groups.

Terms and People

EU	WTO
NAFTA	ethnic cleansing
GATT	al Qaeda

NoteTaking

Reading Skill: Identify Main Ideas
Complete a flowchart like this one to help you identify main ideas about global politics and economics.

U.S. Global Policy		
Free Trade	Foreign Intervention	Middle East
• NAFTA	•	•
•	•	•

Why It Matters With the end of the Cold War, the United States was the sole superpower in a dramatically changing world. No longer defined by its opposition to communism, the United States had to carve out new roles for itself in a world of globalization and increasing regional conflict. President Clinton, the nation's first baby-boomer President, ushered in this new period of American soul-searching. **Section Focus Question: What role did the United States take on in global politics and economics following the Cold War?**

Competing in the Global Economy

In the 1990s, the United States was both an important promoter of global trade and an example for newly industrializing nations. As more nations participated in economic globalization, the United States tinkered with its own policies to ensure it remained an economic powerhouse.

The Role of Free Trade As an economic leader, America has had a major role in globalization. Free trade—the guiding principle of globalization—has been hotly debated in American politics. Americans want the lower costs that free trade creates but worry about the loss of American jobs to other countries. Generally, Republicans have supported the interests of big business and free trade agreements. Democrats have been more sympathetic to labor interests and have often opposed legislation that would cost American workers' jobs. Depending on which party has been in power, free trade has either been encouraged or hindered.

Vocabulary Builder

Use the information below and the following resource to teach students the high-use word from this section. Teaching Resources, Vocabulary Builder, p. 11

High-Use Word	Definition and Sample Sentence
intervention	*n.* becoming involved in the affairs of another nation, often by force The instability of a nation's government has sometimes led to American **intervention** in that country.

Bill Clinton challenged the traditional Democratic thinking by supporting free trade blocs, which in theory would increase the economic prosperity of particular regions. Europe was an example of such a bloc. In 1993, a number of European nations established the **European Union (EU)** to coordinate monetary and economic policies. By the end of the century, the EU had adopted a single currency, the euro, to promote economic efficiency. The EU's combined resources both encouraged trade among its members and challenged the economic leadership of the United States. North American free trade proponents believed a similar bloc would stimulate their own region.

America Joins NAFTA The **North American Free Trade Agreement (NAFTA)**, a direct response to the EU was originally proposed during the Bush administration. President Bush and leaders of the other nations signed the agreement in 1992, but Congress blocked it. It called for a gradual removal of trade restrictions among the United States, Canada, and Mexico. NAFTA's supporters maintained that creating a free trade zone in North America would promote economic growth, reduce prices, increase exports, and encourage economic investment. Most labor leaders, environmentalists, and liberal Democrats argued that NAFTA would force American manufacturers to relocate to Mexico, where wages were lower and environmental controls were less rigid. They feared that hundreds of thousands of American jobs would be lost. President Clinton embraced NAFTA and pushed it through Congress. It went into effect in 1994, and since then the three countries have also signed agreements covering environmental protection, safety standards, and workers' rights.

Fourteen years later, with the removal of remaining trade restrictions between the United States and Mexico, the final provisions of NAFTA went into effect in January 2008.

Expanding Global Trade Clinton signed a total of 270 free trade agreements, including the revision of the **General Agreement on Tariffs and Trade (GATT)** in 1994 and the accords of the **World Trade Organization (WTO)** in 1995. GATT's goal was to reduce tariffs to promote free trade. The WTO replaced GATT, expanding the organization's authority to negotiate trade agreements, settle disputes, and enforce compliance with them. Clinton also continued the strong U.S. support of the World Bank.

Critics complain that the WTO and World Bank favor business interests over environmental concerns and workers' rights. At the 1999 WTO meeting in Seattle, protesters filled the streets, disrupting the proceedings. Yet most people agree that economic globalization has often had positive effects by exposing people to new ideas, technology, and communications. Nations involved in free trade have often become more democratic. Normalizing trade—engaging in free trade with countries rather than imposing sanctions based on disagreements—can strengthen economic ties. For example, normalizing trade with China has encouraged that country to adopt free market reforms.

✔ **Checkpoint** Which trade blocs has the United States become involved with?

Analyzing Political Cartoons

This political cartoon appeared as part of an intense national debate about the United States joining NAFTA.
1. What is the cartoonist's opinion about joining NAFTA?
2. Based on the cartoon, how would joining NAFTA affect the United States?

Americans on the Global Stage

L3

Instruct

- **Introduce: Key Term** Explain that Yugoslavia was made up of different geographic regions and that people in each region were divided along ethnic lines. Have students locate the term *ethnic cleansing* (in bold) and predict its meaning.

- **Teach** List each red heading under "Americans on the Global Stage" on the board. For each, list why the United States got involved, the type of intervention, and its results. Display Color Transparency: *Ethnicity in Yugoslavia*. Discuss the different ethnic groups and the issues that led to this conflict. Ask **How did the breakup of Yugoslavia lead to ethnic cleansing in Bosnia and Kosovo?** (*Serbs had dominated Yugoslavia. With the fall of Communism, there was no central government to unite the ethnic groups. The Serbs feared a loss of power in Bosnia, so they killed non-Serbs or drove them from Bosnia.*) Color Transparencies **A-143**

- **Analyzing the Visuals** Direct students' attention to the circle graph in the Infographic on this page. Ask **Which country has the greatest influence over the World Bank?** (*the United States*) Then, have students read the information in the feature or listen to the audio and answer the questions.

Independent Practice

Have students begin to fill in the worksheet *Outline Map: Global Conflicts*. Students should complete the maps as they work through this section. Teaching Resources, **p. 21**

Monitor Progress

Circulate to make sure that students are accurately filling in their Outline Maps and are able to create a map key.

Answers

Thinking Critically

1. helps countries with reconstruction, healthcare, human rights, debt relief, economic growth, education, and alleviating poverty

2. The work of the World Bank supports the American economy, considering that 45 percent of U.S. exports go to developing countries. Helping improve the strength and stability of other nations also helps increase U.S. security.

Americans on the Global Stage

When Bill Clinton became President, the more than 40-year-old American foreign policy of fighting communism had just ended. The United States needed to develop a role for itself in the post–Cold War world. Americans were willing to provide economic aid, as they did to nations of the former Soviet Union. But many of them questioned military <u>intervention</u> abroad, fearing a costly commitment like the Vietnam War. With violence surging in regional conflicts throughout the world, however, Clinton found it necessary to intervene. He did so with mixed success.

Vocabulary Builder
<u>intervention</u>–(ihn tuhr VEHN shuhn) *n.* becoming involved in the affairs of another nation, often by force

INFOGRAPHIC

The World Bank

The World Bank was founded in 1944 to help rebuild war-torn Europe. It still handles reconstruction efforts, as it did in India following a 2001 earthquake. ❶ Yet it has increasingly focused on issues facing developing countries, such as healthcare, human rights, debt relief, economic growth, and poverty. In Latin America, the Bank gives loans to people like this Peruvian man so they can own their own homes and businesses. ❷ Throughout the developing world, the Bank works to promote education for people like this Bulgarian girl. ❸

The U.S. has taken a primary role in the financing and management of the Bank. The Bank has its headquarters in Washington, D.C. As one of the Bank's most important partners, the U.S. has long seen the Bank and its work as integral to the American economy. Forty-five percent of U.S. exports go to developing countries in which the Bank is active, supporting American jobs. The U.S. also believes that strong and stable developing countries are vital to its own security.

Voting Power by Country

- United States
- Japan
- Germany
- United Kingdom
- France
- Other

16.39%
7.87%
4.49%
62.63%
4.30%
4.30%

SOURCE: The World Bank

▲ Five of the Bank's 184 member countries take the lead in setting its direction. The chart shows the voting power for the Bank's Reconstruction and Development department. As with the World Bank's four other departments, the United States has the most voting power.

▼ A Senegalese family picks tomatoes on land that used to be plagued by drought. The Bank worked with governments and local communities to make the land usable and promote agriculture.

Thinking Critically
1. **Analyze Information** What kinds of work does the World Bank do?
2. **Draw Inferences** Why is it in America's interest to support the World Bank?

Differentiated Instruction   Solutions for All Learners

L4 **Advanced Readers**   L4 **Gifted and Talented Students**

Have students conduct library or Internet research to learn more about one of the conflicts discussed in this section. Ask them to research the conflict's historical roots, its key events, the efforts made to resolve it, and its current status.

Have students present their research to the class in a timeline that highlights key historical processes and events or in the form of a poster that uses short paragraphs, images, a map, and an optional graph to summarize what they have learned.

Intervening in Somalia and Haiti In the late 1980s, civil war broke out in Somalia. By 1991, the government had disintegrated and the fighting had caused widespread famine. In 1992, the United States led a multinational force, later joined by the UN, to bring about peace and distribute food. The coalition fell apart in 1994 when several countries, including the United States, suffered steep casualty rates and withdrew their troops. Eventually, the UN also withdrew, and civil war dragged on for several more years in the devastated country.

Meanwhile, conflict was simmering in Haiti. In 1990, Haitians brought Jean-Bertrand Aristide to the presidency, in the nation's first free elections. Less than a year later, a military coup overthrew Aristide, plunging the country into turmoil. Thousands of Haitians left the country by boat to immigrate to the United States as political refugees. Many were sent back by American immigration officials, causing a public outcry. In 1994, Clinton sent American troops to Haiti to restore Aristide to power. Although American action improved the situation, within a decade Haiti faced a sinking economy and rising rates of disease and crime.

NATO in the Balkans
American soldiers monitor a border crossing between Serbia and Kosovo in 2001.

Fighting Ethnic Cleansing in Eastern Europe
In the Balkans, the collapse of communism broke up the country of Yugoslavia. For decades, the communist leader Tito had contained ethnic and religious strife. But his death in 1980, and the collapse of communism in 1989, left the country with no unifying forces. Soon, four of Yugoslavia's six major republics formed their own states, and long-suppressed ethnic and religious hostilities came boiling to the surface.

In newly independent Bosnia, ethnic and religious rivalries among Eastern Orthodox Serbs, Catholic Croats, and Bosnian Muslims eventually led to civil war. Serbs, with the help of Serbia-dominated Yugoslavia, attacked Bosnians and Croats. In many cases, they forcibly removed Bosnians and Croats from their homes and later murdered them. This state-sanctioned mass murder, violence, and rape, known as **ethnic cleansing,** shocked the world. The UN intervened with humanitarian aid. Yet atrocities continued on all sides of the struggle, and years went by before the world community intervened to stop the slaughter.

Galvanizing NATO Forces Finally, in the late summer of 1995, Clinton encouraged NATO to bomb Serbian strongholds. This was the first time the organization had gone into combat, and its use of force quickly brought about a cease-fire. In December 1995, the Dayton Accords established a federated, multinational Bosnia. Although the ethnic cleansing had ended, the enforced peace had not solved the problems of the region. In 1998, violence flared up anew—this time in Kosovo, a Serbian province on the Adriatic Sea. The fighting once again involved ethnic cleansing and also spread to the neighboring countries of Macedonia and Albania. NATO forced Serbs to withdraw from Kosovo.

✓ **Checkpoint** How did Clinton involve the United States in foreign conflicts?

America and the Middle East

In the 1990s, the Israel military responded to attacks by Palestinians. The level of violence grew increasingly fierce. Meanwhile, instability had increased in the region as a whole. As Clinton worked to address it, violence originating in the region spread outward, with the United States increasingly a target.

History Background

Slobodan Milosevic Serbian president and extreme nationalist Slobodan Milosevic, often called the "Butcher of the Balkans," oppressed majority ethnic Albanians in Kosovo leading to four wars during the 1990s. Peaceful protests led to more repression. In turn, small armies of ethnic Albanians began to respond with armed attacks on Serbian targets. Milosevic rejected international peace efforts and stepped up his program of ethnic cleansing. By the late 1990s, he had already served the legal two terms as president of Serbia, but he retained his power by having the federal legislature elect him president of Yugoslavia. However, this made him vulnerable to prosecution by the UN's International Criminal Tribunal for the Former Yugoslavia (ICTY) for war crimes perpetrated by Yugoslavs in Bosnia. In 2001, he was arrested and given into the custody of the ICTY in The Hague, Netherlands. There, he became the first head of state to be tried by an international court on charges of war crimes, crimes against humanity, and genocide. After many delays, the trial ended when Milosevic died of a heart attack in March 2006.

Instruct

- **Introduce: Key Term** Have students locate the term *al Qaeda* (in bold) in the text. Ask them to share their prior knowledge about this terrorist group, and record their responses in a concept web on the board.

- **Teach** Explain that both Israelis and Palestinians claim land in Israel. Some Israelis and some Palestinians base their feelings on religious grounds and some on nationalistic ideologies, with some Palestinians opposed to the very existence of a state of Israel. Discuss with students how these ideas and feelings have led to conflict. Ask **What were the main ideas in the Declaration of Principles?** *(self-rule for the Palestinians in Jericho and the Gaza Strip and security for the Israelis)* **What do you think must occur to secure peace in Israel?** *(Possible answer: Both sides must be willing to compromise, cease hostilities, find a means for reparations on both sides, and address long-term settlement issues.)* **Why did violence in the Middle East begin to affect the United States directly?** *(The combination of escalating violence in the Middle East and resentment at American involvement there led to more direct attacks on the U.S.)*

Independent Practice

- Have students find news articles describing the current situation in the Middle East. Have students write a paragraph comparing recent events with the situation described in the text. How has the situation in the Middle East changed? How has it remained the same? Who are the current leaders, and what are their positions?

- Have students complete the flowchart by recording the main ideas about the U.S. policy in the Middle East.

Monitor Progress

Read aloud the red and blue headings in this section. Ask students to briefly summarize the information under each red and blue heading.

Answer

✓ Clinton intervened in Somalia and Haiti to end the famine and civil war there. Clinton also encouraged NATO to use force to end the violence in Bosnia and Kosovo.

Camp David Talks
President Clinton walks with Ehud Barak and Yasir Arafat in the woods of Camp David in July 2000.

Trying for Peace in Israel In 1993, Palestinians and Israelis conducted secret negotiations in Oslo, Norway. The resulting Declaration of Principles promised Palestinian self-rule in Jericho and the Gaza Strip, as well as security for the Israelis. The declaration did not adequately address the issues of Israeli settlements in the West Bank, nor did it placate extremists on both sides, who had no interest in compromise. Chronic violence continued even though Israel withdrew from much of the West Bank, and later from Gaza. Israeli prime minister Yitzhak Rabin, who had signed the declaration, fell victim to the fury in 1995 when an Israeli religious fundamentalist assassinated him.

In 2000, Clinton invited Palestinian leader Yasir Arafat and Israeli prime minister Ehud Barak to Camp David to work on a peace agreement. They came close to signing one, but Arafat was not satisfied with any of the proposals. Back in Israel, Barak was ousted by Ariel Sharon, a "hawk" who opposed any concessions to the Palestinians and who withdrew all Israelis from Gaza. Nonetheless, Palestinian suicide bombings increased, and with them so did crackdowns by the Israeli military.

Dealing With Terrorism In 1993, a terrorist group called **al Qaeda** exploded a bomb in the World Trade Center in New York City, killing six people and injuring more than one thousand others. Al Qaeda was led by a wealthy Saudi businessman named Osama bin Laden. Bin Laden had fought in Afghanistan in the 1980s on the side of Islamic fundamentalists who sought to expel the Soviet Union. By the late 1990s, he had formed al Qaeda with the purpose of ending American involvement in Muslim countries. Five years after the U.S. bombing, al Qaeda set off car bombs at American embassies in Nairobi, Kenya, and in Dar es Salaam, Tanzania. The blasts killed 225 people and injured more than 5,500 others. In 2000, al Qaeda bombed the USS *Cole,* an American warship anchored off the coast of Yemen, killing 17 American sailors. These attacks angered Americans and frustrated politicians, who were learning that fighting terrorism would be extremely difficult.

✓ **Checkpoint** What strategic, political, and economic interests did the United States have in the Middle East?

SECTION **3** Assessment

Progress Monitoring *Online*
For: Self-test with vocabulary practice
www.pearsonschool.com/ushist

Comprehension

1. **Terms and People** For each term below, write a sentence describing what effect it has on the global economy or global society.
   - EU
   - NAFTA
   - GATT
   - WTO
   - ethnic cleansing
   - al Qaeda

2. **NoteTaking Reading Skill: Identify Main Ideas** Use your completed flowchart to answer the Section Focus Question: What role did the United States take on in global politics and economics following the Cold War?

Writing About History

3. **Quick Write: Plan a Structure** Compare the issue of America and the world in the context of this section with how it related to an earlier period in American history. Choose the best way to structure your comparison, such as point by point or topic by topic.

Critical Thinking

4. **Identify Central Issues** Why have efforts to reduce tariffs and trade barriers often been controversial in the United States?

5. **Identify Assumptions** What basic assumption about the U.S. role as sole superpower underlies American peacekeeping efforts of the 1990s?

6. **Analyze Information** For what various reasons has the United States become involved in Middle Eastern affairs?

▲ Bush's casual style attracted voters in both of his presidential races. By his reelection in 2004, he was often referred to simply as "W."

WITNESS HISTORY

A Two-Term President

In 2005, George W. Bush was sworn in as President for a second term. In his inaugural address, he alluded to a remarkable shift in traditional American foreign policy, saying that the cause of advancing freedom and democracy abroad was sufficient reason for the United States to involve itself in conflict overseas.

❝All who live in tyranny and hopelessness can know: the United States will not ignore your oppression, or excuse your oppressors. When you stand for your liberty, we will stand with you.❞
—George W. Bush, Second Inaugural Address, 2005

The Bush and Obama Presidencies

Objectives

- Assess the outcome of the 2000 presidential election.
- Explain the goals and achievements of George W. Bush's domestic policy.
- Analyze the impact of terrorist attacks on the United States.
- Summarize the policy goals and actions of the Obama administration.

Terms and People

George W. Bush	Department of
No Child Left Behind	Homeland Security
Act	WMD
Taliban	Barack Obama
Patriot Act	Tea Party Movement

NoteTaking

Reading Skill: Recognize Sequence Record the sequence of events in Bush's presidency in a flowchart like the one below.

```
┌────────────────────────────────────┐
│ The 2000 election is disputed but leads │
│ to victory for George W. Bush.      │
└────────────────────────────────────┘
      ↓        ↓        ↓
┌────────────────────────────────────┐
│ Bush launches an ambitious agenda including │
│ tax cuts and education legislation. │
└────────────────────────────────────┘
```

Why It Matters The election of George W. Bush in 2000 assured Republican domination of the White House and Congress. When the United States was attacked on September 11, 2001, Bush would use this unity to move the nation in a new direction. But a severe financial crisis late in Bush's presidency paved the way for the election of Barack Obama. **Section Focus Question: What was the impact of the terrorist attack against the United States and of the 2008 financial crisis?**

An Election Controversy

The year 2000 brought an end to Clinton's two terms as President. Clinton's legacy of a strong economy coupled with personal scandal polarized voters. As candidates geared up for the 2000 presidential race, it promised to be a close election.

The Candidates Clinton's Vice President, Al Gore, Jr., of Tennessee, ran for the Democrats. Gore selected Connecticut Senator Joseph Lieberman as his Vice President. Lieberman was the first Jewish person to be on the ticket of a major party.

The Republicans chose **George W. Bush** as their candidate. A son of George H. W. Bush and a former governor of Texas, Bush was popular with conservatives. As governor, Bush had worked with Democrats as well as Republicans. He struck many Americans as sincere.

A Tight Race The campaigns focused mainly on how to spend the federal budget surplus. Bush favored widespread tax cuts. Gore proposed strengthening Social Security and paying down the national debt. On election night, Americans voted mainly by party affiliation.

Objectives

As you teach this section, keep students focused on the following objectives to help them answer the Section Focus Question and master core content.

- Assess the outcome of the 2000 presidential election.
- Explain the goals and achievements of George W. Bush's domestic policy.
- Analyze the impact of terrorist attacks on the United States.
- Summarize the policy goals and actions of the Obama Administration.

Prepare to Read

Background Knowledge L3

Ask students to recall the dangers of the Cold War and the problems that developed in the Middle East at the end of the era. Explain that, today, the world faces attacks by terrorists, or violent extremists. Ask students to list some recent examples of terrorism.

Set a Purpose L3

- **WITNESS HISTORY** Read the selection aloud.

  Ask **How does this statement define Bush's foreign policy?** *(It indicates that he will involve the United States in foreign conflicts whenever necessary to promote or restore liberty.)*

- **Focus** Point out the Section Focus Question, and write it on the board. Tell students to refer to this question as they read. *(Answer appears with Section 4 Assessment answers.)*

- **Preview** Have students preview the Section Objectives and the list of Terms and People.

- **NoteTaking** Using the Structured Read Aloud strategy (TE, p. T20), have students read this section. As they read, have students sequence events under Bush and Obama. Reading and Note Taking Study Guide

Vocabulary Builder

Use the information below and the following resource to teach students the high-use word from this section. Teaching Resources, Vocabulary Builder, p. 11

High-Use Word	Definition and Sample Sentence
priority	*n.* degree of importance or urgency
	President Clinton delivered a speech in which he set education as a top **priority**.

An Election Controversy/The Bush Agenda (L3)

Instruct

- **Introduce: Key Term** After a contested election, George W. Bush became President in 2001. One of his priorities was the *No Child Left Behind Act*. Explain that this law was intended to improve education. Ask students how they think the law received its name.

- **Teach** Discuss with students the political situation surrounding the 2000 election. Ask **How did Bush and Gore separate themselves ideologically?** *(Bush advocated using the federal budget surplus to institute tax cuts. Gore advocated using the money to strengthen Social Security and pay down the national debt.)* Display Color Transparency: *The Election of 2000.* Discuss how the cartoon reflects the turmoil surrounding the election recount in Florida. Color Transparencies A-144

- **Quick Activity** Have students access **www.pearsonschool.com/ushist** to use the Geography Interactive map and then answer the map skills questions in the text.

Answers

Map Skills

1. Bush: Midwest, West and South, Gore: Northeast and Pacific coast

2. The voting process may change so that there are fewer errors in vote counting; the electoral college may be dropped in favor of the popular vote.

✓ Because the election was so close, the Democrats sued for a hand recount in certain Florida counties. Republicans sued to prevent it. The Supreme Court determined that the recount should end, and Bush won the presidency.

✓ financing tax cuts, improving education, and extending Medicare to cover prescription drugs for senior citizens

---

Geography *Interactive.*
For: Interactive map
www.pearsonschool.com/ushist

Presidential Election of 2000

Candidate (Party)	Electoral Vote	Popular Vote	% Electoral Vote	% Popular Vote
☐ George W. Bush (Republican)	271	50,456,062	50.5	47.9
☐ Albert Gore (Democratic)	266	50,996,582	49.5	48.4
☐ Ralph Nader (Green)	—	2,858,843	—	2.7
☐ Other	—	1,051,811	—	1

*One elector from Washington, D.C., abstained from voting

Map Skills In the 2000 presidential election, the votes were so close in the state of Florida that officials recounted ballots by hand. Although Al Gore won the popular vote, George Bush captured a greater number of electoral votes and won the presidency.

1. **Identify** In general, which regions voted for Bush? Which voted for Gore?

2. **Predict Consequences** How might the dispute over the 2000 election affect future elections?

Vocabulary Builder
priority –(prī ôr ə tē) *n.* a thing that is considered more important than another.

The vote margin in the Electoral College was razor thin. Although Gore received a half million more votes than Bush, both fell short of winning the 270 electoral votes needed to capture the presidency. The issue was Florida's 25 electoral votes. The popular vote in Florida was so close that a state law mandated an automatic statewide recount. Bush led by a margin of 537 popular votes. He was awarded 271 electoral votes, one more than was needed to win the election.

The Supreme Court Intervenes Given the extreme closeness of the votes, Democrats demanded a hand recount in several Florida counties. Republicans countered by suing in a Miami court to prevent the recount. For more than a month, confusion reigned.

Finally, the Supreme Court ruled on the issue. In the case of *Bush v. Gore*, the court ended the re-recounting by a 5-to-4 decision. On December 12, 2000, Gore conceded defeat, and Bush delivered a conciliatory victory speech.

The election showed an interesting geographical pattern. The Democrats captured votes in their traditional strongholds: the two coasts and large cities. Republicans won a large bloc of voters in the Midwest and the South.

✓ **Checkpoint** Why did the Supreme Court decide the 2000 presidential election?

The Bush Agenda

Once in office, Bush turned his attention to domestic issues. Like most Republicans, Bush believed that tax cuts would stimulate the economy and create new jobs. In 2001, Bush pushed a highly controversial $1.3 trillion tax cut through Congress. The tax cut put more money in the hands of consumers. But most of the benefits of the tax cut went to the wealthiest Americans. As a result, the federal budget deficit increased.

Bush's other domestic priority was education. He supported legislation that tied the federal funding of schools to academic achievement. The 2002 **No Child Left Behind Act** penalized schools that did not reach federal performance standards. It also called for improving teacher quality and other reforms.

Bush also addressed the concerns of older Americans who faced rising costs for prescription drugs. In 2003, Congress extended Medicare to cover prescription drugs for senior citizens. The measure was controversial. It was expensive, and many seniors found its provisions confusing and its coverage inadequate.

✓ **Checkpoint** What were Bush's domestic priorities?

Differentiated Instruction   Solutions for All Learners

L1 Special Needs Students   **L2 English Language Learners**   **L2 Less Proficient Readers**

To help students master vocabulary, have them make a list of this section's high-use words and key terms and people. Encourage students to include in the list additional terms that may be new to them, such as *intervene, campaign,* and *bipartisan.* Then, have them create flashcards with the term on one side and its definition (or, in the case of key people, one sentence identifying who the person is) on the other. For

English Language Learners, you may wish to have students add explanations in their first language on the flashcards. Pair students, and have them quiz each other, using the flashcards.

To help students better comprehend the results of the 2000 presidential election, have them complete the worksheet *History Comics: The 2000 Election.* Teaching Resources, **p. 22**

America's War on Terror

On September 11, 2001, terrorists hijacked four commercial passenger airplanes and crashed two of them into the World Trade Center in New York City and one into the Pentagon in northern Virginia. A fourth plane crashed in a Pennsylvania field after passengers rushed the hijackers in the cockpit. That day, President Bush addressed a shaken nation:

Primary Source "Today, our fellow citizens, our way of life, our very freedom came under attack in a series of deliberate and deadly terrorist acts. . . . Thousands of lives were suddenly ended by evil, despicable acts of terror. . . . These acts of mass murder were intended to frighten our nation into chaos and retreat. But they have failed. . . . "

—President George W. Bush, September 11, 2001

Independent Practice

Have students complete *History Comics: Bush* v. *Gore* to gain additional understanding of the results of the 2000 presidential election. Teaching Resources, **p. 23**

Monitor Progress

As students complete the flowchart, circulate to make sure that they are correctly ordering events. For a completed version of the flowchart, see Note Taking Transparencies, **B-152**.

Events That Changed America

The Terrorist Attacks of 9/11

Shortly before 9 a.m. Eastern time on September 11, 2001, American Airlines Flight 11 slammed into the north tower of the World Trade Center in New York City. The crash was the first of four airplane crashes in an orchestrated attack against the United States. Less than an hour after the second plane hit the south tower, the World Trade Center began to collapse. Hundreds of firefighters and police officers were trapped inside. Meanwhile, passengers on another hijacked plane learned of the crashes through their cellphones, and bravely stormed the cockpit to prevent another attack.

It was the first aerial attack on American soil since the Japanese bombed Pearl Harbor 60 years earlier. Nearly 3,000 Americans died in the attacks. Americans' confidence in their nation's security was deeply shaken.

◄ Terrified workers run away from the collapsing World Trade towers.

Thinking Critically

1. **Expressing Problems Clearly** Why was September 11, 2001, an "event that changed America"?
2. **Draw Inferences** After the attacks, a French newspaper declared, "We are all Americans." What was meant by this statement?

Differentiated Instruction   Solutions for All Learners

L4 Advanced Readers   **L4 Gifted and Talented Students**

The complicated and ever-changing nature of national security in the age of terrorism presents an opportunity for more in-depth analysis of the issues presented in this section. Consider having these students read all or parts of Thomas Friedman's book *Longitude and Attitudes: Exploring the World After September 11th.* This collection of Friedman's newspaper columns delves into the roots of modern global terrorism and the battle to stop it. Students can write a review of the book following their reading. Alternatively, have students consult a variety of print and online sources on issues surrounding the war on terrorism and then present a critical review of their findings to the class.

Answers

Thinking Critically

1. September 11 changed America because it had been 60 years since an external enemy had attacked the United States. Thousands of innocent Americans were killed, and the rest of the nation suffered and empathized with those families. People felt that they were no longer safe just going about their daily lives.
2. It meant that people of all nations empathized with the pain and fear that Americans felt.

America's War on Terror/ Bush's Second Term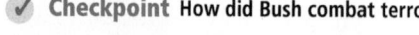

Instruct

- **Introduce** Write the word *terrorism* on the board. Work as a class to agree on a definition. Ask: **How does an act of terrorism differ from an act of war?** *(An act of terrorism is usually a surprise, is aimed to frighten and kill civilians and destroy nonmilitary targets, and usually is not carried out in the name of a national government or by a nation's armed forces.)*

- **Teach** Tell students that after September 11, 2001, U.S. leaders sought ways to increase the nation's security. Debates arose about which methods were effective or in the nation's best interest. Using the Think-Write-Pair-Share strategy (TE p. T23), have students answer the following questions: **Why did the United States invade Afghanistan?** *(to overthrow the Taliban government, which was supporting and hiding Osama bin Laden)* **Why did the United States invade Iraq?** *(as part of the war on terrorism and to search for WMD)* Have students identify steps the United States has taken to improve security within the nation. Ask **Why were some people critical of the Patriot Act?** *(They believed that it could be used to violate Americans' civil liberties.)*

- **Quick Activity** Have students read the HISTORY MAKERS biography of Condoleezza Rice and write a paragraph identifying the character traits that enabled Rice to achieve the position of Secretary of State.

Answer

✓ Bush declared war on terrorism. He sent American forces into Afghanistan to strike terrorist bases and Taliban strongholds. He also worked to improve national security on the home front by establishing the Department of Homeland Security and working to pass the Patriot Act.

As it became clear that the crashes were part of an organized terrorist attack on the United States, Americans responded as a unified, determined nation. Many rushed to donate services, supplies, and their own blood.

Invading Afghanistan In the wake of September 11, Bush and his advisers agreed that the most important priority should be finding and prosecuting the people behind 9/11. This would be just the first step in what Bush called the "war on terrorism."

American government officials quickly determined that Osama bin Laden's al Qaeda network had been behind the attacks. Bin Laden opposed the presence of American troops in Saudi Arabia, the U.S. economic boycott against Iraq, and U.S. support for Israel. Bin Laden and other al Qaeda leaders were in Afghanistan, where the Islamic fundamentalist **Taliban** government allowed them to operate training camps for terrorists.

Bush believed that any government that sponsored terrorism should be held accountable. He demanded that the Taliban turn bin Laden over to U.S. custody. When the Taliban refused, American forces, joined by Great Britain, invaded Afghanistan. Allied forces quickly overthrew the Taliban. Although American troops captured several of al Qaeda's leaders, Osama bin Laden escaped.

Improving National Security Bush moved quickly to prevent future terrorist attacks. Soon after September 11, Congress passed the **Patriot Act** to give law enforcement broader powers to monitor suspected terrorists. Critics claimed that the Patriot Act violated civil liberties. But many Americans were willing to give up some freedoms in return for improved security. Congress also approved Bush's call for the creation of a new Cabinet-level **Department of Homeland Security** to coordinate security matters among federal, state, and local agencies.

Invading Iraq Bush next contemplated invading Iraq as part of his wider war on terrorism. Many people believed that Iraqi president Saddam Hussein was building nuclear, biological, and chemical **Weapons of Mass Destruction (WMD)**.

Despite many Americans' belief that UN weapons inspectors should be allowed to continue their search for Iraqi WMD, Congress authorized Bush to use military force against Iraq. On March 19, 2003, American and British military forces invaded Iraq in Operation Iraqi Freedom. Saddam's forces collapsed almost immediately. As the Iraqi capital of Baghdad fell, Saddam and other Iraqi leaders went into hiding.

> ### HISTORY MAKERS
>
> **Condoleezza Rice** (born 1954)
> Condoleezza Rice grew up in segregated Birmingham, Alabama. At age 15, she entered college to become a concert pianist but graduated at age 19 with a degree in political science instead. By age 30, she had earned a Ph.D., served as an intern in the Carter administration, and held a professorship at Stanford University. In 2000, Rice was tapped by George W. Bush to become National Security Advisor. In 2004, she became the first African American woman to be named Secretary of State. Dr. Rice has taken an active role in the U.S. rebuilding of Iraq.

✓ **Checkpoint** How did Bush combat terrorism?

Bush's Second Term

The Iraq war, terrorism, and the federal budget deficit weighed heavily on Americans' minds as they voted in the 2004 presidential election. Bush campaigned as a "war president," saying he had proved his competency as commander-in-chief. Bush defeated the Democratic candidate for president, Massachusetts senator John Kerry, by a comfortable margin.

War Continues in Iraq Iraq remained a major focus of Bush's second term as the war raged on. However, by late 2005, Iraq had a new constitution and the beginnings of a democracy. The following year, Saddam

---

Connect to Your World

A Position of Power The Secretary of State heads the U.S. Department of State, often referred to as the State Department. The State Department, the first department created under the U.S. Constitution, is responsible for carrying out U.S. foreign policy. There are State Department embassies and consulates around the world. The Secretary of State is fourth in line in the presidential succession.

The main responsibilities of the Secretary of State are to manage diplomatic relations with other nations and to represent the President in negotiations and at important events or ceremonies. The Secretary of State also advises the President on foreign policy and treaty negotiation. President Bill Clinton appointed the first woman Secretary of State, Madeleine Albright, in 1997. His wife, Hillary Rodham Clinton, became Secretary of State in 2009. The first African American Secretary of State, Colin Powell, was appointed by President George W. Bush in 2001.

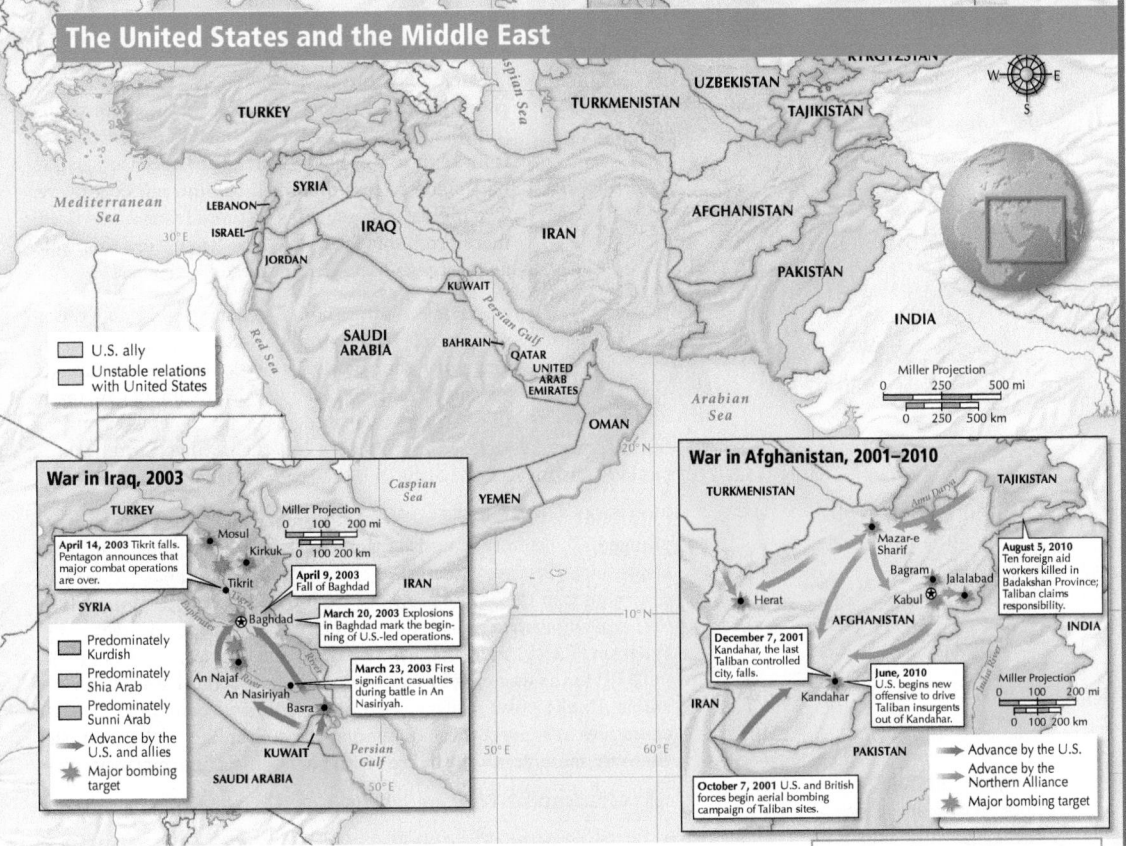

The United States and the Middle East

War in Iraq, 2003

- April 14, 2003 Tikrit falls. Pentagon announces that major combat operations are over.
- April 9, 2003 Fall of Baghdad
- March 20, 2003 Explosions in Baghdad mark the beginning of U.S.-led operations.
- March 23, 2003 First significant casualties during battle in An Nasiriyah.

- Predominately Kurdish
- Predominately Shia Arab
- Predominately Sunni Arab
- Advance by the U.S. and allies
- Major bombing target

War in Afghanistan, 2001–2010

- August 5, 2010 Ten foreign aid workers killed in Badakshan Province; Taliban claims responsibility.
- December 7, 2001 Kandahar, the last Taliban controlled city, falls.
- June, 2010 U.S. begins new offensive to drive Taliban insurgents out of Kandahar.
- October 7, 2001 U.S. and British forces begin aerial bombing campaign of Taliban sites.

- Advance by the U.S.
- Advance by the Northern Alliance
- Major bombing target

U.S. ally
Unstable relations with United States

Hussein was tried, and executed. Saddam's brutal rule had kept fighting in check among Iraq's three major groups: Sunnis, Shi'a, and Kurds. Now these groups fought bitterly for power. An American troop surge in 2007 lessened the violence. However, Iraq's democracy remained fragile.

In 2008, a Senate Intelligence Committee report determined that there was no credible evidence to support claims that Iraq was developing WMD or had ties to terrorist groups. Some accused the Bush administration of deliberately misleading Congress and the American people to win support for the war.

Troubles at Home Meanwhile, Bush faced domestic challenges. In August 2005, Hurricane Katrina hit the Gulf Coast. Katrina caused much destruction in New Orleans. The government's slow response to the damage was widely criticized. National discontent was reflected in the 2006 elections. For the first time in 12 years, Democrats won control of the House and the Senate. Bush's approval ratings fell dramatically during his final two years. The ongoing wars, the threat of terrorist attacks, and the high cost of gasoline were major concerns. Even worse, a serious economic crisis loomed.

✓ **Checkpoint** What challenges did Bush face in his second term?

Map Skills In the early 2000s, the United States waged two wars in the Middle East.

1. **Locate:** (a) Baghdad, (b) Kabul, (c) Pakistan, (d) Syria

2. **Location** Describe the location of Baghdad. What difficulty might a Baghdad-based government have keeping peace?

3. **Draw Inferences** Notice the location of Pakistan. Why is it important to the United States that Pakistan remain a reliable ally?

Geography *Interactive*
For: Interactive map
www.pearsonschool.com/ushist

Independent Practice

- Use the images from the Events That Changed America on page 865 to help students understand the shock to the nation caused by the terrorist attacks of September 11, 2001. Have students search the Internet for more images of that day. Remind them to look for pictures taken at the Pentagon in Virginia and in the field near Shanksville, Pennsylvania, as well as at the World Trade Center site in New York City. Ask students to share their reactions to events by posing questions such as: **What do your family members remember about the events of 9/11? How might this event change people's views of America's role in the world?**

- To further understanding of U.S. responses to the September 11, 2001, attacks, have students access **www.pearsonschool.com/ushist** to use the **Geography Interactive map** and then answer the map skills questions.

Monitor Progress

As students complete their flowcharts, circulate to make sure that they correctly identify and sequence events in Bush's presidency.

Differentiated Instruction — Solutions for All Learners

L1 Special Needs Students   **L2 English Language Learners**   **L2 Less Proficient Readers**

Have students study the map and key. Explain that the inset maps show the same areas in the larger map but in greater detail. Have students match each inset map to its area on the larger map. Ask questions that lead students to study and understand the map, such as the following: **Where did the United States fight first—Iraq or Afghanistan?** *(Afghanistan)* **In which direction did the United States advance in Afghanistan?** *(northeast)* **According**

to the map, **what was achieved by the war in Afghanistan?** *(The Taliban government was ousted.)* **According to the map, what event marked the beginning of U.S.-led operations in Iraq in 2003?** *(the bombing of Baghdad on March 20)* **How many days passed between the fall of Baghdad and the Pentagon's announcement that the major combat operations were over?** *(5 days)*

Answers

Map Skills

1. Review locations with students.

2. Baghdad is located in the center of Iraq. Keeping the peace may be difficult when the government is sandwiched between different ethnic groups competing with one another for control.

3. Pakistan can provide a launching point for U.S. military actions in the Middle East and Central Asia.

✓ the continuing war in Iraq; the damage caused by Hurricane Katrina; a serious economic crisis

Financial Crisis/The 2008 Election

Instruct

- **Introduce** Review the meaning of the term *subprime mortgage*. Explain that people are considered poor credit risks for many reasons, such as having little cash or property, having no credit history, or having a history of missing payments. Ask: **Why would such people be attracted by the chance to get a subprime home loan at high interest?** (*People with a bad credit history might be willing to pay higher rates because they might not get another chance to buy a home.*) **What are the risks of borrowing money you might not be able to repay?** (*If you can't repay the loan, you could lose both your money and your home.*)

- **Teach** Using your chalkboard or white board, help students create a flowchart showing the steps of the 2008 financial crisis. Guide students to consider how unemployment led to foreclosures, which led to the failure of banks and investment firms, and how these failures led to further unemployment. Ask: **What effect did the crisis have on the 2008 election?** (*Unemployment and concern about the economy made voters dissatisfied with the existing Republican leadership.*) Then, ask a volunteer to read aloud the excerpt from Barack Obama's victory rally on this page. Ask volunteers to explain what he meant in their own words.

Independent Practice

Have students write a brief opinion essay for or against the following statement: The economy should be the single most important factor in determining how you vote.

Monitor Progress

As students complete their responses, circulate to make sure they support their responses with logical arguments.

Answer

Caption The unemployment rate more than doubled.

✓ Subprime loans are high-interest loans made to less-qualified borrowers.

Unemployment Rate, 2004–2010

SOURCE: Bureau of Labor Statistics

The Great Recession
Unemployed workers attend a job fair in St. Petersburg, Florida, in 2009. The recession that began in 2007 and the financial crisis that followed led to the country's highest unemployment rate since the Great Depression. *What happened to the unemployment rate between 2007 and 2009?*

Financial Crisis

During the autumn of 2008, Americans faced a potentially disastrous economic crisis centered on the financial industry. The crisis stemmed in part from "subprime" home mortgage loans that banks had made to less-qualified, low-income borrowers. The higher interest rates on these loans made them more profitable for banks. The loans were then sold as mortgage-backed securities to investors.

Recession After the U.S. economy slid into a recession in late 2007, unemployed Americans could no longer pay their mortgages. Foreclosures—seizures of property from borrowers who are unable to repay their loans—increased. As a result, housing prices fell and mortgage-related investments lost their value. Several large banking and investment firms collapsed or were sold.

Financial Industry Bailout In September 2008, the stock market plunged. The country faced its worst economic crisis since the Great Depression. Treasury Secretary Henry Paulson and Federal Reserve chairman Ben Bernanke proposed a $700 billion bailout of the banks that had engaged in risky lending practices. The Troubled Asset Relief Program (TARP) was supported by Bush and approved by Congress.

TARP funds were used to make multibillion-dollar loans to at-risk banks. Public outrage over the taxpayer-funded bailout grew after executives at some of these companies got multimillion-dollar bonuses. However, many credit the bailout with preventing a financial meltdown.

✓ **Checkpoint** What are subprime loans?

The 2008 Election

The 2008 election broke new ground in American politics. Democratic senator **Barack Obama** of Illinois became the first African American to be nominated for president by a major party. Arizona senator John McCain, the Republican nominee for president, chose Governor Sarah Palin of Alaska to be his running mate. Palin was only the second woman to be selected as a vice-presidential nominee. The first, Geraldine Ferraro, ran with Walter Mondale in 1984.

The Candidates John McCain, the son and grandson of navy admirals, served as a pilot in the Vietnam War. He endured six years as a prisoner of war after his plane was shot down. He won election to the House of Representatives in 1982. McCain was elected to the United States Senate in 1986.

A graduate of Columbia University and Harvard Law School, Barack Obama had been a community organizer in Chicago. The son of a white woman from Kansas and a black man from Kenya, Obama served in the Illinois state legislature before being elected to the United States Senate.

A Historic Moment On January 20, 2009, Barack Obama became the 44th U.S. President and the first African American to hold the office. At a huge victory rally in Chicago in November, his words captured the historic moment: "If there is anyone out there who still doubts that America is a place where all things are possible, who still wonders if the dream of our founders is alive in our time, who still questions the power of our democracy, tonight is your answer."

History Background

Women on the Ticket As of the 2008 election, Geraldine Ferraro and Sarah Palin were the only two women ever nominated for Vice President by a major party. Ferraro was nominated as a Democrat. Palin was nominated as a Republican. However, other women had run for President before. Before women could even vote, the Equal Rights Party nominated suffragist Victoria Woodhull for President in 1872. However, her name was not printed on official ballots, and she received few votes. The first woman whose name appeared on an official ballot was Belva Ann Bennett Lockwood, who was nominated by the Equal Rights Party in 1884 and 1888. A noted lawyer, Lockwood was the first woman to argue a case before the Supreme Court. In 1964, Senator Margaret Chase Smith of Maine became the first woman to have her name placed in nomination for President at a major party's convention. Smith lost the Republican nomination to Barry Goldwater.

The election drew a large voter turnout, with 62 percent of voters citing the economy as their main concern. Bush's low approval ratings, combined with McCain's missteps, made a Republican victory seem almost impossible. In Congress, Democrats expanded their majority.

✓ **Checkpoint** Why was the election of 2008 historic?

President Obama Takes Action

Before taking office, President Obama had developed an economic stimulus package to pump money into the sinking economy. The $787 billion bill, the American Recovery and Reinvestment Act, was approved by Congress in February 2009. The stimulus package included tax cuts, aid to state and local governments, and funds for infrastructure projects.

Healthcare Reform In 2008, more than 46 million Americans had no health insurance. During the campaign, Obama had pledged to create a national health plan to provide affordable coverage. He assigned Congress the job of fixing the healthcare system.

In November 2009, the House approved an overhaul of the nation's health care system. The Senate passed its own healthcare bill in December. However, after Democrats lost their filibuster-proof majority in the Senate, healthcare reform was in jeopardy. President Obama campaigned for the bill and won the support of wavering Democrats. In March 2010, in a dramatic vote, the House approved the Senate's healthcare bill. Despite unanimous Republican opposition in the House and Senate, it was the most significant federal healthcare legislation since Medicare was passed in 1965.

The bill extends coverage to the uninsured, prevents insurance companies from denying coverage to patients with pre-existing medical conditions, and provides subsidies to help low-income earners buy insurance. Still, many Americans opposed the new plan. They argued that it cost too much, put too great a burden on small businesses, and gave the federal government too much power.

Iraq and Afghanistan In August 2010, Obama announced, "The American combat mission in Iraq has ended." More than 4,000 Americans had been killed and more than 31,000 wounded during the war. Thanks to the American troop surge, Iraq was significantly more stable, although acts of terrorism continued. About 50,000 American troops remained behind in support roles.

At the same time, Obama increased the American military presence in Afghanistan. American and allied troops had gone into Afghanistan shortly after the 9/11 terrorist attacks, but they had never rid the country of the Taliban forces that had supported Osama bin Laden. Now, Obama asserted, American forces would focus on the Taliban in Afghanistan and their allies in Pakistan.

In May 2011, President Obama announced the death of al Qaeda leader Osama bin Laden. In a secret operation lasting less than an hour, Navy SEALS raided a compound in Pakistan and killed bin Laden, the mastermind behind the 9/11 terrorist attacks. However, Americans knew that the death of bin Laden did not end the threat of terrorism. Intelligence officers examined computer files and other evidence seized at bin Laden's compound in the hopes that it would aid the continuing war on terrorism.

Economic Issues and Reforms America's economic problems continued. Unemployment had risen throughout 2009, peaking at 10.2 percent. Although the economy had stabilized by the spring of 2010, sluggish economic growth and a high unemployment rate left many Americans fearful about the future.

In a decisive victory, Barack Obama became the nation's first African American President.

Assess and Reteach

Assess Progress **L3**

- Have students complete the Section Assessment.

- Administer the Section Quiz. *Teaching Resources*, **p. 28**

- To further assess student understanding, use *Progress Monitoring Transparencies*, **148**.

Reteach

If students need more instruction, have them read the section summary.

Reading and Note Taking Study Guide **L3**

Adapted Reading and Note Taking Study Guide **L1 L2**

Spanish Reading and Note Taking Study Guide **L2**

Extend **L4**

Organize students into discussion groups. Ask them to consider the security measures the United States has taken within its borders since September 11, 2001. Are the measures necessary? Are they enough to prevent future terrorist attacks? How does the issue of privacy during a state of emergency or war figure into this discussion?

Answer

 The goal of the plan was to provide affordable coverage for uninsured Americans.

Environmental Disaster

When this oil rig exploded in the Gulf of Mexico in April 2010, it killed eleven people and caused an environmental disaster. For three months, an estimated 172 million gallons of crude oil spilled into the Gulf, killing wildlife and destroying natural habitats. The oil spill also hurt the seafood and tourism industries in Louisiana, Alabama, and Florida.

In July 2010, Obama signed into law a sweeping financial reform bill aimed at changing the Wall Street practices that contributed to the 2008 financial crisis. The new law increased federal oversight of banks, hedge funds, and other financial institutions. It also created a consumer protection agency to oversee credit card rates, bank fees, mortgages, and car loans.

Critics argued that the 2,300-page bill was too complex and too confusing to yield significant results. They said it would tighten credit and lead to further economic woes.

The 2010 Elections As the 2010 congressional elections approached, the nation seemed increasingly divided. While many Americans supported President Obama, others were angered by his actions. The strongest challenge came from the **Tea Party Movement** which emerged during Obama's first year in office. The movement took its name from the Boston Tea Party, a colonial protest against British taxes. The Tea Party Movement was made up of many local groups, united by a common desire to reduce the size and scope of the federal government.

Although they ran as Republicans, they were not traditional party candidates. They criticized Republicans as big spenders and urged a phase-out of programs such as Social Security and Medicare. In the 2010 elections, more than 40 candidates endorsed by the Tea Party were elected to the House and Senate.

Republicans won back control of the House of Representatives in the 2010 midterm elections. Leaders of the new Republican-controlled House announced that their first priority would be to repeal Obama's healthcare bill. Meanwhile, in the final months of 2010, Congress passed a number of important measures, including extensions of the Bush tax cuts and an arms-control treaty with Russia.

✔ **Checkpoint** What was the goal of Obama's healthcare reform bill?

SECTION 4 Assessment

Progress Monitoring Online
For: Self-test with vocabulary practice
www.pearsonschool.com/ushist

Comprehension

1. Terms and People Using complete sentences, relate each of the following items to the presidency of George W. Bush or Barack Obama.
- No Child Left Behind Act
- Taliban
- Patriot Act
- Department of Homeland Security
- WMD
- Tea Party Movement

2. NoteTaking Reading Skill: Recognize Sequence Use your completed flowchart to answer the Section Focus Question: What was the impact of the terrorist attack against the United States and of the 2008 financial crisis?

Writing About History

3. Quick Write: Provide Details Choose an American issue that has relevance both to the Bush presidency and to an earlier period of American history. Analyze the issue in both time periods, including details that define the issue and support your points.

Critical Thinking

4. Compare Points of View Compare how Democrats and Republicans viewed the initial results of the 2000 election.

5. Analyzing Effects Why do you think the economic crisis in the United States in 2008 had a global effect? Explain.

6. Identify Assumptions What assumptions about the United States were conveyed in Bush's speech to the nation on September 11?

7. Apply Information How did Americans disagree about the role of the federal government under Obama? Give two examples of policies that caused disagreement.

Section 4 Assessment

1. Sentences should reflect an understanding of how each term relates to the presidency of George W. Bush or Barack Obama.

2. When terrorists attacked the United States, Bush immediately invaded Afghanistan to attempt to locate bin Laden; Bush later ordered the invasion of Iraq. The financial crisis increased unemployment; the government spent billions of dollars on bailouts and economic stimulus programs.

3. Students should select an appropriate issue and define the issue in two time periods, using relevant supporting details.

4. Because of the extremely close results, Democrats wanted a recount. Republicans, satisfied that they had won with a narrow margin, did not want a recount.

5. Globalization has unified the people of the world. With financial and economic markets globally dependent, the economic crisis of the United States soon affected the stock markets and financial stability of other countries. Some would say that is one of the negative effects of globalization.

6. that the United States is strong, is unified, and can overcome adversity

7. Some Americans felt that large programs such as the economic stimulus package and healthcare reform were necessary. Others, such as the Tea Party Movement, thought they were too costly and gave the federal government too much power over people's lives.

For additional assessment, have students access **Progress Monitoring Online** at **www.pearsonschool.com/ushist.**

WITNESS HISTORY

Finding the American Dream

In 1990, Eddie (Duc) and Linda (Lieu) Tran left Vietnam with their young son to start over in Columbus, Ohio. Sponsored by Linda's brother, who had fled Vietnam by boat during the fall of Saigon in 1975, the Trans were aware of the obstacles that faced them in their new country.

❝Learning the English language and finding jobs were our biggest challenges. We listened to the radio and tried to converse as much as possible with our co-workers to learn English. Everyone was helpful. And we were determined never to receive welfare. Linda got a job as a tailor ten days after we arrived. I owned a manufacturing business in Vietnam, but it took me six months to get employed here. Times were hard, and we still work 12-hour days in our restaurant now. But the best thing about this country is freedom. If you work hard, you can achieve the American dream.❞

—Eddie and Linda Tran, 2005

▲ The Trans today (above) with their sons and at their wedding in Vietnam (left).

Americans Look to the Future

Objectives
- Analyze the impact of immigration on American society.
- Summarize the causes and effects of changing demographics.

Terms and People

Immigration Act of 1990
bilingual education
Immigration and Control Act of 1986
affirmative action
Violence Against Women Act
privatize

NoteTaking

Reading Skill: Identify Supporting Details
Record supporting details about the changing American society in a table like this one.

A Changing Society	
Immigration	**Demographics**
• Immigration policies relax •	• Family structures change •

Why It Matters As the twenty-first century dawned, American society looked very different from the way it had during the previous century. It also faced different challenges. As the nation entered the new millennium, it sought ways to preserve its heritage while at the same time adapting to rapid social, political, and technological change. **Section Focus Question: How was American society changing at the beginning of the twenty-first century?**

Immigrants Shape a Nation

For two centuries, American protection of religious and personal freedom, along with opportunities for social and economic mobility, has attracted huge numbers of immigrants. Over time, however, the nature of immigration has changed.

Immigration Policies Change For years, the government limited immigration to mainly northern and western Europeans. In the 1960s, however, laws began to relax immigration limitations. The **Immigration Act of 1990** increased quotas by 40 percent and eased most remaining restrictions. As a result, the period from the 1990s to the 2000s saw the largest numbers of immigrants in the country's history. During that time, almost one million immigrants arrived in America each year from all over the globe, representing a wide variety of cultures and religions. Today, immigrants account for more than 10 percent of the total American population.

Vocabulary Builder

Use the information below and the following resource to teach students the high-use word from this section. Teaching Resources, Vocabulary Builder, p. 11

High-Use Word	Definition and Sample Sentence
discrimination	*n.* unfair bias in the treatment of a particular group Sometimes, newcomers to the United States must overcome **discrimination** to find jobs and housing.

Objectives

As you teach this section, keep students focused on the following objectives to help them answer the Section Focus Question and master core content.

- Analyze the impact of immigration on American society.
- Summarize the causes and effects of changing demographics.

Prepare to Read

Background Knowledge

Remind students that the terrorist attacks of 2001 shifted Bush's focus to foreign policy, while changes were occurring at home. Ask students to suggest some of the issues that began to surface in the twenty-first century.

Set a Purpose

- **WITNESS HISTORY** Read the selection aloud.

  Ask **What challenges did the Trans face when they arrived?** *(the language barrier, a lack of employment for Eddie)* **What does Eddie Tran say is the key to achieving the American dream?** *(hard work)*

- **Focus** Point out the Section Focus Question, and write it on the board. Tell students to refer to this question as they read. *(Answer appears with Section 5 Assessment answers.)*

- **Preview** Have students preview the Section Objectives and the list of Terms.

- **NoteTaking** Using the Structured Read Aloud strategy (TE, p. T20), have students read this section. As they read, have students record supporting details about the changing American society. Reading and Note Taking Study Guide

Immigrants Shape a Nation L3

Instruct

- **Introduce: Key Term** Write the key term *bilingual education* on the board. Explain that there is an ongoing debate in the United States regarding *bilingual education.* Some people believe that schools should teach in only the English language. Others believe that immigrants must be taught, at least initially, in their native language as well as in English. Have students offer their opinions in an informal classroom debate on the issue.

- **Teach** Ask **Why was there an increase in immigration to the United States in the 1990s?** *(The Immigration Act of 1990 increased immigration quotas.)* Ask **What is cultural assimilation?** *(A process of consistent integration in which a minority group is absorbed into a larger group. This presumes a loss of some or all of the characteristics that make the newcomers different.)*

- **Analyzing the Visuals** Have students work in pairs and examine the circle graphs on this page. One student should present a "mini-lesson" to the other, explaining one of the graphs, and then the second student should present a similar lesson on the other graph.

Independent Practice

Have students write a few paragraphs about the changes in U.S. immigration as they relate either to Latinos or Asians.

Monitor Progress

As students fill in the table for this section, circulate to make sure that they understand the concepts. For a completed version of the details chart, see Note Taking Transparencies, **B-153**.

Answers

Graph Skills The recent influx of immigrants, mainly Hispanics from the Americas, supports the population graph, which shows Hispanics as the largest group.

✔ The Immigration Act of 1990 allowed many more immigrants into the nation than ever before. Also, most of the new immigrants were now Latinos or Asians.

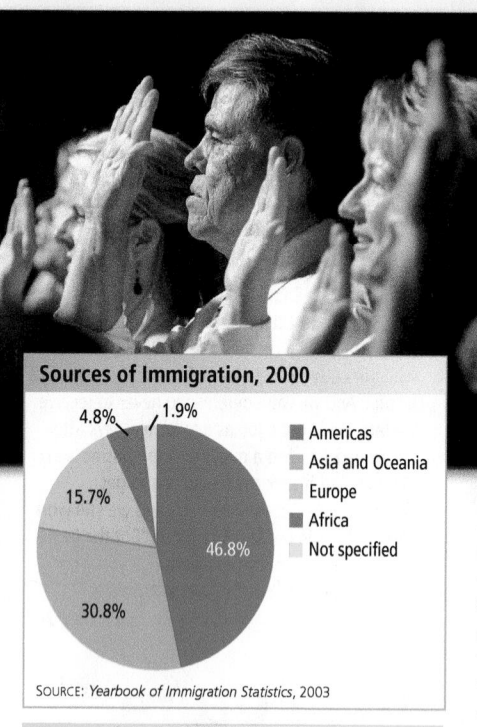

Sources of Immigration, 2000

- Americas — 46.8%
- Asia and Oceania — 30.8%
- Europe — 15.7%
- Africa — 4.8%
- Not specified — 1.9%

SOURCE: *Yearbook of Immigration Statistics,* 2003

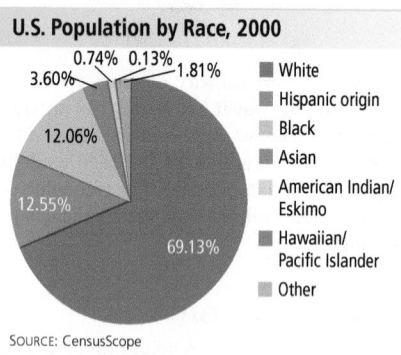

U.S. Population by Race, 2000

- White — 69.13%
- Hispanic origin — 12.55%
- Black — 12.06%
- Asian — 3.60%
- American Indian/ Eskimo — 0.74%
- Hawaiian/ Pacific Islander — 0.13%
- Other — 1.81%

SOURCE: CensusScope

Graph Skills Every year, people from all backgrounds are sworn in as U.S. citizens. Study the two pie charts. What was the largest minority group in 2000? How does the Sources of Immigration graph support the data in the U.S. Population by Race graph?

Latinos Exert Their Influence Most of the new immigrants were Latinos. In 2000, 27 percent of the total immigrant population were Mexicans, with people from the Caribbean and Central America making up almost 17 percent. Mexicans and Central Americans settled largely in the South and Southwest. Caribbean immigrants, many of them Cubans, settled in Florida. The census of 2000 showed that a third or more of the residents of Texas, New Mexico, Arizona, and California were Latinos.

Like all immigrants, Latinos have varying educational and employment backgrounds. Often they are forced to take lower-paying jobs with no healthcare benefits. However, Latino immigrants have had a profound social, cultural, and political impact. By 2001, Latinos held about 5,000 political offices and 4 percent of the seats in Congress, primarily as Democrats. Cuban Americans in Florida, generally Republican, have had an enormous influence on American political policy concerning Cuba.

A Surging Asian Population Asians make up the second-largest source of the new immigration. In 2000, they were nearly 23 percent of the total immigrant population, with the largest numbers coming from China, the Philippines, and India. The majority of Asian immigrants have settled in California, adding to the large Asian population in that state. As a group, Asian immigrants have had widely varying backgrounds, but overall they have the highest level of education. Some came to America with college degrees and marketable skills and found professional jobs. Others came from war-torn countries, with very little education.

Debating Immigration Immigration has long been debated in this country. People who would restrict it worry that immigrants take jobs and social services away from native-born Americans. They generally oppose **bilingual education,** in which students are taught in their native languages as well as in English, saying that immigrants must learn English in order to assimilate into American society. Proponents point out that immigrants contribute to the economy, often by taking jobs no one else wants. They also argue that with the U.S. birthrate falling, immigrants help the country by maintaining its population.

Much of the debate concerns illegal immigrants. A large number of immigrants to the United States, especially Latinos, have come illegally. They labor in low-paying jobs, such as migrant farmwork, and receive no benefits. The goal of the **Immigration Reform and Control Act of 1986** was to stop the flow of illegal immigrants by penalizing employers who hired them and by granting resident status to those living in the United States since 1982. But illegal immigrants still regularly cross U.S. borders. How to treat these illegal—but often necessary—workers is an ongoing debate. In 2008, the Bush administration proposed changes that would make it easier for farm employers to legally hire immigrant workers. He also proposed a process by which illegal immigrants could eventually gain citizenship.

✔ **Checkpoint** How has immigration to America changed over time?

Connect to Your World

Religious Pluralism in the United States
Pluralism is a condition in which numerous distinct ethnic, religious, and/or cultural groups coexist within a society. Asian, Middle Eastern, and Latin American countries have led the rest of the world in immigration to the United States since 1981, increasing religious diversity in the United States.

Although Muslims make up only about .5 percent of the total U.S. population, their number increased from about 500,000 in 1990 to more than 1,100,000 in 2001. The number of people who identified themselves as Hindus almost tripled in the same amount of time.

California, which in 2003 led the country in immigration, stands as a benchmark for religious pluralism in the United States. According to some reports, almost half of all Muslims living in the United States call California home. Also, California is home to about 40 percent of all Buddhists in the country. In 2004, California had more than 100 religious centers for each of the following faiths: Hinduism, Islam, and Buddhism.

Changing American Demographics

At the beginning of 2000, Americans were on the move more than ever. Coastal cities as well as the Sunbelt, or the region of warm southern and southwestern states, saw rapid population and economic growth as people left the cold Northeast and the Rust Belt. Meanwhile, the family itself was changing.

The Changing Family In 1960, more than 70 percent of American households were headed by a working father and a nonworking mother, neither of whom had ever been divorced. By 2000, fewer than 15 percent of households fit this model. In 2000, one out of every two marriages ended in divorce, and in a high percentage of households both parents worked outside the home. Single-parent households were far more common, with a quarter of all children growing up in a single-parent household. The number of children born to unmarried mothers also rose. In 1960, only 5 percent of children were born out of wedlock. In 2000, one out of every four white babies, one out of every three Latino babies, and two out of every three African American babies were born to unmarried mothers.

Debating Affirmative Action In the 1960s, President Johnson introduced the idea of **affirmative action,** or improving opportunities for women and minorities by giving preference to them in school admissions and job applications. Since that time, affirmative action has been hotly debated. Proponents argue that without such initiatives, minorities cannot overcome generations of discrimination. Opponents say that the policy is unfair and discriminates against nonminorities. In 1996, Californians voted to end affirmative action in state hiring and education. That same year, a federal court struck down an affirmative action admissions program at the University of Texas. In 2003, however, the Supreme Court decided in two cases involving the University of Michigan that while race could not be the deciding factor in admissions, it could be one of several factors.

Expanding Rights for All At the turn of the new century, African Americans and women continued to make social and political gains. By 2002, 33 percent of African American families enjoyed incomes of at least $50,000, placing them in the middle class. Also in 2002, 17 percent of African Americans over the age of 25 held bachelor's degrees. At the same time, legislation to enforce equal pay for equal work, address child care needs for working women, and end sexual harassment in the workplace has improved the lives of working women. Outside of the world of work, women have also achieved victories. Issues such as spouse abuse and date rape are now widely discussed. Incidents of violence against women are more often reported and more often punished than ever before.

Vocabulary Builder
discrimination–(dih skrihm ih NAY shuhn) *n.* unfair bias in the treatment of a particular group

Graph Skills While the income gap is slowly narrowing, wages among ethnic groups still vary widely. Study the graph. Which group enjoyed the highest income in the period shown? What might explain this?

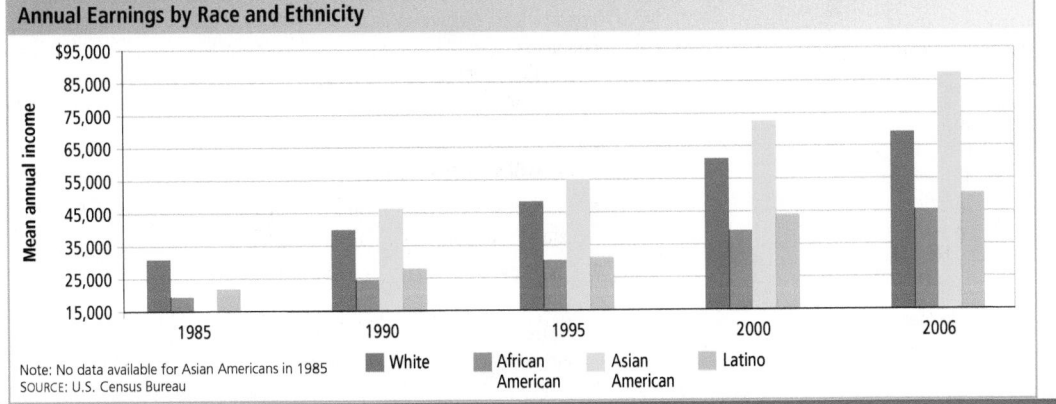

Annual Earnings by Race and Ethnicity

Mean annual income (in dollars): $95,000, 85,000, 75,000, 65,000, 55,000, 45,000, 35,000, 25,000, 15,000

Years: 1985, 1990, 1995, 2000, 2006

■ White ■ African American ■ Asian American ■ Latino

Note: No data available for Asian Americans in 1985
SOURCE: U.S. Census Bureau

Instruct

- **Introduce: Vocabulary Builder** Have students locate the vocabulary term *discrimination* (in bold) in the text. Have students read to find out how people can claim that affirmative action both ends and initiates *discrimination.*

- **Teach** Using the Idea Wave strategy (TE, p. T22), have students describe twenty-first century demographic changes. Ask **How have families changed?** *(More children are being raised by a single parent; in two-parent households, more mothers and fathers work outside the home than previously; more babies are born out of wedlock.)* **How have these changes affected society?** *(Children need childcare both before and after they reach school age. Welfare provides help for struggling parents. Schools are often expected to take on parental roles.)*

Independent Practice

- Refer students to the graph on this page. Have them study the graph and write two questions and answers about it.

- Have students read the HISTORY MAKERS feature at the end of this section. Ask students to identify the qualities that would make Sonia Sotomayor a good Supreme Court justice.

Monitor Progress

Circulate to make sure that students are correctly identifying the main ideas under each blue heading as they fill in their Note Taking table.

Differentiated Instruction   Solutions for All Learners

Special Needs Students
English Language Learners

Have students conduct research to create a line graph that shows changes in life expectancy for men and women in the United States between 1900 and 2000. Ask students to write a summary that explains the data in their graphs.

Advanced Readers
Gifted and Talented Students

Discuss the term *demographics* with students. Organize students in pairs or small groups. Have each group construct a concept map of information about the changes in American demographics since 1990. Students should begin by determining the main idea(s) of each subsection and use the main ideas to complete the concept map.

Answer

Graph Skills Asian workers; overall, Asian immigrants have high levels of education, so they are able to obtain higher-paying jobs.

Objectives

- Understand the historical and modern changes in the goals and approaches of American education.
- Understand differences in opinion regarding the current trend of evaluating student performance through standardized testing.

Background Knowledge (L3)

Ask students to offer some of their goals for their own high school education. Explore with students how standardized tests may or may not help determine if they are meeting their goals.

Instruct (L3)

- Draw students' attention to the timeline. Ask **How has the goal of American education changed over time?** *(American education once focused on religion-based education. Beginning in the 1920s, there was a shift toward measuring performance through standardized tests.)* Have students debate the benefits and disadvantages of standardized testing.

Monitor Progress

- Have students complete the American Issues Journal Worksheet, *Education and American Society.* Check students' work to make sure that they grasp the aspects of the issue. **Teaching Resources, pp. 15–18**

- Remind students to complete their American Issues Journal notes. Review their work for accuracy. **Reading and Note Taking Study Guide**

Answers

Transfer Activities

1. Bizar believes that standardized tests do not accurately evaluate student knowledge. Lemann believes that schools need some way to measure performance.

2. Sample answer: Yes; students will become better test-takers with practice.

3. Students' arguments should present a single distinct viewpoint and support it with logical reasoning and facts. For more information, have students access **www.pearsonschool.com/ushist**.

TRACK THE ISSUE

What should be the goals of American education?

Over time, the purpose of American education has changed. From an early focus on religion, schools turned to the promotion of democratic values. Today, they are placing a strong emphasis on performance standards. Use the timeline below to explore this enduring issue.

1600s–1700s Colonial Education
Schools emphasize religious study.

1852 Public Schools
Massachusetts passes first compulsory school attendance law in the United States.

1903 Du Bois-Washington Debate
Scholars debate the role of education in improving African Americans' lives.

1926 Scholastic Aptitude Test
The Scholastic Aptitude Test (SAT) is first administered.

2001 No Child Left Behind Act
Federal law tries to raise student performance through standardized testing and other measures.

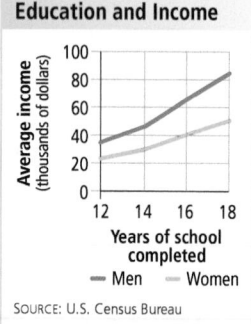

Education and Income

Average income (thousands of dollars) vs. Years of school completed (12, 14, 16, 18)

— Men — Women

SOURCE: U.S. Census Bureau

Students taking a standardized test

DEBATE THE ISSUE

Standardized Testing Standardized tests are used both to assess students and to hold teachers accountable for meeting standards. But critics argue that an emphasis on testing is hurting American schools.

"We have learned a great deal about the nature of teaching and learning, and we know that students need to have opportunities to construct knowledge and connect that knowledge to what they already know. However, many . . . [standardized tests] still continue to focus on the memory of isolated facts which are destined to be forgotten."

—Marilyn Bizar, North Central Regional Educational Laboratory

"You can't figure out whether schools are doing a good job unless you have some way of measuring how much their students are learning. . . . A guarantee by the national government of a decent education for every child is a noble cause, and so is the idea that all Americans will acquire a common body of skills and knowledge as they come of age."

—Nicholas Lemann, writer, *The New Yorker*

? TRANSFER Activities

1. **Compare** Why does Bizar oppose standardized testing? Why does Lemann support standardized testing?

2. **Analyze** Do you think that the increase in standardized testing will cause students' achievement scores to rise? Explain.

3. **Transfer** Use the following Web site to see a video, try a WebQuest, and write in your journal. www.pearsonschool.com/ushist

History Background

The Origins of Standardized Testing In the United States, the first documented achievement tests were administered in the mid-nineteenth century as public education became more widespread. In addition, large immigrant populations led American education reformers to turn to such tests as a way to ensure that all children received the same standard of education. In 1904, under the direction of the French government, French psychologist Alfred Binet developed the first IQ, or intelligence quotient, test for school children. His test was brought to the United States by a Stanford University psychologist named Lewis Terman. Terman then created the Stanford-Binet Test, which, with many revisions, is still in use today. During World War I, the U.S. Army tested recruits with the Army Alpha test, the first mass-administered, standardized IQ test. In the late 1920s, one of the administrators of this test, Carl Brigham of Princeton University, went on to develop the SAT, or Scholastic Aptitude Test, which for years has helped colleges and universities make admission decisions.

The 1994 **Violence Against Women Act** increased federal resources to apprehend and prosecute men guilty of violent acts against women.

America Grows Older While the life expectancy of an American born in 1900 was less than 50 years, an American born in 2000 can expect to live to age 77. By 2000, older Americans tended to retire earlier, live longer, and exert more political influence. These factors have strained the country's social welfare system, especially Social Security and Medicare. In 1960, the federal government spent less than $100 billion on social welfare. By 2003, the amount had increased to $1.4 trillion.

With the large baby-boom generation reaching retirement age, the issue of elder care has become critical. Falling birthrates over the past two decades have meant that when the huge population of baby boomers retires, there will not be enough workers to cover their Social Security benefits. Politicians have been debating how to deal with this impending reality. In his second term, President Bush called for **privatizing** Social Security by allowing younger workers to invest some of their earnings in individual retirement accounts. Critics defeated the measure, saying that it would put younger workers at the mercy of fluctuating stock market returns without addressing the shortfall of funds. As Americans get older, the debate continues.

Facing the Future As the new millennium began, Americans looked back at a century of great change and technological progress. Looking forward, immense challenges remain. Americans still struggle with basic problems with which societies throughout history have struggled, as well as some new problems unique to the time. Yet with its greatest resource—the American people—the United States faces this new century with strength and optimism.

✓ **Checkpoint** What challenges have changing American demographics brought?

HISTORY MAKERS

Sonia Sotomayor (born 1954)
When President Obama nominated Sonia Sotomayor to the Supreme Court, he said she would bring more "varied experience on the bench than anyone currently serving on the United States Supreme Court had when they were appointed." The daughter of Puerto Rican parents, Sotomayor grew up in a public housing project in the Bronx. Despite a childhood diagnosis of diabetes and the death of her father when she was nine, Sotomayor earned scholarships to Princeton and Yale Law School. She began her career as an assistant district attorney in New York City. After serving as a federal judge, Sotomayor became a judge on the Court of Appeals for the Second Circuit in New York. During her confirmation hearings, Sotomayor described her philosophy of judging as "applying the law to the facts at hand." Confirmed in August 2009, Sotomayor is the first Latina to serve as a Supreme Court justice.

Progress Monitoring *Online*
For: Self-test with vocabulary practice
www.pearsonschool.com/ushist

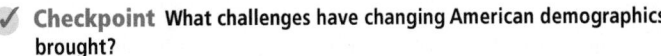

SECTION **5 Assessment**

Comprehension

1. Terms and People For each term below, write a sentence explaining its significance to American society in the twenty-first century.
- Immigration Act of 1990
- bilingual education
- Immigration and Control Act of 1986
- affirmative action
- Violence Against Women Act
- privatize

2. NoteTaking Reading Skill: Identify Supporting Details Use your completed table to answer the Section Focus Question: How was American society changing at the beginning of the twenty-first century?

Writing About History

3. Quick Write: List Details You are writing an essay that analyzes the American issue of education and American society. List details from this section that support your analysis.

Critical Thinking

4. Draw Inferences How can a nation's immigration policies affect its economy?

5. Identify Central Issues Why is an aging population a problem for a society?

Section 5 Assessment

1. Sentences should reflect an understanding of how each term relates to changes in American society in the twenty-first century.

2. More immigrants from around the world came to the United States. American families changed as more parents divorced, more women worked, and more babies were born out of wedlock. In addition, the population was aging.

3. Listed details should support a logical analysis of education and American society.

4. When immigrants enter a country, legally or illegally, they affect the economy in several ways. They compete for and fill jobs, spend money, and require social and other services.

5. An aging population requires support and financial assistance from its younger members who are still able to earn income. When there are more elderly people than working-age people, this puts a huge burden on the younger generation.

Quick Study Guide

- Have students use the Quick Study Guide to prepare for the chapter test. Students may wish to refer to the following sections as they review:

World Trade Organization Members and Observers
Section 3

Major Events in the Clinton and Bush Presidencies
Section 2
Section 3
Section 4

Major Issues of American Society in the New Millennium
Section 1
Section 3
Section 4
Section 5

U.S. Response to September 11
Section 4

Key Events in Contemporary America
Section 1
Section 2
Section 3
Section 4
Section 5

- For additional review, remind students to refer to the Reading and Note Taking Study Guide
Section Note Taking
Section Summaries

- Have students access **www.pearsonschool.com/ushist** for this chapter's History Interactive timeline, which includes expanded entries and additional events.

- If students need more instruction on analyzing graphic data, have them read the Skills Handbook, p. SH21.

For **Progress Monitoring Online,** refer students to the Self-test with vocabulary practice at **www.pearsonschool.com/ushist.**

Quick Study Guide

Progress Monitoring Online
For: Self-test with vocabulary practice
www.pearsonschool.com/ushist

■ World Trade Organization Members and Observers

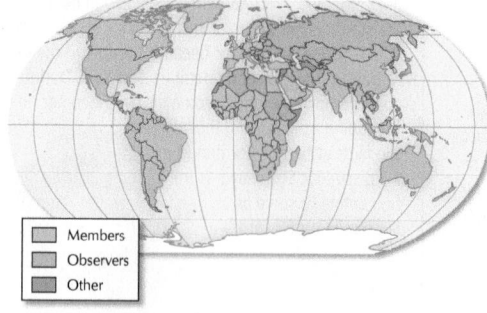

- Members
- Observers
- Other

■ Major Events in the Clinton and Bush Presidencies

President	Event
Clinton	**1992** Signed NAFTA; sent forces into Somalia
	1993 Signed Brady Bill; helped negotiate Declaration of Principles
	1994 Sent troops to Haiti
	1995 Sent forces into Bosnia as part of NATO
	1996 Signed bill to reform welfare
	1999 Impeached; cleared of charges
Bush	**2001** Pushed for major tax cuts; sent troops to war in Afghanistan; signed Patriot Act
	2002 Signed No Child Left Behind Act
	2003 Sent troops to war in Iraq
	2004 Bush reelected

✓ Quick Study Timeline

In America

1992	1994	1996	1998
Bill Clinton is elected President	**Republicans win control of Congress**	**Congress passes Welfare Reform Act**	**President Clinton is impeached**

Presidential Terms George H. W. Bush 1989–1993   William J. Clinton 1993–2001

1992	1994	1996	1998

Around the World

1993	1994	1995	1998
European Union forms	**Mandela is elected President of South Africa**	**NATO forces restore order in Bosnia; WTO is established**	**Indonesian dictator Suharto steps down**

■ Major Issues of American Society in the New Millennium

Technology—Computers, satellites, and advances in agriculture raise productivity and efficiency, but challenge many workers and industries.

Globalization—Globalization brings consumers more choices and opportunities, but can result in the loss of American jobs.

Terrorism—After September 11, government must work to make America more secure.

Immigration—Immigrants continue to enrich American society and fuel its economy, but their increasing numbers spark debate.

Demographics—Federal and local governments must find ways to support older Americans, Americans on the move, and nontraditional families.

Differentiated Instruction Solutions for All Learners

L1 Special Needs Students **L2 English Language Learners** **L2 Less Proficient Readers**

Use the following study guide resources to help students acquiring basic skills:
Adapted Reading and Note Taking Study Guide
- Section Note Taking
- Section Summaries

Use the following study guide resources to help Spanish-speaking students:
Spanish Reading and Note Taking Study Guide
- Section Note Taking
- Section Summaries

American Issues
•—•—•—• Connector

By connecting prior knowledge with what you have learned in this chapter, you can gradually build your understanding of enduring questions that still affect America today. Answer the questions below. Then, use your American Issues Connector study guide (or go online: www.pearsonschool.com/ushist).

Issues You Learned About

● **Education and American Society** American leaders continually try to find new ways to improve the quality of the American education system.

1. Name and describe an educational reform in the United States that you have already learned about.

2. Why do you think the No Child Left Behind Act attracted the support of both Republicans and Democrats?

3. As part of the No Child Left Behind Act, schools must demonstrate success in order to receive federal funding. What are some ways that schools can demonstrate success?

● **Technology and Society** The development of the modern computer has changed the way people live, work, and play.

4. Prior to the computer, what do you think was the most important technological development, and why?

5. What spurred the development of the modern computer?

6. What are some ways that you use personal computers?

● **Global Interdependence** The United States economy depends on trade with countries around the world.

7. What are some of the issues that have caused a debate in the United States over free trade?

8. Why was Clinton's support of NAFTA controversial?

9. What are some of the benefits and drawbacks of globalization?

Connect to Your World	Activity

Politics and Presidential Polls A President's approval can vary over the years. Go online or to the local library to find out the approval rating of the current President. Look for statistics that relate to the current period as well as the President's past tenure in office. Once you have compiled your figures, continue your research to learn more about the events that may have led to changing approval levels. Finally, create a chart that shows your results and write a paragraph or two explaining your analysis of these results.

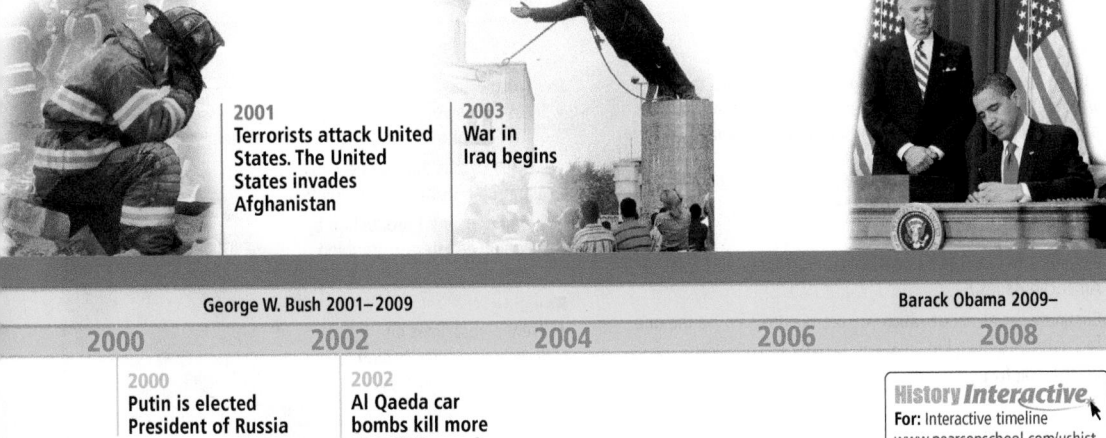

2001 Terrorists attack United States. The United States invades Afghanistan

2003 War in Iraq begins

George W. Bush 2001–2009

Barack Obama 2009–

2000   2002   2004   2006   2008

2000 Putin is elected President of Russia

2002 Al Qaeda car bombs kill more than 200 people in Indonesia

History Interactive
For: Interactive timeline
www.pearsonschool.com/ushist

Differentiated Instruction   Solutions for All Learners

L1 Special Needs Students   **L2 English Language Learners**   **L2 Less Proficient Readers**

Use the following study guide resource to help students acquiring basic skills:
Adapted Reading and Note Taking Study Guide
• American Issues Journal

Use the following study guide resource to help Spanish-speaking students:
Spanish Reading and Note Taking Study Guide
• American Issues Journal

American Issues
——•—• Connector

Tell students that the main issues for this chapter are Education and American Society, Technology and Society, and Global Interdependence. Then, ask them to answer the Issues You Learned About questions on this page. Discuss the Connect to Your World topics, and ask students to complete the project that follows.

American Issues Connector

1. Sample answer: educating boys and girls in the same ways

2. Both parties believed in reforming education to provide for accountability and to ensure that all children learn certain information.

3. Students achieve a certain score on a standardized test; teachers receive a certain amount of training.

4. Possible response: Television; People could learn about and actually watch world events faster than ever before.

5. warfare

6. Possible answer: to do research, to communicate, to shop

7. Sample responses: loss of American jobs, especially in industry; increased environmental pollution caused by the growth of businesses into nations with fewer environmental controls

8. Supporters said that NAFTA would promote economic growth and encourage economic investment. Opponents argued that it would force American manufacturers to relocate to Mexico, where wages were lower.

9. Benefits: lower costs of products and an increase in exports; stronger economic ties; Drawbacks: loss of American jobs; lessened political power for national governments as opposed to international organizations and corporations

Connect to Your World

Students' paragraphs and charts should reflect sound research and a clear understanding of a President's approval rating.

For additional review of this chapter's enduring issues, remind students to refer to the Reading and Note Taking Study Guide American Issues Journal.

Terms and People

1. Mechanical devices orbiting Earth; they relay information to televisions, telephones, and computers.

2. former member of Congress who led the opposition during Clinton's presidency; authored the Contract With America

3. the removal or killing of one ethnic or religious group by another in the same area; used in the Balkans by the Serbs

4. legislation that allowed law enforcement broader powers to monitor suspected terrorists and their activities; the terrorist attacks on September 11, 2001

5. The education of English Language Learners in both English and their native languages; some people believe that the main language of the United States is English and that bilingual education impedes immigrants from learning English.

Focus Questions

6. The U.S. economy has become a service-based system with the advancement of satellites and the Internet and the development of free trade and globalization.

7. Clinton successfully passed the Family Medical Leave Act and anti-crime laws. However, he failed to institute healthcare reform, and his presidency was plagued by scandal.

8. Economically, the U.S. took the lead in globalization and free trade; politically, the U.S. intervened for purposes of peacekeeping and humanitarian relief.

9. Bush passed a tax cut and education and Medicare reform. The acts were met with controversy, and results have been mixed. Following the September 11, 2001, terrorist attack, Bush invaded Afghanistan to seek Osama bin Laden and to punish the Taliban, who were protecting bin Laden. Then, he attacked Iraq. Bush also established the Department of Homeland Security and worked for passage of the Patriot Act.

10. There had been a huge influx of immigrants in the 1990s; the

Chapter Assessment

Terms and People

1. Define **satellite.** What role does satellite technology play in everyday life?

2. Who is **Newt Gingrich**? What were some of his specific proposals during the Clinton presidency?

3. Define **ethnic cleansing.** Where was it used, and by whom?

4. What was the **Patriot Act**? What caused Congress to pass this legislation?

5. What is **bilingual education**? Why are some people opposed to it?

Focus Questions

The focus question for this chapter is **What political, social, technological, and economic trends have shaped American life since 1990?** Build an answer to this question by answering the focus questions for Sections 1 through 5 and the Critical Thinking questions that follow.

Section 1
6. How have technological changes and globalization transformed the American economy?

Section 2
7. What were the successes and failures of the Clinton presidency?

Section 3
8. What role did the United States take on in global politics and economics following the Cold War?

Section 4
9. What was the impact of the terrorist attack against the United States and of the 2008 financial crisis?

Section 5
10. How was American society changing at the beginning of the twenty-first century?

Writing About History

Writing for Assessment As Americans head into the new millennium, many of the major issues that have been part of American history for over two centuries remain relevant. Write an essay that traces an important American issue over time. Explain why it became an American issue and how its relevance has changed or remained the same over time.

Prewriting
• Go online to www.pearsonschool.com/ushist to find a list of American issues.

• Eliminate issues about which you are unsure. Choose the one for which you have the most background information or ideas.

• Identify the focus of your essay by forming a main idea.

Critical Thinking

11. **Identify Central Issues** How did the rise of the service sector benefit some Americans and harm others?

12. **Draw Inferences** In the 1988 presidential election, 57.4 percent of Americans voted; in 1992, 61.3 percent voted, and in 1996, 54.2 percent voted. What may have contributed to the 1992 spike in voter participation?

13. **Analyze Evidence** In 1996, during his reelection campaign, Clinton announced, "The era of big government is over." Cite evidence supporting or refuting this statement.

14. **Synthesize Information** What foreign policy did the United States adopt in the post Cold War world?

15. **Determine Relevance** How helpful was the Declaration of Principles in resolving problems in the Middle East?

16. **Analyze Visuals** Study the visual below. What event are these newspaper headlines describing?

17. **Analyze Information** Did Operation Iraqi Freedom succeed at improving the lives of the Iraqi people?

18. **Explain Causes** Why was affirmative action first introduced in the United States?

Drafting
• Sketch out an organizational plan for your essay. Consider using an outline or other graphic organizer to help you.

• Provide details that define, explain, support, or illustrate your points.

• Strengthen your introduction by including an interest-grabbing sentence.

Revising
• Use the guidelines on page SH11 of the Writing Handbook to revise your report.

American family was also changing with an increase in divorce, in the number of single-parent families, in the number of households with two working parents, and in the number of births to unwed mothers. Also, the population was aging.

Critical Thinking

11. More jobs were available, although some were very low-paying. However, millions of people who had been employed in industry lost their jobs, and they were not trained to work in the service sector.

12. Voters were not pleased with the government. More voters turned out to ensure that there was a change in leadership from Republican to Democrat.

13. Possible response: Clinton's actions did not support this statement. He supported healthcare reform that would have added more bureaucracy to the existing "big government."

14. Believing that free trade benefited the economy, the United States took an active role after the Cold War in the World Bank and in "nation-building" and peacekeeping. Following the September 11, 2001,

Document-Based Assessment

Media Influence on Political Issues

News coverage of the war in Iraq became news in itself. While editorial writers strongly supported or opposed American policy, other journalists questioned the way the war was being reported. Was the media too critical—or not critical enough? Use your knowledge of media coverage of the war in Iraq and Documents A, B, C, and D to answer questions 1 through 4.

Document A

"Mr. Bush's 'Plan for Victory' speech was, of course, the usual unadulterated nonsense. Its overarching theme—'We will never accept anything less than complete victory'—was being contradicted even as he spoke by rampant reports of Pentagon plans for stepped-up troop withdrawals between next week's Iraqi Elections and the more important (for endangered Republicans) American Election Day of 2006. The specifics were phony, too. Once again inflating the readiness of Iraqi troops, Mr. Bush claimed that the recent assault on Tal Afar 'was primarily led by Iraqi security forces'—a fairy tale immediately unmasked by Michael Ware, a Time reporter embedded in the battle's front lines, as 'completely wrong.'"
—*Frank Rich,* The New York Times, *December 11, 2005*

Document B

"It's a strange time:
- When a database search of America's leading newspapers turns up literally 10 times as many mentions of one of the soldiers who has been punished for misconduct—10 times more—than the mentions of Sergeant First Class Paul Ray Smith, the first recipient of the Medal of Honor in the Global War on Terror;
- Or when a senior editor at *Newsweek* disparagingly refers to the brave volunteers in our armed forces—the Army, the Navy, the Air Force, the Marines, the Coast Guard—as a "mercenary army;"
- When the former head of CNN accuses the American military of deliberately targeting journalists. . . .

Those who know the truth need to speak out against these kinds of myths and distortions that are being told about our troops and about our country. America is not what's wrong with the world."
—*Secretary of Defense Donald Rumsfeld, Address at the 88th Annual American Legion National Convention, August 29, 2006*

Document C

Document D

Fairness and Accuracy in Reporting did a study. In the week leading up to General Colin Powell going to the Security Council to make his case for the invasions and the week afterwards—this was the period where more than half of the people in this country were opposed to an invasion—they did a study of CBS *Evening News,* NBC *Nightly News,* ABC *World News Tonight,* and the *NewsHour with Jim Lehrer* on PBS. The four major newscasts. Two weeks. Three hundred and ninety-three interviews on war. Three were anti-war voices. Three of almost four hundred, and that included PBS. . . . [T]hey have to provide the diversity of opinion that fully expresses the debate and the anguish and the discussions that are going on all over this country. That is media serving a democratic society.
—*Amy Goodman, "Independent Media in a Time of War," April 21, 2003*

---

1. Which of the documents is critical of the government's positive assessment of the war in Iraq?
  A Document A C Document C
  B Document B D Document D

2. According to Amy Goodman, which of the following statements is the most accurate assessment of media coverage of the invasion of Iraq?
  A All the major newscasts tried to present both points of view about the invasion.
  B The media coverage resulted in a national debate about the invasion.
  C Media coverage favored opponents of the war.
  D Media coverage did not reflect the diversity of opinion about the war.

3. What is the main point of the cartoon in Document C?
  A People generally do not trust the mainstream media.
  B Although people claim to distrust the media, they still rely on it for information.
  C The mainstream media is biased.
  D The mainstream media is unbiased.

4. **Writing Task** Think about the political perspectives on the war in Iraq expressed in the media. Do you think the media has played an influential role in shaping American foreign policy in Iraq? Use your knowledge of media coverage of the war, key events in the war, and specific evidence from the primary sources above to support your opinion.

---

terrorist attacks, U.S. leaders shifted focus to fighting terrorism around the world.

15. It was ineffective. The declaration did not successfully settle some of the major points of conflict between Israel and the Palestinians.

16. the Florida recount of the presidential election votes of 2000

17. In some ways, Operation Iraqi Freedom successfully improved the lives of Iraqis. The dictator Saddam Hussein was removed from power and many of his supporters were captured or killed. Iraqis wrote a new

constitution and established the beginnings of a new democratic government. In spite of these advances, conflict among the Sunnis, the Shi'a, and the Kurds increased, making the country unstable and dangerous, especially for any Iraqis working with Americans.

18. to combat discrimination

Background Knowledge

Point out that the United States is and always has been a nation of immigrants. Explain that people have immigrated to the United States for many reasons, such as for religious freedom or to earn a fair wage. Tell students that immigrants to the United States have come from almost every region of the world. Discuss how the openness of the United States to immigration affects the nation today.

Instruct

Have students read the essay. Ask **According to the author, what is one issue facing the United States today that has emerged time and again?** *(immigration)* **What sort of trends exist in society today that might serve to relieve the pressure on immigrants to give up their heritage?** *(Answers will vary, but students may mention the concept of diversity, especially as it encourages immigrants to retain elements of their birth culture and makes assimilation less of an imperative than it was in the past.)* Lead a class discussion about the ways that immigration brings cultural diversity to the United States and why cultivating diversity is important if the nation is to continue its leadership role into the twenty-first century and beyond.

Looking Ahead

As it did during the 1800s and 1900s, immigration continues to change the cultural, social, and economic makeup of the United States today. In addition to immigration, the United States will meet new challenges that will test the nation's character.

Reflections: Enduring Issues

There is an expression that the more things change the more they remain the same. As we look over the history of our nation, we can find issues that come to the foreground time and again. We struggle with how to use our might as the strongest nation in the world, how to maintain our freedoms while we protect ourselves from those who would do us harm, and how to balance the rights and responsibilities of the government and the people.

One issue that has emerged time and again is that of immigration. Since our country's founding, immigrants have contributed to the growth of the United States. Millions of people from around the globe have come here seeking a better life—religious freedom, an honest wage, security from armed conflict, the opportunity to succeed regardless of gender, ethnic background, or social standing. Some people have welcomed them, and others have feared the changes they might bring.

Early immigrants struggled to Americanize as quickly as possible. Men like my father, Joseph Viola, arrived in this country from Austria alone, penniless, and unable to speak a word of English. After helping build the New York subway, he moved to Chicago where he helped construct the Elevated Train. It was there that he met and married the daughter of an Italian immigrant. I grew up listening to the stories of America being the promised land and was never taught either German or Italian for fear I would betray our foreign roots.

Today, the subject of immigration is once again a heated social and political issue. This time the bulk of the immigrants are not from Europe, as my parents were, but from Asia, South America, Africa, and other regions. Their arrival has brought forth many of the same issues that faced immigrants in the past. While some try to Americanize quickly, others are more reluctant to give up their heritage. In a world that seems more dangerous, the United States continues to be a refuge where people seek to enjoy the freedoms and democratic ideals of our founders.

Reference Section

Five Themes of Geography

The five themes of geography are tools you can use to analyze geographic information given in photographs, charts, maps, and text. Use these themes to determine the role of geography in U.S. history.

Location answers the question, Where is it? The answer might be an absolute location, such as 167 River Lane, or a relative location, such as six miles west of Mill City.

Place identifies natural and human features that make one place different from another. Landforms and buildings are features that can be used to identify a specific place.

Movement answers the question, How do people, goods, and ideas move from place to place?

Human-Environment Interaction explores the relationship between people and the natural world. Humans often modify their environment, and the environment affects how they live.

Regions are areas that share at least one common feature. Climate, culture, and government are features that can be used to define regions.

Profile of the Fifty States

State	Capital	Entered Union	Population (2005)	Population Rank	Land Area (Sq. Mi.)	Electoral Votes
Alabama	Montgomery	1819	4,557,808	23	50,744	9
Alaska	Juneau	1959	663,661	47	571,951	3
Arizona	Phoenix	1912	5,939,292	17	113,635	10
Arkansas	Little Rock	1836	2,779,154	32	52,068	6
California	Sacramento	1850	36,132,147	1	155,959	55
Colorado	Denver	1876	4,665,177	22	103,718	9
Connecticut	Hartford	1788	3,510,297	29	4,845	7
Delaware	Dover	1787	843,524	45	1,954	3
District of Columbia	——	——	550,521	——	——	3
Florida	Tallahassee	1845	17,789,864	4	53,927	27
Georgia	Atlanta	1788	9,072,576	9	57,906	15
Hawaii	Honolulu	1959	1,275,194	42	6,423	4
Idaho	Boise	1890	1,429,096	39	82,747	4
Illinois	Springfield	1818	12,763,371	5	55,584	21
Indiana	Indianapolis	1816	6,271,973	15	35,867	11
Iowa	Des Moines	1846	2,966,334	30	55,869	7
Kansas	Topeka	1861	2,744,687	33	81,815	6
Kentucky	Frankfort	1792	4,173,405	26	39,728	8
Louisiana	Baton Rouge	1812	4,523,628	24	43,562	9
Maine	Augusta	1820	1,321,505	40	30,862	4
Maryland	Annapolis	1788	5,600,388	19	9,774	10
Massachusetts	Boston	1788	6,398,743	13	7,840	12
Michigan	Lansing	1837	10,120,860	8	56,804	17
Minnesota	St. Paul	1858	5,132,799	21	79,610	10
Mississippi	Jackson	1817	2,921,088	31	46,907	6
Missouri	Jefferson City	1821	5,800,310	18	68,886	11
Montana	Helena	1889	935,670	44	145,552	3
Nebraska	Lincoln	1867	1,758,787	38	76,872	5
Nevada	Carson City	1864	2,414,807	35	109,826	5
New Hampshire	Concord	1788	1,309,940	41	8,968	4
New Jersey	Trenton	1787	8,717,925	10	7,417	15
New Mexico	Santa Fe	1912	1,928,384	36	121,356	5
New York	Albany	1788	19,254,630	3	47,214	31
North Carolina	Raleigh	1789	8,683,242	11	48,711	15
North Dakota	Bismarck	1889	636,677	48	68,976	3
Ohio	Columbus	1803	11,464,042	7	40,948	20
Oklahoma	Oklahoma City	1907	3,547,884	28	68,667	7
Oregon	Salem	1859	3,641,056	27	95,997	7
Pennsylvania	Harrisburg	1787	12,429,616	6	44,817	21
Rhode Island	Providence	1790	1,076,189	43	1,045	4
South Carolina	Columbia	1788	4,255,083	25	30,110	8
South Dakota	Pierre	1889	775,933	46	75,885	3
Tennessee	Nashville	1796	5,962,959	16	41,217	11
Texas	Austin	1845	22,859,968	2	261,797	34
Utah	Salt Lake City	1896	2,469,585	34	82,144	5
Vermont	Montpelier	1791	623,050	49	9,250	3
Virginia	Richmond	1788	7,567,465	12	39,594	13
Washington	Olympia	1889	6,287,759	14	66,544	11
West Virginia	Charleston	1863	1,816,856	37	24,078	5
Wisconsin	Madison	1848	5,536,201	20	54,310	10
Wyoming	Cheyenne	1890	509,294	50	97,100	3

SOURCES: U.S. Census Bureau, U.S. National Archives, *World Almanac*

Atlas

The World: Political

Alaska (United States)
CANADA
NORTH AMERICA
Toronto
Chicago
New York
UNITED STATES
Washington, D.C.
Los Angeles
Atlantic Ocean
Houston
Hawaii (United States)
Tropic of Cancer
MEXICO
see inset below
Mexico City
Pacific Ocean
French Guiana (France)
Galápagos Islands (Ecuador)
Bogotá
COLOMBIA
Equator
Line Islands (United States)
SURINAME
ECUADOR
BRAZIL
American Samoa (United States)
PERU
SOUTH AMERICA
SAMOA
BOLIVIA
French Polynesia (France)
Rio de Janeiro
Tropic of Capricorn
TONGA
Pitcairn Islands (U.K.)
PARAGUAY
São Paulo
CHILE
ARGENTINA
URUGUAY
Buenos Aires
Capital
Other city
Antarctic Circle
Southern Ocean
Gulf of Mexico
UNITED STATES
BAHAMAS
Tropic of Cancer
Turks and Caicos Islands (U.K.)
CUBA
U.S. Virgin Islands (U.S.)
British Virgin Islands (U.K.)
Anguilla (U.K.)
St. Martin (St. Maarten) (France & Neth. Antilles)
ANTIGUA AND BARBUDA
MEXICO
Cayman Islands (U.K.)
HAITI
BELIZE
JAMAICA
DOMINICAN REPUBLIC
Puerto Rico (U.S.)
ST. KITTS AND NEVIS
Montserrat (U.K.)
Guadeloupe (France)
DOMINICA
GUATEMALA
HONDURAS
Caribbean Sea
Martinique (France)
ST. LUCIA
BARBADOS
EL SALVADOR
ST. VINCENT AND THE GRENADINES
GRENADA
NICARAGUA
Conic Projection
0 200 400 mi
0 200 400 km
Aruba (Neth.)
Netherlands Antilles (Neth.)
TRINIDAD AND TOBAGO
Caracas
Lake Maracaibo
VENEZUELA
COSTA RICA
PANAMA
COLOMBIA
Pacific Ocean
SOUTH AMERICA
GUYANA

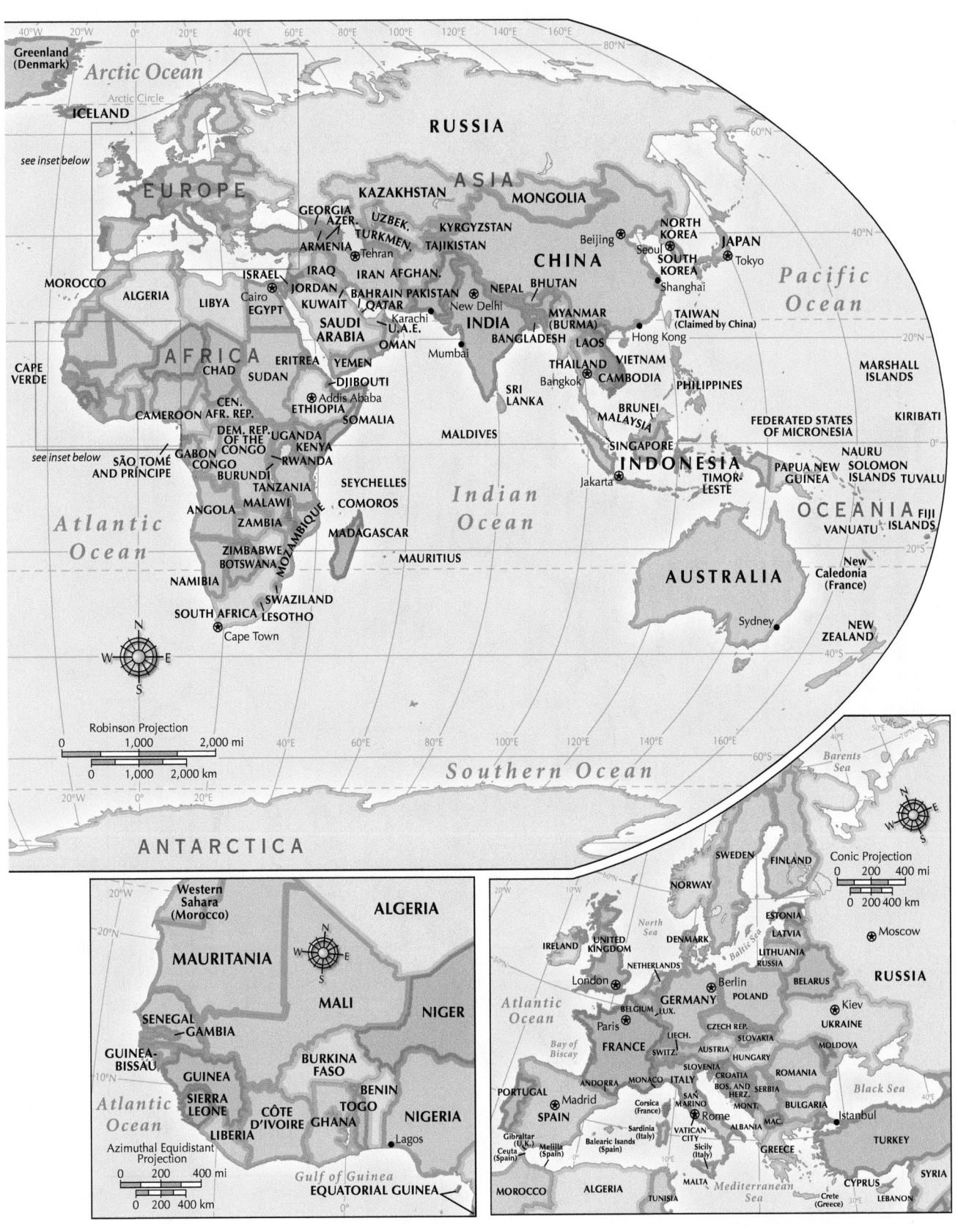

Greenland (Denmark)

Arctic Ocean
Arctic Circle
ICELAND

see inset below

EUROPE

RUSSIA

ASIA

KAZAKHSTAN

MONGOLIA

GEORGIA
AZER.
ARMENIA
Tehran

UZBEK.
TURKMEN.
KYRGYZSTAN
TAJIKISTAN

NORTH KOREA
Beijing
Seoul
SOUTH KOREA
Shanghai

JAPAN
Tokyo

Pacific Ocean

CHINA

MOROCCO

ALGERIA

LIBYA

ISRAEL
Cairo
EGYPT
JORDAN
KUWAIT

IRAQ
BAHRAIN
QATAR
U.A.E.
OMAN

IRAN AFGHAN.

PAKISTAN
Karachi
New Delhi
INDIA
Mumbai

NEPAL BHUTAN
MYANMAR (BURMA)
BANGLADESH
LAOS

TAIWAN
(Claimed by China)
Hong Kong

CAPE VERDE

AFRICA
CHAD

SAUDI ARABIA
ERITREA
SUDAN
YEMEN
DJIBOUTI
Addis Ababa
ETHIOPIA
SOMALIA

CEN. AFR. REP.
CAMEROON

DEM. REP. OF THE CONGO
UGANDA
KENYA
RWANDA
BURUNDI

THAILAND
Bangkok
CAMBODIA
VIETNAM
SRI LANKA

MALDIVES

BRUNEI
MALAYSIA
SINGAPORE

PHILIPPINES

MARSHALL ISLANDS

FEDERATED STATES OF MICRONESIA

KIRIBATI

see inset below
SÃO TOMÉ AND PRÍNCIPE
GABON
CONGO

TANZANIA

SEYCHELLES

COMOROS

Indian Ocean

Jakarta

INDONESIA

TIMOR-LESTE

PAPUA NEW GUINEA

NAURU
SOLOMON ISLANDS TUVALU

Atlantic Ocean

ANGOLA
MALAWI
ZAMBIA
ZIMBABWE
BOTSWANA

MOZAMBIQUE

MADAGASCAR

MAURITIUS

OCEANIA FIJI
VANUATU ISLANDS

New Caledonia (France)

NAMIBIA

SWAZILAND
SOUTH AFRICA LESOTHO
Cape Town

AUSTRALIA

Sydney

NEW ZEALAND

Robinson Projection
0   1,000   2,000 mi
0   1,000   2,000 km

Southern Ocean

Barents Sea

ANTARCTICA

Inset (left):

Western Sahara (Morocco)

ALGERIA

MAURITANIA

MALI

NIGER

SENEGAL
GAMBIA
GUINEA-BISSAU
GUINEA
SIERRA LEONE
LIBERIA

BURKINA FASO

CÔTE D'IVOIRE
GHANA
BENIN
TOGO

NIGERIA

Atlantic Ocean

Azimuthal Equidistant Projection
0   200   400 mi
0   200   400 km

Gulf of Guinea
EQUATORIAL GUINEA
Lagos

Inset (right):

Conic Projection
0   200   400 mi
0   200 400 km

SWEDEN FINLAND
NORWAY
North Sea
IRELAND
UNITED KINGDOM
DENMARK
London
NETHERLANDS
BELGIUM
GERMANY
LUX.
Paris
FRANCE
SWITZ.
LIECH.
PORTUGAL
Madrid
SPAIN

ESTONIA
LATVIA
LITHUANIA
RUSSIA
BELARUS

Moscow

RUSSIA

Kiev
UKRAINE
MOLDOVA
ROMANIA

Black Sea

POLAND
CZECH REP.
SLOVAKIA
AUSTRIA
HUNGARY
SLOVENIA
CROATIA
BOS. AND HERZ.
SERBIA
MONT.
ITALY
SAN MARINO
VATICAN CITY
ANDORRA
MONACO
Corsica (France)
Sardinia (Italy)
Gibraltar (U.K.)
Ceuta (Spain)
Melilla (Spain)
Balearic Islands (Spain)
Rome
Sicily (Italy)
MALTA
ALBANIA
MAC.
BULGARIA
Istanbul
GREECE
Crete (Greece)
TURKEY
CYPRUS
SYRIA
LEBANON

Bay of Biscay

Atlantic Ocean

MOROCCO ALGERIA TUNISIA

Mediterranean Sea

United States: Political

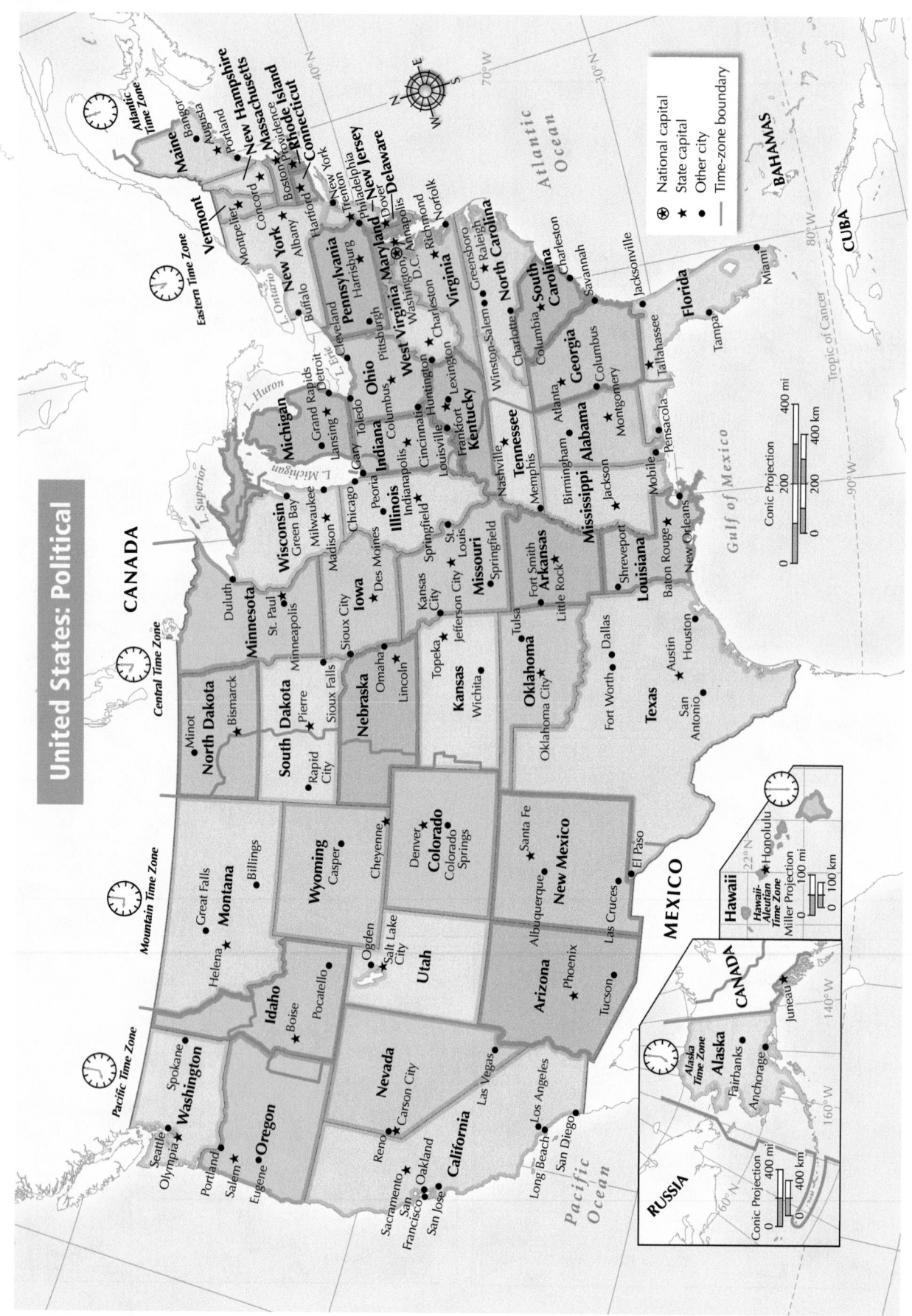

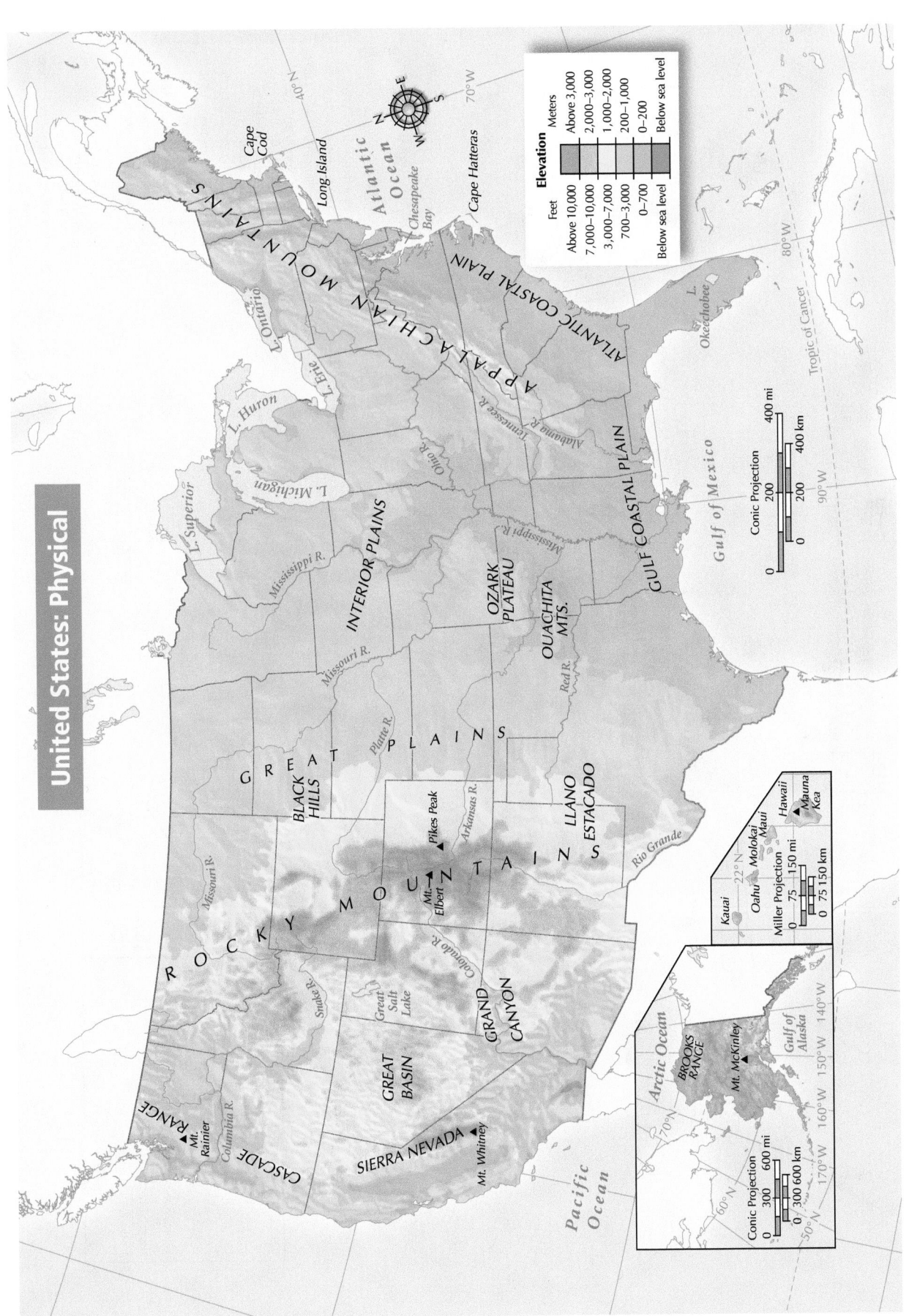

United States: Physical

Elevation

Feet	Meters
Above 10,000	Above 3,000
7,000–10,000	2,000–3,000
3,000–7,000	1,000–2,000
700–3,000	200–1,000
0–700	0–200
Below sea level	Below sea level

Cape Cod

Long Island

Atlantic Ocean

Chesapeake Bay

Cape Hatteras

APPALACHIAN MOUNTAINS

ATLANTIC COASTAL PLAIN

L. Ontario

L. Erie

L. Huron

L. Michigan

L. Superior

Tennessee R.

Ohio R.

INTERIOR PLAINS

Mississippi R.

Mississippi R.

OZARK PLATEAU

OUACHITA MTS.

Alabama R.

GULF COASTAL PLAIN

L. Okeechobee

Tropic of Cancer

Gulf of Mexico

Conic Projection

Missouri R.

Red R.

Arkansas R.

LLANO ESTACADO

Rio Grande

GREAT PLAINS

BLACK HILLS

Platte R.

Pikes Peak

Mt. Elbert

Missouri R.

R O C K Y   M O U N T A I N S

Colorado R.

Snake R.

Great Salt Lake

GREAT BASIN

GRAND CANYON

CASCADE RANGE

Mt. Rainier

Columbia R.

SIERRA NEVADA

Mt. Whitney

Pacific Ocean

Kauai

Oahu

Molokai

Maui

Hawaii

Mauna Kea

Miller Projection

Arctic Ocean

BROOKS RANGE

Mt. McKinley

Gulf of Alaska

Conic Projection

70°W

80°W

90°W

40°N

Atlas

United States: Territorial Expansion from 1763

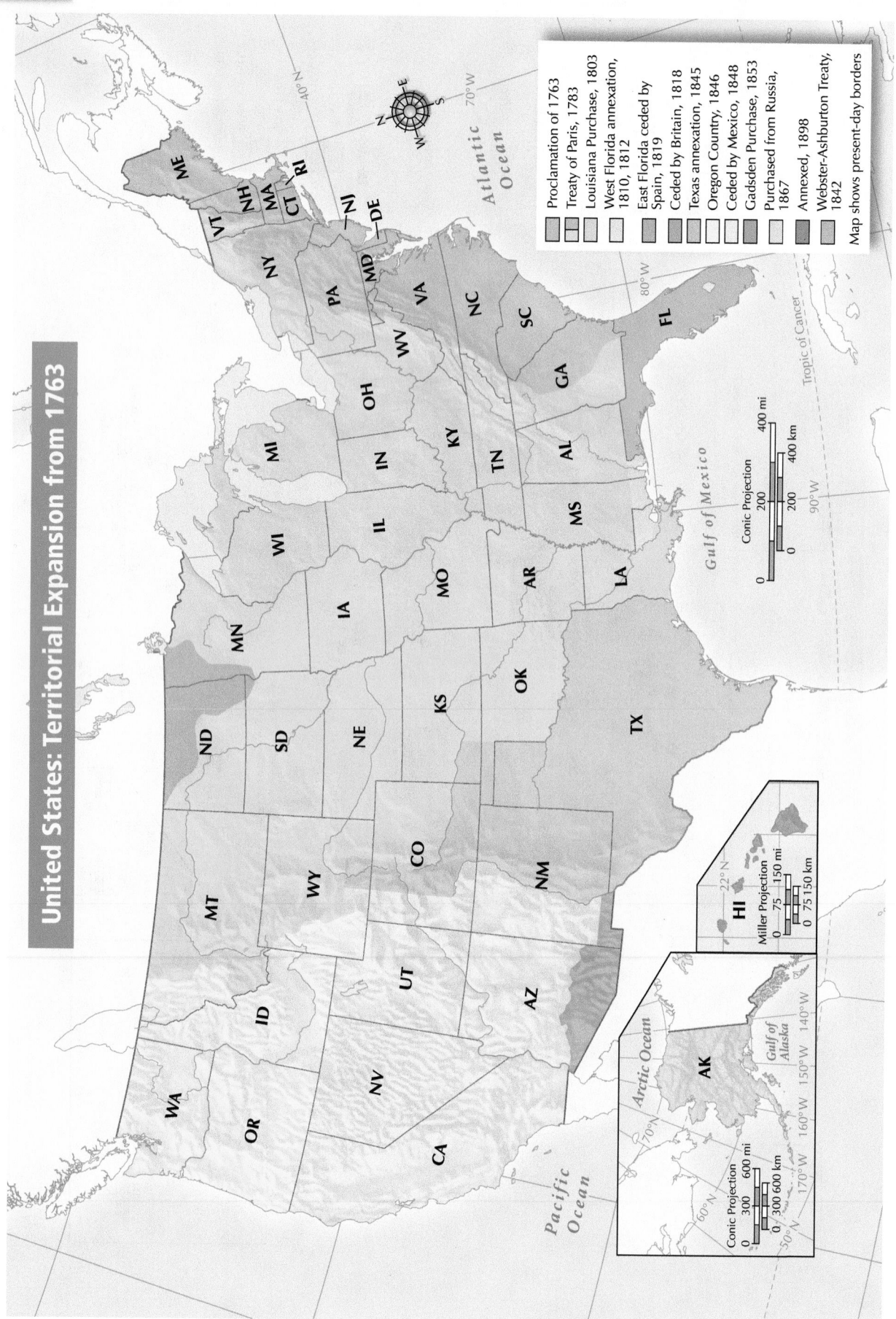

Legend:
- Proclamation of 1763
- Treaty of Paris, 1783
- Louisiana Purchase, 1803
- West Florida annexation, 1810, 1812
- East Florida ceded by Spain, 1819
- Ceded by Britain, 1818
- Texas annexation, 1845
- Oregon Country, 1846
- Ceded by Mexico, 1848
- Gadsden Purchase, 1853
- Purchased from Russia, 1867
- Annexed, 1898
- Webster-Ashburton Treaty, 1842

Map shows present-day borders

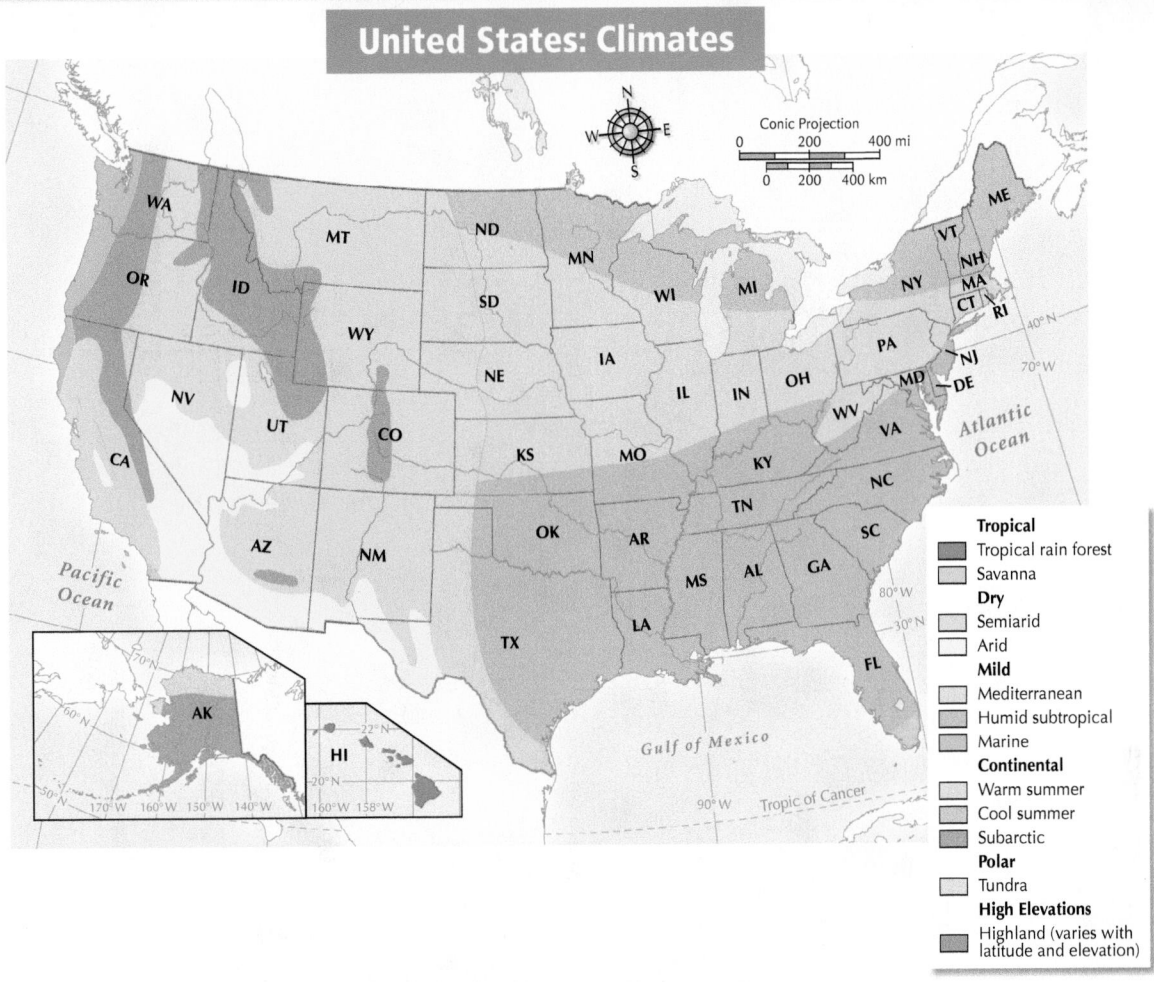

United States: Climates

Tropical
- Tropical rain forest
- Savanna

Dry
- Semiarid
- Arid

Mild
- Mediterranean
- Humid subtropical
- Marine

Continental
- Warm summer
- Cool summer
- Subarctic

Polar
- Tundra

High Elevations
- Highland (varies with latitude and elevation)

Conic Projection
0   200   400 mi
0   200   400 km

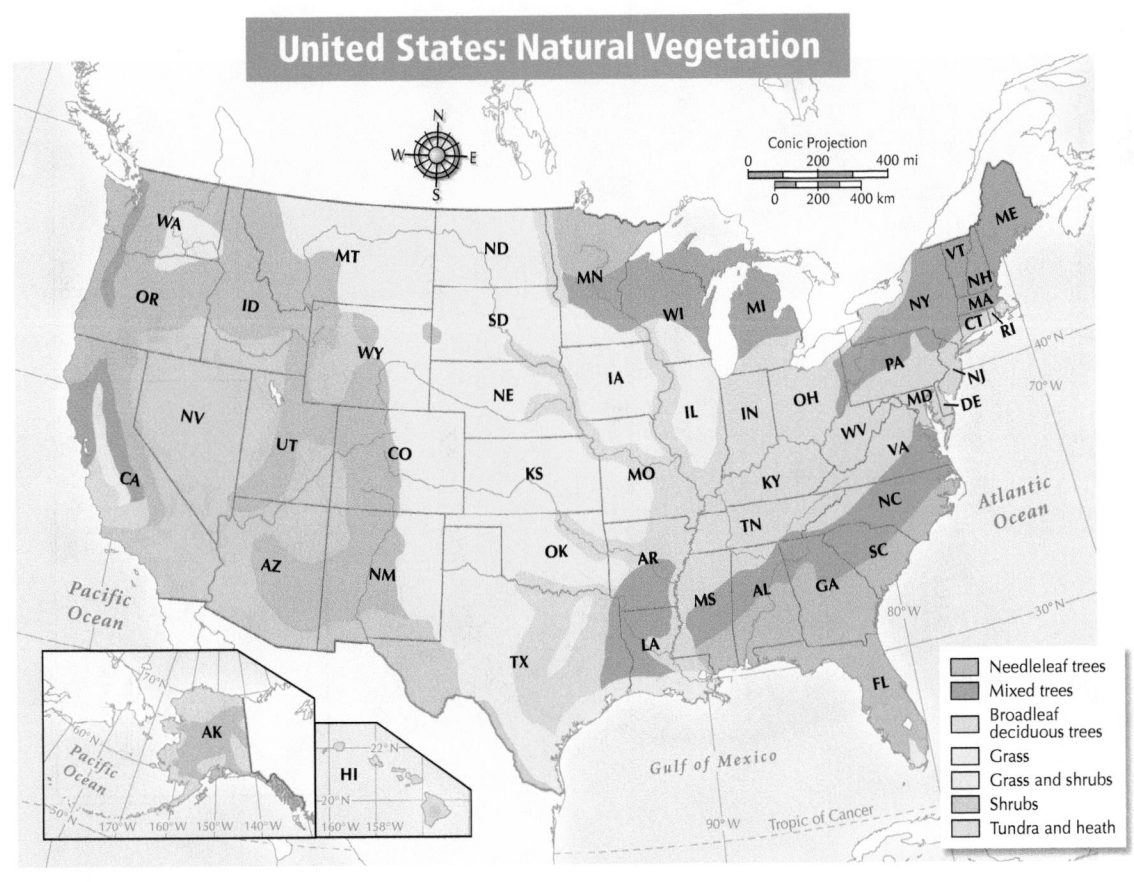

United States: Natural Vegetation

- Needleleaf trees
- Mixed trees
- Broadleaf deciduous trees
- Grass
- Grass and shrubs
- Shrubs
- Tundra and heath

Conic Projection
0   200   400 mi
0   200   400 km

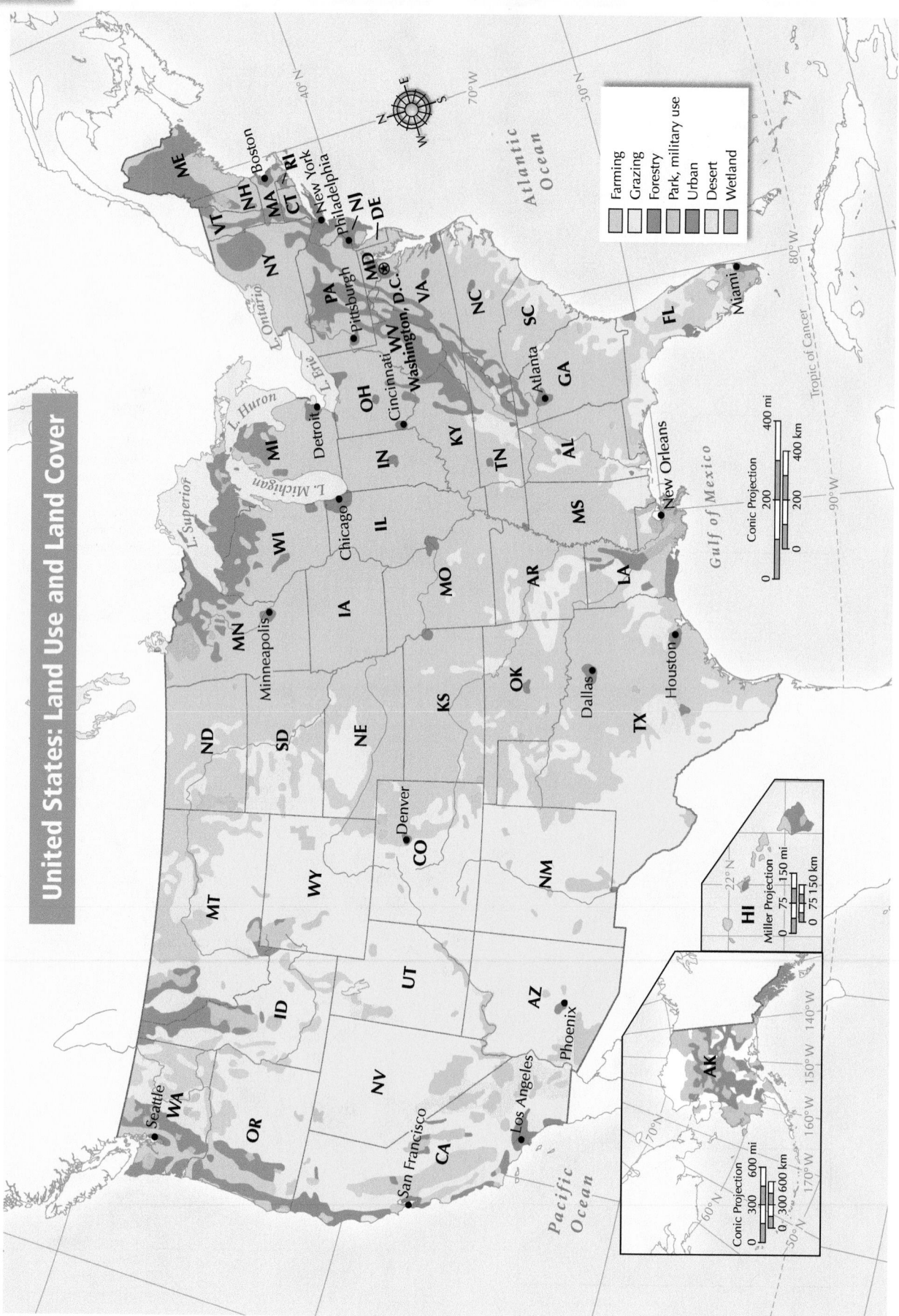

United States: Land Use and Land Cover

Legend:
- Farming
- Grazing
- Forestry
- Park, military use
- Urban
- Desert
- Wetland

Atlantic Ocean

Pacific Ocean

Gulf of Mexico

Tropic of Cancer

Conic Projection

400 mi
400 km
200
200
0
0

HI — Miller Projection
0 75 150 mi
0 75 150 km

AK — Conic Projection
0 300 600 mi
0 300 600 km

L. Superior
L. Michigan
L. Huron
L. Erie
L. Ontario

Cities and states labeled: ME, NH, VT, MA, CT, RI, NY, Boston, New York, Philadelphia, NJ, DE, PA, Pittsburgh, MD, Washington, D.C., WV, VA, NC, SC, GA, Atlanta, FL, Miami, OH, Cincinnati, KY, IN, Detroit, MI, IL, Chicago, WI, MN, Minneapolis, IA, MO, AR, TN, AL, MS, LA, New Orleans, ND, SD, NE, KS, OK, TX, Dallas, Houston, CO, Denver, WY, MT, NM, UT, AZ, Phoenix, NV, ID, OR, WA, Seattle, CA, San Francisco, Los Angeles

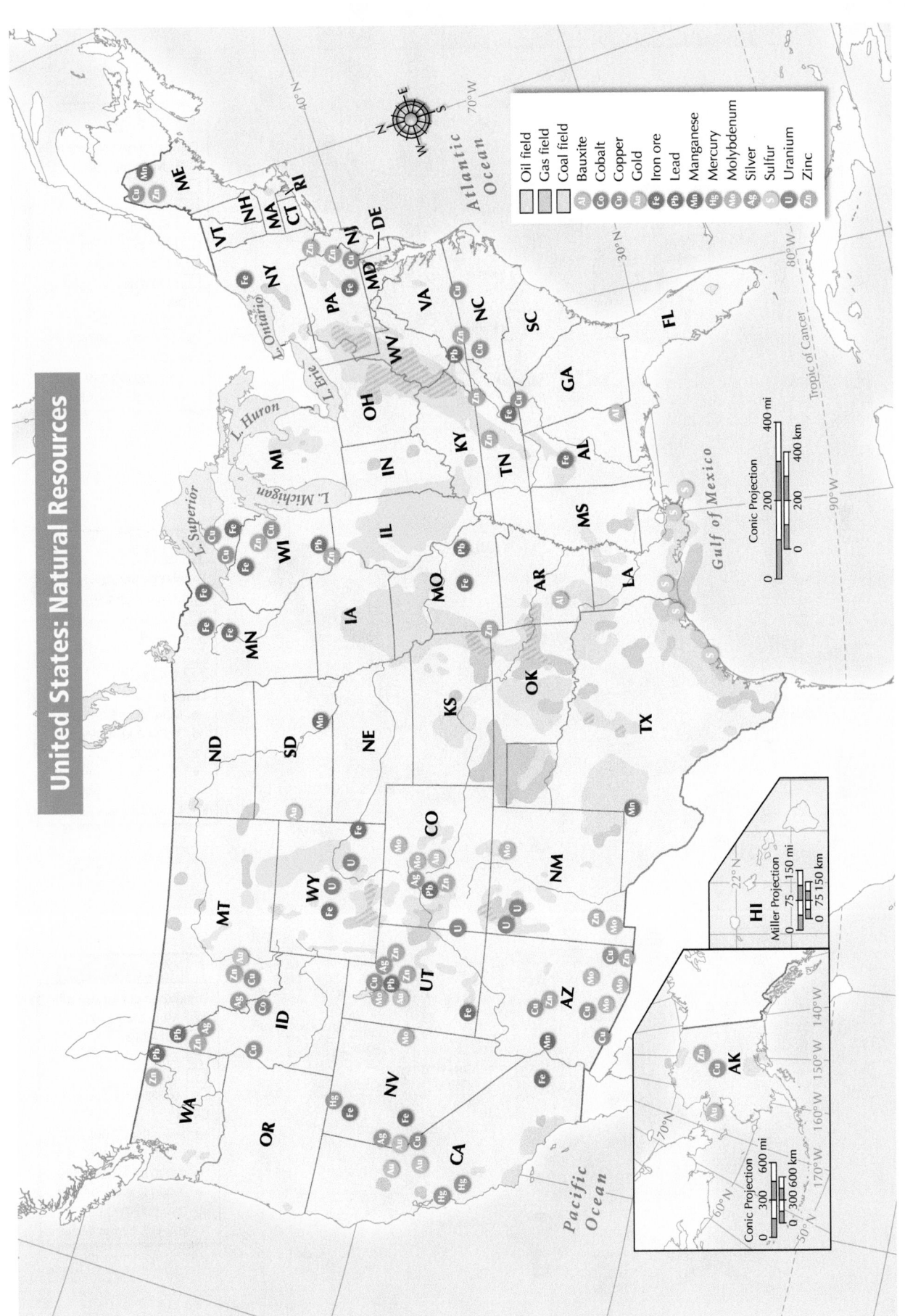

United States: Natural Resources

Legend

- Oil field
- Gas field
- Coal field
- Bauxite
- Cobalt (Co)
- Copper (Cu)
- Gold (Au)
- Iron ore (Fe)
- Lead (Pb)
- Manganese (Mn)
- Mercury (Hg)
- Molybdenum (Mo)
- Silver (Ag)
- Sulfur (S)
- Uranium (U)
- Zinc (Zn)

Conic Projection
0 200 400 mi
0 200 400 km

Miller Projection
0 75 150 mi
0 75 150 km

Conic Projection
0 300 600 mi
0 300 600 km

Atlantic Ocean

Pacific Ocean

Gulf of Mexico

Tropic of Cancer

L. Superior
L. Michigan
L. Huron
L. Erie
L. Ontario

HI

AK

United States: Population Density

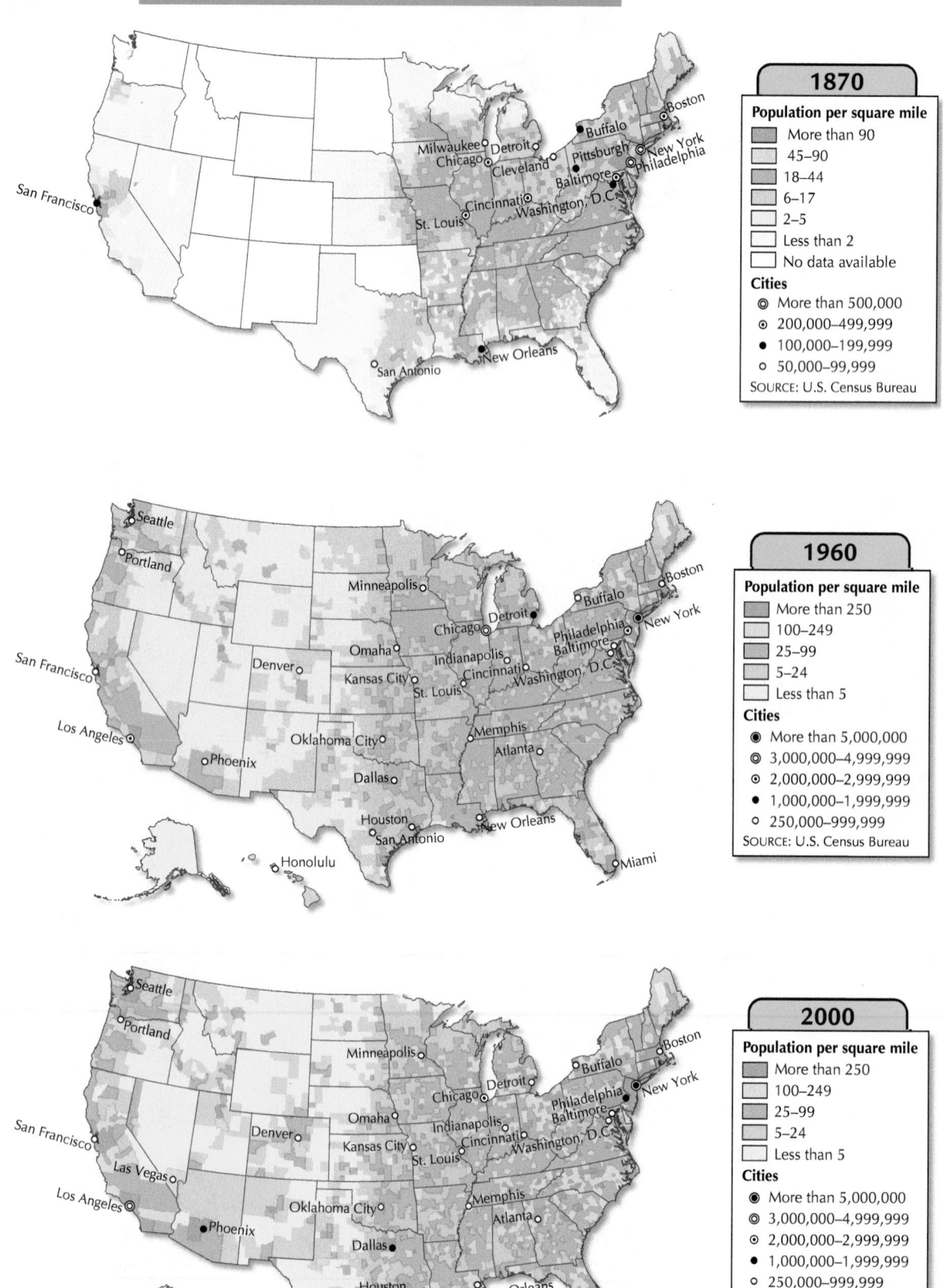

1870

Population per square mile

- More than 90
- 45–90
- 18–44
- 6–17
- 2–5
- Less than 2
- No data available

Cities

- ◉ More than 500,000
- ◉ 200,000–499,999
- ● 100,000–199,999
- ○ 50,000–99,999

SOURCE: U.S. Census Bureau

1960

Population per square mile

- More than 250
- 100–249
- 25–99
- 5–24
- Less than 5

Cities

- ◉ More than 5,000,000
- ◎ 3,000,000–4,999,999
- ◉ 2,000,000–2,999,999
- ● 1,000,000–1,999,999
- ○ 250,000–999,999

SOURCE: U.S. Census Bureau

2000

Population per square mile

- More than 250
- 100–249
- 25–99
- 5–24
- Less than 5

Cities

- ◉ More than 5,000,000
- ◎ 3,000,000–4,999,999
- ◉ 2,000,000–2,999,999
- ● 1,000,000–1,999,999
- ○ 250,000–999,999

SOURCE: U.S. Census Bureau

Presidents of the United States

1
George Washington
(1732-1799)

Years in Office: 1789-1797
No political party

Elected from: Virginia
Vice President: John Adams

2
John Adams
(1735-1826)

Years in Office: 1797-1801
Federalist

Elected from: Massachusetts
Vice President: Thomas Jefferson

3
Thomas Jefferson
(1743-1826)

Years in Office: 1801-1809
Democratic Republican

Elected from: Virginia
Vice Presidents: Aaron Burr,
George Clinton

4
James Madison
(1751-1836)

Years in Office: 1809-1817
Democratic Republican

Elected from: Virginia
Vice Presidents: George
Clinton, Elbridge Gerry

5
James Monroe
(1758-1831)

Years in Office: 1817-1825
National Republican

Elected from: Virginia
Vice President: Daniel Tompkins

6
John Quincy Adams
(1767-1848)

Years in Office: 1825-1829
National Republican

Elected from: Massachusetts
Vice President: John Calhoun

7
Andrew Jackson
(1767-1845)

Years in Office: 1829-1837
Democrat

Elected from: Tennessee
Vice Presidents: John Calhoun,
Martin Van Buren

8
Martin Van Buren
(1782-1862)

Years in Office: 1837-1841
Democrat

Elected from: New York
Vice President: Richard Johnson

9
William Henry Harrison*
(1773-1841)

Year in Office: 1841
Whig

Elected from: Ohio
Vice President: John Tyler

10
John Tyler
(1790-1862)

Years in Office: 1841-1845
Whig

Elected from: Virginia
Vice President: none

11
James K. Polk
(1795-1849)

Years in Office: 1845-1849
Democrat

Elected from: Tennessee
Vice President: George Dallas

12
Zachary Taylor*
(1784-1850)

Years in Office: 1849-1850
Whig

Elected from: Louisiana
Vice President: Millard Fillmore

13
Millard Fillmore
(1800-1874)

Years in Office: 1850-1853
Whig

Elected from: New York
Vice President: none

14
Franklin Pierce
(1804-1869)

Years in Office: 1853-1857
Democrat

Elected from: New Hampshire
Vice President: William King

15
James Buchanan
(1791-1868)

Years in Office: 1857-1861
Democrat

Elected from: Pennsylvania
Vice President: John
Breckinridge

16
Abraham Lincoln**
(1809-1865)

Years in Office: 1861-1865
Republican

Elected from: Illinois
Vice Presidents: Hannibal
Hamlin, Andrew Johnson

Presidents

17

Andrew Johnson
(1808–1875)

Years in Office: 1865–1869
Democrat†

Elected from: Tennessee
Vice President: none

18

Ulysses S. Grant
(1822–1885)

Years in Office: 1869–1877
Republican

Elected from: Illinois
Vice Presidents: Schuyler
Colfax, Henry Wilson

19

Rutherford B. Hayes
(1822–1893)

Years in Office: 1877–1881
Republican

Elected from: Ohio
Vice President: William Wheeler

20

James A. Garfield**
(1831–1881)

Year in Office: 1881
Republican

Elected from: Ohio
Vice President: Chester A.
Arthur

21

Chester A. Arthur
(1830–1886)

Years in Office: 1881–1885
Republican

Elected from: New York
Vice President: none

22

Grover Cleveland
(1837–1908)

Years in Office: 1885–1889
Democrat

Elected from: New York
Vice President: Thomas
Hendricks

23

Benjamin Harrison
(1833–1901)

Years in Office: 1889–1893
Republican

Elected from: Indiana
Vice President: Levi Morton

24

Grover Cleveland
(1837–1908)

Years in Office: 1893–1897
Democrat

Elected from: New York
Vice President: Adlai Stevenson

25

William McKinley**
(1843–1901)

Years in Office: 1897–1901
Republican

Elected from: Ohio
Vice Presidents: Garret Hobart,
Theodore Roosevelt

26

Theodore Roosevelt
(1858–1919)

Years in Office: 1901–1909
Republican

Elected from: New York
Vice President: Charles
Fairbanks

27

William Howard Taft
(1857–1930)

Years in Office: 1909–1913
Republican

Elected from: Ohio
Vice President: James Sherman

28

Woodrow Wilson
(1856–1924)

Years in Office: 1913–1921
Democrat

Elected from: New Jersey
Vice President: Thomas
Marshall

29

Warren G. Harding*
(1865–1923)

Years in Office: 1921–1923
Republican

Elected from: Ohio
Vice President: Calvin Coolidge

30

Calvin Coolidge
(1872–1933)

Years in Office: 1923–1929
Republican

Elected from: Massachusetts
Vice President: Charles Dawes

31

Herbert C. Hoover
(1874–1964)

Years in Office: 1929–1933
Republican

Elected from: New York
Vice President: Charles Curtis

32

Franklin D. Roosevelt*
(1882–1945)

Years in Office: 1933–1945
Democrat

Elected from: New York
Vice Presidents: John Garner,
Henry Wallace, Harry S. Truman

Harry S. Truman
(1884–1972)

Years in Office: 1945–1953
Democrat

Elected from: Missouri
Vice President: Alben Barkley

Dwight D. Eisenhower
(1890–1969)

Years in Office: 1953–1961
Republican

Elected from: New York
Vice President: Richard M. Nixon

John F. Kennedy**
(1917–1963)

Years in Office: 1961–1963
Democrat

Elected from: Massachusetts
Vice President: Lyndon B. Johnson

Lyndon B. Johnson
(1908–1973)

Years in Office: 1963–1969
Democrat

Elected from: Texas
Vice President: Hubert Humphrey

Richard M. Nixon***
(1913–1994)

Years in Office: 1969–1974
Republican

Elected from: New York
Vice Presidents: Spiro Agnew, Gerald R. Ford

Gerald R. Ford
(1913–2006)

Years in Office: 1974–1977
Republican

Elected from: Michigan
Vice President: Nelson Rockefeller

James E. Carter
(1924–)

Years in Office: 1977–1981
Democrat

Elected from: Georgia
Vice President: Walter F. Mondale

Ronald W. Reagan
(1911–2004)

Years in Office: 1981–1989
Republican

Elected from: California
Vice President: George H. W. Bush

George H. W. Bush
(1924–)

Years in Office: 1989–1993
Republican

Elected from: Texas
Vice President: J. Danforth Quayle

William J. Clinton
(1946–)

Years in Office: 1993–2001
Democrat

Elected from: Arkansas
Vice President: Albert Gore, Jr.

George W. Bush
(1946–)

Years in Office: 2001–2009
Republican

Elected from: Texas
Vice President: Richard Cheney

Barack H. Obama
(1961–)

Years in Office: 2009–
Democrat

Elected from: Illinois
Vice President: Joseph R. Biden

* Died in office
** Assassinated
*** Resigned
† Elected Vice President on the coalition Union Party ticket

Adapted from Prentice Hall's *Economics: Principles in Action* by Arthur O' Sullivan and Steven Sheffrin

Step-by-Step Instruction

Objectives

- Define economics and explain the different economic goals of societies.
- Outline three key economic questions.
- Describe three modern economic systems.
- Identify specific nations that operate under the three economic systems.

Key Economic Questions

Background Knowledge ⓛ₃

Ask a volunteer to read aloud the economic goals and their definitions. Then ask students how they would rank the goals in terms of importance. Be sure that students can defend their choices.

Instruct ⓛ₃

Ask **What is economics?** *(the study of how people use their limited resources to meet their wants and needs)* Discuss how the economic goals relate to the economic questions.

Independent Practice

Ask students to select a good or a service that they use or with which they are familiar. Then, have them write a few sentences describing that good or service, how it is produced and by whom (for example, private company or government), and who consumes it.

Monitor Progress

As students write their sentences, circulate to make sure that they have chosen something about which they have adequate knowledge. If not, suggest another good or service.

Key Economic Questions

In every society, people have access to resources such as water, soil, and human labor. Yet all resources are limited. Economics is the study of how people choose to use their limited resources to meet their wants and needs. Every society must answer three basic economic questions. How a society answers these questions depends on how much it values different economic goals.

Economic Goals

Economic efficiency	Making the most of resources
Economic freedom	Freedom from government intervention in the production and distribution of goods and services
Economic security and predictability	Assurance that goods and services will be available, payments will be made on time, and a safety net will protect individuals in times of economic disaster
Economic equity	Fair distribution of wealth
Economic growth and innovation	Innovation leads to economic growth, and economic growth leads to a higher standard of living.
Other goals	Societies pursue additional goals, such as environmental protection.

Three Key Economic Questions

What goods and services should be produced?	How should goods and services be produced?	Who consumes the goods and services?
How much of our resources should we devote to national defense, education, public health, or consumer goods? Which consumer goods should we produce?	Should we produce food on large corporate farms or on small family farms? Should we produce electricity with oil, nuclear power, coal, or solar power?	How do goods and services get distributed? The question of who gets to consume which goods and services lies at the very heart of the differences between economic systems. Each society answers the question of distribution based on its combination of social values and goals.

Choices About How to Produce Goods
This wind farm illustrates a society's decision to produce electricity using the power of the wind. What do you think are the benefits and drawbacks of wind power?

Answer

Caption Benefits: Wind farms do not use fuel and so do not draw on dwindling fossil fuel reserves, nor do they pollute. Drawbacks: The towers are unsightly, and wind power cannot be produced on demand because wind farms are subject to changing weather patterns.

Differentiated Instruction   Solutions for All Learners

ⓛ₁ **Special Needs Students**   ⓛ₂ **English Language Learners**   ⓛ₂ **Less Proficient Readers**

To help students master vocabulary, have them list difficult terms and concepts they encounter as they read the Economics Handbook. For example, on this page, students might select *innovation, production and distribution, safety net, equity, standard of living, consumer goods,* and *corporate*. After they have compiled their lists, have students create flashcards with the term or concept on one side and its definition on the other. For English Language Learners, you may wish to have students add explanations in their first language to the flashcards. Pair students, and have them use their flashcards to quiz each other.

Economic Systems

An economic system is the method used by a society to produce and distribute goods and services. A society's economic system reflects how that society answers the three key economic questions and what its economic goals are. Different systems produce different results in terms of productivity, the welfare of workers, and consumer choice.

Modern Economic Systems

	Description	Origin	Location Today
Market (Capitalist, Free-Enterprise)	Economic decisions are made in the marketplace through interactions between buyers and sellers according to the laws of supply and demand. Individual capitalists own the means of production. Government regulates some economic activities and provides such "public goods" as education.	Capitalism has existed since the earliest buying and selling of goods in a market. The market economic system developed in response to Adam Smith's ideas and the shift from agriculture to industry in the 1800s.	Canada, Germany, Japan, United States, and many other nations
Centrally Planned (Command, Socialist, Communist)	Central government planners make most economic decisions for the people. In theory, the workers own the means of production. In practice, the government does. Some private enterprise, but government dominates.	In the 1800s, criticism of capitalism by Karl Marx and others led to calls for distributing wealth according to need. After the 1917 Russian Revolution, the Soviet Union developed the first command economy.	Communist countries, including China, Cuba, and North Korea
Mixed (Social Democratic, Liberal Socialist)	A mix of socialism and free enterprise in which the government plays a significant role in making economic decisions.	The Great Depression of the 1930s ended laissez-faire capitalism in most countries. People insisted that government take a stronger role in fixing economic problems. The fall of communism in Eastern Europe in the 1990s ended central planning in most countries. People insisted on freer markets.	Most nations, including Brazil, France, India, Italy, Poland, Russia, Sweden, and the United Kingdom

Buyers and Sellers in a Free Market
In a market economy, buyers and sellers make decisions on the basis of their own self-interest. They may freely buy and sell goods. In a voluntary exchange, both parties expect to gain from the transaction.

History Background

Adam Smith and Karl Marx Among the most influential economic writings of all time are Adam Smith's *An Inquiry into the Nature and Causes of the Wealth of Nations* (1776), known as *The Wealth of Nations;* and Karl Marx's *Capital*, published in German as *Das Kapital* (3 volumes, 1867–1894). Both works are extensive and sophisticated theoretical economic analyses. Like many major works, these texts are frequently distorted when interpreted. Over time, such practices have resulted in inaccurate views of the ideas of both Smith and Marx. For example, in *The Wealth of Nations,* Adam Smith posits that property laws have been established for the sole purpose of defending the wealthy people who own property from those people who have little or do not own property. A person with only a superficial knowledge of Smith's work might ascribe this sentiment to Marx. Marx himself, after learning about a particular group's interpretation of his ideas, is reported to have said that if that is Marxism, then he is not a Marxist.

Step-by-Step Instruction

Objectives

- Analyze clauses in the U.S. Constitution that protect free enterprise.
- Understand the flow of goods and services in a market economy.
- Examine key events in U.S. economic history.
- Understand the concept of business cycles.
- Identify and explain leading economic indicators.

The American Economy

Background Knowledge L3

Remind students that the U.S. economy is a free-enterprise system. The visuals on this page will show how this system developed and works today.

Instruct L3

Discuss each chart or graphic on the page. Ask **What are two reasons for the economic success of the United States?** *(the abundance of natural and human resources and the tradition of free enterprise)* **How does the Constitution help safeguard free enterprise?** *(Sample: The Fifth and Fourteenth Amendments safeguard Americans' property rights, and Article 1, Section 10 guarantees the right of individuals and businesses to make binding contracts.)* Ask **According to the circle graph, what occupational group is the largest and which is the smallest?** *(management and professional specialty; natural resources, construction, and maintenance)* Discuss the shift in the United States from a manufacturing economy to a service economy.

Independent Practice

Have students analyze the circular flow model and write paragraphs summarizing the information it presents.

Monitor Progress

As students write their paragraphs, circulate to make sure that they correctly interpret the flow model.

Answer

Caption In 1800, most jobs were in farming. By 1900, most jobs were evenly split between farming and manufacturing.

706

The American Economy

For centuries, people have considered the United States to be a land of opportunity where anyone from any background could achieve success through hard work. Why has the United States been such an economic success? Certainly the open land, natural resources, and uninterrupted flow of immigrant labor have all contributed. But a key factor has also been the tradition of free enterprise—the social and political commitment to giving people the freedom to compete in the marketplace.

Flow of Goods, Services, and Money in a Market Economy

Goods and Services Market

Monetary flow
Physical flow
Taxes
Government purchases

Households — Expenditures — Government — Expenditures — Firms

Government owned factors
Taxes
Physical flow
Monetary flow

Land, Labor, and Capital Market

▲ This circular flow model shows how government typically interacts with households and businesses in the marketplace.

Constitutional Protections of Free Enterprise

Property Rights
Property rights are protected by the Fifth Amendment: "No person shall be deprived of life, liberty, or property, without due process; nor shall private property be taken for public use, without just compensation." The Fourteenth Amendment places the same limitation on state governments.

Taxation
Congress can only tax individuals and businesses in the ways the Constitution allows. Article 1 gives Congress the power to levy taxes, but Sections 2 and 9 require that direct taxes be apportioned according to population. The Sixteenth Amendment gave Congress the right to set taxes based on income.

Binding Contracts
Article 1, Section 10, guarantees people and businesses the right to make binding contracts.

▲ Free enterprise in the United States is founded on ideas so basic to our culture that we tend to take them for granted.

United States Workforce, by Occupation, 2005*

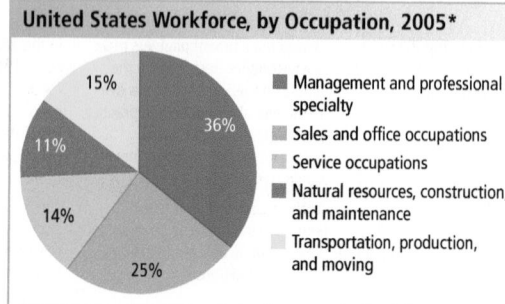

- 36% Management and professional specialty
- 25% Sales and office occupations
- 14% Service occupations
- 11% Natural resources, construction, and maintenance
- 15% Transportation, production, and moving

* Because of rounding, total may be less than or greater than 100 percent.
SOURCE: Bureau of Labor Statistics

▲ How do you think this snapshot of the United States labor force would have looked in 1800? In 1900?

Key Events in American Economic History

| 1791 First Bank of the United States chartered | 1834 Mill girls in Lowell, Massachusetts, protest wage cuts | 1867 Knights of Labor formed | 1886 American Federation of Labor formed |

1780 — **1820** — **1860**

| 1835 Strike for 10-hour workday in Philadelphia | 1869 Financial panic sweeps nation | 1892 Homestead Strike in Pennsylvania |

Differentiated Instruction   Solutions for All Learners

L1 Special Needs Students   **L2 English Language Learners**   **L2 Less Proficient Readers**

To help students understand the categories used in the circle graph, have them work in pairs to list at least three specific jobs for each of the five categories. Encourage students to do research if necessary to complete their lists. As an alternative, you may want to suggest a list of occupations with students, such as *teacher, telemarketer,* or *miner,* and then have them sort each job under one of the five categories.

Measuring the Economy's Performance

A modern industrial economy repeatedly experiences cycles of economic growth and decline. Business cycles are of major interest to macroeconomists, who study their causes and effects. Economists use many tools to predict changes in business cycles. The leading indicators are a set of key economic variables including stock prices, interest rates, and manufacturers' new orders for goods.

▲ **Food Prices** An increase in the price of food can signal inflation. What impact do rising food prices have on families?

Inflation Rate, 1970–2006

SOURCE: Bureau of Labor Statistics

▲ One of the economic indicators economists look at is the economy's level of inflation. Inflation is a general increase in prices. As prices rise, the purchasing power of money declines.

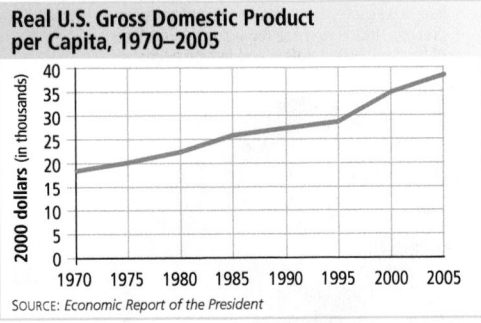

Real U.S. Gross Domestic Product per Capita, 1970–2005

SOURCE: *Economic Report of the President*

▲ Gross Domestic Product is the dollar value of all final goods and services produced within a country's borders in a given year. GDP per capita equals the GDP divided by the country's total population. Long-term increases in GDP allow an entire society to improve its standard of living.

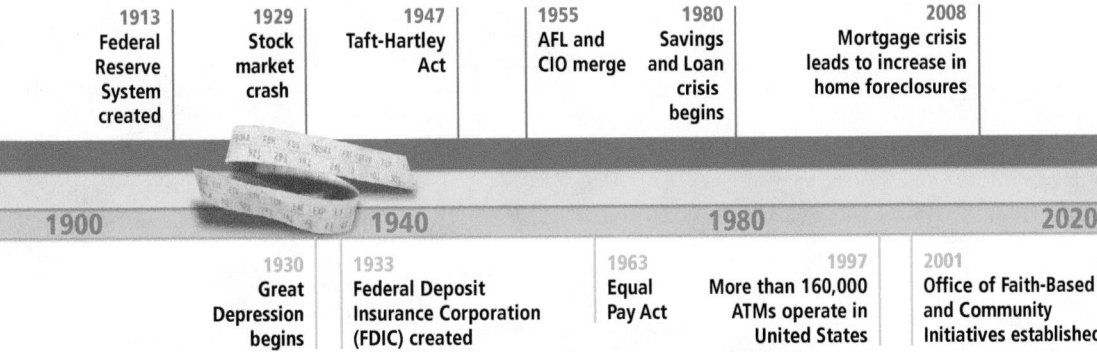

1913	1929	1947	1955	1980	2008
Federal Reserve System created	Stock market crash	Taft-Hartley Act	AFL and CIO merge	Savings and Loan crisis begins	Mortgage crisis leads to increase in home foreclosures

1900 — **1940** — **1980** — **2020**

1930	1933	1963	1997	2001
Great Depression begins	Federal Deposit Insurance Corporation (FDIC) created	Equal Pay Act	More than 160,000 ATMs operate in United States	Office of Faith-Based and Community Initiatives established

Measuring the Economy's Performance

Background Knowledge L3

Point out that nations with different economic systems may measure economic success differently. Ask students to discuss what measurements American economists might use to assess the health of the U.S. economy.

Instruct L3

Ask **What is a business cycle?** (*cycle of economic growth and decline in modern industrial economies*) **What indicators do economists study to understand and explain business cycles?** (*stock prices, interest rates, manufacturers' new orders of goods, rates of inflation, and GDP*) **How does a rising rate of inflation affect the value of a nation's currency?** (*As a nation's rate of inflation increases, the value of its currency decreases.*) **How might inflation affect a nation's GDP?** (*If inflation decreases the value of a nation's currency, the GDP, which is measured in the nation's currency, also decreases.*)

Independent Practice

Ask students to prepare to teach a group of interested fifth graders about inflation and GDP. Tell students to write explanations of these two indicators, and remind them to use simple statements defining or describing any difficult concepts. Encourage students to use visual aids to clarify their explanations.

Monitor Progress

As students prepare their presentations, circulate to make sure that they are keeping their work simple enough for fifth graders to understand.

Answer

Caption All families are affected by rising food prices because they have limited supplies of money, no matter how wealthy they are. However, families that have less money will be more seriously affected by rising food prices.

Differentiated Instruction   Solutions for All Learners

L4 Advanced Readers   L4 Gifted and Talented Students

Governments, businesses, labor organizations, and even individual citizens use measures of inflation to guide their economic decision-making. The Consumer Price Index (CPI) is the most widely used measure of inflation in the United States and serves to assess the average change over time in the prices paid by urban consumers for a representative "basket" of goods and services. Have students do research for more information about the CPI in order to present an approximately three-minute explanation to a peer. (The U.S.

Department of Labor Bureau of Labor Statistics Web site is a good starting point.) Explain that students should identify only the most important and relevant information. Remind students to begin by writing notes to guide their presentations. Then, explain that they should read the presentation aloud, timing themselves to make sure that the delivery takes no longer than three minutes. Tell them to continue practicing until they can deliver the information fluently from memory and within the time limit.

Step-by-Step Instruction

Objectives

- Analyze the importance of trade-offs and opportunity costs in economic decision making.
- Provide examples of cost-benefit analysis.
- Analyze the primary sources of federal revenue and the major areas of federal spending in the United States.
- Explain the terms *budget*, *deficit*, and *national debt*.

Analyzing Costs and Benefits

Background Knowledge ⓛ₃

Ask students to share examples of a recent economic decision in which they opted to buy one thing rather than another on the basis of how they wanted to spend their money. Tell them that businesses and governments make similar choices. Ask students to predict the kinds of economic choices a government must make.

Instruct ⓛ₃

Ask **What are trade-offs and opportunity costs?** *(Trade-offs are what we are willing to give up whenever we choose one course of action over another; opportunity costs are the most desirable alternative given up.)* **Why is it important for decision makers to consider trade-offs and opportunity costs?** *(because it will help them clarify the worth and practicality of various courses of action)* **What are the benefits of auto safety? Are they worth the costs? Explain.** *(Benefits include fewer auto-related deaths, less property damage, lower insurance premiums. Most students will say that, yes, the benefits are worth the costs.)*

Independent Practice

Have students create a three-column chart. In the first column, have them list three or four choices that they made yesterday. In the second column, have them list the trade-offs that correspond to their choices. In the third column, tell them to list the opportunity costs for each choice.

Monitor Progress

Circulate to make sure that students understand the concepts of trade-offs and opportunity costs.

Analyzing Costs and Benefits

Economists point out that all individuals, businesses, and large groups of people make decisions that involve trade-offs. Trade-offs are all the alternatives that we give up whenever we choose one course of action over another. One alternative, though, is usually more desirable than all the others. The most desirable alternative given up as the result of a decision is called the opportunity cost. At times, a decision's opportunity cost may be unclear or complicated. Nonetheless, consumers, businesses, and governments must carefully consider trade-offs and opportunity costs before making a decision.

Safety Versus Cost and Convenience Tens of thousands of people are killed every year in auto accidents in the United States. Safety features like antilock brakes, air bags, and seatbelts may save lives, but they also make cars more expensive. Throughout history, government policymakers have had to weigh the costs and benefits of any policy proposal, including those regarding the regulation of business, health, safety, and foreign policy.

Costs of Auto Safety	
Safety Feature	**Cost**
Antilock brakes	$600.00
Side-impact air bags	$350.00
Traction control	$1,200.00

History Background

Opportunity Cost When economists speak of cost, they are not always talking about price. For economists, cost is not necessarily an intrinsic property of a good or service. Rather, cost is relative; it is the alternative we give up when we choose one option over another—a lost opportunity and lost benefits. A number of earlier writers and thinkers, including philosopher John Stuart Mill (1806–1873) and economist Marie-Ésprit Léon Walras (1834–1910), touched on the notion of opportunity cost. However, it was Austrian economist Friedrich von Wieser (1851–1926) who created a general theory of opportunity cost. Wieser systematically developed the concept in *Der natürliche Wert (Natural Value)*, published in 1889.

The Federal Budget

The federal budget is a written document indicating the amount of money the government expects to receive during a certain year and authorizing the amount the government can spend that year. Government officials who take part in the budgeting process debate how much should be spent on specific programs such as defense, education, and scientific research.

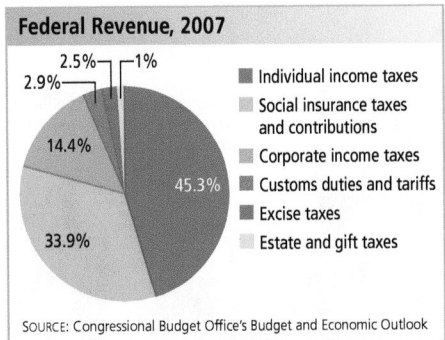

Federal Revenue, 2007

- 45.3% Individual income taxes
- 33.9% Social insurance taxes and contributions
- 14.4% Corporate income taxes
- 2.9% Customs duties and tariffs
- 2.5% Excise taxes
- 1% Estate and gift taxes

SOURCE: Congressional Budget Office's Budget and Economic Outlook

▲ This graph shows the sources of government revenue. What are the largest sources of federal income?

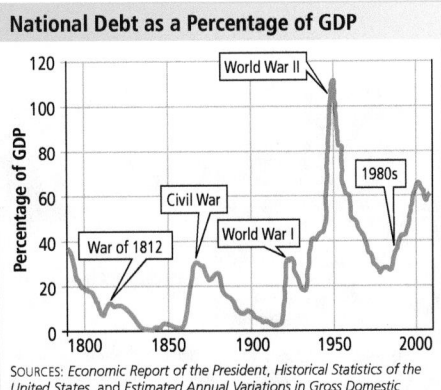

National Debt as a Percentage of GDP

World War II · Civil War · 1980s · War of 1812 · World War I

SOURCES: *Economic Report of the President, Historical Statistics of the United States,* and *Estimated Annual Variations in Gross Domestic Product, 1789–1909* by Thomas Senior Berry

▲ If the federal government's spending is greater than its income in any given year, then the budget is said to be in deficit. The government must then borrow money to pay the shortfall. The total of the government's borrowed money over time is added together to form the national debt.

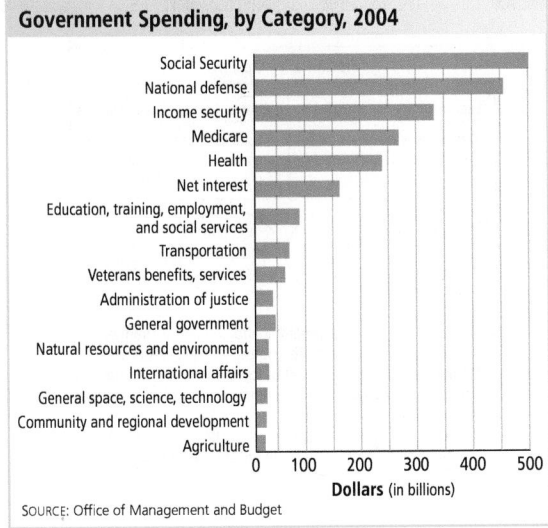

Government Spending, by Category, 2004

Social Security · National defense · Income security · Medicare · Health · Net interest · Education, training, employment, and social services · Transportation · Veterans benefits, services · Administration of justice · General government · Natural resources and environment · International affairs · General space, science, technology · Community and regional development · Agriculture

Dollars (in billions) — 0, 100, 200, 300, 400, 500

SOURCE: Office of Management and Budget

◄ This graph shows how the government spends its money. What are the largest areas of federal spending?

The Federal Budget

Background Knowledge L3

Explain that a budget is a plan that shows how a given amount of money will be spent. Ask students whether they or their families have created a budget. Discuss the benefits of economic planning, and explain that students will learn about the budget of the U.S. government.

Instruct L3

Ask **What is the purpose of the federal budget?** *(to indicate the amount of money the government expects to receive during a certain year and to authorize the amount it can spend in that year)* **How does a budget relate to the concepts of trade-offs and opportunity costs?** *(The government must make economic choices when it decides how to spend its revenue; for example, to meet the budgeted military expenditures in a given year, the government may decide not to fund other programs.)* **What is useful about expressing the national debt as a percentage of GDP rather than as a dollar amount?** *(Possible answer: because a dollar amount gives no context for the relative size of the debt and, therefore, the government's ability to repay it)*

Independent Practice

Have students rearrange the data in the chart "Government Spending, by Category, 2004," and create a new bar graph representing how they think the federal government should spend its revenue.

Monitor Progress

Ask students to compose a short summary in which they describe the historical changes in the U.S. national debt. Ask them to include any generalizations they can make between the debt and historical events.

Differentiated Instruction Solutions for All Learners

L1 Special Needs Students   **L2 English Language Learners**   **L2 Less Proficient Readers**

Read aloud the introductory paragraph on this page. Then, have students examine the three graphs. Ask them to consider how the graphs relate to the passage. Ask **What is helpful about a circle graph showing federal revenue?** *(Without knowing how much money is coming in and from what sources, government leaders would not be able to make responsible decisions about how much to tax various groups and how much to spend.)* **Do the government's revenues always**

cover its expenditures for a given year? *(No; the chart on national debt illustrates that spending is frequently greater than income, resulting in federal deficits and a national debt.)* **How does the category of "net interest" in the chart on government spending relate to the chart on national debt?** *(Because the federal government's spending often exceeds its income, it must borrow money to fund the difference, and interest is the cost of borrowing money.)*

Answers

Caption The largest sources of federal income are individual income taxes and social insurance taxes and contributions.

Caption The largest areas of spending are Social Security, national defense, income security, and Medicare.

Step-by-Step Instruction

Objectives

- Define *fiscal policy.*
- Summarize expansionary and contractionary fiscal policies, and explain how governments use them to influence the economy.
- Describe characteristics of the business cycle.
- Describe the origins and structure of the U.S. Federal Reserve System.
- Introduce the concept of monetary policy and analyze the tools used by the Federal Reserve Board to guide the economy.
- Summarize the differences between fiscal and monetary policy.

Tools for Moderating the Business Cycle: Fiscal Policy

Background Knowledge ⓛ₃

Students have learned that the U.S. government must raise revenue to cover its expenditures. Ask them to predict how revenue and spending decisions might affect economic growth, inflation, and employment.

Instruct ⓛ₃

Ask **What is fiscal policy?** *(use of government spending and revenue collection to influence the economy)* **How does fiscal policy affect the economy?** *(Fiscal policies influence economic growth, control employment rates, maintain price stability.)* **What is the difference between an expansionary and a contractionary fiscal policy?** *(Expansionary policy decreases taxes and increases spending to increase growth or to prevent or reverse a recession; contractionary policy decreases spending and increases taxes to slow the economy in times of increasing demand and inflation.)*

Independent Practice

Have students analyze the business cycle graphic. Then ask them to write a description of one full cycle, including when either expansionary or contractionary policies might apply.

Monitor Progress

Discuss what part of the cycle the country is in today, using signs such as prosperity or unemployment.

Tools for Moderating the Business Cycle: Fiscal Policy

The federal government takes in money to pay for its spending through taxation and borrowing. The decisions the government makes about taxing and spending can have a powerful impact on the overall economy. Fiscal policy is the use of government spending and revenue collection to influence the economy. Fiscal policies are used to achieve economic growth, full employment, and price stability.

▼ Cutting government spending is difficult because some voters will object to cuts that impact their interests.

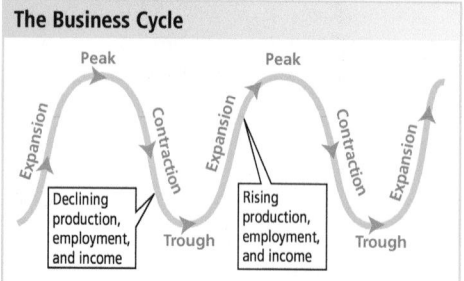

The Business Cycle

Peak — Peak

Expansion / Contraction / Expansion / Contraction / Expansion

Declining production, employment, and income — Trough — Rising production, employment, and income — Trough

▲ In a business cycle, a period of rising real GDP reaches a peak, then falls into a contraction. When the contraction reaches the low point, or trough, a new expansion begins. From 1854 to 1991, the United States experienced 31 business cycles. Excluding wartimes, the cycles averaged 48 months.

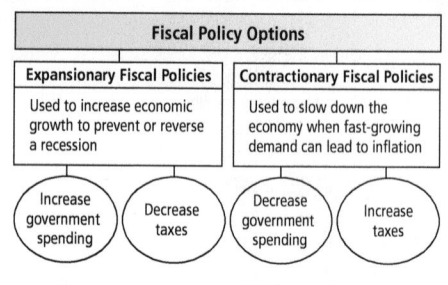

Fiscal Policy Options

Expansionary Fiscal Policies	Contractionary Fiscal Policies
Used to increase economic growth to prevent or reverse a recession	Used to slow down the economy when fast-growing demand can lead to inflation

Increase government spending — Decrease taxes — Decrease government spending — Increase taxes

▲ The total level of government spending can be changed to help increase or decrease the output of the economy. Similarly, taxes can be raised or lowered to help increase or decrease the output of the economy. Fiscal policies are difficult to put into practice because many laws dictate spending. Also, it is difficult to predict the business cycle, and there is a significant lag in time before policies take effect.

History Background

The Multiplier Effect Explain to students that one of the most important aspects of fiscal policy is the *multiplier effect.* The multiplier effect is the idea that every dollar change in fiscal policy—whether an increase in spending or a decrease in taxes—creates a change in the national income greater than one dollar. For example, the government, fearing a recession, stimulates the economy by paying businesses an extra $10 billion to produce more goods and services. However, the GDP will increase by more than $10 billion because the businesses that sold the $10 billion in goods and services to the government have earned an additional $10 billion. These businesses will spend their additional earnings on wages, raw materials, and investment, sending money to workers, suppliers, and stockholders. These recipients will spend some of this money, perhaps as much as 80 percent, or $8 billion. The businesses that benefit from this additional spending will pass it back to households, which will again spend about 80 percent, or $6.4 billion. The next round will add an additional $5.1 billion, and so on. In the final tally, the initial government spending of $10 billion leads to an increase of approximately $50 billion in GDP.

Tools for Moderating the Business Cycle: Monetary Policy

After the charter of the Second Bank of the United States expired, states chartered some banks while the federal government chartered others. Reserve requirements—the amount of money that banks are required to keep on hand—were difficult to enforce, and bank runs often led to panic. After the Panic of 1907, Congress responded with the Federal Reserve Act of 1913. This act created the Federal Reserve System—a group of twelve independent banks that could lend to other banks in times of need. Monetary policy refers to the actions the Federal Reserve Board takes to influence the level of real GDP and the rate of inflation in the economy.

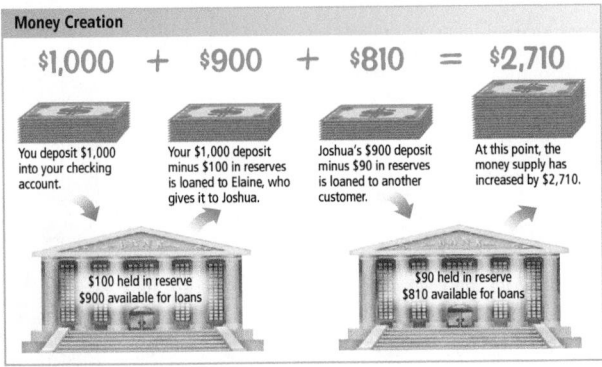

Money Creation

$1,000 + $900 + $810 = $2,710

You deposit $1,000 into your checking account.

Your $1,000 deposit minus $100 in reserves is loaned to Elaine, who gives it to Joshua.

Joshua's $900 deposit minus $90 in reserves is loaned to another customer.

At this point, the money supply has increased by $2,710.

$100 held in reserve
$900 available for loans

$90 held in reserve
$810 available for loans

◄ The Federal Reserve is best known for its role in regulating the nation's money supply. Too much money in the economy leads to inflation. This diagram shows how money is created. By altering the amount of money banks are required to keep in reserve, the Fed can increase or shrink the money supply.

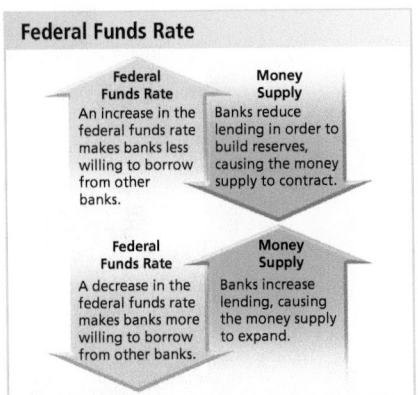

Federal Funds Rate

Federal Funds Rate
An increase in the federal funds rate makes banks less willing to borrow from other banks.

Money Supply
Banks reduce lending in order to build reserves, causing the money supply to contract.

Federal Funds Rate
A decrease in the federal funds rate makes banks more willing to borrow from other banks.

Money Supply
Banks increase lending, causing the money supply to expand.

▲ The federal funds rate is the interest rate that banks charge each other when they lend each other reserves. An increase in the federal funds rate makes borrowing more costly, and the monetary supply contracts. Banks are more willing to borrow and lend money when the federal funds rate is low.

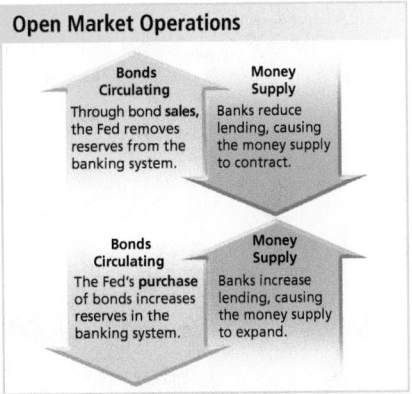

Open Market Operations

Bonds Circulating
Through bond **sales**, the Fed removes reserves from the banking system.

Money Supply
Banks reduce lending, causing the money supply to contract.

Bonds Circulating
The Fed's **purchase** of bonds increases reserves in the banking system.

Money Supply
Banks increase lending, causing the money supply to expand.

▲ When the Fed purchases government bonds on the open market, the bond seller deposits the money from the bond sale in the bank. In this way, funds enter the banking system, setting in motion money creation. When the Fed sells government bonds that it holds, bond buyers pay for the bonds using money from their bank accounts. When the Fed receives this money, it is taken out of circulation.

Step-by-Step Instruction

Objectives

- Explain the importance of foreign trade to the U.S. economy.
- Understand the purposes of free-trade agreements, such as NAFTA.
- Define *balance of trade* and *trade deficit*.
- Identify major trade organizations and their member nations.

U.S. Foreign Trade

Background Knowledge (L3)

Remind students that the United States, like most nations, is engaged in international trade. Ask students to predict how the U.S. economy might be affected by importing more goods and services than it exports.

Instruct (L3)

Have students study the bar graph on this page and the visuals on the following page. Ask **Which four countries are the leading importers to the United States?** (*Canada, China, Mexico, and Japan*) **What is the balance of trade?** (*the difference between the value of a country's exports and the value of its imports*) **In recent years, has the United States had a trade surplus or a trade deficit?** (*a trade deficit*)

U.S. Foreign Trade

Foreign trade has played an important role in the U.S. economy. A free-trade zone is a region where a group of countries agrees to reduce or eliminate trade barriers, such as tariffs or taxes on imports. The North American Free Trade Agreement (NAFTA) set the goal of eliminating all tariffs and trade barriers between Canada, Mexico, and the United States by 2009. Supporters of NAFTA point to increased trade among the countries. About 100 regional trading organizations operate in the world today. Many goods are produced globally by multinational corporations, with parts produced in one country and assembled in another.

U.S. Exports and Imports, by Major Trading Partners, August 2006–August 2007

SOURCE: U.S. Census Bureau

Specialization and Trade International trade occurs when one country provides resources that another country needs. By specializing in the production of certain goods and services, nations can use their resources more efficiently. Do research at the library or online to learn more about absolute and comparative advantage to understand why specialization and trade can benefit all nations—even those with few resources.

Differentiated Instruction   Solutions for All Learners

(L1) Special Needs Students   (L2) English Language Learners   (L2) Less Proficient Readers

Have students examine the photograph of the ship on this page. Ask **What kind of ship is shown in the photograph, and what it is it carrying?** (*Sample: The vessel is a container ship that is loaded with thousands of containers that will be loaded onto trains and trucks when the ship arrives in port.*) Shipping remains a major means of transporting goods and that container ships continue to carry the bulk of the world's dry cargo today. Ask **Why would businesses transport freight by ship when they might choose planes?** (*Possible answer: Because transporting freight by ship is relatively inexpensive compared to shipping freight by airplane*) Tell students that modern container ships are enormous. The largest ships are longer than three football fields and require propellers weighing in excess of 85 tons. Ships of this size can carry approximately 10,000 containers. Even so, these behemoths require relatively small crews of just 13 to 25 people.

Balance of Trade

The **balance of trade** is the relationship between a nation's imports and exports.

Historical Context: According to the theory of mercantilism, a nation could increase its wealth by protecting its own industries from foreign competition through tariffs, or taxes on imports, and by striving to export more than it imports. The American colonies provided a market for British-made goods. American colonists were not permitted to trade with countries other than Britain or to manufacture their own goods.

Today: In recent decades, the United States has had an unfavorable balance of trade. It has imported more than it has exported and experienced annual trade deficits. A trade imbalance can be corrected by limiting imports or increasing exports.

Major Exports and Imports, 2007

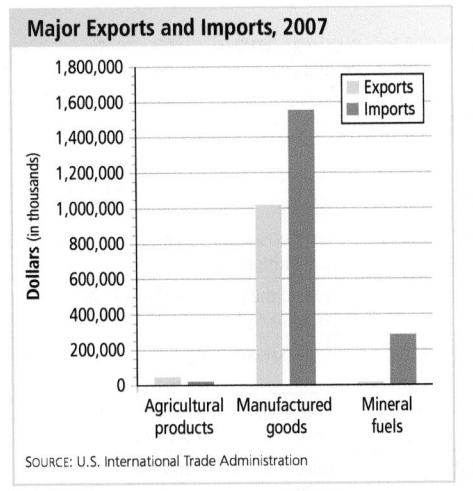

SOURCE: U.S. International Trade Administration

Major Trade Organization Members

Asia-Pacific Economic Cooperation (APEC)

Caribbean Community and Common Market (CARICOM)

European Union (EU)

North American Free Trade Agreement (NAFTA) and APEC

Southern Common Market (MERCOSUR)

Refer students to the visuals on this page. Ask **In 2003, what kind of goods did the United States make the most money exporting?** (*manufactured goods*) **According to the map, which continent has no countries belonging to a major trade organization?** (*Africa*) Ask students to speculate why this is the case.

Independent Practice

Tell students to review the bar graph on the previous page showing major U.S. trading partners. Have each student write a paragraph presenting a theory that explains the high level of imports that the U.S. buys from both Canada and China. Tell students to include in their explanations applicable information from the bar graph on this page.

Monitor Progress

Circulate to make sure that students are able to cite reasons for the importance of U.S. trade with Canada and China. Coach students with questions such as: Where is Canada located? What may be some of its products that the U.S. imports? What do you know about China's economy? What might be some of China's exports?

History Background

NAFTA Although the North American Free Trade Agreement (NAFTA) has won many supporters, it also has a large number of critics. In fact, the debate over the costs and benefits of the agreement continues. For example, in 2004 many of NAFTA's supporters lauded the positive findings of a World Bank report that marked the tenth anniversary of the agreement's implementation (*Lessons From NAFTA for Latin America and the Caribbean Countries: A Summary of Research Findings*). Critics, however, quickly pointed out methodological peculiarities in the finding most often cited by supporters—that NAFTA had increased Mexico's GDP by four to five percent between 1994 and 2002. After a careful review of the report, The Center for Economic and Policy Research concluded that the World Bank used incorrect data as part of its evidence. In fact, the Center pointed out that had the World Bank used different data sources, it would have indicated that in the last 10 years, Mexico experienced slower growth under NAFTA.

Landmark Decisions of the Supreme Court

The table below lists key Supreme Court cases, issues, and decisions that have had a lasting impact on the course of the nation's history. Following the table, you will find a more detailed summary of each of these landmark Supreme Court cases.

The Case	The Issues	The Supreme Court's Decision
Marbury v. *Madison* (1803)	Judicial Review, Checks and Balances	First decision to assert judicial review: the power of the Court to interpret the constitutionality of a law
McCulloch v. *Maryland* (1819)	Federalism, States' Rights	Upheld the power of the national government and denied the right of a state to tax a federal agency.
Gibbons v. *Ogden* (1824)	Federalism, States' Rights, Interstate Commerce	Upheld broad congressional power to legislate and regulate commerce between states.
Worcester v. *Georgia* (1832)	Federalism, States' Rights; Native American Sovereignty	Ruled that Georgia had no power to pass laws affecting the Cherokees because federal jurisdiction over the Cherokees was exclusive.
Dred Scott v. *Sandford* (1857)	Slavery, 5th Amendment, Citizens' Rights	Ruled that slaves were property, not citizens and, therefore, Dred Scott was not entitled to use the courts.
Munn v. *Illinois* (1876)	5th Amendment, Public Interest; States' Rights	Upheld an Illinois law regulating railroad rates because the movement of grain was closely related to public interest.
Civil Rights Cases (1883)	14th Amendment Equal Protection Clause, Racial Discrimination	Stated that the 14th Amendment only applied to discriminatory action taken by states, not to discriminatory actions taken by individuals.
Wabash, St. Louis & Pacific R.R. v. *Illinois* (1886)	Federalism, Interstate Commerce	Struck down an Illinois law regulating interstate railroad rates, ruling that it infringed on the federal government's exclusive control over interstate commerce.
United States v. *E.C. Knight Co.* (1895)	Sherman Antitrust Act, Federalism, States' Rights	The Sherman Antitrust Act does not apply to manufacturers located within a single state, because under the 10th Amendment, states have the right to regulate "local activities."
In Re Debs (1895)	Labor Strikes, Interstate Commerce	Ruled that the federal government had the authority to halt a railroad strike because it interfered with interstate commerce and delivery of the mail.
Plessy v. *Ferguson* (1896)	Segregation, 14th Amendment Equal Protection Clause	Permitted segregated public facilities, arguing that separate but equal accommodations did not violate the equal protection clause of the 14th Amendment.
United States v. *Wong Kim Ark* (1898)	Immigration, citizenship, 14th Amendment	Affirmed that under the 14th Amendment, all persons born in the United States are citizens of the United States.
Northern Securities Co. v. *United States* (1904)	Sherman Antitrust Act, Interstate Commerce	Sherman Antitrust Act could apply to any company that sought to eliminate competition in interstate commerce, including companies chartered within a single state.
Lochner v. *New York* (1905)	Labor conditions, property rights, 14th Amendment	Struck down a state law setting a 10-hour day for employees because the law interfered with an employee's right to contract with an employer and violated the protection of liberty guaranteed by the 14th Amendment.
Muller v. *Oregon* (1908)	Women's rights, Labor Conditions, 14th Amendment	In a departure from the *Lochner* case, the Court upheld a state law limiting women's work hours, viewing women as a special class needing special protections.
Standard Oil of New Jersey v. *United States* (1911)	Antitrust	Ruled that Standard Oil was an illegal monopoly and ordered that it be dissolved into smaller, competing companies.
American Tobacco v. *United States* (1911)	Antitrust	Ruled that American Tobacco was an illegal monopoly and ordered that it be dissolved into smaller, competing companies.
Schenck v. *United States* (1919)	1st Amendment freedom of speech, national security	The Court limited free speech in time of war, reasoning that freedom of speech can be limited if the words present a "clear and present danger" to the country.
Abrams v. *United States* (1919)	1st Amendment freedom of speech, national security	Upheld the convictions of persons who distributed antigovernment literature in violation of the Espionage Act. But Justices Holmes and Brandeis dissented, urging more stringent protection of the 1st Amendment.
Gitlow v. *New York* (1925)	1st Amendment freedoms of speech and press, 14th Amendment	Ruled that the freedoms of speech and press were "incorporated" and protected from impairment by the states by the due process clause of the 14th Amendment.
Stromberg v. *California* (1931)	1st Amendment freedom of speech, 14th Amendment	Overturned an anticommunist law that banned the public display of a red flag. This was the first time the Supreme Court struck down a state law under the 1st Amendment as applied to the states by the 14th Amendment.
Near v. *Minnesota* (1931)	1st Amendment freedom of speech, 14th Amendment	The Supreme Court struck down a Minnesota state law, ruling that it infringed upon freedom of the press, guaranteed by the due process clause of the 14th Amendment.

The Case	The Issues	The Supreme Court's Decision
Schechter Poultry Corporation v. United States (1935)	New Deal, separation of powers, interstate commerce	The Court held that Congress, not the President, has the power to regulate interstate commerce. The National Industrial Recovery Act was declared unconstitutional for exceeding the commerce power that the Constitution had given to Congress.
West Coast Hotel v. Parrish (1937)	Minimum wage laws, 5th Amendment	Ruled that the Constitution allowed the restriction of liberty of contract by state law where such restriction protected the community, health, safety, or vulnerable groups.
West Virginia State Board of Education v. Barnette (1943)	Pledge of Allegiance, 1st Amendment	The Court found that a state law requiring students to pledge allegiance to the flag violated freedom of speech and freedom of religion.
Hirabayashi v. United States (1943)	5th Amendment, civil liberties, national security	The Supreme Court upheld the legitimacy of travel restrictions imposed on Japanese Americans during World War II.
Korematsu v. United States (1944)	5th Amendment, civil liberties, national security	Ruled that the internment of Japanese Americans during World War II did not violate the Constitution.
Everson v. Board of Education (1947)	1st Amendment, establishment clause	The New Jersey law allowing reimbursement of money to parents whose children attended Catholic schools did not violate the 1st amendment. Some services "are separate from the religious function."
Dennis v. United States (1951)	1st Amendment, civil liberties, national security	The Court ruled that the Smith Act, which prohibited advocacy of the overthrow of the U.S. government by force and violence, did not violate the 1st Amendment.
Brown v. Board of Education of Topeka (1954)	School segregation, 14th Amendment	The Court found that segregation itself was a violation of the Equal Protection Clause, commenting that "in the field of public education the doctrine of 'separate but equal' has no place."
Watkins v. United States (1957)	Rights of the accused, 5th Amendment	The Bill of Rights is applicable to congressional investigations, as it is to all forms of governmental action.
Yates v. United States (1957)	1st Amendment freedom of speech, national security	Ruled that the Smith Act did not forbid persons from advocating forcible overthrow of the government; it only forbade actions to achieve that goal.
Cooper v. Aaron (1958)	School segregation, 14th Amendment	The Court ruled unanimously against the Little Rock School Board's efforts to not comply with the Brown decision.
Mapp v. Ohio (1961)	Search and seizure 4th and 14th amendments	Ruled that evidence obtained by searches and seizures in violation of the Constitution is inadmissible.
Baker v. Carr (1962)	Legislative reapportionment, 14th Amendment	Ruled that federal Courts could direct that election-district boundaries be redrawn to ensure citizens' political rights.
Engel v. Vitale (1962)	1st Amendment, establishment clause	Ruled that the recitation of a prayer in a public classroom was a violation of the establishment clause of the 1st Amendment.
Gideon v. Wainwright (1963)	Rights of the accused, 6th and 14th amendments	The Court said that all states must provide an attorney in all felony and capital cases for people who cannot afford one themselves.
Reynolds v. Sims (1964)	Legislative reapportionment, 14th Amendment	Extended the one-person, one-vote principle of *Wesberry* v. *Sanders* (1964) to states, ruling that state legislative districts should be roughly equal in population so that every voter has an equally weighted vote.
Heart of Atlanta Motel v. United States (1964)	Racial segregation, interstate commerce	Racial segregation of private facilities engaged in interstate commerce was found unconstitutional.
Miranda v. Arizona (1966)	Rights of the accused, 5th, 6th, and 14th amendments	Before questioning suspects held in custody, police must inform suspects that they have the right to remain silent, that anything they say may be used against them, and that they have the right to counsel.
Swann v. Charlotte-Mecklenburg Board of Education (1971)	School desegregation, busing	Ruled that busing students to various schools is an acceptable way to integrate segregated school systems. The Court said school districts had broad powers to find solutions to the problem of segregation.
Tinker v. Des Moines (1969)	Students' rights, 1st Amendment freedom of speech	Students in school may exercise freedom of speech as long as they do not disrupt classwork, create substantial disorder, or interfere with the rights of others.
New York Times v. United States (1971)	1st Amendment freedom of the press	The Court limited censorship through "prior restraint" of the press, noting that it is the obligation of the government to prove that actual harm to the nation's security would be caused by the publication.
Roe v. Wade (1973)	Abortion, 9th Amendment, "right to privacy"	Decided that states could regulate abortions only in certain circumstances but otherwise a woman's right to an abortion was protected by her right to privacy.
United States v. Nixon (1974)	Executive privilege, separation of powers	Executive privilege was subordinate to "the fundamental demands of due process of law in the fair administration of criminal justice." President Nixon had to surrender audiotapes to a special prosecutor.
Regents of the University of CA v. Bakke (1978)	Affirmative action, 14th Amendment,	The Court held that a university could consider an applicant's race in making admissions decisions, but the use of strict racial quotas in affirmative action programs was not permissible.
New Jersey v. T.L.O. (1985)	Students' rights, 4th and 14th amendments	School officials, unlike the police, need only "reasonable suspicion" to search students when they believe illegal activity is occurring.
Texas v. Johnson (1989)	1st Amendment freedom of speech	Ruled that desecrating the flag as an act of protest is an act of expression protected by the 1st Amendment.
Cruzan v. Director, Missouri Department of Health (1990)	"Right to die," 9th Amendment, 14th Amendment	Individuals have the right to refuse medical treatment, but the State can preserve life unless there is "clear and convincing" evidence that the patient desires the withdrawal of medical treatment.

Supreme Court Cases

The Case	The Issues	The Supreme Court's Decision
Board of Education of Westside Community Schools v. Mergens (1990)	1st Amendment, Establishment Clause	Allowing students to meet in noncurricular clubs on campus and discuss religion is constitutional because it does not amount to state sponsorship of a religion.
Planned Parenthood of Southeastern Pennsylvania, et al. v. Casey (1992)	Abortion, 14th Amendment, "right to privacy"	The Court upheld a woman's "liberty" to have an abortion but also allowed for restrictive state regulations as long as they did not create an "undue burden" or "substantial obstacle" for a woman.
Vernonia School District v. Acton (1995)	Students' rights, 4th Amendment search and seizure	The Court decided that drug testing of student athletes was constitutional; students' rights can be lessened at school if it is necessary to maintain student safety.
Reno v. American Civil Liberties Union (1997)	Internet, 1st Amendment, freedom of Speech	Ruled that the 1996 Federal Communications Decency Act violated the 1st Amendment's right to freedom of speech by not clearly defining which Internet materials were "indecent."
Bush v. Gore (2000)	Election rules, 14th Amendment	Following the controversial 2000 presidential election, the Supreme Court held that the Florida Supreme Court's plan for recounting ballots was unconstitutional.
Mitchell v. Helms (2000)	1st Amendment, Establishment Clause	Ruled that a federal law providing funds for educational materials to public and private schools, including Catholic parochial schools, does not violate the 1st Amendment's Establishment Clause.
District of Columbia v. Heller (2008)	2nd Amendment	The Court rules that a ban on handguns in the District of Columbia violated the 2nd Amendment right to bear arms.

Abrams v. United States (1919)

(1st Amendment freedom of speech, national security) Jacob Abrams and others distributed leaflets attacking the U.S. decision to send troops to Russia, which was experiencing revolution and civil war. They were found guilty of violating the Espionage Act. The Supreme Court upheld the convictions citing Holmes's "clear and present danger" test. But Justices Holmes and Brandeis published a powerful dissenting opinion. Holmes argued that the "silly leaflet" of "poor and puny anonymities" posed no real danger to U.S. efforts, and thus failed to present a "clear and present danger." He urged his colleagues to enforce the 1st Amendment more stringently.

American Tobacco v. U.S. (1911)

(antitrust) Federal regulators filed an antitrust suit against American Tobacco, controlled by James Buchanan "Buck" Duke. The company controlled more than 90 percent of the world tobacco market. In 1911, the Supreme Court declared the company was a monopoly in violation of the Sherman Antitrust Act and ordered it to be split into five smaller competing companies.

Baker v. Carr (1962)

(legislative reapportionment, 14th Amendment) Rapid population growth had occurred in Tennessee's cities, but the rural-dominated Tennessee legislature did not redraw state legislature districts. Cities with larger populations were underrepresented, while rural communities with smaller populations held the majority of representation. Mayor Baker of Nashville asked for federal court help. The Supreme Court ruled that the apportionment of state legislative districts is within the jurisdiction of federal courts. The Court directed a trial to be held in a Tennessee federal court. The case led to the 1964 *Wesberry* decision, which affirmed voters' right to the equal protection guaranteed by the 14th Amendment and established the principle of "one man, one vote" for the apportionment of congressional districts.

Board of Education of Westside Community Schools v. Mergens (1990)

(1st Amendment, establishment clause) A request by Bridget Mergens to form a student Christian religious group at school was denied by an Omaha high school principal. Mergens took legal action, claiming that a 1984 federal law required "equal access" for student religious groups. The Court ordered the school to permit the club, stating that "a high school does not have to permit any extracurricular activities, but when it does, the school is bound by the . . . [Equal Access] Act of 1984. Allowing students to meet on campus and discuss religion is constitutional because it does not amount to 'State sponsorship of a religion.'"

Brown v. Board of Education of Topeka (1954)

(school segregation, 14th Amendment) Probably no twentieth-century Supreme Court decision so deeply stirred and changed life in the United States as *Brown*. An eight-year-old girl from Topeka, Kansas, was not permitted to attend her neighborhood school because she was an African American. The Court found that segregation was a violation of the Equal Protection Clause, commenting that "in the field of public education the doctrine of 'separate but equal' has no place. . . . Segregation is a denial of the equal protection of the laws." The decision overturned *Plessy*, 1896.

Bush v. Gore (2000)

(election rules, 14th Amendment) Following the controversial 2000 presidential election, the Florida Supreme Court ordered that every county in Florida had to manually recount some ballots. George Bush filed a request for review in the U.S. Supreme Court. The Supreme Court held that the Florida court's plan for recounting ballots was unconstitutional, noting that the Equal Protection Clause guarantees individuals that their ballots cannot be devalued by "later arbitrary and disparate treatment." The Court reasoned that there were too many procedural differences among the various counties for a fair recount to be conducted by the deadline date set by law.

Civil Rights Cases (1883)

(14th Amendment Equal Protection Clause, racial discrimination) The Civil Rights Act of 1875 included punishments for businesses that practiced discrimination. The Court ruled on a number of cases involving the acts in 1883, finding that the Constitution, "while prohibiting discrimination by governments, made no provisions . . . for acts of racial discrimination by private individuals." The decision limited the impact of the Equal Protection Clause, giving tacit approval for segregation in the private sector.

Cooper v. Aaron (1958)

(school segregation, 14th Amendment) President Eisenhower sent troops to Little Rock, Arkansas, to protect black students and enforce court-ordered school integration. But the local school board and state government continued to use delaying tactics. Arkansas officials even claimed that a state governor had the same power as the Supreme Court to interpret the Constitution. African American students appealed to the Supreme Court. The Court reaffirmed the *Brown* ruling that segregation was unconstitutional and boldly affirmed the Supreme Court's authority as the ultimate interpreter of the Constitution.

Cruzan v. Director, Missouri Department of Health (1990)

("right to die," 9th Amendment, 14th Amendment) After Nancy Beth Cruzan was left in a "persistent vegetative state" by a car accident, Missouri officials refused to comply with her parents' request that the hospital terminate life-support. The Court upheld the State policy under which officials refused to withdraw treatment, rejecting the argument that the Due Process Clause of the 14th Amendment gave the parents the right to refuse treatment on their daughter's behalf. Although individuals have the right to refuse medical treatment, "incompetent" persons are not able to exercise this right; without "clear and convincing" evidence that Cruzan desired the withdrawal of treatment, the State could legally act to preserve her life.

Dennis v. United States (1951)

(1st Amendment, civil liberties, national security) Eugene Dennis, a leader of the Communist Party in the United States, was arrested for violation of the Smith Act, which prohibited advocacy of the overthrow of the U.S. government by force and violence. Dennis claimed that the law violated his 1st Amendment right to free speech. Reasoning that the Communist Party is a conspiratorial organization with "evil" intent, the Supreme Court upheld the Smith Act and Dennis's conviction. The Court ruled that free speech may be limited if it presents a clear and present danger to overthrow the government of the United States by force or violence.

District of Columbia v. Heller (2008)

(2nd Amendment, right to bear arms) The Supreme Court upheld a Court of Appeals decision overturning a District of Columbia law that made it illegal for private citizens to own handguns. The law also required that other firearms be kept either unassembled or with trigger locks in place, thus rendering them unusable. The Court ruled, 5–4, that this law violated a person's Second Amendment right to lawfully own a firearm. Justice Antonin Scalia stated in the Court's opinion "Few laws in the history of our Nation have come close to the severe restriction of the District's handgun ban. . . . Undoubtedly some think that the Second Amendment is outmoded in a society . . . where gun violence is a serious problem. That is perhaps debatable, but what is not debatable is that it is not the role of this Court to pronounce the Second Amendment extinct."

Dred Scott v. Sandford (1857)

(slavery, 5th Amendment, citizens' rights) This decision upheld property rights over human rights by saying that Dred Scott, a slave, could not become a free man just because he had traveled in "free soil" states with his master. A badly divided nation was further fragmented by the decision. "Free soil" federal laws and the Missouri Compromise line of 1820 were held unconstitutional because they deprived a slave owner of the right to his "property" without just compensation. This narrow reading of the Constitution, a landmark case of the Court, was most clearly stated by Chief Justice Roger B. Taney, a states' rights advocate.

Engel v. Vitale (1962)

(1st Amendment establishment clause) The State Board of Regents of New York required the recitation of a nonsectarian prayer at the beginning of each school day. A group of parents filed suit against the required prayer. The Supreme Court ruled that the recitation of a prayer in a public classroom was a violation of the establishment clause of the 1st Amendment. The Court ruled New York's action unconstitutional, observing, "There can be no doubt that . . . religious beliefs [are] embodied in the Regents' prayer."

Supreme Court Cases

Everson v. Board of Education (1947)

(1st Amendment, establishment clause) New Jersey allowed for the reimbursement of transportation costs to parents whose children attended private schools, including parochial Catholic schools. Arch Everson, a taxpaying resident of Ewing Township, sued the local school district, insisting that this reimbursement violated both the New Jersey State Constitution and the First Amendment. In a 5–4 ruling, the Supreme Court upheld the law, stating that the "First Amendment has erected a wall between church and state. . . . New Jersey has not breached it here."

Gibbons v. Ogden (1824)

(federalism, states' rights, interstate commerce) Aaron Ogden's exclusive New York ferry license gave him the right to operate steamboats to and from New York. Thomas Gibbons was operating steamboats between New York and New Jersey under a U.S. federal license. Ogden obtained an injunction from a New York court ordering Gibbons to stop operating his boats in New York waters. The Supreme Court invalidated the New York licensing regulations, holding that federal regulations should take precedence under the Constitution's Supremacy Clause (Article VI, Section 2). The decision strengthened the power of the United States to regulate interstate business. Federal regulation of the broadcasting industry, oil pipelines, and banking are all based on *Gibbons*.

Gideon v. Wainwright (1963)

(rights of the accused, 6th and 14th amendments) Gideon was charged with breaking into a poolroom. He could not afford a lawyer, and Florida refused to provide counsel for trials not involving the death penalty. Gideon defended himself poorly and was sentenced to five years in prison. The Court called for a new trial, arguing that the Due Process Clause of the 14th Amendment applied to the 6th Amendment's guarantee of counsel for all poor persons facing a felony charge. Gideon later was found not guilty with the help of a court-appointed attorney.

Gitlow v. New York (1925)

(1st Amendment freedoms of speech and press, 14th Amendment) Gitlow was convicted for distributing a manifesto that called for the establishment of socialism through strikes and other actions. The Supreme Court considered whether the 1st and 14th amendments had influence on state laws. According to what came to be known as the "incorporation" doctrine, the Court argued that the provisions of the 1st Amendment were "incorporated" by the 14th Amendment. The New York law was not overruled, but the decision clearly indicated that the Court could make such a ruling. Later cases extended the incorporation doctrine. Today, the Supreme Court holds that almost every provision of the Bill of Rights applies to both the federal government and the states.

Heart of Atlanta Motel v. United States (1964)

(racial segregation, interstate commerce) The Civil Rights Act of 1964 outlawed racial discrimination in "public accommodations," including motels that refused rooms to blacks. Although local desegregation appeared to fall outside federal authority, the government argued that it was regulating interstate commerce. The Court agreed, declaring, "The power of Congress to promote interstate commerce also includes the power to regulate the local incidents thereof, including local activities . . . which have a substantial and harmful effect upon that commerce." Racial segregation of private facilities engaged in interstate commerce was found unconstitutional.

Hirabayashi v. United States (1943)

(5th Amendment, civil liberties, national security) After the Japanese attack on Pearl Harbor, President Roosevelt issued executive orders to protect the West Coast from espionage and sabotage. As a result of these orders, curfews were established, and Japanese Americans were evacuated to relocation centers. Gordon Kiyoshi Hirabayashi, a student at the University of Washington, was convicted of violating a curfew and relocation order. Did the government policies violate the 5th Amendment rights of Americans of Japanese descent? The Supreme Court upheld the curfew, but evaded ruling on the relocation. The Court considered the vulnerability of military installations on the West Coast and the "solidarity" that persons of Japanese descent felt with their motherland, and reasoned that restrictions served an important national interest. Racial discrimination was justified since "in time of war residents having ethnic affiliations with an invading enemy may be a greater source of danger than those of a different ancestry."

In Re Debs (1895)

(labor strikes, interstate commerce) Eugene V. Debs, a leader of the 1894 Pullman Railroad Car workers' strike, refused to halt the strike as ordered by a federal court. Debs appealed his "contempt of court" conviction. Citing Article 1, Section 8 of the Constitution, the Supreme Court ruled that the government had a right to regulate interstate commerce and ensure the operations of the Postal Service. The federal court had a right to stop the strike because the strikers interfered with the railroad's ability to provide interstate commerce and deliver the mail, which benefited the needs and "general welfare" of all Americans.

Korematsu v. United States (1944)

(5th Amendment, civil liberties, national security) After the Japanese attack on Pearl Harbor, President Roosevelt issued executive orders to protect the West Coast from acts of espionage and sabotage. As a result of these orders, more than 110,000 Japanese Americans living on the West Coast were forced to abandon their property and live in primitive camps far from the coast. Korematsu refused to report to an assembly center and was arrested. The Court rejected his appeal, noting that "pressing public necessity [World War II] may sometimes justify restrictions which curtail the civil rights of a single racial group" but added that "racial antagonism" never can justify such restrictions. The *Korematsu* decision has been widely criticized, particularly since few Americans of German or Italian descent were interned. In 1988, the U.S. government officially apologized for the internment and paid reparations to survivors.

Lochner v. New York (1905)

(labor conditions, property rights, 14th Amendment) A New York law limited bakery employees' working hours to no more than 10 hours a day or 60 hours a week. Lochner claimed that the law infringed on his right to make employer/employee contracts and violated the Due Process Clause of the 14th Amendment. The Supreme Court struck down the New York law, arguing that states have the power to regulate health, safety, and public welfare, but that the New York law was not within the limits of these "police powers." The New York law interfered with citizens' property rights, guaranteed by the 14th Amendment.

Mapp v. Ohio (1961)

(search and seizure, 4th and 14th amendments) Admitting evidence gained by illegal searches was permitted by some states before *Mapp*. Cleveland police raided Dollree Mapp's home without a warrant and found obscene materials. She appealed her conviction, saying that the 4th and 14th amendments protected her against improper police behavior. The Court agreed, extending "exclusionary rule" protections to citizens in state courts, saying that the prohibition against unreasonable searches would be "meaningless" unless evidence gained in such searches was "excluded." *Mapp* developed the concept of "incorporation" begun in *Gitlow* v. *New York*, 1925.

Marbury v. Madison (1803)

(judicial review, checks and balances) After defeat in the 1800 election, President Adams appointed many Federalists to the federal courts, but James Madison, the new Secretary of State, refused to deliver the commissions. William Marbury, one of the appointees, asked the Supreme Court to enforce the delivery of his commission based on a provision of the Judiciary Act of 1789 that allowed the Court to hear such cases on original jurisdiction. The Court refused Marbury's request, finding that the relevant portion of the Judiciary Act was in conflict with the Constitution. This decision, written by Chief Justice Marshall, established the evaluation of federal laws' constitutionality, or "judicial review," as a power of the Supreme Court.

McCulloch v. Maryland (1819)

(federalism, states' rights) This is also known as the "Bank of the United States" case. A Maryland law required federally chartered banks to use only a special paper to print paper money, which amounted to a tax. James McCulloch, the cashier of the Baltimore branch of the bank, refused to use the paper, claiming that states could not tax the federal government. The Court declared the Maryland law unconstitutional, commenting that the "power to tax implies the power to destroy."

Miranda v. Arizona (1966)

(rights of the accused; 5th, 6th, and 14th amendments) Arrested for kidnapping and sexual assault, Ernesto Miranda signed a confession including a statement that he had "full knowledge of [his] legal rights." After conviction, he appealed, claiming that without counsel and without warnings, the confession was illegally gained. The Court agreed with Miranda that "he must be warned prior to any questioning that he has the right to remain silent, that anything he says can be used against him in a court of law, that he has the right to . . . an attorney and that if he cannot afford an attorney one will be appointed for him." Although later modified by *Nix* v. *Williams*, 1984, and other cases, *Miranda* firmly upheld citizen rights to fair trials in state courts.

Mitchell v. Helms (2000)

(1st Amendment Establishment Clause) Chapter 2 of the Education Consolidation and Improvement Act of 1981 provides for the allocation of funds for educational materials and equipment to public and private schools to implement "secular, neutral, and nonideological" programs. In Jefferson Parish, Louisiana, about 30 percent of Chapter 2 funds are allocated for private schools, most of which are Catholic. Mary Helms and other public school parents filed suit alleging that the policy violated the 1st Amendment's Establishment Clause. The Supreme Court disagreed, ruling that Chapter 2, as applied in Jefferson Parish, is not a law respecting an establishment of religion, noting that "the religious, irreligious, and areligious are all alike eligible for governmental aid."

Muller v. Oregon (1908)

(women's rights, labor conditions, 14th Amendment) In 1903, Oregon enacted a law prohibiting women from working in factories or laundries more than 10 hours in any day. After a conviction, Curt Muller claimed that the law violated his freedom of contract, protected by the 14th Amendment. The Court upheld the law, viewing women as a special class that needed special protections. The Court noted that a "woman's physical structure and the functions she performs . . . justify special legislation restricting the conditions under which she should be permitted to toil."

Munn v. Illinois (1876)

(5th Amendment, public interest, states' rights) Responding to farmers' complaints about the exorbitant rates they were paying, Illinois passed laws that set maximum rates that railroads and grain storage companies could charge. Munn, a partner in a Chicago warehouse firm, appealed his conviction, contending that the Illinois regulation constituted a taking of property without due process of law. The Supreme Court upheld the Illinois laws, arguing that states may regulate the use of private property "when such regulation becomes necessary for the public good." The case established as constitutional the principle of public regulation of private businesses involved in serving the public interest.

Near v. Minnesota (1931)

(1st Amendment freedom of speech, 14th Amendment) Jay Near published a Minneapolis newspaper whose articles charged that local government and police officials were implicated with gangsters. A local official filed a complaint against Near under a Minnesota law that provided permanent injunctions against those who created a "public nuisance," by publishing, selling, or distributing a "malicious, scandalous and defamatory newspaper." The Supreme Court held that the Minnesota law was an infringement of freedom of the press guaranteed by the Due Process Clause of the 14th Amendment.

New Jersey v. T.L.O. (1985)

(students' rights, 4th and 14th amendments) After T.L.O., a New Jersey high school student, denied an accusation that she had been smoking in the school lavatory, a vice principal searched her purse and found cigarettes, marijuana, and evidence that T.L.O. had been involved in marijuana dealing at the school. T.L.O. was then sentenced to probation by a juvenile court but appealed on the grounds that the evidence against her had been obtained by an "unreasonable" search. The Court rejected T.L.O.'s arguments, stating that the school had a "legitimate need to maintain an environment in which learning can take place," and that to do this "requires some easing of the restrictions to which searches by public authorities are ordinarily subject." The Court thus created a "reasonable suspicion" rule for school searches, a change from the "probable cause" requirement in the wider society.

New York Times v. United States (1971)

(1st Amendment, freedom of the press) In 1971, *The New York Times* obtained copies of classified Defense Department documents, later known as the "Pentagon Papers," which revealed instances in which the Johnson administration had deceived Congress and the American people regarding U.S. policies during the Vietnam War. A U.S. district court issued an injunction against the publication of the documents, claiming that it might endanger national security. On appeal, the Supreme Court cited the 1st Amendment guarantee of a free press and refused to uphold the injunction against publication. The Court noted that it is the obligation of the government to prove that actual harm to the nation's security would be caused by the publication. The decision limited "prior restraint" of the press.

Northern Securities Co. v. United States (1904)

(Sherman Antitrust Act, interstate commerce) In 1901, financiers formed the Northern Securities Company as a holding company that controlled the stock of the Great Northern Railway, Northern Pacific Railway, the Chicago, Burlington & Quincy Railroad, and other railroads. Fearing a monopoly, President Theodore Roosevelt's trust-busting government applied the Sherman Antitrust Act. In response to the question of whether the Sherman Act applied to a company chartered by one of the states, the Supreme Court ruled "It cannot be said that any state may give a corporation, created under its laws, authority to restrain interstate or international commerce. . . . Every corporation created by a state is necessarily subject to the supreme law of the land."

Planned Parenthood of Southeastern Pennsylvania, et al. v. Casey (1992)

(abortion, 14th Amendment, "right to privacy") The Pennsylvania legislature enacted new regulations limiting abortion. Physicians had to provide patients with antiabortion information and wait at least 24 hours before performing an abortion. In most cases, minors needed the consent of a parent, and married women had to notify their husbands of their intention to abort the fetus. The Supreme Court reaffirmed a woman's "liberty" to have an abortion as it had in the *Roe* decision. However, it upheld most of Pennsylvania's provisions, reasoning that they did not create an "undue burden" or "substantial obstacle" for women seeking an abortion. Under this new "undue burden" test, the only provision to fail was the husband notification requirement.

Plessy v. Ferguson (1896)

(segregation, 14th Amendment equal protection) A Louisiana law required separate seating for white and African American citizens on public railroads, a form of segregation. Herman Plessy argued that his right to "equal protection of the laws" was violated. The Court held that segregation was permitted if facilities were equal. The Court interpreted the 14th Amendment as "not intended to give Negroes social equality but only political and civil equality. . . ." The Louisiana law was seen as a "reasonable exercise of (state) police power. . . ." Segregated public facilities were permitted until *Plessy* was overturned by the *Brown* v. *Board of Education* case of 1954.

Regents of the University of California v. Bakke (1978)

(affirmative action, 14th Amendment) Under an affirmative action program, the medical school of the University of California at Davis reserved 16 of 100 slots in each class for "disadvantaged citizens." When Bakke, a white applicant, was not accepted by the school, he claimed racial discrimination in violation of the 14th Amendment. The Court ruled narrowly, requiring Bakke's admission but not overturning affirmative action, preferring to review such questions on a case-by-case basis.

Reno v. American Civil Liberties Union (1997)

(Internet 1st Amendment, freedom of speech) Seeking to protect minors, the 1996 Federal Communications Decency Act made it a crime to transmit obscene or indecent messages over the Internet. The Supreme Court ruled that the "indecent transmission" provision and the "patently offensive display" provision of the Communications Decency Act violated the 1st Amendment's freedom of speech. The Court reasoned the act did not clearly define "indecent." The Internet does not have the special features (such as historical governmental oversight, limited frequencies, and "invasiveness") that have justified allowing greater regulation of content in radio and television.

Reynolds v. Sims (1964)

(legislative reapportionment, 14th Amendment) Voters of Jefferson County, Alabama, filed a suit challenging the apportionment of the Alabama legislature, which was still based on the 1900 federal census. The Supreme Court extended the "one person, one vote" principle that emerged from *Baker* v. *Carr* (1962) and *Wesberry* v. *Sanders* (1964) and applied it to this case, calling for reapportionment based on current census data. Applying the Equal Protection Clause of the 14th Amendment, the Court ruled that state legislative districts should be roughly equal in population so that every voter has an equally weighted vote.

Roe v. Wade (1973)

(abortion, 9th Amendment, "right to privacy") A Texas woman challenged a state law forbidding the artificial termination of a pregnancy, saying that she "had a fundamental right to privacy." The Court upheld a woman's right to choose in this case, noting that the state's "important and legitimate interest in protecting the potentiality of human life" became "compelling" at the end of the first trimester, and that before then,

". . . the attending physician, in consultation with his patient, is free to determine, without regulation by the state, that . . . the patient's pregnancy should be terminated." The decision struck down the state regulation of abortion in the first three months of pregnancy and was modified by *Planned Parenthood of Southeastern Pennsylvania* v. *Casey*, 1992.

Schechter Poultry Corporation v. United States (1935)

(New Deal, separation of powers, interstate commerce) As part of the New Deal, the National Industrial Recovery Act (NIRA) gave the President authority to regulate aspects of interstate commerce. The government convicted Schechter for not observing minimum wage and hour provisions, selling uninspected chickens, and other violations. The Supreme Court ruled that Congress, not the President, has the power to regulate interstate commerce, and that Congress cannot delegate that power to the President. The Court reversed the conviction of Schechter because his business, which operated almost exclusively in New York State, only indirectly affected interstate commerce. The Court also declared the NIRA to be unconstitutional because it exceeded the commerce power that the Constitution had given to Congress.

Schenck v. United States (1919)

(1st Amendment freedom of speech, national security) Schenck, a member of an antiwar group, urged men drafted into military service in World War I to resist and to avoid induction. He was charged with violating the Espionage Act of 1917, which outlawed active opposition to the war. The Court limited free speech in time of war, stating that Schenck's words presented a "clear and present danger. . . ." Although later decisions modified this one, the *Schenck* case created a precedent that 1st Amendment rights are not absolute.

Standard Oil of New Jersey v. United States (1911)

(antitrust) The Standard Oil Company of New Jersey, controlled by John D. Rockefeller, owned virtually all the oil-refining companies in the United States and was extending its stranglehold over oil exploration and retail distribution of refined products. The government therefore prosecuted Standard Oil under the Sherman Antitrust Act. The Supreme Court found Standard Oil to be an illegal monopoly that restrained free competition. It fined Rockefeller and others, and ordered that the company be dissolved into smaller, competing companies.

Stromberg v. California (1931)

(1st Amendment freedom of speech, 14th Amendment) A California state law, enacted in 1919, prohibited the public display of a red flag. Yetta Stromberg, a member of the Young Communist League and a counselor at a camp for working-class children, was arrested for violating the law. Stromberg had led the youth in raising and pledging allegiance to "the workers' red flag." The Court struck down the law, concluding that a law that permitted the punishment of peaceful opposition exercised in accordance with legal means and constitutional limitations was "repugnant to the guarantee of liberty contained in the 14th Amendment."

Swann v. Charlotte-Mecklenburg Board of Education (1971)

(school desegregation, busing) After the *Brown* decision, school desegregation advanced very slowly. The NAACP took the *Swann* case to the Supreme Court on behalf of six-year-old James Swann and other students in the Charlotte-Mecklenburg, North Carolina, school system where the vast majority of black students attended all-black schools. The Court held that all schools in a district need not reflect the district's racial composition, but that the existence of all-white or all-black schools must be shown not to result from segregation policies. It stated that busing students to various schools is an acceptable way to integrate segregated school systems. The Court said school districts had broad powers to find solutions to the problem of segregation.

Texas v. Johnson (1989)

(1st Amendment freedom of speech) To protest national policies, Johnson doused a U.S. flag with kerosene and burned it outside the 1984 Republican National Convention in Dallas. He was arrested and convicted under a Texas law prohibiting the desecration of the Texas and U.S. flags. The Court ruled that the Texas law placed an unconstitutional limit on "freedom of expression," noting that ". . . nothing in our precedents suggests that a state may foster its own view of the flag by prohibiting expressive conduct relating to it."

Tinker v. Des Moines (1969)

(students' rights, 1st Amendment freedom of speech) Marybeth and John Tinker violated a school rule and wore black armbands to school in protest against the Vietnam War. They were suspended. The Tinkers claimed that their freedom of speech had been violated. The Supreme Court agreed, saying that students do not "shed their constitutional rights to freedom of speech or expression at the schoolhouse gate." Students may express personal opinions as long as they do not disrupt classwork, create substantial disorder, or interfere with the rights of others. Since the wearing of black armbands was a "silent, passive expression of opinion" without these side effects, the Tinkers' action was protected by the 1st Amendment.

United States v. E. C. Knight Co. (1895)

(Sherman Antitrust Act, federalism, states' rights) After gaining control of the E. C. Knight Company, the American Sugar Refining Company controlled more than 90 percent of the American sugar-refining industry. The federal government sued the Knight Company under the provisions of the Sherman Antitrust Act. The Court ruled that the Sherman Antitrust Act does not apply to manufacturers located within a single state, because under the 10th Amendment, states have the right to regulate "local activities," such as manufacturing. In later cases, the Court modified its position and permitted Congress greater power to limit monopolies.

United States v. Nixon (1974)

(executive privilege, separation of powers) During the investigation of the Watergate scandal, journalists discovered that President Nixon had recorded all of his conversations in the White House, including some with administration officials accused of illegal activities. A special prosecutor subpoenaed the tapes. Nixon refused to release them, citing separation of powers, his need for confidentiality, and executive privilege to immunity from court demands for information. The Supreme Court rejected his arguments and ordered him to surrender the tapes. Executive privilege was subordinate to "the fundamental demands of due process of law in the fair administration of criminal justice."

United States v. Wong Kim Ark (1898)

(immigration, citizenship, 14th Amendment) The Chinese Exclusion Act of 1882 denied citizenship to Chinese immigrants. Wong Kim Ark was born in 1873 in California to Chinese parents who were resident aliens. In 1894, Ark visited China. When he returned to the United States, he was denied entrance on grounds that he was not a U.S. citizen. The Supreme Court ruled in favor of Ark. Under the 14th Amendment, all persons born in the United States are citizens of the United States. Since he was born in the United States, Ark was a citizen. The Chinese Exclusion Act could not apply to him because he was a citizen by birth.

Vernonia School District v. Acton (1995)

(students' rights, 4th Amendment, search and seizure) The Vernonia school district of Oregon established a student-athlete drug policy that authorized urinalysis drug testing of student athletes. James Acton refused the urinalysis test and was therefore not allowed to participate in the school's junior high football program. Did the school policy violate the 4th Amendment protection against unreasonable search and seizure? The Supreme Court ruled that the school policy was constitutional. The reasonableness of a search is judged by "balancing the intrusion on the individual's 4th Amendment interests against the promotion of legitimate governmental interests." The school's concern over the safety of students under their supervision overrides the minimal intrusion in student-athletes' privacy.

Wabash, St. Louis & Pacific R.R. v. Illinois (1886)

(federalism, interstate commerce) An Illinois law regulated railroad rates on the intrastate (within one state) portion of an interstate (two or more states) journey. The Supreme Court declared the state law to be invalid, ruling that continuous transportation across the country is essential and that states should not impose restraints on the freedom of commerce. The Court stated that the regulation of interstate railroad rates is a federal power and that states cannot enact statutes interfering or seriously affecting interstate commerce. Soon afterward, Congress created the Interstate Commerce Commission (ICC).

Watkins v. United States (1957)

(rights of the accused, 5th Amendment) In 1954, John Watkins testified in hearings conducted by the House Committee on Un-American Activities. Watkins answered questions about himself but refused to give information on individuals who had left the Communist Party, arguing that such questions were beyond the authority of the committee. After being convicted for refusing to answer the committee's questions, Watkins appealed, arguing that his conviction was a violation of the Due Process Clause of the 5th Amendment. The Supreme Court overturned Watkins's conviction. The Court said that congressional committees had to clearly define the specific purposes of their investigations. Congressional committees must abide by the Bill of Rights. No witness can be made to testify on matters outside the defined scope of a committee's investigation.

West Coast Hotel v. Parrish (1937)

(minimum wage laws, 5th Amendment) The case involved Elsie Parrish, an employee of the West Coast Hotel Company, who received wages below the minimum wage fixed by Washington State law. The issue was whether minimum wage laws violated the liberty of contract as construed under the 5th Amendment and applied by the 14th Amendment. The Supreme Court upheld the constitutionality of the minimum wage legislation, ruling that the Constitution allowed the restriction of liberty of contract by state law where such restriction protected the community, health, safety, or vulnerable groups, as in the case of *Muller* v. *Oregon*, 1908.

West Virginia State Board of Education v. Barnette (1943)

("Pledge of Allegiance," 1st Amendment) The West Virginia Board of Education required that all teachers and pupils salute the flag. Some children did not comply, saying the requirement went against their religious beliefs. The Court held that compelling public schoolchildren to salute the flag was unconstitutional. "Compulsory unification of opinion," the Court held, was antithetical to 1st Amendment values. The decision noted that Americans could not be forced to demonstrate their allegiance to "what shall be orthodox in politics, nationalism, religion, or other matters of opinion."

Worcester v. Georgia (1832)

(federalism, states' rights, Native American sovereignty) Two missionaries were convicted for violating a Georgia law requiring all whites living in Cherokee Indian Territory to obtain a state license. The Supreme Court overturned their convictions, ruling that the state had no power to pass laws affecting the Cherokees because federal jurisdiction over the Cherokees was exclusive. Chief Justice John Marshall argued, "The Cherokee nation, then, is a distinct community occupying its own territory in which the laws of Georgia can have no force. The whole intercourse between the United States and this nation, is, by our constitution and laws, vested in the government of the United States."

Yates v. United States (1957)

(1st Amendment, freedom of speech, national security) In 1951, fourteen members of the Communist Party in California were convicted of violating the Smith Act, which said it was illegal to advocate or organize the forceful overthrow or destruction of the U.S. government. Yates claimed that the law violated his 1st Amendment right to freedom of speech. The Supreme Court reversed the convictions, saying that to violate the Smith Act, a person must urge others to do something, not just believe in something. The Court distinguished between speech promoting an idea and speech advocating direct action.

Documents of Our Nation

The Mayflower Compact

The Pilgrims arrived at Massachusetts in 1620. Before disembarking, they signed a covenant that established a basis for self-government derived from the consent of the governed. Forty-one men signed the compact, agreeing to abide by the laws of the government. Women, who did not enjoy equal rights, were not asked to sign.

In the name of God, Amen. We, whose names are underwritten, the loyal subjects of our dread Sovereign Lord King James, by the grace of God, of Great Britain, France and Ireland king, defender of the faith, etc. Having undertaken, for the glory of God, and advancement of the Christian faith, and honor of our king and country, a voyage to plant the first colony in the Northern parts of Virginia, do by these presents solemnly and mutually in the presence of God and one of another, covenant and combine ourselves together into a civil body politick, for our better ordering and preservation, and furtherance of the ends aforesaid; and by virtue hereof to enacte, constitute, and frame such just and equal laws, ordinances, acts, constitutions and offices, from time to time, as shall be thought most meet and convenient for the general good of the Colony unto which we promise all due submission and obedience.

In witness whereof we have hereunder subscribed our names at Cape Cod the eleventh of November, in the year of the reign of our Sovereign Lord, King James, of England, France and Ireland, the eighteenth, and of Scotland the fifty-fourth. Anno Dom. 1620.

▲ Signing of the Mayflower Compact

Patrick Henry
"Liberty or Death"

On March 23, 1775, Patrick Henry urged a Virginia convention to prepare for war against British forces. Decades later, from the recollections of men like Thomas Jefferson, William Wirt wrote a biography of Henry, including the speech below. Henry's passionate speech caused quite a stir, even if we cannot be certain of his exact words.

. . . It is now too late to retire from the contest. There is no retreat but in submission and slavery! Our chains are forged! Their clanking may be heard on the plains of Boston! The war is inevitable—and let it come! I repeat it, sir, let it come!

It is in vain, sir, to extenuate the matter. Gentlemen may cry, Peace, Peace—but there is no peace. The war is actually begun! The next gale that sweeps from the north will bring to our ears the clash of resounding arms! Our brethren are already in the field! Why stand we here idle? What is it that gentlemen wish? What would they have? Is life so dear, or peace so sweet, as to be purchased at the price of chains and slavery? Forbid it, Almighty God! I know not what course others may take; but as for me, give me liberty or give me death!

▲ Patrick Henry addresses fellow Virginians.

Documents of Our Nation

The Mayflower Compact

Explain to students that the Mayflower Compact is considered the earliest example of democracy in the 13 English colonies. Ask **Who ruled England when the Compact was written?** *(James I, the eighteenth king of England)* **Summarize the stated goals of the colonists.** *(to establish a colony for the glory of God, the advancement of the Christian religion, and the honor of the English monarch)* **What does the phrase "combine ourselves into a civil body politick, for our better ordering and preservation" mean?** *(Sample answer: join together to form a government to keep order and provide for public safety)*

"Liberty or Death"

Tell students that, in this speech, Patrick Henry put into words what many colonists were feeling at the time, and that his words became a rallying cry for those in favor of independence from Great Britain. Ask **According to Henry, where are colonists "enslaved"?** *(in Boston)* **Why does Henry think war is inevitable?** *(He says it has actually already begun, and that fellow colonists are already fighting.)* **What does Henry mean when he asks, "Is life so dear, or peace so sweet, as to be purchased at the price of chains and slavery"?** *(He is asking fellow delegates whether they think it is worth living under tyranny to maintain peace and their safety.)*

Differentiated Instruction   Solves for All Learners

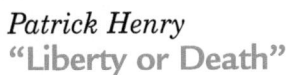

L1 Special Needs Students   L2 English Language Learners   L2 Less Proficient Readers

Explain that language grows and changes over time. The above documents were written hundreds of years ago, and the English during that time was often different in spelling, grammar, and usage from modern English. For example, point out the phrase *dread Sovereigne* in the second line of the Mayflower Compact. Tell students that the word *dread* has undergone a slight change of meaning since the 1620s. In this context, it means "deserving of respect" or "very powerful." Today, its meaning is closer to "terrifying." The spelling of

Sovereigne has also changed since this document was written; it has lost the final *e* and, as it is used here, would probably not be capitalized. Additionally, explain that American and British English still have some different spellings. For example, *honour* is spelled with a *u* in England, but it is spelled *honor* in the United States. Point out other examples of archaic usage of language in either document, such as *raigne* for *reign* or *brethren* for *brothers*. Encourage students to say the words aloud and use the context to determine their meanings.

Common Sense

Explain to students that *Common Sense* was widely read and that it was very influential in persuading Americans to believe that complete independence from Britain was the correct course for the colonies. Ask **What does Paine say will soon make it difficult for Britain to rule the colonies?** *(the complexity of colonial affairs, the distance, and the Britons' ignorance of the colonists' way of life)* **Why does Paine think that the colonists should write their own constitution now, instead of later?** *(because life is precarious, it may not be possible to do this later)* **According to Paine, what should be "King" in a free country? Explain.** *(the law; people should be ruled by law, not by a monarch)*

"Remember the Ladies"

Remind students that women were not allowed to sign the Mayflower Compact and that 150 years later there had still been little progress in equal rights for women. Ask **What does Adams say about "all men"?** *(that they would be tyrants if they could)* **How will women respond if they are not granted the same rights as men?** *(They will rebel.)* **How are Adams's complaints similar to those of the revolutionaries, including those of her husband, who were fighting the British for independence?** *(The Americans claimed that they had a right to rebel against a government that was tyrannical, in part because they had no representation in Parliament. Adams is saying that women will also rebel against laws made by a government in which they have no voice.)*

Thomas Paine
Common Sense

In 1776, after the battles at Lexington and Concord, Thomas Paine published a fiery fifty-page pamphlet that challenged the authority of the British government and the royal monarchy. Paine appealed to the people of America to seek independence from Great Britain.

. . . As to government matters, it is not in the power of Britain to do this continent justice: The business of it will soon be too weighty, and intricate, to be managed with any tolerable degree of convenience, by a power, so distant from us, and so very ignorant of us. . . .

For as in absolute governments the King is law, so in free countries the law ought to be King; and there ought to be no other. But lest any ill use should afterwards arise, let the crown at the conclusion of the ceremony be demolished, and scattered among the people whose right it is.

A government of our own is our natural right: And when a man seriously reflects on the precariousness of human affairs, he will become convinced, that it is infinitely wiser and safer, to form a constitution of our own in a cool deliberate manner, while we have it in our power, than to trust such an interesting event to time and chance. . . .

▲ Abigail Adams

Abigail Adams
"Remember the Ladies"

John and Abigail Adams spent long periods of time apart during the Revolution and the formation of the United States. During this time, they frequently wrote letters to each other, many discussing the politics of the day. In the following letter, written March 31, 1776, Abigail urges her husband to consider the role of women in the new nation.

. . . I long to hear that you have declared an independency—and by the way in the new Code of Laws which I suppose it will be necessary for you to make I desire you would Remember the Ladies, and be more generous and favorable to them than your ancestors. Do not put such unlimited power into the hands of the Husbands. Remember all Men would be tyrants if they could. If particular care and attention is not paid to the Ladies we are determined to foment a Rebellion, and will not hold ourselves bound by any Laws in which we have no voice, or Representation. . . .

History Background

Abigail Smith Adams Wife of one President and mother of another, patriot Abigail Adams was born in Weymouth, Massachusetts, in 1744 to a prominent colonial family. Although her father was a minister, Abigail, like many other girls of her time, received no formal education. However, she had a lively, curious mind, and despite much childhood illness, educated herself. In 1764, she married John Adams who was from the nearby town of Braintree. As John built his law practice in Boston, traveled as a judge, served in the Continental Congress and overseas as a diplomat, Abigail cared for their children and managed the farm, allowing her husband to play a prominent role in our nation's history. Throughout their many long separations, the couple stayed close through a copious and lively correspondence, which today offers unique insights into this crucial period in American history. The letter above is famous because of Abigail's pioneering views on women's rights. At the end of his term, the couple retired to Quincy. Abigail died there in 1818, after spending 54 years in one of the great political partnerships in our nation's early history.

John Adams
"Free and Independent States"

On July 2, 1776, the Second Continental Congress approved a resolution asserting the right of the colonies to be independent of Great Britain. Two days later, Congress would ratify the official Declaration of Independence. In between these two events, John Adams, a member of the Declaration of Independence draft committee, wrote to his wife expressing his excitement.

Yesterday the greatest question was decided, which ever was debated in America, and a greater, perhaps, never was or will be decided among men. A Resolution was passed without one dissenting Colony "that these United Colonies are, and of right ought to be, free and independent States, and as such they have, and of right ought to have, full power to make war, conclude peace, establish commerce, and to do all the other acts and things which other States may rightfully do." You will see, in a few days, a Declaration setting forth the causes which have impelled us to this mighty revolution, and the reasons which will justify it in the sight of God and man. A plan of confederation will be taken up in a few days.

▲ John Adams

Thomas Jefferson
Virginia Statute for Religious Freedom

Thomas Jefferson took great pride in drafting this law in 1777, but it was James Madison who skillfully secured its adoption by the Virginia legislature in 1786. The statute was the basis for the Religion Clauses in the Constitution's Bill of Rights.

. . . Be it enacted by the General Assembly, That no man shall be compelled to frequent or support any religious worship, place, or ministry whatsoever, nor shall be enforced, restrained, molested, or burthened in his body or goods, nor shall otherwise suffer on account of his religious opinions or belief; but that all men shall be free to profess, and by argument to maintain, their opinion in matters of religion, and that the same shall in no wise diminish, enlarge, or affect their civil capacities. . . .

◄ Bruton Parish Church in Virginia

Documents of Our Nation

"Free and Independent States"

Explain to students that when the British colonists in the Americas declared their right to separate from Britain, it was the first time that colonists had ever taken such an action. Ask **How does Adams characterize the resolution?** *(as a decision on "the greatest question" ever debated)* **Why did the delegates propose that the Declaration of Independence be written?** *(to set forth the causes that led to the resolution and the subsequent revolution)* **What is the main idea of the resolution?** *(The colonies will now operate as a nation separate from Great Britain; it also means that the colonies are going to have to fight a war.)*

Virginia Statute for Religious Freedom

Clarify for students that the freedom of religion and the separation of church and state are two of the most important concepts included in the U.S. Constitution, and that those protections have their roots in this document. Ask **What two rights are stated in the first phrase?** *(freedom from being forced to follow a particular religion—meaning a state religion—and freedom to follow one's own beliefs)* **What is the main idea of the second phrase?** *(that it is illegal to punish someone for holding particular beliefs or opinions about religion)* **What is significant about Madison's involvement with the passage of this law in Virginia?** *(He was a main participant in the writing of the Constitution. He obviously felt very strongly about religious freedom and later made sure to include it in the Bill of Rights.)*

Differentiated Instruction   Solutions for All Learners

L4 Advanced Readers   L4 Gifted and Talented Students

Have students conduct research in the library or on the Internet to find the full text of the Virginia Statute for Religious Freedom and the First Amendment. Tell students to analyze the text of the Statute and First Amendment. Finally, ask them to write an essay that explains the Statute's contents and how the ideas it contains are specifically represented in both the Establishment Clause and Free Exercise Clause in the First Amendment to the U.S. Constitution.

The Northwest Ordinance

Explain to students that the Northwest Ordinance was probably the most important achievement of the new government under the Articles of Confederation, and that the basic process for admitting new states outlined within it has since been followed with only slight adjustments. Ask **What rights or concepts are outlined in Articles 1 through 3?** *(1: freedom of worship 2: habeas corpus and trial by jury 3: the idea of education being crucial in a democracy)* **What condition is discussed in Article 6?** *(slavery)* **How do you think this Article may lead to conflict later among slave and non-slave states?** *(Sample answer: No new slave states will be allowed to join the Union, so existing slave states may lose their influence in the federal government, which will cause conflict.)*

The Federalist, No. 51

Explain to students that although most people believed that the government under the Articles of Confederation was unsuccessful, not everyone in 1787 wanted a strong federal government. The authors of the Federalist Papers argued in support of the new Constitution, which proposed a federal system with a strong national government. Ask **According to the essay, what will provide "a great security against a gradual concentration of the several powers in the same department"?** *(giving each branch of government the means to fight off attempts by the other branches to infringe on their respective powers)* **Do you think that the rights of the people are protected under this system?** *(Sample answer: Yes; some of the power of the people is granted to the government at two levels and then further divided among departments so that there is never a concentration of power at any one level or in any one department.)*

The Northwest Ordinance

The Northwest Ordinance

*A*dopted in 1787 by the Second Continental Congress, the Northwest Ordinance created a method for admitting new states to the Union. While the Articles of Confederation lacked a bill of rights, the Ordinance provided one that included many of the basic liberties that would later be included in the Constitution's Bill of Rights.

. . . **ART. 1.** No person, demeaning himself in a peaceable and orderly manner, shall ever be molested on account of his mode of worship or religious sentiments, in the said territory.

ART. 2. The inhabitants of the said territory shall always be entitled to the benefits of the writ of habeas corpus, and of the trial by jury. . . .

ART. 3. Religion, morality, and knowledge, being necessary to good government and the happiness of mankind, schools and the means of education shall forever be encouraged. . . .

ART. 6. There shall be neither slavery nor involuntary servitude in the said territory, otherwise than in the punishment of crimes whereof the party shall have been duly convicted: Provided, always, That any person escaping into the same, from whom labor or service is lawfully claimed in any one of the original States, such fugitive may be lawfully reclaimed and conveyed to the person claiming his or her labor or service as aforesaid.

▲ Settlers moving to the Ohio Territory

The Federalist, No. 51

*T*his Federalist paper was probably written either by James Madison or Alexander Hamilton. It argues that the federal system and the separation of powers proposed in the Constitution provides a system of checks and balances that will protect the rights of the people.

. . . In order to lay a due foundation for that separate and distinct exercise of the different powers of government, which to a certain extent is admitted on all hands to be essential to the preservation of liberty, it is evident that each department should have a will of its own. . . .

But the great security against a gradual concentration of the several powers in the same department, consists in giving to those who administer each department the necessary constitutional means and personal motives to resist encroachments of the others. . . . Ambition must be made to counteract ambition. . . .

The constant aim is to divide and arrange the several offices in such a manner as that each may be a check on the other. . . .

In the compound republic of America, the power surrendered by the people is first divided between two distinct governments, and then the portion allotted to each subdivided among distinct and separate departments. Hence a double security arises to the rights of the people. . . .

History Background

The Federalist Papers The Federalist Papers are a collection of 85 essays written in 1787 and 1788 to convince New Yorkers to ratify the new federal Constitution. The essays were published under the pseudonym Publius, a name chosen to honor one of the founders of the Roman republic Publius Valerius Publicola. (The name *Publicola* means "friend of the people.") For years, authorship of the Federalist Papers was a matter of scholarly debate. However, modern computer analysis and historical evidence has led almost all historians to agree that the essays were written by Alexander Hamilton, James Madison, and John Jay. Most likely, Hamilton wrote 51 of them, Madison wrote 14, and Jay wrote 5; authorship of the remaining 15 is credited to either Hamilton or Madison. All except the last eight were published serially in New York newspapers and then collected for publication in two volumes in 1788. The essays were widely read in their time and remain classics of political science.

Thomas Jefferson
First Inaugural Address

*A*fter the hotly contested presidential election of 1800, some expected that Jefferson's inaugural address would attack the defeated Federalists and their policies. Instead, he extended an olive branch of reconciliation. Jefferson praised a society in which people have full freedom to differ. He urged abidance with the will of the majority and respect for the rights of the minority.

Friends and Fellow Citizens:

... All ... will bear in mind this sacred principle, that though the will of the majority is in all cases to prevail, that will, to be rightful, must be reasonable; that the minority possess their equal rights, which equal laws must protect, and to violate which would be oppression. Let us, then, fellow citizens, unite with one heart and one mind. ... We have called by different names brethren of the same principle. We are all Republicans—we are all Federalists. If there be any among us who would wish to dissolve this Union or to change its republican form, let them stand undisturbed as monuments of the safety with which error of opinion may be tolerated where reason is left free to combat it. ...

Still one thing more, fellow citizens—a wise and frugal government, which shall restrain men from injuring one another, which shall leave them otherwise free to regulate their own pursuits of industry and improvement, and shall not take from the mouth of labor the bread it has earned. This is the sum of good government. ...

You should understand what I deem the essential principles of our government, and consequently those which ought to shape its administration. ... Equal and exact justice to all men, of whatever state or persuasion, religious or political; peace, commerce, and honest friendship, with all nations—entangling alliances with none; the support of the state governments in all their rights ... absolute acquiescence in the decisions of the majority. ...

◄ Campaign banner promoting the election of Thomas Jefferson for President

First Inaugural Address

Explain to students that Thomas Jefferson was a founder of the Democratic-Republican Party, which held that the best government is the least intrusive and that most power should be held by states or even by individuals. At this time, Jefferson's party had just defeated the Federalists in a bitter election and had taken control of Congress, as well as the presidency. Ask **Overall, what is the tone of this address?** *(Sample answer: conciliatory, open, fair, reasonable)* **What does Jefferson say about those who may be in the minority?** *(that their rights must be protected as much as those of the majority)* **According to Jefferson, why are both sides Republicans and Federalists?** *(Both sides support the current Republican form of the Union.)* **What do you think is the significance of this address?** *(Sample answer: It may have set a precedent for post-election cooperation among political parties and helped future governments continue to function even when different parties had control of different branches of the government.)*

Documents of Our Nation

Differentiated Instruction Solutions for All Learners

L1 Special Needs Students   **L2 English Language Learners**   **L2 Less Proficient Readers**

Archaic texts pose a particular challenge to some students. To help students clarify their understanding of this document, work with them in small groups to summarize each paragraph. Have students prepare by listing unfamiliar words, and be sure that several dictionaries are available when you begin. On the board, write "Paragraph 1," and then list students' unfamiliar words or any questions they may have. Begin by discussing the unfamiliar words; have students look

them up, and if the words are no longer in the dictionary or they are unable to locate specific usages, help them use context to figure out their meaning. When all questions are answered and unfamiliar words defined, work with students to trace the meaning of the sentences and write the paragraph's summary statement on the board. Then, write "Paragraph 2" on the board and use the same process until you have summarized each paragraph in the document.

"The Star-Spangled Banner"

Point out to students that shortly before the attack on Fort McHenry was repulsed, the British had captured Washington, D.C., and burned the White House. Ask **What was significant about the events that took place at Fort McHenry?** *(The powerful British were unsuccessful in their attack on the fort, after having captured the nation's capital.)* **How was the fact that the flag was still waving above the fort the next day symbolic?** *(It meant that the Americans still held the fort, and that the British had failed in their attack.)* **Why do you think this song became our national anthem?** *(Sample answer: The story of the less powerful United States defeating or holding back the more powerful Britain is inspirational; also the language is vivid, romantic, and heroic.)*

Independence Day Speech

Remind students that Frederick Douglass was an escaped slave and a famous abolitionist. Ask **What is the tone of this speech?** *(angry, bitter)* **What does Douglass say the Fourth of July represents to enslaved people?** *(the gross injustice of their condition; a sham and a "thin veil" that covers up the crime of slavery)* **What central irony is Douglass pointing out in this speech?** *(the fact that the Fourth of July celebrates liberty and freedom, but is being observed in a nation where hundreds of thousands of people are enslaved)*

▲ Flag that flew over Fort McHenry during the British attack

Francis Scott Key
"The Star-Spangled Banner"

During the War of 1812, a Maryland attorney named Francis Scott Key witnessed the British attack on Fort McHenry, near Baltimore. In the morning, Key was so delighted to see the American flag still flying over the fort that he composed a poem to commemorate the event. Set to the music of a popular folk tune, "The Star-Spangled Banner" was officially made the national anthem by Congress in 1931.

O say, can you see, by the dawn's early light,
What so proudly we hail'd at the twilight's last gleaming?
Whose broad stripes and bright stars, thro' the perilous fight,
O'er the ramparts we watch'd, were so gallantly streaming?
And the rockets' red glare, the bombs bursting in air,
Gave proof thro' the night that our flag was still there.
O say, does that star-spangled banner yet wave
O'er the land of the free and the home of the brave?

▲ Frederick Douglass

Frederick Douglass
Independence Day Speech

In 1852, Douglass accepted an invitation from the leading citizens of Rochester, New York, to speak at their Fourth of July celebration. Douglass delivered a scathing speech in which he attacked the hypocrisy of celebrating independence and freedom in a nation where millions of people were enslaved.

Fellow citizens, pardon me, allow me to ask, why am I called upon to speak here today? What have I, or those I represent, to do with your national independence? Are the great principles of political freedom and of natural justice, embodied in that Declaration of Independence, extended to us? . . .

What, to the American slave, is your Fourth of July? I answer: a day that reveals to him, more than all other days in the year, the gross injustice and cruelty to which he is the constant victim. To him, your celebration is a sham; your boasted liberty, an unholy license; your national greatness, swelling vanity; your sounds of rejoicing are empty and heartless; your denunciation of tyrants, brass-fronted impudence; your shouts of liberty and equality, hollow mockery; your prayers and hymns, your sermons and thanksgivings, with all your religious parade and solemnity, are, to Him, mere bombast, fraud, deception, impiety, and hypocrisy—a thin veil to cover up crimes which would disgrace a nation of savages. There is not a nation of savages. There is not a nation on the earth guilty of practices more shocking and bloody than are the people of the United States at this very hour. . . .

Differentiated Instruction   Solutions for All Learners

L1 Special Needs Students

Have students express the feelings and ideas contained within "The Star-Spangled Banner" in the form of a poster celebrating the song. Have students begin by listing all of the descriptive words in the first verse of the song shown on this page and add their own words to describe the American flag. Encourage students to use words to describe emotions as well as adjectives. Then, have students choose one line from the song and write it neatly using large letters in the center of a sheet of poster board. Have them use art supplies and images to draw or cut out pictures from magazines, and then have them decorate the poster with pictures, other words, or concepts based on their list of descriptive words and their interpretation of the selected verse. When posters are completed, ask volunteers to explain why they chose the verse and how aspects of their poster design support or relate to this verse and to the song as a whole.

Sojourner Truth
"Ain't I a Woman?"

▲ Sojourner Truth

Sojourner Truth, an African American woman prominent in both the abolitionist and early feminist movements, delivered her famous speech at a women's rights convention in Akron, Ohio, in 1851. The version below was first published twelve years later in the Anti-Slavery Standard by Frances Gage, a celebrated antislavery fighter and president of the Convention. Although recent scholarship questions the exact wording of the speech, it made a great impact at the time and has endured as a classic statement of women's rights.

. . . I think that 'twixt the Negroes of the South and the women at the North, all talking about rights, the white men will be in a fix pretty soon. But what's all this here talking about?

That man over there says that women need to be helped into carriages, and lifted over ditches, and to have the best place everywhere. Nobody ever helps me into carriages, or over mud-puddles, or gives me any best place! And ain't I a woman? Look at me! Look at my arm! I have ploughed and planted, and gathered into barns, and no man could head me! And ain't I a woman? I could work as much and eat as much as a man—when I could get it—and bear the lash as well! And ain't I a woman? I have borne thirteen children, and seen most all sold off to slavery, and when I cried out with my mother's grief, none but Jesus heard me! And ain't I a woman? . . .

Elizabeth Cady Stanton
Address to the Legislature of New York

In 1854, Elizabeth Cady Stanton presented this speech to the New York State Legislature. She addressed the inequalities faced by all women under the state laws and discussed the specific challenges met by mothers, wives, and widows.

. . . Gentlemen, in republican America, in the nineteenth century, we, the daughters of the revolutionary heroes of '76, demand at your hands the redress of our grievances—a revision of your State Constitution—a new code of laws. Permit us then, as briefly as possible, to call your attention to the legal disabilities under which we labor.

1st. Look at the position of woman as woman. . . . We are persons; native, free-born citizens; property-holders, tax-payers; yet are we denied the exercise of our right to the elective franchise. We support ourselves, and, in part, your schools, colleges, churches, your poor-houses, jails, prisons, the army, the navy, the whole machinery of government, and yet we have no voice in your councils. We have every qualification required by the Constitution, necessary to the legal voter, but the one of sex. . . .

2nd. Look at the position of woman as wife. . . . The wife who inherits no property holds about the same legal position that does the slave on the Southern plantation. She can own nothing, sell nothing. She has no right even to the wages she earns; her person, her time, her services are the property of another. . . .

"Ain't I a Woman?"

Clarify for students that, like Frederick Douglass, Sojourner Truth was a former slave. Truth escaped from her owner in New York just before the state ended slavery in 1828. Ask **What argument against equal rights for women is Truth refuting?** *(the idea that women are more delicate than men and need protection or cannot cope with equal legal rights and responsibilities)* **How does she effectively support her argument?** *(by pointing out all of the challenges and difficulties she has experienced, which prove that she is as tough as or tougher than a man and so should enjoy equal rights)* **How does the refrain "Ain't I a Woman?" help strengthen Truth's presentation?** *(Sample answer: The repetition of the phrase after each example of how she was brutally or cruelly treated helps underscore the ridiculous quality of the idea that women are more fragile or delicate than men and need protection, not equal rights.)*

Address to the Legislature of New York

Explain that at this time Elizabeth Cady Stanton was one of the most famous women suffragists in America. Ask **What does Stanton want to accomplish by this speech?** *(to persuade the New York legislature to amend the state constitution to give women the right to vote)* **What reasons does Stanton give to support the idea that women should vote?** *(They are citizens and pay taxes, thereby supporting the government, and they have every qualification required by the Constitution to be voters.)* **Do you agree with Stanton's comparison of a wife to a slave?** *(Sample answer: No; women were not sold and forced to work without pay as slaves were.)*

Differentiated Instruction   Solutions for All Learners

L1 Special Needs Students   L2 Less Proficient Readers

Have students create an outline of the text of either "Ain't I a Woman?" or Stanton's address to the New York Legislature on this page. Review with students the outline format and model the first steps. For example:

Ain't I a Woman?
  I. Introduction
    A. African Americans and women are talking about rights.
    B. White men will soon be "in a fix."

When their outlines are complete, ask partners to use their outlines to paraphrase the speech excerpt aloud to one another. Then, have students share their outlines in small groups.

The Gettysburg Address

Tell students that, although some disparaged the speech as too short and therefore disrespectful, today Abraham Lincoln's address at Gettysburg is considered a model of *rhetoric*, or the art of using language to please or persuade. Ask **According to Lincoln, what is being tested by the Civil War?** *(whether or not a democracy can survive for very long without falling apart or destroying itself)* **What does Lincoln say is the task to which the people there should now be dedicated?** *(winning the war to keep the Union intact, so that the dead at Gettysburg will not have died in vain)* **What do you think the phrase "government of the people, by the people, and for the people" means?** *(Sample answer: In general, it refers to the republican form of government—a government formed of citizens and by citizens for the protection of their own rights—and specifically it refers to the U.S. government.)*

Abraham Lincoln
The Gettysburg Address

At the Battle of Gettysburg, more than 51,000 Confederate and Union soldiers were listed as wounded, missing, or dead. President Lincoln gave this brief speech at the dedication of The Gettysburg National Cemetery on November 19, 1863. The five known manuscript copies of the speech differ slightly and historians debate which version Lincoln actually delivered. But the address is considered one of the most eloquent and moving speeches in American history. As Lincoln described the significance of the war, he invoked the Declaration of Independence and its principles of liberty and equality, and he spoke of "a new birth of freedom."

Four score and seven years ago our fathers brought forth on this continent, a new nation, conceived in Liberty, and dedicated to the proposition that all men are created equal.

Now we are engaged in a great civil war, testing whether that nation, or any nation so conceived and so dedicated, can long endure. We are met on a great battle-field of that war. We have come to dedicate a portion of that field, as a final resting place for those who here gave their lives that the nation might live. It is altogether fitting and proper that we should do this.

But, in a larger sense, we can not dedicate—we can not consecrate—we can not hallow—this ground. The brave men, living and dead, who struggled here, have consecrated it, far above our poor power to add or detract. The world will little note, nor long remember what we say here, but it can never forget what they did here. It is for us the living, rather, to be dedicated here to the unfinished work which they who fought here have thus far so nobly advanced. It is rather for us to be here dedicated to the great task remaining before us—that from these honored dead we take increased devotion to that cause for which they gave the last full measure of devotion—that we here highly resolve that these dead shall not have died in vain—that this nation, under God, shall have a new birth of freedom—and that government of the people, by the people, for the people, shall not perish from the earth.

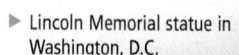

▶ Lincoln Memorial statue in Washington, D.C.

History Background

A Brief Address Most speakers would have used the solemn occasion at Gettysburg to mesmerize spectators for hours, employing all the well worn rhetorical flourishes so loved by nineteenth century orators. Lincoln, however, gave a speech that lasted just minutes—many of those present were not even aware that the president had spoken at all! Yet, he managed to leave a lasting impression on generations with a speech noted for its power and brevity. It was an address that not only honored those who fought and died for union, but also reaffirmed the promise of equality at the foundation of the Declaration of Independence. Some historians contend that Lincoln's famous phrase, "the proposition that all men are created equal," was a bold interpretation of the Constitution as a guarantee of equality for all people regardless of race. At a time of national conflict over this very issue, Lincoln's short address served as a dramatic reminder of what American democracy should strive to be. The keynote speaker at Gettysburg, Edward Everett, a famed orator whose speech lasted two hours, wrote to the president: "I wish that I could flatter myself that I came as near to the central idea of the occasion in two hours as you did in two minutes."

Abraham Lincoln
Second Inaugural Address

*L*incoln delivered his second inaugural address just over a month before his death. He spoke about the war, slavery, and the need "to bind up the nation's wounds." The speech's closing words of reconciliation and healing are today carved in the walls of the Lincoln Memorial.

. . . On the occasion corresponding to this four years ago all thoughts were anxiously directed to an impending civil war. All dreaded it, all sought to avert it. While the inaugural address was being delivered from this place, devoted altogether to saving the Union without war, insurgent agents were in the city seeking to destroy it without war—seeking to dissolve the Union and divide effects by negotiation. Both parties deprecated war, but one of them would make war rather than let the nation survive, and the other would accept war rather than let it perish, and the war came.

One-eighth of the whole population were colored slaves, not distributed generally over the Union, but localized in the southern part of it. These slaves constituted a peculiar and powerful interest. All knew that this interest was somehow the cause of the war. To strengthen, perpetuate, and extend this interest was the object for which the insurgents would rend the Union even by war, while the Government claimed no right to do more than to restrict the territorial enlargement of it. Neither party expected for the war the magnitude or the duration which it has already attained. Neither anticipated that the cause of the conflict might cease with or even before the conflict itself should cease. Each looked for an easier triumph, and a result less fundamental and astounding. Both read the same Bible and pray to the same God, and each invokes His aid against the other. . . . Fondly do we hope, fervently do we pray, that this mighty scourge of war may speedily pass away. Yet, if God wills that it continue until all the wealth piled by the bondsman's two hundred and fifty years of unrequited toil shall be sunk, and until every drop of blood drawn with the lash shall be paid by another drawn with the sword, as was said three thousand years ago, so still it must be said "the judgments of the Lord are true and righteous altogether."

With malice toward none, with charity for all, with firmness in the right as God gives us to see the right, let us strive on to finish the work we are in, to bind up the nation's wounds, to care for him who shall have borne the battle and for his widow and his orphan, to do all which may achieve and cherish a just and lasting peace among ourselves and with all nations.

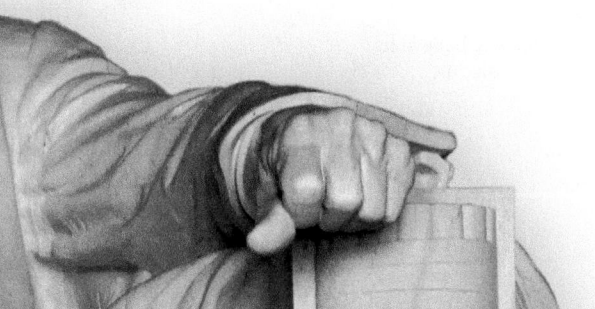

Documents of Our Nation

"I Will Fight No More Forever"

Clarify for students that Chief Joseph gave this very famous speech when he surrendered to the U.S. Army to explain, partly to his subordinate chiefs, why he was doing so. Ask **For what reasons is Chief Joseph surrendering?** *(His people are starving and freezing, and many are missing; he wants to stop running and to find and save as many as he can; he does not want any more to die.)* **What does Chief Joseph mean by "from where the sun now stands"?** *(from this time now)* **What do you think makes this speech poignant or tragic?** *(Sample answer: Chief Joseph was a proud, brave, and extremely able leader, who nearly succeeded in eluding the U.S. Army, but he was willing to surrender in order to avoid further deaths among his people.)*

Preamble to the Constitution of the Knights of Labor

Remind students that the goals of the Knights of Labor were very broad, reaching beyond labor issues to include social and political reforms. Ask **What do the Knights seek to stop, and why?** *(the increase in and unjust accumulation of enormous wealth; to keep the wealthy and powerful from oppressing workers and other less-powerful citizens)* **Why is the organization being formed?** *(to organize and direct the power of the industrial, or working, class)* **Why do you think the power of the Knights might have declined?** *(Sample answer: Their goals were too broad and went far beyond those of labor reforms.)*

Chief Joseph
"I Will Fight No More Forever"

▲ Chief Joseph

*I*n 1877, after being ordered to a reservation, Chief Joseph led some 800 of his Nez Percé people in an attempted escape to Canada. They fled more than 1,000 miles across Idaho and Montana, battling the U.S. Army all along the way. Finally, with fewer than 500 of his people remaining and only 40 miles from Canada, Chief Joseph surrendered. General O.O. Howard reported Chief Joseph's poignant words.

I am tired of fighting. Our chiefs are killed. . . . The old men are all dead. . . . It is cold and we have no blankets. The little children are freezing to death. My people, some of them, have run away to the hills, and have no blankets, no food; no one knows where they are—perhaps freezing to death. I want to have time to look for my children and see how many of them I can find. Maybe I shall find them among the dead. Hear me, my chiefs. I am tired; my heart is sick and sad. From where the sun now stands I will fight no more forever.

Preamble to the Constitution of the Knights of Labor

*T*he Knights of Labor, which adopted its constitution in 1878, was a national labor union that sought the eight-hour day, abolition of child labor, and equal pay for equal work. The organization grew to more than 700,000 workers, but rapidly declined due to unsuccessful strikes and the formation of the American Federation of Labor in 1886.

The recent alarming development and aggression of aggregated wealth, which, unless checked, will inevitably lead to the pauperization and hopeless degradation of the toiling masses, renders it imperative, if we desire to enjoy the blessings of life, that a check should be placed upon its power and upon unjust accumulation, and a system adopted which will secure to the laborer the fruits of his toil; and as this much-desired object can only be accomplished by the thorough unification of labor, and the united efforts of those who obey the divine injunction that "In the sweat of thy brow shalt thou eat bread," we have formed the Noble Order of the Knights of Labor with a view of securing the organization and direction, by co-operative effort, of the power of the industrial classes; and we submit to the world the objects sought to be accomplished by our organization, calling upon all who believe in securing "the greatest good to the greatest number" to aid and assist us. . . .

History Background

Chief Joseph The eloquent chief of the Nez Percé was born In-mut-too-yah-lat-lat ("Thunder Rolling Down the Mountain") around 1840 in Oregon territory. His tribe was one of the most powerful in the Pacific Northwest and also friendly to whites. Joseph was a Christian, as his father had been, and was educated at a Christian school. The pressure of growing white settlement in the western regions led to treaty disputes between Chief Joseph and the U.S. government. In 1877, U.S. officials attempted to move the Nez Percé to a reservation in Idaho. Chief Joseph reluctantly agreed and began preparations for removal. When he heard that a trio of young braves had massacred a group of white settlers, he feared U.S. retaliation and led his followers to Canada instead. All during the summer of 1877, the Nez Percé evaded American troops, Chief Joseph drawing the respect of the enemy for his resourceful strategies and his humane treatment of prisoners. Finally, within 40 miles of the Canadian border, they were forced to surrender. Chief Joseph and his band were sent first to Indian territory (Oklahoma), and later allowed to go to Washington, still in exile from their valley. The tribal leader died at Colville Reservation in Washington State in 1904.

Preamble to the Platform of the Populist Party

*T*he People's, or Populist, Party adopted its party platform in 1892 at its national convention in Omaha, Nebraska. The movement, which emerged from the Farmer's Alliance in the 1880s, sought political reforms and a redistribution of political and economic power.

The conditions which surround us best justify our co-operation; we meet in the midst of a nation brought to the verge of moral, political, and material ruin. Corruption dominates the ballot-box, the Legislatures, the Congress, and touches even the ermine of the bench. . . . The fruits of the toil of millions are boldly stolen to build up colossal fortunes for a few, unprecedented in the history of mankind; and the possessors of these, in turn, despise the Republic and endanger liberty. From the same prolific womb of governmental injustice we breed the two great classes—tramps and millionaires. . . .

We have witnessed for more than a quarter of a century the struggles of the two great political parties for power and plunder, while grievous wrongs have been inflicted upon the suffering people. We charge that the controlling influences dominating both these parties have permitted the existing dreadful conditions to develop without serious effort to prevent or restrain them. . . .

We believe that the power of government—in other words, of the people—should be expanded . . . to the end that oppression, injustice, and poverty shall eventually cease in the land. . . .

Emma Lazarus
"The New Colossus"

*A*t the dedication of the Statue of Liberty in 1886, President Grover Cleveland spoke of the Statue of Liberty as a symbol of Franco-American friendship and American ideals. But Jewish American poet Emma Lazarus saw the statue as a shining beacon to the millions who were migrating to the United States. The poem that she wrote to help raise money for the statue's pedestal is today carved on that pedestal for all to read.

▶ The Statue of Liberty

Not like the brazen giant of Greek fame,
With conquering limbs astride from land to land;
Here at our sea-washed, sunset gates shall stand
A mighty woman with a torch, whose flame
Is the imprisoned lightning, and her name
Mother of Exiles. From her beacon-hand
Glows world-wide welcome; her mild eyes command
The air-bridged harbor that twin cities frame,
"Keep, ancient lands, your storied pomp!" cries she
With silent lips. "Give me your tired, your poor,
Your huddled masses yearning to breathe free,
The wretched refuse of your teeming shore,
Send these, the homeless, tempest-tossed to me,
I lift my lamp beside the golden door!"

Documents of Our Nation

Preamble to the Platform of the Populist Party

Explain that although the Populists did not succeed as a third political party, many of their important ideas were later enacted in the reforms of the Progressive Movement. Ask **What two main social classes of people do the Populists say now exist in America?** *(tramps and millionaires, or the very poor and the very rich)* **Why do you think the Populist Party formed?** *(Sample answer: because some people were unhappy with the political parties that already existed, thinking they were greedy, corrupt, and too wealthy to be concerned with the nation's real social problems)*

"The New Colossus"

Point out that the word *Colossus* and the phrase "brazen giant of Greek fame" both refer to the Colossus of Rhodes, one of the Seven Wonders of the Ancient World. The Colossus was a 110-foot bronze statue of the sun god Helios, which like the Statue of Liberty, stood at the entrance to a harbor—in this case on the Mediterranean island of Rhodes. Ask **According to Lazarus, how is the Statue of Liberty different from the Colossus of Rhodes?** *(She is a welcoming "Mother of Exiles," not a conquering figure.)* **What do you think the "golden door" means?** *(Sample answer: It is a metaphor that describes the harbor or entrance to the United States as a golden doorway to a new, happy, and prosperous life.)*

Differentiated Instruction Solutions for All Learners

L1 Special Needs Students **L2 English Language Learners** **L2 Less Proficient Readers**

Many people think that the imagery in "The New Colossus" is strong and emotionally evocative. Have students reread the poem to select an image or idea that appeals to them, such as "a mighty woman with a torch" or "the golden door," and also look through their textbooks for photographs relating to immigration, especially during the late nineteenth and early twentieth centuries. Discuss with students words that intrigue them but may need clarification, such as "huddled masses." Then, ask students to create a drawing or other visual that illustrates their favorite imagery, word, or idea from the poem. Encourage students to write a title or short caption for their illustration.

The Atlantic Exposition Address

Explain that many African Americans, such as W.E.B. Du Bois, criticized Washington's approach to the fight for civil rights as too mild and accommodating of whites. Ask **What is the main idea of this excerpt?** *(that African Americans can gain equality by developing skills or starting businesses that will bring them economic power first, and then, through this, increased political equality and power)* **What types of pursuits does Washington recommend that African Americans follow to gain equality?** *(skilled work; work in agriculture, mechanics, business, domestic service, and the professions)* **Do you agree or disagree with the statement, "No race can prosper till it learns that there is as much dignity in tilling a field as in writing a poem"? Explain?** *(Answers will vary but should be supported with logical reasoning.)*

"The New Nationalism"

Remind students that in the 1912 election, Roosevelt ran against Republican incumbent William Taft and Democratic challenger Woodrow Wilson as a third-party candidate for the Progressive, or Bull Moose, Party. Ask **How does this speech appeal to the interests and concerns of the Progressives?** *(It advocates legislation to control big business and bring an end to its corrupting influence on government.)* **How do you think Roosevelt views the role of the President under the New Nationalism?** *(He says that it is the role of the President to act as a "steward of the public welfare," so he sees the President as an advocate for and protector of the people.)*

Booker T. Washington
The Atlantic Exposition Address

*I*n 1895, African American leader Booker T. Washington addressed a predominantly white audience in Atlanta. He urged fellow blacks to build friendly relations with whites and to start "at the bottom" by working at "the common occupations of life." Other black leaders rejected Washington's plan and called it the "Atlanta Compromise."

. . . Ignorant and inexperienced, it is not strange that in the first years of our new life we began at the top instead of at the bottom; that a seat in Congress or the state legislature was more sought than real estate or industrial skill; that the political convention or stump speaking had more attractions than starting a dairy farm or truck garden. . . .

To those of my race who depend on bettering their condition in a foreign land or who underestimate the importance of cultivating friendly relations with the Southern white man, who is their next-door neighbor, I would say: "Cast down your bucket where you are"— cast it down in making friends in every manly way of the people of all races by whom we are surrounded.

Cast it down in agriculture, mechanics, in commerce, in domestic service, and in the professions. And in this connection it is well to bear in mind that whatever other sins the South may be called to bear, when it comes to business, pure and simple, it is in the South that the Negro is given a man's chance in the commercial world. . . . Our greatest danger is that in the great leap from slavery to freedom we may overlook the fact that the masses of us are to live by the productions of our hands, and fail to keep in mind that we shall prosper in proportion as we learn to dignify and glorify common labour, and put brains and skill into the common occupations of life. . . . No race can prosper till it learns that there is as much dignity in tilling a field as in writing a poem. It is at the bottom of life we must begin, and not at the top. Nor should we permit our grievances to overshadow our opportunities. . . .

▲ Booker T. Washington

Theodore Roosevelt
"The New Nationalism"

*A*t Ossowatomie, Kansas, in 1910, Theodore Roosevelt formulated the themes that would guide his 1912 campaign for the presidency. He proposed a New Nationalism that would promote human welfare and counter the power of big business.

. . . Now, this means that our government, National and State, must be freed from the sinister influence or control of special interests. Exactly as the special interests of cotton and slavery threatened our political integrity before the Civil War, so now the great special business interests too often control and corrupt the men and methods of government for their own profit. . . .

History Background

Booker Taliaferro Washington Educator, civil rights activist, and author, Booker T. Washington was born into slavery in Virginia in 1856. After emancipation, Washington was forced by his family's poverty to work from the age of nine doing various dangerous and difficult jobs. However, he was determined to learn and, at 16, enrolled at the Hampton Normal and Agricultural Institute, working as a janitor to pay his expenses. Convinced that education was the key to equality, Washington decided to become a teacher. After several different teaching assignments, in 1881, he founded the Tuskegee Normal and Industrial Institute in Alabama. To raise funds for the Institute, Washington began traveling around the country and soon became a celebrated speaker. Washington delivered the above address at the opening of the Cotton States Exposition. Critics such as W.E.B. DuBois dubbed the speech the "Atlanta Compromise," to protest what they felt was Washington's accommodation of whites on the issue of civil rights. Most blacks were comfortable with Washington's words, and he was highly respected by government leaders. He wrote several books, including his 1901 autobiography *Up From Slavery* before his death in 1915.

It has become entirely clear that we must have government supervision of the capitalization, not only of public-service corporations, including, particularly, railways, but of all corporations doing an interstate business. . . .

Combinations in industry are the result of an imperative economic law which cannot be repealed by political legislation. The effort at prohibiting all combination has substantially failed. The way out lies, not in attempting to prevent such combinations, but in completely controlling them in the interest of the public welfare. . . .

This New Nationalism regards the executive power as the steward of the public welfare. It demands of the judiciary that it shall be interested primarily in human welfare rather than in property, just as it demands that the representative body shall represent all the people rather than any one class or section of the people. . . .

▲ Theodore Roosevelt delivering a campaign speech

Woodrow Wilson
"Peace Without Victory"

On January 22, 1917, before the United States entered World War I, President Wilson spoke to the U.S. Senate about his vision for the future. He called for a "peace without victory." His ideas would later influence international cooperation in the League of Nations.

. . . It must be a peace without victory. . . . Victory would mean peace forced upon the loser, a victor's terms imposed upon the vanquished. It would be accepted in humiliation, under duress, at an intolerable sacrifice, and would leave a sting, a resentment, a bitter memory upon which terms of peace would rest, not permanently but only as upon quicksand. Only a peace between equals can last. . . .

No peace can last, or ought to last, which does not recognize and accept the principle that governments derive all their just powers from the consent of the governed, and that no right anywhere exists to hand peoples about from sovereignty to sovereignty as if they were property. . . .

There can be no sense of safety and equality among the nations if great preponderating armaments are henceforth to continue here and there to be built up and maintained. The statesmen of the world must plan for peace, and nations must adjust and accommodate their policy. . . .

I am proposing that all nations henceforth avoid entangling alliances which would draw them into competitions of power, catch them in a net of intrigue and selfish rivalry, and disturb their own. . . . There is no entangling alliance in a concert of power. When all unite to act in the same sense and with the same purpose, all act in the common interest and are free to live their own lives under a common protection. . . .

"Peace Without Victory"

Remind students that the League of Nations was the first international organization established to prevent war. Although the United States did not join the League and it failed to prevent World War II, the concept of global cooperation for peace continued with the formation of the United Nations. Ask **What does Wilson mean by "peace without victory"?** *(that peace must be achieved without forcing humiliating terms on the losers; that there must be equality among all participants at the end of the war for peace to last)* **What does Wilson say must be avoided? Why?** *(entangling alliances; they draw nations into competition and rivalries that lead to war.)* **Why do you think he says that there is a benefit in having a "concert of power"?** *(because if all nations unite to preserve peace, then all nations will benefit from mutual protection)*

Differentiated Instruction   Solutions for All Learners

L1 Special Needs Students   **L2 English Language Learners**   **L2 Less Proficient Readers**

To help students analyze the ideas in this speech, ask them to create a concept web. Have them start with a center oval labeled "Peace Without Victory" and then add subordinate ovals for the main idea of each paragraph in the excerpt. To each of the subordinate ovals, have students add key phrases or words that support the main idea. Ask students to review their concept webs with a partner to be sure that they have included all of the main ideas and important supporting details from the excerpt.

First Inaugural Address

Explain that the Great Depression was a worldwide event that had a devastating effect on the United States. Although Franklin D. Roosevelt did not end the depression, his leadership at this time did much to help people. Ask **What does Roosevelt mean when he says "the only thing we have to fear is fear itself"?** *(that it is the people's fear that will prevent them from working to help themselves or to solve the problems of the depression)* **What effect do you think this speech and Roosevelt's attitude had on the public?** *(By instilling fortitude in the people, Roosevelt's speech also made Americans more hopeful about the future and confident in the government.)* **What leadership traits does Roosevelt exhibit in this speech?** *(Sample answer: strength, determination, action, decisiveness, intelligence, measured optimism, compassion, respect)*

"The Sources of Soviet Conduct"

Explain that at this time, George Kennan was director of the State Department's Policy Planning Staff. In that role, he was instrumental in developing the official U.S. foreign policy regarding the Soviet Union and communism, as described in the Truman Doctrine. Ask **According to Kennan, what is the goal of the Soviet Union?** *(to expand its power around the world wherever possible)* **How does he propose that the United States combat this expansion?** *(through firm and vigilant containment in each area where the Soviets are attempting to exert their influence)* **Describe Kennan's view of the tension between the U.S. and the Soviet Union.** *(Sample: Kennan sees the two countries as so fundamentally different that in order to prevail, the U.S. must prove itself superior morally as well as militarily.)*

Franklin D. Roosevelt
First Inaugural Address

By 1933, the depression had reached its depth. Roosevelt's first inaugural address outlined in broad terms how he hoped to govern. He advised Americans "that the only thing we have to fear is fear itself." He reminded Americans that the nation's "common difficulties" concerned "only material things."

▲ Franklin D. Roosevelt greets supporters.

. . . This great Nation will endure as it has endured, will revive and will prosper. So, first of all, let me assert my firm belief that the only thing we have to fear is fear itself—nameless, unreasoning, unjustified terror which paralyzes needed efforts to convert retreat into advance. In every dark hour of our national life a leadership of frankness and vigor has met with that understanding and support of the people themselves which is essential to victory. I am convinced that you will again give that support to leadership in these critical days. . . .

I am prepared under my constitutional duty to recommend the measures that a stricken nation in the midst of a stricken world may require. These measures, or such other measures as the Congress may build out of its experience and wisdom, I shall seek, within my constitutional authority, to bring to speedy adoption.

But in the event that the Congress shall fail to take one of these two courses, and in the event that the national emergency is still critical, I shall not evade the clear course of duty that will then confront me. I shall ask the Congress for the one remaining instrument to meet the crisis—broad Executive power to wage a war against the emergency, as great as the power that would be given to me if we were in fact invaded by a foreign foe. . . .

George Kennan
"The Sources of Soviet Conduct"

George Kennan published this article anonymously in the July 1947 issue of *Foreign Affairs*. He opposed appeasement and promoted firm opposition to the expansion of communism. His ideas on "containment" became the basis for U.S. policy toward the Soviet Union during the Cold War.

. . . In these circumstances it is clear that the main element of any United States policy toward the Soviet Union must be that of long-term, patient but firm and vigilant containment of Russian expansive tendencies. . . .

The Soviet pressure against the free institutions of the western world is something that can be contained by the adroit and vigilant application of counter-force at a series of constantly shifting geographical and political

---

Differentiated Instruction   Solutions for All Learners

L4 Advanced Readers   **L4 Gifted and Talented Students**

Provide students with a world outline map. From information in their textbook and through additional research, have students make a verbal-visual Cold War containment map. The map should indicate through shading, color, or symbols each area or location in which the United States applied the concept of containment against the Soviet Union or communism in general in the period from 1946 to 1989. Examples include Berlin, Greece, Korea, and Vietnam, among others. Then, have students annotate their maps with explanations and descriptions of each event that they have listed. Remind students to include a key and a title for their maps.

points, corresponding to the shifts and maneuvers of Soviet policy, but which cannot be charmed or talked out of existence. The Russians look forward to a duel of infinite duration, and they see that already they have scored great successes. . . .

The issue of Soviet-American relations is in essence a test of the overall worth of the United States as a nation among nations. To avoid destruction the United States need only measure up to its own best traditions and prove itself worthy of preservation as a great nation. . . .

The Pledge of Allegiance

The Pledge of Allegiance was first written in 1892. It was revised twice before 1954, when the words "under God" were added, and it became the version that is still recited today.

I pledge allegiance to the Flag of the United States of America, and to the Republic for which it stands, one Nation under God, indivisible, with liberty and justice for all.

▲ A new citizen salutes the flag.

Dwight D. Eisenhower
Farewell Address

On January 17, 1961, President Eisenhower delivered his farewell to the American people on national television. To the surprise of the American people, the general who had led America to victory in World War II issued a strong warning about the dangers of the "military-industrial complex."

. . . Until the latest of our world conflicts, the United States had no armaments industry. American makers of plowshares could, with time and as required, make swords as well. But now we can no longer risk emergency improvisation of national defense; we have been compelled to create a permanent armaments industry of vast proportions. . . .

This conjunction of an immense military establishment and a large arms industry is new in the American experience. The total influence—economic, political, even spiritual—is felt in every city, every state house, every office of the Federal government. We recognize the imperative need for this development. Yet we must not fail to comprehend its grave implications. . . .

We must never let the weight of this combination endanger our liberties or democratic processes. We should take nothing for granted. Only an alert and knowledgeable citizenry can compel the proper meshing of huge industrial and military machinery of defense with our peaceful methods and goals, so that security and liberty may prosper together. . . .

Documents of Our Nation

The Pledge of Allegiance

Explain that the Pledge of Allegiance was first published in 1892 and was adopted as the official national pledge by Congress in 1942. Ask **In the phrase "the Republic for which it stands," what does "it" stand for and what is the "Republic"?** *(the flag; the United States)* **What is the meaning of and implication of the word "indivisible"?** *(Not able to be divided; sample: the word implies the indissolubility of the nation and it would be particularly meaningful in the post–Civil War era.)* **Why do you think countries have a national pledge?** *(Sample answer: to foster loyalty, unity, and a sense of national pride)*

Farewell Address

Tell students that the mention by Dwight D. Eisenhower of plowshares and swords refers to a passage from Joel 3:10 in the Bible. It means to turn peacetime articles into weapons. Ask **Why has the United States created a permanent arms industry?** *(because in a modern emergency there will not be time to switch peacetime industries over to making weapons and other war materials)* **What does Eisenhower say is necessary to prevent the military-industrial complex from endangering democracy?** *(an alert and knowledgeable citizenry)* **What might be one of the ways in which a military-industrial complex would "endanger our liberties or democratic processes"?** *(Sample answer: Because of the widespread power of the military-industrial complex, it could become self-sustaining by promoting and encouraging military conflict rather than diplomacy.)*

Inaugural Address

Explain that John F. Kennedy was a dynamic and charismatic public speaker. His inaugural address is considered one of the best in our nation's history, and it inspired a generation of young people to join public service. Ask **To whom do you think the second paragraph may be addressed?** *(the Soviet Union or other communist nations)* **What does Kennedy say are the "common enemies" of all humankind?** *(tyranny, poverty, disease, and war)* Have students read the last two printed sentences of the speech on this page. **Why do you think Kennedy chose to address his "fellow citizens of the world"?** *(because he wanted to call all of the world's citizens to work together for the preservation of freedom)*

Letter from Birmingham Jail

Remind students that Mohandas Gandhi had practiced civil disobedience during India's struggle for independence from Great Britain in the 1940s. Dr. Martin Luther King, Jr., was influenced by Gandhi and by the writings of American philosopher Henry David Thoreau, an advocate and practitioner of the concept. Ask **What have the white clergymen asked King to do? Explain King's response to them.** *(They have asked him to cease leading acts of civil disobedience. He writes that African Americans have been waiting 340 years for equality and that that is long enough.)* **What does King say are the effects of segregation?** *(It distorts the soul and damages the personality of everyone involved by giving the segregator a false sense of superiority and the segregated a false sense of inferiority.)* **Why does King use the metaphor of dark storm clouds?** *(Sample answer: because he sees racial injustice as something that is ominous and a hovering heavy darkness, much like dark clouds during a storm.)* **How does King use the metaphors of "dark clouds" and "deep fog"?** *(He uses the images of threatening weather and opaque fog to indicate the present state of ignorance and prejudice and to contrast it with a future that will be enlightened and beautiful.)*

John F. Kennedy
Inaugural Address

On January 20, 1961, President John F. Kennedy delivered his inaugural address in which he announced to the world that **"we shall pay any price, bear any burden, meet any hardship, support any friend, oppose any foe, in order to assure the survival and success of liberty."**

. . . Let the word go forth from this time and place, to friend and foe alike, that the torch has been passed to a new generation of Americans—born in this century, tempered by war, disciplined by a hard and bitter peace, proud of our ancient heritage—and unwilling to witness or permit the slow undoing of those human rights to which this Nation has always been committed, and to which we are committed today at home and around the world.

Let every nation know, whether it wishes us well or ill, that we shall pay any price, bear any burden, meet any hardship, support any friend, oppose any foe, in order to assure the survival and the success of liberty. . . .

Now the trumpet summons us again—not as a call to bear arms, though arms we need; not as a call to battle, though embattled we are—but a call to bear the burden of a long twilight struggle, year in and year out, "rejoicing in hope, patient in tribulation"—a struggle against the common enemies of man: tyranny, poverty, disease, and war itself. . . .

In the long history of the world, only a few generations have been granted the role of defending freedom in its hour of maximum danger. I do not shrink from this responsibility—I welcome it. . . .

And so, my fellow Americans: ask not what your country can do for you—ask what you can do for your country.

My fellow citizens of the world: ask not what America will do for you, but what together we can do for the freedom of man. . . .

▲ President Kennedy giving his Inaugural Address

Martin Luther King, Jr.
Letter from Birmingham Jail

In 1963, King led a campaign of nonviolent protest against segregation and discrimination in Birmingham, Alabama. Rather than obey a court order to desist, King went to jail. From there, he wrote a response to white Alabama clergymen who were urging King to be more moderate in his struggle. King responded that the wait for civil rights had been too long and that civil disobedience against unjust laws was needed to achieve social justice.

My Dear Fellow Clergymen,

While confined here in the Birmingham City Jail, I came across your recent statement calling our present activities "unwise and untimely." . . .

Differentiated Instruction   Solutions for All Learners

English Language Learners   **Less Proficient Readers**

To enhance students' comprehension of the context of "Letter from the Birmingham Jail" written by Dr. Martin Luther King, Jr., have partners create a timeline of some important events in King's life. Students may use information in the textbook or conduct additional research. Instruct students to start their timelines with King's birth in 1929 and end them with his assassination in 1968. The timelines should also include King's arrest and incarceration in Birmingham City Jail as well as five other events of their choice. Before making the actual timeline, students should first list the events that they will illustrate. Remind them to include a title or short caption as well as a date for each event as well as a title for the timeline itself.

We have waited for more than 340 years for our constitutional and God-given rights. The nations of Asia and Africa are moving with jetlike speed toward the goal of political independence, and we still creep at horse and buggy pace toward the gaining of a cup of coffee at a lunch counter.

I guess it is easy for those who have never felt the stinging darts of segregation to say wait. But when you have seen vicious mobs lynch your mothers and fathers at will and drown your sisters and brothers at whim; when you have seen hate-filled policemen curse, kick, brutalize, and even kill your black brothers and sisters with impunity; when you see the vast majority of your 20 million Negro brothers smothering in an airtight cage of poverty in the midst of an affluent society; when you suddenly find your tongue twisted and your speech stammering as you seek to explain to your six-year-old daughter why she can't go to the public amusement park that has just been advertised on television, and see the tears welling up in her little eyes when she is told that Funtown is closed to colored children, . . . then you will understand why we find it difficult to wait. . . .

You express a great deal of anxiety over our willingness to break laws. . . . The answer is found in the fact that there are two types of laws: There are just and there are unjust laws. I would agree with Saint Augustine that "An unjust law is no law at all." . . .

All segregation statutes are unjust because segregation distorts the soul and damages the personality. It gives the segregator a false sense of superiority, and the segregated a false sense of inferiority. . . .

Let us all hope that the dark clouds of racial prejudice will soon pass away and the deep fog of misunderstanding will be lifted from our fear-drenched communities and in some not too distant tomorrow the radiant stars of love and brotherhood will shine over our great nation with all their scintillating beauty.

Yours for the cause of Peace and Brotherhood,
Martin Luther King, Jr.

▲ A reflective King in his Birmingham jail cell

Betty Friedan
The Feminine Mystique

*B*etty Friedan's book exploded onto the American scene in 1963. Her work sparked a national debate about women's roles and was a pivotal event in the modern women's movement.

. . . It . . . is time to stop giving lip service to the idea that there are no battles left to be fought for women in America, that women's rights have already been won. It is ridiculous to tell girls to keep quiet when they enter a new field, or an old one, so the men will not notice they are there. In almost every professional field, in business and in the arts and sciences, women are still treated as second-class citizens. . . . A girl should not expect special privileges because of her sex, but neither should she "adjust" to prejudice and discrimination.

She must learn to compete then, not as a woman, but as a human being. Not until a great many women move out of the fringes into the mainstream will society itself provide the arrangements for their new plan. . . .

◄ Betty Friedan

The Feminine Mystique

Sometimes considered as the catalyst for the modern women's rights movement, Betty Friedan's book was based on an article she wrote about the unfulfilling lives of her fellow Smith College graduates. Ask **What does Friedan say is needed to further women's equality?** *(Many women must move into the mainstream.)* **What do you think Friedan means by the "fringes" and the "mainstream"?** *(Sample answer: The fringes refers to women still being treated as second-class citizens in the workplace; the mainstream refers to what women can achieve in the workplace once enough women have moved away from those "fringes" and are accepted as equals.)* **How does Friedan say society should react to women in the mainstream?** *(In a sense, women should meet society halfway: they should expect no special privileges because of sex; at the same time, they should work for change and have a right to expect that society will "adjust" or acknowledge the new role of women.)*

Differentiated Instruction   Solutions for All Learners

L2 Special Needs Students   L2 Less Proficient Readers

Have students list challenging or unfamiliar words in the excerpts from "Letter from the Birmingham Jail" and *The Feminine Mystique,* including the words in the titles, and other terms such as *impunity, brutalize, ridiculous, privileges,* and *discrimination.* Then, have students use a dictionary to find and record the definitions and write a sentence using the word. Ask students to review their definitions and share their sentences in small groups. Students might also try to find synonyms for these words in their existing vocabulary.

Voting Rights

Tell students that on March 7, 1965, voting rights activists were assaulted and one was killed in a protest march from Selma, Alabama, to the state capital in Montgomery. These events came to be called "Bloody Sunday." President Lyndon B. Johnson, a civil rights supporter, decided to use his position as President to speak out on this issue. Ask **What is the problem that Johnson addresses?** *(the struggles of African Americans who are being denied the right to vote)* **What legislation is he proposing to Congress?** *(a bill that would eliminate illegal barriers to voting)* **What is Johnson's view of the civil rights struggle?** *(It is not simply a question of race or regional difference. It goes beyond politics and affects all Americans.)*

Resignation Speech

Explain that Richard Nixon's resignation marked the first time in history that a President has voluntarily left office. Clarify that although Nixon was not impeached, it was clear to many that if he did not resign, he might be impeached and charged with wrongdoing. Ask **What reasons does Nixon give for his resignation?** *(that he will not have the support of Congress needed to do his job; that the time taken to deal with "the Watergate matter" will distract his administration and Congress from important national issues.)* **Do you think that these are the real or valid reasons for his resignation? Explain?** *(Sample answer: Yes; he was probably correct. However, he might have resigned to avoid being removed from office.)*

Lyndon Johnson
Voting Rights

President Johnson made this speech to Congress on March 15, 1965, a week after deadly racial violence erupted in Selma, Alabama. He used the phrase "we shall overcome," borrowed from African American leaders struggling for equal rights.

. . . There is no Negro problem. There is no Southern problem. There is no Northern problem. There is only an American problem. And we are met here tonight as Americans—not as Democrats or Republicans—we are met here as Americans to solve that problem. . . .

Many of the issues of civil rights are very complex and most difficult. But about this there can and should be no argument. Every American citizen must have an equal right to vote.

Yet the harsh fact is that in many places in this country men and women are kept from voting simply because they are Negroes. . . .

Wednesday I will send to Congress a law designed to eliminate illegal barriers to the right to vote. . . .

But even if we pass this bill, the battle will not be over. What happened in Selma is part of a far larger movement which reaches into every section and State of America. It is the effort of American Negroes to secure for themselves the full blessings of American life.

Their cause must be our cause too. Because it is not just Negroes, but really it is all of us, who must overcome the crippling legacy of bigotry and injustice.

And we shall overcome. . . .

Richard Nixon
Resignation Speech

In the shadow of the Watergate scandal, President Nixon delivered his resignation speech on August 8, 1974. The next morning, he signed the resignation documents, made a final speech to his staff, and stepped onto the Marine One helicopter for the last time, to begin a trip to California as an ex-President.

. . . I have concluded that because of the Watergate matter I might not have the support of the Congress that I would consider necessary to back the very difficult decisions and carry out the duties of this office in the way the interests of the Nation would require. . . .

To continue to fight through the months ahead for my personal vindication would almost totally absorb the time and attention of both the President and the Congress in a period when our entire focus should be on the great issues of peace abroad and prosperity without inflation at home.

Therefore, I shall resign the Presidency effective at noon tomorrow. Vice President Ford will be sworn in as President at that hour in this office. . . .

▲ Richard Nixon leaves the White House after resigning from the presidency.

History Background

We Shall Overcome The song referred to by President Lyndon B. Johnson had by this time become the anthem of the 1960s African American civil rights movement; however, it had existed long before as a gospel hymn and union song. The lyrics to the modern version of "We Shall Overcome" originate from a gospel song titled, "I'll Overcome Someday," written by Charles Tindley and published in 1900. However, the tune was from a much earlier, pre–Civil War piece, most likely a spiritual. The lyrics were by Zilphia Horton, Frank Hamilton, Guy and Candie Carawan, and Pete Seeger. These singers and songwriters were all associated with the Highlander Center, a social justice organization in Tennessee. Since the civil rights struggles of the 1960s, the hymn has been adopted by many other human and civil rights groups around the world.

Jimmy Carter
"Crisis of Confidence"

*I*n the 1970s, Americans struggled with the aftermath of the Vietnam War and the Watergate scandal. Economic problems and an energy crisis added to the malaise. On July 15, 1979, in a nationally televised address, President Carter identified what he believed to be a "crisis of confidence" among the American people.

. . . I want to talk to you right now about a fundamental threat to American democracy. . . . It is a crisis of confidence . . . that strikes at the very heart and soul and spirit of our national will. We can see this crisis in the growing doubt about the meaning of our own lives and in the loss of a unity of purpose for our nation. . . .

In a nation that was proud of hard work, strong families, close-knit communities, and our faith in God, too many of us now tend to worship self-indulgence and consumption. Human identity is no longer defined by what one does, but by what one owns. But we've discovered that owning things and consuming things does not satisfy our longing for meaning. . . .

As you know, there is a growing disrespect for government and for churches and for schools, the news media, and other institutions. This is not a message of happiness or reassurance, but it is the truth and it is a warning. . . .

Cesar Chavez
Commonwealth Club Address

*T*he Commonwealth Club of California, the nation's oldest public affairs forum, has hosted diverse speakers, including Theodore Roosevelt, Martin Luther King, Jr., Ronald Reagan, and Bill Gates. In 1984, Cesar Chavez spoke about the United Farm Workers and progress for Latinos.

. . . The United Farm Workers is first and foremost a union. . . . But the UFW has always been something more than a union. . . .

The UFW's survival . . . was not in doubt . . . after the union became visible, when Chicanos started entering college in greater numbers, when Hispanics began running for public office in greater numbers, when our people started asserting their rights on a broad range of issues and in many communities across this land. The union survival, its very existence, sent out a signal to all Hispanics that we were fighting for our dignity, that we were challenging and overcoming injustice, that we were empowering the least educated among us, the poorest among us.

The message was clear. If it could happen in the fields, it could happen anywhere: in the cities, in the courts, in the city councils, in the state legislatures. I didn't really appreciate it at the time, but the coming of our union signaled the start of great changes among Hispanics that are only now beginning to be seen. . . .

Like the other immigrant groups, the day will come when we win the economic and political rewards, which are in keeping with our numbers in society. . . .

▲ Cesar Chavez

Documents of Our Nation

Second Inaugural Address

Traditionally, second presidential terms have been more challenging than first terms and Bill Clinton's second term was no exception. Ask **According to Clinton, what is unique about this point in history?** *(More people live under democracy than under dictatorship.)* **What promises to the American people does Clinton make in this speech? Do you think he kept his promises?** *(to meet international obligations, to balance the federal budget, to provide a secure retirement and national health care for people, to fortify the economy while protecting the environment; sample answer: No; he probably could not keep all his promises since his second term was more challenging and filled with more complications than his first.)*

War on Terror Speech

Explain that the September 11, 2001, attacks were a turning point in recent American history. Not only did the attacks cause Americans to reexamine issues of national security and civil liberties, the nation also found itself engaged in the War on Terror, a war directed at a new kind of enemy. Ask **What is al Qaeda?** *(a fringe group of Islamic extremists responsible for the 9/11 attacks)* **How does Bush characterize the coming war on terror?** *(as a lengthy campaign, unlike any other)* **What is the overall tone of this excerpt?** *(Sample answer: grieving, angry, determined)*

President William Clinton

William Clinton
Second Inaugural Address

President Clinton took the oath of office for a second term on January 20, 1997. This was the last inaugural address of the twentieth century, and Clinton looked optimistically to the challenges that lay ahead in the next century.

. . . The world is no longer divided into two hostile camps. Instead, now we are building bonds with nations that once were our adversaries. Growing connections of commerce and culture give us a chance to lift the fortunes and spirits of people the world over. And for the very first time in all of history, more people on this planet live under democracy than dictatorship. . . .

Our land of new promise will be a nation that meets its obligations, a nation that balances its budget, but never loses the balance of its values. A nation where our grandparents have secure retirement and health care, and their grandchildren know we have made the reforms necessary to sustain those benefits for their time. A nation that fortifies the world's most productive economy even as it protects the great natural bounty of our water, air, and majestic land. . . .

George W. Bush
War on Terror Speech

On September 11, 2001, terrorists hijacked and crashed passenger jets into the World Trade Center in New York City and the Pentagon Building in Washington, D.C. On September 20, President Bush addressed a joint session of Congress and announced to the nation a war on terrorism.

. . . Americans have known surprise attacks, but never before on thousands of civilians. All of this was brought upon us in a single day, and night fell on a different world, a world where freedom itself is under attack. . . .

The evidence we have gathered all points to a collection of loosely affiliated terrorist organizations known as al Qaeda.

The terrorists practice a fringe form of Islamic extremism that has been rejected by Muslim scholars and the vast majority of Muslim clerics; a fringe movement that perverts the peaceful teachings of Islam. . . .

Our war on terror begins with al Qaeda, but it does not end there. It will not end until every terrorist group of global reach has been found, stopped and defeated.

Americans are asking "Why do they hate us?" They hate what they see right here in this chamber: a democratically elected government. Their leaders are self-appointed. They hate our freedoms: our freedom of religion, our freedom of speech, our freedom to vote and assemble and disagree. . . .

Our response involves far more than instant retaliation and isolated strikes. Americans should not expect one battle, but a lengthy campaign unlike any other we have ever seen. . . .

We will rally the world to this cause by our efforts, by our courage. We will not tire, we will not falter and we will not fail. . . .

▼ President Bush addresses rescue work at the World Trade Center site.

History Background

The Second Inaugural Only 15 American Presidents have been elected to two terms, and, while some Presidents have achieved greatness in two terms, for others the second term has often proved challenging or scandal-ridden. Originally, the Constitution limited the period of a President's term to four years but put no limits on the number of terms a President could serve. George Washington set the precedent of a two-term limit when he declined to run for a third term. Thomas Jefferson also did not seek a third term. No subsequent President served beyond a second term until Franklin D. Roosevelt was elected to four terms. After his death, Congress and the states approved the 22nd Amendment to the Constitution in 1951, limiting a President to two consecutive terms. The amendment also prohibits a President from running for election more than once if he or she has already served more than two years of a previous President's term.

A

abolitionist reformer who sought to end slavery (p. 36)
abolicionista reformador que abogaba por dar fin a la esclavitud

Acquired Immunodeficiency Syndrome (AIDS) a disease with no known cure that attacks the immune system of its victims. It began spreading in the early 1980s and remains a serious global health crisis today (p. 637)
Síndrome de Inmunodeficiencia Adquirida (SIDA) una enfermedad para la que no se conoce cura que ataca el sistema inmunitario de sus víctimas; empezó a extenderse a principios de la década de 1980 y aún hoy sigue representando una seria crisis de salud mundial

affirmative action policy that gives special consideration to women and minorities to make up for past discrimination (pp. 600, 681)
acción afirmativa política que da trato especial a las mujeres y minorías para resarcirlas de la discriminación del pasado

AFL-CIO in 1955, the American Federation of Labor (AFL) and the Congress of Industrial Organization (CIO) labor unions united (p. 446)
AFL-CIO en 1955 los sindicatos de trabajadores, la Federación Estadounidense del Trabajo y el Congreso de Organización Industrial, se unieron

Alien Act 1798 law that allowed the government to imprison or deport aliens (p. 23)
Ley de Extranjeros ley de 1798 que permitió al gobierno encarcelar o deportar extranjeros

Alliance for Progress President Kennedy's program which provided economic assistance to Latin America (p. 507)
Alianza para el Progreso programa del presidente Kennedy que daba asistencia económica a América Latina

Allies group of countries led by Britain, France, the United States, and the Soviet Union that fought the Axis Powers in World War II (p. 333)
Aliados grupo de países encabezado por Gran Bretaña, Francia, Estados Unidos y la Unión Soviética que peleó contra los Poderes del Eje en la Segunda Guerra Mundial

al Qaeda terrorist group established by Osama bin Laden to rid Muslim countries of Western influence (p. 670)
al Qaida grupo terrorista establecido por Osama bin Laden para eliminar la influencia occidental en los países musulmanes

Alsace-Lorraine territory lost to Germany by France in 1871 (p. 618)
Alsacia y Lorena territorio que Francia perdió ante Alemania en 1871

American Federation of Labor (AFL) labor union that organized skilled workers in a specific trade and focused on specific workers' issues rather than broad issues (p. 71)
Federación Estadounidense del Trabajo sindicato de trabajadores que organizó a los trabajadores calificados en oficios específicos y se enfocó más en los problemas de trabajadores específicos que en aspectos más amplios

American Indian Movement (AIM) group that focused on helping Indians, including the securing of legal rights, land, and self-government for Native Americans (p. 583)
Movimiento de Indígenas Estadounidenses grupo que se concentró en ayudar a los indígenas, incluyendo velar por sus derechos legales, tierra y de autodeterminación

Americanization belief that assimilating immigrants into American society would make them more loyal citizens (p. 116)
americanización creencia que sostenía que la asimilación de los inmigrantes por la sociedad estadounidense los haría ciudadanos más leales

amnesty general pardon for certain crimes (p. 609)
amnistía perdón general de ciertos delitos

Anaconda Plan Northern Civil War strategy to starve the South by blockading seaports and controlling the Mississippi River (p. 49)
Plan Anaconda estrategia del Norte en la Guerra Civil de llevar al Sur a la rendición por inanición al bloquear los puertos marinos y controlar el río Mississippi

anarchist one who opposes all forms of government (p. 71)
anarquista aquél que se opone a todas las formas de gobierno

Angel Island island in San Francisco Bay that served as an immigration station for Asian immigrants (p. 74)
Isla Ángel isla de la bahía de San Francisco que se usó como puesto de migración para los inmigrantes asiáticos

Anschluss union of Germany and Austria in 1933 (p. 330)
Anschluss unión de Alemania y Austria en 1933

Anti-Defamation League organization formed in 1913 to defend Jews against physical and verbal attacks and false statements (p. 119)
Liga Antidifamación organización formada en 1913 para defender a los judíos contra los ataques físicos y verbales y las falsas declaraciones

anti-Semitism prejudice and discrimination against Jewish people (pp. 327, 380)
antisemitismo prejuicios contra las personas judías

apartheid political system of strict segregation by race in South Africa (p. 646)
apartheid sistema político de segregación intransigente basada en la raza, en Sudáfrica

appeasement policy of granting concessions in order to keep the peace (p. 329)
apaciguamiento política de otorgar concesiones a fin de mantener la paz

arms race contest in which nations compete to build more powerful weapons (p. 413)

carrera armamentista competencia en la que las naciones se enfrentan para construir armas más poderosas

assembly line arrangement of equipment and workers in which work passes from operation to operation in direct line until the product is assembled (p. 213)

línea de ensamblaje organización de equipos y trabajadores en la que el trabajo pasa de una operación a otra en una línea directa hasta que el producto queda ensamblado

assimilate to be absorbed into the main culture of a society (p. 84)

asimilarse ser absorbido por la cultura dominante de una sociedad

Atlantic Charter a joint declaration made in August 1941 by Great Britain and the United States, during World War II, that endorsed national self-determination and an international system of general security (p. 338)

Carta del Atlántico declaración conjunta de agosto de 1941 entre Gran Bretaña y Estados Unidos, durante la Segunda Guerra Mundial, que aprobaba la autodeterminación nacional y un sistema internacional de seguridad general

Axis Powers group of countries led by Germany, Italy, and Japan that fought the Allies in World War II (p. 333)

Poderes del Eje grupo de países encabezado por Alemania, Italia y Japón que peleó contra los Aliados en la Segunda Guerra Mundial

B

baby boom increase in births between 1945 and 1964 (p. 435)

baby boom aumento de nacimientos entre 1945 y 1964

Bataan Death March during World War II, the forced march of American and Filipino prisoners of war under brutal conditions by the Japanese military (p. 345)

Marcha de la Muerte de Batán durante la Segunda Guerra Mundial, la marcha forzada de prisioneros de guerra estadounidenses y filipinos en condiciones brutales impuestas por los militares japoneses

Battle of the Bulge in December 1944, Hitler ordered a counterattack on Allied troops in Belgium, but it crippled Germany by using up reserves and demoralizing its troops (p. 375)

batalla de las Ardenas en diciembre de 1944, Hitler ordenó un contraataque contra las tropas aliadas en Bélgica, pero esto debilitó a Alemania al usar todas sus reservas y desmoralizar a sus tropas

Battle of Coral Sea World War II battle that took place in May 1942 in the Pacific theater between Japanese and American aircraft carriers (p. 347)

batalla del Mar del Coral batalla entre aviones japoneses y estadounidenses, durante la Segunda Guerra Mundial, ocurrida en mayo de 1942 en el escenario del Pacífico

Battle of Gettysburg one of the bloodiest battles of the Civil War, it marked the last major Confederate attempt to invade the North (p. 52)

batalla de Gettysburg una de las batallas más sangrientas de la Guerra Civil, marcó el último intento importante de los Confederados por invadir el Norte

Battle of Midway turning point of World War II in the Pacific, in which the Japanese advance was stopped (p. 360)

batalla de Midway momento decisivo de la Segunda Guerra Mundial en el Pacífico, en que se detuvo el avance de los japoneses

Bay of Pigs invasion 1961 failed invasion of Cuba by a CIA-led force of Cuban exiles (p. 508)

invasión de bahía de Cochinos invasión de 1961 por exilados cubanos encabezados por la CIA que fracasaron al tratar de invadir Cuba

beatniks small group of writers and artists, in the 1950s and early 1960s, who were critical of American society (p. 456)

beatniks pequeño grupo de escritores y artistas, en la década de 1950 y principios de los 1960, que criticaban a la sociedad estadounidense

Berlin airlift program in which U.S. and British pilots flew supplies to West Berlin during a Soviet blockade (p. 404)

puente aéreo de Berlín programa en el que pilotos estadounidenses y británicos volaban llevando suministros a Berlín Occidental durante un bloqueo soviético

Berlin Wall dividing wall built by East Germany in 1961 to isolate West Berlin from Communist-controlled East Berlin (p. 510)

Muro de Berlín pared divisoria construida por Alemania Oriental en 1961 para aislar a Berlín Occidental del Berlín Oriental controlado por los comunistas

"big stick" diplomacy Roosevelt's policy of creating and using, when necessary, a strong military to achieve America's goals (p. 157)

diplomacia de "mano dura" política seguida por Roosevelt según la cual se organizaría y usaría, cuando fuera necesario, una fuerza militar poderosa para lograr los objetivos de Estados Unidos

bilingual education system in which students are taught in their native languages as well as in English (p. 680)

educación bilingüe sistema en el que se enseña a los estudiantes en su idioma nativo así como en inglés

bill of rights written list of freedoms guaranteed to citizens by the government (p. 15)

declaración de derechos listado escrito de las libertades que el gobierno garantiza a sus ciudadanos

biotechnology the application of technology to solving problems affecting living organisms (p. 657)

biotecnología aplicación de la tecnología para resolver problemas que afectan a los organismos vivos

Black Cabinet group of African American leaders who served as unofficial advisers to Franklin D. Roosevelt (p. 302)

Gabinete Negro grupo de líderes afroestadounidenses que fungieron como consejeros extraoficiales de Franklin D. Roosevelt

blacklist list of persons who were not hired because of suspected communist ties (p. 422)

lista negra lista de personas que no fueron contratadas por sospechas de vínculos comunistas

Black Panthers organization of militant African Americans founded in 1966 (p. 493)

Panteras Negras organización de militantes afroestadounidenses fundada en 1966

black power movement in the 1960s that urged African Americans to use their collective political and economic power to gain equality (p. 493)

poder negro movimiento de la década de 1960 que exhortó a los afroestadounidenses a usar su poder político y económico colectivo para lograr la igualdad

Black Tuesday October 29, 1929, when stock prices fell sharply in the Great Crash (p. 258)

Martes Negro 29 de octubre de 1929, el día en que los precios de las acciones cayeron precipitadamente en la Gran Caída de la Bolsa

blitzkrieg "lightning war" that emphasized the use of speed and firepower to penetrate deep into the enemy's territory (p. 333)

blitzkrieg "guerra relámpago" que enfatiza el uso de velocidad y capacidad bélica para penetrar muy adentro en el territorio enemigo, usada por Alemania en la Segunda Guerra Mundial

boat people refugees who leave their country by boat (p. 616)

balseros refugiados que dejan su país en bote

Bonus Army a group of World War I veterans who marched on Washington, D.C., in 1932 to demand early payment of a bonus promised them by Congress for their military service (p. 275)

Ejército del Bono grupo de veteranos de la Primera Guerra Mundial que marcharon sobre Washington, D.C., en 1932, para exigir el pago anticipado de un bono que les prometiera el Congreso por sus servicios militares

bootlegger one who sells illegal alcohol (p. 230)

contrabandista quien vende alcohol ilegalmente

Boxer Rebellion violence started by members of a secret society in China, which prompted the governments of Europe and America to send troops to squash the rebellion (p. 154)

Rebelión de los Bóxer actos de violencia iniciados por miembros de una sociedad secreta en China, que

provocó los gobiernos de Europa y América enviaran tropas para sofocar la rebelión

bracero program plan that brought laborers from Mexico to work on American farms (p. 363)

programa de braceros plan que trajo trabajadores de México a trabajar en granjas estadounidenses

Brady Bill law passed in 1993 requiring a waiting period on sales of handguns, along with a criminal background check on the buyer (p. 663)

Ley Brady ley aprobada en 1993 que exige un período de espera de cinco días para la venta de revólveres, junto con una verificación de los antecedentes delictivos del comprador

bread line line of people waiting for food handouts from charities or public agencies (p. 262)

cola de alimentación fila de personas que esperan alimentos gratuitos de obras caritativas o agencias públicas

brinkmanship belief that only by going to the brink of war could the United States protect against communist aggression (p. 414)

teoría del equilibrio del terror creencia según la que sólo estando al borde de la guerra Estados Unidos podía protegerse contra la agresión comunista

budget deficit shortfall between the amount of money spent and the amount taken in by the federal government (p. 634)

déficit presupuestario faltante entre la cantidad de dinero gastado y la cantidad de dinero captado por el gobierno federal

bull market period of rising stock prices (p. 216)

mercado alcista período durante el cual suben los precios de las acciones

business cycle periodic growth and contraction of the economy (p. 258)

ciclo commercial crecimiento y contracción periódicos de la economía

buying on margin margin system of buying stocks in which a buyer pays a small percentage of the purchase price while the broker advances the rest (p. 216)

compra al margen sistema de compra de acciones en el que el comprador paga un pequeño porcentaje del precio de compra mientras que el corredor anticipa el resto

C

California Master Plan called for three tiers of higher education: research universities, state colleges, and community colleges, all of which were to be accessible to all of the state's citizens (p. 447)

Plan Maestro de California hizo un llamado para la creación de tres niveles de educación superior: universidades de investigación, universidades estatales y centros educacionales comunitarios, los cuales deberían ser accesibles para todos los ciudadanos del estado

English/Spanish Glossary

Camp David Accords 1978 agreement brokered by President Jimmy Carter between Egyptian and Israeli leaders that made a peace treaty between the two nations possible (p. 618)

Acuerdos de Camp David acuerdo de 1978 agenciado por el presidente Jimmy Carter, entre los líderes de Egipto e Israel que hizo posible un tratado de paz entre ambas naciones

casualties soldiers killed, wounded, and missing (p. 174)

bajas soldados muertos, heridos y desaparecidos

Central Intelligence Agency (CIA) U.S. intelligence-gathering organization (p. 417)

Agencia Central de Inteligencia organización estadounidense para la recolección de inteligencia

checks and balances system in which each branch of the government has the power to monitor and limit the actions of the other branches (p. 20)

controles y equilibrios sistema en que cada rama del gobierno tiene el poder para vigilar y limitar las acciones de las otras ramas

Chicano movement movement that focused on raising Mexican American consciousness (p. 582)

movimiento chicano movimiento enfocado en despertar la conciencia de los estadounidenses de origen mexicano

Christian fundamentalist individual who believes in a strict, literal interpretation of the Bible as the foundation of the Christian faith (p. 608)

fundamentalista cristiano persona que cree en la interpretación estricta y literal de la Biblia como el fundamento de la fe cristiana

civil disobedience nonviolent refusal to follow laws that one considers to be immoral (p. 36)

desobediencia civil práctica de renuencia pacífica a obedecer las leyes que una persona considera inmorales

Civilian Conservation Corps (CCC) New Deal program that provided young men with relief jobs on environmental conservation projects, including reforestation and flood control (p. 288)

Cuerpos de Conservación Civil programa del Nuevo Trato que proporcionaba ayuda a los jóvenes con trabajo en proyectos de conservación del medio ambiente, incluyendo reforestación y control de inundaciones

Civil Rights Act of 1957 law that established a federal Civil Rights Commission (p. 473)

Ley de Derechos Civiles de 1957 ley que estableció una Comisión Federal de Derechos Civiles

Civil Rights Act of 1964 outlawed discrimination in public places and employment based on race, religion, or national origin (pp. 484, 518)

Ley de Derechos Civiles de 1964 conjunto de leyes que prohibió la discriminación en lugares y empleos públicos con base en la raza, religión o nacionalidad

clan groups of families related through a common ancestor (p. 5)

clan grupo de familias relacionadas a través de un ancestro común

Clayton Antitrust Act 1914 law that strengthened the Sherman Antitrust Act (p. 130)

Ley Clayton Antimonopolio ley de 1914 que fortalecía la Ley Sherman Antimonopolio

Clean Air Act act passed in 1970 that lessened air pollution by limiting the emissions from factories and automobiles (p. 588)

Ley para el Aire Puro ley aprobada en 1970 que buscaba disminuir la contaminación del aire al limitar las emisiones de fábricas y automóviles

Clean Water Act 1973 law that restricted the pollution of water by industry and agriculture (p. 588)

Ley para el Agua Limpia ley aprobada en 1973 que buscaba restringir la contaminación industrial y agrícola del agua

Cold War worldwide rivalry between the United States and the Soviet Union (p. 400)

Guerra Fría rivalidad mundial entre Estados Unidos y la Unión Soviética

collective bargaining process in which employers negotiate with labor unions about hours, wages, and other working conditions (p. 296)

negociación colectiva proceso en el que los patronos negocian con los sindicatos sobre los horarios, salarios y otras condiciones de trabajo

Columbian Exchange the global exchange of goods and ideas between Europe, Africa, and the Americas after Columbus made his first transatlantic voyage in 1492 (p. 8)

intercambio colombino intercambio global de bienes e ideas entre Europa, Africa y las Americas posterior al primer viaje transatlántico de Colón en 1492

Committee on Public Information (CPI) government agency created during World War I to encourage Americans to support the war (p. 182)

Comité de Información Pública organización creada por el gobierno durante la Primera Guerra Mundial para animar al público estadounidense a apoyar la guerra

commune small communities where people share resources (p. 571)

comunas pequeñas comunidades en las que las personas comparten los recursos

Compromise of 1850 agreement designed to ease the controversy over California being admitted as a free state by allowing the residents of other territories to decide the issue of slavery by popular sovereignty (p. 43)

Acuerdo de 1850 acuerdo diseñado para aminorar la controversia sobre la admisión de California como estado libre, que permitía a los residentes de otros territorios decidieran el tema de la esclavitud por soberanía popular

concentration camp camps used by the Nazis to imprison "undesirable" members of society (p. 383)
　campo de concentración campos usados por los nazis para encarcelar a miembros "indeseables" de la sociedad

Congress of Industrial Organization (CIO) a labor organization founded in the 1930s that represents industrial workers (p. 296)
　Congreso de Organización Industrial organización de trabajadores fundada en la década de 1930 que representa a los trabajadores industriales

conquistador one of the sixteenth-century Spanish soldiers who defeated the Indian civilizations of Mexico, Central America, or Peru (p. 8)
　conquistador en particular, uno de los soldados españoles del siglo XVI que derrotaron a las civilizaciones de México, América Central o Perú

conscientious objector person who refuses to fight in a war due to moral or religious beliefs (p. 182)
　objetor de conciencia persona que rehúsa pelear en una guerra por convicciones morales o religiosas

conservative person who tends to support limited government involvement in the economy, favor community help for the needy, and upholds traditional values (p. 628)
　conservador persona que tiende a apoyar una participación gubernamental limitada en la economía, favorece la ayuda comunitaria para los necesitados y mantiene los valores tradicionales

consumerism large-scale buying, much of it on credit (p. 448)
　consumismo compras a gran escala, la mayoría de éstas a crédito

consumer revolution flood of new, affordable goods in the decades after World War I (p. 215)
　revolución de consumo flujo de bienes nuevos y asequibles durante las decadas posteriores a la Primera Guerra Mundial

containment policy of keeping communism contained within its existing borders (p. 402)
　contención política de mantener el comunismo contenido dentro de sus fronteras existentes

Contract With America Republican plan headed by Newt Gingrich that focused on scaling back the government, balancing the budget, and cutting taxes (p. 663)
　Contrato con Estados Unidos plan republicano encabezado por Newt Gingrich enfocado en la reducción del gobierno, el equilibrio del presupuesto y la reducción de los impuestos

contraband during wartime, goods such as weapons and other articles used to fight a war that may be legally confiscated by any belligerent (p. 176)
　contrabando en tiempos de guerra, bienes, como armas y otros artículos, usados para combatir en la guerra que pueden ser confiscados de manera legal por cualesquiera de los beligerantes

Contras anticommunist counterrevolutionaries who opposed the Sandinista government in Nicaragua in the 1980s (p. 640)
　Contras contrarrevolucionarios anticomunistas opuestos al gobierno Sandinista de Nicaragua en la década de 1980

convoy group of merchant ships sailing together, protected by war ships (p. 189)
　convoy grupo de buques mercantes que navegan juntos bajo la protección de buques de guerra

cotton gin machine invented in 1793 to separate the cotton fiber from its hard shell (p. 27)
　desmotadora máquina inventada en 1793 para separar la fibra del algodón de la cáscara

counterculture movement that upheld values different from those of mainstream culture (p. 570)
　contracultura movimiento que mantuvo valores diferentes a los de la cultura tradicional

court packing FDR plan to add up to six new justices to the nine-member Supreme Court after the Court had ruled that some New Deal legislation was unconstitutional (p. 298)
　plan para llenar las cortes plan de FDR para agregar seis nuevos magistrados a los nueve miembros de la Corte Suprema luego de que la Corte dictaminó que algunas leyes del Nuevo Trato eran inconstitucionales

"credibility gap" the American public's growing distrust of statements made by the government during the Vietnam War (p. 546)
　"brecha de credibilidad" creciente desconfianza del público estadounidense ante declaraciones del gobierno durante la Guerra de Vietnam

creditor nation country which is owed more money by other countries than it owes other countries (p. 203)
　nación acreedora país al que otros países le deben más dinero del que éste les debe

Cuban missile crisis 1962 conflict between the U.S. and the Soviet Union resulting from the Soviet installation of nuclear missiles in Cuba (p. 508)
　crisis de los misiles de Cuba conflicto entre Estados Unidos y la Unión Soviética en 1962, como resultado de la instalación de misiles nucleares en Cuba por parte de los soviéticos

D

Dawes Act law enacted in 1887 that divided reservation land into private family plots (p. 84)
　Ley Dawes ley promulgada en 1887 que dividió las tierras de reservación en parcelas privadas para familias

Dawes Plan agreement in which the United States loaned money to Germany, allowing Germany to make reparation payments to Britain and France (p. 222)
　Plan Dawes acuerdo en el que Estados Unidos prestó dinero a Alemania, permitiéndole a ésta hacer

English/Spanish Glossary

pagos de reparación a Gran Bretaña y Francia

D-Day June 6, 1944, the day Allies landed on the beaches of Normandy, France (p. 371)

Día D 6 de junio de 1944, el día en que los Aliados desembarcaron en las playas de Normandía, Francia

death camp Nazi camp designed for the extermination of prisoners (p. 383)

campo de la muerte campo diseñados por los nazis para el exterminio de prisioneros

de facto segregation segregation by unwritten custom or tradition (p. 468)

segregación de facto segregación basada en la costumbre o la tradición no escrita

deficit spending the practice of a nation paying out more money than it is receiving in revenues (p. 513)

déficit de gastos práctica de las naciones que gastan más de lo que reciben por ingresos

de jure segregation segregation imposed by law (p. 468)

segregación de iure segregación impuesta por ley

demobilization sending home members of the army (p. 435)

desmovilización enviar a los miembros del ejército de vuelta a casa

Department of Homeland Security Cabinet-level department created by President Bush to coordinate domestic security efforts (p. 677)

Departamento de Seguridad Nacional departamento a nivel de gabinete creado por el presidente Bush para coordinar los esfuerzos de seguridad interior

deregulation reduction or removal of government controls over an industry (p. 634)

desregulación reducción o eliminación de los controles gubernamentales en una industria

détente flexible diplomacy adopted by Richard Nixon that sought to ease tensions between the United States, the Soviet Union, and the People's Republic of China (p. 562)

distensión diplomacia flexible adoptada por Richard Nixon que buscó aliviar las tensiones entre Estados Unidos, la Unión Soviética y la República Popular China

developing world countries that are less economically and technologically advanced than developed countries such as the United States (p. 617)

mundo en desarrollo países que son menos avanzados económica y tecnológicamente que los países desarrollados como Estados Unidos

direct primary election in which citizens themselves vote to select nominees for upcoming elections (p. 106)

primarias directas elecciones en las que los ciudadanos votan directamente para elegir los candidatos para las siguientes elecciones.

divest to take away or rid oneself of (p. 646)

desposeer quitarse o librarse de algo

"dollar diplomacy" President Taft's policy of expanding American investments abroad (p. 161)

"diplomacia del dólar" política exterior del presidente Taft que buscaba expandir las inversiones estadounidenses en el exterior

domino theory idea that if a nation falls to communism, its closest neighbors will also fall under communist control (p. 534)

teoría dominó idea que estipulaba que si una nación cae ante el comunismo, sus vecinos más cercanos también caerán bajo el control comunista

dove person who opposed U.S. involvement in the Vietnam War (p. 543)

"paloma" persona opuesta a la participación estadounidense en la Guerra de Vietnam

draftee young American man drafted into military service during the Vietnam War (p. 544)

conscripto varón estadounidense joven reclutado para el servicio militar durante la Guerra de Vietnam

Dust Bowl term used for the central and southern Great Plains during the 1930s when the region suffered from drought and dust storms (p. 267)

Cuenco de Polvo término usado para describir las Grandes Planicies durante la década de 1930, cuando la región quedó desolada por la sequía y las tormentas de polvo

E

Earth Day annual event of environmental activism and protest, begun in 1970 (p. 587)

Día de la Tierra evento anual de activismo y protesta ambiental, empezó en 1970

Economic Opportunity Act law passed in 1964 creating the Office of Economic Opportunity to run antipoverty programs (p. 518)

Ley de Igualdad de Oportunidades ley aprobada en 1964 que creo la Oficina de Oportunidades Económicas para dirigir programas contra la pobreza

Eighteenth Amendment constitutional amendment banning the manufacture, distribution, and sale of alcohol in the United States (p. 229)

Decimoctava Enmienda enmienda constitucional que prohibió la fabricación, distribución y venta de alcohol en Estados Unidos

Eisenhower Doctrine policy of President Eisenhower that stated that the United States would use force to help any nation threatened by communism (p. 416)

doctrina Eisenhower política del presidente Eisenhower que indicaba que Estados Unidos usaría la fuerza para ayudar a cualquier nación amenazada por el comunismo

Ellis Island island in New York Harbor that served as an immigration station for millions of immigrants arriving to the United States (p. 74)

Isla Ellis isla en el puerto de Nueva York que se usó como puesto de migración para millones de inmigrantes que llegaron a Estados Unidos

Emancipation Proclamation decree by President Lincoln that freed slaves in all Confederate territory still in rebellion (p. 50)

Proclamación de Emancipación decreto del presidente Lincoln que liberó a los esclavos en todos los territorios confederados aún en rebelión

embargo government ban or restriction on trade (p. 24)

embargo prohibición o restricción gubernamental del comercio

Endangered Species Act law passed in 1973 with the purpose of protecting endangered plants and animals (p. 588)

Ley de Especies en Peligro de Extinción ley aprobada en 1973 con el propósito de proteger las plantas y animales en peligro de extinción

English Bill of Rights 1689 document that guaranteed the rights of English citizens (p. 11)

Declaración de Derechos Inglesa documento de 1689 que garantizó los derechos de los ciudadanos ingleses

Enlightenment eighteenth-century intellectual movement during which European philosophers came to believe that all problems could be solved by reason and science (p. 11)

Ilustración movimiento intelectual del siglo XVIII por el cual los filósofos europeos llegaron a creer que todos los problemas se pueden resolver a través del razón y la ciencia

Environmental Protection Agency (EPA) government agency committed to cleaning up and protecting the environment (p. 588)

Agencia de Protección Ambiental agencia gubernamental comprometida con la limpieza y protección del ambiente

Equal Pay Act law passed in 1963 that required both men and women to receive equal pay for equal work (p. 513)

Ley de Pago Equitativo ley aprobada en 1963 que exigió que hombres y mujeres reciban paga igual por un trabajo igual

Equal Rights Amendment (ERA) proposed amendment to the Constitution that guarantees gender equality (p. 575)

Enmienda de Igualdad de Derechos enmienda propuesta que garantiza la igualdad entre los sexos

Espionage Act act passed by Congress in June 1917 enacting severe penalties for anyone engaged in disloyal or treasonable activities (p. 184)

Ley de Espionaje ley aprobada por el Congreso en junio de 1917 que estableció penas severas para cualquiera que participara en actividades desleales o de traición

ethnic cleansing systematic effort to purge an area or society of an ethnic group through murder or deportation (p. 669)

limpieza étnica esfuerzo sistemático para purgar una zona o sociedad de un grupo étnico mediante el asesinato o la deportación

European Union (EU) economic and political union of European nations established in 1993 (p. 667)

Unión Europea (UE) unión económica y política de las naciones europeas establecida en 1993

Executive Order 8802 World War II measure that assured fair hiring practices in any job funded by the government (p. 362)

Orden Ejecutiva 8802 medida durante la Segunda Guerra Mundial que garantizaba prácticas justas de empleo en cualquier puesto financiado por el gobierno

executive privilege principle that the President has the right to keep certain communications between himself and other members of the executive branch private (p. 604)

privilegio ejecutivo principio que indica que el presidente tiene derecho a mantener en privado ciertas comunicaciones con otros miembros del poder ejecutivo

extractive economy economy in a colony where the colonizing country removed raw materials and shipped them back home to benefit its economy (p. 138)

economía de extracción economía de una colonia donde el país colonizador extraía materias primas y las enviaba a la madre patria para beneficiar su propia economía

F

Fair Deal President Truman's legislative program that would strengthen existing New Deal reforms and establish new programs, such as national health insurance (p. 438)

Trato Justo programa legislativo del presidente Truman que fortalecería las reformas del Nuevo Trato y establecería nuevos programas, tales como el seguro nacional de salud

Fair Labor Standards Act 1938 law that set a minimum wage, a maximum workweek of 44 hours, and outlawed child labor (p. 296)

Ley de Normas Laborales Justas ley aprobada en 1938 que estableció el salario mínimo, y una semana laboral de un máximo de 44 horas, y prohibió el trabajo infantil

Family Medical Leave Act law guaranteeing most full-time employees 12 workweeks of unpaid leave each year for personal or family health reasons (p. 662)

Ley de Permiso Médico Familiar ley que garantiza a la mayoría de los empleados de tiempo completo 12 semanas laborales de permiso sin goce de sueldo cada año por razones personales o de salud familiar

Federal Art Project division of the Works Progress Administration that hired unemployed artists to create artworks for nonfederal public buildings and sponsored art-education programs and exhibitions (p. 313)
Proyecto Federal de Arte división de la Administración de Progreso de Obras que contrató artistas desempleados para crear obras de arte en edificios públicos no federales y patrocinó programas educativos y exhibiciones artísticos

Federal Deposit Insurance Corporation (FDIC) government agency that insures bank deposits, guaranteeing that depositors' money will be safe (p. 287)
Corporación Federal de Aseguramiento de Depósitos agencia gubernamental que asegura los depósitos bancarios, garantizando que el dinero de los depositantes estará seguro

federalism political system in which power is shared between the national government and state governments (p. 20)
federalismo sistema político en el que el poder es compartido entre el gobierno nacional y el gobierno estatal

Federal Reserve Act 1913 law that placed national banks under the control of a Federal Reserve Board, which runs regional banks that hold the reserve funds from commercial banks, sets interest rates, and supervises commercial banks (p. 129)
Ley de Reserva Federal ley de 1913 que sometió a todos los bancos del país bajo el control de una Junta de Reserva Federal; esta última opera los bancos regionales que mantienen un fondo de reserva de los bancos comerciales, fija tasa de intereses y supervisa a los bancos comerciales

Federal Trade Commission (FTC) government agency established in 1914 to identify monopolistic business practices, false advertising, and dishonest labeling (p. 130)
Comisión Federal de Comercio agencia gubernamental establecida en 1914 para identificar las prácticas comerciales monopolistas, falsa propaganda y rótulos deshonestos

feminism theory that women and men should have political, social, and economic equality (p. 574)
feminismo teoría que plantea que las mujeres y los hombres deben tener igualdad política, social y económica

Fifteenth Amendment 1870 constitutional amendment which guaranteed voting rights regardless of race (p. 56)
Decimoquinta Enmienda enmienda constitucional de 1870 que garantizó el derecho al sufragio independientemente de la raza

filibuster tactic by which senators give long speeches to hold up legislative business (p. 484)

obstruccionismo táctica empleada por los senadores que consistió en hacer prolongados discursos para detener los asuntos legislativos

fireside chat informal radio broadcast in which FDR explained issues and New Deal programs to average Americans (p. 287)
"charla junto a la hoguera" transmisión informal de radio en que FDR explicaba asuntos y programas del Nuevo Trato a los estadounidenses promedio

flapper young woman from the 1920s who defied traditional rules of conduct and dress (p. 236)
chica "flapper" mujer joven de la década de 1920 que desafiaba las reglas tradicionales de conducta y atuendo

flexible response defense policy allowing for the appropriate action in any size or type of conflict (p. 507)
respuesta flexible política de defensa que permite acciones apropiadas en conflictos de cualquier tamaño o tipo

Foraker Act law establishing a civil government in Puerto Rico (p. 156)
Ley Foraker ley que estableció un gobierno civil en Puerto Rico

442nd Regimental Combat Team World War II unit made up of Japanese American volunteers (p. 365)
Equipo de Combate del Regimiento 442 unidad de la Segunda Guerra Mundial compuesta por voluntarios estadounidenses de origen japonés

Fourteen Points list of terms for resolving World War I and future wars outlined by American President Woodrow Wilson (p. 193)
Catorce Puntos lista de condiciones planteada por el presidente estadounidense Woodrow Wilson para resolver la Primera Guerra Mundial y guerras futuras

Fourteenth Amendment 1868 constitutional amendment which defined citizenship and guaranteed citizens equal protection under the law (p. 56)
Decimocuarta Enmienda enmienda constitucional de 1868 que definió la ciudadanía y garantizó por ley a los ciudadanos protección ígual

franchise business allows a company to distribute its products or services through retail outlets owned by independent operators (p. 446)
franquicia comercial permiso para que una compañía distribuya sus productos o servicios por medio de establecimientos minoristas e independientes

Freedmen's Bureau federal agency designed to aid freed slaves and poor white farmers and relieve the South's immediate needs after the Civil War (p. 55)
Oficina de Libertos agencia federal diseñada para ayudar a los esclavos liberados y granjeros blancos, y llenar las necesidades inmediatas del Sur luego de la Guerra Civil

freedom rides 1961 protests by black and white activists who rode buses through southern states to test their compliance with the ban on segregation on interstate buses (p. 479)

viaje por la libertad protesta de activistas afro-estadounidense y blancos que en 1961 viajaron en autobús a través de los estados sureños para probar si acataban la prohibición contra la segregación en autobuses interestatales

Freedom Summer 1964 effort to register African American voters in Mississippi (p. 488)

Verano de Libertad esfuerzo de 1964 por empadronar a votantes afroestadounidenses en Mississippi

Free-Soil Party antislavery political party of the mid-1800s (p. 42)

Partido Tierra Libre partido político antiesclavista de mitad del siglo XIX

fundamentalism a movement or attitude stressing strict and literal adherence to a set of basic principles (p. 224)

fundamentalismo movimiento o actitud que enfatiza un cumplimiento estricto y literal a un conjunto de principios básicos

G

General Agreement on Tariffs and Trade (GATT) international agreement first signed in 1947 aimed at lowering trade barriers (pp. 389, 667)

Acuerdo General sobre Aranceles y Comercio tratado internacional firmado originalmente en 1947, diseñado para disminuir las barreras comerciales entre las naciones

generation gap lack of understanding and communication between older and younger members of society (p. 571)

brecha generacional falta de entendimiento y comunicación entre los miembros más viejos y los más jóvenes de la sociedad

Geneva Convention international agreement governing the humane treatment of wounded soldiers and prisoners of war (p. 390)

Convención de Ginebra acuerdo internacional que regula el tratamiento humanitario de soldados heridos y prisioneros de guerra

genocide willful annihilation of a racial, political, or cultural group (p. 383)

genocidio aniquilación intencional de un grupo racial, político o cultural

"Gentlemen's Agreement" pact between the United States and Japan to end segregation of Asian children in San Francisco public schools; in return, Japan agreed to limit the immigration of its citizens to the United States (p. 155)

"Pacto entre Caballeros" acuerdo entre Estados Unidos y Japón para terminar la segregación de niños asiáticos en las escuelas públicas de San Francisco; a cambio, Japón aceptó limitar la migración de sus ciudadanos hacia Estados Unidos

Gettysburg Address speech by President Lincoln in which he dedicated a national cemetery at Gettysburg and reaffirmed the ideas for which the Union was fighting (p. 52)

Discurso de Gettysburg discurso del presidente Lincoln durante la inauguración del cementerio nacional en Gettysburg y que reafirmó las ideas por las que la Unión estaba en lucha

GI Bill of Rights eased the return of World War II veterans by providing education and employment aid (p. 435)

Declaración de Derechos de los Soldados ley que facilitó el retorno de los veteranos de la Segunda Guerra Mundial al brindarles educación y empleo

Gilded Age term used to describe the post-Reconstruction era, which was characterized by a facade of prosperity for the country (p. 87)

Edad Dorada término usado para describir la era después de la Reconstrucción que se caracterizó por una fachada de prosperidad para el país

glasnost Russian term for "new openness," a policy in the Soviet Union in the 1980s calling for open discussion of national problems (p. 640)

glasnost palabra rusa que significa "apertura", política de la Unión Soviética de finales de la década de 1980 con un llamado a la apertura y discusión de los problemas nacionales

globalization process by which national economies, politics, cultures, and societies mix with those of other nations around the world (p. 658)

globalización proceso mediante el cual la economía, política, cultura y sociedad de una nación se mezclan con las de las otras naciones de todo el mundo

gold standard policy of designating monetary units in terms of their value in gold (p. 89)

estándar oro política de designar las unidades monetarias en términos de su valor en oro

Gospel of Wealth Carnegie's doctrine calling for the wealthy to share their riches for the betterment of society (p. 68)

evangelio de la riqueza doctrina de Carnegie con el llamado a que los ricos compartieran su riqueza para mejorar la sociedad

graft acquisition of money through unethical means, such as bribery and corruption (p. 89)

concusión adquisición de dinero por medios no éticos, como sobornos y corrupción

Great Awakening religious movement in the English colonies during the 1730s and 1740s, which was heavily inspired by evangelical preachers (p. 12)

Gran Despertar movimiento religioso en las colonias inglesas durante las décadas de 1730 y 1740, fuertemente inspirado por los predicadores evangélicos

Great Depression period lasting from 1929 to 1941, in which the U.S. economy faltered and unemployment soared (p. 258)

Gran Depresión período entre 1929 y 1941 durante el cual la economía de Estados Unidos falló y el desempleo creció

Great Migration movement of African Americans in the twentieth century from the rural South to the industrial North (p. 186)

    Gran Migración desplazamiento de afroestadounidenses durante el siglo XX desde las zonas rurales del Sur hacia las zonas industrializadas del Norte

Great Society President Johnson's goals for the U.S. in the areas of healthcare, education, the environment, discrimination, and poverty (p. 521)

    Gran Sociedad objetivos del presidente Johnson para Estados Unidos en las áreas de salud, educación, ambiente, discriminación y pobreza

Great White Fleet armada of battleships sent by Roosevelt in 1907 on a "good will cruise" around the world (p. 155)

    Gran Flota Blanca armada de barcos de guerra enviada por Roosevelt en 1907 en una "misión de buena voluntad" alrededor del mundo

guerrilla warfare form of non-traditional warfare generally involving hit-and-run attacks by small bands of fighters (p. 151)

    guerra de guerrillas método de combate no tradicional constituido por ataques de retirada rápida realizados por grupos pequeños de guerreros

Gulf of Tonkin Resolution 1964 Congressional resolution that authorized President Johnson to commit U.S. troops to South Vietnam and fight a war against North Vietnam (p. 536)

    Resolución del Golfo de Tonkin resolución del Congreso de 1964 que autorizó al presidente Johnson a enviar tropas estadounidenses a Vietnam del Sur y entrar en guerra contra Vietnam del Norte

H

habeas corpus constitutional guarantee that no one can be held in prison without charges being filed (p. 51)

    hábeas corpus garantía constitucional para que nadie permanezca en prisión sin que se hayan presentado cargos en su contra

Harlem Renaissance period during the 1920s in which African American novelists, poets, and artists celebrated their culture (p. 245)

    Renacimiento de Harlem período durante la década de 1920 en el que los novelistas, poetas y artistas afroestadounidenses celebraron su cultura

hawk a person who supported U.S. involvement in the Vietnam War (p. 543)

    "halcón" persona que apoyó la participación estadounidense en la Guerra de Vietnam

Hawley-Smoot Tariff protective import tax, authorized by Congress in 1930 (p. 259)

    Arancel Hawley-Smoot impuesto de importaciones aprobado por el Congreso en 1930

Helsinki Accords agreement made in 1975 among the United States, Canada, and European nations, including the Soviet Union, in which all nations agreed to support human rights (p. 615)

    Acuerdos de Helsinki acuerdo realizado en 1975 entre Estados Unidos, Canadá y las naciones de Europa, incluyendo la Unión Soviética, en que todos países acordaron apoyar los derechos humanos

Hepburn Act 1906 law that gave the government the authority to set and limit railroad rates and set maximum prices for ferries, bridge tolls, and oil pipelines (p. 123)

    Ley Hepburn ley de 1906 que otorgó al gobierno la autoridad de fijar y limitar las tarifas ferroviarias y fijar los precios máximos para trasbordadores, peaje de puentes y oleoductos

Hollywood Ten group of movie writers, directors, and producers who refused to answer HUAC questions about alleged communist ties (p. 421)

    diez de Hollywood grupo de guionistas, directores y productores que se rehusaron a contestar preguntas del HUAC sobre supuestos vínculos comunistas

Holocaust name now used to describe the systematic murder of Jews by the Nazis (p. 380)

    Holocausto nombre usado para describir el asesinato sistemático de judíos por los nazis

Hoover Dam dam on the Colorado River, originally named Boulder Dam, that was built during the Great Depression (p. 274)

    Represa Hoover represa en el río Colorado, llamada originalmente Represa Boulder, construida durante la Gran Depresión

Hooverville term used to describe makeshift shantytowns set up by homeless people during the Great Depression (p. 264)

    Hooverville término usado para describir las barriadas de casuchas establecidas por los desposeídos durante la Gran Depresión

hot line direct telephone line between the White House and the Kremlin set up after the Cuban missile crisis (p. 508)

    línea caliente línea de comunicación telefónica directa entre la Casa Blanca y el Kremlin, establecida luego de la crisis de los misiles de Cuba

House of Burgesses representative assembly of colonial Virginia formed in 1619 (p. 11)

    Cámara Baja de Virginia asamblea de representantes en la Virginia colonial formada en 1619

House Un-American Activities Committee (HUAC) congressional committee that investigated possible subversive activities within the United States (p. 421)

    Comité de la Cámara de Representantes contra Actividades AntiEstadounidenses comité del Congreso que investigó posibles actividades subversivas dentro de Estados Unidos

human rights basic rights automatically held by every human being, including religious freedom, education, and equality (p. 615)

    derechos humanos derechos básicos que tiene todo ser humano automáticamente y que incluyen la libertad religiosa, la educación y la igualdad

Immigration Act of 1990 law that increased the number of immigrants allowed in the U.S. per year (p. 679)

Ley de Migración de 1990 ley que aumenta el número de inmigrantes permitidos en Estados Unidos cada año

Immigration and Control Act of 1986 legislation that granted resident status to illegal immigrants residing in the United States since 1982 and penalized employers who hired illegal immigrants (p. 680)

Ley de Migración y Control de 1986 conjunto de leyes que otorgó la condición de residente a los inmigrantes ilegales que vivían en Estados Unidos desde 1982 y penaliza a los patronos que contratan inmigrantes ilegales

Immigration and Nationality Act of 1965 law that changed the national quota system to limits of 170,000 immigrants per year from the Eastern Hemisphere and 120,000 per year from the Western Hemisphere (p. 523)

Ley de Migración y Nacionalidad de 1965 ley que cambió el sistema de cuotas nacionales para limitar a 170,000 por año los inmigrantes del hemisferio oriental y 120,000 por año los del hemisferio occidental

impeachment act of bringing charges against an official to determine whether he or she should be removed from office (pp. 56, 665)

impugnación acción de encausar a un funcionario público para determinar si debe ser dejado en su puesto

imperialism political, military, and economic domination of strong nations over weaker territories (p. 138)

imperialismo dominio político, militar y económico de naciones poderosas sobre territorios más débiles

impressment policy of seizing people or property for military or public service (p. 24)

requisa política de confiscar personas o propiedades para servicio militar o público

Indian New Deal 1930s legislation that gave American Indians greater control over their own affairs and provided funding for construction of schools and hospitals (p. 303)

Nuevo Trato Indígena legislación de 1930 que otorgó mayor control a los indígenas estadounidenses sobre sus propios asuntos y financió la construcción de escuelas y hospitales

inflation rising prices (pp. 52, 200)

inflación aumento de los precios

influenza flu virus (p. 199)

influenza virus de la gripe

information industry businesses that provide informational services (p. 445)

industrias de la información empresas que brindan servicios de información

initiative process in which citizens put a proposed new law directly on the ballot (p. 107)

iniciativa proceso en el que los ciudadanos proponen directamente una nueva ley en la papeleta de una elección

inner city referred to the older, central part of a city with crowded neighborhoods in which low-income, usually minority, groups live (p. 457)

centro de la ciudad la parte más vieja y central de una ciudad, con vecindarios muy poblados en los que viven grupos de bajos recursos, usualmente minorías

installment buying method of purchase in which buyer makes a small down-payment, and then pays off the rest of the debt in regular monthly payments (p. 216)

plan de pago a plazos método de compra mediante el cual el comprador paga un pequeño enganche y luego paga el resto de la deuda con abonos mensuales regulares

insurrection rebellion (p. 151)

insurrección rebelión

Internet a computer network that links people around the world, also called World Wide Web (p. 658)

Internet red de computadoras que enlaza a personas de todo el mundo, también llamada Red Mundial

internment temporary imprisonment of members of a specific group (p. 365)

reclusión encarcelamiento temporal para miembros de un grupo específico

Interstate Highway Act 1956 law that authorized the spending of $32 billion to build 41,000 miles of highway (p. 442)

Ley de Carreteras Interestatales ley de 1956 que autorizó el gasto de $32 mil millones para construir 41,000 millas de carreteras

Iran-Contra affair political scandal under President Reagan involving the use of money from secret arms sales to Iran to illegally support the Contras in Nicaragua (p. 644)

incidente Irán-Contras escándalo político en la administración del presidente Reagan que involucró el uso de dinero procedente de la venta secreta de armas a Irán para apoyar ilegalmente a los Contras en Nicaragua

iron curtain term coined by Winston Churchill to describe the border between the Soviet satellite states and Western Europe (p. 400)

cortina de hierro término acuñado por Winston Churchill para describir la frontera entre los estados satélites soviéticos y Europa Occidental

"irreconcilables" isolationist senators who opposed any treaty ending World War I that had a League of Nations folded into it (p. 196)

"irreconciliables" senadores aislacionistas opuestos a cualquier tratado para finalizar la Primera Guerra Mundial que involucrara una Sociedad de las Naciones

island hopping World War II strategy that involved seizing selected Japanese-held islands in the Pacific while bypassing others (p. 375)

salto de islas estrategia durante la Segunda Guerra Mundial que involucraba capturar islas selectas que mantenía Japón en el Pacífico a la vez que se evitaban otras

English/Spanish Glossary

J

jazz American musical form developed by African Americans, based on improvisation and blending blues, ragtime, and European-based popular music (p. 243)
jazz forma musical estadounidense creada por los afroestadounidenses y europeos, basada en la improvisación y la mezcla de el blues, ragtime y música popular de origen europeo

Jazz Singer, The the first movie with sound synchronized to the action (p. 232)
El Cantante de Jazz primera película con sonido y acción sincronizados

Jim Crow laws laws passed in southern states that separated blacks and whites (p. 87)
Leyes Jim Crow leyes aprobadas en los estados sureños que segregaban a los negros de los blancos

jingoism aggressive nationalism; support for warlike foreign policy (p. 145)
patrioterismo nacionalismo agresivo; apoyo a una política exterior belicosa

judicial review power of the Supreme Court to decide whether the acts of a President or laws passed by Congress are constitutional (p. 23)
revisión judicial poder que le permite a la Corte Suprema decidir si los actos del presidente o las leyes aprobadas por el Congreso son constitucionales

K

kamikazes Japanese pilots who deliberately crashed planes into American ships during World War II (p. 377)
kamikazes pilotos japoneses que deliberadamente chocaban aviones contra buques estadounidenses durante la Segunda Guerra Mundial

Kansas-Nebraska Act 1854 law that divided the Nebraska Territory into Kansas and Nebraska and gave each territory the right to decide whether or not to allow slavery (p. 43)
Ley Kansas-Nebraska ley de 1854 que dividió el territorio de Nebraska en Kansas y Nebraska, dándole a cada territorio el derecho de decidir si permitiría la esclavitud o no

Kellogg-Briand Pact 1928 agreement in which many nations agreed to outlaw war (p. 221)
Pacto Kellogg-Briand acuerdo de 1928 en el que los delegados de muchas naciones estuvieron anuentes a prohibir la guerra

Kerner Commission group set up to investigate the causes of race riots in American cities in the 1960s (p. 492)
Comisión Kerner grupo que se formó para investigar las causas de los disturbios raciales en las ciudades estadounidenses en la década de 1960

Knights of Labor labor union that sought to organize all workers and focused on broad social reforms (p. 71)
Caballeros del Trabajo sindicato de trabajadores que procuró organizar a todos los trabajadores y se enfocó en reformas sociales amplias

Kristallnacht "Night of the Broken Glass," organized attacks on Jewish communities in Germany on November 9, 1938 (p. 381)
Kristallnacht "noche de los cristales rotos", ataques organizados contra comunidades judías en Alemania, el 9 de noviembre de 1938

Ku Klux Klan organization that promotes hatred and discrimination against specific ethnic and religious groups (pp. 58, 227)
Ku Klux Klan organización que promueve el odio y discriminación contra grupos étnicos y religiosos específicos

L

League of Nations world organization established after World War I to promote peaceful cooperation between countries (p. 194)
Sociedad de las Naciones organización mundial establecida después de a la Primera Guerra Mundial para promover la cooperación pacífica entre los países

Lend-Lease Act act passed in 1941 that allowed President Roosevelt to sell or lend war supplies to any country whose defense he considered vital to the safety of the United States (p. 337)
Ley de Préstamo y Arrendamiento ley aprobada por el Congreso en 1941 que permitió al presidente Franklin Roosevelt vender o prestar suministros bélicos a cualquier país cuya defensa se considerara vital para la seguridad de Estados Unidos

liberal a person who tends to support government intervention to help the needy and favor laws protecting the rights of women and minorities (p. 628)
liberal persona que tiende a apoyar la intervención gubernamental en la ayuda a los necesitados y favorece las leyes que protegen los derechos de las mujeres y las minorías

limited war war fought to achieve only specific goals (p. 410)
guerra limitada guerra peleada para alcanzar objetivos específicos

localism policy relied on by President Hoover in the early years of the Great Depression whereby local and state governments act as primary agents of economic relief (p. 273)
localismo política de la que dependió el presidente Hoover a principios de la Gran Depresión para que los gobiernos locales y estatales actuaran como los principales agentes de asistencia económica

"Lost Generation" term for American writers of the 1920s marked by disillusion with World War I and search for new sense of meaning (p. 238)
"Generación Perdida" término usado para referirse a escritores estadounidenses de la década de 1920 marcados por su desilusión con la Primera Guerra Mundial y la búsqueda de un nuevo sentido de la vida

Louisiana Purchase territory between the Mississippi River and the Rocky Mountains, purchased from France in 1803 (p. 24)

Compra de Luisiana territorio entre el río Mississippi y las montañas Rocosas comprado a Francia en 1803

Lusitania British passenger liner sunk by a German U-boat during World War I (p. 176)

Lusitania trasatlántico británico hundido por un submarino alemán en la Primera Guerra Mundial

M

Magna Carta English document from 1215 that limited the power of the king and provided basic rights for citizens (p. 11)

Carta Magna documento inglés de 1215 que limitó el poder del rey y dio derechos básicos a los ciudadanos

Manhattan Project code name of the project that developed the atomic bomb (p. 378)

Proyecto Manhattan nombre en clave del proyecto que desarrolló la bomba atómica

Manifest Destiny doctrine which stated that westward expansion of the United States was inevitable and a God-given right (p. 41)

Destino Manifiesto doctrina que establecía que la expansión de Estados Unidos hacia el Oeste no sólo era inevitable sino un derecho divino

March on Washington 1963 demonstration in which more than 200,000 people rallied for economic equality and civil rights (p. 482)

Marcha en Washington manifestación de más de 200,000 personas que en 1963 marcharon a favor de la igualdad económica y los derechos civiles

Marshall Plan economic and foreign policy that offered aid to Western European countries after World War II (p. 402)

Plan Marshall política económica y exterior que ofreció ayuda a los países de Europa Occidental después de la Segunda Guerra Mundial

mass production rapid manufacture of large numbers of identical products (p. 212)

producción en masa fabricación rápida de grandes cantidades de productos idénticos

massive retaliation policy of threatening to use massive force in response to aggression (p. 414)

represalia masiva política de amenazar con el uso de fuerza masiva en respuesta a una agresión

Mayflower Compact agreement for ruling the Plymouth Colony made in 1620 on the ship the *Mayflower* (p. 11)

Pacto del Mayflower acuerdo para gobernar la colonia de Plymouth alcanzado en 1620 en el barco *Mayflower*

McCarthyism negative catchword for extreme, reckless charges of disloyalty (p. 426)

McCarthyismo lema negativo que expresa acusaciones extremas e irresponsables de deslealtad

Meat Inspection Act 1906 law that allowed the federal government to inspect meat sold across state lines and required federal inspection of meat processing plants (p. 124)

Ley de Inspección de Carnes ley de 1906 que permitió al gobierno federal inspeccionar la carne vendida entre los estados y que exigió la inspección federal de las plantas de procesamiento de carne

median family income measure of average family income (p. 448)

mediana del ingreso familiar medida del ingreso familiar promedio

Medicaid federal program created in 1965 to provide low-cost health insurance to poor Americans of any age (p. 522)

Medicaid programa federal creado en 1965 para brindar seguro de salud de bajo costo a los estadounidenses de escasos recursos de cualquier edad

Medicare federal program created in 1965 to provide basic hospital insurance to most Americans age 65 and over (p. 522)

Medicare programa federal creado en 1965 para brindar seguro hospitalario básico a la mayoría de los estadounidenses mayores de sesenta y cinco años de edad

Middle Passage the forced transport of enslaved persons from Africa to the Americas between the 1500s and the 1800s (p. 6)

Pasaje Medio transporte forzado de esclavos desde África a las Américas entre los siglos XVI y XIX

migrant farmworker person who travels from farm to farm, and sometimes from state to state, to pick fruit and vegetables (p. 581)

trabajador agrícola migratorio persona que viaja de una granja a otra, algunas veces de un estado a otro, para la recolección de frutas y vegetales

militarism glorification of the military (p. 171)

militarismo glorificación de lo militar

Missouri Compromise 1820 agreement calling for the admission of Missouri as a slave state and Maine as a free state, and banning slavery in the Louisiana Purchase territory north of the 36° 30 N latitude (p. 38)

Acuerdo de Missouri acuerdo de 1820 que establecía a Missouri como estado esclavista y a Maine como estado libre, y prohibía la esclavitud en el territorio de la Compra de Luisiana al norte de la latitud 36° 30 N

Model T automobile manufactured by Henry Ford to be affordable on the mass market (p. 213)

Modelo T automóvil fabricado por Henry Ford para que fuera asequible en el mercado masivo

modernism trend that emphasized science and secular values over traditional ideas about religion (p. 223)

modernismo moda que daba énfasis a la ciencia y los valores seculares por sobre las ideas religiosas tradicionales

English/Spanish Glossary

monopoly complete control over an industry by one person or company (p. 68)

monopolio control total de una industria por una persona o compañía

Monroe Doctrine declaration by President Monroe in 1823 that the United States would oppose efforts by any outside power to control a nation in the Western Hemisphere (p. 27)

Doctrina Monroe declaración del presidente Monroe en 1823 en cuanto a que Estados Unidos se opondría a los esfuerzos de cualquier poder extranjero por controlar una nación del hemisferio occidental

Montgomery bus boycott 1955–1956 protest by African Americans in Montgomery, Alabama, against racial segregation in the bus system (p. 474)

boicot de los autobuses de Montgomery protesta de 1955 a 1956 de los afroestadounidenses en Montgomery, Alabama, contra la segregación en el sistema de autobuses

"moral diplomacy" Woodrow Wilson's statement that the U.S. would not use force to assert influence in the world, but would instead work to promote human rights (p. 161)

"diplomacia moral" aseveración de Woodrow Wilson en cuanto a que Estados Unidos no usaría la fuerza para ejercer su influencia en el mundo, sino que trabajaría en la promoción de los derechos humanos

Moral Majority political organization established by Reverend Jerry Falwell in 1979 to advance religious goals (p. 630)

Mayoría Moral organización política establecida por el reverendo Jerry Falwell en 1979 para promover objetivos religiosos

muckraker writer who uncovers and exposes misconduct in politics or business (p. 102)

muckraker escritor que descubre y expone la mala conducta real o aparente de políticos o empresas

multinational corporation companies that produce and sell their goods and services all over the world (pp. 446, 658)

corporaciones multinacionales compañías que producen y venden sus bienes y servicios alrededor del mundo

Munich Pact agreement made between Germany, Italy, Great Britain, and France in 1938 that sacrificed the Sudetenland to preserve peace (p. 330)

Pacto de Munich acuerdo de 1938 entre Alemania, Italia, Gran Bretaña y Francia que sacrificó los Sudetes para preservar la paz

mural a large picture painted directly on a wall or ceiling (p. 313)

mural pintura de grandes dimensiones realizada directamente sobre una pared o cielo raso

mutualistas organized groups of Mexican Americans that make loans and provide legal assistance to other members of their community (p. 119)

mutualistas grupos organizados de estadounidenses de origen mexicano para ofrecer préstamos y asistencia legal a miembros de su comunidad

mutually assured destruction policy in which the United States and the Soviet Union hoped to deter nuclear war by building up enough weapons to destroy one another (p. 413)

destrucción mutua asegurada política con la que Estados Unidos y la Unión Soviética esperaban evitar la guerra nuclear al acumular suficientes armas para destruirse mutuamente

My Lai village in South Vietnam where in 1968 American forces opened fire on unarmed civilians; during the massacre, U.S. soldiers killed between 400 and 500 Vietnamese (p. 555)

My Lai villa en Vietnam del Sur donde en 1968 fuerzas estadounidenses dispararon contra civiles desarmados; durante la masacre, los soldados estadounidenses mataron entre 400 y 500 vietnamitas

napalm jellied gasoline dropped in large canisters that explode on impact and cover large areas in flames; dropped by U.S. planes during the Vietnam War (p. 538)

napalm gasolina gelatinizada lanzada en grandes latas que explotaban al impactar y dejaban en llamas grandes áreas; lanzadas por aviones estadounidenses durante la Guerra de Vietnam

national debt total amount of money that the federal government owes to the owners of government bonds (p. 634)

deuda interna cantidad total de dinero que el gobierno federal debe a los dueños de bonos de gobierno

National Aeronautics and Space Administration (NASA) government agency that coordinates U.S. efforts in space (p. 417)

Administración Nacional de Aeronáutica y del Espacio agencia gubernamental formada para coordinar los esfuerzos estadounidenses en el espacio

National American Woman Suffrage Association (NAWSA) group founded in 1890 that worked on both the state and national levels to earn women the right to vote (p. 111)

Asociación Nacional para el Sufragio de las Mujeres Estadounidenses grupo fundado en 1890 que funcionó a nivel tanto estatal como nacional para que se otorgara a las mujeres el derecho al voto

National Association for the Advancement of Colored People (NAACP) interracial organization founded in 1909 to abolish segregation and discrimination and to achieve political and civil rights for African Americans (p. 119)

Asociación Nacional para el Avance de las Personas de Color organización interracial fundada en 1909 para abolir la segregación y la discriminación y avanzar los derechos políticos y civiles de los afroestadounidenses

National Consumers League (NCL) group organized in 1899 to investigate the conditions under which goods were made and sold and to promote safe working conditions and a minimum wage (p. 110)

Liga Nacional de Consumidores grupo organizado en 1899 para investigar las condiciones en que se fabricaban y vendían los bienes, así como promover condiciones seguras de trabajo y un salario mínimo

nationalize to place a resource under government control (p. 416)

nacionalización poner un recurso bajo control gubernamental

National Organization for Women (NOW) organization established by Betty Friedan to combat discrimination against women in the workplace and education (p. 575)

Organización Nacional de Mujeres organización establecida por Betty Friedan para derribar las barreras de la discriminación en el lugar de trabajo y la educación

National Reclamation Act 1902 law that gave the federal government the power to decide where and how water would be distributed through the building and management of dams and irrigation projects (p. 126)

Ley Nacional de Reclamaciones ley de 1902 que otorgó al gobierno federal el poder para decidir adónde y cómo se distribuiría el agua, mediante la construcción y administración de represas y proyectos de irrigación

National Recovery Administration (NRA) New Deal agency that promoted economic recovery by regulating production, prices, and wages (p. 289)

Administración para la Recuperación Nacional agencia del Nuevo Trato que promovió la recuperación económica al controlar la producción, precios y salarios

Nation of Islam African American religious organization founded in 1930 that advocated separation of the races (p. 492)

Nación Islámica organización religiosa afroestadounidense fundada en 1930 que abogó por la separación de las razas

Neutrality Act of 1939 act that allowed nations at war to buy goods and arms in the United States if they paid cash and carried the merchandise on their own ships (p. 336)

Ley de Neutralidad de 1939 ley que permitió que las naciones en guerra compraran bienes y armas en Estados Unidos siempre que pagaran en efectivo y transportaran la mercancía en sus propios barcos

New Deal programs and legislation enacted by Franklin D. Roosevelt during the Great Depression to promote economic recovery and social reform (p. 285)

Nuevo Trato programas y leyes establecidos por Franklin D. Roosevelt durante la Gran Depresión para promover la recuperación económica y reforma social

New Deal coalition political force formed by diverse groups who united to support Franklin D. Roosevelt and his New Deal (p. 303)

coalición del Nuevo Trato fuerza política formada por grupos diversos unidos para apoyar a Franklin D. Roosevelt y su Nuevo Trato

New Freedom Woodrow Wilson's program to place government controls on corporations in order to benefit small businesses (p. 128)

Nueva Libertad programa de Woodrow Wilson para establecer controles gubernamentales sobre las corporaciones a fin de brindar más oportunidades a las pequeñas empresas

New Frontier President Kennedy's plan aimed at improving the economy, fighting racial discrimination, and exploring space (p. 512)

Nueva Frontera plan doméstico del presidente Kennedy dirigido a mejorar la economía, combatir la discriminación racial y avanzar el programa espacial

New Nationalism President Theodore Roosevelt's plan to restore the government's trustbusting power (p. 127)

Nuevo Nacionalismo plan del presidente Teodoro Roosevelt para restaurar el poder del gobierno de disolver monopolios

New Right political movement supported by reinvigorated conservative groups in the latter half of the twentieth century (p. 629)

Nueva Derecha movimiento político apoyado por grupos conservadores revigorizados durante la última mitad del siglo XX

Niagara Movement group of African American thinkers founded in 1905 that pushed for immediate racial reforms, particularly in education and voting practices (p. 118)

Movimiento Niágara grupo de pensadores afroestadounidenses fundado en 1905 que presionó para obtener reformas raciales inmediatas, particularmente en cuanto a la educación y el voto

Nineteenth Amendment constitutional amendment that gave women the right to vote (p. 113)

Décimonovena Enmienda enmienda constitucional que otorgó a las mujeres el derecho al voto

No Child Left Behind Act 2002 law aimed at improving the performance of primary and secondary schools particularly through mandated sanctions against schools not reaching federal performance standards (p. 673)

Ley Que Ningún Niño Se Quede Atrás ley del año 2002 destinada a mejorar el desempeño de escuelas primarias y secundarias particularmente mediante sanciones por mandato contra las escuelas que no cumplan las normas federales de desempeño

English/Spanish Glossary

North American Free Trade Agreement (NAFTA) agreement signed in 1992 calling for the removal of trade restrictions among Canada, Mexico, and the United States (p. 667)
Tratado de Libre Comercio de América del Norte (TLCAN) acuerdo firmado en 1992 para la remoción de las restricciones comerciales entre Canadá, México y Estados Unidos

North Atlantic Treaty Organization (NATO) military alliance formed to counter Soviet expansion (p. 404)
Organización del Tratado del Atlántico Norte (OTAN) alianza militar creada para parar la expansión soviética

nuclear family ideal or typical household with a father, mother, and children (p. 449)
núcleo familiar hogar ideal o típico formado por un padre, una madre y niños

Nuclear Test Ban Treaty 1963 nuclear-weapons agreement, which prohibited aboveground nuclear tests (p. 510)
Tratado de Prohibición de Pruebas Nucleares acuerdo de 1963 sobre armas nucleares que prohibió las pruebas nucleares en la superficie de la Tierra

Nuremberg Laws laws enacted by Hitler that denied German citizenship to Jews (p. 381)
Leyes de Nuremberg leyes impuestas por Hitler que negaban la ciudadanía alemana a los judíos

Nuremberg Trials trials in which Nazi leaders were charged with war crimes (p. 390)
Juicios de Nuremberg juicios en los que se acusó a los líderes nazis de crímenes de guerra

O

Office of War Information (OWI) government agency that encouraged support of the war effort during World War II (p. 366)
Oficina de Información de Guerra agencia gubernamental que animaba el apoyo al esfuerzo bélico durante la Segunda Guerra Mundial

Okies general term used to describe Dust Bowl refugees during the Great Depression (p. 267)
okies término general usado para describir a los refugiados del Cuenco de Polvo durante la Gran Depresión

Open Door Policy American statement that the government did not want colonies in China, but favored free trade there (p. 154)
política de puertas abiertas declaración estadounidense que proclamaba que el gobierno no deseaba colonias en China, pero favorecía el libre comercio

open range vast area of grassland owned by the federal government (p. 86)
praderas abiertas grandes pastizales propiedad del gobierno federal

Operation Desert Storm 1991 American-led attack on Iraqi forces after Iraq refused to withdraw its troops from Kuwait (p. 649)

Operación Tormenta del Desierto ataque que comandaron los estadounidenses en 1991 contra las fuerzas iraquíes luego que Irak rehusó retirar sus tropas de Kuwait

Organization of Petroleum Exporting Countries (OPEC) group of countries which sell oil to other nations and cooperate to regulate the price and supply of oil (p. 600)
Organización de Países Exportadores de Petróleo (OPEP) grupo de países que venden petróleo a otras naciones y que coopera en la regulación del precio y suministro del crudo

P

Palmer Raids the series of raids in the early 1920s initiated by Attorney General A. Mitchell Palmer, against suspected radicals and communists (p. 201)
Redadas Palmer redadas de principios de la década de 1920 iniciadas por el fiscal general del estado A. Mitchell Palmer contra personas sospechosas de ser radicales o comunistas

Panama Canal human-made waterway linking the Atlantic to the Pacific across the Isthmus of Panama (p. 159)
Canal de Panamá vía acuática hecha por los humanos que une el Atlántico y el Pacífico a través del istmo de Panamá

pardon official forgiveness of a crime and its punishment (p. 608)
indulto perdón oficial de un delito y su castigo

Paris Peace Accords 1973 peace agreement between the United States, South Vietnam, North Vietnam, and the Vietcong that effectively ended the Vietnam War (p. 556)
Acuerdos de Paz de París acuerdo de paz de 1973 entre Estados Unidos, Vietnam del Sur, Vietnam del Norte y el Vietcong que de hecho finalizó la Guerra de Vietnam

Patriot Act law passed following September 11, 2001, giving law enforcement broader powers in monitoring possible terrorist activities (p. 677)
Ley Patriótica ley aprobada después del 11 de septiembre del 2001 que otorgó mayores poderes a los agentes de la ley para vigilar posibles actividades terroristas

Peace Corps American government organization that sends volunteers to provide technical, educational, and medical services in developing countries (p. 507)
Cuerpo de Paz organización del gobierno de Estados Unidos que envía voluntarios para que brinden servicios técnicos, educativos y médicos en países en vías de desarrollo

Pearl Harbor American military base attacked by the Japanese on December 7, 1941 (p. 341)
Peral Harbor base militar estadounidense atacada por los japoneses el 7 de diciembre de 1941

Pendleton Act law that created a civil service system for the federal government in an attempt to hire employees on a merit system rather than on a spoils system (p. 89)

　Ley Pendleton ley que creó un sistema de servicio civil para el gobierno federal en un intento por contratar empleados con un sistema de méritos en lugar de un sistema de clientelismo

Pentagon Papers classified U.S. government study that revealed American leaders intentionally involved the United States in Vietnam without fully informing the American people; leaked to *The New York Times* in 1971 (p. 555)

　Documentos del Pentágono estudio clasificado del gobierno estadounidense que reveló que los líderes estadounidenses intencionalmente involucraron a Estados Unidos en Vietnam sin haber informado completamente a la ciudadanía estadounidense; lo filtró el *The New York Times* en 1971

perestroika policy in the Soviet Union in the late 1980s calling for restructuring of the stagnant Soviet economy (p. 640)

　perestroika política de la Unión Soviética de finales de la década de 1980 que abogó por la reestructuración de la estancada economía soviética

personal computer small computer intended for individual use (p. 657)

　computadora personal computadora pequeña destinada al uso personal

Platt Amendment set of conditions under which Cuba was granted independence in 1902, including restrictions on rights of Cubans and granting to the U.S. the "right to intervene" to preserve order in Cuba (p. 157)

　Enmienda Platt grupo de condiciones con las que se le otorgó la independencia a Cuba en 1902, que incluían restricciones de los derechos de los cubanos y que otorgaban a EE.UU. el "derecho de intervenir" a fin de conservar el orden en Cuba

popular sovereignty concept of permitting the residents of a territory to decide on whether or not to allow slavery (p. 43)

　soberanía popular concepto de permitir a los residentes de un territorio decidir si permiten la esclavitud o no

Populist Party People's Party; political party formed in 1891 to advocate a larger money supply and other economic reforms (p. 89)

　Partido Populista Partido del Pueblo; partido político formado en 1891 para abogar por mayores ofertas monetarias y otras reformas económicas

privatize to transfer from governmental ownership or control to private interests (p. 683)

　privatizar transferir la propiedad o control gubernamental a intereses privados

productivity the rate at which goods are produced or services performed (p. 436)

　productividad velocidad a la que se producen bienes o se brindan servicios

Progressive Party political party that emerged from the Taft-Roosevelt battle that split the Republican Party in 1912 (p. 127)

　Partido Progresivo partido político surgido de la batalla entre Taft y Roosevelt que dividió al Partido Republicano en 1912

Progressivism movement that emerged in response to the pressures of industrialization and urbanization that promoted reforms to bring about social justice (p. 100)

　progresismo movimiento surgido como respuesta a las presiones de la industrialización y urbanización, que promovía nuevas ideas y reformas políticas para alcanzar la justicia social

Prohibition the forbidding by law of the manufacture, transport, and sale of alcohol (p. 229)

　Prohibición ley para prohibir la fabricación, transporte y venta de alcohol

Public Works Administration (PWA) New Deal agency that provided millions of jobs constructing public buildings (p. 289)

　Administración de Obras Públicas agencia del Nuevo Trato que brindó millones de empleos en la construcción de obras públicas

pump priming economic theory that favored public works projects because they put money into the hands of consumers who would buy more goods, stimulating the economy (p. 293)

　cebado de bomba teoría económica que favorece los proyectos de obras públicas porque ponen dinero en manos de los consumidores que comprarán más bienes, estimulando así la economía

Pure Food and Drug Act 1906 law that allowed federal inspection of food and medicine and banned the interstate shipment and sale of impure food and the mislabeling of food and drugs (p. 124)

　Ley de Alimentos y Fármacos Puros ley de 1906 que permitió la inspección federal de los alimentos y medicinas, y prohibió el transporte y venta interestatal de alimentos impuros así como el rotulado erróneo de alimentos y fármacos

Q

quota system arrangement that limited the number of immigrants who could enter the United States from specific countries (p. 225)

　sistema de cuotas acuerdo que limitó el número de inmigrantes provenientes de países específicos que podían ingresar a Estados Unidos

R

Radical Republican congressman who advocated full citizens' rights for African Americans and a harsh Reconstruction policy on the South (p. 56)

　Republicano Radical congresista que abogaba por derechos ciudadanos íntegros para los afroestadounidenses y una política dura de Reconstrucción en el Sur

ratify to approve (p. 17)
ratificar aprobar

rationing government-controlled limits on the amount of certain goods that civilians could buy during wartime (p. 366)
racionamiento límites controlados por el gobierno sobre la cantidad de ciertos bienes que podían comprar los civiles en tiempos de guerra

realpolitik a foreign policy promoted by Henry Kissinger during the Nixon administration based on concrete national interests instead of abstract ideologies (p. 561)
realpolitik política exterior promovida por Henry Kissinger durante la administración Nixon con base en intereses nacionales concretos en lugar de ideologías abstractas

recall process by which voters can remove elected officials from office before their terms end (p. 107)
destitución proceso por el cual los electores pueden remover a funcionarios electos antes de terminar su período

Reconstruction federal program between 1865 and 1877 to repair damage to the South caused by the Civil War and restore the southern states to the Union (p. 55)
Reconstrucción programa instaurado por el gobierno federal entre 1865 y 1877 para reparar los daños que causó la Guerra Civil al Sur y reincorporar los estados sureños a la Unión

Reconstruction Finance Corporation (RFC) federal agency set up by Congress in 1932 to provide emergency government credit to banks, railroads, and other large businesses (p. 274)
Corporación de Financiamiento para la Reconstrucción agencia federal establecida por el Congreso en 1932 para brindar créditos gubernamentales de emergencia a los bancos, ferrocarriles y otras grandes empresas

Red Scare fear that communists were working to destroy the American way of life (pp. 201, 420)
miedo rojo miedo a que los comunistas están empeñados en destruir la forma de vida estadounidense

referendum process that allows citizens to approve or reject a law passed by a legislature (p. 107)
referendo proceso que permite que los ciudadanos aprueben o rechacen una ley que ha aprobado una legislatura

reparations payment for war damages (p. 194)
reparaciones pago por los daños causados por la guerra

repatriation process by which Mexican Americans were encouraged, or forced, by local, state, and federal officials to return to Mexico during the 1930s (p. 269)
repatriación proceso por el cual los estadounidenses de origen mexicano fueron animados, o forzados, por los oficiales locales, estatales y federales a que regresaran a México durante la década de 1930

reservationists a group of Senators, led by Henry Cabot Lodge, who opposed the Treaty of Versailles, to end World War I, unless specific changes were included (p. 196)
reservasionistas grupo de senadores encabezados por Henry Cabot que se oponía a terminar la Primera Guerra Mundial con el Tratado de Versalles a menos que éste inlcuyera ciertos cambios

rock-and-roll music originated in the gospel and blues traditions of African Americans (p. 453)
rock-and-roll música originada en las tradiciones del gospel y blues de los afroestadounidenses

Roosevelt Corollary President Theodore Roosevelt's reassertion of the Monroe Doctrine to keep the Western Hemisphere free from intervention by European powers (p. 159)
Corolario Roosevelt replanteamiento del presidente Teodoro Roosevelt de la Doctrina Monroe, según la cual la política de Estados Unidos era mantener al hemisferio occidental libre de la intervención de las potencias europeas

Rough Riders group of men, consisting of rugged westerners and upper-class easterners who fought during the Spanish-American War and are often remembered for the charge up San Juan Hill (p. 148)
jinetes rudos grupo de hombres fuertes provenientes del Oeste y de la clase alta del Este que pelearon durante la Guerra entre España y Estados Unidos, a quienes se les recuerda principalmente por el ataque a la colina de San Juan

Russo-Japanese War a war between Japan and Russia in 1904 over the presence of Russian troops in Manchuria (p. 155)
Guerra Ruso-Japonesa guerra entre Japón y Rusia durante 1904 por la presencia de tropas rusas en Manchuria

S

sanctions penalties (p. 616)
sanciones castigos

satellite a mechanical device that orbits Earth, receiving and sending communication signals or transmitting scientific data (p. 658)
satélite dispositivo mecánico que orbita la Tierra, y que recibe y envía señales de comunicación o transmite datos científicos

satellite state independent nation under the control of a more powerful nation (p. 399)
estado satélite nación independiente bajo el control de una nación más poderosa

saturation bombing tactic of dropping massive amounts of bombs in order to inflict maximum damage (p. 358)
saturación de bombardeos táctica de dejar caer cantidades masivas de bombas a fin de infligir el máximo daño

Savings and Loan crisis the failure of about 1,000 savings and loan banks as a result of risky business practices (p. 634)

crisis financiera fracaso de cerca de 1,000 bancos de ahorro y préstamo como resultado de prácticas comerciales riesgosas

scientific management approach to improving efficiency, in which experts looked at every step of a manufacturing process, trying to find ways to reduce time, effort, and expense (p. 213)

administración científica enfoque para mejorar la eficiencia, en el que los expertos observaban cada paso de un proceso de manufactura y buscaban formas de reducir el tiempo, esfuerzo y costo

Scopes Trial 1925 trial of a Tennessee schoolteacher for teaching Darwin's theory of evolution (p. 224)

Juicio Scopes juicio al que fue sometido, en 1925, un maestro de Tennessee por enseñar la teoría de Darwin sobre la evolución

secede to withdraw formally from a membership in a group or organization (p. 47)

secesión retiro formal de la membresía en un grupo u organización

Second Great Awakening religious movement in the first half of the 1800s (p. 35)

Segundo Gran Despertar movimiento religioso durante la primera mitad del siglo XIX

Second New Deal legislative activity begun by Franklin D. Roosevelt in 1935 to solve problems created by the Great Depression (p. 292)

Segundo Nuevo Trato actividad legislativa iniciada por Franklin D. Roosevelt en 1935 para lidiar con los problemas económicos y sociales creados por la Gran Depresión

Sedition Act 1798 law that allowed the prosecution of critics of the government (p. 23)

Ley de Sedición ley de 1798 que permitió enjuiciar a quienes criticaran al gobierno

segregation forced separation of one group from another, oftentimes on the basis of race (p. 59)

segregación separación forzada de dos grupos, a menudo con base en la raza

Selective Service Act act passed by Congress in May 1917 authorizing a draft of young men for military service (p. 180)

Ley de Servicio Selectivo ley aprobada por el Congreso en mayo de 1917 que autorizó el reclutamiento de hombres jóvenes para el servicio militar

self-determination the right of people to choose their own form of government (p. 194)

autodeterminación derecho de las personas de elegir su propia forma de gobierno

separation of powers principle by which the powers of government are divided between the executive, legislative, and judicial branches (p. 20)

separación de poderes principio por el cual los poderes de gobierno se dividen entre los poderes ejecutivo, legislativo y judicia

service economy an economic system focused on the buying and selling of services (p. 660)

economía de servicio sistema económico enfocado en la compra y venta de servicios

service sector businesses that provide services rather than manufactured goods (p. 445)

sector de servicios empresas que brindan servicios en lugar de fabricar bienes

settlement house community center organized to provide social services to the urban poor at the turn of the twentieth century (p. 104)

casa de asentamiento centro comunal organizado para ofrecer servicios sociales a los pobres de la ciudad a inicios del siglo XX

sharecropping system in which a farmer tends some portion of a planter's land and receives a share of the crop as payment (pp. 56, 81)

aparcería sistema en el cual un granjero atiende una porción de la tierra del dueño de una plantación y recibe parte de la cosecha como pago

Shays' Rebellion farmers' revolt against high taxes in Massachusetts in 1786 (p. 16)

Rebelión de Shay revuelta de los granjeros contra los altos impuestos de Massachussets en 1786

silent majority phrase introduced by President Richard Nixon to refer to a significant number of Americans who supported his policies but chose not to express their views (p. 599)

mayoría silenciosa frase introducida por el presidente Richard Nixon para referirse a un número significativo de estadounidenses que apoyaban sus políticas pero eligieron no expresar su opinión

sit-down strike labor protest in which workers stop working and occupy the workplace until their demands are met (p. 297)

huelga de brazos caídos protesta laboral en que los trabajadores dejan de trabajar y ocupan el lugar de trabajo hasta que se satisfacen sus demandas

sit-in form of protest where participants sit and refuse to move (p. 477)

sentada forma de protesta en que los participantes se sientan y rehúsan moverse

Sixteenth Amendment 1913 constitutional amendment that gave Congress the authority to levy an income tax (p. 129)

Décimosexta Enmienda enmienda constitucional de 1913 que otorgó al Congreso la autoridad para establecer un impuesto a las rentas

Smith Act law that made it unlawful to teach or advocate the violent overthrow of the United States government (p. 421)

Ley Smith ley que prohibió la enseñanza o defensa de un derrocamiento violento del gobierno estadounidense

Social Darwinism the belief held by some in the late nineteenth century that certain nations and races were superior to others and therefore destined to rule over them (pp. 68, 140)

darwinismo social creencia de algunos a finales del siglo XIX según la que algunas naciones o razas eran superiores a otras y por lo tanto estaban destinadas a gobernar

Social Gospel reform movement that emerged in the late nineteenth century that sought to improve society by applying Christian principles (p. 104)

Evangelio Social movimiento reformista surgido a finales del siglo XIX cuyo fin era mejorar la sociedad al aplicarse principios cristianos

Social Security Act a 1935 law that set up a pension system for retirees, established unemployment insurance, and created insurance for victims of work-related accidents. It also provided aid for poverty-stricken mothers and children, the blind, and the disabled (p. 293)

Ley del Seguro Social ley de 1935 que creó un sistema de pensión para jubilados, estableció un seguro de desempleo y creó seguros para las víctimas de accidentes laborales; también suministra ayuda a las madres y niños pobres, ciegos y discapacitados

Southeast Asia Treaty Organization (SEATO) defensive alliance aimed at preventing communist aggression in Asia (pp. 411, 535)

Organización del Tratado del Sudeste Asiático alianza defensiva orientada a prevenir la agresión comunista en Asia

southern strategy tactic of the Republican Party for winning presidential elections by securing the electoral votes of southern states (p. 600)

estrategia sureña táctica del Partido Republicano para ganar las elecciones presidenciales al asegurarse los votos electorales de los estados del Sur

"space race" the competition between the United States and the Soviet Union to develop the technology to successfully land on the moon (p. 513)

"carrera espacial" competencia entre Estados Unidos y la Unión Soviética en el desarrollo de la tecnología para aterrizar exitosamente en la Luna

Spanish Civil War Nationalist forces led by General Francisco Franco rebelled against the democratic Republican government of Spain (p. 329)

Guerra Civil Española conflicto en España en el que las fuerzas Nacionalistas dirigidas por el General Francisco Franco se rebelaron contra el gobierno democrático Republicano

speculation practice of making high-risk investments in hopes of obtaining large profits (p. 258)

especulación práctica de hacer inversiones de alto riesgo con la esperanza de obtener grandes ganancias

sphere of influence a region dominated and controlled by an outside power (p. 153)

esfera de influencia región dominada y controlada por un poder externo

Square Deal President Theodore Roosevelt's program of reforms to keep the wealthy and powerful from taking advantage of small business owners and the poor (p. 122)

Trato Justo programa de reformas del presidente Teodoro Roosevelt para evitar que los ricos y poderosos se aprovecharan de los propietarios de pequeñas empresas y de los pobres

stagflation term for the economic condition created in the late 1960s and 1970s by high inflation combined with stagnating economic growth and high unemployment (p. 599)

estanflación término para la condición económica creada a finales de las décadas de 1960 y 1970 por una alta inflación combinada con el estancamiento del crecimiento económico y el alto desempleo

Strategic Arms Limitation Treaty (SALT I) 1972 treaty between the United States and the Soviet Union that froze the deployment of intercontinental ballistic missiles and placed limits on antiballistic missiles (p. 562)

Tratado de Limitación de Armas Estratégicas tratado de 1972 entre Estados Unidos y la Unión Soviética que congeló el despliegue de misiles balísticos intercontinentales y puso límites a los misiles antibalísticos

Strategic Arms Limitation Treaty II (SALT II) proposed agreement between the United States and the Soviet Union to limit certain types of nuclear arms production; it was never ratified by the United States Senate (p. 616)

Tratado de Limitación de Armas Estratégicas II acuerdo propuesto entre Estados Unidos y la Unión Soviética para limitar la producción de ciertos tipos de armas nucleares; nunca fue ratificado por el Senado de Estados Unidos

strategic bombing tactic of dropping bombs on key political and industrial targets (p. 359)

bombardeo estratégico táctica de dejar caer bombas en blancos políticos e industriales clave

Strategic Defense Initiative (SDI) nicknamed "Star Wars," President Reagan's plan to develop innovative defenses to guard the United States against nuclear missile attacks (p. 640)

Iniciativa de Defensa Estratégica apodada "Guerra de las Galaxias," plan de 1983 del presidente Reagan para financiar el desarrollo de defensas innovadoras para salvaguardar a Estados Unidos contra ataques con misiles nucleares

Student Nonviolent Coordinating Committee (SNCC) grass-roots movement of young civil rights activists founded in 1960 (p. 478)

Comité Estudiantil Coordinador de la No Violencia movimiento de base compuesto por jóvenes activistas a favor de los derechos civiles fundado en 1960

Students for a Democratic Society (SDS) organization founded in 1960 at the University of Michigan to fight racism and poverty (p. 546)

Estudiantes a Favor de una Sociedad Democrática organización fundada en 1960 en la Universidad de Michigan para combatir el racismo y la pobreza

suburb residential area surrounding a city (p. 76)

suburbio área residencial que rodea a una ciudad

Suez crisis attempt by France and Great Britain to seize control of the Suez Canal in 1956 (p. 416)

crisis de Suez intento de Francia y Gran Bretaña por apoderarse del control del Canal de Suez en 1956

suffrage right to vote (p. 111)

sufragio derecho al voto

Sunbelt name given to the region of states in the South and the Southwest (p. 443)

Cinturón del Sol nombre dado a la región de los estados del sur y suroeste

superpower powerful country that plays a dominant economic, political, and military role in the world (p. 388)

superpotencia país poderoso que juega un papel económico, político y militar dominante en el mundo

supply-side economics economic theory which says that reducing tax rates stimulates economic growth (p. 633)

economía de la oferta teoría económica que dice que reduciendo impuestos estimula el crecimiento conomico

T

Taft-Hartley Act a law that restricted the power of labor unions (p. 437)

Ley Taft Hartley ley que restringió el poder de los sindicatos de trabajadores

Taliban Islamic fundamentalist faction that controlled most of Afghanistan from 1996–2001 (p. 676)

Talibán fracción fundamentalista islámica que controló la mayor parte de Afganistán entre 1996 y 2001

tariff tax on imported goods (p. 35)

arancel impuesto sobre bienes importados

Tea Party Movement informal movement made up of local groups who want to reduce the size and scope of the federal government

movimiento Tea Party movimiento informal compuesto por grupos locales que quieren reducir el tamaño y el alcance del gobierno federal

Teapot Dome scandal scandal during the Harding administration in which the Secretary of the Interior leased government oil reserves to private oilmen in return for bribes (p. 220)

escándalo Teapot Dome escándalo durante la administración Harding en que el secretario del interior arrendó las reservas de petróleo del gobierno a petroleros privados a cambio de un soborno

televangelist minister who uses television to preach (p. 613)

teleevangelista pastor que usa el formato de la television para predicar

temperance movement movement aimed at stopping alcohol abuse and the problems created by it (p. 110)

movimiento por la temperancia movimiento encausado a eliminar el abuso del alcohol y los problemas que éste genera

tenant farmer one who works land owned by another and pays rent either in cash or in shares of produce (p. 265)

agricultor arrendatario aquél que cultiva la tierra propiedad de otro y paga un alquiler en efectivo o en especie con el producto

tenement multistory building divided into apartments to house several families, often in unsanitary conditions (p. 78)

vecindad edificio de varios pisos dividido en departamentos para albergar a varias familias, a menudo en condiciones poco sanitarias

Tennessee Valley Authority (TVA) government agency that built dams in the Tennessee River Valley to control flooding and generate electric power (p. 288)

Autoridad del Valle del Tennessee agencia gubernamental que construye represas en el valle del Río Tennessee para controlar las inundaciones y generar energía eléctrica

termination policy ended all programs monitored by the Bureau of Indian Affairs; also ended federal responsibility for the health and welfare of Native Americans (p. 459)

política de terminación política que cerró todos los programas a cargo de la Oficina de Asuntos Indígenas; también dio por terminada la responsabilidad federal en cuanto a la salud y bienestar de los indígenas estadounidenses

Tet Offensive coordinated communist assault on a large number of South Vietnamese cities in early 1968 (p. 547)

Ofensiva Tet asalto comunista coordinado contra un gran número de ciudades de Vietnam del Sur a principios de 1968

Thirteenth Amendment 1865 constitutional amendment which abolished slavery (p. 56)

Decimotercera Enmienda enmienda constitucional de 1865 que abolió la esclavitud

38th parallel dividing line between North and South Korea (p. 407)

paralelo 38 línea divisoria entre Corea del Norte y Corea del Sur

English/Spanish Glossary

Tiananmen Square site in Beijing where Chinese students' prodemocracy protests were put down by the Chinese government in 1989 (p. 646)
Plaza Tiananmen lugar en Pekín donde las protestas de los estudiantes chinos a favor de la democracia fueron aplacadas por el gobierno chino en 1989

totalitarianism a theory of government in which a single party or leader controls the economic, social, and cultural lives of its people (p. 324)
totalitarismo teoría de gobierno según la que un solo partido o líder controla la vida económica, social y cultural de la población

total war war in which a nation uses all of its resources to destroy enemy troops and their resources (p. 54)
guerra total guerra en la cual una nación usa todos sus recursos para destruir a las tropas enemigas y sus recursos

toxic waste poisonous byproducts of human activity (p. 587)
desechos tóxicos productos de desecho venenosos resultantes de la actividad humana

Treaty of Paris an agreement signed by the United States and Spain in 1898, which officially ended the Spanish-American War (p. 149)
Tratado de París acuerdo firmado por Estados Unidos y España en 1898 que marcó el final oficial de la Guerra entre España y Estados Unidos

trickle-down economics economic theory that holds that money lent to banks and businesses will trickle down to consumers (p. 274)
economía por goteo teoría económica que mantiene que el dinero prestado a los bancos y empresas llegará a los consumidores

Tripartite Pact agreement that created an alliance between Germany, Italy, and Japan during World War II (p. 336)
Pacto Tripartito acuerdo que creó una alianza entre Alemania, Italia y Japón durante la Segunda Guerra Mundial

Truman Doctrine President Truman's promise to help nations struggling against communist movements (p. 400)
doctrina Truman promesa del presidente Truman de ayudar a las naciones en lucha contra los movimientos comunistas

trust a combination of corporations or firms bound by a legal agreement, especially to reduce competition (p. 68)
trust combinación de empresas o firmas vinculadas por un contrato legal, especialmente para reducir la competencia

Tuskegee Airmen African American squadron that escorted bombers in the air war over Europe during World War II (p. 358)
Aviadores de Tuskegee escuadrón de afroestadounidenses que escoltaba a los bombarderos en la guerra aérea en cielos de Europa durante la Segunda Guerra Mundial

Twenty-fifth Amendment constitutional amendment ratified in 1967 that deals with presidential succession, vice presidential vacancy, and presidential inability (p. 603)
Vigésima Quinta Enmienda enmienda constitucional ratificada en 1967 que trata de la sucesión presidencial, vacantes de vicepresidentes e incapacidad presidencial

Twenty-fourth Amendment constitutional amendment that banned the poll tax as a voting requirement (p. 490)
Vigésima Cuarta Enmienda enmienda constitucional que prohibió el impuesto electoral como requisito para votar

U

U-boat German submarine (p. 176)
U boot submarino alemán

unconditional surrender giving up completely without any concessions (p. 357)
rendición incondicional darse por vencido completamente sin concesiones

Underground Railroad support system run by abolitionists to help enslaved people escape to freedom in the North or in Canada (p. 39)
Ferrocarril Subterráneo sistema de apoyo dirigido por los abolicionistas para ayudar a los esclavos en su fuga hacia la libertad en el Norte o en Canadá

unfunded mandate program or action required but not paid for by the federal government (p. 630)
mandatos sin fondos programas o acciones requeridos pero que no paga el gobierno federal

United Farm Workers (UFW) labor union of farm workers that used nonviolent tactics including a workers' strike and a consumer boycott of table grapes (p. 581)
Trabajadores Agrícolas Unidos sindicato de trabajadores agrícolas que usó tácticas pacíficas, incluyendo una huelga de trabajadores y un boicot por los consumidores de uvas

United Nations (UN) organization founded in 1945 to promote peace (p. 389)
Naciones Unidas (ONU) organización fundada en 1945 para promover la paz

Universal Declaration of Human Rights document issued by the UN to promote basic human rights and freedoms (p. 389)
Declaración Universal de los Derechos Humanos documento emitido por la ONU para promover los derechos y libertades humanos básicos

Urban League network of churches and clubs that set up employment agencies and relief efforts to help African Americans get settled and find work in the cities (p. 119)
Liga Urbana red de iglesias y clubes que estableció agencias de empleo y ofreció asistencia para que los afroestadounidenses se asentaran y encontraran empleo en las ciudades

urban renewal government programs for redevelopment of urban areas (p. 457)

renovación urbana programas gubernamentales para el desarrollo de las áreas urbanas

V

Vietcong South Vietnamese communist rebels that waged a guerrilla war against the government of South Vietnam throughout the Vietnam War (p. 535)

Vietcong rebeldes comunistas sudvietnamitas que hicieron guerra de guerrillas contra el gobierno de Vietnam del Sur durante la Guerra de Vietnam

Vietnamization President Nixon's plan for gradual withdrawal of U.S. forces as South Vietnamese troops assumed more combat duties (p. 553)

vietnamización plan del presidente Nixon que planteó un retiro gradual de las fuerzas estadounidenses a medida que las tropas sudvietnamitas asumían más deberes de combate

Violence Against Women Act law passed in 1994 that increased federal resources to apprehend and prosecute men guilty of violent acts against women (p. 683)

Ley contra la Violencia hacia las Mujeres ley aprobada en 1994 que aumentó los recursos federales para arrestar y enjuiciar a los hombres culpables de actos violentos contra las mujeres

Volstead Act law enacted by Congress to enforce the Eighteenth Amendment (p. 229)

Ley Volstead ley impuesta por el Congreso para hacer cumplir la Decimoctava Enmienda

Voting Rights Act law that banned literacy tests and empowered the federal government to oversee voter registration (p. 490)

Ley de Derechos Electorales ley que prohibió las pruebas de alfabetismo y dio poder al gobierno federal de vigilar el empadronamiento de los votantes

voucher certificates or other documents that can be used as money (p. 637)

vales certificados u otros documentos que pueden ser usados como dinero

W

Wagner Act New Deal law that abolished unfair labor practices, recognized the right of employees to organize labor unions, and gave workers the right to collective bargaining (p. 296)

Ley Wagner ley que abolió las prácticas laborales injustas, reconoció el derecho de los trabajadores de organizar sindicatos y dio a los trabajadores el derecho a las negociaciones colectivas

War on Poverty President Johnson's programs aimed at aiding the country's poor through education, job training, proper healthcare and nutrition, and overall community development (p. 518)

Guerra Contra la Pobreza programas del presidente Johnson enfocados en ayudar a los pobres de la nación mediante la educación, entrenamiento laboral, servicios de salud y nutrición adecuadas, y el desarrollo comunitario en general

War Powers Act 1973 law passed by Congress restricting the president's war-making powers; the law requires the President to consult with Congress within 48 hours of committing American forces to a foreign conflict (p. 559)

Ley de Poderes Bélicos ley aprobada por el Congreso en 1973 que restringió los poderes bélicos del presidente; la ley exige que el presidente consulte con el Congreso dentro de un período de 48 horas antes de comprometer fuerzas estadounidenses en un conflicto extranjero

War Refugee Board U.S. government agency founded in 1944 to save Eastern European Jews (p. 384)

Junta de Refugiados de Guerra agencia del gobierno de Estados Unidos fundada en 1944 para salvar a los judíos de Europa Oriental

Warren Commission committee that investigated the assassination of President Kennedy (p. 515)

Comisión Warren comité que investigó el asesinato del presidente Kennedy

"Warren Court" Supreme Court of the 1960s under Chief Justice Earl Warren, whose decisions supported civil rights, civil liberties, voting rights, and personal privacy (p. 523)

"Corte Warren" Corte Suprema de la década de 1960 bajo el mandato del presidente de los magistrados Earl Warren, cuyas decisiones apoyaron los derechos civiles, libertades civiles, derecho al sufragio y privacidad personal

Warsaw Pact military alliance of the Soviet Union and its satellite states (p. 404)

Pacto de Varsovia alianza militar de la Unión Soviética y sus estados satélites

Washington Naval Disarmament Conference meeting held in 1921 and 1922 where world leaders agreed to limit construction of warships (p. 221)

Conferencia de Desarme Naval de Washington reunión realizada en 1921 y 1922 durante la cual los líderes mundiales acordaron limitar la construcción de buques de guerra

Watergate political scandal involving illegal activities that ultimately led to the resignation of President Nixon in 1974 (p. 601)

Watergate escándalo político que involucró actividades ilegales que al final condujeron a la renuncia del presidente Nixon en 1974

Weapons of Mass Destruction (WMD) nuclear, biological, and chemical weapons intended to kill or harm on a large scale (p. 677)

armas de destrucción masiva armas nucleares, biológicas y químicas destinadas a matar o lesionar a gran escala

English/Spanish Glossary

welfare state government that assumes responsibility for providing for the welfare of the poor, elderly, sick, and unemployed (p. 307)
estado de bienestar gobierno que asume la responsabilidad de velar por el bienestar de los pobres, ancianos, enfermos y desempleados

Western Front battle front between the Allies and Central Powers in western Europe during World War I (p. 173)
Frente Occidental frente de batalla entre los Aliados y los Poderes Centrales en Europa Occidental durante la Primera Guerra Mundial

Wilmot Proviso proposed but never approved law that banned slavery in the territory won from Mexico (p. 42)
Condición Wilmot ley propuesta pero no aprobada que prohibía la esclavitud en el territorio ganado a México

Women's Army Corps (WAC) U.S. Army group established during World War II so that women could serve in non combat roles (p. 344)
Cuerpo Femenino del Ejército grupo del Ejército de Estados Unidos establecido durante la Segunda Guerra Mundial para que las mujeres pudieran dar servicio en papeles no combativos

Works Progress Administration (WPA) key New Deal agency that provided work relief through various public-works projects (p. 292)
Administración del Progreso de Obras agencia clave del Nuevo Trato que brindó ayuda laboral a través de varios proyectos de obras públicas

World Trade Organization (WTO) international organization formed in 1995 to encourage the expansion of world trade (p. 667)
Organización Mundial del Comercio (OMC) organización internacional formada en 1995 para estimular la expansión del comercio mundial

Y

Yalta Conference 1945 strategy meeting between Roosevelt, Churchill, and Stalin (p. 386)
Conferencia de Yalta reunión sobre estrategia realizada en 1945 entre Roosevelt, Churchill y Stalin

Yellow Press newspapers that used sensational headlines and exaggerated stories in order to promote readership (p. 145)
prensa amarillista periódicos que utilizaban titulares sensacionales e historias exageradas para promover su circulación

Z

Zimmermann note telegram written by German Foreign Minister Arthur Zimmermann proposing an alliance between Germany and Mexico against the United States during World War I (p. 179)
telegrama de Zimmermann telegrama escrito por el ministro del exterior alemán, Arthur Zimmermann, en el que proponía una alianza entre Alemania y México contra Estados Unidos en la Primera Guerra Mundial

Note: Page numbers followed by *b* refers to box; *c*, chart; *g*, graph; *m*, map; *i*, illustration; *p*, photo; *q*, quotation; *t*, table. Items in blue refer to Teacher's Edition pages.

Index

Index

Index

Index

Index

Index

Index

Index

Index

Index

Index

Index

Acknowledgments

Staff Credits

The people who make up the **United States History** team—representing design services, editorial, editorial services, education technology, manufacturing and inventory planning, research, marketing services and budgeting, product ~~duction~~ services, project ~~~processes~~, project ~~sions~~—are listed ~~denotes core team~~ ... paugh, Diane ...

Ernie Alban ... asjit Arneja, Alimena ...hini, Rosalyn Arcilla, Michele ... Helene Avraham, Penny **Marc** ... ~~Ala~~ ...ee Beach, Peter Brooks, Lois B, Kerry Buckley, Pradeep Byram, ...Camarinha, Lisa Carrillo, Sarah ...arroll, Kerry Cashman, Justin Contursi, Jason Cuoco, Harold DelMonte, **James Doris,** Laura Edgerton-Riser, Leanne Esterly, Anne Falzone, Libby Forsyth, Marianne Frasco, Phillip Gagler, Doreen Galbraith, Joe Galka, Kathy Gavilanes, Julie Gecha, Allen Gold, Holly Gordon, Ellen Welch Granter, Mary Ann Gundersen, Mary Hanisco, Rick Hickox, Karen Holtzman, **Kristan Hoskins,** Beth Hyslip, Katharine Ingram, Linda Johnson, **John Kingston,** Stephanie Krol, Courtney Lane, Mary Sue Langan, Julian Libysen, **Salena LiBritz,** Marian Manners, Grace Massey, Patrick McCarthy, John McClure, Mike McLaughlin, Rich McMahon, Kathleen Mercandetti, Art Mkrtchyan, Karyl Murray, Ken Myett, Deborah Nicholls, Xavier W. Niz, Kim Ortell, Jennifer Paley, Ray Parenteau, **Judi Pinkham,** Linda Punskovsky, Matthew J. Raycroft, Maureen Raymond , **Ryan Richards,** Bruce Rolff, **Laura Ross,** Robyn Salbo, Donna Schindler, Gerry Schrenk, Mildred Schulte, **Melissa Shustyk,** Siri Schwartzman, Ann Shea, Robert Siek, **Laurel Smith,** Lisa Smith-Ruvalcaba, Kara Stokes, Frank Tangredi, Elizabeth Torjussen, Humberto Ugarte, Rachel Winter

Additional Credits

Steve Apple, Karen Beck, Meg Ceccolini, Donna DiCuffa, Lynette Haggard, Stuart Kirschenbaum, Beth Kun, Carol Maglitta, Karen Mancinelli-Paige, Caroline McDonnell, Lesley Pierson, Rachel Ross, Ted Smykal, Alfred Voto, Marc Wezdecki

Art Credits

Kerry Cashman **SH12,** 7, 19, 26, 28–29, 37, 38, 44, 46, 51, 60–61, 68–69, 75, 83, 92–93, 102–103, 112–113, 115, 122–123, 132–133, 142, 146–147, 152–153, 158–159, 162, 164–165, 171, 176–177, 178, 183, 186, 192–193, 204–205, 214, 226, 228–229, 235, 240–241, 263, 266, ~~78~~–279, 285, ~~~~, 316–317, 326–327, ~~348~~–349, 356, 358–359, ~~~~, 372–373, 382, 392–393, ~~~~ 414, 418–419, 422–423, 424, ~~~28~~–429, 436–437, 442–443, 451, 460–461, 474, 479, 482–483, 486–487, 491, 494, 498–499, 514, 519, 520–521, 526–527, 540–541, 549, 556–557, 558, 564–565, 572, 582–583, 590, 592–593, 602–603, 612, 618–619, 620–621, 634, 636, 642–643, 650–651, 668, 674–675, 682, 684–685, 706–707; Ellen Welch Granter **398, 402, 406, 411, 412, 413, 420, 428, 430;** Hefflin Agency/Ilene Winn-Lederer 10; Kevin Jones Associates 358–359; Steve McEntee 659; Rich McMahon **C3, C6, C9, C12, C14, C17,** 92, 443, 598, 601, 607, 615, 620, 640, 707, 708, 709, 710, 711, 712, 713; Jen Paley, **SH11, SH12, SH13, SH14, SH15, SH16, SH17, SH18, SH19, SH20, SH21, SH26, SH27, SH28, SH31,** 4, 9, 13, 15, 18, 20, 21, 28, 29, 31, 34, 35, 42, 48, 50, 54, 55, 59, 60, 62, 66, 73, 80, 87, 92, 100, 105, 106, 109, 116, 121, 126, 128, 130, 132, 135, 138, 140, 144, 147, 149, 151, 156, 159, 161, 164, 165, 166, 170, 174, 180, 181, 183, 189, 193, 194, 198, 199, 204, 212, 213, 216, 217, 218, 221, 223, 224, 231, 234, 235, 238, 240, 241, 242, 248, 254, 256, 257, 259, 260, 261, 262, 263, 266, 272, 274, 278, 280, 284, 286, 292, 293, 295, 296, 297, 299, 300, 303, 305, 308, 309, 310, 316, 318, 324, 325, 329, 331, 337, 340, 344, 345, 348, 350, 351, 354, 358, 361, 365, 370, 377, 380, 384, 386, 390, 392, 395, 400, 423, 428, 434, 435, 437, 440, 441, 448, 455, 458, 460, 463, 468, 476, 477, 488, 490, 496, 498, 504, 505, 508, 511, 512, 517, 518, 526, 528, 529, 532, 537, 539, 544, 545, 549, 552, 553, 559, 560, 564, 566, 570, 572, 574, 578, 580, 581, 583, 584, 586, 589, 592, 594, 599, 603, 605, 609, 610, 611, 628, 629, 633, 639, 644, 645, 648, 650, 652, 653, 656, 658, 660, 661, 663, 664, 666, 668, 671, 678, 679, 680, 681, 682, 684, 691, 704, 705, 706, 710, 714–715; XNR Productions, Inc. **SH22,** 5, 11, 13, 24, 26, 28, 40, 46, 53, 85, 114, 125, 129, 141, 149, 158, 160, 162, 164, 172, 176, 186, 191, 195, 200, 214, 266, 281, 287, 306–307, 328, 333, 343, 346, 356, 364, 372, 374, 376, 383, 388, 401, 403, 408, 409, 416, 428, 438, 444, 460, 470, 479, 500, 509, 533, 539, 547, 550, 564, 565, 588, 601, 611, 632, 646, 648, 650, 669, 672, 676, 684, 692, 693, 694, 695, 696, 697, 698, 699, 700, 713

Photo Credits

Cover and title page: Fox Photos/Getty Images; **Front Endsheet:** L, Library of Congress; **Front Endsheet:** Head, R, Stockdisc/Getty Images; **Front Endsheet:** Body, R, Dirk Anschutz/Getty Images; **vii:** T, © Bettmann/CORBIS; Inset, © Judith Miller/© Dorling Kindersley/Larry & Dianna Elman; **viii:** BL, Tim Ridley © Dorling Kindersley/Louisiana State Museum; TL, Getty Images; M, Getty Images; R, Bettmann/CORBIS; **ix:** © A724/GAMMA; **x:** L, *New York Daily News*; R, ©Nathan Benn/CORBIS; **xi:** L, © Peter Turnley/CORBIS; R, © Reuters/ CORBIS; **xii:** John Dominis/Time Life Pictures/Getty Images; **xxv:** Bettmann/ CORBIS; **xxvii:** © Bettman/CORBIS; **xxviii:** Library of Congress; Head, R, Stockdisc/Getty Images; Body, R, Dirk Anschutz/Getty Images; **xxx:** Brown Brothers; **SH1:** © Darius Ramazani/ zefa/CORBIS; **SH2:** Jose Luis Pelaez, Inc./CORBIS; **SH6:** Tom Stewart/CORBIS; **SH12:** Fox Photos/Getty Images; **SH19:** © Charles Gupton/ CORBIS; **SH23:** Bettmann/CORBIS; **SH24:** The Granger Collection, New York; **SH26:** Library of Congress; **SH30:** © Dynamic Graphics Group/IT Stock Free/Alamy; **SH32:** Background, The Art Archive/National Archives Washington, D.C.; BR, © Bettmann/ CORBIS; TL, © Reuters/CORBIS; BL, © Bettmann/CORBIS; MR, © Bettmann/ CORBIS; TR, The Granger Collection, New York; TM, The Granger Collection, New York; ML, The Granger Collection, New York; **1:** SuperStock, Inc.; **2–3:** Jean Leon Jerome Ferris, ©Private Collection/The Bridgeman Art Library; **3:** M, Colonial Williamsburg Foundation, Williamsburg, VA; T, The Granger Collection, New York; B, National Park Service photo; **4:** The Granger Collection, New York; **6:** T, The Granger Collection, New York; B, The Granger Collection, New York; **7:** T, Sherwin Crasto/Reuters/CORBIS; B, The Granger Collection, New York; **9:** L, The Granger Collection, New York; R, The Granger Collection, New York; **14:** Getty Images; **15:** L, Bettmann/CORBIS; R, National Archives and Records Administration; **16:** © North Wind Picture Archives; **17:** The Granger Collection, New York; **18:** Bettmann/CORBIS; **19:** B, Hulton Archive/Getty Images Inc.; T, Getty Images; **21:** L, The Granger Collection, New York; R, Composite photograph of the almost 200-year-old Star-Spangled Banner, the flag that inspired the national anthem. Smithsonian's National Museum of American History, © 2004; **22:** The Granger Collection, New York; **23:** The Granger Collection, New York; **25:** L, Library of Congress; R, Hulton Archive/ Getty Images Inc.; **26:** The Granger Collection, New York; **28:** The Granger Collection, New York; **29:** L, Getty Images; R, National Park Service photo; **30:** The Granger Collection, New York; **D0–C27:** Border © Photodisc/Getty Images; **D0:** B, Courtesy of The Bostonian Society/Old State House; Frame, © Bruce Burkhardt/CORBIS; R, © NTPL/ Christopher Hurst/The Image Works; **D4:** The Art Archive; **C1:** L, The Signing of the Constitution of the United States in 1787, 1940, Christy, Howard Chandler (1873–1952)/Hall of Representatives, Washington, DC, USA/Bridgeman Art Library; R, The Art Archive/National Archives Washington, D.C.; **C2:** R, © Royalty-Free/CORBIS; L, © Swim Ink 2, LLC/CORBIS; **C4:** courtesy New York State Historical Association; **C7:** T, The Granger Collection, New York; B, © Bettmann/ CORBIS; Inset, The Granger Collection, New York; **C18:** T, ©Michael Kelley/ Getty Images; B, © Royalty-Free/ CORBIS; **C22:** © Bettmann/CORBIS; **32–33:** Illinois State Historical Library; **33:** T, Getty Images; M, Courtesy of The Oakland Museum of California. Collection of Norm Wilson; BR, Larry Sherer/Time-Life Books, Inc./High Impact; BL, © Tria Giovan/ CORBIS; M, Courtesy of The Oakland Museum of California; **34:** T, The Picture Desk/Art Archive; B, © Bettmann/ CORBIS; **35:** The Granger Collection, New York; **37:** T, Steve Liss/Time Life Pictures/Getty Images; B, The Granger Collection, New York; **38:** TM, The Granger Collection, New York; BR, The Granger Collection, New York; TL, The Art Archive/Culver Pictures; BL, Hampton University Museum, Hampton, Virginia; TR, Bettmann/ CORBIS; BM, Getty Images; **39:** The Granger Collection, New York; **41:** California State Library; **42:** T, The Granger Collection, New York; B, The Art Archive/Culver Pictures; **43:** © Bettmann/CORBIS; **44:** T, © Brooks Kraft/CORBIS; B, The Granger Collection, New York; **45:** © Bettmann/CORBIS; **46:** TR, The Lilly Library, Indiana University; BR, The Granger Collection, New York; **47:** United States Dept. of the Interior; **48:** L, © Dorling Kindersley/U.S Army Military History Institute; R, © Bettmann/CORBIS; **49:** Paintings by Don Troiani; historicalartprints.com; **51:** TL, The Granger Collection, New York; BR, The Granger Collection, New York; MR, The Granger Collection, New York; TR, CORBIS; **52:** R, © CORBIS; **54:** © CORBIS; **55:** © 2005 Roger-Viollet/Topham/The Image Works; **57:** T, Corel Professional Photos CD-ROM™; M, istockphoto.com; B, Corel Professional Photos CD-ROM™; BL, The Granger Collection, New York; **58:** © Dallas Historical Society, Texas, USA/Bridgeman Art Library; **60:** © Bettmann/CORBIS; **61:** © Bettmann/

CORBIS; **62:** California State Library; **63:** The Granger Collection, New York; **64–65:** Brown Brothers; **65:** T, Scala/Art Resource, NY; M, © David J. & Janice L. Frent Collection/CORBIS; The Granger Collection, New York; **66:** Brown Brothers; **67:** R, Bettmann/CORBIS; L, CORBIS; **68:** L, CORBIS; **68–69:** M, William J. Gaughan, Archives Service Center, University of Pittsburgh; **69:** TR, Prentice Hall; BR, Mark Gibson/Index Stock Imagery, Inc.; **70:** T, © Royalty-Free/CORBIS; B, © Kellie Strøm-www.balsko.com; **72:** M, © Mary Evans Picture Library/The Image Works; **73:** Library of Congress; **74:** The Granger Collection, New York; **75:** L, Topham/HIP/The Image Works; TMR, © CORBIS; BMR, © Prentice Hall; BR, © Mary Evans Picture Library/Alamy; TR, © Bettmann/CORBIS; **76:** T, CORBIS; B, Bettmann/CORBIS; **77:** T, Bettmann/CORBIS; B, Library of Congress; **78:** © Bettmann/CORBIS; **79:** R, © Bettmann/CORBIS; L, The Granger Collection, New York; **80:** T, © Bettman Corbis; B, The Granger Collection, New York; **81:** The University of Georgia Libraries; **82:** © Christie's Images/CORBIS; **83:** T, AP/Wide World Photos; B, The Granger Collection, New York; **86:** T, Superstock; B, The Granger Collection, New York; **87:** L, Nebraska State Historical Society Photograph Collections; R, © David J. & Janice L. Frent Collection/CORBIS; **88:** The Granger Collection, New York; **89:** Clay County Historical Society, Moorhead MN; **90:** © Bettmann/CORBIS; **91:** T, © Royalty-Free/CORBIS; B, © Bettmann/CORBIS; **92:** The Granger Collection, New York; **93:** L, © Mary Evans Picture Library/The Image Works; R, The Granger Collection, New York; **94:** © Bettman Corbis; **95:** Provided courtesy *HarpWeek*, LLC; **96:** TM, The Granger Collection, New York; TL, © Reuters/CORBIS; TR, The Granger Collection, New York; MR, © Bettmann/CORBIS; ML, The Granger Collection, New York; BL, © Bettmann/CORBIS; BR, © Bettmann/CORBIS; Background, The Art Archive/National Archives Washington, D.C.; **97:** © CORBIS; **98–99:** Brown Brothers; **99:** B, The Granger Collection, New York; T, Dartmouth College Library; M, Getty Images; **100:** Bettmann/CORBIS; **101:** Bettmann/CORBIS; **102:** B, The Granger Collection, New York; TL, Library of Congress; BR, The Granger Collection, New York; **103:** B, Hulton-Deutsch Collection/CORBIS; TR. The Granger Collection, New York; **104:** L, Underwood & Underwood/CORBIS; M, The Granger Collection, New York; R, Brown Brothers; **106:** Courtesy of The Rosenberg Library, Galveston, TX; **108:** TR, Dartmouth College Library; B, Brown Brothers; **109:** TR, Lewis W. Hine/George Eastman House/Getty

Images, Inc.; TL, Prentice Hall School Division; **110:** Minnesota Historical Society/CORBIS; **111:** The Granger Collection, New York; **112:** TR, Underwood & Underwood/CORBIS; BL, © David J. & Janice L. Frent Collection/CORBIS; **112–113:** Foreground, Bettmann/CORBIS; Background, Library of Congress; **113:** TL, Courtesy of the Historic National Woman's Party, Sewall-Belmont House and Museum, Washington, D.C.; TR, Bettmann/CORBIS; **114:** Brown Brothers; **115:** B, National Archives and Records Administration; T, Ariel Skelley/CORBIS; **116:** © San Diego Historical Society, EH Davis Collection; **117:** R, Culver Pictures, Inc.; L, Bettmann/CORBIS; **118:** T, The Granger Collection, New York; B, Courtesy of the Abraham Lincoln Presidential Library; **119:** Library of Congress; **120:** Brown Brothers; **121:** L, Brown Brothers; R, Paul & Rosemary Volpp © Dorling Kindersley; **122:** T, Bettmann/CORBIS; TR, The Granger Collection, New York; TL, Bettmann/CORBIS; **123:** R, CORBIS; BR, Courtesy Kansas State Historical Society; L, The Granger Collection, New York; BR, Science Museum/SSPL/The Image Works; **125:** Library of Congress; **126:** Brown Brothers; **127:** The Granger Collection, New York; **128:** R, Brown Brothers; L, Judith Miller/© Dorling Kindersley/Larry & Dianna Elman; **129:** Getty Images; **130:** The Granger Collection, New York; **132:** Library of Congress; **133:** R, The Granger Collection, New York; L, Bettmann/CORBIS; **134:** © David J. & Janice L. Frent Collection/CORBIS; **136–137:** Bettmann/CORBIS; **137:** M, The Granger Collection/New York; T, Getty Images; B, SCHOMBURG CENTER/Art Resource, NY; **138:** R, Brown Brothers; L, Brown Brothers; **139:** BR, CORBIS; L, Bettmann/CORBIS; **140:** Library of Congress; **141:** Getty Images; **142:** T, Victor Jose Cobo/AP/Wide World Photos; B, COR-BIS; **144:** L, Bettmann/CORBIS; R, Smithsonian Institution; **145:** Pearson Education/PH School; **146:** B, Chicago Historical Society; T, The Granger Collection, New York; **147:** BL, The New York Historical Society; BM, The New York Historical Society; BR, Bettmann/CORBIS; **148:** R, CORBIS; M, SCHOMBURG CENTER/Art Resource, NY; L, © 2002 The Museum of Fine Arts, Houston; **151:** Library of Congress; **152:** R, Bettmann/CORBIS; L, Getty Images; **152–153:** TL, Prentice Hall; **153:** R, Duke University; TM, U.S. Library of Congress; BM, U.S. Library of Congress; **154:** Bettmann/CORBIS; **155:** The Granger Collection, New York; **156:** L, Bettmann/CORBIS; **157:** Bettmann/CORBIS; **159:** L, CORBIS; TR, The Granger Collection, New York; BR, Bettmann/CORBIS; **160:** Bettmann/CORBIS; **162:** M, Getty Images; B, The

Art Archive/Culver Pictures; T, Peter R. Westacott; **164:** R, Bettmann/CORBIS; L, CORBIS; **165:** L, The Granger Collection, New York; R, Getty Images; **166:** Bettmann/CORBIS; **167:** T, The Granger Collection, New York; B, The Granger Collection, New York; **168–169:** National Archives and Records Administration; **169:** B, Brown Brothers; M, Library of Congress; T, © Prentice Hall; **170:** Mary Evans Picture Library; **171:** The Granger Collection, New York; **173:** Bettmann/CORBIS; **174:** Hulton-Deutsch Collection/CORBIS; **175:** The Granger Collection, New York; **176:** T, The Art Archive/Imperial War Museum/Eileen Tweedy; **176–177:** B, Courtesy Motorbuch Verlag and Eberhard Moeller. Photo from *The Encyclopedia of U-Boats; From 1904 to the Present.*; **177:** TR, Three Lions/Getty Images; B, Library of Congress; M, Gary Ombler/Imperial War Museum © Dorling Kindersley; **178:** T, Ceerwan Aziz/Reuters/CORBIS; B, Bettmann/CORBIS; **179:** Hulton Archive/Getty Images Inc.; **180:** R, Stock Montage, Inc.; L, Library of Congress; **181:** Brown Brothers; **182:** Rykoff Collection/CORBIS; **183:** R, Bettmann/CORBIS; BL, CORBIS; TL, Library of Congress; BR, The Granger Collection, New York; **184:** Bettmann/CORBIS; **185:** T, The Granger Collection, New York; B, Culver Pictures, Inc.; **186:** Stock Montage, Inc./Historical Pictures Collection; **188:** T, Library of Congress; B, Bettmann/CORBIS; **189:** L, Library of Congress; R, The Granger Collection, New York; **190:** The Granger Collection, New York; **192:** B, Bettmann/CORBIS; T, Prentice Hall; **192–193:** BL, The Art Archive; **193:** BR, Ann Ronan Picture Library/HIP/The Image Works; M, Liberty Memorial Museum, Kansas City, Missouri; T, Prentice Hall; **194:** CORBIS; **196:** Library of Congress; **198:** Brown Brothers; **199:** R, National Archives and Records Administration; L, Library of Congress; **200:** R, Underwood & Underwood/CORBIS; L, Getty Images; **201:** Bettmann/CORBIS; **202:** Brown Brothers; **203:** T, Bettmann/CORBIS; B, Bettmann/CORBIS; **204:** Liberty Memorial Museum, Kansas City, Missouri; **205:** R, Library of Congress; **206:** T, Library of Congress; B, The Granger Collection, New York; **207:** The Granger Collection, New York; **208:** TM, The Granger Collection, New York; TL, © Reuters/CORBIS; TR, The Granger Collection, New York; MR, © Bettmann/CORBIS; ML, The Granger Collection, New York; BL, © Bettmann/CORBIS; BR, © Bettmann/CORBIS; Background, The Art Archive/National Archives Washington, D.C.; **209:** The Art Archive/Laurie Platt Winfrey; **210–211:** Getty Images; **211:** T, Bettmann/CORBIS; B, The Granger

Br.; M, Getty Images; **214:** sy of The CORBIS Brown Advertisingn/CORBIS; TL, Blue Lan eum/ M, Visions of A s. Inset, © Bettmann/CORL Inset, the City of New York, M, USDA; **218:** L, Bettmann of Getty Images; **219:** The G. Collection, New York; **220:** L, Brothers; R, Bettmann/CORBIS; Library of Congress; R, Getty Image **224:** Brown Brothers; **225:** The Granger Collection, New York; **226:** T, Ramin Talaie/CORBIS; B, Bettmann/CORBIS; **227:** Library of Congress; **228:** BL, Bettmann/CORBIS; BR, Library of Congress; T, Drug Enforcement Administration; **229:** BM, ProQuest Informaton and Learning Co.; TR, Library of Congress; TL, The Art Archive/National Archives Washington; BL, Dave King © Dorling Kindersley, Courtesy of the New York City Police Museum; **230:** K.J. Historical/CORBIS; **231:** R, The Granger Collection, New York; L, Schenectady Museum;Hall of Electrical History Foundation/CORBIS; **232:** L, Image courtesy of The Advertising Archives; R, Bettmann/CORBIS; ML, Image courtesy of The Advertising Archives; MR, Bettmann/CORBIS; **233:** R, Underwood & Underwood/CORBIS; L, Smithsonian Institution Collections, National Museum of American History, Behring Center; **234:** B, © Bettmann/CORBIS; T, The Art Archive/Culver Pictures; **235:** TR, The Jewish Museum, NY/Art Resource, NY; TL, Bettmann/CORBIS; M, The Granger Collection, New York; B, The Art Archive/Culver Pictures; **237:** L, © Francis G. Mayer/CORBIS; R, The Newark Museum/Art Resource, NY; **238:** T, Getty Images; B, AP/Wide World Photos; **239:** Getty Images; **240:** B, John Springer Collection/CORBIS; M, © Bettmann/CORBIS; **240–241:** T, Bettmann/CORBIS; BL, Sarah Fabian-Baddiel/HIP/The Image Works; BM, The Granger Collection, New York; MR, Bettmann/CORBIS; **242:** SCHOMBURG CENTER, The New York Public Library/Art Resource, NY; **243:** Bettmann/CORBIS; **244:** L, Getty Images; R, Getty Images; M, Tim Ridley © Dorling Kindersley/collection of the Louisiana State Museum, Gift of the New Orleans Jazz Club; **245:** Getty Images; **246:** The Granger Collection, New York; **247:** T, Winold Reiss, Portrait of Langston Hughes (1902-1967) ©1925. National Portrait Gallery, Washington, D.C., USA. Art Resource, NY; B, Brown Brothers; **248:** R, Getty Images; L, Bettmann/CORBIS; **249:** L, Bettmann/CORBIS; R, The Granger Collection/New York; **250:** The

Jewish Museum, NY/Art Resource, NY; **251:** Hulton Archive/Getty Images Images; **252–253:** CORBIS; **253:** T, Getty Images; M, Conde Nast Publicat Inc.; B, © Prentice Hall; **254:** Brothers; L, Getty Images; **25** Granger Collection, New Y Bettmann/CORBIS; **257:** Archive/CORBIS; L, M wn Society/CORBIS; **25** Collection, New Y RBIS; T, **259:** Bettmann Granger Brothers; **26** R, Horace Bettmann/**4:** TL, Library of Collectio BIS; **264–265:** T, Bristol istory and Industry/ Con M. **266:** AP/Wide World Photos; he Granger Collection, New ork; **268:** Copyright the Dorothea Lange Collection, Oakland Museum of California, City of Oakland. Gift of Paul S. Taylor; **269:** Library of Congress; **270:** B, © Mary Evans Picture Library/ The Image Works; **270–271:** AP/Wide World Photos; **271:** TL, The Granger Collection, New York; TR, AP/Wide World Photos; BR, Prentice Hall; BL, CORBIS; **272:** T, Hulton Archive/Getty Images Inc.; B, Prentice Hall; **273:** CORBIS; **274:** CORBIS; **275:** M, Prentice Hall; T, Hulton/Getty Images; B, AP/Wide World Photos; BR, Bettmann/CORBIS; **277:** B, Getty Images; T, Peter Anderson/© Dorling Kindersley; **278:** CORBIS; **279:** The Granger Collection, New York; **280:** Minnesota Historical Society/CORBIS; **282–283:** CORBIS; **283:** M, Blank Archives/Getty Images; B, David J. & Janice L. Frent Collection/CORBIS; T, The Granger Collection, New York; **284:** R, Hulton Archive/Getty Images; L, The Granger Collection, New York; **285:** *New York Daily News*; **286:** R, CORBIS; M, The Granger Collection, New York; TL, Topham/The Image Works; BL, CORBIS; **287:** Bettmann/ CORBIS; **288:** R, CORBIS; L, CORBIS; **289:** The Granger Collection, New York; **290:** L, Bettmann/CORBIS; R, Bettmann/CORBIS; **291:** T, AP/Wide World Photos; Inset, no credit neces- sary; **292:** Minnesota Historical Society/CORBIS; **293:** CORBIS; **294:** TL, Bettmann/CORBIS; BL, Associated Press, AP; BR, Bettmann/CORBIS; TR, Library of Congress; **295:** TR, Monika Graff/The Image Works; L, Michael Newman/PhotoEdit; M, Mark Antman/ The Image Works; BR, Dennis MacDonald/PhotoEdit; **296:** B, Bettmann/CORBIS; Inset, CORBIS; **297:** *Celebrate the Century, 1930s FDR's New Deal* © 1998 Used with permis- sion. All rights reserved. Written authorization from the Postal Service is required to use, reproduce, post, trans- mit, distribute, or publicly display these images; **298:** Library of Congress; **299:** AP/Wide World Photos; **300:**

01: L, CORBIS; R, ss; **302:** AP/Wide **303:** AP/Wide World 5: Tim Boyle/Getty Images; **310:** M/THE KOBAL COLLECTION; **311:** L, Getty Images; BR, Bettmann/ CORBIS; M, The Advertising Archive; **312:** BL, CORBIS; **312–313:** B, Smithsonian American Art Museum, Washington, D.C./Art Resource, NY; **313:** BR, Kelly-Mooney Photography/ CORBIS; **314:** The Granger Collection, New York; **315:** ML, SELZNICK/MGM/ THE KOBAL COLLECTION; MR, Everett Collection; TR, The Granger Collection, New York; BL, United Artists/Photofest; **316:** L, Hulton Archive/Getty Images; R, Bettmann/CORBIS; **317:** L, CORBIS; R, SELZNICK/MGM/THE KOBAL COL- LECTION; **318:** CORBIS; **319:** *International Herald Tribune*; **320:** TM, The Granger Collection, New York; TL, © Reuters/CORBIS; TR, The Granger Collection, New York; MR, © Bettmann/CORBIS; ML, The Granger Collection, New York; BL, © Bettmann/ CORBIS; BR, © Bettmann/CORBIS; Background, The Art Archive/National Archives, Washington, D.C.; **321:** Alfred Eisenstaedt/Pix Inc./Time & Life Pictures/Getty Images; **322–323:** Hulton-Deutsch Collection/CORBIS; **323:** T, The Art Archive/Imperial War Museum; B, Deutsches Historisches Museum, Berlin; M, Philip Makanna/ GHOSTS; **324:** R, Bettmann/CORBIS; L, The New York Public Library/Art Resource, NY; **325:** Getty Images; **326:** R, akg-images; L, akg-images; M, Bettmann/CORBIS; **327:** L, Bettmann/ CORBIS; R, Bettmann/CORBIS; M, Mary Evans Picture Library 2005; **329:** Bettmann/CORBIS; **330:** CORBIS; **331:** Bettmann/CORBIS; **332:** L, Bettmann/ CORBIS; R, Bettmann/CORBIS; **333:** Bettmann/CORBIS; **334:** CORBIS; **335:** L, Bettmann/CORBIS; R, Hulton-Deutsch Collection/CORBIS; M, Bettmann/COR- BIS; **336:** The Granger Collection, New York; **337:** B, Bettmann/CORBIS; T, Time Life Pictures/Getty Images; **338:** AP/Wide World Photos; **339:** Printed by permission for the Norman Rockwell Family Agency Copyright © 1943 the Norman Rockwell Family Entities/CORBIS; **340:** Bettmann/ CORBIS; **341:** B, Bettmann/CORBIS; T, The Art Archive/Imperial War Museum; **342:** BL, AP/Wide World Photos; TL, Philip Makanna/GHOSTS; **342–343:** BR, Scott Swanson/Archive Inc.; **343:** L, Photo by Three Lions/Getty Images; R, Photo by Three Lions/Getty Images; M, SuperStock, Inc./SuperStock; **344:** Courtesy National Archives and Records Administration, College Park, Maryland, photo no. (NWDNS-208-AA- 352QQ(5)); **345:** Brown Brothers; **346:** Getty Images; **348:** Bettmann/ CORBIS; **349:** R, Photo by Three Lions/ Getty Images; L, Bettmann/CORBIS;

350: Bettman/CORBIS; **351:** CORBIS; **352–353:** CORBIS; **353:** T, AP/Wide World Photos; M, Getty Images; B, Peter Wilson/© Dorling Kindersley, Courtesy of the Museum of the Regiments, Calgary; **354:** L, Getty Images; R, Getty Images; **355:** CORBIS; **356:** Background, AP/Wide World Photos; R, National Archives; T, DRAGESCO-JOFFE, ALAIN/Animals Animals - Earth Scenes; **357:** BR, Bettmann/CORBIS; **358:** L, AP/Wide World Photos; R, Prentice Hall; **358–359:** Background, National Archives and Records Administration; **359:** R, © A724/GAMMA; **360:** Brown Brothers; **361:** T, Library of Congress; B, Time Life Pictures/National Archives/Getty Images, Inc.; **362:** Hulton Archive/Getty Images Inc.; **363:** CORBIS; **364:** R, AP/Wide World Photos; L, Bettmann/CORBIS; **365:** BR, Peter Wilson/© Dorling Kindersley, Courtesy of the Museum of the Regiments, Calgary; **366:** B, Everett Collection; T, Everett Collection; **367:** T, Brown Brothers; B, AP/Wide World Photos; **368:** TL, National Archives; Background, B, AP/Wide World Photos; BR, AP/Wide World Photos; Inset, BL, SuperStock, Inc.; MR, The Granger Collection, New York; **368–369:** TR, Library of Congress; **369:** R, SuperStock, Inc./SuperStock; Background, AP/Wide World Photos; **370:** L, Brown Brothers; R, Time Life Pictures/Getty Images; **371:** Bettmann/ CORBIS; **372:** BR, KEYSTONE-FRANCE/ ImageState; BL, Prentice Hall; TL, Courtesy Julie Fulmer © Prentice Hall; **372–373:** Background, by ROBERT CAPA © 2001 By Cornell Capa/ Magnum Photos; **373:** T, MYCHELE DANIAU/AFP/Getty Images; **375:** T, Bettmann/CORBIS; B, AP/Wide World Photos; **377:** Brown Brothers; **378:** U.S. Air Force; **379:** T, Bettmann/ CORBIS; B, Andy Crawford/Dorling Kindersley © By kind permission of The Trustees of the Imperial War Museum, London; **380:** CORBIS; **381:** L, Bettmann/CORBIS; R, Andy Crawford/ Dorling Kindersley © Imperial War Museum, London; **382:** M, U.S. Holocaust Memorial Museum. The views or opinions expressed in this book and the context in which the image is used, do not necessarily reflect the views or policy of, nor imply approval or endorsement by The United States Holocaust Memorial Museum.; TL, akg-images; Background, B, USHMM, courtesy of Robert A. Schmuhl; ML, CORBIS; TR, Topham/The Image Works; M, U.S. National Archives/Roger-Viollet/The Image Works; Inset, B, USHMM, courtesy of KZ Gedenkstaette Dachau; Background, T, Keystone/GettyImages; **385:** Vincent Kessler/CORBIS; **386:** LEONE - ullstein bild/The Granger Collection, New York; **387:** Bettmann/

CORBIS; **389:** Bettmann/CORBIS; **391:** Brown Brothers; **392:** R, Peter Wilson/ © Dorling Kindersley, Courtesy of the Museum of the Regiments, Calgary; L, SuperStock, Inc.; **393:** R, CORBIS; L, Bettmann/CORBIS; **394:** T, Used with permission from the *Stars and Stripes*, a DoD publication. @ 2005 *Stars and Stripes*; B, KEYSTONE-FRANCE/ ImageState; **396–397:** Bettmann/ CORBIS; **397:** T, William A. Bake/ CORBIS; M, Getty Images; B, CONEL- RAD Collection; **398:** R, Getty Images; L, Getty Images; **399:** Bettmann/COR- BIS; **401:** Solo Syndication/Associated Newspapers; **402:** Bettmann/CORBIS; **403:** Background, Bettmann/CORBIS; T, Keystone/Getty Images; **405:** T, www.ourdocuments.gov/NARA; B, Bettmann/CORBIS; **406:** L, CORBIS; R, William A. Bake/CORBIS; **407:** AP/ Wide World Photos; **408:** Bettmann/ CORBIS; **410:** Bettmann/CORBIS; **411:** John Nordell/The Image Works; **412:** R, Getty Images; L, CONELRAD Collection; **414:** BL, Jerry Cooke/ CORBIS; MR, Bettmann/CORBIS; TL, Bettmann/CORBIS; TR, Jerry Cooke/ CORBIS; **415:** Time Inc./Time Life Pictures/Getty Images; **417:** B, Getty Images; T, Sovfoto/Eastfoto; **418:** T, CONELRAD Collection; M, CORBIS; BL, Bettmann/CORBIS; BR, Bettmann/ CORBIS; **418–419:** AP/Wide World Photos; **419:** L, BL, Conelrad Collection; TR, Civil Defense Museum; **420:** Conelrad Collection; **421:** The Granger Collection, New York; **422:** Inset, Image courtesy of The Advertising Archives/© 2006 Marvel Characters, Inc. Used with permission; Background, T Conelrad Collection; **422–423:** Conelrad Collection; **423:** R, Allied Artists/The Kobal Collection; L, Courtesy Everett Collection/Everett Collection; Background, T Conelrad Collection; **424:** T, AFP/Getty Images; B, Time Life Pictures/Getty Images; **425:** The Granger Collection, New York; **426:** Marvin Koner/CORBIS; **427:** © Time Life Pictures/Getty Images; **428:** L, Bettmann/CORBIS; R, Bettmann/CORBIS; **429:** B, The Image Works; T, Time Life Pictures/Getty Images; **430:** CORBIS; **431:** The Granger Collection, New York; **432–433:** Getty Images; **433:** M, Dwight D. Eisenhower Library; Bob Paull, Staff Photographer; T, The Granger Collection, New York; B, Bettmann/CORBIS; **434:** Indiana U. Archives & Photoraphic Services(#47- 1082); **435:** Hulton Archive/Getty Images Inc.; **436:** Underwood & Underwood/CORBIS; **437:** L, Associated Press, AP; R, Ewing Galloway/Index Stock Imagery, Inc.; **438:** TL, W. Eugene Smith/Time & Life Pictures/Getty Images; Inset, no credit; **439:** Bettmann/CORBIS; **440:** TL, Photo by J. R. Eyerman/Time Life Pictures/Getty Images; Inset, Richard

Wurts/National Building Museum; **441:** Bettmann/CORBIS; **442:** R, H. Armstrong Roberts/CORBIS; L, H. Armstrong Roberts/Robertstock; **443:** R, Philip Gendreau/CORBIS; L, H. Armstrong Roberts/Robertstock; **444:** R. KRUBNER/H. Armstrong Roberts; **445:** CORBIS; **446:** Bettmann/CORBIS; **447:** Brown Brothers; **448:** TL, John Dominis/Time Life Pictures/Getty Images; Inset, Smithsonian Institution Collections, National Museum of American History, Behring Center.; **449:** BR, Tom Kelley/Hulton Archive/Getty Images; Inset, The Granger Collection, New York; **450:** Bettmann/CORBIS; **451:** BL, Time & Life Pictures/Getty Images; M, Penguin USA; TR, H. Armstrong Roberts/Robertstock; TL, CBS Photo Archive/Getty Images; BR, Getty Images; **452:** TM, Getty Images; M, Image courtesy of The Advertising Archives; TR, CBS Photo Archive/Getty Images; TL, Wrather Corp/Apex Film Corp/The Kobal Collection; **453:** Dunigan/H.Armstrong Roberts; **454:** T, MICHAEL OCHS ARCHIVES.COM; MR, Aardman Animations Ltd.; B, Don Wright/Time & Life Pictures/Getty Images; ML, The Everett Collection, Inc.; **455:** TR, Bettmann/CORBIS; Inset, Touchstone/Simon & Schuster; **456:** Photofest; **457:** L, Bruce Davidson/Magnum Photos; R, AP/Wide World Photos; **458:** Bettmann/CORBIS; **459:** Library of Congress; **460:** L, Library of Congress; R, Richard Wurts/National Building Museum; **461:** B, Touchstone, ©1981; **462:** B, MICHAEL OCHS ARCHIVES.COM; **462:** T, no credit; **463:** R, Collection of the State Museum of Pennsylvania; L, AP/Wide World Photos; **464:** TM, The Granger Collection, New York; TL, © Reuters/CORBIS; TR, The Granger Collection, New York; MR, © Bettmann/CORBIS; ML, The Granger Collection, New York; BL, © Bettmann/CORBIS; ML, The Granger Collection, New York; BR, © Bettmann/CORBIS; Background, The Art Archive/National Archives Washington, D.C.; **465:** © 1976/George Ballis/Take Stock; **466–467:** Bettman/CORBIS; **467:** T, David J. & Janice L. Frent Collections/CORBIS; B, National Museum of American History, Smithsonian Institution; M, Bettman/CORBIS; **468:** B, CORBIS; T, AP/Wide World Photos; **469:** R, Bettman/CORBIS; L, Magnum Photos; **470:** Time Life Pictures/Getty Images; **471:** Time Life Pictures/Getty Images; **472:** Inset, AP/Wide World Photos; Background, AP/Wide World Photos; **473:** Bettman/CORBIS; **474:** B, Time Life Pictures/Getty Images; T, Prentice Hall; M, The Granger Collection, New York; **476:** M, Time Life Pictures/Getty Images; B, Bob Daemmrich/The Image Works; T, CORBIS; **477:** L, AP/Wide World Photos; R, AP/Wide World Photos/Montgomery Advertiser; **478:** R,

Bettman/CORBIS; L Bettman/CORBIS; **479:** BR, Bettmann/CORBIS; Background, B, Bettmann/CORBIS; T, Bruce Davidson/Magnum Photos; **480:** T, AP/Wide World Photos; B, AP/Wide World Photos; **481:** AP/Wide World Photos; **482:** Time & Life Pictures/Getty Images; **482–483:** Background, Flip Schulke/Black Star; **483:** BR, Flip Schulke/CORBIS; BL, John F. Kennedy Library, National Archives, document MS 2003-036; TR, National Museum of American History, Smithsonian Institution; **485:** Inset, Time Life Pictures/Getty Images; Background, Flip Schulke/CORBIS; **486:** L, AP/Wide World Photos; **486–487:** B, AP/Wide World Photos; T, Bettmann/CORBIS; **487:** TR, Bettmann/CORBIS; **488:** R, Time Life Pictures/Getty Images; L, David J. & Janice L. Frent Collections/CORBIS; **489:** AP/Wide World Photos; **490:** Flip Schulke/CORBIS; **491:** T, AP/Wide World Photos; B, Flip Schulke/CORBIS; **492:** B, David J. & Janice L. Frent Collections/CORBIS; **492–493:** TL, Bettmann/CORBIS; **493:** TR, AP/Wide World Photos; Background, T, AP/Wide World Photos; TR, Bob Adelman/Magnum Photos; B, POPPER-FOTO/Alamy; **497:** B, Photofest **498:** R, AP/Wide World Photos; L, Time Life Pictures/Getty Images; **499:** R, Time & Life Pictures/Getty Images; L, Bettmann/CORBIS; **500:** AP/Wide World Photos; **501:** AP Photo/Bill Hudson; **502:** L, © Hulton-Deutsch Collection/CORBIS; **502–503:** Bettmann/Sygma/CORBIS; **503:** M, The Peace Corps; T, David J. and Janice L. Frent Collection/CORBIS; B, Time & Life Pictures/Getty Images; **504:** David J. and Janice L. Frent Collection/CORBIS; **505:** Inset, Bettmann/CORBIS; Getty Images; **506:** CORBIS; **507:** R, Paul Conklin Photography/PhotoEdit; L, JP Laffont/Sygma/CORBIS; **509:** CORBIS; **511:** Bettmann/CORBIS; **512:** T, Bettmann/CORBIS; B, CORBIS; **513:** "Eclipse" from *Straight Herblock* (Simon & Schuster, 1964); **514:** MR, NASA; TL, NIX/NASA Image Exchange; TR, GRIN Great Images in NASA; B, GRIN Great Images in NASA; ML, GRIN Great Images in NASA; **515:** Bettmann/CORBIS; **516:** T, stockphoto.com; B, Larry Kolvoord/The Image Works; **517:** Bettmann/CORBIS; **518:** Bettmann/CORBIS; **519:** T, James Leynse/CORBIS; B, Bettmann/CORBIS; **520:** BL, Marty Heitner/The Image Works; T, AP/Wide World Photos; B, Banana Stock/AGE Fotostock; **521:** TL, Sesame Street and associated characters, trademarks and design elements are owned and licensed by Sesame Workshop.© 2006 Sesame Workshop. All rights reserved.; TR, ArenaPal/Topham/The Image Works; B, Hulton Archive/Getty Images; **522:** L, Getty Images; R, Yoav Levy/Phototake; **523:** Bettmann/CORBIS; **525:** Paul S. Conklin/PhotoEdit; AP/

Wide World Photos; **526:** National Portrait Gallery, Smithsonian Institution/Art Resource, NY; **528:** Bettmann/CORBIS; **530–531:** The Granger Collection, New York; **531:** M, Library of Congress; B, West Point Museum Collection; T, National Museum of American History, Smithsonian Institution; **532:** Topham/The Image Works; **533:** WolfgangKaehler/CORBIS; **534:** TL, AFP/AFP/Getty Images; TR, Topham/The Image Works; **535:** AP/Wide World Photos; **536:** Pierre-Aux wcoutes, Paris/Rothco Cartoons; **537:** TR, National Archives and Records Administration, Records of the U.S. Marine Corps; L, West Point Museum Collection; **539:** B, AP/Wide World Photos; **540:** R, Time Life Pictures/Getty Images; TL, National Archives; BL, AP/Wide World Photos; **541:** R, Ullstein Bild/The Granger Collection, New York; M, Associated Press, AP; **542:** Reuters/CORBIS; **543:** T, "Onward And Upward And Onward And" from *The Herblock Gallery* (Simon & Schuster, 1968); **544:** R, Leif Skoogfors/CORBIS; L, CBS Photo Archive/Getty Images; border, Getty Images; **545:** Topham/The Image Works; **546:** Bernard Gotfryd/Getty Images; **548:** Basset/National Archives and Records Administration; **549:** TR, Associated Press, AP; TL, Time Life Pictures/Getty Images; BL, Getty Images; BR, Bettmann/CORBIS; M, Bettmann/CORBIS; **550:** Photo by Bob Peterson/Time Life Pictures/Getty Images; **551:** B, © David J. & Janice L. Frent Collections; T, © David J. & Janice L. Frent Collections; **552:** L, Leif Skoogfors/CORBIS; R, © David J. & Janice L. Frent Collection/CORBIS; **553:** AP/Wide World Photos/USAF; **554:** Getty Images; **555:** T, Photo by Ronald S. Haeberle/Time Life Pictures/Getty; B, Time Inc./Time Life Pictures/Getty Images; **556:** BL, Getty Images; TL, AbsoluteStockPhoto.com/Alamy; R, Charles E. Pefley/Mira.com; **557:** L, Associated Press, AP; BR, Brand X Pictures/Alamy; TR, Prentice Hall; **558:** T, AHMAD MASOOD/Reuters/Corbis; B, stockphoto.com; **560:** L, Bettmann/CORBIS; R, Corel Professional Photos CD-ROM™; R, Corel Professional Photos CD-ROM™; **561:** Bettmann/CORBIS; **562:** B, National Museum of American History, Smithsonian Institution; T, AP/Wide World Photos; **563:** Dirck Halstead/Liaison/Getty Images; **564:** AP Photo/Malcolm Browne; **565:** L, Photo by Terry Ashe/Time Life Pictures/Getty Images; B, Corel Professional Photos CD-ROM™;R, Corel Professional Photos CD-ROM™; **566:** stockphoto.com; **567:** AP/Wide World Photos; **568–569:** Time Life Pictures/Getty Images; **569:** B, Wally McNamee/CORBIS; T, Charles Gatewood/The

R, k Archives/Getty **571:** nd, Time Life Group; ,Getty Images; Inc.; **572:** Works; New York; Tpublishing Henry Diltz/CORecords, Archives/Getty Image, Armstrong Roberts/R. BL, Jason Reed/Reuters/COR. *Mad* cover #140 image cou. Doug Gilford's *Mad* Cover Site, lectmad.com/madcoversite; TL, Pi Hall; Background R, Prentice Hall; Background L, Prentice Hall; **574:** L, Charles Gatewood/The Image Works; R, Bettmann/CORBIS; **575:** Bettmann/CORBIS; **576:** R, AP/Wide World Photos; L, © *Ms. Magazine*; **577:** L, Bettmann/CORBIS; R, AP/Wide World Photos; **579:** T, © Frank Cantor; B, Mary Kate Denny/PhotoEdit; **580:** © Jack Ramesdale; **581:** B, Time Life Pictures/Getty Images; T, AP Photo/Barry Sweet; **582:** R, Prentice Hall; L, AP Photo; **583:** L, Galen Rowell/CORBIS; Background, AP Photo; R, Ed Kashi/CORBIS; **584:** L, Bettman/CORBIS; R, AP/Worldwide Photos; **585:** AP Photo/*The Post and Courier*, Mic Smith; TR, Photofest; **586:** TL, Library of Congress; **586–587:** BL, Bettmann/CORBIS; **587:** BR, AP Photo/Nature Consortium,Ron Wurzer; **588:** Inset, CORBIS; **588–589:** Background, Ohio EPA; **589:** L, Ohio EPA; R, Ohio EPA; **590:** T, Copyright © John Warden/Alaska Stock LLC; B, Thomas Moran, The Grand Canyon of the Yellowstone, 1872, The U.S. Department of the Interior Museum, Washington, D.C.; **592:** Time Life Pictures/Getty Images; **593:** Henry Diltz/CORBIS; **594:** Photofest; **595:** © 1998 by Lalo Alcaraz, All Rights Reserved; **596–597:** Bettmann/CORBIS; **597:** Dennis Brack/Black Star/stockphoto.com; T, Connie Ricca/CORBIS; M, AP/Wide World Photos; **598:** CORBIS; **599:** Pelican Publications Company, Inc.; **600:** L, Bettmann/CORBIS; R, Bettmann/CORBIS; **602:** MR, Bettmann/CORBIS; BL, AP/Wide World Photos; BR, Mark Godfrey/The Image Works; TM, Prentice Hall; TR, Prentice Hall; TL, Prentice Hall; **603:** TL, AP Photo/National Archives; TR, Bettmann/CORBIS; BR, Mark Godfrey/The Image Works; BL, Charles Gatewood/The Image Works; **604:** B, Nixon Presidential Materials Project, National Archives and Records Administration. Photo by Oliver F. Atkins; T, *New York Daily News*; **606:** Courtesy *Worcester (Mass.) Telegram;* **607:** Mark Godfrey/The Image Works; **608:** T, Bettmann/CORBIS; B, Bettmann/CORBIS; **609:** B, Larry Lee Photography/CORBIS; T, Black Star; **610:** Nathan Benn/CORBIS; **611:**

Acknowledgments

Background, Mark Richards/PhotoEdit; Inset, L, Jeffrey D. Smith/Woodfin Camp; Inset, R, Cleo Photography/PhotoEdit; **612:** #3, Courtesy Everett Collection/Everett Collection; B, Bettmann/CORBIS; #1, CBS/L #2, Courtesy Everett Collection; #5, © ABC-TV Courtesy Everett Collection; #4, CBS/ Collection; BR, © VISION/THE KOB... /Bettmann/CO...ORBIS; CBS/Lando...hotos; **616:** CORBIS; ...**617:** Mark **615:** ...f; **618:** R, Kaveh Bett...RBIS; L, Roger-Viollet/The Pet...rks; **618–619:** Inset, ...ann/CORBIS; **619:** L, Wally McNamee/CORBIS; R, AP/Wide World Photos; **620:** L, Black Star; R, Wally McNamee/CORBIS; **621:** Time & Life Pictures/Getty Images; **622:** Dennis Brack/Black Star/stockphoto.com; **623:** from *Herblock: A Cartoonist's Life* (Time Books, 1998); **624:** TM, The Granger Collection, New York; TL, © Reuters/CORBIS; TR, The Granger Collection, New York; MR, © Bettmann/CORBIS; ML, The Granger Collection, New York; BL, © Bettmann/ CORBIS; ML, The Granger Collection, New York; BR, © Bettmann/CORBIS; Background, The Art Archive/National Archives Washington, D.C.; **625:** Jose L. Pelaez/CORBIS; **626–627:** CORBIS; **627:** M, Bettmann/CORBIS; T, Pearson Education/Prentice Hall School; B, SPELLING/ABC/THE KOBAL COLLEC-TION; **628:** Photo by Time Life Pictures/Time Magazine, Copyright Time Inc./Time Life Pictures/Getty Images; **630:** Wally McNamee/CORBIS; **631:** Bettmann/CORBIS; **633:** L, NARA/Ronald Reagan Presidential Library; R, Pearson Education/Prentice Hall School; **635:** AP/Wide World Photos/Ron Edmonds; **636:** MR, AP Photo/Bruce Weaver; BM, Photos12.com/Polaris; TL, SPELLING/ABC/THE KOBAL COLLECTION; TR, STOCKFOLIO/Alamy; M, AP Photo/Barry Thumma; BL, Prentice Hall; **637:** AP/ Wide World Photos/Charles Tasnadi; **638:** T, AP/Wide World Photos; B, Time Life Pictures/Getty Images; **639:** Leif Skoogfors/CORBIS; **640:** Bill Gentile/ CORBIS; **641:** © Wright, *Providence Journal Bulletin*; **642:** T, CORBIS; M, Prentice Hall; BL, AFP/Getty Images; BR, UK-PRESS/GAMMA; **643:** BR, AP Photo/Lionel Cironneau; TL, Peter Turnley/CORBIS; BL, Charles Steiner/ The Image Works; TR, AP Photo/Doug Mills; **645:** J.L. Atlan/Sygma/CORBIS; **646:** Time Life Pictures/Getty Images; **647:** R, Jacques Langevin/CORBIS SYGMA; L, Bettmann/CORBIS; M, Betty Press/Woodfin Camp; **648:** Ben Gibson-Katz/Woodfin Camp; **649:** J A

...; **650:** NARA/ ...idential Library; ...y Images; B, ...ORBIS; **652:** AP Photo/ ...onneau; **654–655:** AP/Wide ...Photos/Ann Johansson; **655:** M, ...rk Avery/Orange Country Register/ ...ORBIS; B, NASA/Photo Researchers, Inc.; T, Patrick Robert/CORBIS; **656:** T, Courtesy of Dell Inc.; **657:** B, AP Photo/*The Fort Wayne Journal Gazette*, Samuiel Hoffman; T, AP Photo/Steven Senne; **661:** L, Arnie Sachs/CORBIS; R, Pearson Education/PH School Division; **662:** AP/Wide World Photos/Susan Ragan; **663:** Reuters/CORBIS; **664:** T, AP/Wide World Photos/Joe Marquette; B, Najlah Feanny/CORBIS; **666:** AP/ Wide World Photos/Robert Mecea; **667:** Whittemore-Rothco Cartoons; **668:** BL, © Scott Wallace/World Bank; T, ARKO DATTA/AFP/Getty Images; BR, © Scott Wallace/World Bank; M, © Scott Wallace/World Bank; T, Ariadne Van Zandbergen/Lonely Planet/Getty Images; **669:** Tore Bergsaker/Sygma/ CORBIS; **670:** Reuters/CORBIS; **671:** R, Mark Avery/Orange Country Register/CORBIS; L, KEVIN LAMARQUE/Reuters/CORBIS; **672:** RHONA WISE/AFP/Getty Images; **673:** R, © 2001. All rights reserved. Reprint permission provided by Mike Peters in conjunction with the Cartoonist Group.; L, STEVE KELLEY Courtesy *San Diego Union-Tribune*; R, © 2001. All rights reserved. Reprint permission pro-vided by Mike Peters in conjunction with the Cartoonist Group.; **674:** Inset, REUTERS/Sean Adair/Files SV; Background, AP/Wide World Photos; T, Reuters/CORBIS; **675:** BL, Mario Tama/ Getty Images; TL, Patrick Andrade/ Polaris; Background, Steve McCurry/ Magnum Photos; TR, REUTERS/Kai Pfaffenbach; **677:** Martin H. Simon/ CORBIS; **679:** R, Courtesy Linda and Eddie Tran; L, Courtesy Linda and Eddie Tran; **680:** AP Photo/Matt York; **682:** Bob Daemmrich/The Image Works; **683:** SUPRI/Reuters/CORBIS; **684:** AP/Wide World Photos/Susan Ragan; **685:** R, Christophe Calais/In Visu /CORBIS; L, Mario Tama/Getty Images; **686:** T, AP/Wide World Photos; B, AP Photo/Matt York; **687:** © Dan Wasserman, 2005; Courtesy of Tribune Media Services; **688:** Background, The Art Archive/National Archives Washington, D.C.; BR: © Bettmann/ CORBIS; ML, The Granger Collection, New York; TM, The Granger Collection, New York; BL, © Bettmann/CORBIS; MR, © Bettmann/CORBIS; TR, The Granger Collection, New York; TL, © Reuters/CORBIS; **689:** Richard Rowan/ Photo Researchers, Inc.; **690:** TL, Joseph Sohm, ChromoSohm Media Inc./Photo Researchers, Inc.; TR, © Jim Corwin/The Stock Connection; M, Copyright © DEAN RIGGOTT/Grant

Heilman Photography – All rights reserved; TM, © Royalty-Free/CORBIS; B, Jeff Greenberg/Omni-Photo Communications, Inc.; **701:** #1, © National Portrait Gallery, Smithsonian Institution/Art Resource, NY; #2, © National Portrait Gallery, Smithsonian Institution/Art Resource, NY; #3, White House Collection, copyright White House Historical Association; #4, © National Portrait Gallery, Smithsonian Institution/Art Resource, NY; #5, © National Portrait Gallery, Smithsonian Institution/Art Resource, NY; #6, © National Portrait Gallery, Smithsonian Institution/Art Resource, NY; #7, White House Collection, copyright White House Historical Association; #8, White House Collection, copyright White House Historical Association; #9, © National Portrait Gallery, Smithsonian Institution/Art Resource, NY; #10, © National Portrait Gallery, Smithsonian Institution/Art Resource, NY; #11, White House Collection, copyright White House Historical Association; #12, © National Portrait Gallery, Smithsonian Institution/Art Resource, NY; #13, White House Collection, copyright White House Historical Association; #14, © National Portrait Gallery, Smithsonian Institution/Art Resource, NY; #15,© National Portrait Gallery, Smithsonian Institution/Art Resource, NY; #16, White House Collection, copyright White House Historical Association; **701–703:** Background, Corel Professional Photos CD-ROM™; **702:** #17, White House Collection, copyright White House Historical Association; #18, © National Portrait Gallery, Smithsonian Institution/Art Resource, NY; #19, White House Collection, copyright White House Historical Association; #20, © National Portrait Gallery, Smithsonian Institution/Art Resource, NY; #21, © National Portrait Gallery, Smithsonian Institution/Art Resource, NY; #22, White House Collection, copyright White House Historical Association; #23, White House Collection, copyright White House Historical Association; #24, White House Collection, copyright White House Historical Association; #25, © National Portrait Gallery, Smithsonian Institution/Art Resource, NY; #26, © National Portrait Gallery, Smithsonian Institution/Art Resource, NY; #27, © National Portrait Gallery, Smithsonian Institution/Art Resource, NY; #28, White House Collection, copyright White House Historical Association; #29, White House Collection, copyright White House Historical Association; #30, White House Collection, copyright White House Historical Association; #31, White House Collection, copyright White House Historical Association; #32, White House Collection, copyright White House Historical Association;

703: #33, White House Collection, copyright White House Historical Association; #34, White House Collection, copyright White House Historical Association; #35, © National Portrait Gallery, Smithsonian Institution/Art Resource, NY; #36, White House Collection, copyright White House Historical Association; #37: White House Collection, copyright White House Historical Association; #38, White House Collection, copyright White House Historical Association; #39, White House Collection, copyright White House Historical Association; #40, White House Collection, copyright White House Historical Association; #41: White House Collection, copyright White House Historical Association; #42, White House Collection, copyright White House Historical Association; #43, Bob Daemmrich/Stock Boston Inc./PictureQuest; The Granger Collection, New York; **704:** Lester Lefkowitz/CORBIS; **705:** Stockbyte; **706:** © North Wind Picture Archives; **707:** T, Blair Seitz/Stock Connection; B, Getty Images; **708:** Michael Newman/ PhotoEdit; **710:** AP/Wide World Photos; **712:** AP/Wide World Photos; **725:** B, Bettmann/CORBIS; T, The Granger Collection, New York; **726:** Bettmann/CORBIS; **727:** T, Réunion des Musées Nationaux/Art Resource, NY; B, The Colonial Williamsburg Foundation; **728:** Copyright © North Wind/North Wind Picture Archives – All rights reserved; **729:** The Granger Collection, New York; **730:** T, Composite photo-graph of the almost 200-year-old Star-Spangled Banner, the flag that inspired the national anthem. Smithsonian's National Museum of American History, ©2004; B, The Granger Collection, New York; **731:** © Bettmann/CORBIS; **732–733:** AP/Wide World Photos; **734:** © Christie's Images/CORBIS; **735:** Alan Schein/ZEFA/CORBIS; **736:** CORBIS; **737:** Brown Brothers; **738:** Bettmann/CORBIS; **739:** Paul A. Souders/CORBIS; **740:** Bettmann/ CORBIS; **741:** T, Bettmann/CORBIS; B, P Laffont/Sygma/CORBIS; **742:** Reuters/CORBIS; **743:** Time Life Pictures/Getty Images; **744:** T, Reuters/ CORBIS; B, Reuters/CORBIS

Text
Grateful acknowledgement is made to the following for copy-righted material:

Alfred A. Knopf, a division of Random House and Harold Ober Associates
"Beaumont to Detroit: 1943," "My People," "The Negro Speaks of Rivers" from *The Collected Poems Of Langston Hughes* by Langston Hughes, edited by Arnold Rampersad with David Roessel, Associate Editor, copyright © 1994 by

the Estate of Langston Hughes. Used by permission of Alfred A. Knopf, a division of Random House, Inc. and Harold Ober Incorporated.

Alfred Music Publishing Co, Inc.
Over the Rainbow (from "The Wizard of Oz"). Music by HAROLD ARLEN lyrics by E.Y. HARBURG. Copyright © 1938 (Renewed) METRO GOLDWYN MAYER INC. Copyright © 1939 (Renewed) EMI FEIST CATALOG INC. All rights controlled and administered by EMI FEIST CATALOG INC. (Publishing) and ALFRED MUSIC PUB-LISHING CO., INC. (Print). All rights reserved. Used by permission.

Amy Goodman
"Independent Media in a Time of War" by Amy Goodman from *Voices of a People's History of The United States*. Copyright © 2003 by Amy Goodman. Used by permission of the author.

Estate of Lorraine Hansberry, Methuen & Co., Ltd. and Random House, Inc.
A Raisin in the Sun by Lorraine Hansberry. Copyright © 1958 by Robert Nemiroff, as an unpublished work. Copyright © 1959, 1966, 1984 by Robert Nemiroff. Copyright © renewed 1986, 1987 by Robert Nemiroff. Used by permission of the Estate of Lorraine Hansberry, Methuen Drama, an imprint of A&C Black Publishers Ltd and Random House, Inc.

Estate of Michael Harrington and Simon & Schuster, Inc.
The Other American: Poverty In The United States by Michael Harrington. Copyright © 1962, 1969, 1981 by Michael Harrington. Copyright © renewed 1990 by Stephanie Harrington. All rights reserved. Used by permission of the Estate of Michael Harrington and Scribner, a Division of Simon & Schuster, Inc.

Houghton Mifflin Harcourt
"Chicago" from *Chicago Poems* by Carl Sandburg, copyright © 1916 by Holt, Rinehart and Winston and renewed 1944 by Carl Sandburg, reprinted by permission of Houghton Mifflin Harcourt Publishing Company. This material may not be reproduced in any form or by any means without prior written permission of the publisher.

Ludlow Music, Inc.
ROLL ON COLUMBIA by Woody Guthrie. Music based on GOODNIGHT, IRENE by Huddie Ledbetter and John A. Lomax. TRO-©-Copyright 1936 (Renewed) 1957 (Renewed) and 1963 (Renewed). Ludlow Music, Inc., New York, New York. Used by permission.

Next Decade Music, Glocca Morra Music & Gorney Music
"Brother Can You Spare a Dime?" by E.Y. "Yip" Harburg and Jay Gorney. Published by Glocca Morra Music (ASCAP) and Gorney Music (ASCAP). Administered by Next Decade Entertainment, Inc. All rights reserved. Used by permission.

Richard Overy
"World War II: Why the Allies Won" by Professor Richard Overy. Copyright © Professor Richard Overy. Used by permission.

Oxford University Press
Packaging the Presidency 3rd Edition by Jamieson (1996) 66w from p. 451 as an epigraph © 1984, 1992, 1996 by Kathleen Hall Jamieson. Used by permission of Oxford University Press, Inc.

Penguin Books, Ltd., London And Viking Penguin, a division of Penguin Group (USA), Inc.
The Grapes of Wrath by John Steinbeck, copyright © 1939, renewed © 1967 by John Steinbeck. Used by permission of Penguins Books, Ltd. and Viking Penguin, a division of Penguin Group (USA) Inc.

Perseus Books Group
Almost A Woman by Esmeralda Santiago. Copyright © 1994 Esmeralda Santiago. Used by permission of Da Capo Press, a member of Perseus Books Group.

Progressive Labor Party
"The Great Flint Sit Down Strike Against GM 1936 1937" by Walter Linder. Copyright © The Progressive Labor Party. Used by permission of Walter Linder.

The Carl Sandburg Family Trust
Excerpt from "Chicago" from *Chicago Poems*, copyright © by Carl Sandburg, reprinted by permission of the Carl Sandburg Family Trust. This selection may not be reproduced, stored in a retrieval system, or transmitted in any form or by any means without prior written permission.

Simon & Schuster
Manchild in the Promised Land by Claude Brown. Copyright © 1965 by Claude Brown. All rights reserved. Used by permission of Scribner, a Division of Simon & Schuster, Inc., from

University of Exeter Press
"Description of an Early Nazi Rally by Louise Solmitz, Schoolteacher" edited by J. Noakes and G. Pridham from *Nazism Series Volume 1 1919 1945:*

The Rise To Power: A Documentary Reader. Copyright © University of Exeter Press. Used by permission.

Writer's House
"I Have a Dream," "Letter from Birmingham Jail," "Pilgrimage to Non Violence," "A Time to Break Silence" and "When Peace Becomes Obnoxious" by Dr. Martin Luther King Jr. Copyright © 1956, 1958, 1967, 1963 Dr. Martin Luther King Jr., copyright © renewed 1986, 1991, 1995 Coretta Scott King. Used by permission of The Heirs to the Estate of Martin Luther King Jr., c/o Writers House as agent for the proprietor New York, N.Y.

Note: Every effort has been made to locate the copyright owner of material reproduced in this component. Omissions brought to our attention will be corrected in subsequent editions.

Electronic Selections
from *A Raisin in the Sun* by Lorraine Hansberry. Copyright © 1958 by Robert Nemiroff, as an unpublished work. Copyright © 1959, 1966, 1984 by Robert Nemiroff, Random House, Inc. Electronic rights used by permission of the Estate of Jewell Handy Gresham Nemiroff.

Excerpt from "Beaumont to Detroit" from *The Collected Poems of Langston Hughes* by Langston Hughes. Copyright © 1994 by the Estate of Langston Hughes. Reprinted by permission of Harold Ober Associates, Inc.

"My People," Copyright © 1926 by Alfred A. Knopf, Inc. and renewed 1954 by Langston Hughes., from *Selected Poems of Langston Hughes* by Langston Hughes. Reprinted by permission of Harold Ober Associates, Inc.

"The Negro Speaks of Rivers" From *The Collected Poems of Langston Hughes* by Langston Hughes. Copyright © 1994 by the Estate of Langston Hughes. Reprinted by permission of Harold Ober Associates, Inc.

Excerpt From *The Other America: Poverty in the United States* by Michael Harrington. Copyright © 1962, 1969, 1981 by Michael Harrington; Copyright renewed © 1990 by Stephanie Harrington. Spanish Language and Electronic Rights used by permission of Stephanie Harrington.

Excerpt from "The Hashbury is the Capital of the Hippies." First published in *The New York Times*. Copyright © 1979 by Hunter S. Thompson. Used by permission of the Wylie Agency.

has been made
tio... ight owner of
quent, this book.
...our atten-
...subse-

Teacher's Editi...
Photo Credits, T2...
Collection, New York, ...
T34, Library of Congress;
© 2005 Roger-Viollet/Topha...
Image Works; **T42,** Topham/Hl...
Image Works; **T46,** The Granger
Collection, New York; **T50,** © CORB...
T54, The Granger Collection, New
York; **T58,** The Granger Collection,
New York; **T62,** © CORBIS; **T66,**
© CORBIS; **T70,** Photo by Three
Lions/Getty Images; **T74,**
© Bettmann/CORBIS; **T78,** Erich
Lessing/© Magnum Photos;
T82, © Dunigan/H.Armstrong Roberts;
T86, © Bettmann/CORBIS; **T90,** Paul
Conklin Photography/PhotoEdit; **T94,**
National Archives and Records
Administration, Records of the U.S.
Marine Corps; **T98,** Getty Images;
T102, © Mark Richards/PhotoEdit;
T106, AP Photo/Lionel Cironneau;
T110, © Reuters/CORBIS

Text
26, The Washington Post, November 2, 2004; **39,** National Geographic Magazine, September 1, 2003; **215,** Excerpt from 1929 General Electric Refrigerator Advertisement "It's Always Summer-Time in Your Kitchen" Copyright © 1929 General Electric Company; **215,** Excerpt from 1929 General Electric Refrigerator Advertisement "The Food He Eats is the Man He'll Be!" Copyright © 1929 General Electric Company; **363,** The American Experience/PBS; **383,** Never Far Away: The Auschwitz Chronicles of Anna Heilman by Anna Heilman, Sheldon Schwartz, ed.; **495,** Lincoln Lynch, United Black Front Organization; **518,** AmeriCorps. www.americorps.gov